The Broadview Anthology of

BRITISH LITERATURE

Volume 2

The Renaissance and the Early Seventeenth Century

Second Edition

The Broadview Anthology of British Literature

The Medieval Period
The Renaissance and the Early Seventeenth Century
The Restoration and the Eighteenth Century
The Age of Romanticism
The Victorian Era
The Twentieth Century and Beyond

The Broadview Anthology of

BRITISH LITERATURE

Volume 2
The Renaissance and the Early Seventeenth Century
Second Edition

GENERAL EDITORS

Joseph Black, University of Massachusetts, Amherst
Leonard Conolly, Trent University
Kate Flint, University of Southern California
Isobel Grundy, University of Alberta
Don LePan, Broadview Press
Roy Liuzza, University of Tennessee
Jerome J. McGann, University of Virginia
Anne Lake Prescott, Barnard College
Barry V. Qualls, Rutgers University
Claire Waters, University of California, Davis

broadview press

Library and Archives Canada Cataloguing in Publication

The Broadview Anthology of British Literature / general editors, Joseph Black ... [et al.]. —2nd ed.

Includes bibliographical references and indexes.
Partial contents: v.2. The Renaissance and the early seventeenth century.
ISBN 978-1-55481-028-4 (v.2)

1. English literature. I. Black, Joseph Laurence, 1962–

PR1120.B77 2009 820.8 C2009-901366-5

Broadview Press is an independent, international publishing house, incorporated in 1985.

We welcome comments and suggestions regarding any aspect of our publications—please feel free to contact us at the addresses below or at broadview@broadviewpress.com.

North America
PO Box 1243
Peterborough, Ontario
Canada K9J 7H5

2215 Kenmore Avenue
Buffalo, NY, USA 14207
Tel: (705) 743-8990
Fax: (705) 743-8353
customerservice@broadviewpress.com

UK, Europe, Central Asia, Middle East, Africa, India, and Southeast Asia
Eurospan Group
3 Henrietta St.
London WC2E 8LU, UK
Tel: 44 (0) 1767 604972
Fax: 44 (0) 1767 601640
eurospan@turpin-distribution.com

Australia and New Zealand
NewSouth Books
c/o TL Distribution
15-23 Helles Avenue
Moorebank, NSW, Australia 2170
Tel: 02 8778 9999
Fax: 02 8778 9944
orders@tldistribution.com.au

www.broadviewpress.com

Broadview Press gratefully acknowledges the financial support of the Government of Canada through the Canada Book Fund for our publishing activities.

Cover design by Lisa Brawn

PRINTED IN CANADA

Contributing Editors and Writers

Managing Editor Don LePan
Developmental Editors Jennifer McCue, Laura Cardiff
General Academic and Textual Editors Colleen Franklin, Morgan Rooney
Design Coordinator Kathryn Brownsey

Contributing Editors

Katherine O. Acheson
Suzy Anger
Sandra Bell
Emily Bernhard Jackson
Joseph Black
Robert Boenig
Michael Calabrese
Laura Cardiff
Lisa Celovsky
Noel Chevalier
Mita Choudhury
Youngjin Chung
Thomas J. Collins
Leonard Conolly
Dianne Dugaw
Michael Faletra
Christina Fitzgerald
Stephen Glosecki
Amanda Goldrick-Jones
Douglas Hayes
John Holmes
Eleanor Johnson
Michael Keefer
Amy King
Scott Kleinman
Gary Kuchar
Don LePan
Roy Liuzza
Marie Loughlin
D.L. Macdonald
Hugh Magennis
Anne McWhir
Tobias Menely
Britt Mize
Meghan Nieman
David Oakleaf
Jude Polsky
Anne Lake Prescott
Joyce Rappaport
Herbert Rosengarten
Jason Rudy
Janice Schroeder
John T. Sebastian
Emily Steiner
David Swain
Andrew Taylor
Peggy Thompson
Yevgeniya Traps
Fred Waage
Craig Walker
Claire Waters
David Watt
William Weaver
Adrienne Williams Boyarin
James Winny

Contributing Writers

Laura Cardiff
Jude Polsky
Victoria Abboud
Jane Beal
Jennifer Beauvais
Rachel Bennett
Emily Bernhard Jackson
Rebecca Blasco
Julie Brennan
Andrew Bretz
Emily Cargan
Adrienne Eastwood
Wendy Eberle-Sinatra
Peter Enman
Joanne Findon
Jane Grove
Camille Isaacs
Erik Isford
Stephanie King
Gabrielle L'Archeveque
Don LePan
Anna Lepine
John McIntyre
Carrie Nartkler
Byron Nelson
Robin Norris
Kenna Olsen
Kendra O'Neal Smith
Laura Pellerine
Jason Rudy
Anne Salo
Janice Schroeder
Carrie Shanafelt
Nicole Shukin
James Soderholm
Anne Sorbie
Martha Stoddard-Holms
Jenna Stook
Candace Taylor
David van Belle
Shari Watling
Matthew Williams
bj Wray
Nicole Zylstra

Layout and Typesetting

Kathryn Brownsey
Susan Chamberlain

ILLUSTRATION FORMATTING AND ASSISTANCE

Cheryl Baldwin
Lisa Brawn

PRODUCTION COORDINATORS

Barbara Conolly
Chris Griffin
Leonard Conolly
Tara Lowes
Judith Earnshaw
Tara Trueman

PERMISSIONS COORDINATORS

Emily Cargan
Jennifer Elsayed
Amy Nimegeer
Chris Griffin

PROOFREADERS

Jennifer Bingham
Joe Davies
Anne Hodgetts
Martin Boyne
Judith Earnshaw
Amy Neufeld
Lucy Conolly
Lynn Fraser
Lynn Neufeld

EDITORIAL ADVISORS

Rachel Ablow, University of Rochester
Rita Bode, Trent University
Susan Brown, University of Guelph
Catherine Burroughs, Wells College
Elizabeth Campbell, Oregon State University
Nancy Cirillo, University of Illinois, Chicago
David Cowart, University of South Carolina
Alex Dick, University of British Columbia
Len Diepeveen, Dalhousie University
Daniel Fischlin, University of Guelph
Robert Forman, St. John's University
Barbara Gates, University of Delaware
Chris Gordon-Craig, University of Alberta
Stephen Guy-Bray, University of British Columbia
Elizabeth Hodgson, University of British Columbia
John Holmes, University of Reading
Michael Keefer, University of Guelph
Gordon Kipling, University of California, Los Angeles
Emily Kugler, University of California, San Diego
William Liston, Ball State University
Peter Mallios, University of Maryland
Rod Michell, Thompson Rivers University
Byron Nelson, West Virginia University
Michael North, University of California, Los Angeles
Lesley Peterson, University of North Alabama
John Pollock, San Jose State University
Jason Rudy, University of Maryland
Carol Senf, Georgia Tech
Sharon Smulders, Mount Royal College
Goran Stanivukovic, St. Mary's University
Julian Yates, University of Delaware

Contents

APPENDICES

PREFACE

A FRESH APPROACH

The publication of the first edition of this anthology in 2006 was widely hailed as an exciting achievement, with many academics concluding that its comprehensiveness, its consistency, its visual appeal, and its fresh approach made the Broadview the "new standard" in anthologies of British literature. We are also taking a fresh approach in issuing new editions of the anthology's volumes. Rather than publishing a second edition of each of the six volumes simultaneously, we are publishing new editions of the individual volumes at the rate of approximately one per year. If all goes according to plan, each volume will thus appear in a new edition every six years. We recognise that our two main competitors have in recent years made it a practice to issue new editions much more frequently than that, but our feeling is that it is better to allow several years to elapse between editions—not least of all, as a new edition may represent a considerable inconvenience to academics teaching from the anthology. (The approach also has real practical advantages for a smaller publisher such as Broadview; rather than gearing up for a massive process of revision every few years and then gearing down again in the wake of publication, we can proceed at a steady pace with the work of updating and revising.)

For the second edition of this volume a considerable number of changes have been made. William P. Weaver has provided us with a superbly revised and updated translation of More's *Utopia*. We have added several additional sonnets from Sidney's *Astrophil and Stella*, and we now include Spenser's letter to Ralegh along with the selections from *The Fairie Queene*. Isabella Whitney, who has been included in the website component of the anthology, is now included as part of the bound volume. Perhaps the most significant change for the new edition is the inclusion of more Milton. *Samson Agonistes*, which has been part of the website component, is now included in the bound book, and we now include more from *Paradise Lost*; Book 4 and Book 10 now appear in their entirety.

With so much new material added to the bound volume there had to be some cuts as well. The most substantial change in this direction has been to move the excerpts from Cary's *The Tragedy of Mariam* to the website component of the anthology. As before, those wishing to teach the full play may choose one of Broadview's specially-priced combination packages, whereby one or more volumes of *The Broadview Anthology of British Literature* is shrink-wrapped together with one or more volumes from the Broadview Editions series; Stephanie Hodgson-Wright's fine edition of *The Tragedy of Mariam* is one of over 300 titles available in that series.

There have been a range of other additions to the website component of this volume of the anthology since the first edition was published—Thomas Campion and selections from Spenser's *Shepheardes Calender*, for example, are both now included in the website component. So too is Shakespeare's *Twelfth Night*, in a fine edition prepared by David Swain. We decided against including a second Shakespeare play within the boundbook—but *Twelfth Night* is one of several works from the anthology that we are also making available in a stand-alone *Broadview Anthology of British Literature* Edition; those wishing to teach the play will thus have the option of including it in bound book form as part of a specially-priced shrink-wrapped package, together with this volume of the anthology.

As before, Joseph Black and Anne Lake Prescott have taken the lead in preparing the material for this volume—both in making the selections and in much of the hands-on editorial work. But, again as with the first edition, many people outside the General Editors group have also made important contributions to the preparation of the material; for this volume in particular thanks should go to Laura Cardiff and Gary Kuchar as well as to William P. Weaver and David Swain. Enlisting the help of a substantial number of people is entirely consistent with the approach we have followed from the start with *The Broadview Anthology*. Rather than dividing up the vast amount of work entailed in preparing such a large anthology among a relatively small number of academics, and asking each of them to handle on their own the work of choosing, annotating, and preparing introductions to texts in their own areas of specialization, we chose to involve a large number of contributors in the process (as the pages following the title page to this volume attest), and to encourage a high degree of collaboration at every level. First and foremost are the distinguished academics who serve as our General Editors for the project, but in all there have literally been hundreds of people involved at various stages in researching, drafting headnotes or annotations, reviewing material, editing material, and carrying out the work of designing and typesetting the texts and other materials. That approach allowed us to draw on a diverse range of talent, and to prepare the first edition of a large anthology with extraordinary efficiency. It has also facilitated the maintenance of a high degree of consistency. Material has been reviewed and revised in-house at Broadview, by outside editors, by a variety of academics with an extraordinarily diverse range of backgrounds and academic specialities, and by our team of General Editors for the project as a whole. The aim has been not only to ensure accuracy but also to make sure that the same standards be applied throughout the anthology to matters such as coverage provided in introductions, level of annotation, tone of writing, and student accessibility.

As with the first edition, our General Editors have throughout taken the lead in the process of making selections for the anthology. Several core principles have guided those selections. We have endeavoured to provide a selection that is broadly representative, while also being mindful of the importance of choosing texts that have the capacity to engage readers' interest today. We have for the most part made it a policy to include long works in their entirety or not at all; readers will find complete in *The Broadview Anthology* works such as *Utopia*, "Beachy Head," *Lady Susan*, *The History of Mary Prince*, *In Memoriam*, and *A Christmas Carol* that are often excerpted in (or omitted from) other anthologies. Where editions of works are available separately in our acclaimed Broadview Editions series, we have often decided to omit them from the anthology, on the grounds that those wishing to teach one or more such works may easily do so in a combination package with the anthology.

Any discussion of what is distinctive about *The Broadview Anthology of British Literature* must focus above all on the contents. In every volume of the anthology there is material that is distinctive and fresh–including not only selections by lesser-known writers but also less familiar selections from canonical writers. The anthology takes a fresh approach too to a great many canonical texts. The first volume of the anthology includes not only Roy Liuzza's translation of *Beowulf* (widely acclaimed as the most engaging and reliable translation available), but also new translations by Liuzza of many other works of Old English poetry and prose. Unique to the first volume of this anthology are a new verse translation of *Judith* by Stephen Glosecki, and new translations by Claire Waters of several of the *Lais* of Marie de France. The second volume includes *King Lear* not only in the full Folio version but also with three key scenes from the Quarto version; readers are thus invited to engage first-hand with the question of how textual issues may substantially affect larger issues of meaning. And so on through all six volumes.

In a number of these cases the distinctive form of the anthology facilitates the presentation of content in an engaging and practical fashion. Notably, the adoption of a two-column format allows for some translations (the Marie de France *Lais*, the James Winny translation of *Sir Gawain and the Green Knight*) to be presented in parallel column format alongside the original texts, allowing readers to experience something of the flavor of the original, while providing convenient access to an accessible translation. Similarly, scenes from the Quarto version of *King Lear* are presented alongside the comparable sections of the Folio text, and passages from four translations of the Bible are laid out parallel to each other for ready comparison.

The large trim-size, two-column format also allows for greater flexibility in the presentation of visual materials. Throughout our intent is to make this an anthology that is fully alive to the connections between literary and visual culture, from the discussion of the CHI-RHO page of the Lindisfarne Gospels in the first volume of the anthology (and the accompanying color illustration) to the inclusion in Volume 6 of a number of selections (including Graham Greene's "The Basement Room," Hanif Kureishi's "My Son the Fanatic," Tom Stoppard's "Professional Foul," and several skits from "Monty Python's Flying Circus") that may be discussed in connection with film or television versions. Along the way appear several full-page illustrations from the Ellesmere manuscript of Chaucer's *Canterbury Tales* and illustrations to a wide variety of other works, from *Robinson Crusoe* and *Gulliver's Travels* to *A Christmas Carol* and *The Road to Wigan Pier*.

Contextual Materials

Visual materials are also an important component of the background materials that form an important part of the anthology. These materials are presented in two ways. Several "Contexts" sections on particular topics or themes appear in each volume of the anthology, presented independent of any particular text or author. These include broadly based groupings of material on such topics as "Religion and Spiritual Life," "Print Culture," "India and the Orient," "The Abolition of Slavery," "The New Art of Photography," and "The End of Empire." The groups of "In Context" materials each relate to a particular text or author. They range from the genealogical tables provided as a supplement to *Beowulf*; to materials on "The Eighteenth-Century Sexual Imagination" (presented in conjunction with Haywood's *Fantomina*); to a selection of materials relating to the Peterloo massacre (presented in conjunction with Percy Shelley's "The Mask of Anarchy"); to materials on "'The Vilest Scramble for Loot' in Central Africa" (presented in conjunction with Conrad's "An Outpost of Progress"). For the most part these contextual materials are, as the word suggests, included with a view to setting texts in their broader literary, historical, and cultural contexts; in some cases, however, the materials included in "Contexts" sections are themselves literary works of a high order. The autobiographical account by Eliza M. of nineteenth-century life in Cape Town, for example (included in the section in Volume 5 on "Race and Empire"), is as remarkable for its literary qualities as it is for the light it sheds on the realities of colonial life. In the inclusion of texts such as these, as well as in other ways, the anthology aims to encourage readers to explore the boundaries of the literary and the non-literary, and the issue of what constitutes a "literary text."

Women's Place

A central element of the broadening of the canon of British literature in recent generations has of course been a great increase in the attention paid to texts by women writers. As one might expect from a publisher that has played an important role in making neglected works by women writers widely available, this anthology reflects the broadening of the canon quantitatively, by including a substantially larger number of women writers than have earlier anthologies of British literature. But it also reflects this broadening in other ways. In many anthologies of literature (anthologies of British literature, to be sure, but also anthologies of literature of a variety of other sorts) women writers are set somewhat apart, referenced in introductions and headnotes only in relation to issues of gender, and treated as important only for the fact of their being women writers. *The Broadview Anthology* strenuously resists such segregation; while women writers are of course discussed in relation to gender issues, their texts are also presented and discussed alongside those by men in a wide variety of other contexts, including seventeenth-century religious and political controversies, the abolitionist movement and World War I pacifism. Texts by women writers are front and center in the discussion of the development of realism in nineteenth-century fiction. And when it comes to the twentieth century, both Virginia Woolf and Dorothy Richardson are included alongside James Joyce as practitioners of groundbreaking modernist narrative techniques.

"British," "English," "Irish," "Scottish," "Welsh," "Other"

The broadening of English Studies, in conjunction with the expansion and subsequent contraction of British power and influence around the world, has considerably complicated the issue of exactly how inclusive anthologies should be. In several respects this anthology (like its two main competitors) is significantly more inclusive than its title suggests, including a number of non-British writers whose works connect in important ways with the traditions of British literature. We have endeavored first of all to portray the fluid and multilingual reality of the medieval period through the inclusion not only of works in Old and Middle English but also, where other cultures interacted with the nascent "English" language and "British" culture, works in Latin, in French, and in Welsh. In later periods the word "British" becomes deeply problematic in different respects, but on balance we have preferred it to the only obvious alternative, "English." There are several objections to the latter in this context. Perhaps most obviously, "English" excludes authors or texts not only from Ireland but also from Scotland and from Wales, both of which retain to this day cultures quite distinct from that of the English. "English literature," of course, may also be taken to mean "literature written in English," but since the anthology does not cover *all* literature written in English (most obviously in excluding American literature), the ambiguity would not in this case be helpful.

The inclusion of Irish writers presents a related but even more tangled set of issues. At the beginning of the period covered by the six volumes of this anthology we find works, such as the *Book of Kells*, that may have been created in what is now England, in what is now Scotland, in what is now Ireland—or in some combination of these. Through most of the seventeenth, eighteenth, and nineteenth centuries almost the whole of Ireland was under British control—but for the most part unwillingly. In the period covered in the last of the six volumes Ireland was partitioned, with Northern Ireland becoming a part of the United Kingdom and the Republic of Ireland declared independent of Britain on 6 December 1921. Less than two months earlier, James Joyce had completed *Ulysses*, which was first published as a complete work the following year (in Paris, not in Britain). It would be obviously absurd to regard Joyce as a British writer up to just before the publication of *Ulysses*, and an Irish writer thereafter. And arguably he and other Irish writers should never be regarded as British, whatever the politics of the day. If on no other grounds than their overwhelming influence on and connection to the body of literature written in the British Isles, however, we have included Irish writers—among them Swift, Sheridan, Wilde, Shaw, Beckett, Bowen, Muldoon, and Heaney as well as Joyce—throughout this anthology. We have also endeavored to give a real sense in the introductions to the six volumes of the anthology, in the headnotes to individual authors, and in the annotations to the texts themselves, of the ways in which the histories and the cultures of England, Ireland, Scotland and Wales, much as they interact with one another, are also distinct.

Also included in this anthology are texts by writers from areas that are far removed geographically from the British Isles but that are or have been British possessions. Writers such as Mary Rowlandson, Olaudah Equiano, and Phillis Wheatley are included, as they spent all or most of their lives living in what were then British colonial possessions. Writers who came of age in an independent United States, on the other hand, are not included, unless (like T.S. Eliot) they subsequently put down roots in Britain and became important British literary figures. Substantial grey areas, of course, surround such issues. One might well argue, for example, that Henry James merits inclusion in an anthology of British literature, or that W.H. Auden and Thom Gunn are more American poets than British ones. But the chosen subject matter of James's work has traditionally been considered to mark him as having remained an American writer, despite having spent almost two-thirds of his life in England. And both Auden and Gunn so clearly made a mark in Britain before crossing the Atlantic that it would seem odd to exclude them from these pages on the grounds of their having lived the greater part of their adult lives in America. One of our competitors includes Sylvia Plath in their anthology of British literature; Plath lived in England for only five of her thirty years, though, and her poetry is generally agreed to have more in common with the traditions of Lowell, Merwin and Sexton than with the currents of British poetry in the 1950s and '60s.

As a broad principle, we have been open to the inclusion of twentieth and twenty-first century work in English not only by writers from the British Isles but also by writers from British possessions overseas, and by writers from countries that were once British possessions and have remained a part of the British Commonwealth. In such cases we have often chosen selections that relate in one way or another to the tradition of British literature and the British colonial legacy. Of the Judith Wright poems included here, several relate to her coming to terms with the British colonial legacy in Australia; similarly, both the Margaret Atwood and the Alice Munro selections include work in which these Canadian authors attempt to recreate imaginatively the experience of British emigrants to Canada in the nineteenth century; the Chinua Achebe story in the anthology concerns the divide between British colonial culture and traditional Nigerian culture; and so on. For convenience we have also grouped most of the post-World War II non-British authors together, following the "Contexts: The End of Empire" section. (For the most part, the table of contents for the anthology is arranged chronologically according to the birthdate of each author.)

THE HISTORY OF LANGUAGE, AND OF PRINT CULTURE

Among the liveliest discussions we had at meetings of our General Editors were those concerning the issue of whether or not to bring spelling and punctuation into accord with present-day practice. We finally decided that, in the interests of making the anthology accessible to the introductory student, we should *in most cases* bring spelling and punctuation in line with present-day practice. An important exception has been made for works in which modernizing spelling and punctuation would alter the meaning or the aural and metrical qualities. In practice this means that works before the late sixteenth century tend to be presented either in their original form or in translation, whereas later texts tend to have spelling and punctuation modernized. But where spelling and punctuation choices in later texts are known (or believed on reliable authority) to represent conscious choice on the part of the author rather than simply the common practice of the time, we have in those cases, too, made an exception and retained the original spelling and punctuation. (Among these are texts by Edmund Spenser, by William Cowper, by William Blake, John Clare, and several other poets of the Romantic era, by George Bernard Shaw, and by contemporary figures such as Linton Kwesi Johnson.)

Beyond this, we all agreed that we should provide for readers a real sense of the development of the language and of print culture. To that end we have included in each volume examples of texts in their original form—in some cases through the use of pages shown in facsimile, in others by providing short passages in which spelling and punctuation have not been modernized. A list of these appears near the beginning of each volume of the anthology.

We have also included a section of the history of the language as part of the introduction to each volume. And throughout the anthology we include materials—visual as well as textual—relating to the history of print culture.

A DYNAMIC AND FLEXIBLE ANTHOLOGY

Almost all major book publishing projects nowadays are accompanied by an adjunct website, and most large-scale anthologies are accompanied by websites that provide additional background materials in electronic form. The website component of this anthology, on the other hand, is precisely that—a *component* of the anthology itself. The notion of a website of this sort grew organically out of the process of trying to winnow down the contents of the first edition of the anthology to a manageable level—the point at which all the material to be included would fit within the covers of bound books that would not be overwhelmingly heavy. And we simply could not do it. After we had made a very substantial round of cuts we were still faced with a table of contents in which each volume was at least 200 or 300 pages longer than our agreed-upon maximum. Our solution was not to try to cut anything more, but rather to select a range of material to be made available in a website component of the anthology. This material is in every way produced according to the same high standards of the material in the bound books; the editorial standards, the procedures for annotation, the author introductions, and the page design and layout—all are the same. The texts on the web, in short, are not "extra" materials; they are an integral part of the full anthology. In accordance with that principle, we have been careful to include a wide range of texts by lesser-known writers within the bound books, and a number of texts by canonical writers within the web component of the anthology.

The latter may be used in a variety of ways. Most obviously, readings from the web component are available to any purchaser of the book. Instructors who adopt *The Broadview Anthology of British Literature* as a course text are also granted permission to reproduce any web material for which Broadview holds copyright in a supplementary coursepack. An alternative for instructors who want to "create their own" anthology is to provide the publisher with a desired table of contents; Broadview will then make available to students through their university bookstore a custom-made coursepack with precisely those materials included. Other options are available too. Volumes of the anthology itself may of course be shrink-wrapped together at special prices in any desired combination. They may also (for a modest additional charge) be combined in a shrink-wrapped package with one or more of the over 300 volumes in the Broadview Editions series.

We anticipate that over the years the web-based component of the anthology will continue to grow—every year there will be a greater choice of web-based texts in the anthology. But we never foresee a day when the web will be the only option; we expect physical books always to remain central to Broadview's approach to publishing.

THE BROADVIEW LIST

One of the reasons we were able to bring a project of this sort to fruition in such a relatively short time was that we were able to draw on the resources of the full Broadview list: the many titles in the Broadview Editions series, and also the considerable range of other Broadview anthologies. As the contributors' pages and the permissions acknowledgments pages indicate, a number of Broadview authors have acted as contributing editors to this volume, providing material from other volumes that has been adapted to suit the needs of the present anthology; we gratefully acknowledge their contribution.

As it has turned out, the number of cases where we have been able to draw on the resources of the Broadview list in the full sense, using in these pages texts and annotations in very much the same form in which they appear elsewhere, has been relatively small; whether because of an issue such as the level of textual modernization or one of style of annotation, we have more often than not ended up deciding that the requirements of this anthology were such that we could not use material from another Broadview source as-is. But even in these cases we often owe a debt of gratitude to the many academics who have edited outstanding editions and anthologies for Broadview. For even where we have not drawn directly from them, we have often been inspired by them—inspired to think of a wider range of texts as possibilities than we might otherwise have done, inspired to think of contextual materials in places where we might otherwise not have looked, inspired by the freshness of approach that so many of these titles exemplify.

EDITORIAL PROCEDURES AND CONVENTIONS, APPARATUS

The in-house set of editorial guidelines for *The Broadview Anthology of British Literature* runs to over 40 pages, covering everything from conventions for the spacing of marginal notes, to the use of small caps for the abbreviations CE and BCE, to the approach we have adopted to references in author headnotes to name changes. Perhaps the most important core principle in the introductions to the various volumes, in the headnotes for each author, in the introductions in "Contexts" sections, and in annotations throughout the anthology, is to endeavor to provide a sufficient amount of information to enable students to read and interpret these texts, but without making evaluative judgements or imposing particular interpretations. In practice that is all a good deal more challenging than it sounds; it is often extremely difficult to describe why a particular author is considered to be important without using language that verges on the interpretive or the evaluative. But it is fine line that we have all agreed is worth trying to walk; we hope that readers will find that the anthology achieves an appropriate balance.

ANNOTATION: It is also often difficult to make judgments as to where it is appropriate to provide an explanatory annotation for a word or phrase. Our policy as been to annotate where we feel it likely that most first- or second-year students are likely to have difficulty understanding the denotative meaning. (We have made it a practice not to provide notes discussing connotative meanings.) But in practice the vocabularies and levels of verbal facility of first- and second-year students may vary enormously, both from institution to institution and within any given college or university class. On the whole, we provide somewhat more annotation than our competitors, and somewhat less interpretation. Again, we hope that readers will find that the anthology has struck a appropriate balance.

THE ETHICS AND POLITICS OF ANNOTATION: On one issue regarding annotation we have felt that principles are involved that go beyond the pedagogical. Most anthologies of British literature allow many words or phrases of a racist, sexist, anti-Semitic, or homophobic nature either to pass entirely without comment, or to be glossed with apologist comments that leave the impression that such comments were excusable in the past, and may even be unobjectionable in the present. Where derogatory comments about Jewish people and money-lending are concerned, for example, anthologies often leave the impression that money-lending was a pretty unsavory practice that Jewish people entered by choice; it has been all too rare to provide readers with any sense of the degree to which English society consistently discriminated against Jews, expelling them entirely for several centuries, requiring them to wear physical marks identifying their Jewish status, prohibiting them from entering most professions, and so on. *The Broadview Anthology* endeavors in such cases, first of all, not to allow such words and phrases to pass without comment; and second, to gloss without glossing over.

DATES: We make it a practice to include the date when a work was first made public, whether publication in print or, in the case of dramatic works, made public through the first performance of the play. Where that date is known to differ substantially from the date of composition, a note to this effect is included in parentheses. With medieval works, where there is no equivalent to the "publication" of later eras, where texts often vary greatly from one manuscript copy to another, and where knowledge as to date of original composition is usually imprecise, the date that appears at the end of each work is an estimate of the date of the work's origin in the written form included in the anthology. Earlier oral or written versions are of course in some cases real possibilities.

TEXTS: Where translations appear in this anthology, a note at the bottom of the first page indicates what translation is being used. Similar notes also address overall textual issues where choice of copy text is particularly significant. Reliable editions of all works are listed in the bibliography for the anthology, which is included as part of the website component rather than in the bound books, to facilitate ready revision. (In addition to information as to reliable editions, the bibliography provides for each author and for each of the six periods select lists of important or useful historical and critical works.) Copyright information for texts not in the public domain, however, is provided within the bound books in a section listing Permissions Acknowledgments.

INTRODUCTIONS: In addition to the introductory headnotes for each author included in the anthology, each "Contexts" section includes a substantial introduction, and each volume includes an introduction to the period as a whole. These introductions to the six volumes of the anthology endeavor to provide a sense not only of the broad picture of literary developments in the period, but also of the historical, social, and political background, and of the cultural climate. Readers should be cautioned that, while there is inevitably some overlap between information presented here and information presented in the author headnotes, an effort has been made to avoid such repetition as much as possible; the general introduction to each period should thus be read in conjunction with the author headnotes. The general introductions aim not only to provide an overview of ways in which texts and authors included in these pages may connect with one another, but also to give readers a sense of connection with a range of other writers and texts of the period.

READING POETRY: For much of the glossary and for the "Reading Poetry" section that appears as part of the appendices to each volume we have drawn on the superb material prepared by Herbert Rosengarten and Amanda Goldrick-Jones for *The Broadview Anthology of Poetry*; this section provides a concise but comprehensive introduction to the study of poetry. It includes discussions of diction, imagery, poetic figures, and various poetic forms, as well as offering an introduction to prosody.

MAPS: Also appearing within each of the bound books are maps especially prepared for this anthology, including, for each volume, a map of Britain showing towns and features of relevance during the pertinent period; a map showing the counties of Britain and of Ireland; maps both of the London area and of the inner city; and world maps indicating the locations of some of the significant places referenced in the anthology, and for later volumes showing the extent of Britain's overseas territories.

GLOSSARY: Some other anthologies of British literature include both glossaries of terms and essays introducing students to various political and religious categories in British history. Similar information is included in *The Broadview Anthology of British Literature*, but we have adopted a more integrated approach, including political and religious terms along with literary ones in a convenient general glossary. While we recognize that "googling" for information of this sort is often the student's first resort (and we recognize too the value of searching the web for the wealth of background reference information available there), we also recognize that information culled from the Internet is often far from reliable; it is our intent, through this glossary, through our introductions and headnotes, and through the wealth of accessible annotation in the anthology, to provide as part of the anthology a reliable core of information in the most convenient and accessible form possible.

OTHER MATERIALS: A chart of Monarchs and Prime Ministers is also provided within these pages. A range of other adjunct materials may be accessed through *The Broadview Anthology of British Literature* website. "Texts and Contexts" charts for each volume provide a convenient parallel reference guide to the dates of literary texts and historical developments. "Money in Britain" provides a thumbnail sketch of the world of pounds, shillings, and pence, together with a handy guide to estimating the current equivalents of monetary values from earlier eras. And the website offers, too, a variety of aids for the student and the instructor. An up-to-date list of these appears on the site.

Acknowledgments

The names of those on the Editorial Board that shaped this anthology appear on the title page, and those of the many who contributed directly to the writing, editing, and production of the project on the following two pages. Special acknowledgment should go to Jennifer McCue, who as Editorial Coordinator has been instrumental in tying together all the vast threads of this project and in making it a reality; to Laura Cardiff and Jude Polsky, who have carried larger loads than any others in drafting introductory materials and annotations, and who have done so with great skill and unfailing grace; to Kathryn Brownsey, who has been responsible for design and typesetting, and has continued to do a superb job and to maintain her good spirits even when faced with near-impossible demands; to Colleen Franklin, for the range of her scholarship as well as for her keen eye as our primary copy editor for the entire project; to Emily Cargan, Jennifer Elsayed and Amy Nimegeer who have together done superb work on the vast job of clearing permissions for the anthology; and to Michelle Lobkowicz and Anna Del Col, who have ably and enthusiastically taken the lead with marketing matters.

The academic members of the Advisory Editorial Board and all of us in-house at Broadview owe an enormous debt of gratitude to the hundreds of academics who have offered assistance at various stages of this project. In particular we would like to express our appreciation and our thanks to the following:

Rachel Ablow, University of Rochester
Bryan Alexander, Middlebury College
James Allard, Brock University
Sharon Alker, Whitman College
Laurel Amtower, San Diego State University
Rob Anderson, Oakland University
Christopher Armitage, University of North Carolina, Chapel Hill
Clinton Atchley, Henderson State University
John Baird, University of Toronto
William Baker, Northern Illinois University
Karen Bamford, Mount Allison University
John Batchelor, University of Newcastle
Lynn Batten, University of California, Los Angeles
Alexandra Bennett, Northern Illinois University
John Beynon, California State University, Fresno
Robert E. Bjork, Arizona State University
Rita Bode, Trent University
Robert Boenig, Texas A & M University
Rick Bowers, University of Alberta
David Brewer, Ohio State University
William Brewer, Appalachian State University
Susan Brown, University of Guelph
Sylvia Brown, University of Alberta
Sheila Burgar, University of Victoria
Catherine Burroughs, Wells College
Rebecca Bushnell, University of Pennsylvania
Michael Calabrese, California State University
Elizabeth Campbell, Oregon State University
Cynthia Caywood, University of San Diego
Jane Chance, Rice University
Ranita Chatterjee, California State University, Northridge
Nancy Cirillo, University of Illinois, Chicago
Eric Clarke, University of Pittsburgh
Jeanne Clegg, University of Aquila, Italy
Thomas J. Collins, University of Western Ontario
Kevin Cope, Louisiana State University
David Cowart, University of South Carolina
Catherine Craft-Fairchild, University of St. Thomas
Carol Davison, University of Windsor
Alex Dick, University of British Columbia

Len Diepeveen, Dalhousie University
Mary Dockray-Miller, Lesley College
Frank Donoghue, Ohio State University
Chris Downs, Saint James School
Julie Early, University of Alabama, Huntsville
Siân Echard, University of British Columbia
Garrett Epp, University of Alberta
Daniel Fischlin, University of Guelph
Verlyn Flieger, University of Maryland
Robert Forman, St. John's University
Lorcan Fox, University of British Columbia
Roberta Frank, Yale University
Jeff Franklin, University of Colorado, Denver
Maria Frawley, George Washington University
Mark Fulk, Buffalo State College
Andrew Galloway, Cornell University
Michael Gamer, University of Pennsylvania
Barbara Gates, University of Delaware
Daniel Gonzalez, University of New Orleans
Jan Gorak, University of Denver
Chris Gordon-Craig, University of Alberta
Ann-Barbara Graff, Georgia Tech University
Michael Griffin, formerly of Southern Illinois University
Elisabeth Gruner, University of Richmond
Stephen Guy-Bray, University of British Columbia
Ruth Haber, Worcester State College
Dorothy Hadfield, University of Guelph
Margaret Hadley, University of Calgary
Robert Hampson, Royal Holloway University of London
Michael Hanly, Washington State University
Lila Harper, Central Washington State University
Joseph Harris, Harvard University
Anthony Harrison, North Carolina State University
Douglas Hayes, Winona State University
Jennifer Hellwarth, Allegheny University
Peter Herman, San Diego State University
Kathy Hickock, Iowa State University
John Hill, US Naval Academy
Thomas Hill, Cornell University
Elizabeth Hodgson, University of British Columbia
Joseph Hornsby, University of Alabama
Scott Howard, University of Denver
Tara Hyland-Russell, St. Mary's College
Catherine Innes-Parker, University of Prince Edward Island
Jacqueline Jenkins, University of Calgary
John Johansen, University of Alberta
Richard Juang, Susquehanna University
Michael Keefer, University of Guelph
Sarah Keefer, Trent University
Jon Kertzer, University of Calgary
Helen Killoran, Ohio University
Gordon Kipling, University of California, Los Angeles
Anne Klinck, University of New Brunswick
Elizabeth Kraft, University of Georgia
Mary Kramer, University of Massachusetts, Lowell
Linda Leeds, Bellevue Community College
Mary Elizabeth Leighton, University of Victoria
William Liston, Ball State University
Sharon Locy, Loyola Marymount University
Ross MacKay, Malaspina University-College
Peter Mallios, University of Maryland
Arnold Markley, Penn State University
Pamela McCallum, University of Calgary
Kristen McDermott, Central Michigan University
John McGowan, University of North Carolina
Thomas McLean, University of Otago, New Zealand
Susan McNeill-Bindon, University of Alberta
Rod Michell, Thompson Rivers University
Kitty Millett, San Francisco State University
Richard Moll, University of Western Ontario
Monique Morgan, McGill University
Lucy Morrison, Salisbury University
Byron Nelson, West Virginia University
Carolyn Nelson, West Virginia University
Claudia Nelson, Southwest Texas State University
Holly Faith Nelson, Trinity Western University
John Niles, University of Wisconsin, Madison
Michael North, University of California, Los Angeles
Mary Anne Nunn, Central Connecticut State University
David Oakleaf, University of Calgary
Tamara O'Callaghan, Northern Kentucky University
Karen Odden, Assistant Editor for *Victorian Literature and Culture* (formerly of University of Wisconsin, Milwaukee)
Erika Olbricht, Pepperdine University
Patrick O'Malley, Georgetown University
Patricia O'Neill, Hamilton College

Delilah Orr, Fort Lewis College
Cynthia Patton, Emporia State University
Russell Perkin, St. Mary's University
Marjorie G. Perloff, Stanford University
John Peters, University of North Texas
Alexander Pettit, University of North Texas
Jennifer Phegley, The University of Missouri, Kansas City
John Pollock, San Jose State University
Mary Poovey, New York University
Gautam Premnath, University of Massachusetts, Boston
Regina Psaki, University of Oregon
Katherine Quinsey, University of Windsor
Geoff Rector, University of Ottawa
Margaret Reeves, Atkinson College, York University
Cedric Reverand, University of Wyoming
Gerry Richman, Suffolk University
David Robinson, University of Arizona
Laura Rotunno, Pennsylvania State University, Altoona
Nicholas Ruddick, University of Regina
Jason Rudy, University of Maryland
Donelle Ruwe, Northern Arizona University
Michelle Sauer, Minot State University
SueAnn Schatz, Lock Haven University of Pennsylvania
Dan Schierenbeck, Central Missouri State University
Norbert Schürer, California State University, Long Beach
David Seed, University of Liverpool
Karen Selesky, University College of the Fraser Valley
Carol Senf, Georgia Tech University
Judith Slagle, East Tennessee State University
Sharon Smulders, Mount Royal College
Malinda Snow, Georgia State University
Goran Stanivukovic, St. Mary's University
Richard Stein, University of Oregon
Eric Sterling, Auburn University Montgomery
James Stokes, University of Wisconsin, Stevens Point
Mary-Ann Stouck, Simon Fraser University
Nathaniel Strout, Hamilton College
Lisa Surridge, University of Victoria
Beth Sutton-Ramspeck, Ohio State University
Nanora Sweet, University of Missouri, St. Louis
Dana Symons, Simon Fraser University
Andrew Taylor, University of Ottawa
Elizabeth Teare, University of Dayton
Doug Thorpe, University of Saskatchewan
Jane Toswell, University of Western Ontario
Kim Trainor, University of British Columbia
Herbert Tucker, University of Virginia
John Tucker, University of Victoria
Mark Turner, King's College, University of London
Eleanor Ty, Wilfrid Laurier University
Deborah Tyler-Bennett, Loughborough University
Kirsten Uszkalo, University of Alberta
Lisa Vargo, University of Saskatchewan
Gina Luria Walker, The New School, New York City
Kim Walker, Victoria University of Wellington
Miriam Wallace, New College of Florida
Hayden Ward, West Virginia State University
Ruth Wehlau, Queen's University
Lynn Wells, University of Regina
Chris Willis, Birkbeck University of London
Lisa Wilson, SUNY College at Potsdam
Anne Windholz, Augustana College
Susan Wolfson, Princeton University
Kenneth Womack, Pennsylvania State University
Carolyn Woodward, University of New Mexico
Julia Wright, Wilfrid Laurier University
Julian Yates, University of Delaware
Arlene Young, University of Manitoba
Lisa Zeitz, University of Western Ontario

Introduction to the Renaissance and the Early Seventeenth Century

The term "Renaissance" has turned out to be a good deal less stable than was once assumed. The word "Rinascenza" (Italian: "rebirth"), from which "Renaissance" derives, was coined by the Italian historian Giorgio Vasari in 1550 to refer to what Vasari saw as having taken place in Italy over the previous two centuries: a rebirth of the ideas and the aesthetic values associated with the classical cultures of ancient Greece and Rome, after a thousand-year-long era in which civilization had gone into eclipse. By the time of Vasari it had already become conventional to think of that thousand-year period as the "Middle Ages" (or, using the Latinized form of the same phrase, the "medieval period").[1] Subsequently the habit developed of seeing the Renaissance as being followed by another discrete era, the Reformation, a period characterized above all by the challenge presented by Protestantism to the authority of the Church of Rome.

Recent generations of scholarship have done much to destabilize this conceptual framework. Medievalists have located a variety of "renaissances" in, for example, the ninth and the twelfth centuries, and have thoroughly debunked the idea that the supposed "dark ages" were lacking intellectual or cultural life. Scholars have also distinguished among the later renaissances of the fourteenth through sixteenth centuries: a renaissance in Italy that began in the early fourteenth century (with the writings of Dante and Petrarch and the paintings of Giotto) and reached its full flowering in the late fifteenth and early sixteenth centuries (the age of Machiavelli, of Leonardo da Vinci, and of Michelangelo); a renaissance that occurred in northern Europe in the late fifteenth and early sixteenth centuries, especially in the Low Countries but also manifesting itself in France and in England (among the leading figures of this renaissance were the great Humanist thinkers Desiderius Erasmus and Sir Thomas More and the painters Jan van Eyck and Hans Holbein); and a renaissance that occurred in England toward the end of the sixteenth century in the latter part of the reign of Elizabeth I (the age of Edmund Spenser, Sir Philip Sidney, and Christopher Marlowe as well as Shakespeare). Other scholars, though, have questioned whether or not England ever experienced anything that can properly be termed a "Renaissance."

At a minimum, then, the phenomena associated with "the Renaissance" extended over a considerable stretch of time and across much of Europe. But they were not isolated from one another, sharing a tendency to focus on human concerns in new ways (and, in the visual arts, to depict the human form in persuasively realistic if often idealized representations). Historically too, the various renaissances were connected by a variety of direct links, many of them stemming from royal initiatives. The French King Francis I (1494–1547) lent vibrant support to new ideas from Italy and brought to France such renowned Italian artists as Andrea del Sarto and Leonardo da Vinci. In England, Henry VII (1457–1509) and his mother, Margaret, encouraged the "new learning" and brought to England the great Dutch scholar Erasmus; promoted men such as Thomas More, the scholar John Colet, and Bishop John Fisher, who championed better education and classical learning; patronized William Caxton (who in 1476 had set up the first printing press in England); and founded two colleges at Cambridge University.

It was on this foundation that Henry's son, Henry VIII, built his fully developed Renaissance court. The prevailing image of Henry VIII is that of the figure he became in the 1530s and '40s, adding pound upon pound as he accumulated wife after wife. The young Henry—trim and lively, a sporting monarch and a man of culture, the "golden boy" peer of Francis I of France

[1] The earliest recorded expression of the idea of a "Middle Age" between the classical world and the modern one appears in the writing of Flavio Biondo around 1439. Petrarch, writing in the 1330s, is thought to have been the first to characterize what we now term the medieval period as an age of darkness (one which he believed himself still inhabiting).

and Charles V, the Holy Roman Emperor—is a very different figure. Under the young Henry an international culture flourished in which leading continental humanist thinkers and great artists—the Dutch painter Hans Holbein most prominent among them—were persuaded to spend substantial amounts of time in England.

Artist unknown, *Henry VIII*, c. 1509.

Hans Holbein, *Henry VIII*, 1536.

This manifestation of English Renaissance culture in the early sixteenth century was followed near the end of the century by an extraordinary cultural flowering of a different character—the Elizabethan Renaissance. This Renaissance followed the Protestant Reformation, and in consequence took on a different religious coloring from that of the Christian humanism so central to the Italian Renaissance and the early Northern Renaissance, which took shape before Martin Luther launched the Protestant Reformation in 1517. The word "Renaissance" is commonly applied to sixteenth-century and early seventeenth-century English culture, but many historians and even literary historians now prefer to term the era between about 1600 and some time in the eighteenth century the "early modern period."

Regardless of terminology, the period between 1500 and 1660 in Britain[1] saw massive political, social, and religious change, change intimately connected to developments on the continent. The period begins and ends with a country exhausted by war: in 1500 memories of a long series of wars fought over the right of succession to the English throne (the "Wars of the Roses") were still fresh, and in 1660 the return of Charles II from exile marked the end of the republican Commonwealth established after civil wars that had brought tumult to England, Scotland, and Ireland. Over these 160 years the national church—the foundation of the country's devotional practices and beliefs—changed its entire orientation at least four times and was subject to constant debate and evolution. Centuries-old rites and traditions in the countryside, which still resonated strongly throughout society in the early sixteenth century, began to disappear and even to become objects of nostalgia. The world of maypoles and of Morris dancing, of hobbyhorses and bonfires, was bitterly opposed as "pagan" or "papist" by more radical reformers, and while such traditional pastimes were supported by the early Stuart monarchs, they were a thing of the past by the end of the period. Medieval ideals of chivalry were kept alive (or resurrected) largely for political and social purposes even as a developing moneyed economy was refashioning the world. A

[1] "Britain is here used as a term of convenience; strictly speaking there was no "Britain" before 1603 when the accession of King James VI/I brought a *de facto* union of England and Scotland.

succession of monarchs established munificent (if sometimes rough-hewn) court cultures, and a vibrant street life in London and other towns was a vital part of English culture. The English language, though still widely thought inferior to Latin, experienced exuberant growth. Scientific investigations of a recognizably "modern" sort were beginning to be carried out toward the end of the period, even as belief in demons, witches, and astrology increased, as did a more recondite belief in alchemy. For many years a woman reigned as monarch, and in literature a common conceit had it that male lovers were slaves to the females they adored; yet the actual status of women probably did not improve over this period. How did this jumble coalesce in literature? Let us begin by looking more closely at Renaissance humanism and at the Protestant Reformation.

HUMANISM

Nowadays the word *humanist* is often used to imply a "secular" opposition to religion in general and Christianity in particular. The opposite is the case with Renaissance humanism, particularly north of Italy. Humanists were distinguished from other scholars not by exclusive focus on human or secular texts, but rather by their focus on secular writings, particularly classical ones, *as well as* on religious texts and thought. Thus Erasmus produced books on Greco-Roman culture *and* editions of the New Testament in the original Greek and of works by patristic writers. In one key particular, humanism was in accord with Protestant thought: Erasmus and many other humanists supported making the Bible available in the vernacular. But—as attested by Thomas More's willingness to die rather than approve England's separation from the Roman Catholic Church—humanists tended to be more willing than Luther or, later, Calvin to remain connected to Roman Catholic tradition. (Erasmus, for example, favored reform within the Catholic Church but opposed a full Protestant Reformation.)

The recovery and reappraisal of works from classical Greece and Rome was central to Renaissance humanism —as it had been to medieval scholasticism centuries earlier. The recovery of texts by the scholastics, however, had stressed applying classical learning to theological ends, emphasized Aristotle's works, and tended to treat classical writings as authoritative. For Renaissance humanists, classical writings were of interest for many purposes: the epic poems of Homer and Virgil and the erotic poems of Ovid were of as much interest as the writings of the philosophers. And many humanists felt little obligation to demonstrate that a seemingly new idea in fact accorded with ancient authority. Renaissance humanism was often prepared to break new ground, and to acknowledge breaking it.

Of the Greek philosophers, Plato, rather than Aristotle, came to the fore. Of particular importance was the Platonic concept of ideal forms—the notion that for every physical object, metaphysical concept, and ethical principle there is an ideal abstract form that in fact is more "real" than its manifestations in the actual or material world. It is not difficult to see how Platonic "ideas" could be harmonized with Christian ideals, and many humanist thinkers endeavored to do just that.[1] But Platonic philosophy also lent force to the sometime humanist impulse, particularly in Italy, to celebrate humanity itself, if not without reference to a Creator then with unprecedented emphasis on human potential and free will. A groundbreaking text here was the *Oration on the Dignity of Man* (1486) by the Florentine writer Pico della Mirandola. As Pico saw it,

> upon man, at the moment of his creation, God bestowed seeds pregnant with all possibilities, the germs of every form of life. Whichever of these a man shall cultivate, the same will mature and bear fruit in him. If vegetative, he will become a plant; if sensual, he will become brutish; if rational, he will reveal himself as a heavenly being; if intellectual, he will be an angel and the son of God.... Who then will not look with awe upon this our chameleon?

Northern humanists such as Erasmus and More were less optimistic about human nature, but nevertheless the contrast between Pico's confidence and the emphasis on the inherent sinfulness of man (and even more of woman) in both medieval Christianity and the theology of the French Protestant John Calvin (1509–64) could

[1] Some writers (e.g., Spenser and Rabelais) welcomed Platonism's vision of a world of ideas to which we can rise but also stressed God's descent to the world of flesh.

hardly be more marked. It is in the writings of the humanists that we see the possibility of imagining human society as a body independent of the workings of God. The supreme English example is More's *Utopia*, which imagines, although with a countering irony and ambivalence, the transformation of a culture through fundamentally different but entirely human-made social structures and practices.

Though scholars differ as to its extent and influence, most agree that Renaissance humanism helped transform sixteenth-century English literature. The poems of Thomas Wyatt, a member of Henry VIII's court who introduced the Petrarchan sonnet to English literature, show the impact of Renaissance humanism, as do prose works such as Sir Thomas Elyot's *The Book of the Governor* (1531) and Roger Ascham's *The Schoolmaster* (1570). Renaissance humanism is also generally agreed to have contributed to a new exuberance and a new richness in the English language, despite its occasional tendency toward philological pedantry and a sometimes uncomprehending prejudice against medieval scholastic philosophy. One contribution was the introduction of yet more tropes of classical rhetoric into English and an increased attention to English as a language worth study and further polish. According to Ascham, the study of Latin, "wisely brought into schools, truly taught, and constantly used," would "work a true choice [in] placing of words, a right ordering of sentences, and easy understanding of the tongue, a readiness to speak, a facility to write, a true judgement both of his own and other men's doings, what tongue soever he doth use." (Ascham is here practicing what he preaches, using several of the figures of classical rhetoric in the construction of his long and elaborately balanced sentence.)

Humanists such as Erasmus wrote primarily in Latin, but their rhetorical impulse and linguistic exuberance spilled over into the vernacular. Under the influence of Joachim Du Bellay, who had defended French in similar terms, Richard Mulcaster (Edmund Spenser's teacher) asked some pointed questions and gave impassioned answers:

> Is it not indeed a marvellous bondage, to become servants to one tongue for learning's sake the most of our time, with loss of most time, whereas we may have the very same treasure in our own tongue, with the gain of more time? Our own bearing the joyful title of our liberty and freedom, the Latin tongue remembering us of our thraldom and bondage? I love Rome, but London better; I favour Italy, but England more; I honour the Latin, but I worship the English.

Like much else about this period, the extent to which "Renaissance humanism" is a useful concept is subject to debate. Earlier notions of Renaissance humanism often assumed a top-down view of the period in which coherent intellectual movements were prime moving forces of socio-economic as well as political and cultural change. Recent scholars doubt that such movements in intellectual history are often quite so unified and coherent, believing that bottom-up change driven by socio-economic or religious forces may have at least as great an impact. Nevertheless, "Renaissance humanism" remains central to any discussion of the period.

Scientific Inquiry

Science and technology had not been dead in the Middle Ages, as witness developments in, for example, optics. It is the early modern period, however, that saw the start of what was later to be called, with a little exaggeration, "the scientific revolution." And yet the story of scientific development in early modern Europe is one of twists and paradox, not least because the Renaissance saw an increased, not a decreased, interest and belief in astrology, alchemy, and demonology. These fields of exploration are now called "pseudo-sciences," but the observations they entailed and the technology they encouraged, futile though the sciences themselves turned out to be, contributed to what we would call real science. Even the great Isaac Newton believed in the occult. Did Renaissance humanism play a part? Humanist fascination with ancient texts doubtless aided in the recovery or fresh understanding of scientific works by such classical authorities as Aristotle, Euclid, Hippocrates, and Galen (the latter two edited by Rabelais). Even more important was the increased use of Arabic numerals and that mathematically crucial concept, zero (realized in India and perfected by the Arabs).

Although he failed to understand the necessity of mathematics to his dreams of scientific progress, Sir Francis Bacon (1561–1626) was a key figure in formulating new approaches. As his essays demonstrate, Bacon's interests were wide. His *Novum Organum* (1620) was a plan to base scientific endeavor and an understanding of the cosmos more on objective observation and less on armchair theory or the consensus of the past. As Bacon put it, "man, custodian and interpreter of Nature, performs and understands so much as he has collected concerning the order of nature by observation or reason; nor do his powers or his knowledge extend farther." Among those who put into practice the inductive approach advocated by Bacon was William Harvey (1578–1657), an English physician who, through experiment and observation, determined how blood circulates in the human body. As Harvey observed in his *De Motu Cordis et Sanguinis,*[1] *On the Motions of the Heart and Blood* (1628):

> Almost all anatomists, physicians, and philosophers, up to the present time, have supposed with Galen that the object of the pulse was the same as that of respiration.... But as the structure and movements of the heart differ from those of the lungs, and the motions of the arteries from those of the chest, so seems it likely ... that the pulsations and uses of the heart, likewise of the arteries, will differ in many respects from the heavings and uses of the chest and lungs.

What Harvey did for the human body, the astronomers Copernicus, Galileo, and Kepler did for the universe. Galileo provided further proof of the Copernican theory that the cosmos does not revolve around the earth, and Kepler showed that the earth's path is an ellipse (although he continued to believe that the planets make beautiful harmony and tried to work out the musical notation involved). As the poet John Donne put it in his *Anatomy of the World*, if with some exaggeration, the "new philosophy," by which he meant the new natural science, "calls all in doubt":

> The sun is lost, and the earth, and no man's wit,
> Can well direct him where to look for it.

The lines are often quoted, but in truth some welcomed the new astronomy: in the older system, the Earth was at the center of the universe, but that center was a dark, dirty, and unmusical place, unlike the fiery and harmonious planets and stars.

Much as discoveries such as those of Harvey and Galileo affected the intellectual constructs through which people viewed each other and the world, some things remained unchanged from the late-medieval to the Renaissance period. One of these, challenged but persistent, was the habit of thought according to which the macrocosm was made up of four elements—earth, water, air, and fire—and the microcosm of the individual human was made up of four "humors," each with a physical association. Thus a sanguine humor or temperament was associated with blood, a choleric or angry temperament was associated with one sort of bile, a melancholic temperament was associated with a different sort of bile, and a phlegmatic temperament was associated with water. (Melancholia, which often meant what we would call neurosis and which was often thought to be linked to high intelligence and creativity, came in for particular attention in the Jacobean era: Jacques in Shakespeare's *As You Like It* is a paradigm of the type. And, in a different genre, Robert Burton's *The Anatomy of Melancholy* [1621] is a full and entertaining treatise on the subject.) Ideally, all four humors would be balanced. The domination of one humor could be the subject of a medical diagnosis—or of literary satire. Ben Jonson in such plays as *Everyman in his Humour* and *Everyman out of his Humour* was the most notable among many Elizabethan and Jacobean writers to make the "humors" of human individuals the subject of comedy. Such ways of thinking persisted into the late seventeenth century. As so often with scientific or technological developments, there was a lag between a discovery and its general acceptance.

THE REFORMATION IN ENGLAND

The Protestant Reformation was in part about power: would the Roman Catholic Church retain power to act

[1] Like Bacon and like almost all authors of scientific work until the late seventeenth and eighteenth centuries, Harvey wrote in Latin.

as an intermediary between Christians and God, power to define the nature of God, power to control all aspects of worship, power over the legitimacy of marriage and of children, and in many cases vast power over lands and financial resources, including the power to impose tithes and taxes? For centuries the Church of Rome had exerted supreme authority in all these areas.

The spark that set off the Reformation was a challenge put forward by Martin Luther on October 31, 1517 to the long-standing Church practice of selling "indulgences"—certificates granting absolution for sins. Luther saw the practice as a flagrant abuse of Church authority that discouraged people from confessing their sins in a spirit of true repentance. According to tradition, Luther nailed his *Ninety-Five Theses*—a substantial document in which he set out his arguments—to the door of the castle church in Wittenberg. Thanks to the new printing technology, the *Theses* were translated and distributed throughout Europe within two months, and within a year Luther was condemned by the Pope as a heretic.

Before long, the controversy set off by Luther had widened as much conceptually as it had geographically. Luther's protest broadened into a wide-ranging call for reforms in the Church, including the elimination of perceived abuses such as the sale of indulgences as well as a new emphasis on making the Word of God, the Bible—for Luther the one true authority—available directly to all in the vernacular, a new focus on faith alone as the key to salvation, and a denial that human beings have free will (only with grace, he said, and not from the exertion of will, can people choose the good). In 1529, the Diet (or Assembly) of Speyer passed a comprehensive condemnation of Luther and his followers, but a minority of delegates delivered a *Protestatio*—the origin of the term "Protestant" that has come to be applied to the various new churches that sprang up across Europe in opposition to the Church of Rome, and that assumed leading roles in Germany, Holland, and England.

In England, controversies over the use or abuse of power by the Catholic Church were substantially complicated by the fact that this power was exercised from afar, from Italy; even in the Middle Ages such power had been resented in England, and in the early sixteenth century an increased resentment against traditional doctrines and practices can be attributed in part to their origin in Rome (or so said Reformers, for Catholics claimed to have derived them from Scripture, from continued revelation, or from the broader consensus of Christendom). And once the Reformation in England was an established fact, national feeling sometimes played a significant role in fanning the flames of religious hatred. As early as the 1540s, some Protestants had advanced the claim that the Pope was the embodiment of Antichrist, and such sentiment grew when in 1580 Pope Pius V pronounced that assassinating Elizabeth I of England would not constitute a mortal sin. It should nevertheless be remembered, as a number of recent scholars have stressed, that of the large minority of English men and women who remained Catholic and did not move to the continent, most remained loyal to both their faith and their monarch.

In attempting to sort out the causes of the Reformation, what weight should we give to the issue that sparked Luther's rebellion—what many perceived as corruption in the Church, and in particular the sale of indulgences? It is now generally accepted that the degree of corruption in the late-medieval church was exaggerated both at the time and by most later historians; its true extent is still debated. We do know that in the late-medieval period many, including many loyal Catholics, accused the institutional Roman Catholic Church of abandoning its own ideals of concern for the poor, chastity for priests, and Gospel simplicity. Simony—the practice of buying and selling spiritual offices for spiritual benefits—was widespread, as other such abuses were said, not always unjustly, to be. But there were other questions being asked. Should the clergy act as intermediaries in interpreting the Bible for the laity? Or should everyone, even the humble, be allowed to read and interpret the Bible (perhaps even actively encouraged to do so)? Is administering the sacraments and presiding over other rites the most important function of the clergy? (And how many sacraments are there? Catholics said seven; Protestants said only two: baptism and holy communion.) Or is preaching and spreading the word of God the central obligation of a clergyman? Is the sacrament of Confession (the confessing of one's sins to a priest) essential to salvation? Or should confession, no longer a sacrament, be between an individual and God? Is the substance, although not the appearance (the "accidents"), of bread and wine literally transformed during the sacrament of the Eucharist into the body and the blood of Christ by a process called "transubstantiation" that re-enacts Christ's sacrifice? Or are Lutherans right to say that God is "really" but not physically present in the bread and wine? Calvinists (and the Church of England) called the sacrament of the Eucharist a "sign"—connecting signifier to signified so as to make it more than a mere reminder—of God's spiritual presence and His connection to the believer. Not true, said some more radical Protestants, Communion is merely a memorial. Others, even more radical, thought it best to dispense with the ceremony altogether.

There were yet more questions. Are church hierarchies necessary to the carrying out of God's will? Or do they exist only for convenience? Is salvation dependent on good works performed, on sins not committed, and on remaining in communion with God? Or is it dependent purely on one's faith in God, a faith that may in turn be acquired only at God's pleasure? Might the salvation of "the elect" even be predestined by God? Is it a sign of appropriate respect to honor the Virgin Mary and the saints as well as the divinity through splendid displays of devotion? Or does that risk idolatry? (Protestants accused Catholics of actually worshipping saints and of elevating Mary beyond her due as the mother of Christ.) Or does a plain style honor God most fittingly? (In which case elaborate or colorful decoration in churches, let alone beautiful images venerated in themselves, are properly seen as further expressions of idolatry.) Should realism and discretion be exercised in any consideration of measures to "enforce purity" outside the Church? Or is it one's duty as a Christian to pursue purity through restrictions on irresponsible or pleasure-seeking behavior? May we (as King James I was to urge) enjoy a range of traditional practices that probably have pagan roots (maypoles, hobbyhorses, bonfires, bells, Christmas revelry) or must we, as many "Puritans" said, condemn such enjoyments as wicked, even devilish? Divergent answers to such questions separated Catholic from Protestant, and accompanied a number of divisions within Protestantism.

Thomas Wolsey, a butcher's son who became a cardinal of the Roman Catholic Church, and was for many years Lord Chancellor under Henry VIII. Wolsey was as controversial as he was powerful, and his legacy remains controversial today. Widely praised by some for his administrative abilities and his adroitness in foreign affairs, to others he exemplified the corruption of the Church and the dangers of mingling religious office with secular authority. Holding the highest religious position in the land, he was also the King's chief minister, shaping both domestic and foreign policy. He left a lasting legacy in building Hampton Court Palace and founding Cardinal College at Oxford University, but when Henry VIII petitioned the Pope for an annulment of his marriage, Wolsey became caught in the struggle between his two masters. Henry stripped him of his government offices and of most of his property. His servant George Cavendish reported that as he lay dying on his way to what would have doubtless been a trial and execution, he said "If I had served my God as diligently as I have done the King he would not have given me over in my gray hairs."

The Reformation came to England through circuitous means. The rejection by Henry VIII of papal supremacy *led* to a Protestant English Reformation but did not *constitute* a Protestant Reformation of the Church in England; only under Henry's son, Edward VI, was a more explicit Protestantism, both theological and institutional, established in England, and for reasons quite different from those that had motivated Henry. (Likewise, although some in the England of the 1520s and 1530s shared the varieties of Protestantism that were bringing sweeping change in parts of Europe, such beliefs were not yet widespread or powerful enough to establish the Reformation in England. Even when Elizabeth first began her reign it is possible that a majority of her subjects were still loyal to Rome.) Most immediately, Henry's break with Rome was caused by his desire to end his marriage to Catherine of Aragon and obtain a male heir by marrying Anne Boleyn. There is little doubt that he was in love with Anne, but almost certainly he would not have gone to such lengths to marry her had he not become convinced that Catherine would never give him a son.[1]

The key developments in the break from Rome are as follows. In 1533, after Henry had exerted intense pressure on the English clergy to support his course of action, the marriage of Henry and Catherine was annulled, his marriage to (a pregnant) Anne Boleyn was consecrated, and she became Queen. At that point Pope Clement VII, who had been trying diplomatically to placate Henry without doing any violence to Catholic doctrine (or offending Catherine's nephew, the Holy Roman Emperor), now excommunicated Henry: forbidden to receive Communion, Henry was thereby excluded from salvation. Henry's response was to pass an Act of Succession through Parliament, under which all adult males in England would have to swear that they supported the change in the King's marital arrangements. Henry also decreed that the Bible should be made available in English, and that church services should be in English rather than in Latin, a radical break with the practice of the Church of Rome. Later that year the English Church was formally made independent from Rome, and all adult males were additionally required to swear allegiance to the King in his new capacity as "Supreme Head of the Church in England." Among the few who refused so to swear were Sir Thomas More, author of *Utopia* and from 1528 to 1532 Henry's Lord Chancellor, and John Fisher, Bishop of Rochester. In 1535 both were convicted of treason for their refusals and executed. Both were canonized by the Catholic Church in 1935.

As so often with Henry, the personal was entangled with the political. In an effort to build support for the break with Rome, he gave preferment to Protestants who not long before had been labeled heretics. This move helped both to buttress his own authority and to undermine Catholic institutions, most significantly the monasteries, bastions of privilege and possessors of immense wealth. Protestants were fervent in their opposition to the monasteries. Whereas monks had originally been venerated as embodiments of the godly life, they had come to be widely suspected (sometimes rightly) of corrupt and immoral behavior; in some parts of the realm, moreover, they were widely unpopular as landlords despite the role of some monasteries and convents in providing basic schooling and medical aid. In 1535, two years after the break with Rome, Henry appointed commissioners to look into these allegations; as he had doubtless intended them to do, the commissioners confirmed the allegations of corruption, and

[1] The root of Henry VIII's break with Rome may be traced to the desire of Henry VII to improve his standing with the Spanish monarchy by marrying his son to Catherine of Aragon, daughter of Ferdinand and Isabella. Catherine was betrothed to Arthur, Henry's eldest son, in 1488; she was three years old and Arthur a year younger. The two were 15 and 14 respectively when the long-awaited wedding took place in 1501, but within six months Arthur fell sick and died. Henry VII obtained a papal dispensation allowing Catherine to marry Arthur's younger brother Henry; this second marriage for Catherine took place in 1509. She bore several children, but only her daughter Mary survived. Catherine was 42 years old in 1527 when Henry, despairing of her ability to give him a son, and with perhaps some degree of sincerity convinced that his lack of an heir was God's punishment for his living in sin with his deceased brother's wife, began to petition Pope Clement VII to grant him an annulment on the grounds that Catherine's marriage to his brother had made their own union unlawful. Catherine put up strenuous resistance to Henry's petition; she appealed to the Pope herself, insisting that she and Arthur had not consummated their marriage and had therefore never truly been husband and wife. Catherine's nephew was Charles V, the Holy Roman Emperor, whom the Pope had no wish to offend, and the matter was soon at a stalemate—where it remained for six years, while Pope Clement continued to resist Henry's appeals.

beginning in 1536 Henry ordered the dissolution of monasteries throughout England and annexed the land to the Crown. He thus provided himself with a vast and ongoing source of additional revenue, as well as with the ability to extend his generosity more widely to friends and supporters. Through Thomas Cranmer (Archbishop of Canterbury and hence the Primate of the English Church), Henry also broke with Catholic tradition by arranging for the publication of the first English Bible authorized for public use, the 1539 "Great Bible" of Miles Coverdale. The "dissolution" of the monasteries typically entailed their physical destruction, often to provide stones for the Tudor great houses that the gentry and nobility were beginning to build. "Bare, ruined choirs, where late the sweet birds sang" became a common sight in sixteenth-century England.

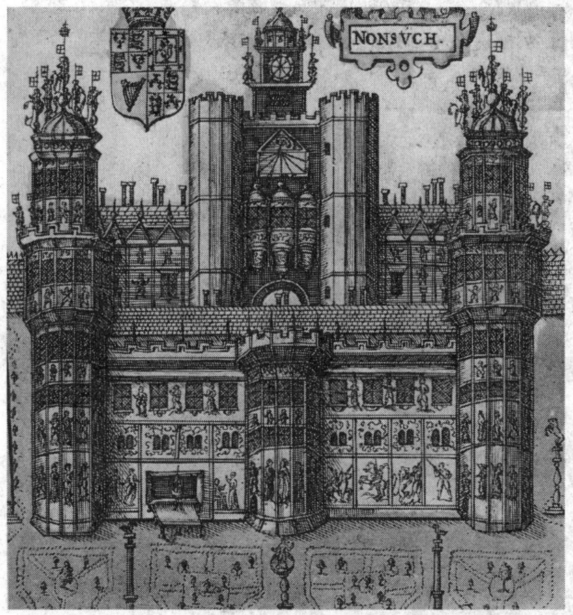

John Speed, vignette of Nonsuch Palace from the map of Surrey in Speed's atlas of Britain, 1616. Nonsuch Palace, the greatest of Henry VIII's edifices and one of the most noted works of Tudor architecture, was begun in 1538, and completed in 1547. It later became a favorite residence of Elizabeth I.

Roger Fenton, *Riveaulx Abbey*. Riveaulx (located in East Yorkshire), once one of the greatest of English monasteries, had subsequently dwindled in importance, and housed fewer than two dozen monks at the time of the Dissolution. In 1538 the remaining monks were forced to leave, and the abbey and surrounding lands were granted to Thomas Manners, who destroyed many of the buildings but left the shell of the early thirteenth-century church standing.

Throughout his reign, Henry, who probably did not consider himself a "Protestant" in any profound or theological sense, attempted to steer a middle course between Protestant demands for further reform and residual Catholic tradition and theology. But for Henry, steering a middle way did not mean conciliation or consensus; it meant veering between censoring, imprisoning, and even executing greater numbers of one side or of the other. Even in the mid-1530s, as he was counting on Protestant support in building a campaign against the monasteries, Henry was also restricting licenses to preach and curtailing other forms of free religious expression that he thought extremist which were being demanded by Protestants.

Wall-painting of the Last Judgment, Stratford Guild Chapel, early sixteenth century. This picture, in which Hell-mouth appears at lower right, is one of a series of wall paintings in the Chapel that were whitewashed over in the later sixteenth century to remove Catholic imagery. The paintings were discovered in 1804, and watercolor copies were published in 1807.

Scholars continue to debate both the manner in which the Reformation came to England and the speed with which it did. Was the Reformation pushed forward primarily by pressure from above—by administrators such as Cranmer? Or was it driven more by pressure from below by a population dissatisfied with the old Church? Was England already Protestant at heart when Mary Tudor began her reign? Or did the Reformation in England remain a work in progress until the 1570s? Just how large was the Catholic minority—and when did it become a minority? Over such issues there is little consensus, although the recent tendency has been to affirm the vitality of the Roman Catholic Church on the eve of Henry's reforms and the continued presence of large numbers of Catholics in officially Protestant England. In any case, the broad outlines of the narrative are clear. For most English people in the sixteenth and seventeenth centuries, matters of faith were intensely felt realities, not abstract theological questions—even if they could be those too. Although educated lay Christians had long practiced versions of piety that included reciting parts of the Bible, we can get some sense of the freshness and the fervency of the feelings aroused by the increased stress on Bible reading through the words of Queen Elizabeth herself:

> I walk many times into the pleasant fields of the Holy Scriptures, where I pluck up the goodly green herbs of sentences, eat them by reading, chew them up musing, and lay them up at length in the seat of memory ... so I may less perceive the bitterness of this miserable life.

It is not difficult to appreciate the aesthetic and cultural importance of religious issues in an age in which everyone was a church-goer (Elizabethan law required it, in part to determine who might be Catholic), in which crucifixes, rosaries, and so on—if now frowned upon by strict Protestants—had long figured in daily life as reminders of Christian doctrine, but in which the practice of reading the Bible had only recently become available to the population at large (if only by hearing it read out loud). The sixteenth and early seventeenth centuries were robustly secular, but they were also passionately religious. Cultures can be both, and it is important not to forget the strength of the religious ferment that extended throughout this period—or the fact that for many of those involved in it, religious matters defined the age and set it off in bold relief from earlier times. Such was the vision of the Protestant reformer John Foxe, whose *Acts and Monuments* (popularly known as the *Book of Martyrs*) was one of the most influential and widely read books of the age. Far from seeing the Middle Ages as a lost Age of Faith, Foxe regarded the thousand years before the Reformation as the millennium of Satan's rule prophesied by the Biblical Book of Daniel.

WALES, SCOTLAND, IRELAND

Henry VIII was an international figure beyond his support of Renaissance humanism; he was also a colonizing monarch, if largely confining his efforts to what is now the United Kingdom and northeast France. A continual thread that runs through the history of the sixteenth and seventeenth centuries is England's conflict with constituent parts of the British Isles. English power reached an early peak around 1300, when the English were able to exert at least loose control over the greater part of Ireland as well as over Scotland and Wales. In all three areas the English faced continuing resistance, however. Scotland was able to re-establish its position as an independent kingdom; in Ireland, the English control diminished to a relatively small area surrounding Dublin known as "the Pale"; and in Wales, though the Normans had managed to install "English" settlers in many of the more fertile lowland areas, those in the mountainous regions remained very largely a traditional society that was effectively independent of English rule. When a Welshman, Henry VII, became King of England in 1485, however, administrative control of Wales from London began to harden. The process culminated under Henry VIII with the Acts of Union of 1536–43: the old Welsh areas of lordships were converted into shires on the English model, and the Welsh code of law was brought into conformity with its English counterpart. The traditional Welsh kinship system, under which equal inheritance among all male children was the norm, was replaced by a system of primogeniture, with land typically held on a freehold basis. Interestingly, though, the Welsh language does not seem to have been threatened during this period, despite English incursions into Welsh custom and culture.

Under Thomas Cromwell, Henry VIII's chief minister in the 1530s, the English attempted the same sort of "reforms" in Ireland that had been imposed in Wales—with much less success. Along with changes to traditional kinship systems, the English attempted to bring about the same religious changes in Ireland that were occurring in England: royal rather than papal supremacy over the Church, the Bible to be read in the vernacular, and the dissolution of the monasteries. These English efforts met with only sporadic success, and Henry did not push the point; it was not until the 1570s, when Elizabeth I's government found itself increasingly threatened by the aggressively expansionist Catholic regime of Philip II in Spain, that a more determined approach was taken toward "stubbornly" Catholic Ireland. Several revolts that had been actively

John Speed, *Wilde Irish Woman* and *Wilde Irish Man*, two of several decorative miniatures surrounding the map of England in Speed's 1616 atlas.

encouraged by Spain were suppressed, and England resumed its efforts to colonize Irish territories (particularly in the north) that had been abandoned in the early fourteenth century. Ireland continued to be a thorn in the side of the English government, however. In one notable episode, Elizabeth's favorite courtier, Robert Devereux, the Earl of Essex, pressed the Queen for permission to lead an army against an Irish rebellion in 1599 led by the Earl of Tyrone. As had many before him, Essex found Irish resistance stronger than he had expected, was forced to make peace with Tyrone (against the Queen's orders), and returned to London in disgrace. (When he responded to his banishment from court by attempting a coup against the Queen, she suppressed his revolt far more successfully than he had managed to suppress that of Tyrone: Essex was beheaded in 1601.)

The English poet Edmund Spenser spent most of the last twenty years of his life in Ireland, where he had gone in 1580 to take up a position as secretary and aide to the Lord Deputy of Ireland. *A View of the Present State of Ireland*, published posthumously as well as anonymously but generally attributed to Spenser, gives a sense of the brutal force to which the English often resorted in their efforts to break Irish resistance and colonize the land: relocation of entire communities to make way for English settlers, acts of wanton destruction aimed at intimidating the population, and even the destruction of crops were common. Things did not improve in the seventeenth century. When Irish forces revolted in the early 1640s against English brutality and the expropriation of the best land for newly arrived English colonists, a considerable number of English settlers were killed. In response, Oliver Cromwell led an army into Ireland that more than matched the killing spree of the rebels, who were completely defeated by 1650. The 1652 Act of Settlement decreed that expropriations be continued until two-thirds of all Ireland was owned by Englishmen, and that the majority of the Irish population be settled in a single county. These terms were never fully enacted, but enough was done to ensure that Irish resentment of and resistance to English colonial policies would continue far into the future.

In the fifteenth and early sixteenth centuries English and Scottish forces had fought a series of battles, perhaps the most important of which was the English victory at Flodden in 1513, a slaughter that put an end to an early Scottish Renaissance. Despite such defeats Scotland remained an independent kingdom. But as the sixteenth century went on, it was more and more a kingdom with significant internal divisions. Throughout these turbulent times, much of the Highlands of Scotland remained out of the fray: it was a world largely separate from the culture of Edinburgh, but unlike Edinburgh's, a traditional and far less literate clan-based culture. In the Lowland areas (most importantly, the east-west stretch of Lowland in which both Glasgow and Edinburgh are located), English had long been the preferred language, a market economy had taken root, and after 1560 John Knox and his Scottish Presbyterian reformers had assumed a dominant position in society. At this point, as a result of royal marriages, Scotland was technically a province of France; Mary Stuart, Queen of Scotland and Queen Consort of France, had assumed the throne in Scotland and was advancing a claim to be Queen of England too. (Mary resided in France, and—somewhat confusingly for the modern student—was represented in Scotland by her mother, Mary of Guise, who acted as regent.) With French troops entering Scotland it indeed seemed that the English throne might be under threat, but with the assistance of English soldiers and English financing, Knox and the Scots Protestant faction won the day; under the terms of the 1560 Treaty of Edinburgh, French troops left Scotland and Knox's Protestants were left in effective control. Mary, Queen of Scots was allowed to hold the throne in Scotland, but only on the condition that she renounce all claims to that of England. (Mary, a Catholic and cousin to Elizabeth I, in fact never renounced that claim, and remained a thorn in Elizabeth's side until England executed Mary for treason.)

When Mary's son came to the throne as James VI of Scotland, however, and particularly when he also assumed the English throne in 1603 as James I of England, Scotland came to be more and more at peace both within itself and with its southern neighbor. Under James the process that would culminate with the Act of Union of 1707 was very much underway.

EDWARD VI, MARY I, AND ELIZABETH I

Henry VIII was succeeded in 1547 by his 10-year-old son, Edward (the third of Henry's wives, Jane Seymour, had finally provided him with a male heir). The boy's uncle, Edward Seymour, Duke of Somerset, acted as Lord Protector. Though Edward's reign was short, it was not uneventful. Edward, his uncle, and other important figures of the time (such as Thomas Cranmer, the Archbishop of Canterbury) were more Protestant than Henry VIII had been, and more influenced by John Calvin. They accelerated the move away from Catholic practices and doctrines that had begun late in Henry's reign.

Edward died in 1553, however, and the move toward Protestantism was thrown into reverse with the accession to the throne of Mary I (not to be confused with the two Marys discussed above, Mary, Queen of Scots and Mary of Guise). Mary, daughter of Henry VIII by Catherine of Aragon, had remained a Roman Catholic and in 1554 married Phillip of Spain (later to become Phillip II). Among the many controversial measures Mary put into effect were the restoration of the Catholic Mass in Latin, the banning of the newly produced Book of Common Prayer, and the reaffirmation of the authority of the Pope over the Church of England. She earned the grim nickname "Bloody Mary" when she authorized the execution of various Protestant leaders, including Thomas Cranmer at Smithfield, from 1555 to 1558. In all, some 300 men and women were burned at the stake during Mary's reign.[1]

Yet the long-term effect of Mary's rule was to strengthen English Protestantism, and English nationalism as well. The image of the martyrs burnt at Smithfield was etched in the English consciousness through the accounts in John Foxe's *Book of Martyrs* as a lasting image of the evils of Catholic rule, and when in 1558 Mary managed to lose Calais, England's last remaining possession on the continent, in an ill-judged attempt to defend some of her husband's interests on the other side of the English Channel, the loss united the country against her. She died in November of that same year; as the Elizabethan historian Raphael Holinshed put it shortly thereafter, she had neither "the favor of God, nor the hearts of her subjects, nor the love of her husband." After 25 years of religious turmoil and violence the stage was set for the religious settlement of 1559 and for the long, stable, relatively consistent, and relatively tolerant Protestant reign of Elizabeth I. The stage was set as well for the English to feel an unprecedented sense of confidence and indeed arrogance as to their place in the world; this, said Foxe in his *Book of Martyrs*, was an "elect nation."

Detail of woodcut illustration showing Thomas Cranmer being burnt at the stake, from the 1563 edition of Foxe's *Book of Martyrs*.

ELIZABETH I AND GENDER

Perhaps the best known gender-related comment of the sixteenth and early seventeenth centuries is John Knox's 1557 outburst against "this monstrous regiment of women" ("regiment" here means rule). Knox, the Scottish Protestant leader, was at odds not only with Mary, Queen of Scots, and her regent, Mary of Guise (Mary's French mother), but also with Mary I, Queen

[1] Appalling as this number is, numbers in some areas of continental Europe were far higher; somewhere in the neighborhood of 6,000 people accused of heresy were burned by Charles V in the Low Countries.

of England: all of them Catholic, all of them opposed to most of the reforms for which Knox was pressing. (Ironically, Knox was one of the very few to advocate universal education for females as well as for males.) He found the Protestant regime of Elizabeth I, who came to the English throne the next year, considerably less monstrous, but his phrase has retained currency as a memorable expression of the almost universal feeling among men in the sixteenth and seventeenth centuries that it was far more appropriate for men to rule over women than for a woman to "reign and have empire above men" (in Knox's words). To the extent that a woman was perceived by men to have intelligence or good judgment in matters of state, men tended also to think of her as manly.

Elizabeth I was a figure who both exemplified conventional notions of gender and stood as the great exception. From the moment she came to the throne in 1558 she ruled with diplomacy, but also with sure-handed authority. Against a background of the violent upheavals of Mary's reign, of many Catholics continuing to hold positions of influence (including control of the House of Lords), of militant Protestants pressing to establish a "perfect school of Christ" throughout the land and controlling the House of Commons, and against threats from abroad (particularly from the powerful Catholic monarchy in Spain), Elizabeth dextrously negotiated a religious settlement that established a stable, relatively moderate Protestant state. She negotiated compromises with Parliament that resulted in a Supremacy Bill of 1559 that established her as "Supreme Governor" of the Church of England (not "Supreme Head," a more controversial title) and reintroduced the Book of Common Prayer. In 1563 she set out the Thirty-Nine Articles, the theological foundation of the Church of England, further establishing religious uniformity. It was mandated that there were to be 9,000 parishes (in theory, enabling everyone in England to walk to church), and a hierarchy was maintained in the Church so that the world of faith continued to mirror the world of politics. The Church of England was established as a national church, and attendance was far from voluntary. By the standards of the time, however, Elizabeth was no extremist: while some "heretics" were executed, the relative religious calm of her reign is set in stark relief by comparison to the continent, where over the same period invasion, slaughter, and religious turmoil remained the norm.

Portrait of Elizabeth I, from the manuscript miscellany of Thomas Trevelyon. Trevelyon's collection includes a record of important events of each year, decorative alphabets, and embroidery patterns, as well as a variety of other portraits.

It should not be imagined that the Elizabethan Settlement satisfied everyone. Many, often called "Recusants," felt varying degrees of loyalty to Rome, a loyalty that led some to flee to the continent and others to risk their lives by committing such crimes as hiding Catholic priests or encouraging the Catholic underground press. Many others, on the other hand, felt strongly that the new Church, with its retention of the old hierarchy of bishops and lower clergy, with a liturgy still closely modeled on that of the Catholic Mass, and with many other trappings of the old Church, had been insufficiently purged of Catholic elements. In such feelings were sown the seeds of Puritanism, the movement for greater "purity" of religion that would form one side of the religious debate that reached its zenith under Oliver Cromwell during the civil wars and led some to leave England for the Americas. Under Elizabeth, though, the tenor of such opposition was as yet one of resentment rather than revolution.

If diplomacy on Elizabeth's part was essential to reach a religious settlement, a willingness to exercise power ruthlessly was sometimes necessary to maintain it. As Elizabeth repeatedly demonstrated (perhaps most dramatically in her reluctant decision to sign the death warrant of her cousin, Mary, Queen of Scots, when evidence seemed to suggest that Mary had been involved in a Catholic plot against her), she was prepared to do whatever was necessary to remain in power and maintain the peace. And when war with Spain became inevitable, she marshaled sufficient financial and military resources to enable her commanders to stave off the threat. After some wavering, she sent troops to France to help Henri IV battle his Catholic enemies and other troops to help the Netherlands in their revolt against Spain.

Yet for all her sure-handedness in exercising power, Elizabeth contrived to remain throughout her reign an icon of female virtues—although of course stressing the virginal ideal, not the maternal, as Elizabeth never married or had children. In part this was possible through a sleight-of-hand accomplished by lawyers and other advisors who, exploiting the old concept of the "king's two bodies," theorized that the Queen embodied an immortal "body politic" that was without gender and without defect, together with a "body natural" that was entirely human in character. Yet despite some grumblings over her refusal to marry and some evidence of exasperation with her tendency to delay, Elizabeth was for the most part admired, even worshipped, as both a woman and a monarch. She built up around her a glittering court and a culture of courtesy, grace, performance, and display that fostered an extraordinarily productive cultural outpouring, and that glorified (if sometimes with subtle reservations) her own person as the center around which all else revolved. Elizabeth, Edmund Spenser explained in the letter to Sir Walter Ralegh that accompanied *The Faerie Queene*, was both Belphœbe, a beautiful maiden who represented the Queen as a woman, and Gloriana, who represented the "most excellent and glorious person of our sovereign the queene and her kingdome in Faery land." Elizabeth was thus both a woman and a queen, a *virgin* queen. Much as she had ample romantic and political opportunity to marry, and much as her advisors pressed her to remember the importance of producing an heir, Elizabeth must have realized that marriage would entail a loss of power, and a loss too of the special aura that had grown up around her. For most women in English society, marriage brought a loss of power: whereas a single woman could act as a legal entity in owning property or being a party to legal agreements, all such rights passed over on marriage to the husband. Elizabeth's situation as monarch was of course different, but even for her, marriage would have brought with it an expectation of submission to male authority.

Nor was it only marriage that would have brought a diminution of authority: for Elizabeth to have openly acknowledged her sexuality in any way other than the virginal would have badly damaged her mystique.

Why did "virgin" resonate so differently in the late sixteenth and early seventeenth centuries than it does today? Some have suggested that the bifurcation in many male minds of opinions concerning woman—a bifurcation that had taken strong hold in the late-medieval period—may have deepened in the sixteenth century. Certainly that was a dichotomy with wide-ranging roots, some of which may be found in Christian traditions of ambivalence toward sex. Along with the growth in the exaltation of the Virgin Mary in the late-medieval period had grown a widespread (albeit far from universal) habit of venerating woman only if in a "pure" or asexual state. Alongside that paradigm had grown its polar opposite, one in which womanhood was associated with temptation, impure sexuality, and fleshly sin. Too often perhaps, little lay in between. Yet the issue is resistant to easy explanation; the dangers of oversimplification in this area cannot be too strongly stressed. The Reformation in general led to an increased emphasis on the virtues of marriage, and Protestant England in particular vigorously privileged marriage. Throughout the period the Church accepted the reality of sexuality for most people (to offer only one example, a marriage could be annulled if a wife refused to have sexual relations with her husband); indeed, outright rejection of the flesh would have been heretical. That said, disgust with the flesh did certainly remain widespread—and some found it easy to project upon the female objects of their lust the disgust or anxiety that their culture had encouraged them to feel not so much about woman *per se*, but about sexual desire. Such misogynistic projections, all too common in other forms around the globe, remained a staple of English culture in the late sixteenth century (and are of course not dead yet). When poets thought of "false love" as Walter Ralegh did, for example, in terms of "a gilded hook that holds a poisoned bait," many found it hard to resist locating the source of the poison in women rather than in their male speakers.[1] Seventeenth-century male writers also not infrequently sexualized religious controversy by reading the religious other as problematically female; Ben Jonson parodies such rhetoric when he has his Puritan character, Tribulation, speak of standing up "against the menstruous cloth and rag of Rome," referring to the deep red vestments worn by the clergy in the Roman Catholic Church. And, as a Contexts section in this volume details, early seventeenth-century popular pamphlets such as Joseph Swetnam's *An Arraignment of Lewd, Idol, Froward, and Unconstant Women* (1615) excited considerable controversy over their attacks on women.

What did women think of all this? The literature of the period is overwhelmingly male-authored, but a few female voices found their way into print. Aemilia Lanyer (1569–1645), for example, one of the first women in England to publish her own poems (and to have obtained patronage in the way that was conventional for male poets), put forward in her *Salve Deus Rex Judaeorum* a bold and cogent denial that Eve was chiefly to blame for the Fall of Man: "Your fault being greater," she asked, "why should you disdain our being your equals, free from tyranny?" Swetnam was also answered directly by Rachel Speght and others, and even figured in a play devoted to his discomfiture. It is probably as unwise to read the texts in this "querelle des femmes" with utter seriousness (some are riotous and hyperbolic in the way of much Renaissance satire) as it would be to dismiss the reality of the issues and the subtle thought that the (often female) defenders of women writers put into their arguments.

English Noblewomen. Detail of an engraving c. 1582 by Flemish artist Georg Hoefnagel.

In sum, expressions of misogyny in Renaissance England were not always utterly serious and were countered by other voices, both male and female—but misogyny was nevertheless a daily reality. Women, even rich and well-born women, lived with what by modern standards were severe restrictions, legally and socially, on what they could do or be. That so many middle- and upper-class women did manage to write, to learn, to influence political, religious, and cultural life is both a testament to their determination and a reminder that social status was often just as important as gender in determining what a person could or could not do.[2]

[1] It should be noted, however, that in many such instances what may look like misogyny in the work of sophisticated poets may be tempered by irony and self-mockery.

[2] The restrictions imposed upon the poor, indeed, were more severe than were gender-based restrictions.

Modern scholarship has extensively explored these issues; in recent years it has also recognized more fully the ways in which sexuality and gender are not entirely essential, but are mediated by the larger culture. For example, recent studies have explored the frequent sixteenth- and seventeenth-century assumption, derived from ancient medical theories, that women are the same as men but, so to speak, inside out and born without enough vital heat to "perfect" them into maleness. And scholars have explored a number of aspects of the history of sexual behavior during the period. It appears, for example, that although sodomy as such was illegal (and loosely defined), the laws against it were not rigorously enforced. Research suggests too that the early modern period was much less anxious than were the next several centuries about the auto-erotic. Thomas Nashe's notorious "Choice of Valentines"—also known as "Nashe's Dildo"—is an important literary example here. (Though Nashe's work was not published at the time, early modern curiosity about masturbation, particularly that by women, is also evident in other literature of the period, both in England and on the continent.)

HOMOEROTICISM AND TRANSGENDERING

Research of the past generation has also increased our appreciation of the ways in which same-sex desire is mediated by history and by culture, and our awareness of the complexity of the issues involved. In any historical or cultural context it is important to distinguish between homosexuality (the definition of which is likely to vary from era to era, even within the same culture), and a broader homoeroticism that might or might not entail physical desire or behavior—and that again is shaped by history and culture. In reading back into history it is far from easy for the modern reader always to draw such distinctions reliably.[1]

[1] For example, the late fourteenth-century expressions of love by the famous theologian Anselm of Bec (that are included in the first volume of this anthology), while making no explicit sexual references, are as fervent when addressed to men as they are when addressed to women; these expressions of love may well have been written without sexual intent, but are likely to seem to modern readers as if they were highly charged with eroticism.

That said, one of the most striking developments of English literature of the early modern period is the widespread appearance of same-sex eroticism. Not surprisingly, given the transgressive nature of such love at the time, it does so in an often conflicted or ambiguous fashion, frequently adopting as a model the conventions of male-female love. In Shakespeare's twentieth sonnet, for example—one of the sonnets that first indicates his speaker's love of another man as a central theme—the poet exploits some of the tropes of Petrarchan poetry in contrasting this love with that of "false" women:

> A woman's face with Nature's own hand painted
> Hast thou, the master-mistress of my passion;
> A woman's gentle heart, but not acquainted
> With shifting change, as is false women's fashion;
> An eye more bright than theirs, less false in rolling.

The poem is perhaps the most famous expression of ambiguity in Shakespeare's sonnets, one that both admits and denies simultaneously. The lover imagines his beloved, the "master mistress of my passion" as once a woman, although less false than women are, but remade by Nature into a man. Since, says the speaker, Nature has "added one thing [i.e., a penis] to my purpose nothing" and "pricked him out" to be male, women can have the use of his body and the speaker can have his love. At first this seems like a denial that the love in question is homosexual or even homoerotic, but as recent critics have been quick to point out, the puns on "nothing" (slang for vagina) and "prick" (slang for a penis) make the denial look far less certain.

The nature of homoeroticism in literature was not always openly acknowledged by the writers of the time even when it was openly expressed. Of some of his clearly homoerotic sonnets, for example, Richard Barnfield offered utterly implausible denials of the clear sense of his verse, saying that he had merely been trying to write like Virgil. (Imitating the classics proved to be useful in giving homoerotic verse a good cover story, so to speak; by taking as his model Virgil's second eclogue, for instance, Marlowe could make his shepherd's invitation to "Come Live with Me" less certainly addressed to a female "nymph.") But the groundbreaking literary expressions are quite real. In this as in so many other respects Shakespeare and Marlowe (in this case along with Barnfield, a much lesser poet) were pioneers; in the 1590s they are the first literary figures we know of to write openly and unequivocally homoerotic literature.[1] Marlowe imagines Neptune making a pass at the naked young Leander as he swims the Hellespont in the poem *Hero and Leander*, and in his play Edward II depicts the King's alienation from his kingdom and his wife in direct consequence of being "love sick for this minion," Lord Gaveston. (In the end Edward is reduced to a despairing hope that he may have "some nook or corner left / To frolic with" his "dearest Gaveston.") Barnfield is more explicit, whatever his odd denials in his prefatory material, about the transgressive nature of the desires being expressed: "If it be sin to love a lovely lad / Oh then sin I."

We have only minimal evidence as to whether the homoerotic expressions of feeling by any of these poets extended beyond the literary. In the case of Shakespeare, at least, we know that such expressions did not preclude marriage and children. More generally, we know that "cross-over" activity of several sorts was characteristic of the age. When Marlowe's Gaveston paints an idyllic picture of the world he desires, for example, it is one featuring "men like satyrs grazing on the lawns" but also young men resembling women:

> Sometime a lovely boy in Diane's shape,
> With hair that guilds the water as it glides,
> Crownets of pearl about his naked arms
> And in his sportful hands an olive tree,
> To hide those parts which men delight to see ...

The place of female homoeroticism, let alone lesbianism, in sixteenth-century England is largely unclear. What we call "lesbianism" was certainly recognized in the early modern period, although the vocabulary differed from our own (a woman involved with another woman was more often called a "tribade" than "lesbian" or "Sapphic"). In general such love seems to have aroused much less anxiety than did male same-sex love. It did arouse curiosity, but there remained a good deal of ignorance as to the realities of same-sex love; it seems to have been a widespread assumption, for example, that same-sex love amongst women would inevitably entail such sex aids as dildos.

Despite some vague flirtations with the topic by Spenser (a woman falls in love with his armed female knight in Book III of *The Faerie Queene*, for example) and by Shakespeare (in whose plays the matter of gender and sexuality is complicated by the fact that boy actors took the roles of women, with effects that are not entirely clear from this historical distance), female-female eroticism is much less evident in the literature of the late sixteenth and early seventeenth centuries than is its male counterpart. One of the few extant literary expressions of such feeling is an elegy by John Donne, that perhaps takes as a model some French poems, in which Sappho expresses her homoerotic longing for her friend "Philaenis." Somewhat later in the seventeenth century, however, representations of such desire begin to appear in some profusion, particularly in the visual arts. In literature the most widely discussed seventeenth-century representations of such desire, more ambiguously expressed, appear in Katherine Philips's poems to her "dearest Lucasia." Philips writes that "there's a religion in our love"; it remains uncertain whether such love is homosexual, homoerotic, or the expression of intense female bonding, a celebration of friendship that may seem more sexual to a modern eye

[1] The importance of this aspect of Shakespeare's writing has only relatively recently begun to be fully and openly acknowledged. The 1609 publication of the sonnets excited no comment that has come down to us. Though some eighteenth-century editions of Shakespeare included the sonnets, others omitted them on clearly homophobic grounds. George Stevens, for example, the editor of a multi-volume edition of Shakespeare's works published in 1793, declared that it was "impossible to read this fulsome panegyric, addressed to a male object, without an equal measure of disgust and indignation." In the nineteenth century some (such as Robert Browning) regarded Shakespeare as representing a pinnacle in the history of sonnet writing in English, but others were distressed. Henry Hallam, for example, found it "impossible not to wish that Shakespeare had never written" the sonnets. And as late as 1930 published comments continued to allude with discomfort to the poems' homoeroticism: as Herbert Thurston wrote in that year, "regretfully as we must say it, the sonnets in their plain and obvious meaning point to a plague spot." It is only relatively recently, then, that the homoeroticism of the sonnets has ceased to be regarded as a taint—and that the poems themselves have been accepted unequivocally and universally as central to the Shakespearian canon. Some in the general public, though, are still taken aback to discover that, for example, the sonnet "Let me not to the marriage of true minds admit impediment" does not refer to heterosexual marriage.

than it seemed at the time. (It is wise to remember that powerful declarations of friendship were less likely to be read as homoerotic in early modern times than they are now, whatever the actual psychodynamics involved.)

A common literary motif throughout the period is the assumption by a protagonist of a transgendered role. One of the male heroes of Sir Philip Sidney's *Arcadia*, for example, assumes a female disguise as an "Amazon" and is even identified as "she" for the greater part of that work. Shakespeare, too, imagines strong and resourceful female figures (played of course by boys) who at some point pretend to be men, such as Viola in *Twelfth Night*, Rosalind in *As You Like It*, Portia in *The Merchant of Venice*, and Helena in *All's Well That Ends Well.* Evidently such behavior existed occasionally in real life as well, although not so much among the well-born: Moll Cutpurse, the lead character of *The Roaring Girl*, a popular 1611 comedy by Thomas Dekker and Thomas Middleton, seems to have been modeled on Mary Frith, a woman notorious for (among other things) dressing as a man.

Economy and Society in the Sixteenth and Seventeenth Centuries

Economic life in Britain over this period was as paradoxical as it was two centuries later during what we now call the Industrial Revolution. Although there was nothing like the explosion of technology in the late eighteenth and nineteenth centuries, there were revolutionary changes in the economy and in industry—"industry" in the sense of how people worked, at what they worked, how much they worked, and what they received in exchange for their labor. The roots of these changes extend back into the fourteenth and fifteenth centuries. The Black Death in 1348–49 wiped out at least a third and perhaps as much as half of the population; the best guess is that the population of Britain did not recover to its pre-1348 levels until the seventeenth century. That catastrophic drop in population led to a surplus of grain (or, to be more precise, a surplus in grain-growing capacity) in the rural areas, and to a labor shortage in the towns as well as on the land. Inevitably, many young people were lured to the towns by the prospect of work in one or another of a variety of trades, and despite the best efforts of the authorities, real wages for such work increased significantly through the later Middle Ages. Whereas in the mid-fourteenth century the economy of England had still been overwhelmingly agricultural, with most rents paid "in kind" (in the form of grain or other agricultural goods) rather than in money, by the end of the sixteenth century approximately half the English population relied entirely on money wages.

But if some were lured to the towns, others were driven there by a process usually referred to as "enclosure." Under the feudal system, those who worked the land did not own it. As large land holders decided that their fields could be put to use more profitably as grazing land for cattle or, especially, sheep, those lands that had typically been without hedges, fences, or other means of enclosure, and farmed on a largely communal basis by the peasant tenantry, were enclosed, thereby depriving many of their livelihood.[1] John Rous, chaplain to the Earl of Warwick in the late fifteenth and early sixteenth centuries, described what happened in such circumstances with chilling concision: "all the inhabitants were expelled." To Rous, the plagues of former times were now being succeeded by a "plague of avarice," and he was far from alone in his outrage; indeed, enclosure was condemned by a chorus of voices in the fifteenth and early sixteenth centuries. When a character in More's *Utopia* says that nowadays sheep eat men, he captures in one comic and yet horrifying expression the full effect of enclosures. The pace of enclosures in fact slowed considerably in the first half of the sixteenth century (with the exception of a period following the dissolution of the monasteries and the distribution by Henry VIII of many of their lands to his allies among the gentry and nobility). But the growth in population now meant that there was often a surplus of labor in the towns. Real wages for the majority were in decline through most of the sixteenth century, reaching their nadir in the late sixteenth and early seventeenth centuries.

[1] Economic matters were of course the primary issues of concern here, but they were not the only ones: in 1514, for example, London apprentices protested the enclosure of open fields outside the city, which they had traditionally used for sports and games, by tearing up the newly planted hedges.

Claes Jansz Visscher, detail from a panoramic view of London (1616). "The Bear Garden" and "The Globe" are both identified on the south bank of the Thames.

The practice of enclosure was particularly common in the south of England; a large proportion of the wool from sheep raised on the enclosed pastureland was exported to Flanders and in particular to Antwerp, center of the cloth industry. By the early sixteenth century the English economy had become to a large degree based on the trade of raw materials—lead, iron, tin, and coal as well as wool and livestock. That pattern now began to change, with considerable growth, particularly in the textile industry. (Many weavers from Flanders had immigrated to England in pursuit of cheaper wool.) Many finished goods were still imported, but towns in both England and Scotland were diversifying and acquiring new economic capabilities. This tendency toward specialization and division of labor often involved entire towns as well as individuals. Thus Newcastle was known for coal production, Coventry and Norwich for textile production, Northampton for leather goods, Glasgow and Perth for various sorts of manufacturing, and Edinburgh for silverware and jewelery. By far the greatest diversification (and the greatest growth) occurred in London, which grew from a population of about 50,000 in 1500, to about 100,000 in 1570, to about 200,000 in 1600, and to 500,000 in 1650, becoming what was probably the largest city in the world.[1] Such growth was a mixed blessing. Despite the "bill of sewers" put forward under the auspices of Thomas More and passed by Parliament in 1531, sanitation could not keep up with population growth, and much of London had a foul smell most of the time. It also became a city largely blackened by soot; the introduction of chimneys in the mid-sixteenth century enabled households and businesses alike to switch from wood fires to coal—a more efficient heat source, but also more polluting.

By comparison, other urban centers, despite their growth, were tiny. In the late sixteenth century Norwich had a population of approximately 13,000; Edinburgh, Dublin, Bristol, and Newcastle each had approximately 10,000; and Glasgow, Exeter, York, Coventry, and Limerick all had about 5,000. The population of England as a whole seems to have risen from something over 2,000,000 in the early sixteenth century, to about 4,000,000 by 1600, to over 5,000,000 in the mid-seventeenth century. Over the same period, the population of Scotland rose from about 600,000 to perhaps 900,000 by 1600; that of Wales went from just under 250,000 to over 400,000; and that of Ireland from around 1,000,000 to around 1,500,000. In England the percentage of the population living in urban areas thus increased from something like 5 per cent in 1500 to between 10 and 15 per cent in the mid-seventeenth century.

This 1762 watercolor by Richard Greene, one of the earliest representations of the house in Stratford-Upon-Avon where Shakespeare was born, provides a clear image of the half-timbered style of sixteenth- and seventeenth-century urban architecture in England.

For city dwellers, even more than for rural folk, life was a perilous business. Roughly half of all those born did not reach adulthood. If one were lucky enough to get through one's teens, one might expect to live until "old age"—but "old age" was typically regarded as beginning at 50. Overall life expectancy with infant mortality taken into account was about 30. As a result of poor sanitation, mortality rates—particularly for infants—were higher in London. And so too was the risk of violence; though the level of violent crime has sometimes been exaggerated, its threat was a real presence, particularly during periods when the population had been swollen even more than usual by impoverished new arrivals, or when a larger than normal number of unemployed apprentices were roaming the streets.

[1] The populations of London and of England as a whole were of course still modest by modern standards, and it is unsurprising that so many of the leading figures of the day were acquainted with one another.

If a shift of people, of economic activity, and of wealth to the cities was one trend throughout the sixteenth and seventeenth centuries, a similar shift from the north to the south of England was another. The Wars of the Roses in the fifteenth century had drained the resources of a substantial proportion of the nobility of northern and western England, and the dissolution of the monasteries (which had been widely distributed throughout the realm) in the 1530s further depleted concentrations of wealth in the North and the Midlands. The southern concentration of the wool and textile industries then had the effect of increasing the shift of wealth from north to south. The merchant traders of Kingston upon Hull voiced a complaint of a sort common throughout the north when they blamed London for the decline of their own business:

> Item, by means of the said companies (the government whereof is ruled only in the city of London) all the whole trade of merchandise is in a manner brought to the city of London; whereby all the wealthy chapmen and the best clothiers are drawn to London, and other ports have in a manner no traffic, but falleth to a great decay, the smart where we feel in our port of Kingston upon Hull.

There was likewise a disparity between social and economic developments in England and those in Scotland, Wales, and Ireland. In the Lowlands of Scotland (and in particular the towns of Edinburgh, Glasgow, and Perth) the pattern of development was not dissimilar to that of southern England, but in the Scottish Highlands small-scale agriculture continued to be the dominant mode of production, and the families of the nobility were often consumed in blood feuds. In Ireland there was a similar dichotomy, with economic growth and diversification in towns such as Cork, Waterford, and Limerick as well as in Dublin (and in the Pale generally), while other areas remained virtually untouched by economic change.

Much as the lot of the dispossessed and of wage laborers was often desperately unhappy, the economic turmoil of the sixteenth and early seventeenth centuries also brought to many others a level of prosperity that by the mid-seventeenth century was unprecedented; per capita, Britain in 1650 was the wealthiest nation in the world. How to explain this extraordinary economic growth? Part of the answer, some have argued, is Protestantism. At the heart of Calvinist belief in predestination and the "community of the elect" lies a widely noted paradox: for all of Luther's and especially Calvin's emphasis on the inherent sinfulness of humanity, the doctrines of predestination and of salvation through faith alone can in practice encourage self-confidence and a focus on the pursuit of prosperity. Not surprisingly, most people preferred to see themselves as elect and, despite warnings of Calvin and others, to read prosperity as a sign of God's approval. As the sociologist Max Weber put it a century ago in his famous analysis of this effect, *The Protestant Ethic and the Spirit of Capitalism*, Calvinist theology "in practice means God helps those who help themselves." (To be sure, primarily Catholic lands such as France and Italy also witnessed an increased accumulation and manipulation of capital; one did not need to be a Calvinist to be a smart merchant or a canny investor.)

The impact of Protestantism—especially in its Calvinist and Puritan strains—on economic life was no less powerful as a result of being indirect in its operation. Protestant cultures often showed an aversion to "sloth," and while many did not share a "Puritan" disapproval of traditional sports, games, the theater, and other pastimes, the period saw a substantial reduction in leisure time. Though "vacations" in the modern sense were unknown, it had become customary by the end of the Middle Ages not only to observe Sunday as a day of rest but also to celebrate a very large number of religious holidays (many of them in honor of saints that Protestants rejected)—so much so that some economic historians have calculated that a third of the year's 365 days may for most people have been leisure time in the early sixteenth century. Such was not the case by the late seventeenth century.

A further indirect but powerful influence on economic life was the Protestant emphasis on literacy. The initial motivation here was religious; in this respect Luther and Calvin (and many later Protestants) followed the evangelical (if also humanist) hopes of scholars such as Erasmus, who had declared that he wished that "even the weakest woman should read the Gospel … and I wish that [the books of the New

Testament] were translated into all the languages so that they might be read and understood, not only by Scots and Irishmen, but also by Turks and Saracens.... I long that the husbandman should sing portions to himself as he follows the plough, that the weaver should hum them to the tune of his shuttle." But the literacy that was useful to a clearer understanding of the faith was also useful at work—for women as well as for men. Erasmus's dream of the rural husbandman who could read did not become a reality in this period; most of the rural population in the sixteenth and early seventeenth centuries remained illiterate. But in the towns there was a steady increase in the percentage of the population that could read and write. Thomas More's estimate in the 1530s that half the population could do so was probably high, but by the mid-sixteenth century almost all the aristocracy and landed gentry were literate, and by the early seventeenth century it is likely that more than half the adult population in the towns could read and write, certainly including a high percentage of merchants, shopkeepers, and their wives, who would often assist with bookkeeping. (Significantly, it was through merchant subsidy that the first municipal libraries in England were started, early in the seventeenth century.)

Religious change may have helped to create a climate conducive to economic transformation, but on its own it could neither create nor maintain the actual engines of capitalism. The sixteenth and seventeenth centuries in England saw these engines—at once exhilarating and appalling in the ferocity of their operation—being forged. At the most fundamental level, capitalism is a series of means of transferring financial resources from those unable or unwilling to use it productively to those who can exploit such resources to create a financial return. Until well into the sixteenth century, the wealthy (like the monarch) tended to store whatever wealth they were not planning to spend in the form of gold in the Tower of London. An important exception was the large stock of gold and silver valuables in the possession of the monasteries. The dissolution of the monasteries in the 1530s—and the distribution of their wealth to various of the nobility and the gentry—substantially increased the available supply of gold and silver, and with it demand for goldsmiths and silversmiths to fashion or refashion precious metal into a variety of forms. Sometime in the early seventeenth century many goldsmiths began as a service to offer to keep supplies of gold in whatever form in their vaults. They soon realized that only a very small percentage of the amounts they were holding for safe keeping would be removed by the owners over the course of any given period; with that in mind they began to lend out the "unused" gold themselves (or, as time went by, use promissory notes in lieu of the gold itself). The precedent for this sort of activity had been set on the continent: the first public bank is thought to have been founded in Venice in 1587, and the Bank of Amsterdam was founded in 1609. The development of banking in England was accelerated by the actions of Charles I in the 1630s. Adamantly refusing to summon Parliament, Charles was thus unable to raise funds to carry on the activities of the government (or of warfare) through what was by then the usual means, by passage of an Act of Parliament. One means to which he resorted in his desperation was simply to appropriate for the Crown gold belonging to others that had been stored in the Tower of London. Not surprisingly, the practice of keeping one's gold in the Tower became much less common thereafter, and the amounts stored with the goldsmiths of London (and thus available to be loaned out) greatly increased. Though the Bank of England itself would not be founded until 1694, in practice something resembling modern banking had by then been present in England for close to a century. Ben Jonson's *Volpone* (1607), set in Venice but informed very largely by the economic realities of the time in England, gives some sense of the workings of the English economic world, or at least of how they could be satirically imagined, and of the importance of credit to their operation. Early in the play Volpone declares that he rejects the "common way" of earning a living:

> ... I use no trade, no venture;
> I ruin no earth with plowshares, Fat no beasts
> To feed the shambles [slaughterhouse]; have no
> mills for iron,
> Oil, corn, or men, to grind them into powder;
> I blow no subtle glass, expose no ships

> To threat'nings of the furrow-faced sea;
> I turn no monies in the public bank,
> Nor usure private....

That "usure private" was a well-known practice in the early seventeenth century is evident from a variety of literary sources. In *The Warring Girl*, for example, Sir Davy Dapper is described as "damned a usurer as ever was among Jews: if he were sure his father's skin would yield him any money, he would, when he dies, flea it off, and sell it to cover drums for children at Bartholomew Fair." Almost always spoken of in derogatory terms, and almost always associated with Jews,[1] money-lending was nevertheless becoming a more and more common practice throughout Christian society—and was thereby facilitating the very substantial economic growth of the seventeenth century.

Economic transformation brought with it massive change to England's class structure, if not always in legal definition then in social reality (to be a gentleman with a right to bear a coat of arms was a legal matter, and only the Crown could create a nobleman no matter what a person's fortune or fame). Much as the physical mobility of the labor force was wrenching and economically unfulfilling for many, for a considerable number of others the turmoil opened possibilities for real if usually limited social mobility. A 1508 legal document gives something of the flavor of what was possible, describing one Thomas Spring of the town of Lavenham in Suffolk as "cloth worker alias yeoman alias gentleman alias merchant." Spring had been accepted into the gentry (with the rank of Esquire) by the time he died, and his son was knighted. Perhaps the fullest literary expression in the late sixteenth century of such aspirations is to be found in the prose fiction of Thomas Deloney. Unlike most of the prose fiction writers from early in the century, Deloney had the benefit neither of a privileged background nor a university education; he was a silk weaver from Norwich who became well-known in the early 1590s as a writer of ballads. Between 1596 and 1600 he produced four short works of prose fiction, all of which were extraordinarily popular. Deloney referred to aristocrats as "idle butterflies" and, whereas the norm for aspiring writers was to dedicate works to prominent members of the nobility in the hope of obtaining patronage from them, Deloney dedicated *Jack of Newbury* "to all famous cloth workers in England":

> Among all manual arts used in this land, none is more famous for desert or more beneficial to the commonwealth than is the most necessary art of clothing; and therefore as the benefit thereof is great, so are the professors of the same to be both loved and maintained.
>
> [... This] excellent commodity ... half being and yet is the nourishing of many thousands of poor people. Wherefore to you, most worthy clothiers, do I dedicate this my rude work, which hath raised out of the dust of forgetfulness a most famous and worthy man, whose name was John Winchcomb, alias Jack of Newbury, of whose life and love I have briefly written, and in a plain and humble manner that it may be the better understood of those for whose sake I take pains to compile it. That is, for the well minded clothiers, that herein they may behold the great worship and credit which men of this trade have in former time come unto.

As the dedication suggests, Deloney challenges both literary convention and the significance of social class not by emphasizing the degree to which a wage worker is downtrodden, but by imagining the possibility that he may rise to become like Jack of Newbury who, although no gentleman born (or even a gentleman made), nevertheless "set continually 500 poor people at work to the great benefit of the commonwealth" through his success as a clothier, and who "had the choice of many wives—men's daughters of good credit and widows of great wealth." To his credit, Newbury chooses none of those but rather "one of his own

[1] Both during the Middle Ages before the expulsion of the Jews under Edward I, and after Cromwell's decision to re-admit them to England, Jews were barred from seeking employment in most occupations (and from all professions considered respectable); one of the few trades a Jew could legally pursue was that of money-lender.

¶ A briefe content of certaine clauses

of the Statutes of King Henrie the eyght, and Queene Marie,

with some moderation thereof, and other prouisions to be obserued, according to her Maiesties Proclamation aboue mentioned.

Mens apparell.

None shal weare in his apparell

- Sylke of the colour Purple, cloth of Golde, or Siluer Tissued, nor Furre of Sables. — Under the degree of an Earle.
- Cloth of Golde, Siluer, or Tinsell Satten. Sylke, Cloth, Canuas, or any stuffe in any apparell, that shalbe myxed or imbrodered with any Gold or Siluer. — Under the degrée of a Baron.
- Woollen clothe made out of the Realme, sauing in Cappes only. Ueluet: Crymson, Carnation, or Blewe. Scarlet cloth. Furres of: Blacke Jenets, or Lusernes. Imbroderie, or Taylers worke, hauing Golde, or Siluer, or Pearle therin. Nor any Enamell, Muske, Ambergrece, Agate, or any other pretious Stone, in Chayne, Button, or Aglet. Nor any Dublet, Jerkin, or other apparel of any stuffe perfumed. — Under the degree of: A Knight of the order, one of the priuie Counsel, or a Gentleman of the priuie Chamber.
- Gownes, Clokes, Capes, or other vppermost garments — of Uelvet. Furres of Libardes. Imbroderie, or Taylers worke like to imbroderie, with Sylke, Bugle, or any other like thing. Nor any Cappes, Hats, Hatbandes, Capbands, Garters, Bootehose, trymmed with — Golde or Syluer. Or Sylke neather Stockes. Shertes, Shertbandes: garnished, mixte, or wrought with Golde. Ruffes made or wrought out of Englande, commonly called Cutworke. — Under the degree of: A Barons sonne, a knight, & Gentleman in ordinarie office, attending vpon her Maiesties person, or persons that are assessed in the last subsidy books at. CC. li. lands, or fees.

None shal weare

- Spurres, Swordes, Rapiers, Skaynes, Woodknyues, or Hangers, Buckles of Gyrdles.
  - Damasked, — vnder the degree of: A Knight of the order. One of the priuie Counsell. A Gentleman of the priuie chamber.
  - Guylte, — vnder the degree of a Knight.
  - Syluered, — vnder the degrees and persons before mentioned.

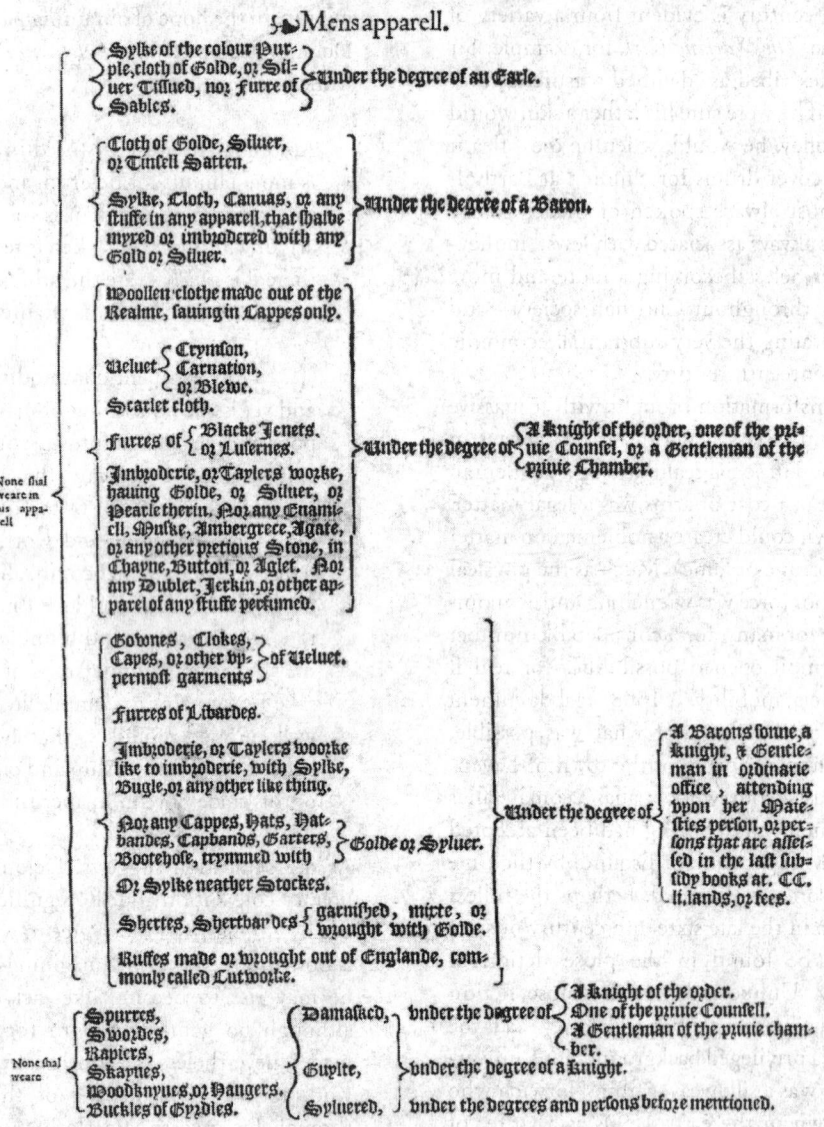

From a proclamation by Elizabeth I concerning apparel, 12 February 1580. For each rank separate restrictions on apparel are given, specifying who is allowed to wear particular colors or forms of decorative clothing ("furre of sables," material "imbroidered with any Gold or Silver," "Ruffes made or wrought out of England," etc.).

servants, … knowing her careful in her business, faithful in her dealing and an excellent good housewife." It is telling from a number of angles that *Jack of Newbury* continued to be enormously popular throughout the seventeenth century.

Much of the social fluidity and economic and social mobility that developed through the sixteenth and early seventeenth centuries came despite efforts by the government to control it. The 1563 statutes of artificers (i.e., concerning apprentices) declared the obligation of everyone to "toil" and declared as well the importance of "degree, priority, and place" as part of the natural order laid down by God. Through the second half of the sixteenth and the first half of the seventeenth centuries, however, it no longer seemed natural that dedication to work would act to support the existing system of "degree, priority, and place."

If the aspiring middle class threatened the old social order, so, too, did the increasing number of landless poor. In the face of the substantial increase in "vagrants and beggars" in the towns in the fifteenth and early sixteenth centuries, authorities began to license beggars and to accept some formal responsibility for the poorest members of society. The culmination of this process came in the 1590s, a decade of extraordinary literary achievement, one that saw some of Shakespeare's greatest plays and his sonnets, the plays and poetry of Marlowe, the early plays of Ben Jonson, much of the secular poetry of John Donne, Spenser's *The Faerie Queene*, and the printing of Philip Sidney's *Arcadia*, *Astrophil and Stella*, and *The Defence of Poesy*. It was also a decade in which the court of Elizabeth I reached its glittering zenith and in which England, fresh from its defeat of the Spanish Armada in 1588, experienced the early stages of its growth into a world power. Elizabeth herself was, wrote John Davies in 1596, "our glorious English court's divine image, / As it should be in this our Golden Age." But this decade was also one of the most economically depressed in English history, with poor harvests causing increased prices and further depressing already-low wages for many of the poor; by one calculation living costs in the late 1590s were in the range of five times as high as they had been at the start of the century, and real wages in 1597 less than a third of what they had been a century earlier. Nor were matters helped by the recurrent visitations of plague, by underemployment souring the temper of some university graduates, and by widespread anger among the well-to-do at Elizabeth's seemingly unfair allotment of economic monopolies. In 1598 the Poor Law Act set out provisions for collecting and distributing a "poor rate" to individual parishes so as to alleviate the worst of the suffering, but improvements in the lot of the poor were at best very gradual over the succeeding decades.

To a considerable degree poverty was structural, relating not only to the substantial degree of control exercised by the authorities over wages and prices, but also to the system of apprenticeship. Unlike modern apprentices, apprentices in the guild system as it had grown up through the later Middle Ages and the sixteenth century were not free to leave the work into which their parents had bound them (typically, by paying a fee of several pounds). They were obligated to serve a master for at least seven years and sometimes many more, in exchange for which they received training and very basic room and board, but no payment beyond that. In 1595 apprentices in London rebelled, with crowds taking large quantities of the food they could not afford to buy and destroying the Cheapside Pillories at which many of them had previously been punished for petty offences.

From about 1600 onwards, however, the old apprenticeship system—and indeed the guild system generally—began to go into decline. The newer (and usually faster-growing) trades tended to be established outside the city boundaries and outside the control of the guilds; apprentices, who made up approximately 15 per cent of the London population in 1600, made up no more than 5 per cent of its much larger population a century later. Apprentices still made their presence felt through much of the seventeenth century (most notably in the turmoil of the 1640s), but by century's end were no longer a significant force; the age of wage labor for all, however young, was by then well underway.

The spread of forward-looking thought was both a cause and a consequence of the economic dynamism of the seventeenth century. Despite the persistence of old prejudices against moneylending and against Jews (witness Shakespeare's Shylock in *The Merchant of Venice* or Marlowe's more satirically imagined Barabas in *The Jew of Malta*), both the lending of money outright and the extension of credit increased fairly steadily through this period, thereby greatly facilitating the expansion of trade and of industry. This expansion of moneylending and credit, it should perhaps be noted, came almost entirely within mainstream Christian society. (Jews had been expelled from England by Edward I in the late thirteenth century, but small numbers returned in the sixteenth and early seventeenth centuries, and in the mid-seventeenth century they were given official sanction to live in England, albeit without all of the rights and privileges enjoyed by Christians.) More and more, habits of thinking into the future were based on calculations of probability rather than on expressions of hope or fear or prophecy. An important indicator of this change was the development in the mid-sixteenth century of insurance. Not until the late seventeenth century, however, were future probabilities calculated for the purpose of insurance in anything like the way they are today; initially, insurance on ships and their cargos (the earliest form of insurance in England) would never be contemplated until a ship was already overdue. Premiums would then be set according to how long overdue the ship was, how dangerous the route was considered to be, and so on.

Although economic change together with higher levels of education and literacy encouraged the spread of rationalist thought, belief in magic and the supernatural barely diminished and in some areas increased (as evidenced, for example, by the proliferation in the seventeenth century of texts on alchemy and astrology). Rationalism and a reliance on supernatural explanations coexisted within most individual minds as well as within society at large. Elizabeth I turned to John Dee for astrological advice, and when the alchemist Cornelius Lannoy could not deliver on his promise to create gold, she made him suffer for his failure. The intellectually lively James I was the author of a treatise on witches (and responsible as well for executing considerable numbers of women alleged to be witches in Scotland). Most people still interpreted unusual occurrences in the heavens as does Gloucester in Shakespeare's *King Lear*: "these late eclipses in the sun and moon portend no good to us." Modern audiences may find it difficult to take seriously the predictions of the witches in Shakespeare's *Macbeth* or the doctor's faith in "demonstrations magical" in Marlowe's *Doctor Faustus*; the skepticism found in Jonson's *The Alchemist* and the disbelieving scoffs that enliven Reginald Scot's *Discoverie of Witchcraft* are more in line with modern sensibilities. But most late sixteenth- and early seventeenth-century people saw such things differently. Indeed, the power to draw simultaneously on rationalist ways of connecting cause and effect *and* on traditional supernatural thought is one reason for the remarkable resonance of much Renaissance drama.

"THE ROUND EARTH'S IMAGINED CORNERS"

Recent scholarship has done much to broaden and to destabilize older notions of Britain and her place in the world. Until the late twentieth century, most accounts of the Renaissance and seventeenth century in England were Anglocentric and, whatever the personal convictions of the historian, apt to ignore English Catholicism and to read the English Reformation as a narrative of obvious progress. Such a perspective, moreover, often accompanied a certain triumphalism in which English history—political, economic, or cultural—was a story of steady movement from one high point to another as the influence of various triumphs radiated outward from their London epicenter. It is now more often recognized that England was then—and as part of the United Kingdom is still—a historical and geographical point connected to a myriad of other points around the globe. At the beginning of the period covered by this volume, England was a small, modestly significant nation on the edge of Europe; by its end, England was Great Britain and a significant world power. But scholars increasingly connect this rise to developments in other countries as much as to developments within Britain itself: in terms of religious, economic, political, and intellectual as well as literary and cultural history, changes in early modern Britain interacted with those in Italy, Holland, France, Germany, and Spain. In addition, as is shown more fully in the "Cultural Encounters" section in this volume, Britain during this period began more significantly to interact with the world beyond Europe.

Throughout this period, the government regulated international trade and settlement with the same care as it regulated wages, prices, or religion. It was often only with the blessing or even sponsorship of the Crown that the great sea voyages of the late sixteenth and early seventeenth centuries could take place, whatever the disappointment on the part of some would-be colonizers with sometimes less than enthusiastic royal support for their overseas projects. Despite the moral qualms Elizabeth is reported to have expressed regarding John Hawkins's pioneering ventures in the slave trade beginning in the 1560s, she became an investor in his ventures. For the most part she supported Sir Walter Ralegh's famous voyages of exploration and sometimes of colonization to Virginia, the West Indies, and South America. She also supported the voyages of plunder carried out against the Spaniards by Sir Francis Drake and others and knighted Drake when he returned to England after voyaging around the world from 1577 to 1580. Unlike the Spanish, English adventurers did not manage to claim any colonies rich with gold. But their failure in this respect was surely a blessing in disguise: Spain's preoccupation with adding to its hoard of precious metals almost certainly contributed to the eventual stagnation of its economy and society.

In the seventeenth century, British arrangements for worldwide trade began to be formalized, largely through the creation of state-sanctioned monopolies. The East India Company was granted its charter in 1600, the Hudson's Bay Company in 1670, and the Royal African Company in 1672; these corporations were to play a vital role not only in establishing trade but also in colonizing India and most of the northwest of North America. Arguably, though, the voyage in this period with the greatest impact on world history was one launched in reaction to the religious policies of the Crown—that of the 102 Protestant sectaries (the "Pilgrims") who, despairing at their religious and political prospects in Jacobean England, left first for the religiously tolerant Netherlands and then, in 1620, set sail on the *Mayflower* for the New World, founding a colony at Plymouth, Massachusetts.

Given this developing engagement with the peoples of the New World, India, and Africa, what of attitudes toward race at this time? From passages such as the following exchange in Ben Jonson's comedy *Volpone* (1607), we may infer that black Africans were commonly regarded with as much derision as other groups against which there was strong prejudice:

> CORVINO. Has he children?
> MOSCA. Bastards,
> Some dozen or more, that he begot on beggars,
> Gypsies, and Jews, and black-moors, when he was drunk.
> Knew you not that, sir? 'Tis the common fable.

Yet we have no evidence to suggest that there was discomfort with Shakespeare's portrayal of the "black-moor" Othello as a tragic hero. (In the eighteenth and nineteenth centuries there was a considerable reaction against any suggestion that such a hero could be black, but we have no record of such a response in the early seventeenth century.) We have noted that Elizabeth invested in John Hawkins's slaving voyages, but she also is said to have described such activity as "detestable" and prophesied it would prompt the "vengeance of Heaven" upon those who participated in it. The problem of determining early modern racial attitudes in Britain is further complicated by shifts in the meaning of the word "race" and the use of the word "black" to mean what we would call "brunette" or "dark." In any case, there was to many minds something of the exotic about almost any dark skin: Henry VIII, Elizabeth I, and James I all included a few African servants in their entourages, and a good portion of the nobility seems to have followed their lead in the late sixteenth century. There can be no question, though, that racial prejudice existed during this period even if evolving in its nature and assumptions. In some cases distinctions appear to have been made based on gradations of color. Some, for example, distinguished "black-moor" from the "white-moor," or drew a tripartite division of black-moor, tawny-moor, and white-moor. Others, however, seem to have used "moor" as synonymous with "black-moor" and, indeed, to have seen all dark skins in very much the same light. Even the native peoples of North America are sometimes described as "black creatures."

THE STUARTS AND THE CIVIL WARS

Elizabeth's decision to remain unmarried helped her negotiate delicate political and religious balances through out her reign. But her lack of a direct heir meant that at her death in 1603 the crown passed to her distant cousin, James VI of Scotland, now also James I of England, son of the executed Mary, Queen of Scots. Elizabeth was the last of the Tudors, the royal family that had ruled England since 1485. James was a Stuart, the royal family that would rule through direct succession until the early eighteenth century, and whose descendants wear the English crown today. The accession of James united the crowns of England and Scotland. With Wales already annexed officially to England under Henry VIII, this union with Scotland was widely celebrated as the revival of the ancient, undivided island realm of Britain (though the country did not officially become "Great Britain" until 1707). The shift from England to Britain marked a new phase of the English Renaissance in the early seventeenth century. But this "British factor" also introduced a new set of political, religious, and social tensions that would in a few decades help tear the country apart in civil wars, wars that would eventually usher in the changed political and cultural world of the Restoration and eighteenth century.

James came to the English throne an experienced king: monarch of Scotland in name from the age of one, he had been educated for the role since childhood and had in his own right successfully ruled his fractious northern kingdom since the mid-1580s. His ascent to the throne was in consequence widely welcomed. While the later 1590s had been a period of astonishing cultural accomplishment in England, these years had also been marked by deep frustration with an aging queen increasingly reluctant to make decisions: most members of the English political class looked optimistically to James for a renewal of energy and action. James, however, would not always live up to these expectations. To begin with, any change in monarchs meant a change in the respective political fortunes of the ruling elite. One observer of the London court commented dryly that as soon as James was named King, would-be courtiers began to race north toward Edinburgh, "as if it were nothing else but first come first served, or that preferment were a goal to be got by footmanship." Some members of the Elizabethan court would keep their positions: Robert Cecil, Secretary of State from 1596, continued to hold the same office under James. Some individuals (like Sir Francis Bacon) and families who had not thrived politically under Elizabeth found great success under James. Others saw their power decline or disappear into the hands of Scottish favorites who happily left their estates in impoverished Scotland and descended hungrily on London. James generously shared his good fortune. While the parsimonious Elizabeth had been served by 18 "gentlemen of the privy chamber," James provided for 48, and appointed as well 200 "gentlemen extraordinary." Many had little to offer the country except charm and beauty, good legs and skilled dancing—qualities that could take a courtier far in the Jacobean court. As funds started to dwindle, new money-making schemes flourished, with James in effect selling aristocratic titles (including a new one, the baronetcy) by the score, and knighthoods by the hundreds. The figure of the newly jumped-up knight or minor aristocrat soon appeared as a satirical target on the London stage.

Religious reformers—Presbyterians and Separatists, collectively known as "Puritans" despite their widely differing ideas about church government—were another disappointed constituency. The Scottish Reformation of 1560 had been a Presbyterian Reformation, producing a church government that, officially at least, did not recognize the authority of bishops. While the Scottish episcopate never quite disappeared, its existence from 1560 to about 1610 was always precarious. English Presbyterians consequently hoped that James, up to that point the monarch of a "reformed" national church, would move the Church of England in a more strongly Protestant direction. But when they petitioned James in 1604, he flatly rejected their request for a church with an egalitarian structure along the lines of the Presbyterian kirk. "No bishop, no king," he replied, voicing the analogical thinking so characteristic of the period: a challenge to hierarchy in the religious sphere threatened the idea of political hierarchy. Within a few decades, he would be proved right: Scottish revolutionaries in the late 1630s and English revolutionaries in the

1640s both abolished episcopacy as soon as they had the power to do so, as a prelude to their attacks on the authority of the Crown.

James did agree to sponsor a new translation of the Bible, in a project that is probably one of the very few masterpieces ever produced by committee. The King James (or "Authorized") version of 1611 for the most part retained the language of Tyndale's version from the 1530s, but in terms of religious politics it represented an important step forward: it was the product of years of collective negotiation over controversial phrases. This translation would shape literary language for centuries

Though the proportion of Catholics in early seventeenth-century Britain is thought to have been low, some Catholics still hoped for an overthrow of Protestant rule and a re-establishing of the Roman Catholic Church. In 1605 extremist Catholics, among them one Guy Fawkes, were reported to have been discovered to be plotting acts of terrorism; bombs, officials claimed, had been discovered beneath the House of Lords. Though James at first noted that not "all professing the Romish religion were guilty of the same," he soon made clear that he had no more tolerance for Catholic dissent than he did for the Puritan variety. Many priests suspected of Catholic leanings were stripped of their posts and/or imprisoned. As for Guy Fawkes, James authorized his torture (he confessed after two days on the rack) and his subsequent execution. To this day November 5, the anniversary of the discovery of the Gunpowder Plot, is celebrated with bonfires and merrymaking through much of England. Some scholars claim that evidence for this conspiracy was exaggerated, perhaps even planted, by officials who sought to fan the flames of anti-Catholic sentiment.

to follow, and retain (with some revisions) its primacy in the Church of England through to the second half of the twentieth century. But James did not succeed in mollifying the more extreme Puritans, and indeed had no intention of trying to do so. Within a few years, some Separatists (later called Independents or Congregationalists, in that they denied the legitimacy of any state church) left for the toleration of Amsterdam and Leiden, and in 1620 sailed to the New World to found their colony in Massachusetts. But on the whole the English church was less divided and contentious under James than under Elizabeth, and scholars refer to a broad "Calvinist consensus" in his reign. It was probably not until the 1630s that debates between "Anglican" and "Puritan" once again became a central component of national debates about the powers of church and state.

James's relationship with his House of Commons was complex, and scholars continue to disagree over how to characterize the politics of his reign. In principle, James was an absolutist, and his reign saw the popularization in England of theories of "divine right" monarchy. But in practice, James was a canny negotiator, and seemed to have good instincts for when to push his theoretical claims for absolute power and when to make concessions (see his 1610 speech to Parliament included in this anthology). Some scholars read this period as marking the beginnings of parliamentary and democratic rebellion that would lead to civil war; others argue that James was on the whole a politically successful monarch, and that the real political challenges developed in reaction to the far less flexible absolutism of his son, Charles I. Certainly, many members of Parliament and the population were exasperated by James's financial extravagances. But they were also exasperated by his refusal to incur the further expense of intervening in the religious wars that devastated Europe after 1618—a decision many saw as particularly irresponsible since James's own daughter, Elizabeth, was Queen of Bohemia and had been compelled to abandon her throne when Bohemia was invaded by a Catholic army. But whatever his motives, James, much like Elizabeth, managed largely to keep Britain out of wars during a period in which warfare consumed Europe. As far as internal politics are concerned, James kept the affairs of his English and Scottish kingdoms quite separate: he had originally favored union between England and Scotland but came to accept that this would be impracticable. But he perhaps sowed the seeds of future trouble by his attempts to impose rule on Scotland from afar, and by encouraging mass emigration by English and particularly by Scots (later called the "Scots-Irish") to Ireland, where he authorized them to dispossess local inhabitants of their lands.

With the death of James and the accession of his son Charles I in 1625, cracks began to appear in the political and religious consensus that James had managed to maintain. Charles's court was far more refined than that of his father, and was artistically brilliant: Charles amassed one of the greatest art collections in Europe. But he lacked his father's willingness to compromise. What Charles looked for in his advisors and his people was primarily obedience, and he believed more firmly than his father in the divine right of kings. When Parliament challenged royal prerogatives with the "Petition of Right" (1628), a declaration of the "rights and liberties of the subject," Charles eventually assented—but within a year he in effect shut down Parliament and ruled without it for the next decade. Since Parliament traditionally voted the funds that supported the monarchy, throughout the 1630s Charles was compelled to rely on increasingly resented alternative means of raising money, such as legally dubious taxes. When he was forced by an invading Scottish army to recall Parliament in 1640, he found himself facing a body interested in little but confronting him with the grievances that had accumulated in the previous decade.

Religious reformers who remained discontented with the Elizabethan Settlement and James's "Calvinist consensus" were outraged—and radicalized—by changes in the Church under Charles and William Laud, named Archbishop of Canterbury in 1633. Many were suspicious (possibly legitimately) of Charles's own religious beliefs: his Queen, Henrietta Maria, was a French Catholic, and her personal priests were widely thought to have too much power in the court. While Laud was not looking to reimpose Catholicism on the Church of England, as his enemies maintained, he was very concerned to introduce a greater degree of ritual, ceremony, and uniformity in Church practice, and many people in England saw Laud's "High Church" innovations as at least Catholicizing. When John Milton writes that he had been prevented from entering the ministry because he was "church-outed by prelates," he was referring to the Laudian Church and its increased emphasis on obedience to hierarchy: to Milton and many others, bishops had become worldly, powerful prelates. Laud himself had been a member of the King's Privy Council since 1628, and many disapproved of this intermingling of religious and secular power.

In the summer of 1637, Charles I and Laud attempted to introduce a revised (Anglican) prayer book for use in Presbyterian Scotland. Many Scots, however, failed to see why an English desire for uniformity of worship meant that they were the ones who needed to change. The new liturgy consequently became a focus of discontent with decades of royal policy. Well-planned riots greeted readings of the new service, followed over the next two years by a chain of events often termed the Scottish Revolution. In 1638, Scots drafted the National Covenant, vowing to withstand innovations and maintain the Presbyterian cause. Charles raised an army to subdue the "Covenanters" by force, but a series of compromises and humiliations for the English culminated in the Scottish occupation of Newcastle in the summer of 1640. These "Bishops' Wars" of 1639–40, named for the perception that they were the result of Laud's Church policies, played a significant role in the buildup to the civil wars that followed.

Charles called Parliament back into session, but found himself compelled to make humiliating concessions: the Scots were not his only subjects with grievances. The King eventually agreed to hand over to Parliament the two men most closely identified with his political and religious policies: his chief advisor, Sir Thomas Wentworth, was tried and executed in 1641, and Archbishop William Laud was imprisoned in 1641 and executed four years later. A 1641 rebellion in Ireland, the third country Charles ruled, further weakened his position. The Irish who had been dispossessed in the wave of emigration begun under James rose against the Protestant usurpers, and killed considerable numbers (though not nearly as many as people in England believed at the time). When Charles asked Parliament for funds to invade Ireland, they feared he in fact planned to form an alliance with Irish Catholics, invade England, and re-establish absolute rule. Mobs of apprentices (who began to be referred to derogatively as "roundheads" in reference to their shorn heads) began to demonstrate for the overthrow of episcopacy. Debates in 1641 over the "Grand Remonstrance," a Parliamentarian manifesto, hardened divisions between those loyal to Parliament and those loyal to the King,

Anthony Van Dyck, *Charles I in Three Positions*, 1635–36. Van Dyck's painting was intended to provide an Italian sculptor with the visual information he needed to prepare a bust of the English king in absentia.

now beginning to be called "cavaliers" (originally a term for an armed horseman, but by this time a word with implications of roistering, swaggering gallantry). An attempt by Charles to arrest five members of Parliament in January 1642 backfired by uniting members of both parliamentary Houses, Lords and Commons, against the King. In the turmoil that followed, Charles fled to the north of England, Parliament began to raise its own army, and war officially broke out when Charles raised his standard at Nottingham in August 1642.

The causes of the civil wars of the 1640s continue to be one of the most heatedly debated subjects in British history. Scholars have argued that the wars were primarily about religion, and that the 1640s were a "puritan" revolution; many contemporaries certainly saw religion as a central issue in the conflict. Others see the wars as the inevitable outgrowth of political tensions between king and parliament, or of long-term social or economic factors such as a declining aristocracy or a rising middle class. Other historians point out that the conflict divided families (John Milton's younger brother, Christopher Milton, was a Royalist), a complication for broad social or economic theories. These historians have focused instead on shorter-term explanations, often the disastrous decisions made by Charles himself, or the sequence of events created by the inherent tensions of having one king ruling three quite different countries. Many scholars see some combination of ideological and circumstantial factors at work. The idea that a civil war might break out in their lifetimes, resulting in the execution of the monarch by his own subjects, would probably have been dismissed as ridiculous by most people in England even just a few years earlier. Yet somehow it happened, and over the next decade about 100,000 people died as a result of the war, with many more wounded, in a country with a population of about 5 million. When Milton describes the destruction and violence of even heavenly warfare in *Paradise Lost*, he expected that almost all his readers would have had their lives touched in some way by war.

The "first" civil war raged from 1642 to 1646, and ended with the defeat of the Royalist armies and left Parliament, dominated by Presbyterians, in charge. They were supported by the victorious New Model Army, formed in 1645, commanded by Sir Thomas Fairfax, and led in battle by a brilliant general named Oliver Cromwell. Many of the more radicalized members of the population resisted the rule of newly empowered Presbyterians, finding them to be as authoritarian as the Laudian bishops they had fought to overthrow. By 1647, the Army had managed to become the dominant power in the country, and the Army, Parliament, and King, each distrusting the other two, attempted to negotiate a political and religious settlement. More radical voices began to join the conversation, expressing ideas created by the intellectual hothouse of the previous half-decade, a period in which the most fundamental political and social certainties seemed suddenly open to debate. Groups such as the Levellers argued for universal manhood suffrage, a written constitution, freedom of worship, and equality before the law; soon enough groups such as the Diggers were arguing that property is theft. When the Leveller Colonel Thomas Rainsborough argued that "every man that is to live under a government ought first by his own consent to put himself under that government," he was articulating an idea that would have been almost unthinkable before 1640. The Levellers are widely regarded as founding voices in the development of modern democracy. But they were not allowed to speak for long: a Leveller mutiny in the Army was crushed by Cromwell, the captured king soon afterward escaped, and a "second" civil war (in effect, a series of Royalist uprisings) broke out in 1648, culminating with the recapture, trial, and execution of King Charles in January 1649 by a Parliament purged by the Army of all but its own supporters. In May 1649, England officially became a Commonwealth, though open hostilities only ended after Cromwell, now commander-in-chief, won bloody campaigns in Ireland (1649–50) and against Scottish Royalists (1650–51).

Oliver Cromwell was now the most powerful man in Britain and effectively ruler (though in theory the "Rump" Parliament held political control). But "the inglorious arts of peace" (as Andrew Marvell termed them) were not always his strength. Cromwell responded to widespread discontent with the Rump Parliament by forcibly dissolving it and replacing it with one nominated by religious congregations; this Parliament proving a failure, Cromwell gave himself the title of "Lord Protector" in late 1653 and over the next few years ruled increasingly by decree. Had he lived, Cromwell might have retained a strong grip on power for many years. While he can be described as a kind of benevolent despot, he was not a tyrant: he attempted to demilitarize the government, and he introduced a great degree of religious freedom, including the readmission of Jews to England. In 1657 he refused Parliament's offer to make him king, and he died in 1658. Oliver Cromwell continues to be an ambivalent figure in the British cultural imagination: he is both admired and condemned, and his character, his motives, and many of his actions remain surrounded by controversy.

Cromwell's regime could not survive without him: his son Richard assumed power on his father's death, and proved unable to hold the nation together. A period of chaos was finally ended with the restoration of the monarchy in 1660. Charles II was proclaimed king by a new Parliament called by General George Monck, a man who had fought for Charles I in the first civil war, but for Cromwell in Ireland, and who was commander-in-chief of the Cromwellian army in Scotland. But Monck returned to his Royalist beginnings, and marched south from Scotland and took control in London. On May 25th Charles landed at Dover, and four days later he received a tumultuous welcome in the capital. The restored monarchy, however, was a very different thing from that which had operated under Charles I. Never again would Parliament be trifled with: Britain was now a parliamentary monarchy. For a brief period following the death of Charles II in 1685 there was again a crisis of power and religion, as Charles had died with no heir and his brother, the Catholic James II, came to the throne. Anti-Catholic sentiment, however, made it impossible for James to rule long, and the bloodless "Glorious Revolution" of 1688 forced James into exile and restored Protestant rule in the person of the Dutch Protestant William of Orange and his wife Mary (daughter of James II).

Literary Genres

The course of British literature over the sixteenth and early seventeenth centuries is marked by the transformation of a number of literary genres, by the creation of others, and by massive changes in the relationships among authors, texts, and readers and audiences. This overview is intended to provide a broad outline of some of the more important changes, and some sense as well of the range of writing within the various genres. A cautionary note at the outset may be appropriate: the amount of space devoted here to individual authors should not be taken as a measure of their importance. In many cases, more attention is given here to writers not included in the anthology than to indisputably major figures. The student is thus advised to read this introduction in conjunction with the substantial headnotes devoted to individual authors, particularly the longer headnotes on such major authors as More, Spenser, Sidney, Marlowe, Shakespeare, Donne, Jonson, Bacon, Marvell, Cavendish, and Milton.

Literature in Prose, and the Development of Print Culture

Arguably the development most important to the literature of this period occurred not in the sixteenth or seventeenth centuries but in the 1450s, with the invention of moveable type and of the printing press by the German craftsman and entrepreneur Johann Gutenberg. In 1476, William Caxton became the first to print books in England, and Caxton was instrumental in the publication of a number of important works of English literature (including Malory's *Morte Darthur*) using the new technology. But in the late fifteenth and early sixteenth centuries a great deal of writing in England retained an "un-English" character. The most important prose work in this period, Sir Thomas More's *Utopia* (1516), was first printed not in England but in Flanders (where More had lived and worked for some time the previous year), and was written not in English but in Latin. In this respect at least, *Utopia* was representative: in the late fifteenth and early sixteenth centuries the majority of books were published in Latin. Even in the late fifteenth century, however, publication in English was more common than is often supposed: of the 90 books printed by Caxton between 1477 and his death in 1491, 74 were in English. And by the second half of the sixteenth century, the movement away from Latin had become much stronger. The Latin edition of *Utopia* lost currency in England upon the publication of an English translation (by Ralph Robinson) in 1551. John Foxe published an early version of his *Book of Martyrs* in Latin in 1559; from 1563 onward editions were published only in English. The market for books in Latin diminished over the course of the seventeenth century, aided by the appearance of English translations of most of the important classical and continental texts. The lone category in which a majority of works continued to be written in Latin was that of scientific writing—ironically, as a result of their authors' belief that they would be more accessible to serious readers in centuries to come if they were written in Latin rather than in English.

More's *Utopia* resonates widely as an expression of the interests of its age. Its tone, at once playful and deeply serious, parallels that of the great work of the northern Renaissance in continental Europe, Erasmus's *In Praise of Folly.* More's focus on the fundamental nature of government follows on important work by writers of the Italian Renaissance (Niccolo Machiavelli most prominently), and foreshadows the considerable attention that would be paid to this issue in England in the later sixteenth and seventeenth centuries. In addition, More's investigation of society on the level of first principles, and his imaginative curiosity about the possibilities offered by a wider world, are deeply characteristic of the Renaissance. Finally, and not least of all, *Utopia* anticipates the great growth in prose fiction that occurred later in the century.

Utopia gave its name to a new genre defined by subject matter: works presenting an imagined world in such a way as to prompt reflection upon the inadequacies and absurdities of the present world. In this period, works wholly or largely "utopian" in character include Francis Bacon's *The New Atlantis* and Margaret Cavendish's *The Description of a New World, Called the Blazing World.* In Bacon's work, European travelers discover Bensalem, an idealized community devoted to scientific pursuits and to enlarging "the bounds of Human Empire" over the natural world. In Cavendish's alternative fantasy, nature is presented in a more unstable fashion: the protagonist discovers a "Blazing World" of extraordinary light, in which the laws of space and time do not apply—a world that evidently cannot be contained by "human empire" or indeed within any system of human thought. In later eras the utopian (and "dystopian") tradition of imagined worlds extends through works such as Jonathan Swift's *Gulliver's Travels* (1726), in which four separate worlds are imagined; to William Morris's late Victorian anti-capitalist utopia, *News from Nowhere* (1872); to twentieth-century works such as Aldous Huxley's *Brave New World* (1932) and George Orwell's *1984* (1949) that project the extension of some of the most disturbing social tendencies of their day into horrific imagined futures.

While utopian fiction is defined by its subject matter, the genre of prose fiction as a whole also came into its own in sixteenth-century British literature: a wide variety of prose fiction in English had appeared by the end of the century, aimed at the increasingly wide variety of audiences that the printing press had made possible. At one end of the spectrum are writers who consciously appealed to a popular audience—writers such as Thomas Deloney, whose commoner protagonists and dedication to "all famous cloth workers in England" have already been touched on. Another writer who appealed to a broad public in some of his work was Thomas Nashe, whose *The Unfortunate Traveler* is a work of prose fiction that has proven almost impossible to classify. At once an exuberant satire of the literary and court conventions of the time, it has also been variously termed a tragicomedy, a picaresque novel, a pioneering work of travel literature, and a celebration of violence. It is also a work alive with the possibilities and tensions of the new print culture. The tensions between the old court culture and a nascent culture of broad-based literacy emerge in the book's wordplay as well as its storyline: pages are related to printing as well as to princes as Jack Wilton, a humble page, bequeaths to the "pages of the court" certain "pages of his misfortune."

If the popular fiction of Deloney and Nashe stands at one end of the spectrum of late sixteenth- and early seventeenth-century prose fiction, another is perhaps most clearly exemplified by John Lyly. Lyly had been a young man of fashion at university, and for a time his *Euphues* (1578) set a fashion too—a fashion that drew attention above all to highly refined and rhetorical prose style. Lyly sets the tone in his dedicatory epistle:

> How so ever the case standeth, I look for no praise for my labour, but pardon for my goodwill; it is the greatest reward that I dare ask, and the least that they can offer. I desire no more, I deserve no less. Should the style nothing delight the dainty ear of the curious sifter, yet will the matter recreate the mind of the courteous reader.

The same style of ornamented sentences, with clauses precisely balanced in supporting or antithetical relationships, is carried through the narrative itself as it tells the story of "a young gentleman of great patrimony, and of so comely a personage, that it was doubted whether he were more bound to nature for the lineaments of his person, or through fortune for the increase of his possessions." This expansive style, which came to be called "Euphuism" after Lyly's title, was for a time very popular, especially among the women at court, where it was reported in 1632 that in the 1590s "the beauty in court who could not parley Euphuism was as little regarded as she which now there speaks not French." Within a few years the style had come to be widely parodied, including by Shakespeare, as for example when Falstaff "elevates" his speech while pretending to be the King addressing Prince Hal in *Henry IV, Part 1*: "Harry, I do not only marvel where thou spendest thy time, but also how thy art accompanied, for though the camomile, the more it is trodden on the faster it grows, yet youth, the more it is wasted, the sooner it wears."

What was satirized by Shakespeare (as well as by Nashe, Ben Jonson, and others) was not the use of balance or antithesis *per se*, but rather their excessive and repetitive use, and the habit of using a great many words to say very little. Shakespeare, Nashe, Jonson, and virtually every other late sixteenth- and early seventeenth-century writer of any significance also employed a great number of rhetorical figures, but aimed more for variety, concision, and pointedness than for abundance of expression. John Donne may command our attention with his colloquial directness of language in lines such as "For God's sake hold your tongue, and let me love," but his poems are filled with parallel structures ("My face in thine eye, thine in mine appears," "With wealth your state, your mind with arts improve") that embody the dichotomies and paradoxes of which he speaks. Ben Jonson may begin his play *The Alchemist* with a crude verbal slanging match in which one character says to another "I fart at thee," but in speeches throughout the play he also draws substantially on the Renaissance traditions of rhetorical figures ("Your fortunes may make me a man, As mine have preserved you a woman").

Like so many other sixteenth-century developments, the growth of prose fiction drew substantially on texts from ancient Greece and Rome, and from Renaissance Italy and France. Compilations of short fiction such as William Painter's *The Palace of Pleasure* (1566) and George Pettie's *A Petite Palace of Pettie His Pleasure* (1576) began to make translations and adaptations of French and Italian tales of romance and adventure much more widely available, and by the end of the century the genre of prose romance was becoming well established in English. Writers of prose romances often borrowed freely from earlier materials, and their works were in turn borrowed from freely, by dramatists and poets as well as by other writers of prose fiction. Thus, for example, Robert Greene's *Pandosto* (1588), which drew on an Italian source, provided the story material for Shakespeare's comedy *The Winter's Tale*, and Thomas Lodge's *Rosalynde* (1590), a prose fiction that drew on a Middle English romance called *Gamelyn* for its story material, provided Shakespeare with material for his comedy *As You Like It.* There was no shame attached to such borrowing: aesthetic value was located in the way in which one told or retold a tale and combined different elements of story material into a pleasing whole, not in whether one had thought up the stories oneself.

In the 1590s, Greene and Nashe, together with George Peele and a few others, constituted a group known as the "university wits." Like Christopher Marlowe and Edmund Spenser, they had attended university on scholarships or with the financial assistance of others, and the three lived something of a precarious existence after leaving Oxford or Cambridge; these were among the earliest English writers to try to earn their living entirely through their writing. Such a goal was still impossible to achieve directly through payments made by printers or publishers; it remained necessary to seek the support of wealthy patrons. That such support was often anything but reliable is evidenced from the dedications to their works. Greene's 17 different books are dedicated to a total of 16 different patrons; Nashe's dedication for the first edition of *The Unfortunate Traveler* to Henry Wriothesley, Earl of Southampton, is dropped in subsequent editions; and so on.

A very different writer of prose fiction was Sir Philip Sidney. Sidney's *Arcadia* (1590, 1593), an engaging and elegantly written pastoral prose romance, drew substantially on continental and classical models, and was instrumental in popularizing in England the genre of heroic Hellenistic prose romance—stories of romance and adventure set in imagined and "timeless" locales, featuring shepherds, damsels, and noblemen in disguise. The work remained immensely popular through the seventeenth century both in England (where it was issued in ten authorized printings) and abroad (where it was translated into French, German, and Dutch). Works inspired by Sidney's *Arcadia* include Lady Mary Wroth's *The Countess of Montgomery's Urania* (1621), the first published work of fiction by an Englishwoman, which mixes pastoral narrative with pointed political commentary, and Anna Weamys's sequel, *A Continuation of Sir Philip Sidney's Arcadia* (1651), less of a hybrid than Wroth's work, but like hers a romance narrative with some political overtones.

Sidney was a central figure not only in the development of prose romance: he was also a pioneer in the use of the sonnet sequence, and as the author of *The Defense of Poesie* (written 1583) he produced the first extended work of literary theory and criticism in English. Sidney's approach embraced both structural analysis from an aesthetic point of view and moral commentary—though that is to put his design very much in modern terms. In general, neither Sidney nor his contemporaries saw a clear boundary between the moral and the aesthetic: what was considered aesthetically good was considered so in large part for its perceived efficacy in conveying moral principles. The occasion for Sidney's *Defense* was a rambling and vituperative attack on the stage by Stephen Gosson entitled *The School of Abuse* (1579), and Sidney's focus is very largely on the drama. In the next generation, his *Defense* was followed by a number of works focused on other genres, among them George Puttenham's *The Art of English Poesie* (1589), noteworthy in particular for its discussion of rhetorical figures, and Thomas Campion's *Observations in the Art of English Poesie* (1602), a groundbreaking work relating the prosody of classical Greece and Rome to that of English poetry.

Arguably the most important prose writings of the late sixteenth and early seventeenth centuries were religious non-fiction works; certainly these were far and away the most popular. Aside from the Bible itself (first made available in the complete English-language printed edition in 1535 by Miles Coverdale) and such masterpieces of liturgical prose as the Book of Common Prayer, the most popular book in England through most of the sixteenth century was the English translation of *The Golden Legend*, by the thirteenth-century Italian scholar Jacobus de Voragine, a collection of narratives of the lives of Christian saints organized so as to be read in conjunction with the feast associated with each saint over the course of the year. In the first hundred years after the appearance of the printing press, more than 150 different editions of *The Golden Legend* appeared across Europe in various languages. William Caxton translated *The Golden Legend* himself and published it in 1483: "in likewise as gold is most noble above all other metals," he declared in his foreword to the book, "in likewise is this legend holden most noble above all other works."

In the wake of the Protestant Reformation, the most widely read book aside from the Bible seems to have been for many decades John Foxe's *Acts and Monuments*, first published in English in 1563. There are significant parallels between this work and *The Golden Legend*. Whereas the earlier work provided in convenient form the lives of saints of the Roman Catholic Church, many of whom attained cult-like status, Foxe's book performed the same function for Protestant religious figures, especially those martyred at the stake by Henry VIII or by Mary I. By the late sixteenth century these figures had also attained cult-like status, and Foxe's book was repeatedly issued in new editions, each time in an expanded form. In addition to these biographical texts, the genre of the sermon was, in the hands of a John Donne or a Lancelot Andrewes, the site of some of the finest prose of the Renaissance; even works of theology and religious controversy could enter what we now consider the "literary" realm when written by Anglican divines such as Richard Hooker or Jeremy Taylor, or by nonconforming radicals such as the pseudonymous satirist Martin Marprelate.

Throughout this period substantial increases in literacy were accompanied by increases in the number of households that possessed books. In 1560 roughly one in ten English households possessed at least one book; by 1640 this figure had risen to approximately 50 per cent of all households. Not surprisingly, such figures were higher in the late sixteenth and early seventeenth centuries in Protestant nations. In the late sixteenth century there was a higher percentage of households in Germany that possessed books than in any other part of Europe, but by 1640 that distinction belonged to England. If the printing press was one engine for the expansion of literacy, the expansion of formal education was another, and with the considerable increase in the number of schools over the course of the period came a demand for textbooks. Of these there were few, but one above all appears to have been almost universally studied—a Latin grammar text by William Lily (grandfather of John Lyly of *Euphues* fame). Indeed, it is possible that more copies were printed of this book than of any other during this period save the Bible.

Throughout this period there was also a growing readership for works that celebrated national accomplishment. Raphael Holinshed's *Chronicles of England, Scotland, and Ireland* (1587) drew on many sources to present a compilation of stories of early Britain, some based on fact, some purely legendary. Holinshed is best known nowadays as the source on which Shakespeare drew for his history plays; in these dramatized versions as well as more directly, the portrait Holinshed sketched of earlier eras exerted a wide influence. Similarly, William Camden's *Britannia* (1586), a "description of the most flourishing kingdoms, England, Scotland, and Ireland, and the islands adjoining," was immensely popular in its English translation, entitled simply *Britain* (1610). Like the "Britain" of many Englishmen, that of Camden was overwhelmingly southern English in character; Camden in fact had little to say about Wales, Scotland, or Ireland, and for the purposes of his county-by-county survey did not travel north of Hadrian's Wall. But such works helped to feed a growing sense among the English that England could be more or less equated with "the British Isles" or "Britain." Popular too was Richard Hakluyt's *Principal Navigations, Voyages and Discoveries of the English Nation* (1589), a unique compilation of more or less accurate accounts of true voyages of English explorers and merchants, combined with accounts based purely on myth and imagination. Nationality was the key criterion for inclusion: "I meddle in this work with the navigations only of our own nation," Hakluyt declares in his preface to the first edition. Ironically enough, "Hakluyt's Voyages," the work's popular title, retained a place in history not so much for the historical accounts it presented but rather for the inspiration it gave Englishmen to embark on the sorts of voyages Hakluyt had only imagined—and in the inspiration it gave Shakespeare for some of the stories in his plays. Furthermore, the kind of writing exemplified by Hakluyt's mariners and merchants, with their straightforward "plain" prose, sustained narratives, and detailed descriptions of the places and people they encountered, would (some scholars argue) eventually contribute as much to the development of the narrative style and strategy of the English novel as the classically inspired romances of Sidney and Lyly.

More's extraordinary vision of human government in *Utopia* was followed in the sixteenth century by a number of influential non-fiction works on the nature of government—works of political theory, we would call them today. A recurrent focus of such work was the relationship of a monarch and his or her subjects to God and to the body of law. Sir Thomas Elyot's *The Book of the Governor* (1531) saw a universe ordered by nature in hierarchical fashion:

> … undoubtedly the best governance is by one king or prince.… For who can deny that all thing in heaven and earth is governed by one God, by one perpetual order, by one Providence? One sun ruleth over the day, one moon over the night. And to descend down to the earth … the bees … hath among them one principal bee for their governor, who excelleth all other in greatness.

The Laws of Ecclesiastical Polity by Richard Hooker (1593–1614), which aimed in large part to justify the

Of Truth.

I.

HAT *is Truth*; ſaid jeſting *Pilate*; And would not ſtay for an Anſwer. Certainly there be, that delight in Giddineſſe; And count it a Bondage, to fix a Beleefe; Affecting Free-will in Thinking, as well as in Acting. And though the Sects of Philoſophers of that Kinde be gone, yet there remaine certaine diſcourſing Wits, which are of the ſame veines, though there be not ſo much Bloud in them, as was in thoſe of the Ancients. But it is not

B onely

Page from the 1625 edition of Francis Bacon's *Essays*.

position of the monarch in England as head of the established Church, also appealed to nature, distinguishing between universal natural law ("nature herself teacheth laws and statutes to live by") and "positive" law (the written body of human law that varies from one jurisdiction to another). Hooker saw the position of monarch as consistent with natural law, but he also thought it highly desirable that the monarch should abide by "positive" law, rather than regarding himself as above the law: "where the king doth guide the state, and the law the king, that commonwealth is like a harp or melodious instrument."

The most important writer of non-fiction prose of the age was Francis Bacon, the writer renowned today both for introducing the essay form into English, and for the contribution he made to the development of research based on experimentation and inductive reasoning—popularly termed the "scientific method." Bacon wrote in both Latin and English. Ironically, the works by Bacon that continue to be widely read are the works in English that he considered less significant: his essays; his short work on the classification of knowledge, *The Advancement of Learning*; and his unfinished scientific utopian fantasy, *The New Atlantis*.

As the religious controversies of the age again became more heated during the Jacobean period and later Interregnum (the period "between kings," 1649–60), so too did the volume of political and religious writing increase. The collapse of censorship laws in the early 1640s led to the appearance of a vast volume of pamphlet literature that represented all points of view; much of this writing was addressed to a popular audience and remains readable for its interest as rhetorical prose as well for its historical influence. Some of the most interesting of these texts are the work of political and religious radicals such as the Levellers, Diggers, Ranters, and later Quakers, in particular writers such as William Walwyn and Richard Overton. But the era also brought forth a number of more substantial works of prose non-fiction. On the Royalist side perhaps the most influential of these was *Eikon Basilike* ("The Image of the King") (1649), a self-justifying overview of key events of the war from the point of view of Charles I. Supposedly written by Charles himself, the treatise was almost certainly ghostwritten by the clergyman John Gauden, and John Milton would call attention to his own anti-monarchical credentials by responding with *Eikonoklastes* (1649; his Greek title means "Image Breaker"). Of far greater influence over the course of succeeding centuries was Thomas Hobbes's *Leviathan* (1651), now recognized as a central document of political philosophy in the Western tradition. Hobbes wrote *Leviathan* while acting as secretary to a Royalist family, the Cavendishes, who were in exile in Paris during the Interregnum;

unsurprisingly in the circumstances, his arguments provide support to the claims of a monarch wishing to exercise absolute sovereignty. But whereas monarchs such as Charles I (and sixteenth-century political theorists such as Elyot and Hooker) had claimed that such power stemmed directly from God, Hobbes saw it as the embodiment of a social contract, under the terms of which the people agree to submit themselves to the authority of a ruler in order to obtain the benefits of social order. By shifting the ground on which arguments for the unfettered authority of rulers were founded, Hobbes's great work in the end had the effect of undermining all claims to a right of absolute rule: if power was ultimately derived from the people, then why should not the people have an ongoing say in how that power was to be exercised, and by whom?

Many of the most important works of prose non-fiction by writers on the Royalist side were not overtly political documents—yet even non-political works were almost inevitably tinged with the controversies of the age. Thomas Browne's 1642–43 work *Religio Medici* ("The Religion of a Doctor") endeavored to present religion from a personal rather than a polemical point of view, adopting a tolerant and sympathetic attitude toward those of all religious backgrounds, while maintaining a strong attachment to the formal structures and rituals of the Church of England. Izaak Walton's most lasting work of prose non-fiction, *The Compleat Angler* (1653), might seem on the face of it to be even further from political or religious advocacy than *Religio Medici.* But this treatise on the art of fishing carries with it a running subtext that celebrates the wise, peaceful, open-hearted, and contemplative values of Piscator (Latin: the fisher), representing the values of the Church of England, in which each member of the clergy acts as a fisher of souls.

Perhaps the most remarkable of all writers of non-fiction prose in the mid-seventeenth century was Margaret Cavendish, Duchess of Newcastle (of the same family to whom Hobbes acted as secretary)—called "Mad Madge" by some dismissive contemporaries. Cavendish's writings are as remarkable for their breadth as they are for originality and for their accomplished writing: her works include scientific and philosophical essays, utopian fantasy, poetry, numerous plays, a biography of her husband, William Cavendish, and *A True Relation of My Birth, Breeding and Life* (1656), one of the most original and important works of a genre still in its infancy during the seventeenth century—autobiography. For most of the Middle Ages the practice of writing autobiographically (with the exception of some writing in a confessional vein) seems to have virtually disappeared, as indeed did biographical writing, with the exception of the lives of saints or martyrs. It is an important indicator of the increased emphasis on the individual in the Renaissance that the writing of such works, as well as the practice of writing diaries, appears to have grown steadily through the seventeenth century. One important element that contributed to this new focus on interiority and the self was the Protestant insistence on documenting the internal, spiritual life. But as so often in the sixteenth and seventeenth centuries, the new practices were also justified by an appeal to classical models. Cavendish expressed the hope that "my readers will not think me vain for writing my life, since there have been many that have done the like, as Caesar, Ovid, and many more, both men and women, and I know no reason I may not do it as well as they." The confidence as well as the individualism of the age finds no fuller expression than it does in the writings of Margaret Cavendish.

Other members of the nobility on the Royalist side (notably Anne Fanshaw and Anne Halkett) followed Cavendish in writing autobiographically during the Interregnum. And such writing appears to have flourished to some extent too among the revolutionaries; perhaps the most notable examples on that side are the writings of Lucy Hutchinson, who, like Cavendish, balanced a memoir recounting the life of her husband with a separate account of her own life. Anna Trapnel, perhaps best known for her extraordinary religious prophecies, also left a remarkable autobiographical account "of her journey from London into Cornwall" during which she was arrested and interrogated on suspicion of witchcraft. Much non-fiction prose writing among those on the revolutionary side tended to address directly the religious and political issues of the time. James Harrington's *The Commonwealth of Oceana* (1656), for example, employs the structure of a utopian vision to address the pressing contemporary issue of how a republic may be founded so as to ensure the perpetuation of government that is both representative and fair.

The leading light of revolutionary writing is unquestionably John Milton, whose non-fiction prose includes not only a wide range of essays and tracts in defense of Parliamentary and Puritan causes, but also groundbreaking treatises in defense of divorce and, perhaps, most importantly, *Areopagitica* (1644), an extended argument for toleration and freedom of expression. It is difficult for those living in the present-day liberal democracies of the Western world to appreciate fully the degree to which societies such as that of sixteenth- and seventeenth-century Britain may operate without any reference to any presumed right of free speech—or, indeed, any reference to any human "rights" at all. Censorship of texts is almost symbiotic in Europe with the invention of the printing press. In England, Henry VIII required that all book publications be approved by the Privy Council, and Elizabeth I instituted a system under which books could not be published without the approval of either the Archbishop of Canterbury or the Bishop of London. The punishments for those who defied the rules were occasionally extreme: John Stubbs, for example, who had the temerity in 1579 to publish a work warning the Queen against marrying the brother of the King of France, was punished by having one of his hands cut off. King James I banned the publication of pamphlets of news, and these early forms of the newspaper would not appear again until the 1640s. For much of the period a system of registration through the Stationers' Company was in essence a comprehensive system of censorship. Admittedly, enforcement of the rules governing printing had always been erratic, and there are not very many examples of actual censorship of books in this period; it has even been argued that many of the laws governing printing were not imposed upon printers but were in fact requested by them as a means of protecting their economic monopoly. But it was the idea of pre-publication licensing of books that was the particular focus of Milton's arguments in *Areopagitica*, and his arguments have been turned to again and again over the intervening centuries by those endeavoring to defend freedom of expression.

Detail from the frontispiece to Margaret Cavendish's *Philosophical and Physical Opinions* (1655). According to the poem accompanying the likeness of Cavendish, "studious she is and all alone ... Her library on which she looks, it is her head, her thoughts, her books ... Her own flames do her inspire."

POETRY

A comparison with medieval poetry reveals the remarkable changes the Renaissance brought to poetic form in English verse. Late-medieval poets used many different verse forms, ranging from alliterative accentual patterns with anywhere from three to six beats in each line, to complex rhyming stanzaic patterns in lyric poems with a dance-like variety of accentual rhythms, to Chaucer's ten-syllable lines, sometimes more loosely organized around stress rather than a strict number of syllables. But strictly accentual-syllabic verse was rare in the medieval English period, whereas from the Renaissance to the early twentieth century it was the dominant poetic form in English.

The late fifteenth- and early sixteenth-century poetry of John Skelton still has one foot in the medieval period, at least as far as meter is concerned. Lines such as the following are written in accentual verse—that is to say, each contains a set number of accented syllables (in this case three), but has no set number of total syllables, and no regular arrangement of stressed and unstressed syllables:

> Then will he rout;
> Then sweetly together we lie,
> As two pigs in a sty.

Only a decade or so after Skelton was writing, other poets—most notably Sir Thomas Wyatt and his contemporary Henry Howard, Earl of Surrey—began to draw on classical and Italian forms of a quite different nature, forms that would dominate English poetry for the next four centuries. Wyatt and Surrey are most often given credit for introducing to English literature the sonnet form that Petrarch and others had established in Italy. Of broader importance was the tradition they established of writing in accentual-syllabic meters. Of these, iambic pentameter was the most frequent choice, whether in sonnets (such as Wyatt's "I find no peace, and all my war is done"), in unrhymed (or "blank") verse of the sort that Surrey was the first to write in English, or in other forms. Iambic tetrameter (i.e., having four "feet" or groups of stressed and unstressed syllables in every line, rather than five) was also common: for example, Surrey's "My friend, the things that do attain" is among the examples included in this volume. (A fuller description of the various forms of accentual-syllabic verse is provided in the "Reading Poetry" section at the end of this volume.) Where Wyatt and Surrey led, others followed; the great outpouring of poetry in the 1580s and 1590s by Sidney, Spenser, Marlowe, Shakespeare, and the rest was entirely an outpouring of accentual-syllabic verse.

Accentual-syllabic meters were structured according to classical principles, with regular patternings of syllables forming poetic "feet," and a set number of feet in every line. But along the way the classical principles were transformed in one crucial respect. Unlike English, classical Greek and Latin are not characterized by large variations in the degree of stress placed on different syllables: there are no distinctions between accented (or stressed) syllables and unaccented (or unstressed) syllables. Distinctions between syllables for the purposes of their arrangement in poetic meter were in ancient times based on *duration* of sound—some syllables taking a shorter time to say, others a longer time—rather than on degrees of stress. In English, however, where the alternation of stressed and unstressed syllables is fundamental to the natural spoken rhythms of the language, the Greek framework and terminology came to be applied to alternations between stressed and unstressed (or "accented" and "unaccented") syllables rather than long or short syllables. Whereas the Greeks had used the term "iambic" to describe verse in which a syllable that took a short time to say was followed by a syllable that took a long time to say, English verse took an iamb to consist of an unstressed syllable followed by a stressed syllable. And so on for trochees (one long syllable followed by one short became one stressed syllable followed by one unstressed); dactyls (one long syllable followed by two short became one stressed syllable followed by two unstressed); anapests (two short followed by one long syllable became two unstressed followed by one stressed syllable); and spondees (two long syllables became two stressed syllables). Regular patterning of what the late sixteenth-century poet, musician, and poetic theorist Thomas Campion referred to as "the heaviness of the syllables" became the ruling principle of English poetic meter.

Borrowing from—and transforming—classical poetic models was a central feature of English poetry throughout the late sixteenth and early seventeenth centuries. From Spenser's *The Shepheardes Calender* to Milton's "Lycidas" and beyond, the pastoral poem, with its conventions of musical shepherds singing songs of love and of sorrow, was a poetic staple. Classical poetic models for satires, for wedding songs (as with Spenser's *Epithalamion*), for elegies, and for love poetry in lyric form were also widely imitated and adapted. And the two great long poems of the period—Spenser's *The Faerie Queene* and Milton's *Paradise Lost*—so different in some respects, are alike in drawing substantially on classical models.

Just as romance narratives were an important subgenre of late sixteenth-century prose, so too was verse romance important to the poetry of the late sixteenth century. The 1590s opened with the publication of the greatest of all verse romances in English, *The Faerie Queene*, which Spenser had begun in 1580. No other verse romance of the period attempted anything so ambitious, but a remarkable succession of shorter verse romances appeared over the course of a few years in the late 1580s and early 1590s: Marlowe's *Hero and Leander* (1598); Lodge's *Scylla's Metamorphosis* (1589); Daniel's *The Complaint of Rosamond* (1592); Shakespeare's *Venus and Adonis* (1593); and Drayton's *Endymion and Phoebe* (1595). These poems draw heavily on the mythological stories recounted by the Roman poet Ovid in his *Metamorphoses*, *Heroides*, and *Amores*, though in form and tone they all bear a decidedly Elizabethan stamp. They all bear the stamp of the court, as well: these were poems intended for the aristocracy and, indeed, for the monarch herself.

The Renaissance was an age of artifice ("artificial" was during this period used exclusively as a term of praise), and much of the poetry of the 1580s and 1590s is given to imagery that is extravagant in its inventiveness. Some of the extravagance is tongue-in-cheek, as is surely the case with Shakespeare's evident lampooning in his early comedy *Love's Labour's Lost* of the verbal excess of the character Holofernes, whose "gift" is "a foolish extravagant spirit, full of forms, figures, shapes, objects, ideas, apprehensions, motions, revolutions: these are begot in the ventricle of memory, nourished in the womb of *pia mater*, and delivered upon the mellowing of occasion." In his poetry of the later 1590s and of the early seventeenth century, Shakespeare tamed his earlier tendency toward extravagant cleverness, though he never abandoned artifice. Much the same may be said of Ben Jonson, who advocated "plain language" and told poets to take care of their style in writing: "Be not winding, or wanton with far-fetched descriptions," he advised.

Many of the most important poets of the early seventeenth century, however, aspired to new heights of inventiveness. Chief among these was John Donne. Donne's early verse in particular often plays in elaborate fashion with extraordinary comparisons. It also twists and turns syntactically, mirroring in its form the surprising paradoxes or contradictions conveyed in the sense of the lines. These sorts of images, drawing extreme comparisons, have come to be known as "conceits." In some cases a conceit may be extended over several lines, or indeed a full poem. So, for example, Donne compares a tear to the globe, and his mistress's body to his "America," his "new-found land." The seventeenth-century poets who have been most often associated with these poetic tendencies—Donne

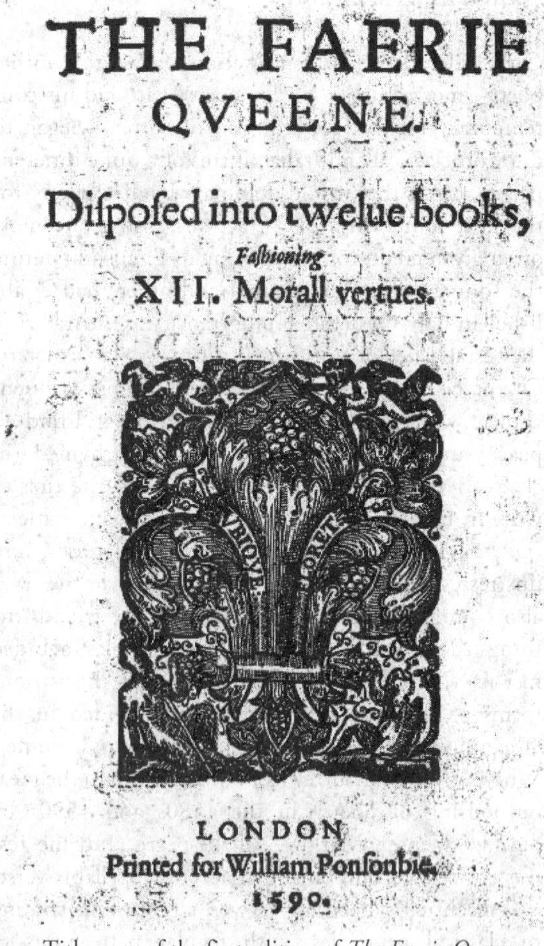

Title page of the first edition of *The Faerie Queene* (1590).

Artist unknown, *Henry VIII at the Opening of Parliament*, 1523. In this watercolor drawing the King is seated below the royal coat of arms, wearing his crown and holding the scepter, his feet resting on a cushion. To his right (i.e., to the left of the picture) are Archbishop Warham of Canterbury and Cardinal Wolsey. Before him two earls hold the cap of maintenance and the sword of state. Dukes wear coronets; other peers of the realm wear hats; to the left nine bishops (in red) and seventeen black abbots wear their miters.

Detail from *Londinum Feracissimi Angliae Regni Metropolis*, the bird's eye view of London in Georg Braun's atlas *Orbis Terrarum*, c. 1574. The view is believed to show London as it was c. 1558. An image of the full map appears on the facing page.

Map of London from *Orbis Terrarum*, c. 1574. (A detail is enlarged on the facing page.)

Artist unknown, untitled watercolour depicting food being served during a game of cards, early seventeenth century (Folger Shakespeare Library). A companion watercolor image is reproduced in the "Culture: A Portfolio" section elsewhere in this volume.

Artist unknown, *Queen Elizabeth I.*

Artist unknown, *William Cecil, Lord Burghley*, c. 1585. Burghley was for many years Queen Elizabeth's most trusted and powerful civil servant.

Artist unknown, *Lady Jane Dudley* (*née Grey*), c. 1550.

Artist unknown, detail of *The Thames at Richmond with a View of Richmond Palace*, c. 1620. The palace had been destroyed by fire in 1497 and rebuilt by Henry VII. It remained one of the royal residences until the time of Charles I. In the foreground a gentleman appears to be offering coins as a token of appreciation for the performance of an impromptu entertainment.

Attributed to David des Granges, *The Salsonstall Family*, 1630s. The painting anachronistically shows Sir Richard Salsonstall together with both his first wife (who died in childbirth) and his second wife (shown at right holding her child), as well as his two children.

Anthony Van Dyck, *Charles I on Horseback with Seigneur de St. Antoine*, 1633. De St. Antoine was the King's riding master. This portrait was widely admired in its time; one contemporary commented that, "if our eyes alone were to be believed they would boldly assert that the king himself is alive in the portrait."

Samuel Cooper, *Oliver Cromwell*, 1649. This, the earliest portrait of Cromwell known to exist, dates from the year in which Charles I was executed.

and Abraham Cowley chief among them, with the devotional poets George Herbert, Richard Crashaw, and Henry Vaughan rather more loosely associated—have since the time of Samuel Johnson in the eighteenth century been referred to as "the metaphysical poets." Johnson's unfavorable assessment of such poetry has been rejected by most critics and scholars for the past century or more; T.S. Eliot, in particular, famously praised the metaphysical poets for uniting feeling and intellect in their verse. Yet Johnson captured something of the truth in his description of metaphysical poets as endeavoring "to be singular in their thoughts," and of the ideas produced through the intellectual gymnastics of many metaphysical poems as "often new, but seldom natural." Eventually Donne turned away from extravagance, abandoning much of the sensual content as well as the extreme conceits of his early verse as he turned to religion and to religious poetry, and Herbert made his efforts to suppress his own skills in rhetorical ornamentation a subject of his poetry:

> My thoughts began to burnish, sprout, and swell,
> Curling with metaphors a plain intention,
> Decking the sense, as if it were to sell.

Yet the audacity of the metaphysical poets has left a lasting mark on English literature: the ways of talking about religious faith and about love of God in the language of human physical love and vice versa; the ways of talking *to* God that Herbert developed; and the extremity of the conceits themselves have all found imitators as well as admirers in subsequent eras.

Lively debates have taken place over the past generation about whether or not the term "metaphysical poetry" in fact conveys something meaningful about a diverse body of work; it is often argued in particular that grouping Herbert with "the metaphysicals" brings us no closer to what is unique and interesting about his poetry. So too has it been debated whether the term "cavalier poetry" as an umbrella term to identify a group of poets from later in the seventeenth century conveys much that is meaningful. Certainly there is a common tendency among poets such as Thomas Carew (pronounced "Carey"), Sir John Denham, Robert Herrick, Richard Lovelace, James Shirley, Sir John Suckling, and Edmund Waller toward smooth rhythms and mellifluous sounds. And they are inevitably associated with one another simply by having been on the Royalist side—though only some were given to infusing verse with a strong political or religious content. (The strongest poetic statement on a Royalist theme may well be Katherine Philips's "Upon the Double Murder of King Charles," in which she poses the following question: "He broke God's laws, and therefore he must die, / and what shall then become of thee and I?") The cavalier poets all tend to write frequently of the good life and of love—but there the similarities largely end. Interestingly, though, the love poetry of the cavalier poets—whether the highly charged eroticism of poets such as Carew and Suckling or the more chaste and chivalrous variety of Lovelace—is unequivocally heterosexual. The homoeroticism that infuses so much of the finest poetry of the 1590s, and that was a significant presence in the court of James I in the early seventeenth century, is nowhere evident in the verse of these later poets.

Few seventeenth-century poets, even the most courtly and cavalier, failed to produce at least some devotional poems. In literature as in life, the seventeenth century mixes devotional and secular responses to the world, inextricably intertwining the language of religion with the language of social life and politics. An increasingly important reference point in devotional poetry as the century wore on became the attitude one held toward prelapsarian existence—humankind before the Fall. Whereas Aemilia Lanyer, writing in 1611, took the Fall as an occasion for weighing the relative merits of man and woman, Lovelace paints an idyllic version of love before the fall of Adam and Eve:

> No serpent kiss poisoned the taste,
> Each touch was naturally chaste,
> And their mere sense a miracle.

Henry Vaughan, a Royalist who saw himself as a "son of George Herbert," took a more gloomy view, and one that partook only of a male perspective. For Vaughan, writing in 1650, it is impossible to conceive of the prelapsarian state in a tone other than that of melancholy: "He sighed for Eden, and would often say, / 'Ah! what bright days were those!'"

There are fewer Puritan or Parliamentary poets of note than there are Royalist ones, but among them are the two pre-eminent poets of the age: Andrew Marvell and John Milton. Milton, indeed, has often been regarded as towering above not only his contemporaries but also over all other English poets, with the sole exception of Shakespeare. Milton is the supremely paradoxical figure of English literature. He was a devout Christian who more or less abandoned institutionalized religion in favor of a "church of one"; he wrote what remains the great Christian epic poem in English, *Paradise Lost*—but gave Satan the leading role; he was a Puritan who eschewed plain style for Latinate inversions and epic grandeur. Milton managed to convey perhaps more fully than any other writer in English both prelapsarian innocence in the "heav'n on earth" of Eden and the "guilty shame, dishonest shame" of humans after their Fall.

Like Milton, Marvell supported the "Good Old Cause" of Cromwell and political Republicanism. To the extent that we can be sure about Marvell's thoughts on any subject, however, Marvell appears to have seen Cromwell more as the embodiment of a pure force of nature than as a representative of pure moral and religious values: his "An Horatian Ode upon Cromwell's Return from Ireland" is among the most subtly balanced pieces of English political verse of any era. Even more than Milton, however, Marvell was a poet of the garden—a garden in which a sense of the Fall was never far away, but yet one of surpassing beauty and innocence. To the contemplation of such scenes Marvell brought his own unique perspective; rather than focus on prelapsarian pleasure, Marvell imagined the supreme joys to be those of solitary contemplation of the beauties of nature:

> Two Paradises 'twere in one
> To live in Paradise alone.

THE DRAMA

The flowering of drama in England from the late 1580s to the 1620s is widely accepted as the greatest cultural achievement in the history of English literature. The list of important dramatists who flourished during this period includes not only Marlowe, Shakespeare, and Jonson but also Thomas Kyd, John Lyly, George Peele, John Webster, Cyril Tourneur, Francis Beaumont, John Fletcher, Thomas Middleton, John Ford, James Shirley, John Marston, Thomas Dekker, Thomas Heywood, and Philip Massinger. It is an outpouring the more remarkable for there being so few advance signs of its coming. In the middle years of the sixteenth century, the main forms of medieval drama were very much alive: audiences were still watching guild-sponsored biblical plays, allegorical dramas such as *Everyman*, and various kinds of (generally crude) secular comedy performed by traveling troupes of players or local inhabitants as part of feast-day celebrations. As the forces behind the Protestant Reformation gathered steam, however, a substantial body of opinion became convinced that neither the popular secular drama nor the often irreverent representations of religious material in the biblical plays were proper to be played at all: a key factor in the demise of the biblical plays is thought to have been hostility from those sympathetic to the Protestant Reformation.

As the biblical plays were dying out, the revival of classical literature ushered in by humanism helped give birth to new forms of English drama. The first phase in the introduction of these new models was the translation of classical plays, particularly Roman tragedies by Seneca and Roman comedies by Plautus and Terence. Of the two, it was Roman comedy that first had an impact in England, with English schools and colleges presenting comedies by Plautus or Terence to school audiences (or occasionally to aristocratic ones, by invitation). The earliest known adaptation into English of one of these comedies is Nicholas Udall's *Ralph Roister Doister*, probably written by Udall during the years when he was the headmaster of Eton, 1534 to 1541. Such performances typically involved scenery painted on canvas stretched out behind the acting area, the canvas often painted so as to represent a street in perspective according to what was believed to be "the manner of the ancients." The play itself is lively, but adds little to its Roman model; it lacks any of the depth that characterizes so much of the drama of the late 1580s to the 1620s.

Of classical models for tragedy the most highly esteemed were the tragedies of Seneca; these began to be performed in Latin on the Italian stage very early in the sixteenth century, and by 1551 are known to have been performed in England at Trinity College, Cambridge. Seneca's tragedies began to be translated into English by Jasper Haywood in the late 1550s, and within 20 years all of Seneca's plays had been translated into English. Ironically, these plays had almost certainly not been acted out fully on the Roman stage: they are filled with set-piece speeches, and are believed by classical scholars to have been recited by a single actor. The Elizabethans, however, took Seneca's plays as a model for lively action, borrowing not only their five-act structure but also their preponderance of long set-piece speeches. Such borrowings were at first very much an upper-class phenomenon: English Senecan plays such as *Gorboduc*, *Jocasta*, *Tancred*, and *Gismunda* were performed in the houses of the nobility or at the Inns of Court on special occasions. To Sir Philip Sidney, endeavoring to apply as a matter of literary theory the rules of classical drama to the English stage, Thomas Norton and Thomas Sackville's *Gorboduc* was particularly deserving of praise. Only the fact of its being "very defectious in the circumstances"—in other words, of its not conforming closely enough to the classical ideal of the "unities," in which a play's action occurred in one setting and over a length of time not exceeding one day—prevented *Gorboduc* from being taken "as an exact model of all tragedies." To later ages, by contrast, it is almost unimaginable that *Gorboduc* could be a model for anything dramatic. Its long speeches seem static; extraordinary and violent actions are reported but never displayed before the audience; and the play is never structured so as to arouse audience expectations.

How did the most dynamic and open period of theater in the history of the English stage develop so quickly out of such a static and restrictive background? A key moment in this extraordinary development was the decision by a London businessman, James Burbage, to build a playhouse northeast of London—outside the city limits, so as to be outside the regulatory authority of the city, but close enough to enable Londoners to attend performances. "The Theatre," as Burbage rather unimaginatively called the new playhouse, became a model for other theaters such as the Globe and the Swan, the latter two both constructed in Southwark, just across the Thames from London—again, outside the London city limits. Before this time such "professional" actors as there had been belonged to troupes that traveled from town to town, typically performing old plays again and again in different venues. The establishment of permanent theaters in the London area reflected the demographic shifts of the time—not only the rapid growth of population, but also its increasing concentration in and around London. But the presence of these playing spaces had a number of important effects. Perhaps most obviously, they suddenly created a steady and ongoing demand for new plays: if Londoners were to be enticed to the new playhouses, the theater companies could not simply keep playing nothing but old standards. And London audiences were the most literate and the most diverse of any in Britain; though the monarch never deigned to attend performances in such venues, audiences certainly included all other elements of the population. Apprentices and others of scant means would pay a penny to stand on the ground in front of and on both sides of the stage (the members of the audience Hamlet calls "groundlings"). Levels of seating, protected from the elements, rose around on all sides; a covered seat for a performance typically cost twopence. Or a performance could be observed from the privacy of a "lord's room" for sixpence. (In Renaissance London, as in London or New York today, the most expensive seats in the theater were sold for the equivalent of a day's wage for a common laborer.)

A theater soon grew up that differed substantially from both the performances of the traveling troupes and the academic theater that had been imitating Roman models. For this "theater in the round," little or no attempt was made to provide realistic sets or backdrops: most props were handheld. There was a good deal of rapid movement and rapid dialogue, and long set speeches became a rarity. Comic characters and comic scenes were introduced into tragedies (a practice strictly forbidden according to Sidney or the classical theorists). And plays began more and more to depict all strata of society, and to depict women as well as men in leading roles. (Throughout this period, it was considered unseemly for women to appear on the public stage, though they did perform in court masques. In public theaters in England, female roles were played by adolescent boy actors, a practice that provided for multiple opportunities for complex layering in storylines such as those of Shakespeare's *Twelfth Night* and *The Merchant of Venice* involving females pretending to be males.)

Playwrights, for their part, were paid a flat fee for their work, typically six pounds per play. Popular plays were performed again and again over many years, but the playwright would receive no additional income from these performances; the incentive for playwrights was thus to produce new work. And produce they did: the 37 plays that Shakespeare is known to have written over the course of approximately 25 years may seem extraordinary by modern standards, but it pales by comparison with the productivity of Thomas Heywood, now best known as the author of the domestic tragedy *A Woman Killed with Kindness* (1603) and of a defense of the theater, *An Apology for Actors* (1612). In an address to the reader prefacing *The English Traveler* (1633), Heywood refers to the "two hundred and twenty plays in which I have had either an entire hand or at least the main finger" (of these, only about 20 survive). In the press to complete more work, collaboration of the sort that Heywood alludes to was frequent. Shakespeare collaborated with other playwrights on at least two projects; Ben Jonson collaborated with Thomas Dekker; Dekker collaborated with Thomas Middleton; Francis Beaumont and John Fletcher usually wrote in collaboration with each other; Philip Massinger collaborated with Dekker and with Nathaniel Field; and so on. In its modes of composition as much as in other respects, then, the Elizabethan drama was fluid and dynamic.

It should not be supposed that classical models were altogether abandoned in this flurry of creative activity; far from it. Comedies of the late 1580s and early 1590s (such as Shakespeare's *The Comedy of Errors*) were in many ways closely modeled on the comedies of Plautus, and tragedies from the same period (such as Thomas Kyd's *The Spanish Tragedy*, Marlowe's *Tamburlaine*, and Shakespeare's *Titus Andronicus*) borrowed extensively from Senecan tragedy. But Shakespeare and other comic dramatists quickly left behind the more formulaic aspects of Plautine comedy. They changed the shape of Senecan tragedy, too; a certain amount of static speechifying was still featured, but now the violence that in Seneca was typically reported as having occurred offstage began to be performed before the eyes of the audience. Audiences remained rapt: *The Spanish Tragedy*, *Tamburlaine*, and *Titus Andronicus* were all enormously popular.

For ten years or more following the establishment of the first permanent theater outside London, most of the plays produced seem to have been fairly crude in their construction. (Since few plays from this period have survived, generalizations must be advanced with caution.) Certainly plays such as those by George Peele from the 1580s and early 1590s, the anonymous *Mucedorus* (c. 1590)—and for that matter *Tamburlaine* and *Titus Andronicus*—are loosely constructed on episodic principles, with nothing to facilitate any sense of awareness in the audience of a concatenation of events unfolding. But by the early 1590s, Marlowe and Shakespeare in particular had refined the craft of playwriting so as to create through their plotting an ongoing sense of the future action as well as of the present. When a character such as Richard III (in the opening scene of Shakespeare's *Richard III*) expresses his intentions to the audience ("Plots I have laid, inductions dangerous ..."), the speech itself is not dissimilar to the set-piece speeches in *Gorboduc*. But here the intentions of Richard III are woven into the plot so as to become a driving force behind the play—a play that was performed more frequently than any other on the Elizabethan and Jacobean stage.

The theaters "in the round" outside the city limits were not the only venues for drama in London during this period. Notably, the old monastery at Blackfriars in London had begun as early as the 1550s to be used as a venue for the production of plays, and by the early seventeenth century it was a leading London theater. As a former monastic area it enjoyed, through a legal loophole, the same immunity from regulation and taxation by the city of London that the theaters outside the city limits enjoyed. The Blackfriars stage, though, was indoors, not outdoors like the public theaters; the stage itself was not surrounded by members of the audience on three sides as were the stages in the other theaters; and the audiences themselves were less diverse: there were no groundlings in the audience at private theaters such as Blackfriars and the Royal Court.

Even when outside the jurisdiction of the city, dramatic performances in the Elizabethan and Jacobean age entailed considerable risk. When in 1605 James I was apprised of the satirical treatment accorded the Scottish court in a play by Ben Jonson, John Marston, and George Chapman (*Eastward Ho!*), he disbanded the company that had mounted the production—even though his wife, Queen Anne, was its patron. Because of the potentially transgressive content of many Elizabethan and Jacobean plays, few were given a local and contemporary setting; even if one wished to convey pointed messages about contemporary politics, it was safer to do so elliptically, by setting the action of a play in Italy and in a vaguely defined past rather than in London in the present.

Title page, *The Workes of Benjamin Jonson* (1616). The publication in 1616 of Jonson's collected works is a landmark in the history of English drama as literature.

The range of the drama in the early years of the seventeenth century is, if anything, even broader than that of the 1590s. This is the era of Shakespeare's great tragedies and of his dark comedies as well as his late romances; of many of Ben Jonson's finest comedies; of a group of violent "revenge tragedies" by Webster and Tourneur; and of a group of "city comedies" concerning London society by Dekker, Middleton, and others. Overall, the tone of the Jacobean drama is darker than that of the Elizabethan stage—the satire more biting, the tragedy more bleak. This is also the era of the masque, a form of court drama that stands in marked contrast to that of "theater in the round." Masques were as much spectacle as drama. They were astonishingly expensive productions performed for the aristocracy by a mixture of professionals and members of the court itself; they typically drew on pastoral or mythological themes; they often involved interaction between performers and spectators; they usually featured elaborate costumes, painted scenery, special effects, and set-piece displays; and they always included a good deal of song, music, and dance.

As the seventeenth century wore on, the theater came more and more frequently under attack by Puritans. Since the late 1580s dramatists had walked a fine line, desiring always to give to those elements of the crowd that were entertained by displays of bawdiness and violence a good deal of what they were looking for, while still insisting that such displays fulfilled a didactic purpose. The description of the action of the domestic tragedy *Arden of Faversham* (c. 1585–90) gives something of the flavor:

> The lamentable and true tragedy of M. Arden of Faversham of Kent. Who was most wickedly murdered by the means of his disloyal and wanton wife.... Wherein is showed the great malice and dissimulation of a wicked woman, the unsatiable desire of filthy lust and the shameful end of all murderers.

Wickedness, in other words, is shown to be punished, but along the way a good deal of titillation for the audience is provided. The theaters managed to resist the

From the frontispiece to William Alabaster, *Roxana Tragedia* (1632). This is one of the earliest printed representations of an English dramatic performance.

criticisms from the Puritans for more than five decades. But when Charles I was forced from London and the Puritans took control at the onset of the civil war in 1642, the theaters were closed by city officials—at the time, probably for political as much as moral reasons (the first thing all authorities traditionally do in a time of revolution is close the sites where large groups of people can meet together). They remained closed for almost two decades, until the Restoration in 1660. The most remarkable era in the history of the English stage was at an end.

THE ENGLISH LANGUAGE IN THE SIXTEENTH AND SEVENTEENTH CENTURIES

If the rediscovery of Greek and Latin literature was a central element of the Renaissance in England, the increased currency of the Greek and Latin languages—and of Latin especially—was central to the changes that occurred in the English language in this period. Of the thousands of new English words imported from Greek and Latin, many were words that named new concepts or things for which no English equivalent existed (from *area* and *equilibrium* to *vacuum*). Such words enlarged the expressive capacity of the English language in several directions, increasing the stock of scientific, mathematical, rhetorical, and philosophical terms, and more broadly increasing the capacity of the language to express abstract concepts. (The word "abstraction" itself is first recorded as having been used in 1547.) Many Latin words remained intact as they entered the English language, including *antenna, apparatus, cerebellum, militia,* and *tedium.* Others became reshaped, often losing their original suffixes, as with, for example, the Latin words *complexus* and *desperatus.* On the other hand, Latin prefixes (among the most common of which are *ob-*, from; *post-*, after; *pre-*, before; and *sub-*, under) tended more often than not to be retained without alteration. In some cases words with Latin roots that had originally entered the English language in an altered form from the French now had a form closer to the Latin original "restored" in English.

There were also extensive borrowings during this period from the French (e.g., *bayonet, muscle*), from the Italian (e.g., *argosy, squadron*), from the Spanish (e.g., *cargo, sherry*), and from the Dutch (e.g., *deck, dock,* and *yacht*). In these borrowings one can see something of the pattern of interaction between Britons and these other nationalities, with borrowings from the Spanish often concerned with warfare, and from the Dutch often concerned with commerce, the sea, and painting (e.g., *easel, sketch,* and *landscape*).

Among the educated classes there were always those who resisted or mocked aspects of this "invasion" of foreign words. Thomas Wilson, for example, lamented in his *Art of Rhetoric* (1553) the use of "inkhorn terms" that were regarded as signs of scholarly affectation. Ralph Lever, responding to the wholesale importation of Latin terms, suggested in 1573 that the existing resources of native English could be adapted in ways that would be preferable to the Latin terms—that *endsay*, for example, should be preferred to *conclusion*, *saywhat* should be preferred to *definition*, and so on. And Ben Jonson in his play *Poetaster* mocked the excessive use of real or presumptive foreign imports such as *defunct*, *fatuate*, *furibund*, *inflate*, *prorumpted* ("What a noise it made!" comments one character at the mention of this word), *strenuous*, *turgidious*, and *ventositous*. "O terrible windy words," laments one character. "A sign of a windy brain," agrees another. We may safely infer that such satire (like that by Shakespeare in *Love's Labours Lost*) had a recognizable referent in real life—that some did indeed use the new coinages in an affected or pompous fashion. But some of the resistance appears to have represented no more than the prejudice that seems inevitable in any age against linguistic change. Just as William Strunk and E.B. White fulminated in the 1950s against the new word *finalize*, unable to recognize how it might fulfill a useful linguistic function, so Jonson and the others made fun of words such as *defunct* and *strenuous* that have ended up taking a permanent (and permanently useful) place in the English language.

The fact that more new words appear in the works of Shakespeare than in those of any other writer from this period has prompted the unjustified assumption that Shakespeare "introduced" more new words to the English language than anyone else. That claim may well be true, but we can of course speak with certainty only of first written occurrences of words and phrases; it is in almost every case entirely possible that a word or phrase had been in common currency for some time before it appears in a piece of writing that has survived. At the very least, however, we may confidently say that Shakespeare was extraordinarily receptive to new coinages, and that his works played a role in helping to shape the changing language during this period. It is noteworthy that among the many words that first appear in English in Shakespeare there are not only a great many borrowings from Latin (e.g., *abstemious*, *arose*, *assignation*) but also a number of words formed by inventive re-combinations of English words, or through part of speech conversions (e.g., *gloomy*, *leapfrog*, *lonely*). In his place in the history of the language as in other respects, Shakespeare stands pre-eminent.

It is worth noting here that many phrases or expressions that we now think of as proverbial also originated in Shakespeare's works. The phrase "vanish into thin air," for example, is used on a daily basis, so much so that it is difficult to recapture a fresh sense of the aptness of the image. Other expressions that make their first appearance in Shakespeare include *come full circle*, *eaten out of house and home*, *has seen better days*, *the livelong day*, and *there's method in his madness*.

Though the printing press had been introduced in 1476, the regularization of spelling that one might have expected to follow as a natural consequence of the spread of printing began to happen only very slowly over the course of the sixteenth and seventeenth centuries. Certainly through to the early seventeenth century it remained common for writers to spell the same word in different ways in the same document, and even for individuals to spell their name in different ways at different times. Pronunciation also began to move toward a common standard as London became more and more dominant in English life, but these changes too, occurred slowly; there remained several distinct dialects of English in the mid-seventeenth century. The great vowel shift (described in the introduction to the first volume of this anthology) was virtually complete by the early sixteenth century, as was the change in habits of pronunciation of the final *e* in many English words; by the end of the fifteenth century that practice had almost entirely died out.

The Renaissance brought several changes in English grammar and syntax. In the sixteenth and seventeenth centuries the *–eth* third person singular verb ending (e.g., *followeth*, *thinketh*) began to die out, though some common contractions of these forms (e.g., *hath* for *haveth*, *doth* for *doeth*) persisted into the late seventeenth century. There were changes, too, in the formation of pronouns. In the third person plural, the forms *ey / them / their* replaced the old *they / hem / hire* that we find in Chaucerian English. And the second person *you* replaced the old *ye* during this period. With second person pronouns, however, the situation is complicated by changes in usage involving the second person pronoun *thou* (and its object form *thee*). These forms were used when one was addressing another in a more familiar or less respectful fashion, whether because of the circumstances or because of the relative social standing of the individuals in conversation. (A child or an animal would also typically be addressed as *thou.*) In less familiar and more respectful contexts *you* would be used. (The distinction here resembles that still existing in languages such as French, in which one may choose when addressing an individual between the more familiar *tu* and the more formal *vous*, which also serves as the second person plural form.) The use of the familiar *thou* and *thee* began to die out early in the sixteenth century, and by the seventeenth century *you* was used almost universally as the second person pronoun in all circumstances.

Finally, there were significant changes during the sixteenth and early seventeenth centuries in the formation of negatives and interrogatives, and in the use of *do* as an auxiliary verb. Instead of saying *we went not* or asking *know you her?* it became common to say *we did not go* and to ask *do you know her?* The use of *do* as an auxiliary spread quickly, and indeed for much of the early modern period came to be used in ways that have since died out; in the sixteenth century the forms *I think* and *I do think* were used interchangeably where now (unless we wish to add emphasis) we would use only the former.

History of the Language and of Print Culture

In an effort to provide for readers a direct sense of the development of the language and of print culture, examples of texts in their original form (and of illustrations) have been provided in each volume. A list of these within the present volume, arranged chronologically, appears below. John Foxe's 1570 comments on "The benefit and invention of printing" appear on pages 96–97.

William Shakespeare, *Sonnets*, facsimile reproductions of pages from 1609 edition, pp. 467–68; title pages of quarto editions of *Romeo and Juliet, A Midsummer Night's Dream, King Lear*, pp. 554–55; title page and facing page, 1623 Folio edition of the plays, p. 555.

Katherine Philips, "Friendship's Memory, To my Dearest Lucasia," poem in original spelling and punctuation, pp. 786–87.

John Milton, *Paradise Lost*, passage in original spelling and punctuation, pp. 827–28.

John Skelton
c. 1460 – 1529

John Skelton was one of the most prominent writers of his time. Friendly with the royal family, he influenced both literary and political spheres. As a poet he was known for his breezy but cutting satirical writing. Politically, however, his most notable trait was outspokenness—a quality that sometimes got him into trouble. Not much is known about his childhood and adolescence beyond the fact that his family was from Yorkshire. He was educated at Cambridge University, then at Oxford. Oxford conferred on him the honorific title "poet laureate" in 1488, as did the University of Louvain in 1492 and Cambridge in 1493.

Skelton began his career as a rhetorician and translator. His translations of texts by such classical writers as Cicero and Diodorus Siculus (albeit from Latin versions, not from the Greek originals) associate him with early Tudor humanist admirers of ancient letters and learning. In 1488 he joined the court of King Henry VII as an official poet; thus began a connection with the court that would last for forty years. The next year he published the first work that can reliably be ascribed to him, an "Elegy on the Death of the Earl of Northumberland" (1489). Between 1496 and 1501 he served as a tutor for Prince Arthur (who died young) and Prince Henry (later Henry VIII); around 1501 he wrote for them his *Speculum Principis* (1501), a "mirror for Princes" on the nature of good rulership that he later revised and presented to Henry on the new king's accession to the throne in 1509.

In 1498 Skelton started a new phase in his professional life. He began studying for the priesthood and, once ordained, rapidly advanced through the lower hierarchy of the church, serving as subdeacon, deacon, and then finally a priest of the Abbey of St. Mary Grace. Despite being a priest, and perhaps because of a satirist's tendency to attract jest and anecdote, he eventually acquired a probably undeserved and largely posthumous reputation for drunkenness and womanizing. Some sources say that he was suspended briefly from serving his church in 1511 for having a wife. He began writing in earnest at this time, and in 1498 published "The Bowge of Courte" (the rewards of court), a biting satire on court politics.

In 1503 Skelton retired briefly from court life to become rector of the parish church in Diss, Norfolk, where he stayed until 1512. While serving this parish, he wrote one of his best-known works, "Phyllyp Sparrowe," a young girl's lament for her dead pet bird. Although Skelton was not a courtier during these years, he continued to address the court in works such as "A Lawde and Prayse Made for Our Soureeigne Lord the King" (1509) and an elegy in Latin on the death of Henry VII (commissioned by the Abbot of Westminster in 1512). After Henry VII's death, Skelton returned to the court, now in the employ of his former pupil, Henry VIII, who gave him the title *Orator regius*, the King's Orator.

During the next few years Skelton served as a poet-propagandist for the court, celebrating England's military victories over the French and the Scots. His "Ballad of the Scottysshe Kynge" was released and distributed throughout England just days after Henry VIII defeated James IV of Scotland, and thus served simultaneously as a poetic reflection on the victory and as a news bulletin.

Skelton's courtly writing also focused on kingship. One of his most elaborate works, a drama called *Magnyfycence* (1515?), is a morality play that explores the qualities to which a king should aspire: generosity, good sense, and grandeur. The main character, Magnificence, is a kingly figure tempted by political vices such as Folly and Counterfeit Countenance but restrained by courtly virtues such as Measure and Perseverance. It is possible that Shakespeare was influenced by this work; the narrative of Prince Hal in *Henry IV.I* and *II* somewhat resembles *Magnyfycence*'s dramaturgical structure.

In 1518 Skelton moved to a house in the Sanctuary of Westminster in London. He began a series of literary attacks on Cardinal Wolsey, England's highest-ranking church official, who had political power commensurate to his station. Skelton's attacks include "Speke, Parrot" (1521?), "Colin Cloute" (1521–22), and "Why Come Ye Nat to Courte" (1522). Wolsey, as Henry VIII's chief minister, had Skelton imprisoned briefly and then released him. In 1523, Skelton appears to have made peace with the cardinal and wrote *The Garlande of Laurell*, which is part autobiography, part lyric, and part apology to Wolsey. In this poem, however, Skelton resumed his vitriolic tone. Written while England was still Catholic, his "Replycacion Against Certayne Yong Scolers Abjured of Late" (1527) scolds two Cambridge graduates for what Skelton thought were their heretical opinions. The poet's outspokenness was not just reserved for political figures, for he maintained a long-standing feud with Alexander Barclay, a rival poet-priest. The two ridiculed each other mercilessly in their poems.

Although he imitated Chaucer's seven-line stanza in some early works, Skelton could also deploy a literary style all his own. His verse often has a peculiar pattern of short, rapid-fire alliterative lines with two or three heavy stresses per line, together with end rhymes that can continue for upwards of seven or eight lines; so distinctive is this manner that scholars have named it "Skeltonic." The subject matter of his writing varied widely—although he wrote frequently for and of the court, many of his works (such as "The Tunnyng of Elynour Rummyng," a satirical poem in Skeltonic lines on female brewers) have commoners as their subjects. Similarly, despite his experiments with Latinate ("aureate") style or the macaronic multi-lingual juxtapositions of his "Speke, Parrot," his writing is grounded in colloquial English. A number of commonplace phrases such as "I smell a rat" and "by hook or by crook" have their earliest recorded literary appearances in his work.

Skelton's work marks a point of transition for English literature. He lived at a time when a medieval mindset was evolving into that of the Renaissance, and his writing has elements of both periods. Bitterly opposed to the Reformation and even to some parts of the new humanist learning, his many classical allusions and his translations demonstrate an interest in exploiting and valuing the culture of the ancient Greeks and Romans.

Skelton died 21 June 1529. He is buried at St. Margaret's Church, Lee Green, London.

⌘⌘⌘

The Tunning° of Elinour Rumming — *brewing*

Tell you I chill,[1]
If that ye will
Awhile be still,
Of a comely Gill° — *woman*
That dwelt on a hill:
But she is not gryl,° — *harsh*
For she is somewhat sage
And well worn in age.
For her viságe° — *face*
It would assuage
A man's coráge. — *courage*
Her loathly lere[2]
Is nothing clear,
But ugly of cheer,° — *expression*

[1] *I chill* I will (from "Ich will").

[2] *loathly lere* Disgusting complexion.

Droopy and drowsy,
Scurvy and lowsy,
Her face all bowsy,° *boozy*
Comely crinkléd,
Woundrously wrinkléd,
Like a roast pig's ear,
Bristléd with hair.
    Her lewd lippes twain,
They slaver, men sayne,
Like a ropy° rain, *stringy*
A gummy glair.[1]
She is ugly fair.
Her nose somedele° hookéd, *somewhat*
And camously crooked,[2]
Never stopping,
But ever dropping;
Her skin, loose and slack,
Grainéd like a sack;
With a crooked back.
    Her eyen° gowndy° *eyes / bleary*
Are full unsowndy,° *unhealthy*
For they are bleared;
And she gray-haired,
Jawéd like a jetty;[3]
A man would have pity
To see how she is gumméd,
Fingered and thumbéd,
Gently jointed,
Greased and annointed
Up to the knuckles;
The bones of her huckles° *hips*
Like as they were with buckles
Together made fast.
Her youth is far past.
Footed like a plane,
Leggéd like a crane,
And yet she will jet° *strut*
Like a jollivet,[4]
In her furréd flocket,[5]
And gray russet rocket,[6]
With simper and cocket.[7]
Her hood of Lincoln green
It had been hers, I ween,° *imagine*
More than forty year;
And so doth it appear,
For the green bare threadës
Look like sere° weedës, *dry*
Witheréd like hay,
The wool worn away.
And yet, I dare say,
She thinketh herself gay
Upon the holy day
When she doth her array[8]
And girdeth in her geets° *garments*
Stitched and pranked with pleats;
Her kirtle° Bristol-red, *dress*
With clothes upon her head
That weigh a sow of lead,[9]
Writhen° in wondrous wise *twisted*
After the Saracen's guise,[10]
With a whim-wham° *fancy detail*
Knit with a trim-tram° *ornament*
Upon her brain-pan;° *skull*
Like an Egyptian
Cappéd about.
When she goeth out
Herself for to shew,
She driveth down the dew
With a pair of heelës
As broad as two wheelës;
She hobbles as a goose
With her blanket hose
Over the fallow;
Her shoon° smeared with tallow, *shoes*
Greaséd upon dirt
That baudeth° her skirt. *dirties*

[1] *glair* Substance resembling egg white.

[2] *camously crooked* Awkwardly turned up.

[3] *Jawéd lyke a jetty* With a jaw that sticks out like a pier.

[4] *jollivet* Neatly dressed woman.

[5] *flocket* Loose tunic with long sleeves.

[6] *russet rocket* Cloak made out of homespun fabric.

[7] *With simper and cocket* With an affected, simpering manner.

[8] *doth her array* Dresses herself.

[9] *weigh a sow of lead* Weighs as much as a lead ingot.

[10] *After the Saracen's guise* Like the turban worn by the "Saracen," a term used in the period to refer to an Arab, a Turk, or a Muslim.

FIT° THE FIRST *part*

And this comely dame,
I understand, her name
Is Elinour Rumming,
At home in her wonning;° *dwelling*
And as men say
She dwelt in Surrey,
In a certain stead
Beside Leatherhead.
She is a tonnish gib,[1]
The devil and she be sib.° *siblings*

But to make up my tale,
She breweth nappy° ale, *strong*
And maketh thereof pot-sale[2]
To travellers, to tinkers,
To sweaters, to swinkers,° *laborers*
And all good ale-drinkers,
That will nothing spare
But drink till they stare
And bring themselves bare,
With *"Now away the mare!*[3]
And let us slay care."
As wise as an hare!

Come whoso will
To Elinour on the hill
With "Fill the cup, fill!"
And sit there by still,
Early and late.
Thither cometh Kate,
Cisly and Sarah,
With their legs bare,
And alsó their feet
Hardely full unsweet;
With their heelës daggéd,° *dirty*
Their kirtles all to-jaggéd,
Their smockës all to-ragged,
With titters and tatters,
Bring dishes and platters,
With all their might running
To Elinour Rumming
To have of her tunning.
She lendeth them on the same,[4]
And thus beginneth the game.
Some wenches come unlacéd,
Some housewives come unbracéd,[5]
With their naked pappes,° *breasts*
That flippës and flappës,
That wiggës and waggës
Like tawny° saffron baggës; *light brown*
A sort of foul drabbës
All scurvy with scabbës.
Some be flybitten,
Some skewéd as a kitten;
Some with a shoe-clout[6]
Bind their headës about;
Some have no hair-lace,
Their locks about their face,
Their tresses untrussed
All full of unlust;
Some look strawry,
Some cawry-mawry;[7]
Full untidy teggës,[8]
Like rotten eggës.
Such a lewd sort
To Elinour resort
From tide to tide.
Abide, abide!
And to you shall be told
How her ale is sold
To Maud and to Mold.

FIT THE SECOND

Some have no money
That thither comë

[1] *tonnish gib* Literally "fashionable cat."

[2] *maketh thereof pot-sale* Makes it available for sale.

[3] *away the mare* Away with sadness.

[4] *She lendeth them on the same* She loans them beer with their clothes as collateral.

[5] *unbracéd* With their garments open.

[6] *shoe clout* Cloth used for wiping shoes.

[7] *cawry-mawry* Like rough material.

[8] *teggës* Contemptuous term for the women (literally "young unshorn sheep").

For their ale to pay.
That is a shrewd array!
Elinour swearéd, "Nay,
Ye shall not bear away
My ale for nought,
By Him that me bought!"[1]
With "Hey, dog, hey!
Have these hogs away!"
With "Get me a staff,
The swine eat my draff![2]
Strike the hogs with a club,
They have drunk up my swilling-tub!"
For, be there never so much press,[3]
These swine go to the high dais,
The sow with her pigs,
The boar his tail wrigs,° *wriggles*
His rump alsó he frigs° *rubs*
Against the high bench!
With, "Fo, there's a stench!
Gather up, thou wench;
Seest thou not what is fall?° *happening*
Take up dirt and all,
And bear out of the hall:
God give it ill-preving,[4]
Cleanly as evil 'chieving!"

But let us turn plain,
There we left again.
For, as ill a patch as that,
The hens run in the mash-vat;
For they go to roost
Straight over the ale-joust,° *ale-pot*
And dung, when it comës,
In the ale-tunnës.° *ale-casks*
Then Elinour taketh
The mash-bowl, and shaketh
The hens' dung away,
And skimmeth it into a tray
Whereas the yeast is,
With her mangy° fistës: *scabby*
And sometime she blens
The dung of her hens
And the ale together,
And sayeth, "Gossip,° come hither, *friend*
This ale shall be thicker,
And flower° the more quicker; *froth*
For I may tell yóu
I learned it of a Jew
When I began to brew,
And I have found it true.
Drink now while it is new:
An ye may it brook,° *enjoy*
It shall make you look
Younger than ye be
Yearës two or three,
For ye may prove it by me."
"Behold," she said, "and see
How bright I am of ble!° *complexion*
Ich am not cast away,
That can my husband say,
When we kiss and play
In lust and in likíng;
He calleth me his whiting,[5]
His mulling° and his miting,° *darling / little one*
His nobbës° and his coney,° *sweetheart / rabbit*
His sweeting and his honey,
With 'Buss,° my pretty bonny, *kiss me*
Thou art worth goods and money!'
Thus make I my fellow fonny,° *foolish*
Till that he dream and drony;° *becomes sluggish*
For, after all our sport,
Then will he rout° and snort: *bellow*
Then sweetly together we lie
As two pigs in a sty."

To cease meseemeth best,
And of this tale to rest,
And for to leave this letter
Because it is no better,
And because it is no sweeter;
We will no further rime
Of it at this time,
But we will turnë plain
Where we left again.

---

[1] *By him that me bought* By Christ.

[2] *draff* Leftover brewing grains, often used as hogs' swill.

[3] *be there never so much press* If the establishment is not busy.

[4] *God give it ill-preving* May God bring it to ruin.

[5] *whiting* Species of fish (a term of endearment).

FIT THE THIRD

Instead of coin and money
Some bringë her a coney,° *rabbit*
And some a pot with honey,
Some a salt, and some a spoon,
Some their hose, some their shoon;° *shoes*
Some run a good trot
With a skillet or a pot;
Some fill their pot full
Of good Lemster wool:
An housewife of trust,
When she is athirst,
Such a web can spin,
Her thrift is full thin.[1]

Some go straight thither,
Be it slaty or slither:[2]
They hold the highway,
They care not what men say,
Be that as be may.
Some, loth to be espied,
Start in at the backë-side
Over the hedge and pale,
And all for the good ale.
Some runnë till they sweat,
Bring with them malt or wheat,
And Dame Elinour entreat
To birle them of the best.[3]

Then cometh another guest:
She sweareth by the rood of rest[4]
Her lippës are so dry
Without drink she must die,
"Therefore fill it by and by,
And have here a peck of rye."

Anon cometh another,
As dry as the other,
And with her doth bring
Meal, salt, or other thing,
Her harvest girdle, her wedding-ring,
To pay for her scot° *bill*
As cometh to her lot.
One bringeth her husband's hood
Because the ale is good;
Another brought her his cap
To offer to the ale-tap,
With flax and with tow;° *unprepared flax*
And some brought sour dough
With "Hey" and with "Ho!
Sit we down a row,
And drink till we blow,° *argue, boast*
And pipe 'Tirly Tirlow!'"[5]

Some laid to pledge
Their hatchet and their wedge,
Their heckle[6] and their reel,
Their rock,[7] their spinning-wheel;
And some went so narrow
They laid to pledge their wharrow,[8]
Their ribskin[9] and their spindle,
Their needle and their thimble.
Here was scant thrift
When they made such shift.° *trade*
Their thirst was so great
They asked never for meat,
But "Drink, still drink,
And let the cat wink![10]
Let us wash our gums
From the dry crumbs!"

FIT THE FOURTH

Some for very need
Laid down a skein° of thread, *length*

[1] *Her thrift is full thin* Her thriftiness goes away.

[2] *slaty or slither* On smooth roads or on stony roads.

[3] *To birle them of the best* To pour them a drink of her best.

[4] *rood of rest* Cross of salvation.

[5] *Tirly Tirlow* Nonsense singing.

[6] *heckle* Comb used in spinning.

[7] *rock* Staff used in spinning.

[8] *wharrow* Pulley on a spinning wheel.

[9] *ribskin* Leather apron used in preparing flax for spinning.

[10] *let the cat wink* A proverb: "let the cat wink and let the mouse run."

And some a skein of yarn;
Some brought from the barn
Both beanës and peas;
Small chaffer° doth ease *trades*
Sometime, now and then;
Another there was that ran
With a good brass-pan,
Her colour was full wan;° *pale*
She ran in all the haste,
Unbracéd and unlaced;
Tawny, swart,° and sallow *dark-skinned*
Like a cake of tallow.
I swear by all hallow
It was a stale° to take *lure*
The devil in a brake!° *cage*
 And then came halting° Joan, *limping*
And brought a gambone[1]
Of bacon that was reasty:° *rancid*
But, Lord, as she was testy,
Angry as a waspy!
She began to gape and gaspy,
And bade Elinour go bet° *quicker*
And fill in good met;° *measure*
It was dear that was far-fet.° *far-fetched*

 Another brought a spick° *fat portion*
Of a bacon flick,
Her tongue was very quick
But she spake somewhat thick.
Her fellow did stammer and stut,
But she was a foul slut,
For her mouth foaméd
And her belly groanéd:
Joan sayn she had eaten a fiest.
"By Christ," said she, "thou liest,
I have as sweet a breath
As thou, with shameful death!"
 Then Elinour said, "Ye callets,° *whores*
I shall break your palates,° *heads*
Without° ye now cease!" *unless*
And so was made the peace.
 Then thither came drunken Alice,
And she was full of talës,
Of tidings in Walës,
And of Saint James in Galës,[2]
And of the Portingalës,° *Portuguese*
With "Lo, gossip, ywis,° *truly*
Thus and thus it is:
There hath been great war
Between Temple Bar
And the Cross in Cheap,[3]
And there came an heap
Of mill-stones in a rout ..."[4]
She speaketh thus in her snout,
Snivelling in her nose
As though she had the pose.° *a head cold*
"Lo, here is an old tippet,° *stole, scarf*
An ye will give me a sippet
Of your stale ale,
God send you good sale!"
And as she was drinking
She fell in a winking
With a barlichood,° *fit of drunkenness*
She pissed where she stood.
Then began she to weep,
And forthwith fell asleep.
Elinour took her up
And blessed her with a cup
Of newë ale in cornës:[5]
Alice found therein no thornës,
But supped it up at onës,
She found therein no bonës.

Fit the Fifth

 Now in cometh another rabble:
First one with a ladle,
Another with a cradle,

[1] *gambone* Bottom of a "side."

[2] *Saint James in Galës* Saint James (d. 44 CE), patron saint of Spain. Many Christians made pilgrimages to his shrine in the Spanish province of Galicia.

[3] *Temple Bar ... Cheap* Temple Bar and Cheapside, areas of London.

[4] *great war ... rout* Reference to riots which began on "Evil May Day" (1 May 1517) in which residents of London's East End rose up against immigrant workers, particularly wealthy French and Flemish merchants.

[5] *newë ale in cornës* Ale drawn off the malt.

And with a side-saddle:
And there began a fabble,° *fable*
A clattering and a babble
Of foolish Philly
That had a foal with Willy,
With "'Jast you!" and "Gup gilly!"[1]
She could not lie stilly.

Then came in a jennet° *horseman*
And swore, "By Saint Bennet,[2]
I drank not this sennight° *week*
A draught to my pay!
Elinour, I thee pray,
Of thine ale let us essay,° *try*
And have here a pilch[3] of gray:
I wear skinnes of coney,° *rabbit*
That causeth I look so dony!"° *drab*

Another then did hitch° her, *jerk*
And brought a pottle-pitcher,
A tunnel° and a bottle, *funnel*
But she had lost the stopple:
She cut off her shoe-sole,
And stoppéd therewith the hole.

Amongë all the blommer° *uproar, confusion*
Another brought a skommer,° *ladle with a sieve*
A frying-pan, and a slicer:
Elinour made the pricë
For good ale each wit.° *offering*

Then start in mad Kit
That had little wit:
She seeméd somedele sick
And brought a penny chick
To Dame Elinour
For a draught of liquor.

Then Margery Milkduck
Her kirtle she did uptuck
An inch above her knee,
Her legs that ye might see;
But they were sturdy and stubbéd,
Mighty pestles and clubbed,
As fair and as white
As the foot of a kite.[4]
She was somewhat foul,
Crooken-neckéd like an owl;
And yet she brought her fees,
A cantle° of Essex cheese,[5] *piece*
Was well a foot thick
Full of maggots quick:° *live*
It was huge and great,
And mighty strong meat° *food*
For the devil to eat:
It was tart and pungete!° *sharp*

Another set of sluts:
Some brought walnuts,
Some apples, some pears,
Some brought their clipping shears,
Some brought this and that,
Some brought I wot° ne'er what; *knew*
Some brought their husband's hat,
Some puddings and links,° *sausages*
Some tripes that stinks.
But of all this throng
One came them among,
She seeméd half a leech° *doctor*
And began to preach
Of the Tuesday in the week
When the mare doth kick;
Of the virtue of an unset leek,[6]
Of her husband's breek;° *breeches*
With the feathers of a quail
She could to Bordeaux sail;
And with good ale barmë° *yeast*
She could make a charmë
To help withal a stitch:
She seemed to be a witch.
Another brought two goslings

[1] *"Jast you!" and "Gup, gilly!"* Exclamations generally used in handling a horse.

[2] *Saint Bennet* Saint Benedict (c. 480–543), the founder of Western monasticism.

[3] *pilch* Coat made up of both the skin and fur of the animal.

[4] *kite* Small bird of prey.

[5] *Essex cheese* Type of cheese prone to maggot infestation.

[6] *the virtue of an unset leek* Young leeks were thought to have strong medicinal properties.

That were noughty frostlings;[1]
She brought them in a wallet,° *knapsack*
She was a comely callet:° *lewd woman*
The goslings were untied;
Elinour began to chide,
"They be wretchocks° thou hast brought, *runts*
They are sheer shaking nought!"[2]

Fit the Sixth

Maud Ruggy thither skippéd:
She was ugly hippéd,
And ugly thick lippéd,
Like an onion sided,
Like tan leather hided.
She had her so guided
Between the cup and the wall
That she was there withal
Into a palsy fall;
With that her head shakéd,
And her handes quakéd,
One's head would have achéd
To see her naked.
She drank so of the dreggës,
The dropsy was in her leggës;
Her face glistering like glass,
All foggy fat she was.
She had alsó the gout
In all her joints about;
Her breath was sour and stale,
And smelléd all of ale:
Such a bedfellaw
Would make one cast his craw.[3]
But yet for all that
She drank on the mash-vat.
  There came an old ribibe:° *woman*
She halted of a kibe,[4]
And had broken her shin
At the threshold coming in,
And fell so wide open
That one might see her token,
The devil thereon be wroken!° *unleashed*
What need all this be spoken?
She yelléd like a calf.
"Rise up, on God's half!"
Said Elinour Rumming,
'I beshrew thee for thy coming!'
And as she at her did pluck,
"Quack, quack!" said the duck
In that lampatram's lap;
With "Fie, cover thy shap
With some flip flap!
God give it ill hap,"° *fortune*
Said Elinour, "for shame!"—
Like an honest dame.
Up she start, half lame,
And scantly could go
For pain and for woe.
  In came another dant,° *loose woman*
With a goose and a gant:° *yawn*
She had a wide weasant;° *windpipe*
She was nothing pleasant,
Neckéd like an elephant;
It was a bulliphant,
A greedy cormorant.[5]

  Another brought her garlic heads,
Another brought her beads
(Of jet or of coal)
To offer to the ale pole.
Some brought a wimble,° *hand drill*
Some brought a thimble,
Some brought a silk lace,
Some brought a pincase,
Some her husband's gown,
Some a pillow of down,
Some of the napery° *table linen*
. . . .[6]
And all this shift° they make *trade*
For the good ale sake.

[1] *noughty frostlings* I.e., of poor quality.

[2] *sheer shaking nought* Diseased.

[3] *cast his craw* Vomit.

[4] *kibe* Ulcer on the heel.

[5] *cormorant* Sea bird known for swallowing fish whole.

[6] Line missing.

"A straw!°" said Bely, "stand utter,° *nonsense! / back*
For we have eggs and butter,
. . . .[1]
And of pigeons a pair."

Then start forth a fizgig,° *giddy girl*
And she brought a boar pig,
The flesh thereof was rank,
And her breath strongly stank;
Yet, ere she went, she drank,
And gat° her great thank *got*
Of Elinour for her ware
That she thither bare
To pay for her share.
Now truly, to my thinking,
This is a solemn drinking!

Fit the Seventh

"Soft!" quod one hight° Sybil, *named*
"And let me with you bibble."° *drink*
She sat down in the place
With a sorry face
Whey-wormed about.[2]
Garnished was her snout
With here and there a pustule
Like a scabbed mussel.
"This ale," said she, "is noppy;
Let us suppë° and soppy° *eat / drink*
And not spill a droppy,
For, so may I hoppy,° *hope*
It cooleth well my croppy.° *stomach*

"Dame Elinour," said she,
"Have here is for me—
A clout° of London pins!" *bag*
And with that she begins
The pot to her pluck
And drank a "good-luck."
She swinged up a quart
At once for her part:
Her paunch was so puffed,
And so with ale stuffed,
Had she not hied° apace *gone*
She had defiled the place.

Then began the sport
Among that drunken sort.
"Dame Elinour," said they,
"Lend here a cock° of hay *stack*
To make all thing clean—
Ye wot° well what we mean!" *know*

But, sir, among all
That sat in that hall
There was a prick-me-dainty[3]
Sat like a sainty
And began to painty° *pant*
As though she would fainty:
She made it as coy
As a *lege de moy*;[4]
She was not half so wise
As she was peevish nice.
She said never a word,
But rose from the board
And called for our dame,
Elinour by name.
We supposed, ywis,
That she rose to piss:
But the very ground
Was for to compound[5]
With Elinour in the spence,° *liquor pantry*
To pay for her expense.
"I have no penny nor groat[6]
To pay," she said, "God wote,° *knows*
For washing of my throat,
But my beads of amber
Bear them to your chamber."
Then Elinour did them hide
Within her beddës side.

[1] Line missing.

[2] *Whey-wormed about* Pimple-faced.

[3] *prick-me-dainty* One who dresses in an affected manner.

[4] *lege de moy* Kind of dance.

[5] *ground ... compound* The very ground would settle their dispute.

[6] *groat* Coin worth one eighth of an ounce of silver.

But some then sat right sad
That nothing had,
There of their own,
Neither gelt nor pawn:[1]
Such were there many
That had not a penny.
But, when they should walk,
Were fain° with a chalk[2] *glad*
To score on the balk,° *wood beam*
Or score on the tail:° *tally*
God give it ill hail!° *bad luck*
For my fingers itch,
I have written too much
Of this mad mumming
Of Elinour Rumming.
Thus endeth the geste° *tale*
Of this worthy feast.
—1521? (WRITTEN C. 1517)

To Mistress Isabell Pennell

By Saint Mary, my lady,
Your mammy and your dady
Brought forth a goodly baby!
My maiden Isabel,
Reflaring° rosabell,° *sweet smelling / rose*
The flagrant° camamell,° *fragrant / chamomile*
The ruddy rosary,
The sovereign° rosemary, *healing*
The pretty strawberry,
The columbine, the nepte,° *catnip*
The jeloffer° well set,° *gillyflower / adorned*
The proper violet;
Ennewéd° your colowre *renewed*
Is like the daisy flower
After the April shower;
Star of the morrow gray,[3]
The blossom on the spray,° *branch*
The freshest flower of May:
Maidenly demure,
Of womanhood the lure;
Wherefore I make you sure
It were an heavenly health,
It were an endless wealth,
A life for God himself,
To hear this nightingale
Among the birdës smale° *small*
Warbeling in the vale,—
Dug, dug, jug, jug,
Good year and good luck,
With chuck, chuck, chuck, chuck!
—1523

[1] *Neither gelt nor pawn* Neither money nor something to trade.

[2] *a chalk* Account of credit written in chalk, a tab.

[3] *Star of the morrow gray* Venus.

Sir Thomas More

1478 – 1535

Thomas More was one of the most impressive figures of the English Renaissance. His writings on politics, religion, faith, and history, his translations of Lucian from the Greek, and his witty Latin epigrams, together with his activities as lawyer, parliamentarian, and Lord Chancellor, won him international fame as an author, a vigorous polemicist, an influential statesman, and, eventually, a Catholic martyr. He is remembered above all for his *Utopia*, an important work of satirical political speculation, and for maintaining his principles during one of the nastiest political struggles in English history—a moral choice that cost him his life.

More was born in London on 7 February 1478, the son of Agnes and Sir John More, a lawyer and judge. As a boy, he studied at St. Anthony's School in London before leaving at age 13 to become a page in the household of John Morton, Archbishop of Canterbury and a future cardinal. Morton recognized More as a promising, intelligent boy, and had him sent to Oxford around 1492. While there, More immersed himself in Greek, Latin, French, history, mathematics, and philosophy. He stayed for two years and then was compelled by his father to leave in order to study law at New Inn in London. In February 1496, he was admitted as a student to Lincoln's Inn, another London law school; once he had qualified as a lawyer, he stayed on as a popular lecturer.

Although law absorbed much of More's time (as he laments in a preface to *Utopia*), he continued to pursue his studies and in 1497 was delighted to meet the famous Dutch scholar Desiderius Erasmus, with whom he became good friends; many of their letters survive. More had, he claimed, considered becoming a monk, living for a while in the London Charterhouse, a monastery for Carthusian monks. Eventually he decided, as he put it, to be "a chaste husband rather than an impure priest." But his early attraction to communal and penitential ways did not disappear; it may well underlie More's wearing a hair shirt—and *Utopia*'s stress on a communal way of life.

In 1504, More was elected to Parliament, where he defended the free speech of Members and opposed Henry VII's demand for a heavy round of taxation. The taxes were reduced, but an angry King arranged to have More's father arrested on a trumped-up charge and More himself expelled. More returned to public life only in 1509, when Henry VIII came to the throne. In 1505, he married Jane Colt; theirs was a happy marriage that produced four children before Jane's death six years later. Grieving, but wanting a mother for his children, More married Alice Middleton, a widow, a month after his first wife's death. He arranged an excellent education for all his children, including his daughters, and was particularly proud of young Margaret's scholarly accomplishments.

In succeeding years, More held several political offices. In 1515, he joined a trade embassy that spent six months in Flanders, where he used his leisure time to begin *Utopia*, which was published the following year. Upon his return to England, More joined the court of Henry VIII. He developed a warm but uneasy relationship with the King, and over the next two decades he received many honors: knighted in 1521, he was elected Speaker of the House in 1523 and appointed High Steward of Cambridge University in 1525. In 1529, More succeeded Cardinal Wolsey as Lord Chancellor,

England's highest political position next to the king's. His first responsibility was to serve as Chief Justice, a position he filled with skill and honesty, introducing reforms that streamlined the judicial system. More was also responsible for enforcing anti-heresy laws (like many at the time, More believed that heresy threatened political stability as well as souls). He not only prosecuted some he called "heretics" but wrote strident denunciations of Martin Luther, William Tyndale, and others, becoming in turn a target of Protestant polemics.

More's greatest challenge was to deal with the "King's great matter," Henry's claim that his marriage to Catherine of Aragon was invalid and that he was free to marry Anne Boleyn. Pope Clement VII refused to agree to an annulment or a divorce and Henry eventually renounced papal authority and declared himself to be head of the English Church. More could not support the King's actions, although he did not publicly reject them and indeed insisted on his right to keep his opinions private. In May 1532, he resigned.

In March 1534, Parliament passed Henry's Act of Succession. This legislation required certain of the King's ministers and subjects to take the Oath of Supremacy, which stated that the King's children by Anne Boleyn were legitimate heirs to the throne. Those who took the Oath were also required to repudiate all foreign authority, including that of the Pope. On 14 April 1534, More was asked to swear. He refused and was sent to the Tower of London. There he wrote letters and religious works, including the serene and surprisingly funny *Dialogue of Comfort Against Tribulation*, until the authorities confiscated his writing implements. On 1 July 1535, More was indicted for high treason, found guilty, and sentenced to hang, although the king commuted the sentence to a more humane method of execution, beheading. More was executed on Tower Hill on 6 July, reportedly saying, "I die the King's good servant but God's first." His body was buried in the Church of St. Peter and his head was displayed on London Bridge for a month. On 19 May 1935, Pope Pius XI declared More a saint.

⌘⌘⌘

Utopia

Even a brief look at the variety—and the interconnectedness—of the life More led during the period leading up to the writing of *Utopia* may offer illuminating perspectives on the work. A lawyer by training, More had attended parliament as a representative of the London merchants. In 1510 he was appointed to the post of under-sheriff in London (one of two such positions); his responsibility was to act on behalf of the sheriff at the Sheriff's Court, held once a week at the Guildhall. Acting in this capacity until 1518, he dealt with a wide variety of matters and had a great deal of contact with the criminal elements of society; theft, assault, rape, and arson were among the many sorts of cases he tried; many of those convicted were sentenced to death (even petty theft could be a capital offence). According to Erasmus he developed a reputation for fairness, and was widely regarded with affection as well as respect. He must also have developed a keen sense of the issues surrounding capital punishment, and inevitably, he would have developed a knowledge of the effects that poverty and disease may have on human lives. But at the same time he was becoming more and more well-connected with people of influence and power both in London and in the country as a whole. He advised various city bodies on legal matters; he acted as a spokesman and legal representative for groups as diverse as the fishmongers, the mercers, the bakers, and various groups of tradesmen, and he began frequently to play a significant negotiating role in the concluding of agreements involving these groups. He was appointed as a commissioner of sewers along the Thames; he lectured regularly on legal matters at Lincoln's Inn; he maintained his own (increasingly flourishing) legal practice; he met frequently with the archbishop of Canterbury and became intimately familiar with many Church affairs; he maintained contact with many of the leading thinkers of the day; he wrote his *History of Richard III*; he began too to become involved in Court and diplomatic circles. Given the scope of his experience, it is hardly surprising that, when an English delegation was being formed in 1515 to try to resolve various commercial disputes with Flanders over the vital wool trade, both the king's council and the Merchant Adventurers asked that More be a part of the delegation.

The negotiations turned out to be far more protracted than had been expected—they dragged on intermittently for several months—but they were far from all-consuming, particularly for someone as used to a busy schedule as More was. He spent some time complaining about the lack of activity (and about the meager pay for those attached to the delegation), but he also spent a great deal of time engaged in intellectual pursuits. Aside from *Utopia*, the most notable of his 1515 writings is perhaps a long letter he wrote to the theologian Martin Dorp in defense of Erasmus, whose projects at the time included a comparison of the then-standard Latin (Vulgate) text of the New Testament with that of the original Greek with a view to identifying misleading or erroneous passages in the Vulgate. Dorp was among those conservative voices in the Church who were suspicious of such work, seeing no need for scholarly initiatives that might lead to challenges to traditional interpretations of Christian texts. But More's arguments for the value of such scholarship were effective; Dorp withdrew his criticisms, and Erasmus's work went forward.

While in Flanders More stayed for several weeks in Antwerp with Peter Giles, Chief Secretary to the city and, like More, a good friend of Erasmus. Like More too, Giles was concerned with questions of justice and fairness; with economic matters and with civic governance; with crime and punishment; and with international affairs. The two spent a good deal of time in conversation, and became friends. It was during his time in Antwerp that More conceived of the idea of writing *De Optimo Reipublicae Statu* (as the work that came to be known as *Utopia* was originally entitled)— "The Best Condition of a Society." Eventually, More made Giles a central figure in *Utopia*, and Giles played an important role in arranging for the printing and dissemination of the work.

More's *Utopia* has given its name to an entire genre (though many would argue that the genre of utopian fiction predates *Utopia*); "utopia" has come to signify any work describing a seemingly idyllic, fictional society. But to what extent is More's *Utopia* a utopia? This elusive and sometimes playful text resists any simple categorization or interpretation. The text can be read convincingly as moral allegory, political manifesto, or elaborate literary joke. And if *Utopia* is indeed meant to illustrate an ideal, it is a matter of much debate what that ideal is; the text has frequently been read as presenting an idealized version of (what we now refer to as) socialist or communist society, but it has also been read as presenting an idealized version of classical Greek society, and as presenting an idealized version of Catholic society. Conflicting interpretations of More's life and beliefs have been brought into the debate as historians and literary critics have attempted to solve the puzzle of the work's meaning through appeals to authorial intention. But *Utopia* has stubbornly resisted efforts to fix its meaning. In part this resistance to fixity may be attributed to the work's form. More seems to have written the second part of the work first, and some time later to have added the opening book, setting the second in the context, but also problematizing any interpretation tending towards taking Book 2 at face value; the two-book structure of the final work militates against interpretations that would resolve its meaning into a neatly unified whole. In part, too, *Utopia*'s elusiveness may be attributed to complexity of narrative viewpoint; multiple layers of narrative voice allow ample space for multiple readings (for example, of the degree to which irony may be at play), and work to steer readers away from readings that exclusively privilege a single point of view.

More's *Utopia* (like other Renaissance texts with utopian themes, such as Francis Bacon's *The New Atlantis* and Henry Neville's *The Isle of Pines*), is deeply steeped in classical tradition: More's text serves as a commentary on classical meditations on the characteristics of an ideal commonwealth—most notably that of Plato in his *Republic*, *Timaeus*, and *Laws*. (More was no doubt aware as well of the views of Aristotle on such matters, as set out in his *Politics*, but the Platonic influence clearly predominates over the Aristotelian.) In Plato's *Republic* the guardians of an ideal society are obliged to ensure that property is held in common, everyone is obliged to work, and the ideal ruler is a philosopher. Other classical texts are also relevant; the often playful spirit of *Utopia* seems indebted to Lucian's *Satirical Sketches* and Horace's *Satires*, both of which aim to combine humor and instruction. A satirical sketch by Lucian, which was translated from Greek to Latin by More and Erasmus around 1505, may have suggested the structure of *Utopia*; in the first part of the sketch a serious issue is discussed from different points of view, and in the second the character Menippus throws light on the issue by telling the tale of a journey to an imaginary land. In other formal aspects too *Utopia* recalls classical authors: Book 1's dialogue form is indebted to the Dialogues of Plato and of Cicero. In the degree to which it both relies upon and reappraises classical works, then, *Utopia* is very much a characteristic work of its time.

Another key influence for *Utopia* was the burgeoning genre of travel literature. During the Renaissance, as European countries competed to explore and lay claim to large parts of Asia, Africa, and the New World, the proliferation of printed material made accounts of many voyages readily available to the literate public. Tales of incredible journeys ranged from the completely fabricated to the accurately documented, and readers had to sift the truth from the fiction. *Utopia* plays with this genre of travel narrative, purporting to be an account of a voyage undertaken by real-life explorer Amerigo Vespucci. In Book 1 Raphael Hythloday is introduced as a sailor with Vespucci, who has encountered the island of Utopia on one of his trips to the New World. The language and tone of Book 2's description of Utopia are suggestive of a travel narrative, while the playful paratexts (prefaces, maps, marginalia, and even a poem in Utopian) that accompanied early editions of *Utopia* resemble the sorts of materials that often accompanied accounts of real voyages. In the context of the possibilities presented by Renaissance exploration, the discovery of such an island would have seemed almost plausible, and this plausibility is played upon throughout the text.

Deliberate gestures towards potential reality are considered one of the defining elements of utopian texts; such works tend to go to great lengths to highlight the plausibility of the lands they describe even while, paradoxically, presenting themselves as works of fiction. Utopias are generally not set in fictional lands, or in distant past or future times. (It is a common mistake to imagine that utopias are typically set in the future.) Instead, these ideal societies tend to neighbor our own; explanations are typically provided as to why they have remained hidden for so long, and how they were discovered. Further, human nature is generally shown to be as we sense it to be from our own experience—members of society are as likely to put their own needs first as they are to give preference to the collective well-being. Economic realities relating to supply and demand still apply, and the same problems of limited resources present themselves. What makes a utopia ideal, then, is not its citizens or its superior environment, but its superior social organization.

The social organization of Utopia—and the ways in which it contrasts with that of England—is the central focus of More's work. Book 1 is set up as a conversation between More, his friend Peter Giles, and Raphael Hythloday, to whom More is introduced by Giles. The three debate the social problems of England, with Raphael denouncing many aspects of the way in which society is organized, from the system of land ownership to the practice of executing thieves when the poor have often been forced by poverty to turn to theft or begging for survival. In Book 2 Raphael provides, by way of contrast, a glowing description of the island of Utopia's social structures and customs. A central principle is collective ownership; private property has been abolished in order to end poverty and curb human greed and pride. (This economic system is presented in contrast to that of England, in which supposedly holy men "enclose every bit of land for pasture, pull down houses, and destroy

> "I can't agree," I said. "Life can never be happy or satisfactory **where all things are held in common.**"

Similarly, the translation of the distinguished More scholar George Logan has

> "But I don't see it that way," I replied. "It seems to me that people cannot possibly live well **when all things are held in common.**"

The popular Paul Turner translation, in contrast, uses phrasing that suggests a stronger connection to the nineteenth-century ideas of Karl Marx than it does to Platonic or Christian notions:

> "I disagree. I don't believe you'd ever have a reasonable standard of living **under a communist system.**"

There can be no doubt that parallels between ideas found in *Utopia* and those of modern socialists and Marxists make for fruitful discussion—and an argument may be made that embedding such parallels in the text makes for a livelier read today. The present editors have felt it preferable, however, not to embed such parallels in the translation.

A notable feature of early editions of *Utopia* is the inclusion of numerous annotations in the margins. These marginal glosses are generally believed to have been added by Peter Giles and/or by Erasmus. Often interesting in themselves, they also provide a real sense of the way in which the intellectual community of the time operated in a collaborative fashion. This edition includes all the significant glosses, albeit in the form of footnotes rather than marginal notations; each such note begins with the heading [marginal note] in square brackets.

Utopia[1]

The Best State of a Commonwealth and the New Island of Utopia

A Truly Golden Handbook, No Less Beneficial than Entertaining, By the Distinguished and Eloquent Author.

THOMAS MORE

Citizen and Sheriff[2] *of the Famous City of London*

Thomas More to Peter Giles[3]

I am almost ashamed, my dear Peter Giles, to send you this little book about the Utopian commonwealth after nearly a year, for I am sure you expected it within a month and a half. Certainly you know that I was relieved of all the labor of gathering materials for it and had to give no thought to their arrangement. I had only to repeat what in your company I had heard Raphael relate. There was no reason for me to take trouble over the style of the narrative; first, his language was, hurried and impromptu, and then, to make matters worse, spoken by one who was, as you know, less acquainted with Latin than with Greek. Therefore the

[1] *Utopia* The present text has been prepared for *The Broadview Anthology of British Literature* by William P. Weaver. The translation from the Latin is that of G.C. Richards, considerably revised and modernized for this anthology.

[2] *Sheriff* More had been appointed Undersheriff of London in 1510. The position sometimes entailed acting in the capacity of a judge as well as representing the Sheriff.

[3] *Peter Giles* Giles (c. 1486–1533), a friend of More's, was a scholar who also worked for the city of Antwerp. As has been noted by scholars of More, in this letter and in *Utopia* More plays with words meaning "all," "nothing," and "nowhere" often exploiting, in the letter to Giles, the rhetorical figure "litotes" (denying the contrary, as in "not nowhere" to mean "somewhere"). Even at the lexical level, then, More's text is a not unsmiling venture into paradox of the sort Renaissance humanists found not unappealing.

nearer my style resembles his careless simplicity the closer it comes to the truth, which here is my main concern.

I confess my dear Peter, that all these considerations relieved me of so much trouble that scarcely anything remained for me to do. Otherwise gathering and arranging materials would have required much time and attention from someone with wits neither the slightest nor the most ignorant. Had the task required writing down the material not only accurately but eloquently, I could not have performed it, no matter how much time and effort I might expend. But, as it was, since those burdensome cares had been removed and it remained only to write out simply what I had heard, I had no difficulty at all. And yet my other obligations left me practically no leisure to finish this trifling task. I am constantly engaged in legal business, either pleading or hearing, either giving an award as arbiter or deciding a case as judge. I pay a courtesy visit to one person and go on business to another. I devote almost the whole day to other people's affairs and what little is left to my own. For myself, that is for learning, I leave nothing at all. When I have return home I must talk with my wife, chat with my children, and confer with my servants. All this activity I count as business if it must be done—and it must be done, unless you want to be a stranger in your own home. Besides, one must take care to be as agreeable as possible to those whom nature has supplied, chance has made, or you yourself have chosen to be the companions of your life, provided you do not spoil them by kindness or through indulgence make masters of your servants.

Amid such occupations, the day, the month, and the year slip away. When, then, can I find time to write? Nor have I said a word about sleep, nor even about food, which for many people takes up as much time as sleep—and sleep takes up almost half a man's life. So I have for myself only the time I filch from sleep and food. Slowly, therefore, because this time is so little, and yet at last, because this time is something, I have finished *Utopia* and sent it to you, my dear Peter, to read—and to remind me of anything that has escaped me.

In this respect I do not entirely distrust myself, wishing only that I were as nimble in intelligence and learning as I am not altogether deficient in memory. Nevertheless, I am not so confident as to believe that I have forgotten nothing. As you know, John Clement,[1] my pupil-servant, was also present at the conversation. Indeed I do not allow him to absent himself from any profitable talk, for from this young plant, which has begun to put forth green shoots in Greek and Latin literature, I expect no small harvest someday. He has made very doubtful concerning one point: according to my own recollection, Hythlodaeus[2] declared that the bridge spanning the river Anydrus[3] at Amaurotum[4] is five hundred paces in length. But my John says that two hundred must be subtracted, for the river there is not more than three hundred paces in breadth. Please recall the matter to mind. If you agree with him, I shall adopt the same view and think myself mistaken. If you do not remember, I shall put down, as I have actually done, what I myself seem to remember. Just as I shall take great pains to have nothing incorrect in the book, so, if there is doubt about anything, I would rather tell an objective falsehood than an intentional lie—for I would rather be honest than clever.

It would be easy for you to remedy this defect if you were to ask Raphael himself, either in person or by letter. You must do so because of another doubt that has arisen, whether through my fault or through yours or through Raphael's I do not know. We forgot to ask, and he forgot to say, where in the New World Utopia is located. I am sorry that point got omitted, and I would be willing to pay a considerable sum to purchase the information, partly because I am somewhat embarrassed not to know in what sea lies the very island of which I am saying so much, and partly because there are several among us (and one in particular, a devout man and a theologian by profession) burning with an extraordinary desire to visit Utopia. The theologian wishes to go not from an idle taste for sight-seeing in novel places, but in order to foster and promote our religion, begun there so felicitously. To carry out this plan properly, he has decided to ask the Pope to

[1] *John Clement* Clement (d. 1572), later a leading scholar and physician to Henry VIII, was at this time tutor to More's children.

[2] *Hythlodaeus* Greek: knowledgeable about nonsense.

[3] *Anydrus* Greek: without water.

[4] *Amaurotum* Greek: made dim.

send him there and, what is more, to name him Bishop of Utopia. He has no scruple in pressing for this appointment, since he considers it a holy suit, motivated not by desire for honor or gain but by piety.

Therefore I beg you, my dear Peter, either in person, if you conveniently can, or by letter if he has gone, to reach Hythlodaeus and make sure that my work includes nothing false and omits nothing true. I am inclined to think that it would be better to show him the book itself. No one else is so well able to correct any mistake, and he cannot do me this favor unless he reads through what I have written. In this way, moreover, you will determine whether he accepts with pleasure or suffers with annoyance my composition of this work. If he has decided to write about his adventures himself, perhaps he might not want me to do so. In making known the commonwealth of Utopia, I certainly do not wish to forestall him or to rob his own narrative of novelty's flower and charm. Nevertheless, to tell the truth, I have not yet made up my own mind whether or not to publish this. So varied are the tastes of mortals, so peevish the characters of some, so ungrateful their dispositions and wrongheaded their judgments, that those who blithely indulge their desires seem better off than those who torment themselves with anxiety in order to publish something meant to bring profit or pleasure to those who all too often receive it with disdain or ingratitude.

Many are ignorant of learning; many despise it. The barbarian rejects as harsh whatever is not utterly barbarian. Those with pretensions to learning despise as trite whatever is not packed with obsolete expressions. Some approve only of what is old; many admire only their own work. This fellow is so grim he will not hear of a joke; that fellow is too insipid to endure wit. Some are so dull-minded that they fear all satire as much as someone bitten by a rabid dog fears water. Others are so fickle that when sitting they praise one thing and when standing praise another. Some lounge in taverns and over their cups criticize the talents of authors. With much pontificating and self-indulgence, they condemn each one for his writings, plucking each one, as it were, by the hair. They themselves remain under cover and, as the saying goes, out of range. They are so smooth and shaven that they present not even one honest hair by which they might be caught. Others are so ungrateful that although delighted with the work they do not love the author any the better. They are not unlike discourteous guests who, after being freely entertained at a rich banquet, go home well filled but without thanking the host who invited them. So go ahead and spread a feast at your own expense for men of such dainty palates, of such varied tastes, and of such unforgetful and grateful natures!

At any rate, my dear Peter, consult with Hythlodaeus on the matter I mentioned. Later I shall be fully free to reopen that case for new debate. Now that I have gone through the labor of writing, however, it is too late for me to be wise. Therefore, provided it be done with the consent of Hythlodaeus, in the matter of publishing in everything that remains I shall follow the advice of my friends—and above all yours. Good-bye, my sweetest friend, and my regards to your excellent wife. Love me as you have ever done, for I love you more than ever.

The Best State of a Commonwealth,
The Discourse of the Extraordinary
Character, Raphael Hythlodaeus, as
Reported by the Renowned Figure,
Thomas More,
Citizen and Sheriff
of the Famous City of
Great Britain,
London.

Utopia

Book 1

The most invincible King of England, Henry VIII, a prince adorned with incomparable virtues, recently found himself involved in a dispute, over matters of no little weight, with His Serene Highness Charles, King of Castile.[1] To discuss these things and negotiate a settlement he sent me on an embassy to Flanders, along with the peerless Cuthbert Tunstall, whom recently, to the

[1] *Charles ... Castile* Charles V (1500–58), Holy Roman Emperor (1519–58), was also King of Spain (1516–56), but at the time referred to here had not yet risen to such heights. The "weighty matters" were commercial matters concerning the prohibition of wool sales to the Netherlands.

great satisfaction of all,[1] he has named Master of the Rolls.[2] Of his praises I shall say nothing, not because I fear that the testimony of a friend might be disbelieved, but because his merit and his learning are too much for me to describe and too well known for me to attempt the task, lest I should display the brightness of the sun with a candle, as the proverb has it.[3]

We were greeted at Bruges, the place appointed for our meeting, by the king of Castile's commissioners, all notable men, at the head of whom was the great Margrave of Bruges.[4] But the chief speaker, and the ablest of them all, was George de Theimsecke, Provost of Cassel,[5] a man not only trained in eloquence but a natural orator, highly learned in the law, moreover, and a clever diplomat of much experience. When after several meetings there were certain points on which we could not agree, they bade us farewell for a few days and left for Brussels to learn their king's will. Meanwhile I myself, as my business led me, made my way to Antwerp.

While I stayed there I had various visitors. Most welcome of all[6] was Peter Giles, a native of Antwerp, where he is highly esteemed and respectably employed (somewhat beneath his merit), a young man both learned and prudent. He is most virtuous, cultured, and courteous, and to his friends so open-hearted, affectionate, loyal and sincere, that you will scarcely find his match in all the annals of friendship. He is unusually modest, exceptionally honest, and second to none for plain good sense. In conversation he is so polished and so witty (without ever giving offence) that though I missed hearth and home, wife and children terribly (for it had been more than four months since I left), his delightful society and charming discourse relieved me of my homesickness.

One day I had been at divine service in Notre Dame, the finest church in the city and the most crowded with worshippers. Mass being over, I was about to return to my lodging when I happened to see Peter conversing with a stranger, a man of advanced years with sunburnt countenance and long beard, his cloak hanging carelessly from his shoulder; his appearance and dress looked to me like those of a seafarer. When Peter saw me, he came up to greet me, but before I could return his salutation he drew me a little aside and said, pointing to the one with whom I had seen him talking, "Do you see this man? I was on the point of taking him straight to you."

"He would have been very welcome," said I, "for your sake."

"No," said he, "if you knew him, then for his own sake. There is no man alive today who can give you such an account of unknown peoples and lands. I know you're passionate to hear such tales."

"Well, then," said I, " my guess was not a bad one. The moment I saw him, I was sure he was a ship's captain."

"But you are quite mistaken," said he, "for his sailing has not been like that of Palinurus but of Ulysses, or rather like that of Plato.[7] Now this Raphael, for that was his name (Hythlodaeus was his family name), was something of a Latinist, but an expert in Greek. He was less studious of the Roman tongue because he was entirely devoted to philosophy and knew that Latin had little to offer him there, except for a few things by Seneca and Cicero.[8] Eager to see the world, he left his worldly goods at home with his brothers (he is Portuguese) and joined Amerigo Vespucci.[9] He was his constant companion on the last three of those four

[1] [marginal note] Cuthbert Tunstall. [More published *Utopia* through his friend Peter Giles, a humanist scholar city official in Antwerp; Erasmus was also consulted. Early editions of the work include numerous marginal glosses, which, it has been widely speculated, were additions by Giles and/or Erasmus. The more significant of these glosses are included in the present volume in the footnotes rather than in the margin.]

[2] *Cuthbert Tunstall* Prominent member of the clergy (1474–1559) who was appointed Archdeacon of Chester at the time of this diplomatic mission; *Master of the Rolls* Principal Clerk of the Chancery Court (a court of appeals).

[3] [marginal note] Adage.

[4] *Bruges* Significant port for the wool trade.

[5] *Provost of Cassel* I.e., Chief Magistrate of Cassel.

[6] [marginal note] Peter Giles.

[7] *Palinurus* Aeneas's steersman, who falls asleep at the helm and is tossed overboard in the *Aeneid*; *Ulysses* His story is told variously in the *Iliad*, the *Odyssey* and the *Aeneid*; *Plato* Greek philosopher (c. 427–347 BCE).

[8] *Seneca* Roman philosopher, playwright and orator (c. 4 BCE–65 CE); *Cicero* Roman statesman, philosopher, and orator, who was stoical in many of his attitudes (c. 106–43 BCE).

[9] *Amerigo Vespucci* Noted Italian explorer (1451–1512), Vespucci was one of the explorers of the "New World," for whom it is named America.

voyages about which everyone has read. In the end, he did not accompany him home, for he pestered, even harassed Amerigo to let him be one of the twenty-four left behind at the fort during the last voyage. And so, to let him have his way, they left him behind, more anxious for travel than over the place of his death; for these two sayings are constantly on his lips: 'He who has no grave is covered by the sky,' and, 'From all places it is the same distance to heaven.'[1] But for the grace of God, this determination of his would have cost him dear. In any case, after Amerigo had set sail, Raphael traveled with five companions from the fort through many countries and came by sheer luck to Ceylon, and thence to Calcutta,[2] where by good fortune he found some Portuguese ships. And so, after much time and beyond all exectation, he returned home."

After Peter finished his story, I thanked him for his kindness in going to such lengths to introduce me to one whose conversation he hoped would give me pleasure; then I turned to Raphael. We greeted each other, exchanging the civilities that commonly pass at the first meeting of strangers, and then went off to my house,where we sat down to talk in the garden, on a bench covered with turves of grass.

Raphael told us how, after the departure of Vespucci, he and the friends who had stayed behind in the fort slowly ingratiated themselves with the natives. Little by little, after continued meetings and civilities, they were not only welcome but even treated as familiars. They were, moreover, in favor and good repute with a chief (whose name and country I have forgotten). He said that the chief, out of generosity, provided him and his five companions with ample provisions and travel money, as well as with a trusty guide for their journey (which was partly by water and partly in carriages over land) who could take them to other princes bearing careful recommendations in their favor.

After traveling many days, he said, they found towns and cities and very populous commonwealths with excellent institutions. To be sure, under the Equator, and on both sides of it as far as the sun's orbit extends, there lie waste deserts, scorched with continual heat. This offers an altogether sad and desolate sight, rough and uncultivated, inhabited by wild animals, snakes, and men as savage and dangerous as animals. But when you have gone a little farther, gradually the country assumes a milder aspect, the climate is less fierce, the ground covered with a pleasant green herbage, and the living creatures less wild. At length you reach peoples, cities and towns that maintain a continual traffic by sea and land, not only with each other and their neighbors but also with far-off countries. This gave him the chance to visit many countries in all directions, for there was not a ship trimmed to sail, no matter where, that did not welcome him and his companions. The ships they saw first were flat-bottomed, with the sails made of sheets of papyrus, and sometimes of leather, stitched together on willow branches. Afterwards they found ships with pointed keels and canvas sails, in all respects like ours. The mariners were skilled in dealing with the sea and weather, although he won their favor by showing them how to use a compass. Because they had not known about such an instrument before, they had hesitated to trust themselves to the sea, doing so only in the summer; but now, trusting the compass, they no longer fear stormy weather and have become dangerously confident. So this instrument, expected to be of great use, may turn out to be one of great mischief because of their lack of prudence.

It would be a long tale to report what Raphael said he saw in each place, and that is not the purpose of this book. Perhaps on another occasion I shall tell his story, especially concerning those good and wise institutions that he noticed in civilized nations. We asked him eagerly about such things, and he was more than willing to converse at length, leaving out, however, the sort of marvelous reports that are really old news. For Scyllas and greedy Harpies and cannibal Laestrygonians[3] are common enough, but well and wisely trained citizens are not to be found everywhere. Just as he noted many ill-advised customs among these strange nations, however, so too he mentioned not a few matters from which our own cities, nations, races, and kingdoms could use as models in correcting our own errors. These, as I said,

[1] [marginal note] Aphorism. [These are paraphrases of Lucan's *Pharsalia*, 8.819, and Cicero's *Tusculan Disputations* 1.43.104, respectively.]

[2] *Ceylon* Island (now the nation of Sri Lanka) located in the Indian Ocean off the coast of India; *Calcutta* Port city on the eastern coast of India.

[3] *Scyllas ... Harpies ... Laestrygonians* Monsters of classical myth.

I must save for another occasion. For now, I will merely relate what he told us of the manners and customs of the Utopians, first, however, recounting the conversation that led him to mention that commonwealth.

Raphael touched with wisdom on the faults of this part of the world and of that, finding many in both, and compared the wiseer measures that have been taken by us and by them; for he remembered the manners and customs of each nation he visited as well as if he had lived there all his life. Peter expressed his surprise as follows: "Why, Master Raphael, I wonder that you do not attach yourself to the court of some king. I am sure there is none of them to whom you would not be very welcome, for you are capable not only of entertaining a ruler with this learning and experience of countries and people, but also of furnishing him with examples and assisting him with counsel. Thus you would not only help advance your own interests but also those of your relatives and friends."

"As for my relatives and friends," Raphael said, "I'm not much troubled about them; for I think I have pretty well performed my duty to them already. Whereas other men don't usually give up their possessions unless they are sick and old, and even then do so unwillingly, I divided my wealth among my relatives and friends when I was not just hale and hearty but young. I think they ought to be satisfied with such generosity and not ask or expect that for their sakes I would become the slave of kings."

"Well said, my good sir!" Peter replied. " But I meant not that you should be in *servitude*, only in *service* to kings."

"One word is but a syllable shorter than the other,"[1] said Raphael.

"Whatever name you call it," said Peter, "I think it is just the right way not only to improve things for individuals and the commonwealth alike, but also to make your own condition more prosperous."

"Would I really be better off," asked Raphael, "with a way of life I completely detest? Right now I live as I please, which is more than could be said for those courtiers of yours. Besides, there are plenty of those who court the friendship of the great; and so you need not think it any great loss if they have to do without me or a few others like me."

"Well," said I, "it is plain, Master Raphael, that you desire neither riches nor power. Assuredly, I admire and look up to a man of your mind, just as much as I do to any of the high and mighty. But, I think, you will do what is worthy of you and of this generous and truly philosophic spirit of yours, if you order your life so as to apply your talent and industry to the public interest, even if so doing involves some disadvantage to yourself. This you could never do more profitably than if you were counselor to some great prince and make him follow, as I am sure you would, a straightforward and honorable course. For from the prince, as from a never failing spring, flows a stream of all that is good or evil over the whole nation. But you have such learning that even without experience of affairs you would make an excellent member of any king's council as well as such experience that even if you had no learning the same would be true."

"You are twice mistaken," said Raphael, "first in me, and then in the matter in question. For I have no such ability as you ascribe to me, and even if I did, and surrendered my leisure to affairs of state, I would not promote the public interest. For in the first place, almost all princes prefer to occupy themselves in the pursuits of war (with which I have no acquaintance nor desire any) rather than in the honorable activities of peace, and they care much more for how, by hook or by crook, they may win fresh kingdoms than how to administer well those they already have."

"In the second place," Raphael continued, "a king's courtiers are so wise that they do not need a second opinion, or so confident that they do not want one—unless, of course, it be the opinion of one of the king's favorites. In that case, one and all eagerly approve and applaud even the stupidest of opinions, for they are studious to gain his favor by such approval. Granted, it is only natural for everyone to like his own brainchild best: the crow is delighted with his chick, the ape pleased with his cub. But if in the company of such self-seeking, such jealous men, someone should propose something that he has read was done in former times or that he has seen done in other places, they try to find fault with it, believing their whole reputation for wisdom endangered if they do not. If all else fails, they

[1] *One … other* In the original Latin, the words for "in servitude to" and "in service to" are "servias" and "inservias."

take refuge in this as a last resort: 'These things,' they say, 'were good enough for our ancestors, and we wish only we were as wise as they were.' With this argument, which they regard as unanswerable and a conclusion of the whole matter, they resume their seats, as if it were dangerous for anyone to be wiser than his forebears. It is curious—we seem to be completely oblivious of the sound opinions of our ancestors until somebody suggests something better. Then, oh, how zealously, how religiously we adhere to them! Such proud, ridiculous and obstinate prejudices I have encountered in many places, and once even in England."

"What?" I asked. "You were in our country?"

"Yes," Raphael said, "I once spent several months there, not long after the disastrous end of the Cornish revolt against the King put down with such horrible bloodshed.[1] During that time I was much indebted to the Right Reverend Father, Cardinal John Morton, Archbishop of Canterbury, at that point also Lord Chancellor of England.[2] Here was a man, Master Peter, (for Master More knows about him and needs no information from me) who deserved no less respect for his wisdom and virtue than for his authority. He was of middle stature and showed no sign of his advanced age; his countenance inspired respect rather than fear; his conversation was agreeable, although serious and dignified. He sometimes liked to speak sharply to petitioners, although not rudely, so as to bring out their spirit and presence of mind. Provided these capacities did not become impudence, they gave him pleasure, for he shared them and thought that they well suit those holding public office. His speech was polished and to the point and his knowledge profound; he was very able, and his memory amazingly retentive, while by learning and practice he improved his natural qualities. The King placed much confidence in his advice, and when I was there, the state seemed to depend upon him. In early youth he had been taken straight from school to court, and there he had spent his whole life in important public affairs. He suffered many turns of fortune, so that through many and great dangers he had acquired that level-headedness which, once learned, is not easily forgotten.

"One day I was at his table,"[3] continued Raphael, "when a layman, who happened to be there and was learned in the laws of your country, took some occasion to launch into a precise encomium of the severe punishments that were then meted out to thieves.[4] They were executed everywhere, he said, with as many as twenty being hanged on one gallows at a time. With so few escaping execution, he wondered by what bad luck they still so infested the country. Being free to speak my mind in front of the Cardinal, I said, 'You need not wonder; for this manner of punishing thieves goes beyond justice and is not in the public interest. It is both too harsh a penalty for theft and an insufficient deterrent. For theft is not so hideous a crime that it should cost someone his life, and no punishment, however great, will deter that man from stealing, who has no other means of getting food. In this practice, you and the greater part of the world resemble bad schoolmasters, who would rather beat than teach their scholars. You ordain grievous and terrible punishments for theft, when it would be much better to provide some means of employment; then no one would be under this terrible necessity of first stealing and then dying for it.'[5]

"'We have,' the layman said, 'made sufficient provision for this. There are handicrafts and there is agriculture; they might maintain themselves by these, if they did not prefer to be rascals.'

"'No,' I said. 'You don't get away so easily. Let's say nothing of those who often come home maimed from foreign or civil wars, such as the recent fight with the

---

[1] *disastrous … bloodshed* In 1497, in response to harsh tax burdens imposed by Henry VII, about 15,000 Cornishmen (men from Cornwall) marched on London and were brutally defeated at Blackheath.

[2] *Cardinal John Morton* Cardinal, Archbishop of Canterbury, and Lord Chancellor, Morton (1420–1500) was an early patron of More and a lifelong friend; *Archbishop of Canterbury* Highest church official in England; *Lord Chancellor* High-ranking official in the House of Lords, the Lord Chancellor is the Keeper of the Great Seal of England and chief administrator of the judicial system.

[3] *One day … his table* The dialogue over the course of the following pages is sometimes difficult to follow. Raphael recounts a long dinner-table conversation with the Cardinal, with a "layman learned in the laws" of England, with a friar, and briefly with various others. The long digression ends with Raphael's apology for telling such a lengthy tale.

[4] [marginal note] Of unjust laws.

[5] [marginal note] How to reduce the number of thieves.

Cornishmen and before that with France.[1] They have lost limbs for country and king, and now their infirmity prevents them from exercising their old crafts even while their age prevents them from learning a new one. These, I say, we can ignore, for wars come intermittently; but let us consider what happens every day. Now there are a great many idle noblemen who not only live like drones off the labors of others, such as their tenants, whom they squeeze to the utmost by raising their rents (for that is the ony way to get money they know, being otherwise so extravagant as to beggar themselves), but also carry about with them a huge crowd of parasites who have never learnt a trade by which to live. When their master dies, or they themselves fall ill, they are soon turned out, for it is easier to maintain the idle than the sick, and in any case the heir can't always support as big a household as had his father. So in the meantime their energies turn to starving, if not to thieving. For what can they do? When by a vagabond life they have worn out both clothes and health, sickly and ragged as they are, gentlemen will not engage them and country folk dare not, knowing well that someone softly brought up in idleness and luxury and has been wont to strut around in sword and buckler,[2] looking down with a swaggering expression on the whole neighborhood, and thinking himself miles above everyone, is not fit to render honest service to a poor man with spade and hoe, for scanty wage, and on frugal fare.'

"'But these' the layman replied, 'are just the men we ought to encourage and make much of; on them, who have spirits loftier and more manly those of artisans and husbandmen, depend the strength and sinews of our army when we have to wage war,'

"'Indeed,' I said, 'you might as well say that for the sake of war we should encourage thieves. For as long as you have these men, you will never be without thieves. Just as robbers are not bad soldiers, so soldiers are not the most cowardly of robbers—so well do these two lines of argument agree. But this defect, though frequent with you, is not yours alone, being common to almost all nations. France in particular is sick with another more grievous plague. Even in peace (if you can call it peace) the whole country is crowded and beset with mercenaries, for the French, like you, think it smart to keep these idle retainers. These wiseacres think the public safety means having a standing army, strong and reliable, and made up chiefly of veterans, for they have no confidence in untrained men.[3] So they must always be finding an excuse for war, lest they have men without experience. They must also make sure that they are not unskilled at cutting throats, lest, as Sallust says wittily, "the hand or mind through lack of practice[4] get dull." Yet France has learned how dangerous it is to rear such wild beasts, and the examples of Rome, Carthage, Syria, and other nations show the same: not only their empires, but also their land and even their cities have been more than once destroyed by their own standing armies. How unnecessary it is to maintain them is clearly proved by this: not even the French soldiers, trained in arms from infancy, can boast that they have very often bested your fresh recruits.[5] I shall say no more, for fear of seeming to flatter you to your faces.

"'At any rate,' I went on, 'neither your town workers nor your rough and untrained farm laborers are supposed to fear the idle followers of gentlemen, unless perhaps their bodies are unfitted for strength and bravery, or whose spirits are broken by poverty. So there is no danger that those, whose bodies, once strong and vigorous (for it is only such men whom gentlemen deign to corrupt), would become weakened by idleness or enfeebled by womanly occupations if they were trained to earn their living by honest pursuits and exercised some manly toil. But, however this may be, it seems to me by in no way helpful to the commonweal to keep for the emergency of a war such a multitude of those who trouble and disturb the peace. You never have war unless you choose it, and you ought to think far more of peace. But this is not the only thing that makes thieving necessary; there is another, one I believe peculiar to you Englishmen alone.'

"'What is that?' said the Cardinal.

"'Your sheep,' I replied, 'which used to be so mild and content, are now, it is said, so greedy and wild that they

[1] *not long ago … France* A reference to the battle at Dixmude (1489) and that at Boulogne (1492).

[2] *buckler* Small shield, usually round, that can be carried or buckled to the arm.

[3] [marginal note] The mischief of standing armies.

[4] *Sallust* Roman politician and historian (86–34 BCE); *hand or … practice* Cf. Sallust's *Cataline Conspiracy*.

[5] *not even … recruits* The English had won several decisive victories over the French.

devour men, laying waste and depopulating fields, houses, and towns.[1] For in those parts of the realm that produce the finest and therefore most costly wool, nobles and gentlemen, and even holy abbots, are unsatisfied with the revenues and annual profits they derive from their estates.[2] No longer content with merely leading an idle life and contributing nothing good to their country, they must also do it real harm. They leave no ground to be tilled, enclose every bit of land for pasture, pull down houses, and destroy towns, leaving only a church for a barn. And, as if not enough English land were already wasted on deer parks and game preserves, these holy men turn all human habitations and cultivated land into a wilderness. Thus so that one fat cat, an insatiable and terrible scourge to his homeland, might enclose some thousand acres of tillable land in a single fence, many tenants are ejected. Some, through fraud or violence, lose their goods. Others are so wearied by oppression that they are driven to sell. Thus by hook or by crook poor wretches are compelled to leave their homes—men, women, husbands, wives, orphans, widows, parents with little children and a family not rich but numerous (for farm work requires many hands). Away they must go, I say, from hearth and home, and find no shelter. All their household furniture, which would not fetch a great price even if they could wait for a purchaser, must be sold for a trifling profit. Then as soon as they've gone through their last penny (near the beginning of their migration), what's left but to steal and hang—with justice, mind you—or wander and beg? But even wandering might land you in prison these days, for it is an "idle loitering." Nobody wants to hire their services, which they desperately offer. Why? They're accustomed to farming, and there's no need for a plow where nothing's to be sowed. It used to take several workers to cultivate a field until it was ripe for the harvest; the same field now requires only a single shepherd or rancher.

"'And so it is because of this,' I continued, 'that the price of food has risen in many parts. Wool too has gone up in price. So much so that the poor, who used to make cloth in England, cannot now afford to buy it, and so are driven from work to idleness. For after the great increase in pastureland a plague killed off a vast number of sheep. Perhaps God, vexed by the owners' display of greed, sent a murrain.[3] It might have fallen more justly on their own heads. In any case, even if the number of sheep had risen, the price wouldn't have fallen, because of the monopoly—excuse me, the *oligopoly*,[4] for there are more than one of them. Wealth stays in the hands of the same few, who are not obliged to sell before they wish, and they do not wish to sell until they get the price they ask. All other kinds of livestock are also high-priced for the same reasons, and all the more so, because as the farmhouses have been pulled down and the tillage is lessened, there are none left to raise livestock. These rich men will not rear calves as they do lambs, but buy them lean and cheap elsewhere and then, having fattened them up in their own pastures, resell them again at a tidy profit. I fear that the full mischief of this system has not yet been felt. Thus far it has raised the prices only where the animals are sold; over time, though, if the buyers remove them faster than they can be bred, then as the supply gradually diminishes in the areas where they are bought, there will be great shortages. Thus the unscrupulous greed of a few is ruining the very thing for which your island was once counted most fortunate. The high price of food is causing everyone to get rid of as many servants as possible, and what, I ask you, can they do but to beg, or, if more courageous, to rob?

"'What, moreover, is found alongside this wretched need and poverty but wanton luxury? For not only the servants of noblemen but craftsmen and farmers, indeed all classes alike, are given to flashy dress and fancy dining. Do not brothels, wine-shops, ale houses, and all those games of chance, cards, dicing, tennis, bowls, and quoits,[5] soon drain the purses of those who cannot resist

[1] *Your sheep ... and towns* Reference to the practice of enclosure, starting in the thirteenth century, in which wealthy landlords would fence off lands previously set aside for common use, using them instead for raising sheep. This practice dislocated rural laborers and sent some into beggary, vagabondage, and even thieving.

[2] *even holy abbots ... estates* The Church frequently enclosed land for its own use.

[3] *murrain* Infectious disease, usually of animals, especially sheep.

[4] *oligopoly* Control of prices by a handful of owners. Drawing on an analogy with "monopoly," More invents a word to satirize landowners.

[5] *quoits* Game in which flat rings of stone, iron, or rope are pitched at a stake.

them, sending them off to rob others when their money is gone? Cast out these ruinous plagues; make laws that those who have destroyed farmhouses and country towns must either restore them or hand them over to those who will do so and are ready to build. Restrict this right of the rich to buy up everything and maintain a kind of monopoly. Let fewer be brought up in idleness. Let farming be restored. Let wool-manufacturing be reintroduced so that there may be honest occupations for the idle crowd of those whom poverty has already made thieves or who are currently vagabonds or lazy servants, and thus likely in any case to become such. Unless you remedy these evils, it is useless for you to boast of the justice you mete out in punishing theft. Such justice is for show, not truly fair or useful. For when you let your young be brought up badly, with their characters corrupted, and then penalize them when as adults they commit the very crimes that from their boyhood they had shown every prospect of committing, what else are you doing but first creating thieves and then punishing them?'"

"Even while I was speaking," Raphael said, "the lawyer had been preparing his reply, determined to adopt the usual method of disputants, who are more careful in repeating what has been said than in answering it, so highly do they regard memory.

"'Certainly, sir,' the lawyer said, 'you have spoken well, considering that you are but a stranger, and have been able only to hear something about these matters, not to get exact knowledge of them. I will briefly make things clear. First I will repeat in order what you have said; then I will show in what respects ignorance of our conditions has deceived you; finally I will demolish and destroy all your arguments. So to begin with what I promised first, in four respects you seemed to me—'

"'Hold your tongue,' said the Cardinal, interrupting the lawyer, 'for it looks as if your reply will be lengthy, if you begin thus.[1] We will relieve you of the trouble of making your answer now and postpone that duty until your next meeting, which I would like to schedule for tomorrow, if, of course, you are both free. But now I should very much like to hear, Raphael, your reasons why we should not punish theft with death. What penalty more beneficial to the commonweal would you recommend? For you must think some punishment is necessary. Even with the death penalty, men still rush into stealing. Give them a guarantee that they will live, then what force, what threat could deter the criminals? They would regard a lighter punishment as a reward, an invitation to commit more crime.'

"'Certainly,' I said to the Cardinal, 'most kind and reverend father, I think it quite unjust that what cost one person some money should cost another his life. Indeed, I do not think that all the goods in the world can equal a man's life in value. But some will say it is not about the money, but about the laws that have been assaulted, the justice that has been violated. They call this "extreme justice"—extreme wrong is more like it. For we ought not to approve such severe Manlian[2] laws that justify drawing the sword against even the slightest infraction. On the other hand, nor should we accept Stoical rulings that count all offences equal, so that there would be no difference between killing a man and taking his coin. If equity has any meaning, there is no similarity or connection between the two cases. God has said, "Thou shalt not kill," and shall we so lightly kill a man for taking a little money? And if the divine commandment does not stop us when we legalize killing, what prevents us from also legalizing adultery, rape and perjury? Now God forbids a man to take another's life—forbids him to take even his own. But certain men have mutually agreed to laws that do allow taking human life. If this exempts their agents from having to observe God's law, killing others without any divine example, will not human law then take precedent over that of God? And so men will obey God in the same way they manage everything else: as it suits them. Finally, the law of Moses, though severe and harsh (being made for an enslaved and stubborn people), nevertheless punishes theft by fine, not death. Let's not suppose that God's new law of mercy, in which He gives commands as a father to his children, allows us greater license to be cruel to one another. These are my reasons for thinking this treatment unlawful. Surely everyone knows how absurd and even dangerous to the commonwealth it is to penalize thief and a murderer with the same punishment. For as soon as a robber sees that he faces no

1 [marginal note] Illustrates the Cardinal's way of interrupting a babbler.

2 *Manlian* Roman general Manlius (4th century BCE) executed his own son for breaking the law.

more penalty for a murder conviction than for the mere guilt of theft, he would not hesitate to kill a man he might otherwise just rob. Because he is in no more danger if caught, it is safer for him to cover up the offence by making sure that there is no one left alive to tell the tale. And so even as we try to frighten thieves with excessive cruelty we also urge them on to the destruction of honest people.

"'Now, as to determining what punishment might be better,' I continued to the Cardinal; 'that is an easy task. It would be much harder to find a worse! But why should we doubt the effectiveness of those punishments that worked for so long for the Romans, those experts in government? When men were convicted of great crimes they were condemned to a lifetime of working, shackled, in stone quarries or mines. Yet I can find no better custom in any nation than that which during my travels I noticed in Persia among the people commonly called the Polylerites.[1] Theirs is a large and well-governed nation. They pay an annual tribute to the Persian ruler, but they are in all other respects free and autonomous.[2] Living far from the sea, almost surrounded by mountains, and satisfied with what their own bounteous land yields, they neither visit others often nor receive visits. In accord with their ancient custom, they do not try to enlarge their territory. Their boundaries, moreover, are protected from all aggression by their mountains and by the tribute they pay to their overlord, and so they live free from military service, not at all extravagantly but comfortably, more in happiness than in fame or honor. Only their immediate neighbors even know their names.

"'In their land,' I went on, 'those who are convicted of theft repay what they have taken to the owner and, not, as is usual elsewhere, to the ruler, who they think has no more right to the stolen thing than do the thieves.[3] If the thing is lost, the value is made up and paid out of the thieves' belongings, the rest is given to their wives and children, and the thieves themselves are condemned to hard labor. Unless the theft was outrageous, they are neither shackled nor jailed but employed in public works, unbound and unguarded. If they refuse to work or if they slack off, they are whipped but not put in chains. If they do a good day's work, they need fear no humiliation. Every night after roll call, they are locked into their sleeping quarters. Aside from its constant toil, their life is not hard. As servants to the commonwealth, they are fed well at public expense, though the arrangement varies in different places. In some parts what is spent on them is raised by donations, and though this method is unpredictable, the people are so kind hearted that the criminals' needs are plentifully supplied. Elsewhere public revenues are set aside to cover the cost, while in yet other places everyone pays a fixed tax. In some parts the offenders do no work for the community, but when someone needs a hired hand he can go to the marketplace and hire a convict for a day at a fixed wage that is less than what he would have had to pay a free man—and it is lawful to whip these servants if they become lazy. So the convicted thieves are never out of work, and beyond the cost of their keep each brings a little daily profit to the public treasury. They are all dressed in clothes of the same color,[4] with hair not shaved off but cropped a little above their ears and the tip of one ear cut off. Their friends may give them food, drink and the appropriately colored clothes, but it is a capital offence to give them money, both for the giver and the receiver. It is just as perilous for a free man to receive money for any reason from one of these slaves, as the convicts are called, as it is for the slaves to touch weapons. A special badge distinguishes each district's slaves. It is a capital offence for slaves to throw away this badge, to go beyond their own bounds, or to talk to a slave from another district. And it is no less risky to plan an escape than actually to run away. Indeed, aiding and abetting an escape means death for a slave, and slavery for a free man. For an informer, however, there is a reward: money for a free man, liberty for a slave. Both are pardoned and given immunity for their help, thus ensuring that it is never safer to follow a wicked purpose than to repent it.

"'This is their way of arranging things,' I continued, 'as I have described it to you. You can easily see how humane and advantageous it is. The object of this punishment is to destroy the vice and save the person. The treatment of the criminals is necessary to make them

[1] *Polylerites* People of much nonsense, one of More's many invented Greek compounds: *polus* (much) and *leros* (nonsense).

[2] [marginal note] The Polylerlite society near the Persians.

[3] [marginal note] To be noted by us, who do otherwise.

[4] [marginal note] Yet modern servants exult in livery of the same sort.

good, and they have the rest of their lives to repair the damage they have done. There is so little fear of their backsliding that even travelers feel safe having these slaves as guides on their journeys, changing them for new ones as they arrive in new districts. Look, there are all sorts of obstacles to their committing a robbery: they are unarmed, money would simply betray them, penalties await them if caught, and there is absolutely no hope of escape. For how could a man expect to escape detection in clothes unlike those of anyone else in the country, unless he were to run away naked—and even then his ear would betray him? It may be objected that convicts might get together and conspire against the state—as if any group of slaves could have a prayer without first tempting and persuading those of many other districts. But this could not happen, because they may not meet and converse, or even greet one another. It is unlikely that they would tell others of a plot when they know that plotting is dangerous if concealed but profitable to anyone who divulges it to the authorities. On the other hand, no one is quite without hope of some day recovering his liberty through obedience and patience, and by showing that he is capable of one day living a reformed life. For no year passes in which some are not restored to freedom, recommended by their patient endurance.'

"After saying this," Raphael continued, "I added that I saw no reason why this method might not also be adopted in England, and be more beneficial than the system of justice that my lawyerly opponent had praised so highly. The lawyer replied that it could never be established in England without seriously endangering the state. He shook his head, screwed up his face, and held his peace. And everyone there agreed with him. Then the Cardinal said, 'It is not easy to guess if it would turn out well without hazarding the attempt. But say a death penalty has been pronounced, and the King postpones its execution and suspends the right to sanctuary[1] in order to try this method. If the experiment works, it is only right to make it law. If it fails, putting to death those already condemned would be no less for the public good and no more unjust than to do so right away. In the meantime, no danger can come of the experiment. Moreover, I am sure that vagabonds might quite well be treated in the same way, for in spite of repeated legislation, we have not made much progress in dealing with them.'

"After the Cardinal said this, they all took turns praising the very plan they ridiculed when I suggested it. They were especially enthusiastic about the part concerning vagabonds, because it was the Cardinal's own addition.

"Perhaps it would be better to omit what followed, it was so absurd," said Raphael, "but I will relate it. It was not bad in itself and had some bearing on the matter.[2] There was present a hanger-on who apparently wanted to adopt the role of fool, but what he said was too near the truth to be funny. His ill-timed jokes were meant to raise a laugh, but he himself was more often the object of laughter than were his jests. Sometimes the fellow made clever observations, however, thus confirming the proverb that if a man throws the dice often he will sooner or later get lucky. So it happened when one of the guests remarked that because my proposal provided well for thieves and the Cardinal had taken precautions for vagabonds, it remained only to make some provision for the poor, who were unable to earn a living because of sickness or old age.

"'Give me leave,' said the hanger-on, 'and I will see that this, too, is set right. For I am very anxious to get this sort of person out of my sight. They have often harassed me with their pitiful whinings, begging for money, but they could never pitch a tune that would get a coin out of my pocket. For one of two things always happens: either I do not want to give, or I cannot because I have nothing to give. So now they have begun to wise up, for when they see me pass by they say nothing, and spare their pains, expecting no more from me than they would from a priest.[3] But I would like to see a law that would distribute all those beggars among the Benedictine monasteries, where the men could become lay brothers,[4] as they call them, and the women could become nuns.'

[1] *right to sanctuary* Right whereby criminals (or those accused of crimes) could demand asylum in churches, escaping—for a time at least—potential penalties imposed by law.

[2] [marginal note] The friar and the fool: a merry dialogue.

[3] [marginal note] A common saying of beggars.

[4] *Benedictine monasteries* Monasteries of the Benedictine religious order, an order of monks founded in the sixth century by St. Benedict, notable for their influence on medieval education; *lay brothers* Men living and working in the monastery but who have not taken vows for clerical orders.

"The Cardinal smiled and allowed it in jest. The others took it seriously—except for a certain friar, who was learned in theology. He was so delighted by this jest at the expense of priests and monks that he too began to laugh, though usually he was serious almost to the point of sourness.

"'Indeed,' said the friar,[1] 'you will not be rid of beggars, unless you make provision for us friars too.'

"'Already done,' said the hanger-on. 'His Eminence made excellent provision for you when he determined that vagabonds should be arrested and made to work. For you are the greatest vagabonds of all.'

"After the company saw by looking at the Cardinal that he did not object to this joke any more than he had to the other, they all began to commend it vigorously. But not the friar, for he—and I do not wonder why—was stung by this taunt. He became so furious and enraged that he could not hold himself back from abuse. He called the man a rascal, a slanderer, a sneak, and a son of perdition, all the while quoting terrible denunciations out of Holy Scripture. Now the hanger-on began to laugh in earnest and was quite in his element.

"'Don't be angry, good friar,' he said, 'for it is written "In your patience ye shall possess your souls."'[2]

"To which the Friar replied—I will repeat his very words—'I am not angry, rogue, or at least I do not sin; for the Psalmist says, "Be ye angry, and sin not."'[3]

"Then the Cardinal gently cautioned the friar to calm himself, but he replied, 'No, my lord, I speak only from good zeal, as holy men should, as it says in the Scriptures, "The zeal of thy house hath consumed me," and we sing in Church—"The scorners of Elisha, while he went up to the house of God, felt the zeal[4] of the bald head,"[5] as perchance this vulgar scoffer shall feel it.'

"'Perhaps,' said the Cardinal, 'you mean well, but I think it would be wiser, though perhaps no holier, to keep from matching wits with a silly fellow or picking a foolish fight with a fool.'

"'No, my lord,' the friar said, 'it would not be wiser. As the wise Solomon saith, "Answer a fool according to his folly."[6] So I do now, and show him the pit into which he will fall, if he take not good heed. For if many scoffers at Elisha, who was only one bald head, felt the zeal of a bald head, how much more will be felt by one scorner of many friars, among whom are many bald men? Moreover, we have a Papal bull[7] by which all who scoff at us are excommunicated.'

"When the Cardinal saw there was no end to the matter in sight, he dismissed the hanger-on with a motion of his head and turned the conversation to a more suitable subject. Soon afterwards he rose from table, dismissed us, and went to hear what the petitioners[8] had to say.

"There, Master More," concluded Raphael, "what a long tale I have burdened you with, one that I would never have told at such length if you had not in the first place so eagerly pestered me and then listened as if you did not want me to leave out a thing. I could have told it more briefly, but I had to tell it in every point to show the judgment of those who initially rejected what I said but then immediately supported it when the Cardinal did not disapprove. They flattered him so much that they even encouraged and almost took in earnest the suggestions of the hanger-on, which the Cardinal took as a joke. So from this you may judge how little regard courtiers would pay me and my advice."

"To be sure, Raphael," I said, "you have given me great pleasure, so wise and clever is everything you have said. Besides, while listening to you I felt not only as if

[1] *friar* Member of one of the four mendicant orders—Franciscans, Dominicans, Carmelites, or Augustinians. Friars are not allowed private property, but must instead beg or work for their sustenance.

[2] *In your … souls* Luke 21.19.

[3] [marginal note] How his people speak in character! [*Be ye … not* Psalms 4.4.]

[4] [marginal note] Out of ignorance, the friar uses "zelus" as if it were a neuter noun, like "scelus." [In the original Latin, the friar incorrectly says "zelus" instead of "zelum," using the wrong form of the noun.]

[5] *The zeal … me* Psalms 69.9; *The scorners … bald head* In II Kings 2.23–24, Elisha, the heir of the prophet Elijah, curses a group of children who have mocked his baldness. Two bears attack the children, killing forty-two of them.

[6] *Solomon* King of Israel noted for his wisdom; *Answer a … folly* Proverbs 26.5.

[7] *Papal bull* Decree issued by the Pope, so called because it was closed by a lead *bulla*, or seal.

[8] *petitioners* Those asking for favors from the Church authorities.

I were at home in my native country, but also as if I had gone back to the days of my youth, for I was pleasantly reminded of the Cardinal in whose household I was brought up as a boy. And since you so highly honor his memory, you cannot think how much more attached I am to you for that than I was already. But my mind is still not changed, and I continue to think that if you could persuade yourself not to shun the courts of kings, you could do the greatest good to the commonwealth through your advice. This is the most important part of your duty, as it that of every good man. For since your favorite writer, Plato, believes that states will be happy only if philosophers are kings or kings turn to philosophy, what a faint hope there will be of happiness if philosophers will not share their advice with kings."[1]

"Philosophers are not so ungracious," Raphael said, "as to refuse to advise monarchs—indeed, many have done so through published books. But rulers must be ready to take good advice. Doubtless Plato was right that unless kings become philosophical they will never take the advice of real philosophers. From their youth, most are infected by and saturated with wrong ideas. Plato experienced this with Dionysius.[2] So if I were to give wise advice to some king, trying to remove the seeds of evil and corruption from his mind, do you not think that as a result, I would be at once banished or ridiculed?

"Come now, imagine me at the French king's court, sitting with the most trusted members of his Privy Council. Imagine the king presiding as they all set their wits to determine by what crafty means he might keep his hold on Milan, bring Naples (which has for the time eluded his grasp) back into his power, destroy Venice, subjugate the whole of Italy, and then add to his rule Flanders, Brabant and the whole of Burgundy, as well as other lands.[3] And suppose that someone advises that he should sign a treaty with the Venetians meant to last only so long as he thought convenient, and that he should develop a common strategy with them, even allowing them to keep part of the booty, which, when all has gone as he wished, he could reclaim. While one counselor recommends the hiring of German lanzknechts,[4] another suggests winning over the Swiss with money,[5] and a third advises appeasing the offended majesty of the Emperor with gold. A fourth thinks that a settlement should be made with the King of Aragon, to whom the independent kingdom of Navarre would be ceded as a guarantee of peace, while still another proposes that the king of Castile should be lured by the prospect of a marriage alliance and that the offer of money would draw some Castilian nobles over to the French side.

"The most perplexing question is what to do with England. The advisers agree that peace should be made and that the alliance, which may be weak at first, should be strengthened as much as possible so that the English could be called friends and suspected as enemies. The Scots therefore must be posted in readiness, ready for any opportunity to be let loose on the English should the latter make any move. Moreover, some exiled noble must be encouraged (secretly, for treaties prevent this being done openly) to maintain a claim to the throne so that he may keep in check a king he does not trust.

"In a case like this, with such plans afoot and each vying with the other in making warlike proposals, what do you suppose would happen if an insignificant person like myself got up and advised another tack: leave Italy alone and stay at home, for as it is, the kingdom of France is almost too large to be well governed by a single man, and so the king should not think of adding another dominion. Suppose I then put before them the decisions taken by the Achorians,[6] who live on the mainland southeast of the Island of Utopia?[7] They went to war to win their king another kingdom, one he claimed because of an old marriage alliance. After securing it they saw it would take no less trouble to keep it than it had taken to obtain it, for there were constant rebellions and foreign invasions. So the Achorians had to keep an army in constant readiness, either to defend them or in case of an attack by them. In the meantime

[1] *For since … kings* See Plato's *Republic* 5.473.

[2] *Dionysius* Dionysus II, tyrant of Syracuse (c. 397–343 BCE). Plato unsuccessfully attempted to instruct him in philosophy.

[3] [marginal note] Indirectly he discourages the French from seizing Italy.

[4] *lanzknechts* German infantry (literally "lance knights").

[5] [marginal note] Swiss mercenaries.

[6] *Achorians* People with no country; another invented Greek compound: *a* (without) and *xoros* (country).

[7] [marginal note] A notable example.

they were being plundered, money was leaving the country, they were losing their lives for the glory of others, and peace was no more secure than before. War corrupted their citizens' morals and they developed a lust for robbery and murder, holding laws in contempt because the king, distracted by governing two kingdoms, could not properly attend to either. Eventually, seeing no other way to end this mischief, the Achorians rallied together and courteously but firmly offered their king his choice of whichever kingdom he preferred. He could not keep both because each had too many people to be ruled by half a king. For who would hire a mule-driver if he worked half the time for somebody else? So the worthy king was forced to be content with his own realm. He handed over the new one to one of his friends, who was soon afterwards driven out.

"Furthermore, imagine I proved that all this warfare, by which so many nations would be kept in turmoil on the French king's account, would, after draining his resources and destroying his people, come to nothing in the end. So it would be more beneficial for him to look after his own kingdom and make it as rich and as flourishing as possible: loving his subjects, being loved by them, living with them, and ruling them gently with no designs upon other kingdoms since what he has is more than enough for him. Now what reception, friend More, do you think this advice of mine would find?"

"To be sure, not a very favorable one," I said.

"Well, then, let us proceed," he said. "Suppose the King and his counselors are debating and calculating how they might heap up treasure for him. One advises raising the value of money when he has to pay off debts and lowering it when he has to receive any. Thus he could settle a large debt with a small sum but receive a large one when only a small one is due him. Another suggests a make-believe war as a pretext for raising money. Then when he saw fit, he could make peace with great solemnity, misleading the people into believing that their king was compassionate, eagerly avoiding bloodshed. Another reminds him of old moth-eaten laws that no one remembers and so everyone has broken. He could exact fines for such infractions, there being no better source of profit—nor any more honorable, for such an approach can outwardly resemble justice. Another says that the king should prohibit many common activities under threat of heavy fines, and then, for large sums of money, allow exceptions to those whose interests are hampered by the prohibition. Thus favor is won from the people, and a double profit is made, first by the exaction of fines from those whose greed has entangled them in the snare, and then by selling privileges to others at a higher price. In fact, the higher the price the better the prince: since he dislikes making exceptions harmful to the common welfare, he will not do so except for much money.

"Another counselor persuades him that he must befriend judges who always decide in favor of the royal prerogative. He must summon them to the palace and invite them to debate his affairs in his presence. In even the most unfair of charges, the judges will all, from a desire to contradict, to be original, or to win favor, find some loophole whereby a false accusation may be set up. If the judges can be made to differ, even the clearest claim will need to be debated and truth becomes a matter of doubt. A convenient handle will be given to the king to interpret the law in his own interest, and everyone else will acquiesce from shame or fear. The sentence will boldly be pronounced from the Bench, and then a pretext can never be lacking for deciding for the king. To such a judge it is enough to have on his side either the letter of the law, or a twisted reading of it, or (what outweighs all law with conscientious judges) the undoubted prerogative of the King's majesty.

"Thus all the counselors agree, consenting to the saying of Crassus:[1] no amount of gold is enough for a king who must keep an army.[2] A king, however much he might want to, can do nothing wrong, for all that men possess is his—they themselves are his—and a man's own is only what the king's generosity does not take away. It is much to the king's interest to leave him as little as possible, so that the people do not threaten him by growing wanton with riches and freedom. Freedom and riches would make them less willing to endure harsh and unjust commands, whereas poverty and need depress

[1] *Crassus* Roman statesman (d. 53 BCE) who—along with Caesar and Pompey—made up the first triumvirate. According to Cicero, Crassus said that only those who had the money to maintain an army should take part in government.

[2] [marginal note] Saying of Crassus the Rich.

them, encouraging their patience and taking away from the oppressed the lively spirit of rebellion.

"Suppose again I rose and maintained that this advice was both dishonorable and dangerous for the king, whose very safety, as well as his honor, rested on the people's resources and not on his own. Suppose I argued that people choose their king for their own sake and not for his, that he has a duty to ensure that they live well, safe from injustice and wrong. That it is the king's responsibility to take more care for the welfare of his people than for his own, just as it is the duty of a shepherd, insofar as he is a shepherd, to feed his flock rather than himself.[1] That whoever thinks the stability of the kingdom rests in the poverty of the people is way off the mark, proved wrong by the facts. For where do you see more quarrelling than among beggars? Who is more eager for revolution than a man discontented with his state of life? Who is more reckless in upsetting order in the hope of profiting by any means or other than someone with nothing to lose? Now if there was a king so despised and hated by his subjects, that the only way he could maintain order would be to oppress, plunder, and harass them, and so reduce them to poverty, it would surely be better for him to resign his throne than to keep it by such means. Otherwise, though he might retain the name of ruler he loses its majesty. For it is not a king's part to reign over beggars, but rather over the prosperous and happy. This was certainly the opinion of that noble and lofty spirit Fabricius,[2] who said that he would rather rule rich men than be rich himself.

"If one man lives a life of pleasure and self-indulgence amidst the groans and lamentations of all around him, he is the keeper of a prison, not of a kingdom. Just as a doctor who cannot cure one disease except by creating another must admit he is incompetent, so a monarch who cannot correct the lives of citizens except by depriving them of the good things of life must admit that he does not know how to govern free men.

"Such a king should rule his own self-indulgence or pride, for it is generally as a result of these vices that the people either scorn or hate him. Let him live harmlessly on what is his own and limit his expenses to his revenues. Let him put a stop to evildoers, and by training his subjects well prevent new evils rather than allow them to develop and then have to punish them. Let him not be hasty in putting into force laws long since fallen into disuse, especially those that were never needed.[3] And let him never confiscate property that no judge would allow a private person to appropriate; it would be crafty and unjust to act that way.

"What if I then recommended to them a law of the Macarians,[4] a people not very far from Utopia? Their king, on the day he first takes office, after solemn sacrifices, is bound by an oath that he will never have in his treasury more than a thousand pounds of gold, or its equivalent in silver.[5] They say that this law was instituted by an excellent king who cared more for his country's good than for his own wealth; his aim was to prevent any ruler from hoarding so much money that he would impoverish his people. He saw that his present wealth was enough to quell a rebellion or defend the kingdom against invasion but not large enough to tempt him to invade the lands of others. This was the law's main purpose; it also provided sufficient funds for daily transactions with the citizenry. Finally, a king who has to pay out to the people whatever exceeds the limit prescribed by law, he is less likely to oppress them. Such a king will be a terror to the evil and be loved by the good. But if I tried to tell these truths to men strongly inclined to the opposite way of thinking, would I not be telling my tale to deaf ears?"[6]

"Deaf indeed, without a doubt," I said, "and by Heaven I am not surprised. Nor, to tell the truth, do I think such talk should be thrust on people, nor such advice given to those who will never listen to it. What good could such novel ideas do? How could they pene-

[1] *That it is … himself* See Plato's *Republic* 1.343, which argues that the true ruler always acts in his subjects' best interest, not his own. Also see Aristotle's *Politics* 4.8.3, which defines a tyrant as one who rules with his own private interests in mind, rather than those of his people.

[2] *Fabricius* Roman general and statesman (d. 275 BCE), noted for his incorruptibility.

[3] *Let him … needed* Some counselors to Henry VII were notorious for fining citizens for breaking laws so old they did not know of their existence.

[4] *Macarians* "Happy ones," from the Greek *makarios* (blessed or happy).

[5] [marginal note] Wonderful law of the Macarians.

[6] [marginal note] Proverb.

trate minds of those entirely possessed by the opposite view? In private conversation among friends this academic sort of philosophizing is not without its charm, but in the councils of kings, where great matters are debated with great authority, there is no room for such things."

"That is just what I meant," he said, "by saying there is no room for philosophy in dealing with kings."

"Yes there is," I said, "but not for this academic philosophy that thinks every thing suited to every place.[1] There is another philosophy, however, a practical one better suiting political life, one that knows its cues, adapts itself to them, and in the play at hand performs its own part neatly and fittingly. This is the one you must use.[2] Suppose a comedy of Plautus is being performed, and just as the household slaves are making trivial jokes at each other you come on the stage in a philosopher's getup and spoke those lines from the *Octavia* in which Seneca is arguing with Nero. Would it not be better to have a non-speaking part than to recite something inappropriate and thus mangle a perfectly good comedy?[3] You spoil and unbalance the play by bringing in irrelevant matter, even if your own lines are superior. Whatever drama is being staged, perform it as well as you can and don't try to wreck it just because you think of another that has more charm.

"So it is in the commonwealth and in the deliberations of kings. Suppose wrong opinions cannot be pulled up by the root and that you cannot cure, as you would wish, vices of long standing. You must not on that account abandon the ship of state during a storm just because you cannot control the winds. Neither must you try to impose upon ministers of state strange and untested notions that you know will carry no weight with those of opposite conviction. You must do your best with an indirect approach and with covert suggestions. And when you cannot ensure a good outcome you must make it as little bad as you can. It is impossible that all can be well until all people are entirely good, something I do not expect for a great many years to come."

"By such means," Raphael said, "I would accomplish nothing except to share the madness of others while attempting to cure their lunacy. If I wish to speak the truth, I must do so in the manner I have described. For all I know, it may be the role of a philosopher to speak falsely, but it is not mine. Although my language may be unwelcome and disagreeable, I cannot see why it should seem so strange that they would think me foolish. It's not as if I told them the kind of things that Plato imagines in his *Republic*, or that the Utopians actually put in practice in theirs.[4] Though such institutions might seem superior (as in fact they are) they might also seem bizarre, because here we have private property, whereas there everything is held in common.

"My advice, in that case, would surely not be accepted—not only because it would be addressed to those who had made up their minds to go headlong down the opposite path, but also because people tend to resent it. But leaving that aside, what have I recommended that would not be appropriate or desirable everywhere? Truly, if all things that to the perverse ways of humanity have come to seem peculiar must be dismissed as unusual and absurd, we must also suppress almost all the doctrines of Christ. And He forbade us to suppress them—so much so that what He whispered in the ears of His disciples, He ordered them to proclaim openly from the housetops.[5] The greater part of His teaching is far more alien to our customary ways than anything I said. But preachers, crafty men that they are, and I suppose following your advice, found that people did not wish to change their ways so as to fit the words of Christ, and so they adapted them to human behavior as if His were a rule of lead, not of iron, in the hope that somehow the two might be reconciled. I cannot see what they have gained except to allow us to be bad with a good conscience. I would achieve no more in the councils of kings. Either I would offer a different opinion, which would be overruled, or I would voice the same opinion as the others, in which case I would, like Mitio in Terence,[6]

1 [marginal note] Philosophy of the Schools.

2 [marginal note] A striking comparison.

3 *Plautus* Roman playwright (c. 254–184 BCE) known for his low-brow, farcical comedies; *Octavia* Grave play in the tragic historical mode, spuriously attributed to Seneca; *comedy* [marginal note] A mute part.

4 [marginal note] Utopian institutions.

5 *what He ... housetops* See Matthew 10.27 and Luke 12.3.

6 *Mitio* Character in a comedy (*The Brothers*) by Terence (c. 190–158 BCE), a Roman playwright. In the speech referred to here, Mitio declares, "Still, if I inflamed or even fell in with his passionate temper, I should surely give him another madman for company" (1.145–47).

share their madness. As to the indirect approach you suggested, saying that if all things cannot be made good, they must at least be so handled as to be made, as far as can be done, as little bad as possible, I do not see the use. At court there is no room for dissembling, nor can you shut your eyes to things; you must openly approve the worst advice, and subscribe to the most ruinous decrees. He will be counted as a spy, almost a traitor, who even stutters in his praise of evil advice. Moreover, you have no chance to do any good when you mix with colleagues more likely to corrupt the best of men than to be reformed. Their evil conversation will either seduce you or turn your integrity and innocence into a screen for the wickedness and folly of others. Thus you are far from being able to make anything better by your indirect approach and your covert suggestions.

"For this reason, Plato shows in a wonderful analogy why philosophers are right to stay away from political life. Although they observe people rushing into the streets and getting soaked by constant showers, they cannot induce them to come in out of the rain. Knowing that they will accomplish nothing by going out, other than to get soaked with the rest, they stay put under cover, content that though they cannot cure the stupidity of others, they can at least save their own heads.[1]

"My dear More, to speak frankly from the heart, it seems to me that wherever you have private property, and all men measure all things by money, it is scarcely possible to have justice or prosperity. Surely you don't think there is justice when all good things come into the hands of the worst people, or that there is prosperity where a very few own everything. Even then those few are not fully content, while the many are downright wretched.

"Consider the wise and holy institutions of the Utopians, among whom, and with very few laws, affairs are so well ordered that virtue is rewarded and yet everyone has an equal abundance of everything. Contrast this with the situation of those many nations that keep creating fresh laws yet never manage to create good order—states in which whatever a man has grabbed he calls his own property but in which all these laws still do not help him secure or defend his goods or distinguish them from those of others (and notice the ever rising number of interminable lawsuits in such nations over what belongs to whom). I tell you, when I consider all this I become more partial to Plato and understand why he disdained to make laws for those who refused to accept the principle of granting an equal share of good things to everyone.[2] The wise philosopher foresaw that the one and only road to the general welfare of a commonwealth would be to enforce equality in all respects.

"I doubt that such well being could be achieved where there is private property. For when everyone aims to have as much of it as possible, even where there is a great wealth it is divvied up among a few, who leave nothing to the rest but poverty. And it generally happens that one class deserves the lot of the other, for the rich tend to be greedy, unscrupulous and useless, while the poor tend to be well behaved, simple and useful—more useful, by their daily labor, to the community than to themselves. I am entirely convinced that no just and even distribution of goods can be made, nor any perfect happiness be found among human beings, until private property is utterly abolished. While it lasts, for most of mankind, and not the worst, there will remain a heavy and intolerable burden of poverty and anxiety. I admit that this can be relieved to some extent, but I maintain that it cannot be removed. A statute might be made that no one be allowed to hold more than a certain amount of land, and that no one might have an income beyond a certain maximum. Laws could be passed to prevent the king from becoming too powerful and the people from becoming arrogant. There might also be legislation to stop public offices from being bought and sold, or held only at great personal expense. Otherwise, officials might take the chance to recoup by fraud and robbery what they spent to gain office, and then the rich would hold offices that should be held by the wise. Laws such as these can alleviate and lessen these evils, just as sick bodies that are past cure can still be kept going by constant medical treatment. There is no hope of a cure or a return to health, however, while each man is master of his own property. Indeed, while you are occupied with the curing of one part, you make the sores of the other worse; thus the disease of the one arises from the healing of the other, since nothing can

[1] *Plato ... their own heads* See *Republic* 6.469 D-E.

[2] *he refused ... everyone* This was Plato's reason for refusing to rule the Arcadians and the Thebans when the possibility was offered to him.

be added to one man without being subtracted from another."

"I can't agree," I said. "Life can never be happy or satisfying where all things are held in common. How could a sufficient supply of goods be kept up? Each person would spend less time working. If hope of personal gain does not motivate a man, he becomes lazy and relies on the industry of others. But when people are driven to labor by poverty and are not allowed to keep what they have worked for, is there not bound to be continual trouble, bloodshed, and revolution? Not to mention that magistrates must lose both authority and dignity, for how there can be any place for them among men who are all on the same level escapes me."

"I am not surprised that you think so," Raphael said, " for you have either have no conception, or a false one, of the sort of state I describe. If you had been with me in Utopia and had yourself seen how people behave, as I did (for I lived there more than five years, and would never have wished to leave except for the desire to make that new world widely known), you certainly would admit that you had never seen a more well-ordered people anywhere."

"Yet surely," said Peter Giles, "it will be hard for you to convince me that one might find in that new world a people better ordered than in our own familiar one. I imagine our governments are older and our minds at least equal in intelligence. Long experience has helped us to invent many conveniences for human life, not to speak of the things we discovered by pure luck and that no amount of intelligence could have devised."

"As for the age of states," said Raphael, "you could give a better opinion if you had read the world's histories; if we may believe them, there were cities there before there were men here. As to what intelligence has invented or chance discovered, that might have happened equally in both places. But even if it's true that we surpass the Utopians in intelligence, I am sure they leave us far behind in perseverance and industry. For according to their chronicles, up to our arrival they had never heard anything about us, whom they call the *Ultraequinoctials*, except that 1,200 years ago a ship driven by tempests to the island of Utopia was wrecked there. Some Romans and Egyptians were cast on shore and never left the island. Now mark with what industry they exploited this one opportunity. There was no useful art in the Roman empire that the Utopians did not either learn from the shipwrecked strangers or discover themselves after making some inquiries. What advantage they took of the chance arrival of a few men there! But if the same fortune has ever carried someone from their country to ours, it is completely forgotten, as perhaps it will be forgotten in times to come that I was ever at Utopia. At our first encounter they immediately took up any good invention of ours, yet I suppose it will be a long time before we receive and adopt anything that is better ordered by them. This, I think, is the chief reason why, though we are inferior to them neither in intelligence nor in wealth, their commonwealth is more wisely governed and more prosperous than ours."

"Well, Raphael," I said, "I insist that you give us a description of the island, and do not be brief, but set forth in order the land, the rivers, the cities, the inhabitants, the manners, customs and laws—in fact everything that you think we would like to know. And you may imagine we'd like to know everything of which we are as yet ignorant."

"There is nothing," he said, "I would be more pleased to do, for I have the facts ready to hand. But it will take time."

"Then," I said, "let us go in to dinner, and afterwards we will take up as much time as we like."

"So be it," he said.

So we went in and dined, and then returned to the same spot, sat down on the same bench, and having given orders to the servants that we must not be interrupted, Peter Giles and I urged Raphael to fulfill his promise. When he saw us intent and eager to listen, after sitting in silent thought for a time, he thus began his tale.

Book 2

Chapter 1

The island of Utopia extends in the center (where it is broadest) for two hundred miles, and this breadth continues for the greater part of the island, but towards both ends it begins gradually to taper.[1] These ends form a circuit of about 500 miles, so that the island resembles

---

[1] [marginal note] Site and shape of Utopia and the new island.

a new moon with horns divided by a strait about eleven miles across that then opens out into a wide expanse. The land that almost surrounds the bay keeps the winds off the water, making it seem like a huge lake, unruffled and not subject to storms. Thus almost all the center of the island makes a harbor, one in which ships can go in every direction to the great convenience of the inhabitants. Shallows and rocks make the mouth of this sea (which is situated between the horns) dangerous. Near the center of the gap stands one great cliff, which is not dangerous because clearly visible. On it stands a tower, manned by a garrison.[1] The other rocks are hidden, and therefore treacherous. Only the natives know the channels, so very few foreigners enter the gulf without a Utopian pilot. Even for them the entrance is hardly safe, but they are guided by landmarks on the shore. If these were removed and resituated, the shoals could easily destroy an enemy fleet, however large.[2]

On the opposite coast there are numerous harbors, but the landing is everywhere so well defended by nature or by art that it would take only a few men to prevent a strong force from invading. As is recorded, and as the appearance of the ground shows, the island was not surrounded by sea until the time of Utopus, who conquered it and gave it its name (up to then it was called "Abraxa").[3] He brought a rude and rustic people to such a degree of civilization and refinement that they now excel almost all others. After a victory on his first landing, he ordered the land excavated for fifteen miles where it was connected to the mainland, thus letting the sea flow round it.[4] He set to the task not only the inhabitants but his own soldiers, and so he prevented anyone from thinking the task imposed upon him a disgrace. By dividing the work equally among so many hands, he ensured that it was finished with astonishing speed. The neighbors, who had at first ridiculed the undertaking as vain, were struck with wonder and terror at his success.[5] The island contains 54 cities or county towns, all large and fine, identical in language, manners, customs and laws,[6] similar in situation, and everywhere, so far as the nature of the ground permits, the same in appearance.[7] None of them is less than twenty-four miles from the next, but none is so isolated that you cannot go from it to another in a day's journey on foot.[8] From each city three senior and experienced citizens meet once a year at Amaurote,[9] the capital, to discuss affairs of common interest to the island, for the city's central location makes it the most conveniently situated place to which representatives of all parts can travel.

The land is so well distributed that each city has at least twenty miles of it on every side, and on some sides more, where the towns are farther apart.[10] No town has any desire to extend its territory, for its citizens consider themselves to be cultivators, not owners, of what they hold.[11] Everywhere in the country they have provided, at suitable distances from each other, farmhouses well equipped with farming tools.[12] These are inhabited by citizens who come in succession to live there. No rural household numbers fewer than forty men and women, besides two slaves attached to the soil, and over each are set a responsible master and mistress of mature years. A Phylarch[13] rules over every thirty households. Twenty from each household return every year to the city, after completing two years in the country. In their place the same number are sent fresh from the city to be instructed by those who have already been there a year and are therefore more experienced in husbandry. They themselves teach others the following year; so there is no danger of any mistake or ineptitude causing scarcity, as

[1] [marginal note] Being naturally safe, the entry is defended by a single fort.

[2] [marginal note] The trick of shifting landmarks.

[3] [marginal note] Utopia named for King Utopia.

[4] [marginal note] This was a bigger job than digging across the Isthmus. [Several unsuccessful attempts had been made to dig a canal across the Isthmus of Corinth, which joins the Peloponnesian peninsula to the rest of Greece. As a result of these repeated failures, this was a proverbially difficult task.]

[5] [marginal note] Many hands make light work.

[6] [marginal note] The towns of Utopia.

[7] [marginal note] Likeness breeds concord.

[8] [marginal note] A middling distance between towns.

[9] *Amaurote* Dim or dark; from the Greek *amauroton*, meaning "made dark."

[10] [marginal note] Distribution of land.

[11] [marginal note] But today this is the curse of all countries.

[12] [marginal note] Farming is the prime occupation.

[13] *Phylarch* Leader of the tribe, from the Greek *phylarchos*, meaning "head of a group."

might happen if all at one time were newcomers without knowledge of husbandry.

Though this system of changing the cultivators of the soil is the rule, designed to prevent anyone being forced to continue long in a life of hard work, men who take a natural pleasure in agriculture can obtain leave to stay several years. The job of the cultivator is to till the ground, to feed the animals, and to get wood, getting it to town by land or water, as is most convenient.[1] Cultivators breed a great quantity of poultry by a wonderful device.[2] The hens do not sit on the eggs; instead, a great number of eggs are kept at a uniform heat until they come to life and hatch. As soon as they have come out of the shell, the chicks follow and recognize human beings instead of hens. They breed very few horses and these only high-spirited ones, which they use for no other purpose than to exercise their young men in horsemanship.[3] All the labor of cultivation and transport is performed by oxen, which may be inferior to horses in a sprint, but are far superior to them in staying power and endurance and not susceptible to so many diseases.[4] Moreover, it takes less trouble and expense to feed them, and when they are past work can be eaten.

Utopians grow grain only for bread.[5] They drink wine, made of grapes or of apples and pears, or else pure water infused with honey or licorice, which they have in abundance.[6] Though they know for certain how much grain the city and its adjacent lands require, they produce far more grain and cattle than they need and distribute the surplus among their neighbors.[7] Whenever they require anything not found in the country, they requisition it from the city, and without having to give anything in exchange easily obtain it from the town officials and have it brought to them every month on a recurring holiday, when many people go to the city and can help transport the needed materials. When the time of harvest is at hand, the Phylarchs in the country tell the city officials how many citizens they need. These harvesters, arriving at the appointed time, and weather permitting, complete almost all the harvest work in a single day.[8]

Chapter 2
The Cities, and Especially Amaurote

If you know one of the cities, you know them all, for as far as the landscape permits they are almost identical, so I could describe this one or that—it does not matter which I would choose—but nothing could be better than Amaurote.[9] None is worthier, for the others defer to it as the place where the Council meets; and none is better known to me, for I lived there for a full five years.

Built on the gentle slope of a hill, Amaurote is almost square-shaped. Its breadth is about two miles starting from just below the crest of the hill and running down to the river Anyder;[10] its length along the river is rather more than its breadth.[11] The river, which rises eighty miles beyond Amaurote from a small spring, is augmented by various tributaries, two of which are fairly large, so that by the time it reaches the city it is half a mile across. It becomes even broader as it flows a further sixty miles and then falls into the ocean. Through the whole distance between the city and the sea, and even above the city for some miles, the tide flows in rapidly for six hours at a time and then recedes with equal speed. When the sea comes in it fills the whole bed of the Anyder with its water for a distance of thirty miles and drives the river back.[12] At such times it turns its water salt for some distance farther, but after that the river becomes gradually fresh and passes the city untainted. When the ebb comes, the fresh water extends almost down to the mouth of the river.

Amaurote is joined to the opposite bank of the river not by a wooden bridge but by a stone one with fine

[1] [marginal note] Farmers' jobs.

[2] [marginal note] A notable way of hatching eggs.

[3] [marginal note] Uses of the horse.

[4] [marginal note] Uses of oxen.

[5] *Utopians … bread* Rather than for making ale or beer.

[6] [marginal note] Food and drink.

[7] [marginal note] Planned planting.

[8] [marginal note] The value of collective labor.

[9] [marginal note] Description of Amaurote, first city of Utopia.

[10] *Anyder* Without water, from the Greek *anydros*, meaning "waterless."

[11] [marginal note] The river Anyder.

[12] [marginal note] Just like the Thames in England.

arches.[1] It is placed at the corner of the city farthest from the sea so that sea-going ships may easily pass along almost the whole town. There is also another river, not large but very gentle and pleasant, which rises out of the same hill on which the town is built and flows through it into the Anyder. The Amaurotians have fortified the source of this river with walls connecting it to the city so that no invading enemy can divert or pollute their drinking water.[2] From where it enters, the water is distributed by brick channels into various parts of the lower town. Where the ground makes that impossible, rainwater collected in big cisterns serves the purpose. A high and broad wall with many towers and battlements surrounds the town.[3] A ditch, dry but deep, broad, and made impassable by thorn hedges, surrounds the walls on three sides; on the fourth side is the river.

The streets are well laid out both for traffic and to avoid the winds.[4] The houses, which are in no way shabby, are set together in long continuous rows facing one another, with twenty-foot wide streets in between.[5] Behind the houses, along the whole length of each street, lies a broad garden enclosed on all sides.[6] Every house has not only a door onto the street but also a back door into the garden. Folding doors, opening easily by hand and closing automatically, give admission to anyone, so that nothing at all is private.[7] Indeed, every ten years citizens exchange their houses by lot. Utopians are very fond of their gardens. These have vines, fruits, herbs, and flowers, so well kept and flourishing that I had never seen anything so fruitful or elegant. They take great pleasure in the gardens themselves but also in keen competition among streets as to which block will have the best ones. Certainly you cannot find anything in the whole city more profitable and enjoyable to the citizens, and there was nothing that the first founder cared more for than these gardens.[8]

They say that Utopus himself first laid out the whole city but left its adornment and improvement to future generations, knowing that there was too much to be done in one lifetime. According to their chronicles (which cover 1,760 years of history and are most carefully preserved), their first houses were low, mere hovels and cabins with mud walls and thatched roofs. But now all the houses are handsome, with three stories and walls faced by flint, plaster, or brick. The roofs are flat and covered with a cement that is inexpensive yet so well mixed that it is fire-resistant and better than lead in resisting the violence of storms. Utopians keep the wind out of their windows by glass, which is in very common use, or sometimes by thin cloth smeared with translucent oil or amber. This has two advantages: more light is let in, and the winds are better kept out.[9]

Chapter 3
The System of Local Government

Each year every thirty families choose a representative whom in their old language they had called a "Syphogrant"[10] but now call a "Phylarch."[11] Over every ten Syphogrants with their families is set a Tranibor,[12] or chief Phylarch. Then the whole body of two hundred Syphogrants, having sworn to pick the one best qualified for the position, chooses by secret ballot a chief executive from four candidates nominated by the citizens[13] in each quarter of the city.

The chief governor holds office for life unless suspected of trying to make himself a dictator.[14] The Tranibors are elected annually and are not changed without good reason, but other administrators hold office for one year. The Tranibors consult the governor every other day, more often if need be. They discuss the affairs of the

[1] [marginal note] Here too London is just like Amaurote.

[2] [marginal note] A source of drinking water.

[3] [marginal note] City walls.

[4] [marginal note] Streets, of what sort.

[5] [marginal note] Buildings.

[6] [marginal note] Gardens next to the houses.

[7] [marginal note] This smacks of Plato's community.

[8] [marginal note] Virgil also wrote in praise of gardens. [See *Georgics*, 4.16–48.]

[9] [marginal note] Windows of glass or oiled linen.

[10] *Syphogrant* Wiseman, from the Greek *sophos* (wise) and *gerontes* (old men).

[11] [marginal note] In the Utopian tongue "tranibor" means "chief official."

[12] *Tranibor* Plain-glutton, from the Greek *tranos* (plain, clear) and *boros* (devouring, gluttonous).

[13] [marginal note] A notable way of electing officials.

[14] [marginal note] Tyranny hateful to the well-ordered commonwealth.

commonwealth, and if there are disputes between private persons—which happen rarely—they settle them quickly.[1] Each day the Tranibors invite two different Syphogrants into the chamber. Nothing concerning the commonwealth may be ratified unless it has been discussed by the Senate on three different days,[2] and talking about public affairs outside the Senate or the electoral body is a capital offence. These rules, Utopians say, make it harder for governor and Tranibors to plot a tyranny and change the nature of the commonwealth. And so important matters are referred to the assembly of Syphogrants, who after informing their families confer and then report their decision to the Senate. Sometimes the matter is laid before the council of the whole island. By custom, the Senate postpones debate on a new matter until the next day, so that no one will blurt out what first comes into his mind and then put all his effort into defending what he had said rather than into thinking of the commonweal, willing to sacrifice the public good if he might save his reputation from seeming to have had so little foresight. He should have taken care at the outset to speak with wisdom rather than in haste.[3]

Chapter 4
Crafts and Occupations

Agriculture is the one pursuit common to all, both men and women, without exception.[4] Everyone is trained in it from early years, partly in school and partly by being taken for an outing to the nearby farmland, where students don't just watch but get their exercise by lending a hand.

Besides agriculture, which as I said is common to all, each person is taught some craft, generally wool working, preparing linen, masonry, carpentry, blacksmith's work, or silk weaving.[5] No other pursuit occupies very many people.[6] Each family makes its own clothes, which are in the same style throughout the island except for distinctions between the sexes and between the married and the single.[7] The garments please the eye, allow the body to move easily, and suit both summer and winter. Everyone, man and woman alike, learns one of these crafts.[8] But women, the weaker sex, take on the lighter tasks, generally working with wool and linen, while the men do the heavy labor. As a rule, a son is brought up in his father's craft, for which he usually has a natural inclination, but anyone attracted to another sort of work is adopted by a family pursuing it.[9] Parents and officials strive to ensure that such a child joins a serious and honest household. Moreover, those already expert in one craft who want to learn a second may do so; having acquired both, they practice whichever they please unless the city has more need of one than the other.

The chief and almost only function of the Syphogrants is to see that no one sits idle but pursues a craft zealously.[10] No one, however, is wearied like a beast of burden by constant toil from early morning till late at night, a wretchedness worse than slavery. Outside Utopia, that is the usual lot of laborers.[11] Utopians divide the day and night into twenty-four equal hours, assigning only six to labor. People work for three hours before noon, after which they go to dinner. After resting for two hours, they do three more and then go to supper.[12] At about 8 p.m. they go to bed and sleep for eight hours. Each person decides how to pass the leisure hours, so long as he does not fritter them away in sloth and roistering but pursues some interest to which he is inclined. Many devote these breaks to literature and

[1] [marginal note] A quick ending to disputes, which now are endlessly and deliberately prolonged.

[2] [marginal note] No abrupt decisions.

[3] [marginal note] This is the old saying, "Do your thinking overnight."

[4] [marginal note] Agriculture is everyone's business, though now we put it off on a despised few.

[5] *Besides ... weaving* In contrast to Plato's conception of an ideal republic, in which order would be maintained only if each individual had only one task.

[6] [marginal note] Trades taught to satisfy need, not greed.

[7] [marginal note] A uniform dress code.

[8] [marginal note] No citizen without a trade.

[9] [marginal note] Everyone to learn the trade for which his nature fits him.

[10] [marginal note] The idle are expelled from society.

[11] *Outside ... laborers* In England at that time, laborers worked from sunrise to sunset.

[12] [marginal note] Workmen not to be overtasked.

learning.[1] For their custom is to hold daily public lectures in the early morning, and although only those specially chosen to devote themselves to learning have to attend, a great number of men and women from every line of work go to hear whichever lecture appeals to them. They do not blame those many who prefer spending time on their craft rather than on intellectual matters, and in fact commend them as useful citizens. After supper they spend one hour in recreation, in summer in the gardens and in winter in the common halls where they have their meals.[2] There they either practice music or entertain themselves with conversation. They know nothing of throwing the dice and other such stupid and hurtful pursuits.[3] They do play two games not unlike chess—one a battle of numbers in which one number takes another, the other a game in which vices fight a pitched battle with virtues.[4] The game cleverly shows the strife among the vices and their concerted opposition to the virtues. It shows which vices oppose which virtues; by what means they attack openly, and by what contrivances they do so indirectly; by what reinforcement the virtues break the power of the vices and by what arts they frustrate their designs; and, finally, by what means one side gains the victory.[5]

But here, lest you misunderstand, there is one matter to which we should return. Since Utopians spend only six hours working, you might think that some scarcity of goods must follow. But this is far from the case: the time is more than ample to supply a wealth of necessities, even of conveniences. You must bear in mind that a large part of the population in other countries does not work.[6] First, almost no women (half of the population) do so, and where the women are busy, almost as a rule, the men are snoring. Second, there is the great and idle company of secular priests and the so-called "religious" clergy. Add to them the rich, and especially the landowners commonly called gentlemen and noblemen. Now add their retainers—I mean that rabble of good-for-nothing swaggering bullies.[7] Finally, add those beggars who are perfectly able to work but who fake some disease as an excuse for laziness, and you will certainly find that those who produce everything that people need for daily use are fewer by far than you had supposed.[8] Now, of those who do work calculate how few ply essential trades. In a society that makes money the standard of everything, inevitably many crafts are vain and superfluous, serving luxury and extravagance. If the number of those who now work were assigned to only those few crafts supplying the needs and conveniences that Nature demands, there would be such a flood of goods that prices would fall drastically and many would lose their jobs. But if all those now busied with unneeded labor, together with all the lazy and idle crowd (each one of whom now consumes as much of the fruits of other men's efforts as any two laborers), were made to do something useful, you would easily see how little time it would take to produce all that is required by necessity, comfort, or even pleasure.

The experience of Utopia makes all this clear. In any city and its immediate neighborhood, exemption from work is granted to no more than five hundred of those men and women whose age and strength makes them fit for toil. The Syphogrants, though released by law from work, take no advantage of this privilege, so that by their example they may inspire others to labor.[9] Others, on the recommendation of priests and by a secret vote of the Syphogrants are granted permanent freedom from labor so that they might devote themselves to study, although anyone who disappoints the hopes placed in him must become a laborer once more. On the other hand, it often happens that someone so industriously devotes his spare hours to learning and makes such progress that he is relieved of manual labor and promoted to the scholarly order. It is out of this group that

1 [marginal note] The study of letters.

2 [marginal note] Diversion after supper.

3 [marginal note] But now gambling is the sport of kings.

4 *vices fight ... virtues* In More's England the most familiar vices were the seven deadly sins (pride, envy, wrath, sloth, greed, gluttony, and lust) and their opposite virtues (the biblical trio faith, hope, and charity, together with the Aristotelian prudence, temperance, fortitude, and justice); in still pagan Utopia, the virtues are more likely to be those of Aristotle, and their opposing vices the many mentioned by Roman moral philosophers. Moralized chess was found also in Europe. Numbers were on European minds, for the Arabic numerals were still new to many places.

5 [marginal note] Their games are useful too.

6 [marginal note] Kinds of idlers.

7 [marginal note] Noblemen's bodyguards.

8 [marginal note] A very shrewd observation.

9 [marginal note] Not even officials dodge work.

Utopians choose ambassadors, priests, Tranibors, and finally the governor himself,[1] whom in their ancient tongue was the "Barzanes," but who is now called the "Ademos."[2]

Because the rest of the people are neither idling nor busied with useless occupations, it is easy to reckon what good work can be accomplished in a few hours. In addition to what I have mentioned, there is the further convenience that most of the necessary crafts do not require as much work as they do in other nations.[3] Take, for example, the building or repair of houses. In most places, this requires the constant labor of a great many men simply because what a father builds his extravagant heir lets decay. Consequently, what might have been kept up at small cost must now be rebuilt at great expense. Even if a house has cost one man a large sum, another man is so fastidious that he thinks little of it, lets it crumble, and then builds another elsewhere at no less cost. But in the Utopians' well-ordered and well-regulated commonwealth, people seldom find new sites for new houses. Not only do they quickly remedy present defects, they also prevent future damages. So with little labor, houses last a long time and masons and carpenters sometimes have scarcely anything to do, although they are told to prepare timber at home and use the time gained to square stone, so that if any work is required they can do it quickly.

As for clothing, see again how little labor is required.[4] While Utopians are at work they dress casually in hide or skins that last for seven years. When they go outdoors they put on a cloak to hide their working clothes; all over the island, this garment has the same natural color. Thus they need much less woolen cloth than is required elsewhere and what they have is less expensive; such cloth is made with less labor, and less of it is consumed. For linen cloth, they care only that it be clean and white; they don't worry about the fineness of thread. So whereas elsewhere one man is not satisfied with four or five woolen gowns of different colors and as many silk coats (and for the more demanding not even ten is enough), in Utopia a man is content with one coat, generally for two years. There is no reason to desire more, for more would not better fortify him against the cold or make him appear better dressed.

With everyone devoted to useful work and satisfied with few goods, sometimes when there is a superabundance of supplies, a great number of citizens are set to fixing roads that are in bad shape. Or, if there is nothing of that kind that needs doing, the officials announce that there will be fewer hours of work. For they do not keep the citizens against their will at unnecessary labor. The constitution of the commonwealth has one objective: that so far as public needs permit, as much time as possible should be taken from serving the body and devoted to the freedom and cultivation of the mind. In that, they believe, consists the happiness of life.

Chapter 5
Their Dealings with One Another

Now I should explain the relations of the citizens one to another, how they treat each other, and how they distribute goods.

Because a city consists of families, the households for the most part consist of those related by blood, although women, when they arrive at maturity and get married, go live in their husbands' houses. Male children and the next generation remain in the family and answer to the oldest parent, unless his mind has become unfit from age, in which case the next oldest is put in his place. Lest any city either be depopulated or grow beyond measure, though, no family of the six thousand that each city (apart from the surrounding district) contains may have fewer than ten or more than sixteen adults.[5] No number can be fixed for underage children. This rule is easily observed by transferring some members of overly large families to those that have too few. If the whole number of citizens surpasses the fixed limit, then they make up any deficient population of other cities. But if the whole island becomes overpopulated they select citizens from each city to go to the mainland nearest them and found a colony wherever the inhabitants have unoccupied and

[1] [marginal note] Only the learned hold public office.

[2] *Barzanes* Probably from the Hebrew *bar* (son of) and *Zanos* (of Zeus); *Ademos* "Peopleless," from the Greek *a* (without) and *demos* (people).

[3] [marginal note] Avoiding expense in building.

[4] [marginal note] Avoiding expense in clothing.

[5] [marginal note] The number of citizens.

unused land. There they live under their own laws, letting the natives who wish to do so join them. When the two groups do blend, the two peoples easily grow into the same way of life and manners, to the great advantage of both. Using Utopian methods, they make the land sufficient for both groups whereas it had once seemed barely adequate for one. If the natives refuse to live according to Utopian laws, the settlers drive them out of the territory that they have claimed. If such natives resist, they fight them, for they think it a most just cause for war whenever a people does not use its soil but keeps it vacant and even forbid others, whose natural right it is to be nourished by it, to use and possess it. If an accident diminishes the citizenry of any Utopian city so badly that the loss cannot be made up by people from other parts of the island without bringing their cities, too, below their proper strength (this has happened only once in all the ages, when a fierce plague raged), they bring back settlers from the colony. They would rather lose colonies than let any of the island's cities weaken.

To return to the family life of the citizens: the oldest, as I said, rules the family. Wives serve their husbands, children their parents, and generally the younger minister to their elders.[1] Every city is divided into four quarters. In the middle of each quarter is a market for all kinds of goods. There the products of each family are conveyed and each kind of is put in separate storehouses. From these, any father of a family takes what he and his family require, and without money or any kind of payment he carries it off. Why should anything be refused? All things are plentiful, and there is no fear that anyone will demand more than he needs. Why should he, when he knows he will never lack anything?[2] In all creatures, only fear of want causes greed; only in human beings does pride lead some to think it glorious to excel in displays of excess. This vice can have no place among Utopians.

Next to the marketplaces I have mentioned are provision markets to which are brought, from sites outside the city where running water washes away all disease and filth,[3] vegetables, fruit, and bread, as well as fish and all edible beasts and birds. In those outer areas, slaves clean the animal carcasses, for Utopians do not allow free citizens to accustom themselves to butchering animals, thinking that such a practice erodes mercy, the finest quality of our nature.[4] Nor do they allow inside the city anything dirty or unclean lest the air be tainted by putrefaction and spread disease.

Every street has spacious halls at equal distance from one another and with special names. In these live the Syphogrants, to each of whom are appointed thirty families, fifteen on either side, with whom to share meals. The caterers of each hall meet at a fixed time in the market and get enough food for the appropriate number of people.

Special care is taken of the sick, who are looked after in one of the four public hospitals that are spaced out at the edges of town, a little outside the walls.[5] These are so roomy that they seem like small towns;[6] the purpose is to prevent the sick, however numerous, from being packed close in discomfort, and also to isolate the contagious and thus prevent their passing on their maladies to others. These hospitals are so well furnished and equipped with everything conducive to health, and the expert attending physicians provide such delicate and careful treatment, that although no one is sent there involuntarily there is hardly anybody in the whole city who, when ill, does not prefer to be cared for there rather than at home.

When the hospital caterer has received the food prescribed by the physicians, the rest is equally distributed among the halls according to the number in each, except that special consideration is given to the Governor, the Bishop, the Tranibors, and to ambassadors and foreigners, if any. Foreigners seldom visit, but when they do, they have special housing.

A trumpet blast summons the whole Syphogranty to assemble in these halls at the fixed hours for dinner and supper, except for those who are in hospital or who take their meals at their own houses.[7] No one is forbidden to bring extra food from the market to his house after the halls have been served. Utopians know that this is never

[1] [marginal note] Thus they eliminate crowds of idle servants.

[2] [marginal note] The sources of greed.

[3] [marginal note] Filth and garbage spread disease in cities.

[4] [marginal note] By butchering beasts we learn to slaughter men.

[5] [marginal note] Caring for the sick.

[6] *These ... towns* England at this time had a number of hospitals, but none on this scale.

[7] [marginal note] Meals in common, mixing all groups.

done without good reason,[1] for while no one is forbidden to dine at home, no one does so willingly—it is seen as inappropriate. It seems foolish to bother preparing an inferior dinner when a rich and sumptuous one is all ready in a nearby hall. In the hall slaves perform all tasks that demand heavy work and soil the hands. The women, from each family by turns, cook and serve the food and arrange the whole meal.[2] They sit down at three or more tables according to the number of the company, the men with their backs to the wall and the women on the outside, so that if any they feel any sudden sickness or pangs, as often happens during pregnancy, they may easily rise and go see the nurses without disturbing others.

The nurses sit apart with the infants in a special room supplied with a fire, clean water, and cradles, so that when they wish they can lay the infants down or take them by the fire and let them play. Each woman nurses her own child unless prevented by death or disease. When that happens, the wives of the Syphogrants quickly provide a nurse and find no difficulty in doing so.[3] Those who can do the service offer themselves with the greatest readiness, since everyone values this kind of charity and the child sees his nurse as his natural mother. In the nurses' quarters are all the children up to five years old;[4] all the others below the age of marriage either wait on their elders or, if not old and strong enough, stand by in absolute silence. Both groups of children eat what is handed to them from the table and have no other separate mealtimes.

The Syphogrant and his wife sit in the middle of the high table, the place of honor, from which they can view the whole company, their table standing crosswise at the end of the room. Alongside sit two of the elderly, for there are always four at a table. If there is a temple in the Syphogranty, the priest and his wife sit with the Syphogrant and preside.[5] On both sides of them sit the younger and next to them, old men again, and so it is throughout the house that those of the same age sit together, and yet still associate with those of a different age.[6] The reason, they say, is to let the grave and reverend behavior of the senior restrain the junior from mischievous words and gestures, since nothing can be done or said at the table that escapes the notice of older neighbors.

The courses are not served in order from the top place down; rather, old men, seated in specially marked places, are served first, with the best food, and then equal portions go to the rest.[7] But the senior, at their discretion, give a share of their delicacies to their neighbors if there are not enough of these for everyone. Thus due respect is paid to age and yet equality is honored. Every meal starts with some reading conducive to morality but brief enough not to become boring.[8] Next the elders introduce good topics of conversation, not too serious or devoid of wit.[9] But they do not take up the whole dinner with long speeches, for they enjoy hearing the young men too, and indeed, try to draw them out, testing the ability and talent that are revealed in the freedom of conversation. Their dinners are somewhat short, their suppers more prolonged, because the first are followed by labor, the latter by sleep and rest, which they think more effective for wholesome digestion.[10] No supper passes without music, nor does any meal lack dessert.[11] They burn spices, and scatter perfumes, and omit nothing that might cheer the company; for they enjoy such things, and regard no pleasure as illicit that does no harm.[12]

Life in the city is communal, but in the country those who live far from others take their meals in their own homes. No family lacks any kind of food, however, for whatever the city-dwellers eat comes from the country.

[1] [marginal note] Note how freedom is granted everywhere, lest people act under compulsion.

[2] [marginal note] Women prepare the meals.

[3] [marginal note] Honor and praise incite people to act properly.

[4] [marginal note] Raising the young.

[5] [marginal note] Priest before prince. But now even bishops act as servants to royalty.

[6] [marginal note] Young mixed with old.

[7] [marginal note] Respect for the elderly.

[8] [marginal note] Not even monks do this now.

[9] [marginal note] Table talk.

[10] [marginal note] Modern doctors think ill of this practice.

[11] [marginal note] Music at mealtimes.

[12] [marginal note] Innocent pleasures are not to be rejected.

Chapter 6
Traveling

Those struck with a desire to visit friends in another city or to see the country may easily get leave from their Syphogrants and Tranibors unless there is good reason against it. Right away a party is formed and departs, bearing a letter from the Governor certifying their permission to travel and naming the day of their return. They are given a wagon with a community slave to drive it and to tend to the oxen, but unless they have women with them they leave the carriage behind as a burden and hindrance.

Throughout their journey, although carrying nothing with them, they lack for nothing, being at home everywhere. If they stay longer than a day in any one place, each plies his trade and finds warm hospitality among his brethren of the same craft. Anyone caught outside his territory's limits without a certificate, however, is scorned as a runaway and punished severely; should he rashly repeat the offence he is made a slave. If anyone wants to explore the country around his own city, though, he may do so if he gets his father's leave and his wife's consent. Wherever he goes, however, he is given no food until he completes a morning's worth of work, or so much work as is usually performed between dinner and supper. If he fulfills his responsibility, he may go where he please within the city's territorial limits, for he will be just as useful to it there as if he were in town. So you can see that there is no way of evading work and no pretext for idleness: no wine shop, no ale house, no brothel, no occasion for depravity, no lurking holes, no secret meetings.[1] Everything is open to everyone, and everyone is bound either to do the usual work or to take lawful and not indecent recreation.

A people following such customs inevitably produce an ample store of everything. And because it is distributed evenly to everyone, nobody is forced into poverty or beggary.[2] The Senate of Amaurote, to which as I have said every city annually sends three members, determines what goods abound in one place or are lacking in another, then fills the shortage in one place with the overflow from another. There is no payment, no taking of anything from those to whom is given, and those who have given freely from their surplus to one city can in turn get what they need from another, thus the whole island is like a single family.[3]

When the Utopians have laid up enough for themselves (figuring that it should last for two years in case of crop failure), then they export to other countries a great deal of grain, honey, wool, linen, wood, scarlet and purple dye, fleeces, wax, tallow,[4] leather, and surplus livestock. They give one-seventh of these goods to the poor of that region and sell the rest at a moderate price.[5] By this exchange they import not only whatever they lack themselves—and practically everything is found in Utopia except iron—but also a great deal of silver and gold. The custom has stood so long that now they have everywhere plenty of these things—more than one would believe—so they care little whether they are paid immediately or later, and usually have much owed to them.

Whenever they are not paid at once, they do not trust the credit of individuals but rather that of a city, as a rule requiring signed promises.[6] When the day for payment arrives, the city collects the money owed by private debtors, puts it into the treasury, and enjoys the use of it until the Utopians claim payment.[7] But for the most part they do not demand repayment, thinking it unfair to take away something useful to others when they do not require it themselves. If other people do need it, however, they call in their debts so as to make a new loan. They do the same whenever a war impends, for war is the only reason for keeping treasure at home and thus available for use in extreme peril or a sudden emergency.[8] They primarily use such treasure to pay

---

[1] [marginal note] O sacred society, worthy of imitation, especially by Christians!

[2] [marginal note] Equality for all results in enough for each.

[3] [marginal note] The commonwealth is nothing but a kind of extended family.

[4] *tallow* Animal fat used in soap and candle production.

[5] [marginal note] Utopian business dealings.

[6] [marginal note] Never do they fail to be mindful of the community.

[7] [marginal note] How money can be useful.

[8] [marginal note] Better to avoid war by bribery or guile than to wage it with great bloodshed.

extravagant sums to foreign mercenaries, whom they would rather hazard than their own citizens, knowing that with such huge cash reserves even their enemies might be purchased and set to fight one another by deceit or open warfare. For this reason they keep a vast treasure, but not *as* treasure. I almost blush to say how they keep it, lest I be disbelieved. Had I not been there and witnessed it, I would have difficulty crediting it myself,[1] for in general the more alien something is to the manners and ways of those who hear, the farther it is from what they can believe. An impartial judge, though, knowing that their other customs are so unlike our own, will not be surprised that their treatment of gold and silver suits their way of life, not ours. And, again, they do not use money themselves but keep it for emergencies that may or may not come.

In the meantime, gold and silver, of which money is made, are treated so that no one values them more than they merit by their nature. Anyone can see that gold and silver are less useful than iron, for iron is as vital to human life, by Heaven, as are fire and water. Nature gave gold and silver no utility—it is only our folly that makes them seem precious.[2] Rather, like a kind and indulgent parent, she exposed to our sight all that is best, such as air, water, and earth itself, and has hidden away as far as possible all vain and unprofitable things.

Now if in Utopia these metals were kept locked up in a tower, it might be suspected—for such is the foolish imagination of the common people—that the Governor and the Council were craftily deceiving the public and profiting at its expense. Moreover, Utopians know that if they turned the metal into drinking cups or other objects of skilful handiwork, then, if they needed to melt them down again so as to hire soldiers, people would be unwilling to lose what they had begun to treasure. To avoid these dangers, they have devised a method that fits their own culture but would seem incredible to anyone who had not been there, so much do we value gold and so careful are we to hoard it. They themselves eat and drink from earthenware and glass of fine workmanship if of little value. But to make chamberpots and other indecent containers for both public halls and private houses they use gold and silver.[3] They use the same metals for their slaves' chains, and they make those who are to be publicly shamed for some offence wear gold earrings, finger rings, necklaces, and coronets. Thus by every means in their power they turn gold and silver into marks of disgrace.[4] Some nations take the loss of these same metals harder than they would a disemboweling, but in Utopia, if all gold and silver were taken in a single crisis, no one would feel that he had lost as much as a penny.

Utopians do gather pearls by the seashore, and value certain stones such as diamonds and garnets, but they do not go searching for them. When they chance upon them, they polish them up and give them to children, who when they are little take delight and pride in such ornaments.[5] After they grow up, however, and see that only children value these toys, they lay them aside, not thanks to orders from their parents but through their own sense of adult self-respect, just as our young, when they grow up, lay aside their marbles, rattles, and dolls.

Different customs, different attitudes.[6] This struck me forcibly during a visit by the Anemolian[7] ambassadors, who came to Amaurote during my stay there. In their honor, the city had assembled ahead of time three representatives of each city in the island. Now, the ambassadors of nearby nations, who had already visited Utopia and knew its customs, were well aware that Utopians have no respect for costly clothes, look with contempt on silk, and regard gold as a badge of disgrace, so they usually arrived in the simplest possible dress. But the Anemolians lived farther off and had had fewer dealings with Utopians. Knowing that in Utopia all dressed alike and with equal simplicity, they had assumed that Utopians must not have what they do not wear, and so, being more proud than wise, they had planned to play the gods by the fineness of their clothing and thus dazzle the eyes of the poor natives. And so the three ambassadors made a grand entry with an entourage of a hundred followers, all in multicolored

[1] [marginal note] O crafty fellow!

[2] [marginal note] As far as utility goes, gold is inferior to iron.

[3] [marginal note] O magnificent scorn for gold!

[4] [marginal note] Gold the mark of infamy.

[5] [marginal note] Gems the playthings of children.

[6] [marginal note] A neat tale.

[7] *Anemolian* Windy; from the Greek *anemolios*.

clothes, mostly of silk. The ambassadors themselves, who were noblemen at home, were splendid in cloth of gold, with big chains of gold and gold earrings, with gold rings on their fingers, and with strings of pearls and precious stones upon their caps—in short, decked out with the very things that in Utopia are used to punish slaves, stigmatize evildoers, or amuse children. And so it was a sight to see how they strutted when they compared their grand clothing with the dress of the Utopians, who had poured into the streets to see them pass. It was no less amusing to notice how mistaken they were in their overconfidence and how far from winning the admiration they had expected. For the Utopians, with the exception of those very few who had visited other countries, found all this gaudy show disgraceful. So they bowed to the lowest of the party but ignored the ambassadors and paid them no deference, thinking them slaves because of their gold. Indeed, you might have seen those children who had discarded pearls and precious stones nudge their mothers at the sight of such things on the caps of the ambassadors and say, "Look at that big idiot, Mother, still wearing pearls and gems like a kid."[1] The mothers in all seriousness would answer, "Hush, son, I think he's one of the ambassadors' jesters." Others called the gold chains useless: so slender that a slave could easily break them, or so loose that he could slip them off and escape. For a couple of days the ambassadors watched as their stupendous show of gold was slighted— indeed, disregarded to the same degree that they had hoped for honor. Then they observed that there was more gold and silver in the chains and fetters of a single runaway slave than in all of their finery put together. Crestfallen and ashamed, all the more so as they became more familiar with the Utopians and their ways, they put away all the finery with which they had made themselves so conspicuous.

The Utopians wonder how any mortal can take pleasure in the uncertain sparkle of a tiny gem or shiny pebble stone when he can look at a star or at the sun itself.[2] They wonder how anyone can be lunatic enough to think himself grander than others because he wears wool of a thinner thread: however finely spun it is, a sheep once wore it and the sheep is still just a sheep. They wonder, too, that gold, in its own nature so useless, is now everywhere valued so highly that humanity itself, by whom and for whose use it got its value, is priced far below gold. They cannot comprehend that a leaden-head who has no more wit than a post and is no less wicked than foolish can keep in bondage many wise and good men merely because he has a great heap of gold coins.[3] Yet if this dolt, by chance or legal chicanery, loses that gold to the lowest rascal of the household (for the law can reverse the high and low as arbitrarily as can fortune), he will surely become a slave of his former servant, as if he had been a mere appendage or adjunct of the money. Much more are they aghast at the madness of those who almost worship the rich even though neither owing them anything nor being in any fashion beholden to them and impressed only by their wealth.[4] This especially surprises the Utopians, for they know that these men are so mean and miserly that probably of all that pile of cash, so long as the rich men live, not a penny will ever come their way. These and similar opinions they have derived partly from their upbringing in a commonwealth with institutions free from such folly and partly from reading books.

Only a few in each city are relieved from other work so as to devote themselves exclusively to study: those who have shown from childhood talent, high intelligence, and a fine disposition. Nevertheless, all children are trained in good letters, and many people, men and women alike, throughout their lives spend those hours that I said were free from manual labor on learning. They study the various branches of knowledge in their own language, for it is rich in vocabulary, pleasing to the ear, and well adapted for expressing thought.[5] Much of that part of the world has the same language, though sometimes in a variety of corrupted forms.

Philosophers whose names are famous to us were unknown to Utopians before our arrival, yet in music, dialectic, arithmetic and geometry they have made almost the same discoveries as our forebears.[6] Just as

[1] [marginal note] The rascal!

[2] [marginal note] "Weak" because the gems are false, or the glitter is feeble and scanty.

[3] [marginal note] How true and how apt!

[4] [marginal note] How much wiser are the Utopians than the common sort of Christians.

[5] [marginal note] Training and studies of the Utopians.

[6] [marginal note] Music, dialectic, and mathematics.

they equal the ancients in almost all respects, however, so they fall far short of our inventive modern logicians,[1] for they have not discovered a single one of those ingeniously derived rules about restrictions, amplifications, and suppositions that our children learn in the *Parva Logicalia.*[2] They are so far from being able to find out second intentions,[3] that not one of them was able to catch sight of "Humanity" in the abstract, even after we pointed at him with our fingers, though "Humanity" is, as you know, a Colossus greater than any giant. But they are most expert in the paths of the stars and the movements of the celestial bodies.[4] Furthermore, they have cleverly devised instruments of different shapes by which they have most exactly understood the movements and positions of the sun and moon and the other stars they see in the sky. But of the agreements and discords of the planets, and of all deceitful divination by the stars, they do not even dream.[5] They forecast rain, wind and changes in the weather by certain signs that they have learned to recognize after long practice. As for the causes of all these things, however, or on the flow of the sea and its saltiness, or in sum on the origin and nature of the heavens and the universe, they sometimes agree with our ancient natural philosophers or, like our own experts, sometimes introduce new theories that disagree with all earlier ones—nor do they always agree with each other.[6]

As for moral philosophy, they discuss the same topics that we do.[7] They inquire into the goods of the soul, goods of the body, and external goods.[8] They also wonder whether the name of "good" may be rightly applied to all three or belongs only to the endowments of the soul.[9] They discuss virtue and pleasure, but chiefly they discuss in what thing—or things— happiness consists.[10] In this matter they seem to lean more than they should to the school that defends pleasure, since they believe it to be the whole or at least chief cause of human happiness.[11] More astonishing, they try to defend this soft philosophy with principles taken from their religion, which is grave and strict, even stern and rigid.[12] They never discuss happiness without joining some principles derived from religion to reasoning drawn from philosophy.[13] Without these principles, they think, reason is too weak and insufficient to investigate true happiness.

These principles are that the soul is immortal, that thanks to God's goodness it is born to be happy, and that after this life our virtues and good deeds are rewarded and our crimes punished.[14] Although these principles are matters of faith, Utopians think that reason leads us to believe and acknowledge them.[15] If they were set aside, they hasten to add, nobody would be so stupid as not to seek pleasure by means fair or foul. He should take care only to stop a lesser pleasure from interfering with a greater one, or to avoid pleasure that leads to pain.[16] For to seek a hard and painful virtue, and not only drive away all enjoyment but voluntarily to suffer pain that without later profit—for what profit can there be if after death you get nothing for having spent your whole life unpleasantly, even wretchedly?—this

[1] [marginal note] The passage seems a bit satiric.

[2] *Parva Logicalia* Latin: Little Logical Works. Texts with this or similar titles were made by Medieval Nominalist philosophers, for whom Renaissance humanists had little liking, although they still studied them. Hence More's allusion to "good letters"—to some extent what we call "literature" and a contrast to the late medieval stress on logic.

[3] *second intentions* "First intentions" are the direct apprehensions of material objects; "second intentions" are abstract conceptions derived from generalizations upon first intentions.

[4] [marginal note] The study of the stars.

[5] [marginal note] Yet these astrologers are revered by Christians to this very day.

[6] [marginal note] Physics the most uncertain study of all.

[7] [marginal note] Ethics.

[8] [marginal note] Higher and lower goods.

[9] *They also wonder ... soul* This first position is that of the Aristotelians; the second is held by the Stoics.

[10] [marginal note] Supreme goods.

[11] *In this ... happiness* This reflects an Epicurean position that sensual pleasures were the only happiness available in the material world.

[12] [marginal note] The Utopians consider honest pleasure the measure of happiness.

[13] [marginal note] First principles of philosophy to be sought in religion.

[14] [marginal note] Utopian theology.

[15] [marginal note] The immortality of the soul, on which nowadays no small number even of Christians have their doubts.

[16] [marginal note] Not every pleasure is desirable, neither is pain to be sought, except for the sake of virtue.

they hold to be utter nonsense. But as it is, the Utopians think happiness rests not in *all* kinds of pleasure, but rather in those that are good and honorable. To these, as to the supreme good, our nature is drawn by virtue itself (to which alone the opposite school of philosophy attributes happiness).[1]

Utopians define virtue as living according to nature, since God created us to that end.[2] Whoever obeys the dictates of reason in desiring one thing and avoiding another, they say, follows the guidance of nature. Reason, first of all, inspires us to love and venerate the Divine Majesty who gave us our lives and our capacity for happiness. Second, reason urges and admonishes us to lead lives as free from care and as full of joy as possible, and, because of our natural fellowship, to help others do likewise. No one was ever such a solemn and strict follower of virtue and hater of pleasure that however hard the labor, wakefulness, and discomfort he urged on you he would not also tell you to do your best to relieve the poverty and discomfort of others. He would tell you to think it praiseworthy, in the name of humanity, for one person to provide for another's health and comfort. Now, if it is especially humane (and this is the virtue most peculiar to humankind) to relieve the misery of others, to take away sorrow from their lives, and to restore enjoyment and pleasure, why should not nature urge us to do the same for ourselves? For if a joyous and pleasurable life is evil, then you should not only not help anyone experience joy and pleasure, you should even try to take these away from everyone else on the grounds that they are harmful and deadly.[3] On the other hand, if you feel bound to praise such a life as good for them, then you should do the same for yourself, to whom you should show no less favor than to others. When nature bids you to be good to others, she does not command you to be cruel and merciless to yourself. Nature herself, the Utopians say, calls us to a merry life, so that, in sum, pleasure is the end of all activity, and to live according to her prescriptions is virtue. But even though Nature calls us all to help each other to a merrier life (for she regards no one as raised so far above the common human lot as to be the sole object of her care), she surely bids you take constant care not to favor yourself so much that you put others at a disadvantage.

Utopians think not only that all bargains between individuals should be observed, but also that the common laws should be obeyed by everyone. Provided that they have been proclaimed by a just ruler and ratified by common consent, such laws provide just rules for the fair distribution of material goods, or, in other words, the means of pleasure.[4] So long as these laws are not broken, it is wisdom to look after your own interests and your duty to take care of the public interest as well. To deprive others of their pleasure so as to secure your own is injustice, while to take away something from yourself to give to others is a duty of humanity and kindness, which never takes away as much as it gives back. First, you are for the most part eventually compensated by a return of benefits. Second, the consciousness of having done a good deed is a benefit in itself. And receiving the love and goodwill of those whom you have benefited gives your mind a greater pleasure than the bodily pleasure you have given up.[5] Finally—this is brought home to those of a religious bent—in return for a brief and small pleasure God repays you with great and endless joy. So the Utopians, having carefully considered and weighed the matter, believe that all our actions and even our virtues have pleasure as their final purpose.

By pleasure they understand every activity or state of body or mind in which a person delights under the guidance of nature.[6] They are right to specify a person's *natural* inclinations.[7] The senses and right reason aim at whatever is naturally pleasant—that is, at whatever is

[1] *school ... happiness* This is the Stoic view, which emphasizes morality, virtue, and duty over material pleasures.

[2] [marginal note] This is like Stoic doctrine.

[3] [marginal note] But now some people cultivate pain as if it were the essence of religion, rather than incidental to performance of a pious duty or the result of natural necessity—and thus to be borne, not pursued.

[4] [marginal note] Contracts and laws.

[5] [marginal note] Mutual assistance.

[6] [marginal note] What is pleasure?

[7] *By pleasure ... inclinations* The following discussion reflects both Plato's and Aristotle's praise of physical and mental pleasures and their distinctions between true pleasures (those "pleasant by nature") and false ones. See Plato's *Philebus* and Aristotle's *Nicomachean Ethics*. Many of the false pleasures listed here are discussed in More's friend Erasmus's *The Praise of Folly* (1511).

not achieved by wrong-doing, does not involve the loss of something more pleasant, and is not followed by pain. But there are some disagreeable things that mortals unnaturally imagine by a foolish consensus to be agreeable (as though mortals could change the nature of things as easily as they do their names).[1] Not only do these things not cause any happiness, they seriously hinder it, for once rooted in the mind they possess it with a false idea of pleasure, leaving no room for true and natural delights. There are many things which by nature are not sweet—indeed, are usually very bitter—yet which through the perversity of our evil desires we regard as the greatest pleasures and even count among those things that make life most worth living. Among those who follow false pleasure the Utopians include the people I mentioned who think themselves better because they wear better clothes.[2] In this one thing such people make two mistakes, for they are just as deceived in thinking their clothes better as in thinking themselves better. If you consider clothing's use, why is fine-spun wool superior to thicker? And yet snobs think not only that the thread is better but also that some extra value thereby attaches to themselves. Dressed in finer threads, they demand a level of respect that they would never hope for if dressed in shabbier clothing. If passed by without visible respect, they get indignant.

And does it not show the same folly to think so much of empty and unprofitable honors?[3] What true and natural pleasure can the bared head or bent knees of another give you? Will this cure the pain in your own knees or relieve the madness in your own head? In this fantasized view of pleasure, men who imagine themselves noble show a strange lunacy, pride themselves on it, and applaud themselves because it has been their fortune to be born of a long succession of rich ancestors (for that is now the only nobility), rich especially in land.[4] But they think themselves not a whit less noble even if their ancestors have not left them an acre, or if they themselves have used up their inheritance through extravagant living.

The Utopians also see as chasing a false pleasure those who dote on jewels and gems, thinking themselves gods if they acquire a fine specimen.[5] They especially ridicule those who most value the most fashionable stones—for the same kinds are not always and everywhere the most highly prized.[6] Such people will not buy gems unless they can see them out of their gold settings, and even then they make the seller swear and offer some security that it is a genuine jewel, a true gem, so anxious are they lest a fake deceive their eyes. But why should a counterfeit stone give less pleasure to the eye if the eye cannot tell it from a true one? Both should be of equal value to you, even as they would be to a blind man.

What can be said of people who keep a surplus of wealth for no other use than to look at? Do they feel any real pleasure, or are they not in fact cheated by an unreal one? And what of people who have the opposite folly and hide away gold that they will never use and may never see again? In their fear of losing it, they lose it indeed—for what else is it to put it back in the ground and thus deprive themselves (and all others) of its use? And still they exult over their hidden treasure as though quite free of all anxiety. Yet suppose someone were to take it, and the miser then were to die ten years later knowing nothing of the theft. During all those ten years, what would it matter to him whether it was stolen or safe? In either case it would have been of equally little use to him.[7]

Also among those who indulge in senseless delights Utopians number those who turn to gambling, and to hunting and hawking. What true pleasure can there be, they ask, in casting dice into a box?[8] To do it so often, even if there is some pleasure in it, must eventually lead to boredom. Or what true pleasure can there be (and not disgust) in hearing the barking and howling of dogs?[9] How is it more pleasurable if a dog chases a hare than if a dog runs after a dog? The same thing happens in either case. Each has fast running, if that's what you like. Only if you are drawn by the hope of slaughter and

[1] [marginal note] False pleasures.

[2] [marginal note] Mistaken pride in fancy dress.

[3] [marginal note] Foolish titles.

[4] [marginal note] Empty nobility.

[5] [marginal note] The silliest pleasures of all: gemstones.

[6] [marginal note] Popular opinion gives gemstones their value or takes it away.

[7] [marginal note] A strange fancy, and much to the point.

[8] [marginal note] Dicing.

[9] [marginal note] Hunting.

the sight of a creature being torn apart in front of you will the former give you more pleasure than the latter. Rather, you should feel pity when you see a poor, weak, timid, and innocent hare rent in pieces by a strong, fierce, and cruel dog. That is why the Utopians have handed over the whole business of hunting, a job unworthy of free citizens, to the butchers (as I said before, they make their slaves butchers).[1] They regard hunting as the most ignoble part of the butcher's craft, and the other parts of his job as more useful and honorable. The butcher does much good and kills animals from necessity, whereas the hunter seeks nothing but pleasure from killing and mangling some poor creature. Utopians think a hunter's desire to see bloodshed either arises from a cruel disposition or creates one as the effect of constant practice in savage pleasure.

Although these and innumerable related pursuits count as pleasures to the common crowd, Utopians hold that they have absolutely nothing to do with real pleasure, since there is nothing *naturally* agreeable in them. That they commonly inspire a feeling of enjoyment (which seems to be the function of pleasure) does not alter this opinion, for the enjoyment does not arise from the nature of the thing but from a perverse habit that leads people to take what is really bitter to be sweet, just as pregnant women with a distorted taste think pitch and tallow sweeter than honey.[2] And yet no person's judgment, however depraved by disease or habit, could change the true nature of pleasure any more than it could change the nature of other things.

The Utopians divide pleasures that they consider genuine into various classes, some belonging to the soul and others to the body.[3] To the soul they ascribe intelligence and the delight that comes from contemplating the truth; to these they add the pleasant recollection of a well-spent life and the confident hope of happiness to come. Bodily pleasure they divide into two categories.[4] The first is that which fills the senses with a perceptible sweetness. This may come by the renewing of those parts that have been emptied by our natural exertion and are restored by food and drink. Sometimes this agreeable sensation comes when some excess is relieved from the overloaded body, as when we move our bowels, engage in the procreative act, or relieve an itch by rubbing or scratching. But sometimes pleasure comes neither from restoring what our bodies lack nor from removing what causes discomfort, for there is a pleasure that tickles and moves us with a secret but remarkable force and attracts the senses: the pleasure engendered by music.

The second category of bodily pleasure, they say, comes from a calm and harmonious state of the body—in a word, health, uninterrupted by any disorder. This is itself delightful, even when not activated by any pleasure applied from without. Although it is less obvious and less perceptible to the senses than the coarser delights of eating and drinking, nonetheless good health is held by many to be the greatest of pleasures. Almost all Utopians so regard it, and it is practically the basis and foundation of all other pleasures, because it alone can make life peaceful and desirable; without it there is no room for any enjoyment.[5] Being without pain but also without health they consider mere dullness, not pleasure.

Utopians long ago rejected the position of those who hold that a state of tranquil and stable health (for this question, too, they have actively discussed) is not to be counted as a pleasure on the grounds that its presence cannot be felt except in contrast with its opposite.[6] Utopians now almost all agree that health is above all things conducive to pleasure. For in disease there is pain, which is pleasure's bitter enemy, just as disease is the enemy of health. So why should we not take pleasure in the complacency of health? Utopians think that it makes no difference whether you call disease pain or pain disease. Both come to the same thing. For if you believe that health is either a pleasure itself or the necessary cause of pleasure, as fire is of heat, in both cases it follows that those in good health cannot be without pleasure. Besides, they say, when we eat, what is that but health fighting against hunger with the aid of food when it was fading? While the body gradually regains strength, the process itself supplies the pleasure

[1] [marginal note] Yet today this is the chosen art of our court-divinities.

[2] [marginal note] Morbid tastes of pregnant women.

[3] [marginal note] Varieties of true pleasure.

[4] [marginal note] Bodily pleasures.

[5] [marginal note] To enjoy anything, one should be in good health.

[6] *Utopians ... opposite* The position is discussed in Plato's *Republic* 9.583 C-E.

by which we are restored. Shall health, which delights in the struggle, not rejoice when it has gained the victory? And, when at last health has successfully found its old strength, which was its sole aim all along, shall it then become insensible and not recognize nor embrace its own good? It is quite false to say that the senses cannot perceive health, the Utopians think, for who when awake does not *feel* that he is in health (unless he is not)? Who is so insensible or lethargic that he does not confess health to be pleasurable and delightful? And what is delight except pleasure under another name?

Above all, Utopians value the pleasures of the mind (they hold them to be the founts and heads of all), and of these the most important arise from the exercise of virtues and the consciousness of a good life.[1] Of all the bodily pleasures, they give the first place to health. Other delights—eating and drinking, and anything that gives the same kind of enjoyment—they also think desirable, but only for the sake of health. For such things are not pleasurable in themselves but only insofar as they resist the secret assaults of disease. And just as a wise man should rather try to prevent disease than seek a remedy for it, so it would be better to have this kind of pleasure than to be eased of pain. If a man thinks that happiness consists in this kind of pleasure, he must admit that the greatest happiness would be to spend his life in perpetual hunger, thirst, itching, eating, drinking, scratching and rubbing. What could be more disgusting or pathetic? These pleasures must be the lowest of all because they are the least pure, never occurring unless joined with their respective pain.[2] Thus to the pleasure of eating is joined hunger (and on no fair terms: the pain is the stronger and lasts longer, for it comes into being before the pleasure and does not end until the pleasure dies with it.) Such pleasures should not be highly valued except in so far as they are necessary. Yet Utopians enjoy even these, gratefully acknowledging the kindness of Mother Nature, who with enticing sweetness coaxes her offspring into doing what by necessity they must constantly perform. In what discomfort would we live if, like the sicknesses that less frequently assail us, these daily diseases of hunger and thirst could be cured only by bitter medications?

Utopians value beauty, strength and nimbleness as special and pleasant gifts of nature. They also prize even those pleasures that enter by the ears, eyes and nose, pleasures that nature designed to be peculiarly characteristic of our species—for no other kind of living creature takes in the fairness and form of the universe, is affected by the pleasantness of smell (except in connection with food), or distinguishes concordant and discordant musical intervals. But in all these matters Utopians make this limitation: the lesser pleasure must not interfere with the greater, and pleasure must not produce pain. They think the latter inevitable if the pleasure in question is base. But to disdain physical beauty, to waste the body and turn agility into sluggishness, to starve oneself to death, to neglect health and all other favors of Mother Nature—to do any of these things for any reason other than the public good and a greater reward from God they consider extreme madness. It is a delusional pleasure to afflict oneself when this doesn't serve anyone, and self-torment does nothing to alleviate future sufferings that may never come. It is above all an offense to nature to reject her benefits so that one might owe her nothing.

This is their understanding of virtue and pleasure, and they believe that human reason can find nothing truer unless some Heaven-sent religion inspires them with something holier.[3] Whether in this they are right or wrong, time does not permit us to examine now, and in any case I have undertaken only to describe their principles, not to defend them, yet of this I am sure: whatever you think of their views, there is nowhere in the world a more excellent people nor a happier commonwealth.[4]

Utopians are active and nimble of body, and stronger than you would expect from their generally short although not minuscule stature. And though their soil is not very fertile nor is their climate very wholesome, they protect themselves by living temperately and repair the defects of the land by hard work. Thus nowhere in

[1] *Above all ... life* See Cicero, *On Old Age* 3.4: "The most suitable defenses of old age are the principles and practice of the virtues, which, if cultivated in every period of life, bring forth wonderful fruits at the close of a long and busy career."

[2] *These pleasures ... pain* See Plato, *Gorgias* 494 C.

[3] [marginal note] Note this and note it well.

[4] [marginal note] The happiness of the Utopians, and a description of them.

the world is there a better supply of grain and cattle, nor a people more vigorous of body and less subject to disease. And so you may behold in Utopia not only farming that improves poor soil by intelligence and industry, but also a whole forest uprooted in one place by human labor and replanted in another. In this they were thinking not so much of abundance as of transport, so that they might have wood closer to the sea, rivers, or the cities themselves. It takes less work to convey grain a long distance by land than it does timber.

The people are in general easy-going, good tempered, skillful with their hands, and fond of leisure but doing their share of manual labor when occasion requires (at other times they are not fond of it). In their devotion to mental study they are unwearied. When they heard from us about Greek learning and letters (except for historians and poets, there was not much in Latin we thought they would like), they were very keen to have us teach them the language and instruct them in the literature.[1] We therefore began to give them lessons, at first more to avoid seeming reluctant to take the trouble than with expectation of success. But soon their progress and diligence showed that our efforts would not be in vain.[2] They began so easily to imitate the shapes of the letters, so readily to pronounce the words, so quickly to learn by heart, and so faithfully to reproduce what they learned, that it would have seemed a miracle, except that we knew most of them signed on not by choice but by an order of the senate, selected from among the scholars of exceptional talent and advanced years.[3] In less than three years they were perfect in the language and able to read good authors without difficulty except when the text was faulty. I imagine that they grasped Greek literature all the more easily because it is so allied to their own. Indeed, I suspect that their race is derived from the Greek, because their language, which in other respects resembles Persian, retains some traces of Greek in the names of their cities and officers.

When I was about to set out on my fourth voyage to Utopia, instead of putting on board goods to sell, I took a fairly large bundle of books, having decided not to leave any time soon, and perhaps not at all. I have given them most of Plato, almost all of Aristotle, and Theophrastus[4] on plants. This last, I regret to say got damaged during the voyage when someone left it lying around and an ape who picked it up to play with carelessly tore out several pages from different parts of the book. Of grammarians they have only Lascaris, for I did not take Gaza with me, and no lexicographer but Hesychius and Dioscorides.[5] They are very fond of Plutarch's works and delight in Lucian's pleasantry and wit.[6] Of the poets they have Aristophanes, Homer, Euripides, and Sophocles in the small Aldine editions;[7] of historians they have Thucydides, Herodotus and also Herodian.[8] As for medicine, my companion Tricius Apinatus had brought along some small treatises of Hippocrates and the *Microtechne* of Galen, which they valued highly,[9] for though there is scarcely any nation that needs medicine less, nowhere is it held in greater honor. For them, medical knowledge is one of the finest and most useful parts of philosophy.[10] When they practice this philosophy and search out the hidden secrets of nature, they not only enjoy it but also believe

1 [marginal note] The usefulness of the Greek tongue.

2 [marginal note] Their wonderful aptitude for learning.

3 [marginal note] But now clods and dullards are taught letters, while the best minds are corrupted by pleasures.

4 *Theophrastus* Student of Aristotle (d. 287 BCE), whose works on botany were still current during More's time.

5 *Lascaris* Constantine Lascaris (1434–1501), who wrote the first "modern" Greek grammar; *Gaza* Theodore of Gaza (d. 1478), a translator of Aristotle who also published a Greek grammar; *Hesychius* Hesychius of Alexandria (c. fifth century CE), noted for his Greek dictionary; *Dioscorides* Greek physician of the first century who wrote *De Materia Medica*, the first systematic pharmacological text outlining descriptions and uses for plants and medications.

6 *Plutarch* Greek biographer (c. 45–125 CE); *Lucian* Greek rhetorician and satirist (c. 120–180 CE).

7 *Aristophanes* Greek comedy writer (c. 448–380 BCE); *Euripides* Greek tragedian (c. 480–406 BCE); *Sophocles* Greek tragedian (c. 495–406 BCE); *Aldine editions* Editions published by Aldus Manutius (1449–1515), noted Italian printer.

8 *Thucydides* Greek historian (c. 471–400 BCE) who wrote *The History of the Peloponnesian War*; *Herodotus* Herodotus of Halicarnassus (c. fifth century BCE), author of *The Histories*; *Herodian* Roman historian (c. 170–240 CE) noted for his *History of the Empire*.

9 *Tricius Apinatus* Fictitious character; *Hippocrates* Greek physician (c. 460–377 BCE); *Microtechne … Galen* Treatise by Roman physician (c. 131–201 CE).

10 [marginal note] Medicine most useful of all studies.

that they win the approval of the Author and Maker of all things.[1] They think that He, like all artificers, set forth the visible mechanism of the world as a spectacle for human beings, whom alone He made capable of appreciating such wonder. He therefore prefers a careful and diligent beholder and admirer of His work to one who like a brute beast passes by so great and marvelous a spectacle ignorant and unimpressed.

The Utopian mind, then, being trained in all learning, is exceedingly successful in the invention of arts that bring pleasure and convenience. Two of these, however, they owe to us: printing and the manufacture of paper. Not entirely to us, for when we showed them our Aldine editions and talked about (since none of us was an expert, I cannot say *explained*) the material of which paper is made and the art of printing, they promptly and accurately guessed how it was done. Though they had earlier written only on skins, bark and papyrus,[2] they now attempted to manufacture paper and print books. Their first attempts were not very successful, but through trial and error they soon mastered both, so that if they had the texts of Greek writers, they would have no lack of books. At present they have nothing more than I have mentioned, but what they have, they now have in many thousands of printed copies.

Whoever visits their country is gladly received if knowledgeable about many nations, gifted in intellect, or experienced in wide travel, for they delight in hearing what is going on in every country, which is why we were so welcome. But few merchants come there. What could they bring to trade except the same iron, or gold and silver that they would rather take back home? And as for what Utopia exports Utopians think it wiser to transport it themselves than to let others come and fetch it, so that by traveling they might acquire more information about foreign nations while also honing their navigational skills.

[1] [marginal note] Contemplation of nature.

[2] *skins ... papyrus* Writing materials made of animal skins (predominantly calf and sheep and called vellum), the outer portion of trees, and fibers of the papyrus (an Egyptian rush plant), respectively.

CHAPTER 7
SLAVERY

They do not enslave prisoners of war except those they take themselves.[3] Nor do they force the children of slaves into bondage, nor slaves whom they could get in other countries. Their slaves are either made such in their own country for heinous crimes or have been condemned to death elsewhere for some offence; most of their slaves are of this latter kind. Utopians bring away many such people from other lands, sometimes buying them cheaply or, often, just asking for them and getting them for nothing. Both sorts of slaves, foreigners and Utopians, are kept at work and in chains, but Utopians treat their own countrymen more harshly. These they regard as more deserving of exemplary punishment because despite their good education in virtuous living they could not restrain themselves from crime. There is also another sort of slave: poor laborers in other countries who voluntarily exchange their drudgery for slavery in Utopia. Except for having somewhat more work assigned to them, these are treated almost as well as are citizens. If anyone of this class of slave wishes to leave, which seldom happens, he is not detained against his will or sent away empty handed.

The sick, as I said, are very lovingly cared for; nothing is left undone that might restore them to health, whether medicine or diet.[4] Those suffering from incurable disease they console by sitting and conversing with them and by applying all possible alleviations. But if the disease brings unceasingly pain and trauma, the priests and the magistrates urge the sufferer, now unfit for all the duties of life and become a living burden to himself as well as a distress to others, to cease fostering disease and plague and be willing to die, now that living is an anguish, and so liberate himself from a life as bitter as imprisonment or torture—or let others liberate him.[5] In this the sufferer will act wisely, since death will put an end not to enjoyment but to torment, and since in so doing he will be obeying the counsels of the priests, interpreters of God's will, his death would be a pious and devout act.

[3] [marginal note] The wonderful fairness of these people.

[4] [marginal note] The sick.

[5] [marginal note] Deliberate death.

Those convinced by these arguments either starve themselves to death or, being put to sleep, are released without the sensation of dying. But they do not do away with anyone against his will; nor in such a case do they at all relax their care. They think a death sanctioned by authority is honorable but that anyone who kills himself without the consent of priests and Council is unworthy of fire or earth; without a proper burial, his disgraced body is tossed into a marsh.

Women may not marry before eighteen, men not until they are four years older.[1] Anyone convicted of premarital intercourse is punished severely; such people are forbidden to marry altogether unless pardoned by the governor. The father and mother in whose house such an offence was committed incur great disgrace for having been neglectful. Utopians made this severe law because they foresaw that few would join in conjugal love, spend all of life with one companion, and bear the vexations and troubles that are incident to marriage unless all were restrained from sexual promiscuity.

In choosing mates they seriously and strictly follow a custom that we thought idiotic and utterly ridiculous.[2] The woman, whether maiden or widow, is shown naked to her suitor by a worthy and respectable matron, and so too a discreet man shows her suitor naked to the woman.[3] We laughed at this custom and condemned it as foolish, but they themselves marvel at the notable folly of other nations. In buying a pony, where there is just a little money involved, people in other nations are so cautious that though the animal is practically naked they will not buy until they have taken off the saddle and removed all the harness lest they conceal some sore. Yet in choosing a wife, a choice on which hangs lifelong pleasure or disgust, the same people are so careless that while the rest of her body is covered with clothes they judge the whole woman from one handbreadth, only her face being visible, and take her to themselves even though there is a high chance that two will find each other unattractive. Not every man is so wise as to care only for the woman's character, and even wise men find good looks no small enhancement of the mind's virtues. Certainly a deformity hidden beneath these coverings may be so foul that it alienates a man's mind from his wife, bodily separation being no longer possible. If such a deformity comes by chance after the marriage contract, each must endure his own fate; but until then the law should protect him against being taken in by deceit.

This provision was all the more urgent, because the Utopians are the only people in that part of the world who are satisfied with one wife; marital bonds are seldom broken except by death, though on rare occasions a marriage may also end because of adultery or an intolerable offensiveness in the mate's disposition.[4] When either spouse is thus offended, the Council gives permission to take another mate while the rejected partner lives in disgrace and perpetual celibacy. But the Utopians think it wrong to divorce a wife because of some physical problem for which she is in no way to blame. They think it cruel to abandon anyone in need of comfort; if that sort of behavior were condoned, there would be little protection against the insecurities of age, which brings disease and is itself a disease.

But sometimes, when a married couple does not accord in dispositions and both find others with whom they hope they might live more agreeably, they part by mutual consent and contract fresh unions. This may not be done without the permission of the Council, which forbids divorce until it and the spouses have carefully reviewed the matter. Even then, it is reluctant to give consent, knowing that to feed hopes of remarriage is hardly a way to reinforce the marital bond.

Those who break that bond are punished by the strictest slavery. If both parties to an adultery were married, the injured spouses, if they so desire, may divorce their mates and marry each other or whomever they wish. If one of them still feels affection for the adulterous mate, the marriage shall continue in force if such a spouse is willing to accompany and share the labor of the one now condemned to slavery. Sometimes the penitence of the one partner and the dutiful persistence of the other move Governor's compassion and they are freed. But those who repeat the offence risk being executed.

For other offences there is no fixed legal penalty, but in each case the Council appoints a punishment according to the seriousness of the crime.[5] Husbands chastise

[1] [marginal note] Marriages.

[2] [marginal note] Not very modest, but not so impractical either.

[3] *The woman ... man* Plato advocates this practice in his *Laws*.

[4] [marginal note] Divorce.

[5] [marginal note] Degrees of punishment left to magistrates.

by exposing their lives they soon spend on riot and wretchedness.

This people will fight for the Utopians against any enemies whatsoever because paid more than they can get anywhere else. The Utopians, just as they seek good men to use, so they enlist these bad men to abuse. For when the need arises, they send them into great peril with the tempting bait of big promises. A large proportion never returns to claim their wages, but the survivors are honestly paid what has been promised in order to incite them to repeat similar deeds of daring. The Utopians do not care how many of them they lose, thinking that it would benefit the whole human race if they could relieve the world of this abominable and shameful people.

Next in order of preference after these mercenaries, the Utopians employ the soldiers of the people for whom they are fighting; then auxiliary squadrons of other allies; and finally a contingent of their own citizens, out of whom they appoint some man of tried valor to command the entire army. They add two potential replacements; these hold no rank while he lives, but if he is taken prisoner or killed then one becomes, as it were, his heir and successor, and then he, if things fall out this way, is succeeded by the third.[1] Thus the death of the commander, the fortunes of war being always incalculable, will not bring the whole military into disorder.

Each city chooses from its volunteers. No one is forced to fight abroad against his will, because the Utopians are convinced that anyone who is timid by nature is unlikely to acquit himself manfully and may make his companions more timid. However, should any enemy assail their own country, they put the faint-hearted, provided that they are physically fit, on shipboard among the braver sort, or put them here and there to man the walls where they cannot run away. Thus the continual regard of their comrades, the looming threat of their enemies, and the impossibility of escape combine to overpower their timidity, and often extreme danger makes them brave.

Just as no one is forced to go fight abroad, so if wives want to go with their husbands to war, not only do the Utopians not forbid it, they even encourage and spur them on by praise. The pair leaves for battle together and wives fight next to their husbands, surrounded by their children, relations and connections, so that those to whom nature has given the strongest motive to help one another may be closest and offer mutual assistance It is the greatest reproach for a husband to return without his wife, a wife without her husband, or a son without his father; so in hand-to-hand fighting, if the enemy stand his ground, the fight is long and desperate, and ends only when all are dead.

Though Utopians bend every effort not to have to fight themselves so long as they can finish the war by hiring substitutes, when personal service is inevitable they prove just as courageous in fighting as they had been prudent when trying to avoid it, not so fierce in the first onslaught as stubborn in the protraction and duration of the fight, more likely to be cut to pieces than to relent. The absence of that anxiety over a man's livelihood or his family's future, which everywhere else breaks the highest spirit, makes a Utopian hold his head high and disdain the foe. The Utopians' training in military discipline gives them confidence, moreover, and the good and sound opinions in which they have been trained from childhood, both in school and through good institutions of the commonweal, give them added courage. So although they do not hold their lives so cheap as to throw them away carelessly, neither do they hold them so excessively dear as to keep them at the price of shame when duty bids them sacrifice themselves.

When the battle is everywhere hottest, a picked band of young men who have sworn themselves to the mission seek out the enemy general, and openly assault or secretly ambush him.[2] They assail him from afar and at close range, as a long chain of men, with fresh comers taking the place of the exhausted, keep up the attack. Almost always, unless he saves himself by running away, he is killed or falls alive into Utopian hands. If the victory rests with the Utopians, they do not revenge themselves with blood, for they would rather take a defeated foe prisoner than kill him, and they never pursue the flying enemy without always keeping one division ready for engagement. Even if they win the battle with this reserve force after the rest of the army

[1] *They add ... third* Strategy practiced by the Spartans.

[2] [marginal note] The enemy general to be most fiercely attacked, so as to end the war sooner.

has been beaten, they prefer to let the whole hostile force escape rather than get into the habit of pursuing the foe in a disorderly way. They remember that on occasion, with most of their army beaten and routed, and while the enemy was flushed with victory and pursuing the fugitives in all directions, a few of their own number, held in reserve for emergencies, had suddenly counter-attacked the scattered enemy, who believing themselves quite safe were off their guard, and had changed the whole fortune of the battle. Thus the Utopians wrest back from the enemy's hand a certain and undoubted victory, conquering their seeming conquerors.

It is not easy to say whether the Utopians are more cunning in laying ambushes or more cautious in avoiding them. You would think them about to turn tail, when that is the last thing they intend. Then, when they do decide to retreat, you would imagine they were planning anything but that. For if they find themselves inferior in number or position, they noiselessly move away by night and set up camp elsewhere, or they evade the enemy by some stratagem, or by daylight withdraw so imperceptibly and in such regular order that it would be as risky to attack them in retreat as it would be if they were advancing. They carefully protect their camps by digging a deep and broad ditch, tossing aside the dirt. They do not use laborers for this. Rather, the soldiers make the ditch with their own hands, and so the whole army is kept at work except for those who keep armed watch in front of the rampart in case of emergencies. Thanks to the work of many hands they can create impressive fortifications, enclosing a large space with amazing speed.

They wear armor strong enough to ward off blows but so well adapted to their body's movements and gestures that they can even swim in it. (Learning to swim armed is part of their military training.)[1] The weapons they use at a distance are arrows, which they shoot with great strength and sureness of aim, both on foot and on horseback, while at close quarters they use not swords but axes, which deal a deadly blow either with blade or through sheer weight, depending on whether they are used to cut or thrust. They are ingenious in inventing weapons, carefully concealing them lest, if seen before needed, they become objects of laughter rather than instruments of war. In making them, their first criteria are maneuverability and ease of transport.

If they make a truce, they keep it so religiously that they will not break it under any provocation.[2] They do not ravage the enemy's country or burn his fields. Indeed, as far as possible they do not allow crops to be crushed by the feet of their men or horses, thinking them grown for their own benefit. They injure no non-combatant unless he is a spy. They keep intact any city that yields. They do not even plunder the ones they have stormed, but merely put to death the men who blocked a surrender and make slaves of the rest, leaving civilians unharmed. If they can locate those who had urged the city to yield they give them a share in the property of the condemned, presenting the rest of the confiscated goods to their auxiliaries; no Utopian touches the booty.

When the war is over, they do not ask the friends for whom they have borne its cost to repay any of it, but rather they make the conquered pay reparations with cash, setting it aside for use in future wars, and also get them to hand over estates from which Utopia itself can get a large annual income, indefinitely.[3] They now have such varied sources of revenue in so many countries that the proceeds have grown to over seven hundred thousand ducats[4] a year. To administer these estates they send some of their own citizens, called Quaestors,[5] to live in grand style and play the part of great lords. Much is left over for the Utopians' common treasury, however, unless they prefer, as they often do, to give the defeated nation credit until the money is needed, and even then they almost never call in the whole sum. Out of these estates they confer a part on those who at their request undertake the dangerous mission that I described earlier. If any king arms himself against Utopia and is about to invade, they immediately march out in great strength beyond their own borders and meet him there, for they prefer not to fight on their own country, nor is any emergency so pressing as to make them let foreign auxiliaries into their island.

[1] [marginal note] The variety of their weapons.

[2] [marginal note] Truces.

[3] [marginal note] But today the victors foot most of the bill.

[4] *ducats* European gold coins of varying value depending on the nation of origin.

[5] *Quaestors* Agents.

CHAPTER 9
THE RELIGIONS IN UTOPIA

There are different religions in different parts of the island and also within each city. Some worship the Sun, others the Moon, and yet others one of the planets. Some people reverence a man who was in former times conspicuous for virtue or glory, not just as *a* god, but also as the supreme God. But the most people, especially the wiser, do nothing of the kind, believing in one unknown Divine Power, eternal, incomprehensible, inexplicable, far beyond the reach of human intellect, diffused throughout the universe as a powerful force. Him they call Father, to Him alone they attribute the beginnings, the growth, the progress, the changes and the ends of all things, and to no other do they give divine honors.

Although all the others believe different things, they agree with the majority in thinking there is one Supreme Being to Whom we owe the creation and maintenance of the world. In their native language all call Him Mithra.[1] Different people define Him differently, however, each thinking that whatever they regard as supreme is that same nature, but all attribute the sum of all things to His unique power and majesty. Gradually, indeed, they are all beginning to depart from their variety of superstitions and are uniting in one religion that seems to surpass the rest in rationality. No doubt the other beliefs would have all disappeared long ago, had not some misfortune happened to those considering changing their religion. Their misfortune was read not as a work of chance but as the work of the deity they had been planning to leave and who wanted to punish their impiety against himself.

But when they heard from us the name of Christ, His teaching, His example, His miracles, and the no less wonderful constancy of the many martyrs whose blood, freely shed, has brought together so many nations in so many parts of the world, you cannot imagine how willing they were to embrace Christianity at once, either secretly inspired by God or because they found it similar to their own most influential beliefs. I think, though, that what carried a lot of weight was our report that Christ approved his disciples' communal way of life,[2] one that the truest Christian communities continue to practice.[3] Whatever it was that affected them, not a few agreed to adopt our faith and were baptized.

But among the four of us (all that remained of our company, two having died), I am sorry to say there was no priest. We gave the Utopians religious instruction, but not those sacraments that we believe only a priest can administer;[4] they understand what they are, however, and are eager to receive them. Indeed, they are even debating earnestly among themselves whether, if no Christian bishop were sent, they might choose one of their own number who could take on valid holy orders. It seemed that they would choose someone, but by the time I left they had not yet done so.

Utopians who do not accept Christianity nevertheless do not try to deter others from doing so or oppose their conversion. Only one of our community was disciplined while I was there. As soon as he had been baptized, and despite our protests, he began to speak publicly of Christianity with more zeal than discretion, so much so that he not only set our religion above any other but condemned outright all others as profane. He loudly called those of other faiths impious, sacrilegious, and worthy of eternal fire. After he had been preaching in this style for some time, he was arrested, not for despising their religion but for stirring up strife. Tried and convicted, he was sentenced to exile. Indeed, among the most ancient Utopian principles is one holding that no one should be made to suffer for his religion.[5]

Before his arrival at the island, King Utopus had heard that the natives were constantly quarrelling over religion. Such dissension among the various sects fighting for their country, he realized, gave him an opportunity to subdue them all. After he had won, he first declared everyone free to follow the religion of his own liking and even to strive to convert others, provided he did so modestly and peaceably, with reasonable arguments, and with no attempt bitterly to discredit the

[1] *Mithra* Persian god of truth and light.

[2] *Christ ... follow* See Acts 2.44–5 and 4.32–5.

[3] [marginal note] Monasteries.

[4] *those Sacraments ... administer* The administration of the Eucharist, Confession, Confirmation, Ordination, and Extreme Unction (the last rites of the Church before death) must be conducted by a priest, while Baptism and Marriage may be performed by non-clergy in extreme or emergency circumstances.

[5] [marginal note] Men must be drawn to religion by its merits.

beliefs of others. Should his efforts fail, he was not to use violence and must refrain from abuse. Those arguing too vehemently would be subject to exile or enslavement. Utopus made this rule not merely for the sake of peace, so easily destroyed by constant religious wrangling and hatred, but also because he thought it in the interest of religion itself. He did not dogmatize concerning faith, thinking that perhaps God desires a varied and manifold worship and so has inspired different people with different views. In any case Utopus thought it arrogant and foolish to insist, with violence and threats, that everyone else must agree with what you believe to be true. He quickly perceived, moreover, that if one religion is true and the others false, then, if religious questions are dealt with reasonably and moderately, by its own natural force truth will emerge into clear visibility. But if such matters are to be decided by force and armed violence, he thought, then the best and holiest religion would be overwhelmed by false ones, like grain overtaken by thorns and bushes, for the worst men are always the most obstinate. So he left the matter open, making it clear that all were free to decide what to believe. The one rule on which he insisted unrelentingly was that no one should sink so far beneath the dignity of human nature as to believe that the soul dies with the body or that mere chance, and not divine providence, rules the world.

This is why Utopians believe that after this life our vices are punished and virtues rewarded; if anyone thinks otherwise they do not regard him as even human, seeing that he has debased the lofty nature of his soul to that of a brute. Still less do they count him as a citizen, for as far as he dared he would thumb his nose at their laws and customs. No one, after all, can doubt that such a person would attempt either to evade by craft the common laws of his country or to break them by violence so as to serve his greed; he would have nothing to fear but the law and no hope beyond the grave. So the Utopians forbid anyone of this mind to hold office; they do not entrust him with any public function and regard him as having a mean and low disposition. They do not punish him in any way, however, convinced that people cannot help what they believe. They neither use threats to make him disguise his views nor allow deceptions or lies in the matter, for they hate mendacity almost as much as they hate actual wrongdoing. They forbid such a person to argue for his opinion publicly, but they encourage him to do so in front of priests and citizens of weight and importance, convinced that such madness will in the end yield to reason.

Another group of people, on the other hand, and a fairly large one, believes that even animals have immortal souls, although not comparable to ours in dignity and not destined for an equal happiness.[1] The Utopians do not find such people bad, and even think that there is something to be said for such a belief. Almost all are absolutely convinced that human bliss in the afterlife will be measureless, so that although they lament everyone's illness, they regret the death of no one unless they see him leave life anxiously or reluctantly. That they take as a very bad omen, as though the unwilling soul, without hope and with a guilty conscience, had a secret premonition of impending punishment. Besides, they think, God will not be pleased by the arrival of one who, when summoned, does not gladly hasten to obey but is drawn unwillingly. Horrified whenever they see this kind of death, they carry the departed to burial in melancholy silence, and then after praying that God might be merciful to the soul and graciously pardon its infirmities, they lay the corpse in the ground. On the other hand, over one who has died full of cheer and good hope, they do not mourn but attend the funeral with singing and affection, commending the soul to God. Then, with more reverence than sorrow, they burn the body[2] and on the spot erect a pillar inscribed with the virtues of the deceased. On returning home they speak of the person's character and deeds, no part of which is more frequently or gladly mentioned than the cheerful death.

They think this memorial to virtue both the best way to inspire the living to good deeds and the best way to honor the dead, who they think are present when talked about, even though invisible to weak mortal sight. For it would be inconsistent with the bliss of the departed not to be able to go where they please, and it would be ungrateful of them absolutely to reject all desire of revisiting their friends, to whom they were

[1] [marginal note] A strange opinion on the souls of animals.

[2] *burn the body* Before the nineteenth century Christians did not practice cremation.

bound during their lives with mutual love and affection (which, like other good things, the Utopians believe does not diminish in the good but even increases posthumously). Thinking that their dead move among them, witnessing their words and actions, Utopians go about their business confident of their protection and convinced that the presence of their ancestors keeps them from all dishonesty.

They utterly despise and mock fortune-telling and all the superstitious divinations taken so seriously in many other places. But miracles, which occur without Nature's assistance, they revere as manifestations of divine power; such, they say, often occur in Utopia. Sometimes when in the midst of great danger they pray publicly for a sign, which they confidently expect and receive.

They think that to contemplate Nature and praise God in His works is a service acceptable to Him. There are some, and not so very few, who for religious reasons give up learning, pursue no science, and take no leisure, but pour themselves into work and other good deeds in order to win happiness after death.[1] Some tend the sick, others repair roads, clean out ditches, rebuild bridges, dig turf, sand and stone, fell and cut up trees, or cart wood, grain, or other materials into the cities. They serve not only the public but also individuals, working harder than slaves. If anywhere there is a task so rough, hard and repulsive that most are deterred by the toil, disgust and despair involved, these people gladly and cheerfully claim it for themselves. Engaged in endless hard work, and claiming no credit, they secure leisure for others, neither denigrating other peoples' lives nor extolling their own. The more they perform like slaves, the more everyone honors them.

These people are of two sorts, with differing opinions and practices. One group includes those who remain single, abstaining not only from sex but also from meat and even, in some cases, all animal food. They completely reject this world's pleasures as harmful and focus only on the life to come, hoping to obtain it soon, by prayer and labor; in the meantime, they are cheerful and lively. Those of the other sort are just as fond of hard labor, but they prefer marriage to the single life. They do not despise the comfort that marriage brings, and think that they owe it to nature to labor, and owe it to their country to have children. They refuse no pleasure that does not interfere with their work, eating meat only because they believe it makes them stronger for their tasks. Most Utopians think this group wiser and the other one holier. If the holier sect tried to defend their preference for celibacy and a hard life with arguments drawn from reason, most would laugh them to scorn; but since they say that their faith prompts them, other Utopians look up to and revere them, (Utopians are exquisitely careful not to jump to conclusions over any point of religion.) Such, then, are these who in their language are given a special name, Buthrescae, or "the particularly religious."

Utopian priests are people of great holiness, so there are very few of them, not more than thirteen in each city, with the same number of churches. When Utopians go to war, seven priests accompany the army, and seven substitutes are appointed until the priests return and take up their former duties. The substitutes then return to their earlier tasks until the priests die, after which they succeed to their places. Until then they assist the Bishop, who is the head of all. Like other officials, priests are elected by secret ballot, so as to prevent politicizing the process, and winners are then ordained by their colleagues. They preside over worship, conduct religious ceremonies, and provide moral guidance. It is a great disgrace for a man to be summoned before them, or reproved for immorality. It is their part to give advice and admonition, whereas the Governor and the other magistrates correct and punish offenders. The priests do, however, excommunicate those whom they determine to be evildoers, and there is no punishment more dreaded. The excommunicated incur very great disgrace and are tortured by inner religious fear; even their bodies do not go scot-free, for unless they quickly satisfy the priests that they are truly repentant, the Council arrests and punishes them for impiety.

The education of the young is entrusted to the priests, whose first concern is not learning, but behavior and virtue. They take the greatest pains to instill into the minds of children, while they are still tender and pliable, attitudes that will help preserve the commonwealth. When firmly implanted, such principles will accompany them all their lives and strengthen the commonwealth, which decays only through vices rooted

[1] [marginal note] The active life.

in distorted thinking. The priests have the most desirable women in the country for wives. (Women are not debarred from the priesthood, but they are only seldom chosen, and none except widows and the elderly.)[1] To no other office in Utopia is so much honor given as to the priesthood—so much so that even priests who have committed a crime are not tried before a public tribunal, but left to God and to themselves.[2] Utopians think it wrong to lay mortal hands on a priest, however guilty, who has been specially consecrated to God as a holy offering. It is easier for them to observe this custom because their priests are few and carefully chosen. Only seldom does anyone elevated to such dignity for being the best of the good, for nothing but virtue sink into corruption and vice. Even if priests do sin (which is bound to happen, given the fallibility of human nature), Utopians need not fear that this will bring ruin to the commonwealth, because priests are few and because their positions carry honor but no real power. Indeed, they keep the number of priests low in order to preserve the order's dignity; they think it hard to find many good enough for so honorable a post, one that requires a more than everyday virtue.[3]

Utopian priests are esteemed just as much in foreign countries as they are among their own people. When the armies are fighting, the priests are to be found not far off, kneeling, dressed in their sacred vestments with hands outstretched to heaven, and praying first of all for peace, then for victory, but without bloodshed on either side.[4] When their own people are winning, the priests run among the combatants and restrain the fury of their own men against the routed enemy. The enemy soldiers see this and appeal to the priests, which is enough to save many lives. To touch their flowing garments protects the supplicant's goods from spoliation. This has brought them such veneration among all nations, and given them so real a majesty, that they have saved their own citizens from the enemy as often as they have protected the enemy from their own men. It has even happened that after the Utopians' own line was broken and things looked grim, while they were retreating and the enemy was rushing on, the priests intervened and brought an end to the carnage, and the armies parted and settled on equal terms. For never was there any nation so savage, cruel, and barbarous that it has not regarded their bodies as sacred and inviolable.

They keep as holy days the first and the last of each month, and also the first and last days of the year, which they divide into months.[5] These they measure by the orbit of the moon, just as they determine the year by the course of the sun. In their language they call the first days Cynemernes, and the last days Trapemernes, which may be interpreted as "First Feasts" and "Last Feasts." Their churches are fine sights, elaborate in workmanship and able to hold vast congregations—a necessity, granted that there are so few of them.[6] They are all fairly dark, not because of the builders' ignorance but because the priests think that dazzle makes the thoughts wander, whereas sparse and dim light concentrates the mind and encourages earnest devotion.

As I have said, not everyone has the same religion, and yet because all the different faiths tend to the same end, the worship of the Divine Nature, nothing is seen or heard in the churches that does not seem to agree with this common belief. If any sect has a rite of its own, its adherents perform it within the walls of their own houses. No image of God is seen in a church, therefore, so that all may be free to conceive of Him according to their own beliefs, in any likeness they please. The priests have no special name for God except "Mithra," by which word they agree to represent the one nature of the Divine Majesty, whatever it might be, and prayers are phrased so that everyone may recite them without offense.

The priests come to the church in the evening of the last day of the month or year, fasting, to thank God for the prosperity they have enjoyed in the past year or month. On the next day, or "first feast," they assemble at the churches in the morning to pray for happiness and prosperity in the following year or month. At a "last feast," before they go to church, wives fall at the feet of their husbands and children at those of their parents, confessing how they have offended, whether by losing something or carelessly performing some duty, and pray

1 [marginal note] Female priests.

2 [marginal note] Unworthy priests.

3 [marginal note] But what a crowd of them we have!

4 [marginal note] O priests far more holy than our own!

5 [marginal note] Holidays observed by the Utopians.

6 [marginal note] What their churches are like.

for pardon.[1] If any cloud of quarrel in the family has arisen, it is dispelled by this penance, so that with clear and pure minds they may attend the divine service; their religion forbids them to attend with a troubled conscience.[2] If aware of hatred or anger against anyone, they do not come to until reconciled and with cleansed hearts; otherwise they risk swift and severe punishment. When they reach the church, men go to the right, women to the left, and arrange themselves so that the males in each house sit in front of the father while the mother of the family sits behind the females. This system allows parents to make sure that those responsible for domestic discipline may observe every visible gesture. They also carefully see to it that everywhere the younger ones are placed in the company of the older, in order to keep children from spending in childish folly time they should pass in developing the respect for God that is the greatest (if not the only) stimulus to virtuous living.

The Utopians never sacrifice animals; they cannot believe that the Divine Being, who gave life to animals, delights in bloodshed and slaughter. They burn incense and other sweet savors, as well as a great many devotional candles. Not that they think these things add anything to the divine nature, any more than do the prayers of men, but they like this harmless kind of worship, and believe that these perfumes and lights and other ceremonies somehow uplift and impel them to a devotion to God's worship. The people wear white in church, and the priest wears vestments of various colors and wonderful design, but not of the costly material one might expect; these are not decorated with gold or precious stones but with different feathers, so cleverly and skillfully done that no costly material would have added to the value. According to the Utopians, the feathers, together with their arrangement on the priest's vestment, contain hidden mysteries with meanings carefully handed down by the priests and designed to remind Utopians of God's loving kindness to them, their own piety in return, and finally their duty to one another.

When the priest thus arrayed first comes out of the inner sanctum, the people fall on the ground in reverence with such deep silence everywhere that the very character of the proceeding fills them with holy awe and feel that God is truly present. After remaining awhile on the ground, at a signal from the priest they rise; then they sing praises to God, often to the accompaniment of musical instruments fashioned differently, for the most part, than those in our part of the world.[3] Many of these surpass our own in sweetness of sound, though some are not as good. In one thing they are undoubtedly far ahead of us: all their music, whether instrumental or vocal, so renders and expresses the natural feelings, the sound suiting the matter (prayer, joy, supplication, trouble, mourning, or anger), and so communicates in the rising of the melody a certain understanding, that it wonderfully seizes, penetrates, and influences the minds of the hearers. At last the priest and people together repeat solemn prayers, each worded so that all may apply individually what all request together.

In these prayers, all recognize God as the Author of the creation, of government, and of every other blessing, thanking Him for all His gifts particular for the favor of life in the happiest of commonwealths and for the truest religion. If this is mistaken, or if there is anything better of which God approves more, then may He of His goodness bring them to its knowledge, for they are ready to follow in whatever direction He may lead. If the Utopian system is the best, however, and one's religion the truest, then may God grant steadfastness in the same and bring all others to the same way of living and the same understanding—unless God in His wisdom prefers a variety of religions. Finally they pray that He will grant an easy death, however soon, or late. But if it is God's will, they are much readier to die a hard death and go to God than to be kept for long away from Him by a prosperous course of life. After this prayer, the people fall down on the ground again. Then, after an interval, they rise and go away to dinner, and the rest of the day they pass in games and military training.

Now I have described to you, as truly as I could, the constitution of that commonwealth, which I think is not only the best but indeed the only one that deserves the name "commonwealth." For everywhere else, although people talk freely of the common good they think only of their own, whereas there, where there is no private property, citizens seriously care for the commonweal. No

[1] [marginal note] The Utopian confession.

[2] [marginal note] But among us the worst sinners try to crowd closest to the altar.

[3] [marginal note] Utopian music.

wonder: in other countries, who doesn't know that he has to look out for himself? If he doesn't, no matter how much the community as a whole may flourish, he will die of hunger, and so necessity compels him, he believes, to think of himself rather than of others.

In Utopia, on the other hand, where everything is shared, no one fears not having enough, provided the common warehouses are well filled. The distribution of good things is not ungenerous, and there are no poor people or beggars: though nobody can have just anything he wants, everyone is rich. For what greater wealth can there be than to live in joy and peace, with no fear for the future, untroubled about food, not harassed by the querulous demands of his wife, not afraid for his son's well-being or worried about his daughter's dowry, and thus without anxiety concerning his and his own, his wife, sons, grandsons, great-grandsons, great-great-grandsons and all the long succession of descendants to which people look forward?

Then recall that there is no less provision for those who have been laborers but are now unable to be such than for those who are still working. Here I would challenge anyone to compare the so-called justice practiced in other nations (among whom, I swear, I cannot discover a trace of justice or fairness) with the Utopian system. For what kind of justice is it for a nobleman or a goldsmith or a money-lender or any of those who do nothing (nothing of use to the commonwealth, anyway) to receive a grand and luxurious living in return for their leisure and pointless work? In the meantime, the day laborer, the carter, the smith, or the farmer, in return for continuous toil that beasts of burden could scarcely endure, and toil so essential that no state could last for a year without it, gets such a poor living and leads such a miserable life that the condition of beasts of burden might seem far preferable. For beasts do not have to work so incessantly, are not much worse fed, derive more pleasure from their lives, and have no fear for the future. The laborers not only must work here and now with little reward but are agonized by the thought of a helpless and indigent old age. Given that their daily wage does not even buy their daily bread, how could they possibly spare anything to put away for buying such bread when they are old?

Is it not unjust and ungrateful to lavish huge rewards on so-called gentlefolk, on goldsmiths, the idle, the parasites, the suppliers of empty pleasures? Is it not unjust to care nothing for those farmers, coal miners, day laborers, carters and smiths without whom there would be no commonwealth at all? But after such a system has used up laborers in their prime, and then, when they are weighed down by age and disease, and in their utter need, forgets all the benefits it has received from them it pays them back with a wretched death. Worse, every day the rich skim off part of the daily assistance to the poor, and not fraudulently but in ways sanctioned by the law itself. And so what was unjust to begin with—a pitiful allowance for those who deserve the best from the commonwealth—they have managed to make a complete travesty by enshrining their injustice in the laws they pass. So when I reflect on the state of all nations flourishing today, so help me God, I can see nothing but a conspiracy of the rich, seeking their own advantage under the name and pretext of the commonwealth.[1] They invent and devise all ways and techniques by which they may keep everything they have amassed by evil means and have no fear of losing their power to drive down wages and profit by the sweat and toil of the poor.

These sinister devices, as soon as the rich declare them to be in the public interest, even in the interest of the poor, finally become laws. But when these evil men, out of their insatiable greed, have divided among themselves what would have been enough for everyone, how far they fall short of the happiness of Utopia! When in Utopia all greed for money was abolished by abolishing money itself, what a mass of troubles was eliminated, and what a great crop of crimes was pulled up by the roots! For who does not know that fraud, theft, robbery, quarrels, disorder, strife, sedition, murder, treason, poisoning, avenged but not deterred by the daily executions, vanish with the death of money, and that fear, anxiety, worries, toils and watching will perish along with it? Although money is often thought to be the solution, take money away, and the problem itself disappears and dies away. To illustrate, imagine a barren year, with failed crops, in which many thousands have died of hunger. I'm sure that after the famine was over, if you searched the rich man's warehouses you would so

[1] [marginal note] Reader, note well!

much grain that, had it been distributed to the poor, those killed by hunger and disease would not have even noticed the fury of the sky and soil. How easily might men get their living, if that much-lauded money, that grand invention meant to open the way to a living, was not itself the only barrier to our getting a living! Even the rich should see that it would be better not to lack necessities than to have a great heap of superfluities, better to escape the many troubles caused by need than be hemmed in by great riches. Nor do I doubt that caring for our own advantage or for the authority of our Savior Christ (Whose wisdom could not fail to know what is best, and Whose goodness would not advise what He knew not to be best) would long ago have brought the world to adopt the laws of this commonwealth had not one single monster, the chief and originator of all plagues, stood in the way—Pride.[1] She measures prosperity not by her own good but by the harm of others. She would not even want to be made a goddess if she had no poor wretches to lord it over. Let her prosperity vex and aggravate their poverty so long as their poverty amplifies and sets off her prosperity. This serpent of Hell slithers into human hearts and stops us, like a suckfish attached to a ship, from following life's better course, sticking on us too tightly to be easily pulled off.

Pride is too deeply rooted in us to be readily plucked out, so I rejoice that at least the Utopians have a system that I wish everyone everywhere would imitate. They have established institutions as the basis of their commonwealth that will produce the greatest possible happiness and that, as far as human foresight can tell, could last forever. At home they have pulled up the roots of ambition and faction, along with other vices, so there is no danger of trouble from the internal strife that has been the only cause for the ruin of many cities' well-established prosperity. So long as the Utopians preserve their internal harmony and keep institutions healthy, not all the envy of neighboring kings can shake or endanger that nation, although such has often been attempted—with no success.

When Raphael had finished his story, I was left thinking that not a few of that people's customs and laws were absurd—not only their method of waging war, their rites and religion, and their other institutions, but above all that which is the chief foundation of their entire system: their communal life with shared goods and no money. This alone utterly overthrows the nobility, magnificence, splendor, and majesty that are, in the opinion of the common people, the true glories and ornaments of a commonwealth. Yet I knew that he was wearied by telling his tale, and I myself had not had enough time to think it over. I doubted, too, wheth er he could brook any opposition to his views, particularly as I remembered how he had censured those who feared that they might not seem wise enough unless they could find fault with other men's thoughts. And so I praised the Utopian way of life, and also Raphael's account of it, and took him by the hand and led him in to supper, first saying that there would be time to think more deeply about these matters and to discuss them more fully. I hope that will indeed happen. In the meantime, while Raphael is in other ways a man of most undoubted learning, one with wide knowledge of the world, I cannot agree with all he said. And yet I readily admit that there are many features of the Utopian commonwealth that I can more easily wish for in our own societies than hope to see realized.

—1516

[1] [marginal note] A striking phrase.

In Context

Illustration of Utopia

Ambrosius Holbein, *Map of the Island of Utopia*. This illustration appeared in the 1518 edition (the 1516 edition includes a less fully-developed illustration by an unknown artist).

Utopian Language

THE UTOPIAN ALPHABET

a b c d e f g h i k l m n o p q r s t u x y

A QUATRAIN IN THE UTOPIAN LANGUAGE

Vtopos ha Boccas peula chama.
polta chamaan
Bargol he maglomi baccan
ſoma gymnoſophaon
Agrama gymnoſophon labarem
bacha bodamilomin
Voluala barchin heman la
lauoluola dramme pagloni.

A Literal Translation of These Verses

Utopus it was who redrew the map,
And made me an island instead of a cape:
Alone among nations resplendent I stand,
Making virtue as plain as the back of your hand—
Displaying to all without argumentation
The shape of a true philosophical nation.
Profusely to all of my own store I give;
What is shown me that's better, I gladly receive.

Poems in the Utopian Tongue

The first poem in Utopian was published with the 1516 edition of *Utopia*, together with a translation into Latin. Several later writers found it amusing to write in Utopian, although not using the original Utopian alphabet. For an example of Utopian in prose, see François Rabelais's *Pantagruel*, chapter 9.

Henry Peacham, epigrammatist and author of a book on drawing, contributed to the many friendly but mocking poems that prefaced *Coryate's Crudities* (1611) by Thomas Coryate of Odcomb, famous for his foreign travels and sometimes clownish behavior. Here the joke is the imaginary language that more or less lists real places:

In the Utopian Tongue

Ny thalonin ythsi Coryate lachmah babowans
O Asiam Europam Americ-werowans
Poph-himgi Savoya, Hessen, Rhetia, Ragonzie
France, Germanien dove Anda-louzie[1]
Not A-rag-on[2] ô Coryate, ô hone vilascar
Einen trunk Od-combe ny Venice Berga-mascar.

John Taylor, "The Water Poet," was by profession a waterman, ferrying customers up and down the Thames, and by avocation the author of many comic tracts and poems. One of his poems in Utopian appears in *Laugh, and be Fat* (1612), reprinted in his 1630 *Works*. It too is about Thomas Coryate and incorporates fragments of English words, usually as implied insults:

The Utopian Tongue

Thoyton Asse Coria Tushrump[3] codsheadirustie,
Mungrellimo whish whap ragge dicete tottrie,
Mangelusquem verminets nipsem barelybittimsore
Culliandolt travellerebumque, graiphone trutchmore.
Pusse per mew (Odcomb) gul abelgrik foppery shig shag
Cock a peps Comb[4] sottishamp, Idioshte momulus[5] tag rag.

A poem by Taylor from *Odcomb's Complaint* (1613; for sale, says the title page, in Utopia) and reprinted in 1630 comes right after a poem in the "Barmooda" tongue (ostensibly the language of the pigs found by the first European visitors to Bermuda). It is also on Coryate and incorporates place names and words from real languages:

---

[1] *Anda-louzie* Andalusia, in Spain, but also "And lousy"—having lice.

[2] *A-rag-on* Aragon (part of Spain) but also not even wearing a rag, naked.

[3] *Thoyton Asse Coria Tushrump* "Thomas Coryat" is embedded in the nonsense words.

[4] *Cock a peps Comb* A phrase incorporating "cockscomb."

[5] *momulus* A "momulus" would be a little "Momus," traditional Greek god of mockery.

Epitaph in the Utopian tongue

Nortumblum callimumquash omystoliton quashte burashte,
Scribuke woshtay solusbay per ambulatushte;
Grekay sons Turkay Paphay zums Jerusalushte.
Neptus esht Ealors Interremoy diz Dolorushte,
Confabuloy Odcumbay Prozeugmolliton tymorumynoy,
Omulus oratushte paralescus tolliton umbroy.

The Same in English,
Translated by Caleb Quishquash, an Utopian Born
and Principal Secretary to the Great Adelontado of Barmoodoes

Here lies the wonder of the English nation,
Involved in Neptune's brinish vasty maw:
For fruitless travel, and for strange relation,
He passed and repassed all that e're eye saw.
Odcomb produced him; many nations fed him,
And worlds of writers, through the world have spread him.

William Tyndale

1494? – 1536

The English phrases that we now think of when we hear the term "Biblical language" are very largely the product of the work of one individual: William Tyndale. Tyndale met constant opposition from church and government officials throughout the course of his adult life. The work of translating the scriptures into the vernacular—English—was so dangerous that he went into hiding in continental Europe while trying to complete it. He was finally executed for his work, but within a few years of his death, his Bible was becoming widely read throughout England.

Tyndale was born in the mid-1490s, most likely in Stinchcombe, Gloucestershire, near the Welsh border. Not much is known about his early life and parentage. We do know that he attended Magdalen Hall, Oxford, was awarded a B.A. in 1512 and was incepted as M.A. in 1515, and was ordained a priest in London that same year. While at Oxford he was greatly influenced by the work of the Dutch philosopher Desiderius Erasmus—particularly by the venerable scholar's study of the *Septuagint*, the original Greek version of the books that Christians now refer to as the New Testament.

After graduation Tyndale returned to Gloucestershire, serving as household chaplain to Sir John and Lady Anne Walsh and as tutor to their children. During this period he began studying Erasmus's Greek New Testament and considered attempting his own English translation, which he hoped would enable local lay people to read the Scriptures for themselves. His translation of Erasmus's *Enchiridion militis Christiani* (*Manual of the Christian Knight*), which encourages the study the New Testament, helped gain the Walshs' support of his position. At this time Tyndale was also in demand as a preacher, but his sermons offended the local clergy, and he was brought before the Bishop's Chancellor on charges of heresy.

Tyndale left the area in 1523 and headed for London, hoping to find support for his translation work. He approached Bishop Cuthbert Tunstall, Erasmus's friend and Bishop of London, hoping he would serve as patron for the project. The Bishop not only refused his request, but became a vocal opponent of any plan to translate the Bible into the vernacular. Tyndale was forced to leave London in May 1524. With the sponsorship of Sir Humphrey Monmouth, a London merchant, he went to Germany, which at the time was more open to the ideas of the Protestant Reformation. He never returned to England.

The details of Tyndale's life in Germany are sketchy. His status as intellectual outlaw meant that he moved around considerably. He stayed in Hamburg for a while and then went to Wittenberg, where it is likely that he met with the famous Reformation leader Martin Luther. Eventually he settled in Cologne, where he set about having his translation of the *New Testament* published. Before it was finished, however, city magistrates caught wind of the project and ordered the printing house raided. Tyndale was able to escape with a portion of his printed New Testament, and this "Cologne Fragment" (which included most of the first Gospel, that of Matthew) circulated throughout England, accompanied by a prologue and marginal notes by Luther. Tyndale fled to Worms, a

Tyndale's *English Bible*

GENESIS: CHAPTER I

In the beginning God created heaven and earth. The earth was void and empty, and darkness was upon the deep, and the spirit of God moved upon the water.

Then God said: let there be light and there was light. And God saw the light that it was good: and divided the light from the darkness, and called the light day, and the darkness night: and so of the evening and morning was made the first day.

And God said: let there be a firmament between the waters, and let it divide the waters asunder. Then God made the firmament and parted the waters which were under the firmament, from the waters that were above the firmament: And it was so. And God called the firmament heaven. And so of the evening and morning was made the second day.

And God said, let the waters that are under heaven gather themselves unto one place, that the dry land may appear: And it came so to pass. And God called the dry land the earth and the gathering together of waters called he the sea. And God saw that it was good.

And God said: let the earth bring forth herb and grass that sow seed, and fruitful trees that bear fruit every one in his kind, having their seed in themselves upon the earth. And it came so to pass: and the earth brought forth herb and grass sowing seed every one in his kind and trees bearing fruit and having their seed in themselves every one in his kind. And God saw that it was good: and then of the evening and morning was made the third day.

King James Bible

GENESIS: CHAPTER I

In the beginning God created the heaven and the earth. And the earth was without form, and void; and darkness *was* upon the face of the deep. And the spirit of God moved upon the face of the waters.

And God said, Let there be light: and there was light. And God saw the light, that *it was* good: and God divided the light from the darkness. And God called the light Day, and the darkness he called Night. And the evening and the morning were the first day.

And God said, Let there be a firmament in the midst of the waters, and let it divide the waters from the waters. And God made the firmament, and divided the waters which *were* under the firmament from the waters which *were* above the firmament: and it was so. And God called the firmament Heaven. And the evening and the morning were the second day.

And God said, Let the waters under the heaven be gathered together unto one place, and let the dry *land* appear: and it was so. And God called the dry *land* Earth; and the gathering together of the waters called he Seas: and God saw that it *was* good.

And God said, Let the earth bring forth grass, the herb yielding seed, *and* the fruit tree yielding fruit after his kind, whose seed *is* in itself, upon the earth: and it was so. And the earth brought forth grass, *and* herb yielding seed after his kind, and the tree yielding fruit, whose seed *was* in itself, after his kind: and God saw that it *was* good. And the evening and the morning were the third day.

Geneva Bible

Genesis: Chapter 1

In the beginning God created the heaven and the earth. And the earth was without form and void, and darkness was upon the deep, and the Spirit of God moved upon the waters.

Then God said, Let there be light: and there was light. And God saw the light that it was good, and God separated the light from the darkness. And God called the light, Day, and the darkness, He called Night. So the evening and the morning were the first day.

Again God said, Let there be a firmament in the midst of the waters: and let it separate the waters from the waters. Then God made the firmament, and parted the waters, which were under the firmament, from the waters which were above the firmament: and it was so. And God called the firmament, Heaven. So the evening and the morning were the second day.

God said again, Let the waters under the heaven be gathered into one place, and let the dry land appear: and it was so. And God called the dry land, Earth, and He called the gathering together of the waters, Seas: and God saw that it was good.

Then God said, Let the earth bud forth the bud of the herb, that seedeth seed, the fruitful tree, which beareth fruit according to his kind, which may have his seed in itself upon the earth: and it was so. And the earth brought forth the bud of the herb, that seedeth seed according to his kind, also the tree that yieldeth fruit, which hath his seed in itself according to his kind: and God saw that it was good. So the evening and the morning were the third day.

Douay-Rheims Bible

Genesis: Chapter 1

In the beginning God created heaven, and earth. And the earth was void and empty, and darkness was upon the face of the deep; and the spirit of God moved over the waters.

And God said: Be light made. And light was made. And God saw the light that it was good; and He divided the light from the darkness. And He called the light Day, and the darkness Night; and there was evening and morning one day.

And God said: Let there be a firmament made amidst the waters: and let it divide the waters from the waters. And God made a firmament, and divided the waters that were under the firmament, from those that were above the firmament, and it was so. And God called the firmament, Heaven; and the evening and morning were the second day.

God also said: Let the waters that are under the heaven, be gathered together into one place: and let the dry land appear. And it was so done. And God called the dry land, Earth; and the gathering together of the waters, He called Seas. And God saw that it was good.

And He said: let the earth bring forth the green herb, and such as may seed, and the fruit tree yielding fruit after its kind, which may have seed in itself upon the earth. And it was so done.

And the earth brought forth the green herb, and such as yieldeth seed according to its kind, and the tree that beareth fruit, having seed each one according to its kind. And God saw that it was good. And the evening and the morning were the third day.

Tyndale's *English Bible*	*King James Bible*
Then said God: let there be lights in the firmament of heaven to divide the day from the night, that they may be unto signs, seasons, days and years. And let them be lights in the firmament of heaven, to shine upon the earth. And so it was. And God made two great lights: A greater light to rule the day, and a less light to rule the night, and he made stars also. And God put them in the firmament of heaven to shine upon the earth, and to rule the day and the night, and to divide the light from darkness. And God saw that it was good: and so of the evening and morning was made the fourth day.	And God said, Let there be lights in the firmament of the heaven to divide the day from the night; and let them be for signs, and for seasons, and for days, and years. And let them be for lights in the firmament of the heaven to give light upon the earth: and it was so. And God made two great lights; the greater light to rule the day, and the lesser light to rule the night: *He made* the stars also. And God set them in the firmament of the heaven to give light upon the earth, and to rule over the day and over the night, and to divide the light from the darkness: and God saw that *it was* good. And the evening and the morning were the fourth day.
And God said, let the water bring forth creatures that move and have life, and fowls for to fly over the earth under the firmament of heaven. And God created great whales and all manner of creatures that live and move, which the waters brought forth in their kinds, and all manner of feathered fowls in their kinds. And God saw that it was good: and God blessed them saying: Grow and multiply and fill the waters of the seas, and let the fowls multiply upon the earth. And so of the evening and morning was made the fifth day.	And God said, Let the waters bring forth abundantly the moving creature that hath life, and fowl *that* may fly above the earth in the open firmament of heaven. And God created great whales, and every living creature that moveth, which the waters brought forth abundantly, after their kind, and every winged fowl after his kind: and God saw that *it was* good. And God blessed them, saying, Be fruitful, and multiply, and fill the waters in the seas, and let fowl multiply in the earth. And the evening and the morning were the fifth day.
And God said: let the earth bring forth living creatures in their kinds: cattle and worms and beasts of the earth in their kinds, and so it came to pass. And God made the beasts of the earth in their kinds and cattle in their kinds, and all manner worms of the earth in their kinds: and God saw that it was good.	And God said, Let the earth bring forth the living creature after his kind, cattle, and creeping thing, and beast of the earth after his kind: and it was so. And God made the beast of the earth after his kind, and cattle after their kind, and every thing that creepeth upon the earth after his kind: and God saw that *it was* good.
And God said: let us make man in our similitude and after our likeness: that he may have rule over the fish of the sea, and over the fowls of the air, and over cattle, and over all the earth, and over all worms that creep on the earth. And God created man after His likeness, after the likeness of God created He Him: male and female created He them.	And God said, Let us make man in our image, after our likeness: and let them have dominion over the fish of the sea, and over the fowl of the air, and over the cattle, and over all the earth, and over every creeping thing that creepeth upon the earth. So God created man in His own image, in the image of God created He him; male and female created He them.

Geneva Bible

And God said, Let there be lights in the firmament of the heaven, to separate the day from the night, and let them be for signs, and for seasons, and for days and years. And let them be for lights in the firmament of the heaven to give light upon the earth: and it was so. God then made two great lights: the greater light to rule the day, and the less light to rule the night: He made also the stars. And God set them in the firmament of the heaven, to shine upon the earth, And to rule in the day, and in the night, and to separate the light from the darkness: and God saw that it was good. So the evening and the morning were the fourth day.

Afterward God said, Let the waters bring forth in abundance every creeping thing that hath life: and let the fowl fly upon the earth in the open firmament of the heaven. Then God created the great whales, and every thing living and moving, which the waters brought forth in abundance, according to their kind, and every feathered fowl according to his kind: and God saw that it was good. Then God blessed them, saying, Bring forth fruit and multiply, and fill the waters in the seas, and let the fowl multiply in the earth. So the evening and the morning were the fifth day.

Moreover God said, Let the earth bring forth the living thing according to his kind, cattle, and that which creepeth, and the beast of the earth, according to his kind: and it was so. And God made the beast of the earth according to his kind, and the cattle according to his kind, and every creeping thing of the earth according to his kind: and God saw that it was good.

Furthermore God said, Let us make man in our image according to our likeness, and let them rule over the fish of the sea, and over the fowl of the heaven, and over the beasts, and over all the earth, and over every thing that creepeth and moveth on the earth. Thus God created the man in his image: in the image of God created He him: He created them male and female.

Douay-Rheims Bible

And God said: Let there be lights made in the firmament of heaven, to divide the day and the night, and let them be for signs, and for seasons, and for days and years: To shine in the firmament of heaven, and to give light upon the earth. And it was so done. And God made two great lights: a greater light to rule the day; and a lesser light to rule the night: and the stars. And He set them in the firmament of heaven to shine upon the earth. And to rule the day and the night, and to divide the light and the darkness. And God saw that it was good. And the evening and morning were the fourth day.

God also said: let the waters bring forth the creeping creature having life, and the fowl that may fly over the earth under the firmament of heaven. And God created the great whales, and every living and moving creature, which the waters brought forth, according to their kinds, and every winged fowl according to its kind. And God saw that it was good. And He blessed them, saying: Increase and multiply, and fill the waters of the sea: and let the birds be multiplied upon the earth. And the evening and morning were the fifth day.

And God said: Let the earth bring forth the living creature in its kind, cattle and creeping things, and beasts of the earth, according to their kinds. And it was so done. And God made the beasts of the earth according to their kinds, and cattle, and every thing that creepeth on the earth after its kind. And God saw that it was good.

And He said: Let us make man to our image and likeness: and let him have dominion over the fishes of the sea, and the fowls of the air, and the beasts, and the whole earth, and every creeping creature that moveth upon the earth. And God created man to His own image: to the image of God He created him: male and female He created them.

Tyndale's *English Bible*

Therefore when thou offerest thy gift at the altar, and there rememberest that thy brother hath aught against thee: leave there thine offering before the altar, and go thy way first and be reconciled to thy brother, and then come and offer thy gift.

Agree with thine adversary quickly, while thou art in the way with him, lest that adversary deliver thee to the judge, and the judge deliver thee to the minister, and then thou be cast into prison. I say unto thee verily: thou shalt not come out thence till thou have paid the utmost farthing.[1]

Ye have heard how it was said to them of old time, Thou shalt not commit adultery. But I say unto you, that whosoever looketh on a wife, lusting after her, hath committed adultery with her already in his heart....

Ye have heard how it is said, an eye for an eye: a tooth for a tooth. But I say to you, that ye resist not wrong. But whosoever give thee a blow on thy right cheek, turn to him the other. And if any man will sue thee at the law, and take away thy coat, let him have thy cloak also. And whosoever will compel thee to go a mile, go with him twain.[2] Give to him that asketh, and from him that would borrow turn not away.

Ye have heard how it is said: thou shalt love thine neighbour, and hate thine enemy. But I say unto you, love your enemies. Bless them that curse you. Do good to them that hate you. Pray for them which do you wrong and persecute you, that ye may be the children of your father that is in heaven: for he maketh his sun to arise on the evil, and on the good, and sendeth his rain on the just and unjust. For if ye love them, which love you: what reward shall ye have? Do not the Publicans[3] even so? And if ye be friendly to your brethren only: what singular thing do ye? Do not the Publicans likewise? Ye shall therefore be perfect, even as your Father which is in heaven, is perfect.

—1534

King James Bible

Therefore if thou bring thy gift to the altar, and there rememberest that thy brother hath aught against thee; Leave there thy gift before the altar, and go thy way; first be reconciled to thy brother, and then come and offer thy gift.

Agree with thine adversary quickly, whiles thou art in the way with him; lest at any time the adversary deliver thee to the judge, and the judge deliver thee to the officer, and thou be cast into prison. Verily I say unto thee, Thou shalt by no means come out thence, till thou hast paid the uttermost farthing.

Ye have heard that it was said by them of old time, Thou shalt not commit adultery: But I say unto you, That whosoever looketh on a woman to lust after her hath committed adultery with her already in his heart.

Ye have heard that it hath been said, An eye for an eye, and a tooth for a tooth: But I say unto you, That ye resist not evil: but whosoever shall smite thee on thy right cheek, turn to him the other also. And if any man will sue thee at the law, and take away thy coat, let him have thy cloak also. And whosoever shall compel thee to go a mile, go with him twain. Give to him that asketh thee, and from him that would borrow of thee turn not thou away.

Ye have heard that it hath been said, Thou shalt love thy neighbour, and hate thine enemy. But I say unto you, Love your enemies, bless them that curse you, do good to them that hate you, and pray for them which despitefully use you, and persecute you; That ye may be the children of your Father which is in heaven: for he maketh his sun to rise on the evil and on the good, and sendeth rain on the just and on the unjust. For if ye love them which love you, what reward have ye? do not even the publicans the same? And if ye salute your brethren only, what do ye more *than others*? do not even the publicans so? Be ye therefore perfect, even as your Father which is in heaven is perfect.

—1611

[1] *farthing* Coin of little value.

[2] *twain* Two.

[3] *publican* Tax-gatherer, a derogatory epithet.

Geneva Bible

If then thou bring thy gift to the altar, and there rememberest that thy brother hath aught against thee, Leave there thine offering before the altar, and go thy way: first be reconciled to thy brother, and then come and offer thy gift.

Agree with thine adversary quickly, while thou art in the way with him, lest thine adversary deliver thee to the judge, and the judge deliver thee to the sergeant, and thou be cast into prison. Verily I say unto thee, thou shalt not come out thence, till thou hast paid the utmost farthing.

Ye have heard that it was said to them of old time, Thou shalt not commit adultery. But I say unto you, that whosoever looketh on a woman to lust after her, hath committed adultery with her already in his heart....

Ye have heard that it hath been said, An eye for an eye, and a tooth for a tooth. But I say unto you, Resist not evil: but whosoever shall smite thee on thy right cheek, turn to him the other also. And if any man will sue thee at the law, and take away thy coat, let him have thy cloak also. And whosoever will compel thee *to go* a mile, go with him twain. Give to him that asketh, and from him that would borrow of thee, turn not away.

Ye have heard that it hath been said, Thou shalt love thy neighbour, and hate thine enemy. But I say unto you, Love your enemies: bless them that curse you: do good to them that hate you, and pray for them which hurt you, and persecute you, That ye may be the children of your father that is in heaven: for he maketh his sun to arise on the evil, and the good, and sendeth rain on the just, and unjust.

For if ye love them, which love you, what reward shall you have? Do not the Publicans even the same? And if ye be friendly to your brethren only, what singular thing do ye? do not even the Publicans likewise? Ye shall therefore be perfect, as your Father which is in heaven, is perfect.
—1599

Douay-Rheims Bible

If therefore thou offer thy gift at the altar, and there thou remember that thy brother hath anything against thee; Leave there thy offering before the altar, and go first to be reconciled to thy brother: and then coming thou shalt offer thy gift.

Be at agreement with thy adversary betimes, whilst thou art in the way with him: lest perhaps the adversary deliver thee to the judge, and the judge deliver thee to the officer, and thou be cast into prison. Amen I say to thee, thou shalt not go out from thence till thou repay the last farthing.

You have heard that it was said to them of old: Thou shalt not commit adultery. But I say to you, that whosoever shall look on a woman to lust after her, hath already committed adultery with her in his heart....

You have heard that it hath been said, An eye for an eye, and a tooth for a tooth. But I say to you not to resist evil: but if one strike thee on thy right cheek, turn to him also the other: And if a man will contend with thee in judgment, and take away thy coat, let go thy cloak also unto him. And whosoever will force thee one mile, go with him other two. Give to him that asketh of thee and from him that would borrow of thee turn not away.

You have heard that it hath been said, Thou shalt love thy neighbour, and hate thy enemy. But I say to you, Love your enemies: do good to them that hate you: and pray for them that persecute and calumniate[1] you: That you may be the children of your Father who is in heaven, who maketh his sun to rise upon the good, and bad, and raineth upon the just and the unjust. For if you love them that love you, what reward shall you have? do not even the publicans this? And if you salute your brethren only, what do you more? do not also the heathens this? Be you therefore perfect, as also your heavenly Father is perfect.
—1582

[1] *calumniate* Slander.

Deathbed of Henry VIII, c. 1549. Henry is shown pointing towards his heir, the young Edward. Members of the Council of Regency (Edward Seymour, John Dudley, Thomas Cranmer, and John Russell), who together acted on the young King's behalf, are shown to the right of the picture. The Pope is shown at the bottom of the picture, with the new *Book of Common Prayer* pressing down on his neck.

Religion and Devotional Life

CONTEXTS

After Henry VIII's break with the Roman Catholic Church in 1533 and the "Elizabethan Settlement" of 1558 that set the liturgical, ecclesiastical, and theological foundations of the Church of England, a majority of the English eventually came to accept, and many to love, the established Church. Others remained Catholic ("recusant") to varying degrees: some outwardly conformed; some risked their lives and fortunes to collaborate with a small but determined underground of priests who brought the sacraments and, often, texts printed in secret or smuggled in from abroad; yet others emigrated to the Continent, where some joined religious houses; and some changed allegiances—Ben Jonson changed twice, becoming a Catholic for a while and reverting. It is also wise to remember that, despite the period's religious hatreds and angry polemics, some Protestants had Catholic friends and a great many people in 1600 could still remember older relatives who had been raised Catholic.

Within the Church of England itself, on the other hand, a loud minority, although having little *theological* objection to the Elizabethan Settlement, demanded that religious practices and church government needed to be further "purified" of such "papist" elements as stained glass, fancy clerical costume, complex church music, altars, and even bishops. Those who rejected such demands sometimes scoffed at those who made them as "Puritans," and the name stuck. Eventually many "Puritans" left the Church of England altogether; these "Separatists," later called "Congregationalists," "Independents," "Nonconformists" or "Dissenters," were related to, although by no means identical with, the Presbyterians of Scotland. But the story does not end there, for beyond the edge of Protestantism a number of radical sects moved much further away from the practice and sometimes the theology of the established church. The political upheavals of the 1640s and 1650s in particular produced a great deal of religious radicalism: some were religious communists (the "Diggers"); some believed in the imminent coming of Christ ("The Fifth Monarchy Men"); some illegally preached to crowds, while others waited for an inward sense of God's presence that could even their bodies shake (the "Quakers"). Most of these movements disappeared; some, such as the Quakers and the Baptists, remain today. But while such people never held power in the period, their radical religious and political thought affected future developments in British devotional and intellectual culture.

Henry VIII broke with Rome but did not think himself thereby a Protestant. Particularly after 1540, with his Reformation in place, he became more conservative, restricting Bible reading and, in 1546, authorizing the torture and execution of those he thought "heretics." One of these was Anne Askew, whose suffering and death are described below. After his persecutions caused protest he swerved again toward the Protestants, and when his young son Edward VI took the throne in 1548, guided by Thomas Cranmer, the Archbishop of Canterbury, and Edward Seymour, the Duke of Somerset, the English Reformation took an explicitly Protestant, indeed a Calvinist, direction. The year 1549 saw the first version of Cranmer's masterpiece, the Book of Common Prayer, which gave the new church a vernacular liturgy that everybody could understand and that, thanks in part to the printing press, could be uniform throughout the realm. Aside from William Tyndale, whose translations of the Bible in the 1520s and 1530s provided most of the language in the King James Version of 1611, there is no other writer whose prose played such a vital role in shaping the aesthetics of English Christian practice (or, nowadays, despite some modernization, that of the Anglican community globe-wide).

With the accession of the Catholic Mary I in 1553 and then of the Protestant Elizabeth I in 1558, religious and political oscillation continued. Under Mary the Catholic service was restored. Some Protestants fled abroad (a number to Geneva) but several hundred who stayed behind, some of them women, were burned at the stake or otherwise executed. Among these were Bishops Hugh Latimer and Nicholas Ridley in 1555 and Cranmer himself in 1556. Elizabeth restored English Protestantism (a slightly more mellow Protestantism than what Edward preferred, for the new queen could be conservative in her religious views and tastes), which began to put down deep roots. By the 1570s England was effectively a Protestant country, albeit one with a Catholic minority. Aside from the Bible and the Book of Common Prayer, the text most important to the establishing the culture of the new religious order was John Foxe's *Acts and monuments* 1563), a vivid account of the persecution and execution of various Protestants. Foxe includes some early Christian martyrs (he was trying to establish Protestantism as the ancient and hence true Christianity) as well as accounts of some earlier Reformers such as John Wycliffe and Martin Luther, but his focus is on the reigns of Henry VIII and Mary. Foxe's *Book of Martyrs*, as it came to be called, went through four editions in his lifetime and many thereafter; his work continued to fan the flames of anti-Catholic feeling for decades and indeed centuries after his death.

If John Foxe provides a vivid sense of the anti-Catholic streak in English Protestantism during this period, Lady Margaret Hoby (1571–1633) provides an equally vivid picture of the importance of religion to daily life in the sixteenth and early seventeenth centuries. Educated in a Puritan family and heir to a substantial estate, Margaret Dakins was eventually married (following the deaths of her first two husbands) to Thomas Hoby. The couple had no children, and she devoted herself to helping run their country estate, to providing medical services to the community—and to religious devotion.

The last of the texts below shows that some could respond to religious polemics in a moderate voice. Well before the seventeenth century, Puritan aims had broadened to include not just the hope (shared with less militant Protestants) that the Bible would be widely read, but also the elimination from the English Church of all remaining traces of Catholicism—in the liturgy, the physical appearance of churches, and church government—and the reformation of English manners and morals. This last aim included the elimination of many traditional practices, such as country dances, maypoles, bonfires, Mayday celebrations, bell-ringing, and games, that Puritans called "papist" or even "pagan." Puritans stressed sobriety of clothing and manner (they also objected to long hair), insisted on a strict observance of the Sabbath, and denounced drunkenness and other signs of immorality. Owen Felltham (?1602–68) was a widely-read essayist and poet; his "Of Puritans" (1623) explores the issues behind the rhetoric, notes the different meanings different people had attached to the label "Puritan," and resolves to admire what should be admired but not to deny life's pleasures. "Be merry, but sin not," he concludes, in a quintessential gesture of Anglican compromise.

⌘⌘⌘

The Martyrdom of Anne Askew

Anne Askew was among the Protestant reformers persecuted for their religious beliefs under Henry VIII. Some issues that excited controversy (particularly over precisely what happens to the consecrated bread and wine at Communion), although still important, now seem less urgent to many people. Others, such as the degree to which Christians need priests to act as intermediaries when they confess their sins or interpret the Bible, or if a Christian church needs a hierarchal clergy, or what should be the role of the government in church affairs, remain live issues for Christians today.

Askew wrote two accounts of the examinations to which she was subjected ("The First Examination" and "The Latter Examination"). She somehow arranged to have these smuggled out of the prison in which she was confined, and they were published in Germany by John Bale in his *Examinations*, and later incorporated by John Foxe into his *Acts and Monuments*. The versions differ somewhat, and in both cases it has been suggested that the mediating voices may have shaped Askew's accounts somewhat for their own purposes. There is no doubt, however, that both Bale's and Foxe's versions of the accounts are based on originals by Askew herself. The text below is that provided by Foxe, and has traditionally been considered the more reliable of the two.

Also included below are the description by Foxe of her death and a ballad alleged to have been written by Askew.

from Anne Askew, "The First Examination of Anne Askew" (1546)

To satisfy your expectation, good people (sayeth she), this was my first examination in the year of our Lord 1545, and in the month of March. First Christopher Dare examined me at Saddlers' Hall, being one of the quest,[1] and asked if I did not believe that the sacrament hanging over the altar[2] was the very body of Christ really. Then I demanded this question of him: wherefore Saint Stephen was stoned to death. And he said he could not tell. Then I answered that no more would I assoil[3] his vain question....

Thirdly, he asked me wherefore I said that I had rather to read five lines in the Bible, than to hear five masses in the temple. I confessed that I said no less. Not for the dispraise of either the Epistle or Gospel, but because the one did greatly edify me, and the other nothing at all....

Fourthly, he laid unto my charge that I should say: "If an ill[4] priest ministered, it was the Devil and not God." My answer was that I never spake such thing. But this was my saying: "That whatsoever he were which ministered unto me, his ill conditions could not hurt my faith, but in spirit I received nevertheless the body and blood of Christ." He asked me what I said concerning confession.[5] I answered him my meaning, which was as Saint James sayeth, that every man ought to knowledge[6] his faults to other, and the one to pray for the other....

Seventhly, he asked me if I had the spirit of God in me. I answered if I had not, I was but reprobate or cast away. Then he said he had sent for a priest to examine me, which was there at hand. The priest asked me what I said to the sacrament of the altar. And required much to know therein my meaning. But I desired him again to hold me excused concerning that matter. None other answer would I make him, because I perceived him a papist.

Eighthly, he asked me if I did not think that private masses did help souls departed.[7] And I said it was great idolatry to believe more in them than in the death which Christ died for us. Then they had me thence unto my Lord Mayor and he examined me, as they had before, and I answered him directly in all things as I answered the quest afore. Besides this my Lord Mayor laid one thing unto my charge which was never spoken of me but of them. And that was whether a mouse eating the host received God or no. This question did I never ask, but indeed they asked it of me, whereunto I made them no answer but smiled. Then the Bishop's Chancellor rebuked me and said that I was much to blame for uttering the Scriptures. For Saint Paul (he said) forbade women to speak or to talk of the word of God. I answered him that I knew Paul's meaning as well as he, which is, 1 Corinthians 14, that a woman ought not to speak in the congregation by the way of teaching. And then I asked him how many women he had seen go into the pulpit and preach? He said he never saw none.

[1] *being one of the quest* I.e., being one of those conducting the inquest or examination.

[2] *Sacrament hanging over the altar* Communion bread or wafers. According to the Catholic doctrine of transubstantiation, first asserted by the Fourth Lateran Council (1215), the substance, but not the "accidental" appearance and taste, of the bread and wine consecrated at the sacrament of Holy Communion are miraculously changed into the body and blood of Christ. In the sixteenth century holy wafers sometimes hung in a container above the altar.

[3] *assoil* Refute.

[4] *ill* Ill in spirit; sinful.

[5] *confession* According to Catholic doctrine, it was essential that Christians confess to a priest at least once a year. For Protestants the confession of sins did not require an intermediary between oneself and God; confession could be conducted privately.

[6] *knowledge* Acknowledge; make known.

[7] *Private masses ... departed* Arranging for a private Mass to be held was one means whereby Catholics hoped to receive benefits in the afterlife—the benefit in the case of these private services being a reduction of time to be served in Purgatory before ascending to Heaven.

Then I said, he ought to find no fault in poor women, except[1] they had offended the law. Then my Lord Mayor commanded me to ward. I asked him if sureties would not serve me, and he made me short answer, that he would take none.

Then was I had to the Counter,[2] and there remained eleven days, no friend admitted to speak with me. But in the meantime there was a priest sent to me which said that he was commanded of the Bishop to examine me, and to give me good counsel, which he did not. But first he asked me for what cause I was put in the Counter. And I told him I could not tell. Then he said it was great pity that I should be there without cause, and concluded that he was very sorry for me.

Secondly, he said it was told him that I should deny the sacrament of the altar. And I answered him again that, that I had said, I had said. Thirdly, he asked me if I were shriven.[3] I told him so that[4] I might have one of these three, that is to say, Doctor Crome, Sir William, or Huntingdon,[5] I was contented, because I knew them to be men of wisdom. "As for you or any other I will not dispraise, because I know ye not."...

Fourthly, he asked me if the Host should fall, and a beast did eat it, whether the beast did receive God or no. I answered, "Seeing ye have taken the pains to ask this question I desire you also to assoil it yourself. For I will not do it, because I perceive ye come to tempt me." And he said it was against the order of schools[6] that he which asked the question should answer it. I told him I was but a woman and knew not the course of schools. Fifthly, he asked me if I intended to receive the sacrament at Easter or no. I answered that else I were no[7] Christian woman, and there I did rejoice, that the time was so near at hand. And then he departed thence with many fair words....

In the meanwhile he commanded his archdeacon to common with me, who said unto me, "Mistress, wherefore are ye accused and thus troubled here before the Bishop?"

To whom I answered again and said, "Sir, ask, I pray you, my accusers, for I know not as yet."

Then took he my book out of my hand and said, "Such books as this hath brought you to the trouble you are in. Beware," sayeth he, "beware, for he that made this book and was the author thereof was an heretic, I warrant you, and burnt in Smithfield."

Then I asked him if he were certain and sure that it was true that he had spoken. And he said he knew well the book was of John Frith's[8] making. Then I asked him if he were not ashamed for to judge of the book before he saw it within or yet knew the truth thereof. I said also that such unadvised and hasty judgment is token apparent of a very slender wit. Then I opened the book and showed it to him. He said he thought it had been another, for he could find no fault therein. Then I desired him no more to be so unadvisedly rash and swift in judgment, till he thoroughly knew the truth, and so he departed from me.

from John Foxe, *Acts and Monuments of These Latter and Perilous Days* (1563)

In a passage separate from his version of Askew's own narrative, Foxe presents the following account of her death.

Hitherto we have entreated of this good woman, now it remaineth that we touch somewhat as touching her end and martyrdom. She being born of such stock and kindred that she might have lived in great wealth and prosperity, if she would rather have followed the world than Christ, but now she was so tormented, that she could neither live long in so great distress, neither yet by the adversaries be suffered to die in secret. Wherefore the day of her execution was appointed, and she brought into Smithfield in a chair, because she could not go on her feet, by means of her great torments. When she was brought unto the stake she was tied by the middle with a chain that held up her body. When all things were thus prepared to the fire, the King's letters of pardon were brought, whereby to

[1] *except* Unless.

[2] *the Counter* Prison in London.

[3] *if I were shriven* I.e., if I had received the Sacrament of Confession.

[4] *so that* So long as.

[5] *Doctor Crome, Sir William, or Huntingdon* All reformist preachers.

[6] *order of schools* Principles of scholastic theology.

[7] *else I were no* Unless I received the sacrament at Easter I would not be a Christian.

[8] *John Frith* Protestant reformer, executed in 1533.

offer her safeguard of her life if she would recant, which she would neither receive, neither yet vouchsafe once to look upon. Shaxton[1] also was there present who, openly that day recanting his opinions, went about with a long oration to cause her also to turn, against whom she stoutly resisted. Thus she being troubled so many manner of ways, and having passed through so many torments, having now ended the long course of her agonies, being compassed in with flames of fire, as a blessed sacrifice unto God, she slept in the Lord, in anno[2] 1546, leaving behind her a singular example of Christian constancy for all men to follow.

Woodcut, *The Burning of Anne Askew and her Fellow Martyrs, July 1546* (1563).

This woodcut appears in the first edition of Foxe's *Acts and Monuments*. As the illustration shows, a grandstand had been built specially for the occasion. A sermon was preached before the pyre was lit, and the Lord Mayor and other officials were among the many spectators.

Anonymous, "I Am a Woman Poor and Blind" (16th century)

The following ballad, commonly attributed to Anne Askew, survives in a number of versions; evidently it was widely known throughout the sixteenth century.

[1] *Shaxton* Nicholas Shaxton, a preacher.

[2] *anno* Latin: year.

I am a Woman Poor and Blind

I am a woman poor and blind,
And little knowledge remains in me,
Long have I sought, but fain would find,
What herb in my Garden were best to be.

A Garden I have which in unknown,
which God of his goodness gave to me,
I mean my body, where I should have sown
The seed of Christ's true verity.

My spirit within me is vexed sore,
My spirit striveth against the same,
My sorrows do increase more and more,
My conscience suffereth most bitter pain.

I with myself being thus at strife
Would fain have been at rest,
Musing and studying, in mortal life,
What things I might do to please God best.

With whole intent and one accord,
Unto a Gardiner[3] that I did know,
I desired him, for the love of the Lord,
True seed in my garden for to sow,

Then this proud Gardener, seeing me so blind,
He thought on me to work his will,
And flattered me with words so kind,
To have me continue in my blindness still.

He fed me then with lies and mocks,
For venial sins[4] he bid me go;
To give my money to stones and stocks,[5]
Which was stark lies and nothing so.[6]

With stinking meat then was I fed,
For to keep me from my Salvation,

[3] *Gardiner* The poet puns here and in the next verse with the name of Stephen Gardiner, Bishop of Winchester and a chief councillor to Henry VIII.

[4] *venial sins* Roman Catholic doctrine makes a distinction between pardonable (or "venial") and deadly (or "mortal") sins.

[5] *stones and stocks* Images made of stone and of wood (for example, of saints).

[6] *nothing so* None of it true.

I had Trentals of mass, and balls of lead,[1]
Not one word spoke of Christ's passion.

In me was sown all kind of feigned seeds,
With Popish Ceremonies many a one,
Masses of Requiem,[2] with other juggling deeds,
Still God's Spirit out of my garden was gone.

Then was I commanded most strictly,
If of my Salvation I would be sure,
To build some Chapel or Chauntry,[3]
To be prayed for while the earth doth endure.

"Beware of new learning," quoth he, "it lyes,
Which in the thing I most abhor,
Meddle not with it in any manner of wise,° *ways*
But do as your fathers have done before."

My trust I did put in the Devil's works,
Thinking sufficient my Soul to save,
Being worse than either Jews or Turks,
Thus Christ of his merits I did deprave, *deprive*

I might liken myself, with a woeful heart,
Unto the Dumb man, in Luke the eleven,[4]
From whence Christ caused the Devil to depart,
But, shortly after, he took the other seven.

My time thus, good Lord, so quickly I spent,
Alas! I shall die the sooner therefore;
O Lord, I find it written in thy Testament,
That thou hast mercy enough in store

For such Sinners, as the Scripture saith,
That would gladly repent and follow Thy word,
Which I'll not deny, whilst I have breath,
For prison, fire, faggot,[5] or fierce sword.

Strengthen me, good Lord, thy truth to stand,
For the bloody butchers have me at their will,
With their slaughter knives ready drawn in their hands,
My simple carcass to devour and kill.

O Lord, forgive me my offence,
For I offended thee very sore;
Take therefore my sinful body from hence,
Then shall I, vile Creature, offend thee no more.

I would wish all creatures, and faithful friends,
For to keep from this Gardener's hands,
For he will bring them soon unto their ends,
With cruel torments of fierce fire brands.

I dare not presume for him to pray,
Because the truth of him it was well known,
But, since that time, he had gone astray,
And much pestilent seed abroad he hath sown.

Because that now I have so space
The cause of my death truly to show,
I trust hereafter that, by God's holy Grace,
That all faithful men shall plainly know.

To Thee, O Lord, I bequeath my spirit,
That art the Work-master of the same,
It is Thine, Lord, therefore take it of right,
My carcass on earth I leave, from whence it came.

Although to ashes it can be now burned,
I know Thou can'st raise it again

[1] *Trentals of mass* Long series of masses; *balls of lead* Papal bulls, or commands.

[2] *Masses of Requiem* Requiem masses are Roman Catholic services on behalf of the souls of the dead, during which the congregation is exhorted to pray that the soul now departed this life not be required to remain in Purgatory for a protracted period before being released to Heaven. Early Christine doctrine conceived of Heaven and Hell as stark alternatives. Belief in Purgatory seems to have developed or at least to have been affirmed in the twelfth century. The doctrine holds that whereas the most sinful souls are sent to Hell for eternal punishment, all souls are in fact sinful to some degree and hence even those who are not damned, with the exception of the particularly good, need a period of purgative suffering before they are ready for God's presence. The clergy was thought able to intercede with God on behalf of such souls so as to reduce their time in Purgatory; sacrifices, including financial sacrifice in aid of the poor or the Church, please God and allow the donor future relief from time in Purgatory. This whole doctrine was roundly condemned by Protestants, both because the corruption that they (and some Catholics) said it fostered and because Protestant belief holds that salvation depends on faith alone, not on good works. Nor, said Protestants, can Purgatory be found in the Bible, for them the only true source of doctrine.

[3] *Chauntry* Chapel specially endowed by its founder, for whom prayers are to be said during services held there.

[4] *Unto … eleven* See Luke 11.

[5] *faggot* Pile of kindling.

In the same likeness as Thou it formed,
In Heaven with Thee evermore to remain.

from Thomas Cranmer, *The Book of Common Prayer* (1552)

Thomas Cranmer's *Book of Common Prayer*, one of English literature's glories and the source of many common phrases still in use today, first came into use in 1549 as part of Edward VI's establishment of a fully Protestant Reformation in England. The book, much of it translated from the Catholic "Sarum" prayer book, was welcomed by some, but also criticized—from two directions. Conservatives such as Princess Mary (and an unknown percentage of the population) grieved that it deserted so much Catholic tradition and doctrine. Radical Protestants, such as John Hooper, said it did not go far enough; Hooper even refused to undergo the ritual making him bishop of Gloucester if his consecration had to follow the form in the new prayer book. Cranmer responded by sending Hooper to prison, and after three weeks of rethinking his objections, the radical relented and was consecrated bishop according to the new fashion. Cranmer himself, however, shared the view of some Reformers that the 1549 book had not moved far enough from its Catholic origins, and under his leadership substantial revisions were undertaken. The resulting 1552 *Book of Common Prayer*, although unable fully to escape the heritage of prayer and biblical texts that it shared with Catholic liturgical practice, was more fully Protestant.

The 1552 edition remained in use for only a very short period; when Queen Mary assumed the throne following the death of young Edward VI in 1553 she immediately brought back the Catholic (and Latin) services. In 1556 Cranmer himself was burnt at the stake for heresy. But when Elizabeth I succeeded Mary in 1558, use of the second prayer book soon resumed, although in the somewhat more moderate revised version of 1559. Further minor revisions to the *Book* were made by order of Elizabeth and James I; those made under Charles II in 1661–62, however, more significantly tilted the doctrinal balance of the prayer book toward Catholic tradition. The 1552 Book of Common Prayer, together with the modifications of 1559, nevertheless remains the basis of the Anglican services.

The Solemnization of Matrimony

First the banns must be asked three several Sundays or holy days, in the time of service, the people being present after the accustomed manner.

And if the persons that would be married dwell in diverse parishes, the banns must be asked in both parishes, and the curate of the one parish shall not solemnize matrimony betwixt them, without a certificate of the banns being thrice asked, from the curate of the other parish. At the day appointed for Solemnization of Matrimony, the persons to be married shall come into the body of the church, with their friends and neighbours. And there the Priest shall thus say,

Dearly beloved friends, we are gathered together here in the sight of God, and in the face of His congregation, to join together this man and this woman in holy matrimony, which is an honorable estate, instituted of God in Paradise, in the time of man's innocency, signifying unto us the mystical union that is betwixt Christ and His Church: which holy estate Christ adorned and beautified with his presence, and first miracle that He wrought, in Cana of Galilee, and is commended of Saint Paul to be honourable among all men; and therefore is not to be enterprised, nor taken in hand unadvisedly, lightly, or wantonly, to satisfy men's carnal lusts and appetites, like brute beasts that have no understanding: but reverently, discreetly, advisedly, soberly, and in the fear of God: duly considering the causes for which Matrimony was ordained. One was the procreation of children, to be brought up in the fear and nurture of the Lord, and praise of God. Secondly it was ordained for a remedy against sin, and to avoid fornication, that such persons as have not the gift of continency might marry, and keep themselves undefiled members of Christ's body. Thirdly, for the mutual society, help, and comfort, that the one ought to have of the other, both in prosperity and adversity; into the which holy estate these two persons present come now to be joined. Therefore if any man can show any just cause, why they may not lawfully be joined together: let him now speak, or else hereafter for ever hold his peace....

If no impediment be alleged, then shall the Curate say unto the man,

Name, Wilt thou have this woman to thy wedded wife, to live together after God's ordinance in the holy estate of matrimony? Wilt thou love her, comfort her, honour, and keep her in sickness and in health? And forsaking all other keep thee only to her, so long as you both shall live?

The man shall answer,

I will.

Then shall the Priest say to the woman,

Name, Wilt thou have this man to thy wedded husband, to live together after God's ordinance, in the holy estate of matrimony? Wilt thou obey him, and serve him, love, honor, and keep him, in sickness and in health? and forsaking all other keep thee only unto him, so long as you both shall live?

The woman shall answer,

I will.

Then shall the Minister say,
Who giveth this woman to be married unto this man?

And the Minister receiving the woman at her father or friend's hands, shall cause the man to take the woman by the right hand, and so either to give their troth to other. The man first saying,

I *Name* take thee *Name* to my wedded wife, to have and to hold from this day forward, for better, for worse, for richer, for poorer, in sickness, and in health, to love, and to cherish, till death us depart, according to God's holy ordinance: And thereto I plight thee my troth.

Then shall they loose their hands, and the woman taking again the man by the right hand shall say,

I *Name* take thee *Name* to my wedded husband, to have and to hold from this day forward, for better, for worse, for richer, for poorer, in sickness, and in health, to love, cherish, and to obey, till death us depart, according to God's holy ordinance: And thereto I give thee my troth.

Then shall they again loose their hands, and the man shall give unto the woman a ring, laying the same upon the book, with the accustomed duty to the priest and clerk. And the priest taking the ring shall deliver it unto the man, to put it upon the fourth finger of the woman's left hand. And the man taught by the priest, shall say,

With this ring I thee wed: with my body I thee worship: and with all my worldly goods I thee endow. In the name of the Father, and of the Son, and of the Holy Ghost. Amen.

Then the man leaving the ring upon the fourth finger of the woman's left hand, the Minister shall say,

Let us pray.
O Eternal God, Creator and Preserver of all mankind, Giver of all spiritual grace, the Author of everlasting life: Send Thy blessing upon these Thy servants, this man and this woman, whom we bless in Thy name, that as Isaac and Rebecca lived faithfully together; so these persons may surely perform and keep the vow and covenant betwixt them made, whereof this ring given and received is a token and pledge: and may ever remain in perfect love and peace together; and live according unto Thy laws; through Jesus Christ our Lord. Amen.

Then shall the Priest join their right hands together, and say,

Those whom God hath joined together, let no man put asunder.

The Order for the Burial of the Dead

The Priest meeting the corpse at the Church stile, shall say, Or else the priests and clerks shall sing, and so go either unto the church or towards the grave,

I am the Resurrection and the Life (sayeth the Lord): he that believeth in Me, yea though he were dead, yet shall he live. And whosoever liveth and believeth in Me, shall not die for ever. (John 11.)

I know that my Redeemer liveth, and that I shall rise out of the earth in the last day, and shall be covered again with my skin, and shall see God in my flesh: yea, and I my self shall behold Him, not with other but with these same eyes. (Job 19.)

We brought nothing into this world, neither may we carry any thing out of this world. 1 Tim. 6. The Lord giveth, and the Lord taketh away. Even as it hath pleased the Lord, so cometh things to pass: blessed be the name of the Lord. (Job 1.)

When they come at the grave, whiles the corpse is made ready to be laid into the earth, the Priest shall say, or the priest and clerks shall singe,

Man that is born of a woman, hath but a short time to live, and is full of misery: he cometh up and is cut down like a flower; he flieth as it were a shadow, and never continueth in one stay. (Job 9.) In the midst of life we be in death: of whom may we seek for succour, but of Thee, O Lord, which for our sins justly art displeased? yet, O Lord God most holy, O Lord most mighty, O holy and most merciful Saviour, deliver us not into the bitter pains of eternal death. Thou knowest, Lord, the secrets of our hearts: shut not up Thy merciful eyes to our prayers: But spare us, Lord most holy, O God most mightie, O holy and merciful Saviour, Thou most worthy judge eternal, suffer us not at our last hour for any pains of death to fall from Thee.

Then while the earth shall be cast upon the body, by some standing by, the priest shall say,

Forasmuch as it hath pleased almighty God of His great mercy to take unto Himself the soul of our dear brother here departed: we therefore commit his body to the ground, earth to earth, ashes to ashes, dust to dust, in sure and certain hope of resurrection to eternal life, through our Lord Jesus Christ, who shall change our vile body, that it may be like to His glorious body, according to the mighty working whereby He is able to subdue all things to himself.

Then shall be said or sung,

I heard a voice from heaven, saying unto me: Write from henceforth, blessed are the dead which die in the Lord. Even so sayth the spirit, that they rest from their labours. (Job 11.) …

The Collect

O Merciful God, the Father of our Lord Jesus Christ, who is the resurrection and the life, in whom whosoever believeth, shall live though he die; and whosoever liveth and believeth in Him, shall not die eternally: who also taught us (by His holy Apostle Paul) not to be sorry, as men without hope, for them that sleep in Him: We meekly beseech Thee (O Father) to raise us from the death of sin unto the life of righteousness, that when we shall depart this life, we may rest in Him, as our hope is this our brother doeth; and that at the general resurrection in the last day, we may be found acceptable in Thy sight, and receive that blessing which Thy well beloved Son shall then pronounce to all that love and fear Thee, saying: Come, ye blessed children of My Father, receive the kingdom prepared for you from the beginning of the world. Grant this we beseech Thee, O merciful Father, through Jesus Christ our mediator and redeemer. Amen.

John Foxe

John Foxe (1516–87) wrote an extended (though unfinished) martyrology in Latin when he was living on the Continent during the reign of Queen Mary; it was published under the title *Rerum in Ecclesia Gestorum ... Commentari* ("Commentary on the Story of Things Ecclesiastial") in 1559. The first English edition of the *Actes and Monuments of these Latter and Perilous Dayes, Touching Matters of the Church* appeared in 1563. Titles of subsequent editions varied considerably (*Actes and Monuments of Things Passed in Every King's Time, in this Realm, Especially in the Church of England*; *Acts and Monuments of Martyrs, with a General Discourse of these Latter Persecutions and Tumults, Stirred up by Roman Prelates in the Church*) but were always extensive. Not surprisingly, the work has come to be referred to simply as *Acts and Monuments*, or alternatively as Foxe's *Book of Martyrs*.

Included below are a few brief excerpts dealing with generalities, including an influential essay Foxe added to the 1570 edition arguing that the invention of the printing press was a gift from God to further the spread of Protestantism. These selections are followed by Foxe's famous account of the martydom of Bishops Ridley and Latimer in 1555. Also included are several illustrations; it has been widely speculated that the visual depictions of martyrdom that accompanied Foxe's text contributed significantly to the continuing popularity of the book.

from John Foxe, *Acts and Monuments of These Latter and Perilous Days* (1563)

... King Henry by Parliament according to God's Word put down the Pope: the clergy consented, and all men openly by oath refused this usurped supremacy, knowing by God's Word Christ to be Head of the Church, and every king in his realm to have under and next unto Christ, the chief sovereignty. King Edward also by Parliament according to God's Word, set the marriage of priests at liberty, abolished the popish and idolatrous Mass, changed the Latin service, and set up the holy Communion: the whole clergy consented hereunto: many of them set it forth by their preaching: and all they by practicing confirmed the same.

Notwithstanding, now when the state is altered, and the laws changed, the Papistical clergy, with other, like worldlings, as men neither fearing God, neither fleeing worldly shame, neither yet regarding their consciences, oaths, or honesty, like wavering weathercocks, turn round about, and putting on harlots' foreheads, sing a new song, and cry with an impudent mouth: come again, come again to the Catholic Church, meaning the anti-Christian Church of Rome which is the synagogue of Satan, and the very sink of all superstition, heresy, and idolatry....

The Apostles were beaten for their boldness, and they rejoiced that they suffered for Christ's cause. Ye have also provided rods for us, and bloody whips: yet when ye have done that which God's hand and counsel hath determined that ye shall do, be it life or death, I trust that God will so assist us by His holy spirit, and grace, that we shall patiently suffer it, and praise God for it.

THE BENEFIT AND INVENTION OF PRINTING (added in 1570)

In following the course and order of years, we find this foresaid Year of Our Lord 1450 to be famous and memorable, for the divine and miraculous invention of printing.... The first inventor thereof (as most agree) is thought to be a German dwelling first in Strasbourg, afterward citizen of Mainz, named John Faustus, a goldsmith. The occasion of this invention first was by engraving the letters of the alphabet in metal: who then laying black ink upon the metal, gave the form of the letters in paper. The man being industrious and active perceiving that, thought to proceed further, and to prove whether it would frame as well in words and in whole sentences as it did in letters. Which when he perceived to come well to pass, he made certain other of his counsel, one John Gutenberg and Peter Schaeffer, binding them by their oath to keep silence for a season. After 10 years, John Gutenberg, copartner with Faustus, began then first to broach the matter at Strasbourg. The

Art being yet but rude, in process of time was set forward by inventive wits, adding more and more to the perfection thereof....

Printing came of God. Notwithstanding what man soever was the instrument, without all doubt God Himself was the ordainer and disposer thereof.... Now to consider to what end and purpose the Lord hath given this gift of printing to the earth, and to what great utility and necessity it serveth, it is not hard to judge.... God of His secret judgement, seeing time to help His church, hath found a way by this faculty of printing, not only to confound his[1] life and conversation, which before he could not abide to be touched, but also to cast down the foundation of his standing, that is, to examine, confute, and detect his doctrine, laws, and institution most detestable, in such sort, that though his life were never so pure: yet his doctrine standing, as it doth, no man is so blind, but may see, that either the Pope is Antichrist, or else that Antichrist is near cousin to the Pope: And all this doth, and will hereafter more and more appear, by printing.

The reason whereof is this: for that hereby tongues are known, knowledge groweth, judgement increaseth, books are dispersed, the Scripture is seen, the doctors be read, stories be opened, times compared, truth discerned, falsehood detected, and with finger pointed, and all (as I said) through the benefit of printing. Wherefore I suppose that either the Pope must abolish printing, or he must seek a new world to reign over: for else, as this world standeth, printing, doubtless, will abolish him. Both the Pope, and all his College of Cardinals, must this understand, that through the light of printing, the world beginneth now to have eyes to see, and heads to judge. He can not walk so invisible in a net, but he will be spied.... So that either the Pope must abolish knowledge and printing, or printing at length will root him out. By reason whereof, as printing of books ministered matter of reading: so reading brought learning: learning showed light, by the brightness whereof blind ignorance was suppressed, error detected, and finally God's glory, with truth of His word, advanced.

[1] *his* I.e., the Pope's.

Bishop Ridley and Bishop Latimer

These reverend prelates suffered October 17, 1555, at Oxford, on the same day Wolsey and Pygott[2] perished at Ely. Pillars of the Church and accomplished ornaments of human nature, they were the admiration of the realm, amiably conspicuous in their lives, and glorious in their deaths.

Dr. Ridley was born in Northumberland, was first taught grammar at Newcastle, and afterward removed to Cambridge, where his aptitude in education raised him gradually until he came to be the head of Pembroke College, where he received the title of Doctor of Divinity. Having returned from a trip to Paris, he was appointed chaplain by Henry VIII and Bishop of Rochester, and was afterwards translated to the see of London in the time of Edward VI.

To his sermons the people resorted, swarming about him like bees, coveting the sweet flowers and wholesome juice of the fruitful doctrine, which he did not only preach, but showed the same by his life, as a glittering lantern to the eyes and senses of the blind, in such pure order that his very enemies could not reprove him in any one jot....

Dr. Ridley was first in part converted by reading Bertram's book on the Sacrament, and by his conferences with Archbishop Cranmer and Peter Martyr.

When Edward VI was removed from the throne, and the bloody Mary succeeded, Bishop Ridley was immediately marked as an object of slaughter. He was first sent to the Tower, and afterward, at Oxford, was consigned to the common prison of Bocardo, with Archbishop Cranmer and Mr. Latimer. Being separated from them, he was placed in the house of one Irish, where he remained until the day of his martyrdom, from 1554, until October 16, 1555....

This old practiced soldier of Christ, Master Hugh Latimer, was the son of one Hugh Latimer, of Thurkesson in the county of Leicester, a husbandman,

[2] *Wolsey and Pygott* William Wolsey and Robert Pygott were burnt at the stake for their Protestant beliefs at Ely in 1555.

of a good and wealthy estimation; where also he was born and brought up until he was four years of age, or thereabout: at which time his parents, having him as then left for their only son, with six daughters, seeing his ready, prompt, and sharp wit, purposed to train him up in erudition, and knowledge of good literature; wherein he so profited in his youth at the common schools of his own country, that at the age of fourteen years, he was sent to the University of Cambridge; where he entered into the study of the school divinity of that day, and was from principle a zealous observer of the Romish superstitions of the time. In his oration when he commenced bachelor of divinity, he inveighed against the reformer Melanchthon,[1] and openly declaimed against good Mr. Stafford, divinity lecturer in Cambridge.

Mr. Thomas Bilney, moved by a brotherly pity towards Mr. Latimer, begged to wait upon him in his study, and to explain to him the groundwork of his (Mr. Bilney's) faith. This blessed interview effected his conversion: the persecutor of Christ became his zealous advocate, and before Dr. Stafford died he became reconciled to him.

Once converted, he became eager for the conversion of others, and commenced to be public preacher, and private instructor in the university. His sermons were so pointed against the absurdity of praying in the Latin tongue, and withholding the oracles of salvation from the people who were to be saved by belief in them, that he drew upon himself the pulpit animadversions of several of the resident friars and heads of houses, whom he subsequently silenced by his severe criticisms and eloquent arguments. This was at Christmas, 1529. At length Dr. West preached against Mr. Latimer at Barwell Abbey, and prohibited him from preaching again in the churches of the university, notwithstanding which, he continued during three years to advocate openly the cause of Christ, and even his enemies confessed the power of those talents he possessed. Mr. Bilney remained here some time with Mr. Latimer, and thus the place where they frequently walked together obtained the name of Heretics' Hill.

Mr. Latimer at this time traced out the innocence of a poor woman, accused by her husband of the murder of her child. Having preached before King Henry VIII at Windsor, he obtained the unfortunate mother's pardon. This, with many other benevolent acts, served only to excite the spleen of his adversaries. He was summoned before Cardinal Wolsey for heresy, but being a strenuous supporter of the King's supremacy, in opposition to the Pope's, by favor of Lord Cromwell and Dr. Buts (the king's physician), he obtained the living of West Kingston, in Wiltshire. For his sermons here against Purgatory, the immaculacy of the Virgin, and the worship of images, he was cited to appear before Warham, Archbishop of Canterbury, and John, Bishop of London. He was required to subscribe certain articles, expressive of his conformity to the accustomed usages; and there is reason to think, after repeated weekly examinations, that he did subscribe, as they did not seem to involve any important article of belief.

Guided by Providence, he escaped the subtle nets of his persecutors, and at length, through the powerful friends before mentioned, became Bishop of Worcester, in which function he qualified or explained away most of the papal ceremonies he was for form's sake under the necessity of complying with. He continued in this active and dignified employment some years.

Beginning afresh to set forth his plow he labored in the Lord's harvest most fruitfully, discharging his talent as well in diverse places of this realm, as before the King at the court. In the same place of the inward garden, which was before applied to lascivious and courtly pastimes, there he dispensed the fruitful Word of the glorious Gospel of Jesus Christ, preaching there before the King and his whole court, to the edification of many....

By the strength of his own mind, or of some inward light from above, he had a prophetic view of what was to happen to the Church in Mary's reign, asserting that he was doomed to suffer for the truth ... Soon after Queen Mary was proclaimed, a messenger was sent to summon Mr. Latimer to town, and there is reason to believe it was wished that he should make his escape.

Thus Master Latimer coming up to London, through Smithfield (where merrily he said that Smithfield had long groaned for him), was brought before the Council, where he patiently bore all the

[1] *Melanchthon* Philip Melanchthon (1497–1560), a leading Lutheran reformer.

mocks and taunts given him by the scornful papists. He was cast into the Tower, where he, being assisted with the heavenly grace of Christ, sustained imprisonment a long time, notwithstanding the cruel and unmerciful handling of the lordly papists, which thought then their kingdom would never fall; he showed himself not only patient, but also cheerful in and above all that which they could or would work against him. Yea, such a valiant spirit the Lord gave him, that he was able not only to despise the terribleness of prisons and torments, but also to laugh to scorn the doings of his enemies.

Mr. Latimer, after remaining a long time in the Tower, was transported to Oxford, with Cranmer and Ridley, the disputations at which place have been already mentioned in a former part of this work. He remained imprisoned until October, and the principal objects of all his prayers were three—that he might stand faithful to the doctrine he had professed, that God would restore His Gospel to England once again, and preserve the Lady Elizabeth to be queen; all of which happened. When he stood at the stake without the Bocardo gate,[1] Oxford, with Dr. Ridley, and fire was putting to the pile of faggots, he raised his eyes benignantly towards heaven, and said, "God is faithful, who will not suffer you to be tempted above that ye are able." His body was forcibly penetrated by the fire, and the blood flowed abundantly from the heart; as if to verify his constant desire that his heart's blood might be shed in defence of the Gospel. His polemical and friendly letters are lasting monuments of his integrity and talents. It has been before said, that public disputation took place in April, 1554, new examinations took place in October, 1555, previous to the degradation and condemnation of Cranmer, Ridley, and Latimer. We now draw to the conclusion of the lives of the two last.

Dr. Ridley, the night before execution, was very facetious, had himself shaved, and called his supper a marriage feast; he remarked upon seeing Mrs. Irish (the keeper's wife) weep, "Though my breakfast will be somewhat sharp, my supper will be more pleasant and sweet."

The place of death was on the north side of the town, opposite Balliol College. Dr. Ridley was dressed in a black gown furred, and Mr. Latimer had a long shroud on, hanging down to his feet. Dr. Ridley, as he passed Bocardo, looked up to see Dr. Cranmer, but the latter was then engaged in disputation with a friar. When they came to the stake, Mr. Ridley embraced Latimer fervently, and bid him: "Be of good heart, brother, for God will either assuage the fury of the flame, or else strengthen us to abide it." He then knelt by the stake, and after earnestly praying together, they had a short private conversation. Dr. Smith then preached a short sermon against the martyrs, who would have answered him, but were prevented by Dr. Marshal, the vice-chancellor. Dr. Ridley then took off his gown and tippet, and gave them to his brother-in-law, Mr. Shipside. He gave away also many trifles to his weeping friends, and the populace were anxious to get even a fragment of his garments. Mr. Latimer gave nothing, and from the poverty of his garb, was soon stripped to his shroud, and stood venerable and erect, fearless of death.

Dr. Ridley being unclothed to his shirt, the smith placed an iron chain about their waists, and Dr. Ridley bid him fasten it securely; his brother having tied a bag of gunpowder about his neck, gave some also to Mr. Latimer.

Dr. Ridley then requested of Lord Williams, of Fame, to advocate with the Queen the cause of some poor men to whom he had, when bishop, granted leases, but which the present bishop refused to confirm. A lighted faggot was now laid at Dr. Ridley's feet, which caused Mr. Latimer to say: "Be of good cheer, Ridley; and play the man. We shall this day, by God's grace, light up such a candle in England, as I trust, will never be put out."

When Dr. Ridley saw the fire flaming up towards him, he cried with a wonderful loud voice, "Lord, Lord, receive my spirit." Master Latimer, crying as vehemently on the other side, "Father of heaven, receive my soul!" received the flame as it were embracing of it. After that he had stroked his face with his hands, and as it were, bathed them a little in the fire, he soon died (as it appeareth) with very little pain or none.

Well! dead they are, and the reward of this world they have already. What reward remaineth for them in heaven, the day of the Lord's glory, when He cometh

[1] *Bocardo gate* Gate of the Bocardo prison, demolished in 1771.

with His saints, shall declare.

In the following month died Stephen Gardiner, Bishop of Winchester and Lord Chancellor of England. This papistical monster was born at Bury, in Suffolk, and partly educated at Cambridge. Ambitious, cruel, and bigoted, he served any cause; he first espoused the King's part in the affair of Anne Boleyn: upon the establishment of the Reformation he declared the supremacy of the Pope an execrable tenet; and when Queen Mary came to the crown, he entered into all her papistical bigoted views, and became a second time Bishop of Winchester. It is conjectured it was his intention to have moved the sacrifice of Lady Elizabeth, but when he arrived at this point, it pleased God to remove him.

It was on the afternoon of the day when those faithful soldiers of Christ, Ridley and Latimer, perished, that Gardiner sat down with a joyful heart to dinner. Scarcely had he taken a few mouthfuls, when he was seized with illness, and carried to his bed, where he lingered fifteen days in great torment, unable in any wise to evacuate, and burnt with a devouring fever, that terminated in death. Execrated by all good Christians, we pray the Father of mercies, that he may receive that mercy above he never imparted below.

Anonymous, *Nicholas Ridley, Bishop of London* (1555).

Anonymous, *Hugh Latimer, Bishop of Worcester* (1555).

Anonymous woodcut, *The Burning of Latimer and Ridley at Oxford, October 1555.* This illustration was allotted a full page in the 1563 edition of Foxe's *Acts and Monuments.*

Anonymous woodcut, *Bishop Bonner Flogging a Protestant.* Edmund Bonner, Archbishop of London during the reign of Queen Mary, played a leading role in the persecution of Protestants—and is a chief villain of Foxe's. This illustration appeared in the original 1570 edition of *Acts and Monuments.*

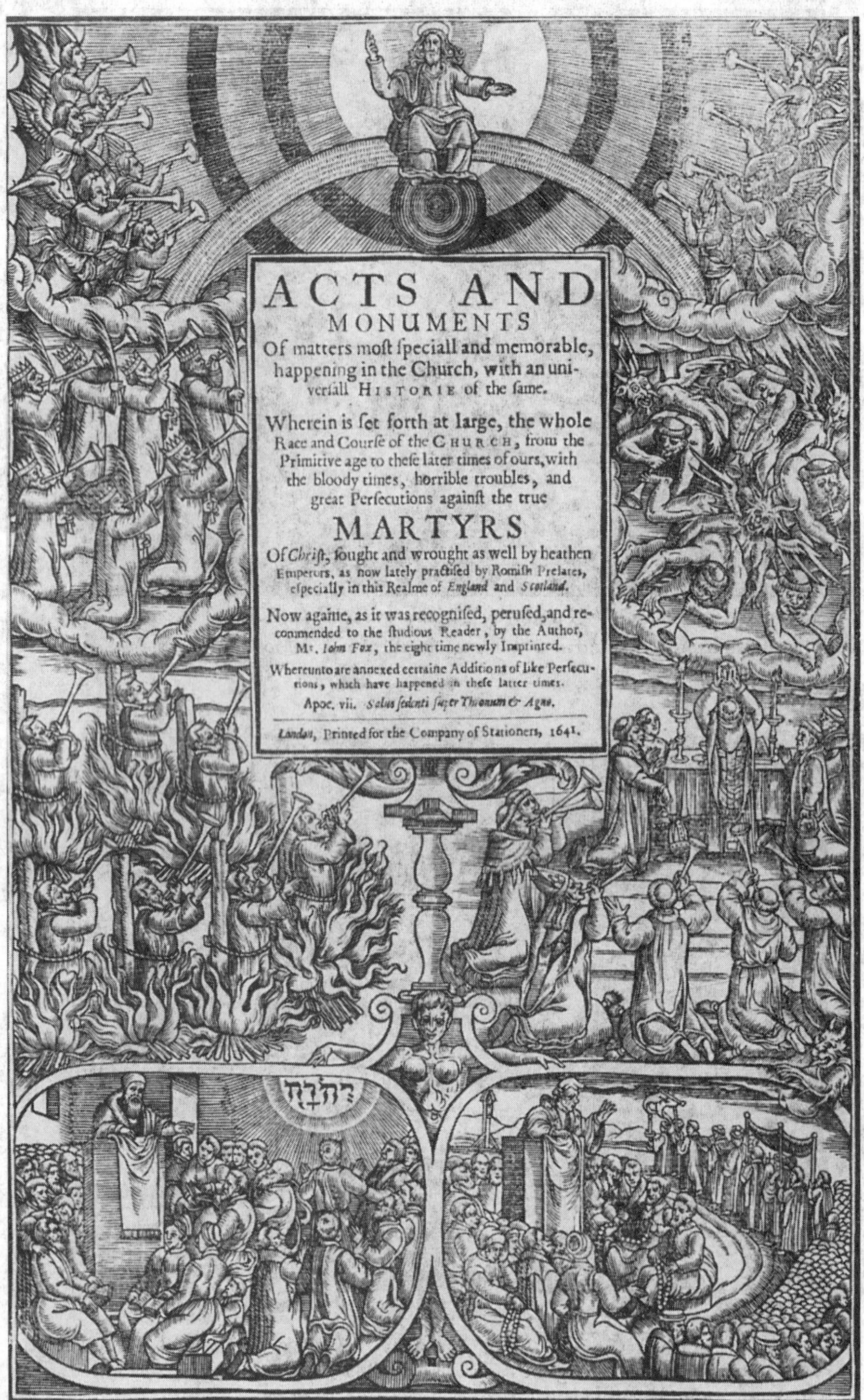

ACTS AND MONUMENTS

Of matters most speciall and memorable, happening in the Church, with an universall HISTORIE of the same.

Wherein is set forth at large, the whole Race and Course of the CHURCH, from the Primitive age to these later times of ours, with the bloody times, horrible troubles, and great Persecutions against the true

MARTYRS

Of *Christ*, sought and wrought as well by heathen Emperors, as now lately practised by Romish Prelates, especially in this Realme of *England* and *Scotland*.

Now againe, as it was recognised, perused, and recommended to the studious Reader, by the Author, Mr. *John Fox*, the eight time newly Imprinted.

Whereunto are annexed certaine Additions of like Persecutions, which have happened in these latter times.

Apoc. vii. *Salus sedenti super Thronum & Agno.*

London, Printed for the Company of Stationers, 1641.

Title page, Foxe's *Acts and Monuments*, 1641 edition.

from Lady Margaret Hoby, Diaries (1599–1603)

Hoby's diaries extend from 1599 to 1605; she is the first English woman whose diaries have survived. (The practice of diary writing was rare or non-existent before the sixteenth century.)

1599

[Friday August 17]
After private prayers I went about the house and read of the Bible and wrought[1] till dinner time: and after dinner it pleased for a just punishment to correct my sins to send me feebleness of stomach and pain of my head that kept me upon my bed till five o'clock: at which time I arose, having release of my sickness, according to the wonted kindness of the Lord who after He had let me see how I had offended, that so I might take better heed to my body and soul hereafter, with a gentle correction let me feel He was reconciled to me: at which time I went to private prayer and praises, examination, and so to work till supper time: which done I heard the lecture and after I had walked an hour with Mr. Hoby I went to bed.

[Monday September 10]
After private prayers I went about the house, and then ate my breakfast: then I walked to the church with Mr. Hoby: after that I wrought a little and neglected my custom of prayer for which as for many other sins it pleased the Lord to punish me with an inward assault: But I know the Lord hath pardoned it because He is true of His promise, and if I had not taken this course of examination I think I had forgotten it: after dinner I walked with Mr. Hoby and after he was gone I went to get tithe apples:[2] after I came home, I prayed with Mr. Rhodes,[3] and after that privately by myself and took examination of myself: and so after I had walked a while I went to supper, after that to the lecture and so to bed.

[The Lord's Day, September 16]
After I had prayed privately I went to church and from thence returning I praised God both for the enabling the minister so profitably to declare the word as he had, and my self to hear with that comfort and understanding I did: after dinner I walked with Mr. Hoby till catechizing was done and then I went to church: after the sermon I looked upon a poor man's leg[4] and after that I walked and read a sermon of Gifford upon the Song of Solomon: then I examined myself and prayed: after supper I was busy with Mr. Hoby till prayer time after which I went to bed.

[Thursday, December 20]
After private prayers, I did eat my breakfast then I writ in my sermon book: after I prayed then I dined, and almost I writ in my Bible all the afternoon: then I dispatched some business in the house and then prayed and examined myself ...

1600

[The 5 day of the week February 1]
After I was ready I went about the house and then prayed, brake my fast, dressed a poor boy's leg that was hurt, and Jurden's[5] hand: after took a lecture, read of the Bible, prayed and so went to dinner: after, I went down a while, then wrought till four o'clock and took order for supper, and then talked a while with Mr. Hoby and after went to private prayer and meditation: after to supper then to public prayers and lastly to bed.

[The 4 day after the Lord's Day, April 10]
After private prayers I went to the minister where I heard Mr. Smith defend the truth against the papist: The question being whether the regenerate do sin: after I came home I went to dinner: I went to the church where I heard Mr. Stuart handle this question between the papists and us—whether we were justified by faith

[1] *wrought* Worked (probably at needlepoint or embroidery).

[2] *tithe apples* Of all agricultural produce a tenth (or tithe) was typically paid to support the local church.

[3] *Mr. Rhodes* Chaplain to Lady Hoby.

[4] *looked upon a poor man's leg* I.e., with a view to providing medical assistance. At the time most small communities lacked trained physicians.

[5] *Jurden's* A servant of Lady Hoby's.

or work:[1] after I came to my lodging and after I had prayed I went and talked with my cousin Bouser: then I went to Mr. Doctor Benet's and after supper I prayed publicly with Mr. Rhodes, and so went to bed.

1601

[The 5 day of May 1601]
After prayers I went to the church where I heard a sermon: after I came home and heard Mr. Rhodes read: after dinner I went abroad and when I was come home I dressed some sores: after I heard Mr. Rhodes read and wrought within a while: after I went to see a calf at Munckman's which had two great heads, four ears, and had to either head a throat pipe besides: the heads had long hairs like bristles about the mouths, such as no other cow hath: the hinder legs had no parting from the rump, but grew backward, and were no longer but from the first joint: also the back bone was parted about the middest of the back, and a round hole was in the midst in to the body of the calf: but one would have thought that to have come of some stroke it might get in the cow's belly: after this I came in to private meditation and prayer.

[August 26]
This day in the afternoon I had had a child brought to see that was born at Silpho, one Talliour's son who had no fundament, and had no passage for excrements but at the mouth: I was earnestly entreated to cut the place to see if any passage could be made, but although I cut deep and searched there was none to be found.

[December 26]
Was young Farley slain by his father's man one that the young man had before threatened to kill and for that end prosecuting him: the man, having a pike staff in his hand, run him into the eye and so into the brain: he never spoke after: this judgment is worth noting, this young man being extraordinary profane, as once causing a horse to be brought into the church of God and there christening him with a name which horrible blasphemy the Lord did not leave unrevenged, even in this world, for example t'others.

1602

[May 6]
I praise God I had health of body: howsoever justly God hath suffered Satan to afflict my mind, yet my hope is that my Redeemer will bring my soul out of troubles, that it may praise His name: and so I will wait with patience for deliverance.

[The Lord's Day, June 27]
Until this day I have continued in bodily health notwithstanding Satan hath not ceased to cast his malice upon me: but temptations hath exercised me, and it hath pleased my God to deliver me from all: Mrs. Girlington with her daughter and son-in-law came but after the sermon: and so, when the Communion was ended and after dinner, we all heard the afternoon exercises[2] together.

1603

[March 26]
This day being the Lord's Day was the death of the Queen published and our now King James of Scotland proclaimed King to succeed her: God send him a long and happy reign, Amen.

[October 23]
This day I heard the plague was so great at Whitby that those which were clear shut themselves up, and the infected that escaped did go abroad: likewise it was reported that, at London, the number was taken of the living and not of the dead: Lord grant that these judgments may cause England with speed to turn to the Lord.

---

[1] *faith or work* A key difference between Protestant and Roman Catholic faiths was (and is) that Protestants believe in salvation on the basis of faith alone, Roman Catholics on the basis of both faith and the "works" (good deeds) one has done while on earth.

[2] *exercises* Religious exercises or devotions.

from Owen Felltham, *Resolves* (1623)

Felltham's *Resolves* brings together reflective essays on a broad variety of topics, including poverty, differences between men and women, and the nature of poetry. The following excerpt is from the essay entitled "Of Puritans."

I find many that are called *Puritans*; yet few, or none that will own the name. Whereof the reason sure is this; that 'tis for the most part held a name of infamy; and is so new, that it hath scarcely yet obtained a definition: nor is it an appellation derived from one man's name, whose tenets we may find, digested into a volume: whereby we do much err in the application. It imports a kind of excellency above another; which man (being conscious of his own frail bendings) is ashamed to assume to himself. So that I believe there are men which *would be* Puritans: but indeed not any that *are*. One will have him one that lives religiously, and will not revel it in a shoreless excess. Another, him that separates from our divine assemblies. Another, him that in some tenets only is peculiar. Another, him that will not swear.[1] Absolutely to define him is a work, I think, of difficulty; some I know that rejoice in the name; but sure they be such, as least understand it. As he is more generally in these times taken, I suppose we may call him a Church-rebel, or one that would exclude order, that his brain might rule. To decline offences; to be careful and conscionable in our several actions, is a purity that every man ought to labour for, which we may well do, without a sullen segregation from all society.... If mirth and recreations be lawful, sure such a one may lawfully use it. If wine were given to cheer the heart, why should I fear to use it for that end? Surely, the merry soul is freer from intended mischief, than the thoughtful man. A bounded mirth, is a patent adding time and happiness to the crazed life of man.... God delights in nothing more than in a cheerful heart, careful to perform him service. What parent is it, that rejoiceth not to see his child pleasant, in the limits of a filial duty? I know, we read of Christ's weeping, not of his laughter: yet we see, he graceth a feast with his first miracle; and that a feast of joy: And can we think that such a meeting could pass without the noise of laughter? What a lump of quickened care is the melancholic man! Change anger into mirth, and the precept will hold good still: Be merry, but sin not. As there be many, that in their life assume too great a liberty; so I believe there are some, that abridge themselves of what they might lawfully use. Ignorance is an ill steward, to provide for either soul, or body. A man that submits to reverent order, that sometimes unbends himself in a moderate relaxation; and in all, labours to approve himself, in the sereneness of a healthful conscience: such a Puritan I will love immutably. But when a man, in things but ceremonial,[2] shall spurn at the grave authority of the Church, and ... out of a blind and uncharitable pride, censure and scorn others as reprobates: or out of obstinacy, fill the world with brawls about undeterminable tenets: I shall think him one of those, whose opinion hath fevered his zeal to madness and distraction. I have more faith in one Solomon, than in a thousand Dutch parlours of such opinionists.[3] Behold then, what I have seen good! That it is comely to eat, and to drink, and to take pleasure in all his labour wherein he travaileth under the sun, the whole number of the days of his life, which God giveth him. For, this is his portion. Nay, "there is no profit to man, but that he eat, and drink, and delight his soul with the profit of his labour." For, he that saw other things but vanity, saw this also, that it was the hand of God. Me thinks the reading of Ecclesiastes, should make a Puritan undress his brain, and lay off all those fanatic toys that jingle about his understanding. For my own part, I think the world hath not better men, than some that suffer under that name: nor withal, more scelestic[4] villainies.[5] For, when they are once elated with that pride, they so contemn others, that they infringe the laws of all human society.

[1] *One will ... will not swear* Felltham is suggesting through these examples that it is extremely difficult to find full agreement as to the consistent parts of the "purity" in Puritanism.

[2] *but ceremonial* Merely ceremonial. (Many of the issues that Puritans raised concerned church ceremony.)

[3] *Dutch parlours of such opinionists* At this time the Dutch were more fervently Protestant than the English, and many English Puritans and radicals travelled to (or emigrated to) Holland.

[4] *scelestic* Wicked.

[5] *the world ... villainies* Some of the world's best people are Puritans—and also some of the most wickedly villainous.

A
DISCOVERY
OF
Six Women-Preachers, in *Middlesex*, *Kent*, *Cambridge*, and *Salisbury*.
WITH
A Relation of their Names, Manners, Life, and Doctrine.

Their Names.

Anne Hempstall. *Mary Bilbrow.* *Joane Banford.* *Susan May.* *Elisa. Bancroft.* *Arabella Thomas.*

Printed, 1641.

Cover, anonymous pamphlet, *A Discovery of Six Women Preachers, in Middlesex, Kent, Cambridge, and Salisbury* (c. 1641). "Discovery" in such contexts means "revelation of illicit activity." By 1641, when England was in the early stages of civil war, there had been an explosion of quasi-revolutionary activities, texts, prophecies, and sermons, many not by "Puritans," whose leaders tended to be respectable propertied gentlemen, but by members of radical sects more open to the participation of women as preachers and prophets filled with "zeal." Royal and ecclesiastical authorities tried to discredit such radicals by publicizing what they saw as their ridiculous radical excesses, whether real or not."

Sir Thomas Wyatt

c. 1503 – 1542

During Thomas Wyatt's brief, 39-year lifespan, English men and women served two kings; three lord chancellors were executed; England waged war in four other lands (Scotland, Wales, Ireland, and France); and Henry VIII married five of his six wives, most of whom met sorry ends. Wyatt lived his entire adult life in service to the court, amidst the political intrigue and turmoil that accompanied the reign of King Henry VIII, and was twice imprisoned in the Tower of London. A few of his poems portray an idyllic life in the countryside away from the machinations of the king and his courtiers, yet they can carry a subtext about the ambient political disorder or the court's political dramas. One of his most famous poems, "Whoso list to hunt," based on a sonnet written by Petrarch (1304–74), is thought to express longing for Anne Boleyn, Henry's future second wife. Wyatt wrote in many poetic forms, but he is best known for the artistry of his satires and songs and, along with Henry Howard, Earl of Surrey (1517–47), for introducing the Italian sonnet to England.

Son of Anne Skinner and Sir Henry Wyatt, Thomas Wyatt was born in 1503 into wealth and status at Allington Castle in Kent, England. His later career as a statesman followed that of his father, as did his political trials and tribulations. Henry Wyatt had been imprisoned and tortured for over two years by the court of King Richard III for his loyalty to the Tudors. When Henry Tudor became King Henry VII, the elder Wyatt was made a Privy Councillor, and he was later knighted by Henry VIII.

Although it is not certain, it appears that Thomas Wyatt entered St. John's College, Cambridge at age twelve, and that he may have graduated by the age of sixteen. He was a man of many accomplishments, adept at music and poetry as well as politics, and he soon became a valued member of King Henry's court. After serving in various minor positions, Wyatt began his diplomatic career in 1526 with missions to France, Rome, and Venice, where, we may surmise, he acquired his knowledge of Italian sonnets. (At about this time Wyatt became estranged from his wife, Elizabeth Brooke, daughter of Lord Cobham, whom he had married at a young age.) He was knighted in 1536 but soon afterward had his first falling out with King Henry and was imprisoned in the Tower of London. Wyatt might have been under suspicion of having had an affair with Anne Boleyn when she was still unmarried; Henry VIII had divorced Catherine of Aragon for Boleyn and thereby provoked England's break with the Roman Catholic Church. Although Anne and five (almost certainly wrongly accused) lovers were all executed, Wyatt was released after a month.

Most of Wyatt's work to this point had been love poems, often containing themes of disappointment or unrequited love but rarely dark in tone. By contrast, poems written after his imprisonments can express bitterness.

Wyatt eventually regained both the king's favor and his diplomatic status. Unfortunately, though, he lost a great ally upon the fall and execution of the statesman Thomas Cromwell, in 1540, and in 1541 he was imprisoned again, this time on trumped-up charges of treason. Once again he was spared and was briefly in favor with the king. Wyatt succumbed to fever the next year, however, and died in Dorset in 1542.

Few of Wyatt's poems were printed in his lifetime, but many appeared in Richard Tottel's 1557 volume *Songes and Sonettes* (later to become known as *Tottel's Miscellany*); a third of the volume is made up of Wyatt's work. Some years later, the Elizabethan critic George Puttenham summarized Sir Thomas Wyatt's importance to the English literary tradition in terms that remain broadly accepted today: "[Wyatt and Surrey] travailed into Italie, and there tasted the sweet and stately measures and stile of the Italian Poesie as novices newly crept out of the schooles of Dante, Arioste and Petrarch. They greatly pollished our rude & homely maner of vulgar Poesie, from that it had been before, and for that cause may justly be said the first reformers of our English meetre and stile."

⌘⌘⌘

Sonnets[1]

10[2]

The long love that in my thought doth harbour
And in mine heart doth keep his residence
Into my face presseth with bold pretence
And therein campeth, spreading his banner.
She that me learneth° to love and suffer *teaches*
And will° that my trust and lust's negligence *wishes*
Be reined by reason, shame,° and reverence, *modesty*
With his hardiness° taketh displeasure. *daring*
Wherewithal unto the heart's forest he fleeth,
Leaving his enterprise with pain and cry,
And there him hideth and not appeareth.
What may I do when my master feareth,
But in the field with him to live and die?
For good is the life ending faithfully.
—1557

29[3]

The pillar perished is whereto I leant,
The strongest stay of mine unquiet mind;
The like of it no man again can find—
From east to west still seeking though he went—
To mine unhap,° for hap° away hath rent *misfortune / chance*
Of all my joy the very bark and rind,
And I, alas, by chance am thus assigned
Dearly to mourn till death do it relent.° *abate*
But since that thus it is by destiny,
What can I more but have a woeful heart,
My pen in plaint,° my voice in woeful cry, *complaint, lament*
My mind in woe, my body full of smart,° *pain*
And I myself, myself always to hate
Till dreadful death do cease my doleful state?
—1557

31

Farewell, Love, and all thy laws forever.
Thy baited hooks shall tangle me no more.
Senec[4] and Plato call me from thy lore
To perfect wealth my wit for to endeavour.[5]
In blind error when I did persevere,
Thy sharp repulse, that pricketh ay so sore,
Hath taught me to set in trifles no store
And 'scape forth, since liberty is lever.° *dearer*
Therefore, farewell. Go trouble younger hearts
And in me claim no more authority.

[1] *Sonnets* For additional sonnets by Sir Thomas Wyatt, please refer to the Elizabethan Sonnet and Lyric section in this anthology.

[2] *10* This poem is an adaptation of sonnet 140 from Petrarch's *Rime sparse* (*Scattered Rhymes*), also translated by Wyatt's friend Henry Howard, Earl of Surrey.

[3] *29* An imitation of Petrarch's *Rime* 269. There has been some speculation that Wyatt here laments the execution of Thomas Cromwell, Wyatt's former patron.

[4] *Senec* Seneca, a Roman essayist and philosopher (c. 4 BCE—65 CE).

[5] *wealth* Well-being; *wit* Intellect; *endeavour* Exert.

With idle youth go use thy property,
And thereon spend thy many brittle darts.
For hitherto, though I have lost all my time,
Me lusteth° no longer rotten boughs to climb. *desire*
—1557

Epigrams

38

Alas, madam, for stealing of a kiss
Have I so much your mind there offended?
Have I then done so grievously amiss
That by no means it may be amended?
Then revenge you, and the next[1] way is this:
Another kiss shall have my life ended.
For to my mouth the first my heart did suck;
The next shall clean out of my breast it pluck.
—1557

48[2]

Vulcan[3] begat me; Minerva[4] me taught.
Nature my mother; craft nourished me year by year.[5]
Three bodies[6] are my food. My strength is in naught.[7]
Slaughter, wrath, waste, and noise are my children dear.
Guess, friend, what I am and how I am wrought:
Monster of sea or of land or of elsewhere?
Know me and use me, and I may thee defend
And, if I be thine enemy, I may thy life end.[8]
—1557

[1] *next* Nearest, most convenient.

[2] *48* The first six lines of this riddle are a translation of a Latin riddle found in *Bombarda*, by Pandolfo Collinutio.

[3] *Vulcan* The Roman god of fire and metal working.

[4] *Minerva* The Roman goddess of war, as well as wisdom.

[5] *Nature … year* I.e., the materials come from nature, but are formed through craft.

[6] *Three bodies* The ingredients of gunpowder.

[7] *is in naught* I.e., the "O" of the gun's mouth.

[8] This riddle was titled "Description of a gun" when first published in *Tottel's Miscellany*.

60

Tagus,[9] farewell, that westward with thy streams
Turns up the grains of gold already tried,° *refined*
With spur and sail for I go seek the Thames,
Gainward° the sun that show'th her wealthy pride[10] *toward*
And to the town which Brutus sought by dreams[11]
Like bended moon doth lend her lusty° side. *pleasant*
My king, my country, alone for whom I live,
Of mighty love the wings for this me give.
—1557

Ballads

80

They flee from me that sometime did me seek
With naked foot stalking° in my chamber. *treading softly*
I have seen them gentle, tame, and meek
That now are wild and do not remember
That sometime they put themself in danger
To take bread at my hand; and now they range,
Busily seeking with a continual change.

Thanked be fortune it hath been otherwise
Twenty times better; but once in special,
In thin array after° a pleasant guise,° *in accordance with / style*
When her loose gown from her shoulders did fall
And she me caught in her arms long and small,
Therewithal sweetly did me kiss
And softly said, "Dear heart, how like you this?"

It was no dream; I lay broad waking.° *wide awake*
But all is turned, through my gentleness,
Into a strange fashion of forsaking.
And I have leave to go of her goodness,[12]
And she also to use newfangleness.° *inconstancy*

[9] *Tagus* River in Spain, where Wyatt spent several months as a diplomat. The Tagus is known for its gold colored sand.

[10] *Gainward … pride* Unlike the Tagus, which flows westward, the Thames flows "against" the sun's path, or eastward.

[11] *the town … dreams* London. According to Geoffrey of Monmouth, Brutus, a Trojan hero and descendant of Aeneas, was visited in a dream by the goddess Diana and told to sail to the cliffs of Albion, where he could build another Troy. When he landed, he proceeded inland and founded the city that became London.

[12] *I have … goodness* I have her permission to go from her.

But since that I so kindly[1] am served,
I would fain° know what she hath deserved. *gladly*
—1557

94

Blame not my lute, for he must sound
Of this or that as liketh° me. *pleases*
For lack of wit the lute is bound
To give such tunes as pleaseth me.
Though my songs be somewhat strange,
And speaks such words as touch thy change,[2]
Blame not my lute.

My lute, alas, doth not offend,
Though that perforce he must agree
To sound such tunes as I intend
To sing to them that heareth me.
Then though my songs be somewhat plain
And toucheth° some that use to feign,[3] *comments on*
Blame not my lute.

My lute and strings may not deny,
But as I strike they must obey;
Break not them then so wrongfully,
But wreak° thyself some wiser way. *avenge*
And though the songs which I indite° *compose*
Do quit° thy change with rightful spite, *requite*
Blame not my lute.

Spite asketh spite, and changing change,
And falsed faith must needs be known;
The faults so great, the case so strange
Of right it must abroad be blown.° *proclaimed*
Then since that by thine own desert
My songs do tell how true thou art,
Blame not my lute.

Blame but thyself, that hast misdone
And well deserved to have blame;
Change thou thy way so evil begun,
And then my lute shall sound that same.

But if till then my fingers play
By thy desert their wonted way,
Blame not my lute.

Farewell, unknown, for though thou break
My strings in spite with great disdain,
Yet have I found out for thy sake
Strings for to string my lute again.
And if perchance this foolish rhyme
Do make thee blush at any time,
Blame not my lute.
—1557

Songs

109

My lute, awake! Perform the last
Labour that thou and I shall waste,
And end that I have now begun;
For when this song is sung and past,
My lute, be still for I have done.

As to be heard where ear is none,
As lead to grave in marble stone,[4]
My song may pierce her heart as soon.
Should we then sigh or sing or moan?
No, no, my lute, for I have done.

The rocks do not so cruelly
Repulse the waves continually
As she my suit and affection,
So that I am past remedy,
Whereby my lute and I have done.

Proud of the spoil that thou hast got
Of simple hearts thorough° Love's shot *through*
By whom, unkind, thou hast them won,
Think not he hath his bow forgot,
Although my lute and I have done.

Vengeance shall fall on thy disdain
That makest but game on earnest pain.
Think not alone under the sun

[1] *kindly* Naturally, according to natural laws (i.e., that women are fickle). The word also ironically suggests the modern "with kindness." Tottel amends this to "unkindly," removing the irony.

[2] *change* Change of heart.

[3] *use to feign* Wont to dissemble.

[4] *As to … stone* When sound is heard where there are no ears to hear it, or when lead (the softest metal) is able to engrave on stone.

Unquit° to cause thy lovers plain,° *unrequited / to lament*
Although my lute and I have done.

May chance[1] thee lie withered and old
The winter nights that are so cold,
Plaining in vain unto the moon.
Thy wishes then dare not be told.
Care then who list,° for I have done. *likes*

And then may chance thee to repent
The time that thou hast lost and spent
To cause thy lovers sigh and swoon.
Then shalt thou know beauty but lent,
And wish and want as I have done.

Now cease, my lute. This is the last
Labour that thou and I shall waste,
And ended is that we begun.
Now is this song both sung and past.
My lute, be still, for I have done.
—1557

123

V. Innocentia
Veritas Viat Fides
Circumdederunt me inimici mei[2]

Who list° his wealth° and ease retain, *desires / well-being*
Himself let him unknown contain.° *keep*
Press not too fast in at that gate
Where the return stands by disdain,[3]
For sure, *circa Regna tonat.*[4]

The high mountains are blasted oft
When the low valley is mild and soft.
Fortune with Health° stands at debate.° *well-being / odds*
The fall is grievous from aloft.
And sure, *circa Regna tonat.*

These bloody days have broken my heart.
My lust,° my youth did them depart, *pleasure*
And blind desire of estate.° *high status*
Who hastes to climb seeks to revert.° *fall back down*
Of truth, *circa Regna tonat.*

The Bell Tower showed me such sight
That in my head sticks day and night.
There did I learn out of a grate,° *barred window*
For all favour, glory, or might,[5]
That yet *circa Regna tonat.*

By proof, I say, there did I learn:
Wit helpeth not defence too yerne,° *willingly*
Of innocency to plead or prate.[6]
Bear low,[7] therefore; give God the stern.° *tiller*
For sure, *circa Regna tonat.*
—1969 (written 1536)

Epistolary Satires

149[8]

Mine own John Poyns,[9] since ye delight to know
The cause why that homeward I me draw
(And flee the press of courts, whereso they go,
Rather than to live thrall° under the awe *enslaved*
Of lordly looks) wrapped within my cloak,
To will and lust° learning to set a law, *pleasure*
It is not because I scorn or mock
The power of them to whom Fortune hath lent
Charge over us, of right to strike the stroke;

---

[1] *May chance* It may chance that.

[2] *V. Innocentia ... mei* This is a rebus, a puzzle in which Wyatt has arranged words to suggest a phrase. Translated from Latin, the rebus reads:
W[yatt] Innocence
Truth Wyatt Faith
My enemies surround me.
It is believed that Wyatt wrote this poem in 1536, while he was imprisoned in the Bell Tower. In May of that year, Wyatt may have witnessed Anne Boleyn's execution from his cell.

[3] *Where ... disdain* From which your forced exit will be disdained.

[4] *circa Regna tonat* Latin: [He] thunders around thrones. This line, referring to Jupiter, is taken from Seneca's *Phaedra*. The first two stanzas of Wyatt's poem are imitations of lines from that play.

[5] *For all ... might* Regardless of one's favor, glory, or might.

[6] *Wit ... prate* Intellect does not help one to earn a defense, or to plead or prattle of one's innocence.

[7] *Bear low* Keep yourself in a humble position. Also a nautical term meaning "sail with the wind."

[8] *149* This poem is an imitation of *Satira 10* (1532), by Luigi Alamanni.

[9] *John Poyns* A fellow member of the court of Henry VIII and a friend of Wyatt's.

But true it is that I have always meant
Less to esteem them than the common sort,
Of outward things that judge in their intent[1]
Without regard what doth inward resort.° *reside*
I grant sometime that of glory the fire
Doth touch my heart; me list not to report
Blame by honour and honour to desire.[2]
But how may I this honour now attain
That cannot dye the colour black a liar?[3]
My Poyns, I cannot frame my tune to feign,
To cloak the truth for praise, without desert,[4]
Of them that list all vice for to retain.
I cannot honour them that sets their part
With Venus and Bacchus[5] all their life long,
Nor hold my peace of them although I smart.
I cannot crouch nor kneel to do such wrong
To worship them like God on earth alone
That are like wolves these silly[6] lambs among.
I cannot with my words complain and moan
And suffer naught, nor smart without complaint,
Nor turn the word that from my mouth is gone.
I cannot speak and look like a saint,
Use wiles for wit° and make deceit a pleasure *intellect*
And call craft counsel, for profit still to paint.
I cannot wrest the law to fill the coffer,
With innocent blood to feed myself fat,
And do most hurt where most help I offer.
I am not he that can allow° the state *praise*
Of high Caesar and damn Cato[7] to die,
That with his death did 'scape out of the gate
From Caesar's hands, if Livy doth not lie,
And would not live where liberty was lost,
So did his heart the common wealth[8] apply.° *serve*
I am not he such eloquence to boast
To make the crow singing as the swan,
Nor call the lion of coward beasts the most,[9]
That cannot take a mouse as the cat can;
And he that dieth for hunger of the gold,
Call him Alexander,[10] and say that Pan
Passeth Apollo in music many fold;[11]
Praise Sir Thopas for a noble tale
And scorn the story that the knight told;[12]
Praise him for counsel that is drunk of ale;
Grin when he laugheth that beareth all the sway,[13]
Frown when he frowneth and groan when he is pale,
On other's lust to hang both night and day.
None of these points would ever frame° in me. *fit, prosper*
My wit is naught. I cannot learn the way.
And much the less of things that greater be,
That asken help of colours of device
To join the mean with each extremity:
With the nearest virtue to cloak alway the vice
And, as to purpose, likewise it shall fall,[14]
To press the virtue,[15] that it may not rise.
As° drunkenness good fellowship to call; *for example,*
The friendly foe with his double face
Say he is gentle and courteous therewithal;
And say that Favel° hath a goodly grace *flattery*

[1] *I have ... their intent* I.e., I have always intended to esteem the great and powerful people less than do the common sort (of people), who form their opinions ("intent") based on external appearances.

[2] *me list ... desire* I do wish to cast blame on honor, or attack honor, while at the same time desiring it.

[3] *cannot dye ... liar* Cannot see black as anything but black.

[4] *without desert* Without its being worthy or deserving.

[5] *Venus and Bacchus* Goddess of love and god of drink, here representing lust and debauchery.

[6] *silly* Simple, helpless, pitiable.

[7] *Cato* Marcus Porcius Cato, the uncle of Brutus and an opponent of Caesar's who, after Caesar's victory, committed suicide rather than submit to his tyrannical authority. The story is recorded by the historian Titus Livius (Livy), mentioned on line 40.

[8] *common wealth* Public welfare, the common good, or the state.

[9] *of coward beasts the most* King of the (cowardly) beasts.

[10] *he that ... Alexander* Alexander the Great conquered the known world. Wyatt says he will not call such a man "Alexander," a name that means "defender or protector of mankind."

[11] *Pan ... many fold* Pan, half man, half goat, was the Greek god of shepherds and flocks. He played simple music on his "Pan's pipes," or "shepherd's pipes." Apollo was the great god of, among other things, poetry, music, and the sun.

[12] *Praise ... knight told* In Chaucer's *Canterbury Tales*, Sir Thopas's tale is so ridiculous that the host asks him to stop before the end, while the knight's tale is considered by all to be the most noble.

[13] *beareth all the sway* Holds all the power.

[14] *as to ... shall fall* As shall likewise be opportune.

[15] *press the virtue* Oppress virtue, condemn it as a vice.

In eloquence; and cruelty to name
Zeal of justice and change in time and place;[1]
And he that suffereth offence without blame,[2]
Call him pitiful,° and him true and plain *compassionate*
That raileth reckless to every man's
shame;° *modesty, decency*
Say he is rude that cannot lie and feign,
The lecher a lover, and tyranny
To be the right of a prince's reign.
I cannot, I! No, no, it will not be!
This is the cause that I could never yet
Hang on their sleeves that weigh, as thou mayst see,
A chip of chance° more than a pound of wit. *good fortune*
This maketh me at home to hunt and to hawk
And in foul weather at my book to sit;
In frost and snow then with my bow to stalk.
No man doth mark whereso I ride or go;
In lusty° leas° in liberty I walk. *pleasant / pastures*
And of these news I feel nor weal° nor woe, *happiness*
Save that a clog[3] doth hang yet at my heel.
No force for that,[4] for it is ordered so
That I may leap both hedge and dike full well.
I am not now in France to judge the wine,
With savoury sauce the delicates to feel;° *smell and taste*
Nor yet in Spain where one must him incline,
Rather than to be, outwardly to seem.
I meddle not with wits that be so fine.
Nor Flanders' cheer[5] letteth not my sight to deem[6]
Of black and white, nor taketh my wit away
With beastliness they, beasts,[7] do so esteem.
Nor I am not where Christ is given in prey
For money, poison, and treason at Rome—
A common practice used night and day.
But here I am in Kent and Christendom
Among the muses, where I read and rhyme,
Where if thou list,° my Poyns, for to come, *desire*
Thou shalt be judge how I do spend my time.
—1557

IN CONTEXT

Epistolary Advice

Below is a letter from Thomas Wyatt to his son, who had recently married (at age fifteen). The letter was sent from Paris on 15 April 1537. Although a personal letter that mentions Wyatt's failed marriage, this exhortation also draws on a long tradition of epistolary advice to the young; William Cecil and Walter Ralegh contributed to the genre and Shakespeare parodies its sententiousness in *Hamlet* when Polonius gives fatherly counsel to Laertes.

In as much as now you are come to some years of understanding, and that you should gather within yourself some frame of honesty, I thought that I should not lose my labor wholly if now I did

[1] *change in time and place* I.e., the time and place in which the law was made differ from those of the crime.

[2] *suffereth ... blame* Allows offences against those who are innocent.

[3] *clog* Heavy block of wood, attached to impede motion.

[4] *No force for that* No matter.

[5] *Flanders' cheer* The Flemish were known for their love of drinking.

[6] *letteth not* Prevents; *deems* Distinguish.

[7] *beastliness* Drunkenness; *beasts* Drunks.

something advertise[1] to you to take the sure foundations and established opinions that leadeth to honesty. And here I call not "honesty" what men commonly call honesty, as reputation for riches, for authority, or some like thing, but that honesty that I dare well say your grandfather (whose soul God pardon) had rather left to me than all the lands he did leave me—that was wisdom, gentleness, soberness, desire to do good, friendliness to get the love of many, and truth[2] above all the rest. A great part to have all these things is to desire to have them: and although glory and honest name are not the very ends wherefore these things are to be followed, yet surely they must needs follow them, as light followeth fire, though it were kindled for warmth. Out of these things the chiefest and infallible ground is the dread and reverence of God, whereupon shall ensue the eschewing of the contraries of these said virtues—that is to say, ignorance, unkindness, rashness, desire of harm, unquiet enmity, hatred, many and crafty falsehood, the very root of all shame and dishonesty.

I say the only dread and reverence of God that seeth all things is the defense of the creeping in of all these mischiefs into you. As for my part, although I do not say there is no man that would his son better than I,[3] yet on my faith I had rather have you lifeless than subject to these vices. Think and imagine always that you are in [the] presence of some honest man that you know, as Sir John Russell, your father-in-law, your uncle, parson, or some other such, and you shall, if at any time you find a pleasure in naughty touches, remember what shame it were before these men to do naughtily. And sure this imagination shall cause you remember that the pleasure of a naughty deed is soon past, and that rebuke, shame, and the note[4] thereof shall remain ever. Then, if these things you take for vain imaginations, yet remember that it is certain and no imagination that you are always in the presence and sight of God: and though you see Him not, so much is the reverence the more to be had, for that He seeth and is not seen. Men punish with shame as [the] greatest punishment on earth, yea greater than death, but His punishment is first the withdrawing of His favour and grace, and in leaving His hand to rule the stern,[5] to let the ship run without guide to your own destruction, and suffereth[6] so the man that He forsaketh to run headlong, as subject to all mishaps, and at last with shameful end to everlasting shame and death. You may see continual examples both of one sort and th'other, and the better if you mark them well that yourself are come of.[7] And consider well your good grandfather what things that were in him, and his end; and they that knew him noted him thus: first and chiefly to have a great reverence of God and good opinion of Godly things, next that there was no man more pitiful,[8] no man more true of his word, no man faster to his friend, no man diligenter nor more circumspect, which thing both the kings his masters noted in him greatly. And if these things, and especially the grace of God that the fear of God always kept with him, had not been, the chances of this troublesome world that he was in had long ago overwhelmed him. This preserved him in prison from the hands of the tyrant[9] that could find in his heart to see him racked, from two years and more imprisonment in Scotland, in irons and stocks, from the danger of sudden changes and commotions diverse, until that well beloved of many, hated of none, in his fair age and good reputation, Godly and Christianly he went to Him that loved him for that he always had Him in reverence. And of myself

---

1 *advertise* Advise, counsel, explain.

2 *truth* Wyatt's word is "trougth," which suggests both "truth" and "troth"—i.e., a trustworthy integrity.

3 *that … than I* That is, would wish better for his son.

4 *rebuke … note* Notice, reputation.

5 *His … stern* In withdrawing his hand from (the ship's) steering wheel, the tiller.

6 *suffereth* Allows.

7 *better … of* If you observe well those from whom you derive—your family.

8 *pitiful* Full of pity, merciful.

9 *tyrant* Richard III.

I may be a mere example unto you of my folly and unthriftiness[1] that hath as I well deserved brought me into a thousand dangers and hazards, enmities, hatreds, imprisonments, despites[2] and indignations: but that God hath of His goodness chastised me and not cast me clean out of His favour, which thing I can impute to nothing but to the goodness of my good father, that I dare well say purchased with continual request of God His grace towards me more than I regarded or considered myself, and a little part to the small fear that I had of God in the most of my rage[3] and the little delight that I had in mischief. You therefore, if you be sure and have God in your sleeve, to call you to His grace at last, venture not hardily[4] by mine example upon naughty unthriftiness in trust of His goodness; and, besides the shame, I dare lay ten to one you shall perish in the adventure: for trust not that my wish or desire of God for you shall stand you in as much effect as I think my father's did for me: we are not all accepted of Him. Begin therefore betimes, make God and goodness your foundations. Make your examples of wise and honest me; shoot at the mark; be no mocker—mocks follow them that delight therein. He shall be sure of shame that feeleth no grief in other men's shames. Have your friends in a reverence and think unkindness to be the greatest offence, and least punished amongst men, but so much the more to be dreaded, for God is Justiser[5] upon that alone. Love well and agree with your wife, for where is noise and debate in the house, there is unquiet dwelling. And much more where it is in one bed. Frame well yourself to love, and rule well and honestly your wife as your fellow, and she shall love and reverence you as her head. Such as you are unto her, such shall she be unto you. Obey and reverence your father-in-law as you would me; and remember that long life followeth them that reverence their fathers and elders. And the blessing of God for good agreement between the wife and husband is fruit of many children, which I for the like thing do lack, and the fault is both in your mother and me, but chiefly in her.

Read oft this my letter and it shall be as though I had often written unto you. And think that I have herein printed a fatherly affection to you. If I may see that I have not lost my pain(s), mine shall be the contentation[6] and yours the profit. And upon condition that you follow my advertisement I send you God's blessing and mine, and as well to come to honesty as to increase of years.

At Paris the 15th of April, your loving father, Thomas Wyatt.

[1] *And ... unthriftiness* Prodigality and imprudence.

[2] *despites* Scorn.

[3] *rage* Irrationality, madness.

[4] *hardily* Boldly, incautiously.

[5] *Justiser* Judge, justice-maker.

[6] *contentation* Payment, satisfaction, contentment.

Henry Howard, Earl of Surrey

1517 – 1547

Like a number of other aristocrats, Henry Howard, Earl of Surrey, largely confined his literary writings to manuscript circulation among his friends and fellow members of Henry VIII's court; it was the posthumous appearance of his works in the printer Richard Tottel's *Miscellany* (1557) that won him widespread readership. His work is a landmark in the development of English literature, for he was among the first in England to import the Petrarchan sonnet, and, in his translation of Books II and IV of Virgil's *Aeneid*, the first to deploy blank verse. As a writer, Surrey was innovative; as a courtier, he was imprudent, and paid the price when the king had him beheaded.

Surrey was born in Hunsdon, Hertfordshire in 1517, eldest son of Lord Thomas Howard, third duke of Norfolk, and Lady Elizabeth Stafford. Surrey's ancestors on both sides of his family included royalty, and as a boy this talented member of one of England's greatest families spent some time at Windsor Castle with Henry VIII's illegitimate son, Henry Fitzroy, Duke of Richmond, and in 1524 was granted the title of earl. He received a sound humanist education and had early experience living abroad when his father served as Lord Lieutenant in Ireland. One of his cousins was Anne Boleyn, second of Henry VIII's six wives, who managed to prevent a proposed marriage between Surrey and the king's daughter, Mary Tudor. Instead, in 1533, Surrey married Lady Frances de Vere, the earl of Oxford's daughter, by whom he had five children. As an adult, Surrey served as a courtier and soldier; his travels in France on diplomatic or military ventures doubtless had an impact on his understanding of the Continental Renaissance in art and letters. Service to the King was a risky business during the King's later years, however, for the King was increasingly suspicious and the court, especially after the Reformation, was split into competing factions. The balance had tipped against Surrey's family in 1536 when Henry VIII married Jane Seymour, his third wife, for the Seymours, who welcomed Henry's break with the Church of Rome, were bitter rivals of the Catholic Howards and took advantage of their new power (Surrey himself seems to have leaned toward Reform, although his exact views can be debated and perhaps shifted). Thanks to probably false accusations that he had sided with a rebellion against the King, the so-called Pilgrimage of Grace, Surrey was imprisoned between 1537 and 1539. His misfortune did not last, however, for Jane Seymour died shortly after giving birth. The King married Catherine Howard, another of Surrey's cousins, bringing the Howard family back into favor, at least until Catherine was found guilty of adultery and executed in early 1542. In 1541 the King named Surrey a Knight of the Garter, and for the next five years Surrey served the King in various English wars or administrative capacities.

During these years Surrey wrote verse (including love poems, elegies, satire, Biblical paraphrases, translated sections of Virgil's *Aeneid*, and a poignant meditation on Windsor Castle). During his lifetime he published only one poem, in praise of the deceased Sir Thomas Wyatt. Shakespeare and others would often adopt his sonnet structure, which instead of Petrarch's pattern—an octave followed by a sestet—most often has three quatrains (four lines usually rhyming alternately) and a couplet (a pair of lines). We call this the Shakespearean or English form, but it was Surrey who invented it. Even more important for the future of English literature is the blank verse that Surrey developed for his translations from Virgil, a flexible and harmonious meter that English writers such as Marlowe, Shakespeare, and Milton found the best equivalent for the dactylic hexameter of Latin epic.

In 1546, Surrey was involved in another political struggle. Henry VIII's health was bad, and the court was thinking about who might be regent for his little son, the future Edward VI. Surrey dared suggest openly that his father, the earl of Norfolk, would be Protector. Norfolk was next in the line of succession after Edward, and the Seymour family convinced the King that he was planning to depose the prince after Henry died and make himself king instead. Surrey was put on trial, the legal excuse being that he had treasonably placed the royal arms and insignia on his own coat of arms. He and his father were imprisoned in the Tower and there Surrey lost his head on 10 January 1547—the last person to be executed during Henry's reign. Norfolk was also condemned to die, but the death of Henry on January 28 voided the sentence at the last minute. Surrey is buried in Framlington, Suffolk.

⌘⌘⌘

Love, that Doth Reign and Live within My Thought[1]

Love, that doth reign and live within my thought,
And built his seat within my captive breast,
Clad in the arms wherein with me he fought,
Oft in my face he doth his banner rest.
But she that taught me love and suffer pain,
My doubtful hope and eke° my hot desire *also*
With shamefast° look to shadow and refrain, *modest*
Her smiling grace converteth straight to ire.
And coward Love, then, to the heart apace
Taketh his flight, where he doth lurk and plain,° *complain*
His purpose lost, and dare not show his face.
For my lord's guilt thus faultless bide° I pain; *endure*
Yet from my lord shall not my foot remove:
Sweet is the death that takes end by love.
—1557

Set Me Whereas the Sun Doth Parch the Green[2]

Set me whereas the sun doth parch the green,
Or where his beams may not dissolve the ice,
In temperate heat where he is felt and seen;
With proud people, in presence sad and wise;
Set me in base, or yet in high degree,
In the long night or in the shortest day,
In clear weather or where mists thickest be,
In lusty° youth or when my hairs be gray; *vigorous*
Set me in earth, in heaven, or yet in hell,
In hill, in dale, or in the foaming flood;
Thrall° or at large, alive whereso I dwell, *captive*
Sick or in health, in ill fame° or in good: *repute*
Yours will I be, and with that only thought
Comfort myself when that my hap° is nought. *luck*
—1557

[1] *Love ... Thought* This sonnet is a translation of Petrarch's *Rima* 140, which Surrey's friend Wyatt also translated.

[2] *Set ... Green* Adaptation of Petrarch's *Rima* 145.

Alas! So All Things Now Do Hold Their Peace[1]

Alas! so all things now do hold their peace,
Heaven and earth disturbed in nothing.
The beasts, the air, the birds their song do cease;
The nightès chair[2] the stars about doth bring;
Calm is the sea, the waves work less and less:
So am not I, whom love, alas, doth wring,
Bringing before my face the great increase
Of my desires, whereat I weep and sing
In joy and woe, as in a doubtful ease.
For my sweet thoughts sometime do pleasure bring,
But by and by the cause of my disease° *uneasiness, distress*
Gives me a pang that inwardly doth sting,
When that I think what grief it is again
To live and lack the thing should rid my pain.

So Cruel Prison How Could Betide[3]

So cruel prison how could betide, alas,
As proud Windsor, where I, in lust and joy,
With a king's son my childish years did pass
In greater feast than Priam's sons of Troy?[4]

Where each sweet place returns a taste full sour:
The large green courts, where we were wont to hove,° *linger*
With eyes cast up unto the maidens' tower,
And easy sighs, such as folk draw in love.

The stately sales,[5] the ladies bright of hue,
The dances short, long tales of great delight,
With words and looks that tigers could but rue,[6]
Where each of us did plead the other's right.

The palm play,[7] where, despoiled° for the game, *stripped*
With dazed eyes oft we by gleams of love
Have missed the ball and got sight of our dame,
To bait° her eyes, which kept the leads[8] above. *attract*

The gravelled ground,° with sleeves tied on the helm,[9] *jousting ground*
On foaming horse, with swords and friendly hearts,
With cheer° as though the one should overwhelm,
Where we have fought and chased oft with darts.° *javelins*

With silver drops the meads yet spread for ruth,[10]
In active games of nimbleness and strength,
Where we did strain, trained by swarms of youth,
Our tender limbs that yet shot up in length.

The secret groves, which oft we made resound
Of pleasant plaint,° and of our ladies' praise, *lament*
Recording soft what grace each one had found,
What hope of speed, what dread of long delays.

The wild forest, the clothed holts° with green; *wooded hills*
With reins avaled, and swift ybreathed horse,[11]
With cry of hounds and merry blasts between,
Where we did chase the fearful hart° a force.[12] *male deer*

The void[13] walls eke° that harboured us each night; *also*
Wherewith, alas, revive within my breast

---

[1] *Alas ... Peace* Surrey's version of Petrarch's *Rima* 164.

[2] *nightès chair* The constellation Ursa Major.

[3] *So ... Betide* In 1537 Surrey was imprisoned in Windsor Castle for having struck a courtier and broken the peace in the king's domain. In this poem he remembers his earlier stay at the castle (1530–32) with Henry Fitzroy, Duke of Richmond and illegitimate son of Henry VIII. Richmond (who had married Surrey's sister in 1533) died in 1536.

[4] *Priam's ... Troy* Priam, the king of Troy at the time of the Trojan war, had fifty sons.

[5] *sales* Halls or spacious chambers (from the French "salle").

[6] *rue* Regard with compassion.

[7] *palm play* Game in which the ball was hit with the palms.

[8] *leads* Sheets of metal that covered the roofs of the courts. Spectators would watch the game from these.

[9] *helm* Helmet, to which jousters would tie a lady's sleeve (then a separate, ornamental covering) as a token of her favor.

[10] *With ... ruth* I.e., the meadows (meads) were still covered with dew; *ruth* Compassion.

[11] *avaled* Slackened; *swift ybreathed* Panting.

[12] *chase ... a force* Run down.

[13] *void* I.e., empty. In royal houses it was customary for all tapestries and wall-hangings to be taken down when the resident members of the court were not at home.

The sweet accord, such sleeps as yet delight,
The pleasant dreams, the quiet bed of rest;

The secret thoughts imparted with such trust,
The wanton talk, the divers change of play,
The friendship sworn, each promise kept so just,
Wherewith we past the winter night away.

And with this thought the blood forsakes my face,
The tears berain° my cheeks of deadly hue, *rain upon*
The which, as soon as sobbing sighs, alas,
Upsupped° have, thus I my plaint renew: *swallowed*

"O place of bliss! renewer of my woes!
Give me accompt,° where is my noble fere,° *account/ companion*
Whom in thy walls thou didst each night enclose,
To other lief;° but unto me most dear?" *precious*

Each stone, alas, that doth my sorrow rue,
Returns thereto a hollow sound of plaint.
Thus I alone, where all my freedom grew,
In prison pine with bondage and restraint;

And with remembrance of the greater grief,
To banish the less, I find my chief relief.
—1557

Wyatt Resteth Here

Wyatt resteth here, that quick° could never rest; *alive*
Whose heavenly gifts increased by disdain,° *malice*
And virtue sank the deeper in his breast:
Such profit he by envy could obtain.

A head where wisdom mysteries° did frame, *profound thoughts*
Whose hammers beat still in that lively brain
As on a stith,° where that some work of fame *anvil*
Was daily wrought to turn to Britain's gain.

A visage stern and mild, where both did grow
Vice to contemn,° in virtue to rejoice; *scorn*
Amid great storms, whom grace assured so,
To live upright and smile at fortune's choice.

A hand that taught what might be said in rhyme;
That reft° Chaucer the glory of his wit— *robbed*
A mark the which (unperfected for time[1])
Some may approach, but never none shall hit.

A tongue that served in foreign realms his king;
Whose courteous talk to virtue did inflame
Each noble heart: a worthy guide to bring
Our English youth, by travail, unto fame.° *good character*

An eye whose judgment no affect° could blind, *affection*
Friends to allure and foes to reconcile;
Whose piercing look did represent a mind
With virtue fraught, reposed, void of guile.

A heart where dread yet never so impressed
To hide the thought that might the truth advance;
In neither fortune loft,° nor yet repressed, *lifted*
To swell in wealth or yield unto mischance.

A valiant corps° where force and beauty met, *body*
Happy—alas, too happy, but for foes;
Lived and ran the race that nature set,
Of manhood's shape, where she the mold did lose.

But to the heavens that simple° soul is fled, *free from guile*
Which left with such as covet° Christ to know[2] *desire*
Witness of faith that never shall be dead;
Sent for our health, but not received so.

Thus, for our guilt, this jewel have we lost;
The earth his bones, the heavens possess his ghost.
—1542

from *Certain Books of Virgil's Aeneis: Book 2*

The Greekës chieftains, all irked° with the war *wearied*
Wherein they wasted had so many years,
And oft repulsed by fatal destiny,
A huge horse made, high raised like a hill,

[1] *for time* For want of time.

[2] *such as covet Christ to know* I.e., Christians.

By the divine science of Minerva;[1]
Of cloven fir compacted were his ribs;
For their return a feigned sacrifice,
The fame whereof so wandered it at point.[2]
In the dark bulk they closed bodies of men,
Chosen by lot, and did enstuff[3] by stealth
The hollow womb with armed soldiers.
There stands in sight an isle hight° Tenedos, *called*
Rich and of fame while Priam's[4] kingdom stood,
Now but a bay and road[5] unsure for ship.
Hither them secretly the Greeks withdrew,
Shrouding themselves under the desert shore;
And, weening° we they had been fled and gone, *believing*
And with that wind had fet° the land of Greece, *reached*
Troia discharged her long continued dole.° *grief*
The gates cast up, we issued out to play,
The Greekish camp desirous to behold,
The places void, and the forsaken coasts.
Here Pyrrhus' band, there fierce Achilles', pight;[6]
Here rode their ships; there did their battles[7] join.
Astonnied,° some the scathful° gift beheld, *astonished / harmful*
Behight° by vow unto the chaste Minerve, *dedicated*
All wond'ring at the hugeness of the horse.
And first of all Timœtes gan° advise *did*
Within the walls to lead and draw the same,
And place it eke° amid the palace court— *moreover*
Whether of guile, or Troia's fate it would.[8]
Capys, with some of judgment more discreet,
Willed° it to drown, or underset with flame *desired*
The suspect present of the Greeks' deceit,
Or bore and gauge the hollow caves uncouth:° *unknown*
So diverse ran the giddy people's mind.
Lo! foremost of a rout° that followed him, *company*
Kindled° Laöcoön[9] hasted from the tower, *inflamed*
Crying far off, "O wretched citizens!
What so great kind of frenzy fretteth° you? *consumes*
Deem ye the Greeks, our enemies, to be gone?
Or any Greekish gifts can you suppose
Devoid of guile? Is so Ulysses[10] known?
Either the Greeks are in this timber hid,
Or this an engine° is to annoy our walls, *instrument of war*
To view our towers, and overwhelm our town.
Here lurks some craft. Good Trojans! give no trust
Unto this horse, for, whatsoever it be,
I dread the Greeks, yea[11] when they offer gifts."
—1557

---

[1] *Minerva* Goddess of wisdom, invention, the arts, and war.

[2] *the fame ... point* I.e., the story (of the supposed sacrifice) travelled ("wandered it") conveniently ("at point").

[3] *enstuff* Fill, garrison.

[4] *Priam* King of Troy.

[5] *road* Sheltered area of water, close to shore, where boats can anchor.

[6] *Pyrrhus* Achilles's son. He became the new leader of the Myrmidons, Achilles's followers; *band* troop; *Achilles* Greatest Greek warrior; *pight* Were pitched.

[7] *battles* Bodies of troops in battle array.

[8] *Whether ... would* I.e., either this idea was a result of Timœtes's treachery, or it was merely Troy's fate that the horse would enter the walls of Troy.

[9] *Laöcoön* A Trojan priest.

[10] *Ulysses* Odysseus, the king of Ithaca and the hero of Homer's *Odyssey*. Odysseus was the warrior who suggested the construction of the horse.

[11] *yea* Especially, even more.

The Elizabethan Sonnet and Lyric

Developed first in thirteenth-century Italy and wildly popular in Renaissance Europe, the sonnet (or "little song") became one of the most enduring forms of English verse. A lyric poem in fourteen lines, usually with ten or twelve syllables to a line, the standard sonnet follows one of several rhyme schemes. The most important are the Italian or "Petrarchan," the English (often referred to as the "Shakespearean," although it was Henry Howard, Earl of Surrey, who first developed it), and the Spenserian. The Petrarchan form, introduced by the Italian writer Francesco Petrarch in the fourteenth century, has two parts: first comes the "octave" of eight lines, which usually sets forth some situation, argument, narrative, analogy, comment, wish, or other thought. This is followed by the "sestet," six lines that often perform a volta, or turn, that gives some resolution, further elaboration, counter-argument, or other contrast to the octave. The rhyme scheme ordinarily is *abba abba cde cde,* although variations for the sestet (such as *cdc dcd or cde cde*) are acceptable.

The English poets Thomas Wyatt and Henry Howard, Earl of Surrey first introduced the sonnet into English, translating some of Petrarch's sonnets in the 1520s and 1530s and, in the case of Surrey, writing a few more in the Petrarchan manner. They were not published until 1557, but they circulated in manuscript. By the 1580s the popularity of the sonnet on the Continent led to its revival in England, and the posthumous publication in 1591 of Sir Philip Sidney's *Astrophil and Stella* started a fashion for the form and for the sonnet sequence that blazed for a few years with extraordinary intensity.

Shakespeare's sonnets (some of which certainly, and many others probably, were written in the 1590s although Shakespeare may well have revised them before they were published, well after the fashion was over, in 1609) typically have four parts: three "quatrains" (a set of four lines) each rhyming *abab cdcd efef* and then a couplet rhyming *gg.* The quatrains may trace the development of an idea, state the same notion several times, or describe a situation from several angles—the possibilities of this flexible form are nearly endless. The couplet may be a logical conclusion, a further thought, or even a dramatic denial of what has come before.

Edmund Spenser's *Amoretti* (1595) have yet another scheme, a sort of compromise between the Petrarchan and the Shakespearean, interlocking its quatrains with the rhyme scheme *abab bcbc cdcd* concluding with a couplet *ee.* Substantial selections from the sonnets by Wyatt, Surrey, Sidney, Shakespeare, and Spenser appear elsewhere in this volume, thus the sonnets in this section are designed to provide further insight into the origins and range of the form; the lyrics by Gascoigne and by an anonymous poet are meant to extend the reader's sense of how the short Elizabethan lyric could handle some of the themes—age, absence—found in the sonnets.

⌘⌘⌘

The Continental Background

Francesco Petrarch (1304–1374)

The influence of Petrarch's sonnet sequence, about his unfulfilled love for Laura, was immense, and provided European love poets with a way to shape the erotic experience in terms of frustration, self-scrutiny, self-division, praise, and longing and to express this through elaborate metaphor, paradox, and an intense focus on detail. Whether the object of imitation, revision, or satire, Petrarch's approach to love long remained the discourse against which and through which poets defined themselves when writing on love.

from *Rime Sparse*

134

Pace non trovo et non ò da far guerra,
e temo et spero, et ardo et son un ghiaccio,
et volo sopra 'l cielo et giacco in terra,
et nulla stringo et tutto 'l mondo abbraccio.
Tal m'à in pregion, che non m'apre né serra,
né per suo mi riten né sciolglie il laccio,
et non m'ancide Amore et non mi sferra,
né mi vuol vivo, né mi trae d'impaccio.
Veggio senza occhi, et non ò lingua et grido,
et bramo di perir, et cheggio aita,
et ò in odio me stesso et amo altrui.
Pascomi di dolor, piangendo rido,
egualmente mi spiace morte et vita.
In questo stato son, Donna, per vui.
—WRITTEN MID-14TH CENTURY

134

I find no peace and all my war is done,
I fear and hope, I burn and freeze like ice;
I fly above the wind yet can I not arise;
And naught I have and all the world I season° *seize upon*
That[1] looseth nor locketh holdeth me in prison
And holdeth me not, yet can I 'scape no wise,
Nor letteth me live nor die at my device.° *own choice*
And yet of death it giveth none occasion.
Without eyen° I see and without tongue I plain;° *eyes / complain*
I desire to perish, and yet I ask health;
I love another, and thus I hate myself;
I feed me in sorrow and laugh in all my pain;
Likewise displeaseth me both death and life:
And my delight[2] is causer of this strife.
—C. 1520S (TRANS. SIR THOMAS WYATT)

140

Amor, che nel penser mio vive et regna
e 'l suo seggio maggior nel mio cor tene,
talor armato ne la fronte vene;
ivi si loca et ivi pon sua insegna.
Quella ch' amare et sofferir ne 'nsegna
e vol che 'l gran desio, l'accesa spene
ragion, vergogna, et reverenza affrene,
di nostro ardir fra se stessa si sdegna.
Onde Amor paventoso fugge al core,
Lasciando ogni sua impresa, et piange et trema;
ivi s'asonde et non appar più fore.
Che poss' io far, temendo il mio signore,
se non star seco infin a l'ora estrema?
ché bel fin fa chi ben amando more.
—WRITTEN MID-14TH CENTEURY

140

Love, that doth reign and live within my thought
And built his seat° within my captive breast, *dwelling*
Clad in the arms wherein with me he fought
Oft in my face he doth his banner rest.
But she that taught me love and suffer pain,
My doubtful hope and eke° my hot desire *also*
With shamefast° look to shadow° and refrain,° *modest / conceal / hold back*
Her smiling grace converteth straight to ire.
And coward Love then to the heart apace
Taketh his flight, where he doth lurk and plain;° *complain*
His purpose lost, and dare not show his face.
For my lord's guilt thus faultless bide I pain,
Yet from my lord[3] shall not my foot remove.
Sweet is the death that taketh end by love.
—C. 1530S (TRANS. HENRY HOWARD, EARL OF SURREY)

189

Passa la nave mia colma d'oblio
per aspro mare a mezza notte il verno

189

My galley chargèd with forgetfulness
Through sharp seas in winter nights doth pass

[1] *That* Which (i.e., Love).

[2] *my delight* His paradoxical pleasure in loving but also the lady—Laura, in Petrarch's poem.

[3] *lord* I.e., Love—the speaker's feudal lord.

enfra Scilla et Caribdi, et al governo
siede 'l signore anzi 'l nimico mio;
à ciascun remo un penser pronto et rio
che la tempesta e 'l fin par ch' abbi a scherno;
la vela rompe un vento umido eterno
di sospir, di speranze et di desio;
pioggia di lagrimar, nebbia di sdegni
bagna et rallenta la già stanche sarte
che son d'error con ignoranzia attorto.
Celansi i duo mei dolci usati segni,
morta fra l'onde è la ragion et l'arte
tal ch' i' 'ncomincio a desperar del porto.

—WRITTEN MID-14TH CENTURY

'Tween rock and rock;[1] and eke° mine enemy, alas, *also*
That is my lord,[2] steereth with cruelness;
And every oar a thought in readiness,
As though that death were light° in such a case. *easy*
An endless wind doth tear the sail apace
Of forcèd sighs and trusty fearfulness.
A rain of tears, a cloud of dark disdain,
Hath done the wearied cords° great hinderance, *ship's rigging*
Wreathèd with error and eke with ignorance
The stars be hid that led me to this pain;
Drownèd is reason that should me consort,° *accompany*
And I remain despairing of the port.

—C. 1520S (TRANS. SIR THOMAS WYATT)

190

Una candida cerva sopra l'erba
verde m'apparve con duo corna d'oro,
fra due riviere all'ombra d'un alloro,
levando 'l sole a la stagione acerba.
Era sua vista sì dolce superba
ch' i' lasciai per seguirla ogni lavoro,
come l'avaro che 'n cercar tesoro
con diletto l'affanno disacerba.
"Nessun mi tocchi," al bel collo d'intorno
scritto avea di diamanti et di topazi.
"Libera farmi al mio Cesare parve."
Et era 'l sol già vòlto al mezzo giorno,
gli occhi miei stanchi di mirar, non sazi,
quand' io caddi ne l'acqua et ella sparve.

—WRITTEN MID-14TH CENTURY

190

Whoso list° to hunt, I know where is a hind,° *wishes* / *female deer*
But as for me, alas, I may° no more: *can*
The vain travail° hath wearied me so sore *effort*
I am of them that farthest come behind.
Yet may I by no means my wearied mind
Draw from the deer: but, as she fleeth afore,
Fainting I follow. I leave off therefore,
Since in a net I seek to hold the wind.
Who list her hunt, I put him out of doubt,
As well as I may spend his time in vain.
And, graven with diamonds in letters plain,
There is written her fair neck round about:
"Noli me tangere,[3] for Caesar's I am,
And wild for to hold, although I seem tame."

—C. 1520S (ADAPTED BY SIR THOMAS WYATT)

---

[1] *'Tween rock and rock* Petrarch specifies Scylla and Charybdis, the dangerous monster who lived on a rock and the whirlpool on either side of a narrow channel through which Ulysses must sail in Homer's *Odyssey*.

[2] *lord* I.e., Cupid, Love.

[3] *Noli me tangere* "Do not touch me," words said by Christ after the Resurrection. Early commentators on Petrarch often read this as signifying that Laura considered herself bound by the laws of chaste marriage as decreed by Augustus Caesar. Wyatt's readers who identified the deer with Anne Boleyn (whom Wyatt knew and perhaps loved), would have read the lines as suggesting that the "hind" belongs to Henry VIII.

GASPARA STAMPA (1523–1554)

132

Quando io dimando nel mio pianto Amore,
Che cosí male il mio parlar ascolata,
Mille fate il dí, non una volta,
Ché mi fere e trafigge a tutte l'ore:
"Come esser può, s'io diedi l'alma e 'l core
al mio signor dal dí ch'a me l'ho tolta,
e se ogni cosa dentro a lui raccolta
è riso e gioia, è scema di dolore,
ch'io senta gelosia fredda e temenza,
e d'allegrezza e gioia resti priva,
s'io vivo in lui, e in me di me son senza?"
"Vo' che tu mora al bene ed al mal viva,"
mi risponde egli in ultima sentenza;
"Questa ti basti, e questo fa' che scriva."
—1554 (*Rime*, NO. 132 IN A. SALZA ED., 1913)

132

When in my weeping I inquire of Love[2]
(Who so unwillingly gives ear to me)
A thousand times a day—never just once—
Why he will wound and pierce me all the time:
"How can it be, since I gave heart and soul
To him,[3] the day I took them both from me;
If everything enclosed within his breast
Is only joy and laughter, never sorrow,
How can I feel cold jealousy and fear
And be deprived of all my joyfulness,
Living in him, and never in myself?"
"I bid you die to joy and live in grief,"
Love answers me in his hard final sentence:
"Let this suffice you, that it makes you write."
—1997 (TRANS. LAURA ANNA STORTONI AND MARY PRENTICE LILLIE)

JOACHIM DU BELLAY (?1522–1560)

113

Si nostre vie est moins qu'une journée
En l'eternel, si l'an qui faict le tour
Chasse noz jours sans espoir de retour,
Si perissable est toute chose née,
Que songes-tu, mon ame emprisonée?
Pourquoy te plaist l'obscur de nostre jour
Si pour voler en un plus cler sejour,
Tu as au dos l'aele bien empanée?
La, est le bien que tout esprit desire,
La, le repos ou tout le monde aspire,
La, est l'amour, la, le plaisir encore.
La, ô mo name au plus hault ciel guide!
Tu y pouras recongnoistre l'Idée
De la beauté, qu'en ce monde j'adore.[1]
—1550

113

If this, our life, be less than but a day
In the eternal; if each circling year
Bears off our days, never to reappear;
If every creature born must death obey,
Why then, my prisoned soul, should you delay?
How can it please you thus to tarry here,
In darkness, when unto a brighter sphere,
Your well-plumed wings would carry you away?
There is the good that man's mind hungers for;
There, the repose he seeks, forevermore;
There, love and joy abound, their bliss bestow.
There, O my soul, as you reach heaven's height,
Beauty ideal will loom within your sight,
That beauty that I worship here below.
—2002 (TRANS. NORMAN R. SHAPIRO)

---

[1] *De la ... j'adore* A Neoplatonic sonnet adapted from a sonnet by Bernardino Daniello.

[2] *Love* The personified god of love, Cupid, Eros.

[3] *To him* Stampa refers to her beloved and social superior, Count Collatino di Collalto, on whose name, "high hill," she often puns, and who seems for a while to have reciprocated her love.

PIERRE DE RONSARD (1524–1585)

Je vouldroy bien richement jaunissant
En pluye d'or goute à goute descendre
Dans le giron de ma belle Cassandre,
Lors qu'en ses yeux le somne va glissant.[1]
Puis je vouldroy bien en toreau blandissant[2]
Me transformer pour finement la prendre,
Quand elle va par l'herbe la plus tendre
Seule à l'escart mille fleurs ravissant.
Je vouldroy bien afin d'aiser ma peine
Estre un Narcisse, & elle une fontaine
Pour m'y plonger une nuict à sejour:
Et vouldroy bien que ceste nuict encore
Durast toujours sans que jamais l'Aurore[4]
D'un front nouveau nous r'allumast le jour.
—1552 (*Amours* I.20)

I would in rich and golden coloured rain,
With tempting showers in pleasant sort descend
Into fair Phyllis' lap (my lovely friend)
When sleep her sense with slumber doth restrain.
I would be changed to a milk-white bull,
When midst the gladsome fields she should appear,
By pleasant sweetness to surprise my dear,
Whilst from their stalks she pleasant flowers did pull.
I were content to weary out my pain,
To be Narcissus so she were a spring
To drown in her those woes my heart do wring:
And, more, I wish transformed to remain:
That whilst I thus in pleasures' lap did lie,
I might refresh desire, which else would die.
—1593 (TRANS. THOMAS LODGE, *Phillis* 34)

Quand vous serez bien vielle, au soir à la chandelle,
Assise aupres du feu, devidant & filant,
Direz, chantant mes vers, en vous esmerveillant,
"Ronsard me celebroit du temps que j'estois belle."
Lors vous n'aurez servante oyant telle nouvelle,
Desja sous le labeur à demy sommeillant,
Qui au bruit de "Ronsard" ne s'aille resveillant,
Benissant vostre nom de louange immortelle.
Je seray sous la terre, & fantaume sans os:
Par les ombres Myrtheux je prendray mon repos.
Vous serez au fouyer une vielle accroupie,
Regrettant mon amour, & vostre fier disdain.
Vivez, si m'en croyez, n'attendez à demain:
Cueillez dés aujourdhuy les roses de la vie.
—1578 (SONNETS FOR HÉLÈNE II, 43)

When you are very old, by candle's flame,
Spinning beside the fire, at end of day,
Singing my verse, admiring, you will say:
"When I was fair, Ronsard's muse I became."
Your servant then, some weary old beldame—
Whoever she may be—nodding away,
Hearing "Ronsard," will shake off sleep, and pray
Your name be blessed, to live in deathless fame.
Buried, I shall a fleshless phantom be,
Hovering by the shadowed myrtle tree;
You, by the hearth, a pining crone, bent low,
Whose pride once scorned my love, much to your sorrow.
Heed me, live for today, wait not the morrow:
Gather life's roses while still fresh they grow.
—2002 (TRANS. NORMAN R. SHAPIRO)

---

[1] *je vouldroy … glissant* In this poem, popular in England, Ronsard wishes to become golden rain like that into which Zeus changed himself so as to visit the imprisoned Danaë, into a white bull like the one Zeus became when he seduced and kidnapped young Europa, and a pool like the one in which Narcissus saw himself and fell in love.

[2] *blandissant* Later editions have "blanchissant"—"white."

[3] *l'Aurore* The dawn goddess.

SAMUEL DANIEL (1562–1619)

from *Delia*

6[1]

Fair is my love, and cruel as she's fair;
  Her brow shades frowns, although her eyes are
    sunny;
  Her smiles are lightning, though her pride despair;
  And her disdains are gall, her favours honey.
A modest maid, decked with a blush of honour,
  Whose feet do tread green paths of youth and love;
  The wonder of all eyes that look upon her:
  Sacred on earth, designed a saint above.
Chastity and Beauty, which were deadly foes,
  Live reconciled friends within her brow:
  And had she pity to conjoin° with those, *join*
  Then who had heard the plaints I utter now?
O had she not been fair, and thus unkind,
My Muse had slept, and none had known my mind.
—1592

28[2]

Raising my hopes on hills of high desire,
  Thinking to scale the heaven of her heart,
  My slender means presumed too high a part;
  Her thunder of disdain forced me retire,
And threw me down to pain in all this fire,
  Where, lo, I languish in so heavy smart,
  Because th'attempt was far above my art:
  Her pride brooked not poor souls should come so
    nigh her.
Yet I protest my high aspiring will
  Was not to dispossess her of her right:
  Her sovereignty should have remained still,
  I only sought the bliss to have her sight.
Her sight, contented thus to see me spill,
Framed my desires fit for her eyes to kill.
—1592

[1] *6* The numbering here follows that in the edition edited by A.C. Sprague (Cambridge, Mass., 1930). Because Daniel frequently revised his poetry, numbering varies in the editions published during his lifetime.

[2] *28* First printed in a collection of sonnets appended to the 1591 unauthorized edition of Sir Philip Sidney's *Astrophil and Stella*.

33

When men shall find thy flower, thy glory pass,
  And thou with careful° brow *full of cares*
    sitting alone
  Received hast this message from thy glass,
  That tells thee truth, and says that all is gone;
Fresh shalt thou see in me the wounds thou madest,
  Though spent thy flame, in me the heat remaining:
  I that have loved thee thus before thou fadest,
  My faith shall wax, when thou art in thy waning.
The world shall find this miracle in me,
  That fire can burn when all the matter's spent:
  Then what my faith hath been thy self shalt see,
  And that thou wast unkind thou mayst repent.
Thou mayst repent that thou hast scorned my tears,
When winter snows upon thy golden hairs.
—1592

MICHAEL DRAYTON (1563–1631)

from *Idea*

6

How many paltry, foolish, painted things,
  That now in coaches trouble every street,
Shall be forgotten, whom no poet sings,
Ere they be well wrapped in their winding sheet?
Where I to thee eternity shall give,
When nothing else remaineth of these days,
And queens hereafter shall be glad to live
Upon the alms of thy superfluous praise;
Virgins and matrons reading these my rhymes,
Shall be so much delighted with thy story,
That they shall grieve they lived not in these times,
To have seen thee, their sex's only glory:
So shalt thou fly above the vulgar throng,
Still to survive in my immortal song.
—1619

61

Since there's no help, come let us kiss and part;
  Nay, I have done: you get no more of me,
And I am glad, yea glad with all my heart,
That thus so cleanly I myself can free;
Shake hands for ever, cancel all our vows,
And when we meet at any time again,

Be it not seen in either of our brows
That we one jot of former love retain.
Now at the last gasp of Love's latest breath,
When his pulse failing, Passion speechless lies,
When Faith is kneeling by his bed of death,
And Innocence is closing up his eyes,
Now if thou would'st, when all have given him over,
From death to life, thou might'st him yet recover.
—1619

63

Truce, gentle Love, a parley now I crave:
Methinks 'tis long since first these wars begun.
Nor thou, nor I, the better yet can have;
Bad is the match, where neither party won.
I offer free conditions of fair peace,
My heart for hostage that it shall remain.
Discharge our forces, here let malice cease,
So for my pledge thou give me pledge again.
Or if no thing but death will serve thy turn,
Still thirsting for subversion of my state,
Do what thou canst, raze, massacre, and burn,
Let the world see the utmost of thy hate:
I send defiance, since if overthrown,
Thou vanquishing, the conquest is mine own.
—1599

WILLIAM SHAKESPEARE (1564–1616)

from *Romeo and Juliet* (Act 1, Scene 5)

ROMEO. If I profane with my unworthiest hand
This holy shrine,[1] the gentle fine is this,
My lips, two blushing pilgrims, ready stand
To smooth that rough touch with a tender kiss.
JULIET. Good pilgrim, you do wrong your hand too much,
Which mannerly devotion shows in this;
For saints[2] have hands that pilgrims' hands do touch,
And palm to palm is holy palmers' kiss.[3]
ROMEO. Have not saints lips, and holy palmers too?
JULIET. Aye, pilgrim, lips that they must use in prayer.
ROMEO. Oh then, dear saint, let lips do what hands do.
They pray. Grant thou, lest faith turn to despair.
JULIET. Saints do not move, though grant for prayers' sake.
ROMEO. Then move not while my prayer's effect I take.
[He kisses her]
—1597 (WRITTEN C. 1595)

SIR JOHN DAVIES (1569–1626)

from *Gulling Sonnets*[4]

3

What eagle can behold her sun-bright eye,
Her sun-bright eye that lights the world with love,
The world of Love wherein I live and die,
I live and die and diverse changes prove,
I changes prove, yet still the same am I,
The same am I and never will remove,
Never remove until my soul doth fly,
My soul doth fly and I surcease to move,
I cease to move which now am moved by you,
Am moved by you that move all mortal hearts,
All mortal hearts whose eyes your eyes doth view,
Your eyes doth view whence Cupid shoots his darts,
Whence Cupid shoots his darts and woundeth those
That honor you, and never were his foes.
—1594

JOHN DAVIES OF HEREFORD (1565–1618)

from *The Scourge of Villany*

The author loving these homely meats[5] specially, viz: cream, pancakes, buttered pippin pies[6] (laugh, good people) and tobacco; writ to that worthy and virtuous gentlewoman, whom he calleth mistress, as followeth:

[1] *holy shrine* Juliet's hand.

[2] *saints* That is, images or statues of saints, venerated by pilgrims.

[3] *palmers' kiss* Palmers were pilgrims who have been to the Holy Land; their emblem was the palm frond (hence Juliet's pun on "palm").

[4] *Gulling Sonnets* Davies's *Gulling Sonnets*, parodying the conventions and clichés of the sonnet form, circulated in manuscript.

[5] *meats* Foods, consumables; Davies, too, is writing parody.

[6] *pippin pies* Apple pies.

If there were, oh! an Hellespont[1] of cream
Between us, milk-white mistress, I would swim
To you, to show to both my love's extreme,
Leander-like—yea! dive from brim to brim.
But met I with a buttered pippin pie
Floating upon't, that would I make my boat
To waft me to you without jeopardy,
Though sea-sick I might be while it did float.
Yet if a storm should rise, by night or day,
Of sugar-snows and hail of caraways,
Then, if I found a pancake in my way,
It like a plank should bring me to your quays;
Which having found, if they tobacco kept,
The smoke should dry me well before I slept.
—1611

RICHARD BARNFIELD (1574–1620)

from *Cynthia*

14

Here, hold this glove (this milk-white cheverel° glove) *leather*
Not quaintly over-wrought with curious knots,
Not decked° with golden spangs,° nor silver spots, *decorated / decorative metal*
Yet wholesome for thy hand as thou shalt prove.
Ah no (sweet boy)[2] place this glove near thy heart,
Wear it, and lodge it still within thy breast,
So shalt thou make me (most unhappy) blest.
So shalt thou rid my pain, and ease my smart:
How can that be (perhaps) thou wilt reply,
A glove is for the hand not for the heart,
Nor can it well be proved by common art,
Nor reason's rule. To this, thus answer I:
If thou from glove dost take away the "g,"
Then glove is love: and so I send it thee.
—1595

[1] *Hellespont* Older name for the Dardanelles, the strait between European and Asian Turkey. The Leander of line 4 is the young man in classical legend who swam across the Hellespont to meet his mistress Hero.

[2] *sweet boy* Barnfield's sonnets are the only extant ones in Renaissance England, other than Shakespeare's, in which a male speaker addresses another man in a homoerotic manner.

17

Cherry-lipped Adonis[3] in his snowy shape,
Might not compare with his pure ivory white,
On whose fair front° a poet's pen may write, *forehead*
Whose roseate red excels the crimson grape,
His love-enticing delicate soft limbs,
Are rarely° framed t' entrap poor gazing eyes: *wonderfully*
His cheeks, the lily and carnation dyes
With lovely tincture, which Apollo's dims.[4]
His lips ripe strawberries in nectar wet,
His mouth a hue, his tongue a honey-comb,
Where muses (like bees) make their mansion.
His teeth pure pearl in blushing coral set.
Oh how can such a body sin-procuring,
Be slow to love, and quick to hate, enduring?
—1595

GEORGE GASCOIGNE (1539–1578)

Gascoigne's Lullaby

Sing lullaby, as women do,
Wherewith they bring their babes to rest,
And lullaby can I sing too
As womanly as can the best.
With lullaby they still the child,
And if I be not much beguiled,
Full many wanton babes have I
Which must be stilled with lullaby.

First lullaby my youthful years,
It is now time to go to bed,
For crooked age and hoary hairs
Have won the haven within my head:
With lullaby then youth be still,
With lullaby content thy will,
Since courage quails, and comes behind,
Go sleep, and so beguile thy mind.

Next lullaby my gazing eyes,
Which wonted were to glance apace.° *directly*

[3] *Adonis* The young man beloved by the goddess Venus.

[4] *Apollo* God of the sun: the beloved's color "dims" even the sun.

For every glass may now suffice,
To show the furrows in my face:
With lullaby then wink awhile,
With lullaby your looks beguile:
Let no fair face, nor beauty bright,
Entice you eft° with vain delight. *again*

And lullaby my wanton will,
Let reasons rule now reign thy thought,
Since all too late I find by skill,
How dear I have thy fancies bought.
With lullaby now take thine ease,
With lullaby thy doubts appease:
For trust to this, if thou be still,
My body shall obey thy will.

Eke° lullaby my loving boy, *also*
My little Robin[1] take thy rest,
Since age is cold, and nothing coy,
Keep close thy coin, for so is best:
With lullaby be thou content,
With lullaby thy lusts relent,
Let others pay which hath mo° pence, *more*
Thou art too poor for such expense.

Thus lullaby my youth, mine eyes,
My will, my ware, and all that was,
I can no mo delays devise,
But welcome pain, let pleasure pass:
With lullaby now take your leave,
With lullaby your dreams deceive,
And when you rise with waking eye,
Remember Gascoigne's lullaby.

[1] *Robin* Slang for penis.

Anonymous[2]

Ode[3]

That time and absence proves[4]
Rather helps than hurts to loves.

Absence, hear thou my protestation
Against thy strength,
Distance and length:
Do what you can for alteration,
For hearts of truest mettle
Absence doth join and time doth settle.

Who loves a mistress of such quality,
He soon hath found
Affection ground[5]
Beyond time, place, and all mortality;
To hearts that cannot vary,
Absence is present, time doth tarry.

My senses want° their outward motions, *lack*
Which now within
Reason doth win,
Redoubled in her[6] secret notions,
Like rich men that take pleasure
In hiding, more than handling, treasure.

By absence, this good means I gain:
That I can catch her,
Where none can watch her,
In some close corner of my brain.
There I embrace and kiss her,
And so I both enjoy and miss her.
—1611

[2] *Anonymous* The authorship is uncertain. This is one of a number of Renaissance love poems celebrating the triumph of the waking or dreaming imagination over the beloved's absence or, in some cases, rejection.

[3] *Ode* From Francis Davison et al., *A Poetical Rhapsody* (1611 ed.).

[4] *That time and absence proves* I.e., prove: a singular verb after a double subject was then common.

[5] *Affection ground* The wording is condensed, but the idea is that love for an admirable lady is a ground, a base, for an affection that does not change because of absence.

[6] *Redoubled in her* I.e., Reason's.

Lady Jane Grey

1537 – 1554

Lady Jane Grey's short, tragic life and nine-day reign as Queen of England have provided matter for novels, plays, and films. These events have enough adventure and intrigue to warrant such attention, but the sensational facts often overshadow the writings that provide a window into the young woman's character and into the political conditions under which she lived.

Jane was the eldest child of Lord Henry and Lady Frances Grey, the Duke and Duchess of Suffolk. Born in October 1537 in Bradgate Park, near Leicester, she was raised in the highest aristocratic circles: her maternal grandmother was Mary Tudor, sister of Henry VII and widow of Louis XII of France. As a granddaughter of Henry VII she was in the line of succession to the throne of England after Henry's children Edward, Mary, and Elizabeth, a situation complicated by political and religious controversies concerning the legitimacy and hence the rights of Henry's two daughters (Protestants might think Mary born to an invalid union, and Catholics might think Elizabeth illegitimate). Jane's position as a possible heir to the throne proved catastrophic.

Although she was raised in luxury, Jane's life was unhappy. A bookish child, she was not close to her unsympathetic parents, whom she called "sharp and severe." They and other members of the aristocracy saw her as a possible bride for her cousin, Edward VI, who became king at a young age upon the death of Henry VIII in 1547. Edward did not want to marry Jane, however, so her parents betrothed her to Guildford Dudley, the youngest son of John Dudley, Duke of Northumberland. Jane tried to refuse the match, but was beaten until she submitted, and was married to Guildford in May 1553 at the age of fifteen. On the urging of her parents, a month after the ceremony she and Guildford consummated their marriage (thus making it legally binding), but the two lived apart.

In July 1553 Jane's life was thrown into chaos. Young Edward VI, who had long been sickly, died before his sixteenth birthday on July 6. A firm Protestant, he did not want his Catholic sister Mary to inherit the throne, so on July 3, three days before he died, he complied with a request by the Duke of Northumberland, Jane's father-in-law and Lord Chamberlain, to name Jane as his successor. Jane opposed the idea at first but finally consented. She was made Queen of England on 10 July 1553, but her coronation was extremely unpopular with the English people, most of whom regarded Mary as the rightful heir. It soon became apparent, moreover, that Jane had been set up as a puppet queen through whom the Duke of Northumberland could rule the country. Mary herself was of course outraged. She declared herself queen on 9 July, as soon as she heard of her brother's death, and raised an army to march on London. Northumberland responded by raising his own army and leaving London to meet Mary's forces in battle. In his absence, his scheme fell apart when the royal council wavered, naming Mary queen instead of Jane. Jane was abandoned by her parents and by Northumberland, who attempted (unsuccessfully) to save his own life by pledging allegiance to Mary and converting to Catholicism. Jane and her husband were charged with treason and imprisoned in the Tower of London.

On 13 November 1553, Jane and Guildford were sentenced to death. Jane expected a pardon from her cousin, Queen Mary, but a revolt in early February 1554 and perhaps an understanding of political necessity hardened the new queen's heart and she signed the couple's death warrants. Mary offered Jane a reprieve if she converted to Catholicism, but the young woman refused, and she was beheaded on 12 February 1554. In his *Book of Martyrs* (1563), John Foxe quotes her final prayers and conversations and describes her execution, including her pathetic request for help as, blindfolded, she groped for the block on which to lay her head.

Jane's surviving letters and other writings document both her domestic life and taste for learning, as well as her experiences as the "nine days' queen." They vividly show the terror felt by a teenage girl caught up in a political power struggle, but they also show that same girl's remarkable clarity of vision and the firmness with which she held to her own convictions in the face of death.

⌘⌘⌘

Letters

Lady Jane Grey to her Father[1]

9 February 1554

Father, although it hath pleased God to hasten my death by you, by whom my life should rather have been lengthened;[2] yet can I so patiently take it, that I yield God more hearty thanks for shortening my woeful days, than if the world had been given unto my possession, with life lengthened at my own will, and albeit I am very well assured of your impatient dolours,[3] redoubled in many ways, both in bewailing your own woe, and especially, as I am informed, my woeful state, yet, my dear father, if I may without offence rejoice in my own mishap, herein I may account myself blessed, that, washing my hands with the innocence of my fact, my guiltless blood may cry before the Lord, "Mercy to the innocent."

And yet though I must needs acknowledge that being constrained, and, as you know well enough, continually assayed,[4] yet in taking upon me I seemed to consent, and therein grievously offended the queen and her laws; yet do I assuredly trust that this my offence towards God is so much the less, in that, being in so royal estate as I was, mine enforced honour blended never with mine innocent heart. And thus, good father, I have opened unto you the state wherein I at present stand; my death at hand, although to you perhaps it may seem woeful, yet to me there is nothing that can be more welcome than from this vale of misery to aspire to that heavenly throne of all joy and pleasure, with Christ our Saviour; in whose steadfast faith, if it may be lawful for the daughter so to write to the father, the Lord that hitherto hath so strengthened you, so continue to keep you, that at the last we may meet in heaven with the Father, the Son, and the Holy Ghost.

I am,

Your obedient daughter till death,

JANE DUDLEY

[1] *Lady Jane Grey to her Father* Here and throughout, the titles given to Grey's writings are those used by John Foxe when they were first published, in Foxe's *Book of Martyrs*.

[2] *by you … lengthened* I.e., as his daughter, Jane should have outlived him. He should, she suggests, have nurtured and protected her.

[3] *dolours* Sorrows, sufferings.

[4] *assayed* Tried, i.e., experiencing trials.

A Letter written by the Lady Jane in the end of the New Testament in Greek, the which she sent unto her Sister Lady Katherine[5] Immediately before she Suffered

I have here sent you, good sister Katherine, a book: which although it be not outwardly trimmed with

[5] *Greek* Refers to the language of the book Jane Grey sends, and not the language in which her letter was written; *Katherine* Jane's middle sister, born in 1540.

gold, yet inwardly it is more worth than precious stones. It is the book, dear sister, of the law of the Lord. It is His testament and last will, which He bequeathed unto us wretches, which shall lead you to the path of eternal joy. And if you with a good mind read it, and with an earnest mind do follow it, it shall bring you to an immortal and everlasting life. It will teach you to live, and learn you to die. It shall win you more, than you should have gained by the possession of your woeful father's lands. For, as if God had prospered him, you should have inherited his lands, so if you apply diligently this book, seeking to direct your life after it, you shall be an inheritor of such riches, as neither the covetous shall withdraw from you, neither the thief shall steal, neither yet the moths corrupt.

Desire with David,[1] good sister, to understand the law of the Lord your God. Live still[2] to die, that you (by death) may purchase eternal life. And trust not, that the tenderness of your age shall lengthen your life. For as soon (if God call) goeth the young, as the old: and labour always to learn to die, defy the world, deny the devil, and despise the flesh, and delight yourself only in the Lord. Be penitent for your sins, and yet despair not. Be strong in faith, and yet presume not. And desire with Saint Paul, to be dissolved and to be with Christ,[3] with whom even in death there is life. Be like the good servant, and even at midnight be waking, lest when death cometh and stealeth upon you like a thief in the night, you be with the evil servant found sleeping, and lest for lack of oil ye be found like the five foolish women, and like him that had not on the wedding garment, and then ye be cast out from the marriage.[4] Rejoice in Christ, as I trust I do. Follow the steps of your master Christ, and take up your cross, lay your sins on His back, and always embrace Him. And as touching my death, rejoice as I do (good sister) that I shall be delivered of this corruption, and put on incorruption. For I am assured, that I shall for losing of a mortal life, win an immortal life. The which I pray God grant you, send you of His grace to live in His fear, and to die in the true Christian faith: from the which (in God's name) I exhort you, that you never swerve, neither for hope of life, nor fear of death. For if ye will deny His truth to lengthen your life, God will deny you, and yet shorten your days. And if you will cleave[5] to Him, He will prolong your days to your comfort and his glory. To the which glory God bring me now, and you hereafter, when it pleaseth Him to call you. Fare you well (good sister) and put your only trust in God, who only must help you.

—PUBLISHED 1563

A Certain Prayer of the Lady Jane in the Time of Her Trouble

O Lord thou God and Father of my life, hear me poor and desolate woman, which fleeth unto thee only in all troubles and miseries. Thou O Lord art the only defender and deliverer of those that put their trust. And therefore, I, being defiled with sin, encumbered with afflictions, unquieted with troubles, wrapped in cares, overwhelmed with miseries, vexed with temptation, and grievously tormented with the long imprisonment of this vile mass of clay, my sinful body, do come unto Thee, O merciful Saviour, craving Thy mercy and help, without the which so little hope of deliverance is left, that I may utterly despair of my liberty. Albeit, it is expedience, that seeing our life standeth upon trying, we should be visited some time with some adversity, whereby we might both be tried whether we be of Thy flock or no, and also know Thee and ourselves the better: yet Thou that saidst Thou wouldst not suffer us to be tempted above our power, be merciful unto me, now a miserable wretch, I beseech Thee; which, with Solomon, do cry unto Thee, humbly desiring Thee, that I may neither be too much puffed up with prosperity, neither too much depressed with adversity; lest I, being too full, should deny Thee, my God; in being too low brought, should despair and blaspheme Thee, my Lord and Saviour.[6] O merciful

[1] *David* Cf. 2 Samuel 11.

[2] *still* Always.

[3] *Saint Paul ... Christ* Cf. Philippians 1.23.

[4] *good servant ... sleeping* Cf. Mark 13.33–37; *lack ... women* Cf. Matthew 25.1–13; *him ... marriage* Cf. Matthew 22.1–14 and Luke 14.16–24.

[5] *cleave* Cling.

[6] *Solomon ... Saviour* Cf. Proverbs 30.7–9.

God, consider my misery, best known unto Thee; and be Thou now unto me a strong tower of defence, I humbly require Thee. Suffer me not to be tempted above my power, but wither be Thou a deliverer unto me out of this great misery, or else give me grace patiently to bear Thy heavy hand and sharp correction. It was Thy right hand that delivered the people of Israel out of the hands of Pharaoh, which for the space of four hundred years did oppress them, and keep them in bondage; let it therefore likewise seem good to Thy fatherly goodness, to deliver me, sorrowful wretch, for whom Thy son Christ shed His precious blood on the cross, out of this miserable captivity and bondage, wherein I am now. How long wilt Thou be absent? Forever? Oh, Lord hast Thou forgotten to be gracious, and hast Thou shut up Thy loving kindness in displeasure? Wilt Thou be no more entreated? Is Thy mercy clear gone forever, and Thy promise come utterly to an end forevermore? Why dost Thou make so long tarrying? Shall I despair of Thy mercy? Oh God, far be that from me; I am Thy workmanship, created in Christ Jesus; give me grace therefore to tarry at Thy leisure, and patiently to bear Thy works, assuredly knowing, that as Thou canst, so Thou wilt deliver me, when it shall please Thee, nothing doubting or mistrusting Thy goodness towards me; for Thou knowest better what is good for me than I do; therefore do with me in all things what Thou wilt, and plague me what way Thou wilt. Only, in the meantime, arm me, I beseech Thee, with Thy armour, that I may stand fast, my loins being girded with verity, having on the breast-plate of righteousness, and shod with the shoes prepared by the gospel of peace; above all things, taking to me the shield of faith, wherewith I may be able to quench all the fiery darts of the wicked; and taking the helmet of salvation, and the sword of Thy spirit, which is Thy most holy word; praying always, with all manner of prayer and supplication, that I may refer myself wholly to Thy will, abiding Thy pleasure, and comforting myself in those troubles that it shall please Thee to send me; seeing such troubles be profitable for me, and seeing I am assuredly persuaded that it cannot but be well all Thou doest. Hear me, O merciful Father, for His sake, whom thou wouldst should be a sacrifice for my sins; to whom with Thee and the Holy Ghost, be all honour and glory. Amen!

—1563

Certain Pretty Verses Written by the Said Lady Jane with a Pin

Non aliena putes homini quae obtingere possunt,
Sors hodierna mihi, tunc erit illa tibi.[1]

Do never think it strange,
Though now I have misfortune
For if that fortune change,
The same to thee may happen.

JANE DUDLEY

Deo juvante nil nocet livor malus.
Et non juvante nil juvat labor gravis;
Post tenebras spero lucem.[2]

If God do help thee,
Hate shall not hurt thee.
If God do fail thee,
Then shall not labour prevail thee.

—1563

[1] *Non ... tibi* Latin; paraphrased below.

[2] *Deo ... lucem* Again, a paraphrase of the Latin follows.

IN CONTEXT

Lady Jane Grey

from John Foxe, *Acts and Monuments of These Latter and Perilous Days* (1563)

In November the Archbishop Cranmer[1] (notwithstanding he had earnestly refused to subscribe to the King's will, in disinheriting his sister Mary, alleging many and pithy reasons for her legitimation) was in the Guildhall of London, arraigned and attainted of high treason, with the Lady Jane, and three of the Duke of Northumberland's sons, which all at the entreaty of certain persons were had again to the Tower.

In this mean while Cardinal Poole[2] being sent for by Queen Mary, was by the Emperor[3] requested to stay with him, to the intent (as some think) that his presence in England should not be a let[4] to the marriage, which he intended between Philip[5] his son and Queen Mary: for the making whereof, he sent a most ample ambassade,[6] with full power to make up the marriage betwixt them: which took such success, that after they had communed of the matter a few days, they knit up the knot.

This was done about the beginning of January, and was very evil taken of the people, and of many of the nobility: who for this and for religion, conspiring among themselves, made a rebellion, whereof Sir Thomas Wyatt,[7] knight, was one of the chief beginners: who being in Kent, said, that the Queen and the counsel would by foreign marriages bring upon this realm most miserable servitude, and establish popish religion. About the 25 of January, news came to London of this stir in Kent, and shortly after of the Duke of Suffolk, who was fled into Warwickshire and Leicestershire, there to gather a power. The Queen, therefore, caused them both with the two Carews of Devonshire to be proclaimed traitors: and sent into Kent against Wyatt, Thomas Duke of Norfolk,[8] who being about Rochester bridge, forsaken of them that went with him, returned safe again to London, without any harm done unto him, and without bloodshed of either party. After the Duke of Norfolk was sent the Earl of Huntington in post, who entering the city of Coventry before the Duke, disappointed[9] him of his purpose. Wherefore the Duke in great distress committed himself to the keeping of a servant of his own in a park, who like a false traitor betrayed him. And so he was brought up to the Tower of London.

In the mean while Peter Carew,[10] hearing of that was done, fled into France: but the other were taken, and Wyatt came towards London in the beginning of February, from whom the Emperor's ambassadors sped themselves away in haste all by water. The Queen, hearing of Wyatt's coming, came

---

[1] *Archbishop Cranmer* Thomas Cranmer (1489–1556), Archbishop of Canterbury who, against his better judgment, signed the document making Jane Grey the successor to Edward VI's throne.

[2] *Cardinal Poole* Reginald Pole (1500–58), Roman Catholic Cardinal and near relative of the Tudor monarchs.

[3] *Emperor* Charles V (1500–58), Holy Roman Emperor (1519–58), and King of Spain (1516–56).

[4] *let* Hindrance.

[5] *Philip* Prince of Spain (1527–98), son of Charles V.

[6] *ambassade* Emissary and his staff.

[7] *Sir Thomas Wyatt* Son of the poet famous for developing the English sonnet, Wyatt (1521?–54) organized an armed rebellion against Queen Mary's marriage to Philip of Spain.

[8] *Thomas … Norfolk* Thomas Howard (1473–1554), leader of Mary's forces against Wyatt.

[9] *disappointed* Thwarted.

[10] *Peter Carew* British nobleman (1514?–75) who supported the Wyatt rebellion.

into the city into the Guildhall, where she made a vehement oration against Wyatt, declaring that she neither had, not would consent to marry otherwise than should seem to the Council to be for the wealth of the realm. Wherefore she desired them of the city to stick to her in the suppressing of rebellious Traitors, and defending her royal estate.

As concerning Wyatt, after that he coming to Southwark could not be received that way into London, returning another way by Kingston with his army, he came up through the streets to Ludgate, whereas returning thence, was resisted at Temple Bar and there apprehended, which was upon Ash Wednesday: at what time at the apprehension of the said Wyatt there was a general pardon by the Herald proclaimed, promising generally pardon of life. Yet that notwithstanding, gallows and gibbets were erected in all parts of the city and suburbs of London to the number of twenty or thereabouts (three being set up in Cheapside). Whereupon, diverse of the captains and soldiers of Wyatt were hanged, and he himself afterward executed at Tower Hill and then quartered, whose head after being set up upon the gallows at Hayhill, was there stolen away, and great search made for the same: concerning whose cause and matter I partly refer them to the English Chronicles, such as list more fully to be satisfied therein, and partly hereafter more shall be touched among other things done in the month of April.

The 12 day of February was beheaded the Lady Jane, to whom was sent Master Fecknam alias Howman,[1] from the Queen, two days before her death, to commune with her, and to reduce[2] her from the doctrine of Christ to Queen Mary's religion, the effect of which communication here followeth.

THE COMMUNICATION HAD BETWEEN THE LADY JANE AND FECKNAM

FECKNAM. Madame, I lament your heavy case,[3] and yet I doubt not but that you bear out this sorrow of yours with a constant and patient mind.

JANE. You are welcome unto me, Sir, if your coming be to give Christian exhortation. And as for my heavy case, (I thank God) I do so little lament it, that rather I accompt[4] the same for a more manifest declaration of God's favour toward me, than ever He showed me any time before. And therefore there is no cause why either you or other which bear me good will, should lament or be grieved with this my case, being a thing so profitable for my soul's health.

FECKNAM. I am here come to you at this present sent from the Queen and her Council, to instruct you in the true doctrine of the right faith: although I have so great confidence in you, that I shall have (I trust) little need to travail with you much therein.

JANE. Forsooth, I heartily thank the Queen's Highness, which is not unmindful of her humble subject: and I hope likewise that you no less will do your duty therein both truly and faithfully, according to that you were sent for.

FECKNAM. What is then required of a Christian?

JANE. That he should believe in God, the Father, the Son, and the Holy Ghost, three persons and one God.

FECKNAM. What? Is there nothing else to be required or looked for in a Christian, but to believe in God?

JANE. Yes, we must believe in Him, we must love Him with all our heart, with all our soul, and with all our mind, and our neighbour as ourself.

---

[1] *Fecknam … Howman* John de Feckenham (1515?–85), prominent clergyman sent to give spiritual counsel to Jane Grey in the final hours before her execution.

[2] *reduce* Restore (to Catholicism).

[3] *case* Circumstance.

[4] *accompt* Account.

FECKNAM. Why? Then faith justifieth not, nor saveth not.

JANE. Yes verily, faith (as Saint Paul[1] sayeth) only justifieth.

FECKNAM. Why? Saint Paul sayeth, if I have all faith without love, it is nothing.

JANE. True it is, for how can I love him, whom I trust not, or how can I trust him whom I love not? Faith and love goeth both together, and yet love is comprehended in faith.

FECKNAM. How shall we love our neighbour?

JANE. To love our neighbour, is to feed the hungry, to clothe the naked, and give drink to the thirsty, and to do to him as we would do to ourselves.

FECKNAM. Why? Then it is necessary unto salvation to do good works also, and it is not sufficient only to believe.[2]

JANE. I deny that, and I affirm that faith only saveth, but it is mete[3] for a Christian, in token that he doth follow his master Christ, to do good works: yet may we not say that they profit to salvation. For when we have done all, yet we be unprofitable servants, and faith only in Christ's blood saveth.

FECKNAM. How many sacraments are there?

JANE. Two. The one, the sacrament of Baptism, and the other the sacrament of the Lord's Supper.

FECKNAM. No, there are seven.[4]

JANE. By what scripture find ye that?

FECKNAM. Well, we will talk of that hereafter, but what is signified by your two sacraments?

JANE. By the sacrament of Baptism, I am washed with water, and regenerated by the spirit, and that washing is a token to me that I am the child of God. The sacrament of the Lord's Supper offered unto me, is a sure seal and testimony that I am by the blood of Christ, which He shed for me on the cross, made partaker of the everlasting Kingdom.

FECKNAM. Why? What do you receive in that sacrament? Do you not receive the very body and blood of Christ?

JANE. No surely I do not so believe. I think that in the supper, I neither receive flesh nor blood, but only bread and wine:[5] which bread when it is broken, and the wine when it is drunken, putteth me in remembrance how that for my sins the body of Christ was broken, and His blood shed on the cross. And with that bread and wine I receive the benefits that cometh by the breaking of His body, and shedding of His blood for our sins on the cross.

FECKNAM. Why? Doth not Christ speak these words: "Take, eat, this is my body?"[6] Require we any plainer words? Doth He not say it is his body?

JANE. I grant He sayeth so: and so He sayeth I am the vine, I am the door,[7] but He is never the more for that the door nor the vine. Doth not Saint Paul say that He calleth things that are not, as though

---

[1] *Saint Paul* The Apostle Paul, author of a number of epistles in the new Testament, spread Christian teachings and helped unite congregations of Christians into a unified Church.

[2] *good works ... believe* The primacy of faith vs good works in the salvation of the soul was a major point of contention between Protestants and Catholics.

[3] *mete* Appropriate, fitting.

[4] *seven* Catholicism recognizes seven sacraments: Baptism, Confirmation, Confession, the Eucharist, Marriage, Holy Orders, and Last Rites.

[5] *the supper ... wine* This refers to the Protestant denial of transubstantiation (the Catholic belief that the bread and wine of communion physically become the body and blood of Christ when consecrated). Protestant belief varied, with Lutherans affirming Christ's "real presence" in the bread and wine and Calvinists claiming they are sacramental signs only.

[6] *Take ... body* Cf. Mark 14.22.

[7] *I am ... door* Cf. John 10.9 and 15.1–10.

they were?[1] God forbid that I should say that I eat the very natural body or blood of Christ. For then either I should pluck away my redemption, either else there were two bodies, or two Christs, or else twelve bodies. One body was tormented on the cross. And then if they did eat another body: then either He had two bodies, either else if His body were eaten, then it was not broken upon the cross: or else if it were broken upon the cross, it was not eaten of His disciples.

Fecknam. Why? Is it not as possible that Christ by his power could make His body both to be eaten and broken, as to be borne of a woman without seed of a man, and as to walk upon the sea having a body, and other such like miracles as He wrought by His power only?

Jane. Yes verily: if God would have done at His supper any miracle He might have done so: but I say that then He minded no work nor miracle, but only to break His body, and shed His blood on the cross for our sins. But I pray you answer me to this one question: where was Christ when He said, "Take, eat, this is my body?" was He not at table when He said so? He was at that time alive, and suffered not till the next day. Well, what took He but bread, what brake[2] He but bread, and what gave He but bread? Look what He took, He brake, and look what He brake He gave, and look what He gave, they did eat, and yet all this while He Himself was alive and at supper before His disciples, or else they were deceived.

Fecknam. You ground your faith upon such authors as say and unsay both with a breath, and not upon the church to whom ye ought to give credit.

Jane. No, I ground my faith on God's word, and not upon the church, for if the church be a good church, the faith of the church must be tried by God's word, and not God's word by the church, neither yet my faith. Shall I believe the church because of antiquity, or shall I give credit to the church that taketh away from me the half part of the Lord's Supper, and will not let any layman receive it in both kinds but themselves: which thing if they deny to us, then deny they to us part of our salvation? And I say that is an evil church, and not the spouse of Christ, but the spouse of the devil that altereth the Lord's Supper, and both taketh from it and addeth to it. To that church (say I) God will add plagues, and from that church will he take their part out of the book of life. Do they learn that of St. Paul when he ministered to the Corinthians in both kinds? Shall I believe this church? God forbid.

Fecknam. That was done for a good intent of the church, to avoid an heresy that sprung on it.

Jane. Why shall the church alter God's will and ordinance for a good intent? How did King Saul?[3] God the Lord defend.

With these and such like persuasions he would have had her lean to the church, but it would not be. There were many more things whereof they reasoned, but these were the chiefest.

These words following were
spoken openly.

After this Fecknam took his leave saying that he was sorry for her. "For I am sure," quoth he, "that we two shall never meet."

Jane. "True it is," said she, "that we shall never meet, except[4] God turn your heart. For I am assured, unless you repent and turn to God, ye are in an evil case: and I pray God in the bowels of His mercy to send you His holy spirit, for He hath given you His great gift of utterance, if it please Him to open the eyes of your heart."

---

[1] *He calleth … were* Cf. Romans 4.17.

[2] *brake* Broke.

[3] *King Saul* King of Israel who persecuted David, violated God's commandments, and had his kingdom taken away.

[4] *except* Unless.

Edmund Spenser

1552? – 1599

Edmund Spenser has consistently been accorded a special place in the history of English literature. In the seventeenth century John Milton, as much impressed by *The Faerie Queene*'s subtle treatment of the moral virtues as by its aesthetic charm, called him "our sage and serious Spenser, whom I dare to name a better teacher than Scotus or Aquinas." In the nineteenth, Wordsworth wrote of "Sweet Spenser, moving through his clouded heaven / With the moon's beauty and the moon's soft pace." And in the twentieth and twenty-first centuries poets and critics have continued to hold Spenser and *The Faerie Queene* in extraordinarily high regard.

Spenser's career as a servant of the Crown was less glorious. He was not the moping failure some have thought him (he had steady work in Ireland helping the English govern its often rebellious and resentful population), but in England he was never the courtier that he seems to have wanted to be. His bid for more direct royal patronage was the first part of *The Faerie Queene* (1590). This is an allegorical epic poem with debts to Virgil, elements of Arthurian and Italian epic or romance, traces of medieval pilgrimage allegory, Chaucerian moments, and passages indebted to a range of other genres from the fabliau to the pastoral. The central if often absent figure is Prince Arthur, the future British king, who is seeking the always absent heroine, Gloriana, queen of Fairyland and an allegorical "mirror," Spenser told his friend Sir Walter Ralegh in a letter published at the end of the volume, of Queen Elizabeth in her public role as ruler. Modern scholars may perceive veiled criticisms of Elizabeth in the poetry, but the queen either did not notice or thought it wise to read the epic as purely complimentary, so she gave the author a generous yearly pension of fifty pounds.

Little is known with any certainty of Spenser's early life, although his writings provide some information. He was born, probably in London, to parents of modest means, and it was as an "impoverished" student that he entered the Merchant Taylors' School, headed by the scholar Richard Mulcaster, remembered today for his impassioned defense of the English language. There Spenser studied Latin, Greek, and possibly Hebrew; he also learned French and Italian. From there he went to Pembroke Hall (now Pembroke College) at Cambridge University, where he was registered as a "sizar," a poor student who was required to work for his keep, earning his bachelor's degree in 1573 and his M.A. in 1576. While at Pembroke, Spenser made friends with Gabriel Harvey, soon to be a prominent Cambridge don, who introduced him to useful patrons and whose correspondence with the young poet demonstrates a shared interest in poetic theory, genres, and metrics.

In 1579 Spenser produced his first significant, if pseudonymous, publication, *The Shepheardes Calender*, a set of illustrated pastoral poems for each month of the year and written, says a prefatory poem, by one "Immerito." The work, dedicated to Philip Sidney, comes with a preface and annotations by the still unidentified "E.K." In this innovative work, which saw a number of editions, Spenser exploits a genre that hearkened back to Theocritus and Virgil in the third and first centuries BCE but that had since added the potential for religious and political commentary because of the Christian associations of "pastor" and "flock." The book's presentation is fashionably Continental and the metrical variation innovative, yet the language is deliberately old-fashioned, reminiscent of

Chaucer and with a name for the protagonist—Colin Clout—taken from the work of an earlier poet, John Skelton.

In that same year, 1579, Spenser was in the service, as secretary, of the Earl of Leicester, an important royal advisor and at one point suitor to Queen Elizabeth. There he would have met Sidney, Leicester's nephew, and Edward Dyer, both poets and both eventually knighted, whose friendship, or at least notice, would have seemed valuable. Sidney may have helped Spenser later gain an appointment as secretary to Lord Grey, the Lord Deputy of Ireland. It is not quite clear how Spenser regarded Grey's brutality against the Spanish troops who supported the Irish rebels, but his later tract, *A Vewe of the Present State of Ireland* (printed 1633), whatever the ambiguities of its dialogue form and a few residual doubts about its authorship, displays little regard for the Irish and even less for the insurgents. After Grey was recalled to England, Spenser remained in Ireland and continued to work as a civil servant, gaining considerable acreage and a small castle.

In 1589 Spenser traveled with Sir Walter Ralegh to England, where in 1590 he published the first three books of *The Faerie Queene*, on which he had been working for about a decade. Politically as well as poetically motivated, this Protestant, but hardly "Puritan," epic creates a romance world filled with monsters, giants, knights, and enchanters, allegorical personifications who enact a subtle, complex, and often elusive interplay between the Aristotelian or Christian virtues and their enemies, both those active out in the world and those operating within the leading figures' own souls. According to his letter to Ralegh, Spenser hoped to write twelve books, but only six were completed (the second set being published in the 1596 edition): the "legends" of holiness, temperance, chastity, friendship, justice, and courtesy, as well as a fragment on "Mutabilitie." Spenser won his pension, but Elizabeth's patronage seems to have gone no further, perhaps because his satirical "Mother Hubberds Tale," included in his *Complaints* (1591), angered the authorities.

In between the first and second installments of *The Faerie Queene* Spenser published his *Complaints*, a collection of poems; *Colin Clouts Come Home Againe* (1595), a sometimes satirical anti-court pastoral; *Astrophel*, an elegy for Philip Sidney (1596); and *Amoretti and Epithalamion* (1595), sonnets that commemorate Spenser's courtship of Elizabeth Boyle, followed by a magnificently stately marriage hymn celebrating their marriage. The sonnets, which depart from the Petrarchan tradition of adulterous or futile desire, are structured by allusions to the liturgical year; the twenty-four stanzas of the "Epithalamion" allude to the day (June 11, then the summer solstice), and its 365 long lines recall the year.

In 1597 Spenser became Sheriff of Cork, but later that year Irish rebels ransacked and burned his castle. He returned to London carrying dispatches for the Privy Council, but his time there was to be short. He died early in 1599 and is buried in Westminster Abbey, next to Chaucer. A memorial erected in 1620 reads, in part, "Heare lyes ... the body of Edmond Spencer, the prince of poets in his tyme; whose divine spirit needs noe other witnesse then the works which he left behinde him."

⌘⌘⌘

The Faerie Queene

In a letter to his friend Sir Walter Ralegh, Spenser writes that his unfinished *Faerie Queene* aimed to "fashion" a gentleman or noble person who would combine the virtues represented by twelve knightly heroes. In his epic poem, each of the books features one of these knights, who represents a virtue and struggles to fight the specific vices that threaten his quest. The hero of Book 1's "Legend of Holinesse," is Saint George (the Redcrosse Knight), patron saint of England and, with God's help, slayer of a satanic dragon that has been threatening a royal family and its kingdom, Eden. In the legend as it came down to Spenser, George rescues the royal maiden and the kingdom by defeating the dragon but then leaves, soon to be martyred. In Spenser's Protestant version, however, the knight will marry the princess, Una (representing the One, the Truth, and the True Church), although not until his earthly service to the Fairy Queen, Gloriana (who represents, among other things, Queen Elizabeth), is finished. Then, at the end of human time, the marriage of Christ and his Church can be completed.

The somewhat chilly hero of Book 2 is Sir Guyon, Knight of Temperance, who with the intermittent guidance of a Palmer (usually a religious figure, but here signifying rectified reason) seeks not so much a middle way as a dynamic mixture of positive and negative energies, fire and water, excess and lack—a mixture that parallels the healthy body's balance of elements and the cosmos's own tense harmony. The villain is the seductively beautiful but murderous Acrasia ("Excess") who, like Homer's Circe, turns men to beasts. After a journey recalling that of Odysseus, Guyon arrives at her island, a pseudo-paradise of sensuous but sterile pleasures and largely artificial beauty.

The Garden of Adonis is the Bower's parallel and correction, made beautiful by Nature's own art. To this garden will come the lovely Amoret to be raised by Venus in "goodly womanhed." The Garden is the center, structurally and conceptually, of Book 3, the Legend of Chastity. For Spenser, Chastity (represented by the armed lady knight, Britomartis) is an energetic love that embraces a sexuality culminating in faithful marriage. In all the books, the epic's chief hero is Prince Arthur, a Briton who is in love with Gloriana and who will, in Spenser's version of the tale, establish the royal line from which will eventually derive the Welsh Tudor dynasty.

Book 1 derives from a saint's legend, a genre that many Protestants contemptuously dismissed as medieval and Catholic. It is also a dynastic epic, as loosely defined in the Renaissance: its opening lines signal Spenser's aims, and his ambition to be a national poet, through paraphrasing the cancelled start of Virgil's *Aeneid* and the opening of Ariosto's *Orlando Furioso*. Spenser takes his structure of twelve books, each consisting of twelve cantos, from Virgil's *Aeneid*, but his rhyme scheme is distinctly his own. Each nine-line stanza (later referred to as the Spenserian stanza) consists of eight lines of iambic pentameter and a final line of iambic hexameter (an alexandrine) with an interlocking rhyme scheme (*ababbcbcc*). Structurally, the poem follows a pattern set by St. Bernard of Clairvaux (1090– 1153) in a sermon that allegorizes the parable of the Prodigal Son: a young man on an impatient horse journeys with a number of personifications through Error, to Pride, to Despair, and finally to a house where he recovers and is ready for Heaven. Spenser also borrows heavily from Ariosto, Tasso's *Jerusalem Delivered*, Virgil, Chaucer, Arthurian legend, and Tudor anti-Catholic polemic, so that the poem incorporates epic, romance, legend, personification allegory, satire, and pastoral. The Bible figures too, for the narrative moves from a besieged Eden through a fall into error and eventually by way of a victory over the old dragon, Satan, to the promise of the New Jerusalem and the union of God and humanity at the end of time. George's very name, from the Greek for farmer, or "earth-worker," parallels that of Adam (Hebrew for "red earth"), because the Legend of Holinesse also narrates the conversion by God's grace of earthly flesh into Saint George of "merry" England.

Book 1 also allegorizes England's loss of the true Church to Catholicism—just when this had occurred, historically, was a matter of debate at the time, and Spenser is not clear on that point—and its recovery under the Protestant Tudors. In this regard, Spenser's poem exemplifies the anti-Catholicism common in his time and place. Yet he also incorporates a number of Catholic touches, from the hermit who instructs Redcrosse to elements of the Catholic Easter Eve liturgy that deepen the concluding betrothal ceremony. Indeed, in recent years Spenser has seemed less urgently Protestant, and although there can be no doubt that he feared and detested the might of Catholic Spain (allegorized by the giant Orgoglio) and what he saw as the mendaciously seductive powers of the Papacy (allegorized by the magician Archimago and the witch Duessa), his theology has been read as less rigidly Calvinist, with at least a little more room for a free human will than strict Protestants would have liked, and with an acceptance of formal and communal ceremony that would make radical Puritans wince.

In recent years, then, Spenser's moral and religious understanding has come to seem more flexible. Similarly, his treatment of the virtues that his knightly heroes represent has been seen as less illustrative or demonstrative and more interrogative or exploratory. In all the books, even Book 1 (which deals with a virtue hard to live by but easy for readers to value), Spenser is willing to show the problems and paradoxes attendant upon the six virtues he examines: holiness, temperance, chastity, friendship, justice, and courtesy. Although few at his time would deny the virtue of holiness, Spenser can still suggest that it might need, or lead to, the other virtues, and when he comes to the remaining five he is willing to show their limits and their need of correction by yet others. In all cases his knights, and especially the usually less than brilliant St. George, make terrible mistakes. Through these knights' errors Spenser implies that we live in a world that makes virtuous action difficult because perceiving what is good, or even simply knowing what is going on, is often harder than wanting to be good. Spenser's readers may (and perhaps should) find his allegory confusing, but his knights are usually just as confused. Eventually both hero and reader realize what is happening, but each experiences the error and puzzlement that, for Spenser, characterize human life.

The first three books of *The Faerie Queene* were published in 1590 with an appended letter to Sir Walter Ralegh in which Spenser outlines his designs for the epic; some modern editions print it as a preface and others, including this anthology, as the "annex" Spenser himself called it.

---

from *The Faerie Queene*

The First Booke of the Faerie Queene Contayning The Legende of the Knight of the Red Crosse, or Of Holinesse

1

Lo I the man, whose Muse[1] whilome° did maske, *formerly*
As time her taught, in lowly Shepheards weeds,° *garments*
Am now enforst a far unfitter taske,
For trumpets sterne to chaunge mine Oaten reeds,[2]
And sing of Knights and Ladies gentle° deeds; *noble*
Whose prayses having slept in silence long,
Me, all too meane,° the sacred Muse areeds° *common / advises*
To blazon° broad° emongst her learned throng: *proclaim / abroad*
Fierce warres and faithfull loves shall moralize my song.

2

Helpe then, O holy Virgin chiefe of nine,
Thy weaker° Novice to performe thy will, *weak*
Lay forth out of thine everlasting scryne[3]
The antique rolles, which there lye hidden still,
Of Faerie knights and fairest Tanaquill,[4]
Whom that most noble Briton Prince° so long *Arthur*
Sought through the world, and suffered so much ill,
That I must rue his undeservèd wrong:
O helpe thou my weake wit, and sharpen my dull tong.

3

And thou most dreaded impe° of highest Jove,[5] *child*
Faire Venus sonne, that with thy cruell dart
At that good knight so cunningly didst rove,° *shoot*
That glorious fire it kindled in his hart,
Lay now thy deadly Heben° bow apart, *ebony*
And with thy mother milde come to mine ayde:

---

[1] *Muse* One of the nine goddesses who preside over the arts and sciences. In line 10 it seems that Spenser is referring either to Clio, the Muse of history, or Calliope, the Muse of epic.

[2] *Oaten reeds* I.e, the shepherd's pipe, the symbol of pastoral poetry. Spenser exchanges these pipes for the trumpet, the symbol of heroic poetry.

[3] *scryne* Chest for valuables, especially sacred objects such as saints' relics.

[4] *Tanaquill* I.e., Gloriana, a symbolic representation of Queen Elizabeth I.

[5] *And thou … Jove* Here Cupid is the son of Jove, Roman King of the gods, and Venus, goddess of beauty and love. Cupid's father is sometimes said to be Hermes or Mars rather than Jove.

Come both, and with you bring triumphant Mart,[1]
In loves and gentle jollities arrayd,
After his murdrous spoiles and bloudy rage allayd.

4

And with them eke,° O Goddesse heavenly bright, *also*
Mirrour of grace and Majestie divine,
Great Lady of the greatest Isle, whose light
Like Phoebus lampe[2] throughout the world doth shine,
Shed thy faire beames into my feeble eyne,° *eyes*
And raise my thoughts too humble and too vile,
To thinke of that true glorious type[3] of thine,
The argument° of mine afflicted° stile:° *topic / humble / work*
The which to heare, vouchsafe, O dearest dred[4] a-while.

Canto I

The Patron of true Holinesse,
Foule Errour doth defeate:
Hypocrisie him to entrappe,
Doth to his home entreate.

1

A Gentle Knight was pricking° on the plaine, *galloping*
Y cladd in mightie armes and silver shielde,
Wherein old dints of deepe wounds did remaine,
The cruell markes of many a bloudy fielde;
Yet armes till that time did he never wield:[5]
His angry steede did chide his foming bitt,
As much disdayning to the curbe to yield:
Full jolly° knight he seemd, and faire did sitt, *handsome*
As one for knightly giusts° and fierce encounters fitt. *jousts*

2

But on his brest a bloudie Crosse he bore,
The deare remembrance of his dying Lord,
For whose sweete sake that glorious badge he wore,
And dead as living ever him ador'd:
Upon his shield the like was also scor'd,
For soveraine° hope, which in his helpe he had: *greatest*
Right faithfull true he was in deede and word,
But of his cheere° did seeme too solemne sad;° *demeanor / serious*
Yet nothing did he dread, but ever was ydrad.° *dreaded*

3

Upon a great adventure he was bond,
That greatest Gloriana to him gave,
That greatest Glorious Queene of Faerie lond,
To winne him worship,° and her grace to have, *renown*
Which of all earthly things he most did crave;
And ever as he rode, his hart did earne° *yearn*
To prove his puissance° in battell brave *strength*
Upon his foe, and his new force to learne;
Upon his foe, a Dragon horrible and stearne.

4

A lovely Ladie rode him faire beside,
Upon a lowly Asse more white then snow,
Yet she much whiter, but the same did hide
Under a vele, that wimpled° was full low, *folded*
And over all a blacke stole she did throw,
As one that inly mournd: so was she sad,
And heavie sat upon her palfrey slow:
Seemèd in heart some hidden care she had,
And by her in a line a milke white lambe she lad.

5

So pure and innocent, as that same lambe,
She was in life and every vertuous lore,
And by descent from Royall lynage came
Of ancient Kings and Queenes, that had of yore
Their scepters stretcht from East to Westerne shore,
And all the world in their subjection held;
Till that infernall feend with foule uprore
Forwasted° all their land, and them expeld: *lay waste*
Whom to avenge, she had this Knight from far compeld.

6

Behind her farre away a Dwarfe did lag,
That lasie seemd in being ever last,
Or wearied with bearing of her bag

[1] *Mart* Mars, god of war and one of Venus's lovers.

[2] *Phoebus lampe* I.e., the sun (Phoebus Apollo is god of the sun).

[3] *that … type* Gloriana.

[4] *dred* Object of reverence.

[5] *Y cladd … wield* The knight wears the "whole armor of God" (Ephesians 13-17), worn by those who struggle against sin. Though the armor itself bears marks from many battles, this particular knight has never fought in it before.

Of needments at his backe. Thus as they past,
The day with cloudes was suddeine overcast,
And angry Jove an hideous storme of raine
Did poure into his Lemans lap[1] so fast,
That every wight° to shrowd° it did
constrain,° *creature / cover / impel*
And this faire couple eke to shroud themselves were
fain.° *eager*

7

Enforst to seeke some covert° nigh at hand, *shelter*
A shadie grove not far away they spide,
That promist ayde° the tempest to withstand: *aid*
Whose loftie trees yclad with sommers pride,
Did spred so broad, that heavens light did hide,
Not perceable[2] with power of any starre:
And all within were pathes and alleies wide,
With footing worne, and leading inward farre:
Faire harbour that them seemes; so in they entred arre.

8

And foorth they passe, with pleasure forward led,
Joying to heare the birdes sweete harmony,
Which therein shrouded from the tempest dred,
Seemd in their song to scorne the cruell sky.
Much can° they prayse the trees so straight and hy, *did*
The sayling Pine, the Cedar proud and tall,
The vine-prop Elme, the Poplar never dry,
The builder Oake, sole king of forrests all,
The Aspine good for staves, the Cypresse funerall.

9

The Laurell, meed° of mightie Conquerours *reward*
And Poets sage, the Firre that weepeth[3] still,° *continuously*
The Willow worne of forlorne Paramours,
The Eugh° obedient to the benders will, *yew*
The Birch for shaftes,° the Sallow for the mill, *lances*
The Mirrhe sweete bleeding in the bitter wound,
The warlike Beech, the Ash for nothing ill,
The fruitfull Olive, and the Platane° round, *plane-tree*
The carver Holme,° the Maple seeldom inward
sound. *holly*

10

Led with delight, they thus beguile the way,
Untill the blustring storme is overblowne;
When weening° to returne, whence they *expecting*
did stray,
They cannot finde that path, which first was showne,
But wander too and fro in wayes unknowne,
Furthest from end then, when they neerest weene,
That makes them doubt, their wits be not their owne:
So many pathes, so many turnings seene,
That which of them to take, in diverse doubt they been.

11

At last resolving forward still to fare,
Till that some end they finde or in or out,
That path they take, that beaten seemd most bare,
And like to lead the labyrinth about;° *out from*
Which when by tract they hunted had throughout,
At length it brought them to a hollow cave,
Amid the thickest woods. The Champion stout
Eftsoones° dismounted from his courser
brave, *soon afterwards*
And to the Dwarfe a while his needlesse spere he gave.

12

Be well aware, quoth then that Ladie milde,
Least suddaine mischiefe ye too rash provoke:
The danger hid, the place unknowne and wilde,
Breedes dreadfull doubts: Oft fire is without smoke,
And perill without show: therefore your stroke
Sir knight with-hold, till further triall made.
Ah Ladie (said he) shame were to revoke° *withdraw*
The forward footing for° an hidden shade: *because of*
Vertue gives her selfe light, through darkenesse for to
wade.

13

Yea but (quoth she) the perill of this place
I better wot° then you, though now too late *know*
To wish you backe returne with foule disgrace,
Yet wisedome warnes, whilest foot is in the gate,
To stay the steppe, ere forcèd to retrate.
This is the wandring wood, this Errours den,
A monster vile, whom God and man does hate:

---

[1] *his Lemans lap* His beloved's lap; i.e., the earth.

[2] *perceable* Able to be perceived.

[3] *weepeth* I.e., by exuding resin.

Therefore I read° beware. Fly fly (quoth then *declare*
The fearefull Dwarfe:) this is no place for living men.

14

But full of fire and greedy hardiment,° *daring*
The youthfull knight could not for ought be staide,
But forth unto the darksome hole he went,
And looked in: his glistring armor made
A litle glooming light, much like a shade,
By which he saw the ugly monster plaine,
Halfe like a serpent horribly displaide,
But th'other halfe did womans shape retaine,
Most lothsom, filthie, foule, and full of vile disdaine.° *loathsomeness*

15

And as she lay upon the durtie ground,
Her huge long taile her den all overspred,
Yet was in knots and many boughtes° upwound, *coils*
Pointed with mortall sting. Of her there bred
A thousand yong ones, which she dayly fed,
Sucking upon her poisonous dugs, each one
Of sundry shapes, yet all ill favorèd:
Soone as that uncouth° light upon them shone, *unfamiliar*
Into her mouth they crept, and suddain all were gone.

16

Their dam° upstart, out of her den effraide,° *mother / alarmed*
And rushèd forth, hurling her hideous taile
About her cursèd head, whose folds displaid
Were stretcht now forth at length without entraile.° *coil*
She lookt about, and seeing one in mayle
Armèd to point,° sought backe to turne againe; *completely*
For light she hated as the deadly bale,° *injury*
Ay° wont° in desert darknesse to remaine, *ever / accustomed*
Where plaine° none might her see, nor she see any plaine. *plainly*

17

Which when the valiant Elfe[1] perceiv'd, he lept
As Lyon fierce upon the flying pray,
And with his trenchand° blade her boldly kept *cutting*
From turning backe, and forcèd her to stay:
Therewith enrag'd she loudly gan to bray,
And turning fierce, her speckled taile advaunst,
Threatning her angry sting, him to dismay:° *defeat*
Who nought aghast, his mightie hand° enhaunst: *raised up*
The stroke down from her head vnto her shoulder glaunst.

18

Much daunted with that dint, her sence was dazd,
Yet kindling rage, her selfe she gathered round,
And all attonce° her beastly body raizd *at once*
With doubled forces high above the ground:
Tho° wrapping up her wrethèd° sterne arownd, *then / coiled*
Lept fierce upon his shield, and her huge traine° *tail*
All suddenly about his body wound,
That hand or foot to stirre he strove in vaine:
God helpe the man so wrapt in Errours endlesse traine.

19

His Lady sad to see his sore constraint,
Cride out, Now now Sir knight, shew what ye bee,
Add faith unto your force, and be not faint:
Strangle her, else she sure will strangle thee.
That when he heard, in great perplexitie,
His gall° did grate for griefe and high disdaine, *spirit / anger*
And knitting all his force got one hand free,
Wherewith he grypt her gorge with so great paine,
That soone to loose her wicked bands did her constraine.

20

Therewith she spewd out of her filthy maw° *mouth*
A floud of poyson horrible and blacke,
Full of great lumpes of flesh and gobbets raw,
Which stunck so vildly,° that it forst him slacke *vilely*
His grasping hold, and from her turne him backe:

[1] *valiant Elfe* I.e., the Redcrosse Knight (who is from Fairyland, and not yet discovered to be English).

Her vomit full of bookes and papers was,[1]
With loathly frogs and toades, which eyes did lacke,
And creeping sought way in the weedy gras:
Her filthy parbreake° all the place defilèd has. *vomit*

21

As when old father Nilus° gins to swell *Nile river*
With timely° pride above the Aegyptian vale, *seasonal*
His fattie° waves do fertile slime outwell, *rich / gush forth*
And overflow each plaine and lowly dale:
But when his later spring gins to avale,° *subside*
Huge heapes of mudd he leaves, wherein there breed
Ten thousand kindes of creatures, partly male
And partly female of his fruitfull seed;
Such ugly monstrous shapes elswhere may no man reed.° *see*

22

The same so sore annoyèd has the knight,
That welnigh chokèd with the deadly stinke,
His forces faile, ne can no longer fight.
Whose corage when the feend perceiv'd to shrinke,
She pourèd forth out of her hellish sinke
Her fruitfull cursèd spawne of serpents small,
Deformèd monsters, fowle, and blacke as inke,
Which swarming all about his legs did crall,
And him encombred sore, but could not hurt at all.

23

As gentle Shepheard in sweete even-tide,
When ruddy Phoebus gins to welke° in west, *set*
High on an hill, his flocke to vewen wide,
Markes° which do byte their hasty supper best; *notes*
A cloud of combrous gnattes do him molest,
All striving to infixe their feeble stings,
That from their noyance he no where can rest,
But with his clownish° hands their tender wings *rustic*
He brusheth oft, and oft doth mar their murmurings.

24

Thus ill bestedd,° and fearefull more of shame, *situated*
Then of the certaine perill he stood in,
Halfe furious unto his foe he came,
Resolv'd in minde all suddenly to win,
Or soone to lose, before he once would lin;° *cease*
And strooke at her with more then manly force,
That from her body full of filthie sin
He raft° her hatefull head without remorse; *cut off*
A streame of cole black bloud forth gushed from her corse.

25

Her scattred brood, soone as their Parent deare
They saw so rudely° falling to the ground, *violently*
Groning full deadly, all with troublous feare,
Gathred themselves about her body round,
Weening° their wonted entrance to have found *believing*
At her wide mouth: but being there withstood
They flockèd all about her bleeding wound,
And suckèd up their dying mothers blood,
Making her death their life, and eke her hurt their good.

26

That detestable sight him much amazde,
To see th'unkindly Impes° of heaven accurst, *unnatural offspring*
Devoure their dam; on whom while so he gazd,
Having all satisfide their bloudy thurst,
Their bellies swolne he saw with fulnesse burst,
And bowels gushing forth: well worthy end
Of such as drunke her life, the which them nurst;
Now needeth him no lenger labour spend,
His foes have slaine themselves, with whom he should contend.

27

His Ladie seeing all, that chaunst, from farre
Approcht in hast to greet his victorie,
And said, Faire knight, borne under happy starre,
Who see your vanquisht foes before you lye:
Well worthy be you of that Armorie,° *armor*
Wherein ye have great glory wonne this day,
And proov'd your strength on a strong enimie,
Your first adventure: many such I pray,
And henceforth ever wish, that like succeed it may.

28

Then mounted he upon his Steede againe,
And with the Lady backward sought to wend;° *travel*

[1] *Her vomit ... was* I.e., works of Roman Catholic propaganda.

That path he kept, which beaten was most plaine,
Ne ever would to any by-way bend,
But still did follow one unto the end,
The which at last out of the wood them brought.
So forward on his way (with God to° frend°) *as / friend*
He passèd forth, and new adventure sought;
Long way he travellèd, before he heard of ought.

29

At length they chaunst to meet upon the way
An agèd Sire, in long blacke weedes yclad,
His feete all bare, his beard all hoarie gray,
And by his belt his booke he hanging had;
Sober he seemde, and very sagely sad,° *serious*
And to the ground his eyes were lowly bent,
Simple in shew, and voyde of malice bad,
And all the way he prayèd, as he went,
And often knockt his brest, as one that did repent.

30

He faire the knight saluted, louting° low, *bowing*
Who faire him quited,° as that courteous was: *returned*
And after askèd him, if he did know
Of straunge adventures, which abroad did pas.
Ah my deare Sonne (quoth he) how should, alas,
Silly° old man, that lives in hidden cell, *simple*
Bidding his beades[1] all day for his trespas,
Tydings of warre and worldly trouble tell?
With holy father sits not with such things to
mell.° *meddle*

31

But if of daunger which hereby doth dwell,
And homebred evill ye desire to heare,
Of a straunge man I can you tidings tell,
That wasteth all this countrey farre and neare.
Of such (said he) I chiefly do inquere,
And shall you well reward to shew the place,
In which that wicked wight his dayes doth weare:° *spend*
For to all knighthood it is foule disgrace,
That such a cursèd creature lives so long a space.

32

Far hence (quoth he) in wastfull° wildernesse *barren*
His dwelling is, by which no living wight
May ever passe, but thorough great distresse.
Now (sayd the Lady) draweth toward night,
And well I wote,° that of your later° fight *know / recent*
Ye all forwearied be: for what so strong,
But wanting rest will also want of might?
The Sunne that measures heaven all day long,
At night doth baite° his steedes the Ocean *refresh*
waves emong.

33

Then with the Sunne take Sir, your timely rest,
And with new day new worke at once begin:
Untroubled night they say gives counsell best.
Right well Sir knight ye have advisèd bin,
(Quoth then that agèd man;) the way to win
Is wisely to advise:° now day is spent; *consider*
Therefore with me ye may take up your In
For this same night. The knight was well content:
So with that godly father to his home they went.

34

A little lowly Hermitage it was,
Downe in a dale, hard by a forests side,
Far from resort of people, that did pas
In travell to and froe: a little wyde° *apart*
There was an holy Chappell edifyde,° *built*
Wherein the Hermite dewly wont° to say *was accustomed*
His holy things each morne and eventyde:
Thereby a Christall streame did gently play,
Which from a sacred fountaine wellèd forth alway.

35

Arrivèd there, the little house they fill,
Ne looke for entertainement, where none was:
Rest is their feast, and all things at their will;
The noblest mind the best contentment has.
With faire discourse the evening so they pas:
For that old man of pleasing wordes had store,
And well could file his tongue as smooth as glas;
He told of Saintes and Popes, and evermore
He strowd an *Ave-Mary*[2] after and before.

[1] *Bidding his beades* I.e., praying with the aid of rosary beads. These beads, each of which represents a prayer, are counted off as each prayer is completed.

[2] *Ave-Mary* I.e., "Hail, Mary!," a prayer to the Virgin Mary.

36

The drouping Night thus creepeth on them fast,
And the sad humour[1] loading their eye liddes,
As messenger of Morpheus on them cast
Sweet slombring deaw,° the which to sleepe them biddes. *dew*
Unto their lodgings then his guestes he riddes:° *leads*
Where when all drownd in deadly° sleepe he findes, *death-like*
He to his study goes, and there amiddes
His Magick bookes and artes of sundry kindes,
He seekes out mighty charmes, to trouble sleepy mindes.

37

Then choosing out few wordes most horrible,
(Let none them read) thereof did verses frame,
With which and other spelles like terrible,
He bad awake blacke Plutoes griesly Dame,[2]
And cursèd heaven, and spake reprochfull shame
Of highest God, the Lord of life and light;
A bold bad man, that dar'd to call by name
Great Gorgon,[3] Prince of darknesse and dead night,
At which Cocytus quakes, and Styx[4] is put to flight.

38

And forth he cald out of deepe darknesse dred
Legions of Sprights, the which like little flyes
Fluttring about his ever damnèd hed,
A-waite whereto their service he applyes,
To aide his friends, or fray° his enimies: *frighten*
Of those he chose out two, the falsest twoo,
And fittest for to forge true-seeming lyes;
The one of them he gave a message too,
The other by him selfe staide other worke to doo.

39

He making speedy way through spersèd° ayre, *dispersed*
And through the world of waters wide and deepe,
To Morpheus house doth hastily repaire.
Amid the bowels of the earth full steepe,
And low, where dawning day doth never peepe,
His dwelling is; there Tethys[5] his wet bed
Doth ever wash, and Cynthia[6] still° doth steepe *continually*
In silver deaw his ever-drouping hed,
Whiles sad° Night over him her mantle black doth spred. *grave*

40

Whose double gates he findeth lockèd fast,
The one faire fram'd of burnisht Yvory,
The other all with silver overcast;
And wakefull dogges before them farre do lye,
Watching to banish Care their enimy,
Who oft is wont to trouble gentle Sleepe.
By them the Sprite doth passe in quietly,
And unto Morpheus comes, whom drownèd deepe
In drowsie fit he findes: of nothing he takes keepe.° *notice*

41

And more, to lulle him in his slumber soft,
A trickling streame from high rocke tumbling downe
And ever-drizling raine upon the loft,
Mixt with a murmuring winde, much like the sowne° *sound*
Of swarming Bees, did cast him in a swowne:° *swoon*
No other noyse, nor peoples troublous cryes,
As still are wont t'annoy the wallèd towne,
Might there be heard: but carelesse° Quiet lyes, *without care*
Wrapt in eternall silence farre from enemyes.

42

The messenger approching to him spake,
But his wast° wordes returnd to him in vaine: *wasted*
So sound he slept, that nought mought° him awake. *might*
Then rudely he him thrust, and pusht with paine,
Whereat he gan to stretch: but he againe
Shooke him so hard, that forcèd him to speake.
As one then in a dreame, whose dryer braine
Is tost with troubled sights and fancies weake,
He mumbled soft, but would not all his silence breake.

[1] *sad humour* Heavy moisture, sent by Morpheus, god of sleep.

[2] *Plutoes griesly Dame* Persephone, or Proserpine, wife of Pluto and goddess of the underworld.

[3] *Gorgon* Demogorgon, a pseudo-classical demon of the underworld, associated with the early days of creation.

[4] *Cocytus … Styx* Two rivers of the underworld.

[5] *Tethys* Goddess of the sea.

[6] *Cynthia* Goddess of the moon.

43

The Sprite then gan more boldly him to wake,
And threatned unto him the dreaded name
Of Hecate:[1] whereat he gan to quake,
And lifting up his lumpish head, with blame
Halfe angry asked him, for what he came.
Hither (quoth he) me Archimago[2] sent,
He that the stubborne Sprites can wisely tame,
He bids thee to him send for his intent
A fit false dreame, that can delude the sleepers sent.

44

The God obayde, and calling forth straight way
A diverse° dreame out of his prison darke, *diverting*
Delivered it to him, and downe did lay
His heavie head, devoide of carefull carke,[3]
Whose sences all were straight benumbd and starke.
He backe returning by the Yvorie dore,
Remounted up as light as chearefull Larke,
And on his litle winges the dreame he bore
In hast unto his Lord, where he him left afore.

45

Who all this while with charmes and hidden artes,
Had made a Lady of that other Spright,
And fram'd of liquid ayre her tender partes
So lively, and so like in all mens sight,
That weaker sence it could have ravisht quight:
The maker selfe for all his wondrous witt,
Was nigh beguilèd with so goodly sight:
Her all in white he clad, and over it
Cast a blacke stole, most like to seeme for Una[4] fit.

46

Now when that ydle dreame was to him brought,
Unto that Elfin knight he bad him fly,
Where he slept soundly void of evill thought,
And with false shewes abuse his fantasy,
In sort as he him schoolèd privily:
And that new creature borne without her dew,[5]
Full of the makers guile, with usage sly
He taught to imitate that Lady trew,
Whose semblance she did carrie under feignèd hew.° *figure*

47

Thus well instructed, to their worke they hast,
And comming where the knight in slomber lay,
The one upon his hardy head him plast,
And made him dreame of loves and lustfull play,
That nigh his manly hart did melt away,
Bathèd in wanton blis and wicked joy:
Then seemèd him his Lady by him lay,
And to him playnd,° how that false wingèd boy,[6] *complained*
Her chast hart had subdewd, to learne Dame pleasures toy.° *play*

48

And she her selfe of beautie soveraigne Queene,
Faire Venus seemde unto his bed to bring
Her, whom he waking evermore did weene,
To be the chastest flowre, that ay° did spring *ever*
On earthly braunch, the daughter of a king,
Now a loose Leman to vile service bound:
And eke the Graces[7] seemèd all to sing,
Hymen iô Hymen, dauncing all around,
Whilst freshest Flora[8] her with Yvie girlond crownd.

49

In this great passion of unwonted lust,
Or wonted feare of doing ought amis,
He started up, as seeming to mistrust,
Some secret ill, or hidden foe of his:
Lo there before his face his Lady is,
Under blake stole hyding her bayted hooke,
And as halfe blushing offred him to kis,
With gentle blandishment and lovely looke,
Most like that virgin true, which for her knight him took.

[1] *Hecate* Greek goddess of the crossroads, often perceived as evil and linked to witchcraft.

[2] *Archimago* Meaning both arch-image maker and arch-magician in Latin.

[3] *carefull* I.e., full of care; *carke* Anxiety, distress.

[4] *Una* From *unus*, the Latin word for one or unity.

[5] *without her dew* I.e., unnaturally.

[6] *wingèd boy* I.e., Cupid.

[7] *the Graces* Handmaids of Venus who personify pleasure, courtesy, and beauty. Here they sing a hymn to Hymen, the god of weddings, in celebration of the pleasures of the marriage bed.

[8] *Flora* Goddess of flowers.

50

All cleane dismayd to see so uncouth sight,
And halfe enragèd at her shamelesse guise,
He thought have slaine her in his fierce despight:° *indignation*
But hasty heat tempring with sufferance wise,
He stayde his hand, and gan himselfe advise
To prove his sense, and tempt her faignèd truth.
Wringing her hands in wemens pitteous wise,
Tho can° she weepe, to stirre up gentle ruth,° *did / compassion*
Both for her noble bloud, and for her tender youth.

51

And said, Ah Sir, my liege Lord and my love,
Shall I accuse the hidden cruell fate,
And mightie causes wrought in heaven above,
Or the blind God, that doth me thus amate,° *dismay*
For° hopèd love to winne me certaine hate? *in place of*
Yet thus perforce he bids me do, or die.
Die is my dew:° yet rew° my wretched state *due / pity*
You, whom my hard avenging destinie
Hath made judge of my life or death indifferently.

52

Your owne deare sake forst me at first to leave
My Fathers kingdome,—There she stopt with teares;
Her swollen hart her speach seemd to bereave,
And then againe begun, My weaker yeares
Captiv'd to fortune and frayle worldly feares,
Fly to your faith for succour and sure ayde:
Let me not dye in languor° and long teares. *distress*
Why Dame (quoth he) what hath ye thus dismayd?
What frayes° ye, that were wont to comfort me affrayd? *frightens*

53

Love of your selfe, she said, and deare° constraint *dire*
Lets me not sleepe, but wast the wearie night
In secret anguish and unpittied plaint,
Whiles you in carelesse sleepe are drownèd quight.
Her doubtfull words made that redoubted° knight *distinguished*
Suspect her truth: yet since no untruth he knew,
Her fawning love with foule disdainefull spight
He would not shend,° but said, Deare dame I rew, *reprove*
That for my sake unknowne such griefe unto you grew.

54

Assure your selfe, it fell not all to ground;
For all so deare as life is to my hart,
I deeme your love, and hold me to you bound;
Ne let vaine feares procure your needlesse smart,° *suffering*
Where cause is none, but to your rest depart.
Not all content, yet seemd she to appease
Her mournefull plaintes, beguilèd° of her art, *foiled*
And fed with words, that could not chuse but please,
So slyding softly forth, she turnd as to her ease.

55

Long after lay he musing at her mood,
Much griev'd to thinke that gentle Dame so light,° *immoral*
For whose defence he was to shed his blood.
At last dull wearinesse of former fight
Having yrockt a sleepe his irkesome° spright,° *weary / spirit*
That troublous dreame gan freshly tosse his braine,
With bowres, and beds, and Ladies deare delight:
But when he saw his labour all was vaine,
With that misformèd spright[1] he backe returnd againe.

CANTO 2

The guilefull great Enchaunter parts
The Redcrosse Knight from Truth:
Into whose stead faire falshood steps,
And workes him wofull ruth.

1

By this the Northerne wagoner[2] had set
His sevenfold teme behind the stedfast starre,
That was in Ocean waves yet never wet,
But firme is fixt, and sendeth light from farre

[1] *that misinformèd spright* I.e., the spirit disguised as Una.

[2] *Northerne wagoner* Constellation, probably Ursa Major (in England also called "Charles's Wain," or cart), imagined as a farmer guiding a wagon. The "steadfast starre" that never sets in the ocean, however, is the North Star, in the nearby Ursa Minor.

To all, that in the wide deepe wandring arre:
And chearefull Chaunticlere° with his note shrill *rooster*
Had warned once, that Phoebus fiery carre° *chariot*
In hast was climbing up the Easterne hill,
Full envious that night so long his roome did fill.

2

When those accursèd messengers of hell,
That feigning dreame, and that faire-forgèd Spright
Came to their wicked maister, and gan tell
Their bootelesse° paines, and ill succeeding night: *useless*
Who all in rage to see his skilfull might
Deluded so, gan threaten hellish paine
And sad Proserpines wrath, them to affright.
But when he saw his threatning was but vaine,
He cast about, and searcht his balefull° bookes againe. *destructive*

3

Eftsoones he tooke that miscreated faire,
And that false other Spright, on whom he spred
A seeming body of the subtile aire,
Like a young Squire, in loves and lusty-hed
His wanton dayes that ever loosely led,
Without regard of armes and dreaded fight:
Those two he tooke, and in a secret bed,
Covered with darknesse and misdeeming° night, *misleading*
Them both together laid, to joy in vaine delight.

4

Forthwith he runnes with feignèd faithfull hast
Unto his guest, who after troublous sights
And dreames, gan now to take more sound repast,° *repose*
Whom suddenly he wakes with fearefull frights,
As one aghast with feends or damnèd sprights,
And to him cals, Rise rise unhappy Swaine,° *lover*
That here wex° old in sleepe, whiles wicked wights *grow*
Have knit themselves in Venus shamefull chaine;
Come see, where your false Lady doth her honour staine.

5

All in amaze he suddenly up start
With sword in hand, and with the old man went;
Who soone him brought into a secret part,
Where that false couple were full closely ment° *joined*
In wanton lust and lewd embracèment:
Which when he saw, he burnt with gealous fire,
The eye of reason was with rage yblent,° *blinded*
And would have slaine them in his furious ire,
But hardly was restreinèd of° that agèd sire. *by*

6

Returning to his bed in torment great,
And bitter anguish of his guiltie sight,
He could not rest, but did his stout heart eat,
And wast his inward gall with deepe despight,
Yrkesome of life, and too long lingring night.
At last faire Hesperus[1] in highest skie
Had spent his lampe, and brought forth dawning light,
Then up he rose, and clad him hastily;
The Dwarfe him brought his steed: so both away do fly.

7

Now when the rosy-fingred Morning faire,
Weary of agèd Tithones[2] saffron bed,
Had spred her purple robe through deawy aire,
And the high hils Titan° discovered, *the sun*
The royall virgin shooke off drowsy-hed,
And rising forth out of her baser bowre,
Lookt for her knight, who far away was fled,
And for her Dwarfe, that wont to wait each houre;
Then gan she waile and weepe, to see that woefull stowre.° *plight*

8

And after him she rode with so much speede
As her slow beast could make; but all in vaine:
For him so far had borne his light-foot steede,
Prickèd with wrath and fiery fierce disdaine,
That him to follow was but fruitlesse paine;
Yet she her weary limbes would never rest,

[1] *Hesperus* Venus as the morning or evening star.

[2] *agèd Tithones* Husband of the goddess of the dawn, Aurora. Aurora asked Jupiter to give the mortal Tithonus eternal life, but forgot to ask for eternal youth.

But every hill and dale, each wood and plaine
Did search, sore grievèd in her gentle brest,
He so ungently left her, whom she lovèd best.

9

But subtill Archimago, when his guests
He saw divided into double parts,
And Una wandring in woods and forrests,
Th'end of his drift,° he praisd his divelish arts, *scheme*
That had such might over true meaning harts;
Yet rests not so, but other meanes doth make,
How he may worke unto her further smarts:
For her he hated as the hissing snake,
And in her many troubles did most pleasure take.

10

He then devisde himselfe how to disguise;
For by his mightie science° he could take *knowledge*
As many formes and shapes in seeming wise,[1]
As ever Proteus[2] to himselfe could make:
Sometime a fowle, sometime a fish in lake,
Now like a foxe, now like a dragon fell,° *fierce*
That of himselfe he oft for feare would quake,
And oft would flie away. O who can tell
The hidden power of herbes, and might of Magicke spell?

11

But now seemde best, the person to put on
Of that good knight, his late beguilèd guest:
In mighty armes he was yclad anon,
And silver shield upon his coward brest
A bloudy crosse, and on his craven° crest° *cowardly / head*
A bounch of haires discolourd diversly:
Full jolly knight he seemde, and well addrest,° *armed*
And when he sate upon his courser free,
Saint George himself ye would have deemèd him to be.

12

But he the knight, whose semblaunt he did beare,
The true Saint George was wandred far away,
Still flying from his thoughts and gealous feare;
Will was his guide, and griefe led him astray.
At last him chaunst to meete upon the way
A faithlesse Sarazin[3] all arm'd to point,
In whose great shield was writ with letters gay
Sans foy:[4] full large of limbe and every joint
He was, and carèd not for God or man a point.

13

He had a faire companion of his way,
A goodly Lady clad in scarlot red,
Purfled° with gold and pearle of rich assay,° *decorated / quality*
And like a Persian mitre° on her hed *headdress*
She wore, with crownes and owches° garnishèd, *brooches*
The which her lavish lovers to her gave;
Her wanton palfrey all was overspred
With tinsell trappings, woven like a wave,
Whose bridle rung with golden bels and bosses° brave.° *studs / handsome*

14

With faire disport° and courting dalliaunce *amusement*
She intertainde her lover all the way:
But when she saw the knight his speare advaunce,
She soone left off her mirth and wanton play,
And bad her knight addresse him to the fray:
His foe was nigh at hand. He prickt with pride
And hope to winne his Ladies heart that day,
Forth spurrèd fast: adowne his coursers side
The red bloud trickling staind the way, as he did ride.

15

The knight of the Redcrosse when him he spide,
Spurring so hote with rage dispiteous,° *merciless*
Gan fairely couch his speare, and towards ride:
Soone meete they both, both fell and furious,
That daunted with their forces hideous,
Their steeds do stagger, and amazed stand,
And eke themselves too rudely rigorous,
Astonied with the stroke of their owne hand,
Do backe rebut,° and each to other yeeldeth land. *retreat*

16

As when two rams stird with ambitious pride,
Fight for the rule of the rich fleecèd flocke,

[1] *in seeming wise* In the matter of seeming; i.e., in appearance.

[2] *Proteus* Sea god able to change his shape at will.

[3] *Sarazin* I.e., Saracen, a Muslim (but representing Catholicism).

[4] *Sans foy* French: without faith.

Their hornèd fronts so fierce on either side
Do meete, that with the terrour of the shocke
Astonied both, stand sencelesse as a blocke,
Forgetfull of the hanging victory:
So stood these twaine, unmovèd as a rocke,
Both staring fierce, and holding idely
The broken reliques of their former cruelty.

17

The Sarazin sore daunted with the buffe
Snatcheth his sword, and fiercely to him flies;
Who well it wards, and quyteth° cuff with cuff: *requites*
Each others equall puissaunce envies,
And through their iron sides with cruell spies° *glances*
Does seeke to perce: repining courage yields
No foote to foe. The flashing fier flies
As from a forge out of their burning shields,
And streames of purple bloud new dies the verdant fields.

18

Curse on that Crosse (quoth then the Sarazin)
That keepes thy body from the bitter fit;[1]
Dead long ygoe I wote thou haddest bin,
Had not that charme from thee forwarnèd° it: *prevented*
But yet I warne thee now assurèd sitt,
And hide thy head. Therewith upon his crest
With rigour so outrageous he smitt,
That a large share it hewd out of the rest,
And glauncing downe his shield, from blame° him fairely blest.° *harm / protected*

19

Who thereat wondrous wroth, the sleeping spark
Of native vertue° gan eftsoones revive, *strength*
And at his haughtie helmet making mark,
So hugely stroke, that it the steele did rive,° *rend*
And cleft his head. He tumbling downe alive,
With bloudy mouth his mother earth did kis,
Greeting his grave: his grudging ghost did strive
With the fraile flesh; at last it flitted is,
Whither the soules do fly of men, that live amis.

[1] *bitter fit* I.e., death.

20

The Lady when she saw her champion fall,
Like the old ruines of a broken towre,
Staid not to waile his woefull funerall,
But from him fled away with all her powre;
Who after her as hastily gan scowre,° *run*
Bidding the Dwarfe with him to bring away
The Sarazins shield, signe of the conqueroure.
Her soone he overtooke, and bad to stay,
For present cause was none of dread her to dismay.

21

She turning backe with ruefull countenaunce,
Cride, Mercy mercy Sir vouchsafe to show
On silly Dame, subiect to hard mischaunce,
And to your mighty will. Her humblesse low
In so ritch weedes° and seeming glorious show, *clothes*
Did much emmove his stout heroicke heart,
And said, Deare dame, your suddein overthrow
Much rueth° me; but now put feare apart, *grieves*
And tell, both who ye be, and who that tooke your part.

22

Melting in teares, then gan she thus lament;
The wretched woman, whom unhappy howre
Hath now made thrall° to your commandèment, *slave*
Before that angry heavens list to lowre,° *scowl*
And fortune false betraide me to your powre,
Was, (O what now availeth that I was!)
Borne the sole daughter of an Emperour,
He that the wide West under his rule has,
And high hath set his throne, where Tiberis doth pas.[2]

23

He in the first flowre of my freshest age,
Betrothèd me unto the onely haire
Of a most mighty king, most rich and sage;
Was never Prince so faithfull and so faire,
Was never Prince so meeke and debonaire;
But ere my hopèd day of spousall shone,
My dearest Lord fell from high honours staire,

[2] *where ... pas* Rome (the seat of Roman Catholicism), through which the river Tiber runs. The prince to whom the lady claims to have been betrothed is Christ.

Into the hands of his accursèd fone,° *foes*
And cruelly was slaine, that shall I ever mone.

24

His blessed body spoild of lively breath,
Was afterward, I know not how, convaid
And fro me hid: of whose most innocent death
When tidings came to me unhappy maid,
O how great sorrow my sad soule assaid.° *assailed*
Then forth I went his woefull corse to find,
And many yeares throughout the world I straid,
A virgin widow, whose deepe wounded mind
With love, long time did languish as the striken
hind.° *female deer*

25

At last it chauncèd this proud Sarazin
To meete me wandring, who perforce° me led *by force*
With him away, but yet could never win
The Fort, that Ladies hold in soveraigne dread.
There lies he now with foule dishonour dead,
Who whiles he liv'de, was callèd proud Sans foy,
The eldest of three brethren, all three bred
Of one bad sire, whose youngest is Sans joy,° *without joy*
And twixt them both was borne the bloudy bold Sans
loy.° *without law*

26

In this sad plight, friendlesse, unfortunate,
Now miserable I Fidessa[1] dwell,
Craving of you in pitty of my state,
To do none ill, if please ye not do well.
He in great passion all this while did dwell,
More busying his quicke eyes, her face to view,
Then his dull eares, to heare what she did tell;
And said, Faire Lady hart of flint would rew
The undeservèd woes and sorrowes, which ye shew.

27

Henceforth in safe assuraunce may ye rest,
Having both found a new friend you to aid,
And lost an old foe, that did you molest:
Better new friend then an old foe is said.
With chaunge of cheare the seeming simple maid
Let fall her eyen, as shamefast to the earth,
And yeelding soft, in that she nought gain-said,
So forth they rode, he feining seemely merth,
And she coy lookes: so dainty° they say maketh
derth.° *valuable / rare*

28

Long time they thus together travelèd,
Till weary of their way, they came at last,
Where grew two goodly trees, that faire did spred
Their armes abroad, with gray mosse overcast,
And their greene leaves trembling with every
blast,° *gust of wind*
Made a calme shadow far in compasse round:
The fearefull Shepheard often there aghast° *frightened*
Under them never sat, ne wont there sound
His mery oaten pipe, but shund th'unlucky ground.

29

But this good knight soone as he them can° spie, *did*
For the coole shade him thither hastly got:
For golden Phoebus now ymounted hie,
From fiery wheeles of his faire chariot
Hurlèd his beame so scorching cruell hot,
That living creature mote it not abide;
And his new Lady it endured not.
There they alight, in hope themselves to hide
From the fierce heat, and rest their weary limbs a tide.

30

Faire seemely pleasaunce° each to other makes, *pleasantry*
With goodly purposes there as they sit:
And in his falsèd° fancy he her takes *deceived*
To be the fairest wight, that livèd yit;
Which to expresse, he bends his gentle wit,
And thinking of those braunches greene to frame
A girlond for her dainty forehead fit,
He pluckt a bough; out of whose rift there came
Small drops of gory bloud, that trickled downe the same.

31

Therewith a piteous yelling voyce was heard,
Crying, O spare with guilty hands to teare
My tender sides in this rough rynd embard,° *enclosed*
But fly, ah fly far hence away, for feare

[1] *Fidessa* Fidelity.

Least° to you hap, that happened to me heare, *lest*
And to this wretched Lady, my deare love,
O too deare love, love bought with death too deare.
Astond he stood, and up his haire did hove,° *raise*
And with that suddein horror could no member move.

32

At last whenas the dreadfull passion
Was overpast, and manhood well awake,
Yet musing at the straunge occasiön,
And doubting much his sence, he thus bespake;
What voyce of damnèd Ghost from Limbo lake,[1]
Or guilefull spright wandring in empty aire,
Both which fraile men do oftentimes mistake,° *mislead*
Sends to my doubtfull eares these speaches rare,
And ruefull plaints, me bidding guiltlesse bloud to spare?

33

Then groning deepe, Nor damned Ghost, (quoth he,)
Nor guilefull sprite, to thee these wordes doth speake,
But once a man Fradubio,[2] now a tree,
Wretched man, wretched tree; whose nature weake,
A cruell witch her cursèd will to wreake,
Hath thus transformd, and plast in open plaines,
Where Boreas[3] doth blow full bitter bleake,
And scorching Sunne does dry my secret vaines:
For though a tree I seeme, yet cold and heat me paines.

34

Say on Fradubio then, or man, or tree,
Quoth then the knight, by whose mischievous arts
Art thou misshapèd thus, as now I see?
He oft finds med'cine, who his griefe imparts;
But double griefs afflict concealing harts,
As raging flames who striveth to suppresse.
The author then (said he) of all my smarts,
Is one Duessa[4] a false sorceresse,
That many errant° knights hath brought to wretchednesse. *wandering*

35

In prime of youthly yeares, when corage hot
The fire of love and joy of chevalree
First kindled in my brest, it was my lot
To love this gentle Lady, whom ye see,
Now not a Lady, but a seeming tree;
With whom as once I rode accompanyde,
Me chauncèd of a knight encountred bee,
That had a like faire Lady by his syde,
Like a faire Lady, but did fowle Duessa hyde.

36

Whose forgèd beauty he did take in hand,[5]
All other Dames to have exceeded farre;
I in defence of mine did likewise stand,
Mine, that did then shine as the Morning starre:
So both to battell fierce arraungèd arre,
In which his harder fortune was to fall
Under my speare: such is the dye of warre:
His Lady left as a prise martiall,
Did yield her comely person, to be at my call.

37

So doubly lov'd of Ladies unlike° faire, *differently*
Th'one seeming such, the other such indeede,
One day in doubt I cast° for to compare, *resolved*
Whether in beauties glorie did exceede;
A Rosy girlond was the victors meede:
Both seemde to win, and both seemde won to bee,
So hard the discord was to be agreede.
Frælissa[6] was as faire, as faire mote bee,
And ever false Duessa seemde as faire as shee.

38

The wicked witch now seeing all this while
The doubtfull ballaunce equally to sway,
What not by right, she cast to win by guile,
And by her hellish science raisd streightway
A foggy mist, that overcast the day,
And a dull blast, that breathing on her face,
Dimmed her former beauties shining ray,
And with foule ugly forme did her disgrace:
Then was she faire alone, when none was faire in place.

[1] *Limbo lake* Part of hell to which the unbaptized are sent.

[2] *Fradubio* Italian: literally, Brother Doubt.

[3] *Boreas* North wind.

[4] *Duessa* Implies two, doubleness.

[5] *take in hand* Maintain.

[6] *Frælissa* Frailty.

39

Then cride she out, Fye, fye, deformèd wight,
Whose borrowed beautie now appeareth plaine
To have before bewitchèd all mens sight;
O leave her soone, or let her soone be slaine.
Her loathly visage viewing with disdaine,
Eftsoones I thought her such, as she me told,
And would have kild her; but with faignèd paine,
The false witch did my wrathfull hand with-hold;
So left her, where she now is turnd to treen mould.

40

Thensforth I tooke Duessa for my Dame,
And in the witch unweeting° joyd long time, *unknowingly*
Ne ever wist, but that she was the same,
Till on a day (that day is every Prime,[1]
When Witches wont do penance for their crime)
I chaunst to see her in her proper hew,
Bathing her selfe in origane and thyme:
A filthy foule old woman I did vew,
That ever to have toucht her, I did deadly rew.

41

Her neather partes misshapen, monstruous,
Were hidd in water, that I could not see,
But they did seeme more foule and hideous,
Then womans shape man would beleeve to bee.
Thensforth from her most beastly companie
I gan refraine, in minde to slip away,
Soone as appeard safe opportunitie:
For danger great, if not assur'd decay
I saw before mine eyes, if I were knowne to stray.

42

The divelish hag by chaunges of my cheare
Perceiv'd my thought, and drownd in sleepie night,
With wicked herbes and ointments did besmeare
My bodie all, through charmes and magicke might,
That all my senses were bereavèd quight:
Then brought she me into this desert waste,
And by my wretched lovers side me pight,° *planted*
Where now enclosd in wooden wals full faste,
Banisht from living wights, our wearie dayes we waste.

[1] *Prime* First day of a new moon.

43

But how long time, said then the Elfin knight,
Are you in this misformèd house to dwell?
We may not chaunge (quoth he) this evil plight,
Till we be bathèd in a living well;[2]
That is the terme prescribèd by the spell.
O how, said he, mote I that well out find,
That may restore you to your wonted well?° *well-being*
Time and suffisèd° fates to former kind *satisfied*
Shall us restore, none else from hence may us unbynd.

44

The false Duessa, now Fidessa hight,° *called*
Heard how in vaine Fradubio did lament,
And knew well all was true. But the good knight
Full of sad feare and ghastly dreriment,° *gloom*
When all this speech the living tree had spent,
The bleeding bough did thrust into the ground,
That from the bloud he might be innocent,
And with fresh clay did close the wooden wound:
Then turning to his Lady, dead with feare her found.

45

Her seeming dead he found with feignèd feare,
As all unweeting° of that well she knew, *unknowing*
And paynd himselfe with busie care to reare
Her out of carelesse° swowne. Her eylids blew *unconscious*
And dimmèd sight with pale and deadly hew
At last she up gan lift: with trembling cheare
Her up he tooke, too simple and too trew,
And oft her kist. At length all passèd feare,
He set her on her steede, and forward forth did beare.

Canto 3

Forsaken Truth long seekes her love,
And makes the Lyon mylde,
Marres blind Devotions mart,° and fals trade
In hand of leachour vylde.

[2] *Till ... well* See 1 John 4.14, which describes Christ as the Well of Life, a "well of water, springing up into eternal life," for those who believe in Christ and follow his teachings.

1

Nought there under heav'ns wilde hollownesse,
That moves more deare compassiön of mind,
Then beautie brought t'unworthy wretchednesse
Through envies snares or fortunes freakes unkind:
I, whether lately through her brightnesse blind,
Or through alleageance and fast fealtie,
Which I do owe unto all woman kind,
Feele my heart perst with so great agonie,
When such I see, that all for pittie I could die.

2

And now it is empassionèd so deepe,
For fairest Unaes sake, of whom I sing,
That my fraile eyes these lines with teares do steepe,
To thinke how she through guilefull handeling,
Though true as touch, though daughter of a king,
Though faire as ever living wight was faire,
Though nor in word nor deede ill meriting,
Is from her knight divorcèd in despaire
And her due loves deriv'd to that vile witches share.

3

Yet she most faithfull Ladie all this while
Forsaken, wofull, solitarie mayd
Farre from all peoples prease,° as in exile, *press*
In wildernesse and wastfull deserts strayd,
To seeke her knight; who subtilly betrayd
Through that late vision, which th'Enchaunter wrought,
Had her abandond. She of nought affrayd,
Through woods and wastnesse wide him daily sought;
Yet wishèd tydings none of him unto her brought.

4

One day nigh wearie of the yrkesome way,
From her unhastie beast she did alight,
And on the grasse her daintie limbes did lay
In secret shadow, farre from all mens sight:
From her faire head her fillet° she undight,° *headband / undid*
And laid her stole aside. Her angels face
As the great eye of heaven shyned bright,
And made a sunshine in the shadie place;
Did never mortall eye behold such heavenly grace.

5

It fortuned out of the thickest wood
A ramping Lyon rushed suddainly,
Hunting full greedie after salvage° blood; *savage*
Soone as the royall virgin he did spy,
With gaping mouth at her ran greedily,
To have attonce devour'd her tender corse:
But to the pray when as he drew more ny,
His bloudie rage aswaged with remorse,
And with the sight amazd, forgat his furious forse.

6

In stead thereof he kist her wearie feet,
And lickt her lilly hands with fawning tong,
As he her wrongèd innocence did weet.° *understand*
O how can beautie maister the most strong,
And simple truth subdue avenging wrong?
Whose yeelded pride and proud submissiön,
Still dreading death, when she had markèd long,
Her hart gan melt in great compassiön,
And drizling teares did shed for pure affection.

7

The Lyon Lord of everie beast in field,
Quoth she, his princely puissance doth abate,
And mightie proud to humble weake does yield,
Forgetfull of the hungry rage, which late
Him prickt, in pittie of my sad estate:° *state*
But he my Lyon, and my noble Lord,
How does he find in cruell hart to hate
Her that him lov'd, and ever most adord,
As the God of my life? why hath he me abhord?

8

Redounding° teares did choke th'end of her plaint, *overflowing*
Which softly ecchoed from the neighbour wood;
And sad to see her sorrowfull constraint
The kingly beast upon her gazing stood;
With pittie calmd, downe fell his angry mood.
At last in close hart shutting up her paine,
Arose the virgin borne of heavenly brood,
And to her snowy Palfrey got againe,
To seeke her strayèd Champion, if she might attaine.° *overtake*

9

The Lyon would not leave her desolate,
But with her went along, as a strong gard
Of her chast person, and a faithfull mate
Of her sad troubles and misfortunes hard:
Still° when she slept, he kept both watch and ward, *always*
And when she wakt, he waited diligent,
With humble service to her will prepard:
From her faire eyes he tooke commaundèment,
And ever by her lookes conceivèd her intent.

10

Long she thus traveilèd through deserts wyde,
By which she thought her wandring knight shold pas,
Yet never shew of living wight espyde;
Till that at length she found the troden gras,
In which the tract of peoples footing was,
Under the steepe foot of a mountaine hore;° *grey*
The same she followes, till at last she has
A damzell spyde slow footing her before,
That on her shoulders sad° a pot of water bore. *stooped*

11

To whom approching she to her gan call,
To weet, if dwelling place were nigh at hand;
But the rude wench her answer'd nought at all,
She could not heare, nor speake, nor understand;[1]
Till seeing by her side the Lyon stand,
With suddaine feare her pitcher downe she threw,
And fled away: for never in that land
Face of faire Ladie she before did vew,
And that dread Lyons looke her cast in deadly hew.

12

Full fast she fled, ne ever lookt behynd,
As if her life upon the wager lay,
And home she came, whereas her mother blynd
Sate in eternall night: nought could she say,
But suddaine catching hold, did her dismay
With quaking hands, and other signs of feare:
Who full of ghastly fright and cold affray,° *fear*
Gan shut the dore. By this arrivèd there
Dame Una, wearie Dame, and entrance did requere.° *request*

[1] *She … understand* The girl is both deaf and mute.

13

Which when none yeelded, her unruly Page
With his rude° clawes the wicket open rent, *rough*
And let her in; where of his cruell rage
Nigh dead with feare, and faint astonishment,
She found them both in darkesome corner pent;
Where that old woman day and night did pray
Upon her beades devoutly penitent;
Nine hundred *Pater nosters*[2] every day,
And thrise nine hundred *Aves* she was wont to say.

14

And to augment her painefull pennance more,
Thrise every weeke in ashes she did sit,
And next her wrinkled skin rough sackcloth wore,
And thrise three times did fast from any bit:
But now for feare her beads she did forget.
Whose needlesse dread for to remove away,
Faire Una framèd words and count'nance fit:
Which hardly° doen, at length she gan them pray, *with difficulty*
That in their cotage small, that night she rest her may.

15

The day is spent, and commeth drowsie night,
When every creature shrowded is in sleepe;
Sad Una downe her laies in wearie plight,
And at her feet the Lyon watch doth keepe:
In stead of rest, she does lament, and weepe
For the late losse of her deare lovèd knight,
And sighes, and grones, and evermore does steepe
Her tender brest in bitter teares all night,
All night she thinks too long, and often lookes for light.

16

Now when Aldeboran was mounted hie
Above the shynie Cassiopeias chaire,[3]
And all in deadly sleepe did drowèd lie,
One knockèd at the dore, and in would fare;
He knockèd fast,° and often curst, and sware, *vigorously*
That readie entrance was not at his call:

[2] *Pater nosters* Latin: Our Fathers; i.e., repetitions of the Lord's Prayer.

[3] *Aldeboran … chaire* Aldeboran, a star in the constellation Taurus, rises above the northern constellation Cassiopeia.

For on his backe a heavy load he bare
Of nightly stelths and pillage severall,
Which he had got abroad by purchase criminall.

17

He was to weete° a stout and sturdie thiefe, *wit*
Wont to robbe Churches of their ornaments,
And poore mens boxes of their due reliefe,
Which given was to them for good intents;
The holy Saints of their rich vestiments
He did disrobe, when all men carelesse slept,
And spoild the Priests of their habiliments,° *robes*
Whiles none the holy things in safety kept;
Then he by cunning sleights in at the window crept.

18

And all that he by right or wrong could find,
Unto this house he brought, and did bestow
Upon the daughter of this woman blind,
Abessa daughter of Corceca[1] slow,
With whom he whoredome usd, that few did know,
And fed her fat with feast of offerings,
And plentie, which in all the land did grow;
Ne sparèd he to give her gold and rings:
And now he to her brought part of his stolen things.

19

Thus long the dore with rage and threats he bet,° *beat*
Yet of those fearefull women none durst rize,
The Lyon frayèd° them, him in to let: *frightened*
He would no longer stay him to advize,° *consider*
But open breakes the dore in furious wize,
And entring is; when that disdainfull° beast *indignant*
Encountring fierce, him suddaine doth surprize,
And seizing cruell clawes on trembling brest,
Under his Lordly foot him proudly hath suppres.

20

Him booteth not resist,[2] nor succour call,
His bleeding hart is in the vengers hand,
Who streight him rent in thousand peeces small,
And quite dismembred hath: the thirstie land
Drunke up his life; his corse° left on the strand.° *body / ground*
His fearefull friends weare out the wofull night,
Ne dare to weepe, nor seeme to understand
The heavie hap,° which on them is alight, *occurrence*
Affraid, least to themselves the like mishappen might.[3]

21

Now when broad day the world discovered has,
Up Una rose, up rose the Lyon eke,
And on their former journey forward pas,
In wayes unknowne, her wandring knight to seeke,
With paines farre passing that long wandring Greeke,
That for his love refusèd deitie;[4]
Such were the labours of this Lady meeke,
Still seeking him, that from her still did flie,
Then furthest from her hope, when most she weenèd° nie. *believed*

22

Soone as she parted thence, the fearefull twaine,° *pair*
That blind old woman and her daughter deare
Came forth, and finding Kirkrapine[5] there slaine,
For anguish great they gan to rend their heare,° *hair*
And beat their brests, and naked flesh to teare.
And when they both had wept and wayld their fill,
Then forth they ranne like two amazèd deare,
Halfe mad through malice, and revenging will,
To follow her, that was the causer of their ill.

23

Whom overtaking, they gan loudly bray,
With hollow howling, and lamenting cry,
Shamefully at her rayling° all the way, *insulting*
And her accusing of dishonesty,° *lewdness*
That was the flowre of faith and chastity;

[1] *Abessa ... Corceca* Abessa's name derives from the word abbess and associates her with Roman Catholic abbey, monasteries, and absence (from the Latin *abesse*, to be absent). Corceca suggests blindness of heart.

[2] *Him ... resist* It did no good for him to resist.

[3] *least ... might* I.e., lest the same mishap befall them.

[4] *that long ... deitie* Odysseus, King of Ithaca who, according to Homer's *Odyssey*, wandered for ten years seeking his home after the Trojan War. On the way, he was detained by the sea nymph Calypso, who offered him immortality if he would stay with her.

[5] *Kirkrapine* Church robber.

And still amidst her rayling, she° did pray, *Corceca*
That plagues, and mischiefs, and long misery
Might fall on her, and follow all the way,
And that in endlesse error° she might ever stray. *roaming*

24

But when she saw her prayers nought prevaile,
She backe returnèd with some labour lost;
And in the way as she did weepe and waile,
A knight her met in mighty armes embost,° *covered*
Yet knight was not for all his bragging bost,° *boast*
But subtill Archimag, that Una sought
By traynes into new troubles to have tost:
Of that old woman tydings he besought,
If that of such a Ladie she could tellen ought.° *anything*

25

Therewith she gan her passion to renew,
And cry, and curse, and raile, and rend her heare,
Saying, that harlot she too lately knew,
That causd her shed so many a bitter teare,
And so forth told the story of her feare:
Much seemèd he to mone her haplesse chaunce,
And after for that Ladie did inquere;
Which being taught, he forward gan advaunce
His fair enchaunted steed, and eke his charmèd launce.

26

Ere long he came, where Una traveild slow,
And that wilde Champion wayting her besyde:
Whom seeing such, for dread he durst not show
Himselfe too nigh at hand, but turnèd wyde
Unto an hill; from whence when she him spyde,
By his like seeming shield, her knight by name
She weend it was, and towards him gan ryde:
Approching nigh, she wist it was the same,
And with faire fearefull humblesse° towards *humility*
him shee came.

27

And weeping said, Ah my long lackèd Lord,
Where have ye bene thus long out of my sight?
Much fearèd I to have bene quite abhord,
Or ought° have done, that ye displeasen might, *aught*
That should as death unto my deare° hart
light:° *heavy / descend*
For since mine eye your joyous sight did mis,
My chearefull day is turnd to chearelesse night,
And eke my night of death the shadow is;
But welcome now my light, and shining lampe of blis.

28

He thereto meeting[1] said, My dearest Dame,
Farre be it from your thought, and fro my will,
To thinke that knighthood I so much should shame,
As you to leave, that have me lovèd still,
And chose in Faery court of meere° goodwill, *absolute*
Where noblest knights were to be found on earth:
The earth shall sooner leave her kindly° skill *natural*
To bring forth fruit, and make eternall derth,° *famine*
Then I leave you, my liefe,° yborne of *beloved*
heavenly berth.

29

And sooth to say, why I left you so long,
Was for to seeke adventure in strange place,
Where Archimago said a felon strong
To many knights did daily worke disgrace;
But knight he now shall never more deface:
Good cause of mine excuse; that mote° ye please *may*
Well to accept, and evermore embrace
My faithfull service, that by land and seas
Have vowd you to defend. Now then your plaint
appease.° *cease*

30

His lovely words her seemd due recompence
Of all her passèd paines: one loving howre° *hour*
For many yeares of sorrow can dispence:° *compensate*
A dram of sweet is worth a pound of sowre:
She has forgot, how many a wofull stowre° *time of turmoil*
For him she late endur'd; she speakes no more
Of past: true is, that true love hath no powre
To looken backe; his eyes be fixt before.
Before her stands her knight, for whom she
toyld° so sore. *toiled*

[1] *thereto meeting* Meeting her manner; i.e., answering in a like fashion.

31

Much like, as when the beaten marinere,
That long hath wandred in the Ocean wide,
Oft soust° in swelling Tethys saltish teare, *soaked*
And long time having tand his tawney hide
With blustring breath of heaven, that none can bide,
And scorching flames of fierce Orions hound,[1]
Soone as the port from farre he has espide,
His chearefull whistle merrily doth sound,
And Nereus crownes with cups;[2] his mates him pledg° around. *toast*

32

Such joy made Una, when her knight she found;
And eke th'enchaunter joyous seemd no lesse,
Then the glad marchant, that does vew from ground
His ship farre come from watrie wildernesse,
He hurles out vowes, and Neptune oft doth blesse:
So forth they past, and all the way they spent
Discoursing of her dreadfull late distresse,
In which he askt her, what the Lyon ment:
Who told her all that fell in journey as she went.

33

They had not ridden farre, when they might see
One pricking° towards them with hastie heat, *galloping*
Full strongly armd, and on a courser free,
That through his fiercenesse fomed all with sweat,
And the sharpe yron° did for anger eat, *bit*
When his hot ryder spurd his chauffed° side; *chafed*
His looke was sterne, and seemèd still to threat
Cruell revenge, which he in hart did hyde,
And on his shield Sans loy in bloudie lines was dyde.

34

When nigh he drew unto this gentle payre
And saw the Red-crosse, which the knight did beare,
He burnt in fire, and gan eftsoones prepare
Himselfe to battell with his couchèd speare.
Loth was that other, and did faint through feare,
To taste th'untryed dint of deadly steele;
But yet his Lady did so well him cheare,
That hope of new good hap he gan to feele;
So bent his speare, and spurnd his horse with yron heele.

35

But that proud Paynim° forward came so fierce, *pagan*
And full of wrath, that with his sharp-head speare
Through vainely crossèd shield[3] he quite did pierce,
And had his staggering steede not shrunke for feare,
Through shield and bodie eke he should him beare:
Yet so great was the puissance of his push,
That from his saddle quite he did him beare:
He tombling rudely downe to ground did rush,
And from his gorèd wound a well of bloud did gush.

36

Dismounting lightly from his loftie steed,
He to him lept, in mind to reave° his life, *take*
And proudly said, Lo there the worthie meed° *recompense*
Of him, that slew Sans foy with bloudie knife;
Henceforth his ghost freed from repining strife,
In peace may passen over Lethe[4] lake,
When morning altars purgd with enemies life,
The blacke infernall Furies[5] doen aslake:° *appease*
Life from Sansfoy thou tookst, Sansloy shall from thee take.

37

Therewith in haste his helmet gan unlace,
Till Una cride, O hold that heavie hand,
Deare Sir, what ever that thou be in place:
Enough is, that thy foe doth vanquisht stand
Now at thy mercy: Mercie not withstand:
For he is one the truest knight alive,
Though conquered now he lie on lowly land,
And whilest him fortune favourd, faire did thrive
In bloudie field: therefore of life him not deprive.

[1] *Orions hound* Sirius, the dog star, brightest star in the constellation Canis Major. The ancient Egyptians, who observed the star shining for most of the summer months, believed its rays caused the extreme heat, hence the "dog days" of summer.

[2] *Nereus … cups* He toasts Nereus, a sea god.

[3] *vainely … shield* "Vainely" bearing the mere image of a cross and not accompanied by true faith, the shield does not offer Archimago protection.

[4] *Lethe* River in Hades whose waters bring forgetfulness.

[5] *Furies* Three terrible winged goddesses who punish those who commit unavenged crimes.

38

Her piteous words might not abate his rage,
But rudely rending up his helmet, would
Have slaine him straight: but when he sees his age,
And hoarie head of Archimago old,
His hastie hand he doth amazèd hold,
And halfe ashamèd, wondred at the sight:
For the old man well knew he, though untold,[1]
In charmes and magicke to have wondrous might,
Ne ever wont in field, ne in round lists[2] to fight.

39

And said, Why Archimago, lucklesse syre,
What doe I see? what hard mishap is this,
That hath thee hither brought to taste mine yre?
Or thine the fault, or mine the error is,
In stead of foe to wound my friend amis?
He answered nought, but in a traunce still lay,
And on those guilefull dazed eyes of his
The cloud of death did sit. Which doen away,
He left him lying so, ne would no lenger stay.

40

But to the virgin comes, who all this while
Amasèd stands, her selfe so mockt to see
By him, who has the guerdon° of his guile, *recompense*
For so misfeigning her true knight to bee:
Yet is she now in more perplexitie,
Left in the hand of that same Paynim bold,
From whom her booteth not at all to flie;
Who by her cleanly° garment catching hold, *pure*
Her from her Palfrey pluckt, her visage to behold.

41

But her fierce servant full of kingly awe
And high disdaine, whenas his soveraine Dame
So rudely handled by her foe he sawe,
With gaping jawes full greedy at him came,
And ramping° on his shield, did weene° *charging / hope*
the same
Have reft away with his sharpe rending clawes:
But he was stout, and lust did now inflame
His corage more, that from his griping pawes
He hath his shield redeem'd, and foorth his sword he
drawes.

42

O then too weake and feeble was the forse
Of salvage beast, his puissance to withstand:
For he was strong, and of so mightie corse,
As ever wielded speare in warlike hand,
And feates of armes did wisely understand.
Eftsoones he perced through his chaufèd° chest *angry*
With thrilling° point of deadly yron brand, *piercing*
And launcht° his Lordly hart: with death opprest *slit*
He roar'd aloud, whiles life forsooke his stubborne brest.

43

Who now is left to keepe the forlorne maid
From raging spoile of lawlesse victors will?
Her faithfull gard remov'd, her hope dismaid,
Her selfe a yeelded pray to save or spill.° *ruin*
He now Lord of the field, his pride to fill,
With foule reproches, and disdainfull spight
Her vildly° entertaines, and will or nill,[3] *vilely*
Beares her away upon his courser light:° *quick*
Her prayers nought prevaile, his rage is more of might.

44

And all the way, with great lamenting paine,
And piteous plaints she filleth his dull° eares, *deaf*
That stony hart could riven have in twaine,
And all the way she wets with flowing teares:
But he enrag'd with rancor, nothing heares.
Her servile beast[4] yet would not leave her so,
But followes her farre off, ne ought he feares,
To be partaker of her wandring woe,
More mild in beastly kind,° then that her beastly
foe. *nature*

---

[1] *though untold* I.e., without being told.

[2] *round lists* Arenas in which tournaments were held.

[3] *will or nill* Expression meaning willingly or not; i.e., whether she will or won't.

[4] *Her ... beast* I.e., her palfrey.

CANTO 4

To sinfull house of Pride, Duessa
Guides the faithfull knight,
Where brothers death to wreak° Sansjoy — *avenge*
Doth chalenge him to fight.

1

Young knight, what ever that dost armes professe,
And through long labours huntest after fame,
Beware of fraud, beware of ficklenesse,
In choice, and change of thy deare lovèd Dame,
Least thou of her beleeve too lightly blame,
And rash misweening doe thy hart remove:
For unto knight there is no greater shame,
Then lightnesse and inconstancie in love;
That doth this Redcrosse knights ensample° plainly prove. — *example*

2

Who after that he had faire Una lorne,° — *deserted*
Through light misdeeming of her loialtie,
And false Duessa in her sted had borne,
Called Fidess', and so supposd to bee;
Long with her traveild, till at last they see
A goodly building, bravely garnishèd,
The house of mightie Prince it seemd to bee:
And towards it a broad high way that led,
All bare through peoples feet, which thither traveilèd.

3

Great troupes of people traveild thitherward
Both day and night, of each degree and place,
But few returnèd, having scapèd hard,° — *with difficulty*
With balefull° beggerie, or foule disgrace, — *miserable*
Which ever after in most wretched case,
Like loathsome lazars,° by the hedges lay. — *lepers*
Thither Duessa bad him bend his pace:
For she is wearie of the toilesome way,
And also nigh consumèd is the lingring day.

4

A stately Pallace built of squarèd bricke,
Which cunningly was without morter laid,
Whose wals were high, but nothing strong, nor thick,
And golden foile[1] all over them displaid,
That purest skye with brightnesse they dismaid:
High lifted up were many loftie towres,
And goodly galleries farre over laid,
Full of faire windowes, and delightfull bowres;
And on the top a Diall° told the timely howres. — *clock, timepiece*

5

It was a goodly heape° for to behould, — *edifice*
And spake the praises of the workmans wit;
But full great pittie, that so faire a mould
Did on so weake foundation ever sit:
For on a sandie hill, that still did flit,° — *shift*
And fall away, it mounted was full hie,
That every breath of heaven shakèd it:
And all the hinder parts, that few could spie,
Were ruinous and old, but painted cunningly.

6

Arrivèd there they passèd in forth right;
For still to all the gates stood open wide,
Yet charge of them was to a Porter hight° — *designated*
Cald Maluenù, who entrance none denide:
Thence to the hall, which was on every side
With rich array and costly arras dight:° — *decorated*
Infinite sorts of people did abide
There waiting long, to win the wishèd sight
Of her, that was the Lady of that Pallace bright.

7

By them they passe, all gazing on them round,
And to the Presence[2] mount; whose glorious vew
Their frayle amazèd senses did confound:
In living Princes court none ever knew
Such endlesse richesse, and so sumptuous shew;
Ne Persia selfe, the nourse° of pompous pride — *nurse*
Like ever saw. And there a noble crew
Of Lordes and Ladies stood on every side
Which with their presence faire, the place much beautifide.

---

[1] *golden foile* Thin layer of gold.

[2] *Presence* Presence-chamber, where members of the royalty receive guests.

8

High above all a cloth of State was spred,
And a rich throne, as bright as sunny day,
On which there sate most brave° embellished *handsomely*
With royall robes and gorgeous array,
A mayden Queene, that shone as Titans ray,
In glistring gold, and peerelesse pretious stone:
Yet her bright blazing beautie did assay
To dim the brightnesse of her glorious throne,
As envying her selfe, that too exceeding shone.

9

Exceeding shone, like Phoebus fairest childe,[1]
That did presume his fathers firie wayne,° *chariot*
And flaming mouthes of steedes unwonted° *unusually*
wilde
Through highest heaven with weaker hand to rayne;
Proud of such glory and advancement vaine,
While flashing beames do daze his feeble eyen,
He leaves the welkin° way most beaten plaine, *heavenly*
And rapt with whirling wheeles, inflames the skyen,
With fire not made to burne, but fairely for to shyne.

10

So proud she shynèd in her Princely state,
Looking to heaven; for earth she did disdayne,
And sitting high; for lowly she did hate:
Lo underneath her scornefull feete, was layne
A dreadfull Dragon with an hideous trayne,° *tail*
And in her hand she held a mirrhour bright,
Wherein her face she often vewèd fayne,° *gladly*
And in her selfe-lov'd semblance tooke delight;
For she was wondrous faire, as any living wight.

11

Of griesly Pluto she the daughter was,
And sad Proserpina the Queene of hell;
Yet did she thinke her pearelesse worth to pas
That parentage, with pride so did she swell,
And thundring Jove, that high in heaven doth dwell,
And wield the world, she claymèd for her syre,
Or if that any else did Jove excell:
For to the highest she did still aspyre,
Or if ought higher were then that, did it desyre.

12

And proud Lucifera men did her call,
That made her selfe a Queene, and crownd to be,
Yet rightfull kingdome she had none at all,
Ne heritage of native soveraintie,
But did usurpe with wrong and tyrannie
Upon the scepter, which she now did hold:
Ne ruld her Realmes with lawes, but
pollicie,° *political cunning*
And strong advizement of six wisards old,
That with their counsels bad her kingdome did uphold.

13

Soone as the Elfin knight in presence came,
And false Duessa seeming Lady faire,
A gentle Husher,° Vanitie by name *usher*
Made rowme, and passage for them did prepaire:
So goodly brought them to the lowest staire
Of her high throne, where they on humble knee
Making obeyssance, did the cause declare,
Why they were come, her royall state to see,
To prove° the wide report of her great Majestee. *confirm*

14

With loftie eyes, halfe loth to looke so low,
She thankèd them in her disdainefull wise,° *fashion*
Ne other grace vouchsafèd them to show
Of Princesse worthy, scarse them bad arise.
Her Lordes and Ladies all this while devise° *prepare*
Themselves to setten forth to straungers sight:
Some frounce° their curlèd haire in courtly guise, *frizz*
Some prancke° their ruffes, and others trimly dight *pleat*
Their gay attire: each others greater pride does spight.

15

Goodly they all that knight do entertaine,
Right glad with him to have increast their crew:
But to Duess' each one himselfe did paine
All kindnesse and faire courtesie to shew;
For in that court whylome° her well they knew: *previously*
Yet the stout Faerie mongst the middest° crowd *central*
Thought all their glorie vaine in knightly vew,

---

[1] *Phoebus ... childe* Phaeton, son of Apollo, tried to drive his father's chariot (by which the sun was pulled across the sky), but he lost control of the horses and was hurled down by Jove.

And that great Princesse too exceeding prowd,
That to strange knight no better countenance allowd.

16

Suddein upriseth from her stately place
The royall Dame, and for her coche doth call:
All hurtlen° forth, and she with Princely pace, *rush*
As faire Aurora in her purple° pall,° *crimson / robe*
Out of the East the dawning day doth call:
So forth she comes: her brightnesse brode° doth blaze; *abroad*
The heapes of people thronging in the hall,
Do ride each other, upon her to gaze:
Her glorious glitterand light doth all mens eyes amaze.

17

So forth she comes, and to her coche does clyme,
Adornèd all with gold, and girlonds gay,
That seemd as fresh as Flora in her prime,
And strove to match, in royall rich array,
Great Junoes golden chaire, the which they say
The Gods stand gazing on, when she does ride
To Joves high house through heavens bras-pavèd way
Drawne of faire Pecocks, that excell in pride,
And full of Argus eyes[1] their tailes dispredden wide.

18

But this was drawne of six unequall beasts,
On which her six sage Counsellours did ryde,[2]
Taught to obay their bestiall beheasts,
With like conditions to their kinds° applyde: *natures*
Of which the first, that all the rest did guyde,
Was sluggish Idlenesse the nourse of sin;
Upon a slouthfull Asse he chose to ryde,
Arayd in habit blacke, and amis[3] thin,
Like to an holy Monck, the service to begin.

19

And in his hand his Portesse° still he bare, *prayer book*
That much was worne, but therein little red,
For of devotion he had little care,
Still drownd in sleepe, and most of his dayes ded;
Scarse could he once uphold his heavie hed,
To looken, whether it were night or day:
May seeme the wayne was very evill led,
When such an one had guiding of the way,
That knew not, whether right he went, or else astray.

20

From worldy cares himselfe he did esloyne,° *remove*
And greatly shunnèd manly exercise,
From every worke he chalengèd° essoyne,° *claimed / exemption*
For contemplation sake: yet otherwise,
His life he led in lawlesse riotise;° *riot*
By which he grew to grievous malady;
For in his lustlesse limbs through evill guise
A shaking fever raignd continually:
Such one was Idlenesse, first of this company.

21

And by his side rode loathsome Gluttony,
Deformèd creature, on a filthie swyne,
His belly was up-blowne with luxury,° *indulgence*
And eke with fatnesse swollen were his eyne,
And like a Crane[4] his necke was long and fyne,
With which he swallowd up excessive feast,
For want whereof poore people oft did pyne;
And all the way, most like a brutish beast,
He spuèd° up his gorge, that° all did him deteast. *vomited / so that*

22

In greene vine leaves he was right fitly clad;
For other clothes he could not weare for heat,
And on his head an yvie girland had,
From under which fast trickled downe the sweat:
Still as he rode, he somewhat still did eat,
And in his hand did beare a bouzing° can, *drinking*
Of which he supt so oft, that on his seat

[1] *full of Argus eyes* The monster Argus, who had one hundred eyes, was sent by Juno to watch Io, who was loved by Juno's husband, Jove. When Argus was killed, Juno placed his eyes in the tail-feathers of a peacock.

[2] *six unequal beasts* Lucifera, the personification of Pride, worst of the Seven Deadly Sins, leads her counselors, who personify the other six. They ride symbolically relevant animals.

[3] *amis* I.e., amice, priestly vestment.

[4] *Crane* Symbol of gluttony; it was thought the crane's long neck gave it increased pleasure in swallowing.

His dronken corse he scarse upholden can,
In shape and life more like a monster, then a man.

23

Unfit he was for any worldy thing,
And eke unhable once to stirre or go,
Not meet to be of counsell to a king,
Whose mind in meat and drinke was drownèd so,
That from his friend he seldome knew his fo:
Full of diseases was his carcas blew,
And a dry dropsie[1] through his flesh did flow:
Which by misdiet daily greater grew:
Such one was Gluttony, the second of that crew.

24

And next to him rode lustfull Lechery,
Upon a bearded Goat, whose rugged haire,
And whally° eyes (the signe of gelosy,) *glaring*
Was like the person selfe, whom he did beare:
Who rough, and blacke, and filthy did appeare,
Unseemely man to please faire Ladies eye;
Yet he of Ladies oft was lovèd deare,
When fairer faces were bid standen by:° *away*
O who does know the bent of womens fantasy?

25

In a greene gowne he clothèd was full faire,
Which underneath did hide his filthinesse,
And in his hand a burning hart he bare,
Full of vaine follies, and new fanglenesse:
For he was false, and fraught with ficklenesse,
And learnèd had to love with secret lookes,
And well could daunce, and sing with
ruefulnesse,° *dejection*
And fortunes tell, and read in loving° bookes, *erotic*
And thousand other wayes, to bait his fleshly hookes.

26

Inconstant man, that lovèd all he saw,
And lusted after all, that he did love,
Ne would his looser life be tide to law,
But joyd weake wemens hearts to tempt, and prove° *test*
If from their loyall loves he might then move;
Which lewdnesse fild him with reprochfull paine
Of that fowle evill, which all men reprove,
That rots the marrow, and consumes the braine:[2]
Such one was Lecherie, the third of all this traine.

27

And greedy Avarice by him did ride,
Upon a Camell loaden all with gold;
Two iron coffers hong on either side,
With precious mettall full, as they might hold,
And in his lap an heape of coine he told;° *counted*
For of his wicked pelfe° his God he made, *riches*
And unto hell him selfe for money sold;
Accursèd usurie was all his trade,
And right and wrong ylike in equall ballaunce waide.

28

His life was nigh unto deaths doore yplast,
And thred-bare cote, and cobled shoes he ware,
Ne scarse good morsell all his life did tast,
But both from backe and belly still did spare,
To fill his bags, and richesse to compare;° *obtain*
Yet chylde ne kinsman living had he none
To leave them to; but thorough daily care
To get, and nightly feare to lose his owne,
He led a wretched life unto him selfe unknowne.

29

Most wretched wight, whom nothing might suffise,
Whose greedy lust did lacke in greatest store,° *plenty*
Whose need had end, but no end covetise,° *covetousness*
Whose wealth was want, whose plenty made him pore,
Who had enough, yet wishèd ever more;
A vile disease, and eke in foote and hand
A grievous gout tormented him full sore,
That well he could not touch, nor go, nor stand:
Such one was Avarice, the fourth of this faire band.

30

And next to him malicious Envie rode,
Upon a ravenous wolfe, and still did chaw° *chew*
Betweene his cankred° teeth a venemous tode, *infected*
That all the poison ran about his chaw;° *jaw*
But inwardly he chawèd his owne maw° *guts*

[1] *dropsie* I.e., dropsy, disease in which fluid accumulates in the bodily tissue and causes bloating.

[2] *that fowle … braine* I.e., syphilis.

At neighbours wealth, that made him ever sad;
For death it was, when any good he saw,
And wept, that cause of weeping none he had,
But when he heard of harme, he wexèd wondrous glad.

31

All in a kirtle° of discolourd° say[1] *tunic / multicolored*
He clothed was, ypainted full of eyes;
And in his bosome secretly there lay
An hatefull Snake, the which his taile uptyes
In many folds, and mortall sting implyes.
Still as he rode, he gnasht his teeth, to see
Those heapes of gold with griple° Covetyse,° *grasping / avarice*
And grudgèd at the great felicitie
Of proud Lucifera, and his owne companie.

32

He hated all good workes and vertuous deeds,
And him no lesse, that any like did use,° *perform*
And who with gracious bread the hungry feeds,
His almes for want of faith he doth accuse;[2]
So every good to bad he doth abuse:° *misrepresent*
And eke the verse of famous Poets witt
He does backebite, and spightfull poison spues
From leprous mouth on all, that ever writt:
Such one vile Envie was, that fifte in row did sitt.

33

And him beside rides fierce revenging Wrath,
Upon a Lion, loth for to be led;
And in his hand a burning brond° he hath, *sword*
The which he brandisheth about his hed;
His eyes did hurle forth sparkles fiery red,
And starèd sterne on all, that him beheld,
As ashes pale of hew and seeming ded;
And on his dagger still his hand he held,
Trembling through hasty rage, when choler° in him sweld. *anger*

34

His ruffin° raiment all was staind with blood, *disordered*
Which he had spilt, and all to rags yrent,
Through unadvizèd rashnesse woxen° wood;° *grew / mad*
For of his hands he had no governement,° *control*
Ne car'd for bloud in his avengement:
But when the furious fit was overpast,
His cruell facts° he often would repent; *deeds*
Yet wilfull man he never would forecast,° *foresee*
How many mischieves should ensue his heedlesse hast.

35

Full many mischiefes follow cruell Wrath;
Abhorrèd bloudshed, and tumultuous strife,
Unmanly murder, and unthrifty° scath,° *wasteful / damage*
Bitter despight,° with rancours rusty knife, *contempt*
And fretting griefe the enemy of life;
All these, and many evils moe haunt ire,
The swelling Splene,[3] and Frenzy raging rife,
The shaking Palsey, and Saint Fraunces fire:[4]
Such one was Wrath, the last of this ungodly tire.° *procession*

36

And after all, upon the wagon beame
Rode Sathan, with a smarting whip in hand,
With which he forward lasht the laesie teme,
So oft as Slowth still in the mire did stand.
Huge routs° of people did about them band, *crowds*
Showting for joy, and still° before their way *always*
A foggy mist had covered all the land;
And underneath their feet, all scattered lay
Dead sculs & bones of men, whose life had gone astray.

37

So forth they marchen in this goodly sort,
To take the solace of the open aire,
And in fresh flowring fields themselves to sport;
Emongst the rest rode that false Lady faire,
The fowle Duessa, next unto the chaire
Of proud Lucifera, as one of the traine:
But that good knight would not so nigh repaire,° *approach*

[1] *say* Fine cloth, usually made of a mixture of silk and wool.

[2] *His almes ... accuse* Envy accuses those who give to the poor of doing so in an attempt to hide their lack of faith.

[3] *Splene* I.e., spleen, ill-humor or violent temper.

[4] *Saint Fraunces fire* Erysipelas; also known as wildfire or St. Anthony's fire, an inflammatory disease of the skin which produces a red rash.

Him selfe estraunging from their joyaunce vaine,
Whose fellowship seemd far unfit for warlike swaine.

38

So having solacèd themselves a space
With pleasaunce of the breathing° fields yfed *fragrant*
They backe returned to the Princely Place;
Whereas° an errant knight in armes ycled, *where*
And heathnish shield, wherein with letters red
Was writ Sans joy, they new arrivèd find:
Enflam'd with fury and fiers hardy-hed,° *hardihood*
He seemd in hart to harbour thoughts unkind,
And nourish bloudy vengeaunce in his bitter mind.

39

Who when the shamèd shield of slaine Sans foy
He spide with that same Faery champions page,
Bewraying him, that did of late destroy
His eldest brother, burning all with rage
He to him leapt, and that same envious°
gage° *envied / token*
Of victors glory from him snatcht away:
But th'Elfin knight, which ought° that warlike°
wage,° *owned / of war / spoil*
Disdaind to loose the meed° he wonne in fray, *prize*
And him rencountring fierce, reskewd° the *rescued*
noble pray.

40

Therewith they gan to hurtlen° greedily, *rush*
Redoubted battaile ready to darrayne,° *engage*
And clash their shields, and shake their swords on hy,
That with their sturre they troubled all the traine;
Till that great Queene upon eternall paine
Of high displeasure, that ensewen might,
Commaunded them their fury to refraine,
And if that either to that shield had right,
In equall lists they should the morrow next it fight.

41

Ah dearest Dame, (quoth then the Paynim bold,)
Pardon the errour of enragèd wight,
Whom great griefe made forget the raines to hold
Of reasons rule, to see this recreant° knight, *faint-hearted*
No knight, but treachour° full of false despight *traitor*
And shamefull treason, who through guile hath slayn
The prowest knight, that ever field did fight,
Even stout Sans foy (O who can then refrayn?)
Whose shield he beares renverst, the more to heape
disdayn.[1]

42

And to augment the glorie of his guile,
His dearest love the faire Fidessa loe° *look*
Is there possessèd of° the traytour vile, *by*
Who reapes the harvest sowen by his foe,
Sowen in bloudy field, and bought with woe:
That brothers hand shall dearely well requight
So be,[2] O Queene, you equall favour showe.
Him litle answerd th'angry Elfin knight;
He never meant with words, but swords to plead his
right.

43

But threw his gauntlet as a sacred pledge,
His cause in combat the next day to try:
So been they parted both, with harts on edge,
To be aveng'd each on his enimy.
That night they pas in joy and jollity,
Feasting and courting both in bowre and hall;
For Steward was excessive Gluttonie,
That of his plenty poured forth to all:
Which doen, the Chamberlain Slowth did to rest
them call.

44

Now whenas darkesome night had all displayd
Her coleblacke curtein over brightest skye,
The warlike youthes on dayntie couches layd,
Did chace away sweet sleepe from sluggish eye,
To muse on meanes of hopèd victory.
But whenas Morpheus had with leaden mace
Arrested[3] all that courtly company,
Up-rose Duessa from her resting place,
And to the Paynims lodging comes with silent pace.

---

[1] *Whose ... disdayn* Carrying a shield upside down was considered a great insult.

[2] *So be* If.

[3] *Arrested* I.e., put to sleep.

45

Whom broad awake she finds, in troublous fit,
Forecasting, how his foe he might annoy,° *harm*
And him amoves° with speaches seeming fit: *arouses*
Ah deare Sans joy, next dearest to Sans foy,
Cause of my new griefe, cause of my new joy,
Joyous, to see his ymage in mine eye,
And greev'd, to thinke how foe did him destroy,
That was the flowre of grace and chevalrye;
Lo his Fidessa to thy secret faith I flye.

46

With gentle wordes he can° her fairely greet, *did*
And bad° say on the secret of her hart. *bade*
Then sighing soft, I learne that litle sweet
Oft tempred is (quoth she) with muchell° smart:° *much / pain*
For since my brest was launcht with lovely° dart *of love*
Of deare Sans foy, I never joyèd howre,
But in eternall woes my weaker° hart *too weak*
Have wasted, loving him with all my powre,
And for his sake have felt full many an heavie stowre.° *turmoil*

47

At last when perils all I weenèd past,
And hop'd to reape the crop of all my care,
Into new woes unweeting I was cast,
By this false faytor,° who unworthy ware *imposter*
His worthy shield, whom he with guilefull snare
Entrappèd slew, and brought to shamefull grave.
Me silly° maid away with him he bare, *helpless*
And ever since hath kept in darksome cave,
For that I would not yeeld, that to Sans-foy I gave.

48

But since faire Sunne hath sperst° that lowring clowd, *dispersed*
And to my loathèd life now shewes some light,
Under your beames I will me safely shrowd,
From dreaded storme of his disdainfull spight:
To you th'inheritance belongs by right
Of brothers prayse, to you eke longs° his love. *belongs*
Let not his love, let not his restlesse spright° *spirit*
Be unreveng'd, that calles to you above
From wandring Stygian shores,[1] where it doth endlesse move.

49

Thereto said he, Faire Dame be nought dismaid
For sorrowes past; their griefe is with them gone:
Ne yet of present perill be affraid;
For needlesse feare did never vantage none,
And helplesse hap it booteth not to mone.° *bemoan*
Dead is Sans-foy, his vitall° paines are past, *living*
Though greevèd ghost for vengeance deepe do grone:
He lives, that shall him pay his dewties° last, *rites*
And guiltie Elfin bloud shall sacrifice in hast.

50

O but I feare the fickle° freakes° (quoth shee) *unpredictable / whims*
Of fortune false, and oddes° of armes in field. *advantages*
Why dame (quoth he) what oddes can ever bee,
Where both do fight alike, to win or yield?
Yea but (quoth she) he beares a charmèd shield,
And eke enchaunted armes, that none can perce,
Ne none can wound the man, that does them wield.
Charmd or enchaunted (answerd he then ferce)° *fiercely*
I no whit reck,° ne you the like need to reherce. *care / recount*

51

But faire Fidessa, sithens fortunes guile,
Or enimies powre hath now captivèd you,
Returne from whence ye came, and rest a while
Till morrow next, that I the Elfe subdew,
And with Sans-foyes dead dowry you endew.
Ay me, that is a double death (she said)
With proud foes sight my sorrow to renew:
Where ever yet I be, my secrete aid
Shall follow you. So passing forth she him obaid.

---

[1] *Stygian shores* Shores of the river Styx, across which (according to classical mythology) all souls had to travel to reach Hades. Those who were not given a proper funeral were condemned to wander the banks of the river for one hundred years.

CANTO 5

The faithfull knight in equall field
Subdewes his faithlesse foe,
Whom false Duessa saves, and for
His cure to hell does goe.

1

The noble hart, that harbours vertuous thought,
And is with child of glorious great intent,
Can never rest, untill it forth have brought
Th'eternall brood of glorie excellent:
Such restlesse passion did all night torment
The flaming corage of that Faery knight,
Devizing, how that doughtie° tournament *worthy*
With greatest honour he atchieven might;
Still did he wake, and still did watch for dawning light.

2

At last the golden Orientall° gate *eastern*
Of greatest heaven gan to open faire,
And Phoebus fresh, as bridegrome to his mate,
Came dauncing forth, shaking his deawie haire:
And hurld his glistring° beames through gloomy aire. *glistening*
Which when the wakeful Elfe perceiv'd, streight way
He started up, and did him selfe prepaire,
In sun-bright armes, and battailous array:
For with that Pagan proud he combat will that day.

3

And forth he comes into the commune hall,
Where earely waite him many a gazing eye,
To weet what end to straunger knights may fall.
There many Minstrales maken melody,
To drive away the dull melancholy,
And many Bardes, that to the trembling chord
Can tune their timely voyces cunningly,
And many Chroniclers, that can record
Old loves, and warres for Ladies doen by many a Lord.

4

Soone after comes the cruell Sarazin,
In woven maile all armèd warily,
And sternly lookes at him, who not a pin
Does care for looke of living creatures eye.
They bring them wines of Greece and Araby,
And daintie spices fetcht from furthest Ynd,° *India*
To kindle heat of corage privily:° *internally*
And in the wine a solemne oth they bynd
T'observe the sacred lawes of armes, that are assynd.

5

At last forth comes that far renowmèd Queene,
With royall pomp and Princely majestie;
She is ybrought unto a palèd° greene, *enclosed*
And placèd under stately canapee,
The warlike feates of both those knights to see.
On th'other side in all mens open vew
Duessa placèd is, and on a tree
Sans-foy his shield is hangd with bloudy hew:
Both those the lawrell girlonds[1] to the victor dew.

6

A shrilling trompet sownded from on hye,
And unto battaill bad them selves addresse:
Their shining shieldes about their wrestes° they tye, *wrists*
And burning blades about their heads do blesse,[2]
The instruments of wrath and heavinesse:
With greedy force each other doth assayle,
And strike so fiercely, that they do impresse
Deepe dinted furrowes in the battred mayle;
The yron walles[3] to ward their blowes are weake & fraile.

7

The Sarazin was stout, and wondrous strong,
And heapèd blowes like yron hammers great:
For after bloud and vengeance he did long.
The knight was fiers, and full of youthly heat:
And doubled strokes, like dreaded thunders threat:
For all for prayse and honour he did fight.
Both stricken strike, and beaten both do beat,
That from their shields forth flyeth firie light,
And helmets hewen deepe, shew marks of eithers might.

---

[1] *lawrell girlonds* Laurel wreaths were awarded to victorious athletes.

[2] *blesse* Brandish (by making the sign of the cross).

[3] *yron walles* I.e., of their armor.

8

So th'one for wrong, the other strives for right:
As when a Gryfon[1] seizèd° of his pray, *having seized*
A Dragon fiers encountreth in his flight,
Through widest ayre making his ydle way,
That would his rightfull ravine° rend away: *spoils*
With hideous horrour both together smight,
And souce° so sore, that they the heavens affray: *smite*
The wise Southsayer seeing so sad sight,
Th'amazèd vulgar tels of warres and mortall fight.

9

So th'one for wrong, the other strives for right,
And each to deadly shame would drive his foe:
The cruell steele so greedily doth bight
In tender flesh, that streames of bloud down flow,
With which the armes, that earst so bright did show,
Into a pure vermillion now are dyde:
Great ruth° in all the gazers harts did grow, *compassion*
Seeing the gorèd woundes to gape so wyde,
That victory they dare not wish to either side.

10

At last the Paynim chaunst to cast his eye,
His suddein° eye, flaming with wrathfull fyre, *quickly glancing*
Upon his brothers shield, which hong thereby:
Therewith redoubled was his raging yre,
And said, Ah wretched sonne of wofull syre,
Doest thou sit wayling by black Stygian lake,
Whilest here thy shield is hangd for victors hyre,° *reward*
And sluggish german° doest thy forces slake, *brother*
To after-send his foe, that him may overtake?

11

Goe caytive° Elfe, him quickly overtake, *servile*
And soone redeeme from his long wandring woe;
Goe guiltie ghost,° to him my message make, *spirit*
That I his shield have quit from dying foe.
Therewith upon his crest he stroke him so,
That twise he reelèd, readie twise to fall;
End of the doubtfull battell deemèd tho
The lookers on, and lowd to him gan call
The false Duessa, Thine the shield, and I, and all.

12

Soone as the Faerie heard his Ladie speake,
Out of his swowning dreame he gan awake,
And quickning faith, that earst was woxen weake,
The creeping deadly cold away did shake:
Tho mov'd with wrath, and shame, and Ladies sake,
Of all attonce he cast° avengd to bee, *resolved*
And with so'exceeding furie at him strake,
That forcèd him to stoupe upon his knee;
Had he not stoupèd so, he should have cloven bee.

13

And to him said, Goe now proud Miscreant,° *infidel*
Thy selfe thy message doe° to german deare, *bring*
Alone he wandring thee too long doth want:
Goe say, his foe thy shield with his doth beare.
Therewith his heavie hand he high gan reare,
Him to have slaine; when loe a darkesome clowd
Upon him fell: he no where doth appeare,
But vanisht is. The Elfe him cals alowd,
But answer none receives: the darknes him does shrowd.

14

In haste Duessa from her place arose,
And to him running said, O prowest knight,
That ever Ladie to her love did chose,
Let now abate the terror of your might,
And quench the flame of furious despight,
And bloudie vengeance; lo th'infernall powres
Covering your foe with cloud of deadly night,
Have borne him hence to Plutoes balefull° bowres. *deadly*
The conquest yours, I yours, the shield, and glory yours.

15

Not all so satisfide, with greedie eye
He sought all round about, his thirstie blade
To bath in bloud of faithlesse enemy;
Who all that while lay hid in secret shade:
He standes amazèd, how he thence should fade.
At last the trumpets Triumph sound on hie,
And running Heralds humble homage made,

[1] *Gryfon* I.e., griffin, gryphon, or griffon: mythical monster with the head and wings of an eagle and the body of a lion.

Greeting him goodly with new victorie,
And to him brought the shield, the cause of enmitie.

16

Wherewith he goeth to that soveraine Queene,
And falling her before on lowly knee,
To her makes present of his service seene:
Which she accepts, with thankes, and goodly gree,° *favor*
Greatly advauncing° his gay chevalree. *extolling*
So marcheth home, and by her takes the knight,
Whom all the people follow with great glee,
Shouting, and clapping all their hands on hight,
That all the aire it fils, and flyes to heaven bright.

17

Home is he brought, and laid in sumptuous bed:
Where many skilfull leaches° him abide,° *doctors / attend*
To salve his hurts, that yet still freshly bled.
In wine and oyle they wash his woundes wide,
And softly can embalme on every side.
And all the while, most heavenly melody
About the bed sweet musicke did divide,° *play*
Him to beguile of griefe and agony:
And all the while Duessa wept full bitterly.

18

As when a wearie traveller that strayes
By muddy shore of broad seven-mouthèd Nile,
Unweeting of the perillous wandring wayes,
Doth meet a cruell craftie Crocodile,
Which in false griefe hyding his harmefull guile,
Doth weepe full sore, and sheddeth tender teares:
The foolish man, that pitties all this while
His mournefull plight, is swallowd up unwares,
Forgetfull of his owne, that mindes anothers cares.

19

So wept Duessa untill eventide,
That shyning lampes in Joves high house were light:
Then forth she rose, ne lenger would abide,
But comes unto the place, where th'Hethen knight
In slombring swownd° nigh voyd of vitall spright, *swoon*
Lay cover'd with inchaunted cloud all day:
Whom when she found, as she him left in plight,[1]
To wayle his woefull case she would not stay,
But to the easterne coast of heaven makes speedy way.

20

Where griesly Night, with visage deadly sad,
That Phoebus chearefull face durst never vew,
And in a foule blacke pitchie mantle clad,
She findes forth comming from her darkesome mew,° *den*
Where she all day did hide her hated hew.
Before the dore her yron charet stood,
Alreadie harnessèd for journey new;
And coleblacke steedes yborne of hellish brood,
That on their rustie bits did champ, as they were wood.° *crazy*

21

Who when she saw Duessa sunny bright,
Adornd with gold and jewels shining cleare,
She greatly grew amazèd at the sight,
And th'unacquainted light began to feare:
For never did such brightnesse there appeare,
And would have backe retyred to her cave,
Untill the witches speech she gan to heare,
Saying, Yet O thou dreaded Dame, I crave
Abide, till I have told the message, which I have.

22

She stayd, and foorth Duessa gan proceede,
O thou most auncient Grandmother of all,[2]
More old then Jove, whom thou at first didst breede,
Or that great house of Gods cælestiall,
Which wast begot in Dæmogorgons[3] hall,
And sawst the secrets of the world unmade,
Why suffredst thou thy Nephewes° deare to fall *grandsons*
With Elfin sword, most shamefully betrade?
Lo where the stout Sansjoy doth sleepe in deadly shade.

---

[1] *in plight* In the same condition in which she found him.

[2] *O … all* According to myth, Night existed before the world was formed and the rest of the gods were born.

[3] *Dæmogorgons* I.e., Demogorgons.

23

And him before, I saw with bitter eyes
The bold Sansfoy shrinke underneath his speare;
And now the pray of fowles in field he lyes,
Nor wayld of friends, nor laid on groning beare,[1]
That whylome was to me too dearely deare.
O what of Gods then boots it to be borne,
If old Aveugles sonnes so evill heare?[2]
Or who shall not great Nightes children scorne,
When two of three her Nephews are so fowle forlorne?

24

Up then, up dreary Dame, of darknesse Queene,
Go gather up the reliques of thy race,
Or else goe them avenge, and let be seene,
That dreaded Night in brightest day hath place,
And can the children of faire light deface.
Her feeling speeches some compassion moved
In hart, and chaunge in that great mothers face:
Yet pittie in her hart was never proved° *known*
Till then: for evermore she hated, never loved.

25

And said, Deare daughter rightly may I rew
The fall of famous children borne of mee,
And good successes, which their foes ensew:
But who can turne the streame of destinee,
Or breake the chayne of strong necessitee,
Which fast is tyde to Joves eternall seat?
The sonnes of Day he favoureth, I see,
And by my ruines thinkes to make them great:
To make one great by others losse, is bad excheat.° *exchange*

26

Yet shall they not escape so freely all;
For some shall pay the price of others guilt:
And he the man that made Sansfoy to fall,
Shall with his owne bloud price° that he hath spilt. *pay for*
But what art thou, that telst of Nephews kilt?
I that do seeme not I, Duessa am,
(Quoth she) how ever now in garments gilt,
And gorgeous gold arayd I to thee came;
Duessa I, the daughter of Deceipt and Shame.

27

Then bowing downe her agèd backe, she kist
The wicked witch, saying; In that faire face
The false resemblance of Deceipt, I wist° *knew*
Did closely° lurke; yet so true-seeming grace *secretly*
It carried, that I scarse in darkesome place
Could it discerne, though I the mother bee
Of falshood, and root of Duessaes race.
O welcome child, whom I have longd to see,
And how have seene unwares. Lo now I go with thee.

28

Then to her yron wagon she betakes,
And with her beares the fowle welfavourd witch:
Through mirkesome° aire her readie way she makes. *murky*
Her twyfold° Teme, of which two blacke as pitch, *twofold*
And two were browne, yet each to each unlich,° *unlike*
Did softly swim away, ne ever stampe,
Unlesse she chaunst their stubborne mouths to twitch;
Then foming tarre, their bridles they would champe,
And trampling the fine element,° would fiercely rampe.° *air / rear*

29

So well they sped, that they be come at length
Unto the place, whereas the Paynim lay,
Devoid of outward sense, and native strength,
Coverd with charmèd cloud from vew of day,
And sight of men, since his late luckelesse fray.
His cruell wounds with cruddy bloud congealed,
They binden up so wisely,° as they may, *skillfully*
And handle softly, till they can be healed:
So lay him in her charet, close in night concealed.

30

And all the while she stood upon the ground,
The wakefull dogs did never cease to bay,
As giving warning of th'unwonted° sound, *unaccustomed*

---

[1] *groning beare* That is, the bier would be attended by moaning or weeping mourners.

[2] *If … heare* If the sons of Aveugle are so poorly thought of. Aveugle (French for blind) is the son of Night and the father of Sansfoy, Sansjoy, and Sansloy.

With which her yron wheeles did them affray,
And her darke griesly looke them much dismay;
The messenger of death, the ghastly Owle
With drearie shriekes did also her bewray;° *expose*
And hungry Wolves continually did howle,
At her abhorred face, so filthy and so fowle.

31

Thence turning backe in silence soft they stole,
And brought the heavie corse with easie pace
To yawning gulfe of deepe Avernus hole.[1]
By that same hole an entrance darke and bace° *low*
With smoake and sulphure hiding all the place,
Descends to hell: there creature never past,
That backe returnèd without heavenly grace;
But dreadfull Furies, which their chaines have brast,° *burst*
And damnèd sprights sent forth to make ill men aghast.

32

By that same way the direfull° dames doe drive *dreadful*
Their mournefull charet, fild° with rusty blood, *defiled*
And downe to Plutoes house are come bilive:° *immediately*
Which passing through, on every side them stood
The trembling ghosts with sad amazèd mood,
Chattring their yron teeth, and staring wide
With stonie eyes; and all the hellish brood
Of feends infernall flockt on every side,
To gaze on earthly wight, that with the Night durst° ride. *dared*

33

They pas the bitter waves of Acheron,
Where many soules sit wailing woefully,
And come to fiery flood of Phlegeton,[2]
Whereas the damnèd ghosts in torments fry,
And with sharpe shrilling shriekes doe bootlesse cry,
Cursing high Jove, the which them thither sent.
The house of endlesse paine is built thereby,
In which ten thousand sorts of punishment
The cursèd creatures doe eternally torment.

34

Before the threshold dreadfull Cerberus[3]
His three deformèd heads did lay along,
Curled with thousand adders venemous,
And lillèd° forth his bloudie flaming tong: *lolled*
At them he gan to reare his bristles strong,
And felly gnarre,° untill dayes enemy *fiercely snarl*
Did him appease; then downe his taile he hong
And suffered them to passen quietly:
For she in hell and heaven had power equally.

35

There was Ixion turnèd on a wheele,
For daring tempt the Queene of heaven to sin;
And Sisyphus an huge round stone did reele
Against an hill, ne might from labour lin;° *cease*
There thirstie Tantalus hong by the chin;
And Tityus fed a vulture on his maw;
Typhoeus joynts were stretchèd on a gin,° *rack*
Theseus condemned to endlesse slouth° by law, *sloth*
And fifty sisters water in leake vessels draw.[4]

36

They all beholding worldly° wights in place, *mortal*
Leave off their worke, unmindfull of their smart,
To gaze on them; who forth by them doe pace,
Till they be come unto the furthest part:
Where was a Cave ywrought by wondrous art,
Deepe, darke, uneasie, dolefull, comfortlesse,
In which sad Æsculapius[5] farre a part

[1] *Avernus hole* Hell.

[2] *Acheron … Phlegeton* Two rivers of the underworld.

[3] *Cerberus* Three-headed dog that guards the entrance to the underworld.

[4] *Ixion* King of Thessaly who attempted to seduce Hera and, as punishment, was bound to an ever-revolving wheel; *Sisyphus* Punished for his greed and cruelty by being forced to push a boulder continually up a hill, only to have it roll back down whenever he reached the top; *Tantalus* After committing a variety of sins, Tantalus was forced to stand chin-deep in water that receded whenever he attempted to drink and with branches of fruit that receded when he attempted to grasp them; *Tityus* A vulture constantly fed on Tityus's liver as punishment for his attempted seduction of Leto; *Theseus* Greek hero who tried to steal Persephone from Hades and instead was trapped in a chair of forgetfulness; *fifty sisters* Daughters of King Danaus who all killed their husbands on their wedding nights, and for this were condemned to forever collect water in leaky vessels.

[5] *Æsculapius* God of medicine.

Emprisond was in chaines remedilesse,
For that Hippolytus rent corse he did redresse.° *restore*

37

Hippolytus a jolly huntsman was,
That wont° in charet chace the foming
Bore;° *was accustomed to / boar*
He all his Peeres in beautie did surpas,
But Ladies love as losse of time forbore:° *abstained from*
His wanton stepdame[1] lovèd him the more,
But when she saw her offred sweets refused
Her love she turnd to hate, and him before
His father fierce of treason false accused,
And with her gealous° termes his open eares
abused. *causing jealousy*

38

Who all in rage his Sea-god syre[2] besought,
Some cursèd vengeance on his sonne to cast:
From surging gulf two monsters straight were brought,
With dread whereof his chasing steedes aghast,
Both charet swift and huntsman overcast.
His goodly corps on ragged cliffs yrent,
Was quite dismembred, and his members chast
Scattered on every mountaine, as he went,
That of Hippolytus was left no moniment.

39

His cruell stepdame seeing what was donne,
Her wicked dayes with wretched knife did end,
In death avowing th'innocence of her sonne.
Which hearing his rash Syre, began to rend
His haire, and hastie tongue, that did offend:
Tho° gathering up the relicks of his smart *then*
By Dianes[3] meanes, who was Hippolyts frend,
Them brought to Æsculape, that by his art
Did heale them all againe, and joyned every part.

40

Such wondrous science in mans wit to raine
When Jove avizd,° that could the dead revive, *observed*
And fates expirèd could renew againe,
Of endlesse life he might him not deprive,
But unto hell did thrust him downe alive,
With flashing thunderbolt ywounded sore:
Where long remaining, he did alwaies strive
Himselfe wilth salves to health for to restore,
And slake the heavenly fire, that raged evermore.

41

There auncient Night arriving, did alight
From her nigh wearie waine, and in her armes
To Æsculapius brought the wounded knight:
Whom having softly disarayd of armes,
Tho gan to him discover all his harmes,
Beseeching him with prayer, and with praise,
If either salves, or oyles, or herbes, or charmes
A fordonne° wight from dore of death *overcome*
mote raise,
He would at her request prolong her nephews daies.

42

Ah Dame (quoth he) thou temptest me in vaine,
To dare the thing, which daily yet I rew,
And the old cause of my continued paine
With like attempt to like end to renew.
Is not enough, that thrust from heaven dew° *due*
Here endlesse penance for one fault I pay,
But that redoubled crime with vengeance new
Thou biddest me to eeke?° Can Night
defray° *augment / appease*
The wrath of thundring Jove, that rules both night
and day?

43

Not so (quoth she) but sith that heavens king
From hope of heaven hath thee excluded quight,
Why fearest thou, that canst not hope for thing,
And fearest not, that more thee hurten might,
Now in the powre of everlasting Night?
Goe to then, O thou farre renowmèd sonne
Of great Apollo, shew thy famous might
In medicine, that else° hath to thee wonne *already*
Great paines, & greater praise, both never to be
donne.° *finished*

[1] *His wanton stepdame* I.e., his stepmother, Phaedra, wife of Theseus.

[2] *Sea-god syre* I.e., Poseidon.

[3] *Dianes* Virgin goddess of the hunt and of the moon.

44

Her words prevaild: And then the learnèd leach
His cunning hand gan to his wounds to lay,
And all things else, the which his art did teach:
Which having seene, from thence arose away
The mother of dread darknesse, and let stay
Aveugles sonne there in the leaches cure,° *care*
And backe returning tooke her wonted way,
To runne her timely race, whilst Phoebus pure
In westerne waves his wearie wagon did recure.

45

The false Duessa leaving noyous° Night, *noxious*
Returnd to stately pallace of dame Pride;
Where when she came, she found the Faery knight
Departed thence, albe his woundès wide
Not throughly heald, unreadie were to ride.
Good cause he had to hasten thence away;
For on a day his wary Dwarfe had spide,
Where in a dongeon deepe huge numbers lay
Of caytive wretched thrals,° that waylèd night and day. *slaves*

46

A ruefull sight, as could be seene with eie;° *eyes*
Of whom he learnèd had in secret wise° *manner*
The hidden cause of their captivitie,
How mortgaging their lives to Covetise,
Through wastfull Pride, and wanton Riotise,
They were by law of that proud Tyrannesse
Provokt with Wrath, and Envies false surmise,
Condemned to that Dongeon mercilesse,
Where they should live in woe, & die in wretchednesse.

47

There was that great proud king of Babylon,[1]
That would compell all nations to adore,
And him as onely God to call upon,
Till through celestiall doome throwne out of dore,
Into an Oxe he was transform'd of yore:
There also was king Croesus,[2] that enhaunst° *exalted*
His heart too high through his great riches store;
And proud Antiochus,[3] the which advaunst
His cursèd hand gainst God, and on his altars daunst.

48

And them long time before, great Nimrod[4] was,
That first the world with sword and fire warrayd;° *ravaged*
And after him old Ninus[5] farre did pas
In princely pompe, of all the world obayd;
There also was that mightie Monarch[6] layd
Low under all, yet above all in pride,
That name of native syre did fowle upbrayd,
And would as Ammons sonne be magnifide,
Till scornd of God and man a shamefull death he dide.

49

All these together in one heape were throwne,
Like carkases of beasts in butchers stall.
And in another corner wide were strowne
The antique ruines of the Romaines fall:
Great Romulus the Grandsyre of them all,
Proud Tarquin, and too lordly Lentulus,
Stout Scipio, and stubborne Hanniball,
Ambitious Sylla, and sterne Marius,
High Cæsar, great Pompey, and fierce Antonius.[7]

50

Amongst these mighty men were wemen mixt,
Proud wemen, vaine, forgetfull of their yoke:° *place*

---

[1] *great ... Babylon* I.e., Nebuchadnezzar, who made his people worship a golden image of himself. See Daniel 3–4.

[2] *king Croesus* Ancient king of Lydia, famous for his wealth.

[3] *Antiochus* King of Syria (215–164 BCE).

[4] *Nimrod* First tyrant to rule after the flood. He ordered the building of the Tower of Babylon. See Genesis 10–11.

[5] *Ninus* Founder of Ninevah, the wicked city. See the Book of Jonah.

[6] *that mightie Monarch* Alexander the Great (356–323 BCE), who claimed to be descended from Jupiter (also called Jupiter Ammon).

[7] *Romulus* Traditional founder of Rome; *Tarquin* Cruel Roman tyrant and the last king of Rome (534–510 BCE); *Lentulus* Roman who conspired against Rome (d. 63 BCE); *Scipio* Roman general who conquered Africa (236–183 BCE); *Hannibal* Renowned general from Carthage (247–183/182 BCE); *Sylla* Sulla, a Roman general who engaged in civil war with Marius (138–78 BCE); *Caesar* Roman (100–44 BCE) who fought with, and defeated, Pompey (106–47 BCE); *Antonius* Marc Antony (83–31 BCE), who fought Caesar's heir, Octavian, for control of the Roman Empire.

The bold Semiramis,[1] whose sides transfixt
With sonnes owne blade, her fowle reproches spoke;
Faire Sthenoboea,[2] that her selfe did choke
With wilfull cord, for wanting of her will;
High minded Cleopatra,[3] that with stroke
Of Aspes sting her selfe did stoutly kill:
And thousands moe the like, that did that dongeon fill.

51

Besides the endlesse routs of wretched thralles,
Which thither were assembled day by day,
From all the world after their wofull falles,
Through wicked pride, and wasted wealthes decay.
But most of all, which in the Dongeon lay
Fell from high Princes courts, or Ladies bowres,
Where they in idle pompe, or wanton play,
Consumèd had their goods, and thriftlesse howres,
And lastly throwne themselves into these heavy stowres.° *troubles*

52

Whose case when as the carefull° Dwarfe had tould, *troubled*
And made ensample of their mournefull sight
Unto his maister, he no lenger would
There dwell in perill of like painefull plight,
But early rose, and ere that dawning light
Discovered had the world to heaven wyde,
He by a privie° Posterne° tooke his flight, *secret / back door*
That of no envious eyes he mote be spyde:
For doubtlesse death ensewd, if any him descryde.

53

Scarse could he footing find in that fowle way,
For many corses, like a great Lay-stall
Of murdred men which therein strowèd° lay, *strewn*
Without remorse, or decent funerall:
Which all through that great Princesse pride did fall
And came to shamefull end. And them beside
Forth ryding underneath the castell wall,
A donghill of dead carkases he spide,
The dreadfull spectacle of that sad house of Pride.

[1] *Semiramus* Wife of King Ninus who disguised herself as her son in an attempt to gain the throne, but was then killed by her son.

[2] *Sthenoboea* Wife of King Proteus of Argos who committed suicide when her brother-in-law refused her advances.

[3] *Cleopatra* Queen of Egypt who committed suicide by allowing herself to be bitten by poisonous snakes when her kingdom was defeated by the Romans (c. 69–30 BCE).

Canto 6

From lawlesse lust by wondrous grace
Fayre Una is releast:
Whom salvage° nation does adore, *savage*
And learnes her wise beheast.

1

As when a ship, that flyes faire under saile,
An hidden rocke escapèd hath unwares,° *unexpectedly*
That lay in waite her wrack° for to bewaile, *destruction*
The Marriner yet halfe amazèd stares
At perill past, and yet in doubt ne dares
To joy at his foole-happie oversight:
So doubly is distrest twixt joy and cares
The dreadlesse° courage of this Elfin knight, *fearless*
Having escapt so sad ensamples in his sight.

2

Yet sad he was that his too hastie speed
The faire Duess' had forst him leave behind;
And yet more sad, that Una his deare dreed[4]
Her truth had staind with treason so unkind;° *unnatural*
Yet crime in her could never creature find,
But for his love, and for her owne selfe sake,
She wandred had from one to other Ynd,[5]
Him for to seeke, ne ever would forsake,
Till her unwares the fierce Sansloy did overtake.

3

Who after Archimagoes fowle defeat,
Led her away into a forrest wilde,
And turning wrathfull fire to lustfull heat,
With beastly sin thought her to have defilde,
And made the vassall of his pleasures vilde.
Yet first he cast by treatie,° and by traynes,° *entreaty / tricks*
Her to perswade, that stubborne fort to yilde:

[4] *dreed* Object of reverence.

[5] *from … Ynd* From one India to the other; i.e., from the East to the West Indies.

For greater conquest of hard love he gaynes,
That workes it to his will, then he that it
constraines.° *forces*

4

With fawning wordes he courted her a while,
And looking lovely,° and oft sighing sore, *lovingly*
Her constant hart did tempt with diverse guile:
But wordes, and lookes, and sighes she did abhore,
As rocke of Diamond stedfast evermore.
Yet for to feed his fyrie lustfull eye,
He snatcht the vele, that hong her face before;
Then gan her beautie shine, as brightest skye,
And burnt his beastly hart t'efforce° her chastitye. *force*

5

So when he saw his flatt'ring arts to fayle,
And subtile engines bet° from batteree, *beaten*
With greedy force he gan the fort assayle,
Whereof he weend possessèd soone to bee,
And win rich spoile of ransackt chastetee.
Ah heavens, that do this hideous act behold,
And heavenly virgin thus outragèd see,
How can ye vengeance just so long withhold,
And hurle not flashing flames upon that Paynim bold?

6

The pitteous maiden carefull° comfortlesse, *troubled*
Does throw out thrilling° shriekes, & *penetrating*
shrieking cryes,
The last vaine helpe of womens great distresse,
And with loud plaints importuneth the skyes,
That molten starres do drop like weeping eyes;
And Phoebus flying so most shamefull sight,
His blushing face in foggy cloud implyes,° *enfolds*
And hides for shame. What wit of mortall wight
Can now devise to quit a thrall° from such a plight? *victim*

7

Eternall providence exceeding thought,
Where none appeares can make her selfe a way:
A wondrous way it for this Lady wrought,
From Lyons clawes to pluck the gripèd pray.
Her shrill outcryes and shriekes so loud did bray,
That all the woodes and forestes did resownd;
A troupe of Faunes and Satyres[1] far away
Within the wood were dauncing in a rownd,
Whiles old Sylvanus[2] slept in shady arber sownd.

8

Who when they heard that pitteous strainèd voice,
In hast forsooke their rurall meriment,
And ran towards the far rebownded°
noyce,° *reverberating / noise*
To weet, what wight so loudly did lament.
Unto the place they come incontinent:° *headlong*
Whom when the raging Sarazin espide,
A rude, misshapen, monstrous rablement,
Whose like he never saw, he durst not bide,
But got his ready steed, and fast away gan ride.

9

The wyld woodgods arrivèd in the place,
There find the virgin dolefull desolate,
With ruffled rayments, and faire blubbred° face, *teary*
As her outrageous foe had left her late,
And trembling yet through feare of former hate;
All stand amazed at so uncouth° sight, *strange*
And gin to pittie her unhappie state,
All stand astonied at her beautie bright,
In their rude eyes unworthie of so wofull plight.

10

She more amaz'd, in double dread doth dwell;
And every tender part for feare does shake:
As when a greedie Wolfe through hunger fell
A seely° Lambe farre from the flocke does *innocent*
take,
Of whom he meanes his bloudie feast to make,
A Lyon spyes fast running towards him,
The innocent pray in hast he does forsake,
Which quit from death yet quakes in every lim
With chaunge of feare, to see the Lyon looke so grim.

11

Such fearefull fit assaid° her trembling hart, *assailed*
Ne word to speake, ne joynt to move she had:
The salvage nation feele her secret smart,

[1] *Satyres* Wood deities that are half man and half goat.

[2] *Sylvanus* God of the forest.

And read her sorrow in her count'nance sad;
Their frowning forheads with rough hornes yclad,
And rusticke horror° all a side doe lay, *roughness*
And gently grenning, shew a semblance glad
To comfort her, and feare to put away,
Their backward bent knees teach her humbly to obay.

12

The doubtfull Damzell dare not yet commit
Her single person to their barbarous truth,
But still twixt feare and hope amazd does sit,
Late learnd what harme to hastie trust ensu'th,
They in compassion of her tender youth,
And wonder of her beautie soveraine,
Are wonne with pitty and unwonted ruth,
And all prostrate upon the lowly plaine,
Do kisse her feete, and fawne on her with count'nance
faine.° *joyful*

13

Their harts she ghesseth by their humble guise,
And yieldes her to extremitie of time;
So from the ground she fearelesse doth arise,
And walketh forth without suspect of crime:
They all as glad, as birdes of joyous Prime,° *spring*
Thence lead her forth, about her dauncing round,
Shouting, and singing all a shepheards ryme,
And with greene braunches strowing all the ground,
Do worship her, as Queene, with olive girlond cround.

14

And all the way their merry pipes they sound,
That all the woods with doubled Eccho ring,
And with their hornèd feet do weare the ground,
Leaping like wanton kids in pleasant Spring.
So towards old Sylvanus they her bring;
Who with the noyse awakèd, commeth out,
To weet° the cause, his weake steps governing, *know*
And agèd limbs on Cypresse stadle[1] stout,
And with an yvie twyne his wast is girt about.

15

Far off he wonders, what them makes so glad,
If Bacchus merry fruit[2] they did invent,° *find*
Or Cybeles franticke rites[3] have made them mad;
They drawing nigh, unto their God present
That flowre of faith and beautie excellent.
The God himselfe vewing that mirrhour[4] rare,
Stood long amazd, and burnt in his intent;° *concentration*
His owne faire Dryope[5] now he thinkes not faire,
And Pholoe[6] fowle, when her to this he doth compaire.

16

The woodborne people fall before her flat,
And worship her as Goddesse of the wood;
And old Sylvanus selfe bethinkes not, what
To thinke of wight so faire, but gazing stood,
In doubt to deeme her borne of earthly brood;
Sometimes Dame Venus selfe he seemes to see,
But Venus never had so sober mood;
Sometimes Diana he her takes to bee,
But misseth bow, and shaftes, and buskins° to *boots*
her knee.

17

By vew of her he ginneth to revive
His ancient love, and dearest Cyparisse,[7]
And calles to mind his pourtraiture alive,° *when alive*
How faire he was, and yet not faire to this,
And how he slew with glauncing dart amisse
A gentle Hynd, the which the lovely boy
Did love as life, above all worldly blisse;
For griefe whereof the lad n'ould° after joy, *never would*
But pynd away in anguish and selfe-wild° annoy. *self-willed*

18

The wooddy Nymphes, faire Hamadryades[8]
Her to behold do thither runne apace,
And all the troupe of light-foot Naiades,
Flocke all about to see her lovely face:

[1] *stadle* Young tree or tree trunk; here probably a staff.

[2] *Bacchus merry fruit* Wine grapes (Bacchus is the god of wine).

[3] *Cybeles franticke rites* Cybele is goddess of the harvest and fertility whose worshipers celebrated her with frenzied dances.

[4] *mirrhour* I.e., of heaven's beauty.

[5] *Dryope* Greek wood nymph.

[6] *Pholoe* Naiad, or water nymph.

[7] *Cyparisse* Young boy loved by Sylvanus. When Sylvanus accidentally killed the boy's doe, Apollo turned Cyparisse into a Cyprus tree to alleviate his pain.

[8] *Hamadryades* Tree spirits.

But when they vewèd have her heavenly grace,
They envie her in their malitious mind,
And fly away for feare of fowle disgrace:
But all the Satyres scorne their woody kind,
And henceforth nothing faire, but her on earth they find.

19

Glad of such lucke, the luckelesse lucky maid,
Did her content to please their feeble eyes,
And long time with that salvage people staid,
To gather breath in many miseries.
During which time her gentle wit she plyes,
To teach them truth, which worshipt her in vaine,
And made her th'Image of Idolatryes;
But when their bootlesse zeale she did restraine
From her own worship, they her Asse would worship fayn.

20

It fortunèd a noble warlike knight
By just occasion to that forrest came,
To seeke his kindred, and the lignage right,
From whence he tooke his well deservèd name:
He had in armes abroad wonne muchell fame,
And fild far landes with glorie of his might,
Plaine, faithfull, true, and enimy of shame,
And ever lov'd to fight for Ladies right,
But in vaine glorious frayes he litle did delight.

21

A Satyres sonne yborne in forrest wyld,
By straunge adventure as it did betyde,
And there begotten of a Lady myld,
Faire Thyamis the daughter of Labryde,[1]
That was in sacred bands of wedlocke tyde
To Therion,[2] a loose unruly swayne;
Who had more joy to raunge the forrest wyde,
And chase the salvage beast with busie payne,
Then serve his Ladies love, and wast in pleasures vayne.

22

The forlorne mayd did with loves longing burne,
And could not lacke her lovers company, *go without*
But to the wood she goes, to serve her turne,
And seeke her spouse, that from her still does fly,
And followes other game and venery:
A Satyre chaunst her wandring for to find,
And kindling coles of lust in brutish eye,
The loyall links of wedlocke did unbind,
And made her person thrall unto his beastly kind.

23

So long in secret cabin there he held
Her captive to his sensuall desire,
Till that with timely fruit her belly sweld,
And bore a boy unto that salvage sire:
Then home he suffred her for to retire,
For ransome leaving him the late borne childe;
Whom till to ryper yeares he gan aspire,
He noursled° up in life and manners wilde, *raised*
Emongst wild beasts and woods, from lawes of men
exilde.

24

For all he taught the tender ymp,° was but *child*
To banish cowardize and bastard° feare; *base*
His trembling hand he would him force to put
Upon the Lyon and the rugged Beare,
And from the she Beares teats her whelps to teare;
And eke wyld roring Buls he would him make
To tame, and ryde their backes not made to beare;
And the Robuckes[3] in flight to overtake,
That every beast for feare of him did fly and quake.

25

Thereby so fearelesse, and so fell° he grew, *deadly*
That his owne sire and maister of his guise
Did often tremble at his horrid vew,
And oft for dread of hurt would him advise,
The angry beasts not rashly to despise,
Nor too much to provoke; for he would learne° *teach*
The Lyon stoup to him in lowly wise,
(A lesson hard) and make the Libbard° sterne *leopard*
Leave roaring, when in rage he for revenge did
earne.° *yearn*

[1] *Thyamis* Passion; *Labryde* Turbulence.

[2] *Therion* Wild beast.

[3] *Robuckes* Bucks of the roe species of deer, known for their speed.

26

And for to make his powre approvèd° more, *clear*
Wyld beasts in yron yokes he would compell;
The spotted Panther, and the tuskèd Bore,
The Pardale° swift, and the Tigre cruell; *female leopard*
The Antelope, and Wolfe both fierce and fell;
And them constraine in equall teme to draw.
Such joy he had, their stubborne harts to quell,
And sturdie courage tame with dreadfull aw,
That his beheast they feared, as tyrans law.

27

His loving mother came upon a day
Unto the woods, to see her little sonne;
And chaunst unwares to meet him in the way,
After his sportes, and cruell pastime donne,
When after him a Lyonesse did runne,
That roaring all with rage, did lowd requere
Her children deare, whom he away had wonne:° *stolen*
The Lyon whelpes she saw how he did beare,
And lull in rugged armes, withouten childish feare.

28

The fearefull Dame all quakèd at the sight,
And turning backe, gan fast to fly away,
Untill with love revokt° from vaine affright, *recalled*
She hardly yet perswaded was to stay,
And then to him these womanish words gan say;
Ah Satyrane, my dearling, and my joy,
For love of me leave off this dreadfull play;
To dally thus with death, is no fit toy,° *pastime*
Go find some other play-fellowes, mine own sweet boy.

29

In these and like delights of bloudy game
He traynèd was, till ryper yeares he raught,° *reached*
And there abode, whilst any beast of name
Walkt in that forest, whom he had not taught
To feare his force: and then his courage haught° *high*
Desird of forreine foemen to be knowne,
And far abroad for straunge adventures sought:
In which his might was never overthrowne,
But through all Faery lond his famous worth was
blown.° *proclaimed*

30

Yet evermore it was his manner faire,
After long labours and adventures spent,
Unto those native woods for to repaire,
To see his sire and ofspring° auncient. *lineage*
And now he thither came for like intent;
Where he unwares the fairest Una found,
Straunge Lady, in so straunge habiliment,° *clothing*
Teaching the Satyres, which her sat around,
Trew sacred lore, which from her sweet lips did
redound.° *flow*

31

He wondred at her wisedome heavenly rare,
Whose like in womens wit he never knew;
And when her curteous deeds he did compare,
Gan her admire, and her sad sorrowes rew,
Blaming of Fortune, which such troubles threw,
And joyd to make proofe of her crueltie
On gentle Dame, so hurtlesse,° and so trew: *innocent*
Thenceforth he kept her goodly company,
And learnd her discipline of faith and veritie.

32

But she all vowd unto the Redcrosse knight,
His wandring perill closely° did lament, *secretly*
Ne in this new acquaintaunce could delight,
But her deare° heart with anguish did torment, *loving*
And all her wit in secret counsels spent,
How to escape. At last in privie° wise° *private / manner*
To Satyrane she shewèd her intent:
Who glad to gain such favour, gan devise,
How with that pensive Maid he best might thence
arise.° *depart*

33

So on a day when Satyres all were gone,
To do their service to Sylvanus old,
The gentle virgin left behind alone
He led away with courage stout and bold.
Too late it was, to Satyres to be told,
Or ever hope recover her againe:
In vaine he seekes that having cannot hold.
So fast he carried her with carefull paine,
That they the woods are past, & come now to the plaine.

34

The better part now of the lingring day,
They traveild had, when as they farre espide
A wearie wight forwandring by the way,
And towards him they gan in hast to ride,
To weet° of newes, that did abroad betide,° *learn / occur*
Or tydings of her knight of the Redcrosse.
But he them spying, gan to turne aside,
For feare as seemd, or for some feignèd losse;
More greedy they of newes, fast towards him do crosse.

35

A silly° man, in simple weedes forworne,° *simple / worn*
And soild with dust of the long drièd way;
His sandales were with toilesome travell torne,
And face all tand with scorching sunny ray,
As he had traveild many a sommers day,
Through boyling sands of Arabie and Ynde;
And in his hand a Jacobs° staffe, to stay *pilgrim's*
His wearie limbes upon: and eke behind,
His scrip° did hang, in which his needments he did bind. *bag*

36

The knight approching nigh, of him inquerd
Tydings of warre, and of adventures new;
But warres, nor new adventures none he herd.
Then Una gan to aske, if ought he knew,
Or heard abroad of that her champion trew,
That in his armour bare a croslet° red. *small cross*
Aye me, Deare dame (quoth he) well may I rew
To tell the sad sight, which mine eies have red:° *seen*
These eyes did see that knight both living and eke ded.

37

That cruell word her tender hart so thrild,° *penetrated*
That suddein cold did runne through every vaine,
And stony horrour all her sences fild
With dying° fit,° that downe she fell for paine. *deathlike / faint*
The knight her lightly° rearèd up againe, *swiftly*
And comforted with curteous kind reliefe:
Then wonne from death, she bad him tellen plaine
The further processe° of her hidden griefe; *tale*
The lesser pangs can beare, who hath endur'd the chiefe.

38

Then gan the Pilgrim thus, I chaunst this day,
This fatall day, that shall I ever rew,
To see two knights in travell on my way
(A sory sight) arraung'd in battell new,
Both breathing vengeaunce, both of wrathfull hew:
My fearefull flesh did tremble at their strife,
To see their blades so greedily imbrew,° *stain themselves*
That drunke with bloud, yet thristed after life:
What more? the Redcrosse knight was slaine with Paynim knife.

39

Ah dearest Lord (quoth she) how might that bee,
And he the stoutest knight, that ever wonne?° *lived*
Ah dearest dame (quoth he) how might I see
The thing, that might not be, and yet was donne?
Where is (said Satyrane) that Paynims sonne,
That him of life, and us of joy hath reft?
Not far away (quoth he) he hence doth wonne° *remain*
Foreby° a fountaine, where I late him left *near*
Washing his bloudy wounds, that through° the steele were cleft. *by*

40

Therewith the knight thence marchèd forth in hast,
Whiles Una with huge heavinesse opprest,
Could not for sorrow follow him so fast;
And soone he came, as he the place had ghest,° *guessed*
Whereas that Pagan proud him selfe did rest,
In secret shadow by a fountaine side:
Even he it was, that earst would have suppress° *ravished*
Faire Una: whom when Satyrane espide,
With fowle reprochfull words he boldly him defide.

41

And said, Arise thou cursèd Miscreaunt,
That hast with knightlesse° guile and trecherous train° *unknightly / trickery*
Faire knighthood fowly shamed, and doest vaunt° *boast*
That good knight of the Redcrosse to have slain:
Arise, and with like treason now maintain

Thy guilty wrong, or else thee guilty yield.
The Sarazin this hearing, rose amain,
And catching up in hast his three square[1] shield,
And shining helmet, soone him buckled° to the field. *equipped*

42

And drawing nigh him said, Ah misborne Elfe,
In evill houre thy foes thee hither sent,
Anothers wrongs to wreake upon thy selfe:
Yet ill thou blamest me, for having blent° *tainted*
My name with guile and traiterous intent;
That Redcrosse knight, perdie,° I never slew, *by God*
But had he beene, where earst his armes were lent,° *borrowed*
Th'enchaunter vaine his errour should not rew:
But thou his errour shalt, I hope now proven trew.

43

Therewith they gan, both furious and fell,° *fierce*
To thunder blowes, and fiersly to assaile
Each other bent his enimy to quell,° *kill*
That with their force they perst both plate and maile,
And made wide furrowes in their fleshes fraile,
That it would pitty° any living eie. *cause pity in*
Large floods of bloud adowne their sides did raile;° *run*
But floods of bloud could not them satisfie:
Both hungred after death: both chose to win, or die.

44

So long they fight, and fell revenge pursue,
That fainting each, themselves to breathen let,
And oft refreshèd, battell oft renue:
As when two Bores with rancling malice met,
Their gory sides fresh bleeding fiercely fret,° *gnaw*
Til breathlesse both them selves aside retire,
Where foming wrath, their cruell tuskes they whet,
And trample th'earth, the whiles they may respire;
Then backe to fight againe, new breathèd and entire.° *fresh*

45

So fiersly, when these knights had breathèd once,
They gan to fight returne, increasing more
Their puissant force, and cruell rage attonce,
With heapèd strokes more hugely, then before,
That with their drerie° wounds and bloudy gore *gory*
They both deformèd, scarsely could be known.
By this sad Una fraught with anguish sore,
Led with their noise, which through the aire was thrown:
Arriv'd, where they in erth their fruitles bloud had sown.

46

Whom all so soone as that proud Sarazin
Espide, he gan revive the memory
Of his lewd lusts, and late attempted sin,
And left the doubtfull° battell hastily, *undecided*
To catch her, newly offred to his eie:
But Satyrane with strokes him turning, staid,
And sternely bad him other businesse plie,
Then hunt the steps of pure unspotted Maid:
Wherewith he all enrag'd, these bitter speaches said.

47

O foolish faeries sonne, what furie mad
Hath thee incenst, to hast thy dolefull fate?
Were it not better, I that Lady had,
Then that thou hadst repented it too late?
Most sencelesse man he, that himselfe doth hate,
To love another. Lo then for thine ayd
Here take thy lovers token on thy pate.° *head*
So they to fight; the whiles the royall Mayd
Fled farre away, of that proud Paynim sore afrayd.

48

But that false Pilgrim, which that leasing° told, *falsehood*
Being in deed old Archimage, did stay
In secret shadow, all this to behold,
And much rejoycèd in their bloudy fray:
But when he saw the Damsell passe away
He left his stond,° and her pursewd apace, *place*
In hope to bring her to her last decay.° *death*
But for to tell her lamentable cace,
And eke this battels end, will need another place.

[1] *three square* Triangular.

CANTO 7

The Redcrosse knight is captive made
By Gyaunt proud opprest,° *vanquished*
Prince Arthur meets with Una greatly
With those newes distrest.

1

What man so wise, what earthly wit so ware,° *wary*
As to descry° the crafty cunning traine,° *perceive / trickery*
By which deceipt doth maske in visour° faire, *mask*
And cast her colours dyed deepe in graine,
To seeme like Truth, whose shape she well can faine,
And fitting gestures to her purpose frame;
The guiltlesse man with guile to entertaine?
Great maistresse of her art was that false Dame,
The false Duessa, cloked with Fidessaes name.

2

Who when returning from the drery Night,
She fownd not in that perilous house of Pryde,
Where she had left, the noble Redcrosse knight,
Her hopèd pray,° she would no lenger bide, *prey*
But forth she went, to seeke him far and wide.
Ere long she fownd, whereas° he wearie sate, *where*
To rest him selfe, foreby a fountaine side,
Disarmèd all of yron-coted Plate,
And by his side his steed the grassy forage ate.

3

He feedes upon the cooling shade, and bayes° *bathes*
His sweatie forehead in the breathing wind,
Which through the trembling leaves full gently playes
Wherein the cherefull birds of sundry kind
Do chaunt sweet musick, to delight his mind:
The Witch approching gan him fairely° greet, *courteously*
And with reproch of carelesnesse unkind
Upbrayd, for leaving her in place unmeet,° *unfitting*
With fowle words tempring faire, soure gall with hony sweet.

4

Unkindnesse past, they gan of solace treat,° *speak*
And bathe in pleasaunce of the joyous shade,
Which shielded them against the boyling heat,
And with greene boughes decking a gloomy glade,
About the fountaine like a girlond made;
Whose bubbling wave did ever freshly well,
Ne ever would through fervent sommer fade:° *dry up*
The sacred Nymph, which therein wont to dwell,
Was out of Dianes favour, as it then befell.° *so happened*

5

The cause was this: one day when Phoebe[1] fayre
With all her band was following the chace,° *hunt*
This Nymph, quite tyr'd with heat of scorching ayre,
Sat downe to rest in middest of the race:
The goddesse wroth° gan fowly her disgrace, *angry*
And bad the waters, which from her did flow,
Be such as she her selfe was then in place.
Thenceforth her waters waxèd dull and slow,
And all that drunke thereof, did faint and feeble grow.

6

Hereof this gentle knight unweeting was,
And lying downe upon the sandie graile,° *gravel*
Drunke of the streame, as cleare as cristall glas;
Eftsoones his manly forces gan to faile,
And mightie strong was turnd to feeble fraile.
His chaunged powres at first them selves not felt,
Till crudled° cold his corage gan assaile, *curdled*
And chearefull° bloud in faintnesse chill did melt, *lively*
Which like a fever fit through all his body swelt.° *raged*

7

Yet goodly court he made still to his Dame,
Pourd° out in loosnesse on the grassy grownd, *stretched*
Both carelesse of his health, and of his fame:[2]
Till at the last he heard a dreadfull sownd,
Which through the wood loud bellowing, did rebownd,
That all the earth for terrour seemd to shake,
And trees did tremble. Th'Elfe therewith astownd,
Upstarted lightly° from his looser make,° *quickly / mate*
And his unready weapons gan in hand to take.

8

But ere he could his armour on him dight,° *place*

---

[1] *Phoebe* Diana, goddess of the moon, chastity, and the hunt.

[2] *fame* Good reputation or character.

Or get his shield, his monstrous enimy
With sturdie steps came stalking in his sight,
An hideous Geant horrible and hye,
That with his talnesse seemd to threat the skye,
The ground eke groned under him for dreed;
His living like saw never living eye,
Ne durst behold: his stature did exceed
The hight of three the tallest sonnes of mortall seed.

9

The greatest Earth his uncouth mother was,
And blustring Aeolus[1] his boasted sire,
Who with his breath, which through the world doth pas,
Her hollow womb did secretly inspire,° *blow in to*
And fild her hidden caves with stormie yre,
That she conceiv'd; and trebling the dew time,
In which the wombes of women do expire,° *bring forth*
Brought forth this monstrous masse of earthly slime,
Puft up with emptie wind, and fild with sinfull crime.

10

So growen great through arrogant delight
Of th'high descent, whereof he was yborne,
And through presumption of his matchlesse might,
All other powres and knighthood he did scorne.
Such now he marcheth to this man forlorne,
And left to losse: his stalking steps are stayde° *supported*
Upon a snaggy Oke, which he had torne
Out of his mothers bowelles, and it made
His mortall° mace,° wherewith his foemen he dismayde. *deadly / weapon*

11

That when the knight he spide, he gan advance
With huge force and insupportable° mayne,° *irresistable / strength*
And towardes him with dreadfull fury praunce;
Who haplesse, and eke hopelesse, all in vaine
Did to him pace, sad battaile to darrayne,° *engage*
Disarmd, disgrast, and inwardly dismayde,
And eke so faint in every joynt and vaine,° *vein*
Through that fraile° fountaine, which him feeble made,
That scarsely could he weeld his bootlesse° single blade. *useless*

12

The Geaunt strooke so maynly° mercilesse, *fiercely*
That could have overthrowne a stony towre,
And were not heavenly grace, that him did blesse,
He had beene pouldred° all, as thin as flowre:° *pulverized / flour*
But he was wary of that deadly stowre,° *danger*
And lightly lept from underneath the blow:
Yet so exceeding was the villeins powre,
That with the wind it did him overthrow,
And all his sences stound,° that still he lay full low. *stunned*

13

As when that divelish yron Engin[2] wrought
In deepest Hell, and framd by Furies skill,
With windy Nitre° and quick Sulphur fraught,° *gunpowder / filled*
And ramd with bullet round, ordaind to kill,
Conceiveth fire, the heavens it doth fill
With thundring noyse, and all the ayre doth choke,
That none can breath, nor see, nor heare at will,
Through smouldry cloud of duskish° stincking smoke, *dark*
That th'onely° breath° him daunts,° who hath escapt the stroke. *alone / smell / overcomes*

14

So daunted when the Geaunt saw the knight,
His heavie hand he heavèd up on hye,
And him to dust thought to have battred quight,
Untill Duessa loud to him gan crye;
O great Orgoglio,[3] greatest under skye,
O hold thy mortall hand for Ladies sake,
Hold for my sake, and do him not to dye,
But vanquisht thine eternall bondslave make,
And me thy worthy meed° unto° thy Leman take. *prize / as*

15

He hearkned, and did stay from further harmes,
To gayne so goodly guerdon, as she spake:
So willingly she came into his armes,

[1] *Aeolus* Keeper of the winds.

[2] *yron Engin* I.e., the cannon.

[3] *Orgoglio* Italian: pride, disdain.

Who her as willingly to grace did take,
And was possessèd of his new found make.
Then up he tooke the slombred sencelesse corse,
And ere he could out of his swowne awake,
Him to his castle brought with hastie forse,
And in a Dongeon deepe him threw without remorse.

16

From that day forth Duessa was his deare,
And highly honourd in his haughtie eye,
He gave her gold and purple pall to weare,
And triple crowne[1] set on her head full hye,
And her endowd with royall majestye:
Then for to make her dreaded more of men,
And peoples harts with awfull terrour tye,° *enthrall*
A monstrous beast[2] ybred in filthy fen
He chose, which he had kept long time in darksome den.

17

Such one it was, as that renowmèd Snake
Which great Alcides in Stremona slew,[3]
Long fostred in the filth of Lerna lake,
Whose many heads out budding ever new,
Did breed him endlesse labour to subdew:
But this same Monster much more ugly was;
For seven great heads out of his body grew,
An yron brest, and backe of scaly bras,
And all embrewd° in bloud, his eyes did shine as glas. *stained*

18

His tayle was stretched out in wondrous length,
That to the house of heavenly gods it raught,° *reached*
And with extorted powre, and borrow'd strength,
The ever-burning lamps[4] from thence it braught,
And prowdly threw to ground, as things of naught;
And underneath his filthy feet did tread
The sacred things, and holy heasts° foretaught. *doctrines*
Upon this dreadfull Beast with sevenfold head
He set the false Duessa, for more aw and dread.

19

The wofull Dwarfe, which saw his maisters fall,
Whiles he had keeping of his grasing steed,
And valiant knight become a caytive thrall,° *slave*
When all was past, tooke up his forlorne weed,
His mightie armour, missing most at need;
His silver shield, now idle maisterlesse;
His poynant° speare, that many made to bleed, *piercing*
The ruefull moniments of heavinesse,° *grief*
And with them all departes, to tell his great distresse.

20

He had not travaild long, when on the way
He wofull Ladie, wofull Una met,
Fast flying from the Paynims greedy pray,° *grasp*
Whilest Satyrane him from pursuit did let:° *prevent*
Who when her eyes she on the Dwarf had set,
And saw the signes, that deadly tydings spake,
She fell to ground for sorrowfull regret,
And lively° breath her sad brest did forsake, *of life*
Yet might her pitteous hart be seene to pant and quake.

21

The messenger of so unhappie newes
Would faine have dyde: dead was his hart within,
Yet outwardly some little comfort shewes:
At last recovering hart, he does begin
To rub her temples, and to chaufe her chin,
And every tender part does tosse and turne:
So hardly° he the flitted life does win, *with difficulty*
Unto her native prison to retourne:
Then gins her grievèd ghost thus to lament and mourne.

22

Ye dreary instruments of dolefull sight,
That doe this deadly spectacle behold,
Why do ye lenger° feed on loathèd light, *longer*
Or liking° find to gaze on earthly mould,° *pleasing / shapes*
Sith cruell fates the carefull threeds unfould,
The which my life and love together tyde?
Now let the stony dart of senselesse cold
Perce to my hart, and pas through every side,
And let eternall night so sad sight fro me hide.

---

[1] *triple crown* Like that worn by the pope.

[2] *beast* The description of Duessa and her beast echo several passages in the Book of Revelation (esp. 17.3, 12.3–4, 9).

[3] *Such one ... slew* Alcides (Hercules) had to kill the nine-headed Hydra of Lerna as one of his twelve labors. Each time he cut off one head, several more would grow in its place.

[4] *ever-burning lamps* I.e., the stars.

23

O lightsome day, the lampe of highest Jove,
First made by him, mens wandring wayes to guyde,
When darknesse he in deepest dongeon drove,
Henceforth thy hated face for ever hyde,
And shut up heavens windowes shyning wyde:
For earthly sight can nought but sorow breed,
And late repentance, which shall long abyde.
Mine eyes no more on vanitie shall feed,
But seelèd up with death, shall have their deadly meed.

24

Then downe againe she fell unto the ground;
But he her quickly rearèd up againe:
Thrise did she sinke adowne in deadly swownd,
And thrise he her reviv'd with busie paine:
At last when life recover'd had the raine,
And over-wrestled his strong enemie,
With foltring tong, and trembling every vaine,
Tell on (quoth she) the wofull Tragedie,
The which these reliques sad present unto mine eie.

25

Tempestuous fortune hath spent all her spight,
And thrilling sorrow throwne his utmost dart;
Thy sad tongue cannot tell more heavy plight,
Then that I feele, and harbour in mine hart:
Who hath endur'd the whole, can beare each part.
If death it be, it is not the first wound,
That launchèd° hath my brest with bleeding smart. *pierced*
Begin, and end the bitter balefull stound;[1]
If lesse, then that I feare, more favour I have found.

26

Then gan the Dwarfe the whole discourse declare,
The subtill traines of Archimago old;
The wanton loves of false Fidessa faire,
Bought with the bloud of vanquisht Paynim bold:
The wretched payre° transform'd to treen mould; *pair*
The house of Pride, and perils round about;
The combat, which he with Sansjoy did hould;
The lucklesse conflict with the Gyant stout,
Wherein captiv'd, of life or death he stood in doubt.

[1] *stound* Time of pain.

27

She heard with patience all unto the end,
And strove to maister sorrowfull assay,° *tribulation*
Which greater grew, the more she did contend,
And almost rent her tender hart in tway;° *two*
And love fresh coles unto her fire did lay:
For greater love, the greater is the losse.
Was never Ladie lovèd dearer day,° *life*
Then she did love the knight of the Redcrosse;
For whose deare sake so many troubles her did tosse.

28

At last when fervent sorrow slakèd was,
She up arose, resolving him to find
A live or dead: and forward forth doth pas,
All as the Dwarfe the way to her assynd:° *indicated*
And evermore in constant carefull mind
She fed her wound with fresh renewèd bale;° *misery*
Long tost with stormes, and bet° with bitter wind, *beaten*
High over hils, and low adowne the dale,
She wandred many a wood, and measurd many a vale.

29

At last she chauncèd by good hap to meet
A goodly knight, faire marching by the way
Together with his Squire, arayèd meet:° *suitably*
His glitterand armour shinèd farre away,
Like glauncing° light of Phoebus brightest ray; *shining*
From top to toe no place appearèd bare,
That deadly dint of steele endanger may:
Athwart his brest a bauldrick[2] brave he ware,
That shynd, like twinkling stars, with stons most pretious rare.

30

And in the midst thereof one pretious stone
Of wondrous worth, and eke of wondrous mights,
Shapt like a Ladies head, exceeding shone,
Like Hesperus emongst the lesser lights,
And strove for to amaze the weaker sights;
Thereby his mortall blade full comely hong
In yvory sheath, ycarv'd with curious slights;° *designs*

[2] *bauldrick* Belt or sash worn to support a sword.

Whose hilts were burnisht gold, and handle strong
Of mother pearle, and buckled with a golden tong.° *pin*

31

His haughtie° helmet, horrid° all with gold, *high / bristling*
Both glorious brightnesse, and great terrour bred;
For all the crest a Dragon did enfold
With greedie pawes, and over all did spred
His golden wings: his dreadfull hideous hed
Close couchèd on the bever,° seem'd to throw *visor*
From flaming mouth bright sparkles fierie red,
That suddeine horror to faint harts did show;
And scaly tayle was stretcht adowne his backe full low.

32

Upon the top of all his loftie crest,° *helmet*
A bunch of haires discolourd° diversly, *dyed*
With sprincled pearle, and gold full richly drest,
Did shake, and seem'd to daunce for jollity,
Like to an Almond tree ymounted hye
On top of greene Selinis[1] all alone,
With blossomes brave bedeckèd daintily;
Whose tender locks do tremble every one
At every little breath, that under heaven is blowne.

33

His warlike shield all closely cover'd was,
Ne might of mortall eye be ever seene;
Not made of steele, nor of enduring bras,
Such earthly mettals soone consumèd bene:
But all of Diamond perfect pure and cleene
It framèd was, one massie entire mould,[2]
Hewen out of Adamant rocke with engines
keene,° *sharp*
That point of speare it never percen could,
Ne dint of direfull sword divide the substance would.

34

The same to wight he never wont disclose,
But° when as monsters huge he would dismay, *except*
Or daunt unequall armies of his foes,
Or when the flying° heavens he would affray; *revolving*
For so exceeding shone his glistring ray,
That Phoebus golden face it did attaint,° *sully*
As when a cloud his beames doth over-lay;
And silver Cynthia wexèd pale and faint,
As when her face is staynd with magicke arts constraint.[3]

35

No magicke arts hereof had any might,
Nor bloudie wordes of bold Enchaunters call,
But all that was not such, as seemd in sight,
Before that shield did fade, and suddeine fall:
And when him list the raskall routes appall,
Men into stones therewith he could transmew,° *transform*
And stones to dust, and dust to nought at all;
And when him list the prouder lookes subdew,
He would them gazing blind, or turne to other
hew.° *shape*

36

Ne let it seeme, that credence this exceedes,
For he that made the same, was knowne right well
To have done much more admirable deedes.
It Merlin was, which whylome did excell
All living wightes in might of magicke spell:
Both shield, and sword, and armour all he wrought
For this young Prince, when first to armes he
fell;° *came*
But when he dyde, the Faerie Queene it brought
To Faerie lond, where yet it may be seene, if sought.[4]

37

A gentle youth, his dearely lovèd Squire
His speare of heben° wood behind him bare, *ebony*
Whose harmefull head, thrice heated in the fire,
Had riven many a brest with pikehead square;
A goodly person, and could menage° faire *manage*
His stubborne steed with curbèd canon bit,[5]
Who under him did trample as the aire,

[1] *Selinis* Town in Italy.

[2] *one … mould* I.e., one solid, unbroken piece of diamond.

[3] *with … constraint* I.e., by a lunar eclipse, believed by some to be caused by magic.

[4] *But when … sought* I.e., this knight's armor (and hence his virtues) can still be found in England. From the references to Merlin and the Faerie Queene, it is clear that the unnamed knight is Arthur.

[5] *canon bit* Type of round, smooth bit.

And chauft, that any on his backe should sit;
The yron rowels[1] into frothy fome he bit.

38

When as this knight nigh to the Ladie drew,
With lovely° court he gan her entertaine; *kindly*
But when he heard her answeres loth,° he knew *reluctant*
Some secret sorrow did her heart distraine:° *afflict*
Which to allay, and calme her storming paine,
Faire feeling words he wisely gan display,
And for her humour fitting purpose° faine, *manner*
To tempt the cause it selfe for to bewray;° *reveal*
Wherewith emmov'd, these bleeding words she gan to say.

39

What worlds delight, or joy of living speach
Can heart, so plung'd in sea of sorrowes deepe,
And heapèd with so huge misfortunes, reach?
The carefull cold beginneth for to creepe,
And in my heart his yron arrow steepe,
Soone as I thinke upon my bitter bale:° *sorrow*
Such helplesse harmes yts better hidden keepe,
Then rip up griefe, where it may not availe,
My last left comfort is, my woes to weepe and waile.

40

Ah Ladie deare, quoth then the gentle knight,
Well may I weene, your griefe is wondrous great;
For wondrous great griefe groneth in my spright,
Whiles thus I heare you of your sorrowes treat.
But wofull Ladie let me you intrete,
For to unfold the anguish of your hart:
Mishaps are maistred by advice discrete,
And counsell mittigates the greatest smart;
Found never helpe, who never would his hurts impart.

41

O but (quoth she) great griefe will not be tould,
And can more easily be thought, then said.
Right so; (quoth he) but he, that never would,
Could never: will to might gives greatest aid.
But griefe (quoth she) does greater grow displaid,
If then it find not helpe, and breedes despaire.
Despaire breedes not (quoth he) where faith is staid.° *firm*
No faith so fast (quoth she) but flesh does paire.° *impaire*
Flesh may empaire (quoth he) but reason can repaire.

42

His goodly reason, and well guided speach
So deepe did settle in her gratious thought,
That her perswaded to disclose the breach,
Which love and fortune in her heart had wrought,
And said; faire Sir, I hope good hap hath brought
You to inquere the secrets of my griefe,
Or that your wisedome will direct my thought,
Or that your prowesse can me yield reliefe:
Then heare the storie sad, which I shall tell you briefe.

43

The forlorne Maiden, whom your eyes have seene
The laughing stocke of fortunes mockeries,
Am th'only daughter of a King and Queene,
Whose parents deare, whilest equall destinies
Did runne about,° and their felicities *their course*
The favourable heavens did not envy,
Did spread their rule through all the territories,
Which Phison and Euphrates floweth by,
And Gehons[2] golden waves doe wash continually.

44

Till that their cruell cursèd enemy,
An huge great Dragon horrible in sight,
Bred in the loathly lakes of Tartary,° *Hell*
With murdrous ravine,° and devouring might *violence*
Their kingdome spoild, and countrey wasted quight:
Themselves, for feare into his jawes to fall,
He forst to castle strong to take their flight,
Where fast embard° in mightie brasen wall, *imprisoned*
He has them now foure yeres besiegd to make them thrall.

45

Full many knights adventurous and stout
Have enterprizd that Monster to subdew;

[1] *rowels* Knobs on the ends of a horse's bit.

[2] *Phison ... Gehons* Three of the four rivers of Eden. Thus Una's parents were Adam and Eve, the rulers of Eden.

From every coast that heaven walks about,
Have thither come the noble Martiall crew,
That famous hard atchievements still pursew,
Yet never any could that girlond win,
But all still shronke,° and still he greater grew: *cowered*
All they for want of faith, or guilt of sin,
The pitteous pray of his fierce crueltie have bin.

46

At last yledd° with farre reported praise, *led by*
Which flying fame throughout the world had spred,
Of doughtie° knights, whom Faery land did raise, *worthy*
That noble order hight° of Maidenhed,° *named / virginity*
Forthwith to court of Gloriane I sped,
Of Gloriane great Queene of glory bright,
Whose kingdomes seat Cleopolis[1] is red,° *called*
There to obtaine some such redoubted knight,
That Parents deare from tyrants powre deliver might.

47

It was my chance (my chance was faire and good)
There for to find a fresh unprovèd knight,
Whose manly hands imbrew'd in guiltie blood
Had never bene, ne ever by his might
Had throwne to ground the unregarded right:
Yet of his prowesse proofe he since hath made
(I witnesse am) in many a cruell fight;
The groning ghosts of many one dismaide
Have felt the bitter dint of his avenging blade.

48

And ye the forlorne reliques of his powre,
His byting sword, and his devouring speare,
Which have endurèd many a dreadfull stowre,
Can speake his prowesse, that did earst you beare,
And well could rule: now he hath left you heare,
To be the record of his ruefull losse,
And of my dolefull disaventurous°
deare:° *unfortunate / dear one*
O heavie record of the good Redcrosse,
Where have you left your Lord, that could so well you
tosse?° *wield*

49

Well hopèd I, and faire beginnings had,
That he my captive° langour should redeeme, *inescapable*
Till all unweeting, an Enchaunter bad
His sence abusd, and made him to misdeeme
My loyalty, not such as it did seeme;
That rather death desire, then such despight.° *treachery*
Be judge ye heavens, that all things right esteeme,
How I him lov'd, and love with all my might,
So thought I eke of him, and thinke I thought aright.

50

Thenceforth me desolate he quite forsooke,
To wander, where wilde fortune would me lead,
And other bywaies he himselfe betooke,
Where never foot of living wight did tread,
That brought not backe the balefull body dead;
In which him chauncèd false Duessa meete,
Mine onely foe, mine onely deadly dread,
Who with her witchcraft and misseeming sweete,
Inveigled° him to follow her desires
unmeete.° *deceived / inappropriate*

51

At last by subtill sleights she him betraid
Unto his foe, a Gyant huge and tall,
Who him disarmèd, dissolute,° dismaid, *weakened*
Unwares surprisèd, and with mightie mall° *mallet*
The monster mercilesse him made to fall,
Whose fall did never foe before behold;
And now in darkesome dungeon, wretched thrall,
Remedilesse, for aie° he doth him hold; *ever*
This is my cause of griefe, more great, then may be told.

52

Ere she had ended all, she gan to faint:
But he her comforted and faire bespake,
Certes, Madame, ye have great cause of plaint,
That stoutest heart, I weene, could cause to quake.
But be of cheare, and comfort to you take:
For till I have acquit° your captive knight, *freed*
Assure your selfe, I will you not forsake.
His chearefull words reviv'd her chearelesse spright,
So forth they went, the Dwarfe them guiding ever
right.

[1] *Cleopolis* From Greek: famous city.

Canto 8

Faire virgin to redeeme her deare
Brings Arthur to the fight,
Who slayes the Gyant, wounds the beast,
And strips Duessa quight.

1

Ay me, how many perils doe enfold
The righteous man, to make him daily fall?
Were not, that heavenly grace doth him uphold,
And stedfast truth acquite him out of all.
Her love is firme, her care continuall,
So oft as he through his owne foolish pride,
Or weaknesse is to sinfull bands° made thrall: *bonds*
Else should this Redcrosse knight in bands have dyde,
For whose deliverance she this Prince doth thither guide.

2

They sadly traveild thus, untill they came
Nigh to a castle builded strong and hie:
Then cryde the Dwarfe, lo yonder is the same,
In which my Lord my liege° doth lucklesse lie, *master*
Thrall to that Gyants hatefull tyrannie:
Therefore, deare Sir, your mightie powres assay.
The noble knight alighted by and by
From loftie steede, and bad the Ladie stay,
To see what end of fight should him befall that day.

3

So with the Squire, th'admirer of his might,
He marchèd forth towards that castle wall;
Whose gates he found fast shut, ne living wight
To ward° the same, nor answere commers call. *guard*
Then tooke that Squire an horne of bugle° small, *hunting horn*
Which hong adowne his side in twisted gold,
And tassels gay. Wyde wonders over all
Of that same hornes great vertues weren told,
Which had approvèd° bene in uses manifold. *proven*

4

Was never wight, that heard that shrilling sound,
But trembling feare did feele in every vaine;
Three miles it might be easie heard around,
And Ecchoes three answerd it selfe againe:
No false enchauntment, nor deceiptfull traine
Might once abide the terror of that blast,
But presently was voide and wholly vaine:
No gate so strong, no locke so firme and fast,
But with that percing noise flew open quite, or brast.° *burst*

5

The same before the Geants gate he blew,
That all the castle quakèd from the ground,
And every dore of freewill open flew.
The Gyant selfe dismaièd with that sownd,
Where he with his Duessa dalliance° fownd, *amorous toying*
In hast came rushing forth from inner bowre,
With staring countenance sterne, as one astownd,
And staggering steps, to weet, what suddein stowre
Had wrought that horror strange, and dar'd his dreaded powre.

6

And after him the proud Duessa came,
High mounted on her manyheaded beast,
And every head with fyrie tongue did flame,
And every head was crownèd on his creast,
And bloudie mouthèd with late cruell feast.
That when the knight beheld, his mightie shild
Upon his manly arme he soone addrest,° *prepared*
And at him fiercely flew, with courage fild,
And eger greedinesse° through every member thrild. *readiness*

7

Therewith the Gyant buckled° him to fight, *engaged*
Inflam'd with scornefull wrath and high disdaine,
And lifting up his dreadfull club on hight,
All arm'd with ragged snubbes° and knottie graine, *stumps*
Him thought at first encounter to haue slaine,
But wise and warie was that noble Pere,° *peer*
And lightly leaping from so monstrous maine,° *force*
Did faire avoide the violence him nere;
It booted nought, to thinke, such thunderbolts to beare.° *withstand*

8

Ne shame he thought to shunne so hideous might:
The idle stroke, enforcing furious way,
Missing the marke of his misaymèd sight
Did fall to ground, and with his heavie sway
So deepely dinted in the driven clay,
That three yardes deepe a furrow up did throw:
The sad earth wounded with so sore assay,° *assault*
Did grone full grievous underneath the blow,
And trembling with strange feare, did like an earthquake show.

9

As when almightie Jove in wrathfull mood,
To wreake° the guilt of mortall sins is bent, *punish*
Hurles forth his thundring dart with deadly food,° *hatred*
Enrold in flames, and smouldring° dreriment,° *suffocating / darkness*
Through riven cloudes and molten firmament;
The fierce threeforkèd engin° making way, *weapon*
Both loftie towres and highest trees hath rent,
And all that might his angrie passage stay,
And shooting in the earth, casts up a mount of clay.

10

His boystrous° club, so buried in the ground, *unwieldy*
He could not rearen up againe so light,° *easily*
But that the knight him at avantage found,
And whiles he strove his combred° clubbe to quight° *encumbered / free*
Out of the earth, with blade all burning bright
He smote off his left arme, which like a blocke
Did fall to ground, depriv'd of native might;
Large streames of bloud out of the trunckèd stocke° *stump*
Forth gushèd, like fresh water streame from riven rocke.

11

Dismaièd with so desperate deadly wound,
And eke impatient of[1] unwonted paine,
He loudly brayd with beastly yelling sound,
That all the fields rebellowèd againe;
As great a noyse, as when in Cymbrian plaine[2]
An heard of Bulles, whom kindly° rage doth sting, *natural*
Do for the milkie mothers want complaine,
And fill the fields with troublous bellowing,
The neighbour woods around with hollow murmur ring.

12

That when his deare Duessa heard, and saw
The evill stownd,° that daungerd her estate,° *peril / condition*
Unto his aide she hastily did draw
Her dreadfull beast, who swolne with bloud of late
Came ramping forth with proud presumpteous gate,
And threatned all his heads like flaming brands.° *torches*
But him the Squire made quickly to retrate,
Encountring fierce with single sword in hand,
And twixt him and his Lord did like a bulwarke stand.

13

The proud Duessa full of wrathfull spight,
And fierce disdaine, to be affronted so,
Enforst her purple beast with all her might
That stop° out of the way to overthroe, *obstacle*
Scorning the let° of so unequall foe: *hindrance*
But nathemore° would that courageous swayne *never the more*
To her yeeld passage, gainst his Lord to goe,
But with outrageous strokes did him restraine,
And with his bodie bard the way atwixt them twaine.

14

Then tooke the angrie witch her golden cup,
Which still she bore, replete with magick artes;
Death and despeyre did many thereof sup,
And secret poyson through their inner parts,
Th'eternall bale of heavie wounded harts;
Which after charmes and some enchauntments said,
She lightly sprinkled on his weaker° parts; *too weak*

[1] *impatient of* Unable to endure.

[2] *Cymbrian plaine* Jutland, a peninsula comprising Northern Germany and most of Denmark and formerly inhabited by the ancient European tribe the Cimbri.

Therewith his sturdie courage soone was quayd,° *quelled*
And all his senses were with suddeine dread dismayd.

15

So downe he fell before the cruell beast,
Who on his necke his bloudie clawes did seize,
That life nigh crusht out of his panting brest:
No powre he had to stirre, nor will to rize.
That when the carefull knight gan well avise,° *perceived*
He lightly left the foe, with whom he fought,
And to the beast gan turne his enterprise;
For wondrous anguish in his hart it wrought,
To see his lovèd Squire into such thraldome brought.

16

And high advauncing his bloud-thirstie blade,
Stroke one of those deformèd heads so sore,
That of his puissance proud ensample made;
His monstrous scalpe downe to his teeth it tore,
And that misformèd shape mis-shapèd more:
A sea of bloud gusht from the gaping wound,
That her gay garments staynd with filthy gore,
And overflowèd all the field around;
That over shoes in bloud he waded on the ground.

17

Thereat he roarèd for exceeding paine,
That to have heard, great horror would have bred,
And scourging th'emptie ayre with his long traine,
Through great impatience of his grievèd hed
His gorgeous ryder from her loftie sted
Would have cast downe, and trod in durtie myre,
Had not the Gyant soone her succoured;
Who all enrag'd with smart and franticke yre,
Came hurtling in full fierce, and forst the knight retyre.

18

The force, which wont in two to be disperst,
In one alone left hand he now unites,
Which is through rage more strong then both were erst;
With which his hideous club aloft he dites,° *raises*
And at his foe with furious rigour smites,
That strongest Oake might seeme to overthrow.
The stroke upon his shield so heavie lites,
That to the ground it doubleth him full low
What mortall wight could ever beare so monstrous blow?

19

And in his fall his shield, that covered was,
Did loose his vele° by chaunce, and open flew: *covering*
The light whereof, that heavens light did pas,° *surpass*
Such blazing brightnesse through the aier threw,
That eye mote not the same endure to vew.
Which when the Gyaunt spyde with staring eye,
He downe let fall his arme, and soft withdrew
His weapon huge, that heavèd was on hye
For to have slaine the man, that on the ground did lye.

20

And eke the fruitfull-headed° beast, amaz'd *many-headed*
At flashing beames of that sunshiny shield,
Became starke blind, and all his senses daz'd,
That downe he tumbled on the durtie field,
And seem'd himselfe as conquerèd to yield.
Whom when his maistresse proud perceiv'd to fall,
Whiles yet his feeble feet for faintnesse reeld,
Unto the Gyant loudly she gan call,
O helpe Orgoglio, helpe, or else we perish all.

21

At her so pitteous cry was much amoov'd
Her champion stout, and for to ayde his frend,° *lover*
Againe his wonted angry weapon proov'd:° *tried*
But all in vaine: for he has read his end
In that bright shield, and all their forces spend
Themselves in vaine: for since that glauncing° sight, *gleaming*
He hath no powre to hurt, nor to defend;
As where th'Almighties lightning brond does light,
It dimmes the dazèd eyen, and daunts the senses quight.

22

Whom when the Prince, to battell new addrest,
And threatning high his dreadfull stroke did see,
His sparkling blade about his head he blest,° *brandished*
And smote off quite his right leg by the knee,
That downe he tombled; as an agèd tree,

High growing on the top of rocky clift,
Whose hartstrings with keene steele nigh hewen be,
The mightie trunck halfe rent, with ragged rift° *split*
Doth roll adowne the rocks, and fall with fearefull drift.° *force*

23

Or as a Castle rearèd high and round,
By subtile° engins and malitious slight° *clever / strategy*
Is underminèd from the lowest ground
And her foundation forst,° and feebled quight, *broken*
At last downe falles, and with her heapèd hight
Her hastie ruine does more heavie make,
And yields it selfe unto the victours might;
Such was this Gyaunts fall, that seemd to shake
The stedfast globe of earth, as it for feare did quake.

24

The knight then lightly leaping to the pray,
With mortall steele him smot againe so sore,
That headlesse his unweldy bodie lay,
All wallowd in his owne fowle bloudy gore,
Which flowèd from his wounds in wondrous store,° *plenty*
But soone as breath out of his breast did pas,
That huge great body, which the Gyaunt bore,
Was vanisht quite, and of that monstrous mas
Was nothing left, but like an emptie bladder was.

25

Whose grievous fall, when false Duessa spide,
Her golden cup she cast unto the ground,
And crownèd mitre rudely threw aside;
Such percing griefe her stubborne hart did wound,
That she could not endure that dolefull stound,
But leaving all behind her, fled away:
The light-foot Squire her quickly turnd around,
And by hard meanes enforcing her to stay,
So brought unto his Lord, as his deservèd pray.

26

The royall Virgin, which beheld from farre,
In pensive° plight, and sad perplexitie, *apprehensive*
The whole atchievement° of this doubtfull warre, *progress*
Came running fast to greet his victorie,
With sober gladnesse, and myld modestie,
And with sweet joyous cheare him thus bespake;
Faire braunch of noblesse, flowre of chevalrie,
That with your worth the world amazèd make,
How shall I quite° the paines, ye suffer for my sake? *requite*

27

And you fresh bud of vertue springing fast,
Whom these sad eyes saw nigh unto deaths dore,
What hath poore Virgin for such perill past,
Wherewith you to reward? Accept therefore
My simple selfe, and service evermore;
And he that high does sit, and all things see
With equall eyes, their merites to restore,° *reward*
Behold what ye this day have done for mee,
And what I cannot quite, requite with usuree.° *interest*

28

But sith the heavens, and your faire handeling° *actions*
Have made you maister of the field this day,
Your fortune maister° eke with governing, *secure*
And well begun end all so well, I pray,
Ne let that wicked woman scape away;
For she it is, that did my Lord bethrall,
My dearest Lord, and deepe in dongeon lay,
Where he his better dayes hath wasted all.
O heare, how piteous he to you for ayd does call.

29

Forthwith he gave in charge unto his Squire,
That scarlot whore to keepen carefully;
Whiles he himselfe with greedie° great desire *eager*
Into the Castle entred forcibly,
Where living creature none he did espye;
Then gan he lowdly through the house to call:
But no man car'd to answere to his crye.
There raignd a solemne silence over all,
Nor voice was heard, nor wight was seene in bowre or hall.

30

At last with creeping crooked pace forth came
An old old man, with beard as white as snow,

That on a staffe his feeble steps did frame,° *support*
And guide his wearie gate° both too and fro: *steps*
For his eye sight him failèd long ygo,
And on his arme a bounch of keyes he bore,
The which unusèd rust did overgrow:
Those were the keyes of every inner dore,
But he could not them use, but kept them still in store.

31

But very uncouth sight was to behold,
How he did fashion his untoward° pace, *awkward*
For as he forward moov'd his footing old,
So backward still was turnd his wrincled face,
Unlike to men, who ever as they trace,
Both feet and face one way are wont to lead.
This was the auncient keeper of that place,
And foster father of the Gyant dead;
His name Ignaro[1] did his nature right aread.° *make known*

32

His reverend haires and holy gravitie
The knight much honord, as beseemèd well,° *proper*
And gently° askt, where all the people bee, *politely*
Which in that stately building wont to dwell.
Who answerd him full soft, he could not tell.
Againe he askt, where that same knight was layd,
Whom great Orgoglio with his puissaunce fell° *deadly*
Had made his caytive thrall; againe he sayde,
He could not tell: ne ever other answere made.

33

Then askèd he, which way he in might pas:
He could not tell, againe he answerèd.
Thereat the curteous knight displeasèd was,
And said, Old sire, it seemes thou hast not red° *noted*
How ill it sits with that same silver hed
In vaine to mocke, or mockt in vaine to bee:
But if thou be, as thou art pourtrahèd° *represented*
With natures pen, in ages grave degree,° *dignity*
Aread° in graver wise, what I demaund of thee. *state*

34

His answere likewise was, he could not tell.
Whose senceless speach, and doted° ignorance *foolish*
When as the noble Prince had markèd well,
He ghest his nature by his countenance,
And calmd his wrath with goodly temperance.
Then to him stepping, from his arme did reach
Those keyes, and made himselfe free enterance.
Each dore he opened without any breach;° *breakage*
There was no barre to stop, nor foe him to empeach.

35

There all within full rich arayd he found,
With royall arras° and resplendent gold. *tapestries*
And did with store of every thing abound,
That greatest Princes presence° might behold. *person*
But all the floore (too filthy to be told)
With bloud of guiltlesse babes, and innocents trew,
Which there were slaine, as sheepe out of the fold,
Defilèd was, that dreadfull was to vew,
And sacred ashes over it was strowèd° new. *scattered*

36

And there beside of marble stone was built
An Altare,[2] carv'd with cunning imagery,
On which true Christians bloud was often spilt,
And holy Martyrs often doen° to dye,° *put / death*
With cruell malice and strong tyranny:
Whose blessed sprites from underneath the stone
To God for vengeance cryde continually,
And with great griefe were often heard to grone,
That hardest heart would bleede, to heare their piteous
mone.

37

Through every rowme he sought, and every bowr,
But no where could he find that wofull thrall:° *slave*
At last he came unto an yron doore,
That fast was lockt, but key found not at all
Emongst that bounch, to open it withall;
But in the same a little grate was pight,° *placed*
Through which he sent his voyce, and lowd did call
With all his powre, to weet, if living wight
Were housèd therewithin, whom he enlargen° *liberate*
might.

[1] *Ignaro* Ignorance.

[2] *Altare* See Revelation 6.9–10. The echo reinforces the association of Arthur with Christ.

38

Therewith an hollow, dreary, murmuring voyce
These piteous plaints and dolours° did resound; *laments*
O who is that, which brings me happy choyce° *chance*
Of death, that here lye dying every stound,° *moment*
Yet live perforce in balefull darkenesse bound?
For now three Moones have changèd thrice their
hew,° *shape*
And have beene thrice hid underneath the ground,
Since I the heavens chearefull face did vew,
O welcome thou, that doest of death bring tydings trew.

39

Which when that Champion heard, with percing point
Of pitty deare his hart was thrillèd sore,
And trembling horrour ran through every joynt,
For ruth of gentle knight so fowle forlore:
Which shaking off, he rent that yron dore,
With furious force, and indignation fell;
Where entred in, his foot could find no flore,
But all a deepe descent, as darke as hell,
That breathèd ever forth a filthie banefull° smell. *poisonous*

40

But neither darkenesse fowle, nor filthy bands,° *bonds*
Nor noyous° smell his purpose could withhold, *noxious*
(Entire affection hateth nicer° hands) *too fastidious*
But that with constant zeale, and courage bold,
After long paines and labours manifold,
He found the meanes that Prisoner up to reare;
Whose feeble thighes, unhable to uphold
His pinèd° corse, him scarse to light could beare, *wasted*
A ruefull spectacle of death and ghastly drere.

41

His sad dull eyes deepe sunck in hollow pits,
Could not endure th'unwonted sunne to view;
His bare thin cheekes for want of better bits,° *sustenance*
And empty sides deceivèd° of their dew,° *deprived / due*
Could make a stony hart his hap to rew;
His rawbone armes, whose mighty brawnèd
bowrs° *muscles*
Were wont to rive steele plates, and helmets hew,
Were cleane consum'd, and all his vitall powres
Decayd, and all his flesh shronk up like withered flowres.

42

Whom when his Lady saw, to him she ran
With hasty joy: to see him made her glad,
And sad to view his visage pale and wan,
Who earst in flowres of freshest youth was clad.
Tho when her well of teares she wasted had,
She said, Ah dearest Lord, what evill starre
On you hath frownd, and pourd his influence bad,
That of your selfe ye thus berobbèd arre,
And this misseeming hew your manly looks doth marre?

43

But welcome now my Lord, in wele or woe,
Whose presence I have lackt too long a day;
And fie on Fortune mine avowèd foe,
Whose wrathfull wreakes° them selves *punishments*
do now alay.
And for these wrongs shall treble penaunce pay
Of treble good: good growes of evils priefe.° *endured*
The chearelesse man, whom sorrow did dismay,
Had no delight to treaten° of his griefe; *tell*
His long endurèd famine needed more reliefe.

44

Faire Lady, then said that victorious knight,
The things, that grievous were to do, or beare,
Them to renew,° I wote,° breeds no delight: *relate / know*
Best musicke breeds delight in loathing eare:
But th'onely good, that growes of passèd feare,
Is to be wise, and ware° of like agein. *wary*
This dayes ensample hath this lesson deare
Deepe written in my heart with yron pen,
That blisse may not abide in state of mortall men.

45

Henceforth sir knight, take to you wonted strength,
And maister these mishaps with patient might;
Loe where your foe lyes stretcht in monstrous length,
And loe that wicked woman in your sight,
The roote of all your care, and wretched plight,
Now in your powre, to let her live, or dye.
To do her dye (quoth Una) were despight,° *spiteful*
And shame t'avenge so weake an enimy;
But spoile° her of her scarlot robe, and let her fly. *strip*

46

So as she bad,° that witch they disaraid, *ordered*
And robd of royall robes, and purple pall,
And ornaments that richly were displaid;
Ne sparèd they to strip her naked all.
Then when they had despoild her tire° and call,° *attire / headdress*
Such as she was, their eyes might her behold,
That her misshapèd parts did them appall,
A loathly, wrinckled hag, ill favoured, old,
Whose secret filth good manners biddeth not be told.

47

Her craftie head was altogether bald,
And as in hate of honorable eld,° *age*
Was overgrowne with scurfe° and filthy scald;[1] *scabs*
Her teeth out of her rotten gummes were feld,° *fallen*
And her sowre breath abhominably smeld;
Her drièd dugs,° like bladders lacking wind, *breasts*
Hong downe, and filthy matter from them weld;° *flowed*
Her wrizled° skin as rough, as maple rind,° *wrinkled / bark*
So scabby was, that would have loathd all womankind.

48

Her neather parts, the shame of all her kind,
My chaster Muse for shame doth blush to write;
But at her rompe she growing had behind
A foxes taile, with dong all fowly dight;° *covered*
And eke her feete most monstrous were in sight;
For one of them was like an Eagles claw,
With griping talaunts armd to greedy fight,
The other like a Beares uneven° paw: *rough*
More ugly shape yet never living creature saw.

49

Which when the knights beheld, amazd they were,
And wondred at so fowle deformèd wight.
Such then (said Una) as she seemeth here,
Such is the face of falshood, such the sight
Of fowle Duessa, when her borrowed light
Is laid away, and counterfesaunce° knowne. *fraud*
Thus when they had the witch disrobèd quight,
And all her filthy feature° open showne, *form*
They let her goe at will, and wander wayes unknowne.

50

She flying fast from heavens hated face,
And from the world that her discovered wide,
Fled to the wastfull° wildernesse apace, *barren*
From living eyes her open shame to hide,
And lurkt in rocks and caves long unespide.
But that faire crew of knights, and Una faire
Did in that castle afterwards abide,
To rest them selves, and weary powres repaire,
Where store they found of all, that dainty was and rare.

CANTO 9

His loves and lignage Arthur tells
The knights knit friendly bands:
Sir Trevisan flies from Despayre,
Whom Redcrosse knight withstands.

1

O goodly golden chaine, wherewith yfere° *together*
The vertues linkèd are in lovely wize:° *ways*
And noble minds of yore allyed were,
In brave poursuit of chevalrous emprize,
That none did others safety despize,
Nor aid envy to him, in need that stands,
But friendly each did others prayse devize
How to advaunce with favourable hands,
As this good Prince redeemd the Redcrosse knight from bands.

2

Who when their powres, empaird through labour long,
With dew repast they had recurèd well, *refreshed*
And that weake captive wight now wexèd strong,
Them list no lenger there at leasure dwell,
But forward fare, as their adventures fell,
But ere they parted, Una faire besought
That straunger knight his name and nation tell;
Least so great good, as he for her had wrought,
Should die unknown, & buried be in thanklesse thought.

[1] *scald* Disease of the skin that causes scabbing and flaking, usually on the scalp.

3

Faire virgin (said the Prince) ye me require
A thing without° the compas of my wit: *beyond*
For both the lignage and the certain Sire,
From which I sprong, from me are hidden yit.
For all so soone as life did me admit
Into this world, and shewèd heavens light,
From mothers pap I taken was unfit:[1]
And streight delivered to a Faery knight,
To be upbrought in gentle thewes° and martiall might. *manners*

4

Unto old Timon[2] he me brought bylive,° *directly*
Old Timon, who in youthly yeares hath beene
In warlike feates th'expertest man alive,
And is the wisest now on earth I weene;
His dwelling is low in a valley greene,
Under the foot of Rauran[3] mossy hore,° *gray*
From whence the river Dee[4] as silver cleene° *clear*
His tombling billowes rolls with gentle rore:
There all my dayes he traind me up in vertuous lore.

5

Thither the great Magicien Merlin came,
As was his use,° ofttimes to visit me: *habit*
For he had charge my discipline° to frame, *education*
And Tutours nouriture° to oversee. *upbringing*
Him oft and oft I askt in privitie,
Of what loines and what lignage I did spring:
Whose aunswere bad me still assurèd bee,
That I was sonne and heire unto a king,
As time in her just terme the truth to light should bring.

6

Well worthy impe, said then the Lady gent,° *noble*
And Pupill fit for such a Tutours hand.
But what adventure, or what high intent
Hath brought you hither into Faery land,
Aread° Prince Arthur, crowne of Martiall band? *declare*
Full hard it is (quoth he) to read aright
The course of heavenly cause, or understand
The secret meaning of th'eternall might,
That rules mens wayes, and rules the thoughts of living wight.

7

For whither he through fatall° deepe foresight *fated*
Me hither sent, for cause to me unghest,
Or that fresh bleeding wound, which day and night
Whilome° doth rancle in my riven brest, *all the while*
With forcèd fury following his° behest, *its*
Me hither brought by wayes yet never found,
You to have helpt I hold my selfe yet blest.
Ah curteous knight (quoth she) what secret wound
Could ever find, to grieve the gentlest hart on ground?

8

Deare Dame (quoth he) you sleeping sparkes awake,
Which troubled once, into huge flames will grow,
Ne ever will their fervent fury slake,
Till living moysture into smoke do flow,
And wasted life do lye in ashes low.
Yet sithens silence lesseneth not my fire,
But told it flames, and hidden it does glow,
I will revele, what ye so much desire:
Ah Love, lay downe thy bow, the whiles I may respire.° *breathe*

9

It was in freshest flowre of youthly yeares,
When courage first does creepe in manly chest,
Then first the coale of kindly° heat appears *natural*
To kindle love in every living brest;
But me had warnd old Timons wise behest,
Those creeping flames by reason to subdew,
Before their rage grew to so great unrest,
As miserable lovers use° to rew, *are used*
Which still wex° old in woe, whiles woe still wexeth new. *grow*

10

That idle name of love, and lovers life,
As losse of time, and vertues enimy

[1] *From … unfit* He was taken from his mother's breast before he was weaned.

[2] *Timon* Honor.

[3] *Rauran* Hill in Wales.

[4] *Dee* River that flows along part of the boundary between England and Wales.

I ever scornd, and joyd to stirre up strife,
In middest of their mournfull Tragedy,
Ay wont to laugh, when them I heard to cry,
And blow the fire, which them to ashes brent:° *burned*
Their God° himselfe, griev'd at my libertie, *Cupid*
Shot many a dart at me with fiers intent,
But I them warded all with wary government.° *self-discipline*

11

But all in vaine: no fort can be so strong,
Ne fleshly brest can armèd be so sound,
But will at last be wonne with battrie long,
Or unawares at disavantage found;
Nothing is sure, that growes on earthly ground:
And who most trustes in arme of fleshly might,
And boasts, in beauties chaine not to be bound,
Doth soonest fall in disaventrous° fight, *disastrous*
And yeeldes his caytive neck to victours most°
despight.° *greatest / malice*

12

Ensample make of him your haplesse joy,
And of my selfe now mated,° as ye see; *beaten*
Whose prouder° vaunt° that proud
avenging boy *too proud / boast*
Did soone pluck downe, and curbd my libertie.
For on a day prickt° forth with jollitie *spurred*
Of looser life, and heat of hardiment,
Raunging the forest wide on courser free,
The fields, the floods, the heavens with one consent
Did seeme to laugh on me, and favour mine intent.

13

For-wearied with my sports, I did alight
From loftie steed, and downe to sleepe me layd;
The verdant gras my couch did goodly dight,° *form*
And pillow was my helmet faire displayd:
Whiles every sence the humour[1] sweet embayd,° *imbued*
And slombring soft my hart did steale away,
Me seemèd, by my side a royall Mayd
Her daintie limbes full softly down did lay:
So faire a creature yet saw never sunny day.

14

Most goodly glee and lovely blandishment° *flattery*
She to me made, and bad me love her deare,
For dearely sure her love was to me bent,
As when just time expirèd° should appeare. *had expired*
But whether dreames delude, or true it were,
Was never hart so ravisht with delight,
Ne living man like words did ever heare,
As she to me delivered all that night;
And at her parting said, She Queene of Faeries
hight.° *was called*

15

When I awoke, and found her place devoyd,° *empty*
And nought but pressèd gras, where she had lyen,
I sorrowed all so much, as earst I joyd,
And washèd all her place with watry eyen.
From that day forth I lov'd that face divine;
From that day forth I cast in carefull° mind, *care-filled*
To seeke her out with labour, and long tyne,° *affliction*
And never vow to rest, till her I find,
Nine monethes I seeke in vaine yet ni'll° that *never will*
vow unbind.

16

Thus as he spake, his visage wexèd pale,
And chaunge of hew great passion did bewray;° *betray*
Yet still he strove to cloke his inward bale,° *sorrow*
And hide the smoke, that did his fire display,
Till gentle Una thus to him gan say;
O happy Queene of Faeries, that hast found
Mongst many, one that with his prowesse may
Defend thine honour, and thy foes confound:
True Loves are often sown, but seldom grow on ground.

17

Thine, O then, said the gentle Redcrosse knight,
Next to that Ladies love, shalbe the place,
O fairest virgin, full of heavenly light,
Whose wondrous faith, exceeding earthly race,
Was firmest fixt in mine extremest case,° *plight*
And you, my Lord, the Patrone° of my life, *protector*
Of that great Queene may well gaine worthy grace:
For onely worthy you through prowes priefe° *proven*

---

[1] *humour* Dew of sleep.

Yf living man mote° worthy be, to be her
liefe.° *may / beloved*

18

So diversly discoursing of their loves,
The golden Sunne his glistring head gan shew,
And sad remembraunce now the Prince amoves,
With fresh desire his voyage to pursew:
Als Una earnd° her traveill to renew. *yearned*
Then those two knights, fast friendship for to bynd,
And love establish each to other trew,
Gave goodly gifts, the signes of gratefull mynd,
And eke as pledges firme, right hands together joynd.

19

Prince Arthur gave a boxe of Diamond sure,° *true*
Embowd° with gold and gorgeous ornament, *wrapped*
Wherein were closd few drops of liquor pure,
Of wondrous worth, and vertue excellent,
That any wound could heale incontinent:° *immediately*
Which to requite, the Redcrosse knight him gave
A booke, wherein his Saveours testament
Was writ with golden letters rich and brave;° *handsome*
A worke of wondrous grace, and able soules to save.

20

Thus beene they parted, Arthur on his way
To seeke his love, and th'other for to fight
With Unaes foe, that all her realme did pray.° *plunder*
But she now weighing the decayèd plight,
And shrunken synewes of her chosen knight,
Would not a while her forward course pursew,
Ne bring him forth in face of dreadfull fight,
Till he recovered had his former hew:
For him to be yet weake and wearie well she knew.

21

So as they traveild, lo they gan espy
An armèd knight towards them gallop fast,
That seemèd from some fearèd foe to fly,
Or other griesly thing, that him agast.
Still as he fled, his eye was backward cast,
As if his feare still followed him behind;
Als flew his steed, as he his bands had brast,° *burst*
And with his wingèd heeles did tread the wind,
As he had beene a fole° of Pegasus his kind. *foal*

22

Nigh as he drew, they might perceive his head
To be unarmd, and curld uncombèd heares
Upstaring stiffe, dismayd with uncouth° dread; *unknown*
Nor drop of bloud in all his face appeares
Nor life in limbe: and to increase his feares,
In fowle reproch° of knighthoods faire degree, *disgrace*
About his neck an hempen rope he weares,
That with his glistring armes does ill agree;
But he of rope or armes has now no memoree.

23

The Redcrosse knight toward him crossed fast,
To weet, what mister° wight was so dismayd: *sort of*
There him he finds all sencelesse and aghast,
That of him selfe he seemd to be afrayd;
Whom hardly he from flying forward stayd,
Till he these wordes to him deliver might;
Sir knight, aread who hath ye thus arayd,° *afflicted*
And eke from whom make ye this hasty flight:
For never knight I saw in such misseeming° *unseemly*
plight.

24

He answerd nought at all, but adding new
Feare to his first amazment, staring wide
With stony° eyes, and hartlesse hollow hew, *staring*
Astonisht stood, as one that had aspide
Infernall furies, with their chaines untide.
Him yet againe, and yet againe bespake
The gentle knight; who nought to him replide,
But trembling every joynt did inly quake,
And foltring tongue at last these words seemd forth to
shake.

25

For Gods deare love, Sir knight, do me not stay;
For loe he comes, he comes fast after mee.
Eft° looking backe would faine have runne away; *again*
But he him forst to stay, and tellen free
The secret cause of his perplexitie:° *anxiety*
Yet nathemore° by his bold hartie speach, *not at all*

Could his bloud-frosen hart emboldned bee,
But through his boldnesse rather feare did reach,
Yet forst, at last he made through silence suddein breach.

26

And am I now in safetie sure (quoth he)
From him, that would have forcèd me to dye?
And is the point of death now turnd fro mee,
That I may tell this haplesse history?
Feare nought: (quoth he) no daunger now is nye.
Then shall I you recount a ruefull cace,° *occurrence*
(Said he) the which with this unlucky eye
I late beheld, and had not greater grace
Me reft from it, had bene partaker of the place.

27

I lately chaunst (Would I had never chaunst)
With a faire knight to keepen companee,
Sir Terwin hight,° that well himselfe advaunst *called*
In all affaires, and was both bold and free,
But not so happie as mote happie bee:
He lov'd, as was his lot, a Ladie gent,
That him againe lov'd in the least degree:[1]
For she was proud, and of too high intent,
And joyd to see her lover languish and lament.

28

From whom returning sad and comfortlesse,
As on the way together we did fare,
We met that villen (God from him me blesse°) *protect*
That cursèd wight, from whom I scapt whyleare,° *earlier*
A man of hell, that cals himselfe Despaire:
Who first us greets, and after faire areedes° *relates*
Of tydings strange, and of adventures rare:
So creeping close, as Snake in hidden weedes,
Inquireth of our states, and of our knightly deedes.

29

Which when he knew, and felt our feeble harts
Embost° with bale, and bitter byting griefe, *fatigued*
Which love had launchèd° with his deadly darts, *penetrated*
With wounding words and termes of foule repriefe
He pluckt from us all hope of due reliefe,
That earst° us held in love of lingring life;° *first*
Then hopelesse hartlesse, gan the cunning thiefe
Perswade us die, to stint° all further strife: *cease*
To me he lent this rope, to him a rustie knife.

30

With which sad instrument of hastie death,
That wofull lover, loathing lenger light,
A wide way made to let forth living breath.
But I more fearefull, or more luckie wight,
Dismayd with that deformèd dismall sight,
Fled fast away, halfe dead with dying feare:° *fear of*
Ne yet assur'd of life by you, Sir knight,
Whose like infirmitie like chaunce may beare:
But God you never let his charmèd speeches heare.

31

How may a man (said he) with idle speach
Be wonne, to spoyle the Castle of his health?
I wote (quoth he) whom triall late did teach,
That like would not for all this worldes wealth:
His subtill tongue, like dropping honny, mealt'th° *melts*
Into the hart, and searcheth every vaine,
That ere one be aware, by secret stealth
His powre is reft, and weaknesse doth remaine.
O never Sir desire to try° his guilefull traine.° *test / deceit*

32

Certes° (said he) hence shall I never rest, *certainly*
Till I that treachours art have heard and tride;
And you Sir knight, whose name mote I request,
Of grace° do me unto his cabin° guide. *a favor / cave*
I that hight Trevisan (quoth he) will ride
Against my liking backe, to doe you grace:
But nor for gold nor glee° will I abide *song*
By you, when ye arrive in that same place;
For lever° had I die, then see his deadly face. *rather*

33

Ere long they come, where that same wicked wight
His dwelling has, low in an hollow cave,
Farre underneath a craggie clift ypight,° *placed*
Darke, dolefull, drearie, like a greedie grave,
That still for carrion carcases doth crave:

[1] *That him ... degree* I.e., did not return his love.

On top whereof aye° dwelt the ghastly Owle,[1] *ever*
Shrieking his balefull note, which ever drave
Farre from that haunt all other chearefull fowle;
And all about it wandring ghostes did waile and howle.

34

And all about old stockes° and stubs of trees, *stumps*
Whereon nor fruit, nor leafe was ever seene,
Did hang upon the ragged rocky knees;° *crags*
On which had many wretches hangèd beene,
Whose carcases were scattered on the greene,
And throwne about the cliffs. Arrivèd there,
That bare-head knight for dread and dolefull
teene,° *suffering*
Would faine have fled, ne durst approchen neare,
But th'other forst him stay, and comforted in feare.

35

That darkesome cave they enter, where they find
That cursèd man, low sitting on the ground,
Musing full sadly in his sullein mind;
His griesie° lockes, long growen, and unbound, *grizzled*
Disordred hong about his shoulders round,
And hid his face; through which his hollow eyne
Lookt deadly dull, and starèd as astound;
His raw-bone cheekes through penurie° and
pine,° *poverty / starvation*
Were shronke into his jawes, as he did never dine.

36

His garment nought but many ragged clouts,° *rags*
With thornes together pind and patchèd was,
The which his naked sides he wrapt abouts;
And him beside there lay upon the gras
A dreárie corse, whose life away did pas,
All wallowd in his owne yet luke-warme blood,
That from his wound yet wellèd fresh alas;
In which a rustie knife fast fixèd stood,
And made an open passage for the gushing flood.

37

Which piteous spectacle, approving° trew *proving*
The wofull tale that Trevisan had told,
When as the gentle Redcrosse knight did vew,
With firie zeale he burnt in courage bold,
Him to avenge, before his bloud were cold,
And to the villein said, Thou damnèd wight,
The author of this fact,° we here behold, *act*
What justice can but judge against thee right,
With thine owne bloud to price° his bloud, *pay for*
here shed in sight.

38

What franticke fit (quoth he) hath thus distraught
Thee, foolish man, so rash a doome to give?
What justice ever other judgement taught,
But he should die, who merites not to live?
None else to death this man despayring drive,° *drove*
But his owne guiltie mind deserving death.
Is then unjust to each his due to give?
Or let him die, that loatheth living breath?
Or let him die at ease, that liveth here uneath?° *with difficulty*

39

Who travels by the wearie wandring way,
To come unto his wishèd home in haste,
And meetes a flood, that doth his passage stay,
Is not great grace to helpe him over past,
Or free his feet, that in the myre sticke fast?
Most envious man, that grieves at neighbours good,
And fond,° that joyest in the woe thou hast, *foolish*
Why wilt not let him passe, that long hath stood
Upon the banke, yet wilt thy selfe not passe the flood?

40

He there does now enjoy eternall rest
And happie ease, which thou doest want and crave,
And further from it daily wanderest:
What if some litle paine the passage have,
That makes fraile flesh to feare the bitter wave?
Is not short paine well borne, that brings long ease,
And layes the soule to sleepe in quiet grave?
Sleepe after toyle, port after stormie seas,
Ease after warre, death after life does greatly please.

41

The knight much wondred at his suddeine wit,° *intelligence*
And said, The terme of life is limited,
Ne may a man prolong, nor shorten it;

[1] *Owle* Owls were believed to bring tidings of death.

The souldier may not move from watchfull sted,
Nor leave his stand, untill his Captaine bed.° *bid*
Who life did limit by almightie doome,
(Quoth he) knowes best the termes establishèd;
And he, that points the Centonell his roome,° *position*
Doth license him depart at sound of morning
droome.° *drum*

42

Is not his deed, what ever thing is donne,
In heaven and earth? did not he all create
To die againe? all ends that was begonne.
Their times in his eternall booke of fate
Are written sure, and have their certaine date.
Who then can strive with strong necessitie,
That holds the world in his still chaunging state,
Or shunne the death ordaynd by destinie?
When houre of death is come, let none aske whence,
nor why.

43

The lenger life, I wote the greater sin,
The greater sin, the greater punishment:
All those great battels, which thou boasts to win,
Through strife, and bloud-shed, and avengement,
Now praysd, hereafter deare thou shalt repent:
For life must life, and bloud must bloud repay.
Is not enough thy evill life forespent?° *spent previously*
For he, that once hath missed the right way,
The further he doth goe, the further he doth stray.

44

Then do no further goe, no further stray,
But here lie downe, and to thy rest betake,
Th'ill to prevent, that life ensewen may.
For what hath life, that may it lovèd make,
And gives not rather cause it to forsake?
Feare, sicknesse, age, losse, labour, sorrow, strife,
Paine, hunger, cold, that makes the hart to quake;
And ever fickle fortune rageth rife,
All which, and thousands mo° do make a *more*
loathsome life.

45

Thou wretched man, of death hast greatest need,
If in true ballance thou wilt weigh thy state:
For never knight, that darèd warlike deede,
More lucklesse disaventures° did
amate:° *misfortunes / dismay*
Witnesse the dongeon deepe, wherein of late
Thy life shut up, for death so oft did call;
And though good lucke prolongèd hath thy date,
Yet death then, would the like mishaps forestall,
Into the which hereafter thou maiest happen fall.

46

Why then doest thou, O man of sin, desire
To draw thy dayes forth to their last degree?
Is not the measure of thy sinfull hire° *work*
High heapèd up with huge iniquitie,° *sin*
Against the day of wrath,[1] to burden thee?
Is not enough, that to this Ladie milde
Thou falsèd° hast thy faith with perjurie, *betrayed*
And sold thy selfe to serve Duessa vilde,° *vile*
With whom in all abuse thou hast thy selfe defilde?

47

Is not he just, that all this doth behold
From highest heaven, and beares an equall° eye? *impartial*
Shall he thy sins up in his knowledge fold,
And guiltie be of thine impietie?
Is not his law, Let every sinner die:
Die shall all flesh? what then must needs be donne,
Is it not better to doe willinglie,
Then linger, till the glasse be all out ronne?
Death is the end of woes: die soone, O faeries sonne.

48

The knight was much enmovèd with his speach,
That as a swords point through his hart did perse,
And in his conscience made a secret breach,
Well knowing true all, that he did reherse,° *recount*
And to his fresh remembrance did reverse° *recall*
The ugly vew of his deformèd crimes,
That all his manly powres it did disperse,
As° he were charmèd with inchaunted rimes, *as if*
That oftentimes he quakt, and fainted oftentimes.

[1] *day of wrath* Judgment Day.

49

In which amazement, when the Miscreant
Perceivèd him to waver weake and fraile,
Whiles trembling horror did his conscience dant,° *daunt*
And hellish anguish did his soule assaile,
To drive him to despaire, and quite to quaile,
He shew'd him painted in a table° plaine, *picture*
The damnèd ghosts, that doe in torments waile,
And thousand feends that doe them endlesse paine
With fire and brimstone, which for ever shall remaine.

50

The sight whereof so throughly him dismaid,
That nought but death before his eyes he saw,
And ever burning wrath before him laid,
By righteous sentence of th'Almighties law:
Then gan the villein him to overcraw,° *overpower*
And brought unto him swords, ropes, poison, fire,
And all that might him to perdition draw;
And bad him choose, what death he would desire:
For death was due to him, that had provokt Gods ire.

51

But when as none of them he saw him take,
He to him raught° a dagger sharpe and keene, *reached*
And gave it him in hand: his hand did quake,
And tremble like a leafe of Aspin greene,
And troubled bloud through his pale face was seene
To come, and goe with tydings from the hart,
As it a running messenger had beene.
At last resolv'd to worke his finall smart,
He lifted up his hand, that backe againe did start.

52

Which when as Una saw, through every vaine
The crudled° cold ran to her well of life,[1] *curdled*
As in a swowne: but soone reliv'd° againe, *revived*
Out of his hand she snatcht the cursèd knife,
And threw it to the ground, enragèd rife,° *deeply*
And to him said, Fie, fie, faint harted knight,
What meanest thou by this reprochfull strife?
Is this the battell, which thou vauntst to fight
With that fire-mouthèd Dragon, horrible and bright?

[1] *well of life* Heart.

53

Come, come away, fraile, seely, fleshly wight,
Ne let vaine words bewitch thy manly hart,
Ne divelish thoughts dismay thy constant spright.
In heavenly mercies hast thou not a part?
Why shouldst thou then despeire, that chosen art?
Where justice growes, there grows eke greater grace,
The which doth quench the brond of hellish smart,
And that accurst hand-writing doth deface,
Arise, Sir knight arise, and leave this cursèd place.

54

So up he rose, and thence amounted° streight. *mounted*
Which when the carle° beheld, and saw his guest *villain*
Would safe depart, for° all his subtill sleight, *in spite of*
He chose an halter from among the rest,
And with it hung himselfe, unbid° unblest. *unprayed for*
But death he could not worke himselfe thereby;
For thousand times he so himselfe had drest,° *prepared*
Yet nathelesse it could not doe° him die, *make*
Till he should die his last, that is eternally.

CANTO 10

Her faithfull knight faire Una brings
To house of Holinesse,
Where he is taught repentance, and
The way to heavenly blesse.

1

What man is he, that boasts of fleshly might,
And vaine assurance of mortality,
Which all so soone, as it doth come to fight,
Against spirituall foes, yeelds by and by,
Or from the field most cowardly doth fly?
Ne let the man ascribe it to his skill,
That thorough grace hath gainèd victory.
If any strength we have, it is to ill,
But all the good is Gods, both power and eke will.

2

By that, which lately hapned, Una saw,
That this her knight was feeble, and too faint;
And all his sinews woxen° weake and raw,° *grown / inexperienced*

Through long enprisonment, and hard constraint,° *misfortune*
Which he endurèd in his late restraint,
That yet he was unfit for bloudie fight:
Therefore to cherish° him with diets daint, *nourish / choice*
She cast to bring him, where he chearen° might, *be cheered*
Till he recouered had his° late decayèd plight. *from his*

3

There was an auntient house not farre away,
Renowmd throughout the world for sacred lore,° *wisdom*
And pure unspotted life: so well they say
It governd was, and guided evermore,
Through wisedome of a matrone grave and hore;° *venerable*
Whose onely joy was to relieve the needes
Of wretched soules, and helpe the helpelesse pore:
All night she spent in bidding of her bedes,° *beads*
And all the day in doing good and godly deedes.

4

Dame Cælia[1] men did her call, as thought
From heaven to come, or thither to arise,
The mother of three daughters, well upbrought
In goodly thewes, and godly exercise:
The eldest two most sober, chast, and wise,
Fidelia and Speranza[2] virgins were,
Though spousd,° yet wanting wedlocks solemnize; *engaged*
But faire Charissa[3] to a lovely° fere° *loving / spouse*
Was linckèd, and by him had many pledges° dere. *children*

5

Arrivèd there, the dore they find fast lockt;
For it was warely watchèd night and day,
For feare of many foes: but when they knockt,
The Porter opened unto them streight way:
He was an agèd syre, all hory gray,
With lookes full lowly cast, and gate° full slow, *gait*
Wont on a staffe his feeble steps to stay,
Hight Humilta.[4] They passe in stouping low;
For streight & narrow was the way, which he did show.

6

Each goodly thing is hardest to begin,
But entred in a spacious court they see,
Both plaine, and pleasant to be walkèd in,
Where them does meete a francklin[5] faire and free,
And entertaines with comely° courteous glee, *appropriate*
His name was Zele,[6] that him right well became,
For in his speeches and behaviour hee
Did labour lively to expresse the same,
And gladly did them guide, till to the Hall they came.

7

There fairely them receives a gentle Squire,
Of milde demeanure, and rare courtesie,
Right cleanly clad in comely sad° attire; *sober*
In word and deede that shew'd great modestie,
And knew his good° to all of each degree, *proper courtesy / rank*
Hight Reverence. He them with speeches meet
Does faire entreat; no courting° nicetie,° *courtly / flattery*
But simple true, and eke unfainèd sweet,
As might become a Squire so great persons to greet.

8

And afterwards them to his Dame he leades,
That agèd Dame, the Ladie of the place:
Who all this while was busie at her beades:
Which doen, she up arose with seemely grace,
And toward them full matronely did pace.
Where when that fairest Una she beheld,
Whom well she knew to spring from heavenly race,
Her hart with joy unwonted° inly sweld, *unaccustomed*
As feeling wondrous comfort in her weaker eld.

9

And her embracing said, O happie earth,
Whereon thy innocent feet doe ever tread,
Most vertuous virgin borne of heavenly berth,
That to redeeme thy woefull parents head,

---

1 *Caelia* Heavenly.

2 *Fidelia and Speranza* Faith and Hope.

3 *Charissa* Charity.

4 *Humilta* Humility.

5 *francklin* I.e., franklin; freeholder, one who owns his own land.

6 *Zele* Zeal.

From tyrans rage, and ever-dying dread,[1]
Hast wandred through the world now long a day;
Yet ceasest not thy wearie soles to lead,
What grace hath thee now hither brought this way?
Or doen thy feeble feet unweeting hither stray?

10

Strange thing it is an errant knight to see
Here in this place, or any other wight,
That hither turnes his steps. So few there bee,
That chose the narrow path, or seeke the right:
All keepe the broad high way, and take delight
With many rather for to go astray,
And be partakers of their evill plight,
Then with a few to walke the rightest way;
O foolish men, why haste ye to your owne decay?

11

Thy selfe to see, and tyred limbs to rest,
O matrone sage (quoth she) I hither came,
And this good knight his way with me addrest,
Led with thy prayses and broad-blazèd fame,
That up to heaven is blowne. The auncient Dame
Him goodly greeted in her modest guise,
And entertaynd them both, as best became,
With all the court'sies, that she could devise.
Ne wanted ought, to shew her bounteous° or wise. *generous*

12

Thus as they gan of sundry things devise,° *discuss*
Loe two most goodly virgins came in place,
Ylinkèd arme in arme in lovely° wise,° *loving / manner*
With countenance demure, and modest grace,
They numberd even steps and equall pace:
Of which the eldest, that Fidelia hight,
Like sunny beames threw from her Christall face,
That could have dazd the rash beholders sight,
And round about her head did shine like heavens light.

13

She was araièd all in lilly white,
And in her right hand bore a cup of gold,
With wine and water fild up to the hight,
In which a Serpent did himselfe enfold,[2]
That horrour made to all, that did behold;
But she no whit did chaunge her constant mood:
And in her other hand she fast did hold
A booke, that was both signd and seald with blood,
Wherein darke things were writ, hard to be understood.[3]

14

Her younger sister, that Speranza hight,
Was clad in blew, that her beseemèd well;
Not all so chearefull seemèd she of sight,
As was her sister; whether dread° did dwell, *fear*
Or anguish in her hart, is hard to tell:
Upon her arme a silver anchor[4] lay,
Whereon she leanèd ever, as befell:° *was appropriate*
And ever up to heaven, as she did pray,
Her stedfast eyes were bent, ne swarvèd other way.

15

They seeing Una, towards her gan wend,° *proceed*
Who them encounters with like courtesie;
Many kind speeches they betwene them spend,
And greatly joy each other well to see:
Then to the knight with shamefast° modestie *humble*
They turne themselves, at Unaes meeke request,
And him salute with well beseeming glee:
Who faire them quites,° as him beseemèd best, *returns*
And goodly gan discourse of many a noble gest.° *deed*

16

Then Una thus; But she your sister deare;
The deare Charissa where is she become?
Or wants she health, or busie is elsewhere?
Ah no, said they, but forth she may not come:
For she of late is lightned of her wombe,
And hath encreast the world with one sonne more,
That her to see should be but troublesome.
Indeede (quoth she) that should her trouble sore,
But thankt be God, and her encrease so evermore.

[1] *ever-dying dread* Ever-present fear of death.

[2] *cup … enfold* The cup of wine and water is the sacrament of Holy Communion, and the serpent is an ancient symbol of renewal and rebirth.

[3] *A booke … understood* The New Testament.

[4] *silver anchor* Symbol of hope.

17

Then said the agèd Caelia, Deare dame,
And you good Sir, I wote that of your toyle,
And labours long, through which ye hither came,
Ye both forwearied be: therefore a whyle
I read° you rest, and to your bowres recoyle.° *advise / retire*
Then called she a Groome, that forth him led
Into a goodly lodge, and gan despoile° *undress*
Of puissant armes, and laid in easie bed;
His name was meeke Obedience rightfully arèd. *understood*

18

Now when their wearie limbes with kindly rest,
And bodies were refresht with due repast,
Faire Una gan Fidelia faire request,
To have her knight into her schoolehouse plaste,
That of her heauenly learning he might taste,
And heare the wisedome of her words divine.
She graunted, and that knight so much agraste,° *favored*
That she him taught celestiall discipline,
And opened his dull eyes, that light mote in them shine.

19

And that her sacred Booke, with bloud ywrit,
That none could read, except she did them teach,
She unto him disclosèd every whit,
And heavenly documents° thereout did preach, *doctrines*
That weaker wit of man could never reach,
Of God, of grace, of justice, of free will,
That wonder was to heare her goodly speach:
For she was able, with her words to kill,
And raise againe to life the hart, that she did thrill.° *pierce*

20

And when she list° poure out her larger° spright, *desired to / greater*
She would commaund the hastie Sunne to stay,
Or backward turne his course from heavens hight;
Sometimes great hostes of men she could dismay,
Dry-shod to passe, she parts the flouds in tway;
And eke huge mountaines from their native seat
She would commaund, themselves to beare away,
And throw in raging sea with roaring threat.
Almightie God her gave such powre, and puissance great.

21

The faithfull knight now grew in litle space,
By hearing her, and by her sisters lore,
To such perfection of all heavenly grace,
That wretched world he gan for to abhore,
And mortall life gan loath, as thing forlore,° *confounded*
Greev'd with remembrance of his wicked wayes,
And prickt with anguish of his sinnes so sore,
That he desirde to end his wretched dayes:
So much the dart of sinfull guilt the soule dismayes.

22

But wise Speranza gave him comfort sweet,
And taught him how to take assurèd hold
Upon her silver anchor, as was meet;
Else had his sinnes so great, and manifold
Made him forget all that Fidelia told.
In this distressèd doubtfull agonie,
When him his dearest Una did behold,
Disdeining life, desiring leave° to die, *permission*
She found her selfe assayld with great perplexitie.

23

And came to Caelia to declare her smart,
Who well acquainted with that commune plight,
Which sinfull horror workes in wounded hart,
Her wisely comforted all that she might,
With goodly counsell and advisement right;
And streightway sent with carefull diligence,
To fetch a Leach, the which had great insight
In that disease of grievèd conscience,
And well could cure the same; His name was Patience.

24

Who comming to that soule-diseasèd knight,
Could hardly him intreat, to tell his griefe:
Which knowne, and all that noyd° his heavie spright *troubled*
Well searcht,° eftsoones he gan apply reliefe *examined*
Of salves and med'cines, which had passing° priefe, *superior*
And thereto added words of wondrous might:
By which to ease he him recurèd° briefe,° *cured / quickly*
And much asswag'd the passion° of his plight, *suffering*
That he his paine endur'd, as seeming now more light.

25

But yet the cause and root of all his ill,
Inward corruption, and infected sin,
Not purg'd nor heald, behind remainèd still,
And festring sore did rankle yet within,
Close creeping twixt the marrow and the skin.
Which to extirpe,° he laid him privily *remove*
Downe in a darkesome lowly place farre in,
Whereas he meant his corrosives to apply,
And with streight° diet tame his stubborne malady. *strict*

26

In ashes and sackcloth he did array
His daintie corse, proud humors to abate,
And dieted with fasting every day,
The swelling of his wounds to mitigate,
And made him pray both earely and eke late:
And ever as superfluous flesh did rot
Amendment readie still at hand did wayt,
To pluck it out with pincers firie whot,° *hot*
That soone in him was left no one corrupted jot.

27

And bitter Penance with an yron whip,
Was wont him once to disple° every day: *discipline*
And sharpe Remorse his hart did pricke and nip,
That drops of bloud thence like a well did play;
And sad Repentance usèd to embay° *bathe*
His bodie in salt water smarting sore,
The filthy blots of sinne to wash away.
So in short space they did to health restore
The man that would not live, but earst° lay at deathes dore. *now*

28

In which his torment often was so great,
That like a Lyon he would cry and rore,
And rend his flesh, and his owne synewes eat.
His owne deare Una hearing evermore
His ruefull shriekes and gronings, often tore
Her guiltlesse garments, and her golden heare,
For pitty of his paine and anguish sore;
Yet all with patience wisely she did beare;
For well she wist, his crime could else be never cleare.

29

Whom thus recover'd by wise Patience,
And trew Repentance they to Una brought:
Who joyous of his curèd conscience,
Him dearely kist, and fairely° eke besought *courteously*
Himselfe to chearish, and consuming thought
To put away out of his carefull brest.
By this° Charissa, late in child-bed brought, *this time*
Was woxen strong, and left her fruitfull nest;
To her faire Una brought this unacquainted guest.

30

She was a woman in her freshest age,
Of wondrous beauty, and of bountie rare,
With goodly grace and comely personage,
That was on earth not easie to compare;
Full of great love, but Cupids wanton snare
As hell she hated, chast in worke and will;
Her necke and breasts were ever open bare,
That ay thereof her babes might sucke their fill;
The rest was all in yellow robes arayèd still.

31

A multitude of babes about her hong,
Playing their sports, that joyd her to behold,
Whom still she fed, whiles they were weake & young,
But thrust them forth still, as they wexèd old:
And on her head she wore a tyre° of gold, *headdress*
Adornd with gemmes and owches wondrous faire,
Whose passing° price° uneath° was to be told; *surpassing / value / scarcely*
And by her side there sate a gentle paire
Of turtle doves, she sitting in an yvorie chaire.

32

The knight and Una entring, faire her greet,
And bid her joy of that her happie brood;
Who them requites with court'sies seeming meet,
And entertaines with friendly chearefull mood.
Then Una her besought, to be so good,
As in her vertuous rules to schoole her knight,
Now after all his torment well withstood,
In that sad house of Penaunce, where his spright
Had past the paines of hell, and long enduring night.

33

She was right joyous of her just request,
And taking by the hand that Faeries sonne,
Gan him instruct in every good behest,
Of love, and righteousnesse, and well to donne,[1]
And wrath, and hatred warely to shonne,
That drew on men Gods hatred, and his wrath,
And many soules in dolours had fordonne:° *overcome*
In which when him she well instructed hath,
From thence to heaven she teacheth him the ready° path. *direct*

34

Wherein his weaker wandring steps to guide,
An auncient matrone she to her does call,
Whose sober lookes her wisedome well descride:° *revealed*
Her name was Mercie, well knowne over all,
To be both gratious, and eke liberall:
To whom the carefull charge of him she gave,
To lead aright, that he should never fall
In all his wayes through this wide worldès wave,° *changing conditions*
That Mercy in the end his righteous soule might save.

35

The godly Matrone by the hand him beares° *leads*
Forth from her presence, by a narrow way,
Scattred with bushy thornes, and ragged breares,° *briars*
Which still before him she remov'd away,
That nothing might his ready passage stay:
And ever when his feet encombred were,
Or gan to shrinke, or from the right to stray,
She held him fast, and firmely did upbeare,
As carefull Nourse her child from falling oft does reare.

36

Eftsoones unto an holy Hospitall,° *hostel*
That was fore° by the way, she did him bring, *close*
In which seven Bead-men[2] that had vowèd all
Their life to service of high heavens king
Did spend their dayes in doing godly thing:
Their gates to all were open evermore,
That by the wearie way were traveiling,
And one sate wayting ever them before,
To call in-commers by, that needy were and pore.

37

The first of them that eldest was, and best,° *foremost*
Of all the house had charge and governement,
As Guardian and Steward of the rest:
His office was to give entertainement
And lodging, unto all that came, and went:
Not unto such, as could him feast againe,° *in return*
And double quite,° for that he on them spent, *repay*
But such, as want of harbour° did constraine: *shelter*
Those for Gods sake his dewty was to entertaine.

38

The second was as Almner[3] of the place,
His office was, the hungry for to feed,
And thristy give to drinke, a worke of grace:
He feard not once him selfe to be in need,
Ne car'd to hoord for those, whom he did breede:
The grace of God he layd up still in store,
Which as a stocke° he left unto his seede;° *inheritance / children*
He had enough, what need him care for more?
And had he lesse, yet some he would give to the pore.

39

The third had of their wardrobe custodie,
In which were not rich tyres,° nor garments gay, *attire*
The plumes of pride, and wings of vanitie,
But clothes meet to keepe keene could° away, *cold*
And naked nature seemely° to aray; *appropriately*
With which bare wretched wights he dayly clad,
The images of God in earthly clay;
And if that no spare cloths to give he had,
His owne coate he would cut, and it distribute glad.

40

The fourth appointed by his office was,
Poore prisoners to relieve with gratious ayd,
And captives to redeeme with price° of bras, *payment*
From Turkes and Sarazins, which them had stayd;° *taken prisoner*

[1] *well to done* Good deeds.

[2] *seven Bead-men* These men of prayer perform the seven works of charity, which are described in the following stanzas.

[3] *Almner* One who distributes alms.

And though they faultie° were, yet well he
wayd,° *sinful / judged*
That God to us forgiveth every howre
Much more then that, why° they in bands° were
layd, *for which / bonds*
And he that harrowd hell with heavie stowre,
The faultie soules from thence brought to his heavenly
bowre.[1]

41

The fift had charge sicke persons to attend,
And comfort those, in point of death which lay;
For them most needeth comfort in the end,
When sin, and hell, and death do most dismay
The feeble soule departing hence away.
All is but lost, that living we bestow,° *store up*
If not well ended at our dying day.
O man have mind of that last bitter throw;° *throe*
For as the tree does fall, so lyes it ever low.

42

The sixt had charge of them now being dead,
In seemely sort their corses to engrave,° *bury*
And deck with dainty flowres their bridall bed,
That to their heavenly spouse both sweet and
brave° *handsome*
They might appeare, when he their soules shall save.
The wondrous workemanship of Gods owne mould,
Whose face he made, all beasts to feare, and gave
All in his hand, even dead we honour should.
Ah dearest God me graunt, I dead be not defould.

43

The seventh now after death and buriall done,
Had charge the tender Orphans of the dead
And widowes ayd, least they should be undone:° *ruined*
In face of judgement[2] he their right would plead,
Ne ought° the powre of mighty men did dread *at all*
In their defence, nor would for gold or fee° *bribe*
Be wonne their rightfull causes downe to tread:
And when they stood in most necessitee,
He did supply their want, and gave them ever free.

44

There when the Elfin knight arrivèd was,
The first and chiefest of the seven, whose care
Was guests to welcome, towardes him did pas:
Where seeing Mercie, that his steps up bare,
And alwayes led, to her with reverence rare
He humbly louted° in meeke lowlinesse, *bowed*
And seemely welcome for her did prepare:
For of their order she was Patronesse,
Albe° Charissa were their chiefest founderesse. *although*

45

There she awhile him stayes, him selfe to rest,
That to the rest more able he might bee:
During which time, in every good behest
And godly worke of Almes and charitee
She him instructed with great industree;
Shortly therein so perfect he became,
That from the first unto the last degree,
His mortall life he learnèd had to frame
In holy righteousnesse, without rebuke or blame.

46

Thence forward by that painfull way they pas,
Forth to an hill, that was both steepe and hy;
On top whereof a sacred chappell was,
And eke a litle Hermitage thereby,
Wherein an agèd holy man did lye,° *live*
That day and night said his devotion,
Ne other worldly busines did apply;° *conduct*
His name was heavenly Contemplation;
Of God and goodnesse was his meditation.

47

Great grace that old man to him given had;
For God he often saw from heavens hight,
All° were his earthly eyen both blunt° *although / dim*
and bad,
And through great age had lost their kindly sight,
Yet wondrous quick and persant° was his spright, *keen*
As Eagles eye, that can behold the Sunne:

---

[1] *And he … bowre* According to some Christian tradition, Christ descended into Hell after his crucifixion in order to release all the good Israelites who had lived before his earthly sufferings opened the gate of Heaven. In traditional terminology, this was known as the Harrowing of Hell, described in *The Golden Legend.*

[2] *judgement* I.e., in a court of law.

That hill they scale with all their powre and might,
That his frayle thighes nigh wearie and fordonne
Gan faile, but by her helpe the top at last he wonne.

48

There they do finde that godly agèd Sire,
With snowy lockes adowne his shoulders shed,
As hoarie frost with spangles° doth attire *icicles*
The mossy braunches of an Oke halfe ded.
Each bone might through his body well be red,
And every sinew seene through his long fast:
For nought he car'd his carcas long unfed;
His mind was full of spirituall repast,
And pyn'd° his flesh, to keepe his body low° and chast. *starved / humble*

49

Who when these two approching he aspide,
At their first presence grew agrievèd sore,° *sorely*
That forst him lay his heavenly thoughts aside;
And had he not that Dame respected more,° *greatly*
Whom highly he did reverence and adore,
He would not once have movèd for the knight.
They him saluted standing far afore;° *away*
Who well them greeting, humbly did requight,° *return*
And askèd, to what end they clomb that tedious height.

50

What end (quoth she) should cause us take such paine,
But that same end, which every living wight
Should make his marke,° high heaven to attaine? *object*
Is not from hence the way, that leadeth right
To that most glorious house, that glistreth bright
With burning starres, and everliving fire,
Whereof the keyes are to thy hand behight° *granted*
By wise Fidelia? she doth thee require,
To shew it to this knight, according° his desire. *granting*

51

Thrise happy man, said then the father grave,
Whose staggering steps thy steady hand doth lead,
And shewes the way, his sinfull soule to save.
Who better can the way to heaven aread,° *counsel*
Then thou thy selfe, that was both borne and bred
In heavenly throne, where thousand Angels shine?
Thou doest the prayers of the righteous sead° *seed*
Present before the majestie divine,
And his avenging wrath to clemencie incline.

52

Yet since thou bidst, thy pleasure shalbe donne.
Then come thou man of earth, and see the way,
That never yet was seene of Faeries sonne,
That never leads the traveiler astray,
But after labours long, and sad delay,
Brings them to joyous rest and endlesse blis.
But first thou must a season fast and pray,
Till from her bands the spright assoilèd° is, *freed*
And have her strength recur'd° from fraile infirmitis. *recovered*

53

That done, he leads him to the highest Mount;
Such one, as that same mighty man of God,
That bloud-red billowes like a wallèd front
On either side disparted° with his rod, *parted*
Till that his army dry-foot through them yod,° *went*
Dwelt fortie dayes upon; where writ in stone
With bloudy letters by the hand of God,
The bitter doome of death and balefull mone
He did receive, whiles flashing fire about him shone.[1]

54

Or like that sacred hill, whose head full hie,
Adornd with fruitfull Olives all arownd,[2]
Is, as it were for endlesse memory
Of that deare Lord, who oft thereon was fownd,
For ever with a flowring girlond crownd:
Or like that pleasaunt Mount,[3] that is for ay
Through famous Poets verse each where[4] renownd,
On which the thrise three learnèd Ladies play

[1] *That done ... shone* References to Mount Sinai, upon which Moses lived for 40 days before receiving the Ten Commandments ("bloody letters"), to Moses's parting of the Red Sea to allow the Israelites to escape from Egypt, and to the burning bush through which God spoke to Moses. See the Book of Exodus.

[2] *Or like ... arownd* The Mount of Olives, upon which Jesus delivered the "Sermon on the Mount" (see Matthew 5–7).

[3] *that pleasaunt Mount* Mount Parnassus, sacred to the Nine Muses.

[4] *each where* Everywhere.

Their heavenly notes, and make full many a lovely
lay.° *verse*

55

From thence, far off he unto him did shew
A litle path, that was both steepe and long,
Which to a goodly Citie led his vew;
Whose wals and towres were builded high and strong
Of perle and precious stone, that earthly tong
Cannot describe, nor wit of man can tell;
Too high a ditty° for my simple song; *theme*
The Citie of the great king hight it well,
Wherein eternall peace and happinesse doth dwell.

56

As he thereon stood gazing, he might see
The blessed Angels to and fro descend
From highest heaven, in gladsome companee,[1]
And with great joy into that Citie wend,
As commonly° as friend does with his frend. *familiarly*
Whereat he wondred much, and gan enquere,
What stately building durst so high extend
Her loftie towres unto the starry sphere,
And what unknowen nation there empeopled were.

57

Faire knight (quoth he) Hierusalem° that is, *Jerusalem*
The new Hierusalem, that God has built
For those to dwell in, that are chosen his,
His chosen people purg'd from sinfull guilt,
With pretious bloud, which cruelly was spilt
On cursèd tree, of that unspotted lam,° *lamb*
That for the sinnes of all the world was kilt:
Now are they Saints all in that Citie sam,° *same*
More deare unto their God, then younglings to their
dam.

58

Till now, said then the knight, I weenèd well,
That great Cleopolis, where I have beene,
In which that fairest Faerie Queene doth dwell,
The fairest Citie was, that might be seene;
And that bright towre all built of christall cleene,
Panthea, seemd the brightest thing, that was:
But now by proofe all otherwise I weene;
For this great Citie that does far surpas,
And this bright Angels towre quite dims that towre of
glas.

59

Most trew, then said the holy agèd man;
Yet is Cleopolis for earthly frame,° *structure*
The fairest peece, that eye beholden can:
And well beseemes all knights of noble name,
That covet in th'immortall booke of fame
To be eternizèd, that same to haunt,
And doen their service to that soveraigne Dame,
That glorie does to them for guerdon graunt:
For she is heavenly borne, and heaven may justly
vaunt.° *boast*

60

And thou faire ymp, sprong out from English race,
How ever now accompted° Elfins sonne, *considered*
Well worthy doest thy service for her grace,
To aide a virgin desolate foredonne.° *undone*
But when thou famous victorie hast wonne,
And high emongst all knights hast hong thy shield,
Thenceforth the suit of earthly conquest shonne,° *shun*
And wash thy hands from guilt of bloudy field:
For bloud can nought but sin, & wars but sorrowes yield.

61

Then seeke this path, that I to thee presage,° *point out*
Which after all to heaven shall thee send;
Then peaceably thy painefull pilgrimage
To yonder same Hierusalem do bend,
Where is for thee ordaind a blessed end:
For thou emongst those Saints, whom thou doest see,
Shalt be a Saint, and thine owne nations frend
And Patrone: thou Saint George shalt callèd bee,
Saint George of mery England, the signe of victoree.

62

Unworthy wretch (quoth he) of so great grace,
How dare I thinke such glory to attaine?
These that have it attaind, were in like cace
(Quoth he) as wretched, and liv'd in like paine.

[1] *The blessed … companee* Jacob had a vision of a ladder that connected earth and heaven. See Genesis 28.12.

But deeds of armes must I at last be faine,° *willing*
And Ladies love to leave so dearely bought?
What need of armes, where peace doth ay remaine,
(Said he) and battailes none are to be fought?
As for loose loves they are vaine, and vanish into nought.

63

O let me not (quoth he) then turne againe
Backe to the world, whose joyes so fruitlesse are;
But let me here for aye in peace remaine,
Or streight way on that last long voyage fare,
That nothing may my present hope empare.
That may not be (said he) ne maist thou yit
Forgo that royall maides bequeathèd care,
Who did her cause into thy hand commit,
Till from her cursèd foe thou have her freely quit.° *released*

64

Then shall I soone, (quoth he) so God me grace,
Abet° that virgins cause disconsolate, *support*
And shortly backe returne unto this place,
To walke this way in Pilgrims poore estate.
But now aread,° old father, why of late *state*
Didst thou behight° me borne of English blood, *call*
Whom all a Faeries sonne doen nominate?
That word shall I (said he) avouchen° good, *prove*
Sith to thee is unknowne the cradle of thy brood.

65

For well I wote, thou springst from ancient race
Of Saxon kings, that have with mightie hand
And many bloudie battailes fought in place° *that place*
High reard° their royall throne in Britane land, *erected*
And vanquisht them, unable to withstand:
From thence a Faerie thee unweeting° reft, *secretly*
There as thou slepst in tender swadling band,
And her base Elfin brood there for thee left.
Such men do Chaungelings call, so chaungd by Faeries theft.

66

Thence she thee brought into this Faerie lond,
And in an heapèd furrow did thee hyde,
Where thee a Ploughman all unweeting fond,
As he his toylesome teme that way did guyde,
And brought thee up in ploughmans state to byde,
Whereof Georgos[1] he thee gave to° name; *as*
Till prickt with courage, and thy forces pryde,
To Faery court thou cam'st to seeke for fame,
And prove thy puissaunt armes, as seemes thee best became.° *suited*

67

O holy Sire (quoth he) how shall I quight° *repay*
The many favours I with thee have found,
That hast my name and nation red aright,
And taught the way that does to heaven bound?
This said, adowne he lookèd to the ground,
To have returnd, but dazèd were his eyne,
Through passing° brightnesse, which did quite confound *exceeding*
His feeble sence, and too exceeding shyne.
So darke are earthly things compard to things divine.

68

At last whenas himselfe he gan to find,° *recover*
To Una back he cast him to retire;
Who him awaited still with pensive° mind. *apprehensive*
Great thankes and goodly meed° to that good syre, *recompense*
He thence departing gave for his paines hyre.° *reward*
So came to Una, who him joyd to see,
And after litle rest, gan him desire,
Of her adventure° mindfull for to bee. *quest*
So leave they take of Caelia, and her daughters three.

Canto II

The knight with that old Dragon fights
Two dayes incessantly:
The third him overthrowes, and gayns
Most glorious victory.

1

High time now gan it wex[2] for Una faire,
To thinke of those her captive Parents deare,
And their forwasted kingdome to repaire:

---

[1] *Georgos* Farmer.

[2] *gan it wex* It began to grow.

Whereto whenas they now approchèd neare,
With hartie words her knight she gan to cheare,
And in her modest manner thus bespake;
Deare knight, as deare, as ever knight was deare,
That all these sorrowes suffer for my sake,
High heaven behold the tedious toyle, ye for me take.

2

Now are we come unto my native soyle,
And to the place, where all our perils dwell;
Here haunts that feend, and does his dayly spoyle,
Therefore henceforth be at your keeping well,[1]
And ever ready for your foeman fell.
The sparke of noble courage now awake,
And strive your excellent selfe to excell;
That shall ye evermore renowmèd make,
Above all knights on earth, that batteill undertake.

3

And pointing forth, lo yonder is (said she)
The brasen towre in which my parents deare
For dread of that huge feend emprisond be
Whom I from far see on the walles appeare
Whose sight my feeble soule doth greatly cheare:
And on the top of all I do espye
The watchman wayting tydings glad to heare,
That O my parents might I happily
Unto you bring, to ease you of your misery.

4

With that they heard a roaring hideous sound,
That all the ayre with terrour fillèd wide,
And seemd uneath° to shake the stedfast ground. *almost*
Eftsoones that dreadfull Dragon they espide,
Where stretcht he lay upon the sunny side
Of a great hill, himselfe like a great hill.
But all so soone, as he from far descride
Those glistring armes, that heaven with light did fill,
He rousd himselfe full blith,° and hastned them
untill.° *gladly / towards*

5

Then bad the knight his Lady yede° aloofe, *go*
And to an hill her selfe with draw aside,
From whence she might behold that battailles
proof° *outcome*
And eke be safe from daunger far descryde:° *observed*
She him obayd, and turnd a little wyde.
Now O thou sacred Muse, most learnèd Dame,
Faire ympe of Phoebus, and his agèd bride,[2]
The Nourse of time, and everlasting fame,
That warlike hands ennoblest with immortall name;

6

O gently come into my feeble brest,
Come gently, but not with that mighty rage,
Wherewith the martiall troupes thou doest
infest,° *arouse*
And harts of great Heroës doest enrage,
That nought their kindled courage may aswage,
Soone as thy dreadfull trompe° begins to sownd; *trumpet*
The God of warre with his fiers equipage
Thou doest awake, sleepe never he so sownd,
And scarèd nations doest with horrour sterne
astownd.° *astonish*

7

Faire Goddesse lay that furious fit° aside, *music*
Till I of warres and bloudy Mars do sing,
And Briton fields with Sarazin bloud bedyde,
Twixt that great faery Queene and Paynim king,
That with their horrour heaven and earth did ring,
A worke of labour long, and endlesse prayse:
But now a while let downe that haughtie string,
And to my tunes thy second tenor rayse,
That I this man of God his godly armes may
blaze.° *proclaim*

8

By this the dreadfull Beast drew nigh to hand,
Halfe flying, and halfe footing in his hast,
That with his largenesse measurèd much land,
And made wide shadow under his huge wast;° *girth*
As mountaine doth the valley overcast.
Approching nigh, he rearèd high afore
His body monstrous, horrible, and vast,

[1] *at your keeping well* Well on your guard.

[2] *his agèd bride* Mnemosyne, or Memory, the mother of the Muses.

Which to increase his wondrous greatnesse more,
Was swolne with wrath, & poyson, & with bloudy gore.

9

And over, all with brasen scales was armd,
Like plated coate of steele, so couchèd° neare,° *set / closely*
That nought mote perce, ne might his corse be harmd
With dint of sword, nor push of pointed speare;
Which as an Eagle, seeing pray appeare,
His aery plumes doth rouze, full rudely° dight, *roughly*
So shakèd he, that horrour was to heare,
For as the clashing of an Armour bright,
Such noyse his rouzèd scales did send unto the knight.

10

His flaggy° wings when forth he did display, *pendulous*
Were like two sayles, in which the hollow wynd
Is gathered full, and worketh speedy way:
And eke the pennes, that did his pineons° *quills / wings*
bynd,
Were like mayne-yards, with flying canvas lynd,
With which whenas him list the ayre to beat,
And there by force unwonted° passage find, *unaccustomed*
The cloudes before him fled for terrour great,
And all the heavens stood still amazèd with his threat.

11

His huge long tayle wound up in hundred foldes,
Does overspred his long bras-scaly backe,
Whose wreathèd boughts° when ever he unfoldes, *coils*
And thicke entangled knots adown does slacke.
Bespotted all with shields° of red and blacke, *scales*
It sweepeth all the land behind him farre,
And of three furlongs[1] does but litle lacke;
And at the point two stings in-fixèd arre,
Both deadly sharpe, that sharpest steele exceeden farre.

12

But stings° and sharpest steele did far exceed *spears*
The sharpnesse of his cruell rending clawes;[2]
Dead was it sure, as sure as death in deed,
What ever thing does touch his ravenous pawes,
Or what within his reach he ever drawes.
But his most hideous head my toung to tell
Does tremble: for his deepe devouring jawes
Wide gapèd, like the griesly mouth of hell,
Through which into his darke abisse all ravin° fell. *prey*

13

And that more wondrous was, in either jaw
Three ranckes of yron teeth enraungèd were,
In which yet trickling bloud and gobbets° raw *chunks*
Of late devourèd bodies did appeare,
That sight thereof bred cold congealèd feare:
Which to increase, and as atonce to kill,
A cloud of smoothering smoke and sulphur seare° *searing*
Out of his stinking gorge forth steemèd still,
That all the ayre about with smoke and stench did fill.

14

His blazing eyes, like two bright shining shields,
Did burne with wrath, and sparkled living fyre;
As two broad Beacons, set in open fields,
Send forth their flames farre off to every shyre,° *district*
And warning give, that enemies conspyre,
With fire and sword the region to invade;
So flam'd his eyne with rage and rancorous yre:
But farre within, as in a hollow glade,
Those glaring lampes were set, that made a dreadfull
shade.

15

So dreadfully he towards him did pas,
Forelifting up aloft his speckled brest,
And often bounding on the brusèd gras,
As for great joyance of his newcome guest.
Eftsoones he gan advance his haughtie crest,
As chauffèd° Bore his bristles doth upreare, *angered*
And shoke his scales to battell readie drest;
That made the Redcrosse knight nigh quake for feare,
As bidding° bold defiance to his foeman neare. *inviting*

16

The knight gan fairely couch° his steadie speare, *aim*
And fiercely ran at him with rigorous might:
The pointed steele arriving rudely theare,

---

[1] *furlong* Agricultural measurement presently equal to 220 yards; originally the length of a furrow in a common field.

[2] *but stings … clawes* I.e., the sharpness of his claws far exceeded that of spears and the sharpest steel.

His harder hide would neither perce, nor bight,
But glauncing by forth passèd forward right;
Yet sore amovèd with so puissant push,
The wrathfull beast about him turnèd light,° *swiftly*
And him so rudely passing by, did brush
With his long tayle, that horse and man to ground did rush.

17

Both horse and man up lightly rose againe,
And fresh encounter towards him addrest:
But th'idle° stroke yet backe recoyld in vaine, *futile*
And found no place his deadly point to rest.
Exceeding rage enflam'd the furious beast,
To be avengèd of so great despight;° *outrage*
For never felt his imperceable brest
So wondrous force, from hand of living wight;
Yet had he prov'd the powre of many a puissant knight.

18

Then with his waving wings displayèd wyde,
Himselfe up high he lifted from the ground,
And with strong flight did forcibly divide
The yielding aire, which nigh° too feeble found *almost*
Her flitting partes, and element unsound,
To beare so great a weight: he cutting way
With his broad sayles, about him soarèd round:
At last low stouping with unweldie sway,° *force*
Snatcht up both horse & man, to beare them quite away.

19

Long he them bore above the subject plaine,
So farre as Ewghen[1] bow a shaft may send,
Till struggling strong did him at last constraine,
To let them downe before his flightès end:
As hagard° hauke presuming to contend *wild*
With hardie fowle, above his hable° might,° *proper / strength*
His wearie pounces° all in vaine doth spend, *talons*
To trusse the pray too heavie for his flight;
Which comming downe to ground, does free it selfe by fight.

20

He so disseizèd of his gryping° grosse,° *freed / grip / heavy*
The knight his thrillant° speare againe assayd *penetrating*
In his bras-plated body to embosse,° *plunge*
And three mens strength unto the stroke he layd;
Wherewith the stiffe beame quaked, as affrayd,
And glauncing from his scaly necke, did glyde
Close under his left wing, then broad displayd.
The percing steele there wrought a wound full wyde,
That with the uncouth° smart the Monster lowdly cryde. *unknown*

21

He cryde, as raging seas are wont to rore,
When wintry storme his wrathfull wreck does threat,
The rolling billowes° beat the ragged shore, *waves*
As they the earth would shoulder from her seat,
And greedie gulfe does gape, as he would eat
His neighbour element in his revenge:
Then gin the blustring brethren° boldly threat, *winds*
To move the world from off his stedfast henge,° *hinge*
And boystrous battell make, each other to avenge.

22

The steely head stucke fast still in his flesh,
Till with his cruell clawes he snatcht the wood,
And quite a sunder broke. Forth flowèd fresh
A gushing river of blacke goarie blood,
That drownèd all the land, whereon he stood;
The streame thereof would drive a water-mill.
Trebly augmented was his furious mood
With bitter sense of his deepe rooted ill,° *wound*
That flames of fire he threw forth from his large nosethrill.

23

His hideous tayle then hurlèd he about,
And therewith all enwrapt the nimble thyes° *thighs*
Of his froth-fomy steed, whose courage stout
Striving to loose the knot, that fast him tyes,
Himselfe in streighter° bandes too rash implyes,° *tighter / entangles*
That to the ground he is perforce° constraynd *thereby*
To throw his rider: who can quickly ryse
From off the earth, with durty bloud distaynd,° *dirtied*
For that reprochfull fall right fowly he disdaynd.

[1] *Ewghen* Made of wood from the yew tree.

24

And fiercely tooke his trenchand° blade in hand, *cutting*
With which he stroke so furious and so fell,
That nothing seemd the puissance could withstand:
Upon his crest the hardned yron fell,
But his more hardned crest was armd so well,
That deeper dint therein it would not make;
Yet so extremely did the buffe° him quell, *blow*
That from thenceforth he shund the like to take,
But when he saw them come, he did them still forsake.° *avoid*

25

The knight was wrath to see his stroke beguyld,° *foiled*
And smote againe with more outrageous might;
But backe againe the sparckling steele recoyld,
And left not any marke, where it did light;
As if in Adamant° rocke it had bene pight.° *hardest / pitched*
The beast impatient of his smarting wound,
And of so fierce and forcible despight,
Thought with his wings to stye° above the ground; *rise*
But his late wounded wing unserviceable found.

26

Then full of griefe and anguish vehement,
He lowdly brayd, that like was never heard,
And from his wide devouring oven sent
A flake° of fire, that flashing in his beard, *stream*
Him all amazd, and almost made affeard:
The scorching flame sore swingèd° all his face, *singed*
And through his armour all his bodie seard,
That he could not endure so cruell cace,
But thought his armes to leave, and helmet to unlace.

27

Not that great Champion[1] of the antique world,
Whom famous Poetes verse so much doth vaunt,
And hath for twelve huge labours high extold,
So many furies and sharpe fits did haunt,
When him the poysoned garment did enchaunt
With Centaures bloud, and bloudie verses charm'd,
As did this knight twelve thousand dolours daunt,
Whom fyrie steele now burnt, that earst him arm'd,
That erst him goodly arm'd, now most of all him harm'd.

28

Faint, wearie, sore, emboylèd, grievèd, brent
With heat, toyle, wounds, armes, smart, & inward fire
That never man such mischiefes did torment;
Death better were, death did he oft desire,
But death will never come, when needes require.
Whom so dismayd when that his foe beheld,
He cast to suffer him no more respire,° *live*
But gan his sturdie sterne° about to weld, *tail / swing*
And him so strongly stroke, that to the ground him feld.

29

It fortunèd (as faire it then befell)
Behind his backe unweeting, where he stood,
Of auncient time there was a springing well,
From which fast trickled forth a silver flood,
Full of great vertues, and for med'cine good.
Whylome, before that cursèd Dragon got
That happie land, and all with innocent blood
Defyld those sacred waves, it rightly hot° *was called*
The well of life, ne yet his vertues had forgot.

30

For unto life the dead it could restore,
And guilt of sinfull crimes cleane wash away,
Those that with sicknesse were infected sore,
It could recure,° and agèd long decay *heal*
Renew, as one were borne that very day.
Both Silo this, and Jordan did excell,
And th'English Bath, and eke the german Spau,
Ne can Cephise, nor Hebrus match this well:[2]
Into the same the knight backe overthrowèn, fell.

[1] *that great Champion* Hercules, who successfully completed twelve labors. His death occurred when his wife inadvertently presented him with a poisoned shirt. The pain was so intense that he caused a funeral pyre to be built so that he could cast himself upon it. He was, however, rescued from the pyre and brought to dwell on Mount Olympus, the home of the gods.

[2] *Both Silo ... well* These waters have all been said to have healing powers. In John 9.7 a blind man is cured in the waters of the Siloam; Christ was baptized in the river Jordan; the supposedly medicinal waters of Bath and Spa were visited by those suffering from a variety of ailments; the waters of Cephise and Hebrus are praised in classical mythology for their purifying powers.

31

Now gan the golden Phoebus for to steepe
His fierie face in billowes of the west,
And his faint steedes watred in Ocean deepe,
Whiles from their journall° labours they did rest, *daily*
When that infernall Monster, having kest° *cast*
His wearie foe into that living well,
Can° high advance his broad discoloured brest, *did*
Above his wonted pitch,° with countenance fell,° *height / fierce*
And clapt his yron wings, as victor he did dwell.° *stay*

32

Which when his pensive Ladie saw from farre,
Great woe and sorrow did her soule assay,
As weening that the sad end of the warre,
And gan to highest God entirely° pray, *earnestly*
That fearèd chance from her to turne away;
With folded hands and knees full lowly bent
All night she watcht, ne once adowne would lay
Her daintie limbs in her sad dreriment,° *peril*
But praying still did wake, and waking did lament.

33

The morrow next gan early to appeare,
That Titan rose to runne his daily race:
But early ere the morrow next gan reare
Out of the sea faire Titans deawy face,
Up rose the gentle virgin from her place,
And lookèd all about, if she might spy
Her lovèd knight to move his manly pace:
For she had great doubt of his safety,
Since late she saw him fall before his enemy.

34

At last she where he upstarted brave
Out of the well, wherein he drenchèd lay;
As Eagle fresh out of the Ocean wave,
Where he hath left his plumes all hoary gray,
And deckt himselfe with feathers youthly gay,
Like Eyas hauke° up mounts unto the skies, *young hawk*
His newly budded pineons to assay,
And marveiles at himselfe, still as he flies:
So new this new-borne knight to battell new did rise.

35

Whom when the damnèd feend so fresh did spy,
No wonder if he wondred at the sight,
And doubted, whether his late enemy
It were, or other new supplièd knight.
He, now to prove his late renewèd might,
High brandishing his bright deaw-burning[1] blade,
Upon his crested scalpe so sore did smite,
That to the scull a yawning wound it made:
The deadly dint his dullèd senses all dismaid.

36

I wote not, whether the revenging steele
Were hardned with that holy water dew,
Wherein he fell, or sharper edge did feele,
Or his baptizèd hands now greater grew;
Or other secret vertue° did ensew; *power*
Else never could the force of fleshly arme,
Ne molten mettall in his bloud embrew:° *thrust*
For till that stownd° could never wight him harme, *time*
By subtilty, nor slight, nor might, nor mighty charme.

37

The cruell wound enragèd him so sore,
That loud he yelded for exceeding paine;
As hundred ramping Lyons seem'd to rore,
Whom ravenous hunger did thereto constraine:
Then gan he tosse aloft his stretchèd traine,° *tail*
And therewith scourge the buxome° aire so sore,° *pliant / violently*
That to his force to yeelden it was faine;
Ne ought° his sturdie strokes might stand afore, *aught*
That high trees overthrew, and rocks in peeces tore.

38

The same advauncing high above his head,
With sharpe intended° sting so rude him smot, *extended*
That to the earth him drove, as stricken dead,
Ne living wight would have him life behot:° *expected*
The mortall sting his angry needle shot
Quite through his shield, and in his shoulder seasd,° *fastened*
Where fast it stucke, ne would there out be got:

[1] *deaw-burning* I.e., the sword is so bright that its light, like that of the sun, burns up the dew.

The griefe thereof him wondrous sore diseasd,
Ne might his ranckling paine with patience be appeasd.

39

But yet more mindfull of his honour deare,
Then of the grievous smart, which him did wring,° *vex*
From loathèd soile he can him lightly reare,
And strove to loose the farre infixèd sting:
Which when in vaine he tryde with struggeling,
Inflam'd with wrath, his raging blade he heft,° *raised*
And strooke so strongly, that the knotty string
Of his huge taile he quite a sunder cleft,
Five joynts thereof he hewd, and but the stump him left.

40

Hart cannot thinke, what outrage, and what cryes,
With foule enfouldred[1] smoake and flashing fire,
The hell-bred beast threw forth unto the skyes,
That all was coverèd with darknesse dire:
Then fraught° with rancour, and engorgèd ire, *filled*
He cast at once him to avenge for all,
And gathering up himselfe out of the mire,° *mud*
With his uneven wings did fiercely fall
Upon his sunne-bright shield, and gript it fast withall.

41

Much was the man encombred with his hold,
In feare to lose his weapon in his paw,
Ne wist yet, how his talants° to unfold; *talons*
Nor harder was from Cerberus greedie jaw
To plucke a bone, then from his cruell claw
To reave° by strength the gripèd gage away: *wrest*
Thrise he assayd it from his foot to draw,
And thrise in vaine to draw it did assay,
It booted nought to thinke, to robbe him of his pray.

42

Tho° when he saw no power might prevaile, *then*
His trustie sword he cald to his last aid,
Wherewith he fiercely did his foe assaile,
And double blowes about him stoutly laid,
That glauncing fire out of the yron plaid;° *danced*
As sparckles from the Andvile° use to fly, *anvil*
When heavie hammers on the wedge° are swaid;° *i.e., anvil / struck*
Therewith at last he forst him to unty° *release*
One of his grasping feete, him to defend thereby.

43

The other foot, fast fixèd on his shield,
Whenas no strength, nor stroks mote° him constraine *could*
To loose, ne yet the warlike pledge to yield,
He smot thereat with all his might and maine,
That nought so wondrous puissance might sustaine;
Upon the joynt the lucky steele did light,
And made such way, that hewd it quite in twaine;
The paw yet missèd not his minisht° might, *diminished*
But hong still on the shield, as it at first was pight.° *placed*

44

For griefe thereof, and divelish despight,
From his infernall fournace forth he threw
Huge flames, that dimmèd all the heavens light,
Enrold in duskish smoke and brimstone° blew;° *sulphur / blue*
As burning Aetna[2] from his boyling stew
Doth belch out flames, and rockes in peeces broke,
And ragged ribs of mountaines molten new,
Enwrapt in coleblacke clouds and filthy smoke,
That all the land with stench, and heaven with horror choke.

45

The heate whereof, and harmefull pestilence° *injury*
So sore him noyd,° that forst him to retire *vexed*
A little backward for his best defence,
To save his bodie from the scorching fire,
Which he from hellish entrailes did expire.° *exhale*
It chaunst (eternall God that chaunce did guide)
As he recoylèd backward, in the mire
His nigh forwearied feeble feet did slide,
And downe he fell, with dread of shame sore terrifide.

46

There grew a goodly tree him faire beside,
Loaden with fruit and apples rosie red,

[1] *enfouldred* Charged with lightning.

[2] *Aetna* Volcano in eastern Sicily.

As they in pure vermilion had beene dide,
Whereof great vertues over all were red:° *told*
For happie life to all, which thereon fed,
And life eke everlasting did befall:
Great God it planted in that blessed sted° *place*
With his almightie hand, and did it call
The tree of life,[1] the crime of our first fathers fall.

47

In all the world like was not to be found,
Save in that soile, where all good things did grow,
And freely sprong out of the fruitfull ground,
As incorrupted Nature did them sow,
Till that dread Dragon[2] all did overthrow.
Another like faire tree eke grew thereby,
Whereof who so did eat, eftsoones did know
Both good and ill: O mornefull memory:
That tree through one mans fault hath doen us all to dy.

48

From that first tree forth flowd, as from a well,
A trickling streame of Balme, most soveraine° *powerful*
And daintie° deare,° which on the ground still fell, *particularly / precious*
And overflowèd all the fertill plaine,
As it had deawèd bene with timely° raine: *seasonal*
Life and long health that gratious° ointment gave, *pleasing*
And deadly woundes could heale, and reare againe
The senselesse corse appointed for the grave.
Into that same he fell: which did from death him save.

49

For nigh thereto the ever damnèd beast
Durst not approch, for he was deadly° made, *of death*
And all that life preservèd, did detest:
Yet he it oft adventur'd to invade.
By this the drouping day-light gan to fade
And yeeld his roome to sad succeeding night,
Who with her sable mantle gan to shade
The face of earth, and wayes of living wight,
And high her burning torch set up in heaven bright.

50

When gentle Una saw the second fall
Of her deare knight, who wearie of long fight,
And faint through losse of bloud, mov'd not at all,
But lay as in a dreame of deepe delight,
Besmeard with pretious Balme, whose vertuous might
Did heale his wounds, and scorching heat alay,
Againe she stricken was with sore affright,
And for his safetie gan devoutly pray;
And watch the noyous° night, and wait for joyous day. *harmful*

51

The joyous day gan early to appeare,
And faire Aurora from the deawy bed
Of agèd Tithone gan her selfe to reare,
With rosie cheekes, for shame as blushing red;
Her golden lockes for haste were loosely shed
About her eares, when Una her did marke
Clymbe to her charet, all with flowers spred;
From heaven high to chase the chearelesse darke,
With merry note her loud salutes the mounting larke.

52

Then freshly up arose the doughtie knight,
All healèd of his hurts and woundès wide,
And did himselfe to battell readie dight;
Whose early foe awaiting him beside
To have devourd, so soone as day he spyde,
When now he saw himselfe so freshly reare,
As if late fight had nought him damnifyde,° *hurt*
He woxe° dismayd, and gan his fate to feare; *grew*
Nathlesse with wonted rage he him advauncèd neare.

53

And in his first encounter, gaping wide,
He thought attonce him to have swallowd quight,
And rusht upon him with outragious pride;
Who him r'encountring fierce, as hauke in flight,
Perforce° rebutted backe. The weapon bright *forcibly*
Taking advantage of his open jaw,
Ran through his mouth with so importune° might, *exacting*
That deepe emperst his darksome hollow maw,° *mouth*

---

[1] *tree of life* This tree grows in the Garden of Eden, from which Adam and Eve were expelled for eating from the Tree of Knowledge.

[2] *that dread Dragon* I.e., Satan.

And back retyrd,° his life bloud forth with all did draw. *withdrawn*

54

So downe he fell, and forth his life did breath,
That vanisht into smoke and cloudès swift;
So downe he fell, that th'earth him underneath
Did grone, as feeble so great load to lift;
So downe he fell, as an huge rockie clift,
Whose false° foundation waves have washt away, *defective*
With dreadfull poyse° is from the mayneland rift, *weight*
And rolling downe, great Neptune doth dismay;
So downe he fell, and like an heapèd mountaine lay.

55

The knight himselfe even trembled at his fall,
So huge and horrible a masse it seem'd;
And his deare Ladie, that beheld it all,
Durst not approch for dread, which she misdeem'd,° *misjudged*
But yet at last, when as the direfull feend
She saw not stirre, off-shaking vaine° affright, *empty*
She nigher drew, and saw that joyous end:
Then God she praysd, and thankt her faithfull knight,
That had atchiev'd so great a conquest by his might.

Canto 12

Faire Una to the Redcrosse knight
Betrouthèd is with joy:
Though false Duessa it to barre° *stop*
Her false sleights doe imploy.

1

Behold I see the haven nigh at hand,
To which I meane my wearie course to bend;
Vere° the maine shete, and beare up with[1] the land, *release*
The which afore is fairely to be kend,° *recognized*
And seemeth safe from stormes, that may offend;
There this faire virgin wearie of her way
Must landed be, now at her journeyes end:
There eke my feeble barke° a while may stay, *vessel*
Till merry° wind and weather call her thence away. *favorable*

2

Scarsely had Phoebus in the glooming° East *glowing*
Yet harnessèd his firie-footed teeme,
Ne reard aboue the earth his flaming creast,° *crest*
When the last deadly smoke aloft did steeme,
That signe of last outbreathèd life did seeme,
Unto the watchman on the castle wall;
Who thereby dead that balefull° Beast did deeme, *destructive*
And to his Lord and Ladie lowd gan call,
To tell, how he had seene the Dragons fatall fall.

3

Uprose with hastie joy, and feeble speed
That agèd Sire, the Lord of all that land,
And lookèd forth, to weet, if true indeede
Those tydings were, as he did understand,
Which whenas true by tryall he out fond,
He bad to open wyde his brazen gate,
Which long time had bene shut, and out of hond[2]
Proclaymèd joy and peace through all his state;
For dead now was their foe, which them forrayèd° late. *pillaged*

4

Then gan triumphant Trompets sound on hie,
That sent to heaven the ecchoèd report
Of their new joy, and happie victorie
Gainst him, that had them long opprest with tort,° *injury*
And fast imprisonèd in siegèd fort.
Then all the people, as in solemne feast,
To him assembled with one full consort,[3]
Rejoycing at the fall of that great beast,
From whose eternall bondage now they were releast.

5

Forth came that auncient Lord and agèd Queene,
Arayd in antique robes downe to the ground,
And sad habiliments right well beseene;° *appropriate*
A noble crew about them waited round

[1] *beare up with* Steer toward.

[2] *out of hond* Immediately.

[3] *one full consort* All at once.

Of sage and sober Peres,° all gravely gownd; *peers*
Whom farre before did march a goodly band
Of tall young men, all hable° armes to sownd,° *able / wield*
But now they laurell braunches bore in hand;
Glad signe of victorie and peace in all their land.

6

Unto that doughtie° Conquerour they came, *valiant*
And him before themselves prostrating low,
Their Lord and Patrone° loud did him proclame, *protector*
And at his feet their laurell boughes did throw.
Soone after them all dauncing on a row
The comely virgins came, with girlands dight,
As fresh as flowres in medow greene do grow,
When morning deaw upon their leaves doth light:
And in their hands sweet Timbrels° all *tambourines*
upheld on hight.

7

And them before, the fry° of children young *group*
Their wanton sports and childish mirth did play,
And to the Maydens sounding tymbrels sung
In well attunèd notes, a joyous lay,
And made delightfull musicke all the way,
Untill they came, where that faire virgin stood;
As faire Diana in fresh sommers day
Beholds her Nymphes, enraung'd° in shadie *spread out*
wood,
Some wrestle, some do run, some bathe in christall flood.

8

So she beheld those maydens meriment
With chearefull vew; who when to her they came,
Themselves to ground with gratious humblesse bent,
And her ador'd by honorable name,° *titles*
Lifting to heaven her everlasting fame:
Then on her head they set a girland greene,
And crownèd her twixt earnest and twixt game;
Who in her selfe-resemblance well beseene,
Did seeme such, as she was, a goodly maiden Queene.

9

And after, all the raskall many ran,
Heapèd together in rude° rabblement° *disorganized / swarm*
To see the face of that victorious man:
Whom all admired, as from heaven sent,
And gazd upon with gaping wonderment.
But when they came, where that dead Dragon lay,
Stretcht on the ground in monstrous large extent,
The sight with idle feare did them dismay,
Ne durst approch him nigh, to touch, or once assay.

10

Some feard, and fled; some feard and well it faynd;° *hid*
One that would wiser seeme, then all the rest,
Warnd him not touch, for yet perhaps remaynd
Some lingring life within his hollow brest,
Or in his wombe might lurke some hidden nest
Of many Dragonets, his fruitfull seed;
Another said, that in his eyes did rest
Yet sparckling fire, and bad thereof take heed;
Another said, he saw him move his eyes indeed.

11

One mother, when as her foolehardie chyld
Did come too neare, and with his talants° play, *claws*
Halfe dead through feare, her litle babe
revyld,° *reprimanded*
And to her gossips gan in counsell say;
How can I tell, but that his talants may
Yet scratch my sonne, or rend his tender hand?
So diversly themselves in vaine they fray;° *frighten*
Whiles some more bold, to measure him nigh stand,
To prove how many acres he did spread of land.

12

Thus flockèd all the folke him round about,
The whiles that hoarie° king, with all his *gray-headed*
traine,
Being arrivèd, where that champion stout
After his foes defeasance° did remaine, *defeat*
Him goodly greetes, and faire does entertaine,
With princely gifts of yvorie and gold,
And thousand thankes him yeelds for all his paine.
Then when his daughter deare he does behold,
Her dearely doth imbrace, and kisseth
manifold.° *many times*

13

And after to his Pallace he them brings,
With shaumes,[1] & trompets, & with Clarions sweet;
And all the way the joyous people sings,
And with their garments strowes the pavèd street:
Whence mounting up, they find purveyance° meet *provisions / fitting*
Of all, that royall Princes court became,° *suited*
And all the floore was underneath their feet
Bespred with costly scarlot[2] of great name,
On which they lowly sit, and fitting purpose° frame. *conversation*

14

What needs me tell their feast and goodly guize,° *behavior*
In which was nothing riotous nor vaine?
What needs of daintie dishes to devize,° *recount*
Of comely services, or courtly trayne?
My narrow leaves cannot in them containe
The large discourse of royall Princes state.
Yet was their manner then but bare and plaine:
For th'antique world excesse and pride did hate;
Such proud luxurious pompe is swollen up but late.

15

Then when with meates and drinkes of every kinde
Their fervent appetites they quenchèd had,
That auncient Lord gan fit occasion finde,
Of straunge adventures, and of perils sad,
Which in his travell him befallen had,
For to demaund of his renowmèd guest:
Who then with utt'rance grave, and count'nance sad
From point to point, as is before exprest,
Discourst his voyage long, according his request.

16

Great pleasure mixt with pittifull° regard, *compassionate*
That godly King and Queene did passionate,° *feel*
Whiles they his pittifull° adventures heard, *deplorable*
That oft they did lament his lucklesse state,
And often blame the too importune° fate, *exacting*
That heapd on him so many wrathfull wreakes:° *injuries*
For never gentle knight, as he of late,
So tossèd was in fortunes cruell freakes;° *vagaries*
And all the while salt teares bedeawd the hearers cheaks.

17

Then said that royall Pere in sober wise;
Deare Sonne, great beene the evils, which ye bore
From first to last in your late enterprise,
That I note,° whether prayse, or pitty more: *could not*
For never living man, I weene, so sore
In sea of deadly daungers was distrest;
But since now safe ye seisèd have the shore,
And well arrivèd are, (high God be blest)
Let us devize° of ease and everlasting rest. *talk*

18

Ah dearest Lord, said then that doughty knight,
Of ease or rest I may not yet devize;
For by the faith, which I to armes have plight,
I bounden am streight after this emprize,° *enterprise*
As that your daughter can ye well advize,
Backe to returne to that great Faerie Queene,
And her to serve six yeares in warlike wize,° *ways*
Gainst that proud Paynim king, that workes her teene:° *sorrow*
Therefore I ought crave pardon, till I there have beene.

19

Unhappie falles that hard necessitie,
(Quoth he) the troubler of my happie peace,
And vowèd foe of my felicitie;
Ne I against the same can justly preace:° *contend*
But since that band° ye cannot now release, *bond*
Nor doen undo; (for vowes may not be vaine°) *empty*
Soone as the terme of those six yeares shall cease,
Ye then shall hither backe returne againe,
The marriage to accomplish vowd betwixt you twain.

20

Which for my part I covet to performe,
In sort as through the world I did proclame,
That who so kild that monster most deforme,
And him in hardy battaile overcame,
Should have mine onely daughter to his Dame,
And of my kingdome heire apparaunt bee:
Therefore since now to thee perteines the same,

[1] *shaumes* Older instruments resembling the oboe.

[2] *scarlot* Rich type of cloth, usually of a vivid red color.

By dew desert of noble chevalree,
Both daughter and eke kingdome, lo I yield to thee.

21

Then forth he callèd that his daughter faire,
The fairest Un' his onely daughter deare,
His onely daughter, and his onely heyre;
Who forth proceeding with sad° sober cheare, *serious*
As bright as doth the morning starre appeare
Out of the East, with flaming lockes bedight,° *bedecked*
To tell that dawning day is drawing neare,
And to the world does bring long wishèd light;
So faire and fresh that Lady shewd her selfe in sight.

22

So faire and fresh, as freshest flowre in May;
For she had layd her mournefull stole° aside, *cloak*
And widow-like sad wimple° throwne away, *veil*
Wherewith her heavenly beautie she did hide,
Whiles on her wearie journey she did ride;
And on her now a garment she did weare,
All lilly white, withoutten spot, or pride,° *adornment*
That seemd like silke and silver woven neare,° *tightly*
But neither silke nor silver therein did appeare.

23

The blazing brightnesse of her beauties beame,
And glorious light of her sunshyny face
To tell, were as to strive against the streame.
My ragged rimes are all too rude and bace,
Her heavenly lineaments for to enchace.° *portray*
Ne wonder; for her owne deare lovèd knight,
All° were she dayly with himselfe in place, *although*
Did wonder much at her celestiall sight:
Oft had he seene her faire, but never so faire dight.

24

So fairely dight, when she in presence came,
She to her Sire made humble reverence,
And bowèd low, that her right well became,
And added grace unto her excellence:
Who with great wisedome, and grave eloquence
Thus gan to say. But eare he thus had said,
With flying speede, and seeming great pretence,° *purpose*
Came running in, much like a man dismaid,
A Messenger with letters, which his message said.

25

All in the open hall amazèd stood,
At suddeinnesse of that unwarie° sight, *unexpected*
And wondred at his breathlesse hastie mood.
But he for nought would stay his passage right,° *straight*
Till fast before the king he did alight;
Where falling flat, great humblesse he did make,
And kist the ground, whereon his foot was pight;
Then to his hands that writ he did betake,° *deliver*
Which he disclosing,° red thus, as the paper spake. *unfolding / said*

26

To thee, most mighty king of Eden faire,
Her greeting sends in these sad lines addrest,
The wofull daughter, and forsaken heire
Of that great Emperour of all the West;
And bids thee be advizèd for the best,
Ere thou thy daughter linck in holy band
Of wedlocke to that new unknowen guest:
For he already plighted his right hand
Unto another love, and to another land.

27

To me sad mayd, or rather widow sad,
He was affiauncèd° long time before, *engaged*
And sacred pledges he both gave, and had,
False erraunt knight, infamous, and forswore:
Witnesse the burning Altars,[1] which° he swore, *by which*
And guiltie° heavens of his bold perjury, *polluted*
Which though he hath polluted oft of yore,
Yet I to them for judgement just do fly,
And them conjure t'avenge this shamefull injury.

28

Therefore since mine he is, or free or bond,
Or false or trew, or living or else dead,
Withhold, O soveraine Prince, your hasty hond
From knitting league with him, I you aread;

[1] *burning Altars* In classical Greece and Rome, the union of two persons in marriage was confirmed by burning sacrifices.

Ne weene° my right with strength adowne to tread, *think*
Through weakenesse of my widowhed, or woe:
For truth is strong, her rightfull cause to plead,
And shall find friends, if need requireth soe,
So bids thee well to fare, Thy neither friend, nor foe,
Fidessa.

29

When he these bitter byting words had red,
The tydings straunge did him abashèd make,
That still he sate long time astonishèd
As in great muse,° ne word to creature spake. *perplexity*
At last his solemne silence thus he brake,
With doubtfull eyes fast fixèd on his guest;
Redoubted° knight, that for mine onely sake *respected*
Thy life and honour late adventurest,
Let nought be hid from me, that ought to be exprest.

30

What meane these bloudy vowes, and idle threats,
Throwne out from womanish impatient mind?
What heavens? what altars? what enragèd heates° *passions*
Here heapèd up with termes of love unkind,° *unnatural*
My conscience cleare with guilty bands would bind?
High God be witnesse, that I guiltlesse ame.
But if your selfe, Sir knight, ye faultie find,
Or wrappèd be in loves of former Dame,
With crime do not it cover, but disclose the same.

31

To whom the Redcrosse knight this answere sent,
My Lord, my King, be nought hereat dismayd,
Till well ye wote by grave intendiment,° *consideration*
What woman, and wherefore doth me upbrayd
With breach of love, and loyalty betrayd.
It was in my mishaps, as hitherward
I lately traveild, that unwares I strayd
Out of my way, through perils straunge and hard;
That day should faile me, ere I had them all declard.

32

There did I find, or rather I was found
Of this false woman, that Fidessa hight,
Fidessa hight the falsest Dame on ground,
Most false Duessa, royall richly dight,
That easie° was t'invegle° weaker sight: *eager / blind*
Who by her wicked arts, and wylie skill,
Too false and strong for earthly skill or might,
Unwares me wrought unto her wicked will,
And to my foe betrayd, when least I fearèd ill.

33

Then steppèd forth the goodly royall Mayd,
And on the ground her selfe prostrating low,
With sober countenaunce thus to him sayd;
O pardon me, my soveraigne Lord, to show
The secret treasons, which of late I know
To have bene wroght by that false sorceresse.
She onely she it is, that earst° did throw *once*
This gentle knight into so great distresse,
That death him did awaite in dayly wretchednesse.

34

And now it seemes, that she subornèd hath
This craftie messenger with letters vaine,
To worke new woe and improvided° scath, *unforeseen / damage*
By breaking of the band betwixt us twaine;
Wherein she usèd hath the practicke° paine° *cunning / care*
Of this false footman, clokt with simplenesse,
Whom if ye please for to discover plaine,
Ye shall him Archimago find, I ghesse,
The falsest man alive; who tries shall find no lesse.

35

The king was greatly movèd at her speach,
And all with suddein indignation fraight,° *laden*
Bad on that Messenger rude hands to reach.
Eftsoones° the Gard, which on his state did wait, *at once*
Attacht° that faitor° false, and bound him strait: *seized / imposter*
Who seeming sorely chauffèd at his band,
As chainèd Beare, whom cruell dogs do bait,
With idle force did faine them to withstand,
And often semblaunce made to scape out of their hand.

36

But they him layd full low in dungeon deepe,
And bound him hand and foote with yron chains.
And with continuall watch did warely keepe;
Who then would thinke, that by his subtile trains
He could escape fowle death or deadly paines?
Thus when that Princes wrath was pacifide,
He gan renew the late forbidden banes,° *banns*
And to the knight his daughter deare he tyde,
With sacred rites and vowes for ever to abyde.

37

His owne two hands the holy knots did knit,
That none but death for ever can devide;
His owne two hands, for such a turne most fit,
The housling° fire did kindle and provide, *sacramental*
And holy water thereon sprinckled wide;[1]
At which the bushy Teade° a groome did light, *torch*
And sacred lampe in secret chamber hide,
Where it should not be quenchèd day nor night,
For feare of evill fates, but burnen ever bright.

38

Then gan they sprinckle all the posts with wine,[2]
And made great feast to solemnize that day;
They all perfumde with frankincense divine,
And precious odours fetcht from far away,
That all the house did sweat with great aray:° *festivities*
And all the while sweete Musicke did apply
Her curious° skill, the warbling notes to play, *complex*
To drive away the dull Melancholy;
The whiles one sung a song of love and jollity.

39

During the which there was an heavenly noise
Heard sound through all the Pallace pleasantly,
Like as it had bene many an Angels voice,
Singing before th'eternall maiesty,
In their trinall triplicities[3] on hye;
Yet wist no creature, whence that heavenly sweet
Proceeded, yet each one felt secretly
Himselfe thereby reft of his sences meet,
And ravishèd with rare impression in his sprite.

40

Great joy was made that day of young and old,
And solemne feast proclaimd throughout the land,
That their exceeding merth may not be told:
Suffice it heare by signes to understand
The usuall joyes at knitting of loves band.
Thrise happy man the knight himselfe did hold,
Possessèd of his Ladies hart and hand,
And ever, when his eye did her behold,
His heart did seeme to melt in pleasures manifold.

41

Her joyous presence and sweet company
In full content he there did long enioy,
Ne wicked envie, ne vile gealosy
His deare delights were able to annoy:
Yet swimming in that sea of blisfull joy,
He nought forgot, how he whilome had sworne,
In case he could that monstrous beast destroy,
Unto his Farie Queene backe to returne:
The which he shortly did, and Una left to mourne.

42

Now strike your sailes ye jolly Mariners,
For we be come unto a quiet rode,° *harbor*
Where we must land some of our passengers,
And light this wearie vessell of her lode.
Here she a while may make her safe abode,
Till she repairèd have her tackles spent,° *worn out*
And wants supplide. And then againe abroad
On the long voyage whereto she is bent:
Well may she speede and fairely finish her intent.

[1] *The housing ... wide* The king is blessing the marriage with sacramental fire and water, as was common in ancient Roman marriage rituals.

[2] *Then gan ... wine* Sprinkling doorways with wine was meant to bring fertility.

[3] *trinall triplicities* The triple triad (nine orders) of angels, which correspond to the nine spheres of the universe. Thus the music described is that of the spheres, an extraordinarily beautiful harmony that humankind has been unable to hear since the Fall.

from THE SECOND BOOKE OF THE FAERIE QUEENE CONTAYNING THE LEGEND OF SIR GUYON, OR OF TEMPERAUNCE

from CANTO 12[1]

42

Thence passing forth, they shortly do arrive,
Whereas° the Bowre of Blisse was situate; *where*
A place pickt out by choice of best alive,
That natures worke by art can imitate:[2]
In which what ever in this worldly state
Is sweet, and pleasing unto living sense,
Or that may dayntiest fantasie aggrate,° *please*
Was pourèd forth with plentifull dispence,° *liberality*
And made there to abound with lavish affluence.

43

Goodly it was enclosèd round about,
Aswell their entred guestes to keepe within,
As those unruly beasts to hold without;
Yet was the fence thereof but weake and thin;
Nought° feard their force, that fortilage° *naught / fortress*
to win,
But wisedomes powre, and temperaunces might,
By which the mightiest things efforcèd° bin:° *compelled / are*
And eke° the gate was wrought of substaunce light, *also*
Rather for pleasure, then for battery or fight.

44

Yt° framèd was of precious yvory, *it*
That seemd a worke of admirable wit;° *skill*
And therein all the famous history
Of Jason and Medæa was ywrit;
Her mighty charmes, her furious loving fit,
His goodly conquest of the golden fleece,
His falsèd° faith, and love too lightly flit,° *violated / changing*
The wondred Argo, which in venturous°
peece° *adventurous / ship*
First through the Euxine seas bore all the flowr of Greece.[3]

45

Ye might have seene the frothy billowes fry° *foam*
Under the ship, as thorough them she went,
That seemd the waves were into yvory,
Or yvory into the waves were sent;
And other where[4] the snowy substaunce sprent° *sprinkled*
With vermell,° like the boyes bloud[5] *vermillion*
therein shed,
A piteous spectacle did represent,
And otherwhiles° with gold besprinkelèd; *elsewhere*
Yt seemd th'enchaunted flame, which did Creüsa wed.[6]

46

All this, and more might in that goodly gate
Be red; that ever open stood to all,
Which thither came: but in the Porch there sate
A comely personage of stature tall,
And semblaunce° pleasing, more then naturall, *appearance*
That travellers to him seemd to entize;° *entice*
His looser garment to the ground did fall,
And flew about his heeles in wanton wize,° *manner*
Not fit for speedy pace, or manly exercize.

47

They in that place him Genius did call:
Not that celestiall powre,[7] to whom the care
Of life, and generation of all
That lives, pertaines in charge particulare,
Who wondrous things concerning our welfare,

---

[1] *Canto 12* So far in Book 2, Sir Guyon has tried to exemplify Temperance. To do so he has had to exercise self-control in the face of all passions. Led by his guide, the Palmer, he travels to the Bower of Bliss, ruled by the murderous witch Acrasia, in order to destroy it. Palmers were those who wore palm leaf badges to show that they had made the pilgrimage to Jerusalem.

[2] *best alive ... imitate* I.e., the best artists.

[3] *famous history ... Greece* Jason sailed on his ship the Argo to steal the Golden Fleece, which belonged to the King of Colchis. The King's daughter, Medea, fell in love with Jason and used her magical powers to betray her father and assist Jason. After obtaining the fleece, Jason broke his promise of fidelity to Medea.

[4] *other where* Elsewhere.

[5] *boyes blood* Referring to the blood of Medea's brother, whom she murdered and chopped into pieces. She then scattered the pieces to distract her father as she and Jason escaped with the Fleece.

[6] *Yt ... wed* When Jason abandoned Medea in favor of Creüsa, the vengeful Medea sent Creüsa an enchanted dress that burned her to death when she put it on.

[7] *celestiall powre* God of birth and generation.

And straunge phantome° doth let us oft forsee, *images*
And oft of secret ill bids us beware:
That is our Selfe, whom though we do not see,
Yet each doth in him selfe it well perceive to bee.

48

Therefore a God him sage Antiquity
Did wisely make, and good Agdistes[1] call:
But this same was to that quite contrary,
The foe of life, that good envyes° to all, *begrudges*
That secretly doth us procure° to fall, *arrange*
Through guilefull semblaunts,° which he makes us see. *illusions*
He of this Gardin had the governall,° *rule*
And Pleasures porter was devizd to bee,
Holding a staffe in hand for more formalitee.

49

With diverse flowres he daintily was deckt,
And strowèd° round about, and by his side *strewn*
A mighty Mazer bowle° of wine was set, *goblet*
As if it had to him bene sacrifide;
Wherewith all new-come guests he gratifide:
So did he eke Sir Guyon passing by:
But he his idle curtesie defide,
And overthrew his bowle disdainfully;
And broke his staffe, with which he charmèd semblants sly.[2]

50

Thus being entred, they behold around
A large and spacious plaine, on every side
Strowed with pleasauns,° whose faire grassy ground *pleasure-grounds*
Mantled° with greene, and goodly beautified *covered*
With all the ornaments of Floraes[3] pride,
Wherewith her mother Art, as halfe in scorne
Of niggard° Nature, like a pompous bride *stingy*
Did decke her, and too lavishly adorne,
When forth from virgin bowre she comes in th'early morne.

51

Thereto the Heavens alwayes Joviall,
Lookt on them lovely,° still° in stedfast state, *lovingly / always*
Ne suffred storme nor frost on them to fall,
Their tender buds or leaves to violate,
Nor scorching heat, nor cold intemperate
T'afflict the creatures, which therein did dwell,
But the milde air with season moderate
Gently attempred,° and disposd so well, *temperate*
That still it breathèd forth sweet spirit & holesome smell.

52

More sweet and holesome, then the pleasaunt hill
Of Rhodope, on which the Nimphe, that bore
A gyaunt babe, her selfe for griefe did kill;
Or the Thessalian Tempe, where of yore
Faire Daphne Phoebus hart with love did gore;
Or Ida, where the Gods lov'd to repaire,° *retire*
When ever they their heavenly bowres forlore;°[4] *left*
Or sweet Parnasse, the haunt of Muses faire;
Or Eden selfe, if ought with Eden mote compaire.

53

Much wondred Guyon at the faire aspect° *appearance*
Of that sweet place, yet suffred no delight
To sincke into his sence, nor mind affect,
But passèd forth, and lookt still forward right,° *straight*
Bridling his will, and maistering his might:
Till that he came unto another gate,
No gate, but like one, being goodly dight° *decorated*
With boughes and braunches, which did broad dilate° *spread*
Their clasping armes, in wanton wreathings intricate.

54

So fashionèd a Porch with rare device,° *design*
Archt over head with an embracing vine,
Whose bounches° hanging downe, seemed to entice *bunches*

---

[1] *Agdistes* I.e., Agdistis, originally a mother-goddess.

[2] *his staffe … sly* His magic staff, with which he raised deceitful apparitions.

[3] *Flora* Goddess of flowers.

[4] *More sweet … fair* References to Rhodope, a nymph who bore a child by Neptune and was turned into a mountain; Daphne, a nymph who was pursued by the god Phoebus Apollo, and who was turned into a laurel tree when she prayed to escape him; and Mount Ida, which was the location of Jupiter's rape of Ganymede and of the beauty contest among Juno, Venus, and Minerva.

All passers by, to tast their lushious wine,
And did themselves into their hands incline,
As freely offering to be gatherèd:
Some deepe empurpled as the Hyacint,[1]
Some as the Rubine,° laughing sweetly red, *ruby*
Some like faire Emeraudes, not yet well ripenèd.

55

And them amongst, some were of burnisht gold,
So made by art, to beautifie the rest,
Which did themselves emongst the leaves enfold,
As lurking from the vew of covetous guest,
That the weake bowes,° with so rich load opprest, *boughs*
Did bow adowne, as over-burdened.
Under that Porch a comely dame did rest,
Clad in faire weedes,° but fowle disorderèd, *garments*
And garments loose, that seemd unmeet° for womanhed.° *unsuitable / womanhood*

56

In her left hand a Cup of gold she held,
And with her right the riper fruit did reach,
Whose sappy liquor, that with fulnesse sweld,
Into her cup she scruzd,° with daintie breach° *squeezed / breaking*
Of her fine fingers, without fowle empeach,° *injury*
That so faire wine-presse made the wine more sweet:
Thereof she usd to give to drinke to each,
Whom passing by she happenèd to meet:
It was her guise,° all Straungers goodly so to greet. *habit*

57

So she to Guyon offred it to tast;
Who taking it out of her tender hond,
The cup to ground did violently cast,
That all in peeces it was broken fond,° *found*
And with the liquor stainèd all the lond:
Whereat Excesse exceedingly was wroth,
Yet no'te° the same amend, ne yet withstond,° *could not / prevent*
But suffered him to passe, all were she loth;° *although / reluctant*
Who nought regarding her displeasure forward goth.

58

There the most daintie Paradise on ground,
It selfe doth offer to his sober eye,
In which all pleasures plenteously abound,
And none does others happinesse envye:
The painted° flowres, the trees upshooting hye, *variegated*
The dales for shade, the hilles for breathing space,
The trembling groves, the Christall° running by; *clear water*
And that, which all faire workes doth most aggrace,° *add grace*
The art, which all that wrought, appeared° in no place. *was visible*

59

One would have thought, (so cunningly, the rude,
And scornèd parts were mingled with the fine,)
That nature had for wantonesse ensude° *imitated*
Art, and that Art at nature did repine;° *fret*
So striving each th'other to undermine,
Each did the others worke more beautifie;
So diff'ring both in willes,° agreed in fine:° *wills / the conclusion*
So all agreed through sweete diversitie,
This Gardin to adorne with all varietie.

60

And in the midst of all, a fountaine stood,
Of richest substaunce, that on earth might bee,
So pure and shiny, that the silver flood
Through every channell running one might see;
Most goodly it with curious imageree
Was over-wrought, and shapes of naked boyes,
Of which some seemd with lively jollitee,
To fly about, playing their wanton toyes,° *games*
Whilest others did them selves embay° in liquid joyes. *bathe*

61

And over all, of purest gold was spred,
A trayle of yvie in his native hew:
For the rich mettall was so colourèd,
That wight,° who did not well avis'd° it vew, *creature / attentively*

[1] *Hyacint* Jacinth, a sapphire-colored stone.

Would surely deeme it to be yvie trew:
Low his lascivious armes adown did creepe,
That themselves dipping in the silver dew,
Their fleecy flowres they tenderly did steepe,
Which drops of Christall seemd for
wantones° to weepe. *wantonness*

62

Infinit streames continually did well
Out of this fountaine, sweet and faire to see,
The which into an ample laver° fell, *basin*
And shortly grew to so great quantitie,
That like a little lake it seemd to bee;
Whose depth exceeded not three cubits[1] hight,
That through the waves one might the bottom see,
All pav'd beneath with Jaspar[2] shining bright,
That seemd the fountaine in that sea did sayle upright.

63

And all the margent° round about was set, *border*
With shady Laurell trees, thence to defend° *protect from*
The sunny beames, which on the billowes bet,° *beat*
And those which therein bathèd, mote offend.° *bother*
As Guyon hapned by the same to wend,° *pass*
Two naked Damzelles he therein espyde,
Which therein bathing, seemèd to contend,
And wrestle wantonly,° ne car'd to hyde, *lasciviously*
Their dainty parts from vew of any, which them eyde.

64

Sometimes the one would lift the other quight
Above the waters, and then downe againe
Her plong,° as over maisterèd by might, *plunge*
Where both awhile would coverèd remaine,
And each the other from to rise restraine;
The whiles their snowy limbes, as through a vele,
So through the Christall waves appearèd plaine:
Then suddeinly both would themselves unhele,° *display*
And th'amarous sweet spoiles to greedy eyes revele.

65

As that faire Starre, the messenger of morne,
His deawy face out of the sea doth reare:
Or as the Cyprian goddesse,[3] newly borne
Of th'Oceans fruitfull froth, did first appeare:
Such seemèd they, and so their yellow heare
Christalline° humour° droppèd downe apace. *clear / water*
Whom such when Guyon saw, he drew him neare,
And somewhat gan° relent his earnest pace, *began*
His stubborne brest gan secret pleasaunce to embrace.

66

The wanton Maidens him espying, stood
Gazing a while at his unwonted°
guise;° *unfamiliar / appearance*
Then th'one her selfe low duckèd in the flood,
Abasht, that her a straunger did avise:° *observe*
But th'other rather higher did arise,
And her two lilly paps° aloft displayd, *breasts*
And all, that might his melting hart entise
To her delights, she unto him bewrayd:° *revealed*
The rest hid underneath, him more desirous made.

67

With that, the other likewise up arose,
And her faire lockes, which formerly were bownd
Up in one knot, he low adowne did lose:° *loosen*
Which flowing long and thick, her cloth'd arownd,
And th'yvorie in golden mantle gownd:° *covered*
So that faire spectacle from him was reft,° *taken*
Yet that, which reft it, no lesse faire was fownd:
So hid in lockes and waves from lookers theft,
Nought but her lovely face she for his looking left.

68

Withall she laughèd, and she blusht withall,
That blushing to her laughter gave more grace,
And laughter to her blushing, as did fall:
Now when they spide the knight to slacke his pace,
Them to behold, and in his sparkling face
The secret signes of kindled lust appeare,
Their wanton meriments they did encreace,
And to him beckned, to approch more neare,
And shewd him many sights, that courage° cold could
reare.° *lust / arouse*

[1] *cubits* Units of measurement equal to approximately 20 inches.

[2] *Jaspar* Precious stone.

[3] *that fair starre ... Cyprian goddesse* Venus, the morning star, referred to as the Cyprian goddess because one of her main shrines was on the island of Cyprus.

69

On which when gazing him the Palmer saw,
He much rebukt those wandring eyes of his,
And counseld well, him forward thence did draw.
Now are they come nigh to the Bowre of blis
Of her fond favorites so nam'd amis:
When thus the Palmer; Now Sir, well avise;° *consider*
For here the end of all our travell is:
Here wonnes° Acrasia,[1] whom we must surprise, *lives*
Else she will slip away, and all our drift° despise. *purpose*

70

Eftsoones° they heard a most melodious sound, *soon afterwards*
Of all that mote delight a daintie eare,
Such as attonce might not on living ground,
Save in this Paradise, be heard elswhere:
Right hard it was, for wight, which did it heare,
To read,° what manner musicke that mote bee: *interpret*
For all that pleasing is to living eare,
Was there consorted° in one harmonee, *combined*
Birdes, voyces, instruments, windes, waters, all agree.

71

The joyous birdes shrouded in chearefull shade,
Their notes unto the voyce attempred° sweet; *attuned*
Th'Angelicall soft trembling voyces made
To th'instruments divine respondence° meet:° *response / fitting*
The silver sounding instruments did meet° *join*
With the base murmure of the waters fall:
The waters fall with difference discreet,° *distinct*
Now soft, now loud, unto the wind did call:
The gentle warbling wind low answerèd to all.

72

There, whence that Musick seemèd heard to bee,
Was the faire Witch her selfe now solacing,° *entertaining*
With a new Lover, whom through sorceree
And witchcraft, she from farre did thither bring:
There she had him now layd a slombering,
In secret shade, after long wanton joyes:
Whilst round about them pleasauntly did sing
Many faire Ladies, and lascivious boyes,
That ever mixt their song with light licentious toyes.

73

And all that while, right over him she hong,
With her false° eyes fast fixèd in his sight, *treacherous*
As seeking medicine, whence she was stong,
Or greedily depasturing° delight: *grazing on*
And oft inclining downe with kisses light,
For feare of waking him, his lips bedewd,
And through his humid eyes did sucke his spright,
Quite molten into lust and pleasure lewd;
Wherewith she sighèd soft, as if his case she rewd.° *pitied*

74

The whiles some one did chaunt this lovely lay;° *song*
Ah see, who so faire thing doest faine° to see, *desire*
In springing flowre the image of thy day;
Ah see the Virgin Rose, how sweetly shee
Doth first peepe forth with bashfull modestee,
That fairer seemes, the lesse ye see her may;
Lo see soone after, how more bold and free
Her barèd bosome she doth broad display;
Loe see soone after, how she fades, and falles away.

75

So passeth, in the passing of a day,
Of mortall life the leafe, the bud, the flowre,
Ne more doth flourish after first decay,
That earst° was sought to decke both bed and bowre, *formerly*
Of many a Ladie, and many a Paramowre:° *lover*
Gather therefore the Rose, whilest yet is prime,° *spring*
For soone comes age, that will her pride deflowre:
Gather the Rose of love, whilest yet is time,
Whilest loving thou mayst lovèd be with equall crime.

76

He ceast, and then gan all the quire° of birdes *choir*
Their diverse notes t'attune unto his lay,
As in approvance of his pleasing words.
The constant paire heard all, that he did say,
Yet swarvèd° not, but kept their forward way, *swerved*
Through many covert groves, and thickets close,
In which they creeping did at last display° *discover*

[1] *Acrasia* Meaning ill-temper (from Greek: excess, or badly "tempered").

That wanton Ladie, with her lover lose,° *wanton*
Whose sleepie head she in her lap did soft dispose.° *place*

77

Upon a bed of Roses she was layd,
As faint through heat, or dight° to° pleasant sin, *prepared / for*
And was arayd, or rather disarayd,
All in a vele of silke and silver thin,
That hid no whit her alablaster skin,
But rather shewd more white, if more might bee:
More subtile web Arachne[1] can not spin,
Nor the fine nets, which oft we woven see
Of scorchèd° deaw, do not in th'aire more lightly flee.° *dried / float*

78

Her snowy brest was bare to readie spoyle
Of hungry eies, which n'ote° therewith be fild, *could not*
And yet through languour° of her late sweet toyle, *fatigue*
Few drops, more cleare then Nectar, forth distild,° *gathered*
That like pure Orient perles adowne it trild,° *dripped*
And her faire eyes sweet smyling in delight,
Moystened their fierie beames, with which she thrild° *pierced*
Fraile harts, yet quenchèd° not; like starry light *killed*
Which sparckling on the silent waves, does seeme more bright.

79

The young man sleeping by her, seemd to bee
Some goodly swayne° of honorable place,° *young man / rank*
That certès it great pittie was to see
Him his nobilitie so foule deface;
A sweet regard,° and amiable grace, *manner*
Mixèd with manly sternnesse did appeare
Yet sleeping, in his well proportiond face,
And on his tender lips the downy heare
Did now but freshly spring, and silken blossomes beare.

80

His warlike armes, the idle instruments
Of sleeping praise,° were hong upon a tree, *merit*
And his brave shield, full of old moniments,° *marks of honor*
Was fowly ra'st,° that none the signes might see; *erased*
Ne for them, ne for honour carèd hee,
Ne ought, that did to his advauncement tend,
But in lewd loves, and wastfull luxuree,° *licentiousness*
His dayes, his goods, his bodie he did spend:
O horrible enchantment, that him so did blend.° *blind*

81

The noble Elfe, and carefull Palmer drew
So nigh them, minding nought, but lustfull game,
That suddein forth they on them rusht, and threw
A subtile net, which onely for the same
The skilfull Palmer formally° did frame. *expressly*
So held them under fast, the whiles the rest
Fled all away for feare of fowler° shame. *fouler*
The faire Enchauntresse, so unwares opprest,° *overwhelmed*
Tryde all her arts, & all her sleights, thence out to wrest.° *escape*

82

And eke her lover strove: but all in vaine;
For that same net so cunningly was wound,
That neither guile, nor force might it distraine.° *rend*
They tooke them both, & both them strongly bound
In captive bandes, which there they readie found:
But her in chaines of adamant° he tyde; *diamond*
For nothing else might keepe her safe and sound;
But Verdant (so he hight°) he soone untyde, *was called*
And counsell sage in steed[2] thereof to him applyde.

83

But all those pleasant bowres and Pallace brave,° *grand*
Guyon broke downe, with rigour pittilesse;
Ne ought their goodly workmanship might save
Them from the tempest of his wrathfulnesse,
But that their blisse he turn'd to balefulnesse:° *sadness*
Their groves he feld, their gardins did deface,
Their arbers spoyle, their Cabinets° suppresse, *bowers*

[1] *Arachne* According to myth, Arachne challenged Athena (goddess of wisdom and practical arts) to a weaving contest and was turned into a spider as punishment.

[2] *in steed* Instead.

Their banket° houses burne, their buildings race,° *banquet / raze*
And of the fairest late, now made the fowlest place.

84

Then led they her away, and eke that knight
They with them led, both sorrowfull and sad:
The way they came, the same retourn'd they right,
Till they arrivèd, where they lately had
Charm'd those wild-beasts, that rag'd with furie mad.
Which now awaking, fierce at them gan fly,
As in their mistresse reskew,° whom they lad;° *rescue / led*
But them the Palmer soone did pacify.
Then Guyon askt, what meant those beastes, which there did ly.

85

Said he, These seeming beasts are men indeed,
Whom this Enchauntresse hath transformèd thus,
Whylome° her lovers, which her lusts did feed, *previously*
Now turned into figures hideous,
According to their mindes like monstruous.
Sad end (quoth he) of life intemperate,
And mournefull meed° of joyes delicious: *reward*
But Palmer, if it mote° thee so aggrate, *may*
Let them returnèd be unto their former state.

86

Streight way he with his vertuous° staffe them strooke, *powerful*
And streight of beasts they comely men became;
Yet being men they did unmanly looke,
And starèd ghastly, some for inward shame,
And some for wrath, to see their captive Dame:
But one above the rest in speciall,
That had an hog beene late, hight Grille[1] by name,
Repinèd° greatly, and did him miscall,° *complained / abuse*
That had from hoggish forme him brought to naturall.

87

Said Guyon, See the mind of beastly man,
That hath so soone forgot the excellence
Of his creation, when he life began,
That now he chooseth, with vile difference,° *preference*
To be a beast, and lacke intelligence.
To whom the Palmer thus, The donghill kind
Delights in filth and foule incontinence:
Let Grill be Grill, and have his hoggish mind,
But let us hence depart, whilest wether° serves and wind. *weather*

[1] *Grille* Fierce or cruel. In *The Odyssey*, Grille is one of Odysseus's men whom Circe turns into a pig. In one of Plutarch's dialogues, Grille then refuses to be returned to human form.

from THE THIRD BOOKE OF THE FAERIE QUEENE CONTAYNING THE LEGEND OF BRITOMARTIS[2] OR OF CHASTITIE

CANTO 6

The birth of faire Belphoebe and
Of Amoret is told.
The Gardins of Adonis fraught
With pleasures manifold.

1

Well may I weene, faire Ladies, all this while
Ye wonder, how this noble Damozell
So great perfections did in her compile,
Sith that in salvage° forests she did dwell, *wild*
So farre from court and royall Citadell,
The great schoolmistresse of all curtesy:
Seemeth that such wild woods should far expell
All civill usage and gentility,
And gentle sprite deforme with rude rusticity.

2

But to this faire Belphoebe[3] in her berth
The heavens so favourable were and free,° *liberal*
Looking with myld aspect upon the earth,
In th'Horoscope of her nativitee,[4]
That all the gifts of grace and chastitee

[2] *Britomartis* Her name is a combination of the words Britain and Mars (god of war).

[3] *Belphoebe* Her name associates her with the goddess Diana (also called Phoebe).

[4] *The heavens … nativitee* I.e., the planets were favorably arranged at the time of her birth. Any combination of Jupiter (Jove) and Venus was believed to bring particular luck.

On her they pourèd forth of plenteous horne;[1]
Jove laught on Venus from his soveraigne see,° *throne*
And Phoebus[2] with faire beames did her adorne,
And all the Graces[3] rockt her cradle being borne.

3

Her berth was of the wombe of Morning dew,[4]
And her conception of the joyous Prime,
And all her whole creation did her shew
Pure and unspotted from all loathly crime,
That is ingenerate° in fleshly slime. *innate*
So was this virgin borne, so was she bred,
So was she traynèd up from time to time,[5]
In all chast vertue, and true bounti-hed° *goodness*
Till to her dew perfection she was ripenèd.

4

Her mother was the faire Chrysogonee,
The daughter of Amphisa,[6] who by race
A Faerie was, yborne of high degree,
She bore Belphoebe, she bore in like cace
Faire Amoretta[7] in the second place:
These two were twinnes, & twixt them two did share
The heritage of all celestiall grace.
That all the rest it seem'd they robbèd bare
Of bountie,° and of beautie, and all vertues rare. *goodness*

5

It were a goodly storie, to declare,
By what straunge accident faire Chrysogone
Conceiv'd these infants, and how them she bare,
In this wild forrest wandring all alone,
After she had nine moneths fulfild and gone:
For not as other wemens commune brood,
They were enwombèd in the sacred throne
Of her chaste bodie, nor with commune food,
As other wemens babes, they suckèd vitall blood.

6

But wondrously they were begot, and bred
Through influence of th'heavens fruitfull ray,
As it in antique bookes is mentionèd.
It was upon a Sommers shynie day,
When Titan[8] faire his beamès did display,
In a fresh fountaine, farre from all mens vew,
She bath'd her brest, the boyling heat t'allay;
She bath'd with roses red, and violets blew,
And all the sweetest flowres, that in the forrest grew.

7

Till faint through irkesome wearinesse, adowne
Upon the grassie ground her selfe she layd
To sleepe, the whiles a gentle slombring swowne° *sleep*
Upon her fell all naked bare displayd;
The sunne-beames bright upon her body playd,
Being through former bathing mollifide,° *made soft*
And pierst into her wombe, where they
embayd° *permeated*
With so sweet sence° and secret power unspide, *sensation*
That in her pregnant flesh they shortly fructifide.

8

Miraculous may seeme to him, that reades
So straunge ensample of conception;
But reason teacheth that the fruitfull seades
Of all things living, through impression
Of the sunbeames in moyst complexion,
Doe life conceive and quickned are by kynd:° *nature*
So after Nilus° inundation, *the Nile's*
Infinite shapes of creatures men do fynd,
Informèd° in the mud, on which the Sunne *formed*
hath shynd.

9

Great father he of generation
Is rightly cald, th'author of life and light;

[1] *plenteous horne* Horn of plenty.

[2] *Phoebus* I.e., Phoebus Apollo, god of the sun.

[3] *the Graces* Three sister goddesses who dispense the gifts of pleasure, beauty, and charm.

[4] *Her ... dew* Cf. Psalm 110.3, describing the reign of the Messiah: "Thy people shall be willing in the day of thy power, in the beauties of holiness from the womb of the morning: thou hast the dew of thy youth."

[5] *from time to time* Continuously.

[6] *Chrysogonee* Golden-born (Danaë conceived when Jove came to her as a golden shower); *Amphisa* Of double nature.

[7] *Amoretta* Italian: little love.

[8] *Titan* The sun.

And his faire sister[1] for creation
Ministreth matter fit, which tempred right
With heate and humour,° breedes the living
wight.° *moisture / creature*
So sprong these twinnes in wombe of Chrysogone,
Yet wist° she nought thereof, but sore affright, *knew*
Wondred to see her belly so upblone,
Which still increast, till she her terme had full outgone.

10

Whereof conceiving shame and foule disgrace,
Albe° her guiltlesse conscience her cleard, *although*
She fled into the wildernesse a space,
Till that unweeldy burden she had reard,° *brought forth*
And shund dishonor, which as death she feard:
Where wearie of long travell, downe to rest
Her selfe she set, and comfortably cheard;[2]
There a sad cloud of sleepe her overkest,° *covered*
And seizèd every sense with sorrow sore opprest.

11

It fortunèd, faire Venus having lost
Her little sonne, the wingèd god of love,
Who for some light displeasure, which him crost,
Was from her fled, as flit° as ayerie Dove, *quick*
And left her blisfull bowre of joy above,
(So from her often he had fled away,
When she for ought him sharpely did reprove,
And wandred in the world in strange aray,
Disguiz'd in thousand shapes, that none might him
bewray.°) *reveal*

12

Him for to seeke, she left her heavenly hous,
The house of goodly formes and faire aspects,
Whence all the world derives the glorious
Features of beautie, and all shapes select,° *choice*
With which high God his workmanship hath deckt;
And searchèd every way, through which his wings
Had borne him, or his tract° she mote° *path / might*
detect:
She promist kisses sweet, and sweeter things
Unto the man, that of him tydings to her brings.

13

First she him sought in Court, where most he used
Whylome° to haunt, but there she found *previously*
him not;
But many there she found, which sore accused
His falsehood, and with foule infamous blot
His cruell deedes and wicked wyles did spot:° *reproach*
Ladies and Lords she every where mote heare
Complayning, how with his empoysned shot
Their wofull harts he wounded had
whyleare,° *a while earlier*
And so had left them languishing twixt hope and feare.

14

She then the Citties sought from gate to gate,
And every one did aske, did he him see;
And every one her answerd, that too late° *recently*
He had him seene, and felt the crueltie
Of his sharpe darts and whot° artillerie; *hot*
And every one threw forth reproches rife
Of his mischievous deedes, and said, that hee
Was the disturber of all civill life,
The enimy of peace, and author of all strife.

15

Then in the countrey she abroad him sought,
And in the rurall cottages inquired,
Where also many plaints to her were brought,
How he their heedlesse harts with love had fyred,
And his false venim through their veines inspyred;
And eke the gentle shepheard swaynes,° *country laborers*
which sat
Keeping their fleecie flockes, as they were hyred,
She sweetly heard complaine, both how and what
Her sonne had to them doen; yet she did smile thereat.

16

But when in none of all these she him got,
She gan avize,° where else he mote him hyde: *reflect*
At last she her bethought, that she had not
Yet sought the salvage woods and forrests wyde,
In which full many lovely Nymphes abyde,
Mongst whom might be, that he did closely lye,
Or that the love of some of them him tyde:° *bound*

[1] *his fair sister* The moon.

[2] *comfortably cheard* I.e., was cheered by this comfort.

For thy,[1] she thither cast° her course t'apply, *resolved*
To search the secret haunts of Dianes company.

17

Shortly unto the wastefull° woods she came, *wild*
Whereas she found the Goddesse with her crew,
After late chace of their embrewèd° game, *bloodstained*
Sitting beside a fountaine in a rew,° *row*
Some of them washing with the liquid dew
From off their dainty limbes the dustie sweat,
And soyle which did deforme their lively hew;
Others lay shaded from the scorching heat;
The rest upon her person gave attendance great.

18

She having hong upon a bough on high
Her bow and painted quiver, had unlaste° *untied*
Her silver buskins° from her nimble thigh, *boots*
And her lancke° loynes ungirt, and brests unbraste, *slender*
After her heat the breathing cold to taste;
Her golden lockes, that late in tresses bright
Embreaded° were for° hindring of her haste, *braided / to prevent*
Now loose about her shoulders hong undight,° *unbound*
And were with sweet Ambrosia° all bespinckled light. *perfume*

19

Soone as she Venus saw behind her backe,
She was asham'd to be so loose surprized,
And woxe° halfe wroth against her damzels slacke, *grew*
That had not her thereof before avized,° *warned*
But suffred her so carelesly disguized
Be overtaken. Soone her garments loose
Upgath'ring, in her bosome she comprized,° *gathered*
Well as she might, and to the Goddesse rose,
Whiles all her Nymphes did like a girlond her enclose.

20

Goodly° she gan faire Cytherea[2] greet, *politely*
And shortly askèd her, what cause her brought
Into that wildernesse for her unmeet,° *unsuitable*
From her sweet bowres, and beds with pleasures fraught:
That suddein change she strange adventure° thought. *chance*
To whom halfe weeping, she thus answerèd,
That she her dearest sonne Cupido sought,
Who in his frowardnesse° from her was fled; *naughtiness*
That she repented sore, to have him angerèd.

21

Thereat Diana gan to smile, in scorne
Of her vaine plaint, and to her scoffing sayd;
Great pittie sure, that ye be so forlorne
Of your gay sonne, that gives ye so good ayd
To your disports:° ill mote ye bene apayd.° *amusements / repaid*
But she was more engrievèd, and replide;
Faire sister, ill beseemes it to upbrayd
A dolefull heart with so disdainfull pride;
The like that mine, may be your paine another tide.° *time*

22

As you in woods and wanton wildernesse
Your glory set, to chace the salvage beasts,
So my delight is all in joyfulnesse,
In beds, in bowres, in banckets,° and in feasts: *banquets*
And ill becomes you with your loftie creasts,° *helmets*
To scorne the joy, that Jove is glad to seeke;
We both are bound to follow heavens beheasts,
And tend our charges with obeisance meeke:
Spare, gentle sister, with reproch my paine to eeke.° *increase*

23

And tell me, if that ye my sonne have heard,
To lurke emongst your Nymphes in secret wize;
Or keepe their cabins:° much I am affeard, *caves*
Least he like one of them him selfe disguize,
And turne his arrowes to their exercize:
So may he long himselfe full easie hide:
For he is faire and fresh in face and guize,
As any Nymph (let not it be envyde),° *begrudged*
So saying every Nymph full narrowly she eyde.

---

[1] *For thy* Therefore.

[2] *Cytherea* Venus, who, according to myth, first rose out of the sea near the island of Cythera.

24

But Phoebe therewith sore was angered,
And sharply said; Goe Dame, goe seeke your boy,
Where you him lately left, in Mars[1] his bed;
He comes not here, we scorne his foolish joy,
Ne lend we leisure to his idle toy:° *play*
But if I catch him in this company,
By Stygian lake[2] I vow, whose sad annoy° *affliction*
The Gods doe dread, he dearely shall abye:° *atone for it*
Ile clip his wanton wings, that he no more shall fly.

25

Whom when as Venus saw so sore displeased,
She inly sory was, and gan relent,
What she had said: so her she soone appeased,
With sugred words and gentle blandishment,° *flattery*
Which as a fountaine from her sweet lips went,
And wellèd goodly forth, that in short space
She was well pleasd, and forth her damzels sent,
Through all the woods, to search from place to place,
If any tract° of him or tydings they mote trace. *trace*

26

To search the God of love, her Nymphes she sent
Throughout the wandring forrest every where:
And after them her selfe eke with her went
To seeke the fugitive, both farre and nere,
So long they sought, till they arrivèd were
In that same shadie covert, whereas lay
Faire Crysogone in slombry traunce whilere:
Who in her sleepe (a wondrous thing to say)
Unwares had borne two babes, as faire as
springing° day. *dawning*

27

Unwares she them conceiv'd, unwares she bore:
She bore withouten paine, that she conceived
Withouten pleasure: ne her need implore
Lucinaes[3] aide: which when they both perceived,
They were through wonder nigh° of sense
bereaved, *almost*
And gazing each on other, nought bespake:° *spoke*
At last they both agreed, her seeming grieved° *afflicted*
Out of her heavy swowne not to awake,
But from her loving side the tender babes to take.

28

Up they them tooke, each one a babe uptooke,
And with them carried, to be fosterèd;
Dame Phoebe to a Nymph her babe betooke,
To be upbrought in perfect Maydenhed,° *virginity*
And of her selfe her name Belphoebe red:° *declared*
But Venus hers thence farre away convayd,
To be upbrought in goodly womanhed,
And in her litle loves stead, which was strayd,
Her Amoretta cald, to comfort her dismayd.

29

She brought her to her joyous Paradize,
Where most she wonnes,° when she on earth
does dwel. *resides*
So faire a place, as Nature can devize:
Whether in Paphos, or Cytheron hill,
Or it in Gnidus[4] be, I wote not well;
But well I wote by tryall, that this same
All other pleasant places doth excell,
And callèd is by her lost lovers name,[5]
The Gardin of Adonis, farre renowmd by fame.

30

In that same Gardin all the goodly flowres,
Wherewith dame Nature doth her beautifie,
And decks the girlonds° of her paramoures, *garlands*
Are fetcht: there is the first seminarie° *seed-plot*
Of all things, that are borne to live and die,
According to their kindes. Long worke it were,
Here to account° the endlesse progenie *enumerate*
Of all the weedes, that bud and blossome there;
But so much as doth need, must needs be
counted° here. *listed*

[1] *Mars* God of war and Venus's lover.

[2] *Stygian lake* The Styx, a river of the underworld. Oaths made on the Styx were especially sacred; even the gods would not break them.

[3] *Lucinaes* Goddess of childbirth.

[4] *Paphos ... Gnidus* Locations of three major shrines to Venus.

[5] *her ... name* Venus loved a beautiful boy named Adonis, who was killed by a boar while hunting one day. His blood was transformed into a flower, the anemone.

31

It sited° was in fruitfull soyle of old, *located*
And girt in with two walles on either side;
The one of yron, the other of bright gold,
That none might thorough breake, nor over-stride:
And double gates it had, which opened wide,
By which both in and out men moten pas;
Th'one faire and fresh, the other old and dride:
Old Genius[1] the porter of them was,
Old Genius, the which a double nature has.

32

He letteth in, he letteth out to wend,° *come*
All that to come into the world desire;
A thousand thousand naked babes attend
About him day and night, which doe require,
That he with fleshly weedes would them attire:
Such as him list,° such as eternall fate *likes*
Ordainèd hath, he clothes with sinfull mire,[2]
And sendeth forth to live in mortall state,
Till they againe returne backe by the hinder gate.

33

After that they againe returnèd beene,
They in that Gardin planted be againe;
And grow afresh, as they had never seene
Fleshly corruption, nor mortall paine.
Some thousand yeares so doen they there remaine;
And then of him are clad with other hew,° *form*
Or sent into the chaungefull world againe,
Till thither they returne, where first they grew:
So like a wheele around they runne from old to new.

34

Ne needs there Gardiner to set, or sow,
To plant or prune: for of their owne accord
All things, as they created were, doe grow,
And yet remember well the mightie word,
Which first was spoken by th'Almightie lord,
That bad them to increase and multiply:[3]
Ne doe they need with water of the ford,° *stream*
Or of the clouds to moysten their roots dry;
For in themselves eternall moisture they imply.° *contain*

35

Infinite shapes of creatures there are bred,
And uncouth° formes, which none yet ever knew, *unfamiliar*
And every sort is in a sundry° bed *separate*
Set by it selfe, and ranckt° in comely rew:° *arranged / row*
Some fit for reasonable[4] soules t'indew,° *assume*
Some made for beasts, some made for birds to weare,
And all the fruitfull spawne of fishes hew
In endlesse rancks along enraungèd were,
That seem'd the Ocean could not containe them there.

36

Daily they grow, and daily forth are sent
Into the world, it to replenish more;
Yet is the stocke not lessenèd, nor spent,
But still remaines in everlasting store,
As it at first created was of yore.
For in the wide wombe of the world there lyes,
In hatefull darkenesse and in deepe horrore,
An huge eternall Chaos, which supplyes
The substances of natures fruitfull progenyes.

37

All things from thence doe their first being fetch,
And borrow matter, whereof they are made,
Which when as forme and feature it does ketch,° *take*
Becomes a bodie, and doth then invade° *enter*
The state of life, out of the griesly shade.
That substance is eterne, and bideth so,
Ne when the life decayes, and forme does fade,
Doth it consume, and into nothing go,
But chaungèd is, and often altred to and fro.

38

The substance is not chaunged, nor alterèd,
But th'only forme and outward fashion;
For every substance is conditionèd° *bound*
To change her hew, and sundry formes to don,
Meet for her temper and complexion:
For formes are variable and decay,

[1] *Genius* I.e., Janus, the Roman god of doors and gates.

[2] *sinfull mire* Flesh.

[3] *increase and multiply* See Genesis 1.28.

[4] *reasonable* Rational; i.e., human.

By course of kind,° and by occasion; *nature*
And that faire flowre of beautie fades away,
As doth the lilly fresh before the sunny ray.

39

Great enimy to it, and to all the rest,
That in the Gardin of Adonis springs,
Is wicked Time, who with his scyth addrest,° *armed*
Does mow the flowring herbes and goodly things,
And all their glory to the ground downe flings,
Where they doe wither, and are fowly mard:° *marred*
He flyes about, and with his flaggy wings
Beates downe both leaves and buds without regard,
Ne ever pittie may relent° his malice hard. *soften*

40

Yet pittie often did the gods relent,
To see so faire things mard, and spoylèd quight:
And their great mother Venus did lament
The losse of her deare brood, her deare delight:
Her hart was pierst with pittie at the sight,
When walking through the Gardin, them she spyde,
Yet no'te she find redresse for such despight.
For all that lives, is subject to that law:
All things decay in time, and to their end do draw.

41

But were it not, that Time their troubler is,
All that in this delightfull Gardin growes,
Should happie be, and have immortall blis:
For here all plentie, and all pleasure flowes,
And sweet love gentle fits° emongst them throwes, *impulses*
Without fell rancor, or fond° gealosie; *foolish*
Franckly each paramour his leman knowes,
Each bird his mate, ne any does envie
Their goodly meriment, and gay felicitie.

42

There is continuall spring, and harvest there
Continuall, both meeting at one time:
For both the boughes doe laughing blossomes beare,
And with fresh colours decke the wanton Prime,
And eke attonce the heavy trees they clime,
Which seeme to labour under their fruits lode:
The whiles the joyous birdes make their pastime
Emongst the shadie leaves, their sweet abode,
And their true loves without suspition tell abrode.

43

Right in the middest of that Paradise,
There stood a stately Mount, on whose round top
A gloomy° grove of mirtle trees[1] did rise, *shady*
Whose shadie boughes sharpe steele did never lop,° *cut*
Nor wicked beasts their tender buds did crop,
But like a girlond compassèd the hight,
And from their fruitfull sides sweet gum did drop,
That all the ground with precious deaw bedight,° *bedecked*
Threw forth most dainty odours, & most sweet delight.

44

And in the thickest covert of that shade,
There was a pleasant arbour, not by art,
But of the trees owne inclination made,
Which knitting their rancke° braunches part to part, *dense*
With wanton yvie twyne entrayld° athwart,° *entwined / across*
And Eglantine,° and Caprifole° emong, *sweet-briar / honeysuckle*
Fashiond above within their inmost part,
That nether Phoebus beams could through them throng,
Nor Aeolus sharp blast could worke them any wrong.

45

And all about grew every sort of flowre,
To which sad lovers were transformd of yore;
Fresh Hyacinthus,[2] Phoebus paramoure,
And dearest love:
Foolish Narcisse,[3] that likes the watry shore,
Sad Amaranthus, made a flowre but late,° *recently*
Sad Amaranthus, in whose purple gore

[1] *mirtle trees* Myrtle was sacred to Venus.

[2] *Hyacinthus* Apollo accidentally killed his young lover Hyacinth, and the hyacinth flower sprang up from the drops of his blood.

[3] *Narcisse* Narcissus, who fell in love with his own reflection in a pool of water and pined away when he realized it. A narcissus sprang up at the poolside when he died.

Me seemes I see Amintas[1] wretched fate,
To whom sweet Poets verse hath given endlesse date.

46

There wont° faire Venus often to enioy *was accustomed*
Her deare Adonis joyous company,
And reape sweet pleasure of the wanton boy;
There yet, some say, in secret he does ly,
Lappèd in flowres and pretious spycery,° *spices*
By her hid from the world, and from the skill° *knowledge*
Of Stygian Gods, which doe her love envy;
But she her selfe, when ever that she will,
Possesseth him, and of his sweetnesse takes her fill.

47

And sooth° it seemes they say: for he may not *truly*
For ever die, and ever buried bee
In balefull night, where all things are forgot;
All° be he subject to mortalitie, *although*
Yet is eterne in mutabilitie,
And by succession made perpetuall,
Transformèd oft, and chaungèd diverslie:
For him the Father of all formes they call;
Therefore needs mote he live, that living gives to all.

48

There now he liveth in eternall blis,
Joying° his goddesse, and of her enjoyd: *enjoying*
Ne feareth he henceforth that foe of his,
Which with his cruell tuske him deadly cloyd:° *pierced*
For that wilde Bore, the which him once annoyd,° *harmed*
She firmely hath emprisoned for ay,° *ever*
That her sweet love his malice mote avoyd,
In a strong rocky Cave, which is they say,
Hewen underneath that Mount, that none him losen may.

49

There now he lives in everlasting joy,
With many of the Gods in company,
Which thither haunt, and with the wingèd boy
Sporting himselfe in safe felicity:
Who when he hath with spoiles and cruelty
Ransackt the world, and in the wofull harts
Of many wretches set his triumphes hye,
Thither resorts, and laying his sad darts
Aside, with faire Adonis playes his wanton parts.

50

And his true love faire Psyche[2] with him playes,
Faire Psyche to him lately reconcyld,
After long troubles and unmeet upbrayes,° *reproofs*
With which his mother Venus her revyld,° *reproached*
And eke himselfe her cruelly exyld:
But now in stedfast love and happy state
She with him lives, and hath him borne a chyld,
Pleasure, that doth both gods and men aggrate,° *gratify*
Pleasure, the daughter of Cupid and Psyche late.

51

Hither great Venus brought this infant faire,
The younger daughter of Chrysogonee,
And unto Psyche with great trust and care
Committed her, yfosterèd to bee,
And traind up in true feminitee:
Who no lesse carefully her tenderèd,° *cared for*
Then her owne daughter Pleasure, to whom shee
Made her companion, and her lessonèd° *taught*
In all the lore of love, and goodly womanhead.

52

In which when she to perfect ripenesse grew,
Of grace and beautie noble Paragone,° *model*
She brought her forth into the worldès vew,
To be th'ensample of true love alone,
And Lodestarre° of all chaste affectione, *guiding star*
To all faire Ladies, that doe live on ground.
To Faery court she came, where many one
Admyrd her goodly haveour,° and found *bearing*
His feeble hart wide launchèd° with loves cruell wound. *cut*

[1] *Amintas* Man who died for the love of a woman named Phillis and was changed into an Amaranthus flower.

[2] *Psyche* Wife of Cupid who, when she disobeyed his orders never to look at his face, was punished by Venus, who set her several seemingly impossible tasks. Finally the gods mercifully granted Psyche immortality, allowing her to become a suitable partner for Cupid. See Apoleius's *Golden Ass* (second century CE).

53

But she to none of them her love did cast,
  Save to the noble knight Sir Scudamore,
  To whom her loving hart she linkèd fast
  In faithfull love, t'abide for ever more,
  And for his dearest sake endurèd sore,
  Sore trouble of an hainous enimy;
  Who her would forcèd have to have forlore° *abandoned*
  Her former love, and stedfast loyalty,
As ye may elsewhere read that ruefull history.

54

But well I weene, ye first desire to learne,
  What end unto that fearefull Damozell,
  Which fled so fast from that same foster°
    stearne,° *forester / cruel*
  Whom with his brethren Timias slew, befell:
  That was to weet, the goodly Florimell;
  Who wandring for to seeke her lover deare,
  Her lover deare, her dearest Marinell,
  Into misfortune fell, as ye did heare,
And from Prince Arthur fled with wings of idle feare.[1]
—1590, 1596

Letter to Sir Walter Ralegh *on* The Faerie Queene

Spenser's letter to Sir Walter Ralegh, an important colleague in England's efforts to govern the often rebellious Irish, was first published, together with a large number of dedicatory sonnets, as an explanatory "annex" to the 1590 *Faerie Queene.* The 1596 edition dropped it, possibly because Ralegh had recently earned the queen's displeasure or perhaps because, or so think many scholars, what the letter says about the plot sits problematically alongside the poem itself. Nor is it clear how the "virtues" on which Spenser tells Ralegh he would base his projected twelve books in fact relate to those of Aristotle, particularly since Aristotelian tradition had been modified by a still lively Medieval Scholastic and Christian understanding of that Greek philosopher. The Letter reappeared near the end of the 1690 *Faerie Queene*, and since then it has been routinely printed with the poem, often as a preface even though Spenser wrote it as an appendix. Authorities on Spenser, who read the Letter with interest, caution, and sometimes puzzlement, disagree as to where it should be placed. In this edition we retain it as an "annex," but readers should remember that it is an anomaly—a prefatory afterword.

Letter to Sir Walter Ralegh *on* The Faerie Queene

A Letter of the author's expounding his whole intention in the course of this work: which, for that it giveth great light to the reader, for the better understanding is hereunto annexed.[2]

To the right noble, and valorous, Sir Walter Ralegh, knight, Lord Warden of the Stanneries,[3] and Her Majesty's lieutenant of the County of Cornwall.

Sir: Knowing how doubtfully all Allegories may be construed, and this book of mine, which I have entitled the *Faery Queene*, being a continued allegory, or dark conceit,[4] I have thought good, as well for avoiding of jealous opinions and misconstructions, as also for your better light in reading thereof (being so by you commanded), to discover unto you the general intention and meaning which in the whole course thereof I have fashioned, without expressing of any particular purposes or by-accidents[5] therein occasioned. The general end therefore of all the book is to fashion a

[1] *But well ... feare* In Canto 1, Britomart, Arthur, and Timias (meaning honored), his squire, encounters the lovely Florimell (whose name combines the words flower and honey and who is associated with Beauty) fleeing from a cruel forester. Timias pursues and eventually slays the forester, along with his two brothers, though he is seriously wounded in the process. In Canto 4, we learned that Florimell is seeking her beloved, Marinell (whose name associates him with the sea). Marinell, however, has been told by his mother that a woman will cause him mortal harm and therefore has rejected Florimell's love.

[2] *Annexed* Added.

[3] *Stanneries* Mines in Cornwall and Devon.

[4] *dark conceit* Semi-concealed or difficult poetic notion, plan, or conception.

[5] *by-accidents* Secondary narratives or descriptions.

gentleman or noble person in virtuous and gentle[1] discipline: which for that I conceived should be most plausible and pleasing being coloured with an historical fiction,[2] the which the most part of men delight to read rather for variety of matter than for profit of the ensample,[3] I chose the history of King Arthur, as most fit for the excellency of his person, being made famous by many men's former works, and also furthest from the danger of envy, and suspicion of present time.[4] In which I have followed all the antique poets historical: first Homer, who in the persons of Agamemnon and Ulysses hath ensampled[5] a good governor and a virtuous man, the one in his Ilias, the other in his Odysseus; then Virgil, whose like intention was to do[6] in the person of Æneas; after him Ariosto comprised them both in his Orlando; and lately Tasso dissevered them again and formed both parts in two persons, namely that part which they in philosophy call Ethice, or virtues of a private man, coloured[7] in his Rinaldo; the other named Politice in his Godfredo.[8] By ensample of which excellent poets, I labour to portrait[9] in Arthur, before he was king, the image of a brave knight perfected in the twelve private moral virtues as Aristotle hath devised, the which is the purpose of these first twelve books:[10] which if I find to be well accepted, I may be perhaps encouraged to frame the other part of politic virtues in his person after that he came to be king. To some, I know, this method will seem unpleasant, who had rather have good discipline delivered plainly in way of precepts,[11] or sermoned at large, as they use, than thus cloudily enwrapped in allegorical devises. But such, meseems, should be satisfied with the use[12] of these days, seeing all things accounted by their shows and nothing esteemed of that is not delightful and pleasing to common sense.[13] For this cause is Xenophon preferred before Plato,[14] for that the one, in the exquisite depth of his judgement, formed a commonwealth such as it should be, but the other in the person of Cyrus and the Persians fashioned a government such as might best be: so much more profitable and gracious is doctrine by ensample than by rule. So have I laboured to do in the person of Arthur: whom I conceive, after his long education by Timon, to whom he was by Merlin delivered to be brought up so soon as he was born of the Lady Igrayne, to have seen in a dream or vision the Faery Queene, with whose excellent beauty ravished, he awaking resolved to seek her out, and so being by Merlin armed, and by Timon thoroughly instructed, he went to seek her forth in Faery Land. In that Faery Queene I mean glory in my general intention, but in my particular I conceive the most excellent and glorious person of our sovereign the Queene,[15] and her kingdom in Faery Land. And yet, in some places else[16] I do otherwise shadow[17] her. For considering she beareth two persons, the one of a most royal queene or empress, the

[1] *fashion* Represent; also form, educate; *gentle* As befits the gentry class, the well-born.

[2] *historical fiction* Imaginary narrative, fiction.

[3] *ensample* Example, model.

[4] *suspicion of present time* Potential accusations related to current political controversies or government censorship.

[5] *ensampled* Exemplified.

[6] *like intention was to do* I.e., "intention was to do something similar."

[7] *coloured* Illustrated, demonstrated.

[8] *Ariosto* Lodovico Ariosto (1474–1533) wrote the epic romance *Orlando Furioso* (1532); *Tasso* Torquato Tasso (1544–95) published *Rinaldo*, a chivalric romance, in 1562, and *Gerusalemme Liberata* (which follows the epic adventures of Count Godfredo) in 1581.

[9] *portrait* Portray.

[10] *first twelve books* Evidently, Spenser planned for *The Faerie Queene* to comprise 12 books and then perhaps a sequel of another 12; so far as we know, he completed only six.

[11] *precepts* Principles, advice.

[12] *use* Custom.

[13] *shows* Outward appearances; *common sense* Popular opinion, or less pejoratively, the consensus.

[14] *Xenophon preferred before Plato* Spenser contrasts Xenophon's *Cyropaedia* (early 4th century BCE), with its narrative excitement, compelling characters, and greater political realism, to Plato's more abstract ideal *Republic* (c. 380 BCE).

[15] *our sovereign the Queene* Elizabeth I (reigned 1558–1603); Spenser exploits the older conception of the monarch's two bodies, one public and continuing, the other private, individual, and mortal.

[16] *places else* Other places.

[17] *shadow* Indirectly represent.

other of a most virtuous and beautiful lady, this latter part in some places I do express in Belphœbe, fashioning her name according to your own excellent conceit of Cynthia[1] (Phoebe and Cynthia being both names of Diana). So in the person of Prince Arthur I set forth magnificence[2] in particular, which virtue for that (according to Aristotle and the rest) it is the perfection of all the rest and containeth in it them all, therefore in the whole course I mention the deeds of Arthur applicable to that virtue which I write of in that book. But of the 12 other virtues I make 12 other knights the patrons, for the more variety of the history: of which these three books contain three. The first of the Knight of the Redcrosse, in whom I express holiness. The second of Sir Guyon, in whom I set forth temperance.[3] The third of Britomart, a lady knight, in whom I picture chastity.[4] But because the beginning of the whole work seemeth abrupt and as depending upon other antecedents, it needs that ye know the occasion of these three knights' several adventures. For the method of a poet historical is not such as of an historiographer.[5] For an historiographer discourseth[6] of affairs orderly as they were done, accounting as well the times as the actions; but a poet thrusteth into the midst, even where it most concerneth him, and there recoursing to the things forepast,[7] and divining of things to come, maketh a pleasing analysis of all.

The beginning therefore of my history, if it were to be told by an historiographer, should be the twelfth book, which is the last, where I devise that the Faery Queene kept her annual feast 12 days, upon which 12 several[8] days, the occasions of the 12 several adventures happened, which being undertaken by 12 several knights, are in these 12 books severally handled and discoursed. The first was this: In the beginning of the feast, there presented himself a tall clownish[9] young man, who falling before the Queen of Faries desired a boon[10] (as the manner then was), which during that feast she might not refuse: which was that he might have the achievement of any adventure which during that feast should happen; that being granted, he rested him on the floor, unfit through his rusticity for a better place. Soon after entered a fair lady in mourning weeds,[11] riding on a white ass, with a dwarf behind her leading a warlike steed that bore the arms of a knight, and his spear in the dwarf's hand. She, falling before the Queene of Faeries, complained that her father and mother, an ancient king and queene, had been by an huge dragon many years shut up in a brasen[12] castle, who thence suffered them not to issue;[13] and therefore besought the Faery Queene to assign her some one of her knights to take on him that exploit. Presently that clownish person, upstarting, desired that adventure, whereat the Queene much wondering and the lady much gainsaying,[14] yet he earnestly importuned[15] his desire. In the end the lady told him that unless that

[1] *Cynthia* Probably as an effort to soften her anger, Ralegh's poem *The Ocean to Cynthia* (1592?) praises the still-offended Queen Elizabeth. Cynthia, Phoebe, and Diana were all names for the Greco-Roman virgin goddess of the hunt and the moon.

[2] *magnificence* "Greatness in action," specifically a princely and protective liberality suiting a great ruler. How Magnificence relates to the Aristotelian "Magnanimity" (greatness of soul) has been debated, as has the relation of either virtue to Christian thinking, especially granted Medieval interpretations of Aristotle.

[3] *temperance* Moderation and self restraint, but also the dynamic fusion of opposites (one "tempers" a sword with fire and cold water).

[4] *chastity* Not to be confused with virginity; chastity includes faithful married sexuality.

[5] *historiographer* Writer of factual chronicles.

[6] *discourseth* Tells.

[7] *recoursing to things forepast* Returning to past events; like Homer and Virgil, Spenser begins his poem *in medias res* (in the middle) and then indicates what has come before.

[8] *several* Separate.

[9] *clownish* Rustic-looking.

[10] *boon* Favor.

[11] *weeds* Clothes.

[12] *brasen* Strong.

[13] *issue* Emerge.

[14] *gainsaying* Opposing.

[15] *importuned* Begged for.

armour which she brought would serve him (that is, the armour of a Christian man specified by Saint Paul, vi Ephes.),[1] that he could not succeed in that enterprise: which being forthwith put upon him with due furnitures[2] thereunto, he seemed the goodliest man in all that company, and was well liked of the lady. And soon after taking on him knighthood, and mounting on that strange courser,[3] he went forth with her on that adventure, where beginneth the first book, vz.[4] "A gentle knight was pricking on the plain," &c.

The second day there came in a palmer[5] bearing an infant with bloody hands, whose parents he complained to have been slain by an enchantress called Acrasia, and therefore craved of the Faery Queene to appoint him some knight to perform that adventure, which being assigned to Sir Guyon, he presently went forth with that same palmer, which is the beginning of the second book and the whole subject thereof. The third day there came in a groom,[6] who complained before the Faery Queene, that a vile enchanter called Busirane had in hand a most fair lady, called Amoret, whom he kept in most grievous torment because she would not yield him the pleasure of her body. Whereupon Sir Scudamour, the lover of that lady, presently took on him that adventure. But being unable to perform it by reason of the hard[7] enchantments, after long sorrow, in the end met with Britomart, who succoured[8] him, and rescued his love.

But by occasion hereof, many other adventures are intermedled, but rather as accidents than intendments,[9] as the love of Britomart, the overthrow of Marinell, the misery of Florimell, the virtuousness of Belphœbe, the lasciviousness[10] of Hellenora, and many the like.

Thus much, Sir, I have briefly overrun[11] to direct your understanding to the well-head of the history, that from thence gathering the whole intention of the conceit ye may, as in a handful, grip all the discourse, which otherwise may happily[12] seem tedious and confused. So humbly craving the continuance of your honourable favour towards me, and th'eternal establishment of your happiness, I humbly take leave.

23 January, 1589[13]

Yours most humbly affectionate,

Ed. Spenser

[1] *Saint Paul, vi Ephes.* Ephesians 6 in which Paul commands, "Put on the whole armor of God, that ye may be able to stand against the wiles of the devil." The parts specified are the loins girt about with truth; the breastplate of righteousness; feet shod with the gospel of peace; the shield of faith "wherewith ye shall be able to quench all the fiery darts of the wicked"; the helmet of salvation; and "the sword of the Spirit, which is the word of God."

[2] *due furnitures* Suitable equipment, supplies.

[3] *courser* Swift horse.

[4] *vz.* Latin: Namely, to wit (Videlicet. Abbreviation: viz).

[5] *palmer* Pilgrim, especially one who has returned from the Holy Land.

[6] *groom* Manservant.

[7] *hard* Persistent, powerful.

[8] *succoured* Assisted.

[9] *accidents than intendments* Episodes not part of the main story-lines.

[10] *lasciviousness* Unrestrained sensuality, especially lustful behavior.

[11] *overrun* Described rapidly.

[12] *happily* By chance.

[13] *23 January, 1589* By the modern (i.e., Gregorian) calendar, 3 February 1590; England did not abandon the old Julian Calendar until 1752, and in Spenser's day March 25 was still the official start of the new year.

IN CONTEXT

The Redcrosse Knight

This illustration of the Redcrosse Knight is from the 1590 edition of *The Faerie Queene*.

Christian Armor

The opening stanza of Book 1 presents a riddle: how can Redcrosse Knight's armor be dented and battle scarred when the Knight has yet to see battle? Spenser expected his readers to realize that the Knight's armor is allegorical, the Christian armor specified by Saint Paul in Ephesians 6.11–17. The idea of spiritual armor for the spiritual warfare of everyday life was a popular trope in Renaissance theology and literature, and one of the best known treatments appeared in the *Handbook of the Christian Soldier* by the great Dutch humanist Desiderius Eramsus (c. 1469–1546).

from Paul's Epistle to the Ephesians, 6.11–17 (Geneva Bible, modernized spelling)

Put on the whole armour of God, that ye may be able to stand against the assaults of the devil.
For we wrestle not against flesh and blood, but against principalities, against powers, and against the worldly governors, the princess of the darkness of this world, against spiritual wickednesses, which are in the high places.

For this cause take unto you the whole armour of God, that ye may be able to resist in the evil day, & having finished all things, stand fast.

Stand therefore, and your loins gird about with verity, & having on the breast plate of righteousness,

And your feet shod with the preparation of the Gospel of peace.

Above all, take the shield of faith, wherewith ye may quench all the fiery darts of the wicked,

And take the helmet of salvation, and the sword of the Spirit, which is the word of God.

from Desiderius Erasmus, *Enchiridion militis Christiani* [Handbook of the Christian Soldier] (1504), first translated into English in 1533, probably by William Tyndale. The following excerpt is a modern spelling version of the 1533 translation.

ON THE ARMOR OF THE CHRISTIAN KNIGHT

Wilt thou hear the instruments or artillery of Christian men's war? And the zeal of him (saith scripture) shall take harness, and shall harness his creature to avenge his enemies; he will put on justice for his breast plate, and take for his helmet sure and true judgement; he will take a shield of equity impenetrable or that cannot be pierced, yea and he will sharpen or fashion cruel wrath into a spear. Thou readest also in Isaiah he is armed with justice as with an habergeon,[1] and a sallet[2] of health upon his head; he is clothed with the vestures[3] of vengeance, and covered as it were with a cloak of zeal.

Now if thou list, go thee to the storehouse of Paul that valiant captain, certainly thou shalt also find there the armour of war, not carnal things but valiant in God to destroy fortresses and counsels, and every high thing that exalteth himself against the doctrine of God. Thou shalt find there the armour of God, by the which thou mayest resist in a woeful day. Thou shalt find the harness of justice on the right hand, and on the left thou shalt find the defense of thy sides' verity, and the habergeon of justice, the buckler[4] of faith wherewith thou mayest quench all the hot and fiery weapons of thy cruel adversary. Thou shalt find also the helmet of health and the sword of the spirit, which is the word of God, with the which all, if a man shall be diligently covered and fenced, he may boldly without fear bring forth the bold saying of Paul: who shall separate us from the love of God? shall tribulation? shall straitness or difficulty? shall hunger? shall nakedness? shall peril? shall persecution? shall a sword? Behold how mighty enemies and how much feared of all men he setteth at nought.

---

[1] *habergeon* Sleeveless coat or jacket of mail or scale armor.

[2] *sallet* Light headpiece, with the lower part curving out behind.

[3] *vestures* Clothing, apparel.

[4] *buckler* Small round shield.

But hear also a certain greater thing, for it followeth. But in all things we have overcome by his help which loved us. And I am assured (saith he) that neither death nor life, nor angels, neither principates, neither virtues, neither present things, neither things to come, neither strength, neither highness, neither lowness, nor none other creature shall or may separate us from the love of God which is in Christ Jesu. O happy trust and confidence which the weapons or armour of light giveth to Paul, that is by interpretation a little man, which calleth himself the refuse or outcast of the world. Of such armour therefore abundantly shall holy scripture minister to thee, if thou wilt occupy thy time in it with all thy might: so that thou shalt not need our counsel or admonitions. Nevertheless, seeing it is thy mind, lest I should seem not to have obeyed thy request, I have forged for thee this little treatise called *Enchiridion*, that is to say, a certain little dagger, whom never lay out of thy hand, no not when thou art at meat, or in thy chamber. Insomuch that if at any time thou shalt be compelled to make a pilgrimage in these worldly occupations, and shalt be accumbered to bear about with the whole and complete armour and harness of holy scripture, yet commit not that the sutler[1] in wait at any season should come upon thee and find thee utterly unarmed, but at the least let it not grieve thee to have with them this little hanger,[2] which shall not be heavy to bear, nor unprofitable for thy defense, for it is very little, yet if thou use it wisely, and couple with it the buckler of faith, thou shalt be able to withstand the fierce and raging assault of thine enemy: so that thou shalt have no deadly wound.

Spirituality and *The Faerie Queene*

The Bible's Song of Solomon, a quasi-dialogue of lovers filled with sensuous metaphors, had long been read in both Jewish and Christian tradition as allegorizing the marriage between God and humanity, or God and the soul, or Christ and the Church (the body of all believers). For writers such as Spenser and Donne, the tradition further legitimized the crossover between the spiritual and the erotic found in much Renaissance art and literature.

Heading to the Song of Solomon (Geneva Bible, modernized spelling)

In this song, Salomon by most sweet and comfortable allegories and parables describeth the perfect love of Jesus Christ, the true Salomon and King of peace, and the faithful soul of his church which he hath sacrificed and appointed to be his spouse, holy, chaste, and without reprehension. So that here is declared the singular love of the bridegroom toward the bride, and his great and excellent benefits wherewith he doth enrich her of his pure bounty and grace without any of her deservings. Also the earnest affection of the church which is inflamed with the love of Christ desiring to be more and more joined to him in love, and not to be forsaken for any spot or blemish that is in her.

[1] *sutler* One who sells provisions to soldiers.

[2] *hanger* Short sword.

from *Amoretti* [1]

1

Happy ye leaves° when as those lilly hands, *pages*
which hold my life in their dead doing[2] might,
shall handle you and hold in loves soft bands,° *bonds*
lyke captives trembling at the victors sight.
And happy lines, on which with starry light,
those lamping° eyes will deigne sometimes to look *blazing*
and reade the sorrowes of my dying spright,° *spirit*
written with teares in harts close bleeding book.
And happy rymes bath'd in the sacred brooke,
of Helicon[3] whence she derivèd is,
when ye behold that Angels blessèd looke,
my soules long lackèd foode, my heavens blis.
Leaves, lines, and rymes, seeke her to please alone,
whom if ye please, I care for other none.

3

The soverayne beauty which I doo admyre,
witnesse the world how worthy to be prayzed:
the light wherof hath kindled heavenly fyre,
in my fraile spirit by her from basenesse raysed.
That being now with her huge brightnesse dazed,
base thing I can no more endure to view:
but looking still on her I stand amazed,
at wondrous sight of so celestiall hew.° *form*
So when my toung would speak her praises dew,° *due*
it stoppèd is with thoughts astonishment:
and when my pen would write her titles true,
it ravisht is with fancies wonderment:
Yet in my hart I then both speake and write,
The wonder that my wit cannot endite.

6

Be nought dismayd that her unmovèd mind
doth still persist in her rebellious pride:
such love not lyke to lusts of baser kynd,
the harder wonne, the firmer will abide.
The duresull° Oake, whose sap is not yet dride, *durable*
is long ere it conceive the kindling fyre:
but when it once doth burne, it doth divide,
great heat, and makes his flames to heaven aspire.
So hard it is to kindle new desire,
in gentle brest that shall endure for ever:
deepe is the wound, that dints° the parts entire *strikes*
with chast affects, that naught but death can sever.
Then thinke not long in taking litle paine,
to knit the knot, that ever shall remaine.

15

Ye tradefull° Merchants, that with weary toyle,° *engaged in trading / toil*
do seeke most pretious things to make your gain;
and both the Indias[4] of their treasures spoile,
what needeth you to seeke so farre in vaine?
For loe° my love doth in her selfe containe *behold*
all this worlds riches that may farre be found,
if Saphyres, loe her eies be Saphyres plaine,
if Rubies, loe hir lips be Rubies sound:° *pure*
If Pearles, hir teeth be pearles both pure and round;
if Yvorie, her forhead yvory weene;° *seems*
if Gold, her locks are finest gold on ground;
if silver, her faire hands are silver sheene.° *beautiful*
But that which fairest is, but few behold,
her mind adornd with vertues manifold.

22

This holy season fit to fast and pray,[5]
Men to devotion ought to be inclynd:
therefore, I lykewise on so holy day,[6]
for my sweet Saynt some service fit will find.
Her temple fayre is built within my mind,
in which her glorious ymage placèd is,
on which my thoughts doo day and night attend
lyke sacred priests that never thinke amisse.
There I to her as th'author of my blisse,
will builde an altar to appease her yre:
and on the same my hart will sacrifise,

---

[1] *Amoretti* Italian: little loves. This sonnet sequence is generally read as a description of Spenser's courtship of and marriage to Elizabeth Boyle (whom he had married in the previous year, 1594).

[2] *dead doing* Death-dealing.

[3] *Helicon* One of the mountains sacred to the Nine Muses, the goddesses of the arts and sciences. The sacred spring which flows from Helicon is the Hippocrene.

[4] *both the Indias* I.e., the East and West Indies.

[5] *This holy season* Lent.

[6] *holy day* Ash Wednesday.

burning in flames of pure and chast desyre:
The which vouchsafe O goddesse to accept,
amongst thy deerest relicks to be kept.

26

Sweet is the Rose, but growes upon a brere;° *thorny bush*
Sweet is the Junipere, but sharpe his bough;
sweet is the Eglantine,° but pricketh nere; *sweet-briar*
sweet is the firbloome,[1] but his braunches rough.
Sweet is the Cypresse, but his rynd° is tough, *bark*
sweet is the nut, but bitter is his pill;° *shell*
sweet is the broome-flowre,[2] but yet sowre enough;
and sweet is Moly,[3] but his root is ill.
So every sweet with soure is tempred still,
that maketh it be coveted the more:
for easie things that may be got at will,
most sorts of men doe set but little store.
Why then should I accoumpt° of little paine, *think much*
that endlesse pleasure shall unto me gaine.

34[4]

Lyke as a ship that through the Ocean wyde,
by conduct of some star doth make her way,
whenas a storme hath dimd her trusty guyde,
out of her course doth wander far astray.
So I whose star, that wont with her bright ray,
me to direct, with cloudes is overcast,
doe wander now in darknesse and dismay,
through hidden perils round about me plast.° *placed*
Yet hope I well, that when this storme is past
my Helice the lodestar of my lyfe[5]
will shine again, and looke on me at last,
with lovely light to cleare my cloudy grief,
Till then I wander carefull° comfortlesse, *full of cares*
in secret sorow and sad pensivenesse.

37

What guyle is this, that those her golden tresses,
She doth attyre under a net of gold:
and with sly° skill so cunningly them dresses, *dexterous*
that which is gold or heare,° may scarse be told? *hair*
Is it that mens frayle eyes, which gaze too bold,
she may entangle in that golden snare:
and being caught may craftily enfold,
theyr weaker harts, which are not wel aware?
Take heed therefore, myne eyes, how ye doe stare
henceforth too rashly on that guilefull net,
in which if ever ye entrappèd are,
out of her bands° ye by no meanes shall get. *bonds*
Fondnesse° it were for any being free, *foolishness*
to covet fetters, though they golden bee.

54

Of this worlds Theatre in which we stay,
My love lyke the Spectator ydly sits
beholding me that all the pageants° play, *parts*
disguysing diversly my troubled wits.
Sometimes I joy when glad occasion fits,
and mask in myrth lyke to a Comedy:
soone after when my joy to sorrow flits,
I waile and make my woes a Tragedy.
Yet she beholding me with constant eye,
delights not in my merth nor rues° my smart:° *pities / pain*
but when I laugh she mocks, and when I cry
she laughes, and hardens evermore her hart.
What then can move her? if nor merth nor mone,° *moan*
she is no woman, but a sencelesse stone.

64

Comming to kisse her lyps, (such grace I found)
Me seemd I smelt a gardin of sweet flowres:
that dainty odours from them threw around
for damzels fit to decke their lovers bowres.
Her lips did smell lyke unto Gillyflowers,° *carnations*
her ruddy cheekes lyke unto Roses red:
her snowy browes lyke budded Bellamoures,[6]
her lovely eyes lyke Pincks[7] but newly spred,
Her goodly bosome lyke a Strawberry bed,

[1] *firbloome* Fruit of the fir tree.

[2] *broome-flowre* Large yellow flower of the broom shrub, a common English plant.

[3] *Moly* Mythical herb with a white flower and black root, taken by Odysseus to ward off the spells of the witch Circe.

[4] *34* From Petrarch's *Rima* 189, or one of the many adaptations.

[5] *Helice* The constellation Ursa Major; *lodestar* North Star, Polaris, in the constellation Ursa Major.

[6] *Bellamoures* Unidentified.

[7] *Pincks* Dianthus plants, the flowers of which can be red, white, pink, or variegated.

her neck lyke to a bounch of Cullambynes:° *columbines*
her brest lyke lillyes, ere theyr leaves be shed,
her nipples lyke yong blossomd Jessemynes,° *jasmines*
Such fragrant flowres doe give most odorous smell,
but her sweet odour did them all excell.

67[1]

Lyke as a huntsman after weary chace,
Seeing the game from him escapt away,
sits downe to rest him in some shady place,
with panting hounds beguilèd of their pray:
So after long pursuit and vaine° assay,° *fruitless / attempt*
when I all weary had the chace forsooke,
the gentle deare returnd the selfe-same way,
thinking to quench her thirst at the next brooke.
There she beholding me with mylder looke,
sought not to fly, but fearelesse still did bide:
till I in hand her yet halfe trembling tooke,
and with her owne goodwill hir fyrmely tyde.
Strange thing me seemd to see a beast so wyld,
so goodly wonne with her owne will beguyld.° *deluded*

68

Most glorious Lord of lyfe that on this day,[2]
Didst make thy triumph, over death and sin:
and having harrowd hell didst bring away[3]
captivity thence captive us to win:
This joyous day, deare Lord, with joy begin,
and grant that we for whom thou diddest dye
being with thy deare blood clene washt from sin,
may live for ever in felicity.
And that thy love we weighing worthily,
may likewise love thee for the same againe:
and for thy sake that all lyke deare[4] didst buy,
with love may one another entertayne.
So let us love, deare love, lyke as we ought,
love is the lesson which the Lord us taught.

69

The famous warriors of the anticke world,[5]
Used Trophees to erect in stately wize:° *ways*
in which they would the records have enrold,
of theyr great deeds and valarous emprize.
What trophee then shall I most fit devize,
in which I may record the memory
of my loves conquest, peerelesse beauties prise,
adorn'd with honour, love, and chastity.
Even this verse vowd to eternity,
shall be thereof immortall moniment:
and tell her prayse to all posterity,
that may admire such worlds rare wonderment.
The happy purchase of my glorious spoile,
gotten at last with labour and long toyle.

70

Fresh spring the herald of loves mighty king,
In whose cote armour richly are displayd
all sorts of flowers the which on earth do spring
in goodly colours gloriously arrayd.
Goe to my love, where she is carelesse layd,
yet in her winters bowre not well awake:
tell her the joyous time wil not be staid° *halted*
unlesse she doe him by the forelock take.[6]
Bid her therefore her selfe soone ready make,
to wayt on love amongst his lovely crew:
where every one that misseth then her make,° *mate*
shall be by him amearst° with penance dew.° *immersed / due*
Make hast therefore sweet love, whilest it is prime,° *spring*
for none can call againe the passèd time.

74

Most happy letters fram'd by skilfull trade,° *application*
with which that happy name[7] was first desynd:
the which three times thrise happy hath me made,
with guifts of body, fortune and of mind.
The first my being to me gave by kind,° *nature*

---

[1] *67* An adaptation of the Italian poet Petrarch's *Rima* 190 (also adapted by Thomas Wyatt, Torquato Tasso, and Marguerite de Navarre). Spenser significantly changes Petrarch's original ending, turning Petrarch's lament into a happy celebration of the realization of his desires.

[2] *this day* Easter.

[3] *having ... away* Before his Resurrection, Christ descended into Hell to rescue the good Israelites who had died before his birth—an event referred to as the Harrowing of Hell.

[4] *lyke deare* At the same cost. I.e., Christ redeemed all people at the same cost.

[5] *anticke world* I.e., antique world, classical Greece and Rome.

[6] *by ... take* Seize the time or take the opportunity.

[7] *that happy name* Elizabeth, the name shared by Spenser's mother, Queen and wife.

from mothers womb deriv'd by dew° descent, *due*
the second is my sovereigne Queene most kind,
that honour and large richesse to me lent.
The third my love, my lives last ornament,
by whom my spirit out of dust was raysed:° *raised*
to speake her prayse and glory excellent,
of all alive most worthy to be praysed.
Ye three Elizabeths for ever live,
that three such graces[1] did unto me give.

75

One day I wrote her name upon the strand,° *shore*
but came the waves and washèd it away:
agayne I wrote it with a second hand,
but came the tyde, and made my paynes his pray.° *prey*
Vayne man, sayd she, that doest in vaine assay,° *attempt*
a mortall thing so to immortalize.
for I my selve shall lyke to this decay,
and eek° my name bee wypèd out lykewize. *also*
Not so, (quod° I) let baser things devize *said / plan*
to dy in dust, but you shall live by fame:
my verse your vertues rare shall eternize,
and in the hevens wryte your glorious name.
Where whenas death shall all the world subdew,
our love shall live, and later life renew.

80

After so long a race as I have run
Through Faery land, which those six books[2] compile,
give leave to rest me being halfe fordonne,° *overcome*
and gather to my selfe new breath awhile.
Then as a steed refreshèd after toyle,
out of my prison I will breake anew:
and stoutly will that second worke assoyle,° *discharge*
with strong endevour and attention dew.° *due*
Till then give leave to me in pleasant mew,° *seclusion*
to sport my muse and sing my loves sweet praise:
the contemplation of whose heavenly hew,° *form*
my spirit to an higher pitch will rayse.
But let her prayses yet be low and meane,° *common*
fit for the handmayd of the Faery Queene.

82

Joy of my life, full oft for loving you
I blesse my lot, that was so lucky placed:
but then the more your owne mishap I rew,° *pity*
that are so much by so meane° love
embased.° *common / lowered*
For had the equall hevens so much you graced
in this as in the rest, ye mote invent
som hevenly wit, whose verse could have
enchased° *engraved*
your glorious name in golden moniment.
But since ye deignd so goodly to relent
to me your thrall,° in whom is little worth, *bondage*
that little that I am, shall all be spent,
in setting your immortall prayses forth.
Whose lofty argument° uplifting me, *theme*
shall lift you up unto an high degree.

89

Lyke as the Culver° on the barèd bough, *dove*
Sits mourning for the absence of her mate:
and in her songs sends many a wishfull vow,
for his returne that seemes to linger late.
So I alone now left disconsolate,
mourne to my selfe the absence of my love:
and wandring here and there all desolate,
seek with my playnts° to match that *laments*
mournful dove
Ne joy of ought° that under heaven doth
hove,° *anything / dwell*
can comfort me, but her owne joyous sight:
whose sweet aspect both God and man can move,
in her unspotted° pleasauns° to delight. *pure / pleasure*
Dark is my day, whyles her fayre light I mis,
and dead my life that wants such lively° blis. *vital*
—1594

[1] *three such graces* I.e., Three Graces, sister goddesses of beauty, mirth, and bounty.

[2] *those six books* The six completed books of *The Faerie Queene.*

Epithalamion[1]

Ye learnèd sisters[2] which have oftentimes
Beene to me ayding, others to adorne:° *praise*
Whom ye thought worthy of your gracefull rymes,
That even the greatest did not greatly scorne
To heare theyr names sung in your simple layes,° *songs*
But joyèd in theyr prayse.
And when ye list° your owne mishaps to mourne, *desire*
Which death, or love, or fortunes wreck did rayse,
Your string could soone to sadder tenor turne,
And teach the woods and waters to lament
Your dolefull dreriment.° *misery*
Now lay those sorrowfull complaints aside,
And having all your heads with girland crownd,
Helpe me mine owne loves prayses to resound,
Ne let the same of any be envide:
So Orpheus did for his owne bride,[3]
So I unto my selfe alone will sing,
The woods shall to me answer and my Eccho ring.

Early before the worlds light giving lampe,
His golden beame upon the hils doth spred,
Having disperst the nights unchearefull dampe,
Doe ye awake, and with fresh lusty hed[4]
Go to the bowre° of my belovèd love, *bedroom*
My truest turtle dove
Bid her awake; for Hymen[5] is awake,
And long since ready forth his maske° to
move, *wedding procession*
With his bright Tead° that flames with many a
flake,° *torch / spark*
And many a bachelor to waite on him,
In theyr fresh garments trim.
Bid her awake therefore and soone her dight,° *prepare*
For lo the wishèd day is come at last,
That shall for al the paynes and sorrowes past,
Pay to her usury° of long delight, *interest*
And whylest she doth her dight,
Doe ye to her of joy and solace sing,
That all the woods may answer and your eccho ring.

Bring with you all the Nymphes that you can heare[6]
Both of the rivers and the forrests greene:
And of the sea that neighbours to her neare,
Al with gay girlands goodly wel beseene.° *befit*
And let them also with them bring in hand,
Another gay girland
For my fayre love of lillyes and of roses,
Bound true love wize[7] with a blew silke riband.° *ribbon*
And let them make great store of bridale poses,° *posies*
And let them eeke° bring store of other flowers *also*
To deck the bridale bowers.
And let the ground whereas her foot shall tread,
For feare the stones her tender foot should wrong
Be strewed with fragrant flowers all along,
And diapred° lyke the discolored°
mead.° *adorned / multicoloured / meadow*
Which done, doe at her chamber dore awayt,
For she will waken strayt,° *at once*
The whiles doe ye this song unto her sing,
The woods shall to you answer and your Eccho ring.

Ye Nymphes of Mulla[8] which with carefull heed,
The silver scaly trouts doe tend full well,
And greedy pikes which use therein to feed,
(Those trouts and pikes all others doo excell)
And ye likewise which keepe the rushy lake,
Where none doo fishes take
Bynd up the locks the which hang scatterd light,

[1] *Epithalamion* Meaning "at the bedroom" (Greek), an epithalamion is a wedding song, normally written by an outsider to celebrate a marriage. Classical poets including Sappho and Catullus wrote poems in this genre, which always begin with an invocation of the Muses, proceed through a full description of the wedding ceremony and celebration, and end with a reference to the consummation of the marriage. In Spenser's poem, each of the twenty-four sections corresponds to an hour of the wedding day.

[2] *learnèd sisters* The Nine Muses, goddesses of the arts and sciences.

[3] *So ... bride* One of the earliest and most celebrated poets of Greek mythology, Orpheus was famous for the magical power of his music and his passion for his wife, Eurydice, whom he attempted to rescue from the underworld after her death.

[4] *lusty hed* Vigor.

[5] *Hymen* God of marriage.

[6] *that you can heare* I.e., that can hear you.

[7] *true love wize* I.e., in a truelove's knot, an ornamental, double-looped knot.

[8] *Mulla* Poetic name of the River Awbeg in Ireland, near Spenser's home.

And in his waters which your mirror make,
Behold your faces as the christall bright,
That when you come whereas° my love doth lie, *to where*
No blemish she may spie.
And eke ye lightfoot mayds which keepe the deere,
That on the hoary° mountayne use to towre, *ancient*
And the wylde wolves which seeke them to devoure,
With your steele darts doo chace fro comming neer
Be also present heere,
To helpe to decke her and to help to sing,
That all the woods may answer and your eccho ring.

Wake now my love, awake; for it is time,
The Rosy Morne long since left Tithones[1] bed,
All ready to her silver coche° to clyme, *coach*
And Phoebus[2] gins to shew his glorious hed.
Hark how the cheerefull birds do chaunt theyr laies
And carroll of loves praise.
The merry Larke hir mattins° sings aloft, *morning prayers*
The thrush replyes, the Mavis descant playes,[3]
The Ouzell° shrills, the Ruddock° warbles soft, *blackbird / robin*
So goodly all agree with sweet consent,
To this dayes merriment.
Ah my deere love why doe ye sleepe thus long,
When meeter° were that ye should now awake, *more suitable*
T'awayt the comming of your joyous make,° *mate*
And hearken to the birds lovelearnèd song,
The deawy leaves among.
For they of joy and pleasance to you sing,
That all the woods them answer & theyr eccho ring.

My love is now awake out of her dreame,
And her fayre eyes like stars that dimmèd were
With darksome cloud, now shew theyr goodly beams
More bright then Hesperus[4] his head doth rere.
Come now ye damzels, daughters of delight,
Helpe quickly her to dight,
But first come ye fayre houres which were begot
In Joves[5] sweet paradice, of Day and Night,
Which doe the seasons of the yeare allot,
And al that ever in this world is fayre
Doe make and still° repayre.° *always / recreate*
And ye three handmayds of the Cyprian Queene,[6]
The which doe still adorne her beauties pride,
Helpe to addorne my beautifullest bride:
And as ye her array, still throw betweene° *occasionally*
Some graces to be seene,
And as ye use° to Venus, to her sing, *are accustomed*
The whiles the woods shal answer & your eccho ring.

Now is my love all ready forth to come,
Let all the virgins therefore well awayt,
And ye fresh boyes that tend upon her groome
Prepare your selves; for he is comming strayt.° *immediately*
Set all your things in seemely° good aray° *suitable / order*
Fit for so joyfull day,
The joyfulst day that ever sunne did see.
Faire Sun, shew forth thy favourable ray,
And let thy lifull° heat not fervent be *life-giving*
For feare of burning her sunshyny face,
Her beauty to disgrace.
O fayrest Phoebus, father of the Muse,[7]
If ever I did honour thee aright,
Or sing the thing, that mote° thy mind delight, *might*
Doe not thy servants simple boone° refuse, *request*
But let this day let this one day be myne,
Let all the rest be thine.
Then I thy soverayne prayses loud wil sing,
That all the woods shal answer and theyr eccho ring.

Harke how the Minstrels gin to shrill aloud
Their merry Musick that resounds from far,
The pipe, the tabor,° and the trembling Croud,° *drum / fiddle*
That well agree withouten breach° or jar. *break*
But most of all the Damzels doe delite,
When they their tymbrels° smyte, *tambourines*
And thereunto doe daunce and carrol sweet,

[1] *Tithones* I.e., Tithonus, husband of Aurora, goddess of the dawn.

[2] *Phoebus* Phoebus Apollo, god of the sun.

[3] *Mavis* Song thrush; *descant* Accompaniment.

[4] *Hesperus* Morning star.

[5] *Jove* King of the gods.

[6] *ye three … Queene* The Cyprian Queen is Venus, goddess of love, and her handmaids are the Three Graces, who embody beauty, love, and pleasure.

[7] *father … Muse* Apollo was god of music and poetry.

That all the sences they doe ravish quite,
The whyles the boyes run up and downe the street,
Crying aloud with strong confusèd noyce,° *noise*
As if it were one voyce.
Hymen[1] io° Hymen, Hymen they do shout, *dear*
That even to the heavens theyr shouting shrill
Doth reach, and all the firmament doth fill,
To which the people standing all about,
As in approvance doe thereto applaud
And loud advaunce her laud,° *praise*
And evermore they Hymen Hymen sing,
That al the woods them answer and theyr eccho ring.

Loe where she comes along with portly° pace *majestic*
Lyke Phoebe[2] from her chamber of the East,
Arysing forth to run her mighty race,
Clad all in white, that seemes° a virgin best. *suits*
So well it her beseemes that ye would weene° *believe*
Some angell she had beene.
Her long loose yellow locks lyke golden wyre,
Sprinckled with perle, and perling flowres a tweene,° *between*
Doe lyke a golden mantle her attyre,
And being crownèd with a girland greene,
Seeme lyke some mayden Queene.
Her modest eyes abashèd to behold
So many gazers, as on her do stare,
Upon the lowly ground affixèd are.
Ne dare lift up her countenance too bold,
But blush to heare her prayses sung so loud,
So farre from being proud.
Nathlesse doe ye still loud her prayses sing.
That all the woods may answer and your eccho ring.

Tell me ye merchants daughters did ye see
So fayre a creature in your towne before,
So sweet, so lovely, and so mild as she,
Adornd with beautyes grace and vertues store,
Her goodly eyes lyke Saphyres shining bright,
Her forehead yvory white,
Her cheekes lyke apples which the sun hath rudded,° *reddened*
Her lips lyke cherryes charming men to byte,
Her brest like to a bowle of creame uncrudded,° *unclotted*
Her paps° lyke lyllies budded, *breasts*
Her snowie necke lyke to a marble towre,
And all her body like a pallace fayre,
Ascending uppe with many a stately stayre,
To honors seat and chastities sweet bowre.
Why stand ye still ye virgins in amaze,
Upon her so to gaze,
Whiles ye forget your former lay to sing,
To which the woods did answer and your eccho ring.

But if ye saw that which no eyes can see,
The inward beauty of her lively° spright,° *living / spirit*
Garnisht with heavenly guifts of high degree,
Much more then would ye wonder at that sight,
And stand astonisht lyke to those which red° *beheld*
Medusaes mazeful hed.[3]
There dwels sweet love and constant chastity,
Unspotted fayth and comely womanhood,
Regard of honour and mild modesty,
There vertue raynes as Queene in royal throne,
And giveth lawes alone.
The which the base affections doe obay,
And yeeld theyr services unto her will,
Ne thought of thing uncomely° ever may *unseemly*
Thereto approch to tempt her mind to ill.
Had ye once seene these her celestial threasures,
And unrevealèd pleasures,
Then would ye wonder and her prayses sing,
That al the woods should answer and your echo ring.

Open the temple gates unto my love,
Open them wide that she may enter in,
And all the postes adorne as doth behove,
And all the pillours deck with girlands trim,
For to recyve this Saynt with honour dew,
That commeth in to you.
With trembling steps and humble reverence,
She commeth in, before th'almighties vew,
Of her ye virgins learne obedience,

[1] *Hymen* God of marriage.

[2] *Phoebe* Another name for Diana, virgin goddess of the moon.

[3] *Medusaes mazeful head* Medusa was one of the Gorgons, three sister monsters, terrible to behold. Medusa's hair was made up of intertwined serpents, and when she was looked upon, her beholder would turn to stone. Renaissance commentators often read her as symbolizing amazing chastity.

When so ye come into those holy places,
To humble your proud faces:
Bring her up to th'high altar that she may
The sacred ceremonies there partake,
The which do endlesse matrimony make,
And let the roring Organs loudly play
The praises of the Lord in lively notes,
The whiles with hollow throates
The Choristers the joyous Antheme sing,
That al the woods may answere and their eccho ring.

Behold whiles she before the altar stands
Hearing the holy priest that to her speakes
And blesseth her with his two happy hands,
How the red roses flush up in her cheekes,
And the pure snow with goodly° vermill° stayne, *fair / scarlet*
Like crimsin dyde in grayne,[1]
That even th'Angels which continually,
About the sacred Altare doe remaine,
Forget their service and about her fly,
Ofte peeping in her face that seemes more fayre,
The more they on it stare.
But her sad° eyes still fastened on the ground, *dignified*
Are governèd with goodly modesty,
That suffers not one looke to glaunce awry,
Which may let in a little thought unsownd.
Why blush ye love to give to me your hand,
The pledge of all our band?° *bond*
Sing ye sweet Angels, Alleluya sing,
That all the woods may answere and your eccho ring.

Now al is done; bring home the bride againe,
Bring home the triumph of our victory,
Bring home with you the glory of her gaine,° *having gained*
With joyance bring her and with jollity.
Never had man more joyfull day then this,
Whom heaven would heape with blis.
Make feast therefore now all this live long day,
This day for ever to me holy is,
Poure out the wine without restraint or stay,° *pause*
Poure not by cups, but by the belly full,
Poure out to all that wull,° *will*
And sprinkle all the postes and wals with wine,
That they may sweat, and drunken be withall.

[1] *in grayne* Fast dyed.

Crowne ye God Bacchus[2] with a coronall,° *garland*
And Hymen also crowne with wreathes of vine,
And let the Graces daunce unto the rest;
For they can doo it best:
The whiles the maydens doe theyr carroll sing,
To which the woods shal answer & theyr eccho ring.

Ring ye the bels, ye yong men of the towne,
And leave your wonted° labors for this day: *habitual*
This day is holy; doe ye write it downe,
That ye for ever it remember may.
This day the sunne is in his chiefest hight,
With Barnaby the bright,[3]
From whence declining daily by degrees,
He somewhat loseth of his heat and light,
When once the Crab[4] behind his back he sees.
But for this time it ill ordainèd was,
To chose the longest day in all the yeare,
And shortest night, when longest fitter weare:° *were*
Yet never day so long, but late° would passe. *finally*
Ring ye the bels, to make it weare° away, *wear*
And bonefiers° make all day, *bonfires*
And daunce about them, and about them sing:
That all the woods may answer, and your eccho ring.

Ah when will this long weary day have end,
And lende° me leave to come unto my love? *grant*
How slowly do the houres theyr numbers spend?
How slowly does sad Time his feathers move?
Hast thee O fayrest Planet[5] to thy home
Within the Westerne fome:° *ocean*
Thy tyred steedes long since have need of rest.
Long though it be, at last I see it gloome,° *become dusk*
And the bright evening star with golden creast° *crest*
Appeare out of the East.
Fayre childe of beauty, glorious lampe of love
That all the host of heaven in rankes doost lead,
And guydest lovers through the nightès dread,

[2] *Bacchus* God of wine.

[3] *Barnaby the bright* In the Julian Calendar St. Barnaby's Day, June 11, was the longest day of the year.

[4] *the Crab* Cancer, the constellation through which the sun passes toward the end of July.

[5] *fayrest Planet* The sun, which the god Apollo pulls in his horse-drawn chariot.

How chearefully thou lookest from above,
And seemst to laugh atweene thy twinkling light
As joying in the sight
Of these glad many which for joy doe sing,
That all the woods them answer and their echo ring.

Now ceasse ye damsels your delights forepast;° *past*
Enough is it, that all the day was youres:
Now day is doen, and night is nighing° fast: *coming*
Now bring the Bryde into the brydall boures.
Now night is come, now soone her disaray,
And in her bed her lay;
Lay her in lillies and in violets,
And silken courteins over her display,
And odourd sheetes, and Arras° coverlets, *tapestry*
Behold how goodly my faire love does ly
In proud humility;
Like unto Maia,[1] when as Jove her tooke,
In Tempe,[2] lying on the flowry gras,
Twixt sleepe and wake, after she weary was,
With bathing in the Acidalian brooke.
Now it is night, ye damsels may be gon,
And leave my love alone,
And leave likewise your former lay to sing:
The woods no more shal answere, nor your echo ring.

Now welcome night, thou night so long expected,
that long daies labour doest at last defray,° *repay*
And all my cares, which cruell love collected,
Hast sumd in one, and cancellèd for aye:° *ever*
Spread thy broad wing over my love and me,
That no man may us see,
And in thy sable mantle us enwrap,
From feare of perrill and foule horror free.
Let no false treason seeke us to entrap,
Nor any dread disquiet once annoy
The safety of our joy:
But let the night be calme and quietsome,
Without tempestuous storms or sad afray:° *fear*
Lyke as when Jove with fayre Alcmena[3] lay,
When he begot the great Tirynthian groome:
Or lyke as when he with thy selfe° did lie, *i.e., night*
And begot Majesty.
And let the mayds and yongmen cease to sing:
Ne let the woods them answer, nor theyr eccho ring.

Let no lamenting cryes, nor dolefull teares,
Be heard all night within nor yet without:
Ne let false whispers, breeding hidden feares,
Breake gentle sleepe with misconceivèd dout.
Let no deluding dreames, nor dreadful sights
Make sudden sad affrights;
Ne let house fyres, nor lightnings helpelesse harmes,
Ne let the Pouke,[4] nor other evill sprights,
Ne let mischivous witches with theyr charmes,
Ne let hob Goblins, names whose sence we see not,
Fray us with things that be not.
Let not the shriech° Oule, nor the Storke be heard: *screech*
Nor the night Raven that still° deadly yels,[5] *always*
Nor damnèd ghosts cald up with mighty spels,
Nor griesly° vultures make us once affeard: *ghastly*
Ne let th'unpleasant Quyre° of Frogs still croking *choir*
Make us to wish theyr choking.
Let none of these theyr drery accents sing;
Ne let the woods them answer, nor theyr eccho ring.

But let stil Silence trew night watches keepe,
That sacred peace may in assurance rayne,
And tymely sleep, when it is tyme to sleepe,
May poure his limbs forth on your pleasant playne,
The whiles an hundred little wingèd loves,[6]
Like divers° fethered doves, *diverse*
Shall fly and flutter round about your bed,
And in the secret darke, that none reproves,
Their prety stealthes shal worke, & snares shal spread
To filch away sweet snatches of delight,
Conceald through covert night.
Ye sonnes of Venus, play your sports at will,
For greedy pleasure, carelesse of your toyes,° *games*
Thinks more upon her paradise of joyes,

[1] *Maia* Eldest daughter of Atlas, who gave birth to Mercury after being seduced by Jove.

[2] *Tempe* Vale of Tempe, in Thessaly.

[3] *Alcmena* Mother of Hercules, with whom Jove lay for three nights.

[4] *Pouke* Puck, or Robin Goodfellow, a mischievous fairy.

[5] *Let not … yels* The owl was said to be a harbinger of death and the raven to be a bad omen; the stork, according to Chaucer, was an avenger of adultery.

[6] *wingèd loves* Cupids.

Then what ye do, albe it good or ill.
All night therefore attend your merry play,
For it will soone be day:
Now none doth hinder you, that say or sing,
Ne will the woods now answer, nor your Eccho ring.

Who is the same, which at my window peepes?
Or whose is that faire face, that shines so bright,
Is it not Cinthia,[1] she that never sleepes,
But walkes about high heaven al the night?
O fayrest goddesse, do thou not envy
My love with me to spy:
For thou likewise didst love, though now unthought,
And for a fleece of woll,° which privily, *wool*
The Latmian shephard[2] once unto thee brought,
His pleasures with thee wrought.
Therefore to us be favorable now;
And sith° of wemens labours thou hast charge, *since*
And generation goodly dost enlarge,
Encline thy will t'effect our wishfull vow,
And the chast wombe informe° with timely seed, *impregnate*
That may our comfort breed:
Till which we cease our hopefull hap° to sing, *hoped for good fortune*
Ne let the woods us answere, nor our Eccho ring.

And thou great Juno,[3] which with awful might
The lawes of wedlock still dost patronize,
And the religion° of the faith first plight *worship*
With sacred rites hast taught to solemnize:
And eeke for comfort often callèd art
Of women in their smart,° *pain*
Eternally bind thou this lovely band,
And all thy blessings unto us impart.
And thou glad Genius, in whose gentle hand,
The bridale bowre and geniall° bed remaine, *nuptial*
Without blemish or staine,
And the sweet pleasures of theyr loves delight.
With secret ayde doest succour° and supply, *assist*
Till they bring forth the fruitfull progeny,
Send us the timely fruit of this same night.
And thou fayre Hebe,[4] and thou Hymen free,
Grant that it may so be.
Til which we cease your further prayse to sing,
Ne any woods shal answer, nor your Eccho ring.

And ye high heavens, the temple of the gods,
In which a thousand torches flaming bright
Doe burne, that to us wretched earthly clods:
In dreadful darknesse lend desirèd light;
And all ye powers which in the same remayne,
More then we men can fayne,° *desire*
Poure out your blessing on us plentiously,
And happy influence upon us raine,
That we may raise a large posterity,
Which from the earth, which they may long possesse,
With lasting happinesse,
Up to your haughty° pallaces may mount, *lofty*
And for the guerdon° of theyr glorious merit *reward*
May heavenly tabernacles there inherit,
Of blessed Saints for to increase the count.
So let us rest, sweet love, in hope of this,
And cease till then our tymely joyes to sing,
The woods no more us answer, nor our eccho ring.

Song made in lieu of many ornaments,
With which my love should duly have bene dect,° *decked*
Which cutting off through hasty accidents,
Ye would not stay your dew time to expect,° *await*
But promist both to recompens,
Be unto her a goodly ornament,
And for short time an endlesse moniment.
—1594

[1] *Cinthia* Diana, goddess of the moon and childbirth.

[2] *Latmian shephard* Endymion, whom Diana loved.

[3] *Juno* Goddess of marriage and wife of Jove.

[4] *Hebe* Goddess of youth and spring.

Sir Philip Sidney

1554 – 1586

Sir Philip Sidney remains not only a famous writer but an example of the complete Renaissance courtier. He was the author of the sonnet sequence *Astrophil and Stella*, of the prose romance *Arcadia*, and of *An Apology for Poetry* (also known as *A Defence of Poesy*), the first extended work of literary criticism in English. Sidney's writings are witty, eloquent, and imaginative in their marriage of English style and the Renaissance genres and ideals embraced by artists in Italy, France, and Spain. Sidney was also a courtier, diplomat, and gentleman-soldier renowned for his courtesy; according to a probably apocryphal story, when wounded on the battlefield and offered water, he saw a thirsty foot-soldier eying the bottle longingly and told him to take it, saying "Thy necessity is yet greater than mine."

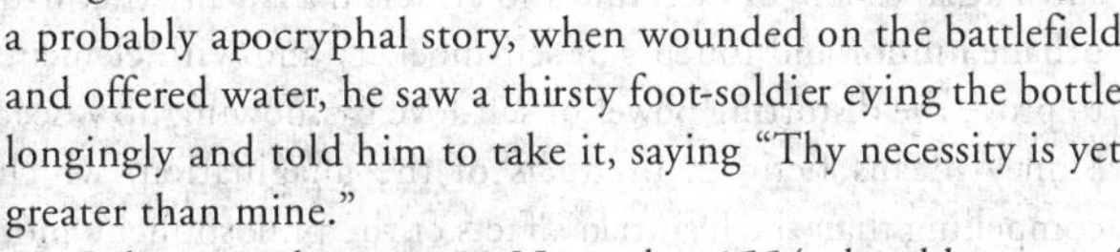

Sidney was born on 30 November 1554, the eldest son of Sir Henry Sidney and Lady Mary Dudley. Although his family was not rich by the standards of the nobility, his birth placed him in an élite circle: his father, at one point Viceroy of Ireland, had been a friend of Edward VI; his godfather was Philip II of Spain, for whom he was named; and his uncle, Robert Dudley, was the powerful Earl of Leicester, the royal favorite who had courted Elizabeth and whom the Queen certainly loved. Sidney's education befitted one of his class. He entered Shrewsbury School in 1564, was taught there by the learned Thomas Ashton, and in 1568 entered Christ Church, Oxford, where he remained until he was 17. He left without a degree, as was often done, and was sent on a tour of Europe to learn about the languages and circumstances of other countries. This trip was to be highly beneficial for the young Sidney: it sparked a fascination with Continental ideas, and the important figures he befriended in the political, philosophical, and scholarly worlds helped shape his mind and career.

Sidney's cosmopolitanism also earned him some favor at court. In 1572 he was a junior member of a special embassy to France's Charles IX. While in Paris, Sidney witnessed the horrifying St. Bartholomew's Day massacre in which many Huguenots (French Protestants) were slaughtered. The event left its mark on him, confirming his passionate, if hardly narrow-minded, Protestantism. He continued his travels around Europe, studying for a while at the University of Padua and visiting Vienna, Frankfurt, and Prague. He returned to England in May 1575, finding service with the Queen and gaining a reputation as an excellent diplomat.

Although Sidney's writing took second place to his political service, he influenced the literary world by encouraging other writers such as Edward Dyer, Fulke Greville (who later wrote his biography), and the young Edmund Spenser, who dedicated his *Shepheardes Calender* (1579) to him. Sidney's own first known work is *The Lady of May* (1578), a masque he composed for a royal visit; it featured the Queen herself.

Knowing his talent as a persuasive writer, the political faction headed by the Earl of Leicester and Sir Francis Walsingham, an important royal advisor and director of the secret service whose daughter was to marry Sidney, asked Philip to write a letter to Elizabeth opposing her marriage plans. Throughout the 1570s Spain had been gathering political and military power, so as a counterbalance some in England and France suggested an alliance between the two nations to be cemented by a match between Elizabeth and the Duke of Alençon, brother of the French king (who had himself once courted the English queen). In his letter Sidney reminds the queen of the duke's role in the murder of Huguenots and urges her not to marry a foreign and Catholic prince. It used to be thought that Elizabeth was highly displeased at this gesture: John Stubbs, Puritan gentleman, printed a pamphlet that contained similar advice and was severely punished. Sidney, however, was doing his duty as a courtier, and there is no evidence that the Queen resented his letter. He did fall out with the Earl of Oxford in a tennis-court quarrel and, given the Earl's murderous proclivities, seems to have thought it safer to stay with his sister Mary and her husband, the Earl of Pembroke, at their Wiltshire manor for a year. There he composed verses, translated a few Huguenot texts and some psalms, and wrote *A Defence of Poesy* (published in 1595). In this last, Sidney sets out a more wide-ranging and substantial theory of literature and criticism than any that had yet appeared in English, lightened by urbane humor and touches of self-mockery and with elements of paradox (Sidney smilingly claims to prove the distorting power of self-love by showing how he, a poet, can praise poetry). By "poetry" Sidney means fictions, products of the imagination, which he insists are more psychologically compelling than the historian's facts or the philosopher's moral abstractions. He also comments on particular authors and works, and compares modern English literature to that of ancient Greece and Rome. His assessment of the English play *Gorboduc* is the first sustained critical discussion of a literary work in English.

In writing his poetic work *Astrophil and Stella*, and despite his claim not to be a "pickpurse of another's wit," Sidney had before him a major Continental model—the Petrarchan sonnet sequence. Although Sidney's own contribution to, and revision of, the genre was not printed until five years after his death, the sonnets had been circulating in manuscript. Their publication in 1591 launched a brief but intense fashion for sonnet sequences. Sidney's longest work, *The Countess of Pembroke's Arcadia*, a pastoral romance with elements of epic and drama, recounts the romantic and martial adventures of two Greek princes, Musidorus and Pyrocles. Mixed in with the five books of prose narrative are a number of pastoral poems that sometimes experiment with classical meters. Ostensibly begun as entertainment for the author's sister, Sidney revised what is now called "The Old Arcadia" (lost until 1908), increasing the work's epic possibilities and political significance; he was part way through this version, now called "The New Arcadia," when he died. In 1590 his sister Mary published *The Countess of Pembroke's Arcadia*, a hybrid volume with the revised first part and the unrevised later part; it was this version that became popular and influential in England and even on the Continent.

In the early 1580s Sidney was knighted, named Joint Master of the Ordnance, and later charged with helping the English prepare an expedition to aid the Dutch in their revolt against Spain. In 1585 he was appointed Governor of Flushing, a town in the Netherlands that the English used as a base of operations, where he participated in several successful armed forays against the Spanish. On 22 September 1586, during a skirmish with Spanish forces outside the Dutch town of Zutphen, Sidney was shot in the thigh. The wound became gangrenous, and Sidney died of the infection on 17 October 1586. A flurry of grieving poetry was to follow and in February 1587 the body was brought home and given a magnificent funeral—an occasion designed in part to stir public patriotism and encourage support for the struggle against Spain. A fine poet had died but a legend had been born.

⌘⌘⌘

from *Astrophil and Stella*

1

Loving in truth, and fain° in verse my love to show, *desiring*
That she, dear she,[1] might take some pleasure of my pain,
Pleasure might cause her read, reading might make her know,
Knowledge might pity win, and pity grace obtain,
I sought fit words to paint the blackest face of woe,
Studying inventions fine, her wits to entertain,
Oft turning others' leaves, to see if thence would flow
Some fresh and fruitful showers upon my sun-burned brain.
But words came halting forth, wanting Invention's stay;° *support*
Invention, Nature's child, fled step-dame Study's blows,
And others' feet still seemed but strangers in my way.
Thus, great with child to speak, and helpless in my throes,
Biting my truant pen, beating myself for spite,
"Fool," said my Muse to me, "look in thy heart and write."

2

Not at first sight, nor with a dribbèd° shot, *faulty*
Love[2] gave the wound which while I breathe will bleed.
But known worth did in mine[3] of time proceed,
'Till by degrees it had full conquest got.
I saw and liked, I liked but lovèd not,
I loved, but straight did not what Love decreed.
At length to Love's decrees I—forced—agreed,
Yet with repining at so partial° lot. *unequal*
Now even that footstep of lost liberty
Is gone, and now like slave-born Muscovite.
I call it praise to suffer tyranny;
And now employ the remnant of my wit.
To make myself believe that all is well,
While with a feeling skill I paint my hell.

[1] *That she, dear she* In the 1591 edition, this phrase is "That the dear she."

[2] *Love* Cupid.

[3] *mine* Subterranean passage dug under an enemy fortress.

7

When Nature made her chief work, Stella's eyes,
In colour black, why wrapped she beams so bright?
Would she in beamy black, like painter wise,
Frame daintiest lustre mixed of shades and light?
Or did she else that sober hue devise,
In object[4] best to knit and strength our sight,
Lest if no veil these brave gleams did disguise,
They, sun-like, should more dazzle than delight?
Or would she her miraculous power show,
That whereas black seems beauty's contrary,
She e'en in black doth make all beauties flow?
Both so, and thus, she, minding° Love, should be *remembering*
Placed ever there, gave him this mourning weed° *garment*
To honour all their deaths who for her bleed.

18

With what sharp checks I in myself am shent[5]
When into Reason's audit I do go,
And by just counts myself a bankrout° know *bankrupt*
Of all those goods which Heaven to me hath lent.
Unable quite to pay even Nature's rent,
Which unto it by birthright I do owe.
And which is worse, no good excuse can show,
But that my wealth I have most idly spent.
My youth doth waste, my knowledge brings forth toys,[6]
My wit doth strive those passions to defend,
Which for reward spoil it with vain annoys.[7]
I see my course to lose myself doth bend.
I see, and yet no greater sorrow take
Than that I lose no more for Stella's sake.

20

Fly, fly, my friends, I have my death wound; fly!
See there that boy, that murdering boy° I say, *Cupid*
Who like a thief, hid in dark bush doth lie,
Till bloody bullet get him wrongful prey.
So tyrant he no fitter place could spy,

[4] *In object* With the goal.

[5] *sharp checks* Reproaches; *shent* Disgraced.

[6] *toys* Frivolous pieces of writing.

[7] *annoys* Irritations.

Nor so fair level[1] in so secret stay,
As that sweet black which veils the heav'nly eye:
There himself with his shot he close doth lay.
Poor passenger,° pass now thereby I did, *passer-by*
And stayed pleased with the prospect of the place,
While that black hue from me the bad guest hid:
But straight I saw motions of lightning grace,
And then descried the glist'ring of his dart:
But ere I could fly hence, it pierced my heart.

21

Your words, my friend, (right healthful caustics[2]) blame
My young mind marred, whom Love doth
  windlass° so, *ensnare*
That mine own writings like bad servants show
My wits, quick in vain thoughts, in virtue lame;
That Plato[3] I read for nought, but if° he tame *unless*
Such doltish gyres;° that to my birth I owe *circles*
Nobler desires, lest else that friendly foe,
Great expectation, were a train of shame.
For since mad March great promise made of me,
If now the May of my years much decline,
What can be hoped my harvest time will be?
Sure you say well, "Your wisdom's golden mine,
Dig deep with learning's spade." Now tell me this,
Hath this world aught so fair as Stella is?

22

In highest way of heav'n the Sun did ride,
Progressing then from fair twins' golden place:[4]
Having no scarf of clouds before his face,
But shining forth of heat in his chief pride;
When some fair ladies by hard promise tied,
On horseback met him in his furious race,
Yet each prepared with fan's well-shading grace
From that foe's wounds° their tender skins *sunburn*
  to hide.
Stella alone with face unarmed marched.
Either to do like him which open shone,
Or careless of the wealth because her own:
Yet were the hid and meaner beauties parch'd,
Her daintiest bare went free; the cause was this,
The Sun, which others burned, did her but kiss.

23

The curious wits seeing dull pensiveness
Bewray° itself in my long settled eyes, *reveal*
Whence those same fumes of melancholy rise,
With idle pains, and missing aim, do guess.
Some that know how my spring I did address,
Deem that my Muse some fruit of knowledge plies:
Others, because the Prince° my service tries, *the Queen*
Think that I think state errors to redress.
But harder judges judge ambition's rage,
Scourge of itself, still climbing slipp'ry place,
Holds my young brain cativ'd° in golden cage. *captive*
Oh fools, or over-wise, alas the race
Of all my thoughts hath neither stop nor start,
But only Stella's eyes and Stella's heart.

24

Rich fools there be, whose base and filthy heart
Lies hatching still the goods wherein they flow:
And damning their own selves to Tantal's smart,[5]
Wealth breeding want, more blist° more *blessed*
  wretched grow.
Yet to those fools heav'n such wit doth impart
As what their hands do hold, their heads do know,
And knowing love, and loving, lay apart,
As sacred things, far from all danger's show.
But that rich fool[6] who by blind Fortune's lot
The richest gem of love and life enjoys,
And can with foul abuse such beauties blot;
Let him, deprived of sweet but unfelt joys,
(Exiled for aye° from those high treasures, which *ever*
He knows not) grow in only folly rich.

[1] *so fair level* So well take aim.

[2] *right healthful caustics* Truly life-giving corrosives.

[3] *Plato* Plato likened reason to a charioteer of the passions.

[4] *fair twins' golden place* Gemini, the sign from which the sun emerges in June.

[5] *Tantal's smart* The torment of Tantalus, the miser, who was condemned to perpetual thirst even amid water.

[6] *that rich fool* Lord Rich, the husband of Penelope Devereaux (Sidney's Stella).

25

The wisest scholar[1] of the wight° most wise *man*
By Phoebus' doom,[2] with sugared sentence says,
That Virtue, if it once met with our eyes,
Strange flames of love it in our souls would raise;
But for that man with pain his truth descries,
While he each thing in sense's balance weighs,
And so nor will, nor can behold those skies
Which inward sun to *heroic* mind displays,
Virtue of late with virtuous care to stir° *encourage*
Love of herself, took Stella's shape, that she
To mortal eyes might sweetly shine in her.
It is most true, for since I her did see,
Virtue's great beauty in that face I prove,
And find th'effect, for I do burn in love.

26

Though dusty° wits dare scorn astrology, *earthbound*
And fools can think those lamps° of purest light *stars*
Whose numbers, ways, greatness, eternity,
Promising wonders, wonder do invite,
To have for no cause birthright in the sky,
But for to spangle the black weeds of night:
Or for some brawl,° which in that chamber high, *country dance*
They should still dance to please a gazer's sight;
For me, I do Nature unidle know,
And know great causes, great effects procure:
And know those bodies high reign on the low.
And if these rules did fail, proof° makes me sure, *experience*
Who oft fore-judge my after-following race,
By only those two stars in Stella's face.

27

Because I oft in dark abstracted guise
Seem most alone in greatest company,
With dearth of words, or answers quite awry,
To them that would make speech of speech arise,
They deem, and of their doom the rumour flies,
That poison foul of bubbling pride doth lie
So in my swelling breast that only I
Fawn on myself, and others do despise:
Yet pride I think doth not my soul possess,
Which looks too oft in his unflatt'ring glass:° *mirror*
But one worse fault, ambition, I confess,
That makes me oft my best friends overpass,
Unseen, unheard, while though to highest place
Bends all his powers, even° unto Stella's grace. *only*

31

With how sad steps, oh Moon, thou climb'st the skies,
How silently, and with how wan° a face. *pale*
What, may it be, that even in heav'nly place
That busy archer° his sharp arrows tries? *Cupid*
Sure, if that long-with-love-acquainted eyes
Can judge of love, thou feel'st a lover's case;
I read it in thy looks; thy languished grace
To me that feel the like, thy state descries.° *reveals*
Then ev'n of fellowship, oh Moon, tell me
Is constant love deemed there but want of wit?
Are beauties there as proud as here they be?
Do they above love to be loved, and yet
Those lovers scorn whom that love doth possess?
Do they call virtue there ungratefulness?

34

Come, let me write. "And to what end?" To ease
A burdened heart. "How can words ease, which are
The glasses of thy daily vexing care?"
Oft cruel fights well-pictured forth do please.
"Art not ashamed to publish[3] thy disease?"
Nay, that may breed my fame, it is so rare.
"But will not wise men think thy words fond ware?"[4]
Then be they close,° and so none shall displease. *concealed*
"What idler thing than speak and not be heard?"
What harder thing than smart and not to speak?
Peace, foolish wit, with wit my wit is marred.
Thus write I while I doubt[5] to write, and wreak
My harms on ink's poor loss. Perhaps some find
Stella's great pow'rs that so confuse my mind.

39

Come, Sleep! O Sleep, the certain knot of peace,
The baiting place of wit, the balm of woe,

[1] *wisest scholar* Plato was the pupil of Socrates.

[2] *By Phoebus' doom* Judged most wise by the oracle of Apollo at Delphi.

[3] *publish* Make public.

[4] *fond ware* Frivolities.

[5] *doubt* Hesitate.

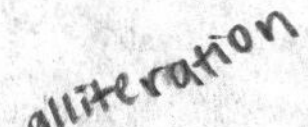

The poor man's wealth, the prisoner's release,
Th' indifferent° judge 'tween the high and low. *impartial*
With shield of proof shield me from out the press
Of those fierce darts Despair at me doth throw.
O make in me those civil wars to cease;
I will good tribute pay, if thou do so.
Take thou of me smooth pillows, sweetest bed,
A chamber deaf to noise and blind to light,
A rosy garland, and a weary head.
And if these things, as being thine by right,
Move not thy heavy grace, thou shalt in me,
Livelier than elsewhere, Stella's image see.

41

Having this day my horse, my hand, my lance
Guided so well, that I obtained the prize,
Both by the judgment of the English eyes,
And of some sent from that sweet enemy France;[1]
Horsemen my skill in horsemanship advance,
Town-folks my strength; a daintier° judge applies *more discerning*
His praise to sleight,° which from good use doth rise; *dexterity*
Some lucky wits impute it but to chance;
Others, because of both sides I do take
My blood from them who did excel in this,[2]
Think Nature me a man of arms did make.
How far they shot awry! The true cause is,
Stella looked on, and from her heav'nly face
Sent forth the beams, which made so fair my race.

45

Stella oft sees the very face of woe
Painted in my beclouded stormy face,
But cannot skill[3] to pity my disgrace,
Not though thereof the cause herself she know.
Yet hearing late a fable which did show
Of lovers never known a grievous case,
Pity thereof gate° in her breast such place *got*
That, from that sea derived, tears' spring did flow.
Alas, if fancy, drawn by imagined things,
Though false, yet with free scope more grace doth breed
Than servant's[4] wrack, where new doubts honor brings,
Then think, my dear, that you in me do read
Of lover's ruin some sad tragedy:
I am not I; pity the tale of me.

47

What, have I thus betrayed my liberty?
Can those black beams such burning marks[5] engrave
In my free side? or am I born a slave,
Whose neck becomes[6] such yoke of tyranny?
Or want° I sense to feel my misery? *lack*
Or sprite,° disdain of such disdain to have, *spirit*
Who for long faith, though daily help I crave,
May get no alms but scorn of beggery?
Virtue awake, beauty but beauty is;
I may, I must, I can, I will, I do
Leave following that, which it is gain to miss.
Let her go. Soft, but here she comes. "Go to,
Unkind, I love you not." Oh me, that eye
Doth make my heart give to my tongue the lie.

48

Soul's joy, bend not those morning stars from me,
Where Virtue is made strong by Beauty's might,
Where Love is chasteness, Pain doth learn delight,
And Humbleness grows one with Majesty.
Whatever may ensue, oh let me be
Copartner of the riches of that sight:
Let not mine eyes be hell-driv'n from that light:
Oh look, oh shine, oh let me die and see.
For though I oft my self of them bemoan,
That through my heart their beamy darts be gone,
Whose cureless wounds ev'n now most freshly bleed:
Yet since my death-wound is already got,
Dear killer, spare not thy sweet cruel shot:
A kind of grace it is to slay with speed.

[1] *that sweet enemy France* French emissaries sent by the Duke of Anjou to negotiate a match with Queen Elizabeth. Sidney participated in a tournament at court to honor the delegation in April, 1581.

[2] *both sides … this* Both sides of Sidney's family were distinguished in war and chivalry.

[3] *cannot skill* Is unable.

[4] *servant's* I.e., the lover's.

[5] *burning marks* Permanent scars seared into him by Stella's eyes.

[6] *becomes* Is suited to.

49

I on my horse, and Love on me doth try
Our horsemanships, while by strange work I prove
A horseman to my horse, a horse to Love;
And now man's wrongs in me, poor beast,
descry.° *discover*
The reins wherewith my rider doth me tie,
Are humbled thoughts, which bit of reverence move,
Curbed in with fear, but with gilt boss[1] above
Of hope, which makes it seem fair to the eye.
The wand° is will; thou, fancy, saddle art,[2] *crop*
Girt° fast by memory; and while I spur *fastened*
My horse, he spurs with sharp desire my heart:
He sits me fast, however I do stir:
And now hath made me to his hand so right,[3]
That in the manage[4] myself takes delight.

50

Stella, the fullness of my thoughts of thee
Cannot be stayed within my panting breast,
But they do swell and struggle forth of me,
Till that in words thy figure be expressed.
And yet as soon as they so formed be,
According to my Lord Love's own behest:
With sad eyes I their weak proportion see,
To portrait° that which in this world is best. *portray*
So that I cannot choose but write my mind,
And cannot choose but put out what I write,
While these poor babes[5] their death in birth do find:
And now my pen these lines had dashed quite,
But that they stopped his fury from the same,
Because their forefront bare sweet Stella's name.[6]

51

Pardon mine ears, both I and they do pray,° *ask earnestly*
So may your tongue still fluently proceed,
To them that do such entertainment need,
So may you still have somewhat new to say.
On silly me do not the burden lay
Of all the grave conceits[7] your brain doth breed;
But find some Hercules to bear, instead
Of Atlas tired, your wisdom's heav'nly sway.
For me, while you discourse of courtly tides,
Of cunning fishers in most troubled streams,[8]
Of straying ways, when valiant error guides:
Meanwhile my heart confers with Stella's beams,
And is even irked that so sweet comedy,[9]
By such unsuited speech should hindered be.

52

A strife is grown between Virtue and Love,
While each pretends° that Stella must be his. *declares*
Her eyes, her lips, her all, saith Love, do this
Since they do wear his badge, most firmly prove.
But Virtue thus that title doth disprove:
That Stella (oh dear name) that Stella is
That virtuous soul, sure heir of heav'nly bliss,
Not this fair outside, which our hearts doth move.
And therefore, though her beauty and her grace
Be Love's indeed, in Stella's self he may
By no pretense claim any manner° place. *kind of*
Well, Love, since this demur our suit doth stay,[10]
Let Virtue have that Stella's self; yet thus,
That Virtue but that body grant to us.

53

In martial sports I had my cunning tried,
And yet to break more staves° did me address: *lances*
While, with the people's shouts, I must confess,
Youth, luck, and praise, ev'n filled my veins with pride;
When Cupid having me his slave descried,° *discerned*
In Mars's livery, prancing in the press:[11]
"What now, Sir Fool," said he; I would no less.[12]
"Look here, I say." I look'd and Stella spied,

[1] *gilt boss* Metal knob on the bit.

[2] *thou, fancy, saddle art* You, imagination, are the saddle.

[3] *to his hand so right* Respond so sensitively to his hand.

[4] *the manage* The process of training, management.

[5] *these poor babes* The poems.

[6] *Because their ... name* Because Stella is the first word of the sonnet, it preserves the poem from destruction.

[7] *grave conceits* Serious ideas.

[8] *cunning fishers ... streams* Courtiers currying favor amid political turmoil.

[9] *sweet comedy* Pleasant reflections.

[10] *demur* Objection; *stay* Halt.

[11] *livery* Uniform; *press* Throng.

[12] *I would no less* I would like the same attention that you give Mars.

Who hard by made a window send forth light.
My heart then quaked, then dazzled were mine eyes;
One hand forgot to rule,[1] th'other to fight.
Nor trumpet's sound I heard, nor friendly cries;
My foe came on, and beat the air for me,[2]
Till that her blush taught me my shame to see.

54

Because I breathe not love to every one,
Nor do not use set colours[3] for to wear,
Nor nourish special locks of vowed hair,[4]
Nor give each speech the full point of a groan,
The courtly nymphs,[5] acquainted with the moan
Of them, who in their lips Love's
standard° bear; *distinctive flag*
"What he?" say they of me. "Now I dare swear,
He cannot love. No, no, let him alone."
And think so still, so Stella know my mind.
Profess indeed I do not Cupid's art;
But you, fair maids, at length this true shall find:
That his right° badge is worn but in the heart; *true*
Dumb swans, not chatt'ring pies,[6] do lovers prove;
They love indeed, who quake to say they love.

55

Muses, I oft invoked your holy aid,
With choicest flow'rs my speech t'engarland so
That it, despised in true but naked show,[7]
Might win some grace in your sweet skill arrayed.
And oft whole troops of saddest words I stayed,° *held back*
Striving abroad a-foraging to go,
Until by your inspiring I might know
How their black banner° might be best displayed. *sad aspect*
But now I mean no more your help to try,
Nor other sug'ring of my speech to prove,
But on her name incessantly to cry:
For let me but name her whom I do love,
So sweet sounds straight mine ear and heart do hit,
That I well find no eloquence like it.

61

Oft with true sighs, oft with uncallèd tears,
Now with slow words, now with dumb eloquence,
I Stella's eyes assail, invade her ears,
But this at last is her sweet-breathed defense:
That who indeed in-felt affection bears,
So captives to his saint both soul and sense,
That wholly hers, all selfness° he forbears; *self-centeredness*
Thence his desires he learns, his life's course thence.
Now, since her chaste mind hates this love in me,
With chastened mind I straight must show that she
Shall quickly me from what she hates remove.
O Doctor[8] Cupid, thou for me reply,
Driven else to grant, by angel's sophistry,[9]
That I love not without I leave to love.

69

O joy too high for my low style to show!
O bliss fit for a nobler state than me!
Envy, put out thine eyes, lest thou do see
What oceans of delight in me do flow.
My friend, that oft saw, through all masks, my woe,
Come, come, and let me pour myself on thee.
Gone is the winter of my misery,
My spring appears, O see what here doth grow.
For Stella hath with words where faith doth shine,
Of her high heart given me the monarchy.
I, I, O I may say that she is mine!
And though she give but thus condition'ly
This realm of bliss, while virtuous course I take,
No kings be crowned but they some covenants make.

71

Who will in fairest book of Nature know
How Virtue may best lodged in beauty be,
Let him but learn of love to read in thee,
Stella, those fair lines which true goodness show.
There shall he find all vices' overthrow,
Not by rude force, but sweetest sovereignty

[1] *to rule* To control the horse.

[2] *beat the air for me* Struck at the empty air instead of me.

[3] *set colours* The usual colors of a lover.

[4] *nourish special ... hair* Keep special locks of hair given as a pledge.

[5] *courtly nymphs* Women at court.

[6] *dumb* Silent; *pies* Magpies.

[7] *despised in ... show* Despised for being plain, though sincere.

[8] *Doctor* One who is well educated and highly knowledgeable.

[9] *sophistry* Clever but fallacious reasoning.

Of reason, from whose light those night-birds fly,
That inward sun in thine eyes shineth so.
And not content to be Perfection's heir,
Thyself, dost strive all minds that way to move,
Who mark in thee what is in thee most fair.
So while thy beauty draws thy heart to love,
As fast thy virtue bends that love to good.
"But ah," Desire still cries, "Give me some food."

94

Grief find the words, for thou hast made my brain
So dark with misty vapours, which arise
From out thy heavy mould, that inbent[1] eyes
Can scarce discern the shape of mine own pain.
Do thou then (for thou canst), do thou complain,° *lament*
For my poor soul, which now that sickness tries,[2]
Which ev'n to sense, sense of itself denies,
Though harbingers of death lodge there his train.
Or if thy love of plaint° yet mine forbears, *lamentation*
As of a caitiff[3] worthy so to die,
Yet wail thyself, and wail with causeful tears,
That though in wretchedness thy life doth lie,
Yet growest more wretched than thy nature bears,
By being placed in such a wretch as I.

95

Yet Sighs, dear Sighs, indeed true friends you are,
That do not leave your least friend at the worst,
But as you with my breast I oft have nursed,
So grateful now you wait upon my care.
Faint coward Joy no longer tarry dare,
Seeing Hope yield when this woe strake° him first: *struck*
Delight protests he is not for th'accursed,
Though oft himself my mate-in-arms he sware.[4]
Nay Sorrow comes with such main rage, that he
Kills his own children, Tears, finding that they
By love were made apt to consort with me.
Only, true Sighs, you do not go away;
Thank may you have for such a thankful part,
Thank-worthiest yet when you shall break my heart.

96

Thought, with good cause thou lik'st so well the Night,
Since kind or chance gives both one livery,[5]
Both sadly black, both blackly darkened be,
Night barred from sun, thou from thy own sunlight;
Silence in both displays his sullen might,
Slow Heaviness in both holds one degree—[6]
That full of doubts, *thou* of perplexity;
Thy tears express Night's native moisture right.[7]
In both a mazeful° solitariness: *bewildering*
In Night of sprites° the ghastly powers to stir, *spirits*
In thee, or sprites or sprited ghastliness.
But, but (alas) Night's side the odds hath, fur,°[8] *far*
For that° at length yet doth invite some rest, *night*
Thou, though still tired, yet still dost it° detest. *rest*

97

Dian,[9] that fain would cheer her friend the Night,
Shows her oft at the full her fairest face,
Bringing with her those starry nymphs, whose chase° *arrows*
From heav'nly standing hits each mortal wight.[10]
But ah, poor Night, in love with Phoebus'[11] light,
And endlessly despairing of his grace,
Herself (to show no other joy hath place)
Silent and sad in mourning weeds doth dight:[12]
Ev'n so (alas) a lady, Dian's peer,
With choice delights and rarest company
Would fain° drive clouds from out my heavy cheer. *gladly*
But woe is me, though Joy itself were she,
She could not show my blind brain ways of joy,
While I despair my[13] Sun's sight to enjoy.

---

[1] *inbent* Inward-looking.

[2] *sickness tries* Lovesickness triumphs.

[3] *caitiff* Despicable person.

[4] *sware* Swore he was.

[5] *kind* Nature; *livery* Aspect.

[6] *one degree* Similar sway.

[7] *Thy tears … right* Thought's tears reveal night's natural dampness.

[8] *fur* Far. (Spelled by Sidney this way to rhyme with "stir.")

[9] *Dian* Diana, goddess of the moon.

[10] *standing* Position; *wight* Man.

[11] *Phoebus'* The sun god's.

[12] *weeds* Clothes; *dight* Dress.

[13] *despair my* Despair of my.

98

Ah bed, the field where joy's peace some do see,
The field where all my thoughts to war be trained,° *drawn*
How is thy grace by my strange fortune stained!
How thy lee° shores by my sighs stormed be! *sheltered*
With sweet soft shades° thou oft invitest me *shadows*
To steal some rest, but wretch I am constrained
(Spurred with Love's spur, though galled and shortly
  reined[1]
With Care's hard hand) to turn and toss in thee.
While the black horrors of the silent night
Paint woe's black face so lively to my sight,
That tedious leisure marks each wrinkled line.
But when Aurora leads out Phoebus' dance,[2]
Mine eyes then only wink,° for spite perchance, *close*
That worms should have their Sun, and I want mine.

99

When far-spent night persuades each mortal eye,
To whom nor° art nor nature granteth light, *neither*
To lay his then mark-wanting° shafts of sight, *aimless*
Closed with their quivers, in sleep's armory;
With windows° ope then most my mind doth lie, *eyes*
Viewing the shape of darkness and delight,
Takes in that sad hue, which the inward night
Of his mazed powers[3] keeps perfect harmony.
But when birds charm,[4] and that sweet air which is
Morn's messenger, with rose enamel'd skies,
Calls each wight° to salute the flower of bliss: *person*
In tomb of lids then buried are mine eyes,
Forced by their lord, who is ashamed to find
Such light in sense,[5] with such a darkened mind.

100

Oh tears, no° tears, but rain from Beauty's skies, *not*
Making those lilies and those roses[6] grow,
Which aye° most fair, now more than most *always*
  fair show,
While graceful Pity Beauty beautifies.
Oh honeyed sighs, which from that breast do rise,
Whose pants do make unspilling cream to flow,
Winged with whose breath, so pleasing zephyrs blow,
As can refresh the hell where my soul fries.
Oh plaints° conserved in such a sugared phrase *complaints*
That Eloquence itself envies your praise
While sobbed-out words a perfect music give.
Such tears, sighs, plaints, no sorrow is, but joy:
Or if such heav'nly signs must prove annoy,
All mirth farewell, let me in sorrow live.

101

Stella is sick, and in that sickbed lies
Sweetness, that breathes and pants as oft as she;
And Grace, sick too, such fine conclusions[7] tries
That Sickness brags itself best graced to be.[8]
Beauty is sick, but sick in so fair guise
That is that paleness Beauty's white we see;
And Joy, which is inseparate° from those eyes, *inseparable*
Stella now learns (strange case) to weep in thee.
Love moves[9] thy pain, and like a faithful page,
As thy looks stir, runs up and down to make
All folks pressed° at thy will thy pain t'assuage. *eager*
Nature with care sweats for her darling's sake,
Knowing worlds pass, ere she enough can find
Of such heav'n stuff,° to clothe so heav'nly mind. *matter*

102

Where be those roses gone, which sweetened so our eyes?
Where those red cheeks, which oft with fair increase
  did frame
The height of honour in the kindly° badge *pleasant*
  of shame?
Who hath the crimson weeds° stol'n from my *clouds*
  morning skies?
How doth the colour fade of those vermilion° dyes *scarlet*
Which Nature's self did make, and self
  engrained° the same? *dyed fast*
I would know by what right this paleness overcame

[1] *galled* Sore, chafed; *shortly reined* Reined in tight.

[2] *Aurora* Goddess of the dawn; *Phoebus' dance* The sun's dance, daylight.

[3] *mazed powers* Bewildered thoughts.

[4] *charm* Sing in chorus.

[5] *light in sense* Light available to the senses.

[6] *those lilies and those roses* The colors of Stella's cheeks.

[7] *fine conclusions* Delicate trials.

[8] *best graced to be* In the most graced of states.

[9] *moves* Is animated by.

That hue, whose force my heart still unto thraldom ties.
Galen's adoptive sons,[1] who by a beaten way
Their judgments hackney on, the fault of sickness lay;
But feeling proof makes me say they mistake it fur:° *far*
It is but Love, which makes his paper perfect white
To write therein more fresh the story of delight,
While Beauty's reddest ink Venus for him doth stir.

103

Oh happy Thames, that didst my Stella bear,
I saw thyself with many a smiling line
Upon thy cheerful face,[2] Joy's livery° wear, *uniform*
While those fair planets[3] on thy streams did shine.
The boat for joy could not to dance forbear,
While wanton winds with beauties so divine
Ravished, stayed not, till in her golden hair
They did themselves (oh sweetest prison) twine.
And fain° those Aeol's youths[4] there would their stay *gladly*
Have made, but, forced by Nature still to fly,
First did with puffing kiss those locks display:° *blow about*
She so disheveled, blushed; from window I
With sight thereof cried out, "oh fair disgrace;
Let Honour's self to thee grant highest place."

104

Envious wits,° what hath been mine offence, *minds*
That with such poisonous care my looks you mark,
That to each word, nay, sigh of mine you hark,
As grudging me my sorrow's eloquence?
Ah, is it not enough that I am thence?[5]
Thence, so far thence, that scarcely any spark
Of comfort dare come to this dungeon dark,
Where rigorous exile locks up all my sense?
But if I by a happy window pass,
If I but stars[6] upon mine armour bear
—Sick, thirsty, glad (though but of empty glass):
Your moral notes straight my hid meaning tear
From out my ribs, and puffing prove that I
Do Stella love. Fools, who doth it deny?

105

Unhappy sight, and hath she vanished by
So near, in so good time, so free° a place? *open*
Dead glass,[7] dost thou thy object so embrace,
As what my heart still sees thou canst not spy?
I swear by her I love and lack, that I
Was not in fault, who bend thy dazzling race[8]
Only unto the heav'n of Stella's face,
Counting but dust what in the way did lie.
But cease, mine eyes; your tears do witness well
That you, guiltless thereof, your nectar missed:
Cursed be the page from whom the bad torch fell,
Cursed be the night which did your strife° resist, *objective*
Cursed be the coachman which did drive so fast,
With no worse curse than absence makes me taste.

106

Oh absent presence, Stella is not here;
False flattering Hope, that with so fair a face
Bare me in hand,[9] that in this orphan place,
Stella, I say my Stella, should appear:
What say'st thou now? Where is that dainty cheer
Thou told'st mine eyes should help their famished case?
But thou art gone, now that self-felt disgrace
Doth make me most to wish thy comfort near.
But here I do store of[10] fair ladies meet,
Who may with charm° of conversation sweet *harmony*
Make in my heavy mould new thought to grow:
Sure they prevail as much with me, as he
That bade his friend, but then new maimed, to be
Merry with him, and not think of his woe.

[1] *Galen's adoptive sons* Doctors; followers of Aelius Galenus (131?–201? CE), probably the most accomplished medical researcher of the Roman period.

[2] *many a … face* Water is conceived as having a human face elsewhere by Sidney; in the *Countess of Pembroke's Arcadia*, for example, he describes blood as filling "the wrinkles of the sea's visage."

[3] *fair planets* Stella's eyes.

[4] *Aeol's youths* Breezes; sons of Aeolus, ruler of the winds in Greek mythology.

[5] *thence* Away from where I want to be.

[6] *stars* Stella's emblems.

[7] *Dead glass* Astrophil's eyes.

[8] *dazzling race* Lantern, torch.

[9] *Bare me in hand* Deceived me.

[10] *store of* Many.

107

Stella, since thou so right a princess art
Of all the powers which life bestows on me,
That ere by them aught undertaken be[1]
They first resort unto that sovereign part;[2]
Sweet, for a while give respite to my heart,
Which pants as though it still should leap to thee,
And on my thoughts give thy lieutenancy° *authority*
To this great cause,[3] which needs both use° *experience*
    and art.
And as a queen, who from her presence sends
Whom she employs, dismiss from thee my wit,
Till it have wrought what thy own will attends.[4]
On servants' shame oft master's blame doth sit;
Oh let not fools in me thy works° reprove, *actions*
And scorning say, "See what it is to love."

108

When Sorrow (using mine own fire's might)
Melts down his lead into my boiling breast,
Through that dark furnace to my heart oppressed
There shines a joy from thee, my only light;
But soon as thought of thee breeds my delight,
And my young soul flutters to thee, his nest,
Most rude Despair, my daily unbidden guest,
Clips straight my wings, straight wraps me in his night,
And makes me then bow down my head and say,
"Ah, what doth Phoebus' gold° that wretch avail *sunlight*
Whom iron doors do keep from use of[5] day?"
So strangely (alas) thy works in me prevail,[6]
That in my woes for thee thou art my joy,
And in my joys for thee my only annoy.
—1591

[1] *ere by ... be* Before they undertake anything.

[2] *resort unto ... part* Refer to your sovereign direction.

[3] *this great cause* Perhaps the composition of the *Arcadia.*

[4] *wrought* Created; *attends* Waits for.

[5] *use of* Enjoying.

[6] *thy works ... prevail* Your actions rule me.

The Defence of Poesy

When the right virtuous Edward Wotton[7] and I were at the Emperor's Court together, we gave ourselves to learn horsemanship of John Pietro Pugliano, one that with great commendation had the place of an esquire[8] in his stable; and he, according to the fertileness of the Italian wit, did not only afford us the demonstration of his practise, but sought to enrich our minds with the contemplations therein, which he thought most precious. But with none I remember mine ears were at any time more laden, than when (either angered with slow payment, or moved with our learner-like admiration) he exercised his speech in the praise of his faculty.[9] He said soldiers were the noblest estate of mankind, and horsemen the noblest of soldiers. He said they were the masters of war and ornaments of peace, speedy goers and strong abiders, triumphers both in camps and courts. Nay, to so unbelieved a point he proceeded as that no earthly thing bred such wonder to a prince as to be a good horseman. Skill of government was but a pedanteria[10] in comparison. Then would he add certain praises by telling us what a peerless beast the horse was, the one serviceable courtier without flattery, the beast of most beauty, faithfulness, courage, and such more, that if I had not been a piece of a logician[11] before I came to him, I think he would have persuaded me to have wished myself a horse. But thus much at least with his no few words he drove into me that self-love is better than any gilding to make that seem gorgeous wherein ourselves be parties. Wherein, if Pugliano's strong affection and weak arguments will not satisfy you, I will give you a nearer example of myself, who (I know not by what mischance) in these my not old years and idlest times having slipped into the title of a poet, am provoked to say something unto you in the defence of that my un-elected vocation, which if I handle with more good will than good reasons, bear with me,

[7] *Edward Wotton* Statesman and courtier with whom Sidney developed a friendship while they were both serving as diplomats at the court of Holy Roman Emperor Maxmillian II in Vienna.

[8] *esquire* Equerry, manager of a nobleman's stable and horses.

[9] *faculty* Area of expertise or learning; ability.

[10] *pedanteria* Pedantry.

[11] *if ... logician* I.e., if I had not been somewhat proficient in logic.

since the scholar is to be pardoned that followeth the steps of his master. And yet I must say that, as I have more just cause to make a pitiful defence of poor poetry, which from almost the highest estimation of learning is fallen to be the laughingstock of children, so have I need to bring some more available proofs: since the former is by no man barred of his deserved credit, the silly latter hath had even the names of philosophers used to the defacing of it, with great danger of civil war among the Muses.

And first, truly, to all them that, professing learning, inveigh against poetry, may justly be objected that they go very near to ungratefulness, to seek to deface that which, in the noblest nations and languages that are known, hath been the first light-giver to ignorance, and first nurse, whose milk little & little enabled them to feed afterwards of tougher knowledges. And will you play the hedgehog, that, being received into the den, drive out his host? Or rather the vipers, that with their birth kill their parents?

Let learned Greece in any of his manifold sciences be able to show me one book before Musaeus, Homer, & Hesiod,[1] all three nothing else but poets. Nay, let any history be brought that can say any writers were there before them, if they were not men of the same skill, as Orpheus, Linus,[2] and some other are named, who, having been the first of that country that made pens deliverers of their knowledge to the posterity, may justly challenge to be called their fathers in learning. For not only in time they had this priority (although in itself antiquity be venerable), but went before them as causes to draw with their charming sweetness the wild untamed wits to an admiration of knowledge. So, as Amphion[3] was said to move stones with his poetry to build Thebes, and Orpheus to be listened to by beasts—indeed stony and beastly people—so among the Romans were Livius Andronicus, and Ennius.[4] So in the Italian language the first that made it aspire to be a treasure-house of science, were the poets Dante, Bocaccio, and Petrarch.[5] So in our English were Gower[6] and Chaucer, after whom, encouraged & delighted with their excellent fore-going, others have followed to beautify our mother tongue as well in the same kind as other arts.

This did so notably show itself that the Philosophers of Greece durst not a long time appear to the world but under the mask of poets. So Thales, Empedocles, and Parmenides[7] sang their natural philosophy in verses; so did Pythagoras and Phocylides[8] their moral counsels; so did Tyrtaeus in war matters, and Solon[9] in matters of policy: or rather they, being poets, did exercise their delightful vein in those points of highest knowledge, which before them lay hidden to the world. For that wise Solon was directly a poet, it is manifest, having written in verse the notable fable of the Atlantic Island, which was continued by Plato.[10] And truly even Plato

[1] *Musaeus* Fifth-century BCE Greek priest and poet who was said to have been either the son or student of Orpheus; *Homer* Eighth-century BCE Greek poet credited with authoring the epic poems *The Iliad* and *The Odyssey*; *Hesiod* Greek poet known for *Works and Days* and *The Theogony* (eighth century BCE).

[2] *Orpheus* In Greek mythology, poet whose songs possessed the uncanny ability to charm; *Linus* Mythical poet and musician, said to be Orpheus's teacher.

[3] *Amphion* Son of Zeus whose magical lyre could move stones. The walls of Thebes were said to have built themselves by the music of his lyre.

[4] *Livius Andronicus* Roman playwright (third century BCE) who composed the first tragedy and the first comedy in Latin; *Ennius* Highly influential Latin poet (239–169 BCE) known as the father of Latin poetry.

[5] *Dante* Dante Alighieri, an Italian poet (1265–1321) best known for the poem *The Divine Comedy*; *Bocaccio* Giovanni Bocaccio (1313–75), an Italian author and poet known for his collection of tales *The Decameron*; *Petrarch* Francesco Petrarch, Italian author (1304– 74) best known for his sonnets, which were a source of influence for many poets of the early modern period, including Sidney, Henry Howard, Thomas Wyatt, and Edmund Spenser.

[6] *Gower* John Gower, English author and poet (1330–1408).

[7] *Thales* Greek geometrician, scientist, and philosopher of the sixth century BCE; *Empedocles* Greek philosopher of the fifth century BCE; *Parmenides* Greek philosopher (c. fifth century BCE) who appears as a character in one of Plato's dialogues.

[8] *Pythagoras* Greek mathematician (c. fifth century BCE) influential in the development of mathematics; *Phocylides* Greek moralist of the sixth century BCE.

[9] *Tyrtaeus* Poet whose surviving elegiac verses extol the military virtues of the Spartans (c. seventh century BCE.); *Solon* Athenian statesman of the sixth century BCE who was believed to have written an epic (now lost) about Atlantis.

[10] *fable … Plato* Plato wrote two dialogues which refer to the lost civilization of Atlantis.

whosoever well considereth shall find that in the body of his work, though the inside & strength were philosophy, the skin, as it were, and beauty depended most of[1] poetry; for all standeth upon dialogues, wherein he feigneth many honest burgesses of Athens speak of such matters, that, if they had been set on the rack, they would never have confessed them, besides his poetical describing the circumstances of their meetings, as the well ordering of a banquet, the delicacy of a walk, with interlacing mere tales, as Gyges' ring and others,[2] which who knoweth not to be flowers of poetry did never walk into Apollo's Garden.[3]

And even historiographers (although their lips sound of things done, and verity be written in their foreheads) have been glad to borrow both fashion and, perchance, weight of the poets. So Herodotus entitled his History by the name of the nine Muses;[4] and both he and all the rest that followed him either stole or usurped of poetry their passionate describing of passions, the many particularities of battles which no man could affirm, or, if that be denied me, long orations put in the mouths of great kings and captains, which it is certain they never pronounced.

So that truly neither philosopher nor historiographer could at the first have entered into the gates of popular judgments if they had not taken a great passport of poetry, which in all nations at this day where learning flourisheth not, is plain to be seen; in all which they have some feeling of poetry.

In Turkey, besides their lawgiving divines, they have no other writers but poets. In our neighbour country Ireland, where truly learning goes very bare, yet are their poets held in a devout reverence. Even among the most barbarous and simple Indians where no writing is, yet they have their poets who make & sing songs, which they call *areytos*,[5] both of their ancestor's deeds and praises of their gods—a sufficient probability that, if ever learning come among them, it must be by having their hard dull wits softened and sharpened with the sweet delights of poetry, for until they find a pleasure in the exercise of the mind, great promises of much knowledge will little persuade them that know not the fruits of knowledge. In Wales, the true remnant of the ancient Britons, as there are good authorities to show the long time they had poets, which they called bards, so through all the conquests of Romans, Saxons, Danes, and Normans, some of whom did seek to ruin all memory of learning from among them, yet do their poets even to this day last; so as it is not more notable in the soon beginning, than in long continuing.

But since the authors of most of our sciences[6] were the Romans, and before them the Greeks, let us a little stand upon their authorities, but even so far as to see what names they have given unto this now scorned skill.

Among the Romans a poet was called *vates*, which is as much as a diviner, foreseer, or prophet, as by his conjoined words *vaticinium* and *vaticinari*[7] is manifest: so heavenly a title did that excellent people bestow upon this heart-ravishing knowledge. And so far were they carried into the admiration thereof that they thought in the chanceable hitting upon any of such verses great foretokens of their following fortunes were placed. Whereupon grew the word of *Sortes Vergilianae*,[8] when by sudden opening Virgil's book they lighted upon some verse of his, as it is reported by many, whereof the histories of the emperors' lives are full: as of Albinus, the governor of our island, who in his childhood met with this verse

Arma amens capio, nec sat rationis in armis[9]

[1] *of* On.

[2] *well ... banquet* *The Symposium* is set during a banquet; *delicacy ... walk* In *The Phaedrus* the two speakers discuss their ideas while taking a walk; *Gyges' ring* In Plato's *Republic*, a shepherd uses a magic ring to make himself invisible for self-gain.

[3] *which who ... garden* I.e., whoever does not recognize these works as the flowers of poetry must know nothing of poetry (Apollo was the classical god of poetry).

[4] *Muses* Greek goddesses who presided over learning and the arts.

[5] *areytos* Song-dance performances of the Taino people that recounted past histories and legends.

[6] *sciences* Branches of knowledge; fields of study.

[7] *vaticinium* Latin: prophecy; *vaticinari* Latin: to predict.

[8] *Sortes Virgilianae* Practice of opening at random one of the works of the Latin poet Virgil and using the text as a means of divination.

[9] *Arma ... armis* Latin: "Frantically I seized my arms, though there is little reason in arms." (*Aeneid* 2.314).

and in his age performed it. Although it were a very vain and godless superstition, as also it was to think spirits were commanded by such verses—whereupon this word "charms," derived of *carmina*,[1] cometh—so yet serves it to show the great reverence those wits were held in; and altogether not without ground, since both by the oracles of Delphos and Sybilla's prophesies[2] were wholly delivered in verses. For that same exquisite observing of number and measure in the words, and that high flying liberty of conceit[3] proper to the poet, did seem to have some divine force in it.

And may not I presume a little farther, to show the reasonableness of this word *vates*, and say that the holy David's Psalms[4] are a divine poem? If I do, I shall not do it without the testimony of great learned men, both ancient and modern. But even the name of Psalms will speak for me, which being interpreted, is nothing but songs; then that it is fully written in meter, as all learned Hebraists agree, although the rules be not yet fully found.[5] Lastly and principally, his handling his prophecy, which is merely[6] poetical: for what else is the awaking his musical instruments, the often and free changing of persons, his notable *prosopopeias*,[7] when he makes you as it were see God coming in His majesty, his telling of the beasts' joyfulness and hills leaping, but a heavenly poesy, wherein almost he shows himself a passionate lover of that unspeakable and everlasting beauty to be seen by the eyes of the mind, only cleared by faith? But truly now having named him, I fear I seem to profane that holy name, applying it to poetry, which is among us thrown down to so ridiculous an estimation. But they that with quiet judgments will look a little deeper into it, shall find the end & working of it such as, being rightly applied, deserves not to be scourged out of the Church of God.

But now let us see how the Greeks have named it, and how they have deemed of it. The Greeks named him ποιητήν,[8] which name hath, as the most excellent, gone through other languages. It cometh of this word ποιεῖν, which is "to make": wherein, I know not whether by luck or wisdom, we Englishmen have met with the Greeks in calling him a maker, which name, how high and incomparable a title it is, I had rather were known by marking the scope of other sciences than by any partial allegation.

There is no art delivered unto mankind that hath not the works of nature for his principal object, without which they could not consist, and on which they so depend, as they become actors & players, as it were of what nature will have set forth. So doth the astronomer look upon the stars, and, by that he sees, set down what order nature hath taken therein. So doth the geometrician & arithmetician in their diverse sorts of quantities. So doth the musicians in time tell you which by nature agree, which not. The natural philosopher thereon hath his name, and the moral philosopher standeth upon the natural virtues, vices, or passions of man; and follow nature (saith he) therein, and thou shalt not err. The lawyer saith what men have determined; the historian, what men have done. The grammarian speaketh only of the rules of speech; and the rhetorician and logician, considering what in nature will soonest prove and persuade, thereon give artificial rules, which still are compassed within the circle of a question according to the proposed matter. The physician weigheth the nature of man's body, & the nature of things helpful or hurtful unto it. And the metaphysic, though it be in the second & abstract notions, and therefore be counted supernatural, yet doth he indeed build upon the depth of nature. Only the poet, disdaining to be tied to any such subjection, lifted up with the vigour of his own invention, doth grow in effect into another nature, in making things either better than nature bringeth forth, or, quite anew, forms such as never were in nature, as the Heroes,

1 *carmina* Latin: songs.

2 *oracles of Delphos* Greek oracle of the god Apollo; *Sybilla* Female prophet of the oracle.

3 *conceit* Conception; signification.

4 *David's Psalms* Book of Psalms, thought to be written by the biblical King David of Israel.

5 *then that ... found* Many Renaissance scholars believed that the psalms were written in verse forms that closely resembled classical Greek and Latin meters.

6 *merely* Solely.

7 *prosopopoeias* Greek: personifications.

8 ποιητήν Greek: poet.

Demigods, Cyclops, Chimeras, Furies,[1] and such like: so as he goes hand in hand with nature, not enclosed within the narrow warrant of her gifts, but freely ranging within the zodiac of his own wit. Nature never set forth the earth in so rich tapestry as diverse poets have done: neither with so pleasant rivers, fruitful trees, sweet-smelling flowers, nor whatsoever else may make the too much loved earth more lovely. Her world is brazen, the poets only deliver a golden.

But let those things alone and go to man—for whom as the other things are, so it seemeth in him her uttermost cunning is employed—& know whether she have brought forth so true a lover as Theagenes, so constant a friend as Pylades, so valiant a man as Orlando, so right a prince as Xenophon's Cyrus, so excellent a man every way as Virgil's Aeneas.[2] Neither let this be jestingly conceived, because the works of the one be essential, the other in imitation or fiction: for every understanding knoweth the skill of each artificer standeth in that *idea* or fore-conceit[3] of the work, and not in the work itself. And that the poet hath that *idea* is manifest by delivering them forth in such excellency as he had imagined them. Which delivering forth also is not wholly imaginative, as we are wont to say by them that build castles in the air, but so far substantially it worketh, not only to make a Cyrus, which had been but a particular excellency as nature might have done, but to bestow a Cyrus upon the world to make many Cyruses, if they will learn aright why and how that maker made him.

Neither let it be deemed too saucy a comparison to balance the highest point of man's wit with the efficacy of nature; but rather give right honor to the heavenly maker of that maker, who, having made man to his own likeness, set him beyond and over all the works of that second nature: which in nothing he showeth so much as in poetry, when with the force of a divine breath he bringeth things forth surpassing her doings—with no small arguments to the incredulous of that first accursed fall of Adam, since our erected wit maketh us know what perfection is, and yet our infected will keepeth us from reaching unto it. But these arguments will by few be understood, and by fewer granted. This much I hope will be given me, that the Greeks with some probability of reason gave him the name above all names of learning.

Now let us go to a more ordinary opening[4] of him, that the truth may be the more palpable: and so I hope, though we get not so unmatched a praise as the etymology of his names will grant, yet his very description, which no man will deny, shall not justly be barred from a principal commendation.

Poesy therefore is an art of imitation: for so Aristotle termeth it in the word μιμησις,[5] that is to say, a representing, counterfeiting, or figuring forth—to speak metaphorically, a speaking picture—with this end, to teach and delight.

Of this there have been three general kinds. The chief, both in antiquity and excellency, were they that did imitate the unconceivable excellencies of God. Such were David in his Psalms; Solomon in his Song of Songs, in his Ecclesiastes and Proverbs; Moses and Deborah in their Hymns; and the writer of Job: which, beside other, the learned Immanuel Tremellius and Franciscus Junius[6] do entitle the poetical part of the Scripture. Against these none will speak that hath the Holy Ghost in due holy reverence. (In this kind, though in a full wrong divinity, were Orpheus, Amphion, Homer in his hymns, and many other, both Greeks and Romans.) And this poesy must be used by whosoever will follow St. James's counsel in singing psalms when

[1] *Cyclops* Mythical race of giants, each of whom has only one eye; *Chimeras* Mythological fire-breathing monsters, part goat, part lion, and part serpent; *Furies* Three avenging winged goddesses.

[2] *Theagenes* Hero in Heliodorus's prose romance *Theagenes and Chariclea*; *Pylades* Character in Aeschylus's play *Oresteia* who helped his friend Orestes avenge his father Agamemnon's death; *Orlando* Character of exemplary valor and heroism in *Orlando Furioso*, Ariosto's epic romance; *Xenophon's Cyrus* In his *Cyropaedia*, the Greek historian Xenophon recounts the education of Cyrus the Great, first Achaemenian Emperor of Persia; *Aeneas* Hero who led his fellow Trojans to Italy; protagonist of Virgil's epic *The Aeneid*.

[3] *fore-conceit* Plan.

[4] *opening* Examination.

[5] μιμησις Greek: mimesis, the concept of poetry as primarily imitative. (See Aristotle's *Poetics* 1.2.)

[6] *Immanuel … Junius* Two theologians who produced a Latin translation of the Hebrew and Greek Bible first published in 1575.

they are merry,[1] and I know is used with the fruit of comfort by some, when, in sorrowful pangs of their death-bringing sins, they find the consolation of the never-leaving goodness.

The second kind is of them that deal with matters philosophical; either moral, as Tyrteus, Phocylides, Cato; or natural, as Lucretius and Virgil's Georgics; or astronomical, as Manilius and Pontanus; or historical, as Lucan:[2] which who mislike, the fault is in their judgment quite out of taste, & not in the sweet food of sweetly uttered knowledge.

But because this second sort is wrapped within the fold of the proposed subject, and takes not the free course of his own invention, whether they properly be poets or no let grammarians dispute, and go to the third, indeed right poets, of whom chiefly this question ariseth: betwixt whom and these second is such a kind of difference as betwixt the meaner sort of painters, who counterfeit only such faces as are set before them, and the more excellent, who, having no law but wit, bestow that in colours upon you which is fittest for the eye to see: as the constant, though lamenting look of Lucretia[3] when she punished in herself another's fault, wherein he painteth not Lucretia whom he never saw, but painteth the outward beauty of such a virtue. For these third be they which most properly do imitate to teach & delight, and to imitate borrow nothing of what is, hath been, or shall be; but range, only reined with learned discretion, into the divine consideration of what may be and should be. These be they that, as the first and most noble sort may justly be termed *vates*, so these are waited on in the excellentest languages and best understandings with the fore-described name of poets. For these indeed do merely make to imitate; and imitate both to delight & teach; and delight, to move men to take that goodness in hand, which without delight they would fly as from a stranger; and teach, to make them know that goodness whereunto they are moved—which being the noblest scope to which ever any learning was directed, yet want there not idle tongues to bark at them.

These be subdivided into sundry more special denominations. The most notable be the heroic, lyric, tragic, comic, satiric, iambic, elegiac, pastoral, and certain others, some of these being termed according to the matter they deal with, some by the sort of verse they liked best to write in; for indeed the greatest part of poets have apparelled their poetical inventions in that numbrous kind of writing which is called verse—indeed but apparelled, verse being but an ornament and no cause to poetry, since there have been many most excellent poets that never versified, and now swarm many versifiers that need never answer to the name of poets. For Xenophon, who did imitate so excellently as to give us *effigiem iusti imperii*, the portraiture of a just empire, under the name of Cyrus (as Cicero saith of him), made therein an absolute heroical poem. So did Heliodorus in his sugared invention of that picture of love in Theagenes & Chariclea;[4] and yet both these wrote in prose, which I speak to show that it is not rhyming and versing that makes a poet (no more than a long gown makes an advocate,[5] who, though he pleaded in armour, should be an advocate and no soldier). But it is that feigning notable images of virtues, vices, or what else, with that delightful teaching, which must be the right describing note to know a poet by. Although indeed the senate of poets hath chosen verse as their fittest raiment, meaning, as in matter they passed all in all, so in manner to go beyond them: not speaking (table-talk fashion or like men in a dream) words as they chanceably fall from the mouth, but peising[6] each syllable of each word by just proportion, according to the dignity of the subject.

[1] *whosoever … merry* "Is any among you afflicted? Let him pray. Is any merry? Let him sing psalms" (James 5.13).

[2] *Cato* Dionysus Cato (234–149 BCE), author of *The Distichs*, a collection of proverbial wisdom used in moral education; *Lucretius* First-century BCE Epicurean poet, author of *De Rerum Natura* (*On the Nature of Things*); *Georgics* Virgil's instructive poems on farming; *Manilius* First-century CE Stoic, author of the *Astronomica*, an astrological poem; *Pontanus* Fifteenth-century Italian humanist Giovanni Pontano, author of an astrological poem entitled *Urania*; *Lucan* Roman poet of the first century CE who never finished his epic *Pharsalia*, on Rome's civil wars.

[3] *Lucretia* Beautiful wife of Tarquinius Collatinus, a Roman noble, whose suicide after she was raped by Sextus Tarquinius, a Roman prince, led to political revolt and the creation of the Roman Republic.

[4] *Theagenes & Chariclea* Lovers in *The Aethiopica* by Heliodorus.

[5] *advocate* Lawyer.

[6] *peising* Weighing.

Now, therefore, it shall not be amiss first to weigh this latter sort of poetry by his works, and then by his parts; and if in neither of these anatomies he be condemnable, I hope we shall obtain a more favorable sentence.

This purifying of wit—this enriching of memory, enabling of judgment, and enlarging of conceit—which commonly we call learning, under what name soever it come forth, or to what immediate end soever it be directed, the final end is to lead and draw us to as high a perfection as our degenerate souls, made worse by their clayey lodgings, can be capable of.

This, according to the inclination of man, bred many-formed impressions. For some, that thought this felicity principally to be gotten by knowledge, and no knowledge to be so high or heavenly as acquaintance with the stars, gave themselves to astronomy. Others, persuading themselves to be demigods if they knew the causes of things, became natural and supernatural philosophers. Some an admirable delight drew to music, and some the certainty of demonstration to the mathematics. But all, one and other, having scope to know, & by knowledge to lift up the mind from the dungeon of the body to the enjoying his own divine essence.

But when by the balance of experience it was found that the astronomer, looking to the stars, might fall in a ditch, that the inquiring philosopher might be blind in himself, & the mathematician might draw forth a straight line with a crooked heart, then lo, did proof, the overruler of opinions, make manifest that all these are but serving sciences, which, as they have each a private end in themselves, so yet are they all directed to the highest end of the mistress-knowledge, by the Greeks called ἀρχίτεκτονικη,[1] which stands, as I think, in the knowledge of a man's self, in the ethic and politic consideration, with the end of well-doing and not of well-knowing only—even as the saddler's next end is to make a good saddle, but his further end to serve a nobler faculty, which is horsemanship, so the horseman's to soldiery, and the soldier not only to have the skill, but to perform the practise of a soldier. So that, the ending end of all earthly learning being virtuous action, those skills that most serve to bring forth that have a most just title to be princes over all the rest.

Wherein, if we can, show we the poet is worthy to have it before any other competitors, among whom principally to challenge it step forth the moral philosophers, whom me thinketh I see coming towards me with a sullen gravity, as though they could not abide vice by daylight, rudely clothed for to witness outwardly their contempt of outward things, with books in their hands against glory, whereto they set their names, sophistically speaking against subtlety, and angry with any man in whom they see the foul fault of anger. These men casting largess as they go, of definitions, divisions, and distinctions, with a scornful interrogative do soberly ask whether it be possible to find any path so ready to lead a man to virtue as that which teacheth what virtue is, & teacheth it not only by delivering forth his very being, his causes and effects, but also by making known his enemy, vice, which must be destroyed, and his cumbersome servant, passion, which must be mastered; by showing the generalities that containeth it and the specialties that are derived from it; lastly, by plain setting down how it extendeth itself out of the limits of a man's own little world to the government of families and maintaining of public societies.

The historian scarcely gives leisure to the moralist to say so much, but that he, laden with old mouse-eaten records, authorizing himself for the most part upon other histories, whose greatest authorities are built upon the notable foundation hearsay, having much ado to accord differing writers & to pick truth out of partiality; better acquainted with a thousand years ago than with the present age, and yet better knowing how this world goeth than how his own wit runneth; curious for antiquities and inquisitive of novelties; a wonder to young folks and a tyrant in table talk, denieth, in a great chafe,[2] that any man for teaching of virtue, and virtuous actions, is comparable to him. "I am *testis temporum, lux veritatis, vita memoriae, magistra vitae, nuncia vetustatis.*[3] The philosopher," saith he, "teacheth a disputative virtue, but I do an active. His virtue is excellent in the dangerless Academy of Plato, but mine showeth forth

[1] ἀρχίτεκτονικη Greek: architectonics (the science of architecture, or more broadly, of structure) is perhaps the closest modern equivalent to this Greek word.

[2] *chafe* Temper, passion.

[3] *testis … vetustatis* Latin: "The witness of time, the light of truth, the life of memory, the instructor of life, the herald of old age" (Cicero, *De Oratore*, 2.9.36).

her honorable face in the battles of Marathon, Pharsalia, Poitiers, and Agincourt.[1] He teacheth virtue by certain abstract considerations, but I only follow the footing of them that have gone before you. Old-aged experience goeth beyond the fine-witted philosopher, but I give the experience of many ages. Lastly, if he make the songbook, I put the learner's hand to the lute; and if he be the guide, I am the light." Then he would allege you innumerable examples, confirming story by stories, how much the wisest senators and princes have been directed by the credit of history, as Brutus, Alphonsus of Aragon,[2] and who not, if need be. At length the long line of their disputation maketh a point in this, that the one giveth the precept, & the other the example.

Now whom shall we find (since the question stands for the highest form in the school of learning) to be moderator? Truly as me seemeth, the poet; and if not a moderator, even the man that ought to carry the title from them both, & much more from all the other serving sciences. Therefore compare we the poet with the historian & with the moral philosopher; and if he go beyond them both, no other human skill can match him. For as for the divine, with all reverence it is ever to be excepted, not only for having his scope as far beyond any of these as eternity exceeds a moment, but even for passing each of these in themselves. And for the lawyer, though *Ius*[3] be the daughter of Justice, the chief of virtues, yet because he seeketh to make men good rather *formidine poenae* than *virtutis amore*;[4] or, to say righter, doth not endeavour to make men good, but that their evil hurt not others; having no care so he be a good citizen, how bad a man he might be. Therefore, as our wickedness maketh him necessary, and necessity maketh him honorable, so he is not in the deepest truth to stand in rank with these who all endeavour to take naughtiness away and plant goodness even in the secretest cabinet of our souls. And these four are all that any way deal in the consideration of men's manners, which being the supreme knowledge, they that best breed it deserve the best commendation.

The philosopher, therefore, and the historian are they which would win the goal, the one by precept, the other by example. But both, not having both, do both halt.[5] For the philosopher, setting down with thorny arguments the bare rule, is so hard of utterance and so misty to be conceived, that one that hath no other guide but him shall wade in him till he be old before he shall find sufficient cause to be honest. For his knowledge standeth so upon the abstract and general that happy is that man who may understand him, and more happy that can apply what he doth understand. On the other side, the historian, wanting the precept, is so tied, not to what should be but to what is, to the particular truth of things and not to the general reason of things, that his example draweth no necessary consequence, and therefore a less fruitful doctrine.

Now doth the peerless poet perform both: for whatsoever the philosopher says should be done, he gives a perfect picture of it by someone by whom he presupposes it was done, so as he coupleth the general notion with the particular example. A perfect picture I say, for he yieldeth to the powers of the mind an image of that whereof the philosopher bestoweth but a wordish description, which doth neither strike, pierce, nor possess the sight of the soul so much as that other doth. For as in outward things, to a man that had never seen an elephant or a rhinoceros, who should tell him most exquisitely all their shape, colour, bigness, and particular marks, or of a gorgeous palace an architect, who, declaring the full beauties, might well make the hearer able to repeat, as it were by rote, all he had heard, yet should never satisfy his inward conceit with being witness to itself of a true lively knowledge; but the same man, as

[1] *Marathon* Site of the Greeks' victory over the Persians in 490 BCE; *Pharsalia* Site of Pompey's loss to Caesar in 48 BCE; *Poitiers* Site of the French defeat by Edward, England's Black Prince, in 1356; *Agincourt* Battlefield on which the French were again defeated by the English in 1415.

[2] *Brutus* Roman politician who conspired to assassinate Caesar, and was inspired to do so by the history of his ancestor, Junius Brutus, who defeated the Tarquin kings; *Alphonsus of Aragon* King of Aragon who carried the histories of Livy and Caesar with him into battle and who, according to Jacques Amyot, recovered from a severe illness upon being read aloud the deeds of Alexander the Great.

[3] *Ius* Latin: right.

[4] *formidine ... amore* Latin: "By fear of punishment" than "by love of virtue" (Horace, *Epistles,* 1.6.52–53).

[5] *halt* Limp; proceed unsteadily or imperfectly.

soon as he might see those beasts well painted, or that house well in model, should straightaways grow without need of any description, to a judicial comprehending of them: so no doubt the philosopher with his learned definitions—be it of virtues or vices, matters of public policy or private government—replenisheth the memory with many infallible grounds of wisdom, which, notwithstanding, lie dark before the imaginative and judging power, if they be not illuminated or figured forth by the speaking picture of poesy.

Tully[1] taketh much pains, and many times not without poetical helps, to make us know the force love of our country hath in us. Let us but hear old Anchises speaking in the midst of Troy's flames, or see Ulysses in the fullness of all Calypso's delights bewail his absence from barren and beggarly Ithaca.[2] Anger, the Stoics said, was a short madness: let but Sophocles bring you Ajax on a stage, killing or whipping sheep and oxen, thinking them the army of Greeks with their chieftains Agamemnon and Menelaus,[3] and tell me if you have not a more familiar insight into anger than finding in the schoolmen his genus and difference.[4] See whether wisdom and temperance in Ulysses and Diomedes, valour in Achilles, friendship in Nisus and Euryalus,[5] even to an ignorant man carry not an apparent shining; and, contrarily, the remorse of conscience in Oedipus; the soon repenting pride in Agamemnon; the self-devouring cruelty in his father Atreus; the violence of ambition in the two Theban brothers; the sour sweetness of revenge in Medea; and, to fall lower, the Terentian Gnatho and our Chaucer's Pandar[6] so expressed that we now use their names to signify their trades: and finally, all virtues, vices, and passions so in their own natural states laid to the view that we seem not to hear of them, but clearly to see through them.

But even in the most excellent determination of goodness, what philosopher's counsel can so readily direct a prince, as the feigned Cyrus in Xenophon; or a virtuous man in all fortunes, as Aeneas in Virgil; or a whole commonwealth, as the way of Sir Thomas More's *Utopia*? I say the way, because where Sir Thomas More erred, it was the fault of the man and not of the poet, for that way of patterning a commonwealth was most absolute, though he perchance hath not so absolutely performed it. For the question is, whether the fashioned image of poetry or the regular instruction of philosophy hath the more force in teaching: wherein if the philosophers have more rightly showed themselves philosophers than the poets have attained to the high top of their profession, as in truth

> *Mediocribus esse poetis non Dii, non homines,*
> *non concessere columnae,*[7]

it is, I say again, not the fault of the art, but that by few men that art can be accomplished.

Certainly, even our Saviour Christ could as well have given the moral commonplaces of uncharitableness and humbleness as the divine narration of Dives and Lazarus; or of disobedience and mercy, as the heavenly discourse of the lost child and the gracious father;[8] but that his thorough-searching wisdom knew the estate of

[1] *Tully* First-century BCE Roman rhetorician Marcus Tullius Cicero.

[2] *Anchises … flames* In *The Aeneid* 2.634–49; *Ulysses … Ithaca* *Odyssey* 5.149–59.

[3] *Sophocles … Menelaus* In *Ajax* by Sophocles.

[4] *difference* Attribute that distinguishes one species from others in the same genus.

[5] *Diomedes* Achaean warrior, see *Iliad* 5.114; *Achilles* Primary Greek hero of Homer's *Iliad*; *Nisus and Euryalus* Two Trojan warriors and fast friends who die together in battle (*Aeneid* 9.443–45).

[6] *Agamemnon* Greek king whose pride causes the dispute with Achilles that results in Achilles's temporary withdrawal from battle; *Atreus* King of Mycenae who, after being challenged for the throne by his brother, Thyestes, got revenge by banishing Thyestes and gruesomely murdering his sons; *Theban brothers* Polynices and Eteocles, the children of Oedipus and his mother Jocasta. The brothers agreed to rule their father's kingdom jointly, but neither respected their agreement; *Terentian Gnatho* Fawning, obsequious character in *The Eunuch*, a comedy by the Roman playwright Terence; *Pandar* Machinating character who serves as go-between for the lovers in Chaucer's *Troilus and Criseyde*.

[7] *Mediocribus … columnae* Latin: "Neither gods nor men nor booksellers allow poets to be ordinary" (Horace, *Ars Poetica* 372–73).

[8] *Dives and Lazarus* See Luke 16.20–31. Dives is a rich man condemned to hell after refusing to help the beggar Lazarus; *lost … father* See Luke 15.11–32, in which the Prodigal Son is welcomed home by his father.

Dives burning in hell, and of Lazarus in Abraham's bosom, would more constantly, as it were, inhabit both the memory and judgment. Truly, for myself, meseems I see before mine eyes the lost child's disdainful prodigality, turned to envy a swine's dinner: which by the learned divines are thought not to be historical acts, but instructing parables.

For conclusion, I say the philosopher teacheth, but he teacheth obscurely, so as the learned only can understand him; that is to say, he teacheth them that are already taught. But the poet is the food for the tenderest stomachs; the poet is indeed the right popular philosopher, whereof Aesop's tales give good proof, whose pretty allegories, stealing under the formal tales of beasts, makes many, more beastly than beasts, begin to hear the sound of virtue from those dumb speakers.

But now it may be alleged that if this imagining of matters be so fit for the imagination, then must the historian needs surpass, who bringeth you images of true matters, such as indeed were done, and not such as fantastically or falsely may be suggested to have been done. Truly Aristotle himself, in his discourse of poesy, plainly determines this question, saying that poetry is φιλοσοφωτερων and σπουδαιοτερον that is to say, it is more philosophical and more studiously serious than history. His reason is, because poesy dealeth with καθόλου;[1] that is to say, with the universal consideration, and the history with καθ' ἑκαστον,[2] the particular. Now, saith he, the universal ways what is fit to be said or done, either in likelihood or necessity (which the poesy considers in his imposed names), and the particular only marketh whether Alcibiades[3] did, or suffered, this or that. Thus far Aristotle: which reason of his (as all his) is most full of reason. For indeed, if the question were whether it were better to have a particular act truly or falsely set down, there is no doubt which is to be chosen, no more than whether you had rather have Vespasian's[4] picture right as he was, or, at the painter's pleasure, nothing resembling. But if the question be for your own use and learning, whether it be better to have it set down as it should be, or as it was, then certainly is more doctrinable the feigned Cyrus in Xenophon than the true Cyrus in Justin, and the feigned Aeneas in Virgil than the right Aeneas in Dares Phrygius:[5] as to a lady that desired to fashion her countenance to the best grace, a painter should more benefit her to portrait a most sweet face, writing Canidia upon it, than to paint Canidia as she was, who, Horace sweareth, was full ill-favored.[6]

If the poet do his part aright, he will show you in Tantalus,[7] Atreus, and such like, nothing that is not to be shunned; in Cyrus, Aeneas, Ulysses, each thing to be followed; where the historian, bound to tell things as things were, cannot be liberal (without he will be poetical) of a perfect pattern, but, as in Alexander or Scipio himself, show doings, some to be liked, some to be misliked. And then how will you discern what to follow but by your own discretion, which you had without reading Quintus Curtius.[8] And whereas a man may say, though in universal consideration of doctrine the poet prevaileth, yet that the history, in his saying such a thing was done, doth warrant a man more in that he shall follow—the answer is manifest: that, if he stand upon that was (as if he should argue, because it rained yesterday, therefore it should rain today), then indeed hath it some advantage to a gross conceit. But if he know an example only informs a conjectured likelihood, and so go by reason, the poet doth so far exceed him as he is to frame his example to that which is most

[1] καθόλου Greek: universal, Catholic (in the sense of universal or worldwide).

[2] καθ'ἑκαστον Greek: detailed, or particular account or list.

[3] *Alcibiades* Greek statesman and friend of Achilles. (See *Poetics* 9.145.)

[4] *Vespasian* First-century CE Roman emperor, reported to have been very ugly.

[5] *Justin* Marcus Justinus, whose c. second-century BCE *Histories* provide an account of Cyrus' actions; *Dares Phrygius* Supposed author of an account of the Trojan War, probably in fact written after the second century CE.

[6] *Horace ... ill-favored* Cf. *Epodes* 5, in which Horace attacks the Roman prostitute Canidia; she had apparently rejected him.

[7] *Tantalus* When invited to dine with the gods, Tantalus served them pieces of his own murdered son, Pelops.

[8] *Quintus Curtius* Roman historian who wrote a multi-volume biography of Alexander the Great.

reasonable (be it in warlike, politic, or private matters), where the historian in his bare *was* hath many times that which we call fortune to overrule the best wisdom. Many times he must tell events whereof he can yield no cause; or, if he do, it must be poetically.

For that a feigned example hath as much force to teach as a true example (for as for to move, it is clear, since the feigned may be tuned to the highest key of passion) let us take one example wherein an historian and a poet did concur. Herodotus and Justin doth both testify that Zopirus, King Darius's faithful servant, seeing his master long resisted by the rebellious Babylonians, feigned himself in extreme disgrace of his king; for verifying of which he caused his own nose and ears to be cut off, and so flying to the Babylonians was received, and for his known valour so far credited that he did find means to deliver them over to Darius. Much like matter doth Livy record of Tarquinius and his son.[1] Xenophon excellently feigneth such another stratagem performed by Abradates in Cyrus' behalf.[2] Now would I fain know, if occasion be presented unto you to serve your prince by such an honest dissimulation, why you do not as well learn it of Xenophon's fiction as of the others verity; and truly so much the better, as you shall save your nose by the bargain: for Abradates did not counterfeit so far. So then the best of the historian is subject to the poet; for whatsoever action, or faction, whatsoever counsel, policy, or war stratagem the historian is bound to recite, that may the poet (if he list[3]) with his imitation make his own, beautifying it both for further teaching, and more delighting, as it please him: having all, from Dante's heaven to his hell, under the authority of his pen.[4] Which if I be asked what poets have done so, as I might well name some, so yet say I, and say again, I speak of the art, and not of the artificer.

Now to that which commonly is attributed to the praise of history, in respect of the notable learning, is got by marking the success, as though therein a man should see virtue exalted & vice punished—truly that commendation is peculiar to poetry, and far off from history. For indeed poetry ever sets Virtue so out in her best colours, making Fortune her well-waiting handmaid, that one must needs be enamoured of her. Well may you see Ulysses in a storm and in other hard plights, but they are but exercises of patience and magnanimity, to make them shine the more in the near following prosperity. And of the contrary part, if evil men come to the stage, they ever go out (as the tragedy writer answered to one that misliked the show of such persons) so manacled as they little animate folks to follow them. But the history, being captived to the truth of a foolish world, is many times a terror from well-doing, and an encouragement to unbridled wickedness. For see we not valiant Miltiades[5] rot in his fetters? The just Phocion[6] and the accomplished Socrates put to death like traitors? The cruel Severus[7] live prosperously? The excellent Severus[8] miserably murdered? Sulla and Marius[9] dying in their beds? Pompey and Cicero[10] slain then, when they would have thought exile a happiness? See we not virtuous Cato[11] driven to kill himself, and rebel Caesar so advanced that his name yet, after 1600 years, lasteth in the highest honor? And mark but even Caesar's own words

[1] *Livy … son* Tarquinius Superbus, last king of Rome (534–510 BCE), and his son, who pretended to be an ally of the Gabians in order to deliver them over to his father. See Titus Livius's *Early History of Rome*.

[2] *Xenophon … behalf* Abradates, the fifth-century BCE viceroy of Shushan who gave his allegiance to Cyrus, King of Persia. See Xenophon's *Cyropaedia*.

[3] *list* Desires.

[4] *from Dante's … pen* Reference to Dante's *Divine Comedy*, which describes its narrator's journey through hell, purgatory, and heaven.

[5] *Miltiades* Fifth-century BCE Athenian general who was imprisoned by his own people after leading a failed naval attack.

[6] *Phocion* Athenian statesman (402–318 BCE).

[7] *cruel Severus* Lucius Septimius Severus, second-century BCE Roman emperor known for his cruelty.

[8] *excellent Severus* Alexander Severus (208–235 CE), noble and virtuous Roman emperor who was nevertheless killed by his troops.

[9] *Sulla and Marius* Lucius Sulla (138–78 BCE) and Gaius Marius (157–83 BCE), two rival Roman generals and politicians whose disputes brought civil war to Rome.

[10] *Pompey* Gnaeus Pompeius, first-century BCE Roman general who was murdered after opposing Caesar in battle; *Cicero* Marcus Tullius Cicero was murdered by order of Marcus Antonius.

[11] *Cato* Marcus Porcius Cato (95–46 BCE), Roman aristocrat who opposed both Pompey and Caesar and who committed suicide rather than submit to Caesar's authority.

of the forenamed Sulla (who in that only did honestly, to put down his dishonest tyranny), *literas nescivet*,[1] as if want of learning caused him to do well. He meant it not by poetry, which, not content with earthly plagues, deviseth new punishments in hell for tyrants, nor yet by philosophy, which teacheth *occidendos esse*; but no doubt by skill in history, for that indeed can afford you Cypselus, Periander, Phalaris, Dionysius,[2] and I know not how many more of the same kennel, that speed well enough in their abominable injustice of usurpation.

I conclude, therefore, that he excelleth history, not only in furnishing the mind with knowledge, but in setting it forward to that which deserves to be called and accounted good: which setting forward, and moving to well-doing, indeed setteth the laurel crown upon the poets as victorious, not only of the historian, but over the philosopher, howsoever in teaching it may be questionable.

For suppose it be granted (that which I suppose with great reason may be denied) that the philosopher, in respect of his methodical proceeding, doth teach more perfectly than the poet, yet do I think that no man is so much φιλοφιλοσοφος[3] as to compare the philosopher in moving with the poet. And that moving is of a higher degree than teaching, it may by this appear, that it is well nigh both the cause and effect of teaching. For who will be taught, if he be not moved with desire to be taught? And what so much good doth that teaching bring forth (I speak still of moral doctrine) as that it moveth one to do that which it doth teach. For, as Aristotle saith, it is not γνωσις but πραχις[4] must be the fruit. And how πραχις can be, without being moved to practice, it is no hard matter to consider.

The philosopher showeth you the way; he informeth you of the particularities, as well of the tediousness of the way, as of the pleasant lodging you shall have when your journey is ended, as of the many by-turnings that may divert you from your way. But this is to no man but to him that will read him, and read him with attentive studious painfulness; which constant desire whosoever hath in him, hath already passed half the hardness of the way, and therefore is beholding to the philosopher but for the other half. Nay truly, learned men have learnedly thought that where once reason hath so much over-mastered passion as that the mind hath a free desire to do well, the inward light each mind hath in itself is as good as a philosopher's book; since in nature we know it is well to do well, and what is well, and what is evil, although not in the words of art which philosophers bestow upon us; for out of natural conceit the philosophers drew it. But to be moved to do that which we know, or to be moved with desire to know, *hoc opus, hic labor est*.[5]

Now therein of all sciences (I speak still of human, and according to the human conceit) is our poet the monarch. For he doth not only show the way, but giveth so sweet a prospect into the way, as will entice any man to enter into it. Nay, he doth, as if your journey should lie through a fair vineyard, at the very first give you a cluster of grapes, that full of the taste, you may long to pass further. He beginneth not with obscure definitions, which must blur the margin with interpretations and load the memory with doubtfulness, but he cometh to you with words set in delightful proportion, either accompanied with, or prepared for, the well enchanting skill of music; and with a tale forsooth he cometh unto you, with a tale which holdeth children from play and old men from the chimney corner. And, pretending no more, doth intend the winning of the mind from wickedness to virtue—even as the child is often brought to take most wholesome things by hiding them in such other as have a pleasant taste, which, if one should begin to tell them the nature of the *aloes* or *rhabarbarum*[6] they should receive, would

[1] *literas nescivet* Latin: "He knew nothing of letters" (Suetonius, *Life of Caesar*, ch. 77).

[2] *occidentos esse* Latin: "They are to be killed"; *Cypselus, Periander, Phalaris, Dionysius* Tyrannical rulers remembered for the brutality of their crimes and the impunity with which those crimes were committed.

[3] φιλοφιλοσοφος Greek: one who loves philosophy.

[4] γνωσις Greek: theory, knowing; πραχις Greek: practice. (See *Nicomachean Ethics*, 1.1.)

[5] *hoc ... est* Latin: "This is the task, this is the work" (Virgil, *Aeneid* 6.129).

[6] *aloes or rhabarbarum* Aloe and rhubarb, two bitter-tasting plants often taken as medicines.

sooner take their physic at their ears than at their mouth. So it is in men (most of which are childish in the best things, till they be cradled in their graves): glad they will be to hear the tales of Hercules, Achilles, Cyrus, Aeneas; and, hearing them, must needs hear the right description of wisdom, value, and justice; which, if they had been barely (that is to say philosophically) set out, they would swear they be brought to school again.

That imitation whereof poetry is, hath the most conveniency to nature of all other, insomuch that, as Aristotle saith, those things which in themselves are horrible, as cruel battles, unnatural monsters, are made in poetical imitation delightful.[1] Truly, I have known men that even with reading *Amadis de Gaule*[2] (which God knoweth wanteth much of a perfect poesy) have found their hearts moved to the exercise of courtesy, liberality, and especially courage. Who readeth Aeneas carrying old Anchises on his back, that wisheth not it were his fortune to perform so excellent an act? Whom doth not those words of Turnus move, the tale of Turnus having planted his image in the imagination,

> *Fugientam haec terra videbit?*
> *Usque adeone mori miserum est?*[3]

Where the philosophers, as they scorn to delight, so must they be content little to move—saving wrangling whether *virtus*[4] be the chief or the only good, whether the contemplative or the active life do excel—which Plato and Boethius well knew, and therefore made mistress Philosophy very often borrow the masking raiment of poesy.[5] For even those hard-hearted evil men who think virtue a school name, and know no other good but *indulgere genio*,[6] and therefore despise the austere admonitions of the philosopher, and feel not the inward reason they stand upon, yet will be content to be delighted—which is all the good-fellow poet seemeth to promise—and so steal to see the form of goodness, (which seen, they cannot but love) ere themselves be aware, as if they took a medicine of cherries.

Infinite proofs of the strange effects of this poetical invention might be alleged; only two shall serve, which are so often remembered as I think all men know them. The one of Menenius Agrippa,[7] who, when the whole people of Rome had resolutely divided themselves from the Senate, with apparent show of utter ruin, though he were (for that time) an excellent orator, came not among them upon trust either of figurative speeches or cunning insinuations, and much less with far-fet[8] maxims of philosophy, which (especially if they were Platonic) they must have learned geometry before they could well have conceived; but forsooth he behaves himself like a homely and familiar poet. He telleth them a tale, that there was a time when all the parts of the body made a mutinous conspiracy against the belly, which they thought devoured the fruits of each other's labour; they concluded that they would let so unprofitable a spender starve. In the end, to be short (for the tale is notorious, and as notorious that it was a tale), with punishing the belly they plagued themselves. This, applied by him, wrought such effect in the people, as I never read that only words brought forth but then so sudden and so good an alteration; for upon reasonable conditions a perfect reconcilement ensued. The other is of Nathan the prophet, who, when the holy David had so far forsaken God as to confirm adultery with murder, when he was to do the tenderest office of a friend in laying his own shame before his eyes, sent by God to call again so chosen a servant, how doth he it but by telling of a man whose beloved lamb was ungratefully taken from his

[1] *as Aristotle ... delightful* Cf. *Poetics* Part 4.

[2] *Amadis de Gaule* Spanish chivalric romance written by Vasco de Lobeyra.

[3] *Fugientam ... est* Latin. In Virgil's *Aeneid*, Turnus, when attempting to defend his home from the invading Trojans, cries, "Shall this land see him [Turnus] run away? / Is it so hard to die?" (*Aeneid* 12.645–46).

[4] *virtus* Latin word that carries with it the sense of courage and strength of purpose as well as the quality we now use the word "virtue" to denote.

[5] *which ... poesy* Both Plato and Boethius were philosophers who believed in the superiority of a contemplative life.

[6] *indulgere genio* Latin: "To indulge your appetite"; i.e., self-indulgence (Persius, *Satires* 5.151).

[7] *Menenius Agrippa* Roman consul of the fifth century BCE. See Livy, *Histories* 2.32.

[8] *far-fet* Far-fetched.

bosom: the application most divinely true, but the discourse itself feigned; which made David (I speak of the second and instrumental cause) as in a glass see his own filthiness, as that heavenly psalm of mercy[1] well testifieth.

By these, therefore, examples and reasons, I think it may be manifest that the poet, with that same hand of delight, doth draw the mind more effectually than any other art doth. And so a conclusion not unfitly ensue: that, as virtue is the most excellent resting place for all worldly learning to make his end of, so poetry, being the most familiar to teach it, and most princely to move towards it, in the most excellent work is the most excellent workman.

But I am content not only to decipher him[2] by his works (although works, in commendation and dispraise, must ever hold a high authority), but more narrowly will examine his parts; so that (as in a man) though all together may carry a presence full of majesty and beauty, perchance in some one defectuous[3] piece we may find blemish.

Now in his parts, kinds, or species (as you list to term them), it is to be noted that some poesies have coupled together two or three kinds, as the tragical and comical, whereupon is risen the tragicomical. Some, in the manner, have mingled prose and verse, as Sannazaro[4] and Boethius; some have mingled matters heroical and pastoral. But that cometh all to one in this question; for, if severed they be good, the conjunction cannot be hurtful. Therefore, perchance forgetting some and leaving some as needless to be remembered, it shall not be amiss in a word to cite the special kinds, to see what faults may be found in the right use of them.

Is it then the Pastoral poem which is misliked? (For perchance where the hedge is lowest[5] they will soonest leap over.) Is the poor pipe[6] disdained, which sometimes out of Meliboeus' mouth can show the misery of people under hard lords and ravening soldiers, and again, by Tityrus,[7] what blessedness is derived to them that lie lowest from the goodness of them that sit highest; sometimes, under the pretty tales of wolves and sheep, can include the whole considerations of wrongdoing and patience; sometimes show that contentions for trifles can get but a trifling victory: where perchance a man may see that even Alexander & Darius, when they strove who should be cock of this world's dunghill, the benefit they got was that the after-livers may say

> *Haec memini & victum frustra contendere Thyrsin:*
> *Ex illo Corydon, Corydon est tempore nobis.*[8]

Or is it the lamenting Elegiac, which in a kind heart would move rather pity than blame; who bewails with the great philosopher Heraclitus[9] the weakness of mankind and the wretchedness of the world; who surely is to be praised either for compassionate accompanying just causes of lamentations, or for rightly painting out how weak be the passions of woefulness? Is it the bitter but wholesome Iambic,[10] who rubs the galled mind, in making shame the trumpet of villainy, with bold and open crying out against naughtiness? Or the Satiric, who

> *Omne vafer vitium ridenti tangit amico;*[11]

[1] *heavenly psalm of mercy* Cf. Psalm 51.

[2] *him* I.e., poet.

[3] *defectuous* Defective.

[4] *Sannazaro* Italian poet Jacopo Sannazaro, author of the pastoral romance *Arcadia,* which mixes poetry and prose.

[5] *lowest* Pastoral poetry was considered the lowest and least technically advanced of the poetic genres.

[6] *pipe* Shepherd's pipe, the symbol of pastoral poetry.

[7] *Meliboeus ... Tityrus* Meliboeus and Tityrus are two shepherds in Virgil's *Eclogues.*

[8] *Haec ... nobis* Latin: "These things I remember, how Thyrsis, vanquished, strove in vain. From that time it is Corydon, Corydon with us." From Virgil, *Eclogues* 7.69–70, in which the pastoral poets Thyrsis and Corydon challenge one another to a singing contest—an event which, Sidney says, is comparable to the victory of Alexander the Great over Darius of Persia.

[9] *Heraclitus* Fifth-century BCE Greek philosopher who believed that everything in the universe is subject to constant change and strife.

[10] *Iambic* Verse form typically used in satire and direct attacks.

[11] *Omne ... amico* Latin: "The crafty man probes every fault while making his friends laugh" (Persius, *Satires* 1.116–17).

who sportingly never leaveth till he make a man laugh at folly, and at length ashamed, to laugh at himself, which he cannot avoid without avoiding the folly; who, while

circum praecordia ludit,[1]

giveth us to feel how many headaches a passionate life bringeth us to; how, when all is done,

Est Ulubris, animus si nos non deficit aequus.[2]

No, perchance it is the Comic, whom naughty play-makers and stage-keepers have justly made odious. To the arguments of abuse I will after answer. Only thus much now is to be said, that the comedy is an imitation of the common errors of our life, which he representeth in the most ridiculous and scornful sort that may be, so as it is impossible that any beholder can be content to be such a one. Now, as in geometry the oblique must be known as well as the right, and in arithmetic the odd as well as the even, so in the actions of our life who seeth not the filthiness of evil wanteth a great folly to perceive the beauty of virtue. This doth the comedy handle so in our private and domestical matters as with hearing it we get, as it were, an experience what is to be looked for of a niggardly Demea, of a crafty Davus, of a flattering Gnatho, of a vain-glorious Thraso;[3] and not only to know what effects are to be expected, but to know who be such, by the signifying badge given them by the comedian. And little reason hath any man to say that men learn the evil by seeing it so set out, since, as I said before, there is no man living but, by the force truth hath in nature, no sooner seeth these men play their parts, but wisheth them *in pistrinum*;[4] although perchance the sack of his own faults lie so behind his back that he seeth not himself to dance the same measure;[5] whereto yet nothing can more open his eyes than to see his own actions contemptibly set forth.

So that the right use of comedy will, I think, by nobody be blamed; and much less of the high and excellent Tragedy, that openeth the greatest wounds, and showeth forth the ulcers that are covered with tissue; that maketh kings fear to be tyrants, and tyrants manifest their tyrannical humours; that, with stirring the affects of admiration and commiseration, teacheth the uncertainty of this world, and upon how weak foundations gilded roofs are builded; that maketh us know

Qui sceptra saevus duro imperio regit
Timet timentes; metus in auctorem redit.[6]

But how much it can move, Plutarch yieldeth a notable testimony of the abominable tyrant Alexander Pheraeus,[7] from whose eyes a tragedy, well made and represented, drew abundance of tears, who without all pity had murdered infinite numbers, and some of his own blood: so as he, that was not ashamed to make matters for tragedies, yet could not resist the sweet violence of a tragedy. And if it wrought no further good in him, it was that he, in despite of himself, withdrew himself from hearkening to that which might mollify his hard heart.

But it is not the tragedy they do mislike; for it were too absurd to cast out so excellent a representation of whatsoever is most worthy to be learned.

Is it the Lyric that most displeaseth, who with his tuned lyre and well-accorded voice giveth praise, the

[1] *Circum praecordia ludit* Latin: "He plays about the heart" (Persius, *Satires*, 1.117).

[2] *Est … aequus* Latin: "[What you are seeking] is at Ulubrae, if a well-balanced mind does not fail us" (Adaptation of Horace, *Epistles*, 1.11.30). Ulubrae was a small, notoriously dull town bordered by marshlands.

[3] *Demea … Thraso* Four stock characters from the plays of Terence.

[4] *in pistrinum* Latin: in the mill (where Roman slaves and criminals were forced to work as punishment).

[5] *the sack … measure* Reference to one of Aesop's fables, in which every person is given two sacks to carry. One, which is slung behind the back, out of sight, contains one's own faults. The other, hung in front of one's neck, contains all the faults of others.

[6] *Qui … redit* Latin: "The cruel man who rules his kingdom with harsh sway / Fears those who fear him; terror returns upon the author" (Seneca, *Oedipus* 3.705–06).

[7] *Alexander Pheraeus* Tyrant who, according to Plutarch, wept to see the suffering of Hecuba and Andromache in Euripides's tragedy *Troades*.

reward of virtue, to virtuous acts; who gives moral precepts, and natural problems; who sometimes raiseth up his voice to the height of the heavens in singing the lauds of the immortal God? Certainly I must confess mine own barbarousness, I never heard the old song of Percy and Douglas[1] that I found not my heart moved more than with a trumpet; and yet is it sung but by some blind crowder,[2] with no rougher voice than rude style; which, being so evil apparelled in the dust and cobwebs of that uncivil age, what would it work trimmed in the gorgeous eloquence of Pindar?[3] In Hungary I have seen it the manner at all feasts, and other such like meetings, to have songs of their ancestors' valour, which that right soldier-like nation think one of the chiefest kindlers of brave courage. The incomparable Lacedemonians[4] did not only carry that kind of music ever with them to the field, but even at home, as such songs were made, so were they all content to be singers of them—when the lusty men were to tell what they did, the old men what they had done, and the young what they would do. And where a man may say that Pindar many times praiseth highly victories of small moment, rather matters of sport than virtue; as it may be answered, it was the fault of the poet, and not of the poetry, so indeed the chief fault was in the time and custom of the Greeks, who set those toys at so high a price that Philip of Macedon[5] reckoned a horserace won at Olympus among his three fearful felicities. But as the unimitable Pindar often did, so is that kind most capable and most fit to awake the thoughts from the sleep of idleness to embrace honorable enterprises.

There rests the Heroical[6]—whose very name, I think, should daunt all backbiters. For by what conceit can a tongue be directed to speak evil of that which draweth with him no less champions than Achilles, Cyrus, Aeneas, Turnus, Tydeus, Rinaldo[7]—who doth not only teach and move to a truth, but teacheth and moveth to the most high and excellent truth; who maketh magnanimity and justice shine through all misty fearfulness and foggy desires; who, if the saying of Plato and Tully be true, that who could see virtue would be wonderfully ravished with the love of her beauty—this man sets her out to make her more lovely in her holiday apparel, to the eye of any that will deign not to disdain until they understand. But if anything be already said in the defence of sweet poetry, all concurreth to the maintaining the heroical, which is not only a kind, but the best and most accomplished kinds of poetry. For, as the image of each action stirreth and instructeth the mind, so the lofty image of such worthies most inflameth the mind with desire to be worthy, and informs with counsel how to be worthy. Only let Aeneas be worn in the tablet of your memory, how he governeth himself in the ruin of his country; in the preserving his old father, and carrying away his religious ceremonies; in obeying God's commandment to leave Dido,[8] though not only all passionate kindness, but even the human consideration of virtuous gratefulness, would have craved other of him; how in storms, how in sports, how in war, how in peace, how a fugitive, how victorious, how besieged, how besieging, how to strangers, how to allies, how to enemies, how to his own; lastly, how in his inward self, and how in his outward government—and, I think, in a mind most prejudiced with a prejudicating humour, he will be found in excellency fruitful. Yea as Horace saith,

---

1 *old song ... Douglas* *The Ballad of Chevy Chase.*

2 *crowder* One who would play the Celtic instrument called the "crowd," an early form of the fiddle.

3 *Pindar* Famous Greek lyric poet (d. c. 443 BCE) whose odes celebrated victorious athletes.

4 *Lacedemonians* Spartans.

5 *Philip of Macedon* Father of Alexander the Great. According to Plutarch's *Life of Alexander*, Philip received three wonderful tidings in one day—that his wife had given birth to a son, that his general had been victorious in battle, and that his horse had won a race at Olympia.

6 *Heroical* Epic.

7 *Turnus* Great adversary of Aeneas in Virgil's *Aeneid*; *Tydeus* Hero of Statius's *Thebaid*; *Rinaldo* Hero of Ariosto's *Orlando Furioso.*

8 *Aeneas ... Dido* See *Aeneid* 2.705–20; 4.23–34. When Aeneas leads his people from Troy to Carthage, Dido, Queen of Carthage, becomes his lover until the gods order Aeneas to leave her and continue on his mission to build a new city for his people.

melius Chrisippo & Crantore.[1]

But truly I imagine it falleth out with these poet-whippers, as with some good women, who often are sick, but in faith they cannot tell where; so the name of poetry is odious to them, but neither his cause nor effects, neither the sum that contains him, nor the particularities descending from him, give any fast handle to their carping dispraise.

Since then poetry is of all human learnings the most ancient and of most fatherly antiquity, as from whence other learnings have taken their beginnings; since it is so universal that no learned nation doth despise it, nor barbarous nation is without it; since both Roman & Greek gave such divine names unto it, the one of prophesying, the other of making; and that indeed the name of making is fit for him, considering that where all other arts retain themselves within their subject, and receive, as it were, their being from it, the poet only bringeth his own stuff, and doth not learn a conceit out of a matter, but maketh matter for a conceit; since neither his description nor end containing any evil, the thing described cannot be evil; since his effects be so good as to teach goodness and delight the learners of it; since therein (namely in moral doctrine, the chief of all knowledges) he doth not only far pass the historian, but, for instructing, is well nigh comparable to the philosopher, for moving, leaves him behind him; since the Holy Scripture (wherein there is no uncleanness) hath whole parts in it poetical, and that even our Saviour Christ vouchsafed to use the flowers of it; since all his kinds are not only in their united forms, but in their severed dissections, fully commendable; I think (and think I think rightly) the laurel crown appointed for triumphant captains doth worthily (of all other learnings) honor the poet's triumph.

But because we have ears as well as tongues, and that the lightest reasons that may be will seem to weigh greatly, if nothing be put in the counterbalance, let us hear, and, as well as we can, ponder what objections be made against this art, which may be worthy either of yielding or answering.

First, truly I note not only in these μισομουσι, poet-haters, but in all that kind of people who seek a praise by dispraising others, that they do prodigally spend a great many wandering words in quips and scoffs, carping and taunting at each thing which, by stirring the spleen, may stay the brain from a thorough-beholding the worthiness of the subject. Those kind of objections, as they are full of a very idle easiness, since there is nothing of so sacred a majesty but that an itching tongue may rub itself upon it, so deserve they no other answer, but, instead of laughing at the jest, to laugh at the jester. We know a playing wit can praise the discretion of an ass, the comfortableness of being in debt, and the jolly commodities of being sick of the plague. So of the contrary side, if we will turn Ovid's verse,

Ut lateat virtus, proximitate mali,[2]

that good lie hid in nearness of the evil, Agrippa will be as merry in showing the vanity of science as Erasmus was in the commending of folly.[3] Neither shall any man or matter escape some touch of these smiling railers. But for Erasmus and Agrippa, they had another foundation than the superficial part would promise. Marry, these other pleasant fault-finders, who will correct the verb before they understand the noun, and confute others knowledge before they confirm their own, I would have them only remember that scoffing cometh not of wisdom; so as the best title in true English they get with their merriments is to be called good fools, for so have our grave forefathers ever termed that humorous kind of jesters.

But that which giveth greatest scope to their scorning humour is rhyming and versing. It is already said (and, as I think, truly said) it is not rhyming and versing that makes poesy. One may be a poet without versing,

[1] *melius … Crantore* Latin: "Better than Chrysippus and Crantor" (*Epistles*, 1.2.4); *Chrysippus* Third-century BCE Stoic philosopher; *Crantor* Greek philosopher of the fourth century BCE and the first commentator on Plato.

[2] *Ut … mali* Latin: "That virtue may lurk next to evil" (Ovid, *The Art of Love* 2.662).

[3] *Agrippa* German philosopher and author of *On the Uncertainty and Vanity of the Sciences and the Arts* (1526); *Erasmus* Dutch humanist who wrote *The Praise of Folly* (1509).

and a versifier without poetry. But yet, presuppose it were inseparable (as indeed it seemeth Scaliger[1] judgeth), truly it were an inseparable commendation. For if *oratio* next to *ratio*, speech next to reason, be the greatest gift bestowed upon mortality, that cannot be praiseless which doth most polish that blessing of speech; which considers each word, not only (as a man may say) by his forcible quality, but by his best measured quantity, carrying even in themselves a harmony—without, perchance, number, measure, order, proportion be in our time grown odious. But lay aside the just praise it hath by being the only fit speech for music (music, I say, the most divine striker of the senses), thus much is undoubtedly true, that if reading be foolish without remembering, memory being the only treasure of knowledge, those words which are fittest for memory are likewise most convenient for knowledge. Now, that verse far exceedeth prose in the knitting up of the memory, the reason is manifest: the words (besides their delight, which hath a great affinity to memory) being so set as one cannot be lost but the whole work fails; which accusing itself, calleth the remembrance back to itself, and so most strongly confirmeth it. Besides, one word so, as it were, begetting another, as, be it in rhyme or measured verse, by the former a man shall have a near guess to the follower. Lastly, even they that have taught the art of memory have showed nothing so apt for it as a certain room divided into many places well & thoroughly known. Now, that hath the verse in effect perfectly, every word having his natural seat, which seat must needs make the word remembered. But what needeth more in a thing so known to all men? Who is it that ever was scholar that doth not carry away some verse of Virgil, Horace, or Cato, which in his youth he learned, and even to his old age serve him for hourly lessons; as

Percontatorem fugito nam garrulus idem est;
Dum tibi quisque placet credula turba sumas.[2]

But the fitness it hath for memory is notably proved by all delivery of arts, wherein, for the most part, from grammar to logic, mathematics, physic, and the rest, the rules chiefly necessary to be borne away are compiled in verses. So that, verse being in itself sweet and orderly, and being best for memory, the only handle of knowledge, it must be in jest that any man can speak against it.

Now then go we to the most important imputations laid to the poor poets. For aught I can yet learn, they are these. First, that there being many other more fruitful knowledges, a man might better spend his time in them than in this. Secondly, that it is the mother of lies. Thirdly, that it is the nurse of abuse, infecting us with many pestilent desires; with a siren's sweetness drawing the mind to the serpent's tail of sinful fancies (and herein, especially, comedies give the largest field to ear,[3] as Chaucer saith); how, both in other nations and in ours, before poets did soften us, we were full of courage, given to martial exercises, the pillars of man-like liberty, and not lulled asleep in shady idleness with poets' pastimes. And lastly and chiefly, they cry out with open mouth, as if they had shot Robin Hood, that Plato banished them out of his commonwealth. Truly this is much, if there be much truth in it.

First, to the first. That a man might better spend his time, is a reason indeed; but it doth, as they say, but *petere principium*.[4] For if it be as I affirm, that no learning is so good as that which teacheth and moveth to virtue; and that none can both teach and move thereto so much as poesy, then is the conclusion manifest that ink and paper cannot be to a more profitable purpose employed. And certainly, though a man should grant their first assumption, it should follow (methinks) very unwillingly, that good is not good, because better is better. But I still and utterly deny that there is sprung out of the earth a more fruitful knowledge.

To the second, therefore, that they should be the principal liars, I answer paradoxically, but truly, I think truly, that of all writers under the sun, the poet is the least liar; and, though he would, as a poet can scarcely

[1] *Scaliger* Julius Caesar Scaliger, Italian scholar of the sixteenth century who wrote *Seven Books on Poetry*.

[2] *Percontatorem ... est* Latin: "Flee the inquisitive man, for he is sure to be garrulous" (Horace, *Epistles* 1.18.69); *Dum ... sumas* Latin: "While each pleases himself we are a credulous mob" (Ovid, *Remedia Amoris* 686).

[3] *comedies ... ear* See "The Knight's Tale" 1.28, in Chaucer's *Canterbury Tales*: "a large feeld to ere" ("ere" meaning "to plow").

[4] *petere principium* Latin: to beg the question.

be a liar. The astronomer, with his cousin the geometrician, can hardly escape, when they take upon them to measure the height of the stars. How often, think you, do the physicians lie, when they aver things good for sicknesses, which afterwards send Charon[1] a great number of souls drowned in a potion before they come to his ferry? And no less of the rest, which take upon them to affirm. Now, for the poet, he nothing affirms, and therefore never lieth. For, as I take it, to lie is to affirm that to be true which is false. So as the other artists, and especially the historian, affirming many things, can, in the cloudy knowledge of mankind, hardly escape from many lies. But the poet, as I said before, never affirmeth. The poet never maketh any circles about your imagination, to conjure you to believe for true what he writes. He citeth not authorities of other histories, but even for his entry calleth the sweet Muses to inspire unto him a good invention; in truth, not labouring to tell you what is or is not, but what should or should not, be. And therefore, though he recount things not true, yet because he telleth them not for true, he lieth not—without we will say that Nathan lied in his speech before alleged to David; which as a wicked man durst scarce say, so think I none so simple would say that Aesop lied in the tales of his beasts; for who thinks Aesop wrote it for actually true were well worthy to have his name chronicled among the beasts he writeth of. What child is there that, coming to a play and seeing "Thebes" written in great letters upon an old door, doth believe that it is Thebes? If then a man can arrive to the child's age to know that the poets' persons and doings are but pictures what should be, and not stories what have been, they will never give the lie to things not affirmatively but allegorically and figuratively written. And therefore, as in history, looking for truth, they may go away full fraught with falsehood, so in poesy, looking but for fiction, they shall use the narration but as an imaginative ground-plot of a profitable invention. But hereto is replied that the poets give names to men they write of, which argueth a conceit of an actual truth, and so, not being true, proves a falsehood. And doth the lawyer lie then, when under the names of *John-a-stiles* and *John-a-nokes*[2] he putteth his case? But that is easily answered. Their naming of men is but to make their picture the more lively, and not to build any history: painting men, they cannot leave men nameless. We see we cannot play at chess but that we must give names to our chessmen; and yet, methinks, he were a very partial champion of truth that would say we lied for giving a piece of wood the reverend title of a bishop. The poet nameth Cyrus and Aeneas no other way than to show what men of their fames, fortunes, and estates should do.

Their third is, how much it abuseth men's wit, training it to wanton sinfulness and lustful love. For indeed that is the principal, if not only, abuse I can hear alleged. They say the comedies rather teach than reprehend amorous conceits. They say the lyric is larded with passionate sonnets, the elegiac weeps the want of his mistress, and that even to the heroical, Cupid hath ambitiously climbed. Alas, Love, I would thou couldst as well defend thyself as thou canst offend others. I would those on whom thou doest attend could either put thee away, or yield good reason why they keep thee. But grant love of beauty to be a beastly fault (although it be very hard, since only man, and no beast, hath that gift to discern beauty); grant that lovely name of Love to deserve all hateful reproaches (although even some of my masters the philosophers spent a good deal of their lamp-oil in setting forth the excellency of it); grant, I say, whatsoever they will have granted, that not only love, but lust, but vanity, but (if they list) scurrility, possesseth many leaves of the poets' books; yet, think I, when this is granted, they will find their sentence may with good manners put the last words foremost, and not say that poetry abuseth man's wit, but that man's wit abuseth poetry.

For I will not deny but that man's wit may make poesy, which should be εἰκαστική[3] (which some learned have defined, "figuring forth good things"), to be φανταστική[4] (which doth, contrariwise, infect the fancy

[1] *Charon* Greek mythological ferryman of the underworld who transports the souls of the dead across the River Styx.

[2] *John ... nokes* Fictitious names, like John Doe.

[3] εἰκαστική Greek: representing real things.

[4] φανταστική Greek: representing imaginary things.

with unworthy objects), as the painter should give to the eye either some excellent perspective, or some fine picture fit for building or fortification, or containing in it some notable example (as Abraham sacrificing his son Isaac, Judith killing Holofernes, David fighting with Goliath),[1] may leave those, and please an ill-pleased eye with wanton shows of better hidden matters. But what, shall the abuse of a thing, make the right use odious? Nay, truly, though I yield that poesy may not only be abused, but that, being abused, by the reason of his sweet charming force, it can do more hurt than any other army of words: yet shall it be so far from concluding that the abuse should give reproach to the abused, that, contrariwise, it is a good reason that whatsoever, being abused, doth most harm, being rightly used (and upon the right use, each thing receives his title), doth most good. Do we not see skill of physic, the best rampire[2] to our often-assaulted bodies, being abused, teach poison, the most violent destroyer? Doth not knowledge of law, whose end is to even & right all things, being abused, grow the crooked fosterer of horrible injuries? Doth not (to go to the highest) God's word, abused, breed heresy, and his name, abused, become blasphemy? Truly, a needle cannot do much hurt, and as truly (with leave of ladies be it spoken) it cannot do much good: with a sword thou mayst kill thy father, and with a sword thou mayst defend thy prince and country. So that, as in their calling poets fathers of lies they said nothing, so in this their argument of abuse they prove the commendation.

They allege herewith, that before poets began to be in price, our nation had set their hearts' delight upon action, and not imagination: rather doing things worthy to be written, than writing things fit to be done. What that before-time was, I think scarcely Sphinx[3] can tell, since no memory is so ancient that hath not the precedent of poetry. And certain it is that, in our plainest homeliness, yet never was the Albion nation[4] without poetry. Marry, this argument, though it be levelled against poetry, yet is it indeed a chainshot[5] against all learning, or "bookishness," as they commonly term it. Of such mind were certain Goths, of whom it is written that, having in the spoil of a famous city taken a fair library, one hangman (belike fit to execute the fruits of their wits), who had murdered a great number of bodies, would have set fire in it. "No," said another very gravely, "take heed what you do; for while they are busy about those toys, we shall with more leisure conquer their countries." This indeed is the ordinary doctrine of ignorance, and many words sometimes I have heard spent in it. But because this reason is generally against all learning, as well as poetry, or rather, all learning but poetry; because it were too great a digression to handle it, or at least too superfluous (since it is manifest that all government of action is to be gotten by knowledge, and knowledge best by gathering many knowledges, which is reading), I only, with Horace, to him that is of that opinion

jubeo stultum esse libenter;[6]

for as for poetry itself, it is the freest from this objection.

For poetry is the companion of camps. I dare undertake Orlando Furioso, or honest King Arthur, will never displease a soldier; but the quiddity of *ens* and *prima materia* will hardly agree with a corselet;[7] and therefore, as I said in the beginning, even Turks and Tartars are delighted with poets. Homer, a Greek, flourished before Greece flourished. And if to a slight conjecture a conjecture may be opposed, truly it may seem that, as by him their learned men took almost their first light of knowledge, so their active men received

[1] *as Abraham … Goliath* See Genesis 22, Judith 2–14, and 1 Samuel 17, respectively.

[2] *rampire* Rampart; bulwark.

[3] *Sphinx* Mythical creature with the head of a woman and the body of a lion who posed riddles to humans.

[4] *Albion nation* England.

[5] *chainshot* Weapon used in naval warfare to destroy ships; it consists of two cannon balls joined by a chain.

[6] *jubeo … libenter* Latin: "I order him to be gladly foolish" (Horace, *Satires* 1.1.63).

[7] *quiddity* Subtlety; *ens* Latin: essential nature; *prima materia* Latin: primary, original matter of the universe; *corselet* Soldier (literally, a corselet is a piece of body armor worn by soldiers).

their first motions of courage. Only Alexander's example may serve, who by Plutarch is accounted of such virtue, that Fortune was not his guide but his footstool; whose acts speak for him, though Plutarch did not: indeed the phoenix[1] of warlike princes. This Alexander left his schoolmaster, living Aristotle, behind him, but took dead Homer with him. He put the philosopher Callisthenes to death for his seeming philosophical, indeed mutinous, stubbornness, but the chief thing he was ever heard to wish for was that Homer had been alive. He well found he received more bravery of mind by the pattern of Achilles than by hearing the definition of fortitude. And therefore, if Cato misliked Fulvius for carrying Ennius with him to the field,[2] it may be answered that, if Cato misliked it, the noble Fulvius liked it, or else he had not done it; for it was not the excellent Cato Uticensis[3] (whose authority I would much more have reverenced), but it was the former, in truth a bitter punisher of faults (but else a man that had never sacrificed to the Graces:[4] he misliked and cried out against all Greek learning, and yet, being four score years old, began to learn it, belike fearing that Pluto[5] understood not Latin). Indeed, the Roman laws allowed no person to be carried to the wars but he that was in the soldiers' role; and therefore, though Cato misliked his unmustered[6] person, he misliked not his work. And if he had, Scipio Nasica, judged by common consent the best Roman, loved him. Both the other Scipio brothers, who had by their virtues no less surnames than of Asia and Afric,[7] so loved him that they caused his body to be buried in their sepulture.[8] So as Cato's authority, being but against his person, and that answered with so far greater than himself, is herein of no validity.

But now indeed my burden is great, that Plato's name is laid upon me, whom, I must confess, of all philosophers, I have ever esteemed most worthy of reverence; and with good reason, since of all philosophers he is the most poetical. Yet if he will defile the fountain out of which his flowing streams have proceeded, let us boldly examine with what reasons he did it. First, truly, a man might maliciously object that Plato, being a philosopher, was a natural enemy of poets. For indeed, after the philosophers had picked out of the sweet mysteries of poetry the right discerning true points of knowledge, they forthwith, putting it in method, and making a school-art of that which the poets did only teach by a divine delightfulness, beginning to spurn at their guides like ungrateful apprentices, were not content to set up shop for themselves, but sought by all means to discredit their masters; which by the force of delight being barred them, the less they could overthrow them, the more they hated them. For indeed, they found for Homer seven cities strove who should have him for their citizen; where so many cities banished philosophers as not fit members to live among them. For only repeating certain of Euripides's verses, many Athenians had their lives saved of the Syracusans, where the Athenians themselves thought many philosophers unworthy to live.[9] Certain poets, as Simonides and Pindarus, had so prevailed with Hiero the First that of a tyrant they made him a just king; where Plato could do so little with Dionysus,[10] that he himself of a philosopher was made a slave. But who should do thus, I confess, should requite the objections made against poets with like cavillations[11] against philosophers; as likewise one should

[1] *phoenix* Mythical unique bird said to be eternally reborn from its own ashes.

[2] *Cato ... field* Marcus Portius Cato the Censor objected to his general, Marcus Flavius Nobilior, bringing the poet Quintus Ennius (not merely his poetry) with him into battle.

[3] *Cato Uticensis* Great-grandson of Cato the Censor and famous political opponent of Julius Caesar.

[4] *the Graces* Three mythological goddesses, daughters of Zeus and Eurynome who bestow joy, beauty, and charm.

[5] *Pluto* God of the underworld.

[6] *unmustered* I.e., not officially enrolled in the army.

[7] *Scipio Nasica* Second-century BCE consul of Rome; *other Scipio brothers* Scipio Asiaticus and Scipio Africanus, two skilled and noble generals.

[8] *sepulture* Sepulcher.

[9] *Athenians ... live* Plutarch, in his *Life of Nicias*, ch. 29, claims that a group of Greek slaves won their freedom as a reward for having taught their masters the poetry of Euripides.

[10] *Hiero the First* Despotic ruler of Syracuse who was also a patron of Greek poets; *Simonides* Greek lyric poet (c. 556–468 BCE); *Dionysus* Fourth-century BCE tyrant of Syracuse who is said to have indirectly caused Plato to be sold into slavery.

[11] *cavillations* Meritless objections.

do that should bid one read *Phaedrus* or *Symposium* in Plato, or the discourse of love in Plutarch, and see whether any poet do authorize abominable filthiness, as they do. Again, a man might ask out of what commonwealth Plato did banish them:[1] in sooth, thence where himself alloweth community of women—so as belike this banishment grew not for effeminate wantonness, since little should poetical sonnets be hurtful when a man might have what woman he listed.[2] But I honor philosophical instructions, and bless the wits which bred them: so as they be not abused, which is likewise stretched to poetry.

St. Paul himself setteth a watch-word upon philosophy, indeed upon the abuse.[3] So doth Plato upon the abuse, not upon poetry. Plato found fault that the poets of his time filled the world with wrong opinions of the gods, making light tales of that unspotted essence, and therefore would not have the youth depraved with such opinions. Herein may much be said. Let this suffice: the poets did not induce such opinions, but did imitate those opinions already induced; for all the Greek stories can well testify that the very religion of that time stood upon many, and many-fashioned, gods, not taught so by poets, but followed according to their nature of imitation. Who list may read in Plutarch the discourses of Isis and Osiris, of the cause why Oracles ceased, of the divine providence, & see whether the theology of that nation stood not upon such dreams which the poets indeed superstitiously observed—and truly (since they had not the light of Christ) did much better in it than the philosophers, who, shaking off superstition, brought in atheism. Plato therefore (whose authority I had much rather justly construe than unjustly resist) meant not in general of poets, in those words of which Julius Scaliger saith, *Qua authoritate barbari quidam atque hispidi abuti velint ad poetas e republica exigendos*;[4] but only meant to drive out those wrong opinions of the Deity (whereof now, without further law, Christianity hath taken away all the hurtful belief), perchance (as he thought) nourished by then-esteemed poets. And a man need go no further than to Plato himself to know his meaning: who, in his dialogue called *Ion*, giveth high and rightly divine commendation unto poetry. So as Plato, banishing the abuse, not the thing, not banishing it, but giving due honor unto it, shall be our patron, and not our adversary. For indeed I had much rather, since truly I may do it, show their mistaking of Plato (under whose lion's skin they would make an ass-like braying against poesy) than go about to overthrow his authority; whom the wiser a man is, the more just cause he shall find to have in admiration; especially since he attributeth unto poesy more than myself do, namely, to be a very inspiring of a divine force, far above man's wit, as in the forenamed dialogue is apparent.

Of the other side, who would show the honors have been by the best sort of judgments granted them, a whole sea of examples would present themselves: Alexanders, Caesars, Scipios, all favorers of poets; Laelius,[5] called the Roman Socrates, himself a poet, so as part of *Heautontimorumenos* in Terence was supposed to be made by him; and even the Greek Socrates, whom Apollo confirmed to be the only wise man, is said to have spent part of his old time in putting Aesop's fables into verses. And therefore, full evil should it become his scholar Plato to put such words in his master's mouth against poets. But what need more? Aristotle writes the Art of Poesy; and why, if it should not be written? Plutarch teacheth the use to be gathered of them;[6] and how, if they should not be read? And who reads Plutarch's either history or philosophy shall find he trimmeth both their garments with guards of poesy. But I list not to defend poesy with the help of his underling

[1] *them* I.e., poets.

[2] *community of women* Cf. Plato's *Republic*, 5.449–62, in which he proposes that in an ideal republic, women would not marry, but would be shared equally by all men.

[3] *St. Paul ... abuse* See Colossus 2.8: "Beware lest any man spoil you through philosophy and vain deceit, after the tradition of men, after the rudiments of the world, and not after Christ."

[4] *Qua ... exigendos* Latin: "By the abuse of which authority [i.e., Plato's] some barbarous and crude men seek to expel poets from the Republic" (Scaliger, *Poetics* 5.a.1).

[5] *Laelius* Roman soldier and politician Gaius Laelius (d. 160 BCE).

[6] *Plutarch ... them* See Plutarch's *Moralia* 17, "How the Young Man Should Study Poetry."

historiography. Let it suffice to have showed it is a fit soil for praise to dwell upon; and what dispraise may set upon it, is either easily overcome, or transformed into just commendation.

So that, since the excellencies of it may be so easily and so justly confirmed, and the low-creeping objections so soon trodden down—it not being an art of lies, but of true doctrine; not of effeminateness, but of notable stirring of courage; not of abusing man's wit, but of strengthening man's wit; not banished, but honored, by Plato—let us rather plant more laurels for to engarland the poets' heads (which honor of being laureate, as besides them only triumphant captains were, is a sufficient authority to show the price they ought to be held in) than suffer the ill-favored breath of such wrong-speakers once to blow upon the clear springs of poesy.

But since I have run so long a career in this matter, methinks, before I give my pen a full stop, it shall be but a little more lost time to enquire why England, the mother of excellent minds, should be grown so hard a stepmother to poets, who certainly in wit ought to pass all other, since all only proceedeth from their wit, being indeed makers of themselves, not takers of others. How can I but exclaim

Musa, mihi causas memoria, quo numine laeso?[1]

Sweet poesy, that hath anciently had kings, emperors, senators, great captains, such as—besides a thousands others—David, Adrian, Sophocles, Germanicus, not only to favor poets, but to be poets; and of our nearer times can present for her patrons a Robert, King of Sicily, the great King Francis of France, King James of Scotland; such cardinals as Bembus and Bibbiena; such famous preachers and teachers as Beza and Melanchthon; so learned philosophers as Fracastorius and Scaliger; so great orators as Pontanus and Muretus; so piercing wits as George Buchanan; so grave counsellors as, besides many, but before all, that Hospital of France,[2] than whom (I think) that realm never brought forth a more accomplished judgment, more firmly built upon virtue: I say these, with numbers of others, not only to read others' poesies, but to poetize for others' reading—that poesy, thus embraced in all other places, should only find in our time a hard welcome in England. I think the very earth lamenteth it, and therefore decks our soil with fewer laurels than it was accustomed. For heretofore poets have in England also flourished, and which is to be noted, even in those times when the trumpet of Mars[3] did sound loudest. And now that an over-faint quietness should seem to strew the house for poets, they are almost in as good reputation as the mountebanks[4] at Venice. Truly even that, as of the one side it giveth great praise to poesy, which like Venus (but to better purpose) had rather be troubled in the net with Mars than enjoy the homely quiet of Vulcan:[5] so serves it for a piece of a reason why they are less grateful to idle England, which now can scarce endure the pain of a pen.

Upon this necessarily followeth, that base men with evil wits undertake it, who think it enough if they can

[1] *Musa ... laeso* Latin: "O Muse, tell me the cause by which the divine has been offended?" (*Aeneid* 1.8).

[2] *David* King David of Israel; *Adrian* Roman emperor Hadrian (76–138 CE), a patron of the arts and also a writer; *Germanicus* Roman general (d. 19 CE), known for conquering Germany and said to have written verse; *Robert* King Robert II of Anjou (1275–1343), patron to Petrarch; *Francis* King Francis I of France (1494–1547), under whose patronage many French poets flourished; *James* King James VI of Scotland (later James I of England), author, and patron of other poets; *Bembus* The Roman Catholic cardinal, philosopher, and poet Pietro Bembo (1470–1547); *Bibbiena* Cardinal and author of the comedy *Calandria* (1513); *Beza* Theodore Beza (1519–1605), Calvinist reformer, theologian, and author; *Melanchthon* Philip Melanchthon (1497–1560), theologian, author, and friend and supporter of Martin Luther; *Fracastorius* The Italian physician Girolamo Fracastoro, known for writing the *Naugerius* (1555); *Pontanus* The poet Giovanni Pontano (1426–1503); *Muretus* The French humanist Marc-Antoine de Muret (1526–85); *George Buchanan* Scottish humanist, poet, and playwright (1506–82); *Hospital of France* Michel de L'Hôpital (1505–73), reformist French Chancellor and Latin poet.

[3] *Mars* Roman god of war.

[4] *mountebanks* Charlatans.

[5] *Venus ... Vulcan* Vulcan, the Roman god of fire, forged a net to catch his wife, Venus, goddess of love and beauty, in adultery with Mars.

be rewarded of the printer. And so as Epaminondas[1] is said with the honor of his virtue to have made an office, by his exercising it, which before was contemptible, to become highly respected; so these men, no more but setting their names to it, by their own disgracefulness disgrace the most graceful poesy. For now, as if all the Muses were got with child to bring forth bastard poets, without any commission they do post over the banks of the Helicon,[2] till they make the readers more weary than post-horses; while, in the meantime, they

Queis meliore luto finxit praecordia Titan[3]

are better content to suppress the outflowings of their wit, than, by publishing them, to be accounted knights of the same order. But I that, before ever I durst aspire unto the dignity, am admitted into the company of the paper-blurrers, do find the very true cause of our wanting estimation is want of desert—taking upon us to be poets in despite of Pallas.

Now, wherein we want desert were a thankworthy labour to express; but if I knew, I should have mended myself. But as I never desired the title, so have I neglected the means to come by it. Only, overmastered by some thoughts, I yielded an inky tribute unto them. Marry, they that delight in poesy itself should seek to know what they do, and how they do; and especially look themselves in an unflattering glass of reason, if they be inclinable unto it. For poesy must not be drawn by the ears; it must be gently led, or rather it must lead—which was partly the cause that made the ancient-learned affirm it was a divine gift, & no human skill: since all other knowledges lie ready for any that have strength of wit. A poet no industry can make, if his own genius be not carried into it; and therefore it is an old proverb, *orator fit, poeta nascitur.*[4]

Yet confess I always, that as the fertilest ground must be manured, so must the highest flying wit have a Daedalus[5] to guide him. That Daedalus, they say, both in this and in other, hath three wings to bear itself up into the air of due commendation: that is, art, imitation, and exercise. But these, neither artificial rules nor imitative patterns, we much cumber[6] ourselves with all. Exercise indeed we do, but that very fore-backwardly: for where we should exercise to know, we exercise as having known; and so is our brain delivered of much matter which never was begotten by knowledge. For there being two principal parts, matter to be expressed by words, and words to express the matter: in neither, we use art or imitation rightly. Our matter is *quodlibet*[7] indeed, though wrongly performing Ovid's verse,

Quicquid conabar dicere, Versus erit.[8]

never marshalling it into any assured rank, that almost the readers cannot tell where to find themselves.

Chaucer, undoubtedly, did excellently in his Troilus and Criseyde; of whom, truly, I know not whether to marvel more, either that he in that misty time could see so clearly, or that we in this clear age go so stumblingly after him. Yet had he great wants, fit to be forgiven in so reverent an antiquity. I account the Mirror of Magistrates[9] meetly furnished of beautiful parts, and in the Earl of Surrey's lyrics many things tasting of a noble birth, and worthy of a noble mind. The *Shepherd's Calendar*[10] hath much poetry in his eclogues, indeed worthy the reading, if I be not deceived. (That same framing of his style to an old rustic language I dare not allow, since neither Theocritus in Greek, Virgil in Latin, nor Sannazaro[11] in Italian did affect it.) Besides these, I

[1] *Epaminondas* Theban general of the fourth century BCE.

[2] *Helicon* Mountain sacred to the Muses.

[3] *Queis… Titan* Latin: "whose breasts the Titan [Prometheus] has fashioned from finer clays" (Juvenal, *Satires* 14.36).

[4] *orator… nascitur* Latin: "The orator is made, the poet is born."

[5] *Daedalus* Mythical inventor who escaped prison on wings made of wax and feathers.

[6] *cumber* Encumber.

[7] *quodlibet* Latin: anything you wish.

[8] *Quicquid … erit* Latin: "Whatever I shall try to say, it will be verse" (Ovid, *Tristia* 4.10.26).

[9] *Mirror of Magistrates* Collection of poems imagined said by various fallen political figures (1559).

[10] *Shepherd's Calendar* Twelve pastoral poems by Edmund Spenser (1552–99), dedicated to Sidney.

[11] *Theocrites, Virgil, Sannazaro* Pastoral poets.

do not remember to have seen but few (to speak boldly) printed that have poetical sinews in them; for proof whereof, let but most of the verses be put in prose, and then ask the meaning, and it will be found that one verse did but beget another, without ordering at the first what should be at the last; which becomes a confused mass of words with a tingling sound of rhyme, barely accompanied with reason.

Our tragedies and comedies (not without cause cried out against), observing rules neither of honest civility, nor skilful poetry—excepting *Gorboduc*[1] (again, I say, of those that I have seen), which notwithstanding as it is full of stately speeches and well-sounding phrases, climbing to the height of Seneca's style, and as full of notable morality, which it doth most delightfully teach, and so obtain the very end of poesy, yet in truth it is very defectuous in the circumstances, which grieveth me, because it might not remain as an exact model of all tragedies. For it is faulty both in place and time, the two necessary companions of all corporal actions. For where the stage should always represent but one place, and the uttermost time presupposed in it should be, both by Aristotle's precept and common reason, but one day, there is both many days and places inartificially imagined.

But if it be so in *Gorboduc*, how much more in all the rest, where you shall have Asia of the one side, and Africa of the other, and so many other under-kingdoms that the player, when he cometh in, must ever begin with telling where he is, or else the tale will not be conceived? Now you shall have three ladies walk to gather flowers: and then we must believe the stage to be a garden. By and by we hear news of shipwreck in the same place: and then we are to blame if we accept it not for a rock. Upon the back of that comes out a hideous monster with fire and smoke: and then the miserable beholders are bound to take it for a cave. While in the meantime two armies fly in, represented with four swords & bucklers: and then what hard heart will not receive it for a pitched field?

[1] *Gorboduc* 1561 tragedy by Thomas Norton and Thomas Sackville.

Now, of time they are much more liberal: for ordinary it is that two young princes[2] fall in love; after many traverses[3] she is got with child, delivered of a fair boy; he is lost, groweth a man, falls in love, and is ready to get another child; and all this is in two hours' space: which, how absurd it is in sense, even sense may imagine, and art hath taught, and all ancient examples justified—and at this day, the ordinary players in Italy will not err in. Yet will some bring in an example of *Eunuchus* in Terence, that containeth matter of two days, yet far short of twenty years. True it is, and so was it to be played in two days, and so fitted to the time it set forth. And though Plautus[4] have in one place done amiss, let us hit with him, & not miss with him.

But they will say, how then shall we set forth a story which containeth both many places and many times? And do they not know that a tragedy is tied to the laws of poesy, and not of history; not bound to follow the story, but having liberty either to feign a quite new matter or to frame the history to the most tragical conveniency? Again, many things may be told which cannot be showed, if they know the difference betwixt reporting and representing. As, for example, I may speak (though I am here) of Peru, and in speech digress from that to the description of Calcutta; but in action I cannot represent it without Pacolet's horse.[5] And so was the manner the ancients took, by some *nuntius*[6] to recount things done in former time or other place. Lastly, if they will represent a history, they must not (as Horace saith) begin *ab ovo*,[7] but they must come to the principal point of that one action which they will represent.

By example this will be best expressed. I have a story of young Polydorus,[8] delivered for safety's sake, with great riches, by his father Priam to Polymnester, King of

[2] *princes* I.e., children of kings, both male and female.

[3] *traverses* Trials; tribulations.

[4] *Plautus* Roman writer whose play *The Menaechmi or the Twin Brothers* provided the basis for Shakespeare's *Comedy of Errors*.

[5] *Pacolet's horse* Enchanted flying horse in the French romance *Valentine and Orson*.

[6] *nuntius* Latin: messenger.

[7] *ab ovo* Latin: From the egg; i.e., from the beginning.

[8] *story … Polydorus* Euripedes tells this story in his play *Hecuba*.

Thrace, in the Trojan war time. He, after some years, hearing the overthrow of Priam, for to make the treasure his own, murdereth the child; the body of the child is taken up by Hecuba; she, the same day, findeth a sleight to be revenged most cruelly of the tyrant. Where now would one of our tragedy writers begin, but with the delivery of the child? Then should he sail over into Thrace, and so spend I know not how many years, and travel numbers of places. But where doth Euripides? Even with the finding of the body, the rest leaving to be told by the spirit of Polydorus. This needs no further to be enlarged; the dullest wit may conceive it.

But besides these gross absurdities, how all their plays be neither right tragedies, nor right comedies, mingling kings and clowns, not because the matter so carrieth it, but thrust in the clown by head and shoulders to play a part in majestical matters with neither decency nor discretion, so as neither the admiration and commiseration, nor the right sportfulness, is by their mongrel tragicomedy obtained. I know Apuleius[1] did somewhat so, but that is a thing recounted with space of time, not represented in one moment; and I know the ancients have one or two examples of tragicomedies, as Plautus hath *Amphitryo*;[2] but, if we mark them well, we shall find that they never, or very daintily, match hornpipes and funerals. So falleth it out that, having indeed no right comedy, in that comical part of our tragedy we have nothing but scurrility, unworthy of any chaste ears, or some extreme show of doltishness, indeed fit to lift up a loud laughter, and nothing else: where the whole tract of a comedy should be full of delight, as the tragedy should be still maintained in a well-raised admiration.

But our comedians think there is no delight without laughter, which is very wrong; for though laughter may come with delight, yet cometh it not of delight, as though delight should be the cause of laughter; but well may one thing breed both together. Nay, rather in themselves they have, as it were, a kind of contrariety: for delight we scarcely do but in things that have a conveniency to ourselves, or to the general nature; laughter almost ever cometh of things most disproportioned to ourselves and nature. Delight hath a joy in it, either permanent or present. Laughter hath only a scornful tickling.

For example, we are ravished with delight to see a fair woman, and yet are far from being moved to laughter. We laugh at deformed creatures, wherein certainly we cannot delight. We delight in good chances, we laugh at mischances. We delight to hear the happiness of our friends and country, at which he were worthy to be laughed at that would laugh; we shall, contrarily, laugh sometimes to find a matter quite mistaken and go down the hill against the bias[3] in the mouth of some such men—as for the respect of them one shall be heartily sorry, he cannot choose but laugh, and so is rather pained than delighted with laughter.

Yet deny I not but that they may go well together. For as in Alexander's picture well set out we delight without laughter, and in twenty mad antics we laugh without delight; so in Hercules, painted with his great beard and furious countenance, in a woman's attire, spinning at Omphale's commandment,[4] it breedeth both delight and laughter: for the representing of so strange a power in love procureth delight, and the scornfulness of the action stirreth laughter. But I speak to this purpose, that all the end of the comical part be not upon such scornful matters as stir laughter only, but, mixed with it, that delightful teaching which is the end of poesy. And the great fault even in that point of laughter, and forbidden plainly by Aristotle,[5] is that they stir laughter in sinful things, which are rather execrable than ridiculous, or in miserable, which are rather to be pitied than scorned. For what is it to make folks gape at a wretched beggar and a beggarly clown; or, against law of hospitality, to jest at strangers because they speak not English so well as we do? What do we learn, since it is certain

Nil habet infoelix paupertas durius in se,

[1] *Apuleius* Author of the Latin work *The Golden Ass* (translated into English in 1566 by William Adlington).

[2] *Amphitryo* Tragicomedy by the Roman playwright Plautus, in which the gods trick Alcmena, the heroine, into sleeping with Jupiter.

[3] *go down ... bias* End disastrously.

[4] *Omphale's commandment* Hercules, in love with Queen Omphale, agreed to dress as a woman and complete various tasks for her.

[5] *laughter ... Aristotle* See *Nicomachean Ethics* 4.8 (1128a).

Quam quod ridiculos homines facit?[1]

But rather, a busy loving courtier and a heartless threatening Thraso; a self-wise-seeming schoolmaster; an awry transformed traveller. These, if we saw walk in stage names, which we play naturally, therein were delightful laughter, and teaching delightfulness—as in the other, the tragedies of Buchanan do justly bring forth a divine admiration.

But I have lavished out too many words of this play matter. I do it because, as they are excelling parts of poesy, so is there none so much used in England, and none can be more pitifully abused; which, like an unmannerly daughter showing a bad education, causeth her mother Poesy's honesty to be called in question.

Other sort of poetry almost have we none, but that lyrical kind of songs and sonnets: which, Lord, if He gave us so good minds, how well it might be employed, and with how heavenly fruits, both private and public, in singing the praises of the immortal beauty: the immortal goodness of that God who giveth us hands to write and wits to conceive; of which we might well want words, but never matter; of which we could turn our eyes to nothing, but we should ever have new-budding occasions. But truly many of such writings as come under the banner of unresistible love, if I were a mistress, would never persuade me they were in love: so coldly they apply fiery speeches, as men that had rather read lovers' writings—and so caught up certain swelling phrases which hang together like a man that once told me the wind was at northwest and by south, because he would be sure to name winds enough—than that in truth they feel those passions, which easily (as I think) may be bewrayed[2] by that same forcibleness, or *energia* (as the Greeks call it), of the writer. But let this be a sufficient though short note, that we miss the right use of the material point of poesy.

Now, for the outside of it, which is words, or (as I may term it) *diction*, it is even well worse. So is it that honey-flowing matron, Eloquence, apparelled, or rather disguised, in a courtesan-like painted affectation. One time, with so far-fet words that many seem monsters, but must seem strangers to any poor Englishman; another time, with coursing of a letter,[3] as if they were bound to follow the method of a dictionary: another time, with figures and flowers, extremely winter-starved. But I would this fault were only peculiar to versifiers, and had not as large possession among prose-printers: and (which is to be marvelled) among many scholars; & (which is to be pitied) among some preachers. Truly I could wish, if at least I might be so bold to wish in a thing beyond the reach of my capacity, the diligent imitators of Tully & Demosthenes[4] (most worthy to be imitated) did not so much keep Nizolian paper-books[5] of their figures and phrase, as by attentive translation, as it were, devour them whole, and make them wholly theirs: for now they cast sugar and spice upon every dish that is served to the table—like those Indians, not content to wear earrings at the fit and natural place of the ears, but they will thrust jewels through their nose and lips, because they will be sure to be fine. Tully, when he was to drive out Catiline, as it were with a thunderbolt of eloquence, often used the figure of repitition, as *Vivit & vincit, imo in senatum. Venit imo, in senatum venit, &c.*[6] Indeed, inflamed with a well grounded rage, he would have his words (as it were) double out of his mouth, and so do that artificially[7] which we see men in choler do naturally. And we, having noted the grace of those words, hale them in sometimes to a familiar epistle, when it were too much choler to be choleric. How well store of *similiter*[8] *cadences* doth sound with the gravity of the pulpit, I would but invoke Demosthenes' soul to tell, who with a rare daintiness useth them. Truly they have made me think of the sophister[9] that with too much subtlety

[1] *Nil ... facit* Latin: "Luckless poverty has in itself nothing harder than that it makes men ridiculous" (Juvenal, *Satires* 3.152–53).

[2] *bewrayed* Betrayed.

[3] *coursing of a letter* Repetition of a letter; i.e., alliteration.

[4] *Demosthenes* Famous Athenian orator of the fifth century BCE.

[5] *Nizolian paper-books* Selection of Cicero's phrases and sayings compiled by sixteenth-century Italian humanist Mario Nizolio.

[6] *Vivit ... venit* Latin: "He lives and he comes, indeed he comes into the Senate. He indeed comes, into the Senate he comes." Adaptation of Cicero, *Catiline* 1.1.2.

[7] *artificially* Artfully; skillfully.

[8] *similiter* I.e., in like manner.

[9] *sophister* One who values rhetoric over veracity.

would prove two eggs three, and though he might be counted a sophister, had none for his labour. So these men bringing in such a kind of eloquence, well may they obtain an opinion of a seeming finesse, but persuade few—which should be the end of their finesse. Now for similitudes, in certain printed discourses, I think all herbarists, all stories of beasts, fowls, and fishes, are rifled up,[1] that they may come in multitudes to wait upon any of our conceits; which certainly is as absurd a surfeit to the ears as is possible. For the force of a similitude not being to prove anything to a contrary disputer, but only to explain to a willing hearer, when that is done, the rest is a most tedious prattling, rather over-swaying the memory from the purpose whereto they were applied, than any whit informing the judgment, already either satisfied, or by similitudes not to be satisfied. For my part, I do not doubt, when Antonius and Crassus,[2] the great forefathers of Cicero in eloquence, the one (as Cicero testifieth of them) pretended not to know art, the other not to set by it, because with a plain sensibleness they might win credit of popular ears (which credit is the nearest step to persuasion, which persuasion is the chief mark of oratory), I do not doubt (I say) but that they used these knacks very sparingly; which who doth generally use, any man may see doth dance to his own music, and so to be noted by the audience more careful to speak curiously than truly. Undoubtedly (at least to my opinion undoubtedly), I have found in divers small learned courtiers a more sound style than in some professors of learning; of which I can guess no other cause, but that the courtier, following that which by practice he findeth fittest to nature, therein (though he know it not) doth according to art, though not by art: where the other, using art to show art, and not hide art (as in these cases he should do), flieth from nature, & indeed abuseth art.

But what? Methinks I deserve to be pounded for straying from poetry to oratory. But both have such an affinity in the wordish consideration, that I think this digression will make my meaning receive the fuller understanding: which is not to take upon me to teach poets how they should do, but only, finding myself sick among the rest, to show some one or two spots of the common infection grown among the most part of writers, that, acknowledging ourselves somewhat awry, we may bend to the right use both of matter and manner: whereto our language giveth us great occasion, being indeed capable of any excellent exercising of it. I know some will say it is a mingled language: and why not, so much the better, taking the best of both the other? Another will say it wanteth grammar. Nay truly, it hath that praise, that it wants not grammar: for grammar it might have, but it needs it not, being so easy in itself, and so void of those cumbersome differences of cases, genders, moods, & tenses, which I think was a piece of the Tower of Babylon's[3] curse, that a man should be put to school to learn his mother tongue. But for the uttering sweetly and properly the conceit of the mind, which is the end of speech, that hath it equally with any other tongue in the world; and is particularly happy in compositions of two or three words together, near the Greek, far beyond the Latin, which is one of the greatest beauties can be in a language.

Now, of versifying there are two sorts, the one ancient, the other modern. The ancient marked the quantity of each syllable, and according to that, framed his verse; the modern, observing only number (with some regard of the accent) the chief life of it standeth in that like sounding of the words, which we call rhyme. Whether of these be the more excellent, would bear many speeches: the ancient no doubt more fit for music, both words and time observing quantity, and more fit lively to express divers passions by the low or lofty sound of the well-weighed syllable; the latter likewise with his rhyme striketh a certain music to the ear, and, in fine, since it doth delight, though by an other way, it obtains the same purpose, there being in either sweetness, and wanting in neither majesty. Truly the English, before any vulgar language[4] I know, is fit for both sorts: for, for the ancient, the Italian is so full of vowels that it must ever be cumbered with elisions; the Dutch so of the other side, with consonants, that they cannot yield the sweet sliding fit for a verse; the

[1] *rifled up* Searched through.

[2] *Antonius and Crassus* Two Roman consuls (of 99 and 175 BCE, respectively).

[3] *Tower of Babylon* I.e., the Tower of Babel.

[4] *vulgar language* Vernacular.

French in his whole language hath not one word that hath his accent in the last syllable, saving two, called *antepenultima*; and little more hath the Spanish, and therefore very gracelessly may they use dactyls. The English is subject to none of these defects. Now for rhyme, though we do not observe quantity, yet we observe the accent very precisely, which other languages either cannot do, or will not do so absolutely. That *caesura*, or breathing place in the midst of the verse, neither Italian nor Spanish have, the French and we never almost fail of. Lastly, even the very rhyme itself, the Italian cannot put it in the last syllable, by the French named the masculine rhyme, but still in the next to the last, which the French call the female, or the next before that, which the Italian term *sdrucciola*. The example of the former, is *buono, suono*, of the *sdrucciola*, is *femina, semina*. The French, of the other side, hath both the male, as *bon, son*; and the female, as *plaise, taise*; but the *sdrucciola* he hath not: where the English hath all three, as due, true; father, rather; motion, potion[1]—with much more which might be said, but that already I find the triflingness of this discourse is much too much enlarged.

So that since the ever-praiseworthy Poesy is full of virtue-breeding delightfulness, and void of no gift that ought to be in the noble name of learning; since the blames laid against it are either false or feeble; since the cause why it is not esteemed in England is the fault of poet-apes, not poets; since, lastly, our tongue is most fit to honor poesy, and to be honored by poesy; I conjure you all that have had the evil luck to read this ink-wasting toy of mine, even in the name of the nine Muses, no more to scorn the sacred mysteries of poesy; no more to laugh at the name of poets, as though they were next inheritors to fools; no more to jest at the reverent title of a rhymer; but to believe, with Aristotle, that they were the ancient treasurers of the Grecians' divinity; to believe, with Bembus, that they were the first bringers-in of all civility; to believe, with Scaliger, that no philosopher's precepts can sooner make you an honest man than the reading of Virgil; to believe, with Clauserus, the translator of Cornatus,[2] that it pleased the heavenly Deity, by Hesiod and Homer, under the veil of fables to give us all knowledge, logic, rhetoric, philosophy natural and moral, and *quid non*?[3] To believe, with me, that there are many mysteries contained in poetry, which of purpose were written darkly, lest by profane wits it should be abused; to believe, with Landino,[4] that they are so beloved of the gods that whatsoever they write proceeds of a divine fury; lastly, to believe themselves when they tell you they will make you immortal by their verses. Thus doing, your name shall flourish in the printers' shops; thus doing, you shall be of kin to many a poetical preface; thus doing, you shall be most fair, most rich, most wise, most all: you shall dwell upon superlatives; thus doing, though you be *libertino patre natus*, you shall suddenly grow *Herculea proles*,

Si quid mea carmina possunt;[5]

thus doing, your soul shall be placed with Dante's Beatrice, or Virgil's Anchises. But if (fie of such a but) you be born so near the dull-making cataract of Nilus[6] that you cannot hear the planet-like music[7] of poetry; if you have so earth-creeping a mind that it cannot lift itself up to look to the sky of poetry, or rather, by a certain rustical disdain, will become such a mome as to be a Momus[8] of poetry; then, though I will not wish unto you the ass's ears of Midas,[9] nor to be driven by a

[1] *motion, potion* Pronounced with three syllables.

[2] *Clauserus* Conrad Clauser (1826–91), German scholar who translated the work of Cornatus, a Stoic philosopher of the first century.

[3] *quid non?* Latin: what not?

[4] *Landino* Cristoforo Landino (1424–1504), Italian humanist and literary critic best known for his highly acclaimed annotated edition of Dante's *Divine Comedy*.

[5] *libertino ... natus* Latin: Born of a freed slave; *Herculea proles* Latin: Descendant of Hercules; *Si ... possunt* Latin: "If my songs are able to do anything" (Virgil, *Aeneid* 9.446).

[6] *so near ... poetry* Cicero believed that the sound of the Nile's cataracts caused deafness to those nearby.

[7] *planet-like music* Many had long believed that the movement of the various planets' spheres produced a beautiful and perfectly harmonious music.

[8] *mome* Fool; *Momus* God of mockery and unfair criticism; he was exiled from Mt. Olympus as a result of his constant criticism.

[9] *ass's ears of Midas* Apollo, god of music, punished King Midas by giving him the ears of an ass after Midas judged the rustic pipe playing of Pan to be superior to that of Apollo.

poet's verses, as Bubonax[1] was, to hang himself, nor to be rhymed to death, as is said to be done in Ireland;[2] yet thus much curse I must send you in the behalf of all poets: that while you live, you live in love, and never get favor, for lacking skill of a sonnet; and when you die, your memory die from the earth for want of an epitaph.

—1595

In Context

The Abuse of Poesy

The attacks against which Sidney and others were defending poetry have important roots in ancient philosophy. They stem in particular from the Platonic arguments that storytelling is in some ways morally akin to lying, and that in so far as fictions are to be allowed (whether spoken, written in prose, or acted upon the stage) they should embody human notions of moral justice, with the wicked shown to be punished, and so on. In the sixteenth century some Protestants expanded upon these arguments from Plato, contending that the representation of wickedness in artistic form was itself immoral—regardless of whether wickedness was represented as leading in the end to reward or punishment. The most famous of these attacks was *The School of Abuse* by Stephen Gosson (1554–1624). Gosson, who had himself been a playwright as well as a writer of pamphlets, and who would later become a clergyman, was commissioned by the authorities in London to write an attack on what were perceived to be the excesses and immoralities of the commercial drama. Gosson's style of attack itself ran to excess—as is evident in the excerpt below.

from Plato, *The Republic* (c. 375 BCE)[3]

In this excerpt the philosopher Socrates (who is assumed to be speaking for Plato) is discussing with Adeimantus the education of a leader. In the course of the discussion he puts forward the argument that the sorts of stories that poets and dramatists are allowed to recount should be restricted, and that certain subjects should be censored.

from Book 2:

...

Socrates. You know also that the beginning is the most important part of any work, especially in the case of a young and tender thing; for that is the time at which the character is being formed and the desired impression is more readily taken.

Adeimantus. Quite true.

[1] *Bubonax* Combination of the name of the sculptor Bupalus and that of the Greek poet Hipponax. Hipponax mocked Bupalus in verse after seeing an unflattering portrait the sculptor had made of him. His satiric attack was so biting that Bupalus was driven to hang himself.

[2] *rhymed ... Ireland* Irish poets bragged that their magical rhymes could cause death.

[3] *The Republic* Translated by Benjamin Jowett (1894).

SOCRATES. And shall we just carelessly allow children to hear any casual tales which may be devised by casual persons, and to receive into their minds ideas for the most part the very opposite of those which we should wish them to have when they are grown up?

ADEIMANTUS. We cannot.

SOCRATES. Then the first thing will be to establish a censorship of the writers of fiction, and let the censors receive any tale of fiction which is good, and reject the bad; and we will desire mothers and nurses to tell their children the authorized ones only. Let them fashion the mind with such tales, even more fondly than they mold the body with their hands; but most of those which are now in use must be discarded.

ADEIMANTUS. Of what tales are you speaking?

SOCRATES. You may find a model of the lesser in the greater, for they are necessarily of the same type, and there is the same spirit in both of them.

ADEIMANTUS. Very likely, but I do not as yet know what you would term the greater.

SOCRATES. Those which are narrated by Homer and Hesiod,[1] and the rest of the poets, who have ever been the great story-tellers.

ADEIMANTUS. But which stories do you mean; and what fault do you find with them?

SOCRATES. A fault which is most serious—the fault of telling a lie, and, what is more, a bad lie.

ADEIMANTUS. But when is this fault committed?

SOCRATES. Whenever an erroneous representation is made of the nature of gods and heroes —as when a painter paints a portrait not having the shadow of a likeness to the original. [...] God, if He be good, is not the author of all things, as the many assert, but He is the cause of a few things only, and not of most things that occur to men. For few are the goods of human life, and many are the evils, and the good is to be attributed to God alone; of the evils the causes are to be sought elsewhere, and not in Him.

ADEIMANTUS. That appears to me to be most true.

SOCRATES. Then we must not listen to Homer or to any other poet who is guilty of the folly of saying that two casks lie at the threshold of Zeus,[2] full of lots, one of good, the other of evil lots, and that he to whom Zeus gives a mixture of the two sometimes meets with evil fortune, at other times with good; but that he to whom is given the cup of unmingled ill, him wild hunger drives o'er the beauteous earth. And if anyone assert that the violation of oaths and treaties, which was really the work of Pandarus,[3] was brought about by Athene[4] and Zeus, or that the strife and contention of the gods was instigated by Themis[5] and Zeus, he shall not have our approval; neither will we allow our young men to hear the words of Aeschylus,[6] that God plants guilt among men when he desires utterly to destroy a house. And if a poet writes of the sufferings of Niobe—the subject of the tragedy in

---

[1] *Homer* Eighth-century BCE Greek poet credited with authoring the epic poems *The Iliad* and *The Odyssey*; Hesiod Eighth-century BCE Greek poet known for *Works and Days* and *The Theogeny*.

[2] *Zeus* King of the Greek gods.

[3] Pandarus Trojan warrior in Homer's *Iliad* who broke the truce between Greece and Troy by wounding Menelaus, the king of Sparta.

[4] *Athene* Athena, the Greek goddess of wisdom and warfare and the protectress of Athens.

[5] *Themis* In Greek mythology, a Titan and the goddess of order and justice.

[6] *Aeschylus* Athenian tragic dramatist of the fifth century BCE.

which these iambic verses occur—or of the house of Pelops,[1] or of the Trojan war or on any similar theme, either we must not permit him to say that these are the works of God, or if they are of God, he must devise some explanation of them such as we are seeking; he must say that God did what was just and right, and they were the better for being punished; but that those who are punished are miserable, and that God is the author of their misery, the poet is not to be permitted to say; though he may say that the wicked are miserable because they require to be punished, and are benefitted by receiving punishment from God; but that God being good is the author of evil to anyone is to be strenuously denied, and not to be said or sung or heard in verse or prose by anyone whether old or young in any well-ordered commonwealth. Such a fiction is suicidal, ruinous, impious.

from Stephen Gosson, *The School of Abuse* (1579)

I must confess that poets are the whetstones of wit, notwithstanding that wit is dearly bought. Where honey and gall are mixed, it will be hard to sever the one from the other. The deceitful physician giveth sweet syrups to make his poison go down the smoother; the juggler casteth a mist to work the close; the Siren's song[2] is the sailor's wreck; the fowler's whistle, the bird's death; the wholesome bait, the fish's bane; the Harpies[3] have virgins' faces and vultures' talons; Hyena speaks like a friend, and devours like a foe; the calmest seas hide dangerous rocks; the wolf jets in weathers fells. Many good sentences are spoken by Davus[4] to shadow his knavery, and written by poets as ornaments to beautify their works and set their trumpery to sale without suspect.

But if you look well to Epeus's horse, you find in his bowels the destruction of Troy;[5] open the sepulchre of Semiramis,[6] whose title promiseth such wealth to the kings of Persia, you shall see nothing but dead bones; rip up the golden ball that Nero[7] consecrated to Jupiter Capitolinus, you shall have it stuffed with the shavings of his beard; pull off the vizard that poets mask in, you shall disclose their reproach, bewray their vanity, loath their wantonness, lament their folly, and perceive their sharp sayings to be placed as pearls in dunghills, fresh pictures on rotten walls, chaste matrons' apparel on common courtesans. These are the cups of Circe that turn reasonable creatures into brute beasts, the

[1] *Niobe* Queen of Thebes who boasted of her fruitfulness, angering the gods Apollo and Artemis and causing them to murder her children; *Pelops* Son of Tantalus who won his wife, Hippodamia, by defeating her father, the king of Pisa, in a chariot race. To ensure his victory, Pelops bribed the king's charioteer to betray his master. After the race, Pelops was unable to pay the reward, and threw the charioteer in the lake instead. Before drowning, the charioteer cursed the house of Pelops.

[2] *Siren's song* In Greek mythology the Sirens—creatures that were half woman, half bird—would sing in a captivating fashion that would lead sailors to destroy themselves, whether by jumping overboard or by running their ships aground.

[3] *Harpies* Greek mythological creatures with women's faces and bodies, wings, and sharp claws.

[4] *Davus* Servant in *Andria*, a comedy by the Roman second-century BCE dramatist Terence.

[5] *Epeus's horse ... Troy* According to Greek legend, the Greeks pretended to retreat after having attacked the city of Troy for many years, but they left behind a huge wooden horse, supposedly as a gift. When the Trojans moved the horse inside the city walls, Greek warriors who had hidden themselves inside the structure attacked the Trojans and conquered the city. Epeus had taken the lead in constructing the horse.

[6] *Semiramis* Mythical Assyrian queen who was said to have conquered many lands and founded the city of Babylon.

[7] *Nero* Tyrannical Roman emperor of the first century CE.

balls of Hippomenes that hinder the course of Atalanta,[1] and the blocks of the Devil that are cast in our ways to cut off the race of toward wits. No marvel though Plato shut them out of his school and banished them quite from his commonwealth as effeminate writers, unprofitable members, and utter enemies to virtue.

The Romans were very desirous to imitate the Greeks, and yet very loath to receive their poets. Insomuch that Cato[2] layeth it in the dish of Marcus the noble as a foul reproach that in the time of his consulship he brought Ennius the poet into his province. Tully,[3] accustomed to read them with great diligence in his youth, but when he waxed graver in study, elder in years, riper in judgment, he accompted them the fathers of lies, the pipes of vanity, and schools of abuse. Maximus Tyrius[4] taketh upon him to defend the discipline of these doctors under the name of Homer, wresting the rashness of Ajax to valor, the cowardice of Ulysses to policy,[5] the dotage of Nestor to grave counsel, and the battle of Troy to the wonderful conflict of the four elements, where Juno, which is counted the air, sets in her foot to take up the strike and steps boldly betwixt them to part the fray. It is a pageant worth the sight, to behold how he labors with mountains to bring forth mice, much like to some of those players that come to the scaffold[6] with drum and trumpet to proffer skirmish, and when they have sounded alarm, off go the pieces to encounter a shadow, or conquer a paper monster. You will smile, I am sure, if you read it, to see how this moral philosopher toils to draw the lion's skin upon Aesop's ass, Hercules' shoes on a child's feet, amplifying that which the more it is stirred, the more it stinks, the less it is talked of, the better it is liked, and as wayward children, the more they be flattered, the worse they are, or as cursed sores with often touching wax angry, and run the longer without healing. He attributeth the beginning of virtue to Minerva, if friendship to Venus, and the root of all handicrafts to Vulcan, but if he had broke his arm as well as his leg when he fell out of heaven into Lemnos,[7] either Apollo must have played the bonesetter, or every occupation been laid a-water.[8]

[1] *cups of Circe* In Homer's *Odyssey*, the enchantress Circe gives Odysseus's men a potion that turns them into swine; *balls of Hippomenes* According to Greek mythology, Atalanta was a huntress who was famous for her speed, and who would only marry the suitor who could beat her in a race. Hippomenes did so by dropping three golden apples, which Atalanta stopped to retrieve.

[2] *Cato* The Roman statesman Cato the Younger (95-46 BCE), whose great-grandfather, the statesman Cato the Elder (Marcus Porcius Cato), brought the poet Ennius from Sardinia to Rome.

[3] *Tully* Marcus Tullius Cicero, a great Roman orator and politician (106-43 BCE).

[4] *Maximus Tyrius* See Oration 26 of the *Philosophical Orations* of Maximus of Tyre, a second-century CE Greek philosopher.

[5] *policy* Political cunning.

[6] *scaffold* Stage.

[7] *Lemnos* Island in the northern part of the Aegean Sea.

[8] *laid a-water* Made of no effect.

Elizabeth I, Queen of England

1533 – 1603

One of the most famous monarchs in European history, Queen Elizabeth I presided over a vigorous culture that saw notable accomplishments in the arts, voyages of discovery, the "Elizabethan settlement" that created the Church of England, and the defeat of military threats from Spain. Her shrewd political mind helped sustain her country in a time of occasional famine, widespread poverty, intermittent plague, and deep religious and political divisions; she also, if sometimes reluctantly, supported the beginnings of an empire that would flourish over the next 350 years. Elizabeth was also a precocious writer, penning translations even in her childhood and later composing poetry and speeches.

Elizabeth was the product of a controversial union, that of Henry VIII and Anne Boleyn. Some months before giving birth on 7 September 1533 Boleyn became the king's second wife. In 1534, Pope Clement VII, who had waffled for a few years, officially confirmed his refusal to annul Henry's marriage to his first wife, Catherine of Aragon. Henry responded by declaring himself head of the English Church, but many in and out of the government refused to recognize either his right to do this or the validity of his new marriage. A significant portion of the population therefore considered Elizabeth illegitimate, and throughout her reign many of those loyal to the Roman Catholic Church continued to dispute her right to the throne.

At first Henry designated Elizabeth as his heir. However, after her mother fell from favor and was executed in 1536, Elizabeth's political fortunes turned (much as they had for her older half-sister, Mary). Henry married Jane Seymour and had a son, Edward, who was named King after Henry died in 1547. Orphaned, Elizabeth was cared for by Henry's last wife, Catherine Parr, and her new husband, Thomas Seymour. Catherine made sure that Elizabeth received a fine education, hiring a number of prominent tutors, including the distinguished humanist Roger Ascham.

Young Edward VI proved to be sickly, dying in 1553 before his sixteenth birthday. Various political maneuvers ensued, but eventually Elizabeth's half-sister Mary was crowned Queen. Mary I was a staunch Catholic who wanted to undo the reforms of her father as well as the explicitly Protestant changes made by Edward, and she attempted to convince Elizabeth to convert to Catholicism. Whether from sincere reluctance or awareness that she was the Protestant hope, or both, Elizabeth was prudently ambiguous about her religious beliefs, so on 17 March 1554, fearful of plots against her throne, Mary had her imprisoned in the Tower of London. There she stayed for two months before being transferred into custody at Woodstock Castle, a dilapidated hunting lodge in Oxfordshire, where she remained for almost a year.

When Mary died on 17 November 1558, childless in her marriage to Philip II of Spain, Elizabeth was named Queen. She was crowned on 15 January 1559, after elaborate London celebrations, in Westminster Abbey. As Queen, Elizabeth proved to be a strong and cunning leader. Early in her reign she worked hard to solidify her rule, thwarting assassination attempts and Catholic plots to install her cousin, Mary Stuart, as queen. Elizabeth took a more moderate approach to England's religious conflicts than had her predecessors. She reinstated the reforms instituted by her father and brother, but she eschewed Edward's Calvinist militancy as well as Mary's punitive conservatism. She also displayed her acumen in domestic politics, manipulating her advisors as a means of maintaining her own control and playing the Petrarchan mistress or virgin goddess to encourage her courtiers' and subjects' loyalty and affection. Internationally, although she did send money and men to help Henri IV to the French throne and to help the Dutch expel the Spanish, she largely withdrew England from costly involvement in foreign conflicts. Ireland was another matter, and Elizabeth's government engaged in an often bloody struggle to suppress Irish revolts against English rule.

Throughout the first half of her reign, Elizabeth was under pressure from advisors and Parliament to marry and produce an heir. She resisted, no doubt aware that any spouse would exert considerable influence over her. She entertained many suitors, English and foreign, but declared that she preferred being married to England.

Elizabeth's writings provide glimpses into her mind, although as a princess or queen she knew she was always on stage and without real privacy. Her lines written on a window frame during her captivity at Woodstock (1555) cry for justice, for example, while "On Monsieur's Departure" (c. 1581; "Monsieur" is almost certainly her suitor the Duc d'Anjou, brother to the French king) shows her romantic side—or its political simulation. In her so-called "Golden Speech," her farewell speech to Parliament given on 30 November 1601, Elizabeth speaks frankly about the burdens of queenship: "to be a king and wear a crown is a thing more glorious to them that see it than it is pleasant to them that bear it." The queen also translated various works, including passages from Boethius' *Consolation of Philosophy*, and made the first English translation of Horace's "Art of Poetry."

Elizabeth overcame the uncertainty that surrounded her accession to become enormously popular, even with many Catholics; she came to be known to her subjects as "Good Queen Bess." She died on 24 March 1603 at almost seventy, having ruled England for nearly 45 years. She was buried in Westminster Abbey and was succeeded by James VI of Scotland, the Protestant son of Mary Stuart, who reigned as James I.

⌘⌘⌘

Written on a Wall at Woodstock[1]

Oh fortune, thy wresting[2] wavering state
Hath fraught with cares my troubled wit,
Whose witness this present prison late
Could bear, where once was joy's loan quit.[3]
Thou causedst the guilty to be loosed
From bands where innocents were enclosed,
And caused the guiltless to be reserved,
And freed those that death had well deserved.
But herein can be nothing wrought,
So God send to my foes as they have thought.
—c. 1554–55

[1] *Wall* This poem is variously noted as being written on a wall, a shutter, and a window frame. Writing poetry or proverbs on these surfaces was not uncommon in the period; *Woodstock* Elizabeth, under suspicion for involvement in Sir Thomas Wyatt the Younger's plots against Mary, was placed under house arrest at Woodstock.

[2] *wresting* Struggling, twisting.

[3] *joy's loan quit* The lease of joy repaid.

Written in Her French Psalter[4]

No crooked leg, no bleared eye,
No part deformed out of kind,

[4] *Psalter* Translation or version of the Book of Psalms. This poem is inscribed in the last leaf of Elizabeth's French psalter.

Nor yet so ugly half can be
As is the inward suspicious mind.
—1565

The Doubt of Future Foes[1]

The doubt of future foes exiles my present joy,
And wit me warns to shun such snares as threaten mine annoy,
For falsehood now doth flow, and subjects' faith doth ebb,
Which should not be if reason ruled or wisdom weaved the web.
But clouds of joys untried do cloak aspiring minds,
Which turn to rain of late repent by changed course of winds.
The top of hope supposed the root upreared shall be,
And fruitless all their grafted guile, as shortly ye shall see.
Their dazzled eyes with pride, which great ambition blinds,
Shall be unsealed by worthy wights° whose foresight falsehood finds. *people*
The daughter of debate[2] that discord aye doth sow
Shall reap no gain where former rule still peace hath taught to grow.
No foreign banished wight shall anchor in this port;
Our realm brooks° not seditious sects, let them elsewhere resort. *tolerates*
My rusty sword through rest[3] shall first his edge employ
To poll° their tops that seek such change or gape for future joy. *crop or cut*
—c. 1568–71

[1] *Doubt* Dread or fear; *Future Foes* This poem was written in response to the threat to Elizabeth's rule from Mary, Queen of Scots. Mary believed she had a legitimate claim to the throne of England and became the focal point of Catholic protests against Elizabeth. This was probably written shortly after Mary's flight from Scotland to England in 1568, as it appeared in commonplace books early in the 1570s, though the poem has been understood as a response to Mary's execution in 1587.

[2] *The daughter of debate* Mary, Queen of Scots.

[3] *rusty sword through rest* The sword is rusty because unused.

On Monsieur's Departure[4]

I grieve, and dare not show my discontent,
I love, and yet am forced to seem to hate,
I do, yet dare not say I ever meant,
I seem stark mute, but inwardly do prate.
I am and not, I freeze and yet am burned,
Since from myself another self I turned.

My care is like my shadow in the sun,
Follows me flying, flies when I pursue it,
Stands and lies by me, doth what I have done.
His too familiar care doth make me rue° it. *regret*
No means I find to rid him from my breast,
Till by the end of things it be suppressed.

Some gentler passion slide into my mind,
For I am soft and made of melting snow,
Or be more cruel, love, and so be kind.
Let me or float or sink, be high or low,[5]
Or let me live with some more sweet content,
Or die, and so forget what love ere meant.
—c. 1582

When I Was Fair and Young[6]

When I was fair and young, and favour graced me,
Of many was I sought their mistress for to be,
But I did scorn them all and answered them therefore,
"Go, go, go, seek some other where. Importune me no more."
How many weeping eyes I made to pine with woe,
How many sighing hearts I have no skill to show,
But I the prouder grew and still this spake therefore,
"Go, go, go, seek some other where. Importune me no more."

[4] *On Monsieur's Departure* This poem was written in response to the final departure of Elizabeth's French suitor, François, duc d'Anjou, in 1582.

[5] *or ... or* Either ... or.

[6] *When I was Fair and Young* The date of this poem is uncertain, and some editors have doubted its authenticity.

Then spake fair Venus' son,[1] that proud victorious boy,
Saying, "You dainty dame, for that you be so coy,
I will so pluck your plumes as you shall say no more,
'Go, go, go, seek some other where. Importune me no more.'"

When he had spoke these words, such change grew in my breast
That neither night nor day since that I could take any rest.
Wherefore I did repent that I had said before,
"Go, go, go, seek some other where. Importune me no more."

—1589–90

To Our Most Noble and Virtuous Queen Katherine, Elizabeth Her Humble Daughter Wishes Perpetual Felicity and Everlasting Joy[2]

Not only knowing the affectionate will and fervent zeal which your highness hath toward all godly learning, as also my duty toward you (most gracious and sovereign princess), but knowing also that pusillanimity[3] and idleness are most repugnant unto a reasonable creature and that (as the philosopher[4] saith) even as an instrument of iron or of other metal waxeth soon rusty unless it be continually occupied,[5] even so shall the wit of a man or woman wax dull and unapt to do or understand anything perfectly unless it be always occupied upon some manner of study, which things considered hath moved so small a portion as God hath lent me to prove what I could do. And therefore have I as for assay[6] or beginning (so following the right noble saying of the proverb aforesaid) translated this little book out of French rhyme into English prose, joining the sentences together as well as the capacity of my simple wit and small learning could extend themselves. The which book is entitled, or named, *The Mirror or Glass of the Sinful Soul*, wherein is contained how she[7] (beholding and contemplating what she is) doth perceive how of herself and of her own strength she can do nothing that good is, or prevaileth for her salvation, unless it be through the grace of God, whose mother, daughter, sister, and wife by the scriptures she proveth herself to be. Trusting also that through His incomprehensible love, grace, and mercy she (being called from sin to repentance) doth faithfully hope to be saved. And although I know that as for my part which I have wrought in it (as well spiritual as manual) there is nothing done as it should be, nor else worthy to come in your grace's hands, but rather all unperfect and uncorrect, yet do I trust also that albeit it is like a work which is but new begun and shaped, that the file of your excellent wit and godly learning in the reading of it (if so it vouchsafe your highness to do) shall rub out, polish, and mend (or else cause to mend) the words (or rather the order of my writing), the which I know in many places to be rude, and nothing done as it should be. But I hope that after having been in your grace's hands there shall be nothing in it worthy of reprehension and that in the meanwhile no other (but your highness only) shall read it or see it, lest my faults be known of many. Then shall they be better excused (as my confidence is in your grace's accustomed benevolence) than if I should bestow a whole year in writing or inventing ways to excuse them.

Praying God almighty, the maker and creator of all things, to grant unto your highness this same New Year's day a lucky and prosperous year with prosperous issue and continuance of many years in good health and continual joy and all to His honour, praise, and glory.

—1548 (31 DECEMBER 1544)

---

1 *Venus' son* Cupid.

2 *To our most … joy* This is the prefatory letter to Elizabeth's English translation of Marguerite de Navarre's *Miroir de l'Ame Récheresse*, given as a New Year's gift to Catherine Parr, Henry VIII's last wife.

3 *pusillanimity* Lack of courage and strength of mind.

4 *the philosopher* Aristotle, but the thought is proverbial.

5 *occupied* Used.

6 *assay* Attempt.

7 *she* Marguerite de Navarre.

To the Troops at Tilbury[1]

My loving people, we have been persuaded by some that are careful of our safety to take heed how we commit ourself to armed multitudes for fear of treachery, but I assure you, I do not desire to live to distrust my faithful and loving people. Let tyrants fear. I have always so behaved myself that under God I have placed my chiefest strength and safeguard in the loyal hearts and good will of my subjects. And therefore I am come amongst you as you see at this time not for my recreation and disport, but being resolved in the midst and heat of the battle to live or die amongst you all, to lay down for God and for my kingdom and for my people my honour and my blood even in the dust. I know I have the body of a weak and feeble woman, but I have the heart and stomach of a king, and of a king of England too, and think foul scorn that Parma[2] or Spain or any prince of Europe should dare invade the borders of my realm, to which, rather than any dishonour shall grow by me, I myself will take up arms; I myself will be your general, judge, and rewarder of every one of your virtues in the field. I know already for your forwardness you have deserved rewards and crowns, and we do assure you in the word of a prince, they shall be duly paid you.

In the meantime my lieutenant-general[3] shall be in my stead, than whom never prince commanded a more noble or worthy subject. Not doubting but by your obedience to my general, by your concord in the camp and your valour in the field, we shall shortly have a famous victory over these enemies of God, of my kingdom, and of my people.

—1588

[1] *To the Troops at Tilbury* In July 1588, the Spanish Armada sailed toward England intending to invade. As the Armada entered the English Channel it was attacked by an English fleet led by Sir Francis Drake. Although at this point in the fighting the Spanish ships had been dissipated, there were fears they would regroup; as preparations continued at Tilbury, one observer noted that Elizabeth "rode through all the squadrons of her army as armed Pallas attended by noble footmen" before she gave this speech.

[2] *Parma* Duke of Parma, who was regent of the Spanish Netherlands at the time.

[3] *lieutenant-general* Robert Dudley, the Earl of Leicester and Elizabeth's favorite, who would die a few months later.

Two Letters from Elizabeth to Catherine de Bourbon, Sister of Henri IV of France[4]

Madame,

If my paper had the color of my heart, I would not dare to show it to you, the color black suiting too ill with the young. It is, I thank God, in no way for myself that I feel regret, but for him[5] for whom I wish the greatest good, [and] upon whom I see so many misfortunes fall that I feel them too much to [want to] be part of them. And in response to your desire to be able to serve me in place of [or perhaps "close to"] the king your brother, nothing you could do for me would so please me as to purchase for him so much honor and security that whatever harm he has wished to do to himself may not crush him through his forgetting the care of those of the true religion[6] who for so many years have consumed their means [and] poured out their blood to safeguard his cause. Not only does he owe this in good conscience, policy of state invites him to it, which is so uncertainly grounded on marshlands that he needs to grasp some very strong poles to get himself out. Remind him, Madam my good sister, in God's honor, that he must keep so much reputation even among his enemies that at no price should he abandon those devoted to him just to please wickedness. Rest assured that if you do this you will oblige me to remain

[4] *Henry IV of France* Henri de Navarre became Henri IV, King of France, upon the assassination in 1589 of his childless cousin, Henri III. Because Navarre was the leader of the Huguenot (Protestant) side in a three-sided civil war among supporters of Henri III, Huguenots, and ultra-papist supporters of the Duc de Guise, his accession merely led to further fighting. To prevent more bloodshed and to strengthen his position, Navarre announced his conversion to Catholicism in the summer of 1593; his sincerity has been doubted, but perhaps unjustly, and there is in fact no firm evidence that he ever said "Paris is worth a mass." His conversion had been widely anticipated, but after hearing the news Elizabeth wrote to him in an anguish of reproach, making sure that the letter circulated widely. A little later she also wrote Henri's still Protestant sister, Catherine. Catherine was herself an experienced politician, having at times served her brother as regent in his ancestral domains.

[5] *him* Henri IV.

[6] *those of the true religion* Huguenots.

Your most faithful sister. ER.
—1593 (AUGUST 25)

Madam,

As I am sending this gentleman[1] to the King, I have been unable to restrain my pen from revealing to you one of the urgent reasons for sending him at once: he must serve as tablets to remind him[2] of the important reasons why he must have consideration for those of the Religion,[3] not only for the danger to their lives, bodies, and goods when he was not too near his [current] dignity to reward them for it, but for his own salvation and the firm maintenance of his state. For if his enemies see him even slightly leaning on them, they make sport of him, knowing he has lost all other hope. Behold here, Madame, my boldness in minding somebody else's business: if this is a sin, I merit pardon for acknowledging it. Nevertheless, I beg you to add your urging [to mine]. And rest assured always to have in me

Your most faithful sister. ER.
—1593 (NOVEMBER)

The Golden Speech[4]

Mr. Speaker,[5] we have heard your declaration and perceive your care of our state, by falling into the consideration of a grateful acknowledgement of such benefits as you have received, and that your coming is to present thanks unto us, which I accept with no less joy than your loves can have desire to offer such a present.

I do assure you that there is no prince that loveth his subjects better, or whose love can countervail[6] our love. There is no jewel, be it of never so rich a price, which I prefer before this jewel—I mean your love—for I do more esteem it than any treasure or riches: for that we know how to prize, but love and thanks I count inestimable. And though God has raised me high, yet this I count the glory of my crown: that I have reigned with your loves. This makes me that I do not so much rejoice that God hath made me to be a queen, as to be a queen over so thankful a people. Therefore I have cause to wish nothing more than to content the subjects, and that is a duty which I owe. Neither do I desire to live longer days than that I may see your prosperity, and that is my only desire. And as I am that person that still yet under God hath delivered you, so I trust by the almighty power of God that I still shall be His instrument to preserve you from envy, peril, dishonour, shame, tyranny, and oppression, partly by means of your intended helps, which we take very acceptably, because it manifests the largeness of your loves and loyalties unto your sovereign.

Of myself I must say this: I never was any greedy, scraping grasper, nor a strait,[7] fast-holding prince, nor yet a waster; my heart was never set on worldly goods, but only for my subjects' good. What you do bestow on me I will not hoard up, but receive it to bestow on you again. Yea, mine own properties I account yours, to be expended for your good. Therefore render unto them, I beseech you, Mr. Speaker, such thanks as you imagine my heart yieldeth, but my tongue cannot express.

Mr. Speaker, I would wish you and the rest to stand up, for I shall yet trouble you with longer speech.[8]

Mr. Speaker, you give me thanks, but I doubt me[9] I have more cause to thank you all than you me: and I charge you to thank them of the Lower House[10] from me, for had I not received a knowledge from you, I

[1] *gentleman* Presumably a messenger or diplomat.

[2] *him* I.e., Henri.

[3] *those of the Religion* Huguenots.

[4] *The Golden Speech* This text is based on a transcription by one of the members of parliament, Hayward Townshend. This parliamentary speech was Elizabeth's most celebrated, and in it she states her recognition of the people's right—and even duty—to raise grievances over royal policies. Here, Elizabeth addresses grievances raised over monopolies, which, because they favored certain individuals, were often economically detrimental to many.

[5] *Mr. Speaker* The speaker of the house at the time was Sir John Croke (1553–1620).

[6] *countervail* Equal.

[7] *strait* Severe, strict.

[8] Townshend's transcription here indicates that all listeners have been kneeling so far.

[9] *doubt me* Do not doubt.

[10] *Lower House* House of Commons.

might have fallen into the lapse of an error only for lack of true information.

Since I was queen, yet never did I put my pen to any grant but that upon pretext and semblance made unto me that it was both good and beneficial to the subjects in general, though a private profit to some of my ancient servants who had deserved well. But the contrary being found by experience, I am exceedingly beholding to such subjects as would move the same at first. And I am not so simple to suppose but that there be some of the Lower House whom these grievances never touched, and from them I think they speak out of zeal to their countries[1] and not out of spleen or malevolent affection, as being parties grieved. And I take it exceedingly grateful from them, because it gives us to know that no respects or interests had moved them other than the minds they bear to suffer no diminution of our honour and our subjects' love unto us, the zeal of which affection, tending to ease my people and knit their hearts unto me, I embrace with a princely care.

Far above all earthly treasure I esteem my people's love, more than which I desire not to merit. That my grants should be grievous to my people and oppressions to be privileged under colour of our patents, our kingly dignity shall not suffer it. Yea, when I heard it, I could give no rest to my thoughts until I had reformed it. Shall they think to escape unpunished that have thus oppressed you and have been respectless of their duty and regardless of our honour? No, Mr. Speaker, I assure you, were it not more for conscience' sake than for any glory or increase of love that I desire, these errors, troubles, vexations, and oppressions done by these varlets[2] and lewd persons, not worthy the name of subjects, should not escape without condign[3] punishment. But I perceive they dealt with me like physicians who, ministering a drug, make it more acceptable by giving it a good aromatical savour, or, when they give pills, do gild[4] them all over.

I have ever used to set the last judgement day before my eyes and so to rule as I shall be judged to answer before a higher judge. To whose judgement seat I do appeal that never thought was cherished in my heart that tended not unto my people's good. And if my kingly bounty have been abused and my grants turned to the hurt of my people, contrary to my will and meaning, or if any in authority under me have neglected or perverted what I have committed to them, I hope God will not lay their culps[5] and offenses to my charge. And though there were danger in repealing our grants, yet what danger would not I rather incur for your own good, than I would suffer them still to continue?

I know the title of a king is a glorious title, but assure yourself that the shining glory of princely authority hath not so dazzled the eyes of our understanding but we well know and remember that we also are to yield an account of our actions before the great judge. To be a king and wear a crown is a thing more glorious to them that see it than it is pleasant to them that bear it. For myself, I was never so much enticed with the glorious name of a king or royal authority of a queen as delighted that God hath made me His instrument to maintain His truth and glory, and to defend this kingdom, as I said, from peril, dishonour, tyranny, and oppression.

There will never queen sit in my seat with more zeal to my country or care to my subjects, and that will sooner with willingness venture her life for your good and safety than myself. For it is not my desire to live nor reign longer than my life and reign shall be for your good. And though you have had and may have many princes more mighty and wise sitting in this seat, yet you never had or shall have any that will be more careful and loving.

Should I ascribe anything to myself and my sexly weakness, I were not worthy to live then, and of all most unworthy of the mercies I have had from God, who hath ever yet given me a heart which never yet feared foreign or home enemies. I speak it to give God the praise as a testimony before you, and not to attribute anything unto myself. For I, O Lord, what am I, whom practices and perils past should not fear? Or what can I

[1] *countries* Counties.

[2] *varlets* Knaves, rogues.

[3] *condign* Appropriate, deserved.

[4] *gild* Cover with gold.

[5] *culps* Guilt, sins.

do? That I should speak for any glory, God forbid.

This, Mr. Speaker, I pray you deliver unto the House, to whom heartily recommend me. And so I commit you all to your best fortunes and further counsels. And I pray you, Mr. Comptroller, Mr. Secretary, and you of my Council, that before these gentlemen depart into their countries, you bring them all to kiss my hand.

—30 NOVEMBER 1601

IN CONTEXT

The Defeat of the Spanish Armada

Tensions between England and Spain rose through the 1580s primarily as a result of raids on Spanish shipping and the looting of Spanish settlements in the Americas (largely by Sir Francis Drake), and religious differences between Catholic Spain and Protestant England. Finally, on 30 May 1588, Philip II of Spain launched an Armada of 130 ships, which, together with the army of Philip's nephew the Duke of Parma (then stationed across the English Channel in Flanders), was to invade and conquer England. The English fleet (under Lord Howard and Drake) of 197 smaller and more maneuverable ships engaged the Spanish in a battle that began on 29 July and extended over many days, culminating in a Spanish defeat at Gravesend and made more decisive by a gale that drove the remnants of the Spanish fleet north, up the English coast. Meanwhile an English army of 22,000 troops had gathered at Tilbury (east of London on the Thames). Under the command of Robert Dudley, the Earl of Lecister, it prepared to engage the army of the Duke of Parma—but with the defeat of the armada was never called upon to fight. Leicester, the Queen's favorite, died of natural causes only 28 days later.

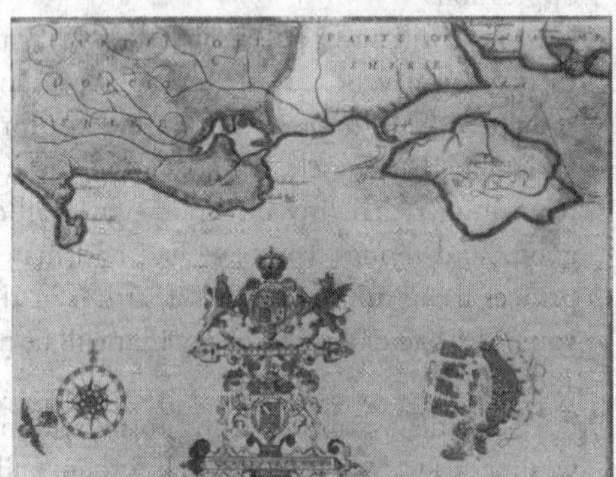

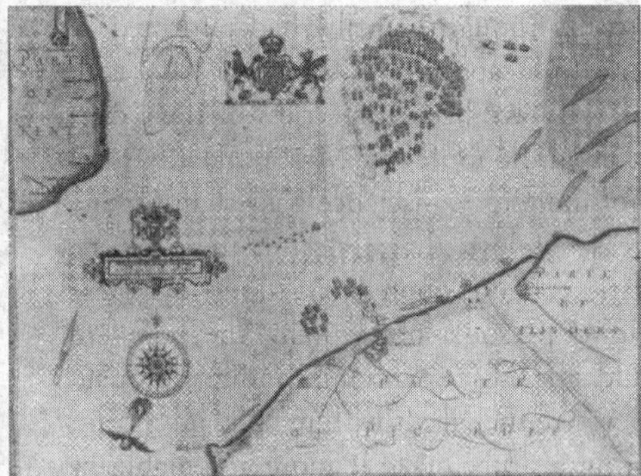

These engravings (by Augustine Ryther, based on illustrations by Robert Adams to the 1588 book *Expeditionis Hispanorum*), depict battles between the English fleet and the Spanish Armada on 4 August off the Isle of Wight (left) and on 8 August off Gravelines, Flanders (right).

The Ark Royal, flagship of the English fleet, commanded by Lord Howard against the Armada in 1588.

Sir William Segar, *Robert Dudley, Earl of Leicester*, c. 1583.

Culture: A Portfolio

CONTEXTS

As in any period, the culture of the sixteenth and early seventeenth centuries was not monolithic and uniform: the "high" culture of the nobility was largely foreign to the rural laborers (although the élite was often familiar with popular culture), various cultural phenomena were peculiar to the citizens and merchants in the social class below the nobility and gentry, or to the yeomen in the social class above the laborers, and so on. It varied substantially by gender: the culture of women was different from that of men, and women were effectively excluded from participation in many activities. Culture varied too from place to place: the culture of London (and to a lesser extent that of other cities, such as Bristol and York) differed from that of the rural areas of England or that of smaller centers, and that of Scotland, of Wales, and of other regions was different again. Of necessity, then, the following can provide only limited impressions of the culture of Britain during this period.

⌘⌘⌘

Music

Over the sixteenth and early seventeenth centuries, home performance from printed or manuscript music began to play a much larger role in daily life than it had in earlier periods. The work of composers and musicians such as John Dowland (1563–1626), William Byrd (1539–1623) and Thomas Campion (1567–1620) was highly regarded, and their compositions, whether for stringed instruments such as the lute (in Dowland's case), or keyboard instruments such as the virginal and the harpsichord (as with Byrd) began to be printed and distributed. Among the common people music continued to play an integral part of daily life; most communities possessed shared knowledge of a body of popular song, as this excerpt from Walton's *Compleat Angler* (1653) indicates.

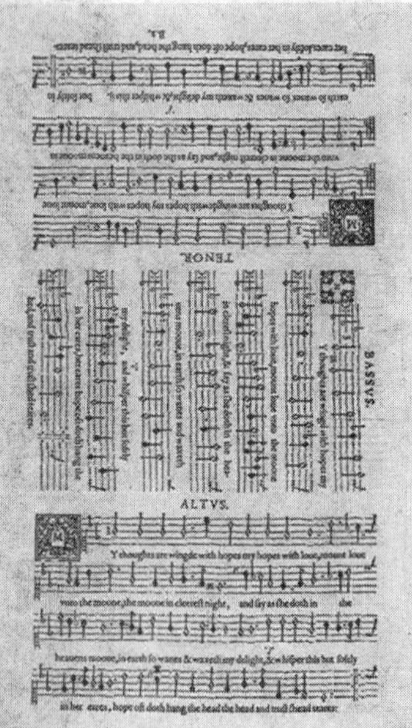

from John Dowland, *First Booke of Songs or Ayres*, 1597.

The book of songs, each written for four-part singing, was printed to allow each of the four singers to face his or her own part.

PARTHENIA
or
THE MAYDENHEAD
of the first musicke that
euer was printed for the VIRGINALLS.
COMPOSED
By three famous Masters: William Byrd, Dr: John Bull, & Orlando Gibbons,
Gentilmen of his Ma:tie most Illustrious Chappell.
Ingrauen
by William Hole.
for
DORETHIE EUANS.
Cum
Priuilegio.
Printed at LONDON by G: Lowe and are to be soulde
at his howse in Loathberry.

Advertisement for William Byrd, *Parthenia*, a collection of songs by William Byrd and others, c. 1611.

from Izaak Walton, *The Compleat Angler, or, The Contemplative Man's Recreation* (1653)

PISCATOR.[1] I pray, do us a courtesy that shall stand you and your daughter in nothing, and yet we will think ourselves something in your debt. It is but to sing a song that was sung by your daughter when I last passed over this meadow, about eight or nine days since.

MILK-WOMAN: What song was it, pray? Was it "Come Shepherds, deck your herds"? or "As at noon Dulcina rested"? or "Phillida flouts me"? or "Chevy Chace"? or "Johnny Armstrong"? or "Troy Town?

PISCATOR. No, it is none of those; it is a song that your daughter sung the first part, and you sung the answer to it.

MILK-WOMAN. Come, Maudlin, sing the first part to the gentleman with a merry heart; and I'll sing the second when you have done.

[The song that follows is Christopher Marlowe's "Come live with me and be my love."]

Painting

The emphasis throughout this period was on portraiture; in the sixteenth century, it was common for portraits to depict the subject's face naturalistically so as to suggest three dimensions, while the portrayal of the rest of the figure was rendered in a flatter, decorative fashion. (The portrait of Edward Alleyn below is a good example.)

Some of the best-known "English" paintings of the period were painted by leading artists from the Continent: Hans Holbein the Younger (1497–1543) became court painter to Henry VIII, and Anthony Van Dyck court painter to Charles I. Among sixteenth- and early seventeenth-century painters of English nationality, Nicholas Hilliard may have been the best known—for his *Treatise Concerning the Art of Limning* as well as for his miniature cameos and other portraits. ("Limning," as a later seventeenth-century definition explains, is an "Art whereby in Water Colours, we strive to resemble Nature in every thing to the life.")

The two passages ending this section present contrasting attitudes of the subjects of portraits as to how they should be painted. The quotation attributed to Oliver Cromwell is the source of the famous phrase "warts and all" (Cromwell did indeed have several warts on his face, and they are shown in the Lely portrait.)

[1] *Piscator* Latin: fisher.

Rowland Lockey, copy of Hans Holbein the Younger, *Sir Thomas More and his Family*, detail, 1593, original c. 1527.

The original of this large portrait (the full picture includes eleven figures) is now lost; it is the first known example by a northern European artist of a large group portrait in which the figures are all shown standing (rather than most or all being shown kneeling).

Nicholas Hilliard, *A Youth Leaning Against a Tree Among Roses*, c. 1590.

from Nicholas Hilliard, *A Treatise Concerning the Art of Limning* (1624)

I wish it were so that none should meddle with limning but gentlemen alone, for that it is a kind of gentle painting of less subjection than any other; for one may leave when he will, his colours nor his work taketh any harm by it. Moreover it is secret, a man may use it and scarcely be perceived of his own folk; it is sweet and cleanly to use, and it is a thing apart from all other painting or drawing, and tendeth not to common men's use, either for furnishing of houses or any patterns for tapestries, or building, or any other work whatsoever, and yet it excelleth all other painting whatsoever in sundry points, in giving the true lustre to pearl and precious stone, and worketh the metals gold or silver with themselves, which so enricheth and ennobleth the work that it seemeth to be the thing itself.

from A Letter to F.P. Verney from the Countess of Sussex (1639)

Sweet Mr. Verney, the picture came very well, many hearty thanks to you for it. The frame is a little hurt, the gilt being rubbed off. The picture is very ill favoured, makes me quite out of love with myself, the face is so big and so fat that it pleases me not at all. It looks like one of the winds puffing—but truly I think it is like the original. If ever I come to London before Sir Vandyck go, I will get him to mend my picture, for though I be ill favoured I think that makes me worse than I am.

Oliver Cromwell, Instructions to His Painter, as Reported by George Vertue, *Notebooks* (c. 1720)

Mr. Lilly,[1] I desire you would use all your skill to paint my picture truly like me and not flatter me at all but [pointing to his own face] remark all these roughnesses, pimples, warts and everything as you see me; otherwise I will never pay a farthing for it.

[1] *Mr. Lilly* I.e., Peter Lely (1618–80), later Sir Peter Lely.

Sir Peter Lely, *Portrait of Oliver Cromwell*, c. 1653.

Games and Pastimes

Considerable attention was paid to games and pastimes in the sixteenth century. Skill in archery was considered to be of particular importance to the defence of the realm—so much so that Henry VIII passed several statutes to enforce its practice and ensure that "every man having a man-child or men-children in his house, shall provide, ordain, and have in his house for every man-child being of the age of seven years and above, till he come to the age of seventeen years, a bow and two shafts to induce and learn them, and bring them up in shooting." The statutes appear to have been widely ignored, and it is probable that archery became slowly less popular over this period.

Sports, games, and entertainments pursued purely for pleasure, on the other hand, clearly gained in popularity. Bear-baiting is of special interest because of the surprising degree to which connections existed between bear-baiting and the theater in the late-sixteenth and early-seventeenth centuries. Philip Henslowe, a prominent theater manager, and Edward Alleyn, a leading actor, were from 1594 onwards two of the leading figures in the sport. For some years they controlled both the Bear Garden and the Paris Garden, the two sites for bear-baiting in London, and they eventually built a new theater, the Hope, designed to house both bear-baiting and stage plays. Both Elizabeth I and James I encouraged the practice, and royal exhibitions of bear-baiting (at venues such as Whitehall and Greenwich Park) to entertain foreign visitors were frequent occurrences; though the monarch is never recorded to have attended public performances of plays during this period, Elizabeth is known to have visited the Paris Garden in 1599.

Though most sports, games and pastimes were heavily male-oriented, there are some exceptions among the more gentle pastimes. Queen Elizabeth is known to have played draughts (checkers) and chess with Roger Ascham, and Arthur Saul dedicated *The Famous Game of Chess-Play* (1614) to Lucy, Countess of Bedford.

Frontispiece, Gervase Markham, *The Art of Archery*, 1634. The woodcut depicts Charles I.

A Game of Tennis, early seventeenth century.
The early version of the game was played indoors with short-handled racquets and leather balls packed with hair. (The modern game of "lawn tennis" dates from the nineteenth century.)

THE NOBLE ARTE OF
VENERIE OR HVNTING.

VVherein is handled and ſet out the Vertues, Nature, and Properties of fiuetene ſundrie Chaces togither, with the order and maner how to Hunte and kill euery one of them.

Tranſlated and collected for the pleaſure of all Noblemen and Gentlemen, out of the beſt approued Authors, which haue written any thing *concerning the ſame: And reduced into ſuch order and proper termes* as are vſed here, in this noble Realme of England.

The Contentes vvhereof ſhall more playnely appeare in the Page next followyng.

Title page, George Turberville, *The Noble Art of Venerie or Hunting*, 1575.

The Booke of Faulconrie or Hau-
KING, FOR THE ONELY DE-
light and pleaſure of all Noblemen and Gentlemen:
Collected out of the beſt aucthors, aſvvell Italians as Frenchmen, and ſome Engliſh practiſes withall concernyng Faulconrie, the contentes whereof are to be ſeene in the next page folowyng.
By *George Turberuile* Gentleman.
NOCET EMPTA DOLORE VOLVPTAS.

Imprinted at London for Chriſtopher Barker, at the ſigne of the Graſhopper in Paules Churchyarde. *Anno.* 1575.

Title page, George Turberville, *The Book of Falconry or Hawking*, 1575.

Anonymous, *Edward Alleyn*, detail (early seventeenth century).

In addition to being one of the most important bear-baiting impresarios of the age, Alleyn (1566–1626) was widely considered to be the era's greatest actor. Among his leading parts were the title roles in *Tamburlaine* and *Doctor Faustus*; in 1592 Thomas Nashe wrote that no one "could ever perform more in action than famous Ned Allen."

The famous game
of Cheſſe-play,
Truely diſcouered, and all doubts resolued;
So that by reading this ſmall Booke thou
ſhalt profit more then by the playing
a thouſand *Mates.*
An Exerciſe full of delight, fit for Princes, or any
perſon of what qualitie ſoeuer.
Newly publiſhed by A. S. Gent.

Printed at London for *Roger Iackson*, and are to be
ſould at his ſhop neere Fleetſtreet-Conduit. 1614.

Title page, *The Famous Game of Chess-Play.*

Food and Drink

In this as in many other things, the sixteenth and early-seventeenth century point of comparison was often Italy. The first of the passages below gives an early impression of the comparison from an Italian point of view, the second a seventeenth-century view from an English gentleman. Moryson's comment that the English eat "more flesh" than the Italians may be something of an understatement: the 1589 records preserved of the food and drink purchased for a well-off bachelor in London show a diet of almost nothing but meat. On May 11, for example, the following were purchased for the midday dinner:

a piece of beef	xviiid.
a loin of veal	iis.
2 chickens	xiiiid.
oranges	iid
for dressings ye veal & chickens & sauce	xiid

The following items were purchased for supper the same day:

a shoulder of mutton	xvid.
2 rabbits	xd.
for dressing ye mutton, rabbits & a pigges pettie toes	viiid.
cold beef	viiid.
cheese	iid.

The diet of commoners, in contrast, included a good deal of bread and cheese but relatively little meat through much of the year. Even in towns most families kept chickens (and sometimes pigs) and maintained a small plot of land. Animals were slaughtered in the late autumn, and salted or smoked meat was consumed in the winter. At all levels of society the Church requirement that fish be eaten on Fridays was observed; for those living at any significant distance from the sea, salt rather than fresh fish was usually the only option. Neither potatoes nor tomatoes were yet a part of the English diet, and green vegetables do not seem to have figured very prominently in most people's diet; fruit was common, however.

Many remarked on the liberal consumption of beer and ale throughout the sixteenth century and into the seventeenth, and clearly women as well as men were known to frequent taverns. Indeed, if the the catalogue of tavern types in John Skelton's account of "The Tunning of Elynour Rumming" (with its account of "wenches unlaced" and "housewives unbraced") is to be believed even in part, that was far from a rare occurrence. As the early seventeenth-century watercolor reproduced below illustrates, wine was often the preferred drink of the better-off classes of society. Beginning in the late 1560s the smoking of tobacco—described below by William Harrison—also became common. By the early 1600s there was also a strong reaction against the "stinking smoke" of tobacco—expressed most powerfully in James I's *A Counterblast to Tobacco* (an excerpt from which is included elsewhere in this anthology).

from An Anonymous Venetian Official Traveling in England, *A Relation, or Rather a True Account, of the Island of England* (1497)

The English are, for the most part, both men and women of all ages, handsome and well-proportioned; though not quite so much so, in my opinion, as it had been asserted to me, before your magnificence went to that kingdom; and I have understood from persons acquainted with these countries, that the Scotch are much handsomer; and that the English are great lovers of themselves, and of everything belonging to them; they think that there are no other men than themselves, and no other world but England; and whenever they see a handsome foreigner, they say that "he looks like an Englishman," and that "it is a great pity that he should not be an Englishman;" and when they partake of any delicacy with a foreigner, they ask him, "whether such a thing is made in *their* country?" They take great pleasure in having a quantity of excellent victuals, and also in remaining a long time at table, being very sparing of wine when they drink it at their own expense. And this, it is said, they do in order to induce their other English guests to drink wine in moderation also; not considering it any inconvenience for three or four persons to drink out of the same cup. Few people keep wine in their own houses, but buy it, for the most part, at a tavern; and when they mean to drink a great deal, they go to the tavern, and this is done not only by the men, but by ladies of distinction. The deficiency of wine, however, is amply supplied by the abundance of ale and beer, to the use of which these people are become so habituated, that, at an entertainment where there is plenty of wine, they will drink them in preference to it, and in great quantities.

from Fynes Moryson, *Itinerary* (1617)

England abounds in cattle of all kinds, and particularly hath very great oxen, the flesh whereof is so tender, as no meat is more desired ... The flesh of hogs and swine is more savoury than in any other parts, excepting the bacon of Westphalia. ... English husbandmen eat barley and rye brown bread, and prefer it to white bread as abiding longer in the stomach, and not so soon digested with their labour....

The Italian Sansovino is much deceived, writing, that in general the English eat and cover the table at least four times in the day; for howsoever those that journey and some sickly men staying at home may perhaps take a small breakfast, yet in general the English eat but two meals (of dinner and supper) each day. And I profess for myself and other Englishmen, passing through Italy so famous for temperance, that we often observed, that, howsoever we might have a pullet and some flesh[1] prepared for us, eating it with a moderate proportion of bread, the Italians at the same time, with a charger[2] full of herbs for a salad, and with roots,[3] like meats of small price, would each of them eat two or three penny-worth of bread. And since all fulness is ill, and that of bread worst, I think we were more temperate in our diet, though eating more flesh, than they eating so much more bread than we did....

I observed a custom in all those Italian cities and towns through which I passed that is not used in any

[1] *a pullet and some flesh* A chicken and some red meat.

[2] *charger* Large plate or dish.

[3] *roots* I.e., root vegetables such as carrots, parsnips, or beetroot.

other country that I saw in my travels, neither do I think that any other nation in Christendom use it, but only Italy. The Italians ... do always at their meals use a little fork when they cut their meat.... The reason for this their curiosity[1] is because the Italian cannot endure by any means to have his dish touched by fingers, seeing that all men's fingers are not alike clean.

Anonymous, Miniature watercolor depicting eating and drinking, c. 1610.

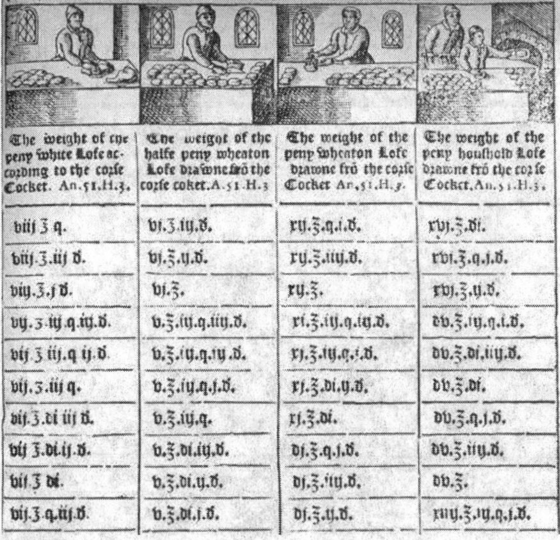

The weight of the peny white Lofe according to the corse Cocket. An.51.H.3.	The weight of the halfe peny wheaton Lofe drawne frō the corse coket.A.51.H.3	The weight of the peny wheaton Lofe drawne frō the corse Cocket An.51.H.3.	The weight of the peny houshold Lofe drawne frō the corse Cocket.An.51.H.3.
viij ℥ q.	vj.℥.iij.d.	xij.℥.q.i.d.	xvj.℥.di.
viij.℥.iij d.	vj.℥.ij.d.	xij.℥.iiij.d.	xvi.℥.q.j.d.
viij.℥.j d.	vj.℥.	xij.℥.	xvj.℥.ij.d.
vij.℥.iij.q.iij.d.	v.℥.iij.q.iiij.d.	xi.℥.iij.q.iij.d.	xv.℥.iij.q.i.d.
vij.℥.iij.q ij.d.	v.℥.iij.q.iij.d.	xj.℥.iij.q.i.d.	xv.℥.di.iiij.d.
vij.℥.iij q.	v.℥.iij.q.j.d.	xj.℥.di.ij.d.	xv.℥.di.
vij.℥.di iij d.	v.℥.iij.q.	xj.℥.di.	xv.℥.q.j.d.
vij ℥.di.ij.d.	v.℥.di.iij.d.	xj.℥.q.j.d.	xv.℥.iiij.d.
vij ℥ di.	v.℥.di.ij.d.	xj.℥.iiij.d.	xv.℥.
vij.℥.q.iij.d.	v.℥.di.j.d.	xj.℥.ij.d.	xiiij.℥.iij.q.j.d.

The Assize of Bread, London, 1600. The chart sets out the prices to be charged for different sorts of loaves of bread, depending on the price of wheat at the time.

[1] *curiosity* Curious or unusual behavior.

from Sarah Longe, *Mrs. Sarah Longe Her Receipt Book* (manuscript c. 1610)

Medieval recipes (or "receipts") are typically as vague as is Longe about cooking times, but many published recipes from the late sixteenth and early seventeenth centuries include references to time ("cook it a quarter of an hour ..." etc.).

To make cherry marmalet

Take 5 pound of cherries, you must weigh them with their stones in them, after stone them, then take one pound of sugar such as you make marmalet with, and put your cherries and your sugar both together into the pan, or skillet which you will make it in, but beat your sugar very well, and so let it boil as you do other marmalets, and when you think it is boiled enough, put it into your boxes or glasses as fast as you can.

from William Harrison, *Chronologie* (1573)

In these days, the taking-in of the smoke of the Indian herb called tobacco by an instrument formed like a little ladle, whereby it passeth from the mouth into the head and stomach, is greatly taken up and used in England, against rheums and some other diseases engendered in the lungs.

Children and Education

There was little support for compulsory or state-supported education in the British Isles before the late-seventeenth century, except in Scotland, but with the tide of Protestantism came much greater interest in education. The Convocation of Canterbury in 1529 ordered all parish priests to teach children to read and write, and, while it is certain not all did so, it may be that close to half of the population were at least barely literate by the end of the sixteenth century. Under the Tudors, Parliament expressed its support for educational ideals, and acted to regulate grammar schools in such matters as the prescribing of textbooks. (Lily's *Short Intro-*

duction of Grammar remained the standard for Latin grammar until well into the nineteenth century.) Boys from well-off families aged five to seven attended a Petty (from the French "petit," or small) School; they then attended a grammar school from ages seven through fourteen; only a few would follow on to one of the two universities. Boys (and often girls) of noble birth were educated by a tutor at home; girls of other social classes were generally not provided with any formal education. Male children of laborers and poor townsfolk were also effectively denied an education for, although schools were officially open to all boys, in practice the fees that were charged (often a pound or more per year, even in the mid-sixteenth century) put education out of reach of those of modest means.

from John Baidon, *New Book containg All Sorts of Hands* (revised edition 1611), first published c. 1570), woodcut, "How you ought to hold your pen."

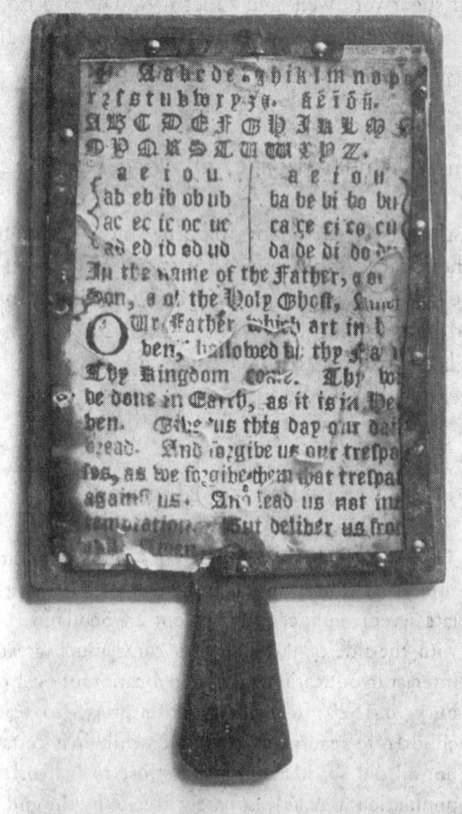

A hornbook from the early seventeenth century. Hornbooks typically included the letters of the alphabet and the text of the Lord's Prayer, framed in wood and covered by a thin layer of transparent horn.

Anonymous woodcut, a Petty School
(early seventeenth century).

Edward IV Grammar School, Stratford-upon-Avon.

Attributed to the Master of the Countess of Warwick, *Lord Cobham and his Family*, 1567. Cobham's wife is shown opposite him; her sister is to the left. The age of each child is painted above the head.

Artist unknown, *Portrait of John Donne*, c. 1595.

Anthony Van Dyck, *George and Francis Villiers*, 1635. After their father, the Duke of Buckingham, was assassinated, these children were raised in the household of Charles I. Francis was killed in battle during the Civil War; following the Restoration George became a leading politician. (George is portrayed by John Dryden in "Absalom and Architophel" in the character of Zimri, "stiff in opinions, always in the wrong.")

Sir Peter Lelly, *George Villiers, Second Duke of Buckingham*, c. 1675.

The Supernatural and the Miraculous

The supernatural was the subject of ongoing controversy in the sixteenth and early seventeenth centuries. Belief in astrology, in witchcraft, and in a wide range of supernatural or miraculous occurrences was widespread throughout society. Though repeated efforts were made by writers such as Joseph Hall to associate such "superstitions"[1] with the uneducated or simple of mind, Elizabeth I is known to have had her own astrologer, and (as the account below records) James I regarded witchcraft with the utmost seriousness. The writings on witchcraft of George Gifford, from which an excerpt appears below, give an almost anthropological analysis of how allegations of witchcraft took root and grew in a community.

[1] *superstitions* The word "superstition" first appeared in the fifteenth century, and it gained wide currency in the sixteenth; Richard Hooker in his *Ecclesiastical Polity*, 1597 defines it thus: "superstition is, when things are either abhorred or observed, with a zealous or fearful, but erroneous relation to God." As time went on the term started to be less and less frequently applied to perceived Christian heresies, and to become reserved more and more for denoting (and ridiculing) supernatural beliefs outside of a Christian context.

ASTROLOGASTER,
OR,
THE FIGVRE-CASTER.

Rather the Arraignment of Artlesse Astrologers, and Fortune-tellers, that cheat many ignorant people vnder the pretence of foretelling things to *come, of telling things that are past, finding out things that are lost*, expounding Dreames, calculating Deaths and Natiuities, *once againe brought to the Barre.*

By Iohn Melton.

Cicero. *Stultorum plena sunt omnia.*

Imprinted at London by *Barnard Alsop*, for *Edward Blackmore*, and are to be sold in *Paules* Churchyard, at the Signe of the *Blazing-Starre.* 1620.

Title page, John Melton, *Astrologastor, or, the Figurecaster*, 1620. Included in the text of Melton's book is the following reference to the stage:

> Another [astrologer] will foretell of lightning and thunder that shall happen such a day, when there are no such inflammations seen, except[2] men go to the Fortune in Golding Lane, to see the tragedy of *Doctor Faustus.* There indeed a man may behold shag-haired devils run roaring over the stage with squibs[3] in their mouths, while drummers make thunder in the tiring-house,[4] and the twelve-penny hirelings make artificial lightning in their heavens.

[2] *except* Unless.

[3] *squibs* Fireworks.

[4] *tiring-house* Room in which actors dressed for the stage.

from Reginald Scot, *The Discovery of Witchcraft* (1584)

Who they be that are called witches, with a manifest declaration of the cause that moveth men so commonly to think, and witches themselves to believe that they can hurt children, cattle, &c. with words and imaginations: and of cozening witches.

One sort of such as are said to be witches, are women which be commonly old, lame, blear-eyed, pale, foul, and full of wrinkles; poor, and sullen, superstitious, and papists; or such as know no religion: in whose drowsy minds the devil hath gotten a fine seat; so as, what mischief, mischance, calamity, or slaughter is brought to pass, they are easily persuaded the same is done by themselves; imprinting in their minds an earnest and constant imagination hereof. They are lean and deformed, showing melancholy in their faces, to the horror of all that see them. They are doting, scolds, mad, devilish; and not much differing from them that are thought to be possessed with spirits; so firm and steadfast in their opinions, as whosoever shall only have respect to the constancy of their words uttered, would easily believe they were true indeed.

These miserable wretches are so odious unto all their neighbors, and so feared, as few dare offend them, or deny them any thing they ask: whereby they take upon them; yea, and sometimes think, that they can do such things as are beyond the ability of human nature. These go from house to house, and from door to door for a pot full of milk, yeast, drink, pottage, or some such relief; without the which they could hardly live: neither obtaining for their service and pains, nor by their art, nor yet at the devil's hands (with whom they are said to make a perfect and visible bargain) either beauty, money, promotion, wealth, worship, pleasure, honor, knowledge, learning, or any other benefit whatsoever.

from George Gifford, *A Discourse of the Subtle Practices of Devils by Witches and Sorcerers* (1587)

In a later text, *A Dialogue Concerning Witches and Witchcraft* (1593), Gifford summarized the purpose of the work from which the following excerpt is taken: "certain years now past ... I published a small Treatise concerning witches, to lay open some of Satan's sleights, and subtle practices, lest the ignoranter sort should be carried awry and seduced more and more by them."

Some woman doth fall out bitterly with her neighbour: there followeth some great hurt, either that God hath permitted the devil to vex him: or otherwise. There is a suspicion conceived. Within few years after she is in some jar with an other. He is also plagued. This is noted of all. Great fame is spread of the matter. Mother W. is a witch. She hath bewitched goodman B. Two hogs which died strangely: or else he is taken lame. Well, mother W. doth begin to be very odious and terrible unto many. Her neighbours dare say nothing but yet in their hearts they wish she were hanged. Shortly after another falleth sick and doth pine, he can have no stomach unto his meat, now he can not sleep. The neighbours come to visit him. "Well, neighbour," sayeth one, "do ye not suspect some naughty dealing: did ye never anger mother W.?" "Truly neighbour" (sayth he), "I have not liked the woman a long time. I can not tell how I should displease her, unless it were this other day, my wife prayed her, and so did I, that she would keep her hens out of my garden. We spake her as fair as we could for our lives. I think verily she hath bewitched me." Every body sayeth now that mother W. is a witch in deed, and hath bewitched the good man E. He cannot eat his meat. It is out of all doubt: for there were (those) which saw a weasel run from her house-ward into his yard even a little before he fell sick. The sick man dieth, and taketh it upon his death that he is bewitched: then is mother W. apprehended, and sent to prison.

from Joseph Hall, *Characters of Virtues and Vices* (1608)

Joseph Hall (1574–1656) was a moral philosopher well known for his attempts to reconcile the ideas of the ancient Stoics with those of Christianity. In later life he was appointed Bishop of Exeter (in 1627) and became heavily embroiled in the conflicts between Anglican and Puritan factions.

Superstition is godless religion, devout impiety. The superstitious is fond in observation, servile in fear; he worships God but as he lists; he gives God what he asks not, more than he asks, and all but what he should give, and makes more sins than the Ten Commandments. This man dares not stir forth till his breast be crossed and his face sprinkled. If but an hare cross him the way, he returns; or if his journey began, unawares, on the dismal day; or, if he stumbled at the threshold. If he see a snake unkilled, he fears a mischief; if the salt fall towards him, he looks pale and red, and is not quiet till one of the waiters have poured wine on his lap; and when he sneezeth, thinks them not his friends that uncover not. In the morning, he listens whether the crow crieth even or odd, and by that token presages of the weather. If he hear but a raven croak from the next roof, he makes his will; or if a bittour[1] fly over his head by night: but if his troubled fancy shall second his thoughts with the dream of a fair garden, or green rushes, or the salutation of a dead friend, he takes leave of the world, and says he cannot live. He will never set to sea but on a Sunday.… When he lies sick on his deathbed, no sin troubles him so much, as that he did once eat flesh on a Friday: no repentance can expiate that; the rest need none. There is no dream of his without an interpretation, without a prediction; and if the event answer not his exposition, he expounds it according to the event.… Old wives and stars are his counsellors: his nightspell is his guard; and charms, his physicians.… This man is strangely credulous, and calls impossible things miraculous: if he hear that some sacred block speaks, moves, weeps, smiles, his bare feet carry him thither with an offering; and if a danger miss him in the way, his saint hath the thanks. Some ways he will not go, and some he dares not; either there are bugs, or he feigneth them; every lantern is a ghost, and every noise is of chains. He knows not why, but his custom is to go a little about, and to leave the cross still on the right hand. One event is enough to make a rule: out of these rules he concludes fashions, proper to himself; and nothing can turn him out of his own course.

[1] *bittour* Bittern (a species of large heron).

from Sir John Harington, "Account of an Audience with King James I" (1604), as recorded in *Nugae Antiquae*

Soon upon this, the Prince his Highness did enter, and in much good humour asked if I was "cousin to Lord Harrington of Exton?" I humbly replied [that] His Majesty did me some honour in enquiring my kin to one whom he had so late honoured and made a baron; and moreover did add, "we were both branches of the same tree." Then he enquired much of learning, and showed me his own in such sort, as made me remember my examiner at Cambridge aforetime. He sought much to know my advances in philosophy, and uttered profound sentences of Aristotle, and such like writers, which I had never read, and which some are bold enough to say, others do not understand: but this I must pass by. The Prince did now press my reading to him part of a canto in Ariosto; praised my utterance, and said he had been informed of many, as to my learning, in the time of the Queen. He asked me what I thought pure wit was made of; and whom it did best become? Whether a King should not be the best clerk in his own country; and, if this land did not entertain good opinion of his learning and wisdom. His Majesty did much press for my opinion touching the power of Satan in matter of witchcraft; and asked me, with much gravity, if I did "truly understand, why the devil did work more with ancient women than others."

More serious discourse did next ensue, wherein I wanted room to continue, and sometime room to escape; for the Queen was not forgotten, nor Davison[2] neither. His Highness told me her death was visible in Scotland before it did really happen, being, as he said, "spoken of in secret by those whose power of sight

[2] *Davison* William Davison (c. 1541–1608), a courtier.

presented to them a bloody head dancing in the air." He then did remark much on this gift, and said he had sought out of certain books a sure way to attain knowledge of future chances. Hereat, he named many books, which I did not know, nor by whom written; but advised me not to consult some authors which would lead me to evil consultations. I told his Majesty, "the power of Satan had, I much feared, damaged my bodily frame; but I had not farther will to court his friendship, for my soul's hurt." We next discoursed somewhat on religion, when at length he said: "Now, Sir, you have seen my wisdom in some sort, and I have pried into yours. I pray you, do me justice in your report, and in good season, I will not fail to add to your understanding, in such points as I may find you lack amendment." I made courtesy hereat, and withdrew down the passage, and out at the gate, amidst the many varlets and lordly servants who stood around.

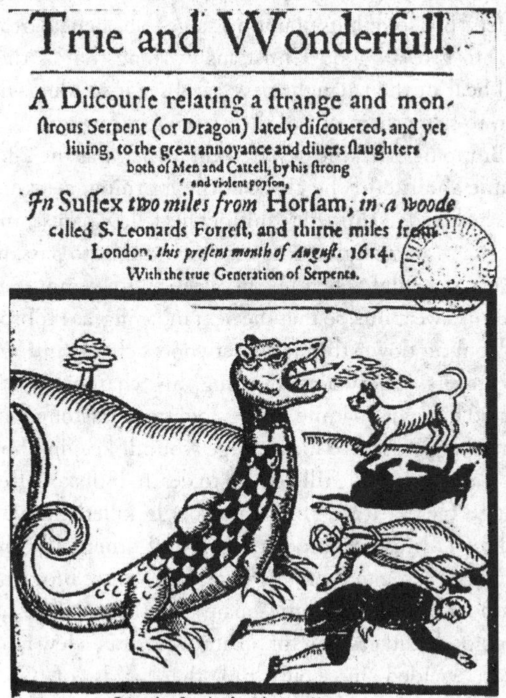

True and Wonderfull.

A Discourse relating a strange and monstrous Serpent (or Dragon) lately discouered, and yet liuing, to the great annoyance and diuers slaughters both of Men and Cattell, by his strong and violent poyson,

In Sussex two miles from Horsam, in a woode called S. Leonards Forrest, and thirtie miles from London, this present month of August. 1614.

With the true Generation of Serpents.

Printed at London by Iohn Trundle.

Title page, *True and Wonderfull: A Discourse Relating a Strange and Monstrous Serpent (or Dragon) Lately Discovered*, 1614.

Anonymous Broadsheet, "The Form and Shape of a Monstrous Child Born at Maidstone in Kent, the 24th of October, 1568"

At Maidstone in Kent there was one Margaret Mere, daughter to Richard Mere of the said town of Maidstone, who being unmarried, played the naughty pack,[1] and was gotten with child, being delivered of the same child the 24th day of October last past, in the year of our Lord 1568 at seven of the clock in the afternoon of the same day, being Sunday. Which child, being a man child, had first the mouth slitted on the right side like a leopard's mouth, terrible to behold, the left arm lying upon the breast, fast thereto joined, having as it were stumps on the hands, the left leg growing upward toward the head, and the right leg bending toward the left leg, the foot thereof growing into the buttock of the said left leg. In the middest of the back there was a broad lump of flesh in fashion like a rose, in the middest whereof was a hole, which voided like an issue. This said child was born alive, and lived 24 hours, and then departed this life. Which may be a terror as well to all such workers of filthiness and iniquity, as to those ungodly livers. Who (if in them any fear of God be) may move them to repentance and amendment of life. Which God for Christ's sake grant both to them and us. Amen.

Witnesses hereof were these: William Plomer, John Squier Glasier, John Sadler Goldsmith, beside diverse other credible persons both men and women.

Crime

In the late sixteenth century many publications offered accounts of crimes. Some, such as Robert Greene's *Notable Discovery of Coosenage, Now Daily Practised by Sundry lewd persons, called Connie-Catchers, and Cross-Biters* (1593) aimed to warn the populace of the methods adopted by petty crooks and confidence tricksters. Others provided lurid accounts of violent crime. As the excerpt below from the pamphlet describing the murder of Richard

[1] *played the naughty pack* Engaged in immoral behavior (slang term of unknown origin).

Hobson illustrates, these were often colored with religious or political bias.

THE BELMAN
OF LONDON.
Bringing to light the moſt notorious
villanies that are now practiſed
in the KINGDOME.
Profitable for Gentlemen, Lawyers, Merchants, Citizens, Farmers,
Maſters of Houſholds, and all ſortes of ſeruants, to marke,
and delightfull for all men to Reade.
Lege, Perlege, Relege.

Printed at London for NATHANIEL BVTTER. 1608.

Title page, Thomas Dekker, *The Belman*[1] *of London,* 1608.

With the temporary closing of the theaters in 1603 due to the plague, the playwright Thomas Dekker turned to writing pamphlets. In *The Belman of London* he promised to the reader that he would "bring to light a number of more notable enormities (daily hatched in this Realm) than ever have yet been published to the open eye of the world."

[1] *Belman* Man employed to walk the streets of a town making public announcements, or simply "calling the hours."

from "A True Report of the late Horrible Murder Committed by William Sherwood, upon Richard Hobson, Gentleman, both Prisoners in the Queen's Bench, for the profession of Popery, the 18th of June, 1581"

I am the more loath at this time, to lay open unto the view of the whole world that late foul murder committed by Sherwood, because I would not speak much of them which be gone, and be thought to bite them by the back which are dead, and so be like unto those papists which being hot in cruelty did not only curse the dead continually, but did take up and burn the bones of diverse good men into ashes, to signify unto the world that no drink could cool their thirst but blood, no sacrifice could content them but the warm heart blood of martyrs and the death of the saints of God. But my intent is this: for as much as their scabs now break out, and that their cruelty seeketh no corners[2] but setteth itself upon a stage to be beheld of all men, to give all good Christians warning that as they shall hear of their naughtiness,[3] and see it so, they will learn to spew them out of their stomachs forever....

But to be brief: the day grew on, which was the 28th of June about 8 of the clock in the morning, at which time he had determined to murder his fellow papist, and that the matter might more easy be brought to pass, he caused the night before the keeper to remove all Hobson's weapons, so that the next morning, as Hobson was coming down through Sherwood's chamber, from his prayers, Sherwood shutting his chamber door, assailed him with a knife, and a stool trestle, astonishing him, afterwards gave him a large wound, keeping him down and struggling till he bled to death, Hobson often crying, "Help, Father Throckmorton, he killeth me with his knife!" Master Throckmorton and others, hearing this noise, came upon Sherwood and by force broke up his doors, found the young man all to befouled in his own blood, and gasping for breath: who after a few faint words, yielded his soul into the hands of God. Sherwood perceived a great many busy about Hobson, began to practice to escape, but by heed taking of one Master Smith's man, he was brought to the marshal's

[2] *corners* I.e., places to hide.

[3] *naughtiness* Wickedness, evil.

hands, and imbrued in his fellow's blood: who being examined, he denied that manifest murder, which by witness was proved, and he being brought to the slain body, the blood which was settled, issued out afresh. Thus he slew this young man, in deed and cause miserably, in form and fashion cruelly and beastly.

Let us advisedly now weigh and consider what manner of razor this is that cutteth so sharp: if they be thus unable to master their passions, and thus like bloodsuckers do open them against their own fellow prisoners, what shall we look for at their hands? …

Print Culture

Mechanical print technology originated in Germany in the mid-fifteenth century and the printing press was introduced to the British Isles by William Caxton in 1476. The illustrations that follow give some sense of the range of print culture in the sixteenth and early seventeenth centuries beyond what has been presented under the headings above.

from Jan van der Straet, *Nova Reperta.* This engraving by a Flemish artist of a printing shop was one of a series published in Antwerp in the 1580s; no comparable illustration of the technology of printing from Elizabethan England is known.

¶Here begynneth a newe tracte or treatyse moost pfytable for all husbāde men/and very frutefull for all other persones to rede/newly correcte & amended by the auctour/with dyuerse other thynges added therunto.

Husbondrye

Title page, attributed to Anthony Fitzherbert, *The Book of Husbandry*, c. 1523.

In 1598 the eleventh edition of this work was published; it appears to have been one of the most popular books of the age. In all probability the primary audience for the work was the yeoman farmer; laborers were in most cases illiterate. The book offers advice on such matters as whether to plough with horses or oxen, how to sow oats or barley, how to make simple farm implements, and how to care for animals, including how to treat their diseases. Advice on highway repair is also included; throughout the sixteenth century husbandmen were required to devote several days per year to road work in their area. Gender roles were strictly differentiated; women are advised to clean the house, feed the animals, prepare meals, and make butter and cheese. In only a few areas are the roles allowed to overlap; the wife is advised to go to market if her husband is unable to do so, and to assist him in filling "the muck wain or dung cart." Each spouse is advised to provide an honest account to the other of money spent.

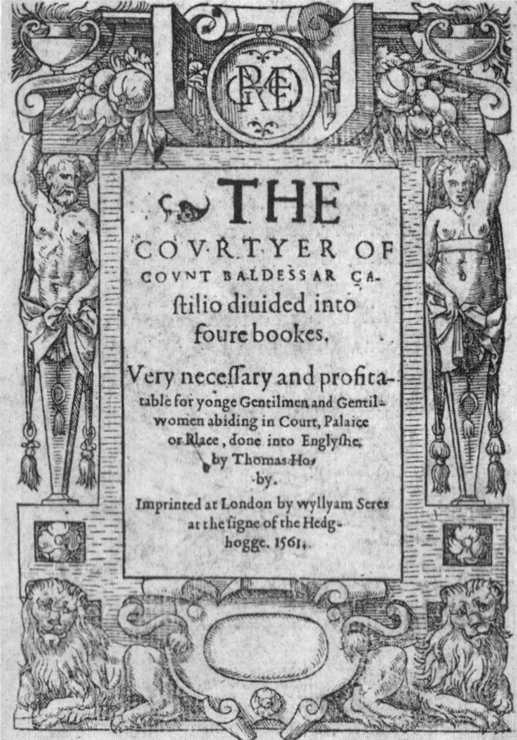

THE
COVRTYER OF
COVNT BALDESSAR CA-
ſtilio diuided into
foure bookes.
Very neceſſary and profita-
table for yonge Gentilmen and Gentil-
women abiding in Court, Palaice
or Place, done into Englyſhe
by Thomas Ho-
by.
Imprinted at London by wyllyam Seres
at the ſigne of the Hedg-
hogge. 1561.

Title page, Baldassare Castiglione, *The Courtier*, translated by Thomas Hoby (first English edition, 1561). Castiglione's work (often referred to as *The Book of the Courtier*), was first published in Venice in 1528. It quickly became influential throughout Europe in its many translations.

Crispin van de Passe the Elder, engraving after a drawing by Isaac Oliver, *Queen Elizabeth*, 1603. This engraving is thought to have been published in commemoration of the Queen's death.

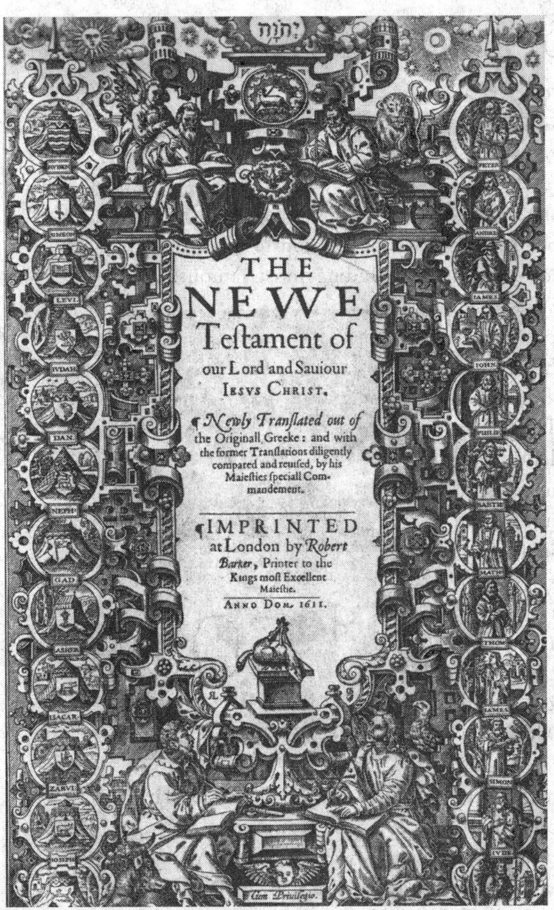

THE NEWE Testament of our Lord and Sauiour IESVS CHRIST.

Newly Translated out of the Originall Greeke: and with the former Translations diligently compared and reuised, by his Maiesties speciall Commandement.

IMPRINTED at London by Robert Barker, Printer to the Kings most Excellent Maiestie.

ANNO DOM. 1611.

Title page, *New Testament, King James Bible* (first edition, 1611).

The Fearefull Summer: OR, Londons Calamitie, The Countries Discourtesie, And both their Miserie.

Printed by Authoritie in Oxford, in the last great Infection of the Plague, 1625. And now reprinted with some Editions, concerning this present yeere, 1636.

With some mention of the grievous and afflicted estate of the famous Towne of New-Castle upon Tine, with some other visited Townes of this Kingdome.

By IOHN TAYLOR.

Title page, John Taylor, *The Fearful Summer: or London's Calamity* (1625, reprinted 1636). The plague of 1665 remains the most famous of the seventeenth century, but it was one of many—including those of 1603, 1625 and 1636.

Mary Stuart, Queen of Scots

1542 – 1587

The life of Mary, Queen of Scots, also known as Mary I of Scotland and Mary Stuart, was the stuff of melodrama: violent, traumatic, and often shaped by forces beyond her control. In a time of fierce antagonism between traditional Catholics and Protestants (including most famously the Calvinist John Knox), Mary, although herself a Catholic, attempted to find a middle course and keep peace amongst her subjects. The task proved impossible, in part because she had also to deal with an ancient nobility and clan leaders who feared that a strong monarchy would diminish their own power. The poetry and letters of this embattled and sometimes imprudent queen portray a sorrowful woman trying desperately to bring peace to her life if also, her enemies insisted (rightly or more often wrongly), resorting on occasion to political and personal crime.

Mary was born in the castle of Linlithgow, in West Lothian, Scotland, on 8 December 1542, the only legitimate child of James V of Scotland and his French wife, Mary of Guise, whose family would soon lead the ultra-conservative Catholic faction in France's religious civil wars. On 14 December James V died, leaving his wife as regent and his daughter a six-day-old queen. In 1548, hoping to strengthen an alliance with France and thus help protect the realm against the English, the Regent and her government negotiated little Mary's betrothal to the French Crown Prince, himself only four. Mary went to live in France to be brought up at the dazzling court of Henry II, where she had a fine education and was tutored in poetry by Pierre de Ronsard, the most famous French poet of his generation (and who had briefly been in Scotland with Mary's mother). Mary seems to have gradually forgotten her native language and for the rest of her life spoke and wrote primarily in French. In 1558 she married Francis, who unexpectedly inherited the French throne when his father was killed in a jousting accident in 1559. Mary was now Queen of Scotland and Queen Consort of France, even if then and for many years the French government was effectively run by Mary's mother-in-law, Catherine de Medici. After young Francis II died of an infection in December of 1560, however, Mary found herself a seventeen-year-old widow and in 1561 she returned to Scotland.

In Scotland, Mary attempted to be a moderate leader, particularly in religious matters, and to promote the peace and prosperity of her realm. Although a devoted Catholic, she encouraged mutual tolerance, a policy that merely made her unpopular with the more militant members of both religious groups. She seems to have been liked, at first, by most of her subjects, but her efforts to consolidate the power of the throne infuriated many of the nobility.

Mary now attempted to arrange an advantageous match for herself, after several setbacks finally marrying her handsome English cousin, Henry Stewart, Lord Darnley, on 29 July 1565. The marriage was a disaster: Darnley proved to be self-centered, ruthless, and afflicted by syphilis. In March 1566, when Mary was six months pregnant, he was one of a group of nobles said to have broken into her supper-room at Holyrood Palace in Edinburgh and before her eyes stabbed to death her confidant and private secretary, David Riccio (or Rizzio). The lords, who resented this ugly but charming Italian musician for his influence over Mary, had encouraged Darnley to suspect an adulterous relationship for which there is in fact little convincing evidence. After Riccio's murder, Mary was for a time a virtual prisoner in her own palace. Her baby (named James) was born in June, but the addition to the family did little to reconcile Mary and Darnley; by the autumn she was considering divorcing him.

In February of 1567 a group of nobles hostile to Darnley conspired to blow up a house near Edinburgh where the young man was staying. Darnley tried to flee but was strangled on the grounds just as the house itself exploded. Understandably, Mary's enemies suspected her of having a hand in the assassination but again there is no evidence of her guilt. Soon afterward one noble, James Hepburn, Earl of Bothwell, who had assembled a small army, convinced the queen to marry him, possibly after raping her, and assured her that he would help her to keep her nobles in line. Terrified, and with an infant son to worry about, Mary thought she had no choice, and that May they were married. Fearing that Bothwell now had too much power, however, a group of other lords confronted Mary while she was traveling and told her to abandon him. She refused. Despite the presence of her own troops, Mary declined an armed battle and accompanied the lords to Edinburgh. Imprisoned in Lochleven Castle, she was now forced to abdicate. In July 1567 her one-year-old son became James VI of Scotland.

After ten months of captivity, Mary escaped. Attempting to regain her crown, she raised an army but was defeated near Glasgow. In May 1568 Mary fled south, hoping for help from her cousin Elizabeth, unaware that the English queen saw her as a danger to her own throne. Many English Catholics, who thought Elizabeth was not only a heretic but illegitimate, with no right to her throne, considered Mary the rightful heir. As soon as Mary arrived, Elizabeth had her imprisoned. She remained a prisoner for the next nineteen years and, despite her repeated pleas, she never saw Elizabeth face to face.

Mary's writings provide a personal parallel, or sometimes a counterpoint, to the external facts of her life (since she wrote in French, selections appear here in translation). Her letters reveal an articulate woman with some measure of political astuteness, yet her letter of 1 October 1569 to Elizabeth shows how badly she could misjudge her situation. Her poems—perhaps only seemingly more private, for queens have little personal life—provide a glimpse of tragedy's toll on their author.

In October 1586 Mary was sent to trial at Fotheringhay Castle, accused of complicity in plots against Elizabeth. The result was inevitable: she was allowed no witnesses on her behalf and was found guilty after two days. On 8 February 1587, after a long delay during which Elizabeth dithered (and apparently tried to arrange for an assassination), the Queen of Scots was beheaded. Sixteen years later her son became James I of England; in 1612 he had her remains reburied in Westminster Abbey. All English monarchs since the death of Elizabeth descend from Mary Stuart.

⌘⌘⌘

Sonnet to Elizabeth

A single thought that haunts me, day and night,
Bitter and sweet, torments my heart, without cease,
Between fear and hope it oppresses me
So that peace and rest flee me.
So, dear sister, if this paper reveals
The desire to see you that oppresses me,
That is because I live in pain and sadness,
So long as my suit[1] is not quickly granted.
I have seen a ship freed from constraint
On the high seas, near to entering a port,
And the calm sea turned to storms:
Likewise, I am troubled and in fear,
Not because of you, but because Fortune
Often wrongly rips sails and rigging.

Une seul penser qui me profite le jour et la nuit
Amer et doux, change en mon coeur sans cesse,
Entre le doubte et l'espoir il m'oppresse
Tant que la paix et le repos me fuient.
Donc, chère soeur, si cette carte suit
L'affection de vous voir qui me presse,
C'est que je vis en peine et en tristesse,
Si promptement l'effect ne s'en ensuit.
J'ai vu la nef relâcher par contrainte
En haute mer proche d'entrer au port,
Et le serein se convertir en trouble.
Ainsi je suis en souci et en crainte,
Non pas de vous mais quant aux fois à tort
Fortune rompe voile et cordage double.
—1568

Sonnets to Bothwell[2]

O gods, have of me compassion,
And show what certain proof
I may give, which shall not seem to him vain,
Of my love and fervent affection.
Alas, is he not already in possession
Of my body, of heart that refuses no pain,
Nor dishonour in this life uncertain,
Offence of friends, nor worse affliction?
For him I esteem all my friends less than nothing,
And I will have good hope of my enemies.
I have put in hazard for him both fame and conscience,[3]
I will die to set him forward.[4]
What remains to give proof of my constancy?

O Dieux ayez de moy compassion,
Et m'enseignez quelle preuve certain
Je puis donner qui ne luy semble vain
De mon amour & ferme affection.
Las! n'est il pas ja en possession
Du corps, du coeur qui ne refuse paine
Ny dishonneur, en la vie incertaine,
Offense de parents, ne pire affliction?
Pour luy tous mes amis j'estime moins que rien
Et de mes ennemis je veux esperer bien.
J'ay hazardé pour luy & nom & conscience:
Je veux pour luy au monde renoncer:
Je veux mourir pour luy avancer.
Que reste il plus pour prouver ma constance?

In his hands and in his full power,
I put my son, my honour, and my life,
My country, my subjects, my soul all subdued
To him, and have no other will

Entre ses mains & en son plein pouvoir
Je metz mon filz, mon honneur, & ma vie,
Mon pais, mes subjectz, mon ame assubjectie
Est tout à luy, & n'ay autre voulloir

[1] *my suit* Plea. In 1568 Mary came to Elizabeth, seeking asylum.

[2] *Sonnets to Bothwell* The sonnets included here were published by George Buchanan in *A Detection of the Doings of Mary, Queen of Scots, Touching the murder of her husband* (1571). This anthology includes the sixteenth-century French "originals" of sonnets 1, 2, 6, and 7, as well as their modernized and anglicized Scottish translations. The authenticity of these poems is sometimes questioned.

[3] *fame* The French has "nom" (name) here: the royal name upon which all Mary's "fame" rests.

[4] *I will ... forward* The twelfth line from the French is not translated in the original Scottish translation: "I will renounce the world for him."

For my scope,[1] which without deceit,
I will follow in spite of all envy
That may ensue. For I have no other desire
But to make him perceive my faithfulness;
For storm or fair weather that may come,
Never will it change dwelling or place.
Shortly I shall give of my truth such proof,
That he shall know my constancy without fiction,
Not by my weeping, or feigned obedience,
As others have done, but by other experience.

And now she[2] begins to see
That she was of very evil judgement,
To esteem the love of such a lover,
And would feign[3] deceive my love,
By writings and painted learning,
Which, not the less, did not breed in her brain,[4]
But borrowed from some feat° author, *accomplished, successful*
To feign one story and have none.
And for all that, her painted words,
Her tears, her plaints° full of dissimulation, *complaints*
And her high cries and lamentations
Have won that point: that you keep in store
Her letters and writings, to which you give trust,
Yea, and love and believe her more than me.

You believe her (alas) I perceive it too well,
And call in doubt my firm constancy
(O my only wealth, and my only hope)
And I cannot assure you of my truth.
I see that you esteem me light,
And be no way assured of me,
And do suspect (my heart) without any appearing cause,
Discrediting me wrangously.° *wrongly*
You do not know the love I bear to you.
You suspect that other love transports me.
You think my words be but wind.
You paint my very heart as it were of wax.
You imagine me a woman without judgment.
And all that encreases my burning.

[1] *no other … scope* No other desire for my object.

[2] *she* Bothwell's first wife. He divorced her very shortly before marrying Mary.

[3] *would feign* "Desires to," but this also plays with the meaning of "feign" as "pretend."

Pour mon object que sans le decevoir
Suivre je veux malgré tout l'envie
Qu'issir en peult, car je n'ay autre envie
Que de ma foy, luy faire appercevoir
Que pour tempeste ou bonnace qui face,
Jamais ne veux changer demeure ou place.
Brief je feray de may foy telle preuve,
Qu'il cognoistra sans fainte ma constance,
Non par mes pleurs ou fainte obeyssance,
Comme autres ont fait, mais par divers espreuve.

Et maintenant elle commence à voir
Qu'elle estoit bien de mauvais jugement
De n'estimer l'amour d'un tel amant
Et voudroit bien mon amy decevoir,
Par les escriptz tout fardez de sçavoir
Qui pourtant n'est en son esprit croissant
Ains emprunté de quelque autheur luissant,
A faint tresbien un envoy sans l'avoir
Et toutefois ses parolles fardez,
Ses pleurs, ses plaincts remplis de fictions,
Et ses hauts cris & lamentations
Ont tant gaigné qui par vous sont gardez
Ses lettres escriptes ausquelles vous donnez foy
Et si l'aymez & croyez plus que moy.

Vous la croyez, las! trop je l'apperçoy
Et vous doutez de ma ferme constance,
O mon seul bien & mon seul esperance,
Et ne vous puis j'asseurer de ma foy
Vous m'estimez leger qui le voy,
Et si n'avez en moy nul asseurance
Et soupçonnez mon coeur sans apparence,
Vous deffiant à trop grand tort de moy.
Vous ignorez l'amour que je vous porte,
Vous soupçonnez qu'autre amour me transporte,
Vous estimez mes parolles du vent,
Vous depeignez de cire mon las coeur,
Vous me pensez femme sans jugement.
Et tout cela augmente mon ardeur.
—1571

[4] *Which … brain* A somewhat confusing double negative, meaning "which her brain did not create."

Letters

In 1567, Mary's enemies seized from one of Bothwell's servants letters written by Mary to Bothwell that appeared to prove both her adultery and her complicity in the murder of her husband Darnley; they are known as the "casket letters" from the silver box in which they were ostensibly discovered. The originals were probably written in French—but the originals were never produced by officials at the time, and they are not extant; one theory has it that they were destroyed by James I. But contemporary copies, in manuscript and in print, exist in Latin, English, Scots, and French. Mary's defenders and detractors have debated the authenticity of these letters ever since, with her defenders arguing that the letters, or at least the more incriminating elements within them, were forgeries. Most scholars agree that at least four of the letters are undoubtedly Mary's, but that the versions that survive have possibly been tampered with.

from LETTER TWO

I went to my supper. The bearer of these letters[1] will inform you of my arrival. He[2] begged me to come back and I did so. He told me how ill he was and said that he would make no last will but simply leave everything to me; adding that I was the cause of his sickness because of his distress on account of my strangeness toward him. And then he said, "You ask me what were the cruelties which I mentioned in my letters? The reference was to you alone who will not accept my repentance or my promises. I admit that I have greatly offended but not in the matter which I have always denied. I have also sinned against some of your subjects and this you have forgiven."

"I am young."

"You will say that you have often forgiven me, and that I repeat my offences. May not a man of my age, lacking good counsel, fall twice or thrice and fail in his promises, and afterwards repent of his fault and chasten himself by experience? If I can win forgiveness, I promise not to offend hereafter. I will ask for nothing except that we may be at bed and board together as husband and wife; and if you do not consent to that, I shall never rise from this bed again. I beg you to let me hear your decision, for God knows what grief I have suffered by making you into a god and by thinking of nothing else but you: and should I at any time give you offence, you yourself will be the cause thereof; for if I knew that, when somebody offends against *me,* I had the refuge of being able to take my trouble to you, I would make no complaint to any other: but now if I hear anything I am compelled to keep it shut within my breast, since I am not on easy terms with yourself. This troubles me so direly that it deprives me of wisdom and good understanding."

I answered him all the time, but it would be a long business to write it all down. I asked him why he had considered going away in that English ship. This he denied under oath but admitted that he had talked with the English. Then I enquired about the interrogation of William Highgate.[3] This he also denied till I repeated the very words which he had uttered. He then said that Minto[4] had informed him that they said that one of the council had sent for my signature to letters which would put him in prison or, if he did not obey, would send him to death. And that he had addressed the same enquiries to Minto who answered that he thought this was true. As for the rest, concerning William Highgate, he has confessed to it, but not till the day after my arrival.

In the end he desired much that I would lodge in his lodging. I have refused, and told him that he must be disinfected and that this could not be done here. He said to me that he had heard that I had brought the litter[5] but would have liked much better to go with me. I believe he feared that I might take him prisoner. I answered that I would carry him away with me to Craigmillar[6] where the doctors and I could look after him without my being too far away from my son. He replied that he was ready to go wherever I wished, provided that I would assure him of what he had required of me.

---

[1] *bearer of these letters* Nicolas Hubert, a French page (d. 1569), who was also known as French Paris.

[2] *He* Darnley. Henry Stuart, Lord Darnley (1545–67), Mary's second husband.

[3] *William Highgate* Town Clerk of Glasgow, an ally of Mary's.

[4] *Minto* The Laird of Minto.

[5] *litter* Framework supporting a bed for transport of the sick.

[6] *Craigmillar* Castle near Edinburgh.

He wanted not to be seen by anybody. He gets angry whenever I speak of Walker, and says that he will pluck his ears from his head and that he lies: because I had asked him about that matter and also why he had complained of some of the lords and had threatened them. He denied it, and said that he liked all of them, and begged me not to believe anyone but himself; and that as for me, he would rather lose his life than give me displeasure.

At this point he employed so many little flatteries, so adroitly and with such weight, as would have astonished you. I had almost forgotten that he said he could not suspect me in the Highgate affair and will never believe that I, his own flesh and blood, would do him any injury, and that he knew well that I had refused to subscribe[1] to it. That if anybody aimed at his life, he would sell it dearly, but that he neither did nor would suspect anyone but would love all those whom I loved.

He would not let me go but wanted me to sit up with him. I pretended that it all seemed to me quite genuine, and said I would think it over, and when I had excused myself from staying up with him that night, he said that he cannot sleep. I have never known him to speak more mildly or to behave so well; and if I had not learned by experience that his will is as weak as wax, and that mine is hard as a diamond which no arrow could pierce unless it were shot by your hand, it might well have chanced that I should have pitied him. However, have no fears, this fortress will be held to the death: but look to it lest your own be surprised by that faithless nation which with no less pertinacity[2] will contend for it against you.

I think they[3] have been taught at the same school. The one here has always a tear or two in his eye; he greets everybody, down to the meanest,[4] and flatters them in a pitiable manner in order that he may prevail on them to be sorry for him. Today his father[5] bled at the nose and at the mouth, and you can guess the significance of that.[6] I have seen nothing of him[7] since, because he has remained in his room. The King requires that I should give him[8] his food with my own hands: but believe no more where you are than I do here.

There—that is the end of my first day's work. I hope to finish the rest tomorrow. I write everything down, no matter how unimportant, so that by choosing out the best you may be able to form your judgement. I am busy here with a task which is infinitely uncongenial: but would you not like to see how trimly[9] I lie or at least how well I dissimulate while speaking the truth? He has given away to me everything that is in the name of the Bishop[10] and of Sutherland,[11] although I have not spoken to him or said a single word of what you reported to me: so do I merely by the power of flattery and coaxing cause him to feel sure of me. And by complaining about the Bishop I have got everything from him, and the rest is taken for granted....

LETTER THREE

My Lord,

Whether the strain of your absence and your forgetfulness, added to the fear of danger threatening your beloved person from everybody, affords me much consolation I will leave you to judge, especially in view of the unhappiness which my cruel lot and continual misadventure seem to promise me on top of all those mischances and fears both recent and in bygone days of which you so well know. But for all that, I will not accuse you of remembering me so little or of caring so little, still less of your broken promises (or of the coldness in your writing), since what pleases you is acceptable to me and because my thoughts are so willingly subdued to yours that I take for granted that whatever proceeds from you does not really come from any of the

[1] *subscribe* Agree.

[2] *pertinacity* Stubborn adherence.

[3] *they* Darnley and Lady Bothwell.

[4] *meanest* Lowest, in terms of social status.

[5] *his father* Lennox. Matthew Stewart, fourth Earl of Lennox (1516–71), Mary's father-in-law.

[6] *bled...that* To "bleed at the nose" was also a sixteenth-century French euphemism for being afraid.

[7] *him* I.e., Lennox.

[8] *him* I.e., Darnley.

[9] *trimly* Cleverly.

[10] *Bishop* Perhaps the Bishop of Mondavi, the papal nuncio with whom Mary had recently consulted, or one of the Scottish bishops.

[11] *Sutherland* John Gordon, eleventh Earl of Sutherland (1525–67).

causes which I have mentioned but from such as are just and reasonable and of a kind which I would myself desire. And that is the understanding upon which I have based my actions as coming from the only Sustainer of my life. And it is only for this that I want to preserve my life because without this I should desire nothing but a sudden death. And to show you how far I humble myself before your commandments, I have sent you—by Paris—as a token of my homage an ornament for the head, seeing that the head is the leader of the other members,[1] signifying thereby that by investing you with the spoils of that which is uppermost, the rest must necessarily be subject to you and with a consenting heart. In place of which, since you have it,[2] I send you a sepulchre of hard stone painted black and sown with tears and bones. This stone I liken to my heart which, like it, is carven into a safe tomb or receptacle for your commands and, above all, for your name and your memory which lie therein, just as my heart is enclosed within this ring, never to come forth from it until death enables you to use my bones as trophies. Just as the ring is filled up, so have you made complete conquest of me and my heart and even my bones, which will be left to you in remembrance of your victory and of my happy and willing defeat, so to be better bestowed than I deserve. The surrounding enamel is black, signifying the steadfastness of her who sends it. The tears are beyond numbering as are also my fears of displeasing you; tears for your absence and tears of vexation because I cannot be yours in outward show as I am unfeignedly in heart and soul, and rightly so even if my merits were greater than the greatest that I ever had, and were such as I wish they might be and which I shall strive to emulate in order that they may be worthy of your rule. Receive it, my only treasure, in good part as I with such extreme joy did accept our marriage which, until the marriage of our bodies be made public news, shall not go forth from my bosom as the essence of all that I hope or desire of happiness in this world. Now, fearing to displease you in the reading of this as much as I have enjoyed the writing of it, I will make an end, first having kissed your hands with such deep affection as I pray God (O you only Sustainer of my life!) to give you a long and happy life, and to me your good favour, as being the only good that I desire and for which I starve. I have told the bearer of this letter all that I have learned, relying upon him because I know how well he stands with you, as he does also with her who will be to you for ever a humble and obedient wife and your chosen friend, dedicating altogether to you her heart, her body, unalterably, as to him whom I made possessor of a heart whereof you may be certain that it will never change until death, nor shall evil or good have power to estrange it.

[1] *members* Parts of the body.

[2] *it* I.e., the heart.

LETTER FOUR

I have sat up there[3] later than I would have done if it were not for drawing out that which the bearer will relate to you,—that I have found the best possible way of excusing your business. I have promised to bring him away tomorrow. If it seems to you good, therefore, see to it.

Now I have broken my promise that I would neither write nor send messages to you. But not in order to annoy you: and if you realised how much I am afraid just now you would not have so many contrary suspicions in your mind, suspicions which, all the same, I put up with and take in good part as coming from the thing which I most desire and most earnestly seek of all things under heaven, which is your good grace—which I will earn by my own behaviour. As for me, I will never despair of winning it, and I beg you to fulfil those promises which made me believe in your affection. Otherwise, I should consider that it had made for my unhappiness, and that the favour of the stars toward other women, who nonetheless have not a third part of the loyalty and obedience which I bear to you, must have won the advantage over me which the second love of Jason[4] won: not that I want to compare you with such an ill-fated person nor myself to such an entirely pitiless woman. However, you do cause me to be something like her in any matter that touches you or that may preserve you and keep you to her to whom alone you belong by right: if I may so appropriate to

[3] *up there* I.e., in Darnley's room.

[4] *second ... Jason* In Greek mythology, Jason left his first wife, Medea, for Glauce. Glauce was killed when she touched a poisoned dress that Medea had sent her.

myself that which is won by having loved you loyally, having loved you only, as I say, and as I shall always do while I live, no matter what ills or perils may come. And for all these mishaps, of which you are the cause, give me a recompense—by keeping in mind the place which is close to here.

I do not ask that you keep your promise tomorrow. But let us be together and do not put any trust in those suspicions unless they are proved by experience to be facts. I ask nothing else of God but that you may realise that my heart is yours, and that He may guard you from all evils at least so long as I am alive, nor do I hold my life at all precious except insofar as it and I are pleasing to you. I am going to bed and will say goodnight. Let me know in good time to-morrow how you are faring, for I shall be anxious until I hear. As a bird escaped from the cage or the turtle who has no companion, I shall be alone, lamenting your absence howsoever short it may be. This letter will happily do something which I cannot do as I am afraid perchance that you may be asleep. I did not dare to write while Joseph, Sebastian and Joachim[1] were about, and they had only just gone when I began to write this letter.

Letter Seven

As to the time and the place, I leave them to your brother and you. I will follow him, and there shall be no blunder on my part. He finds many difficulties. I think he has told you about them and about all that he requires for playing his part well. As for my own role, I realise that I must act in accordance with what has been arranged.

It seems to me that your long service, and the high opinion which the Lords have of you, ought to gain you forgiveness even if you should advance yourself beyond the status of a subject. You hazarded this venture[2] not in order to ravish me and to hold me captive but to be sure of a place near to me, nor can the arguments or remonstrances of other people stop me from consenting to that which you hope that your service to me will some day enable you to secure. In a word, it is for you to make sure of the Lords and to become free to marry: since for your own support you can, after such loyal service, reasonably proffer this humble request always accompanied by your persistency.

Make your excuses, therefore, and persuade them as best you may that you are compelled to chase your enemies. You will speak well enough if the matter and the theme are to your taste: and give Lethington[3] many fair words. If this does not seem good to you, let me know, and do not throw all the blame onto me.

Letter Eight

My Lord, since my last letter, your brother-in-law, as he was, has asked my advice as to what he should do after tomorrow because there are many people here, including the Earl of Sutherland, who would sooner die, on account of the benefits which they have lately received from me, than suffer me to be carried away while they are acting as my bodyguard. On the other hand, he is afraid that if there is trouble it will be said that he was ungrateful in having betrayed me. I told him that he ought to have arranged for all that with you, and that he should get rid of all those whom he most mistrusts.

Following my advice he has decided to write to you about it; and I am astonished to see how irresolute he is in the hour of need. I say to myself that he will play the man; but I thought it would be well to let you know of his fear that he may be charged and accused of treason so that, without distrusting him, you may be the more careful and be the better equipped. Yesterday we had more than three hundred horse—his and Livingstone's. For the love of God, see that you are accompanied by more rather than by less; that, indeed, is my chief anxiety.

I must go to write my despatches, and I pray God that we may soon have a happy meeting. I write in haste so that you may be warned in good time.

—1571 (1947 this translation)

---

[1] *Joseph … Joachim* Three of Mary's servants.

[2] *this venture* In early 1567, Mary was abducted, or possibly went away consensually, with Bothwell.

[3] *Lethington* William Maitland of Lethington (c. 1528–73), Mary's Secretary of State.

Aemilia Lanyer

1569 – 1645

Aemilia Lanyer published her one book of poetry at a time when it was unusual for an English woman to publish her writing, especially under her full name. It was even more unusual for a middle-class woman to approach publication as a means of making money; to choose herself female patrons; and to make carefully planned use of poems addressed to them in order to raise the status of her work. Lanyer did all of these things.

Because Lanyer was not born into the nobility, many of the details of her personal life are sketchy, cobbled together from court and church records, information gleaned from her poems, and the professional journals of Simon Forman, an astrologer whom she consulted in 1597. She was born to Baptista Bassano and Margaret Johnson, a couple in a common-law marriage, in January 1569. Her father was an Italian musician in the courts of Edward VI and Elizabeth I, so although Aemilia Bassano was not of noble birth, she had access to aristocratic circles and was probably educated along with the young ladies of the court, likely in classical literature and rhetoric.

At age 18, Aemilia Bassano became the mistress of Henry Carey, Lord Hunsdon, who was then serving as Lord Chamberlain to Queen Elizabeth. The affair continued for five years, until she became pregnant. To avoid embarrassment, Carey married her off to another court musician, Alfonso Lanyer, on 18 October 1592, and provided her with an annual stipend of £40. Lanyer bore a son in early 1593, and named him Henry. Lanyer's marriage to Alfonso was not happy: according to Simon Forman's journals, "her husband hath dealt hardly with her and spent and consumed her goods and she is now ... in debt." The couple had one child together in December 1598, named Odillya, who died at the age of ten months.

Despite her domestic situation, Lanyer maintained her connection with aristocratic families, particularly with a circle of intellectual court women, to whom she later dedicated many poems. Some time before 1609, she stayed with Margaret Clifford, Countess of Cumberland, and her daughter Anne at the estate where they were then living, Cookham Dean. The visit influenced Lanyer profoundly, as she relates in "The Description of Cooke-ham," the first "country house" poem published in English. While at Cookham Dean, she says, she experienced a spiritual awakening, inspired by the piety of the countess.

In 1611, at age 42, she published her volume of verse, *Salve Deus Rex Judæorum* (*Hail, God, King of the Jews*). Although the book focuses on virtue and religion, topics considered appropriate for a woman, it is nevertheless a radical (although not unprecedented) work for its time. Among its topics is the traditional and misogynistic maltreatment of women. The title poem, a lively narrative of the passion of Christ, interrupts its story once to argue that Eve, and, by extension, womankind, have been unjustly made to bear the chief responsibility for eating the fruit of the forbidden tree: that sin pales in comparison to the sin of the men who deliberately sentenced Christ to death. She commends the intervention of Pilate's wife and contrasts the behavior of Christ's male disciples, who forsook or denied him, with that of the women who stayed with him to the end.

After her husband died in 1613, Lanyer founded a school for the children of nobility and other wealthy families as a means of supporting herself. The only details concerning the remainder of her life come from court records, which indicate that she had considerable legal troubles, first concerning her school, then regarding the estate of her son, Henry, who died in October 1633. Lanyer died at age 76, and was buried 3 April 1645, at St. James Church, Clerkenwell.

⌘⌘⌘

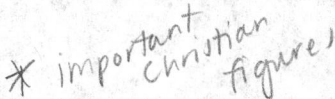

* important christian figures

To the Virtuous Reader

Often have I heard that it is the property[1] of some women not only to emulate the virtues and perfections of the rest, but also by all their powers of ill-speaking to eclipse the brightness of their deserved fame; now contrary to this custom, which men I hope unjustly lay to their charge, I have written this small volume or little book, for the general use of all virtuous ladies and gentlewomen of this kingdom; and in commendation of some particular persons of our own sex, such as for the most part are so well known to myself and others, that I dare undertake fame dares not to call any better. And this have I done to make known to the world that all women deserve not to be blamed, though some forgetting they are women themselves, and in danger to be condemned by the words of their own mouths, fall into so great an error, as to speak unadvisedly against the rest of their sex; which if it be true, I am persuaded they can show their own imperfection in nothing more; and therefore could wish (for their own ease, modesties and credit) they would refer such points of folly to be practised by evil-disposed men, who forgetting they were born of women, nourished of women, and that if it were not by the means of women, they would be quite extinguished out of the world, and a final end of them all, do like vipers deface the wombs wherein they were bred,[2] only to give way and utterance to their want of discretion and goodness. Such as these, were they that dishonoured Christ, his apostles and prophets, putting them to shameful deaths. Therefore we are not to regard any imputations, that they undeservedly lay upon us, no otherwise than to make use of them to our own benefits, as spurs to virtue, making us fly all occasions that may colour their unjust speeches to pass current.[3] Especially considering that they have tempted even the patience of God himself, who gave power to wise and virtuous women to bring down their pride and arrogance. As was cruel Cesarius by the discreet counsel of noble Deborah,[4] judge and prophetess of Israel, and resolution of Jael,[5] wife of Heber the Kenite; wicked Haman, by the divine prayers and prudent proceedings of beautiful Hester;[6] blasphemous Holofernes, by the invincible courage, rare wisdom, and confident carriage of Judith;[7] and the unjust judges, by the innocence of chaste Susanna;[8] with infinite others, which for brevity's sake I will omit. As also in respect it pleased our Lord and Saviour Jesus Christ, without the assistance of man, being free from original and all other sins, from the time of his conception till the hour of his death, to be begotten of a woman, born of a woman, nourished of a woman, obedient to a woman; and that he healed women, pardoned women, comforted women, yea, even when he was in his greatest agony and bloody sweat, going to be crucified, and also in the last hour of his death, took care to dispose of a woman; after his resurrection, appeared first to a woman, sent a woman to declare his most glorious resurrection to the rest of his disciples. Many other examples I could allege of diverse faithful and virtuous women, who have in all ages not only been confessors, but also endured most cruel martyrdom for their faith in Jesus Christ. All which is sufficient to enforce all good Christians and honourable-minded men to speak reverently of our sex, and especially of all virtuous and good women. To the modest censures of both which I refer these my imperfect endeavours, knowing that according to their own excellent dispositions they will rather cherish, nourish, and increase the least spark of virtue where they find it, by their favourable and best interpretations, than quench it by wrong constructions. To whom I wish with all increase of virtue, and desire their best opinions.

---

[1] *property* Habit.

[2] *vipers … bred* It was thought that at birth the viper's young bit through the sides of the mother in order to be born, killing her.

[3] *pass current* Seem legitimate.

[4] *Deborah* Ruler of Israel who defeated the army of Sisera (Cesarius), a Canaanite general (see Judges 4).

[5] *Jael* Woman who killed Sisera by driving a tent peg through his head (see Judges 4).

[6] *Hester* Jewish queen (also called Esther) who saved the Jews from a genocidal plot concocted by Haman by appealing to Xerxes, King of Persia (see Esther 3–7).

[7] *Judith* Woman who killed the Babylonian general Holofernes by cutting off his head (see Judith 8–12).

[8] *Susanna* Woman who resisted the advances of two judges, who then unjustly charged her with adultery (see Daniel and Susanna 13).

from *Salve Deus Rex Judæorum*

"Invocation"

Sith° *Cynthia*[1] is ascended to that rest *since*
Of endless joy and true eternity,
That glorious place that cannot be expressed
By any wight° clad in mortality, *creature*
In her almighty love so highly blest,
And crowned with everlasting sovereignty;
  Where saints and angels do attend her throne,
  And she gives glory unto God alone.

To thee, great Countess,[2] now I will apply
My pen, to write thy never dying fame;
That when to heaven thy blessed soul shall fly,
These lines on earth record thy reverend name:
And to this task I mean my muse to tie,
Though wanting skill I shall but purchase blame:
  Pardon (dear Lady) want of woman's wit
  To pen thy praise, when few can equal it.

* * *

"Eve's Apology in Defense of Women"

Now Pontius Pilate[3] is to judge the cause
Of faultless Jesus, who before him stands,
Who neither hath offended prince, nor laws,
Although he now be brought in woeful bands.
O noble governor, make thou yet a pause,
Do not in innocent blood inbrue° thy hands;[4] *defile*
  But hear the words of thy most worthy wife,
  Who sends to thee, to beg her Savior's life.[5]

Let barb'rous cruelty far depart from thee,
And in true justice take affliction's part;
Open thine eyes, that thou the truth may'st see.
Do not the thing that goes against thy heart,
Condemn not him that must thy Savior be;
But view his holy life, his good desert.° *merit*
  Let not us women glory in men's fall.[6]
  Who had power given to overrule us all.

Till now your indiscretion sets us free.
And makes our former fault much less appear;
Our mother Eve, who tasted of the tree,[7]
Giving to Adam what she held most dear,
Was simply good, and had no power to see;
The after-coming harm did not appear:
  The subtle serpent that our sex betrayed
  Before our fall so sure a plot had laid.

That undiscerning ignorance perceived
No guile or craft that was by him intended;
For had she known of what we were bereaved,[8]
To his request she had not condescended.
But she, poor soul, by cunning was deceived;
No hurt therein her harmless heart intended:
  For she alleged° God's word, which he[9] denies, *affirmed*
  That they should die, but even as gods be wise.

But surely Adam cannot be excused;
Her fault though great, yet he was most to blame;
What weakness offered, strength might have refused,
Being lord of all, the greater was his shame.
Although the serpent's craft had her abused,
God's holy word ought all his actions frame,° *shape*
  For he was lord and king of all the earth,
  Before poor Eve had either life or breath,

[1] *Cynthia* Goddess of the moon, often identified with Queen Elizabeth I, who died in 1603.

[2] *Countess* Margaret Clifford, Countess of Cumberland (1560–1616), Lanyer's patroness.

[3] *Pontius Pilate* Roman governor of Judea, who presided over the trial of Jesus (see Matthew 27.11–26).

[4] *Do ... hands* Reference to Matthew 27.24, in which Pilate washes his hands to demonstrate that he does not consider himself responsible for what happens to Jesus.

[5] *hear ... life* Pilate received a message from his wife, urging him not to convict Jesus (see Matthew 27.19).

[6] *men's fall* Fall into a sin, by crucifying Christ, greater than Eve's "original" sin.

[7] *Eve ... tree* According to Genesis 3.6, Eve ate the fruit of the tree of the knowledge of good and evil. She shared the fruit with Adam, and as a consequence the two were banished from the Garden of Eden.

[8] *bereaved* Robbed (of eternal life).

[9] *he* I.e., the serpent (see Genesis 3.4–5).

Who being framed° by God's eternal hand *formed*
The perfectest man that ever breathed on earth;
And from God's mouth received that strait° command, *strict*
The breach whereof he knew was present death;
Yea, having power to rule both sea and land,
Yet with one apple won to lose that breath[1]
Which God had breathed in his beauteous face,
Bringing us all in danger and disgrace.

And then to lay the fault on Patience' back,
That we (poor women) must endure it all.
We know right well he did discretion lack,
Being not persuaded thereunto at all.
If Eve did err, it was for knowledge sake;
The fruit being fair persuaded him to fall:
No subtle serpent's falsehood did betray him;
If he would eat it, who had power to stay° him? *stop*

Not Eve, whose fault was only too much love,
Which made her give this present to her dear,
That what she tasted he likewise might prove,° *experience*
Whereby his knowledge might become more clear;
He never sought her weakness to reprove
With those sharp words which he of God did hear;
Yet men will boast of knowledge, which he took
From Eve's fair hand, as from a learned book.

If any evil did in her remain,
Being made of him,[2] he was the ground of all.
If one of many worlds[3] could lay a stain
Upon our sex, and work so great a fall
To wretched man by Satan's[4] subtle train,
What will so foul a fault amongst you all?
Her weakness did the serpent's words obey,
But you in malice God's dear Son betray,

Whom, if unjustly you condemn to die,
Her sin was small to what you do commit;
All mortal sins that do for vengeance cry
Are not to be compared unto it.
If many worlds would altogether try
By all their sins the wrath of God to get,
This sin of yours surmounts them all as far
As doth the sun another little star.[5]

Then let us have our liberty again,
And challenge° to yourselves no sovereignty. *attribute*
You came not in the world without our pain,
Make that a bar against your cruelty;
Your fault being greater, why should you disdain
Our being your equals, free from tyranny?
If one weak woman simply did offend,
This sin of yours hath no excuse nor end,

To which, poor souls, we never gave consent.
Witness, thy wife, O Pilate, speaks for all,
Who did but dream, and yet a message sent
That thou shouldest have nothing to do at all
With that just man[6] which, if thy heart relent,
Why wilt thou be a reprobate[7] with Saul[8]
To seek the death of him that is so good,
For thy soul's health to shed his dearest blood?

The Description of Cooke-ham[9]

Farewell (sweet Cooke-ham) where I first obtained
Grace from that grace where perfect grace remained;
And where the muses gave their full consent,
I should have power the virtuous to content;
Where princely palace willed me to indite° *write*

[1] *breath* God breathed life into Adam (see Genesis 2.7).

[2] *made ... him* According to Genesis 2.21–22, Eve was made from one of Adam's ribs.

[3] *many worlds* As the first man, Adam was the father of all humans. Human beings were sometimes likened to individual worlds in the literature of the time.

[4] *Satan's* Belonging to the serpent, traditionally identified with Satan.

[5] *sun ... star* As the sun outshines the other stars in the sky, so the sin of killing Jesus is greater in magnitude. In earlier understandings of astronomy, the sun was thought to be much larger than the stars.

[6] *just man* I.e., Jesus.

[7] *a reprobate* Damned.

[8] *Saul* King of Israel, who tried to kill David (see 1 Samuel 19.9–24).

[9] *Cooke-ham* Cookham Dean, a country house in Berkshire, UK, leased by the brother of Lanyer's patroness, Margaret Clifford, Countess of Cumberland.

The sacred story of the soul's delight.[1]
Farewell (sweet place) where virtue then did rest,
And all delights did harbour in her breast;
Never shall my sad eyes again behold
Those pleasures which my thoughts did then unfold;
Yet you (great lady) mistress of that place,[2]
From whose desires did spring this work of grace,
Vouchsafe° to think upon these pleasures past *are prepared*
As fleeting, worldly joys that could not last,
Or as dim shadows of celestial pleasures,
Which are desired above all earthly treasures.
Oh how (methought) against you thither came
Each part did seem some new delight to frame!
The house received all ornaments to grace it,
And would endure no foulness to deface it.
The walks put on their summer liveries,° *uniforms*
And all things else did hold like similes:
The trees with leaves, with fruits, with flowers clad,
Embraced each other, seeming to be glad,
Turning themselves to beauteous canopies
To shade the bright sun from your brighter eyes;
The crystal streams with silver spangles graced,
While by the glorious sun they were embraced;
The little birds in chirping notes did sing,
To entertain both you and that sweet spring;
And Philomela[3] with her sundry lays,
Both you and that delightful place did praise.
Oh, how methought each plant, each flower, each tree
Set forth their beauties then to welcome thee;
The very hills right humbly did descend,
When you to tread upon them did intend.
And as you set your feet, they still did rise,
Glad that they could receive so rich a prize.
The gentle winds did take delight to be
Among those woods that were so graced by thee
And in sad murmur uttered pleasing sound,
That pleasure in that place might more abound;
The swelling banks delivered all their pride,
When such a phoenix once they had espied.
Each arbour, bank, each seat, each stately tree
Thought themselves honoured in supporting thee.
The pretty birds would oft come to attend thee,
Yet fly away for fear they should offend thee;
The little creatures in the burrow by
Would come abroad to sport them in your eye;[4]
Yet fearful of the bow in your fair hand
Would run away when you did make a stand.
Now let me come unto that stately tree,
Wherein such goodly prospects you did see;
That oak that did in height his fellows pass,
As much as lofty trees, low-growing grass;
Much like a comely cedar, straight and tall,
Whose beauteous stature far exceeded all;
How often did you visit this fair tree,
Which seeming joyful in receiving thee,
Would like a palm tree spread his arms abroad,
Desirous that you there should make abode;
Whose fair green leaves much like a comely veil
Defended Phoebus[5] when he would assail;
Whose pleasing boughs did lend a cool fresh air,
Joying his happiness when you were there;
Where being seated, you might plainly see
Hills, vales and woods, as if on bended knee
They had appeared, your honour to salute,
Or to prefer° some strange unlooked-for suit;° *proffer / request*
All interlaced with brooks and crystal springs,
A prospect fit to please the eyes of kings;
And thirteen shires appear all in your sight,
Europe could not afford much more delight.
What was there then but gave you all content,
While you the time in meditation spent,
Of their creator's power, which there you saw
In all his creatures held a perfect law,
And in their beauties did you plain descry° *discern*
His beauty, wisdom, grace, love, majesty.
In these sweet woods how often did you walk
With Christ and his apostles there to talk;
Placing his holy writ° in some fair tree, *scripture*
To meditate what you therein did see;

[1] *sacred … delight* *Salve Deus Rex Judeaeorum*, to which this poem is appended.

[2] *you … place* Margaret Clifford, Countess of Cumberland (1560-1616).

[3] *Philomela* Nightingale. In Greek mythology, Philomela was a woman who was changed into a nightingale.

[4] *sport … eye* Entertain you.

[5] *Phoebus* Sun. "Phoebus" is an epithet for Apollo, Greek and Roman god of the sun.

With Moses you did mount his holy hill,[1]
To know his pleasure and perform his will.
With lovely David you did often sing,
His holy hymns to heaven's eternal king.[2]
And in sweet music did your soul delight,
To sound his praises, morning, noon and night.
With blessed Joseph you did often feed
Your pined brethren when they stood in need.[3]
And that sweet lady sprung from Clifford's race,
Of noble Bedford's blood, fair stem of grace,
To honourable Dorset now espoused,[4]
In whose fair breast true virtue then was housed;
Oh, what delight did my weak spirits find
In those pure parts of her well-framed mind;
And yet it grieves me that I cannot be
Near unto her, whose virtues did agree
With those fair ornaments of outward beauty,
Which did enforce from all both love and duty.
Unconstant fortune, thou art most to blame,
Who casts us down into so low a frame,° *state*
Where our great friends we cannot daily see,
So great a difference is there in degree.° *social status*
Many are placed in those orbs of state,
Parters° in honour, so ordained by fate, *dividers*
Nearer in show, yet farther off in love,
In which the lowest always are above.
But whither am I carried in conceit?° *thought*
My wit too weak to conster° of the great. *understand*
Why not? although we are but born of earth,
We may behold the heavens, despising death;
And loving heaven that is so far above,
May in the end vouchsafe° us entire love. *grant*
Therefore sweet memory, do thou retain
Those pleasures past, which will not turn again;
Remember beauteous Dorset's[5] summer sports,[6]
So far from being touched by ill reports;
Wherein myself did always bear a part,
While reverend love presented my true heart;
Those recreations let me bear in mind,
Which her sweet youth and noble thoughts did find;
Whereof deprived, I evermore must grieve,
Hating blind fortune, careless to relieve.
And you, sweet Cooke-ham, whom these ladies leave,
I now must tell the grief you did conceive
At their departure; when they went away,
How everything retained a sad dismay;
Nay long before, when once an inkling came,
Methought each thing did unto sorrow frame;
The trees that were so glorious in our view,
Forsook both flowers and fruit, when once they knew
Of your depart, their very leaves did wither,
Changing their colours as they grew together.
But when they saw this had no power to stay you,
They often wept, though speechless, could not pray you;
Letting their tears in your fair bosoms fall,
As if they said: "Why will ye leave us all?"
This being vain, they cast their leaves away,
Hoping that pity would have made you stay;
Their frozen tops, like age's hoary hairs,
Shows their disasters, languishing in fears;
A swarthy rivelled rine[7] all overspread
Their dying bodies, half-alive, half-dead.
But your occasions called you so away,
That nothing there had power to make you stay;
Yet did I see a noble, grateful mind,
Requiting each according to their kind;
Forgetting not to turn and take your leave
Of these sad creatures, powerless to receive
Your favour, when with grief you did depart,
Placing their former pleasures in your heart;
Giving great charge to noble memory,
There to preserve their love continually;
But specially the love of that fair tree,
That first and last you did vouchsafe to see;
In which it pleased you oft to take the air,

[1] *Moses … hill* In Exodus 24.9 Moses climbs Mount Sinai in order to see God.

[2] *With … king* David was then supposed to be the author of most or all of Psalms, songs written in praise of God.

[3] *With … need* Reference to Genesis 42.25, in which Joseph, as governor of Egypt, provides his deceitful brothers with food in order to save them from starvation.

[4] *sweet lady … espoused* Margaret Clifford's daughter, Lady Anne Clifford (1589–1675), married Richard Sackville, Earl of Dorset (1589–1624). Lady Anne's maternal grandfather was Francis Russell, Earl of Bedford (1527–85). A selection from her diary is in this anthology.

[5] *Dorset* Lady Anne Clifford.

[6] *summer sports* E.g., country dances and outdoor games.

[7] *rivelled rine* Wrinkled bark.

With noble Dorset, then a virgin fair;
Where many a learned book was read and scanned;
To this fair tree, taking me by the hand,
You did repeat the pleasures which had passed,
Seeming to grieve they could no longer last.
And with a chaste, yet loving kiss took leave,
Of which sweet kiss I did it soon bereave;° *rob*
Scorning a senseless creature should possess
So rare a favour, so great happiness.
No other kiss it could receive from me,
For fear to give back what it took of thee;
So I, ungrateful creature, did deceive it,
Of that which you vouchsafed in love to leave it.
And though it oft had giv'n me much content,
Yet this great wrong I never could repent;
But of the happiest made it most forlorn,
To show that nothing's free from fortune's scorn,
While all the rest with this most beauteous tree,
Made their sad consort sorrow's harmony.
The flowers that on the banks and walks did grow,
Crept in the ground, the grass did weep for woe.
The winds and waters seemed to chide together,
Because you went away, they knew not whither.
And those sweet brooks that ran so fair and clear,
With grief and trouble wrinkled did appear.
Those pretty birds that wonted° were to sing, *accustomed*
Now neither sing, nor chirp, nor use their wing;
But with their tender feet on some bare spray,° *branch*
Warble forth sorrow, and their own dismay.
Fair Philomela leaves her mournful ditty,
Drowned in dead sleep, yet can procure no pity;
Each arbour, bank, each seat, each stately tree
Looks bare and desolate now, for want of thee;
Turning green tresses° into frosty grey, *hair*
While in cold grief they wither all away.
The sun grew weak, his beams no comfort gave,
While all green things did make the earth their grave;
Each briar, each bramble, when you went away,
Caught fast your clothes, thinking to make you stay;
Delightful Echo,[1] wonted to reply
To our last words, did now for sorrow die;
The house cast off each garment that might grace it,
Putting on dust and cobwebs to deface it.
All desolation then there did appear,
When you were going whom they held so dear.
This last farewell to Cooke-ham here I give;
When I am dead thy name in this may live,
Wherein I have performed her noble hest,° *command*
Whose virtues lodge in my unworthy breast,
And ever shall, so long as life remains,
Tying my heart to her by those rich chains.

To the Doubtful[2] *Reader*

Gentle reader, if thou desire to be resolved,[3] why I give this title, *Salve Deus Rex Judæorum*,[4] know for certain, that it was delivered unto me in sleep many years before I had any intent to write in this manner, and was quite out of my memory, until I had written the Passion of Christ, when immediately it came into my remembrance, what I had dreamed long before; and thinking it a significant token, that I was appointed to perform this work, I gave the very same words I received in sleep as the fittest title I could devise for this book.

—1611

[1] *Echo* Nymph in Greek mythology who was prevented by a curse from saying anything other than what others said.

[2] *Doubtful* Curious.

[3] *be resolved* Understand.

[4] *Salve ... Judæorum* Latin: Hail, God, King of the Jews.

Sir Walter Ralegh

1554 – 1618

Sir Walter Ralegh was one of the leading courtiers, adventurers, and literary figures of the Elizabethan era. Intermittently regarded as a hero and a traitor in his lifetime, Ralegh profited richly and suffered considerably from his proximity to Elizabeth I—but fared considerably worse after James I replaced Elizabeth on the throne. Known for his gallantry, for his fighting ability, for his effort at colonization in Virginia, and for bringing the practice of smoking tobacco into European culture, Ralegh was also the author of literary work that ranged from love poetry to exploration narratives to an unfinished history of the world.

Born into the lesser gentry at Hayes Barton, Devon, Ralegh went to France in 1569 to fight for the Huguenots in the French religious civil wars. By 1572, he was studying at Oriel College, Oxford, only to leave over a year later without a degree. Ralegh finished his education in the Inns of Court, including Lyon's Inn and the Middle Temple, and it was during these years that his first poem was probably printed. It is often difficult to date or even attribute Ralegh's poems accurately, for like many courtiers, Ralegh generally circulated his verses in manuscript.

Ralegh's poetry is characterized by an intensely personal treatment of such conventional themes as love, loss, beauty, and time. The majority of his poems are short lyrics—many of them occasional, written in response to particular events.

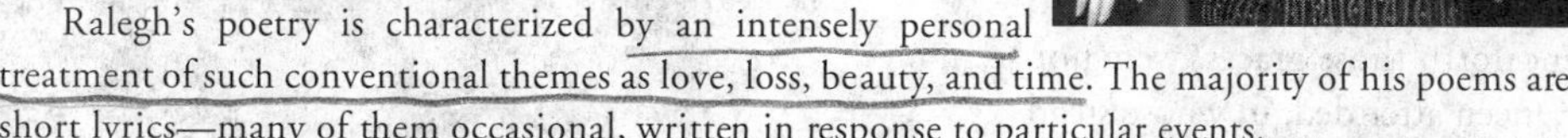

After embarking with his stepbrother, Humphrey Gilbert, on an unsuccessful colonizing expedition to North America in 1578, Ralegh spent a year and a half fighting in Ireland. He returned to England in 1581 and caught the Queen's attention, eventually emerging as her new favorite and reaping substantial rewards, including a monopoly over wine licences in 1583 and a knighthood in 1585. A grant of 42,000 Irish acres on which to establish English colonists, made in 1587, brought Ralegh back to Ireland several times, and he was responsible for bringing an acquaintance, Edmund Spenser, back to England and introducing him to the Queen in 1589.

Ralegh's rapid rise to prominence at Elizabeth I's court was abruptly halted in 1592 after the discovery of his secret marriage to Elizabeth Throckmorton, one of the Queen's attendants. The Queen had him imprisoned in the Tower of London for several months—the occasion for his long poem, *The Ocean to Cynthia*, Ralegh's lament over Elizabeth's displeasure. This, Ralegh's most ambitious and sprawling poem, is a work that exists only in fragments, the longest of them over five hundred lines long. Five years elapsed before Ralegh was again in the Queen's good graces, a period during which he traveled to Guiana (1595), published a report on his adventures entitled *The Discoverie of the Large, Rich, and Bewtiful Empyre of Guiana* (1596), developed his Irish plantations, and participated in the attack on Cadiz (1596). Always critical of Spain's colonial and naval power, Ralegh never lost interest in North America, sponsoring reconnaissance and colonizing expeditions in the late 1580s to the areas now known as Virginia and the Carolinas.

Following James I's accession in 1603, Ralegh returned to the Tower of London for nearly thirteen years after a dubious treason conviction for allegedly supporting Arabella Stuart's claim to the throne. Rarely idle, Ralegh kept abreast of the political and intellectual climate during his imprisonment by entertaining numerous visitors (including James's son, Prince Henry), conducting scientific experiments, compounding drugs, and writing. His most notable work from this period is *The Historie of the World* (1614), a three-volume overview of world events from creation to the second century BCE. Ralegh was released in 1617 to make a second journey to Guiana in search of the gold mine that he claimed to have found on his first voyage. Returning empty-handed in 1618, he was imprisoned under his former sentence for disobeying James's orders to avoid any acts of violence against the Spanish, and then beheaded. Despite a reputation for unorthodoxy and even atheism, Ralegh made a pious if showy end and replied, when asked if he should not face east (toward Jerusalem), "What matter how the head lie, so the heart be right?"

⌘⌘⌘

A Vision Upon This Conceit of the Fairy Queen[1]

Methought I saw the grave where Laura[2] lay,
Within that temple where the vestal flame[3]
Was wont to burn: and, passing by that way,
To see that buried dust of living fame,
Whose tomb fair Love and fairer Virtue kept,
All suddenly I saw the Faery Queen,° *Elizabeth I*
At whose approach the soul of Petrarch wept;
And from thenceforth those graces[4] were not seen,
For they this Queen attended; in whose stead
Oblivion laid him down on Laura's hearse.
Hereat the hardest stones were seen to bleed,
And groans of buried ghosts the heavens did pierce:
Where Homer's spright° did tremble all for grief, *spirit*
And cursed the access[5] of that celestial thief.[6]
—1590

[1] *A Vision … Queen* Ralegh's poem was printed in the first edition of Spenser's *The Fairie Queene* (1590).

[2] *Laura* The subject of Petrarch's love poems of the fourteenth century.

[3] *vestal flame* Reference to the Roman goddess of the hearth, Vesta, whose temple was maintained by vestal virgins guarding an eternal flame.

[4] *those graces* I.e., "Fair Love and fairer Virtue."

[5] *access* To achieve an honour or office (accession).

[6] *Homer's spright … celestial thief* The Queen has usurped Laura's reputation for purity and chastity, and Spenser has stolen Petrarch's artistic legacy and even threatened the place of Homer in the literary pantheon; *Homer* Author of *The Iliad* and *The Odyssey*.

Detail from a portrait of Sir Walter Ralegh and His Son, 1602 (artist unknown).

Sir Walter Ralegh to His Son[7]

Three things there be that prosper up apace° *quickly*
And flourish, whilst they grow asunder° far, *apart*
But on a day, they meet all in one place,
And when they meet, they one another mar;° *damage*
And they be these: the wood, the weed, the wag.[8]
The wood is that which makes the gallow tree;

[7] *Sir Walter Ralegh to His Son* Ralegh's son, Wat, had a reputation for being wild. He died during his father's second voyage to Guiana.

[8] *wag* Joker, mischievous boy.

The weed is that which strings the hangman's bag;
The wag, my pretty knave, betokeneth thee.
Mark well, dear boy, whilst these assemble not,
Green springs the tree, hemp grows, the wag is wild,
But when they meet, it makes the timber rot,
It frets the halter, and it chokes the child.
Then bless thee, and beware, and let us pray
We part not with thee at this meeting day.
—c. 1600

The Nymph's Reply to the Shepherd[1]

If all the world and love were young,
And truth in every shepherd's tongue,
These pretty pleasures might me move
To live with thee and be thy love.

Time drives the flocks from field to fold
When rivers rage and rocks grow cold,
And Philomel[2] becometh dumb;
The rest complains of cares to come.

The flowers do fade, and wanton° fields *unrestrained, unruly*
To wayward winter reckoning yields;
A honey tongue, a heart of gall,° *bitterness, rancor*
Is fancy's spring, but sorrow's fall.

Thy gowns, thy shoes, thy beds of roses,
Thy cap, thy kirtle,° and thy posies *tunic or skirt*
Soon break, soon wither, soon forgotten—
In folly ripe, in reason rotten.

Thy belt of straw and ivy buds,
Thy coral clasps and amber studs,
All these in me no means can move
To come to thee and be thy love.

But could youth last and love still breed,
Had joys no date nor age no need,[3]
Then these delights my mind might move
To live with thee and be thy love.
—1600

[1] *The Nymph's ... Shepherd* Response to Christopher Marlowe's "The Passionate Shepherd to His Love."

[2] *Philomel* I.e., the nightingale doesn't sing. In classical mythology, Philomela, the daughter of the King of Athens, was transformed into a nightingale after being pursued and raped by her brother-in-law, Tereus, King of Thrace.

[3] *Had joys ... no need* If joys had no ending, and aging did not bring with it its own needs.

The Lie

Go, soul, the body's guest,
Upon a thankless errand;
Fear not to touch the best;
The truth shall be thy warrant.
Go, since I needs must die,
And give the world the lie.

Say to the court, it glows
And shines like rotten wood;
Say to the church, it shows
What's good, and doth no good.
If church and court reply,
Then give them both the lie.

Tell potentates° they live *powerful rulers*
Acting by others' action;
Not loved unless they give,
Not strong but by a faction.
If potentates reply,
Give potentates the lie.

Tell men of high condition,
That manage the estate,° *the state or body politic*
Their purpose is ambition,
Their practice only hate.
And if they once reply,
Then give them all the lie.

Tell them that brave it most,[4]
They beg for more by spending,

[4] *brave it most* Dress extravagantly.

Who, in their greatest cost,
Seek nothing but commending.
And if they make reply,
Then give them all the lie.

Tell zeal it wants° devotion; *lacks*
Tell love it is but lust;
Tell time it is but motion;
Tell flesh it is but dust.
And wish them not reply,
For thou must give the lie.

Tell age it daily wasteth;° *fades, diminishes*
Tell honour how it alters;
Tell beauty how she blasteth;
Tell favour how it falters.
And as they shall reply,
Give every one the lie.

Tell wit° how much it wrangles *intelligence, understanding*
In tickle points of niceness;[1]
Tell wisdom she entangles
Herself in overwiseness.
And when they do reply,
Straight give them both the lie.

Tell physic° of her boldness;° *medicine / presumption*
Tell skill it is pretension;
Tell charity of coldness;
Tell law it is contention.
And as they do reply,
So give them still the lie.

Tell fortune of her blindness;
Tell nature of decay;
Tell friendship of unkindness;
Tell justice of delay.
And if they will reply,
Then give them all the lie.

[1] *wrangles … niceness* To waste time with trivial, or overly subtle matters.

Tell arts[2] they have no soundness,
But vary by esteeming;[3]
Tell schools[4] they want profoundness,
And stand too much on seeming.
If arts and schools reply,
Give arts and schools the lie.

Tell faith it's fled the city;
Tell how the country erreth;
Tell manhood shakes off pity
And virtue least preferreth.[5]
And if they do reply,
Spare not to give the lie.

So when thou hast, as I
Commanded thee, done blabbing—
Although to give the lie
Deserves no less than stabbing—[6]
Stab at thee he that will,
No stab the soul can kill.
—1608 (WRITTEN C. 1592)

Nature That Washed Her Hands in Milk

Nature that washed her hands in milk
And had forgot to dry them,
Instead of earth[7] took snow and silk,
At love's request to try° them, *test*

[2] *arts* The seven liberal arts: grammar, rhetoric, logic, arithmetic, geometry, astronomy, and music; *soundness* Freedom from weakness, based on fact.

[3] *they have … esteeming* They have no basis in solid and unchanging fact; they are subject to opinion.

[4] *schools* Systems of philosophy.

[5] *Tell manhood … virtue least preferreth* Tell humanity that it refuses to feel pity, and that it prefers virtue less than all other things.

[6] *Deserves no less than stabbing* To accuse someone of lying would likely cause a duel.

[7] *Instead of earth* The Bible recounts the creation of Adam out of the dust of the earth. See Genesis 2.7.

If she a mistress could compose
To please love's fancy out of those.[1]

Her eyes he would° should be of light, *wanted*
A violet breath and lips of jelly,
Her hair not black nor over-bright,
And of the softest down her belly;
As for her inside he would have it
Only of wantonness° and wit.° *sexual appetite / intelligence, understanding*

At love's entreaty, such a one
Nature made, but with her beauty
She hath framed a heart of stone,
So as love by ill destiny
Must die for her whom nature gave him
Because her darling would not save him.

But time, which nature doth despise,
And rudely gives her love the lie,[2]
Makes hope a fool, and sorrow wise,
His hands doth neither wash nor dry,
But being made of steel and rust,
Turns snow, and silk, and milk to dust.

The light, the belly, lips, and breath
He dims, discolors, and destroys,
With those he feeds, but fills not death,
Which sometimes were the food of joys;
Yea, time doth dull each lively wit
And dries all wantonness with it.

Oh cruel time which takes in trust
Our youth, our joys, and all we have,
And pays us but with age and dust,
Who in the dark and silent grave,
When we have wandered all our ways,
Shuts up the story of our days.[3]

—early 17th century

[1] *To please love's fancy out of those* At the request of love, Nature attempted to make a mistress out of snow and silk.

[2] *gives … the lie* Offers a challenge; in this period, to a duel.

[3] *Oh cruel time … shuts up the story of our days* The night before he died, Ralegh wrote this final stanza, with alterations, in his Bible. He changed the first three words to "Even such is time," and added a final couplet, "But from which earth and grave and dust / The Lord shall raise me up, I trust."

from *The Discovery of the Large, Rich, and Beautiful Empire of Guiana;*[4] *with a relation of the great and golden City of Manoa,*[5] *which the Spaniards call El Dorado …*

To the Right Honourable my singular good Lord and kinsman Charles Howard,[6] *Knight of the Garter, Baron, and Councillor, and of the Admirals of England the most renowned; and to the Right Honourable Sir Robert Cecil,*[7] *Knight, Councillor in her Highness's Privy Councils.*

Part 1, Preface

For your Honours' many honourable and friendly parts, I have hitherto only returned promises; and now, for answer of both your adventures,[8] I have sent you a bundle of papers, which I have divided between your Lordship and Sir Robert Cecil, in these two respects chiefly; first, for that it is reason that wasteful factors,[9] when they have consumed such stocks as they had in trust, do yield some colour[10] for the same in their account; secondly, for that I am assured that whatsoever shall be done, or written, by me, shall need a double protection and defence. The trial that I had of both your loves, when I was left of all but of malice and revenge,

[4] *Empire of Guiana* Ralegh's Guiana is located predominately in the Orinoco basin of present-day eastern Venezuela.

[5] *Manoa* The European myth of El Dorado, "the gilded one," resulted from conflated reports of several indigenous peoples' practices. Once a year, a king, or a chief, was anointed with gold dust and paddled to the center of a lake, believed to be in an upland area beside the golden city of Manoa, where he would make gold offerings. The location of El Dorado, or Manoa, was variously held to be in Colombia, Surinam, Guyana, and Venezuela.

[6] *Charles Howard* Baron Howard of Effingham (1536–1624), Earl of Nottingham, Lord High Admiral, Commander-in-chief of the English fleet against the Spanish Armada in 1588. Howard contributed a ship, the *Lion's Whelp*, to Ralegh's expedition.

[7] *Sir Robert Cecil* Earl of Salisbury (1563–1612), Secretary of State. Although an ally of Ralegh's at the time of the Guiana expedition, Cecil would later turn James I against Ralegh by suggesting his involvement in the plot to place Arabella Stuart on the throne.

[8] *adventures* Commercial investments in Ralegh's voyage.

[9] *factors* Those who buy or sell for others, agents.

[10] *colour* Specious or plausible reason, pretext.

makes me still presume that you will be pleased (knowing what little power I had to perform aught,[1] and the great advantage of forewarned enemies) to answer that out of knowledge, which others shall but object out of malice. In my more happy times as I did especially honour you both, so I found that your loves sought me out in the darkest shadow of adversity, and the same affection which accompanied my better fortune soared not away from me in my many miseries; all which though I cannot requite, yet I shall ever acknowledge; and the great debt which I have no power to pay, I can do no more for a time but confess to be due. It is true that as my errors were great, so they have yielded very grievous effects; and if aught might have been deserved in former times, to have counterpoised[2] any part of offences, the fruit thereof, as it seemeth, was long before fallen from the tree, and the dead stock only remained. I did therefore, even in the winter of my life, undertake these travails,[3] fitter for bodies less blasted with misfortunes, for men of greater ability, and for minds of better encouragement, that thereby, if it were possible, I might recover but the moderation of excess, and the least taste of the greatest plenty formerly possessed. If I had known other way to win, if I had imagined how greater adventures might have regained, if I could conceive what farther means I might yet use but even to appease so powerful displeasure,[4] I would not doubt but for one year more to hold fast my soul in my teeth till it were performed. Of that little remain I had, I have wasted in effect all herein. I have undergone many constructions;[5] I have been accompanied with many sorrows, with labour, hunger, heat, sickness, and peril; it appeareth, notwithstanding, that I made no other bravado of going to the sea, than was meant, and that I was never hidden in Cornwall, or elsewhere, as was supposed. They have grossly belied me that forejudged that I would rather become a servant to the Spanish king than return; and the rest were much mistaken, who would have persuaded that I was too easeful and sensual to undertake a journey of so great travail. But if what I have done receive the gracious construction of a painful pilgrimage, and purchase the least remission,[6] I shall think all too little, and that there were wanting to the rest many miseries. But if both the times past, the present, and what may be in the future, do all by one grain of gall[7] continue in eternal distaste, I do not then know whether I should bewail myself, either for my too much travail and expense, or condemn myself for doing less than that which can deserve nothing. From myself I have deserved no thanks, for I am returned a beggar, and withered; but that I might have bettered my poor estate, it shall appear from the following discourse, if I had not only respected her Majesty's future honour and riches.…

from PART 5

… To speak of what passed homeward were tedious, either to describe or name any of the rivers, islands, or villages of the Tivitivas, which dwell on trees; we will leave all those to the general map. And to be short, when we were arrived at the sea-side, then grew our greatest doubt, and the bitterest of all our journey forepassed; for I protest before God, that we were in a most desperate estate. For the same night which we anchored in the mouth of the river of Capuri, where it falleth into the sea, there arose a mighty storm, and the river's mouth was at least a league broad, so as we ran before night close under the land with our small boats, and brought the galley as near as we could. But she had as much ado to live as could be, and there wanted little of her sinking, and all those in her; for mine own part, I confess I was very doubtful which way to take, either to go over in the pestered[8] galley, there being but six foot water over the sands for two leagues together, and that also in the channel, and she drew five; or to adventure in so great a billow, and in so doubtful weather, to cross the seas in my barge. The longer we tarried the worse it was, and therefore I took Captain Gifford, Captain Caulfield, and my cousin Greenvile into my

[1] *aught* Anything.

[2] *counterpoised* Bring to or keep in a state of balance.

[3] *travails* Labor.

[4] *powerful displeasure* Ralegh's secret marriage to Elizabeth Throckmorton in 1592 incurred Queen Elizabeth's wrath; he was imprisoned in the Tower of London for several months and did not regain the queen's favor for some years.

[5] *constructions* Trials.

[6] *remission* Pardon.

[7] *gall* Bitterness, rancor.

[8] *pestered* Troubled.

barge; and after it cleared up about midnight we put ourselves to God's keeping, and thrust out into the sea, leaving the galley at anchor, who durst not adventure but by daylight. And so, being all very sober and melancholy, one faintly cheering another to shew courage, it pleased God that the next day about nine o'clock, we descried[1] the island of Trinidad; and steering for the nearest part of it, we kept the shore till we came to Curiapan, where we found our ships at anchor, than which there was never to us a more joyful sight.

Now that it hath pleased God to send us safe to our ships, it is time to leave Guiana to the sun, whom they worship, and steer away towards the north. I will, therefore, in a few words finish the discovery thereof. Of the several nations which we found upon this discovery I will once again make repetition, and how they are affected. At our first entrance into Amana, which is one of the outlets of the Orinoco, we left on the right hand of us in the bottom of the bay, lying directly against Trinidad, a nation of inhuman Cannibals, which inhabit the rivers of Guanipa and Berbeese.[2] In the same bay there is also a third river, which is called Areo, which riseth on Paria side towards Cumana, and that river is inhabited with the Wikiri, whose chief town upon the said river is Sayma. In this bay there are no more rivers but these three before rehearsed and the four branches of Amana, all which in the winter thrust so great abundance of water into the sea, as the same is taken up fresh two or three leagues from the land. In the passages towards Guiana, that is, in all those lands which the eight branches of the Orinoco fashion into islands, there are but one sort of people, called Tivitivas, but of two castes, as they term them, the one called Ciawani, the other Waraweeti,[3] and those war one with another.

On the hithermost[4] part of the Orinoco, as at Toparimaca and Winicapora, those are of a nation called Nepoios, and are the followers of Carapana, lord of Emeria. Between Winicapora and the port of Morequito, which standeth in Aromaia, and all those in the valley of Amariocapana are called Orenoqueponi, and did obey Morequito and are now followers of Topiawari. Upon the river of Caroli are the Canuri, which are governed by a woman who is inheritrix[5] of that province; who came far off to see our nation, and asked me divers questions of her Majesty, being much delighted with the discourse of her Majesty's greatness, and wondering at such reports as we truly made of her Highness' many virtues. And upon the head of Caroli and on the lake of Cassipa are the three strong nations of the Cassipagotos. Right south into the land are the Capurepani and Emparepani, and beyond those, adjoining to Macureguarai, the first city of Inca, are the Iwarawakeri. All these are professed enemies to the Spaniards, and to the rich Epuremei also. To the west of Caroli are divers nations of Cannibals and of those Ewaipanoma without heads. Directly west are the Amapaias and Anebas, which are also marvellous rich in gold. The rest towards Peru we will omit. On the north of the Orinoco, between it and the West Indies, are the Wikiri, Saymi, and the rest before spoken of, all mortal enemies to the Spaniards. On the south side of the main mouth of the Orinoco are the Arawaks; and beyond them, the Cannibals; and to the south of them, the Amazons.

To make mention of the several beasts, birds, fishes, fruits, flowers, gums, sweet woods, and of their several religions and customs, would for the first require as many volumes as those of Gesnerus,[6] and for the next another bundle of Decades.[7] The religion of the Epuremei is the same which the Incas, emperors of Peru, used, which may be read in Cieza[8] and other Spanish stories; how they believe the immortality of the soul, worship the sun, and bury with them alive their best beloved wives and treasure, as they likewise do in Pegu[9] in the East Indies, and other places. The poni bury not their

[1] *descried* Caught sight of.

[2] *Berbeese* Berbice River in eastern Guyana.

[3] *Ciawani ... Waraweeti* Warao sub-groups, now called Siawani and Waraowitu.

[4] *hithermost* Nearest.

[5] *inheritrix* Female heiress.

[6] *Gesnerus* Conrad Gesner (1516–65), Swiss zoologist, author of *Historia animalium* (1551), a compilation of information, both ancient and contemporary, concerning animals.

[7] *bundle of Decades* Richard Eden's *The Decades of the Newe World of West India* (1555), was a translation of Pietro Martire d'Anghiera's *De Orbe Novo* (1511–30); the first printed book to use the name "America" is the anonymous *Of the newe landes* (1520).

[8] *Cieza* Pedro Cieza de Leon (1518?–60), Spanish soldier and explorer, author of *Chronicle of Peru* (1553?).

[9] *Pegu* Capital of the United Burmese kingdom during the sixteenth century.

wives with them, but their jewels, hoping to enjoy them again. The Arawaks dry the bones of their lords, and their wives and friends drink them in powder. In the graves of the Peruvians the Spaniards found their greatest abundance of treasure. The like, also, is to be found among these people in every province. They have all many wives, and the lords five-fold to the common sort. Their wives never eat with their husbands, nor among the men, but serve their husbands at meals and afterwards feed by themselves. Those that are past their younger years make all their bread and drink, and work their cotton-beds, and do all else of service and labour; for the men do nothing but hunt, fish, play, and drink, when they are out of the wars.

I will enter no further into discourse of their manners, laws, and customs. And because I have not myself seen the cities of Inca I cannot avow on my credit what I have heard, although it be very likely that the emperor Inca hath built and erected as magnificent palaces in Guiana as his ancestors did in Peru; which were for their riches and rareness most marvellous, and exceeding all in Europe, and, I think, of the world, China excepted, which also the Spaniards, which I had, assured me to be true, as also the nations of the borderers, who, being but savages to those of the inland, do cause much treasure to be buried with them. For I was informed of one of the caciques of the valley of Amariocapana which had buried with him a little before our arrival a chair of gold most curiously wrought, which was made either in Macureguarai adjoining or in Manoa. But if we should have grieved them in their religion at the first, before they had been taught better, and have digged up their graves, we had lost them all. And therefore I held my first resolution, that her Majesty should either accept or refuse the enterprise before anything should be done that might in any sort hinder the same. And if Peru had so many heaps of gold, whereof those Incas were princes, and that they delighted so much therein, no doubt but this which now liveth and reigneth in Manoa hath the same humour,[1] and, I am assured, hath more abundance of gold within his territory than all Peru and the West Indies.

For the rest, which myself have seen, I will promise these things that follow, which I know to be true. Those that are desirous to discover and to see many nations may be satisfied within this river, which bringeth forth so many arms and branches leading to several countries and provinces, above 2,000 miles east and west and 800 miles south and north, and of these the most either rich in gold or in other merchandises. The common soldier shall here fight for gold, and pay himself, instead of pence, with plates of half-a-foot broad, whereas he breaketh his bones in other wars for provant[2] and penury. Those commanders and chieftains that shoot at honour and abundance shall find there more rich and beautiful cities, more temples adorned with golden images, more sepulchres[3] filled with treasure, than either Cortés[4] found in Mexico or Pizarro[5] in Peru. And the shining glory of this conquest will eclipse all those so far-extended beams of the Spanish nation. There is no country which yieldeth more pleasure to the inhabitants, either for those common delights of hunting, hawking, fishing, fowling, and the rest, than Guiana doth; it hath so many plains, clear rivers, and abundance of pheasants, partridges, quails, rails, cranes, herons, and all other fowl; deer of all sorts, porks, hares, lions, tigers, leopards, and divers other sorts of beasts, either for chase or food. It hath a kind of beast called cama or anta,[6] as big as an English beef, and in great plenty. To speak of the several sorts of every kind I fear would be troublesome to the reader, and therefore I will omit them, and conclude that both for health, good air, pleasure, and riches, I am resolved it cannot be equalled by any region either in the east or west. Moreover the country is so healthful, as of an hundred persons and more, which lay without shift most sluttishly, and were every day almost melted with heat in rowing and marching, and suddenly wet again with great showers, and did eat of all sorts of corrupt fruits, and made meals of fresh fish without seasoning, of tortugas,[7] of lagartos or crocodiles, and of all sorts good and bad, without either order or measure,

[1] *humour* State of mind.

[2] *provant* Allowance of food.

[3] *sepulchres* Tombs.

[4] *Cortés* Hernán Cortés (1485–1547), Spanish conquistador, conqueror of Mexico.

[5] *Pizarro* Francisco Pizarro (1476–1541), Spanish conquistador, conqueror of Peru.

[6] *anta* Tapir.

[7] *tortugas* Turtles.

and besides lodged in the open air every night, we lost not any one, nor had one ill-disposed to my knowledge; nor found any calentura[1] or other of those pestilent diseases which dwell in all hot regions, and so near the equinoctial line.

Where there is store of gold it is in effect needless to remember other commodities for trade. But it hath, towards the south part of the river, great quantities of brazil-wood,[2] and divers berries that dye a most perfect crimson and carnation; and for painting, all France, Italy, or the East Indies yield none such. For the more the skin is washed, the fairer the colour appeareth, and with which even those brown and tawny women spot themselves and colour their cheeks. All places yield abundance of cotton, of silk, of balsamum,[3] and of those kinds most excellent and never known in Europe, of all sorts of gums, of Indian pepper; and what else the countries may afford within the land we know not, neither had we time to abide the trial and search. The soil besides is so excellent and so full of rivers, as it will carry sugar, ginger, and all those other commodities which the West Indies have.

The navigation is short, for it may be sailed with an ordinary wind in six weeks, and in the like time back again; and by the way neither lee-shore,[4] enemies' coast, rocks, nor sands. All which in the voyages to the West Indies and all other places we are subject unto; as the channel of Bahama, coming from the West Indies, cannot well be passed in the winter, and when it is at the best, it is a perilous and a fearful place; the rest of the Indies for calms and diseases very troublesome, and the sea about the Bermudas a hellish sea for thunder, lightning, and storms.

This very year (1595) there were seventeen sail of Spanish ships lost in the channel of Bahama, and the great Philip, like to have sunk at the Bermudas, was put back to St. Juan de Puerto Rico; and so it falleth out in that navigation every year for the most part. Which in this voyage are not to be feared; for the time of year to leave England is best in July, and the summer in Guiana is in October, November, December, January, February, and March, and then the ships may depart thence in April, and so return again into England in June. So as they shall never be subject to winter weather, either coming, going, or staying there: which, for my part, I take to be one of the greatest comforts and encouragements that can be thought on, having, as I have done, tasted in this voyage by the West Indies so many calms, so much heat, such outrageous gusts, such weather, and contrary winds.

To conclude, Guiana is a country that hath yet her maidenhead,[5] never sacked, turned, nor wrought;[6] the face of the earth hath not been torn, nor the virtue and salt of the soil spent by manurance. The graves have not been opened for gold, the mines not broken with sledges, nor their images pulled down out of their temples. It hath never been entered by any army of strength, and never conquered or possessed by any Christian prince. It is besides so defensible, that if two forts be builded in one of the provinces which I have seen, the flood setteth in so near the bank, where the channel also lieth, that no ship can pass up but within a pike's length of the artillery, first of the one, and afterwards of the other. Which two forts will be a sufficient guard both to the empire of Inca, and to an hundred other several kingdoms, lying within the said river, even to the city of Quito in Peru.

There is therefore great difference between the easiness of the conquest of Guiana, and the defence of it being conquered, and the West or East Indies. Guiana hath but one entrance by the sea, if it hath that, for any vessels of burden. So as whosoever shall first possess it, it shall be found unaccessible for any enemy, except he come in wherries, barges, or canoes, or else in flat-bottomed boats; and if he do offer to enter it in that manner, the woods are so thick 200 miles together upon the rivers of such entrance, as a mouse cannot sit in a boat unhit from the bank. By land it is more impossible to approach; for it hath the strongest situation of any region under the sun, and it is so environed with impassable mountains on every side, as it is impossible to victual any company in the passage. Which hath been

[1] *calentura* Disease experienced by sailors in the tropics, characterized by fever and delirium.

[2] *brazil-wood* Brownish hardwood used to make a red dye.

[3] *balsamum* Aromatic resin of the balsam tree used for medicines.

[4] *lee-shore* Shore on which the wind blows.

[5] *maidenhead* Literally, hymen; i.e., Guiana is still a virgin country.

[6] *wrought* Worked.

well proved by the Spanish nation, who since the conquest of Peru have never left five years free from attempting this empire, or discovering some way into it; and yet of three-and-twenty several gentlemen, knights, and noblemen, there was never any that knew which way to lead an army by land, or to conduct ships by sea, anything near the said country. Orellana,[1] of whom the river of the Amazon taketh name, was the first, and Don Antonio de Berreo, whom we displanted, the last: and I doubt much whether he himself or any of his yet know the best way into the said empire. It can therefore hardly be regained, if any strength be formerly set down, but in one or two places, and but two or three crumsters[2] or galleys built and furnished upon the river within. The West Indies have many ports, watering places, and landings; and nearer than 300 miles to Guiana, no man can harbour a ship, except he know one only place, which is not learned in haste, and which I will undertake there is not any one of my companies that knoweth, whosoever hearkened most after it.

Besides, by keeping one good fort, or building one town of strength, the whole empire is guarded; and whatsoever companies shall be afterwards planted within the land, although in twenty several provinces, those shall be able all to reunite themselves upon any occasion either by the way of one river, or be able to march by land without either wood, bog, or mountain. Whereas in the West Indies there are few towns or provinces that can succour or relieve one the other by land or sea. By land the countries are either desert, mountainous, or strong enemies. By sea, if any man invade to the eastward, those to the west cannot in many months turn against the breeze and eastern wind. Besides, the Spaniards are therein so dispersed as they are nowhere strong, but in Nueva Espana only; the sharp mountains, the thorns, and poisoned prickles, the sandy and deep ways in the valleys, the smothering heat and air, and want of water in other places are their only and best defence; which, because those nations that invade them are not victualled or provided to stay, neither have any place to friend adjoining, do serve them instead of good arms and great multitudes.

The West Indies were first offered her Majesty's grandfather[3] by Columbus, a stranger, in whom there might be doubt of deceit; and besides it was then thought incredible that there were such and so many lands and regions never written of before. This Empire is made known to her Majesty by her own vassal,[4] and by him that oweth to her more duty than an ordinary subject; so that it shall ill sort with the many graces and benefits which I have received to abuse her Highness, either with fables or imaginations. The country is already discovered, many nations won to her Majesty's love and obedience, and those Spaniards which have latest and longest laboured about the conquest, beaten out, discouraged, and disgraced, which among these nations were thought invincible. Her Majesty may in this enterprise employ all those soldiers and gentlemen that are younger brethren, and all captains and chieftains that want employment, and the charge will be only the first setting out in victualling and arming them; for after the first or second year I doubt not but to see in London a Contractation-House[5] of more receipt for Guiana than there is now in Seville for the West Indies.

And I am resolved that if there were but a small army afoot in Guiana, marching towards Manoa, the chief city of Inca, he would yield to her Majesty by composition so many hundred thousand pounds yearly as should both defend all enemies abroad, and defray all expenses at home; and that he would besides pay a garrison of three or four thousand soldiers very royally to defend him against other nations. For he cannot but know how his predecessors, yea, how his own great uncles, Guascar and Atabalipa,[6] sons to Guiana-Capac, emperor of Peru, were, while they contended for the empire, beaten out by the Spaniards, and that both of

[1] *Orellana* Francesco de Orellana was the first Spaniard to descend the entire length of the Amazon river in 1541–42. Orellana renamed the river "Amazon" from "Marañon" after encountering a group of female warriors.

[2] *crumsters* Merchant ships used as warships that accompanied Spanish galleons. The crumster could carry a great deal of cargo and firepower.

[3] *her Majesty's grandfather* Bartholomew Columbus, brother of Christopher, approached Henry VII of England to raise money for Columbus's western route to India, but Columbus had already contracted his services to Queen Isabella of Spain.

[4] *vassal* Humble servant.

[5] *Contractation-House* Seville's Casa de Contractacion controlled all aspects of the Spanish trade with the Americas.

[6] *Atabalipa* Atahualpa.

late years and ever since the said conquest, the Spaniards have sought the passages and entry of his country; and of their cruelties used to the borderers he cannot be ignorant. In which respects no doubt but he will be brought to tribute with great gladness; if not, he hath neither shot nor iron weapon in all his empire, and therefore may easily be conquered.

And I further remember that Berreo confessed to me and others, which I protest before the Majesty of God to be true, that there was found among the prophecies in Peru, at such time as the empire was reduced to the Spanish obedience, in their chiefest temples, amongst divers others which foreshadowed the loss of the said empire, that from Inglatierra[1] those Incas should be again in time to come restored, and delivered from the servitude of the said conquerors. And I hope, as we with these few hands have displanted the first garrison, and driven them out of the said country, so her Majesty will give order for the rest, and either defend it, and hold it as tributary,[2] or conquer and keep it as empress of the same. For whatsoever prince shall possess it, shall be greatest; and if the King of Spain enjoy it, he will become unresistible. Her Majesty hereby shall confirm and strengthen the opinions of all nations as touching her great and princely actions. And where the south border of Guiana reacheth to the dominion and empire of the Amazons, those women shall hereby hear the name of a virgin, which is not only able to defend her own territories and her neighbours, but also to invade and conquer so great empires and so far removed.

To speak more at this time I fear would be but troublesome: I trust in God, this being true, will suffice, and that he which is King of all Kings, and Lord of Lords, will put it into her heart which is Lady of Ladies to possess it. If not, I will judge those men worthy to be kings thereof, that by her grace and leave will undertake it of themselves.

—1596

[1] *Inglatierra* England.

[2] *tributary* I.e., tributary nation, one which pays tribute in the form of goods or money to a sovereign nation.

Letter to His Wife[3]

original spelling

You shall now receive (my deare wife) my last words in these last lines. My love I send you that you may keep it when I am dead, and my councell that you may remember it when I am no more. I would not by my will present you with sorrowes (dear Besse) let them go to the grave with me and be buried in the dust. And seeing that it is not Gods will that I should see you any more in this life, beare it patiently, and with a heart like thy selfe.

First, I send you all the thankes which my heart can conceive, or my words can rehearse for your many travailes, and care taken for me, which though they have not taken effect as you wished, yet my debt to you is not the lesse: but I pay it I never shall in this world.

Secondly, I beseech you for the love you beare me living, do not hide your selfe many dayes, but by your travailes seeke to helpe your miserable fortunes and the right of your poor childe. Thy mourning cannot availe me, I am but dust.

Thirdly, you shall understand, that my land was conveyed *bona fide*[4] to my childe; the writings were drawne[5] at midsumer was twelve months, my honest cosen Brett can testify so much, and Dolberry too, can remember somewhat therein. And I trust my blood will quench their malice that have cruelly murthered me: and that they will not seek also to kill thee and thine with extreme poverty.

To what friend to direct thee I know not, for all mine have left me in the true time of tryall. And I perceive that my death was determined from the first day. Most sorry I am God knowes that being thus surprised with death I can leave you in no better estate. God is my witnesse I meant you all my office of wines or all that I could have purchased by selling it, halfe of my stuffe, and all my jewels, but some one for the boy,

[3] *Letter to His Wife* The following letter was written after Ralegh had been convicted of attempting to conspire against the Crown, and sent to the Tower of London; he believed he would be executed the next day. That did not happen, but he did remain imprisoned in the Tower for most of the rest of his life, and was finally executed in 1618.

[4] *bona fide* Latin: in good faith.

[5] *the writings were drawne* The documents were made out.

but God hath prevented all my resolutions. That great God that ruleth all in all, but if you live free from want, care for no more, for the rest is but vanity. Love God, and begin betimes to repose your selfe upon him, have travailed and wearied your thoughts over all sorts of worldly cogitations, you shall but sit downe by sorrowe in the end.

Teach your son also to love and feare God while he is yet young, that the feare of God may grow with him, and then God will be a husband to you, and a father to him; a husband and a father which cannot be taken from you.

Baily oweth me 200 pounds, and Adrian Gilbert 600. In Jersey I also have much owing me besides. The arrearages of the wines will pay my debts. And howsoever you do, solues sake,[1] pay all poore men. When I am gone, no doubt you shall be sought for my many, for the world thinkes that I was very rich. But take heed of the pretences of men, and their affections, for they last not but in honest and worthy men, and no greater misery can befall you in this life, than to become a prey, and afterwards to be despised. I speake not this (God knowes) to dissuade you from marriage, for it will be best for you, both in respect of the world and of God. As for me, I am no more yours, nor you mine, death hath cut us asunder: and God hath divided me from the world, and your from me.

Remember your poor childe for his father's sake, who chose you, and loved you in his happiest times. Get those letters (if it be possible) which I write to the Lords, wherein I sued for my life: God is my witnesse it was for you and yours that I desired life, but it is true that I disdained my self for begging of it: for know it (my deare wife) that your son is the son of a true man, and one who in his owne respect despiseth death and all his misshapen & ugly formes.

I cannot write much, God he knows how hardly I steale time while others sleep, and it is also time that I should separate my thoughts from the world. Begg my dead body which living was denied thee; and either lay it at Sherburne (and if the land continue) or in Exeter-Church, by my Father and Mother; I can say no more, time and death call me away.

The everlasting God, powerfull, infinite, and omnipotent God, That Almighty God, who is goodnesse it selfe, the true life and true light keep thee and thine: have mercy on me, and teach me to forgive my persecutors and false accusers, and send us to meet in his glorious Kingdome. My deare wife farewell. Blesse my poore boy. Pray for me, and let my good God hold you both in his arms.

Written with the dying hand of sometimes thy Husband, but now alasse overthrowne.

Yours that was, but now not my own.

Walter Rawleigh

—1603

original spelling

[1] *solues sake* So long as you are solvent.

Other Lands, Other Cultures

CONTEXTS

Trade and exploration eastward was a preoccupation of many in mid-sixteenth century England; the Muscovy Company was formed in 1555 for the purposes of trading with Russia, and Elizabeth I's Act for the Corporation of Merchant Adventurers for the Discovery of New Trades (1566) makes reference far more frequently to dealings with Russia and eastern Europe than it does to trade or exploration in other parts of the world. Among the most readable of the narratives of discovery in Hakluyt's *Voyages* are the accounts by Anthony Jenkinson of his various expeditions to Russia, central Asia, and Persia, excerpts from which are included here. Jenkinson's comments on the cultures of the "Mohammedans" may be of particular interest.

One of the most interesting and influential pieces of late sixteenth-century writing about distant cultures is the essay "Of Cannibals" by Michel de Montaigne. Montaigne's essay was prompted by published accounts of French travelers to Brazil, who had reported that some native peoples practiced cannibalism. The Montagne essay is accompanied here by relevant excerpts from Shakespeare's *The Tempest*.

The first permanent English settlement in North America was established at Annapolis Royal in what is now Nova Scotia, in 1605. Two years later the East India Company established a post on the west coast of India, and colonists landed in Virginia, on the east coast of America. The Virginia colony was central to English presence in North America, and certain episodes connected with its establishment—notably the story of John Smith and Pocahontas—remain a central part of American legend. The documents below present a variety of different points of view of the Virginia colony, including that of Pocahontas as she looked back on the events years later in London.

The portrayal of distant lands as forms of Paradise was a common theme in the literature of exploration—particularly when the intent was to interest potential settlers in leaving the British Isles. A striking example is Richard Whitbourne's *A Discourse and Discovery of Newfoundland* (1620), from which it would be impossible to divine that "the Rock" (as Newfoundland came to be known) is a place of bleak landscapes, poor farming conditions, and harsh winters. Robert Hayman's amusing poem on the same subject is not quite so disingenuous as to the "wild, savage" aspect of the land, but holds out the hope that "good husbandry" will make the place far more attractive.

Exploration and colonization continued to be carried out through Royal Charter following the Restoration, with the Royal Charter of the Hudson's Bay Company the most important case in point. Excerpts from the charter, which granted a variety of rights and privileges to the Governor and Company of Adventurers of England trading into Hudson Bay, are reprinted below.

The captivity narrative is coming to be recognized as an important sub-genre of English literature. Perhaps the best known of late seventeenth-century accounts of life in captivity is that of Mary Rowlandson, a Puritan English woman who spent several weeks among the Pequot Indians of Massachusetts in 1675.

⌘⌘⌘

from Anthony Jenkinson, "The Voyage of Master Anthony Jenkinson, made from the city of Moscow in Russia, to the city of Boghar in Bactria, in the year 1558: written by himself to the Merchants of London of the Moscovy Company," as printed in Richard Hakluyt, *Principal Navigations, Voyages, Traffics and Discoveries of the English Nation* (1589–90)

The excerpts below chiefly concern various encounters with other peoples during Jenkinson's 1558 expedition to central Asia. The trip was not a great success in terms of opening up potential trading connections, and after Jenkinson's trip no other Englishman traveled to central Asia for more than 200 years.

The 23rd day of April, in the year 1558. (Having obtained the Emperor of Russia his letters, directed unto sundry kings and princes, by whose dominions I should pass) I departed from Moscow by water, having with me two of your servants, namely, Richard Johnson, and Robert Johnson, and a Tartar Tolmach, with diverse parcels of wares, as by the inventory appeareth: and the 28th day we came to a town called Collom, distant from Moscow 20 leagues, and passing one league beyond the said Collom, we came unto a river called Occa, into the which the river Moscow falleth, and loseth his name....

Thus proceeding on our journey the 25th day of May aforesaid, we came to another castle called Sabowshare, which we left on our right hand, distant from Vasiliagorod 16 leagues. The country hereabout is called Mordouits, and the habitants did profess the law of the Gentiles. But now, being conquered by this Emperor of Russia, most of them are christened, but lie in the woods and wilderness, without town or habitation....

[The river of Cama.]

Thus proceeding forward the 14th day, we passed by a goodly[1] river called Cama, which we left on our left hand. The river falleth out of the country of Permia into the river of Volga, and is from Cazan 15 leagues, and the country lying betwixt the said Cazan and the said river Cama on the left hand of Volga is called Vachen, and the inhabitants be Gentiles, and live in the wilderness without house or habitation. And the country on the other side of Volga over against the said river Cama is called the land of Cheremizes, half Gentiles, half Tartars, and all the land on the left hand of the said Volga from the said river unto Astracan, and so following the North and Northeast side of the Caspian sea, to a land of the Tartars called Turkemen, is called the country of Magnat or Nagay, whose inhabitants are of the law of Mahomet, and were all destroyed in the year 1558, at my being at Astracan, through civil wars among them, accompanied with famine, pestilence, and such plagues, in such sort that in the said year there were consumed of the people, in one sort and another, above one hundred thousand. The like plague was never seen in those parts, so that the said country of Nagay, being a country of great pasture, remaineth now unreplenished to the great contentation of the Russes,[2] who have had cruel wars a long time together.

The Nagayans, when they flourished, lived in this manner: they were divided into diverse companies called hordes, and every horde had a ruler, whom they obeyed as their king, and was called a Murse. Town or house they had none, but lived in the open fields, every Murse or King having his hordes or people about him, with their wives, children and cattle, who having consumed the pasture in one place, removed unto another; and when they remove they have houses like tents set upon wagons or carts, which are drawn from place to place with camels, and therein their wives, children, and all their riches, which is very little, is carried about, and every man hath at the least four or five wives, besides concubines. Use of money they have none, but do barter their cattle for apparel and other necessaries. They delight in no art nor science, except the wars, wherein they are expert, but for the most part they be pasturing people, and have great store of cattle, which is all their riches. They eat much flesh, and especially the horse, and they drink mare's milk, wherewith they be oftentimes drunk. They are seditious and inclined to theft and murder. Corn they sow not, neither do eat any bread, mocking the Christians for the same, and disabling our strengths, saying we live by eating the top of

[1] *goodly* Large.

[2] *Russes* Russians.

a weed, and drink a drink made out of the same, allowing their great devouring of flesh and drinking of milk to be the increase of their strength. But now to proceed forward to my journey.

[The Crimean Tartars.]
All the country upon our right hand the river Volga, from over against the river Cama, unto the town of Astracan, is the land of Crimme,[1] whose inhabitants be also of the law of Mahomet, and live for the most part according to the fashions of the Nagayes, having continual wars with the Emperor of Russia, and are valiant in the field, having countenance, and support from the great Turke....

The 14th day of July passing by an old castle, which was Old Astracan, and leaving it upon our right hand, we arrived at New Astracan, which this Emperor of Russia conquered six years past, in the year 1552. It is from the Moscow unto Astracan six hundred leagues, or thereabout. The town of Astracan is situated in an Island upon a hillside, having a castle within the same, walled about with earth and timber, neither fair nor strong: The town is also walled about with earth; the buildings and houses (except[2] it be the captain's lodging, and certain other gentlemen's) most base and simple. The island is most destitute and barren of wood and pasture, and the ground will bear no corn; the air is there most infected, by reason (as I suppose) of much fish, and specially sturgeon, by which only the inhabitants live, having great scarcity of flesh and bread. They hang up their fish in their streets and houses to dry for their provision, which causeth such abundance of flies to increase there, as the like was never seen in any land, to their great plague. And at my being at the said Astracan, there was a great famine and plague among the people, and specially among the Tartars called Nagayans, who the same time came thither in great numbers to render themselves to the Russes their enemies, and to seek succor at their hands, their country being destroyed, as I said before. But they were but ill entertained or relieved, for there died a great number of them for hunger, which lay all the island through in heaps dead and like to beasts unburied, very pitiful to behold. Many of them were also sold by the Russes, and the rest were banished from the island. At that time it had been an easy thing to have converted that wicked nation to the Christian faith, if the Russes themselves had been good Christians; but how should they shew compassion unto other nations, when they are not merciful unto their own? At my being there I could have bought many goodly Tartars' children, if I would have had a thousand, of their own fathers and mothers, to say a boy or a wench for a loaf of bread worth sixpence in England, but we had more need of victuals at that time then of any such merchandise....

This Astracan is the furthest hold that this Emperor of Russia has conquered of the Tartars towards the Caspian Sea, which he keepeth very strong, sending thither every year provision of men and victuals, and timber to build the castle.... There is a certain trade of merchandise there used, but as yet so small and beggarly, that it is not worth the making mention, and yet there come merchants thither from diverse places. The chiefest commodities that the Russes bring thither are red hides, red sheep's skins, wooden vessels, bridles, and saddles, knives, and other trifles, with corn, bacon, and other victuals. The Tartars bring thither diverse kinds of wares made of cotton wool, with diverse kinds of wrought silks: and they that come out of Persia, namely from Shamacki do bring sewing silk, which is the coarsest that they use in Russeland, Crasco, diverse kinds of pied silks for girdles, shirts of mail, bows, swords, and such like things; and some years corn, and walnuts, but all such things in such small quantity, the merchants being so beggarly and poor that bring the same, that it is not worth the writing, neither is there any hope of trade in all those parts worth the following....

[Urgence.]
The 14th day of the month we departed from this Castle of Sellizure, and the 16th of the same we arrived at a city called Urgence, where we paid custom as well for our own heads, as for our camels and horses.... This city or town of Urgence standeth in a plain ground, with walls of the earth, by estimation four miles about it. The buildings within it are also of earth, but ruined

[1] *Crimme* Crimea.

[2] *except* Unless.

and out of good order: it hath one long street that is covered above, which is the place of their market. It hath been won and lost four times within seven years by civil wars, by means whereof there are but few merchants in it, and they very poor, and in all that town I could not sell about four. The chiefest commodities there sold are such wares as come from Boghar, and out of Persia, but in most small quantity not worth the writing.

[The country of Turkeman.]
All the land from the Caspian Sea to this City of Urgence is called the land of Turkeman, and is subject to the said Azim Can, and his brethren which be five in number, and one of them hath the name of the chief king called Can, but he is little obeyed saving in his own Dominion, and where he dwelleth: for every one will be King of his own portion, and one brother seeketh always to destroy another, having no natural love among them, by reason that they are begotten of diverse women, and commonly they are the children of slaves, either Christians or Gentiles, which the father doth keep as concubines, and every Can or Sultan hath at least four or five wives, besides young maidens and boys, living most viciously. And when there are wars betwixt these brethren (as they are seldom without), he that is overcome if he be not slain, flieth to the field with such company of men as will follow him, and there liveth in the wilderness resorting to watering places, and so robbeth and spoileth as many Caravans of Merchants and others as they be able to overcome, continuing in this sort his wicked life, until such time as he may get power and aid to invade some of his brethren again. From the Caspian Sea unto the Castle of Sellizure aforesaid, and all the countries about the said sea, the people live without town or habitation in the wild fields, removing from one place to another in great companies with their cattle, whereof they have great store, as camels, horses, and sheep both tame and wild. Their sheep are of great stature with great buttocks, weighing 60 or 80 pounds. There are many wild horses which the Tartars do many times kill with their hawks, and that in this order: the hawks are lured to seize upon the beasts' necks or heads, which with chafing of themselves and sore beating of the hawks are tired; then the hunter, following his game, doth slay the horse with his arrow or sword. In all this land there groweth no grass, but a certain brush or heath, whereon the cattle feeding become very fat.

The Tartars never ride without their bow, arrows, and sword, although it be on hawking, or at any other pleasure, and they are good archers both on horseback, and on foot also. These people have not the use of gold, silver, or any other coin, but when they lack apparel or other necessaries, they barter their cattle for the same. Bread they have none, for they neither till nor sow. They be great devourers of flesh, which they cut in small pieces, and eat it by handfuls most greedily, and especially the horseflesh. Their chiefest drink is mare's milk soured, as I have said before of the Nagayans, and they will be drunk with the same. They have no rivers nor places of water in this country, until you come to the aforesaid gulf, distant from the place of our landing 20 day's journey, except it be[1] in wells, the water whereof is saltish, and yet distant the one from the other two days' journey and more. They eat their meat upon the ground, sitting with their legs double under them, and so also when they pray. Art or science they have none, but live most idly, sitting round in great companies in the fields, devising, and talking most vainly....

from Michel de Montaigne, "Of Cannibals" (1588)

In keeping with his concept of "essays" (or "attempts"), Montaigne returned to this piece several times, publishing versions in 1580, 1588, and 1595. The first English translation, by John Florio, was published in 1603, and appears to have been quite influential in England; Shakespeare's *The Tempest* is the best known of the many works that were influenced by "Of Cannibals."

When King Pyrrhus invaded Italy,[2] having viewed and considered the order of the army the Romans sent out to meet him; "I know not," said he, "what kind of barbarians" (for so the Greeks called all other nations), "these may be; but the disposition of this army, that I see, has nothing of barbarism in it." As much said

[1] *except it be* Unless it is.

[2] *When King Pyrrhus invaded Italy* In the third century CE.

the Greeks of that which Flaminius[1] brought into their country; and Philip, beholding from an eminence the order and distribution of the Roman camp formed in his kingdom by Publius Sulpicius Galba,[2] spake to the same effect. By which it appears how cautious men ought to be of taking things upon trust from vulgar opinion, and that we are to judge by the eye of reason, and not from common report.

I long had a man in my house that lived ten or twelve years in the New World, discovered in these latter days, and in that part of it where Villegaignon landed,[3] which he called Antarctic France. This discovery of so vast a country seems to be of very great consideration. I cannot be sure that hereafter there may not be another, so many wiser men than we having been deceived in this. I am afraid our eyes are bigger than our bellies, and that we have more curiosity than capacity, for we grasp at all, but catch nothing but wind.

... I find that there is nothing barbarous and savage in this nation, by anything that I can gather, excepting, that everyone gives the title of barbarism to everything that is not in use in his own country. As, indeed, we have no other level of truth and reason, than the example and idea of the opinions and customs of the place wherein we live; there is always the perfect religion, there the perfect government, there the most exact and accomplished usage of all things. They are savages at the same rate that we say fruit are wild, which nature produces of herself and by her own ordinary progress, whereas in truth, we ought rather to call those wild, whose natures we have changed by our artifice, and diverted from the common order.

These nations then seem to me to be so far barbarous, as having received but very little form and fashion from art and human invention, and consequently to be not much remote from their original simplicity. The laws of nature, however, govern them still, not as yet much vitiated with any mixture of ours; but 'tis in such purity that I am sometimes troubled we were not sooner acquainted with these people, and that they were not discovered in those better times, when there were men much more able to judge of them than we are. I am sorry that Lycurgus[4] and Plato had no knowledge of them, for to my apprehension, what we now see in those nations does not only surpass all the pictures with which the poets have adorned the golden age, and all their inventions in feigning a happy state of man, but, moreover, the fancy and even the wish and desire of philosophy itself; so native and so pure a simplicity, as we by experience see to be in them, could never enter into their imagination, nor could they ever believe that human society could have been maintained with so little artifice and human patchwork....

This is a people amongst whom there is no commerce; no knowledge of letters; no science of numbers; no judges or politicians; no habit of service; no riches and no poverty; no contracts, no inheritance; no property; no employments, except those of leisure; no respect for authority except within the family; no clothing; no agriculture; no metal; no use of wheat or of wine. The very words that signify lying, treachery, dissimulation, avarice, envy, detraction, pardon, are all unknown. How far short do imaginary republics fall from such perfection!...

They have I know not what kind of priests and prophets, who very rarely present themselves to the people, having their abode in the mountains. At their arrival, there is a great feast, and solemn assembly of many villages. Each house, as I have described, makes a village, and they are about a French league distant from one another. This prophet declaims to them in public, exhorting them to virtue and their duty; but all their ethics are comprised in these two articles, resolution in war, and affection to their wives. He also prophesies to them events to come, and the issues they are to expect from their enterprises, and prompts them to or diverts them from war. But let him look to't; for if he fail in his divination, and anything happen otherwise than he has foretold, he is cut into a thousand pieces, if he be caught, and condemned for a false prophet. For that reason, if any of them has been mistaken, he is no more heard of....

[1] *Flaminius* Roman statesman of the third century.

[2] *Philip ... Publius Sulpicius Galba* In the sixth century CE.

[3] *Villegaignon landed* In 1555 Nicolas Durand Villegaignon landed in the Bay of Rio de Janeiro, Brazil, and set up a French colony on a neighboring island.

[4] *Lycurgus* Famed lawgiver to the Spartans of ancient Greece, as related in Plutarch's *Lives*.

They have continual war with the nations that live further within the mainland, beyond their mountains, to which they go naked, and without other arms than their bows and wooden swords, fashioned at one end like the heads of our javelins. The obstinacy of their battles is wonderful, and they never end without great effusion of blood: for as to running away, they know not what it is. Everyone for a trophy brings home the head of an enemy he has killed, which he fixes over the door of his house. After having a long time treated their prisoners very well, and given them all the regales they can think of, he to whom the prisoner belongs, invites a great assembly of his friends. They being come, he ties a rope to one of the arms of the prisoner, of which, at a distance, out of his reach, he holds the one end himself, and gives to the friend he loves best the other arm to hold after the same manner; which being done, they two, in the presence of all the assembly, despatch him with their swords. After that they roast him, eat him among them, and send some chops to their absent friends. They do not do this, as some think, for nourishment, as the Scythians anciently did, but as a representation of an extreme revenge, as will appear by this: that having observed the Portuguese, who were in league with their enemies, to inflict another sort of death upon any of them they took prisoners, which was to set them up to the girdle in the earth, to shoot at the remaining part till it was stuck full of arrows, and then to hang them, they thought those people of the other world (as being men who had sown the knowledge of a great many vices among their neighbors, and who were much greater masters in all sorts of mischief than they) did not exercise this sort of revenge without a meaning, and that it must needs be more painful than theirs, they began to leave their old way, and to follow this.

I am not sorry that we should here take notice of the barbarous horror of so cruel an action; but, seeing so clearly into their faults, we should not be so blind to our own. I conceive there is more barbarity in eating a man alive, than when he is dead; in tearing the body limb from limb by racks and torments while the person remains conscious; in roasting it by degrees; in causing it to be bitten and worried by dogs and swine (as we have not only read, but lately seen, not among inveterate and mortal enemies, but among neighbors and fellow citizens, and, which is worse, under color of piety and religion); than there is barbarity in roasting and eating a person after he is dead....

We may then call these people barbarous, in respect to the rules of reason, but not in respect to ourselves, who in all sorts of barbarity exceed them. Their wars are throughout noble and generous, and are fought for reasons as good as that human malady is capable of; having with them no other foundation than the urge to valour. Their disputes are not for the conquest of new lands, for those they already possess are sufficiently fruitful by nature to supply their needs in such abundance that they have no need to enlarge their borders. And they are, moreover, happy in this, that they wish for only so much as their natural necessities require; all beyond that is superfluous to them; men of the same age call one another generally brothers, those who are younger, children; and the old men are fathers to all. These leave to their heirs in common the full possession of goods, without any manner of division, or other title than what nature bestows upon her creatures, in bringing them into the world. If their neighbors pass over the mountains to assault them, and obtain a victory, all the victors gain by it is glory, and the advantage of having proved themselves the better in valor and virtue, for they never meddle with the goods of the conquered, but presently return into their own country, where they have no want of anything necessary, nor of this greatest of all goods, to know happily how to enjoy their condition and to be content....

from William Shakespeare, *The Tempest* (1612–13)

In Shakespeare's *The Tempest*, Alonzo, King of Naples and Antonio, Duke of Milan, together with others of their party, are shipwrecked on a mysterious island controlled by Prospero, a magician who turns out to be of royal Milanese blood as well. Also on the island is Caliban (whose name is an anagram of "cannibal"), a native of the island who has been enslaved by Prospero. Excerpts from two passages that draw on Montaigne are included below. In the first, Caliban and Prospero exchange words over the reality of Caliban's situation; in the second Gonzalo, "an honest old councillor," jests about an imagined ideal society as he banters with Antonio and Sebastian.

from ACT 1, SCENE 2

… PROSPERO. Thou poisonous slave, got° by the devil himself *begotten*
Upon thy wicked dam,° come forth! *mother*

(*Enter Caliban.*)

CALIBAN. As wicked dew as e'er my mother brushed
With raven's feather from unwholesome fen
Drop on you both! A southwest ° blow on ye *unhealthy wind*
And blister you all o'er!
PROSPERO. For this, be sure, to-night thou shalt have cramps,
Side-stitches that shall pen thy breath up; urchins
Shall, forth at vast of night that they may work,
All exercise on thee;[1] thou shalt be pinched
As thick as honeycomb, each pinch more stinging
Than bees that made 'em.
CALIBAN. I must eat my dinner.
This island's mine, by Sycorax my mother,
Which thou takest from me. When thou cam'st first,
Thou strok'st me and madest much of me, wouldst give me
Water with berries in't, and teach me how
To name the bigger light, and how the less,
That burn by day and night. And then I loved thee
And showed thee all the qualities° o' the isle, *features*
The fresh springs, brine-pits, barren place and fertile:
Cursed be I that did so! All the charms° *spells*
Of Sycorax, toads, beetles, bats, light on you!
For I am all the subjects[2] that you have,
Which first was mine own king: and here you stay° me *keep*
In this hard rock, whiles you do keep from me
The rest o' the island.
PROSPERO. Thou most lying slave,
Whom stripes° may move, not kindness! I have used thee, *lashes*
Filth as thou art, with human care, and lodged thee
In mine own cell, till thou didst seek to violate
The honour of my child.
CALIBAN. O ho, O ho! Would't had been done!
Thou didst prevent me; I had peopled else[3]
This isle with Calibans.
MIRANDA. Abhorrèd slave,
Which any print° of goodness wilt not take, *imprint*
Being capable of all ill! I pitied thee,
Took pains to make thee speak, taught thee each hour
One thing or other: when thou didst not, savage,
Know thine own meaning, but wouldst gabble like
A thing most brutish, I endowed thy purposes
With words[4] that made them known. But thy vile race,° *nature*
Though thou didst learn, had that in't which good natures
Could not abide to be with; therefore wast thou
Deservedly confined into this rock,
Who hadst deserved more than a prison.[5]
CALIBAN. You taught me language; and my profit on't
Is, I know how to curse. The red plague rid° you *get rid of*
For learning me your language!
PROSPERO. Hag-seed, hence!
Fetch us in fuel; and be quick, thou'rt best,[6]
To answer other business. Shrug'st thou, malice?
If thou neglect'st or dost unwillingly
What I command, I'll rack thee with old cramps,
Fill all thy bones with aches, make thee roar
That beasts shall tremble at thy din.
CALIBAN. No, pray thee.
(*Aside.*) I must obey: His art is of such power,
It would control my dam's god, Setebos,[7]
And make a vassal° of him. *servant, slave*
PROSPERO. So, slave, hence!

(*Exit Caliban.*)…

[1] *urchins … on thee* Goblins shall go out in the dead of night to work evil on you.

[2] *all the subjects* The only subject.

[3] *had peopled else* Would otherwise have populated.

[4] *endow'd thy purposes with words* I was able to express what you meant in words.

[5] *Abhorrèd slave … a prison* These lines have frequently been assigned by editors to Prospero rather than to his daughter.

[6] *thou'rt best* You would be best advised.

[7] *Setebos* God of a South American native people.

from ACT 2, SCENE 1

... GONZOLO. Had I plantation of this isle,[1] my lord—
ANTONIO. (To Sebastian.) He'd sow't with nettle-seed.
SEBASTIAN. Or docks, or mallows.[2]
GONZOLO. And were I th'king on't, what would I do?
SEBASTIAN. 'Scape being drunk for want of wine.[3]
GONZOLO. I' the commonwealth I would by contraries
Execute all things;[4] for no kind of traffic° *trade*
Would I admit; no name of magistrate;
Letters ° should not be known; riches, poverty *learning*
And use of service,° none; contract, *servants*
succession,° *inheritance*
Bourn,° bound of land, tilth,° vineyard, *borders / tilled land*
none;
No use of metal, corn,° or wine, or oil; *grain*
No occupation; all men idle, all;
And women too, but innocent and pure;
No sovereignty—
SEBASTIAN. Yet he would be king on't.
ANTONIO. The latter end of his commonwealth forgets
the beginning.
GONZOLO. All things in common nature should produce
Without sweat or endeavour: treason, felony,
Sword, pike,° knife, gun, or need of any *pikestaff*
engine,° *weapon*
Would I not have; but nature should bring forth,
Of its own kind, all foison,° all abundance, *plenty*
To feed my innocent people.
SEBASTIAN. No marrying 'mong his subjects?
ANTONIO. None, man, all idle: whores and knaves.
GONZOLO. I would with such perfection govern, sir,
T' excel the golden age.[5]
SEBASTIAN. God save his majesty!
ANTONIO. Long live Gonzolo!
GONZOLO. And,—do you mark° me, sir? *pay attention to*
ALONZO. Prithee, no more: thou dost talk nothing to me.
GONZOLO. I do well believe your highness; and did it to minister occasion[6] to these gentlemen, who are of such sensible and nimble[7] lungs that they always use to laugh at nothing.
ANTONIO. 'Twas you we laughed at.
GONZOLO. Who in this kind of merry fooling am nothing to you: so you may continue and laugh at nothing still....

[1] *had I plantation of this isle* Were I able to colonize this island.

[2] *docks* Coarse wildflowers; *mallows* Wildflowers typically found in waste places.

[3] *'Scape being drunk ... wine* Escape drunkenness only because you would lack wine.

[4] *I would ... all things* I would have everything done in the opposite way from the way it is.

[5] *T' excel the golden age* I would govern so well that my rule would excel the Golden Age of the world, i.e., the first and best age of the world, according to the Greek and Roman poets.

[6] *minister occasion* Provide an opportunity.

[7] *sensible and nimble* Easily affected by the urge to laugh.

Elizabethan Adventurers

Sir Francis Drake (1542–96). Drake first took to sea with his cousin, Sir John Hawkins, in the 1560s, on Hawkins's pirating and slave trading voyages. His ship and that of Hawkins were the only English vessels to escape when the Spanish caught an English fleet by surprise at San Juan de Ulua in 1568. In the 1570s Drake became England's most successful sea-pirate, capturing vast hoards of treasure for himself and for his sovereign. From 1577–81 he circumnavigated the globe (becoming the first Englishman to do so) and his ships again returned laden with stolen treasure. At the Queen's behest, he raided several Spanish settlements in the Caribbean in the 1580s. In the battle against the Spanish Armada in 1588 he was Vice-Admiral of the fleet, captaining the *Revenge*. Both he and Hawkins died during an ill-fated 1595–96 voyage to South America.

Sir Martin Frobisher (1535–94). A seaman from an early age, Frobisher was captured by a native chief in Guinea at age 18. He spent much of his twenties and thirties engaged in piracy against Spanish ships. In 1576 he sailed in search of the Northwest Passage; he returned with samples of ore that he believed contained gold, and with optimistic reports suggesting that the body of Arctic water he had discovered (now known as Frobisher Bay) might lead to the Orient. He formed the Cathay Company and made two other North American voyages (during which he claimed Labrador for the English), but the ore was not gold and Frobisher Bay did not lead to Cathay. Frobisher took up piracy again in the 1580s (including on one very successful voyage with Drake in 1586), and was Captain of the *Triumph* in the battle against the Spanish Armada in 1588. He died of wounds suffered during a battle with the French as he was attempting to facilitate the emigration of French Protestants (Hugenots).

Sir Richard Grenville (1541–91). An experienced and headstrong sailor, Grenville also fought in Ireland against rebel forces, and was for a time a Member of Parliament. In 1591 he commanded *The Revenge* in an action against the Spaniards off the Azores in 1591. The ship was one of a squadron that sought (with the blessing of Queen Elizabeth) to intercept Spanish ships returning from the West Indies laden with treasure. On this occasion the English were outnumbered; Grenville died when his ship was lost.

Sir John Hawkins (c. 1562–1622). The most enduring of Elizabeth's pirates, Hawkins made a name for himself in the 1560s, both by attacking Spanish ships and stealing the treasure they were carrying, and by initiating the trade in African slaves. In the 1570s he became a shipbuilder and treasurer of the Navy, and in the 1580s played a key role in rebuilding the English fleet with smaller, more maneuverable ships. Hawkins was Rear-Admiral of the fleet during the victory over the Spanish Armada. He died aboard ship in 1595, on a voyage to South America with his cousin and old friend Sir Francis Drake.

The English in Virginia, the Powhatans in London

Perhaps the most significant English colonization initiatives of the late sixteenth and early seventeenth centuries were those involving the territory that had been named "Virginia" in honor of the virgin queen, Elizabeth. Arthur Barlow, together with Philip Amadas, was commissioned in 1585 by Sir Walter Ralegh to explore the territory in order to ascertain the prospects for settlement. Barlow's account of that voyage is excerpted below; it provided a range of interesting comments on the native peoples of the territory, as well as an optimistic assessment of the chances English settlers would have of flourishing in these environs. The first effort at settlement began the next year at Roanoke, but ended badly, with all the settlers either dead or unaccounted for.

In 1606 efforts for settlement were renewed when the Virginia Company was established as a joint stock company under the auspices of James I with a new mandate to colonize "Virginia"—defined as all the territory between Florida and Massachusetts, together with the Bermuda Islands. As may be inferred from the tone of Drayton's poem "To the Virginian Voyage," the endeavor was attended by considerable fanfare—and this time the colonization effort succeeded, albeit with enormous hardship, as Captain John Smith recorded in his *History of Virginia and the Summer Isles* (1623). Smith himself was at the center of the most famous incident of the colony's early history, in which his life was reportedly saved by a young native woman, Pocahontas.[1] He was then released, on the understanding that he and the colony would relocate from their initial settlement place, Jamestown, to a location known as Tsenacommacah, and would turn over to the Powhatans "two great guns, and a grindstone." The English colonists did neither of those things, and hostilities commenced that ended only many years later with the forced subjugation of the Native peoples of the territory. During this period, however, there were frequently times of guarded friendliness between the Jamestown colony and Powhatans—as, for example, the 1609 feast described below at which Smith and Chief Powhatan discuss the English intentions in America.

Pocahontas herself became a captive of the English in 1613. While being held by them, she met John Rolfe, the farmer who had introduced the Caribbean variety of tobacco to the colony (which eventually became its staple crop). The two fell in love and in 1614 were married; Rolfe's letter to Sir Thomas Dale (excerpted below) describes the effect of the marriage on the community, while rejecting any suggestion that he entered into matrimony for

[1] *Smith himself … Pocahontas* Beginning in the nineteenth century there have been various suggestions that Smith might have invented key parts of this story. Most present-day historians accept that Smith's story is not completely invented—but the degree to which Smith was in danger is unclear. As historians such as Fredrik Gleach have pointed out, the events as described by Smith are entirely consistent with the ceremonial sequence of many Native adoption rituals; the Powhatans may have intended the extraordinary (to European eyes) sequence as a ceremonial adoption of Smith and of the English colony as a whole.

primarily lustful motives. In 1616 Rolfe and his wife sailed for England in a party that included Uttamatomakkin, a Powhatan councillor who had been instructed by his chief to report on the number and condition of the English people, as well as on the whereabouts of John Smith (who had himself left Virginia for England in 1609). For a time they all moved in high circles of London society (among those Pocahontas met were the Bishop of London and Ben Jonson, and Uttamatomakkin is known to have met King James). Smith's description of meeting Pocahontas again is included below. Pocahontas became seriously ill in England, however; she died shortly after she and Rolfe sailed again for Virginia in 1617, and was buried in Gravesend, just east of London.

from Arthur Barlow, "The first voyage made to the coasts of America, with two barks,[1] wherein were Captains M. Philip Amadas, and M. Arthur Barlow, who discovered part of the country now called Virginia, Anno[2] 1584. Written by one of the said Captains, and sent to Sir Walter Raleigh, Knight, at whose charge and direction the said voyage was set forth" (1584)

The second of July, we found shoal water, where we smelled so sweet, and so strong a smell, as if we had been in the midst of some delicate garden abounding with all kind of odoriferous flowers, by which we were assured, that the land could not be far distant; and keeping good watch, and bearing but slack sail, the fourth of the same month we arrived upon the coast, which we supposed to be a continent and firm land, and we sailed along the same a hundred and twenty English miles before we could find any entrance, or river issuing into the sea. The first that appeared unto us, we entered, though not without some difficulty, and cast anchor about three harquebus-shot[3] within the haven's mouth, on the left hand of the same. And after thanks given to God for our safe arrival thither, we manned our boats, and went to view the land next adjoining, and to take possession of the same, in the right of the Queen's most excellent Majesty, as rightful Queen, and Princess of the same, and after delivered the same over to your use, according to her Majesty's grant, and letters patents, under her Highness's great seal. Which being performed, according to the ceremonies used in such enterprises, we viewed the land about us, being, whereas we first landed, very sandy and low towards the water's side, but so full of grapes, as the very beating and surge of the sea overflowed them, of which we found such plenty, as well there as in all places else, both on the sand and on the green soil on the hills, as in the plains, as well on every little shrub, as also climbing towards the tops of high cedars, that I think in all the world the like abundance is not to be found....

This island had many goodly woods full of deer, hares, and fowl, even in the midst of summer in incredible abundance. The woods are not such as you find in Bohemia, Muscovia, or Hercynia, barren and fruitless, but rather having the highest and reddest cedars[4] of the world, far bettering the cedars of the Azores, of the Indies.... We remained by the side of this island two whole days before we saw any people of the country: the third day we spied one small boat rowing towards us having in it three persons....

The next day there came unto us diverse boats, and in one of them the King's brother, accompanied with forty or fifty men, very handsome and goodly people, and in their behaviour as mannerly and civil as any of Europe. His name was Granganimeo, and the King is called Wingina, the country Wingandacoa, and now by her Majesty Virginia. The manner of his coming was in this sort: he left his boats altogether as the first man did a little from the ships by the shore, and came along to the place over against the ships, followed with forty men. When he came to the place, his servants spread a long mat upon the ground, on which he sat down, and at the other end of the mat four others of his company did the like, the rest of his men stood round about him, somewhat afar off. When we came to the shore to him with our weapons, he never moved from his place, nor any of the other four, nor never mistrusted any harm to be offered from us, but sitting still he beckoned us to come and sit by him, which we performed; and being

[1] *barks* Ships.

[2] *Anno* Latin: in the year.

[3] *harquebus-shot* Early portable gun.

[4] *cedars* Barlow appears to use "cedars" here as synonymous with "coniferous trees."

set he made all signs of joy and welcome, striking on his head and his breast and afterwards on ours, to show we were all one, smiling and making show the best he could of all love, and familiarity. After he had made a long speech unto us, we presented him with diverse things, which he received very joyfully, and thankfully. None of the company dared speak one word all the time; only the four which were at the other end, spoke one in the other's ear very softly....

We exchanged our tin dish for twenty skins, worth twenty crowns,... and a copper kettle for fifty skins worth fifty crowns. They offered us good exchange for our hatchets, and axes, and for knives, and would have given anything for swords, but we would not part with any. After two or three days the King's brother came aboard the ships, and drank wine, and ate of our meat and of our bread, and liked exceedingly thereof; and after a few days overpassed, he brought his wife with him to the ships, his daughter and two or three children. His wife was very well favoured, of mean stature and very bashful; she had on her back a long cloak of leather, with the fur side next to her body, and before her a piece of the same. About her forehead she had a band of white coral, and so had her husband many times. In her ears she had bracelets of pearls hanging down to her middle (whereof we delivered your worship a little bracelet), and those were of the bigness of good peas. The rest of her women of the better sort had pendants of copper hanging in either ear, and some of the children of the King's brother and other noblemen, have five or six in either ear. He himself had upon his head a broad plate of gold or copper for being unpolished we knew not what metal it should be, neither would he by any means suffer[1] us to take it off his head, but feeling it, would bow very easily. His apparel was as that of his wives, only the women wear their hair long on both sides, and the men but on one. They are of colour yellowish, and their hair black for the most part, and yet we saw children that had very fine auburn and chestnut coloured hair.

After that these women had been there, there came down from all parts great store of people, bringing with them leather, coral, diverse kinds of dyes very excellent, and exchanged with us. But when Granganimeo the King's brother was present, none dared trade but himself except such as wear red pieces of copper on their heads like himself; for that is the difference between the noblemen and the governors of the countries, and you have understood since by these men, which we brought home, that no people in the world carry more respect to their King, nobility, and governors, than these do. The King's brother's wife, when she came to us (as she did many times) was followed with forty or fifty women always; and when she came into the ship, she left them all on land, saving[2] her two daughters, her nurse, and one or two more. The King's brother always kept this order, as many boats as he would come withal to the ships, so many fires would he make on the shore afar off, to the end[3] we might understand with what strength and company he approached. Their boats are made of one tree, either of pine or of pitch trees, a wood not commonly known to our people, nor found growing in England. They have no edge-tools to make them withal; if they have any they are very few, and those it seems they had twenty years since, which, as those two men declared, was out of a wreck which happened upon their coast of some Christian ship, being beaten that way by some storm and outrageous weather, whereof none of the people were saved, but only the ship, or some part of her being cast upon the sand, out of whose sides they drew the nails and the spikes, and with those they made their best instruments. The manner of making their boats is thus: they burn down some great tree, or take such as are wind fallen, and putting gum and rosin upon one side thereof, they set fire into it, and when it had burnt it hollow, they cut out the coal with their shells, and ever where they would burn it deeper or wider they lay on gums, which burn away the timber, and by these means they fashion very fine boats, and such as will transport twenty men. Their oars are like scoops, and many times they set with long poles, as the depth serveth....

After they had been diverse times aboard our ships, myself, with seven more, went twenty miles into the river that runs toward the city of Skicoak, which river they call Occam; and the evening following, we came to an island, which they call Roanoke, distant from the

[1] *suffer* Allow.

[2] *saving* Except.

[3] *to the end* With the intention that.

harbour by which we entered, seven leagues; and at the north end thereof was a village of nine houses, built of cedar, and fortified round about with sharp trees, to keep out their enemies, and the entrance into it made like a turnpike very artificially;[1] when we came towards it, standing near unto the water's side, the wife of Granganimo, the King's brother, came running out to meet us very cheerfully and friendly. Her husband was not then in the village; some of her people she commanded to draw our boat on shore…; others she appointed to carry us on their backs to the dry ground, and others to bring our oars into the house for fear of stealing. When we were come into the other room, having five rooms in her house, she caused us to sit down by a great fire, and after took off our clothes and washed them, and dried them again. Some of the women plucked off our stockings and washed them, some washed our feet in warm water, and she herself took great pains to see all things ordered in the best manner she could, making great haste to dress some meat for us to eat.

After we had thus dried ourselves, she brought us into the inner room, where she set on the board standing along the house, some venison, and roasted fish … and melons raw, and sodden roots of diverse kinds. Their drink is commonly water, but while the grape lasts, they drink wine, and for want of casks to keep it, all the year after they drink water, but it is sodden with ginger in it, and black cinnamon, and sometimes sassafras, and diverse other wholesome and medicinable herbs and trees. We were entertained with all love and kindness, and with as much bounty (after their manner) as they could possibly devise. We found the people most gentle, loving, and faithful, void of all guile and treason, and such as live after the manner of the golden age. The people only care how to defend themselves from the cold in their short winter, and to feed themselves with such meat as the soil affords.…

Within the place where they feed was their lodging, and within that their Idol, which they worship, of whom they speak incredible things. While we were at meat, there came in at the gates two or three men with their bows and arrows from hunting, whom when we spied, we began to look one towards another, and offered to reach our weapons; but as soon as the wife of Granganimo, the King's brother spied our mistrust, she was very much moved, and caused some of her men to run out, and take away their bows and arrows and break them, and withal beat the poor fellows out of the gate again. When we departed in the evening and would not tarry all night, she was very sorry, and gave us into our boat our supper half dressed, pots and all, and brought us to our boatside, in which we lay all night, removing the same a pretty distance from the shore. She perceiving our situation was much grieved, and sent diverse men and thirty women to sit all night on the bank side by us, and sent us into our boats five mats to cover us from the rain, using very many words to entreat us to rest in their houses. But because we were few men, and if we had miscarried, the voyage had been in very great danger, we dared not adventure[2] anything, though there was no cause of doubt; for a more kind and loving people there can not be found in the world, as far as we have hitherto had trial.

[1] *artificially* With great artifice; skilfully.

Michael Drayton, "To the Virginian Voyage" (1606)

You brave heroic minds,
Worthy your country's name,
That honour still pursue,
Go, and subdue,
Whilst loit'ring hinds[3]
Lurk here at home, with shame.

Britons, you stay too long,
Quickly aboard bestow you,
And with a merry gale
Swell your stretch'd sail,
With vows as strong,
As the winds that blow you.

Your course securely steer,
West and by south forth keep,
Rocks, lee shores, nor shoals,

[2] *adventure* Risk.

[3] *hinds* People of low estate.

When Aeolus[1] scowls,
You need not fear,
So absolute the deep.[2]

And cheerfully at sea,
Success you still entice,
To get the pearl and gold,
And ours to hold,
Virginia,
Earth's only paradise.

Where nature hath in store,
Fowl, venison, and fish,
And the fruitfull'st soil,
Without your toil,
Three harvests more,
All greater then you wish.

And the ambitious vine
Crowns with his purple mass,
The Cedar reaching high
To kiss the sky,
The Cypress, pine
And useful Sassafras.[3]

To whose, the golden age
Still nature's laws doth give,
No other cares that tend,
But them to defend
From winter's age,
That long there doth not live.

When as the luscious smell
Of that delicious land,
Above the seas that flows,
The clear wind throws,
Your hearts to swell
Approaching the dear strand.° *coast*

In kenning° of the shore *seeing*
(Thanks to God first given,)
O you the happy'st men,
Be frolic then,
Let cannons roar,
Frighting the wide heaven.

And in regions far
Such heroes bring ye forth,
As those from whom we came,
And plant our name,
Under that star
Not known unto our north.

And as there plenty grows
Of laurel everywhere,
Apollo's sacred tree,[4]
You it may see,
A poet's brows
To crown, that may sing there.

Thy voyages attend,
Industrious Hakluyt,[5]
Whose reading shall inflame
Men to seek fame,
And much commend
To after-times thy wit.° *intelligence, far-sightedness*
—1606

from John Smith, *General History of Virginia and the Summer Isles* (1623)

Throughout his history of the colony, Smith writes of all individuals, including himself, in the third person. His use of direct speech for the words of Chief Powhatan has excited considerable discussion; it is known that Smith did learn to speak the language, but the extent to which Smith may be a mediating voice in the speeches of Powhatan is impossible to establish.

[1] *Aeolus* In Greek mythology, the god of wind.

[2] *absolute the deep* I.e.,the water is so deep there will be no danger of running aground.

[3] *Sassafras* The sassafras tree has a variety of medicinal purposes.

[4] *laurel … tree* In Greek mythology, the laurel was the sacred tree of the god Apollo; a crown of laurels may be worn either as a sign of victory or in recognition of poetic achievement.

[5] *Industrious Hakluyt* Richard Hakluyt (c. 1522–1616), compiler of a widely read collection of accounts of English voyages of discovery, was also one of the investors in the 1606 Virginian voyage.

And now [in December 1607], the winter approaching, the rivers became so covered with swans, geese, ducks, and cranes, that we daily feasted with good bread, Virginia peas, pumpkins, ... fish, fowl, and diverse sorts of wild beasts as fat as we could eat them; so that none of our tuftaffaty[1] humorists desired to go for England....

But our comedies never endured long without a tragedy [while Captain Smith was in search of the head of the Chickahamania River], when his barge could pass no farther, he left her in a broad bay out of danger of shot, commanding none should go ashore till his return. Himself with two English and two savages went up higher in a canoe; but he was not long absent but his men went ashore, whose want of government gave both occasion and opportunity to the savages to surprise one George Cassen, whom they slew, and much failed not to have cut off the boat and all the rest.

Smith, little dreaming of that accident, being got to the marshes at the river's head,... finding he was beset with 200 savages, two of them he slew, still defending himself with the aid of a savage his guide, whom he bound to his arm with his garters, and used him as a buckler,[2] yet he was shot in his thigh a little, and had many arrows that stuck in his clothes; but no great hurt, till at last they took him prisoner. When this news came to Jamestown, much was their sorrow for his loss, few expecting what ensued.

Six or seven weeks those barbarians kept him prisoner, many strange triumphs and conjurations[3] they made of him, yet he so demeaned[4] himself amongst them, as he not only diverted them from surprising the fort but procured his own liberty, and got himself and his company such estimation amongst them that those savages admired him more than their own Quiyouckosucks.

He demanding for their captain, they showed him Opechankanough, King of Pamaunkee, to whom he gave a round ivory double compass dial. Much they marveled at the playing of the fly and needle, which they could see so plainly and yet not touch it because of the glass that covered them. But when he demonstrated by that globe-like jewel the roundness of the earth and skies, the sphere of the sun, moon, and stars, and how the sun did chase the night round about the world continually; the greatness of the land and sea, the diversity of nations, variety of complexions, and how we were to them antipodes, and many other such like matters, they all stood as amazed with admiration. Notwithstanding, within an hour after they tied him to a tree, and as many as could stand about him prepared to shoot him; but the King, holding up the compass in his hand, they all laid down their bows and arrows, and in a triumphant manner led him to Orapaks, where he was after their manner kindly feasted, and well used.[5]

At last they brought him to Werowocomoco, where was Powhatan, their emperor. Here more than two hundred of those grim courtiers stood wondering at him, as[6] he had been a monster, till Powhatan and his train had put themselves in their greatest braveries.[7] Before a fire, upon a seat like a bedstead, he sat covered with a great robe, made of raccoon skins, and all the tails hanging by. On either hand did sit a young wench[8] of sixteen or eighteen years, and along on each side the house, two rows of men, and behind them as many women, with all their heads and shoulders painted red, many of their heads bedecked with the white down of birds, but every one with something, and a great chain of white beads about their necks. At his entrance before the King, all the people gave a great shout. The Queen of Appamatuck was appointed to bring him water to wash his hands, and another brought him a bunch of feathers, instead of a towel to dry them. Having feasted him after the best barbarous manner they could, a long consultation was held, but the conclusion was, two great stones were brought before Powhatan. Then as many as could laid hands on him dragged him to them, and thereon laid his head, and being ready with their clubs to beat out his brains, Pocahontas, the King's dearest daughter, when no entreaty could prevail, got his head

[1] *tuftaffaty* Luxuriously dressed.

[2] *buckler* Shield.

[3] *conjurations* Invocations of spirits.

[4] *demeaned* Conducted.

[5] *used* Treated.

[6] *as* As if.

[7] *had put themselves in their greatest braveries* Had put on their most impressive dress.

[8] *wench* Woman.

in her arms, and laid her own upon his to save his from death: whereat the Emperor was contented he should live to make him hatchets, and her bells, beads, and copper; for they thought him as well of all occupations as themselves. For the King himself will make his own robes, shoes, bows, arrows, pots; plant, hunt, or do anything so well as the rest.

Two days after, Powhatan having disguised himself in the most fearfulest manner he could, caused Captain Smith to be brought forth to a great house in the woods, and there upon a mat by the fire to be left alone. Not long after, from behind a mat that divided the house was made the most dolefullest[1] noise he ever heard; then Powhatan, more like a devil than a man, with some two hundred more as black as himself, came unto him and told him now they were friends, and presently he should go to Jamestown, to send him two great guns, and a grindstone, for which he would give him the county of Capahowosick, and for ever esteem him as his son Nantaquoud....

The next day [13 January, 1609], having feasted us after his ordinary manner, Chief Powhatan began to ask us when we would be gone, feigning he sent not for us, neither had he any corn, and his people much less—yet for forty swords he would procure us forty baskets. The president of the Jamestown colony, showing him the men there present that brought him the message and conditions, asked Powhatan how it chanced he became so forgetful. Thereat the King concluded the matter with a merry laughter, asking for our commodities. But none he liked without guns and swords, valuing a basket of corn more precious than a basket of copper, saying he could rate his corn but not the copper.

Captain Smith, seeing the intent of this subtle[2] savage, began to deal with him after this manner: "Powhatan, though I had many courses to have made my provision, yet believing your promises to supply my wants, I neglected all to satisfy your desire. And to testify my love, I send you my men for your building, neglecting mine own. What your people had you have engrossed, forbidding them our trade; and now you think by consuming the time we shall consume for want, not having to fulfill your strange demands. As for swords and guns, I told you long ago I had none to spare. And you must know those I have can keep me from want. Yet steal or wrong you I will not, nor dissolve that friendship we have mutually promised, except you constrain me by our bad usage."[3]

The King, having attentively listened to this discourse, promised that both he and his country would spare him what he could, the which within two days they should receive.

"Yet Captain Smith," saith the King, "some doubt I have of your coming hither that makes me not so kindly seek to relieve you as I would. For many do inform me your coming hither is not for trade but to invade my people and possess my country, who dare not come to bring you corn, seeing you thus armed with your men. To free us of this fear, leave aboard your weapons, for here they are needless, we being all friends and forever Powhatans."

With many such discourses they spent the day, quartering that night in the King's houses....

King Powhatan commands C. Smith to be slayne, his daughter Pokahontas begs his life (engraving by Robert Vaughan from *Smith's General History of Virginia*, 1624).

[1] *dolefullest* Saddest.

[2] *subtle* Devious.

[3] *except you constrain me by our bad usage* Unless you force me to dissolve our friendship by treating us badly.

from John Rolfe, "Letter to Sir Thomas Dale" (1615, written 1614)

The bruit[1] of this proposed marriage came soon to Powhatan's knowledge, a thing acceptable to him, as appeared by his sudden consent thereunto, who some ten days after sent an old uncle of hers, named Opachisco, to give her as his deputy in the Church, and two of his sons to see the marriage solemnized, which was accordingly done about the fifth of April, and ever since we have had friendly commerce and trade, not only with Powhatan himself, but also with his subjects round about us; so as now I see no reason why the colony should not thrive apace....

Now if the vulgar sort, who square all men's actions by the base rule of their own filthiness, shall tax or taunt me in this my godly labour; let them know, it is not any hungry appetite, to gorge myself with incontinency;[2] sure (if I would, and were so sensually inclined) I might satisfy such desire, though not without a seared conscience, yet with Christians more pleasing to the eye, and less fearful in the offence unlawfully committed. Nor am I in so desperate an estate that I regard not what becometh of me; nor am I out of hope but one day to see my country, nor so void of friends, nor mean in birth, but there to obtain a match to my great content; nor have I ignorantly passed over my hopes there, or regardlessly seek to lose the love of my friends, by taking this course: I know them all, and have not rashly overslipped any....

from John Smith, *General History of Virginia and the Summer Isles* (1623)

Hearing that Pocahontas was at Branford with diverse of my friends, I went to see her. After a modest salutation, without any word, she turned about, obscured her face, as not seeming well contented; and in that humour her husband, with diverse others, we all left her two or three hours, repenting myself to have writ she could speak English. But not long after, she began to talk, and remembered me well what courtesies she had done, saying, "you did promise Powhatan what was yours should be his, and he the like to you; you called him father being in his land a stranger, and by the same reason so must I do you;" which though I would have excused, I durst not allow of that title, because she was a King's daughter. With a well-set countenance she said, "were you not afraid to come into my father's country, and did you not cause fear in him and all his people (but me); and fear you here that I should call you father. I tell you then I will, and you shall call me child, and so I will be for ever and ever your countryman. They did tell us always you were dead, and I knew no other till I came to Plymouth; yet Powhatan did command Uttamatomakkin to seek you, and know the truth, because your countrymen will lie much." ...

Pocahontas (1616 engraving by Simon van de Passe, reproduced in Smith's *General History of Virginia*, 1624).

[1] *bruit* News.

[2] *incontinency* Lack of sexual restraint.

Newfoundland "With Good Clothes On"

Richard Whitbourne first visited Newfoundland in 1580, and had maintained a connection with the island once it had been established as a colony (beginning in 1583). In 1618 he was appointed Governor of Newfoundland. The Hayman poem was published in his book *Quodlibets,* in which he promotes the settlement of Newfoundland. Interestingly, the frontispiece depicts an iguana, or what is here called "the West-Indian Guane."

from Richard Whitbourne, *A Discourse and Discovery of Newfoundland* (1620)

Most dread Sovereign, it is to be seen by the cosmographers' maps, and well approved, that the Newfoundland is an island, bordering upon the continent of America, from which it is divided by sea: so far distant as England is from the nearest part of France, and lieth between 46 and 53 degrees north latitude. It is as spacious as Ireland, and lies near the course that ships usually hold in their return from the West Indies, and near half the way between Ireland and Virginia.

I shall not much need to commend the wholesome temperature of that country, seeing the greatest part thereof lieth about four degrees nearer the south than any part of England doth. And it hath been well approved by some of our nation, who have lived there many years, that in the winter season it is as pleasant and healthful as England is. And although the example of one summer be no certain rule for other years, yet thus much also can I truly affirm, that in the year 1615 of the many thousands of English, French, Portugals, and others, that were then upon that coast (amongst whom I sailed to and fro more than one hundred and fifty leagues), I neither saw nor heard in all that travel, of any man or boy of either of these nations that died there during the whole voyage; neither was there so much as any one of them sick....

The soil of this country is so fruitful as that in any diverse places; there the summer naturally produces out of the fruitful womb of the earth, without the labour of man's hand, great plenty of green peas and vetches, fair, round, full and wholesome as our vetches are in England; of which I have there fed on many times. The hawmes[1] of them are good fodder for cattle and other beasts in the winter, with the help of hay, of which there may be made great store with little labour, in divers places of the country. Then have you there fair strawberries, red and white, and fair raspberries, and gooseberries, as there be in England, as also multitudes of bilberries, which are called by some, worts, and many other delicate berries (which I cannot name) in great abundance. There are also many other fruits, as small pears, cherries, filberts, etc. And of these berries and fruits the store is there so great that the mariners of my ship and barque's company have gathered at once more than half a hogshead would hold of which diverse times, eating their fill, I never heard of any man whose health was thereby any way impaired.

There are also herbs, for salads and broth, as[2] parsley, alexander, sorrel, etc. And also flowers, as the red and white damask rose, with other kinds; which are most beautiful and delightful, both to the sight and smell. And questionless the country is stored with many physical herbs and roots, albeit their virtues are not known, because not sought after; yet within these few years, many of our nation finding themselves ill, have bruised some of the herbs and strained the juice into beer, wine or aqua-vitae, and by God's assistance, after a few drinkings, it hath restored them to their former health. The like virtue it hath to cure a wound, or any swelling, either by washing the grieved places with some of the herbs boiled, or by applying them so thereunto (plaster-wise) which I have seen by often experience.

This being the natural fruitfulness of the earth, producing such variety of things fit for food without the labour of man, I might in reason hence infer that if the same were manured and husbanded in some places, as our grounds are, it would be apt to bear corn no less fertile than the English soil. But I need not confine myself to probabilities therein: seeing our men that have wintered there diverse years did for a trial and experiment thereof sow some small quantity of corn which I saw growing very fair; and they found the increase to be great, and the grain very good; and it is well known to me and diverse that trade there yearly, how that cab-

[1] *hawmes* Pods.

[2] *as* Such as.

bage, turnips, lettuce, parsley, and such like, prove so well there as elsewhere....

Robert Hayman, "To My Very Good friend Mr. John Poynts, Esquire, one of the Planters of Newfoundland" (1628)

'Tis said wise Socrates look'd like an ass,
Yet he with wondrous sapience fillèd was;
So, though our *Newfound-Land* look wild, savage,
She hath much wealth penn'd in her rusty cage.
So have I seen a lean-cheeks, bare and raggèd,
Who of his private thousands could have braggèd.
Indeed, she now looks rude, untowardly—
She must be deckèd with good husbandry.
So have I seen a plain, swart sluttish Joan
Look pretty pert and neat with good clothes on.

from "The Royal Charter for Incorporating the Hudson's Bay Company" (1670)

Hudson Bay was initially valued as a potential entrance to a Northwest Passage to the Orient; with this end in mind it was explored by Martin Frobisher in 1576, by Henry Hudson in 1610–11, and by many others. It was not until much later in the seventeenth century that the English began to realize that the value of the wilderness adjacent to Hudson Bay might lie in its natural resources as well as in its proximity to the Orient. But it took a squabble among the French in Canada to spark action on the part of the English. Pierre-Esprit Radisson and Médart Chouart, Sieur des Groseilliers, had explored vast tracts of territory northwest of the Great Lakes, and had confirmed that the area was rich in furs. But they were refused a licence to trade in furs both by the Governor of New France and, on appeal, by the authorities in France. In response they made contacts among the English with a view to obtaining permission from the English to trade in furs via Hudson Bay rather than by the French-controlled Great Lakes. An Englishman, Colonel George Cartwright, eventually took up their cause and presented them to King Charles II. In due course Prince Rupert, cousin of the King, became involved in the project. Radisson and Groseilliers set out on an initial voyage with two ships, the *Eaglet* and the *Nonsuch*; the *Eaglet* suffered storm damage and was forced to return early, but the *Nonsuch* returned to England in 1669 laden with furs, and the following year a charter for the Hudson's Bay Company was granted; the charter is of as much interest for what it says about other peoples as for what it says about territory and trade. At one time the territory controlled by the Company encompassed much of what is now the United States and Canada.

Charles the Second, By the Grace of God King of England, Scotland, France, and Ireland. Defender of the Faith &c.

To all to whom these presents shall come, greeting.

Whereas our dear and entirely beloved cousin Prince Rupert Count Paladin of the Rhine, Duke of Bavaria and Cumberland &c, Christopher Duke of Albemarle, William Earle of Craven, Henry Lord Arlington, Anthony Lord Ashley,... Sir John Robinson, and Sir Robert Viner; Knights and Baronets Sir Peter Colliton Baronet, Sir Edward Hungerford Knight of the Bath, Sir Paul Neele Knight, Sir John Griffith and Sir Phillip Carteret Knights, James Hayes, John Kirke, Francis Millington, William Prettyman, John Fenn Esquire and John Portman Citizen and Goldsmith of London, have at their own great cost and charge undertaken an expedition for Hudson's Bay in the northwest part of America for the discovery of a new passage into the South Sea and for the finding some trade for furs, minerals, and other considerable commodities and by such their undertaking have already made such discoveries as do encourage them to proceed further in pursuance of their said design by means whereof there may probably arise very great advantage to us and our kingdom;

And whereas the said undertakers for their further encouragement in the said design have humbly besought us to incorporate them and grant unto them and their successors the sole trade and commerce of all those seas, straits, bays, rivers, lakes, creeks, and sounds in whatsoever latitude they shall be that lie within the the entrance of the straits commonly called Hudson's Straits, together with all the lands, countries, and territories upon the coasts and confines of the seas, straits, bays, rivers, lakes, creeks, and sounds aforesaid which are not now actually possessed by any of our subjects or by the subjects of any other Christian prince or state;

Now know ye that we … do give, grant, ratify and confirm unto our said cousin Prince Rupert, [same names as above repeated] that they and such others as shall be admitted into the said society as is hereafter expressed shall be one body corporate and politic in deed and in name by the name of the Governor and Company of Adventurers of England trading into Hudson's Bay, … really and fully forever, for us, our heirs and successors; do make, ordain, constitute, establish, confirm, and declare by these presents and that by the same name of Governor and Company of Adventurers of England Trading into Hudson's Bay they shall have perpetual succession.

We do assign, nominate, constitute, and make our said cousin Prince Rupert to be the first and present governor of the said Company and to continue in the said office from the date of these presents until the tenth of November next. Then following if he the said Prince Rupert shall so long live and so until a new Governor be chosen by the said Company in form hereafter expressed.…

We have given, granted, and confirmed, and by these presents for us, our heirs and successors, do give, grant, and confirm unto the said Governor and Company and their successors the sole trade and commerce of all those seas, straits, bays, rivers, lakes, creeks, and sounds in whatsoever latitude they shall be that lie within the entrance of the straits commonly called Hudson's Straits, together with all the lands and territories upon the countries, coasts, and confines of the seas, bays, lakes, rivers, creeks, and sounds aforesaid that are not already actually possessed by or granted to any of our subjects or possessed by the subjects of any other Christian prince or state.

With the fishing of all sorts of fish, whales, sturgeons, and all other royal fishes in the seas, bays, inlets, and rivers within the premises and the fish therein, taken together with the royalty of the sea upon the coasts with the limits aforesaid, and all mines royal as well discovered as not discovered of gold, silver, gems, and precious stones to be found or discovered within the territories, limits, and places aforesaid. And that the said land be from henceforth reckoned and reputed as one of our plantations or colonies in America, called Rupert's Land.

And further we do by these presents for us our heirs and successors make, create and constitute the said Governor and Company for the time being and their successors the true and absolute lords and proprietors of the same territory limits and places aforesaid.…

Saving the faith and allegiance due to be performed to us our heirs and successors as aforesaid and that the said Governor and Company shall have liberty full power and authority to appoint and establish governors and all other officers to govern them. And that the Governor and his council of the several and respective places where the said Company shall have plantations, forts, factories,[1] colonies, or places of trade within any the countries, lands or territories hereby granted may have power to judge all persons belonging to the said Governor and Company or that shall live under them in all causes, whether civil or criminal, according to the laws of this kingdom, and to execute justice accordingly.

And by these presents for us our heirs and successors we do give and grant unto the said Governor and Company and their successors free liberty and licence in case they conceive it necessary to send either ships of war, men, or ammunition unto any of their plantations, forts, factories, or places of trade aforesaid for the security and defence of the same, and to choose commanders and officers over them, and to give them power and authority by commission under their common seal, or otherwise to continue or make peace or war with any prince or people whatsoever that are not Christians in any places where the said company shall have any plantations, forts, or factories or adjacent thereunto as shall be most for the advantage and benefit of the said Governor and Company and of their trade and also to right and recompense themselves upon the goods, estates, or people of those parts by whom the said Governor and Company shall sustain any injury, loss, or damage, or upon any other people whatsoever that shall any way contrary to the intent of these presents

[1] *factories* Places where mercantile activity was carried out (not, in the case of Hudson's Bay Company outposts, centers of manufacturing activity).

interrupt, wrong, or injure them in their said trade within the said places, territories, and limits granted by this Charter.

In witness whereof we have caused these our letters to be made patents,

Witness ourself at Westminster the second day of May in the two and twentieth year of our reign.

By Writ of Privy Seal

from Mary Rowlandson, *A Narrative of the Captivity and Restoration of Mrs. Mary Rowlandson* (1682)

Like other English settlers, the Puritans had few qualms about taking land from the native North American peoples and calling it their own. Puritan colonizers arrived in what became the Massachusetts Bay Colony in 1629, and numerous groups followed in the decades between then and the 1675 attack during which Rowlandson was captured. The English intruders faced stiffer and more persistent resistance than did English colonizers in many other areas along the east coast of North America, but by the 1670s the English had for the most part gained the upper hand. The Pequot attacks on English settlements of 1675 were among the last such episodes; the English sold many Pequot (primarily women and children) into slavery in Bermuda, and killed many more. Pequot reservations were finally established in the nineteenth century; today approximately one thousand Pequot survive. Rowlandson, for her part, was ransomed after seven weeks of captivity, and lived well into her eighties; she died in 1711.

On the tenth of February, 1675, came the Indians with great number upon Lancaster. Their first coming was about sun-rising. Hearing the noise of some guns, we looked out; several houses were burning, and the smoke ascending to Heaven. There were five persons taken in one house, the father and the mother, and a sucking child, they knocked on the head; the other two they took, and carried away alive. There were two others, who, being out of their garrison upon some occasion, were set upon; one was knocked on the head, the other escaped. Another there was, who, running along, was shot and wounded, and fell down; he begged of them his life, promising them money (as they told me), but they would not hearken to him, but knocked him on the head, stripped him naked, and split open his bowels. Another, seeing many of the Indians about his barn, ventured and went out, but was quickly shot down. There were three others belonging to the same garrison who were killed. The Indians, getting up upon the roof of the barn, had advantage to shoot down upon them over their fortification. Thus these murderous wretches went on, burning and destroying before them.

At length they came and beset our own house, and quickly it was the dolefullest[1] day that ever mine eyes saw. The house stood upon the edge of a hill; some of the Indians got behind the hill, others into the barn, and others behind any thing that would shelter them; from all which places they shot against the house, so that the bullets seemed to fly like hail; and quickly they wounded one man among us, then another, and then a third. About two hours (according to my observation in that amazing time) they had been about the house before they could prevail to fire it (which they did with flax and hemp, which they brought out of the barn, and there being no defense about the house, only two flankers, at two opposite corners, and one of them not finished). They fired it once, and one ventured out and quenched it; but they quickly fired it again, and that took. Now is that dreadful hour come that I have often heard of (in the time of the war, as it was the case of others) but now mine eyes see it. Some in our house were fighting for their lives, others wallowing in their blood; the house on fire over our heads, and the bloody heathen ready to knock us on the head if we stirred out. Now might we hear mothers and children crying out for themselves and one another, *Lord, what shall we do?* Then I took my children (and one of my sister's, hers) to go forth and leave the house; but as soon as we came to the door and appeared, the Indians shot so thick that the bullets rattled against the house as if one had taken an handful of stones and threw them; so that we were fain to give back.... The bullets flying thick, one went through my side, and the same (as would seem) through the bowels and hand of my dear child in my arms. One of my eldest sister's children (named William) had then

[1] *dolefullest* Saddest.

his leg broken, which the Indians perceiving, they knocked him on the head. Thus were we butchered by those merciless heathen, standing amazed, with the blood running down to our heels.

My elder sister, being yet in the house, and seeing those woeful sights, the infidels hauling mothers one way and children another, and some wallowing in their blood, and her elder son telling her that (her son) William was dead, and myself was wounded; she said, *Lord, let me die with them!*, which was no sooner said but she was struck with a bullet, and fell down dead over the threshold. I hope she is reaping the fruit of her good labours, being faithful to the service of God in her place. In her younger years she lay under much trouble upon spiritual accounts, till it pleased God to make that precious Scripture take hold of her heart, 2 Cor. 12.9, *And he said unto me, My grace is sufficient for thee.* More than twenty years after, I have heard her tell how sweet and comfortable that place was to her.

But to return: the Indians laid hold of us, pulling me one way and the children another, and said, *Come, go along with us.* I told them they would kill me. They answered, *If I were willing to go along with them, they would not hurt me.* I had often before this said, that if the Indians should come, I should choose rather to be killed by them than taken alive; but when it came to the trial my mind changed; their glittering weapons so daunted my spirit, that I chose rather to go along with those (as I may say) ravenous bears, than that moment to end my days. And that I may the better declare what happened to me during that grievous captivity, I shall particularly speak of the several removes we had up and down the wilderness.

The first remove: Now away we must go with those barbarous creatures, with our bodies wounded and bleeding, and our hearts no less than our bodies. About a mile we went that night; up upon a hill, within sight of the town, where they intended to lodge. There was hard by[1] a vacant house (deserted by the English before, for fear of the Indians) I asked them whether I might not lodge in the house that night to which they answered, *What, will you love English-men still?* This was the dolefullest night that ever my eyes saw: oh the roaring, and singing, and dancing, and yelling of those black creatures in the night, which made the place a lively resemblance of hell! And as miserable was the waste that was there made of horses, cattle, sheep, swine, calves, lambs, roasting pigs, and fowls (which they had plundered in the town), some roasting, some lying and burning, and some boiling, to feed our merciless enemies; who were joyful enough, though we were disconsolate....

There remained nothing to me but one poor wounded babe, and it seemed at present worse than death that it was in such a pitiful condition, bespeaking compassion, and I had no refreshing for it, nor suitable things to revive it. Little do many think what is the savageness and brutishness of this barbarous enemy, even those that seem to profess more than others among them, when the English have fallen into their hands....

The second remove: But now (the next morning) I must turn my back upon the town, and travel with them into the vast and desolate wilderness, I know not whither. It is not my tongue or pen can express the sorrows of my heart and bitterness of my spirit that I had at this departure. But God was with me in a wonderful manner, carrying me along, and bearing up my spirit, that it did not quite fail. One of the Indians carried my poor wounded babe upon a horse: it went moaning all along, *I shall die, I shall die!* I went on foot after it, with sorrow that cannot be expressed. At length I took it off the horse, and carried it in my arms, till my strength failed, and I fell down with it. Then they set me upon a horse, with my wounded child in my lap; and there being no furniture[2] upon the horseback; as we were going down a steep hill, we both fell over the horse's head, at which they, like inhuman creatures, laughed, and rejoiced to see it, though I thought we should there have ended our days, as overcome with so many difficulties. But the Lord renewed my strength still, and carried me along, that I might see more of his power, yea, so much that I could never have thought of, had I not experienced it.

After this it quickly began to snow; and when night came on they stopped; and now down I must sit in the snow (by a little fire and a few boughs behind me), with my sick child in my lap; and calling much for water, being now (through the wound) fallen into a violent fever (my own wound also growing so stiff that I could

[1] *hard by* Nearby.

[2] *furniture* Covering (such as a saddle).

scarce sit down or rise up). Yet so it must be, that I must sit all this cold winter night upon the cold snowy ground, with my sick child in my arms, looking that every hour would be the last of its life; and having no Christian friend near me, either to comfort or help me. Oh, I may see the wonderful power of God, that my spirit did not utterly sink under my affliction! Still the Lord upheld me with his gracious and merciful Spirit, and we were both alive to see the light of the next morning....

The fourth remove: And now must I part with that little company that I had. Here I parted from my daughter Mary (whom I never saw again till I saw her in Dorchester, returned from captivity), and from four little cousins and neighbours, some of which I never saw afterward; the Lord only knows the end of them. Amongst them also was that poor woman before mentioned, who came to a sad end, as some of the company told me in my travel: she having much grief upon her spirit about her miserable condition, being so near her time, she would be often asking the Indians to let her go home; they, not being willing to that, and yet vexed with her importunity, gathered a great company together about her, and stripped her naked, and set her in the midst of them; and when they had sung and danced about her (in their hellish manner) as long as they pleased; they knocked her on the head, and the child in her arms with her. When they had done that they made a fire, and put them both into it; and told the other children that were with them, that if they attempted to go home, they would serve them in like manner. The children said she did not shed one tear, but prayed all the while. But, to return to my own journey: we travelled about half a day, or a little more, and came to a desolate place in the wilderness, where there were no wigwams or inhabitants before. We came about the middle of the afternoon to this place; cold, and wet, and snowy, and hungry, and weary, and no refreshing (for man) but the cold ground to sit on, and our poor Indian cheer....

The fifth remove: The occasion (as I thought) of their moving at this time was the English army, its being near and following them; for they went as if they had gone for their lives for some considerable way; and then they made a stop, and chose out some of their stoutest men, and sent them back to hold the English army in play whilst the rest escaped; and then, like Jehu,[1] they marched on furiously, with their old and with their young: some carried their old decrepit mothers, some carried one and some another. Four of them carried a great Indian upon a bier; but going through a thick wood with him they were hindered, and could make no haste; whereupon they took him upon their backs, and carried him, one at a time, till we came to Bacquaug River....

The first week of my being among them I hardly ate anything; the second week I found my stomach grow very faint for want of something; and yet 'twas very hard to get down their filthy trash; but the third week (though I could think how formerly my stomach would turn against this or that, and I could starve and die before I could eat such things, yet) they were pleasant and savory to my taste. I was at this time knitting a pair of white cotton stockings for my mistress; and I had not yet wrought[2] upon the Sabbath-day. When the Sabbath came, they bade me go to work; I told them it was Sabbath-day, and desired them to let me rest, and told them I would do as much more tomorrow; to which they answered me, they would break my face.

And here I cannot but take notice of the strange providence of God in preserving the heathen. They were many hundreds, old and young, some sick and some lame; many had papooses[3] at their backs, the greatest number (at this time with us) were squaws;[4] and they travelled with all they had, bag and baggage, and yet they got over this river aforesaid; and on Monday they set their wigwams on fire, and away they went: on that very day came the English army after them to this river, and saw the smoke of their wigwams; and yet this river put a stop to them. God did not give them courage or activity to go after us; we were not ready for so great a

[1] *like Jehu* Extremely fast. The allusion is to 2 Kings 9.20: "the driving is like the driving of Jehu, the son of Nimshi, for he driveth furiously."

[2] *wrought* Made anything.

[3] *papooses* Native North American babies (now generally regarded as an offensive term).

[4] *squaws* Native North American women; specifically wives (now acknowledged to be a derogatory term).

mercy as victory and deliverance; if we had been, God would have found out a way for the English to have passed this river, as well as for the Indians, with their squaws and children, and all their luggage. *Oh that my people had harkened to me, and Israel had walked in my ways, I should soon have subdued their enemies, and turned my hand against their adversaries, Psalm* 81 13, 14....

The sixth remove: On Monday (as I said) they set their wigwams on fire and went away. It was a cold morning, and before us there was a great brook with ice on it; some waded through it, up to the knees and higher, but others went till they came to a beaver dam, and I amongst them, where through the good providence of God, I did not wet my foot. I went along that day, mourning and lamenting, leaving farther my own country, and traveling into a vast and howling wilderness, and I understood something of Lot's wife's temptation, when she looked back.[1]

We came that day to a great swamp, by the side of which we took up our lodging that night. When I came to the brow of the hill, that looked toward the swamp, I thought we had come to a great Indian town (though there were none but our own company). The Indians were as thick as the trees: it seemed as if there had been a thousand hatchets going at once. If one looked before one there was nothing but Indians, and behind one, nothing but Indians, and so on either hand, I myself in the midst, and no Christian soul near me, and yet how hath the Lord preserved me in safety? Oh the experience that I have had of the goodness of God, to me and mine!...

The nineteenth remove: My master had three squaws; living sometimes with one, and sometimes with another. One was this old squaw at whose wigwam I was, and with whom my master had been those three weeks. Another was Wettimore, with whom I had lived and served all this while. A severe and proud dame she was, bestowing every day in dressing herself near as much time as any of the gentry of the land; powdering her hair and painting her face, going with her necklaces, with jewels in her ears, and bracelets upon her hands. When she had dressed herself, her work was to make girdles of wampum[2] and beads. The third squaw was a younger one, by whom he had two papooses. By that time I was refreshed by the old squaw, with whom my master was, Wettimore's maid came to call me home, at which I fell a weeping; then the old squaw told me, to encourage me, that if I wanted victuals I should come to her, and that I should lie there in her wigwam. Then I went with the maid, and quickly came again and lodged there. The squaw laid a mat under me and a good rug over me; the first time I had any such kindness showed me. I understood that Wettimore thought that if she should let me go and serve with the old squaw she would be in danger to lose not only my service, but the redemption-pay also. And I was not a little glad to hear this; being by it raised in my hopes that in God's due time there would be an end of this sorrowful hour. Then came an Indian, and asked me to knit him three pair of stockings, for which I had a hat and a silk handkerchief. Then another asked me to make her a shift, for which she gave me an apron.

Then came Tom and Peter, with the second letter from the council about the captives. Though they were Indians, I got them by the hand, and burst out into tears; my heart was so full that I could not speak to them. But recovering myself, I asked them how my husband did, and all my friends and acquaintance. They said, they were well, but very melancholy. They brought me two biscuits and a pound of tobacco. The tobacco I quickly gave away; when it was all gone, one asked me to give him a pipe of tobacco; I told him all was gone; then began he to rant and to threaten; I told him when my husband came I would give him some. "Hang him, rogue," (says he), "I will knock out his brains if he comes here." And then again, in the same breath, they would say, that if there should come an hundred without guns they would do them no hurt. So unstable and like madmen they were, so that, fearing the worst, I durst not send to my husband, though there were some thoughts of his coming to redeem and fetch me, not knowing what might follow; for there was little more to trust them than to the master they served.

When the letter was come, the Saggamores met to

[1] *Lot's wife's temptation ... looked back* According to the story recounted in Genesis 19.15–23, God allowed Lot and his family to escape from Sodom and Gomorrah as those cities were being destroyed, saying, "'Escape for thy life; look not behind thee, neither stay thou in all the plain; escape to the mountain, lest thou be consumed.'... But his wife looked back from behind him, and she became a pillar of salt."

[2] *wampum* Beads made from shells, used as currency by various North American Native peoples.

consult about the captives, and called me to them to enquire how much my husband would give to redeem me. When I came, I sat down among them, as I was wont to do, as their manner is. Then they bade me stand up, and said, they were the general court. They bid me speak what I thought he would give. Now, knowing that all we had was destroyed by the Indians, I was in a great strait. I thought if I should speak of but little it would be slighted, and hinder the matter; if of a great sum, I knew not where it would be procured; yet at a venture, I said *twenty pounds,* yet desired them to take less. But they would not hear of that, but sent that message to Boston, that for *twenty pounds* I should be redeemed....

But to return again to my going home, where we may see a remarkable change of Providence. At first they were all against it, except my husband would come for me; but afterwards they assented to it, and seemed much to rejoice in it; some asking me to send them some bread, others some tobacco, others shaking me by the hand, offering me a hood and scarf to ride in; not one moving hand or tongue against it. Thus hath the Lord answered my poor desires, and the many requests of others put up unto God for me. In my travels an Indian came to me, and told me, if I were willing, he and his squaw would run away, and go home along with me. I told him, no, I was not willing to run away, but desired to wait God's time, that I might go home quietly, and without fear. And now God hath granted me my desire. Oh the wonderful power of God that I have seen, and the experiences that I have had! I have been in the midst of those roaring lions and savage bears, that feared neither God nor man, nor the Devil, by night and day, alone and in company, sleeping all sorts together; and yet not one of them ever offered the least abuse or unchastity to me in word or action....

The twenty pounds, the price of my redemption, was raised by some Boston gentlewomen, and M. Usher, whose bounty and religious charity I would not forget to make mention of. Then Mr. Thomas Shepherd of Charlestown received us into his house, where we continued eleven weeks; and a father and mother they were unto us. And many more tender-hearted friends we met with in that place. We were now in the midst of love, yet not without much and frequent heaviness of heart for our poor children and other relations who were still in affliction.

The week following, after my coming in, the governor and council sent forth to the Indians again, and that not without success; for they brought in my sister and Goodwife Kettle; their not knowing where our children were was a sore trial to us still, and yet we were not without secret hopes that we should see them again.... About this time the council had ordered a day of public thanksgiving; though I thought I had still cause of mourning; and being unsettled in our minds, we thought we would ride toward the eastward, to see if we could hear anything concerning our children. And as we were riding along (God is the wise disposer of all things) between Ipswich and Rowly we met with Mr. William Hubbard, who told us our son Joseph was come in to Major Waldrens, and another with him, which was my sister's son.... Now we were between them, the one on the east, and the other on the west; our son being nearest we went to him first, to Portsmouth; where we met with him, and with the Major also, who told us he had done what he could, but could not redeem him under seven pounds, which the good people thereabouts were pleased to pay. The Lord reward the Major and all the rest, though unknown to me, for their labour of love. My sister's son was redeemed for four pounds, which the Council gave order for the payment of. Having now received one of our children, we hastened towards the other; going back through Newbury, my husband preached there on the Sabbath-day, for which they rewarded him manifold....

Our family being now gathered together (those of us that were living), the South Church in Boston hired an house for us; then we removed from Mr. Shepherd's (those cordial friends) and went to Boston, where we continued about three quarters of a year; still the Lord went along with us, and provided graciously for us. I thought it somewhat strange to set up housekeeping with bare walls; but, as Solomon says, *Money answers all things,* and that we had, through the benevolence of Christian friends, some in this town and some in that, and others, and some from England, that in a little time we might look and see the house furnished with love....
—1682

"View of the New World of America, Newly Described," a map from the London 1606 edition of *Theatrum Orbis Terrarum* ("Theatre of the entire World"), an atlas prepared by Abraham Ortelius.

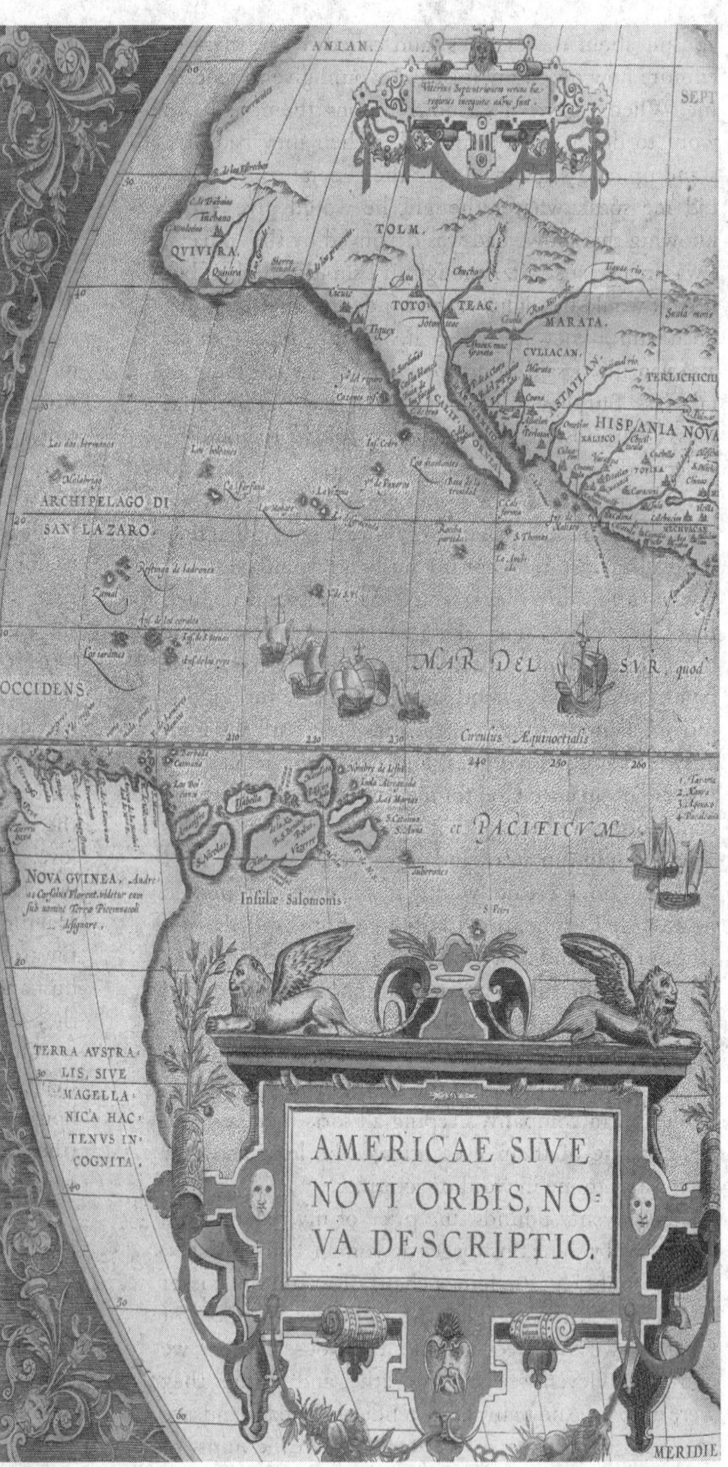

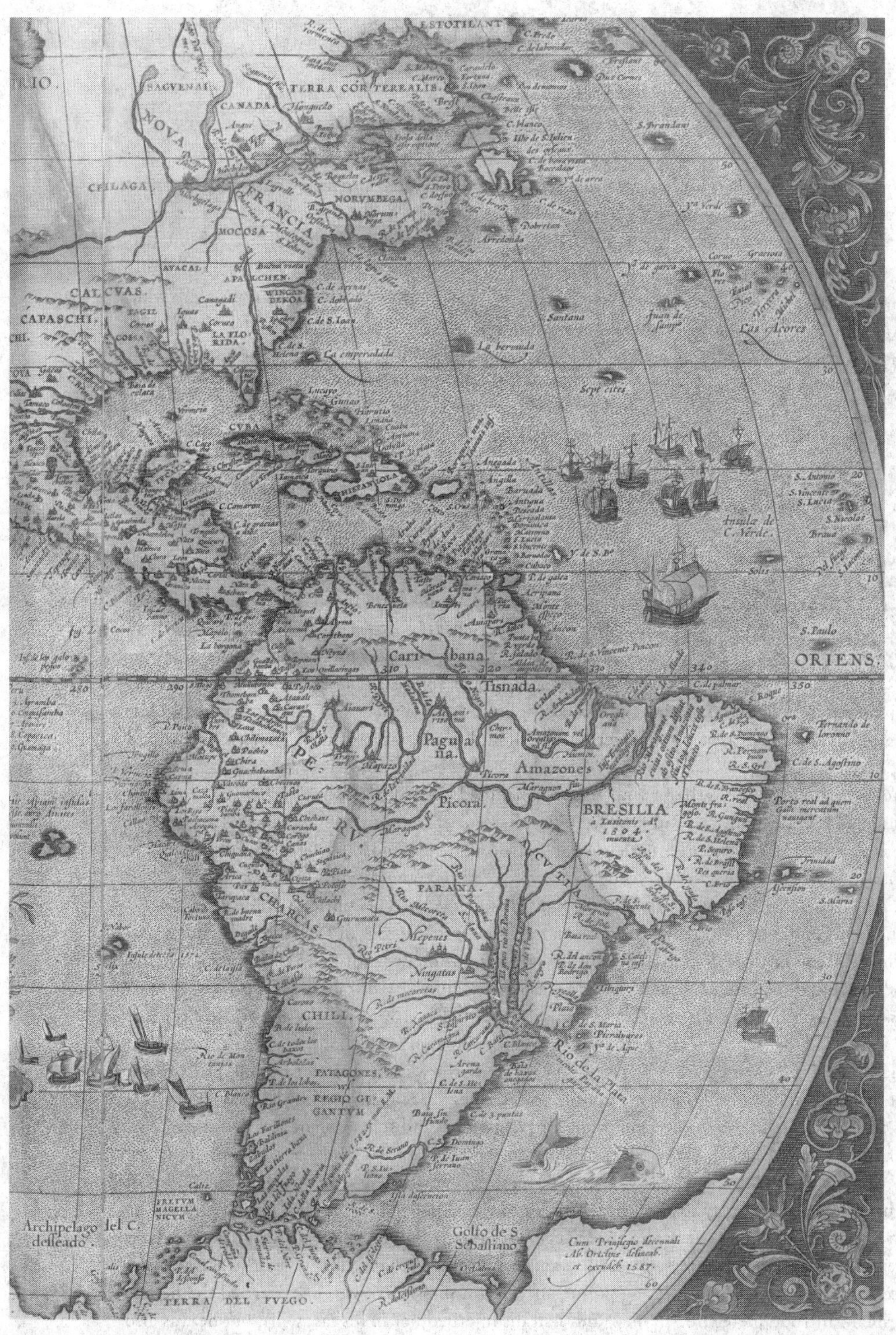
TERRA CORTEREALIS
SAGVENAI
CANADA
NOVA FRANCIA
CHILAGA
NORVMBEGA
MOCOSA
CAPASCHI
LA FLORIDA
Las Acores
CVBA
Insula de C. Verde
ORIENS
Caribana
Tisnada
Amazones
Picora
PERV
BRESILIA
PARANA
CHARCAS
CHILI
PATAGONES
REGIO GIGANTVM
Rio de la Plata
Archipelago del C. desseado
Golfo de S. Sebastiano
Cum Privilegio decennali Ab. Ortelius delineab. et excudeb. 1587
TERRA DEL FVEGO

Francis Bacon

1561 – 1626

Philosopher, essayist, jurist, politician, naturalist, classicist, historian, and utopian fantasist, Francis Bacon had an extraordinary capacity to range throughout the world of learning while keeping a focus on the practical uses of knowledge, able not only to master the traditions of the past but also to combine, manipulate, and consolidate old concepts into fruitful new ideas. His essays, memorable distillations of his wide reading and worldly experience, are still widely read and enjoyed. His philosophical writings, in both Latin and English, aim at nothing less than the reformation of humanity's approach to understanding nature and society. Ironically, it can be hard for us now, reading from the other side of the revolution he helped accelerate, to appreciate the full impact of Bacon's philosophy. He did not fully develop what some call "the scientific method" or anticipate the crucial role of mathematics in later scientific developments. What he did accomplish, in his philosophy and in his often terse style (deliberately free, usually, from flights of metaphor or fancy), was to anchor the mind more firmly in experience and to lend momentum to a new sense of worldly inquiry and expectation. It would be unfair to hold him responsible, as some have done, for the dangers and excesses inherent in modern science and its assumptions; indeed, in *The New Atlantis* Bacon himself hints presciently that increased power over nature should be accompanied by increased love and gratitude.

"I had rather studied books than men," Bacon concluded late in his life, but his origins made vast ambitions in both the political and intellectual spheres seem almost inevitable. His father, Sir Nicholas Bacon, was Lord Keeper of the Great Seal, one of the most powerful ministers in the Elizabethan government. His mother, Ann Cook, was an erudite and devout Calvinist who instilled in her son a deep sense of purpose and a passion for knowledge. Cambridge student at twelve, Assistant to the Ambassador to France at sixteen, barrister and Member of Parliament by the age of twenty-three, Bacon achieved much early, but his father's untimely death in 1579 left him short of funds and without direct influence at court. He was not well liked by Elizabeth, and it was not until the accession of James I that his star began to rise. Knighted in 1603, he was appointed Solicitor General in 1607, Attorney General in 1613, Privy Councillor in 1616, Lord Keeper of the Seal in 1617, and finally Lord Chancellor in 1618, acquiring along the way the titles of Baron Verulam and Viscount St. Albans. "By indignities men come to dignities," Bacon wrote in his essay "Of Great Place"—conscious, no doubt, of the reputation for sycophancy and scheming he had acquired in his quest for power and position—and "the standing is slippery." In 1621, Bacon lost his political footing. Caught on the wrong side of a dispute between Parliament and his ally the Duke of Buckingham, he pleaded guilty to accepting bribes and was expelled for life from public office. The bribes do not seem to have dulled Bacon's keen legal mind: John Aubrey could report fifty years later that "there are fewer of his decrees reversed than of any other Chancellor." Bacon was variously denounced as a spendthrift, a calculating politician, and a homosexual who had married the heiress Alice Barnham in 1606 merely for money (and had disinherited her in his last will), but he was also respected as an able administrator and advisor and a consummate orator whose audiences, Ben Jonson testified, were unwilling to accept that his speeches must end.

Until his death in 1626 (reputedly from a chill caught while investigating the preservative properties of snow), Bacon concentrated on expanding and refining his intellectual project. A third edition of his *Essays* appeared in 1625 with a new subtitle, *Counsels, Civil and Moral.* Bacon was the first to import the term "essai" into English from Montaigne for this new form, but as the subtitle indicates, his orientation was more public and impersonal than Montaigne's, based more in the tradition of the commonplace book and the manual of conduct than in discursive meditation. The first edition of 1597 was composed of terse, aphoristic observations organized under ten topics. The final edition of 1625 had grown to 58 essays. The overall style is one of brevity, curtness, and sagacity, with fluid transitions between subjects. Bacon employs to great effect aphoristic devices such as observations in parallel series of twos and threes, and he is fond of antitheses, "the case exaggerated both ways, with the utmost force of the wit," which have the effect of encouraging a balanced consideration of the issues by the reader. A notable exception is "Of Gardens," in which Bacon, an avid gardener, indulges in a didactic and uncharacteristically opinionated exhortation concerning his lifelong passion.

To the end of his life Bacon pursued another passion, his grand design for the renewal of knowledge, the Great Instauration, which he had already outlined in the preface to his aphoristic Latin treatise *Novum Organum* (New Instrument) in 1620. Only a few of the many volumes he conceived for this project were actually completed, though others exist in partial form, or as prefaces or proposals. He wrote many of these in Latin, still considered the international language of scholarship. Bacon now expanded and translated *The Advancement of Learning*, which had appeared in English in 1605, as *De Augmentis*. Its vital innovation was a reclassification of knowledge so as to separate theology from natural philosophy. Bacon was no atheist, but he insisted that the deductive, syllogistic methods applied by the Aristotelian Schoolmen to theological speculation would not succeed in unlocking nature's secrets. Rather than perceiving the natural world through the lens of unproven axioms and generalizations, we must begin with nature itself, gathering facts, sorting and analyzing them using inductive methods, and only then deriving principles which may be used to enhance further investigation: "Nature cannot be commanded except by being obeyed."

In fact, the pure induction favored by Bacon did not suffice for fruitful experimental investigation; the scientific method still needs room for intuitive guesses and intermediate deduction. But if Bacon's methodology and philosophy was not in accord with twenty-first century practices, he was certainly rhetorically skillful and inspiring on the topic to a degree unmatched by his contemporaries. His *New Atlantis*, a fragment written in 1610 and published after his death in 1626, imagines in vivid and beguiling detail a utopian community of dynamic technical and spiritual progress founded upon bureaucratic and co-operative science. The power of Bacon's prose fired the imagination of seventeenth-century English readers and sparked widespread public interest in scientific undertakings. In 1662, the Royal Society, the first concrete realization of Bacon's dream of a scientific bureaucracy, acclaimed him as their model and prophet; a century later, Diderot adopted Bacon's classification of learning and dedicated the Encyclopedia to him, as did Kant his *Critique of Pure Reason*. Bacon's ambition, announced in *The Advancement of Learning*, to "ring a bell to call other wits together," has been fulfilled.

⌘⌘⌘

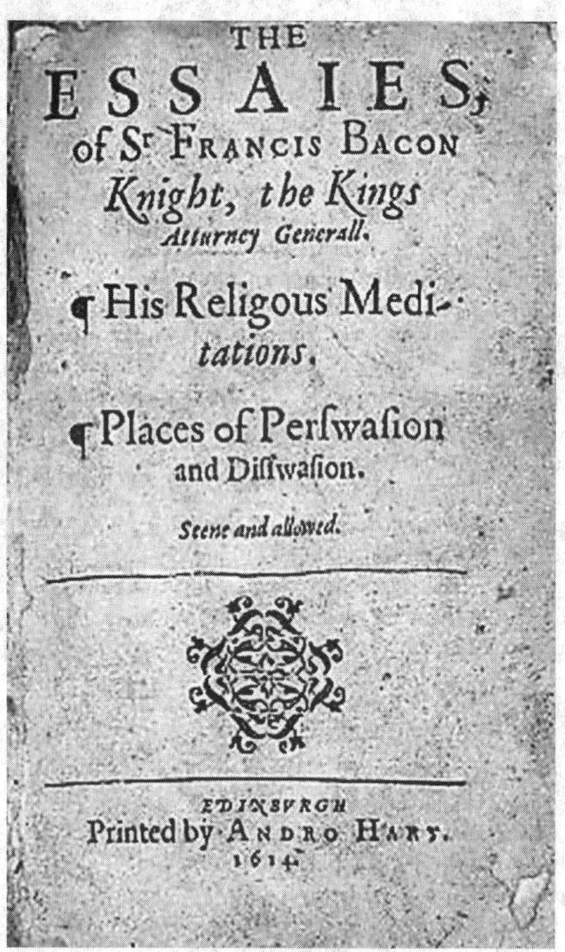

THE
ESSAIES,
of Sr FRANCIS BACON
Knight, the Kings
Atturney Generall.

¶ His Religous Medi-
tations.

¶ Places of Perſwaſion
and Diſſwaſion.

Seene and allowed.

EDINBVRGH
Printed by ANDRO HART.
1614.

Title page of the 1614 edition of Bacon's *Essays.*

from *Essays*

OF TRUTH

"What is truth?" said jesting Pilate,[1] and would not stay for an answer. Certainly there be that delight in giddiness, and count it a bondage to fix a belief; affecting free-will in thinking, as well as in acting. And though the sects of philosophers of that kind[2] be gone, yet there remain certain discoursing wits, which are of the same veins, though there be not so much blood in them, as was in those of the ancients. But it is not only the difficulty and labor which men take in finding out of truth, nor again that when it is found it imposeth upon men's thoughts, that doth bring lies in favor; but a natural though corrupt love of the lie itself. One of the later school of the Grecians examineth the matter,[3] and is at a stand to think what should be in it, that men should love lies, where neither they make for pleasure, as with poets, nor for advantage, as with the merchant; but for the lie's sake. But I cannot tell: this same truth is a naked and open day-light, that doth not show the masks and mummeries and triumphs[4] of the world half so stately and daintily as candle-lights. Truth may perhaps come to the price of a pearl, that showeth best by day; but it will not rise to the price of a diamond or carbuncle,[5] that showeth best in varied lights. A mixture of a lie doth ever add pleasure.

Doth any man doubt, that if there were taken out of men's minds vain opinions, flattering hopes, false valuations, imaginations as one would, and the like, but it would leave the minds of a number of men poor shrunken things, full of melancholy and indisposition,[6] and unpleasing to themselves? One of the fathers, in

[1] *What is truth* Cf. John 18.38; *Pilate* Pontius Pilate, Roman governor of Judea from 26–36 CE, who presided over Christ's trial.

[2] *of that kind* I.e., Skepticism, a mid-fourth century BCE philosophy positing the uncertainty of all knowledge.

[3] *One of … matter* See the *Philopseudes* (*The Lover of Lies*) by Lucian of Samosata (c. 120–180 CE).

[4] *masks* I.e., masques, elaborate court pageants; *mummeries* Popular plays or ceremonies; *triumphs* Ceremonial processions of victorious military commanders and their forces.

[5] *carbuncle* Ruby.

[6] *melancholy* Brooding sadness; in Bacon's day the word could also denote neurosis; *indisposition* Hesitancy or reluctance.

great severity, called poesy *vinum daemonum*,[1] because it filleth the imagination; and yet it is but with the shadow of a lie. But it is not the lie that passeth through the mind, but the lie that sinketh in and settleth in it, that doth the hurt; such as we spake of before. But howsoever these things are thus in men's depraved judgments and affections, yet truth, which only doth judge itself, teacheth that the inquiry of truth, which is the love-making, or wooing of it, the knowledge of truth, which is the presence of it, and the belief of truth, which is the enjoying of it, is the sovereign good of human nature.

The first creature of God, in the works of the days, was the light of the sense; the last, was the light of reason; and His sabbath work[2] ever since, is the illumination of his Spirit. First He breathed light upon the face of the matter or chaos; then He breathed light into the face of man; and still He breatheth and inspireth light into the face of His chosen. The poet that beautified the sect that was otherwise inferior to the rest[3] saith yet excellently well: "It is a pleasure to stand upon the shore, and to see ships tossed upon the sea; a pleasure to stand in the window of a castle, and to see a battle and the adventures thereof below: but no pleasure is comparable to the standing upon the vantage ground of Truth" (a hill not to be commanded, and where the air is always clear and serene), "and to see the errors, and wanderings, and mists, and tempests, in the vale below";[4] so always that this prospect be with pity, and not with swelling or pride. Certainly, it is heaven upon earth to have a man's mind move in charity, rest in Providence, and turn upon the poles of truth.

[1] *One of … fathers* St. Augustine (354–430 CE) or St. Jerome (340?–420 CE); *vinum daemonum* Latin: wine of devils. This reference likely combines passages from St. Jerome's Epistle 146 and St. Augustine's *Confessions* 1.16.26.

[2] *sabbath work* God's work on the seventh ("sabbath") day, here imagined as the ongoing period of divine rest after the initial six days' work of creation. Bacon's paradox is that God "works" daily even if rigorous Puritans objected to all labor on the Sabbath.

[3] *The poet* Lucretius (c. 99–c. 55 BCE), Roman poet who expressed the Epicurean world view in his *De Rerum Natura* (*On the Nature of Things*); *the sect … rest* The Epicureans, philosophers who taught that the highest pursuit involved avoiding pain and pursuing pleasures, which they identified with the practice of virtue.

[4] *"It is … below"* Cf. Lucretius's *De Rerum Natura* 2.1–13.

To pass from theological, and philosophical truth to the truth of civil business; it will be acknowledged even by those that practise it not that clear and round[5] dealing is the honor of man's nature; and that mixture of falsehood is like alloy in coin of gold and silver, which may make the metal work the better, but it embaseth[6] it. For these winding and crooked courses are the goings of the serpent, which goeth basely upon the belly, and not upon the feet. There is no vice that doth so cover a man with shame as to be found false and perfidious. And therefore Montaigne[7] saith prettily, when he inquired the reason, why the word of the lie should be such a disgrace and such an odious charge? Saith he, "If it be well weighed, to say that a man lieth, is as much to say, as that he is brave towards God and a coward towards men."[8] For a lie faces God, and shrinks from man. Surely the wickedness of falsehood and breach of faith cannot possibly be so highly expressed, as in that it shall be the last peal to call the judgments of God upon the generations of men; it being foretold, that when Christ cometh, "He shall not find faith upon the earth."[9]

Of Marriage and Single Life

He that hath wife and children hath given hostages to fortune; for they are impediments to great enterprises, either of virtue or mischief. Certainly the best works, and of greatest merit for the public, have proceeded from the unmarried or childless men; which both in affection and means have married and endowed the public. Yet it were great reason that those that have children should have greatest care of future times; unto which they know they must transmit their dearest pledges. Some there are, who though they lead a single life, yet their thoughts do end with themselves, and account future times impertinences.[10] Nay, there are

[5] *round* Honest.

[6] *alloy* Metal added to strengthen gold or silver; *embaseth* Makes less pure.

[7] *Montaigne* Michel de Montaigne (1533–1592), French writer commonly credited as the originator of the personal essay.

[8] *"If it … men"* Cf. Montaigne's *Essays* 2.18, "Of Giving the Lie."

[9] *"He shall … earth"* Cf. Luke 18.8.

[10] *impertinences* Things that are trivial and irrelevant.

some other that account wife and children but as bills of charges. Nay more, there are some foolish rich covetous men, that take a pride in having no children, because they may be thought so much the richer. For perhaps they have heard some talk, "Such an one is a great rich man," and another except[1] to it, "Yea, but he hath a great charge of children"; as if it were an abatement[2] to his riches. But the most ordinary cause of a single life is liberty, especially in certain self-pleasing and humorous minds, which are so sensible of every restraint, as they will go near to think their girdles and garters[3] to be bonds and shackles.

Unmarried men are best friends, best masters, best servants; but not always best subjects; for they are light to run away; and almost all fugitives are of that condition. A single life doth well with churchmen; for charity will hardly water the ground where it must first fill a pool. It is indifferent for judges and magistrates; for if they be facile[4] and corrupt, you shall have a servant five times worse than a wife. For soldiers, I find the generals commonly in their hortatives[5] put men in mind of their wives and children; and I think the despising of marriage amongst the Turks maketh the vulgar soldier more base. Certainly wife and children are a kind of discipline of humanity; and single men, though they may be many times more charitable, because their means are less exhaust, yet, on the other side, they are more cruel and hardhearted (good to make severe inquisitors), because their tenderness is not so oft called upon. Grave natures, led by custom, and therefore constant, are commonly loving husbands; as was said of Ulysses, *vetulam suam praetulit immortalitati*.[6] Chaste women are often proud and froward,[7] as presuming upon the merit of their chastity. It is one of the best bonds both of chastity and obedience in the wife, if she think her husband wise; which she will never do if she find him jealous. Wives are young men's mistresses; companions for middle age; and old men's nurses. So as a man may have a quarrel to marry when he will. But yet he was reputed one of the wise men,[8] that made answer to the question, when a man should marry?—"A young man not yet, an elder man not at all." It is often seen that bad husbands have very good wives; whether it be that it raiseth the price of their husband's kindness when it comes; or that the wives take a pride in their patience. But this never fails, if the bad husbands were of their own choosing, against their friends' consent; for then they will be sure to make good their own folly.

[1] *except* Object.

[2] *abatement* Reduction.

[3] *humorous* Fanciful, whimsical; *girdles* Belts; *garters* Bands that keep stockings from coming down.

[4] *facile* Yielding, compliant.

[5] *hortatives* Speeches meant to exhort or encourage.

[6] *Ulysses* Wily, well-traveled character of Greek legend, his story is told variously in the *Iliad*, the *Odyssey* and the *Aeneid*; *vetulam … immortalitati* Latin: he preferred his old wife to immortality.

[7] *froward* Headstrong and obstinate.

OF TRAVEL

Travel, in the younger sort, is a part of education; in the elder, a part of experience. He that travelleth into a country before he hath some entrance into the language, goeth to school,[9] and not to travel. That young men travel under some tutor, or grave servant, I allow[10] well; so that he be such a one that hath the language, and hath been in the country before; whereby he may be able to tell them what things are worthy to be seen in the country where they go; what acquaintances they are to seek; what exercises or discipline, the place yieldeth. For else young men shall go hooded,[11] and look abroad little. It is a strange thing, that in sea voyages, where there is nothing to be seen but sky and sea, men should make diaries; but in land-travel, wherein so much is to be observed, for the most part they omit it; as if chance were fitter to be registered than observation. Let diaries, therefore, be brought in use.

The things to be seen and observed are: the courts of princes, specially when they give audience to ambassadors; the courts of justice, while they sit and

[8] *he … wise men* Thales (b. seventh century BCE), one of the Seven Sages of ancient Greece. When a young man was asked by his mother when he would marry, he reputedly responded, "I'm too young," and when an older man, responded to the same question, "I am too old."

[9] *goeth … school* I.e., goes to learn.

[10] *allow* Approve of.

[11] *hooded* Blindfolded.

hear causes; and so of consistories ecclesiastic;[1] the churches and monasteries, with the monuments which are therein extant; the walls and fortifications of cities and towns, and so the havens[2] and harbors; antiquities and ruins; libraries; colleges, disputations,[3] and lectures, where any are; shipping and navies; houses and gardens of state and pleasure, near great cities; armories; arsenals; magazines;[4] exchanges; bourses;[5] warehouses; exercises of horsemanship, fencing, training of soldiers, and the like; comedies, such whereunto the better sort of persons do resort; treasuries of jewels and robes; cabinets[6] and rarities; and, to conclude, whatsoever is memorable in the places where they go. After all which the tutors or servants ought to make diligent inquiry. As for triumphs, masks,[7] feasts, weddings, funerals, capital executions, and such shows, men need not to be put in mind of them; yet are they not to be neglected.

If you will have a young man to put his travel into a little room, and in short time to gather much, this you must do. First, as was said, he must have some entrance into the language before he goeth. Then he must have such a servant or tutor as knoweth the country, as was likewise said. Let him carry with him also some card[8] or book describing the country where he travelleth; which will be a good key to his inquiry. Let him keep also a diary. Let him not stay long in one city or town; more or less as the place deserveth, but not long; nay, when he stayeth in one city or town, let him change his lodging from one end and part of the town to another; which is a great adamant[9] of acquaintance. Let him sequester himself from the company of his countrymen, and diet in such places where there is good company of the nation where he travelleth. Let him upon his removes from one place to another, procure recommendation to some person of quality residing in the place whither he removeth; that he may use his favour in those things he desireth to see or know. Thus he may abridge[10] his travel with much profit.

As for the acquaintance which is to be sought in travel; that which is most of all profitable, is acquaintance with the secretaries and employed men of ambassadors: for so in travelling in one country, he shall suck the experience of many. Let him also see and visit eminent persons in all kinds, which are of great name abroad; that he may be able to tell how the life agreeth with the fame. For quarrels, they are with care and discretion to be avoided. They are commonly for mistresses, healths, place, and words. And let a man beware how he keepeth company with choleric[11] and quarrelsome persons; for they will engage him into their own quarrels. When a traveller returneth home, let him not leave the countries where he hath travelled altogether behind him; but maintain a correspondence by letters with those of his acquaintance which are of most worth. And let his travel appear rather in his discourse[12] than his apparel or gesture; and in his discourse let him be rather advised in his answers, than forward to tell stories; and let it appear that he doth not change his country manners for those of foreign parts; but only prick in some flowers of that he hath learned abroad into the customs of his own country.

OF PLANTATIONS[13]

Plantations are amongst ancient, primitive, and heroical works. When the world was young it begat more children; but now it is old it begets fewer: for I may justly account new plantations to be the children of former kingdoms. I like a plantation in a pure soil; that is, where people are not displanted to the end to plant in others. For else it is rather an extirpation[14] than a

[1] *consistories ecclesiastic* Church councils.

[2] *havens* Ports.

[3] *disputations* Debates.

[4] *magazines* Storehouses.

[5] *bourses* Exchanges, or money-markets.

[6] *cabinets* Places devoted to displaying artistic and historical objects.

[7] *triumphs* Ceremonial processions of victorious military commanders and their forces; *masks* I.e., masques, or plays.

[8] *card* Map.

[9] *adamant* Here, magnet.

[10] *abridge* Shorten.

[11] *choleric* Bad-tempered.

[12] *discourse* Conversation.

[13] *Plantations* Colonies.

[14] *extirpation* Rooting out, extermination.

plantation. Planting of countries is like planting of woods; for you must make account to lease almost twenty years' profit, and expect your recompense in the end. For the principal thing that hath been the destruction of most plantations, hath been the base[1] and hasty drawing of profit in the first years. It is true, speedy profit is not to be neglected, as far as may stand with the good of the plantation, but no further.

It is a shameful and unblessed thing to take the scum of people, and wicked condemned men, to be the people with whom you plant; and not only so, but it spoileth the plantation; for they will ever live like rogues, and not fall to work, but be lazy, and do mischief, and spend victuals, and be quickly weary, and then certify over to their country[2] to the discredit of the plantation. The people wherewith you plant ought to be gardeners, ploughmen, laborers, smiths, carpenters, joiners, fishermen, fowlers, with some few apothecaries,[3] surgeons, cooks, and bakers.

In a country of plantation, first look about, what kind of victual the country yields of itself to hand; as chestnuts, walnuts, pine-apples,[4] olives, dates, plums, cherries, wild honey, and the like; and make use of them. Then consider what victual or esculent[5] things there are, which grow speedily, and within the year; as parsnips, carrots, turnips, onions, radish, artichokes of Hierusalem, maize,[6] and the like. For wheat, barley, and oats, they ask too much labour; but with peas and beans you may begin, both because they ask less labour, and because they serve for meat as well as for bread. And of rice likewise cometh a great increase, and it is a kind of meat. Above all, there ought to be brought store of biscuit, oatmeal, flour, meal, and the like, in the beginning, till bread may be had. For beasts, or birds, take chiefly such as are least subject to diseases, and multiply fastest; as swine, goats, cocks, hens, turkeys, geese, housedoves, and the like. The victual in plantations ought to be expended almost as in a besieged town; that is, with certain allowance.[7] And let the main part of the ground employed to gardens or corn, be to a common stock; and to be laid in, and stored up, and then delivered out in proportion; besides some spots of ground that any particular person will manure for his own private.[8]

Consider likewise what commodities the soil where the plantation is doth naturally yield, that they may some way help to defray the charge of the plantation (so it be not, as was said, to the untimely prejudice of the main business), as it hath fared with tobacco in Virginia. Wood commonly aboundeth but too much; and therefore timber is fit to be one. If there be iron ore, and streams whereupon to set the mills, iron is a brave[9] commodity where wood aboundeth. Making of bay-salt,[10] if the climate be proper for it, would be put in experience. Growing silk likewise, if any be, is a likely commodity. Pitch and tar, where store of firs and pines are, will not fail. So drugs and sweet woods, where they are, cannot but yield great profit. Soap-ashes[11] likewise, and other things that may be thought of. But moil[12] not too much under ground; for the hope of mines is very uncertain, and useth to make the planters lazy in other things.

For government, let it be in the hands of one, assisted with some counsel; and let them have commission to exercise martial laws, with some limitation. And above all, let men make that profit of being in the wilderness, as they have God always, and His service, before their eyes. Let not the government of the plantation depend upon too many counsellors and undertakers in the country that planteth, but upon a temperate[13] number; and let those be rather noblemen

[1] *base* Lowly.

[2] *spend victuals* Waste food or provisions; *certify ... country* Send reports back to their country.

[3] *joiners* Cabinet-makers; *apothecaries* Preparers and sellers of drugs.

[4] *pine-apples* Pine-cones, in particular the edible kernel or pine-nuts.

[5] *esculent* Edible.

[6] *artichokes of Hierusalem* Jerusalem artichokes, sunflowers having edible bulbs; *maize* Corn.

[7] *with certain allowance* I.e., rationed.

[8] *private* I.e., private use.

[9] *brave* Worthy.

[10] *bay-salt* Coarse salt evaporated from saltwater ponds.

[11] *Soap-ashes* Ashes from certain trees that are used to produce lye, a necessary ingredient for making soap.

[12] *moil* Work.

[13] *undertakers* Partners in an enterprise, shareholders; *temperate* Moderate.

and gentlemen, than merchants; for they look ever to the present gain. Let there be freedoms from custom,[1] till the plantation be of strength; and not only freedom from custom, but freedom to carry their commodities where they may make their best of them, except there be some special cause of caution.

Cram not in people, by sending too fast company after company; but rather hearken how they waste,[2] and send supplies proportionably; but so as the number may live well in the plantation, and not by surcharge be in penury.[3]

It hath been a great endangering to the health of some plantations, that they have built along the sea and rivers, in marish[4] and unwholesome grounds. Therefore, though you begin there, to avoid carriage and like discommodities,[5] yet build still rather upwards from the streams, than along. It concerneth likewise the health of the plantation that they have good store of salt with them, that they may use it in their victuals, when it shall be necessary.

If you plant where savages are, do not only entertain them with trifles and gingles;[6] but use them justly and graciously, with sufficient guard nevertheless; and do not win their favor by helping them to invade their enemies, but for their defence it is not amiss; and send oft of them over to the country that plants,[7] that they may see a better condition than their own, and commend it when they return. When the plantation grows to strength, then it is time to plant with women as well as with men; that the plantation may spread into generations, and not be ever pieced from without. It is the sinfullest thing in the world to forsake or destitute a plantation once in forwardness; for besides the dishonor, it is the guiltiness of blood of many commiserable[8] persons.

[1] *custom* Taxes on imported goods.

[2] *waste* Consume.

[3] *surcharge* Excessive charge; *penury* Poverty.

[4] *marish* Marshy.

[5] *carriage* Cost of transport; *discommodities* Inconveniences.

[6] *trifles* Toys or trinkets; *gingles* Jingling baubles.

[7] *send … plants* I.e., often send some of them to the plantation's home country.

[8] *commiserable* Pitiable.

OF STUDIES
(1597 version, original spelling)

original spelling

Studies serve for pastimes, for ornaments and for abilities. Their chiefe use for pastime is in privateness and retiring; for ornamente is in discourse, and for abilitie is in judgement. For expert men can execute, but learned men are fittest to judge or censure.

To spend too much time in them is slouth, to use them too much for ornament is affectation: to make judgement wholly by their rules, is the humour of a Scholler.

They perfect *Nature*, and are perfected by experience.

Craftie men contemn them, simple men admire them, wise men use them: For they teach not their owne use, but that is a wisedome without them: and above them wonne by observation.

Reade not to contradict, nor to believe, but to waigh and consider.

Some bookes are to bee tasted, others are to bee swallowed, and some few to bee chewed and disgested: That is, some bookes are to be read only in partes; others to be read, but cursorily, and some few to be read wholly and with diligence and attention.

Reading maketh a full man, conference a readye man, and writing an exacte man. And therefore if a man write little, he had neede have a great memorie, if he conferre little, he had neede have a present wit, and if he reade little, hee had neede have much cunning, to seeme to know that he doth not.

Histories make men wise, Poets wittie: the Mathematickes subtle, naturall Phylosophie deepe: Morall grave, Logicke and Rhetoricke able to contend.

OF STUDIES
(1625 version, modernized)

Studies serve for delight, for ornament, and for ability. Their chief use for delight, is in privateness and retiring;[9] for ornament, is in discourse;[10] and for ability, is in the judgment and disposition of business. For

[9] *retiring* Removing oneself from public life.

[10] *discourse* Conversation.

expert men can execute, and perhaps judge of particulars, one by one; but the general counsels, and the plots and marshalling of affairs, come best from those that are learned. To spend too much time in studies is sloth; to use them too much for ornament, is affectation; to make judgment wholly by their rules, is the humor of a scholar. They perfect nature, and are perfected by experience: for natural abilities are like natural plants, that need pruning by study; and studies themselves do give forth directions too much at large, except they be bounded in by experience. Crafty men contemn[1] studies, simple men admire them, and wise men use them; for they teach not their own use; but that is a wisdom without them, and above them, won by observation. Read not to contradict and confute; nor to believe and take for granted; nor to find talk and discourse; but to weigh and consider. Some books are to be tasted, others to be swallowed, and some few to be chewed and digested; that is, some books are to be read only in parts; others to be read but not curiously;[2] and some few to be read wholly, and with diligence and attention. Some books also may be read by deputy,[3] and extracts made of them by others; but that would be only in the less important arguments, and the meaner[4] sort of books; else distilled books are like common distilled waters, flashy[5] things. Reading maketh a full man; conference a ready man; and writing an exact man. And therefore, if a man write little, he had need have a great memory; if he confer little, he had need have a present wit: and if he read little, he had need have much cunning, to seem to know that he doth not. Histories make men wise; poets witty; the mathematics subtle; natural philosophy deep; moral grave; logic and rhetoric able to contend. *Abeunt studia in mores*.[6] Nay there is no stond or impediment in the wit, but may be wrought[7] out by fit studies; like as diseases of the body may have appropriate exercises. Bowling is good for the stone and reins;[8] shooting for the lungs and breast; gentle walking for the stomach; riding for the head; and the like. So if a man's wit be wandering, let him study the mathematics; for in demonstrations, if his wit be called away never so little, he must begin again. If his wit be not apt to distinguish or find differences, let him study the schoolmen;[9] for they are *cymini sectores*.[10] If he be not apt to beat over matters, and to call up one thing to prove and illustrate another, let him study the lawyers' cases. So every defect of the mind, may have a special receipt.[11]

OF SIMULATION AND DISSIMULATION[12]

Dissimulation is but a faint kind of policy or wisdom; for it asketh a strong wit and a strong heart to know when to tell truth, and to do it. Therefore it is the weaker sort of politiques,[13] that are the great dissemblers.

Tacitus saith, "Livia sorted well with the arts of her husband and dissimulation of her son"; attributing arts or policy to Augustus, and dissimulation to Tiberius.[14] And again, when Mucianus encourageth Vespasian to take arms against Vitellius, he saith, "We rise not against

[1] *crafty* Artful, cunning; *contemn* Scorn.

[2] *curiously* Carefully, attentively.

[3] *by deputy* Second-hand, as in extracts or commentaries.

[4] *meaner* More common, less significant.

[5] *distilled waters* Medicinal waters made from plant and vegetable essences; *flashy* Dull, tasteless.

[6] *Abeunt ... mores* Latin: Studies influence manners; see Ovid's *Heroides* 15.83.

[7] *stond* Obstacle; *wrought* Worked.

[8] *stone and reins* Kidney stones and the kidneys.

[9] *schoolmen* Medieval scholastic theologians and philosophers, whose practices were characterized by systematic rigor.

[10] *cymini sectores* Latin: literally, dividers of cumin seeds. I.e., close and careful arguers; hair-splitters.

[11] *receipt* Recipe, prescription.

[12] *simulation* Explicit, outright lying; *dissimulation* Disguising intentions or feelings with a false appearance.

[13] *politiques* Politicians, here dependent on cunning and strategy.

[14] *Tacitus* Prominant Roman historian (55?–120? CE); *Livia* Notable Roman empress (58 BCE–29 CE), married to Octavian of Rome and mother to Tiberius; *"Livia ... son"* Cf. Tacitus *Annals* Book 1; *sorted* Partook of; *Augustus* Octavian (63 BCE–14 CE), first emperor of Rome and arguably the most important figure in Roman history; *Tiberius* Augustus' successor (14–37 CE); his reign was characterized by his own dark moodiness and manipulation by unscrupulous politicians.

the piercing judgment of Augustus, nor the extreme caution or closeness of Tiberius."[1] These properties, of arts or policy and dissimulation or closeness, are indeed habits and faculties several,[2] and to be distinguished. For if a man have that penetration of judgment as he can discern what things are to be laid open, and what to be secreted, and what to be showed at half lights, and to whom and when (which indeed are arts of state and arts of life, as Tacitus well calleth them), to him a habit of dissimulation is a hindrance and a poorness. But if a man cannot obtain to that judgment, then it is left to him generally to be close, and a dissembler. For where a man cannot choose or vary in particulars, there it is good to take the safest and wariest way, in general; like the going[3] softly, by one that cannot well see. Certainly the ablest men that ever were have had all an openness and frankness of dealing; and a name of certainty[4] and veracity; but then they were like horses well managed; for they could tell passing well when to stop or turn; and at such times when they thought the case indeed required dissimulation, if then they used it, it came to pass that the former opinion spread abroad of their good faith and clearness of dealing made them almost invisible.

There be three degrees of this hiding and veiling of a man's self. The first, closeness, reservation, and secrecy; when a man leaveth himself without observation, or without hold to be taken, what he is. The second, dissimulation, in the negative; when a man lets fall signs and arguments, that he is not that[5] he is. And the third, simulation, in the affirmative; when a man industriously and expressly feigns and pretends to be that he is not.

[1] *Mucianus* Gaius Licinius Mucianus (c. first century CE), Roman statesman and general; *Vespasian* Caesar Vespasian Augustus (9–79 CE), succeeded Vitellius as Roman Emperor at the end of the civil war known as the Year of the Four Emperors. He restored the discipline and order his predecessor eroded among the Roman military; *Vitellius* Aulus Vitellius (15–69 CE), Vespasian's predecessor, known for his luxurious excesses; *"We rise ... Tiberius"* See Tacitus, *Histories* 1.10.

[2] *several* Separate.

[3] *going* Walking.

[4] *name of certainty* Reliable reputation.

[5] *that* What.

For the first of these, secrecy; it is indeed the virtue of a confessor. And assuredly the secret man heareth many confessions. For who will open himself to a blab or a babbler? But if a man be thought secret, it inviteth discovery; as the more close air sucketh in the more open; and as in confession the revealing is not for worldly use, but for the ease of a man's heart, so secret men come to the knowledge of many things in that kind; while men rather discharge their minds than impart their minds. In few words, mysteries are due to secrecy. Besides (to say truth) nakedness is uncomely,[6] as well in mind as body; and it addeth no small reverence to men's manners and actions, if they be not altogether open. As for talkers and futile persons, they are commonly vain and credulous withal.[7] For he that talketh what he knoweth, will also talk what he knoweth not. Therefore set it down, that an habit of secrecy is both politic[8] and moral. And in this part, it is good that a man's face give his tongue leave to speak. For the discovery of a man's self by the tracts of his countenance is a great weakness and betraying; by how much it is many times more marked and believed than a man's words.

For the second, which is dissimulation; it followeth many times upon secrecy by a necessity; so that he that will be secret must be a dissembler in some degree. For men are too cunning to suffer a man to keep an indifferent carriage between both, and to be secret, without swaying the balance on either side. They will so beset a man with questions, and draw him on, and pick it out of him, that, without an absurd silence, he must show an inclination one way; or if he do not, they will gather as much by his silence as by his speech. As for equivocations, or oraculous[9] speeches, they cannot hold out long. So that no man can be secret, except he give himself a little scope of dissimulation; which is, as it were, but the skirts or train[10] of secrecy.

[6] *uncomely* Unlovely.

[7] *futile* Extremely talkative; *withal* As well, also.

[8] *politic* Sagacious, clever.

[9] *oraculous* Oracle-like, cunningly ambiguous.

[10] *train* Trailing part of skirt or dress.

But for the third degree, which is simulation and false profession; that I hold more culpable, and less politic; except it be in great and rare matters. And therefore a general custom of simulation (which is this last degree) is a vice, rising either of a natural falseness or fearfulness, or of a mind that hath some main faults, which because a man must needs disguise, it maketh him practise simulation in other things, lest his hand should be out of ure.[1]

The great advantages of simulation and dissimulation are three. First, to lay asleep opposition, and to surprise. For where a man's intentions are published, it is an alarum to call up all that are against them. The second is, to reserve to a man's self a fair retreat. For if a man engage himself by a manifest declaration, he must go through or take a fall. The third is, the better to discover the mind of another. For to him that opens himself men will hardly show themselves adverse; but will (fair) let him go on, and turn their freedom of speech to freedom of thought. And therefore it is a good shrewd proverb of the Spaniard, "Tell a lie and find a truth." As if there were no way of discovery but by simulation. There be also three disadvantages, to set it even. The first, that simulation and dissimulation commonly carry with them a show of fearfulness, which in any business doth spoil the feathers of round flying up to the mark. The second, that it puzzleth and perplexeth the conceits[2] of many, that perhaps would otherwise co-operate with him; and makes a man walk almost alone to his own ends. The third and greatest, is, that it depriveth a man of one of the most principal instruments for action; which is trust and belief. The best composition and temperature is to have openness in fame[3] and opinion; secrecy in habit; dissimulation in seasonable use; and a power to feign, if there be no remedy.

OF LOVE

The stage is more beholding to love, than the life of man. For as to the stage, love is ever matter of comedies, and now and then of tragedies; but in life it doth much mischief; sometimes like a siren, sometimes like a fury.[4] You may observe, that amongst all the great and worthy persons whereof the memory remaineth, either ancient or recent, there is not one that hath been transported to the mad degree of love: which shows that great spirits and great business do keep out this weak passion. You must except nevertheless Marcus Antonius, the half-partner of the empire of Rome, and Appius Claudius, the decemvir[5] and lawgiver; whereof the former was indeed a voluptuous man, and inordinate;[6] but the latter was an austere and wise man: and therefore it seems (though rarely) that love can find entrance not only into an open heart, but also into a heart well fortified, if watch be not well kept. It is a poor saying of Epicurus, *Satis magnum alter alteri theatrum sumus*;[7] as if man, made for the contemplation of heaven and all noble objects, should do nothing but kneel before a little idol, and make himself a subject, though not of the mouth (as beasts are), yet of the eye; which was given him for higher purposes.

It is a strange thing to note the excess of this passion, and how it braves the nature and value of things, by this: that the speaking in a perpetual hyperbole is comely[8] in nothing but in love. Neither is it merely in the phrase; for whereas it hath been well said that the arch-flatterer, with whom all the petty flatterers have

---

[1] *ure* Practice.

[2] *conceits* Ideas, thoughts.

[3] *fame* Reputation.

[4] *siren* One of the mythical sea nymphs who lure sailors to destruction with their sweet singing voices; *fury* One of the three winged goddesses of Greek mythology who punish those who commit unavenged crimes.

[5] *Marcus Antonius* Roman general (83–30 BCE) known for his disastrous love affair with Cleopatra, the Egyptian queen; *Appius Claudius* Leader of the Roman Republic (c. fifth century BCE), whose love affair with Verginia led to his murder (by her father), which incited a commoner revolt; *decemvir* One of ten officials responsible for administration in the Roman Republic. This term literally means "man of ten."

[6] *voluptuous* Devoted to sensuality or pleasure; *inordinate* Disorderly.

[7] *Epicurus* Ancient Greek philosopher (341–270 BCE) who founded Epicureanism, the philosophy that advocated avoiding pain and pursuing pleasure, which he linked to virtue; *Satis magnum ... sumus* Latin: Each of us is enough of an audience for another. See Seneca, *Epistles*, 7.2.

[8] *comely* Pleasing.

intelligence,[1] is a man's self; certainly the lover is more. For there was never proud man thought so absurdly well of himself, as the lover doth of the person loved; and therefore it was well said, that "it is impossible to love and to be wise."[2] Neither doth this weakness appear to others only, and not to the party loved; but to the loved most of all, except the love be reciproque.[3] For it is a true rule, that love is ever rewarded either with the reciproque or with an inward and secret contempt. By how much the more men ought to beware of this passion, which loseth not only other things, but itself. As for the other losses, the poet's relation doth well figure them; that he that preferred Helena, quitted the gifts of Juno and Pallas.[4] For whosoever esteemeth too much of amorous affection quitteth both riches and wisdom.

This passion hath his floods in very times of weakness, which are great prosperity and great adversity, though this latter hath been less observed: both which times kindle love, and make it more fervent, and therefore show it to be the child of folly. They do best, who if they cannot but admit love, yet make it keep quarter,[5] and sever it wholly from their serious affairs, and actions of life; for if it check[6] once with business, it troubleth men's fortunes, and maketh men that they can no ways be true to their own ends. I know not how, but martial men are given to love: I think it is but as they are given to wine; for perils commonly ask to be paid in pleasures. There is in man's nature a secret inclination and motion towards love of others, which if it be not spent upon some one or a few, doth naturally spread itself towards many, and maketh men become humane and charitable; as it is seen sometime in friars. Nuptial love maketh mankind; friendly love perfecteth it; but wanton love corrupteth and embaseth[7] it.

Of Masks and Triumphs[8]

These things are but toys, to come amongst such serious observations. But yet, since princes will have such things, it is better they should be graced with elegancy than daubed[9] with cost.

Dancing to song is a thing of great state and pleasure. I understand it, that the song be in choir, placed aloft, and accompanied with some broken music,[10] and the ditty fitted to the device. Acting in song, especially in dialogues, hath an extreme good grace; I say acting, not dancing (for that is a mean[11] and vulgar thing); and the voices of the dialogue would be strong and manly (a bass and a tenor, no treble); and the ditty high and tragical, not nice or dainty. Several choirs placed one over against another and taking the voice by catches,[12] anthem-wise, give great pleasure. Turning dances into figure is a childish curiosity.[13] And generally let it be noted, that those things which I here set down are such as do naturally take the sense, and not respect petty wonderments. It is true, the alterations of scenes, so it be quietly and without noise, are things of great beauty and pleasure; for they feed and relieve the eye, before it be full of the same object.

Let the scenes abound with light, specially colored and varied; and let the maskers, or any other, that are to

[1] *intelligence* Communication.

[2] *it is ... wise* Classical saying most notably quoted in Bacon's time in Erasmus's *Adagia*.

[3] *reciproque* Reciprocal.

[4] *he ... Helena* Paris, who chose Venus's prize (the love of Helen) over the power and riches offered by Juno and the wisdom offered by Minerva; *Helena* Helen of Troy, reputedly the most beautiful woman in the world, whose abduction by Paris spurred the Trojan War between Greece and Troy; *quitted* Renounced; *Juno* Queen of the Gods and wife of Jupiter in the Roman pantheon; *Pallas* Athena in the Greek tradition, or Minerva in the Roman, goddess of wisdom.

[5] *keep quarter* Keep to its own place.

[6] *check* Collides.

[7] *embaseth* Degrades.

[8] *Masks* I.e., masques: elaborate theatrical spectacles; *Triumphs* Here, chivalric jousts and tournaments, often with theatrical elements. While Bacon affects to dismiss these court entertainments as "toys," the essay reveals his first-hand knowledge of them: Bacon wrote several masque-like "devices" in the 1590s, and organized two magnificently expensive entertainments in 1613–14.

[9] *daubed* Plastered over.

[10] *broken music* Music produced by a broken consort—a small group of musicians who play different kinds of instruments.

[11] *mean* Common.

[12] *catches* Intricate, rhyming compositions for three or more voices.

[13] *figure* Form; *curiosity* Interest.

come down from the scene, have some motions upon the scene itself before their coming down; for it draws the eye strangely, and makes it with great pleasure to desire to see that it cannot perfectly discern. Let the songs be loud and cheerful, and not chirpings or pulings.[1] Let the music likewise be sharp and loud, and well placed. The colors that show best by candle-light are white, carnation, and a kind of sea-water-green; and oes, or spangs,[2] as they are of no great cost, so they are of most glory. As for rich embroidery, it is lost and not discerned. Let the suits of the maskers be graceful, and such as become the person when the vizards[3] are off; not after examples of known attires, Turks, soldiers, mariners, and the like.

Let anti-masks[4] not be long; they have been commonly of fools, satyrs, baboons, wild-men, antics, beasts, sprites, witches, Ethiops, pygmies, turquets, nymphs, rustics,[5] cupids, statues moving, and the like. As for angels, it is not comical enough to put them in anti-masks; and any thing that is hideous, as devils, giants, is on the other side as unfit. But chiefly, let the music of them be recreative, and with some strange changes. Some sweet odors suddenly coming forth, without any drops falling, are, in such a company as there is steam and heat, things of great pleasure and refreshment. Double masks, one of men, another of ladies, addeth state[6] and variety. But all is nothing except the room be kept clear and neat.

For jousts, and tourneys, and barriers:[7] the glories of them are chiefly in the chariots, wherein the challengers make their entry; especially if they be drawn with strange beasts, as lions, bears, camels, and the like; or in the devices[8] of their entrance; or in the bravery of their liveries; or in the goodly furniture of their horses and armor. But enough of these toys.

OF DEATH

Men fear death as children fear to go in the dark; and as that natural fear in children is increased with tales, so is the other. Certainly, the contemplation of death, as the wages of sin, and passage to another world, is holy and religious; but the fear of it, as a tribute due unto nature, is weak. Yet in religious meditations there is sometimes mixture of vanity and of superstition. You shall read in some of the friars' books of mortification, that a man should think with himself, what the pain is, if he have but his finger's end pressed or tortured; and thereby imagine what the pains of death are, when the whole body is corrupted and dissolved; when many times death passeth with less pain than the torture of a limb, for the most vital parts are not the quickest of sense.[9] And by him that spake only as a philosopher and natural man, it was well said, *Pompa mortis magis terret, quam mors ipsa*.[10] Groans and convulsions, and a discolored face, and friends weeping, and blacks and obsequies,[11] and the like, show death terrible. It is worthy the observing that there is no passion in the mind of man so weak but it mates and masters the fear of death; and therefore death is no such terrible enemy when a man hath so many attendants about him that can win the combat of him. Revenge triumphs over death; love slights it; honor aspireth to it; grief flieth to it; fear preoccupateth it; nay, we read, after Otho the emperor[12] had slain himself, pity (which is the tenderest of affections) provoked many to die out of

[1] *pulings* Whinings.

[2] *oes ... spangs* Spangles, or glittering ornaments. "Oes" is the plural of the letter "O," suggesting their round shapes.

[3] *vizards* Masks.

[4] *anti-masks* I.e., anti-masques: grotesquely comic scenes of chaos contrasting with the opulent order of the main masque.

[5] *fools* Jesters; *satyrs* Mythical woodland creatures with human torsos and legs of a goat; *antics* Grotesque figures often combining animal and vegetable elements; *sprites* Elf or pixie-like creatures; *Ethiops* Ethiopians, commonly used to denote any individual of African descent; *pygmies* Dwarfish figures; *turquets* Players dressed as little Turks; *nymphs* Woodland fairies usually represented as beautiful maidens; *rustics* Clownish countryfolk.

[6] *state* Magnificence or solemnity.

[7] *jousts ... barriers* Chivalric martial competitions, respectively on horseback with lances; on horseback with swords; and on foot with swords, usually with a barrier partially separating combatants.

[8] *devices* Personal emblems, heraldric displays.

[9] *quickest of sense* Most alive with feeling.

[10] *him ... man* Seneca (4 BCE–65 CE), Roman philosopher and writer; *Pompa ... ipsa* Latin: The trappings of death alarm us more than death itself.

[11] *blacks* Funeral clothes; *obsequies* Funeral ceremonies.

[12] *Otho ... emperor* Roman emperor (69 CE).

mere compassion to their sovereign, and as the truest sort of followers. Nay Seneca adds niceness[1] and satiety: *Cogita quamdiu eadem feceris; mori velle, non tantum fortis aut miser, sed etiam fastidiosus potest.*[2] A man would die, though he were neither valiant nor miserable, only upon a weariness to do the same thing so oft, over and over. It is no less worthy to observe how little alteration in good spirits the approaches of death make, for they appear to be the same men till the last instant. Augustus Caesar died in a compliment: *Livia, conjugii nostri memor, vive et vale.*[3] Tiberius in dissimulation, as Tacitus saith of him, *Jam Tiberium vires et corpus, non dissimulatio, deserebant.*[4] Vespasian in a jest, sitting upon the stool, *Ut puto deus fio.*[5] Galba with a sentence, *Feri, si ex re sit populi Romani,*[6] holding forth his neck. Septimius Severus in dispatch, *Adeste, si quid mihi restat agendum,*[7] and the like. Certainly the Stoics[8] bestowed too much cost upon death, and by their great preparations made it appear more fearful. Better, saith he, *Qui finem vitae extremum inter munera ponat naturae.*[9] It is as natural to die as to be born; and to a little infant, perhaps, the one is as painful as the other. He that dies in an earnest pursuit is like one that is wounded in hot blood who, for the time, scarce feels the hurt; and therefore a mind fixed and bent upon somewhat that is good doth avert the dolors[10] of death; but, above all, believe it, the sweetest canticle is, *Nunc dimittis,*[11] when a man hath obtained worthy ends and expectations. Death hath this also, that it openeth the gate to good fame, and extinguisheth envy: *Extinctus amabitur idem.*[12]

—1625

[1] *niceness* Fastidiousness.

[2] *Cogita ... potest* Latin: Think about for how long you have done the same; one may wish to die not so much because he is brave or miserable, but because he is discriminating. See Seneca, *Epistles* 10.1.6.

[3] *Livia ... vale* Latin: Livia, remember our marriage, live and farewell. Cf. Suetonius, *Augustus* 99.

[4] *Tiberius* Roman emperor 14–37 ce); *Tacitus* Prominant Roman historian (55?–120? CE); *Jam ... deserebant* Latin: His strength and body deserted him, but not his deceit. See Tacitus, *Annals* 6.50.

[5] *Vespasian* Roman emperor 69–79 CE; *stool* Toilet; *Ut ... fio* Latin: I think I am becoming a God. Cf. Suetonius, *Vespasian* 23.

[6] *Galba* Roman emperor 68–69 CE, who was executed by the military after ruling for only seven months; *Feri ... Romani* Latin: Strike, if it be in the public interest of the Roman people. Suetonius, *Galba* 20.

[7] *Septimius Severus* Roman emperor 193–211 CE; *Adeste ... agendum* Latin: Hurry, if there is more for me to do. See Dio Cassius 67.17.

[8] *Stoics* Followers of stoicism, a popular ancient Greek philosophy advocating making virtue the focus of one's life and preferring intellectual pursuits over those of the body.

[9] *he* Juvenal, Roman satiric poet (c. first century CE); *Qui ... naturae* Latin: Who values the end of life as one of nature's gifts. See Juvenal, *Satires* 10.358.

[10] *dolors* Sorrows.

[11] *canticle* Song; *Nunc dimittis* Latin: literally "thou dost dismiss." From Luke 2.29, *Nunc dimittis servun tuum Domine,* "And, now lettest thou they servant depart," used in the Anglican service for Evening prayer.

[12] *fame* Reputation; *Extinctus ... idem* Latin: When dead, that same man will be loved. See Horace, *Epistles* 2.1.14.

Robert Southwell

1561 – 1595

Robert Southwell wrote in early modern England as a religious outlaw. Serving as a Jesuit priest of the Roman Catholic faith in Protestant England, Southwell composed poems, prose homilies, and treatises, as part of an illegal missionary project to further the interests of the underground Catholic community in England. Because the outward practice of Roman Catholicism was a crime in Elizabethan England, uncensored versions of Southwell's work were initially read in secret through manuscripts that circulated privately among Catholics. Somewhat surprising, however, is the fact that anonymous versions of his work, which had explicitly Catholic elements excised so as not to offend Protestant authorities, flourished in England. The popularity of Southwell's works is significant given that even these slightly censored, anonymous print editions contained coded expressions of Catholic experience in early modern England that were legible to those who knew what to look for. Even though the works did not identify Southwell as their author, there seems to have been a general understanding among readers as to their authorship.

P. ROBERTVS SOVTHVELL Soc. Iesu
Londini pro Cath. fide suspensus et sectus. 3. mar. 1595.

The popularity of Southwell's works testifies to the significant impact he had on English literary history. His long poem *St. Peter's Complaint* (1595) is perhaps his most widely known and often imitated work. Allusions to this and other of Southwell's texts have been identified in William Shakespeare, George Herbert, Richard Crashaw, and many other English Renaissance writers. Imitations of his poetry, particularly his representations of repentance for sins, also appear throughout the seventeenth century.

Stylistically, Southwell helped introduce so-called "metaphysical poetry" into England—a mode of writing often associated with John Donne and George Herbert, in which paradox and outlandish metaphors are used to express, among other things, key aspects of Christian faith. He also played a significant role in the rise of religious verse at the end of the sixteenth and into the seventeenth century. The full extent and the precise nature of his influence on various poets and playwrights (most notably William Shakespeare) has only recently begun to be seriously explored.

Born at Horsham St. Faith's, Norfolk, in 1561, Southwell was the son of a well-to-do Protestant convert and a Catholic mother who was descended from the Copley and Shelley families. There is a distant relation between Southwell and P.B. Shelley, both of whom wrote poems about the alpine landscape, albeit, in very different ways and in very different contexts. Raised in his mother's faith, Southwell was sent to the Continent as a boy to be educated by leading Catholic scholars. His education began at the college in Douai, which was founded by Cardinal William Allen, a major Catholic apologist during Elizabeth's reign. At the age of 17. Southwell sought admission into the Society of Jesus but was initially rejected. Although Southwell took the rejection hard, he was admitted soon thereafter. Southwell's training as a Jesuit took him to Rome where he was ordained a priest in 1584, becoming director of the English College.

Southwell returned to England in July 1586 with his Jesuit superior, Henry Garnet, as part of the Catholic mission. Knowing that he would likely be captured and executed, Southwell worked secretly as a chaplain for powerful Catholic families, administering to the spiritual needs of those still committed to the "old faith." During this time, Southwell helped popularize St. Ignatius's *Spiritual Exercises* (c. 1522–24), a work setting out a rigorous program of spiritual meditation in which believers visualize themselves as participating in central biblical events. The highly visual nature of this Jesuit form of meditation informs the themes and structures of Southwell's poetry and prose, and also likely influenced work by subsequent writers of devotional literature.

Southwell's clandestine life as a Jesuit priest came to an end when he was arrested in 1592 by the priest-hunter, Richard Topcliffe. After long periods of torture and confinement, Southwell was executed in 1595 for treason, suffering the penalty then usual for the crime—hanging, disembowelment, and quartering. He was beatified by the Roman Catholic Church in 1927 and canonized in 1970.

⌘⌘⌘

The Burning Babe

As I in hoary[1] Winter's night
Stood shivering in the snow,
Surprised I was with sudden heat,
Which made my heart to glow;

And lifting up a fearful eye,
To view what fire was near,
A pretty Babe all burning bright
Did in the air appear;

Who, scorched with excessive heat,
Such floods of tears did shed,
As though his floods should quench his flames,
Which with his tears were fed:

Alas, (quoth he) but newly born,
In fiery heats I fry,
Yet none approach to warm their hearts,
Or feel my fire, but I;

My faultless breast the furnace is,
The fuel wounding thorns:
Love is the fire, and sighs the smoke,
The ashes, shame and scorns;

The fuel Justice layeth on,
And Mercy blows the coals,
The metal in this furnace wrought,
Are men's defiled souls:

For which, as now on fire I am
To work them to their good,
So will I melt into a bath,
To wash them in my blood.

With this he vanished out of sight,
And swiftly shrunk away,
And straight I called unto mind,
That it was Christmas day.

[1] *hoary* Grayish-white, as in the white of frozen dew also known as hoar-frost; also associated with age and venerability.

The Nativity of Christ

Behold the father, is his daughter's son:
The bird that built the nest, is hatched therein:
The old of years, an hour hath not outrun:
Eternal life, to live doth now begin.
The word is dumb:° the mirth of heaven doth weep: *silent*
Might feeble is: and force doth faintly creep.

O dying souls, behold your living spring:
O dazzled eyes, behold your son of grace:
Dull ears, attend what word this word doth bring:
Up heavy hearts: with joy your joy embrace.

From death, from dark, from deafness, from despairs:
This life, this light, this word, this joy repairs.

Gift better than himself. God doth not know:
Gift better than his God, no man can see:
This gift doth here the giver given bestow:
Gift to this gift let each receiver be.
God is my gift, himself he freely gave me:
God's gift am I and none but God shall have me.

Man altered was by sin from man to beast:
Beast's food is hay, hay is all mortal flesh:
Now God is flesh and lies in Manger pressed:
As hay, the brutest° sinner to refresh *most brutish*
O happy field wherein this fodder grew,
Whose taste, doth us from beasts to men renew.

His Circumcision

The head is lanced to work the body's cure,
With angring[1] salve[2] it smarts to heal our wound,
To faultless son from all offences pure
The faulty vassals scourges do redound,
The Judge is cast the guilty to acquit,
The son defaced to lend the star his light,

The vein[3] of life distilleth drops of grace,
Our rock gives issue to an heavenly spring,
Tears from his eyes, blood runs from wounded place,
Which showers to heaven of joy a harvest bring,
This sacred dew let angels gather up,
Such dainty drops best fit their nectared cup.

With weeping eyes his mother rued° his smart, *pitied*
If blood from him, tears came from her as fast,
The knife that cut his flesh did pierce her heart,
The pain that Jesus felt did *Mary* taste,
His life and hers hung by one fatal twist,
No blow that hit the son the mother missed.

[1] *angring* Smarting, used in relation to inflamed or painful wounds.

[2] *salve* A healing ointment for wounds; a remedy, especially of spiritual sorrows.

[3] *vein* Likely with a pun on "vine."

Christ's Bloody Sweat

Fat soil, full spring, sweet olive, grape of bliss,
That yields, that streams, that pours,[4] that dost distil,
Untilled, undrawn, unstamped, untouched of press,
Dear fruit, clear brooks, fair oil, sweet wine at will:
Thus Christ unforced prevents in shedding blood
The whips, the thorns, the nails, the spear, and rood.

He Pelican's, he Phoenix fate doth prove,
Whom flames consume, whom streams enforce to die,
How burneth blood, how bleedeth burning love?
Can one in flame and stream both bathe and fry?
How could he join a Phoenix fiery pains
In fainting Pelican's still bleeding veins?

Elias once to prove god's sovereign power
By prayer procured a fire of wondrous force
That blood and wood and water did devour,
Yea stones and dust beyond all nature's course:
Such fire is love that fed with gory blood
Doth burn no less than in the driest wood.[5]

O sacred Fire come show thy force on me
That sacrifice to Christ I may return,
If withered wood for fuel fittest be,
If stones and dust, if flesh and blood will burn,
I withered am and stony to all good,
A sack of dust, a mass of flesh and blood.

[4] *pours* With a pun on "powers."

[5] *Elias once … wood* See 1 Kings 18.21–39; "Elias" is the Latinized form of "Elijah."

A Vale of Tears

A Vale there is enwrapped with dreadful shades,
Which thick of mourning pines shrouds from the sun,
Where hanging cliffs yield short and dumpish° glades,[1] *sad, dejected*
And snowy floods with broken streams do run,

Where eye-roam is from rocks to cloudy sky,
From thence to dales with stony ruins strow'd,°[2] *strewn*
Then to the crushed waters frothy fry,
Which tumbleth from the tops where snow is thaw'd:

Where ears of other sound can have no choice,
But various blustering of the stubborn wind
In trees, in caves, in straits[3] with diverse noise,
Which now doth hiss, now howl, now roar by kind:

Where waters wrestle with encountering stones,
That break their streams, and turn them into foam,
The hollow clouds full fraught with thundering groans,
With hideous thumps discharge their pregnant womb.

And in the horror of this fearful choir,
Consists the music of this doleful° place: *sad, mournful*
All pleasant birds their tunes from thence retire,
Where none but heavy° notes have any grace. *profound, grave*

Resort there is of none but pilgrim wights,° *living creatures*
That pass with trembling foot and panting heart,
With terror cast in cold and shivering frights
They judge the place to terror framed by art:

Yet nature's work it is of art untouched,
So strait indeed, so vast unto the eye,
With such disordered order strangely couched,
And so with pleasing horror low and high,

That who it views must needs remain aghast,
Much at the work, more at the maker's might,
And muse how Nature such a plot could cast,
Where nothing seemed wrong, yet nothing right:

A place for mated[4] minds, an only[5] bower,
Where every thing doth sooth[6] a dumpish mood.
Earth lies forlorn, the cloudy sky doth lower,[7]
The wind here weeps, here sighs, here cries aloud.

The struggling flood between the marble groans,
Then roaring beats upon the craggy sides,
A little off amidst the pebble stones,
With bubbling streams and purling noise it glides.

The pines thick set, high grown, and ever green,
Still clothe the place with shade and mourning veil.
Here gaping cliffs, there moss grown plain is seen,
Here hope doth spring, and there again doth quail.° *fail, give way*

Huge massy stones that hang by tickle[8] stay
Still threaten fall, and seem to hang in fear:
Some withered trees ashamed of their decay,
Beset with green, are forced gray coats to wear.

---

[1] *glades* A clear, open space or passage in a wood or wild area.

[2] *strow'd* Print editions of the poem that were published in England and that underwent scrutiny by Protestant censors of the period are different from manuscript versions that circulated privately amongst Catholic readers. In editions of the poem that were printed in England and deemed acceptable by the Protestant censor, this line reads, "From thence to dales which stormy ruins shroud." The published editions of the poem thus soften, if not totally efface, Southwell's apparent allusion to the dissolution of the monasteries at the beginning of the English Reformation under Henry VIII, a highly traumatic event for English Catholics.

[3] *straits* Narrow places, such as passes or gorges between mountains. Also used figuratively for psychological or spiritual states of feeling confined or overwhelmed.

[4] *mated* Confounded, amazed; matched, fitted or fitting together.

[5] *only* Solitary, lonely; unique.

[6] *sooth* Confirm, verify; also, to restore to a more tranquil condition.

[7] *lower* With a pun on "lower/lour."

[8] *hang by tickle* Precarious, insecure; in danger of falling.

Here crystal springs crept out of secret vein,[1]
Straight find some envious hole that hides their grace.
Here seared tufts lament the want of rain,
There thunder wrack gives terror to the place.

All pangs and heavy passions here may find
A thousand motives[2] suitly to their griefs,[3]
To feed the sorrows of their troubled mind,
And chase away dame pleasure's vain reliefs.

To plaining thoughts this vale a rest may be,
To which from worldly joys they may retire,
Where sorrow springs from water, stone, and tree,
Where every thing with mourners doth conspire.

Set here my soul main streams of tears afloat,
Here all thy sinful foils° alone recount, *disgraces, stigmas*
Of solemn tunes make thou the dolefulest note,
That to thy ditties dolor may amount.

When *Echo* doth repeat thy plainful cries,
Think that the very stones thy sins bewray,° *betray*
And now accuse thee with their sad replies,
As heaven and earth shall in the latter day,

Let former faults be fuel of the fire,
For grief in Limbeck[4] of thy heart to still
Thy pensive thoughts, and dumps of thy desire,
And vapour tears up to thy eyes at will.

Let tears to tunes, and pains to plaints be pressed,
And let this be the burden[5] of thy song,
Come deep remorse, possess my sinful breast:
Delights adieu, I harboured you too long.

[1] *secret vein* A channel from which water flows out of the earth.

[2] *motives* Denotes a movement of emotion.

[3] *suitly to their griefs* Signifies "appropriate to" or "in sympathy with."

[4] *Limbeck* Alembic, an apparatus used for the process of distillation.

[5] *burden* The refrain or chorus of a song; a set of words at the end of each verse.

Mary Magdalen's Complaint at Christ's Death

Sith° my life from life is parted: *since*
Death come take thy portion.
Who survives, when life is murdered,
Lives by mere extortion.
All that live, and not in God:
Couch their life in death's abode.

Silly[6] stars must needs leave shining,
When the sun is shadowed.
Borrowed streams refrain their running,
When head springs are hindered.
One that lives by other's breath,
Dieth also by his death.

O true life, sith thou hast left me,
Mortal life is tedious.
Death it is to live without thee,
Death, of all most odious.
Turn again or take me to thee,
Let me die or live thou in me.

Where the truth once was, and is not,
Shadows are but vanity:
Showing want, that help they cannot:
Signs, not salves of misery.
Painted meat no hunger feeds,
Dying life each death exceeds.

With my love, my life was nestled
In the sum of happiness:
From my love, my life is wrested° *taken by force*
To a world of heaviness.
O, let love my life remove
Sith I live not where I love.

[6] *Silly* In sixteenth-century usage, silly or "seely" meant not only foolish or simple but also punctual; blissful, lucky; spiritually blessed; pious, holy, good; deserving of pity or sympathy; frail, worn out.

O my soul, what did unloose thee
From thy sweet captivity?
God, not I, did still possess thee:
His, not mine, thy liberty.
O, too happy thrall thou wert,° *were*
When thy prison, was his heart.

Spiteful spear,[1] that break'st° this prison, *broke*
Seat of all felicity,
Working thus, with double treason,
Love's and life's delivery:° *surrender*
Though my life thou drav'st° away, *drove*
Maugre° thee my love shall stay. *In spite of*

Lewd Love Is Loss

Misdeeming° eye that stoopest to the lure *Misjudging, Mistaking*
Of mortal worths not worth so worthy love:
All beauties base, all graces are impure:
That do thy erring thoughts from God remove.
Sparks to the fire, the beams yield to the sun,
All grace to God from whom all graces run.

If picture move, more should the pattern please,
No shadow can with shadowed things compare,
And fairest shapes whereon our loves do seize,
But silly° signs of God's high beauties are. *weak, frail*
Go starving sense, feed thou on earthly mast,° *animal feed*
True love in Heav'n, seek thou thy sweet repast.

Glean not in barren soil these offal° ears,° *worthless / corn*
Sith reap thou mayest whole harvests of delight.
Base joys with griefs, bad hopes do end in fears:
Lewd love with loss, evil peace with deadly fight:
God's love alone doth end with endless ease,
Whose joys in hope, whose hope concludes in peace.

Let not the luring train[2] of Fancy's[3] trap,
Or gracious features proofs of nature's skill,
Lull Reason's force asleep in Error's lap,
Or draw thy wit to bent of wanton will;[4]
The fairest flowers have not the sweetest smell,
A seeming heaven proves oft a damning hell.

Self-pleasing souls that play with beauty's bait,
In shining shroud may swallow fatal hook,
Where eager sight, or semblant° fair doth wait, *appearance*
A lock it proves that first was but a look.
The fish with ease into the Net doth glide,
But to get out the way is not so wide.

So long the fly doth dally with the flame,
Until his singed wings do force his fall:
So long the eye doth follow Fancy's game,
Till love hath left the heart[5] in heavy thrall.
Soon may the mind be cast in Cupid's jail,
But hard it is imprisoned thoughts to bail.

O loath that love whose final aim is lust,
Moth of the mind, eclipse of reason's light:
The grave of grace, the mole of nature's rust,
The wrack of wit, the wrong of every right.
In sum an evil whose harms no tongue can tell,
In which to live is death, to die is hell.

[1] *Spiteful spear* I.e., the spear that penetrated Christ's side.

[2] *luring train* Pieces of meat laid in a line or trail for luring wild beasts such as wolves or foxes into a trap.

[3] *of Fancy's* A personification of the mind's ability to construct and become enamored with delusional images.

[4] *Or draw … will* The mind is being described here through a comparison with an archery bow, where the faculty of thought (or wit) is the bowstring and the faculty of will is the bow that bends when the string is pulled taut.

[5] *heart* With a pun on "hart" or deer.

Christopher Marlowe
1564 – 1593

Christopher Marlowe's small body of work—seven plays, as well as a number of poems written during six productive years—profoundly influenced the course of English Renaissance drama. His plays set precedents for English history plays, tragedy, and heroic drama, while his newly supple and powerful blank verse (unrhymed iambic pentameter) impressed Ben Jonson as Marlowe's "mighty line." Had his writing career not been cut so short by a lethal tavern brawl he might have rivaled Shakespeare as the finest dramatist of his age.

Marlowe was born in Canterbury on 26 February 1564, in the same year as Shakespeare. His father was a shoemaker and a bondsman but also an actor; his mother was the daughter of a clergyman—and both theater and theology would help shape him. Despite his father's fairly humble occupation, Marlowe was well educated, first at King's School, in Canterbury, and then at Cambridge University's Corpus Christi College. His education at Cambridge, which was paid for by a foundation set up by Matthew Parker, Archbishop of Canterbury, included history, philosophy, and the theology of the Protestant Reformation, one version of which, despite a large and sometimes surreptitiously active Catholic minority, was now the orthodoxy of the officially established Church of England. In 1584 he earned his B.A.

During the latter part of his time at Cambridge, Marlowe frequently disappeared for extended periods. It is likely, some historians believe, that Marlowe had been recruited as a spy by Queen Elizabeth's Privy Council, which had longstanding fears of subversive Catholic activity at home and abroad. He spent time in the French city of Rheims, a refuge for many English Catholic expatriates, and perhaps helped uncover a Catholic plot to assassinate Elizabeth. This theory is strengthened by the actions of the Council upon Marlowe's return to England. Marlowe applied for his M.A., a degree normally granted automatically upon application once a certain amount of time had elapsed since the granting of a B.A., but the university refused him on multiple grounds. Not only had Marlowe failed to pursue ordination after his theological studies (as was expected of theology students); he had also spent considerable time among Catholics in France, and was therefore suspected of Catholic sympathies. Marlowe asked the Privy Council to intercede on his behalf and it obliged by sending a letter to the Cambridge authorities indicating that Marlowe "had done Her Majesty good service, & deserved to be rewarded for his faithful dealing." Moreover, says the letter severely, "it was not Her Majesty's pleasure that anyone employed, as [Marlowe] had been, in matters touching the benefit of his country, should be defamed by those that are ignorant in th' affairs he went about." Marlowe was granted his M.A. in 1587.

In the same year, Marlowe left Cambridge and moved to London to pursue his career as a playwright. His London years were marked by violence. In 1589 he spent two weeks in Newgate Prison, charged with the murder of one William Bradley, although he was acquitted and released, and in 1592 court records indicate that he was implicated in a street fight in which another man was killed. Through these same years, however, Marlowe's career soared. He had the luxury of being hired by the Lord Admiral's Company, which meant that the finest of London's actors would perform his plays. His first major plays, including *Tamburlaine the Great*—a grandiloquently written and violence-filled play—were produced in 1587 and were wildly popular. Over the next six years Marlowe completed at least five more plays: *The Jew of Malta* (c.1589), *Edward II* (c.1592), *The Massacre of Paris* (printed c. 1593), *Dido, Queen of Carthage* (printed in 1594), and *The Tragical History of Doctor Faustus* (?1593). In recent decades *Edward II* has drawn critical notice for its ambivalent portrayal of homoerotic love in conflict with political and marital duty, while the darkly comic *Jew of Malta*, whose Christians are quite as wicked as the Jewish protagonist, is significant in understanding early modern English views of the Jew as "other." *Faustus*, however, remains the most widely read and performed of Marlowe's plays. Based on an old Czech and German legend, the play presents a scholar who sells his soul to the devil in exchange for knowledge and power. As always, this proves a bad bargain: Faustus fritters away his power on pointless magic tricks and must, eventually, disappear in anguish into Hell. Marlowe's sympathies are hard to identify: the play may be read as orthodox (the anti-Catholic humor would not displease audiences or ecclesiastical authorities in England) but it may also raise difficult questions about free will and an implacable God.

Marlowe is also known for his poetry, including translations from Lucan's *Pharsalia* and Ovid's *Amores*. His most famous English poems are the unfinished "Hero and Leander," a tragic love story lightened by witty rhymes, outrageous metaphors, and a view of erotic love at once skeptical and sympathetic, and "The Passionate Shepherd to His Love," a poem based in part on Virgil's homoerotic Second Eclogue (Marlowe's version was soon treated as entirely heterosexual but recent criticism has noted its ambiguity in this regard). Unfortunately, piecing together Marlowe's *oeuvre* is a complicated matter. We have, for example, two quite different versions of *Doctor Faustus* (1604 and 1616).

Marlowe's death on 30 May 1593 has been the subject of much controversy. According to the coroner's report, Marlowe and a number of his acquaintances were dining at Eleanor Bull's House, a tavern just outside London. A heated argument arose between Marlowe and a fellow diner, Ingram Frizer, over the bill. The report states that Marlowe attacked Frizer with a knife and injured him on the back of the head. Frizer wrested the knife from Marlowe's grasp and sank its blade two inches into Marlowe's skull, just above the right eye. Marlowe died instantly. Was there a conspiracy behind this? Marlowe had maintained connections from his spying days and at the time of his death was in the presence of men with connections to his former employer, Sir Francis Walsingham, who as Secretary of State was responsible for the government's intelligence operations. Marlowe had recently been arrested on charges of atheism (an imprecisely defined offence which could be laid against anyone expressing unorthodox theological opinions) and was due to go on trial in a few days. Some scholars have speculated that members of the government feared that Marlowe would identify other "atheists" in high positions or perhaps reveal espionage secrets should he appear in a court of law, and so had him assassinated.

Marlowe was buried in an unmarked grave on the grounds of St. Nicholas's Church, Deptford, on 1 June 1593. Not until July 2002, more than 400 years after he died, was he memorialized in the prestigious Poet's Corner of Westminster Abbey.

⌘⌘⌘

Hero and Leander

On Hellespont,[1] guilty of true-loves' blood,
In view and opposite, two cities stood,
Sea-borderers, disjoined by Neptune's[2] might;
The one Abydos,[3] the other Sestos[4] hight.° *named*
At Sestos Hero dwelt; Hero the fair,
Whom young Apollo[5] courted for her hair,
And offered as a dower his burning throne,
Where she should sit for men to gaze upon.
The outside of her garments were of lawn,[6]
The lining purple silk, with gilt stars drawn;
Her wide sleeves green, and bordered with a grove
Where Venus in her naked glory strove
To please the careless and disdainful eyes
Of proud Adonis, that before her lies;[7]
Her kirtle° blue, whereon was many a stain, *skirt*
Made with the blood of wretched lovers slain.
Upon her head she ware° a myrtle wreath, *wore*
From whence her veil reached to the ground beneath.
Her veil was artificial flowers and leaves,
Whose workmanship both man and beast deceives;
Many would praise the sweet smell as she passed,
When 'twas the odor which her breath forth cast;
And there for honey, bees have sought in vain,
And, beat from thence, have lighted there again.
About her neck hung chains of pebble-stone,
Which, lightened° by her neck, like diamonds shone. *lit up*
She ware no gloves, for neither sun nor wind
Would burn or parch her hands, but to her mind[8]
Or° warm or cool them, for they took delight *either*
To play upon those hands, they were so white.
Buskins° of shells all silvered usèd she, *boots*
And branched with blushing coral to the knee,
Where sparrows perched, of hollow pearl and gold,
Such as the world would wonder to behold;
Those with sweet water oft her handmaid fills,
Which, as she went, would chirrup through the bills.
Some say, for her the fairest Cupid pined,
And looking in her face, was strooken° blind. *struck*
But this is true: so like was one the other,
As he imagined Hero was his mother;[9]
And oftentimes into her bosom flew,
About her naked neck his bare arms threw,
And laid his childish head upon her breast,
And with still° panting rocked, there took his rest. *continual*
So lovely fair was Hero, Venus' nun,[10]
As Nature wept, thinking she was undone,
Because she took more from her than she left
And of such wondrous beauty her bereft;
Therefore, in sign her treasure suffered wrack,
Since Hero's time hath half the world been black.
Amorous Leander, beautiful and young,
(Whose tragedy divine Musaeus[11] sung)
Dwelt at Abydos; since him dwelt there none
For whom succeeding times make greater moan.
His dangling tresses that were never shorn,
Had they been cut and unto Colchos[12] borne,
Would have allured the vent'rous youth of Greece
To hazard more than for the Golden Fleece.
Fair Cynthia[13] wished his arms might be her sphere;° *orbit*
Grief makes her pale, because she moves not there.
His body was as straight as Circe's wand;[14]
Jove might have sipped out nectar from his hand.
Even as delicious meat is to the taste,
So was his neck in touching, and surpassed

[1] *Hellespont* Narrow strait in Turkey between the Aegean Sea and the Marmara sea, now called the Dardanelles. One bank lies in Europe, one in Asia.

[2] *Neptune* Roman god of the sea.

[3] *Abydos* Ancient city on the Asian bank.

[4] *Sestos* Ancient city on the European bank.

[5] *Apollo* Greek and Roman sun god.

[6] *lawn* Fine linen.

[7] *bordered ... lies* Description of an embroidered pattern depicting the story of Venus and Adonis, told by both the Roman writer Ovid in his *Metamorphoses* (1 CE) and by Shakespeare in his *Venus and Adonis* (1593).

[8] *to her mind* As she chose.

[9] *Hero ... mother* Cupid's mother was Venus, Roman goddess of love and beauty.

[10] *Venus' nun* Hero was a priestess of Venus.

[11] *Musaeus* Greek poet (fifth century CE) who wrote an early version of the Hero and Leander story.

[12] *Colchos* Colchis, a country now in western Georgia, where the Argonauts (the "vent'rous youths") were said to have found the Golden Fleece.

[13] *Cynthia* Moon.

[14] *Circe's wand* In Homer's *Odyssey*, Circe turns Odysseus's crew into pigs with her wand.

The white of Pelops' shoulder.[1] I could tell ye
How smooth his breast was, and how white his belly,
And whose immortal fingers did imprint
That heavenly path, with many a curious° dint, *artful*
That runs along his back; but my rude[2] pen
Can hardly blazon forth the loves of men,
Much less of powerful gods; let it suffice
That my slack° muse sings of Leander's eyes, *weak*
Those orient° cheeks and lips, exceeding his *lustrous*
That leapt into the water for a kiss
Of his own shadow, and despising many,
Died ere he could enjoy the love of any.[3]
Had wild Hippolytus[4] Leander seen,
Enamored of his beauty had he been;
His presence made the rudest peasant melt,
That in the vast uplandish country dwelt;
The barbarous Thracian soldier, moved with naught,
Was moved with him, and for his favor sought.
Some swore he was a maid in man's attire,
For in his looks were all that men desire:
A pleasant smiling cheek, a speaking° eye, *expressive*
A brow for love to banquet royally;
And such as knew he was a man, would say,
"Leander, thou art made for amorous play;
Why art thou not in love, and loved of all?
Though thou be fair, yet be not thine own thrall."
The men of wealthy Sestos every year,
For his sake whom their goddess held so dear,
Rose-cheeked Adonis,[5] kept a solemn feast.
Thither resorted many a wandering guest
To meet their loves; such as had none at all
Came lovers home from this great festival;
For every street, like to a firmament,
Glistered with breathing stars, who, where they went,
Frighted the melancholy earth, which deemed
Eternal heaven to burn, for so it seemed
As if another Phaëton[6] had got
The guidance of the sun's rich chariot.
But, far above the loveliest, Hero shined,
And stole away th' enchanted gazer's mind;
For like sea nymphs'[7] inveigling harmony,
So was her beauty to the standers by.
Nor that night-wandering pale and watery star[8]
(When yawning dragons draw her thirling° car *hurtling*
From Latmos' mount[9] up to the gloomy sky,
Where, crowned with blazing light and majesty,
She proudly sits) more over-rules the flood
Than she the hearts of those that near her stood.
Even as when gaudy nymphs pursue the chase,° *hunt*
Wretched Ixion's shaggy-footed race,[10]
Incensed with savage heat, gallop amain
From steep pine-bearing mountains to the plain,
So ran the people forth to gaze upon her,
And all that viewed her were enamored on her.
And as in fury of a dreadful fight,
Their fellows being slain or put to flight,
Poor soldiers stand with fear of death dead-strooken,
So at her presence all, surprised and tooken,
Await the sentence of her scornful eyes;
He whom she favors lives, the other dies.
There might you see one sigh, another rage,
And some, their violent passions to assuage,
Compile sharp satires; but alas, too late,
For faithful love will never turn to hate.
And many, seeing great princes were denied,
Pined as they went, and thinking on her, died.
On this feast day, oh, cursèd day and hour!
Went Hero thorough° Sestos, from her tower *through*
To Venus' temple, where unhappily,
As after chanced, they did each other spy.
So fair a church as this had Venus none;

[1] *Pelops' shoulder* In Ovid, Pelops was cut into pieces by his father, Tantalus, and served to the gods. The gods put him back together, except for his shoulder, which had already been eaten. They fashioned a new one out of ivory for him.

[2] *rude* Lacking in elegance.

[3] *his ... any* Reference to Narcissus, who fell in love with his own reflection in the water and drowned.

[4] *Hippolytus* Exceedingly beautiful young man in Greek mythology.

[5] *Adonis* Beautiful boy beloved by Aphrodite, Greek goddess of love.

[6] *Phaëton* Son of the Greek sun god Apollo. Phaëton drives the sun chariot so badly that Zeus blasts him from the sky.

[7] *sea nymphs* I.e., the Sirens.

[8] *night-wandering ... star* Moon.

[9] *Latmos' mount* Diana, the Greek moon goddess, nightly visited her sleeping beloved Eudymion on Mount Latmos.

[10] *Ixion's ... race* Centaurs, fathered by Ixion, who was condemned to be bound to a burning wheel for all eternity.

The walls were of discolored° jasper stone, *multicolored*
Wherein was Proteus[1] carvèd, and o'erhead
A lively° vine of green sea-agate spread, *lifelike*
Where, by one hand, light-headed Bacchus[2] hung,
And with the other, wine from grapes out-wrung.
Of crystal shining fair the pavement was;
The town of Sestos called it Venus' glass;° *mirror*
There might you see the gods in sundry shapes,
Committing heady riots, incest, rapes:
For know that underneath this radiant floor
Was Danaë's statue in a brazen tower,
Jove slyly stealing from his sister's bed
To dally with Idalian Ganymede,
And for his love Europa bellowing loud,
And tumbling with the rainbow in a cloud;[3]
Blood-quaffing Mars heaving the iron net
Which limping Vulcan and his Cyclops set;[4]
Love kindling fire to burn such towns as Troy;[5]
Silvanus weeping for the lovely boy[6]
That now is turned into a cypress tree,
Under whose shade the wood-gods love to be.
And in the midst a silver altar stood;
There Hero sacrificing turtles'[7] blood,
Vailed° to the ground, veiling her eyelids close, *bowed*
And modestly they opened as she rose;
Thence flew love's arrow with the golden head,
And thus Leander was enamorèd.
Stone still he stood, and evermore he gazed,
Till with the fire that from his countenance blazed,
Relenting Hero's gentle heart was strook;
Such force and virtue° hath an amorous look. *power*
It lies not in our power to love or hate,
For will in us is overruled by fate.
When two are stripped, long ere the course[8] begin
We wish that one should lose, the other win;
And one especially do we affect° *prefer*
Of two gold ingots, like in each respect.
The reason no man knows, let it suffice,
What we behold is censured° by our eyes. *judged*
Where both deliberate, the love is slight;
Who ever loved, that loved not at first sight?[9]
He kneeled, but unto her devoutly prayed.
Chaste Hero to herself thus softly said,
"Were I the saint he worships, I would hear him,"
And as she spake those words, came somewhat near him.
He started up; she blushed as one ashamed,
Wherewith Leander much more was inflamed.
He touched her hand; in touching it she trembled:
Love deeply grounded hardly is dissembled.[10]
These lovers parlèd° by the touch of hands; *spoke*
True love is mute, and oft amazèd stands.
Thus, while dumb signs their yielding hearts entangled,
The air with sparks of living fire was spangled,
And Night, deep drenched in misty Acheron,[11]
Heaved up her head, and half the world upon
Breathed darkness forth. (Dark night is Cupid's day.)
And now begins Leander to display
Love's holy fire, with words, with sighs and tears,
Which like sweet music entered Hero's ears,
And yet at every word she turned aside
And always cut him off as he replied.
At last, like to a bold sharp sophister,[12]
With cheerful hope thus he accosted her:
"Fair creature, let me speak without offense;
I would my rude words had the influence
To lead thy thoughts as thy fair looks do mine;
Then shouldst thou be his prisoner, who is thine.

[1] *Proteus* Greek lesser sea god able to change his shape rapidly.

[2] *Bacchus* Greek god of wine.

[3] *Danaë's … cloud* Chronicle of the amorous exploits of Zeus (called Jove in Roman mythology). He impregnated Danaë as a shower of gold while she was locked in a tower, married his sister Juno, kidnapped the beautiful young man Ganymede on Mount Ida, seduced Europa while in the form of a bull, and had a tryst with Iris, goddess of the rainbow (although this last conquest is a Renaissance addition to the myth).

[4] *Blood … set* Vulcan, god of fire, used a net to catch his wife Venus in an affair with Mars, god of war. The Cyclopes were his assistants.

[5] *Love … Troy* Paris's abduction of Helen of Troy caused the Trojan Wars.

[6] *lovely boy* Cyparissus, who was turned into a cypress tree by Apollo.

[7] *turtles* Turtledoves, a symbol of fidelity.

[8] *course* I.e., race course.

[9] *Who … sight?* Shakespeare quotes this line in *As You Like It* 3.5.87.

[10] *hardly is dissembled* Is difficult to disguise.

[11] *Acheron* River in the underworld.

[12] *sophister* Here, student or scholar adept at rhetoric.

Be not unkind and fair—misshapen stuff[1]
Are of behavior boisterous and rough.
O shun me not, but hear me ere you go;
God knows I cannot force° love, as you do. *compel*
My words shall be as spotless as my youth,
Full of simplicity and naked truth.
This sacrifice, whose sweet perfume descending
From Venus' altar to your footsteps bending,° *turning*
Doth testify that you exceed her far
To whom you offer and whose nun you are.
Why should you worship her? Her you surpass
As much as sparkling diamonds flaring° glass. *gaudy*
A diamond set in lead his worth retains;
A heavenly nymph, beloved of human swains,
Receives no blemish but ofttimes more grace;
Which makes me hope, although I am but base—
Base in respect of[2] thee, divine and pure—
Dutiful service may thy love procure;
And I in duty will excel all other,
As thou in beauty dost exceed Love's mother.
Nor heaven, nor thou, were made to gaze upon;
As heaven preserves all things, so save thou one.
A stately builded ship, well rigged and tall,
The ocean maketh more majestical:
Why vowest thou then to live in Sestos here,
Who on Love's seas more glorious wouldst appear?
Like untuned golden strings all women are,
Which, long time lie untouched, will harshly jar.[3]
Vessels of brass, oft handled, brightly shine;
What difference betwixt the richest mine
And basest mold,° but use? for both not used *earth*
Are of like worth. Then treasure is abused
When misers keep it; being put to loan,[4]
In time it will return us two for one.
Rich robes themselves and others do adorn;
Neither themselves nor others, if not worn.
Who builds a palace and rams up the gate
Shall see it ruinous and desolate.
Ah, simple Hero, learn thyself to cherish;
Lone women, like to empty houses, perish.
Less sins the poor rich man that starves himself
In heaping up a mass of drossy pelf,[5]
Than such as you: his golden earth remains,
Which after his decease some other gains.
But this fair gem, sweet in the loss alone,
When you fleet hence[6] can be bequeathed to none.
Or if it could, down from th' enameled° sky *multi-colored*
All heaven would come to claim this legacy,
And with intestine broils[7] the world destroy
And quite confound Nature's sweet harmony.
Well therefore by the gods decreed it is,
We human creatures should enjoy that bliss.
One is no number;[8] maids are nothing then
Without the sweet society of men.
Wilt thou live single still? One shalt thou be,
Though never-singling Hymen[9] couple thee.
Wild savages, that drink of running springs,
Think water far excels all earthly things;
But they that daily taste neat° wine despise it. *pure*
Virginity, albeit some highly prize it,
Compared with marriage, had you tried them both,
Differs as much as wine and water doth.
Base bullion for the stamp's sake we allow:[10]
Even so for men's impression do we you;
By which alone, our reverend fathers[11] say,
Women receive perfection every way.
This idol which you term Virginity,
Is neither essence,° subject to the eye— *real*
No, nor to any one exterior sense;
Nor hath it any place of residence,
Nor is 't of earth or mold° celestial, *form*
Or capable of any form at all.
Of that which hath no being do not boast:
Things that are not at all are never lost.
Men foolishly do call it virtuous:

[1] *misshapen stuff* Human beings.

[2] *in respect of* Compared to.

[3] *harshly jar* Be out of tune.

[4] *put to loan* Invested.

[5] *drossy pelf* Gold ore that has not yet been refined.

[6] *fleet hence* Die.

[7] *intestine broils* Civil wars.

[8] *One … number* Aristotelian mathematical idea.

[9] *Hymen* Greek god of weddings.

[10] *Base … allow* We allow poorer metal to gain worth by being stamped as coins.

[11] *reverend fathers* Early Christian theologians.

What virtue is it that is born with us?[1]
Much less can honor be ascribed thereto:
Honor is purchased by the deeds we do.
Believe me, Hero, honor is not won
Until some honorable deed be done.
Seek you for chastity, immortal fame,
And know that some have wronged Diana's name?[2]
Whose name is it, if she be false or not,
So she be fair, but some vile tongues will blot?
But you are fair, aye me! so wondrous fair,
So young, so gentle, and so debonair,° *pleasant*
As Greece will think, if thus you live alone,
Some one or other keeps you as his own.
Then, Hero, hate me not, nor from me fly
To follow swiftly-blasting infamy.
Perhaps thy sacred priesthood makes thee loath.
Tell me, to whom madest thou that heedless oath?"
"To Venus," answered she, and as she spake,
Forth from those two tralucent cisterns[3] brake
A stream of liquid pearl, which down her face
Made milk-white paths whereon the gods might
trace° *follow*
To Jove's[4] high court. He thus replied:
"The rites in which Love's beauteous empress most delights
Are banquets, Doric music,[5] midnight revel,
Plays, masques, and all that stern age counteth evil.
Thee as a holy idiot doth she scorn;
For thou, in vowing chastity, hast sworn
To rob her name and honor, and thereby
Commit'st a sin far worse than perjury—
Even sacrilege against her Deity,
Through regular and formal purity.
To expiate which sin, kiss and shake hands;
Such sacrifice as this Venus demands."
Thereat she smiled and did deny him so
As, put° thereby, yet might he hope for mo.° *put aside / more*
Which makes him quickly reinforce his speech
And her in humble manner thus beseech:
"Though neither gods nor men may thee deserve,
Yet for her sake whom you have vowed to serve,
Abandon fruitless, cold Virginity,
The gentle Queen of Love's sole enemy.
Then shall you most resemble Venus' nun,
When Venus' sweet rites are performed and done.
Flint-breasted Pallas[6] joys in single life,
But Pallas and your mistress are at strife.
Love, Hero, then, and be not tyrannous,
But heal the heart that thou hast wounded thus,
Nor stain thy youthful years with avarice;
Fair fools delight to be accounted nice.° *shy*
The richest corn° dies, if it be not reaped; *grain*
Beauty alone is lost, too warily kept."
These arguments he used, and many more,
Wherewith she yielded, that was won before.[7]
Hero's looks yielded, but her words made war:
Women are won when they begin to jar.° *argue*
Thus, having swallowed Cupid's golden hook,
The more she strived, the deeper was she strook.
Yet, evilly feigning anger, strove she still
And would be thought to grant against her will.
So having paused a while, at last she said:
"Who taught thee rhetoric to deceive a maid?
Aye me, such words as these should I abhor,
And yet I like them for the orator."
With that, Leander stooped to have embraced her,
But from his spreading arms away she cast her,° *herself*
And thus bespake him: "Gentle youth, forbear
To touch the sacred garments which I wear.
"Upon a rock, and underneath a hill,
Far from the town, where all is whist° and still, *hushed*
Save that the sea, playing on yellow sand,
Sends forth a rattling murmur to the land,
Whose sound allures the golden Morpheus[8]
In silence of the night to visit us,
My turret stands, and there, God knows, I play
With Venus' swans and sparrows[9] all the day.

[1] *What ... us?* Virtues can only be acquired. One is not born with them.

[2] *Seek ... name?* Even Diana, the goddess of chastity, could not prove her chastity when it was slandered.

[3] *tralucent cisterns* Translucent eyes.

[4] *Jove* Chief in the pantheon of Roman gods (Greek Zeus).

[5] *Doric music* Form of music with a military feel to it. This may not be the association that Leander (or Marlowe) had intended.

[6] *Pallas* Athena, Greek goddess of wisdom, was, in one of her roles, a goddess of war, and was thus depicted dressed in armor.

[7] *that ... before* I.e., she was, privately, already convinced.

[8] *Morpheus* Greek god of dreams, whose gift was golden slumbers.

[9] *swans and sparrows* Venus's chariot was drawn by swans and sparrows.

A dwarfish beldame° bears me company, *old woman*
That hops about the chamber where I lie
And spends the night, that might be better spent,
In vain discourse and apish° merriment. *foolish*
Come thither." As she spake this, her tongue tripped,
For unawares "Come thither" from her slipped;
And suddenly her former color changed
And here and there her eyes through anger ranged.
And like a planet, moving several ways,[1]
At one self° instant, she, poor soul, assays° *same / tries*
Loving, not to love at all, and every part
Strove to resist the motions of her heart;
And hands so pure, so innocent, nay, such
As might have made heaven stoop to have a touch,
Did she uphold to Venus, and again
Vowed spotless chastity, but all in vain.
Cupid beat down her prayers with his wings;
Her vows above the empty air he flings.
All deep enraged, his sinewy° bow he bent, *strong*
And shot a shaft that burning from him went,
Wherewith she, strooken, looked so dolefully
As made Love sigh to see his tyranny.
And as she wept, her tears to pearl he turned,
And wound them on his arm, and for her mourned.
Then towards the palace of the Destinies,[2]
Laden with languishment and grief, he flies,
And to those stern nymphs humbly made request
Both might enjoy each other and be blessed.
But with a ghastly dreadful countenance,
Threatening a thousand deaths at every glance,
They answered Love, nor would vouchsafe so much
As one poor word, their hate to him was such.
Harken a while, and I will tell you why:
Heaven's wingèd herald, Jove-born Mercury,[3]
The selfsame day that he asleep had laid
Enchanted Argus,[4] spied a country maid
Whose careless hair, instead of pearl t' adorn it,
Glistered with dew, as one that seemed to scorn it;[5]
Her breath as fragrant as the morning rose,
Her mind pure, and her tongue untaught to glose.° *flatter*
Yet proud she was, for lofty pride that dwells
In towered courts is oft in shepherds' cells,
And too-too well the fair vermilion[6] knew,
And silver tincture of her cheeks, that drew
The love of every swain. On her, this god
Enamored was, and with his snaky rod[7]
Did charm her nimble feet and made her stay;
The while upon a hillock down he lay,
And sweetly on his pipe began to play,
And with smooth speech, her fancy to assay,
Till in his twining arms he locked her fast,
And then he wooed with kisses, and at last,
As shepherds do, her on the ground he laid,
And tumbling in the grass, he often strayed
Beyond the bounds of shame, in being bold
To eye those parts which no eye should behold;
And, like an insolent commanding lover,
Boasting his parentage, would needs discover
The way to new Elysium;[8] but she,
Whose only dower was her chastity,
Having striven in vain, was now about to cry
And crave the help of shepherds that were nigh.
Herewith he stayed his fury,° and began *passion*
To give her leave to rise. Away she ran;
After went Mercury, who used such cunning
As she, to hear his tale, left off her running.
Maids are not won by brutish force and might,
But speeches full of pleasure and delight.
And knowing Hermes courted her, was glad
That she such loveliness and beauty had
As could provoke his liking, yet was mute,
And neither would deny nor grant his suit.
Still vowed he love; she, wanting no excuse
To feed him with delays, as women use,° *do*
Or thirsting after immortality

[1] *several ways* In older astronomy, the planets moved around the earth within their own orbits and were also affected by the movement of other heavenly bodies; *several* Different.

[2] *Destinies* Fates, three female entities in Greek mythology who controlled the destiny of all humans.

[3] *Mercury* Roman messenger god, called Hermes by the Greeks. Mercury was depicted with winged feet.

[4] *Enchanted Argus* Monster placed by Juno as a guard over Io to keep her away from Jupiter. Mercury put Argus to sleep.

[5] *it* Pearls, jewelry.

[6] *vermilion* Red.

[7] *snaky rod* Caduceus, held by Mercury. Now the symbol for medicine.

[8] *Elysium* Section of the underworld in Greek mythology reserved for heroes. In the Renaissance could apply to Paradise.

(All women are ambitious naturally),
Imposed upon her lover such a task
As he ought not perform, nor yet she ask.
A draft of flowing nectar she requested,
Wherewith the king of gods and men is feasted.
He, ready to accomplish what she willed,
Stole some from Hebe[1] (Hebe Jove's cup filled)
And gave it to his simple rustic love,
Which being known (as what is hid from Jove?)
He inly° stormed and waxed more furious *inwardly*
Than for the fire filched by Prometheus,[2]
And thrusts him down from heaven. He, wandering here,
In mournful terms, with sad and heavy cheer,[3]
Complained to Cupid. Cupid, for his sake,
To be revenged on Jove did undertake;
And those on whom heaven, earth, and hell relies
(I mean the adamantine° Destinies) *immovable*
He wounds with love and forced them equally
To dote upon deceitful Mercury.
They offered him the deadly fatal knife
That shears the slender threads of human life;[4]
At his fair feathered feet the engines laid
Which th' earth from ugly Chaos' den upweighed.[5]
These he regarded not, but did entreat
That Jove, usurper of his father's seat,
Might presently be banished into hell
And agèd Saturn in Olympus dwell.
They granted what he craved, and once again
Saturn and Ops began their golden reign.
Murder, rape, war, lust, and treachery
Were with Jove closed in Stygian empery.
But long this blessèd time continued not;
As soon as he his wishèd purpose got,
He, reckless of his promise, did despise
The love of th' everlasting Destinies.
They seeing it, both Love and him abhorred,
And Jupiter unto his place restored.[6]
And but that Learning, in despite of Fate,
Will mount aloft and enter heaven gate,
And to the seat of Jove itself advance,
Hermes had slept in hell with Ignorance.
Yet as a punishment they added this,
That he and Poverty should always kiss.[7]
And to this day is every scholar poor;
Gross gold from them runs headlong to the boor.
Likewise the angry sisters, thus deluded,
To venge themselves on Hermes, have concluded
That Midas' brood[8] shall sit in Honor's chair,
To which the Muses' sons are only heir.
And fruitful wits, that inaspiring[9] are
Shall discontent run into regions far;
And few great lords in virtuous deeds shall joy,
But be surprised with every garish toy,
And still enrich the lofty servile clown,° *boor*
Who, with encroaching guile, keeps learning down.
Then muse not[10] Cupid's suit no better sped,
Seeing in their loves the Fates were injurèd.
By this, sad Hero, with love unacquainted,
Viewing Leander's face, fell down and fainted.
He kissed her and breathed life into her lips,
Wherewith, as one displeased, away she trips.
Yet as she went, full often looked behind,
And many poor excuses did she find
To linger by the way, and once she stayed,
And would have turned again, but was afraid,

[1] *Hebe* Greek goddess of youth, cupbearer for the gods.

[2] *Prometheus* Greek Titan who stole fire from the gods.

[3] *terms* Condition; *cheer* Expression.

[4] *knife ... life* The Fate Atropos caused a human death by cutting the thread of life.

[5] *engines ... upweighed* The Fates were also said to be in charge of the pillars that held the world up ("upweighed") out of Chaos, the primeval disordered matter from which the gods first came.

[6] *These he regarded ... his place restored* Mythical story in which Mercury rejects the gifts of the Fates, requesting instead that Jove be overthrown as king of the gods and thrown down into Hades. Jove's father, Saturn, the original ruler of heaven during the Golden Age, returns with his wife Ops and begins a second Golden Age, where all the negative elements associated with Jove ("Murder, rape, war, lust and treachery") are similarly banished to Hades (the "Stygian empery"). The second Golden Age does not last long, for Mercury quickly forgets the Fates, who restore Jove to his throne.

[7] *Learning ... kiss* Myth invented by Marlowe. Mercury (referred to here by his Greek name Hermes) is identified as god of learning. Mercury sleeps "in hell with Ignorance," yet Learning is so great a power that it raises him up to heaven ("the seat of Jove") despite the wishes of the Fates. The Fates punish Mercury for his inconstancy, linking Learning with Poverty.

[8] *Midas' brood* I.e., the rich and the foolish.

[9] *inaspiring* I.e., those that do not aspire toward wealth.

[10] *muse not* Do not wonder that.

In offering parley to be counted light.[1]
So on she goes, and in her idle flight
Her painted fan of curlèd plumes let fall,
Thinking to train° Leander therewithal. *lure*
He, being a novice, knew not what she meant
But stayed, and after her a letter sent,
Which joyful Hero answered in such sort
As he had hope to scale the beauteous fort
Wherein the liberal Graces[2] locked their wealth,
And therefore to her tower he got by stealth.
Wide open stood the door; he need not climb,
And she herself before the pointed° time *appointed*
Had spread the board,[3] with roses strewed the room,
And oft looked out, and mused he did not come.
At last he came; O who can tell the greeting
These greedy lovers had at their first meeting?
He asked, she gave, and nothing was denied;
Both to each other quickly were affied.° *betrothed*
Look how their hands, so were their hearts united,
And what he did, she willingly requited.
(Sweet are the kisses, the embracements sweet,
When like desires and affections meet,
For from the earth to heaven is Cupid raised
Where fancy is in equal balance peised.)° *weighed*
Yet she this rashness suddenly repented
And turned aside and to herself lamented,
As if her name and honor had been wronged
By being possessed of him for whom she longed.
Ay, and she wished, albeit not from her heart,
That he would leave her turret and depart.
The mirthful god of amorous pleasure smiled
To see how he this captive nymph beguiled,
For hitherto he did but fan the fire
And kept it down that it might mount the higher.
Now waxed she jealous lest his love abated,
Fearing her own thoughts made her to be hated.
Therefore unto him hastily she goes
And, like light Salmacis,[4] her body throws
Upon his bosom where, with yielding eyes,
She offers up herself a sacrifice
To slake his anger; if he were displeased,
O what god would not therewith be appeased?
Like Aesop's cock,[5] this jewel he enjoyed,
And as a brother with his sister toyed,
Supposing nothing else was to be done,
Now he her favor and good will had won.
But know you not that creatures wanting sense° *intelligence*
By nature have a mutual appetence,° *attraction*
And wanting organs to advance a step,
Moved by love's force, unto each other leap?
Much more in subjects having intellect
Some hidden influence breeds like effect.
Albeit Leander, rude° in love and raw, *unsophisticated*
Long dallying with Hero, nothing saw
That might delight him more, yet he suspected
Some amorous rites or other were neglected.
Therefore unto his body, hers he clung;
She, fearing on the rushes[6] to be flung,
Strived with redoubled strength; the more she strived,
The more a gentle, pleasing heat revived,
Which taught him all that elder lovers know.
And now the same gan° so to scorch and glow, *began*
As, in plain terms, yet cunningly, he craved it.
(Love always makes those eloquent that have it.)
She, with a kind of granting, put him by it,
And, ever as he thought himself most nigh it,
Like to the tree of Tantalus,[7] she fled,
And, seeming lavish, saved her maidenhead.
Ne'er king more sought to keep his diadem° *crown*
Than Hero this inestimable gem.
Above our life we love a steadfast friend;
Yet, when a token of great worth we send,
We often kiss it, often look thereon,
And stay the messenger that would be gone.
No marvel then, though Hero would not yield
So soon to part from that she dearly held.
Jewels being lost are found again, this never;
'Tis lost but once, and once lost, lost forever.

[1] *In offering … light* By conversing to be considered improper.

[2] *Graces* Three Greek goddesses of joy, charm and beauty.

[3] *spread the board* Set the table.

[4] *Salmacis* Nymph who falls in love with Hermaphroditus. He rejects her, but she clings to him and prays that they will never be parted. The gods grant her wish by fusing their two bodies together.

[5] *Aesop's cock* In Aesop's "The Cock and the Jewel" a rooster finds a jewel but sees no value in it, preferring barleycorns.

[6] *rushes* Floors in Renaissance houses and castles were often strewn with reeds.

[7] *Tantalus* Tantalus was cursed to stand under a tree whose fruit remained just out of reach and to stand in water, unable to drink.

Now had the Morn espied her lover's steeds,[1]
Whereat she starts, puts on her purple weeds,° *clothes*
And, red for anger that he stayed so long,
All headlong throws herself the clouds among.
And now Leander, fearing to be missed,
Embraced her suddenly, took leave, and kissed;
Long was he taking leave, and loath to go,
And kissed again, as lovers use to do.
Sad Hero wrung him by the hand and wept,
Saying, "Let your vows and promises be kept."
Then, standing at the door, she turned about,
As loath to see Leander going out.
And now the sun that through th' horizon peeps,
As pitying these lovers, downward creeps,
So that in silence of the cloudy night,
Though it was morning, did he take his flight.
But what the secret trusty night concealed,
Leander's amorous habit° soon revealed. *clothing*
With Cupid's myrtle[2] was his bonnet° crowned; *hat*
About his arms the purple riband° wound *ribbon*
Wherewith she wreathed her largely spreading hair;
Nor could the youth abstain but he must wear
The sacred ring wherewith she was endowed
When first religious chastity she vowed;
Which made his love through Sestos to be known,
And thence unto Abydos sooner blown
Than he could sail, for incorporeal Fame,
Whose weight consists in nothing but her name,
Is swifter than the wind, whose tardy plumes
Are reeking water and dull earthly fumes.[3]
Home when he came, he seemed not to be there,
But like exilèd air thrust from his sphere,
Set in a foreign place, and straight from thence,
Alcides-like,[4] by mighty violence
He would have chased away the swelling main
That him from her unjustly did detain.
Like as the sun in a diameter[5]
Fires and inflames objects removèd far,
And heateth kindly, shining lat'rally,
So beauty sweetly quickens when 'tis nigh,
But being separated and removed,
Burns where it cherished, murders where it loved.[6]
Therefore, even as an index to a book,
So to his mind was young Leander's look.
O none but gods have power their love to hide:
Affection by the count'nance is descried.[7]
The light of hidden fire itself discovers,
And love that is concealed betrays poor lovers.
His secret flame apparently° was seen; *clearly*
Leander's father knew where he had been,
And for the same mildly rebuked his son,
Thinking to quench the sparkles new begun.
But love, resisted once, grows passionate,
And nothing more than counsel lovers hate.
For as a hot, proud horse highly disdains
To have his head controlled, but breaks the reins,
Spits forth the ringled° bit, and with his hooves *ringed*
Checks° the submissive ground; so he that loves, *paws*
The more he is restrained, the worse he fares.
What is it now but mad Leander dares?[8]
"O Hero, Hero!" thus he cried full oft,
And then he got him to a rock aloft,
Where, having spied her tower, long stared he on't
And prayed the narrow toiling Hellespont
To part in twain, that he might come and go;
But still the rising billows answered "No!"
With that he stripped him to the ivory skin,
And crying, "Love, I come!" leapt lively in.
Whereat the sapphire-visaged god[9] grew proud,
And made his capering Triton[10] sound aloud;
Imagining that Ganymede,[11] displeased,
Had left the heavens, therefore on him seized.
Leander strived; the waves about him wound
And pulled him to the bottom, where the ground
Was strewed with pearl, and in low coral groves

[1] *lover's steeds* Horses that pull the sun's chariot.

[2] *myrtle* Plant symbolic of love, which Cupid wears on his head.

[3] *Are ... fumes* I.e., are as fleeting as mist.

[4] *Alcides-like* Like Hercules.

[5] *in a diameter* I.e., shining directly.

[6] *being separated ... loved* I.e., inaccessible love can be a destructive force.

[7] *Affection ... descried* Love is visible on the face.

[8] *but mad ... dares?* That Leander won't do?

[9] *sapphire-visaged god* Neptune.

[10] *Triton* Son of Neptune, who blew on a conch shell to raise the waves.

[11] *Ganymede* Young man abducted by Jove and taken to the heavens to be the gods' cupbearer.

Sweet singing mermaids sported with their loves
On heaps of heavy gold and took great pleasure
To spurn in careless sort the shipwrack treasure;
For here the stately azure palace stood
Where kingly Neptune and his train abode.
The lusty god embraced him, called him love,
And swore he never should return to Jove.
But when he knew it was not Ganymede,
For under water he was almost dead,
He heaved him up, and looking on his face,
Beat down the bold waves with his triple mace,[1]
Which mounted up, intending to have kissed him,
And fell in drops like tears because they missed him.
Leander being up, began to swim,
And, looking back, saw Neptune follow him;
Whereat aghast, the poor soul gan to cry,
"O let me visit Hero ere I die!"
The god put Helle's bracelet[2] on his arm,
And swore the sea should never do him harm.
He clapped his plump cheeks, with his tresses played,
And, smiling wantonly, his love bewrayed.° *exposed*
He watched his arms, and as they opened wide,
At every stroke betwixt them he would slide
And steal a kiss, and then run out and dance
And, as he turned, cast many a lustful glance
And throw him gaudy toys to please his eye,
And dive into the water and there pry
Upon his breast, his thighs, and every limb,
And up again and close beside him swim,
And talk of love. Leander made reply,
"You are deceived; I am no woman, I."
Thereat smiled Neptune, and then told a tale
How that a shepherd, sitting in a vale,
Played with a boy so lovely fair and kind,
As for his love both earth and heaven pined;
That of the cooling river durst not drink,
Lest water nymphs should pull him from the brink.
And when he sported in the fragrant lawns,
Goat-footed satyrs and up-staring fawns[3]
Would steal him thence. Ere half this tale was done
"Ay me!" Leander cried, "th' enamored sun
That now should shine on Thetis' glassy bower[4]
Descends upon my radiant Hero's tower.
O that these tardy arms of mine were wings!"
And as he spake, upon the waves he springs.
Neptune was angry that he gave no ear,
And in his heart revenging malice bare.
He flung at him his mace, but as it went
He called it in, for love made him repent.
The mace returning back, his own hand hit,
As meaning to be venged for darting it.
When this fresh bleeding wound Leander viewed,
His color went and came, as if he rued
The grief which Neptune felt. In gentle breasts
Relenting thoughts, remorse, and pity rests;
And who have hard hearts and obdurate minds
But vicious, harebrained, and illit'rate hinds?° *boors*
The god, seeing him with pity to be moved,
Thereon concluded that he was beloved.
(Love is too full of faith, too credulous,
With folly and false hope deluding us.)
Wherefore Leander's fancy to surprise,
To the rich ocean for gifts he flies.
'Tis wisdom to give much; a gift prevails
When deep persuading oratory fails.
By this[5] Leander, being near the land,
Cast down his weary feet and felt the sand.
Breathless albeit he were, he rested not
Till to the solitary tower he got,
And knocked and called; at which celestial noise
The longing heart of Hero much more joys
Than nymphs and shepherds when the timbrel[6] rings,
Or crooked dolphin when the sailor sings.[7]
She stayed not for her robes, but straight arose
And, drunk with gladness, to the door she goes;

[1] *triple mace* Three-pointed trident.

[2] *Helle's bracelet* Fleeing a cruel stepmother on a flying ram, Helle fell into the Hellespont and in most versions drowns. She gave her name to the Hellespont. The bracelet appears to be Marlowe's invention.

[3] *Goat-footed ... fawns* Fauns; wood creatures who divined the future by looking up at the stars.

[4] *Thetis' glassy bower* Sea. Thetis was a sea nymph.

[5] *By this* By this time.

[6] *timbrel* Tambourine.

[7] *crooked dolphin ... sings* Arion, the musician, was saved from drowning by a dolphin (swimming in leaps, hence "crooked") that was charmed by his music.

Where, seeing a naked man, she screeched for fear
(Such sights as this to tender maids are rare)
And ran into the dark herself to hide.
Rich jewels in the dark are soonest spied.
Unto her was he led, or rather drawn
By those white limbs which sparkled through the lawn.
The nearer that he came, the more she fled,
And, seeking refuge, slipped into her bed.
Whereon Leander sitting, thus began,
Through numbing cold, all feeble, faint, and wan:
"If not for love, yet, love, for pity's sake
Me in thy bed and maiden bosom take;
At least vouchsafe these arms some little room,
Who, hoping to embrace thee, cheerly° swum. *gladly*
This head was beat with many a churlish billow,[1]
And therefore let it rest upon thy pillow."
Herewith affrighted Hero shrunk away
And in her lukewarm place Leander lay;
Whose lively heat, like fire from heaven fet,° *fetched*
Would animate gross clay, and higher set
The drooping thoughts of base declining souls
Than dreary° Mars carousing nectar bowls. *gory*
His hands he cast upon her like a snare;
She, overcome with shame and sallow fear,
Like chaste Diana when Actaeon spied her,[2]
Being suddenly betrayed, dived down to hide her,
And as her silver body downward went,
With both her hands she made the bed a tent,
And in her own mind thought herself secure,
O'ercast with dim and darksome coverture.° *covering*
And now she lets him whisper in her ear,
Flatter, entreat, promise, protest, and swear;
Yet ever as he greedily assayed
To touch those dainties, she the Harpy[3] played,
And every limb did, as a soldier stout,
Defend the fort and keep the foeman out.
For though the rising ivory mount he scaled,
Which is with azure circling lines empaled,° *surrounded*
Much like a globe (a globe may I term this,
By which love sails to regions full of bliss),
Yet there with Sisyphus[4] he toiled in vain,
Till gentle parley did the truce obtain.
Wherein Leander on her quivering breast,
Breathless spoke something, and sighed out the rest;
Which so prevailed, as he, with small ado,
Enclosed her in his arms and kissed her, too.
And every kiss to her was as a charm,
And to Leander as a fresh alarm,[5]
So that the truce was broke, and she, alas,
Poor silly° maiden, at his mercy was. *defenseless*
Love is not full of pity, as men say,
But deaf and cruel, where he means to prey.
Even as a bird which in our hands we wring
Forth plungeth and oft flutters with her wing,
She trembling strove; this strife of hers, like that
Which made the world,[6] another world begat
Of unknown joy. Treason was in her thought,
And cunningly to yield herself she sought.
Seeming not won, yet won she was, at length.
(In such wars women use but half their strength.)
Leander now, like Theban Hercules,[7]
Entered the orchard of th' Hesperides,
Whose fruit none rightly can describe but he
That pulls or shakes it from the golden tree.[8]
And now she wished this night were never done,
And sighed to think upon th' approaching sun,
For much it grieved her that the bright daylight
Should know the pleasure of this blessèd night,
And them like Mars and Erycine[9] displayed,
Both in each other's arms chained as they laid.
Again she knew not how to frame her look

---

[1] *churlish billow* Angry wave.

[2] *Diana ... spied her* The hunter Actaeon was punished for seeing Diana while she was bathing in a woodland pool.

[3] *Harpy* Monster, half-bird, half-woman. Although a banquet was set for the mythical character Phineus, the harpies continually stole the food out of his hands before he could put it in his mouth.

[4] *Sisyphus* Sisyphus was forever condemned to roll a stone up a hill; as he brought it to the top, it would roll down again.

[5] *alarm* Call to arms.

[6] *like ... world* The Greek philosopher Empedocles held that the world was created out of the tension between love and strife.

[7] *Hercules* Hercules's eleventh task was to steal the golden apples of the Hesperides, nymphs who tended a beautiful garden.

[8] Some scholars have suggested that an error occurred during the first printing of this poem, in which two pages of Marlowe's original manuscript were reversed. If this is the case, lines 775–84 were intended to follow line 762.

[9] *Erycine* Another name for Venus, caught in bed with Mars by her husband Vulcan.

Or speak to him who in a moment took
That which so long so charily° she kept; *carefully*
And fain by stealth away she would have crept
And to some corner secretly have gone,
Leaving Leander in the bed alone.
But as her naked feet were whipping out,
He on the sudden clinged her so about
That mermaid-like unto the floor she slid:
One half appeared, the other half was hid.
Thus near the bed she blushing stood upright;
And from her countenance behold ye might
A kind of twilight break, which through the hair,
As from an orient cloud, glims° here and there, *glimmers*
And round about the chamber this false morn
Brought forth the day before the day was born.
So Hero's ruddy cheek Hero betrayed,
And her all naked to his sight displayed,
Whence his admiring eyes more pleasure took
Than Dis[1] on heaps of gold fixing his look.
By this Apollo's golden harp began
To sound forth music to the Ocean,
Which watchful Hesperus[2] no sooner heard
But he the day's bright-bearing car prepared,
And ran before, as harbinger of light,
And with his flaring beams mocked ugly Night
Till she, o'ercome with anguish, shame, and rage,
Danged° down to hell her loathsome carriage. *threw*
Desunt nonnulla.[3]
—1598

The Passionate Shepherd to His Love

Come live with me and be my love,
And we will all the pleasures prove° *experience*
That valleys, groves, hills, and fields,
Woods, or steepy mountain yields.

And we will sit upon the rocks,
Seeing the shepherds feed their flocks,
By shallow rivers to whose falls
Melodious birds sing madrigals.[4]

And I will make thee beds of roses
And a thousand fragrant posies,
A cap of flowers, and a kirtle° *skirt*
Embroidered all with leaves of myrtle;

A gown made of the finest wool
Which from our pretty lambs we pull;
Fair linèd slippers for the cold,
With buckles of the purest gold;

A belt of straw and ivy buds,
With coral clasps and amber studs:
And if these pleasures may thee move,
Come live with me, and be my love.

The shepherd swains° shall dance and sing *rustic lovers*
For thy delight each May morning:
If these delights thy mind may move,
Then live with me and be my love.
—1599

[1] *Dis* Another name for Pluto, god of the underworld.

[2] *Hesperus* Evening star, the planet Venus.

[3] *Desunt nonnulla* "Something is missing." Inserted by the first printer. Marlowe does not include the tragic end of the story as related by other authors. It is possible that he died before finishing the poem.

[4] *madrigals* Part-songs for several voices, often with pastoral or amatory associations.

The Tragical History of Doctor Faustus

The Tragical History of Doctor Faustus is a work that employs belief from both the medieval and modern worlds. At its core is a story, of which there are various medieval versions, of a man selling his soul to the devil. Yet the play is plotted in a way that differs strikingly from the conventions of most medieval drama with, for example, a progression of scenes structured to suggest the passage of time in the real world. (Whereas in most medieval plays characters may exit at the end of one scene and reappear immediately at the beginning of the next in a different place or at a different time, Marlowe and Shakespeare broke new ground in the early 1590s, always providing for some passage of time in such circumstances.) The play posits sinister magical worlds that may seem far-fetched to the modern mind; in the late sixteenth century the lines that now divide what we term "science" from "superstition" had barely begun to be drawn and—again like Shakespeare—Marlowe mixes the comic and the tragic in ways that may jar on some modern sensibilities. Yet its treatment of the connections between the worlds of religion, magic, and science; of the connections between knowledge and power; and of the bitter fruits of excessive ambition resonate deeply with modern readers and modern audiences. So too does the material of the story itself, which has been recast by many authors in the intervening centuries—most notably by Goethe in the eighteenth century (*Faust*, 1790) and by Thomas Mann in the twentieth century (*Dr. Faustus*, 1947).

Not surprisingly, a somewhat uneasy relationship exists between *Dr. Faustus* and traditional Christian doctrine, Protestant or Catholic. However much the ambition of Faustus leads to damning sin, we are made to sense something attractive in his soaring visions. And in numerous other respects, too, the play puts forward religious notions from outside the mainstream (that hell may also be a state of mind, for example, and that there may be legitimate ties between the practices of magic and those of Christianity). Yet the play remains a memorable and provocative literary exploration of Christian doctrine. Do we have free will? What are the limits of God's forgiveness?

Marlowe's *Dr. Faustus* exists in two substantially different versions. There has been a great deal of scholarly discussion of the differences between the two, and debate over which is closest to what Marlowe himself wrote.

Marlowe probably completed the play in 1592 or early 1593 (he died on 30 May of that year). We know that between September of 1594 and October of 1597 the play was performed 25 times at the Rose Theatre by the Admiral's Men, with Edward Alleyn playing Faustus. The same company added the play to their repertory again when they opened the Fortune Theatre as their new house in late 1602. (Payment of £4 was made at this time on behalf of the Admiral's Men to two individuals "for there adicyones in doctor fostes.")

The first printed text that has come down to us is that of 1604 (commonly known as the "A" text). A much longer version was published in 1616; it included numerous new scenes (the majority of them comic) and a variety of other revisions throughout. Some of these revisions were evidently forced by the 1606 "Act to restrain Abuses of Players," which forbad actors "in any Stage play ... jestingly or prophanely" from speaking or using "the holy Name of God or of Christ Jesus, or of the Holy Ghoste or of the Trinitie, which are not to be spoken but with feare and reverence." Thus Faustus's characterization of God as "unpleasant, harsh, contemptible, and vile" 1.1.110 is cut from the 1616 (or "B") text; similarly, his vision of Christ's blood and the frowns of an angry God (5.2.70–77) are radically altered. The reasons for and the source of the various other differences between the A and B texts remain in dispute among scholars. Michael Keefer, whose edition of the play appears in these pages, has argued persuasively not only that the "A" text is "shorter, harsher, more focused, and more disturbing" than the 1616 "B" text but also that it is much closer to the play as it was performed in the 1590s. The edition here has been adapted from Keefer's edition, which is based on the 1604 "A" text. For the text of all the 1616 revisions, together with a full scholarly discussion of the differences between the two versions, readers are invited to consult Keefer's full edition of the play, which appears as part of the Broadview Editions series.

The Tragical History of Doctor Faustus

("A" Text)

DRAMATIS PERSONAE

John Faustus, *doctor of theology*
Wagner, *a student, and Faustus's servant; also speaks the part of Chorus*
Good Angel
Evil Angel
Valdes and Cornelius, *magicians*
Three Scholars, *colleagues of Faustus at Wittenberg University*
Mephastophilis, *a devil*
Clown (Robin)
Rafe, *another clown*
Lucifer
Belzebub
The Seven Deadly Sins
Pope
Cardinal of Lorraine
Friar
Vintner
Charles V, Emperor of Germany
Knight
Alexander the Great and his Paramour, *spirits*
Horse-courser
Duke of Vanholt and his Duchess
Helen of Troy, a spirit
Old Man
Devils, Friars, Attendants

PROLOGUE

(*Enter Chorus.*)

CHORUS. Not marching now in fields of Thracimene
Where Mars did mate[1] the Carthaginians,
Nor sporting in the dalliance of love
In courts of kings where state is overturn'd,
Nor in the pomp of proud audacious deeds
Intends our muse to vaunt° his heavenly verse. *display proudly*
Only this, gentlemen: we must perform
The form of Faustus' fortunes, good or bad.
To patient judgments we appeal our plaud,[2]
And speak for Faustus in his infancy:
Now is he born, his parents base of stock,
In Germany, within a town call'd Rhodes;[3]
Of riper years to Wittenberg[4] he went,
Whereas his kinsmen chiefly brought him up.
So soon he profits in divinity,
The fruitful plot of scholarism grac'd,
That shortly he was grac'd[5] with doctor's name,
Excelling all whose sweet delight disputes[6]

[1] *Mars did mate* Mars "allied himself with" or "rivaled." Hannibal's Carthaginian army inflicted a crushing defeat upon the Romans at the battle of Lake Trasummenus in 217 BCE.

[2] *appeal our plaud* Appeal for our applause.

[3] *Rhodes* Roda (now Stadtroda), near Weimar.

[4] *Wittenberg* The University of Wittenberg was famous under Martin Luther as a Protestant center of learning.

[5] *grac'd* At Cambridge it was and still is by the "grace" or decree of the university Senate that degrees are conferred; Marlowe's name appears in the Grace Book in 1584 and 1587 for the B.A. and M.A. degrees respectively.

[6] *whose ... disputes* It is possible to construe "disputes" as a verb; more probably the expression is elliptical and means "whose sweet delight consists in disputes."

In heavenly matters of theology,
Till swoll'n with cunning[1] of a self-conceit,
His waxen wings[2] did mount above his reach
And melting heavens conspir'd his overthrow.
For falling to a devilish exercise,
And glutted now with learning's golden gifts,
He surfeits upon cursed necromancy;
Nothing so sweet as magic is to him,
Which he prefers before his chiefest bliss:
And this the man that in his study sits.

(*Exit.*)

ACT 1, SCENE 1[3]

(*Faustus in his study.*)

FAUSTUS. Settle thy studies, Faustus, and begin
To sound the depth of that thou wilt profess.[4]
Having commenc'd,[5] be a divine in show,
Yet level at the end of every art,[6]
And live and die in Aristotle's works:
Sweet *Analytics*,[7] 'tis thou hast ravish'd me—
Bene disserere est finis logices.[8]
Is to dispute well logic's chiefest end?
Affords this art no greater miracle?
Then read no more, thou hast attain'd the end.
A greater subject fitteth Faustus' wit:° understanding
Bid *on kai me on*[9] farewell; Galen[10] come,
Seeing *ubi desinit philosophus, ibi incipit medicus.*[11]
Be a physician Faustus, heap up gold,
And be eterniz'd for some wondrous cure!
Summum bonum medicinae sanitas:[12]
The end of physic° is our bodies' health. medicine
Why Faustus, hast thou not attain'd that end?
Is not thy common talk sound aphorisms?[13]
Are not thy bills hung up as monuments,
Whereby whole cities have escap'd the plague,
And thousand desperate maladies been eas'd?
Yet art thou still but Faustus, and a man.
Couldst thou make men to live eternally,
Or being dead, raise them to life again,
Then this profession were to be esteem'd.
Physic farewell; where is Justinian?
Si una eademque res legatur duobus,
alter rem, alter valorem rei,[14] *etc.*
A petty case of paltry legacies!
Exhereditare filium non potest pater, nisi—[15]
Such is the subject of the *Institute*[16]
And universal body of the law.
This study fits a mercenary drudge
Who aims at nothing but external trash—

---

[1] *cunning* Knowledge, erudition, cleverness; sometimes with negative connotations.

[2] *waxen wings* Allusion to the story of Icarus (cf. Ovid, *Metamorphoses* 8.183–235): escaping with his father Daedalus from Minos's island kingdom of Crete, Icarus ignored his father's warning about the wings he had made for them and flew too close to the sun.

[3] *Act 1, Scene 1.* Neither the 1604 nor the 1616 texts of the play contains any act or scene divisions; all such divisions in modern editions of the play are therefore editorial.

[4] *profess* Affirm faith in or allegiance to.

[5] *commenc'd* Taken a degree.

[6] *level ... art* Take aim at the final purpose or limit of every discipline.

[7] *Analytics* Name of two treatises on logic by Aristotle, whose works still dominated the university curriculum.

[8] *Bene ... logices* Latin: "To argue well is the end or purpose of logic" (a definition derived not from Aristotle but from Cicero).

[9] *on kai me on* Transliteration of Greek words meaning "being and not being," the subject of an ancient Greek philosophical treatise.

[10] *Galen* Claudius Galenus (c. 130–200 CE), most famous of ancient writers on medicine.

[11] *ubi ... medicus* Latin: "Where the philosopher leaves off, there the physician begins." Freely translated from Aristotle, *Sense and Sensibilia* 436a.

[12] *Summum ... sanitas* Latin: "The supreme good of medicine is health." Translated from Aristotle, *Nicomachean Ethics* 1094a.

[13] *sound aphorisms* Reliable medical precepts.

[14] *Si ... rei* Latin: "If one and the same thing is bequeathed to two persons, one of them shall have the thing, the other the value of the thing." Derived in part from 2.20 of the *Institutes*, a compilation of Roman law carried out at the command of the emperor Justinian in the sixth century.

[15] *Exhereditare ... nisi—* Latin: "A father cannot disinherit his son except—." An incomplete formulation of a rule from Justinian's *Institutes* 2.12.

[16] *Institute* "Institute" here means "founding principle," and may refer also to Justinian's *Institutes*.

Too servile[1] and illiberal for me.
When all is done, divinity is best:
Jerome's Bible,[2] Faustus, view it well.
Stipendium peccati mors est.[3] Ha! *Stipendium, etc.*
The reward of sin is death? That's hard.
Si peccasse negamus, fallimur,
et nulla est in nobis veritas.[4]
If we say that we have no sin
We deceive ourselves, and there's no truth in us.
Why then belike we must sin,
And so consequently die.
Ay, we must die, an everlasting death.
What doctrine call you this? *Che sarà, sarà,*
What will be, shall be? Divinity, adieu!
These metaphysics[5] of magicians
And necromantic books are heavenly!
Lines,[6] circles,[7] seals, letters and characters:[8]
Ay, these are those that Faustus most desires,
O, what a world of profit and delight,
Of power, of honor, of omnipotence,
Is promis'd to the studious artisan![9]
All things that move between the quiet poles[10]
Shall be at my command. Emperors and kings
Are but obey'd in their several provinces,
Nor can they raise the wind, or rend the clouds;[11]
But his dominion that exceeds° in this *excels*
Stretcheth as far as doth the mind of man!
A sound magician is a mighty god:
Here tire, my brains, to get° a deity! *beget*

(*Enter Wagner.*)

Wagner, commend me to my dearest friends,
The German Valdes and Cornelius;
Request them earnestly to visit me.
WAGNER. I will, sir.

(*Exit.*)

FAUSTUS. Their conference will be a greater help to me
Than all my labors, plod I ne'er so fast.

(*Enter the Good Angel and the Evil Angel.*)

GOOD ANGEL. O Faustus, lay that damned book aside,
And gaze not on it, lest it tempt thy soul
And heap God's heavy wrath upon thy head!
Read, read the Scriptures; that is blasphemy.
EVIL ANGEL. Go forward, Faustus, in that famous art
Wherein all nature's treasury is contain'd:
Be thou on earth as Jove[12] is in the sky,
Lord and commander of these elements![13]

(*Exeunt Angels.*)

---

[1] *Too servile* To contrast the liberal arts with "servile" or "mechanical" studies and practices is an Elizabethan commonplace.

[2] *Jerome's Bible* Vulgate, prepared mainly by St. Jerome in the fourth century, was the Latin text of the Bible used by the Roman Catholic church.

[3] *Stipendium … est* This is the first of several quotations from the Latin Vulgate Bible. This quotation is the first half of Romans 6.23, a verse which in the Geneva Bible (1560) is translated as follows: "For the wages of sin is death: but the gift of God is eternal life through Jesus Christ our Lord."

[4] *Si peccasse … veritas* 1 John 1.8. Faustus has again quoted only the first half of an antithetical statement: he notices the condemnation of sinners by the law of God, but not the conditional promise of divine mercy which immediately follows in 1 John 1.9. In the Geneva Bible, 1 John 1.8–9 is rendered as follows: "If we say that we have no sin, we deceive our selves, and truth is not in us. If we acknowledge our sins, he is faithful and just, to forgive us our sins, and to cleanse us from all unrighteousness."

[5] *metaphysics* Science of the supernatural.

[6] *lines* Reference to the occult art of geomancy, or divination by means of astrologically determined patterns of points and lines.

[7] *circles* Magic circles protected the practitioner of ceremonial magic from evil spirits.

[8] *seals, letters and characters* Talismanic symbols of the planets and of the angels, spiritual intelligences, and daemons that were believed to govern them.

[9] *artisan* Practitioner of an art.

[10] *quiet poles* This could refer either to the poles of the outermost celestial sphere or, more probably, to those of the earth.

[11] *raise … clouds* Blasphemous echo of Jeremiah 10.13 (which speaks of God's power over clouds, lightning and wind).

[12] *Jove* The substitution of the supreme god of the pagan Roman pantheon for the Christian God is common in Renaissance texts and in Elizabethan poetry.

[13] *these elements* Earth, water, air and fire, here used as a metonymy for the world contained by the sphere of the moon which these elements were thought to constitute.

FAUSTUS. How am I glutted with conceit[1] of this!
Shall I make spirits fetch me what I please,
Resolve me of all ambiguities,
Perform what desperate enterprise I will?
I'll have them fly to India for gold,
Ransack the ocean for orient pearl
And search all corners of the new found world
For pleasant fruits and princely delicates;
I'll have them read me strange philosophy
And tell the secrets of all foreign kings;
I'll have them wall all Germany with brass
And make swift Rhine[2] circle fair Wittenberg;
I'll have them fill the public schools with silk
Wherewith the students shall be bravely[3] clad;
I'll levy soldiers with the coin they bring,
And chase the Prince of Parma[4] from our land
And reign sole king of all our provinces;
Yea, stranger engines for the brunt° of war *assault, onset*
Than was the fiery keel at Antwerp's bridge[5]
I'll make my servile spirits to invent.
Come, German Valdes and Cornelius,
And make me blest with your sage conference!

(*Enter Valdes and Cornelius.*)

Valdes, sweet Valdes, and Cornelius,
Know that your words have won me at the last
To practise magic and concealed arts:
Yet not your words only, but mine own fantasy,
That will receive no object, for my head
But ruminates on necromantic skill.[6]
Philosophy is odious and obscure;
Both law and physic are for petty wits;
Divinity is basest of the three,
Unpleasant, harsh, contemptible and vile;
'Tis magic, magic, that hath ravish'd me.
Then, gentle friends, aid me in this attempt,
And I, that have with concise syllogisms[7]
Gravell'd° the pastors of the German church *confounded*
And made the flowering pride of Wittenberg
Swarm to my problems as the infernal spirits
On sweet Musaeus[8] when he came to hell,
Will be as cunning as Agrippa was,
Whose shadows[9] made all Europe honor him.

VALDES. Faustus, these books, thy wit, and our experience
Shall make all nations canonize us.
As Indian Moors[10] obey their Spanish lords,
So shall the subjects[11] of every element
Be always serviceable to us three:
Like lions shall they guard us when we please,
Like Almain rutters[12] with their horsemen's staves,° *lances*
Or Lapland giants trotting by our sides;
Sometimes like women, or unwedded maids,
Shadowing° more beauty in their airy brows *harboring*
Than has the white breasts of the queen of love.[13]
From Venice shall they drag huge Argosies,[14]

[1] *conceit* Thought, notion.

[2] *Rhine* River in Germany.

[3] *bravely* Splendidly. University regulations forbade students to wear fine clothing: their scholars' gowns were to be made of woolen cloth in somber colors, and silk-lined hoods could only be worn by the holders of doctoral degrees.

[4] *Prince of Parma* Alessandro Farnese, Duke of Parma, a grandson of the emperor Charles V and the foremost general of his time. Parma served as Spanish governor of the Netherlands from 1578 until his death in 1592; he was hated by Protestants as a tyrant. He commanded the force that the Spanish Armada was to have transported across the Channel in 1588 for the invasion of England.

[5] *fiery ... bridge* On 4 April 1585 the Netherlanders sent two fireships loaded with explosives against the pontoon bridge over the river Scheldt which formed part of Parma's siegeworks around Antwerp; one of them reached its target and destroyed part of the bridge, killing many Spanish soldiers. Parma had the bridge rebuilt, and Antwerp subsequently surrendered.

[6] *Yet ... skill* Faustus is saying that his imagination is so preoccupied with thoughts of magic that he can think of no other subjects.

[7] *syllogisms* Particular form of argument from logic.

[8] *Musaeus* Legendary pre-Homeric Greek poet, a pupil of Orpheus. In Virgil's *Aeneid*, Musaeus is represented as standing in the midst of a crowd of spirits in the underworld, head and shoulders above the rest.

[9] *Agrippa ... shadows* Henricus Cornelius Agrippa of Nettesheim (1486–1535), said to be "the greatest conjurer in Christendom." Agrippa distinguished between two kinds of necromancy: *necyomantia,* the reviving of corpses by means of a blood sacrifice, and *scyomantia*, in which only the shadow of a dead person is invoked.

[10] *Indian Moors* Native peoples of the Americas.

[11] *subjects* Spirits. "Subjects" carries the additional implication of subjection to a sovereign will (here, that of the magician).

[12] *Almain rutters* German soldiers.

[13] *queen of love* Venus, Roman goddess of love.

[14] *Argosies* Richly laden merchant ships.

And from America the golden fleece[1]
That yearly stuffs old Philip's treasury,[2]
If learned Faustus will be resolute.

FAUSTUS. Valdes, as resolute am I in this
As thou to live, therefore object it not.

CORNELIUS. The miracles that magic will perform
Will make thee vow to study nothing else.
He that is grounded in[3] astrology,
Enrich'd with tongues,[4] well seen in minerals,[5]
Hath all the principles magic doth require.
Then doubt not, Faustus, but to be renown'd
And more frequented° for this mystery *sought out*
Than heretofore the Delphian oracle.[6]
The spirits tell me they can dry the sea
And fetch the treasure of all foreign wrecks,
Ay, all the wealth that our forefathers hid
Within the massy° entrails of the earth. *heavy, massive*
Then tell me Faustus, what shall we three want?

FAUSTUS. Nothing, Cornelius. O, this cheers my soul!
Come, show me some demonstrations magical,
That I may conjure in some lusty grove
And have these joys in full possession.

VALDES. Then haste thee to some solitary grove,
And bear wise Bacon's and Albanus' works,[7]
The Hebrew Psalter, and New Testament;
And whatsoever else is requisite
We will inform thee ere our conference cease.

CORNELIUS. Valdes, first let him know the words of art,
And then, all other ceremonies learn'd,
Faustus may try his cunning by himself.

VALDES. First I'll instruct thee in the rudiments,
And then wilt thou be perfecter than I.

FAUSTUS. Then come and dine with me, and after meat
We'll canvas every quiddity[8] thereof.
For ere I sleep I'll try what I can do;
This night I'll conjure though I die therefore.

(*Exeunt.*)

ACT 1, SCENE 2

(*Enter two scholars.*)

FIRST SCHOLAR. I wonder what's become of Faustus, that was wont to make our schools ring with *sic probo*.[9]

SECOND SCHOLAR. That shall we presently° know, for see: here comes his boy. *at once*

(*Enter Wagner.*)

FIRST SCHOLAR. How now sirrah,[10] where's thy master?

WAGNER. God in heaven knows.

SECOND SCHOLAR. Why, dost not thou know?

WAGNER. Yes, I know, but that follows not.

FIRST SCHOLAR. Go to sirrah, leave your jesting, and tell us where he is.

WAGNER. That follows not necessary by force of argument, which you, being licentiate,[11] should stand upon;[12] therefore acknowledge your error and be attentive.

SECOND SCHOLAR. Why, didst thou not say thou knew'st?

WAGNER. Have you any witness on't?

FIRST SCHOLAR. Yes, sirrah, I heard you.

WAGNER. Ask my fellow if I be a thief!

SECOND SCHOLAR. Well, you will not tell us.

---

[1] *golden fleece* In Greek mythology, Jason and his crew sailed in the Argo on a quest for the Golden Fleece.

[2] *golden ... treasury* Annual fleet that shipped gold and silver from the Americas to Spain.

[3] *grounded in* Firmly established in.

[4] *enrich'd with tongues* Improved by knowledge of (ancient) languages.

[5] *well ... minerals* Well versed in the properties of minerals.

[6] *Delphian oracle* Oracle of Apollo at Delphi, the most famous and authoritative of ancient Greek oracles.

[7] *wise Bacon's and Albanus's works* Roger Bacon (c. 1214–94), an English Franciscan philosopher, was reputed also to have been a magician "Albanus" is an error for Pietro d'Abano or Petrus de Aponus (c. 1250–1316), a physician who was posthumously convicted of sorcery and burned in effigy by the Inquisition.

[8] *canvass every quiddity* Discuss every essential particular.

[9] *sic probo* Latin: "Thus I prove"; the cry of triumph with which Faustus would have clinched his victories in disputation.

[10] *sirrah* Term of address that expresses the speaker's contempt, the addressee's social inferiority, or both.

[11] *licentiate* Licensed by an academic degree to proceed to further studies.

[12] *stand upon* Insist on.

WAGNER. Yes sir, I will tell you; yet if you were not dunces[1] you would never ask me such a question, for is not he *corpus naturale*, and is not that *mobile*?[2] Then wherefore should you ask me such a question? But that I am by nature phlegmatic, slow to wrath and prone to lechery (to love I would say), it were not for you to come within forty foot of the place of execution[3]—although I do not doubt but to see you both hanged the next sessions. Thus having triumphed over you, I will set my countenance like a precisian,[4] and begin to speak thus: Truly, my dear brethren, my master is within at dinner with Valdes and Cornelius, as this wine if it could speak would inform your worships; and so the Lord bless you, preserve you, and keep you,[5] my dear brethren, my dear brethren.

(*Exit.*)

FIRST SCHOLAR. Nay then, I fear he is fallen into that damned art, for which they two are infamous through the world.

SECOND SCHOLAR. Were he a stranger, and not allied to me, yet should I grieve for him. But come, let us go and inform the Rector, and see if he by his grave counsel can reclaim him.

FIRST SCHOLAR. O, but I fear me nothing can reclaim him.

SECOND SCHOLAR. Yet let us try what we can do.

(*Exeunt.*)

[1] *dunces* Renaissance humanists opposed both the hair-splitting complexity of scholastic logic. As a result, the name of Johannes Duns Scotus (c. 1265 –1308), one of the most subtle medieval logicians, came to connote sophistical quibbling and, by extension, stupidity.

[2] *corpus naturale … mobile* Latin: "A body that is natural or subject to change"—an adaptation of Aristotle's statement of the subject-matter of physics.

[3] *place of execution* Scene of action; in this case, the dining-room.

[4] *precisian* Puritan, one who is precise and scrupulous about religious observances. Having parodied the logic of scholastic disputation, Wagner proceeds to parody the discourse of excessive piety.

[5] *the Lord … keep you* Numbers 6.24. In quoting these words as an exit line, Wagner is mocking the language with which religious services were (and are) commonly brought to a close.

ACT 1, SCENE 3

(*Enter Faustus to conjure.*)

FAUSTUS. Now that the gloomy shadow of the earth,
Longing to view Orion's drizzling look,[6]
Leaps from th'antarctic world unto the sky[7]
And dims the welkin° with her pitchy breath, *sky*
Faustus, begin thine incantations,
And try if devils will obey thy hest,° *command*
Seeing thou hast pray'd and sacrific'd to them.
Within this circle is Jehovah's name,
Forward and backward anagrammatiz'd,[8]
The breviated° names of holy saints, *abbreviated*
Figures of every adjunct to[9] the heavens,
And characters of signs and erring stars[10]
By which the spirits are enforc'd to rise;
Then fear not, Faustus, but be resolute,
And try the uttermost magic can perform.
Sint mihi dei Acherontis propitii! Valeat numen triplex Iehovae! Ignei, aerii, aquatici spiritus salvete! Orientis princeps Belzebub, inferni ardentis monarcha, et Demogorgon, propitiamus vos ut appareat et surgat Mephastophilis. Quid tu moraris? Per Iehovam, Gehennam et consecratam aquam quam nunc spargo, signumque crucis quod nunc facio, et per vota nostra, ipse nunc surgat nobis dicatus Mephastophilis.[11]

[6] *Orion's drizzling look* Constellation of Orion associated in classical poetry with winter storms.

[7] *th'antarctic world* If one believes the sun to revolve around the earth, and lives in the northern hemisphere, then the sun will be conceived of as shining on the southern hemisphere when it is night in the northern, and re-emerging from "th'antarctic world" at dawn.

[8] *anagrammatiz'd* Cabalist mystics believed that hidden meanings were present in every possible recombination of letters in the Hebrew scriptures, and practitioners of Cabalistic magic saw the names of God in particular as containing occult secrets of divine power and knowledge.

[9] *adjunct to* Heavenly body attached to.

[10] *characters … stars* Diagrams representing the constellations of the zodiac (one Latin term for which was *signa*) and the planets.

[11] *Sint … Mephastophilis* Latin: "May the gods of Acheron be propitious to me. Away with the threefold divinity of Jehovah! Hail, spirits of fire, air, and water! Belzebub, Prince of the East, monarch of burning hell, and Demogorgon, we invoke your favor that Mephastophilis may appear and ascend. Why do you delay? By Jehovah, Gehenna, and the holy water which I now sprinkle, by the sign of the cross which I now make, and by our vows, may Mephastophilis himself now rise to serve us!"; *Mephasto-*

(*Enter a devil.*)

I charge thee to return and change thy shape.
Thou art too ugly to attend on me;
Go, and return an old Franciscan friar:
That holy shape becomes a devil best.

(*Exit devil.*)

I see there's virtue[1] in my heavenly words,
Who would not be proficient in this art?
How pliant is this Mephastophilis,
Full of obedience and humility:
Such is the force of magic and my spells!
Now, Faustus, thou art conjurer laureate[2]
That canst command great Mephastophilis!
Quin redis, Mephastophilis, fratris imagine![3]

(*Enter Mephastophilis.*)

MEPHASTOPHILIS. Now, Faustus, what wouldst thou have me do?
FAUSTUS. I charge thee wait upon me whilst I live
To do whatever Faustus shall command,
Be it to make the moon drop from her sphere
Or the ocean to overwhelm the world.
MEPHASTOPHILIS. I am a servant to great Lucifer,[4]
And may not follow thee without his leave;
No more than he commands must we perform.
FAUSTUS. Did not he charge thee to appear to me?
MEPHASTOPHILIS. No, I came hither of my own accord.
FAUSTUS. Did not my conjuring speeches raise thee? Speak.
MEPHASTOPHILIS. That was the cause, but yet *per accidens*,[5]
For when we hear one rack° the name of God, *torture*
Abjure the Scriptures and his saviour Christ,
We fly, in hope to get his glorious[6] soul;
Nor will we come unless he use such means
Whereby he is in danger to be damn'd.
Therefore the shortest cut for conjuring
Is stoutly[7] to abjure the Trinity,[8]
And pray devoutly to the prince of hell.
FAUSTUS. So Faustus hath already done,
And holds this principle:
There is no chief but only Belzebub,
To whom Faustus doth dedicate himself.
This word "damnation" terrifies not him,
For he confounds hell in Elysium:[9]
His ghost be with the old philosophers!
But leaving these vain trifles of men's souls,
Tell me, what is that Lucifer thy lord?
MEPHASTOPHILIS. Arch-regent and commander of all spirits.
FAUSTUS. Was not that Lucifer an angel once?
MEPHASTOPHILIS. Yes Faustus, and most dearly lov'd of God.
FAUSTUS. How comes it then that he is prince of devils?
MEPHASTOPHILIS. O, by aspiring pride and insolence,
For which God threw him from the face of heaven.
FAUSTUS. And what are you that live with Lucifer?
MEPHASTOPHILIS. Unhappy spirits that fell with Lucifer,
Conspir'd against our God with Lucifer,
And are for ever damn'd with Lucifer.
FAUSTUS. Where are you damn'd?
MEPHASTOPHILIS. In hell.
FAUSTUS. How comes it then that thou art out of hell?
MEPHASTOPHILIS. Why this is hell, nor am I out of it:
Think'st thou that I who saw the face of God
And tasted the eternal joys of heaven

philis Compound of three Greek words indicating negation (*me*), light (*phos*), and loving (*philis*); in its original form, the name thus means "not-light-loving"—perhaps parodying the Latin "Lucifer," or "light-bearer."

[1] *virtue* Power.

[2] *laureate* Crowned with laurel; of proved distinction.

[3] *Quin ... imagine* Latin: "Why do you not return, Mephastophilis, in the shape of a friar!"

[4] *Lucifer* The name appears in Isaiah 14.12.

[5] *per accidens* Scholastics distinguished between an efficient cause, i.e., an agent which itself produced an effect, and a cause *per accidens*, which was related to the final effect only in having provided an occasion for the intervention of some external agent.

[6] *glorious* Splendid; possibly also boastful.

[7] *stoutly* Courageously, resolutely.

[8] *Trinity* In orthodox Christian belief, the three persons (God the Father, Son, and Holy Spirit) of the Godhead.

[9] *confounds ... Elysium* Identifies Hell with Elysium; confuses the two; undoes Hell through belief in Elysium (in ancient Greece, the place in the afterworld reserved for heroes).

Am not tormented with ten thousand hells
In being depriv'd of everlasting bliss?
O Faustus, leave these frivolous demands,
Which strike a terror to my fainting soul.

FAUSTUS. What, is great Mephastophilis so passionate
For being deprived of the joys of heaven?
Learn thou of Faustus manly fortitude
And scorn those joys thou never shalt possess.
Go, bear these tidings to great Lucifer:
Seeing Faustus hath incurr'd eternal death
By desperate thoughts against Jove's deity,
Say he surrenders up to him his soul,
So[1] he will spare him four and twenty years,
Letting him live in all voluptuousness,
Having thee ever to attend on me
To give me whatsoever I shall ask,
To tell me whatsoever I demand,
To slay mine enemies and aid my friends,
And always be obedient to my will.
Go, and return to mighty Lucifer,
And meet me in my study at midnight,
And then resolve me of thy master's mind.

MEPHASTOPHILIS. I will, Faustus.

(*Exit.*)

FAUSTUS. Had I as many souls as there be stars
I'd give them all for Mephastophilis!
By him I'll be a great emperor of the world,
And make a bridge thorough[2] the moving air
To pass the ocean with a band of men;
I'll join the hills that bind the Afric shore,
And make that country continent to[3] Spain,
And both contributory to my crown;
The emperor shall not live but by my leave,
Nor any potentate of Germany.
Now that I have obtain'd what I desire,
I'll live in speculation of this art
Till Mephastophilis return again.

(*Exit.*)

[1] *So* On condition that.

[2] *thorough* I.e., through.

[3] *continent to* Continuous with.

ACT 1, SCENE 4

(*Enter Wagner and the Clown.*)[4]

WAGNER. Sirrah boy, come hither.

CLOWN. How, "boy"? Swowns[5] boy, I hope you have seen many boys with such pickadevaunts[6] as I have. "Boy," quotha?

WAGNER. Tell me sirrah, hast thou any comings in?[7]

CLOWN. Ay, and goings out[8] too, you may see else.

WAGNER. Alas, poor slave: see how poverty jesteth in his nakedness. The villain is bare, and out of service,[9] and so hungry that I know he would give his soul to the devil for a shoulder of mutton, though it were blood raw.

CLOWN. How, my soul to the devil for a shoulder of mutton though 'twere blood raw? Not so, good friend: b'urlady[10] I had need have it well roasted, and good sauce to it, if I pay so dear.

WAGNER. Well, wilt thou serve me, and I'll make thee go like *Qui mihi discipulus?*[11]

CLOWN. How, in verse?

WAGNER. No sirrah, in beaten silk[12] and stavesacre.[13]

CLOWN. How, how, knave's acre? Ay, I thought that was all the land his father left him. Do ye hear, I would be sorry to rob you of your living.

WAGNER. Sirrah, I say in stavesacre!

[4] *Clown* Boorish rustic, a fool. This character is presumably to be identified with the Robin of 2.2 and 3.2.

[5] *Swowns* Contraction of "God's wounds" (a mild oath).

[6] *pickadevaunts* Short beards trimmed to a point; apparently from the French *piqué devant*, "peaked in front," possibly with an obscene *double entendre*.

[7] *comings in* Earnings.

[8] *goings out* Expenses; a punning reference to the fact that the Clown is bursting out of his tattered clothes.

[9] *out of service* Unemployed.

[10] *b'urlady* Contraction of "by Our Lady."

[11] *Qui mihi discipulus* Latin: "You who are my pupil." The opening words of a didactic poem which appeared in the standard elementary Latin textbook used in Elizabethan schools.

[12] *beaten silk* Embroidered silk; with a punning suggestion that Wagner will thrash his servant.

[13] *stavesacre* Preparation against lice made from the seeds of a plant related to the delphinium.

Clown. Oho, oho, stavesacre! Why then belike,[1] if I were your man I should be full of vermin.

Wagner. So thou shalt, whether thou beest with me or no. But sirrah, leave your jesting, and bind yourself presently unto me for seven years,[2] or I'll turn all the lice about thee into familiars,[3] and they shall tear thee to pieces.

Clown. Do you hear, sir? You may save that labor: they are too familiar with me already, swowns they are as bold with my flesh as if they had paid for my meat and drink.

Wagner. Well, do you hear, sirrah? Hold, take these guilders.

Clown. Gridirons, what be they?

Wagner. Why, French crowns.

Clown. Mass, but for the name of French crowns, a man were as good have as many English counters.[4] And what should I do with these?

Wagner. Why now, sirrah, thou art at an hour's warning whensoever or wheresoever the devil shall fetch thee.

Clown. No, no; here, take your gridirons again.

Wagner. Truly, I'll none of them.

Clown. Truly, but you shall.

Wagner. Bear witness I gave them him!

Clown. Bear witness I give them you again!

Wagner. Well, I will cause two devils presently to fetch thee away. Baliol,[5] and Belcher!

Clown. Let your Balio and Belcher come here, and I'll knock them, they were never so knocked since they were devils! Say I should kill one of them, what would folks say? "Do ye see yonder tall[6] fellow in the round slop,[7] he has killed the devil": so I should be called "kill-devil" all the parish over.

(*Enter two devils, and the clown runs up and down crying.*)

Wagner. Balio and Belcher, spirits away!

(*Exeunt.*)

Clown. What, are they gone? A vengeance on them, they have vile long nails. There was a he-devil and a she-devil. I'll tell you how you shall know them: all he-devils has horns,[8] and all she-devils has clefts[9] and cloven feet.

Wagner. Well sirrah, follow me.

Clown. But do you hear: If I should serve you, would you teach me to raise up Banios and Belcheos?

Wagner. I will teach thee to turn thyself to anything: to a dog, or a cat, or a mouse, or a rat, or any thing.

Clown. How? A Christian fellow to a dog or a cat, a mouse or a rat? No, no, sir. If you turn me into anything, let it be in the likeness of little pretty frisking flea, that I may be here and there and everywhere: O, I'll tickle the pretty wenches' plackets,[10] I'll be amongst them i'faith!

Wagner. Well sirrah, come.

Clown. But do you hear, Wagner?

Wagner. How? Baliol and Belcher!

Clown. O Lord! I pray sir, let Banio and Belcher go sleep.

Wagner. Villain, call me Master Wagner, and see that you walk attentively, and let your right eye be always diametrally fixed upon my left heel, that thou mayest *quasi vestigiis nostris insitere*.[11]

---

[1] *belike* In all likelihood.

[2] *seven years* Standard period of time for an apprenticeship or a contract of indentured labor.

[3] *familiars* Attendant spirits of witches and sorcerers, who took the form of animals.

[4] *guilders ... English counters* Wagner professes to give the Clown Dutch guilders. Observing, it would seem, that the coins have holes punched in them, the Clown mis-hears the word as "gridirons"—whereupon Wagner re-identifies the coins as French crowns. A proclamation of 1587 authorized members of the public to strike holes in French crowns, which in the late 1580s and early 1590s were notoriously debased, and often counterfeit. From the sixteenth until the early nineteenth century, English merchants issued privately minted counters or tokens which circulated without having any officially accepted value; "counter" often denoted a debased or counterfeit coin; *Mass* An oath: "by the Mass."

[5] *Baliol* Deformation of "Belial," a name which occurs in the Bible (e.g., 2 Cor. 6.15).

[6] *tall* Valiant, handsome.

[7] *round slop* Baggy breeches.

[8] *horns* Standard demonic equipment, perhaps with an overtone of cuckoldry.

[9] *clefts* Vulvas.

[10] *plackets* Pockets in women's skirts; metaphorically, a woman's genitals.

[11] *quasi vestigiis nostris insitere* Latin: "As if walking in our footsteps."

(*Exit.*)

CLOWN. God forgive me, he speaks Dutch fustian.[1]
Well, I'll follow him, I'll serve him, that's flat.

(*Exit.*)

ACT 2, SCENE 1

(*Enter Faustus in his study.*)

FAUSTUS. Now Faustus, must thou needs be damn'd,
And canst thou not be saved.
What boots° it then to think of God or heaven? *avails*
Away with such vain fancies, and despair,
Despair in God, and trust in Belzebub.
Now go not backward: no Faustus, be resolute.
Why waverest thou? O, something soundeth in mine ears:
"Abjure this magic, turn to God again."
Ay, and Faustus will turn to God again.
To God? He loves thee not;
The god thou serv'st is thine own appetite,
Wherein is fix'd the love of Belzebub:
To him I'll build an altar and a church,
And offer lukewarm blood of new-born babes!

(*Enter Good Angel, and Evil.*)

GOOD ANGEL. Sweet Faustus, leave that execrable art.
FAUSTUS. Contrition, prayer, repentance: what of these?
GOOD ANGEL. O, they are means to bring thee unto heaven.
EVIL ANGEL. Rather illusions, fruits of lunacy,
That makes men foolish that do trust them most.
GOOD ANGEL. Sweet Faustus, think of heaven and heavenly things.
EVIL ANGEL. No Faustus, think of honor and of wealth.

(*Exeunt Angels.*)

FAUSTUS. Of wealth?
Why, the signory° of Emden[2] shall be mine! *lordship, rule*
When Mephastophilis shall stand by me
What God can hurt me?[3] Faustus, thou art safe;
Cast° no more doubts. Come, Mephastophilis, *emit, ponder*
And bring glad tidings[4] from great Lucifer!
Is't not midnight? Come Mephastophilis,
Veni, veni, Mephastophilis![5]

(*Enter Mephastophilis.*)

Now tell me, what says Lucifer thy lord?
MEPHASTOPHILIS. That I shall wait on Faustus whilst he lives,
So he will buy my service with his soul.
FAUSTUS. Already Faustus hath hazarded that for thee.
MEPHASTOPHILIS. But now thou must bequeath it solemnly,
And write a deed of gift with thine own blood,
For that security craves great Lucifer.
If thou deny it I will back to hell.
FAUSTUS. Stay Mephastophilis, and tell me,
What good will my soul do thy lord?
MEPHASTOPHILIS. Enlarge his kingdom.
FAUSTUS. Is that the reason why he tempts us thus?
MEPHASTOPHILIS. *Solamen miseris socios habuisse doloris.*[6]
FAUSTUS. Why, have you any pain that tortures others?
MEPHASTOPHILIS. As great as have the human souls of men.
But tell me, Faustus, shall I have thy soul?
And I will be thy slave and wait on thee,
And give thee more than thou hast wit to ask.
FAUSTUS. Ay Mephastophilis, I give it thee.
MEPHASTOPHILIS. Then stab this arm courageously,
And bind thy soul, that at some certain day
Great Lucifer may claim it as his own:

[1] *fustian* Bombast, nonsense. Fustian was a coarse cloth made of cotton and flax; the word was metaphorically applied to inflated or inappropriately lofty language.

[2] *Emden* Prosperous port in northwest Germany which conducted an extensive trade with England.

[3] *When … me?* Blasphemous distortion of Romans 8.31: "If God be on our side, who can be against us?"

[4] *glad tidings* Cf. Luke 2.10: "I bring you glad tidings of great joy."

[5] *Veni, veni, Mephastophilis!* Latin: "Come, O come, Mephastophilis!"—a blasphemous echo of the twelfth-century Advent hymn *Veni, veni, Emmanuel* (Come, O Come Redeemer).

[6] *Solamen … doloris* Latin: "It is a comfort to the wretched to have had companions in misfortune."

And then be thou as great as Lucifer!
FAUSTUS. Lo Mephastophilis, for love of thee
I cut mine arm, and with my proper° blood *own*
Assure my soul to be great Lucifer's,
Chief lord and regent of perpetual night.
View here the blood that trickles from mine arm,
And let it be propitious for my wish.
MEPHASTOPHILIS. But Faustus, thou must
Write it in manner of a deed[1] of gift.
FAUSTUS. Ay, so I will. But Mephastophilis,
My blood congeals, and I can write no more.
MEPHASTOPHILIS. I'll fetch thee fire to dissolve it straight.

(*Exit.*)

FAUSTUS. What might the staying of my blood portend?
Is it unwilling I should write this bill?° *contract*
Why streams it not, that I may write afresh?
"Faustus gives to thee his soul": ah, there it stay'd.
Why should'st thou not? Is not thy soul thine own?
Then write again: "Faustus gives to thee his soul."

(*Enter Mephastophilis with a chafer*[2] *of coals.*)

MEPHASTOPHILIS. Here's fire: come Faustus, set it on.
FAUSTUS. So: now the blood begins to clear again;
Now will I make an end immediately.
MEPHASTOPHILIS. (*Aside.*) O, what will not I do to obtain his soul!
FAUSTUS. *Consummatum est*:[3] this bill is ended,
And Faustus hath bequeath'd his soul to Lucifer.
But what is this inscription on mine arm?
Homo fuge![4] Whither should I fly?
If unto God he'll throw thee down to hell.
My senses are deceiv'd: here's nothing writ.
O yes, I see it plain! Even here is writ
Homo fuge; yet shall not Faustus fly.
MEPHASTOPHILIS. I'll fetch him somewhat to delight his mind.

(*Exit. Enter with devils, giving crowns and rich apparel to Faustus, and dance, and then [the devils] depart.*)

FAUSTUS. Speak Mephastophilis: what means this show?
MEPHASTOPHILIS. Nothing, Faustus, but to delight thy mind,
And let thee see what magic can perform.
FAUSTUS. But may I raise such spirits when I please?
MEPHASTOPHILIS. Ay Faustus, and do greater things than these.
FAUSTUS. Then there's enough for a thousand souls!
Here Mephastophilis, receive this scroll,
A deed of gift, of body and of soul:
But yet conditionally, that thou perform
All articles prescrib'd between us both.
MEPHASTOPHILIS. Faustus, I swear by hell and Lucifer
To effect all promises between us made.
FAUSTUS. Then hear me read them.
On these conditions following:
First, that Faustus may be a spirit in form and substance;
Secondly, that Mephastophilis shall be his servant, and at his command;
Thirdly, that Mephastophilis shall do for him, and bring him whatsoever;
Fourthly, that he shall be in his chamber or house invisible;
Lastly, that he shall appear to the said John Faustus at all times, in what form or shape soever he please;
I, John Faustus of Wittenberg, Doctor, by these presents[5] *do give both body and soul to Lucifer, Prince of the East, and his minister Mephastophilis, and furthermore grant unto him that four and twenty years being expired, and these articles above written being inviolate, full power to fetch or carry the said John Faustus, body and soul, flesh, blood, or goods, into their habitation wheresoever.*
By me, John Faustus.

MEPHASTOPHILIS. Speak Faustus, do you deliver this as your deed?
FAUSTUS. Ay, take it, and the devil give thee good on't.

[1] *deed* Legally binding document.

[2] *chafer* Saucepan or chafing-dish.

[3] *Consummatum est* "It is finished." According to the Gospel of John, these were the last words of Jesus on the cross (John 19.30).

[4] *Homo fuge* Latin: "Man, flee!" The words occur in the Vulgate text of 1 Timothy 6.11, but this line as a whole alludes more distinctly to Psalm 139.7–8: "Whither shall I go from thy spirit? or whither shall I flee from thy presence? If I ascend into heaven, thou art there: if I lie down in hell, thou art there."

[5] *these presents* Legal articles being presented.

MEPHASTOPHILIS. So. Now, Faustus, ask me what thou wilt.
FAUSTUS. First will I question with thee about hell.
Tell me, where is the place that men call hell?
MEPHASTOPHILIS. Under the heavens.
FAUSTUS. Ay, so are all things else; but whereabouts?
MEPHASTOPHILIS. Within the bowels of these elements,
Where we are tortur'd and remain forever.
Hell hath no limits, nor is circumscrib'd
In one self° place, but where we are is hell, *single, particular*
And where hell is there must we ever be;
And to be short, when all the world dissolves
And every creature shall be purify'd,
All places shall be hell that is not heaven.
FAUSTUS. Come, I think hell's a fable.
MEPHASTOPHILIS. Ay, think so still, till experience change thy mind.
FAUSTUS. Why, think'st thou then that Faustus shall be damn'd?
MEPHASTOPHILIS. Ay, of necessity, for here's the scroll
Wherein thou hast given thy soul to Lucifer.
FAUSTUS. Ay, and body too, but what of that?
Think'st thou that Faustus is so fond° to imagine *foolish*
That after this life there is any pain?
Tush, these are trifles and mere old wives' tales.
MEPHASTOPHILIS. But I am an instance to prove the contrary,
For I tell thee I am damn'd, and now in hell.
FAUSTUS. Nay, and this be hell, I'll willingly be damn'd!
What, sleeping, eating, walking and disputing?
But leaving this, let me have a wife, the fairest maid in Germany, for I am wanton and lascivious, and cannot live without a wife.

MEPHASTOPHILIS. How, a wife? I prithee Faustus, talk not of a wife.

FAUSTUS. Nay, sweet Mephastophilis, fetch me one, for I will have one.

MEPHASTOPHILIS. Well, thou wilt have one. Sit there till I come; I'll fetch thee a wife in the devil's name.

(*Enter a devil dressed like a woman, with fireworks.*)[1]

MEPHASTOPHILIS. Tell, Faustus: how dost thou like thy wife?

FAUSTUS. A plague on her for a hot whore!

(*Exit devil.*)

MEPHASTOPHILIS. Tut, Faustus, marriage is but a ceremonial toy.° *trifle*
If thou lov'st me, think no more of it.
I'll cull thee out the fairest courtesans
And bring them every morning to thy bed.
She whom thine eye shall like, thy heart shall have,
Be she as chaste as was Penelope,[2]
As wise as Saba,[3] or as beautiful
As was bright Lucifer before his fall.
Hold, take this book: peruse it thoroughly.
The iterating of these lines brings gold;
The framing of this circle on the ground
Brings whirlwinds, tempests, thunder and lightning.
Pronounce this thrice devoutly to thyself,
And men in armor shall appear to thee,
Ready to execute what thou desir'st.

FAUSTUS. Thanks, Mephastophilis; yet fain would I have a book wherein I might behold all spells and incantations, that I might raise up spirits when I please.

MEPHASTOPHILIS. Here they are in this book.

(*There turn to them.*)

FAUSTUS. Now would I have a book where I might see all characters[4] and planets of the heavens, that I might know their motions and dispositions.

MEPHASTOPHILIS. Here they are too.

(*Turn to them.*)

FAUSTUS. Nay, let me have one book more, and then I have done, wherein I might see all plants, herbs, and trees that grow upon the earth.

MEPHASTOPHILIS. Here they be.

[1] *fireworks* In the comic sequences of sixteenth-century pageants and plays, fireworks were often attached to the costumes of devils and clowns in ways designed to make fun of sexual and excretory functions.

[2] *Penelope* Faithful wife of Odysseus, hero of the Trojan War and Homer's *Odyssey*.

[3] *Saba* Queen of Sheba, who in 1 Kings 10.1–13 comes to Jerusalem to test King Solomon's knowledge of God.

[4] *characters* Talismanic symbols of the planets and of the spiritual powers that govern them.

FAUSTUS. O, thou art deceived.
MEPHASTOPHILIS. Tut, I warrant thee.[1]

(*Turn to them. Exeunt.*)

ACT 2, SCENE 2[2]

(*Enter Robin the ostler with a book in his hand.*)

ROBIN. O, this is admirable! Here I ha' stolen one of Doctor Faustus' conjuring books, and i'faith I mean to search some circles[3] for my own use: now will I make all the maidens in our parish dance at my pleasure stark naked before me, and so by that means I shall see more than I ever felt, or saw yet.

(*Enter Rafe, calling Robin.*)

RAFE. Robin, prithee come away! There's a gentleman tarries to have his horse, and he would have his things rubbed and made clean: he keeps such a chafing with my mistress about it, and she has sent me to look thee out; prithee come away!

ROBIN. Keep out, keep out, or else you are blown up, you are dismembered. Rafe! Keep out, for I am about a roaring[4] piece of work.

RAFE. Come, what dost thou with that same book? Thou canst not read.

ROBIN. Yes, my master and mistress shall find that I can read: he for his forehead,[5] she for her private study.[6] She's born to bear with[7] me, or else my art fails.

RAFE. Why Robin, what book is that?

ROBIN. What book? Why, the most intolerable book for conjuring that e'er was invented by any brimstone devil!

RAFE. Canst thou conjure with it?

ROBIN. I can do all these things easily with it: first, I can make thee drunk with hippocras[8] at any tavern in Europe for nothing; that's one of my conjuring works.

RAFE. Our master parson says that's nothing.

ROBIN. True, Rafe. And more, Rafe, if thou hast any mind to Nan Spit our kitchen maid, then turn her and wind her[9] to thine own use, as often as thou wilt, and at midnight.

RAFE. O brave Robin, shall I have Nan Spit, and to mine own use? On that condition I'll feed thy devil with horse-bread[10] as long as he lives, of free cost.

ROBIN. No more, sweet Rafe: let's go and make clean our boots which lie foul upon our hands; and then to our conjuring, in the devil's name!

(*Exeunt.*)

ACT 2, SCENE 3

(*Enter Faustus in his study, and Mephastophilis.*)

FAUSTUS. When I behold the heavens then I repent
And curse thee, wicked Mephastophilis,
Because thou hast depriv'd me of those joys.
MEPHASTOPHILIS. Why Faustus,
Think'st thou heaven is such a glorious thing?
I tell thee 'tis not half so fair as thou
Or any man that breathes on earth.
FAUSTUS. How prov'st thou that?
MEPHASTOPHILIS. 'Twas made for man,
Therefore is man more excellent.
FAUSTUS. If it were made for man, 'twas made for me:
I will renounce this magic and repent.

---

[1] *I warrant thee* I assure you.

[2] *Act 2, Scene 2.* In both the 1604 and the 1616 texts of the play this scene, together with the scene numbered Act 3, Scene 2 in the present edition, appear in succession.

[3] *circles* Magic circles, and also women's vaginas.

[4] *roaring* Noisy, riotous.

[5] *forehead* Deceived husbands or cuckolds were said to wear horns on their foreheads.

[6] *private study* With a quibble on private parts.

[7] *to bear with* To put up with; also (another bawdy quibble) to lie under, to bear the weight of his body.

[8] *hippocras* Wine flavored with spices.

[9] *Nan Spit … wind her* One of the humblest occupations in the kitchen of a large household or inn was that of the turnspit, whose job was to stand by the open fireplace and crank the horizontally mounted spit on which roasting meat was impaled. Robin tempts Rafe with the thought of sexually impaling and "turning" this kitchen maid—of treating her, in effect, as she treats a roast of meat.

[10] *horse-bread* Bread made of beans, bran, etc. for horses—but apparently sometimes eaten also by the very poor. Rafe seems to be aware of the popular superstition according to which familiar spirits took the form of animals, and were fed like pets by the witches to whom they attached themselves.

(*Enter Good Angel and Evil Angel.*)

GOOD ANGEL. Faustus, repent yet, God will pity thee.
EVIL ANGEL. Thou art a spirit, God cannot pity thee.
FAUSTUS. Who buzzeth° in mine ears I am a spirit? *whispers*
Be I a devil, yet God may pity me.
Ay, God will pity me if I repent.
EVIL ANGEL. Ay, but Faustus never shall repent.

(*Exeunt Angels.*)

FAUSTUS. My heart's so harden'd I cannot repent.
Scarce can I name salvation, faith, or heaven,
But fearful echoes thunders in mine ears,
"Faustus, thou art damn'd!" Then swords and knives,
Poison, guns, halters,[1] and envenom'd steel
Are laid before me to dispatch myself,
And long ere this I should have done the deed
Had not sweet pleasure conquer'd deep despair.
Have I not made blind Homer sing to me
Of Alexander's love and Oenone's death?[2]
And hath not he that built the walls of Thebes
With ravishing sound of his melodious harp[3]
Made music with my Mephastophilis?
Why should I die, then, or basely despair?
I am resolv'd: Faustus shall ne'er repent.
Come Mephastophilis, let us dispute again,
And reason of divine astrology.[4]
Speak, are there many spheres above the moon?
Are celestial bodies but one globe,
As is the substance of this centric earth?[5]
MEPHASTOPHILIS. As are the elements, such are the heavens,
Even from the moon unto the empyreal orb,
Mutually folded on each other's spheres,
And jointly move upon one axle-tree
Whose termine is term'd the world's wide pole.
Nor are the names of Saturn, Mars, or Jupiter
Feign'd, but are erring stars.
FAUSTUS. But tell me, have they all one motion, both *situ et tempore?*[6]
MEPHASTOPHILIS. All jointly move from east to west in four and twenty hours upon the poles of the world, but differ in their motions upon the poles of the zodiac.
FAUSTUS. These slender questions Wagner can decide:
Hath Mephastophilis no greater skill?
Who knows not the double notion of the planets?[7]
The first is finish'd in a natural day,
The second thus: Saturn in thirty years,
Jupiter in twelve, Mars in four, the Sun, Venus, and Mercury in a year, the Moon in twenty-eight days.[8]

[1] *halters* Hangman's nooses.

[2] *Alexander's ... death* These are matters which Homer left unsung; Faustus would have been the first to hear them from his lips. Paris (also named Alexandros), a son of King Priam and Queen Hecuba of Troy, was cast out by his parents (for it was prophesied that he should cause the destruction of Troy) and brought up among the shepherds of Mount Ida, where he won the love of Oenone. Asked by Hera, Athena, and Aphrodite to award a golden apple to the most beautiful goddess, he succumbed to Aphrodite's bribe of the love of the fairest woman alive, abandoned Oenone and abducted Helen from Sparta, thus provoking the Trojan War. Later, having been wounded by a poisoned arrow, he could have been healed only by Oenone; after jealously refusing to cure him, she was overwhelmed with remorse and threw herself onto his funeral pyre.

[3] *he ... harp* Amphion and his brother built the walls of Thebes; the music of Amphion's lyre magically moved huge stones into place.

[4] *astrology* Not clearly distinguished from astronomy until the seventeenth century.

[5] *the substance of this centric earth* The elements (earth, water, air, and fire) that make up "the substance of this centric earth" were thought to be concentrically disposed; so also, in the old geocentric cosmology, were the spheres that governed the motions of those wandering or "erring" stars, the planets. Mephastophilis says there are nine spheres: those of the planets, including the moon and the sun; the firmament, to which the fixed stars are attached; and the empyrean, the outermost and motionless sphere of the universe. (He apparently conflates the *primum mobile*, thought of by some astronomers as a distinct sphere that imparts motion to the heavens, with the firmament.) All of this is utterly commonplace. The systems developed by ancient astronomers were enormously more complex: Eudoxus (fourth century BCE) required twenty-seven, and Ptolemy (second century CE) more than eighty variously revolving spheres, including epicyclic and eccentric ones, to explain the motions of the planets.

[6] *situ et tempore* Latin: "In position and time"; i.e., in the direction of their revolutions around the earth and in the time these take.

[7] *poles ... planets* The apparent diurnal motion of the planetary spheres "upon one axle-tree" (the northern "termine" of which nearly coincides with the star Polaris) is of course due, in post-Copernican terms, to the earth's rotation upon its axis. The second component of the planets' apparent "double motion" is an effect of the differences between the earth's period of revolution around the sun and theirs.

[8] *first ... days* The periods of planetary revolution given by Faustus correspond for the most part to the then-accepted figures: Saturn 28 years, Jupiter 12 years, Mars 2 years, Venus, Mercury, and, of course,

Tush, these are freshmen's suppositions! But tell me, hath every sphere a dominion or *intelligentia?*[1]

MEPHASTOPHILIS. Ay.

FAUSTUS. How many planets or spheres are there?

MEPHASTOPHILIS. Nine: the seven planets, the firmament, and the empyreal heaven.

FAUSTUS. But is there not *coelum igneum, et crystallinum?*[2]

MEPHASTOPHILIS. No, Faustus, they be but fables.

FAUSTUS. Resolve me then in this one question: Why are not conjunctions, oppositions, aspects,[3] eclipses all at one time, but in some years we have more, in some less?

MEPHASTOPHILIS. *Per inaequalem motum respectu totius.*[4]

FAUSTUS. Well, I am answered. Now tell me who made the world.

MEPHASTOPHILIS. I will not.

FAUSTUS. Sweet Mephastophilis, tell me.

MEPHASTOPHILIS. Move° me not, Faustus. *anger*

FAUSTUS. Villain, have I not bound thee to tell me any thing?

MEPHASTOPHILIS. Ay, that is not against our kingdom. This is. Thou are damn'd, think thou of hell.

FAUSTUS. Think, Faustus, upon God that made the world!

MEPHASTOPHILIS. Remember this.

(*Exit.*)

FAUSTUS. Ay, go accursed spirit to ugly hell:
'Tis thou hast damn'd distressed Faustus' soul.
Is't not too late?

(*Enter Good Angel and Evil Angel.*)

EVIL ANGEL. Too late.

GOOD ANGEL. Never too late, if Faustus can repent.

EVIL ANGEL. If thou repent, devils shall tear thee in pieces.

GOOD ANGEL. Repent, and they shall never raze° thy skin. *graze*

(*Exeunt Angels.*)

FAUSTUS. Ah Christ, my Saviour,
Seek to save distressed Faustus' soul!

(*Enter Lucifer, Belzebub, and Mephastophilis.*)

LUCIFER. Christ cannot save thy soul, for he is just;
There's none but I have interest in[5] the same.

FAUSTUS. O, what art thou that look'st so terribly?

LUCIFER. I am Lucifer, and this is my companion prince in hell.

FAUSTUS. O Faustus, they are come to fetch away thy soul!

LUCIFER. We come to tell thee thou dost injure us.
Thou talk'st of Christ, contrary to thy promise.

BELZEBUB. Thou should'st not think of God.

LUCIFER. Think of the devil.

BELZEBUB. And of his dam° too. *woman*

FAUSTUS. Nor will I henceforth:[6] pardon me in this,
And Faustus vows never to look to heaven,
Never to name God or to pray to him,
To burn his Scriptures, slay his ministers,
And make my spirits pull his churches down.

LUCIFER. So shalt thou show thyself an obedient servant, and we will highly gratify thee for it.

BELZEBUB. Faustus, we are come from hell to show thee some pastime. Sit down, and thou shalt behold the Seven Deadly Sins appear to thee in their own proper shapes and likeness.

FAUSTUS. That sight will be as pleasing unto me as Paradise was to Adam, the first day of his creation.

LUCIFER. Talk not of Paradise, or creation, but mark the show.
Go, Mephastophilis, fetch them in.

(*Enter the Seven Deadly Sins.*)

---

the sun 1 year, and the moon 1 month. The actual—as opposed to apparent—periods for the inner planets are of course much less: $7^1/_2$ and 3 months respectively.

[1] *dominion or intelligentia* It was widely believed that the planets were moved or guided by angels or intelligences.

[2] *coelum igneum, et crystallinum* Latin: "A fiery, and a crystalline heaven."

[3] *conjunctions ... aspects* Astrological terms referring respectively to the apparent proximity of two planets, to their positioning on opposite sides of the sky, and to any other angular relation between their positions.

[4] *Per inaequalem motum respectu totius* Latin: "Through an unequal motion with respect to the whole."

[5] *interest in* Legal claim upon.

[6] *Nor ... henceforth* I.e., think of God.

BELZEBUB. Now Faustus, question them of their names and dispositions.

FAUSTUS. That shall I soon: what art thou, the first?

PRIDE. I am Pride. I disdain to have any parents. I am like Ovid's flea,[1] I can creep into every corner of a wench: sometimes like a periwig I sit upon her brow; next like a necklace I hang about her neck; then like a fan of feathers I kiss her lips; and then, turning myself to a wrought smock, do what I list. But fie, what a smell is here? I'll not speak a word more, unless the ground be perfumed and covered with a cloth of arras.[2]

FAUSTUS. Thou art a proud knave indeed. What art thou, the second?

COVETOUSNESS. I am Covetousness, begotten of an old churl in an old leathern bag; and might I have my wish, I would desire that this house and all the people in it were turned to gold, that I might lock you up in my good chest. O, my sweet gold!

FAUSTUS. What art thou, the third?

WRATH. I am Wrath. I had neither father nor mother; I leapt out of a lion's mouth when I was scarce half an hour old, and ever since I have run up and down the world with this case[3] of rapiers, wounding myself when I had nobody to fight withal. I was born in hell, and look to it: for some of you shall be my father.

FAUSTUS. What art thou, the fourth?

ENVY. I am Envy, begotten of a chimney-sweeper and an oyster wife.[4] I cannot read, and therefore wish all books were burned; I am lean with seeing others eat. O, that there would come a famine through all the world, that all might die, and I live alone: then thou should'st see how fat I would be. But must thou sit and I stand? Come down, with a vengeance![5]

FAUSTUS. Away, envious rascal! What art thou, the fifth?

GLUTTONY. Who I, sir? I am Gluttony. My parents are all dead, and the devil a penny they have left me, but a bare pension, and that buys me thirty meals a day and ten bevers:[6] a small trifle to suffice nature. O, I come of a royal parentage: my grandfather was a gammon of bacon,[7] my grand-mother a hogshead[8] of claret[9] wine. My god-fathers were these: Peter Pickleherring[10] and Martin Martlemas-beef.[11] O, but my godmother she was a jolly gentlewoman, and well-beloved in every good town and city: her name was Mistress Margery March-beer.[12] Now, Faustus, thou hast heard all my progeny, wilt thou bid me to supper?

FAUSTUS. No, I'll see thee hanged: thou wilt eat up all my victuals.

GLUTTONY. Then the devil choke thee.

FAUSTUS. Choke thyself, glutton! What art thou, the sixth?

SLOTH. I am Sloth. I was begotten on a sunny bank, where I have lain ever since, and you have done me great injury to bring me from thence. Let me be carried thither again by Gluttony and Lechery. I'll not speak another word for a king's ransom.

FAUSTUS. What are you, mistress minx,[13] the seventh and last?

LECHERY. Who I, sir? I am one that loves an inch of raw mutton[14] better than an ell[15] of fried stock-fish,[16] and the first letter of my name begins with Lechery.

LUCIFER. Away, to hell, to hell.

---

[1] *Ovid's flea* *Elegia de pulice*, a poem written in imitation of Ovid, was wrongly ascribed to him. In it is a line addressed to the flea: "You go wherever you wish; nothing, savage, is hidden from you."

[2] *cloth of arras* Tapestry fabric of the kind woven at Arras in Flanders; to use it as a floor covering would be grossly ostentatious.

[3] *case* Pair.

[4] *begotten ... wife* I.e., filthy and foul-smelling woman.

[5] *with a vengeance* With a curse on you.

[6] *bevers* Drinks; also light meals or snacks.

[7] *gammon of bacon* Bottom piece of a flitch of bacon.

[8] *hogshead* Wine-barrel of a standard size, holding (in modern terms) 225 liters or 63 American gallons—the equivalent of 25 cases of a dozen bottles of wine.

[9] *claret* Light red wine from the Bordeaux region.

[10] *Pickleherring* Clown figure associated with carnival festivities and popular farces.

[11] *Martlemas-beef* Martinmas, or St. Martin's Day (November 11), was the traditional time to slaughter cattle that could not be fed over the winter, and to commence the production of salt beef; it was therefore also a time for feasting on "green" or unsalted beef.

[12] *March-beer* Strong beer brewed in March.

[13] *minx* Hussy, wanton woman.

[14] *raw mutton* Metaphor for prostitutes; the expression here takes on a phallic meaning.

[15] *ell* Measure of length (equal in England to some forty-five inches), commonly contrasted to an inch.

[16] *stock-fish* Unsalted dried fish, sometimes abusively associated with the flaccid male organ.

(*Exeunt the Sins.*)

Now Faustus, how dost thou like this?
FAUSTUS. O, this feeds my soul.
LUCIFER. Tut, Faustus, in hell is all manner of delight.
FAUSTUS. O, might I see hell, and return again, how happy were I then!
LUCIFER. Thou shalt. I will send for thee at midnight. In mean time, take this book, peruse it thoroughly, and thou shalt turn thyself into what shape thou wilt.
FAUSTUS. Great thanks, mighty Lucifer:
This will I keep as chary° as my life. *carefully*
LUCIFER. Farewell, Faustus, and think on the devil.
FAUSTUS. Farewell, great Lucifer. Come, Mephastophilis.

(*Exeunt all.*)

ACT 3, CHORUS.

(*Enter the Chorus [Wagner].*)

WAGNER. Learned Faustus,
To know the secrets of astronomy
Graven in the book of Jove's high firmament,
Did mount him up to scale Olympus' top,[1]
Where sitting in a chariot burning bright,[2]
Drawn by the strength of yoked dragons' necks,
He views the clouds, the planets and the stars,
The tropics, zones, and quarters[3] of the sky,
From the bright circle of the horned moon
Even to the height of *primum mobile*;[4]
And whirling round with this circumference
Within the concave compass of the pole,
From east to west his dragons swiftly glide,

[1] *to scale Olympus' top* I.e., to ascend to the dwelling-place of the gods, on the top of Mount Olympus.

[2] *chariot … bright* Parodic echo of the vision of the divine chariot-throne in Ezekiel 1.13–28.

[3] *tropics … quarters* Tropics of Cancer and Capricorn, the arctic and antarctic circles and the equator divided the celestial sphere into five belts or zones; traditional astronomy also quartered the celestial sphere with two other circles that passed through its north and south poles: the solstitial colure, which intersects the two tropics at the solstitial points (those at which the ecliptic meets the tropics); and the equinoctial colure, which intersects the equator at the equinoctial points (those at which the ecliptic crosses the equator).

[4] *From … mobile* From the lowest to the highest of the spheres.

And in eight days did bring him home again.
Not long he stay'd within his quiet house
To rest his bones after his weary toil,
But new exploits do hale him out again,
And mounted then upon a dragon's back
That with his wings did part the subtle° air, *rarified*
He now is gone to prove cosmography,[5]
That measures coasts and kingdoms of the earth.
And as I guess, will first arrive at Rome
To see the Pope, and manner of his court,
And take some part of holy Peter's[6] feast,
The which this day is highly solemniz'd.
(*Exit.*)

ACT 3, SCENE 1

(*Enter Faustus and Mephastophilis.*)

FAUSTUS. Having now, my good Mephastophilis,
Pass'd with delight the stately town of Trier,[7]
Environ'd round with airy mountain tops,
With walls of flint, and deep entrenched lakes,
Not to be won by any conquering prince;
From Paris next, coasting the realm of France,
We saw the river Main fall into Rhine,
Whose banks are set with groves of fruitful vines;
Then up to Naples, rich Campania,[8]
Whose buildings, fair and gorgeous to the eye
(The streets are straightforth and pav'd with finest brick),
Quarters the town in four equivalents.
There saw we learned Maro's[9] golden tomb,

[5] *to prove cosmography* To put geography to the test. Cosmography was sometimes thought of as a science that maps the universe as a whole, thus incorporating geography and astronomy.

[6] *holy Peter* St. Peter.

[7] *Trier* City on the Moselle River, capital of an electoral state of the Holy Roman Empire, which under the rule of Elector-Archbishop Johann von Schönenburg was subjected during the 1580s and 1590s to a violent wave of witch-hunts.

[8] *Campania* In ancient usage, the plain surrounding the city of Capua; since medieval times, Naples has been the principal city of this region. (In modern Italy the name Campania is applied to a much larger area.)

[9] *Maro* Virgil, or Publius Vergilius Maro, died at Naples in 19 BCE. In part because his fourth Eclogue was interpreted as a prophecy of the coming of Christ, he acquired a reputation during the medieval period as a necromancer. His supposed (continued)

The way[1] he cut, an English mile in length,
Thorough a rock of stone in one night's space.
From thence to Venice, Padua, and the rest,
In midst of which a sumptuous temple stands,
That threats the stars[2] with her aspiring top.
Thus hitherto hath Faustus spent his time.
But tell me now, what resting place is this?
Hast thou, as erst° I did command, *first*
Conducted me within the walls of Rome?

MEPHASTOPHILIS. Faustus, I have, and because we will not be unprovided,
I have taken up his Holiness' privy chamber[3] for our use.
FAUSTUS. I hope his Holiness will bid us welcome.
MEPHASTOPHILIS. Tut, 'tis no matter, man, we'll be bold with his good cheer.
And now my Faustus, that thou may'st perceive
What Rome containeth to delight thee with,
Know that this city stands upon seven hills
That underprop the groundwork of the same;
Just through the midst runs flowing Tiber's stream,
With winding banks that cut it in two parts,
Over the which four stately bridges lean,
That make safe passage to each part of Rome.
Upon the bridge call'd Ponte Angelo
Erected is a castle passing strong,[4]
Within those walls such stores of ordnance are,
And double cannons,[5] fram'd of carved brass,
As match the days within one complete year—
Besides the gates and high pyramides[6]
Which Julius Caesar brought from Africa.
FAUSTUS. Now, by the kingdoms of infernal rule,
Of Styx, Acheron, and the fiery lake
Of ever-burning Phlegethon,[7] I swear
That I do long to see the monuments
And situation of bright splendent Rome.
Come therefore, let's away.
MEPHASTOPHILIS. Nay Faustus, stay: I know you'd fain see the Pope,
And take some part of° holy Peter's feast, *in*
Where thou shalt see a troop of bald-pate friars
Whose *summum bonum*[8] is in belly-cheer.
FAUSTUS. Well, I am content to compass° then some sport, *contrive*
And by their folly make us merriment.
Then charm me, that I may be invisible,
To do what I please
Unseen of any whilst I stay in Rome.

(*Mephastophilis charms him.*)[9]

MEPHASTOPHILIS. So, Faustus: now
Do what thou wilt, thou shalt not be discern'd.

(*Sound a sennet.*[10] *Enter the Pope and the Cardinal of Lorraine*[11] *to the banquet, with Friars attending.*)

POPE. My lord of Lorraine, will't please you draw near?
FAUSTUS. Fall to, and the devil choke you and you spare.[12]

---

tomb stands on the promontory of Posilipo on the Bay of Naples, at the Naples end of a tunnel, nearly half a mile in length, which cuts through the promontory—and which, as Petrarch wrote, "the insipid masses conclude was made by Virgil with magical incantations."

[1] *way* Road. The tunnel is in fact some seven yards wide.

[2] *sumptuous … stars* Saint Mark's in Venice. The "aspiring top" would have to be that of the campanile, which stands at some distance from the church.

[3] *privy chamber* Bedchamber.

[4] *castle … strong* Papal fortress of Castel San Angelo.

[5] *double cannons* Cannons of very large caliber.

[6] *pyramides* Obelisk, in this case the one brought to Rome from Egypt by the emperor Caligula (not Julius Caesar), and moved to its present site in the Piazza San Pietro in 1586. The word is singular, not plural.

[7] *Styx, Acheron … Phlegethon* Three of the four rivers of Hades, the Greek underworld.

[8] *summum bonum* Latin: highest good.

[9] *Mephastophilis charms him* According to Henslowe's *Diary* the Admiral's Men owned a "robe for to go invisible," a prop which may have been used here.

[10] *sennet* Flourish on the trumpet to announce a ceremonial entrance.

[11] *Cardinal of Lorraine* This position was held during the sixteenth century by several members of the powerful Guise family: Jean de Guise (1498–1550); Charles de Guise (1524–74), who helped foment the wars of religion that convulsed France for decades after 1562 and acquired a reputation for dissimulation and cruelty; and Louis de Guise (1555–88), who along with his brother, Henri, third Duc de Guise (1550–88), was assassinated by King Henri III. As leaders of the pro-Spanish and ultra-Catholic Ligue, and thus major figures in the Spanish-led campaign against Protestantism, Louis and Henri de Guise were feared and detested in England.

[12] *and you spare* If you eat sparingly.

POPE. How now, who's that which spake? Friars, look about!

FRIAR. Here's nobody, if it like[1] your Holiness.

POPE. My lord, here is a dainty dish was sent me from the Bishop of Milan.

FAUSTUS. I thank you, sir.

(*Snatch it.*)

POPE. How now, who's that which snatched the meat from me? Will no man look? My lord, this dish was sent me from the Cardinal of Florence.

FAUSTUS. You say true, I'll ha' it.

(*Snatch it.*)

POPE. What, again! My lord, I'll drink to your grace.

FAUSTUS. I'll pledge your grace.

(*Snatch it.*)

LORRAINE. My lord, it may be some ghost newly crept out of purgatory come to beg a pardon of your Holiness.

POPE. It may be so. Friars, prepare a dirge[2] to lay the fury of this ghost. Once again, my lord, fall to. (*The Pope crosses himself.*[3])

FAUSTUS. What, are you crossing your self? Well, use that trick no more, I would advise you.

(*Cross again.*)

FAUSTUS. Well, there's the second time. Aware the third, I give you fair warning.

(*Cross again, and Faustus hits him a box of the ear, and they all run away.*)

Come on, Mephastophilis, what shall we do?

MEPHASTOPHILIS. Nay, I know not; we shall be cursed with bell, book and candle.[4]

FAUSTUS. How? Bell, book and candle, candle, book and bell,
Forward and backward, to curse Faustus to hell.
Anon you shall hear a hog grunt, a calf bleat, and an ass bray,
Because it is Saint Peter's holy day!

(*Enter all the Friars to sing the dirge.*)

FRIAR. Come brethren, let's about our business with good devotion.

(*They sing this:*)

Cursed be he that stole away his Holiness' meat from the table.
Maledicat dominus![5]
Cursed be he that struck his Holiness a blow on the face.
Maledicat dominus!
Cursed be he that took Friar Sandelo a blow on the pate.
Maledicat dominus!
Cursed be he that disturbeth our holy dirge.
Maledicat dominus!
Cursed be he that took away his Holiness' wine.
Maledicat dominus! Et omnes sancti![6] *Amen.*

(*Faustus and Mephastophilis beat the Friars and fling fireworks among them, and so exeunt.*)

ACT 3, SCENE 2

(*Enter Robin and Rafe with a silver goblet.*)

ROBIN. Come Rafe, did I not tell thee we were for ever made by this Doctor Faustus' book? *Ecce signum,*[7] here's

---

[1] *like* Please.

[2] *dirge* Originally "dirige," the first word of the Latin antiphon at matins in the Office of the Dead ("Dirige, Domine, Deus meus, in conspectu tuo viam meum": "Direct, O Lord, my God, my way in thy sight").

[3] *crosses himself* Makes the sign of the cross, the preliminary to Roman Catholic prayer.

[4] *bell, book and candle* At the end of the ritual of excommunication, which is performed to debar a member of the Church from the sacraments, the bell is tolled, the book closed, and the candle extinguished. That ritual is confused here with the office of exorcism, performed to banish evil spirits.

[5] *Maledicat dominus* Latin: "May the Lord curse him."

[6] *et omnes sancti!* Latin: "And (may) all the saints (curse him)."

[7] *Ecce signum* Latin: "Behold the sign."

a simple purchase for horse-keepers! Our horses shall eat no hay as long as this lasts.

(*Enter the Vintner.*)

RAFE. But Robin, here comes the Vintner.

ROBIN. Hush, I'll gull[1] him supernaturally. Drawer,[2] I hope all is paid. God be with you; come Rafe.

VINTNER. Soft,[3] sir; a word with you. I must yet have a goblet paid from you ere you go.

ROBIN. I a goblet? Rafe, I a goblet? I scorn you, and you are but a etc.[4] I a goblet? Search me!

VINTNER. I mean so, sir, with your favor.

(*Searches Robin.*)

ROBIN. How say you now?

VINTNER. I must say somewhat to your fellow. You, sir.

RAFE. Me, sir? Me, sir! Search your fill! Now, sir, you may be ashamed to burden honest men with a matter of truth.

VINTNER. Well, t'one of you hath this goblet about you.

ROBIN. You lie, drawer, 'tis afore me. Sirrah you, I'll teach ye to impeach[5] honest men: stand by, I'll scour you for a goblet. Stand aside, you had best, I charge you in the name of Belzebub! Look to the goblet, Rafe.[6]

VINTNER. What mean you, sirrah?

ROBIN. I'll tell you what I mean.

(*He reads.*)

Sanctabulorum periphrasticon—Nay, I'll tickle you, Vintner! Look to the goblet, Rafe. *Polypragmos Belseborams framanto pacostiphos tostu Mephastophilis, etc.*[7]

(*Enter Mephastophilis; sets squibs*[8] *at their backs; they run about.*)

VINTNER. *O nomine Domine!* What mean'st thou, Robin? Thou hast no goblet!

RAFE. *Peccatum peccatorum!* Here's thy goblet, good Vintner!

ROBIN. *Misericordia pro nobis!*[9] What shall I do? Good devil, forgive me now, and I'll never rob thy library more!

MEPHASTOPHILIS. Monarch of hell, under whose black survey
Great potentates do kneel with awful fear,
Upon whose altars thousand souls do lie,
How am I vexed with these villains' charms!
From Constantinople am I hither come
Only for pleasure of these damned slaves.

ROBIN. How, from Constantinople? You have had a great journey, will you take sixpence in your purse to pay for your supper, and be gone?

MEPHASTOPHILIS. Well villains, for your presumption, I transform thee into an ape, and thee into a dog, and so be gone!

(*Exit.*)

ROBIN. How, into an ape? That's brave, I'll have fine sport with the boys; I'll get nuts and apples enow.[10]

RAFE. And I must be a dog.

ROBIN. I'faith, thy head will never be out of the pottage pot.

(*Exeunt.*)

---

[1] *gull* Trick.

[2] *Drawer* An insult: Robin pretends to mistake the Vintner (or innkeeper) for his employee, the tapster or drawer who serves the customers.

[3] *Soft* Softly, slowly; here carrying an imperative force, as in "not so fast!"

[4] *etc.* Substitute for a scatological or obscene expression.

[5] *impeach* Accuse.

[6] *Look ... Rafe* Robin and Rafe are apparently passing the goblet back and forth between them.

[7] *Sanctabulorum ... Mephastophilis, etc.* Robin's incantation is gibberish, though some of it comes close to deviating into sense. The Greek *periphrastikos* means "circumlocutory." In Greek *polypragmosyne* means "curiosity" or "meddlesomeness," and a *polypragmon* is a "busybody." The first four words of the invocation might then be translated as "Busy-body Belseborams ... of beating-around-the-bush holy-molydoms!"

[8] *squibs* Fireworks.

[9] *O ... nobis* Garbled scraps of liturgical Latin.

[10] *enow* Enough.

ACT 4, CHORUS

(*Enter Chorus.*)

CHORUS. When Faustus had with pleasure ta'en the view
Of rarest things and royal courts of kings,
He stay'd his course, and so returned home,
Where such as bear his absence but with grief,
I mean his friends and nearest companions,
Did gratulate his safety with kind words,
And in their conference of what befell
Touching his journey through the world and air
They put forth questions of astrology,
Which Faustus answer'd with such learned skill
As[1] they admir'd and wonder'd at his wit.
Now is his fame spread forth in every land;
Amongst the rest of Emperor is one,
Carolus the Fifth,[2] at whose palace now
Faustus is feasted 'mongst his noblemen.
What there he did in trial of his art
I leave untold, your eyes shall see perform'd.

(*Exit.*)

ACT 4, SCENE 1

(*Enter Emperor, Faustus, and a Knight, with attendants.*)

EMPEROR. Master Doctor Faustus, I have heard strange report of thy knowledge in the black art, how that none in my empire, nor in the whole world, can compare with thee for the rare[3] effects of magic: they say thou hast a familiar spirit, by whom thou canst accomplish what thou list.[4] This therefore is my request: that thou let me see some proof of thy skill, that mine eyes may be witnesses to confirm what mine ears have heard reported; and here I swear to thee, by the honor of mine imperial crown, that whatever thou doest, thou shalt be no ways prejudiced or endamaged.[5]

KNIGHT. (*Aside.*) I'faith, he looks much like a conjurer.

FAUSTUS. My gracious sovereign, though I must confess myself far inferior to the report men have published, and nothing answerable[6] to the honor of your imperial Majesty, yet for that[7] love and duty binds me thereunto, I am content to do whatsoever your Majesty shall command me.

EMPEROR. Then Doctor Faustus, mark what I shall say.
As I was sometime solitary set
Within my closet,[8] sundry thoughts arose
About the honor of mine ancestors:
How they had won by prowess such exploits,
Got riches, subdu'd so many kingdoms,
As we that do succeed,[9] or they that shall
Hereafter possess our throne shall,
I fear me, never attain to that degree
Of high renown and great authority;
Amongst which kings is Alexander the Great,
Chief spectacle of the world's pre-eminence,[10]
The bright shining of whose glorious acts
Lightens the world with his reflecting beams,
As when I hear but motion° made of him *mention*
It grieves my soul I never saw the man.
If therefore thou, by cunning of thine art,
Canst raise this man from hollow vaults below
Where lies entomb'd this famous conqueror,
And bring with him his beauteous paramour,[11]
Both in their right shapes, gesture, and attire
They us'd to wear during their time of life,
Thou shalt both satisfy my just desire
And give me cause to praise thee whilst I live.

FAUSTUS. My gracious lord, I am ready to accomplish your request, so far forth as by art and power of my spirit I am able to perform.

KNIGHT. (*Aside.*) I'faith that's just nothing at all.

---

[1] *As* That.

[2] *Carolus the Fifth* Charles V (1500–58), King of Spain and Holy Roman Emperor from 1518 and 1519 respectively until his abdication in 1555. The historical Doctor Faustus never made an appearance at the imperial court. Contemporary *magi*, however, had connections with the courts of both the emperor Maximilian (Charles V's grandfather and immediate predecessor) and Charles V.

[3] *rare* Remarkable, extraordinary.

[4] *what thou list* Whatever you wish.

[5] *endamaged* Harmed.

[6] *nothing answerable* Quite unequal.

[7] *for that* Because.

[8] *closet* Study, inner chamber.

[9] *succeed* Follow in dynastic succession.

[10] *pre-eminence* Pre-eminent people.

[11] *paramour* Mistress, consort (i.e., Roxane of Oxyartes).

FAUSTUS. But if it like your Grace, it is not in my ability to present before your eyes the true substantial bodies of those two deceased princes, which long since are consumed to dust.

KNIGHT. (*Aside.*) Ay, marry[1] Master Doctor, now there's a sign of grace in you when you will confess the truth.

FAUSTUS. But such spirits as can lively resemble Alexander and his paramour shall appear before your Grace, in that manner that they best lived in, in their most flourishing estate, which I doubt not shall sufficiently content your imperial Majesty.

EMPEROR. Go to,[2] Master Doctor, let me see them presently.[3]

KNIGHT. Do you hear, Master Doctor? You bring Alexander and his paramour before the Emperor?

FAUSTUS. How then, sir?

KNIGHT. I'faith, that's as true as Diana turned me to a stag.

FAUSTUS. No sir, but when Actaeon[4] died, he left the horns for you. Mephastophilis, be gone.

(*Exit Mephastophilis.*)

KNIGHT. Nay, and[5] you go to conjuring, I'll be gone.

(*Exit Knight.*)

FAUSTUS. I'll meet with[6] you anon for interrupting me so. Here they are, my gracious lord.

(*Enter Mephastophilis with Alexander and his paramour.*)

EMPEROR. Master Doctor, I heard this lady while she lived had a wart or mole in her neck. How shall I know whether it be so or no?

FAUSTUS. Your highness may boldly go and see.

(*Emperor does so; then spirits exeunt.*)

EMPEROR. Sure these are no spirits, but the true substantial bodies of these two deceased princes.[7]

FAUSTUS. Will't please your highness now to send for the knight that was so pleasant with me here of late?

EMPEROR. One of you call him forth.

(*Enter the Knight with a pair of horns on his head.*)

How now, sir knight? Why, I had thought thou had'st been a bachelor, but now I see thou hast a wife, that not only gives thee horns but makes thee wear them. Feel on thy head!

KNIGHT. Thou damned wretch and execrable dog,
Bred in the concave of some monstrous rock,
How dar'st thou thus abuse a gentleman?
Villain, I say, undo what thou hast done!

FAUSTUS. O not so fast, sir; there's no haste but good.[8] Are you remembered how you crossed me in my conference with the Emperor? I think I have met with you for it.

EMPEROR. Good Master Doctor, at my entreaty release him. He hath done penance sufficient.

FAUSTUS. My gracious lord, not so much for the injury[9] he offered me here in your presence, as to delight you with some mirth, hath Faustus worthily requited this injurious knight; which being all I desire, I am content to release him of his horns. And sir knight, hereafter speak well of scholars. Mephastophilis, transform him straight.[10] Now, my good lord, having done my duty, I humbly take my leave.

EMPEROR. Farewell, Master Doctor; yet ere you go, expect from me a bounteous reward.

(*Exeunt Emperor, Knight, and attendants.*)

ACT 4, SCENE 2

FAUSTUS. Now Mephastophilis, the restless course

---

[1] *marry* Here, expression used to give emphasis to a statement.

[2] *Go to* Normally an expression of incredulity, it appears here to express mild demurral, or perhaps encouragement, with the same range of meanings as "Come, come."

[3] *presently* At once.

[4] *Diana ... Actaeon* Actaeon, a hunter, witnessed the goddess Diana and her nymphs bathing; the goddess transformed him into a stag and he was torn to pieces by his own dogs.

[5] *and* If.

[6] *meet with* Get even with.

[7] *princes* Used in this period to refer, not to a male ruler, but any ruler.

[8] *there's ... good* Common proverb: "No haste but good (speed)."

[9] *injury* Insult.

[10] *straight* At once.

That time doth run with calm and silent foot,
Shortening my days and thread of vital life,
Calls for the payment of my latest years.
Therefore, sweet Mephastophilis,
Let us make haste to Wittenberg.

MEPHASTOPHILIS. What, will you go on horseback, or on foot?

FAUSTUS. Nay, till I am past this fair and pleasant green
I'll walk on foot.

(*Enter a Horse-courser.*)[1]

HORSE-COURSER. I have been all this day seeking one Master Fustian; mass,[2] see where he is. God save you, Master Doctor.

FAUSTUS. What, horse-courser, you are well met.

HORSE-COURSER. Do you hear, sir? I have brought you forty dollars for your horse.

FAUSTUS. I cannot sell him. If thou lik'st him for fifty, take him.

HORSE-COURSER. Alas sir, I have no more. I pray you, speak for me.

MEPHASTOPHILIS. I pray you, let him have him. He is an honest fellow, and he has a great charge,[3] neither wife nor child.

FAUSTUS. Well, come, give me your money. My boy will deliver him to you. But I must tell you one thing before you have him: ride him not into the water at any hand.[4]

HORSE-COURSER. Why sir, will he not drink of all waters?

FAUSTUS. O yes, he will drink of all waters, but ride him not into the water. Ride him over hedge or ditch, or where thou wilt, but not into the water.

HORSE-COURSER. Well, sir, now am I a made man for ever! I'll not leave[5] my horse for forty. If he had but the quality of hey ding ding, hey ding ding, I'd make a brave living on him: he has a buttock so slick as an eel.[6] Well, God-bye[7] sir, your boy will deliver him me. But hark ye sir, if my horse be sick or ill at ease, if I bring his water[8] to you, you'll tell me what it is?

FAUSTUS. Away, you villain! What, dost thou think I am a horse-doctor?

(*Exit Horse-courser.*)

What art thou, Faustus, but a man condemn'd to die?
Thy fatal time[9] doth draw to final end;
Despair doth drive distrust into my thoughts.
Confound these passions with a quiet sleep:
Tush, Christ did call the thief upon the cross.[10]
Then rest thee, Faustus, quiet in conceit.

(*Sleeps in his chair. Enter Horse-courser all wet, crying.*)

HORSE-COURSER. Alas, alas, Doctor Fustian, quotha? Mass, Doctor Lopus[11] was never such a doctor: has given me a purgation,[12] has purged me of forty dollars, I shall never see them more. But yet like an ass as I was, I would not be ruled by him, for he bade me I should ride him into no water. Now I, thinking my horse had some rare quality that he would not have had me know of, I like a venturous youth rid him into the deep pond at the town's end. I was no sooner in the middle of the pond, but my horse vanished away, and I sat upon a bottle[13] of hay, never so near drowning in my life! But I'll seek out my doctor, and have my forty dollars again, or I'll make

---

[1] *Horse-courser* Horse dealer.

[2] *Fustian* Clownish deformation of "Faustus"; bombast, nonsense; *mass* Contraction of "By the Mass."

[3] *charge* Burden (of family responsibilities).

[4] *at any hand* Under any circumstances.

[5] *leave* Sell.

[6] *hey ding ding … eel* "Hey ding-a-ding" is a common refrain in popular songs. The phrase has sexual overtones, and "buttock so slick as an eel" implies sexual potency; thus, the "brave living" that the horse-courser anticipates will presumably come from stud fees.

[7] *God-bye* Contraction of "God be with you."

[8] *water* Urine.

[9] *fatal time* Time allotted by fate.

[10] *the thief … cross* See Luke 23.43.

[11] *Doctor Lopus* Doctor Roderigo Lopez, a Portuguese *marrano*, or Christianized Jew, and personal physician to Queen Elizabeth. Lopez incurred the enmity of the Earl of Essex, who in January 1594 accused him of high treason; he was tried (and convicted) on February 28 on charges that included attempting to poison the queen, and was executed on June 7—more than a year after Marlowe's death. Although Lopez was well-known even before his appointment as the queen's physician in 1586 (he had previously been household physician to the Earl of Leicester), the past-tense allusion to him suggests that in its present form this scene must have been written after Marlowe's death.

[12] *purgation* Emetic.

[13] *bottle* From the French "botte," meaning bundle.

it dearest[1] horse. O, yonder is his snipper-snapper.[2] Do you hear? you, hey-pass,[3] where's your master?

MEPHASTOPHILIS. Why sir, what would you? You cannot speak with him.

HORSE-COURSER. But I will speak with him.

MEPHASTOPHILIS. Why, he's fast asleep; come some other time.

HORSE-COURSER. I'll speak with him now, or I'll break his glass windows[4] about his ears.

MEPHASTOPHILIS. I tell thee, he hath not slept this eight nights.

HORSE-COURSER. And he have not slept this eight weeks I'll speak with him.

MEPHASTOPHILIS. See where he is, fast asleep.

HORSE-COURSER. Ay, this is he. God save ye Master Doctor! Master Doctor, Master Doctor Fustian, forty dollars, forty dollars for a bottle of hay!

MEPHASTOPHILIS. Why, thou seest he hears thee not.

HORSE-COURSER. So ho, ho! So ho, ho![5] (*Hallow in his ear.*) No, will you not wake? I'll make you wake ere I go!

(*Pull him by the leg, and pull it away.*)

Alas, I am undone! What shall I do?

FAUSTUS. O my leg, my leg! Help, Mephastophilis! Call the officers, my leg, my leg!

MEPHASTOPHILIS. Come villain, to the constable.

HORSE-COURSER. O Lord, sir: let me go, and I'll give you forty dollars more.

MEPHASTOPHILIS. Where be they?

HORSE-COURSER. I have none about me; come to my ostry,[6] and I'll give them you.

MEPHASTOPHILIS. Be gone, quickly.

(*Horse-courser runs away.*)

FAUSTUS. What, is he gone? Farewell he, Faustus has his leg again, and the horse-courser, I take it, a bottle of hay for his labor. Well, this trick shall cost him forty dollars more.

(*Enter Wagner.*)

How now, Wagner, what's the news with thee?

WAGNER. Sir, the Duke of Vanholt doth earnestly entreat your company.

FAUSTUS. The Duke of Vanholt! An honorable gentleman, to whom I must be no niggard[7] of my cunning. Come Mephastophilis, let's away to him.

(*Exeunt.*)

ACT 4, SCENE 3

(*Enter to them the Duke, and the Duchess; the Duke speaks.*)

DUKE. Believe me, Master Doctor, this merriment hath much pleased me.

FAUSTUS. My gracious lord, I am glad it contents you so well. But it may be, madam, you take no delight in this. I have heard that great-bellied[8] women do long for some dainties or other: what is it, madam? Tell me, and you shall have it.

DUCHESS. Thanks, good Master Doctor, and for I see your courteous intent to pleasure me, I will not hide from you the thing my heart desires; and were it now summer, as it is January, and the dead time of winter, I would desire no better meat[9] than a dish of ripe grapes.

FAUSTUS. Alas, madam, that's nothing. Mephastophilis, be gone.

(*Exit Mephastophilis.*)

Were it a greater thing than this, so it would content you, you should have it.

(*Enter Mephastophilis with the grapes.*)

Here they be, madam, will't please you to taste on them?

DUKE. Believe me, Master Doctor, this makes me wonder above the rest, that being in the dead time of

---

[1] *dearest* Most expensive. If the horse-courser can't have his money back, he'll take revenge.

[2] *snipper-snapper* Conceited young fellow, smart-aleck.

[3] *hey-pass* Expression used by fairground conjurors or jugglers.

[4] *glass windows* Spectacles.

[5] *So ho, ho* Huntsman's cry.

[6] *ostry* Hostelry, inn.

[7] *niggard* Parsimonious person, one who shares only grudgingly.

[8] *great-bellied* Pregnant.

[9] *meat* Food.

winter, and in the month of January, how you should come by these grapes.

FAUSTUS. If it like your Grace, the year is divided into two circles over the whole world, that when it is here winter with us, in the contrary circle it is summer with them, as in India, Saba, and farther countries in the east;[1] and by means of a swift spirit that I have, I had them brought hither, as ye see. How do you like them, madam, be they good?

DUCHESS. Believe me, Master Doctor, they be the best grapes that e'er I tasted in my life before.

FAUSTUS. I am glad they content you so, madam.

DUKE. Come, madam, let us in, where you must well reward this learned man for the kindness he hath showed to you.

DUCHESS. And so I will, my lord, and whilst I live rest beholden for this courtesy.

FAUSTUS. I humbly thank your Grace.

DUKE. Come Master Doctor, follow us, and receive your reward.

(*Exeunt.*)

ACT 5, SCENE 1

(*Enter Wagner alone.*)

WAGNER. I think my master means to die shortly,
For he hath given to me all his goods;
And yet methinkes[2] if that death were near
He would not banquet and carouse and swill
Amongst the students, as even now he doth,
Who are at supper with such belly-cheer
As Wagner ne'er beheld in all his life.
See where they come: belike the feast is ended.

(*Exit. Enter Faustus with two or three scholars.*)

FIRST SCHOLAR. Master Doctor Faustus, since our conference about fair ladies, which was the beautiful'st in all the world, we have determined with[3] our selves that Helen of Greece was the admirablest lady that ever lived. Therefore, Master Doctor, if you will do us so much favor as to let us see that peerless dame of Greece, whom all the world admires for majesty, we should think ourselves much beholding unto you.

FAUSTUS. Gentlemen,
For that[4] I know your friendship is unfeign'd
(And Faustus' custom is not to deny
The just requests of those that wish him well),
You shall behold that peerless dame of Greece
No otherways for pomp and majesty
Than when Sir Paris cross'd the seas with her
And brought the spoils to rich Dardania.[5]
Be silent then, for danger is in words.

(*Music sounds, and Helen passeth over the stage.*)

SECOND SCHOLAR. Too simple is my wit to tell her praise,
Whom all the world admires for majesty.

THIRD SCHOLAR. No marvel though the angry Greeks pursued[6]
With ten years' war the rape° of such a queen, *abduction*
Whose heavenly beauty passeth all compare.

FIRST SCHOLAR. Since we have seen the pride of nature's works,
And only paragon of excellence,

(*Enter an old man.*)

Let us depart, and for this glorious deed
Happy and blest be Faustus evermore.

FAUSTUS. Gentlemen, farewell, the same I wish to you.

(*Exeunt scholars.*)

OLD MAN. Ah, Doctor Faustus, that I might prevail
To guide thy steps unto the way of life,
By which sweet path thy may'st attain the goal
That shall conduct thee to celestial rest.
Break heart, drop blood, and mingle it with tears,
Tears falling from repentant heaviness

---

[1] *two circles ... east* The two "circles" should of course be the northern and southern hemispheres. Saba is the land of the Queen of Sheba, now Yemen.

[2] *methinkes* Modernized spelling would upset the rhythm of this line.

[3] *determined with* Settled among.

[4] *for that* Because.

[5] *Dardania* Troy, referred to here by the name of the founder of the Trojan dynasty, Dardanus.

[6] *pursued* Sought to avenge.

Of thy most vile and loathsome filthiness,
The stench whereof corrupts the inward soul
With such flagitious[1] crimes of heinous sins
As no commiseration may expel
But mercy, Faustus, of thy Saviour sweet,
Whose blood alone must wash away thy guilt.[2]

FAUSTUS. Where art thou, Faustus?[3] wretch, what hast thou done?
Damn'd art thou, Faustus, damn'd, despair and die!
Hell claims his right, and with a roaring voice
Says, "Faustus, come, thine hour is almost come!"

(*Enter Mephastophilis, who gives him a dagger.*)

And Faustus now will come to do thee right.

OLD MAN. Ah stay, good Faustus, stay thy desperate steps:
I see an angel hovers o'er thy head,
And with a vial full of precious grace[4]
Offers to pour the same into thy soul:
Then call for mercy and avoid despair.

FAUSTUS. Ah my sweet friend, I feel thy words
To comfort my distressed soul.
Leave me awhile to ponder on my sins.

OLD MAN. I go, sweet Faustus, but with heavy cheer,
Fearing the ruin of thy hopeless soul.

(*Exit.*)

FAUSTUS. Accursed Faustus, where is mercy now?
I do repent, and yet I do despair:
Hell strives with grace for conquest in my breast;
What shall I do to shun the snares of death?

MEPHASTOPHILIS. Thou traitor, Faustus, I arrest thy soul
For disobedience to my sovereign lord.
Revolt,[5] or I'll in piece-meal tear thy flesh!

FAUSTUS. I do repent I e'er offended him.
Sweet Mephastophilis, entreat thy lord
To pardon my unjust presumption,
And with my blood again I will confirm
My former vow I made to Lucifer.

MEPHASTOPHILIS. Do it then quickly, with unfeigned heart,
Lest greater danger do attend thy drift.[6]

FAUSTUS. Torment, sweet friend, that base and crooked age
That durst dissuade me from thy Lucifer,
With greatest torments that our hell affords.

MEPHASTOPHILIS. His faith is great, I cannot touch his soul.
But what I may afflict his body with
I will attempt, which is but little worth.

FAUSTUS. One thing, good servant, let me crave of thee
To glut the longing of my heart's desire:
That I might have unto° my paramour *as*
That heavenly Helen which I saw of late,
Whose sweet embracings may extinguish clean
These thoughts that do dissuade me from my vow,
And keep mine oath I made to Lucifer.

MEPHASTOPHILIS. Faustus, this, or what else thou shalt desire
Shall be perform'd in the twinkling of an eye.

(*Enter Helen.*)

FAUSTUS. Was this the face that launch'd a thousand ships
And burnt the topless° towers of Ilium?° *soaring / Troy*
Sweet Helen, make me immortal with a kiss;
Her lips suck forth my soul, see where it flies!
Come Helen, come, give me my soul again;
Here will I dwell, for heaven be in these lips,
And all is dross that is not Helena.

(*Enter old man.*)

I will be Paris, and for love of thee
Instead of Troy shall Wittenberg be sack'd,
And I will combat with weak Menelaus[7]

[1] *flagitious* Extremely wicked, infamous.

[2] *no ... guilt* Cf. Revelation 1.5: "Jesus Christ ... loved us, and washed us from our sins in his own blood." *The Prayer-Book of Queen Elizabeth* (1559) specifies that if a person in "extremity of sickness ... do truly repent him of his sins, and steadfastly believe that Jesus Christ ... shed his blood for his redemption" (135), this is the equivalent of taking communion.

[3] *Where ... Faustus?* Cf. Genesis 3.9: "The Lord God called to the man, and said unto him, Where art thou?"

[4] *vial ... grace* The old man here individualizes an image from Revelation 5.8, in which elders worshiping before the throne of God carry "golden vials full of odors, which are the prayers of saints."

[5] *Revolt* Reverse your course of action.

[6] *drift* Conscious or unconscious tendency or aim.

[7] *weak Menelaus* Book 3 of Homer's *Iliad* recounts the duel between Alexandros or Paris and Menelaus. Paris challenged all the best of the Achaeans to single combat, but recoiled in fear from Menelaus. Having agreed that Helen and her possessions should go to the victor, Paris was defeated, but saved from death by Aphrodite,

And wear thy colours on my plumed crest;
Yea, I will wound Achilles in the heel
And then return to Helen for a kiss.
O, thou art fairer than the evening air
Clad in the beauty of a thousand stars;
Brighter art thou than flaming Jupiter
When he appear'd to hapless Semele,[1]
More lovely than the monarch of the sky
In wanton Arethusa's[2] azur'd arms,
And none but thou shalt be my paramour.

(*Exeunt.*)

OLD MAN. Accursed Faustus, miserable man,
That from thy soul exclud'st the grace of heaven
And fliest the throne of his tribunal seat!

(*Enter the devils.*)

Satan begins to sift me[3] with his pride;
As in this furnace God shall try my faith,
My faith, vile hell, shall triumph over thee!
Ambitious fiends, see how the heaven smiles
At your repulse, and laughs your state to scorn:
Hence, hell, for hence I fly unto my God.

(*Exeunt.*)

ACT 5, SCENE 2

(*Enter Faustus with the scholars.*)

FAUSTUS. Ah, gentlemen!

FIRST SCHOLAR. What ails Faustus?

FAUSTUS. Ah, my sweet chamber-fellow, had I lived with thee, then had I lived still, but now I die eternally. Look, comes he not, comes he not?

SECOND SCHOLAR. What means Faustus?

THIRD SCHOLAR. Belike he is grown into some sickness, by being over-solitary.

FIRST SCHOLAR. If it be so, we'll have physicians to cure him. 'Tis but a surfeit,[4] never fear, man.

FAUSTUS. A surfeit of deadly sin, that hath damned both body and soul.

SECOND SCHOLAR. Yet Faustus, look up to heaven; remember, God's mercies are infinite.

FAUSTUS. But Faustus' offence can ne'er be pardoned: the serpent that tempted Eve may be saved, but not Faustus. Ah gentlemen, hear me with patience, and tremble not at my speeches. Though my heart pants and quivers to remember that I have been a student here these thirty years, O would I had never seen Wittenberg, never read book: and what wonders I have done, all Germany can witness, yea all the world, for which Faustus hath lost both Germany and the world, yea heaven itself, heaven the seat of God, the throne of the blessed, the kingdom of joy, and must remain in hell for ever—hell, ah, hell, for ever! Sweet friends, what shall become of Faustus, being in hell for ever?

THIRD SCHOLAR. Yet Faustus, call on God.

FAUSTUS. On God, whom Faustus hath abjured? on God, whom Faustus hath blasphemed? Ah my God, I would weep, but the devil draws in my tears. Gush forth blood instead of tears, yea life and soul! Oh, he stays my tongue; I would lift up my hands, but see, they hold them, they hold them!

ALL. Who, Faustus?

FAUSTUS. Lucifer and Mephastophilis. Ah, gentlemen, I gave them my soul for my cunning.[5]

ALL. God forbid!

FAUSTUS. God forbade it indeed, but Faustus hath done it: for the vain pleasure of four and twenty years hath Faustus lost eternal joy and felicity. I writ them a bill with mine own blood, the date is expired, the time will come, and he will fetch me!

FIRST SCHOLAR. Why did not Faustus tell of this before, that divines might have prayed for thee?

FAUSTUS. Oft have I thought to have done so, but the devil threatened to tear me in pieces if I named God, to fetch both body and soul if I once gave ear to divinity,

---

who carried him in a mist into his own bedchamber. There, although shamed in Helen's eyes as in everyone else's, he promptly took her to bed.

[1] *hapless Semele* One of Jupiter's human mistresses, she was persuaded by Juno to ask him to come to her in the same form in which he embraced Juno in heaven, and was consumed by fire.

[2] *Arethusa* Nymph who, bathing in the river Alpheus, aroused the river-god's lust; fleeing from him, she was transformed into a fountain. No classical myth links her with Jupiter or the sun-god.

[3] *sift me* Cf. Christ's words to Peter at the last supper: "Simon, Simon, behold, Satan hath desired to have you, and he may sift you as wheat" (Luke 22.31).

[4] *surfeit* Excessive indulgence in food or drink, and the resulting disorder of the system.

[5] *cunning* Knowledge.

and now 'tis too late: gentlemen, away, lest you perish with me.

SECOND SCHOLAR. O what may we do to save Faustus?

FAUSTUS. Talk not of me, but save yourselves, and depart.

THIRD SCHOLAR. God will strengthen me, I will stay with Faustus.

FIRST SCHOLAR. Tempt not God, sweet friend, but let us into the next room, and there pray for him.

FAUSTUS. Ah, pray for me, pray for me; and what noise soever[1] ye hear, come not unto me, for nothing can rescue me.

SECOND SCHOLAR. Pray thou, and we will pray that God may have mercy upon thee.

FAUSTUS. Gentlemen, farewell. If I live till morning, I'll visit you; if not, Faustus is gone to hell.

ALL. Faustus, farewell.

(*Exeunt scholars. The clock strikes eleven.*)

FAUSTUS. Ah Faustus,
Now hast thou but one bare hour to live,
And then thou must be damn'd perpetually.
Stand still, you ever-moving spheres of heaven.
That time may cease, and midnight never come!
Fair nature's eye, rise, rise again, and make
Perpetual day, or let this hour be but a year,
A month, a week, a natural day,
That Faustus may repent, and save his soul.
O lente lente currite noctis equi![2]
The stars move still, time runs, the clock will strike,
The devil will come, and Faustus must be damn'd.
O, I'll leap up to my God: who pulls me down?
See, see where Christ's blood streams in the firmament:
One drop would save my soul, half a drop! Ah, my Christ,
Ah rend not my heart for the naming of my Christ,[3]
Yet I will call on him, oh spare me Lucifer!
Where is it now? 'tis gone,
And see where God stretcheth out his arm
And bends his ireful brows!
Mountains and hills, come, come, and fall on me
And hide me from the heavy wrath of God.[4]
No, no?
Then will I headlong run into the earth.
Earth, gape! O no, it will not harbor me.
You stars that reign'd at my nativity,
Whose influence hath allotted death and hell,
Now draw up Faustus like a foggy mist
Into the entrails of yon laboring cloud,
That when you vomit forth into the air
My limbs may issue from your smoky mouths,
So that my soul may but ascend to heaven.

(*The watch*° *strikes.*) *clock*

Ah, half the hour is past: 'twill all be past anon.
Oh God, if thou wilt not have mercy on my soul,
Yet for Christ's sake, whose blood hath ransom'd me,
Impose some end to my incessant pain:
Let Faustus live in a hell a thousand years,
A hundred thousand, and at last be sav'd.
O, no end is limited to damned souls.[5]
Why wert thou not a creature wanting soul?
Or why is this immortal that thou hast?
Ah, Pythagoras' metempsychosis,[6] were that true
This soul should fly from me, and I be chang'd
Unto some brutish beast.
All beasts are happy, for when they die
Their souls are soon dissolv'd in elements,
But mine must live still to be plagu'd in hell.
Curst be the parents that engender'd me;
No Faustus, curse thyself, curse Lucifer
That hath depriv'd thee of the joys of heaven!

(*The clock strikes twelve.*)

O it strikes, it strikes, now body, turn to air
Or Lucifer will bear thee quick° to hell! *alive*

(*Thunder and lightning.*)

O soul, be changed into little water drops
And fall into the ocean, ne'er be found;
My God, my God, look not so fierce on me!

[1] *soever* I.e., whatsoever.

[2] *O lente ... equi* Latin: "O gallop slowly, slowly, you horses of the night!" Ovid, *Amores* 1.8.40.

[3] *rend ... Christ* Cf. Joel 2.12–13, where, faced by a terrifying prospect of destruction that makes the earth quake and the heavens tremble, and that darkens the sun, moon and stars, the Israelites are exhorted to "rend their hearts in repentance."

[4] *Mountains ... God* Cf. Luke 23.30, Revelation 6.16, Hosea 10.8.

[5] *no end ... souls* I.e., damnation is endless.

[6] *metempsychosis* Doctrine of the transmigration of souls.

(*Enter devils.*)

Adders and serpents, let me breathe awhile!
Ugly hell gape not, come not Lucifer,
I'll burn my books, ah Mephastophilis!

(*Exeunt with him.*)

EPILOGUE

(*Enter Chorus.*)

CHORUS. Cut is the branch that might have grown full straight,
And burned is Apollo's laurel bough
That sometime grew within this learned man:
Faustus is gone, regard his hellish fall,
Whose fiendful fortune may exhort the wise
Only to wonder[1] at unlawful things,
Whose deepness doth entice such forward wits
To practice more than heavenly power permits.

(*Exit.*)

Terminat hora diem, terminat Author opus.[2]
—1604, 1616

In Context

Dr. Faustus

from Anonymous, *The History of the Damnable Life, and Deserved Death of Dr. John Faustus* (1592)

Though much of the story of Marlowe's *Dr. Faustus* and of its principal source, the prose *History of the Damnable Life, and Deserved Death of Dr. John Faustus*, are obviously legendary or mythic in nature, there was indeed a historical Dr. Faustus. Like Marlowe himself, the historical Faustus was, in Michael Keefer's words, "a transgressor both of sexual and of ideological codes."

The historical Faustus was Georgius of Helmstadt (c. 1466–c. 1537), a magician from the village of Helmstadt who attended the University of Heidelberg from 1483 until 1489 or thereabouts, and who by 1507 had established himself as a magician styling himself as "Magister Georgius Sabellicus, the younger Faustus, Chief of Necromancers, Astrologer, the Second Magus, Palmist, Diviner by Earth and Fire, Second in the Art of Divination by Water." Georgius Faustus seems to have had a very mixed career; he was hired in 1520 to cast the horoscope of the Bishop of Bamberg, and consulted in 1536 by a close associate of Erasmus's to predict the fortunes of an expedition to the new world—but he was also accused of being a braggart, a blasphemer, and worse. (When, in 1507, Faustus for a time took an appointment as a schoolmaster, he was accused of having indulged "in the most abominable kind of fornication with the boys," and fled to escape punishment.)

There was no suggestion during the life of the historical Faustus of a pact with the devil. Even before his death, however, the historical figure had evidently become something of a magnet for anecdotes of all sorts about sorcerers, charlatans, and demons. Interestingly, Martin Luther seems to have played a key role in the formation of the Faustus legend; the earliest record that survives of many of the anecdotes about Faustus is the written record of the "table talk" of Luther in the 1530s.

---

[1] *Only to wonder* To be content with wondering.

[2] *Terminat … opus* Latin: "The hour ends the day; the author ends his work."

The direct source of the legend of Faustus selling his soul to the devil is the *Historia von D. Johann Fausten* of 1587, translated into English as *The History of the Damnable Life, and Deserved Death of Dr. John Faustus* in 1592. Marlowe evidently drew on this work extensively for his *Dr. Faustus*; a few key passages are reproduced below, with parallel passages from the play noted.

from CHAPTER 1. John Faustus, born in the town of Rhode, lying in the province of Weimar in Germ[any], his father a poor husbandman and not [able] well to bring him up: but having an uncle at Wittenberg, a rich man and without issue, took this J. Faustus from his father and made him his heir, in so much that his father was no more troubled with him, for he remained with his uncle at Wittenberg, where he was kept at the university in the same city to study divinity. But Faustus, being of a naughty mind and otherwise addicted, applied not his studies, but took himself to other exercises: the which his uncle oftentimes hearing, rebuked him for it, as Eli oft times rebuked his children for sinning against the Lord: even so this good man labored to have Faustus apply his study of divinity, that he might come to the knowledge of God and his laws. But it is manifest that many virtuous parents have wicked children, as Cain, Reuben, Absolom and such like have been to their parents: so this Faustus having godly parents, and seeing him to be of a toward wit, were very desirous to bring him up in those virtuous studies, namely, of divinity: but he gave himself secretly to study necromancy and conjuration, in so much that few or none could perceive his profession.

But to the purpose: Faustus continued at study in the university, and was by the Rectors and sixteen Masters afterwards examined how he had profited in his studies; and being found by them that none for his time were able to argue with him in divinity, or for the excellency of his wisdom to compare with him, with one consent they made him Doctor of Divinity. But Doctor Faustus, within short time after he had obtained his degree, fell into such fantasies and deep cogitations that he was marked of many, and of the most part of the students was called the Speculator; and sometime he would throw the scriptures from him as though he had no care of his former profession: so that he began a very ungodly life, as hereafter more at large may appear; for the old proverb saith, Who can hold that will away? So who can hold Faustus from the devil, that seeks after him with all his endeavor? For he accompanied himself with divers that were seen in those devilish arts, and that had the Chaldean, Persian, Hebrew, Arabian, and Greek tongues, using figures, characters, conjurations, incantations, with many other ceremonies belonging to these infernal arts, as necromancy, charms, soothsaying, witchcraft, enchantment, being delighted with their books, words, and names so well that he studied day and night therein: in so much that he could not abide to be called doctor of divinity, but waxed a worldly man, and named himself an astrologian, and a mathematician: and for a shadow sometimes a physician, and did great cures, namely with herbs, roots, waters, drinks, receipts, and clisters. And without doubt he was passing wise, and excellent perfect in the holy scriptures: but he that knoweth his master's will and doth it not, is worthy to be beaten with many stripes. It is written, No man can serve two masters, and Thou shalt not tempt the Lord thy God: but Faustus threw all this in the wind, and made his soul of no estimation, regarding more his worldly pleasure than the joys to come: therefore at the day of judgment there is no hope of his redemption.

CHAPTER 2. You have heard before, that all Faustus' mind was set to study the arts of necromancy and conjuration, the which exercise he followed day and night: and taking to him the wings of an eagle, thought to fly over the whole world, and to know the secrets of heaven and earth; for his speculation was so wonderful, being expert in using his *vocabula*, figures, characters, conjurations, and other ceremonial actions, that in all the haste he put in practice to bring the devil before him. And taking his way to a thick wood near to Wittenberg, called in the German tongue *Spisser Waldt*..., he came into the same wood towards evening into a cross way, where he made with a wand a circle in the dust, and within that many more circles and characters: and thus he passed away the time, until it was nine or ten of the clock in the night, then began Doctor Faustus to call for Mephostophiles the spirit, and to charge him in the name of Beelzebub to appear there personally without any long stay: then presently the devil began so great a rumor in the wood, as if heaven and earth would have come together with wind, the trees bowing their tops to the ground; then fell the devil to bleat as if the whole wood had been full of lions, and suddenly about the circle ran the devil as if a thousand wagons had been running together on paved stones.... Faustus commanded that the next morning at twelve of the clock he should appear to him at his house, but the devil would in no wise grant. Faustus began again to conjure him in the name of Beelzebub, that he should fulfil his request: whereupon the spirit agreed, and so they departed each one his way.

from CHAPTER 3. Doctor Faustus having commanded the spirit to be with him, at his hour appointed he came and appeared in his chamber, demanding of Faustus what his desire was: then began Doctor Faustus anew with him to conjure him that he should be obedient unto him, and to answer him certain articles, and to fulfil them in all points.

1. That the spirit should serve him and be obedient unto him in all things that he asked of him from that hour until the hour of his death.
2. Farther, any thing that he desired of him he should bring it to him.
3. Also, that in all Faustus his demands or interrogations the spirit should tell him nothing but that which is true.

Hereupon the spirit answered and laid his case forth, that he had no power of himself, until he had first given his prince (that was ruler over him) to understand thereof, and to know if he could obtain so much of his lord: Therefore speak farther that I may do thy whole desire to my prince: for it is not in my power to fulfil without his leave....

Doctor Faustus upon this arose where he sat, and said, I will have my request, and yet I will not be damned. The spirit answered, Then shalt thou want thy desire, and yet art thou mine notwithstanding: if any man would detain thee it is in vain, for thine infidelity hath confounded thee.

Hereupon spake Faustus: Get thee hence from me, and take Saint Valentine's farewell and Crisam with thee, yet I conjure thee that thou be here at evening, and bethink thyself on that I have asked thee, and ask thy prince's counsel therein. Mephostophiles the spirit, thus answered, vanished away, leaving Faustus in his study, where he sat pondering with himself how he might obtain his request of the devil without loss of his soul: yet fully he was resolved in himself rather than to want his pleasure, to do whatsoever the spirit and his lord should condition upon.

from CHAPTER 4. Faustus continuing in his devilish cogitations, never moving out of the place where the spirit left him (such was his fervent love to the devil), the night approaching, this swift flying spirit appeared to Faustus, offering himself with all submission to his service, with full authority from his prince to do whatsoever he would request, if so be Faustus would promise to be his: This answer I bring thee, and an answer must thou make by me again, yet will I hear what is thy desire, because thou hast sworn me to be here at this time. Doctor Faustus gave him this answer, though faintly (for his soul's sake): That his request was none other but to become a devil, or at least a limb of him, and that the spirit should agree unto these articles as followeth.

1. That he might be a spirit in shape and quality.
2. That Mephostophiles should be his servant, and at his commandment.
3. That Mephostophiles should bring him any thing, and do for him whatsoever.
4. That at all times he should be in his house, invisible to all men, except only to himself, and at his commandment to show himself.

5. Lastly, that Mephostophiles should at all times appear at his command, in what form or shape soever he would.

Upon these points the spirit answered Doctor Faustus, that all this should be granted him and fulfilled, and more if he would agree unto him upon certain articles as followeth.

First, that Doctor Faustus should give himself to his lord Lucifer, body and soul.
Secondly, for confirmation of the same, he should make him a writing, written with his own blood.
Thirdly, that he would be an enemy to all Christian people.
Fourthly, that he would deny his Christian belief.
Fifthly, that he let not any man change his opinion, if so be any man should go about to dissuade or withdraw him from it.

Further, the spirit promised Faustus to give him certain years to live in health and pleasure, and when such years were expired, that then Faustus should be fetched away, and if he should hold these articles and conditions, then he should have all whatsoever his heart would wish or desire; and that Faustus should quickly perceive himself to be a spirit in all manner of actions whatsoever. Hereupon Doctor Faustus his mind was so inflamed that he forgot his soul, and promised Mephostophiles to hold all things as he had mentioned them: he thought the devil was not so black as they use to paint him, nor hell so hot as the people say, etc.

from CHAPTER 6. *How Doctor Faustus set his blood in a saucer on warm ashes, and writ as followeth.* ... [N]ow have I, Doctor John Faustus, unto the hellish prince of Orient and his messenger Mephostophiles, given both body and soul, upon such condition that they shall learn me, and fulfil my desire in all things, as they have promised and vowed unto me, with due obedience unto me, according to the articles mentioned between us.

Further, I covenant and grant them by these presents, that at the end of 24 years next ensuing the date of this present letter ... I give them full power to do with me at their pleasure, to rule, to send, fetch, or carry me or mine, be it either body, soul, flesh, blood, or goods, into their habitation, be it wheresoever: and hereupon, I defy God and his Christ, all the host of heaven, and all living creatures that bear the shape of God, yea all that lives; and again I say it, and it shall be so. And to the more strengthening of this writing, I have written it with mine own hand and blood....

from Henricus Cornelius Agrippa, *De Occulta Philosophia* (Of Occult Philosophy),[1] 1533

Early in *Dr. Faustus* Faustus imagines that he "will be as cunning as Agrippa was, / Whose shadows made all Europe honour him." Agrippa (1486–1535) was a contemporary of the historical Dr. Faustus, and the two names were often linked in sixteenth century attacks on magic. Agrippa's *De Occulta Philosophia* is an encyclopaedic survey of magical beliefs and practices which also expounds a magical form of Christianity; Agrippa draws on Hermetic, Cabalistic, and Neoplatonic writings as well as on the canonical scriptures in developing his own notions of rebirth and deification. Not surprisingly, his efforts to associate non-Christian magical practices and traditions with the Christian scriptures were widely denounced. The groundbreaking Protestant thinker Jean Calvin termed him an atheist (1550), and André Thevet described his doctrines as "mortal poison" in 1584.

[1] *Of Occult Philosophy* Translated by Michael Keefer, originally published as part of Appendix 3 to Keefer's edition of *Dr. Faustus* (Peterborough: Broadview, 1991, second edition 2006).

from Author's Preface

I do not doubt but that the title of our book, *Of Occult Philosophy, or of Magic*, may by its rarity entice a large number to read it, among whom some twisted, feeble-minded people, and also many ill-disposed and hostile to my talents, will approach: these, in their rash ignorance taking the name of magic in the worse sense, will cry out, hardly having beheld the title, that I teach forbidden arts, sow the seed of heresy, am an offence to pious ears and to outstanding minds a stumbling block; that I am a sorcerer, a superstitious man, and a demoniac, because I am a magician. To these people I would reply that *magus* among learned men does not signify a sorcerer, nor a superstitious man, nor one possessed, but one who is a wise man, a priest, a prophet. The Sibyls were magicians; hence they prophesied most plainly of Christ. And indeed the Magi knew by the wonderful secrets of the world that Christ the author of the world itself was born, and were the first of all to come and worship him. And the name itself of magic was accepted by philosophers, extolled by theologians, and was also not displeasing to the gospel itself. Yet I believe those censors to be of such steadfast arrogance that they will forbid themselves the Sibyls and the holy magicians, and even the gospel itself, sooner than that the name of magic should be admitted into favour; to such a degree are they careful of their conscience, that neither Apollo, nor all the Muses, nor an angel from heaven would be able to deliver me from their curse. And I advise them now that they neither read, nor understand, nor remember our treatise, for it is harmful, it is poisonous, the gate of Acheron is in this book, it speaks stones: let them take heed lest it beat out their brains....

Dr. Faustus

The title pages of the 1604 and 1616 editions of *Dr. Faustus* are reproduced below.

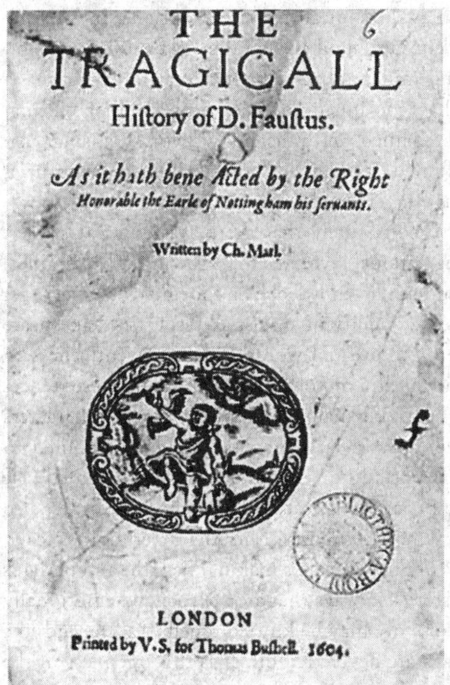

THE TRAGICALL Hiſtory of D. Fauſtus.

As it hath bene Acted by the Right Honorable the Earle of Nottingham his ſeruants.

Written by Ch. Marl.

LONDON

Printed by V.S. for Thomas Buſhell. 1604.

The Tragicall Hiſtorie of the Life and Death of Doctor Fauſtus.

With new Additions.

Written by Ch. Mar.

Printed at London for *Iohn Wright*, and are to be ſold at his ſhop without Newgate. 1631.

William Shakespeare

1564 – 1616

The plays of Shakespeare are foundational works of Western culture; in the English-speaking world they have influenced subsequent literary culture more broadly and more deeply than any other group of texts except the books of the Bible. The language and imagery of the plays; their ways of telling stories; their innovative dramatic qualities; the characters that populate them (and the ways in which these characters are created); the issues and ideas the plays explore (and the ways in which they explore them)—all these have powerfully shaped English literature and culture over the past four centuries. And this shaping influence has continually touched popular culture as well as more "elevated" literary and academic worlds. From the eighteenth century on Shakespeare's plays have held the stage with far greater frequency than those of any other playwright, and in the twentieth century many have been made into popular films (some of the best of which are films in Japanese and in Russian). Even outside the English-speaking world the plays of Shakespeare receive unparalleled exposure; in the Netherlands, for example, his plays have been performed in the late twentieth and early twenty-first centuries more than twice as often as those of any other playwright. In 2000 he headed the list both on the BBC "person of the millennium" poll and on the *World Almanac*'s poll listing the 10 "most influential people of the second millennium." The fact that a playwright, a member of the popular entertainment industry, has continued to enjoy this kind of cultural status—ranked above the likes of Newton, Churchill, Galileo, and Einstein—is worth pausing over. Why are these plays still performed, read, watched, filmed, studied, and appropriated four centuries after they were written? What is the source of his ongoing cultural currency?

There are many ways to answer this question. One is surely that the plays tell great stories. Fundamental, psychologically sophisticated stories, about love, death, growing up, families, communities, guilt, revenge, jealousy, order and disorder, self-knowledge and identity. Another, just as surely, is that they tell them with extraordinary verbal facility in almost all respects: Shakespeare is generally regarded as unsurpassed in his choice of individual words and his inventiveness in conjuring up striking images; in his structuring of the rhythm of poetic lines; in balancing sentences rhetorically; in shaping long speeches; and in crafting sparkling dialogue. A third is that the characters within the stories are uniquely engaging and memorable. In large part this can be attributed to Shakespeare's ingenuity: within the English literary tradition he more or less invented the psychologically realistic literary character; within the European literary tradition he more or less also invented the strong, independent female character. The bare bones of his characters are typically provided by other sources, but the flesh and blood is of Shakespeare's making. Fourth, and perhaps most important of all, Shakespeare's plays tell their stories in ways that are open-ended emotionally and intellectually: no matter how neatly the threads of story may be knitted together at the end, the threads of idea and of emotion in Shakespeare's plays are never tied off. It is this openness of the plays, their availability for reinterpretation, that enables them to be endlessly re-staged, rewritten, re-interpreted—and to yield fresh ideas and fresh feelings time and time again.

Given the centrality of Shakespeare to Western culture, the wish of many readers to know far more than we do about his life is understandable. In fact we do know a fair amount about the facts of his life—given late sixteenth- and early seventeenth-century norms, perhaps more than we might expect to know of someone of his class and background. But we know a good deal less of Shakespeare than we do of some other leading writers of his era—Ben Jonson, for example, or John Donne. And, perhaps most frustrating of all, we know almost nothing of an intimate or personal nature about Shakespeare.

Shakespeare (whose surname also appears on various documents as Shakespear, Shakspere, Shaxpere, and Shagspere) was baptized in Stratford-upon-Avon on 26 April 1564. Reasonable conjecture, given the customs of the time, suggests that he was born two-to-four days earlier; the date that has been most frequently advanced is 23 April (the same day of the year on which he died in 1616, and also the day on which St. George, England's patron saint, is traditionally honored). His father, John, was a glove-maker and also a local politician: first an alderman and then bailiff, a position equivalent to mayor. Some scholars have argued that he had remained a Catholic in newly-Protestant England, and that Shakespeare thus grew up in a clandestinely Catholic home; though the evidence for this is suggestive, it is not conclusive. (If Shakespeare had grown up Catholic, that background might lead readers to see some of his history plays in a different perspective, and might lend even greater poignancy to images such as that of the "bare ruined choirs" of Sonnet 73, with its suggestion of the destruction of the monasteries destroyed by Henry VIII following the break with Rome.)

Stratford-upon-Avon had a good grammar school, which is generally presumed to have provided William's early education, though no records exist to confirm this. Not surprisingly, he did not go on to university, which at the time would have been unusual for a person from the middle class. (Even Ben Jonson, one of the finest classicists of the period, did not attend university.) Shakespeare's first exposure to theater was probably through the troupes of traveling players that regularly toured the country at that time.

On 28 November 1562, when Shakespeare was eighteen, he was married to Anne Hathaway, who was eight years his senior. Six months later, in May of 1583, Anne gave birth to their first daughter, Susanna; given the timing, it seems reasonable to speculate that an unexpected pregnancy may have prompted a sudden marriage. In February 1585, twins, named Hamnet (Shakespeare's only son, who was to die at the age of eleven) and Judith, were born. Some time later, probably within the next three years, Shakespeare moved to London, leaving his young family behind. There has been considerable speculation as to his reasons for leaving Stratford-upon Avon, but no solid evidence has been found to support any of the numerous theories. Certainly London was then (as now) a magnet for ambitious young men, and in the late 1580s it was effectively the only English city conducive to the pursuit of a career as a writer or in the theater.

It is not known exactly when Shakespeare joined the professional theater in London, but by 1592 several of his plays had reached the stage–the three parts of *Henry VI*, probably *The Comedy of Errors* and *Titus Andronicus*, possibly others. The earliest extant mention of him in print occurs in 1592: a sarcastic jibe by an embittered older playwright, Robert Greene. Greene calls Shakespeare "an upstart crow beautified with our feathers," probably referring to Shakespeare's work on the series of *Henry VI* plays, which may well have involved the revision of material by other writers who had originally worked on the play. In any case, from 1594 on, Will Shakespeare is listed as a member of the company called The Lord Chamberlain's Men (later called The King's Men, when James I became their patron).

Professional theater in London did not become firmly established until 1576, when the first permanent playhouses opened. By the late 1580s four theaters were in operation—an unprecedented level of activity, and one that in all probability helped to nurture greater sophistication on the part of audiences. Certainly it was a hothouse that nurtured an extraordinary growth of theatrical agility on the part of Elizabethan playwrights. Shakespeare, as both playwright and actor in The Lord Chamberlain's Men, was afforded opportunities of forging, testing and reworking his written work in the heat of rehearsals and performances—opportunities that were not open to other playwrights.[1] And in Christopher Marlowe he had a rival playwright of a most extraordinary sort. It seems safe to conjecture that the two learned a good deal about play construction from each other. In the late 1580s and early 1590s they both adopt virtually simultaneously the practice of having their characters express their intentions in advance of the unfolding action, thereby encouraging the formation of audience expectations; they also begin to make it a practice to interpose some other action between the exit and the re-entry of any character, thereby further fostering the creation of a sense of temporal and spatial illusion of a sort quite new to the English stage.

In his early years in London Shakespeare also established himself as a non-dramatic poet—and sought aristocratic patronage in doing so. In the late sixteenth century the writing of poetry was accorded considerable respect, the writing of plays a good deal less. It was conventional for those not of aristocratic birth themselves to seek a patron for their writing—as Shakespeare evidently did with the Earl of Southampton, a young noble to whom he dedicated two substantial poems of mythological narrative, *Venus and Adonis* (1593) and *The Rape of Lucrece* (1594). (It is a measure of the enormity of Shakespeare's achievement that these poems, which would be regarded as major works of almost any other writer of the period, are an afterthought in most considerations of Shakespeare's work.) Before the end of the century Shakespeare was also circulating his sonnets, as we know from the praise of Francis Meres, who wrote in 1598 that the "sweet, witty soul" of the classical poet of love, Ovid, "lives in mellifluous and honey-tongued Shakespeare, witness his Venus and Adonis, his Lucrece, his sugared sonnets among his private friends, etc." Such circulation among "private friends" was common practice at the time, and was not necessarily followed by publication. When Shakespeare's sonnets were finally published, in 1609, the dedication was from the printer rather than the author, suggesting that Shakespeare may not have authorized their publication.

There are thirty-eight extant plays by Shakespeare (if *Two Noble Kinsmen* is included in the total). Unlike most other playwrights of the age, he wrote in every major dramatic genre. His history plays (most of them written in the 1590s) include *Richard III, Henry IV, Part 1 and Part 2*, and *Henry V*. He wrote comedies throughout his playwriting years; the succession of comedies that date from the years 1595–1601, including *Much Ado About Nothing*, *As You Like It* and *Twelfth Night*, may represent his most successful work in this genre, though some have argued that *The Merchant of Venice* (c. 1596) and the "dark comedies" which date from between 1601 and 1604 (including *All's Well That Ends Well* and *Measure for Measure*) resonate even more deeply. The period of the "dark comedies" substantially overlaps with the period in which Shakespeare wrote a succession of great tragedies. *Hamlet* may have been written as early as 1598–99, but *Othello*, *King Lear*, and *Macbeth* were written in succession between 1601 and1606. Several of his last plays are romance-comedies—notably *Cymbeline*, *The Winter's Tale* and *The Tempest* (all of which date from the period 1608–11).

Shakespeare was a shareholder in The Lord Chamberlain's Men, and it was in that capacity rather than as a playwright or actor that he made a good deal of money. There was at the time no equivalent

[1] From the nineteenth century onwards (though, perhaps tellingly, never before that), the suggestion has occasionally been put forward that Shakespeare never wrote the plays attributed to him, and that someone else–perhaps Francis Bacon, perhaps Edward de Vere, 17th Earl of Oxford–was actually the author. These conspiracy theories have sometimes gained popular currency, but scholars have never found any reason whatsoever to credit any of them. One of the many reasons such theories lack credibility follows from our sure knowledge that Shakespeare was an actor in many of the plays that bear his name as author. If Shakespeare had not written the plays himself it would surely have been impossibly difficult to conceal that fact from all the members of the rest of the company, in rehearsal as well as in performance, over the course of many, many years.

to modern laws of copyright, or to modern conventions of payment to the authors of published works. Nineteen of Shakespeare's plays were printed individually during Shakespeare's lifetime, but it is clear that many of these publications did not secure his co-operation. It has often been hypothesized that some of the printers of the most obviously defective texts (referred to by scholars as "bad quartos") are pirated editions dictated from memory to publishers by actors; there is some evidence to support this theory, though even if correct it leaves many textual issues unresolved.

The first publication of Shakespeare's collected works did not occur until 1623, several years after his death, when two of his fellow actors, John Heminges and Henry Condell, arranged to have printed the First Folio, a carefully prepared volume (by the standards of the time) that included thirty-six of Shakespeare's plays. Eighteen of these were appearing for the first time, and four others for the first time in a reliable edition. (*Two Noble Kinsmen*, which was written in collaboration with a younger playwright, John Fletcher, and *Pericles*, of which it appears Shakespeare was not the sole author, were both excluded, although the editors did include *Henry VIII*, which is now generally believed to have been another work in which Fletcher had a hand.)

A vital characteristic of Shakespeare's plays is their extraordinary richness of language. After several centuries of forging a new tongue out of its polyglot sources, the English language in the sixteenth century had entered a period of steady growth in its range, as vocabulary expanded to meet the needs of an increasingly complex society. Yet its structure over this same time (no doubt in connection with the spread of print culture) was becoming increasingly stable. When we compare the enormous difference between the language of Chaucer, who was writing in the late fourteenth century, and that of Shakespeare, writing in the late sixteenth century, it is remarkable to see how greatly the language changed over those two centuries—considerably more than it has changed in the four centuries from Shakespeare's time to our own. English was still effectively a new language in his time, with immense and largely unexplored possibilities for conveying subtleties of meaning. More than any other, Shakespeare embarked on that exploration; his reading was clearly very wide,[1] as was his working vocabulary. But he expanded the language as well as absorbing it; a surprising number of the words Shakespeare used are first recorded as having been used in his work.

The popular image of Shakespeare's last few years is that first expressed by Nicholas Rowe in 1709:

> The latter part of his life was spent, as all men of good sense wish theirs may be, in ease, retirement, and the conversation of his friends. He had the good fortune to gather together an estate equal to his occasion, and, in that, to his wish; and is said to have spent some years before his death at his native Stratford.

We know for a fact that around 1610 Shakespeare moved from London to Stratford, where his family had continued to live throughout the years he had spent in London, and the move has often been referred to as a "retirement." Shakespeare did not immediately give up playwriting, however: *The Tempest* (1611), *Henry VIII* (c. 1612) and *Two Noble Kinsmen* (c. 1613) all date from after his move to Stratford. By the time he left London Shakespeare was indeed a relatively wealthy man, with

[1] In his early years in London Shakespeare may well have acquired much of his reading material from Richard Field, a man from Stratford-upon-Avon of about Shakespeare's age who was in the book trade. Field printed Shakespeare's early poems, *Venus and Adonis* and *The Rape of Lucrece*, and it is certainly possible that the two men had some understanding by which Shakespeare borrowed some of the books he read, which otherwise might have been prohibitively expensive. (Among the works printed by Field was a multi-volume Thomas North translation of Plutarch's *Lives*, of which Shakespeare made extensive use.) Shakespeare also lodged for a time in London with a French Huguenot family named Montjoy, whose home may have been the source for some of the French books that his plays demonstrate a familiarity with. And he may also have had the use of the libraries of one or more of his aristocratic patrons.

substantial investments both in real estate and in the tithes of the town (an arrangement that would be comparable to buying government bonds today).

After 1613 we have no record of any further writing; he died on 23 April 1616, aged 52. In his will, Shakespeare left his extensive property to the sons of his daughter, Susanna (described in her epitaph as "witty above her sex"). To his wife, he left his "second-best bed"—a bequest which many have found both puzzling and provocative. He was buried as a respectable citizen in the chancel of the parish church, where his gravestone is marked not with a name, but a simple poem:

Good friend, for Jesus' sake forbear
To dig the dust enclosed here.
Blest be the man that spares these stones,
And curst be he that moves my bones.

Shakespeare's work appears to have been extremely well regarded in his lifetime; soon after his death a consensus developed that his work—his plays in particular—constitute the highest achievement in English literature. In some generations he has been praised most highly for the depth of his characterization, in others for the dense brilliance of his imagery, in others for the extraordinary intellectual suggestiveness of the ideas that his characters express (and occasionally embody). But in every generation since the mid-seventeenth century a consensus has remained that Shakespeare stands without peer among English authors.

In most generations the study of Shakespeare has also helped to shape the development of literary criticism and theory. From John Dryden and Samuel Johnson to Samuel Taylor Coleridge to Northrop Frye, works central to the development of literary theory and criticism have had Shakespeare as their subject. And in the past 50 years Shakespeare has been a vital test case in the development of feminist literary theory, of post-colonial theory, and of political, cultural, and new historicist criticism: just as with each generation people of the theater develop new ways of playing Shakespeare that yield fresh insight, so too do scholars develop new ways of reading texts through reading Shakespeare.

The Sonnets

Begun in the 1590s, intermittently revised, and with some of its contents already circulating, Shakespeare's *Sonnets* was printed in 1609 under obscure circumstances. Did Shakespeare authorize publication by the printer Thomas Thorpe? Did he organize the sonnets himself? Is there a pattern to them? The 154 sonnets, concluding with two light poems on Cupid, are followed by a long "Lover's Complaint" in a female voice. How does this poem fit the volume, and do we know with any certainty that Shakespeare is the author of it as well?

The volume's structure parallels that of sonnet collections in the 1590s, such as Samuel Daniel's *Delia* and Spenser's *Epithalamion and Amoretti*. Is Shakespeare merely following this example or subtly commenting on it? Who is the "W.H." whom the printer Thorpe calls "the only begetter" of the sonnets? No one knows. Nor, despite sometimes wild speculation, do we know the identity of the beautiful but faithless young man to whom many of the sonnets are addressed (or if there is only one young man), or that of the "dark lady" whom the lover treats with erotic admiration and moral contempt, or that of the rival poet to whom some sonnets allude. Is the lady always the same woman? Sonnet 145 seems to pun on "Hathaway," maiden name of Shakespeare's wife, Anne. Who is the presumed speaker of these sonnets? Several sonnets pun on the "Will"—a useful name, for it could also denote a faculty of the soul, sexual desire, and even the genitals.

For many years the sonnets received little attention or respect. The second edition of Shakespeare's poems, a shabby volume published by John Benson (1640), feminizes some pronouns, runs some sonnets together, and plagiarizes some commentary; it did the sonnets' reputation no good, and it was not until relatively recently that their splendor and power was fully acknowledged.

One source of older generations' unease with the sonnets was the passion with which the speaker addresses a younger man. It is conventional to think that the first 126 sonnets are to or about this youth and most of the remainder to or about a "dark lady," but many of the sonnets leave the gender of the addressee unspecified. Some of those undeniably involving the young man are clearly expressive of strong homoerotic desire, but the extent to which such desire is acted upon is much less clear. Sonnet 20 seems to say that a sexual relation between the speaker and his friend is impossible, but for some recent critics the poem's puns hint at the opposite. However we read them, such ardent expressions of love and longing for a fellow man are unusual, although not unparalleled, in the literature either of Renaissance England or the Continent.

Also unusual is the lover's sexually reciprocated but problematic love for a compliant if unfaithful woman. This is another respect in which Shakespeare makes a show of revising the Petrarchan tradition familiar to him from Renaissance poetry, in which the love of the male wooer was typically not reciprocated by his female beloved. Much as Shakespeare was clearly indebted to the Petrarchan tradition, he departed from it in a variety of ways.

In form, Petrarch and most other Italian poets had made it a practice to divide their sonnets formally into an octave followed by a sestet. Henry Howard, Earl of Surrey, had been instrumental in the development of an "English" sonnet pattern of three quatrains followed by a couplet. Shakespeare varies the structure of his sonnets in a number of ways, but generally employs rhyme schemes deriving from the "English" pattern (most commonly: *abab cdcd efef gg*).

Whether or not we read *Sonnets* as a sequence, certain recurrent motifs are worth noticing: desire and "will" in every sense, the ruinous passage of time together with the physical and poetic means of surmounting its ravages, the cyclical and poignant beauty of the natural world, and the paradoxes involved in loving the unworthy. Just as notable is the language, which offers an astonishing array of puns, syntactic or lexical ambiguities, and metaphors that evolve through associative connections with a logic just below the surface sense of the verse. Note, for example, how Sonnet 60 moves from ocean waves, to crooked eclipses that must involve the moon (which affects the ocean), to the (curved) plow that makes agricultural furrows, that parallels the wrinkles of bent age, and to Time's curved scythe. Shakespeare can also be funny, though—as witness Sonnet 135's bawdy insinuations, or the resigned (bitter? amused?) puns in Sonnet 138 on lying to and lying with a lover.

⌘⌘⌘

Sonnets

1

From fairest creatures we desire increase,° *progeny*
That thereby beauty's rose might never die,
But as the riper should by time[1] decease
His tender° heir might bear his memory: *young*
But thou, contracted[2] to thine own bright eyes,
Feed'st thy light's flame with self-substantial fuel,[3]
Making a famine where abundance lies,[4]
Thyself thy foe, to thy sweet self too cruel.
Thou that art now the world's fresh° ornament, *unspoiled*
And only herald to the gaudy[5] spring,
Within thine own bud buriest thy content,[6]
And, tender churl, mak'st waste in niggarding.[7]
Pity the world, or else this glutton[8] be,
To eat the world's due, by the grave and thee.[9]

2

When forty[10] winters shall besiege thy brow,
And dig deep trenches in thy beauty's field,
Thy youth's proud livery,° so gazed on now, *uniform*
Will be a tattered weed° of small worth held: *garment*
Then being asked, where all thy beauty lies,
Where all the treasure of thy lusty° days, *vigorous*
To say, within thine own deep-sunken eyes,
Were an all-eating shame and thriftless[11] praise.
How much more praise deserved thy beauty's use[12]
If thou couldst answer, "This fair child of mine
Shall sum my count, and make my old excuse,"[13]
Proving his beauty by succession° thine: *legal inheritance*
This were to be new made when thou art old,
And see thy blood warm when thou feel'st it cold.

12

When I do count the clock[14] that tells the time,
And see the brave° day sunk in hideous night; *splendid*
When I behold the violet past prime,
And sable curls all silvered o'er with white:
When lofty trees I see barren of leaves,
Which erst from heat did canopy the herd,[15]
And summer's green all girded° up in sheaves *bundled*
Borne on the bier with white and bristly beard:[16]
Then of thy beauty do I question make,
That thou among the wastes of time must go,
Since sweets and beauties do themselves forsake,[17]
And die as fast as they see others grow,
And nothing 'gainst time's scythe can make defence
Save breed° to brave° him, when he takes thee hence. *reproduce / defy*

15

When I consider° everything that grows *consider that*
Holds in perfection but a little moment;
That this huge stage presenteth naught but shows[18]

---

[1] *But* But rather that; *riper* Older; *by time* Because of the passage of time.

[2] *contracted* Betrothed; also confined.

[3] *Feed'st ... fuel* Like a candle, you consume your own substance with self-love; cf. the story of Narcissus in Ovid, *Metamorphoses* 3.464 ("I am burned by love of myself / I produce and am consumed by flames").

[4] *Making ... lies* Cf. *Metamorphoses* 3.466 ("my very abundance makes me poor").

[5] *only* Chief; *gaudy* Brightly colored, but not in the modern pejorative sense.

[6] *content* Contentment; also, essence.

[7] *churl* Here, miser; *mak'st ... niggarding* Cf. *Romeo and Juliet* 1.1.223; *niggarding* Behaving in a miserly fashion.

[8] *this glutton* This kind of glutton.

[9] *To ... thee* What should belong to the world will be consumed first by yourself, then by death.

[10] *forty* Number signifying many and, in Shakespeare's time, corresponding to late middle age.

[11] *thriftless* Wasteful or unprofitable.

[12] *deserved ... use* Would thy beauty's use deserve; *use* Proper employment, also engagement for profit, as in money on loan.

[13] *sum my count* Display the total of my assets; *make ... excuse* Justify or make reparation for my old age.

[14] *count the clock* Count the sounds of the clock.

[15] *erst* Formerly; *canopy the herd* Provide shade for livestock.

[16] *bier* Barrow or litter for carrying crops, but more often associated with the bearing of a corpse to the grave; *white ... beard* As on wheat or barley after harvest.

[17] *sweets* Pleasures, or people or things affording pleasure; *themselves forsake* Lose their essence through time.

[18] *this huge stage* The world as stage was a common notion in the Renaissance; cf. Shakespeare's *As You Like It* 2.7.139–40: "All the world's a stage / And all the men and women merely players"; *shows* Theatrical displays.

Whereon the stars in secret influence[1] comment;
When I perceive that men as plants increase,
Cheered and checked even by the self-same sky,
Vaunt° in their youthful sap, at height decrease, *exult*
And wear their brave state out of memory:[2]
Then the conceit of this inconstant stay[3]
Sets you, most rich in youth, before my sight,
Where wasteful[4] time debateth with decay
To change your day of youth to sullied[5] night:
And all in war with time for love of you
As he takes from you, I engraft[6] you new.

16

But wherefore° do not you a mightier way *why*
Make war upon this bloody tyrant, time,
And fortify yourself in your decay
With means more blessed than my barren rhyme?
Now stand you on the top of happy hours,
And many maiden gardens, yet unset,° *unplanted*
With virtuous wish would bear your living flowers,
Much liker[7] than your painted counterfeit:
So should the lines of life that life repair,[8]
Which this, time's pencil or my pupil pen,
Neither in inward worth nor outward fair,° *beauty*
Can make you live yourself in eyes of men:
To give away yourself[9] keeps yourself still,° *always*
And you must live drawn by your own sweet skill.

18

Shall I compare thee to a summer's day?
Thou art more lovely and more temperate:
Rough winds do shake the darling buds of May,
And summer's lease hath all too short a date:
Sometime too hot the eye of heaven shines,
And often is his gold complexion dimmed;
And every fair° from fair sometime declines, *beauty*
By chance, or nature's changing course, untrimmed:
But thy eternal summer shall not fade,
Nor lose possession of that fair thou ow'st,° *own*
Nor shall death brag thou wander'st in his shade
When in eternal lines to time thou grow'st:
So long as men can breathe or eyes can see,
So long lives this, and this gives life to thee.

19

Devouring time, blunt thou the lion's paws,
And make the earth devour her own sweet brood;
Pluck the keen teeth from the fierce tiger's jaws,
And burn the long-lived Phoenix in her blood;[10]
Make glad and sorry seasons as thou fleet'st,
And do whate'er thou wilt, swift-footed time,
To the wide world and all her fading sweets:° *pleasures*
But I forbid thee one most heinous crime,
O carve not with thy hours my love's fair brow,
Nor draw no lines there with thine antique[11] pen;
Him in thy course untainted[12] do allow
For beauty's pattern to succeeding men.
Yet do thy worst, old Time, despite thy wrong,
My love shall in my verse ever live young.

20

A woman's face with nature's own hand painted
Hast thou, the master mistress of my passion;
A woman's gentle heart, but not acquainted
With shifting change, as is false women's fashion;
An eye more bright than theirs, less false in rolling,[13]
Gilding the object whereupon it gazeth;
A man in hue,° all hues in his controlling, *appearance*
Which steals men's eyes and women's souls amazeth;
And for a woman wert thou first created,

[1] *secret influence* The supposed life effects of the stars on human life and temperament.

[2] *wear ... memory* Decay until their glory fades from memory.

[3] *conceit* Thought; conception; *inconstant stay* Constant state ("stay") of inconstancy, or change, as in the aging process.

[4] *wasteful* In the sense of wasting or destructive.

[5] *sullied* Tarnished; made gloomy or dull.

[6] *engraft* Insert a scion, or shoot, from one tree into the bark of another, from which it gains sustenance.

[7] *liker* More like you.

[8] *lines of life* Bloodlines of your descendants, or the outlines of you reflected in them; *repair* Restore.

[9] *give away yourself* Marry.

[10] *Phoenix* Mythical bird that after living five or six centuries burns itself in a nest of spices and then rises from the ashes renewed to begin another cycle; *in her blood* Alive.

[11] *antique* Ancient.

[12] *untainted* Unmarked, unhurt.

[13] *rolling* Glancing at lovers.

Till nature as she wrought thee fell a-doting,
And by addition[1] me of thee defeated,
By adding one thing to my purpose nothing:
    But since she pricked[2] thee out for women's pleasure,
    Mine be thy love, and thy love's use[3] their treasure.

23

As an unperfect actor[4] on the stage,
Who with his fear is put besides[5] his part;
Or some fierce thing, replete with too much rage,
Whose strength's abundance weakens his own heart;
So I, for fear of trust,[6] forget to say
The perfect ceremony[7] of love's right,° *due*
And in mine own love's strength seem to decay,
O'ercharged with burden of mine own love's might:
O let my books be then the eloquence
And dumb presagers[8] of my speaking breast,
Who plead for love, and look for recompense,
More than that tongue that more hath more expressed:
    O learn to read what silent love hath writ!
    To hear with eyes belongs to love's fine wit.[9]

29

When in disgrace with fortune and men's eyes
I all alone beweep my outcast state,
And trouble deaf heav'n with my bootless° cries, *unavailing*
And look upon myself, and curse my fate,
Wishing me like to one more rich in hope,
Featured like him,[10] like him with friends possessed,
Desiring this man's art° and that man's scope, *skill*
With what I most enjoy contented least;
Yet in these thoughts myself almost despising,
Haply° I think on thee, and then my state, *by chance*

[1] *by addition* I.e., of male genitals.

[2] *pricked* Selected; "prick" was also slang for penis.

[3] *love's use* Sexual pleasure and probably the suggestion of reproduction and increase, with a pun on "usury."

[4] *unperfect actor* Actor who does not remember his lines accurately.

[5] *is put besides* Loses track of, forgets.

[6] *for … trust* Afraid to trust myself, or perhaps afraid of not being trusted.

[7] *perfect ceremony* Precise words demanded by the situation.

[8] *dumb presagers* Silent signals.

[9] *belongs … wit* Is characteristic of love's subtle intelligence.

[10] *featured like him* With physical attractions like his.

Like to the lark at break of day arising,
From sullen° earth sings hymns at *dark, gloomy*
        heaven's gate;
    For thy sweet love remembered such wealth brings
    That then I scorn to change my state with kings.

30

When to the sessions° of sweet silent *judicial sittings*
thought
I summon up remembrance of things past,[11]
I sigh the lack of many a thing I sought,
And with old woes new wail my dear time's waste;
Then can I drown an eye (unused to flow)
For precious friends hid in death's dateless night,
And weep afresh love's long since cancelled woe,
And moan th'expense° of many a vanished sight. *loss*
Then can I grieve at grievances foregone,° *past*
And heavily from woe to woe tell° o'er *count*
The sad account of fore-bemoanéd moan,
Which I new pay, as if not paid before;
    But if the while I think on thee, dear friend,
    All losses are restored, and sorrows end.

33

Full many a glorious morning have I seen
Flatter the mountain tops with sovereign eye,
Kissing with golden face the meadows green,
Gilding pale streams with heavenly alchemy;
Anon° permit the basest clouds to ride *soon*
With ugly rack[12] on his celestial face,
And from the forlorn world his visage hide,
Stealing unseen to west with this disgrace:
Even so my sun one early morn did shine
With all triumphant splendour on my brow;
But out alack,[13] he was but one hour mine,
The region cloud[14] hath masked him from me now.
    Yet him for this, my love no whit[15] disdaineth:

[11] *summon* Call to court; *remembrance … past* Cf. Geneva Bible (1560), *Wisdom* 11.10: "For their grief was double with mourning, and the remembrance of things past."

[12] *rack* Mass of clouds driven by the wind in the upper air.

[13] *out alack* An expression of sharp regret.

[14] *region cloud* Clouds of the upper air.

[15] *no whit* Not the least bit.

Suns of the world may stain,[1] when heaven's sun
staineth.

35

No more be grieved at that which thou hast done;
Roses have thorns, and silver fountains mud;
Clouds and eclipses stain both moon and sun,
And loathsome canker° lives in sweetest bud. *caterpillar*
All men make faults, and even I, in this,
Authorizing thy trespass with compare,° *comparisons*
Myself corrupting, salving thy amiss,[2]
Excusing these sins more than these sins are:[3]
For to thy sensual fault I bring in sense;[4]
Thy adverse party is thy advocate,[5]
And 'gainst myself a lawful plea commence:
Such civil war is in my love and hate
That I an accessary needs must be
To that sweet thief which sourly robs from me.

36

Let me confess that we two must be twain,° *separate*
Although our undivided loves are one;
So shall those blots° that do with me remain, *disgraces*
Without thy help, by me be borne alone.
In our two loves there is but one respect,[6]
Though in our lives a separable spite;[7]
Which, though it alter not love's sole effect,[8]
Yet doth it steal sweet hours from love's delight.
I may not evermore acknowledge[9] thee,
Lest my bewailed guilt should do thee shame,
Nor thou with public kindness honour me,
Unless thou take[10] that honour from thy name:
But do not so;[11] I love thee in such sort,
As thou being mine, mine is thy good report.

55

Not marble, nor the gilded monuments
Of princes, shall outlive this powerful rhyme;
But you shall shine more bright in these contents[12]
Than unswept stone, besmeared with sluttish time.[13]
When wasteful war shall statues overturn
And broils° root out the work of masonry, *violent quarrels*
Nor Mars[14] his sword, nor war's quick° fire, *vigorous*
shall burn
The living record of your memory:
'Gainst death, and all oblivious[15] enmity,
Shall you pace forth; your praise shall still find room
Even in the eyes of all posterity
That wear this world out to the ending doom.[16]
So till the judgement that yourself arise,[17]
You live in this, and dwell in lovers' eyes.

60

Like as the waves make towards the pebbled shore,
So do our minutes hasten to their end,
Each changing place with that which goes before,
In sequent toil all forwards do contend.
Nativity, once in the main° of light, *broad expanse*
Crawls to maturity; wherewith being crowned
Crooked eclipses 'gainst his glory fight,
And time, that gave, doth now his gift confound.° *ruin*
Time doth transfix° the flourish set on youth, *pierce*
And delves the parallels[18] in beauty's brow;
Feeds on the rarities of nature's truth,
And nothing stands[19] but for his scythe to mow.

---

[1] *stain* Lose luster or brightness.

[2] *salving thy amiss* Excusing or explaining away your wrong.

[3] *Excusing ... are* My making excuses for your sins is worse than the actual sins themselves.

[4] *bring in sense* Add spurious reasoning.

[5] *adverse party* Legal opponent; *advocate* Legal defender.

[6] *one respect* A single, and hence mutual, regard.

[7] *a separable spite* An injury or misfortune capable of separating us.

[8] *love's sole effect* Our unity in love.

[9] *acknowledge* Greet or recognize in public.

[10] *Unless thou take* Without taking.

[11] *do not so* Do not display such public kindness toward me.

[12] *these contents* The contents of these poems.

[13] *Than ... time* Than in dust-covered stone dirtied by the passage of time, which is dirty and grimy ("sluttish") in its effects.

[14] *Mars* Roman god of war.

[15] *oblivious* Bringing about oblivion.

[16] *ending doom* Last Judgment at the end of the world.

[17] *That ... arise* When you yourself are resurrected.

[18] *delves the parallels* Digs the trenches, i.e., forms the wrinkled lines; cf. Sonnet 2.2: "... dig deep trenches in thy beauty's field."

[19] *stands* Grows to full height, as a plant ready for harvest.

And yet to times in hope my verse shall stand,
Praising thy worth, despite his cruel hand.

64

When I have seen by time's fell hand defaced
The rich proud cost[1] of outworn buried age;[2]
When sometime lofty towers I see down razed,
And brass eternal slave to mortal rage;[3]
When I have seen the hungry ocean gain
Advantage on the kingdom of the shore,
And the firm soil win of the wat'ry main,° *ocean*
Increasing store° with loss, and loss with store; *gain*
When I have seen such interchange of state,
Or state itself confounded,° to decay, *ruined*
Ruin hath taught me thus to ruminate:
That time will come and take my love away.
This thought is as a death, which cannot choose
But weep[4] to have that which it fears to lose.

65

Since brass, nor stone, nor earth, nor boundless sea,
But sad mortality o'er-sways° their power, *overcomes*
How with this rage[5] shall beauty hold a plea,[6]
Whose action is no stronger than a flower?
O how shall summer's honey breath hold out
Against the wrackful° siege of batt'ring days *destructive*
When rocks impregnable are not so stout,
Nor gates of steel so strong, but time decays?
O fearful meditation! Where, alack,
Shall time's best jewel from time's chest lie hid?
Or what strong hand can hold his swift foot back,
Or who his spoil° o'er beauty can forbid? *plunder*
O none, unless this miracle have might:
That in black ink my love may still shine bright.

71

No longer mourn for me when I am dead
Than you shall hear[7] the surly sullen bell[8]
Give warning to the world that I am fled
From this vile world, with vilest worms to dwell:
Nay, if you read this line, remember not
The hand that writ it, for I love you so
That I in your sweet thoughts would be forgot,
If thinking on me then should make you woe.[9]
O if (I say) you look upon this verse,
When I, perhaps, compounded am with clay,
Do not so much as my poor name rehearse,° *utter*
But let your love even° with my life decay; *along*
Lest the wise world should look into your moan,[10]
And mock you with me[11] after I am gone.

73

That time of year thou mayst in me behold,
When yellow leaves, or none, or few do hang
Upon those boughs which shake against the cold,
Bare ruined choirs[12] where late the sweet birds sang;
In me thou seest the twilight of such day
As after sunset fadeth in the west,
Which by and by black night doth take away,
Death's second self[13] that seals up all in rest;
In me thou seest the glowing of such fire
That on the ashes of his youth doth lie,
As the deathbed, whereon it must expire,
Consumed with that which it was nourished by;
This thou perceiv'st, which makes thy love more
strong,
To love that well, which thou must leave° *lose*
ere long.

[1] *rich ... cost* Prideful and extravagant splendor.

[2] *outworn ... age* Antiquity worn out and obscured by time.

[3] *Brass ... rage* Brass, known for its durability, but also subject ultimately to the fatally destructive effects of time.

[4] *cannot ... weep* Can only weep.

[5] *with this rage* Against this destructive action.

[6] *hold a plea* Present a legal case.

[7] *you shall hear* The span of time during which you hear.

[8] *surly ... bell* Passing-bell, rung solemnly from the church to announce a death, customarily one chime for each year of the deceased's lifespan.

[9] *make you woe* Cause you grief.

[10] *look ... moan* Question the cause of your grief.

[11] *with me* Along with me, and perhaps in the same manner.

[12] *choirs* Parts of churches designated for singers.

[13] *Death's second self* Sleep.

74

But be contented when that fell° arrest *cruel*
Without all bail shall carry me away.[1]
My life hath in this line some interest,[2]
Which for memorial still[3] with thee shall stay.
When thou reviewest this, thou dost review
The very part was consecrate to thee.
The earth can have but earth, which is his due;
My spirit is thine, the better part of me.
So then thou hast but° lost the dregs of life, *only*
The prey of worms, my body being dead,
The coward conquest of a wretch's knife,
Too base of thee to be remembered.
The worth of that is that which it contains,[4]
And that is this, and this with thee remains.

80

O how I faint° when I of you do write, *lose heart*
Knowing a better spirit[5] doth use your name,
And in the praise thereof spends all his might,
To make me tongue-tied speaking of your fame.
But since your worth, wide as the ocean is,
The humble as the proudest sail doth bear,° *carry along*
My saucy bark,[6] inferior far to his,
On your broad main° doth wilfully appear. *ocean*
Your shallowest help will hold me up afloat,
Whilst he upon your soundless° deep doth ride; *immeasurable*
Or, being wracked, I am a worthless boat,
He of tall building, and of goodly pride.
Then if he thrive, and I be cast away,
The worst was this: my love was my decay.

87

Farewell—thou art too dear[7] for my possessing,
And like enough thou know'st thy estimate.° *value*
The charter of thy worth gives thee releasing;[8]
My bonds in thee are all determinate.° *expired*
For how do I hold thee but by thy granting,
And for that riches where is my deserving?[9]
The cause of this fair gift in me is wanting,
And so my patent° back again is swerving. *title to property*
Thyself thou gav'st, thy own worth then not knowing,
Or me to whom thou gav'st it else mistaking;
So thy great gift, upon misprision° growing, *error*
Comes home again, on better judgement making.
Thus have I had thee as a dream doth flatter:
In sleep a king, but waking no such matter.

93

So shall I live supposing thou art true
Like a deceived husband; so love's face
May still seem love to me, though altered new—
Thy looks with me, thy heart in other place.
For there can live no hatred in thine eye,
Therefore in that I cannot know thy change.[10]
In many's looks the false heart's history
Is writ in moods and frowns and wrinkles strange;
But heav'n in thy creation did decree
That in thy face sweet love should ever dwell;
Whate'er thy thoughts or thy heart's workings be,
Thy looks should nothing thence but sweetness tell.
How like Eve's apple doth thy beauty grow
If thy sweet virtue answer not thy show![11]

---

[1] *But be … away* Some modern editors punctuate these lines with a semi-colon after "contented" and a comma after "away."

[2] *in this line* I.e., in this verse.

[3] *for memorial still* As a remembrance always.

[4] *The worth of that … contains* The value of the body is that it contains the spirit.

[5] *a better spirit* A rival poet of superior gifts, referred to in Sonnet 79.

[6] *bark* Small boat.

[7] *too dear* Both "too expensive" and "too much loved."

[8] *The character … releasing* The document stating your value releases you (from any associated debts).

[9] *for that riches … deserving?* How do I deserve the rich reward (of being granted your affection)?

[10] *in that … change* From your eye I cannot know that your heart has changed.

[11] *How like … thy show* How much your beauty grows to resemble the attractiveness of the apple to Eve (i.e., that it will lead to the downfall of the one attracted to it) if your virtue does not match your appearance.

94

They that have power to hurt and will do none,
 That do not do the thing they most do show,[1]
Who, moving others, are themselves as stone,
Unmovèd, cold, and to temptation slow—[2]
They rightly do inherit heaven's graces,
And husband° nature's riches from expense;° *conserve / spending*
They are the lords and owners of their faces,
Others but stewards° of their excellence. *managers*
The summer's flower is to the summer sweet
Though to itself it only live and die,
But if that flower with base infection meet
The basest weed outbraves his dignity;[3]
 For sweetest things turn sourest by their deeds:
 Lilies that fester smell far worse than weeds.

97

How like a winter hath my absence been
 From thee, the pleasure of the fleeting year!
What freezings have I felt, what dark days seen,
What old December's bareness everywhere!
And yet this time removed[4] was summer's time,
The teeming autumn big with[5] rich increase
Bearing the wanton burden of the prime,[6]
Like widowed wombs after their lords' decease:
Yet this abundant issue° seemed to me *offspring*
But hope of orphans, and unfathered fruit;
For summer and his pleasures wait on thee,[7]
And thou away, the very birds are mute;
 Or if they sing, 'tis with so dull a cheer
 That leaves look pale, dreading the winter's near.

98

From you have I been absent in the spring,
 When proud pied° April, dressed in all his trim,° *particolored / adornment*
Hath put a spirit of youth in everything,
That° heavy Saturn[8] laughed, and leaped with him. *such that*
Yet nor the lays° of birds, nor the sweet smell *songs*
Of different flowers in odour and in hue,
Could make me any summer's story tell,
Or from their proud lap[9] pluck them where they grew;
Nor did I wonder at the lily's white,
Nor praise the deep vermilion in the rose;
They were but° sweet, but figures of delight, *merely*
Drawn after you, you pattern of all those.
 Yet seemed it winter still, and, you away,
 As with your shadow I with these did play.

105

Let not my love be called idolatry,
 Nor my beloved as an idol show,[10]
Since all alike my songs and praises be
To one, of one, still such, and ever so.
Kind is my love today, tomorrow kind,[11]
Still constant in a wondrous excellence.
Therefore my verse, to constancy confined,
One thing expressing, leaves out difference.
"Fair, kind, and true" is all my argument,
"Fair, kind, and true" varying to other words,
And in this change is my invention spent,[12]
Three themes in one, which wondrous scope affords.
Fair, kind, and true have often lived alone,
Which three till now never kept seat in one.

---

[1] *the thing they most do show* It is not entirely clear what this thing is, but it probably relates to romantic or sexual activity; "though they inspire love, they do not reciprocate," is one possible paraphrase.

[2] *to temptation slow* Slow to respond to temptation.

[3] *But if that flower ... dignity* The most common weed will outshine a lovely flower that has been infected by disease.

[4] *time removed* Time of my absence.

[5] *big with* Great with, about to give birth to.

[6] *burden* Contents of a womb; *prime* Spring.

[7] *wait on thee* Hold themselves in abeyance until you are present.

[8] *Saturn* Planetary God associated astrologically with the melancholy humor.

[9] *their proud lap* The rich earth that nurtures them.

[10] *as an idol show* Seem to be (perhaps also with a pun on "idle"—"be called an insignificant creature of appearances").

[11] *Kind ... kind* Both "of one sort today, and the same tomorrow," and "kind" in the sense of "having a gentle and sympathetic nature."

[12] *varying ... spent* My inventiveness is used up in finding other words (to express the same thought).

106

When in the chronicle of wasted time[1]
I see descriptions of the fairest wights,[2]
And beauty making beautiful old rhyme,
In praise of ladies dead, and lovely knights;
Then in the blazon[3] of sweet beauties best,
Of hand, of foot, of lip, of eye, of brow,
I see their antique pen would have expressed
Even such a beauty as you master° now: *possess*
So all their praises are but prophecies
Of this our time, all you prefiguring;
And for° they looked but with divining eyes *since*
They had not skill enough your worth to sing;
For we which now behold these present days
Have eyes to wonder, but lack tongues to praise.

109

O never say that I was false of heart,
Though absence seemed my flame to qualify;
As easy might I from myself depart
As from my soul which in thy breast doth lie:
That is my home of love; if I have ranged,
Like him that travels I return again,
Just to the time,[4] not with the time exchanged,[5]
So that myself bring water for my stain;[6]
Never believe, though in my nature reigned
All frailties that besiege all kinds of blood,
That it could so preposterously be stained,° *corrupted*
To leave for nothing all thy sum of good:
For nothing this wide universe I call,
Save thou, my rose; in it thou art my all.

[1] *wasted time* Time gone by, with "chronicles" suggesting previous eras, or "olden times."

[2] *fairest wights* Most beautiful people, again with an archaic flavor by Shakespeare's time.

[3] *blazon* Description catalogue of a beloved's body.

[4] *Just ... time* Exactly on time.

[5] *not ... exchanged* Not changed during the time spent away.

[6] *So ... stain* So that my return, unchanged, might erase the fault of my absence; *water* Possibly, tears of repentence.

110

Alas, 'tis true, I have gone here and there,
And made myself a motley to the view,[7]
Gored[8] mine own thoughts, sold cheap what is most dear,
Made old offences of affections new.[9]
Most true it is that I have looked on truth° *constancy*
Askance and strangely°; but by all above, *coldly*
These blenches[10] gave my heart another youth,[11]
And worse essays[12] proved thee my best of love.
Now all is done, save what shall have no end;
Mine appetite I never more will grind° *whet*
On newer proof,° to try° an older friend, *experience / test*
A god in love, to whom I am confined:° *devoted*
Then give me welcome, next my heaven the best,
Even to thy pure and most most loving breast.

116

Let me not to the marriage of true minds
Admit impediments;[13] love is not love
Which alters when it alteration finds,
Or bends with the remover[14] to remove.
O no, it is an ever-fixed mark,
That looks on tempests and is never shaken;
It is the star to every wand'ring bark,° *boat*
Whose worth's unknown, although his height be taken.[15]
Love's not Time's fool, though rosy lips and cheeks

[7] *motley* Fool (from the motley, or particolored clothing traditionally worn by jesters); *to the view* In appearance, in the eyes of society.

[8] *gored* Altered, as a garment is altered by inserting a gore, or wedge-shaped piece of cloth, and perhaps even mutilated, like a person gored by a horned animal.

[9] *Made ... new* Committed infidelity by pursuing new relationships.

[10] *blenches* Flinchings or deviations (from constancy).

[11] *gave ... youth* Rejuvenated my affections for you.

[12] *worse essays* Experiments with inferior loves.

[13] *impediments* Cf. the marriage service in the Book of Common Prayer (c. 1552): "If any of you know cause, or just impediment, why these two persons should not be joined together in holy Matrimony, ye are to declare it."

[14] *remover* One who changes, e.g., ceases to love.

[15] *Whose ... taken* Referring to the "star" of the previous line, most likely the North Star, whose altitude can be reckoned for navigation purposes using a sextant, but whose essence remains unknown.

Within his bending sickle's compass° come; *sweep*
Love alters not with his brief hours and weeks,
But bears it out even to the edge of doom.
If this be error and upon me proved,
I never writ, nor no man ever loved.

117

Accuse me thus: that I have scanted[1] all
Wherein I should your great deserts repay,
Forgot upon your dearest love to call,
Whereto all bonds do tie me day by day;
That I have frequent been with unknown minds,
And given to time your own dear-purchased right;[2]
That I have hoisted sail to all the winds
Which should transport me farthest from your sight.
Book° both my wilfulness and errors down, *record*
And on just proof surmise accumulate;[3]
Bring me within the level° of your frown, *aim*
But shoot not at me in your wakened hate:
Since my appeal says[4] I did strive to prove° *test*
The constancy and virtue of your love.

127

In the old age[5] black was not counted fair,° *beautiful*
Or if it were, it bore not beauty's name;
But now is black beauty's successive° heir, *legitimate*
And beauty slandered with a bastard shame:[6]
For since each hand hath put on nature's power,[7]
Fairing the foul with art's false borrowed face,
Sweet beauty hath no name, no holy bower,[8]
But is profaned, if not lives in disgrace.
Therefore my mistress' eyes are raven black,
Her eyes so suited,° and they mourners seem *attired*
At such who, not born fair, no beauty lack,[9]
Sland'ring creation with a false esteem;[10]
Yet so they mourn, becoming of[11] their woe,
That every tongue says beauty should look so.

128

How oft when thou, my music, music play'st
Upon that blessed wood[12] whose motion sounds
With thy sweet fingers, when thou gently sway'st° *direct*
The wiry concord[13] that mine ear confounds,° *dazzles*
Do I envy those jacks° that nimble leap, *keys*
To kiss the tender inward° of thy hand, *palm*
Whilst my poor lips, which should that harvest reap,
At the wood's boldness by thee blushing stand?
To be so tickled they would change their state
And situation with those dancing chips,[14]
O'er whom thy fingers walk with gentle gait,
Making dead wood more blessed than living lips.
Since saucy jacks[15] so happy are in this,
Give them thy fingers, me thy lips to kiss.

129

Th'expense of spirit in a waste° of shame *desolation*
Is lust in action; and till action, lust
Is perjured, murd'rous, bloody, full of blame,
Savage, extreme, rude, cruel, not to trust;° *be trusted*
Enjoyed no sooner but despised straight;
Past reason hunted, and no sooner had,
Past reason hated as a swallowed bait,
On purpose laid to make the taker mad;
Mad in pursuit, and in possession so,
Had, having, and in quest to have, extreme;
A bliss in proof,° and proved, a very woe; *experience*
Before, a joy proposed; behind, a dream.

---

[1] *scanted* Provided grudgingly or insufficently for.

[2] *given ... right* Spent elsewhere the time you had a right to expect I should spend with you.

[3] *on ... accumulate* On the basis of my proven misdeeds, add others on suspicion.

[4] *my appeal says* My defense is that.

[5] *the old age* Earlier times.

[6] *beauty ... shame* The former (fair) conception of beauty has been discredited as illegitimate and false.

[7] *each ... power* Everyone has assumed the power to mimic natural beauty (through cosmetics).

[8] *name* Legitimate title; *holy bower* Sacred dwelling-place.

[9] *who ... lack* (1) Who, lacking natural beauty, have acquired it artificially; (2) Who, not being of fair coloration, are in accord with current ideals of beauty.

[10] *Sland'ring ... esteem* Devaluing natural beauty with false praise accorded to the artificial.

[11] *becoming of* Suiting well.

[12] *blessed wood* Probably a virginal, a small, legless harpsichord on which the strings were plucked rather than struck.

[13] *wiry concord* Harmony produced by the plucking of the strings.

[14] *dancing chips* The keys.

[15] *saucy jacks* Common slang for impertinent fellows, but here referring also to the aforementioned keys.

All this the world well knows, yet none knows well
To shun the heaven that leads men to this hell.

130

My mistress' eyes are nothing like the sun;
Coral is far more red than her lips' red;
If snow be white, why then her breasts are dun;
If hairs be wires, black wires grow on her head;
I have seen roses damasked,° red and white, *parti-colored*
But no such roses see I in her cheeks;
And in some perfumes is there more delight
Than in the breath that from my mistress reeks.
I love to hear her speak, yet well I know
That music hath a far more pleasing sound;
I grant I never saw a goddess go;° *walk*
My mistress when she walks treads on the ground.
And yet, by heaven, I think my love as rare
As any she[1] belied with false compare.

135

Whoever hath her wish,[2] thou hast thy Will,[3]
And Will to boot, and Will in overplus;° *superabundance*
More than enough am I, that vex thee still,
To thy sweet will making addition thus.
Wilt thou, whose will is large and spacious,
Not once vouchsafe to hide my will in thine?
Shall will in others seem right gracious,
And in my will no fair acceptance shine?
The sea, all water, yet receives rain still,
And in abundance addeth to his store;
So thou, being rich in Will, add to thy Will
One will of mine, to make thy large Will more:
Let no unkind,° no fair beseechers kill; *unkindness*
Think all but one,[4] and me in that one Will.

136

If thy soul check[5] thee that I come so near,
Swear to thy blind[6] soul that I was thy Will,
And will, thy soul knows, is admitted there;
Thus far for love my love-suit sweet fulfil.
Will will fulfil the treasure of thy love,
Ay, fill it full with wills, and my will one;
In things of great receipt° with ease we prove *capacity*
Among a number one is reckoned none.
Then in the number let me pass untold,
Though in thy store's account I one must be.
For nothing hold° me, so it please thee hold *regard*
That nothing, me, a something sweet to thee.
Make but my name thy love, and love that still;° *always*
And then thou lov'st me, for my name is Will.

138

When my love swears that she is made of truth,
I do believe her, though I know she lies,
That she might think me some untutored youth
Unlearnèd in the world's false subtleties.
Thus vainly thinking that she thinks me young,
Although she knows my days are past the best,
Simply I credit her false-speaking tongue;
On both sides thus is simple truth suppressed.
But wherefore says she not she is unjust?° *unfaithful*
And wherefore say not I that I am old?
O love's best habit is in seeming trust,
And age in love[7] loves not t'° have years told: *to*
Therefore I lie with her, and she with me,
And in our faults by lies we flattered be.

143

Lo, as a careful housewife[8] runs to catch
One of her feathered creatures broke away,
Sets down her babe, and makes all swift dispatch° *haste*
In pursuit of the thing she would have stay;
Whilst her neglected child holds her in chase,[9]
Cries to catch her whose busy care is bent° *determined*
To follow that which flies before her face,
Not prizing° her poor infant's discontent: *considering*

---

[1] *any she* Any woman.

[2] *Whoever … wish* No matter what other women may wish for or attain.

[3] *Will* In Shakespeare's time, the word could also refer to sexual desire and even to the genitals.

[4] *Think … one* Think of all your suitors as one.

[5] *check* Restrain or rebuke.

[6] *blind soul* Blind by nature, being enclosed within the body, or blinded by passion.

[7] *age in love* An older person in love, or in matters of love.

[8] *careful* Attentive, but also perhaps "full of cares," or anxious; *housewife* Pronounced "hussif" in Shakespeare's time.

[9] *holds … chase* Chases after her.

So run'st thou after that which flies from thee,
Whilst I, thy babe, chase thee afar behind.
But if thou catch thy hope,[1] turn back to me,
And play the mother's part, kiss me, be kind:
So will I pray that thou mayst have thy Will,
If thou turn back and my loud crying still.° *soothe*

144

Two loves I have, of comfort and despair,
Which, like two spirits, do suggest° me still:° *tempt / always*
The better angel is a man right fair,
The worser spirit a woman coloured ill.[2]
To win me soon to hell[3] my female evil
Tempteth my better angel from my side,
And would corrupt my saint to be a devil,
Wooing his purity with her foul pride;
And whether that[4] my angel be turned fiend
Suspect I may, yet not directly° tell; *exactly*
But being both from me both to each friend,[5]
I guess one angel in another's hell.
Yet this shall I ne'er know, but live in doubt,
Till my bad angel fire my good one out.[6]

147

My love is as a fever, longing still° *continually*
For that which longer nurseth the disease,
Feeding on that which doth preserve the ill,
Th'uncertain° sickly appetite to please: *fitful*
My reason, the physician to my love,
Angry that his prescriptions are not kept,
Hath left me, and I, desperate, now approve° *accept that*
Desire is death, which physic did except.[7]
Past cure I am, now reason is past care,
And frantic mad with ever more unrest;
My thoughts and my discourse as madmen's are,
At random[8] from the truth vainly expressed:[9]
For I have sworn thee fair, and thought thee bright,
Who art as black as hell, as dark as night.

153

Cupid laid by his brand,[10] and fell asleep;
A maid of Dian's[11] this advantage° found, *opportunity*
And his love-kindling fire did quickly steep° *plunge*
In a cold valley-fountain[12] of that ground,
Which borrowed from this holy fire of love
A dateless° lively heat still° to endure, *endless / always*
And grew° a seething bath, which yet men prove *grew into*
Against strange maladies a sovereign° cure: *potent*
But at my mistress' eye love's brand new fired,[13]
The boy for trial needs would[14] touch my breast;
I, sick withal, the help of bath desired,
And thither hied,[15] a sad distempered guest,
But found no cure; the bath for my help lies
Where Cupid got new fire: my mistress' eye.

154

The little love-god° lying once asleep, *Cupid*
Laid by his side his heart-inflaming brand,[16]
Whilst many nymphs, that vowed chaste life to keep,[17]
Came tripping by; but in her maiden hand
The fairest votary[18] took up that fire

---

[1] *thy hope* The object of your hope.

[2] *coloured ill* Of a dark or ugly complexion or temperament.

[3] *hell* For the equation of hell with sexual intercourse, cf. Sonnet 129.14: "… the heaven that leads men to this hell."

[4] *whether that* Whether or not.

[5] *being … friend* Both spirits being apart from me and together (and friendly) with each other.

[6] *fire … out* Expel or reject my good angel; to "fire out" meant to drive someone or something away from a place by setting a fire, as, e.g., in fox hunting; *fire* Possibly "fever," with perhaps a glancing reference to venereal disease.

[7] *Desire … except* The sexual desire objected to by my physician is deadly.

[8] *At random* Wandering.

[9] *vainly expressed* Expressing myself foolishly or fecklessly.

[10] *Cupid … brand* Cupid, Roman god of love, often pictured as a small boy carrying a torch (brand) used to kindle erotic love in the hearts of mortals; *laid by* Set aside.

[11] *maid of Dian's* Diana, Roman goddess of the moon and the hunt, known for her chastity, was attended by young virgin nymphs (maids).

[12] *cold valley-fountain* One of the cool springs associated with the dwelling-place of Diana.

[13] *new fired* Reignited.

[14] *for trial* To test the flame; *needs would* Wanted to.

[15] *thither hied* Hastened there.

[16] *heart-inflaming brand* Torch used by Cupid to kindle erotic love in the hearts of mortals.

[17] *nymphs … keep* Attendants of the chaste goddess Diana, who themselves took a vow of chastity.

[18] *fairest votary* Most beautiful of those vowed to chastity.

Which many legions of true hearts had warmed;
And so the general of hot desire[1]
Was, sleeping, by a virgin hand disarmed.
This brand she quenched in a cool well by,° *nearby*
Which from love's fire took heat perpetual,
Growing° a bath and healthful remedy *growing into*
For men diseased; but I, my mistress' thrall,
  Came there for cure, and this by that I prove:
    Love's fire heats water, water cools not love.

—1609

On this and the following page appear facsimile reproductions of two pages from the 1609 quarto edition of Shakespeare's sonnets. The facsimile pages include some sonnets that may be compared with annotated texts in modernized spelling appearing elsewhere in these pages, and others that are provided here only in this facsimile form, without mediation.

SHAKE-SPEARES

70

THat thou are blam'd ſhall not be thy defect,
For ſlanders marke was euer yet the faire,
The ornament of beauty is ſuſpect,
A Crow that flies in heauens ſweeteſt ayre.
So thou be good,ſlander doth but approue,
Their worth the greater beeing woo d of time,
For Canker vice the ſweeteſt buds doth loue,
And thou preſent'ſt a pure vnſtayined prime.
Thou haſt paſt by the ambuſh of young daies,
Either not aſſayld,or victor beeing charg'd,
Yet this thy praiſe cannot be ſoe thy praiſe,
To tye vp enuy,euermore inlarged,
  If ſome ſuſpect of ill maskt not thy ſhow,
  Then thou alone kingdomes of hearts ſhouldſt owe.

71

NOe Longer mourne for me when I am dead,
Then you ſhall heare the ſurly ſullen bell
Giue warning to the world that I am fled
From this vile world with vildeſt wormes to dwell:
Nay if you read this line,remember not,
The hand that writ it,for I loue you ſo,
That I in your ſweet thoughts would be forgot,
If thinking on me then ſhould make you woe.
O if(I ſay)you looke vpon this verſe,
When I (perhaps) compounded am with clay,
Do not ſo much as my poore name reherſe;
But let your loue euen with my life decay.
  Leaſt the wiſe world ſhould looke into your mone,
  And mocke you with me after I am gon.

72

O Leaſt the world ſhould taske you to recite,
What merit liu'd in me that you ſhould loue
After my death(deare loue)for get me quite,
For you in me can nothing worthy proue.
Vnleſſe you would deuiſe ſome vertuous lye,

To

[1] *general ... desire* Cupid, pictured as the commander of erotic passion.

SONNETS.

To doe more for me then mine owne desert,
And hang more praise vpon deceased I,
Then nigard truth would willingly impart:
O least your true loue may seeme falce in this,
That you for loue speake well of me vntrue,
My name be buried where my body is,
And liue no more to shame nor me, nor you.
For I am shamd by that which I bring forth,
And so should you, to loue things nothing worth.

73

THat time of yeeare thou maist in me behold,
When yellow leaues, or none, or few doe hange
Vpon those boughes which shake against the could,
Bare rn'wd quiers, where late the sweet birds sang.
In me thou seest the twi-light of such day,
As after Sun-set fadeth in the West,
Which by and by blacke night doth take away,
Deaths second selfe that seals vp all in rest.
In me thou seest the glowing of such fire,
That on the ashes of his youth doth lye,
As the death bed, whereon it must expire,
Consum'd with that which it was nurrisht by.
This thou perceu'st, which makes thy loue more strong,
To loue that well, which thou must leaue ere long.

74

BVt be contented when that fell arest,
With out all bayle shall carry me away,
My life hath in this line some interest,
Which for memoriall still with thee shall stay.
When thou reuewest this, thou doest reuew,
The very part was consecrate to thee,
The earth can haue but earth, which is his due,
My spirit is thine the better part of me,
So then thou hast but lost the dregs of life,
The pray of wormes, my body being dead,
The coward conquest of a wretches knife,

To

King Lear

Most scholars and critics of the past century or so would agree that *King Lear* is Shakespeare's greatest play. That doesn't make it his most popular play: *King Lear* is difficult to stage, hard to film, and intimidating to read. With its reputation as the greatest work by the greatest writer in English, it bears the weight of great expectations.

King Lear was probably written in 1605, which makes it one of Shakespeare's later plays, from about four-fifths of the way though his career. The story of Lear had been around since at least the twelfth century, when it appeared in Geoffrey of Monmouth's *Historia regum Britanniae* (c. 1135–39), and had been retold in Holinshed's *Chronicles* (1577), in the multiple-authored *The Mirror for Magistrates* (1574–87), in Book II, Canto X of Spenser's *The Fairie Queene* (1589) and, most relevantly, in an anonymous play, *King Leir*, which had been first performed in 1594 and was published in 1605, the same year Shakespeare's play was first performed. Today, Lear is regarded by historians as based more upon legend than upon fact (he appears to have been derived from the Celtic god, Llyr); but Shakespeare's audience believed Lear to have been a historical figure. That fact makes Shakespeare's alterations to the story seem strikingly audacious—most notably, his changing of the ending; in earlier versions the main protagonists all survive.

Assertions of *King Lear*'s supremacy among Shakespeare's works chiefly begin to appear within the twentieth century; for most of the eighteenth and nineteenth centuries *Hamlet* held pride of place, with *Lear* ranked somewhat below it as literature, and rated a good deal below it as drama. Indeed, for much of the more than four hundred years of its history, *King Lear* was regarded as being virtually unplayable in its unaltered form—unplayable less on the conventional grounds of its being difficult to stage convincingly (though it surely is that), than on the grounds of its tragic ending embodying too massive an assault on our sensibilities and our belief in a just universe. In 1681—seventy-five years after Shakespeare's version was first published—the poet laureate, Nahum Tate, published a radically revised version of *King Lear* that would hold the stage until well into the nineteenth century. In Tate's version, the Fool has been eliminated, and there is a happy ending: neither Lear nor Cordelia dies, and Gloucester is blinded but spared death. Cordelia loves not the King of France but Edgar, whom she marries at the end of the play, the pair becoming the new monarchs of Britain while Lear goes off into a happy retirement with his friends Gloucester and Kent. Tate's revised text of *Lear* has become a favourite bête noir among historians of drama, but we should beware of jeering; a reluctance to embrace tragic endings is widespread in many eras, including our own, and in Tate's day many demanded "poetic justice" in drama. Moreover, in sparing the lives of the main protagonists and eliminating the Fool Tate was essentially returning the story to its original pattern.

In the preface to his 1681 revision of *King Lear*, Tate explained some of his reasons for undertaking an alteration of Shakespeare's play, describing the original as

> a Heap of Jewels, unstrung and unpolisht; yet so dazling in their Disorder, that I soon perceiv'd I had seiz'd a Treasure. 'Twas my good Fortune to light on one Expedient to rectifie what was wanting in the Regularity and Probability of the Tale, which was to run through the whole A Love betwixt Edgar and Cordelia, that never chang'd word with each other in the Original. This renders Cordelia's Indifference and her Father's Passion in the first Scene probable. It likewise gives Countenance to Edgar's Disguise, making that a generous Design that was before a poor Shift to save his Life.

In large part, then, Tate's revision was his attempt to rationalize the play, to tie up some of what he regarded as its loose ends. It is indeed a play that leaves a number of outstanding questions of this kind. Why does Cordelia not find a gentler way of answering Lear while still avoiding the hypocrisy of her sisters? Why does Edgar keep up his Poor Tom disguise with the mad Lear, and in the presence of his blinded and remorseful father? Why does Kent maintain his disguise until the last scene of the play? Why does the Fool appear only at the beginning of Lear's trials and then disappear in Act Three? Interestingly, in the old anonymous play, *King Leir*—so much cruder a work in many respects—far greater care is taken to give apprehensible motives to the characters in many of these instances. Shakespeare seems to have deliberately stripped these from his play; it is as if the characters were saying to us, as Edmund (or, in the Quarto, Goneril) says, near the end of the play, "Ask me not what I know."

If *King Lear* leaves a number of small questions unanswered, far more so does it leave unanswered the many large questions it raises. What is the play about? At one level, it tells a very simple story, almost like a folktale. Once upon a time there was a foolish king, who decided to divide his kingdom into three parts, and give one part to each of his three daughters. At this level, as George Orwell observed, "*Lear* is one of the minority of Shakespeare's plays that are unmistakably *about* something. For example, *Macbeth* is about ambition, *Othello* is about jealousy, and *Timon of Athens* is about money. The subject of *Lear* is renunciation." But from its simple beginning the play expands in resonance to become a work about life, about the universe, about everything. *King Lear* is a play about growing old, and about death; about the relations between parents and children; about power, and rule, and justice; about the bonds of human love; about the depths of human despair, and the depths of human cruelty and evil of which humans are capable; about the difficulty of achieving knowledge of other humans, and perhaps even more the difficulty of achieving knowledge of oneself. It explores what it means to be human, and it asks what remains when everything that gives us identity is taken away. Above all, *King Lear* asks: does life have meaning? Is humanity ultimately the victim of a cruel, indifferent, or meaningless universe? Are we defined only by suffering?

The story of Gloucester, Edmund and Edgar (which is based on that of the King of Paphlagonia and his sons, Plexirtus and Leonatus in Philip Sidney's *Arcadia*) was added by Shakespeare to the plot of *King Leir*. It is the most highly developed subplot in Shakespearean drama, and opens up a variety of thematic and theatrical parallels with the main story—parallels that substantially broaden and deepen the impact of the play as a whole. On the practical plane the interweaving of the two stories and the oscillation between settings it entails help Shakespeare to add scope to a story that otherwise (as it does in the anonymous *King Leir*) might unfold with undue rapidity. But the addition of a story that in large part parallels that of Lear also considerably expands the play's intellectual and emotional range. The story of filial betrayal and loyalty in Gloucester's case, for example, adds to our understanding of Lear's. Gloucester's loss of sight and Lear's loss of reason each gain in force for being juxtaposed with one another. The bleak vision that Lear gives voice to is echoed by that of the more innocent Gloucester; it is through Gloucester rather than Lear that perhaps the bleakest vision is presented: "as flies to wanton boys are we to the gods: they kill us for their sport." And elements in one line of story sometimes cast a different and surprising light on both narrative and thematic narrative elements in the other. Edmund's worship of nature, for example, may lead us to question the degree to which the selfishness of Lear's two eldest daughters really should be considered "unnatural," as Lear calls it. Is goodness natural, or is it merely part of a veneer of civilization that we have been taught? That is one more of the large questions that this play, perhaps more than any other work of English literature, spins off in rich profusion.

THE TEXT

Every modern edition of *King Lear* depends to varying degrees on the two first published texts, the Quarto edition of 1608 and the First Folio of 1623. These words, "Quarto" and "Folio," refer to how a book's paper was folded. A standard sized sheet of paper folded once to make two pages would be a folio; if it were folded twice to make four pages, it would be a quarto. Quarto books were used in the publication of single plays. The folio format was generally used for large, authoritative works (works of theology, editions of classical literature, certain sorts of Bibles); Ben Jonson set a precedent for playwrights by publishing his collected plays in a folio edition in 1616.

There are often substantial differences between the Quarto and the Folio texts of Shakespeare's plays; *King Lear* is an extreme case. To begin with, there are 300 lines which appear in the Quarto but not in the Folio, and there are 100 lines which appear in the Folio, but not in the Quarto. There are also many smaller differences; some are negligible (it hardly matters, for instance, whether one spells the expletive "Oh" or "O"), but others may be important to the interpretation of the play. There are a number of cases in which a difference in a particular word or phrase alters the meaning of a speech; and on several occasions a particular speech is assigned to different characters in the two editions. An early instance of this is the assignment of a line in the first scene: "Here's France and Burgundy, my noble Lord." In the Quarto edition this line is assigned to Gloucester, but in the Folio it is assigned to Cordelia. Whoever says the line, the same information is given to Lear, but it makes a difference to the way in which we may interpret the character of Cordelia whether the announcement is made by Gloucester or by Cordelia (whom Lear has at this point banished). Most editors have preferred the Quarto's assignment in this instance, but the Folio offers a provocative dramatic possibility.

For many years editors generally assumed that each of the two editions represented an imperfect version of Shakespeare's intended text. Accordingly, the usual practice was to blend the two editions into one slightly longer play, choosing between the specific variations by using one's judgement as to which was the stronger text in any given instance, and attempting to include all or nearly all the lines that Shakespeare had written. However, scholarly opinion is now largely in agreement that the two editions represent two different versions of the play, each of which is legitimate (although each does include some obvious errors). Most probably the Quarto was printed from an early version of Shakespeare's uncorrected papers, and the Folio was an attempt to revise the Quarto edition, with reference to an altered and shortened version in a promptbook that had been prepared for performance.

The Folio edition has usually been preferred to the Quarto, quite simply because it contains a number of clear improvements. This anthology, too, presents the Folio text in the first instance, but with substantial reference made to the Quarto throughout. The notes indicate all instances where the Quarto contains important differences, and for three scenes where the Folio and Quarto are markedly different both versions are presented side by side, enabling readers conveniently to explore issues of text and meaning.

In declaring that the Folio edition is preferable, it is important to exercise considerable caution, in large part because we cannot be sure that all the revisions found in the Folio were indeed the work of Shakespeare himself. While it seems that many of these were made for performance (including additional passages which are certainly of the same quality as the rest of what Shakespeare had written), others are clearly editorial attempts to clarify and normalize certain passages for publication. In the former case, it is likely that Shakespeare himself made the revisions, so as to improve the play in performance. But in the case of those revisions which seem to have been made for publication, there are a number of reasons to suspect a hand other than Shakespeare's. First, we know that Shakespeare was dead by the time that the First Folio was prepared, and it seems unlikely that he would have concerned himself with the preparation of one of his plays for publication on a speculative basis. And there is also some evidence that some person or persons—perhaps Heminge and Condell—exercised personal judgement over many of the revisions.

⌘⌘⌘

King Lear[1]

DRAMATIS PERSONAE

Lear, *King of Britain*
King of France
Gonerill, *Lear's eldest daughter*
Duke of Albany, *Gonerill's husband*
Regan, *Lear's second daughter*
Duke of Cornwall, *Regan's husband*
Cordelia, *Lear's youngest daughter*
Duke of Burgundy
Earl of Kent
Earl of Gloucester
Edgar, *Gloucester's elder son, later disguised as Tom o' Bedlam*
Edmund, *Gloucester's younger, bastard son*
Oswald, *Gonerill's steward*
Old Man, *Gloucester's tenant*
Curan, *Gloucester's servant*
Fool, *attending on Lear*
Doctor
Servants, Captains, Herald, Knight, Messenger, Gentlemen, Soldiers, etc.

ACT 1, SCENE 1

(*Enter Kent, Gloucester*[2] *and Edmund.*[3])

KENT. I thought the King had more affected the Duke of Albany than Cornwall.[4]

GLOUCESTER. It did always seem so to us, but now, in the division of the kingdoms, it appears not which of the Dukes he values most, for equalities are so weighed, that curiosity in neither can make choice of either's moiety.[5]

KENT. Is not this your son, my Lord?

GLOUCESTER. His breeding, Sir, hath been at my charge.[6] I have so often blushed to acknowledge him, that now I am brazed to it.[7]

KENT. I cannot conceive you.[8]

GLOUCESTER. Sir, this young fellow's mother could; whereupon she grew round wombed; and had indeed, Sir, a son for her cradle, ere she had a husband for her bed. Do you smell a fault?

KENT. I cannot wish the fault undone, the issue of it being so proper.

GLOUCESTER. But I have a son, Sir, by order of law,[9] some year elder then this—who, yet is no dearer in my account. Though this knave came something saucily to the world before he was sent for, yet was his mother fair; there was good sport at his making; and the whoreson[10] must be acknowledged. (*To Edmund.*)[11] Do you know this noble gentleman, Edmund?

EDMUND. No, my Lord.

GLOUCESTER. (*To Edmund.*) My Lord of Kent. Remember him hereafter, as my honourable friend.

EDMUND. (*To Kent.*) My services to your Lordship.

KENT. (*To Edmund.*) I must love you, and sue to know you better.

EDMUND. Sir, I shall study deserving.[12]

---

[1] *King Lear* The present text has been prepared for *The Broadview Anthology of British Literature* by Craig Walker. The first Folio edition is used as the copy text; the more significant differences between the Folio and Quarto texts are detailed in the notes, and for the scenes in which the degree of divergence between the two is greatest both versions are provided in parallel column format.

[2] *Gloucester* Occasionally in the first Folio edition (hereafter F) and throughout the first Quarto edition (hereafter Q), the name is spelled phonetically as "Gloster."

[3] *Bastard/Edmund* In Q, the stage directions and tag-lines begin by referring to the character as "Bastard" (or "Bast."), and then maintain this practice throughout most of the rest of the play. F begins by using the character's name, at first spelling it "Edmond," then "Edmund," but then also uses "Bastard" for much of the play.

[4] *affected* Favored.

[5] *equalities … moiety* Their shares have been apportioned so equally that close examination of one or the other cannot show that either has a preferable share.

[6] *breeding … charge* A pun: I have been charged with having begotten him / he has been raised at my expense.

[7] *brazed* Brazened.

[8] *conceive* Understand; Gloucester then puns on the word in the sense of "become pregnant by."

[9] *by order of law* Legitimately born.

[10] *whoreson* Bastard (jocular).

[11] (*To Edmund.*) All stage directions or parts of stage directions appearing in square brackets have been inserted by the current editor; those appearing in round parentheses are derived from the source text.

[12] *study deserving* Attempt to prove worthy of your kindness.

GLOUCESTER. (*To Kent.*) He hath been out[1] nine years, and away he shall again. The King is coming.

(*Sennet.*[2] *Enter King Lear, Cornwall, Albany, Gonerill,*[3] *Regan, Cordelia, and attendants.*)

LEAR. Attend the Lords of France and Burgundy,
Gloucester.
GLOUCESTER. I shall, my Lord.

(*Exit.*)

LEAR. Meantime we shall express our darker purpose.[4]
Give me the map there. Know, that we have divided
In three our kingdom; and 'tis our fast° intent, *firm*
To shake all cares and business from our age,
Conferring them on younger strengths, while we
Unburdened crawl toward death. Our son of Cornwall,
And you, our no less loving son of Albany:
We have this hour a constant will to publish[5]
Our daughters' several[6] dowers, that future strife
May be prevented now. The Princes, France and
Burgundy,
Great rivals in our youngest daughter's love,
Long in our court, have made their amorous sojourn,[7]
And here are to be answered. Tell me, my daughters—
Since now we will divest us both of rule,
Interest° of territory, cares of state— *ownership*
Which of you shall we say doth love us most,
That we, our largest bounty may extend
Where nature doth with merit challenge. Gonerill,[8]
Our eldest born, speak first.
GONERILL. Sir, I love you more than word can
wield° the matter; *convey*
Dearer than eye-sight, space, and liberty;
Beyond what can be valued, rich or rare;
No less than life, with grace, health, beauty, honour;
As much as child e'r loved, or father found;° *experienced*
A love that makes breath poor, and speech unable;
Beyond all manner of so much, I love you.
CORDELIA. What shall Cordelia speak? Love, and be
silent.
LEAR. Of all these bounds even from this line, to this,
With shadowy forests, and with champains° *open plains*
riched
With plenteous rivers, and wide-skirted meads,[9]
We make thee Lady. To thine and Albany's
issues° *descendants*
Be this perpetual. What says our second daughter?
Our dearest Regan, wife of Cornwall?
REGAN. I am made of that self-mettle as my sister,[10]
And prize me[11] at her worth. In my true heart,
I find she names my very deed[12] of love;
Only she comes too short, that I profess[13]
Myself an enemy to all other joys,
Which the most precious square of sense professes,[14]
And find I am alone felicitate° *made happy*
In your dear Highness' love.
CORDELIA. Then poor Cordelia!
And yet not so, since I am sure my love's
More ponderous than my tongue.
LEAR. To thee, and thine hereditary ever,

[1] *out* Away from home (presumably at school or some similar arrangement).

[2] *Sennet* Notes played on trumpet or cornet to signal a royal entrance.

[3] *Gonerill* While it has become common to spell this character's name "Goneril" (with an e and one l), apparently that was not the spelling used by Shakespeare. In F, the name is consistently spelt "Gonerill"; in Q it is usually spelt "Gonorill."

[4] *darker purpose* Hidden intention. The equivalent speech in the Quarto version is substantially shorter. It reads as follows: "Meantime we will express our darker purposes. / The map there; know we have divided / In three, our kingdom; and 'tis our first intent, / To shake all cares and business of our state, / Confirming them on younger years. / The two great Princes France and Burgundy, / Great rivals in our youngest daughter's love, / Long in our Court have made their amorous sojourn, / And here are to be answered. Tell me my daughters, / Which of you shall we say doth love us most, / That we our largest bounty may extend, / Where merit doth most challenge it. / Gonorill, our eldest born, speak first."

[5] *constant ... publish* Resolute intention to announce.

[6] *several* Separate, individual.

[7] *amorous sojourn* Visit for the purpose of courtship.

[8] *Where nature ... challenge* Where natural affection is equal to merit.

[9] *wide-skirted meads* Widely spread meadows.

[10] *self-mettle* Same spirit (with perhaps a pun on "metal").

[11] *And prize me* I.e., and I do prize me.

[12] *deed* Pun on action and document of real estate ownership.

[13] *that I profess* In that I recognize.

[14] *most precious square of sense professes* Invaluable state of the well-balanced mind.

Remain this ample third of our fair kingdom;
No less in space, validity, and pleasure
Than that conferred on Gonerill.[1] Now our joy,
Although our last and least; to whose young love,
The vines of France, and milk of Burgundy,
Strive to be interest. What can you say, to draw
A third more opulent than your sisters'? Speak.

CORDELIA. Nothing my Lord.

LEAR. Nothing?

CORDELIA. Nothing.

LEAR. Nothing will come of nothing; speak again.

CORDELIA. Unhappy that I am, I cannot heave
My heart into my mouth. I love your Majesty
According to my bond,[2] no more nor less.

LEAR. How, how Cordelia? Mend your speech a little,
Lest you may mar your fortunes.

CORDELIA. Good my Lord,
You have begot me, bred me, loved me.
I return those duties back as are right fit:
Obey you, love you, and most honour you.
Why have my sisters husbands, if they say
They love you all? Happily, when I shall wed,
That Lord, whose hand must take my plight,[3] shall carry
Half my love with him, half my care, and duty.
Sure I shall never marry like my sisters.

LEAR. But goes thy heart with this?

CORDELIA. Aye, my good Lord.

LEAR. So young, and so untender?

CORDELIA. So young, my Lord, and true.

LEAR. Let it be so: thy truth then be thy dower;
For by the sacred radiance of the sun,
The mysteries of Hecate[4] and the night;
By all the operation of the orbs,[5]
From whom we do exist, and cease to be:
Here I disclaim all my paternal care,
Propinquity and property of blood,[6]
And as a stranger to my heart and me,
Hold thee from this forever. The barbarous Scythian,[7]
Or he that makes his generation messes[8]
To gorge his appetite, shall to my bosom
Be as well neighboured, pitied, and relieved,
As thou my sometime° daughter. *former*

KENT. Good my Liege—

LEAR. Peace, Kent!
Come not between the dragon[9] and his wrath.
I loved her most, and thought to set my rest[10]
On her kind nursery. Hence, and avoid my sight!
So be my grave, my peace, as here I give
Her father's heart from her. Call France! Who stirs?[11]
Call Burgundy! (*To his sons-in law.*) Cornwall, and Albany:
With my two daughters' dowers, digest the third.[12]
Let pride, which she calls plainness, marry her![13]
I do invest you jointly with my power,
Preeminence, and all the large effects
That troop with majesty.[14] Ourself, by monthly course,
With reservation of an hundred knights,[15]
By you to be sustained, shall our abode
Make with you by due turn. Only we shall retain
The name, and all th'addition[16] to a king. The sway,° *management*
Revenue, execution of the rest,
Belovèd sons, be yours; which to confirm,
This coronet part between you.[17]

KENT. Royal Lear,

---

[1] The following lines are substantially different in the Quarto text. The Quarto reads as follows: "Than that confirmed on Gonorill. But now our joy, / Although the last, not least in our dear love, / What can you say to win a third more opulent / Than your sisters'?"

[2] *bond* Bond between daughter and father, but also carrying the implication of legal obligation.

[3] *plight* Oath of marriage.

[4] *mysteries of Hecate* Rites of the goddess of witchcraft and crossroads (F reads "miseries," clearly an error).

[5] *operation … orbs* Movement of the planetary spheres (i.e., astrological influence).

[6] *propinquity … blood* Relationship and shared blood.

[7] *Scythian* Literally, an inhabitant of what is now Russia, but established by Roman poets as a byword for savage.

[8] *makes … messes* Makes meals of his parents or children.

[9] *dragon* Heraldic emblem of Britain.

[10] *set my rest* Pun: build my retiring years; stake everything (a term drawn from *primero*, a card game).

[11] *Who stirs?* Move it!

[12] *digest* Swallow (i.e. split the third between the first two).

[13] *Let pride … her* Let her pridefulness, which she insists is merely plain-speaking, stand as her dowry and find her a husband.

[14] *large effects … majesty* Splendid retinues and display of pomp.

[15] *with reservation of* Reserving the privilege of having.

[16] *addition* Additional honors.

[17] *This coronet … you* This crown be split between you.

Whom I have ever honoured as my King,
Loved as my father, as my master followed,
As my great patron thought on in my prayers—
LEAR. The bow is bent and drawn; make from the shaft.[1]
KENT. Let it fall rather, though the fork° invade *arrow-head*
The region of my heart. Be Kent unmannerly,
When Lear is mad.[2] What wouldest thou do, old man?
Think'st thou that duty shall have dread to speak,
When power to flattery bows?
To plainness honour's bound,
When Majesty falls to folly. Reserve thy state;[3]
And in thy best consideration check° *stop*
This hideous rashness. Answer my life, my judgement:[4]
Thy youngest daughter does not love thee least;
Nor are those empty hearted, whose low sounds
Reverb no hollowness.[5]
LEAR. Kent, on thy life no more!
KENT. My life I never held but as pawn[6]
To wage against thine enemies, ne'r feared to lose it,
Thy safety being motive.
LEAR. Out of my sight!
KENT. See better Lear, and let me still remain
The true blank of thine eye.
LEAR. Now by Apollo—[7]
KENT. Now by Apollo, King
Thou swear'st thy gods in vain.
LEAR. O, Vassal! Miscreant!
ALBANY and CORDELIA. Dear sir, forbear.[8]
KENT. Kill thy physician, and thy fee bestow
Upon the foul disease![9] Revoke thy gift,
Or whil'st I can vent clamour[10] from my throat,
I'll tell thee thou dost evil.
LEAR. Hear me, recreant; on thine allegiance, hear me!
That thou hast sought to make us break our vows,
Which we durst° never yet; and with strained° pride, *dared* *forced*
To come betwixt our sentences, and our power,
Which, nor our nature, nor our place can bear;
Our potency made good,[11] take thy reward.
Five days we do allot thee for provision,
To shield thee from disasters of the world,
And on the sixth to turn thy hated back
Upon our kingdom; if on the tenth day following,
Thy banished trunk° be found in our dominions, *body*
The moment is thy death. Away! By Jupiter,[12]
This shall not be revoked.
KENT. Fare thee well King; sith thus thou wilt appear,
Freedom lives hence, and banishment is here.

(*To Cordelia.*)

The gods to their dear shelter take thee maid,
That justly think'st, and hast most rightly said.

(*To Gonerill and Regan.*)

And your large speeches, may your deeds approve,
That good effects may spring from words of love.

(*To Albany and Cornwall and the others.*)

Thus Kent, O Princes, bids you all adieu,
He'll shape his old course,[13] in a country new.

(*Exit.*)

[1] *The bow … shaft* Lear suggests that he is figuratively an archer who has drawn his bow, so Kent should get out of the arrow's way.

[2] *Be Kent … mad* When you behave insanely, it calls for a breach of manners on my part.

[3] *Reserve thy state* Hold on to your power.

[4] *Answer … judgment* I'll answer with my life if I am wrong in this judgement.

[5] *Nor … hollowness* Nor does the lack of a loud rhetorical expression of emotion from someone suggest that she has nothing in her heart.

[6] *pawn* Least valuable piece in a chess game.

[7] *Apollo* God associated not only with clear sight, but also with archery (the world of the play is nominally pagan).

[8] *Dear Sir, forbear* Many editors follow Nicholas Rowe (1709) in inserting, prior to this line, the stage direction for Lear: "laying his hand on his sword." It is possible, however, that they would suggest Lear restrain himself from violent outbursts, without his having made any threat of actual violence. It is also possible that Kent's continued defiance of the King could provide sufficient motivation for Albany and Cordelia to address the line to him.

[9] *Kill … disease* Sarcastic reference to the way Lear is punishing those who are loyal to him and rewarding those who are disloyal.

[10] *vent clamour* Cry out.

[11] *Our … good* My royal authority now having been asserted.

[12] *Jupiter* Supreme Roman god.

[13] *shape his old course* Resume his accustomed (truthful) behavior.

(*Flourish.*[1] *Enter Gloucester with [the King of] France, and [the Duke of] Burgundy, Attendants.*)

CORDELIA. Here's France and Burgundy, my noble Lord.[2]

LEAR. My Lord of Burgundy,
We first address toward you, who with this King
Hath rivalled for our daughter. What, in the least,
Will you require in present dower with her,
Or cease your quest of love?

BURGUNDY. Most Royal Majesty,
I crave no more than hath your Highness offered—
Nor will you tender less?

LEAR. Right noble Burgundy,
When she was dear to us, we did hold her so,
But now her price is fallen. Sir, there she stands;
If aught within that little seeming substance—
Or all of it, with our displeasure pieced
And nothing more[3]—may fitly like your Grace,
She's there, and she is yours.

BURGUNDY. I know no answer.

LEAR. Will you, with those infirmities she owes,° *owns*
Unfriended, new adopted to our hate,
Dow'rd with our curse, and strangered[4] with our oath,
Take her or, leave her?

BURGUNDY. Pardon me, Royal Sir,
Election makes not up in such conditions.[5]

LEAR. Then leave her, Sir, for by the power that made me,
I tell you all her wealth. (*To France.*) For you, great King,
I would not from your love make such a stray,
To match you where I hate; therefore, beseech you
T'avert your liking a more worthier way,
Than on a wretch whom Nature is ashamed
Almost t'acknowledge hers.

FRANCE. This is most strange,
That she—whom even but now, was your object,
The argument of your praise,[6] balm of your age,
The best, the dearest—should in this trice of time
Commit a thing so monstrous to dismantle
So many folds of favour. Sure her offence
Must be of such unnatural degree
That monsters it[7]—or your fore-vouched affection
Fall into taint[8]—which to believe of her
Must be a faith that reason without miracle
Should never plant in me.[9]

CORDELIA. I yet beseech your Majesty—
If, for I want that glib and oily art,
To speak and purpose not; since what I will intend,
I'll do't before I speak—that you make known
It is no vicious blot, murder, or foulness,
No unchaste action or dishonoured step
That hath deprived me of your grace and favour,
But even for want of that for which I am richer:
A still soliciting eye,[10] and such a tongue,
That I am glad I have not, though not to have it,
Hath lost me in your liking.

LEAR. Better thou had'st
Not been born, than not t'have pleased me better.

FRANCE. Is it but this? A tardiness in nature,[11]
Which often leaves the history unspoke
That it intends to do. My Lord of Burgundy,
What say you to the lady? Love's not love
When it is mingled with regards that stands
Aloof from th'entire point;[12] will you have her?
She is herself a dowry.[13]

BURGUNDY. Royal King,
Give but that portion which your self proposed,

[1] *Flourish* Fanfare to mark the entrance of important persons.

[2] *Here's France ... Lord* Most editors regard the assignment of this line to Cordelia as an error, and assign it either to Gloucester, as the Quarto does, or to Cornwall. But to have Cordelia helpfully speak to her father in a moment when he is upset and distracted is far from implausible, and could have dramatic force.

[3] *with our ... nothing more* With the addition of my displeasure and nothing else (i.e., without any dowry).

[4] *strangered* Made a stranger, disowned.

[5] *Election ... conditions* One cannot make a choice in such circumstances.

[6] *object ... praise* Both the object of your praise and the example of how it should be bestowed.

[7] *must ... monsters it* Must be so outlandish as to be monstrous.

[8] *or your ... taint* Either that or your previously expressed affection must be suspected.

[9] *faith ... in me* A belief that I could never arrive at rationally without some miracle to prove it.

[10] *still soliciting eye* Eye that is always looking for advantage.

[11] *tardiness in nature* Reserved character.

[12] *with regards ... point* With matters, such as a dowry, that have nothing to do with love.

[13] *she ... dowry* Her own person is a great treasure.

And here I take Cordelia by the hand,
Duchess of Burgundy.
LEAR. Nothing, I have sworn. I am firm.
BURGUNDY. (*To Cordelia.*) I am sorry then you have so lost a father,
That you must lose a husband.
CORDELIA. Peace be with Burgundy,
Since that respect and fortunes are his love,
I shall not be his wife.
FRANCE. Fairest Cordelia, that art most rich being poor,
Most choice forsaken, and most loved despised,
Thee and thy virtues here I seize upon,
Be it lawful I take up what's cast away.
Gods, Gods! 'Tis strange, that from their cold'st neglect
My love should kindle to inflamed respect.

(*To Lear.*)

Thy dowerless daughter, King, thrown to my chance,
Is Queen of us, of ours, and our fair France.
Not all the Dukes of wat'rish Burgundy,[1]
Can buy this unprized precious maid of me.
Bid them farewell Cordelia; though unkind,
Thou losest here, a better where to find.
LEAR. Thou hast her France; let her be thine, for we
Have no such daughter, nor shall ever see
That face of hers again. Therefore be gone,
Without our grace, our love, our benison.° *blessing*
Come, noble Burgundy.

(*Flourish. Exeunt [all but France, Cordelia, Regan and Gonerill].*)

FRANCE. Bid farewell to your sisters.
CORDELIA. The jewels of our father, with washed° eyes *tearful*
Cordelia leaves you. I know you what you are,
And like a sister am most loath to call
Your faults as they are named.[2] Love well our father:
To your professèd bosoms[3] I commit him.
But yet alas, stood I within his grace,
I would prefer° him to a better place. *recommend*
So farewell to you both.
REGAN. Prescribe not us our duty.
GONERILL. Let your study
Be to content your Lord, who hath received you
At Fortune's alms.[4] You have obedience scanted,
And well are worth the want that you have wanted.[5]
CORDELIA. Time shall unfold what plighted cunning[6] hides:
Who covers faults, at last with shame derides.[7]
Well may you prosper!
FRANCE. Come, my fair Cordelia.

(*Exit France and Cordelia.*)

GONERILL. Sister, it is not little I have to say, of what most nearly appertains to us both. I think our father will hence tonight.

REGAN. That's most certain, and with you; next month with us.

GONERILL. You see how full of changes his age is; the observation we have made of it hath been little.[8] He always loved our sister most, and with what poor judgement he hath now cast her off, appears too grossly.[9]

REGAN. 'Tis the infirmity of his age; yet he hath ever but slenderly known himself.

GONERILL. The best and soundest of his time hath been but rash.[10] Then must we look from his age to receive not alone the imperfections of long ingrafted condition, but therewithal the unruly waywardness that infirm and choleric years bring with them.[11]

---

[1] *wat'rish Burgundy* The insult is meant to suggest that Burgundy is weak in character, like watered down Burgundy wine.

[2] *as ... named* By their proper (ugly) names.

[3] *professèd bosoms* Hearts that claim to love him.

[4] *at Fortune's alms* As a charity case.

[5] *are worth ... wanted* Have deserved the lack of affection which you yourself lacked.

[6] *plighted cunning* Manipulative oath-taking (with a pun on "pleated," folded).

[7] *Who covers ... derides* Time conceals faults at first, but eventually exposes the sinner to scorn.

[8] *the observation ... little* We hadn't much noticed [how far his mind had slipped].

[9] *grossly* Obviously.

[10] *the best ... rash* At even his best moments, he's been imprudent.

[11] *Then must ... them* So, with his advancing years, we should expect not merely the faults that have always been in his character, but also the difficulties that are associated with troublesome old age.

REGAN. Such unconstant starts[1] are we like to have from him, as this of Kent's banishment.

GONERILL. There is further complement of leave-taking[2] between France and him. Pray you, let us sit together; if our father carry authority with such disposition as he bears, this last surrender of his will but offend us.[3]

REGAN. We shall further think of it.

GONERILL. We must do something, and i'th' heat.° *quickly*

(*Exeunt.*)

ACT 1, Scene 2

(*Enter Edmund.*)

EDMUND. Thou, Nature,[4] art my goddess; to thy law
My services are bound. Wherefore should I
Stand in the plague of custom,[5] and permit
The curiosity of nations[6] to deprive me?
For that I am some twelve, or fourteen moonshines° *months*
Lag of[7] a brother? Why bastard? Wherefore base?
When my dimensions are as well compact,° *formed*
My mind as generous, and my shape as true
As honest madam's issue? Why brand they us
With base? With baseness, bastardy? Base, base?
Who in the lusty stealth of Nature, take
More composition, and fierce quality,
Than doth within a dull, stale, tired bed[8]
Go to th' creating a whole tribe of fops[9]
Got[10] 'tween a sleep, and wake? Well then,
Legitimate Edgar, I must have your land.
Our father's love is to the bastard Edmund,
As to th' legitimate. Fine word: legitimate.
Well, my legitimate, if this letter speed,° *prosper*
And my invention° thrive, Edmund the base *plan*
Shall to'th' legitimate.[11] I grow, I prosper.
Now gods, stand up for bastards.

(*Enter Gloucester.*)

GLOUCESTER. Kent banished thus? And France in choler parted?
And the King gone tonight? Prescribed[12] his power,
Confined to exhibition?[13] All this done
Upon the gad?[14] Edmund, how now? What news?

EDMUND. (*Conspicuously hiding a letter.*) So please your Lordship, none.

GLOUCESTER. Why so earnestly seek you to put up[15] the letter?

EDMUND. I know no news, my Lord.

GLOUCESTER. What paper were you reading?

EDMUND. Nothing my Lord.

GLOUCESTER. No? What needed then that terrible dispatch of it into your pocket? The quality of nothing hath not such need to hide itself. Let's see; come, if it be nothing, I shall not need spectacles.

EDMUND. I beseech you Sir, pardon me; it is a letter from my brother, that I have not all o'er-read; and for so much as I have perused, I find it not fit for your o'er-looking.

GLOUCESTER. Give me the letter, Sir.

EDMUND. I shall offend, either to detain or give it. The contents, as in part I understand them, are to blame.

GLOUCESTER. Let's see, let's see.

---

1 *unconstant starts* Sudden jerks, impulsive acts.

2 *further … leave-taking* More diplomatic ceremonies connected with the King of France's departure.

3 *sit together* I.e., during the leave-taking ceremony to follow; *if our … but offend us* If our father attempts to act officially in the mood he is in, his leaving us his property and authority is going to be nothing but trouble (e.g., if Lear should declare war on France).

4 *Nature* The material world, as distinct not only from the spiritual realm, but also from civilized order (a realm in which Edmund, being "illegitimately born," is legally disenfranchised).

5 *stand … custom* Accept a deplorable convention.

6 *curiosity of nations* Arbitrary distinctions established by law.

7 *Lag of* Behind, born later than.

8 *dull stale tired bed* Bed of a married couple who have grown sexually bored with each other through long familiarity.

9 *fops* Affected aristocratic fools.

10 *Got* Begotten.

11 *Shall to th'legitimate* Will become legitimate; usually emended to "shall top."

12 *Prescribed* Limited.

13 *exhibition* Pension.

14 *upon the gad* On the spur of the moment, impulsively.

15 *put up* Put away.

EDMUND. I hope, for my brother's justification, he wrote this but as an essay, or taste[1] of my virtue.

GLOUCESTER. (*Reads.*)
"This policy and reverence of age makes the world bitter to the best of our times: keeps our fortunes from us, till our oldness cannot relish them.[2] I begin to find an idle and fond bondage in the oppression of aged tyranny, who sways not as it hath power, but as it is suffered.[3] Come to me, that of this I may speak more. If our father would sleep till I waked him,[4] you should enjoy half his revenue for ever, and live the beloved of your brother. Edgar."

Hum? Conspiracy? "... sleep till I wake him ... you should enjoy half his revenue ..." My son Edgar—had he a hand to write this? A heart and brain to breed it in? When came you to this? Who brought it?

EDMUND. It was not brought me, my Lord; there's the cunning of it. I found it thrown in at the casement of my closet.[5]

GLOUCESTER. You know the character[6] to be your brother's?

EDMUND. If the matter[7] were good my Lord, I durst swear it were his; but in respect of that,[8] I would fain[9] think it were not.

GLOUCESTER. It is his.

EDMUND. It is his hand, my Lord; but I hope his heart is not in the contents.

GLOUCESTER. Has he never before sounded you in this business?

EDMUND. Never my Lord. But I have heard him oft maintain it to be fit, that sons at perfect age, and fathers declined, the father should be as ward to the son, and the son manage his revenue.

GLOUCESTER. O villain, villain! His very opinion in the letter! Abhorred villain; unnatural, detested, brutish villain—worse than brutish! Go, sirrah, seek him! I'll apprehend him. Abominable villain! Where is he?

EDMUND. I do not well know my Lord. If it shall please you to suspend your indignation against my brother, til you can derive from him better testimony of his intent, you should run a certain course: where, if you violently proceed against him, mistaking his purpose, it would make a great gap in your own honour, and shake in pieces, the heart of his obedience. I dare pawn down[10] my life for him, that he hath writ this to feel my[11] affection to your Honour, and to no other pretence of danger.[12]

GLOUCESTER. Think you so?

EDMUND. If your Honour judge it meet,[13] I will place you where you shall hear us confer of this, and by an auricular assurance[14] have your satisfaction, and that without any further delay, than this very evening.

GLOUCESTER. He cannot be such a monster. Edmund, seek him out; wind me into him,[15] I pray you. Frame the business after your own wisdom. I would unstate my self to be in a due resolution.[16]

EDMUND. I will seek him, Sir, presently; convey the business as I shall find means;[17] and acquaint you withal.

GLOUCESTER. These late[18] eclipses in the sun and moon portend no good to us. Though the wisdom of Nature[19] can reason it thus and thus; yet Nature finds itself scourged by the sequent effects.[20] Love cools, friendship falls off, brothers divide. In cities, mutinies; in countries, discord; in palaces, treason; and the bond cracked 'twixt son and father. This villain of mine comes under the

[1] *as an essay ... taste* As a trial, or test.

[2] *This policy ... times* This custom of deferring to old age makes life unpleasant when we are in the prime of our life.

[3] *sways ... suffered* Is influential not because of any inherent power, but because it is indulged by those who suffer under it.

[4] *If our father ... sleep till I waked him* Were it up to me when he should awake (i.e., never, from death).

[5] *casement of my closet* Window of my bedroom.

[6] *character* Hand-writing.

[7] *matter* Content.

[8] *in respect of that* In view of the content, such as it is.

[9] *fain* Prefer to.

[10] *pawn down* Stake.

[11] *feel my* Feel out my.

[12] *pretence of danger* Dangerous possibility.

[13] *meet* Appropriate.

[14] *auricular assurance* Audible proof.

[15] *wind me into him* Worm your (and my) way into his confidence.

[16] *unstate ... resolution* Give up my earldom to be resolved of all doubt.

[17] *convey ... means* Manage the business as best as I can.

[18] *late* Recent.

[19] *wisdom of Nature* Natural science (as opposed to astrology).

[20] *yet ... effects* The natural world nevertheless suffers the subsequent effects (of the eclipses).

prediction:[1] there's son against father; the King falls from bias of Nature: there's father against child. We have seen the best of our time. Machinations, hollowness,[2] treachery, and all ruinous disorders follow us disquietly[3] to our graves. Find out this villain, Edmund; it shall lose thee nothing. Do it carefully. And the noble and true-hearted Kent banished; his offence, honesty. 'Tis strange.

(*Exit.*)

EDMUND. This is the excellent foppery[4] of the world, that when we are sick in Fortune,[5] often the surfeits of our own behaviour,[6] we make guilty of our disasters the sun, the moon, and stars, as if we were villains on necessity; fools by heavenly compulsion; knaves, thieves, and treachers by spherical predominance;[7] drunkards, liars and adulterers by an enforced obedience of planetary influence; and all that we are evil in, by a divine thrusting on. An admirable evasion of whoremaster man, to lay his goatish disposition on the charge of a star.[8] (*Sarcastically.*) "My father compounded with my mother under the dragon's tail; and my nativity was under Ursa major, so that it follows, I am rough and lecherous." I should have been that I am, had the maidenliest star in the firmament twinkled on my bastardizing.[9]

(*Enter Edgar.*)

(*Aside.*) Pat[10] he comes, like the catastrophe of the old comedy.[11] My cue[12] is villainous melancholy, with a sigh like Tom o' Bedlam.[13] (*Aloud.*) O, these eclipses do portend these divisions. (*Sings.*) Fa, Sol, La, Mi![14]

EDGAR. How now, brother Edmund, what serious contemplation are you in?

EDMUND. I am thinking, brother, of a prediction I read this other day, what should follow these eclipses.

EDGAR. Do you busy your self with that?

EDMUND. I promise you, the effects he writes of succeed unhappily.
When saw you my Father last?

EDGAR. The night gone by.

EDMUND. Spake you with him?

EDGAR. Aye, two hours together.[15]

EDMUND. Parted you in good terms? Found you no displeasure in him, by word, nor countenance?

EDGAR. None at all.

EDMUND. Bethink your self wherein you may have offended him; and at my entreaty forbear his presence, until some little time hath qualified the heat of his displeasure; which at this instant so rageth in him, that

[1] *This villain ... prediction* The behavior of this villainous son of mine was predicted by the astrological portents.

[2] *hollowness* Insincerity.

[3] *disquietly* Disturbingly.

[4] *excellent foppery* Splendid foolishness.

[5] *sick in Fortune* Having bad luck.

[6] *the surfeits ... behaviour* Caused by our own excesses.

[7] *treachers ... predominance* Traitors because a certain planet was in ascendancy at our birth.

[8] *an admirable ... of a star* It is admirable that men evade responsibility for their lecherous natures by blaming astrology.

[9] *I should ... bastardizing* I'd be who I am if the most virginal star in the heavens had presided over my conception.

[10] *Pat* Right on time.

[11] *like ... comedy* As the climax of an old comedy might be contrived to arrive coincidentally at the perfect moment.

[12] *My cue* The part I must play.

[13] *Tom o' Bedlam* Archetypal madman, named from the Bethlehem (pronounced and often written "Bedlam") Hospital in London.

[14] *Fa ... Mi* Edmund appears to be mocking the neo-Pythagorean notion of a connection between music and the order of the cosmos. Several critics have attempted to show special significance to these notes, but this seems out of keeping with anything the character might be attempting.

[15] *I promise you ... two hours together* The equivalent passage in the Quarto version is longer, and substantially different: "BASTARD. I promise you the effects he writ of succeed unhappily: as of unnaturalness between the child and the parent; death, dearth; dissolutions of ancient amities; divisions in state; menaces and maledictions against King and nobles; needless diffidences; banishment of friends; dissipation of cohorts; nuptial breaches; and I know not what.
EDGAR. How long have you been a sectary astronomical?
BASTARD. Come, come, when saw you my father last?
EDGAR. Why, the night gone by.
BASTARD. Spake you with him?
EDGAR. Two hours together."

with the mischief of your person, it would scarcely allay.[1]

EDGAR. Some villain hath done me wrong.

EDMUND. That's my fear. I pray you have a continent forbearance[2] till the speed of his rage goes slower; and as I say, retire with me to my lodging, from whence I will fitly bring you to hear my Lord speak. Pray ye, go. (*Hands him a key.*) There's my key. If you do stir abroad, go armed.

EDGAR. Armed, brother?

EDMUND. Brother,[3] I advise you to the best. I am no honest man, if there be any good meaning toward you. I have told you what I have seen, and heard but faintly: nothing like the image, and horror of it. Pray you, away!

EDGAR. Shall I hear from you anon?

EDMUND. I do serve you in this business.

(*Exit [Edgar].*)

A credulous father, and a brother noble,
Whose nature is so far from doing harms,
That he suspects none; on whose foolish honesty
My practises° ride easy: I see the business. *schemes*
Let me, if not by birth, have lands by wit,° *intelligence*
All with me's meet, that I can fashion fit.[4]

(*Exit.*)

ACT 1, SCENE 3

(*Enter Gonerill, and [Oswald, her] Steward.*[5])

GONERILL. Did my father strike my gentleman for chiding of his fool?

OSWALD. Aye, Madam.

GONERILL. By day and night, he wrongs me; every hour
He flashes into one gross crime, or other,
That sets us all at odds. I'll not endure it.
His knights grow riotous, and himself upbraids us
On every trifle. When he returns from hunting,
I will not speak with him. Say I am sick.
If you come slack of former services,[6]
You shall do well. The fault of it,[7] I'll answer.

OSWALD. He's coming Madam, I hear him.

GONERILL. Put on what weary negligence you please,
You and your fellows; I'd have it come to question.
If he distaste it, let him to my sister,
Whose mind and mine, I know, in that are one.[8]
Remember what I have said.

OSWALD. Well Madam.

GONERILL. And let his Knights have colder looks among you. What grows of it, no matter; advise your fellows so. I'll write straight to my sister to hold my course.[9] Prepare for dinner.

(*Exeunt.*)

ACT 1, SCENE 4[10]

(*Enter Kent.*)

KENT. If, but as well, I other accents borrow,[11]
That can my speech defuse, my good intent
May carry through itself to that full issue
For which I razed my likeness.[12] Now, banished Kent,
If thou canst serve where thou dost stand condemned,
So may it come, thy master whom thou lov'st,
Shall find thee full of labours.

(*Horns within.*[13] *Enter Lear and Attendants.*)

[1] *with the mischief … allay* With the additional provocation of your physical presence, his displeasure would be unlikely to ease.

[2] *have a continent forbearance* Control your feelings and keep your distance.

[3] *Pray ye … Brother* These lines do not appear in the Quarto version.

[4] *All … fit* Everything is acceptable to me, so long as I can shape it to my purposes.

[5] *Steward* Oswald is identified only as "Steward" during this scene in F.

[6] *If you … services* If you fall short of serving him as well as you have.

[7] *The fault of it* The blame for it.

[8] *If he … that are one* If things are not to his taste, let him go to my sister; I know that she and I are of one mind about this.

[9] *straight … to hold my course* I will write immediately to my sister, and advise her to do the same thing as I am doing.

[10] *Scene 4* F indicates a definite scene break here, unlike Q.

[11] *other accents borrow* I am able to disguise my way of speaking by putting on other accents.

[12] *razed my likeness* Concealed my appearance.

[13] *within* I.e., offstage.

LEAR. Let me not stay a jot[1] for dinner; go get it ready. (*To Kent.*) How now, what art thou?

KENT. A man, Sir.

LEAR. What dost thou profess?[2] What would'st thou with us?

KENT. I do profess to be no less than I seem; to serve him truly that will put me in trust; to love him that is honest; to converse with him that is wise and says little; to fear judgement; to fight when I cannot choose; and to eat no fish.[3]

LEAR. What art thou?

KENT. A very honest hearted fellow, and as poor as the King.

LEAR. If thou be'st as poor for a subject, as he's for a King, thou art poor enough. What would'st thou?

KENT. Service.

LEAR. Who would'st thou serve?

KENT. You.

LEAR. Do'st thou know me fellow?

KENT. No Sir, but you have that in your countenance which I would fain call Master.[4]

LEAR. What's that?

KENT. Authority.

LEAR. What services canst thou do?

KENT. I can keep honest counsel; ride; run; mar a curious tale in telling it and deliver a plain message bluntly. That which ordinary men are fit for, I am qualified in; and the best of me is diligence.

LEAR. How old art thou?

KENT. Not so young, Sir, to love a woman for singing, nor so old to dote on her for anything. I have years on my back forty-eight.

LEAR. Follow me, thou shalt serve me, if I like thee no worse after dinner. I will not part from thee yet. Dinner, ho, dinner! Where's my knave, my Fool?[5] Go you and call my fool hither. (*To Oswald who is passing through.*) You, you sirrah! Where's my daughter?

OSWALD. So please you …[6]

(*Exit.*)

LEAR. What says the fellow there? Call the clot-poll[7] back! (*A Knight pursues Oswald.*) Where's my Fool? Ho! I think the world's asleep! (*Knight re-enters.*) How now? Where's that mongrel?

KNIGHT. He says, my Lord, your daughter is not well.

LEAR. Why came not the slave back to me when I called him?

KNIGHT. Sir, he answered me in the roundest manner, he would not.

LEAR. He would not?

KNIGHT. My Lord, I know not what the matter is; but to my judgement your Highness is not entertained with that ceremonious affection as you were wont. There's a great abatement of kindness appears as well in the general dependants, as in the Duke himself also, and your daughter.

LEAR. Ha? Sayst thou so?

KNIGHT. I beseech you pardon me, my Lord, if I be mistaken; for my duty cannot be silent, when I think your Highness wronged.

LEAR. Thou but remem'brest me of mine own conception.[8] I have perceived a most faint neglect of late, which I have rather blamed as mine own jealous curiosity,[9] than as a very pretence and purpose of unkindness. I will look further into't. But where's my Fool? I have not seen him this two days.

---

[1] *not stay a jot* Not wait a moment.

[2] *What … profess* What do you do for a living? (Kent's response puns on the word "profess" as also meaning "claim.")

[3] *eat no fish* The humor of this self-deflating claim has proved effective in performance regardless of whether its sense is understood; but the fact remains that it has yet to be satisfactorily explained. The most frequently cited explanation is that in abjuring fish, Kent is claiming to be a Protestant. Another suggestion is that fish-eating might have been regarded as a less manly taste, so Kent is claiming not to be a weakling. Perhaps the line should be read in the context of the regional dialect Kent has just adopted to disguise himself, for a certain dialect (Cornish, for example) could imply that he is a former fisher—a profession in which, proverbially, people grow sick of eating fish. The line might also be a bawdy joke (often the case with "fish" in Shakespeare).

[4] *that in your countenance … call Master* Something in your appearance that leads me to want to call you Master.

[5] *Fool* For the sake of clarity, the word has been capitalized wherever it refers directly to the character so named.

[6] *So please you …* The incomplete sentence may indicate inaudibility, either due to mumbling or because Oswald walks out of the room while speaking.

[7] *clot-poll* Block head (literally, lump-of-dirt-head).

[8] *Thou … conception* You have reminded me of a notion I'd had earlier.

[9] *as mine own jealous curiosity* As the result of my being excessively on the lookout for signs of ill-will in others.

KNIGHT. Since my young Lady's going into France, Sir, the Fool hath much pined away.

LEAR. No more of that; I have noted it well. Go you and tell my daughter I would speak with her. Go you call hither my Fool.

(*Exit Servant; Enter [Oswald].*)

Oh you, Sir, you; come you hither, Sir. Who am I, Sir?

OSWALD. My Lady's father.

LEAR. "My Lady's father"? My Lord's knave, you whoreson dog, you slave, you cur.

OSWALD. I am none of these my Lord; I beseech your pardon.[1]

LEAR. Do you bandy[2] looks with me, you rascal? (*Strikes him.*)

OSWALD. I'll not be strucken, my Lord.

KENT. (*Tripping him.*) Nor tripped neither, you base football player.

LEAR. I thank thee, fellow. Thou serv'st me, and I'll love thee.

KENT. Come sir, arise; away. I'll teach you differences! Away, away! If you will measure your lubber's length[3] again, tarry; but away, go to; have you wisdom, so.[4]

(*Exit Oswald.*)

LEAR. (*To Kent.*) Now my friendly knave, I thank thee. (*Giving him money.*) There's earnest of thy service.[5]

(*Enter Fool.*)

FOOL. Let me hire him too; here's my coxcomb.[6]

LEAR. How now my pretty knave, how dost thou?

FOOL. Sirrah, you were best take my coxcomb.

LEAR. Why, my boy?

FOOL. Why? For taking one's part that's out of favour.[7] (*To Kent.*) Nay, and thou canst not smile as the wind sits,[8] thou'lt catch cold shortly. There, take my coxcomb. Why, this fellow has banished two on's[9] daughters, and did the third a blessing against his will; if thou follow him, thou must needs wear my coxcomb. (*To Lear.*) How now, Nuncle?[10] Would I had two coxcombs and two daughters.

LEAR. Why, my boy?

FOOL. If I gave them all my living, I'd keep my coxcombs myself.[11] There's mine; beg another of thy daughters.

LEAR. Take heed Sirrah; the whip.[12]

FOOL. Truth's a dog must to kennel; he must be whipped out, when the Lady Brach[13] may stand by'th' fire and stink.

LEAR. A pestilent gall[14] to me.

FOOL. Sirrah, I'll teach thee a speech.

LEAR. Do.

FOOL. Mark it, Nuncle:
Have more than thou showest,
Speak less than thou knowest,
Lend less than thou owest,
Ride more than thou goest,
Learn more than thou trowest,° *believe*
Set less than thou throwest;[15]
Leave thy drink and thy whore,
And keep in a door,° *indoors*
And thou shalt have more,
Than two tens to a score.[16]

---

[1] *beseech ... pardon* I.e., for contradicting Lear, not for past behavior.

[2] *bandy* Insolently exchange, toss back-and-forth.

[3] *lubber's length* Lubber is a sailor's term for a clumsy person; his length is measured when he is spread out on the floor.

[4] *have you wisdom, so* Many editors propose adding a question mark after "wisdom." Others suggest that it is an imperative: "have wisdom enough to do as I say."

[5] *earnest of thy service* A token of thanks for serving me.

[6] *coxcomb* Traditional cap of a fool, resembling the crest (comb) of a rooster (cock).

[7] *For taking ... favour* I.e., Kent should be awarded with the cap of a fool for siding with someone (Lear) who is currently in disgrace with the host.

[8] *and ... sits* If you are not perfectly happy to have the wind blow as hard and cold as it likes.

[9] *on's* Of his.

[10] *Nuncle* The Fool's pet name for Lear derives from "mine uncle."

[11] *If I ... myself* If I gave them everything by which I made my living, then I would be a fool indeed.

[12] *the whip* I.e., you'll be whipped if you aren't careful.

[13] *Lady Brach* Tongue-in-cheek title; a brach is a female hound.

[14] *pestilent gall* I.e., the Fool is a bitter source of affliction.

[15] *Set ... throwest* Stake less than you may win in a game.

[16] *two tens ... score* More than you started with (twenty shillings made an old English pound).

KENT. This is nothing, Fool.

FOOL. Then 'tis like the breath of an unfeed lawyer;[1] you gave me nothing for't. (*To Lear.*) Can you make no use of nothing, Nuncle?

LEAR. Why, no boy; nothing can be made out of nothing.

FOOL. (*To Kent.*) Prithee, tell him, so much the rent of his land comes to. He will not believe a fool.

LEAR. A bitter fool.

FOOL. Do'st thou know the difference my boy, between a bitter fool, and a sweet one?

LEAR. No lad, teach me.

FOOL. Nuncle, give me an egg, and I'll give thee two crowns.

LEAR. What two crowns shall they be?

FOOL. Why, after I have cut the egg i'th' middle and eat[2] up the meat, the two crowns of the egg: when thou clovest[3] thy crowns i'th' middle, and gav'st away both parts, thou bor'st thine ass on thy back o'r the dirt. Thou had'st little wit in thy bald crown, when thou gav'st thy golden one away. If I speak like myself[4] in this, let him be whipped that first finds it so.[5] (*Sings.*)

Fools had ne'r less grace in a year,
For wisemen are grown foppish,
And know not how their wits to wear,
Their manners are so apish.

LEAR. When were you wont to be so full of songs, sirrah?

FOOL. I have used it Nuncle, e'r since thou mad'st thy daughters thy mothers; for when thou gav'st them the rod, and put'st thine own breeches, (*Sings.*)

Then they for sudden joy did weep,
And I for sorrow sung,
That such a King should play bo-peep,
And go the fool among.

Prithee, Nuncle, keep a schoolmaster that can teach thy Fool to lie; I would fain learn to lie.

LEAR. And[6] you lie, Sirrah, we'll have you whipped.

FOOL. I marvel what kin thou and thy daughters are: they'll have me whipped for speaking true; thou'lt have me whipped for lying; and sometimes I am whipped for holding my peace. I had rather be any kind o' thing than a fool. And yet I would not be thee Nuncle: thou hast pared thy wit o' both sides, and left nothing i'th'middle. Here comes one o'the parings.

(*Enter Gonerill.*)

LEAR. How now daughter? What makes that frontlet[7] on? You are too much of late i'th' frown.

FOOL. Thou wast a pretty fellow when thou hadst no need to care for her frowning; now thou art an O without a figure.[8] I am better than thou art now: I am a fool; thou art nothing. (*To Gonerill.*) Yes, forsooth, I will hold my tongue, so your face bids me, though you say nothing.

Mum, mum,
He that keep nor° crust, nor crumb,[9] *neither*
Weary of all, shall want some.

[*Indicating Lear.*] That's a shelled peascod.[10]

GONERILL. Not only, Sir, this, your all-licenced[11] fool,
But other of your insolent retinue
Do hourly carp and quarrel, breaking forth
In rank, and (not to be endured) riots, Sir.
I had thought by making this well known unto you,
To have found a safe° redress; but now grow fearful, *certain*
By what yourself too late° have spoke and done, *recently*
That you protect this course, and put it on
By your allowance; which, if you should, the fault
Would not 'scape censure, nor the redresses sleep,[12]
Which in the tender of a wholesome weal,[13]
Might in their working do you that offence,
Which else were shame, that then necessity

[1] *like the breath of an unfeed lawyer* I.e., worth nothing because unpaid.

[2] *eat* Have eaten.

[3] *clovest* Cut.

[4] *speak like myself* Speak seriously.

[5] *let him ... so* I.e., because to suggest that what the Fool says is not nonsense, but sense, would be impudent.

[6] *And* If.

[7] *frontlet* I.e., frown (literally, an ornamental band).

[8] *an O without a figure* A zero without a numeral before it.

[9] *crumb* The soft inside of the bread.

[10] *shelled peascod* Empty peapod.

[11] *all-licenced* Indulged in all liberties.

[12] *nor ... sleep* Nor would your attempts to make amends pause until they had been fulfilled.

[13] *in the tender of a wholesome weal* Out of concern to bring about healthy state of affairs.

Will call discreet proceeding.[1]
FOOL. (*To Lear.*) For you know, Nuncle:
The hedge-sparrow fed the cuckoo so long,
That it had its head bit off by its young.[2]
So, out went the candle, and we were left darkling.[3]
LEAR. (*To Gonerill.*) Are you our daughter?
GONERILL. I would you would make use of your good wisdom
Whereof I know you are fraught,° and put away *supplied*
These dispositions, which of late transport you
From what you rightly are.
FOOL. May not an ass know when the cart draws the horse? (*Sings.*) Whoop, Jug, I love thee.[4]
LEAR. Does any here know me? This is not Lear.
Does Lear walk thus? Speak thus? Where are his eyes?
Either his notion° weakens, or's discernings *thinking*
Are lethargied. Ha! Waking? 'Tis not so?
Who is it that can tell me who I am?
FOOL. Lear's shadow.
LEAR. Your name,[5] fair gentlewoman?
GONERILL. This admiration Sir, is much o'th'savour[6]
Of other your new pranks. I do beseech you
To understand my purposes aright;
As you are old, and reverend, should be wise.[7]
Here do you keep a hundred knights and squires:
Men so disordered, so debauched and bold,
That this our court, infected with their manners,
Shows like a riotous inn; epicurism° and lust *hedonism*
Makes it more like a tavern, or a brothel,
Than a graced palace. The shame itself doth speak° *calls out*
For instant remedy. Be then desired—
By her that else will take the thing she begs—
A little to disquantity your train,[8]
And the remainders that shall still depend,[9]
To be such men as may besort° your age, *be suitable to*
Which know themselves, and you.
LEAR. Darkness and devils!
Saddle my horses; call my train together.
(*To Gonerill.*) Degenerate bastard, I'll not trouble thee;
Yet have I left a daughter.
GONERILL. You strike my people, and your disordered rabble make servants of their betters.

(*Enter [Duke of] Albany.*)

LEAR. (*To Albany.*) Woe, that too late repents.[10]
Is it your will? Speak , Sir! (*To followers.*)—Prepare my horses.—
(*Spoken at large.*) Ingratitude! Thou marble-hearted fiend,
More hideous when thou show'st thee in a child,
Than the sea-monster.
ALBANY. Pray, Sir, be patient.
LEAR. (*To Gonerill.*) Detested kite,[11] thou liest!
My train are men of choice, and rarest parts,[12]
That all particulars of duty know,
And in the most exact regard, support
The worships of their name.[13] O most small fault,

[1] *Might ... proceeding* The redresses might, in the doing, cause you a sense of embarrassment and humiliation, were it not that they were necessary and therefore the discreet thing to do.

[2] *hedge-sparrow fed the cuckoo* Cuckoos lay their eggs in the nests of other birds, including the smaller hedge-sparrow. The "host" bird then feeds the young cuckoo until it has grown so large that it endangers the host, and is allegedly able to devour it.

[3] *So ... darkling* Thus, the life upon which we (the Fool imagines himself to be one of the sparrow's chicks) depended was snuffed out, and we were left facing death.

[4] *Whoop ... thee* Apparently the refrain of a lost comic song, which may be sung in response from some threatening gesture from Gonerill. Jug is an affectionate variation on Joan, a common name for a girl, used as Australians now use "Sheila."

[5] *Who is it that can tell me ... Your name* Additional text appears here in the Quarto version, with Lear answering his own question: "Who is it that can tell me who I am? Lear's shadow? I would learn that; for by the marks of sovereignty, knowledge, and reason, I should be false persuaded I had daughters.
FOOL. Which they will make an obedient father.
LEAR. Your name, fair gentlewoman?"

[6] *This admiration ... much o'th'savour* This show of bewilderment has much the same taste to it.

[7] *As ... wise* Given your age and status, you should show an appropriate wisdom.

[8] *disquantity your train* Reduce the number of your followers.

[9] *still depend* Continue to stay with you.

[10] *Woe ... repents* Woe to the person (i.e., Albany) who comes too late to make amends.

[11] *kite* Bird of prey associated with cowardice and treachery.

[12] *of choice, and rarest parts* Having highly valuable virtues.

[13] *support ... name* Show themselves worthy of their title (Knight).

How ugly did'st thou in Cordelia show!
Which like an engine,[1] wrenched my frame of nature[2]
From the fixed place,[3] drew from my heart all love,
And added to the gall.[4] O Lear, Lear, Lear!
Beat at this gate[5] that let thy folly in,
And thy dear judgement out. (*To followers.*)—Go, go,
my people.

ALBANY. My Lord, I am guiltless, as I am ignorant
Of what hath moved you.

LEAR. It may be so, my Lord.
(*Lyrically.*) Hear Nature, hear dear Goddess, hear:
Suspend thy purpose, if thou did'st intend
To make this creature fruitful;
Into her womb convey sterility;
Dry up in her the organs of increase,° *womb*
And from her derogate° body, never spring *debased*
A babe to honour her. If she must teem,° *bear life*
Create her child of spleen,[6] that it may live
And be a thwart disnatured° torment to her. *unnatural*
Let it stamp wrinkles in her brow of youth,
With cadent° tears fret channels in her cheeks, *dropping*
Turn all her mother's pains and benefits
To laughter, and contempt: that she may feel,
How sharper than a serpent's tooth it is,
To have a thankless child!—Away, away!

(*Exit [Lear with Kent, Fool and Others].*)

ALBANY. Now Gods that we adore, whereof comes this?

GONERILL. Never afflict your self to know more of it:
But let his disposition have that scope
As dotage gives it.

(*[Re-]enter Lear [with Fool].*)

LEAR. What! fifty of my followers at a clap?
Within a fortnight?[7]

ALBANY. What's the matter, Sir?

LEAR. I'll tell thee. Life and death, I am ashamed
That thou hast power to shake my manhood thus,
That these hot tears, which break from me perforce
Should make thee worth them.[8]
Blasts and fogs upon thee:
Th'untented° woundings of a father's *unbandaged, raw*
curse
Pierce every sense about thee. Old fond eyes:
Beweep this cause again, I'll pluck ye out,
And cast you with the waters that you loose
To temper clay.[9] Ha? Let it be so.
I have another daughter,
Who I am sure is kind and comfortable:
When she shall hear this of thee, with her nails
She'll flay thy wolfish visage. Thou shalt find
That I'll resume the shape which thou dost think
I have cast off for ever.

(*Exit [Lear].*)

GONERILL. Do you mark that?

ALBANY. I cannot be so partial, Gonerill,
To the great love I bear you.

GONERILL. Pray you, content. (*Calls.*)—What,
Oswald, ho? (*To Fool.*)
You, Sir, more knave than fool: after your master.

FOOL. Nuncle Lear, Nuncle Lear! Tarry, take the Fool
with thee!
A fox, when one has caught her,
And such a daughter,
Should sure to the slaughter
If my cap would buy a halter.
So the Fool follows after.

(*Exit.*)

[1] *engine* War machine (such as a battering ram or a crane used in a siege).

[2] *frame of nature* Natural disposition.

[3] *fixed place* Natural location.

[4] *added to the gall* Increased the amount of bile (thus making him, according to the medical concepts of the day, uncharacteristically bitter and angry).

[5] *this gate* I.e., his skull.

[6] *of spleen* Entirely malicious.

[7] *What! fifty ... fortnight* In F's revision, Lear leaves briefly, and discovers that half of his followers have already been dismissed while he has been arguing with Gonerill.

[8] *That these hot tears ... worth them* That my involuntary tears should choose to be prompted by so unworthy a cause as you are.

[9] *Old fond eyes ... clay* Eyes, if you should ever betray me by weeping again, I will pluck you out and, along with the tears you shed, consign you to an early grave.

GONERILL. This man hath had good counsel: a hundred Knights?
'Tis politic, and safe to let him keep
At point a hundred Knights! Yes, that on every dream,
Each buzz, each fancy, each complaint, dislike,
He may enguard his dotage[1] with their powers,
And hold our lives in mercy! —Oswald, I say!

ALBANY. Well, you may fear too far.

GONERILL. Safer than trust too far;
Let me still take away the harms I fear,
Not fear still to be taken.[2] I know his heart,
What he hath uttered, I have writ my sister;
If she sustain him, and his hundred Knights
When I have showed th'unfitness—

(Enter [Oswald].)

How now, Oswald?[3]
What, have you writ that letter to my sister?

OSWALD. Aye, Madam.

GONERILL. Take you some company, and away to horse,
Inform her full of my particular fear,
And thereto add such reasons of your own,
As may compact it more.[4] Get you gone,
And hasten your return. *(Exit Oswald.)*
(To Albany.) No, no, my Lord,
This milky gentleness, and course of yours,
Though I condemn not, yet, under pardon,
You are much more at task[5] for want of wisdom,
Than praised for harmful mildness.

ALBANY. How far your eyes may pierce I cannot tell;
Striving to better, oft we mar what's well.

GONERILL. Nay then—

ALBANY. Well, well, th' event.[6]

(Exeunt.)

ACT 1, SCENE 5

(Enter Lear, Kent, Gentleman, and Fool.)

LEAR. Go you before to Gloucester with these letters; acquaint my daughter no further with anything you know than comes from her demand out of the letter.[7] If your diligence be not speedy, I shall be there afore you.

KENT. I will not sleep, my Lord, till I have delivered your letter.

(Exit.)

FOOL. If a man's brains were in's heels, were't not in danger of kibes?[8]

LEAR. Aye, boy.

FOOL. Then I prithee, be merry; thy wit shall not go slipshod.[9]

LEAR. Ha, ha, ha!

FOOL. Shalt see thy other daughter will use thee kindly; for though she's as like this as a crabbe's like an apple,[10] yet I can tell what I can tell.

LEAR. What canst tell boy?

FOOL. She will taste as like this, as a crabbe does to a crab.[11] Thou canst tell why one's nose stands i'th'middle on's face?

LEAR. No.

FOOL. Why, to keep one's eyes of either side's nose, that what a man cannot smell out, he may spy into.

LEAR. I did her wrong—

FOOL. Can'st tell how an oyster makes his shell?

LEAR. No.

FOOL. Nor I neither; but I can tell why a snail has a house.

LEAR. Why?

FOOL. Why to put's head in, not to give it away to his daughters, and leave his horns without a case.

---

[1] *enguard his dotage* Protect his senile whims.

[2] *Let me ... taken* Let me remove anything I fear rather than fear to be removed myself.

[3] *This man ... How now, Oswald?* The equivalent speech in the Quarto version is one line only: "GONERILL. What Oswald, ho!"

[4] *As may compact it more* As may give the argument more force.

[5] *at task* To be blamed, taken to task.

[6] *Well ... event* Well, we shall see what happens in the event.

[7] *than ... letter* Than her reading of the letter leads her to ask.

[8] *kibes* Chilblains (inflammation of the feet).

[9] *thy wit ... slipshod* You won't have to worry about protecting your brains with slippers, for walking to Regan's shows you have no brains in your feet.

[10] *as a crabbe's ... apple* As similar as a crab-apple is (in appearance) to a regular apple.

[11] *She will taste ... crab* She will be that much more sour and unpleasant than Gonerill as a crab-apple is than a crab.

LEAR. I will forget my nature. So kind a father? —Be my horses ready?

FOOL. Thy asses[1] are gone about 'em. The reason why the seven stars are no mo than seven, is a pretty reason.

LEAR. Because they are not eight.

FOOL. Yes indeed; thou would'st make a good fool.

LEAR. To take't again perforce[2]—monster ingratitude!

FOOL. If thou wert my fool, Nuncle, I'd have thee beaten for being old before thy time.

LEAR. How's that?

FOOL. Thou shouldst not have been old, till thou had'st been wise.

LEAR. O let me not be mad, not mad, sweet heaven!
Keep me in temper, I would not be mad.

(*Enter a Gentleman.*)

How now? Are the horses ready?

GENTLEMAN. Ready, my Lord.

LEAR. Come, boy.

FOOL. She that's a maid now, and laughs at my departure,
Shall not be a maid long, unless things be cut shorter.[3]

(*Exeunt.*)

ACT 2, SCENE 1

(*Enter Bastard, and Curan, severally.*)

EDMUND. Save thee, Curan.

CURAN. And you, Sir. I have been with your father, and given him notice that the Duke of Cornwall, and Regan, his Duchess, will be here with him this night.

EDMUND. How comes that?

CURAN. Nay, I know not. You have heard of the news abroad?—I mean the whispered ones, for they are yet but ear-kissing arguments.[4]

EDMUND. Not I; pray you, what are they?

CURAN. Have you heard of no likely wars toward, 'twixt the Dukes of Cornwall and Albany?

EDMUND. Not a word.

CURAN. You may do then in time. Fare you well, Sir.

(*Exit.*)

EDMUND. The Duke be here tonight? The better best;[5]
This weaves itself perforce into my business.
My father hath set guard to take my brother,
And I have one thing of a queasy question[6]
Which I must act. Briefness and Fortune work.

(*Enter Edgar [above].*)

Brother, a word. Descend, brother, I say!
My father watches. O Sir, fly this place;
Intelligence is given where you are hid.
You have now the good advantage of the night.
Have you not spoken 'gainst the Duke of Cornwall?
He's coming hither; now, i'th'night, i'th'haste,
And Regan with him. Have you nothing said
Upon his party 'gainst the Duke of Albany?
Advise yourself.[7]

EDGAR. I am sure on't, not a word.

EDMUND. I hear my father coming. Pardon me:
In cunning,[8] I must draw my sword upon you.
Draw, seem to defend yourself,
Now quit you well.—
Yield! Come before my Father! Light! Hoa, here!
—Fly brother— Torches, Torches!— So farewell.

(*Exit Edgar.*)

Some blood drawn on me would beget opinion
Of my more fierce endeavour. (*Cuts himself.*) I have seen drunkards
Do more than this in sport. —Father, Father!
Stop, stop! No help?

[1] *asses* I.e., Lear's servants.

[2] *to take't ... perforce* I.e., to re-take the kingdom forcibly.

[3] *She that's ... shorter* A crude sexual gibe: she who finds this situation comic will have the seriousness of things thrust upon her, unless the fool loses his virility. (Note that in Shakespeare's time "departure" was pronounced so as to rhyme with "shorter.")

[4] *ear-kissing arguments* Whispered rumors.

[5] *The better best* Better and better.

[6] *of a queasy question* Of a precarious sort.

[7] *advise yourself* Think carefully.

[8] *In cunning* In order to maintain the deception.

(*Enter Gloucester, and Servants with torches.*)

GLOUCESTER. Now Edmund, where's the villain?
EDMUND. Here stood he in the dark, his sharp sword out,
Mumbling of wicked charms, conjuring the moon
To stand auspicious mistress.[1]
GLOUCESTER. But where is he?
EDMUND. Look sir, I bleed.
GLOUCESTER. Where is the villain, Edmund?
EDMUND. Fled this way, Sir, when by no means he could—
GLOUCESTER. (*To Servants.*) Pursue him, ho; go after!
—By no means, what?
EDMUND. Persuade me to the murder of your Lordship.
But that I told him the revenging gods,
'Gainst parricides did all the thunder bend,
Spoke with how manifold and strong a bond
The child was bound to'th'father. Sir, in fine,[2]
Seeing how loathly opposite[3] I stood
To his unnatural purpose, in fell[4] motion
With his preparèd[5] sword, he charges home[6]
My unprovided body, latched[7] mine arm;
And when he saw my best alarumed spirits[8]
Bold in the quarrels right, roused to th' encounter—
Or whether gasted[9] by the noise I made—
Full suddenly he fled.
GLOUCESTER. Let him fly far:
Not in this land shall he remain uncaught;
And found, dispatch. The noble Duke, my master,
My worthy arch and patron comes tonight,
By his authority I will proclaim it:
That he which finds him shall deserve our thanks,
Bringing the murderous coward to the stake;
He that conceals him, death.

EDMUND. When I dissuaded him from his intent,
And found him pight[10] to do it, with cursed speech[11]
I threatened to discover him. He replied:
"Thou unpossessing bastard: dost thou think,
If I would stand against thee, would the reposal[12]
Of any trust, virtue, or worth in thee
Make thy words faithed?[13] No, what should I deny,
(As this I would, though thou didst produce
My very character)[14] I'd turn it all
To thy suggestion, plot, and damnèd practise.[15]
And thou must make a dullard of the world,[16]
If they not thought the profits of my death
Were very pregnant and potential spirits[17]
To make thee seek it."

(*Tucket*[18] *within.*)

GLOUCESTER. O strange and fastened[19] villain! Would he
deny his letter, said he? —Hark, the Duke's trumpets.
I know not wherefore he comes.
All ports I'll bar; the villain shall not scape.
The Duke must grant me that. Besides, his picture
I will send far and near, that all the kingdom
May have due note of him. And of my land—
Loyal and natural boy!—I'll work the means
To make thee capable.

(*Enter Cornwall, Regan, and Attendants.*)

CORNWALL. How now, my noble friend, since I came hither—
Which I can call but now—I have heard strangeness.

---

[1] *Mumbling ... mistress* Invoking black magic.

[2] *in fine* In short.

[3] *loathly opposite* Horrified and opposed.

[4] *fell* Lethal.

[5] *preparèd* Ready at hand.

[6] *charges home* Swings directly at.

[7] *latched* Nicked, cut.

[8] *best alarumed spirits* Best energies aroused by the prospect of battle.

[9] *gasted* Frightened by.

[10] *pight* Pitched, fixed.

[11] *cursed speech* Speech full of angry curses.

[12] *reposal* Investment.

[13] *If I ... faithed?* If I were to contradict you, do you think that any amount of virtue in you is going to be sufficient for anyone to believe your word against mine?

[14] *very character* Actual handwriting.

[15] *I'd ... practise* I'd make out that it was you that thought of it, planned it and did it.

[16] *thou must ... world* You must think the world stupid.

[17] *very pregnant ... spirits* Full and powerful motives.

[18] *Tucket* Flourish of trumpets.

[19] *strange and fastened* Unnatural and obstinate.

REGAN. If it be true, all vengeance comes too short
Which can pursue th' offender. How dost my Lord?
GLOUCESTER. O Madam, my old heart is cracked, it's cracked.
REGAN. What, did my father's godson seek your life?
He whom my father named, your Edgar?
GLOUCESTER. O Lady, Lady, shame would have it hid.
REGAN. Was he not companion with the riotous knights
That tended upon my father?
GLOUCESTER. I know not Madam. 'Tis too bad, too bad.
EDMUND. Yes, Madam; he was of that consort.
REGAN. No marvel then; though he were ill affected,[1]
'Tis they have put him on the old man's death,
To have th' expense[2] and waste of his revenues.
I have this present evening from my sister
Been well informed of them,[3] and with such cautions,
That if they come to sojourn at my house,
I'll not be there.
CORNWALL. Nor I, I assure thee Regan.
Edmund, I hear that you have shown your father
A child-like[4] office.
EDMUND. It was my duty, Sir.
GLOUCESTER. He did bewray his practise,[5] and received
This hurt you see, striving to apprehend him.
CORNWALL. Is he pursued?
GLOUCESTER. Aye, my good Lord.
CORNWALL. If he be taken, he shall never more
Be feared of doing harm. Make your own purpose
How in my strength you please.[6] For you, Edmund,
Whose virtue and obedience doth this instant
So much commend itself, you shall be ours.[7]
Natures of such deep trust, we shall much need;
You, we first seize on.
EDMUND. I shall serve you Sir,
Truly, however else.
GLOUCESTER. For him I thank your Grace.
CORNWALL. You know not why we came to visit you?
REGAN. —Thus out of season, threading dark-eyed night?[8]
Occasions, noble Gloucester, of some prize:
Wherein we must have use of your advice.
Our father he hath writ, so hath our sister,
Of differences,[9] which I best thought it fit
To answer from our home;[10] the several messengers
From hence attend dispatch.[11] Our good old friend,
Lay comforts to your bosom,[12] and bestow
Your needful counsel to our businesses,
Which craves the instant use.[13]
GLOUCESTER. I serve you Madam.
Your Graces are right welcome.

(*Exeunt. Flourish.*)

ACT 2, SCENE 2

(*Enter Kent, and [Oswald], severally.*)

OSWALD. Good dawning to thee, friend. Art of this house?[14]
KENT. Aye.
OSWALD. Where may we set our horses?
KENT. I'th' mire.
OSWALD. Prithee, if thou lov'st me, tell me.
KENT. I love thee not.
OSWALD. Why then I care not for thee.
KENT. If I had thee in Lipsbury pinfold,[15] I would make thee care for me.
OSWALD. Why do'st thou use me thus? I know thee not.

[1] *ill affected* Disposed to wickedness.

[2] *expense* Spending.

[3] *them* I.e., Lear's knights.

[4] *child-like* Appropriately filial.

[5] *bewray his practise* Expose Edgar's plot.

[6] *Make your … please* Do what you need to do, making as much use of my forces as you require.

[7] *ours* The "royal we" is being used.

[8] *threading … night* Finding our way through the darkness with difficulty (the metaphor is from threading the eye of a needle).

[9] *differences* Disagreements between them.

[10] *answer from our home* Reply to not from our own home but from elsewhere (Regan and Cornwall have left their home empty so they will not be obliged to host Lear and his retinue when they arrive).

[11] *attend dispatch* Await our instructions.

[12] *Lay … bosom* Console yourself.

[13] *Which … use* Which is needed immediately.

[14] *Art of this house?* Do you live here?

[15] *Lipsbury pinfold* A pinfold is a place in which stray animals are kept. Lipsbury appears to be a made up place name, though the word might be slang for "space between the lips," so that the sentence would mean: "If I had you between my teeth, I'd make you care."

KENT. Fellow I know thee.

OSWALD. What do'st thou know me for?

KENT. A knave, a rascal, an eater of broken meats;[1] a base, proud, shallow, beggarly, three-suited,[2] hundred-pound,[3] filthy worsted-stocking[4] knave; a lily-livered, action-taking,[5] whoreson, glass-gazing,[6] super-serviceable,[7] finical[8] rogue; one-trunk-inheriting[9] slave; one that would'st be a bawd in way of good service, and art nothing but the composition of a knave, beggar, coward, pander, and the son and heir of a mongrel bitch—one whom I will beat into clamorous whining, if thou deniest the least syllable of thy addition.[10]

OSWALD. Why, what a monstrous fellow art thou, thus to rail on one, that is neither known of thee, nor knows thee?

KENT. What a brazen-faced varlet art thou, to deny thou knowest me? Is it two days since I tripped up thy heels, and beat thee before the King? Draw, you rogue; for though it be night, yet the moon shines; I'll make a sop o' th' moonshine[11] of you! You whoreson cullionly barber-monger,[12] draw.

OSWALD. Away, I have nothing to do with thee.

KENT. Draw you rascal; you come with letters against the King, and take vanity-the-puppet's[13] part, against the royalty of her father! Draw, you rogue; or I'll so carbonado[14] your shanks—! Draw, you rascal; come your ways!

OSWALD. Help, ho, murder, help!

KENT. Strike, you slave! Stand, rogue; stand, you neat[15] slave, strike!

OSWALD. Help, hoa! Murder, murder!

(*Enter Bastard, Cornwall, Regan, Gloucester, Servants.*)

EDMUND. How now, what's the matter? Part.

KENT. With you[16] goodman boy,[17] if you please; come, I'll flesh[18] ye! Come on young master.

GLOUCESTER. Weapons? Arms? What's the matter here?

CORNWALL. Keep peace upon your lives.[19] He dies that strikes again. What is the matter?

REGAN. The messengers from our sister, and the King.

CORNWALL. What is your difference, speak?

OSWALD. I am scarce in breath, my Lord.

KENT. No marvel, you have so bestirred your valour, you cowardly rascal, nature disclaims in thee.[20] A tailor made thee.

CORNWALL. Thou art a strange fellow: a tailor make a man?

KENT. A tailor, Sir. A stone-cutter, or a painter, could not have made him so ill, though they had been but two years o'th' trade.

CORNWALL. Speak yet, how grew your quarrel?

OSWALD. This ancient ruffian, Sir, whose life I have spared at suit of his gray-beard—

KENT. Thou whoreson zed![21] Thou unnecessary letter! My Lord, if you will give me leave, I will tread this

---

[1] *broken meats* Left-overs.

[2] *three-suited* Serving men would be given three suits in a year.

[3] *hundred-pound* The price for which one could buy a knighthood at this time, implying that Oswald has purchased his position, and is not a born gentleman.

[4] *worsted-stocking* Cheap substitute for silk stockings.

[5] *action-taking* Inclined to resort to the law rather than to fight.

[6] *glass-gazing* Inclined to admire oneself in mirrors.

[7] *super-serviceable* Sycophantic.

[8] *finical* Overly fastidious.

[9] *one-trunk-inheriting* Owning only a trunkful of property.

[10] *addition* Titles just bestowed.

[11] *sop o' th' moonshine* Sponge to soak up the moonshine (because of the holes he will leave in Oswald's body).

[12] *cullionly barbermonger* Wretched, effeminate patron of barbershops. Barbers doubled as surgeons who could medicate you for venereal disease.

[13] *vanity-the-puppet* I.e., the part of Gonerill, here identified with a stock vain and selfish character seen in morality plays.

[14] *carbonado* Cut cross-wise (as meat before grilling).

[15] *neat* Unadulterated or foppish.

[16] *With you* Let's have you.

[17] *goodman boy* Peasant boy (contemptuously).

[18] *flesh* Let you smell blood (a term from hunting, when the hounds are allowed to smell a piece of meat).

[19] *upon your lives* I.e., or suffer the punishment of execution.

[20] *you have ... in thee* You have so overtaxed your courage that nature wants nothing to do with you.

[21] *zed* I.e., the last letter of the alphabet (US: zee), often left out of dictionaries at the time; superfluous non-entity.

unbolted[1] villain into mortar, and daub the wall of a jakes[2] with him. Spare my gray-beard, you wagtail?

CORNWALL. Peace, Sirrah!
You beastly knave, know you no reverence?

KENT. Yes, Sir, but anger hath a privilege.

CORNWALL. Why art thou angry?

KENT. That such a slave as this should wear a sword,
Who wears no honesty! Such smiling rogues as these—
Like rats oft bite the holy cords atwain,[3]
Which are too intrinced[4] unloose—smooth every passion
That in the natures of their lords rebel,[5]
Being oil to fire, snow to the colder moods,
Revenge, affirm, and turn their halcyon beaks[6]
With every gall,[7] and vary of their Masters,
Knowing naught (like dogs) but following.
(*To Oswald.*) A plague upon your epileptic[8] visage!
Smile you my speeches, as I were a fool?
Goose, if I had you upon Sarum Plain,
I'd drive ye cackling home to Camelot.[9]

CORNWALL. What art thou mad, old fellow?

GLOUCESTER. How fell you out, say that?

KENT. No contraries hold more antipathy
Than I, and such a knave.

CORNWALL. Why dost thou call him knave?
What is his fault?

KENT. His countenance likes me not.

CORNWALL. No more perchance does mine; not his, nor hers.

KENT. Sir, 'tis my occupation to be plain,
I have seen better faces in my time,
Than stands on any shoulder that I see
Before me, at this instant.

CORNWALL. This is some fellow,
Who having been praised for bluntness, doth affect
A saucy roughness,[10] and constrains the garb
Quite from his nature.[11] He cannot flatter, he!
An honest mind and plain; he must speak truth.
And they will take it so. If not, he's plain.
These kind of knaves I know, which in this plainness
Harbour more craft, and more corrupter ends,
Than twenty silly-ducking observants,[12]
That stretch their duties nicely.[13]

KENT. Sir, in good faith, in sincere verity,
Under th'allowance of your great aspect,
Whose influence, like the wreath of radiant fire
On flickering Phoebus' front—[14]

CORNWALL. What mean'st by this?

KENT. To go out of my dialect, which you discommend so much. I know, Sir—I am no flatterer—he that beguiled you in a plain accent, was a plain knave; which, for my part, I will not be, though I should win your displeasure to entreat me to't.[15]

CORNWALL. What was th'offence you gave him?

OSWALD. I never gave him any.
It pleased the King, his master, very late
To strike at me upon his misconstruction,[16]
When he (*Indicating Kent.*), compact,[17] and flattering his displeasure[18]

---

[1] *unbolted* Unsifted, unrefined, a pure villain.

[2] *jakes* Outdoor toilet.

[3] *holy cords atwain* Sacred bond in two.

[4] *intrinced* Entangled.

[5] *smooth ... rebel* Humor every foolish whimsical notion their masters have.

[6] *halcyon beaks* Those of the kingfisher, which was proverbially regarded as changeable; according to superstition, the kingfisher would serve as a weathervane when hung by its neck.

[7] *gall* Difficult moment.

[8] *epileptic* Contorted (presumably Oswald is moving through various expressions of incredulity, indignation and forced laughter).

[9] *Goose ... Camelot* Goose, presumably because of Oswald's cackling; *Sarum Plain* Salisbury Plain, the site of Stonehenge, which was associated with King Arthur because it was said to have been built by Merlin; *Camelot* Legendary home of King Arthur. Kent's threat appears to allude to some Arthurian legend which is now lost; the general idea is that he would thrash Oswald from one place to the next, thus knocking the foolishness out of him.

[10] *saucy roughness* Cheeky rudeness.

[11] *constrains the garb ... his nature* Keeps any cloak of civility away from him.

[12] *silly-ducking observants* Foolishly bowing attendants.

[13] *stretch ... nicely* Bend over backwards to be precise in their work.

[14] *Sir ... front* Kent assumes an absurdly flattering attitude to mock Cornwall's preference for servitude, identifying Cornwall with a planetary influence and with the sun itself.

[15] *I know ... me to't* I know, and will say so bluntly, that whoever it was that deceived you by putting on plain speech was simply a knave; that's something I won't be, even if you were made cross by trying to persuade me to take on that attitude.

[16] *upon his misconstruction* Because of his (Lear's) misunderstanding.

[17] *compact* In league (with the King).

[18] *flattering his displeasure* Playing to Lear's bad mood.

Tripped me behind; being down,[1] insulted, railed,
And put upon him such a deal of man,
That worthied him,[2] got praises of the King,
For him attempting who was self-subdued,[3]
And in the fleshment° of this dread exploit,[4] *excitement*
Drew on me here again.

KENT. None of these rogues and cowards
But Ajax is their fool.[5]

CORNWALL. Fetch forth the stocks.
You stubborn ancient knave; you reverend braggart,[6]
We'll teach you!

KENT. Sir, I am too old to learn:
Call not your stocks for me; I serve the King,
On whose employment I was sent to you.
You shall do small respects, show too bold malice
Against the grace and person of my master,
Stocking his messenger.

CORNWALL. Fetch forth the stocks.
As I have life and honour, there shall he sit till noon.

REGAN. Till noon? Till night, my Lord; and all night too.

KENT. Why Madam, if I were your father's dog,
You should not use me so.

REGAN. Sir, being his Knave, I will.

CORNWALL. This is a fellow of the self-same colour
Our sister speaks of.[7] Come, bring away the stocks.

(*Stocks brought out.*)

GLOUCESTER. Let me beseech your Grace not to do so.
The King his master, needs must take it ill
That he so slightly valued in his messenger,
Should have him thus restrained.[8]

CORNWALL. I'll answer that.

REGAN. My sister may receive it much more worse,
To have her gentleman abused, assaulted.

(*Kent is put in the stocks.*)

CORNWALL. (*To Gloucester.*) Come my Lord, away.

(*Exit [Cornwall and Regan].*)

GLOUCESTER. I am sorry for thee friend. 'Tis the
Duke's pleasure,
Whose disposition, all the world well knows,
Will not be rubbed[9] nor stopped. I'll entreat for thee.

KENT. Pray, do not, Sir. I have watched[10] and travelled
hard;
Some time I shall sleep out, the rest I'll whistle.
A good man's fortune may grow out at heels.[11]
Give you good morrow.

GLOUCESTER. The Duke's to blame in this.
'Twill be ill taken.

(*Exit.*)

KENT. Good King, that must approve the common
saw:° *saying, proverb*
Thou out of heaven's benediction com'st
To the warm sun.[12]
Approach thou beacon to this under globe,[13]
That by thy comfortable beams I may

---

[1] *being down* I.e., me being down.

[2] *put upon … worthied him* Acted like such a hero that he was regarded as being of great worth in the eyes of others.

[3] *For him … self-subdued* For overcoming someone who had put up no struggle.

[4] *dread exploit* Heroic deed (ironic).

[5] *None … fool* This sort of person inevitably plays upon and prevails with the Ajax type (the boastful idiot described in Homer's *Iliad*, implicitly compared here to Cornwall).

[6] *ancient … braggart* The thrust of Cornwall's name-calling lies in what he regards as the inappropriateness of Kent's insubordination to his advanced age.

[7] *This is … speaks of* This is the same sort of person that Gonerill complained of (i.e., Lear's followers).

[8] *Let me beseech … thus restrained* The equivalent speech in the Quarto version is several lines longer: "GLOUCESTER. Let me beseech your Grace not to do so. / His fault is much, and the good King his master / Will check him for't. Your purposed low correction / Is such as basest and damnest wretches for pilf'rings / And most common trespasses are punished with. / The King must take it ill, that he's so slightly valued / In his messenger; should have him thus restrained."

[9] *rubbed* Diverted (a term used in lawn bowling).

[10] *watched* Stayed awake.

[11] *A … heels* Even a good man has bad luck sometimes (as one's shoes must wear out).

[12] *Thou … sun* One has to leave good things and come to unpleasant things (the heat of the sun being regarded as an uncomfortable affliction).

[13] *Approach … globe* Rise, sun, and shine on the earth.

Peruse this letter. Nothing almost sees miracles
But misery.[1] I know 'tis from Cordelia,
Who hath most fortunately been informed
Of my obscured course;[2] and shall find time
From this enormous state, seeking to give
Losses their remedies.[3] All weary and o'er-watched.[4]
Take vantage, heavy eyes, not to behold
This shameful lodging.[5] Fortune, goodnight;
Smile once more, turn thy wheel.[6]

(*Sleeps.*)
(*Enter Edgar.*)[7]

EDGAR. I heard myself proclaimed,[8]
And by the happy° hollow of a tree, *lucky*
Escaped the hunt. No port is free; no place
That guard, and most unusual vigilance,
Does not attend my taking.[9] Whiles I may 'scape
I will preserve myself: and am bethought° *have decided*
To take the basest, and most poorest shape
That ever penury, in contempt of man,
Brought near to beast.[10] My face I'll grime with filth,
Blanket[11] my loins; elf all my hairs in knots,[12]
And with presented° nakedness out-face° *exposed / defy*
The winds, and persecutions of the sky.
The country gives me proof° and precedent *example*
Of Bedlam beggars who, with roaring voices,
Strike in their numbed and mortified arms
Pins, wooden-pricks, nails, sprigs of rosemary.
And with this horrible object,° from low farms, *spectacle*
Poor pelting° villages, sheep-cotes, and mills— *paltry*
Sometimes with lunatic bans,° sometime with *curses*
prayers—
Enforce their charity. "Poor Turlygod, poor Tom!"[13]
That's something yet. Edgar I nothing am.
(*Exit.*)

(*Enter Lear, Fool, and Gentleman.*)[14]

LEAR. 'Tis strange that they should so depart from home,
And not send back my messengers.[15]
GENTLEMAN. As I learned,
The night before, there was no purpose in them
Of this remove.[16]
KENT. Hail to thee, noble master.
LEAR. Ha? Maks't thou this shame thy pastime? [17]
KENT. No, my Lord.
FOOL. Ha, ha! He wears cruel garters![18] Horses are tied by the heads; dogs and bears by th'neck; monkeys by

---

[1] *Nothing ... misery* Only those who are miserable can see the possibility of miracles happening.

[2] *obscured course* Disguised journey.

[3] *shall find ... remedies* Shall take the time from the (French) affairs of state to come and remedy the problems here.

[4] *o'er-watched* Awake too long.

[5] *Take ... lodging* Take advantage of the opportunity presented by sleep not to have to look at these disgraceful circumstances in which I have been left.

[6] *Fortune ... wheel* Fortune was depicted as a goddess with a large wheel which represented the cyclical turns of a person's luck or misfortune.

[7] *Enter Edgar* Though many editions mark a new scene (Act 2, Scene 3) at this point, in the Folio there is no scene break; Kent, in stocks, is unable to leave the stage, so technically the scene is continuous. However, we are to understand that Edgar is at some distance from the place where Kent has been stocked.

[8] *proclaimed* I.e., publicly proclaimed an outlaw.

[9] *attend my taking* Wait to arrest me.

[10] *That ever ... beast* That poverty, in stripping away the veneer of civilization, has been able to use to demonstrate how close a human still is to an animal.

[11] *blanket* Cover only with a blanket.

[12] *elf ... knots* As mischievous elves were reputed to do, tangle the hair into matted lumps.

[13] *Poor ... Tom* Edgar is trying out the voice for his new character. The origin of the name Turlygod is unknown, and continues to be debated.

[14] *Enter ... Gentleman* Many editions mark a new scene (Act 2, Scene 4) as starting here, but in the Folio text there is no scene break. (As noted above, Kent remains onstage.)

[15] *'Tis ... messengers* I.e., Regan and Cornwall have left their own house to come to Gloucester's without sending Lear's messenger (Kent) back to tell him where they are so as to save him the journey.

[16] *there was ... remove* They did not declare any intention of making this move.

[17] *Maks't ... pastime* Is this shameful thing your idea of a game?

[18] *cruel garters* Pun on the cruelty of the stocks and on crewel (slack woolen yarn, worsted) stockings.

th'loins; and men by th'legs. When a man's over-lusty[1]
at legs, then he wears wooden nether-stocks.[2]

LEAR. What's he that hath so much thy place mistook[3]
To set thee here?

KENT. It is both he and she,
Your son and daughter.

LEAR. No.

KENT. Yes.

LEAR. No I say.

KENT. I say yea.

LEAR. By Jupiter, I swear no.

KENT. By Juno,[4] I swear aye.

LEAR. They durst not do't:
They could not, would not do't! 'Tis worse than murder,
To do upon respect such violent outrage!
Resolve me with all modest haste, which way
Thou might'st deserve, or they impose this usage,[5]
Coming from us.[6]

KENT. My Lord, when at their home
I did commend your Highness' letters to them.
Ere I was risen from the place, that showed
My duty kneeling, came there a reeking post,
Stewed in his haste,[7] half breathless, panting forth
From Gonerill, his mistress, salutations;
Delivered letters spite of intermission,° *without pausing*
Which presently they read. On those contents[8]
They summoned up their many, straight took horse,[9]
Commanded me to follow, and attend
The leisure of their answer;[10] gave me cold looks.
And meeting here the other messenger,
Whose welcome I perceived had poisoned mine,
Being the very fellow which of late
Displayed so saucily[11] against your Highness,
Having more man than wit[12] about me, drew.
He raised° the house, with loud and coward *aroused*
cries.
Your son and daughter found this trespass worth
The shame which here it suffers.

FOOL. Winter's not gone yet, if the wild geese fly that
way.[13]
Fathers that wear rags,
do make their children blind,[14]
But fathers that bear bags,[15]
shall see their children kind.
Fortune, that arrant whore,
ne'r turns the key[16] to th'poor.
But for all this thou shalt have as many dolours[17] for thy
daughters, as thou canst tell° in a year.[18] *count*

LEAR. Oh how this mother[19] swells up toward my heart!
Hysterica passio:[20] down thou climbing sorrow;
Thy element's below.[21] Where is this daughter?

KENT. With the Earl, Sir, here within.

LEAR. Follow me not, stay here.

(*Exit.*)

GENTLEMAN. Made you no more offence, but what you
speak of?

---

[1] *over-lusty* Irrepressibly active (either just physically or sexually).

[2] *nether-stocks* Pun on nether (lower) stockings (as opposed to upper stocks, or breeches).

[3] *thy place mistook* Misunderstood your rank (as the King's servant).

[4] *Jupiter/Juno* Chief Roman god, and his consort.

[5] *which way ... usage* What you have done to deserve, or what their reasons are for imposing.

[6] *Coming from us* I.e., given that you are my servant.

[7] *reeking ... haste* Perspiring messenger (Oswald), steaming in the sweat which his haste had produced.

[8] *On those contents* On the basis of what they had read.

[9] *straight took horse* Assembled their many followers and immediately mounted their horses.

[10] *attend ... answer* Wait until they were ready to reply.

[11] *Displayed so saucily* Showed off so insolently.

[12] *more man than wit* More manliness than sense.

[13] *Winter's ... way* If these acts are the signs we are to judge by (like geese flying south), more trouble is yet to come.

[14] *blind* I.e., to the needs of their fathers.

[15] *bags* I.e., of money.

[16] *turns the key* Opens the door.

[17] *dolours* Sorrows (with a pun on dollars).

[18] *Winter's not gone yet ... in a year* This speech does not appear in the Quarto version; Lear's line "Oh how this mother ..." follows directly after Kent's speech.

[19] *mother* Hysteria; the word is derived from the Greek *hysteria* (womb), which was thought to be mobile within the body and a physical source for feelings of hysteria, especially in women.

[20] *Hysterica passio* Medical term in the early seventeenth century for a feeling of rising panic and suffocation.

[21] *thy element's below* Your proper place is in the viscera (not climbing the throat and threatening to take hold of the mind).

KENT. None. How chance the King comes with so small a number?

FOOL. And[1] thou hadst been set i'th' stocks for that question, thoud'st well deserved it.

KENT. Why, Fool?

FOOL. We'll set thee to school to an ant,[2] to teach thee there's no labouring i'th' winter. All that follow their noses, are led by their eyes, but blind men; and there's not a nose among twenty, but can smell him that's stinking.[3] Let go thy hold when a great wheel runs down a hill, least it break thy neck with following; but the great one that goes upward, let him draw thee after.[4] When a wise man gives thee better counsel, give me mine again. I would ha' none but knaves use it, since a Fool gives it.

That Sir which serves and seeks for gain,
And follows but for form[5]
Will pack, when it begins to rain,
And leave thee in the storm.
But I will tarry, the Fool will stay,
And let the wise man fly.
The knave turns fool that runs away,
The Fool no knave perdy.[6]

KENT. Where learned you this, Fool?

FOOL. Not i'th' stocks, fool.

(*Enter Lear and Gloucester.*)

LEAR. Deny to speak with me? They are sick! They are weary!
They have travelled all the night? Mere fetches,[7]
The images of revolt and flying off.° *desertion*
Fetch me a better answer.

GLOUCESTER. My dear Lord,
You know the fiery quality of the Duke,
How unremovable and fixed he is
In his own course.

LEAR. Vengeance, plague, death, confusion!
"Fiery?" What quality? Why Gloucester, Gloucester!
I'd speak with the Duke of Cornwall and his wife.

GLOUCESTER. Well, my good Lord, I have informed them so.

LEAR. Informed them? Dost thou understand me, man?[8]

GLOUCESTER. Aye, my good Lord.

LEAR. The King would speak with Cornwall! The dear father
Would with his daughter speak; commands, tends service.[9]
Are they informed of this? My breath and blood!
Fiery? The fiery Duke! Tell the hot Duke that—
No, but not yet; maybe he is *not* well.
Infirmity doth still neglect all office,
Whereto our health is bound.[10] We are not ourselves,
When nature, being oppressed, commands the mind
To suffer with the body. I'll forbear,
And am fallen out with my more headier° will, *headstrong*
To take the indisposed and sickly fit
For the sound man.[11] (*Noticing Kent again.*)
Death on my state![12] Wherefore° *why*
Should he sit here? This act persuades me,
That this remotion° of the Duke and her *removal*
Is practise° only. Give me my servant forth! *stratagem*
Go tell the Duke and's wife I'd speak with them
Now, presently! Bid them come forth and hear me,

---

[1] *And* If.

[2] *set thee ... ant* Have an ant be your tutor. The allusion is to the ant and the grasshopper fable, wherein the ant labors through the summer and then has food in the winter. So Lear has failed to make prudent provision for his old age (his "winter").

[3] *All that ... stinking* Anyone who has eyes to see knows that Lear is in trouble, and even a blind man would know the smell of a corpse.

[4] *Let go ... after* Cynical summary of the opportunistic policy of most of Lear's followers: to latch onto winners and to abandon losers.

[5] *for form* Out of convention (rather than loyalty).

[6] *perdy* By God (from the French, *par Dieu*). The disloyal servant will be recognized as lacking in wisdom, but the fool, at least, will remain loyal in the eyes of God.

[7] *fetches* Deceptions, excuses (literally, a nautical term describing tacking away from the direct course).

[8] *Well my good Lord ... understand me, man?* These two short speeches do not appear in the Quarto version.

[9] *tends service* Waits to be served.

[10] *Infirmity ... bound* When we are sick, we neglect responsibilities that we would never think of neglecting when we are in health.

[11] *To take ... man* To assume that someone disabled by sickness has the same abilities as someone healthy.

[12] *Death on my state* May my royal power end (an oath similar to "I'll be damned").

Or at their chamber door I'll beat the drum,
Till it cry sleep to death![1]

GLOUCESTER. I would have all well betwixt you.

(*Exit.*)

LEAR. Oh me, my heart! My rising heart! But down.

FOOL. Cry to it, Nuncle, as the cockney did to the eels,[2] when she put 'em i'th'paste[3] alive. She knapped[4] 'em o'th'coxcombs[5] with a stick, and cried: "Down wantons,[6] down!" 'Twas her brother that, in pure kindness to his horse, buttered his hay.[7]

(*Enter Cornwall, Regan, Gloucester, Servants.*)

LEAR. Good morrow to you both.
CORNWALL. Hail to your Grace.

(*Kent here set at liberty.*)

REGAN. I am glad to see your Highness.
LEAR. Regan, I think you are. I know what reason
I have to think so. If thou should'st not be glad,
I would divorce me from thy mother's tomb—
Sepulch'ring an adulteress.[8] (*To Kent.*) O, are you free?
Some other time for that. — Belovèd Regan,
Thy sister's naught!° Oh Regan, she hath tied *wicked*
Sharp-toothed unkindness, like a vulture, here![9]
I can scarce speak to thee. Thou'lt not believe

[1] *cry sleep to death* I.e., Like a pack of hounds in pursuit of Sleep, intent on killing it.

[2] *as the cockney ... eels* This may be a reference to a story now lost. In the early seventeenth century "cockney" could mean "Londoner," "child," or "poor woman."

[3] *paste* Pastry.

[4] *knapped* Rapped.

[5] *coxcombs* Heads.

[6] *wantons* Naughty, playful things. The gist of the story is that the cockney woman, too squeamish to kill the eels before baking them, then fruitlessly attempts to scold them for their natural reaction, like Lear, who, having foolishly given his two selfish daughters power, now attempts to scold them into being kind to him.

[7] *'Twas ... hay* I.e., the foolish gesture was unappreciated, and aroused only ingratitude.

[8] *adulteress* I.e., because Regan could not be Lear's own child.

[9] *here* I.e., his chest.

With how depraved a quality° — Oh, Regan! *nature*
REGAN. I pray you, Sir, take patience. I have hope
You less know how to value her desert,
Than she to scant her duty.
LEAR. Say? How is that?
REGAN. I cannot think my sister in the least
Would fail her obligation. If, Sir, perchance
She have restrained the riots of your followers,
'Tis on such ground, and to such wholesome end,
As clears her from all blame.[10]
LEAR. My curses on her!
REGAN. O, Sir, you are old.
Nature in you stands on the very verge
Of his confine.[11] You should be ruled and led
By some discretion that discerns your state
Better than you yourself.[12] Therefore, I pray you,
That to our sister you do make return.
Say you have wronged her.
LEAR. Ask her forgiveness?
Do you but mark how this becomes the house:[13]
(*Kneeling.*) "Dear daughter, I confess that I am old;
Age is unnecessary: on my knees I beg,
That you'll vouchsafe me raiment,° bed, and food." *clothing*
REGAN. Good Sir, no more: these are unsightly tricks:
Return you to my sister.
LEAR. (*Rises.*) Never, Regan.
She hath abated° me of half my train; *cut off*
Looked black upon me, struck me with her tongue
Most serpent-like upon the very heart.
All the stored vengeances of heaven fall
On her ingrateful top!° Strike her young bones, *head*
You taking airs, with lameness.[14]
CORNWALL. Fie sir, fie.
LEAR. You nimble lightnings, dart your blinding flames
Into her scornful eyes! Infect her beauty,

[10] *Say? How is that? ... from all blame* These six lines do not appear in the Quarto version.

[11] *Nature ... confine* I.e., you cannot live much longer.

[12] *some ... yourself* Some discreet mind that understands your condition better than you do.

[13] *Do you ... the house* Just think how becoming that would be to my royal state.

[14] *Strike ... lameness* "Young bones" was a colloquial expression for "unborn child"; Lear is calling for her progeny to be struck with disease (causing lameness) by the infected air.

You fen-sucked fogs,[1] drawn by the powerful sun,
To fall, and blister.
REGAN. O the blest Gods!
So will you wish on me, when the rash mood is on.
LEAR. No, Regan, thou shalt never have my curse.
Thy tender-hearted nature shall not give
Thee o'er to harshness. Her eyes are fierce, but thine
Do comfort, and not burn. 'Tis not in thee
To grudge my pleasures, to cut off my train,
To bandy hasty words, to scant my sizes,[2]
And in conclusion, to oppose the bolt[3]
Against my coming in. Thou better know'st
The offices of nature,[4] bond of childhood,
Effects° of courtesy, dues of gratitude. *demonstrations*
Thy half o'th' kingdom hast thou not forgot,
Wherein I thee endowed.
REGAN. Good Sir, to'th' purpose.[5]

(*Tucket within.*)

LEAR. Who put my man i'th' stocks?

(*Enter [Oswald.]*)

CORNWALL. What trumpet's that?
REGAN. I know't, my sister's. This approves[6] her letter,
That she would soon be here. (*To Oswald.*) Is your Lady come?
LEAR. (*Of Oswald.*) This is a slave, whose easy borrowed[7] pride
Dwells in the sickly grace[8] of her he follows.
(*To Oswald.*) Out varlet, from my sight!
CORNWALL. What means your Grace?

(*Enter Gonerill.*)

LEAR. Who stocked my servant? Regan, I have good hope
Thou did'st not know on't.[9]—Who comes here? O, heavens,
If you do love old men; if your sweet sway
Allow[10] obedience; if you yourselves are old,
Make it your cause; send down, and take my part.
(*To Gonerill.*) Art not ashamed to look upon this beard?
O Regan, will you take her by the hand?
GONERILL. Why not by th'hand, Sir? How have I offended?
All's not offence that indiscretion finds,
And dotage terms so.[11]
LEAR. O sides, you are too tough!
Will you yet hold? —How came my man i'th'stocks?
CORNWALL. I set him there, Sir, but his own disorders[12]
Deserved much less advancement.[13]
LEAR. You? Did you?
REGAN. I pray you father, being weak, seem so.[14]
If, till the expiration of your month,
You will return and sojourn with my sister,
Dismissing half your train, come then to me.
I am now from home, and out of that provision
Which shall be needful for your entertainment.[15]
LEAR. Return to her? And fifty men dismissed?
No, rather I abjure all roofs, and choose
To wage against the enmity o'th'air,
To be a comrade with the wolf and owl—
Necessity's sharp pinch![16] Return with her?
Why, the hot-bloodied France, that dowerless took
Our youngest born: I could as well be brought

[1] *fen-sucked fogs* Fogs that have risen from noxious swamps.

[2] *scant my sizes* Reduce my allowances.

[3] *oppose the bolt* Bolt the door.

[4] *offices of nature* Natural obligations.

[5] *to'th' purpose* Come to the point.

[6] *approves* Confirms the content of.

[7] *easy borrowed* Facile and not earned.

[8] *sickly grace* Feeble favor.

[9] *Who stocked ... did'st not know on't* In the Quarto version almost identical lines are given to Gonerill rather than to Lear: "GONERILL. Who struck my servant? Regan I have good hope Thou didst no know on't. LEAR. Who comes here?"

[10] *If you ... Allow* If your authority approve of.

[11] *All's ... terms so* Not everything is offensive which the foolish and the senile call so.

[12] *disorders* Misbehaviors.

[13] *Deserved much less advancement* Deserved even worse.

[14] *being weak, seem so* I.e., don't pretend to a strength you no longer possess.

[15] *needful ... entertainment* Necessary to host you.

[16] *Necessity's ... pinch* The pain of not having enough.

To knee his[1] throne, and squire-like[2] pension beg,
To keep base life afoot![3] Return with her?
Persuade me rather to be slave and sumpter° *laborer*
To this detested groom. (*Indicates Oswald.*)
GONERILL. At your choice, Sir.
LEAR. I prithee, daughter do not make me mad.
I will not trouble thee, my child. Farewell.
We'll no more meet, no more see one another.
But yet thou art my flesh, my blood, my daughter—
Or rather a disease that's in my flesh,
Which I must needs call mine. Thou art a bile,
A plague sore, or embossèd carbuncle° *swollen boil*
In my corrupted blood. But I'll not chide thee.
Let shame come when it will, I do not call it.
I do not bid the thunder-bearer shoot,
Nor tell tales of thee to high-judging Jove.[4]
Mend when thou canst, be better at thy leisure.
I can be patient, I can stay with Regan,
I and my hundred knights.
REGAN. Not altogether so.
I looked not for you yet, nor am provided
For your fit welcome. Give ear, Sir, to my sister;
For those that mingle reason with your passion,[5]
Must be content to think you old, and so—
But she knows what she does.
LEAR. Is this well spoken?
REGAN. I dare avouch it, Sir. What, fifty followers?
Is it not well? What should you need of more?
Yea, or so many? Sith that both charge and danger[6]
Speak 'gainst so great a number? How, in one house,
Should many people under two commands
Hold amity?[7] 'Tis hard, almost impossible.
GONERILL. Why might not you, my Lord, receive attendance
From those that she calls servants, or from mine?
REGAN. Why not, my Lord? If, then, they chanced to slack ye,[8]
We could control them. If you will come to me—
For now I spy a danger[9]—I entreat you
To bring but five and twenty. To no more
Will I give place or notice.[10]
LEAR. I gave you all—
REGAN. And in good time you gave it.
LEAR. —Made you my guardians, my depositaries,° *trustees*
But kept a reservation[11] to be followed
With such a number. What, must I come to you
With five and twenty? Regan, said you so?
REGAN. And speak't again my Lord: no more with me.
LEAR. Those wicked creatures yet do look well favoured
When others are more wicked.[12] Not being the worst
Stands in some rank of praise. (*To Gonerill.*) I'll go with thee,
Thy fifty yet doth double five and twenty,
And thou art twice her love.
GONERILL. Hear me my Lord;
What need you five and twenty? Ten? Or five?
To follow in a house, where twice so many
Have a command to tend you?
REGAN. What need one?
LEAR. O, reason not the need! Our basest beggars
Are in the poorest thing superfluous.[13]
Allow not nature more than nature needs,
Man's life is cheap as beast's. Thou art a lady;
If only to go warm were gorgeous,
Why nature needs not what thou gorgeous wear'st,
Which scarcely keeps thee warm.[14] But for true need—
You heavens, give me that patience, patience I need!

[1] *knee his* Go on my knees before.

[2] *squire-like* As if I were his servant.

[3] *To … afoot* Just to keep my miserable life going.

[4] *high-judging Jove* Jupiter/Zeus, the chief god of the Greek and Roman pantheon, who judges from on high.

[5] *mingle … passion* I.e., take your emotional outbursts with a grain of salt.

[6] *Sith … danger* Since both the expense and the risks involved.

[7] *Hold amity* Remain friendly.

[8] *slack ye* Show you poor service.

[9] *For now … danger* For I now see that there is a risk (in what I had previously agreed to).

[10] *place or notice* Lodging or acknowledgment.

[11] *kept a reservation* Specified a condition.

[12] *Those … wicked* Even the wicked start to look good when others are worse.

[13] *Our … superfluous* Even the poorest person possesses some small thing that is beyond absolute necessity.

[14] *If only … warm* If being warm were your only concern, if that's what you thought gorgeous, then you would have no need of those gorgeous things you wear, which can hardly be said to keep you warm.

You see me here, you gods, a poor old man,
As full of grief as age, wretchèd in both.
If it be you that stirs these daughters' hearts
Against their father, fool me not so much[1]
To bear it tamely; touch me with noble anger,
And let not women's weapons, water drops,
Stain my man's cheeks. No, you unnatural hags,
I will have such revenges on you both,
That all the world shall— I will do such things—
What they are yet, I know not, but they shall be
The terrors of the earth! You think I'll weep.
No, I'll not weep! I have full cause of weeping,

(*Storm and tempest [is heard].*)[2]

But this heart shall break into a hundred thousand
flaws° *pieces*
Or ere[3] I'll weep! O, Fool, I shall go mad.

(*Exeunt [Lear, Gentleman, Kent and Fool].*)

CORNWALL. Let us withdraw; 'twill be a storm.
REGAN. This house is little, the old man and's people,
Cannot be well bestowed.° *lodged*
GONERILL. 'Tis his own blame hath put himself from
rest,
And must needs taste his folly.[4]
REGAN. For his particular,[5] I'll receive him gladly,
But not one follower.
GONERILL. So am I purposed.
Where is my Lord of Gloucester?

(*Enter Gloucester.*)

CORNWALL. Followed the old man forth; he is returned.
GLOUCESTER. The King is in high rage.
CORNWALL. Whether is he going?
GLOUCESTER. He calls to horse, but will I know not
whither.
CORNWALL. 'Tis best to give him way; he leads himself.[6]
GONERILL. My Lord, entreat him by no means to stay.
GLOUCESTER. Alack, the night comes on, and the high
winds
Do sorely ruffle.° For many miles about *threaten, agitate*
There's scarce a bush.
REGAN. O Sir, to willful men,
The injuries that they themselves procure,
Must be their schoolmasters. Shut up your doors,
He is attended with a desperate train,
And what they may incense him to, being apt
To have his ear abused,[7] wisdom bids fear.
CORNWALL. Shut up your doors, my Lord, 'tis a wild
night.
My Regan counsels well; come out o'th'storm.

(*Exeunt.*)

ACT 3, SCENE 1

(*Storm still.*[8] *Enter Kent, and a Gentleman, severally.*)

KENT. Who's there besides foul weather?
GENTLEMAN. One minded like the weather: most
unquietly.
KENT. I know you. Where's the King?
GENTLEMAN. Contending with the fretful elements;
Bids the wind blow the earth into the sea,
Or swell the curlèd waters 'bove the main,° *land*
That things might change, or cease.[9]
KENT. But who is with him?[10]

[1] *fool … much* Don't make me such a fool.

[2] *Storm and tempest* The two words now tend to be regarded as synonymous, but in the early seventeenth century "tempest" signified a more violent storm, including thunder and lightning; a "storm" might involve merely wind and rain, without any electrical activity.

[3] *Or ere* Before.

[4] *'Tis … folly* It's his own fault that he's so upset, and now he's going to have to suffer the consequences.

[5] *For his particular* As far as he himself is concerned.

[6] *leads himself* He'll have his own will.

[7] *being apt … abused* Being susceptible to the knights' perverse advice.

[8] *Storm still* Here the stage direction may simply be a note to the reader that the storm continues, but in subsequent appearances, it may be a surviving backstage direction to those who were providing the noise of the storm.

[9] *change or cease* Exchange places or end altogether (returning to chaos by reversing the process described in Genesis 1.1–10).

[10] *But who is with him?* An additional eight lines appear immediately before this line in the Quarto version.

GENTLEMAN. None but the Fool, who labours to out-jest
His heart-struck injuries.[1]
KENT. Sir, I do know you,
And dare, upon the warrant of my note
Commend a dear thing to you. There is division—
Although as yet the face of it is covered
With mutual cunning—'twixt Albany, and Cornwall,
Who have—as who have not, that their great stars
Throned and set high[2]—servants, who seem no less,[3]
Which are to France the spies and speculations[4]
Intelligent of our state. What hath been seen,
Either in snuffs and packings[5] of the Dukes,
Or the hard rein[6] which both of them hath borne
Against the old kind King—or something deeper,
Whereof, perchance, these are but furnishings—[7]
GENTLEMAN. I will talk further with you.[8]
KENT. No, do not.[9]
For confirmation that I am much more
Than my out-wall,[10] open this purse, and take
What it contains. If you shall see Cordelia—
As fear not but you shall—show her this ring,
And she will tell you who that fellow is
That yet you do not know.[11] Fie on this storm!
I will go seek the King.
GENTLEMAN. Give me your hand,
Have you no more to say?
KENT. Few words, but to effect more than all yet:[12]
That when[13] we have found the King. In which your pain[14]
That way, I'll this. He that first lights on° him, *sees*
Holla the other.

(*Exeunt.*)

ACT 3, Scene 2

(*Storm still. Enter Lear, and Fool.*)

LEAR. Blow, winds, and crack your cheeks! Rage, blow!
You cataracts and hurricanoes, spout
Till you have drenched our steeples; drown the cocks![15]
You sulph'rous and thought-executing fires,[16]
Vaunt-couriers[17] of oak-cleaving thunder-bolts,
Singe my white head. And thou, all-shaking thunder,
Strike flat the thick rotundity o'th' world!
Crack Nature's moulds, all germens[18] spill at once
That makes ingrateful man.
FOOL. O Nuncle, court holy-water in a dry house, is better than this rain-water out o' door.[19] Good Nuncle, in, ask thy daughters' blessing. Here's a night pities neither wisemen nor fools.

[1] *heart-struck injuries* Sufferings which have struck him to the heart.

[2] *as who ... set high* As who doesn't, who has been brought by their lucky stars into a state of great power.

[3] *who seem no less* Who look like ordinary servants.

[4] *speculations* What the modern military calls "intelligence advisors": those who, even in the absence of direct information, are able to offer informed speculation about the enemy.

[5] *snuffs and packings* Huffing (exchanging angry words) and plotting.

[6] *hard rein* Cruel treatment (a metaphor from horse-riding).

[7] *Who have ... furnishings* The equivalent passage in the Quarto version is longer and substantially different. In the Quarto version the French are said to have already landed: "With mutual cunning—'twixt Albany and Cornwall. / But true it is, from France there comes a power / Into this scattered kingdom, who already wise in our negligence, / Have secret feet in some of our best ports, / And are at point to show their open banner. / Now, to you: if on my credit you dare build so far / To make your speed to Dover, you shall find / Some that will thank you, making just report / Of how unnatural and bemadding sorrow / The King hath cause to 'plain. / I am a gentleman of blood and breeding, / And from some knowledge and assurance, / Offer this office to you."

[8] *I will talk further with you* Let's discuss this later.

[9] *No, do not* I.e., do not brush me off and assume you can talk to me later.

[10] *out-wall* Outward appearance.

[11] *who that fellow ... know* I.e., who I am.

[12] *to effect ... yet* More important in consequence than anything I have said thus far.

[13] *That when* That I will tell you when.

[14] *In which your pain* Towards the accomplishment of which, please take the trouble to go.

[15] *cocks* I.e., those on weather vanes.

[16] *thought-executing fires* Mind-numbing lightning.

[17] *Vaunt-couriers* Advance guard.

[18] *Nature's moulds* Forms Nature uses to make human beings; *germens* Seeds, life.

[19] *court holy water* Phrase used to describe flattery (because the blessings offered in court are so often empty of sincerity). The Fool suggests Lear might be better off being insincere.

LEAR. Rumble thy belly full; spit fire, spout rain!
Nor rain, wind, thunder, fire are my daughters;
I tax° not you, you elements, with unkindness. *accuse*
I never gave you kingdom, called you children;
You owe me no subscription.° Then let fall *allegiance*
Your horrible pleasure!° Here I stand, your slave: *will*
A poor, infirm, weak, and despised old man.
But yet I call you servile ministers,° *agents*
That will with two pernicious daughters join
Your high-engendered battles 'gainst a head
So old, and white as this! O, ho! 'Tis foul!

FOOL. He that has a house to put's head in, has a good head-piece.[1]

The codpiece[2] that will house[3]
before the head has any,
The head, and he shall louse:[4]
so beggars marry many.[5]
The man who makes his toe,
what he his heart should make,[6]
Shall of a corn cry woe,
and turn his sleep to wake.

For there was never yet fair woman, but she made mouths in a glass.[7]

(*Enter Kent.*)

LEAR. No, I will be the pattern of all patience;[8]
I will say nothing.

KENT. Who's there?

FOOL. Marry here's grace and a codpiece—that's a wiseman, and a fool.

KENT. Alas, Sir, are you here? Things that love night,
Love not such nights as these. The wrathful skies
Gallow° the very wanderers of the dark *terrify*
And make them keep their caves. Since I was man,
Such sheets of fire, such bursts of horrid thunder,
Such groans of roaring wind and rain, I never
Remember to have heard. Man's nature cannot carry
Th'affliction, nor the fear.

LEAR. Let the great goddess
That keep this dreadful pudder° o'er our heads, *racket*
Find out their enemies now. Tremble, thou wretch,
That hast within thee undivulgèd crimes
Unwhipped of[9] justice. Hide thee, thou bloody hand;
Thou perjured, and thou, simular° of virtue *counterfeit*
That art incestuous. Caitiff,° to pieces shake, *low wretch*
That under covert, and convenient seeming[10]
Has practised[11] on man's life. Close pent-up guilts,
Rive° your concealing continents,° *split / containers*
and cry
These dreadful summoners' grace.[12] I am a man
More sinned against, than sinning.

KENT. Alack, bare-headed?
Gracious my Lord, hard by here is a hovel,
Some friendship will it lend you 'gainst the tempest.
Repose you there, while I to this hard[13] house—
More harder than the stones whereof 'tis raised,
Which even but now, demanding after you,[14]
Denied me to come in—return, and force
Their scanted courtesy.

(*Exit.*)

LEAR. My wits begin to turn.
Come on, my boy. How dost my boy? Art cold?
I am cold myself. Where is this straw, my fellow?
The art of our necessities is strange,
And can make vile things precious. Come, your hovel;
Poor Fool and knave, I have one part in my heart
That's sorry yet for thee.

FOOL. (*Sings.*) He that has and a little tiny wit,
With heigh-ho, the wind and the rain,

[1] *head-piece* Pun on "helmet" and "brain."

[2] *codpiece* Often ostentatious covering for male genitals, sometimes, as here, standing for the penis itself.

[3] *house* Find a home (i.e., a vagina, etc.).

[4] *louse* Get a case of lice.

[5] *so ... many* In this way, the poor have many partners (the lice).

[6] *The man ... make* The man who mistakenly sets a higher premium on lesser concerns rather than focusing on what is most essential to him.

[7] *For there ... glass* I.e., vanity is a thing to which we are all prone.

[8] *No ... patience* Lear has resolved to bear his sufferings stoically rather than complain.

[9] *Unwhipped of* Unpunished by.

[10] *convenient seeming* Opportunistic deception.

[11] *practised* Plotted against.

[12] *cry ... grace* Call for mercy from the awful agents who summon you before heaven's court.

[13] *hard* I.e., hard-hearted.

[14] *demanding after you* Seeking to know if you were there.

Must make content with his fortunes fit,
Though the rain it raineth every day.[1]

LEAR. True, boy. Come, bring us to this hovel.

(*Exit.*)

FOOL. This is a brave night[2] to cool a courtesan.[3]
I'll speak a prophecy ere I go:
When priests are more in word than matter;
When brewers mar their malt with water;
When nobles are their tailors' tutors,
No heretics burned, but wenches' suitors;[4]
When every case in law is right;
No squire in debt, nor no poor knight;
When slanders do not live in tongues;
Nor cut-purses come not to throngs;
When usurers tell their gold i'th'field,
And bawds and whores do churches build,
Then shall the realm of Albion come to great confusion.
Then comes the time, who lives to see't,
That going shall be used with feet.[5]
This prophecy Merlin shall make, for I live before his time.

(*Exit.*)

ACT 3, SCENE 3

(*Enter Gloucester, and Edmund.*)

GLOUCESTER. Alack, alack, Edmund, I like not this unnatural dealing. When I desired their leave[6] that I might pity[7] him, they took from me the use of mine own house, charged me, on pain of perpetual displeasure, neither to speak of him, entreat for him, or any way sustain[8] him.

EDMUND. Most savage and unnatural.

GLOUCESTER. Go to; say you nothing. There is division between the Dukes, and a worse matter than that: I have received a letter this night—'Tis dangerous to be spoken; I have locked the letter in my closet. These injuries the King now bears, will be revenged home;[9] there is part of a power already footed.[10] We must incline to the King. I will look[11] him, and privily relieve[12] him. Go you and maintain talk with the Duke, that my charity be not of him perceived. If he ask for me, I am ill, and gone to bed. If I die for it—as no less is threatened me—the King my old master must be relieved. There is strange things toward,[13] Edmund; pray you, be careful.

(*Exit.*)

EDMUND. This courtesy forbid thee,[14] shall the Duke
Instantly know, and of that letter too.
This seems a fair deserving,[15] and must draw[16] me
That which my father loses: no less than all.
The younger rises when the old doth fall.

(*Exit.*)

ACT 3, SCENE 4

(*Enter Lear, Kent, and Fool. Storm still.*)

KENT. Here is the place,[17] my Lord. Good my Lord, enter;
The tyranny of the open night's too rough
For nature to endure.

LEAR. Let me alone.

[1] *He that … day* This song is derived from the song that Feste sings at the end of *Twelfth Night*. The lyrics are slightly different in Q and in F, but the meaning is substantially the same: for the person who has little reason, it is necessary to find contentment in whatever fortune brings, because misfortunes will come steadily.

[2] *brave night* Pun on "brave knight."

[3] *cool a courtesan* Bring a quick end to lascivious enthusiasm.

[4] *When … suitors* When priests are hypocrites, brewers water their beer, noblemen know more about clothes than tailors do, and the only people punished by "burning" are young men with syphilis.

[5] *going … feet* People will walk on their feet (obviously an absurd truism).

[6] *leave* Permission.

[7] *pity* Show pity towards.

[8] *sustain* Help.

[9] *home* To the utmost.

[10] *footed* Landed, or possibly only mobilized.

[11] *look* Seek.

[12] *privily relieve* Secretly assist.

[13] *toward* Coming.

[14] *forbid thee* Which you have already been forbidden to exercise.

[15] *fair deserving* Act likely to earn me favor.

[16] *draw* Win.

[17] *the place* The hovel spoken of in 3.2.

KENT. Good my Lord, enter here.
LEAR. Wilt break my heart?
KENT. I had rather break mine own. Good my Lord, enter.
LEAR. Thou think'st 'tis much that this contentious storm
Invades us to the skin; so 'tis to thee.
But where the greater malady is fixed,[1]
The lesser is scarce felt. Thou'dst shun a bear,
But if thy flight lay toward the roaring sea,
Thou'dst meet the bear i'th' mouth. When the mind's free[2]
The body's delicate. The tempest in my mind,
Doth from my senses take all feeling else,
Save what beats there: filial ingratitude.
Is it not as this mouth should tear this hand
For lifting food to't? But I will punish home—
No, I will weep no more! In such a night,
To shut me out? Pour on, I will endure!
In such a night as this?[3] O, Regan, Gonerill,
Your old kind father, whose frank heart gave all—
O, that way madness lies! Let me shun that;
No more of that.
KENT. Good my Lord, enter here.
LEAR. Prithee, go in thyself; seek thine own ease.
This tempest will not give me leave to ponder
On things would hurt me more— But I'll go in.
[*To Fool.*] In, boy, go first.
[*Begins to soliloquize.*]—You houseless poverty—
[*To others.*] Nay get thee in; I'll pray, and then I'll sleep.[4]

(*Exit [Fool].*)

—Poor naked wretches, wheresoe'er you are
That bide the pelting of this pitiless storm,
How shall your house-less heads, and unfed sides,
Your looped and windowed[5] raggedness defend you
From seasons such as these? O I have ta'en
Too little care of this. Take physic, pomp;[6]
Expose thyself to feel what wretches feel,
That thou mayst shake the superflux° to them, *excess*
And show the heavens more just.

(*Enter Edgar [disguised], and Fool.*)

EDGAR. Fathom and half,[7] fathom and half! Poor Tom!
FOOL. Come not in here, Nuncle; here's a spirit! Help me, help me!
KENT. Give my thy hand. Who's there?
FOOL. A spirit, a spirit! He says his name's Poor Tom.
KENT. What art thou that dost grumble there i'th' straw? Come forth.
EDGAR. Away, the foul fiend follows me. (*Sings.*) "Through the sharp hawthorn blow the winds—"[8]
Humh, go to thy bed and warm thee.
LEAR. Did'st thou give all to thy daughters? And art thou come to this?
EDGAR. Who gives anything to Poor Tom?—whom the foul fiend hath led through fire and through flame,[9] through sword, and whirlpool, o'er bog, and quagmire; that hath laid knives under his pillow, and halters[10] in his pew, set ratsbane[11] by his porridge, made him proud of heart, to ride on a bay trotting-horse over four-inched[12] bridges, to course[13] his own shadow for a traitor? Bless thy five wits,[14] Tom's a cold. (*Humming.*)

---

1 *fixed* Lodged in the mind.

2 *free* I.e., from care.

3 *But I will punish ... such a night as this* The Quarto version is at this point slightly shorter: "For lifting food to't? But I will punish sure—/ No! I will weep no more, in such a night as this! / O, Regan, Gonorill, your old kind father / Whose frank heart gave you all— / O, that way madness lies! Let me shun that; / No more of that."

4 *In, boy ... then I'll sleep* These lines do not appear in the Quarto version.

5 *looped and windowed* Loosely wrapped and full of holes.

6 *Take physic, pomp* Take this medicine, great ones.

7 *Fathom and half* Sailor's cry of the depth of water in a channel (presumably a comment on the rain).

8 *Through ... winds* Probably a line from a melancholy old song, though the source is unknown.

9 *fire and through flame* The redundancy suggests there may have been a compositor's error. The Quarto version has "ford" for "fire."

10 *halters* Nooses.

11 *ratsbane* Poison (along with the knives and halters, emblematic means by which the Devil was said to tempt a person to suicide).

12 *four-inched* Four inches wide (thus risking his life).

13 *course* To hunt down.

14 *Bless ... wits* Not to be confused with the five senses, the five wits were said to be common wit, imagination, fantasy, estimation, and memory. To have them disordered or disproportionate (i.e., unblessed) would effectively mean madness.

O, do de, do de, do de! Bless thee from whirlwinds, star-blasting,[1] and taking! Do poor Tom some charity, whom the foul fiend vexes. There could I have him now! And there! And there again! And there!

(*Storm still.*)

LEAR. Has his daughters brought him to this pass? Could'st thou save nothing? Would'st thou give 'em all?

FOOL. Nay, he reserved a blanket, else we had been all shamed.[2]

LEAR. Now all the plagues that, in the pendulous° air, *hanging*
Hang fated o'er men's faults, light on thy daughters!

Kent. He hath no daughters, Sir.

LEAR. Death, traitor! Nothing could have subdued nature
To such a lowness but his unkind daughters.
Is it the fashion, that discarded fathers,
Should have thus little mercy on their flesh?
Judicious punishment:[3] 'twas this flesh begot
Those pelican daughters.[4]

EDGAR. (*Sings.*) "Pillicock sat on Pillicock Hill: alow, alow, loo, loo."[5]

FOOL. This cold night will turn us all to fools and madmen.

EDGAR. Take heed o'th'foul fiend! Obey thy parents; keep thy word's justice;[6] swear not; commit not[7] with man's sworn spouse; set not thy sweet heart on proud array. Tom's a cold.

LEAR. What hast thou been?

EDGAR. A servingman? Proud in heart and mind; that curled my hair, wore gloves in my cap;[8] served the lust of my mistress' heart, and did the act of darkness with her; swore as many oaths as I spake words, and broke them in the sweet face of heaven. One that slept in the contriving of lust, and waked to do it. Wine loved I dearly, dice dearly; and in woman, out-paramoured the Turk.[9] False of heart, light of ear,[10] bloody of hand; hog in sloth, fox in stealth, wolf in greediness, dog in madness, lion in prey. Let not the creaking of shoes, nor the rustling of silks, betray thy poor heart to woman. Keep thy foot out of brothels, thy hand out of plackets,[11] thy pen from lenders' books,[12] and defy the foul fiend! (*Sings.*) "Still through the hawthorn blows the cold wind" says: (*Sings.*)

Suum, mun, nonny,
Dolphin[13] my boy;
Boy, sessa:[14] let him trot by.[15]

(*Storm still.*)

LEAR. Thou wert better in a grave, than to answer with thy uncovered body, this extremity of the skies. Is man no more than this? Consider him well. Thou ow'st the worm no silk; the beast, no hide; the sheep, no wool; the cat, no perfume.[16] Ha? Here's three on's[17] are sophisticated; thou art the thing itself. Unaccommodated man is no more but such a poor, bare, forked animal as thou art. (*Begins to remove his clothing.*) Off, off you lendings![18] Come, unbutton here.

(*Enter Gloucester with a torch.*)

---

1 *star-blasting* Unwholesome effects of malignant stars.

2 *shamed* Embarrassed (by his nakedness).

3 *Judicious punishment* (On second thought) a just punishment.

4 *pelican daughters* According to legend, the young of the pelican would feed by sucking blood directly from the breast of the parents.

5 *Pillicock ... loo* This song has survived in the somewhat altered form of a nursery rhyme known from the nineteenth century: "Pillicock, pillicock, sat on a hill / If he's not gone, he sits there still." The name is probably related to "pillock," slang for penis, also applied to a young boy and a fool.

6 *keep thy word's justice* Don't break your promises.

7 *commit not* I.e., adultery.

8 *gloves ... cap* A dandy's pledge to his mistress.

9 *out-paramoured the Turk* Had more lovers than a Turkish Sultan has concubines.

10 *light of ear* Ready to believe slander.

11 *plackets* Openings in the front of women's skirts.

12 *thy pen from lenders' books* Do not sign your name to money-lenders.

13 *Dolphin* The usual English version of the French *dauphin*, prince, here, apparently the name of a horse.

14 *sessa* Possibly "sa, sa!" an exhortation to a horse (like giddyup), possibly a corruption of the French "cessez."

15 In the Quarto version these three lines read as follows: Hey no nonny, / Dolphin my boy, my boy! / Cease, let him trot by.

16 *cat, no perfume* Civet perfumes are made from the anal glands of the civet cat (a creature found in Asia and Africa, related to the common cat, but more similar to the mongoose).

17 *on's* Of us.

18 *lendings* Borrowed clothes.

FOOL. Prithee, Nuncle, be contented; 'tis a naughty night to swim in. Now a little fire in a wild field were like an old lecher's heart: a small spark, all the rest on's[1] body, cold. Look, here comes a walking fire.

EDGAR. This is the foul Flibbertigibbet![2] He begins at curfew, and walks at first cock. He gives the web and the pin;[3] squints the eye, and makes the harelip; mildews the white wheat, and hurts the poor creature of earth.

S'withold footed thrice the old,[4]
He met the night mare, and her nine-fold;
Bid her alight, and her troth plight,
And aroint thee, witch, aroint thee![5]

KENT. How fares your Grace?
LEAR. What's he?
Kent. Who's there? What is't you seek?
GLOUCESTER. What are you there? Your names?

EDGAR. Poor Tom, that eats the swimming frog, the toad, the tadpole, the wall-newt[6] and the water; that, in the fury of his heart, when the foul fiend rages, eats cow-dung for sallets;[7] swallows the old rat and the ditch-dog;[8] drinks the green mantle[9] of the standing pool; who is whipped from tithing to tithing,[10] and stocked,[11] punished, and imprisoned; who hath three suits to his back, six shirts to his body—

Horse to ride, and weapon to wear:
But mice, and rats, and such small deer,[12]
Have been Tom's food for seven long year:

Beware my follower![13] Peace, Smulkin![14] Peace, thou fiend!

GLOUCESTER. (*To Lear.*) What, hath your Grace no better company?

EDGAR. The Prince of Darkness[15] is a gentleman. Modo he's called, and Mahu.[16]

GLOUCESTER. (*To Lear.*) Our flesh and blood, my Lord, is grown so vile, that it doth hate what gets it.[17]

EDGAR. Poor Tom's a cold.
GLOUCESTER. (*To Lear.*)
Go in with me; my duty cannot suffer° *allow me*
T'obey in all your daughters' hard commands:
Though their injunction be to bar my doors,
And let this tyrannous night take hold upon you,
Yet have I ventured to come seek you out,
And bring you where both fire and food is ready.
LEAR. First, let me talk with this philosopher.
(*To Edgar.*) What is the cause of thunder?
KENT. Good my Lord take his offer; go into th' house.
LEAR. I'll talk a word with this same learnèd
Theban.° *Greek*
(*To Edgar.*) What is your study?
EDGAR. How to prevent the fiend, and to kill vermin.
LEAR. Let me ask you one word in private.
KENT. Importune him once more to go, my Lord.
His wits begin t'unsettle.
GLOUCESTER. Canst thou blame him?
His daughters seek his death. Ah, that good Kent;
He said it would be thus. Poor banished man.
Thou sayest the King grows mad; I'll tell thee, friend
I am almost mad myself. I had a son,
Now outlawed from my blood:[18] he sought my life

---

[1] *on's* Of his.

[2] *Flibbertigibbet* Name of a devil, according to Elizabethan demonology.

[3] *web and the pin* Cataracts of the eye.

[4] *S'withold ... old* Saint Withold, a Saxon saint, was said to have walked three times across Britain, banishing demons, as is remembered in this rhyme.

[5] *night mare ... thee* The word "nightmare" originally denoted a monster from folklore known as the night mare (with "mare" deriving not from the word for female horse but from the Old Norse word for incubus, a demon that preyed on one during sleep). Here it appears that the night mare is imagined as a female demon mounted on a horse; Saint Withold forces her to dismount, together with her nine children, and swear allegiance to heaven, so that the witch is commanded to depart (aroint).

[6] *wall-newt* Lizard that inhabits a stone wall; *water* I.e., water newt.

[7] *sallets* Salads.

[8] *ditch-dog* Dead dog left in a ditch.

[9] *green mantle* Pond scum.

[10] *tithing* Rural district defined by ten families.

[11] *stocked* Put in stocks (as Kent had been).

[12] *small deer* Small game.

[13] *follower* Familiar, enslaved spirit.

[14] *Smulkin* Devil from Elizabethan demonology.

[15] *Prince of Darkness* The Devil (Edgar is directly contradicting Gloucester's suggestion that Lear is keeping poor company).

[16] *Modo ... Mahu* Devils from Elizabethan demonology, here spoken of by Edgar as if they were titled nobles.

[17] *Our flesh ... gets it* We have grown so debased as human beings that children hate their parents who begot them (Gloucester is consoling Lear with his shared misfortune, his betrayal—as he thinks—by Edgar).

[18] *outlawed ... blood* Disowned.

But lately, very late.° I loved him, friend— *recently*
No father his son dearer. True to tell thee,
The grief hath crazed my wits.

(*Storm still.*)

What a night's this?
I do beseech your grace.

LEAR. O, cry you mercy,[1] Sir.
Noble philosopher, your company.

EDGAR. Tom's a cold.

GLOUCESTER. In fellow there, into th' hovel; keep thee warm.

LEAR. Come, let's in all.

KENT. This way, my Lord.

LEAR. With him;
I will keep still with my philosopher.

KENT. Good my Lord, soothe him; let him take the fellow.

GLOUCESTER. Take him you on.° *with you*

KENT. Sirrah, come on. Go along with us.

LEAR. Come, good Athenian.[2]

GLOUCESTER. No words, no words, hush.

EDGAR. Child Rowland[3] to the dark tower came,
His word was still: "Fie, fo, and fum,
I smell the blood of a British man."[4]

(*Exeunt.*)

ACT 3, SCENE 5

(*Enter Cornwall and Edmund.*)

CORNWALL. I will have my revenge, ere I depart his house.

EDMUND. How, my Lord, I may be censured, that nature thus gives way to loyalty,[5] something fears me to think of.

CORNWALL. I now perceive, it was not altogether your brother's evil disposition made him seek his death, but a provoking merit set a-work by a reprovable badness in himself.[6]

EDMUND. How malicious is my fortune, that I must repent to be just? This is the letter which he spoke of, which approves him an intelligent party[7] to the advantages[8] of France. O, heavens! That this treason were not; or not I the detector.

CORNWALL. Go with me to the Duchess.

EDMUND. If the matter of this paper be certain, you have mighty business in hand.

CORNWALL. True or false, it hath made thee Earl of Gloucester. Seek out where thy father is, that he may be ready for our apprehension.

EDMUND. (*Aside.*) If I find him comforting the King, it will stuff his suspicion more fully.[9] I will persevere in my course of loyalty, though the conflict be sore between that and my blood.[10]

CORNWALL. I will lay trust upon thee; and thou shalt find a dear father in my love.

(*Exeunt.*)

---

[1] *cry you mercy* I beg your pardon. (In the Quarto version this line is addressed to Edgar, not to Gloucester.)

[2] *Athenian* I.e., because a Greek philosopher.

[3] *Child Rowland* Hero of the French medieval epic, *Chanson de Roland* ("Child" being the term used to denote a candidate for knighthood), and later stories and ballads.

[4] *Fie … man* The giant's lines from such tales as "Jack-and-the-Beanstalk," and "Jack the Giant-Killer." The juxtaposition of the two stories is incongruous, and helps indicate Edgar's "madness."

[5] *that nature … loyalty* That I have allowed my natural affections to be superseded by my loyalty to you.

[6] *it was … himself* It was not Edgar's wickedness that made him plot to kill Gloucester, but his good qualities, which were activated by the badness in Gloucester.

[7] *intelligent party* Spy.

[8] *to the advantages* In the service.

[9] *stuff his suspicion more fully* Make him more of a suspect.

[10] *though … blood* Though it is a great hardship to maintain my loyalty to you when it conflicts with my natural affection for my father.

ACT 3, SCENE 6
(FOLIO EDITION)

(*Enter Kent and Gloucester.*)

GLOUCESTER. Here[1] is better than the open air; take it thankfully. I will piece out the comfort with what addition I can. I will not be long from you.

KENT. All the power of his wits have given way to his impatience. The gods reward your kindness.

(*Exit Gloucester.*)
(*Enter Lear, Edgar and Fool.*)

parallel texts

EDGAR. Fraterretto[2] calls me, and tells me Nero[3] is an angler in the lake of darkness. Pray, innocent; and beware the foul fiend!

FOOL. Prithee, Nuncle, tell me whether a madman be a gentleman or a yeoman.

LEAR. A King, a King.

FOOL. No, he's a yeoman that has a gentleman to his[4] son; for he's a mad yeoman that sees his son a gentleman before him.

LEAR. To have a thousand with red burning spits
Come hissing in upon 'em![5]

[1] *Here* Apparently one of the outlying buildings on Gloucester's estate—likely imagined as a barn or stable.

[2] *Fraterretto* Shakespeare borrows names for his demons from accounts of exorcisms in Samuel Harsnett's *A Declaration of Egregious Popish Impostures (1603).*

[3] *Nero* Villainous Roman emperor. The gist seems to be that Edgar is aware that the tyrants are looking for victims.

[4] *to his* For a.

[5] *To have ... 'em* Lear is evidently fantasizing about a legion of devils punishing his daughters in the after-life.

(QUARTO EDITION)

(*Enter Gloucester, Lear, Kent, Fool, and [Edgar, still disguised as] Tom.*)

GLOUCESTER. Here is better than the open air; take it thankfully. I will piece out the comfort with what addition I can. I will not be long from you.

KENT. All the power of his wits have given way to impatience. The gods deserve your kindness.

(*Exit Gloucester.*)

EDGAR. Frateretto calls me, and tells me Nero is an angler in the lake of darkness. Pray, innocent, beware the foul fiend.

FOOL. Prithee, Nuncle, tell me whether a madman be a gentleman or a yeoman.

LEAR. A King, a King, to have a thousand with red burning spits come hissing in upon them.

EDGAR. The foul fiend bites my back.

FOOL. He's mad, that trusts in the tameness of a wolf, a horse's health, a boy's love, or a whore's oath.

LEAR. It shall be done; I will arraign them straight. (*To Edgar.*) Come sit, thou here, most learned justice. (*To Fool.*) Thou, sapient[6] sir, sit here. (*To his imaginary daughters.)*—No, you she-foxes—!

EDGAR. (*To the imaginary daughters.*) Look where he stands and glares. Want'st thou eyes?[7] At trial,[8] madam! "Come o'er the broom, Bessy, to me."[9]

FOOL. (*Sings.*)

Her boat hath a leak,
And she must not speak,
Why she dares not come over to thee.[10]

[6] *sapient* Wise.

[7] *Want'st thou eyes?* Are you blind?

[8] *At trial* Take your place in the defence stand.

[9] *Come ... to me* Edgar quotes a line altered from an old song, "Come over the bourn (stream), Bessy, to me," here presumably adjusted to suit their location, in which we may imagine straw (broom) on the floor.

[10] *Her boat ... thee* The Fool joins in by parodying the song in reply.

EDGAR. The foul fiend haunts poor Tom in the voice of a nightingale. Hoppedance[1] cries in Tom's belly for two white herring. Croak[2] not, black angel, I have no food for thee.

KENT. (*To Lear.*) How do you sir? Stand you not so amazed.
Will you lie down and rest upon the cushions?

LEAR. I'll see their trial first. Bring in their evidence.
(*To Edgar.*) Thou robèd man of justice, take thy place.
(*To Fool.*) And thou, his yokefellow[3] of equity,
Bench by his side. (*To Kent.*) You are o'th' commission,
Sit you, too.

EDGAR. Let us deal justly.
(*Sings.*) Sleepest or wakest, thou jolly shepherd?
Thy sheep be in the corn,
And for[4] one blast of thy minikin mouth,[5]
Thy sheep shall take no harm.[6]
Purr[7] the cat is gray.

LEAR. (*Indicating a stool.*) Arraign her first. 'Tis Gonorill. I here take my oath before this honourable assembly, she kicked the poor king her father.

FOOL. Come hither, mistress. Is your name Gonorill?

LEAR. She cannot deny it.

FOOL. Cry you mercy, I took you for a join stool.[8]

LEAR. And here's another whose warped looks proclaim

parallel texts

[1] *Hoppedance* Another name of a demon taken from Harsnett.

[2] *Croak* Sound of a demon, and of the growling of a stomach.

[3] *yokefellow* Partner.

[4] *for* In exchange for you making.

[5] *minikin* Shrill.

[6] *Sleepest … harm* Variation on the nursery rhyme: "Little Boy Blue, come blow your horn / The sheep's in the meadow, the cow's in the corn. / But where is the boy who looks after the sheep? / He's under a haystack, fast asleep."

[7] *Purr* A pun: the name of a devil drawn from Elizabethan demonology, and also the sound a cat makes.

[8] *join stool* Stool made of jointed pieces of wood. "I took you for a join stool" was a common jocular way of claiming not to have noticed someone.

parallel texts

EDGAR. Bless thy five wits.
KENT. O, pity! Sir, where is the patience now
That you so oft have boasted to retain?
EDGAR. (*Aside.*) My tears begin to take his part so much,
They mar my counterfeiting.[1]
LEAR. The little dogs, and all—
Trey, Blanch, and Sweetheart—see, they bark at me.
EDGAR. Tom will throw his head[2] at them.—Avaunt you curs!

Be thy mouth or black or white,
Tooth that poisons if it bite:
Mastiff, grey-hound, mongrel, grim,
Hound or spaniel, brach° or him,° *bitch / male*
Or bobtail tight, or trundle tail,[3]
Tom will make him weep and wail,
For with throwing thus my head;
Dogs leapt the hatch, and all are fled.

Do, de, de, de! Sesa![4] Come, march to wakes and fairs and market towns. Poor Tom, thy horn[5] is dry.

LEAR. Then let them anatomize[6] Regan; see what breeds about her heart. Is there any cause in nature that makes these hard-hearts? (*To Edgar.*) You sir, I entertain for one of my hundred; only I do not like the fashion of your garments. You will say they are Persian;[7] but let them be changed.

(*Enter Gloucester.*)

KENT. (*To Lear.*) Now good my Lord, lie here and rest awhile.

What store her heart is made on.[8] Stop her there!
Arms, arms, sword, fire, corruption in the place!
False justicer,[9] why hast thou let her 'scape?
EDGAR. Bless thy five wits.
KENT. O, pity! Sir, where is the patience now
That you so oft have boasted to retain.
EDGAR. (*Aside.*) My tears begin to take his part so much,
They'll mar my counterfeiting.
LEAR. The little dogs and all—Trey, Blanch, and Sweetheart—see, they bark at me.
EDGAR. Tom will throw his head at them.—Avaunt, you curs!

Be thy mouth or black or white,
Tooth that poisons if it bite,
Mastiff, greyhound, mongrel grim
Hound or spaniel, brach or him,
Bobtail tyke, or trundle-tail,
Tom will make them weep and wail,
For with throwing thus my head,
Dogs leap the hatch and all are fled!

Loudla doodla![10] Come march to wakes and fairs, and market towns! Poor Tom, thy horn is dry.

LEAR. Then let them anatomize Regan; see what breeds about her heart. Is there any cause in nature that makes this hardness? (*To Edgar.*) You sir, I entertain you for one of my hundred. Only I do not like the fashion of your garments. You'll say they are Persian attire; but let them be changed.

KENT. Now good my Lord, lie here awhile.

---

[1] *mar my counterfeiting* Make it difficult to keep up the deception.

[2] *throw his head* Meet their aggression with his own (throwing his head forward as an aggressive dog does).

[3] *Bobtail … tail* Short-tailed or long-tailed.

[4] *Do, de, de, de! Sesa!* Presumably the sound is an imitation of a trumpet used to announce a public attraction with a following shout to the horses as they set off on their imaginary tour.

[5] *horn* Hollowed out horns were often hung about the necks of Bedlam beggars and used as cheap vessels for water.

[6] *anatomize* Dissect.

[7] *Persian* Persians were known for their elaborate and exotic finery (ironic).

[8] *whose … made on* Whose wicked expression shows the material her heart is made out of.

[9] *justicer* Judge.

[10] *Loudla doodla* Presumably an imitation of a trumpet used to announce a public attraction.

LEAR. Make no noise, make no noise, draw the curtains:[1] so, so.
We'll go to supper i'th' morning.
FOOL. And I'll go to bed at noon.

GLOUCESTER. Come hither, friend. Where is the King my master?
KENT. Here Sir, but trouble him not. His wits are gone.
GLOUCESTER. Good friend, I prithee take him in thy arms;
I have o'er-heard a plot of death upon him.
There is a litter[2] ready; lay him in't,
And drive toward Dover, friend, where thou shalt meet
Both welcome, and protection. Take up thy master,
If thou should'st dally half an hour, his life
With thine, and all that[3] offer to defend him,
Stand in assurèd loss. Take up, take up,
And follow me, that will to some provision° *supplies*
Give thee quick conduct.

Come, come away.

(*Exeunt.*)

[1] *curtains* Presumably imaginary.

[2] *litter* Mobile couch enclosed with curtains.

[3] *and all that* And the lives of all those who.

LEAR. Make no noise, make no noise. Draw the curtains.
So, so, so. We'll go to supper i'th morning. So, so, so.

(*Enter Gloucester.*)

GLOUCESTER. Come hither, friend. Where is the King my master?
KENT. Here sir, but trouble him not. His wits are gone.
GLOUCESTER. Good friend, I prithee, take him in thy arms.
I have o'erheard a plot of death upon him.
There is a litter ready; lay him it't.
And drive towards Dover, friend, where thou shalt meet
Both welcome and protection. Take up thy master.
If thou should'st daily half an hour, his life
With thine, and all that offer to defend him.
Stand in assurèd loss. Take up the King
And follow me, that will to some provision
Give thee quick conduct.
KENT. Oppressèd nature sleeps.
This rest might yet have balmed° thy broken sinews,[4] *healed*
Which, if convenience will not allow, stand in hard cure.[5]
(*To Fool.*) Come, help to bear thy master. Thou must not stay behind.
GLOUCESTER. Come, come away.

(*Exit [Lear, Kent, Gloucester and the Fool].*)

EDGAR. When we our betters see bearing our woes,
We scarcely think our miseries our foes.[6]
Who alone suffers, suffers most i'th' mind,
Leaving free things and happy shows behind.[7]
But then the mind much sufferance doth o'erskip
When grief hath mates; and bearing fellowship,
How light and portable my pain seems now,

[4] *broken sinews* Figuratively, shattered nerves.

[5] *stand … cure* Will be hard to cure.

[6] *When … foes* It is so upsetting to see our superiors suffer that we begin to forget our own misfortunes.

[7] *free* Carefree; *happy shows* Displays of happiness; *Who … behind* The worst thing about suffering alone is the mental anguish at having left behind ordinary happiness (that others still enjoy).

When that which makes me bend, makes the King bow.[2]
He childed as I fathered. Tom, away:[3]
Mark the high noises[4] and thyself bewray° *reveal*
When false opinion, whose wrong
thoughts° defile thee, *misconceptions*
In thy just proof repeals and reconciles thee.[5]
What will hap more tonight, safe 'scape the King.[6]
Lurk, lurk.

(*Exit.*)

ACT 3, SCENE 7

(*Enter Cornwall, Regan, Gonerill, Bastard, and Servants.*)

CORNWALL. (*To Gonerill.*) Post speedily to my Lord your husband; show him this letter. The army of France is landed. (*To Servants.*) Seek out the traitor Gloucester.

(*Exeunt some servants.*)

REGAN. Hang him instantly.
GONERILL. Pluck out his eyes.
CORNWALL. Leave him to my displeasure. Edmund, keep you our sister company: the revenges we are bound to take upon your traitorous Father, are not fit for your beholding. Advise the Duke where you are going—to a most festinate[1] preparation. We are bound to the like. Our posts shall be swift and intelligent betwixt us. (*To Gonerill.*) Farewell, dear sister. (*To Bastard.*) Farewell, my Lord of Gloucester.

(*Enter [Oswald, the] Steward.*)

How now? Where's the King?
OSWALD. My Lord of Gloucester hath conveyed him hence.
Some five or six and thirty of his knights,
Hot questrists° after him, met him at gate, *seekers*
Who, with some other of the Lord's dependents,[7]
Are gone with him toward Dover, where they boast
To have well armed friends.
CORNWALL. Get horses for your Mistress.

---

[1] *festinate* Hasty.

[2] *But ... bow* But suffering is much lessened when misery has company, and now that I'm no longer alone, I find my own suffering much easier to bear, by seeing how much more deeply affected the King is by his own troubles.

[3] *He childed ... fathered* I.e., he had children who now seek his death, as I have a father who now seeks mine.

[4] *Mark the high noises* Keep your eye on the brewing problems amongst those in power (i.e., Gonorill and Regan and their husbands).

[5] *In thy ... thee* In proving your true innocence, ends your sentence of banishment and reconciles you to your father.

[6] *What ... King* Whatever else happens, may the King escape safely.

[7] *Lord's dependents* Gloucester's attendants.

(*Exit Oswald.*)

GONERILL. Farewell sweet Lord, and Sister.

(*Exit [Gonerill and Edmund].*)

CORNWALL. Edmund, farewell. (*To Servants.*) Go seek the traitor Gloucester.
Pinion him like a thief; bring him before us.

(*Exit Servants.*)

Though well we may not pass upon his life
Without the form of justice, yet our power
Shall do a court'sy to our wrath, which men
May blame, but not control.

(*Enter Gloucester [brought in by] Servants.*)

Who's there? The traitor?
REGAN. Ingrateful fox, 'tis he.
CORNWALL. (*To Servants.*) Bind fast his corky[1] arms.
GLOUCESTER. What means your Graces?
Good my friends, consider: you are my guests!
Do me no foul play, friends.
CORNWALL. (*To Servants.*) Bind him, I say.
REGAN. Hard, hard! O, filthy traitor.
GLOUCESTER. Unmerciful lady, as you are,[2] I'm none.
CORNWALL. (*To Servants.*) To this chair bind him.
Villain, thou shalt find—

(*Regan plucks Gloucester's beard.*)

GLOUCESTER. By the kind gods, 'tis most ignobly done
To pluck me by the beard.
REGAN. So white, and such a traitor?
GLOUCESTER. Naughty[3] lady,
These hairs which thou dost ravish from my chin
Will quicken[4] and accuse thee. I am your host.
With robbers' hands my hospitable favours
You should not ruffle thus. What will you do?
CORNWALL. Come, Sir: what letters had you late from France?
REGAN. Be simple answered,[5] for we know the truth.
CORNWALL. And what confederacy have you with the traitors
Late footed[6] in the kingdom?
REGAN. To whose hands
You have sent the lunatic King? Speak.
GLOUCESTER. I have a letter guessingly set down[7]
Which came from one that's of a neutral heart,
And not from one opposed.
CORNWALL. Cunning.
REGAN. And false.
CORNWALL. Where hast thou sent the King?
GLOUCESTER. To Dover.
REGAN. Wherefore to Dover? Wast thou not charged,[8] at peril—[9]
CORNWALL. Wherefore to Dover? Let him answer that.
GLOUCESTER. I am tied to'th'stake, and I must stand the course.[10]
REGAN. Wherefore to Dover?
GLOUCESTER. Because I would not see thy cruel nails
Pluck out his poor old eyes, nor thy fierce sister,
In his anointed[11] flesh, stick boarish fangs!
The sea, with such a storm as his bare head,
In hell-black night endured, would have buoyed up
And quenched the stellèd° fires. *starry*
Yet poor old heart, he holp° the heavens to rain.[12] *helped*
If wolves had at thy gate howled that stern time,
Thou should'st have said "Good porter, turn the key."

---

[1] *corky* Dry (because old).

[2] *as you are* I.e., a traitor.

[3] *Naughty* Evil (the word "naughty" did not have then the playful connotation it has now).

[4] *quicken* Come to life.

[5] *Be simple answered* Answer straightforwardly.

[6] *late footed* Who have recently gained a foothold.

[7] *guessingly set down* Written speculatively.

[8] *charged* Ordered.

[9] *at peril* On peril (of losing your life).

[10] *stand the course* Endure the assaults to come.

[11] *anointed* Consecrated. Kings and Queens of England were anointed with holy oil at their coronations as a sign that they were sanctified by God as lawful rulers.

[12] *he holp the heavens to rain* The Quarto version here reads, "he helped the heavens to rage."

All cruels else subscribe;[1] but I shall see
The wingèd[2] vengeance overtake such children.
CORNWALL. See't shalt thou never. (*To Servants.*) Fellows, hold the chair.
(*To Gloucester.*) Upon these eyes of thine, I'll set my foot.
GLOUCESTER. He that will think to live, till he be old,
Give me some help!

(*Cornwall forces out one of Gloucester's eyes.*)

—O, cruel! O, ye gods!
REGAN. One side will mock another: Th' other too.
CORNWALL. (*To Gloucester.*)
If you see vengeance—
SERVANT. Hold your hand, my Lord:
I have served you ever since I was a child;
But better service have I never done you,
Than now to bid you hold.
REGAN. How now, you dog?
SERVANT. If you did wear a beard upon your chin,
I'd shake it on this quarrel.[3] (*To Cornwall.*) What do you mean?
CORNWALL. My villain?
SERVANT. Nay then, come on, and take the chance of anger.

(*They begin to fight; Cornwall is wounded.*)

REGAN. (*To another Servant.*) Give me thy sword. A peasant stand up thus?

(*Kills him.*)

SERVANT. Oh, I am slain! (*To Gloucester.*) My Lord, you have one eye left
To see some mischief on him. Oh.

(*He dies.*)

CORNWALL. Lest it see more, prevent it. Out, vile jelly.
(*He forces out Gloucester's other eye.*) Where is thy luster now?
GLOUCESTER. All dark and comfortless? Where's my son Edmund?
Edmund, enkindle all the sparks of nature
To quit this horrid act.
REGAN. Out, treacherous villain!
Thou call'st on him that hates thee. It was he
That made the overture of thy treasons to us,
Who is too good to pity thee.
GLOUCESTER. O, my follies! Then Edgar was abused,
Kind Gods, forgive me that, and prosper him.
REGAN. (*To Servants.*) Go thrust him out at gates, and let him smell
His way to Dover.

(*Exit [Servants] with Gloucester.*)

How is't my Lord? How look you?
CORNWALL. I have received a hurt. Follow me, Lady.
Turn out that eyeless villain. Throw this slave
Upon the dunghill. Regan, I bleed apace,
Untimely comes this hurt. Give me your arm.[4]

(*Exeunt.*)

[1] *All cruels else subscribe* All other cruelties tolerate. (Gloucester addresses the heavens.)

[2] *wingèd* I.e., that of Furies, whose assigned role included the punishing of ill-behaved children, as well as those who damaged familial bonds.

[3] *If you … quarrel* If you were a man, I'd challenge you to a duel.

[4] *Give me your arm* Following this line in the Quarto version, the scene concludes with an exchange between two servants, who have remained on the stage: "Untimely comes this hurt. Give me your arm. / (*Exit [Cornwall and Regan]*.) / 2nd SERVANT. I'll never care what wickedness I do, / If this man come to good.
3rd SERVANT. If she live long, / And in the end meet the old course of death, / Women will all turn monsters.
2nd SERVANT. Let's follow the old Earl, and get the bedlam / To lead him where he would. His roguish madness / Allows itself to anything.
3rd SERVANT. Go thou; I'll fetch some flax and whites of eggs / To apply to his bleeding face. Now heaven help him / (*Exeunt*)."

ACT 4, SCENE 1

(*Enter Edgar.*)

EDGAR. Yet better thus, and known to be condemned,
Than still condemned and flattered.[1] To be worst,
The lowest and most dejected thing of Fortune,
Stands still in esperance, lives not in fear.[2]
The lamentable change is from the best;
The worst returns to laughter.[3] Welcome then,
Thou unsubstantial air that I embrace;
The wretch that thou hast blown unto the worst,
Owes nothing to thy blasts.[4]

(*Enter Gloucester and an Old Man.*)

But who comes here?
My father, poorly[5] led? World, world, O world![6]
But that thy strange mutations make us hate thee,
Life would not yield to age.[7]
OLD MAN. O, my good Lord, I have been your tenant,
And your father's tenant, these fourscore years.
GLOUCESTER. Away, get thee away. Good friend, be gone.
Thy comforts can do me no good at all,
Thee, they may hurt.
OLD MAN. You cannot see your way.
GLOUCESTER. I have no way, and therefore want no eyes;
I stumbled when I saw. Full oft, 'tis seen,
Our means secure us, and our mere defects
Prove our commodities.[8] Oh, dear son Edgar—
The food[9] of thy abusèd father's wrath:
Might I but live to see thee in my touch,
I'd say I had eyes again.
OLD MAN. How now? who's there?
EDGAR. (*Aside.*) O gods! Who is't can say I am at the worst?
I am worse than e'er I was.
OLD MAN. 'Tis poor mad Tom.
EDGAR. (*Aside.*) And worse I may be yet; the worst is not,
So long as we can say: "This is the worst."
OLD MAN. Fellow, where goest?
GLOUCESTER. Is it a beggar-man?
OLD MAN. Madman, and beggar too.
GLOUCESTER. He has some reason, else he could not beg.
I'th'last night's storm I such a fellow saw;
Which made me think a man a worm. My son
Came then into my mind, and yet my mind
Was then scarce friends with him. I have heard more since.
As flies to wanton boys, are we to th'gods,
They kill us for their sport.
EDGAR. (*Aside.*) How should this be?[10]
Bad is the trade[11] that must play fool to sorrow,
Ang'ring itself and others. (*To Old Man.*) Bless thee, master.
GLOUCESTER. Is that the naked fellow?
OLD MAN. Aye, my Lord.

---

[1] *better … flattered* Better to be a despised madman and beggar and know it than to be secretly despised yet openly flattered.

[2] *Stands … fear* Still exists within the realm of hope (*esperance*: French for hope) yet with no more fear of things becoming worse.

[3] *The lamentable … laughter* The change to be lamented is descending from good fortune to bad; once one is at bottom, one can look forward to laughing again.

[4] *The wretch … blasts* Because it has caused nothing but harm to him, Edgar owes the air no debt of gratitude.

[5] *poorly* By a poor person.

[6] *Welcome then … O world!* In the Quarto version Gloucester and the Old Man do not enter until after Edgar's speech, which is at this point somewhat different and shorter: "The worst returns to laughter. / Who's here? / My father, parti-eyed? World, world, O world!"

[7] *But that … age* Were it not that the grotesque changes of the world make us hate it, we would not succumb to death in our old age.

[8] *Our means … commodities* Our livelihood gives us a false sense of security, whereas our simple defects turn out to be to our advantage.

[9] *food* I.e., the object on which Gloucester's wrath nourished itself.

[10] *How should this be* How is this to be done? (I.e., playing the part of Poor Tom under these circumstances.)

[11] *trade* Line of work (i.e., pretending to be Poor Tom).

GLOUCESTER. Get thee away. If for my sake
Thou wilt o'er-take us hence a mile or twain
I'th'way toward Dover,[1] do it for ancient° love; *long-surviving*
And bring some covering for this naked soul,
Which I'll entreat to lead me.

OLD MAN. Alack sir, he is mad.

GLOUCESTER. 'Tis the time's plague,[2] when madmen lead the blind.
Do as I bid thee; or rather, do thy pleasure;
Above the rest, be gone.[3]

OLD MAN. I'll bring him the best 'parel° *apparel* that I have,
Come on't what will.

(*Exit.*)

GLOUCESTER. Sirrah, naked fellow—

EDGAR. Poor Tom's a cold. (*Aside.*) I cannot daub it further.[4]

GLOUCESTER. Come hither fellow.

EDGAR. (*Aside.*) And yet I must. (*Aloud.*) Bless thy sweet eyes, they bleed.

GLOUCESTER. Know'st thou the way to Dover?

EDGAR. Both stile and gate; horse-way and foot-path. Poor Tom hath been scared out of his good wits. Bless thee, good man's son, from the foul fiend.[5]

GLOUCESTER. Here take this purse, thou whom the heavens' plagues
Have humbled to all strokes.[6] That I am wretchèd
Makes thee the happier. Heavens, deal so still:[7]
Let the superfluous[8] and lust-dieted man
That slaves your ordinance,[9] that will not see
Because he does not feel, feel your power quickly;
So distribution should undo excess,
And each man have enough. Dost thou know Dover?

EDGAR. Aye, master.

GLOUCESTER. There is a cliff, whose high and bending° head *overhanging*
Looks fearfully in the confinèd deep:
Bring me but to the very brim of it,
And I'll repair the misery thou dost bear
With something rich about me. From that place,
I shall no leading need.

EDGAR. Give me thy arm.
Poor Tom shall lead thee.

(*Exeunt.*)

[1] *o'er take ... Dover* Catch up with us a mile or two along the road towards Dover.

[2] *time's plague* Misfortune characteristic of the age.

[3] *Above ... gone* Whatever else [you do].

[4] *daub it further* Paint (i.e., dissemble, put on the assumed identity) any longer.

[5] *from the foul fiend* This speech of Edgar's is extended in the Quarto version as follows: "Bless the good man from the foul fiend! Five fiends have been in poor Tom at once: of lust, as Obidicut; Hobbididence, prince of dumbness; Mahu, of stealing; Modo, of murder; Flibbertigibbet of mobbing and mowing, who since possesses chambermaids and waiting women. So, bless thee master."

[6] *humbled ... strokes* Reduced to suffering all humiliations.

[7] *heavens ... still* May the heavens continue to do this.

[8] *superfluous* Possessing too much.

[9] *slaves your ordinance* Enslaves, uses to his own ends injunctions from heaven.

ACT 4, SCENE 2 (FOLIO EDITION)

(*Enter Gonerill and Edmund.*)

GONERILL. Welcome my Lord. I marvel our mild husband
Not met° us on the way. *did not meet*

(*Enter Oswald.*)

—Now, where's your master?
OSWALD. Madam, within; but never man so changed.
I told him of the army that was landed;
He smiled at it. I told him you were coming,
His answer was "The worse." Of Gloucester's treachery,
And of the loyal service of his son
When I informed him, then he called me "sot,"
And told me I had turned the wrong side out.
What most he should dislike, seems pleasant to him;
What like,[1] offensive.
GONERILL. (*To Edmund.*) Then shall you go no further.
It is the cowish terror of his spirit
That dares not undertake. He'll not feel[2] wrongs
Which tie him to an answer. Our wishes on the way[3]
May prove effects. Back, Edmund, to my brother,
Hasten his musters, and conduct his powers.[4]
I must change names[5] at home, and give the distaff[6]
Into my husband's hands. This trusty servant
Shall pass between us. Ere long you are like to hear—
If you dare venture in your own behalf—
A mistress's command.

(*Presenting him with a locket.*)

Wear this—spare speech;
Decline your head. This kiss, if it durst speak
Would stretch thy spirits up into the air.

[1] *What like* What he should like.

[2] *not feel* I.e., not acknowledge that he feels.

[3] *Our wishes on the way* What we were wishing on the way here.

[4] *Hasten … powers* Get him to hurry the readying of his troops, and then lead them back here.

[5] *change names* I.e., master for mistress.

[6] *distaff* Staff on which wool is wound for spinning (a symbol of womanhood).

(QUARTO EDITION)

(*Enter Gonorill and Bastard.*)

GONORILL. Welcome my Lord, I marvel our mild husband
Not met us on the way.

(*Enter [Oswald the] Steward.*)

Now where's your master?
OSWALD. Madame, within; but never man so changed.
I told him of the army that was landed;
He smiled at it. I told him you were coming;
His answer was "The worse." Of Gloucester's treachery,
And of the loyal service of his son
When I informed him, then he called me "sot,"
And told me I had turned the wrong side out.
What he should most despise seems pleasant to him,
What like, offensive.
GONORILL. (*To Bastard.*) Then shall you go no further,
It is the cowish cure[7] of his spirit
That dares not undertake. He'll not feel wrongs
Which tie him to an answer. Our wishes on the way
May prove effects. Back, Edmund, to my brother;
Hasten his musters, and conduct his powers.
I must change arms[8] at home, and give the distaff
Into my husband's hands. This trusty servant
Shall pass between us, ere long you are like to hear—
If you dare venture in your own behalf—
A mistress's command.

(*Presenting him with a locket.*)

Wear this—spare speech;
Decline your head. This kiss, if it durst speak,
Would stretch thy spirits up into the air.

[7] *cure* Conditioning (as leather is "cured").

[8] *change arms* I.e., pick up the sword and hand off the distaff.

parallel texts

Conceive, and fare thee well.
EDMUND. Yours in the ranks of death.

(*Exit.*)

GONERILL. My most dear Gloucester.
Oh, the difference of man, and man,
To thee a woman's services are due.
My fool usurps my body.
OSWALD. Madam, here comes my Lord.

(*Enter Albany [and exit Oswald].*)

GONERILL. I have been worth the whistle.[1]
ALBANY. Oh, Gonerill,
You are not worth the dust which the rude wind
Blows in your face.

[1] *I have ... whistle* "So, you decided to come and look for me after all." The allusion is to a proverb: "It is a poor dog that is not worth the whistling."

Conceive, and fare you well.
BASTARD. Yours in the ranks of death.

GONORILL. My most dear Gloucester:
To thee, woman's services are due.

(*Exit Bastard.*)

My foot usurps my body.[2]
OSWALD. Madam, here comes my Lord.

(*Exit Oswald [and enter Albany].*)

GONORILL. I have been worth the whistle.
ALBANY. O Gonorill,
You are not worth the dust which the rude wind
Blows in your face. I fear your disposition.
That nature which contemns its origin[3]
Cannot be bordered certain[4] in itself.
She that herself will sliver and disbranch
From her material sap,[5] perforce must wither,
And come to deadly use.[6]
GONORILL. No more, the text[7] is foolish.
ALBANY. Wisdom and goodness to the vile seem vile;
Filths savour but themselves. What have you done?
Tigers, not daughters! What have you performed?
A father, and a gracious agèd man,
Whose reverence even the head-lugged[8] bear would
lick—

[2] *My foot usurps my body* "A fool usurps my bed" in the "corrected version of the Quarto edition; "My foot usurps my head" in later Quarto editions.

[3] *contemns its origin* Despises the source from which it sprung (as Gonorill has Lear).

[4] *bordered certain* Confidently defined.

[5] *material sap* Life-giving substance (i.e., family blood).

[6] *deadly use* To be used as one does dead branches, for burning.

[7] *text* Figuratively, the biblical text that is used as the basis for a sermon.

[8] *head-lugged* Pulled by the head (usually with a ring through its nose) into the bear-baiting pit, where, naturally, it was furious.

GONERILL. Milk-livered[1] man,
That bear'st a cheek for blows, a head for wrongs,
Who hast not in thy brows an eye discerning
Thine honour from thy suffering—[2]

ALBANY. See thyself, devil;
Proper deformity[3] seems not in the fiend
So horrid as in woman.
GONERILL. Oh, vain fool—

Most barbarous, most degenerate!—have you madded.[4]
Could my good brother[5] suffer you to do it?
A man, a prince, by him so benefacted?[6]
If that the heavens do not their visible spirits
Send quickly down to tame the vile offences,
It will come: humanity must perforce
Prey on itself, like monsters of the deep![7]
GONORILL. Milk livered man!
That bearest a cheek for blows, a head for wrongs,
Who hast not in thy brows an eye deserving thine honour!
From thy suffering, that not know'st fools, do those villains pity
Who are punished ere they have done their mischief![8]
Where's thy drum?
France spreads his banners in our noiseless land!
With plumèd helm, thy slayer begins threats[9]
Whil'st thou, a moral fool, sits still and cries
"Alack, why does he so?"
ALBANY. See thyself, devil!
Proper deformity seems not in the fiend
So horrid as in woman.
GONORILL. O vain fool!

parallel texts

[1] *Milk-livered* Cowardly, lily-livered (the liver was regarded as the source of courage).

[2] *Who hast … thy suffering* Who doesn't have the eyes to see the difference between doing something honorable and simply suffering.

[3] *Proper deformity* Deformity, appropriate to the fiend, seems horrid in a woman.

[4] *have you madded* You have made (this father) mad, insane.

[5] *good brother* I.e., brother-in-law—Cornwall.

[6] *so benefacted* From whom he had received so many benefits.

[7] *If that … deep* If heaven does not send some clear vengeance, humanity will descend into a subhuman savagery.

[8] *Milk livered … mischief* You gutless man, who turns the other cheek to blows, and who tolerates wrongs done to you; who lacks the sense befitting one of your rank; out of your compassion for suffering—which you don't seem to know is self-deceptive—go ahead and pity those villains, who are simply receiving pre-emptive justice before they can commit crimes.

[9] *With plumèd … threats* Wearing a plumed helmet (i.e., with a display of aristocratic bellicosity), the adversary who will kill you has begun to make open threats. Gonorill speaks of Albany, a head of state (one of two, as far as these two know), as if he were a single knight challenging his opponent to chivalric combat. This is substantially the text as it originally appeared in the first Quarto (an "s" has been added to "begin"). The speculative emendation embraced by almost all editors since Charles Jennens introduced it in 1770—"thy state begins to threat"—seems unnecessary, and tends to weaken the synecdoche (a poetic figure in which a part is taken for the whole).

parallel texts

(*Enter a Messenger.*)

MESSENGER. Oh my good Lord: the Duke of Cornwall's dead,
Slain by his servant, going to[1] put out
The other eye of Gloucester.
ALBANY. Gloucester's eyes?
MESSENGER. A servant that he bred,[2] thrilled with[3] remorse,
Opposed against the act, bending his sword
To his great master, who, threat-enraged[4]
Flew on him, and amongst them[5] felled him dead;
But not without that harmful stroke, which since
Hath plucked him after.[6]
ALBANY. (*To gods.*) This shows you are above,
You justices, that these our nether[7] crimes
So speedily can venge. —But O, poor Gloucester!
Lost he his other eye?

[1] *going to* While about to.

[2] *he bred* Cornwall had raised.

[3] *thrilled with* Deeply affected by.

[4] *threat-enraged* Infuriated by being threatened.

[5] *amongst them* With assistance from others.

[6] *plucked him after* Dragged him behind the servant into death.

[7] *nether* Below (committed on earth).

ALBANY. Thou changèd, and self-covered[8] thing, for shame
Be-monster not thy feature![9] Wer't my fitness[10]
To let these hands obey my blood,° *impulses*
They are apt enough to dislocate and tear
Thy flesh and bones! Howe'er thou art[11] a fiend,
A woman's shape doth shield thee.
GONORILL. Marry your manhood now—[12]

(*Enter a Gentleman.*)

ALBANY. What news?
GENTLEMAN. O my good Lord: the Duke of Cornwall's dead,
Slain by his servant, going to put out
The other eye of Gloucester.
ALBANY. Gloucester's eyes?
GENTLEMAN. A servant that he bred, thralled with remorse,
Opposed against the act, bending his sword
To his great master, who, thereat enraged,[13]
Flew on him, and amongst them, felled him dead;
But not without that harmful stroke, which since
Hath plucked him after.
ALBANY. (*To gods.*) This shows you are above,
You justices, that these our nether crimes
So speedily can venge. —But O, poor Gloucester!
Lost he his other eye?

[8] *changèd and self-covered* Transformed and self-deluded.

[9] *Be-monster … feature* Don't let your inner monster show externally.

[10] *my fitness* Appropriate for me.

[11] *Howe'er thou art* However much you may be.

[12] *Marry … now* This is the Q1 reading, the sense of which is: "try to wed your womanly disposition to your male sex, and—" (the rest of the line, which would presumably have to do with Gonorill urging Albany to get ready to fight, is cut off my the messenger's appearance). In Q2, "now" was changed to "mew," an alteration which has become widely accepted, though it is arguably the weaker of the two versions. In that revised reading, "Marry" becomes an exclamation and with "mew," usually Gonorill is assumed to imitate a cat, so that the sense of the line becomes: "Honestly, what is one to say about your masculinity, except that it is cat-like." Another reading glosses "mew" as "coop up," so that the sense of the line is: "Go ahead and hide your manhood away."

[13] *thereat enraged* Infuriated by that (being opposed).

MESSENGER. Both, both, my Lord.
(*To Gonerill.*) This letter, Madam, craves a speedy answer:
'Tis from your sister.
GONERILL. (*Aside.*) One way I like this well.
But being widow, and my Gloucester with her,

May all the building in my fancy pluck
Upon my hateful life.[1] Another way
The news is not so tart. (*Aloud.*)—I'll read, and answer.

ALBANY. Where was his son, when they did take his eyes?
MESSENGER. Come with my Lady hither.
ALBANY. He is not here.
MESSENGER. No my good Lord, I met him back again.[2]
ALBANY. Knows he the wickedness?
MESSENGER. Aye, my good Lord: 'twas he informed against him,[3]
And quit the house on purpose that their punishment
Might have the freer course.
ALBANY. Gloucester, I live
To thank thee for the love thou showedst the King,
And to revenge thine eyes. —Come hither, friend,
Tell me what more thou know'st.

(*Exeunt.*)

GENTLEMAN. Both, both my Lord.
(*To Gonorill.*) This letter, madam, craves a speedy answer:
'Tis from your sister.
GONORILL. (*Aside.*) One way I like this well;
But, being widow, and my Gloucester with her,
Another way the news is not so took.[4]
May all the building on my fancy pluck
Upon my hateful life.[5] (*Aloud.*)—I'll read and answer.

(*Exit.*)

ALBANY. Where was his son when they did take his eyes?
GENTLEMAN. Come with my Lady hither.
ALBANY. He is not here.
GENTLEMAN. No, my good Lord. I met him back again.
ALBANY. Knows he the wickedness?
GENTLEMAN. Aye, my good Lord: 'twas he informed against him,
And quit the house on purpose that their punishment
Might have the freer course.
ALBANY. Gloucester, I live
To thank thee for the love thou showedst the King,
And to revenge thy eyes.—Come hither, friend;
Tell me what more thou knowest.

(*Ex[eun]t.*)

[1] *May … life* (This situation) may bring all the building of dreams (of marrying Edmund) which I have been doing in my imagination crashing down onto my horrible life. (This sense requires reading "pluck" as "pluck down.")

[2] *back again* On his way back again.

[3] *he … him* Edmund who informed against his father.

[4] *One way … took* On the one hand, this is good news (that Cornwall is dead because it likely means that Albany—and therefore Regan—will likely take over the rule of the entire kingdom), but given that Edmund is now with the newly available Gonorill, this is not such good news. *Another … took* This line has been placed here by the current editor; in Q the line appears, as it does in F, after "hateful life." Compare F for an unamended reading.

[5] *May … hateful life* I pray that all the planning I have been doing in my imagination (about marrying Edmund and becoming Queen) will pull upon (as one plucks on a thread of yarn and thereby unravels a sweater) my hateful life. Again, compare F for a very different reading.

parallel texts

Act 4, Scene 3

(*Enter Kent and a Gentleman.*[1])

Kent. Why the King of France is so suddenly gone back, know you no reason?
Gentleman. Something he left imperfect in the state,[2]
Which since his coming forth is thought of, which
Imports° to the kingdom so much fear and danger *would mean*
That his personal return was most required and necessary.
Kent. Who hath he left behind him general?
Gentleman. The Marshall of France, Monsier la Far.
Kent. Did your letters pierce° the queen to any demonstration of grief? *move*
Gentleman. Aye, sir. She took them, read them in my presence,
And now and then an ample tear trilled down
Her delicate cheek. it seemed she was a queen
Over her passion, who[3] most rebel-like,
Sought to be King o'er her.
Kent. O, then it moved her.
Gentleman. Not to a rage; patience and sorrow strove
Who should express her goodliest.[4] You have seen
Sunshine and rain at once? Her smiles and tears
Were like—a better way.[5] Those happy smilets,[6]
That played on her ripe lip seemed not to know
What guests were in her eyes, which parted thence,
As pearls from diamonds dropped. In brief,
Sorrow would be a rarity most belovèd,
If all could so become it.[7]

---

[1] *Gentleman* This is not the same gentleman who was speaking to Albany in the last scene.

[2] *imperfect in the state* Unresolved in his own kingdom.

[3] *who* Which (the passion).

[4] *patience … goodliest* Her patience and her solemn grief competed as to which was the most accurate (and most moral) expression of her character.

[5] *Were like … way* Were similar to that—only in an improved manner.

[6] *smilets* Little smiles.

[7] *Sorrow … become it* Sadness would be a precious commodity if it were as becoming (flattering) to others as it was to her.

KENT. Made she no verbal question?
GENTLEMAN. Faith, once or twice she heaved the name of "father"
Pantingly forth as if it pressed her heart;
Cried "Sisters, sisters! Shame of ladies, sisters!
Kent! Father! Sisters! What, i'th'storm? I'th'night?
Let pity not be believed!" There she shook
The holy water from her heavenly eyes,
And clamour moistened her.[1] Then away she started[2]
To deal with grief alone.
KENT. It is the stars,
The stars above us govern our conditions.[3]
Else one self mate and make could not beget
Such different issues.[4] You spoke not with her since?
GENTLEMAN. No.
KENT. Was this before the King returned?
GENTLEMAN. No, since.
KENT. Well sir, the poor distressèd Lear's i'th'town,
Who some time in his better tune[5] remembers
What we are come about, and by no means
Will yield to see his daughter.
GENTLEMAN. Why good sir?
KENT. A sovereign shame so elbows him.[6] His own unkindness
That stripped her from his benediction, turned her
To foreign casualties,[7] gave her dear rights
To his dog-hearted daughters—These things sting
His mind so venomously that burning shame
Detains him from Cordelia.
GENTLEMAN. Alack, poor gentleman!
KENT. Of Albany's and Cornwall's powers[8] you heard not?
GENTLEMAN. 'Tis so: they are afoot.
KENT. Well sir, I'll bring you to our master, Lear,

parallel texts

[1] *clamour moistened her* She began to weep openly.

[2] *started* Moved quickly.

[3] *govern our conditions* Determine our characters.

[4] *Else ... issues* Otherwise it wouldn't be possible for the same husband and wife to produce such completely different daughters.

[5] *better tune* Saner moments (his insanity being compared to a musical instrument that has fallen out of tune).

[6] *sovereign ... him* Overpowering shame prods him.

[7] *turned her to foreign casualties* Cast her to the fortune she would find in a foreign land.

[8] *powers* Troops.

And leave you to attend him. Some dear cause,[10]
Will in concealment wrap me up awhile.
When I am known aright you shall not grieve
Lending me this acquaintance.
I pray you go along with me.

(*Ex[eun]t.*)

Act 4, Scene 4[1]

(*Enter with Drum and Colours, Cordelia, Gentlemen, and Soldiers.*)

Cordelia. Alack, 'tis he! Why, he was met even now,
As mad as the vexèd sea, singing aloud,
Crowned with rank fumitor,[2] and furrow weeds,[3]
With hardocks,[4] hemlock,[5] nettles, cuckoo flowers,[6]
Darnel,[7] and all the idle weeds that grow
In our sustaining corn. A century[8] send forth;
Search every acre in the high-grown field,
And bring him to our eye. What can man's wisdom
In the restoring his bereavèd sense?[9]
He that helps him, take all my outward worth.

Gentleman. There is means, Madam.
Our foster nurse of nature is repose:
The which he lacks. That to provoke in him
Are many simples operative, whose power
Will close the eye of anguish.[11]

Cordelia. All blest secrets,
All you unpublished virtues[12] of the earth
Spring with my tears; be aidant, and remediate
In the goodman's desires.[13] Seek, seek for him,
Lest his ungoverned rage dissolve the life
That wants the means to lead it.

(*Enter Messenger.*)

Messenger. News, Madam:
The British[14] powers are marching hitherward.

Cordelia. 'Tis known before; our preparation stands
In expectation of them. O, dear father,
It is thy business that I go about:
Therefore great France
My mourning, and importuned tears hath pitied.
No blown° ambition doth our arms incite, *inflated*
But love, dear love, and our aged father's right.
Soon may I hear, and see him.

(*Exeunt.*)

[1] Since the Folio does not include the preceeding scene, this scene is numbered 4.3 in the Folio, and there are corresponding differences in scene numbering through to the end of Act 4.

[2] *rank fumitor* Thick climbing vine (now known as fumitory).

[3] *furrow weeds* Weeds growing in the furrows of ploughed fields.

[4] *hardocks* Prickly, burr-bearing weed more commonly known as burdock.

[5] *hemlock* Fern-like, poisonous plant with white flowers (not related to the spruce trees known as hemlock in North America).

[6] *cuckoo flowers* Wildflowers with white or pink petals that bloom in the Spring, when the cuckoo bird is heard.

[7] *Darnel* Grass-like weed.

[8] *century* One hundred soldiers.

[9] *What can ... sense* The verb "do" is understood, following "wisdom."

[10] *dear cause* Important reason.

[11] *Our foster ... anguish* The natural means of curing a disordered mind is rest; this is all he lacks; but we can remedy that by giving him any of several simple sedative medicines that will allow the suffering person to sleep.

[12] *unpublished virtues* Undiscovered medicinal properties.

[13] *aidant and remediate in the goodman's desires* Helpful and curative in the hopes of the gentleman (to find an herbal cure).

[14] *British* I.e., those of Cornwall (now under the command of Edmund) and Albany.

ACT 4, SCENE 5

(*Enter Regan, and Steward.*)

REGAN. But are my brother's[1] powers set forth?
OSWALD. Aye, Madam.
REGAN. Himself in person there?
OSWALD. Madam, with much ado. Your sister is the better soldier.
REGAN. Lord Edmund spake not with your Lord at home?
OSWALD. No, Madam.
REGAN. What might import my sister's letter to him?
OSWALD. I know not, Lady.
REGAN. Faith, he is posted hence on serious matter.
It was great ignorance, Gloucester's eyes being out
To let him live. Where he arrives, he moves
All hearts against us.[2] Edmund, I think, is gone
In pity of his misery, to dispatch
His nighted[3] life; moreover to descry
The strength o'th'enemy.
OSWALD. I must needs after him, Madam, with my Letter.
REGAN. Our troops set forth tomorrow; stay with us;
The ways are dangerous.
OSWALD. I may not, Madam.
My Lady charged my duty[4] in this business.
REGAN. Why should she write to Edmund?
Might not you transport her purposes by word?
Belike,° *probably*
Some things—I know not what. I'll love thee much;
Let me unseal the letter.
OSWALD. Madam, I had rather—
REGAN. I know your Lady does not love her husband.
I am sure of that; and at her late being here,
She gave strange *oeillades*,° and most speaking looks *stares*
To noble Edmund. I know you are of her bosom.
OSWALD. I, Madam?
REGAN. I speak in understanding. Y'are; I know't.
Therefore, I do advise you, take this note:[5]
My Lord is dead; Edmund and I have talked,
And more convenient is he for my hand
Than for your Lady's: You may gather more.
If you do find him, pray you give him this,[6]
And when your mistress hears thus much[7] from you,
I pray, desire her call her wisdom to her.
So, fare you well.
If you do chance to hear of that blind traitor,
Preferment[8] falls on him that cuts him off.[9]
OSWALD. Would I could meet him Madam; I should show
What party I do follow.
REGAN. Fare thee well.

(*Exeunt.*)

ACT 4, SCENE 6

(*Enter Gloucester and Edgar.*)

GLOUCESTER. When shall I come to th'top of that same hill?
EDGAR. You do climb up it now. Look how we labour.
GLOUCESTER. Methinks the ground is even.
EDGAR. Horrible steep.
Hark, do you hear the sea?
GLOUCESTER. No, truly.
EDGAR. Why, then your other senses grow imperfect
By your eyes' anguish.
GLOUCESTER. So may it be indeed.
Methinks thy voice is altered, and thou speak'st
In better phrase and matter than thou did'st.
EDGAR. Y'are much deceived; in nothing am I changed
But in my garments.
GLOUCESTER. Methinks y'are better spoken.
EDGAR. Come on, Sir. Here's the place. Stand still. How fearful
And dizzy 'tis, to cast ones eyes so low!
The crows and choughs,[10] that wing the midway air

[1] *brother's* I.e., brother-in-law's (Albany's).

[2] *Where … us* Wherever Gloucester goes, the people's pity for him incites their anger against Regan and her allies.

[3] *nighted* Darkened (because blinded).

[4] *charged my duty* Commanded me to be strictly obedient.

[5] *take this note* Note what I am about to say.

[6] *this* Probably a token such as a ring.

[7] *thus much* I.e., that I have asked you to give Edmund this token.

[8] *Preferment* Promotion.

[9] *cuts him off* Kills him (before he reaches Dover).

[10] *choughs* Crow-like birds.

Show scarce so gross° as beetles. Half-way down *large*
Hangs one that gathers samphire[1]—dreadful trade!
Methinks he seems no bigger than his head.
The fishermen that walked upon the beach
Appear like mice; and yond tall anchoring bark° *ship*
Diminished to her cock;[2] her cock a buoy
Almost too small for sight. The murmuring surge,
That on th' unnumbered idle pebble chafes
Cannot be heard so high. I'll look no more,
Lest my brain turn, and the deficient sight
Topple down headlong.[3]

GLOUCESTER. Set me where you stand.

EDGAR. Give me your hand. You are now within a foot
Of th' extreme verge. For all beneath the moon
Would I not leap upright.

GLOUCESTER. Let go my hand.
Here, friend, 's another purse; in it, a jewel
Well worth a poor man's taking. Fairies and gods
Prosper it[4] with thee. Go thou further off.
Bid me farewell, and let me hear thee going.

EDGAR. (*Pretending to move much farther away.*)
Now fare ye well, good Sir.

GLOUCESTER. With all my heart.[5]

EDGAR. (*Aside.*) Why I do trifle thus with his despair
Is done to cure it.

GLOUCESTER. (*On his knees.*) O you mighty Gods!
This world I do renounce, and in your sights
Shake patiently my great affliction off:
If I could bear it longer, and not fall
To quarrel with your great opposeless wills,
My snuff, and loathèd part of nature,[6] should
Burn itself out. If Edgar live, O bless him!
—Now fellow, fare thee well!

EDGAR. Gone Sir, farewell!

(*Gloucester falls forward.*)

(*Aside.*) And yet I know not how conceit may rob
The treasury of life, when life[7] itself
Yields to the theft. Had he been where he thought,
By this,[8] had thought been past. —Alive, or dead?
(*To Gloucester.*) Hoa, you Sir! Friend! Hear you, Sir?
Speak![9]
(*Aside.*) Thus might he pass indeed; yet he revives.
What are you Sir?

GLOUCESTER. Away, and let me die.

EDGAR. Had'st thou been aught but gossamer,
feathers, air,
So many fathom down precipitating
Thou'dst shivered° like an egg! But thou *shattered*
dost breathe,
Hast heavy substance, bleed'st not, speak'st, art
sound!
Ten masts at each,[10] make not the altitude
Which thou hast perpendicularly fell,
Thy life's a miracle. Speak yet again.

GLOUCESTER. But have I fall'n, or no?

EDGAR. From the dread summit of this chalky
bourn!° *boundary*
Look up a height, the shrill-gorged° *throated*
lark so far
Cannot be seen, or heard. Do but look up!

GLOUCESTER. Alack, I have no eyes:
Is wretchedness deprived that benefit
To end itself by death? 'Twas yet some comfort,
When misery could beguile the tyrant's rage,
And frustrate his proud will.[11]

EDGAR. Give me your arm.
Up, so. How is't? Feel you your legs? You stand.

GLOUCESTER. Too well, too well.

EDGAR. This is above all strangeness.
Upon the crown o'th'cliff, what thing was that

---

[1] *samphire* Carrot-like plant that grows on cliffs near the seashore and can be eaten if pickled; gathering it was considered a "dreadful trade" because, notoriously, one risked one's life in clambering down the cliffs to get to it.

[2] *cock* Small dinghy attached to a large ship.

[3] *Lest my brain … headlong* Lest I am overcome by vertigo, and with my vision having failed, fall over the edge.

[4] *Prosper it* Make it multiply (a talent which fairies were said to possess).

[5] *With all my heart* I.e., and I return the same sentiments to you with all my heart.

[6] *snuff … nature* Spirit (seen as the flickering wick of a candle) and body.

[7] *I know not … life* I wonder to what degree imagination can bring one close to death.

[8] *this* This point.

[9] *Friend … Speak:!* Beginning with this line, Edgar drops the Poor Tom disguise, and pretends to be a resident of Dover.

[10] *at each* Placed end to end.

[11] *frustrate his proud will* I.e., by committing suicide.

Which parted from you?
GLOUCESTER. A poor unfortunate beggar.
EDGAR. As I stood here below, methought his eyes
Were two full moons; he had a thousand noses,
Horns whelked[1] and waved like the enragèd sea:
It was some fiend. Therefore, thou happy father,
Think that the clearest° gods, who make them honours *purest*
Of men's impossibilities, have preserved thee.[2]
GLOUCESTER. I do remember now; henceforth I'll bear
Affliction till it do cry out itself:
"Enough, enough!" and die. That thing you speak of,
I took it for a man; often 'twould say
"The fiend, the fiend." He led me to that place.
EDGAR. Bear free[3] and patient thoughts.

(*Enter Lear.*)

But who comes here?
The safer sense will ne'er accommodate
His master thus.[4]
LEAR. No, they cannot touch me for crying.[5] I am the King himself.
EDGAR. O thou side-piercing[6] sight!
LEAR. Nature's above art, in that respect.[7]—There's your press-money.[8] That fellow handles his bow like a crow-keeper![9] Draw me a clothier's yard![10]—Look, look, a mouse! Peace, peace. This piece of toasted cheese will do't.[11] There's my gauntlet; I'll prove it on a giant.[12] Bring up the brown bills![13]—O ,well flown bird! I'th' clout, i'th'clout![14] Hewgh! (*To Edgar.*) Give the word![15]
EDGAR. Sweet marjoram.[16]
LEAR. Pass.
GLOUCESTER. I know that voice.
LEAR. Ha! Gonerill with a white beard? They flattered me like a dog,[17] and told me I had the white hairs[18] in my beard, ere the black ones were there. To say aye and no, to every thing that I said—aye and no too!—was no good divinity.[19] When the rain came to wet me once, and the wind to make me chatter; when the thunder would not peace at my bidding, there I found 'em, there I smelt 'em out.[20] Go to, they are not men o'their words; they told me I was everything. 'Tis a lie! I am not ague-proof.[21]
GLOUCESTER. The trick of that voice, I do well remember:
Is't not the King?
LEAR. Aye, every inch a King.
When I do stare, see how the subject quakes.
I pardon that man's life. What was thy cause?

[1] *whelked* Shaped like the shell of a whelk (large marine snail with a pointed, spiral shell).

[2] *who ... thee* Who become honored and revered because they accomplish that which it is impossible for human beings to achieve. Edgar is trying to persuade Gloucester that he was literally led towards his suicide attempt by a devil, and to remind Gloucester that his life is, religiously speaking, not his own to take.

[3] *free* I.e., free according to Christian and Stoic doctrine, i.e., free of despair.

[4] *The safer ... thus* Gloucester's newly regained senses will not be able to withstand the blow of encountering Lear in his present state.

[5] *touch ... crying* Censure me for weeping in public. Q's "coining" may be preferable for reasons mentioned below.

[6] *side-piercing* Heart-rending (with an overtone of the piercing of the side of Jesus by the Roman soldier—John 19.34).

[7] *Nature's ... respect* Allusion to the ongoing Renaissance debate as to the superiority of nature or art.

[8] *press-money* Money paid out to men who were forced, or "pressed," into service as sailors or soldiers.

[9] *crow-keeper* Scarecrow.

[10] *clothier's yard* Tailor's measurement of a yard of fabric, achieved by holding the fabric from his breastbone to his outstretched wrist. (Lear imagines himself pressing soldiers; one holds his bow weakly, as if he is made of straw; in drill-sergeant fashion, Lear demands that the bow be stretched to the utmost limit.)

[11] *do't* I.e., a sufficiently large fee to entice the mouse into joining his imaginary army.

[12] *prove it on a giant* Maintain my challenge even against a giant (let alone a mouse).

[13] *brown bills* Troops carrying the weapon so named—a sort of shorter version of the pike.

[14] *well-flown ... clout* Probably the "bird" is an imaginary arrow which hits its target (clout), but Lear may be remarking on the flight of an actual bird, seeking prey.

[15] *word* I.e., password.

[16] *Sweet marjoram* Herb thought to have medicinal values for mental illness.

[17] *like a dog* I.e., as a dog flatters its master.

[18] *white hairs* I.e., the sign of wisdom (more flattery).

[19] *no good divinity* Distorted theology.

[20] *there I smelt 'em out* In this I was able to detect their deceptiveness.

[21] *ague-proof* Immune to fevers.

Adultery? Thou shalt not die. Die for adultery?
No, the wren goes to't, and the small gilded fly
Does lecher in my sight. Let copulation thrive!
For Gloucester's bastard son was kinder to his father,
Than my daughters got° 'tween the lawful sheets.[1] *begotten*
To't! Luxury pell-mell, for I lack soldiers.[2]
Behold yond simp'ring dame, whose face between
Her forks presages snow;[3] that minces virtue,
And does shake the head to hear of pleasure's name.[4]
The fitchew,[5] nor the soilèd horse[6] goes to't with
A more riotous appetite. Down from the waist
They are centaurs,[7] though women all above;
But° to the girdle do the gods inherit; *only*
Beneath is all the fiends. There's hell; there's darkness;
There is the sulphurous pit: burning, scalding,
Stench, consumption! Fie, fie, fie; pah, pah!—Give me
An ounce of civet,° good apothecary; *perfume*
Sweeten my imagination. There's money for thee.

GLOUCESTER. O let me kiss that hand.

LEAR. Let me wipe it first. It smells of mortality.

GLOUCESTER. O ruined piece of nature! This great world
Shall so wear out to naught.[8]—Dost thou know me?

LEAR. I remember thine eyes well enough. Dost thou squiny at me? No, do thy worst blind Cupid, I'll not love. Read thou this challenge;[9] mark but the penning of it.

GLOUCESTER. Were all thy letters suns, I could not see.

EDGAR. I would not take this from report; it is, and my heart breaks at it.

LEAR. Read.

GLOUCESTER. What! With the case[10] of eyes?

LEAR. Oh ho, are you there with me? No eyes in your head, nor no money in your purse? Your eyes are in a heavy case, your purse in a light; yet you see how this world goes.

GLOUCESTER. I see it feelingly.

LEAR. What, art mad? A man may see how this world goes, with no eyes. Look with thine ears. See how yond justice rails upon yond simple[11] thief. Hark in thine ear: change places, and handy-dandy, which is the justice, which is the thief? Thou hast seen a farmer's dog bark at a beggar?

GLOUCESTER. Aye, Sir.

LEAR. And the creature run from the cur? There thou might'st behold the great image of authority: a dog's obeyed in office. Thou, rascal beadle,[12] hold thy bloody hand; why dost thou lash that whore? Strip thy own back; thou hotly lusts to use her in that kind, for which thou whip'st her. The usurer hangs the cozener.[13] Through tattered clothes, great vices do appear; robes and furred gowns hide all. Plate sins with gold, and the strong lance of justice hurtless breaks; arm it in rags, a pigmy's straw does pierce it.[14] None does offend; none, I say none. I'll able 'em.[15] Take that of me, my friend, who have the power to seal th'accuser's lips.[16] Get thee glass-eyes, and like a scurvy[17] politician, seem to see the things thou dost not. Now, now, now, now. Pull off my boots. Harder, harder—so.

EDGAR. O matter and impertinency[18] mixed.
Reason in madness.

LEAR. If thou wilt weep my fortunes, take my eyes.

---

[1] *For Gloucester's ... sheets* Lear does not yet know of Edmund's treachery.

[2] *Luxury ... soldiers* Let people indulge their lechery in any which way, because they may beget me children who will become my army.

[3] *whose face ... snow* Who, judging by the look on her face, would be frigid between her legs.

[4] *does shake ... name* Shakes her head in disapproval merely to hear the word "pleasure" spoken.

[5] *fitchew* Polecat (a member of the weasel family, reputed to be lecherous, and its name accordingly applied to prostitutes).

[6] *soilèd horse* Horse left to run in pasture and therefore more sexually enthusiastic than a stabled horse.

[7] *Down ... centaurs* They have bestial appetites below the waist, like centaurs, who have the torsos of men and the bodies of horses.

[8] *Shall so ... naught* Shall come to nothing (in the same way that Lear has).

[9] *challenge* The paper may be imaginary.

[10] *case* Empty eye-sockets.

[11] *simple* Petty.

[12] *beadle* Constable.

[13] *the usurer ... cozener* The moneylender hangs the petty cheat.

[14] *Plate ... pierce it* Cover sinfulness with wealth (plate it with gold) and it acts as armour; but sinfulness in rags has no protection, and can be penetrated by the merest trifle.

[15] *able 'em* Vouch for them.

[16] *Plate sins ... th'accuser's lips* These four sentences do not appear in the Quarto version.

[17] *scurvy* Corrupt.

[18] *matter and impertinency* Sense and nonsense.

I know thee well enough; thy name is Gloucester.
Thou must be patient. We came crying hither;
Thou know'st, the first time that we smell the air
We wail and cry. I will preach to thee. Mark:
GLOUCESTER. Alack, alack the day.
LEAR. When we are born, we cry that we are come
To this great stage of fools. This a good block.[1]
It were a delicate stratagem to shoe
A troop of horse with felt![2] I'll put't in proof,
And when I have stol'n upon these son-in-laws,
Then kill, kill, kill, kill, kill, kill!

(Enter a Gentleman.)

GENTLEMAN. Oh here he is. *(To Edgar.)* Lay hand upon him, Sir.
(To Lear.) Your most dear daughter—
LEAR. No rescue? What, a prisoner? I am even
The natural fool[3] of Fortune. Use me well;
You shall have ransom. Let me have surgeons;
I am cut to'th' brains.
GENTLEMAN. You shall have anything.
LEAR. No seconds?[4] All myself?
Why, this would make a man a man of salt,[5]
To use his eyes for garden water-pots.
I will die bravely, like a smug bridegroom.[6]
What? I will be jovial. Come, come.
I am a king, masters, know you that?
GENTLEMAN. You are a royal one, and we obey you.
LEAR. Then there's life in't.[7] Come, and you get it,
You shall get it by running: Sa, sa, sa, sa![8]

(Exit.)

GENTLEMAN. A sight most pitiful in the meanest wretch,
Past speaking of in a king. Thou hast a daughter
Who redeems nature from the general curse
Which twain have brought her to.[9]
EDGAR. Hail gentle° Sir. *noble*
GENTLEMAN. Sir, speed you.[10] What's your will?
EDGAR. Do you hear ought, Sir, of a battle toward.[11]
GENTLEMAN. Most sure, and vulgar:[12]
Every one hears that, which can distinguish sound.
EDGAR. But, by your favour, how near's the other army?
GENTLEMAN. Near, and on speedy foot: the main descry
Stands on the hourly thought.[13]
EDGAR. I thank you Sir, that's all.
GENTLEMAN. Though that the Queen on special cause is here
Her army is moved on.
EDGAR. I thank you Sir.

(Exit [Gentleman].)

GLOUCESTER. You ever gentle gods, take my breath from me,
Let not my worser spirit[14] tempt me again
To die before you please.
EDGAR. Well pray you,[15] father.[16]
GLOUCESTER. Now good sir, what are you?
EDGAR. A most poor man, made tame to Fortune's blows[17]
Who, by the art of known and feeling sorrows,
Am pregnant to good pity.[18] Give me your hand;
I'll lead you to some biding.° *abode*
GLOUCESTER. Hearty thanks;
The bounty, and the benison° of heaven *blessing*

[1] *This a good block* The meaning is debated.

[2] *shoe ... felt* I.e., so their approaching hooves could not be heard.

[3] *the natural fool* Born to be a fool ("a natural" was an expression for those born mentally challenged).

[4] *seconds* Assistants, as in a duel.

[5] *make a man a man of salt* Make a man cry salt tears.

[6] *die bravely ... smug bridegroom* Embrace death as if it were a bride.

[7] *there's life in't* There's hope yet.

[8] *Sa, sa, sa, sa* Cry used to urge on horses when hunting.

[9] *general curse ... her to* Pun: the curse of family blood which Gonerill and Regan have brought upon her, and the state of original sin left us by Adam and Eve.

[10] *speed you* God speed you.

[11] *battle toward* Impending battle.

[12] *vulgar* Common knowledge.

[13] *main descry ... thought* Sighting of the main part of the army is expected any hour.

[14] *worser spirit* Bad angel, wicked side.

[15] *Well pray you* That's a good prayer.

[16] *father* Though ambiguous, used here as a manner of addressing an older man who is a stranger (Edgar has yet to reveal himself).

[17] *tame ... blows* As a dog or horse is made timid by a cruel master.

[18] *by the art ... pity* Having been instructed by the sorrows I have known and deeply felt, I am susceptible to feeling sympathy for others.

To boot, and boot.[1]

(*Enter [Oswald].*)

OSWALD. A proclaimed prize![2] Most happy!
That eyeless head of thine, was first framed[3] flesh
To raise my fortunes, thou old, unhappy traitor!
Briefly thyself remember;[4] the sword is out
That must destroy thee.
GLOUCESTER. Now let thy friendly[5] hand
Put strength enough to't.

(*Edgar intervenes.*)

OSWALD. Wherefore, bold peasant,
Dar'st thou support a published[6] traitor? Hence,
Lest that th'infection of his fortune take
Like hold on thee. Let go his arm.
EDGAR. Chill not let go, Zir, without vurther 'casion.[7]
OSWALD. Let go, slave, or thou diest.
EDGAR. Good Gentleman, go your gate, and let poor volk pass. And 'chud ha'bin zwaggerd out of my life, 'twould not ha'bin zo long as 'tis, by a vortnight.[8] Nay, come not near th'old man. Keep out che vor'ye, or I'ce try whether your costard,[9] or my ballow[10] be the harder, chill be plain with you.
OSWALD. Out, dunghill.
EDGAR. Chill pick your teeth,[11] Zir. Come, no matter vor your foins.[12]

(*They fight.*)

OSWALD. Slave, thou hast slain me. Villain, take my purse;
If ever thou wilt thrive, bury my body,
And give the letters which thou find'st about me,
To Edmund, Earl of Gloucester. Seek him out
Upon the English party.[13] Oh, untimely death! Death!

(*He dies.*)

EDGAR. I know thee well: serviceable[14] villain,
As duteous to the vices of thy mistress,
As badness would desire.
GLOUCESTER. What, is he dead?
EDGAR. Sit you down, father; rest you.—(*Aside.*)
Let's see these pockets; the letters that he speaks of
May be my friends.—(*To Gloucester.*) He's dead; I am only sorry
He had no other deathsman. (*Aside.*)—Let us see;
Leave gentle wax; and manners blame us not[15]
To know our enemies' minds. We rip their hearts;
Their papers is more lawful.

(*Reads the letter.*)

"Let our reciprocal vows be remembered. You have

---

[1] *To boot, and boot* To reward you, and again. (Boot can mean both to reward and again or in addition.)

[2] *proclaimed prize* Wanted man with a price on his head.

[3] *framed* Created.

[4] *Briefly … remember* Say your prayers quickly.

[5] *friendly* Welcome (because it brings death).

[6] *published* Publicly declared.

[7] *Chill … 'casion* I will not let go, Sir, without being given further occasion to do so (i.e., without hearing an explanation of why I should). The line is written in a rural dialect more reminiscent of today's Somerset than Kent. The convention does not appear in Edgar's lines immediately preceding these, but, because we cannot know how closely the Folio and Quarto texts conform to Shakespeare's intentions, we can only speculate as to whether he meant Edgar to have been using the same dialect to deceive Gloucester since his attempted suicide, or whether Edgar actually only adopts the dialect here to deceive Oswald. While readers can side-step the question, an actor performing the role must make a definite choice.

[8] *And … vortnight* If it were possible for me to have been swaggered to death, I would have died some time ago; *vortnight* I.e., fortnight, two weeks.

[9] *costard* Literally, apple, but in this case, slang for head.

[10] *ballow* Cudgel.

[11] *pick your teeth* Slug you in the jar (a figurative threat, like "kick butt").

[12] *foins* Thrusts (with a sword).

[13] *Upon … party* Amongst the English troops (as opposed to Cordelia's French party).

[14] *serviceable* Unscrupulously ready to be employed in anyone's service.

[15] *Leave gentle wax and manners blame us not* I ask your leave (permission), noble sealing wax (which must be broken to read the letter) let it not be considered ill-mannered that we open another's letter.

many opportunities to cut him off; if your will want not,[1] time and place will be fruitfully offered. There is nothing done if he return the conqueror; then am I the prisoner, and his bed, my gaol—from the loathèd warmth whereof, deliver me, and supply the place for your labour.[2]

Your (wife, so I would[3] say) affectionate servant, Gonerill."

Oh indistinguished space[4] of woman's will!
A plot upon her virtuous husband's life;
And the exchange my brother! (*To Oswald's corpse.*)
Here, in the sands
Thee I'll rake up, the post unsanctified[5]
Of murderous lechers; and in the mature time,[6]
With this ungracious paper strike the sight
Of the death-practised Duke.[7] For him, 'tis well,
That of thy death, and business, I can tell.

(*Exit Edgar, with the body of Oswald.*)

GLOUCESTER. The King is mad; how stiff is my vile sense,
That I stand up, and have ingenious feeling
Of my huge sorrows?[8] Better I were distract,° *insane*
So should my thoughts be severed from my griefs,

(*Drum afar off. [Re-enter Edgar.]*)

And woes, by wrong imaginations,[9] lose
The knowledge of themselves.

EDGAR. Give me your hand;
Far off methinks I hear the beaten drum.
Come, father; I'll bestow you with a friend.

(*Exeunt.*)

[1] *if your will want not* If you are not lacking in resolve.

[2] *supply … labour* By killing him, make room for yourself to have sex.

[3] *would* Would like to.

[4] *indistinguished space* Unfathomable scope.

[5] *post unsanctified* Wicked messenger (about to be buried in unsanctified ground).

[6] *in the mature time* At the most opportune time (when the time is ripe).

[7] *death-practised Duke* Duke whose death is plotted (i.e., Albany).

[8] *The King … sorrows* "Given that the King is insane, how cunningly contrived my senses be that I can still bear up and have an acute awareness of my immense misfortunes."

[9] *wrong imaginations* Deluded imaginings.

ACT 4, SCENE 7

(*Enter Cordelia, Kent, and Gentleman.*)

CORDELIA. O, thou good Kent! How shall I live and work
To match thy goodness? My life will be too short,
And every measure° fail me. *attempt*

KENT. To be acknowledged, Madam, is o'er-paid.
All my reports go with the modest truth,
Nor more, nor clipped,[10] but so.

CORDELIA. Be better suited.[11]
These weeds° are memories of those worser hours; *clothes*
I prithee, put them off.

KENT. Pardon, dear Madam;
Yet to be known shortens my made° intent. *deliberate*
My boon I make it,[12] that you know me not,
Till time, and I, think meet.° *appropriate*

CORDELIA. Then be't so. (*To Gentleman.*) My good Lord, how does the King?

GENTLEMAN. Madam, sleeps still.

CORDELIA. O you kind Gods!
Cure this great breach in his abusèd nature,
Th'untuned and jarring senses, O wind up,[13]
Of this child-changed[14] father.

GENTLEMAN. So please your Majesty,
That we may wake the King? He hath slept long.

CORDELIA. Be governed by your knowledge, and proceed
I'th'sway of your own will. Is he arrayed?

GENTLEMAN. Aye, Madam; in the heaviness of sleep,
We put fresh garments on him.

(*Enter Lear in a chair carried by Servants.*)

Be by, good Madam, when we do awake him.

[10] *No more, not clipped* Not exaggerated, nor cut short.

[11] *suited* Clothed (Kent is still wearing the servant costume he assumed in his "Caius" disguise).

[12] *My boon … it* The favor I request is.

[13] *Th'untuned … wind up* Tighten the untuned strings of his mind (as one might tune a lyre), so that they are restored to sense and harmony.

[14] *child-changed* Become child-like (or changed thanks to children).

I doubt of his temperance.[1]
CORDELIA. O my dear Father! Restoration[2] hang
Thy medicine on my lips, and let this kiss
Repair those violent harms that my two sisters
Have in thy reverence[3] made.
KENT. Kind and dear princess!
CORDELIA. Had you not been their father, these white flakes[4]
Did challenge[5] pity of them. Was this a face
To be opposed against the jarring winds?
Mine enemy's dog, though he had bit me,
Should have stood that night against my fire,[6]
And was't thou fain, poor father,
To hovel thee with swine and rogues forlorn,
In short[7] and musty straw? Alack, alack!
'Tis wonder that thy life and wits at once
Had not concluded all. (*To Gentleman.*) He wakes, speak to him.
GENTLEMAN. Madam do you, 'tis fittest.
CORDELIA. How does my Royal Lord? How fares your Majesty?
LEAR. You do me wrong to take me out o'th'grave.
Thou art a soul in bliss; but I am bound
Upon a wheel of fire,[8] that mine own tears
Do scald, like molten lead.
CORDELIA. Sir, do you know me?
LEAR. You are a spirit I know. Where did you die?
CORDELIA. (*To Gentleman.*) Still, still, far wide.[9]
GENTLEMAN. He's scarce awake. Let him alone a while.
LEAR. Where have I been? Where am I? Fair daylight?
I am mightily abused.° I should e'en die with pity *deluded*
To see another thus. I know not what to say:
I will not swear these are my hands. Let's see:
I feel this pin prick. Would I were assured
Of my condition.
CORDELIA. O look upon me, Sir,
And hold your hand in benediction o'er me.
You must not kneel.
LEAR. Pray do not mock me:
I am a very foolish fond old man—
Fourscore and upward;[10] not an hour more, nor less—
And to deal plainly,
I fear I am not in my perfect mind.
Methinks I should know you, (*Of Kent.*) and know this man;
Yet I am doubtful. For I am mainly ignorant
What place this is; and all the skill I have
Remembers not these garments; nor I know not
Where I did lodge last night. Do not laugh at me,
For, as I am a man, I think this lady
To be my child, Cordelia.
CORDELIA. And so I am. I am.
LEAR. Be your tears wet? Yes, faith. I pray, weep not;
If you have poison for me, I will drink it.
I know you do not love me, for your sisters
Have, as I do remember, done me wrong.
You have some cause, they have not.
CORDELIA. No cause, no cause.
LEAR. Am I in France?
KENT. In your own kingdom, Sir.
LEAR. Do not abuse° me. *deceive*
GENTLEMAN. Be comforted good Madam, the great rage,
You see, is killed in him. Desire him to go in;
Trouble him no more till further settling.
CORDELIA. Wilt please your Highness walk?
LEAR. You must bear with me.
Pray you now, forget, and forgive:
I am old and foolish.[11]

[1] *I doubt ... temperance* I'm not sure how self-controlled he will be.

[2] *Restoration* I.e., the powers of restoration to health.

[3] *reverence* Dignity, venerable state.

[4] *flakes* Wisps of hair.

[5] *Did challenge* Would have demanded.

[6] *against my fire* By my fireplace.

[7] *short* Broken, much used.

[8] *wheel of fire* Binding a person on a wheel and breaking his bones was a form of execution. There's a sort of wheel of fire in Hell in the illustrated Kalendar of Shepherds (1498).

[9] *wide* I.e., wide of the mark.

[10] *Fourscore and upward* Over eighty.

[11] In the Quarto version Kent and a Gentleman remain on stage after the others exit here, and conclude the scene as follows: "GENTLEMAN. Holds it true, Sir, that the Duke of Cornwall was so slain?
KENT. Most certain, Sir.
GENTLEMAN. Who is conductor of his people?
KENT. As 'tis said, the bastard son of Gloucester.
GENTLEMAN. They say Edgar, his banished son, is with the Earl of Kent in Germany.
KENT. Report is changeable. 'Tis time to look about. The powers of the kingdom approach apace.
GENTLEMAN. The arbitrament is like to be bloody. Fare you well, Sir. (*Exit.*)

(*Exeunt.*)

ACT 5, SCENE 1

(*Enter with Drum and Colours, Edmund, Regan, Gentlemen, and Soldiers.*)

EDMUND. Know of the Duke if his last purpose hold,
Or whether since he is advised by ought
To change the course. He's full of alteration,
And self-reproving. Bring his constant pleasure.[1]

(*Exit Messenger.*)

REGAN. Our sister's man is certainly miscarried.[2]
EDMUND. 'Tis to be doubted, Madam.
REGAN. Now, sweet Lord,
You know the goodness I intend upon you;
Tell me but truly—but then speak the truth—
Do you not love my sister?
EDMUND. In honoured love.
REGAN. But have you never found my brother's way[3]
To the forfended° place? *forbidden*
EDMUND. No,[4] by mine honour, Madam.
REGAN. I never shall endure her. Dear my Lord,
Be not familiar with her.
EDMUND. Fear not—
She and the Duke her husband.

(*Enter, with drum and colours, Albany, Gonerill, Soldiers.*)

ALBANY. (*To Regan.*) Our very loving sister, well be-met.[5]
(*To Edmund.*)[6] Sir, this I heard: the King is come to his daughter
With others, whom the rigour of our state[7]
Forced to cry out.[8]
REGAN. Why is this reasoned?[9]
GONERILL. Combine together 'gainst the enemy;
For these domestic and particular broils[10]
Are not the question here.
ALBANY. Let's then determine with th'ancient of war[11]
On our proceeding.
REGAN. Sister, you'll go with us?[12]
GONERILL. No.
REGAN. 'Tis most convenient, pray go with us.
GONERILL. Oh ho, I know the riddle,[13] I will go.

(*Exeunt both the armies [except Albany].*)
(*Enter Edgar [still disguised].*)

EDGAR. If e'er your Grace had speech with man so poor,
Hear me one word.
ALBANY. (*To those departing.*) I'll overtake you.
(*To Edgar.*) Speak.
EDGAR. Before you fight the battle, ope this letter.
If you have victory, let the trumpet sound
For him that brought it:[14] Wretchèd though I seem,
I can produce a champion, that will prove[15]
What is avouchèd° there. If you miscarry, *maintained*
Your business of° the world hath so an end, *in*

KENT. My point and period will be throughly wrought, Or well, or ill, as this day's battle's fought. (*Exit.*)"

[1] *constant pleasure* Final decision.

[2] *is ... miscarried* Has definitely come to some harm.

[3] *But have ... way* But have you never followed the path of my brother-in-law (Albany); i.e., have you never had sex with her?

[4] *To the forfended place ... No* The Quarto version here includes an additional exchange, as follows: "REGAN. But have you never found my brother's way / To the forfended place?
BASTARD. That thought abuses you.
REGAN. I am doubtful that you have been conjunct / And bosomed with her, as far as we call her's.
BASTARD. No, by mine honour Madam.
REGAN. I never shall endure her. Dear my Lord, / Be not familiar with her.
BASTARD. Fear me not— / She and the Duke her husband."

[5] *well be-met* It is good to see you.

[6] *to Edmund* Albany addresses Edmund in F, though he ignores him in Q.

[7] *rigour of our state* Tyranny of our governance.

[8] *Forced to cry out* The Quarto version here includes several additional lines, as follows: "Forced to cry out. Where I could not be honest / I never yet was valiant. For this business, / It touches us, as France invades our land, / Now bolds the King, with others whom I fear. / Most just and heavy causes make oppose."

[9] *Why is this reasoned* Why do you think to bring this up (now)?

[10] *domestic and particular broils* Personal quarrels.

[11] *th'ancient of war* Those with experience of war.

[12] *us* Me (rather than Edmund).

[13] *riddle* Secret (reason for asking).

[14] *him that brought it* I.e., me.

[15] *prove* I.e., by combat.

And machination ceases.[1] Fortune loves you.

(*He begins to leave.*)

ALBANY. Stay till I have read the letter.
EDGAR. I was forbid it.
When time shall serve, let but the herald cry,
And I'll appear again.

(*Exit.*)

ALBANY. Why, fare thee well. I will o'er-look thy paper.

(*Enter Edmund.*)

EDMUND. The enemy's in view; draw up your powers.

(*Hands Albany a paper.*)

Here is the guess of their true strength and forces
By diligent discovery; but your haste
Is now urged on you.[2]
ALBANY. We will greet the time.

(*Exit.*)

EDMUND. To both these sisters have I sworn my love:
Each jealous° of the other, as the stung *suspicious*
Are of the adder. Which of them shall I take?
Both? One? Or neither? Neither can be enjoyed
If both remain alive: To take the widow,
Exasperates, makes mad her sister Gonerill.
And hardly[3] shall I carry out my side,[4]
Her husband being alive. Now then, we'll use
His countenance[5] for the battle; which being done,
Let her who would be rid of him devise
His speedy taking off.° As for the mercy *murder*
Which he intends to Lear and to Cordelia:
The battle done, and they within our power,
Shall never see his pardon; for my state
Stands on me to defend, not to debate.[6]

(*Exit.*)

ACT 5, SCENE 2

(*Alarum within. Enter, with drum and colours, Lear, Cordelia, and Soldiers, over the stage, and exeunt.*)

(*Enter Edgar and Gloucester.*)

EDGAR. Here, father, take the shadow of this tree
For your good host.[7] Pray that the right° *righteous*
may thrive;
If ever I return to you again,
I'll bring you comfort.
GLOUCESTER. Grace go with you Sir.

(*Exit Edgar.*)
(*Alarum and retreat within. [Re-]enter Edgar.*)

EDGAR. Away, old man! Give me thy hand; away!
King Lear hath lost; he and his daughter ta'en.[8]
Give me thy hand; come on.
GLOUCESTER. No further, Sir! A man may rot even here.
EDGAR. What in ill thoughts again? Men must endure
Their going hence, even as their coming hither.
Ripeness is all. Come on.
GLOUCESTER. And that's true too.

(*Exeunt.*)

[1] *If you ... ceases* If, on the other hand, you lose the battle, you won't be worried about what is happening in the world, and this plan will be called off.

[2] *Here is ... on you* This is the best estimate of the size of the enemy's numbers according to careful spying; but don't read it now, you need to hurry.

[3] *hardly* With difficulty.

[4] *my side* I.e., of the bargain.

[5] *use his countenance* Use him as a figurehead (to muster the troops).

[6] *my state ... debate* My circumstances make it imperative for me to defend myself, not to weigh questions of right and wrong.

[7] *For ... host* As shelter.

[8] *ta'en* Have been taken (prisoner).

ACT 5, Scene 3 (Folio Edition)

(*Enter in conquest, with drum and colours, Edmund; Lear and Cordelia, as prisoners; Soldiers, Captain.*)

EDMUND. Some officers take them away. Good guard,[1]
Until their greater pleasures first be known
That are to censure them.[2]
CORDELIA. (*To Lear.*) We are not the first,
Who with best meaning have incurred the worst.
For thee, oppressèd King, I am cast down;° *desolate*
Myself could else out-frown false Fortune's frown.
Shall we not see these daughters, and these sisters?
LEAR. No, no, no, no; come let's away to prison.
We two alone will sing like birds i'th'cage.
When thou dost ask me blessing, I'll kneel down
And ask of thee forgiveness. So we'll live
And pray, and sing, and tell old tales, and laugh
At gilded butterflies; and hear (poor rogues)
Talk of court news; and we'll talk with them too—
Who loses, and who wins; who's in, who's out—
And take upon's the mystery of things,[3]
As if we were God's spies. And we'll wear out,° *outlast*
In a walled prison, packs and sects of great ones
That ebb and flow by th'moon.[4]
EDMUND. (*To Soldiers.*) Take them away.[5]
LEAR. (*To Cordelia.*) Upon such sacrifices,[6] my Cordelia,
The gods themselves throw incense.[7] Have I caught
thee?

(Quarto Edition)

parallel texts

(*Enter Edmund [and Soldiers], with Lear and Cordelia prisoners.*)

BASTARD. Some officers take them away. Good guard
Untill their greater pleasures best be known
That are to censure them.
CORDELIA. (*To Lear.*) We are not the first
Who with best meaning have incurred the worst.
For thee, oppressèd King, am I cast down;
Myself could else out-frown false Fortune's frown.
Shall we not see these daughters, and these sisters?
LEAR. No, no; come let's away to prison.
We two alone will sing like birds i'th'cage.
When thou dost ask me blessing, I'll kneel down
And ask of thee forgiveness. So we'll live
And pray, and sing, and tell old tales, and laugh
At gilded butterflies; and hear poor rogues
Talk of court news; and we'll talk with them too—
Who loses, and who wins; who's in, who's out—
And take upon's the mystery of things
As if we were God's spies. And we'll wear out,
In a walled prison, packs and sects of great ones
That ebb and flow by th'moon.
BASTARD. (*To Soldiers.*) Take them away.
LEAR. (*To Cordelia.*) Upon such sacrifices, my Cordelia,
The gods themselves throw incense. Have I caught
thee?

---

[1] *Good guard* Guard them well.

[2] *Until ... them* Until the will of those who will be passing judgement upon these prisoners (i.e., Albany, Gonerill and Regan) is known.

[3] *take upon's ... things* Observe and comment upon the wonders of life and death.

[4] *packs ... th'moon* The cliques and factions of the powerful that rise and fall like the (moon-influenced) tides.

[5] *Take them away* Evidently, the soldiers are reluctant to obey; they have already been given the order at the top of the scene.

[6] *such sacrifices* I.e., as Lear and Cordelia will make in turning our backs on the world.

[7] *throw incense* Cast incense, an act normally performed by a priest.

He that parts us,[1] shall bring a brand° from heaven, *torch*
And fire us hence, like foxes![2] Wipe thine eyes,
The good years[3] shall devour them, flesh and fell,° *skin*
Ere they shall make us weep! We'll see 'em starved first!
Come.

(*Ex[eunt Lear and Cordelia under guard]*.)

EDMUND. Come hither, Captain. Hark:
Take thou this note; go follow them to prison.
One step I have advanced thee;[4] if thou dost
As this instructs thee, thou dost make thy way
To noble fortunes.[5] Know thou this: that men
Are as the time is; to be tender minded
Does not become a sword. Thy great employment
Will not bear question; either say thou'lt do't,
Or thrive by other means.
CAPTAIN. I'll do't my Lord.
EDMUND. About it, and write happy,[6] when th'hast done.
Mark, I say: instantly, and carry it so
As I have set it down.[7]

(*Exit Captain.*)
(*Flourish. Enter Albany, Gonerill, Regan, Soldiers.*)

ALBANY. (*To Edmund.*) Sir, you have showed today your valiant strain

parallel texts

He that parts us shall bring a brand from heaven,
And fire us hence like foxes! Wipe thine eyes;
The good shall devour 'em, flesh and fell,
Ere they shall make us weep! We'll see 'em starve first.
Come.

(*Exeunt Lear and Cordelia, under guard.*)

BASTARD. Come hither, Captain. Hark:
Take thou this note; go follow them to prison.
One step I have advanced thee; if thou dost
As this instructs thee, thou dost make thy way
To noble fortunes. Know thou this: that men
Are as the time is; to be tender minded
Does not become a sword. Thy great employment
Will not bear question; either say thou'lt do't,
Or thrive by other means.
CAPTAIN. I'll do't, my Lord.
BASTARD. About it, and write happy when thou hast done.
Mark, I say: instantly, and carry it so
As I have set it down.
CAPTAIN. I cannot draw a cart,
Nor eat dried oats; if it be man's work, I'll do't.[8]

(*Exit.*)
(*Enter [Albany, Gonorill, Regan] and others.*)

ALBANY. (*To Bastard.*) Sir, you have showed today your valiant strain;

[1] *He that parts us* I.e., the only person able to part us (will be divine).

[2] *fire … foxes* The reference is to a hunting technique in which a fire is lit at one or more holes of a den to force the fox out another opening.

[3] *good years* Perhaps a reference to Biblical years of God's favor in which enemies are afflicted (Genesis 41).

[4] *One step … thee* I have promoted you once.

[5] *make … fortunes* You will have earned promotion to the ranks of the nobility.

[6] *About it, and write happy* Go to it immediately, and call yourself fortunate.

[7] *set it down* Written it down.

[8] *I cannot … do't* I cannot do honest drudge work as an animal can; being a human being, I will do the sort of work (i.e., evil) that human beings do.

And Fortune led you well. You have the captives
Who were the opposites° of this day's strife; *opponents*
I do require them of you, so to use them,
As we shall find their merits and our safety
May equally determine.
EDMUND. Sir, I thought it fit
To send the old and miserable King to some retention—
Whose age had charms[1] in it, whose title, more,
To pluck the common bosom on his side,[2]
And turn our impressèd lances[3] in our eyes
Which do command them. With him I sent the
Queen—
My reason all the same—and they are ready
Tomorrow, or at further space, t'appear
Where you shall hold your session.[4]
ALBANY. Sir, by your patience,
I hold you but a subject of[5] this war,
Not as a brother.
REGAN. That's as we list[6] to grace him.
Methinks our pleasure might have been demanded
Ere you had spoke so far. He led our powers,
Bore the commission of my place and person,[7]
The which immediacy may well stand up,
And call itself your brother.[8]

And Fortune led you well. You have the captiues
That were the opposites of this day's strife;
We do require then, of you, so to use them,
As we shall find their merits and our safety
May equally determine.
BASTARD. Sir, I thought it fit
To save the old and miserable King to some retention—
Whose age has charms in it, whose title, more,
To pluck the coren bosom of his side,
And turn our impressèd lances in our eyes
Which do command them. With him I sent the
Queen—
My reason all the same—and they are ready
Tomorrow, or at further space, to appear
Where you shall hold your session. At this time,
We sweat and bleed; the friend hath lost his friend
And the best quarrels in the heat are curst
By those that feel their sharpness.[9]
The question of Cordelia and her father
Requires a fitter place.
ALBANY. Sir, by your patience,
I hold you but a subject of this war,
Not as a brother.
REGAN. That's as we list to grace him.
Methinks our pleasure should have been demanded
Ere you had spoke so far. He led our powers,
Bore the commission of my place and person,
The which immediate may well stand up,
And call itself your brother.

parallel texts

[1] *charms* Persuasive power.

[2] *Whose age … on his side* I.e., if Lear is not locked away, the hearts of the common people might be swayed by sympathy for him (as an old man) and respect for him (as king) such that they would turn against the rebels (and convince the soldiers to do the same).

[3] *impressèd lances* Conscripted ordinary soldiers (and their lances, in the eye-piercing metaphor).

[4] *session* Trial.

[5] *hold you but a subject of* Consider you only as a subordinate in.

[6] *we list* I choose (the royal pronoun is used here and below).

[7] *Bore … person* Represented my personal, royal authority.

[8] *The which … brother* The temporary expedient of which may be made permanent, which would demand that you consider Edmund a sort of brother.

[9] *At this time … sharpness* In circumstances such as these, when suffering and passion abound, it is inadvisable to go to trial, because even a righteous argument (i.e., against Lear and Cordelia) is going to be difficult to bear.

parallel texts

GONERILL. Not so hot.
In his own grace he doth exalt himself,
More than in your addition.[1]
REGAN. In my rights,
By me invested,[2] he compeers° the best. *equals*
ALBANY. That were the most, if he should husband you.
REGAN. Jesters do oft prove prophets.
GONERILL. Hola, hola![3]
That eye that told you so, looked but asquint.
REGAN. Lady, I am not well; else I should answer
From a full-flowing stomach.[4] (*To Edmund.*) General:
Take thou my soldiers, prisoners, patrimony.
Dispose of them, of me; the walls[5] are thine.
Witness the world, that I create thee here
My Lord and Master.
GONERILL. Mean you to enjoy him?
ALBANY. The let-alone[6] lies not in your good will.
EDMUND. Nor in thine, Lord.
ALBANY. Half-blooded[7] fellow, yes.
REGAN. Let the drum strike, and prove my title[8] thine.
ALBANY. Stay yet, hear reason. Edmund, I arrest thee
On capital treason; and in thy arrest,[9] (*Indicating Gonerill.*)
This gilded serpent. (*To Regan.*) For your claim, fair sister,

[1] *In his ... addition* His own merits demand his promotion and respect more than any title you give him.

[2] *In my rights ... invested* In the rights belonging to me that I have conferred on him.

[3] *Hola, hola* Expostulation roughly equivalent to "now, now" or "hang on."

[4] *full-flowing stomach* Bellyful of rage.

[5] *walls* Regan speaks figuratively, as if she were a fortress taken by Edmund after a long siege.

[6] *let-alone* Say-so, permission.

[7] *Half-blooded* Illegitimate.

[8] *my title* I.e., the title I have given you.

[9] *in thy arrest* In connection with your arrest (i.e., as accessory to your crimes).

GONORILL. Not so hot.
In his own grace he doth exalt himself
More than in your advancement.
REGAN. In my right,
By me invested, he compeers the best.
GONORILL. That were the most, if he should husband you.
REGAN. Jesters do oft prove prophets.
GONORILL. Hola, hola!
That eye that told you so, looked but asquint.
REGAN. Lady, I am not well; else I should answer
From a full-flowing stomach. (*To Bastard.*) General:
Take thou my soldiers, prisoners, patrimony.

Witness the world that I create thee here
My lord and master.
GONORILL. Mean you to enjoy him, then?
ALBANY. The let-alone lies not in your good will.
BASTARD. Nor in thine, Lord.
ALBANY. Half-blooded fellow, yes.
BASTARD. Let the drum strike, and prove my title good.
ALBANY. Stay yet, hear reason. Edmund, I arrest thee
On capital treason; and in thine attaint,[10] (*Indicating Gonorill.*)
This gilded serpent. (*To Regan.*) For your claim, fair sister,

[10] *in thine attaint* Sharing your corruption.

I bar it in the interest[1] of my wife.
'Tis *she* is sub-contracted to this Lord;
And I, her husband, contradict your banns.[2]
If you will marry, make your loves to me.[3]
My Lady is bespoke.
GONERILL. An interlude![4]
ALBANY. (*To Edmund.*) Thou art armed Gloucester; let the trumpet sound.[5]
If none appear to prove[6] upon thy person
Thy heinous, manifest, and many treasons,

(*He throws down his glove.*)

There is my pledge. I'll make it[7] on thy heart,
Ere I taste bread, thou art in nothing less
Than I have here proclaimed thee.
REGAN. Sick, O sick!
GONERILL. (*Aside.*) If not, I'll ne'er trust medicine.
EDMUND. (*To Albany, throwing down his own glove.*)
There's my exchange.[8] What in the world[9] he is
That names me traitor, villain-like he lies.
Call by the trumpet. He that dares approach—
On him, on you; who not?—I will maintain
My truth and honour firmly.
ALBANY. A herald, ho!

(*Enter a Herald.*)

Trust to thy single virtue, for thy soldiers
All levied in my name, have in my name

I bar it in the interest of my wife.
'Tis *she* is subcontracted to this lord,
And I, her husband, contradict the banns.
If you will marry, make your love to me.
My Lady is bespoke.

(*To Bastard.*) Thou art armed, Gloucester;

If none appear to prove upon thy head
Thy heinous, manifest, and many treasons,

(*He throws down his glove.*)

There is my pledge. I'll prove it on thy heart,
Ere I taste bread, thou art in nothing less
Than I have here proclaimed thee.
REGAN. Sick, o sick.
GONORILL. (*Aside.*) If not, I'll ne'er trust poison.
BASTARD. (*To Albany, throwing down his own glove.*)
There's my exchange. What in the world he is
That names me traitor, villain-like he lies.
Call by thy trumpet. He that dares approach—
On him, on you; who not?—I will maintain
My truth and honour firmly.
ALBANY. A herald, ho!
BASTARD. A herald ho! A herald!

ALBANY. Trust to thy single virtue, for thy soldiers,
All levied in my name, have in my name

parallel texts

[1] *in the interest of* On behalf of.

[2] *banns* Formal declaration of the intent to marry.

[3] *to me* I.e., because if Gonerill can make a sub-contract, so can Albany (spoken facetiously).

[4] *interlude* Short farcical play, by now old-fashioned.

[5] *let the trumpet sound* I.e., to announce a challenge to a duel.

[6] *prove* I.e., by combat.

[7] *make it* Make it good, prove it.

[8] *exchange* Acceptance of the duel (symbolized through the exchange of gloves).

[9] *What in the world* Whoever in the world.

Took their discharge.[1]

REGAN. My sickness grows upon me.

ALBANY. She is not well, convey her to my tent.

(*Exit Regan with one or more soldiers.*)

Come hither, herald. Let the trumpet sound,
And read out this.

(*A trumpet sounds.*)

HERALD. (*Reads.*) "If any man of quality or degree,[2] within the lists[3] of the army, will maintain upon Edmund, supposèd Earl of Gloucester, that he is a manifold traitor, let him appear by the third sound of the trumpet. He is bold in his defence.

(*1st trumpet.*)

HERALD. Again.

(*2nd trumpet.*)

HERALD. Again.

(*3rd trumpet. Trumpet answers within.*)
(*Enter Edgar, armed.*[4])

ALBANY. Ask him his purposes, why he appears
Upon this call o'th'trumpet.

HERALD. What are you?
Your name, your quality, and why you answer
This present summons?

Took their discharge.

REGAN. This sickness grows upon me.

ALBANY. She is not well; convey her to my tent.

(*Exit Regan with one or more soldiers. Enter a Herald.*)

Come hither, herald. Let the trumpet sound,
And read out this.

CAPTAIN. Sound trumpet!

(*A trumpet sounds.*)

HERALD. (*Reads.*) "If any man of quality or degree, in the host[5] of the army, will maintain upon Edmund, supposèd Earl of Gloucester, that he's a manifold traitor, let him appear at the third sound of the trumpet. He is bold in his defence."

BASTARD. Sound!

(*Trumpeter sounds a second time.*[6])

Again!

(*Trumpeter sounds a third time.*)
(*Enter Edgar [armed] at the third sound, a trumpet before him.*[7])

ALBANY. Ask him his purposes, why he appears
Upon this call o'th'trumpet.

HERALD. (*To Edgar.*) What are you?
Your name and quality, and why you answer
This present summons?

---

[1] *Trust … discharge* You're on your own, because all of your soldiers, who were recruited using my name, have been discharged by my authority.

[2] *quality or degree* Noble rank or important position.

[3] *lists* Rolls.

[4] *armed* A helmet conceals his face.

[5] *host* Body.

[6] *second time* In Q, the trumpets are counted from that which preceded the herald; in F, from after the herald's announcement.

[7] *before him* I.e., sound in response, just before his entrance.

EDGAR. Know my name is lost
By treason's tooth: bare-gnawn, and canker-bit.[1]
Yet am I noble as the adversary
I come to cope.[2]
ALBANY. Which is that adversary?
EDGAR. What's he that speaks for Edmund, Earl of
Gloucester?
EDMUND. Himself, what say'st thou to him?
EDGAR. Draw thy sword,
That, if my speech offend a noble heart,
Thy arm may do thee justice. Here is mine.

(*He draws his sword.*)

Behold; it is my privilege,
The privilege of mine honours,
My oath, and my profession.[3] I protest—[4]
Malgré[5] thy strength, place, youth, and eminence,
Despite thy victor-sword,[6] and fire-new fortune,
Thy valour, and thy heart—thou art a traitor:
False to thy gods, thy brother, and thy father,
Conspirant 'gainst this high illustrious Prince,[7]
And from th'extremest upward of thy head,
To the descent and dust below thy foot,
A most toad-spotted traitor. Say thou "no":
This sword, this arm, and my best spirits are bent
To prove upon thy heart, whereto I speak,
Thou liest.
EDMUND. In wisdom I should ask thy name,[8]
But since thy outside looks so fair and warlike,
And that thy tongue (some say)[9] of breeding breathes,

EDGAR. O know, my name is lost;
By treason's tooth, bare-gnawn and canker-bit.
Yet, ere I move't,[10] where is the adversary
I come to cope withal?[11]
ALBANY. Which is that adversary?
EDGAR. What's he that speaks for Edmund, Earl of
Gloucester?
BASTARD. Himself, what sayest thou to him?
EDGAR. Draw thy sword,
That, if my speech offend a noble heart, thy arm
May do thee justice. Here is mine.

(*He draws his sword.*)

Behold; it is the privilege of my tongue,

My oath, and my profession. I protest—
Malgré thy strength, youth, place and eminence;
Despite thy victor-sword, and fire-new fortune,
Thy valour and thy heart—thou art a traitor:
False to thy gods, thy brother, and thy father;
Conspirate 'gainst this high, illustrious prince,
And from th'extremest upward of thy head,
To the descent and dust beneath thy feet,
A most toad-spotted traitor. Say thou "no":
This sword, this arm—and my best spirit—is bent
To prove upon thy heart, whereto I speak,
Thou liest.
BASTARD. In wisdom I should ask thy name;
But since thy outside looks so fair and warlike,
And that thy being some say[12] of breeding breathes,

[1] *canker-bit* Worm-eaten.

[2] *cope* Deal with; encounter in battle.

[3] *profession* Vows and role as a knight.

[4] *protest* Claim.

[5] *Malgré* Despite.

[6] *victor-sword* Victorious sword (in the battle just fought).

[7] *Prince* I.e., Albany.

[8] *In wisdom … name* It would be prudent because, if his adversary were a man of lower social rank, according to the rules of chivalry he could honorably refuse combat.

[9] *(some say)* This provides an interesting example of the effect of a compositor's punctuation on the sense of a line. While in most cases, the punctuation of both Q and F has been altered to make the best sense to a contemporary reader, the parentheses around "some say" have been left here to show the transformation of the meaning according to the original compositor's understanding of the line. While in Q, "some say" is to be understood as "some assay" (or hint), the object of "breathes," in F Edmund appears to be reporting the rumors he has heard; but there has been no such opportunity for him to hear anything said about his masked adversary.

[10] *ere I move't* Before I declare my case against him.

[11] *cope withal* Encounter by means of this (challenge).

[12] *some say* Some hint, or taste (i.e., "given that your being breathes a hint of breeding").

parallel texts

What safe and nicely I might well delay° *avoid*
By rule of knighthood, I disdain and spurn.
Back do I toss these treasons to thy head.
With the hell-hated[1] lie, o'er-whelm thy heart,
Which, for they yet glance by and scarcely bruise,
This sword of mine shall give them instant way,[2]
Where they shall rest for ever. Trumpets, speak!

(*The trumpets sound. Edgar and Edmund fight; Edgar wounds and overcomes Edmund and holds him at his mercy.*)

ALBANY. Save him, save him.[3]
GONERILL. (*To Edmund.*) This is practice,[4] Gloucester.
By th'law of war, thou wast not bound to answer
An unknown opposite! Thou art not vanquished,
But cozened, and beguiled.
ALBANY. Shut your mouth, dame,
Or with this paper[5] shall I stop it! —Hold, Sir.—[6]
Thou worse than any name, read thine own evil.
No tearing Lady, I perceive you know it.
GONERILL. Say if I do, the laws are mine not thine,[7]
Who can arraign me for't?[8]

(*Exit.*)

ALBANY. Most monstrous! (*To Edmund.*)
O, know'st thou this paper?
EDMUND. Ask me not what I know.

[1] *hell-hated* Hated as much as hell.

[2] *give … way* Make a passage for them (to your heart).

[3] *save him* Spare him (i.e., not a cry for help, but a request that Edgar allow Edmund to live—presumably so he can make a full confession).

[4] *practice* Trickery.

[5] *this paper* The letter from Gonerill to Edmund that Oswald was carrying when Edgar killed him.

[6] *Hold, Sir* Perhaps addressed to Edgar, who stands ready to kill Edmund, or perhaps to Edmund, who is trying to rise.

[7] *mine and not thine* Gonerill is of royal blood; although Albany is the effective ruler, technically, he is only the consort.

[8] *Who … for't* I.e., there is no one of higher rank to bring a sovereign to trial.

My right of knighthood, I disdain and spurn.
Here do I toss those treasons to thy head.
With the hell hated lie o'er-turn thy heart,
Which, for they yet glance by and scarcely bruise,
This sword of mine shall give them instant way,
Where they shall rest for ever. Trumpets, speak!

(*The trumpets sound. Edgar and Bastard fight; Edgar wounds and overcomes Bastard and holds him at his mercy.*)

ALBANY. Save him, save him.
GONORILL. (*To Bastard.*) This is mere practice, Gloucester!
By the law of arms, thou art not bound to answer
An unknown opposite! Thou art not vanquished,
But cozened and beguiled!
ALBANY. Stop your mouth, dame,
Or with this paper shall I stopple it![9]
Thou, worse than anything, read thine own evil.
Nay, no tearing, Lady; I perceive you know't.
GONORILL. Say if I do: the laws are mine, not thine;
Who shall arraign me for't?

ALBANY. Most monstrous!
Know'st thou this paper?
GONORILL. Ask me not what I know.[10]

(*Exit Gonorill.*)

[9] *stopple it* Put a stopper in it (as a cork is put in a bottle).

[10] *Ask … know* Cf. F's assignment of this line to Edmund.

ALBANY. (*To Soldiers.*) Go after her. She's desperate;
govern her.
EDMUND. What you have charged me with, that have
I done;
And more, much more; the time will bring it out.
'Tis past, and so am I.[1] But what art thou
That hast this fortune on me? If thou'rt noble,
I do forgive thee.
EDGAR. Let's exchange charity:
I am no less in blood than thou art, Edmund;
If more,[2] the more th'hast wronged me.

(*Removes his helmet.*)

My name is Edgar, and thy father's son.
The gods are just, and of our pleasant vices
Make instruments to plague us;
The dark and vicious place[3] where thee he got,° *begot*
Cost him his eyes.
EDMUND. Th'hast spoken right; 'tis true;
The wheel is come full circle;[4] I am here.
ALBANY. (*To Edgar.*) Methought thy very gait did
prophesy
A royal nobleness. I must embrace thee.
Let sorrow split my heart, if ever I
Did hate thee, or thy father.
EDGAR. Worthy Prince, I know't.
ALBANY. Where have you hid yourself?
How have you known the miseries of your father?
EDGAR. By nursing them, my Lord. List[5] a brief tale;
And when 'tis told, O that my heart would burst!
The bloody proclamation[6] to escape
That followed me so near—O, our lives' sweetness,
That we the pain of death would hourly die,

ALBANY. (*To Soldiers.*) Go after her. She's desperate;
govern her.
BASTARD. What you have charged me with, that have I
done;
And more, much more; the time will bring it out.
'Tis past, and so am I. But what art thou
That hast this fortune on me? If thou be'st noble
I do forgive thee.
EDGAR. Let's exchange charity.
I am no less in blood than thou art, Edmund;
If more, the more thou hast wronged me.

(*Removes his helmet.*)

My name is Edgar, and thy father's son.
The gods are just, and of our pleasant virtues
Make instruments to scourge us;
The dark and vicious place where thee he got
Cost him his eyes.
BASTARD. Thou hast spoken truth;
The wheel is come full circled; I am here.
ALBANY. (*To Edgar.*) Methought thy very gait did
prophesy
A royal nobleness. I must embrace thee.
Let sorrow split my heart if I did ever hate
Thee or thy father.
EDGAR. Worthy Prince, I know[1]t.
ALBANY. Where have you hid yourself?
How have you known the miseries of your father ?
EDGAR. By nursing them, my Lord. List a brief tale;
And when 'tis told, O that my heart would burst!
The bloody proclamation to escape
That followed me so near—O, our lives, sweetness,
That with the pain of death would hourly die,

parallel texts

[1] *so am I* He is dying from a wound he received in the fight.

[2] *If more* In that he is legitimate.

[3] *dark and vicious place* Place of sin (adultery).

[4] *wheel … circle* I.e., just as Gloucester's dark sin left him with darkened sight, so has Edmund's plan to overcome Edgar resulted in Edgar's overcoming him.

[5] *List* I.e., listen to.

[6] *bloody proclamation* Announcement that he was a traitor and was wanted dead or alive.

parallel texts

Rather then die at once![1]—taught me to shift
Into a mad-man's rags, t'assume a semblance
That very dogs disdained. And in this habit° *costume*
Met I my father with his bleeding rings,
Their precious stones° new lost; became his guide, *eyes*
Led him, begged for him, saved him from despair.
Never—O fault!—revealed myself unto him,
Until some half hour past, when I was armed.
Not sure, though hoping of this good success,
I asked his blessing, and from first to last
Told him our pilgrimage. But his flawed heart—
Alack, too weak the conflict to support!—
Twixt two extremes of passion, joy and grief,
Burst smilingly.
EDMUND. This speech of yours hath moved me,
And shall perchance do good. But speak you on;
You look as you had something more to say.
ALBANY. If there be more, more woeful, hold it in,
For I am almost ready to dissolve,[2]
Hearing of this.

[1] *our lives' ... once* This is a sign of how dearly we value life, that we would accept a situation so painful that it felt as if we were dying every hour rather than confronting certain death and thereby getting it over and done with.

[2] *dissolve* I.e., into tears.

Rather than die at once!—taught me to shift
Into a mad-man's rags, to assume a semblance
That very dogs disdained. And in this habit
Met I my father with his bleeding rings,
The precious stones new lost; became his guide,
Led him, begged for him, saved him from despair.
Never—O Father!—revealed myself unto him,
Until some half hour past, when I was armed.
Not sure, though hoping of this good success,
I asked his blessing, and from first to last,
Told him my pilgrimage. But his flawed heart—
Alack, too weak the conflict to support!—
Twixt two extremes of passion, joy and grief,
Burst smilingly.
BASTARD. This speech of yours hath moved me,
And shall perchance do good. But speak you on;
You look as you had something more to say,
ALBANY. If there be more, more woeful, hold it in,
For I am almost ready to dissolve,
Hearing of this.
EDGAR. This would have seemed a period° *ending*
To such as love not sorrow;
But another to amplify—too much
Would make much more and top extremity—[3]
Whil'st I was big in clamour,[4] came there in a man,
Who having seen me in my worst estate,° *condition*
Shunned my abhorred society; but then, finding
Who 'twas that so endured,[5] with his strong arms
He fastened on my neck and bellowed out
As he'd burst heaven; threw him on my father,[6]
Told the most piteous tale of Lear and him
That ever ear received—which, in recounting,
His grief grew puissant° and the strings of life[7] *overpowering*
Began to crack. Twice, then, the trumpets sounded,
And there I left him tranced.

[3] *This would ... extremity* This incident would have seemed a tragic enough ending for those with no taste for tragedies, but to tell (amplify) another story—if I were to add much more than this, it would surpass the utmost of what humans can bear.

[4] *big in clamour* Weeping loudly.

[5] *so endured* Had been forced to be Poor Tom.

[6] *my father* The body of Gloucester.

[7] *strings of life* Heart-strings.

(*Enter a Gentleman.*)

GENTLEMAN. Help, help! O help!
EDGAR. What kind of help?
ALBANY. Speak, man.
EDGAR. What means this bloody knife?
GENTLEMAN. 'Tis hot, it smokes!
It came even from the heart of—O, she's dead!

ALBANY. Who dead? Speak, man!
GENTLEMAN. Your Lady, Sir, your Lady! And her sister
By her is poisoned; she confesses it.
EDMUND. I was contracted to them both, all three
Now marry in an instant.
EDGAR. Here comes Kent

(*Enter Kent.*)

ALBANY. Produce the bodies, be they alive or dead.

(*Some Soldiers go to recover the bodies.*[1])

This judgement of the heavens that makes us tremble.
Touches us not with pity. (*Of Kent.*) O, is this he?

The time will not allow the compliment
Which very manners urges.[2]
KENT. I am come
To bid my King and Master aye° good night. *forever*
Is he not here?

ALBANY. But who was this?
EDGAR. Kent sir, the banished Kent; who, in disguise,
Followed his enemy king and did him service
Improper for a slave.[3]

(*Enter one with a bloody knife.*)

GENTLEMAN. Help, help!

ALBANY. What kind of help? What means that bloody knife?
GENTLEMAN. It's hot, it smokes! It came even from the heart of …
ALBANY. Who, man, speak?
GENTLEMAN. Your Lady, Sir, your Lady! And her sister
By her is poisoned; she hath confessed it.
BASTARD. I was contracted to them both, all three
Now marry in an instant.

ALBANY. Produce their bodies, be they alive or dead.

(*Some Soldiers go to recover the bodies.*)

This justice of the heavens that makes us tremble,
Touches us not with pity.
EDGAR. Here comes Kent, Sir.

(*Enter Kent.*)

ALBANY. O, 'tis he! The time will not allow
The compliment that very manners urges.
KENT. I am come
To bid my King and master aye good night.
Is he not here?

parallel texts

[1] *Some … bodies* F has the next stage direction (*Gonerill and Regan's bodies brought out*) placed at this point, though it is clear that the action of retrieving the bodies merely begins here.

[2] *compliment … urges* Formal greeting which mere manners would dictate.

[3] *Improper … slave* Entailing more hardship than would be expected of a slave.

ALBANY. Great thing of us forgot,
Speak, Edmund, where's the King? And where's
Cordelia?

(*Gonerill and Regan's bodies brought out.*)

ALBANY. Seest thou this object, Kent?[1]
KENT. Alack, why thus?
EDMUND. Yet Edmund was beloved:
The one the other poisoned for my sake,
And after slew herself.
ALBANY. Even so. Cover their faces.
EDMUND. I pant for life; some good I mean to do
Despite of mine own nature. Quickly send—
Be brief in it!—to'th'castle; for my writ
Is on the life of Lear and on Cordelia!
Nay, send in time.
ALBANY. (*To Soldiers.*) Run, run, O run!
EDGAR. (*Stopping them.*) To who my Lord? (*To Edmund.*) Who has the office?[2]
Send thy token of reprieve.
EDMUND. Well thought on.
Take my sword; give it the Captain.
EDGAR. (*Giving the sword to the Soldiers.*) Haste thee, for thy life!

(*Exit one or more Soldiers.*)[3]

EDMUND. (*To Albany.*) He hath commission from thy wife and me,
To hang Cordelia in the prison, and
To lay the blame upon her own despair,
That she fordid herself.[4]
ALBANY. The gods defend her!
Bear him hence awhile.

(*Soldiers bear Edmund off.*)

[1] *Seest ... Kent* In both Q and F, this line is assigned to Albany, but for reasons of dramatic effectiveness, it is occasionally reassigned in performance to Edmund.

[2] *office* Orders (to kill Lear and Cordelia).

[3] *Exit ... Soldiers* Cf. Q and note.

[4] *fordid herself* Committed suicide.

ALBANY. Great thing of us forgot!
Speak Edmund, where's the King? And where's
Cordelia?

(*The bodies of Gonorill and Regan are brought in.*)

BASTARD. Seest thou this object, Kent?[5]
KENT. Alack, why thus?
BASTARD. Yet Edmund was beloved,
The one the other poisoned for my sake,
And after slew herself.
ALBANY. Even so. Cover their faces.
BASTARD. I pant for life; some good I mean to do,
Despite of my own nature. Quickly send—
Be brief, in't!—to th'castle; for my writ,
Is on the life of Lear and on Cordelia,
Nay send in time.
ALBANY. (*To Edgar.*) Run, run, O run!
EDGAR. To who my Lord? (*To Edmund.*) Who hath the office?
Send thy token of reprieve.
BASTARD. Well thought on.
Take my sword— the Captain; give it the Captain!
ALBANY. (*To Edgar*) Haste thee, for thy life!

(*Exit Edgar.*[6])

BASTARD. He hath commission from thy wife and me,
To hang Cordelia in the prison, and to lay
The blame upon her own despair,
That she fordid her self.
ALBANY. The gods defend her!
Bear him hence a while.

(*Soldiers bear Bastard off.*)

[5] *Seest ... Kent* See note on this line in F.

[6] *To Edgar ... Exit Edgar* No stage directions are offered here in either Q or F. Most editors suppose that it is the Second Captain, who appears shortly thereafter, who is sent. But an exit here could not plausibly give him time to witness Lear's killing of the first Captain. Furthermore, the assignment of "Haste thee for thy life" to Albany in Q, together with Edgar's preceding dialogue, suggests that it is more probably Edgar who goes.

(*Enter Lear with Cordelia in his arms, [followed by a Gentleman].*)

LEAR. Howl, howl, howl! O, you are men of stones!
Had I your tongues and eyes,[1] I'd use them so
That heavens' vault[2] should crack! She's gone for ever.
I know when one is dead, and when one lives;
She's dead as earth. Lend me a looking-glass.
If that her breath will mist or stain the stone,
Why then, she lives.
KENT. Is this the promised end?[3]
EDGAR. Or image of that horror.
ALBANY. Fall and cease.[4]
LEAR. This feather stirs;[5] she lives! If it be so,
It is a chance which does redeem all sorrows
That ever I have felt.
KENT. O, my good Master—
LEAR. Prithee, away.
EDGAR. 'Tis noble Kent, your friend.
LEAR. A plague upon you; murderers, traitors all!
I might have saved her; now she's gone for ever!—
Cordelia, Cordelia, stay a little— Ha?
What is't thou say'st? —Her voice was ever soft,
Gentle, and low: an excellent thing in woman.—
I killed the slave that was a-hanging thee.
GENTLEMAN. 'Tis true, my Lords, he did.
LEAR. Did I not, fellow?
I have seen the day, with my good biting falchion[6]
I would have made him skip. I am old now,
And these same crosses spoil me.[7] (*To Kent.*) Who are you?
Mine eyes are not o'th'best, I'll tell you straight.

[1] *tongues and eyes* I.e., eyes for seeing the horror, tongues for protesting it.

[2] *heavens' vault* The sky (conceived up as an arched roof in which the stars were fixed).

[3] *promised end* Generally taken as an allusion to Judgement Day, the end of the world prophesied in the Bible (Mark 13, Revelations 16, etc.), but see the note on this line in Q.

[4] *Fall and cease* Let the heavens fall and the world cease.

[5] *feather stirs* Lear mistakenly believes a feather is stirred by Cordelia's breath.

[6] *biting falchion* Sharp curved sword.

[7] *these ... spoil me* These sorts of confrontation ruin my strength.

(*Enter Lear with Cordelia in his arms.*)
(*Edgar follows behind with the Second Captain.*)

LEAR. Howl, howl, howl, howl! O you are men of stones!
Had I your tongues and eyes, I would use them so
That heavens' vault should crack! She's gone for ever.
I know when one is dead, and when one lives;
She's dead as earth. Lend me a looking-glass;
If that her breath will mist or stain the stone,
Why then, she lives.
KENT. Is this the promised end?[8]
EDGAR. Or image of that horror.
ALBANY. Fall and cease.
LEAR. This feather stirs; she lives! If it be so,
It is a chance which does redeem all sorrows
That ever I have felt.
KENT. Ah, my good master—
LEAR. Prithee, away!
EDGAR. 'Tis noble Kent, your friend.
LEAR. A plague upon you, murderous traitors all!
I might have saved her; now she's gone for ever!—
Cordelia, Cordelia, stay a little— Ha?
What is't thou sayest? —Her voice was ever soft,
Gentle and low: an excellent thing in women.—
I killed the slave that was a-hanging thee.
[2ND] CAPTAIN. 'Tis true my Lords, he did.
LEAR. Did I not, fellow?
I have seen the day, with my good biting falchion
I would have made them skip. I am old now,
And these same crosses spoil me. (*To Kent.*) Who are you?
Mine eyes are not o'the best, I'll tell you straight.

[8] *promised end* Kent may be speaking of Judgement Day, the end of the world, but there remain the possibilities that he is referring either (as some critics have argued) to the end of the chain of events begun in the first scene of the play with the abdication of Lear, or to the "top [ping of] extremity" mentioned earlier in this scene (in Q, though not in F), when Edgar had talked about the consequences of adding one sad story on top of another. In any case, Edgar certainly takes Kent's line as an apocalyptic reference.

Kent. If Fortune brag of two she loved and hated,
One of them we behold.[1]
Lear. This is a dull sight, are you not Kent?
Kent. The same—
Your servant Kent. Where is your servant Caius?[2]
Lear. He's a good fellow, I can tell you that,
He'll strike and quickly too. He's dead and rotten.
Kent. No my good Lord, I am the very man—
Lear. I'll see that straight.[3]
Kent. —that from your first of difference and decay,[4]
Have followed your sad steps.
Lear. You are welcome hither.
Kent. Nor no man else.[5] All's cheerless, dark, and deadly.
Your eldest daughters have fordone themselves,
And desperately° are dead. *in despair*
Lear. Aye, so I think.
Albany. He knows not what he says; and vain is it
That we present us to him.
Edgar. Very bootless.° *useless*

(*Enter a Messenger.*)

Messenger. Edmund is dead, my Lord.
Albany. That's but a trifle here.
You Lords and noble friends, know our intent:
What comfort to this great decay may come,[6]
Shall be applied. For us, we[7] will resign,
During the life of this old majesty,
To him our absolute power. (*To Edgar and Kent.*) You
to your rights,
With boot,[8] and such addition as your honours
Have more than merited. All friends shall
Taste the wages of their virtue, and all foes
The cup of their deservings. —O see, see.

Kent. If Fortune bragged of two she loved or hated,
One of them we behold.
Lear. Are not you Kent?
Kent. The same, your servant Kent. Where is your
servant, Caius?
Lear. He's a good fellow, I can tell that,
He'll strike and quickly too. He's dead and rotten.
Kent. No my good Lord, I am the very man—
Lear. I'll see that straight.
Kent. —that from your life of difference and decay,
Have followed your sad steps.
Lear. You're welcome hither.
Kent. Nor no man else. All's cheerless, dark and deadly.
Your eldest daughters have fordone themselves,
And desperately are dead.
Lear. So think I, too.
Albany. He knows not what he sees; and vain it is,
That we present us to him.
Edgar. Very bootless.

(*Enter [another] Captain.*)

[3rd]Captain. Edmund is dead my Lord.
Albany. That's but a trifle here.
You Lords and noble friends, know our intent:
What comfort to this decay may come,
Shall be applied. For us, we will resign
During the life of this old majesty
To him our absolute power. (*To Edgar and Kent.*)

You to your rights with boot, and such addition
As your honour have more than merited.
All friends shall taste the wages of their virtue,
And all foes the cup of their deservings—
(*Looking at Lear.*) O see, see!

[1] *If Fortune … behold* Kent offers Lear a clue in a sort of riddle: i.e., "If Fortune brought her greatest extremes to two people, each of us beholds one of them."

[2] *Caius* This is the only mention of the name Kent took when in disguise.

[3] *I'll … straight* I'll look into that in a moment.

[4] *first … decay* First days of your change and decline in fortune.

[5] *Nor no man else* This line could finish off Kent's previous speech (i.e., "the very man, and no one else") or it could be a response to Lear's line (i.e., "No, I don't suppose I am welcome, nor is anyone else").

[6] *What comfort … come* Whatever may be done to help the general disaster we have experienced.

[7] *us, we* Albany is using "the royal we" to refer to himself.

[8] *boot* Extra measure.

LEAR. And my poor fool[1] is hanged. No, no, no life?
Why should a dog, a horse, a rat have life,
And thou, no breath at all? Thou'lt come no more.
Never, never, never, never, never.
Pray you, undo this button.[2] Thank you, Sir.
Do you see this? Look on her? Look her lips,
Look there, look there—
(*He dies.*)

EDGAR. He faints. (*To Lear.*) My Lord? My Lord?
KENT. Break heart, I prithee break.
EDGAR. Look up, my Lord.
KENT. Vex not his ghost. O let him pass. He hates him,
That would upon the rack[3] of this tough world
Stretch him out longer.

EDGAR. He is gone indeed.
KENT. The wonder is, he hath endured so long,
He but usurped his life.[4]
ALBANY. (*To Soldiers.*) Bear them from hence. Our present business
Is general woe. (*To Edgar and Kent*) Friends of my soul, you twain
Rule in this realm, and the gored state sustain.
KENT. I have a journey, Sir, shortly to go;
My master calls me; I must not say no.
EDGAR.[5] The weight of this sad time we must obey,° *submit to*
Speak what we feel, not what we ought to say.
The oldest hath borne° most; we that are young, *suffered*
Shall never see so much, nor live so long.

(*Exeunt with a dead march.*)

[*End of Play.*]
—1623

LEAR. And my poor fool is hanged. No, no life.
Why should a dog, a horse, a rat have life,
And thou, no breath at all? O, thou wilt come no more.
Never, never, never. Pray you:
Undo this button? Thank you sir. O, o, o, o.

EDGAR. He faints. (*To Lear.*) My Lord? My Lord?
LEAR. Break heart, I prithee break.
EDGAR. Look up, my Lord.
KENT. Vex not his ghost. O, let him pass. He hates him
That would upon the rack of this tough world
Stretch him out longer.

(*Lear dies.*[6])

EDGAR. O, he is gone indeed.
KENT. The wonder is, he hath endured so long.
He but usurped his life.
ALBANY. (*To Soldiers.*) Bear them from hence. Our present business
Is to general woe. (*To Edgar and Kent.*) Friends of my soul, you 'twain
Rule in this kingdom, and the gored state sustain.
KENT. I have a journey, Sir, shortly to go;
My master calls, and I must not say no.
ALBANY.[7] The weight of this sad time we must obey,
Speak what we feel, not what we ought to say.
The oldest have borne most; we that are young,
Shall never see so much, nor live so long.

(*Exeunt, bearing the bodies.*)

([*End of Play*].)
—1608

[1] *fool* Likely a term of endearment, used with reference to Cordelia, but possibly also a reference to the Fool, absent from the play since Act 3. The line has been much discussed, with some critics suggesting that Lear's madness leads him to conflate the two.

[2] *button* Presumably the button at his own throat.

[3] *rack* Instrument of torture on which the limbs of victims were painfully stretched.

[4] *usurped his life* Kept life longer than he was entitled to.

[5] *EDGAR* Note that this last speech is assigned to Albany in Q. By convention, the last speech in most tragedies is given to the character of highest social rank. But the references within the speech itself, to youth, and to speaking from the heart rather than according to protocol, have been cited by some critics as evidence that the speech is, indeed, intended for Edgar.

[6] *Lear dies* This is the latest the death might take place; unlike F, Q does not include a stage direction to mark the exact point of Lear's death.

[7] *ALBANY* Note that this last speech is assigned to Edgar in F.

IN CONTEXT

The Shakespearean Theater

The Swan Theatre

The illustration below, a "Sketch of The Swan Theatre" by Johannes De Witt, is the best visual guide we have of the physical arrangement of the interior of London's four playhouses of the late sixteenth century. The sketch, by a Dutch visitor, is accompanied by the following note (translated here from the Latin):

> There are four amphitheatres in London of notable beauty, which from their diverse signs bear diverse names. In each of them a different play is daily exhibited to the populace. The two more magnificent of these are situated to the southward beyond the Thames, and from the signs suspended before them are called the Rose and Swan. The two others are outside the city towards the north on the highway which issues through the Episcopal Gate, called in the vernacular Bishopsgate. There is also a fifth, but of dissimilar structure, devoted to the baiting of beasts, where are maintained in separate cages and enclosures many bears and dogs of stupendous size, which are kept for fighting, furnishing thereby a most delightful spectacle to men. Of all the theatres, however, the largest and the most magnificent is that one of which the sign is a swan, called in the vernacular the Swan Theatre; for it accommodates in its seats three thousand persons, and is built of a mass of flint stones (of which there is a prodigious supply in Britain), and supported by wooden columns painted in such excellent imitation of marble that it is able to deceive even the most cunning. Since its form resembles that of a Roman work, I have made a sketch of it above.

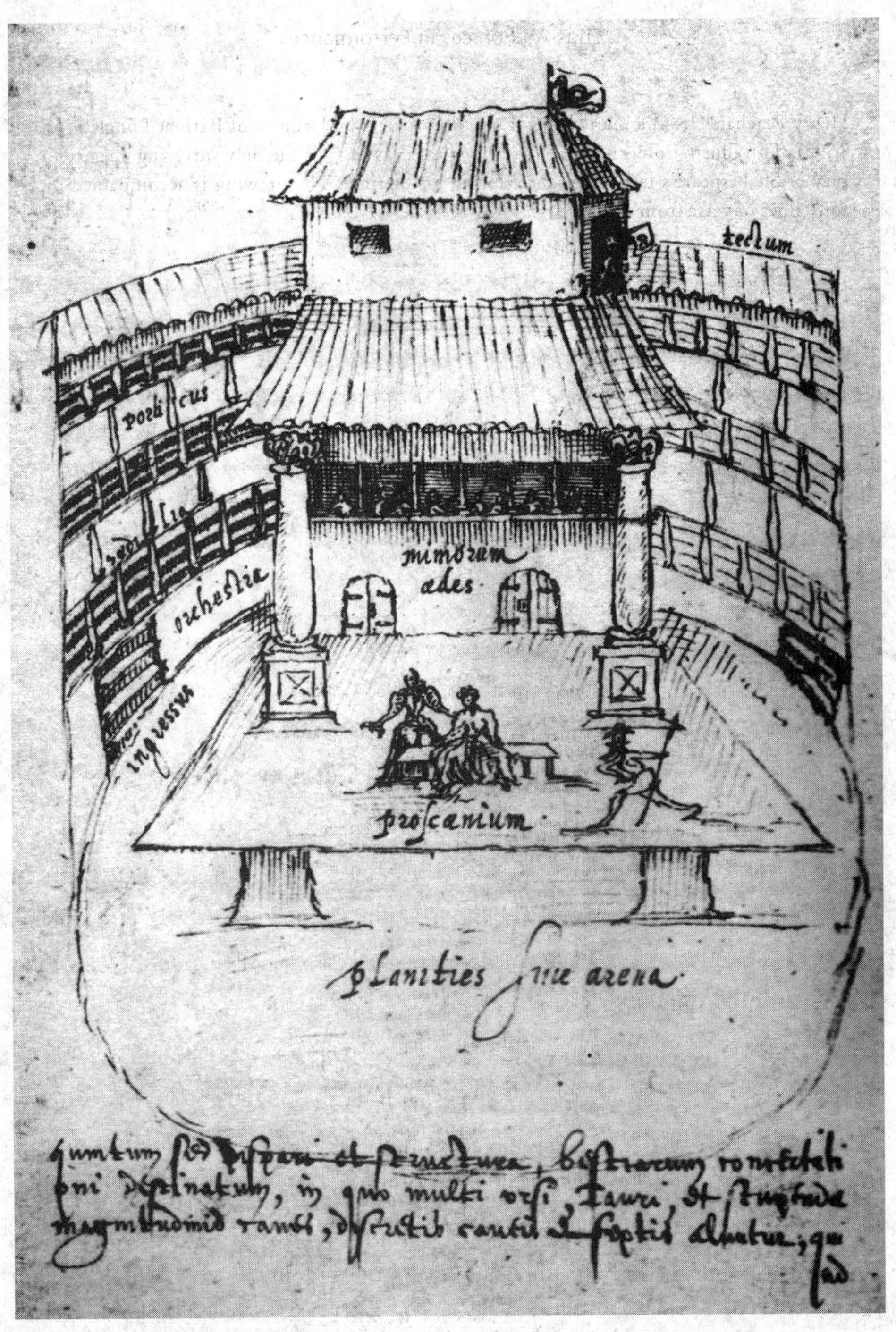

Johannes De Witt, Sketch of the Swan Theatre, as copied by Arend van Buchell (c. 1596).

Titus Andronicus in Performance

Henry Peacham, from a manuscript in the library of the Marquess of Bath at Longleat (c. 1595). This illustration (known as "the Longleat drawing") is the only surviving image of a play of Shakespeare's in performance during his lifetime. The drawing is accompanied by forty lines of verse from the play.

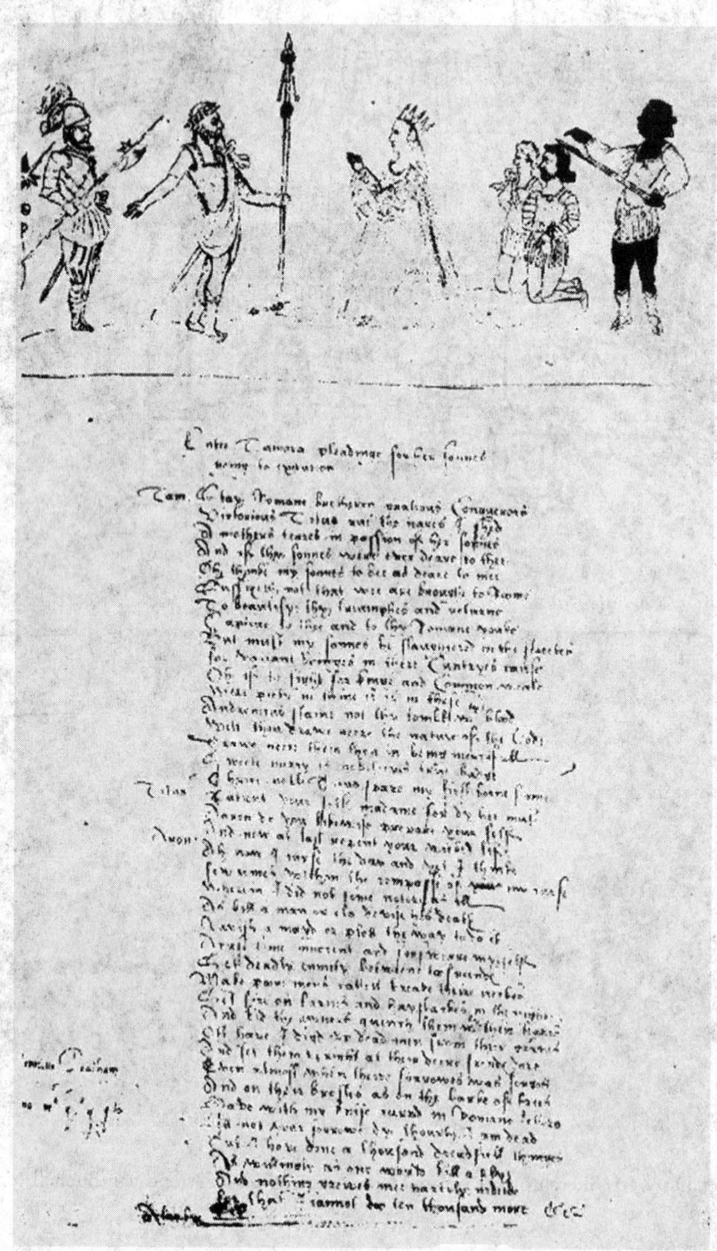

The Plot of an Elizabethan Play

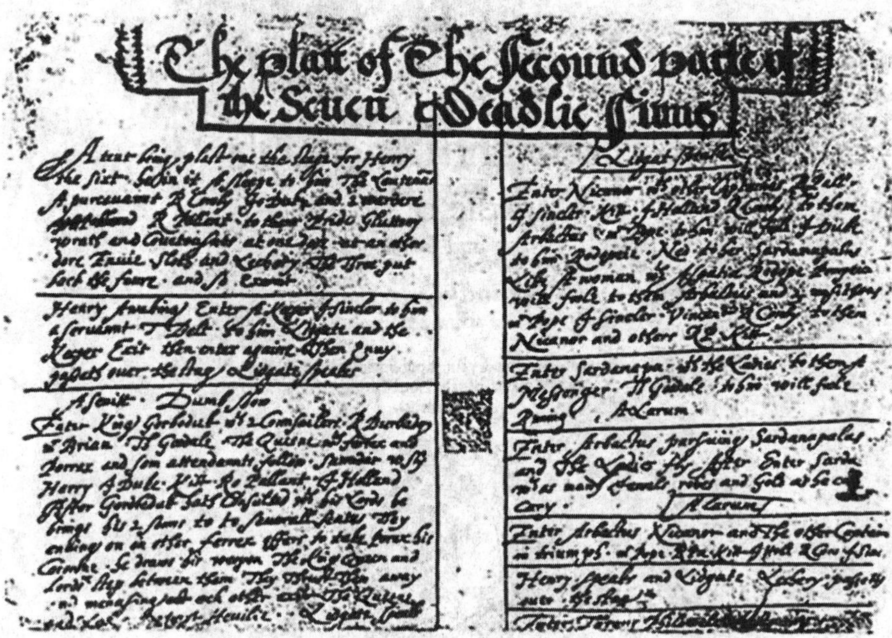

The plott of The secound parte of the Seven Deadlie sinns

The plot of *The Seven Deadly Sins* (c. 1590). Originally the "plot" was a physical object listing the scenes of a play, which was hung backstage as an aid for the actors. In this detail of the plot of *The Seven Deadly Sins, Part Two* the square from which the plot hung during a performance is visible.

Early Editions of Shakespeare's Plays

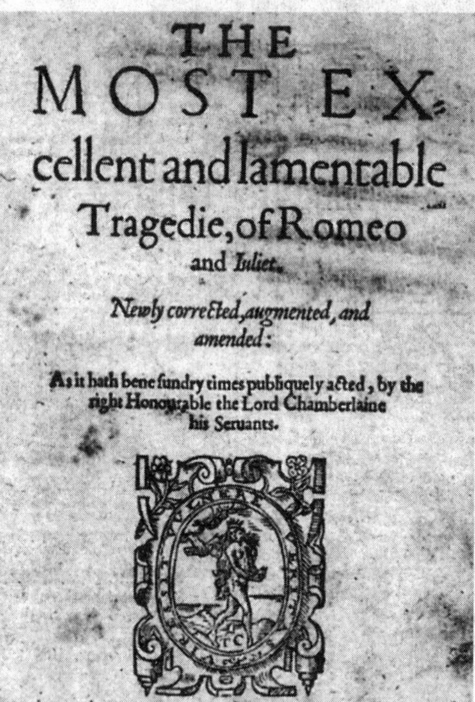

THE
MOST EX-
cellent and lamentable
Tragedie, of Romeo
and *Iuliet*.

Newly corrected, augmented, and amended:

As it hath bene ſundry times publiquely acted, by the right Honourable the Lord Chamberlaine his Seruants.

Romeo and Juliet, good Second Quarto edition (1599).

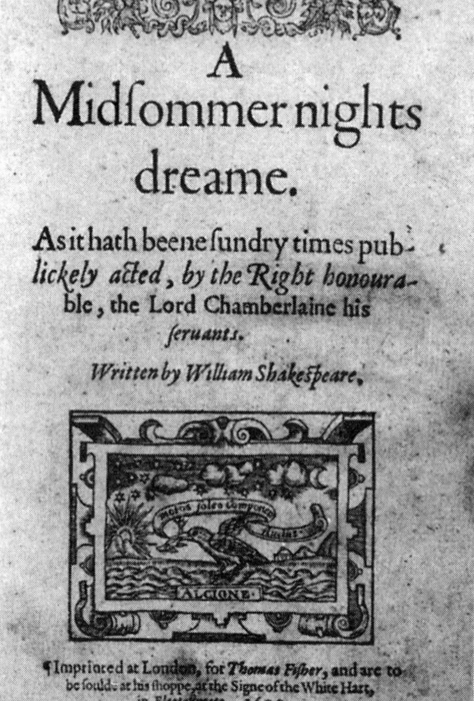

A
Midſommer nights
dreame.

As it hath beene ſundry times publickely *acted, by the Right honourable*, the Lord Chamberlaine his *ſeruants.*

Written by William Shakeſpeare.

¶ Imprinted at London, for *Thomas Fisher*, and are to be soulde at his ſhoppe, at the Signe of the White Hart, in *Fleeteſtreete*. 1600.

A Midsummer Night's Dream, good First Quarto edition (1600).

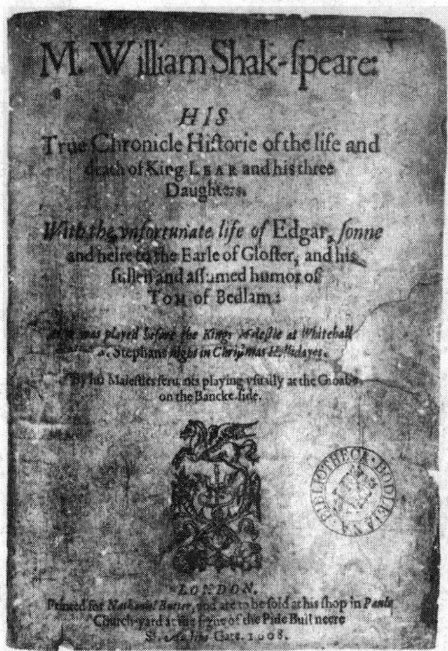

M. William Shak-speare:

HIS

True Chronicle Historie of the life and death of King LEAR and his three Daughters.

With the unfortunate life of Edgar, *sonne* and heire to the Earle of Gloster, and his sullen and assumed humor of TOM of Bedlam:

As it was played before the Kings Maiestie at Whitehall upon S. Stephans night in Christmas Hollidayes.

By his Maiesties seruants playing vsually at the Gloabe on the Bancke-side.

LONDON,

Printed for *Nathaniel Butter*, and are to be sold at his shop in *Pauls* Church-yard at the signe of the Pide Bull neere St. *Austins* Gate. 1608.

King Lear, First Quarto edition (1608).

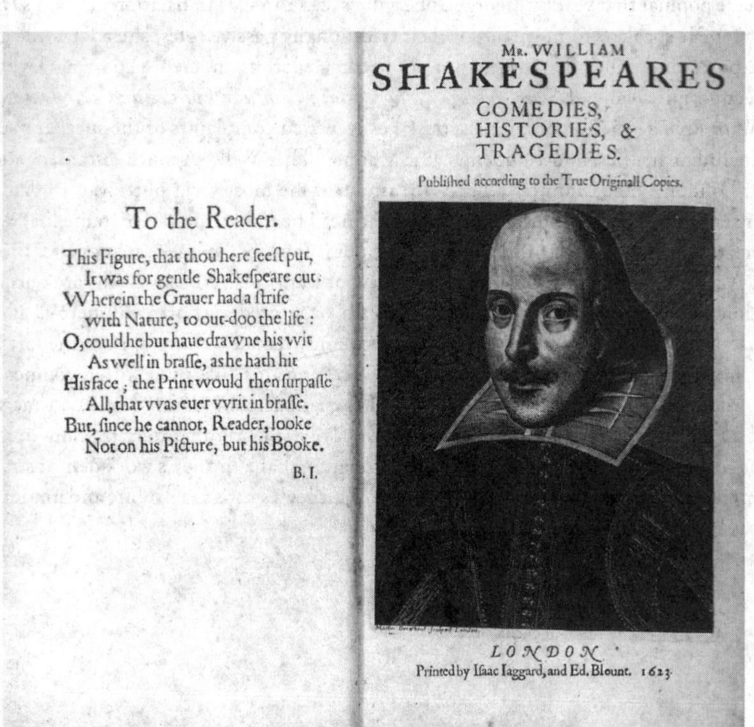

To the Reader.

This Figure, that thou here seest put,
It was for gentle Shakespeare cut;
Wherein the Grauer had a strife
with Nature, to out-doo the life:
O, could he but haue drawne his wit
As well in brasse, as he hath hit
His face; the Print would then surpasse
All, that vvas euer vvrit in brasse.
But, since he cannot, Reader, looke
Not on his Picture, but his Booke.

B. I.

MR. WILLIAM SHAKESPEARES COMEDIES, HISTORIES, & TRAGEDIES.

Published according to the True Originall Copies.

LONDON

Printed by Isaac Iaggard, and Ed. Blount. 1623.

Title page, Folio edition (1623). The page facing the title page includes a prefatory poem by Ben Jonson.

Isabella Whitney
fl. 1566 – 1573

Little record remains of the life of poet Isabella Whitney, and scholars cannot even estimate the dates of her birth and death. It is certain that she was alive and writing between the years 1566 and 1573, and that she spent a significant portion of her life in London, perhaps all of it. By cross-referencing names that appear in her poetry with names that appear in the will of one Geoffrey Whitney (c. 1548–1601), another minor writer, scholars guess that the two writers were siblings.

Although little is known about the woman behind the poetry, it is evident that, as a writer, Whitney was extraordinary for her time. She is the author of the earliest printed volume of secular poetry by a woman in England. While female writers of the sixteenth century were generally noblewomen or women of influence whose verses focused on pious themes, Whitney is not thought to have been well connected, and her verse is characterized by a uniquely public, informal tone. Her poems, often written in popular ballad measure, give easy expression to common secular concerns and engage with popular London literary trends.

The Copy of a Letter (1566–67), Whitney's first known miscellany, contains four jocular complaints from lovers—two female and two male—that play on contemporary debates about the nature of women. The female-narrated poems lament the misuse of women, while the male-narrated poems bemoan female rebelliousness. Whitney's poems play with the genre of the female love lament, which was made popular that year by George Tuberville's (c. 1543–97) translation of Ovid's *Heroides*. Allowing the female speakers to move out of their traditionally passive roles, she adapts the genre to her own purposes and cautions women not to become victims in men's sporting love affairs. Whitney's second miscellany, *A Sweet Nosegay and Certain Familiar Epistles and Friendly Letters by the Author: With Replies* (1573), contains a series of exaggerated complaints of the speaker's suffering and illness, including her best known poem, "The Manner of her Will." A mock testament addressed to the city of London, "The Manner of her Will" is one of the most vivid portrayals of daily life in sixteenth-century London to be found in British literature. The unique narrative frame that Whitney gives her mock testament may have influenced contemporary author George Gascoigne (c. 1534–77), whose "Last Will and Testament of Dan Bartholomew of Bath" (1573) uses a similar conceit.

In addition to her two miscellanies, Whitney is the suspected author of numerous additional poems in various miscellanies by other writers. She is the only female to have written the sort of verse that popular male writers of the period, including Gascoigne and Tuberville, often composed, and her poetry is thought to have influenced the work of these male contemporaries. In a time when it was unusual for any but the most privileged women to have even a rudimentary training in rhetoric, much less the sort of familiarity with contemporary literature that Whitney's work demonstrates, her accomplishments are all the more impressive. Despite Whitney's status as a prolific and unique female writer, she has been neglected by scholars until recently.

⌘⌘⌘

Is. W. to Her Unconstant Lover

As close° as you your wedding kept, *secret*
yet now the truth I hear,
Which you (ere now) might me have told—
what need you nay to swear?

You know I always wisht you well,
so will I during life;
But sith° you shall a husband be, *since*
God send you a good wife.

And this (whereso you shall become)
full boldly may you boast:
That once you had as true a love,
as dwelt in any coast.

Whose constantness had never quailed° *failed*
if you had not begon;° *left*
And yet it is not so far past
but might again be won.

If you so would, yea, and not change
so long as life would last,
But if that needs you marry must?
then farewell, hope is past.

And if you cannot be content
to lead a single life?
(Although the same right quiet be)
then take me to your wife.

So shall the promises be kept
that you so firmly made;
Now choose whether ye will be true,
or be of Sinon's trade.[1]

Whose trade if that you long shall use,
it shall your kindred stain;[2]
Example take by many a one
whose falsehood now is plain.

As by Aeneas first of all,
who did poor Dido[3] leave,
Causing the Queen by his untruth
with sword her heart to cleave.

Also I find that Theseus[4] did
his faithful love forsake,
Stealing away within the night,
before she did awake.

Jason[5] that came of noble race,
two ladies did beguile.
I muse how he durst show his face,
to them that knew his wile.

For when he by Medea's art
had got the Fleece of Gold
And also had of her that time,
all kind of things he wold.° *would, wished*

He took his ship and fled away,
regarding not the vows
That he did make so faithfully
unto his loving spouse.

How durst he trust the surging seas
knowing himself forsworn?

[1] *Sinon's trade* I.e., treachery. In Homer's *Odyssey*, Sinon is a Greek who allowed himself to be captured by the Trojans. Then, when the Greeks offered the "gift" of the wooden horse, he convinced the Trojans to accept it, allowing the Greeks hidden inside it to attack the city.

[2] *kindred stain* Belief that one's ancestors would be punished for one's evil deeds, as a result of the shame attached to the family name.

[3] *Aeneas* Son of Priam (king of Troy) who escaped the defeated Troy and founded Rome in Virgil's *Aeneid*; *Dido* Queen of Carthage, seduced and then abandoned by Aeneas on his way to found Rome.

[4] *Theseus* King of Athens who slew the monstrous Minotaur. He was able to escape from the Minotaur's labyrinth only by the help of Ariadne, daughter of the king of Crete, whom he brought with him when he left Crete but afterwards abandoned.

[5] *Jason* Leader of the Argonauts who captured the Golden Fleece with the help of the sorceress Medea. She was his mistress for some time, but he later abandoned her to marry Glauce, daughter of the king of Corinth.

Why did he 'scape safe to the land
before the ship was torn?

I think King Aeolus[1] stayed the winds
and Neptune[2] ruled the sea;
Then might he boldly pass the waves
no perils could him slee.° *slay*

But if his falsehood had to them
been manifest before,
They would have rent the ship as soon
as he had gone from shore.

Now may you hear how falseness is
made manifest in time,
Although they that commit the same
think it a venial° crime. *pardonable*

For they, for their unfaithfulness,
did get perpetual fame.
Fame? wherefore did I term it so?
I should have called it shame.

Let Theseus be, let Jason pass,
let Paris[3] also 'scape,
That brought destruction unto Troy
all through the Grecian rape.

And unto me a Troilus[4] be,
if not you may compare
With any of these persons that
above expressed are.

But if I cannot please your mind
for wants° that rest in me, *deficiencies*
Wed whom you list;° I am content, *desire*
your refuse for to be.

It shall suffice me, simple soul,
of thee to be forsaken:
And it may chance, although not yet,
you wish you had me taken.

But rather than you should have cause
to wish this through° your wife, *as a result of*
I wish to her, ere you her have,
no more but love of life.

For she that shall so happy be,
of thee to be elect,° *chosen*
I wish her virtues to be such,
she need not be suspect.

I rather wish her Helen's face
than one of Helen's trade,[5]
With chasteness of Penelope,[6]
the which did never fade.

A Lucres[7] for her constancy,
and Thisbie[8] for her truth:
If such thou have, then Peto[9] be,
not Paris, that were ruth.[10]

Perchance ye will think this thing rare
in one woman to find:
Save Helen's beauty, all the rest
the Gods have me assigned.

These words I do not speak, thinking
from thy new love to turn thee:

[1] *King Aeolus* God of the winds.

[2] *Neptune* God of the sea.

[3] *Paris* Son of Priam, the king of Troy, who stole Helen, the wife of King Menelaus of Greece, thus prompting the Greeks to invade Troy.

[4] *Troilus* Another son of Priam who was famously faithful to Cressida, who in turn deserted him for a Greek warrior.

[5] *one of Helen's trade* I.e., a seductress.

[6] *Penelope* Wife of Odysseus who waited faithfully for several years for his return from the Trojan War.

[7] *Lucres* Lucretia, a Roman whose husband boasted to his friends that his wife would always remain chaste in his absence. His friend Tarquin, challenged by this declaration, stole into Lucretia's bedchamber and raped her. Lucretia committed suicide out of shame.

[8] *Thisbie* Woman who killed herself in order to be with her dying lover, Pyramus, in death.

[9] *Peto* Cardinal William Peto (d. 1558), who openly argued against King Henry VIII's plan to divorce Catherine of Aragon.

[10] *ruth* Feelings of sorrow or regret.

Thou know'st by proof what I deserve;
I need not to inform thee.

But let that pass. Would God I had
Cassandra's gift[1] me lent;
Then either thy ill chance or mine
my foresight might prevent.

But all in vain for this I seek;
wishes may not attain it.
Therefore may hap° to me what shall, *happen*
and I cannot refrain° it. *prevent*

Wherefore I pray God be my guide
and also thee defend;
No worser than I wish myself,
until thy life shall end.

Which life, I pray God, may again
King Nestor's[2] life renew;
And after that your soul may rest
amongst the heavenly crew.

Thereto I wish King Xerxes' wealth
or else King Cressus'[3] gold,
With as much rest and quietness
as man may have on mould.° *earth*

And when you shall this letter have,
let it be kept in store,
For she that sent the same hath sworn
as yet to send no more.

And now farewell, for why at large
my mind is here exprest,
The which you may perceive if that
you do peruse the rest.

Finis.
—1567

[1] *Cassandra's gift* Clairvoyance. Cassandra, the daughter of Priam who had prophetic powers, predicted the fall of Troy but was not believed.

[2] *King Nestor* Greek king famous for his wisdom and longevity.

[3] *King Xerxes* Wealthy king of Persia; *King Cressus* Wealthy king of Lydia.

The Admonition by the Author to all Young Gentlewomen, and to all Other Kinds of Maids Being in Love

Ye Virgins, ye from Cupid's[4] tents
do bear away the foil,[5]
Whose hearts as yet with raging love
most painfully do boil.

To you I speak, for you be they
that good advice do lack;
Oh, if I could good counsel get,° *produce*
my tongue should not be slack.° *idle*

But such as I can give, I will.
Here in few words express,
Which, if you do observe, it will
some of your care redress.

Beware of fair and painted° talk, *false*
beware of flattering tongues:
The mermaids[6] do pretend no good
for all their pleasant songs.

Some use the tears of crocodiles,
contrary to their heart,
And if they cannot always weep,
they wet their cheeks by art.

Ovid, within his Art of Love,[7]
doth teach them this same knack,
To wet their hand and touch their eyes,
so oft as tears they lack.

Why have ye such deceit in store?
have you such crafty wile?
Less craft than this, God knows, would soon
us simple souls beguile.

[4] *Cupid* God of love.

[5] *foil* Sword used in fencing.

[6] *mermaids* According to myth, these creatures would lure sailors to shore with their beautiful singing, and the sailors' boats would be smashed on rocky shores.

[7] *Ovid ... Love* Ovid's *Ars Amatoria* (*The Art of Love*, c. 1 CE), a facetious treatise giving advice on how to woo one's love.

And will ye not leave off? but still
delude us in this wise?
Sith° it is so, we trust we shall *Since*
take heed to feigned lies.

Trust not a man at the first sight,
but try him well before;
I wish all maids within their breasts
to keep this thing in store.

For trial shall declare his truth
and show what he doth think,
Whether he be a lover true,
or do intend to shrink.

If Scilla[1] had not trust too much
before that she did try,
She could not have been clean forsake
when she for help did cry.

Or if she had had good advice,
Nisus had lived long:
How durst she trust a stranger and
do her dear father wrong.

King Nisus had a hair by fate,
which hair, while he did keep,
He never should be overcome,
neither on land nor deep.

The stranger that the daughter loved
did war against the King
And always sought how that he might
them in subjection bring.

This Scylla stole away the hair,
for to obtain her will,
And gave it to the stranger that
did straight her father kill.

Then she, who thought her self most sure
to have her whole desire,
Was clean reject and left behind
when he did home retire.

Or if such falsehood had been once
unto Oenone[2] known,
About the fields of Ida wood,
Paris had walkt alone.

Or if Demophoon's[3] deceit
to Phillis had been told,
She had not been transformed so,
as Poets tell of old.[4]

Hero did try Leander's truth[5]
before that she did trust:
Therefore she found him unto her
both constant, true, and just.

For he always did swim the sea
when stars in sky did glide,
Till he was drowned by the way
near hand unto the side.

She scrat° her face, she tore her hair *scratched*
(it grieveth me to tell)
When she did know the end of him
that she did love so well.

But like Leander there be few,
therefore in time take heed
And always try before ye trust,
so shall you better speed.

[1] *Scilla* Daughter of Nisus, the king of Megera whose magical purple locks protected his kingdom against attack. Scilla fell in love with the beseiging enemy King Minos of Crete and cut off a lock of her father's hair for him. Minos then conquered Megaera, but rejected Scilla.

[2] *Oenone* Nymph who lived on Mount Ida; she loved and was abandoned by Paris, son of the king of Troy.

[3] *Demophoon* Son of Theseus and the lover of Phillis, daughter of the king of Thrace. When Demophoon, a Greek warrior, neglected to return to her, Phillis, believing he had forsaken her, committed suicide and was turned into a tree.

[4] *as Poets … old* See Ovid, *Heroides*, Book 2.

[5] *Hero did … truth* Hero's beloved, Leander, would swim across the Hellespont nightly to be with her. When he drowned one night, she threw herself into the sea to join him.

The little fish that careless is
within the water clear,
How glad is he, when he doth see,
a bait for to appear.

He thinks his hap° right good to be, *luck*
that he the same could spy,
And so the simple fool doth trust
too much before he try.

O little fish, what hap hadst thou?
to have such spiteful fate,
To come into one's cruel hands
out of so happy state?

Thou didst suspect no harm when thou
upon the bait didst look:
O that thou hadst had Linceus'[1] eyes
for to have seen the hook.

Then hadst thou with thy pretty mates
been playing in the streams
Whereas Sir Phoebus[2] daily doth
show forth his golden beams.

But sith thy fortune is so ill
to end thy life on shore,
Of this thy most unhappy end
I mind to speak no more.

But of thy fellow's chance that late
such pretty° shift° did make, *clever / movement*
That he from fishers' hook did spirit
before he could him take.

And now he pries° on every bait, *looks closely*
suspecting still that prick
(for to lie hid in every thing)
wherewith the fishers strick.° *strike*

And since the fish that reason lacks
once warnèd doth beware,
Why should not we take heed to that
that turneth us to care?

And I who was deceived late
by one's unfaithful tears
Trust now for to beware, if that
I live this hundreth years.

FINIS. Is. W.
—1567

A Careful Complaint by the Unfortunate Author[3]

Good Dido[4] stint° thy tears *stop*
and sorrows all resign
To me: that born was to augment,
misfortune's luckless line.
Or being still the same,
good Dido do thy best:
In helping to bewail the hap,° *occurrence*
that furthereth mine unrest.
For though thy Trojan mate
that Lord Aeneas hight:° *was called*
Requiting ill thy steadfast love
from Carthage took his flight
And foully broke his oath
and promise made before,
Whose falsehood finished thy delight,
before thy hairs were hoar;° *gray*
Yet greater cause of grief
compels me to complain,
For Fortune fell° converted hath *cruel*
my health to heaps of pain.
And that she swears my death
too plain it is (alas),
Whose end let malice still attempt
to bring the same to pass.
O Dido, thou hadst lived
a happy Woman still
If fickle fancy had not thralled° *enslaved*
thy wits: to retchless° will. *reckless*

[1] *Linceus* One of the Argonauts, famed for his keen sight.

[2] *Phoebus* I.e., the sun. Phoebus Apollo was god of the sun.

[3] *A Careful ... Author* Apparently written after Whitney lost her position as a servant in London.

[4] *Dido* Queen of Carthage who was abandoned by her lover, Aeneas. She married him in a vain attempt to keep him in Carthage, and when he left she killed herself.

For as the man by whom
    thy deadly dolors° bred, *sorrows*
Without regard of plighted° troth° *pledged / faithfulness*
    from Carthage city fled,
So might thy cares in time
    be banished out of thought:
His absence might well salve° the sore *heal*
    that erst° his presence wrought. *first*
For fire no longer burns
    than° Faggots° feed the flame; *except when / sticks*
The want of things that breed annoy
    may soon redress the same.
But I unhappy most
    and gripped with endless griefs,
Despair (alas) amid my hope
    and hope without relief.
And as the sweltering heat
    consumes the War away,
So do the heaps of deadly harms
    still threaten my decay.
O Death delay not long
    thy duty to declare:
Ye Sisters three[1] dispatch my days
    and finish all my care.
—1573

In Answer to Comfort Her, by Showing His Haps[2] to be Harder

Friend Is., be now content and let my sorrows quell
    the extreme rage and care thou restest in:
For wailing sprites, ne° furies fierce in hell, *nor*
    nor grisly souls that still in woe have been,
Have ever felt like storms that I sustain,
    frownst so I am, and dulled in deep despair,
That sure (me thinks) my extreme raging pain
    might gain thee health and set thee free from fear.
For Dido, thou, and many thousands more,
    which living feel the pangs of extreme care,
Though tortured much and torn in pieces small:
    whom ever griping, death doth never spare,
Nor he that falsely Carthage City fled,
    so fraught with wiles, nor the such sorrows taste
By thousand parts as I who rightly said,
    do pine as wax before the fire wastes.
I freeze to ICE, I heat with parching SUN,
    and torn with teen,° thus languishing in pain, *suffering*
Do feel my sorrows ever fresher run
    to flowing cares that endless sorrows gain.
For what, for whom, and why this evil works,
    friend Is. W., time, nor silence, may it show;
But once ere many days, my care that lurks
    shall blown be and thou the same shall know.
Till then, with silly Dido be content
    and rip° no more thy wrongs in such excess: *disclose*
Thy FORTUNE rather wills thee so lament,
    with speedy wit, till hope may have redress.

Finis T.B.[3]
—1573

A Reply to the Same

The bitter force of *Fortune's* frowardness° *perversity*
  Is painted out by B.,[4] his changéd hue:
Report bewrays° that tyrant's doubleness, *reveals*
    Which I by trial prove (alas) too true;
    Constrained I am, on thy mishaps to rue
As oft as I consider thine estate.° *condition*
Which differs far, from that thou wast of late.

Where be thy wonted° lively looks become; *customary*
    Or what mischance hath dimmed thy beauty so?
There is no God that deals such doubtful doom;
    No *Jupiter*[5] hath brought thee down so low:
    Thy hapless° fate hath wrought thy overthrow. *luckless*
For as *Saturnus*[6] reaves° the *Berry's* joy, *robs*
So Fortune strives to further thine annoy.

---

[1] *Ye Sisters three* The three Fates, sister goddesses who, according to classical mythology, determine the course of human life.

[2] *Haps* Mischances.

[3] *T.B.* Believed to be Whitney's literary friend Thomas Berrie.

[4] *B.* Thomas Berrie, the author of "In Answer to Comfort her, by Showing his Haps to be Harder."

[5] *Jupiter* In classical mythology, king of the gods.

[6] *Saturnus* Saturn, classical god of agriculture and father of Jupiter.

O Fortune false, O thrice unsteady joys,
Why doth not man mistrust thy subtle shows,
Whose proffers° prove in time to be but toys *offers*
As this the fruit that from your blossom grows?
Then may you rightly be compared with those
Whose painted speech professeth friendship still,
But time bewrays the meaning to be ill.

For time that shows what erst I could not see
Hath brought about that I suspected least:
Complaining still on our simplicity,
Who headlong runs, as doth the careless beast
Till hunter's snares have laid his limbs to rest,
For when we least mistrust and dread deceit,
Then are we snared with unsuspected bait.

As lately unto thee it did befall,
Whose hap enforceth me to rue thy chance,
For thou that florisht erst° at beauty's stall *before*
Hath felt the force of froward *Fortune's* lance,
Compelled to furnish out misfortune's dance;
See here the surety that belongeth aye° *always*
To mortal joys whereon the world doth stay.

But live in hope that better hap may light,
For after storms Sir *Phoebus's*[1] force is seen;
So when *Saturnus* hath declared his might,
And *Winter* stints° to turn the world to *ceases*
teen,° *suffering*
Then pleasant *Ver*° shall clothe the ground *Spring*
in green
And lusty *May* shall labour to restore
The things that *Winter's* spit had spoiled before.

Then shall the *Berry* cleave her wonted hue,
And eke° my B. that long hath tasted pain, *also*
When Fortune doth her former grace renew,
Shall hoisted be to happy state again
In ***[2]

Delighting oft among his friends and kin,
To tell what danger erst his life was in.

Which happy sight of mortal creatures, who
Shall more rejoice? Than I thy friend to see
And while dame Fortune yielded not thereto
But doth proceed to prove her suite on thee,
Yet shalt thou not so ill belovéd be,
But that thy Fame forever flourish shall
If *Is.*, her pen, may promise ought at all.

Farewell.
—1573

The Manner of Her Will

The Author (though loath to leave the City) upon her friend's procurement[3] *is constrained to depart: wherefore (she feigneth as she would die) and maketh her will and testament, as followeth, with large legacies of such goods and riches which she most abundantly hath left behind her, and thereof maketh London sole executor to see her legacies performed.*

A communication which the Author had to London, before she made her will.

The time is come I must depart,
from thee ah famous city.
I never yet to rue° my smart,° *regret / suffering*
did find that thou hadst pity.
Wherefore small cause there is, that I
should grieve from thee go;
But many women foolishly,
like me, and other mo'e,° *more*
Do such a fixèd fancy set,
on those which least deserve,
That long it is ere wit we get
away from them to swerve.° *turn away*
But time with pity oft will tell
to those that will her try,
Whether it best be more to mell,° *mix*
or utterly defy.

[1] *Sir Phoebus* I.e., the sun. Phoebus Apollo is the classical god of the sun.

[2] *In **** There appears to be a line missing here. Although "Delighting oft among ..." begins a new page of the printed text, the previous page (which ends with the line "shall hoisted be ...") indicated that the following page should begin with "In." In addition, following the pattern of the rest of the poem's stanzas, an indented line should occur here.

[3] *procurement* Arrangement, contrivance.

And now hath time me put in mind
of thy great cruelness,
That never once a help would find
to ease me in distress.
Thou never yet wouldst credit give
to board° me for a year, *feed*
Nor with apparel me relieve
except thou payèd were.
No, no, thou never didst me good,
nor ever wilt I know;
Yet am I in no angry mood,
but will, or ere I go,
In perfect love and charity
my testament here write,
And leave to thee such treasury,° *wealth*
as I in it recite.
Now stand aside and give me leave
to write my latest will,
And see that none° you do deceive,° *i.e., no one / cheat*
of that I leave them till.

The Manner of Her Will, and What She Left to London and all Those in it at Her Departing

I whole in body, and in mind,
but very weak in purse,
Do make and write my testament
for fear it will be worse.
And first I wholly do commend
my soul and body eke,° *also*
To God the Father and the Son,
so long as I can speak.
And after speech, my soul to him,
and body to the grave,
'Till time that all shall rise again,
their judgement for to have.
And then I hope they both shall meet,
to dwell for aye° in joy; *ever*
Whereas I trust to see my friends
releast from all annoy.° *discomfort, vexation*
Thus have you heard touching my soul
and body what I mean;
I trust you all will witness bear,
I have a steadfast[1] brain.
And now let me dispose such things
as I shall leave behind,
That those which shall receive the same
may know my willing mind.
I first of all to London leave,
because I there was bred,
Brave buildings rare, of churches store,° *plenty*
and Paul's to the head.[2]
Between the same, fair streets there be,
and people goodly store.
Because their keeping craveth° cost, *demands*
I yet will leave him more.
First for their food, I butchers leave,
that every day shall kill;
By Thames you shall have brewers store,
and bakers at your will.
And such as orders do observe,[3]
and eat fish thrice a week,
I leave two streets,[4] full fraught therewith,
they need not far to seek.
Watling Street, and Canwick° Street, *Candlewick*
I full of woollen leave:
And linen store in Friday Street,
if they me not deceive.
And those which are of calling such
that costlier they require,
I mercers[5] leave, with silk so rich,
as any would desire.
In Cheap of them,[6] they store shall find,
and likewise in that street,
I goldsmiths leave, with jewels such
as are for ladies meet.° *suitable*

---

[1] *steadfast* I.e., sane.

[2] *Paul's* St. Paul's Cathedral, in the center of the City of London. The cathedral's roof and part of its spire had been destroyed by lightning in 1561. It burnt to the ground in the Great Fire of London in 1666 and was rebuilt in the seventeenth century by Sir Christopher Wren; *to the head* Foremost; as chief.

[3] *such as orders do observe* I.e., those who have taken religious orders; priests.

[4] *two streets* Fish Street Hill, which led to London Bridge, and Billingsgate Market on Lower Thames Street.

[5] *mercers* Dealers in silk and other luxury cloths.

[6] *In Cheap of them* On Cheapside Street were many cloth stores.

And plate[1] to furnish cupboards with,
full brave there shall you find,
With purl[2] of silver and of gold,
to satisfy your mind.
With hoods, bongraces,[3] hats or caps,
such store are in that street,
As if on t'one° side you should miss *one*
the t'other° serves your feat. *other*
For nets[4] of every kind of sort,
I leave within the pawn,[5]
French ruffs, high purls,° gorgets° *frills / collars*
and sleeves
of any kind of lawn.° *linen*
For purse or knives, for comb or glass,° *mirror*
or any needful knack,° *knick-knack*
I by the Stocks[6] have left a boy
will ask you what you lack.
I hose° do leave in Birchin Lane, *stockings*
of any kind of size,
For women stitcht, for men both trunks° *short breeches*
and those of Gascoigne guise.[7]
Boots, shoes, or pantables° good store, *slippers*
Saint Martin's[8] hath for you.
In Cornwall, there I leave you beds,
and all that 'longs° thereto. *belongs*
For women shall you tailors have,
by Bow,[9] the chiefest dwell.
In every lane you some shall find,
can do indifferent well.
And for the men, few streets or lanes,
but bodymakers[10] be,
And such as make the sweeping cloaks,
with guards[11] beneath the knee.
Artillery at Temple Bar,[12]
and dagges° at Tower Hill;[13] *pistols*
Swords and bucklers° of the best, *small shields*
are nigh the Fleet[14] until.
Now when thy folk are fed and clad
with such as I have named,
For dainty mouths, and stomachs weak
some junckets[15] must be framed.° *prepared*
Wherefore I 'pothicaries° leave, *apothecaries*
with banquets in their shop;
Physicians also for the sick,
Diseases for to stop.
Some roisters° still must bide in thee, *bullies*
and such as cut it out,[16]
That with the guiltless quarrel will,
to let their blood about.
For them I cunning surgeons leave,
some plasters° to apply, *bandages*
That ruffians may not still be hanged,
nor quiet persons die.
For salt, oatmeal, candles, soap,
or what you else do want,
In many places, shops are full;
I left you nothing scant.° *lacking*
If they that keep what I you leave,
ask money, when they sell it,
At Mint,[17] there is such store, it is
impossible to tell it.
At Steelyard[18] store of wines there be,
your dullèd minds to glad,

[1] *plate* Vessels or utensils made of gold or silver.

[2] *purl* Ornamental border.

[3] *bongraces* Large bonnets used to shade women's faces from the sun.

[4] *nets* Fine mesh used for veils or hair.

[5] *pawn* Gallery or covered walk, especially one in a market where sellers display their goods.

[6] *Stocks* A fish and meat market.

[7] *of Gascoigne guise* I.e., resembling natives of Gascony (who were stereotypically known as being braggarts).

[8] *Saint Martin's* St. Martin's was a precinct famous for its tailors.

[9] *Bow* St. Mary-le-Bow, where numerous churchyards had stalls where clothing was sold.

[10] *bodymakers* Bodice-makers, or tailors. (The "body," or bodice, was the part of the dress that covered the body above the skirt.)

[11] *guards* Ornamental edges.

[12] *Temple Bar* Gate that divided the western edge of the City of London from the Strand.

[13] *Tower Hill* An open space within the City of London, on a hill, that had a view of the Tower of London just to the south.

[14] *the Fleet* Prison on the west edge of London (also the name of a river and a street in London).

[15] *junckets* Cakes, sweets.

[16] *cut it out* Possibly a reference to cutting purses (a method of robbery).

[17] *Mint* The Royal Mint.

[18] *Steelyard* Area of wharves west of London Bridge.

And handsome men,[1] that must not wed
 except they leave their trade.
They oft shall seek for proper girls,
 and some perhaps shall find.
(That need compels, or lucre° lures *money*
 to satisfy their mind.)
And near the same, I houses leave,
 for people to repair,° *go to*
To bathe themselves, so to prevent
 infection of the air.
On Saturdays I wish that those,
 which all the week do drug° *drag, drudge*
Shall thither trudge, to trim them up
 on Sundays to look smug.° *smart*
If any other thing be lackt
 in thee, I wish them look,
For there it is: I little brought
 but nothing from thee took.
Now for the people in thee left,
 I have done as I may,
And that the poor, when I am gone,
 have cause for me to pray.
I will to prisons portions° leave, *amounts*
 what though but very small;
Yet that they may remember me,
 occasion be it shall,
And first the counter° they shall have, *debtors' prison*
 least they should go to wrack.° *ruin*
Some coggers,° and some honest men, *cheats*
 that sergeants draw aback.° *restrain*
And such as friends will not them bail,
 whose coin is very thin,
For them I leave a certain hole,° *cell*
 and little ease within.
The Newgate[2] once a month shall have
 a sessions° for his share: *court hearing*
Least being heapt,° infection might *i.e., overcrowded*
 procure a further care.
And at those sessions some shall 'scape,
 with burning° near the thumb, *branding*
And afterward to beg their fees,
 till they have got the sum.
And such whose deeds deserveth death,
 and twelve° have found the same, *i.e., a jury*
they shall be drawn up Holburn Hill,[3]
 to come to further shame.
Well, yet to such I leave a nag° *horse*
 shall soon their sorrows cease,
For he shall either break their necks
 or gallop from the preace.° *crowd*
The Fleet not in their circuit is,[4]
 yet if I give him naught,
It might procure his curse, ere I
 unto the ground be brought.
Wherefore I leave some papist° old *Catholic*
 to underprop[5] his roof:
And to the poor within the same,
 A box° for their behoof.° *alms box / benefit*
What makes you standers by to smile,
 and laugh so in your sleeve.
I think it is, because that I
 to Ludgate[6] nothing give.
I am not now in case° to lie, *a position*
 here is no place of jest;
I did reserve that for myself,
 if I my health possest.
And ever came in credit so
 a debtor for to be;
When days of payment did approach,
 I thither meant to flee.
To shroud° myself amongst the rest, *hide*
 that choose to die in debt,
Rather than any creditor,
 should money from them get.
Yet 'cause I feel myself so weak
 that none me credit[7] dare,
I here revoke, and do it leave,
 some bankrupts to his share.
To all the bookbinders by Paul's,[8]
 because I like their art,

[1] *handsome men* I.e., apprentices, bound to tradesmen.

[2] *The Newgate* London's main prison, located on Newgate Street.

[3] *Holburn Hill* Place of execution.

[4] *The Fleet ... is* Fleet prison was for people convicted of crimes of the conscience, such as treason or religious dissent. It is not in the same "circuit" as Newgate because it is not for prisoners convicted under common law.

[5] *underprop* Support (financially).

[6] *Ludgate* A debtors' prison.

[7] *me credit* I.e., to give me credit.

[8] *Paul's* St. Paul's Cathedral. Many booksellers were located in the surrounding churchyards.

They every week shall money have,
when they from books depart.
Amongst them all, my printer[1] must
have somewhat to his share;
I will° my friends there books to buy *desire*
of him, with other ware.
For maidens poor, I widowers rich
do leave, that oft shall dote,
And by that means shall marry them,
to set the girls afloat.
And wealthy widows will I leave,
to help young gentlemen,
Which when you have in any case
be courteous to them then,
And see their plate and jewels eke
may not be marred with rust;
Nor let their bags[2] too long be full,
for fear that they do burst.
To every gate under the walls,
that compass thee about,
I fruit-wives[3] leave to entertain
such as come in and out.
To Smithfield[4] I must something leave
my parents there did dwell;
So careless for to be of it,
none would accompt° it well. *account*
Wherefore it thrice a week shall have,
of horse and meat° good store, *cattle*
And in his 'spitle,[5] blind and lame,
to dwell for evermore.
And Bedlem[6] must not be forgot,
for that was oft my walk;
I people there too many leave,
that out of tune do talk.
At Bridewell[7] there shall beadles[8] be,
and matrons that shall still
See chalk well chopt, and spinning plied,
and turning of the mill.
For such as cannot quiet be,
but strive for house or land,
At th'Inns of Court,[9] I lawyers leave
to take their cause in hand.
And also leave I at each Inn
of Court, or Chancery,° *court*
Of gentlemen, a youthful root,
full of activity,
For whom I store of books have left,
at each bookbinder's stall,
And part of all that London hath
to furnish them withal.° *therewith*
And when they are with study cloyed,° *burdened, tired*
to recreate their mind,
Of tennis courts, of dancing schools,
and fence° they store shall find. *fencing*
And every Sunday at the least,
I leave to make them sport,
In diverse places players, that
of wonders shall report.
Now London have I (for thy sake)
within thee, and without,
As comes into my memory,
dispersed round about
Such needful things, as they should have,
here left now unto thee.
When I am gone, with conscience
let them dispersed be.
And though I nothing named have,
to bury me withal,
Consider that above the ground,
annoyance be I shall.
And let me have a shrouding sheet[10]
to cover me from shame,
And in oblivion bury me
and never more me name.
Ringings[11] nor other ceremonies,
use you not for cost,
Nor at my burial make no feast;
your money were but lost.

[1] *my printer* Richard Jones.

[2] *bags* Probably of money.

[3] *fruit-wives* Women who sell fruit.

[4] *Smithfield* Horse and cattle market, located northeast of the city walls, where animals were slaughtered.

[5] *'spitle* Hospital; St. Bartholomew Hospital in Smithfield.

[6] *Bedlem* St. Mary of Bethlehem, a mental hospital.

[7] *Bridewell* A prison and poorhouse.

[8] *beadles* Under-bailiffs; constables.

[9] *Inns of Court* Legal colleges.

[10] *shrouding sheet* Sheet in which a body was wrapped before burial.

[11] *Ringings* I.e., of the church bells, to mark a death.

Rejoice in God that I am gone,
out of this vale[1] so vile.
And that of each thing, left such store,
as may your wants exile.
I make thee sole executor, because
I loved thee best.
And thee I put in trust, to give
the goods unto the rest.
Because thou shalt a helper need,
In this so great a charge,
I wish good Fortune be thy guide, lest
thou shouldst run at large.
The happy days and quiet times,
they both her servants be
Which well will serve to fetch and bring,
such things as need to thee.
Wherefore (good London) not° refuse, *do not*
for helper her to take;
Thus being weak and weary both
an end here will I make.
To all that ask what end I made,
and how I went away,
Thou answer may'st like those which here,
no longer tarry may.
And unto all that wish me well,
or rue that I am gone,
Do me commend, and bid them cease
my absence for to moan.
And tell them further, if they would,
my presence still have had,
They should have sought to mend my luck,
which ever was too bad.
So fare thou well a thousand times,
God shield thee from thy foe,
And still make thee victorious,
of those that seek thy woe.
And (though I am persuade°) that I *persuaded*
shall never more thee see,
Yet to the last, I shall not cease
to wish much good to thee.
This twenty of October, I,
in Anno Domini
A thousand five hundred seventy three,
as almanacs descry,
Did write this will with mine own hand
and it to London gave,
In witness of the standers by,
whose names if you will have,
Paper, Pen, and Standish° were *inkpot*
at that same present by,
With Time, who promised to reveal,
so fast as she could hie,
The same, lest of my nearer kin
for anything should vary.
So finally I make an end
no longer can I tarry.

Finis, by Is. W.
—1573

[1] *vale* Valley (i.e., of tears).

"Unconstant Women," "Excellent Women": A Seventeenth-Century Debate

CONTEXTS

Early Modern England saw a continuation of medieval arguments—sometimes serious, sometimes for rhetorical show—concerning the nature and value of women. Men did not monopolize this debate, which is often called the "querelle des femmes" (the argument over women); as early as Christine de Pizan's protofeminist *Cité des Dames* (written in 1405), women had replied in a range of voices from defensive argument to swaggering displays of scorn for those who limited and denigrated them. The "querelle" did not change much until the uproars and changes of the seventeenth century profoundly reshaped European culture. With women playing an increasing role in religious and political conflicts as well as in the world of literature, arguments over their nature took new forms and tones.

Throughout these debates, many women stood their ground against attacks on their sex. Nor did all men denigrate them. In the sixteenth century, women were denied equal status and opportunities and (unless widowed) had few legal rights, yet some did receive excellent educations. In the Humanist tradition of Erasmus and Sir Thomas More, women were legally subordinate but were not thought morally inferior. Thomas More could imagine, for his ideal world of Utopia if not in real life, divorce by mutual consent and an equal punishment for adultery, while Erasmus blamed men disproportionately for trouble between man and wife: "No man," he asserted, "ever had a shrew for a wife except through his own fault." In France, Rabelais agreed: the best way to keep a wife faithful, one character is told, is to be faithful yourself. In seventeenth-century Britain, too, men could come to women's defense, as witness such writers as Daniel Tuvill, whose *Asylum Veneris* (1616), directed against Joseph Swetnam (see below), describes good and accomplished women from the past. The essayist Owen Felltham, whose work concludes this selection of texts, accepts some Renaissance assumptions about gender but questions many others: he asks commonsense questions and is willing to look beyond stereotypes.

But it remains true that in some ways the situation of women declined during the Renaissance. The closing of the convents removed one possible means by which women could exercise social power; changes in manufacturing would eventually mean less economic independence for women; and later in the period, male doctors began to replace midwives, displacing women from one of their traditional positions of expertise and social power. The horrifying executions of women accused of witchcraft, moreover, took place largely after the Middle Ages. Some scholars have also wondered if religious difference affected arguments over gender. Did the Protestant stress on the role of the family in religious life also shift attitudes toward gender? Certainly some Catholic women who refused to conform to the Church of England experienced, in their own minds, an obligation to dissent from male-dominated authority.

Attacks on women in the seventeenth century could come from several directions. On the one hand, Protestant moralists tended to allocate greater blame to woman than to man for the original sin in the Garden of Eden (although such accusations had ample precedent in earlier centuries). On the other hand, some men, often half-seriously, could adopt a cavalier (in both senses of the word) licentiousness, especially if they had connections at Court or were writing to impress the mostly male worlds of law schools and universities. The latter manner can be seen in the "problems" and "paradoxes" of John Donne, whose misogyny is generally regarded as springing from a playful and rhetorically showy cynicism rather than genuine contempt for women. By contrast, the intemperate polemic of Joseph Swetnam's *An Arraignment of Lewd, Idle, Froward, and Unconstant Women* seems less playful, although the degree of his seriousness can be hard to gauge—the work's hyperbole seems designed in part for strutting display.

Seventeenth-century attacks such as those of Swetnam were met by strong replies in verse by poets such as Aemilia Lanyer and, later in the century, Katherine Phillips. More directly, Swetnam's essay brought responses in prose from at least two sources. Rachel Speght, nineteen years old, daughter of one clergyman and married to another, and also a poet, uncovered Swetnam's authorship (the work had been published anonymously) and published her reply in 1616. Shortly thereafter another response to Swetnam appeared, under the pen name "Ester Sowernam." Sowernam, whose pseudonym plays her "Sower/Sour" against "Swet/Sweetnam," argues that Speght, though defending women against Swetnam's allegations, was herself too willing to assign them blame; Sowernam's own defense ranges more broadly, and is founded less than is Speght's on overtly Christian arguments. This particular phase of the controversy did not end there. A 1620 play, *Swetnam the Woman-hater, Arraigned by Women* (attributed to Thomas Heywood), dramatized this pamphlet war, depicting Swetnam and "Amazon Atalanta" as engaged in a court battle with each other.

⌘⌘⌘

from John Donne, *Paradoxes and Problems* (written c. 1600)

from PARADOX I, "A DEFENSE OF WOMEN'S INCONSTANCY"

That women are inconstant, I with any man confess, but that inconstancy is a bad quality, I against any man will maintain: for every thing as it is one better than another, so is it fuller of change. The heavens themselves continually turn, the stars move, the moon changeth; fire whirleth, air flyeth, water ebbs and flows, the face of the earth altereth her looks, time stays not; the colour that is most light will take most dyes: so in men, they that have the most reason are the most alterable in their designs, and the darkest or most ignorant do seldomest change; therefore women changing more than men have also more reason. They cannot be immutable like stocks, like stones, like the earth's dull center; gold that lieth still, rusteth; water, corrupteth; air that moveth not, poisoneth; then why should that which is the perfection of other things be imputed to women as greatest imperfection? Because thereby they deceive men. Are not your wits pleased with those jests which cozen[1] your expectation? You can call it pleasure to be beguiled in troubles, and in the most excellent toy in the world, you call it treachery: I would you had your mistresses so constant that they would never change, no not so much as their smocks, then should you see what sluttish virtue constancy were. Inconstancy is a most commendable and cleanly quality, and women in this quality are far more absolute than the heavens, than the stars, moon, or any thing beneath it; for long observation hath picked certainty out of their mutability. The learned are so well acquainted with the stars, signs, and planets that they make them but characters, to read the meaning of the heaven in his own forehead. Every simple fellow can bespeak the change of the moon a great while beforehand: but I would fain have the learnedest man so skilfull as to tell when the simplest woman meaneth to vary....

[1] *cozen* Cheat, deceive.

Paradox 6, "That it is Possible to Find Some Virtue in Some Women"

I am not of that seared[1] impudence that I dare defend women, or pronounce them good; yet we see physicians allow some virtue in every poison. Alas! why should we except women? Since certainly, they are good for physic[2] at least, so as some wine is good for a fever. And though they be the occasioners of many sins, they are also the punishers and revengers of the same sins: for I have seldom seen one which consumes his substance and body upon them, escape diseases, or beggary; and this is their justice. And if *suum cuique dare*[3] be the fulfilling of all civil justice, they are most just; for they deny that which is theirs to no man:

Tanquam non liceat nulla puella negat.[4]

And who may doubt of great wisdom in them, that doth but observe with how much labour and cunning our justicers and other dispensers of the laws study to embrace them: and how zealously our preachers dehort[5] men from them, only by urging their subtleties and policies, and wisdom, which are in them? Or who can deny them a good measure of fortitude, if he consider how valiant men they have overthrown, and being themselves overthrown, how much and how patiently they bear? And though they be most intemperate, I care not, for I undertook to furnish them with some virtue, not with all. Necessity, which makes even bad things good, prevails also for them, for we must say of them, as of some sharp pinching laws: if men were free from infirmities, they were needless. These or none must serve for reasons, and it is my great happiness that examples prove not rules, for to confirm this opinion, the world yields not one example.

[1] *seared* Unfeeling.

[2] *physic* Medicine.

[3] *suum ... dare* Latin: "To give to each his own."

[4] *Tanquam ... negat* Latin: "As long as it is forbidden no girl will deny it."

[5] *dehort* Dissuade.

Problem 6, "Why Hath the Common Opinion Afforded Women Souls?"

It is agreed that we have not so much from them as any part of either our mortal souls of sense or growth,[6] and we deny souls to others equal to them in all but in speech for which they are beholding to their bodily instruments: for perchance an ox's heart, or a goat's, or a fox's, or a serpent's would speak just so, if it were in the breast, and could move that tongue and jaws. Have they so many advantages and means to hurt us (for, ever their loving destroyed us) that we dare not displease them, but give them what they will? And so when some call them angels, some goddesses, and the Peputian heretics[7] made them bishops, we descend so much with the stream, to allow them souls? Or do we somewhat (in this dignifying of them) flatter princes and great personages that are so much governed by them? Or do we in that easiness and prodigality, wherein we daily lose our own souls to we care not whom, so labour to persuade ourselves that since a woman hath a soul, a soul is no great matter? Or do we lend them souls but for use,[8] since they for our sakes give their souls again, and their bodies to boot? Or perchance because the Devil (who is all soul) doth most mischief, and for convenience and proportion, because they would come nearer him, we allow them some souls: and so as the Romans naturalized some provinces in revenge, and made them Romans, only for the burthen of the Commonwealth; so we have given women souls only to make them capable of damnation?

[6] *mortal souls ... growth* According to a tradition still alive in the Renaissance, plants have a "vegetable soul" making them capable of growth; animals have that plus an "animal soul" permitting motion and perception; and humans have those two and also a "rational soul" which makes us able to understand God's world.

[7] *Peputian heretics* Ancient heretical group denounced by St. Augustine.

[8] *use* Interest (at the extreme, usury).

from Joseph Swetnam, *The Arraignment of Lewd, Idle, Froward, and Unconstant Women* (1615)

from CHAPTER 2

The Second Chapter showeth the manner of such women as live upon evil report: it also showeth that the beauty of women has been the bane of many a man, for it hath overcome valiant and strong men, eloquent and subtle men.

... Men, I say, may live without women, but women cannot live without men. For Venus,[1] whose beauty was excellent fair, yet when she needeth man's help she took Vulcan,[2] a clubfooted smith. And therefore if a woman's face glister, and her gesture pierce the marble wall, or if her tongue be as smooth as oil or as soft as silk, and her words so sweet as honey, or if she were a very ape for wit, or a bag of gold for wealth, or if her personage have stolen away all that nature can afford, and if she be decked up in gorgeous apparel, then a thousand to one she will love to walk where she may get acquaintance, and acquaintance bringeth familiarity, and familiarity setteth all follies abroach,[3] and twenty to one that if a woman love gadding[4] but that she will pawn her honor to please her fantasy.

Man must be at all the cost and yet live by the loss. A man must take all the pains and women will spend all the gains. A man must watch and ward, fight and defend, till the ground, labor in the vineyard, and look what he getteth in seven years; a woman will spread it abroad with a fork in one year, and yet little enough to serve her turn but a great deal too little to get her good will. Nay, if thou give her ever so much and yet if thy person please not her humor, then will I not give a half-penny for her honesty at the year's end.

For then her breast will be the harborer of an envious heart, and her heart the storehouse of poisoned hatred; her head will devise villainy, and her hands are ready to practice that which their heart desireth. Then who can but say that women are sprung from the devil, whose heads, hands and hearts, minds and souls are evil, for women are called the hook of all evil, because men are taken by them as a fish is taken in with the hook.

For women have a thousand ways to entice thee, and ten thousand ways to deceive thee and all such fools as are suitors unto them; some they keep in hand with promises, and some they feed with flattery, and some they delay with dalliances, and some they please with kisses. They lay out the folds of their hair to entangle men into their love; betwixt their breasts is the vale of destruction, and in their beds there is hell, sorrow, and repentance. Eagles do not eat men till they are dead, but women devour them alive, for a woman will pick thy pocket and empty thy purse, laugh in thy face and cut thy throat. They are ungrateful, perjured, full of fraud, flouting, and deceit, unconstant, waspish, toyish,[5] light, sullen, proud, discourteous and cruel, and yet they were by God created, and by nature formed, and therefore by policy and wisdom to be avoided, for good things abused are to be refused. Or else for a month's pleasure, she may make thee go stark naked. She will give thee roast meat, but she will beat thee with the spit. If thou hast crowns in thy purse, she will be thy heart's gold until she leave thee not a whit of white money. They are like summer birds, for they will abide no storm, but flock about thee in the pride of thy glory, and fly from thee in the storms of affliction; for they aim more at thy wealth than at thy person, and esteem more thy money than any man's virtuous qualities; for they esteem of a man without money as a horse does a fair stable without meat. They are like eagles which will always fly where the carrion is.

They will play the horse-leech to suck away thy wealth, but in the winter of thy misery, she will fly from thee. Not unlike the swallow, which in the summer harboreth herself under the eaves of a house, and against winter flieth away, leaving nothing but dirt behind her....

Plato saith that women are either angels or devils, and that they either love dearly or hate bitterly, for a woman hath no mean in her love, nor mercy in her hate, no pity in revenge, nor patience in her anger; therefore it is said that there is nothing in the world which both pleases and displeases a man more than a

[1] *Venus* Roman goddess of love.

[2] *Vulcan* Roman god of fire and metallurgy, husband of Venus.

[3] *set ... abroach* Set loose, or afoot.

[4] *gadding* Wandering.

[5] *toyish* Frivolous.

woman, for a woman most delighteth a man and yet most deceiveth him, for as there is nothing more sweet to a man than a woman when she smiles, even so there is nothing more odious than the angry countenance of a woman.

from Rachel Speght, *A Muzzle for Melastomus,*[1] *The Cynical Baiter of, and Foul-Mouthed Barker Against Eve's Sex. Or, an Apologetical Answer to that Irreligious and Illiterate Pamphlet made by Joseph Swetnam Entitled The Arraignment of Women* (1617)

To all virtuous Ladies, Honorable or Worshipful, and to all other of Eve's sex fearing God, and loving just reputation, grace and peace through Christ, to eternal glory:

It was the simile of that wise and learned *Lactantius*[2] that if fire, though but with a final spark kindled, be not at the first quenched, it may work great mischief and damage: so likewise may the scandals and defamations of the malevolent in time prove pernicious, if they be not nipped in the head at their first appearance. The consideration of this (right Honorable and Worshipful Ladies) has incited me (though young, and the unworthiest of thousands) to encounter with a furious enemy to our sex, lest if his unjust imputations should continue without answer, he might insult and account himself a victor....

Not unto the veriest idiot that ever set pen to paper, but to the cynical baiter of women, or metamorphosed misogynes, Joseph Swetnam:

From standing water, which soon putrefies, can no good fish be expected; for it produces no other creatures but those that are venomous or noisome, as snakes, adders, and such like. Semblably,[3] no better stream can we look should issue from your idle corrupt brain, then that whereto the ruff of your fury (to use your own words) has moved you to open the sluice....

Many propositions have you framed, which (as you think) make much against women, but if one would make a logical assumption, the conclusion would be flat against your own sex. Your dealing wants so much discretion that I doubt whether to bestow so good a name as the dunce upon you: but minority bids me keep within my bounds; and therefore I only say unto you, that your corrupt heart, and railing tongue, has made you a fit scribe for the Devil.

In that you have termed your virulent foam *the bear-baiting of women*, you have plainly displayed your own disposition to be cynical, in that there appears no other dog or bull to bait them but yourself. Good had it been for you to have put on that muzzle, which Saint James would have all Christians to wear; "Speak not evil one of another":[4] and then had you not seemed so like the serpent Porphirus, as now you do; which, though full of deadly poison, yet being toothless, hurts none so much as himself. For you having gone beyond the limits not of humanity alone, but of Christianity, have done greater harm unto your own soul than unto women, as may plainly appear. First, in dishonoring God by palpable blasphemy, wresting and perverting every place of Scripture that you have alleged; which by the testimony of Saint Peter,[5] is to the destruction of them that so do. Secondly, it appears by your disparaging of, and opprobrious speeches against, that excellent work of God's hands, which in His great love He perfected for the comfort of man. Thirdly, and lastly, by this your hodge-podge of heathenish sentences, similes, and examples, you have set forth yourself in your right colors, unto the view of the world: and I doubt not but the judicious will account of you according to your demerit. As for the vulgar sort, which have no more learning than you have showed in your book, it is likely they will applaud you for your pains....

In your title leaf you arraign none but the lewd, idle, forward, and inconstant women, but in the sequel (though defect of memory as it seems), forgetting that you had made a distinction of good from bad, condemning all in general, you advise men to beware of, and not to match with, any of these six sorts of women,

[1] *Melostomus* Latin: black (or evil) mouth.

[2] *Lactantius* Third-century CE Christian author and teacher of rhetoric in the Roman Empire.

[3] *Semblably* Similarly.

[4] *Speak not evil ... another* See James 4.11.

[5] *testimony ... Peter* See 1 Peter 3.16.

viz. *good* and *bad, fair* and *foul, rich* and *poor.* But this doctrine of devils, Saint Paul foreseeing would be broached in the latter times, gives warning of.[1] There also you promise a commendation of wise, virtuous, and honest women, when as in the subsequent, the worst words, and filthiest epithets that you can devise, you bestow on them in general, excepting no sort of women....

Proverbs 18.22: "*He that finds a wife, finds a good thing, and receives favor of the Lord.*"

... Almighty God, who is rich in mercy,[2] having made all things of nothing, created man in His own image: that is (as the Apostle expounds it), "*In wisdom, righteousness and true holiness,*[3] *making him Lord over all*": to avoid that solitary condition that he was then in, having none to commerce or converse withal but dumb creatures, it seemed good unto the Lord, that as of every creature He had made male and female, and man only being alone without mate, so likewise to form an help meet for him.[4] Adam for this cause being cast into a heavy sleep, God extracting a rib from his side, thereof made, or built, Woman; showing thereby that man was as an imperfect building before woman was made; and, bringing her unto Adam, united and married them together.

Thus the resplendent love of God toward man appeared, in taking care to provide him a helper before he saw his own want, and in providing him such a helper as should be meet[5] for him. Sovereignty had he over all creatures, and they were all serviceable unto him; but yet before woman was formed, there was not a meet help found for Adam. Man's worthiness not meriting this great favor at God's hands, but His mercy only moving him thereunto: I may use those words which the Jews uttered when they saw Christ weep for Lazarus, "Behold how He loved him."[6] Behold, and that with good regard, God's love; yea His great love, which from the beginning He has borne unto man: which, as it appears in all things, so next, His love in Christ Jesus apparently in this; that for man's sake, that he might not be an unity, when all other creatures were for procreation dual, He created woman to be a solace unto him, to participate of his sorrows, partake of his pleasures, and as a good yoke-fellow bear part of his burden. Of the excellencies of this structure, I mean of women, whose foundation and original of creation was God's love, do I intend to dilate.

Of woman's excellency, with the causes of her creation, and of the sympathy which ought to be in man and wife each toward other.

The work of creation being finished, this approbation thereof was given by God Himself, that "*All was very good*":[7] If all, then woman, who, excepting man, is the most excellent creature under the canopy of heaven. But if it be objected by any: first, that woman, though created good, yet by giving ear to Satan's temptations brought death and misery upon her posterity....

To the first of these objections, I answer that Satan first assailed the woman because where the hedge is lowest, most easy it is to get over, and she being the weaker vessel[8] was with more facility to be seduced—like as a crystal glass sooner receives a crack then a strong stone pot. Yet we shall find the offense of Adam and Eve almost to parallel: for as an ambitious desire of being made like unto God was the motive which caused her to eat, so likewise was it his; as may plainly appear by that *ironia*,[9] "*Behold, man is become as one of us.*"[10] Not that he was so indeed, but hereby his desire to attain a greater perfection than God had given him was reproved. Woman sinned, it is true, by her infidelity in not believing the word of God, but giving credit to Satan's fair promises that "*she should not die*"[11]—but so did the man, too. And if Adam had not approved of that deed

[1] *this doctrine ... of* See 1 Timothy 4.3.

[2] *who is ... mercy* From Ephesians 2.4.

[3] *righteousness ... holiness* See Ephesians 4.24.

[4] *that as ... him* See Genesis 2.20.

[5] *meet* Appropriate.

[6] *Behold ... him* From John 11.36.

[7] *All ... good* From Genesis 1.31.

[8] *weaker vessel* From 1 Peter 3.7.

[9] *ironia* Latin: irony.

[10] *Behold ... us* From Genesis 3.22.

[11] *she should not die* From Genesis 3.4.

which Eve had done, and been willing to tread the steps which she had gone, he, being her head, would have reproved her and have made the commandment a bit to restrain him from breaking his Maker's injunction. For if a man burn his hand in the fire, the bellows that blew the fire are not to be blamed, but himself rather, for not being careful to avoid the danger. Yet if the bellows had not blown, the fire had not burnt; no more is woman simply to be condemned for man's transgression: for by the free will, which before his fall he enjoyed, he might have avoided, and been free from, being burnt or singed with that fire which was kindled by Satan and blown by Eve. It therefore served not his turn a whit afterwards to say, "*The woman which thou gavest me, gave me of the tree, and I did eat.*"[1] For a penalty was inflicted upon him, as well as on the woman, the punishment of her transgression being particular to her own sex, and to none but the female kind; but for the sin of man the whole earth was cursed. And he being better able than the woman to have resisted temptation, because the stronger vessel, was first called to account, to show that to whom much is given, of them much is required; and that he who the sovereign of all creatures visible, should have yielded greatest obedience to God.

True it is (as is already confessed) that woman first sinned, yet find we no mention of spiritual nakedness till man sinned: then it is said, "*Their eyes were opened*,"[2] the eyes of their mind and conscience; and then perceived they themselves naked, that is, not only bereft of that integrity which they originally had, but felt the rebellion and disobedience of their members in the disordered motions of their now corrupt nature, which made them for shame to cover their nakedness. Then (and not before) is it said that they saw it, as if sin were imperfect and unable to bring a deprivation of a blessing received, or death on all mankind, till man (in whom lay the active power of generation) had transgressed. The offense, therefore, of *Adam* and *Eve* is by Saint *Austin*[3] thus distinguished: "*the man sinned against God and himself, the woman against God, herself, and her husband*"; yet in her giving of the fruit to eat had she no malicious intent towards him, but did therein show a desire to make her husband partaker of that happiness which she thought by their eating they should both have enjoyed. This her giving Adam of the sauce, wherewith Satan had served her, whose sourness, afore he had eaten, she did not perceive, was that which made her sin to exceed his. Wherefore, that she might not of him who ought to honor her be abhorred,[4] the first promise that was made in Paradise, God makes to woman, that by her seed should the serpent's head be broken.[5] Whereupon Adam calls her *Hevah*, Life, that as the woman had been an occasion of his sin, so should woman bring forth the Savior from sin, which was in the fullness of time accomplished;[6] by which was manifested that he is a Savior of believing women no less than of men, that so the blame of sin may not be imputed to his creature which is good, but to the will by which Eve sinned; and yet by Christ's assuming the shape of a man was it declared that His mercy was equivalent to both sexes. So that by Hevah's blessed Seed (as Saint Paul affirms), it is brought to pass, that "*male and female are all one in Christ Jesus.*"[7] …

The Epilogue or Upshot of the Premises

… Ingratitude is, and always has been, accounted so odious a vice that Cicero[8] said, "*If one doubt what name to give a wicked man, let him call him an ungrateful person, and then he had said enough.*" It was so detested among the Persians, as that by a law they provided that such should suffer death as felons, which proved unthankful for any gift received. And "love" (said the Apostle) "is the fulfilling of the law."[9] But where ingratitude is harbored, there love is banished. Let men therefore beware of all unthankfulness, but especially of the superlative ingratitude—that which is towards God—which is no way more palpably declared than by

[1] *The woman … eat* From Genesis 3.21.

[2] *Their … opened* From Genesis 3.7.

[3] *Saint Austin* I.e., Saint Augustine (354–430). The following quotation echoes part of his sermon on Adam and Eve.

[4] *that she … abhorred* See 1 Peter 3.7.

[5] *by her … broken* See Genesis 3.15.

[6] *which was … accomplished* See Galatians 4.4.

[7] *male and … Jesus* From Galatians 3.28.

[8] *Cicero* Great Roman orator, philosopher, and writer of the first century BCE.

[9] *is the … law* From Romans 13.10.

the contemning of, and railing against, women; which sin of some men (if to be termed men) no doubt but God will one day avenge, when they shall plainly perceive that it had been better for them to have been born dumb and lame than to have used their tongues and hands, the one in repugning, the other in writing against God's handiwork, their own flesh—women I mean, whom God has made equal with themselves in dignity, both temporally and eternally, if they continue in the faith. Which God for His mercy sake grant they always may, to the glory of their Creator, and comfort of their own souls, through Christ. Amen.

from Ester Sowernam, *Ester Hath Hanged Haman: An Answer to a Lewd Pamphlet, Entitled The Arraignment of Women* (1617)

To all right honorable, noble, and worthy ladies, gentlewomen, and others, virtuously disposed, of the feminine sex.

Right honorable, and all others of our sex, upon my repair to London this last Michaelmas term,[1] being at supper among friends, where the number of each sex were equal, as nothing is more usual for table-talk, there fell out a discourse concerning women, some defending, others objecting against our sex. Upon which occasion, there happened a mention of a pamphlet entitled *The Arraignment of Women*, which I was desirous to see. The next day a gentleman brought me the book, which when I had superficially run over, I found the discourse as far off from performing what the title promised as I found it scandalous and blasphemous. For where the author pretended to write against lewd, idle, and unconstant women, he doth most impudently rage and rail generally against all the whole sex of women. Whereupon, I, in defense of our sex, began an answer to that full pamphlet, in which, after I had spent some small time, word was brought me that an apology for women was already undertaken, and ready for the press, by a minister's daughter. Upon this news, I stayed my pen, as I did expect some fitting performance of what was undertaken. At last the maiden's book was brought me, which when I had likewise run over, I did observe that whereas the maid doth many times excuse her tenderness of years, I found it to be true in the slenderness of her answer. For she, undertaking to defend women, doth rather charge and condemn women, as in the ensuing discourse shall appear. So that, whereas I expected to be eased of what I began, I do now find myself double charged, as well to make reply to the one, as to add supply to the other.

In this my apology, right honorable, right worshipful, and all others of our sex, I do in the first part of it plainly and resolutely deliver the worthiness and worth of women, both in respect of their creation, as in the work of redemption. Next I do show, in examples out of both Testaments, what blessed and happy choice has been made of women, as gracious instruments to derive God's blessings and benefits to mankind.

In my second part I do deliver of what estimate women have been valued in all ancient and modern times, which I prove by authorities, customs, and daily experiences. Lastly, I do answer all material objections which have or can be alleged against our sex; in which also I do arraign such kind of men which correspond the humor and disposition of the author—lewd, idle, furious, and beastly disposed persons.

This being performed, I doubt not but such as heretofore have been so froward and lavish against women will hereafter pull in their horns, and have as little desire, and less cause, so scandalously and slanderously to write against us than formerly they have....

CHAPTER 2

What incomparable and excellent prerogatives God hath bestowed upon women, in their first creation.

In this ensuing chapter I determine briefly to observe (not curiously to discourse at large) the singular benefits and graces bestowed upon women. In regard of which, it is first to be considered that the Almighty God, in the world's frame in His divine wisdom, designed to Himself a main end to which He ordained all the works of His Creation, in which He being a most excellent workmaster, did so create His works, that every succeeding

[1] *Michaelmas term* Term of the High Court of Justice in England and of schools and universities, starting soon after Michaelmas (the feast of St. Michael, on September 29).

work was more excellent than what was formerly created. He wrought by degrees, providing in all for that which was and should be the end.

It appeareth, by that sovereignty which God gave to Adam over all the creatures of sea and land, that man was the end of God's Creation, whereupon it doth necessarily, without exception, follow that Adam, being the last work, is therefore the most excellent work of Creation. Yet Adam was not so absolutely perfect, but that in the sight of God he wanted an *helper*; whereupon God created the woman His last work, as to supply and make absolute that imperfect building which was unperfected in man, as all Divines do hold, till the happy creation of the woman. Now, of what estimate that creature is and ought to be which is the last work, upon whom the Almighty set up His last rest, whom He made to add perfection to the end of all Creation, I leave rather to be acknowledged by others, than resolved by myself.

CHAPTER 4

What excellent blessings and graces have been bestowed upon women in the Law of Grace

The first which cometh in this place to be mentioned is that blessed mother and mirror of all womanhood, the Virgin Mary, who was magnified in the birth of Jesus, glorified by angels, chosen by the Almighty to bear in her womb the Savior of mankind....

I might hereunto add those wives, widows, and virgins, which flourished in the primitive church and all succeeding ages since, who in all virtues have excelled, and honored both their sex in general, and themselves in particular, who in their martyrdoms, in their confession of Jesus, and in all Christian and divine virtues, have in no respect been inferior unto men.

Thus out of the second and third chapters of Genesis, and out of the Old and New Testaments, I have observed in proof of the worthiness of our sex. First, that woman was the last work of Creation, I dare say the best. She was created out of the chosen and best refined substance. She was created in a more worthy country. She was married by a most holy priest. She was given by a most gracious Father. Her husband was enjoined to a most inseparable and affectionate care over her. The first promise of salvation was made to a woman. There is inseparable hatred and enmity put betwixt the woman and the serpent. Her first name, *Eve*, does presage the nature and disposition of all women, not only in respect of their bearing, but further, for the life and delight of heart and soul to all mankind.

CHAPTER 6

The arraignment of Joseph Swetnam, who was the author of the Arraignment of Women; *and under his person, the arraignment of all idle frantic, froward, and lewd men.*

Joseph Swetnam having written his rash, idle, furious, and shameful discourse against women, it was at last delivered into my hands. Presently I did acquaint some of our sex with the accident, with whom I did advise what course we should take with him.... As he had arraigned women at the bar of fame and report, we resolved, at the same bar where he did us the wrong, to arraign him, that thereby we might defend our assured right: and withal (respecting ourselves) we resolved to favor him so far in his trial that the world might take notice there was no partial or indirect dealing, but that he had as much favor as he could desire, and far more than he did or could deserve.

So that we brought him before two judges, *Reason* and *Experience*, who being in place, no man can suspect them with any indirect proceedings: For, albeit *Reason* of itself may be blinded by passion, yet when she is joined with *Experience* she is known to be absolute, and without compare. As for *Experience*, she is known of herself to be admirable excellent in her courses. She knoweth how to use every man in her courses; she will whip the fool to learn him more wit; she will punish the knave to practice more honestly; she will curb in the prodigal, and teach him to be wary; she will trip up the heels of such as are rash and giddy, and bid them hereafter look before they leap. To be sure, there is not in all the world, for all estates, degrees, qualities, and conditions of men, so singular a mistress, or so fit to be a judgess as she. Only one property she hath above the rest: no man cometh before her but she maketh him ashamed, and she will call and prove almost every man a fool, especially such who are wise in their own conceits.

CHAPTER 7

Joseph Swetnam his Indictment

Joseph Swetnam, thou art indicted by the name of *Joseph Swetnam* of *Bedlemmore*, in the County of *Onopolie*, for that thou the twentieth day of *December*, in the year &c. diddest most wickedly, blasphemously, falsely, and scandalously publish a lewd pamphlet, entitled the *Arraignment* of Women, in which, albeit, thou diddest honestly pretend to arraign lewd, idle, froward, and inconstant women, yet contrary to thy pretended promise thou diddest rashly and maliciously rail and rage against all women, generally writing and publishing most blasphemously that women by their Creator were made for *helpers*, for *helpers* (thou sayest) "*to spend and consume that which man painfully getteth.*" Furthermore, thou dost write, "*That being made of a rib, which was crooked, they are therefore crooked and froward in conditions, and that woman was no sooner made, but her heart was set upon mischief*," which thou doest derive to all the sex generally, in these words: "And therefore ever since they have been a woe unto man, and follow the line of their first leader." Further than all this, thou dost affirm an impudent lie upon Almighty God, in saying that God calleth them "necessary evils, and that therefore they were created to be a plague unto man." Thou writest also, "That women are proud, lascivious, froward, curst, unconstant, idle, impudent, shameless, and that they deck and dress themselves to tempt and allure men to lewdness," with much and many more foul, intemperate, and scandalous speeches, &c.

CHAPTER 8

The answer to all objections which are material, made against women

Right honourable and worshipful, and you of all degrees, it hath ever been a common custom amongst idle and humorous poets, pamphleteers, and rhymers, out of passionate discontents, or having little otherwise to employ themselves about, to write some bitter satire-pamphlet or rhyme against women, in which argument he who could devise anything more bitterly or spitefully against our sex hath never wanted the liking, allowance, and applause of giddy headed people.... I will at this present examine all the objections which are most material, which our adversary hath vomited out against woman....

It is the main end that our adversary aimeth at in all his discourse, to prove and say that women are bad. If he should offer this upon particulars, no one would deny it; but to lavish generally against all women, who can endure it? You might, Mr. Swetnam, with some show of honesty have said some women are bad, both by custom and company, but you cannot avoid the brand both of blasphemy and dishonesty to say of women generally they are all naught, both in their creation and by nature, and to ground your inferences upon Scriptures....

A man and a woman talk in the fields together. An honest mind will imagine of their talk answerable to his own disposition, whereas an evil disposed mind will censure according to his lewd inclination. When men complain of beauty and say, "That women's dressings and attire are provocations to wantonness, and baits to allure men," it is a direct means to know of what disposition they are. It is a shame for men in censuring of women to condemn themselves; but a common inn cannot be without a common sign; it is a common sign to know a lecher by complaining upon the cause and occasion of his surfeit. Who had known his disease but by his own complaint? It is extreme folly to complain of another when the root of all resteth within himself. Purge an infected heart, and turn away a lascivious eye, and then neither their dressings nor their beauty can any ways hurt you.... Bad minds are discovered by bad thoughts and hearts. Do not say and rail at women to be the cause of men's overthrow, when the original root and cause is in yourselves. If you be so affected that you cannot look but you must forthwith be infected, I do marvel, Joseph Swetnam, you set down no remedies for that torment of love, as you call it. You bid men shun and avoid it, but those be common and ordinary rules and instructions; yet not so ordinary, as able to restrain the extraordinary humors of your giddy company....

And experience proveth. It is a shame for a man to

complain of a froward woman, in many respects all concerning himself. It is a shame he hath no more government over the weaker vessel. It is a shame he hath hardened her tender sides and gentle heart with his boisterous and northern blasts. It is a shame for a man to publish and proclaim household secrets, which is a common practice amongst men, especially drunkards, lechers, and prodigal spend-thrifts. These, when they come home drunk, or are called in question for their riotous misdemeanors, they presently show themselves, the right children of Adam. They will excuse themselves by their wives, and say that their unquietness and frowardness at home is the cause that they run abroad. …

And this shall appear in the imputation which our adversary chargeth upon our sex, to be lascivious, wanton and lustful. He sayeth, "Women tempt, allure, and provoke men." How rare a thing is it for women to prostitute and offer themselves? How common a practice is it for men to seek and solicit women to lewdness? What charge do they spare? What travel do they bestow? What vows, oaths, and protestations do they spend, to make them dishonest? They hire panders,[1] they write letters, they seal them with damnations and execrations, to assure them of love, when the end proves but lust. They know the flexible disposition of women, and, the sooner to overreach them, some will pretend they are so plunged in love that except they obtain their desire they will seem to drown, hang, stab, poison, or banish themselves from friends and country. What motives are these to tender dispositions? Some will pretend marriage, another offer continual maintenance, but when they have obtained their purpose, what shall a woman find? Just that which is her everlasting shame and grief: she hath made herself the unhappy subject to a lustful body, and the shameful stall of a lascivious tongue. Men may with foul shame charge women with this sin which they had never committed if she had not trusted, nor had ever trusted if she had not been deceived with vows, oaths, and protestations. To bring a woman to offend in one sin, how many damnable sins do they commit? I appeal to their own consciences.…

Our adversary bringeth many examples of men which have been overthrown by women. It is answered, before the fault is their own. But I would have him, or anyone living, to show any woman that offended in this sin of lust, but that she was first solicited by a man.

Helen was the cause of Troy's burning. First, Paris did solicit her; next, how many knaves and fools of the male kind had Troy, which to maintain whoredom would bring their city to confusion?…

Hitherto I have so answered all your objections against women, that as I have not defended the wickedness of any, so I have set down the true state of the question. As Eve did not offend without the temptation of a serpent, so women do seldom offend but it is by provocation of men. Let not your impudence, nor your consorts' dishonesty, charge our sex hereafter with those sins of which you yourselves were the first procurers. I have, in my discourse, touched you and all yours to the quick. I have taxed you with bitter speeches; you will (perhaps) say I am a railing scold. In this objection, Joseph Swetnam, I will teach you both wit and honesty. The difference betwixt a railing scold and an honest accuser is this: the first rageth upon passionate fury without bringing cause or proof, the other bringeth direct proof for what she allegeth. You charge women with clamorous words and bring no proof; I charge you with blasphemy, with impudence, scurrility, foolery, and the like. I show just and direct proof for what I say. It is not my desire to speak so much; it is your desert to provoke me upon just cause so far. It is no railing to call a crow black, or a wolf a ravener, or a drunkard a beast; the report of the truth is never to be blamed. The deserver of such a report deserveth the shame.

Now, for this time to draw to an end, let me ask according to the question of Cassian, "Cui bono?"[2] What have you gotten by publishing your pamphlet? Good I know you can get none. You have (perhaps) pleased the humors of some giddy, idle, conceited persons, but you have dyed yourself in the colours of shame, lying, slandering, blasphemy, ignorance, and the like.

The shortness of time and the weight of business call me away and urge me to leave off thus abruptly; but assure yourself, where I leave now, I will by God's grace

[1] *panders* Go-betweens in clandestine love affairs; pimps.

[2] *Cassian … bono* Cassian (360–435 CE) was an Eastern Christian monk who brought Eastern spirituality to the West. *Cui bono* Latin: To whom is the good?

supply the next term, to your small content. You have exceeded in your fury against widows, whose defense you shall hear of at the time aforesaid. In the mean space recollect your wits, write out of deliberation, not out of fury; write out of advice, not out of idleness; forbear to charge women with faults which come from the contagion of masculine serpents.

Owen Felltham, "Of Woman," from *Resolves* (1628)[1]

Some are so uncharitable, as to think all women bad; and others are so credulous, as they believe they all are good. Sure: though every man speaks as he finds, there is reason to direct our opinion without experience of the whole sex; which in a strict examination, makes more for their honour than most men have acknowledged. At first, she was created his equal, only the difference was in the sex: otherwise, they both were Man. If we argue from the text, that male and female made man, so the man being put first was worthier: I answer, "So the evening and the morning was the first day," yet few will think the night the better.[2] That man is made her governor, and so above her, I believe rather the punishment of her sin, than the prerogative of his worth. Had they both stood, it may be thought, she had never been in that subjection: for then had it been no curse, but a continuance of her former estate: which had nothing but blessedness in it. Peter Martyr indeed is of opinion that man before the fall had priority. But Chrysostom, he says, does doubt it.[3]

All will grant her body more admirable, more beautiful than man's: fuller of curiosities, and noble nature's wonders: both for conception, and fostering the producted birth. And can we think God would put a worser soul into a better body? When man was created, 'tis said, "God made man": but when woman, 'tis said, "God builded her": as if he had then been about a frame of rarer rooms, and more exact composition.[4] And, without doubt, in her body, she is much more wonderful: and by this, we may think her so in her mind. Philosophy tells us, though the soul be not caused by the body, yet in the general it follows the temperament of it: so the comeliest outsides are naturally (for the most part) more virtuous within. If place can be any privilege, we shall find her built in Paradise, when man was made without it.[5]

'Tis certain, they are by constitution colder than the boiling man:[6] so by this, more temperate: 'tis heat that transports man to immoderation and fury: 'tis that, which hurries him to a savage and libidinous violence. Women are naturally the more modest: and modesty is the seat and dwelling place of virtue. Whence proceed the most abhorred villainies, but from a masculine unblushing impudence? What a deal of sweetness do we find in a mild disposition? When a woman grows bold and daring, we dislike her, and say, "she is too like a man": yet in our selves, we magnify what we condemn in her. Is not this injustice? Every man is so much the better, by how much he comes nearer to God. Man in nothing is more like Him, than in being merciful. Yet woman is far more merciful than man: it being a sex, wherein pity and compassion have dispersed far brighter rays. God is said to be love; and I am sure, everywhere woman is spoken of, for transcending in that quality. It was never found, but in two men only, that their love exceeded that of the feminine sex: and if you observe them, you shall find they were both of melting dispositions.[7]

I know, when they prove bad, they are a sort of the vilest creatures: yet still the same reason gives it: for, *Optima corrupta, pessima*: the best things corrupted,

---

[1] Owen Felltham (1604?–68) published the first edition of *Resolves* in 1623, before he was twenty years old. The essays in this collection, which he revised and expanded over subsequent years, played an important role in the development of the English essay.

[2] *So the evening ... better* See Genesis 1.27 and 1.5.

[3] *Peter ... Chrysostom* Peter Martyr Vermigli (1500–62), Italian theologian and religious reformer; Saint John Chrysostom (347?–407), Patriarch of Constantinople.

[4] *When man ... composition* Felltham quotes Genesis 2.22, using the Geneva translation, which glossed "made he a woman" as "built."

[5] *without it* I.e., outside Paradise.

[6] *colder than the boiling man* In medieval and Renaissance physiology, women were associated with cold and moist qualities, men with hot and dry.

[7] *two men only* The Biblical friends David and Jonathan; see especially II Samuel 1.26.

become the worst. They are things, whose souls are of a more ductible[1] temper than the harder metal of man: so may be made both better and worse. The representations of Sophocles and Euripides may be both true:[2] and for the tongue-vice, talkativeness, I see not but at meetings men may very well vie words with them. 'Tis true, they are not of so tumultuous a spirit, so not so fit for great actions. Natural heat does more actuate the stirring genius of man. Their easy natures make them somewhat more unresolute; whereby men have argued them of fear and inconstancy. But men have always held the Parliament, and have enacted their own wills, without ever hearing them speak: and then, how easy is it to conclude them guilty? Besides, education makes more difference between men and them, than nature: and all their aspersions are less noble, for that they are only from their enemies, men.

Diogenes[3] snarled bitterly when, walking with another, he spied two women talking, and said, "See, the viper and the asp are changing poison." The poet[4] was conceited that said, after they were made ill, that God made them fearful, that man might rule them; otherwise they had been past dealing with. Catullus[5] his conclusion was too general, to collect a deceit in all women, because he was not confident of his own:

Nulli se dicit mulier mea nubere malle
Quàm mihi: non si se Jupiter ipse petat.
Dicit: sed mulier Cupido quod dicit amanti,
In vento, & rapida scribere oportet aqua.

My mistress swears, she'd leave all men for me:
Yea, though that Jove himself should suitor be.
She says it: but, what women swear to kind
Loves, may be writ in rapid streams, and wind.

I am resolved to honour virtue, in what sex soever I find it. And I think, in the general, I shall find it more in women, than men; though weaker, and more infirmly guarded. I believe, they are better, and may be wrought to be worse. Neither shall the faults of many, make me uncharitable to all: nor the goodness of some, make me credulous of the rest. Though hitherto, I confess, I have not found more sweet and constant goodness in man than I have found in woman: and yet of these, I have not found a number.

---

[1] *ductible* Malleable, pliable.

[2] *Sophocles … Euripedes* Probably referring to the differing characterizations by these ancient Greek playwrights of the tragic figure of Electra, who is more sympathetic in Sophocles's tragedy of that name than in Euripedes's.

[3] *Diogenes* Classical Greek philosopher.

[4] *The poet* Unidentified; probably classical. Felltham often does not identify his sources; he believed that the essay was like a conversation in which notes would be pedantic.

[5] *Catullus* Roman lyric poet (first century BCE). Feltham quotes *Poems* lxx and provides his own translation.

BEN JONSON

1572 –1637

Ben Jonson was an innovator in poetry, drama, and criticism. In 1616 he became the first Englishman to edit and publish not just his own poetry but his own drama. King James I awarded him a pension and he was, in effect, England's Poet Laureate although there was as yet no such official position. He presided over a literary following that in one poem he calls the "tribe of Ben," members of which included some of the best Cavalier poets. Like Shakespeare a pioneer in the transition from verse to prose in comic dialogue, with a particular talent for shaping social and moral satire into comedy, Jonson also preferred to create his own plots rather than to borrow stories from earlier sources, as was a common practice. With inventive and lyrical virtuosity, he also accumulated a supple and diverse body of poetry. His reputation came to be partially eclipsed by that of Shakespeare, for his humanist erudition and the frequent comic realism of his drama made him seem flat and pedantic beside what was read as Shakespeare's genial inspiration (what Milton called his "native woodnotes wild")—a writer for scholars, to be respected and admired sooner than loved and enjoyed. The twentieth century, though, felt an affinity for what appeared to be the anticipatory modern elements in Jonson—his "plain style," his acute social observation, and his audacity in manipulating dramatic and classical conventions. T.S. Eliot, one of the first to sense this affinity, called Jonson's works "a part of our literary inheritance that craves further expression."

Jonson's grounding in the classics began in adolescence at Westminster School under the noted scholar and antiquarian William Camden, a lifelong friend whom Jonson later praised as the teacher "to whom I owe all that I am in arts." After brief stints as an apprentice bricklayer and a soldier, Jonson (like Shakespeare) joined the developing theater world as an actor. *Every Man in his Humour* (1598), in which Shakespeare acted, established Jonson as master of the new "comedy of humors," which lampoons eccentricities of character, called "humors" because diagnosable as an imbalance of the four humors that make up the body and affect the mind. Jonson also announced himself as an innovator with a mission. His prologue to the play—one of many such overt statements and justifications of his art that he eventually learned to dramatize more indirectly—sets out what remained the core of his dramatic philosophy; in it he advocates direct and realistic language ("deeds and language such as men do use") and a return to classical unities of time and space, eschewing the elaborate fantasies and distortions common in Elizabethan comedy and even more common in Jacobean romance and tragicomedy. A more satirical sequel, *Every Man out of his Humour* (1599), proved so popular that Jonson took the unorthodox step of personally supervising its publication, thereby establishing a double precedent—the play as property of its author rather than of the acting company, and the popular stage play as literary document.

Jonson's high opinion of his art proved justified; his plays *Volpone* (1606) and *The Alchemist* (1610) remain two of the best-loved comedies in British literature. *Volpone* chronicles a scheming miser's deception of a series of legacy hunters; in *The Alchemist*, various vain and gullible types are exploited by three servants posing as musicians in their master's absence. Both are comedies of intrigue, and in both Jonson set new standards in incisive, naturalistic dialogue and intricate plot construction. (Coleridge judged the plot of *The Alchemist* "absolute perfection.") These comedies show Jonson able to turn his ferocious satirical gifts to a coherent purpose, what he called "high moral" comedy, and, in the case of *The Alchemist*, to attain perfect classical unities of time and space: its action takes place in real time in a set built to actual size.

Jonson also scored hits with *Epicoene* (1612), a sportive exploration of sexual politics, and *Bartholomew Fair* (1614), a broad, slice-of-life portrait of London holiday street life. His attempts at tragedy, *Sejanus* (1603) and *Catiline* (1612), were judged too ponderous and pedantic, though Jonson, who well understood the power of print, was convinced his reading public would overleap what he saw as the deficiencies of his playgoing audiences. In the case of *Catiline*, he was right: though never a performance success, it was the most-quoted English play of the seventeenth century.

Posterity has since consigned Jonson's tragedies to relative obscurity but has shown increased regard for the limpid and clever verse he contributed to the Jacobean court masques. These were entertainments, commissioned to celebrate special events, that were danced and acted by members of the court. They featured increasingly elaborate costumes, scenery, and special effects, all designed by Jonson's collaborator, the court architect Inigo Jones. Such spectacles as the *Masque of Blackness* (1605) and the *Masque of Beauty* (1608) played off antique myths, providing a venue for Jonson to display his classical learning and sharpen his lyrical gifts. Jonson also introduced, in such flattering yet admonitory court masques as *Pleasure Reconciled to Virtue* and *Love Restored* (1612), the intriguing device of the "antimasque," a more rough-and-tumble moment with comic images of irrationality or grotesquerie that the surrounding masque both absorbs and exorcizes. Between them, Jonson and Jones took the masque from transitory amusement into a high art that in its multimedia form in some ways anticipates the opera and even film.

Jonson considered himself above all a poet. His poetry follows his dramas and masques in the 1616 folio of his collected works, which was the culmination of his career to that point, "the ripest of my studies." When, in his "Epistle to the Countess of Rutland" (1600), he introduced his "strange poems, which as yet / Had not their form touched by an English wit," Jonson was referring to such classical forms as the ode, epistle, epitaph, and epigram that he intended to revive or invigorate with a more crystalline yet colloquial style. His two best-loved lyrics, "To Celia" and "Drink to Me Only With Thine Eyes," written for *Volpone*, are not mere translations of Catullus and Philostrates; they are quintessentially Jonsonian, bringing to mind Oscar Wilde's assertion that Jonson "made the poets of Greece and Rome terribly modern."

These classical poetic genres were well suited to the intensely personal and yet social nature of Jonson's poetry, and it is here that his turbulent life and personality are reflected most vividly. We see in his many commissioned occasional pieces the cultivation of the aristocratic patronage on which he depended—as in "To Penshurst," his eloquent tribute to the estate of the Sidney family. We witness his capacity for generous friendship in his epigrams to John Donne and his preface to Shakespeare's First Folio, and his capacity for grief in the restrained eloquence of his epitaphs on his young son and infant daughter. We even glean hints of his legendary appetite for food and drink in "Inviting a Friend to Supper," which celebrates the sort of literary camaraderie Jonson found (and read about in his beloved Horace) in his early years, at the Mermaid Tavern, where he held court with a coterie of wits and fellow writers. Other early literary friends included Ralegh, Bacon, Chapman, Beaumont, and Fletcher, while later in his career, he mentored younger poets such as Herrick, Suckling, and Carew, presiding over a literary cult of sorts, the "sons [or sometimes "tribe"] of Ben," at the Devil Tavern in the 1620s. Jonson had enemies, too; he could be vain, arrogant and quarrelsome, especially in defense of his literary principles and reputation, as in his legendary feud with his rival playwrights Dekker and Marston early in his career. Indeed, in 1598 he got into a fight with an actor and killed him (a crime for which he was branded and sent for a while to prison, where he became a Catholic, reconverting some years later).

The royal pension bestowed on him in 1616 enabled Jonson to leave the stage and concentrate largely on his poetry for a decade. In 1618, he traveled to Scotland, where he visited the poet William Drummond, who left a record of their conversations and Jonson's often imperious opinions. The following year he was awarded an honorary M.A. from Oxford. Such triumphs and his "tribe" or "sons" notwithstanding, the 1620s brought a gradual decline in Jonson's health and fortunes. A fire destroyed his library, along with several manuscripts, in 1623. The death of King James in 1625 left him without a place at court, necessitating a return to the stage in 1626 with *The Staple of News*, a satire on the emerging newspaper business; it was not well-received. In fact, he was never again to attain success as a playwright; Dryden was later to refer to these late plays as "Jonson's dotages." His masque-writing career ended with the culmination in 1631 of a long-running feud with Inigo Jones. Even though disabled and confined to his house after a stroke in 1628, however, and though no longer the influential lion of his youth, Jonson did not lack for admirers or companionship. When he died in August 1637, most of London's literary and social elite attended his funeral.

Ben Jonson did not leave the world of letters as he found it. His assertion of ownership and careful editing of his own works affected the development of modern authorship and certainly influenced the publication of Shakespeare's First Folio. His satirical comedies provided a significant model for Restoration and eighteenth-century drama, and even for later comic writers in other genres such as Fielding and Dickens. In numerous justificatory prologues to his plays, and in his commonplace book, *Timber, or Discoveries*, he left behind a striking record of a writer's mind at work. And, just as important, the muscular yet supple "plain style" of his poetry was pivotal in deflecting a late Elizabethan taste for the highly wrought and decorative towards a more direct and colloquial manner that became one major strand of late seventeenth-century (and modern) aesthetics.

⌘⌘⌘

To the Reader

Pray thee take care, that tak'st my book in hand,
To read it well: that is, to understand.
—1616

To My Book

It will be looked for, book, when some but see
Thy title, *Epigrams,* and named of me,
Thou should'st be bold, licentious, full of gall,
Wormwood and sulphur, sharp and toothed withal;[1]
Become a petulant thing, hurl ink and wit
As madmen stones, not caring whom they hit.
Deceive their malice who could wish it so,
And by thy wiser temper let men know
Thou are not covetous of least self-fame
Made from the hazard of another's shame;
Much less with lewd, profane and beastly phrase,
To catch the world's loose laughter or vain gaze.
He that departs with his own honesty
For vulgar praise, doth it too dearly buy.
—1616

On Something that Walks Somewhere

At court I met it, in clothes brave enough
To be a courtier, and looks grave enough
To seem a statesman: as I near it came,
It made me a great face; I asked the name.
"A lord," it cried, "buried in flesh and blood,
And such from whom let no man hope least good,

[1] *Thou should'st ... toothed withal* Characteristics of late Elizabethan verse satire, a mode of poetry with which epigrams were associated.

For I will do none; and as little ill,
For I will dare none." Good lord, walk dead still.
—1616

To William Camden[1]

Camden, most reverend head, to whom I owe
All that I am in arts, all that I know
(How nothing's that?), to whom my country owes
The great renown and name wherewith she goes;[2]
Than thee the age sees not that thing more grave,
More high, more holy, that she more would crave.
What name, what skill, what faith hast thou in things!
What sight in searching the most antique springs!
What weight, and what authority in thy speech!
Man scarce can make that doubt, but thou canst teach.
Pardon free truth, and let thy modesty,
Which conquers all, be once overcome by thee.
Many of thine this better could than I;
But for their powers, accept my piety.
—1616

On My First Daughter

Here lies, to each her parents' ruth,
Mary, the daughter of their youth;
Yet, all heaven's gifts being heaven's due,
It makes the father less to rue.
At six months' end she parted hence
With safety of her innocence;
Whose soul heaven's queen (whose name she bears)
In comfort of her mother's tears,
Hath placed amongst her virgin train:
Where, while that severed doth remain,[3]
This grave partakes the fleshly birth;
Which cover lightly, gentle earth.
—1616

[1] *Camden* William Camden (1551–1623), historian and schoolmaster; Jonson's teacher at Westminster School.

[2] *name* Punning reference to Camden's great historical work *Britannia* (1586).

[3] *that severed doth remain* Her soul, severed from the body, remains in heaven.

To John Donne[4]

Donne, the delight of Phoebus[5] and each muse,
Who, to thy one, all other brains refuse;[6]
Whose every work of thy most early wit
Came forth example, and remains so yet;
Longer a-knowing than most wits do live,
And which no affection praise enough can give!
To it, thy language, letters, arts, best life,
Which might with half mankind maintain a strife;
All which I meant to praise, and yet I would,
But leave, because I cannot as I should.
—1616

On My First Son

Farewell, thou child of my right hand,[7] and joy;
My sin was too much hope of thee, loved boy.
Seven years thou wert lent to me, and I thee pay,
Exacted by thy fate, on the just day.[8]
Oh, could I lose all father, now! For why
Will man lament the state he should envy?
To have so soon 'scaped world's and flesh's rage,
And, if no other misery, yet age?
Rest in soft peace, and, asked, say here doth lie
Ben Jonson his best piece of poetry;
For whose sake, henceforth, all his vows be such,
As what he loves may never like too much.
—1616 (WRITTEN 1603)

[4] *To John Donne* For biographical information on Donne, see the introduction to the selection of his works; for some of Jonson's informal opinions on Donne, see the selection from his "Conversations with William Drummond."

[5] *Phoebus* Apollo, god of poetry.

[6] *refuse* Jonson's syntax here is compact: Apollo and the Muses refuse to bestow on other brains the gifts they've given Donne, or they reject all brains in favor of his.

[7] *right hand* The name "Benjamin," which was also the name of Jonson's dead son, means "son of the right hand" in Hebrew (see Genesis 35), implying right-handedness, and good luck, also being placed in a position of privilege and paternal favor.

[8] *Seven years ... just day* Jonson's first son (b. 1596) died at the age of seven, and seven years was the traditional length of time for which loans were extended.

On Lucy, Countess of Bedford[1]

This morning, timely rapt with holy fire,
I thought to form unto my zealous muse
What kind of creature I could most desire
To honour, serve and love, as poets use.
I meant to make her fair, and free,° and wise, *generous*
Of greatest blood, and yet more good than great;
I meant the day-star[2] should not brighter rise,
Nor lend like influence from his lucent° seat. *shining*
I meant she should be courteous, facile,° sweet, *affable*
Hating that solemn vice of greatness, pride;
I meant each softest virtue there should meet,
Fit in that softer bosom to reside.
Only a learnèd and a manly soul
I purposed her; that should, with even powers,
The rock, the spindle and the shears control
Of destiny,[3] and spin her own free hours.
Such when I meant to feign, and wished to see,
My muse bade, *Bedford* write, and that was she.
—1616

Inviting a Friend to Supper

Tonight, grave sir, both my poor house and I
Do equally desire your company:
Not that we think us worthy such a guest,
But that your worth will dignify our feast
With those that come; whose grace may make that seem
Something, which else could hope for no esteem.
It is the fair acceptance, sir, creates
The entertainment perfect, not the cates.° *food*
Yet shall you have, to rectify your palate,
An olive, capers, or some better salad
Ushering the mutton; with a short-legged hen,
If we can get her, full of eggs, and then
Lemons, and wine for sauce; to these, a coney° *rabbit*
Is not to be despaired of, for our money;
And though fowl now be scarce, yet there are clerks,[4]
The sky not falling, think we may have larks.[5]
I'll tell you of more, and lie, so you will come:
Of partridge, pheasant, woodcock, of which some
May yet be there; and godwit, if we can;
Knat, rail and ruff, too.[6] Howsoe'er, my man
Shall read a piece of Virgil, Tacitus,
Livy, or of some better book to us,
Of which we'll speak our minds, amidst our meat;
And I'll profess no verses to repeat;
To this, if aught appear which I not know of,
That will the pastry, not my paper, show of.[7]
Digestive cheese and fruit there sure will be;
But that which most doth take my muse and me
Is a pure cup of rich Canary wine,[8]
Which is the Mermaid's now,[9] but shall be mine;
Of which had Horace or Anacreon tasted,[10]
Their lives, as do their lines, till now had lasted.
Tobacco,[11] nectar, or the Thespian Spring[12]

[1] *Lucy, Countess of Bedford* (1581–1627), friend and patron of Ben Jonson and other writers, including John Donne, Samuel Daniel, and Michael Drayton.

[2] *day-star* Often the morning star or planet Venus, but sometimes, as here, the sun (the next line indicates that this day-star is figured as masculine).

[3] *rock ... of destiny* Referring to the three Fates of classical myth: Clotho spun the thread of life (a "rock" is a distaff), Lachesis measured its length on her spindle, and Atropos cut the thread. Jonson's ideal patron controls her own destiny, and so spins for herself her "free" (unmeasured) hours.

[4] *clerks* Pronounced "clarks."

[5] *larks* Playing on a proverb: "if the sky falls, we shall have larks." Here, some "clerks" (knowledgeable people) think Jonson's supper will feature larks even if the sky does not fall. Not figurative: to "have larks" in the sense of to "have fun" first appears in the nineteenth century.

[6] *knat ... too* All edible birds. Jonson is not offering his guest an expensive feast: by the standards of the gentry of the time, the food on offer is simple and inexpensive, though well chosen.

[7] *if aught appear ... show of* That is, if Jonson's own poems do make a surprise appearance, it will only be because they are on paper used to wrap the pastries.

[8] *Canary wine* Light, sweet wine from the Canary Islands, off the west coast of Africa.

[9] *Mermaid's* The Mermaid Tavern in Cheapside, Jonson's favorite place to meet friends and drink.

[10] *Horace or Anacreon* Respectively, a Roman and an ancient Greek lyric poet; both wrote in praise of wine.

[11] *Tobacco* Tobacco was described as being "drunk" rather than "smoked" in the period.

[12] *Thespian Spring* Stream at the foot of Mount Helicon sacred to the classical Muses.

Are all but Luther's beer[1] to this I sing.
Of this we will sup free, but moderately;
And we will have no Poley or Parrot by;[2]
Nor shall our cups make any guilty men,
But at our parting we will be as when
We innocently met. No simple word
That shall be uttered at our mirthful board
Shall make us sad next morning, or affright
The liberty that we'll enjoy tonight.
—1616

To Penshurst[3]

Thou art not, Penshurst, built to envious show
Of touch° or marble, nor canst boast a row *black stone*
Of polished pillars, or a roof of gold;
Thou hast no lantern whereof tales are told,[4]
Or stair, or courts; but standst an ancient pile,
And these grudged at, art reverenced the while.
Thou joy'st in better marks, of soil, of air,
Of wood, of water; therein thou art fair.
Thou hast thy walks for health as well as sport:
Thy Mount, to which the dryads° do resort, *wood nymphs*
Where Pan and Bacchus their high feasts have made,[5]
Beneath the broad beech and the chestnut shade;
That taller tree, which of a nut was set
At his great birth,[6] where all the Muses met.
There, in the writhèd° bark, are cut the names *twisted*
Of many a sylvan, taken with his flames;[7]
And thence the ruddy satyrs oft provoke
The lighter fauns to reach thy lady's oak.[8]
Thy copse, too, named of Gamage,[9] thou hast there,
That never fails to serve thee seasoned° deer *of suitable age*
When thou wouldst feast or exercise thy friends.
The lower land, that to the river bends,
Thy sheep, thy bullocks, kine and calves do feed;
The middle grounds thy mares and horses breed.
Each bank doth yield thee conies,° and the tops, *rabbits*
Fertile of wood, Ashour and Sidney's copse,[10]
To crown thy open table, doth provide
The purpled pheasant with the speckled side;
The painted partridge lies in every field,
And for thy mess° is willing to be killed. *meal*
And if the high-swoll'n Medway[11] fail thy dish,
Thou hast thy ponds that pay thee tribute fish:
Fat, agèd carps, that run into thy net;
And pikes, now weary their own kind to eat,[12]
As loath the second draught or cast to stay,
Officiously,° at first, themselves betray; *obligingly*
Bright eels, that emulate them, and leap on land
Before the fisher, or into his hand.
Then hath thy orchard fruit, thy garden flowers,
Fresh as the air and new as are the hours:
The early cherry, with the later plum,
Fig, grape and quince, each in his time doth come;

[1] *Luther's beer* Beer brewed in Germany and thought to be weaker than and inferior to English beer.

[2] *Poley or Parrot* Two well known government spies or informers; Robert Poley (or Pooly) and Henry Parrot. Pooly was present when Christopher Marlowe was fatally stabbed in a Deptford tavern. Jonson also plays on these men's names: a "Polly" or Parrot is a talkative bird.

[3] *To Penshurst* Penshurst Place, in Kent, was the home of Sir Robert Sidney, Viscount Lisle (1563–1626) and his wife, Barbara Gamage (c. 1559–1621); Robert was the younger brother of Sir Philip Sidney (1554–86) and, in 1618, was made Earl of Leicester. Penshurst had been given to the Sidney family by King Edward VI in 1552, but, as Jonson points out, parts of the manor were much older: the Great Hall was built in 1340–41, and remains today as one of England's finest examples of fourteenth-century domestic architecture.

[4] *lantern* Windowed turret or similar structure; the new, lavish manors with which Jonson compares Penshurst featured such "talked about" architectural features.

[5] *Pan and Bacchus* Greek gods: Pan was the half man, half goat deity of the pastoral world; Bacchus was the god of wine. Both were also associated with song and poetic inspiration, and their presence is an implicit tribute to the Sidneys as a family of poets (Philip in particular; see line 14) and patrons of poetry.

[6] *his great birth* Sir Philip Sidney (b. 1554).

[7] *sylvan* Rural lover, inspired by the flames of love (or by the passions in Sidney's love poetry).

[8] *satyrs … lady's oak* Satyrs and fauns are ancient woodland deities: the satyrs challenge the (smaller) fauns in races to an oak tree named for a Lady Leicester who went into labor while sitting under it.

[9] *Gamage* Named for Barbara Gamage, Lady Leicester.

[10] *tops … copse* Like other parts of the estate, nature in the "tops" (high grounds) bears the names of people.

[11] *Medway* River near the estate.

[12] *And pikes … to eat* Pikes were reputed to be particularly voracious fish.

The blushing apricot and woolly peach
Hang on thy walls, that every child may reach.
And though thy walls be of the country° stone, *local*
They're reared with no man's ruin, no man's groan;
There's none that dwell about them wish them down,
But all come in, the farmer and the clown,° *rustic*
And no one empty-handed, to salute
Thy lord and lady, though they have no suit.° *request*
Some bring a capon, some a rural cake,
Some nuts, some apples; some that think they make
The better cheeses, bring 'em; or else send
By their ripe daughters, whom they would commend
This way to husbands; and whose baskets bear
An emblem of themselves, in plum or pear.
But what can this (more than express their love)
Add to thy free provisions, far above
The need of such? whose liberal board doth flow
With all that hospitality doth know!
Where comes no guest but is allowed to eat
Without his fear, and of thy lord's own meat;
Where the same beer and bread and self-same wine
That is his lordship's shall be also mine;
And I not fain to sit, as some this day
At great men's tables, and yet dine away.
Here no man tells° my cups, nor, standing by, *counts*
A waiter, doth my gluttony envy,
But gives me what I call, and lets me eat;
He knows below he shall find plenty of meat,
Thy tables hoard not up for the next day.
Nor, when I take my lodging, need I pray
For fire or lights or livery:° all is there, *provisions*
As if thou then wert mine, or I reigned here;
There's nothing I can wish, for which I stay.° *wait*
That found King James, when, hunting late this way
With his brave son, the Prince,[1] they saw thy fires
Shine bright on every hearth as the desires
Of thy Penates[2] had been set on flame
To entertain them; or the country came
With all their zeal to warm their welcome here.
What (great, I will not say, but) sudden cheer
Didst thou then make 'em! and what praise was heaped
On thy good lady then! who therein reaped
The just reward of her high housewifery:
To have her linen, plate, and all things nigh
When she was far; and not a room but dressed
As if it had expected such a guest!
These, Penshurst, are thy praise, and yet not all.
Thy lady's noble, fruitful, chaste withal;
His children thy great lord may call his own,
A fortune in this age but rarely known.
They are and have been taught religion; thence
Their gentler spirits have sucked innocence.
Each morn and even they are taught to pray
With the whole household, and may every day
Read in their virtuous parents' noble parts
The mysteries of manners, arms, and arts.
Now, Penshurst, they that will proportion° thee *compare*
With other edifices, when they see
Those proud, ambitious heaps, and nothing else,
May say, their lords have built, but thy lord dwells.
—1616 (WRITTEN 1611/12)

Song: To Celia[3]

Drink to me only, with thine eyes,
And I will pledge with mine;
Or leave a kiss but in the cup,
And I'll not look for wine.
The thirst that from the soul doth rise
Doth ask a drink divine;
But might I of Jove's nectar sup,
I would not change for thine.
I sent thee late a rosy wreath,
Not so much honouring thee
As giving it a hope that there
It could not withered be.
But thou thereon didst only breathe,
And sent'st it back to me;
Since when it grows, and smells, I swear,
Not of itself, but thee.
—1616

[1] *The Prince* Prince Henry; he died in November 1612.

[2] *Penates* Roman household divinities.

[3] *Song: To Celia* Much of this poem consists of Jonson's translations of prose fragments by the ancient Greek writer Philostratus.

To the Memory of My Beloved, The Author, Mr. William Shakespeare, And What He Hath Left Us[1]

To draw no envy, Shakespeare, on thy name,
Am I thus ample to thy book and fame;
While I confess thy writings to be such
As neither man nor Muse can praise too much:
'Tis true, and all men's suffrage. But these ways
Were not the paths I meant unto thy praise:
For silliest ignorance on these may light,
Which, when it sounds at best, but echoes right;
Or blind affection, which doth ne'er advance
The truth, but gropes, and urgeth all by chance;
Or crafty malice might pretend this praise,
And think to ruin where it seemed to raise.
These are as some infamous bawd or whore
Should praise a matron: what could hurt her more?
But thou art proof against them, and indeed
Above the ill fortune of them, or the need.
I therefore will begin. Soul of the age!
The applause, delight, the wonder of our stage!
My Shakespeare, rise: I will not lodge thee by
Chaucer or Spenser, or bid Beaumont[2] lie
A little further, to make thee a room;
Thou art a monument without a tomb,
And art alive still while thy book doth live,
And we have wits to read, and praise to give.
That I not mix thee so, my brain excuses:
I mean with great, but disproportioned, Muses;
For if I thought my judgement were of years
I should commit thee surely with thy peers:
And tell how far thou didst our Lyly outshine,
Or sporting Kyd, or Marlowe's mighty line.[3]
And though thou hadst small Latin, and less Greek,[4]
From thence to honour thee I would not seek
For names, but call forth thundering Aeschylus,
Euripides, and Sophocles to us,[5]
Pacuvius, Accius, him of Cordova dead,[6]
To life again, to hear thy buskin[7] tread
And shake a stage; or, when thy socks[8] were on,
Leave thee alone for the comparison
Of all that insolent Greece or haughty Rome
Sent forth, or since did from their ashes come.
Triumph, my Britain, thou hast one to show
To whom all scenes of Europe homage owe.
He was not of an age, but for all time!
And all the Muses still were in their prime
When like Apollo he came forth to warm
Our ears, or like a Mercury to charm![9]
Nature herself was proud of his designs,
And joyed to wear the dressing of his lines,
Which were so richly spun and woven so fit
As, since, she will vouchsafe no other wit.
The merry Greek, tart Aristophanes,
Neat Terence, witty Plautus,[10] now not please,
But antiquated and deserted lie
As they were not of nature's family.
Yet must I not give nature all: thy art,
My gentle Shakespeare, must enjoy a part.
For though the poet's matter nature be,
His art doth give the fashion. And that he
Who casts to write a living line must sweat
(Such as thine are) and strike the second heat
Upon the Muses' anvil: turn the same
(And himself with it) that he thinks to frame;
Or for the laurel he may gain a scorn:
For a good poet's made, as well as born;
And such wert thou.[11] Look how the father's face

[1] *To the Memory … Left Us* Published in the first folio edition of Shakespeare's *Works* (1623).

[2] *Beaumont* Playwright Francis Beaumont (1584–1616), buried, like Chaucer and Spenser, in Westminster Abbey.

[3] *our Lyly … mighty line* Playwrights John Lyly (c. 1554–1606), Thomas Kyd (1558–94), and Christopher Marlowe (1564–93).

[4] *small Latin, and less Greek* By Jonson's standards, this means something less than erudite and expert fluency.

[5] *Aeschylus, Euripides, and Sophocles* Ancient Greek dramatists.

[6] *Pacuvius … Cordova dead* Ancient Roman playwrights. No works are extant by Pacuvius or Accius; "him of Cordova" is Seneca.

[7] *buskin* Boot worn by actors in Greek tragedies, and so a metonym for tragic drama.

[8] *Socks* Shoes worn by actors in Greek and Roman comedies, and so a metonym for comic drama.

[9] *Apollo … Mercury* Gods of poetry and eloquence.

[10] *tart Aristophanes … Plautus* Aristophanes was a Greek dramatist known for satirical comedies; Plautus and Terence were both Roman playwrights known for comedies.

[11] *thy art … wert thou* Jonson in fact seems to have resented the ease with which Shakespeare wrote: see his comments in the "Conversations with Drummond" and *Timber, or, Discoveries*.

Lives in his issue: even so, the race
Of Shakespeare's mind and manners brightly shines
In his well-turned and true-filed lines:
In each of which he seems to shake a lance,
As brandished at the eyes of ignorance.
Sweet swan of Avon! What a sight it were
To see thee in our waters yet appear,
And make those flights upon the banks of Thames
That so did take Eliza, and our James![1]
But stay, I see thee in the hemisphere
Advanced, and made a constellation there!
Shine forth, thou star of poets, and with rage
Or influence chide or cheer the drooping stage;
Which, since thy flight from hence, hath mourned like night
And despairs day, but for thy volume's light.
—1623

Ode to Himself[2]

Come leave the loathèd stage,
And the more loathsome age,
Where pride and impudence, in faction knit,
Usurp the chair of wit:
Indicting and arraigning every day
Something they call a play.
Let their fastidious, vain
Commission of the brain
Run on, and rage, sweat, censure, and condemn:
They were not made for thee, less thou for them.

Say that thou pour'st them wheat,
And they will acorns eat:
'Twere simple fury, still, thyself to waste
On such as have no taste:
To offer them a surfeit of pure bread,
Whose appetites are dead.
No, give them grains their fill,
Husks, draff° to drink and swill. *dregs*
If they love lees, and leave the lusty wine,
Envy them not, their palate's with the swine.

No doubt some mouldy tale,
Like Pericles,[3] and stale
As the shrieve's crusts,[4] and nasty as his fish-
Scraps out of every dish
Thrown forth, and raked into the common tub,
May keep up the play-club:
There, sweepings do as well
As the best ordered meal.
For, who the relish of these guests will fit,
Needs set them but the alms-basket of wit.

And much good do't you then:
Brave plush and velvet-men;
Can feed on orts:° and safe in your stage-clothes, *scraps*
Dare quit, upon your oaths,
The stagers and the stage-wrights too (your peers)
Of larding your large ears
With their foul comic socks,
Wrought upon twenty blocks:
Which if they are torn, and turned, and patched enough,
The gamesters share your guilt, and you their stuff.

Leave things so prostitute,
And take the Alcaic lute;
Or thine own Horace or Anacreon's lyre;
Warm thee by Pindar's fire:[5]
And though thy nerves be shrunk, and blood be cold,
Ere years have made thee old,
Strike that disdainful heat
Throughout, to their defeat:

[1] *Eliza ... James* I.e., Queen Elizabeth I and King James I of England.

[2] *Ode to Himself* Written in response to the poor reception of his play *The New Inn*, which was hissed off stage in 1629. Jonson first published this ode with the printed version of the play in 1631; the version here, slightly revised, appeared in his 1640 *Works*.

[3] *Pericles* Usually read as a reference to the play by Shakespeare, performed in 1607–08; Jonson would have disapproved of the play (a romance with a very loose structure, based on old narrative elements), but he also refers to the taste of his audience, which apparently still preferred to watch a play first performed two decades earlier.

[4] *shrieve's crusts* Sheriff's crusts; referring to the leftover food collected to feed poor prisoners.

[5] *Alcaic... Pindar* Jonson tells himself to return to classical literary genres, as represented by such renowned ancient poets as the Greeks Alcaeus, Pindar, and Anacreon, and the Roman Horace.

As curious fools, and envious of thy strain,
May, blushing, swear no palsy's in thy brain.

But when they hear thee sing
The glories of thy King,
His zeal to God, and his just awe o'er men:
They may, blood-shaken, then,
Feel such a flesh-quake to possess their powers
As they shall cry, "Like ours
In sound of peace or wars,
No harp e'er hit the stars,
In tuning forth the acts of his sweet reign:
And raising Charles's chariot 'bove his Wain."[1]
—1631, 1640

My Picture Left in Scotland

I now think Love is rather deaf than blind,
For else it could not be,
That she
Whom I adore so much, should so slight me,
And cast my suit behind:
I'm sure my language to her was as sweet,
And every close[2] did meet
In sentence of as subtle feet,
As hath the youngest he
That sits in shadow of Apollo's tree.

Oh, but my conscious fears,
That fly my thoughts between,
Tell me that she hath seen
My hundreds of gray hairs
Told seven and forty years,
Read so much waist, as she cannot embrace
My mountain belly, and my rocky face,
And all these, through her eyes, have stopped her ears.
—1640 (WRITTEN 1619)

[1] *Charles ... his Wain* "Charles's Wain" is the constellation the Big Dipper, named for Charlemagne; a "wain" is a chariot or cart. Jonson's poetry will elevate King Charles above the stars.

[2] *close* Conclusion of a musical theme or phrase

To the Immortal Memory and Friendship of That Noble Pair, Sir Lucius Cary and Sir H. Morison[3]

The Turn[4]

Brave infant of Saguntum,[5] clear° *explain*
Thy coming forth in that great year
When the prodigious Hannibal did crown
His rage with razing your immortal town.
Thou, looking then about,
Ere thou wert half got out,
Wise child, didst hastily return,
And mad'st thy mother's womb thine urn.
How summed° a circle didst thou leave
mankind *complete*
Of deepest lore, could we the centre find!

The Counter-Turn

Did wiser nature draw thee back
From out the horror of that sack?
Where shame, faith, honour, and regard of right
Lay trampled on; the deeds of death and night
Urged, hurried forth, and hurled
Upon the affrighted world:
Sword, fire, and famine with fell fury met,

[3] *Noble Pair ... Morison* Sir Lucius Cary (1609/10–43), second Viscount Falkland, famed for his learning and for the intellectual and literary circle that met at his estate of Great Tew, outside of Oxford. A peaceable, moderate Royalist who fell into despair with the outbreak of civil war, Cary would die in battle when he more or less deliberately exposed himself to enemy fire. Sir Henry Morison (1608–29), Cary's brother-in-law, probably died of smallpox.

[4] *The Turn* This poem is one of the earliest attempts in English to imitate the Greek Pindaric ode., and the most successful. Pindar (518–438 BCE) composed choral odes that commemorate winners at the Olympic games. His language is allusive and his form and meter complex. His structure is tripartite: the chorus sings a "strophe" (Jonson's "turn") while moving in one direction, then reverses direction and sings a structurally identical "antistrophe" (Jonson's "counter-turn"), then stops and sings the "epode" (Jonson's "stand"), which differs structurally from the other parts.

[5] *infant of Saguntum* According to the Roman writer Pliny, an infant born in Sagunto (in Spain) while it was being sacked by the Carthaginian general Hannibal in 219 BCE returned immediately to its mother's womb.

And all on utmost ruin set;
As, could they but life's miseries foresee,
No doubt all infants would return like thee?

The Stand

For what is life, if measured by the space,
Not by the act?
Or maskèd man, if valued by his face
Above his fact?
Here's one outlived his peers
And told forth fourscore years;
He vexèd time, and busied the whole state;
Troubled both foes and friends,
But ever to no ends;
What did this stirrer,° but die late? *agitator*
How well at twenty had he fallen or stood!
For three of his fourscore he did no good.

The Turn

He entered well by virtuous parts,
Got up and thrived with honest arts;
He purchased friends and fame and honours then,
And had his noble name advanced with men;
But weary of that flight,
He stooped in all men's sight
To sordid flatteries, acts of strife,
And sunk in that dead sea of life
So deep, as he did then death's waters sup,
But that the cork of title buoyed him up.

The Counter-Turn

Alas, but Morison fell young!
He never fell: thou fall'st, my tongue.
He stood, a soldier to the last right end,
A perfect patriot, and a noble friend;
But most, a virtuous son.
All offices were done
By him so ample, full, and round,
In weight, in measure, number, sound,
As, though his age imperfect might appear,
His life was of humanity the sphere.

The Stand

Go now, and tell out days summed up with fears,
And make them years;
Produce thy mass of miseries on the stage,
To swell thine age;
Repeat of things a throng,
To show thou hast been long,
Not lived; for life doth her great actions spell
By what was done and wrought
In season, and so brought
To light: her measures are, how well
Each syllabe answered, and was formed, how fair;
These make the lines of life, and that's her air.

The Turn

It is not growing like a tree
In bulk, doth make man better be;
Or standing long an oak, three hundred year,
To fall a log at last, dry, bald, and sere:
A lily of a day
Is fairer far, in May,
Although it fall and die that night;
It was the plant and flower of light.
In small proportions we just beauty see,
And in short measures life may perfect be.

The Counter-Turn

Call, noble Lucius, then for wine,
And let thy looks with gladness shine;
Accept this garland, plant it on thy head;
And think, nay know, thy Morison's not dead.
He leaped the present age,
Possessed with holy rage
To see that bright eternal day,
Of which we priests and poets say
Such truths as we expect for happy men;
And there he lives with memory, and Ben

The Stand

Jonson, who sung this of him, ere he went
Himself to rest,

Or taste a part of that full joy he meant
To have expressed
In this bright asterism;° *constellation*
Where it were friendship's schism
(Were not his Lucius long with us to tarry)
To separate these twi-
Lights, the Dioscuri;[1]
And keep the one half from his Harry.
But fate doth so alternate the design,
Whilst that in heaven, this light on earth must shine.

The Turn

And shine as you exalted are;
Two names of friendship, but one star:
Of hearts the union. And those not by chance
Made, or indentured, or leased out to advance
The profits for a time.
No pleasures vain did chime,
Of rhymes, or riots, at your feasts,
Orgies of drink, or feigned protests:
But simple love of greatness, and of good;
That knits brave minds and manners, more than blood.

The Counter-Turn

This made you first to know the why
You liked; then after to apply
That liking; and approach so one the t'other,
Till either grew a portion of the other:
Each styled, by his end,
The copy of his friend.
You lived to be the great surnames
And titles by which all made claims
Unto the virtue. Nothing perfect done
But as a Cary, or a Morison.

The Stand

And such a force the fair example had,
As they that saw
The good and durst not practise it, were glad
That such a law
Was left yet to mankind;
Where they might read and find
Friendship in deed was written, not in words;
And with the heart, not pen,
Of two so early men
Whose lines her rolls were, and records.
Who, ere the first down bloomèd on the chin,
Had sowed these fruits, and got the harvest in.
—1640 (WRITTEN 1629?)

Karolin's Song[2]

Though I am young, and cannot tell
Either what Death or Love is well,
Yet I have heard they both bear darts,
And both do aim at human hearts;
And then again, I have been told,
Love wounds with heat, as Death with cold;
So that I fear they do but bring
Extremes to touch, and mean one thing.

As in a ruin we it call
One thing to be blown up, or fall;
Or to our end, like way may have,
By flash of lightning, or a wave:
So Love's inflamèd shaft or brand,
May kill as soon as Death's cold hand;
Except Love's fires the virtue have
To fright the frost out of the grave.
—1640

Hymn to Cynthia[3]

Queen and huntress, chaste and fair,
Now the sun is laid to sleep,
Seated in thy silver chair,

[1] *Dioscuri* Castor and Pollux, twins set among the stars as the constellation Gemini.

[2] *Karolin's Song* From Jonson's final, unfinished play *The Sad Shepherd* (1640), 1.5; the speaker, Karolin, is a kind but naive shepherd.

[3] *Hymn to Cynthia* From Jonson's play *Cynthia's Revels* (1601), 5.6. Cynthia is Diana, goddess of the moon, of chastity, and of hunting; in the literature of the English Renaissance generally, and in this poem, Diana is also a figure for Queen Elizabeth.

State in wonted manner keep:
Hesperus entreats thy light,[1]
Goddess excellently bright.

Earth, let not thy envious shade
Dare itself to interpose;
Cynthia's shining orb was made
Heaven to clear, when day did close:
Bless us then with wishèd sight,
Goddess excellently bright.

Lay thy bow of pearl apart,
And thy crystal-shining quiver;
Give unto the flying hart° *deer*
Space to breathe, how short soever:
Thou that mak'st a day of night,
Goddess excellently bright.
—1601

Clerimont's Song[2]

Still° to be neat, still to be dressed, *always*
As you° were going to a feast; *as if you*
Still to be powdered, still perfumed:
Lady, it is to be presumed,
Though Art's hid causes are not found,
All is not sweet, all is not sound.

Give me a look, give me a face,
That makes simplicity a grace;
Robes loosely flowing, hair as free:
Such sweet neglect more taketh me,
Than all the adulteries of Art;
They strike mine eyes, but not my heart.
—1609

[1] *Hesperus* The planet Venus (when it appears after sunset); in the play, the song is sung by Hesperus.

[2] *Clerimont's Song* From Jonson's play *Epicoene: or, The Silent Woman* (1609), 1.1; in the play, the song is written by Clerimont, a young male gallant, about a woman named Lady Haughty.

Volpone

If Jonson is to be believed, *Volpone* was written in a few weeks in very early 1606. If so, the result is nevertheless remarkably polished. It has also been remarkably popular: Jonson's career as a playwright took off after the warm reception of *Volpone*, and the play has continued to be produced through the English-speaking world in every century since, if sometimes in a modernized form.

The play contains an abundance of both classical and contemporary references. Virtually all of the former are drawn from texts that would have been familiar, in the original or in translation, to any Englishman who attended a good grammar school in the 1590s: the verse satires of Horace and Juvenal, the Greek dialogues and prose satires by Lucian, and the fables of Aesop. These influences run throughout the play; Jonson drew the idea for his legacy-hunting plot out of Horace, while the intolerable Lady Politic Would-be recalls Juvenal's misogynist sixth satire. Animal names are used for nearly all the characters (even Sir Politic's nickname "Pol" suggests a parrot), although Bonario and Celia, as decent people, are exempt; the naming owes something to medieval bestiaries, Erasmus's *Praise of Folly* and the medieval legends of Raynard the Fox, as well as to Aesop. Some of the characters and scenes appear modeled on those of the Italian commedia dell'arte; in Act 2, for example, Corbaccio directly compares himself to the stock character Pantalone.

The lasting appeal of the play rests less on its dense web of allusion than on its humor, which is both subtle and broad. The play does not shy away from scatological invective, as in Act 2's reference to "turdy-facy-nasty-paty-lousy-fartical rogues," but its effective satire is more pointedly witty. And doubtless some of the play's enduring attraction rests on a tension between the infectious allure of Volpone's machinations against corrupt victims and our abhorrence of his amorality. To see a fox outfoxed is deeply satisfying even if the play also discourages easy moralizing.

The play was published in 1607 in a quarto edition dedicated to the universities of Cambridge and Oxford. With only a few changes, it was reprinted in Jonson's 1616 *Works*.

Volpone: or, The Fox

THE PERSONS OF THE PLAY

Volpone,[1] *a magnifico*[2]
Mosca,[3] *his parasite*
Voltore,[4] *an advocate*[5]
Corbaccio,[6] *an old gentleman*
Corvino,[7] *a merchant*
Avocatori,[8] *four magistrates*
Notario, *the register*
Nano, *a dwarf*
Castrone, *an eunuch*
Grege[9] (the crowd)
Sir Politic Would-be, *a knight*
Peregrine,[10] *a gentleman traveller*
Bonario,[11] *son to Corbaccio*
Fine Madam Would-be, *Sir Politic's wife*
Celia,[12] *the merchant's wife*
Commandatori, *officers of justice*
Mercatori, *three merchants*
Androgyno, *a hermaphrodite*
Servitori, *a servant*
Women, *two*

(*The Scene: Venice.*)

[1] *Volpone* "Old fox."

[2] *Magnifico* Rich, distinguished man.

[3] *Mosca* Italian form of the Latin "musca," meaning fly or parasite. Flies were often associated with carrion and sometimes with the devil.

[4] *Voltore* Vulture.

[5] *Advocate* Lawyer, barrister.

[6] *Corbaccio* Raven.

[7] *Corvino* Crow.

[8] *Avocatori* These officials were not magistrates in early modern Venice, but rather public prosecutors.

[9] *Grege* From the Latin, *grex, gregis.*

[10] *Peregrine* Hunting hawk.

[11] *Bonario* Honest.

[12] *Celia* Heavenly one.

THE ARGUMENT

V olpone, childless, rich, feigns sick, despairs,° *is despaired of*
O ffers his state° to hopes of several heirs, *estate*
L ies languishing: his parasite receives
P resents of all, assures, deludes; then weaves
O ther cross plots, which ope themselves, are told.° *exposed*
N ew tricks for safety are sought; they thrive: when bold,
E ach tempts the other again, and all are sold.° *betrayed*

PROLOGUE[13]

Now, luck yet[14] send us, and a little wit
Will serve to make our play hit;
(According to the palates of the season)
Here is rhyme, not empty of reason.[15]
This we were bid to credit from our poet,
Whose true scope, if you would know it,
In all his poems still hath been this measure,
To mix profit with your pleasure;
And not as some, whose throats their envy failing,
Cry hoarsely, "All he writes is railing,"
And when his plays come forth, think they can flout them,
With saying, 'He was a year about them.'[16]
To this there needs no lie,[17] but this his creature,
Which was two months since no feature;
And though he dares give them five lives to mend it,
'Tis known, five weeks fully penned it,
From his own hand; without a co-adjutor,° *collaborator*
Novice, journey-man, or tutor.
Yet thus much I can give you as a token

[13] *Prologue* Volpone was also prefaced in its original publication by a substantial dedication to "the two famous universities." The full text of the dedication is available on the adjunct website associated with this anthology.

[14] *yet* This appears in the 1606 Quarto as "God," and was possibly amended to abide by the 1606 Act against Blasphemy.

[15] *Now … reason* I.e., "Given public taste, we need only luck and a little cunning to make our play a hit, so here is a rhyme not empty of reason."

[16] *He was … them* Jonson was a notoriously slow writer.

[17] *needs no lie* Needs no challenge or nothing to show that they lie.

Of his play's worth, no eggs are broken,
Nor quaking custards with fierce teeth affrighted,
Wherewith your rout are so delighted;
Nor hales he in a gull old ends reciting,
To stop gaps in his loose writing;[1]
With such a deal of monstrous and forced action,
As might make Bedlam[2] a faction:
Nor made he his play for jests stolen from each table,[3]
But makes jests to fit his fable;
And so presents quick comedy refined,
As best critics have designed;
The laws of time, place, persons he observeth,
From no needful rule he swerveth.
All gall and copperas[4] from his ink he draineth,
Only a little salt remaineth,
Wherewith he'll rub your cheeks, till red, with laughter,
They shall look fresh a week after.

ACT 1, SCENE 1

(*Enter Volpone and Mosca.*)

VOLPONE. Good morning to the day; and next, my gold!—
Open the shrine, that I may see my saint.

[*Mosca reveals the treasure.*]

Hail the world's soul,[5] and mine! more glad than is
The teeming earth to see the longed-for sun
Peep through the horns of the celestial Ram,[6]
Am I, to view thy splendour darkening his;
That lying here, amongst my other hoards,
Show'st like a flame by night, or like the day
Struck out of chaos,[7] when all darkness fled
Unto the centre. O thou son of Sol,
But brighter than thy father, let me kiss,
With adoration, thee, and every relic
Of sacred treasure in this blessed room.
Well did wise poets, by thy glorious name,
Title that age[8] which they would have the best;
Thou being the best of things, and far transcending
All style of joy, in children, parents, friends,
Or any other waking dream on earth:
Thy looks when they to Venus did ascribe,
They should have given her twenty thousand Cupids;
Such are thy beauties and our loves! Dear saint,
Riches, the dumb god, that giv'st all men tongues,
Thou canst do naught, and yet mak'st men do all things;[9]
The price of souls; even hell, with thee to boot,[10]
Is made worth heaven. Thou art virtue, fame,
Honour, and all things else. Who can get thee,
He shall be noble valiant, honest, wise—

MOSCA. And what he will, sir. Riches are in fortune
A greater good than wisdom is in nature.[11]

VOLPONE. True, my beloved Mosca. Yet I glory
More in the cunning purchase° of my wealth, *acquisition*
Than in the glad possession, since I gain
No common way; I use no trade, no venture;
I wound no earth with plough-shares, fat no beasts,
To feed the shambles;° have no mills for iron, *slaughterhouse*
Oil, corn, or men, to grind them into powder:
I blow no subtle glass, expose no ships
To threat'nings of the furrow-faced sea;
I turn no monies in the public bank,[12]

[1] *nor hales... writing* He does not fill in the empty spaces in his writing with old jokes.

[2] *Bedlam* St. Mary's of Bethlehem, "Bedlam," a lunatic asylum.

[3] *Nor ... table* I.e., nor does the poet steal jokes from others.

[4] *gall and copperas* Oak-apple and iron sulphate used in the manufacture of ink; also rancor and bitterness.

[5] *world's soul* Perhaps with a pun on the Latin Sol, sun, and sol, a gold coin.

[6] *celestial Ram* As it moves north the sun enters the constellation Aries (the "Ram") at the Spring equinox.

[7] *day struck out of chaos* The creation of the world. See Genesis 1.2–4.

[8] *that age* The Golden Age.

[9] *thou canst do all things* Reference to Aristotle's concept of the Unmoved Mover, from which all things in the universe get their motion.

[10] *to boot* Into the bargain. The New Testament emphasizes that the rich will find it difficult to enter heaven.

[11] *Riches are in fortune... in nature* I.e., it is better to be rich by chance than wise by nature.

[12] *public bank* The Banco della Piazza di Rialto was the first public bank, opened in Venice in 1587.

Nor usure private.[1]
MOSCA. No, sir, nor devour
Soft prodigals. You shall have some will swallow
A melting heir as glibly° as your Dutch *readily*
Will pills of butter,[2] and ne'er purge for it;
Tear forth the fathers of poor families
Out of their beds, and coffin them alive
In some kind clasping prison, where their bones
May be forthcoming, when the flesh is rotten:
But your sweet nature doth abhor these courses;
You loathe the widow's or the orphan's tears
Should wash your pavements, or their piteous cries
Ring in your roofs, and beat the air for vengeance.
VOLPONE. Right, Mosca; I do loathe it.
MOSCA. And besides, sir,
You are not like the thresher that doth stand
With a huge flail, watching a heap of corn,
And, hungry, dares not taste the smallest grain,
But feeds on mallows, and such bitter herbs;
Nor like the merchant, who hath filled his vaults
With Romagnia,[3] and rich Candian[4] wines,
Yet drinks the lees of Lombard's vinegar:[5]
You will lie not in straw, whilst moths and worms
Feed on your sumptuous hangings and soft beds;
You know the use of riches, and dare give now
From that bright heap, to me, your poor observer,
Or to your dwarf, or your hermaphrodite,
Your eunuch, or what other household
trifle° *worthless person*
Your pleasure allows maintenance—
VOLPONE. Hold thee, Mosca,

[*Gives him money.*]

Take of my hand; thou strik'st on truth in all,
And they are envious term° thee parasite. *who term*
Call forth my dwarf, my eunuch, and my fool,
And let them make me sport. [*Exit Mosca.*] What
should I do,
But cocker up my genius,[6] and live free
To all delights my fortune calls me to?
I have no wife, no parent, child, ally,
To give my substance to; but whom I make° *designate*
Must be my heir: and this makes men
observe° me: *be submissive to*
This draws new clients daily to my house,
Women and men of every sex and age,
That bring me presents, send me plate, coin, jewels,
With hope that when I die (which they expect
Each greedy minute) it shall then return
Ten-fold upon them; whilst some, covetous
Above the rest, seek to engross me whole,[7]
And counter-work the one unto the other,
Contend in gifts, as they would seem in love:
All which I suffer,° playing with their hopes, *allow*
And am content to coin them into profit,
And look upon their kindness, and take more,
And look on that; still bearing them in hand,[8]
Letting the cherry knock against their lips,[9]
And draw it by their mouths, and back again.—How
now!

ACT 1, SCENE 2

(*Enter Mosca with Nano, Androgyno, and Castrone.*)

NANO. Now, room° for fresh gamester, who *make room*
do will you to know,
They do bring you neither play nor university show;[10]
And therefore do entreat you, that whatsoever they
rehearse,° *recite*

[1] *usure private* Lend money privately.

[2] *Dutch ... of butter* Cheese and butter were famously produced by the Dutch, so the Dutch were often mocked as "butter-eaters."

[3] *Romagnia* Sweet wine from Greece, also known as Rumney.

[4] *Candian* Wines from Candia in Crete, commonly shortened to "Candy" by the Elizabethans.

[5] *Lombard's vinegar* The wines of Lombardy in northern Italy were of notoriously poor quality.

[6] *cocker up my genius* Indulge my inclination and nature.

[7] *engross me whole* Take advantage of me completely. "Engrossers" monopolized or purchased commodities in large quantities.

[8] *bearing them in hand* Leading them on.

[9] *Letting the cherry ... their lips* The game of bob-cherry or chop-cherry involved players trying to bite a dangling cherry.

[10] *neither play nor university show* Not a play intended for public theaters or as an entertainment for the university.

May not fare a whit the worse, for the false pace of the verse.[1]
If you wonder at this, you will wonder more ere we pass,
For know, here is enclosed the soul of Pythagoras,[2]
That juggler divine, as hereafter shall follow;
Which soul, fast and loose,[3] sir, came first from Apollo,
And was breathed into Aethalides,[4] Mercurius, his son,
Where it had the gift to remember all that ever was done.
From thence it fled forth, and made quick transmigration
To goldilocked Euphorbus,[5] who was killed in good fashion,
At the siege of old Troy, by the cuckold of Sparta.[6]
Hermotimus[7] was next (I find it in my charta)[8]
To whom it did pass, where no sooner it was missing
But with one Pyrrhus of Delos[9] it learned to go a-fishing;
And thence did it enter the sophist of Greece.[10]
From Pythagore, she went into a beautiful piece,
Hight° Aspasia, the meretrix;[11] and the next toss of her *named*
Was again of° a whore, she became a philosopher, *became*
Crates the cynic,[12] as itself[13] doth relate it:
Since kings, knights, and beggars, knaves, lords, and fools gat it,
Besides ox and ass, camel, mule, goat, and brock,
In all which it hath spoke, as in the cobbler's cock.[14]
But I come not here to discourse of that matter,
Or his one, two, or three, or his great oath, "By quarter!"[15]
His musics, his trigon,[16] his golden thigh,[17]
Or his telling how elements shift,[18] but I
Would ask, how of late thou hast suffered translation,
And shifted thy coat in these days of reformation.[19]

ANDROGYNO. Like one of the reformed, a fool, as you see,
Counting all old doctrine heresy.

NANO. But not on thine own forbid meats hast thou ventured?

ANDROGYNO. On fish, when first a Carthusian I entered.[20]

NANO. Why, then thy dogmatical silence hath left thee?[21]

---

[1] *false pace of the verse* Irregular poetic meter and line length. Nano's verse here is reminiscent of that of Tudor "Interludes." On the other hand, the dense classical references here suggest university comedies, known for their learned parodies.

[2] *Pythagoras* Greek mathematician and philosopher known for his doctrine of the transmigration of souls. The entirety of Nano's interlude is an indictment of such thought. Nano is referring to Androgyno as the receptacle of Pythagoras's soul.

[3] *fast and loose* Hard to catch. From a gambling trick where a leather belt with a hidden layer was folded several times and then the mark was asked to thrust a dagger through the belt. The extra layer made it next to impossible to thrust the dagger "fast."

[4] *Aethalides* Herald to the Argonauts, famed for his memory.

[5] *goldilocked Euphorbus* A Trojan who wounded Patroclus, favorite of Achilles.

[6] *cuckold of Sparta* Menelaus, whose wife, Helen, left him for the Trojan prince, Paris, thus starting the Trojan War.

[7] *Hermotimus* Greek philosopher and prophet.

[8] *charta* Latin: letter, paper, i.e., document.

[9] *Pyrrhus of Delos* Greek philosopher, who started life as a fisher.

[10] *sophist of Greece* Pythagoras.

[11] *Aspasia, the meretrix* The mistress of Pericles, leader of Athens.

[12] *Crates the cynic* Crates of Thebes, founder of the Cynic school of philosophy.

[13] *itself* According to Pythagorean thought the soul is neuter and may be either sex when it is incarnated.

[14] *cobbler's cock* A cock is the narrator of Lucian's *The Dream*.

[15] *by quarter* Pythagorean thought held that the all of the universe could be understood in terms of a permutation of the numeric series 1, 2, 3, 4. Thus, Pythagoreans swore their most important oaths by the sign of the quarter.

[16] *trigon* A triangle. The famous "Pythagorean theorem" defines the relation of the hypotenuse to the other two sides of a right triangle.

[17] *golden thigh* Pythagoras was supposed to have had a thigh made of gold.

[18] *elements shift* In Pythagorean thought, each of the four elements was held to be transmutable into any of the others.

[19] *reformation* It is not clear whether the reference here is to the Protestant Reformation as a whole (Jonson was still a Catholic in 1606), or the further reformation of Protestantism that Puritans were striving for in the early seventeenth century.

[20] *But not on ... I entered* Pythagoras forbade his followers to eat fish, flesh and beans. Carthusians were allowed to eat only fish, no meat.

[21] *dogmatical silence hath left thee* Pythagoreans supposedly were to undergo a period of five years of silence.

ANDROGYNO. Of that an obstreperous lawyer bereft me.
NANO. O wonderful change, when sir lawyer forsook thee!
For Pythagore's sake, what body then took thee?[1]
ANDROGYNO. A good dull mule.
NANO. And how! by that means
Thou wert brought to allow of the eating of beans?[2]
ANDROGYNO. Yes.
NANO. But from the mule into whom didst thou pass?
ANDROGYNO. Into a very strange beast, by some writers called an ass;
By others, a precise, pure, illuminate brother,
Of those° devour flesh, and sometimes one another; *those that*
And will drop you forth a libel, or a sanctified lie,
Betwixt every spoonful of a nativity-pie.[3]
NANO. Now quit thee, for heaven, of that profane nation,
And gently report thy next transmigration.
ANDROGYNO. To the same that I am.
NANO. A creature of delight,
And, what is more than a fool, an hermaphrodite!
Now, prithee, sweet soul, in all thy variation,
Which body would'st thou choose, to keep up thy station?
ANDROGYNO. Troth, this I am in: even here would I tarry.
NANO. 'Cause here the delight of each sex thou canst vary?
ANDROGYNO. Alas, those pleasures be stale and forsaken;
No, 'tis your fool wherewith I am so taken,
The only one creature that I can call blessed;
For all other forms I have proved most distressed.
NANO. Spoke true, as thou wert in Pythagoras still.
This learned opinion we celebrate will,
Fellow eunuch, as behoves us, with all our wit and art,
To dignify that whereof ourselves are so great and special a part.
VOLPONE. Now, very, very pretty! Mosca, this
Was thy invention?
MOSCA. If it please my patron,
Not else.
VOLPONE. It doth, good Mosca.
MOSCA. Then it was, sir.

(*Song.*)

Fools, they are the only nation° *tribe*
Worth men's envy or admiration:
Free from care or sorrow-taking,
Selves and others merry making:
All they speak or do is sterling.° *accepted as excellent*
Your fool he is your great man's darling,
And your ladies' sport and pleasure;
Tongue and bauble are his treasure.
E'en his face begetteth laughter,
And he speaks truth free from slaughter;[4]
He's the grace of every feast,
And sometimes the chiefest guest;
Hath his trencher and his stool,
When wit waits upon the fool.[5]
O, who would not be
He, he, he?

(*One knocks wihout.*)

VOLPONE. Who's that? Away!

[*Exeunt Nano and Castrone.*]

Look, Mosca.

[*Exit Androgyno.*]

MOSCA. Fool, begone!
'Tis Signior Voltore, the advocate;

[1] *What body then took thee?* A pun. Lawyers would travel in their robes to the courts at Westminster on the backs of mules.

[2] *beans* See above note. Eating beans was forbidden by Pythagoras.

[3] *Into a very strange … nativity-pie* This whole speech is an indictment of English Puritans. They were often attacked for their allegedly libelous publishing practices, their sense of religious superiority, and their refusal to use the word "Mass" even in compound words such as Christmas—hence, Nativity.

[4] *free from slaughter* Free from punishment.

[5] *wit waits upon the fool* The fool is served by the wit, as at the Feast of Fools. Also, when the witty attend to the words of the foolish.

I know him by his knock.
VOLPONE. Fetch me my gown,
My furs[1] and night-caps; say, my couch is changing,
And let him entertain himself awhile
Without i' the gallery. [*Exit Mosca.*] Now, now, my clients
Begin their visitation! Vulture, kite,
Raven, and gor-crow,° all my birds of prey, *carrion crow*
That think me turning carcass, now they come;
I am not for them yet—

[*Re-enter Mosca, with the gown, etc.*]

How now! the news?
MOSCA. A piece of plate,[2] sir.
VOLPONE. Of what bigness?
MOSCA. Huge,
Massy, and antique, with your name inscribed,
And arms engraven.
VOLPONE. Good! and not a fox
Stretched on the earth, with fine delusive sleights,
Mocking a gaping crow? ha, Mosca!
MOSCA. Sharp, sir.
VOLPONE. Give me my furs. Why dost thou laugh so, man?
MOSCA. I cannot choose, sir, when I apprehend
What thoughts he has without now, as he walks:
That this might be the last gift he should give;
That this would fetch you; if you died to-day,
And gave him all, what he should be to-morrow;
What large return would come of all his ventures;
How he should worshipped be, and reverenced;
Ride with his furs, and foot-cloths;[3] waited on
By herds of fools, and clients; have clear way
Made for his mule, as lettered as himself;
Be called the great and learned advocate:
And then concludes, there's naught impossible.
VOLPONE. Yes, to be learned, Mosca.
MOSCA. O, no: rich
Implies it. Hood an ass with reverend purple,[4]
So you can hide his two ambitious ears,
And he shall pass for a cathedral doctor.
VOLPONE. My caps, my caps, good Mosca. Fetch him in.
MOSCA. Stay, sir; your ointment[5] for your eyes.
VOLPONE. That's true;
Dispatch, dispatch: I long to have possession
Of my new present.
MOSCA. That, and thousands more,
I hope to see you lord of.
VOLPONE. Thanks, kind Mosca.
MOSCA. And that, when I am lost in blended dust,
And hundred such as I am, in succession—
VOLPONE. Nay, that were too much, Mosca.
MOSCA. You shall live,
Still, to delude these harpies.
VOLPONE. Loving Mosca!
'Tis well: my pillow now, and let him enter.

[*Exit Mosca.*]

Now, my feigned cough, my phthisic,° and my gout, *asthma*
My apoplexy,[6] palsy, and catarrhs,[7]
Help, with your forced functions, this my posture,
Wherein, this three year, I have milked their hopes.
He comes; I hear him—Uh! [*Coughing.*] uh! uh! uh! O—

ACT 1, SCENE 3

[*Enter Mosca, ushering in Voltore, carrying a platter.*]

MOSCA. You still are what you were, sir. Only you,
Of all the rest, are he° commands his love, *he who*
And you do wisely to preserve it thus,
With early visitation, and kind notes° *indications*
Of your good meaning to him, which, I know,
Cannot but come most grateful. Patron! sir!
Here's Signior Voltore is come—
VOLPONE. [*Faintly.*] What say you?
MOSCA. Sir, Signior Voltore is come this morning
To visit you.

[1] *furs* Worn by the sick for warmth.

[2] *plate* Gold or silver plated vessels, platters, tableware, etc.

[3] *foot-cloths* Pageant draperies for a horse.

[4] *reverend purple* The crimson robes of a Doctor of Divinity.

[5] *ointment* To make his eyes run.

[6] *apoplexy* Stroke.

[7] *catarrhs* Inflammations of the nose and eyes.

VOLPONE. I thank him.
MOSCA. And hath brought
A piece of antique plate, bought of St. Mark,[1]
With which he here presents you.
VOLPONE. He is welcome.
Pray him to come more often.
MOSCA. Yes.
VOLTORE. What says he?
MOSCA. He thanks you, and desires you see him often.
VOLPONE. Mosca.
MOSCA. My patron!
VOLPONE. Bring him near, where is he?
I long to feel his hand.
MOSCA. The plate is here, sir.
VOLTORE. How fare you, sir?
VOLPONE. I thank you, Signior Voltore;
Where is the plate? Mine eyes are bad.
VOLTORE. [*Putting it into his hands.*] I'm sorry,
To see you still thus weak.
MOSCA. [*Aside.*] That he's not weaker.
VOLPONE. [*Taking hold of the platter.*] You are too munificent.
VOLTORE. No, sir; would to heaven,
I could as well give health to you, as that plate!
VOLPONE. You give, sir, what you can: I thank you. Your love
Hath taste in this, and shall not be unanswered:
I pray you see me often.
VOLTORE. Yes, I shall, sir.
VOLPONE. Be not far from me.
MOSCA. [*To Voltore.*] Do you observe that, sir?
VOLPONE. Hearken unto me still; it will concern you.
MOSCA. [*To Voltore.*] You are a happy man, sir; know your good.
VOLPONE. I cannot now last long—
MOSCA. (*To Voltore.*) You are his heir, sir.
VOLTORE. Am I?
VOLPONE. I feel me going; uh! uh! uh! uh!
I'm sailing to my port, uh! uh! uh! uh![2]
And I am glad I am so near my haven.
MOSCA. Alas, kind gentleman! Well, we must all go—
VOLTORE. But, Mosca—
MOSCA. Age will conquer.
VOLTORE. Pray thee, hear me:
Am I inscribed his heir[3] for certain?
MOSCA. Are you!
I do beseech you, sir, you will vouchsafe
To write me in your family.[4] All my hopes
Depend upon your worship: I am lost,
Except the rising sun do shine on me.
VOLTORE. It shall both shine, and warm thee, Mosca.
MOSCA. Sir,
I am a man, that hath not done your love
All the worst offices: here I wear your keys,[5]
See all your coffers and your caskets locked,
Keep the poor inventory of your jewels,
Your plate and monies; am your steward, sir,
Husband your goods here.
VOLTORE. But am I sole heir?
MOSCA. Without a partner, sir; confirmed this morning:
The wax[6] is warm yet, and the ink scarce dry
Upon the parchment.
VOLTORE. Happy, happy, me!
By what good chance, sweet Mosca?
MOSCA. Your desert, sir;
I know no second cause.
VOLTORE. Thy modesty
Is not to know it; well, we shall requite it.
MOSCA. He ever liked your course,° sir; that first took him. *course of action*
I oft have heard him say, how he admired
Men of your large profession, that could speak
To every cause, and things mere contraries,[7]
Till they were hoarse again, yet all be law;
That, with most quick agility, could turn,
And return; make knots, and undo them;
Give forkèd° counsel; take provoking gold *equivocal*
On either hand, and put it up:[8] these men,

[1] *bought of St. Mark* The goldsmith shops in the Piazza di San Marco were famous.

[2] *uh! uh! uh! uh!* Volpone is feigning his last breath.

[3] *inscribed his heir* Officially entered as his heir in a will.

[4] *write me in your family* Admit me to your household (as a servant).

[5] *your keys* By looking after Volpone's property Mosca is supposedly looking after Voltore's.

[6] *wax* Used to seal the will.

[7] *that could speak … mere contraries* That are able to argue any cause, even contradictory ones.

[8] *put it up* Pocket it.

He knew, would thrive with their humility.[1]
And, for his part, he thought he should be blest
To have his heir of such a suffering spirit,
So wise, so grave, of so perplexed a tongue,[2]
And loud withal, that would not wag, nor scarce
Lie still, without a fee; when every word
Your worship but lets fall, is a cecchine![3]

(*Another knocks.*)

Who's that? one knocks; I would not have you seen, sir.
And yet—pretend you came, and went in haste:
I'll fashion an excuse—and, gentle sir,
When you do come to swim in golden lard,
Up to the arms in honey, that your chin
Is borne up stiff, with fatness of the flood,
Think on your vassal; but remember me:
I have not been your worst of clients.
VOLTORE. Mosca!—
MOSCA. When will you have your inventory brought, sir?
Or see a copy of the will?—Anon!—° *coming, immediately*
I'll bring them to you, sir. Away, be gone,
Put business in your face.

[*Exit Voltore.*]

VOLPONE. [*Springing up.*] Excellent Mosca!
Come hither, let me kiss thee.
MOSCA. Keep you still, sir.
Here is Corbaccio.
VOLPONE. Set the plate away:
The vulture's gone, and the old raven's come!

ACT 1, SCENE 4

(MOSCA.) Betake you to your silence, and your sleep.
[*Putting the plate aside.*] Stand there and multiply.
Now, we shall see
A wretch who is indeed more impotent
Than this can feign to be; yet hopes to hop
Over his grave—

(*Enter Corbaccio.*)

Signior Corbaccio!
You're very welcome, sir.
CORBACCIO. How does your patron?
MOSCA. Troth, as he did, sir; no amends.
CORBACCIO. What! mends he?
MOSCA. No, sir: he's rather worse.
CORBACCIO. That's well. Where is he?
MOSCA. Upon his couch, sir, newly fallen asleep.
CORBACCIO. Does he sleep well?
MOSCA. No wink, sir, all this night.
Nor yesterday; but slumbers.
CORBACCIO. Good! He should take
Some counsel of physicians: I have brought him
An opiate here, from mine own doctor.
MOSCA. He will not hear of drugs.
CORBACCIO. Why? I myself
Stood by while it was made, saw all the ingredients:
And know, it cannot but most gently work:
My life for his, 'tis but to make him sleep.
VOLPONE. [*Aside.*] Aye, his last sleep, if he would take it.
MOSCA. Sir,
He has no faith in physic.
CORBACCIO. Say you, say you?
MOSCA. He has no faith in physic: he does think
Most of your doctors are the greater danger,
And worse disease, to escape. I often have
Heard him protest, that your physician
Should never be his heir.
CORBACCIO. Not I his heir?
MOSCA. Not your physician, sir.
CORBACCIO. O, no, no, no,
I do not mean it.
MOSCA. No, sir, nor their fees
He cannot brook: he says, they flay a man,
Before they kill him.
CORBACCIO. Right, I do conceive° you. *understand*
MOSCA. And then they do it by experiment;[4]

[1] *humility* A pun based on the Latin *humilitas*, meaning "close to the ground."

[2] *perplexed a tongue* Intricate way of speaking.

[3] *cecchine* A sequin or zecchino, a Venetian gold coin worth about seven shillings.

[4] *experiment* I.e., by experimenting upon the patient.

For which the law not only doth absolve them,
But gives them great reward: and he is loath
To hire his death, so.
CORBACCIO. It is true, they kill
With as much license as a judge.
MOSCA. Nay, more;
For he but kills, sir, where the law condemns,
And these can kill him too.
CORBACCIO. Aye, or me;
Or any man. How does his apoplex?
Is that strong on him still?
MOSCA. Most violent.
His speech is broken, and his eyes are set,
His face drawn longer than 'twas wont—
CORBACCIO. How! how!
Stronger than he was wont?
MOSCA. No, sir: his face
Drawn longer than 'twas wont.
CORBACCIO. O, good!
MOSCA. His mouth
Is ever gaping, and his eyelids hang.
CORBACCIO. Good.
MOSCA. A freezing numbness stiffens all his joints,
And makes the colour of his flesh like lead.
CORBACCIO. 'Tis good.
MOSCA. His pulse beats slow, and dull.
CORBACCIO. Good symptoms still.
MOSCA. And from his brain—[1]
CORBACCIO. Ha? how? not from his brain?
MOSCA. Yes, sir, and from his brain—
CORBACCIO. I conceive you; good.
MOSCA. Flows a cold sweat, with a continual rheum,
Forth the resolved corners of his eyes.
CORBACCIO. Is't possible? Yet° I am better, ha! *again*
How does he, with the swimming of his head?
MOSCA. O, sir, 'tis past the scotomy;° he now *dizziness from poor eyesight*
Hath lost his feeling, and hath left° to snort: *ceased*
You hardly can perceive him, that he breathes.
CORBACCIO. Excellent, excellent! sure I shall outlast him:
This makes me young again, a score of years.
MOSCA. I was a coming for you, sir.
CORBACCIO. Has he made his will?
What has he given me?
MOSCA. No, sir.
CORBACCIO. Nothing! ha?
MOSCA. He has not made his will, sir.
CORBACCIO. Oh, oh, oh!
What then did Voltore, the lawyer, here?
MOSCA. He smelt a carcass, sir, when he but heard
My master was about his testament;
As I did urge him to it for your good—
CORBACCIO. He came unto him, did he? I thought so.
MOSCA. Yes, and presented him this piece of plate.
CORBACCIO. To be his heir?
MOSCA. I do not know, sir.
CORBACCIO. True:
I know it too.
MOSCA. [*Aside.*] By your own scale,[2] sir.
CORBACCIO. Well,
I shall prevent him, yet. See, Mosca, look,
Here, I have brought a bag of bright cecchines,
Will quite weigh down[3] his plate.
MOSCA. (*Taking the bag.*) Yea, marry, sir.
This is true physic, this your sacred medicine;
No talk of opiates, to this great elixir!
CORBACCIO. 'Tis *aurum palpabile*, if not *potabile*.[4]
MOSCA. It shall be ministered to him, in his bowl.
CORBACCIO. Aye, do, do, do.
MOSCA. Most blessed cordial!° *medicine*
This will recover him.
CORBACCIO. Yes, do, do, do.
MOSCA. I think it were not best, sir.
CORBACCIO. What?
MOSCA. To recover him.
CORBACCIO. O, no, no, no; by no means.
MOSCA. Why, sir, this
Will work some strange effect, if he but feel it.
CORBACCIO. 'Tis true, therefore forbear; I'll take my venture:
Give me it again.
MOSCA. At no hand; pardon me:
You shall not do yourself that wrong, sir. I

[1] *from his brain* The last stage of apoplexy was held to be marked by fluid leaking from the brain.

[2] *by your own scale* In your own estimation.

[3] *weigh down* Outweigh, overpower.

[4] *aurum palpabile ... potabile* Latin: This is gold that can be touched, if not drunk. (Potions infused with gold were commonly prescribed for a bad heart.)

Will so advise you, you shall have it all.
CORBACCIO. How?
MOSCA. All, sir; 'tis your right, your own: no man
Can claim a part: 'tis yours, without a rival,
Decreed by destiny.
CORBACCIO. How, how, good Mosca?
MOSCA. I'll tell you, sir. This fit he shall recover.
CORBACCIO. I do conceive you.
MOSCA. And, on first advantage° *opportunity*
Of his gained° sense, will I re-importune him *regained*
Unto the making of his testament:
And show him this.

[*Pointing to the money.*]

CORBACCIO. Good, good.
MOSCA. 'Tis better yet,
If you will hear, sir.
CORBACCIO. Yes, with all my heart.
MOSCA. Now, would I counsel you, make home with speed;
There, frame° a will; whereto you shall inscribe *create*
My master your sole heir.
CORBACCIO. And disinherit
My son!
MOSCA. O, sir, the better: for that colour° *semblance*
Shall make it much more taking.° *attractive*
CORBACCIO. O, but colour?
MOSCA. This will, sir, you shall send it unto me.
Now, when I come to enforce,° as I will do, *urge*
Your cares, your watchings, and your many prayers,
Your more than many gifts, your this day's present,
And last, produce your will; where, without thought,
Or least regard, unto your proper issue,° *own offspring*
A son so brave, and highly meriting,
The stream of your diverted love hath thrown you
Upon my master, and made him your heir:
He cannot be so stupid, or stone-dead,
But out of conscience, and mere gratitude—
CORBACCIO. He must pronounce me his?
MOSCA. 'Tis true.
CORBACCIO. This plot
Did I think on before.
MOSCA. I do believe it.
CORBACCIO. Do you not believe it?
MOSCA. Yes, sir.
CORBACCIO. Mine own project.
MOSCA. Which, when he hath done, sir—
CORBACCIO. Published me his heir?
MOSCA. And you so certain to survive him—
CORBACCIO. Aye.
MOSCA. Being so lusty a man—
CORBACCIO. 'Tis true.
MOSCA. Yes, sir—
CORBACCIO. I thought on that too. See, how he should be
The very organ to express my thoughts!
MOSCA. You have not only done yourself a good—
CORBACCIO. But multiplied it on my son.
MOSCA. 'Tis right, sir.
CORBACCIO. Still, my invention.[1]
MOSCA. 'Las,° sir! heaven knows, *alas*
It hath been all my study, all my care
(I e'en grow gray withal), how to work things—
CORBACCIO. I do conceive, sweet Mosca.
MOSCA. You are he,
For whom I labour here.
CORBACCIO. Aye, do, do, do:
I'll straight about it.

[*Going.*]

MOSCA. [*Aside.*] Rook go with you,[2] raven!
CORBACCIO. I know thee honest.
MOSCA. You do lie, sir!
CORBACCIO. And—
MOSCA. Your knowledge is no better than your ears, sir.[3]
CORBACCIO. I do not doubt, to be a father to thee.
MOSCA. Nor I to gull my brother of his blessing.[4]
CORBACCIO. I may have my youth restored to me, why not?
MOSCA. Your worship is a precious ass!

[1] *Still my invention* Corbaccio claims Mosca's ideas as his own.

[2] *Rook go with you* May you be cheated, cheat. This plays on the fact that both "to rook" and "raven" were terms for cheat.

[3] *Your knowledge is ... ears, sir* This is both a taunt and a strict truth.

[4] *gull my brother* Reference to Genesis 27, in which Jacob cheats Esau out of his inheritance.

CORBACCIO. What say'st thou?
MOSCA. I do desire your worship to make haste, sir.
CORBACCIO. 'Tis done, 'tis done; I go.

[*Exit.*]

VOLPONE. [*Leapingup.*] O, I shall burst!
Let out my sides, let out my sides—
MOSCA. Contain
Your flux° of laughter, sir: you know this hope *flow*
Is such a bait, it covers any hook.
VOLPONE. O, but thy working, and thy placing it!
I cannot hold; good rascal, let me kiss thee:
I never knew thee in so rare a humour.[1]
MOSCA. Alas, sir, I but do as I am taught;
Follow your grave instructions; give them words;[2]
Pour oil° into their ears, and send them hence. *flattery*
VOLPONE. 'Tis true, 'tis true. What a rare punishment
Is avarice to itself!
MOSCA. Aye, with our help, sir.
VOLPONE. So many cares, so many maladies,
So many fears attending on old age,
Yea, death so often called on, as no wish
Can be more frequent with them, their limbs faint,
Their senses dull, their seeing, hearing, going,
All dead before them; yea, their very teeth,
Their instruments of eating, failing them:
Yet this is reckoned life! nay, here was one,
Is now gone home, that wishes to live longer!
Feels not his gout, nor palsy; feigns himself
Younger by scores of years, flatters his age
With confident belying it, hopes he may,
With charms, like Aeson,[3] have his youth restored:
And with these thoughts so battens,° as if fate *prospers*
Would be as easily cheated on, as he,
And all turns air! (*Another knocks.*) Who's that there, now? a third!
MOSCA. Close, to your couch again; I hear his voice:
It is Corvino, our spruce° merchant. *dapper*
VOLPONE. Dead.

[1] *so rare a humour* So inventive a mood.

[2] *give them words* I.e., deceive them with words.

[3] *Aeson* Jason's father, who was given his youth back by the magic of Medea.

MOSCA. Another bout, sir, with your eyes.[4] Who's there?

ACT 1, SCENE 5

(*Enter Corvino.*)

MOSCA Signior Corvino! Come most wished for! O,
How happy were you, if you knew it, now!
CORVINO Why? what? wherein?
MOSCA. The tardy hour is come, sir.
CORVINO He is not dead?
MOSCA. Not dead, sir, but as good;
He knows no man.
CORVINO. How shall I do then?
MOSCA. Why, sir?
CORVINO. I have brought him here a pearl.[5]
MOSCA. Perhaps he has
So much remembrance left, as to know you, sir:
He still calls on you; nothing but your name
Is in his mouth. Is your pearl orient,[6] sir?
CORVINO. Venice was never owner of the like.
VOLPONE. (*Faintly.*) Signior Corvino!
MOSCA. Hark.
VOLPONE. Signior Corvino!
MOSCA. He calls you; step and give it him.—He's here, sir,
And he has brought you a rich pearl.
CORVINO. [*To Volpone.*] How do you, sir?
[*To Mosca.*] Tell him, it doubles the twelfth carat.
MOSCA. Sir,
He cannot understand, his hearing's gone;
And yet it comforts him to see you—
CORVINO. Say,
I have a diamond for him, too.
MOSCA. Best show it, sir;
Put it into his hand; 'tis only there
He apprehends: he has his feeling, yet.

[4] *Another bout … your eyes* Mosca reapplies the ointment to Volpone's eyes.

[5] *pearl* The gifts of the three "heirs" reflect their characters: the socially aspiring lawyer gives a plate with Volpone's coat of arms, the miser gives coins, and the cuckold gives his family jewels.

[6] *orient* Asian pearls were considered of superior value.

See how he grasps it!
CORVINO. 'Las, good gentleman!
How pitiful the sight is!
MOSCA. Tut! forget, sir.
The weeping of an heir should still be laughter
Under a visor.° *mask*
CORVINO. Why, am I his heir?
MOSCA. Sir, I am sworn, I may not show the will
Till he be dead; but here has been Corbaccio,
Here has been Voltore, here were others too,
I cannot number 'em, they were so many;
All gaping here for legacies: but I,
Taking the vantage of his naming you,
"Signior Corvino, Signior Corvino," took
Paper, and pen, and ink, and there I asked him,
Whom he would have his heir. "Corvino." Who
Should be executor? "Corvino." And,
To any question he was silent to,
I still interpreted the nods he made,
Through weakness, for consent: and sent home th' others,
Nothing bequeathed them, but to cry and curse.

[*They embrace.*]

CORVINO. O, my dear Mosca! Does he not perceive us?
MOSCA. No more than a blind harper.[1] He knows no man,
No face of friend, nor name of any servant,
Who 'twas that fed him last, or gave him drink:
Not those he hath begotten, or brought up,
Can he remember.
CORVINO. Has he children?
MOSCA. Bastards,
Some dozen, or more, that he begot on beggars,
Gypsies, and Jews, and black-moors,[2] when he was drunk.
Knew you not that, sir? 'tis the common fable.[3]
The dwarf, the fool, the eunuch, are all his;
He's the true father of his family,° *household*
In all, save me:—but he has given them nothing.
CORVINO. That's well, that's well! Art sure he does not hear us?
MOSCA. Sure, sir! why, look you, credit your own sense.

[*Shouts in Volpone's ear.*]

The pox° approach, and add to your diseases, *syphilis*
If it would send you hence the sooner, sir,
For your incontinence, it hath deserved it
Thoroughly, and thoroughly, and the plague to boot!—[4]
You may come near, sir.—Would you would once close
Those filthy eyes of yours, that flow with slime,
Like two frog-pits; and those same hanging cheeks,
Covered with hide instead of skin—Nay, help, sir—
That look like frozen dish-clouts set on end!
CORVINO. Or like an old smoked wall, on which the rain
Ran down in streaks!
MOSCA. Excellent, sir! speak out:
You may be louder yet; a culverin° *handgun*
Discharged in his ear would hardly bore° it. *penetrate*
CORVINO. His nose is like a common sewer, still running.
MOSCA. 'Tis good! And what° his mouth? *what of*
CORVINO. A very draught.° *cesspool*
MOSCA. O, stop it up—
CORVINO. By no means.
MOSCA. 'Pray you, let me:
Faith, I could stifle him rarely° with a pillow, *excellently*
As well as any woman that should keep him.
CORVINO. Do as you will; but I'll begone.
MOSCA. Be so:
It is your presence makes him last so long.

---

[1] *blind harper* The image of a blind harp player was evidently intended to suggest both randomness and incompetence; it was something of a proverbial expression in the sixteenth and seventeenth centuries.

[2] *beggars ... black-moors* Lines such as these are illuminating markers of the various cultural, racial, and religious prejudices that held sway in the sixteenth and early seventeenth century; here the categories of beggar, gypsy, Jew, and "black-moor" are all evidently regarded as equally deserving of derision. The term "moor" more often than not was assumed in itself to imply darkness of skin; sometimes, however, distinctions were made between "black-moors" and Africans of lighter skin, who were referred to as "white moors" or occasionally as "tawny moors."

[3] *'tis the common fable* That is the story generally told.

[4] *For your incontinence ... to boot* You have deserved to get syphilis—and the plague as well—on account of your loose sexual behavior.

CORVINO. I pray you, use no violence.
MOSCA. No, sir! Why?
Why should you be thus scrupulous, pray you, sir?
CORVINO. Nay, at your discretion.
MOSCA. Well, good sir, begone.
CORVINO. I will not trouble him now, to take my pearl.[1]
MOSCA. Puh! nor your diamond. What a needless care
Is this afflicts you? Is not all here yours?
Am not I here, whom you have made your creature?
That owe my being to you?
CORVINO. Grateful Mosca!
Thou art my friend, my fellow, my companion,
My partner, and shalt share in all my fortunes.
MOSCA. Excepting one.
CORVINO. What's that?
MOSCA. Your gallant° wife, sir,— *beautiful*

[*Exit Corvino*]

Now is he gone: we had no other means
To shoot him hence, but this.
VOLPONE. My divine Mosca!
Thou hast to-day outgone thyself. (*Another knocks.*)
Who's there?
I will be troubled with no more. Prepare
Me music, dances, banquets, all delights;
The Turk is not more sensual in his pleasures,
Than will Volpone. [*Exit Mosca.*] Let me see; a pearl!
A diamond! plate! cecchines! Good morning's
purchase.° *haul*
Why, this better than rob churches, yet;
Or fat, by eating, once a month, a man—

[*Re-enter Mosca.*]

Who is't?
MOSCA. The beauteous Lady Would-be, sir,
Wife to the English knight, Sir Politic Would-be,
(This is the style, sir, is directed me,)[2]
Hath sent to know how you have slept to-night,
And if you would be visited?
VOLPONE. Not now:
Some three hours hence—
MOSCA. I told the squire so much.
VOLPONE. When I am high with mirth and wine;
then, then:
'Fore heaven, I wonder at the desperate valour
Of the bold English, that they dare let loose
Their wives to all encounters![3]
MOSCA. Sir, this knight
Had not his name for nothing, he is politic,
And knows, howe'er his wife affect strange airs,
She hath not yet the face to be dishonest:[4]
But had she Signior Corvino's wife's face—
VOLPONE. Has she so rare a face?
MOSCA. O, sir, the wonder,
The blazing star of Italy! a wench
Of the first year! a beauty ripe as harvest!
Whose skin is whiter than a swan all over,
Than silver, snow, or lilies! a soft lip,
Would tempt you to eternity of kissing!
And flesh that melteth in the touch to blood!
Bright as your gold, and lovely as your gold!
VOLPONE. Why had not I known this before?
MOSCA. Alas, sir,
Myself but yesterday discovered it.
VOLPONE. How might I see her?
MOSCA. O, not possible;
She's kept as warily as is your gold;
Never does come abroad,[5] never takes air,
But at a window. All her looks are sweet,
As the first grapes or cherries, and are watched
As near° as they are. *closely*
VOLPONE. I must see her.
MOSCA. Sir,
There is a guard of spies ten thick upon her,
All his whole household; each of which is set
Upon his fellow, and have all their charge,
When he goes out, when he comes in, examined.
VOLPONE. I will go see her, though but at her window.
MOSCA. In some disguise, then.
VOLPONE. That is true; I must

[1] *take my pearl* Volpone already has the pearl and the diamond.

[2] *This is the style ... directed me* This is the way in which I have been directed to refer to them.

[3] *'Fore heaven ... all encounters* English women were considered by the Italians to have too much freedom.

[4] *she hath not ... dishonest* She is too ugly to be unfaithful.

[5] *come abroad* Go out of the house.

Maintain mine own shape° still the same: we'll
think. *disguise*

[*Exeunt.*]

ACT 2, SCENE 1

(*Enter Sir Politic Would-be, Peregrine.*)

SIR POLITIC. Sir, to a wise man, all the world's his soil:
It is not Italy, nor France, nor Europe,
That must bound me, if my fates call me forth.
Yet, I protest, it is no salt° desire *wanton*
Of seeing countries, shifting a religion,
Nor any disaffection to the state
Where I was bred, and unto which I owe
My dearest plots, hath brought me out; much less,
That idle, antique, stale, gray-headed project
Of knowing men's minds and manners, with Ulysses![1]
But a peculiar humour of my wife's
Laid for this height of Venice, to observe,
To quote, to learn the language, and so forth—
I hope you travel, sir, with license?[2]
PEREGRINE. Yes.
SIR POLITIC. I dare the safelier converse—How long, sir,
Since you left England?
PEREGRINE. Seven weeks.
SIR POLITIC. So lately!
You have not been with my Lord Ambassador?
PEREGRINE. Not yet, sir.
SIR POLITIC. Pray you, what news, sir, vents our climate?[3]
I heard last night a most strange thing reported
By some of my lord's followers, and I long
To hear how 'twill be seconded.
PEREGRINE. What was't, sir?
SIR POLITIC. Marry, sir, of a raven that should[4] build
In a ship royal of the king's.
PEREGRINE. [*Aside.*] This fellow,
Does he gull° me, trow? or is gulled?—Your name, sir? *fool*
SIR POLITIC. My name is Politic Would-be.
PEREGRINE. [*Aside.*] O, that speaks him.—
A knight, sir?
SIR POLITIC. A poor knight, sir.
PEREGRINE. Your lady
Lies° here in Venice, for intelligence *stays*
Of tires,° and fashions, and behaviour, *clothing*
Among the courtesans? The fine Lady Would-be?
SIR POLITIC. Yes, sir; the spider and the bee, oft times,
Suck from one flower.
PEREGRINE. Good Sir Politic,
I cry you mercy; I have heard much of you:
'Tis true, sir, of your raven.
SIR POLITIC. On your knowledge?
PEREGRINE. Yes, and your lion's whelping in the Tower.[5]
SIR POLITIC. Another whelp!
PEREGRINE. Another, sir.
SIR POLITIC. Now heaven!
What prodigies be these? The fires at Berwick![6]
And the new star![7] These things concurring, strange,
And full of omen! Saw you those meteors?
PEREGRINE. I did, sir.
SIR POLITIC. Fearful! Pray you, sir, confirm me,
Were there three porpoises[8] seen above the Bridge,° *London Bridge*
As they give out?
PEREGRINE. Six, and a sturgeon,[9] sir.
SIR POLITIC. I am astonished.
PEREGRINE. Nay, sir, be not so;
I'll tell you a greater prodigy than these.

---

[1] *Ulysses* Roman form of Odysseus, protagonist of *The Odyssey*.

[2] *license* A passport issued from the Privy Council.

[3] *vents our climate* Comes out of our country.

[4] *should* I.e., that a raven is said to have built.

[5] *whelp at the Tower* King James's lionesses at the menagerie of the Tower of London gave birth to cubs on 5 August 1604 and 26 February 1605.

[6] *fires at Berwick* The town of Berwick on the Scottish border witnessed a ghostly battle on a nearby hill in 1604. The phenomenon, probably the result of particularly violent aurora borealis, was reported throughout the land, and provided fuel for the witch craze.

[7] *new star* In 1604 a supernova appeared in the constellation Serpens; it lasted for two years.

[8] *three porpoises* On 19 January 1606, a porpoise was discovered in a small creek in West Ham (well below London Bridge), and shortly afterwards, a whale swam up the Thames to within sight of London.

[9] *and a sturgeon* The sturgeon was a common fish in the Thames at the time; hence the joke.

SIR POLITIC. What should these things portend?
PEREGRINE. The very day
(Let me be sure) that I put forth from London,
There was a whale discovered in the river,
As high as Woolwich, that had waited there,
Few know how many months, for the subversion
Of the Stade fleet.[1]
SIR POLITIC. Is't possible? believe it,
'Twas either sent from Spain, or the archdukes:[2]
Spinola's whale,[3] upon my life, my credit!
Will they not leave these projects? Worthy sir,
Some other news.
PEREGRINE. Faith, Stone the fool[4] is dead,
And they do lack a tavern fool extremely.
SIR POLITIC. Is Mas'° Stone dead? *master*
PEREGRINE. He's dead, sir; why, I hope
You thought him not immortal? [*Aside.*] O, this knight,
Were he well known, would be a precious thing
To fit our English stage: he that should write
But such a fellow, should be thought to feign
Extremely, if not maliciously.
SIR POLITIC. Stone dead!
PEREGRINE. Dead.—Lord! how deeply, sir, you apprehend° it? *feel*
He was no kinsman to you?
SIR POLITIC. That° I know of. *not that*
Well! that same fellow was an unknown fool.[5]
PEREGRINE. And yet you knew him, it seems?
SIR POLITIC. I did so. Sir,
I knew him one of the most dangerous heads
Living within the state, and so I held him.
PEREGRINE. Indeed, sir?
SIR POLITIC. While he lived, in action,[6]
He has received weekly intelligence,
Upon my knowledge, out of the Low Countries,
For all parts of the world, in cabbages;[7]
And those dispensed again to ambassadors,
In oranges, musk-melons,° apricots, *common melons*
Lemons, pome-citrons,° and such-like; sometimes *limes*
In Colchester oysters, and your Selsey cockles.[8]
PEREGRINE. You make me wonder.
SIR POLITIC. Sir, upon my knowledge.
Nay, I've observed him, at your public ordinary,[9]
Take his advertisement from a traveller,
A concealed statesman, in a trencher of meat;
And instantly, before the meal was done,
Convey an answer in a tooth-pick.
PEREGRINE. Strange!
How could this be, sir?
SIR POLITIC. Why, the meat was cut
So like his character,° and so laid, as he *code, cipher*
Must easily read the cipher.
PEREGRINE. I have heard,
He could not read, sir.
SIR POLITIC. So 'twas given out,
In policy, by those that did employ him:
But he could read, and had your languages,[10]
And to't, as sound a noddle—° *head*
PEREGRINE. I have heard, sir,
That your baboons were spies, and that they were
A kind of subtle nation near to China.
SIR POLITIC. Aye, aye, your Mamaluchi.[11] Faith, they had
Their hand in a French plot or two; but they

[1] *the Stade fleet* The Company of the English Merchant Adventurers anchored their fleet at Stade on the Elbe. In 1602, on their way back to England, the fleet famously met a pod of whales that appeared to be impervious to gunshot. This was considered an ominous portent.

[2] *archdukes* I.e., rulers of the Spanish Netherlands, Archduchess Isabella and Archduke Albert.

[3] *Spinola's whale* Ambrosio Spinola, general of the Spanish army in the Netherlands, famed for his use of ingenious secret weapons. One of these was supposed to be (in the words of Charles Herle) "Spinola's whale that should have been hir'd to have drown'd London by snuffing up the Thames and spouting it upon the City."

[4] *Stone the fool* A real person, Stone was whipped to death in spring 1605 for mocking the Earl of Nottingham.

[5] *unknown fool* A fool not appreciated for what he really was. I.e., Sir Politic thinks Stone was a government agent.

[6] *in action* Implying that he was an intelligence agent.

[7] *cabbages* Often exported from Holland at the time.

[8] *Colchester oysters ... Selsey cockles* Colchester has been famous for its oysters since Roman times and Selsey is noted for its shellfish.

[9] *ordinary* Eating house.

[10] *had your languages* Could speak foreign languages.

[11] *Mamaluchi* The Italianate plural of "Mameluk," the ruling dynasty of Egypt from 1254. Peregrine's apparent ignorance of geography and zoology is a device to trick Sir Politic into revealing his own ignorance.

Were so extremely given to women,[1] as
They made discovery of all: yet I
Had my advices here, on Wednesday last.
From one of their own coat,° they were returned, *livery*
Made their relations, as the fashion is,
And now stand fair for fresh employment.

PEREGRINE. [*Aside.*] 'Heart! *God's heart!*
This Sir Pol will be ignorant of nothing.
It seems, sir, you know all.

SIR POLITIC. Not all, sir, but
I have some general notions. I do love
To note and to observe: though I live out,
Free from the active torrent,[2] yet I'd mark
The currents and the passages of things,
For mine own private use; and know the ebbs
And flows of state.

PEREGRINE. Believe it, sir, I hold
Myself in no small tie° unto my fortunes, *obligation*
For casting me thus luckily upon you,
Whose knowledge, if your bounty equal it,
May do me great assistance, in instruction
For my behaviour, and my bearing, which
Is yet so rude and raw.

SIR POLITIC. Why, came you forth
Empty of rules for travel?

PEREGRINE. Faith, I had
Some common ones, from out that vulgar grammar,
Which he that cried° Italian to me, taught me. *spoke*

SIR POLITIC. Why this it is that spoils all our brave bloods,° *gallants*
Trusting our hopeful gentry unto pedants.
Fellows of outside, and mere bark. You seem
To be a gentleman, of ingenuous race:—
I not profess it, but my fate hath been
To be, where I have been consulted with,
In this high kind,[3] touching some great men's sons,
Persons of blood and honour.—

PEREGRINE. Who be these, sir?

[1] *given to women* Baboons were proverbially taken to be lustful creatures.

[2] *I live ... torrent* I.e., I do not engage in politics.

[3] *In this high kind* Regarding important matters of this sort.

ACT 2, SCENE 2

(*Enter Mosca, Nano followed by Grege.*)

MOSCA. Under that window, there it must be. The same. [*They set out a platform.*]

SIR POLITIC. Fellows, to mount a bank.[4] Did your instructor
In the dear tongues, never discourse to you
Of the Italian mountebanks?

PEREGRINE. Yes, sir.

SIR POLITIC. Why,
Here you shall see one.

PEREGRINE. They are quacksalvers;° *quacks*
Fellows, that live by vending oils and drugs.

SIR POLITIC. Was that the character he gave you of them?

PEREGRINE. As I remember.

SIR POLITIC. Pity his ignorance.
They are the only knowing men of Europe!
Great general scholars, excellent physicians,
Most admired statesmen, professed favourites,
And cabinet° counsellors to the greatest princes; *private*
The only languaged men of all the world!

PEREGRINE. And I have heard, they are most lewd° impostors; *ignorant*
Made all of terms and shreds;[5] no less beliers
Of great men's favours, than their own vile med'cines;
Which they will utter upon monstrous oaths:
Selling that drug for two-pence, ere they part,
Which they have valued at twelve crowns before.

SIR POLITIC. Sir, calumnies are answered best with silence.
Yourself shall judge.—Who is it mounts, my friends?

MOSCA. Scoto of Mantua,[6] sir.

SIR POLITIC. Is't he? Nay, then
I'll proudly promise, sir, you shall behold
Another man than has been phant'sied[7] to you.
I wonder yet, that he should mount his bank,

[4] *mount a bank* Referring to the Italian *monta in banco*, "mount a bench." Figuratively, an itinerant quack.

[5] *terms and shreds* Jargon and snatches of medical language.

[6] *Scoto of Mantua* Italian actor of the commedia dell' arte who visited England between 1576–83.

[7] *phant'sied* Suggested to your fancy.

Here in this nook, that has been wont t'appear
In face of the Piazza!—Here he comes.

[*Enter Volpone, disguised as a mountebank doctor, and followed by a crowd of people.*]

VOLPONE. (*To Nano.*) Mount, zany.° *clown, buffoon*
GREGE. Follow, follow, follow, follow, follow!
SIR POLITIC. See how the people follow him! He's a man
May write ten thousand crowns in bank here. Note,

[*Volpone mounts the platform.*]

Mark but his gesture:—I do use to observe
The state° he keeps in getting up. *ceremony*
PEREGRINE. 'Tis worth it, sir.

VOLPONE. Most noble gentlemen, and my worthy patrons! It may seem strange, that I, your Scoto Mantuano, who was ever wont to fix my bank in face of the public Piazza, near the shelter of the Portico to the Procuratia,[1] should now, after eight months' absence from this illustrious city of Venice, humbly retire myself into an obscure nook of the Piazza.

SIR POLITIC. Did not I now object the same?
PEREGRINE. Peace, sir.

VOLPONE. Let me tell you: I am not, as your Lombard proverb saith, cold on my feet;[2] or content to part with my commodities at a cheaper rate, than I accustomed: look not for it. Nor that the calumnious reports of that impudent detractor, and shame to our profession (Alessandro Buttone, I mean), who gave out, in public, I was condemned *a sforzato*[3] to the galleys, for poisoning the cardinal Bembo's ... cook,[4] hath at all attached, much less dejected me. No, no, worthy gentlemen; to tell you true, I cannot endure to see the rabble of these ground *ciarlitani*,[5] that spread their cloaks on the pavement, as if they meant to do feats of activity, and then come in lamely, with their mouldy tales out of Boccacio, like stale Tabarine,[6] the fabulist: some of them discoursing their travels, and of their tedious captivity in the Turks' galleys, when, indeed, were the truth known, they were the Christians' galleys, where very temperately they eat bread, and drunk water, as a wholesome penance, enjoined them by their confessors, for base pilferies.

SIR POLITIC. Note but his bearing, and contempt of these.

VOLPONE. These turdy-facy-nasty-paty-lousy-fartical rogues, with one poor groat's-worth of unprepared antimony,[7] finely wrapped up in several *scartoccios*,[8] are able, very well, to kill their twenty a week, and play; yet, these meagre, starved spirits, who have half stopped the organs of their minds with earthy oppilations,[9] want not their favourers among your shrivelled salad-eating artisans, who are overjoyed that they may have their half-pe'rth[10] of physic; though it purge them into another world, it makes no matter.

SIR POLITIC. Excellent! have you heard better language, sir?

VOLPONE. Well, let them go. And, gentlemen, honourable gentlemen, know, that for this time, our bank, being thus removed from the clamours of the *canaglia*,[11] shall be the scene of pleasure and delight; for I have nothing to sell, little or nothing to sell.

SIR POLITIC. I told you, sir, his end.
PEREGRINE. You did so, sir.

VOLPONE. I protest, I, and my six servants, are not able to make of this precious liquor, so fast as it is fetched away from my lodging by gentlemen of your city; strangers of the terra-firma; worshipful merchants; aye, and senators too: who, ever since my arrival, have detained me to their uses, by their splendidous[12] liberalities. And worthily; for, what avails your rich man to have his magazines[13] stuffed with moscadelli,[14] or of

[1] *portico to the Procuratia* Arcade in the Piazza di San Marco in front of the houses of the rich, in this case, Corvino's house.

[2] *cold on my feet* Forced by poverty to sell cheaply.

[3] *a sforzato* Italian: Against my will.

[4] *Cardinal Bembo's ... cook* The pause suggests that "mistress" will be said instead of "cook."

[5] *ciarlitani* Italian: charlatans.

[6] *Tabarine* Famous clown from an Italian touring acting troupe.

[7] *groat's worth ... antimony* A groat was a four penny piece. Antimony was a white metal used in alchemy.

[8] *scartoccios* A paper package for spices used by apothecaries.

[9] *earthly oppilations* Gross obstructions.

[10] *half-pe'rth* Half-penny worth.

[11] *canaglia* Italian: rascals.

[12] *splendidous* Superlative of "splendid."

[13] *magazines* Storehouses.

[14] *moscadelli* Muscadine wine.

the purest grape, when his physicians prescribe him, on pain of death, to drink nothing but water cocted[1] with aniseeds? O, health! Health! The blessing of the rich! the riches of the poor! Who can buy thee at too dear a rate, since there is no enjoying this world without thee? Be not then so sparing of your purses, honourable gentlemen, as to abridge the natural course of life—

PEREGRINE. You see his end.

SIR POLITIC. Aye, is't not good?

VOLPONE. For, when a humid flux, or catarrh, by the mutability of air, falls from your head into an arm or shoulder, or any other part; take you a ducat,[2] or your cecchine of gold, and apply to the place affected: see what good effect it can work. No, no, 'tis this blessed *unguento*,[3] this rare extraction, that hath only power to disperse all malignant humours, that proceed either of hot, cold, moist, or windy causes—

PEREGRINE. I would he had put in dry too.

SIR POLITIC. Pray you, observe.

VOLPONE. To fortify the most indigest and crude stomach, aye, were it of one that, through extreme weakness, vomited blood, applying only a warm napkin to the place, after the unction and fricace;[4]—for the vertigine[5] in the head, putting but a drop into your nostrils, likewise behind the ears; a most sovereign and approved remedy: the mal caduco,[6] cramps, convulsions, paralyses, epilepsies, tremor-cordia,[7] retired nerves, ill vapours of the spleen, stopping of the liver, the stone, the strangury,[8] hernia ventosa,[9] iliaca passio;[10] stops a dysenteria immediately; easeth the torsion of the small guts; and cures melancholia hypondriaca,[11] being taken and applied according to my printed receipt. (*Pointing to his bill and his glass.*) For, this is the physician, this the medicine; this counsels, this cures; this gives the direction, this works the effect; and, in sum, both together may be termed an abstract of the theoric and practic in the Aesculapian[12] art. 'Twill cost you eight crowns. And,—Zan Fritada,[13] prithee sing a verse extempore in honour of it.

SIR POLITIC. How do you like him, sir?

PEREGRINE. Most strangely, I!

SIR POLITIC. Is not his language rare?

PEREGRINE. But° alchemy, *excepting*
I never heard the like; or Broughton's[14] books.

(*Song.*)

NANO. Had old Hippocrates or Galen,[15]
(That to their books put med'cines all in,)
But known this secret, they had never
(Of which they will be guilty ever)
Been murderers of so much paper,
Or wasted many a hurtless taper;
No Indian drug had e'er been famed,
Tobacco, sassafras not named;
Ne yet, of guacum[16] one small stick, sir,
Nor Raymond Lully's[17] great elixir.
Ne had been known the Danish Gonswart,
Or Paracelsus, with his long sword.[18]

PEREGRINE. All this, yet, will not do; eight crowns is high.

---

[1] *cocted* Boiled.

[2] *ducat* Gold coin.

[3] *ungento* Italian: ointment.

[4] *fricace* Massage.

[5] *vertingine* Dizziness.

[6] *mal caduco* Epilepsy.

[7] *tremor-cordia* Heart palpitations.

[8] *strangury* Impeded and painful urination.

[9] *hernia ventosa* Hernia caused by flatulence.

[10] *iliaca passio* Colic.

[11] *melancholia hypocondriaca* The melancholic humor, once thought to derive from the area immediately under the lower ribs (the hypochondria) that includes the spleen and liver.

[12] *Aesculpian* Referring to Aesculapius, the classical god of medicine.

[13] *Zan Fritada* Volpone refers to Nano by the name of a famous clown, literally, "Jack Pancake."

[14] *Broughton* Hugh Broughton (1549–1612), a scholar of Hebrew and noted Puritan.

[15] *Hippocrates or Galen* European medical practice was primarily founded on the theories of Hippocrates (460–377 BCE) and Galen (131–201 CE).

[16] *Tobacco, sassafras, guacum* "New World" plants considered to have medicinal properties.

[17] *Raymond Lully* Raymond Lull, a thirteenth-century philosopher and alchemist said to have found the Elixir of Life.

[18] *Paracelsus ... long sword* Paracelsus, a famous and controversial medical scholar and occultist, kept his purest elixirs in his sword's pommel.

VOLPONE. No more. Gentlemen, if I had but time to discourse to you the miraculous effects of this my oil, surnamed Oglio del Scoto; with the countless catalogue of those I have cured of the aforesaid, and many more diseases; the patents and privileges of all the princes and commonwealths of Christendom; or but the depositions of those that appeared on my part, before the Signiory of the Sanita[1] and most learned College of Physicians; where I was authorized, upon notice taken of the admirable virtues of my medicaments, and mine own excellency in matter of rare and unknown secrets, not only to disperse them publicly in this famous city, but in all the territories, that happily joy under the government of the most pious and magnificent states of Italy. But may some other gallant fellow say, O, there be diverse that make profession to have as good, and as experimented receipts as yours: indeed, very many have assayed, like apes, in imitation of that, which is really and essentially in me, to make of this oil; bestowed great cost in furnaces, stills, alembics,[2] continual fires, and preparation of the ingredients (as indeed there goes to it six hundred several simples,[3] besides some quantity of human fat, for the conglutination,[4] which we buy of the anatomists), but, when these practitioners come to the last decoction, blow, blow, puff, puff, and all flies in fumo:[5] ha, ha, ha! Poor wretches! I rather pity their folly and indiscretion, than their loss of time and money; for these may be recovered by industry: but to be a fool born, is a disease incurable. For myself, I always from my youth have endeavoured to get the rarest secrets, and book them, either in exchange, or for money: I spared nor cost nor labour, where anything was worthy to be learned. And, gentlemen, honourable gentlemen, I will undertake, by virtue of chemical art, out of the honourable hat that covers your head, to extract the four elements; that is to say, the fire, air, water, and earth, and return you your felt without burn or stain. For, whilst others have been at the Balloo,[6] I have been at my book; and am now past the craggy paths of study, and come to the flowery plains of honour and reputation.

SIR POLITIC. I do assure you, sir, that is his aim.

VOLPONE. But to our price—

PEREGRINE. And that withal, Sir Politic.

VOLPONE. You all know, honourable gentlemen, I never valued this ampulla, or vial, at less than eight crowns; but for this time, I am content to be deprived of it for six: six crowns is the price, and less in courtesy I know you cannot offer me; take it or leave it, howsoever, both it and I am at your service. I ask you not as the value of the thing, for then I should demand of you a thousand crowns, so the Cardinals Montalto, Fernese, the great Duke of Tuscany,[7] my gossip,[8] with diverse other princes, have given me; but I despise money. Only to show my affection to you, honourable gentlemen, and your illustrious state here, I have neglected the messages of these princes, mine own offices, framed my journey hither, only to present you with the fruits of my travels. Tune your voices once more to the touch of your instruments, and give the honourable assembly some delightful recreation.

PEREGRINE. What monstrous and most painful circumstance
Is here, to get some three or four gazets,[9]
Some three-pence in the whole! for that 'twill come to.

(*Song.*)

NANO. You that would last long, list to my song,
Make no more coil,° but buy of this oil. *fuss*
Would you be ever fair and young?
Stout of teeth, and strong of tongue?
Tart of palate? quick of ear?
Sharp of sight? of nostril clear?
Moist of hand? and light of foot?
Or, I will come nearer to't,
Would you live free from all diseases?
Do the act your mistress pleases,

[1] *Signiory of the Santa* Board of Health.

[2] *alembics* Alchemical apparatus.

[3] *simples* Unmixed and medicinal herbal ingredients.

[4] *conglutination* Gluing together.

[5] *in fumo* Up in smoke.

[6] *Balloo* Venetian game.

[7] *Cardinals Montalto ... Tuscany* The two cardinals mentioned both became popes, Sixtus V and Paul III respectively. Cosimo de Medici, the famed aristocrat and patron of the arts, was the Archduke of Tuscany.

[8] *gossip* Godparent for one's child.

[9] *gazets* Venetian coin worth just under a penny.

Yet fright all aches from your bones?
Here's a medicine for the nones.° *occasion*

VOLPONE. Well, I am in a humour at this time to make a present of the small quantity my coffer contains; to the rich in courtesy, and to the poor for God's sake. Wherefore now mark: I asked you six crowns; and six crowns, at other times, you have paid me; you shall not give me six crowns, nor five, nor four, nor three, nor two, nor one; nor half a ducat; no, nor a moccenigo.[1] Six – pence[2] it will cost you, or six hundred pound —expect no lower price, for, by the banner of my front, I will not bate a bagatine,[3]—that I will have, only, a pledge of your loves, to carry something from amongst you, to show I am not contemned by you. Therefore, now, toss your handkerchiefs, cheerfully, cheerfully; and be advertised, that the first heroic spirit that deigns to grace me with a handkerchief, I will give it a little remembrance of something, beside, shall please it better, than if I had presented it with a double pistolet.[4]

PEREGRINE. Will you be that heroic spark,° *gallant*
Sir Politic?

[*Celia throws down her handkerchief from the window above.*][5]

O, see! the window has prevented° you. *anticipated*

VOLPONE. Lady, I kiss your bounty; and for this timely grace you have done your poor Scoto of Mantua, I will return you, over and above my oil, a secret of that high and inestimable nature, shall make you for ever enamoured on that minute, wherein your eye first descended on so mean, yet not altogether to be despised, an object. Here is a powder concealed in this paper, of which, if I should speak to the worth, nine thousand volumes were but as one page, that page as a line, that line as a word; so short is this pilgrimage of man (which some call life) to the expressing of it. Would I reflect on the price? Why, the whole world is but as an empire, that empire as a province, that province as a bank, that bank as a private purse to the purchase of it. I will only tell you; it is the powder that made Venus a goddess (given her by Apollo), that kept her perpetually young, cleared her wrinkles, firmed her gums, filled her skin, coloured her hair; from her derived to Helen, and at the sack of Troy unfortunately lost: till now, in this our age, it was as happily recovered, by a studious antiquary, out of some ruins of Asia, who sent a moiety[6] of it to the court of France (but much sophisticated), wherewith the ladies there, now, colour their hair. The rest, at this present, remains with me; extracted to a quintessence: so that, wherever it but touches, in youth it perpetually preserves, in age restores the complexion; seats your teeth, did they dance like virginal jacks,[7] firm as a wall; makes them white as ivory, that were black as—

ACT 2, SCENE 3

(*Enter Corvino.*)

CORVINO. Spite o' the devil, and my shame! Come
down here;
Come down;—No house but mine to make your scene?
Signior Flaminio, will you down, sir? Down?
What, is my wife your Franciscina,[8] sir?
No windows on the whole Piazza, here,
To make your properties, but mine? but mine?

[*Beats away Volpone, Nano, etc.*]

Heart! ere tomorrow I shall be new-christened,
And called the Pantalone di Besogniosi,[9]
About the town.

PEREGRINE. What should this mean, Sir Pol?

SIR POLITIC. Some trick of state, believe it; I will home.

PEREGRINE. It may be some design on you.

---

[1] *monccenigo* Venetian coin worth about nine pence.

[2] *Six – pence* The dash indicates that Volpone has recognized Sir Politic and Peregrine for Englishmen and switches his appeals to English currency.

[3] *bagatine* Italian coin worth 1/12 of a penny.

[4] *pistolet* Venetian coin worth six shillings.

[5] *her handkerchief* With the money tied into the corner, to effect a purchase.

[6] *moiety* Part or share; often a half.

[7] *virginal jacks* Keys of a virginal, a harpsichord-like instrument.

[8] *Flaminio ... Franciscina* Stock characters from commedia dell' arte plays, a young lover and a saucy maid.

[9] *Pantalone di Besogniosi* Pantalone is the avaricious old man and often cuckolded husband of commedia dell' arte.

SIR POLITIC. I know not,
I'll stand upon my guard.
PEREGRINE. It is your best, sir.
SIR POLITIC. This three weeks, all my advices, all my letters.
They have been intercepted.
PEREGRINE. Indeed, sir!
Best have a care.
SIR POLITIC. Nay, so I will.
PEREGRINE. This knight,
I may not lose him, for my mirth, till night.

[*Exeunt.*]

ACT 2, SCENE 4

(*Enter Volpone, Mosca.*)

VOLPONE. O, I am wounded!
MOSCA. Where, sir?
VOLPONE. Not without;
Those blows were nothing: I could bear them ever.
But angry Cupid, bolting° from her eyes, *shooting arrows*
Hath shot himself into me like a flame;
Where, now, he flings about his burning heat,
As in a furnace an ambitious fire,
Whose vent is stopped. The fight is all within me.
I cannot live, except thou help me, Mosca;
My liver[1] melts, and I, without the hope
Of some soft air, from her refreshing breath,
Am but a heap of cinders.
MOSCA. 'Las, good sir,
Would you had never seen her!
VOLPONE. Nay, would thou
Had'st never told me of her!
MOSCA. Sir, 'tis true;
I do confess I was unfortunate,
And you unhappy: but I'm bound in conscience,
No less than duty, to effect my best
To your release of torment, and I will, sir.
VOLPONE. Dear Mosca, shall I hope?
MOSCA. Sir, more than dear,
I will not bid you to despair of aught
Within a human compass.
VOLPONE. O, there spoke
My better angel. Mosca, take my keys,
Gold, plate, and jewels, all's at thy devotion;
Employ them how thou wilt; nay, coin me too:
So thou, in this, but crown my longings, Mosca.
MOSCA. Use but your patience.
VOLPONE. So I have.
MOSCA. I doubt not
To bring success to your desires.
VOLPONE. Nay, then,
I not repent me of my late disguise.
MOSCA. If you can horn° him, sir, you need not. *cuckold*
VOLPONE. True:
Besides, I never meant him for my heir.
Is not the colour of my beard and eyebrows[2]
To make me known?
MOSCA. No jot.
VOLPONE. I did it well.
MOSCA. So well, would I could follow you in mine,
With half the happiness!—and yet I would
Escape your epilogue.
VOLPONE. But were they gulled
With a belief that I was Scoto?
MOSCA. Sir,
Scoto himself could hardly have distinguished!
I have not time to flatter you now; we'll part;
And as I prosper, so applaud my art.

(*Exeunt.*)

ACT 2, SCENE 5

(*Enter Corvino, Celia.*)

CORVINO. Death of mine honour, with the city's fool!
A juggling, tooth-drawing,[3] prating mountebank!
And at a public window! where, whilst he,
With his strained° action, and his dole of faces, *extravagant*
To his drug-lecture draws your itching ears,

[1] *liver* Thought to be the seat of passion.

[2] *colour of ... eyebrows* I.e., red, the color of a fox.

[3] *tooth-drawing* Dentistry was sometimes performed by mountebanks.

A crew of old, unmarried, noted lechers,
Stood leering up like satyrs; and you smile
Most graciously, and fan your favours forth,
To give your hot spectators satisfaction!
What, was your mountebank their call? Their whistle?
Or were you enamoured on his copper rings,
His saffron jewel, with the toad-stone in't,
Or his embroidered suit, with the cope-stitch,[1]
Made of a hearse cloth?[2] Or his old tilt-feather?[3]
Or his starched beard?[4] Well, you shall have him, yes!
He shall come home, and minister unto you
The fricace for the mother. Or, let me see,
I think you'd rather mount;[5] would you not mount?
Why, if you'll mount, you may; yes, truly, you may:
And so you may be seen, down to the foot.
Get you a cittern,[6] Lady Vanity,[7]
And be a dealer° with the virtuous man; *prostitute*
Make one: I'll but protest myself a cuckold,
And save your dowry.[8] I'm a Dutchman, I!
For, if you thought me an Italian,
You would be damned, ere you did this, you whore!
Thou'ldst tremble, to imagine, that the murder
Of father, mother, brother, all thy race,
Should follow, as the subject of my justice.
CELIA. Good sir, have patience.
CORVINO. What couldst thou propose
Less to thyself, than in this heat of wrath.
And stung with my dishonour, I should strike [*draws his sword*]
This steel into thee, with as many stabs,
As thou wert gazed upon with goatish eyes?
CELIA. Alas, sir, be appeased! I could not think
My being at the window should more now
Move your impatience, than at other times.
CORVINO. No! not to seek and entertain a parley
With a known knave, before a multitude!
You were an actor with your handkerchief,
Which he most sweetly kissed in the receipt,
And might, no doubt, return it with a letter,
And point the place where you might meet; your sister's,
Your mother's, or your aunt's° might serve the turn.[9] *bawd, pimp*
CELIA. Why, dear sir, when do I make these excuses,
Or ever stir abroad, but to the church?
And that so seldom—
CORVINO. Well, it shall be less;
And thy restraint before was liberty,
To what I now decree: and therefore mark me.
First, I will have this bawdy light dammed up;
And till't be done, some two or three yards off,
I'll chalk a line: o'er which if thou but chance
To set thy desperate foot, more hell, more horror,
More wild remorseless rage shall seize on thee,
Than on a conjuror, that had heedless left
His circle's safety ere his devil was laid.
Then here's a lock° which I will hang upon thee, *chastity belt*
And, now I think on't, I will keep thee backwards;[10]
Thy lodging shall be backwards; thy walks backwards;
Thy prospect, all be backwards; and no pleasure,
That thou shalt know but backwards: nay, since you force
My honest nature, know, it is your own,
Being too open, makes me use you thus:
Since you will not contain your subtle nostrils
In a sweet room, but they must snuff the air
Of rank and sweaty passengers° [*knocking*]— One knocks. *passers-by*
Away, and be not seen, pain° of thy life; *on pain*
Nor look toward the window: if thou dost—
Nay, stay, hear this—let me not prosper, whore,

[1] *cope-stitch* Embroidered stitch used to border a cope or long cloak.

[2] *hearse cloth* Coffin drapery, funeral pall.

[3] *tilt-feather* Plume worn in the helmet used when jousting.

[4] *starched beard* Gummed and waxed beards were the height of fashion.

[5] *rather mount* The mountebank's platform and also the mountebank himself.

[6] *cittern* Kind of guitar.

[7] *Lady Vanity* Character from morality plays.

[8] *save your dowry* An adulteress forfeited her dowry to her husband.

[9] *serve the turn* Be to the purpose; also sexually, witness the congress.

[10] *keep thee backwards* Keep at the back of the house, also a pun with the suggestion of buggery.

But I will make thee an anatomy,[1]
Dissect thee mine own self, and read a lecture
Upon thee to the city, and in public.
Away!—

[*Exit Celia.*]

Who's there?

[*Enter Servitore.*]

SERVITORE. 'Tis Signior Mosca, sir.

ACT 2, SCENE 6

CORVINO. Let him come in. His master's dead: there's yet
Some good to help the bad.—

(*Enter Mosca.*)

My Mosca, welcome!
I guess your news.
MOSCA. I fear you cannot, sir.
CORVINO. Is't not his death?
MOSCA. Rather the contrary.
CORVINO. Not his recovery?
MOSCA. Yes, sir.
CORVINO. I am cursed,
I am bewitched, my crosses° meet to vex me. *afflictions*
How? how? how? how?
MOSCA. Why, sir, with Scoto's oil;
Corbaccio and Voltore brought of it,
Whilst I was busy in an inner room—
CORVINO. Death! that damned mountebank; but for the law
Now, I could kill the rascal: it cannot be,
His oil should have that virtue. Have not I
Known him a common rogue, come fiddling in
To the osteria,° with a tumbling whore, *inn*
And, when he has done all his forced tricks, been glad
Of a poor spoonful of dead wine, with flies in't?
It cannot be. All his ingredients
Are a sheep's gall, a roasted bitch's marrow,
Some few sod° earwigs, pounded caterpillars, *boiled*
A little capon's grease, and fasting spittle:[2]
I know them to a dram.
MOSCA. I know not, sir;
But some on't, there, they poured into his ears,
Some in his nostrils, and recovered him;
Applying but the fricace.
CORVINO. Pox o' that fricace!
MOSCA. And since, to seem the more officious
And flattering of his health, there, they have had,
At extreme fees, the College of Physicians
Consulting on him, how they might restore him;
Where one would have a cataplasm° of spices, *poultice*
Another a flayed ape clapped to his breast,
A third would have it a dog, a fourth an oil,
With wild cats' skins: at last, they all resolved
That, to preserve him, was no other means,
But some young woman must be straight sought out,
Lusty, and full of juice, to sleep by him;
And to this service, most unhappily,
And most unwillingly, am I now employed,
Which here I thought to pre-acquaint you with,
For your advice, since it concerns you most;
Because, I would not do that thing might cross
Your ends, on whom I have my whole dependence, sir:
Yet, if I do it not, they may delate° *denounce*
My slackness to my patron, work me out
Of his opinion; and there all your hopes,
Ventures, or whatsoever, are all frustrate!
I do but tell you, sir. Besides, they are all
Now striving, who shall first present him; therefore—
I could entreat you, briefly conclude somewhat;
Prevent° them if you can. *go before*
CORVINO. Death to my hopes,
This is my villainous fortune! Best to hire
Some common courtesan?
MOSCA. Aye, I thought on that, sir;
But they are all so subtle, full of art—
And age again doting and flexible,
So as—I cannot tell—we may, perchance,
Light on a quean° may cheat us all. *prostitute*

[1] *make thee an anatomy* Executed criminals were given to schools to be anatomically studied; also, here, to give a public moral analysis on Celia's failings.

[2] *fasting spittle* Spittle of someone who has been fasting.

CORVINO. 'Tis true.
MOSCA. No, no: it must be one that has no tricks, sir,
Some simple thing, a creature made unto it;
Some wench you may command. Have you no kinswoman?
God's so° — Think, think, think, think, think, think, think, sir. *soul*
One o' the doctors offered there his daughter.
CORVINO. How!
MOSCA. Yes, Signior Lupo,° the physician. *wolf*
CORVINO. His daughter?
MOSCA. And a virgin, sir. Why, alas,
He knows the state of's body, what it is;
That naught can warm his blood, sir, but a fever;
Nor any incantation raise his spirit:
A long forgetfulness hath seized that part.
Besides sir, who shall know it? Some one or two—
CORVINO. I pray thee give me leave. [*Walks aside.*] If any man
But I had had this luck—The thing in itself,
I know, is nothing—Wherefore should not I
As well command my blood and my affections,
As this dull doctor? In the point of honour,
The cases are all one of wife and daughter.
MOSCA. [*Aside.*] I hear him coming.
CORVINO. She shall do't: 'tis done.
'Slight!° if this doctor, who is not engaged, *God's light*
Unless it be for his counsel, which is nothing,
Offer his daughter, what should I, that am
So deeply in? I will prevent him—Wretch!
Covetous wretch! Mosca, I have determined.
MOSCA. How, sir?
CORVINO. We'll make all sure. The party you wot of
Shall be mine own wife, Mosca.
MOSCA. Sir, the thing,
But that I would not seem to counsel you,
I should have motioned° to you, at the first: *suggested*
And make your count,° you have cut all their throats. *count on it*
Why, 'tis directly taking a possession!
And in his next fit, we may let him go.
'Tis but to pull the pillow from his head,
And he is throttled: it had been done before,
But for your scrupulous doubts.
CORVINO. Aye, a plague on't,
My conscience fools my wit! Well, I'll be brief,
And so be thou, lest they should be before us:
Go home, prepare him, tell him with what zeal
And willingness I do it; swear it was
On the first hearing, as thou may'st do, truly,
Mine own free motion.
MOSCA. Sir, I warrant you,
I'll so possess him with it, that the rest
Of his starved clients shall be banished all;
And, only you received. But come not, sir,
Until I send, for I have something else
To ripen for your good—you must not know't.
CORVINO. But do not you forget to send now.
MOSCA. Fear not.

[*Exit Mosca.*]

ACT 2, SCENE 7

CORVINO. Where are you, wife? my Celia! wife!

[*Enter Celia.*]

—What, blubbering
Come, dry those tears. I think thou thought'st me in earnest;
Ha! By this light I talked so but to try thee:
Methinks the lightness of the occasion
Should have confirmed thee. Come, I am not jealous.
CELIA. No!
CORVINO. Faith I am not, I, nor never was;
It is a poor unprofitable humour.
Do not I know, if women have a will,° *sexual appetite*
They'll do 'gainst all the watches of the world,
And that the fiercest spies are tamed with gold?
Tut, I am confident in thee, thou shalt see't;
And see I'll give thee cause too, to believe it.
Come kiss me. Go, and make thee ready, straight,
In all thy best attire, thy choicest jewels,
Put them all on, and, with them, thy best looks:
We are invited to a solemn feast,
At old Volpone's, where it shall appear
How far I am free from jealousy or fear.

[*Exeunt.*]

ACT 3, SCENE 1

[*Enter Mosca.*]

MOSCA. I fear, I shall begin to grow in love
With my dear self, and my most prosperous parts,° *abilities*
They do so spring and burgeon; I can feel
A whimsy° in my blood: I know not how, *giddiness*
Success hath made me wanton. I could skip
Out of my skin, now, like a subtle snake,
I am so limber. O! your parasite
Is a most precious thing, dropt from above,
Not bred 'mongst clods and clotpoles,° here on earth. *idiots*
I muse, the mystery was not made a science,
It is so liberally professed! Almost
All the wise world is little else, in nature,
But parasites or sub-parasites. And yet,
I mean not those that have your bare town-art,[1]
To know who's fit to feed them; have no house,
No family, no care, and therefore mould
Tales[2] for men's ears, to bait that sense; or get
Kitchen-invention,° and some stale receipts *elaborate recipes*
To please the belly, and the groin; nor those,
With their court dog-tricks,[3] that can fawn and fleer,° *smile*
Make their revenue out of legs and faces,
Echo my lord, and lick away a moth:° *mote, speck*
But your fine elegant rascal, that can rise,
And stoop, almost together, like an arrow;
Shoot through the air as nimbly as a star;° *meteor*
Turn short as doth a swallow, and be here,
And there, and here, and yonder, all at once;
Present to any humour, all occasion;
And change a visor, swifter than a thought!
This is the creature had the art born with him;
Toils not to learn it, but doth practice it
Out of most excellent nature: and such sparks
Are the true parasites, others but their zanies.

[1] *bare town-art* Negligible skills of a street parasite, learned in towns.

[2] *mould / Tales* Invent scandals.

[3] *court dog-tricks* To beg like a dog as courtiers do.

ACT 3, SCENE 2

[*Enter Bonario.*]

MOSCA. Who's this? Bonario, old Corbaccio's son?
The person I was bound° to seek.—Fair sir, *on my way*
You are happily met.
BONARIO. That cannot be by thee.
MOSCA. Why, sir?
BONARIO. Nay, pray thee, know thy way, and leave me:
I would be loath to interchange discourse
With such a mate° as thou art. *fellow*
MOSCA. Courteous sir,
Scorn not my poverty.
BONARIO. Not I, by heaven;
But thou shalt give me leave to hate thy baseness.
MOSCA. Baseness!
BONARIO. Aye; answer me, is not thy sloth
Sufficient argument?° Thy flattery? *evidence*
Thy means of feeding?
MOSCA. Heaven be good to me!
These imputations are too common, sir,
And easily stuck on virtue when she's poor.
You are unequal to me, and however
Your sentence may be righteous, yet you are not
That, ere you know me, thus proceed in censure:
St. Mark bear witness 'gainst you, 'tis inhuman.

[*Weeps.*]

BONARIO. What! does he weep? the sign is soft and good:
I do repent me that I was so harsh.
MOSCA. 'Tis true, that, swayed by strong necessity,
I am enforced to eat my careful bread
With too much obsequy;° 'tis true, beside, *humility*
That I am fain° to spin mine own poor raiment *compelled*
Out of my mere observance, being not born
To a free fortune: but that I have done
Base offices, in rending friends asunder,
Dividing families, betraying counsels,
Whispering false lies, or mining° men with praises, *undermining*
Trained° their credulity with perjuries, *led on*

Corrupted chastity, or am in love
With mine own tender ease, but would not rather
Prove the most rugged, and laborious course,
That might redeem my present estimation,
Let me here perish, in all hope of goodness.
BONARIO. [*Aside.*] This cannot be a
personated° passion! *feigned*
I was to blame, so to mistake thy nature;
Prithee, forgive me: and speak out thy business.
MOSCA. Sir, it concerns you; and though I may seem,
At first to make a main offence in manners,
And in my gratitude unto my master;
Yet, for the pure love, which I bear all right,
And hatred of the wrong, I must reveal it.
This very hour your father is in purpose
To disinherit you—
BONARIO. How!
MOSCA. And thrust you forth,
As a mere stranger to his blood; 'tis true, sir,
The work no way engageth° me, but, as *concerns*
I claim an interest in the general state
Of goodness and true virtue, which I hear
To abound in you: and, for which mere respect,
Without a second aim, sir, I have done it.
BONARIO. This tale hath lost thee much of the late trust
Thou hadst with me; it is impossible:
I know not how to lend it any thought,
My father should be so unnatural.
MOSCA. It is a confidence that well becomes,
Your piety;° and formed, no doubt, it is *filial obligation*
From your own simple innocence: which makes
Your wrong more monstrous and abhorred. But, sir,
I now will tell you more. This very minute,
It is, or will be doing; and, if you
Shall be but pleased to go with me, I'll bring you,
I dare not say where you shall see, but where
Your ear shall be a witness of the deed;
Hear yourself written bastard, and professed
The common issue of the earth.
BONARIO. I'm 'mazed!° *amazed*
MOSCA. Sir, if I do it not, draw your just sword,
And score° your vengeance on my front and face: *mark*
Mark me your villain: you have too much wrong,
And I do suffer for you, sir. My heart
Weeps blood in anguish—
BONARIO. Lead; I follow thee.

[*Exeunt.*]

ACT 3, SCENE 3

(*Enter Volpone, Nano, Androgyno, and Castrone.*)

VOLPONE. Mosca stays long, methinks. Bring forth your sports,
And help to make the wretched time more sweet.
NANO. Dwarf, fool, and eunuch, well met here we be.
A question it were now, whether of us three,
Being all the known delicates° of a rich man, *favorites*
In pleasing him, claim the precedency can?
CASTRONE. I claim for myself.
ANDROGYNO. And so doth the fool.
NANO. 'Tis foolish indeed: let me set you both to school.
First for your dwarf, he's little and witty,
And every thing, as it is little, is pretty;
Else why do men say to a creature of my shape,
So soon as they see him, It's a pretty little ape?
And why a pretty ape, but for pleasing imitation
Of greater men's actions, in a ridiculous fashion?
Beside, this feat° body of mine doth not crave *dainty*
Half the meat, drink, and cloth, one of your bulks will have.
Admit your fool's face be the mother of laughter,
Yet, for his brain, it must always come after:[1]
And though that do feed him, it's a pitiful case,
His body is beholding to such a bad face.

(*One knocks.*)

VOLPONE. Who's there? my couch; away! look! Nano, see:
Give me my caps, first—go, enquire. [*Exeunt Nano, Androgyno and Castrone.*] Now, Cupid
Send it be Mosca, and with fair return![2]
NANO. (*Within.*) It is the beauteous madam—
VOLPONE. Would-be—is it?

[1] *come after* Be of less importance.

[2] *fair return* I.e., from a profitable business venture.

NANO. The same.
VOLPONE. Now torment on me! Squire her in;
For she will enter, or dwell here for ever;
Nay, quickly. That my fit were past! I fear
A second hell too, that my loathing this
Will quite expel my appetite to the other:
Would she were taking now her tedious leave.
Lord, how it threats me what I am to suffer!

ACT 3, SCENE 4

(Re-enter Nano, with Lady Politic Would-be.)

LADY POLITIC. I thank you, good sir. Pray you signify
Unto your patron, I am here.—This band° *collar*
Shows not my neck enough.—I trouble you, sir;
Let me request you, bid one of my women
Come hither to me.—In good faith, I am dressed
Most favourably° to-day! It is no matter: *pleasantly*
'Tis well enough.—

[*Enter 1 Woman.*]

Look, see, these petulant things,
How they have done this!
VOLPONE. [*Aside.*] I do feel the fever
Entering in at mine ears; O, for a charm,
To fright it hence!
LADY POLITIC. Come nearer: is this curl
In his° right place, or this? Why is this higher *its*
Than all the rest? You have not washed your eyes, yet!
Or do they not stand even in your head?
Where is your fellow? Call her.

[*Exit 1 Woman.*]

NANO. Now, St. Mark
Deliver us! anon, she'll beat her women,
Because her nose is red.

[*Re-enter 1 with 2 Woman.*]

LADY POLITIC. I pray you, view
This tire, forsooth:° are all things apt, or no? *a refined oath*
1 WOM. One hair a little, here, sticks out, forsooth.
LADY POLITIC. Does't so, forsooth! and where was your dear sight,
When it did so, forsooth! What now! Bird-eyed?[1]
And you, too? Pray you, both approach and mend it.
Now, by that light, I muse you are not ashamed!
I, that have preached these things so oft unto you,
Read you the principles, argued all the grounds,
Disputed every fitness, every grace,
Called you to counsel of so frequent dressings—
NANO. [*Aside.*] More carefully than of your fame or honour.
LADY POLITIC. Made you acquainted, what an ample dowry
The knowledge of these things would be unto you,
Able, alone, to get you noble husbands
At your return:[2] and you thus to neglect it!
Besides you seeing what a curious nation
The Italians are, what will they say of me?
"The English lady cannot dress herself."
Here's a fine imputation to our country!
Well, go your ways, and stay in the next room.
This fucus° was too coarse too; it's no matter.— *cosmetic paste*
Good sir, you'll give them entertainment?

[*Exeunt Nano and Waiting-women.*]

VOLPONE. The storm comes toward me.
LADY POLITIC. How does my Volp?
VOLPONE. Troubled with noise, I cannot sleep; I dreamt
That a strange fury entered, now, my house,
And, with the dreadful tempest of her breath,
Did cleave my roof asunder.
LADY POLITIC. Believe me, and I
Had the most fearful dream, could I remember't—
VOLPONE. [*Aside.*] Out on my fate! I have given her the occasion
How to torment me: she will tell me hers.
LADY POLITIC. Me thought, the golden mediocrity,
Polite and delicate—
VOLPONE. O, if you do love me,
No more: I sweat, and suffer, at the mention

[1] *Bird-eyed* Startled, but possibly short-sighted or timid.
[2] *return* To England.

Of any dream; feel how I tremble yet.
LADY POLITIC. Alas, good soul! the passion of the heart.° *heartburn*
Seed-pearl[1] were good now, boiled with syrup of apples,
Tincture of gold, and coral, citron-pills,
Your elecampane root, myrobalans—[2]
VOLPONE. [*Aside.*] Ah me, I have ta'en a grasshopper by the wing!
LADY POLITIC. Burnt silk,[3] and amber:° *ambergris*
You have muscadel
Good i'the house—
VOLPONE. You will not drink, and part?
LADY POLITIC. No, fear not that. I doubt, we shall not get
Some English saffron, half a dram would serve;
Your sixteen cloves, a little musk, dried mints,
Bugloss,[4] and barley-meal—
VOLPONE. [*Aside.*] She's in again!
Before I feigned diseases, now I have one.
LADY POLITIC. And these applied with a right scarlet cloth.[5]
VOLPONE. [*Aside.*] Another flood of words! a very torrent!
LADY POLITIC. Shall I, sir, make you a poultice?
VOLPONE. No, no, no,
I'm very well, you need prescribe no more.
LADY POLITIC. I have a little studied physic; but now,
I'm all for music, save, in the forenoons,
An hour or two for painting. I would have
A lady, indeed, to have all, letters and arts,
Be able to discourse, to write, to paint,
But principal, as Plato holds, your music,
And so does wise Pythagoras, I take it,
Is your true rapture: when there is concent
In face, in voice, and clothes: and is, indeed,
Our sex's chiefest ornament.
VOLPONE. The poet
As old in time as Plato, and as knowing,
Says, that your highest female grace is silence.
LADY POLITIC. Which of your poets? Petrarch, or Tasso, or Dante?
Guarini? Ariosto? Aretine?[6]
Cieco di Hadria?[7] I have read them all.
VOLPONE. [*Aside.*] Is every thing a cause to my destruction?
LADY POLITIC. I think I have two or three of them about me.
VOLPONE. [*Aside.*] The sun, the sea, will sooner both stand still
Than her eternal tongue! nothing can 'scape it.
LADY POLITIC. Here's Pastor Fido—[8]
VOLPONE. [*Aside.*] Profess obstinate silence;
That's now my safest.
LADY POLITIC. All our English writers,
I mean such as are happy in the Italian, ° *to know Italian*
Will deign to steal out of this author, mainly:
Almost as much as from Montagnié:[9]
He has so modern and facile a vein,
Fitting the time, and catching the court-ear!
Your Petrarch is more passionate, yet he,
In days of sonnetting, trusted them with much:
Dante is hard, and few can understand him.
But, for a desperate wit, there's Aretine;
Only, his pictures are a little obscene—
You mark me not.
VOLPONE. Alas, my mind's perturbed.
LADY POLITIC. Why, in such cases, we must cure ourselves,
Make use of our philosophy—
VOLPONE. Ohimè![10]
LADY POLITIC. And as we find our passions do rebel,

[1] *Seed-pearl* A home remedy for heart stimulation.

[2] *elecampane … myrobalans* Alecampane is also known as horse-heal, the leaves of which were used as a stimulant tonic. Myrobalans is a plum-like fruit from India hailed for its efficacy in curing melancholy and agues.

[3] *Burnt silk* Considered a cure for smallpox when boiled in water.

[4] *Bugloss* Herb used as a heart stimulant.

[5] *scarlet cloth* Believed to be a cure for small pox when the patient was wrapped in it.

[6] *Aretine* I.e., Pietro Aretino (1492–1557), Italian satirical poet noted for his lewd writing.

[7] *Cieco di Hadria* Luigi Groto, "The Blind Man of Adria," a minor poet compared to the others listed.

[8] *Pastor Fido* A pastoral tragic-comedy by G.B. Guarini, translated into English as *The Faithful Shepherd* in 1602.

[9] *Montagnié* The terminal accent shows Lady Politic's ignorance of the proper pronunciation of the name (Montaigne, i.e., Michel de Montaigne), but fits with the meter of the line.

[10] *Ohimè!* Italian: alas!

Encounter them with reason, or divert them,
By giving scope unto some other humour
Of lesser danger: as, in politic bodies,° *astute men*
There's nothing more doth overwhelm the judgment,
And cloud the understanding, than too much
Settling and fixing, and, as 'twere, subsiding[1]
Upon one object. For the incorporating
Of these same outward things, into that part,
Which we call mental, leaves some certain fæces
That stop the organs, and as Plato says,
Assassinates our knowledge.

VOLPONE. [*Aside.*] Now, the spirit
Of patience help me!

LADY POLITIC. Come, in faith, I must
Visit you more a days; and make you well:
Laugh and be lusty.

VOLPONE. [*Aside.*] My good angel save me!

LADY POLITIC. There was but one sole man in all the world,
With whom I e'er could sympathize; and he
Would lie you,° often, three, four hours together *stay*
To hear me speak; and be sometimes so rapt,
As he would answer me quite from the purpose,
Like you, and you are like him, just. I'll discourse,
An't be but only, sir, to bring you asleep,
How we did spend our time and loves together,
For some six years.

VOLPONE. Oh, oh, oh, oh, oh, oh!

LADY POLITIC. For we were coætanei,[2] and brought up—

VOLPONE. Some power, some fate, some fortune rescue me!

ACT 3, SCENE 5

(*Enter Mosca.*)

MOSCA. God save you, madam!

LADY POLITIC. Good sir.

VOLPONE. Mosca! welcome,
Welcome to my redemption.

MOSCA. Why, sir?

VOLPONE. Oh,
Rid me of this my torture, quickly, there;
My madam, with the everlasting voice:
The bells, in time of pestilence, ne'er made
Like noise,[3] or were in that perpetual motion!
The cock-pit comes not near it. All my house,
But now, steamed like a bath with her thick breath,
A lawyer could not have been heard; nor scarce
Another woman, such a hail of words
She has let fall. For hell's sake, rid her hence.

MOSCA. Has she presented?° *given a present*

VOLPONE. O, I do not care;
I'll take her absence, upon any price,
With any loss.

MOSCA. Madam—

LADY POLITIC. I have brought your patron
A toy,° a cap here, of mine own work. *trifle*

MOSCA. 'Tis well.
I had forgot to tell you, I saw your knight.
Where you would little think it.—

LADY POLITIC. Where?

MOSCA. Marry,
Where yet, if you make haste, you may apprehend
Rowing upon the water in a gondola
With the most cunning courtesan of Venice.

LADY POLITIC. Is't true?

MOSCA. Pursue them, and believe your eyes:
Leave me, to make your gift. [*Exit Lady Politic.*] I knew 'twould take:
For, lightly,° they that use themselves most license, *commonly*
Are still most jealous.

VOLPONE. Mosca, hearty thanks,
For thy quick fiction, and delivery of me.
Now to my hopes, what say'st thou?

[*Re-enter Lady Politic.*]

LADY POLITIC. But do you hear, Sir?—

VOLPONE. Again! I fear a paroxysm.

LADY POLITIC. Which way
Rowed they together?

---

[1] *Settling … fixing … subsiding* Alchemical jargon.

[2] *coætanei* Contemporaries.

[3] *The bells … Like noise* During outbreaks of the plague, church bells rang once for each year of the life of every victim, resulting in almost continual ringing.

MOSCA. Toward the Rialto.[1]
LADY POLITIC. I pray you lend me your dwarf.
MOSCA. I pray you, take him.—

[*Exit Lady Politic.*]

Your hopes, sir, are like happy blossoms, fair,
And promise timely fruit, if you will stay
But the maturing; keep you at your couch,
Corbaccio will arrive straight, with the will;
When he is gone, I'll tell you more.

[*Exit Mosca.*]

VOLPONE. My blood,
My spirits are returned; I am alive:
And, like your wanton gamester at primero,[2]
Whose thought had whispered to him, not go less,
Methinks I lie, and draw—for an encounter.

[*Volpone draws the curtains around his bed.*]

ACT 3, SCENE 6

[*Mosca leads Bonario in and hides him.*]

MOSCA. Sir, here concealed, you may hear all. But, pray you,
Have patience, sir. (*One knocks.*) The same's your father knocks:
I am compelled to leave you.

[*Exit.*]

BONARIO. Do so ... Yet
Cannot my thought imagine this a truth.

[1] *Rialto* Rialto Bridge, center of commerce in Venice.

[2] *primero* Card game rather like poker where "go less," "lie," "draw," and "encounter" were all game terms.

ACT 3, SCENE 7

[*Enter Mosca and Corvino, Celia following.*]

MOSCA. Death on me! you are come too soon, what meant you?
Did not I say, I would send?
CORVINO. Yes, but I feared
You might forget it, and then they prevent us.° *get there first*
MOSCA. [*Aside.*] Prevent! Did e'er man haste so, for his horns?[3]
A courtier would not ply it so, for a place.° *place at court*
Well, now there is no helping it, stay here;
I'll presently return.
CORVINO. Where are you, Celia?
You know not wherefore I have brought you hither?
CELIA. Not well, except you told me.
CORVINO. Now, I will:
Hark hither.
MOSCA. [*To Bonario.*] Sir, your father hath sent word,
It will be half an hour ere he come;
And therefore, if you please to walk the while
Into that gallery°—at the upper end, *study, library*
There are some books to entertain the time:
And I'll take care no man shall come unto you, sir.
BONARIO. Yes, I will stay there. [*Aside.*] I do doubt this fellow.
MOSCA. There; he is far enough; he can hear nothing:
And, for his father, I can keep him off.
CORVINO. Nay, now, there is no starting back, and therefore,
Resolve upon it: I have so decreed.
It must be done. Nor would I move't° afore, *have urged it*
Because I would avoid all shifts° and tricks, *evasions*
That might deny me.
CELIA. Sir, let me beseech you,
Affect° not these strange trials; if you doubt *seek*
My chastity, why, lock me up for ever;
Make me the heir of darkness. Let me live,
Where I may please your fears, if not your trust.
CORVINO. Believe it, I have no such humour, I.
All that I speak I mean; yet I'm not mad;

[3] *horns* Cuckold's horns.

Nor horn-mad,[1] see you? Go to, show yourself
Obedient, and a wife.
CELIA. O heaven!
CORVINO. I say it,
Do so.
CELIA. Was this the train?° *trick*
CORVINO. I've told you reasons;
What the physicians have set down: how much
It may concern me; what my engagements are;
My means; and the necessity of those means,
For my recovery: wherefore, if you be
Loyal, and mine, be won, respect my venture.
CELIA. Before your honour?
CORVINO. Honour! Tut, a breath.
There's no such thing in nature; a mere term
Invented to awe fools. What is my gold
The worse for touching, clothes for being looked on?
Why, this is no more. An old decrepit wretch,
That has no sense, no sinew; takes his meat
With others' fingers; only knows to gape,
When you do scald his gums; a voice, a shadow;
And, what can this man hurt you?
CELIA. [*Aside.*] Lord! what spirit
Is this hath entered him?
CORVINO. And for your fame,
That's such a jig;° as if I would go tell it, *trifle*
Cry it on the Piazza! Who shall know it,
But he that cannot speak it, and this fellow,
Whose lips are in my pocket? Save yourself.
If you'll proclaim't, you may! I know no other
Shall come to know it.
CELIA. Are heaven and saints then nothing?
Will they be blind or stupid?
CORVINO. How!
CELIA. Good sir,
Be jealous still, emulate them; and think
What hate they burn with toward every sin.
CORVINO. I grant you: if I thought it were a sin,
I would not urge you. Should I offer this
To some young Frenchman, or hot Tuscan blood
That had read Aretine, conned all his prints,[2]
Knew every quirk° within lust's labyrinth, *sudden turn*
And were professed critic° in lechery; *qualified expert*
And I would look upon him, and applaud him,
This were a sin: but here, 'tis contrary,
A pious work, mere charity for physic,
And honest polity,[3] to assure mine own.
CELIA. O heaven! canst thou suffer such a change?
VOLPONE. Thou art mine honour, Mosca, and my pride,
My joy, my tickling, my delight! Go bring them.
MOSCA. Please you draw near, sir.
CORVINO. Come on, what—
You will not be rebellious? by that light—
MOSCA. Sir, Signior Corvino, here, is come to see you.
VOLPONE. Oh!
MOSCA. And hearing of the consultation had,
So lately, for your health, is come to offer,
Or rather, sir, to prostitute—[4]
CORVINO. Thanks, sweet Mosca.
MOSCA. Freely, unasked, or unentreated—
CORVINO. Well.
MOSCA. As the true fervent instance of his love,
His own most fair and proper wife; the beauty,
Only of price in Venice—
CORVINO. 'Tis well urged.
MOSCA. To be your comfortress, and to preserve you.
VOLPONE. Alas, I am past, already! Pray you, thank him
For his good care and promptness. But, for that,
'Tis a vain labour; e'en to fight 'gainst heaven.
Applying fire to stone—uh, uh, uh, uh—
Making a dead leaf grow again. I take
His wishes gently, though; and you may tell him,
What I have done for him. Marry, my state is hopeless!
Will him to pray for me; and to use his fortune
With reverence, when he comes to't.
MOSCA. Do you hear, sir?
Go to him with your wife.
CORVINO. Heart of my father!
Wilt thou persist thus? Come, I pray thee, come.

[1] *horn-mad* Pun; horn-mad means being angry, so here, also, means being angry at being made a cuckold as well as jealous ("horn-madded").

[2] *prints* Specifically, the erotic illustrations that accompanied Aretino's sexual explicit *Sixteen Postures*, by Guilio Romano.

[3] *polity* Policy, skillful management.

[4] *prostitute* Both the sexual sense and to offer with total submission and devotion.

Thou seest 'tis nothing, Celia. By this hand,
I shall grow violent. Come, do't, I say.
CELIA. Sir, kill me, rather: I will take down poison,
Eat burning coals,[1] do anything—
CORVINO. Be damned!
Heart, I will drag thee hence, home, by the hair;
Cry thee a strumpet through the streets; rip up
Thy mouth unto thine ears; and slit thy nose,
Like a raw rochet![2]—Do not tempt me; come,
Yield, I am loath. Death! I will buy some slave
Whom I will kill, and bind thee to him, alive;[3]
And at my window hang you forth, devising
Some monstrous crime, which I, in capital letters,
Will eat into thy flesh with aquafortis,° *nitric acid*
And burning corsives,° on this stubborn breast. *corrosives*
Now, by the blood thou hast incensed, I'll do it!
CELIA. Sir, what you please, you may, I am your martyr.
CORVINO. Be not thus obstinate, I have not deserved it:
Think who it is entreats you. 'Prithee, sweet;
Good faith, thou shalt have jewels, gowns, attires,
What thou wilt think, and ask. Do but go kiss him.
Or touch him, but. For my sake. At my suit.
This once. No! not! I shall remember this.
Will you disgrace me thus? Do you thirst my undoing?
MOSCA. Nay, gentle lady, be advised.
CORVINO. No, no.
She has watched her time.[4] God's precious,[5] this is scurvy,
'Tis very scurvy; and you are—
MOSCA. Nay, good sir.
CORVINO. An arrant locust, by heaven, a locust!
Whore, crocodile, that hast thy tears prepared,[6]
Expecting how thou'lt bid them flow—
MOSCA. Nay, pray you, sir!
She will consider.
CELIA. Would my life would serve
To satisfy—

[1] *eat burning coals* Proverbial for the actions of a faithful wife, from the death of Portia, Brutus's wife.

[2] *rochet* Red Gurnard, a fish.

[3] *some slave... alive* Tarquin threatens Lucrece in this way in Shakespeare's *Rape of Lucrece*, ll. 515–671.

[4] *watched her time* Waited for the right time to do me a bad turn.

[5] *God's precious* I.e., God's precious blood.

[6] *Crocodile... tears prepared* Crocodiles were believed to lure their victims with feigned tears.

CORVINO. S'death! if she would but speak to him,
And save my reputation, it were somewhat;
But spitefully to affect my utter ruin!
MOSCA. Aye, now you have put your fortune in her hands.
Why i'faith, it is her modesty, I must quit° her. *acquit*
If you were absent, she would be more coming;° *flirtatious*
I know it: and dare undertake for her.
What woman can before her husband? Pray you,
Let us depart, and leave her here.
CORVINO. Sweet Celia,
Thou may'st redeem all, yet; I'll say no more:
If not, esteem yourself as lost. (*Celia starts to leave.*) Nay, stay there.

[*Exeunt Corvino, Mosca.*]

CELIA. O God, and his good angels! whither, whither,
Is shame fled human breasts? that with such ease,
Men dare put off your honours, and their own?
Is that, which ever was a cause of° life, *purpose for*
Now placed beneath the basest circumstance,
And modesty an exile made, for money?
VOLPONE. Aye, in Corvino, and such earth-fed minds,
(*He leaps off from his couch.*) That never tasted the true heaven of love.
Assure thee, Celia, he that would sell thee,
Only for hope of gain, and that uncertain,
He would have sold his part of Paradise
For ready money, had he met a copeman.[7]
Why art thou mazed to see me thus revived?
Rather applaud thy beauty's miracle;
'Tis thy great work: that hath, not now alone,
But sundry times raised me, in several shapes,
And, but this morning, like a mountebank,
To see thee at thy window: aye, before
I would have left my practice,° for thy love, *schemes*
In varying figures, I would have contended
With the blue Proteus,[8] or the horned flood.
Now art thou welcome.
CELIA. Sir!
VOLPONE. Nay, fly me not.
Nor let thy false imagination

[7] *copeman* Merchant, chapman.

[8] *blue Proteus* Proteus was a shape-changing sea god.

That I was bed-rid, make thee think I am so:
Thou shalt not find it. I am, now, as fresh,
As hot, as high, and in as jovial plight,
As when, in that so celebrated scene,
At recitation of our comedy,
For entertainment of the great Valois,[1]
I acted young Antinous;[2] and attracted
The eyes and ears of all the ladies present,
To admire each graceful gesture, note, and
footing.° *dancing*

(*Song.*)

Come, my Celia, let us prove,
While we can, the sports of love,
Time will not be ours for ever,
He, at length, our good will sever;
Spend not then his gifts in vain;
Suns, that set, may rise again;
But if once we lose this light,
'Tis with us perpetual night.
Why should we defer our joys?
Fame and rumour are but toys.
Cannot we delude the eyes
Of a few poor household spies?
Or his easier ears beguile,
Thus removed by our wile?—
'Tis no sin love's fruits to steal:
But the sweet thefts to reveal;
To be taken, to be seen,
These have crimes accounted been.

CELIA. Some serene[3] blast me, or dire lightning strike
This my offending face!

VOLPONE. Why droops my Celia?
Thou hast, in place of a base husband, found
A worthy lover: use thy fortune well,
With secrecy and pleasure. See, behold,
What thou art queen of; not in expectation,
As I feed others: but possessed and crowned.
See, here, a rope of pearl; and each, more orient
Than that the brave Egyptian queen caroused:[4]
Dissolve and drink them. See, a carbuncle,° *garnet*
May put out both the eyes of our St. Mark;
A diamond, would have bought Lollia Paulina,[5]
When she came in like star-light, hid with jewels,
That were the spoils of provinces; take these,
And wear, and lose them: yet remains an ear-ring
To purchase them again, and this whole state.
A gem but worth a private patrimony,
Is nothing: we will eat such at a meal.
The heads of parrots, tongues of nightingales,
The brains of peacocks, and of ostriches,
Shall be our food: and, could we get the phoenix,
Though nature lost her kind,[6] she were our dish.

CELIA. Good sir, these things might move a mind
affected
With such delights; but I, whose innocence
Is all I can think wealthy, or worth the enjoying,
And which, once lost, I have naught to lose beyond it,
Cannot be taken with these sensual baits:
If you have conscience—

VOLPONE. 'Tis the beggar's virtue;
If thou hast wisdom, hear me, Celia.
Thy baths shall be the juice of July-flowers,° *gillyflowers*
Spirit of roses, and of violets,
The milk of unicorns, and panthers' breath[7]
Gathered in bags, and mixed with Cretan wines.
Our drink shall be prepared gold and amber;
Which we will take, until my roof whirl round
With the vertigo: and my dwarf shall dance,
My eunuch sing, my fool make up the
antic,° *grotesque dance*
Whilst we, in changed shapes, act Ovid's tales,
Thou, like Europa now, and I like Jove,[8]

[1] *Valois* France's ruling family in the sixteenth century; Henry de Valois II passed through Venice on his way home to be crowned king in 1574.

[2] *Antinous* Chief suitor for Penelope in Homer's *Odyssey*.

[3] *serene* Noxious mist.

[4] *Egyptian queen caroused* Pliny tells of how, to win a bet with Mark Antony, Cleopatra drank a pearl, worth ten million sesterces, dissolved in vinegar.

[5] *Lollia Paulina* Notoriously avaricious mistress of the Emperor Caligula.

[6] *Though nature lost her kind* There is only one phoenix, so eating it would cause its extinction from nature.

[7] *the panther's breath* The panther was said to attract its victims with its sweet breath, and then to kill them.

[8] *Europa ... Jove* Jupiter (Jove), in the form of a bull, wooed Europa.

Then I like Mars, and thou like Erycine:[1]
So, of the rest, till we have quite run through,
And wearied all the fables of the gods.
Then will I have thee in more modern forms,
Attired like some sprightly dame of France,
Brave Tuscan lady, or proud Spanish beauty;
Sometimes, unto the Persian Sophy's[2] wife;
Or the Grand Signior's[3] mistress; and, for change,
To one of our most artful courtesans,
Or some quick Negro, or cold Russian;
And I will meet thee in as many shapes:
Where we may so transfuse our wandering souls
Out at our lips, and score up sums of pleasures,

[*Sings.*]

That the curious shall not know
How to tell° them as they flow; *count*
And the envious, when they find
What their number is, be pined.

CELIA. If you have ears that will be pierced—or eyes
That can be opened—a heart that may be touched—
Or any part that yet sounds man about you—
If you have touch of holy saints—or heaven—
Do me the grace to let me 'scape—if not,
Be bountiful and kill me. You do know,
I am a creature, hither ill betrayed,
By one, whose shame I would forget it were. —
If you will deign me neither of these graces,
Yet feed your wrath, sir, rather than your lust —
(It is a vice comes nearer manliness) —
And punish that unhappy crime of nature,
Which you miscall my beauty—flay my face,
Or poison it with ointments, for seducing
Your blood to this rebellion. —Rub these hands,
With what may cause an eating leprosy,
E'en to my bones and marrow— any thing,
That may disfavour° me, save in my honour— *disfigure*
And I will kneel to you, pray for you, pay down
A thousand hourly vows, sir, for your health;
Report, and think you virtuous—

VOLPONE. Think me cold,
Frozen and impotent, and so report me?
That I had Nestor's[4] hernia, thou wouldst think.
I do degenerate, and abuse my nation,
To play with opportunity thus long;
I should have done the act, and then have parleyed.
Yield, or I'll force thee.

CELIA. O! just God!

VOLPONE. In vain—

BONARIO. (*He leaps out from where Mosca had placed him.*)
Forbear, foul ravisher, libidinous swine!
Free the forced lady, or thou diest, impostor.
But that I'm loath to snatch thy punishment
Out of the hand of justice, thou shouldst, yet,
Be made the timely sacrifice of vengeance,
Before this altar, and this dross,[5] thy idol.—
Lady, let's quit the place, it is the den
Of villainy; fear naught, you have a guard:
And he, ere long, shall meet his just reward.

[*Exeunt Bonario, Celia.*]

VOLPONE. Fall on me, roof, and bury me in ruin!
Become my grave, that wert my shelter! O!
I am unmasked, unspirited,° undone, *dejected*
Betrayed to beggary, to infamy—

ACT 3, SCENE 8

[*Enter Mosca, bleeding.*]

MOSCA. Where shall I run, most wretched shame of men,
To beat out my unlucky brains?

VOLPONE. Here, here.
What! dost thou bleed?

MOSCA. O that his well-driven sword
Had been so courteous to have cleft me down
Unto the navel, ere I lived to see
My life, my hopes, my spirits, my patron, all
Thus desperately engagèd, by my error!

VOLPONE. Woe on thy fortune!

MOSCA. And my follies, sir.

[1] *Mars ... Erycine* Venus (Erycine, after Eryx in Sicily) and Mars were adulterous lovers.

[2] *Sophy* The Persian Shah or Supreme Ruler.

[3] *Grand Signior* Great Sultan of Turkey.

[4] *Nestor* Elderly king in Homer's *Iliad*; "Nestor's hernia" suggests impotence.

[5] *dross* The scum shaven off metal during the smelting process. In this case, Bonario seems to be referring to Volpone's gold.

VOLPONE. Thou hast made me miserable.
MOSCA. And myself, sir.
Who would have thought he would have hearkened so?
VOLPONE. What shall we do?
MOSCA. I know not; if my heart
Could expiate the mischance, I'd pluck it out.
Will you be pleased to hang me, or cut my throat?
And I'll requite you, sir. Let's die like Romans,
Since we have lived like Grecians.[1]

[*They knock without.*]

VOLPONE. Hark! who's there?
I hear some footing; officers, the Saffi,° *bailiffs*
Come to apprehend us! I do feel the brand
Hissing already at my forehead; now,
Mine ears are boring.[2]
MOSCA. To your couch, sir, you,
Make that place good, however. [*Volpone lies down.*] Guilty men
Suspect what they deserve still. [*Opens door.*] Signior Corbaccio!

ACT 3, SCENE 9

[*Enter Corbaccio.*]

CORBACCIO. Why, how now, Mosca?

[*Enter Voltore, behind.*]

MOSCA. O, undone, amazed, sir.
Your son, I know not by what accident,
Acquainted with your purpose to my patron,
Touching your will, and making him your heir,
Entered our house with violence, his sword drawn
Sought for you, called you wretch, unnatural,
Vowed he would kill you.
CORBACCIO. Me!
MOSCA. Yes, and my patron.
CORBACCIO. This act shall disinherit him indeed;
Here is the will.
MOSCA. 'Tis well, sir.
CORBACCIO. Right and well:
Be you as careful now for me.
MOSCA. My life, sir,
Is not more tendered; I am only yours.
CORBACCIO. How does he? will he die shortly, think'st thou?
MOSCA. I fear
He'll outlast May.
CORBACCIO. To-day?
MOSCA. No, last out May, sir.
CORBACCIO. Could'st thou not give him a dram?[3]
MOSCA. O, by no means, sir.
CORBACCIO. Nay, I'll not bid you.
VOLTORE. [*Aside.*] This is a knave, I see.
MOSCA. [*Aside.*] How! Signior Voltore! Did he hear me?
VOLTORE. Parasite!
MOSCA. Who's that?—O, sir, most timely welcome—[*joins Voltore*]
Voltore. Scarce,
To the discovery of your tricks, I fear.
You are his, only? And mine also, are you not?
MOSCA. Who? I, sir?
VOLTORE. You, sir. What device is this
About a will?
MOSCA. A plot for you, sir.
VOLTORE. Come,
Put not your foists[4] upon me; I shall scent them.
MOSCA. Did you not hear it?
VOLTORE. Yes, I hear Corbaccio
Hath made your patron there his heir.
MOSCA. 'Tis true,
By my device, drawn to it by my plot,
With hope—
VOLTORE. Your patron should reciprocate?
And you have promised?
MOSCA. For your good, I did, sir.
Nay, more, I told his son, brought, hid him here,

---

1 *Romans ... Grecians* Ancient Romans were characterized as being willing to commit suicide rather than face dishonor. Ancient Greeks were often depicted as dissolute and histrionic.

2 *the brand ... boring* Branding on the forehead and cropping the ears were common punishments. Jonson himself had been branded on the thumb for killing the actor Gabriel Spencer in a duel.

3 *a dram* Dose of poison.

4 *foists* Knaveries.

Where he might hear his father pass the deed:
Being persuaded to it by this thought, sir,
That the unnaturalness, first, of the act,
And then his father's oft disclaiming° in him *disowning*
(Which I did mean t'help on), would sure enrage him
To do some violence upon his parent,
On which the law should take sufficient hold,
And you be stated° in a double hope:[1] *instated*
Truth be my comfort, and my conscience,
My only aim was to dig you a fortune
Out of these two old rotten sepulchres—

VOLTORE. I cry thee mercy, Mosca.

MOSCA. Worth your patience,
And your great merit, sir. And see the change!

VOLTORE. Why, what success?

MOSCA. Most hapless! you must help, sir.
Whilst we expected the old raven, in comes
Corvino's wife, sent hither by her husband—

VOLTORE. What, with a present?

MOSCA. No, sir, on visitation—
I'll tell you how anon— and staying long,
The youth he grows impatient, rushes forth,
Seizeth the lady, wounds me, makes her swear—
Or he would murder her, that was his vow—
To affirm my patron to have done her rape:
Which how unlike it is, you see! and hence,
With that pretext he's gone, to accuse his father,
Defame my patron, defeat you—

VOLTORE. Where is her husband?
Let him be sent for straight.

MOSCA. Sir, I'll go fetch him.

VOLTORE. Bring him to the Scrutineo.[2]

MOSCA. Sir, I will.

VOLTORE. This must be stopped.

MOSCA. O you do nobly, sir.
Alas, 'twas laboured all, sir, for your good;
Nor was there want of counsel° in the plot: *deliberation*
But fortune can, at any time, o'erthrow
The projects of a hundred learned clerks, sir.

CORBACCIO. [*Listening.*] What's that?

VOLTORE. Will't please you, sir, to go along?

[*Exit Voltore, Corbaccio.*]

MOSCA. Patron, go in, and pray for our success.

VOLPONE. Need makes devotion: heaven your labour bless!

[*Exeunt.*]

ACT 4, SCENE 1

(*Enter Sir Politic Would-be and Peregrine.*)

SIR POLITIC. I told you, sir, it was a plot:[3] you see
What observation is! You mentioned° me *asked*
For some instructions: I will tell you, sir
(Since we are met here in this height° *latitude*
of Venice),
Some few particulars I have set down,
Only for this meridian, fit to be known
Of your crude° traveller; and they are *inexperienced*
these.
I will not touch, sir, at your[4] phrase, or clothes,
For they are old.

PEREGRINE. Sir, I have better.

SIR POLITIC. Pardon,
I meant, as they are themes.° *topics*

PEREGRINE. O, sir, proceed:
I'll slander you no more of wit, good sir.

SIR POLITIC. First, for your garb,° it *demeanour*
must be grave and serious,
Very reserved and locked;° not tell a secret *enigmatic*
On any terms, not to your father; scarce
A fable, but with caution: make sure choice
Both of your company, and discourse; beware
You never speak a truth—

PEREGRINE. How!

SIR POLITIC. Not to strangers,
For those be they you must converse with most;
Others I would not know,° sir, but at *acknowledge*
distance,
So as I still might be a saver in them:
You shall have tricks else passed upon you hourly.
And then, for your religion, profess none,

---

[1] *double hope* I.e., Both Volpone and Corbaccio's fortunes.

[2] *Scrutineo* The Venetian law courts.

[3] *it was a plot* The mountebank scene, Act 2, Scene 2.

[4] *your* Used impersonally, which Peregrine pretends to misinterpret.

But wonder at the diversity of all:
And, for your part, protest, were there no other
But simply the laws o' the land, you could content you,
Nick Machiavel,[1] and Monsieur Bodin,[2] both
Were of this mind. Then must you learn the use
And handling of your silver fork[3] at meals,
The metal[4] of your glass; (these are main matters
With your Italian;) and to know the hour
When you must eat your melons, and your figs.
PEREGRINE. Is that a point of state too?
SIR POLITIC. Here it is:
For your Venetian, if he see a man
Preposterous in the least, he has him straight;[5]
He has: he strips° him. I'll acquaint you, sir, *ridicules*
I now have lived here, 'tis some fourteen months
Within the first week of my landing here,
All took me for a citizen of Venice,
I knew the forms so well—
PEREGRINE. [*Aside.*] And nothing else.
SIR POLITIC. I had read Contarine,[6] took me a house,
Dealt with my Jews[7] to furnish it with
moveables°— *furniture*
Well, if I could but find one man, one man
To mine own heart, whom I durst trust, I would—
PEREGRINE. What, what, sir?
SIR POLITIC. Make him rich; make him a fortune:
He should not think again. I would command it.
PEREGRINE. As how?
SIR POLITIC. With certain projects that I have;
Which I may not discover.° *reveal*
PEREGRINE. [*Aside.*] If I had
But one to wager with, I would lay odds now,
He tells me instantly.
SIR POLITIC. One is, and that
I care not greatly who knows, to serve the state
Of Venice with red herrings[8] for three years,
And at a certain rate, from Rotterdam,
Where I have correspondence. There's a letter,
Sent me from one o' the states, and to that purpose:
He cannot write his name, but that's his mark.
PEREGRINE. He is a chandler?[9]
SIR POLITIC. No, a cheesemonger.
There are some others too with whom I treat
About the same negotiation;
And I will undertake it: for, 'tis thus.
I'll do't with ease, I have cast° it all: Your hoy[10] *reckoned*
Carries but three men in her, and a boy;
And she shall make me three returns a year:
So, if there come but one of three, I save;
If two, I can defalk.° But this is now, *allow a deduction*
If my main project fail.
PEREGRINE. Then you have others?
SIR POLITIC. I should be loath to draw the subtle air
Of such a place, without my thousand aims.
I'll not dissemble, sir: where'er I come,
I love to be considerative;° and 'tis true, *thoughtful*
I have at my free hours thought upon
Some certain goods unto the state of Venice,
Which I do call my cautions; and, sir, which
I mean, in hope of pension, to propound
To the Great Council, then unto the Forty,
So to the Ten.[11] My means° are made already— *contacts*
PEREGRINE. By whom?
SIR POLITIC. Sir, one that, though his place be
obscure,
Yet he can sway, and they will hear him. He's
A commandatore.
PEREGRINE. What, a common sergeant?° *bailiff*

---

[1] *Nick Machiavel* Niccolò Machiavelli, author of *The Prince*.

[2] *Monsieur Bodin* Jean Bodin advocated religious toleration as imposition of orthodoxy was liable to undermine the state.

[3] *fork* Forks were still rarely used in England.

[4] *metal* Lead is employed in the making of fine crystal glassware.

[5] *If he see … him straight* I.e., if a Venetian comes across a man whose fashion is disordered, he spots him at once for a foreigner.

[6] *Contarine* Translated into English in 1599, *De Magistratibus et Republica Venetorum* was a book on Venetian history and culture, written by Cardinal Gasparo Contarini.

[7] *my Jews* Remarks such as this, which we now consider racist and offensive, were casually made at this time. Jews were frequently associated with the lending of money (for centuries one of the few occupations they were not restricted from entering) and thus with pressing to be paid amounts owed.

[8] *red herrings* Herrings turned red when prepared by smoking. The modern idiomatic use of "red herring" was not current at the time of writing.

[9] *chandler* Candle maker.

[10] *hoy* Small vessel for passengers and goods.

[11] *Great Council … the Ten* The administrative and political hierarchy of Venice.

SIR POLITIC. Sir, such as they are, put it in their mouths,° *the mouths of the great*
What they should say, sometimes; as well as greater:
I think I have my notes to show you—
PEREGRINE. Good sir.
SIR POLITIC. But you shall swear unto me, on your gentry,
Not to anticipate—
PEREGRINE. I, sir!
SIR POLITIC. Nor reveal
A circumstance—My paper is not with me.
PEREGRINE. O, but you can remember, sir.
SIR POLITIC. My first is
Concerning tinder-boxes. You must know,
No family is here without its box.
Now, sir, it being so portable a thing,
Put case, that you or I were ill affected
Unto the state, sir; with it in our pockets,
Might not I go into the Arsenale,[1]
Or you, come out again, and none the wiser?
PEREGRINE. Except yourself, sir.
SIR POLITIC. Go to, then. I therefore
Advertise to the state, how fit it were,
That none but such as were known patriots,
Sound lovers of their country, should be suffered
To enjoy them in their houses; and even those
Sealed at some office, and at such a bigness
As might not lurk in pockets.
PEREGRINE. Admirable!
SIR POLITIC. My next is, how to enquire, and be resolved,
By present demonstration, whether a ship,
Newly arrived from Soria,[2] or from
Any suspected part of all the Levant,[3]
Be guilty of the plague: and where they use
To lie out forty, fifty days, sometimes,
About the Lazaretto,[4] for their trial;
I'll save that charge and loss unto the merchant,
And in an hour clear the doubt.
PEREGRINE. Indeed, sir!
SIR POLITIC. Or—I will lose my labour.
PEREGRINE. My faith, that's much.
SIR POLITIC. Nay, sir, conceive me. It will cost me in onions,[5]
Some thirty livres[6]—
PEREGRINE. Which is one pound sterling.
SIR POLITIC. Beside my water-works: for this I do, sir,
First, I bring in your ship 'twixt two brick walls;
But those the state shall venture: On the one
I strain me a fair tarpaulin, and in that
I stick my onions, cut in halves: the other
Is full of loop-holes, out at which I thrust
The noses of my bellows; and those bellows
I keep, with water-works, in perpetual motion,
Which is the easiest matter of a hundred.
Now, sir, your onion, which doth naturally
Attract the infection, and your bellows blowing
The air upon him, will show, instantly,
By his changed colour, if there be contagion;
Or else remain as fair as at the first.
—Now it is known, 'tis nothing.
PEREGRINE. You are right, sir.
SIR POLITIC. I would I had my note.
PEREGRINE. Faith, so would I:
But you have done well for once, sir.
SIR POLITIC. Were I false,
Or would be made so, I could show you reasons
How I could sell this state now to the Turk,
Spite of their galleys, or their—
PEREGRINE. Pray you, Sir Politic.
SIR POLITIC. I have them not about me.
PEREGRINE. That I feared:
They are there, sir.
SIR POLITIC. No, this is my diary,
Wherein I note my actions of the day.
PEREGRINE. Pray you, let's see, sir. What is here? "Notandum,
A rat had gnawn my spur-leathers; notwithstanding,
I put on new, and did go forth: but first
I threw three beans over the threshold. Item,

[1] *Arsenale* Sir Politic affects the Italian pronunciation here with four syllables. The Arsenal was the storehouse of all the ships and weapons of Venice.

[2] *Soria* Italian pronunciation of "Syria," affected by Sir Politic.

[3] *the Levant* Area including modern day Syria, Lebanon, Israel, Palestine, and Jordan.

[4] *Lazaretto* Literally, leprosy house. One of two quarantined islands where ships suspected of carrying the plague were sent for a period.

[5] *onions* Supposed to protect against the plague.

[6] *livres* French coins.

I went and bought two toothpicks,[1] whereof one
I burst[2] immediately, in a discourse
With a Dutch merchant, 'bout ragion del stato.[3]
From him I went and paid a *mocenigo*[4]
For piecing[5] my silk stockings; by the way
I cheapened sprats;[6] and at St. Mark's I urined."° *urinated*
'Faith these are politic[7] notes!
SIR POLITIC. Sir, I do slip
No action of my life, but thus I quote it.
PEREGRINE. Believe me, it is wise!
SIR POLITIC. Nay, sir, read forth.

ACT 4, SCENE 2

(*Enter Lady Politic Would-be, Nano, and two Women*.)

LADY POLITIC. Where should this loose knight be, trow?[8] Sure he's housed.[9]
NANO. Why, then he's fast.[10]
LADY POLITIC. Aye, he plays both with me.
I pray you stay. This heat will do more harm
To my complexion, than his heart is worth.
I do not care to hinder, but to take him.—
How it comes off!
1 WOM. My master's yonder.
LADY POLITIC. Where?
2 WOM. With a young gentleman.
LADY POLITIC. That same's the party;
In man's apparel! Pray you, sir, jog my knight:
I will be tender to his reputation,
However he demerit.° *merits blame*
SIR POLITIC. My lady!
PEREGRINE. Where?
SIR POLITIC. 'Tis she indeed, sir; you shall know her. She is,
Were she not mine, a lady of that merit,
For fashion and behaviour; and for beauty
I durst compare—
PEREGRINE. It seems you are not jealous,
That dare commend her.
SIR POLITIC. Nay, and for discourse—
PEREGRINE. Being your wife, she cannot miss that.
SIR POLITIC. Madam,
Here is a gentleman, pray you, use him fairly;
He seems a youth, but he is—
LADY POLITIC. None.
SIR POLITIC. Yes, one
Has put his face as soon into the world—
LADY POLITIC. You mean, as early? but to-day?
SIR POLITIC. How's this?
LADY POLITIC. Why, in this habit, sir; you apprehend me:—
Well, Master Would-be,[11] this doth not become you;
I had thought the odour, sir, of your good name
Had been more precious to you; that you would not
Have done this dire massacre on your honour;
One of your gravity and rank besides!
But knights, I see, care little for the oath
They make to ladies; chiefly, their own ladies.
SIR POLITIC. Now, by my spurs, the symbol of my knighthood,—
PEREGRINE. [*Aside*.] Lord, how his brain is humbled for an oath!
SIR POLITIC. I reach° you not. *understand*
LADY POLITIC. Right, sir, your policy
May bear it through thus. [*To Peregrine*.] —Sir, a word with you.
I would be loath to contest publicly
With any gentlewoman, or to seem
Froward,° or violent, as *The Courtier*[12] says; *unreasonable*
It comes too near rusticity in a lady,
Which I would shun by all means: and however
I may deserve from master Would-be, yet

[1] *toothpicks* People carried their own toothpicks at this time. They were sometimes made of gold, silver, or other fine materials.

[2] *burst* Broke.

[3] *ragion del stato* Reason of state (here political affairs).

[4] *mocenigo* Venetian coin.

[5] *piecing* Mending.

[6] *cheapened sprats* Bartered for fish.

[7] *politic* A play on Sir Politic and politically astute.

[8] *trow* Do you suppose?

[9] *housed* I.e., at a bawdy house.

[10] *loose ... fast* The game "fast and loose" is being punned on.

[11] *Master Would-Be* This form of address indicates that the Sir Pol only recently bought his knighthood.

[12] *The Courtier* Baldassare Castiglione's courtesy book, *The Courtier*, was immensely popular.

T'have one fair gentlewoman thus be made
The unkind instrument to wrong another,
And one she knows not, aye, and to persévér;° *persevere*
In my poor judgment, is not warranted
From being a solecism[1] in our sex,
If not in manners.
PEREGRINE. How is this!
SIR POLITIC. Sweet madam,
Come nearer to your aim.
LADY POLITIC. Marry, and will, sir.
Since you provoke me with your impudence,
And laughter of your light° land-siren[2] here, *immoral*
Your Sporus,[3] your hermaphrodite—
PEREGRINE. What's here?
Poetic fury, and historic storms!
SIR POLITIC. The gentleman, believe it, is of worth,
And of our nation.
LADY POLITIC. Aye, your Whitefriars[4] nation.
Come, I blush for you, Master Would-be, I:
And am ashamed you should have no more forehead,[5]
Than thus to be the patron, or St. George,
To a lewd harlot, a base fricatrice,° *prostitute*
A female devil, in a male outside.
SIR POLITIC. Nay,
An you be such a one, I must bid adieu
To your delights. The case appears too liquid.

[*Exit.*]

LADY POLITIC. Aye, you may carry't clear, with your state-face!—
But for your carnival concupiscence,° *lust*
Who here is fled for liberty of conscience,
From furious persecution of the marshal,° *prison officer*
Her will I disple.° *discipline*
PEREGRINE. This is fine, i'faith!
And do you use this° often? Is this part *act this way*
Of your wit's exercise, 'gainst° you have occasion? *whenever*
Madam—
LADY POLITIC. Go to, sir.
PEREGRINE. Do you hear me, lady?
Why, if your knight have set you to beg shirts,
Or to invite me home, you might have done it
A nearer way, by far.
LADY POLITIC. This cannot work you
Out of my snare.
PEREGRINE. Why, am I in it, then?
Indeed your husband told me you were fair.
And so you are; only your nose inclines,
That side that's next the sun, to the queen-apple.° *early variety of apple*
LADY POLITIC. This cannot be endured by any patience.

ACT 4, SCENE 3

(*Enter Mosca.*)

MOSCA. What is the matter, madam?
LADY POLITIC. If the Senate
Right not my quest in this, I will protest them
To all the world, no aristocracy.
MOSCA. What is the injury, lady?
LADY POLITIC. Why, the callet° *prostitute*
You told me of, here I have ta'en disguised.
MOSCA. Who? This! What means your ladyship? The creature
I mentioned to you is apprehended now,
Before the senate; you shall see her—
LADY POLITIC. Where?
MOSCA. I'll bring you to her. This young gentleman,
I saw him land this morning at the port.
LADY POLITIC. Is't possible? How has my judgment wandered?
Sir, I must, blushing, say to you, I have erred;
And plead your pardon.
PEREGRINE. What, more changes yet!
LADY POLITIC. I hope you have not the malice to remember
A gentlewoman's passion. If you stay

---

[1] *solecism* Impropriety.

[2] *land-siren* The Sirens were mythical seductresses of the sea.

[3] *Sporus* Favorite of Nero. Nero castrated Sporus, dressed him as a woman, and married him publicly.

[4] *Whitefriars* Notorious abode of criminals within the city of London.

[5] *forehead* Capacity to blush.

In Venice here, please you to use me,[1] sir—
MOSCA. Will you go, madam?
LADY POLITIC. Pray you, sir, use me; in faith,
The more you see me, the more I shall conceive
You have forgot our quarrel.

[*Exeunt Lady Politic, Mosca, Nano, and Waiting-women.*]

PEREGRINE. This is rare!
Sir Politic Would-be? No; Sir Politic Bawd,
To bring me thus acquainted with his wife!
Well, wise Sir Pol, since you have practised thus
Upon my freshmanship,[2] I'll try your salt-head,[3]
What proof it is against a counter-plot.

ACT 4, SCENE 4

(*Enter Voltore, Corbaccio, Corvino.*)

VOLTORE. Well, now you know the carriage of the business,
Your constancy is all that is required
Unto the safety of it.
MOSCA. Is the lie
Safely conveyed amongst us? is that sure?
Knows every man his burden?° *part in the lie*
CORVINO. Yes.
MOSCA. Then shrink not.
CORVINO. But knows the advocate the truth?
MOSCA. O, sir,
By no means; I devised a formal° tale, *elaborate*
That salved° your reputation. But be valiant, sir. *saved*
CORVINO. I fear no one but him, that this his pleading
Should make him stand for a co-heir—
MOSCA. Co-halter!
Hang him; we will but use his tongue, his noise,
As we do Croaker's[4] here.
CORVINO. Aye, what shall he do?
MOSCA. When we have done, you mean?
CORVINO. Yes.
MOSCA. Why, we'll think:
Sell him for mummia;[5] he's half dust already.
[*To Voltore.*] Do you not smile, to see this buffalo,
How he doth sport it with his head?[6] (*Aside.*) I should,
If all were well and past. (*To Corbaccio.*) Sir, only you
Are he that shall enjoy the crop of all,
And these not know for whom they toil.
CORBACCIO. Aye, peace.
MOSCA. [*To Corvino.*] But you shall eat it.[7] Much!
[*Then to Voltore again.*] —Worshipful sir,
Mercury[8] sit upon your thundering tongue,
Or the French Hercules,[9] and make your language
As conquering as his club, to beat along,
As with a tempest, flat, our adversaries;
But much more yours, sir.
VOLTORE. Here they come, have done.
MOSCA. I have another witness, if you need, sir,
I can produce.
VOLTORE. Who is it?
MOSCA. Sir, I have her.

ACT 4, SCENE 5

(*Enter 4 Avocatori, Bonario, Celia, Notario, Commandatori, and Others.*)

1 AVOCATORI. The like of this the Senate never heard of.
2 AVOCATORI. 'Twill come most strange to them when we report it.
4 AVOCATORI. The gentlewoman has been ever held
Of unreproved name.
3 AVOCATORI. So, the young man.

[1] *use* Be socially useful, but also with the suggestion of sexual licentiousness.

[2] *practiced thus... freshmanship* Contrived against my inexperience. Peregrine mistakenly believes Sir Politic has attempted to trick him.

[3] *salt-head* Experienced head; also, bawdy mind.

[4] *Croaker's* Indicating Corbaccio.

[5] *mummia* Pulverized dust made of supposed Egyptian mummies was thought to have medicinal powers.

[6] *see this buffalo... head* Alluding to the horns of a cuckold (and said while pointing to Corvino).

[7] *eat it* Enjoy Volpone's legacy.

[8] *Mercury* God of eloquence and thieves.

[9] *French Hercules* While returning from his tenth labour, Hercules was supposed to have fathered the Celts in Gaul (modern France). The Gallic Hercules was a symbol of eloquence.

4 AVOCATORI. The more unnatural part that of his father.
2 AVOCATORI. More of the husband.
1 AVOCATORI. I not know to give
His act a name, it is so monstrous!
4 AVOCATORI. But the impostor, he's a thing created
To exceed example!
1 AVOCATORI. And all after-times!° *future examples*
2 AVOCATORI. I never heard a true voluptuary
Described, but him.
3 AVOCATORI. Appear yet those were cited?° *summoned*
NOTARIO. All but the old magnifico, Volpone.
1 AVOCATORI. Why is not he here?
MOSCA. Please your fatherhoods,
Here is his advocate: himself's so weak,
So feeble—
4 AVOCATORI. What are you?
BONARIO. His parasite,
His knave, his pander. I beseech the court,
He may be forced to come, that your grave eyes
May bear strong witness of his strange impostures.
VOLTORE. Upon my faith and credit with your virtues,
He is not able to endure the air.
2 AVOCATORI. Bring him, however.
3 AVOCATORI. We will see him.
4 AVOCATORI. Fetch him.
VOLTORE. Your fatherhoods'[1] fit pleasures be obeyed;
But sure, the sight will rather move your pities,
Than indignation. May it please the court,
In the mean time, he may be heard in me;
I know this place most void of prejudice,
And therefore crave it, since we have no reason
To fear our truth should hurt our cause.
3 AVOCATORI. Speak free.
VOLTORE. Then know, most honoured fathers, I must now
Discover to your strangely abusèd° ears, *deceived*
The most prodigious and most frontless° piece *shameless*
Of solid impudence, and treachery,
That ever vicious nature yet brought forth
To shame the state of Venice. This lewd woman,
That wants no artificial looks or tears
To help the visor° she has now put on, *mask*
Hath long been known a close° adulteress *secret*
To that lascivious youth there; not suspected,
I say, but known, and taken in the act
With him; and by this man, the easy husband,
Pardoned; whose timeless° bounty makes him now *unwise*
Stand here, the most unhappy, innocent person,
That ever man's own goodness made accused.
For these not knowing how to owe° a gift *own*
Of that dear grace, but with their shame; being placed
So above all powers of their gratitude,
Began to hate the benefit; and, in place
Of thanks, devise to extirpe° the memory *extirpate*
Of such an act: wherein I pray your fatherhoods
To observe the malice, yea, the rage of creatures
Discovered in their evils; and what heart° *boldness*
Such take, even from their crimes:—but that anon
Will more appear.—This gentleman, the father,
Hearing of this foul fact, with many others,
Which daily struck at his too tender ears,
And grieved in nothing more than that he could not
Preserve himself a parent, (his son's ills
Growing to that strange flood,) at last decreed
To disinherit him.
1 AVOCATORI. These be strange turns!
2 AVOCATORI. The young man's fame was ever fair and honest.
VOLTORE. So much more full of danger is his vice,
That can beguile so under shade of virtue.
But, as I said, my honoured sires, his father
Having this settled purpose, by what means
To him betrayed, we know not, and this day
Appointed for the deed; that parricide,
I cannot style him better, by confederacy° *conspiracy*
Preparing this his paramour to be there,
Entered Volpone's house, (who was the man,
Your fatherhoods must understand, designed
For the inheritance,) there sought his father:—
But with what purpose sought he him, my lords?
(I tremble to pronounce it, that a son
Unto a father, and to such a father,
Should have so foul, felonious intent)
It was to murder him. When, being prevented
By his more happy absence, what then did he?

[1] *fatherhoods'* The correct form of address, but Volpone later mocks it as pretentious in 5.2.

Not check his wicked thoughts: no, now new deeds:
(Mischief doth never end where it begins)
An act of horror, fathers! he dragged forth
The agèd gentleman that had there lain bed-rid
Three years and more, out of his innocent couch,
Naked upon the floor, there left him; wounded
His servant in the face: and, with this strumpet
The stale[1] to his forged practice, who was glad
To be so active, (I shall here desire
Your fatherhoods to note but my collections,
As most remarkable) thought, at once, to stop
His father's ends;° discredit his free choice, *aims*
In the old gentleman; redeem themselves,
By laying infamy upon this man,
To whom, with blushing, they should owe their lives.
1 AVOCATORI. What proofs have you of this?
BONARIO. Most honoured fathers,
I humbly crave there be no credit given
To this man's mercenary tongue.
2 AVOCATORI. Forbear.
BONARIO. His soul moves in his fee.
3 AVOCATORI. O, sir.
BONARIO. This fellow,
For six sols more, would plead against his maker.
1 AVOCATORI. You do forget yourself.
VOLTORE. Nay, nay, grave fathers,
Let him have scope: can any man imagine
That he will spare his accuser, that would not
Have spared his parent?
1 AVOCATORI. Well, produce your proofs.
CELIA. I would I could forget I were a creature.
VOLTORE. Signior Corbaccio!
4 AVOCATORI. What is he?
VOLTORE. The father.
2 AVOCATORI. Has he had an oath?
NOTARIO. Yes.
CORBACCIO. What must I do now?
NOTARIO. Your testimony's craved.
CORBACCIO. Speak to the knave?
I'll have my mouth first stopped with earth; my heart
Abhors his knowledge: I disclaim in him.
1 AVOCATORI. But for what cause?
CORBACCIO. The mere
portent° of nature! *signs*

[1] *stale* Lure; also, a kind of prostitute used by thieves as a decoy.

He is an utter stranger to my loins.
BONARIO. Have they made° you to this? *forced*
CORBACCIO. I will not hear thee,
Monster of men, swine, goat, wolf, parricide!
Speak not, thou viper.
BONARIO. Sir, I will sit down,
And rather wish my innocence should suffer,
Than I resist the authority of a father.
VOLTORE. Signior Corvino!
2 AVOCATORI. This is strange.
1 AVOCATORI. Who's this?
NOTARIO. The husband.
4 AVOCATORI. Is he sworn?
NOTARIO. He is.
3 AVOCATORI. Speak, then.
CORVINO. This woman, please your fatherhoods, is a whore,
Of most hot exercise, more than a partridge,[2]
Upon record—
1 AVOCATORI. No more.
CORVINO. Neighs like a jennet.° *horse*
NOTARIO. Preserve the honour of the court.
CORVINO. I shall,
And modesty of your most reverend ears.
And yet I hope that I may say, these eyes
Have seen her glued unto that piece of cedar,
That fine well-timbered gallant; and that here
The letters may be read, thorough the horn,[3]
That make the story perfect.
MOSCA. Excellent! sir.
CORVINO. There is no shame in this now, is there?
MOSCA. None.
CORVINO. Or if I said, I hoped that she were onward
To her damnation, if there be a hell
Greater than whore and woman; a good Christian
May make the doubt.
3 AVOCATORI. His grief hath made him frantic.
1 AVOCATORI. Remove him hence.

[2] *partridge* Supposed to be the most lecherous bird.

[3] *thorough the horn* Pun based on the horns of the cuckold and the hornbooks, early grammars and primers, from which children learned to read. Corvino holds his forked fingers up to his head, displaying the horns of the cuckold, thus making himself a "hornbook."

(*Celia swoons.*)

2 AVOCATORI. Look to the woman.
CORVINO. Rare!
Prettily feigned, again!
4 AVOCATORI. Stand from about her.
1 AVOCATORI. Give her the air.
3 AVOCATORI. (*To Mosca.*) What can you say?
MOSCA. My wound,
May it please your wisdoms, speaks for me, received
In aid of my good patron, when he missed
His sought-for father, when that well-taught dame
Had her cue given her, to cry out, "A rape!"
BONARIO. O most laid° impudence! Fathers— *plotted*
3 AVOCATORI. Sir, be silent;
You had your hearing free, so must they theirs.
2 AVOCATORI. I do begin to doubt the imposture here.
4 AVOCATORI. This woman has too many moods.
VOLTORE. Grave fathers,
She is a creature of a most professed
And prostituted lewdness.
CORVINO. Most impetuous,
Unsatisfied, grave fathers!
VOLTORE. May her feignings
Not take your wisdoms: but this day she baited
A stranger, a grave knight, with her loose eyes,
And more lascivious kisses. This man saw them
Together on the water, in a gondola.
MOSCA. Here is the lady herself, that saw them too;
Without; who then had in the open streets
Pursued them, but for saving her knight's honour.
1 AVOCATORI. Produce that lady.
2 AVOCATORI. Let her come.

[*Exit Mosca.*]

4 AVOCATORI. These things,
They strike with wonder!
3 AVOCATORI. I am turned a stone!

ACT 4, SCENE 6

(*Enter Mosca with Lady Politic Would-be.*)

MOSCA. Be resolute, madam.
LADY POLITIC. Aye, this same is she.
Out, thou chameleon harlot! Now thine eyes
Vie tears with the hyena.[1] Dar'st thou look
Upon my wronged face?—I cry your pardons,
I fear I have forgettingly transgressed
Against the dignity of the court—
2 AVOCATORI. No, madam.
LADY POLITIC. And been exorbitant—° *outrageous*
2 AVOCATORI. You have not, lady.
4 AVOCATORI. These proofs are strong.
LADY POLITIC. Surely, I had no purpose
To scandalize your honours, or my sex's.
3 AVOCATORI. We do believe it.
LADY POLITIC. Surely, you may believe it.
2 AVOCATORI. Madam, we do.
LADY POLITIC. Indeed you may; my breeding
Is not so coarse—
4 AVOCATORI. We know it.
LADY POLITIC. To offend
With pertinacy—[2]
3 AVOCATORI. Lady—
LADY POLITIC. Such a presence!
No surely.
1 AVOCATORI. We well think it.
LADY POLITIC. You may think it.
1 AVOCATORI. Let her o'ercome.° *have the last word*
What witnesses have you
To make good your report?
BONARIO. Our consciences.
CELIA. And heaven, that never fails the innocent.
4 AVOCATORI. These are no testimonies.
BONARIO. Not in your courts,
Where multitude,° and clamour overcomes. *numbers*
1 AVOCATORI. Nay, then you do wax insolent.

---

[1] *tears with the hyena* Crocodiles were supposed to shed tears to lure their prey, while hyenas lured prey with their human voices. Lady Politic here confuses the two.

[2] *pertinacy* It seems that Lady Politic means "impertinence."

(*Volpone is brought in, as impotent.*[1])

VOLTORE. Here, here,
The testimony comes, that will convince,
And put to utter dumbness their bold tongues:
See here, grave fathers, here's the ravisher,
The rider on men's wives, the great impostor,
The grand voluptuary! Do you not think
These limbs should affect venery?° Or these eyes *pursuit of sexual pleasure*
Covet a concubine? Pray you mark these hands;
Are they not fit to stroke a lady's breasts?—
Perhaps he doth dissemble!
BONARIO. So he does.
VOLTORE. Would you have him tortured?
BONARIO. I would have him proved.° *tested*
VOLTORE. Best try him then with goads, or burning irons;
Put him to the strappado:[2] I have heard
The rack hath cured the gout;[3] faith, give it him,
And help him of a malady; be courteous.
I'll undertake, before these honoured fathers,
He shall have yet as many left diseases,
As she has known° adulterers, or thou strumpets. *known carnally*
O, my most equal° hearers, if these deeds, *unbiased*
Acts of this bold and most exorbitant strain,
May pass with sufferance, what one citizen
But owes the forfeit of his life, yea, fame,
To him that dares traduce him? Which of you
Are safe, my honoured fathers? I would ask,
With leave of your grave fatherhoods, if their plot
Have any face or colour like to truth?
Or if, unto the dullest nostril here,
It smell not rank, and most abhorrèd slander?
I crave your care of this good gentleman,
Whose life is much endangered by their fable;
And as for them, I will conclude with this,
That vicious persons, when they're hot and fleshed
In impious acts, their constancy° abounds: *resolution*
Damned deeds are done with greatest confidence.
1 AVOCATORI. Take them to custody, and sever them.
2 AVOCATORI. 'Tis pity two such prodigies° should live. *monsters*
1 AVOCATORI. Let the old gentleman be returned with care.
I'm sorry our credulity hath wronged him.

[*Exeunt Officers with Volpone.*]

4 AVOCATORI. These are two creatures!
3 AVOCATORI. I've an earthquake in me.
2 AVOCATORI. Their shame, even in their cradles, fled their faces.
4 AVOCATORI. [*To Voltore.*] You have done a worthy service to the state, sir,
In their discovery.
1 AVOCATORI. You shall hear, ere night,
What punishment the court decrees upon them.
VOLTORE. We thank your fatherhoods.

[*Exeunt Avocatori, Notario, and Officers with Bonario and Celia.*]

How like you it?
MOSCA. Rare.
I'd have your tongue, sir, tipped with gold for this;
I'd have you be the heir to the whole city;
The earth I'd have want men, ere you want living:° *lack livelihood*
They're bound to erect your statue in St. Mark's.
Signior Corvino, I would have you go
And show yourself, that you have conquered.
CORVINO. Yes.
MOSCA. It was much better that you should profess
Yourself a cuckold thus, than that the other[4]
Should have been proved.
CORVINO. Nay, I considered that:
Now it is her fault.
MOSCA. Then it had been yours.
CORVINO. True; I do doubt this advocate still.
MOSCA. I'faith
You need not, I dare ease you of that care.

[1] *impotent* I.e., disabled.

[2] *strappado* Form of torture in which the victim's hands were tied behind his back and secured to a pulley, with which the victim was then lifted.

[3] *rack hath cured the gout* Both a popular belief and a joke, as gout affected the joints in the legs.

[4] *the other* I.e., procuring his wife for Volpone.

CORVINO. I trust thee, Mosca.
MOSCA. As your own soul, sir.

[*Exit Corvino.*]

CORBACCIO. Mosca!
MOSCA. Now for your business, sir.
CORBACCIO. How! Have you business?
MOSCA. Yes, yours, sir.
CORBACCIO. O, none else?
MOSCA. None else, not I.
CORBACCIO. Be careful, then.
MOSCA. Rest you with both your eyes, sir.
CORBACCIO. Dispatch it.
MOSCA. Instantly.
CORBACCIO. And look that all,
Whatever, be put in, jewels, plate, moneys.
Household stuff, bedding, curtains.
MOSCA. Curtain-rings, sir:
Only the advocate's fee must be deducted.
CORBACCIO. I'll pay him now; you'll be too prodigal.
MOSCA. Sir, I must tender it.
CORBACCIO. Two cecchines is well.
MOSCA. No, six, sir.
CORBACCIO. 'Tis too much.
MOSCA. He talked a great while;
You must consider that, sir.
CORBACCIO. Well, there's three—
MOSCA. I'll give it him.
CORBACCIO. Do so, and there's for thee.

[*Exit Corbaccio.*]

MOSCA. Bountiful bones![1] What horrid strange offence
Did he commit 'gainst nature, in his youth,
Worthy this age?[2] (*To Voltore.*) You see, sir, how I work
Unto your ends: take you no notice.
VOLTORE. No,
I'll leave you.

[*Exit Voltore.*]

MOSCA. All is yours, the devil and all:
Good advocate!—Madam, I'll bring you home.
LADY POLITIC. No, I'll go see your patron.
MOSCA. That you shall not:
I'll tell you why. My purpose is to urge
My patron to reform° his will; and for *rewrite*
The zeal you have shown to-day, whereas before
You were but third or fourth, you shall be now
Put in the first: which would appear as begged,
If you were present. Therefore—
LADY POLITIC. You shall sway° me. *persuade*

[*Exeunt.*]

ACT 5, SCENE 1

(*Enter Volpone.*)

VOLPONE. Well, I am here, and all this brunt° *crisis*
is past.
I ne'er was in dislike with my disguise
Till this fled° moment: here 'twas good, in *past*
private;
But in your public,—cavè° whilst I breathe. *beware*
'Fore God, my left leg 'gan to have the cramp,
And I apprehended straight some power had struck me
With a dead palsy: well, I must be merry,
And shake it off. A many of these fears
Would put me into some villainous disease,
Should they come thick upon me: I'll prevent 'em.
Give me a bowl of lusty wine, to fright
This humour from my heart. (*He drinks.*) Hum,
hum, hum!
'Tis almost gone already; I shall conquer.
Any device, now, of rare ingenious knavery,
That would possess me with a violent laughter,
Would make me up again. (*Drinks again.*) So, so, so, so.
This heat is life; 'tis blood by this time:—Mosca!

---

[1] *Beautiful bones* Mosca notes Corbaccio's leanness, avarice and age.

[2] *Worthy this age* To deserve an old age like this.

ACT 5, SCENE 2

(*Enter Mosca.*)

MOSCA. How now, sir? Does the day look clear again?
Are we recovered, and wrought out of error,
Into our way, to see our path before us?
Is our trade free once more?
VOLPONE. Exquisite Mosca!
MOSCA. Was it not carried learnedly?
VOLPONE. And stoutly:
Good wits are greatest in extremities.
MOSCA. It were a folly beyond thought, to trust
Any grand act unto a cowardly spirit:
You are not taken° with it enough, methinks. *pleased*
VOLPONE. O, more than if I had enjoyed the wench:
The pleasure of all woman-kind's not like it.
MOSCA. Why now you speak, sir. We must here
be fixed;
Here we must rest; this is our master-piece;
We cannot think to go beyond this.
VOLPONE. True,
Thou hast played thy prize, my precious Mosca.
MOSCA. Nay, sir,
To gull° the court— *deceive*
VOLPONE. And quite divert the torrent
Upon the innocent.
MOSCA. Yes, and to make
So rare a music out of discords—
VOLPONE. Right.
That yet to me's the strangest, how thou hast
borne° it! *managed*
That these, being so divided 'mongst themselves,
Should not scent somewhat, or in me or thee,
Or doubt their own side.
MOSCA. True, they will not see't.[1]
Too much light blinds them, I think. Each of them
Is so possessed[2] and stuffed with his own hopes,
That any thing unto the contrary,
Never so true, or never so apparent,
Never so palpable, they will resist it—
VOLPONE. Like a temptation of the devil.

MOSCA. Right, sir.
Merchants may talk of trade, and your great signiors
Of land that yields well; but if Italy
Have any glebe° more fruitful than these fellows, *soil*
I am deceived. Did not your advocate rare?[3]
VOLPONE. O—'My most honoured fathers, my
grave fathers,
Under correction of your fatherhoods,
What face of truth is here? If these strange deeds
May pass, most honoured fathers'—I had much ado
To forbear laughing.
MOSCA. It seemed to me, you sweat, sir.
VOLPONE. In troth, I did a little.
MOSCA. But confess, sir,
Were you not daunted?° *dazed*
VOLPONE. In good faith, I was
A little in a mist, but not dejected;
Never, but still my self.
MOSCA. I think° it, sir. *believe*
Now, so truth help me, I must needs say this, sir,
And out of conscience for your advocate,
He has taken pains, in faith, sir, and deserved,
In my poor judgment, I speak it under
favour,° *with permission*
Not to contrary° you, sir, very richly— *contradict*
Well—to be cozened.° *cheated*
VOLPONE. Troth, and I think so too,
By that I heard him, in the latter end.
MOSCA. O, but before, sir: had you heard him first
Draw it to certain heads, then aggravate,[4]
Then use his vehement figures—I looked still
When he would shift a shirt:[5] and, doing this
Out of pure love, no hope of gain—
VOLPONE. 'Tis right.
I cannot answer° him, Mosca, as I would, *repay*
Not yet; but for thy sake, at thy entreaty,
I will begin, even now—to vex them all,
This very instant.
MOSCA. Good sir.
VOLPONE. Call the dwarf

[1] *They will not see't* Proverbial: there is none so blind as a person who will not see.

[2] *possessed* Both "in possession of," and "being possessed by."

[3] *rare* I.e., rear up, attack the case eagerly.

[4] *aggravate* Put weight upon; emphasize through seriousness of tone.

[5] *shift a shirt* Mosca intimates that Voltore's violent gesticulation will cause him to need to change his shirt.

And eunuch forth.
MOSCA. Castrone, Nano!

[*Enter Castrone and Nano.*]

NANO. Here.
VOLPONE. Shall we have a jig now?
MOSCA. What you please, sir.
VOLPONE. Go, straight give out about the streets, you two,
That I am dead; do it with constancy,° *conviction*
Sadly, do you hear? Impute it to the grief
Of this late slander.

[*Exeunt Castrone and Nano.*]

MOSCA. What do you mean, sir?
VOLPONE. O,
I shall have instantly my Vulture, Crow,
Raven, come flying hither, on the news,
To peck for carrion, my she-wolf, and all,
Greedy, and full of expectation—
MOSCA. And then to have it ravished from their mouths?
VOLPONE. 'Tis true. I will have thee put on a gown,
And take upon thee, as thou wert mine heir:
Show them a will: open that chest, and reach
Forth one of those that has the blanks;[1] I'll straight
Put in thy name.
MOSCA. [*Getting a blank will.*] It will be rare,[2] sir.
VOLPONE. Aye,
When they ev'n gape, and find themselves deluded—
MOSCA. Yes.
VOLPONE. And thou use them scurvily!
Dispatch, get on thy gown.
MOSCA. [*Dressing.*] But what, sir, if they ask
After the body?
VOLPONE. Say, it was corrupted.
MOSCA. I'll say, it stunk, sir; and was fain° *obliged* to have it
Coffined up instantly, and sent away.
VOLPONE. Any thing; what thou wilt. Hold, here's my will.
Get thee a cap, a count-book,° pen and ink, *ledger*
Papers afore thee; sit as thou wert taking
An inventory of parcels. I'll get up
Behind the curtain, on a stool, and hearken;
Sometime peep over, see how they do look,
With what degrees their blood doth leave their faces,
O, 'twill afford me a rare meal of laughter!
MOSCA. Your advocate will turn stark dull upon it.
VOLPONE. It will take off his oratory's edge.
MOSCA. But your clarissimo,° *Venetian nobleman* old round-back, he
Will crump you like a hog-louse,° *wood louse* with the touch.
VOLPONE. And what Corvino?
MOSCA. O, sir, look for him,
To-morrow morning, with a rope and dagger,[3]
To visit all the streets; he must run mad.
My lady too, that came into the court,
To bear false witness for your worship—
VOLPONE. Yes,
And kissed me 'fore the fathers, when my face
Flowed all with oils.
MOSCA. And sweat — sir. Why, your gold
Is such another med'cine, it dries up
All those offensive savours: it transforms
The most deformed, and restores them lovely,
As 'twere the strange poetical girdle.[4] Jove
Could not invent t'himself a shroud more subtle
To pass Acrisius' guards.[5] It is the thing
Makes all the world her grace, her youth, her beauty.
VOLPONE. I think she loves me.
MOSCA. Who? the lady, sir?
She's jealous of you.[6]
VOLPONE. Dost thou say so?

[*Knocking outside.*]

[1] *blanks* In pre-made legal documents like wills, spaces were left for the names of heirs to be filled in.

[2] *rare* Here, splendid, fine, i.e., a splendid joke.

[3] *rope and dagger* Stock symbols of suicidal madness.

[4] *poetical girdle* Jonson himself glosses this as "Cestus," or Venus's girdle, which had magical powers to make the wearer irresistible.

[5] *Acrisius' guards* Acrisius was the King of Argos, father of Danaë. According to legend, to keep his daughter from becoming pregnant with a son who had been prophesied to kill him, he locked her in a tower. Zeus then came to Danaë in a shower of gold and impregnated her, and the gold of the shower corrupted Acrisius's guards.

[6] *jealous of you* Devoted to your well being.

MOSCA. Hark,
There's some already.
VOLPONE. Look.
MOSCA. It is the Vulture;
He has the quickest scent.
VOLPONE. I'll to my place,
Thou to thy posture.° *pretence*

[*Conceals himself.*]

MOSCA. I am set.
VOLPONE. But, Mosca,
Play the artificer now, torture them rarely.

ACT 5, SCENE 3

(*Enter Voltore.*)

VOLTORE. How now, my Mosca?
MOSCA. Turkey carpets,[1] nine—
VOLTORE. Taking an inventory! That is well.
MOSCA. Two suits of bedding, tissue—[2]
VOLTORE. Where's the will?
Let me read that the while.

[*Enter Corbaccio in a sedan chair.*]

CORBACCIO. So, set me down,
And get you home.

[*Exeunt Servants.*]

VOLTORE. Is he come now, to trouble us!
MOSCA. Of cloth of gold, two more—
CORBACCIO. Is it done, Mosca?
MOSCA. Of several velvets° eight— *velvet hangings*
VOLTORE. I like his care.
CORBACCIO. Dost thou not hear?

[*Enter Corvino.*]

CORBACCIO. Ha! Is the hour come, Mosca?

(*Volpone peeps from behind a traverse.*)[3]

VOLPONE. (*Aside.*) Aye, now they muster.
CORVINO. What does the advocate here,
Or this Corbaccio?
CORBACCIO. What do these here?

[*Enter Lady Politic Would-be.*]

LADY POLITIC. Mosca!
Is his thread spun?[4]
MOSCA. Eight chests of linen—
VOLPONE. O,
My fine dame Would-be, too!
CORVINO. Mosca, the will,
That I may show it these, and rid them hence.
MOSCA. Six chests of diaper,[5] four of damask.[6]—
There.

[*Gives Corvino the will.*]

CORBACCIO. Is that the will?
MOSCA. Down-beds and bolsters—
VOLPONE. [*Aside.*] Rare!
Be busy still. Now they begin to flutter:
They never think of me. Look, see, see, see!
How their swift eyes run over the long deed,
Unto the name, and to the legacies,
What is bequeathed them there—
MOSCA. Ten suits of hangings—
VOLPONE. [*Aside.*] Aye, in their garters,[7] Mosca. Now their hopes
Are at the gasp.
VOLTORE. Mosca the heir!
CORBACCIO. What's that?

---

1 *Turkey carpets* Used as tapestries and table covers.

2 *suits of bedding* Bed curtains and hangings in expensive materials; *tissue* Rich cloth woven with gold or silver threads.

3 *traverse* Curtain.

4 *If his thread spun?* I.e., is he dead? Reference to the Fates, who spin the thread of life, determine its length, and cut it.

5 *diaper* Linen with a diamond pattern weave.

6 *damask* Fabric with designs figured into its weave.

7 *in their garters* Volpone puns on the saying, "Hang yourself in your own garters."

VOLPONE. [*Aside.*] My advocate is dumb; look to my merchant,
He has heard of some strange storm, a ship is lost,
He faints; my lady will swoon. Old glazen-eyes,[1]
He hath not reached his despair yet.
CORBACCIO. All these
Are out of hope; I am, sure, the man.
CORVINO. But, Mosca—
MOSCA. Two cabinets.
CORVINO. Is this in earnest?
MOSCA. One
Of ebony—
CORVINO. Or do you but delude me?
MOSCA. The other, mother of pearl—I am very busy.
Good faith, it is a fortune thrown° upon me— *thrust*
Item, one salt° of agate—not my seeking. *salt-cellar*
LADY POLITIC. Do you hear, sir?
MOSCA. A perfumed box—Pray you forbear,
You see I'm troubled°—made of an onyx— *busy*
LADY POLITIC. How?
MOSCA. Tomorrow or next day, I shall be at leisure
To talk with you all.
CORVINO. Is this my large hope's issue?
LADY POLITIC. Sir, I must have a fairer answer.
MOSCA. Madam!
Marry, and shall: pray you, fairly° quit my house. *peacefully*
Nay, raise no tempest with your looks; but hark you,
Remember what your ladyship offered me
To put you in an heir; go to, think on it:
And what you said e'en your best madams did
For maintenance; and why not you? Enough.
Go home, and use the poor Sir Pol, your knight, well,
For fear I tell some riddles;° go, be melancholy. *secrets*

[*Exit Lady Politic Would-be.*]

VOLPONE. O, my fine devil!
CORVINO. Mosca, pray you a word.
MOSCA. Lord! Will you not take your dispatch hence yet?
Methinks, of all, you should have been the example.
Why should you stay here? With what thought, what promise?
Hear you; do you not know, I know you an ass,
And that you would most fain have been a wittol,° *willing cuckold*
If fortune would have let you? That you are
A declared cuckold, on good terms? This pearl,
You'll say, was yours? Right. This diamond?
I'll not deny't, but thank you. Much here else?
It may be so. Why, think that these good works
May help to hide your bad. I'll not betray you;
Although you be but extraordinary,
And have it only in title, it sufficeth:
Go home, be melancholy too, or mad.

[*Exit Corvino.*]

VOLPONE. [*Aside.*] Rare Mosca! How his villainy becomes him!
VOLTORE. Certain he doth delude all these for me.
CORBACCIO. Mosca the heir!
VOLPONE. [*Aside.*] O, his four eyes have found it.
CORBACCIO. I am cozened, cheated, by a parasite slave;
Harlot,° thou hast gulled me. *rascal*
MOSCA. Yes, sir. Stop your mouth,
Or I shall draw the only tooth is left.
Are not you he, that filthy covetous wretch,
With the three legs,° that here, in hope of prey, *two legs and a cane*
Have, any time this three years, snuffed about,
With your most grovelling nose, and would have hired
Me to the poisoning of my patron, sir?
Are not you he that have to-day in court
Professed the disinheriting of your son?
Perjured yourself? Go home, and die, and stink.
If you but croak a syllable, all comes out:
Away, and call your porters! Go, go, stink.

[*Exit Corbaccio.*]

VOLPONE. [*Aside.*] Excellent varlet!
VOLTORE. Now, my faithful Mosca,
I find thy constancy.
MOSCA. Sir?
VOLTORE. Sincere.
MOSCA. A table

[1] *glazen-eyes* Corbaccio wears glasses.

Of porphyry—I mar'l° you'll be thus troublesome. *marvel*
VOLTORE. Nay, leave off now, they are gone.
MOSCA. Why, who are you?
What! who did send for you? O, cry you mercy,
Reverend sir! Good faith, I am grieved for you,
That any chance of mine should thus defeat
Your (I must needs say) most deserving travails:
But I protest, sir, it was cast upon me,
And I could almost wish to be without it,
But that the will o' the dead must be observed.
Marry, my joy is that you need it not;
You have a gift, sir (thank your education),
Will never let you want, while there are men,
And malice, to breed causes.° Would I had *law-suits*
But half the like, for all my fortune, sir!
If I have any suits, as I do hope,
Things being so easy and direct, I shall not,
I will make bold with your obstreperous aid,
Conceive me,—for your fee, sir. In mean time,
You that have so much law, I know have the conscience
Not to be covetous of what is mine.
Good sir, I thank you for my plate; 'twill help
To set up a young man. Good faith, you look
As you were costive; best go home and purge, sir.

[*Exit Voltore.*]

VOLPONE. [*Coming forward.*] Bid him eat lettuce[1] well.
My witty mischief,
Let me embrace thee. O that I could now
Transform thee to a Venus!—Mosca, go,
Straight take my habit of clarissimo,[2]
And walk the streets; be seen, torment them more:
We must pursue, as well as plot. Who would
Have lost this feast?
MOSCA. I doubt it will lose them.
VOLPONE. O, my recovery shall recover all.
That I could now but think on some disguise
To meet them in, and ask them questions:
How I would vex them still at every turn!
MOSCA. Sir, I can fit you.
VOLPONE. Canst thou?
MOSCA. Yes, I know
One o' the Commandatori, sir, so like you;
Him will I straight make drunk, and bring you his habit.
VOLPONE. A rare disguise, and answering thy brain!
O, I will be a sharp disease unto them.
MOSCA. Sir, you must look for curses—
VOLPONE. Till they burst;
The Fox fares ever best when he is cursed.

[*Exeunt.*]

ACT 5, SCENE 4

[*Enter Peregrine disguised, and three Merchants.*]

PEREGRINE. Am I enough disguised?
1 MERCHANT. I warrant° you. *assure*
PEREGRINE. All my ambition is to fright him only.
2 MERCHANT. If you could ship him away, 'twere excellent.
3 MERCHANT. To Zant, or to Aleppo?[3]
PEREGRINE. Yes, and have his
Adventures put i'th'*Book of Voyages*,[4]
And his gulled story° registered for truth. *story of his deceiving*
Well, gentlemen, when I am in a while,
And that you think us warm in our discourse,
Know your approaches.
1 MERCHANT. Trust it to our care.

[*Exeunt Merchants. Enter Waiting-woman.*]

PEREGRINE. Save you, fair lady! Is Sir Pol within?
WOMAN. I do not know, sir.
PEREGRINE. Pray you say unto him,
Here is a merchant, upon earnest° business, *important*
Desires to speak with him.
WOMAN. I will see, sir.
PEREGRINE. Pray you.

[1] *Bid him eat lettuce* Lettuce was considered to be a remedy both for constipation and for frenzy.

[2] *habit of clarissimo* Clothing of a gentleman.

[3] *Zant ... Aleppo* Greek island owned by Venice and a town in Syria.

[4] *Book of Voyages* Possibly referring to Hakluyt's *Principal Navigations*, published in 1598–1600; books of voyages were popular throughout the period.

[*Aside.*] I see the family is all female here.[1]
WOMAN. He says, sir, he has weighty affairs of state,
That now require him whole; some other time
You may possess him.
PEREGRINE. Pray you say again,
If those require him whole, these will exact
him,° *demand his attention*
Whereof I bring him tidings. [*Exit Woman.*] What
might be
His grave affair of state now! How to make
Bolognian sausages here in Venice, sparing
One o' the ingredients?

[*Re-enter Woman.*]

WOMAN. Sir, he says, he knows
By your word "tidings," that you are no
statesman,° *agent of the state, spy*
And therefore wills you stay.
PEREGRINE. Sweet, pray you return him;
I have not read so many proclamations,
And studied them for words, as he has done—
But—here he deigns to come.

[*Enter Sir Politic.*]

SIR POLITIC. Sir, I must crave
Your courteous pardon. There hath chanced to-day,
Unkind disaster 'twixt my lady and me;
And I was penning my apology,
To give her satisfaction, as you came now.
PEREGRINE. Sir, I am grieved I bring you worse disaster:
The gentleman you met at the port to-day,
That told you, he was newly arrived—
SIR POLITIC. Aye, was
A fugitive punk?° *prostitute*
PEREGRINE. No, sir, a spy set on you;
And he has made relation to the Senate,
That you professed to him to have a plot
To sell the state of Venice to the Turk.
SIR POLITIC. O me!
PEREGRINE. For which, warrants are signed by
this time,
To apprehend you, and to search your study
For papers—
SIR POLITIC. Alas, sir, I have none, but notes
Drawn out of play-books—
PEREGRINE. All the better, sir.[2]
SIR POLITIC. And some essays.[3] What shall I do?
PEREGRINE. Sir, best
Convey yourself into a sugar-chest;
Or, if you could lie round,° a frail[4] were rare, *curl up*
And I could send you aboard.
SIR POLITIC. Sir, I but talked so,
For discourse sake merely.

(*They knock without.*)

PEREGRINE. Hark! they are there.
SIR POLITIC. I am a wretch, a wretch!
PEREGRINE. What will you do, sir?
Have you ne'er a currant-butt° to leap *cask for currants*
into?
They'll put you to the rack; you must be sudden.° *quick*
SIR POLITIC. Sir, I have an engine—
3 MERCHANT. Sir Politic Would-be!
2 MERCHANT. Where is he?
SIR POLITIC. That I have thought upon
before time.
PEREGRINE. What is it?
SIR POLITIC. I shall ne'er endure the torture.
Marry, it is, sir, of a tortoise-shell,
Fitted for these extremities: Pray you, sir, help me.
[*Gets into the shell.*] Here I've a place, sir, to put back
my legs,
Please you to lay it on, sir. With this cap,
And my black gloves. I'll lie, sir, like a tortoise,
'Till they are gone.
PEREGRINE. And call you this an engine?
SIR POLITIC. Mine own device°— *invention*
Good sir, bid my wife's women
To burn my papers.

[1] *the family…here* Peregrine thinks he has stumbled upon a brothel.

[2] *All the better, sir* Writeres risked imprisonment on evidenced by the authorities "deciphering" their texts. Jonson had been imprisoned twice for "seditious" comments in his plays.

[3] *essays* The essay was a new genre, one that Jonson loathed.

[4] *frail* Basket for raisins and figs.

[*Exit Peregrine and Woman. The three merchants rush in.*]

1 MERCHANT. Where is he hid?
3 MERCHANT We must,
And will sure find him.
2 MERCHANT. Which is his study?

[*Re-enter Peregrine.*]

1 MERCHANT. What
Are you, sir?
PEREGRINE. I am a merchant, that came here
To look upon this tortoise.
3 MERCHANT. How!
1 MERCHANT. St. Mark!
What beast is this!
PEREGRINE. It is a fish.
2 MERCHANT. Come out here!
PEREGRINE. Nay, you may strike him, sir, and tread upon him;
He'll bear a cart.
1 MERCHANT. What, to run over him?
PEREGRINE. Yes.
3 MERCHANT. Let's jump upon him.
2 MERCHANT. Can he not go?
PEREGRINE. He creeps, sir.
1 MERCHANT. Let's see him creep.
PEREGRINE. No, good sir, you will hurt him.
2 MERCHANT. Heart, I will see him creep, or prick his guts.
3 MERCHANT. Come out here!
PEREGRINE. Pray you, sir! (*To Sir Politic.*) Creep a little.
1 MERCHANT. Forth.
2 MERCHANT. Yet farther.
PEREGRINE. Good sir!—Creep.
2 MERCHANT. We'll see his legs.

[*They pull off the shell and discover him.*]

3 MERCHANT. Godso,° he has garters! *God's soul*
1 MERCHANT. Aye, and gloves!
2 MERCHANT. Is this
Your fearful tortoise?
PEREGRINE. Now, Sir Pol, we are even;
For your next project I shall be prepared:
I am sorry for the funeral of your notes, sir.
1 MERCHANT. 'Twere a rare motion° *puppet-show*
to be seen in Fleet-street.
2 MERCHANT. Aye, in the Term.[1]
1 MERCHANT. Or Smithfield,[2] in the fair.
3 MERCHANT. Methinks 'tis but a melancholy sight.
PEREGRINE. Farewell, most politic tortoise!

[*Exeunt Peregrine and Merchants. Re-enter Waiting-woman.*]

SIR POLITIC. Where's my lady?
Knows she of this?
WOMAN. I know not, sir.
SIR POLITIC. Enquire.—
O, I shall be the fable of all feasts,
The freight of the gazetti,° ship-boy's tale; *topic of news reports*
And, which is worst, even talk for ordinaries.° *taverns*
WOMAN. My lady's come most melancholy home,
And says, sir, she will straight to sea, for physic.° *her health*
SIR POLITIC. And I to shun this place and clime for ever,
Creeping with house on back, and think it well
To shrink my poor head in my politic shell.

[*Exeunt.*]

ACT 5, SCENE 5

(*Enter Volpone, Mosca; the first, in the habit of a Commandatore, and the other, of a Clarissimo.*)

VOLPONE. Am I then like him?[3]
MOSCA. O, sir, you are he:
No man can sever° you. *distinguish*
VOLPONE. Good.
MOSCA. But what am I?
VOLPONE. 'Fore heaven, a brave clarissimo; thou

[1] *the Term* Season when the law courts were in session.
[2] *Smithfield* Location of Bartholomew Fair, a large market.
[3] *like him?* I.e., the Commandatore.

becom'st it!
Pity thou wert not born one.
MOSCA. If I hold° *keep*
My made one,° 'twill be well. *feigned status*
VOLPONE. I'll go and see
What news first at the court.

[*Exit.*]

MOSCA. Do so. My Fox
Is out of his hole, and ere he shall re-enter,
I'll make him languish in his borrowed case,
Except he come to composition° with me. *an agreement*
Androgyno, Castrone, Nano!

[*Enter Androgyno, Castrone, and Nano.*]

ALL. Here.
MOSCA. Go, recreate yourselves
abroad;° go sport. *outside*

[*Exeunt Androgyno, Castrone, and Nano.*]

So, now I have the keys, and am possessed.
Since he will needs be dead afore his time,
I'll bury him, or gain by him: I am his heir,
And so will keep me,° till he share at least. *remain*
To cozen him of all, were but a cheat
Well placed; no man would construe it a sin:
Let his sport pay for't. This is called the Fox-trap.

[*Exit.*]

ACT 5, SCENE 6

(*Enter Corbaccio and Corvino.*)

CORBACCIO. They say, the court is set.
CORVINO. We must maintain
Our first tale good, for both our reputations.
CORBACCIO. Why, mine's no tale: my son would
there have killed me.
CORVINO. That's true, I had forgot. Mine is, I'm sure.
But for your will, sir.
CORBACCIO. Aye, I'll come upon him
For that hereafter, now his patron's dead.

[*Enter Volpone.*]

VOLPONE. Signior Corvino! And Corbaccio! sir,
Much joy unto you.
CORVINO. Of what?
VOLPONE. The sudden good
Dropped down upon you—
CORBACCIO. Where?
VOLPONE. And none knows how,
From old Volpone, sir.
CORBACCIO. Out, arrant knave!
VOLPONE. Let not your too much wealth, sir, make you
furious.
CORBACCIO. Away, thou varlet!
VOLPONE. Why, sir?
CORBACCIO. Dost thou mock me?
VOLPONE. You mock the world, sir; did you not
change wills?
CORBACCIO. Out, harlot!
VOLPONE. O! Belike you are the man,
Signior Corvino? Faith, you carry it well;
You grow not mad withal; I love your spirit:
You are not over-leavened° with your fortune. *over inflated*
You should have some would swell now, like a wine-vat,
With such an autumn—Did he give you all, sir?
CORVINO. Avoid,° you rascal! *go away*
VOLPONE. Troth, your wife has shown
Herself a very woman; but you are well,
You need not care, you have a good estate,
To bear it out, sir, better by this chance:
Except° Corbaccio have a share. *unless*
CORBACCIO. Hence, varlet.
VOLPONE. You will not be aknown,° *acknowledged*
sir; why, 'tis wise.
Thus do all gamesters, at all games, dissemble:
No man will seem to win. [*Exeunt Corvino and
Corbaccio.*]
Here comes my vulture,
Heaving his beak up in the air, and snuffing.

ACT 5, SCENE 7

(*Enter Voltore.*)

VOLTORE. Outstripped thus, by a parasite! a slave,
Would run on errands, and make legs for crumbs!
Well, what I'll do—
VOLPONE. The court stays for your worship.
I e'en rejoice, sir, at your worship's happiness,
And that it fell into so learned hands,
That understand the fingering—
VOLTORE. What do you mean?
VOLPONE. I mean to be a suitor to your worship,
For the small tenement, out of reparations,
That, to the end of your long row of houses,
By the Piscaria:[1] it was, in Volpone's time,
Your predecessor, ere he grew diseased,
A handsome, pretty, customed° bawdy-house *patronized*
As any was in Venice, none dispraised;
But fell with him: his body and that house
Decayed together.
VOLTORE. Come, sir, leave your prating.
VOLPONE. Why, if your worship give me but your hand,° *handshake*
That I may have the refusal, I have done.
'Tis a mere toy to you, sir; candle-rents;[2]
As your learned worship knows—
VOLTORE. What do I know?
VOLPONE. Marry, no end of your wealth, sir; God decrease it!
VOLTORE. Mistaking knave! what, mock'st thou my misfortune?
VOLPONE. His blessing on your heart, sir; would 'twere more!—

[*Exit Voltore.*]

Now to my first again, at the next corner.

[1] *Piscaria* Fish market, located on a wharf just south of the Piazza di San Marco.

[2] *candle-rents* Rent from properties that are deteriorating (as a candle burns itself out).

ACT 5, SCENE 8

(*Enter Corbaccio, Corvino, Mosca passant.*)[3]

CORBACCIO. See, in our habit! See the impudent varlet!
CORVINO. That I could shoot mine eyes at him like gunstones!° *cannonballs*
VOLPONE. But is this true, sir, of the parasite?
CORBACCIO. Again, to afflict us! Monster!
VOLPONE. In good faith, sir,
I'm heartily grieved, a beard of your grave length[4]
Should be so over-reached. I never brooked° *endured*
That parasite's hair; methought his nose should cozen:
There still was somewhat in his look, did promise
The bane of a clarissimo.
CORBACCIO. Knave—
VOLPONE. Methinks
Yet you, that are so traded in the world,
A witty merchant, the fine bird, Corvino,
That have such moral emblems[5] on your name,
Should not have sung your shame, and dropped your cheese,
To let the fox laugh at your emptiness.
CORVINO. Sirrah, you think the privilege of the place,[6]
And your red saucy cap, that seems to me
Nailed to your jolt-head° with those two cecchines,[7] *blockhead*
Can warrant your abuses; come you hither:
You shall perceive, sir, I dare beat you; approach.
VOLPONE. No haste, sir, I do know your valour well,
Since you durst publish what you are,[8] sir.
CORVINO. Tarry,
I'd speak with you.
VOLPONE. Sir, sir, another time—
CORVINO. Nay, now.
VOLPONE. O lord, sir! I were a wise man,

[3] *passant* I.e., crosses the stage.

[4] *a beard of … length* I am as old as yourself.

[5] *moral emblems* Allegorical drawings of animals with accompanying verses, on themes such as greed, lechery, love, etc.

[6] *privilege of place* The commandatore uniform that disguises Volpone also protects him.

[7] *red saucy cap … two cecchines* A commandatore wore a red hat with two medallions of St. Mark hanging from either side.

[8] *what you are* I.e., a cuckold.

Would stand the fury of a distracted cuckold.

(*Mosca walks by 'em.*)

CORBACCIO. What, come again!
VOLPONE. Upon 'em, Mosca; save me.
CORBACCIO. The air's infected where he breathes.
CORVINO. Let's fly him.

[*Exeunt Corvino and Corbaccio.*]

VOLPONE. Excellent basilisk![1] Turn upon the vulture.

ACT 5, SCENE 9

(*Enter Voltore.*)

VOLTORE. Well, flesh-fly,° it is summer with you now; *blow-fly*
Your winter will come on.
MOSCA. Good advocate,
Prithee not rail, nor threaten out of place thus;
Thou'lt make a solecism, as madam says.
Get you a biggin° more, your brain breaks loose. *a lawyer's cap*

[*Exit.*]

VOLTORE. Well, sir.
VOLPONE. Would you have me beat the insolent slave,
Throw dirt upon his first good clothes?
VOLTORE. This same
Is doubtless some familiar.
VOLPONE. Sir, the court,
In troth, stays for you. I am mad, a mule
That never read Justinian,[2] should get up,
And ride an advocate. Had you no quirk° *trick*
To avoid gullage,° sir, by such a creature? *being made a fool*
I hope you do but jest; he has not done it,
'Tis but confederacy, to blind the rest.
You are the heir.
VOLTORE. A strange, officious,
Troublesome knave! Thou dost torment me.
VOLPONE. I know—
It cannot be, sir, that you should be cozened;
'Tis not within the wit of man to do it;
You are so wise, so prudent—and 'tis fit
That wealth and wisdom still should go together.—

ACT 5, SCENE 10

(*Enter Avocatori, Notario, Bonario, Celia, Corbaccio, Corvino, Commandatori, Saffi, etc.*)

1 AVOCATORI. Are all the parties here?
NOTARIO. All but the advocate.
2 AVOCATORI. And here he comes.
1 AVOCATORI.[3] Then bring them forth to sentence.
VOLTORE. O, my most honoured fathers, let your mercy
Once win upon° your justice, to forgive— *override*
I am distracted—
VOLPONE. [*Aside.*] What will he do now?
VOLTORE. O,
I know not which to address myself to first;
Whether your fatherhoods, or these innocents—
CORVINO. [*Aside.*] Will he betray himself?
VOLTORE. Whom equally
I have abused, out of most covetous ends—
CORVINO. The man is mad!
CORBACCIO. What's that?
CORVINO. He is possessed.[4]
VOLTORE. For which, now struck in conscience, here, I prostrate
Myself at your offended feet, for pardon.
1, 2 AVOCATORI. Arise.
CELIA. O heaven, how just thou art!
VOLPONE. [*Aside.*] I am caught
In mine own noose—
CORVINO. [*To Corbaccio.*] Be constant, sir: naught now
Can help, but impudence.

---

[1] *basilisk* A mythical reptile that could kill with its gaze.

[2] *Justinian* Roman law code compiled by Justinian.

[3] *1 Avocatori* Both quarto and folio are ambiguous over who should speak this line and it is possible that it was intended for all Avocatori to speak chorally.

[4] *possessed* I.e., by a devil.

1 AVOCATORI. [*To Voltore.*] Speak forward.° *continue speaking*
COMMANDATORI. Silence!
VOLTORE. It is not passion in me, reverend fathers,
But only conscience, conscience, my good sires,
That makes me now tell truth. That parasite,
That knave, hath been the instrument of all.
2 AVOCATORI. Where is that knave? Fetch him.
VOLPONE. I go.

[*Exit.*]

CORVINO. Grave fathers,
This man's distracted; he confessed it now:
For, hoping to be old Volpone's heir,
Who now is dead—
3 AVOCATORI. How?
2 AVOCATORI. Is Volpone dead?
CORVINO. Dead since,[1] grave fathers.
BONARIO. O sure vengeance!
1 AVOCATORI. Stay,
Then he was no deceiver.
VOLTORE. O no, none:
The parasite, grave fathers.
CORVINO. He does speak
Out of mere envy, 'cause the servant's made
The thing he gaped° for: please your fatherhoods, *gasped*
This is the truth, though I'll not justify
The other, but he may be some-deal° faulty. *somewhat*
VOLTORE. Aye, to your hopes, as well as mine, Corvino:
But I'll use modesty.° Pleaseth your wisdoms, *moderation*
To view these certain notes, and but confer° them; *compare*
As I hope favour, they shall speak clear truth.
CORVINO. The devil has entered him!
BONARIO. Or bides in you.
4 AVOCATORI. We have done ill, by a public officer[2]
To send for him, if he be heir.
2 AVOCATORI. For whom?
4 AVOCATORI. Him that they call the parasite.
3 AVOCATORI. 'Tis true,
He is a man of great estate, now left.
4 AVOCATORI. [*To Notario.*] Go you, and learn his name, and say, the court
Entreats his presence here, but to the clearing
Of some few doubts.

[*Exit Notario.*]

2 AVOCATORI. This same's a labyrinth!
1 AVOCATORI. Stand you unto your first report?
CORVINO. My state,° *estate*
My life, my fame—
BONARIO. Where is it?
CORVINO. Are at the stake.
1 AVOCATORI. Is yours so too?
CORBACCIO. The advocate's a knave,
And has a forkèd tongue—
2 AVOCATORI. Speak to the point.
CORBACCIO. So is the parasite too.
1 AVOCATORI. This is confusion.
VOLTORE. I do beseech your fatherhoods, read but those—
CORVINO. And credit nothing the false spirit hath writ:
It cannot be, but he's possessed, grave fathers.

ACT 5, SCENE 11[3]

(*Enter Volpone.*)

VOLPONE. To make a snare for mine own neck! And run
My head into it, wilfully! With laughter!
When I had newly 'scaped, was free, and clear,
Out of mere wantonness! O, the dull devil° *devil of stupidity*
Was in this brain of mine, when I devised it,
And Mosca gave it second; he must now
Help to sear° up this vein, or we bleed dead. *cauterize*

[*Enter Nano, Androgyno, and Castrone.*]

How now! Who let you loose? Whither go you now?
What, to buy gingerbread, or to drown kitlings?° *kittens*
NANO. Sir, master Mosca called us out of doors,
And bid us all go play, and took the keys.

[1] *since* Since the last time the court convened.

[2] *public officer* Volpone, disguised as a commandatore.

[3] *Act 5, Scene 11* Jonson seems to be using split staging here, with two parts of the city represented. No one leaves the stage, but the action of the courtroom scene is not resumed until Scene 12.

ANDROGYNO. Yes.
VOLPONE. Did master Mosca take the keys? Why so!
I'm farther in. These are my fine conceits!
I must be merry, with a mischief to me!
What a vile wretch was I, that could not bear
My fortune soberly? I must have my
crotchets,° *whimsical fantasies*
And my conundrums! Well, go you, and seek him:
His meaning may be truer than my fear.
Bid him, he straight come to me to the court;
Thither will I, and, if't be possible,
Unscrew[1] my advocate, upon° new hopes: *by means of*
When I provoked him, then I lost myself.

[*Exeunt.*]

ACT 5, SCENE 12

[*Avocatori, Bonario, Celia, Corbaccio, Corvino, Commandatori, Saffi, etc., as before.*]

1 AVOCATORI. [*Reading Voltore's notes.*] These things
can ne'er be reconciled. He, here,
Professeth, that the gentleman was wronged,
And that the gentlewoman was brought thither,
Forced by her husband, and there left.
VOLTORE. Most true.
CELIA. How ready is heaven to those that pray!
1 AVOCATORI. But that
Volpone would have ravished her, he holds
Utterly false, knowing his impotence.
CORVINO. Grave fathers, he's possessed; again, I say,
Possessed: nay, if there be possession, and
Obsession,[2] he has both.
3 AVOCATORI. Here comes our officer.

[*Enter Volpone.*]

VOLPONE. The parasite will straight be here, grave
fathers.
4 AVOCATORI. You might invent some other name, sir
varlet.
3 AVOCATORI. Did not the notary meet him?
VOLPONE. Not that I know.
4 AVOCATORI. His coming will clear all.
2 AVOCATORI. Yet,° it is misty. *for now*
VOLTORE. May't please your fatherhoods—

(*Volpone whispers* [*to*] *the Advocate.*)

VOLPONE. Sir, the parasite
Willed me to tell you, that his master lives;
That you are still the man; your hopes the same;
And this was only a jest—
VOLTORE. How?
VOLPONE. Sir, to try
If you were firm, and how you stood affected.
VOLTORE. Art sure he lives?
VOLPONE. Do I live, sir?
VOLTORE. O me!
I was too violent.
VOLPONE. Sir, you may redeem it.
They said, you were possessed; fall down, and seem so:
I'll help to make it good. [*Voltore falls.*]—God bless
the man!—
Stop your wind° hard, and swell— *hold your breath*
See, see, see, see!
He vomits crooked pins! his eyes are set,
Like a dead hare's hung in a poulter's° shop! *poulterer*
His mouth's running away! Do you see, Signior?
Now it is in his belly.[3]
CORVINO. Aye, the devil!
VOLPONE. Now in his throat.
CORVINO. Aye, I perceive it plain.
VOLPONE. 'Twill out, 'twill out! Stand clear. See
where it flies,
In shape of a blue toad, with a bat's wings!
Do you not see it, sir?

[1] *Unscrew* Tell him to change his present course of action.

[2] *obsession* Distinct from possession in that obsession was an attack by a devil from without, whereas possession is an attack from within.

[3] *They said ... his belly* Volpone alternates between coaching Voltore to appear possessed and addressing the court. Accounts of possession and the symptoms thereof were widely available in texts published during the period.

CORBACCIO. What? I think I do.
CORVINO. 'Tis too manifest.
VOLPONE. Look! He comes to himself!
VOLTORE. Where am I?
VOLPONE. Take good heart, the worst is past, sir.
You are dispossessed.
1 AVOCATORI. What accident° is this! *unforeseen event*
2 AVOCATORI. Sudden, and full of wonder!
3 AVOCATORI. If he were
Possessed, as it appears, all this is nothing.
CORVINO. He has been often subject to these fits.
1 AVOCATORI. Show him that writing:—do you know it, sir?
VOLPONE. [*To Voltore.*] Deny it, sir, forswear it; know it not.
VOLTORE. Yes, I do know it well, it is my hand;
But all that it contains is false.
BONARIO. O practice!° *trickery*
2 AVOCATORI. What maze is this!
1 AVOCATORI. Is he not guilty then,
Whom you there name the parasite?
VOLTORE. Grave fathers,
No more than his good patron, old Volpone.
4 AVOCATORI. Why, he is dead.
VOLTORE. O no, my honoured fathers,
He lives.—
1 AVOCATORI. How! lives?
VOLTORE. Lives.
2 AVOCATORI. This is subtler yet!
3 AVOCATORI. You said he was dead.
VOLTORE. Never.
3 AVOCATORI. You said so.
CORVINO. I heard so.
4 AVOCATORI. Here comes the gentleman; make him way.

[*Enter Mosca dressed as a clarissimo.*]

3 AVOCATORI. A stool!
4 AVOCATORI. A proper° man. [*Aside.*] *handsome*
And, were Volpone dead,
A fit match for my daughter.
3 AVOCATORI. Give him way.
VOLPONE. [*To Mosca.*] Mosca, I was almost lost; the advocate
Had betrayed all; but now it is recovered;
All's o'the hinge° again—Say, I am *running smoothly*
living.

(*Aside to Mosca.*)

MOSCA. What busy knave is this! Most reverend fathers,
I sooner had attended your grave pleasures,
But that my order for the funeral
Of my dear patron, did require me—
VOLPONE. Mosca!
MOSCA. Whom I intend to bury like a gentleman.
VOLPONE. Aye, quick,° and cozen me of all. *alive*
2 AVOCATORI. Still stranger!
More intricate!
1 AVOCATORI. And come about[1] again!
4 AVOCATORI. It is a match, my daughter is bestowed.
MOSCA. [*To Volpone.*] Will you give me half?
VOLPONE. [*To Mosca.*] First, I'll be hanged.
MOSCA. I know
Your voice is good, cry not so loud.
1 AVOCATORI. Demand° *ask*
The advocate.—Sir, did you not affirm
Volpone was alive?
VOLPONE. Yes, and he is;
This gentleman told me so. [*To Mosca.*] Thou shalt have half.—
MOSCA. Whose drunkard is this same? Speak, some that know him:
I never saw his face. [*To Volpone.*] I cannot now
Afford it you so cheap.
VOLPONE. No!
1 AVOCATORI. What say you?
VOLTORE. The officer told me.
VOLTORE. I did, grave fathers,
And will maintain he lives, with mine own life,
And that this creature told me. [*Aside.*] I was born
With all good stars my enemies.

---

[1] *come about* Turned around. 1 Avocatori expresses frustration that Volpone is dead, then alive, now dead again.

MOSCA. Most grave fathers,
If such an insolence as this must pass° *be allowed*
Upon me, I am silent: 'twas not this
For which you sent, I hope.
2 AVOCATORI. Take him away.
VOLPONE. [*To Mosca.*] Mosca!
3 AVOCATORI. Let him be whipped.
VOLPONE. Wilt thou betray me?
Cozen me?
3 AVOCATORI. And taught to bear himself
Toward a person of his rank.
4 AVOCATORI. Away.

[*Volpone is seized.*]

MOSCA. I humbly thank your fatherhoods.
VOLPONE. Soft, soft: Whipped!
And lose all that I have! (*Aside.*) If I confess,
It cannot be much more.
4 AVOCATORI. Sir, are you married?
VOLPONE. They'll be allied anon;° I must be resolute: *married soon*
The fox shall here uncase.° *remove his disguise (figuratively his fox's pelt)*

(*He puts off his disguise.*)

MOSCA. Patron![1]
VOLPONE. Nay, now
My ruins shall not come alone; your match
I'll hinder sure: my substance shall not glue you,
Nor screw you into a family.[2]
MOSCA. Why, patron!
VOLPONE. I am Volpone, and this is my knave;

[*Pointing to Mosca, Voltore, Corbaccio, Corvino, in turn.*]

This, his own knave; this, avarice's fool;
This, a chimera of wittol, fool, and knave:
And, reverend fathers, since we all can hope
Naught but a sentence, let's not now despair it.
You hear me brief.

[1] *Patron* Mosca pretends to be startled back into a servile role.

[2] *my substance ... family* You will not use my wealth to insinuate yourself into a marriage by sympathy or guile.

CORVINO. May it please your fatherhoods—
COMMANDATORI. Silence.
1 AVOCATORI. The knot is now undone by miracle.
2 AVOCATORI. Nothing can be more clear.
3 AVOCATORI. Or can more prove
These innocent.
1 AVOCATORI. Give them their liberty.
BONARIO. Heaven could not long let such gross crimes be hid.
2 AVOCATORI. If this be held the high-way to get riches,
May I be poor!
3 AVOCATORI. This is not the gain, but torment.
1 AVOCATORI. These possess wealth, as sick men possess fevers,
Which trulier may be said to possess them.
2 AVOCATORI. Disrobe that parasite.
CORVINO, MOSCA. Most honoured fathers!—
1 AVOCATORI. Can you plead aught to stay the course of justice!
If you, can speak.
CORVINO, VOLTORE. We beg favour.
CELIA. And mercy.
1 AVOCATORI. You hurt your innocence, suing for the guilty.
Stand forth; and first the parasite: You appear
T'have been the chiefest minister, if not plotter,
In all these lewd impostures; and now, lastly,
Have with your impudence abused the court,
And habit of a gentleman of Venice,
Being a fellow of no birth or blood:
For which our sentence is, first, thou be whipped;
Then live perpetual prisoner in our galleys.
VOLPONE. I thank you for him.
MOSCA. Bane to thy wolvish nature!
1 AVOCATORI. Deliver him to the Saffi.[3] By blood and rank a gentleman, canst not fall
Under like censure; but our judgment on thee
Is, that thy substance all be straight confiscate
To the hospital of the Incurabili:[4]
And, since the most was gotten by imposture,

[3] *Deliver him ... Saffi* There is no indication that Mosca or Volpone exit here; tradition has Volpone remain onstage throughout the sentencing.

[4] *Incurabili* The Hospital for Incurables was created for the treatment of sexually transmitted diseases in 1522.

By feigning lame, gout, palsy, and such diseases,
Thou art to lie in prison, cramped with irons,
Till thou be'st sick and lame indeed.—Remove him.
VOLPONE. This is called mortifying[1] of a Fox.
1 AVOCATORI. Thou, Voltore, to take away the scandal
Thou hast given all worthy men of thy profession,
Art banished from their fellowship, and our state.
Corbaccio—bring him near—we here possess
Thy son of all thy state, and confine thee
To the monastery of San Spirito;[2]
Where, since thou knew'st not how to live well here,
Thou shalt be learned to die well.
CORBACCIO. Ah! What said he?
COMMANDATORI. You shall know anon, sir.
1 AVOCATORI. Thou, Corvino, shalt
Be straight embarked from thine own house, and rowed
Round about Venice, through the Grand Canale,[3]
Wearing a cap, with fair long ass's ears,
Instead of horns; and so to mount, a paper
Pinned on thy breast, to the Berlino—° *pillory*
CORVINO. Yes,
And have mine eyes beat out with stinking fish,
Bruised fruit, and rotten eggs—'Tis well. I am glad
I shall not see my shame yet.
1 AVOCATORI. And to expiate
Thy wrongs done to thy wife, thou art to send her
Home to her father, with her dowry trebled:
And these are all your judgments—
ALL. Honoured fathers!
1 AVOCATORI. Which may not be revoked. Now you begin,
When crimes are done, and past, and to be punished,
To think what your crimes are: away with them.
Let all that see these vices thus rewarded,
Take heart and love to study 'em! Mischiefs feed
Like beasts, till they be fat, and then they bleed.

[*Exeunt.*]

VOLPONE. The seasoning of a play, is the applause.
Now, though the Fox be punished by the laws,
He yet doth hope, there is no suffering due,
For any fact° which he hath done 'gainst you; *crime*
If there be, censure him; here he doubtful stands.
If not, fare jovially, and clap your hands.

[*Exit.*]
—1606

[1] *mortifying* A pun: Humiliating; sentencing to death; tenderizing game by hanging it or keeping it alive before slaughtering it; disposing of property for religious or charitable purposes; rendering the flesh dead by spiritual discipline; giving one gangrene.

[2] *San Spirito* The monastery of the Holy Spirit.

[3] *Canale* The Italian pronunciation, with three syllables.

IN CONTEXT

Sources for *Volpone*

The fox as a trickster is a character with deep roots in the stories of many cultures (Aesop himself was said to have been a slave from Africa, eventually freed because of his talent). In writing *Volpone* Jonson also drew on a variety of other classical texts, including Horace's *Satires* (for his portrayals of hunting and of old age); "The Cock" by Lucian, Syrian author of satires in Greek (for the treatment of Pythagoras in the comic byplay of Act 1); and the anti-feminist Latin satires of Juvenal (for the character of Lady Politic Would-be).

from Aesop, *Fables* (6th century BCE)

The raven seized a piece of cheese and carried his spoils up to his perch high in a tree. A fox came up and walked in circles around the raven, planning a trick. "What is this," cried the fox. "O raven, the elegant proportions of your body are remarkable and you have a complexion that is worthy of the king of birds. If only you had a voice to match, you would be the first among the fowl!" The fox said these things to trick the raven, and the raven fell for it; he let out a great squawk and dropped his cheese. By showing off his voice, the raven let go of his spoils. The fox grabbed the cheese and said, "O raven, you do have a voice, but no brains to go with it!"

If you follow your enemies' advice, you will get hurt.

from Thomas Wilson, *Art of Rhetoric* (1553)

Themisticles persuaded the Athenians not to change their officers by rehearsing the fable of the scabbed Fox. For (quoth he) when many flies stood feeding upon his raw flesh and had well fed themselves, he was contented at another's persuasion to have slapped them away: whereupon there ensued such hungry flies afterwards that the sorry Fox, being all alone, was eaten up almost to the hard bone, and therefore cursed the time that ever he agreed to any such evil counsel.

from Horace, *Satires*, 2.5.48–63 (c. 35 BCE)

Then again, if a sickly son,
Has been born the one to be reared in a wealthy household,
Worm your way into the father's good graces, in the hope
Of being named second heir—you mustn't make it obvious
That you specialize mainly in bachelors—and also in the hope
That if some chance spirits the child off to the hereafter,
You may come into the property. This kind of gambit
Seldom fails.
    If someone gives you his will to read,
Refuse, and push the tablets away, with a sidelong
Glance at the second line on page one. Run your eyes
Swiftly across it to see if you are the sole heir

Or share with many co-heirs. Some night-court judge,
Newly tricked out in the professional robes of a scribe,
Will often be able to outwit the ravenous crow,
The way Coranus made a fool of the legacy hunter,
Nasica.

from Lucian, *Gallus* (2nd century CE)

Cock

Have you ever heard of a man named Pythagoras, the son of Mnesarchus, of Samos?

Micyllus

You mean the sophist, the quack, who made laws against tasting meat and eating beans, banishing from the table the food that I for my part like the best of all, and then trying to persuade people that before he became Pythagoras he was Euphorbus (well fed)? They say he was a conjurer and a miracle worker, Cock.

Cock

I am that very Pythagoras, Micyllus, so stop abusing me, my good friend, especially as you do not know what sort of man I really was....

Cock

How my soul originally left Apollo, flew down to earth and entered a human body and what sin it was condemned to expiate in that way would make a long story: besides, it is impious either for me to tell or for you to hear such things. But when I became Euphorbus ... In brief, Micyllus, I was a sophist, for I must tell the truth, I suppose. However, I was not uneducated or unacquainted with the noblest sciences. I even went to Egypt to study with the prophets, penetrated into their sanctuaries and learned the books of Horus and Isis by heart, and then I sailed away to Italy and worked upon the Greeks in that quarter of the world to such an extent that they thought me a god.

Micyllus

So I have heard, and I have also heard that you were thought to have come to life again after dying, and that you once showed them that your thigh was of gold. But, look here, tell me how it occurred to you to make a law against eating either meat or beans?

Cock

It was nothing sensible or wise, but I perceived that if I made laws that were ordinary and just like those of the run of legislators I should not induce men to wonder at me, whereas the more I departed from precedent, the more of a figure I should cut, I thought, in their eyes.... Look here, *you* are laughing at *me*, now.

Micyllus

... But after you put off the part of Pythagoras what other did you assume?

Cock

Aspasia, the courtesan from Miletus....

Micyllus

But what man or woman did you become after Aspasia?

Cock

The Cynic Crates.

Micyllus

Twin brethren! what ups and downs! First a courtesan, then a philosopher!

Cock

Then a king, then a poor man, and soon a satrap; then a horse, a jackdaw, a frog, and a thousand things besides; it would take too long to enumerate them all. But of late I have often been a cock, for I liked that sort of life …

from Juvenal, *Satires*, Satire 10, 2.188–241; 2.434–56 (2nd century CE)

"Grant us a long life, Jupiter, O grant us many years!"
In the bloom of youth it's this which, pale with anxiety,
You pray for, and this alone. Yet how grisly, how unrelenting
Are longevity's ills! Look first at your face, you'll see an ugly
And shapeless caricature of its former self: your skin
Has become a scaly hide, you're all chapfallen, the wrinkles
Scored down your cheeks now make you resemble nothing so much
As some elderly female baboon in darkest Africa.
Young men are all individuals: A will have better looks
Or brains than B, while B will beat A on muscle;
But old men all look alike, all share the same bald pate,
Their noses all drip like an infant's, their voices tremble
As much as their limbs, they mumble their bread with toothless
Gums. It's a wretched life for them, they become a burden
To their wives, their children, themselves; the noblest and best of them
Become so loathsome a sight that even legacy-hunters
Turn queasy. Their taste-buds are ruined, they get scant pleasure
From food or wine, sex lies in long oblivion—
Or if they try, it's hopeless: though they labour all night long
At that limp and shrivelled object, limp it remains.
What can the future hold for these impotent dodderers?
Nothing very exciting. Sex is a pretty dead loss—
The old tag's true—when desire outruns performance.
The other senses deteriorate: take hearing, for instance.
How can the deaf appreciate music? The standard
Of the performance eludes them: a top-line soloist,
Massed choirs in their golden robes, all mean less than nothing.
What does it matter to them where they sit in the concert-hall
When a brass band blowing its guts out is barely audible?
The slave who announces the time, or a visitor, must bawl
At the top of his lungs before they take in the message.

The blood runs thin with age, too: now nothing but fever
Can warm that frigid hulk, while diseases of every type
Assault it by battalions. (If you asked me their names
I'd find it less trouble to list all of Oppia's lovers,
The number of patients Doc Themison kills each autumn,
The partners that X, the wards that Y has defrauded,
The times tall Maura goes down in a day, the pupils
Hamillus has off; I could sooner list all the country houses
Owned by the barber who shaved me when I was a lad.)
One has an arthritic hip, another sciatica,
Lumbago plagues a third, while the totally sightless
Envy the one-eyed. Here's a fellow whose jaws would open
Wide, once long ago, at the prospect of dinner—but now
Those leaden lips must mumble the tit-bits another hand
Feeds to him; when he gapes today, he's like a baby
Swallow that sees its mother approaching, her beak
Well-crammed with grubs. But worse than all bodily ills
Is the senescent mind. Men forget what their own servants
Are called, they can't recognize yesterday's host at dinner,
Or, finally, the children they begot and brought up. A heartless
Codicil to the will disinherits their flesh and blood,
And the whole estate is entailed to some whore, whose expert mouth—
After years in that narrow archway—earns her a rich reward....

Worse still is the well-read menace, who's hardly settled for dinner
Before she starts praising Virgil, making a moral case
For Dido (death justifies all), comparing, evaluating
In opposite scales, weighed up one against the other.
Critics surrender, academics are routed, all
Fall silent, not a word from lawyer or auctioneer—
Or even another woman. Such a rattle or talk,
You'd think all the pots and bells were being clashed together
When the moon's in eclipse. No need now for trumpets or brass:
One woman can act, single-handed, as lunar midwife.
But wisdom imposes limits, even on virtue, and if
She's so determined to prove herself eloquent, learned,
She should hoist up her skirts and gird them above the knee,
Offer a pig to Silvanus (female worshippers banned) and
Scrub off in the penny baths. So avoid a dinner partner
With an argumentative style, who hurls well rounded
Syllogisms like slingshots, who has all history pat:
Choose someone rather who doesn't understand all she reads.
I hate these authority-citers, the sort who are always thumbing
Some standard grammatical treatise, whose every utterance
Observes all the laws of syntax, who with antiquarian zeal
Quote poets I've never heard of. Such matters are men's concerns.
If she wants to correct someone's language, she can always
Start with her unlettered girl-friends. A husband should be allowed
His solecisms in peace.

Venice: Mountebanks and Courtesans

Venice occupied a unique place in the Renaissance imagination and travel narratives that involved Venice were highly popular. These excerpts below are from a travelogue published a few years after *Volpone* appeared.

from Thomas Coryate, *Crudities* (1611)

... I hope it will not be esteemed for an impertinency to my discourse, if I next speak of the mountebanks of Venice, seeing amongst many other things that do much famous this city, these two sorts of people, namely the courtesans and the mountebanks are not the least: for although there are Mountebanks also in other cities of Italy; yet because there is a greater concourse of them in Venice than elsewhere, and also for that there is a larger toleration of them here than in other cities (for in Rome, &c. they are restrained from certain matters as I have heard which are here allowed them) therefore they use to name a Venetian mountebank χατ' ἐζοχηυ for the corphaeus and principal mountebank of all Italy: neither do I much doubt but that this treatise of them will be acceptable to some readers, as being a mere novelty never before heard of (I think) by thousands of our English gallants. Surely the principal reason that hath induced me to make mention of them is, because when I was in Venice, they oftentimes ministered infinite pleasure unto me.

The principal place where they act, is the first part of Saint Mark's Street that reacheth betwixt the west front of St. Mark's Church, and the opposite front of Saint Geminian's Church. In which, twice a day, that is, in the morning and in the afternoon, you may see five or six several stages erected for them: those that act upon the ground, even the foresaid charlatans being the poorer sort of them, stand most commonly in the second part of St. Mark's, not far from the gate of the Duke's Palace. These mountebanks at one end of their stage place their trunk, which is replenished with a world of new fangled trumperies. After the whole rabble of them is gotten up to the stage, whereof some wear vizards being disguised like fools in a play, some that are women (for there are diverse women also amongst them) are attired with habits according to that person that they sustain; after (I say) they are all upon the stage, the music begins. Sometimes vocal, sometimes instrumental, and sometimes both together. This music is a preamble and introduction to the ensuing matter: in the meantime while the music plays, the principal mountebank which is the captain and ring-leader of all the rest, opens his trunk, and sets abroach his wares; after the music hath ceased, he maketh an oration to the audience of half an hour long, or almost an hour. Wherein he doth most hyperbolically extol the virtue of his drugs and confections:

Laudat venales qui vult extrudere merces.[1]

Though many of them are very counterfeit and false. Truly I often wondered at many of these natural orators. For they would tell their tales with such admirable volubility and plausible grace, even extempore, and seasoned with that singular variety of elegant jests and witty conceits, that they did often strike great admiration into strangers that never heard them before: and by how much more eloquent these naturalists are, by so much the greater audience they draw unto them, and the more ware they sell. After the chiefest mountebank's first speech is ended, he delivereth out his commodities by little and little, the jester still playing his part, and the musicians singing and playing upon their instruments. The principal things that they sell are oils, sovereign waters, amorous songs printed, apothecary drugs, and a commonweal of other trifles. The head mountebank at every time

[1] *Laudat ... merces* From Horace, Epistles 2.2.11: "He who praises his merchandise is trying to get rid of it."

that he delivereth out any thing, maketh an extemporal speech, which he doth eftsoons intermingle with such savory jests (but spiced now and then with singular scurrility) that they minister passing mirth and laughter to the whole company, which perhaps may consist of a thousand people that flock together about one of their stages....

As for the number of these Venetian courtesans it is very great ... A most ungodly thing without doubt that there should be a toleration of such licentious wantons in so glorious, so potent, so renowned a city ... For they think that the chastity of their wives would be the sooner assaulted, and so consequently they should be capricornified (which of all the indignities in the world the Venetian cannot patiently endure), were it not for these places of evacuation. But I marvel how that should be true though these courtesans were utterly rooted out of the city. For the gentlemen do even coop up their wives always within the walls of their houses for fear of these inconveniences, as much as if there were no courtesans at all in the city. So that you shall very seldom see a Venetian gentleman's wife but either at a solemnization of a great marriage, or at the christening of a Jew, or late in the evening rowing in a gondola.

John Donne

1572 – 1631

John Donne was an innovator: his work represented something new in poetry, and his contemporaries knew it. Donne set out to startle his readers with his disdain for convention, writing poems that challenged expectations about what was appropriate in poetic subject, form, tone, language, and imagery. He was not afraid of being difficult, or ambiguous, or contradictory from one poem to another: like the speaker of his "Holy Sonnet 19," in Donne "contraries meet in one." Some critics and readers try to smooth out these "contraries" by separating Donne's works into the secular verse written by "Jack Donne" (Donne's own phrase), the witty young man-about-London whose love poems combine erotic energy with high-minded argument; and the religious verse written later in life by Dr. John Donne, Dean of St. Paul's Cathedral, the learned Anglican minister famous for his electrifying sermons. But this neat division is complicated by the fact that many of his poems are impossible to date. Donne wrote primarily for manuscript circulation: only a handful of his poems were printed before he died. Some religious poetry may therefore have been written earlier than once thought, and some love lyrics later. In any case, Donne frequently blurs any differences between the sacred and the secular, erotic love and divine love: he can present erotic love as a form of religious experience, and religious devotion as an erotic experience. Donne's voice, moreover, ranges across a multitude of roles and postures, from misogynist cynicism and self-mocking sophistry to tender idealism and devout if still painfully self-conscious religious passion.

With his colloquial language, rough meter, sometimes swaggeringly masculine persona, and elaborately worked out philosophical (or wittily pseudo-philosophical) conceits, Donne's poetry breaks with the late Elizabethan poets: even when expressing difficult or ambiguous thoughts, they tended to prefer lines of smooth and highly decorated elegance. Donne's new manner caught the imagination of many poets, and his work was immensely influential for much of the seventeenth century. Times and tastes change, however, and what had been thought wit in 1600 by 1700 had come to seem mere fancy, unrestrained by judgment. In 1693, for example, John Dryden argued that Donne "affects the metaphysics ... where nature only should reign," claiming that his love poetry "perplexes [women's minds] ... with nice speculations of philosophy, when he should engage their hearts." In the eighteenth century, Samuel Johnson labeled Donne and his followers "Metaphysical Poets" who "ransacked" nature to create startling and strained conceits. (Because of the objections of scholars who point out that the term is misleading, the long-popular term "metaphysical" is currently losing ground.) Thanks to further shifts in sensibility, and thanks also to the praise of T.S. Eliot, who found in Donne's difficulty and intellectual dazzle a model for modernist poetic practice, Donne's work moved again in the twentieth century to the center of the English poetic canon.

Born in London in 1572, Donne was the son of a prosperous ironmonger. The family was Catholic at a time when the government viewed all Catholics with suspicion and prosecuted those it thought seditious. Donne's mother, Elizabeth, was related to Thomas More, beheaded as a traitor for refusing to support Henry VIII's rejection of the Pope's authority. Two of her uncles lived in exile; another, a Jesuit, was incarcerated; and in 1593 Donne's brother Henry died of a fever while imprisoned for harboring a priest. Thus, Donne well understood religious persecution, which is why some have speculated that his conversion to the Church of England, however sincere, must have felt at times like a betrayal. First educated by Jesuits, at age eleven Donne entered Oxford, and then studied at Cambridge. He took no degree, perhaps because graduation required accepting the Church of England's thirty-nine "articles of religion." In 1592 he began legal studies at Lincoln's Inn, and over the next few years wrote many of the love lyrics that were known at first to a few friends and then, especially in the next century, found a large readership. A set of five satires mocking English life, laws, and mores (including those of courtiers) also dates from these years; they helped intensify a fashion in the late 1590s for biting verse satire. The most powerful, "Satire III," explores with surprising candor, if no conclusion, the risks and dilemmas of choosing a version of Christianity to follow.

After taking part in the 1596 and 1597 anti-Spanish expeditions to Cadiz and the Azores, in 1598 Donne was appointed secretary to Sir Thomas Egerton, Lord Keeper of the Great Seal. By now his future seemed assured—he had distanced himself from the Roman Catholic Church and had served in Parliament. In 1601, however, he nearly wrecked his prospects by a secret marriage to Egerton's 17-year-old-niece, Ann More. When the marriage was discovered, Donne wrote to her father, Sir George More, begging that Ann not "feel the terror of your sudden anger," but Sir George disinherited his daughter and had Donne dismissed from his position and briefly imprisoned. Years of poverty and unemployment lay before the couple and their family (Ann eventually had twelve children, seven of whom survived). Donne found some support, however, from various friends and patrons, among them Sir Robert Drury, for whom he wrote two long "Anniversary" poems (1611-1612) lamenting the death of Sir Robert's daughter, Elizabeth.

During this difficult period Donne finally renounced his Roman Catholicism and within a few years published two anti-Catholic tracts: *Pseudo-Martyr* (1610), which argues that Catholics should take the Oath of Allegiance to the crown, and the satirical *Ignatius his Conclave* (1611), which describes a meeting of Jesuits in Hell. King James was pleased but insisted that Donne be ordained before receiving an appointment. Donne complied and was shortly thereafter made a royal chaplain and a Reader in Divinity at Lincoln's Inn. He soon suffered a personal loss, however, when his wife died during childbirth at age 33, a sorrow to which Donne probably alludes in his seventeenth "Holy Sonnet," when he mentions that "she whom I loved hath paid her last debt." Most of his "Holy Sonnets," however (including "Death be not Proud"), seem to have been written before his ordination and reflect earlier hopes and anguish. In 1621 Donne was appointed Dean of St. Paul's, and attracted large audiences for his intellectually challenging and emotionally stirring sermons, many of which were published, both during and after his life.

During a grave illness in the mid-1620s, Donne wrote his popular *Devotions Upon Emergent Occasions* (1624), a series of prose meditations that include his famous assertion of human interconnectedness ("No man is an island"). Donne survived, but he never lost his fascination with death. He delivered his last sermon, "Death's Duel," early in 1631 before Charles I. His audience, it was later said, sensed that he was in effect preaching his own funeral sermon; he died that March. Donne is buried at St. Paul's Cathedral; his monument is modeled on a portrait of himself taken while he was still alive and dressed for the occasion in his shroud. His collected *Poems* were printed in 1633 and was reprinted several times before his reputation faded with the coming of the Restoration and a new generation's taste for neoclassical poetry.

⌘⌘⌘

from *Songs and Sonnets*[1]

The Good-Morrow

I wonder by my troth, what thou, and I
Did, till we loved? were we not weaned till then?
But sucked on country pleasures, childishly?
Or snorted we in the seven sleepers' den?[2]
'Twas so; but° this, all pleasures fancies be *except for*
If ever any beauty I did see,
Which I desired, and got, 'twas but a dream of thee.

And now good-morrow to our waking souls,
Which watch not one another out of fear;
For love, all love of other sights controls,
And makes one little room, an every where.
Let sea-discoverers to new worlds have gone,
Let maps[3] to others, worlds on worlds have shown,
Let us possess one world,[4] each hath one, and is one.

My face in thine eye, thine in mine appears,
And true plain hearts do in the faces rest,
Where can we find two better hemispheres,
Without sharp North, without declining West?
What ever dies, was not mixed equally;[5]
If our two loves be one, or, thou and I
Love so alike that none do slacken, none can die.
—1633

Song ("Go, and catch a falling star")

Go, and catch a falling star,
Get with child a mandrake root,[6]
Tell me, where all past years are,
Or who cleft the Devil's foot,
Teach me to hear mermaids singing,
Or to keep off envy's stinging,
And find
What wind
Serves to advance an honest mind.

If thou be'st born to strange sights,
Things invisible to see,
Ride ten thousand days and nights,
Till age snow white hairs on thee,
Thou, when thou return'st, wilt tell me
All strange wonders that befell thee,
And swear,
No where
Lives a woman true, and fair.

If thou find'st one, let me know,
Such a pilgrimage were sweet;
Yet do not, I would not go,
Though at next door we might meet;
Though she were true, when you met her,
And last, till you write your letter,
Yet she
Will be
False, ere I come, to two, or three.
—1633

Woman's Constancy

Now thou hast loved me one whole day,
To-morrow when thou leavest, what wilt thou say?
Wilt thou then antedate some new-made vow?
Or, say that now
We are not just those persons, which we were?
Or, that oaths made in reverential fear
Of Love, and his wrath, any may forswear?
Or, as true deaths, true marriages untie,
So lovers' contracts, images of those,
Bind but till sleep, death's image, them unloose?
Or, your own end to justify,
For having purposed change, and falsehood, you
Can have no way but falsehood to be true?

[1] *Sonnets* Donne uses the term as a general one for love poems or love songs, rather than referring specifically to the 14-line sonnet; his secular love poetry includes no traditional 14-line sonnets.

[2] *seven sleepers den* In early Christian legend, seven youths walled up in a cave during a persecution who slept for nearly 200 years.

[3] *maps* Probably astronomical maps.

[4] *one world* Many manuscript versions have "our world."

[5] *Whatever … equally* Classical medical theory held that disease was the result of improper balance among the body's elements.

[6] *mandrake root* Plant whose forked root resembles a human body.

Vain lunatic,[1] against these 'scapes I could
Dispute, and conquer, if I would;
Which I abstain to do,
For by to-morrow, I may think so too.
—1633

The Sun Rising

Busy old fool, unruly Sun,
Why dost thou thus,
Through windows, and through curtains call on us?
Must to thy motions lovers' seasons run?
Saucy pedantic wretch, go chide
Late schoolboys and sour prentices,
Go tell court-huntsmen that the King will ride,
Call country ants to harvest offices;
Love, all alike, no season knows, nor clime,
Nor hours, days, months, which are the rags of time.

Thy beams, so reverend, and strong
Why shouldst thou think?
I could eclipse and cloud them with a wink,
But that I would not lose her sight so long:
If her eyes have not blinded thine,
Look, and tomorrow late, tell me,
Whether both the Indias of spice and mine[2]
Be where thou leftst them, or lie here with me.
Ask for those kings whom thou saw'st yesterday,
And thou shalt hear, All here in one bed lay.

She's all states, and all princes, I,
Nothing else is.
Princes do but play us; compared to this,
All honor's mimic, all wealth alchemy.[3]
Thou sun art half as happy as we,
In that the world's contracted thus:
Thine age asks ease, and since thy duties be
To warm the world, that's done in warming us.
Shine here to us, and thou art everywhere;
This bed thy center is, these walls, thy sphere.
—1633

[1] *lunatic* Under the control of the moon, thus inconstant, subject to change.

[2] *Indias of spice and mine* The East Indies (source of spice and perfume) and West Indies (source of gold and precious metals).

[3] *alchemy* Here, flashy rubbish.

The Canonization

For God's sake hold your tongue, and let me love,
Or chide my palsy, or my gout,
My five gray hairs, or ruined fortune flout,
With wealth your state, your mind with arts improve,
Take you a course, get you a place,[4]
Observe his honour, or his grace,[5]
And the King's real, or his stamped face
Contemplate;[6] what you will, approve,[7]
So you will let me love.

Alas, alas, who's injured by my love?
What merchant's ships have my sighs drowned?
Who says my tears have overflowed his ground?
When did my colds a forward spring remove?
When did the heats which my veins fill
Add one more to the plaguy bill?[8]
Soldiers find wars, and lawyers find out still
Litigious men, which quarrels move,
Though she and I do love.

Call us what you will, we are made such by love;
Call her one, me another fly,[9]
We're tapers too, and at our own cost die,[10]

[4] *course ... place* Take a course of action; get yourself a position.

[5] *his honour ... his grace* Cultivate contacts with political or religious dignitaries.

[6] *stamped face / Contemplate* Look at the king's face stamped on coins: in effect, "go think about money."

[7] *what you will, approve* Do whatever you want.

[8] *plaguy bill* Weekly list of those who had died of the plague.

[9] *me another fly* Call her a fly (butterfly or moth), and call me one too.

[10] *We're tapers ... die* "To die" was slang for reaching orgasm, and each sexual act was popularly believed to shorten one's life by one day. The two lovers are compared to moths attracted to a candle, and to the self-consuming candle (taper) itself: moths, candle, and lovers all pay for doing what they do by their very nature.

And we in us find the eagle and the dove.[1]
The phoenix riddle hath more wit
By us; we two being one, are it.[2]
So, to one neutral thing both sexes fit,
We die and rise the same, and prove
Mysterious by this love.

We can die by it, if not live by love,
And if unfit for tombs and hearse
Our legend be, it will be fit for verse;
And if no piece of chronicle° we prove, *history*
We'll build in sonnets° pretty rooms;[3] *love poems*
As well a well wrought urn becomes
The greatest ashes, as half-acre tombs,
And by these hymns, all shall approve
Us canonized for love.

And thus invoke us: You whom reverend love
Made one another's hermitage;
You, to whom love was peace, that now is rage;
Who did the whole world's soul contract,[4] and drove
Into the glasses of your eyes
(So made such mirrors, and such spies,
That they did all to you epitomize)
Countries, towns, courts: beg from above
A pattern of your love.
—1633

Song ("Sweetest love, I do not go")

Sweetest love, I do not go
For weariness of thee,
Nor in hope the world can show
A fitter love for me;
But since that I
Must die at last, 'tis best
To use my self in jest
Thus by feigned deaths to die.[5]

Yesternight the sun went hence,
And yet is here today,
He hath no desire nor sense,
Nor half so short a way:
Then fear not me,
But believe that I shall make
Speedier journeys, since I take
More wings and spurs than he.

O how feeble is man's power,
That if good fortune fall,
Cannot add another hour,
Nor a lost hour recall!
But come bad chance,
And we join to it our strength,
And we teach it art and length,
Itself o'er us to advance.

When thou sigh'st, thou sigh'st not wind,
But sigh'st my soul away,
When thou weep'st, unkindly kind,
My life's blood doth decay.
It cannot be
That thou lov'st me, as thou say'st,
If in thine my life thou waste,
Thou art the best of me.

Let not thy divining heart
Forethink me any ill,
Destiny may take thy part,
And may thy fears fulfil;
But think that we
Are but turned aside to sleep;
They who one another keep
Alive, ne'er parted be.
—1633

[1] *eagle and the dove* Symbols of (masculine) strength and (feminine) gentleness, now united in the lovers.

[2] *phoenix riddle* Only one mythical phoenix ever lived at a time; the bird mysteriously renewed itself by rising from the ashes of its own funeral pyre. The "riddle" of its unisex existence makes better sense (has "more wit") when compared with the two lovers: like the phoenix, they combine "both sexes" to make "one neutral thing" which dies, then rises the same (with the traditional play on the sexual resonances of dying and rising).

[3] *rooms* In Italian, "stanza" means "room."

[4] *contract* Manuscript versions have "extract."

[5] *feigned deaths* Separations from the beloved.

Air and Angels

Twice or thrice had I loved thee,
Before I knew thy face or name;
So in a voice, so in a shapeless flame,[1]
Angels affect us oft, and worshipped be;
Still when, to where thou wert, I came,
Some lovely glorious nothing I did see.
But since my soul, whose child love is,
Takes limbs of flesh, and else could nothing do,
More subtle than the parent is
Love must not be, but take a body too;
And therefore what thou wert, and who,
I bid Love ask, and now
That it assume thy body, I allow,
And fix itself in thy lip, eye, and brow.

Whilst thus to ballast love, I thought,
And so more steadily to have gone,
With wares which would sink admiration,
I saw I had love's pinnace[2] overfraught;
Ev'ry thy hair for love to work upon
Is much too much, some fitter must be sought;
For, nor in nothing, nor in things
Extreme, and scatt'ring bright, can love inhere;
Then as an angel, face and wings
Of air, not pure as it, yet pure doth wear,
So thy love may be my love's sphere;
Just such disparity
As is 'twixt air and angels' purity,
'Twixt women's love, and men's will ever be.
—1633

Break of Day[3]

'Tis true, 'tis day; what though it be?
O wilt thou therefore rise from me?
Why should we rise because 'tis light?
Did we lie down because 'twas night?
Love, which in spite of darkness brought us hither,
Should in despite of light keep us together.

Light hath no tongue, but is all eye;
If it could speak as well as spy,
This were the worst that it could say,
That being well, I fain would stay,
And that I loved my heart and honor so,
That I would not from him, that had them, go.

Must business thee from hence remove?
Oh that's the worst disease of love,
The poor, the foul, the false, love can
Admit, but not the busied man.
He which hath business, and makes love, doth do
Such wrong, as when a married man doth woo.
—1612, 1633

The Anniversary

All kings, and all their favourites,
All glory of honours, beauties, wits,
The sun itself, which makes times, as they pass,
Is elder by a year, now, than it was
When thou and I first one another saw:
All other things to their destruction draw,
Only our love hath no decay;
This, no tomorrow hath, nor yesterday,
Running it never runs from us away,
But truly keeps his first, last, everlasting day.

Two graves must hide thine and my corse,° *corpse*
If one might, death were no divorce:
Alas, as well as other princes, we
(Who prince enough in one another be)
Must leave at last in death, these eyes, and ears,
Oft fed with true oaths, and with sweet salt tears;
But souls where nothing dwells but love
(All other thoughts being inmates) then shall prove
This, or a love increased there above,
When bodies to their graves, souls from their
graves remove.

---

[1] *shapeless flame* Unsteady, or suddenly flaring, flame.

[2] *pinnace* Small, light ship, unsuited for carrying the figurative cargo of the beloved's many beauties.

[3] *Break of Day* First printed, with a musical setting, in William Corkine's *Second Book of Airs* (1612). The speaker is a woman.

And then we shall be throughly° blest, *thoroughly*
But we no more than all the rest,
Here upon earth, we're kings, and none but we
Can be such kings, nor of such subjects be;
Who is so safe as we? where none can do
Treason to us, except one of us two.
True and false fears let us refrain,
Let us love nobly, and live, and add again
Years and years unto years, till we attain
To write threescore: this is the second of our reign.
—1633

Twicknam Garden[1]

Blasted with sighs, and surrounded with tears,
Hither I come to seek the spring,
And at mine eyes, and at mine ears,
Receive such balms, as else cure everything;
But O, self traitor, I do bring
The spider[2] love, which transubstantiates all,
And can convert manna to gall,
And that this place may thoroughly be thought
True Paradise, I have the serpent[3] brought.

'Twere wholesomer for me, that winter did
Benight the glory of this place,
And that a grave frost did forbid
These trees to laugh and mock me to my face;
But that I may not this disgrace
Endure, nor leave this garden, Love, let me
Some senseless piece of this place be;
Make me a mandrake, so I may groan here,[4]
Or a stone fountain weeping out my year.

Hither with crystal vials, lovers come,
And take my tears, which are love's wine,
And try° your mistress' tears at home, *test*
For all are false, that taste not just like mine;
Alas, hearts do not in eyes shine,
Nor can you more judge woman's thoughts by tears,
Than by her shadow, what she wears.
O perverse sex, where none is true but she,
Who's therefore true, because her truth kills me.
—1633

A Valediction: of Weeping

Let me pour forth
My tears before thy face, whil'st I stay here,
For thy face coins them, and thy stamp they bear,
And by this mintage they are something worth,
For thus they be
Pregnant of thee;
Fruits of much grief they are, emblems of more,
When a tear falls, that thou falls which it bore,
So thou and I are nothing then, when on a diverse shore.

On a round ball[5]
A workman that hath copies by, can lay
An Europe, Afric, and an Asia,[6]
And quickly make that, which was nothing, All,
So doth each tear,
Which thee doth wear,
A globe, yea world by that impression grow,
Till thy tears mixed with mine do overflow
This world, by waters sent from thee, my heaven dissolved so.

O more than Moon,
Draw not up seas to drown me in thy sphere,
Weep me not dead, in thine arms, but forbear
To teach the sea what it may do too soon;
Let not the wind
Example find,
To do me more harm than it purposeth;

[1] *Twicknam Garden* Twickenham Park (pronounced, and often in the period spelled, Twicknam) was the home of Lucy, Countess of Bedford (1581–1627), a friend and patron of Donne and other writers, including Ben Jonson, Samuel Daniel, and Michael Drayton.

[2] *spider* Spiders were believed to transform everything they ate into poison.

[3] *serpent* Emblem of envy, and of temptation.

[4] *mandrake … groan here* Plant whose forked root was thought to resemble the human body, and reputed to shriek or groan; the printed edition has "grow," but many manuscripts have "groan," which better parallels the weeping fountain in the next line.

[5] *round ball* Blank globe, on which printed maps could be placed to make a world.

[6] *Asia* Pronounced in the period as a three-syllable word.

Since thou and I sigh one another's breath,
Who e'r sighs most is cruellest, and hastes the
other's death.[1]
—1633

The Flea

Mark but this flea, and mark in this,
How little that which thou deny'st me is;
It sucked me first,[2] and now sucks thee,
And in this flea our two bloods mingled be;[3]
Thou know'st that[4] this cannot be said
A sin, nor shame, nor loss of maidenhead,
Yet this enjoys before it woo,
And pampered swells with one blood made of two,
And this, alas, is more than we would do.

Oh stay, three lives in one flea spare,
Where we almost, nay more than married are:
This flea is you and I, and this
Our marriage bed, and marriage temple is;
Though parents grudge, and you, we're met
And cloistered in these living walls of jet.° *black stone*
Though use° make you apt to kill me, *habit*
Let not to that, self murder added be,
And sacrilege, three sins in killing three.

Cruel and sudden, hast thou since
Purpled thy nail in blood of innocence?
Wherein could this flea guilty be,
Except in that drop which it sucked from thee?
Yet thou triumph'st, and say'st that thou
Find'st not thy self, nor me the weaker now;
'Tis true, then learn how false, fears be;
Just so much honor, when thou yield'st to me,
Will waste, as this flea's death took life from thee.
—1633

[1] *Who e'r sighs … death* According to folklore, sighing shortened life (each sigh was said to cost one drop of blood).

[2] *It sucked me first* "Me it sucked first" in many manuscripts.

[3] *mingled be* The speaker's subsequent argument hinges on the traditional belief that blood mixed during sexual intercourse.

[4] *Thou know'st that this* "Confess it" in many manuscripts.

A Nocturnal upon St. Lucy's Day, Being the Shortest Day[5]

'Tis the year's midnight, and it is the day's,
Lucy's, who scarce seven hours herself unmasks;
The sun is spent, and now his flasks° *the stars*
Send forth light squibs, no constant rays;
The world's whole sap is sunk:
The general balm[6] the hydroptic° earth hath drunk, *thirsty*
Whither, as to the bed's-feet, life is shrunk,
Dead and interred; yet all these seem to laugh,
Compared with me, who am their epitaph.

Study me then, you who shall lovers be
At the next world, that is, at the next spring:
For I am every dead thing,
In whom Love wrought new alchemy.
For his art did express° *extract*
A quintessence even from nothingness,
From dull privations, and lean emptiness;
He ruined me, and I am re-begot
Of absence, darkness, death; things which are not.

All others, from all things, draw all that's good,
Life, soul, form, spirit, whence they being have;
I, by love's limbeck,[7] am the grave
Of all that's nothing. Oft a flood
Have we two wept, and so
Drowned the whole world, us two; oft did we grow
To be two chaoses, when we did show
Care to aught else; and often absences
Withdrew our souls, and made us carcasses.

But I am by her death (which word wrongs her)
Of the first nothing the elixir grown;
Were I a man, that I were one
I needs must know; I should prefer,
If I were any beast,
Some ends, some means; yea plants, yea stones detest,
And love; all, all some properties invest;

[5] *St Lucy's Day, Being the Shortest Day* December 13, the shortest day of the year in the old Julian calendar.

[6] *general balm* The innate, vital sap believed to preserve all things.

[7] *limbeck* Retort, or still (apparatus for distillation).

If I an ordinary nothing were,
As shadow, a light and body must be here.

But I am none; nor will my sun renew.
You lovers, for whose sake the lesser sun
At this time to the Goat[1] is run
To fetch new lust, and give it you,
Enjoy your summer all;
Since she enjoys her long night's festival,
Let me prepare towards her, and let me call
This hour her vigil, and her eve, since this
Both the year's, and the day's deep midnight is.
—1633

The Bait

Come live with me, and be my love,
And we will some new pleasures prove
Of golden sands, and crystal brooks,
With silken lines, and silver hooks.

There will the river whispering run
Warmed by thy eyes, more than the sun.
And there the enamoured fish will stay,
Begging themselves they may betray.

When thou wilt swim in that live bath,
Each fish, which every channel hath,
Will amorously to thee swim,
Gladder to catch thee, than thou him.

If thou, to be so seen, be'st loth,
By sun or moon, thou dark'nest both,
And if myself have leave to see,
I need not their light, having thee.

Let others freeze with angling reeds,
And cut their legs with shells and weeds,
Or treacherously poor fish beset,
With strangling snare, or windowy net.

[1] *Goat* The constellation Capricorn, into whose sign the sun enters at the winter solstice; goats were associated with lust.

Let coarse bold hands, from slimy nest
The bedded fish in banks out-wrest,
Or curious traitors, sleave-silk[2] flies,
Bewitch poor fishes' wand'ring eyes.

For thee, thou need'st no such deceit,
For thou thyself art thine own bait;
That fish, that is not catched thereby,
Alas, is wiser far than I.
—1633

The Apparition

When by thy scorn, O murd'ress, I am dead,
And that thou thinkst thee free
From all solicitation from me,
Then shall my ghost come to thy bed,
And thee, feigned vestal,[3] in worse arms shall see;
Then thy sick taper will begin to wink,
And he, whose thou art then, being tired before,
Will, if thou stir, or pinch to wake him, think
Thou call'st for more,
And in false sleep will from thee shrink,
And then, poor aspen° wretch, neglected thou *trembling*
Bathed in a cold quicksilver sweat[4] wilt lie,
A verier ghost than I;
What I will say, I will not tell thee now,
Lest that preserve thee; and since my love is spent,
I'd rather thou shouldst painfully repent,
Than by my threatnings rest still innocent.
—1633

A Valediction: Forbidding Mourning

As virtuous men pass mildly away,
And whisper to their souls to go,

[2] *sleave-silk* Silk in the form of fine filaments.

[3] *feigned vestal* Pretended virgin. The original has "fained," the common variant spelling in the period; many editions retain "fained" (eager, glad).

[4] *quicksilver sweat* Shiny coating of sweat; from quicksilvering, the application of a thin coat of an alloy using mercury (quicksilver). That mercury was also used to relieve the symptoms of syphilis adds to Donne's insult.

Whilst some of their sad friends do say,
The breath goes now, and some say, no:

So let us melt, and make no noise,
No tear-floods, nor sigh-tempests move,
'Twere profanation of our joys,
To tell the laity our love.

Moving of the earth° brings harms and fears, *earthquakes*
Men reckon what it did and meant,
But trepidation of the spheres,[1]
Though greater far, is innocent.

Dull sublunary[2] lovers' love
(Whose soul is sense) cannot admit
Absence, because it doth remove
Those things which elemented it.

But we by a love, so much refined
That our selves know not what it is,
Inter-assured of the mind,
Care less, eyes, lips, and hands to miss.

Our two souls therefore, which are one,
Though I must go, endure not yet
A breach, but an expansion,
Like gold to airy thinness beat.

If they be two, they are two so
As stiff twin compasses[3] are two:
Thy soul, the fixed foot, makes no show
To move, but doth, if the other do.

And though it in the center sit,
Yet when the other far doth roam,
It leans, and hearkens after it,
And grows erect, as that comes home.

Such wilt thou be to me, who must
Like the other foot, obliquely run;
Thy firmness makes my circle just,
And makes me end, where I begun.
—1633

[1] *trepidation of the spheres* The precession of the equinox, thought to be caused by movements in the celestial spheres.

[2] *sublunary* Beneath the moon, hence corruptible and subject to change (because subject to the consequences of the Fall from Paradise).

[3] *Twin compasses* Single drawing compass (with twin "feet").

The Ecstasy

Where, like a pillow on a bed,
A pregnant bank swelled up, to rest
The violet's reclining head,
Sat we two, one another's best.
Our hands were firmly cemented
With a fast balm, which thence did spring;
Our eye-beams twisted, and did thread
Our eyes upon one double string.
So to engraft our hands, as yet
Was all our means to make us one,
And pictures in our eyes to get° *beget*
Was all our propagation.
As 'twixt two equal armies, Fate
Suspends uncertain victory,
Our souls (which to advance their state,
Were gone out) hung 'twixt her and me.
And whilst our souls negotiate there,
We like sepulchral statues lay;
All day, the same our postures were,
And we said nothing, all the day.
If any, so by love refined,
That he soul's language understood,
And by good love were grown all mind,
Within convenient distance stood,
He (though he knew not which soul spake,
Because both meant, both spake the same)
Might thence a new concoction take,[4]
And part far purer than he came.
This ecstasy doth unperplex
(We said) and tell us what we love;
We see by this, it was not sex;
We see, we saw not what did move:
But as all several souls contain
Mixture of things, they know not what,

[4] *new concoction take* Be even further refined.

Love, these mixed souls doth mix again,
And makes both one, each this, and that.
A single violet transplant,
The strength, the colour, and the size
(All which before was poor and scant)
Redoubles still, and multiplies.
When love with one another so
Interinanimates two souls,
That abler soul, which thence doth flow,
Defects of loneliness controls.
We then, who are this new soul, know
Of what we are composed, and made,
For the atomies of which we grow
Are souls, whom no change can invade.
But O alas, so long, so far
Our bodies why do we forbear?
They're ours, though they're not we, we are
The intelligences, they the sphere.
We owe them thanks, because they thus
Did us, to us, at first convey,
Yielded their forces, sense, to us,
Nor are dross to us, but allay.° *alloy*
On man heaven's influence works not so,
But that it first imprints the air;
So soul into the soul may flow,
Though it to body first repair.
As our blood labours to beget
Spirits, as like souls as it can,
Because such fingers need to knit
That subtle knot, which makes us man:
So must pure lovers' souls descend
To affections, and to faculties,
Which sense may reach and apprehend,
Else a great prince in prison lies.
To our bodies turn we then, that so
Weak men on love revealed may look;
Love's mysteries in souls do grow,
But yet the body is his book.
And if some lover, such as we,
Have heard this dialogue of one,
Let him still mark us, he shall see
Small change when we're to bodies gone.
—1633

The Relic

When my grave is broke up again
Some second guest to entertain
(For graves have learned that woman-head[1]
To be to more than one a bed)
And he that digs it, spies
A bracelet of bright° hair about the bone, *fair*
Will he not let us alone,
And think that there a loving couple lies,
Who thought that this device might be some way
To make their souls, at the last busy day,
Meet at this grave, and make a little stay?

If this fall in a time, or land,
Where mis-devotion doth command,[2]
Then he that digs us up will bring
Us to the Bishop, and the King,
To make us relics; then
Thou shalt be a Mary Magdalen, and I
A something else thereby;
All women shall adore us, and some men;
And since at such times miracles are sought,
I would have that age by this paper taught
What miracles we harmless lovers wrought.

First, we loved well and faithfully,
Yet knew not what we loved, nor why,
Difference of sex no more we knew,
Than our guardian angels do;
Coming and going, we
Perchance might kiss, but not between those meals;
Our hands ne'er touched the seals,
Which nature, injured by late law,[3] sets free:
These miracles we did; but now, alas,
All measure, and all language, I should pass,
Should I tell what a miracle she was.
—1633

[1] *woman-head* Womanishness (a play on "maidenhead").

[2] *If this fall ... command* That is, in a time or place where people prayed to saints and venerated relics: in effect, were Roman Catholic.

[3] *late law* Human law, which came after the original "law" of nature.

from *Elegies*

Elegy 1. Jealousy[1]

Fond° woman, which wouldst have thy husband die, *foolish*
And yet complain'st of his great jealousy.
If swollen with poison, he lay in his last bed,
His body with a sere-bark° covered, *dry crust*
Drawing his breath as thick and short as can
The nimblest crocheting[2] musician,
Ready with loathsome vomiting to spew
His soul out of one hell into a new,
Made deaf with his poor kindred's howling cries,
Begging with few feigned tears great legacies,
Thou wouldst not weep, but jolly and frolic be,
As a slave which to-morrow should be free.
Yet weep'st thou when thou seest him hungerly
Swallow his own death, heart's-bane jealousy.
Oh give him many thanks, he's courteous,
That in suspecting kindly warneth us.
We must not, as we used, flout openly
In scoffing riddles his deformity;
Nor at his board, together being sat,
With words, nor touch, scarce looks, adulterate.
Nor when he, swol'n and pampered with great fare,
Sits down and snorts, caged in his basket chair,
Must we usurp his own bed any more,
Nor kiss and play in his house, as before.
Now I see many dangers; for that is
His realm, his castle, and his diocese.
But if, as envious men which would revile
Their prince, or coin his gold, themselves exile
Into another country, and do it there,
We play in another house, what should we fear?
There we will scorn his household policies,
His silly plots and pensionary spies,° *servants*
As the inhabitants of Thames' right side[3]
Do London's mayor, or Germans, the Pope's pride.[4]
—1633

[1] *Elegey 1. Jealousy* Numbered "Elegy 4" in some modern editions.

[2] *crotcheting* Crotchets are grace notes; in effect, "quick-fingered."

[3] *Thames' right side* Southwark, where the theaters were, was outside the jurisdiction of London authorities.

Elegy 8. The Comparison[5]

As the sweet sweat of roses in a still,
As that which from chafed musk cat's pores doth trill,° *flow*
As the almighty balm° of the early East, *morning dew*
Such are the sweat drops of my mistress' breast,
And on her neck her skin such lustre sets,
They seem no sweat drops, but pearl carcanets.° *necklaces*
Rank sweaty froth thy mistress' brow defiles,
Like spermatic issue of ripe menstruous boils,
Or like that scum, which, by need's lawless law
Enforced, Sanserra's starved men did draw
From parboiled shoes, and boots, and all the rest
Which were with any sovereign fatness blest,[6]
And like vile lying stones in saffroned tin,[7]
Or warts, or weals, they hang upon her skin.
Round as the world's her head, on every side,
Like to that fatal ball which fell on Ide,[8]
Or that whereof God had such jealousy,
As, for the ravishing thereof we die.[9]

[4] *Pope's pride* Germany was the birthplace of the Reformation, which challenged the authority of the Pope.

[5] *Elegy 8. The Comparison* Numbered "Elegy 2" in some modern editions.

[6] From parboiled shoes ... fatness blest The King's Catholic army laid siege to the Protestants of Sancerre, France, for nine months in 1573; the town's inhabitants were reduced to eating anything made out of leather.

[7] *lying stones in saffroned tin* Artificial jewels set in false gold (gilded tin).

[8] *fatal ball that fell on Ide* The golden apple inscribed "To the fairest" that Eris, goddess of discord, brought to a wedding in revenge for not being invited. Hera, Athena, and Aphrodite competed for the prize, and Paris, a herdsman on Mount Ida (near Troy), had to choose the winner. His choice of Aphrodite led to the Trojan war. The elegy invites the reader to compare that beauty competition with the one it offers.

[9] *ravishing ... we die* The forbidden fruit of the Tree of the Knowledge of Good and Evil in Eden.

Thy head[1] is like a rough-hewn statue of jet,° *black stone*
Where marks for eyes, nose, mouth, are yet scarce set;
Like the first Chaos, or flat seeming face
Of Cynthia,° where the earth's shadows her embrace. *the moon*
Like Proserpine's white beauty-keeping chest,[2]
Or Jove's best fortune's urn,[3] is her fair breast.
Thine's like worm eaten trunks, clothed in seal's skin,
Or grave, that's dirt without, and stink within.
And like that slender stalk, at whose end stands
The woodbine quivering, are her arms and hands,
Like rough-barked elmboughs, or the russet skin
Of men late scourged for madness, or for sin,
Like sun-parched quarters on the city gate,[4]
Such is thy tanned skin's lamentable state.
And like a bunch of ragged carrots stand
The short swoll'n fingers of thy gouty hand.
Then like the chemic's masculine equal° fire, *evenly heating*
Which in the limbeck's[5] warm womb doth inspire
Into the earth's worthless dirt a soul of gold,
Such cherishing heat her best loved part doth hold.
Thine's like the dread mouth of a fired gun,
Or like hot liquid metals newly run
Into clay moulds, or like to that Aetna[6]
Where round about the grass is burnt away.
Are not your kisses then as filthy, and more,
As a worm sucking an envenomed sore?
Doth not thy fearful hand in feeling quake,
As one which gath'ring flowers, still fears a snake?
Is not your last act harsh, and violent,
As when a plough a stony ground doth rent?
So kiss good turtles,° so devoutly nice *turtledoves*
Are priests in handling reverent sacrifice,
And such in searching wounds the surgeon is
As we, when we embrace, or touch, or kiss.
Leave her, and I will leave comparing thus,
She, and comparisons are odious.
—1633

[1] *Thy head* That is, the head of thy mistress, as opposed to "her head" (the speaker's mistress) of line 15. The poem proceeds to contrast the qualities of the speaker's "her" with those of "thy" or "thine" mistress.

[2] *beauty-keeping chest* In classical story, Psyche was required to travel to the underworld and ask Prosperina (Persephone) to place in a box a gift of beauty for Venus.

[3] *Jove's best fortune's urn* From Homer, *Iliad*: Zeus (Jove) kept two urns in his palace, one filled with good gifts, the other with evil ones.

[4] *Like sun-parched ... city gate* The dessicated body parts of "quartered" criminals, impaled as warning to would-be offenders on city gates.

[5] *limbeck* Alchemical still or retort.

[6] *Aetna* Volcano in Sicily.

Elegy 19. To His Mistress Going to Bed[7]

Come Madam, come, all rest my powers defy,
Until I labour, I in labour lie.
The foe oft-times, having the foe in sight,
Is tired with standing though they never fight.
Off with that girdle, like heaven's zone glistering,
But a far fairer world encompassing.
Unpin that spangled breastplate,[8] which you wear
That the eyes of busy fools may be stopped there.
Unlace your self: for that harmonious chime[9]
Tells me from you that now 'tis your bed time.
Off with that happy busk,° which I envy, *corset*
That still can be, and still can stand so nigh.
Your gown's going off, such beauteous state reveals,
As when from flowr'y meads the hill's shadow steals.
Off with that wiry coronet and show
The hairy diadem which on you doth grow.
Now off with those shoes, and then softly tread
In this love's hallowed temple, this soft bed.
In such white robes, Heaven's angels used to be
Received by men: thou, angel, bringst with thee
A heaven like Mahomet's Paradise,[10] and though
Ill spirits walk in white, we easily know
By this these angels from an evil sprite:
Those set our hairs, but these our flesh upright.

[7] *Elegy 19. To His Mistress Going to Bed* Censoring authorities refused to let the publisher include this elegy in early collections of Donne's poems; it was first printed in an anthology, *The Harmony of the Muses* (1654), and did not appear in an edition of Donne's poems until 1669. It is numbered "Elegy 8" in some modern editions.

[8] *spangled breastplate* The stomacher; it covered the chest and was often richly ornamented.

[9] *chime* The lady wears a chiming watch.

[10] *Mahomet's Paradise* Heaven of erotic bliss. The sensual aspects of the Islamic version of Paradise are described in the Koran sura 55, 54–56, sura 56, 12–40, and sura 76, 12–22.

Licence my roving hands, and let them go,
Behind, before, above, between, below.[1]
Oh my America, my newfound land,
My kingdom, safeliest when with one man manned,
My mine of precious stones: my empery,° *empire*
How blest am I in this discovering thee!
To enter in these bonds, is to be free;
Then where my hand is set, my seal shall be.
Full nakedness, all joys are due to thee;
As souls unbodied, bodies unclothed must be
To taste whole joys. Gems which you women use
Are like Atlanta's balls,[2] cast in men's views,
That when a fool's eye lighteth on a gem,
His earthly soul may covet theirs, not them.
Like pictures, or like books' gay coverings, made
For lay-men,[3] are all women thus arrayed;
Themselves are mystic books, which only we
(Whom their imputed grace[4] will dignify)
Must see revealed. Then since I may know,
As liberally as to a midwife show
Thyself: cast all, yea, this white linen hence,
There is no penance, much less innocence.[5]
To teach thee, I am naked first; why then
What needst thou have more covering than a man.
—1654

[1] *Behind, before ... below* The order of the words in this line varies in the manuscripts and printed editions.

[2] *Atlanta's balls* In classical legend, Atalanta said she would only marry a man who could defeat her in footrace. Her suitor Hippomenes won the challenge by dropping three golden balls as he ran; Atalanta stopped to pick them up. The speaker here reverses the story's gender dynamic.

[3] *lay-men* Referring to the traditional use of images to instruct non-clerics ("lay-men") who could not read the Bible itself; and to the ornate bindings commissioned by wealthy owners to cover books they probably would never read. The speaker proceeds to argue that women are like these kinds of pictures or books: externally beautiful, but only a favored few may "read" what lies inside.

[4] *imputed grace* Theological term associated with Protestantism: the justifying grace ascribed to a person through Christ's righteousness.

[5] *this white ... innocence* The color white is associated with both penitence and innocence. In some manuscripts and in the 1654 and 1669 printed editions, this line reads "There is no penance due to innocence," a more theologically conventional reading. Some manuscripts read "Here is no penance, much less innocence."

from *Satires*

Satire 3

Kind pity chokes my spleen; brave scorn forbids
Those tears to issue which swell my eye-lids;
I must not laugh, nor weep sins, and be wise,
Can railing then cure these worn maladies?
Is not our mistress, fair Religion,
As worthy of all our soul's devotion,
As virtue was to the first blinded age?
Are not heaven's joys as valiant to assuage
Lusts, as earth's honour was to them?[6] Alas,
As we do them in means, shall they surpass
Us in the end, and shall thy father's spirit
Meet blind philosophers in heaven, whose merit
Of strict life may be imputed faith,[7] and hear
Thee, whom he taught so easy ways and near
To follow, damned? Oh if thou dar'st, fear this;
This fear great courage, and high valour is.
Dar'st thou aid mutinous Dutch,[8] and dar'st thou lay
Thee in ships, wooden sepulchers, a prey
To leaders' rage, to storms, to shot, to dearth?
Dar'st thou dive seas, and dungeons of the earth?
Hast thou courageous fire to thaw the ice
Of frozen North discoveries? and thrice
Colder than salamanders,[9] like divine
Children in the oven,[10] fires of Spain, and the line,[11]

[6] *them* The virtuous ancients who lived in the "blinded age" before the Christian revelation; their motive for virtue was earthly fame.

[7] *imputed faith* The speaker daringly uses a key term from Protestant theology to suggest that ancient philosophers might be "saved" as a result of their own merits, which might constitute an "imputed faith."

[8] *mutinous Dutch* The (Protestant) Dutch had been in revolt against their (Catholic) Spanish occupiers since 1568.

[9] *salamanders* Reputed to be so naturally cold that they could extinguish fires by contact.

[10] *Children in the oven* children who survived in the fiery furnace into which Nebuchadnezzar cast them. See Daniel 3.11–30.

[11] *fires of Spain, and the line* The tropical heat of the Spanish Main and the equatorial line; possibly also a reference to the "fires" of the Spanish inquisition.

Whose countries' limbecks to our bodies be,[1]
Canst thou for gain bear? and must every he
Which cries not "Goddess" to thy Mistress, draw,
Or eat thy poisonous words? courage of straw!
Oh desperate coward, wilt thou seem bold, and
To thy foes and his (who made thee to stand
Sentinel in his world's garrison) thus yield,
And for forbidden wars, leave the appointed field?
Know thy foes: the foul devil, whom thou
Striv'st to please, for hate, not love, would allow
Thee fain his whole realm to be quit; and as
The world's all parts wither away and pass,
So the world's self, thy other loved foe, is
In her decrepit wane, and thou loving this,
Dost love a withered and worn strumpet; last,
Flesh (itself's death) and joys which flesh can taste,
Thou lovest; and thy fair goodly soul, which doth
Give this flesh power to taste joy, thou dost loathe.
Seek true religion. Oh where? Mirreus[2]
Thinking her unhoused here, and fled from us,
Seeks her at Rome;[3] there, because he doth know
That she was there a thousand years ago;
He loves her rags so, as we here obey
The statecloth[4] where the Prince sat yesterday.
Crants to such brave loves will not be enthralled,
But loves her only, who at Geneva is called
Religion,[5] plain, simple, sullen, young,
Contemptuous, yet unhandsome: as among
Lecherous humors, there is one that judges
No wenches wholesome, but coarse country drudges.
Graius stays still at home here,[6] and because
Some preachers, vile ambitious bauds, and laws
Still new like fashions, bid him think that she
Which dwells with us, is only perfect, he
Embraceth her whom his godfathers will
Tender to him, being tender, as wards still
Take such wives as their guardians offer, or
Pay values.[7] Careless Phrygius doth abhor
All, because all cannot be good, as one
Knowing some women whores, dares marry none.
Graccus loves all as one, and thinks that so
As women do in diverse countries go
In diverse habits, yet are still one kind,
So doth, so is Religion; and this blind-
ness too much light breeds; but unmoved thou
Of force must one, and forced but one allow;
And the right; ask thy father which is she,
Let him ask his; though truth and falsehood be
Near twins, yet truth a little elder is;
Be busy to seek her, believe me this,
He's not of none, nor worst, that seeks the best.
To adore, or scorn an image, or protest,
May all be bad; doubt wisely; in strange way
To stand inquiring right, is not to stray;
To sleep, or run wrong, is. On a huge hill,
Cragged and steep, Truth stands, and he that will
Reach her, about must, and about must go;
And what the hill's suddenness resists, win so;
Yet strive so, that before age, death's twilight,
Thy soul rest, for none can work in that night.
To will implies delay, therefore now do.
Hard deeds, the body's pains; hard knowledge too
The mind's endeavours reach, and mysteries
Are like the sun, dazzling, yet plain to all eyes.
Keep the truth which thou hast found; men do not stand
In so ill case here, that God hath with his hand
Signed kings blank-charters[8] to kill whom they hate,
Nor are they vicars, but hangmen to fate.
Fool and wretch, wilt thou let thy soul be tied
To man's laws, by which she shall not be tried

[1] *limbecks to our bodies be* Because they make our bodies sweat: a limbeck is an alchemical still.

[2] *Mirreus* Some of the proper names the poem assigns to characters who hold various opinions (Mirreus, Graius, Graccus, Phrygius) have classical resonances; "Crants" (l. 49) sounds vaguely Dutch or German; but none appears to hold any particular significance.

[3] *Seeks her at Rome* Mirreus finds "true religion" in Catholicism.

[4] *statecloth* The canopy over the throne, or chair of state, respected as an emblem of the monarch's power.

[5] *But loves ... called / Religion* "Crants" seeks "true religion" in the austere Protestantism of Genevan Calvinism.

[6] *Graius stays still at home here* "Graius" settles for the Church of England, but does so only because those around him do likewise.

[7] *Pay values* A ward who refused a marriage arranged by his or her guardian had to pay the guardian a compensatory fine.

[8] *blank-charters* Originally, legal papers that recorded a promise to supply the king with money: the amount of money was left blank, to be filled in by the king after it was signed. Here, warrants to have people killed, with the space for the victim's name left blank.

At the last day? Will it then boot thee
To say a Philip, or a Gregory,
A Harry, or a Martin taught thee this?[1]
Is not this excuse for mere contraries
Equally strong? Cannot both sides say so?
That thou mayest rightly obey power, her bounds
know;
Those passed, her nature and name is changed; to be
Then humble to her is idolatry;
As streams are, Power is; those blest flowers that dwell
At the rough stream's calm head, thrive and do well,
But having left their roots, and themselves given
To the stream's tyrannous rage, alas are driven
Through mills, and rocks, and woods, and at last,
almost
Consumed in going, in the sea are lost:
So perish souls, which more choose men's unjust
Power from God claimed, than God himself to trust.
—1633

from *Verse Letters*

To Sir Henry Wotton[2]

Sir, more than kisses, letters mingle souls;
For thus, friends absent speak. This ease controls
The tediousness of my life: but for these
I could ideate nothing which could please,
But I should wither in one day, and pass
To a bottle° of hay, that am a lock of grass. *bundle*
Life is a voyage, and in our life's ways
Countries, courts, towns are rocks, or remoras;[3]
They break or stop all ships, yet our state's such,
That though than pitch they stain worse, we must
touch.
If in the furnace of the even line,° *the equator*
Or under the adverse icy pole thou pine,
Thou know'st two temperate regions, girded in,
Dwell there: But Oh, what refuge canst thou win
Parched in the court, and in the country frozen?
Shall cities, built of both extremes, be chosen?
Can dung or garlic be a perfume? Or can
A scorpion and torpedo[4] cure a man?
Cities are worst of all three; of all three
(O knotty riddle) each is worst equally.
Cities are sepulchres; they who dwell there
Are carcasses, as if no such there were.
And courts are theatres, where some men play
Princes, some slaves, all to one end, and of one clay.
The country is a desert, where no good,
Gained (as habits, not born), is understood.
There men become beasts, and prone to more evils;
In cities blocks, and in a lewd court, devils.
As in the first chaos, confusedly,
Each element's qualities were in the other three,
So pride, lust, covetise,° being several *covetousness*
To these three places, yet all are in all,
And mingled thus, their issue is incestuous.
Falsehood is denizened.[5] Virtue is barbarous.
Let no man say there, "Virtue's flinty wall
Shall lock vice in me, I'll do none, but know all."
Men are sponges, which to pour out, receive,
Who know false play, rather than lose, deceive.
For in best understandings sin began,
Angels sinned first, then devils, and then man.
Only perchance beasts sin not; wretched we
Are beasts in all, but white integrity.
I think if men, which in these place live,
Durst look in themselves, and themselves retrieve,
They would like strangers greet themselves, seeing then
Utopian youth, grown old Italian.[6]
Be then thine own home, and in thyself dwell;

[1] *A Philip ... thee this* Respectively, King Philip II of Spain, Pope Gregory (either XIII or XIV), King Henry VIII, and Martin Luther: the group balances two Roman Catholic leaders against two Reformation leaders.

[2] *To Sir Henry Wotton* Administrator, diplomat, poet and writer, Sir Henry Wotton (1568–1639) met Donne at Oxford and was a close friend. This poem appears to have been written in the late 1590s, when both men were looking to win positions at court.

[3] *remoras* Parasitical fish that could attach themselves to the bottom of ships and were thought to slow them down.

[4] *torpedo* Also known as the numbfish or crampfish; the electric ray.

[5] *denizined* Naturalized (as in a "naturalized citizen").

[6] *Utopian youth ... Italian* That is, an ideal youth turned old and depraved (from proverbial expressions concerning Italianate Englishmen, and Machiavelli).

Inn anywhere; continuance maketh hell.
And seeing the snail, which everywhere doth roam,
Carrying his own house still, still is at home,
Follow (for he is easy paced) this snail,
Be thine own palace, or the world's thy jail.
And in the world's sea, do not like cork sleep
Upon the water's face; nor in the deep
Sink like a lead without a line; but as
Fishes glide, leaving no print where they pass,
Nor making sound, so closely thy course go,
Let men dispute, whether thou breathe, or no.
Only in this be no Galenist:[1] to make
Courts' hot ambitions wholesome, do not take
A dram of country's dullness; do not add
Correctives, but, as chemics, purge the bad.
But, sir, I advise not you, I rather do
Say o'er those lessons, which I learned of you:
Whom, free from German schisms, and lightness
Of France, and fair Italy's faithlessness,
Having from these sucked all they had of worth,
And brought home that faith which you carried forth,
I throughly° love; but if myself I've won *thoroughly*
To know my rules, I have, and you have

DONNE.

—1633

An Anatomy of the World

Wherein, by occasion of the untimely death of mistress Elizabeth Drury,[2] the frailty and the decay of this whole world is represented.

[1] *Galenist* Follower of the ancient Roman doctor Galen, who believed that illness was a result of imbalance among the body's four "humors" and who cured an imbalance of one quality with a dose of its opposite.

[2] *Elizabeth Drury* The daughter of Sir Robert Drury; she died in December 1610, aged 14. Donne had never met her, but his sister Anne knew the family and possibly encouraged Donne to write the poem in hopes (ultimately successful) of patronage. A year later, Donne wrote a second poem to commemorate Elizabeth, *The Second Anniversary*. They are two of the few poems Donne published in his lifetime.

THE FIRST ANNIVERSARY

When that rich soul which to her heaven is gone,
Whom all they celebrate, who know they have one,
(For who is sure he hath a soul, unless
It see, and judge, and follow worthiness,
And by deeds praise it? he who doth not this,
May lodge an inmate soul, but 'tis not his.)
When that Queen ended here her progress time,[3]
And, as t' her standing house, to heaven did climb,
Where, loth to make the saints attend her long,
She's now a part both of the choir, and song,
This world, in that great earthquake languished;
For in a common bath of tears it bled,
Which drew the strongest vital spirits out:
But succoured then with a perplexed doubt,
Whether the world did lose or gain in this,
(Because since now no other way there is
But goodness, to see her, whom all would see,
All must endeavour to be good as she,)
This great consumption to a fever turned,
And so the world had fits; it joyed, it mourned;
And, as men think, that agues physic are,
And th' ague being spent, give over care,
So thou, sick world, mistak'st thyself to be
Well, when alas, thou'rt in a lethargy.
Her death did wound and tame thee then, and then
Thou mightst have better spared the sun, or man.
That wound was deep, but 'tis more misery,
That thou hast lost thy sense and memory.
'Twas heavy then to hear thy voice of moan,
But this is worse, that thou art speechless grown.
Thou has forgot thy name thou hadst; thou wast
Nothing but she, and her thou hast o'erpast.
For as a child kept from the font,[4] until
A prince, expected long, come to fulfil
The ceremonies, thou unnamed hadst laid,
Had not her coming, thee her palace made:
Her name defined thee, gave thee form, and frame,
And thou forget'st to celebrate thy name.
Some months she hath been dead (but being dead,

[3] *progress time* Monarch's ceremonial journey through the kingdom.

[4] *font* Baptismal font.

Measures of times are all determined)
But long she hath been away, long, long, yet none
Offers to tell us who it is that's gone.
But as in states doubtful of future heirs,
When sickness without remedy impairs
The present prince, they're loth it should be said,
The prince doth languish, or the prince is dead:
So mankind feeling now a general thaw,
A strong example gone, equal to law,
The cement which did faithfully compact
And glue all virtues, now resolved, and slacked,
Thought it some blasphemy to say sh' was dead;
Or that our weakness was discovered
In that confession; therefore spoke no more
Than tongues, the soul being gone, the loss deplore.
But though it be too late to succour thee,
Sick world, yea dead, yea putrefied, since she
Thy intrinsic balm, and thy preservative,
Can never be renewed, thou never live,
I (since no man can make thee live) will try,
What we may gain by thy anatomy.
Her death hath taught us dearly, that thou art
Corrupt and mortal in thy purest part.
Let no man say, the world itself being dead,
'Tis labour lost to have discovered
The world's infirmities, since there is none
Alive to study this dissection;
For there's a kind of world remaining still,
Though she which did inanimate and fill
The world, be gone, yet in this last long night,
Her ghost doth walk; that is, a glimmering light,
A faint weak love of virtue and of good
Reflects from her, on them which understood
Her worth; and though she have shut in all day,
The twilight of her memory doth stay;
Which, from the carcass of the old world, free,
Creates a new world; and new creatures be
Produced: the matter and the stuff of this,
Her virtue, and the form our practice is.
And though to be thus elemented, arm
These creatures, from home-born intrinsic harm,
(For all assumed unto this dignity,
So many weedless paradises be,
Which of themselves produce no venomous sin,
Except some foreign serpent bring it in)
Yet, because outward storms the strongest break,
And strength itself by confidence grows weak,
This new world may be safer, being told
The dangers and diseases of the old:
For with due temper men do then forgo,
Or covet things, when they their true worth know.
There is no health; physicians say that we
At best, enjoy but a neutrality.
And can there be worse sickness, than to know
That we are never well, nor can be so?
We are born ruinous: poor mothers cry,
That children come not right, nor orderly,
Except they headlong come, and fall upon
An ominous precipitation.
How witty's ruin! how importunate
Upon mankind! it laboured to frustrate
Even God's purpose: and made woman, sent
For man's relief, cause of his languishment.
They were to good ends, and they are so still,
But accessory, and principal in ill.
For that first marriage was our funeral:
One woman at one blow, then killed us all,
And singly, one by one, they kill us now.
We do delightfully ourselves allow
To that consumption; and profusely blind,
We kill ourselves,[1] to propagate our kind.
And yet we do not that; we are not men:
There is not now that mankind, which was then,
When as the sun, and man, did seem to strive,
(Joint tenants of the world) who should survive.
When stag, and raven, and the long-lived tree,
Compared with man, died in minority;
When, if a slow-paced star had stol'n away
From the observer's marking, he might stay
Two or three hundred years to see't again,
And then make up his observation plain;
When, as the age was long, the size was great:
Man's growth confessed, and recompensed the meat:
So spacious and large, that every soul
Did a fair kingdom, and large realm control:
And when the very stature thus erect,
Did that soul a good way towards heaven direct.
Where is this mankind now? who lives to age,

[1] *we kill ourselves* Sex was believed to shorten life.

Fit to be made Methusalem[1] his page?
Alas, we scarce live long enough to try
Whether a new made clock run right, or lie.
Old grandsires talk of yesterday with sorrow,
And for our children we reserve tomorrow.
So short is life, that every peasant strives,
In a torn house, or field, to have three lives.[2]
And as in lasting, so in length is man
Contracted to an inch, who was a span;
For had a man at first in forests strayed,
Or shipwrecked in the sea, one would have laid
A wager, that an elephant, or whale,
That met him, would not hastily assail
A thing so equal to him: now alas,
The fairies and the pygmies well may pass
As credible; mankind decays so soon,
We're scarce our fathers' shadows cast at noon.
Only death adds to our length: nor are we grown
In stature to be men, till we are none.
But this were light, did our less volume hold
All the old text; or had we changed to gold
Their silver; or disposed into less glass
Spirits of virtue, which then scattered was.
But 'tis not so: we're not retired, but damped;
And as our bodies, so our minds are cramped:
'Tis shrinking, not close weaving that hath thus,
In mind and body both bedwarfed us.
We seem ambitious, God's whole work to undo;
Of nothing he made us, and we strive too,
To bring ourselves to nothing back; and we
Do what we can, to do 't so soon as he.
With new diseases on ourselves we war,
And with new physic, a worse engine far.
Thus man, this world's vice-emperor, in whom
All faculties, all graces are at home;
And if in other creatures they appear,
They're but man's ministers, and legates there,
To work on their rebellions, and reduce
Them to civility, and to man's use.
This man, whom God did woo, and loth t'attend
Till man came up, did down to man descend,
This man, so great, that all that is, is his,
Oh what a trifle, and poor thing he is!
If man were anything, he's nothing now:
Help, or at least some time to waste, allow
T' his other wants, yet when he did depart
With her whom we lament, he lost his heart.
She, of whom th' ancients seemed to prophesy,
When they called virtues by the name of *she*;
She in whom virtue was so much refined,
That for allay unto so pure a mind
She took the weaker sex, she that could drive
The poisonous tincture,[3] and the stain of Eve,
Out of her thoughts, and deeds; and purify
All, by a true religious alchemy;
She, she is dead; she's dead: when thou know'st this,
Thou know'st how poor a trifling thing man is.
And learn'st thus much by our anatomy,
The heart being perished, no part can be free.
And that except thou feed (not banquet)[4] on
The supernatural food, religion,
Thy better growth grows withered, and scant;
Be more than man, or thou'rt less than an ant.
Then, as mankind, so is the world's whole frame
Quite out of joint, almost created lame:
For, before God had made up all the rest,
Corruption entered, and depraved the best:
It seized the angels, and then first of all
The world did in her cradle take a fall,
And turned her brains, and took a general maim
Wronging each joint of th' universal frame.
The noblest part, man, felt it first; and then
Both beasts and plants, cursed in the curse of man.
So did the world from the first hour decay,
That evening was beginning of the day,
And now the springs and summers which we see,
Like sons of women after fifty be.
And new philosophy calls all in doubt,
The element of fire is quite put out;[5]
The sun is lost, and th' earth, and no man's wit

[1] *Methusalem* I.e., Methuselah, who lived 969 years (Genesis 5.27).

[2] *three lives* Probably referring to certain kinds of leases, which lasted until the death of three named leasees.

[3] *poisonous tincture* Original sin.

[4] *banquet* That is, feed rather than snack or nibble: a banquet in the period could refer to an appetizer or dessert course.

[5] *The element of fire … put out* The astronomer Johannes Kepler (1571–1630) disproved the traditional belief that the earth was surrounded by a sphere of fire.

Can well direct him where to look for it.[1]
And freely men confess that this world's spent,
When in the planets, and the firmament
They seek so many new; they see that this
Is crumbled out again to his atomies.
'Tis all in pieces, all coherence gone;
All just supply, and all relation:
Prince, subject, father, son, are things forgot,
For every man alone thinks he hath got
To be a phoenix, and that there can be
None of that kind, of which he is, but he.
This is the world's condition now, and now
She that should all parts to reunion bow,
She that had all magnetic force alone,
To draw, and fasten sundered parts in one;
She whom wise nature had invented then
When she observed that every sort of men
Did in their voyage in this world's sea stray,
And needed a new compass for their way;
She that was best, and first original
Of all fair copies; and the general
Steward to Fate; she whose rich eyes, and breast,
Gilt the West Indies, and perfumed the East;
Whose having breathed in this world, did bestow
Spice on those isles, and bade them still smell so,
And that rich Indy which doth gold inter,
Is but as single money, coined from her:
She to whom this world must itself refer,
As suburbs, or the microcosm of her,
She, she is dead; she's dead: when thou know'st this,
Thou know'st how lame a cripple this world is.
And learn'st thus much by our anatomy,
That this world's general sickness doth not lie
In any humour, or one certain part;
But as thou sawest it rotten at the heart,
Thou seest a hectic fever hath got hold
Of the whole substance, not to be controlled,
And that thou hast but one way, not to admit
The world's infection, to be none of it.
For the world's subtlest immaterial parts
Feel this consuming wound, and age's darts.
For the world's beauty is decayed, or gone,
Beauty, that's colour, and proportion.
We think the heavens enjoy their spherical,
Their round proportion embracing all.[2]
But yet their various and perplexed course,
Observed in diverse ages, doth enforce
Men to find out so many eccentric parts,
Such diverse down-right lines, such overthwarts,
As disproportion that pure form. It tears
The firmament in eight and forty shares,
And in these constellations then arise
New stars,[3] and old do vanish from our eyes:
As though heaven suffered earthquakes, peace or war,
When new towns rise, and old demolished are.
They have impaled within a zodiac
The free-born sun, and keep twelve signs awake
To watch his steps; the goat and crab control,
And fright him back, who else to either pole
(Did not these tropics fetter him) might run:
For his course is not round; nor can the sun
Perfect a circle, or maintain his way
One inch direct; but where he rose today
He comes no more, but with a cozening line,
Steals by that point, and so is serpentine:
And seeming weary with his reeling thus,
He means to sleep, being now fall'n nearer us.
So, of the stars which boast that they do run
In circle still, none ends where he begun.
All their proportion's lame, it sinks, it swells.
For of meridians, and parallels,
Man hath weaved out a net, and this net thrown
Upon the heavens, and now they are his own.
Loth to go up the hill, or labour thus
To go to heaven, we make heaven come to us.
We spur, we rein the stars, and in their race

[1] *The sun is lost ... look for it* Referring to the cosmological uncertainty created by the new, heliocentric theories of Copernicus, Brahe, and Kepler.

[2] *Their round proportion embracing all* Beginning in line 251, Donne points to changes in astronomical models as a sign of universal change. Plato had suggested that planetary orbits were perfect circles (lines 251–52); Ptolemy had constructed a more complex model, still geocentric, that accounted for observed movements (line 253 forward). Ptolemy's model was itself under challenge in Donne's time by the work of astronomers such as Copernicus.

[3] *new stars* Brahe and Kepler had observed the appearance of new stars, and Galileo had discovered the moons of Jupiter; these observations all challenged belief in the unchangeableness of the firmament above the moon.

They're diversely content t' obey our pace.
But keeps the earth her round proportion still?
Doth not a Tenerife,[1] or higher hill
Rise so high like a rock, that one might think
The floating moon would shipwreck there, and sink?
Seas are so deep, that whales being struck today,
Perchance tomorrow, scarce at middle way
Of their wished journey's end, the bottom, die.
And men, to sound depths, so much line untie,
As one might justly think that there would rise
At end thereof, one of th' Antipodes:
If under all, a vault infernal be,
(Which sure is spacious, except that we
Invent another torment, that there must
Millions into a strait hot room be thrust)
Then solidness, and roundness have no place.
Are these but warts, and pock-holes in the face
Of th' earth? Think so: but yet confess, in this
The world's proportion disfigured is,
That those two legs whereon it doth rely,
Reward and punishment are bent awry.
And, oh, it can no more be questioned,
That beauty's best, proportion, is dead,
Since even grief itself, which now alone
Is left us, is without proportion.
She by whose lines proportion should be
Examined, measure of all symmetry,
Whom had that ancient[2] seen, who thought souls made
Of harmony, he would at next have said
That harmony was she, and thence infer,
That souls were but resultances from her,
And did from her into our bodies go,
As to our eyes, the forms from objects flow:
She, who if those great Doctors[3] truly said
That the Ark to man's proportions was made,
Had been a type for that, as that might be
A type of her in this, that contrary
Both elements, and passions lived at peace
In her, who caused all civil war to cease.
She, after whom what form soe'er we see
Is discord, and rude incongruity;
She, she is dead, she's dead; when thou know'st this
Thou know'st how ugly a monster this world is:
And learn'st thus much by our anatomy,
That here is nothing to enamour thee:
And that, not only faults in inward parts,
Corruptions in our brains, or in our hearts,
Poisoning the fountains, whence our actions spring,
Endanger us: but that if everything
Be not done fitly and in proportion,
To satisfy wise, and good lookers-on,
(Since most men be such as most think they be)
They're loathsome too, by this deformity.
For good, and well, must in our actions meet;
Wicked is not much worse than indiscreet.
But beauty's other second element,
Colour, and lustre now, is as near spent.
And had the world his just proportion,
Were it a ring still, yet the stone is gone.
As a compassionate turquoise[4] which doth tell
By looking pale, the wearer is not well,
As gold falls sick[5] being stung with mercury,
All the world's parts of such complexion be.
When nature was most busy, the first week,
Swaddling the new born earth, God seemed to like
That she should sport herself sometimes, and play,
To mingle, and vary colours every day:
And then, as though she could not make enow,
Himself his various rainbow did allow.
Sight is the noblest sense of any one,
Yet sight hath only colour to feed on,
And colour is decayed: summer's robe grows
Dusky, and like an oft dyed garment shows.
Our blushing red, which used in cheeks to spread,
Is inward sunk, and only our souls are red.
Perchance the world might have recovered,
If she whom we lament had not been dead:
But she, in whom all white, and red, and blue
(Beauty's ingredients) voluntary grew,

[1] *Tenerife* Mountain on the island of Teneriffe, in the Canary Islands; it rises over 12,000 feet, but was often considered much higher in the period.

[2] *that ancient* Probably the ancient Greek mathematician and philosopher Pythagoras (born c. 560 BCE).

[3] *great Doctors* Church doctors or fathers, the patristic writers; Augustine and Ambrose both make this claim.

[4] *compassionate turquoise* Turquoise was reputed to change lustre according to the health of the wearer.

[5] *gold falls sick* Gold amalgam, a mixture of gold with mercury, is paler than gold.

As in an unvexed paradise; from whom
Did all things verdure, and their lustre come,
Whose composition was miraculous,
Being all colour, all diaphanous,
(For air, and fire but thick gross bodies were
And liveliest stones but drowsy, and pale to her),
She, she, is dead; she's dead: when thou know'st this,
Thou know'st how wan a ghost this our world is:
And learn'st thus much by our anatomy,
That it should more affright, than pleasure thee.
And that, since all fair colour then did sink,
'Tis now but wicked vanity, to think
To colour vicious deeds with good pretense,
Or with bought colours to elude men's sense.
Nor in aught more this world's decay appears,
Than that her influence the heaven forbears,
Or that the elements do not feel this,
The father, or the mother barren is.
The clouds conceive not rain, or do not pour
In the due birth time, down the balmy shower.
Th' air doth not motherly sit on the earth,
To hatch her seasons, and give all things birth.
Spring-times were common cradles, but are tombs;
And false conceptions fill the general wombs.
Th' air shows such meteors, as none can see,
Not only what they mean, but what they be.
Earth such new worms, as would have troubled much
Th' Egyptian Mages[1] to have made more such.
What artist now dares boast that he can bring
Heaven hither, or constellate anything,
So as the influence of those stars may be
Imprisoned in an herb, or charm, or tree,
And do by touch, all which those stars could do?
The art is lost, and correspondence too.
For heaven gives little, and the earth takes less,
And man least knows their trade, and purposes.
If this commerce 'twixt heaven and earth were not
Embarred, and all this traffic quite forgot,
She, for whose loss we have lamented thus,
Would work more fully and powerfully on us.
Since herbs, and roots by dying, lose not all,
But they, yea ashes too, are medicinal,
Death could not quench her virtue so, but that
It would be (if not followed) wondered at:
And all the world would be one dying swan,
To sing her funeral praise, and vanish then.
But as some serpents' poison hurteth not,
Except it be from the live serpent shot,
So doth her virtue need her here, to fit
That unto us; she working more than it.
But she, in whom to such maturity
Virtue was grown, past growth, that it must die,
She, from whose influence all impressions came,
But, by receivers' impotencies, lame,
Who, though she could not transubstantiate
All states to gold, yet gilded every state,
So that some princes have some temperance;
Some counsellors some purpose to advance
The common profit; and some people have
Some stay, no more than kings should give, to crave;
Some women have some taciturnity,
Some nunneries, some grains of chastity.
She that did thus much, and much more could do,
But that our age was iron, and rusty too,
She, she is dead; she 's dead; when thou know'st this,
Thou know'st how dry a cinder this world is.
And learn'st thus much by our anatomy,
That 'tis in vain to dew, or mollify
It with thy tears, or sweat, or blood: nothing
Is worth our travail, grief, or perishing,
But those rich joys, which did possess her heart,
Of which she's now partaker, and a part.
But as in cutting up a man that's dead,
The body will not last out to have read
On every part, and therefore men direct
Their speech to parts, that are of most effect;
So the world's carcass would not last, if I
Were punctual in this anatomy.
Nor smells it well to hearers, if one tell
Them their disease, who fain would think they're well.
Here therefore be the end: and, blessed maid,
Of whom is meant whatever hath been said,
Or shall be spoken well by any tongue,
Whose name refines coarse lines, and makes prose song,
Accept this tribute, and his first year's rent,
Who till his dark short taper's end be spent,
As oft as thy feast sees this widowed earth,

[1] *Egyptian mages* From Exodus 7.10–12; Donne refers to the new snakes ("worms") that explorers in Africa and America were encountering.

Will yearly celebrate thy second birth,
That is, thy death. For though the soul of man
Be got when man is made, 'tis born but then
When man doth die. Our body's as the womb,
And as a midwife death directs it home.
And you her creatures, whom she works upon
And have your last, and best concoction
From her example, and her virtue, if you
In reverence to her, do think it due,
That no one should her praises thus rehearse,
As matter fit for chronicle, not verse,
Vouchsafe to call to mind, that God did make
A last, and lasting'st piece, a song. He spake
To Moses, to deliver unto all,
That song: because he knew they would let fall
The Law, the prophets, and the history,
But keep the song still in their memory.[1]
Such an opinion (in due measure) made
Me this great office boldly to invade.
Nor could incomprehensibleness deter
Me, from thus trying to imprison her.
Which when I saw that a strict grave could do,
I saw not why verse might not do so too.
Verse hath a middle nature: heaven keeps souls,
The grave keeps bodies, verse the fame enrols.
—1611

from *Holy Sonnets*

2[2]

As due by many titles I resign
Myself to thee, O God, first I was made
By thee, and for Thee, and when I was decayed
Thy blood bought that, the which before was Thine;
I am Thy son, made with Thyself to shine,
Thy servant, whose pains Thou hast still repaid,
Thy sheep, Thine image, and, till I betrayed
Myself, a temple of Thy Spirit divine;
Why doth the devil then usurp on me?
Why doth he steal, nay ravish, that's Thy right?
Except Thou rise and for Thine own work fight,
Oh I shall soon despair, when I do see
That Thou lov'st mankind well, yet wilt not choose me,
And Satan hates me, yet is loth to lose me.
—1633

5[3]

I am a little world made cunningly
Of elements, and an angelic sprite,
But black sin hath betrayed to endless night
My world's both parts, and (oh) both parts must die.
You which beyond that heaven which was most high
Have found new spheres, and of new lands can write,
Pour new seas in mine eyes, that so I might
Drown my world with my weeping earnestly,
Or wash it, if it must be drowned no more:
But oh it must be burnt; alas the fire
Of lust and envy have burnt it heretofore,
And made it fouler; let their flames retire,
And burn me O Lord, with a fiery zeal
Of Thee and Thy house, which doth in eating heal.
—1635

6[4]

This is my play's last scene, here heavens appoint
My pilgrimage's last mile; and my race
Idly, yet quickly run, hath this last pace,
My span's last inch, my minute's last point,
And gluttonous death will instantly unjoint
My body and soul, and I shall sleep a space,
But my ever-waking part shall see that face
Whose fear already shakes my every joint:
Then, as my soul, to heaven her first seat, takes flight,
And earth-born body in the earth shall dwell,
So, fall my sins, that all may have their right,
To where they're bred, and would press me, to hell.

[1] *a song* See Deuteronomy 31.19, 31–43.

[2] *2* Numbered as Sonnet 1 in some modern editions.

[3] *5* Numbered as Sonnet 2 (of those added in 1635) in some modern editions.

[4] *6* Numbered as Sonnet 3 in some modern editions.

Impute me righteous,[1] thus purged of evil,
For thus I leave the world, the flesh, and devil.
—1633

7[2]

At the round earth's imagined corners, blow
Your trumpets, angels, and arise, arise
From death, you numberless infinities
Of souls, and to your scattered bodies go,
All whom the flood did, and fire shall o'erthrow,
All whom war, dearth, age, agues, tyrannies,
Despair, law, chance, hath slain, and you whose eyes
Shall behold God and never taste death's woe.[3]
But let them sleep, Lord, and me mourn a space,
For if above all these my sins abound,
'Tis late to ask abundance of Thy grace
When we are there; here on this lowly ground,
Teach me how to repent; for that's as good
As if Thou hadst sealed my pardon with Thy blood.
—1633

9[4]

If poisonous minerals, and if that tree,
Whose fruit threw death on else immortal us,
If lecherous goats, if serpents envious
Cannot be damned, alas, why should I be?
Why should intent or reason, born in me,
Make sins, else equal, in me more heinous?
And mercy being easy, and glorious
To God, in His stern wrath, why threatens He?
But who am I, that dare dispute with Thee?
O God, oh! of Thine only worthy blood
And my tears, make a heavenly Lethean flood,[5]
And drown in it my sins' black memory.
That Thou remember them, some claim as debt,
I think it mercy, if Thou wilt forget.
—1633

10[6]

Death be not proud, though some have called thee
Mighty and dreadful, for thou are not so;
For those whom thou think'st thou dost overthrow
Die not, poor death, nor yet canst thou kill me.
From rest and sleep, which but thy pictures be,
Much pleasure; then from thee, much more must flow,
And soonest our best men with thee do go,
Rest of their bones, and soul's delivery.
Thou art slave to fate, chance, kings, and desperate men,
And dost with poison, war, and sickness dwell;
And poppy, or charms, can make us sleep as well
And better than thy stroke; why swell'st thou then?
One short sleep past, we wake eternally,
And death shall be no more; death, thou shalt die.
—1633

13[7]

What if this present were the world's last night?
Mark in my heart, O soul, where thou dost dwell,
The picture of Christ crucified, and tell
Whether that countenance can thee affright,
Tears in His eyes quench the amazing light,
Blood fills His frowns, which from His pierced head fell,
And can that tongue adjudge thee unto hell,
Which prayed forgiveness for His foes' fierce spite?
No, no; but as in my idolatry
I said to all my profane mistresses,
Beauty, of pity, foulness only is

[1] *Impute me righteous* Key idea of Protestant theology: justifying grace is imputed to a person through Christ's righteousness.

[2] *7* Numbered as Sonnet 4 in some modern editions.

[3] *Shall behold … death's woe* Referring to those mentioned in Luke 9.27, who will "not taste of death, till they have seen the kingdom of God."

[4] *9* Numbered as Sonnet 5 in some modern editions.

[5] *Lethean flood* In classical myth, Lethe is a river in the underworld; those who drink from it forget their earthly life.

[6] *10* Numbered as Sonnet 6 in some modern editions.

[7] *13* Numbered as Sonnet 9 in some modern editions.

A sign of rigour:[1] so I say to thee,
To wicked spirits are horrid shapes assigned,
This beauteous form assures a piteous mind.
—1633

14[2]

Batter my heart, three personed God; for you
As yet but knock, breathe, shine, and seek to mend;
That I may rise and stand, o'erthrow me, and bend
Your force, to break, blow, burn and make me new.
I, like an usurped town, to another due,
Labour to admit You, but oh, to no end:
Reason Your viceroy in me, me should defend,
But is captived, and proves weak or untrue.
Yet dearly I love You, and would be loved fain,
But am betrothed unto your enemy:
Divorce me, untie, or break that knot again,
Take me to You, imprison me, for I
Except You enthral me, never shall be free,
Nor ever chaste, except You ravish me.
—1633

18[3]

Show me, dear Christ, Thy spouse, so bright and clear.
What, is it she which on the other shore
Goes richly painted?[4] or which, robbed and tore,
Laments and mourns in Germany and here?[5]
Sleeps she a thousand, then peeps up one year?
Is she self-truth and errs? now new, now outwore?
Doth she, and did she, and shall she evermore
On one, on seven, or on no hill appear?[6]
Dwells she with us, or like adventuring knights
First travail we to seek and then make love?
Betray, kind husband, Thy spouse to our sights,
And let mine amorous soul court Thy mild dove,
Who is most true and pleasing to Thee then
When she's embraced and open to most men.
—1899

19[7]

Oh, to vex me, contraries meet in one:
Inconstancy unnaturally hath begot
A constant habit; that when I would not
I change in vows, and in devotion.
As humorous is my contrition
As my profane love, and as soon forgot:
As riddlingly distempered, cold and hot,
As praying, as mute; as infinite, as none.
I durst not view heaven yesterday; and today
In prayers and flattering speeches I court God:
Tomorrow I quake with true fear of His rod.
So my devout fits come and go away
Like a fantastic ague: save that here
Those are my best days, when I shake with fear.
—1899

Good Friday, 1613. Riding Westward

Let man's soul be a sphere, and then, in this,
The intelligence that moves, devotion is,[8]
And as the other spheres, by being grown
Subject to foreign motions, lose their own,
And being by others hurried every day,
Scarce in a year their natural form obey:

[1] *A sign of rigour* That is, beauty is a sign of pity (compassion for the lover and his desires), ugliness a sign of rigor (denial of the lover his desires).

[2] *14* Numbered as Sonnet 10 in some modern editions.

[3] *18* Numbered as Sonnet 2 (of the Westmoreland manuscript sonnets) in some modern editions.

[4] *Goes richly painted* The Roman Catholic Church.

[5] *Laments … and here* The Protestant or perhaps, more specifically, Calvinist Church.

[6] *On one … hill appear* Solomon's Temple stood on one hill, Mount Moriah (see 2 Chronicles 3.1); Rome has seven hills; Geneva, the center of Calvinism, has none.

[7] *19* Numbered as Sonnet 3 (of the Westmoreland manuscript sonnets) in some modern editions.

[8] *The intelligence … devotion is* Donne invokes traditional cosmography, in which each heavenly sphere was controlled by its "intelligence" or spirit.

Pleasure or business, so our souls admit
For their First Mover, and are whirled by it.
Hence is't, that I am carried towards the West
This day, when my soul's form bends towards the East.
There I should see a sun, by rising set,
And by that setting endless day beget;
But that Christ on this cross did rise and fall,
Sin had eternally benighted all.
Yet dare I almost be glad, I do not see
That spectacle of too much weight for me.
Who sees God's face, that is self life, must die;
What a death were it then to see God die?
It made His own lieutenant, Nature, shrink,
It made His footstool crack, and the sun wink.
Could I behold those hands which span the poles,
And tune all spheres at once, pierced with those holes?
Could I behold that endless height which is
Zenith to us, and to our antipodes,
Humbled below us? or that blood which is
The seat of all our souls, if not of His,
Made dirt of dust, or that flesh which was worn
By God, for His apparel, ragged and torn?
If on these things I durst not look, durst I
Upon His miserable mother cast mine eye,
Who was God's partner here, and furnished thus
Half of that sacrifice, which ransomed us?
Though these things, as I ride, be from mine eye,
They are present yet unto my memory,
For that looks towards them; and thou look'st
towards me,
O Saviour, as Thou hang'st upon the tree;
I turn my back to Thee, but to receive
Corrections, till Thy mercies bid Thee leave.
O think me worth Thine anger, punish me,
Burn off my rusts, and my deformity,
Restore Thine image, so much, by Thy grace,
That Thou may'st know me, and I'll turn my face.
—1633

A Hymn to God the Father

1

Wilt Thou forgive that sin where I begun,
Which is my sin, though it were done before?
Wilt Thou forgive those sins through which I run,
And do them still, though still I do deplore?
When Thou hast done, Thou hast not done,
For I have more.

2

Wilt Thou forgive that sin which I have won
Others to sin? and made my sin their door?
Wilt Thou forgive that sin which I did shun
A year, or two, but wallowed in, a score?
When Thou hast done, Thou hast not done,
For I have more.

3

I have a sin of fear, that when I have spun
My last thread, I shall perish on the shore;
But swear by Thyself, that at my death Thy sun
Shall shine as he shines now, and heretofore;
And, having done that, Thou hast done,
I have no more.[1]
—1633

from *Devotions*[2]

MEDITATION 17

Nunc Lento Sonitu Dicunt, Morieris
Now, this bell tolling softly for another, says to me:
Thou must die

Perchance he for whom this bell tolls may be so ill, as that he knows not it tolls for him; and perchance I may think myself so much better than I am, as that they who are about me, and see my state, may have caused it to toll for me, and I know not that. The Church is catholic, universal, so are all her actions; all that she does

[1] *I have no more* "I fear no more" in the printed version; "have" in the manuscripts.

[2] *Devotions* Donne wrote *Devotions* (1624) during his convalescence from a dangerous illness. The book consists of 23 "stations," each consisting of a meditation, an expostulation, and a concluding prayer. Each of the meditations explores a stage of his illness (that is, a stage in the story of the little world of the body), by looking for correspondences to and implications of that stage in the larger world.

belongs to all. When she baptizes a child, that action concerns me; for that child is thereby connected to that body which is my head too, and ingrafted into that body whereof I am a member. And when she buries a man, that action concerns me: all mankind is of one author, and is one volume; when one man dies, one chapter is not torn out of the book, but translated into a better language; and every chapter must be so translated; God employs several translators; some pieces are translated by age, some by sickness, some by war, some by justice; but God's hand is in every translation, and His hand shall bind up all our scattered leaves again for that library where every book shall lie open to one another. As therefore the bell that rings to a sermon calls not upon the preacher only, but upon the congregation to come, so this bell calls us all; but how much more me, who am brought so near the door by this sickness. There was a contention as far as a suit (in which both piety and dignity, religion and estimation, were mingled), which of the religious orders should ring to prayers first in the morning; and it was determined, that they should ring first that rose earliest. If we understand aright the dignity of this bell that tolls for our evening prayer, we would be glad to make it ours by rising early, in that application, that it might be ours as well as his, whose indeed it is. The bell doth toll for him that thinks it doth; and though it intermit again, yet from that minute that that occasion wrought upon him, he is united to God. Who casts not up his eye to the sun when it rises? but who takes off his eye from a comet when that breaks out? Who bends not his ear to any bell which upon any occasion rings? but who can remove it from that bell which is passing a piece of himself out of this world? No man is an island, entire of itself; every man is a piece of the continent, a part of the main. If a clod be washed away by the sea, Europe is the less, as well as if a promontory were, as well as if a manor of thy friend's or of thine own were: any man's death diminishes me, because I am involved in mankind, and therefore never send to know for whom the bells tolls; it tolls for thee. Neither can we call this a begging of misery, or a borrowing of misery, as though we were not miserable enough of ourselves, but must fetch in more from the next house, in taking upon us the misery of our neighbours. Truly it were an excusable covetousness if we did, for affliction is a treasure, and scarce any man hath enough of it. No man hath affliction enough that is not matured and ripened by it, and made fit for God by that affliction. If a man carry treasure in bullion, or in a wedge of gold, and have none coined into current money, his treasure will not defray him as he travels. Tribulation is treasure in the nature of it, but it is not current money in the use of it, except we get nearer and nearer our home, heaven, by it. Another man may be sick too, and sick to death, and this affliction may lie in his bowels, as gold in a mine, and be of no use to him; but this bell, that tells me of his affliction, digs out and applies that gold to me: if by this consideration of another's danger I take mine own into contemplation, and so secure myself, by making my recourse to my God, who is our only security.

—1624

John Webster

c. 1578 – c. 1634 or 1638

John Webster's dark brooding tragedies, *The White Devil* and *The Duchess of Malfi*, continue to intrigue readers and playgoers. Webster is often called the last of the great dramatists of the English Renaissance, for after his death in the early 1630s there were no immediate successors who could match his dramatic skill—and in 1642, the authorities, under Puritan influence, closed the theaters.

Little is known about Webster himself. In 1666 the Great Fire of London destroyed many records, including those of St. Sepulchre Parish, which presumably documented Webster's birth, baptism, marriage, and death. Similarly, only three plays have survived that we know to be entirely of his own composition, although there is evidence that he wrote others. We do know that Webster was born some time around 1578, the son of a London carriage maker. His father, also John Webster, occasionally provided local theater companies with transportation for their productions; these business transactions might have provided the young Webster with the first taste of his future career. The elder Webster presumably belonged to the Merchant Taylors' Guild, so his son was educated at the prestigious Merchant Taylors' School. There he would have learned Latin and Greek and read a number of classical works. It is also probable that as a young man Webster studied law at the Middle Temple, a background that helps explain the playwright's frequent references to the law as well as the title of his tragicomedy, *The Devil's Law Case* (c. 1618).

By 1602, Webster had been hired by Philip Henslowe, London's most important theater producer. Henslowe's diaries indicate that he had engaged Webster to work with Thomas Dekker and Thomas Middleton on a play entitled *Caesar's Fall*. Throughout the early stages of his career Webster worked mostly in collaboration with others. But his reputation rests on the first two plays he wrote on his own. In *The White Devil* (c. 1612), a searing tragedy that seems to be based on an actual episode in Italian history, a beautiful but ruthless aristocrat has an adulterous affair and then murders her husband. *The Duchess of Malfi* (c. 1614) dramatizes an independent-minded if imprudent woman's destruction at the hands of her vengeful and selfish brothers. Disturbing, violent, and bloody, these tragedies raise metaphysical questions to which they give no clear answers.

In March of 1606 Webster married sixteen-year-old Sara Peniall. A son, John, was born less than two months later. The marriage appears to have been happy, and three daughters (Margery, Sara, and Elizabeth) followed. Though we know little of Webster's later life, he seems to have remained active as a playwright through much of the 1620s. Webster also wrote the pageant *Monuments of Honour* (1624) and collaborated on other dramatic works with such writers as William Rowley, Thomas Middleton, Thomas Heywood, John Fletcher, Philip Massinger, and John Ford.

As is the case with so many details of Webster's life, we have no reliable information about his death or burial. It is assumed that he died in the mid or late 1630s.

⌘⌘⌘

The Duchess of Malfi

TO THE RIGHT HONOURABLE GEORGE HARDING, BARON BERKELEY, OF BERKELEY CASTLE AND KNIGHT OF THE ORDER OF THE BATH TO THE ILLUSTRIOUS PRINCE CHARLES

My Noble Lord,

That I may present my excuse why, being a stranger to your Lordship, I offer this poem to your patronage, I plead this warrant: men who never saw the sea, yet desire to behold that regiment of waters, choose some eminent river to guide them thither, and make that, as it were, their conduct or postilion:[1] by the like ingenious means has your fame arrived at my knowledge, receiving it from some of worth, who both in contemplation and practice owe to your honour their clearest service. I do not altogether look up at your title; the ancientest nobility being but a relic of time past, and the truest honour indeed being for a man to confer honour on himself, which your learning strives to propagate, and shall make you arrive at the dignity of a great example. I am confident this work is not unworthy your honour's perusal, for by such poems as this poets have kissed the hands of great princes, and drawn their gentle eyes to look down upon their sheets of paper, when the poets themselves were bound up in their winding-sheets.[2] The like courtesy from your Lordship shall make you live in your grave, and laurel spring out of it, when the ignorant scorners of the Muses, that like worms in libraries seem to live only to destroy learning, shall wither neglected and forgotten. This work and myself I humbly present to your approved censure, it being the utmost of my wishes to have your honourable self my weighty and perspicuous[3] comment; which grace so done me shall ever be acknowledged

By your Lordship's in all duty and observance,

John Webster.

[1] *postilion* Guide.

[2] *winding-sheets* Burial shrouds.

[3] *perspicuous* Distinguished.

CHARACTERS

Ferdinand, *Duke of Calabria*
The Cardinal, *Ferdinand's brother*
Daniel de Bosola, *steward of the Duchess's horses*
Antonio Bologna, *steward of the Duchess's household*
Delio, *Antonio's friend*
Castruccio, *a lord*
The Marquis of Pescara, *a soldier*
Count Malateste, *a courtier*
Silvio, *a courtier*
Roderigo, *a courtier*
Grisolan, *a courtier*
Doctor
The Duchess of Malfi
Cariola, *the Duchess's waiting woman*
Julia, *Castruccio's wife and the Cardinal's mistress*
An Old Lady
Two Pilgrims
Three Young Children
Several Madmen
Court Officers

ACT 1, SCENE 1

(*Enter Antonio and Delio.*)

DELIO. You are welcome to your country, dear Antonio;
You have been long in France, and you return
A very formal Frenchman in your habit.° *dress*
How do you like the French court?
ANTONIO. I admire it;
In seeking to reduce both state and people
To a fixed order, their judicious king
Begins at home; quits° first his royal palace *rids*
Of flattering sycophants, of dissolute
And infamous persons, which he sweetly terms
His master's masterpiece, the work of heaven;
Consid'ring duly, that a prince's court
Is like a common fountain, whence should flow
Pure silver drops in general,[4] but if't chance

[4] *in general* Everywhere.

Some cursed example poison't near the head,[1]
Death and diseases through the whole land spread.
And what is't makes this blessed government,
But a most provident council, who dare freely
Inform him the corruption of the times?
Though some o' th' court hold it presumption
To instruct princes what they ought to do,
It is a noble duty to inform them
What they ought to foresee. Here comes Bosola,
The only court-gall;[2] yet I observe his railing
Is not for simple love of piety:
Indeed he rails at those things which he wants;
Would be as lecherous, covetous, or proud,
Bloody, or envious, as any man,
If he had means to be so. Here's the Cardinal.

(*Enter Bosola and Cardinal.*)

BOSOLA. I do haunt you still.

CARDINAL. So.

BOSOLA. I have done you better service than to be slighted thus. Miserable age, where only the reward of doing well, is the doing of it!

CARDINAL. You enforce[3] your merit too much.

BOSOLA. I fell into the galleys in your service, where, for two years together, I wore two towels instead of a shirt, with a knot on the shoulder, after the fashion of a Roman mantle.[4] Slighted thus! I will thrive some way: black-birds fatten best in hard[5] weather; why not I in these dog-days?[6]

CARDINAL. Would you could become honest!

BOSOLA. With all your divinity do but direct me the way to it. I have known many travel far for it, and yet return as arrant knaves as they went forth, because they carried themselves always along with them.

(*Exit Cardinal.*)

Are you gone? Some fellows, they say, are possessed with the devil, but this great fellow were able to possess the greatest devil, and make him worse.

ANTONIO. He hath denied thee some suit?

BOSOLA. He and his brother are like plum-trees that grow crooked over standing-pools;[7] they are rich, and o'erladen with fruit, but none but crows, pies,[8] and caterpillars feed on them. Could I be one of their flattering panders,[9] I would hang on their ears like a horseleech, till I were full, and then drop off. I pray leave me. Who would rely upon these miserable dependencies, in expectation to be advanced to-morrow? What creature ever fed worse, than hoping Tantalus?[10] Nor ever died any man more fearfully, than he that hoped for a pardon. There are rewards for hawks and dogs, when they have done us service; but for a soldier that hazards his limbs in a battle, nothing but a kind of geometry is his last supportation.[11]

DELIO. Geometry!

BOSOLA. Ay, to hang in a fair pair of slings, take his latter swing in the world upon an honourable pair of crutches, from hospital to hospital. Fare ye well, sir. And yet do not you scorn us, for places in the court are but like beds in the hospital, where this man's head lies at that man's foot, and so lower and lower.

(*Exit Bosola.*)

DELIO. I knew this fellow seven years in the galleys
For a notorious murder; and 'twas thought
The Cardinal suborned[12] it: he was released

---

[1] *head* Double entendre, indicating both the source of the fountain and the head of state.

[2] *court-gall* Court malcontent.

[3] *enforce* Emphasize.

[4] *mantle* Here, toga.

[5] *hard* Cold.

[6] *dog-days* Hottest days of the year, coinciding with the August rising of Sirius, the dog star. These days were considered the most unwholesome time of the year.

[7] *standing-pools* Stagnant ponds.

[8] *pies* Magpies.

[9] *panders* Pimps.

[10] *Tantalus* King of Phyrgia in Greek mythology. For revealing the secrets of the gods, Tantalus was condemned to stand up to his chin in water. Whenever he stooped for a drink, the water would recede. Above him, fruit hung on branches just out of his reach.

[11] *nothing ... supportation* His last reward is a stiff and crooked body.

[12] *suborned* Arranged through devious means.

By the French general, Gaston de Foix,[1]
When he recovered Naples.
ANTONIO. 'Tis great pity
He should be thus neglected: I have heard
He's very valiant. This foul melancholy
Will poison all his goodness; for, I'll tell you,
If too immoderate sleep be truly said
To be an inward rust unto the soul,
It then doth follow want of action
Breeds all black malcontents, and their close rearing,[2]
Like moths in cloth, do hurt for want of wearing.

ACT 1, SCENE 2

(*Enter Castruccio, Roderigo, Silvio, and Grisolan.*)

DELIO. The presence[3] 'gins to fill: you promised me
To make me the partaker of the natures[4]
Of some of your great courtiers.
ANTONIO. The Lord Cardinal's,
And other strangers, that are now in court?
I shall: here comes the great Calabrian[5] Duke.

(*Enter Ferdinand.*)

FERDINAND. Who took the ring[6] oftenest?

SILVIO. Antonio Bologna, my Lord.

FERDINAND. Our sister Duchess's great master[7] of her household: give him the jewel. When shall we leave this sportive action and fall to action indeed?

CASTRUCCIO. Methinks, my Lord, you should not desire to go to war in person.

FERDINAND. Now, for some gravity; why, my Lord?

CASTRUCCIO. It is fitting a soldier arise to be a prince, but not necessary a prince descend to be a captain.

FERDINAND. No?

CASTRUCCIO. No, my Lord; he were far better do it by a deputy.

FERDINAND. Why should he not as well sleep, or eat by a deputy? This might take idle, offensive, and base office[8] from him, whereas the other deprives him of honour.

CASTRUCCIO. Believe my experience: that realm is never long in quiet, where the ruler is a soldier.

FERDINAND. Thou toldest me thy wife could not endure fighting.

CASTRUCCIO. True, my Lord.

FERDINAND. And of a jest she broke[9] of a captain she met full of wounds: I have forgot it.

CASTRUCCIO. She told him, my Lord, he was a pitiful fellow, to lie like the children of Ismael,[10] all in tents.[11]

FERDINAND. Why, there's a wit were able to undo all the chirurgeons[12] o' th' city, for although gallants[13] should quarrel, and had drawn their weapons, and were ready to go to it, yet her persuasions would make them put up.[14]

CASTRUCCIO. That she would, my Lord. How do you like my Spanish jennet?[15]

RODERIGO. He is all fire.

FERDINAND. I am of Pliny's[16] opinion, I think he was begot by the wind; he runs as if he were ballassed with quicksilver.[17]

SILVIO. True, my Lord, he reels from the tilt[18] often.

RODERIGO AND GRISOLAN. Ha, ha, ha!

[1] *Gaston de Foix* General (1489–1512) who served in the Italian wars (1494–1559).

[2] *their … rearing* Having been nurtured close at hand.

[3] *presence* Presence chamber, used for reception ceremonies.

[4] *make … natures* Tell me about the characters.

[5] *Calabrian* Calabria is a region in the southernmost "toe" of Italy.

[6] *took the ring* In jousting, where the goal is to thread a lance through a ring.

[7] *great master* Steward.

[8] *base office* Low tasks.

[9] *broke* Made.

[10] *children of Ismael* I.e., the children of Ishmael, a common name for Arabs.

[11] *tents* Reference to Genesis 16.12, concerning a prophecy that Ishmael would become a wild man and live in a tent. "Tents" can also mean "bandages."

[12] *chirurgeons* Surgeons.

[13] *gallants* Gentlemen.

[14] *put up* Sheathe their swords.

[15] *jennet* Horse.

[16] *Pliny* Pliny the Elder (23–79 CE), Roman author and scientist. In his *Naturalis Historia* he states that Portuguese mares were impregnated by the west wind.

[17] *ballassed … quicksilver* Ballasted with mercury.

[18] *reels … tilt* Resists running at the ring in jousting.

FERDINAND. Why do you laugh? Methinks you that are courtiers should be my touchwood,[1] take fire when I give fire; that is, not laugh but when I laugh, were the subject never so witty.

CASTRUCCIO. True, my Lord; I myself have heard a very good jest, and have scorned to seem to have so silly[2] a wit, as to understand it.

FERDINAND. But I can laugh at your fool, my Lord.

CASTRUCCIO. He cannot speak, you know, but he makes faces: my lady cannot abide him.

FERDINAND. No?

CASTRUCCIO. Nor endure to be in merry company; for she says too much laughing, and too much company, fills her too full of the wrinkle.

FERDINAND. I would then have a mathematical instrument made for her face, that she might not laugh out of compass.[3] I shall shortly visit you at Milan, Lord Silvio.

SILVIO. Your Grace shall arrive most welcome.

FERDINAND. You are a good horseman, Antonio: you have excellent riders in France. What do you think of good horsemanship?

ANTONIO. Nobly, my Lord: as out of the Grecian horse issued many famous princes,[4] so out of brave horsemanship arise the first sparks of growing resolution, that raise the mind to noble action.

FERDINAND. You have bespoke it worthily.

SILVIO. Your brother, the Lord Cardinal, and sister Duchess.

(*Enter Cardinal, Duchess, Cariola, and Julia.*)

CARDINAL. Are the galleys come about?

GRISOLAN. They are, my Lord.

FERDINAND. Here's the Lord Silvio is come to take his leave.

DELIO. Now, sir, your promise: what's that Cardinal? I mean his temper?[5] They say he's a brave fellow, will play his five thousand crowns at tennis, dance, court ladies, and one that hath fought single combats.

ANTONIO. Some such flashes[6] superficially hang on him, for form; but observe his inward character: he is a melancholy churchman; the spring[7] in his face is nothing but the engendering[8] of toads; where he is jealous of any man, he lays worse plots for him than ever was imposed on Hercules,[9] for he strews in his way flatterers, panders, intelligencers,[10] atheists, and a thousand such political[11] monsters. He should have been Pope, but instead of coming to it by the primitive decency of the Church, he did bestow bribes so largely, and so impudently, as if he would have carried it away[12] without heaven's knowledge. Some good he hath done—

DELIO. You have given[13] too much of him: what's his brother?

ANTONIO. The Duke there? A most perverse and turbulent nature:
What appears in him mirth is merely outside;
If he laugh heartily, it is to laugh
All honesty out of fashion.

DELIO. Twins?

ANTONIO. In quality.
He speaks with others' tongues, and hears men's suits
With others' ears; will seem to sleep o' th' bench[14]
Only to entrap offenders in their answers;
Dooms men to death by information,[15]
Rewards by hearsay.

DELIO. Then the law to him
Is like a foul black cobweb to a spider,
He makes it his dwelling and a prison
To entangle those shall feed him.

---

[1] *touchwood* Tinder.

[2] *silly* Simple.

[3] *out of compass* Immoderately.

[4] *Grecian … princes* The Trojan horse containing Greek soldiers who crept out at night and sacked Troy.

[5] *temper* Disposition.

[6] *flashes* Instances of showy behavior.

[7] *spring* I.e., of water: his tears.

[8] *engendering* Birthplace.

[9] *Hercules* From Greek and Roman mythology. Hercules was required to complete a series of twelve arduous tasks as penance for murdering his wife and children in a fit of madness.

[10] *intelligencers* Spies.

[11] *political* Scheming.

[12] *carried it away* Done it.

[13] *given* Told.

[14] *bench* Judge's seat.

[15] *information* Testimony provided by paid informants.

ANTONIO. Most true:
He never pays debts unless they be shrewd turns,[1]
And those he will confess that he doth owe.
Last, for his brother there, the Cardinal,
They that do flatter him most say oracles[2]
Hang at his lips; and verily I believe them,
For the devil speaks in them.
But for their sister, the right noble Duchess,
You never fixed your eye on three fair medals
Cast in one figure, of so different temper.
For her discourse, it is so full of rapture,
You only will begin then to be sorry
When she doth end her speech, and wish, in wonder,
She held it less vain-glory,[3] to talk much,
Than your penance to hear her: whilst she speaks,
She throws upon a man so sweet a look,
That it were able to raise one to a galliard[4]
That lay in a dead palsy,° and to dote *paralysis*
On that sweet countenance; but in that look
There speaketh so divine a continence,
As cuts off all lascivious and vain hope.
Her days are practised in such noble virtue,
That sure her nights, nay more, her very sleeps,
Are more in heaven, than other ladies' shrifts.° *confessions*
Let all sweet ladies break their flattering glasses,° *mirrors*
And dress themselves in her.
DELIO. Fie, Antonio,
You play the wire-drawer with her commendation.[5]
ANTONIO. I'll case the picture up: only thus much,
All her particular worth, grows to this sum;
She stains° the time past, lights the time to come. *eclipses*
CARIOLA. You must attend my lady in the gallery,
Some half an hour hence.
ANTONIO. I shall.

(Exeunt Antonio and Delio.)

FERDINAND. Sister, I have a suit to you.[6]
DUCHESS. To me, sir?
FERDINAND. A gentleman here, Daniel de Bosola,
One that was in the galleys—
DUCHESS. Yes, I know him.
FERDINAND. A worthy fellow h'is: pray let me entreat for
The provisorship of your horse.[7]
DUCHESS. Your knowledge of him
Commends him and prefers him.
FERDINAND. Call him hither.

(Exit attendant.)

We are now upon parting. Good Lord Silvio,
Do us commend to all our noble friends
At the leaguer.° *camp*
SILVIO. Sir, I shall.
FERDINAND. You are for Milan?
SILVIO. I am.
DUCHESS. Bring the carroches;° we'll bring you down to the haven.° *carriages / harbor*

(Exeunt all but the Cardinal and Ferdinand.)

CARDINAL. Be sure you entertain that Bosola
For your intelligence:[8] I would not be seen in't;
And therefore many times I have slighted him,
When he did court our furtherance,° as this morning. *help*
FERDINAND. Antonio, the great master of her household,
Had been far fitter.
CARDINAL. You are deceived in him:
His nature is too honest for such business.
He comes: I'll leave you.

(Exit Cardinal. Enter Bosola.)

BOSOLA. I was lured to you.
FERDINAND. My brother here, the Cardinal could never
Abide you.
BOSOLA. Never since he was in my debt.
FERDINAND. Maybe some oblique character[9] in your face
Made him suspect you.
BOSOLA. Doth he study physiognomy?

[1] *shrewd turns* Malicious acts.

[2] *oracles* Words of wisdom.

[3] *vain-glory* Empty pride.

[4] *galliard* Quick dance.

[5] *You ... commendation* You draw out your praise of her unnecessarily.

[6] *suit to you* Favor to ask you.

[7] *let ... horse* Let me ask you to make him the groom of your horse.

[8] *entertain ... intelligence* Use Bosola as your spy.

[9] *oblique character* Hidden expression.

There's no more credit to be given to th' face,
Than to a sick man's urine, which some call
The physician's whore, because she cozens° him. *fools*
He did suspect me wrongfully.
FERDINAND. For that
You must give great men leave to take their times.
Distrust doth cause us seldom be deceived:
You see, the oft shaking of the cedar-tree
Fastens it more at root.
BOSOLA. Yet, take heed;
For to suspect a friend unworthily,
Instructs him the next way to suspect you,
And prompts him to deceive you.
FERDINAND. There's gold.
BOSOLA. So,
What follows? Never rained such showers as these
Without thunderbolts i' th' tail of them:[1]
Whose throat must I cut?
FERDINAND. Your inclination to shed blood rides post
Before my occasion to use you. I give you that
To live i' th' court here, and observe the Duchess;
To note all the particulars of her 'haviour,
What suitors do solicit her for marriage,
And whom she best affects. She's a young widow:
I would not have her marry again.
BOSOLA. No, sir?
FERDINAND. Do not you ask the reason; but be satisfied
I say I would not.
BOSOLA. It seems you would create me
One of your familiars.
FERDINAND. Familiar! What's that?
BOSOLA. Why, a very quaint invisible devil in flesh;
An intelligencer.
FERDINAND. Such a kind of thriving thing
I would wish thee; and ere long, thou may'st arrive
At a higher place by't.
BOSOLA. Take your devils,
Which hell calls angels:[2] these cursed gifts would make
You a corrupter, me an impudent traitor;
And should I take these, they'd take me to hell.
FERDINAND. Sir, I'll take nothing from you, that I have
given:
There is a place that I procured for you
This morning, the provisorship o' th' horse;
Have you heard on't?
BOSOLA. No.
FERDINAND. 'Tis yours: is't not worth thanks?
BOSOLA. I would have you curse yourself now, that your
bounty
(Which makes men truly noble)[3] e'er should make
Me a villain. O, that to avoid ingratitude
For the good deed you have done me, I must do
All the ill man can invent! Thus the devil
Candies all sins o'er; and what heaven terms vile
That names he complemental.° *admirable*
FERDINAND. Be yourself;
Keep your old garb of melancholy; 'twill express
You envy those that stand above your reach,
Yet strive not to come near 'em: this will gain
Access to private lodgings, where yourself
May, like a politic dormouse—
BOSOLA. As I have seen some,
Feed in a lord's dish, half asleep, not seeming
To listen to any talk; and yet these rogues
Have cut his throat in a dream. What's my place?
The provisorship o' th' horse? Say, then, my corruption
Grew out of horse-dung: I am your creature.
FERDINAND. Away.
BOSOLA. Let good men, for good deeds, covet good fame,
Since place[4] and riches, oft are bribes of shame:
Sometimes the devil doth preach.
(*Exit Bosola. Enter Duchess, Cardinal, and Cariola.*)

CARDINAL. We are to part from you; and your own
discretion
Must now be your director.
FERDINAND. You are a widow:
You know already what man is; and therefore
Let not youth, high promotion, eloquence—
CARDINAL. No, nor anything without the addition,
honour,
Sway your high blood.

[1] *never ... them* Reference to classical mythology. Zeus, god of sky and thunder, changes himself into a shower of gold in order to reach Danae, who is confined to a tower.

[2] *angels* Gold coins with an image of the Archangel Michael on them.

[3] *noble* I.e., money grants nobility.

[4] *place* I.e., place at court; office or position.

FERDINAND. Marry! They are most luxurious,[1]
Will wed twice.
CARDINAL. O, fie!
FERDINAND. Their livers[2] are more spotted
Than Laban's sheep.[3]
DUCHESS. Diamonds are of most value,
They say, that have past through most jewellers' hands.
FERDINAND. Whores, by that rule, are precious.
DUCHESS. Will you hear me?
I'll never marry.
CARDINAL. So most widows say;
But commonly that motion lasts no longer
Than the turning of an hour-glass: the funeral sermon
And it, end both together.
FERDINAND. Now hear me:
You live in a rank° pasture here, i' th' court; *lustful*
There is a kind of honey-dew[4] that's deadly;
'Twill poison your fame; look to't: be not cunning;
For they whose faces do belie their hearts,
Are witches ere they arrive at twenty years,
Ay, and give the devil suck.
DUCHESS. This is terrible good counsel.
FERDINAND. Hypocrisy is woven of a fine small thread,
Subtler than Vulcan's[5] engine: yet, believ't,
Your darkest actions, nay, your privat'st thoughts,
Will come to light.
CARDINAL. You may flatter yourself,
And take your own choice; privately be married
Under the eaves of night—
FERDINAND. Think't the best voyage
That e'er you made; like the irregular crab,
Which, though't goes backward, thinks that it goes right,
Because it goes its own way: but observe,
Such weddings may more properly be said
To be executed, than celebrated.
CARDINAL. The marriage night
Is the entrance into some prison.
FERDINAND. And those joys,
Those lustful pleasures, are like heavy sleeps
Which do forerun man's mischief.° *misfortune*
CARDINAL. Fare you well.
Wisdom begins at the end: remember it.

(*Exit Cardinal.*)

DUCHESS. I think this speech between you both was studied,
It came so roundly off.[6]
FERDINAND. You are my sister;
This was my father's poniard,° do you see? *dagger*
I'd be loath to see't look rusty, 'cause 'twas his.
I would have you to give o'er these chargeable revels,[7]
A visor and a mask[8] are whispering rooms
That were never built for goodness—fare ye well,
And beware that part, which like the lamprey,
Hath never a bone in't.
DUCHESS. Fie, sir.
FERDINAND. Nay,
I mean the tongue; variety of courtship;
What cannot a neat knave with a smooth tale
Make a woman believe: Farewell, lusty widow.

(*Exit Ferdinand.*)

DUCHESS. Shall this move me? If all my royal kindred
Lay in my way unto this marriage,
I'd make them my low footsteps; and even now,
Even in this hate, as men in some great battles,
By apprehending danger, have achieved
Almost impossible actions—I have heard soldiers say so—
So I through frights and threatenings will assay° *try*
This dangerous venture. Let old wives report
I winked,[9] and chose a husband. Cariola,
To thy known secrecy I have given up
More than my life—my fame.
CARIOLA. Both shall be safe:

[1] *luxurious* Unchaste.

[2] *livers* The liver was believed to be the source of passion.

[3] *Laban's sheep* Reference to Genesis 30.29–43, in which Jacob creates his own herd by taking the spotted sheep from Laban's herd.

[4] *honey-dew* Substance secreted by some plants which entraps insects.

[5] *Vulcan* In Roman mythology, Vulcan, the god of fire, created a net to catch his wife, Venus, and her lover, Mars. The net was made of threads so fine (or "subtle") that they could not be seen.

[6] *It ... off* It was said with such straightforwardness.

[7] *give ... revels* Abandon these expensive amusements.

[8] *visor ... mask* Disguises worn at revels or masques.

[9] *winked* Turned a blind eye to a misdeed. From an old saying: "let the cat wink and let the mice play."

For I'll conceal this secret from the world,
As warily as those that trade in poison
Keep poison from their children.
DUCHESS. Thy protestation
Is ingenious and hearty: I believe it.
Is Antonio come?
CARIOLA. He attends you.
DUCHESS. Good dear soul,
Leave me; but place thyself behind the arras,[1]
Where thou may'st overhear us. Wish me good speed,
For I am going into a wilderness
Where I shall find no path, nor friendly clew,[2]
To be my guide.

(*Exit Cariola. Enter Antonio.*)

I sent for you: sit down;
Take pen and ink, and write: are you ready?
ANTONIO. Yes.
DUCHESS. What did I say?
ANTONIO. That I should write somewhat.
DUCHESS. O, I remember.
After these triumphs and this large expense,
It's fit, like thrifty husbands,[3] we inquire
What's laid up for tomorrow.
ANTONIO. So please your beauteous excellence.
DUCHESS. Beauteous!
Indeed I thank you: I look young for your sake;
You have ta'en my cares upon you.
ANTONIO. I'll fetch your Grace
The particulars of your revenue and expense.
DUCHESS. O, you are an upright treasurer; but you mistook:
For when I said I meant to make inquiry
What's laid up for to-morrow, I did mean
What's laid up yonder for me.
ANTONIO. Where?
DUCHESS. In heaven.
I am making my will, (as 'tis fit princes should,
In perfect memory,) and, I pray, sir, tell me
Were not one better make it smiling, thus,
Than in deep groans, and terrible ghastly looks,
As if the gifts we parted with procured
That violent distraction?
ANTONIO. O, much better.
DUCHESS. If I had a husband now, this care were quit:° *gone*
But I intend to make you overseer.
What good deed shall we first remember? Say.
ANTONIO. Begin with that first good deed begun i' th' world
After man's creation, the sacrament of marriage:
I'd have you first provide for a good husband;
Give him all.
DUCHESS. All?
ANTONIO. Yes, your excellent self.
DUCHESS. In a winding-sheet?
ANTONIO. In a couple.
DUCHESS. St. Winifred,[4] that were a strange will!
ANTONIO. 'Twere strange
If there were no will in you to marry again.
DUCHESS. What do you think of marriage?
ANTONIO. I take't, as those that deny purgatory,
It locally contains, or heaven, or hell,
There's no third place in't.
DUCHESS. How do you affect[5] it?
ANTONIO. My banishment, feeding my melancholy,
Would often reason thus.
DUCHESS. Pray, let's hear it.
ANTONIO. Say a man never marry, nor have children,
What takes that from him? Only the bare name
Of being a father, or the weak delight
To see the little wanton[6] ride a cock-horse° *hobby-horse*
Upon a painted stick, or hear him chatter
Like a taught starling.
DUCHESS. Fie, fie, what's all this?
One of your eyes is blood-shot; use my ring to't,
They say 'tis very sovereign: 'twas my wedding ring,
And I did vow never to part with it
But to my second husband.
ANTONIO. You have parted with it now.
DUCHESS. Yes, to help your eye-sight.
ANTONIO. You have made me stark blind.
DUCHESS. How?

---

[1] *arras* Hanging tapestry.

[2] *clew* Ball of thread used by Theseus to find his way through the labyrinth. From Greek mythology.

[3] *husbands* Stewards (with an obvious double meaning).

[4] *St. Winifred* Seventh-century Welsh saint, beheaded for rejecting the sexual propositions of Caradog of Hawarden.

[5] *affect* Like.

[6] *wanton* Brat (a term of affection).

ANTONIO. There is a saucy and ambitious devil,
Is dancing in this circle.
DUCHESS. Remove him.
ANTONIO. How?
DUCHESS. There needs small conjuration, when your finger
May do it; thus; is it fit?

(*He kneels.*)

ANTONIO. What said you?
DUCHESS. Sir,
This goodly roof of yours, is too low built;
I cannot stand upright in't nor discourse,
Without° I raise it higher; raise yourself; *unless*
Or, if you please, my hand to help you: so.

(*He stands.*)

ANTONIO. Ambition, madam, is a great man's madness,
That is not kept in chains, and close-pent rooms,
But in fair lightsome lodgings, and is girt° *surrounded*
With the wild noise of prattling visitants,° *visitors*
Which makes it lunatic beyond all cure.
Conceive not I am so stupid but I aim
Whereto your favours tend: but he's a fool,
That being a-cold, would thrust his hands i' th' fire
To warm them.
DUCHESS. So now the ground's broke,
You may discover what a wealthy mine
I make you lord of.
ANTONIO. O, my unworthiness!
DUCHESS. You were ill to sell yourself:
This darkening of your worth is not like that
Which tradesmen use i' th' city; their false lights
Are to rid bad wares off;[1] and I must tell you,
If you will know where breathes a complete man,
(I speak it without flattery,) turn your eyes,
And progress through yourself.
ANTONIO. Were there nor heaven nor hell,
I should be honest: I have long served virtue,
And ne'er ta'en wages of her.
DUCHESS. Now she pays it.
The misery of us that are born great!
We are forced to woo, because none dare woo us;
And as a tyrant doubles with his words,
And fearfully equivocates, so we
Are forced to express our violent passions
In riddles, and in dreams, and leave the path
Of simple virtue, which was never made
To seem the thing it is not. Go, go brag
You have left me heartless; mine is in your bosom:
I hope 'twill multiply love there. You do tremble:
Make not your heart so dead a piece of flesh,
To fear, more than to love me. Sir, be confident:
What is't distracts you? This is flesh and blood sir;
'Tis not the figure[2] cut in alabaster,
Kneels at my husbands tomb. Awake, awake, man!
I do here put off all vain ceremony,
And only do appear to you a young widow
That claims you for her husband, and like a widow,
I use but half a blush in't.[3]
ANTONIO. Truth speak for me:
I will remain the constant sanctuary
Of your good name.
DUCHESS. I thank you, gentle love:
And 'cause you shall not come to me in debt,
Being now my steward, here upon your lips
I sign your *Quietus est.*[4] This you should have begged now;
I have seen children oft eat sweetmeats thus,
As fearful to devour them too soon.
ANTONIO. But for your brothers?
DUCHESS. Do not think of them:
All discord without this circumference[5]
Is only to be pitied, and not feared:
Yet, should they know it, time will easily
Scatter the tempest.
ANTONIO. These words should be mine,
And all the parts you have spoke, if some part of it
Would not have savoured° flattery. *resembled*
DUCHESS. Kneel.

---

[1] *darkening ... off* Reference to shops that kept their lights dim so that their customers would not notice shoddy wares.

[2] *figure* Statue.

[3] *widow ... in't* I am less than embarrassed, having been married before.

[4] *Quietus est* Latin: It is finished, an accounting term indicating that all figures are correct, but also a metaphor for death.

[5] *without this circumference* Outside of the circle of the two of us.

(*Enter Cariola.*)

ANTONIO. Ha!
DUCHESS. Be not amazed, this woman's of my counsel:
I have heard lawyers say, a contract in a chamber
Per verba presenti[1] is absolute marriage.
Bless, heaven, this sacred Gordian,[2] which let violence
Never untwine!
ANTONIO. And may our sweet affections, like the spheres,[3]
Be still° in motion. *always*
DUCHESS. Quickening,[4] and make
The like soft music.
ANTONIO. That we may imitate the loving palms,[5]
Best emblem of a peaceful marriage
That never bore fruit divided.
DUCHESS. What can the Church force more?
ANTONIO. That fortune may not know an accident
Either of joy, or sorrow, to divide
Our fixed wishes.
DUCHESS. How can the Church build faster?
We now are man and wife, and 'tis the Church
That must but echo this.[6] Maid, stand apart:
I now am blind.
ANTONIO. What's your conceit° in this? *idea*
DUCHESS. I would have you lead your fortune by the hand
Unto your marriage bed:
(You speak in me this, for we now are one:)[7]
We'll only lie, and talk together, and plot
T'appease my humourous° kindred; and if you please, *volatile*
Like the old tale in Alexander and Lodowick,
Lay a naked sword between us, keep us chaste.[8]
O, let me shroud my blushes in your bosom,
Since 'tis the treasury of all my secrets!

(*Exeunt.*)

CARIOLA. Whether the spirit of greatness, or of woman
Reign most in her, I know not; but it shows
A fearful madness: I owe her much of pity.

(*Exit.*)

ACT 2, SCENE 1

(*Enter Bosola and Castruccio.*)

BOSOLA. You say, you would fain[9] be taken for an eminent courtier?

CASTRUCCIO. 'Tis the very main[10] of my ambition.

BOSOLA. Let me see: you have a reasonable good face for't already, and your night-cap[11] expresses your ears sufficient largely. I would have you learn to twirl the strings of your band[12] with a good grace, and in a set speech, at th' end of every sentence, to hum three or four times, or blow your nose till it smart again, to recover your memory. When you come to be a president[13] in criminal causes, if you smile upon a prisoner, hang him, but if you frown upon him, and threaten him, let him be sure to 'scape the gallows.

CASTRUCCIO. I would be a very merry president.

BOSOLA. Do not sup a' nights; 'twill beget you an admirable wit.

CASTRUCCIO. Rather it would make me have a good stomach to quarrel; for they say, your roaring boys[14] eat meat seldom, and that makes them so valiant. But how

[1] *Per verba present* Latin: Through words in the present (tense)—a legal verbal contract.

[2] *Gordian* I.e., a Gordian knot, one that is exceedingly difficult to untie. Gordius, king of Phyrgia, was said to have tied a knot so intricate that it remained tied until cut by Alexander the Great.

[3] *spheres* Planets, whose harmonious orbits were thought to make sweet music.

[4] *Quickening* Coming to life.

[5] *palms* Palm trees, it was thought, needed to be fertilized by male palms in order to bear fruit.

[6] *the Church ... echo this* The marriage will be confirmed by a church ceremony.

[7] *we ... one* Reference to Ephesians 5.31, in which a married couple is said to have become one flesh.

[8] *Alexander and Lodowick ... chaste* Old tale about two friends so alike as to be indistinguishable. Lodowick marries the Princess of Hungaria in Alexander's name, but places a sword between himself and his bride in bed, so as not to cuckold Alexander.

[9] *fain* Rather.

[10] *main* Goal.

[11] *night-cap* Skullcup, worn by lawyers.

[12] *band* Neck bank or ruff.

[13] *president* Magistrate.

[14] *roaring boys* Raucous young men, bullies.

shall I know whether the people take me for an eminent fellow?

BOSOLA. I will teach a trick to know it: give out you lie a-dying, and if you hear the common people curse you, be sure you are taken for one of the prime night-caps.[1]

(*Enter an old lady.*)

You come from painting now.

OLD LADY. From what?

BOSOLA. Why, from your scurvy face-physic.[2] To behold thee not painted, inclines somewhat near a miracle: these in thy face here, were deep ruts, and foul sloughs, the last progress. There was a lady in France, that having the small-pox, flayed the skin off her face, to make it more level; and whereas before she looked like a nutmeg-grater, after she resembled an abortive hedgehog.

OLD LADY. Do you call this painting?

BOSOLA. No, no, but you call't careening[3] of an old morphewed[4] lady, to make her disembogue[5] again: there's rough-cast phrase to your plastic.[6]

OLD LADY. It seems you are well acquainted with my closet.

BOSOLA. One would suspect it for a shop of witchcraft, to find in it the fat of serpents, spawn of snakes, Jews' spittle, and their young children's ordure;[7] and all these for the face. I would sooner eat a dead pigeon, taken from the soles of the feet of one sick of the plague, than kiss one of you fasting. Here are two of you, whose sin of your youth is the very patrimony[8] of the physician; makes him renew his foot-cloth[9] with the spring, and change his high-priced courtesan with the fall of the leaf. I do wonder you do not loathe yourselves. Observe my meditation now:
What thing is in this outward form of man
To be beloved? We account it ominous,
If nature do produce a colt, or lamb,
A fawn, or goat, in any limb resembling
A man, and fly from't as a prodigy.
Man stands amazed to see his deformity
In any other creature but himself.
But in our own flesh, though we bear diseases
Which have their true names only ta'en from beasts,
As the most ulcerous wolf and swinish measle,
Though we are eaten up of lice and worms,
And though continually we bear about us
A rotten and dead body, we delight
To hide it in rich tissue; all our fear,
Nay all our terror, is, lest our physician
Should put us in the ground, to be made sweet.
Your wife's gone to Rome: you two couple, and get you
To the wells at Lucca,[10] to recover your aches.

(*Exeunt Castruccio and the old lady.*)

I have other work on foot. I observe our Duchess
Is sick a-days, she pukes, her stomach seethes,
The fins° of her eyelids look most teeming blue,[11] *edges*
She wanes i' th' cheek, and waxes fat i' th' flank,
And, contrary to our Italian fashion,
Wears a loose-bodied gown; there's something in't.
I have a trick may chance discover it,
A pretty one: I have bought some apricocks,[12]
The first our spring yields—

(*Enter Antonio and Delio.*)

DELIO. And so long since married!
You amaze me.

ANTONIO. Let me seal your lips for ever:
For did I think, that anything but th' air

[1] *prime night-caps* Eminent lawyers.

[2] *face-physic* Healing your face; i.e., putting makeup on.

[3] *careening* Scraping paint off a ship.

[4] *morphewed* Skin-diseased.

[5] *disembogue* Leave the harbor for another journey.

[6] *There's … plastic* In contrast to your changeable (or "plastic") face, here is some straight-talking.

[7] *ordure* Feces.

[8] *patrimony* Inheritance.

[9] *foot-cloth* Richly ornamented cloth laid over the back of a horse—a mark of wealth and dignity.

[10] *Lucca* Site of hot springs near Pisa.

[11] *teeming blue* Pregnant women's eyelids were thought to have a blue tinge to them.

[12] *apricocks* I.e., apricots, meant to discover the Duchess's pregnancy by revealing a craving for fruit.

Could carry these words from you, I should wish
You had no breath at all.

(*To Bosola.*)

Now, sir, in your contemplation?
You are studying to become a great wise fellow.

BOSOLA. O, sir, the opinion of wisdom, is a foul tetter,[1] that runs all over a man's body: if simplicity direct us to have no evil, it directs us to a happy being: for the subtlest folly proceeds from the subtlest wisdom: let me be simply honest.

ANTONIO. I do understand your inside.

BOSOLA. Do you so?

ANTONIO. Because you would not seem to appear to th' world
Puffed up with your preferment, you continue
This out-of-fashion melancholy: leave it, leave it.

BOSOLA. Give me leave to be honest in any phrase, in any complement whatsoever. Shall I confess myself to you? I look no higher than I can reach: they are the gods that must ride on winged horses. A lawyer's mule, of a slow pace, will both suit my disposition and business: for, mark me, when a man's mind rides faster than his horse can gallop, they quickly both tire.

ANTONIO. You would look up to heaven, but I think
The devil that rules i' th' air stands in your light.

BOSOLA. O, sir, you are lord of the ascendant, chief man with the Duchess; a Duke was your cousin-german removed.[2] Say you were lineally descended from King Pepin,[3] or he himself, what of this? Search the heads[4] of the greatest rivers in the world, you shall find them but bubbles of water. Some would think the souls of princes were brought forth by some more weighty cause, than those of meaner persons: they are deceived, there's the same hand to them; the like passions sway them; the same reason that makes a vicar to go to law for a tithe-pig,[5] and undo his neighbours, makes them spoil a whole province, and batter down goodly cities with the cannon.

(*Enter Duchess and ladies.*)

DUCHESS. Your arm, Antonio: do I not grow fat?
I am exceeding short-winded. Bosola,
I would have you, sir, provide for me a litter;
Such a one as the Duchess of Florence rode in.

BOSOLA. The Duchess used one when she was great with child.

DUCHESS. I think she did. Come hither, mend my ruff:
Here, when?[6] Thou art such a tedious lady; and
Thy breath smells of lemon pills:[7] would thou hadst done!
Shall I swoon under thy fingers? I am
So troubled with the mother.[8]

BOSOLA. (*Aside.*) I fear too much.

DUCHESS. I have heard you say, that the French courtiers
Wear their hats on 'fore the king.

ANTONIO. I have seen it.

DUCHESS. In the presence?

ANTONIO. Yes.

DUCHESS. Why should not we bring up that fashion?
'Tis ceremony more than duty, that consists
In the removing of a piece of felt:
Be you the example to the rest o' th' court,
Put on your hat first.

ANTONIO. You must pardon me:
I have seen, in colder countries than in France,
Nobles stand bare to th' prince; and the distinction
Methought showed reverently.

BOSOLA. I have a present for your Grace.

DUCHESS. For me, sir?

BOSOLA. Apricocks, madam.

DUCHESS. O, sir, where are they?
I have heard of none to year.[9]

BOSOLA. (*Aside.*) Good, her colour rises.

DUCHESS. Indeed I thank you: they are wondrous fair ones:

---

[1] *tetter* Skin disease.

[2] *Cousin-german removed* First cousin once removed.

[3] *King Pepin* Pippin III (714–768), King of the Franks, and the father of Charlemagne.

[4] *heads* Headwaters.

[5] *go … tithe-pig* Go to court for a pig taken as a tithe (i.e., for nothing).

[6] *when* An expression of impatience.

[7] *lemon pills* Remedy for bad breath. Possibly "lemon peels."

[8] *the mother* Type of hysteria in which the victim feels choked.

[9] *to year* This year.

What an unskilful fellow is our gardner!
We shall have none this month.
BOSOLA. Will not your Grace pare° them? *peel*
DUCHESS. No: they taste of musk,[1] methinks; indeed they do.
BOSOLA. I know not: yet I wish your Grace had pared 'em.
DUCHESS. Why?
BOSOLA. I forgot to tell you, the knave gardener,
Only to raise his profit by them the sooner,
Did ripen them in horse-dung.
DUCHESS. O, you jest.

(*To Antonio.*)

You shall judge: pray, taste one.
ANTONIO. Indeed, madam,
I do not love the fruit.
DUCHESS. Sir, you are loath
To rob us of our dainties: 'tis a delicate fruit;
They say they are restorative.
BOSOLA. 'Tis a pretty art,
This grafting.
DUCHESS. 'Tis so: a bettering of nature.
BOSOLA. To make a pippin grow upon a crab,[2]
A damson on a black-thorn.[3] (*Aside.*) How greedily she eats them!
A whirlwind strike off these bawd farthingales!° *petticoats*
For, but for that, and the loose-bodied gown,
I should have discovered apparently
The young springal cutting a caper[4] in her belly.
DUCHESS. I thank you, Bosola: they were right good ones,
If they do not make me sick.
ANTONIO. How now, madam?
DUCHESS. This green fruit and my stomach are not friends:
How they swell me!
BOSOLA. (*Aside.*) Nay, you are too much swelled already.
DUCHESS. O, I am in an extreme cold sweat!
BOSOLA. I am very sorry.

(*Exit.*)

DUCHESS. Lights to my chamber. O, good Antonio,
I fear I am undone!
DELIO. Lights there, lights.

(*Exit Duchess.*)

ANTONIO. O my most trusty Delio, we are lost!
I fear she's fallen in labour; and there's left
No time for her remove.
DELIO. Have you prepared
Those ladies to attend her? And procured
That politic safe conveyance for the midwife,
Your Duchess plotted?
ANTONIO. I have.
DELIO. Make use then of this forced occasion:
Give out that Bosola hath poisoned her
With these apricocks; that will give some colour° *reason*
For her keeping close.[5]
ANTONIO. Fie, fie, the physicians
Will then flock to her.
DELIO. For that you may pretend
She'll use some prepared antidote of her own,
Lest the physicians should re-poison her.
ANTONIO. I am lost in amazement: I know not what to think on't.

(*Exeunt.*)

[1] *musk* Animal scent.

[2] *pippin ... crab* Two types of apples.

[3] *damson ... black-thorn* Two types of plums.

[4] *young ... caper* Child dancing.

[5] *keeping close* Staying hidden away.

ACT 2, SCENE 2

(*Enter Bosola.*)

BOSOLA. So, so, there's no question but her tetchiness[1] and most vulturous eating of the apricocks, are apparent signs of breeding.

(*Enter an old lady.*)

Now?

OLD LADY. I am in haste, sir.

BOSOLA. There was a young waiting-woman, had a monstrous desire to see the glass-house—[2]

OLD LADY. Nay, pray let me go.

BOSOLA. And it was only to know what strange instrument it was, should swell up a glass to the fashion of a woman's belly.

OLD LADY. I will hear no more of the glass house. You are still abusing women.

BOSOLA. Who I? No, only, by the way, now and then, mention your frailties. The orange-tree bears ripe and green fruit and blossoms, altogether: and some of you give entertainment for pure love, but more, for precious reward. The lusty spring smells well; but drooping autumn tastes well. If we have the same golden showers, that rained in the time of Jupiter[3] the thunderer, you have the same Danaes still, to hold up their laps to receive them. Didst thou never study the mathematics?

OLD LADY. What's that, sir?

BOSOLA. Why, to know the trick how to make a many lines meet in one centre. Go, go, give your foster-daughters good counsel: tell them, that the devil takes delight to hang at a woman's girdle, like a false rusty watch, that she cannot discern how the time passes.

(*Exit old lady. Enter Antonio, Roderigo, Delio, and Grisolan.*)

ANTONIO. Shut up the court-gates.

RODERIGO. Why, sir? What's the danger?

ANTONIO. Shut up the posterns presently,° *immediately*
and call
All the officers o' th' court.

GRISOLAN. I shall instantly.

(*Exit.*)

ANTONIO. Who keeps the key o' th' park gate?

RODERIGO. Forobosco.

ANTONIO. Let him bring't presently.

(*Enter Grisolan and servants.*)

1ST SERVANT. O, gentlemen o' th' court, the foulest treason!

BOSOLA. (*Aside.*) If that these apricocks should be poisoned now, without my knowledge!

1ST SERVANT. There was taken even now
A Switzer[4] in the Duchess's bed-chamber—

2ND SERVANT. A Switzer!

1ST SERVANT. With a pistol in his great cod-piece.[5]

BOSOLA. Ha, ha, ha!

1ST SERVANT. The cod-piece was the case for't.

2ND SERVANT. There was a cunning traitor; who would have searched his cod-piece?

1ST SERVANT. True, if he had kept out of the ladies' chambers: And all the moulds of his buttons were leaden bullets.

2ND SERVANT. O, wicked cannibal! A firelock in's codpiece!

1ST SERVANT. 'Twas a French plot, upon my life.

2ND SERVANT. To see what the devil can do!

ANTONIO. All the officers here?

SERVANTS. We are.

ANTONIO. Gentlemen,
We have lost much plate° you know; and but this
evening *money*
Jewels, to the value of four thousand ducats,
Are missing in the Duchess's cabinet.° *boudoir*
Are the gates shut?

1ST SERVANT. Yes.

ANTONIO. 'Tis the Duchess's pleasure

[1] *tetchiness* Irritability.

[2] *glass-house* Workshop in which glass is produced.

[3] *Jupiter* Jupiter became a shower of gold to impregnate the imprisoned Danae.

[4] *Switzer* Soldier, mercenary from Switzerland.

[5] *cod-piece* Protruding bag on men's tightss, which covered the genitals.

Each officer be locked into his chamber
Till the sun-rising; and to send the keys
Of all their chests, and of their outward doors
Into her bed-chamber. She is very sick.
RODERIGO. At her pleasure.
ANTONIO. She entreats you take 't not ill: the innocent
Shall be the more approved by it.
BOSOLA. Gentlemen o' th' wood-yard,[1] where's your Switzer now?
1ST SERVANT. By this hand 'twas credibly reported by one o' th' blackguard.[2]

(*Exeunt Gentlemen.*)

DELIO. How fares it with the Duchess?
ANTONIO. She's exposed
Unto the worst of torture, pain and fear.
DELIO. Speak to her all happy comfort.
ANTONIO. How I do play the fool with mine own danger!
You are this night, dear friend, to post to Rome:
My life lies in your service.
DELIO. Do not doubt me.
ANTONIO. O, 'tis far from me! And yet fear presents me
Somewhat that looks like danger.
DELIO. Believe it,
'Tis but the shadow of your fear, no more:
How superstitiously we mind our evils!
The throwing down salt, or crossing of a hare,
Bleeding at nose, the stumbling of a horse,
Or singing of a cricket, are of power
To daunt whole man in us.[3] Sir, fare you well:
I wish you all the joys of a blest father;
And, for my faith, lay this unto your breast,
Old friends, like old swords, still are trusted best.

(*Exit Delio. Enter Cariola with a child.*)

CARIOLA. Sir, you are the happy father of a son:
Your wife commends him to you.
ANTONIO. Blessed comfort!
For heaven's sake tend her well: I'll presently
Go set a figure[4] for's nativity.

(*Exeunt.*)

ACT 2, SCENE 3

(*Enter Bosola, with a dark lantern.*)[5]

BOSOLA. Sure I did hear a woman shriek: list, ha!
And the sound came, if I received it right,
From the Duchess's lodgings. There's some stratagem
In the confining all our courtiers
To their several wards: I must have part of it;
My intelligence will freeze else. List, again!
It may be 'twas the melancholy bird,
Best friend of silence and of solitariness,
The owl, that screamed so. Ha! Antonio!

(*Enter Antonio.*)

ANTONIO. I heard some noise. Who's there? What art thou? Speak.
BOSOLA. Antonio? Put not your face nor body
To such a forced expression of fear:
I am Bosola, your friend.
ANTONIO. Bosola!
(*Aside.*) This mole does undermine me. Heard you not
A noise even now?
BOSOLA. From whence?
ANTONIO. From the Duchess's lodging.
BOSOLA. Not I: did you?
ANTONIO. I did, or else I dreamed.
BOSOLA. Let's walk towards it.
ANTONIO. No: it may be 'twas
But the rising of the wind.
BOSOLA. Very likely:
Methinks 'tis very cold, and yet you sweat.
You look wildly.
ANTONIO. I have been setting a figure[6]
For the Duchess's jewels.

[1] *Gentlemen … wood-yard* Men who work in the area where firewood is cut. Generally, "servants."

[2] *blackguard* Kitchen servants.

[3] *daunt … us* Make us afraid.

[4] *set a figure* Create a horoscope.

[5] *dark lantern* Lantern with shutters that open and close to control the amount of light emitted.

[6] *setting a figure* Casting a horoscope.

BOSOLA. Ah, and how falls your question?
Do you find it radical?[1]
ANTONIO. What's that to you?
'Tis rather to be questioned what design,° *intention*
When all men were commanded to their lodgings,
Makes you a night-walker.
BOSOLA. In sooth I'll tell you:
Now all the court's asleep, I thought the devil
Had least to do here; I came to say my prayers,
And if it do offend you I do so,
You are a fine courtier.
ANTONIO. (*Aside.*) This fellow will undo me.
You gave the Duchess apricocks today:
Pray heaven they were not poisoned.
BOSOLA. Poisoned! A Spanish fig[2]
For the imputation.° *accusation*
ANTONIO. Traitors are ever confident,
Till they are discovered. There were jewels stol'n too:
In my conceit, none are to be suspected
More than yourself.
BOSOLA. You are a false steward.
ANTONIO. Saucy slave, I'll pull thee up by the roots.
BOSOLA. Maybe the ruin will crush you to pieces.
ANTONIO. You are an impudent snake indeed, sir.
Are you scarce warm, and do you show your sting?[3]
BOSOLA.—[4]
ANTONIO. You libel well, sir.
BOSOLA. No, sir: copy it out,
And I will set my hand to't.
ANTONIO. My nose bleeds.
One that were superstitious would count
This ominous, when it merely comes by chance:
Two letters, that are wrote here for my name,[5]
Are drowned in blood!
Mere accident. For you, sir, I'll take order
I' th' morn you shall be safe—(*Aside.*) 'tis that must
colour
Her lying in—sir, this door you pass not:
I do not hold it fit that you come near
The Duchess's lodgings, till you have quit° *acquitted*
yourself.
(*Aside.*) The great are like the base; nay, they are the same,
When they seek shameful ways to avoid shame.

(*Exit.*)

BOSOLA. Antonio hereabout did drop a paper.
Some of your help, false friend. O, here it is:
What's here? A child's nativity calculated!
(*Reading.*) "The Duchess was delivered of a son, 'tween the hours twelve and one in the night, *Anno Dom.* 1504," (that's this year) "*decimo nono Decembris,*" (that's this night,) taken according to the Meridian of Malfi" (that's our Duchess: happy discovery!) "The Lord of the first house being combust in the ascendant, signifies short life;[6] and Mars being in a human sign, joined to the tail of the Dragon,[7] in the eighth house, doth threaten a violent death. *Caetera non scrutantur.*"[8]
Why, now 'tis most apparent: this precise fellow
Is the Duchess's bawd—I have it to my wish!
This is a parcel of intelligency
Our courtiers were cased up for: it needs must follow,
That I must be committed, on pretence
Of poisoning her; which I'll endure, and laugh at.
If one could find the father now! But that
Time will discover. Old Castruccio
I' th' morning posts to Rome: by him I'll send
A letter, that shall make her brothers' galls
O'erflow their livers. This was a thrifty way.[9]
Though lust do mask in ne'er so strange disguise,
She's oft found witty, but is never wise.

(*Exit.*)

[1] *radical* Solvable (through astrology).

[2] *Spanish fig* Term of contempt, accompanied by an obscene gesture.

[3] *You ... sting* Reference to Aesop's fable "The Countryman and the Snake." The countryman brings home a nearly-frozen snake out of pity; when the snake revives, it attacks his family.

[4] Line missing.

[5] *Two ... name* Either Antonio's initials embroidered on a handkerchief or two written letters addressed to him.

[6] *The ... life* Astrological terms. The planet dominant at birth on 19 December is too near the sun and hence seemingly burnt up.

[7] *Dragon* No the constellation Draco, but one of the points at which the orbit of the moon intersects that of the sun.

[8] *Caetera non scrutantur* Latin: the rest do not determine.

[9] *thrifty way* Shrewd plan.

ACT 2, SCENE 4

(*Enter Cardinal and Julia.*)

CARDINAL. Sit: thou art my best of wishes. Prithee tell me,
What trick didst thou invent to come to Rome
Without thy husband?
JULIA. Why, my Lord, I told him
I came to visit an old anchorite° *hermit*
Here, for devotion.
CARDINAL. Thou art a witty false one;
I mean, to him.
JULIA. You have prevailed with me
Beyond my strongest thoughts: I would not now
Find you inconstant.
CARDINAL. Do not put thyself
To such a voluntary torture, which proceeds
Out of your own guilt.
JULIA. How, my Lord?
CARDINAL. You fear
My constancy, because you have approved
Those giddy and wild turnings in yourself.
JULIA. Did you ever find them?
CARDINAL. Sooth, generally; for women,
A man might strive to make glass malleable,
Ere he should make them fixed.
JULIA. So, my Lord.
CARDINAL. We had need go borrow that fantastic glass,
Invented by Galileo the Florentine,[1]
To view another spacious world i' th' moon,
And look to find a constant woman there.
JULIA. This is very well, my Lord.
CARDINAL. Why do you weep?
Are tears your justification? The self-same tears
Will fall into your husband's bosom, lady,
With a loud protestation that you love him
Above the world. Come, I'll love you wisely:
That's jealousy; since I am very certain
You cannot make me cuckold.
JULIA. I'll go home
To my husband.
CARDINAL. You may thank me, lady:
I have taken you off your melancholy perch,
Bore you upon my fist, and showed you game,
And let you fly at it.[2] I pray thee kiss me.
When thou was't with thy husband, thou was't watched
Like a tame elephant—still you are to thank me—
Thou hadst only kisses from him, and high feeding;[3]
But what delight was that? 'Twas just like one
That hath a little fingering on the lute,
Yet cannot tune° it—still you are to thank me. *play*
JULIA. You told me of a piteous wound i' th' heart,
And a sick liver, when you wooed me first,
And spake like one in physic.[4]
CARDINAL. Who's that?

(*Enter servant.*)

Rest firm, for my affection to thee,
Lightning moves slow to't.
SERVANT. Madam, a gentleman,
That's come post from Malfi, desires to see you.
CARDINAL. Let him enter: I'll withdraw.

(*Exit.*)

SERVANT. He says,
Your husband, old Castruccio, is come to Rome,
Most pitifully tired with riding post.

(*Exit. Enter Delio.*)

JULIA. Signior Delio! (*Aside.*) 'Tis one of my old suitors.
DELIO. I was bold to come and see you.
JULIA. Sir, you are welcome.
DELIO. Do you lie here?
JULIA. Sure, your own experience
Will satisfy you, no: our Roman prelates[5]
Do not keep lodging for ladies.
DELIO. Very well:

[1] *fantastic ... Florentine* Telescope, credited here to Galileo Galilei (1564–1642), although not actually invented by him. Its mention here is an anachronism—Galileo did not publish his improvements of the telescope until around 1610.

[2] *I ... it* The metaphor is drawn from falconry.

[3] *high feeding* Rich food.

[4] *in physic* Receiving medical treatment.

[5] *Roman prelates* Catholic leaders.

I have brought you no commendations from your husband,
For I know none by him.
JULIA. I hear he's come to Rome.
DELIO. I never knew man and beast, of a horse and a knight,
So weary of each other; if he had had a good back,
He would have undertook to have borne his horse,
His breech° was so pitifully sore. *rump*
JULIA. Your laughter
Is my pity.
DELIO. Lady, I know not whether
You want money, but I have bought you some.
JULIA. From my husband?
DELIO. No, from mine own allowance.
JULIA. I must hear the condition, ere I be bound to take it.
DELIO. Look on't, 'tis gold; hath it not a fine colour?
JULIA. I have a bird more beautiful.
DELIO. Try the sound on't.
JULIA. A lute-spring far exceeds it:
It hath no smell, like cassia,° or civet;° *cinnamon / musk*
Nor is it physical, though some fond doctors
Persuade us seethe't in cullises.[1] I'll tell you,
This is a creature bred by—

(*Enter servant.*)

SERVANT. Your husband's come,
Hath delivered a letter to the Duke of Calabria,
That to my thinking, hath put him out of his wits.

(*Exit.*)

JULIA. Sir, you hear:
Pray let me know your business, and your suit,
As briefly as can be.
DELIO. With good speed, I would wish you,
At such time as you are non-resident
With your husband, my mistress.
JULIA. Sir, I'll go ask my husband if I shall,
And straight return your answer.

(*Exit.*)

[1] *cullises* Broths, especially for the sick.

DELIO. Very fine.
Is this her wit, or honesty, that speaks thus?
I heard one say the Duke was highly moved
With a letter sent from Malfi. I do fear
Antonio is betrayed: how fearfully
Shows his ambition now! Unfortunate fortune!
They pass through whirlpools, and deep woes do shun,
Who the event weigh, ere the action's done.

(*Exit.*)

ACT 2, SCENE 5

(*Enter Cardinal, and Ferdinand with a letter.*)

FERDINAND. I have this night digged up a mandrake.[2]
CARDINAL. Say you?
FERDINAND. And I am grown mad with't.
CARDINAL. What's the prodigy?° *omen*
FERDINAND. Read there, a sister damned: she's loose i' th' hilts;[3]
Grown a notorious strumpet.
CARDINAL. Speak lower.
FERDINAND. Lower!
Rogues do not whisper't now, but seek to publish't
(As servants do the bounty of their lords)
Aloud; and with a covetous searching eye,
To mark who note them. O, confusion seize her!
She hath had most cunning bawds to serve her turn,
And more secure conveyances for lust,
Than towns of garrison for service.
CARDINAL. Is't possible?
Can this be certain?
FERDINAND. Rhubarb, O, for rhubarb,[4]
To purge this choler!° Here's the cursed day *anger*
To prompt my memory; and here't shall stick
Till of her bleeding heart I make a sponge
To wipe it out.
CARDINAL. Why do you make yourself
So wild a tempest?
FERDINAND. Would I could be one,

[2] *mandrake* Plant with magical powers, thought to provoke madness or death when uprooted.

[3] *loose i' th' hilts* Promiscuous.

[4] *rhubarb* Thought to purge anger.

That I might toss her palace 'bout her ears,
Root up her goodly forests, blast her meads,° *meadows*
And lay her general territory as waste,
As she hath done her honours.
CARDINAL. Shall our blood,
The royal blood of Aragon and Castile,
Be thus attainted?
FERDINAND. Apply desperate physic:
We must not now use balsamum,° but fire, *balm*
The smarting cupping-glass,[1] for that's the mean
To purge infected blood, such blood as hers.
There is a kind of pity in mine eye,
I'll give it to my handkerchief; and now 'tis here
I'll bequeath this to her bastard.
CARDINAL. What to do?
FERDINAND. Why, to make soft lint° for his mother's wounds, *bandages*
When I have hewed her to pieces.
CARDINAL. Cursed creature!
Unequal nature, to place women's hearts
So far upon the left side![2]
FERDINAND. Foolish men,
That e'er will trust their honour in a bark° *small ship*
Made of so slight weak bulrush as is woman,
Apt every minute to sink it!
CARDINAL. Thus ignorance, when it hath purchased honour,
It cannot wield it.
FERDINAND. Methinks I see her laughing:
Excellent hyena! Talk to me somewhat, quickly,
Or my imagination will carry me
To see her in the shameful act of sin.
CARDINAL. With whom?
FERDINAND. Happily° with some strong-thighed bargeman, *perhaps*
Or one o' th' wood-yard, that can quoit the sledge,[3]
Or toss the bar, or else some lovely squire
That carries coals up to her privy lodgings.
CARDINAL. You fly beyond your reason.
FERDINAND. Go to, mistress!
'Tis not your whore's milk that shall quench my wild-fire,
But your whore's blood.
CARDINAL. How idly shows this rage, which carries you,
As men conveyed by witches through the air,
On violent whirlwinds! This intemperate noise
Fitly resembles deaf men's shrill discourse,
Who talk aloud, thinking all other men
To have their imperfection.
FERDINAND. Have not you
My palsy?
CARDINAL. Yes; I can be angry
Without this rupture: there is not in nature
A thing that makes man so deformed, so beastly,
As doth intemperate anger. Chide yourself.
You have divers men, who never yet expressed
Their strong desire of rest, but by unrest,
By vexing of themselves. Come, put yourself
In tune.
FERDINAND. So, I will not only study to seem
The thing I am not. I could kill her now,
In you, or in myself; for I do think
It is some sin in us, heaven doth revenge
By her.
CARDINAL. Are you stark mad?
FERDINAND. I would have their bodies
Burnt in a coal-pit with the ventage° stopped, *chimney*
That their cursed smoke might not ascend to heaven;
Or dip the sheets they lie in in pitch or sulphur,
Wrap them in't, and then light them like a match;
Or else to boil their bastard to a cullis
And give't his lecherous father, to renew
The sin of his back.
CARDINAL. I'll leave you.
FERDINAND. Nay, I have done.
I am confident, had I been damned in hell,
And should have heard of this, it would have put me
Into a cold sweat. In, in, I'll go sleep.
Till I know who leaps my sister, I'll not stir:
That known, I'll find scorpions to string my whips,
And fix her in a general eclipse.[4]

(*Exeunt.*)

---

[1] *cupping-glass* Heated glass vessel used to draw blood, in this period a remedy for illness.

[2] *hearts … side* Deceitful people were believed to have their hearts farther to the left or "sinister" (Latin for "left") side.

[3] *quoit the sledge* Throw the hammer.

[4] *fix … eclipse* Put her into a state of darkness.

ACT 3, SCENE 1

(*Enter Antonio and Delio.*)

ANTONIO. Our noble friend, my most beloved Delio!
O, you have been a stranger long at court:
Came you along with the Lord Ferdinand?
DELIO. I did, sir: and how fares your noble Duchess?
ANTONIO. Right fortunately well: she's an excellent
Feeder of pedigrees; since you last saw her,
She hath had two children more, a son and daughter.
DELIO. Methinks 'twas yesterday; but let me wink,
And not behold your face—which to mine eye
Is somewhat leaner—verily I should dream
It were within this half hour.
ANTONIO. You have not been in law,° friend Delio, *court*
Nor in prison, nor a suitor at the court,
Nor begged the reversion° of some great man's place, *inheritance*
Nor troubled with an old wife, which doth make
Your time so insensibly hasten.
DELIO. Pray, sir, tell me,
Hath not this news arrived yet to the ear
Of the Lord Cardinal?
ANTONIO. I fear it hath:
The Lord Ferdinand, that's newly come to court,
Doth bear himself right dangerously.
DELIO. Pray, why?
ANTONIO. He is so quiet, that he seems to sleep
The tempest out, as dormice do in winter:
These houses that are haunted, are most still
Till the devil be up.
DELIO. What say the common people?
ANTONIO. The common rabble do directly say
She is a strumpet.
DELIO. And your graver heads,
Which would be politic, what censure° they? *judge*
ANTONIO. They do observe, I grow to infinite purchase,° *wealth*
The left hand way; and all suppose the Duchess
Would amend it, if she could: for, say they,
Great princes, though they grudge their officers
Should have such large and unconfined means
To get wealth under them, will not complain,
Lest thereby they should make them odious
Unto the people; for other obligation
Of love or marriage, between her and me,
They never dream of.
DELIO. The Lord Ferdinand
Is going to bed.

(*Enter Duchess, Ferdinand, and Bosola.*)

FERDINAND. I'll instantly to bed,
For I am weary. I am to bespeak° *recommend*
A husband for you.
DUCHESS. For me, sir! Pray who is't?
FERDINAND. The great Count Malateste.
DUCHESS. Fie upon him:
A count! He's a mere stick of sugar-candy;
You may look quite through him. When I choose
A husband, I will marry for your honour.
FERDINAND. You shall do well in't. How is't, worthy Antonio?
DUCHESS. But, sir, I am to have private conference with you
About a scandalous report is spread
Touching mine honour.
FERDINAND. Let me be ever deaf to't:
One of Pasquil's paper-bullets,[1] court-calumny,° *slander*
A pestilent air, which princes' palaces
Are seldom purged of. Yet, say that it were true,
I pour it in your bosom: my fixed love
Would strongly excuse, extenuate, nay, deny
Faults, were they apparent in you. Go, be safe
In your own innocency.
DUCHESS. O blessed comfort!
This deadly air is purged.

(*Exeunt all but Ferdinand and Bosola.*)

FERDINAND. Her guilt treads on
Hot burning culters.[2] Now, Bosola,
How thrives our intelligence?
BOSOLA. Sir, uncertainly:

[1] *Pasquil's paper-bullets* Anonymous written satirical attacks, affixed to Pasquil or Pasquin, and hence "by"an Italian statue.

[2] *culters* Cultures, or plough blades. In medieval England, the ability to walk unharmed on red-hot plough blades was an indication of innocence.

'Tis rumoured she hath had three bastards, but
By whom, we may go read i' th' stars.
FERDINAND. Why some
Hold opinion, all things are written there.
BOSOLA. Yes, if we could find spectacles to read them.
I do suspect, there hath been some sorcery
Used on the Duchess.
FERDINAND. Sorcery! To what purpose?
BOSOLA. To make her dote on some desertless° fellow, *undeserving*
She shames to acknowledge.
FERDINAND. Can your faith give way
To think there's power in potions, or in charms,
To make us love whether we will or no?
BOSOLA. Most certainly.
FERDINAND. Away, these are mere gulleries,° *deceptions* horrid things,
Invented by some cheating mountebanks,[1]
To abuse us. Do you think that herbs, or charms,
Can force the will? Some trials have been made
In this foolish practice, but the ingredients
Were lenitive poisons,[2] such as are of force
To make the patient mad; and straight the witch
Swears by equivocation[3] they are in love.
The witch-craft lies in her[4] rank blood. This night
I will force confession from her. You told me
You had got, within these two days, a false key
Into her bed-chamber.
BOSOLA. I have.
FERDINAND. As I would wish.
BOSOLA. What do you intend to do?
FERDINAND. Can you guess?
BOSOLA. No.
FERDINAND. Do not ask then:
He that can compass me, and know my drifts,° *intentions*
May say he hath put a girdle 'bout the world,
And sounded all her quicksands.
BOSOLA. I do not
Think so.
FERDINAND. What do you think, then, pray?
BOSOLA. That you
Are your own chronicle too much, and grossly
Flatter yourself.
FERDINAND. Give me thy hand; I thank thee:
I never gave pension° but to flatterers, *rewards, wages*
Till I entertained thee. Farewell.
That friend a great man's ruin strongly checks,
Who rails into his belief all his defects.

(*Exeunt.*)

ACT 3, SCENE 2

(*Enter Duchess, Antonio, and Cariola.*)

DUCHESS. Bring me the casket hither, and the glass.° *mirror*
You get no lodging here to night, my Lord.
ANTONIO. Indeed, I must persuade one.
DUCHESS. Very good:
I hope in time 'twill grow into a custom,
That noblemen shall come with cap and knee,[5]
To purchase a night's lodging of their wives.
ANTONIO. I must lie here.
DUCHESS. Must! You are a lord of misrule.[6]
ANTONIO. Indeed, my rule is only in the night.
DUCHESS. To what use will you put me?
ANTONIO. We'll sleep together.
DUCHESS. Alas, what pleasure can two lovers find in sleep!
CARIOLA. My Lord, I lie with her often; and I know
She'll much disquiet you.
ANTONIO. See, you are complained of.
CARIOLA. For she's the sprawlingest bedfellow.
ANTONIO. I shall like her the better for that.
CARIOLA. Sir, shall I ask you a question?
ANTONIO. Ay, pray thee, Cariola.
CARIOLA. Wherefore still, when you lie with my lady,
Do you rise so early?
ANTONIO. Labouring men
Count the clock oftenest, Cariola;
Are glad when their task's ended.
DUCHESS. I'll stop your mouth.

[1] *mountebanks* Itinerant peddlers of useless remedies.

[2] *lenitive poisons* Powerful drugs.

[3] *equivocation* Swearing that love and madness are the same thing.

[4] *her* I.e., the Duchess's.

[5] *with cap and knee* Kneeling, with cap in hand.

[6] *lord of misrule* Man of low rank chosen to preside over games at Christmas festivities. The reversal of roles was an important aspect of the revelry.

(*She kisses him.*)

ANTONIO. Nay, that's but one; Venus had two soft doves
To draw her chariot; I must have another.

(*He kisses her.*)

When wilt thou marry, Cariola?
CARIOLA. Never, my Lord.
ANTONIO. O, fie upon this single life! Forego it.
We read how Daphne, for her peevish flight,
Became a fruitless bay-tree; Syrinx turned
To the pale empty reed; Anaxarete
Was frozen into marble: whereas those
Which married, or proved kind unto their friends,
Were by a gracious influence, transhaped
Into the olive, pomegranate, mulberry,
Became flowers, precious stones, or eminent stars.[1]
CARIOLA. This is a vain poetry; but I pray you tell me,
If there were proposed me wisdom, riches, and beauty,
In three several young men, which should I choose?
ANTONIO. 'Tis a hard question: this was Paris's case,[2]
And he was blind in't, and there was great cause;
For how was't possible he could judge right,
Having three amorous goddesses in view,
And they stark naked? 'Twas a motion
Were able to benight the apprehension[3]
Of the severest counsellor of Europe.
Now I look on both your faces so well formed,
It puts me in mind of a question I would ask.
CARIOLA. What is't?
ANTONIO. I do wonder why hard-favoured° ladies, *ugly*
For the most part, keep worse-favoured waiting women,
To attend them, and cannot endure fair ones.
DUCHESS. O, that's soon answered.
Did you ever in your life know an ill painter
Desire to have his dwelling next door to the shop
Of an excellent picture-maker? 'Twould disgrace
His face-making, and undo him. I prithee,
When were we so merry? My hair tangles.
ANTONIO (*Aside to Cariola.*) Pray thee, Cariola, let's steal forth the room,
And let her talk to herself: I have divers times
Served her the like, when she hath chafed extremely.
I love to see her angry. Softly, Cariola.

(*Exeunt Antonio and Cariola.*)

DUCHESS. Doth not the colour of my hair 'gin to change?
When I wax gray, I shall have all the court
Powder their hair with arras[4] to be like me.
You have cause to love me; I entered you into my heart
Before you would vouchsafe to call for the keys.

(*Enter Ferdinand unseen.*)

We shall one day have my brothers take you napping:
Methinks his presence, being now in court,
Should make you keep your own bed; but you'll say
Love mixed with fear is sweetest. I'll assure you,
You shall get no more children till my brothers
Consent to be your gossips. Have you lost your tongue?

(*She sees that Ferdinand holds a poniard.*)

'Tis welcome:
For know, whether I am doomed to live or die,
I can do both like a prince.
FERDINAND. Die then quickly.

(*Ferdinand gives her a poniard.*)

Virtue, where art thou hid? What hideous thing
Is it that doth eclipse thee?
DUCHESS. Pray, sir, hear me.
FERDINAND. Or is it true thou art but a bare name,
And no essential thing?
DUCHESS. Sir—
FERDINAND. Do not speak.
DUCHESS. No, sir:
I will plant my soul in mine ears, to hear you.

---

[1] *Daphne* In Greek mythology, Daphne fled Apollo's advances, and asked to be changed into a laurel tree; *Sirinx* Spurned Pan's love and was turned into a reed; *Anaxarete* Rejected the shepherd Iphis. In despair, he killed himself, yet she did nothing to stop him. Aphrodite punished her by turning her to stone.

[2] *Paris's case* Paris was asked to choose which goddess was most beautiful, Hera, Athena, or Aphrodite; he chose Aphrodite.

[3] *benight the apprehension* Cloud the understanding.

[4] *arras* I.e., orris powder, made from ground orris-root.

FERDINAND. O, most imperfect light of human reason,
That mak'st us so unhappy to foresee
What we can least prevent! Pursue thy wishes,
And glory in them: there's in shame no comfort,
But to be past all bounds and sense of shame.
DUCHESS. I pray, sir, hear me: I am married.
FERDINAND. So.
DUCHESS. Happily, not to your liking: but for that,
Alas, your shears do come untimely now
To clip the bird's wings, that's already flown!
Will you see my husband?
FERDINAND. Yes. If I could change
Eyes with a basilisk.[1]
DUCHESS. Sure, you came hither
By his confederacy.
FERDINAND. The howling of a wolf
Is music to thee, screech-owl: prithee, peace.
Whate'er thou art that hast enjoyed my sister,
For I am sure thou hears't me, for thine own sake
Let me not know thee. I come hither prepared
To work thy discovery; yet am now persuaded
It would beget such violent effects
As would damn us both. I would not for ten millions
I had beheld thee: therefore use all means
I never may have knowledge of thy name;
Enjoy thy lust still, and a wretched life,
On that condition. And for thee, vile woman,
If thou do wish thy lecher may grow old
In thy embracements, I would have thee build
Such a room for him as our anchorites
To holier use inhabit. Let not the sun
Shine on him, till he's dead; let dogs and monkeys
Only converse with him, and such dumb things
To whom nature denies use to sound his name;
Do not keep a paraquito,° lest she learn it; *parrot*
It thou do love him, cut out thine own tongue
Lest it bewray° him. *expose*
DUCHESS. Why might not I marry?
I have not gone about in this to create
Any new world or custom.
FERDINAND. Thou art undone;
And thou hast ta'en that massy sheet of lead[2]
That hid thy husband's bones, and folded it
About my heart.
DUCHESS. Mine bleeds for't!
FERDINAND. Thine! Thy heart!
What should I name't, unless a hollow bullet° *cannonball*
Filled with unquenchable wild-fire?
DUCHESS. You are in this
Too strict; and were you not my princely brother,
I would say, too wilful: my reputation
Is safe.
FERDINAND. Dost thou know what reputation is?
I'll tell thee, to small purpose, since th' instruction
Comes now too late:
Upon a time Reputation, Love, and Death
Would travel o'er the world; and it was concluded
That they should part, and take three several ways.
Death told them, they should find him in great battles,
Or cities plagued with plagues. Love gives them counsel
To enquire for him 'mongst unambitious shepherds,
Where dowries were not talked of, and sometimes
'Mongst quiet kindred, that had nothing left
By their dead parents. "Stay," quoth Reputation,
"Do not forsake me; for it is my nature
If once I part from any man I meet,
I am never found again." And so, for you:
You have shook hands with Reputation,
And made him invisible. So fare you well:
I will never see you more.

(*Exit. Enter Cariola and Antonio with a pistol.*)

DUCHESS. You saw this apparition?
ANTONIO. Yes: we are
Betrayed. How come he hither? I should turn
This to thee, for that.

(*He points the pistol at Cariola.*)

CARIOLA. Pray, sir, do; and when
That you have cleft my heart, you shall read there
Mine innocence.
DUCHESS. That gallery gave him entrance.
ANTONIO. I would this terrible thing would come again,
That, standing on my guard, I might relate
My warrantable° love! Ha! What means this? *genuine*

[1] *change ... basilisk* Looking into the eyes of a basilisk was believed to cause death.

[2] *massy ... lead* Lead lining of her first husband's coffin.

(*She shows the poniard.*)

DUCHESS. He left this with me.
ANTONIO. And it seems, did wish
You would use it on yourself.
DUCHESS. His action seemed
To intend so much.
ANTONIO. This hath a handle to't,
As well as a point: turn it towards him,
And so fasten the keen edge in his rank gall.

(*Knocking.*)

How now! Who knocks? More earthquakes!
DUCHESS. I stand
As if a mine beneath my feet were ready
To be blown up.
CARIOLA. 'Tis Bosola.
DUCHESS. Away.
O misery! Methinks unjust actions
Should wear these masks and curtains, and not we.
You must instantly part hence: I have fashioned it already.

(*Exit Antonio. Enter Bosola.*)

BOSOLA. The Duke your brother is ta'en up in a whirlwind;
Hath took horse, and 's rid post to Rome.
DUCHESS. So late!
BOSOLA. He told me, as he mounted into th' saddle,
You were undone.
DUCHESS. Indeed, I am very near it.
BOSOLA. What's the matter?
DUCHESS. Antonio, the master of our household,
Hath dealt so falsely with me in's accounts:
My brother stood engaged° with me for money *committed*
Ta'en up of[1] certain Neapolitan Jews,[2]
And Antonio lets the bonds be forfeit.
BOSOLA. Strange—(*Aside.*) this is cunning!
DUCHESS. And hereupon
My brother's bills at Naples are protested
Against.[3] Call up our officers.
BOSOLA. I shall.

(*Exit Bosola. Enter Antonio.*)

DUCHESS. The place that you must fly to, is Ancona:
Hire a house there; I'll send after you
My treasure, and my jewels. Our weak safety
Runs upon enginous° wheels: short syllables, *devious*
Must stand for periods.[4] I must now accuse you
Of such a feigned crime, as Tasso[5] calls
Magnanima menzogna, a noble lie,
'Cause it must shield our honours—hark, they are coming!

(*Enter Bosola and officers.*)

ANTONIO. Will your Grace hear me?
DUCHESS. I have got well by[6] you; you have yielded me
A million of loss: I am like to inherit
The people's curses for your stewardship.
You had the trick in audit-time to be sick,
Till I had signed your *Quietus*; and that cured you
Without help of a doctor. Gentlemen,
I would have this man be an example to you all,
So shall you hold my favour; I pray, let° him; *release*
For h'as done that, alas! You would not think of,
And, because I intend to be rid of him,
I mean not to publish. Use your fortune elsewhere.
ANTONIO. I am strongly armed to brook° my overthrow: *endure*
As commonly men bear with a hard year,
I will not blame the cause on't; but do think
The necessity of my malevolent star
Procures this, not her humour. O, the inconstant
And rotten ground of service! You may see,
'Tis even like him, that in a winter night,
Takes a long slumber o'er a dying fire,
A-loath to part from't; yet parts thence as cold,
As when he first sat down.

---

[1] *Ta'en up of* Loaned from.

[2] *Jews* Throughout much of Western European history Jews were excluded from many occupations; money lending, widely considered by Christians to be inherently sinful, was an exception.

[3] *protested /Against* Called due.

[4] *periods* Full sentences.

[5] *Tasso* Torquato Tasso (1544–95), Italian epic poet.

[6] *got well by* Had enough of.

DUCHESS. We do confiscate
Towards the satisfying of your accounts,
All that you have.
ANTONIO. I am all yours; and 'tis very fit
All mine should be so.
DUCHESS. So, sir, you have your pass.
ANTONIO. You may see, gentlemen, what it is to serve
A prince with body and soul.

(*Exit.*)

BOSOLA. Here's an example for extortion: what moisture is drawn out of the sea, when foul weather comes pours down, and runs into the sea again.
DUCHESS. I would know what are your opinions
Of this Antonio.
2ND OFFICER. He could not abide to see a pig's head gaping: I thought your Grace would find him a Jew.
3RD OFFICER. I would you had been his officer, for your own sake.
4TH OFFICER. He stopped his ears with black wool, and to those came to him for money, said he was thick of hearing.
2ND OFFICER. Some said he was an hermaphrodite, for he could not abide a woman.
4TH OFFICER. How scurvy proud he would look, when the treasury was full! Well, let him go.
1ST OFFICER. Yes, and the chippings of the buttery[1] fly after him, to scour his gold chain.[2]
DUCHESS. Leave us.

(*Exeunt officers.*)

What do you think of these?
BOSOLA. That these are rogues, that in's prosperity,
But to have waited on his fortune, could have wished
His dirty stirrup rivetted through their noses;[3]
And followed after 's mule, like a bear in a ring.
Would have prostituted their daughters to his lust;
Made their first-born intelligencers; thought none happy
But such as were born under his blest planet,
And wore his livery:[4] and do these lice drop off now?
Well, never look to have the like again:
He hath left a sort of flattering rogues behind him;
Their doom must follow. Princes pay flatterers
In their own money, flatterers dissemble their vices,
And they dissemble their lies;[5] that's justice.
Alas, poor gentleman!
DUCHESS. Poor! He hath amply filled his coffers.
BOSOLA. Sure he was too honest. Plutus,[6] the god of riches,
When he's sent by Jupiter to any man,
He goes limping, to signify that wealth
That comes on God's name, comes slowly; but when he's sent
On the devil's errand, he rides post and comes in by scuttles.[7]
Let me show you, what a most unvalued jewel
You have in a wanton humour thrown away,
To bless the man shall find him. He was an excellent
Courtier, and most faithful; a soldier, that thought it
As beastly to know his own value too little,
As devilish to acknowledge it too much.
Both his virtue and form deserved a far better fortune.
His discourse° rather delighted to judge itself, than show itself: *conversation*
His breast was filled with all perfection,
And yet it seemed a private whispering-room,
It made so little noise of 't.
DUCHESS. But he was basely descended.
BOSOLA. Will you make yourself a mercenary herald,
Rather to examine men's pedigrees, than virtues?
You shall want him:
For know an honest statesman to a prince,
Is like a cedar planted by a spring:
The spring bathes the tree's root, the grateful tree
Rewards it with his shadow—you have not done so.
I would sooner swim to the Bermoothes[8] on
Two politicians' rotten bladders, tied

[1] *chippings of the buttery* Bread crumbs, used to polish gold.

[2] *gold chain* Indicating the office of steward.

[3] *riveted ... noses* Bears used for bear-baiting were controlled by rings in their noses.

[4] *wore his livery* Were in his service.

[5] *Flatterers ... lies* Flatterers lie about princes' vices, and princes lie about the flatterers' deceptions.

[6] *Plutus* The Greek personification of riches.

[7] *by scuttles* In a hurried run.

[8] *Bermoothes* Bermudas.

Together with an intelligencer's heart-string,
Than depend on so changeable a prince's favour.
Fare thee well, Antonio! Since the malice of the world
Would needs down with thee, it cannot be said yet
That any ill happened unto thee, considering thy fall
Was accompanied with virtue.

DUCHESS. O, you render me excellent music!

BOSOLA. Say you?

DUCHESS. This good one that you speak of, is my husband.

BOSOLA. Do I not dream? Can this ambitious age
Have so much goodness in't, as to prefer
A man merely for worth, without these shadows
Of wealth and painted honours? Possible?

DUCHESS. I have had three children by him.

BOSOLA. Fortunate lady!
For you have made your private nuptial bed
The humble and fair seminary° of peace. *seed bed*
No question but many an unbeneficed° scholar *unsponsored*
Shall pray for you for this deed, and rejoice
That some preferment in the world can yet
Arise from merit. The virgins of your land
That have no dowries, shall hope your example
Will raise them to rich husbands. Should you want
Soldiers, 'twould make the very Turks and Moors
Turn Christians, and serve you for this act.
Last, the neglected poets of your time,
In honour of this trophy of a man,
Raised by that curious engine, your white hand,
Shall thank you, in your grave, for't; and make that
More reverend than all the cabinets
Of living princes. For Antonio,
His fame shall likewise flow from many a pen,
When heralds shall want coats to sell to men.

DUCHESS. As I taste comfort in this friendly speech,
So would I find concealment.

BOSOLA. O, the secret of my prince,
Which I will wear on th' inside of my heart!

DUCHESS. You shall take charge of all my coin and jewels,
And follow him; for he retires himself
To Ancona.

BOSOLA. So.

DUCHESS. Whither, within few days,
I mean to follow thee.

BOSOLA. Let me think:
I would wish your Grace to feign a pilgrimage
To our lady of Loretto,[1] scarce seven leagues
From fair Ancona; so may you depart
Your country with more honour, and your flight
Will seem a princely progress, retaining
Your usual train about you.

DUCHESS. Sir, your direction
Shall lead me by the hand.

CARIOLA. In my opinion,
She were better progress to the baths at Lucca,
Or go visit the Spa
In Germany:[2] for, if you will believe me,
I do not like this jesting with religion,
This feigned pilgrimage.

DUCHESS. Thou art a superstitious fool!
Prepare us instantly for our departure.
Past sorrows, let us moderately lament them,
For those to come, seek wisely to prevent them.

(Exeunt Duchess and Cariola.)

BOSOLA. A politician is the devil's quilted anvil;
He fashions all sins on him, and the blows
Are never heard: he may work in a lady's chamber,
As here for proof. What rests° but I reveal *remains*
All to my Lord? O, this base quality
Of intelligencer! Why, every quality i' th' world
Prefers but[3] gain or commendation.
Now, for this act I am certain to be raised,
And men that paint weeds to the life,[4] are praised.

(Exit.)

ACT 3, SCENE 3

(Enter Cardinal, Ferdinand, Malateste, Pescara, Delio, and Silvio.)

---

[1] *our lady of Loretto* Shrine a few miles south of Ancona.

[2] *Spa / In Germany* Town in what is now Belgium near the German border from which the spa derives its name. Its waters are said to be medicinal.

[3] *Prefers but* Looks for only.

[4] *to the life* That look life-like.

CARDINAL. Must we turn soldier then?
MALATESTE. The Emperor,[1]
Hearing your worth that way, ere you attained
This reverend garment, joins you in commission
With the right fortunate soldier, the Marquess of Pescara,
And the famous Lannoy.[2]
CARDINAL. He that had the honour
Of taking the French king prisoner?
MALATESTE. The same.
Here's a plot drawn for a new fortification
At Naples.
FERDINAND. This great Count Malateste, I perceive,
Hath got employment?
DELIO. No employment, my Lord;
A marginal note in the muster-book,[3] that he is
A voluntary lord.
FERDINAND. He's no soldier.
DELIO. He has worn gunpowder in's hollow tooth,
For the tooth-ache.
SILVIO. He comes to the leaguer with a full intent
To eat fresh beef and garlic, means to stay
Till the scent be gone, and straight return to court.
DELIO. He hath read all the late service,[4]
As the City Chronicle[5] relates it:
And keeps two pewterers[6] going, only to express
Battles in model.
SILVIO. Then he'll fight by the book.
DELIO. By the almanac, I think,
To choose good days, and shun the critical;
That's his mistress's scarf.
SILVIO. Yes, he protests
He would do much for that taffeta.
DELIO. I think he would run away from a battle,
To save it from taking prisoner.
SILVIO. He is horribly afraid
Gunpowder will spoil the perfume on't.
DELIO. I saw a Dutchman break his pate° once *head*
For calling him pot-gun;[7] he made his head
Have a bore in't like a musket.
SILVIO. I would he had made a touchhole[8] to't.
He is indeed a guarded sumpter-cloth,[9]
Only for the remove of the court.

(*Enter Bosola.*)

PESCARA. Bosola arrived! What should be the business?
Some falling out amongst the Cardinals.
These factions amongst great men, they are like
Foxes, when their heads are divided,
They carry fire in their tails, and all the country
About them goes to wrack for't.[10]
SILVIO. What's that Bosola?
DELIO. I knew him in Padua—a fantastical scholar, like such, who study how many knots was in Hercules' club, of what colour Achilles' beard was, or whether Hector were not troubled with the tooth-ache. He hath studied himself half blear-eyed to know the true symmetry of Caesar's nose by a shoeing-horn;[11] and this he did to gain the name of a speculative man.
PESCARA. Mark Prince Ferdinand:
A very salamander[12] lives in's eye,
To mock the eager violence of fire.
SILVIO. That cardinal hath made more bad faces with his oppression than ever Michael Angelo[13] made good ones: he lifts up's nose, like a foul porpoise before a storm.
PESCARA. The Lord Ferdinand laughs.
DELIO. Like a deadly cannon, that lightens ere it

---

[1] *Emperor* Charles V (1500–58), Holy Roman Emperor from 1519–58.

[2] *Marquess of Pescara* Fernando Francesco Davalos (1489–1525), a hero of the Italian wars who captured Francis I of France in 1525; *Lannoy* Charles de Lannoy (1482–1527), appointed Viceroy of Naples by Charles V in 1522.

[3] *muster-book* Register of military personnel.

[4] *late service* Recent military developments.

[5] *City Chronicle* Official report about the affairs of the city.

[6] *pewterers* Workers in pewter, here as makers of figurines.

[7] *pot-gun* Boaster. Literally, a pop gun.

[8] *touchhole* Part of a gun to which fire was applied for ignition.

[9] *sumpter-cloth* Valuable blanket laid over the back of a horse.

[10] *Foxes … for't* Reference to Judges 15.4–5, in which Samson ties pairs of foxes together by their tails. He attaches lit torches to the tails and sets the foxes loose in the Philistines' fields, burning them.

[11] *symmetry … shoeing-horn* How Caesar's nose compared in symmetry to a shoe-horn.

[12] *salamander* Reptile thought to be able to live in fire.

[13] *Michael Angelo* Michaelangelo Buonarroti (1475–1564), Italian painter, sculptor, and poet.

smokes.
PESCARA. These are your true pangs of death,
The pangs of life, that struggle with great statesmen.
DELIO. In such a deformed silence, witches whisper
their charms.
CARDINAL. Doth she make religion her riding hood
To keep her from the sun and tempest?
FERDINAND. That,
That damns her. Methinks her fault and beauty,
Blended together, show like leprosy,
The whiter, the fouler. I make it a question
Whether her beggarly brats were ever christened.
CARDINAL. I will instantly solicit the state of Ancona
To have them banished.
FERDINAND. You are for[1] Loretto:
I shall not be at your ceremony; fare you well.
Write to the Duke of Malfi, my young nephew
She had by her first husband, and acquaint him
With's mother's honesty.
BOSOLA. I will.
FERDINAND. Antonio!
A slave that only smelled of ink and counters
And never in's life looked like a gentleman,
But in the audit-time. Go, go presently,
Draw me out an hundred and fifty of our horse,
And meet me at the fort-bridge.

(*Exeunt.*)

ACT 3, SCENE 4

(*Enter two pilgrims to the Shrine of our Lady of Loretto.*)

1ST PILGRIM. I have not seen a goodlier shrine than this,
Yet I have visited many.
2ND PILGRIM. The Cardinal of Aragon
Is this day to resign his cardinal's hat:
His sister duchess likewise is arrived
To pay her vow of pilgrimage. I expect
A noble ceremony.
1ST PILGRIM. No question. They come.

(*Here the ceremony of the Cardinal's installment, in the habit of a soldier, performed in delivering up his cross, hat, robes, and ring, at the shrine, and investing him with sword, helmet, shield, and spurs: then Antonio, the Duchess, and their children, having presented themselves at the shrine, are [by a form of banishment in dumb-show expressed towards them by the Cardinal and the state of Ancona] banished. During all which ceremony, this ditty is sung, to very solemn music, by diverse churchmen, and then Exeunt all but the two pilgrims, who sing:*)

Arms, and honours deck thy story,
To thy fame's eternal glory:
Adverse fortune ever fly thee;
No disastrous fate come nigh thee.

I alone will sing thy praises,
Whom to honour virtue raises;
And thy study, that divine is,
Bent to martial discipline is.
Lay aside all those robes lie by thee;
Crown thy arts with arms, they'll beautify thee.

O, worthy of worthiest name, adorned in this manner,
Lead bravely thy forces on, under war's warlike banner!
O, may'st thou prove fortunate in all martial courses!
Guide thou still by skill in arts and forces:
Victory attend thee nigh, whilst fame sings loud thy powers;
Triumphant conquest crown thy head, and blessings pour down showers![2]

1ST PILGRIM. Here's a strange turn of state! Who would have thought
So great a lady would have matched herself
Unto so mean a person? Yet the Cardinal
Bears him much too cruel.
2ND PILGRIM. They are banished.
1ST PILGRIM. But I would ask what power hath this state
Of Ancona, to determine of[3] a free prince?
2ND PILGRIM. They are a free state, sir, and her brother showed
How that the Pope fore-hearing of her looseness,
Hath seized into the protection of the Church

---

[1] *for* Leaving for.

[2] *Arms … showers* In the original printings of the play, this song was accompanied by a text note, which read "The Author disclaims this Ditty to be his." The authorship of the song is unknown.

[3] *determine of* Pass judgment on.

The Dukedom, which she held as dowager.
1ST PILGRIM. But by what justice?
2ND PILGRIM. Sure I think by none,
Only her brother's instigation.
1ST PILGRIM. What was it with such violence he took
Off from her finger?
2ND PILGRIM. 'Twas her wedding ring.
Which he vowed shortly he would sacrifice
To his revenge.
1ST PILGRIM. Alas, Antonio!
If that a man be thrust into a well,
No matter who sets hand to't, his own weight
Will bring him sooner to th' bottom. Come, let's hence.
Fortune makes this conclusion general,
All things do help th' unhappy man to fall.

(*Exeunt.*)

ACT 3, SCENE 5

(*Enter Duchess, Antonio, children, Cariola and servants.*)

DUCHESS. Banished Ancona!
ANTONIO. Yes, you see what power
Lightens in great men's breath.
DUCHESS. Is all our train° *entourage*
Shrunk to this poor remainder?
ANTONIO. These poor men,
Which have got little in service, vow
To take your fortune: but your wiser buntings,[1]
Now they are fledged,[2] are gone.
DUCHESS. They have done wisely.
This puts me in mind of death: physicians thus,
With their hands full of money, use to give o'er
Their patients.
ANTONIO. Right° the fashion of the world: *such is*
From decayed fortunes every flatterer shrinks;
Men cease to build where the foundation sinks.
DUCHESS. I had a very strange dream tonight.
ANTONIO. What was't?
DUCHESS. Methought I wore my coronet[3] of state,
And on a sudden[4] all the diamonds
Were changed to pearls.
ANTONIO. My interpretation
Is, you'll weep shortly; for to me the pearls
Do signify your tears.
DUCHESS. The birds that live i' th' field
On the wild benefit of nature, live
Happier than we; for they may choose their mates,
And carol their sweet pleasures to the spring.

(*Enter Bosola with a letter.*)

BOSOLA. You are happily o'erta'en.
DUCHESS. From my brother?
BOSOLA. Yes, from the Lord Ferdinand, your brother.
All love and safety.
DUCHESS. Thou dost blanch° mischief, *hide*
Would'st make it white. See, see, like to calm weather
At sea before a tempest, false hearts speak fair
To those they intend most mischief.

(*She reads the letter.*)

"Send Antonio to me; I want his head in a business."
A politic equivocation!
He doth not want your counsel, but your head;
That is, he cannot sleep till you be dead.
And here's another pitfall that's strewed o'er
With roses; mark it, 'tis a cunning one;
"I stand engaged for your husband, for several debts at Naples: let not that trouble him; I had rather have his heart than his money."
And I believe so too.
BOSOLA. What do you believe?
DUCHESS. That he so much distrusts my husband's love,
He will by no means believe his heart is with him,
Until he see it: the devil is not cunning enough
To circumvent us in riddles.
BOSOLA. Will you reject that noble and free league
Of amity and love, which I present you?
DUCHESS. Their league is like that of some politic kings,
Only to make themselves of strength and power

[1] *buntings* Small birds.

[2] *are fledged* Have grown their adult feathers.

[3] *coronet* Small crown.

[4] *on a sudden* All of a sudden.

To be our after-ruin: tell them so.
BOSOLA. And what from you?
ANTONIO. Thus tell him; I will not come.
BOSOLA. And what of this?
ANTONIO. My brothers have dispersed
Blood-hounds abroad; which till I hear are muzzled,
No truce, though hatched with ne'er such politic skill,
Is safe, that hangs upon our enemies' will.
I'll not come at them.
BOSOLA. This proclaims your breeding:
Every small thing draws a base mind to fear,
As the adamant[1] draws iron. Fare you well, sir:
You shall shortly hear from 's.

(Exit.)

DUCHESS. I suspect some ambush:
Therefore by all my love I do conjure you
To take your eldest son, and fly towards Milan.
Let us not venture all this poor remainder,
In one unlucky bottom.[2]
ANTONIO. You counsel safely.
Best of my life, farewell, since we must part:
Heaven hath a hand in't: but no otherwise,
Than as some curious artist[3] takes in sunder
A clock, or watch, when it is out of frame,
To bring't in better order.
DUCHESS. I know not which is best,
To see you dead, or part with you. Farewell, boy:
Thou art happy, that thou hast not understanding
To know thy misery; for all our wit
And reading brings us to a truer sense
Of sorrow. In the eternal Church, sir,
I do hope we shall not part thus.
ANTONIO. O, be of comfort!
Make patience a noble fortitude,
And think not how unkindly we are used:
Man, like to cassia,[4] is proved best, being bruised.
DUCHESS. Must I, like to a slave-born Russian,
Account it praise to suffer tyranny?
And yet, O heaven, thy heavy hand is in't!
I have seen my little boy oft scourge his top,
And compared myself to't: nought made me e'er go right
But heaven's scourge-stick.
ANTONIO. Do not weep:
Heaven fashioned us out of nothing; and we strive
To bring ourselves to nothing. Farewell, Cariola,
And thy sweet armful. *(To Duchess.)* If I do never see
thee more,
Be a good mother to your little ones,
And save them from the tiger: fare you well.
DUCHESS. Let me look upon you once more, for that
speech
Came from a dying father: your kiss is colder
Than that I have seen an holy anchorite
Give to a dead man's skull.
ANTONIO. My heart is turned to a heavy lump of lead,
With which I sound my danger:[5] fare you well.

(Exit.)

DUCHESS. My laurel is all withered.
CARIOLA. Look, madam, what a troop of armed men
Make toward us.

(Enter Bosola and soldiers, with vizards.)

DUCHESS. O, they are very welcome!
When fortune's wheel is over-charged° *overloaded*
with princes,
The weight makes it move swift: I would have my ruin
Be sudden. I am your adventure,° am I not? *prey*
BOSOLA. You are: you must see your husband no more.
DUCHESS. What devil art thou, that counterfeits
heaven's thunder?
BOSOLA. Is that terrible? I would have you tell me
Whether is that note worse that frights the silly birds
Out of the corn, or that which doth allure them
To the nets? You have hearkened to the last too much.
DUCHESS. O misery! Like to a rusty o'er-charged cannon.[6]
Shall I ne'er fly in pieces? Come, to what prison?
BOSOLA. To none.

[1] *adamant* Lodestone, a stone with magnetic properties.

[2] *bottom* Hold of a ship.

[3] *artist* Artisan, workman.

[4] *cassia* Cinnamon, which must be pounded out of bark.

[5] *lead … danger* Sailors used to lower lumps of lead overboard to check depths, particularly in dangerous shallows.

[6] *o'er-charged cannon* Cannons would explode if packed with too much gunpowder.

DUCHESS. Whither, then?
BOSOLA. To your palace.
DUCHESS. I have heard that Charon's boat[1] serves to convey
All o'er the dismal lake, but brings none back again.
BOSOLA. Your brothers mean you safety and pity.
DUCHESS. Pity!
With such a pity men preserve alive
Pheasants and quails, when they are not fat enough
To be eaten.
BOSOLA. These are your children?
DUCHESS. Yes.
BOSOLA. Can they prattle?° *talk*
DUCHESS. No:
But I intend, since they were born accursed,
Curses shall be their first language.
BOSOLA. Fie, madam,
Forget this base, low fellow.
DUCHESS. Were I a man,
I'd beat that counterfeit face[2] into thy other.
BOSOLA. One of no birth.
DUCHESS. Say that he was born mean,
Man is most happy when's own actions
Be arguments and examples of his virtue.
BOSOLA. A barren, beggarly virtue.
DUCHESS. I prithee who is greatest, can you tell?
Sad tales befit my woe: I'll tell you one.
A salmon, as she swam unto the sea,
Met with a dog-fish, who encounters her
With this rough language: Why art thou so bold
To mix thyself with our high state of floods,
Being no eminent courtier, but one
That for the calmest, and fresh time o' th' year
Dost live in shallow rivers, rank'st thyself
With silly smelts and shrimps? And darest thou
Pass by our dog-ship without reverence?
O, quoth the salmon, sister, be at peace:
Thank Jupiter, we both have passed the net!
Our value never can be truly known,
Till in the fisher's basket we be shown:
I' th' market then my price may be the higher,
Even when I am nearest to the cook and fire.
So, to great men the moral may be stretched;
Men oft are valued high, when th' are most wretched.
But come, whither you please. I am armed 'gainst misery;
Bent to all sways of the oppressor's will:
There's no deep valley but near some great hill.

(*Exeunt.*)

ACT 4, SCENE 1

(*Enter Ferdinand and Bosola.*)

FERDINAND. How doth our sister Duchess bear herself
In her imprisonment?
BOSOLA. Nobly: I'll describe her.
She's sad, as one long used to't, and she seems
Rather to welcome the end of misery,
Than shun it; a behaviour so noble,
As gives a majesty to adversity:
You may discern the shape of loveliness
More perfect in her tears than in her smiles:
She will muse for hours together; and her silence,
Methinks, expresseth more than if she spake.
FERDINAND. Her melancholy seems to be fortified
With a strange disdain.
BOSOLA. 'Tis so; and this restraint,
Like English mastiffs[3] that grow fierce with tying,
Makes her too passionately apprehend
Those pleasures she's kept from.
FERDINAND. Curse upon her!
I will no longer study in the book
Of another's heart. Inform her what I told you.

(*Exit. Enter Duchess with servants.*)

BOSOLA. All comfort to your Grace.
DUCHESS. I will have none.
Pray thee, why dost thou wrap thy poisoned pills
In gold and sugar?
BOSOLA. Your elder brother, the Lord Ferdinand,
Is come to visit you, and sends you word,
'Cause once he rashly made a solemn vow

[1] *Charon's boat* In classical mythology, Charon is the ferryman of Hades, bringing the dead from one side of the River Styx to the other.

[2] *counterfeit face* I.e., masked face.

[3] *mastiffs* Large dogs.

Never to see you more, he comes i' th' night;
And prays you gently neither torch nor taper
Shine in your chamber: he will kiss your hand,
And reconcile himself; but, for his vow,
He dares not see you.
DUCHESS. At his pleasure.
Take hence the lights; he's come.

(*Exit servants with the lights. Enter Ferdinand.*)

FERDINAND. Where are you?
DUCHESS. Here, sir.
FERDINAND. This darkness suits you well.
DUCHESS. I would ask you pardon.
FERDINAND. You have it;
For I account it the honorabl'st revenge,
Where I may kill, to pardon. Where are your cubs?
DUCHESS. Whom?
FERDINAND. Call them your children,
For though our national law distinguish bastards
From true legitimate issue, compassionate nature
Makes them all equal.
DUCHESS. Do you visit me for this?
You violate a sacrament o' th' Church[1]
Shall make you howl in hell for't.
FERDINAND. It had been well,
Could you have lived thus always; for indeed,
You were too much i' th' light[2]—but no more;
I come to seal my peace with you. Here's a hand,

(*He gives her a dead man's hand.*)

To which you have vowed much love; the ring upon't
You gave.
DUCHESS. I affectionately kiss it.
FERDINAND. Pray do, and bury the print of it in your heart.
I will leave this ring with you, for a love-token;
And the hand, as sure as the ring; and do not doubt
But you shall have the heart too: when you need a friend,
Send it to him that owned° it: you shall see
Whether he can aid you.

[1] *sacrament ... Church* I.e., her marriage to Antonio.

[2] *i' th' light* In the public eye.

DUCHESS. You are very cold:
I fear you are not well after your travel.
Ha! Lights! O, horrible!
FERDINAND. Let her have lights enough.

(*Exit. Enter servants with lights.*)

DUCHESS. What witchcraft[3] doth he practise, that he hath left
A dead man's hand here?

(*Here is discovered, behind a traverse, the artificial figures of Antonio and his children,*[4] *appearing as if they were dead.*)

BOSOLA. Look you, here's the piece, from which 'twas ta'en.
He doth present you this sad spectacle,
That, now you know directly they are dead,
Hereafter you may wisely cease to grieve
For that which cannot be recovered.
DUCHESS. There is not between heaven and earth one wish
I stay for after this: it wastes me more
Than were't my picture,° fashioned out of wax, [*image*]
Stuck with a magical needle, and then buried
In some foul dunghill; and yond's an excellent property
For a tyrant, which I would account mercy.
BOSOLA. What's that?
DUCHESS. If they would bind me to that lifeless trunk,[5]
And let me freeze to death.
BOSOLA. Come, you must live.
DUCHESS. That's the greatest torture souls feel in hell,
In hell that they must live, and cannot die.
Portia, I'll new kindle thy coals again,
And revive the rare and almost dead example
Of a loving wife.[6]

[3] *witchcraft* A dead man's hand was thought to be used in witchcraft as a charm to fend off madness.

[4] *traverse* Stage curtain; *Antonio and his children* A discrepancy—their older son went with Antonio, but the rest have apparently remained with the Duchess (see Act 4, scene 2).

[5] *lifeless trunk* I.e., the dead body of Antonio.

[6] *Portia* Portia Catones (d. 42 BCE), wife of Brutus killed herself by swallowing hot coals in despair over her husband's defeat.

BOSOLA. O fie! Despair? Remember
You are a Christian.
DUCHESS. The Church enjoins fasting:
I'll starve myself to death.
BOSOLA. Leave this vain sorrow.
Things being at the worst, begin to mend: the bee
When he hath shot his sting into your hand,
May then play with your eyelid.[1]
DUCHESS. Good comfortable fellow!
Persuade a wretch that's broke upon the wheel[2]
To have all his bones new set; entreat him live
To be executed again. Who must dispatch me?
I account this world a tedious theatre,
For I do play a part in't 'gainst my will.
BOSOLA. Come, be of comfort; I will save your life.
DUCHESS. Indeed I have not leisure to tend so small a business.
BOSOLA. Now, by my life, I pity you.
DUCHESS. Thou art a fool then,
To waste thy pity on a thing so wretched
As cannot pity itself. I am full of daggers.
Puff, let me blow those vipers from me.

(*Enter servant.*)

What are you?
SERVANT. One that wishes you long life.
DUCHESS. I would thou wert hanged for the horrible curse
Thou hast given me: I shall shortly grow° one *become*
Of the miracles of pity. I'll go pray, no,
I'll go curse.
BOSOLA. O, fie!
DUCHESS. I could curse the stars.
BOSOLA. O, fearful!
DUCHESS. And those three smiling seasons of the year
Into a Russian winter: nay the world
To its first chaos.
BOSOLA. Look you, the stars shine still.
DUCHESS. O, but you must
Remember, my curse hath a great way to go:
Plagues, that make lanes through largest families,
Consume them.
BOSOLA. Fie, lady!
DUCHESS. Let them like tyrants
Never be remembered, but for the ill they have done;
Let all the zealous prayers of mortified
Churchmen forget them,—
BOSOLA. O, uncharitable!
DUCHESS. Let heaven, a little while, cease crowning martyrs,
To punish them. Go, howl them this, and say, I long to bleed:
It is some mercy when men kill with speed.

(*Exit Bosola and servant. Enter Ferdinand.*)

FERDINAND. Excellent, as I would wish; she's plagued in art:[3]
These presentations are but framed in wax,
By the curious master in that quality,
Vincentio Lauriola, and she takes them
For true substantial bodies.
BOSOLA. Why do you do this?
FERDINAND. To bring her to despair.
BOSOLA. 'Faith, end here,
And go no farther in your cruelty;
Send her a penitential garment to put on
Next to her delicate skin, and furnish her
With beads, and prayer-books.
FERDINAND. Damn her! That body of hers,
While that my blood ran pure in't, was more worth
Than that which thou wouldst comfort, called a soul.
I will send her masks of common courtesans,
Have her meat served up by bawds and ruffians,
And, 'cause she'll needs be mad, I am resolved
To remove forth the common hospital
All the mad-folk, and place them near her lodging;
There let them practise together, sing and dance,
And set their gambols to the full o' th' moon:[4]
If she can sleep the better for it, let her.
Your work is almost ended.
BOSOLA. Must I see her again?
FERDINAND. Yes.

[1] *bee ... eyelid* Once the bee has stung, it poses no more threat.

[2] *broke ... wheel* Method of torture in which a victim's bones are broken.

[3] *plagued in art* Tormented by the false figures.

[4] *full o'th' moon* The time when lunatics were thought to be at their worst.

BOSOLA. Never.
FERDINAND. You must.
BOSOLA. Never in mine own shape;
That's forfeited by my intelligence,° *spying*
And this last cruel lie: when you send me next,
The business shall be comfort.
FERDINAND. Very likely;
Thy pity is nothing of kin to thee. Antonio
Lurks about Milan: thou shalt shortly thither,
To feed a fire as great as my revenge,
Which never will slack till it have spent his fuel:
Intemperate agues[1] make physicians cruel.

(*Exeunt.*)

ACT 4, SCENE 2

(*Enter Duchess and Cariola.*)

DUCHESS. What hideous noise was that?
CARIOLA. 'Tis the wild consort
Of madmen, lady, which your tyrant brother
Hath placed about your lodging: this tyranny,
I think, was never practised till this hour.
DUCHESS. Indeed, I thank him: nothing but noise and folly
Can keep me in my right wits; whereas reason
And silence make me stark mad. Sit down;
Discourse to me some dismal tragedy.
CARIOLA. O, 'twill increase your melancholy.
DUCHESS. Thou art deceived:
To hear of greater grief would lessen mine.
This is a prison.
CARIOLA. Yes, but you shall live
To shake this durance° off. *imprisonment*
DUCHESS. Thou art a fool:
The robin-red-breast and the nightingale
Never live long in cages.
CARIOLA. Pray, dry your eyes:
What think you of, madam?
DUCHESS. Of nothing;
When I muse thus, I sleep.
CARIOLA. Like a madman, with your eyes open?
DUCHESS. Dost thou think we shall know one another
In th' other world?
CARIOLA. Yes, out of question.
DUCHESS. O, that it were possible we might
But hold some two days' conference with the dead!
From them I should learn somewhat,° I am sure, *something*
I never shall know here. I'll tell thee a miracle;
I am not mad yet, to my cause of sorrow:[2]
Th' heaven o'er my head seems made of molten brass,
The earth of flaming sulphur, yet I am not mad.
I am acquainted with sad misery,
As the tanned galley-slave is with his oar;
Necessity makes me suffer constantly,
And custom makes it easy. Whom do I look like now?
CARIOLA. Like to your picture in the gallery,
A deal of life in show, but none in practice;
Or rather like some reverend monument
Whose ruins are even pitied.
DUCHESS. Very proper;
And fortune seems only to have her eyesight,
To behold my tragedy. How now!
What noise is that?

(*Enter servant.*)

SERVANT. I am come to tell you,
Your brother hath intended you some sport.
A great physician, when the pope was sick
Of a deep melancholy, presented him
With several sorts of madmen, which wild object
Being full of change and sport,° forced him to laugh, *entertainment*
And so th' imposthume° broke: the selfsame cure *illness*
The Duke intends on you.
DUCHESS. Let them come in.

(*Enter madmen.*)

SERVANT. There's a mad lawyer; and a secular priest;
A doctor, that hath forfeited his wits
By jealousy; an astrologian
That in his works said, such a day o' th' month
Should be the day of doom, and failing of't,
Ran mad; an English tailor, crazed i' th' brain

[1] *Intemperate agues* Severe fevers.

[2] *to ... sorrow* And this gives me sorrow.

With the study of new fashion; a gentleman usher,[1]
Quite beside himself with care to keep in mind
The number of his lady's salutations,
Or "How do you," she employed him in each morning;
A farmer too, an excellent knave in grain,
Mad 'cause he was hindered transportation;° *export*
And let one broker° that's mad loose to these, *pawnbroker*
You'd think the devil were among them.

DUCHESS. Sit, Cariola. Let them loose when you please,
For I am chained to endure all your tyranny.

(*Here by a madman this song is sung, to a dismal kind of music:*)

O, let us howl some heavy note,
Some deadly dogged howl,
Sounding, as from the threatening throat
Of beasts and fatal fowl!
As ravens, screech-owls, bulls, and bears,
We'll bell,° and bawl our parts, *bellow*
Till irksome noise have cloyed° your ears, *overloaded*
And corrosived your hearts.
At last, when as our quire° wants breath, *choir*
Our bodies being blest,
We'll sing, like swans, to welcome death,
And die in love and rest.

1ST MADMAN. Doomsday not come yet! I'll draw it nearer by a perspective,[2] or make a glass that shall set all the world on fire upon an instant. I cannot sleep; my pillow is stuffed with a litter of porcupines.

2ND MADMAN. Hell is a mere glass-house, where the devils are continually blowing up women's souls on hollow irons, and the fire never goes out.

3RD MADMAN. I will lie with every woman in my parish the tenth night; I will tithe them over like haycocks.[3]

4TH MADMAN. Shall my 'pothecary[4] outgo me,[5] because I am a cuckold? I have found out his roguery; he makes alum of his wife's urine, and sells it to Puritans that have sore throats with overstraining.[6]

1ST MADMAN. I have skill in heraldry.

2ND MADMAN. Hast?

1ST MADMAN. You do give for your crest a woodcock's head, with the brains picked out on't; you are a very ancient gentleman.

3RD MADMAN. Greek is turned Turk: we are only to be saved by the Helvetian translation.[7]

1ST MADMAN. Come on, sir, I will lay the law to you.

2ND MADMAN. O, rather lay a corrosive; the law will eat to the bone.

3RD MADMAN. He that drinks but to satisfy nature, is damned.

4TH MADMAN. If I had my glass here, I would show a sight should make all the women here call me mad doctor.

1ST MADMAN. What's he, a rope-maker?

2ND MADMAN. No, no, no, a snuffling knave, that while he shows the tombs, will have his hand in a wench's placket.[8]

3RD MADMAN. Woe to the caroch,[9] that brought home my wife from the mask at three a'clock in the morning! It had a large featherbed in it.

4TH MADMAN. I have pared the devil's nails forty time, roasted them in ravens' eggs, and cured agues with them.

3RD MADMAN. Get me three hundred milch[10] bats, to make possets[11] to procure sleep.

4TH MADMAN. All the college may throw their caps at me; I have made a soapboiler costive:[12] it was my masterpiece.

(*Here the dance, consisting of eight madmen, with musicians answerable*[13] *thereunto; after which, Bosola, like*

[1] *gentleman usher* Gentleman who acts as usher to a person of higher rank.

[2] *perspective* Telescope.

[3] *haycocks* Haystacks.

[4] *'pothecary* I.e., apothecary, druggist.

[5] *outgo me* Get the better of me.

[6] *Puritans … overstraining* English Protestants, known for strict reformist views and supposedly nasal singing and preaching voices.

[7] *Greek … translation* The priest decries the new (1611) Authorized or King James translation, preferring instead the Helvetian or "Geneva" Bible, with its "puritan" marginal notes.

[8] *placket* Petticoat.

[9] *caroch* Carriage.

[10] *milch* Milking.

[11] *possets* Curative drinks made of hot milk curdled with liquor.

[12] *costive* Constipated.

[13] *answerable* Appropriate.

an old man, enters.)

DUCHESS. Is he mad too?
1ST SERVANT. Pray question him. I'll leave you.

(*Exeunt all but the Duchess and Bosola.*)

BOSOLA. I am come to make thy tomb.
DUCHESS. Ha! My tomb!
Thou speak'st as if I lay upon my death-bed,
Gasping for breath: dost thou perceive me sick?

BOSOLA. Yes, and the more dangerously, since thy sickness is insensible.

DUCHESS. Thou art not mad sure: dost thou know me?
BOSOLA. Yes.
DUCHESS. Who am I?

BOSOLA. Thou art a box of worm-seed,[1] at best but a salvatory of green mummy.[2] What's this flesh? A little cruded[3] milk, fantastical puff-paste.[4] Our bodies are weaker than those paper-prisons boys use to keep flies in; more contemptible, since ours is to preserve earth-worms. Didst thou ever see a lark in a cage? Such is the soul in the body; this world is like her little turf of grass, and the heaven o'er our heads, like her looking-glass, only gives us a miserable knowledge of the small compass of our prison.

DUCHESS. Am not I thy Duchess?

BOSOLA. Thou art some great woman sure, for riot begins to sit on thy forehead (clad in gray hairs) twenty years sooner than on a merry milkmaid's. Thou sleepest worse than if a mouse should be forced to take up her lodging in a cat's ear: a little infant that breeds its teeth, should it lie with thee, would cry out, as if thou wert the more unquiet bedfellow.

DUCHESS. I am Duchess of Malfi still.
BOSOLA. That makes thy sleep so broken:
Glories, like glowworms afar off shine bright,
But looked to near, have neither heat nor light.
DUCHESS. Thou art very plain.
BOSOLA. My trade is to flatter the dead, not the living;
I am a tomb-maker.
DUCHESS. And thou com'st to make my tomb?
BOSOLA. Yes.
DUCHESS. Let me be a little merry:
Of what stuff wilt thou make it?
BOSOLA. Nay, resolve me first, of what fashion?
DUCHESS. Why, do we grow fantastical[5] in our death-bed?
Do we affect fashion in the grave?
BOSOLA. Most ambitiously. Princes' images on their tombs
Do not lie, as they were wont, seeming to pray
Up to heaven; but with their hands under their cheeks,
As if they died of the tooth-ache: they are not carved
With their eyes fixed upon the stars; but
As their minds were wholly bent upon the world,
The selfsame way they seem to turn their faces.
DUCHESS. Let me know fully, therefore, the effect
Of this thy dismal preparation,
This talk, fit for a charnel.[6]
BOSOLA. Now I shall;

(*Enter executioners with a coffin, cords, and a bell.*)

Here is a present from your princely brothers,
And may it arrive welcome, for it brings
Last benefit, last sorrow.
DUCHESS. Let me see it:
I have so much obedience in my blood,
I wish it in their veins to do them good.
BOSOLA. This is your last presence-chamber.
CARIOLA. O, my sweet lady!
DUCHESS. Peace; it affrights not me.
BOSOLA. I am the common bellman,[7]
That usually is sent to condemned persons
The night before they suffer.
DUCHESS. Even now thou said'st
Thou wast a tomb-maker.
BOSOLA. 'Twas to bring you

[1] *worm-seed* Drugs that fend off intestinal worms, with a double entendre that alludes to a dead body eaten by worms.

[2] *salvatory ... mummy* Another double entendre, meaning both a salve supposedly made from Egyptian mummies and a box containing a mummy.

[3] *cruded* Curdled.

[4] *puff-paste* Puff-pastry.

[5] *fantastical* Preoccupied with fantasies.

[6] *charnel* House of the dead.

[7] *bellman* Person who, at funerals, rings a bell to frighten evil spirits away from the departing soul.

By degrees to mortification.[1] Listen:

(*He rings the bell.*)

Hark, now everything is still,
The screech-owl, and the whistler[2] shrill,
Call upon our dame aloud,
And bid her quickly don her shroud!
Much you had of land and rent;
Your length in clay's now competent:
A long war disturbed your mind;
Here your perfect peace is signed.
Of what is't fools make such vain keeping? ° concern
Sin their conception, their birth weeping;
Their life a general mist of error,
Their death a hideous storm of terror.
Strew your hair with powders sweet,
Don clean linen, bathe your feet,
And (the foul fiend more to check)
A crucifix let bless your neck:
'Tis now full tide 'tween night and day;
End your groan, and come away.

(*The executioners approach.*)

CARIOLA. Hence, villains, tyrants, murderers! Alas!
What will you do with my lady? Call for help.
DUCHESS. To whom, to our next neighbours? They are mad-folks.
BOSOLA. Remove that noise.
DUCHESS. Farewell, Cariola.
In my last will, I have not much to give:
A many hungry guests have fed upon me;
Thine will be a poor reversion.
CARIOLA. I will die with her.
DUCHESS. I pray thee, look thou giv'st my little boy
Some syrup for his cold, and let the girl
Say her prayers ere she sleep.

(*Cariola is forced out.*)

Now what you please:
What death?
BOSOLA. Strangling; here are your executioners.
DUCHESS. I forgive them:
The apoplexy, catarrh, or cough o' th' lungs,
Would do as much as they do.
BOSOLA. Doth not death fright you?
DUCHESS. Who would be afraid on't,
Knowing to meet such excellent company
In th' other world?
BOSOLA. Yet, methinks,
The manner of your death should much afflict you;
This cord should terrify you.
DUCHESS. Not a whit:
What would it pleasure me to have my throat cut
With diamonds? Or to be smothered
With cassia? Or to be shot to death with pearls?
I know death hath ten thousand several doors
For men to take their exits; and 'tis found
They go on such strange geometrical hinges,
You may open them both ways:[3] any way, for heaven sake,
So I were out of your whispering. Tell my brothers,
That I perceive death, now I am well awake,
Best gift is they can give, or I can take.
I would fain put off my last woman's fault,[4]
I'd not be tedious to you.
EXECUTIONERS. We are ready.
DUCHESS. Dispose my breath how please you, but my body
Bestow upon my women, will you?
EXECUTIONERS. Yes.
DUCHESS. Pull, and pull strongly, for your able strength,
Must pull down heaven upon me:
Yet stay, heaven-gates are not so highly arched
As princes' palaces; they that enter there,
Must go upon their knees. Come, violent death,
Serve for mandragora,[5] to make me sleep:
Go, tell my brothers, when I am laid out,
They then may feed in quiet.

(*They strangle her.*)

BOSOLA. Where's the waiting-woman?

[1] *bring ... mortification* Bring you to penitence.

[2] *whistler* Bird whose shrill cry was considered a bad omen.

[3] *both ways* Either through unwilled death or suicide.

[4] *woman's fault* Too much talking.

[5] *mandragora* Sedative made from mandrake root.

Fetch her: some other strangle the children.

(*Exeunt executioners. One enters with Cariola.*)

Look you, there sleeps your mistress.
CARIOLA. O, you are damned
Perpetually for this! My turn is next;
Is't not so ordered?
BOSOLA. Yes, and I am glad
You are so well prepared for't.
CARIOLA. You are deceived, sir,
I am not prepared for't; I will not die:
I will first come to my answer, and know
How I have offended.
BOSOLA. Come, dispatch her.
You kept her counsel, now you shall keep ours.
CARIOLA. I will not die, I must not; I am contracted° *engaged*
To a young gentleman.
EXECUTIONER. Here's your wedding-ring.
CARIOLA. Let me but speak with the Duke; I'll discover
Treason to his person.
BOSOLA. Delays: throttle her.
EXECUTIONER. She bites and scratches.
CARIOLA. If you kill me now,
I am damned; I have not been at confession
This two years.
BOSOLA. When?
CARIOLA. I am quick with child.[1]
BOSOLA. Why then,
Your credit's saved.[2]

(*Cariola is strangled.*)

Bear her into the next room;
Let this lie still.

(*Exeunt executioners with Cariola's body. Enter Ferdinand.*)

FERDINAND. Is she dead?
BOSOLA. She is what
You'd have her. But here begin your pity:

(*Shows the children strangled.*)

Alas! How have these offended?
FERDINAND. The death
Of young wolves is never to be pitied.
BOSOLA. Fix your eye here.
FERDINAND. Constantly.
BOSOLA. Do you not weep?
Other sins only speak; murder shrieks out:
The element of water moistens the earth,
But blood flies upwards and bedews the heavens.
FERDINAND. Cover her face; mine eyes dazzle: she
died young.
BOSOLA. I think not so; her infelicity
Seemed to have years too many.
FERDINAND. She and I were twins;
And should I die this instant, I had lived
Her time to a minute.
BOSOLA. It seems she was born first:
You have bloodily approved the ancient truth,
That kindred commonly do worse agree
Than remote strangers.
FERDINAND. Let me see her face again.
Why didst not thou pity her? What an excellent
Honest man might'st thou have been
If thou hadst borne her to some sanctuary;
Or, bold in a good cause, opposed thyself,
With thy advanced sword above thy head,
Between her innocence and my revenge.
I had thee, when I was distracted of my wits,
Go kill my dearest friend, and thou hast done't.
For let me but examine well the cause:
What was the meanness of her match to me?
Only I must confess I had a hope,
Had she continued widow, to have gained
An infinite mass of treasure by her death;
And that was the main cause, her marriage,
That drew a stream of gall quite through my heart.
For thee, as we observe in tragedies
That a good actor many times is cursed
For playing a villain's part, I hate thee for't,
And for my sake say thou hast done much ill, well.
BOSOLA. Let me quicken your memory, for I perceive
You are falling into ingratitude; I challenge
The reward due to my service.

---

[1] *quick with child* Pregnant women were not executed until they had given birth.

[2] *credit's saved* Your reputation is saved (because you will not bear an illegitimate child).

FERDINAND. I'll tell thee
What I'll give thee.
BOSOLA. Do.
FERDINAND. I'll give thee a pardon
For this murder.
BOSOLA. Ha!
FERDINAND. Yes, and 'tis
The largest bounty I can study to do thee.
By what authority didst thou execute
This bloody sentence?
BOSOLA. By yours.
FERDINAND. Mine! Was I her judge?
Did any ceremonial form of law,
Doom her to not being? Did a complete jury
Deliver her conviction up i' th' court?
Where shalt thou find this judgment registered,
Unless in hell? See, like a bloody fool,
Th' hast forfeited thy life, and thou shalt die for't.
BOSOLA. The office of justice is perverted quite,
When one thief hangs another. Who shall dare
To reveal this?
FERDINAND. O, I'll tell thee;
The wolf shall find her grave, and scrape it up,
Not to devour the corpse, but to discover
The horrid murder.
BOSOLA. You, not I, shall quake for't.
FERDINAND. Leave me.
BOSOLA. I will first receive my pension.
FERDINAND. You are a villain.
BOSOLA. When your ingratitude
Is judge, I am so.
FERDINAND. O horror,
That not the fear of him, which binds the devils,[1]
Can prescribe man obedience!
Never look upon me more.
BOSOLA. Why, fare thee well:
Your brother and yourself are worthy men:
You have a pair of hearts are hollow graves,
Rotten, and rotting others; and your vengeance,
Like two chained bullets,[2] still goes arm in arm.
You may be brothers; for treason, like the plague,
Doth take much in a blood.[3] I stand like one
That long hath ta'en a sweet and golden dream:
I am angry with myself, now that I wake.
FERDINAND. Get thee into some unknown part o' th' world,
That I may never see thee.
BOSOLA. Let me know
Wherefore I should be thus neglected? Sir,
I served your tyranny, and rather strove,
To satisfy yourself, than all the world:
And though I loathed the evil, yet I loved
You that did counsel it; and rather sought
To appear a true servant, than an honest man.
FERDINAND. I'll go hunt the badger by owl-light:
'Tis a deed of darkness.

(*Exit.*)

BOSOLA. He's much distracted. Off, my painted honour!
While with vain hopes our faculties we tire,
We seem to sweat in ice and freeze in fire.
What would I do, were this to do again?
I would not change my peace of conscience
For all the wealth of Europe. She stirs; here's life—
Return, fair soul, from darkness, and lead mine
Out of this sensible hell—she's warm, she breathes—
Upon thy pale lips I will melt my heart,
To store them with fresh colour. Who's there!
Some cordial drink![4] Alas! I dare not call:
So pity would destroy pity. Her eye opes,
And heaven in it seems to ope, that late was shut,
To take me up to mercy.
DUCHESS. Antonio!
BOSOLA. Yes, madam, he is living;
The dead bodies you saw, were but feigned statues;
He's reconciled to your brothers; the Pope hath wrought
The atonement.
DUCHESS. Mercy!

(*She dies.*)

BOSOLA. O, she's gone again! There the cords of life broke.

[1] *him … devils* God.

[2] *two chained bullets* Cannonballs chained together for greater destruction.

[3] *Doth … blood* Runs in the family.

[4] *cordial drink* Reviving medicine.

O, sacred innocence, that sweetly sleeps
On turtles'° feathers, whilst a guilty conscience *turtledoves'*
Is a black register, wherein is writ
All our good deeds and bad, a perspective
That shows us hell! That we cannot be suffered
To do good when we have a mind to it!
This is manly sorrow;
These tears, I am very certain, never grew
In my mother's milk: my estate is sunk
Below the degree of fear: where were
These penitent fountains, while she was living?
O, they were frozen up! Here is a sight
As direful to my soul, as is the sword
Unto a wretch hath slain his father. Come,
I'll bear thee hence,
And execute thy last will; that's deliver
Thy body to the reverend dispose
Of some good women: that, the cruel tyrant
Shall not deny me. Then I'll post to Milan,
Where somewhat I will speedily enact
Worth my dejection.

(*Exit with the Duchess's body.*)

ACT 5, SCENE 1

(*Enter Antonio and Delio.*)

ANTONIO. What think you of my hope of reconcilement
To the Aragonian brethren?
DELIO. I misdoubt it;
For though they have sent letter of safe conduct
For your repair° to Milan, they appear *return*
But nets to entrap you. The Marquis of Pescara,
Under whom you hold certain land in cheat,[1]
Much 'gainst his noble nature hath been moved
To seize those lands, and some of his dependents
Are at this instant making it their suit
To be invested in[2] your revenues.
I cannot think they mean well to you life,
That do deprive you of your means of life,
Your living.
ANTONIO. You are still an heretic° *skeptic*
To any safety I can shape myself.
DELIO. Here comes the Marquis: I will make myself
Petitioner for some part of your land,
To know whither it is flying.[3]
ANTONIO. I pray do.

(*Enter Pescara.*)

DELIO. Sir, I have a suit to you.
PESCARA. To me?
DELIO. An easy one:
There is the citadel of St. Bennet,[4]
With some demesnes,[5] of late in the possession
Of Antonio Bologna—please you bestow them on me.
PESCARA. You are my friend; but this is such a suit,
Nor fit for me to give, nor you to take.
DELIO. No, sir?
PESCARA. I will give you ample reason for't,
Soon in private: here's the Cardinal's mistress.

(*Enter Julia.*)

JULIA. My Lord, I am grown your poor petitioner,
And should be an ill beggar, had I not
A great man's letter here, the Cardinal's,
To court you in my favour.

(*She gives him a letter.*)

PESCARA. He entreats for you
The citadel of St. Bennet, that belonged
To the banished Bologna.
JULIA. Yes.
PESCARA. I could not have thought of a friend I could
Rather pleasure with it: 'tis yours.
JULIA. Sir, I thank you;
And he shall know how doubly I am engaged
Both in your gift, and speediness of giving,
Which makes your grant the greater.

[1] *in cheat* In "escheat": lands held which would revert to the original lord's possession should the holder be convicted of a crime or die without an heir.

[2] *be invested in* Take over.

[3] *whither … flying* How it is being given away.

[4] *St. Bennet* I.e., St. Benedict.

[5] *demesnes* Attached land.

(*Exit.*)

ANTONIO. (*Aside.*) How they fortify
Themselves with my ruin!
DELIO. Sir, I am
Little bound to you.
PESCARA. Why?
DELIO. Because you denied this suit to me, and gave't
To such a creature.
PESCARA. Do you know what it was?
It was Antonio's land; not forfeited
By course of law, but ravished from his throat
By the Cardinal's entreaty: it were not fit
I should bestow so main° a piece of wrong *great*
Upon my friend; 'tis a gratification
Only due to a strumpet, for it is injustice.
Shall I sprinkle the pure blood of innocents
To make those followers I call my friends
Look ruddier upon me? I am glad
This land, ta'en from the owner by such a wrong,
Returns again unto so foul an use,
As salary for his lust. Learn, good Delio,
To ask noble things of me, and you shall find
I'll be a noble giver.
DELIO. You instruct me well.
ANTONIO. (*Aside.*) Why, here's a man now, would fright impudence
From sauciest beggars.
PESCARA. Prince Ferdinand's come to Milan,
Sick, as they give out, of an apoplexy;
But some say, 'tis a frenzy: I am going
To visit him.

(*Exit.*)

ANTONIO. 'Tis a noble old fellow.[1]
DELIO. What course do you mean to take, Antonio?
ANTONIO. This night I mean to venture all my fortune,
Which is no more than a poor lingering life,
To the Cardinal's worst of malice: I have got
Private access to his chamber; and intend
To visit him about the mid of night,
As once his brother did our noble Duchess.
It may be that the sudden apprehension
Of danger, for I'll go in mine own shape,
When he shall see it fraight with[2] love and duty,
May draw the poison out of him, and work
A friendly reconcilement: if it fail,
Yet it shall rid me of this infamous calling;
For better fall once, than be ever falling.
DELIO. I'll second you in all danger, and, howe'er;
My life keeps rank with yours.
ANTONIO. You are still my loved and best friend.

(*Exeunt.*)

ACT 5, SCENE 2

(*Enter Pescara and a doctor.*)

PESCARA. Now, doctor, may I visit your patient?
DOCTOR. If't please your Lordship: but he's instantly
To take the air here in the gallery
By my direction.
PESCARA. Pray thee, what's his disease?
DOCTOR. A very pestilent disease, my Lord,
They call lycanthropia.
PESCARA. What's that?
I need a dictionary to't.
DOCTOR. I'll tell you.
In those that are possessed with't there o'erflows
Such melancholy humour, they imagine
Themselves to be transformed into wolves;
Steal forth to church-yards in the dead of night,
And dig dead bodies up: as two nights since
One met the Duke 'bout midnight in a lane
Behind St. Mark's Church, with the leg of a man
Upon his shoulder, and he howled fearfully;
Said he was a wolf, only the difference
Was, a wolf's skin was hairy on the outside,
His on the inside; bade them take their swords,
Rip up his flesh, and try: straight, I was sent for,
And having ministered unto him, found his Grace
Very well recovered.
PESCARA. I am glad on't.
DOCTOR. Yet not without some fear
Of a relapse. If he grow to his fit again,

[1] *old fellow* The historical Pescara died at age 36.

[2] *fraight with* Full of.

I'll go a nearer[1] way to work with him
Than ever Paracelsus[2] dreamed of; if
They'll give me leave, I'll buffet his madness out of him.
Stand aside; he comes.

(*Enter Ferdinand, Malateste, Cardinal, and Bosola.*)

FERDINAND. Leave me.
MALATESTE. Why doth your Lordship love this solitariness?
FERDINAND. Eagles commonly fly alone: they are crows, daws, and starlings that flock together. Look, what's that follows me?
MALATESTE. Nothing, my Lord.
FERDINAND. Yes.
MALATESTE. 'Tis your shadow.
FERDINAND. Stay it; let it not haunt me.
MALATESTE. Impossible, if you move, and the sun shine.
FERDINAND. I will throttle it.

(*He throws himself on his shadow.*)

MALATESTE. O, my Lord, you are angry with nothing.
FERDINAND. You are a fool: how is't possible I should catch my shadow, unless I fall upon't? When I go to hell, I mean to carry a bribe; for, look you, good gifts evermore make way for the worst persons.
PESCARA. Rise, good my Lord.
FERDINAND. I am studying the art of patience.
PESCARA. 'Tis a noble virtue.
FERDINAND. To drive six snails before me from this town to Moscow; neither use goad nor whip to them, but let them take their own time—the patient'st man i' th' world match me for an experiment—and I'll crawl after like a sheep-biter.[3]
CARDINAL. Force him up.

(*They pick up Ferdinand.*)

FERDINAND. Use me well, you were best.
What I have done, I have done: I'll confess nothing.
DOCTOR. Now let me come to him. Are you mad,
My Lord, are you out of your princely wits?
FERDINAND. What's he?
PESCARA. Your doctor.
FERDINAND. Let me have his beard sawed off, and his eye-brows
Filed more civil.[4]
DOCTOR. I must do mad tricks with him,
For that's the only way on't. I have brought
Your Grace a salamander's skin, to keep you
From sun-burning.
FERDINAND. I have cruel sore eyes.
DOCTOR. The white of a cockatrix's[5] egg is present remedy.
FERDINAND. Let it be new-laid one, you were best.
Hide me from him: physicians are like kings,
They brook no contradiction.
DOCTOR. Now he begins to fear me:
Now let me be alone with him.

(*Ferdinand begins taking off his gown. The Cardinal stops him.*)

CARDINAL. How now? Put off your gown?
DOCTOR. Let me have some forty urinals[6] filled with rose-water: he and I'll go pelt one another with them. Now he begins to fear me. Can you fetch a frisk,[7] sir? Let him go, let him go upon my peril: I find by his eye he stands in awe of me; I'll make him as tame as a dormouse.

(*The Cardinal lets go of Ferdinand.*)

FERDINAND. Can you fetch your frisks, sir! I will stamp him into a cullis, flay off his skin, to cover one of the anatomies this rogue hath set i' th' cold yonder in Barber-Chirurgeon's-hall.[8]

---

1 *nearer* More direct.

2 *Paracelsus* Theophrastus von Hohenheim (1493–1541), an eminent Swiss doctor and alchemist also interested in chemistry and spirits.

3 *sheep-biter* Dog that bites sheep. Also a woman-chaser.

4 *filed more civil* Shaped into a more polite expression.

5 *cockatrix* Cockatrice, a mythical beast combining rooster and snake. As with the basilisk, looking at it is thought to cause death.

6 *urinals* Bottles used to collect urine samples.

7 *fetch a frisk* Dance.

8 *Barber-Chirurgeon's-hall* Contained a museum dedicated to human anatomy.

(*He attacks the doctor.*)

Hence, hence! You are all of you like beasts for sacrifice: there's nothing left of you, but tongue and belly, flattery and lechery.

(*Exit.*)

PESCARA. Doctor, he did not fear you thoroughly.
DOCTOR. True; I was somewhat too forward.
BOSOLA. (*Aside.*) Mercy upon me, what a fatal judgement
Hath fall'n upon this Ferdinand!
PESCARA. Knows your Grace
What accident hath brought unto the prince
This strange distraction?
CARDINAL. (*Aside.*) I must feign somewhat. Thus they say it grew:
You have heard it rumoured for these many years,
None of our family dies but there is seen
The shape of an old woman, which is given
By tradition to us to have been murdered
By her nephews, for her riches. Such a figure
One night, as the prince sat up late at's book,
Appeared to him; when, crying out for help,
The gentleman of's chamber, found his Grace
All on a cold sweat, altered much in face
And language: since which apparition,
He hath grown worse and worse, and I much fear
He cannot live.
BOSOLA. Sir, I would speak with you.
PESCARA. We'll leave your Grace,
Wishing to the sick prince, our noble Lord,
All health of mind and body.
CARDINAL. You are most welcome.

(*Exeunt all but the Cardinal and Bosola.*)

(*Aside.*) Are you come? So—this fellow must not know
By any means I had intelligence
In our Duchess' death; for though I counselled it,
The full of all th' engagement[1] seemed to grow
From Ferdinand. Now, sir, how fares our sister?
I do not think but sorrow makes her look
Like to an oft-dyed garment: she shall now
Taste comfort from me. Why do you look so wildly?
O, the fortune of your master here, the prince,
Dejects you; but be you of happy comfort:
If you'll do one thing for me, I'll entreat,
Though he had a cold tombstone o'er his bones,
I'd make you what you would be.
BOSOLA. Anything,
Give it me in a breath, and fly to't:
They that think long, small expedition win,
For musing much o' th' end, cannot begin.

(*Enter Julia.*)

JULIA. Sir, will you come in to supper?
CARDINAL. I am busy; leave me.
JULIA. (*Aside.*) What an excellent shape hath that fellow!

(*Exit.*)

CARDINAL. 'Tis thus. Antonio lurks here in Milan:
Enquire him out, and kill him. While he lives,
Our sister cannot marry, and I have thought
Of an excellent match for her. Do this, and style me
Thy advancement.
BOSOLA. But by what means shall I find him out?
CARDINAL. There is a gentleman called Delio,
Here in the camp, that hath been long approved[2]
His loyal friend. Set eye upon that fellow;
Follow him to mass; maybe Antonio,
Although he do account religion
But a school-name,[3] for fashion of the world
May accompany him; or else go enquire out
Delio's confessor, and see if you can bribe
Him to reveal it. There are a thousand ways
A man might find to trace him; as to know
What fellows haunt the Jews, for taking up
Great sums of money, for sure he's in want;
Or else to go to th' picture-makers, and learn
Who bought her picture lately: some of these
Happily may take.
BOSOLA. Well, I'll not freeze i' th' business:
I would see that wretched thing, Antonio,
Above all sights i' th' world.

[1] *The full ... engagement* Most of the plot.

[2] *approved* Proved to be.

[3] *But a school-name* Only a theory.

CARDINAL. Do, and be happy.

(*Exit.*)

BOSOLA. This fellow doth breed basilisks in's eyes,
He's nothing else but murder; yet he seems
Not to have notice of the Duchess's death.
'Tis his cunning: I must follow his example;
There cannot be a surer way to trace[1]
Than that of an old fox.

(*Enter Julia, with a pistol.*)

JULIA. So, sir, you are well met.
BOSOLA. How now?
JULIA. Nay, the doors are fast enough:
Now, sir, I will make you confess your treachery.
BOSOLA. Treachery!
JULIA. Yes, confess to me
Which of my women 'twas you hired to put
Love-powder into my drink?
BOSOLA. Love-powder!
JULIA. Yes, when I was at Malfi.
Why should I fall in love with such a face else?
I have already suffered for thee so much pain,
The only remedy to do me good,
Is to kill my longing.
BOSOLA. Sure your pistol holds
Nothing but perfumes, or kissing-comforts.[2] Excellent lady!
You have a pretty way on't to discover° *reveal*
Your longing. Come, come, I'll disarm you,
And arm you thus: yet this is wondrous strange.
JULIA. Compare thy form and my eyes together,
You'll find my love no such great miracle.

(*She kisses him.*)

Now you'll say
I am wanton: this nice modesty in ladies
Is but a troublesome familiar
That haunts them.
BOSOLA. Know you me, I am a blunt soldier.
JULIA. The better;
Sure, there wants fire, where there are no lively sparks
Of roughness.
BOSOLA. And I want[3] compliment.
JULIA. Why, ignorance
In courtship cannot make you do amiss,
If you have a heart to do well.
BOSOLA. You are very fair.
JULIA. Nay, if you lay beauty to my charge,
I must plead unguilty.
BOSOLA. Your bright eyes
Carry a quiver of darts in them, sharper
Than sun-beams.
JULIA. You will mar me with commendation,
Put yourself to the charge of courting me,
Whereas now I woo you.
BOSOLA. (*Aside.*) I have it; I will work upon this creature.
Let us grow most amorously familiar:
If the great Cardinal should see me thus,
Would he not count me a villain?
JULIA. No, he might count me a wanton,
Not lay a scruple° of offence on you; *tiny amount*
For if I see, and steal a diamond,
The fault is not i' th' stone, but in me the thief
That purloins it. I am sudden with you:
We that are great women of pleasure, use to cut off
These uncertain wishes and unquiet longings,
And in an instant join the sweet delight
And the pretty excuse together. Had you been i' th' street
Under my chamber window, even there
I should have courted you.
BOSOLA. O, you are an excellent lady!
JULIA. Bid me do somewhat for you presently,
To express I love you.
BOSOLA. I will, and if you love me,
Fail not to effect it.
The Cardinal is grown wondrous melancholy:
Demand the cause, let him not put you off
With feigned excuse; discover the main ground on't.
JULIA. Why would you know this?
BOSOLA. I have depended on him,
And I hear that he is fall'n in some disgrace

[1] *surer ... trace* Better way to follow.

[2] *kissing-comforts* Breath sweeteners.

[3] *want* Lack.

With the emperor; if he be, like the mice
That forsake falling houses, I would shift
To other dependence.
JULIA. You shall not need follow the wars:[1]
I'll be your maintenance.[2]
BOSOLA. And I your loyal servant;
But I cannot leave my calling.
JULIA. Not leave
An ungrateful general, for the love of a sweet lady!
You are like some cannot sleep in feather-beds,
But must have blocks for their pillows.
BOSOLA. Will you do this?
JULIA. Cunningly.
BOSOLA. Tomorrow, I'll expect th' intelligence.
JULIA. Tomorrow! Get you into my cabinet;
You shall have it with you. Do not delay me,
No more than I do you: I am like one
That is condemned; I have my pardon promised,
But I would see it sealed. Go, get you in:
You shall see me wind my tongue about his heart,
Like a skein of silk.[3]

(*Exit Bosola. Enter Cardinal and servants.*)

CARDINAL. Where are you?
SERVANT. Here.
CARDINAL. Let none, upon your lives
Have conference with the prince Ferdinand,
Unless I know it.

(*Exeunt servants.*)

In this distraction, he may reveal the murder.
Yond's my lingering consumption:° *disease*
I am weary of her, and by any means
Would be quit of.
JULIA. How now, my Lord,
What ails you?
CARDINAL. Nothing.
JULIA. O, you are much altered!
Come, I must be your secretary,° and remove *confidante*
This lead from off your bosom: what's the matter?
CARDINAL. I may not tell you.
JULIA. Are you so far in love with sorrow,
You cannot part with part of it? Or think you
I cannot love your Grace when you are sad
As well as merry? Or do you suspect
I, that have been a secret to your heart
These many winters, cannot be the same
Unto your tongue?
CARDINAL. Satisfy thy longing:
The only way to make thee keep my counsel
Is not to tell thee.
JULIA. Tell your echo this,
Or flatterers, that like echoes still report
What they hear though most imperfect, and not me;
For, if that you be true unto yourself, I'll know.
CARDINAL. Will you rack me?[4]
JULIA. No, judgment shall
Draw it from you: it is an equal fault,
To tell one's secrets unto all or none.
CARDINAL. The first argues folly.
JULIA. But the last tyranny.
CARDINAL. Very well; why, imagine I have committed
Some secret deed, which I desire the world
May not hear of.
JULIA. Therefore may not I know it?
You have concealed for me as great a sin
As adultery. Sir, never was occasion
For perfect trial of my constancy
Till now: sir, I beseech you—
CARDINAL. You'll repent it.
JULIA. Never.
CARDINAL. It hurries thee to ruin: I'll not tell thee.
Be well advised, and think what danger 'tis
To receive a prince's secrets: they that do,
Had need have their breasts hooped with adamant
To contain them. I pray thee yet be satisfied;
Examine thine own frailty; 'tis more easy
To tie knots, than unloose them: 'tis a secret
That, like a lingering poison, may chance lie
Spread in thy veins, and kill thee seven year hence.
JULIA. Now you dally with me.
CARDINAL. No more, thou shalt know it.
By my appointment, the great Duchess of Malfi,
And two of her young children, four nights since,

[1] *need ... wars* Be a mercenary.

[2] *maintenance* Source of income.

[3] *skein of silk* Length of silk thread.

[4] *rack me* Torture me for an answer.

Were strangled.
JULIA. O heaven! Sir, what have you done?
CARDINAL. How now! How settles this?[1] Think you
Your bosom will be a grave dark and obscure enough
For such a secret?
JULIA. You have undone yourself, sir.
CARDINAL. Why?
JULIA. It lies not in me to conceal it.
CARDINAL. No?
Come, I will swear you to't upon this book.[2]
JULIA. Most religiously.
CARDINAL. Kiss it.

(*She kisses the book.*)

Now you shall never utter it; thy curiosity
Hath undone thee: thou art poisoned with that book.
Because I knew thou couldst not keep my counsel,
I have bound thee to't by death.

(*Enter Bosola.*)

BOSOLA. For pity sake, hold.
CARDINAL. Ha, Bosola!
JULIA. I forgive you
This equal piece of justice you have done;
For I betrayed your counsel to that fellow:
He overheard it; that was the cause I said
It lay not in me to conceal it.
BOSOLA. O, foolish woman,
Couldst not thou have poisoned him?
JULIA. 'Tis weakness,
Too much to think what should have been done.
I go, I know not whither.

(*Dies.*)

CARDINAL. Wherefore com'st thou hither?
BOSOLA. That I might find a great man, like yourself,
Not out of his wits, as the Lord Ferdinand,
To remember my service.
CARDINAL. I'll have thee hewed in pieces.
BOSOLA. Make not yourself such a promise of that life,
Which is not yours to dispose of.
CARDINAL. Who placed thee here?
BOSOLA. Her lust, as she intended.
CARDINAL. Very well:
Now you know me for your fellow-murderer.
BOSOLA. And wherefore should you lay your fair marble colours
Upon your rotten purposes to me?[3]
Unless you imitate some that do plot great treasons,
And when they have done, go hide themselves i' th' graves
Of those were actors in't?
CARDINAL. No more: there is a fortune attends thee.
BOSOLA. Shall I go sue to fortune any longer?
'Tis the fool's pilgrimage.
CARDINAL. I have honours in store for thee.
BOSOLA. There are a many ways that conduct to seeming
Honour, and some of them very dirty ones.
CARDINAL. Throw to the devil
Thy melancholy. The fire burns well;
What need we keep a stirring of't, and make
A greater smother? Thou wilt kill Antonio?
BOSOLA. Yes.
CARDINAL. Take up that body.
BOSOLA. I think I shall
Shortly grow the common bier[4] for church-yards.
CARDINAL. I will allow thee some dozen of attendants,
To aid thee in the murder.
BOSOLA. O, by no means. Physicians that apply horseleeches to any rank swelling, use to cut off their tails, that the blood may run through them the faster: let me have no train when I go to shed blood, lest it make me have a greater when I ride to the gallows.
CARDINAL. Come to me after midnight, to help to remove that body
To her own lodging: I'll give out she died o' th' plague;
'Twill breed the less enquiry after her death.
BOSOLA. Where's Castruccio, her husband?
CARDINAL. He's rode to Naples, to take possession
Of Antonio's citadel.
BOSOLA. Believe me, you have done a very happy turn.
CARDINAL. Fail not to come: there is the master-key

[1] *How settles this?* How does this strike you?

[2] *this book* The Bible.

[3] *lay ... colours* Paint over wood to make it appear to be marble.

[4] *bier* Platform used to carry bodies to graveyards.

Of our lodgings; and by that you may conceive
What trust I plant in you.
BOSOLA. You shall find me ready.

(*Exit Cardinal.*)

O, poor, Antonio, though nothing be so needful
To thy estate as pity, yet I find
Nothing so dangerous! I must look to my footing:
In such slippery ice-pavements, men had need
To be frost-nailed[1] well, they may break their necks else;
The precedent's here afore me. How this man
Bears up in blood! Seems fearless! Why, 'tis well:
Security some men call the suburbs of hell,
Only a dead wall between. Well, good Antonio,
I'll seek thee out; and all my cares shall be
To put thee into safety from the reach
Of these most cruel biters, that have got
Some of thy blood already. It may be,
I'll join with thee, in a most just revenge:
The weakest arm is strong enough, that strikes
With the sword of justice. Still methinks the Duchess
Haunts me: there, there! 'Tis nothing but my melancholy.
O Penitence, let me truly taste thy cup,
That throws men down, only to raise them up!

(*Exit.*)

ACT 5, SCENE 3

(*Enter Antonio and Delio.*)

DELIO. Yond's the Cardinal's window. This fortification
Grew from the ruins of an ancient abbey;
And to yond side o' th' river lies a wall,
Piece of a cloister, which in my opinion
Gives the best echo that you ever heard,
So hollow and so dismal, and withal
So plain in the distinction of our words,
That many have supposed it is a spirit
That answers.
ANTONIO. I do love these ancient ruins.
We never tread upon them, but we set
Our foot upon some reverend history:
And, questionless, here in this open court,
Which now lies naked to the injuries
Of stormy weather, some men lie interred
Loved the church so well, and gave so largely to't,
They thought it should have canopied their bones
Till doom's-day; but all things have their end:
Churches and cities, which have diseases like to men,
Must have like death that we have.
ECHO. (*From the Duchess' grave.*) Like death that we have.
DELIO. Now the echo hath caught you.
ANTONIO. It groaned,
Methought, and gave a very deadly accent.
ECHO. Deadly accent.
DELIO. I told you 'twas a pretty one: you may make it
A huntsman, or a falconer, a musician,
Or a thing of sorrow.
ECHO. A thing of sorrow.
ANTONIO. Ay sure, that suits it best.
ECHO. That suits it best.
ANTONIO. 'Tis very like my wife's voice.
ECHO. Ay, wife's voice.
DELIO. Come, let us walk farther from't.
I would not have you go to th' Cardinal's to-night:
Do not.
ECHO. Do not.
DELIO. Wisdom doth not more moderate wasting sorrow,
Than time: take time for't: be mindful of thy safety.
ECHO. Be mindful of thy safety.
ANTONIO. Necessity compels me:
Make scrutiny throughout the passes° *events*
Of your own life, you'll find it impossible
To fly° your fate. *flee*
ECHO. O fly your fate!
DELIO. Hark! The dead stones seem to have pity on you,
And give you good counsel.
ANTONIO. Echo, I will not talk with thee,
For thou art a dead thing.
ECHO. Thou art a dead thing.
ANTONIO. My Duchess is a-sleep now,
And her little ones, I hope sweetly: O heaven,
Shall I never see her more?
ECHO. Never see her more.
ANTONIO. I marked not one repetition of the echo

[1] *frost-nailed* Shoes with nails driven into the soles to prevent slipping.

But that; and on the sudden, a clear light
Presented me a face folded in sorrow.
DELIO. Your fancy merely.
ANTONIO. Come, I'll be out of this ague,
For to live thus, is not indeed to live;
It is a mockery and abuse of life:
I will not henceforth save myself by halves;[1]
Lose all, or nothing.
DELIO. Your own virtue save you!
I'll fetch your eldest son, and second you:
It may be that the sight of his own blood
Spread in so sweet a figure, may beget
The more compassion.
ANTIONIO: However, fare you well.
Though in our miseries fortune have a part,
Yet in our noble sufferings she hath none;
Contempt of pain, that we may call our own.

(*Exeunt.*)

ACT 5 , SCENE 4

(*Enter Cardinal, Pescara, Malateste, Roderigo, and Grisolan.*)

CARDINAL. You shall not watch to-night by the sick prince;
His Grace is very well recovered.
MALATESTE. Good, my Lord, suffer° us. *allow*
CARDINAL. O, by no means:
The noise and change of object in his eye
Doth more distract him: I pray, all to bed;
And though you hear him in his violent fit,
Do not rise, I entreat you.
PESCARA. So, sir; we shall not.
CARDINAL. Nay, I must have you promise
Upon your honours, for I was enjoined to't[2]
By himself; and he seemed to urge it sensibly.
PESCARA. Let our honours bind this trifle.
CARDINAL. Nor any of your followers.
MALATESTE. Neither.
CARDINAL. It may be, to make trial of your promise,
When he's asleep, myself will rise and feign
Some of his mad tricks, and cry out for help,
And feign myself in danger.
MALATESTE. If your throat were cutting,
I'd not come at you, now I have protested against it.
CARDINAL. Why, I thank you.
GRISOLAN. 'Twas a foul storm tonight.
RODERIGO. The Lord Ferdinand's chamber shook like an osier.[3]
MALATESTE. 'Twas nothing but pure kindness in the devil,
To rock his own child.

(*Exeunt all but the Cardinal.*)

CARDINAL. The reason why I would not suffer these
About my brother is because at midnight
I may with better privacy convey
Julia's body to her own lodging. O, my conscience!
I would pray now; but the devil takes away my heart
For having any confidence in prayer.
About this hour I appointed Bosola
To fetch the body: when he hath served my turn,
He dies.

(*Exit. Enter Bosola.*)

BOSOLA. Ha! 'Twas the Cardinal's voice; I heard him name
Bosola, and my death: listen, I hear one's footing.

(*Enter Ferdinand.*)

FERDINAND. Strangling is a very quiet death.
BOSOLA. Nay then, I see I must stand upon my guard.
FERDINAND. What say to that? Whisper softly; do you agree to't?
So, it must be done i' th' dark; the Cardinal
Would not for a thousand pounds the doctor should see it.

(*Exit.*)

BOSOLA. My death is plotted; here's the consequence of murder.

[1] *I … halves* I will not try to remedy my situation bit by bit.

[2] *enjoined to't* Made to promise it.

[3] *osier* Willow tree.

We value not desert nor Christian breath,
When we know black deeds must be cured with death.

(*Enter servant and Antonio.*)

SERVANT. Here stay, sir, and be confident, I pray:
I'll fetch you a dark lantern.

(*Exit.*)

ANTONIO. Could I take him
At his prayers, there were hope of pardon.
BOSOLA. Fall right my sword:

(*He strikes Antonio.*)

I'll not give thee so much leisure as to pray.
ANTONIO. O, I am gone! Thou hast ended a long suit
In a minute.
BOSOLA. What art thou?
ANTONIO. A most wretched thing,
That only have the benefit in death,
To appear myself.

(*Enter servant with a light.*)

SERVANT. Where are you, sir?
ANTONIO. Very near my home. Bosola!
SERVANT. O, misfortune!
BOSOLA. Smother thy pity, thou art dead else. Antonio!
The man I would have saved 'bove mine own life!
We are merely the stars' tennis-balls, struck and banded
Which way please them. O good Antonio,
I'll whisper one thing in thy dying ear,
Shall make thy heart break quickly! Thy fair Duchess
And two sweet children—
ANTONIO. Their very names
Kindle a little life in me.
BOSOLA. Are murdered.
ANTONIO. Some men have wished to die
At the hearing of sad tidings; I am glad
That I shall do't in sadness: I would not now
Wish my wounds balmed nor healed, for I have no use
To put my life to. In all our quest of greatness,
Like wanton boys, whose pastime is their care,
We follow after bubbles blown in th' air.
Pleasure of life, what is't? Only the good hours
Of an ague—merely a preparative to rest,
To endure vexation. I do not ask
The process of my death; only commend me
To Delio.
BOSOLA. Break, heart!
ANTONIO. And let my son fly the courts of princes.

(*Dies.*)

BOSOLA. Thou seem'st to have loved Antonio?
SERVANT. I brought him hither,
To have reconciled him to the Cardinal.
BOSOLA. I do not ask thee that:
Take him up, if thou tender° thy own life, *value*
And bear him where the lady Julia
Was wont to lodge. O my fate moves swift!
I have this Cardinal in the forge already,
Now I'll bring him to th' hammer. O direful
misprision!° *mistake*
I will not imitate things glorious,
No more than base; I'll be mine own example.
On, on, and look thou represent, for silence,
The thing thou bear'st.[1]

(*Exeunt.*)

ACT 5, SCENE 5

(*Enter Cardinal, with a book.*)

CARDINAL. I am puzzled in a question about hell:
He says, in hell there's one material fire,
And yet it shall not burn all men alike.
Lay him by. How tedious is a guilty conscience!
When I look into the fish-ponds in my garden,
Methinks I see a thing armed with a rake,
That seems to strike at me.

(*Enter Bosola and the servant with Antonio's body.*)

Now, art thou come? Thou look'st ghastly;
There sits in thy face some great determination,

[1] *thing thou bear'st* I.e., the body of Antonio.

Mixed with some fear.
BOSOLA. Thus it lightens° into action: *flares*
I am come to kill thee.
CARDINAL. Ha! Help! Our guard!
BOSOLA. Thou art deceived;
They are out of thy howling.
CARDINAL. Hold; and I will faithfully divide
Revenues with thee.
BOSOLA. Thy prayers and proffers
Are both unseasonable.
CARDINAL. Raise the watch!
We are betrayed.
BOSOLA. I have confined your flight:
I'll suffer your retreat to Julia's chamber,
But no further.
CARDINAL. Help! We are betrayed.

(*Enter Malateste, Pescara, Roderigo, and Grisolan, above.*)

MALATESTE. Listen.
CARDINAL. My Dukedom for rescue!
RODERIGO. Fie upon his counterfeiting.
MALATESTE. Why, 'tis not the Cardinal.
RODERIGO. Yes, yes, 'tis he:
But I'll see him hanged ere I'll go down to him.
CARDINAL. Here's a plot upon me; I am assaulted! I am lost
Unless some rescue!
GRISOLAN. He doth this pretty well;
But it will not serve to laugh me out of mine honour.
CARDINAL. The sword's at my throat!
RODERIGO. You would not bawl so loud then.
MALATESTE. Come, come,
Let's go to bed: he told us thus much aforehand.
PESCARA. He wished you should not come at him; but believe't,
The accent of the voice sounds not in jest:
I'll down to him, howsoever, and with engines° *tools*
Force ope the doors.

(*Exit.*)

RODERIGO. Let's follow him aloof,
And note how the Cardinal will laugh at him.

(*Exeunt, above, Malateste, Roderigo, and Grisolan.*)

BOSOLA. There's for you first,
'Cause you shall not unbarricade the door
To let in rescue.

(*He kills the servant.*)

CARDINAL. What cause hast thou to pursue my life?
BOSOLA. Look there.
CARDINAL. Antonio!
BOSOLA. Slain by my hand unwittingly:
Pray, and be sudden: when thou killed'st thy sister,
Thou took'st from justice her most equal balance,
And left her nought but her sword.[1]
CARDINAL. O mercy!
BOSOLA. Now it seems thy greatness was only outward;
For thou fall'st faster of thyself, than calamity
Can drive thee: I'll not waste longer time; there.

(*He stabs the Cardinal.*)

CARDINAL. Thou hast hurt me.
BOSOLA. Again.

(*He stabs him again.*)

CARDINAL. Shall I die like a leveret,° *hare*
Without any resistance? Help, help, help!
I am slain.

(*Enter Ferdinand.*)

FERDINAND. Th' alarum! Give me a fresh horse;
Rally the vaunt-guard,[2] or the day is lost.
Yield, yield: I give you the honours of arms,[3]
Shake my sword over you; will you yield?
CARDINAL. Help me, I am your brother!
FERDINAND. The devil?
My brother fight upon the adverse party?

---

[1] *justice … sword* Commonly portrayed as a blindfolded woman standing with a set of scales in one hand and a sword in the other.

[2] *vaunt-guard* Forward troops, vanguard.

[3] *honours of arms* Right to retain your weapons after you have surrendered.

(*He wounds the Cardinal, and [in the scuffle] gives Bosola his death wound.*)

There flies your ransom.[1]
CARDINAL. O justice!
I suffer now for what hath former been:
Sorrow is held the eldest child of sin.
FERDINAND. Now you're brave fellows. Caesar's fortune was harder than Pompey's; Caesar died in the arms of prosperity, Pompey at the feet of disgrace. You both died in the field. The pain's nothing: pain many time is taken away with the apprehension of greater, as the tooth-ache with the sight of a barber[2] that comes to pull it out: there's philosophy for you.
BOSOLA. Now my revenge is perfect. Sink, thou main cause
Of my undoing. The last part of my life
Hath done me best service.

(*He stabs Ferdinand.*)

FERDINAND. Give me some wet hay,[3] I am broken-winded.
I do account° this world but a dog-kennel: *consider*
I will vault credit[4] and affect high pleasures,
Beyond death.
BOSOLA. He seems to come to himself,
Now he's so near the bottom.
FERDINAND. My sister, O my sister! There's the cause on't.
Whether we fall by ambition, blood, or lust,
Like diamonds, we are cut with our own dust.

(*Dies.*)

CARDINAL. Thou hast thy payment too.
BOSOLA. Yes, I hold my weary soul in my teeth;
'Tis ready to part from me. I do glory
That thou, which stood'st like a huge pyramid
Begun upon a large and ample base,
Shalt end in a little point, a kind of nothing.

(*Enter Pescara, Malateste, Roderigo and Grisolan.*)

PESCARA. How now, my Lord!
MALATESTE. O, sad disaster!
RODERIGO. How comes this?
BOSOLA. Revenge for the Duchess of Malfi, murdered
By the Aragonian brethren; for Antonio,
Slain by this hand; for lustful Julia,
Poisoned by this man; and lastly for myself,
That was an actor in the main of all
Much 'gainst mine own good nature, yet i' th' end
Neglected.
PESCARA. How now, my Lord!
CARDINAL. Look to my brother:
He gave us these large wounds, as we were struggling
Here i' th' rushes.[5] And now, I pray, let me
Be laid by and never thought of.

(*Dies.*)

PESCARA. How fatally, it seems, he did withstand
His own rescue!
MALATESTE. Thou wretched thing of blood,
How came Antonio by his death?
BOSOLA. In a mist: I know not how:
Such a mistake as I have often seen
In a play. O, I am gone!
We are only like dead walls, or vaulted graves,
That ruined, yield no Echo. Fare you well.
It may be pain, but no harm to me to die,
In so good a quarrel. O, this gloomy world!
In what a shadow, or deep pit of darkness,
Doth womanish and feaful mankind live!
Let worthy minds ne'er stagger in distrust
To suffer death or shame for what is just:
Mine is another voyage.

(*Dies.*)

PESCARA. The noble Delio, as I came to th' palace,
Told me of Antonio's being here, and showed me
A pretty gentleman, his son and heir.

(*Enter Delio and Antonio's son.*)

[1] *There ... ransom* There goes your chance to be ransomed.
[2] *barber* Barbers were also surgeons and dentists.
[3] *wet hay* Considered a good remedy for a winded horse.
[4] *vault credit* See Matthew 6.19–21.
[5] *rushes* Reeds were often used to cover castle floors.

Malateste. O sir, you come too late!
Delio. I heard so, and
Was armed for't, ere I came. Let us make noble use
Of this great ruin; and join all our force
To establish this young hopeful gentleman
In's mother's right. These wretched eminent things
Leave no more fame behind 'em, than should one
Fall in a frost, and leave his print in snow:
As soon as the sun shines, it ever melts,
Both form and matter. I have ever thought
Nature doth nothing so great for great men,
As when she's pleased to make them lords of truth:
Integrity of life is fame's best friend,
Which nobly, beyond death, shall crown the end.

(*Exeunt.*)

The End

—1623 (written c. 1614)

Lady Mary Wroth

1587 – 1651

Lady Mary Wroth wrote the first work of prose fiction and the first amatory sonnet sequence published by a woman in English. Her court romance, *The Countess of Montgomery's Urania* (1621) exploits multiple Renaissance genres—sonnet, ballad, madrigal, pastoral narrative and song, among others—with penetrating observation, worldly skepticism, and emotional subtlety. Wroth's work was admired by a number of poets of her day—Ben Jonson, who dedicated his play *The Alchemist* (1610) to her, proclaimed that her verse had made him "a better lover, and much better poet"—and although her reputation faded into oblivion during the ensuing centuries, today Mary Wroth is recognized as a significant Jacobean writer and pioneer.

Born Mary Sidney in 1587, Wroth was a member of an illustrious political and literary family that included her uncle, Sir Philip Sidney, her aunt, Mary Sidney Herbert, Countess of Pembroke (herself a poet and patron of poets), and her father, Sir Robert Sidney, a statesman and minor poet. Educated by tutors, Mary was already an accomplished scholar, musician, and dancer by the time of her arranged marriage in 1604 to a wealthy landowner, Sir Robert Wroth. The union was not a happy one, but it did propel Lady Mary further into the life of the Jacobean court, where she performed in Ben Jonson's *Masque of Blackness* in 1605 and *Masque of Beauty* in 1608, and, in her family's tradition, bestowed friendship and patronage on poets such as Jonson and George Chapman.

On her husband's death in 1614, Wroth was left with an infant son (who died in 1616) and crushing debts. She was also free to pursue more openly a long-time illicit affair with her cousin, William Herbert, with whom she eventually had two illegitimate children. This affair, and financial constraints, may have limited Wroth's access to court and spurred her to write more seriously. She polished her sonnets, already circulating in manuscript as early as 1605, and in 1621 appended them to a 558-page prose romance, *Urania*, dedicated to the Countess of Montgomery. Because of its fictionalized allusions to actual court personages and events, the book offended those who saw themselves depicted too transparently. One such person, Sir William Denny, complained to the King and circulated a scathing poem criticizing Wroth as a "hermaphrodite" and "monster," an "oyster" gaping open to every tide. Denny's attack sparked a wittily vigorous reply in which Wroth mimicked the exact form of Denny's verse, rewriting his lines one by one. But in the end the attacks on her found their mark; she withdrew the edition of *Urania* and published no more work during her lifetime. (A second part of *Urania*, a few other poems, and a pastoral drama, *Love's Victory*, remained unpublished until our own time.)

Scandalous elements aside, *Urania* is a groundbreaking work because it uses a genre traditionally written by men—the episodic pastoral narrative of Philip Sidney's *Arcadia* and the digressive adventures of the Alexandrian romance—in untraditional ways to examine the social situation of women in actual court society. Wroth's prose is plainer than Sidney's and her outlook even more skeptical of romantic ideals. ("Credit no thing" is a typical warning.) Centering on the friendship of the shepherdess Urania (modeled on the Countess of Montgomery) with the princess Pamphilia (modeled on Wroth herself) and Pamphilia's frustrated love for the faithless Amphilanthus (whose name means "lover of two"), the story branches into multiple episodes and characters, interspersed with over fifty poems and songs in various genres. While celebrating the power of female desire, Wroth does not shrink from depicting the casual brutality of relations between the sexes: women seduced and abandoned, the indignity of forced marriages, the tortures of jealousy and deception.

In *Pamphilia to Amphilanthus*, the sequence of 83 sonnets and 20 songs that follows *Urania*, Wroth, no doubt influenced by her famous uncle's *Astrophil and Stella*, again applies herself to a genre traditionally (although by now by no means exclusively) reserved for males. She again deftly employs a somewhat outdated convention—the Petrarchan sonnet—in ways that highlight love's tensions and contradictions. Pamphilia addresses not her beloved, as in many Petrarchan sonnets, but herself ("I with my spirit talk and cry"), as well as Cupid, Time, Fortune, and other personifications of her trials. As Paula Payne observes, "Astrophil is writing to win his love, but Pamphilia is writing to discover her self." If so, she may in this regard be more genuinely and interestingly Petrarchan than some of Petrarch's later and lesser followers. The climax of *Pamphilia to Amphilanthus* is a technical *tour de force*, a "corona" of fourteen sonnets in which the last line of the first becomes the first line of the next. The line that begins and ends it ("In this strange labyrinth how shall I turn?") is emblematic of Wroth's skill in combining the elegant detachment of the Petrarchan form with a heightened emotional urgency: love, it turns out, is not the "thread" that she had expected to lead her from the labyrinth, for the "corona" leaves her there.

Mary Wroth lived her final decades in obscurity, struggling with debt, and died in 1651. In the youthful portrait of her which survives, she is pictured holding, not the gloves or fan customary in female portraits of the time, but an archlute—symbol of the poet.

⌘⌘⌘

from *Pamphilia to Amphilanthus*

1.

When night's black mantle could most darkness prove,° *display*
And sleep death's Image did my senses hire° *engage*
From knowledge of my self, then thoughts did move
Swifter than those most swiftness need require:
In sleep, a Chariot drawn by winged desire
I saw: where sat bright Venus Queen of love,
And at her feet her son,[1] still adding fire
To burning hearts which she did hold above,
But one heart flaming more than all the rest
The goddess held, and put it to my breast,
Dear son, now shoot said she: thus must we win;
He her obeyed, and martyred my poor heart,
I, waking hoped as dreams it would depart
Yet since: O me: a lover I have been.

[1] *her son* Cupid, customarily pictured as a winged infant carrying a bow and a quiver of arrows for piercing hearts, and torches to set them ablaze.

6.

My pain, still smothered in my grieved breast,
Seeks for some ease, yet cannot passage find
To be discharged of this unwelcome guest;
When most I strive, more fast his burdens bind,
Like to a ship, on Goodwins[2] cast by wind
The more she strives, more deep in sand is pressed
Till she be lost; so am I, in this kind° *manner*
Sunk, and devoured, and swallowed by unrest,
Lost, shipwrecked, spoiled, debarred of smallest hope
Nothing of pleasure left; save° thoughts have scope, *unless*
Which wander may: Go then, my thoughts, and cry
Hope's perished; Love tempest-beaten; Joy lost;
Killing despair hath all these blessings crossed
Yet faith still cries, Love will not falsify.

[2] *Goodwins* The Goodwins, or Goodwin Sands, a dangerous shoal off the coast of Kent proverbially associated with shipwrecks in Wroth's time.

7.

Love leave° to urge, thou know'st thou hast the hand;° *cease / upper hand*
'Tis cowardice, to strive where none resist:
Pray thee leave off, I yield unto thy band;° *bond*
Do not thus, still, in thine own power persist,
Behold I yield: let forces be dismissed;
I am thy subject, conquered, bound to stand,
Never thy foe, but did thy claim assist
Seeking thy due of those who did withstand;
But now, it seems, thou would'st I should thee love;
I do confess, 'twas thy will made me choose;
And thy fair shows[1] made me a lover prove
When I my freedom did, for pain, refuse.
Yet this Sir God,[2] your boyship I despise;
Your charms I obey, but love not want of eyes.[3]

13.

Dear, famish not what you your self gave food;
Destroy not what your glory is to save;
Kill not that soul to which you spirit gave;
In pity, not disdain your triumph stood;
An easy thing it is to shed the blood
Of one, who at your will, yields to the grave;
But more you may true worth[4] by mercy crave
When you preserve, not spoil, but nourish good;
Your sight is all the food I do desire;
Then sacrifice me not in hidden fire,
Or stop the breath which did your praises move:
Think but how easy 'tis a sight to give;
Nay ev'n desert; since by it I do live,
I but chameleon-like[5] would live, and love.

14.

Am I thus conquered? have I lost the powers
That to withstand, which joys° to ruin me? *delights*
Must I be still while it my strength devours
And captive leads me prisoner, bound, unfree?
Love first shall leave men's fancies to them free,
Desire shall quench love's flames, spring hate° sweet showers, *shall hate*
Love shall loose all his darts, have sight, and see
His shame, and wishings hinder happy hours;
Why should we not love's purblind° charms resist? *almost blind*
Must we be servile, doing what he list?° *wishes*
No, seek some host to harbour thee: I fly° *flee from*
Thy babish° tricks, and freedom do profess; *babyish*
But O my hurt, makes my lost heart confess
I love, and must: So farewell liberty.

15.

Truly poor Night thou welcome art to me:
I love thee better in this sad attire
Than that which raiseth some men's fancies higher
Like painted outsides which foul inward be;
I love thy grave, and saddest looks to see,
Which seems° my soul, and dying heart entire, *resembles*
Like to the ashes of some happy fire
That flamed in joy, but quenched in misery:
I love thy count'nance, and thy sober pace
Which evenly goes, and as of loving grace
To us, and me among the rest oppressed
Gives quiet, peace to my poor self alone,
And freely grants day leave when thou art gone
To give clear light to see all ill° redressed. *misery*

22.

Like to the Indians, scorched with the sun,
The sun which they do as their God adore
So am I used by love, for ever more
I worship him, less favors have I won,
Better are they who thus to blackness run,
And so can only whiteness' want deplore
Than I who pale, and white am with grief's store,° *abundance*
Nor can have hope, but to see hopes undone;
Besides, their sacrifice received's in sight
Of their chose saint: mine hid as worthless rite;

---

[1] *shows* Displays (of power).

[2] *Sir God* Mocking address to Cupid.

[3] *want of eyes* Blindness, a proverbial attribute of love, and of Cupid.

[4] *worth* Pun on "Wroth," which was pronounced "worth."

[5] *chameleon-like* The chameleon could survive for long periods without food, and was thus reputed to live on air.

Grant me to see where I my offerings give,
Then let me wear the mark of Cupid's might
In heart as they in skin of Phoebus' light[1]
Not ceasing offerings to love while I Live.

23.

When every one to pleasing pastime hies° *hastens*
Some hunt, some hawk, some play, while some delight
In sweet discourse, and music shows joy's might
Yet I my thoughts do far above these prize.
The joy which I take, is that free from eyes[2]
I sit, and wonder at this daylike night
So to dispose themselves, as void° of right; *bereft*
And leave true pleasure for poor vanities;
When others hunt, my thoughts I have in chase;
If hawk,[3] my mind at wished end doth fly,
Discourse,[4] I with my spirit talk, and cry
While others, music choose as greatest grace.
O God, say I, can these fond° pleasures move? *foolish*
Or music be but in sweet thoughts of love?

35.

False hope which feeds but to destroy, and spill
What it first breeds;[5] unnatural to the birth
Of thine own womb; conceiving but to kill,
And plenty gives to make the greater dearth,
So Tyrants do who falsely ruling earth
Outwardly grace them, and with profit's fill
Advance those who appointed are to death
To make their greater fall to please their will.
Thus shadow they their wicked vile intent
Colouring evil with a show of good
While in fair shows° their malice so is spent; *spectacles*
Hope kills the heart, and tyrants shed the blood.
For hope deluding brings us to the pride° *peak*
Of our desires the farther down to slide.
—1621

from *A Crown of Sonnets Dedicated to Love*

77

In this strange labyrinth how shall I turn?
Ways° are on all sides while the way I miss: *paths*
If to the right hand, there in love I burn;
Let me go forward, therein danger is;
If to the left, suspicion hinders bliss;
Let me turn back, shame cries I ought return,
Nor faint, though crosses° with my fortunes kiss; *troubles*
Stand still is harder, although sure to mourn.[6]
Thus let me take the right, or left-hand way,
Go forward, or stand still, or back retire:
I must these doubts endure without allay° *relief*
Or help, but travail[7] find for my best hire.
Yet that which most my troubled sense doth move,
Is to leave all, and take the thread of Love.[8]
—1621

Railing Rhymes Returned upon the Author by Mistress Mary Wroth

Hermaphrodite[9] in sense in Art a monster
As by your railing rhymes the world may conster° *construe*
Your spiteful words against a harmless book
Shows that an ass much like the sire doth look
Men truly noble fear no touch of blood
Nor question make of others much more good
Can such comparisons seem the want° of wit *lack*
When oysters have inflamed your blood with it
But it appears your guiltiness gaped wide
And filled with Dirty doubt your brain's swollen tide
Both friend and foe in deed you use alike
And your mad wit in sherry equal strike

[1] *as … light* As Indians, "scorched with the sun," show "in their skins" the mark of Phoebus, the sun-god.

[2] *eyes* The eyes, or gaze, of others.

[3] *If hawk* If they (others) hawk.

[4] *Discourse* When others discourse.

[5] *spill … breeds* As in a miscarriage.

[6] *although sure to mourn* Although sure to make me mourn.

[7] *travail* Hard work, but also with a pun on "travel."

[8] *thread of Love* Referring to the myth of Ariadne, who gave her beloved Theseus a spool of thread to unwind behind him as he traveled through the labyrinth of the Minotaur; by following the thread he could find his way back out.

[9] *Hermaphrodite* Possessing both male and female sexual organs; often used pejoratively to describe a mannish woman or an effeminate man.

These slanderous flying flames raised from the pot[1]
You know are false and raging makes you hot
How easily now do you receive your own
Turned on your self from whence the squib was thrown
When these few lines not thousands writ at least
Mainly thus prove your self the drunken beast
This is far less to you than you have done
A Thread but of your own all words worse spun
By which you lively see in your own glass[2]
How hard it is for you to lie and pass
Thus you have made yourself a lying wonder
Fools and their pastimes should not part asunder.
—1983 (WRITTEN C. 1621)

IN CONTEXT

The Occasion of "Railing Rhymes"

Wroth's "Railing Rhymes" was written in response to the following attack by Lord Denny.

Edward Denny, Baron of Waltham, To Pamphilia from the Father-in-Law of Seralius (c. 1621)[3]

Hermaphrodite in show, in deed a monster
As by thy words and works all men may conster° *construe*
Thy wrathful spite conceived an Idle° book *worthless*
Brought forth a fool which like the dam doth look
Wherein thou strikes at some man's noble blood
Of kin to thine[4] if thine be counted good
Whose vain comparison for want° of wit *lack*
Takes up the oystershell to play with it
Yet common oysters such as thine gape wide
And take in pearls or worse at every tide
Both friend and foe to thee are even alike
Thy wit runs mad not caring who it strike
These slanderous flying f[l]ames rise from the pot
For potted wits inflamed are raging hot
How easy wer't to pay thee with thine own
Returning that which thou thyself hast thrown
And write a thousand lies of thee at least
And by thy lines describe a drunken beast

[1] *pot* Drinking vessel (for liquor).

[2] *glass* Mirror, but here perhaps also drinking-glass.

[3] *Seralius* A character in Wroth's court pastoral *The Countess of Montgomery's Urania* (1621), whose satirical resemblance to Denny's son-in-law was transparent enough to suggest embarrassing parallels to a recent Denny family scandal. Denny wrote angry letters to Wroth demanding withdrawal of her book and circulated this poem questioning her honesty and the appropriateness of a woman pursuing the vocation of writing.

[4] *Of kin to thine* As good, or noble, as yours.

This were no more to thee than thou hast done
A Thread but of thine own which thou hast spun
By which thou plainly seest in thine own glass
How easy 'tis to bring a lie to pass
Thus hast thou made thyself a lying wonder
Fools and their Babbles seldom part asunder
Work o th' Works leave idle books alone
For wise and worthier women have writ none.
—1983 (WRITTEN C. 1621)

Thomas Hobbes

1588 – 1679

Thomas Hobbes was active in the study of geometry, optics, physics, psychology, language, and religion, but he is best known as the author of *Leviathan*, a seminal work of political and moral philosophy. His writings have remained the subject of controversy—not least of all his contention that the life of one who exists in a state of nature is "solitary, poor, nasty, brutish, and short." In his own time Hobbes had to contend with more severe criticism by the Royalists, the Parliamentarians, and the Church, all of which at various times found his writings to be seditious; the reading of his works was at one time banned by both the Church and Oxford University. Many objected to his materialist assertions that a person attains knowledge only by way of sensory impressions and not by divine transference (Hobbes said "the universe is corporeal; all that is real is material, and what is not material is not real"), and that moral behavior is best only because it is rational to live a moral life and not because God wills people to do so.

Hobbes was born in Wiltshire, England, in the year of the Spanish Armada (1588); rumors had it that his premature birth had been brought on by his mother's fear of an attack. He was raised after the age of seven by his uncle, who took responsibility when Thomas Hobbes Sr., a parson, fled the family after a violent argument with another vicar. Hobbes appears not to have suffered intellectually from this upheaval, however—he translated Euripides's *Medea* from Greek to Latin during his formative years and entered Oxford University at the age of 15. After graduation he became tutor to the son of William Cavendish, Baron Hardwick (later the Earl of Devonshire), and indeed he would spend most of his life as a tutor. Hobbes accompanied the younger Cavendish on a European tour in 1610, and on this and subsequent trips overseas he met and befriended such important thinkers as Galileo and René Descartes (Hobbes wrote a famous refutation of Descartes's *Meditations*), all of whom influenced his theories of mathematics and natural science.

Hobbes continued translating throughout his life, first publishing Thucydides's *Eight Books of the Peloponnesian War* in 1629, long after he had completed the translation. The purpose of the book, he says in the introduction, is to "instruct and enable men, by the knowledge of actions past, to bear themselves prudently in the present and providently towards the future." In one of the first texts authored and published by Hobbes, *Elements of Law, Natural and Politic* (1642), which he called a "scientific treatment of politics," he responded to the political and civil unrest during the reign of Charles I by arguing for the right of the monarchy to absolute power. The contentious nature of the book and its appearance at the time of the King's dissolution of Parliament and the beginning of the Civil War caused Hobbes to flee to Paris, where he lived in exile for over a decade, there tutoring the future king, Charles II, and beginning his work on an important philosophical trilogy concerning politics (*De Cive*, 1642), matter (*De Corpore*, 1655), and human nature (*De Homine*, 1658).

The crux of the argument in *Leviathan* (1651) has its basis in the upheaval of the Civil War in England (1642–48). The work outlines Hobbes's theories about the necessity for a civilized society to live under the rule of government and abide obediently by its laws in order to exist in security. A sovereign power, Hobbes thought, is in the best position to make decisions regarding the welfare of its people and should be given absolute authority to rule over its constituents. He did not, however, specify that the "sovereign power" need be a king or queen, and because of this, when *Leviathan* appeared, Hobbes found himself in danger on the Continent, as the Royalists, who were also living in exile, interpreted his political stance as supportive of Cromwell's reign.

Leviathan's argument was founded on a defense of reason, which Hobbes saw as having as a natural goal self-preservation and the avoidance of war and violent death. Rather than living in a state of nature (i.e., without laws), people are better able in the long term to protect themselves against the threat of anarchy and civil war by banding together and giving themselves up to sovereign rule. They are then obliged to abide unquestioningly by the sovereign's laws, and, in essence, to let government become the "voice of the people." While Hobbes's doctrines were from one angle supportive of the sovereign power of the monarch, they were revolutionary in deriving justifications for that power from the common interests of the people and not from any divine right.

Hobbes lived to 91, an extraordinary age for someone of his day. He did not cease work in his final decade, but wrote his autobiography, translated Homer's *Iliad* and *Odyssey*, and completed work on *Behemoth* (authorized version published 1682), a history of the Civil War period in the form of a dialogue.

⌘⌘⌘

Frontispiece to the 1651 edition of *Leviathan.*

from *Leviathan;*[1] *Or the Matter, Form, & Power of a Commonwealth, Ecclesiastical and Civil*

The Introduction

Nature (the art whereby God hath made and governs the world) is by the art of man, as in many other things, so in this also imitated, that it can make an artificial animal. For seeing life is but a motion of limbs, the beginning whereof is in some principal part within, why may we not say that all automata (engines that move themselves by springs and wheels as doth a watch) have an artificial life? For what is the heart, but a spring; and the nerves, but so many strings; and the joints, but so many wheels, giving motion to the whole body, such as was intended by the Artificer? Art goes yet further, imitating that rational and most excellent work of nature, man. For by art is created that great Leviathan called a Commonwealth, or State (in Latin, *Civitas*), which is but an artificial man, though of greater stature and strength than the natural, for whose protection and

[1] *Leviathan* From Job 41: an enormous primordial sea serpent whose strength is immeasurable and the existence of which attests to God's power and will. The 1651 edition of Hobbes's book pictured the Leviathan as sovereign power, personified by a giant monarch made up of small figures of men.

defense it was intended; and in which the sovereignty is an artificial soul, as giving life and motion to the whole body. The magistrates and other officers of judicature and execution, artificial joints. Reward and punishment (by which fastened to the seat of the sovereignty, every joint and member is moved to perform his duty) are the nerves that do the same in the body natural. The wealth and riches of all the particular members are the strength. *Salus populi* (the people's safety) its business. Counsellors, by whom all things needful for it to know are suggested unto it, are the memory. Equity and laws, an artificial reason and will. Concord, health. Sedition. sickness. And civil war, death. Lastly, the pacts and covenants by which the parts of this body politic were at first made, set together, and united, resemble that fiat,[1] or the "Let us make man,"[2] pronounced by God in the Creation.

To describe the nature of this artificial man, I will consider: first, the matter thereof, and the artificer, both which is Man. Secondly, how, and by what covenants it is made; what are the rights and just power or authority of a sovereign; and what it is that preserveth and dissolveth it. Thirdly, what is a Christian Commonwealth. Lastly, what is the Kingdom of Darkness.

Concerning the first, there is a saying much usurped of late that wisdom is acquired, not by reading of books, but of men. Consequently whereunto, those persons, that for the most part can give no other proof of being wise, take great delight to show what they think they have read in men by uncharitable censures of one another behind their backs. But there is another saying, not of late understood, by which they might learn truly to read one another, if they would take the pains, and that is *nosce teipsum*, read thyself, which was not meant, as it is now used, to countenance either the barbarous state of men in power towards their inferiors or to encourage men of low degree to a saucy behavior towards their betters, but to teach us that for the similitude of the thoughts and passions of one man to the thoughts and passions of another, whosoever looketh into himself and considereth what he doth when he does think, opine, reason, hope, fear, etc., and upon what grounds, he shall thereby read and know what are the thoughts and passions of all other men upon the like occasions. I say the similitude of passions, which are the same in all men, desire, fear, hope, etc., not the similitude of the objects of the passions, which are the things desired, feared, hoped, etc.; for these the constitution individual and particular education do so vary, and they are so easy to be kept from our knowledge that the characters of man's heart, blotted and confounded as they are with dissembling, lying, counterfeiting, and erroneous doctrines are legible only to him that searcheth hearts. And though by men's actions we do discover their design sometimes; yet to do it without comparing them with our own and distinguishing all circumstances by which the case may come to be altered is to decipher without a key and be for the most part deceived by too much trust or by too much diffidence, as he that reads is himself a good or evil man.

But let one man read another by his actions never so perfectly, it serves him only with his acquaintance, which are but few. He that is to govern a whole nation must read in himself, not this or that particular man, but mankind, which though it be hard to do, harder than to learn any language or science; yet when I shall have set down my own reading orderly and perspicuously, the pains left another will be only to consider if he also find not the same in himself. For this kind of doctrine admitteth no other demonstration.

Chapter 13: Of the Natural Condition of Mankind as Concerning their Felicity and Misery

Nature hath made men so equal in the faculties of body and mind, as that, though there be found one man sometimes manifestly stronger in body or of quicker mind than another, yet when all is reckoned together, the difference between man and man is not so considerable as that one man can thereupon claim to himself any benefit to which another may not pretend as well as he. For as to the strength of body, the weakest has strength enough to kill the strongest, either by secret machination or by confederacy with others that are in the same danger with himself.

And as to the faculties of the mind, setting aside the arts grounded upon words, and especially that skill of proceeding upon general and infallible rules, called

[1] *fiat* Decree. Latin: "Let there be."

[2] *"Let us make man"* From Genesis 1.26.

science, which very few have and but in few things, as being not a native faculty born with us, nor attained, as prudence, while we look after somewhat else, I find yet a greater equality amongst men than that of strength. For prudence is but experience, which equal time equally bestows on all men in those things they equally apply themselves unto. That which may perhaps make such equality incredible is but a vain conceit of one's own wisdom, which almost all men think they have in a greater degree than the vulgar, that is, than all men but themselves and a few others, whom by fame or for concurring with themselves, they approve. For such is the nature of men that howsoever they may acknowledge many others to be more witty or more eloquent or more learned, they will hardly believe there be many so wise as themselves, for they see their own wit at hand and other men's at a distance. But this proveth rather that men are in that point equal, than unequal. For there is not ordinarily a greater sign of the equal distribution of anything than that every man is contented with his share.

From this equality of ability ariseth equality of hope in the attaining of our ends. And therefore if any two men desire the same thing, which nevertheless they cannot both enjoy, they become enemies, and in the way to their end (which is principally their own conservation, and sometimes their delectation only) endeavour to destroy or subdue one another. And from hence it comes to pass that where an invader hath no more to fear than another man's single power, if one plant, sow, build, or possess a convenient seat, others may probably be expected to come prepared with forces united to dispossess and deprive him, not only of the fruit of his labour, but also of his life or liberty. And the invader again is in the like danger of another.

And from this diffidence of one another, there is no way for any man to secure himself so reasonable as anticipation, that is, by force or wiles, to master the persons of all men he can so long till he see no other power great enough to endanger him; and this is no more than his own conservation requireth, and is generally allowed. Also, because there be some that, taking pleasure in contemplating their own power in the acts of conquest, which they pursue farther than their security requires, if others, that otherwise would be glad to be at ease within modest bounds, should not by invasion increase their power, they would not be able, long time, by standing only on their defence, to subsist. And by consequence, such augmentation of dominion over men being necessary to a man's conservation, it ought to be allowed him.

Again, men have no pleasure (but on the contrary a great deal of grief) in keeping company where there is no power able to overawe them all. For every man looketh that his companion should value him at the same rate he sets upon himself, and upon all signs of contempt or undervaluing naturally endeavours, as far as he dares (which amongst them that have no common power to keep them in quiet is far enough to make them destroy each other), to extort a greater value from his contemners,[1] by damage; and from others, by the example.

So that in the nature of man, we find three principal causes of quarrel. First, competition; secondly, diffidence; thirdly, glory.

The first maketh men invade for gain; the second, for safety; and the third, for reputation. The first use violence to make themselves masters of other men's persons, wives, children, and cattle; the second, to defend them; the third, for trifles, as a word, a smile, a different opinion, and any other sign of undervalue, either direct in their persons or by reflection in their kindred, their friends, their nation, their profession, or their name.

Hereby it is manifest that during the time men live without a common power to keep them all in awe, they are in that condition which is called war; and such a war as is of every man against every man. For war consisteth not in battle only, or the act of fighting, but in a tract of time, wherein the will to contend by battle is sufficiently known; and therefore the notion of *time* is to be considered in the nature of war, as it is in the nature of weather. For as the nature of foul weather lieth not in a shower or two of rain, but in an inclination thereto of many days together, so the nature of war consisteth not in actual fighting, but in the known disposition thereto during all the time there is no assurance to the contrary. All other time is peace.

Whatsoever therefore is consequent to a time of war, where every man is enemy to every man, the same consequent to the time wherein men live without other

[1] *his contemners* Those who scorn him.

security than what their own strength and their own invention shall furnish them withal. In such condition there is no place for industry, because the fruit thereof is uncertain; and consequently no culture of the earth; no navigation, nor use of the commodities that may be imported by sea; no commodious building; no instruments of moving and removing such things as require much force; no knowledge of the face of the earth; no account of time; no arts; no letters; no society; and which is worst of all, continual fear, and danger of violent death; and the life of man, solitary, poor, nasty, brutish, and short.

It may seem strange to some man that has not well weighed these things that nature should thus dissociate and render men apt to invade and destroy one another; and he may therefore, not trusting to this inference, made from the passions, desire perhaps to have the same confirmed by experience. Let him therefore consider with himself; when taking a journey, he arms himself and seeks to go well accompanied; when going to sleep, he locks his doors; when even in his house he locks his chests; and this when he knows there be laws and public officers, armed to revenge all injuries shall be done him; what opinion he has of his fellow subjects, when he rides armed; of his fellow citizens, when he locks his doors; and of his children, and servants, when he locks his chests. Does he not there as much accuse mankind by his actions as I do by my words? But neither of us accuse man's nature in it. The desires and other passions of man are in themselves no sin. No more are the actions that proceed from those passions till they know a law that forbids them; which, till laws be made, they cannot know; nor can any law be made till they have agreed upon the person that shall make it.

It may peradventure be thought there was never such a time nor condition of war as this; and I believe it was never generally so, over all the world; but there are many places where they live so now. For the savage people in many places of America, except the government of small families, the concord whereof dependeth on natural lust, have no government at all, and live at this day in that brutish manner, as I said before. Howsoever, it may be perceived what manner of life there would be, where there were no common power to fear, by the manner of life which men that have formerly lived under a peaceful government use to degenerate into a civil war.

But though there had never been any time wherein particular men were in a condition of war one against another; yet in all times kings and persons of sovereign authority, because of their independency, are in continual jealousies, and in the state and posture of gladiators, having their weapons pointing and their eyes fixed on one another, that is, their forts, garrisons, and guns upon the frontiers of their kingdoms, and continual spies upon their neighbours, which is a posture of war. But because they uphold thereby the industry of their subjects, there does not follow from it that misery which accompanies the liberty of particular men.

To this war of every man against every man, this also is consequent: that nothing can be unjust. The notions of right and wrong, justice and injustice, have there no place. Where there is no common power, there is no law; where no law, no injustice. Force and fraud are in war the two cardinal virtues. Justice and injustice are none of the faculties neither of the body nor mind. If they were, they might be in a man that were alone in the world, as well as his senses and passions. They are qualities that relate to men in society, not in solitude. It is consequent also to the same condition that there be no propriety,[1] no dominion, no *mine* and *thine* distinct, but only that to be every man's that he can get, and for so long as he can keep it. And thus much for the ill condition which man by mere nature is actually placed in, though with a possibility to come out of it, consisting partly in the passions, partly in his reason.

The passions that incline men to peace are fear of death, desire of such things as are necessary to commodious living, and a hope by their industry to obtain them. And reason suggesteth convenient articles of peace upon which men may be drawn to agreement. These articles are they which otherwise are called the laws of nature, whereof I shall speak more particularly in the two following chapters.

—1651

[1] *propriety* Private property.

Robert Herrick

1591 – 1674

Of the "sons of Ben" who basked in the genius of Ben Jonson in 1620s London, Robert Herrick is the poet most familiar to modern readers—more so, to many readers, than Jonson himself. "Gather ye Rosebuds while ye may," the opening line of Herrick's "To the Virgins, to make much of Time," is the most famous version of a classical refrain, while poems such as "Delight in Disorder" and "The Hock Cart" are fixtures in anthologies. That Herrick's fame rests on a few crystalline lyrics obscures the fact that he possessed a fairly varied repertoire. Herrick emulated Jonson (whom he called "Saint Ben") not only in editing and publishing his own complete works but also in cultivating and "Englishing" a number of classical poets. Herrick's *Hesperides* (1648) contains epigrams, epistles, odes, eclogues, and other lyric forms—over 1,400 poems in all—on a variety of themes. The pastoral features prominently in *Hesperides*, as does the amorous (158 poems are addressed to 14 separate mistresses, most of whom seem to be the products of Herrick's literary imagination) and the political; poems such as "Upon Julia's Clothes" express an aesthetics of sensuality. The best of these poems had been circulating in manuscript for decades before they were published, and some had become popular songs, set to music by Henry Lawes and others.

Hesperides appeared during a period of political upheaval and civil war, and achieved little notice in Herrick's lifetime. Its often light bucolic tone did not match the seriousness of the time; its occasional indecency offended some; and *His Noble Numbers*, the religious verse appended to it, seemed flat and undistinguished. No separate volume of Herrick's poetry was published again until 1810, but once his poetry had been rediscovered the romantic attraction to pastoral and rural themes made Herrick popular with nineteenth-century anthologists. If subsequent critics have never quite endorsed Algernon Charles Swinburne's extravagant praise of Herrick as "the greatest song-writer ever born of English race," recent consensus has raised his status among mid-seventeenth- century poets thanks to a deeper appreciation of his cunning and delicate artistry, the clever scope and organization of *Hesperides*, and the political implications of his celebration of traditional rites and pastimes.

The son of a London goldsmith, Herrick apprenticed in that craft before attending Cambridge, from which he graduated in 1617. After years spent mostly in London, cultivating patrons and literary friendships with Ben Jonson and others, he moved to Devonshire to become vicar of Dean Prior in 1629. Ousted from his living by the triumphant Parliamentary forces in 1647, Herrick, in "His Returne to London," shed no tears for "the dull confines of the drooping West," indeed lamenting the economic necessity that had condemned him to such "a long and irksome banishment." He returned to Dean Prior at his own request after the Restoration in 1660, however, to live out the remainder of his bachelor's life ministering to his "rude" flock.

In "Discontents in Devon," Herrick confesses his ambivalence toward country life: "I ne'er invented such / Ennobled numbers for the Presse / Then where I loath'd so much." In fact, the Epicurean bent of Herrick's classical models had prepared him well for versifying the joys of the natural world and infusing them with the echoes of what Puritans (doubtless correctly) thought the residual paganism he found in rural festivals and rituals, as he does impeccably in "Corinna's Gone A-Maying." In "The Argument of His Book," his verse preface to *Hesperides,* he announces himself as a poet of nature (as it was perceived in his day), ceremony, and "Times trans-shifting," linking natural cycles and the transience of nature's creatures to the inevitability of aging and death. Just as the title of his book recalls the island garden of classical myth (a sea-guarded place of golden apples, maidens, and a vigilant dragon), Herrick views nature and the natural cycles of work and play, including festivals and holidays, as providing shelter against the ravages of time, mortality, and civil strife. An ardent Royalist, Herrick would also have approved of the political role such rural festivals played in reinforcing traditional hierarchies and social stability. Not surprisingly, these holidays (including "Sunday sports") had been espoused and encouraged in the *Book of Sports* issued by the Stuart kings, but deplored and condemned by the Puritans as profanations of the Sabbath and excuses for drunkenness. Herrick's conservative politics and his natural Epicureanism leave no doubt as to his stand on the issue. From his classical models, Herrick had learned to express a carefully cultivated simplicity of outlook that sets him apart from the smooth urbanity and self-conscious sophistication of the Cavalier poets and the strenuous spiritual strivings of the metaphysical poets. For Herrick, or at least for the persona he constructs, mortality must either be confronted by seizing and enjoying the pleasures of today (*Carpe diem*, as the Romans put it) or transcended by achieving poetic immortality. Although he seems to have been a sincere Christian and wrote some fine religious verse, "To live merrily, and to trust to Good Verses," the memorable title of one of his lyrics, might be cited as Herrick's ultimate advice to posterity.

⌘⌘⌘

The Argument[1] of His Book

I sing of brooks, of blossoms, birds, and bowers,
Of April, May, of June, and July flowers.
I sing of Maypoles, hock carts, wassails, wakes,[2]
Of bridegrooms, brides, and of their bridal cakes.
I write of youth, of love, and have access
By these, to sing of cleanly° wantonness. *innocent*
I sing of dews, of rains, and piece by piece,
Of balm, of oil, of spice, and ambergris.[3]
I sing of times trans-shifting; and I write
How roses first came red, and lilies white.
I write of groves, of twilights, and I sing
The court of Mab,[4] and of the fairy king.
I write of hell; I sing (and ever shall)
Of Heaven, and hope to have it after all.
—1648

[1] *Argument* Summary of the subject matter of a book or poem.

[2] *hock carts* Wagons carrying the last of the harvest, associated with rural festivals; *wassails* Toasts drunk to the health of others, especially on Twelfth Night or Christmas Eve; *wakes* Annual parish festivals.

[3] *ambergris* Waxy secretion produced by sperm whales, used in making perfume, and very valuable.

[4] *Mab* Queen of the Fairies.

Delight in Disorder

A sweet disorder in the dress
Kindles in clothes a wantonness:
A lawn[5] about the shoulders thrown
Into a fine distractiòn;
An erring lace, which here and there
Enthralls the crimson stomacher:[6]
A cuff neglectful, and thereby
Ribbons to flow confusedly:

[5] *lawn* Shawl or scarf of finely woven cotton or linen.

[6] *stomacher* Decorative garment worn over the breast and stomach and secured by lacing.

A winning wave, deserving note,
In the tempestuous petticoat;
A careless shoestring, in whose tie
I see a wild civility:
Do more bewitch me than when art
Is too precise in every part.
—1648

His Farewell to Sack

Farewell, thou thing, time-past so known, so dear
To me as blood to life and spirit; near,
Nay, thou more near than kindred, friend, man, wife,
Male to the female, soul to body, life
To quick action, or the warm soft side
Of the resigning yet resisting bride.
The kiss of virgins; first-fruits of the bed;
Soft speech, smooth touch, the lips, the maidenhead;
These and a thousand sweets could never be
So near or dear as thou wast once to me.
O thou, the drink of gods and angels! Wine
That scatterest spirit and lust;° whose purest shine *pleasure*
More radiant than the summer's sunbeams shows,
Each way illustrious, brave;° and like to those *splendid*
Comets we see by night, whose shagg'd[1] portents
Foretell the coming of some dire events,
Or some full flame which with a pride aspires,° *rises*
Throwing about his wild and active fires.
'Tis thou, above nectar, O divinest soul!
(Eternal in thyself) that canst control
That which subverts whole nature: grief and care,
Vexation of the mind, and damned despair.
'Tis thou alone who with thy mystic fan[2]
Work'st more than wisdom, art, or nature can
To rouse the sacred madness, and awake
The frost-bound blood and spirits, and to make
Them frantic with thy raptures, flashing through
The soul like lightning, and as active too.
'Tis not Apollo[3] can, or those thrice three
Castalian sisters[4] sing, if wanting thee.
Horace, Anacreon[5] both had lost their fame
Had'st thou not filled them with thy fire and flame.
Phoebean splendor! and thou Thespian spring![6]
Of which sweet swans° must drink before they sing *poets*
Their true-paced numbers° and their holy lays° *verses / songs*
Which makes them worthy° cedar and the bays.[7] *worthy of*
But why? why longer do I gaze upon
Thee with the eye of admiration?
Since I must leave thee, and enforced must say
To all thy witching beauties, Go, Away.
But if thy whimpering looks do ask me why,
Then know that nature bids thee go, not I.
'Tis her erroneous self has made a brain
Uncapable of such a sovereign
As is thy powerful self. Prithee not smile,
Or smile more inly,° lest thy looks beguile *inwardly*
My vows denounced° in zeal, which thus much show thee, *announced*
That I have sworn but by thy looks to know thee.
Let others drink thee freely, and desire
Thee and their lips espoused, while I admire
And love thee but not taste thee. Let my muse
Fail of thy former helps,° and only use *supports*
Her inadulterate strength. What's done by me
Hereafter shall smell of the lamp,[8] not thee.
—1648

[1] *shagg'd* Shaggy or ragged, as the tail of a comet.

[2] *mystic fan* Winnowing fan for grain, sacred emblem in the rites of Dionysus, Greek god of wine.

[3] *Apollo* Greek sun god, and god of poetry and music.

[4] *Castalian sisters* The nine muses in Greek mythology, who presided over the various arts and sciences. The Castalian spring on Mount Parnassus was sacred to them and to Apollo.

[5] *Horace* Roman poet (65–8 BCE) noted for his satires and odes; *Anacreon* Greek lyric poet (c. 570–480 BCE) celebrated for his drinking songs.

[6] *Phoebean* Bright as the sun, from Phoebus, a common epithet for Apollo; *Thespian spring* Hippocrene spring near Thespiae in Boeotia, sacred to the muses.

[7] *cedar* Cedar oil, used to preserve manuscripts; *the bays* Laurel crown for poetic achievement; poetic renown.

[8] *smell of the lamp* Labored and turgid, the product of study, not inspiration.

Corinna's Going A-Maying[1]

Get up! get up for shame! the blooming morn
Upon her wings presents the god unshorn.[2]
See how Aurora[3] throws her fair
Fresh-quilted colors through the air:
Get up, sweet slug-a-bed, and see
The dew bespangling herb and tree.
Each flower has wept, and bowed toward the east
Above an hour since, yet you not dressed;
Nay, not so much as out of bed?
When all the birds have matins[4] said,
And sung their thankful hymns: 'tis sin,
Nay, profanation to keep in,
Whenas a thousand virgins on this day
Spring, sooner than the lark, to fetch in May.[5]

Rise, and put on your foliage, and be seen
To come forth, like the springtime, fresh and green,
And sweet as Flora.[6] Take no care
For jewels for your gown or hair;
Fear not; the leaves will strew
Gems in abundance upon you;
Besides, the childhood of the day has kept,
Against° you come, some orient pearls unwept; *until*
Come and receive them[7] while the light
Hangs on the dew-locks of the night,
And Titan° on the eastern hill *the sun*
Retires himself, or else stands still
Till you come forth. Wash, dress, be brief in praying:
Few beads[8] are best, when once we go a-Maying.

Come, my Corinna, come; and coming, mark
How each field turns° a street; each street a park *becomes*
Made green and trimmed with trees; see how
Devotion gives each house a bough,
Or branch: each porch, each door, ere this,
An ark, a tabernacle is,
Made up of whitethorn neatly interwove;[9]
As if here were those cooler shades of love.
Can such delights be in the street
And open fields, and we not see 't?
Come, we'll abroad;° and let's obey *go out*
The proclamation[10] made for May,
And sin no more, as we have done, by staying;
But, my Corinna, come, let's go a-Maying.

There's not a budding boy, or girl, this day
But is got up and gone to bring in May;
A deal° of youth, ere this, is come *multitude*
Back, and with whitethorn laden, home.
Some have dispatched their cakes and cream,
Before that we have left to dream:[11]
And some have wept, and wooed, and plighted troth,
And chose their priest, ere we can cast off sloth.
Many a green-gown[12] has been given,
Many a kiss, both odd and even;
Many a glance, too, has been sent
From out the eye, love's firmament;
Many a jest told of the keys betraying
This night, and locks picked; yet we're not a-Maying.

---

[1] *A-Maying* Celebrating May Day, especially by gathering spring flowers and greenery.

[2] *god unshorn* Apollo, the sun god of classical mythology, often pictured with long, brilliant, streaming hair suggesting the rays of the sun, and also often identified with the advent of spring.

[3] *Aurora* Roman goddess of the dawn.

[4] *matins* Morning prayers.

[5] *fetch in May* Bring in the month of May; also a pun on "may" as a common word for the blossoms of the hawthorn, which were gathered ("fetched in") on May Day and whose white or pinkish hue was suggestive of virginity.

[6] *Flora* Roman goddess of flowers and spring.

[7] *receive them* According to English rural tradition, young girls could ensure their future beauty by washing themselves in the dew of the hawthorn on May Day.

[8] *beads* Prayers, or beads of a rosary.

[9] *Devotion … interwove* According to ancient rural custom (eventually tailored to Christian belief), hawthorn boughs were placed above a doorway on May Day to confer blessing on the dwelling.

[10] *proclamation* Referring to a royal "Declaration concerning lawful sports" (1613, 1633), which encouraged traditional pastimes such as maypoles and May games to counter puritan Sabbatarianism.

[11] *Before … dream* Before we have ceased to dream, i.e., awoken.

[12] *green-gown* Gown grass-stained from amorous sport.

Come, let us go while we are in our prime,
And take the harmless folly of the time.
We shall grow old apace, and die
Before we know our liberty.
Our life is short, and our days run
As fast away as does the sun;
And as a vapor or a drop of rain,
Once lost, can ne'er be found again,
So when or you or I are made
A fable, song, or fleeting shade,
All love, all liking, all delight
Lies drowned with us in endless night.
Then while time serves, and we are but decaying,
Come, my Corinna, come, let's go a-Maying.
—1648

To the Virgins, to Make Much of Time

Gather ye rosebuds while ye may,
Old time is still a-flying;[1]
And this same flower that smiles today,
Tomorrow will be dying.

The glorious lamp of heaven, the sun,
The higher he's a-getting;
The sooner will his race be run,[2]
And nearer he's to setting.

That age is best, which is the first,
When youth and blood are warmer;
But being spent, the worse, and worst
Times still succeed the former.

Then be not coy, but use your time,
And while ye may, go marry;
For having lost but once your prime,
You may for ever tarry.
—1648

[1] *Old ... a-flying* Paraphrase of the Latin *tempus fugit* ("time flies").

[2] *his race be run* The sun's movement was pictured in Greek mythology as the chariot of Phoebus Apollo racing across the sky.

The Hock-Cart, or Harvest Home[3]

To the Right Honorable, Mildmay,
Earl of Westmoreland[4]

Come, sons of summer, by whose toil,
We are the lords of wine and oil;
By whose tough labors, and rough hands,
We rip up first, then reap our lands.
Crowned with the ears of corn, now come,
And, to the pipe, sing harvest home.
Come forth, my Lord, and see the cart
Dressed up with all the country art.
See, here a maukin,[5] there a sheet,
As spotless pure, as it is sweet,
The horses, mares, and frisking fillies,
(Clad, all, in linen, white as lilies).
The harvest swains,° and wenches bound *peasant lads*
For joy, to see the hock-cart crowned.
About the cart, hear how the rout° *crowd*
Of rural younglings raise the shout,
Pressing before, some coming after,
Those with a shout and these with laughter.
Some bless the cart, some kiss the sheaves;
Some prank° them up with oaken leaves: *dress*
Some cross° the fill-horse,° *sit astride / shaft-horse*
some with great
Devotion stroke the home-borne wheat:
While other rustics, less attent° *attentive*
To prayers, than to merriment,
Run after with their breeches rent.
Well, on, brave boys, to your Lord's hearth,
Glittering with fire; where, for your mirth,
Ye shall see first the large and chief
Foundation of your feast, fat beef:
With upper stories, mutton, veal,
And bacon,° (which makes full the meal) *pork*
With several dishes standing by,
As here a custard, there a pie,

[3] *Hock-Cart* The hock-cart, or "high cart" (because piled high), was the last wagon load of the harvest.

[4] *Mildmay ... Westmoreland* Mildmay Fane was Herrick's friend and patron; he published a collection of his own poetry, *Otia Sacra* (1648).

[5] *maukin* Rag doll, made of cloths.

And here all tempting frumenty.[1]
And for to make the merry cheer,
If smirking wine be wanting here,
There's that, which drowns all care, stout beer:
Which freely drink to your Lord's health,
Then to the plough, (the common-wealth),
Next to your flails, your fanes, your vats;[2]
Then to the maids with wheaten° hats: *straw*
To the rough sickle, and crook'd sythe,
Drink, frolic boys, till all be blithe.
 Feed, and grow fat; and as ye eat,
Be mindful, that the laboring neat,° *oxen*
As you, may have their fill of meat.
And know, besides, ye must revoke° *recall*
The patient ox unto the yoke,
And all go back unto the plow
And harrow, though they're hanged up now.
And, you must know, your Lord's word's true,
Feed him ye must, whose food fills you,
And that this pleasure is like rain,
Not sent ye for to drown your pain,
But for to make it spring again.
—1648

Upon Julia's Clothes

Whenas° in silks my Julia goes, *whenever*
Then, then, methinks, how sweetly flows
That liquefaction of her clothes.

Next, when I cast mine eyes and see
That brave° vibration each way free, *beautiful*
Oh, how that glittering taketh me!
—1648

[1] *frumenty* Hulled wheat boiled in milk and flavored with sugar and spices.

[2] *fanes* Winnowing fans; *vats* Storage barrels.

George Herbert

1593 – 1633

Although his contribution to English poetry consists of a single volume, *The Temple*, George Herbert stands in the first rank of the poets of the seventeenth century and, indeed, of all English lyric poets. Born into wealth and privilege, he chose instead a life dedicated to the power of faith and poetry, dying a humble country parson. An early friend and poetic disciple of John Donne, he left behind Donne's learned abstruseness and fashioned instead a modestly artful music that overleaps sectarian boundaries. Immensely influential on the devotional poets of his own century, Herbert in the eighteenth century was celebrated perhaps more for his piety than his poetry. (John Wesley, for instance, turned a number of Herbert's lyrics into hymns, some of which are still sung.) In the nineteenth century his reputation waned, though he was deeply admired by a few major figures, including Coleridge, Emerson, and Hopkins. In the twentieth century Herbert rejoined the poetic mainstream when T.S. Eliot, in his influential 1921 essay "The Metaphysical Poets," lamented the modern "dissociation of sensibility" and praised Herbert as one of the last poets to have consummated a true fusion of feeling and intellect.

George Herbert was born in 1593, the fifth son of a prominent landowning family in the Welsh Border Country. His eldest brother, Edward, Lord Herbert of Cherbury, was a noted philosopher and diplomat. Raised by their widowed mother Magdalen, an intelligent and strong-willed woman, the Herbert children benefitted from a sound education and a lively environment that included a close family friendship with John Donne. George Herbert attended Westminster School in London and later Trinity College at Cambridge, where he stayed on as a tutor and lecturer. His appointment as Public Orator there in 1620 made him spokesman for the University. Able, urbane, and ambitious, Herbert aspired to political prominence, and was named as Member of Parliament in 1624. Soon after, however, with the ascension of a new monarch and the fall from favor of influential friends such as Francis Bacon, Herbert's political fortunes dimmed and his health began to fail. A devoted Anglican all his life, he began to turn more seriously toward the Church, and was ordained deacon in 1624. When his mother died in 1627, John Donne delivered her funeral oration, and Herbert commemorated her with a collection of Latin and Greek verse, *Memoriae Matris Sacrum*.

For the next few years Herbert seems to have lived quietly with friends, nursing his health, pursuing his religious vocation, and writing much of the devotional poetry in English for which he was to become famous. He married in 1629, was ordained a priest in 1630, and devoted his remaining years to his small country parish at Bemerton, near Salisbury. Herbert died in 1633, releasing for publication on his deathbed *The Temple*, a meticulously crafted compilation of devotional and meditative verse that was to achieve immediate popularity, running through at least eleven editions in the seventeenth century alone.

Herbert had been writing poetry as early as 1610, when, in two sonnets sent as a gift to his mother, he declared his intention to consecrate his poetic gifts to the glory of God rather than to erotic or romantic love. With the exception of some occasional pieces and a collection of polemical Latin epigrams written during his tenure as Public Orator, he remained true to his word.

As a collection, *The Temple* is an intricately structured whole, with numerous correspondences and connections among its almost 170 poems. Herbert establishes resonant patterns that link the physical space of the church with the interior space of the human heart, and the cycle of the church year with the spiritual journey of both the individual believer and humanity as a whole. The poems themselves reflect the subtle spiritual struggles of the everyday inner life. Herbert shows the influence of John Donne in his affinity for plain diction and the rhythms of colloquial speech, but he consciously avoids the elaborate conceits, scholarly allusions, and self-dramatizing spiritual anguish found in Donne's devotional verse. Simplicity, or the artfulness of seeming artless, is one of the central themes of Herbert's poetry, and generations of readers and poets have admired Herbert's exquisite craftsmanship, emotional directness, modest wit, elegance and concision of language, and ability to create connections among poetic form, language, and meaning.

⌘⌘⌘

The Altar

A broken ALTAR, Lord thy servant rears,
Made of a heart, and cemented with tears:[1]
Whose parts are as thy hand did frame;
No workman's tool hath touched the same.[2]
A HEART alone
Is such a stone,
As nothing but
Thy pow'r doth cut.
Wherefore° each part — *accordingly*
Of my hard heart
Meets in this frame,
To praise thy name.
That, if I chance to hold my peace,
These stones to praise thee may not cease.[3]
O let thy blessed SACRIFICE be mine,
And sanctify this ALTAR to be thine.
—1633

Redemption

Having been tenant long to a rich Lord,
Not thriving, I resolved to be bold,
And make a suit unto him, to afford° — *grant*
A new small-rented lease, and cancel th' old.
In heaven at his manor I him sought:
They told me there, that he was lately gone
About some land, which he had dearly bought
Long since on earth, to take possession.
I straight returned, and knowing his great birth,
Sought him accordingly in great resorts;
In cities, theatres, gardens, parks, and courts:
At length I heard a ragged noise and mirth
Of thieves and murderers: there I him espied,
Who straight, *Your suit is granted*, said, and died.
—1633

[1] *A broken ... tears* Cf. Psalms 51.17.

[2] *No ... same* Cf. Exodus 20.25.

[3] *That ... cease.* From Luke 19.40.

Easter Wings

Lord, who createdst man in wealth and store,
Though foolishly he lost the same,
Decaying more and more,
Till he became
Most poor:
With thee
O let me rise
As larks, harmoniously,
And sing this day thy victories:
Then shall the fall further the flight in me.

My tender age in sorrow did begin:
And still with sicknesses and shame
Thou didst so punish sin,
That I became
Most thin.
With thee
Let me combine,
And feel this day thy victory:
For, if I imp[1] my wing on thine,
Affliction shall advance the flight in me.

—1633

Affliction (1)

When first thou didst entice to thee my heart,
I thought the service brave:° *splendid*
So many joys I writ down for my part,
Besides what I might have
Out of my stock of natural delights,
Augmented with thy gracious benefits.

I looked on thy furniture so fine,
And made it fine to me:
Thy glorious household-stuff did me entwine,
And 'tice° me unto thee. *entice*
Such stars I counted mine: both heav'n and earth
Paid me my wages in a world of mirth.

What pleasures could I want, whose King I served?
Where joys my fellows were.
Thus argued into hopes, my thoughts reserved
No place for grief or fear.
Therefore my sudden[2] soul caught at[3] the place,
And made her youth and fierceness seek thy face,

At first thou gav'st me milk and sweetnesses;
I had my wish and way:
My days were strawed[4] with flow'rs and happiness;
There was no month but May.
But with my years sorrow did twist and grow,
And made a party° unawares° for woe. *faction / unwittingly*

My flesh began unto my soul in pain,
Sicknesses cleave my bones;
Consuming agues° dwell in ev'ry vein, *fevers*
And tune my breath to groans.
Sorrow was all my soul; I scarce believed,
Till grief did tell me roundly, that I lived.

[1] *imp* Graft feathers from one falcon onto the wing of another, a technique used in falconry to mend damaged wings and improve flight.

[2] *sudden* Rash, impetuous.

[3] *caught at* Eagerly sought.

[4] *strawed* Strewn.

When I got health, thou took'st away my life,
        And more; for my friends die:
My mirth and edge was lost; a blunted knife
        Was of more use than I.
Thus thin and lean without a fence or friend,
I was blown through with ev'ry storm and wind.

Whereas my birth and spirit rather took
        The way that takes the town;
Thou didst betray me to a ling'ring book,
        And wrap me in a gown.[1]
I was entangled in the world of strife,
Before I had the power to change my life.

Yet, for I threat'ned oft the siege to raise,
        Not simp'ring all mine age,
Thou often didst with academic praise
        Melt and dissolve my rage.
I took thy sweet'ned pill, till I came where
I could not go away, nor persevere.

Yet lest perchance I should too happy be
        In my unhappiness,
Turning my purge to food, thou throwest me
        Into more sicknesses.
Thus doth thy power cross-bias[2] me, not making
Thine own gift good, yet me from my ways taking.

Now I am here, what thou wilt do with me
        None of my books will show:
I read, and sigh, and wish I were a tree;
        For sure then I should grow
To fruit or shade: at least some bird would trust
Her household to me, and I should be just.

Yet, though thou troublest me, I must be meek;
        In weakness must be stout.
Well, I will change the service,[3] and go seek
        Some other master out.
Ah my dear God! though I am clean forgot,
Let me not love thee, if I love thee not.
—1633

Prayer (1)

Prayer the Church's banquet, Angels' age,
    God's breath in man returning to his birth,
The soul in paraphrase, heart in pilgrimage,
The Christian plummet sounding heav'n and earth;
Engine[4] against th' Almighty, sinners' tower,[5]
    Reversed thunder, Christ-side-piercing spear,[6]
The six-days world transposing in an hour,
A kind of tune, which all things hear and fear;
Softness, and peace, and joy, and love, and bliss,
    Exalted Manna,[7] gladness of the best,
Heaven in ordinary,[8] man well dressed,
The milky way, the bird of Paradise,[9]
    Church-bells beyond the stars heard, the soul's blood,
The land of spices; something understood.
—1633

Jordan[10] (1)

Who says that fictions only and false hair
    Become° a verse? Is there in truth no beauty? *befit*
Is all good structure in a winding stair?

---

[1] *book ... gown* Symbolic book and gown of Herbert's academic life at Cambridge.

[2] *cross-bias* Deflect from straight or intended course (a metaphor from the game of bowls as well as a play on Christ's cross).

[3] *service* As in domestic service; see also line 2 above.

[4] *Engine* Instrument of war, such as a catapult or battering-ram; also, a device, a stratagem.

[5] *sinners' tower* Alluding to the tower of Babel, in Genesis 11.1–9, and also, perhaps, to the siege tower as an engine of war.

[6] *Christ ... spear* From John 19.34.

[7] *Manna* Food supplied by God to the Israelites in Exodus 16.15.

[8] *ordinary* Everyday clothing.

[9] *bird of Paradise* Tropical bird mistakenly believed to reside constantly in the air.

[10] *Jordan* The river associated with entry into the Promised Land and Christ's baptism, here meant also to suggest the purity and simplicity of Christian poetry as opposed to the artificiality of secular verse.

May no lines pass, except they do their duty
Not to a true, but painted chair?[1]

Is it no verse, except enchanted groves
And sudden arbours shadow coarse-spun lines?[2]
Must purling[3] streams refresh a lover's loves?
Must all be veiled, while he that reads, divines, *interprets*
Catching the sense at two removes?

Shepherds are honest people; let them sing:
Riddle who list, for me, and pull for Prime:[4]
I envy no man's nightingale or spring;
Nor let them punish me with loss of rhyme,
Who plainly say, *My God, My King.*
—1633

Church-Monuments

While that my soul repairs to her devotion,
Here I intomb my flesh, that it betimes° *soon*
May take acquaintance of this heap of dust;
To which the blast of death's incessant motion,
Fed with the exhalation of our crimes,
Drives all at last. Therefore I gladly trust

My body to this school, that it may learn
To spell his elements,[5] and find his birth
Written in dusty heraldry and lines:
Which dissolution sure doth best discern,[6]
Comparing dust with dust, and earth with earth.
These laugh at jet° and marble put for signs, *black stone*

To sever the good fellowship of dust,
And spoil the meeting. What shall point out them,
When they shall bow, and kneel, and fall down flat
To kiss those heaps, which now they have in trust?
Dear flesh, while I do pray, learn here thy stem[7]
And true descent; that when thou shalt grow fat,

And wanton in thy cravings, thou mayst know,
That flesh is but the glass,[8] which holds the dust
That measures all our time; which also shall
Be crumbled into dust. Mark here below
How tame these ashes are, how free from lust,
That thou mayst fit thyself against thy fall.[9]
—1633

The Windows

Lord, how can man preach thy eternal word?
He is a brittle crazy° glass: *cracked*
Yet in thy temple thou dost him afford
This glorious and transcendent place,
To be a window, through thy grace.

But when thou dost anneal[10] in glass thy story,
Making thy life to shine within
The holy Preacher's; then the light and glory
More rev'rend grows, and more doth win:
Which else shows wat'rish, bleak, and thin.

Doctrine and life, colours and light, in one
When they combine and mingle, bring
A strong regard and awe: but speech alone
Doth vanish like a flaring thing,
And in the ear, not conscience ring.
—1633

[1] *painted chair* The meaning here is uncertain. This may be a reference to the ideas of Plato regarding the reality of ideal forms. Some have suggested a reference to the English Royal Throne is intended.

[2] *sudden* Unexpected; *shadow* Camouflage; *coarse-spun* Shoddy.

[3] *purling* Rippling; babbling.

[4] *Riddle who list* Let those who enjoy riddling do so; *pull for Prime* Draw for a winning hand at Primero, a fashionable card game.

[5] *elements* Letters of the alphabet.

[6] *Which … discern* The body best comprehends its own decay.

[7] *stem* Line of ancestry.

[8] *flesh is … glass* A play on "All flesh is grass," Isaiah 40.6, with "glass" here meaning "hourglass."

[9] *against thy fall* Against the individual body's fall into death, but also the original Fall of humankind into sin and death. See Genesis 3.19: "… for dust thou art, and unto dust thou shalt return."

[10] *anneal* Apply heat to stained glass to fix the colors painted on it.

Denial

When my devotions could not pierce
Thy silent ears;
Then was my heart broken, as was my verse:
My breast was full of fears
And disorder:

My bent thoughts, like a brittle bow,
Did fly asunder:
Each took his way; some would to pleasures go,
Some to the wars and thunder
Of alarms.

As good go anywhere, they say,
As to benumb
Both knees and heart, in crying night and day,
Come, come my God, O come,
But no hearing.

O that thou shouldst give dust a tongue
To cry to thee,
And then not hear it crying! all day long
My heart was in my knee,
but no hearing.

Therefore my soul lay out of sight,
Untuned, unstrung:
My feeble spirit, unable to look right,
Like a nipped blossom, hung
Discontented.

O cheer and tune my heartless breast,
Defer no time;[1]
That so thy favours granting my request,
They and my mind may chime,
And mend my rhyme.

—1633

[1] *Defer no time* Wait no longer.

Virtue

Sweet day, so cool, so calm, so bright,
The bridal° of the earth and sky: *wedding*
The dew shall weep thy fall tonight;
For thou must die.

Sweet rose, whose hue angry and brave° *beautiful; splendid*
Bids the rash gazer wipe his eye:
Thy root is ever in its grave,
And thou must die.

Sweet spring, full of sweet days and roses,
A box where sweets compacted lie;
My music shows ye have your closes,[2]
And all must die.

Only a sweet and virtuous soul,
Like seasoned timber, never gives;° *gives way*
But though the whole world turn to coal,[3]
Then chiefly lives.

—1633

Man

My God, I heard this day,
That none doth build a stately habitation,
But he that means to dwell therein.
What house more stately hath there been,
Or can be, than is Man? to° whose creation *next to*
All things are in decay.

For Man is ev'ry thing,
And more: He is a tree, yet bears no fruit;
A beast, yet is, or should be more:
Reason and speech we only bring.
Parrots may thank us, if they are not mute,
They go upon the score.[4]

[2] *closes* Conclusions of phrases or themes in music.

[3] *turn to coal* Be destroyed by fire, as predicted in the Bible.

[4] *They … score* They are in our debt.

Man is all symmetry,
Full of proportions, one limb to another,
And all to all the world besides:
Each part may call the farthest, brother:
For head with foot hath private amity,
And both with moons and tides.

Nothing hath got so far,
But Man hath caught and kept it, as his prey.
His eyes dismount° the highest star: *bring down*
He is in little° all the sphere.° *miniature / world*
Herbs gladly cure our flesh; because that they
Find their acquaintance there.

For us the winds do blow,
The earth doth rest, heav'n move, and fountains flow.
Nothing we see, but means our good,
As our delight, or as our treasure:
The whole is, either our cupboard of food,
Or cabinet of pleasure.

The stars have us to bed;
Night draws the curtain, which the sun withdraws;
Music and light attend our head.
All things unto our flesh are kind° *akin*
In their descent° and being; to our mind *becoming*
In their ascent° and cause. *origin*

Each thing is full of duty:
Waters united are our navigation;
Distinguished,[1] our habitation;
Below, our drink; above, our meat;
Both are our cleanliness. Hath one° such beauty? *one thing*
Then how are all things neat?° *excellent*

More servants wait on Man,
Than he'll take notice of: in ev'ry path
He treads down that which doth befriend him,
When sickness makes him pale and wan.[2]
O mighty love! Man is one world, and hath
Another to attend him.

Since then, my God, thou hast
So brave° a Palace built; O dwell in it, *splendid*
That it may dwell with thee at last!
Till then, afford us so much wit;
That, as the world serves us, we may serve thee,
And both thy servants be.
—1633

Jordan (2)

When first my lines of heav'nly joys made mention,
Such was their lustre, they did so excel,
That I sought out quaint words, and trim invention;
My thoughts began to burnish, sprout, and swell,
Curling with metaphors a plain intention,
Decking° the sense, as if it were to sell. *adorning*

Thousands of notions in my brain did run,
Off'ring their service, if I were not sped:° *successful*
I often blotted what I had begun;
This was not quick° enough, and that was dead. *lively*
Nothing could seem too rich to clothe the sun,
Much less those joys which trample on his head.

As flames do work and wind, when they ascend,
So did I weave my self into the sense.
But while I bustled, I might hear a friend
Whisper, *How wide is all this long pretence!*
There is in love a sweetness ready penned;
Copy out only that, and save expense.
—1633

Time

Meeting with Time, slack° thing, said I, *remiss*
Thy scythe is dull; whet it for shame.
No marvel Sir, he did reply,
If it at length deserve some blame:
But where one man would have me grind it,
Twenty for one[3] too sharp do find it.

[1] *Distinguished* Separated.

[2] *He treads … wan* Referring to the herbs mentioned above that "gladly cure our flesh."

[3] *Twenty for one* Twenty men for every one.

Perhaps some such of old did pass,
Who above all things loved this life;
To whom thy scythe a hatchet was,
Which now is but a pruning-knife.
Christ's coming hath made man thy debtor,
Since by thy cutting he grows better.

And in his blessing thou art blessed;
For where thou only wert° before *were*
An executioner at best;
Thou art a gard'ner now, and more,
An usher to convey our souls
Beyond the utmost stars and poles.

And this is that makes life so long,
While it detains us from our God.
Ev'n pleasures here increase the wrong,
And length of days lengthen the rod.° *punishment*
Who wants° the place, where God doth dwell, *lacks*
Partakes already half of hell.

Of what strange length must that needs be,
Which ev'n eternity excludes!
Thus far Time heard me patiently:
Then chafing said, This man deludes:
What do I here before his door?
He doth not crave less time, but more.
—1633

The Bunch of Grapes[1]

Joy, I did lock thee up: but some bad man
Hath let thee out again:
And now, methinks, I am where I began
Sev'n years ago: one vogue and vein,
One air of thoughts usurps my brain.
I did toward Canaan draw; but now I am
Brought back to the Red Sea, the sea of shame.[2]
For as the Jews of old by God's command
Travelled, and saw no town:
So now each Christian hath his journeys spanned:[3]
Their story pens and sets us down.
A single deed is small renown.
God's works are wide, and let in future times;
His ancient justice overflows our crimes.

Then have we too our guardian fires and clouds;[4]
Our Scripture-dew drops fast:
We have our sands and serpents, tents and shrouds;[5]
Alas! our murmurings come not last.
But where's the cluster? where's the taste
Of mine inheritance? Lord, if I must borrow,
Let me as well take up their joy, as sorrow.

But can he want the grape, who hath the wine?
I have their fruit and more.
Blessèd be God, who prospered Noah's vine,[6]
And make it bring forth grapes good store.
But much more him I must adore,
Who of the law's sour juice sweet wine did make,
Ev'n God himself, being pressed for my sake.
—1633

The Collar

I struck the board,° and cried, No more. *table*
I will abroad.° *go abroad; depart*
What? shall I ever° sigh and pine? *always*
My lines and life are free; free as the road,
Loose as the wind, as large as store.° *abundance*
Shall I be still in suit?[7]
Have I no harvest but a thorn
To let me blood,° and not restore *bleed*
What I have lost with cordial fruit?
Sure there was wine
Before my sighs did dry it: there was corn

[1] *Bunch of Grapes* Cluster of grapes brought by scouts to Moses from the Promised Land of Canaan as evidence of its fertility: see Numbers 13.23.

[2] *I did … shame* On the brink of attaining the Promised Land, the Israelites were condemned by the Lord for their faithlessness to wander the desert for 40 years (thus returning in the direction of the Red Sea): see Numbers 14.22–35.

[3] *spanned* Limited.

[4] *guardian … clouds* Cf. Exodus 13.21.

[5] *shrouds* Shelters.

[6] *Noah's vine* Vineyard planted by Noah with the Lord's blessing after the Flood: see Genesis 9.20.

[7] *in suit* In attendance.

Before my tears did drown it.
Is the year only lost to me?
Have I no bays° to crown it? *laurel wreaths*
No flowers, no garlands gay? All blasted?
All wasted?
Not so, my heart: but there is fruit,
And thou hast hands.[1]
Recover all thy sigh-blown age
On double pleasures: leave thy cold dispute
Of what is fit, and not. Forsake thy cage,
Thy rope of sands,[2]
Which petty thoughts have made, and made to thee
Good cable, to enforce and draw,
And be thy law,
While thou didst wink[3] and wouldst not see.
Away; take heed:
I will abroad.
Call in thy death's head° there: tie up thy fears. *skull*
He that forbears° *neglects*
To suit and serve his need,
Deserves his load.
But as I raved and grew more fierce and wild
At every word,
Me thoughts I heard one calling, *Child:*
And I replied, *My Lord.*
—1633

The Pulley

When God at first made man,
Having a glass of blessings standing by,
Let us (said he) pour on him all we can:
Let the world's riches, which dispersed lie,
Contract into a span.[4]

So strength first made a way;
Then beauty flowed, then wisdom, honour, pleasure:
When almost all was out, God made a stay,° *paused*
Perceiving that alone of all his treasure
Rest in the bottom lay.

For if I should (said he)
Bestow this jewel also on my creature,
He would adore my gifts instead of me,
And rest in Nature, not the God of Nature:
So both should losers be.

Yet let him keep the rest,
But keep them with repining° restlessness: *fretful*
Let him be rich and weary, that at least,
If goodness lead him not, yet weariness
May toss him to my breast.
—1633

The Flower

How fresh, O Lord, how sweet and clean
Are thy returns! ev'n as the flowers in spring;
To which, besides their own demean,[5]
The late-past frosts tributes of pleasure bring.
Grief melts away
Like snow in May,
As if there were no such cold thing.

Who would have thought my shrivelled heart
Could have recovered greenness? It was gone
Quite underground; as flowers depart
To see their mother-root, when they have blown;° *bloomed*
Where they together
All the hard weather,
Dead to the world, keep house unknown.

These are thy wonders, Lord of power,
Killing and quick'ning,[6] bringing down to hell
And up to heaven in an hour;

[1] *but ... hands* An echo of the disobedience that led to the original Fall; see Genesis 3.22: " lest he put forth his hand, and take also of the tree of life."

[2] *rope of sands* Delusive security. To "twist a rope of sand" is also a proverbial expression of futility.

[3] *wink* Shut one's eyes.

[4] *span* Distance between the tip of the thumb and little finger of an extended hand.

[5] *demean* Demesne, or estate, where a tenant might pay tributes to the landlord.

[6] *quick'ning* Bringing to life.

Making a chiming of a passing-bell.[1]
We say amiss,
This or that is:
Thy word is all, if we could spell.° *comprehend*

O that I once past changing were,
Fast in thy Paradise, where no flower can wither!
Many a spring I shoot up fair,
Off'ring° at heav'n, growing and groaning thither:
Nor doth my flower
Want° a spring-shower, *lack*
My sins and I joining together:

But while I grow in a straight line,
Still upwards bent, as if heav'n were mine own,
Thy anger comes, and I decline:
What° frost to that? what pole is not the zone,
Where all things burn,
When thou dost turn,
And the least frown of thine is shown?

And now in age I bud again,
After so many deaths I live and write;
I once more smell the dew and rain,
And relish versing: O my only light,
It cannot be
That I am he
On whom thy tempests fell all night.

These are thy wonders, Lord of love,
To make us see we are but flowers that glide:[2]
Which when we once can find and prove,[3]
Thou hast a garden for us, where to bide.
Who° would be more, *those who*
Swelling through store,° *abundance; wealth*
Forfeit their Paradise by their pride.
—1633

[1] *passing-bell* Bell tolled to mark a death.

[2] *flowers that glide* Flowers that pass away silently, imperceptibly. Cf. Job 14.2: "Man cometh forth like a flower, and is cut down; he fleeteth also like a shadow, and continueth not."

[3] *prove* Confirm through experience.

Discipline

Throw away thy rod,
Throw away thy wrath:
O my God,
Take the gentle path.

For my heart's desire
Unto thine is bent:
I aspire
To a full consent.

Not a word or look
I affect to own,
But by book,
And thy book alone.

Though I fail, I weep:
Though I halt in pace,
Yet I creep
To the throne of grace.

Then let wrath remove;° *depart*
Love will do the deed:
For with love
Stony hearts will bleed.

Love is swift of foot;
Love's a man of war,[4]
And can shoot,
And can hit from far.

Who can scape° his bow? *escape*
That which wrought° on thee, *worked*
Brought thee low,
Needs must work on me.

Throw away thy rod;
Though man frailties hath,
Thou art God:
Throw away thy wrath.
—1633

[4] *Love's ... war* Cf. Exodus 15.3: "The Lord is a man of war." Also, an armed naval vessel.

Death

Death, thou wast once an uncouth hideous thing,
Nothing but bones,
The sad effect of sadder groans:
Thy mouth was open, but thou couldst not sing.

For we considered thee as at some six
Or ten years hence,
After the loss of life and sense,
Flesh being turned to dust, and bones to sticks.

We looked on this side of thee, shooting short;
Where we did find
The shells of fledge[1] souls left behind,
Dry dust, which sheds no tears, but may extort.

But since our Saviour's death did put some blood
Into thy face;
Thou art grown fair and full of grace,
Much in request, much sought for, as a good.

For we do now behold thee gay and glad,
As at doomsday;
When souls shall wear their new array,° *clothing*
And all thy bones with beauty shall be clad.

Therefore we can go die as sleep, and trust
Half that we have
Unto an honest faithful grave;
Making our pillows either down, or dust.
—1633

Love (3)

Love bade me welcome: yet my soul drew back,
Guilty of dust and sin.
But quick-eyed Love, observing me grow slack[2]
From my first entrance in,
Drew nearer to me, sweetly questioning,
If I lacked anything.
A guest, I answered, worthy to be here:
Love said, You shall be he.
I the unkind, ungrateful? Ah my dear,
I cannot look on thee.
Love took my hand, and smiling did reply,
Who made the eyes but I?
Truth Lord, but I have marred them: let my shame
Go where it doth deserve.
And know you not, says Love, who bore the blame?
My dear, then I will serve.
You must sit down, says Love, and taste my meat:[3] So
I did sit and eat.
—1633

[1] *fledge* Ready to fly.

[2] *grow slack* Become hesitant or uncertain.

[3] *My dear … my meat.* Cf. Luke 12.37: "Blessed are those servants, whom the Lord when he cometh shall find watching: verily I say unto you, that he shall gird himself, and make them to sit down to meat, and will come forth and serve them."

Andrew Marvell

1621 – 1678

In his life as well as in his writing, Andrew Marvell is elusive. Famous long after his death as a spokesman for political and religious liberty, the intensely private Marvell kept his personal opinions largely to himself. His verse is complex, full of paradoxes and ironies, and is frequently mediated through naive or ambivalent personae who present debates or balance competing claims. His poem "An Horation Ode upon Cromwell's Return from Ireland" oscillates between praise for (and veiled criticism of) both Oliver Cromwell, who choreographed the abolition of the monarchy in 1649, and admiration for King Charles I, who was executed in the process. (Later, he would satirize the restored monarchy of Charles II.) A poet who wrote seductive and titillating love poetry, Marvell was also a politician who lampooned the government in satires for which he was renowned in his day. Even after death, mystery surrounded his life; in order to keep creditors of his estate at bay a few years later, his housekeeper, Mary Palmer, claimed to have been the author's wife and published his *Miscellaneous Poems* (1681), which included a preface by "Mary Marvell" guaranteeing the poems to be the "exact copies of my late dear husband."

Marvell, the son of Anne Pease and the Reverend Andrew Marvell, was born in 1621 in Winestead, but was raised primarily in Hull. At age twelve he was admitted to the University of Cambridge, where he studied for the following seven years and where he published his first poems, written in Latin and Greek. Before he had completed his degree, his father drowned and Marvell left England to travel on the Continent, perhaps to wait out the period of the Civil War (1642–47). In a letter of 1653 proposing that Marvell be given the post of Assistant Latin Secretary to the Council of State, Milton mentioned that Marvell had been abroad for four years and that on this journey he had learned to speak Dutch, French, Italian, and Spanish. (He did not win the appointment at that time, but it was awarded to him four years later.) In 1650 Marvell wrote "An Horation Ode Upon Cromwell's Return from Ireland," one of his best known and most widely studied poems. Written in a complex style that marks much of his subsequent work, the "Ode" defies definitive interpretation but instead raises many political and ideological questions. Scholars continue to disagree over Marvell's allegiance to Cromwell, whose armies had just completed a bloody mission in Ireland.

Later in 1650 Marvell began working as a tutor to the twelve-year-old daughter of Thomas, Lord Fairfax, the retired Commander-in-Chief of the Parliamentary Army. In the poem "Upon Appleton House," Marvell celebrates the architecture and inhabitants of the Fairfax home. It is likely that during his two years on this estate he composed many of his most famous works, including much of his pastoral poetry and the poems "The Definition of Love" and "Dialogue Between the Soul and the Body." In the sensuous and witty *carpe diem* poem "To His Coy Mistress," also likely written in this period, Marvell's speaker tries to convince his love of the brevity of life and the need to seize the moment of passion.

In 1653, the year in which Cromwell declared himself Lord Protector of England, Marvell was appointed tutor to a ward of Cromwell, William Dutton. Along with Milton and Dryden, Marvell took part in Cromwell's 1659 funeral procession, but despite his ties to the republican regime his political career flourished upon the restoration of a Royalist Parliament. In 1659 he was elected Member of Parliament for Hull, a seat he would maintain until his death. While in office, Marvell was outspoken in his contempt for Charles II, who was restored to the monarchy in 1660; in his 1667 satire *The Last Instructions to a Painter*, he ridiculed the King and his government for their ineffectuality. Marvell took part in a diplomatic mission to Holland in 1662–63 and another to Russia, Sweden, and Denmark in 1665; these operations served to strengthen his criticism of corruption in the government, which he recorded in numerous pamphlets and newsletters and circulated to his constituents.

When Marvell died of complications from a fever in 1678, there was still an outstanding government reward offered for the name of the man who had written "An Account of the Growth of Popery and Arbitrary Government in England" a year earlier. More satires and poems were published posthumously as a result of Mary Palmer's efforts, but they fell into relative obscurity in the following century as readers began to perceive his metaphysical conceits as cold and discordant. The nineteenth century saw something of a revival of his poetry; Wordsworth praised his work, and Tennyson recognized him as "the green poet" for his sensuous pastoral poems. In the twentieth century Marvell's reputation was firmly re-established by T.S. Eliot, who championed him as one of the finest of the "metaphysical" poets.

⌘⌘⌘

The Coronet

When for the thorns with which I long, too long,
With many a piercing wound,
My Saviour's head have crowned,
I seek with garlands to redress that wrong:
Through every garden, every mead,° *meadow*
I gather flowers (my fruits are only flowers),[1]
Dismantling all the fragrant towers[2]
That once adorned my shepherdess's head.
And now, when I have summed up all my store,
Thinking (so I myself deceive)
So rich a chaplet thence to weave
As never yet the King of Glory wore:
Alas! I find the serpent old
That, twining in his speckled breast,
About the flowers disguised does fold,
With wreaths of fame and interest.
Ah, foolish man, that wouldst debase with them,
And mortal glory, Heaven's diadem!
But thou[3] who only couldst the serpent tame,
Either his slippery knots at once untie,
And disentangle all his winding snare:
Or shatter too with him my curious frame,[4]
And let these wither, so that he may die,
Though set with skill, and chosen out with care:
That they, while thou on both their spoils dost tread,
May crown thy feet, that could not crown thy head.
—1681 (PROBABLY WRITTEN IN THE 1640S)

[1] *fruits ... flowers* With verbal play on "fruits" as accomplishments, the "fruits" of his efforts (spiritual and literary); and on "flowers" as poems or poetic tropes (anthologies in the period could gather "flowers of poetry" or "flowers of rhetoric").

[2] *fragrant towers* Floral garlands; but also the secular love poems the poet had made for his beloved.

[3] *thou* Christ.

[4] *curious frame* Clever or ingenious structure: the floral garland or chaplet within the fiction of the poem, and the "Coronet" that is the poem itself.

Bermudas

Where the remote Bermudas ride,
In the ocean's bosom unespied,
From a small boat, that rowed along,
The listening winds received this song:
"What should we do but sing his praise
That led us through the watery maze,
Unto an isle so long unknown,[1]
And yet far kinder than our own?
Where He the huge sea-monsters wracks,[2]
That lift the deep upon their backs,
He lands us on a grassy stage,
Safe from the storms, and prelate's rage.[3]
He gave us this eternal spring,
Which here enamels every thing,
And sends the fowls to us in care,
On daily visits through the air.
He hangs in shades the orange bright,
Like golden lamps in a green night,
And does in the pom'granates close° *enclose*
Jewels more rich than Ormus shows.[4]
He makes the figs our mouths to meet,
And throws the melons at our feet;
But apples plants of such a price,
No tree could ever bear them twice;
With cedars chosen by His hand,
From Lebanon, He stores the land,
And makes the hollow seas that roar,
Proclaim the ambergris[5] on shore;
He cast (of which we rather boast)
The Gospel's pearl upon our coast,
And in these rocks for us did frame
A temple where to sound His name.
Oh let our voice His praise exalt,
Till it arrive at heaven's vault,
Which, thence (perhaps) rebounding, may
Echo beyond the Mexique Bay."
Thus sung they, in the English boat,
An holy and a cheerful note;
And all the way, to guide their chime,
With falling oars they kept the time.

—1681 (PROBABLY WRITTEN C. 1653–54)

[1] *Unto an isle ... unknown* Although the Spanish had landed on (and named) Bermuda in 1515, English seafarers first reached the island in 1609, when an expedition on its way to Jamestown landed there during a storm; Shakespeare is thought to have drawn on accounts of their "miraculous" survival for *The Tempest.* An English colony was founded on the island soon after, and early accounts, such as Lewis Hughes's *A letter, sent to England from the Summer Islands* (1615) and John Smith's *General History of Virginia, the Summer Isles, and New England* (1624), stressed Bermuda's paradisal qualities. Bermuda was sometimes called Somers' or Summer Island, after Sir George Somers, the admiral of the first English expedition that landed there.

[2] *wracks* Casts ashore; Marvell is probably referring to a mock-heroic poem by Edmund Waller, "The Battle of the Summer Islands" (1645), which describes attempts by the colonists to kill two stranded whales.

[3] *prelate's rage* This phrase situates the poem in the 1630s, when religious Independents (Congregationalists) left England as a result of attempts by William Laud, Archbishop of Canterbury, to impose uniformity in Church practice. In the early 1650s, Marvell lived in the house of the John Oxenbridge, a religious Independent who had twice been to Bermuda, and who in 1655 would become Governor of the Somers Islands Company. This poem was written at least in part as a compliment to Oxenbridge.

[4] *Ormus* Hormuz, near the entrance to the Persian Gulf, an international market proverbial for the riches on display.

[5] *ambergris* Wax-like substance secreted by sperm whales, valuable for its use in perfume.

A Dialogue between the Soul and Body

SOUL

O, who shall from this dungeon raise
A soul, enslaved so many ways?
With bolts of bones, that fettered stands
In feet, and manacled in hands.
Here blinded with an eye; and there
Deaf with the drumming of an ear.
A soul hung up, as 'twere, in chains
Of nerves, and arteries, and veins,
Tortured, besides each other part,
In a vain head, and double heart.

BODY

O, who shall me deliver whole,
From bonds of this tyrannic soul?
Which, stretched upright, impales me so,

That mine own precipice I go;[1]
And warms and moves this needless frame
(A fever could but do the same),
And, wanting where its spite to try,
Has made me live to let me die,
A body that could never rest,
Since this ill spirit it possessed.

SOUL

What magic could me thus confine
Within another's grief to pine?
Where, whatsoever it complain,
I feel, that cannot feel, the pain.
And all my care itself employs,
That to preserve, which me destroys:
Constrained not only to endure
Diseases, but, what's worse, the cure:
And ready oft the port to gain,[2]
Am shipwrecked into health again.

BODY

But physic yet could never teach
The maladies thou me dost reach:
Whom first the cramp of hope does tear,
And then the palsy shakes of fear;
The pestilence of love does heat,
Or hatred's hidden ulcer eat;
Joy's cheerful madness does perplex,
Or sorrow's other madness vex;
Which knowledge forces me to know,
And memory will not forgo.
What but a soul could have the wit
To build me up for sin so fit?
So architects do square and hew,
Green trees that in the forest grew.[3]

—1681 (PROBABLY WRITTEN AFTER 1652)

[1] *mine own precipice* The body complains that, being upright, it is a moving precipice.

[2] *the port to gain* That is, the death of the body, which "lands" the soul in eternal life.

[3] *What but ... forest grew* These last four lines are crossed out by hand in an important copy of Marvell's 1681 *Poems* that contains several additional poems in manuscript; the annotator has also added the words "desunt multa" ("much is missing").

The Nymph Complaining for the Death of Her Fawn

The wanton troopers[4] riding by
Have shot my fawn, and it will die.
Ungentle men! They cannot thrive
To kill thee. Thou ne'er didst alive
Them any harm; alas, nor could
Thy death yet do them any good.
I'm sure I never wished them ill;
Nor do I for all this, nor will:
But if my simple prayers may yet
Prevail with heaven to forget
Thy murder, I will join my tears
Rather than fail. But, O my fears!
It cannot die so. Heaven's King
Keeps register of every thing:
And nothing may we use in vain.
Even beasts must be with justice slain,
Else men are made their deodands.[5]
Though they should wash their guilty hands
In this warm life-blood which doth part
From thine, and wound me to the heart,
Yet could they not be clean: their stain
Is dyed in such a purple grain.
There is not such another in
The world, to offer for their sin.
Unconstant Sylvio, when yet
I had not found him counterfeit,
One morning (I remember well),
Tied in this silver chain and bell
Gave it to me: nay, and I know
What he said then, I'm sure I do.
Said he, "Look how your huntsman here
Hath taught a fawn to hunt his dear."[6]
But Sylvio soon had me beguiled.

[4] *troopers* Cavalry soldiers; the word was first used of soldiers in the Scottish ("Covenanting") army that invaded England in 1640, and during the civil wars was associated with Parliamentary soldiers.

[5] *deodands* Literally, "things given to God": possessions (including animals) that caused a person's death and were therefore forfeited to the king to be used for pious purposes, for example, to be given to the poor and hungry; the nymph suggests that people who unjustly cause an animal's death should be treated likewise.

[6] *dear* Sylvio makes the obvious pun on "deer."

This waxèd tame, while he grew wild,
And quite regardless of my smart,
Left me his fawn, but took his heart.
Thenceforth I set myself to play
My solitary time away
With this: and very well content,
Could so mine idle life have spent.
For it was full of sport, and light
Of foot and heart, and did invite
Me to its game; it seemed to bless
Itself in me. How could I less
Than love it? O, I cannot be
Unkind to a beast that loveth me.
Had it lived long, I do not know
Whether it too might have done so
As Sylvio did; his gifts might be
Perhaps as false, or more, than he.
But I am sure, for aught that I
Could in so short a time espy,
Thy love was far more better then° *than*
The love of false and cruel men.
With sweetest milk and sugar first
I it at mine own fingers nursed.
And as it grew, so every day
It waxed more white and sweet than they.
It had so sweet a breath! And oft
I blushed to see its foot more soft
And white (shall I say than my hand?
Nay, any lady's of the land).
It is a wondrous thing, how fleet
'Twas on those little silver feet.
With what a pretty skipping grace,
It oft would challenge me the race:
And, when 't had left me far away,
'Twould stay, and run again, and stay.
For it was nimbler much than hinds;
And trod, as on the foúr[1] winds.
I have a garden of my own,
But so with roses overgrown,
And lilies, that you would it guess
To be a little wilderness.
And all the springtime of the year
It only lovèd to be there.
Among the beds of lilies, I
Have sought it oft, where it should lie;
Yet could not, till itself would rise,
Find it, although before mine eyes.
For, in the flaxen lilies' shade,
It like a bank of lilies laid.
Upon the roses it would feed,
Until its lips e'en seem to bleed:
And then to me 'twould boldly trip,
And print those roses on my lip.
But all its chief delight was still
On roses thus itself to fill:
And its pure virgin limbs to fold
In whitest sheets of lilies cold.
Had it lived long, it would have been
Lilies without, roses within.
O help! O help! I see it faint:
And die as calmly as a saint.
See how it weeps. The tears do come
Sad, slowly, dropping like a gum.
So weeps the wounded balsam: so
The holy frankincense doth flow.
The brotherless Heliades[2]
Melt in such amber tears as these.
I in a golden vial will
Keep these two crystal tears; and fill
It till it do o'erflow with mine;
Then place it in Diana's shrine.[3]
Now my sweet fawn is vanished to
Whither the swans and turtles° go: *turtledoves*
In fair Elysium to endure,
With milk-white lambs, and ermines pure.
O do not run too fast: for I
Will but bespeak thy grave, and die.
First, my unhappy statue shall
Be cut in marble; and withal,
Let it be weeping too: but there
The engraver sure his art may spare,
For I so truly thee bemoan,

[1] *foúr* Pronounced as two syllables.

[2] *Heliades* Daughters of Helios, the sun; while weeping over the death of their brother Phaethon they were transformed into poplar trees that wept amber tears (a story from Ovid's *Metamorphoses*).

[3] *Diana* Roman goddess of chastity, the moon, and hunting; according to a story in Ovid's *Metamorphoses*, her pet stag was killed during a hunt.

That I shall weep, though I be stone:[1]
Until my tears, still dropping, wear
My breast, themselves engraving there.
There at my feet shalt thou be laid,
Of purest alabaster made:
For I would have thine image be
White as I can, though not as thee.
—c. 1681

To His Coy Mistress

Had we but world enough, and time,
This coyness Lady were no crime.
We would sit down, and think which way
To walk, and pass our long love's day.
Thou by the Indian Ganges' side
Shouldst rubies find: I by the tide
Of Humber[2] would complain. I would
Love you ten years before the Flood:
And you should, if you please, refuse
Till the conversion of the Jews.[3]
My vegetable love[4] should grow
Vaster than empires, and more slow.
An hundred years should go to praise
Thine eyes, and on thy forehead gaze.
Two hundred to adore each breast:
But thirty thousand to the rest.
An age at least to every part,
And the last age should show your heart:
For Lady you deserve this state;
Nor would I love at lower rate.
  But at my back I always hear
Time's wingèd chariot hurrying near:
And yonder all before us lie
Deserts of vast eternity.
Thy beauty shall no more be found;
Nor, in thy marble vault, shall sound
My echoing song: then worms shall try[5]
That long-preserved virginity:
And your quaint honour turn to dust;
And into ashes all my lust.
The grave's a fine and private place,
But none, I think, do there embrace.
  Now, therefore, while the youthful glew[6]
Sits on thy skin like morning dew,
And while thy willing soul transpires
At every pore with instant fires,
Now let us sport us while we may;
And now, like amorous birds of prey,
Rather at once our time devour,
Than languish in his slow-chapped power.[7]
Let us roll all our strength, and all
Our sweetness, up into one ball:
And tear our pleasures with rough strife,
Thorough° the iron gates[8] of life. *through*

[1] *I shall weep, though I be stone* Like Niobe, who continued to weep after she was turned into stone by Zeus. Niobe wept for the loss of her many children, who died as punishment for Niobe's excessive maternal pride (she had boasted that she was a more impressive mother than Latona, who only had two children, Apollo and Artemis/Diana). From Ovid's *Metamorphoses*.

[2] *Humber* River in northern England; it flowed alongside Hull, Marvell's home town.

[3] *conversion of the Jews* Event supposed to usher in the final Millenium leading to the end of time. Jews were officially readmitted to England in 1655 (after being expelled in 1290), primarily as a result of widespread millenarian hopes that their return would speed up the process of conversion.

[4] *vegetable love* His love (or its physical manifestation) would grow slowly and steadily: Aristotle had defined the vegetative part of the soul as that characterized only by growth.

[5] *try* Test, and taste.

[6] *youthful glew / … morning dew* One of the more famous textual problems in English literature. The 1681 printed edition has "youthful hew / … morning glew." The version of the 1681 text with manuscript corrections changes this reading to "youthful glew / … morning dew." Another manuscript, a transcription of the entire poem dated 1672, reads "youthful glue / … morning dew." Many modern editions conflate the first line of the 1681 edition with the second line from the two manuscript versions, producing the decorous "youthful hue/ … morning dew." But the original manuscript reading does seem to have been "glew," a word then read by one transcriber as "glue," and changed by a puzzled 1681 printer to "hew." "Glew" appears to mean sweat, which sits on the Lady's skin like dewdrops (and is evaporating from her pores in lines 35-36). The image might seem unusual, but is in keeping with the violent, passionate physicality of the poem's final section. "Glew" might be a northern dialect spelling of "glow," a word that could imply sexual ardour.

[7] *slow-chapped* Slowly devouring; "chaps" are jaws.

[8] *gates* "Grates" in the 1681 printed edition with manuscript corrections. But many editors see "gates of life" as a typically Marvellian inversion of the Biblical "gates of death" (Psalm 9.13).

Thus, though we cannot make our sun
Stand still,[1] yet we will make him run.
—1681

The Picture of Little T.C. in a Prospect of Flowers[2]

1

See with what simplicity
This nymph begins her golden days!
In the green grass she loves to lie,
And there with her fair aspect tames
The wilder flowers, and gives them names:[3]
But only with the roses plays;
And them does tell
What colour best becomes them, and what smell.

2

Who can foretell for what high cause
This Darling of the Gods was born!
Yet this is she whose chaster laws
The wanton Love shall one day fear,
And, under her command severe,
See his bow broke and ensigns torn,
Happy, who can
Appease this virtuous enemy of man!

3

O, then let me in time compound,[4]
And parley with those conquering eyes;
Ere they have tried their force to wound,
Ere, with their glancing wheels, they drive
In triumph over hearts that strive,
And them that yield but more despise.
Let me be laid,
Where I may see thy glories from some shade.

4

Meantime, whilst every verdant thing
Itself does at thy beauty charm,
Reform the errors of the spring;
Make that the tulips may have share
Of sweetness, seeing they are fair;
And roses of their thorns disarm:
But most procure
That violets may a longer age endure.

5

But, O young beauty of the woods,
Whom Nature courts with fruits and flowers,
Gather the flowers, but spare the buds;
Lest Flora angry at thy crime,[5]
To kill her infants in their prime,
Do quickly make the example yours;
And, ere we see,
Nip in the blossom all our hopes and thee.
—1681 (PROBABLY WRITTEN IN THE EARLY 1650S)

The Mower against Gardens

Luxurious man, to bring his vice in use,
Did after him the world seduce,
And from the fields the flowers and plants allure,
Where nature was most plain and pure.
He first enclosed within the gardens square
A dead and standing pool of air,
And a more luscious earth for them did knead,
Which stupefied them while it fed.
The pink grew then as double as his mind;
The nutriment did change the kind.
With strange perfumes he did the roses taint,
And flowers themselves were taught to paint.
The tulip, white, did for complexion seek,

[1] *sun / Stand still* Referring ultimately to Joshua 10.12–14, when Joshua made the sun and moon stand still while his army slaughtered the Amorites; but also invoking a traditional trope of love poetry in which lovers ask for time to slow down or stop when in one another's company.

[2] *T.C.* Probably Theophila Cornewall (b. 1644), whose mother was a member of a family, the Skinners, with whom Marvell was familiar. "Darling of the Gods" (line 10) is a literal translation of "Theophila."

[3] *gives them names* Associating "T.C." with Eve, traditionally said to have named the flowers in Eden (*Paradise Lost*, 11.277).

[4] *compound* "Come to terms with." The word also had a political resonance in the period: Royalists "compounded" by paying a fine to avoid confiscation of their estates.

[5] *Flora* Roman goddess of flowers.

And learned to interline its cheek:
Its onion root they then so high did hold,
That one was for a meadow sold.[1]
Another world was searched, through oceans new,
To find the *Marvel of Peru*.[2]
And yet these rarities might be allowed
To man, that sovereign thing and proud,
Had he not dealt between the bark and tree,[3]
Forbidden mixtures there to see.
No plant now knew the stock from which it came;
He grafts upon the wild the tame:
That the uncertain and adulterate fruit
Might put the palate in dispute.
His green seraglio has its eunuchs too,
Lest any tyrant him outdo.
And in the cherry he does nature vex,
To procreate without a sex.[4]
'Tis all enforced, the fountain and the grot,
While the sweet fields do lie forgot:
Where willing Nature does to all dispense
A wild and fragrant innocence:
And fauns and fairies do the meadows till,
More by their presence than their skill.
Their statues, polished by some ancient hand,
May to adorn the gardens stand:
But howsoe'er the figures do excel,
The gods themselves with us[5] do dwell.
—1681 (probably written in the early 1650s)

[1] *for a meadow sold* Referring to the speculative bubble of the "tulip mania" in Holland in the 1630s, during which spectacular prices were paid for some bulbs.

[2] *Marvel of Peru* Much prized multi-colored tropical flower of South America (and possibly with a pun on the poet's name).

[3] *between the bark and tree* "To deal between the bark and the tree" was a proverbial expression for interfering activity, often to interfering between husband and wife; the proverb is here made literal through its reference to grafting.

[4] *And in the cherry ... a sex* Probably referring to attempts to create, through grafting, stoneless cherries (hence "eunuchs").

[5] *with us* With mowers (not with gardeners).

Damon the Mower

1

Hark how the Mower Damon sung,
With love of Juliana stung!
While everything did seem to paint
The scene more fit for his complaint.
Like her fair eyes the day was fair,
But scorching like his am'rous care.
Sharp like his scythe his sorrow was,
And withered like his hopes the grass.

2

"Oh what unusual heats are here,
Which thus our sunburned meadows sear!
The grasshopper its pipe gives o'er;
And hamstringed frogs can dance no more.[6]
But in the brook the green frog wades;
And grasshoppers seek out the shades.
Only the snake, that kept within,
Now glitters in its second skin.

3

"This heat the sun could never raise,
Nor Dog Star[7] so inflame the days.
It from an higher beauty groweth,
Which burns the fields and mower both:
Which mads the dog, and makes the sun
Hotter than his own Phaëton.[8]
Not Jùly causeth these extremes,
But Juliana's scorching beams.

4

"Tell me where I may pass the fires
Of the hot day, or hot desires.
To what cool cave shall I descend,

[6] *hamstringed* Lamed or disabled (figuratively) by the heat.

[7] *Dog Star* Sirius; associated with the "dog days" of July and August, the period when Sirius rises at the same time as the sun.

[8] *Phaëton* Son of the sun god, who set part of the world on fire when driving his father's chariot.

Or to what gelid° fountain bend? *cold*
Alas! I look for ease in vain,
When remedies themselves complain.
No moisture but my tears do rest,
Nor cold but in her icy breast.

5

"How long wilt thou, fair shepherdess,
Esteem me, and my presents less?
To thee the harmless snake I bring,
Disarmèd of its teeth and sting;
To thee chameleons, changing hue,
And oak leaves tipped with honey dew.
Yet thou, ungrateful, hast not sought
Nor what they are, nor who them brought.

6

"I am the Mower Damon, known
Through all the meadows I have mown.
On me the morn her dew distils
Before her darling daffodils.
And, if at noon my toil me heat,
The sun himself licks off my sweat.
While, going home, the evening sweet
In cowslip-water bathes my feet.

7

"What, though the piping shepherd stock
The plains with an unnumbered flock,
This scythe of mine discovers wide
More ground than all his sheep do hide.
With this the golden fleece[1] I shear
Of all these closes° every year. *enclosed fields*
And though in wool more poor than they,
Yet am I richer far in hay.

8

"Nor am I so deformed to sight,
If in my scythe I lookèd right;
In which I see my picture done,
As in a crescent moon the sun.
The deathless fairies takes me oft
To lead them in their dances soft:
And, when I tune myself to sing,
About me they contract their ring.

9

"How happy might I still have mowed,
Had not Love here his thistles sowed!
But now I all the day complain,
Joining my labour to my pain;
And with my scythe cut down the grass,
Yet still my grief is where it was:
But, when the iron blunter grows,
Sighing, I whet my scythe and woes."

10

While thus he threw his elbow round,
Depopulating all the ground,
And, with his whistling scythe, does cut
Each stroke between the earth and root,
The edgèd steel by careless chance
Did into his own ankle glance;
And there among the grass fell down,
By his own scythe, the mower mown.

11

"Alas!" said he, "these hurts are slight
To those that die by love's despite.
With shepherd's-purse, and clown's-all-heal,[2]
The blood I staunch, and wound I seal.
Only for him no cure is found,
Whom Juliana's eyes do wound.
'Tis death alone that this must do:
For Death thou art a mower too."
—1681 (PROBABLY WRITTEN IN THE EARLY 1650S)

[1] *golden fleece* The golden hay he mows, which he implies is superior to the regular fleece of the shepherd's sheep; but also associating himself with the ancient hero Jason, who sought and obtained the Golden Fleece.

[2] *shepherd's-purse, and clown's-all-heal* Herbs traditionally used to stop bleeding and to heal wounds; a "clown" is a country dweller.

The Garden

1

How vainly men themselves amaze
To win the palm, the oak, or bays,[1]
And their uncessant labours see
Crowned from some single herb or tree,
Whose short and narrow vergèd shade
Does prudently their toils upbraid,
While all flow'rs and all trees do close
To weave the garlands of repose.

2

Fair Quiet, have I found thee here,
And Innocence, thy sister dear!
Mistaken long, I sought you then
In busy companies of men.
Your sacred plants, if here below,
Only among the plants will grow.
Society is all but rude,
To this delicious solitude.

3

No white nor red[2] was ever seen
So am'rous as this lovely green.
Fond lovers, cruel as their flame,
Cut in these trees their mistress' name.
Little, alas, they know, or heed,
How far these beauties hers exceed!
Fair trees! wheres'e'er your barks I wound,
No name shall but your own be found.

4

When we have run our passions' heat,
Love hither makes his best retreat.
The gods, that mortal beauty chase,
Still in a tree did end their race.
Apollo hunted Daphne so,
Only that she might laurel grow.
And Pan did after Syrinx speed,
Not as a nymph, but for a reed.[3]

5

What wondrous life is this I lead!
Ripe apples drop about my head;
The luscious clusters of the vine
Upon my mouth do crush their wine;
The nectarine, and curious peach,
Into my hands themselves do reach;
Stumbling on melons, as I pass,
Ensnared with flow'rs, I fall on grass.

6

Meanwhile the mind, from pleasures less,
Withdraws into its happiness:
The mind, that ocean where each kind
Does straight its own resemblance find;[4]
Yet it creates, transcending these,
Far other worlds, and other seas,
Annihilating all that's made
To a green thought in a green shade.

7

Here at the fountain's sliding foot,
Or at some fruit-tree's mossy root,
Casting the body's vest aside,
My soul into the boughs does glide:
There like a bird it sits, and sings,
Then whets,° and combs its silver wings; *preens*
And, till prepared for longer flight,
Waves in its plumes the various light.

---

[1] *the palm, the oak, or bays* Wreaths or garlands; the traditional rewards signifying military (palm leaves), civic or political (oak leaves), or poetic (laurel, or bay, leaves) achievement.

[2] *white nor red* Colors traditionally associated with female beauty.

[3] *Apollo ... Pan* The speaker invokes two classical myths associated with erotic pursuit and the transformation of desire into art. Daphne, chased by Apollo, the god of poetry, was transformed into the laurel tree that became Apollo's sacred emblem. Syrinx, chased by Pan, god of flocks and shepherds, was transformed into a reed, the basis of the pan-pipe, emblem of pastoral poetry. The speaker naively (or mischievously) claims that these gods were really seeking the plants these women transformed into, not the women themselves, and thus asserts the superiority in beauty of plants to women.

[4] *that ocean ... own resemblance find* Alluding to the Renaissance belief that the ocean contains a counterpart for every plant and animal on land.

8

Such was that happy garden-state,
While man there walked without a mate:
After a place so pure, and sweet,
What other help could yet be meet?[1]
But 'twas beyond a mortal's share
To wander solitary there:
Two Paradises 'twere in one
To live in Paradise alone.

9

How well the skilful gardener drew
Of flowers and herbs this dial new,[2]
Where from above the milder sun
Does through a fragrant zodiac run;
And, as it works, the industrious bee
Computes its time as well as we.
How could such sweet and wholesome hours
Be reckoned but with herbs and flowers!

—1681 (PROBABLY WRITTEN IN THE EARLY 1650S)

An Horatian Ode upon Cromwell's Return from Ireland[3]

The forward[4] youth that would appear[5]
Must now forsake his Muses dear,
Nor in the shadows sing
His numbers[6] languishing:
'Tis time to leave the books in dust,
And oil the unused armour's rust:
Removing from the wall
The corslet of the hall.[7]
So restless Cromwell could not cease
In the inglorious arts of peace,
But through adventurous war
Urged his active star:
And, like the three-forked lightning, first
Breaking the clouds where it was nursed,
Did thorough° his own side *through*
His fiery way divide.[8]
(For 'tis all one to courage high
The emulous or enemy:
And with such to enclose
Is more than to oppose.)
Then burning through the air he went,
And palaces and temples rent:
And Caesar's head at last
Did through his laurels blast.[9]
'Tis madness to resist or blame
The force of angry heaven's flame:
And, if we would speak true,
Much to the man is due,
Who, from his private gardens, where
He lived reserved and austere,
As if his highest plot
To plant the bergamot,[10]

[1] *help ... meet* Alluding to Genesis 2.18: "And the Lord God said, It is not good that the man should be alone; I will make him an help meet for him."

[2] *dial* Floral sundial; sometimes read literally (Renaissance gardens did contain floral sundials), but the speaker also likens the entire garden to a sundial, in that it keeps seasonal time as the sun moves through its twelve-part zodiac.

[3] *An Horatian Ode upon Cromwell's Return from Ireland* In May 1650, Oliver Cromwell returned from a military expedition to Ireland, where he had defeated Royalist armies in several bloody battles. At the time he was second-in-command of Parliament's New Model Army, but in June 1650 Sir Thomas Fairfax resigned, and Cromwell became Commander-in-Chief in July, just prior to the invasion of Scotland this poem anticipates in lines 125ff. This poem was typeset for inclusion in the 1681 *Poems,* but the pages on which it was printed were removed before publication ("cancelled") from all but two extant copies.

[4] *forward* Prompt, ready, eager, spirited.

[5] *appear* Emerge to play a role in public life.

[6] *numbers* Metrical numbers: the youth can no longer spend time in the shadows writing love ("languishing") poetry.

[7] *corslet* Piece of armour that covered the body: the youth's "hall" or house had one, hanging on the wall.

[8] *side ... divide* Referring to Cromwell's rise to power through the ranks and past "emulous" (envious) rivals.

[9] *And Caesar's head ... blast* Comparing Charles I to Caesar, and Cromwell to a bolt of lightning: Roman emperors wore laurel wreaths; lightning was thought not to strike laurel trees; but Cromwell's bolt blasted through this protection. Note that Cromwell is figured as Caesar in line 100, and that lines 81-82 remind readers of the historical clash between the Imperial Caesar and the Roman republic.

[10] *bergamot* Variety of pear traditionally known as the pear of kings: a "plot" to "plant" (bury) this fruit was not as innocent sounding as it might seem.

Could by industrious valour climb
To ruin the great work of time,
And cast the kingdoms[1] old
Into another mould.
Though justice against fate complain,
And plead the ancient rights[2] in vain:
But those do hold or break
As men are strong or weak.
Nature, that hateth emptiness,
Allows of penetration less:[3]
And therefore must make room
Where greater spirits come.
What field of all the Civil Wars,
Where his were not the deepest scars?
And Hampton[4] shows what part
He had of wiser art:
Where, twining subtle fears with hope,
He wove a net of such a scope,
That Charles himself might chase
To Carisbrooke's narrow case:° *box, prison*
That thence the royal actor borne
The tragic scaffold might adorn:[5]
While round the armed bands
Did clap their bloody hands.
He nothing common did or mean
Upon that memorable scene:
But with his keener eye[6]
The axe's edge did try:
Nor called the gods with vulgar spite
To vindicate his helpless right,
But bowed his comely head,
Down, as upon a bed.[7]
This was that memorable hour
Which first assured the forced power.
So when they did design
The Capitol's first line,
A bleeding head where they begun,
Did fright the architects to run;
And yet in that the State
Foresaw its happy fate.[8]
And now the Irish are ashamed
To see themselves in one year tamed:[9]
So much one man can do,
That does both act and know.
They can affirm his praises best,
And have, though overcome, confessed
How good he is, how just,
And fit for highest trust:[10]
Nor yet grown stiffer with command,

[1] *kingdoms* Charles was King of three countries: England, Scotland, and Ireland.

[2] *ancient rights* Not the "divine right" of kings, but the place of the monarch in the "ancient" constitution, a place abolished by the English Republic.

[3] *Nature, that hateth ... less* Nature abhors a vacuum, but it also will not let two objects occupy the same place simultaneously: one needs to go.

[4] *Hampton* Hampton Court Palace, where Charles stayed until, fearful of assassination, he fled to Carisbrooke Castle (see line 52) on the Isle of Wight in November 1647. Charles expected to be safe in the Isle of Wight, but the Governor held him prisoner and he was eventually returned to London for trial. The poem voices contemporary rumors that Cromwell had slyly organized the whole train of events; these rumors are now thought to be groundless.

[5] *The tragic scaffold might adorn* The execution of the King (the "royal actor") is presented through a sustained theatrical metaphor. Marvell probably assumed that readers would remember that Charles was beheaded on a scaffold set up outside the Banqueting House, where plays and court entertainments were staged before the war: many of these entertainments, the court masques, celebrated royal power and featured members of the court on stage.

[6] *keener eye* I.e., keener than the blade with which he was to be executed.

[7] *He nothing ... a bed* Charles (the "He" of line 56, though the poem requires the reader to pause a moment to identify the referent) won admiration for his dignified manner throughout his trial and execution.

[8] *And yet ... fate* The "Capitol" is the ancient Roman temple of Jupiter Capitolium: according to Roman historians, workers digging the temple's foundation found a man's undecayed (hence "bleeding") head, which Roman authorities interpreted as a good omen: in Latin, the word head (*caput*) is related to capital, so the head was read as a sign that the temple would be the capital of a great empire. The poem implies that under Cromwell another empire will be founded on another bleeding head.

[9] *And now ... tamed* Cromwell's ferocious campaign against the Irish lasted from August 1649 to May 1650.

[10] *They... trust* The Irish; few if any Irish, then or now, would "confess" any goodness or justice to Cromwell in his campaign in Ireland.

But still in the Republic's hand:[1]
How fit he is to sway
That can so well obey.
He to the Commons' feet presents
A kingdom, for his first year's rents:
And, what he may, forbears
His fame, to make it theirs:
And has his sword and spoils ungirt,
To lay them at the public's skirt.[2]
So when the falcon high
Falls heavy from the sky,
She, having killed, no more does search
But on the next green bough to perch,
Where, when he first does lure,
The falconer has her sure.
What may not then our isle presume
While Victory his crest does plume?
What may not others fear
If thus he crowns each year?
A Caesar, he, ere long to Gaul,[3]
To Italy a Hannibal,[4]
And to all states not free
Shall climacteric be.[5]
The Pict[6] no shelter now shall find
Within his parti-coloured mind,[7]
But from this valour sad[8]
Shrink underneath the plaid:
Happy, if in the tufted brake
The English hunter him mistake,
Nor lay his hounds in near
The Caledonian° deer. *Scottish*
But thou, the Wars' and Fortune's son,
March indefatigably on,
And for the last effect
Still keep thy sword erect:
Besides the force it has to fright
The spirits of the shady night,[9]
The same arts that did gain
A power, must it maintain.
—1681 (BUT CANCELLED FROM MOST COPIES; WRITTEN 1650)

[1] *in ... hand* The next four stanzas figure Cromwell as a falcon (see line 91) under the control of the House of Commons, the Republic's representative body: as a bird of prey he hunts kingdoms, but dutifully brings them back to the "falconer" rather than claiming them for himself.

[2] *public's skirt* He lays his sword, and trophies, at the feet of the "body politic."

[3] *A Caesar ... Gaul* Julius Caesar subdued Gaul (France); the poem implies that Cromwell before long might do likewise.

[4] *Hannibal* Carthaginian general who invaded Italy in 218 BCE, and left, undefeated, fifteen years later. He was later defeated by a Roman army, but the reference is probably not meant ironically: the power to invade, to "be a Hannibal" to Italy, is the key point.

[5] *climacteric be* Be the cause of a critical or crucial moment in the lives of those states.

[6] *Pict* Scot, from the name of the ancient Celtic people who inhabited Scotland when the Romans occupied Britain; the name, with its link to picture and painting, also puns on "parti-coloured" in the next line.

[7] *parti-coloured* Varied in color; the Scots were regarded in the period as politically fickle, prone to change and to variety of opinion.

[8] *sad* Referring to Cromwell's "valor": steadfast and grave; also dark or soberly colored (in contrast with the "parti-coloured" Scots).

[9] *Besides ... night* Cold iron, and the cross-shaped hilt of a sword, were both thought to have the power to protect against evil spirits.

Katherine Philips

1632 – 1664

Katherine Philips, known also by her *nom de plume* "Orinda" whom some called "the Matchless Orinda," was the first Englishwoman to enjoy widespread public acclaim as a poet during her lifetime. Despite prejudice against seeing women's secular works in print, her male peers recognized Philips as a poet of the first rank. As early as 1651, Henry Vaughan paid tribute to her "new miracles in Poetrie," and in 1663 Abraham Cowley proclaimed her verse "then Man more strong, and more then Woman sweet." In the guise of her literary persona Orinda, Philips dramatized, within her self-devised Society of Friendship, the ideals—and the realities and tribulations—of Platonic love with wit, elegance, and clarity. Thus the Society—whether fully actual or partly imaginary—helped establish a literary standard for her generation and Orinda herself a model for the female writers who followed her. Toward the end of her fairly short life Philips also broke new ground as a playwright and translator: although other women had written or translated dramas, her translation of Corneille's neoclassical *Pompey* was the first rhymed version of a French tragedy in English and the first English play written by a woman to be performed on the professional stage.

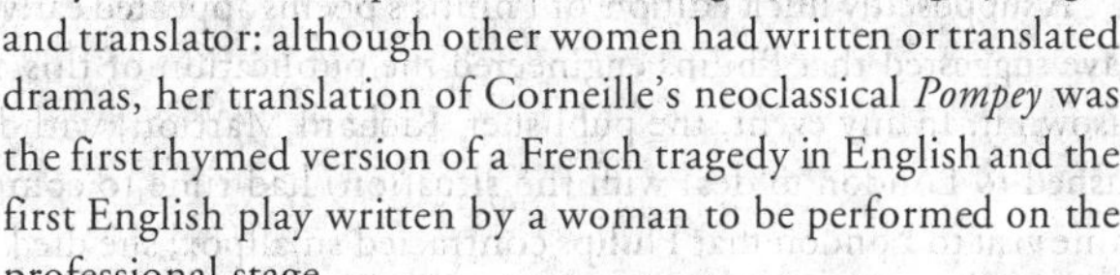

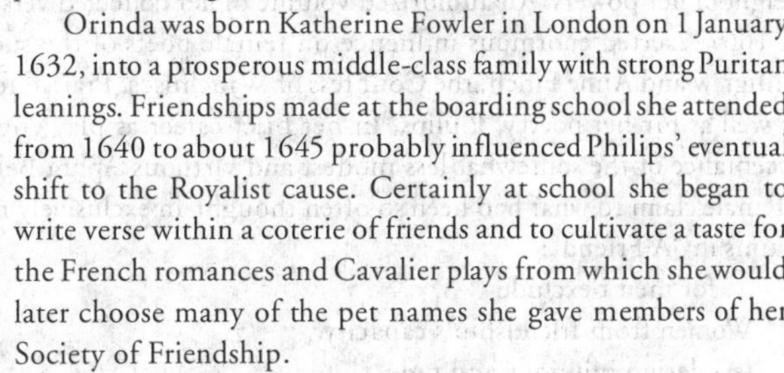

Orinda was born Katherine Fowler in London on 1 January 1632, into a prosperous middle-class family with strong Puritan leanings. Friendships made at the boarding school she attended from 1640 to about 1645 probably influenced Philips' eventual shift to the Royalist cause. Certainly at school she began to write verse within a coterie of friends and to cultivate a taste for the French romances and Cavalier plays from which she would later choose many of the pet names she gave members of her Society of Friendship.

In 1648, Philips, then 16, married James Philips and moved with him to Cardigan in Wales, which was to remain her family home for the rest of her life. Since her husband was a prominent Parliamentarian, however, she accompanied him occasionally on trips to London, where she befriended a circle of Cavalier writers gathered around the composer Henry Lawes and devoted to the memory of William Cartwright, who had died in 1643. It was her prefatory poem to the 1651 edition of Cartwright's works, in fact, that marked Philips' first appearance in print, and she contributed her "To the much honoured Henry Lawes" and "Mutuall Affection between Orinda and Lucasia" (later retitled as "Friendship's Mysterys") to Lawes' *Second Book of Ayres* in 1655. By this time, her poems were being read in manuscript as public chronicles of a literary and social clique.

The Society of Friendship had its origins in the cult of Neoplatonic love imported from the continent in the 1630s by Charles I's French wife, Henrietta Maria. Adherents indulged in elaborate rhetoric about the mingling of souls, and often adopted pseudonyms drawn from French pastoral romances or Cavalier dramas. With her literary gifts, however, and her intuitive sense of the value of deep friendships in a time of war and social schism, Philips enriched this convention as a cultural ideal of harmony and personal friendships to set against the faithless, war-torn public world. At the same time many of her poems (which she herself evidently valued highly) address public, political events.

During the 1650s the Society of Friendship probably numbered at least 20 people of both sexes, but Philips' literary energies were concentrated on her two closest female friends, Mary Aubrey {"Rosania")—until the latter's marriage in 1652 caused an estrangement—and then, in the succeeding decade, Anne Owen Lewis ("Lucasia"). The degree to which these friendships and the poetry that sprang from them include an erotic component is a subject of debate among scholars; what is agreed is that these poems have always attracted the keenest critical attention from readers of Philips's works. Initially strongly influenced by John Donne, Philips eventually matched the best of the Cavalier lyricists in freshness of wit, elegant invention, and pleasing rhythm.

Hoping to bolster her husband's political fortunes after the Restoration in 1660, Philips wrote many Royalist occasional pieces and became a friend of Sir Charles Cotterell, Master of Ceremonies to the King. She dubbed him "Poliarchus" and carried on a lively correspondence with him that was published after her death. While visiting the newly married Anne Owen in Ireland in 1662, Philips translated Corneille's *Mort de Pompée* from French alexandrines into fine English heroic couplets. The play was an instant success in Dublin and London in 1663, introducing Philips to wider celebrity as a playwright. (She left a second Corneille translation, *Horace*, unfinished, however.)

A supposedly illicit edition of Philips's poems appeared early in 1664. Germaine Greer and others have suggested that Philips engineered the publication of this edition in such a way that she could disown it. In any event, the publisher, Richard Marriott, withdrew the edition before Philips (who rushed to London to deal with the situation) had time to compel him to do so. It was during this same visit to London that Philips contracted smallpox; she died in June of that year, seemingly at the height of her powers. An authorized volume of her collected verse, published by Henry Herringman in 1667, exerted enormous influence on female poets of the succeeding generations, such as Anne Killigrew and Anne Finch, the Countess of Winchilsea. Praised for her modesty and Christian virtue as well as for her poetry, Philips, in her brief career as playwright, helped to pave the way for the acceptance of the somewhat less modest and virtuous Aphra Behn. Finally, as Orinda, she asserted a female claim to what had been so often thought an exclusively male sphere: ideal friendship. As she claims in "A Friend":

> ... for men t'exclude
> Women from friendship's capacity,
> Is a design injurious and rude,
> Only maintain'd by partial tyranny.
> Love is allow'd to us, and Innocence,
> And noblest friendships do proceed from thence.

⌘⌘⌘

A Married State

A married state affords but little ease
The best of husbands are so hard to please.
This in wives' careful° faces you may spell° *careworn / discern*
Though they dissemble° their misfortunes well. *conceal*
A virgin state is crowned with much content;° *contentment*
It's always happy as it's innocent.
No blustering husbands to create your fears;
No pangs of childbirth to extort your tears;
No children's cries for to offend your ears;
Few worldly crosses° to distract your prayers: *difficulties*
Thus are you freed from all the cares that do
Attend on matrimony and a husband too.
Therefore Madam, be advised by me
Turn, turn apostate to° loves levity. *reject, forsake*
Suppress wild nature if she dare rebel.

There's no such thing as leading apes in hell.[1]
—c. 1648

Upon the Double Murder of King Charles

In Answer to a Libelous Rhyme made by V. P.[2]

I think not on the state, nor am concerned
Which way soever that great helm is turned,
But as that son whose father's danger nigh
Did force his native dumbness, and untie
His fettered organs:[3] so here is a cause
That will excuse the breach of nature's laws.
Silence were now a sin: nay passion now
Wise men themselves for merit would allow.
What noble eye could see, (and careless pass)
The dying lion kicked by every ass?[4]
Hath Charles so broke God's laws, he must not have
A quiet crown, nor yet a quiet grave?
Tombs have been sanctuaries; thieves lie here
Secure from all their penalty and fear.
Great Charles his double misery was this,
Unfaithful friends, ignoble enemies;
Had any heathen been this prince's foe,
He would have wept to see him injured so.
His title was his crime, they'd reason good
To quarrel at the right they had withstood.
He broke God's laws, and therefore he must die,
And what shall then become of thee and I?
Slander must follow treason; but yet stay,° *stop*
Take not our reason with our king away.
Though you have seized upon all our defense,
Yet do not sequester° our common sense. *confiscate*
But I admire not at this new supply:
No bounds will hold those who at scepters fly.
Christ will be King, but I ne'er understood,
His subjects built his kingdom up with blood
(Except their own) or that he would dispense
With his commands, though for his own defense.
Oh! to what height of horror are they come
Who dare pull down a crown, tear up a tomb![5]
—1667

On the Third of September, 1651[6]

As when the glorious magazine of light[7]
Approaches to his canopy of night,
He with new splendor clothes his dying rays,
And double brightness to his beams conveys;
As if to brave° and check his ending fate, *defy*
Puts on his highest looks in 's lowest state;
Dressed in such terror as to make us all
Be anti-Persians,[8] and adore his fall;
Then quits the world, depriving it of day,
While every herb and plant does droop away:
So when our gasping English royalty
Perceived her period° now was drawing nigh, *end*
She summons her whole strength to give one blow,
To raise her self, or pull down others too.
Big with revenge and hope, she now spake more
Of terror than in many months before;
And musters her attendants, or to save
Her from, or wait upon° her to the grave: *escort / follow*
Yet but enjoyed the miserable fate
Of setting majesty, to die in state.
Unhappy Kings! who cannot keep a throne,
Nor be so fortunate to fall alone!

[1] *leading apes in hell* The proverbial fate of spinsters after death.

[2] *V.P.* Vavasor Powell (1617–70), an itinerant Nonconformist preacher and one of the Fifth Monarchists, who believed in the imminent Second Coming and the illegitimacy of earthly kings. The verses alluded to by Philips have not survived.

[3] *that son … fettered organs* Referring to the ancient Greek tale in which Croesus, King of Lydia, was saved from summary execution during the sack of Sardis by his mute son, who, speaking for the first time, identified his father as King and thus a man to be taken alive (Herodotus 1.85).

[4] *dying lion kicked by every ass* The dying Lion in Aesop's fable "The Sick Lion," who is assaulted in his helplessness by the various beasts, his subjects. On being finally kicked in the face by the Ass, the Lion proclaims, "This is a double death." Aesop's moral reads, "Only cowards insult dying majesty." The Scottish lion was also the dominant figure on the Stuart coat of arms.

[5] *tear up a tomb* Deface the honor and memory of the dead king.

[6] *Third of September, 1651* The date of the Battle of Worcester, in which Oliver Cromwell decisively defeated Charles II and the Royalist cause, bringing the English Civil War to an end.

[7] *magazine of light* The sun, pictured as a storehouse of light.

[8] *anti-Persians* Anti-sun, referring to the ancient Persian worship of Mithra, later identified with the sun.

Their weight sinks others: Pompey could not fly,
But half the world must bear him company;[1]
Thus captive Sampson could not life conclude,
Unless attended with a multitude.[2]
Who'd trust to greatness now, whose food is air,[3]
Whose ruin sudden, and whose end despair?
Who would presume upon his glorious birth,
Or quarrel for a spacious share of earth,
That sees such diadems become thus cheap,
And heroes tumble in the common heap
O! give me virtue then, which sums up° all, *encompasses*
And firmly stands when crowns and scepters fall.
—1667

To My Excellent Lucasia, on Our Friendship

17th. July 1651[4]

I did not live until this time
Crowned my felicity,
When I could say without a crime,
I am not thine, but thee.
This carcass° breathed, and walked, and slept, *body*
So that the world believed
There was a soul the motions kept;
But they were all deceived.
For as a watch by art° is wound *mechanical skill*
To motion, such was mine:
But never had Orinda found
A soul till she found thine;

Which now inspires, cures and supplies,
And guides my darkened breast:
For thou art all that I can prize,
My joy, my life, my rest.
Nor bridegroom's nor crowned conqueror's mirth
To mine compared can be:
They have but pieces of this earth,
I've all the world in thee.
Then let our flame still light and shine,
(And no bold° fear control) *strong*
As innocent as our design,° *intent*
Immortal as our soul.
—1667

Friendship's Mystery, To My Dearest Lucasia

original spelling

Come, my *Lucasia*, since we see
That Miracles Mens faith do move,
By wonder and by prodigy[5]
To the dull angry world let's prove
There's a Religion in our Love.

For though we were design'd t' agree,
That Fate no liberty destroyes,
But our Election is as free
As Angels, who with greedy choice
Are yet determin'd to their joyes.

Our hearts are doubled by the loss,
Here Mixture is Addition grown;
We both diffuse, and both ingross:
And we whose minds are so much one,
Never, yet ever are alone.

We court our own Captivity
Than Thrones more great and innocent:
'Twere banishment to be set free,
Since we wear fetters whose intent
Not Bondage is, but Ornament.

[1] *Pompey...company* The Roman general Pompey fled to Egypt after being defeated by Julius Caesar at Pharsalus (48 BCE), where 15,000 of his men were killed. Pompey's defeat and subsequent assassination in Egypt brought an end to the Civil War of the Triumvirate.

[2] *captive Samson ... multitude* Captured and blinded by the Philistines, the biblical hero Samson brought down the pillars of the temple at Gaza, killing thousands of his enemies along with himself. See Book of Judges 16.

[3] *whose food is air* Who is changeable and inconstant as the chameleon, which had the ability to endure long periods without food, and was thus reputed to live on air.

[4] *Lucasia ... 1651* Philips met her close friend Anne Owen (Lucasia) in 1651.

[5] *prodigy* Miracle or extraordinary event.

Divided joyes are tedious found,
And griefs united easier grow:
We are our selves but by rebound,
And all our Titles shuffled so,

Both Princes, and both Subjects too.
Our Hearts are mutual Victims laid,
While they (such power in Friendship lies)
Are Altars, Priests, and Off'rings made:
And each Heart which thus kindly dies,
Grows deathless by the Sacrifice.
—1667

On the Death of My First and Dearest Child, Hector Philips[1]

1

Twice forty months of wedlock I did stay,[2]
Then had my vows crowned with a lovely boy,
And yet in forty days he dropt away,
O swift vicissitude of human joy.

2

I did but see him and he disappeared,
I did but pluck the rosebud and it fell,
A sorrow unforeseen and scarcely feared,
For ill can mortals their afflictions spell.

3

And now (sweet babe) what can my trembling heart
Suggest to right my doleful fate or thee,
Tears are my Muse and sorrow all my Art,
So piercing groans must be thy eulogy.

4

Thus whilst no eye is witness of my moan,
I grieve thy loss (ah boy too dear to live)
And let the unconcerned world alone,
Who neither will, nor can refreshment give.

5

An off'ring too for thy sad tomb I have,
Too just a tribute to thy early hearse,
Receive these gasping numbers to thy grave,
The last of thy unhappy mother's verse.
—1667 (written 1655)

[1] *Hector Philips* According to a manuscript copy of this poem, Philips's son Hector was born 23 April 1655 and died about ten days later, on 2 May. She would have one other child, a daughter named Katherine, the following year.

[2] *Twice forty ... stay* Philips was married in August 1648, almost seven years before Hector was born.

Royalist and "Cavalier" Poetry

A "cavalier" was originally a mounted soldier or knight, but by the late sixteenth century the term also implied a roistering gallant. When the word was first applied to the gentlemen who fought on behalf of King Charles during the civil wars of the 1640s, it was meant as an insult. But as is often the case with such labels, it was eventually embraced by those to whom it was reproachfully applied.

The "cavalier poets" are writers associated with the Royalist cause; "cavalier poetry" is above all a political category. But not all cavalier poets knew they were cavaliers: Thomas Carew and Sir John Suckling died before the wars began (and so before Royalist cavaliers even existed). A great deal of "cavalier poetry" is in fact court poetry of the 1620s and 1630s, poetry that was subsequently packaged in the 1640s as expressing "Royalist" values. That is, the cavalier mode is in many ways retrospective and nostalgic: it celebrates beauty, love, nature, sensuality, drinking, good fellowship, honor and social life, and it does so in poetry famous for its urbanity, elegance, and often ironic ease. Of course, once the wars got underway, many Royalist poets also wrote explicitly political verse that commented on the conflict. Cavalier poets were all deeply influenced by the wit of John Donne and the craftsmanship of Ben Jonson; at its best, cavalier poetry seems the offspring of a poetic marriage between the work of these two great models. For other Royalist or "cavalier" poetry, see the selections from Robert Herrick and Katherine Philips.

⌘⌘⌘

Thomas Carew[1]

The Spring

Now that the winter's gone, the earth hath lost
Her snow-white robes, and now no more the
frost
Candies the grass, or casts an icy cream
Upon the silver lake or crystal stream;
But the warm sun thaws the benumbed earth,
And makes it tender; gives a sacred birth
To the dead swallow; wakes in hollow tree
The drowsy cuckoo, and the humble-bee.
Now do a choir of chirping minstrels bring
In triumph to the world the youthful Spring.
The valleys, hills, and woods in rich array
Welcome the coming of the longed for May.
Now all things smile, only my *Love* doth lour;
Nor hath the scalding noonday sun the power
To melt that marble ice, which still doth hold
Her heart congealed, and makes her pity cold.
The ox, which lately did for shelter fly
Into the stall, doth now securely lie
In open fields; and love no more is made
By the fireside, but in the cooler shade
Amyntas now doth with his Chloris[2] sleep
Under a sycamore, and all things keep
Time with the season; only she doth carry
June in her eyes, in her heart *January.*
—1640

[1] *Thomas Carew* Carew (1594/95–1640), courtier, masque writer, and one of the most widely read poets of the 1620s and 1630s (in manuscript: most of his poems were not printed until after his death). He joined the King's army for the 1639 expedition to Scotland (the "bishops' war"), but died before the beginning of the civil wars.

[2] *Amyntas … Chloris* Traditional generic names for rural lovers.

A Song[1]

Ask me no more where Jove bestows,
When June is past, the fading rose;
For in your beauty's orient deep
These flowers, as in their causes,[2] sleep.

Ask me no more whither do stray
The golden atoms of the day;
For in pure love heaven did prepare
Those powders to enrich your hair.

Ask me no more whither doth haste
The nightingale when May is past;
For in your sweet dividing[3] throat
She winters and keeps warm her note.

Ask me no more where those stars light
That downwards fall in dead of night;
For in your eyes they sit, and there
Fixèd become as in their sphere.

Ask me no more if east or west
The phoenix builds her spicy nest;
For unto you at last she flies,
And in your fragrant bosom dies.
—1640

An Elegy upon the Death of the Dean of Paul's, Dr. John Donne

Can we not force from widowed poetry
Now thou art dead (great Donne) one elegy
To crown thy hearse? Why yet dare we not trust
Though with unkneaded dough-baked prose thy dust,
Such as the unscissored[4] churchman from the flower
Of fading rhetoric, short lived as his hour,
Dry as the sand that measures it,[5] should lay
Upon thy ashes, on the funeral day?
Have we no voice, no tune? Didst thou dispense
Through all our language, both the words and sense?
'Tis a sad truth. The pulpit may her plain
And sober Christian precepts still retain,
Doctrines it may, and wholesome uses frame,
Grave homilies, and lectures, but the flame
Of thy brave soul (that shot such heat and light,
As burnt our earth, and made our darkness bright,
Committed holy rapes upon our will,
Did through the eye the melting heart distill,
And the deep knowledge of dark truths so teach,
As sense might judge, what fancy could not reach)
Must be desired for ever. So the fire,
That fills with spirit and heat the Delphic choir,[6]
Which kindled first by thy Promethean breath,[7]
Glowed here a while, lies quenched now in thy death.
The Muses' garden, with pedantic weeds
O'erspread, was purged by thee, the lazy seeds
Of servile imitation thrown away,
And fresh invention planted; thou didst pay
The debts of our penurious bankrupt age:
Licentious thefts, that make poetic rage
A mimic fury, when our souls must be
Possessed, or with Anacreon's ecstasy,
Or Pindar's,[8] not their own; the subtle cheat
Of sly exchanges, and the juggling feat
Of two-edged words, or whatsoever wrong
By ours was done the Greek, or Latin tongue,
Thou hast redeemed, and opened us a mine
Of rich and pregnant fancy, drawn a line
Of masculine expression, which had good

[1] *Song* Printed in Carew's *Poems*, this poem might in fact be by William Strode (for Strode see below): it was not unusual for poems that circulated in manuscript to be misattributed when they appeared in printed collections.

[2] *causes* Her beauty is the source of floral beauty (playing on the philosophical meanings of "cause" formulated by Aristotle).

[3] *dividing* Ornamenting notes while singing.

[4] *unscissored* With unshorn hair.

[5] *Dry as the sand that measures it* I.e., in the hourglass that times the sermon.

[6] *Delphic choir* Poets, inspired by Apollo (whose oracle was at Delphi); the lines within the parentheses identify Donne with Apollo.

[7] *Promethean breath* His inspiringly "fiery" verse: Prometheus stole fire from the gods and gave it to humans.

[8] *Anacreon … Pindar* Ancient Greek poets whose work became increasingly influential in the seventeenth century; the poems attributed in the Renaissance to Anacreon (fl. sixth century BCE) were in fact Anacreontic imitations written many centuries after his death.

Old Orpheus[1] seen, or all the ancient brood
Our superstitious fools admire, and hold
Their lead more precious, than thy burnished gold,
Thou hadst been their Exchequer,° and no more *treasury*
They each in other's dust, had raked for ore.
Thou shalt yield no precedence, but of time,
And the blind fate of language, whose tuned chime
More charms the outward sense; yet thou mayst claim
From so great disadvantage greater fame,
Since to the awe of thy imperious wit
Our stubborn language bends, made only fit
With her tough thick-ribbed hoops to gird about
Thy giant fancy, which had proved too stout
For their soft melting phrases. As in time
They had the start, so did they cull the prime
Buds of invention many a hundred year,
And left the rifled fields, besides the fear
To touch their harvest, yet from those bare lands
Of what is purely thine, thy only hands
(And that thy smallest work) have gleaned more
Than all those times, and tongues could reap before.
But thou art gone, and thy strict laws will be
Too hard for libertines in poetry.
They will repeal the goodly exiled train
Of gods and goddesses, which in thy just reign
Were banished nobler poems; now, with these,
The silenced tales of th' *Metamorphoses*[2]
Shall stuff their lines, and swell the windy page,
Till verse refined by thee, in this last age
Turn ballad rhyme, or those old idols be
Adored again, with new apostasy.
    Oh, pardon me that break with untuned verse
The reverend silence that attends thy hearse,
Whose solemn awful° murmurs were to thee *full of awe*
More than these faint lines, a loud elegy,
That did proclaim in a dumb eloquence
The death of all the arts, whose influence
Grown feeble, in these panting numbers lies
Gasping short-winded accents, and so dies.
So doth the swiftly turning wheel not stand
In the instant we withdraw the moving hand,
But some small time maintain a faint weak course
By virtue of the first impulsive force:
And so whilst I cast on thy funeral pile
Thy crown of bays, oh, let it crack a while,
And spit disdain, till the devouring flashes
Suck all the moisture up, then turn to ashes.
    I will not draw the envy to engross° *collect*
All thy perfections, or weep all our loss:
Those are too numerous for an elegy,
And this too great, to be expressed by me.
Though every pen should share a distinct part,
Yet art thou theme enough to tire all art;
Let others carve the rest, it shall suffice
I on thy tomb this epitaph incise:

Here lies a king, that ruled as he thought fit
The universal monarchy of wit;
Here lies two flamens,[3] *and both those, the best,*
Apollo's first, at last the true God's priest.

—1633

[1] *Orpheus* The mythological "father" of poetry.

[2] *Metamorphoses* The mythological stories in Ovid's *Metamorphoses* had appeared in the work of many Renaissance poets.

SIR JOHN SUCKLING[4]

Song

Why so pale and wan fond lover?
    Prithee why so pale?
Will, when looking well can't move her,
    Looking ill prevail?
    Prithee why so pale?

Why so dull and mute young sinner?
    Prithee why so mute?
Will, when speaking well can't win her,
    Saying nothing do't?
    Prithee why so mute?

[3] *Flamens* Priests (that is, Donne was priest of Apollo and of God).

[4] *Sir John Suckling* Poet, playwright, courtier, and gamester, Sir John Suckling (1609–41?) was the "greatest gallant of his time" and the inventor of cribbage. He outfitted his own troop of 100 splendidly dressed men for the 1639 expedition to Scotland; fled to Paris after being implicated in a Royalist plot in 1641; and died there in mysterious circumstances. His poems were printed posthumously.

Quit, quit, for shame, this will not move,
This cannot take her;
If of her self she will not love,
Nothing can make her,
The Devil take her.
—1638

A Ballad. Upon a Wedding[1]

I tell thee Dick, where I have been,
Where I the rarest things have seen,
O things beyond compare!
Such sights again cannot be found
In any part of English ground,
Be it at wake, or fair.

At Charing Cross,[2] hard by the way
Where we (thou know'st) do sell our hay,
There is a house with stairs;
And there did I see coming down
Such folk as are not in our town,
Forty at least, in pairs.

Amongst the rest, one pest'lent fine
(His beard no bigger though than thine)
Walked on before the rest:
Our landlord looks like nothing to him:
The King (God bless him) 'twould undo him,
Should he go still so dressed.[3]

At course-a-park,[4] without all doubt,
He should have first been taken out
By all the maids in th' town;
Though lusty Roger there had been,
Or little George upon the green,
Or Vincent of the crown.

But wot you what? the youth was going
To make an end of all his wooing;
The parson for him stayed:
Yet by his leave (for all his haste)
He did not wish so much all past,
(Perchance) as did the maid.

The maid (and thereby hangs a tale,
For such a maid no Whitsun ale[5]
Could ever yet produce):
No grape that's kindly ripe, could be
So round, so plump, so soft as she,
Nor half so full of juice.

Her finger was so small, the ring
Would not stay on which they did bring,
It was too wide a peck:
And to say truth (for out it must)
It looked like the great collar (just)
About our young colt's neck.

Her feet beneath her petticoat,
Like little mice stole in and out,
As if they feared the light:
But oh, she dances such a way!
No sun upon an Easter day
Is half so fine a sight.

He would have kissed her once or twice,
But she would not, she was so nice,
She would not do't in sight;
And then she looked as who should say
I will do what I list to day;
And you shall do't at night.

Her cheeks so rare a white was on,
No daisy makes comparison
(Who sees them is undone),
For streaks of red were mingled there,

[1] *A Ballad. Upon a Wedding* This poem is a "rustic epithalamion," in which a "rustic" speaker describes a fashionable city wedding in country terms and language. The speaker's friend "Dick" is likely the poet Richard Lovelace, and the poem was probably written for the July 1638 wedding of Suckling's brother, John, Lord Lovelace, to Lady Anne Wentworth.

[2] *Charing Cross* In London, near Haymarket.

[3] *Should he go still so dressed* That is, it would bankrupt the King himself to dress this well.

[4] *course-a-park* Country game in which a girl calls out the name of a boy to chase her.

[5] *Whitsun ale* Parish festival held on Whitsunday, for which a "lord" and "lady" of the ale were chosen.

Such as are on a Katherine pear
    (The side that's next the sun).

Her lips were red, and one was thin,
Compared to that was next her chin
    (Some bee had stung it newly).
But (Dick) her eyes so guard her face;
    I durst no more upon her gaze,
Than on the sun in July.[1]

Her mouth so small when she doth speak,
Thou'dst swear her teeth her words did break,
    That they might passage get;
But she so handles still the matter,
They come as good as ours, or better,
    And are not spoiled one whit.

If wishing should be any sin,
The parson himself had guilty been
    (She looked that day so purely),
And did the youth so oft the feat
At night, as some did in conceit,
    It would have spoiled him, surely.

Passion oh me! how I run on!
There's that that would be thought upon
    (I trow) besides the bride:
The bus'ness of the kitchen great,
For it is fit that men should eat,
    Nor was it there denied.

Just in the nick the cook knocked thrice,
And all the waiters in a trice
    His summons did obey:
Each serving man with dish in hand,
Marched boldly up, like our trained band,[2]
    Presented, and away.

When all the meat was on the table,
What man of knife, or teeth, was able
    To stay to be entreated?
And this the very reason was,
Before the parson could say grace,
    The company was seated.

Now hats fly off, and youths carouse;
Healths first go round, and then the house,
    The brides[3] came thick and thick:
And when 'twas named another's health,
Perhaps he made it hers by stealth.
    (And who could help it, Dick?)

O'th' sudden up they rise and dance,
Then sit again and sigh, and glance;
    Then dance again and kiss:
Thus several ways the time did pass,
Whilst every woman wished her place,
    And every man wished his.

By this time all were stol'n aside
To counsel and undress the bride;
    But that he must not know:
But yet 'twas thought he guessed her mind,
And did not mean to stay behind
    Above an hour or so.

When in he came (Dick) there she lay
Like new-fall'n snow melting away
    ('Twas time I trow to part);
Kisses were now the only stay,
Which soon she gave, as who should say,
    Good-bye, with all my heart.

But just as heavens would have to cross it,
In came the bridemaids with the posset:[4]
    The bridegroom eat in spite;
For had he left the women to't
It would have cost two hours to do't,
    Which were too much that night.

At length the candles out, and now
All that they had not done, they do:
    What that is, who can tell?
But I believe it was no more

[1] *July* Pronounced with the emphasis on the first syllable, like "Julie."

[2] *trained band* Local militia.

[3] *Brides* Toasts to the bride.

[4] *Posset* Sweetened hot milk curdled with ale or wine, ceremonially consumed by the bride and groom before retiring to bed.

Than thou and I have done before
With Bridget, and with Nell.
—1646

"Out upon it, I have loved"

Out upon it, I have loved
Three whole days together;
And am like to love three more,
If it prove fair weather.

Time shall moult away his wings
Ere he shall discover
In the whole wide world again
Such a constant lover.

But the spite on't is, no praise
Is due at all to me:
Love with me had made no stay,
Had it any been but she.

Had it any been but she,
And that very face,
There had been at least ere this
A dozen dozen in her place.
—1659

From an anonymous broadsheet, *The Sucklington Faction, or (Suckling's) Roaring Boyes* (1641). The broadsheet aimed to depict Suckling and his "roaring" cavaliers in a hostile light, as drinking, smoking, card playing, dicing and sexually irresponsible fops. (The curtained bed in the background would have implied a certain set of attitudes towards sexuality.)

RICHARD LOVELACE[1]

To Lucasta, Going to the Wars

1

Tell me not (sweet) I am unkind,
That from the nunnery
Of thy chaste breast, and quiet mind,
To war and arms I fly.

2

True; a new mistress now I chase,
The first foe in the field;
And with a stronger faith embrace
A sword, a horse, a shield.

3

Yet this inconstancy is such,
As you too shall adore:
I could not love thee (dear) so much,
Loved I not honour more.
—1649

To Althea, From Prison
Song

1

When love with unconfinèd wings
Hovers within my gates;
And my divine Althea brings
To whisper at the grates;
When I lie tangled in her hair,
And fettered to her eye;
The gods[2] that wanton in the air,
Know no such liberty.

2

When flowing cups run swiftly round
With no allaying Thames,[3]
Our careless heads with roses bound,
Our hearts with loyal flames;
When thirsty grief in wine we steep,
When healths and draughts go free,
Fishes, that tipple in the deep,
Know no such liberty.

3

When (like committed linnets)[4] I
With shriller throat shall sing
The sweetness, mercy, majesty,
And glories of my King.
When I shall voice aloud, how good
He is, how great should be,
Enlargèd winds, that curl the flood,
Know no such liberty.

4

Stone walls do not a prison make,
Nor iron bars a cage;
Minds innocent and quiet take
That for an hermitage;
If I have freedom in my love,
And in my soul am free,
Angels alone that soar above
Enjoy such liberty.
—1649

WILLIAM STRODE[5]

On Westwell Downs[6]

When Westwell Downs I 'gan to tread,
Where cleanly winds the green did sweep,

[1] *Richard Lovelace* Poet, courtier, and Royalist army officer, Richard Lovelace (1618–57) was a student at Oxford when he was described as "the most amiable and beautiful person that ever eye beheld." Born into a wealthy family in Kent, he joined the King's army for the 1639 "bishops' war"; in the 1640s he sold most of his estates to help the royal cause, and was twice jailed for his efforts.

[2] *gods* Probably Cupids; some manuscript copies read "birds."

[3] *no allaying Thames* No diluting water.

[4] *committed linnets* Caged songbirds.

[5] *William Strode* Church of England minister (1602–45) with a reputation as a witty preacher. Strode's poetry circulated widely in manuscript but was not collected until the twentieth century.

[6] *Westwell Downs* Downs are elevated, undulating, treeless areas of land, usually used for pasturage; Westwell Downs are near Oxford.

Methought a landscape[1] there was spread,
Here a bush and there a sheep:
The pleated wrinkles of the face
Of wave-swollen earth did lend such grace,
As shadowings in imagery
Which both deceive and please the eye.

The sheep sometimes did tread the maze
By often winding in and in,
And sometimes round about they trace
Which milkmaids call a fairy ring:
Such semicircles have they run,
Such lines across so trimly spun,
That shepherds learn whene'er they please
A new geometry with ease.

The slender food upon the down
Is always even, always bare;
Which neither spring nor winter's frown
Can ought improve or ought impair:
Such is the barren eunuch's chin,
Which thus doth evermore begin
With tender down to be o'ercast
Which never comes to hair at last.

Here and there two hilly crests
Amidst them hug a pleasant green,
And these are like two swelling breasts
That close a tender fall between.
Here would I sleep, or read, or pray
From early morn till flight of day;
But hark, a sheep-bell calls me up,
Like Oxford college bells, to sup.
—(WRITTEN 1630S?)

On a Gentlewoman Walking in the Snow

I saw fair Chloris walk alone
Where feathered rain came softly down,
And Jove descended from his tower
To court her in a silver shower:[2]
The wanton snow flew to her breast
Like little birds into their nest,
And overcome with whiteness there
For grief it thawed into a tear;
Thence falling on her garment's hem
To deck her, froze into a gem.
—1655

[1] *landscape* Landscape painting.

THOMAS RANDOLPH[3]

Upon the Loss of His Little Finger

Arithmetic nine digits, and no more
Admits of;[4] then I still have all my store.
For what mischance hath ta'en from my left hand,
It seems did only for a cipher stand.
But this I'll say for thee, departed joint,
Thou wert not given to steal, nor pick, nor point
At any in disgrace; but thou didst go
Untimely to thy death only to show
The other members what they once must do:
Hand, arm, leg, thigh, and all must follow too.
Oft didst thou scan my verse, where, if I miss
Henceforth, I will impute the cause to this.
A finger's loss (I speak it not in sport)
Will make a verse a foot too short.
Farewell, dear finger: much I grieve to see
How soon mischance hath made a hand of[5] thee.
—1638

[2] *Jove ... shower* Jove (or Zeus, in Greek mythology) descended to Danaë in a golden shower and impregnated her.

[3] *Thomas Randolph* Randolph (1605–35), playwright, College Fellow, and one of the poetic "sons" of Ben Jonson. His poems were not published until after his death.

[4] *Admits of* "Arithmetic" is used here as a verb, as in "count nine digits."

[5] *made a hand of* Idiom for "done away with."

RICHARD CORBETT[1]

Upon Fairford Windows[2]

Tell me, you anti-saints, why glass
With you is longer lived than brass?
And why the saints have 'scaped their falls
Better from windows than from walls?
Is it because the brethren's fires
Maintain a glass-house at Blackfriars,
Next which the church stands north and south,
And east and west the preacher's mouth?
Or is't because such painted ware
Resembles something what you are,
So pied, so seeming, so unsound
In manners, and in doctrine, found,
That, out of emblematic wit,
You spare yourselves in sparing it?
If it be so, then, Fairford, boast
Thy church hath kept what all have lost,
And is preserved from the bane
Of either war or Puritan,
Whose life is coloured in thy paint:
The inside dross, the outside saint.
—1648

EDMUND WALLER[3]

Go, Lovely Rose!

Go, lovely rose!
Tell her that wastes her time and me
That now she knows,
When I resemble her to thee,
How sweet and fair she seems to be.

Tell her that's young,
And shuns to have her graces spied,
That hadst thou sprung
In deserts, where no men abide,
Thou must have uncommended died.

Small is the worth
Of beauty from the light retired;
Bid her come forth,
Suffer herself to be desired,
And not blush so to be admired.

Then die! that she
The common fate of all things rare
May read in thee;
How small a part of time they share
That are so wondrous sweet and fair!
—1645

[1] *Richard Corbett* Son of a Surrey gardener, Richard Corbett (1582–1635) rose to be Bishop of Oxford (1628) and later of Norwich (1632). He was well known in the literary circles of Jacobean London, where he enjoyed a reputation for wit and conviviality and was a friend of Ben Jonson's. His poems circulated widely in manuscript, and were published posthumously in 1647 and in an enlarged edition in 1648.

[2] *Upon Fairford Windows* The stained glass windows (ca. 1480) in St. Mary's Church in Fairford, Gloucestershire, were (and still are) one of the only sets to survive the iconoclastic destruction that accompanied both the Reformation and the civil wars of the 1640s.

[3] *Edmund Waller* Member of Parliament in the 1620s and 30s, Edmund Waller (1606–87) published his first collection of poems in 1633 and several more in the mid-1640s. During the civil wars he was caught participating in a plot to secure London for the King, and was imprisoned; he returned to Parliament in 1661. Many Restoration and eighteenth-century poets saw Waller's polish and regularity as an important precursor to their poetic style.

Abraham Cowley[1]

Of Wit

Tell me, O tell, what kind of thing is Wit
Thou who master art of it.[2]
For the first matter loves variety less;
Less women love 't, either in love or dress.
A thousand different shapes it bears,
Comely in thousand shapes appears.
Yonder we saw it plain; and here 'tis now,
Like spirits in a place, we know not how.

London, that vents of false ware so much store,
In no ware deceives us more.
For men led by the colour, and the shape,
Like Zeuxis' birds fly to the painted grape;[3]
Some things do through our judgment pass
As through a multiplying glass.
And sometimes, if the object be too far,
We take a falling meteor for a star

Hence 'tis a Wit, that greatest word of fame,
Grows such a common name.
And Wits by our creation they become,
Just so, as titular bishops made at Rome.[4]
'Tis not a tale, 'tis not a jest
Admired with laughter at a feast,
Nor florid talk which can that title gain;
The proofs of wit forever must remain.

'Tis not to force some lifeless verses meet
With their five gouty feet.
All everywhere, like man's, must be the soul,
And reason the inferior powers control.
Such were the numbers which could call
The stones into the Theban wall.[5]
Such miracles are ceased; and now we see
No towns or houses raised by poetry.

Yet 'tis not to adorn, and gild each part
That shows more cost, than art.
Jewels at nose and lips but ill appear;
Rather than all things Wit, let none be there.
Several lights will not be seen,
If there be nothing else between.
Men doubt, because they stand so thick in th' sky,
If those be stars which paint the galaxy.

'Tis not when two like words make up one noise;
Jests for Dutch men, and English boys.
In which who finds out Wit, the same may see
In anagrams and acrostics poetry.
Much less can that have any place
At which a virgin hides her face,
Such dross the fire must purge away; 'tis just
The author blush, there where the reader must.

'Tis not such lines as almost crack the stage
When Bajazet begins to rage.[6]
Nor a tall metaphor in the Oxford way,[7]
Nor the dry chips of short lunged Seneca.[8]
Nor upon all things to obtrude,
And force some odd similitude.
What is it then, which like the power divine
We only can by negatives define?

---

[1] *Abraham Cowley* Son of a London stationer, Abraham Cowley (1618–67) was writing poems by the age of ten and published his first collection when he was only fifteen years old. A fellow of Trinity College, Cambridge before the civil wars, he joined the court in exile and acted as a Royalist spy in the 1650s, though eventually he was trusted by neither side. After the Restoration he was active in the circle that founded The Royal Society.

[2] *Thou* The poem's addressee is unknown.

[3] *Zeuxis* Ancient artist, whose painted grapes were so convincing that birds tried to eat them.

[4] *titular bishops* Bishops created in title only, without an episcopal see.

[5] *Theban wall* In classical myth, Amphion charmed stones through song into building themselves into a wall around the city of Thebes.

[6] *Bajazet … rage* Referring to the powerful rhetoric of a character in Christopher Marlowe's *Tamburlaine*.

[7] *Oxford way* Changed by Cowley to "bombast way" in a later edition.

[8] *Seneca* The Roman playwright Seneca was known for his "clipped" or choppy style.

In a true piece of Wit all things must be,
Yet all things there agree.
As in the ark, joined without force or strife,
All creatures dwelt; all creatures that had life
Or as the primitive forms of all
(If we compare great things with small)
Which without discord or confusion lie,
In that strange mirror of the deity.

But love that moulds one man up out of two,
Makes me forget and injure you.
I took you for my self sure when I thought
That you in any thing were to be taught.
Correct my error with thy pen;
And if any ask me then,
What thing right Wit, and height of genius is,
I'll only show your lines, and say, 'tis this.
—1656

HENRY VAUGHAN[1]

Regeneration[2]

1

A ward, and still in bonds, one day
I stole abroad,
It was high-spring, and all the way
Primrosed, and hung with shade;
Yet, was it frost within,
And surly winds
Blasted my infant buds, and sin
Like clouds eclipsed my mind.

2

Stormed thus, I straight perceived my spring
Mere stage, and show,
My walk a monstrous, mountained thing
Rough-cast with rocks, and snow;
And as a pilgrim's eye
Far from relief,
Measures the melancholy sky
Then drops, and rains for grief,

3

So sighed I upwards still; at last
'Twixt steps, and falls
I reached the pinnacle, where placed
I found a pair of scales,
I took them up and laid
In the one late pains,
The other smoke, and pleasures weighed
But proved the heavier grains;

4

With that, some cried, *Away;* straight I
Obeyed, and led
Full east, a fair, fresh field could spy
Come called it, *Jacob's bed*;
A Virgin-soil, which no
Rude feet ere trod,
Where (since he stepped there), only go
Prophets, and friends of God.

5

Here, I reposed; but scarce well set,
A grove descried
Of stately height, whose branches met
And mixed on every side;
I entered, and once in
(Amazed to see't),
Found all was changed, and a new spring
Did all my senses greet;

6

The unthrift Sun shot vital gold
A thousand pieces,
And heaven its azure did unfold
Chequered with snowy fleeces,
The air was all in spice
And every bush
A garland wore; thus fed my eyes
But all the ear lay hush.

[1] *Henry Vaughan* An ardent Royalist (though not all Royalist poets were "cavaliers"), Henry Vaughan (1621-95) was a devotional poet whose primary model was George Herbert. His twin brother Thomas was a notable hermetic philosopher and alchemist, and Henry's poetry reveals a similarly mystical and symbolic imagination.

[2] *Regeneration* "Regeneration" is a vision of a journey of spiritual renewal. The poem's language and rhetoric is suffused with scriptural reference.

7

Only a little fountain lent
Some use for ears,
And on the dumb shades language spent
The music of her tears;
I drew her near, and found
The cistern full
Of divers stones, some bright, and round
Others ill-shaped, and dull.

8

The first (pray mark), as quick as light
Danced through the flood,
But, the last more heavy than the night
Nailed to the centre stood;
I wondered much, but tired
At last with thought,
My restless eye that still desired
As strange an object brought;

9

It was a bank of flowers, where I descried
(Though 'twas mid-day,)
Some fast asleep, others broad-eyed
And taking in the ray,
Here musing long, I heard
A rushing wind
Which still increased, but whence it stirred
No where I could not find;

10

I turned me round, and to each shade
Dispatched an eye,
To see, if any leaf had made
Least motion, or reply,
But while I listening sought
My mind to ease
By knowing, where 'twas, or where not,
It whispered; *Where I please.*

Lord, then said I, *On me one breath,*
And let me die before my death!

Song of Solomon 4.16

Arise O north, and come thou south-wind, and blow upon my garden, that the spices thereof may flow out.
—1650

The World

I saw Eternity the other night,
Like a great ring of pure and endless light,
All calm, as it was bright;
And round beneath it, Time in hours, days, years,
Driven by the spheres
Like a vast shadow moved; in which the world
And all her train were hurled.
The doting lover in his quaintest strain
Did there complain;
Near him, his lute, his fancy, and his flights,
Wit's sour delights,
With gloves, and knots, the silly snares of pleasure,
Yet his dear treasure
All scattered lay, while he his eyes did pour
Upon a flower.
The darksome statesman hung with weights and woe,
Like a thick midnight-fog moved there so slow,
He did not stay, nor go;
Condemning thoughts (like sad eclipses) scowl
Upon his soul,
And clouds of crying witnesses without
Pursued him with one shout.
Yet digged the mole, and lest his ways be found,
Worked under ground,
Where he did clutch his prey; but One did see
That policy;
Churches and altars fed him; perjuries
Were gnats and flies;
It rained about him blood and tears, but he
Drank them as free.
The fearful miser on a heap of rust
Sate pining all his life there, did scarce trust
His own hands with the dust,
Yet would not place one piece above, but lives
In fear of thieves.
Thousands there were as frantic as himself,

And hugged each one his pelf;
The downright epicure placed Heaven in sense,
And scorned pretence,
While others, slipped into a wide excess,
Said little less;
The weaker sort slight, trivial wares enslave,
Who think them brave;
And poor despised Truth sat counting by
Their victory.
Yet some, who all this while did weep and sing,
And sing, and weep, soared up into the ring;
But most would use no wing.
O fools (said I) thus to prefer dark night
Before true light,
To live in grots and caves, and hate the day
Because it shows the way,
The way, which from this dead and dark abode
Leads up to God,
A way where you might tread the sun, and be
More bright than he.
But as I did their madness so discuss
One whispered thus,
"This ring the Bridegroom did for none provide,
But for his bride."

All that is in the world, the lust of the flesh, the lust of the eyes, and the pride of life, is not of the father, but is of the world. And the world passeth away, and the lusts thereof, but he that doth the will of God abideth for ever (1 John 2.16–17).

—1650

RICHARD CRASHAW[1]

Saint Mary Magdalene or, The Weeper[2]

Lo where a wounded heart with bleeding eyes conspire.
Is she a flaming fountain, or a weeping fire?

1

Hail sister springs,
Parents of silver-footed rills!
Ever bubbling things!
Thawing crystal! Snowy hills!
Still spending, never spent;
I mean Thy fair eyes, sweet Magdalene.

2

Heavens thy fair eyes be;
Heavens of ever-falling stars;
'Tis seed-time still with thee,
And stars thou sow'st, whose harvest dares
Promise the earth to countershine
Whatever makes Heaven's forehead fine.

3

But we're deceived all:
Stars indeed they are too true,
For they but seem to fall
As Heaven's other spangles do:
It is not for our earth and us,
To shine in things so precious.

[1] *Richard Crashaw* Like Henry Vaughan, a devotional poet, admirer of George Herbert, and political Royalist, Crashaw (1612–49) offers yet a different direction for an English poet in the 1640s: he converted to Catholicism, and died in Rome. Crashaw is often considered the most "baroque" of English Renaissance poets.

[2] *Saint Mary Magdalene or, The Weeper* Crashaw printed this poem with variations in three different collections (1646, 1648, and 1652); this version reflects the last of these three, with corrections from 1648.

4

Upwards thou dost weep;
Heaven's bosom drinks the gentle stream.
Where the milky rivers creep,
Thine floats above and is the cream.
Waters above the heavens, what they be,
We are taught best by thy tears and thee.

5

Every morn from hence,
A brisk cherub something sips,
Whose soft influence
Adds sweetness to his sweetest lips;
Then to his music: and his song
Tastes of this breakfast all day long.

6

Not in the evening's eyes,
When they read with weeping are
For the Sun that dies,
Sits Sorrow with a face so fair.
Nowhere but here did ever meet
Sweetness so sad, sadness so sweet.

7

When Sorrow would be seen
In her brightest majesty,
For she is a Queen,
Then is she dressed by none but thee.
Then, and only then, she wears
Her richest pearls, I mean thy tears.

8

The dew no more will weep,
The primrose's pale cheek to deck;
The dew no more will sleep,
Nuzzled in the lily's neck.
Much rather would it tremble here,
And leave them both to be thy tear.

9

There is no need at all,
That the balsam-sweating bough
So coyly should let fall
His med'cinable tears; for now
Nature hath learnt t'extract a dew
More sovereign and sweet from you.

10

Yet let the poor drops weep,
Weeping is the case of woe;
Softly let them creep,
Sad that they are vanquished so;
They, though to others no relief,
May balsam be for their own grief.

11

Such the maiden gem
By the wanton spring put on,
Peeps from her parent stem,
And blushes at the bridegroom sun:
This watery blossom of thy eyn[1]
Ripe, will make the richer wine.

12

When some new bright guest
Takes up among the stars a room,
And Heaven will make a feast,
Angels with crystal vials come;
And draw from these full eyes of thine
Their Master's water, their own wine.

13

Golden though he be,
Golden Tagus[2] murmurs; though
Were his way by thee,
Content and quiet he would go;
So much more rich would he esteem
Thy silver, than his golden stream.

14

Well does the May that lies
Smiling in thy cheeks, confess
The April in thine eyes;
Mutual sweetness they express.
No April e'er lent kinder showers,
Nor May returned more faithful flowers.

---

[1] *eyn* Eyes.

[2] *Tagus* River in Spain f

15

O cheeks! Beds of chaste loves,
By your own showers seasonably dashed.
Eyes! nests of milky doves,
In your own wells decently washed.
O wit of love! that thus could place
Fountain and garden in one face.

16

O sweet contest; of woes
With loves, of tears with smiles disporting!
O fair and friendly foes,
Each other kissing and comforting!
While rain and sunshine, cheeks and eyes,
Close in kind contrarieties.

17

But can these fair floods be
Friends with the bosom fires that fill ye!
Can so great flames agree
Eternal tears should thus distil thee!
O floods, O fires, O suns, O showers!
Mixed and made friends by love's sweet powers.

18

'Twas his well-pointed dart
That digged these wells, and dressed this vine;
And taught that wounded heart
The way into these weeping eyn.
Vain loves avaunt!° bold hands forbear! *be gone!*
The lamb hath dipped his white foot here.

19

And now where'er he strays
Among the Galilean mountains,
...r more unwelcome ways,
...ollowed by two faithful fountains;
...hs, two weeping motions,
...dious oceans.

...r store,
...ces,
He might provoke the wealth of princes.
What prince's wanton'st pride e'er could
Wash with silver, wipe with gold?

21

Who is that King, but he
Who call'st his crown to be called thine,
Thus can boast to be
Waited on by a wandering mine,
A voluntary mint, that strews
Warm silver showers where'er he goes?

22

O precious prodigal!
Fair spendthrift of thyself! thy measure,
Merciless love! is all
Even to the last pearl in thy treasure.
All places, times, and objects be
Thy tear's sweet opportunity.

23

Does the day-star rise?
Still thy stars do fall, and fall;
Does day close his eyes?
Still the fountain weeps for all.
Let night or day do what they will,
Thou hast thy task, thou weepest still.

24

Does thy song lull the air?
Thy falling tears keep faithful time.
Does thy sweet-breathed prayer
Up in clouds of incense climb?
Still at each sigh, that is, each stop,
A bead, that is, a tear, does drop.

25

At these thy weeping gates,
Watching their wat'ry motion,
Each winged moment waits,
Takes his tear, and gets him gone.
By thine eye's tinct ennobled thus,
Time lays him up: he's precious.

26

Not, so long she lived,
Shall thy tomb report of thee;
But, so long she grieved,
Thus must we date thy memory.
Others by moments, months, and years,
Measure their ages; thou, by tears.

27

So do perfumes expire;
So sigh tormented sweets, oppressed
With proud unpitying fire;
Such tears the suffering Rose that's vexed
With ungentle flames does shed,
Sweating in a too warm bed.

28

Say, ye bright brothers,
The fugitive sons of those fair eyes
Your fruitful mothers,
What make you here? What hopes can 'tice° *entice*
You to be born? What cause can borrow
You from those nests of noble sorrow?

29

Whither away so fast?
For sure the sordid earth
Your sweetness cannot taste,
Nor does the dust deserve your birth.
Sweet, whither haste you then? O, say
Why you trip so fast away?

30

We go not to seek
The darlings of Aurora's bed,
The rose's modest cheek,
Nor the violet's humble head.
Though the field's eyes, too, weepers be,
Because they want such tears as we.

31

Much less mean we to trace
The fortune of inferior gems,
Preferred to some proud face,
Or perched upon feared diadems.
Crowned heads are toys. We go to meet
A worthy object, our Lord's feet.
—1652 (written 1646, revised 1648 and 1652)

JOHN MILTON

1608 – 1674

John Milton aspired to be a writer for the ages—and he succeeded. Almost within his lifetime, Milton was widely considered England's greatest poet and a writer whose only serious rivals were the ancient masters Homer and Virgil. His influence on subsequent English poetry is probably second only to that of Shakespeare: for centuries, major poets struggled to define themselves in relation to Milton's achievement in a literary psychodrama of admiration, emulation, exasperation, and denial. No other English writer appears to have assimilated so thoroughly all the literature, culture, and history that had come before him. Milton first mastered the European artistic tradition, and then out of it made something new, producing magnificent and innovative poems in all the major genres. In addition, had Milton not published a line of verse he would still hold a place in literary history by virtue of his prose. Even though he dismissed these books as the product of "his left hand," Milton was a significant prose writer and a formidable polemicist, in Latin as well as English, producing a wide range of works on political, social, religious, educational, and historical issues.

Of all the major writers in English, Milton was probably the most deeply engaged in the politics of his time. Milton's poetry has consequently been read in light of his active involvement in political, religious, and social revolution. But the nature of Milton's literary engagement with these issues continues to be debated: Milton, like Shakespeare, rarely if ever offers easy answers. Over the centuries, Milton has been championed as both a pillar of religious orthodoxy and as the great dissenter, a religious radical or even heretic. He has been called a proto-feminist and the great patriarchal bogeyman, a radical political egalitarian and a man who did not believe in democracy. His is the greatest voice of "Puritanism" in English literature, but to think of him in anything like the modern sense of "puritanical" is to go immediately off-track. While a profoundly religious man, Milton by the end of his life had almost no use for institutional religion or theological tradition. While a "Puritan," he was also a spokesman for revolution, freedom of the will (which Protestant theory usually denied), and political, social, intellectual, and personal liberty. Thomas Jefferson copied out 48 excerpts from Milton's works into his commonplace book, almost all of them having to do with liberty. Milton's works have been called the culmination of Renaissance humanism and a monument to dead ideas; and they have been celebrated as ushering in the modern world in their complex treatment of human agency, human love, and human political relations.

No writer before Milton fashioned himself quite so insistently and self-consciously as an author: in text after text, Milton invites us to read connections between his life and his writing, and then challenges or complicates our ability to do so. Born the eldest son of a successful scrivener in London in 1608, Milton was surrounded by words from an early age; he began writing seriously at the age of ten. In 1618 he was admitted to Christ's College, Cambridge, where he would remain the next seven years, graduating M.A. in 1632. While Milton did very well in his studies, he also complained repeatedly about the inadequacies of the educational curriculum and requirements: he described his frustration with traditional approaches to education in his treatise *On Education* (1644). Milton entered Cambridge expecting to become a minister in the Church of England (he would later change his mind, probably in the 1630s). In his university writings, however, he talks about himself as a poet and as a scholar, and never as a prospective minister. But he did develop a reputation for erudition and literary skill: during his university years he wrote several poems he would later publish, including the companion poems "L'Allegro" and "Il Penseroso."

After he left Cambridge, Milton spent the next six years in "studious retirement," living with his parents, reading extensively, preparing himself for his vocation—and trying to discover what that vocation was. He published his first poem, an epitaph for Shakespeare included in Shakespeare's second folio (1632); he accepted commissions for two aristocratic entertainments (*Arcades* and *A Maske*, popularly known as *Comus*). He kept a close eye on the changing political and religious conditions of England over the 1630s. Finally, in 1638, he published "Lycidas," one of the most extraordinary poems in English, simultaneously a eulogy for a drowned classmate, a denunciation of current Anglican Church leadership, and a confident assertion of his own poetic vocation, all mediated through the conventions of classical pastoral elegy. Writing "Lycidas" seemed to be the trigger that propelled Milton from his retirement into an active engagement with the world. In 1638 and 1639, he traveled abroad, spending considerable time in Italy, where he was much taken with the intellectual and cultural life. Had not rumors of the impending English Civil War called him home in late 1639, Milton's travels would likely have lasted much longer.

Milton continued to train himself towards his goal of becoming a great poet in the classical tradition of Virgil, becoming familiar with Spanish, Dutch, and Hebrew as well as Latin and Greek, French and Italian, and with the leading works of history, science and philosophy as well as of literature. But after returning to England in 1639 he devoted himself over the next twenty years very largely to the cause of political and religious change. Most of his publications during this period consist of prose polemic, including some anti-episcopal tracts in the early 1640s, several others arguing for an increased freedom to divorce, *Areopagitica* (1644), and works of political theory and argument that hold a central place among the writings of the English civil wars: *The Tenure of Kings and Magistrates* (1649), *Eikonoklastes* (1649), *Defensio pro populo Anglicano* (1651), *Defensio secunda* (1654), and *The Ready and Easy Way to Establish a Free Commonwealth* (1659). Milton's skill as a polemicist brought him to the attention of the revolutionary government, and in the 1650s he served as Secretary for Foreign Tongues in the government of Oliver Cromwell—a job that entailed writing a wide variety of official documents and letters (Latin remained the most important "foreign tongue" for international communication).

Of his prose works, the most widely read in the modern era has been *Areopagitica* (1644), Milton's extended defense of literary and intellectual freedom. The occasion for the work was the effort by Parliament to require books to be licensed prior to publication. Milton did not advocate complete freedom of the press. But his arguments for the necessity of letting readers make up their own minds, of letting arguments fight it out in the public sphere, continue to be cited in legal cases today. At the time, however, Milton was far better known, notorious even, for his books advocating a right to divorce. In June of 1642 Milton (then thirty-six) married Mary Powell, a young woman from a Royalist family. The two proved to be a less than perfect match, and she returned to her family's home in Buckinghamshire two months later. They were eventually reconciled, but many readers see a connection between their apparent difficulties and Milton's publication of *The Doctrine and Discipline of Divorce* (1642), in which he argues that the purpose of marriage is to provide companionship based on affection and like-mindedness, and that divorce should be allowed when a marriage fails to do so. The scandal Milton provoked in England with these arguments was supplanted only by the European-wide scandal he created by defending the execution of King Charles I.

While Milton might not have had time to write much poetry in the 1640s, he did publish the poetry he had written up to the outbreak of war. In 1645, a year that saw some of the bloodiest fighting of the war, Humphrey Moseley, the most prominent literary publisher of the day, produced

The Poems of Mr. John Milton, Both English and Latin. In addition to "On the Morning of Christ's Nativity," "On Shakespeare," "L'Allegro" and "Il Penseroso," "Lycidas," and *A Maske*, the collection included twenty-two other poems in English, including ten sonnets (six of them written in Italian), and twelve Latin poems.

Milton's wife Mary died during childbirth in 1652, and one of the couple's four children died shortly thereafter. At about the same time Milton entirely lost his sight; the sonnet "When I consider how my light is spent" (often referred to as "On His Blindness") was written later that same year. His two daughters were among those who served thereafter as scribes; all of his subsequent works were dictated. In 1656 Milton married Katherine Woodcock; two years later, in 1658, she also died of complications arising from childbirth.

With the Restoration in 1660, Milton went into hiding from the authorities. Eventually he suffered a brief imprisonment, but his freedom was negotiated by friends (notable among them the poet Andrew Marvell). His existence for the final fourteen years of his life was one of relative isolation—but these were also the years of his greatest poetic achievement. Rising early each day and beginning to dictate as soon as his scribe or secretary joined him, he had begun in the late 1650s to compose *Paradise Lost*, a sweeping re-telling of the Biblical story of humanity's expulsion from Paradise; the epic was initially published in 1667 in ten books, and then reissued in a revised twelve-book edition in 1674. Since the early eighteenth century *Paradise Lost* has been almost universally accorded a central place in the English literary canon. Two other major works followed: *Paradise Regained* (1671), which presents in blank verse the story of the temptation of Jesus and of his defeat of Satan; and *Samson Agonistes* (1671), which recounts in the form of a poetic drama the story of the blind and anguished Samson, struggling to understand God's will.

In 1663 Milton married Elizabeth Minshul, who became a scribe, caregiver, and inspiration to him in the last decade of his life. Though *Paradise Lost* sold moderately well from its first publication, and though Milton came to be regarded by many as a "classic" even during his lifetime, his anti-monarchical political views precluded any official honors; when he died in 1674 he was buried not in Westminster Abbey but beside his father in Saint Giles's Church, Cripplegate.

⌘⌘⌘

L'Allegro[1]

Hence loathèd Melancholy
Of Cerberus,[2] and blackest Midnight born,
In Stygian[3] cave forlorn
'Mongst horrid shapes, and shrieks, and sights unholy,
Find out some uncouth cell,
Where brooding Darkness spreads his jealous wings,
And the night-raven sings;
There under ebon shades, and low-browed rocks,
As ragged as thy locks,
In dark Cimmerian[4] desert ever dwell.
But come thou goddess fair and free,
In heaven yclept° Euphrosyne,[5] named
And by men, heart-easing Mirth,
Whom lovely Venus at a birth
With two sister Graces more
To ivy-crownèd Bacchus bore;[6]

[1] *L'Allegro* Italian: the merry or happy man.

[2] *Cerberus* In classical myth, the three-headed dog that guards the entrance to the underworld.

[3] *Stygian* Hellishly black; from Styx, a river that in classical myth leads to the underworld.

[4] *Cimmerian* Densely dark (from the Cimmerians, a people fabled in classical story to live in perpetual darkness).

[5] *Euphrosyne* Classical personification of Joy and one of the three Graces.

[6] *heart-easing Mirth ... Bacchus bore* Milton makes the three Graces the daughters of Venus (goddess of love) and Bacchus (god of wine); Euphrosyne's two sisters were Aglaia (Brightness) and Thalia (Bloom).

Or whether (as some sager sing)
The frolic wind that breathes the spring,
Zephyr with Aurora[1] playing,
As he met her once a-Maying,[2]
There on beds of violets blue,
And fresh-blown roses washed in dew,
Filled her with thee a daughter fair,
So buxom, blithe, and debonair.[3]
Haste thee nymph, and bring with thee
Jest and youthful jollity,
Quips and cranks, and wanton wiles,[4]
Nods, and becks,° and wreathèd smiles, *beckonings*
Such as hang on Hebe's[5] cheek,
And love to live in dimple sleek;
Sport that wrinkled Care derides,
And Laughter holding both his sides.
Come, and trip it as ye go
On the light fantastic toe,
And in thy right hand lead with thee,
The mountain nymph, sweet Liberty;
And if I give thee honour due,
Mirth, admit me of thy crew
To live with her, and live with thee,
In unreprovèd° pleasures free; *free of blame*
To hear the lark begin his flight,
And singing startle the dull night,
From his watch-tower in the skies,
Till the dappled dawn doth rise;
Then to come in spite of sorrow,
And at my window bid good morrow,[6]

[1] *Zephyr ... Aurora* Classical personifications of the west wind and of the dawn.

[2] *a-Maying* Celebrating the arrival of May; May Day was celebrated with various traditional pastimes. Sterner Puritans opposed such revelry as pagan.

[3] *buxom, blithe, and debonair* These three adjectives had overlapping meanings in the period, and were often grouped with one another: *buxom* Easy-going, lively; *blithe* Merry, jolly; *debonair* Affable, kindly, gracious.

[4] *Quips* Witty sayings; *cranks* Plays on words; *wanton wiles* Playful games and tricks.

[5] *Hebe* Classical personification of youth.

[6] *to come ... bid good morrow* That is, L'Allegro comes to his window and bids the day good morrow (though some readers think it is the lark who bids good morrow to L'Allegro): the same, deliberately agentless syntax has L'Allegro "oft list'ning" and "sometime walking" in subsequent lines.

Through the sweet-briar, or the vine,
Or the twisted eglantine.
While the cock with lively din,
Scatters the rear of darkness thin,
And to the stack,° or the barn door, *haystack*
Stoutly struts his dames before,
Oft list'ning how the hounds and horn
Cheerly rouse the slumb'ring morn,
From the side of some hoar° hill, *grey*
Through the high wood echoing shrill.
Sometime walking not unseen
By hedgerow elms, on hillocks green,
Right against the eastern gate,
Where the great sun begins his state,
Robed in flames, and amber light,
The clouds in thousand liveries dight,° *clothed*
While the ploughman near at hand,
Whistles o'er the furrowed land,
And the milkmaid singeth blithe,
And the mower whets his scythe,
And every shepherd tells his tale[7]
Under the hawthorn in the dale.
Straight mine eye hath caught new pleasures
Whilst the landscape round it measures.
Russet lawns, and fallows grey,
Where the nibbling flocks do stray,
Mountains on whose barren breast
The labouring clouds do often rest:
Meadows trim with daisies pied,
Shallow brooks, and rivers wide,
Towers, and battlements it sees
Bosomed high in tufted trees,
Where perhaps some beauty lies,
The cynosure[8] of neighbouring eyes.
Hard by, a cottage chimney smokes,
From betwixt two agèd oaks,
Where Corydon and Thyrsis met,[9]
Are at their savoury dinner set
Of herbs, and other country messes,
Which the neat-handed Phyllis dresses;

[7] *tells his tale* A double meaning: "tells his story" and/or "counts his flock."

[8] *cynosure* Center of attraction or interest.

[9] *Corydon ... Thyrsis* With "Phyllis" and "Thestylis" five lines below, traditional names in classical pastoral poetry.

And then in haste her bower she leaves,
With Thestylis to bind the sheaves;
Or if the earlier season lead
To the tanned haycock in the mead,
Sometimes with secure delight
The upland hamlets will invite,
When the merry bells ring round,
And the jocund rebecks[1] sound
To many a youth, and many a maid,
Dancing in the chequered shade;
And young and old come forth to play
On a sunshine holiday,
Till the livelong daylight fail,
Then to the spicy nut-brown ale,
With stories told of many a feat,
How Fairy Mab[2] the junkets[3] eat,
She was pinched, and pulled she said,
And he by Friar's Lantern[4] led
Tells how the drudging Goblin[5] sweat,
To earn his cream-bowl duly set,
When in one night, ere glimpse of morn,
His shadowy flail hath threshed the corn,
That ten day-labourers could not end;
Then lies him down the lubber fiend,
And stretched out all the chimney's length,
Basks at the fire his hairy strength;
And crop-full[6] out of doors he flings,
Ere the first cock his matin rings.
Thus done the tales, to bed they creep,
By whispering winds soon lulled asleep.
Towered cities please us then,
And the busy hum of men,
Where throngs of knights and barons bold,
In weeds of peace[7] high triumphs hold,
With store of ladies, whose bright eyes
Rain influence, and judge the prize
Of wit, or arms, while both contend
To win her grace, whom all commend.
There let Hymen[8] oft appear
In saffron robe, with taper clear,[9]
And pomp, and feast, and revelry,
With masque, and antique pageantry,
Such sights as youthful poets dream
On summer eves by haunted stream.
Then to the well-trod stage anon,
If Jonson's learnèd sock[10] be on,
Or sweetest Shakespeare, fancy's child,
Warble his native wood-notes wild,
And ever against eating cares,
Lap me in soft Lydian airs,[11]
Married to immortal verse
Such as the meeting soul may pierce
In notes, with many a winding bout
Of linkèd sweetness long drawn out,
With wanton heed, and giddy cunning,
The melting voice through mazes running;
Untwisting all the chains that tie
The hidden soul of harmony.
That Orpheus self[12] may heave his head
From golden slumber on a bed
Of heaped Elysian[13] flowers, and hear
Such strains as would have won the ear
Of Pluto, to have quite set free
His half-regained Eurydice.[14]

---

[1] *rebecks* Three-stringed fiddles.

[2] *Fairy Mab* In English folklore, the Queen of the Fairies.

[3] *junkets* Dishes of sweet curds and cream.

[4] *Friar's Lantern* Folkloric name for the will-o'-the-wisp.

[5] *Goblin* Robin Goodfellow or Hobgoblin; usually a mischievous trickster, he might help with household chores, as here, if propitiated with an offering of cream.

[6] *crop-full* Filled to the brim (here, with cream).

[7] *weeds of peace* Showy tournament outfits, as opposed to real, wartime armor.

[8] *Hymen* Classical god of weddings.

[9] *taper clear* Candle or torch; it was a good omen for the marriage if the flame burned without smoke ("clear").

[10] *sock* Slipper worn by comic actors in ancient Greece (as opposed to the buskin worn by actors in tragedies): L'Allegro suggests going to the theater if one of Ben Jonson's erudite comedies is playing.

[11] *Lydian airs* Soft, convivial songs or melodies ("Lydian" is one of the Greek musical modes).

[12] *Orpheus self* That is, Orpheus's self, or Orpheus himself. For Orpheus, see note below.

[13] *Elysian* From Elysian Fields or Elysium, the resting place of dead heroes in classical myth.

[14] *Orpheus ... Eurydice* In classical myth, Orpheus was the musician who traveled to the underworld to reclaim his wife, Eurydice, after she died. Touched by the beauty of Orpheus's playing, Pluto, god of the underworld, agreed to release her. But he made the condition that Orpheus had to leave the underworld without looking back to

These delights, if thou canst give,
Mirth with thee, I mean to live.
—1645 (WRITTEN C. 1631?)

Il Penseroso[1]

Hence vain deluding joys,
The brood of folly without father bred,
How little you bestead,[2]
Or fill the fixèd mind with all your toys;
Dwell in some idle brain,
And fancies fond with gaudy shapes possess,
As thick and numberless
As the gay motes that people the sunbeams,
Or likest hovering dreams
The fickle pensioners of Morpheus' train.[3]
But hail thou goddess, sage and holy,
Hail divinest Melancholy,
Whose saintly visage is too bright
To hit the sense of human sight;
And therefore to our weaker view,
O'erlaid with black staid Wisdom's hue.
Black, but such as in esteem, Prince
Memnon's sister[4] might beseem,
Or that starred Ethiop queen[5] that strove
To set her beauty's praise above
The sea-nymphs, and their powers offended.
Yet thou art higher far descended,
Thee bright-haired Vesta[6] long of yore,
To solitary Saturn[7] bore;
His daughter she (in Saturn's reign,
Such mixture was not held a stain)
Oft in glimmering bowers, and glades
He met her, and in secret shades
Of woody Ida's[8] inmost grove,
While yet there was no fear of Jove.
Come pensive nun, devout and pure,
Sober, steadfast, and demure,
All in a robe of darkest grain,
Flowing with majestic train,
And sable stole of cypress lawn,[9]
Over thy decent shoulders drawn.
Come, but keep thy wonted state,
With even step, and musing gait,
And looks commercing with the skies,
Thy rapt soul sitting in thine eyes:
There held in holy passion still,
Forget thyself to marble, till
With a sad leaden downward cast,
Thou fix them on the earth as fast.
And join with thee calm Peace, and Quiet,
Spare Fast, that oft with gods doth diet,
And hears the Muses in a ring,
Ay round about Jove's altar sing.
And add to these retired Leisure,
That in trim gardens takes his pleasure;
But first, and chiefest, with thee bring,
Him that yon soars on golden wing,
Guiding the fiery-wheelèd throne,[10]
The cherub Contemplation,
And the mute Silence hist° along, *summon*
'Less Philomel[11] will deign a song,

see if Eurydice was following; at the last minute, he looked, and lost her once again (hence she is "half-regained").

[1] *Il Penseroso* The pensive or contemplative man (Italian).

[2] *bestead* Help, avail, be of service.

[3] *Morpheus' train* Dreams are the attendants of Morpheus, the god of sleep.

[4] *Memnon's sister* In classical story, Memnon was an Ethiopian prince who fought on the side of the Trojans in the Trojan war; his sister was named Himera.

[5] *starred Ethiop queen* Cassiopaeia; in classical myth she was changed into a constellation (hence "starred") as punishment for claiming to be more beautiful than the sea nymphs.

[6] *Vesta* Classical goddess of hearth and home.

[7] *Saturn* In classical myth, father of Jove (mentioned below); traditionally "solitary," he was associated with melancholics (hence the adjective "saturnine") even though his was the Golden Age.

[8] *Ida* Mount Ida, in Crete, the traditional site from which Saturn ruled, before his son Jove overthrew him.

[9] *cypress lawn* Lawn is a fine linen, usually white, but "cypress lawn" is black.

[10] *fiery-wheelèd throne* Apparently referring to the Biblical vision of Ezekiel (Ezekiel 10) of a chariot guided by cherubim (angels).

[11] *Philomel* The nightingale, from a classical story in which a young woman, Philomela, is transformed into the sweet-singing bird after being raped and silenced by having her tongue cut out (hence "saddest plight").

In her sweetest, saddest plight,
Smoothing the rugged brow of night,
While Cynthia[1] checks her dragon yoke,
Gently o'er th' accustomed oak;
Sweet bird that shunn'st the noise of folly,
Most musical, most melancholy!
Thee chauntress oft the woods among,
I woo to hear thy even-song;
And missing thee, I walk unseen
On the dry smooth-shaven green,
To behold the wandering moon,
Riding near her highest noon,[2]
Like one that had been led astray
Through the heaven's wide pathless way;
And oft, as if her head she bowed,
Stooping through a fleecy cloud.
Oft on a plat° of rising ground, *patch*
I hear the far-off curfew sound,
Over some wide-watered shore,
Swinging slow with sullen roar;
Or if the air will not permit,
Some still removèd place will fit,
Where glowing embers through the room
Teach light to counterfeit a gloom,
Far from all resort of mirth,
Save the cricket on the hearth,
Or the bellman's° drowsy charm, *night watchman*
To bless the doors from nightly harm:
Or let my lamp at midnight hour,
Be seen in some high lonely tower,
Where I may oft outwatch the Bear,[3]
With thrice great Hermes,[4] or unsphere
The spirit of Plato[5] to unfold
What worlds, or what vast regions hold
The immortal mind that hath forsook
Her mansion in this fleshly nook:
And of those daemons[6] that are found
In fire, air, flood, or underground,
Whose power hath a true consent
With planet, or with element.
Sometime let gorgeous Tragedy
In sceptred pall come sweeping by,
Presenting Thebes, or Pelops' line,[7]
Or the tale of Troy divine.
Or what (though rare) of later age,
Ennobled hath the buskined stage.[8]
But, O sad virgin, that thy power
Might raise Musaeus[9] from his bower,
Or bid the soul of Orpheus sing
Such notes as warbled to the string,
Drew iron tears down Pluto's cheek,
And made hell grant what love did seek.[10]
Or call up him[11] that left half-told
The story of Cambuscan bold,
Of Camball, and of Algarsife,
And who had Canace to wife,
That owned the virtuous ring and glass,
And of the wondrous horse of brass,
On which the Tartar king did ride;[12]

[1] *Cynthia* Classical goddess of the moon, here imagined as driving across the night sky in a chariot drawn by a dragon.

[2] *highest noon* Highest point, apogee.

[3] *the Bear* The constellation Ursa Major.

[4] *thrice great Hermes* Hermes Trismegistus, the reputed author of the classical *Corpus Hermeticum*, a collection of mystical ("Hermetic") writings that Il Penseroso stays up all night to read.

[5] *Plato* Il Penseroso contemplates reading the works of Plato, whose spirit is imagined as inhabiting a heavenly sphere or star.

[6] *daemons* From neo-Platonic or Hermetic philosophy, spirits that inhabit the four "elements" of fire, air, water, and earth.

[7] *Thebes, or Pelops' line* Two royal families whose stories provided subject matter for classical tragedies: the house of Thebes was that of Oedipus and his family; the house of Pelops was the family of Atreus, Agamemnon, Orestes, Electra, and Iphigenia.

[8] *buskined stage* Tragedies, from the footwear worn by Greek tragic actors; Milton implies that good tragedies were rare in his (as opposed to the classical) period.

[9] *Musaeus* In classical myth, a great singer, sometimes called the son of Orpheus.

[10] *Orpheus ... seek* In classical myth, Orpheus was the master musician who traveled to the underworld to reclaim his wife, Eurydice, after she died. Touched by the beauty of Orpheus's playing, Pluto, god of the underworld, agreed to release her. But he made the condition that Orpheus had to leave the underworld without looking back to see if Eurydice was following; at the last minute, he looked, and lost her once again (hence she is "half-regained").

[11] *him* I.e., Geoffrey Chaucer.

[12] *story of ... ride* The romance of Cambuscan, his children Camball, Algarsife, and Canace, and the gifts of a brass horse and a magic ring, is told in Chaucer's unfinished "Squire's Tale" in the *Canterbury Tales*, and continued by Spenser in Book 4 of *The Faerie*

And if aught else, great bards beside,
In sage and solemn tunes have sung,
Of tourneys and of trophies hung;
Of forest, and enchantments drear,
Where more is meant than meets the ear.[1]
Thus Night oft see me in thy pale career,
Till civil-suited Morn appear,
Not tricked and frounced as she was wont,
With the Attic boy[2] to hunt,
But kerchiefed in a comely cloud,
While rocking winds are piping loud,
Or ushered with a shower still,
When the gust hath blown his fill,
Ending on the rustling leaves,
With minute drops from off the eaves.
And when the sun begins to fling
His flaring beams, me goddess bring
To archèd walks of twilight groves,
And shadows brown that Sylvan[3] loves
Of pine, or monumental oak,
Where the rude axe with heavèd stroke,
Was never heard the nymphs to daunt,
Or fright them from their hallowed haunt.
There in close covert by some brook,
Where no profaner eye may look,
Hide me from day's garish eye,
While the bee with honied thigh,
That at her flowery work doth sing,
And the waters murmuring
With such consort as they keep,
Entice the dewy-feathered Sleep;
And let some strange mysterious dream,
Wave at his wings in airy stream,
Of lively portraiture displayed,
Softly on my eyelids laid.
And as I wake, sweet music breathe
Above, about, or underneath,
Sent by some spirit to mortals good,
Or th' unseen genius° of the wood. *guardian spirit*

But let my due° feet never fail, *dutiful*
To walk the studious cloister's[4] pale,° *enclosure*
And love the high embowèd roof,
With antique pillars' massy proof,
And storied windows[5] richly dight,° *decorated*
Casting a dim religious light.
There let the pealing organ blow,
To the full-voiced choir below,
In service high, and anthems clear,
As may with sweetness, through mine ear,
Dissolve me into ecstasies,
And bring all heaven before mine eyes.
And may at last my weary age
Find out the peaceful hermitage,
The hairy gown and mossy cell,
Where I may sit and rightly spell,[6]
Of every star that heaven doth shew,
And every herb that sips the dew;
Till old experience do attain
To something like prophetic strain.
These pleasures Melancholy give,
And I with thee will choose to live.
—1645 (WRITTEN C.1631?)

Lycidas

In this monody[7] the author bewails a learned friend,[8] unfortunately drowned in his passage from Chester on the Irish Seas, 1637. And by occasion foretells the ruin of our corrupted clergy then in their height.[9]

Queene.

[1] *more is meant than meets the ear* Milton apparently refers to *The Faerie Queene* and Spenser's allegorical method.

[2] *Attic boy* In classical myth, Aurora (Dawn) loved Cephalus, an Athenian (Attic) youth.

[3] *Sylvan* Sylvanus, Roman god of forests.

[4] *cloister* Covered walk; here, probably a university, not a monastic, cloister.

[5] *storied windows* Pictorial stained glass windows.

[6] *spell* Study, decipher.

[7] *monody* Lament sung by one voice.

[8] *friend* Edward King (1612–37), a fellow student of Milton's at Cambridge.

[9] *In this … height* Milton added this headnote to the version in his *Poems* (1645), published when the success of Parliament in the Civil Wars made it possible to publish a comment about the "corrupted clergy." When the poem was first published, in a 1638 collection of poems dedicated to the memory of Edward King, English bishops, under the leadership of Archbishop William Laud, were indeed at the "height" of their power.

Yet once more, O ye laurels, and once more
Ye myrtles brown, with ivy never sere,° *withered*
I come to pluck your berries harsh and crude,
And with forced fingers rude,
Shatter your leaves before the mellowing year.[1]
Bitter constraint, and sad occasion dear,
Compels me to disturb your season due:
For Lycidas[2] is dead, dead ere his prime,
Young Lycidas, and hath not left his peer:
Who would not sing for Lycidas? he knew
Himself to sing, and build the lofty rhyme.
He must not float upon his watery bier
Unwept, and welter[3] to the parching wind,
Without the meed° of some melodious tear. *honour*
Begin then, sisters of the sacred well,[4]
That from beneath the seat of Jove[5] doth spring,
Begin, and somewhat loudly sweep the string.
Hence with denial vain, and coy excuse,
So may some gentle muse
With lucky words favour my destined urn,
And as he passes turn,
And bid fair peace be to my sable shroud.
For we were nursed upon the self-same hill,[6]
Fed the same flock; by fountain, shade, and rill.° *brook*
Together both, ere the high lawns[7] appeared
Under the opening eyelids of the morn,
We drove afield, and both together heard
What time the grey-fly winds[8] her sultry horn,
Battening° our flocks with the fresh dews[9] *feeding*
of night,
Oft till the star that rose, at evening, bright
Toward heaven's descent had sloped his westering
wheel.
Meanwhile the rural ditties were not mute,
Tempered to the oaten flute,
Rough satyrs[10] danced, and fauns with cloven heel,
From the glad sound would not be absent long,
And old Damoetas[11] loved to hear our song.
But O the heavy change, now thou art gone,
Now thou art gone, and never must return!
Thee shepherd, thee the woods, and desert caves,
With wild thyme and the gadding vine o'ergrown,
And all their echoes mourn.
The willows, and the hazel copses green,
Shall now no more be seen,
Fanning their joyous leaves to thy soft lays.° *songs*
As killing as the canker to the rose,
Or taint-worm to the weanling herds that graze,
Or frost to flowers, that their gay wardrobe wear,
When first the whitethorn blows;° *blooms*
Such, Lycidas, thy loss to shepherd's ear.
Where were ye nymphs when the remorseless deep
Closed o'er the head of your loved Lycidas?
For neither were ye playing on the steep,
Where your old bards, the famous Druids[12] lie,
Nor on the shaggy top of Mona high,
Nor yet where Deva spreads her wizard stream:
Ay me, I fondly dream!
Had ye been there … for what could that have done?
What could the Muse herself that Orpheus bore,
The Muse herself, for her enchanting son

[1] *laurels … myrtles … ivy* These three evergreens were emblems of poetic achievement: laurel was sacred to Apollo, so a laurel wreath was the traditional crown of poets; myrtle was sacred to Venus, and so was an emblem of love poetry; ivy was linked with Bacchus, god of wine, and so was associated with poetic ecstasy or inspiration. By saying that he needs to pluck these berries before they are ripe, the speaker implies that he thinks himself unready to write the poetry these plants honored.

[2] *Lycidas* Traditional name in classical and Renaissance pastoral literature.

[3] *welter* Roll or tumble about.

[4] *sisters of the sacred well* The nine Muses; their well is the emblematic source of artistic inspiration.

[5] *seat of Jove* Probably Mt. Olympus, from beneath which one of the muses' sacred springs flowed; possibly Mt. Helicon, the site of another sacred spring.

[6] *nursed upon the self-same hill* Milton uses pastoral conventions to indicate that he and "Lycidas" went to the same school.

[7] *lawns* Open spaces between woods, glades.

[8] *winds* Blows its horn (that is, buzzes).

[9] *dews* Grasses still covered in dew.

[10] *satyrs* Part human, part animal creatures associated with lechery and wildness; when translated from the pastoral fiction, these are Milton's fellow undergraduates at Cambridge.

[11] *Damoetas* Conventional pastoral name, and here a teacher or mentor figure, possibly alluding to a real tutor at Cambridge.

[12] *Druids* The speaker asks if the sea nymphs failed to save King because they were playing in places associated with the Druids, ancient Celtic minstrel-poets or, here, "bards": Bardsey (the "steep" island where they "lie" buried), the island of Mona (Anglesey), and the river Dee (here, Latinized as "Deva") in Chester.

Whom universal nature did lament,
When by the rout that made the hideous roar,
His gory visage down the stream was sent,
Down the swift Hebrus to the Lesbian shore.[1]
  Alas! What boots it with uncessant care
To tend the homely slighted shepherd's trade,
And strictly meditate the thankless Muse,
Were it not better done as others use,
To sport with Amaryllis in the shade,
Or with the tangles of Neaera's hair?[2]
Fame is the spur that the clear spirit doth raise
(That last infirmity of noble mind)
To scorn delights, and live laborious days;
But the fair guerdon° when we hope to find, *reward*
And think to burst out into sudden blaze,
Comes the blind Fury[3] with th' abhorrèd shears,
And slits the thin-spun life. But not the praise,
Phoebus[4] replied, and touched my trembling ears;
Fame is no plant that grows on mortal soil,
Nor in the glistering foil
Set off to the world, nor in broad rumour lies,
But lives and spreads aloft by those pure eyes,
And perfect witness of all-judging Jove;
As he pronounces lastly on each deed,
Of so much fame in heaven expect thy meed.
  O fountain Arethuse,[5] and thou honoured flood,
Smooth-sliding Mincius[6] crowned with vocal reeds,
That strain I heard was of a higher mood:
But now my oat[7] proceeds,
And listens to the herald of the sea° *Triton*
That came in Neptune's plea,
He asked the waves, and asked the felon winds,
What hard mishap hath doomed this gentle swain?
And questioned every gust of rugged wings[8]
That blows from off each beakèd promontory;
They knew not of his story,
And sage Hippotades[9] their answer brings,
That not a blast was from his dungeon strayed,
The air was calm, and on the level brine,
Sleek Panope[10] with all her sisters played.
It was that fatal and perfidious bark
Built in th' eclipse, and rigged with curses dark,
That sunk so low that sacred head of thine.
  Next Camus,[11] reverend sire, went footing slow,
His mantle hairy, and his bonnet sedge,
Inwrought with figures dim, and on the edge
Like to that sanguine flower inscribed with woe.[12]
Ah! who hath reft (quoth he) my dearest pledge?
Last came, and last did go,
The pilot of the Galilean lake,[13]
Two massy keys he bore of metals twain
(The golden opes, the iron shuts amain),
He shook his mitred locks,[14] and stern bespake,
How well could I have spared for thee, young swain,
Enow° of such as for their bellies' sake, *enough*

[1] *What could the Muse ... shore* Orpheus was the greatest musician/poet in the classical tradition; his mother was the Muse Calliope. He met his death at the hands of Maenads, a group of women in an ecstatic frenzy. Orpheus's severed bleeding head ("gory visage") floated down the Hebrus river across the sea and to the island of Lesbos, where the Muses buried it.

[2] *Amaryllis ... Neaera* Conventional names in pastoral poetry for young women.

[3] *Fury* In classical myth, the three Fates respectively spun the thread of life, measured it, and then cut it; the Fate with the cutting shears was named Atropos, or Destiny. The speaker compares her to one of the Furies, another group of mythological sisters, who were snaky-haired agents of vengeance.

[4] *Phoebus* Apollo, god of poetry.

[5] *Arethuse* Fountain on an island near Sicily, associated with pastoral poetry; named for the nymph Arethusa, who was transformed into the fountain while being chased by the river god Alpheus (see below, line 132).

[6] *Mincius* River in Mantua, where the Roman poet Virgil was born.

[7] *oat* Oaten flute (of l. 33); metaphorically, the speaker's song (poem).

[8] *wings* Winds, imagined as birdlike.

[9] *Hippotades* Aeolus, the classical keeper of winds.

[10] *Panope* The chief nymph of fifty sea-nymph sisters, the Nereides.

[11] *Camus* Personification of the River Cam, in Cambridge.

[12] *sanguine flower ... woe* The hyacinth. In classical myth, it sprang from the blood of Hyacinthus, a youth beloved of Apollo; the god recorded his grief by marking the flower with the letters AI AI ("alas").

[13] *pilot of the Galilean lake* Usually identified as St. Peter, speaking as the founder of the Christian Church; he mourns the loss of a young man who had intended to enter the ministry. He holds the keys of the kingdom of Heaven, from Matthew 16.19. Thee pilot is sometimes identified as Christ. But as a (ship) pilot on Galilee, Peter would here appear to be paired with Christ, mentioned in line 173 below as "Him that walked the waves."

[14] *mitred locks* Peter, the first bishop, wears the bishop's mitre (a tall, cleft headdress), and shakes his head.

Creep and intrude, and climb into the fold?° *sheepfold*
Of other care they little reckoning make,
Than how to scramble at the shearers' feast,
And shove away the worthy bidden guest.
Blind mouths! that scarce themselves know how
to hold
A sheep-hook, or have learned aught else the least
That to the faithful herdman's art belongs!
What recks it them?[1] What need they? They are sped;[2]
And when they list,[3] their lean and flashy songs
Grate on their scrannel[4] pipes of wretched straw,
The hungry sheep look up, and are not fed,
But swoll'n with wind, and the rank mist they draw,
Rot inwardly, and foul contagion spread:
Besides what the grim wolf[5] with privy paw[6]
Daily devours apace, and nothing said,[7]
But that two-handed engine[8] at the door,
Stands ready to smite once, and smite no more.
Return Alpheus,[9] the dread voice is past,
That shrunk thy streams; return Sicilian Muse,[10]

[1] *What recks it them* What do they care?

[2] *They are sped* They have done well.

[3] *when they list* When they choose, or please.

[4] *scrannel* Shriveled, thin; an unusual word, probably provincial dialect, apparently chosen for its appropriately ugly sound.

[5] *wolf* Usually identified as an allusion to the threat posed by Catholicism.

[6] *with privy paw* With secret or hidden steps; possibly also an allusion to the Privy Council, and implying that the government under Charles I was helping the Church push a Catholic agenda.

[7] *nothing said* In the manuscript version of this poem, Milton originally wrote "nothing" but then crossed it out and wrote "little"; "nothing" appears in the 1645 edition.

[8] *two-handed engine* The specific reference here continues to be debated. Probably, in one respect, a sword: in *Paradise Lost*, the Archangel Michael wields a "huge two-handed" sword (6.251), which likely refers to the two-edged swords mentioned in Revelation 1.16 and Psalm 149.6. But as an emblem for divine agency or judgment, the "sword of God" can also be interpreted as manifesting itself in many different objects, institutions, or ideas (such as the two keys of line 110 above).

[9] *Alphaeus* River in Greece, and the god of the river (see l. 85 above). The speaker invites the return of sources that inspire the pastoral mode.

[10] *Sicilian Muse* Probably Arethusa (see l. 85 above). Sicily was associated with the pastoral mode: the poet Theocritus (fl. 280 BCE), the creator of pastoral poetry, was Sicilian.

And call the vales, and bid them hither cast
Their bells, and flowrets of a thousand hues.
Ye valleys low where the mild whispers use,
Of shades and wanton winds, and gushing brooks,
On whose fresh lap the swart star[11] sparely looks,
Throw hither all your quaint enamelled eyes,
That on the green turf suck the honied showers,
And purple all the ground with vernal flowers.
Bring the rathe° primrose that forsaken dies, *early blooming*
The tufted crow-toe, and pale jessamine,
The white pink, and the pansy freaked° with jet, *streaked*
The glowing violet,
The musk-rose, and the well-attired woodbine,
With cowslips wan that hang the pensive head,
And every flower that sad embroidery wears:
Bid amaranthus all his beauty shed,
And daffodillies fill their cups with tears,
To strew the laureate[12] hearse where Lycid lies.
For so to interpose a little ease,
Let our frail thoughts dally with false surmise
(Ay me!) Whilst thee the shores, and sounding seas
Wash far away, where'er thy bones are hurled,
Whether beyond the stormy Hebrides
Where thou perhaps under the whelming tide
Visit'st the bottom of the monstrous world;
Or whether thou to our moist vows denied,
Sleep'st by the fable of Bellerus[13] old,
Where the great vision of the guarded mount[14]
Looks toward Namancos and Bayona's hold;° *fortress*
Look homeward angel now, and melt with ruth.
And, O ye dolphins, waft the hapless youth.
Weep no more, woeful shepherds weep no more,
For Lycidas your sorrow is not dead,
Sunk though he be beneath the watery floor,
So sinks the day-star° in the ocean bed, *the sun*

[11] *swart star* Sirius, the Dog Star, associated with the hottest weeks of the year.

[12] *laureate* Decorated with laurel (see line 1).

[13] *Bellerus* Milton apparently invents the name from Bellarium, the Latin name for Land's End in Cornwall, the south-west tip of England.

[14] *guarded mount* St. Michael's Mount in Cornwall, from which the Archangel was traditionally said to guard England; here, Michael looks out toward two places in Spain, but is asked to look "homeward" in pity for Lycidas.

And yet anon repairs his drooping head,
And tricks his beams, and with new spangled ore,
Flames in the forehead of the morning sky:
So Lycidas sunk low, but mounted high,
Through the dear might of Him that walked the waves,
Where other groves, and other streams along,
With nectar pure his oozy locks he laves,
And hears the unexpressive nuptial song,
In the blest kingdoms meek of joy and love.
There entertain him all the saints above,
In solemn troops, and sweet societies
That sing, and singing in their glory move,
And wipe the tears for ever from his eyes.
Now Lycidas the shepherds weep no more;
Henceforth thou art the genius° of the shore, *guardian spirit*
In thy large recompense, and shalt be good
To all that wander in that perilous flood.
Thus sang the uncouth swain to th' oaks and rills,
While the still morn went out with sandals grey,
He touched the tender stops of various quills,° *reeds (flutes)*
With eager thought warbling his Doric[1] lay:
And now the sun had stretched out all the hills,
And now was dropped into the western bay;
At last he rose, and twitched his mantle blue:[2]
Tomorrow to fresh woods, and pastures new.[3]
—1638, 1645

Sonnets

7

How soon hath Time the subtle thief of youth,
Stol'n on his wing my three and twenti'th year!
My hasting days fly on with full career,
But my late spring no bud or blossom shew'th.
Perhaps my semblance might deceive the truth,
That I to manhood am arriv'd so near,
And inward ripeness doth much less appear,
That some more timely-happy spirits indu'th.
Yet be it less or more, or soon or slow,
It shall be still° in strictest measure ev'n, *always*
To that same lot, however mean, or high,
Toward which Time leads me, and the will of Heav'n;
All is, if I have grace to use it so,
As ever in my great task-master's eye.
—1645 (WRITTEN EITHER 1631 OR 1632)

16[4]

TO THE LORD GENERAL CROMWELL[5]

Cromwell, our chief of men, who through a cloud
Not of war only, but detractions rude,
Guided by faith and matchless fortitude,
To peace and truth thy glorious way hast plough'd,
And on the neck of crowned Fortune proud
Hast rear'd God's trophies, and his work pursu'd,
While Darwen stream[6] with blood of Scots imbru'd,
And Dunbar field,[7] resounds thy praises loud,
And Worcester's[8] laureate wreath; yet much remains
To conquer still: peace hath her victories
No less renown'd than war. New foes arise
Threat'ning to bind our souls with secular chains:[9]
Help us to save free Conscience from the paw
Of hireling[10] wolves whose Gospel is their maw.
—1694 (WRITTEN 1652)

[1] *Doric* Musical mode.

[2] *blue* Color traditionally associated with hope.

[3] *Thus song ... new* The final eight lines, rhyming ABABABCC, reflect the form of an *ottava rima* stanza, one pattern associated with epic narrative poetry.

[4] *16* Not published in Milton's lifetime. It is numbered sonnet 16 in Milton's manuscript version, though some modern editions give the number 16 to "When I consider how my light is spent" (Sonnet 19 here). The manuscript dates the poem May 1652, and has a scratched-out subtitle: "On the proposals of certain ministers at the Committee for Propagation of the Gospel."

[5] *to the Lord General Cromwell* Oliver Cromwell (1599–1658), at the time Commander-in-Chief of the Parliamentary Army, and subsequently Lord Protector.

[6] *Darwen stream* The river near Preston, where Cromwell defeated a Scottish army in August 1648.

[7] *Dunbar field* Where Cromwell routed the Scottish army in September 1650.

[8] *Worcester* Where Cromwell defeated the Royalist Army of Charles II, who was crowned in Scotland when in exile after the death of his father.

[9] *To conquer ... secular chains* Referring to the proposals mentioned in the poem's manuscript subtitle (see note above) that sought to reinstall a state-controlled church.

[10] *hireling* Milton disapproved of compulsory tithes, believing that congregations should be able to hire ministers of their own choosing: to him, ministers in a state church are hired state employees.

18[1]

On the Late Massacre in Piedmont[2]

Avenge O Lord the slaughtered saints, whose bones
Lie scattered on the Alpine mountains cold,
Even them who kept thy truth so pure of old
When all our fathers worshipped stocks and stones,
Forget not: in thy book record their groans
Who were thy sheep and in their ancient fold
Slain by the bloody Piedmontese that rolled
Mother with infant down the rocks. Their moans
The vales redoubled to the hills, and they
To heaven. Their martyred blood and ashes sow
O'er all the Italian fields where still doth sway
The triple tyrant:[3] that from these may grow
A hundredfold, who having learnt thy way
Early may fly the Babylonian woe.
—c. 1673 (written 1655)

19[4]

When I consider how my light is spent,
Ere half my days,[5] in this dark world and wide,
And that one talent[6] which is death to hide,
Lodged with me useless, though my soul more bent
To serve therewith my maker, and present
My true account, lest he returning chide,
Doth God exact day-labour, light denied,
I fondly ask; but patience to prevent
That murmur, soon replies, God doth not need
Either man's work or his own gifts, who best
Bear his mild yoke, they serve him best, his state
Is kingly. Thousands at his bidding speed
And post[7] o'er land and ocean without rest:
They also serve who only stand and wait.
—1673 (written c. 1652–55)

23[8]

Methought I saw my late espoused saint[9]
Brought to me, like Alcestis,[10] from the grave,
Whom Jove's great son to her glad husband gave,
Rescued from death by force, though pale and faint.
Mine, as whom washed from spot of child-bed taint
Purification in the old Law[11] did save,
And such as yet once more I trust to have
Full sight of her in Heaven without restraint,
Came vested all in white, pure as her mind;
Her face was veiled,[12] yet to my fancied sight
Love, sweetness, goodness, in her person shined
So clear as in no face with more delight.
But Oh! as to embrace me she inclined,
I waked, she fled, and day brought back my night.
—1673 (written between 1652 and 1658)

---

[1] *18* Some modern editions number this sonnet 15, the number assigned it in the 1673 edition of Milton's *Poems.*

[2] *Massacre in Piedmont* In April 1655, a Catholic army under the command of the Duke of Savoy began a persecution of the Vaudois or Waldensians, a Protestant sect that lived in the mountainous Piedmont region of Italy, near the Swiss border. The Waldensians had broken away from the Catholic Church in the twelfth century. But seventeenth-century Protestants thought they represented a much older tradition, and regarded them as having retained the beliefs of the primitive Church.

[3] *triple tyrant* The Pope, from the three-crowned papal mitre or headdress.

[4] *19* Numbered sonnet 16 in some modern editions. The title "On his blindness" was added in the eighteenth century, and appears in some modern editions.

[5] *half my days* The source of much debate on the date of this poem: Milton was born in December 1608, and it is not clear by what standard he judges the normal length of a life. He was totally blind by early 1652.

[6] *talent* Alluding to the parable of the talents in Matthew 25.14-30.

[7] *post* Ride.

[8] *23* Numbered sonnet 19 in some modern editions.

[9] *late espoused saint* Milton's first wife, Mary Powell, died in May 1652, shortly after giving birth to their daughter Deborah. His second wife, Katherine Woodcock, died in February 1658, several months after giving birth to their daughter Katherine. The sonnet could refer to either wife, or even both (on the grounds that if Milton had wanted to make the reference clear, he could have).

[10] *Alcestis* In classical story, Alcestis sacrificed her life to save her husband, Admetus; Hercules, the son of Jove, repays Admetus's hospitality to him by forcing Death (in a wrestling match) to return her alive. The story is told in the play *Alcestis* by Euripedes.

[11] *Purification in the old Law* Referring to the rites of purification after childbirth detailed in Leviticus 12 (the old Law of the Old Testament, as opposed to the new Law of the New Testament).

[12] *veiled* Like Alcestis, when she returned; but also from the reader.

Areopagitica: A Speech of Mr. John Milton for the Liberty of Unlicensed Printing, to the Parliament of England[1]

They who to states and governors of the Commonwealth direct their speech, High Court of Parliament, or, wanting such access in a private condition, write that which they foresee may advance the public good; I suppose them, as at the beginning of no mean endeavour, not a little altered and moved inwardly in their minds: some with doubt of what will be the success, others with fear of what will be the censure; some with hope, others with confidence of what they have to speak. And me perhaps each of these dispositions, as the subject was whereon I entered, may have at other times variously affected; and likely might in these foremost expressions now also disclose which of them swayed most, but that the very attempt of this address thus made, and the thought of whom it hath recourse to, hath got the power within me to a passion, far more welcome than incidental to a preface....

If ye be thus resolved, as it were injury to think ye were not, I know not what should withhold me from presenting ye with a fit instance wherein to show both that love of truth which ye eminently profess, and that uprightness of your judgment which is not wont to be partial to yourselves; by judging over again that Order which ye have ordained to regulate printing: that no book, pamphlet, or paper shall be henceforth printed, unless the same be first approved and licensed by such, or at least one of such, as shall thereto be appointed. For that part which preserves justly every man's copy to himself, or provides for the poor, I touch not, only wish they be not made pretences to abuse and persecute honest and painful men, who offend not in either of these particulars. But that other clause of licensing books, which we thought had died with his brother quadragesimal and matrimonial[2] when the prelates expired, I shall now attend with such a homily, as shall lay before ye, first the inventors of it to be those whom ye will be loath to own; next what is to be thought in general of reading, whatever sort the books be; and that this Order avails nothing to the suppressing of scandalous, seditious, and libellous books, which were mainly intended to be suppressed. Last, that it will be primely to the discouragement of all learning, and the stop of Truth, not only by disexercising and blunting our abilities in what we know already, but by hindering and cropping the discovery that might be yet further made both in religious and civil wisdom.

I deny not, but that it is of greatest concernment in the Church and Commonwealth to have a vigilant eye how books demean themselves as well as men; and thereafter to confine, imprison, and do sharpest justice on them as malefactors. For books are not absolutely dead things, but do contain a potency of life in them to be as active as that soul was whose progeny they are; nay, they do preserve as in a vial the purest efficacy and extraction of that living intellect that bred them. I know they are as lively, and as vigorously productive, as those fabulous dragon's teeth;[3] and being sown up and down, may chance to spring up armed men. And yet, on the other hand, unless wariness be used, as good almost kill a man as kill a good book. Who kills a man kills a reasonable creature, God's image; but he who destroys a good book, kills reason itself, kills the image of God,

[1] *Areopagitica ... England* Milton's title invokes the *Areopagite Discourse* (c. 355 BCE) by the Greek orator Isocrates, who advocated a return to the days when the Athenian court of the Areopagus (a kind of Supreme Court) was a model of virtue, wisdom, and responsibility. Milton might also expect his readers to remember that Saint Paul delivered an oration on the Areopagus, the hill outside Athens that gave its name to the court that met there (Acts 17.19-34). Milton's text is in the form of an oration to Parliament, the entity the speaker addresses throughout. His motive for writing was a Parliamentary order (June 1643) that banned the publication of any book that had not been licensed before publication: what Milton attacks here is pre-publication censorship, not censorship in general (he does *not* argue for complete freedom of the press). Milton's main strategy is to embarrass Parliament by linking their attempt to control the press to the similar powers wielded by the monarchical government they were battling to overthrow.

[2] *quadragesimal and matrimonial* Referring to powers formerly held by bishops to award dispensations, here specifically those governing dietary restrictions in Lent ("quadragesimal" refers to Lent's forty days) and marriage licenses. Milton's point, a recurring one, is that with this new order, Parliament was giving itself the kind of controlling powers it had abolished when it abolished episcopacy.

[3] *dragon's teeth* In Greek mythology, the teeth of a dragon slain by the hero Cadmus bred armed men when sown in the ground.

as it were in the eye. Many a man lives a burden to the earth; but a good book is the precious life-blood of a master spirit, embalmed and treasured up on purpose to a life beyond life. 'Tis true, no age can restore a life, whereof perhaps there is no great loss; and revolutions of ages do not oft recover the loss of a rejected truth, for the want of which whole nations fare the worse.

We should be wary therefore what persecutions we raise against the living labours of public men, how we spill that seasoned life of man, preserved and stored up in books; since we see a kind of homicide may be thus committed, sometimes a martyrdom, and if it extend to the whole impression, a kind of massacre; whereof the execution ends not in the slaying of an elemental life, but strikes at that ethereal and fifth essence, the breath of reason itself, slays an immortality rather than a life....

Good and evil we know in the field of this world grow up together almost inseparably; and the knowledge of good is so involved and interwoven with the knowledge of evil, and in so many cunning resemblances hardly to be discerned, that those confused seeds which were imposed upon Psyche as an incessant labour to cull out, and sort asunder, were not more intermixed.[1] It was from out the rind of one apple tasted, that the knowledge of good and evil, as two twins cleaving together, leaped forth into the world. And perhaps this is that doom which Adam fell into of knowing good and evil, that is to say of knowing good by evil. As therefore the state of man now is; what wisdom can there be to choose, what continence to forbear without the knowledge of evil? He that can apprehend and consider vice with all her baits and seeming pleasures, and yet abstain, and yet distinguish, and yet prefer that which is truly better, he is the true wayfaring Christian.

I cannot praise a fugitive and cloistered virtue, unexercised and unbreathed, that never sallies out and sees her adversary, but slinks out of the race, where that immortal garland is to be run for, not without dust and heat. Assuredly we bring not innocence into the world, we bring impurity much rather; that which purifies us is trial, and trial is by what is contrary. That virtue therefore which is but a youngling in the contemplation of evil, and knows not the utmost that vice promises to her followers, and rejects it, is but a blank virtue, not a pure; her whiteness is but an excremental[2] whiteness. Which was the reason why our sage and serious poet Spenser, whom I dare be known to think a better teacher than Scotus or Aquinas, describing true temperance under the person of Guyon, brings him in with his Palmer through the cave of Mammon, and the bower of earthly bliss, that he might see and know, and yet abstain.[3] Since therefore the knowledge and survey of vice is in this world so necessary to the constituting of human virtue, and the scanning of error to the confirmation of truth, how can we more safely, and with less danger, scout into the regions of sin and falsity than by reading all manner of tractates and hearing all manner of reason? And this is the benefit which may be had of books promiscuously read....

If we think to regulate printing, thereby to rectify manners, we must regulate all recreations and pastimes, all that is delightful to man. No music must be heard, no song be set or sung, but what is grave and Doric.[4] There must be licensing dancers, that no gesture, motion, or deportment be taught our youth but what by their allowance shall be thought honest; for such Plato was provided of; it will ask more than the work of twenty licensers to examine all the lutes, the violins, and the guitars in every house; they must not be suffered to prattle as they do, but must be licensed what they may say. And who shall silence all the airs and madrigals that whisper softness in chambers? The windows also, and the balconies must be thought on; there are shrewd books, with dangerous frontispieces, set to sale; who

[1] *Psyche* Apuleius (born 125 CE) tells the story of Cupid and Psyche in *The Golden Ass*; Psyche's impossible task was set her by her mother-in-law, Venus.

[2] *excremental* Superficial.

[3] *Which was the reason ... yet abstain* Milton here famously misremembers *The Faerie Queene*. Guyon, the Knight of Temperance in Book 2, does resist the temptation offered by the Bower of Bliss (2.12.42ff.) with the aid of the Palmer (a pilgrim who has been to the Holy Land, and in Spenser a figure for the reason that restrains passion). But Guyon's settled habits of temperance allow him to withstand the temptations of Mammon's cave on his own (2.7.2, 2.8.3).

[4] *Doric* One of the "modes" of ancient music; in his *Republic*, Plato (cited later in the paragraph) used "Doric" to describe poetry that was manly and dignified.

shall prohibit them, shall twenty licensers? The villages also must have their visitors to inquire what lectures the bagpipe and the rebeck[1] reads, even to the ballatry and the gamut of every municipal fiddler, for these are the countryman's Arcadias, and his Montemayors.[2]

Next, what more national corruption, for which England hears ill abroad, than household gluttony: who shall be the rectors of our daily rioting? And what shall be done to inhibit the multitudes that frequent those houses where drunkenness is sold and harboured? Our garments also should be referred to the licensing of some more sober workmasters to see them cut into a less wanton garb. Who shall regulate all the mixed conversation of our youth, male and female together, as is the fashion of this country? Who shall still appoint what shall be discoursed, what presumed, and no further? Lastly, who shall forbid and separate all idle resort, all evil company? These things will be, and must be; but how they shall be least hurtful, how least enticing, herein consists the grave and governing wisdom of a state.

To sequester out of the world into Atlantic and Utopian polities which never can be drawn into use will not mend our condition; but to ordain wisely as in this world of evil, in the midst whereof God hath placed us unavoidably. Nor is it Plato's licensing of books will do this, which necessarily pulls along with it so many other kinds of licensing, as will make us all both ridiculous and weary, and yet frustrate; but those unwritten, or at least unconstraining, laws of virtuous education, religious and civil nurture, which Plato there mentions as the bonds and ligaments of the commonwealth, the pillars and the sustainers of every written statute; these they be which will bear chief sway in such matters as these, when all licensing will be easily eluded. Impunity and remissness, for certain, are the bane of a commonwealth; but here the great art lies, to discern in what the law is to bid restraint and punishment, and in what things persuasion only is to work.

If every action which is good or evil in man at ripe years were to be under pittance and prescription and compulsion, what were virtue but a name, what praise could be then due to well-doing, what gramercy to be sober, just, or continent? Many there be that complain of Divine Providence for suffering Adam to transgress; foolish tongues! When God gave him reason, he gave him freedom to choose, for reason is but choosing; he had been else a mere artificial Adam, such an Adam as he is in the motions. We ourselves esteem not of that obedience, or love, or gift, which is of force: God therefore left him free, set before him a provoking object, ever almost in his eyes; herein consisted his merit, herein the right of his reward, the praise of his abstinence. Wherefore did he create passions within us, pleasures round about us, but that these rightly tempered are the very ingredients of virtue?...

And lest some should persuade ye, Lords and Commons, that these arguments of learned men's discouragement at this your Order are mere flourishes, and not real, I could recount what I have seen and heard in other countries, where this kind of inquisition tyrannizes; when I have sat among their learned men, for that honour I had, and been counted happy to be born in such a place of philosophic freedom, as they supposed England was, while themselves did nothing but bemoan the servile condition into which learning amongst them was brought; that this was it which had damped the glory of Italian wits; that nothing had been there written now these many years but flattery and fustian. There it was that I found and visited the famous Galileo,[3] grown old a prisoner to the Inquisition, for thinking in astronomy otherwise than the Franciscan and Dominican licensers thought.

And though I knew that England then was groaning loudest under the prelatical yoke, nevertheless I took it as a pledge of future happiness, that other nations were so persuaded of her liberty. Yet was it beyond my hope that those worthies were then breathing in her air, who

[1] *bagpipe and the rebeck* Viewed as rustic instruments; a rebeck is a three-stringed fiddle.

[2] *the countryman's Arcadias, and his Montemayors* That is, popular music is the rural equivalent to sophisticated prose romances, such as Sir Philip Sidney's *Arcadia* (1590) and Jorge de Montemayor's *Diana* (c. 1559).

[3] *There it was ... Galileo* Milton visited Italy in 1638-39; there seems no reason to doubt his claim to have visited Galileo, who is the only contemporary Milton names in *Paradise Lost* (5.262). Galileo at the time was under house arrest for having published his *Dialogue Concerning the Two Chief World Systems.*

should be her leaders to such a deliverance, as shall never be forgotten by any revolution of time that this world hath to finish. When that was once begun, it was as little in my fear that, what words of complaint I heard among learned men of other parts uttered against the Inquisition, the same I should hear by as learned men at home uttered in time of Parliament against an order of licensing; and that so generally that, when I had disclosed myself a companion of their discontent, I might say, if without envy, that he whom an honest quaestorship had endeared to the Sicilians was not more by them importuned against Verres,[1] than the favourable opinion which I had among many who honour ye, and are known and respected by ye, loaded me with entreaties and persuasions, that I would not despair to lay together that which just reason should bring into my mind, toward the removal of an undeserved thraldom upon learning. That this is not therefore the disburdening of a particular fancy, but the common grievance of all those who had prepared their minds and studies above the vulgar pitch to advance truth in others, and from others to entertain it, thus much may satisfy....

Truth indeed came once into the world with her Divine Master, and was a perfect shape most glorious to look on: but when He ascended, and His Apostles after Him were laid asleep, then straight arose a wicked race of deceivers, who, as that story goes of the Egyptian Typhon with his conspirators, how they dealt with the good Osiris,[2] took the virgin Truth, hewed her lovely form into a thousand pieces, and scattered them to the four winds. From that time ever since, the sad friends of Truth, such as durst appear, imitating the careful search that Isis made for the mangled body of Osiris, went up and down gathering up limb by limb, still as they could find them. We have not yet found them all, Lords and Commons, nor ever shall do, till her Master's second coming; He shall bring together every joint and member, and shall mold them into an immortal feature of loveliness and perfection. Suffer not these licensing prohibitions to stand at every place of opportunity, forbidding and disturbing them that continue seeking, that continue to do our obsequies to the torn body of our martyred saint.

We boast our light; but if we look not wisely on the Sun itself, it smites us into darkness. Who can discern those planets that are oft combust, and those stars of brightest magnitude that rise and set with the Sun, until the opposite motion of their orbs bring them to such a place in the firmament, where they may be seen evening or morning? The light which we have gained was given us, not to be ever staring on, but by it to discover onward things more remote from our knowledge. It is not the unfrocking of a priest, the unmitring of a bishop, and the removing him from off the Presbyterian shoulders, that will make us a happy nation. No, if other things as great in the Church, and in the rule of life both economical and political, be not looked into and reformed, we have looked so long upon the blaze that Zwinglius and Calvin[3] hath beaconed up to us, that we are stark blind. There be who perpetually complain of schisms and sects, and make it such a calamity that any man dissents from their maxims. 'Tis their own pride and ignorance which causes the disturbing, who neither will hear with meekness, nor can convince; yet all must be suppressed which is not found in their syntagma.[4] They are the troublers, they are the dividers of unity, who neglect and permit not others to unite those dissevered pieces which are yet wanting to the body of Truth. To be still searching what we know not by what we know, still closing up truth to truth as we find it (for all her body is homogeneal and proportional), this is the golden rule in theology as well as in arithmetic, and makes up the best harmony in a Church; not the forced and outward union of cold and neutral, and inwardly divided minds.

Lords and Commons of England, consider what nation it is whereof ye are, and whereof ye are the governors: a nation not slow and dull, but of a quick, ingenious and piercing spirit, acute to invent, subtle and

[1] *he ... Verres* Cicero (106-43 BCE), whose forensic oratory drove the corrupt Gaius Verres from office.

[2] *Typhon ... Osiris* Milton's source for this allegory about the search for the divided body of truth is likely Plutarch's essay "On Isis and Osiris." Typhon (the Egyptian god Set) tore up and scattered the body of Osiris; Isis, Osiris's sister, collected the pieces and put them back together.

[3] *Zwinglius and Calvin* Ulrich Zwingli (1484-1531) and John Calvin (1509-64), two leading figures of the Protestant Reformation.

[4] *syntagma* Systematic treatise or body of doctrine.

sinewy to discourse, not beneath the reach of any point, the highest that human capacity can soar to. Therefore the studies of Learning in her deepest sciences have been so ancient and so eminent among us, that writers of good antiquity and ablest judgment have been persuaded that even the school of Pythagoras and the Persian wisdom took beginning from the old philosophy of this island. And that wise and civil Roman, Julius Agricola, who governed once here for Caesar, preferred the natural wits of Britain before the laboured studies of the French.[1] Nor is it for nothing that the grave and frugal Transylvanian sends out yearly from as far as the mountainous borders of Russia, and beyond the Hercynian wilderness, not their youth, but their staid men, to learn our language and our theologic arts.[2]

Yet that which is above all this, the favour and the love of Heaven, we have great argument to think in a peculiar manner propitious and propending towards us. Why else was this nation chosen before any other, that out of her, as out of Sion, should be proclaimed and sounded forth the first tidings and trumpet of Reformation to all Europe? And had it not been the obstinate perverseness of our prelates against the divine and admirable spirit of Wycliffe,[3] to suppress him as a schismatic and innovator, perhaps neither the Bohemian Huss and Jerome,[4] no nor the name of Luther or of Calvin, had been ever known: the glory of reforming all our neighbours had been completely ours. But now, as our obdurate clergy have with violence demeaned the matter, we are become hitherto the latest and backwardest scholars, of whom God offered to have made us the teachers. Now once again by all concurrence of signs, and by the general instinct of holy and devout men, as they daily and solemnly express their thoughts, God is decreeing to begin some new and great period in his Church, even to the reforming of Reformation itself: what does He then but reveal himself to His servants, and as His manner is, first to his Englishmen? I say, as his manner is, first to us, though we mark not the method of His counsels, and are unworthy.

Behold now this vast city: a city of refuge, the mansion house of liberty, encompassed and surrounded with His protection; the shop of war hath not there more anvils and hammers waking, to fashion out the plates and instruments of armed Justice in defence of beleaguered Truth, than there be pens and heads there, sitting by their studious lamps, musing, searching, revolving new notions and ideas wherewith to present, as with their homage and their fealty, the approaching Reformation: others as fast reading, trying all things, assenting to the force of reason and convincement. What could a man require more from a nation so pliant and so prone to seek after knowledge? What wants there to such a towardly and pregnant soil but wise and faithful labourers, to make a knowing people, a nation of prophets, of sages, and of worthies? We reckon more than five months yet to harvest; there need not be five weeks; had we but eyes to lift up, the fields are white already.[5]

Where there is much desire to learn, there of necessity will be much arguing, much writing, many opinions; for opinion in good men is but knowledge in the making. Under these fantastic terrors of sect and schism, we wrong the earnest and zealous thirst after knowledge and understanding which God hath stirred up in this city. What some lament of, we rather should rejoice at, should rather praise this pious forwardness among men, to reassume the ill-reputed care of their Religion into their own hands again. A little generous prudence, a little forbearance of one another, and some grain of charity might win all these diligences to join, and unite in one general and brotherly search after Truth; could we but forgo this prelatical tradition of crowding free consciences and Christian liberties into canons and precepts of men. I doubt not, if some great and worthy stranger should come among us, wise to discern the mold and temper of a people, and how to govern it,

[1] *And that wise ... the French* Citing a story that appears in the Roman historian Tacitus, *Agricola*, 21.

[2] *Nor is it ... theologic arts* Many theologians from strongly Protestant Transylvania came to study during this period in Western European universities.

[3] *Wycliffe* John Wycliffe (c. 1324-84), an early Church reformer associated with the Lollard movement, often regarded as a proto-Protestant.

[4] *Huss and Jerome* John Huss (c. 1383-1415), founder of an influential reform movement in Bohemia, also often regarded as proto-Protestant; Jerome of Prague (d. 1416) was a disciple of both Wycliffe and Huss.

[5] *We reckon ... white already* Milton here adapts John 4.35.

observing the high hopes and aims, the diligent alacrity of our extended thoughts and reasonings, in the pursuance of truth and freedom, but that he would cry out as Pyrrhus did,[1] admiring the Roman docility and courage: If such were my Epirots, I would not despair the greatest design that could be attempted, to make a Church or Kingdom happy.

Yet these are the men cried out against for schismatics and sectaries; as if, while the temple of the Lord was building, some cutting, some squaring the marble, others hewing the cedars, there should be a sort of irrational men who could not consider there must be many schisms and many dissections made in the quarry and in the timber, ere the house of God can be built. And when every stone is laid artfully together, it cannot be united into a continuity, it can but be contiguous in this world; neither can every piece of the building be of one form; nay rather the perfection consists in this, that, out of many moderate varieties and brotherly dissimilitudes that are not vastly disproportional, arises the goodly and the graceful symmetry that commends the whole pile and structure.

Let us therefore be more considerate builders, more wise in spiritual architecture, when great reformation is expected. For now the time seems come, wherein Moses the great prophet may sit in heaven rejoicing to see that memorable and glorious wish of his fulfilled, when not only our seventy Elders, but all the Lord's people, are become prophets. No marvel then though some men, and some good men too perhaps, but young in goodness, as Joshua then was, envy them. They fret, and out of their own weakness are in agony, lest these divisions and subdivisions will undo us. The adversary again applauds, and waits the hour: When they have branched themselves out, saith he, small enough into parties and partitions, then will be our time. Fool! he sees not the firm root, out of which we all grow, though into branches: nor will beware until he see our small divided maniples[2] cutting through at every angle of his ill-united and unwieldy brigade. And that we are to hope better of all these supposed sects and schisms, and that we shall not need that solicitude, honest perhaps though over-timorous of them that vex in this behalf, but shall laugh in the end at those malicious applauders of our differences, I have these reasons to persuade me.

First, when a city shall be as it were besieged and blocked about, her navigable river infested, inroads and incursions round, defiance and battle oft rumoured to be marching up even to her walls and suburb trenches, that then the people, or the greater part, more than at other times, wholly taken up with the study of highest and most important matters to be reformed, should be disputing, reasoning, reading, inventing, discoursing, even to a rarity and admiration, things not before discoursed or written of, argues first a singular goodwill, contentedness and confidence in your prudent foresight and safe government, Lords and Commons; and from thence derives itself to a gallant bravery and well-grounded contempt of their enemies, as if there were no small number of as great spirits among us, as his was, who when Rome was nigh besieged by Hannibal, being in the city, bought that piece of ground at no cheap rate, whereon Hannibal himself encamped his own regiment.

Next, it is a lively and cheerful presage of our happy success and victory. For as in a body, when the blood is fresh, the spirits pure and vigorous, not only to vital but to rational faculties, and those in the acutest and the pertest operations of wit and subtlety, it argues in what good plight and constitution the body is so when the cheerfulness of the people is so sprightly up, as that it has not only wherewith to guard well its own freedom and safety, but to spare, and to bestow upon the solidest and sublimest points of controversy and new invention, it betokens us not degenerated, nor drooping to a fatal decay, but casting off the old and wrinkled skin of corruption to outlive these pangs and wax young again, entering the glorious ways of truth and prosperous virtue, destined to become great and honourable in these latter ages. Methinks I see in my mind a noble and puissant nation rousing herself like a strong man after sleep, and shaking her invincible locks. Methinks I see her as an eagle mewing[3] her mighty youth, and kindling her undazzled eyes at the full midday beam; purging and unscaling her long-abused sight at the fountain itself of heavenly radiance; while the whole noise of timorous

[1] *Pyrrhus did* Pyrrhus, King of Epirus (his people are the "Epirots" mentioned later in the paragraph) defeated a Roman army in 280 BCE.

[2] *maniples* Infantry companies in the Roman Army.

[3] *mewing* Renewing, from a term in falconry meaning to moult.

and flocking birds, with those also that love the twilight, flutter about, amazed at what she means, and in their envious gabble would prognosticate a year of sects and schisms.

What would ye do then? Should ye suppress all this flowery crop of knowledge and new light sprung up and yet springing daily in this city? should ye set an oligarchy of twenty engrossers[1] over it, to bring a famine upon our minds again, when we shall know nothing but what is measured to us by their bushel? Believe it, Lords and Commons, they who counsel ye to such a suppressing do as good as bid ye suppress yourselves; and I will soon show how. If it be desired to know the immediate cause of all this free writing and free speaking, there cannot be assigned a truer than your own mild and free and humane government. It is the liberty, Lords and Commons, which your own valorous and happy counsels have purchased us, liberty which is the nurse of all great wits; this is that which hath rarefied and enlightened our spirits like the influence of heaven; this is that which hath enfranchised, enlarged and lifted up our apprehensions degrees above themselves.

Ye cannot make us now less capable, less knowing, less eagerly pursuing of the truth, unless ye first make yourselves, that made us so, less the lovers, less the founders of our true liberty. We can grow ignorant again, brutish, formal and slavish, as ye found us; but you then must first become that which ye cannot be, oppressive, arbitrary and tyrannous, as they were from whom ye have freed us. That our hearts are now more capacious, our thoughts more erected to the search and expectation of greatest and exactest things, is the issue of your own virtue propagated in us; ye cannot suppress that, unless ye reinforce an abrogated and merciless law, that fathers may dispatch at will their own children. And who shall then stick closest to ye, and excite others? not he who takes up arms for coat and conduct and his four nobles of Danegelt.[2] Although I dispraise not the defence of just immunities, yet love my peace better, if that were all. Give me the liberty to know, to utter, and to argue freely according to conscience, above all liberties....

For who knows not that Truth is strong, next to the Almighty? She needs no policies, nor stratagems, nor licensings to make her victorious; those are the shifts and the defences that error uses against her power. Give her but room, and do not bind her when she sleeps, for then she speaks not true, as the old Proteus did,[3] who spake oracles only when he was caught and bound, but then rather she turns herself into all shapes, except her own, and perhaps tunes her voice according to the time, as Micaiah did before Ahab, until she be adjured into her own likeness.[4] Yet is it not impossible that she may have more shapes than one. What else is all that rank of things indifferent, wherein Truth may be on this side or on the other, without being unlike herself? What but a vain shadow else is the abolition of those ordinances, that handwriting nailed to the cross? What great purchase is this Christian liberty which Paul so often boasts of? His doctrine is, that he who eats or eats not, regards a day or regards it not, may do either to the Lord. How many other things might be tolerated in peace, and left to conscience, had we but charity, and were it not the chief stronghold of our hypocrisy to be ever judging one another?

I fear yet this iron yoke of outward conformity hath left a slavish print upon our necks; the ghost of a linen decency[5] yet haunts us. We stumble and are impatient at the least dividing of one visible congregation from another, though it be not in fundamentals; and through our forwardness to suppress, and our backwardness to recover any enthralled piece of truth out of the grip of custom, we care not to keep truth separated from truth, which is the fiercest rent and disunion of all. We do not see that, while we still affect by all means a rigid external formality, we may as soon fall again into a gross conforming stupidity, a stark and dead congealment of wood and hay and stubble, forced and frozen together,

[1] *engrossers* Monopolists.

[2] *coat and conduct* Tax that provided clothing and transportation of new troops; *noble* Coin worth six shillings eight pence; *Danegelt* Tax known as "ship money," originally levied to support the building of ships with which to oppose invading Danes but controversially resurrected by King Charles I.

[3] *Proteus* Shape-shifting sea deity in Greek mythology.

[4] *Micaiah … Ahab* See 1 Kings 22.9–28.

[5] *linen decency* Referring to the clerical vestments (with linen sleeves) that Archbishop William Laud insisted ministers wear in the interest of conformity.

which is more to the sudden degenerating of a Church than many subdichotomies of petty schisms.

Not that I can think well of every light separation, or that all in a Church is to be expected gold and silver and precious stones: it is not possible for man to sever the wheat from the tares, the good fish from the other fry; that must be the angels' ministry at the end of mortal things. Yet if all cannot be of one mind—as who looks they should be?—this doubtless is more wholesome, more prudent, and more Christian that many be tolerated, rather than all compelled. I mean not tolerated popery, and open superstition, which, as it extirpates all religions and civil supremacies, so itself should be extirpate, provided first that all charitable and compassionate means be used to win and regain the weak and the misled: that also which is impious or evil absolutely either against faith or manners no law can possibly permit, that intends not to unlaw itself: but those neighbouring differences, or rather indifferences, are what I speak of, whether in some point of doctrine or of discipline, which, though they may be many, yet need not interrupt the unity of Spirit, if we could but find among us the bond of peace.

In the meanwhile if any one would write, and bring his helpful hand to the slow-moving Reformation which we labour under, if Truth have spoken to him before others, or but seemed at least to speak, who hath so bejesuited us that we should trouble that man with asking licence to do so worthy a deed? and not consider this, that if it come to prohibiting, there is not aught more likely to be prohibited than truth itself; whose first appearance to our eyes, bleared and dimmed with prejudice and custom, is more unsightly and unplausible than many errors, even as the person is of many a great man slight and contemptible to see to. And what do they tell us vainly of new opinions, when this very opinion of theirs, that none must be heard, but whom they like, is the worst and newest opinion of all others; and is the chief cause why sects and schisms do so much abound, and true knowledge is kept at distance from us; besides yet a greater danger which is in it? ...

And as for regulating the press, let no man think to have the honour of advising ye better than yourselves have done in that Order published next before this, "that no book be printed, unless the printer's and the author's name, or at least the printer's, be registered."[1] Those which otherwise come forth, if they be found mischievous and libellous, the fire and the executioner will be the timeliest and the most effectual remedy that man's prevention can use. For this authentic Spanish policy of licensing books, if I have said aught, will prove the most unlicensed book itself within a short while; and was the immediate image of a Star Chamber decree to that purpose made in those very times when that Court did the rest of those her pious works, for which she is now fallen from the stars with Lucifer.[2] Whereby ye may guess what kind of state prudence, what love of the people, what care of religion or good manners there was at the contriving, although with singular hypocrisy it pretended to bind books to their good behaviour.
—1644

[1] *And as for regulating ... be registered* Milton cites a Parliamentary Order of January 29, 1642.

[2] *Star Chamber decree* Referring to the 1637 Star Chamber decree for licensing books; the Court of Star Chamber at Westminster Palace was associated with efforts to maintain royal authority before the war, and had been abolished by Parliament in 1641. Milton punningly links the "fallen" Star Chamber with Lucifer, the "morning star" (Isaiah 14.12) and "fallen" angel.

Paradise Lost

While there is some evidence that Milton drafted parts of *Paradise Lost* in the 1640s, he appears to have written most of the poem between about 1658 and about 1663. He thus composed his great epic of human loss followed by the restoration of hope across the Restoration of 1660, an event that marked the collapse of the English Republic and Milton's own hopes for a reformed political and religious structure. *Paradise Lost* was first published in 1667 as a work of ten books. Milton subsequently re-divided the poem (with the original Books 7 and 10 each split into two) and republished it in 1674 as a work in twelve books, thus more closely mirroring the form of Virgil's *Aeneid*. Since Milton had gone completely blind in the early 1650s, he wrote the work through dictation. Interestingly, the one surviving manuscript (which includes only Book 1) reveals that he nevertheless revised with a view to spelling and punctuation.

The epic, written in blank verse (i.e. unrhymed lines of iambic pentameter), draws heavily on classical inspiration and is highly allusive. Scholars estimate that Milton draws on more than 1500 books in *Paradise Lost*, but his primary touchstones are Homer's *Iliad* and *Odyssey*, Virgil's *Aeneid*, Ovid's *Metamorphoses*, Spenser's *Faerie Queene*, and such central works of epic and romance of the European Renaissance as Ludovico Ariosto's *Orlando Furioso*, Torquato Tasso's *Jersualem Delivered*, and Guillaume Du Bartas's *Divine Weeks* (Milton in fact borrows many whole phrases from Joshua Sylvester's 1608 translation of Du Bartas). Milton takes his title from the account in Genesis of the expulsion of humankind from Paradise after Adam and Eve eat from the forbidden Tree of Knowledge. As a retelling of the Biblical Fall, *Paradise Lost* is the best known and most influential literary version of this foundational story of innocence and experience, temptation and expulsion, desire and its consequences.

The poem's dramatic first two books focus not on humanity but on the defeated but still rebellious Satan, cast down from Heaven with his traitor legions for daring to war on God. Satan and his fellows explore Hell, make a home of sorts, and decide to continue their fight with God not in open warfare, but through subverting and corrupting God's new creation, humankind. The rest of *Paradise Lost* follows the enactment of Satan's plan, though in true epic fashion the poem flashes back to the story's beginnings and looks forward to its end, which in this case means the beginning and end of time itself. Critical discussion of the poem has often concerned the extent to which Satan appears to be the driving force behind the epic, sometimes taking as a starting point William Blake's remark that the "reason Milton wrote in fetters when he wrote of Angels & God, and at liberty when of Devils & Hell, is because he was a true Poet and of the Devil's party without knowing it." As a character, Satan is indeed dramatically compelling, if also arguably repellent in his pride and thirst for power: Milton opens his epic by confronting us with the power of the adversary he believed we faced in everyday life. But many readers also find that Satan recedes and shrinks over the whole course of the poem, while Adam and Eve gain in complexity and stature through their conversations with one another and with the angels Raphael and Michael.

The theological heart of *Paradise Lost* is the extended conversation in Book 3 between God and the Son. God addresses the problem of foreknowledge and free will by explaining the central importance in Milton's world of choice and freedom. God anticipates Satan's subsequent actions, yet promises mercy and grace through the Son should humanity fall. In its broad outlines, the theology Milton presents is conventional Christian thought; in some respects though, Milton is less orthodox. His God, for example, is not a Calvinist: there is no predestination in Milton's heaven, because all will hear the call of the Divine, and all those who choose to be saved will be saved. Milton also appears to make the Son subordinate to (rather than co-eternal with) the Father, though scholars argue over the implications (and importance to the poem) of this conception of the divine.

The most frequently debated issue in *Paradise Lost* is probably Milton's depiction of Adam and Eve. Modern readers can feel uncomfortable with the explicit subordination of women in some passages, particularly those that draw on St. Paul's injunctions from the New Testament. Are these moments to be taken as representing the views of Adam, of Raphael, of Milton, or of God? In other passages, however, *Paradise Lost* gives Eve a greater personal, political, and theological equality than she had ever been accorded: in Book 10 in particular, Eve's actions give her a good claim to be the poem's true hero. She even gives names to some of God's creation, a sign of power and capacity to rule that the Bible itself reserves only for Adam. On the subject of Eve, the poem speaks with two voices, and Milton invites readers to work through the implications of the ways Adam and Eve are presented as man and woman, as husband and wife, as humanity in general, and even as different aspects of the individual human psyche.

Despite its daunting erudition and older poetics, *Paradise Lost* still speaks powerfully and directly to modern readers. As Johnson, Coleridge, and many others have pointed out, the verbal acrobatics of the poem may occasionally frustrate, but vested in them is also the capacity to astonish. And the rich poetic texture of the full poem retains the capacity to provoke intellectual inquiry not only concerning theology and gender, but also concerning the human condition, religious faith, responsibility and heroism, politics and hierarchy, and the limits that may exist on the pursuit of knowledge and freedom.

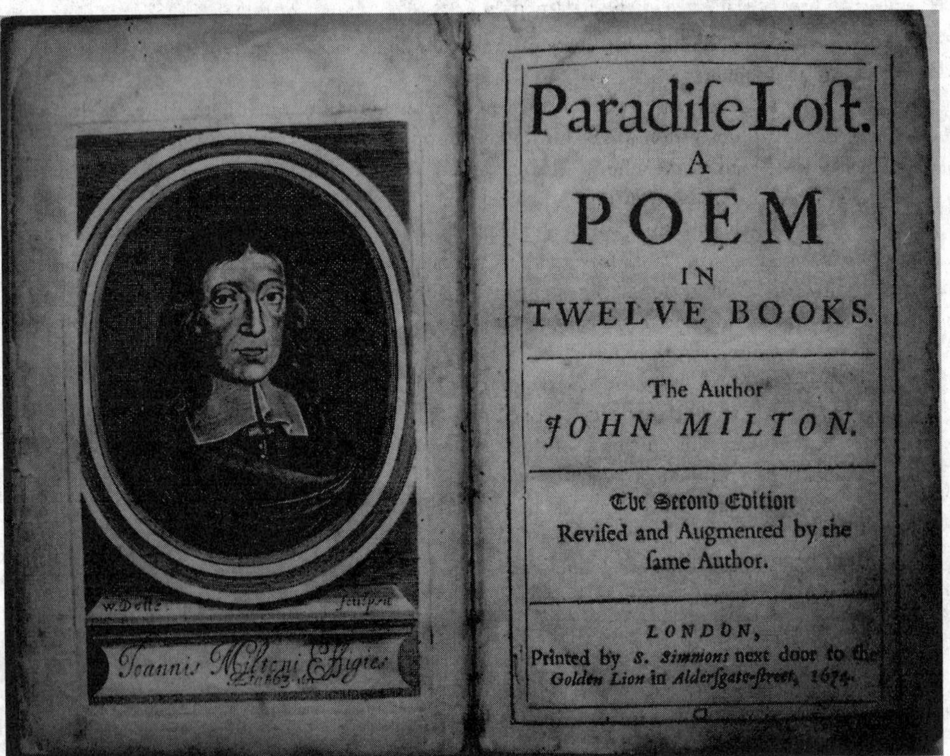

Joannis Miltoni Effigies

Paradiſe Loſt.
A
POEM
IN
TWELVE BOOKS.

The Author
JOHN MILTON.

The Second Edition
Reviſed and Augmented by the
ſame Author.

LONDON,
Printed by S. Simmons next door to the
Golden Lion in Alderſgate-ſtreet, 1674.

Title page of the 1674 edition of *Paradise Lost*.

from *Paradise Lost*

THE VERSE

The measure is English heroic verse without rhyme,[1] as that of Homer in Greek, and Virgil in Latin; rhyme being no necessary adjunct or true ornament of poem or good verse, in longer works especially, but the invention of a barbarous age, to set off wretched matter and lame metre; graced indeed since by the use of some famous modern poets, carried away by custom, but much to their own vexation, hindrance, and constraint to express many things otherwise, and for the most part worse then else they would have expressed them. Not without cause therefore some both Italian, and Spanish poets of prime note have rejected rhyme both in longer and shorter works, as have also long since our best English tragedies, as a thing of itself, to all judicious ears, trivial, and of no true musical delight; which consists only in apt numbers, fit quantity of syllables, and the sense variously drawn out from one verse into another, not in the jingling sound of like endings, a fault avoided by the learned ancients both in poetry and all good oratory. This neglect then of rhyme so little is to be taken for a defect, though it may seem so perhaps to vulgar readers, that it rather is to be esteemed an example set, the first in English, of ancient liberty recovered to heroic poem from the troublesome and modern bondage of rhyming.

ARGUMENT TO BOOK I[2]

This first book proposes first in brief the whole subject, man's disobedience, and the loss thereupon of Paradise wherein he was placed: then touches the prime cause of his fall, the serpent, or rather Satan in the serpent; who revolting from God, and drawing to his side many legions of angels, was by the command of God driven out of Heaven with all his crew into the great deep. Which action past over, the poem hastes into the midst of things, presenting Satan with his angels now fallen into Hell, described here, not in the center (for Heaven and Earth may be supposed as yet not made, certainly not yet accurst) but in a place of utter darkness, fitliest called Chaos: here Satan with his angels lying on the burning lake, thunder-struck and astonished, after a certain space recovers, as from confusion, calls up him who next in order and dignity lay by him; they confer of their miserable fall. Satan awakens all his legions, who lay till then in the same manner confounded; they rise, their numbers, array of battle, their chief leaders named, according to the idols known afterwards in Canaan and the countries adjoining. To these Satan directs his speech, comforts them with hope yet of regaining Heaven, but tells them lastly of a new world and new kind of creature to be created, according to an ancient prophesy or report in Heaven; for that angels were long before this visible creation, was the opinion of many ancient Fathers. To find out the truth of this prophesy, and what to determine thereon, he refers to a full council. What his associates thence attempt. Pandemonium the palace of Satan rises, suddenly built out of the deep: the infernal peers there sit in council.

BOOK I

Of Mans First Disobedience, and the Fruit
Of that Forbidden Tree, whose mortal tast
Brought Death into the World, and all our woe,
With loss of *Eden,* till one greater Man[3]
Restore us, and regain the blissful Seat,
Sing Heav'nly Muse,[4] that on the secret° top   *hidden*
Of *Oreb,* or of *Sinai,*[5] didst inspire
That Shepherd,[6] who first taught the chosen Seed,[7]

— original spelling —

[1] *English ... rhyme* Verse suited to the treatment of heroic or elevated themes; i.e., blank verse in iambic pentameter.

[2] *Argument to Book 1* The Arguments are Milton's own prose summaries of the action in each of the twelve books of *Paradise Lost.* They did not appear in the first edition, but Milton added them in 1668, apparently at the request of his printer.

[3] *one greater Man* Christ, in this poem, or here, the Son of God.

[4] Heav'nly Muse Urania, Muse of astronomy and hence religious poetry.

[5] *Of Oreb, or of Sinai* God delivered the Ten Commandments to Moses on the summit either of Mount Horeb (Deuteronomy 4.10) or Mount Sinai (Exodus 19.10).

[6] *That Shepherd* Moses, who was tending the sheep of his father-in-law, Jethro, when God first appeared to him as a burning bush (Exodus 3.1–4).

[7] *the chosen Seed* The Jewish people. See Deuteronomy 6.6–8.

original spelling

In the Beginning how the Heav'ns and Earth
Rose out of *Chaos.* Or if *Sion* Hill[1]
Delight thee more, and *Siloa's* Brook[2] that flow'd
Fast by the Oracle of God; I thence
Invoke thy[3] aid to my adventrous Song,
That with no middle° flight intends to soar *mediocre*
Above th' *Aonian* Mount,[4] while it pursues
Things unattempted yet in Prose or Rhime.
And chiefly Thou O Spirit, that dost prefer
Before all Temples th' upright heart and pure,
Instruct me, for Thou know'st; Thou from the first
Wast present, and with mighty wings outspread
Dove-like satst brooding on the vast Abyss
And mad'st it pregnant:[5] What in me is dark
Illumine, what is low raise and support;
That to the highth of this great Argument
I may assert th' Eternal Providence,
And justifie the wayes of God to men.

Say first—for Heav'n hides nothing from thy view,
Nor the deep tract of Hell—say first what cause
Moved our grand parents,[6] in that happy state,[7]
Favoured of Heav'n so highly, to fall off
From their Creator, and transgress His will
For one restraint,[8] lords of the world besides.
Who first seduced them to that foul revolt?
Th' infernal Serpent; he it was whose guile,
Stirred up with envy and revenge, deceived
The mother of mankind, what time[9] his pride
Had cast him out from Heav'n, with all his host
Of rebel angels, by whose aid, aspiring
To set himself in glory above his peers,
He trusted to have equalled the Most High,
If he opposed, and with ambitious aim
Against the throne and monarchy of God,
Raised impious war in Heav'n and battle proud,
With vain attempt. Him the Almighty Power
Hurled headlong flaming from th' ethereal sky,
With hideous ruin and combustion, down
To bottomless perdition, there to dwell
In adamantine° chains and penal fire, *unbreakable*
Who dared defy th' Omnipotent to arms.
Nine times the space that measures day and night
To mortal men, he, with his horrid crew,
Lay vanquished, rolling in the fiery gulf,
Confounded, though immortal. But his doom
Reserved him to more wrath;[10] for now the thought
Both of lost happiness and lasting pain
Torments him: round he throws his baleful eyes,
That witnessed huge affliction and dismay,
Mixed with obdurate pride and steadfast hate.
At once, as far as angels ken,° he views *can see*
The dismal situation waste and wild.
A dungeon horrible, on all sides round,
As one great furnace flamed; yet from those flames
No light; but rather darkness visible
Served only to discover sights of woe,
Regions of sorrow, doleful shades, where peace
And rest can never dwell, hope never comes
That comes to all, but torture without end
Still urges, and a fiery deluge,° fed *downpour*
With ever-burning sulphur unconsumed.
Such place Eternal Justice has prepared
For those rebellious; here their prison ordained
In utter darkness, and their portion set,
As far removed from God and light of Heav'n
As from the centre thrice to the utmost pole.[11]
Oh how unlike the place from whence they fell!
There the companions of his fall, overwhelmed

[1] *Sion Hill* Mount Zion, a sacred mountain, site of Solomon's temple and a seat of religious and secular law (Isaiah 2.3).

[2] *Siloa's Brook* The pool of Siloam in the Temple at Jerusalem, mentioned first in Nehemiah 3.15, then used by Jesus to restore a blind man's sight in John 9.1–12.

[3] *thy* I.e., Urania/God.

[4] *th' Aonian Mount* Helicon, a mountain in central Greece sacred to the Muses, and one of their homes.

[5] *O Spirit ... pregnant* The Holy Spirit, specifically in its generative aspect.

[6] *our grand parents* Adam and Eve.

[7] *in that happy state* Simultaneously the state of innocence and the state, or country, of Eden.

[8] *one restraint* God's admonition against eating from the Tree of Knowledge of Good and Evil (Genesis 2.17).

[9] *what time* "When" or "by which time."

[10] *Reserved him to more wrath* Gave Satan yet more pain.

[11] *As far removed ... utmost pole.* In Homer, Hades was as far below Earth as Heaven was above; in Virgil, Tartarus was twice as far below. Milton overdoes his classical predecessors by placing Hell three times as far from Heaven as Earth is.

With floods and whirlwinds of tempestuous fire,
He soon discerns; and, weltering° by his side, *rolling*
One next himself in power, and next in crime,
Long after known in Palestine, and named
Beelzebub.[1] To whom th' arch-enemy,
And thence in Heaven called Satan,[2] with bold words
Breaking the horrid silence, thus began:—
"If thou beest he—but O how fall'n! How changed
From him who, in the happy realms of light
Clothed with transcendent brightness, didst outshine
Myriads, though bright!—if he whom mutual league,
United thoughts and counsels, equal hope
And hazard in the glorious enterprise
Joined with me once, now misery hath joined
In equal ruin; into what pit thou seest
From what height fall'n: so much the stronger proved
He with his thunder; and till then who knew
The force of those dire arms? Yet not for those,
Nor what the potent Victor in his rage
Can else inflict, do I repent, or change,
Though changed in outward lustre, that fixed mind,
And high disdain from sense of injured merit,
That with the mightiest raised me to contend,
And to the fierce contentions brought along
Innumerable force of Spirits armed,
That dared dislike His reign, and, me preferring,
His utmost power with adverse power opposed
In dubious° battle on the plains of Heaven, *uncertain*
And shook His throne. What though the field be lost?
All is not lost—the unconquerable will,
And study of revenge, immortal hate,
And courage never to submit or yield:
And what is else not to be overcome?
That glory never shall His wrath or might
Extort from me. To bow and sue for grace
With suppliant knee, and deify His power
Who, from the terror of this arm, so late
Doubted His empire—that were low indeed;
That were an ignominy and shame beneath
This downfall; since, by fate, the strength of gods,
And this empyreal° substance, cannot fail; *celestial*
Since, through experience of this great event,
In arms not worse, in foresight much advanced,
We may with more successful hope resolve
To wage by force or guile eternal war,
Irreconcilable to our grand foe,
Who now triumphs, and in th' excess of joy
Sole reigning holds the tyranny of Heaven."
So spake th' apostate[3] angel, though in pain,
Vaunting° aloud, but racked with deep despair; *bragging*
And him thus answered soon his bold compeer:[4]
"O Prince, O Chief of many thronèd powers
That led th' embattled seraphim[5] to war
Under thy conduct, and, in dreadful deeds
Fearless, endangered Heav'n's perpetual king,
And put to proof his high supremacy,
Whether upheld by strength, or chance, or fate,
Too well I see and rue the dire event
That, with sad overthrow and foul defeat,
Hath lost us Heav'n, and all this mighty host
In horrible destruction laid thus low,
As far as gods and heavenly essences
Can perish: for the mind and spirit remains
Invincible, and vigour soon returns,
Though all our glory extinct, and happy state
Here swallowed up in endless misery.
But what if He our conqueror (whom I now
Of force[6] believe almighty, since no less
Than such could have o'erpow'red such force as ours)
Have left us this our spirit and strength entire,
Strongly to suffer and support our pains,
That we may so suffice His vengeful ire,
Or do Him mightier service as His thralls
By right of war, whatever His business be,
Here in the heart of Hell to work in fire,
Or do His errands in the gloomy deep?
What can it then avail though yet we feel
Strength undiminished, or eternal being

[1] *Beelzebub* Hebrew for Lord of the Flies, the name is an alteration of Baal, historically the chief male god of Phoenicia and Canaan.

[2] *And thence in Heaven called Satan* Satan is the English transliteration of the Hebrew word for "adversary."

[3] *apostate* One who has abandoned one's faith.

[4] *compeer* Fellow comrade.

[5] *embattled seraphim* Rebelling or persecuted seraphim. Seraphim are the highest-ranked angels in traditional angelology.

[6] *Of force* Of necessity, per force.

To undergo eternal punishment?"[1]
Whereto with speedy words the archfiend replied:
"Fall'n cherub, to be weak is miserable,
Doing or suffering: but of this be sure—
To do aught° good never will be our task, *nothing*
But ever to do ill our sole delight,
As being the contrary to His high will
Whom we resist. If then His Providence
Out of our evil seek to bring forth good,
Our labour must be to pervert that end,
And out of good still to find means of evil;
Which oft times may succeed so as perhaps
Shall grieve Him, if I fail not, and disturb
His inmost counsels from their destined aim.
But see! The angry Victor hath recalled
His ministers of vengeance and pursuit
Back to the gates of Heav'n: the sulphurous hail,
Shot after us in storm, o'erblown has laid
The fiery surge[2] that from the precipice
Of Heav'n received us falling;[3] and the thunder,
Winged with red lightning and impetuous rage,
Perhaps hath spent his shafts, and ceases now
To bellow through the vast and boundless deep.
Let us not slip° th' occasion, whether scorn *miss*
Or satiate° fury yield it from our Foe. *satisfied*
Seest thou yon dreary plain, forlorn and wild,
The seat of desolation, void of light,
Save what the glimmering of these livid flames
Casts pale and dreadful? Thither let us tend[4]
From off the tossing of these fiery waves;
There rest, if any rest can harbour there;
And, re-assembling our afflicted powers,
Consult how we may henceforth most offend
Our enemy, our own loss how repair,
How overcome this dire calamity,
What reinforcement we may gain from hope,
If not, what resolution from despair."
Thus Satan, talking to his nearest mate,
With head uplift above the wave, and eyes
That sparkling blazed; his other parts besides
Prone on the flood, extended long and large,
Lay floating many a rood,[5] in bulk as huge
As whom the fables name of monstrous size,
Titanian or Earth-born, that warred on Jove,
Briareos or Typhon,[6] whom the den
By ancient Tarsus[7] held, or that sea-beast
Leviathan,[8] which God of all His works
Created hugest that swim th' ocean stream.
Him, haply slumbering on the Norway foam,
The pilot of some small night-foundered[9] skiff,
Deeming some island, oft, as seamen tell,
With fixèd anchor in his scaly rind,
Moors by his side under the lee, while night
Invests the sea, and wishèd morn delays.
So stretched out huge in length the arch-fiend lay,
Chained on the burning lake; nor ever thence
Had ris'n, or heaved his head, but that the will
And high permission of all-ruling Heaven
Left him at large to his own dark designs,
That with reiterated crimes he might
Heap on himself damnation, while he sought
Evil to others, and enraged might see
How all his malice served but to bring forth
Infinite goodness, grace, and mercy, shown
On Man by him seduced, but on himself
Treble° confusion, wrath, and vengeance poured. *tripled*
Forthwith upright he rears from off the pool
His mighty stature; on each hand the flames
Driven backward slope their pointing spires, and rolled
In billows, leave i' th' midst a horrid vale.
Then with expanded wings he steers his flight

[1] *What can it … eternal punishment* What good can it do that we don't feel any weaker, or that since we're immortal our punishment can never end?

[2] *surge* Surf, especially a rolling swell.

[3] *the sulphurous hail … received us falling* Satan is pointing out that the fiery lake they fell into in Hell was the product of the fiery hail Heaven shot after them, which passed them and filled the basin below them.

[4] *Thither let us tend* Let us go there.

[5] *rood* Unit of linear measurement from 5.5 to 8 yards long.

[6] *Titanian … Typhon* In Greek mythology, the Titans (children of the sky and earth) and the giants, including Briareos and Typhon, fought and were defeated by Zeus (Jupiter/Jove).

[7] *Tarsus* Ancient city in Southern Turkey.

[8] *Leviathan* Mythological sea creature, supposed to be the largest creature in all creation; mentioned in Job 41.1–8 to illustrate the enormity of God's power, and mentioned in Isaiah 27 as defeated by the promised Messiah.

[9] *night-foundered* Sinking at night.

Aloft, incumbent on the dusky air,
That felt unusual weight; till on dry land
He lights°—if it were land that ever burned *alights*
With solid, as the lake with liquid fire,
And such appeared in hue as when the force
Of subterranean wind transports a hill
Torn from Pelorus, or the shattered side
Of thundering Etna,[1] whose combustible
And fuelled entrails, thence conceiving fire,
Sublimed with mineral fury, aid the winds,
And leave a singèd bottom all involved
With stench and smoke. Such resting found the sole
Of unblessed feet. Him followed his next mate;
Both glorying to have scaped the Stygian[2] flood
As gods, and by their own recovered strength,
Not by the suff'rance of supernal° power. *celestial*
"Is this the region, this the soil, the clime,"
Said then the lost archangel, "this the seat
That we must change for Heav'n? This mournful gloom
For that celestial light? Be it so, since He
Who now is sovereign can dispose and bid
What shall be right: farthest from Him is best
Whom reason has equalled, force has made supreme
Above His equals. Farewell, happy fields,
Where joy forever dwells! Hail, horrors! Hail,
Infernal world! And thou, profoundest Hell,
Receive thy new possessor—one who brings
A mind not to be changed by place or time.
The mind is its own place, and in itself
Can make a Heav'n of Hell, a Hell of Heav'n.
What matter where, if I be still the same,
And what I should be, all but less than He
Whom thunder hath made greater? Here at least
We shall be free; th' Almighty hath not built
Here for His envy, will not drive us hence:
Here we may reign secure; and, in my choice,
To reign is worth ambition, though in Hell:
Better to reign in Hell than serve in Heav'n.
But wherefore let we then our faithful friends,
Th' associates and co-partners of our loss,
Lie thus astonished on th' oblivious pool,
And call them not to share with us their part
In this unhappy mansion, or once more
With rallied arms to try what may be yet
Regained in Heaven, or what more lost in Hell?"
So Satan spake; and him Beelzebub
Thus answered: "Leader of those armies bright
Which, but th' Omnipotent, none could have foiled!
If once they hear that voice, their liveliest pledge
Of hope in fears and dangers—heard so oft
In worst extremes, and on the perilous edge
Of battle, when it raged, in all assaults
Their surest signal—they will soon resume
New courage and revive, though now they lie
Grovelling and prostrate on yon lake of fire,
As we erewhile, astounded and amazed;
No wonder, fall'n such a pernicious height!"
He scarce had ceased when the superior fiend
Was moving toward the shore; his ponderous shield,
Ethereal temper,° massy, large, and round, *strength*
Behind him cast.[3] The broad circumference
Hung on his shoulders like the moon, whose orb
Through optic glass[4] the Tuscan artist[5] views
At ev'ning, from the top of Fesolé,[6]
Or in Valdarno,[7] to descry new lands,
Rivers, or mountains, in her spotty globe.
His spear—to equal which the tallest pine
Hewn on Norwegian hills, to be the mast
Of some great ammiral,[8] were but a wand
He walked with, to support uneasy steps
Over the burning marl,° not like those steps *soil*
On Heaven's azure; and the torrid clime
Smote on him sore besides, vaulted with fire.
Natheless° he so endured, till on the beach *nevertheless*
Of that inflamèd sea he stood, and called
His legions—angel forms, who lay entranced
Thick as autumnal leaves that strew the brooks

[1] *Pelorus … thundering Etna* Cape Pelorus in Sicily, located near volcanic Mount Etna.

[2] *Stygian* I.e., like the river Styx, a river that the dead must cross in order to enter the underworld. The word connotes the river's location in the underworld, but also implies bleakness and darkness.

[3] *Behind him cast* Satan wears his shield slung across his back.

[4] *optic glass* Telescope.

[5] *the Tuscan artist* Galileo (1564–1652), the only contemporary mentioned in the poem.

[6] *Fesolé* Fiesole, a town just outside Florence, Italy.

[7] *Valdarno* Arno Valley, the valley in which Florence is located.

[8] *ammiral* Admiral's flagship. This spelling was standard at the time, and refers specifically to a first-rate ship of the fleet.

In Vallombrosa,[1] where th' Etrurian shades
High over-arched embower;[2] or scattered sedge
Afloat, when with fierce winds Orion[3] armed
Hath vexed the Red Sea coast, whose waves o'erthrew
Busiris and his Memphian chivalry,[4]
While with perfidious hatred they pursued
The sojourners of Goshen,[5] who beheld
From the safe shore their floating carcasses
And broken chariot wheels. So thick bestrewn,
Abject and lost, lay these, covering the flood,
Under amazement of their hideous change.
He called so loud that all the hollow deep
Of Hell resounded: "Princes, potentates,
Warriors, the flower of Heav'n once yours; now lost,
If such astonishment as this can seize
Eternal spirits! Or have ye chos'n this place
After the toil of battle to repose
Your wearied virtue, for the ease you find
To slumber here, as in the vales of Heav'n?
Or in this abject posture have ye sworn
To adore the conqueror who now beholds
Cherub and seraph rolling in the flood
With scattered arms and ensigns,° till anon *flags*
His swift pursuers from Heaven-gates discern
Th' advantage, and descending, tread us down
Thus drooping, or with linkèd thunderbolts
Transfix us to the bottom of this gulf?
Awake, arise, or be forever fall'n!"
They heard, and were abashed, and up they sprung
Upon the wing, as when men wont to watch
On duty, sleeping found by whom they dread,
Rouse and bestir themselves ere well awake.
Nor did they not perceive the evil plight
In which they were, or the fierce pains not feel;
Yet to their General's voice they soon obeyed
Innumerable. As when the potent rod
Of Amram's son, in Egypt's evil day,
Waved round the coast, up-called a pitchy cloud
Of locusts, warping on the eastern wind,
That o'er the realm of impious Pharaoh hung
Like Night, and darkened all the land of Nile;[6]
So numberless were those bad angels seen
Hovering on wing under the cope° of Hell, *vault, canopy*
'Twixt upper, nether,° and surrounding fires; *lower*
Till, as a signal giv'n, th' uplifted spear
Of their great sultan waving to direct
Their course, in even balance down they light
On the firm brimstone, and fill all the plain:
A multitude like which the populous North
Poured never from her frozen loins to pass
Rhene or the Danaw,[7] when her barbarous sons
Came like a deluge on the south, and spread
Beneath Gibraltar to the Libyan sands.
Forthwith, form every squadron and each band,
The heads and leaders thither haste where stood
Their great commander—godlike shapes, and forms
Excelling human; princely dignities;
And powers that erst° in Heav'n sat on thrones, *formerly*
Though on their names in heav'nly records now
Be no memorial, blotted out and razed
By their rebellion from the books of life.[8]
Nor had they yet among the sons of Eve
Got them new names, till, wand'ring ov'r the earth,
Through God's high sufferance for the trial of man,
By falsities and lies the greatest part
Of mankind they corrupted to forsake
God their Creator, and th' invisible
Glory of Him that made them to transform
Oft to the image of a brute, adorned
With gay religions full of pomp and gold,
And devils to adore for deities:
Then were they known to men by various names,
And various idols through the heathen world.

[1] *Vallombrosa* Valley near Florence famous for its arboreal displays; literally, valley of shadow or shadowed valley.

[2] *where th' Etrurian ... embower* Where the leaves of Etruria arch high and densely overhead. Etruria was an ancient region in west-central Italy, the seat of the Etruscan empire.

[3] *Orion* Great hunter whom Diana loved but killed in error and then had made into a constellation in the Northern sky; its appearance above the horizon heralds winter.

[4] *Busiris and his Memphian chivalry* Pharaoh and his horsemen or charioteers, stymied by Moses's parting of the Red Sea (Exodus 14.21–31).

[5] *sojourners of Goshen* Israelites who fled Egypt with Moses.

[6] *As when the potent ... land of Nile* Moses was the son of Amram; God's command to him to reach out with his staff (or rod) summoned the plague of locusts to afflict Egypt (Exodus 10.12–20).

[7] *Rhene or the Danaw* Rhine and Danube Rivers.

[8] *books of life* Books in which are written all the names of God's faithful (Exodus 32.32–33).

Say, Muse, their names then known, who first, who last,
Roused from the slumber on that fiery couch,
At their great emperor's call, as next in worth
Came singly where he stood on the bare strand,
While the promiscuous crowd stood yet aloof?
The chief were those who, from the pit of Hell
Roaming to seek their prey on Earth, dared fix
Their seats, long after, next the seat of God,
Their altars by His altar, gods adored
Among the nations round, and dared abide
Jehovah thundering out of Sion, throned
Between the cherubim; yea, often placed
Within His sanctuary itself their shrines,
Abominations; and with cursèd things
His holy rites and solemn feasts profaned,
And with their darkness dared affront His light.
First, Moloch,[1] horrid king, besmeared with blood
Of human sacrifice, and parents' tears;
Though, for the noise of drums and
    timbrels° loud, *small hand drums*
Their children's cries unheard that passed through fire
To his grim idol. Him the Ammonite[2]
Worshiped in Rabba and her watery plain,
In Argob and in Basan, to the stream
Of utmost Arnon.[3] Nor content with such
Audacious neighbourhood, the wisest heart
Of Solomon he led by fraud to build
His temple right against the temple of God
On that opprobrious hill, and made his grove
The pleasant valley of Hinnom,[4] Tophet[5] thence
And black Gehenna[6] called, the type of Hell.

[1] *Moloch* Heathen god worshipped by sacrificing children in ovens or flame; his name means king or monarch.

[2] *Ammonite* Biblical enemies of the Israelites.

[3] *Rabba ... Argob ... Basan ... Arnon* Lands east of the Dead Sea, in present-day Jordan.

[4] *Hinnom* Valley west and southwest of Jerusalem, mentioned in the Bible as a place of child sacrifice.

[5] *Tophet* City in the valley Hinnom where children of the Israelites were sacrificed in flame.

[6] *Gehenna* Because of the sacrifice of Israelite children at Tophet in Hinnom, Gehenna (a transliteration of the Hebrew for the place-name) became the New Testament word for Hell.

Next Chemos,[7] th' obscene dread of Moab's[8] sons,
From Aroar to Nebo and the wild
Of southmost Abarim; in Hesebon
And Horonaim, Seon's realm, beyond
The flow'ry dale of Sibma clad with vines,
And Eleale to th' Asphaltic Pool:[9]
Peor[10] his other name, when he enticed
Israel in Sittim,[11] on their march from Nile,
To do him wanton rites, which cost them woe.
Yet thence his lustful orgies he enlarged
Even to that hill of scandal, by the grove
Of Moloch homicide, lust hard by hate,
Till good Josiah[12] drove them thence to Hell.
With these came they who, from the bordering flood
Of old Euphrates to the brook that parts
Egypt from Syrian ground, had general names
Of Baalim[13] and Ashtaroth[14]—those male,
These feminine. For spirits, when they please,
Can either sex assume, or both; so soft
And uncompounded° is their essence pure, *unalloyed*
Not tried or manacled with joint or limb,
Nor founded on the brittle strength of bones,
Like cumbrous flesh; but, in what shape they choose,
Dilated or condensed, bright or obscure,
Can execute their airy purposes,
And works of love or enmity fulfil.
For those the race of Israel oft forsook
Their living strength,[15] and unfrequented left

[7] *Chemos* God of war worshipped by the Moabites.

[8] *Moab* Biblical country east of the Dead Sea. The place names that follow are all associated with Moab in various books of the Old Testament.

[9] *Asphaltic Pool* Dead Sea.

[10] *Peor* Diminutive form of Baal-Peor, a Moabite god who appeared both as a sun god and moon goddess.

[11] *Sittim* Site of the last camp of the Israelites before they entered Canaan and were suborned by Baal-Peor (Numbers 25).

[12] *Josiah* Biblical King of Judah who renewed his people's covenant with God and ruined heathen temples (2 Kings 23).

[13] *Baalim* Hebrew: collective term for Phoenician and Canaanite sun gods.

[14] *Ashtaroth* Collective term for variants of Ashtoreth, or Ishtar, a goddess of love, fertility, and war worshipped throughout the Middle East; her classical equivalent is Venus.

[15] *living strength* I.e., God.

His righteous altar, bowing lowly down
To bestial gods; for which their heads as low
Bowed down in battle, sunk before the spear
Of despicable foes. With these in troop
Came Astoreth, whom the Phoenicians called
Astarte, queen of Heaven, with crescent horns;
To whose bright image nightly by the moon
Sidonian[1] virgins paid their vows and songs;
In Sion also not unsung, where stood
Her temple on th' offensive mountain, built
By that uxorious king whose heart, though large,
Beguiled by fair idolatresses, fell
To idols foul.[2] Thammuz came next behind,
Whose annual wound in Lebanon allured
The Syrian damsels to lament his fate
In amorous ditties all a summer's day,
While smooth Adonis from his native rock
Ran purple to the sea, supposed with blood
Of Thammuz yearly wounded:[3] the love-tale
Infected Sion's daughters with like heat,
Whose wanton passions in the sacred porch
Ezekiel saw, when, by the vision led,
His eye surveyed the dark idolatries
Of alienated Judah.[4] Next came one
Who mourned in earnest, when the captive ark
Maimed his brute image, head and hands lopped off,
In his own temple, on the groundsel-edge,° *threshold*
Where he fell flat and shamed his worshippers:[5]
Dagon his name, sea-monster, upward man
And downward fish; yet had his temple high
Reared in Azotus, dreaded through the coast
Of Palestine, in Gath and Ascalon,
And Accaron[6] and Gaza's frontier bounds.
Him followed Rimmon,[7] whose delightful seat
Was fair Damascus, on the fertile banks
Of Abbana and Pharphar, lucid streams.
He also against the house of God was bold:
A leper once he lost, and gained a king—
Ahaz,[8] his sottish conqueror, whom he drew
God's altar to disparage and displace
For one of Syrian mode, whereon to burn
His odious offerings, and adore the gods
Whom he had vanquished. After these appeared
A crew who, under names of old renown,
Osiris, Isis, Orus,[9] and their train,
With monstrous shapes and sorceries abused
Fanatic Egypt and her priests to seek
Their wandering gods disguised in brutish forms[10]
Rather than human. Nor did Israel scape
Th' infection, when their borrowed gold composed
The calf in Oreb;[11] and the rebel king
Doubled that sin in Bethel and in Dan,[12]
Lik'ning his maker to the grazèd ox,
Jehovah, who in one night, when he passed
From Egypt marching, equalled with one stroke

[1] *Sidonian* From Sidonia, a Biblical country north of the Dead Sea, between modern day Lebanon and Syria.

[2] *that uxorious king … idols foul* King Solomon.

[3] *Thammuz came next … yearly wounded* Thammuz's consort of Astarte, identified with the Greek god Adonis. His sacred river runs reddish-purple yearly with silt, marking his feast and commemorating his mortal wounding by a wild boar.

[4] *Whose wanton passions … alienated Judah* See Ezekiel's vision of faithless Israelites in Ezekiel 8.9–15.

[5] *the captive ark … worshippers* After the Philistines captured the Ark of the Covenant and brought it back to the temple of Dagon, the statue of Dagon fell and broke into pieces (1 Samuel 5.1–5).

[6] *Azotus* Philistine city northeast of Gaza, also called Ashdod; *Gath* Now thought to be located at modern Tel es-Safi, west of Jerusalem; *Ascalon* Now called Ashkelon, located southwest of Ashdod; *Accaron* Modern Tel Miqne, located approximately twenty-five miles west of Jerusalem; these four cities plus Gaza were the five major cities of the Philistines.

[7] *Rimmon* Ancient Syrian storm god.

[8] *Ahaz* Also known as Ahaziah, a wicked apostate king of the Israelites (1 Kings 22.51–53, 2 Kings 1.1–17).

[9] *Osiris* Ancient Egyptian chief god, judge of the dead; *Isis* Wife of Osiris and goddess of fertility; *Orus* Horus, ancient Egyptian God of the sun, revenge, and war, son of Osiris and Isis.

[10] *disguised in brutish forms* Ancient Egyptian gods were depicted as having animal heads.

[11] *The calf in Oreb* While waiting for Moses to return from his mountaintop meeting with God, his brother Aaron crafted a golden calf, and the Israelites began to worship it as an idol (Exodus 32).

[12] *the rebel king … and in Dan* Jeroboam is the rebel king who, with the ten tribes of Israel, overthrew King Rehoboam, the son of Solomon (1 Kings 11). He set up two golden bull idols, saying "It is too much for you to go up to Jerusalem. Here are your gods, O Israel, who brought you up out of Egypt" (1 Kings 12.28).

Both her first-born and all her bleating gods.[1]
Belial[2] came last; than whom a Spirit more lewd
Fell not from Heaven, or more gross to love
Vice for itself. To him no temple stood
Or altar smoked; yet who more oft than he
In temples and at altars, when the priest
Turns atheist, as did Eli's sons, who filled
With lust and violence the house of God?[3]
In courts and palaces he also reigns,
And in luxurious cities, where the noise
Of riot ascends above their loftiest tow'rs,
And injury and outrage; and, when night
Darkens the streets, then wander forth the sons
Of Belial,[4] flown° with insolence and wine. *delirious*
Witness the streets of Sodom,[5] and that night
In Gibeah, when the hospitable door
Exposed a matron, to avoid worse rape.[6]
These were the prime in order and in might:
The rest were long to tell; though far renowned
Th' Ionian° gods—of Javan's[7] issue held *Greek*
Gods, yet confessed later than Heav'n and Earth,
Their boasted parents; Titan, Heav'n's first-born,
With his enormous brood, and birthright seized
By younger Saturn: he from mightier Jove,
His own and Rhea's son, like measure found;
So Jove usurping reigned. These, first in Crete
And Ida[8] known, thence on the snowy top
Of cold Olympus ruled the middle air,
Their highest Heav'n; or on the Delphian cliff,[9]
Or in Dodona,[10] and through all the bounds
Of Doric° land; or who with Saturn old *Greek*
Fled over Adria to th' Hesperian fields,
And o'er the Celtic roamed the utmost isles.[11]
All these and more came flocking; but with looks
Downcast and damp; yet such wherein appeared
Obscure some glimpse of joy to have found their chief
Not in despair, to have found themselves not lost
In loss itself; which on his count'nance cast
Like doubtful hue. But he, his wonted pride
Soon recollecting, with high words, that bore
Semblance of worth, not substance, gently raised
Their fainting courage, and dispelled their fears.
Then straight commands that, at the warlike sound
Of trumpets loud and clarions, be upreared
His mighty standard. That proud honour claimed
Azazel[12] as his right, a cherub tall:
Who forthwith from the glittering staff unfurled
Th' imperial ensign; which, full high advanced,
Shone like a meteor streaming to the wind,
With gems and golden lustre rich emblazed,
Seraphic arms and trophies; all the while
Sonorous metal blowing martial sounds:
At which the universal host up-sent
A shout that tore Hell's concave,[13] and beyond
Frighted the reign of chaos and old night.
All in a moment through the gloom were seen
Ten thousand banners rise into the air,
With orient° colours waving: with them rose *exotic*
A forest huge of spears; and thronging helms
Appeared, and serried° shields in thick array *crowded*
Of depth immeasurable. Anon they move
In perfect phalanx to the Dorian mood[14]

[1] *Jehovah … her bleating gods* Jehovah in one night ravaged Egypt and its gods by slaying Egypt's firstborn sons (see Exodus 12:29–33).

[2] *Belial* Personification of defilement, fornication, and wealth. Here a devil; originally a Hebrew word for worthlessness.

[3] *Eli's sons* Eli, the man who raised Samuel in the temple; he had two sons who were lustful and who seduced members of the congregation (1 Samuel 2.12–25).

[4] *sons / Of Belial* I.e., drunken rioters and lechers.

[5] *Sodom* Biblical city that epitomized wickedness and debauchery, destroyed by God (Genesis 19.27–28).

[6] *that night … worse rape* Biblical incident in which a group who demanded to rape an Israelite man traveling through Gibeah settled instead for raping and killing his concubine, whose master then killed her. See Judges 19.16–30.

[7] *Javan* Grandson of Noah.

[8] *Ida* Highest mountain in Crete.

[9] *Delphian cliff* Site of ancient Greece's most important Oracle.

[10] *Dodona* The most ancient Greek oracular site.

[11] *Adria* The Adriatic Sea; *Hesperian fields* Italy; *Celtic* France; *utmost isles* Far reaches of Scotland and Ireland.

[12] *Azazel* Hebrew: scapegoat. Mentioned in Leviticus 16, this name refers either to the scapegoat ritual given to Aaron, the scapegoat itself, or the entity to whom the scapegoat is sacrificed.

[13] *Hell's concave* Roof of Hell seen from underneath resembles an inverted bowl.

[14] *the Dorian mood* Greek musical mode associated with martial valor.

Of flutes and soft recorders—such as raised
To height of noblest temper heroes old
Arming to battle, and instead of rage
Deliberate valour breathed, firm, and unmoved
With dread of death to flight or foul retreat;
Nor wanting power to mitigate and swage[1]
With solemn touches troubled thoughts, and chase
Anguish and doubt and fear and sorrow and pain
From mortal or immortal minds. Thus they,
Breathing united force with fixed thought,
Moved on in silence to soft pipes that charmed
Their painful steps o'er the burnt soil. And now
Advanced in view they stand—a horrid front
Of dreadful length and dazzling arms, in guise
Of warriors old, with ordered spear and shield,
Awaiting what command their mighty chief
Had to impose. He through the armèd files
Darts his experienced eye, and soon traverse° *crosswise*
The whole battalion views—their order due,
Their visages and stature as of gods;
Their number last he sums. And now his heart
Distends with pride, and, hardening in his strength,
Glories: for never, since created Man,
Met such embodied force as, named with these,
Could merit more than that small infantry
Warred on by cranes—[2] though all the giant brood
Of Phlegra[3] with th' heroic race were joined
That fought at Thebes and Ilium,° on each side *Troy*
Mixed with auxiliar gods; and what resounds
In fable or romance of Uther's son,[4]
Begirt with British and Armoric° knights; *Breton*
And all who since, baptized or infidel,
Jousted in Aspramont, or Montalban,
Damasco, or Marocco, or Trebisond,[5]
Or whom Bizerta[6] sent from Afric shore
When Charlemagne with all his peerage fell
By Fontarabbia.[7] Thus far these beyond
Compare of mortal prowess, yet observed
Their dread commander. He, above the rest
In shape and gesture proudly eminent,
Stood like a tow'r. His form had yet not lost
All her original brightness, nor appeared
Less than archangel ruined, and th' excess
Of glory obscured: as when the sun new-ris'n
Looks through the horizontal misty air
Shorn of his beams, or, from behind the moon,
In dim eclipse, disastrous twilight sheds
On half the nations, and with fear of change
Perplexes monarchs.[8] Dark'n'd so, yet shone
Above them all th' archangel: but his face
Deep scars of thunder had entrenched, and care
Sat on his faded cheek, but under brows
Of dauntless courage, and considerate pride
Waiting revenge. Cruel his eye, but cast
Signs of remorse and passion, to behold
The fellows of his crime, the followers rather
(Far other once beheld in bliss), condemned
Forever now to have their lot in pain—
Millions of spirits for his fault amerced
Of Heav'n,[9] and from eternal splendours flung
For his revolt—yet faithful how they stood,
Their glory withered; as, when Heaven's fire
Has scathed° the forest oaks or mountain pines, *blasted*
With singèd top their stately growth, though bare,
Stands on the blasted heath. He now prepared
To speak; whereat their doubled ranks they bend
From wing to wing, and half enclose him round
With all his peers: attention held them mute.
Thrice he assayed, and thrice, in spite of scorn,
Tears, such as angels weep, burst forth: at last
Words interwove with sighs found out their way:

[1] *swage* I.e., assuage: to appease.

[2] *that small infantry / Warred on by cranes* Pygmies. Allusion to the fabled battle between cranes and tiny pygmies often mentioned in classical texts and after.

[3] *Phlegra* Location of the battle between rebellious giants and Zeus.

[4] *Uther's son* King Arthur, son of Uther Pendragon.

[5] *Aspramont ... Montalban ... Damasco ... Marocco ... Trebisond* Sites associated with the Crusades.

[6] *Bizerta* Departure point from which Moorish fleets invaded southern Europe.

[7] *When Charlemagne ... By Fontarabbia* Charlemagne (742–814) did not die at Fontarabia, in Northern Spain, but his troops under the command of Roland (Charlemagne's general) were defeated at Roncesvalles, 40 miles from Fontarabia, in 778.

[8] *from behind the moon ... Perplexes monarchs* Eclipses are traditionally harbingers of disaster or of death, especially of the deaths of monarchs, who were routinely identified with the sun.

[9] *amerced / Of Heaven* Both those banished from Heaven, and those punished by Heaven.

"O myriads of immortal spirits! O powers
Matchless, but with th' Almighty; and that strife
Was not inglorious, though th' event was dire,
As this place testifies, and this dire change,
Hateful to utter. But what power of mind,
Foreseeing or presaging, from the depth
Of knowledge past or present, could have feared
How such united force of gods, how such
As stood like these, could ever know repulse?
For who can yet believe, though after loss,
That all these puissant° legions, whose exile *powerful*
Hath emptied Heaven, shall fail to re-ascend,
Self-raised, and repossess their native seat?
For me, be witness all the host of Heav'n,
If counsels different, or danger shunned
By me, have lost our hopes. But He who reigns
Monarch in Heav'n till then as one secure
Sat on His throne, upheld by old repute,
Consent or custom, and His regal state
Put forth at full, but still His strength concealed—
Which tempted our attempt, and wrought our fall.
Henceforth His might we know, and know our own,
So as not either to provoke, or dread
New war provoked: our better part remains
To work in close design, by fraud or guile,
What force effected not; that He no less
At length from us may find, who overcomes
By force hath overcome but half His foe.
Space may produce new worlds; whereof so rife
There went a fame° in Heav'n that He ere long *rumor*
Intended to create, and therein plant
A generation whom His choice regard
Should favour equal to the sons of Heav'n.
Thither, if but to pry, shall be perhaps
Our first eruption—thither, or elsewhere;
For this infernal pit shall never hold
Celestial spirits in bondage, nor th' abyss
Long under darkness cover. But these thoughts
Full counsel must mature. Peace is despaired;
For who can think submission? War, then, war
Open or understood, must be resolved."
He spake; and, to confirm his words, outflew
Millions of flaming swords, drawn from the thighs
Of mighty cherubim; the sudden blaze
Far round illumined Hell. Highly they raged
Against the highest and fierce with graspèd arms
Clashed on their sounding shields the din of war,
Hurling defiance toward the vault of Heav'n.
There stood a hill not far, whose grisly top
Belched fire and rolling smoke; the rest entire
Shone with a glossy scurf[1]—undoubted sign
That in his womb was hid metallic ore,
The work of sulphur. Thither, winged with speed,
A numerous brigade hastened: as when bands
Of pioneers,[2] with spade and pickaxe armed,
Forerun the royal camp, to trench a field,
Or cast a rampart. Mammon led them on—
Mammon, the least erected[3] spirit that fell
From Heav'n; for even in Heav'n his looks and thoughts
Were always downward bent, admiring more
The riches of Heav'n's pavement, trodden gold,
Than aught divine or holy else enjoyed
In vision beatific. By him first
Men also, and by his suggestion taught,
Ransacked the centre,[4] and with impious hands
Rifled the bowels of their mother Earth
For treasures better hid. Soon had his crew
Op'nd into the hill a spacious wound,
And digged out ribs of gold. Let none admire
That riches grow in Hell; that soil may best
Deserve the precious bane. And here let those
Who boast in mortal things, and wondering tell
Of Babel,[5] and the works of Memphian kings,[6]
Learn how their greatest monuments of fame
And strength and art are easily outdone
By spirits reprobate, and in an hour
What in an age they, with incessant toil
And hands innumerable, scarce perform.

[1] *scurf* Scaly crust.

[2] *pioneers* Advance body of foot-soldiers who prepare for the main body of the army.

[3] *least erected* Lowest-ranked. Mammon is concerned with worldly or material goods and wealth.

[4] *Ransacked the centre* Mined the Earth; "centre" extends the Ptolemaic metaphor.

[5] *Babel* Tower built by men who wished to reach Heaven. For their presumption, God caused them all to speak in different languages, so that they could not communicate well enough to continue to build the city. See Genesis 11.1–9.

[6] *Memphian kings* Egyptian Pharaohs.

Nigh on the plain, in many cells prepared,
That underneath had veins of liquid fire
Sluiced from the lake, a second multitude
With wondrous art founded the massy° ore, *heavy*
Sev'ring each kind, and scummed the bullion dross.
A third as soon had formed within the ground
A various mould, and from the boiling cells
By strange conveyance filled each hollow nook;
As in an organ, from one blast of wind,
To many a row of pipes the soundboard breathes.
Anon out of the earth a fabric huge
Rose like an exhalation, with the sound
Of dulcet symphonies and voices sweet—
Built like a temple, where pilasters[1] round
Were set, and Doric pillars overlaid
With golden architrave;° nor did there want *filigree*
Cornice or frieze, with bossy° sculptures graven; *embossed*
The roof was fretted° gold. Not Babylon *engraved*
Nor great Alcairo° such magnificence *Cairo*
Equalled in all their glories, to enshrine
Belus or Serapis[2] their gods, or seat
Their kings, when Egypt with Assyria strove
In wealth and luxury. Th' ascending pile
Stood fixed her stately height, and straight the doors,
Op'ning their brazen folds, discover, wide
Within, her ample spaces o'er the smooth
And level pavement: from the arched roof,
Pendant° by subtle magic, many a row *hanging*
Of starry lamps and blazing cressets,° fed *torches*
With naptha and asphaltus,° yielded light *pitch*
As from a sky. The hasty multitude
Admiring entered; and the work some praise,
And some the architect. His hand was known
In Heav'n by many a towered structure high,
Where sceptred angels held their residence,
And sat as princes, whom the supreme King
Exalted to such power, and gave to rule,
Each in his hierarchy, the orders bright.
Nor was his name unheard or unadored
In ancient Greece; and in Ausonian° land *Italian*
Men called him Mulciber;[3] and how he fell
From Heav'n they fabled, thrown by angry Jove
Sheer o'er the crystal battlements: from morn
To noon he fell, from noon to dewy eve,
A summer's day, and with the setting sun
Dropt from the zenith, like a falling star,
On Lemnos, th' Aegaean isle.[4] Thus they relate,
Erring; for he with this rebellious rout
Fell long before; nor aught availed him now
To have built in Heav'n high tow'rs; nor did he 'scape
By all his engines, but was headlong sent,
With his industrious crew, to build in Hell.
Meanwhile the wingèd heralds, by command
Of sovereign power, with awful ceremony
And trumpet's sound, throughout the host proclaim
A solemn council forthwith to be held
At Pandemonium,[5] the high capital
Of Satan and his peers. Their summons called
From every band and squarèd regiment
By place or choice the worthiest: they anon
With hundreds and with thousands trooping came
Attended. All access was thronged; the gates
And porches wide, but chief the spacious hall
(Though like a covered field, where champions bold
Wont ride in armed, and at the Soldan's° chair *Sultan's*
Defied the best of paynim° chivalry *pagan*
To mortal combat, or career° with lance), *joust*
Thick swarmed, both on the ground and in the air,
Brushed with the hiss of rustling wings. As bees
In springtime, when the sun with Taurus rides,[6]
Pour forth their populous youth about the hive
In clusters; they among fresh dews and flowers
Fly to and fro, or on the smoothèd plank,
The suburb of their straw-built citadel,
New rubbed with balm, expatiate, and confer
Their state-affairs: so thick the airy crowd
Swarmed and were straightened; till, the signal giv'n,
Behold a wonder! They but now who seemed
In bigness to surpass Earth's giant sons,
Now less than smallest dwarfs, in narrow room

[1] *pilasters* Pillars fixed to the wall.

[2] *Belus* Baal; *Serapis* Egyptian bull god.

[3] *Mulciber* Vulcan, or Hephaestus, the gods' blacksmith.

[4] *and how he fell … Aegaean isle* In some accounts, Hephaestus was thrown out of Heaven for attempting to protect his mother, Hera, from Zeus's (Jove's) anger.

[5] *Pandemonium* Literally, all demonhood or all demons; the word is Milton's invention.

[6] *when the sun with Taurus rides* Springtime, when the sun is in the astrological house of Taurus, the bull.

Throng numberless—like that pygmean race
Beyond the Indian mount; or faery elves,
Whose midnight revels, by a forest-side
Or fountain, some belated peasant[1] sees,
Or dreams he sees, while overhead the moon
Sits arbitress, and nearer to the earth
Wheels her pale course: they, on their mirth and dance
Intent, with jocund music charm his ear;
At once with joy and fear his heart rebounds.
Thus incorporeal spirits to smallest forms
Reduced their shapes immense, and were at large,
Though without number still, amidst the hall
Of that infernal court. But far within,
And in their own dimensions like themselves,
The great seraphic lords and cherubim
In close recess and secret conclave sat,
A thousand demi-gods on golden seats,
Frequent° and full. After short silence then, *many*
And summons read, the great consult began.

THE END OF THE FIRST BOOK

ARGUMENT TO BOOK 2

The consultation begun, Satan debates whether another battle be to be hazarded for the recovery of Heaven: some advise it, others dissuade. A third proposal is preferred, mentioned before by Satan, to search the truth of that prophesy or tradition in Heaven concerning another world, and another kind of creature equal or not much inferior to themselves, about this time to be created; their doubt who shall be sent on this difficult search; Satan their chief undertakes alone the voyage, is honoured and applauded. The council thus ended, the rest betake them several ways and to several employments, as their inclinations lead them, to entertain the time till Satan return. He passes on his journey to Hell gates, finds them shut, and who sat there to guard them, by whom at length they are opened, and discover to him the great gulf between Hell and Heaven; with what difficulty he passes through, directed by Chaos, the power of that place, to the sight of this new world which he sought.

[1] *belated peasant* I.e., a peasant out late.

BOOK 2

High on a throne of royal state, which far
Outshone the wealth of Ormuz and of Ind,[2]
Or where the gorgeous east with richest hand
Showers on her kings barbaric pearl and gold,
Satan exalted sat, by merit raised
To that bad eminence; and, from despair
Thus high uplifted beyond hope, aspires
Beyond thus high, insatiate to pursue
Vain war with Heav'n; and, by success untaught,
His proud imaginations thus displayed:
"Powers and dominions, deities of Heav'n!
For, since no deep° within her gulf can hold *depth*
Immortal vigour, though oppressed and fallen,
I give not Heav'n for lost: from this descent
Celestial virtues rising will appear
More glorious and more dread than from no fall,
And trust themselves to fear no second fate!
Me though just right, and the fixed laws of Heav'n,
Did first create your leader—next, free choice
With what besides in council or in fight
Hath been achieved of merit—yet this loss,
Thus far at least recovered, hath much more
Established in a safe, unenvied throne,
Yielded with full consent. The happier state
In Heav'n, which follows dignity, might draw
Envy from each inferior; but who here
Will envy whom the highest place exposes
Foremost to stand against the Thunderer's aim
Your bulwark, and condemns to greatest share
Of endless pain? Where there is, then, no good
For which to strive, no strife can grow up there
From faction: for none sure will claim in Hell
Precedence; none whose portion is so small
Of present pain that with ambitious mind
Will covet more! With this advantage, then,
To union, and firm faith, and firm accord,
More than can be in Heav'n, we now return
To claim our just inheritance of old,
Surer to prosper than prosperity
Could have assured us; and by what best way,
Whether of open war or covert guile,

[2] *Ormuz* Straight of Hormuz, a waterway linking the Persian Gulf with the Gulf of Oman—traditionally and still a critical waterway for trade and shipping; *Ind* India.

We now debate. Who can advise may speak."
He ceased; and next him Moloch, sceptred king,
Stood up—the strongest and the fiercest spirit
That fought in Heav'n, now fiercer by despair.
His trust was with th' eternal to be deemed
Equal in strength, and rather than be less
Cared not to be at all; with that care lost
Went all his fear: of God, or Hell, or worse,
He recked not, and these words thereafter spake:
"My sentence is for open war. Of wiles,
More unexpert, I boast not: them let those
Contrive who need, or when they need; not now.
For, while they sit contriving, shall the rest—
Millions that stand in arms, and longing wait
The signal to ascend—sit lingering here,
Heav'n's fugitives, and for their dwelling-place
Accept this dark opprobrious den of shame,
The prison of His tyranny who reigns
By our delay? No! Let us rather choose,
Armed with Hell-flames and fury, all at once
O'er Heav'n's high towers to force resistless[1] way,
Turning our tortures into horrid arms
Against the Torturer; when, to meet the noise
Of His almighty engine,[2] He shall hear
Infernal thunder, and, for lightning, see
Black fire and horror shot with equal rage
Among His angels, and His throne itself
Mixed with Tartarean° sulphur and strange fire, *hellish*
His own invented torments. But perhaps
The way seems difficult, and steep to scale
With upright wing against a higher foe!
Let such bethink them, if the sleepy drench
Of that forgetful lake[3] benumb not still,
That in our proper motion we ascend
Up to our native seat; descent and fall
To us is adverse. Who but felt of late,
When the fierce Foe hung on our broken rear
Insulting,[4] and pursued us through the deep,
With what compulsion and laborious flight
We sunk thus low? Th' ascent is easy, then;
Th' event is feared! Should we again provoke
Our stronger, some worse way His wrath may find
To our destruction, if there be in Hell
Fear to be worse destroyed! What can be worse
Than to dwell here, driven out from bliss, condemned
In this abhorred deep to utter woe!
Where pain of unextinguishable fire
Must exercise us without hope of end
The vassals of His anger, when the scourge
Inexorably, and the torturing hour,
Calls us to penance? More destroyed than thus,
We should be quite abolished, and expire.
What fear we then? What doubt we to incense
His utmost ire? Which, to the height enraged,
Will either quite consume us, and reduce
To nothing this essential—happier far
Than miserable to have eternal being—
Or, if our substance be indeed divine,
And cannot cease to be, we are at worst
On this side nothing;[5] and by proof we feel
Our power sufficient to disturb his Heav'n,
And with perpetual inroads[6] to alarm,
Though inaccessible, his fatal throne:
Which, if not victory, is yet revenge."
He ended frowning, and his look denounced
Desperate revenge, and battle dangerous
To less than gods. On th' other side up rose
Belial, in act more graceful and humane.
A fairer person lost not Heav'n; he seemed
For dignity composed, and high exploit.
But all was false and hollow; though his tongue
Dropped manna,[7] and could make the worse appear
The better reason, to perplex and dash
Maturest counsels: for his thoughts were low—
To vice industrious,[8] but to nobler deeds

[1] *resistless* I.e., cannot be resisted.

[2] *engine* I.e., war machine.

[3] *Of that forgetful lake* Lethe, river of oblivion in Hades.

[4] *hung on our broken rear / Insulting* Followed close behind our broken rear ranks, attacking us and exulting; the scatological joke of "broken rear" is intentional.

[5] *What doubt we ... this side nothing* Why do we care if we anger God more? We're immortal, and either God can't hurt us, or He will just completely erase us from existence—either way, we are no worse off than we are right now.

[6] *perpetual inroads* Constant attacks.

[7] *though his tongue / Dropped manna* Though he spoke as sweetly as could be.

[8] *To vice industrious* Quick to commit vice, and hardworking when doing so.

Timorous and slothful. Yet he pleased the ear,
And with persuasive accent thus began:
"I should be much for open war, O peers,
As not behind in hate, if what was urged
Main reason to persuade immediate war
Did not dissuade me most, and seem to cast
Ominous conjecture on the whole success;
When he who most excels in fact of arms,
In what he counsels and in what excels
Mistrustful, grounds his courage on despair
And utter dissolution, as the scope
Of all his aim, after some dire revenge.
First, what revenge? The tow'rs of Heav'n are filled
With armèd watch,° that render all access *guards*
Impregnable: oft on the bordering deep
Encamp their legions, or with obscure wing
Scout far and wide into the realm of night,
Scorning[1] surprise. Or, could we break our way
By force, and at our heels all Hell should rise
With blackest insurrection to confound
Heav'n's purest light, yet our great Enemy,
All incorruptible, would on His throne
Sit unpolluted, and th' ethereal mould,
Incapable of stain, would soon expel
Her mischief, and purge off the baser fire,[2]
Victorious. Thus repulsed, our final hope
Is flat despair: we must exasperate
Th' almighty Victor to spend all his rage;
And that must end us; that must be our cure—
To be no more. Sad cure! For who would lose,
Though full of pain, this intellectual° being, *sentient*
Those thoughts that wander through eternity,
To perish rather, swallowed up and lost
In the wide womb of uncreated night,
Devoid of sense and motion? And who knows,
Let this be good, whether our angry Foe
Can give it, or will ever? How He can
Is doubtful; that He never will is sure.
Will He, so wise, let loose at once His ire,
Belike through impotence or unaware,
To give His enemies their wish, and end
Them in His anger whom His anger saves
To punish endless? 'Wherefore cease we, then?'
Say they who counsel war; 'we are decreed,
Reserved, and destined to eternal woe;
Whatever doing, what can we suffer more,
What can we suffer worse?' Is this, then, worst—
Thus sitting, thus consulting, thus in arms?
What when we fled amain,° pursued *at full speed*
and struck
With Heav'n's afflicting thunder, and besought
The deep to shelter us? This Hell then seemed
A refuge from those wounds. Or when we lay
Chained on the burning lake? That sure was worse.
What if the breath that kindled those grim fires,
Awaked, should blow them into sevenfold rage,
And plunge us in the flames; or from above
Should intermitted° vengeance arm again *paused*
His red right hand to plague us? What if all
Her stores were op'n'd, and this firmament
Of Hell should spout her cataracts of fire,
Impendent° horrors, threatening hideous fall *hanging*
One day upon our heads; while we perhaps,
Designing or exhorting glorious war,
Caught in a fiery tempest, shall be hurled,
Each on his rock transfixed,° the sport and prey *pinned*
Of racking° whirlwinds, or forever sunk *torturing*
Under yon boiling ocean, wrapt in chains,
There to converse with everlasting groans,
Unrespited, unpitied, unreprieved,
Ages of hopeless end?[3] This would be worse.
War, therefore, open or concealed, alike
My voice dissuades; for what can force or guile
With Him, or who deceive His mind, whose eye
Views all things at one view? He from Heav'n's height
All these our motions vain sees and derides,
Not more almighty to resist our might
Than wise to frustrate all our plots and wiles.
Shall we, then, live thus vile—the race of Heav'n
Thus trampled, thus expelled, to suffer here
Chains and these torments? Better these than worse,
By my advice; since fate inevitable
Subdues us, and omnipotent decree,
The Victor's will. To suffer, as to do,

[1] *Scorning* Making impossible.

[2] *th' ethereal mould ... purge off the baser fire* The pure "consuming fire" of God (Exodus 24.17, Numbers 11.1, Deuteronomy 4.24) would quickly defeat and exterminate the merely "flaming fire" of the rebel angels (Exodus 3.2, Psalm 104.4, Hebrews 1.7).

[3] *Ages of hopeless end* An ages-long hopeless fate.

Our strength is equal; nor the law unjust
That so ordains. This was at first resolved,
If we were wise, against so great a foe
Contending, and so doubtful what might fall.
I laugh when those who at the spear are bold
And venturous, if that fail them, shrink, and fear
What yet they know must follow—to endure
Exile, or ignominy, or bonds, or pain,
The sentence of their conqueror. This is now
Our doom; which if we can sustain and bear,
Our supreme Foe in time may much remit
His anger, and perhaps, thus far removed,
Not mind us not offending, satisfied
With what is punished; whence these raging fires
Will slacken, if His breath stir not their flames.
Our purer essence then will overcome
Their noxious vapour; or, inured, not feel;
Or, changed at length, and to the place conformed
In temper and in nature, will receive
Familiar the fierce heat; and, void of pain,
This horror will grow mild, this darkness light;
Besides what hope the never-ending flight
Of future days may bring, what chance, what change
Worth waiting—since our present lot appears
For happy though but ill, for ill not worst,
If we procure not to ourselves more woe."
    Thus Belial, with words clothed in reason's garb,
Counselled ignoble ease and peaceful sloth,
Not peace; and after him thus Mammon spoke:
    "Either to disenthrone the King of Heaven
We war, if war be best, or to regain
Our own right lost. Him to unthrone we then
May hope, when everlasting fate shall yield
To fickle chance, and chaos judge the strife.
The former, vain to hope, argues as vain
The latter; for what place can be for us
Within Heav'n's bound, unless Heav'n's Lord Supreme
We overpower? Suppose He should relent
And publish° grace to all, on promise made *grant*
Of new subjection; with what eyes could we
Stand in His presence humble, and receive
Strict laws imposed, to celebrate His throne
With warbled hymns, and to His godhead sing
Forced hallelujahs, while He lordly sits
Our envied Sovereign, and His altar breathes
Ambrosial odours and ambrosial[1] flowers,
Our servile offerings? This must be our task
In Heav'n, this our delight. How wearisome
Eternity so spent in worship paid
To Whom we hate! Let us not then pursue
By force impossible, by leave obtained
Unacceptable,[2] though in Heav'n, our state
Of splendid vassalage;° but rather seek *servitude*
Our own good from ourselves, and from our own
Live to ourselves, though in this vast recess,
Free and to none accountable, preferring
Hard liberty before the easy yoke
Of servile pomp. Our greatness will appear
Then most conspicuous when great things of small,
Useful of hurtful, prosperous of adverse,
We can create, and in what place soe'er° *whatsoever*
Thrive under evil, and work ease out of pain
Through labour and endurance. This deep world
Of darkness do we dread? How oft amidst
Thick clouds and dark doth Heav'n's all-ruling Sire
Choose to reside, His glory unobscured,
And with the majesty of darkness round
Covers His throne, from whence deep thunders roar.[3]
Must'ring their rage, and Heav'n resembles Hell!
As He our darkness, cannot we His light
Imitate when we please? This desert soil
Wants not her hidden lustre, gems and gold;
Nor want we skill or art from whence to raise
Magnificence; and what can Heav'n show more?
Our torments also may, in length of time,
Become our elements, these piercing fires
As soft as now severe, our temper changed
Into their temper; which must needs remove
The sensible[4] of pain. All things invite
To peaceful counsels, and the settled state
Of order, how in safety best we may

---

[1] *Ambrosial* Ambrosia is the mythical food of the Greek and Roman gods.

[2] *Let us not then pursue ... by leave obtained / Unacceptable* Let us not try and take by considerable force of arms a servitude we would find disgusting and hateful.

[3] *How oft amidst / Thick clouds ... from whence deep thunders roar.* See, for example Exodus 13 and 14, Leviticus 16.2, Numbers 9–16.

[4] *The sensible* Those who feel.

Compose our present evils, with regard
Of what we are and where, dismissing quite
All thoughts of war. Ye have what I advise."
He scarce had finished, when such murmur filled
Th' assembly as when hollow rocks retain
The sound of blustering winds, which all night long
Had roused the sea, now with hoarse cadence lull
Seafaring men o'erwatched,[1] whose bark° by chance *boat*
Or pinnace,° anchors in a craggy bay *ship*
After the tempest. Such applause was heard
As Mammon ended, and his sentence pleased,
Advising peace: for such another field
They dreaded worse than Hell; so much the fear
Of thunder and the sword of Michael[2]
Wrought still within them; and no less desire
To found this nether empire, which might rise,
By policy and long process of time,
In emulation opposite to Heav'n.
Which when Beelzebub perceived—than whom,
Satan except, none higher sat—with grave
Aspect he rose, and in his rising seemed
A pillar of state. Deep on his front° engraven *forehead*
Deliberation sat, and public care;
And princely counsel in his face yet shone,
Majestic, though in ruin. Sage he stood
With Atlantean[3] shoulders, fit to bear
The weight of mightiest monarchies; his look
Drew audience and attention still as night
Or summer's noontide air, while thus he spoke:
"Thrones and imperial powers, offspring of Heav'n,
Ethereal virtues; or these titles now
Must we renounce, and, changing style, be called
Princes of Hell? For so the popular vote
Inclines—here to continue, and build up here
A growing empire; doubtless; while we dream,
And know not that the King of Heav'n hath doomed
This place our dungeon, not our safe retreat
Beyond His potent arm, to live exempt
From Heav'n's high jurisdiction, in new league
Banded against His throne, but to remain
In strictest bondage, though thus far removed,
Under th' inevitable curb, reserved
His captive multitude. For He, to be sure,
In height or depth, still first and last will reign
Sole king, and of His kingdom lose no part
By our revolt, but over Hell extend
His empire, and with iron sceptre rule
Us here, as with His golden those in Heav'n.
What sit we then projecting peace and war?
War hath determined us and foiled with loss
Irreparable; terms of peace yet none
Vouchsafed or sought; for what peace will be given
To us enslaved, but custody severe,
And stripes° and arbitrary punishment *lashes*
Inflicted? And what peace can we return,
But, to our power,[4] hostility and hate,
Untamed reluctance, and revenge, though slow,
Yet ever plotting how the Conqueror least
May reap His conquest, and may least rejoice
In doing what we most in suffering feel?
Nor will occasion want, nor shall we need
With dangerous expedition to invade
Heaven, whose high walls fear no assault or siege,
Or ambush from the deep. What if we find
Some easier enterprise? There is a place
(If ancient and prophetic fame in Heav'n
Err not)—another world, the happy seat
Of some new race called Man, about this time
To be created like to us, though less
In power and excellence, but favoured more
Of Him who rules above; so was His will
Pronounced among the gods, and by an oath
That shook Heav'n's whole circumference confirmed.
Thither let us bend all our thoughts, to learn
What creatures there inhabit, of what mould° *form*
Or substance, how endued, and what their power
And where their weakness: how attempted best,
By force or subtlety. Though Heav'n be shut,
And Heav'n's high Arbitrator sit secure
In His own strength, this place may lie exposed,
The utmost border of His kingdom, left
To their defence who hold it: here, perhaps,
Some advantageous act may be achieved

[1] *o'erwatched* Worn out from having to forgo sleep for watchfulness.

[2] *Michael* Archangel Michael, a general of God's army.

[3] *Atlantean* The Titan Atlas carried the world on his broad shoulders.

[4] *to our power* To our utmost ability.

By sudden onset°—either with Hell-fire *assault*
To waste His whole creation, or possess
All as our own, and drive, as we were driven,
The puny habitants; or, if not drive,
Seduce them to our party, that their God
May prove their Foe, and with repenting hand
Abolish His own works. This would surpass
Common revenge, and interrupt His joy
In our confusion, and our joy upraise
In His disturbance; when his darling sons,
Hurled headlong to partake with us, shall curse
Their frail original, and faded bliss—
Faded so soon! Advise if this be worth
Attempting, or to sit in darkness here
Hatching vain empires." Thus Beelzebub
Pleaded his devilish counsel—first devised
By Satan, and in part proposed: for whence,
But from the author of all ill, could spring
So deep a malice, to confound the race
Of mankind in one root, and earth with Hell
To mingle and involve, done all to spite
The great Creator? But their spite still serves
His glory to augment. The bold design
Pleased highly those infernal states,[1] and joy
Sparkled in all their eyes: with full assent
They vote: whereat his speech he thus renews:
"Well have ye judged, well ended long debate,
Synod[2] of gods, and, like to what ye are,
Great things resolved, which from the lowest deep
Will once more lift us up, in spite of fate,
Nearer our ancient seat—perhaps in view
Of those bright confines, whence, with neighbouring arms,
And opportune excursion, we may chance
Re-enter Heav'n; or else in some mild zone
Dwell, not unvisited of Heav'n's fair light,
Secure, and at the bright'ning orient beam[3]
Purge off this gloom: the soft delicious air,
To heal the scar of these corrosive fires,
Shall breathe her balm. But, first, whom shall we send
In search of this new world? Whom shall we find
Sufficient? Who shall tempt with wandering feet
The dark, unbottomed, infinite abyss,
And through the palpable obscure[4] find out
His uncouth° way, or spread his airy flight, *unknown*
Upborne with indefatigable wings
Over the vast abrupt, ere he arrive
The happy isle? What strength, what art, can then
Suffice, or what evasion bear him safe,
Through the strict sentries and stations thick
Of angels watching round? Here he had need
All circumspection: and we now no less
Choice in our suffrage; for on whom we send
The weight of all, and our last hope, relies."
This said, he sat; and expectation held
His look suspense,[5] awaiting who appeared
To second, or oppose, or undertake
The perilous attempt. But all sat mute,
Pondering the danger with deep thoughts; and each
In other's count'nance read his own dismay,
Astonished. None among the choice and prime
Of those Heav'n-warring champions could be found
So hardy[6] as to proffer or accept,
Alone, the dreadful voyage; till, at last,
Satan, whom now transcendent glory raised
Above his fellows, with monarchal pride
Conscious of highest worth, unmoved thus spake:
"O progeny of Heav'n! Empyreal thrones!
With reason hath deep silence and demur
Seized us, though undismayed. Long is the way
And hard, that out of Hell leads up to light.
Our prison strong, this huge convex° of fire, *dome*
Outrageous° to devour, immures us round *eager*
Ninefold; and gates of burning adamant,[7]
Barred over us, prohibit all egress.
These passed, if any pass, the void profound
Of unessential[8] night receives him next,
Wide-gaping, and with utter loss of being
Threatens him, plunged in that abortive gulf.
If thence he scape, into whatever world,

[1] *states* Heads of state or estates, the hierarchs of Hell.

[2] *Synod* Council or assembly, especially of church officials.

[3] *bright'ning orient beam* Lightening of the eastern horizon; dawn.

[4] *the palpable obscure* Darkness so complete one can feel it.

[5] *expectation held / His look suspense* His look was suspenseful as he waited for their response.

[6] *hardy* Tough, or also possibly "foolhardy."

[7] *adamant* Unbreakable shining metal.

[8] *unessential* Having no substance, absolutely empty.

Or unknown region, what remains him less
Than unknown dangers, and as hard escape?
But I should ill become this throne, O peers,
And this imperial sov'reignty, adorned
With splendour, armed with power, if aught proposed
And judged of public moment° in the shape *importance*
Of difficulty or danger, could deter
Me from attempting. Wherefore do I assume
These royalties, and not refuse to reign,
Refusing to accept as great a share
Of hazard as of honour, due alike
To him who reigns, and so much to him due
Of hazard more as he above the rest
High honoured sits? Go, therefore, mighty powers,
Terror of Heav'n, though fallen; intend at[1] home,
While here shall be our home, what best may ease
The present misery, and render Hell
More tolerable; if there be cure or charm
To respite, or deceive, or slack the pain
Of this ill mansion: intermit no watch[2]
Against a wakeful foe, while I abroad
Through all the coasts of dark destruction seek
Deliverance for us all. This enterprise
None shall partake with me." Thus saying rose
The monarch, and prevented all reply;
Prudent, lest from his resolution raised
Others among the chief might offer now,
Certain to be refused, what erst° they feared, *formerly*
And, so refused, might in opinion stand
His rivals, winning cheap the high repute
Which he through hazard huge must earn. But they
Dreaded not more th' adventure than his voice
Forbidding; and at once with him they rose.
Their rising all at once was as the sound
Of thunder heard remote. Towards him they bend
With awful reverence prone, and as a God
Extol him equal to the high'st in Heav'n.
Nor failed they to express how much they praised
That for the general safety he despised
His own: for neither do the spirits damned
Lose all their virtue; lest bad men should boast
Their specious° deeds on earth, which glory excites, *worthless*
Or close ambition varnished o'er with zeal.
Thus they their doubtful consultations dark
Ended, rejoicing in their matchless chief:
As, when from mountaintops the dusky clouds
Ascending, while the north wind sleeps, o'erspread
Heav'n's cheerful face, the louring element[3]
Scowls o'er the darkened landscape snow or shower,
If chance the radiant sun, with farewell sweet,
Extend his ev'ning beam, the fields revive,
The birds their notes renew, and bleating herds
Attest their joy, that hill and valley rings.
O shame to men! Devil with devil damned
Firm concord holds;[4] men only disagree
Of creatures rational, though under hope
Of heavenly grace, and, God proclaiming peace,
Yet live in hatred, enmity, and strife
Among themselves, and levy cruel wars
Wasting the earth, each other to destroy:
As if (which might induce us to accord)
Man had not hellish foes enow° besides, *enough*
That day and night for his destruction wait!
The Stygian° council thus dissolved; and forth *hellish*
In order came the grand infernal peers:
Midst came their mighty paramount, and seemed
Alone th' antagonist of Heaven, nor less
Than Hell's dread emperor, with pomp supreme,
And God-like imitated state: him round[5]
A globe of fiery seraphim enclosed
With bright emblazonry, and horrent arms.[6]
Then of their session ended they bid cry
With trumpet's regal sound the great result:
Toward the four winds four speedy cherubim
Put to their mouths the sounding alchemy,[7]
By herald's voice explained; the hollow abyss
Heard far and wide, and all the host of Hell
With deaf'ning shout returned them loud acclaim.
Thence more at ease their minds, and somewhat raised
By false presumptuous hope, the rangèd powers

[1] *intend at* Turn your thoughts to.

[2] *intermit no watch* Do not interrupt your vigilance.

[3] *louring element* Darkening sky.

[4] *Devil ... holds* Devils hold firm to their contracts with each other.

[5] *him round* Around him.

[6] *bright emblazonry ... horrent arms* Bright heraldry and bared weapons.

[7] *the sounding alchemy* Trumpets, metal that sings.

Disband; and, wand'ring, each his several way
Pursues, as inclination or sad choice
Leads him perplexed, where he may likeliest find
Truce to his restless thoughts, and entertain
The irksome hours, till his great chief return.
Part° on the plain, or in the air sublime, *some*
Upon the wing or in swift race contend,
As at th' Olympian games or Pythian fields;[1]
Part curb their fiery steeds, or shun the goal
With rapid wheels,[2] or fronted° brigades form: *ranked*
As when, to warn proud cities, war appears
Waged in the troubled sky, and armies rush
To battle in the clouds; before each van° *foremost division*
Prick forth the airy knights, and couch° their spears, *set*
Till thickest legions close; with feats of arms
From either end of Heav'n the welkin° burns. *sky*
Others, with vast Typhoean rage, more fell,[3]
Rend up both rocks and hills, and ride the air
In whirlwind; Hell scarce holds the wild uproar:
As when Alcides,° from Oechalia crowned *Hercules*
With conquest, felt th' envenomed robe, and tore
Through pain up by the roots Thessalian pines,
And Lichas from the top of Oeta threw
Into th' Euboic sea.[4] Others, more mild,
Retreated in a silent valley, sing
With notes angelical to many a harp
Their own heroic deeds, and hapless fall
By doom of battle, and complain that fate
Free virtue should enthral to force or chance.
Their song was partial;[5] but the harmony
(What could it less when spirits immortal sing?)
Suspended Hell, and took with ravishment
The thronging audience. In discourse more sweet
(For eloquence the soul, song charms the sense)[6]
Others apart sat on a hill retired,
In thoughts more elevate, and reasoned high
Of Providence, foreknowledge, will, and fate—
Fixed fate, free will, foreknowledge absolute,
And found no end, in wandering mazes lost.
Of good and evil much they argued then,
Of happiness and final misery,
Passion and apathy, and glory and shame:
Vain wisdom all, and false philosophy!
Yet, with a pleasing sorcery, could charm
Pain for a while or anguish, and excite
Fallacious hope, or arm th' obdured breast[7]
With stubborn patience as with triple steel.
Another part, in squadrons and gross bands,
On bold adventure to discover wide
That dismal world, if any clime° perhaps *region*
Might yield them easier habitation, bend
Four ways their flying march, along the banks
Of four infernal rivers, that disgorge
Into the burning lake their baleful streams—
Abhorred Styx, the flood of deadly hate;
Sad Acheron of sorrow, black and deep;
Cocytus, named of lamentation loud
Heard on the rueful stream; fierce Phlegeton,
Whose waves of torrent fire inflame with rage.
Far off from these, a slow and silent stream,
Lethe, the river of oblivion, rolls
Her watery labyrinth, whereof who drinks
Forthwith his former state and being forgets—
Forgets both joy and grief, pleasure and pain.[8]
Beyond this flood a frozen continent
Lies dark and wild, beat with perpetual storms
Of whirlwind and dire hail, which on firm land
Thaws not, but gathers heap,[9] and ruin seems
Of ancient pile; all else deep snow and ice,

[1] *Pythian fields* Fields below the Temple of the Oracle at Delphi, site of games honoring Apollo's victory over Python, the great serpent that was ravaging the area.

[2] *shun ... wheels* Avoid crashing their chariots into the goalposts they must pass close to in order to score in their games.

[3] *Typhoean* Monstrous, from Typhon the monstrous giant whom Zeus threw into Hades. Some said he lay under Mt. Aetna and caused eruptions; *more fell* Nastier, more evil.

[4] *from Oechalia ... th' Euboic sea* Hercules, after returning from victory in Oechalia, a region in Greece, was presented as a gift a cloak dipped in burning venom. Once he put it on, the pain drove him into a violent rage and he threw Lichas, the innocent and unknowing giver of the fatal gift, into the Euboean Sea.

[5] *partial* Sung in parts, or harmony.

[6] *For eloquence ... sense* Eloquence charms the soul, song charms the senses.

[7] *th' obdured breast* Hardened heart.

[8] *Acheron* River of woe; *Cocytus* River of lamentation; *Phlegeton* River of fire; *Lethe* River from which the dead drink to forget their prior lives; these are four of the five rivers of the underworld in Greek mythology, the fifth being the Styx.

[9] *gathers heap* Gathers into heaps.

A gulf profound as that Serbonian bog
Betwixt Damiata and Mount Casius old,[1]
Where armies whole have sunk: the parching air
Burns frore,° and cold performs th' effect of fire. *frostily*
Thither, by harpy-footed furies[2] haled,° *dragged*
At certain revolutions all the damned
Are brought; and feel by turns the bitter change
Of fierce extremes, extremes by change more fierce,
From beds of raging fire to starve° in ice *i.e., freeze*
Their soft ethereal warmth, and there to pine
Immovable, infixed, and frozen round
Periods of time, thence hurried back to fire.
They ferry over this Lethean sound[3]
Both to and fro, their sorrow to augment,
And wish and struggle, as they pass, to reach
The tempting stream,[4] with one small drop to lose
In sweet forgetfulness all pain and woe,
All in one moment, and so near the brink;
But fate withstands, and, to oppose th' attempt,
Medusa with Gorgonian terror[5] guards
The ford, and of itself the water flies
All taste of living wight,° as once it fled *person*
The lip of Tantalus.[6] Thus roving on
In confused march forlorn, th' adventurous bands,
With shuddering horror pale, and eyes aghast,
Viewed first their lamentable lot, and found
No rest. Through many a dark and dreary vale
They passed, and many a region dolorous,
O'er many a frozen, many a fiery alp,
Rocks, caves, lakes, fens, bogs, dens, and shades
 of death—
A universe of death, which God by curse
Created evil, for evil only good;
Where all life dies, death lives, and nature breeds,
Perverse, all monstrous, all prodigious things,
Abominable, inutterable, and worse
Than fables yet have feigned or fear conceived,
Gorgons, and hydras, and chimeras dire.
 Meanwhile the adversary of God and man,
Satan, with thoughts inflamed of highest design,
Puts on swift wings, and toward the gates of Hell
Explores his solitary flight: sometimes
He scours the right hand coast, sometimes the left;
Now shaves with level wing the deep, then soars
Up to the fiery concave towering high.
As when far off at sea a fleet descried
Hangs in the clouds, by equinoctial winds
Close sailing from Bengala, or the isles
Of Ternate and Tidore,[7] whence merchants bring
Their spicy drugs; they on the trading flood,
Through the wide Ethiopian to the Cape,[8]
Ply stemming nightly toward the pole: so seemed
Far off the flying fiend. At last appear
Hell-bounds, high reaching to the horrid roof,
And thrice threefold the gates; three folds were brass,
Three iron, three of adamantine rock,
Impenetrable, impaled° with circling fire, *fenced*
Yet unconsumed. Before the gates there sat
On either side a formidable shape.
The one seemed woman to the waist, and fair,
But ended foul in many a scaly fold,
Voluminous and vast—a serpent armed
With mortal sting. About her middle round
A cry° of Hell-hounds never-ceasing barked *pack*
With wide Cerberean[9] mouths full loud, and rung
A hideous peal; yet, when they list,° would *wanted to*
 creep,
If aught disturbed their noise, into her womb,
And kennel there; yet there still barked and howled
Within unseen. Far less abhorred than these

[1] *that Serbonian bog ... Mount Casius old* Lake Serbonis (modern Lake Bardawil), located in northern Egypt, is surrounded by quicksand.

[2] *harpy-footed furies* Talon-footed furies. The infernal snake-haired Furies, and Harpies (taloned birds with heads of women) were agents of retribution in classical myth.

[3] *sound* Expanse of water.

[4] *The tempting stream* Lethe, the river of forgetfulness.

[5] *Medusa with Gorgonian terror* Medusa and her sisters were Gorgons, monsters of Greek myth, and Medusa specifically was so terrible that her sight turned men to stone.

[6] *The lip of Tantalus* In Greek myth, Tantalus was condemned to be immersed in water that receded when he tried to drink and was overhung by fruit on a branch that retreated from his reach.

[7] *Bengala ... Ternate ... Tidore* Three eastern Indian ports, source of spices and exotic trade riches.

[8] *the wide Ethiopian to the Cape* The Indian Ocean to the Cape of Good Hope.

[9] *Cerberean* Cerberus, guardian of the underworld in classical mythology, was a dog with three heads.

Vexed Scylla,[1] bathing in the sea that parts
Calabria from the hoarse Trinacrian° shore; *Sicilian*
Nor uglier follow the night-hag, when, called
In secret, riding through the air she comes,
Lured with the smell of infant blood, to dance
With Lapland witches, while the labouring moon
Eclipses at their charms. The other shape—
If shape it might be called that shape had none
Distinguishable in member, joint, or limb;
Or substance might be called that shadow seemed,
For each seemed either—black it stood as night,
Fierce as ten furies, terrible as Hell,
And shook a dreadful dart:° what seemed his head *javelin*
The likeness of a kingly crown had on.
Satan was now at hand, and from his seat
The monster moving onward came as fast
With horrid strides; Hell trembled as he strode.
Th' undaunted fiend what this might be
    admired—° *wondered*
Admired, not feared (God and His Son except,
Created thing naught valued he nor shunned),
And with disdainful look thus first began:
"Whence and what art thou, execrable shape,
That dar'st, though grim and terrible, advance
Thy miscreated front athwart my way
To yonder gates? Through them I mean to pass,
That be assured, without leave asked of thee.
Retire; or taste thy folly, and learn by proof,
Hell-born, not to contend with spirits of Heav'n."
    To whom the goblin,° full of wrath, replied: *monster*
"Are thou that traitor angel? Are thou he,
Who first broke peace in Heav'n and faith, till then
Unbroken, and in proud rebellious arms
Drew after him the third part of Heaven's sons,
Conjured against the highest—for which both thou
And they, outcast from God, are here condemned
To waste eternal days in woe and pain?
And reckon'st thou thyself with spirits of Heav'n
Hell-doomed, and breath'st defiance here and scorn,
Where I reign king, and, to enrage thee more,
Thy king and lord? Back to thy punishment,
False fugitive; and to thy speed add wings,
Lest with a whip of scorpions[2] I pursue
Thy lingering, or with one stroke of this dart
Strange horror seize thee, and pangs unfelt before."
    So spake the grisly terror, and in shape,
So speaking and so threat'ning, grew tenfold,
More dreadful and deform. On th' other side,
Incensed with indignation, Satan stood
Unterrified, and like a comet burned,
That fires the length of Ophiuchus[3] huge
In th' arctic sky, and from his horrid hair
Shakes pestilence and war.[4] Each at the head
Levelled his deadly aim; their fatal hands
No second stroke intend; and such a frown
Each cast at th' other as when two black clouds,
With Heav'n's artillery[5] fraught, came rattling on
Over the Caspian, then stand front to front
Hovering a space, till winds the signal blow
To join their dark encounter in mid-air.
So frowned the mighty combatants that Hell
Grew darker at their frown; so matched they stood;
For never but once more was either like
To meet so great a foe. And now great deeds
Had been achieved, whereof all Hell had rung,
Had not the snaky sorceress, that sat
Fast by Hell-gate and kept the fatal key,
Risen, and with hideous outcry rushed between.
    "O father, what intends thy hand," she cried,
"Against thy only son? What fury, O son,
Possesses thee to bend that mortal dart
Against thy father's head? And know'st for whom?
For Him who sits above, and laughs the while
At thee, ordained His drudge to execute
Whate'er His wrath, which He calls justice, bids—
His wrath, which one day will destroy ye both!"
    She spake, and at her words the hellish pest
Forbore: then these to her Satan returned:
    "So strange thy outcry, and thy words so strange

[1] *Scylla* Nymph transformed by Circe, the Greek enchantress, into a dreadful monster with a lower body composed of savage dogs.

[2] *with a whip of scorpions* Mirrors the words of King Rheoboam, son of Solomon in 1 Kings 12.11, whose promise of harshness sparked a civil war.

[3] *Ophiuchus* The constellation Serpent Bearer, visible in the northern sky from June to October.

[4] *from his horrid hair … war* Comets, with their long luminous tails, or hair, were believed to be harbingers of disaster.

[5] *Heaven's artillery* Lightning.

Thou interposest, that my sudden hand,
Prevented, spares to tell thee yet by deeds
What it intends, till first I know of thee
What thing thou art, thus double-formed, and why,
In this infernal vale first met, thou call'st
Me father, and that phantasm call'st my son.
I know thee not, nor ever saw till now
Sight more detestable than him and thee."
T' whom thus the portress[1] of Hell-gate replied:
"Hast thou forgot me, then; and do I seem
Now in thine eye so foul? Once deemed so fair
In Heaven, when at th' assembly, and in sight
Of all the seraphim with thee combined
In bold conspiracy against Heaven's King,
All on a sudden miserable pain
Surprised thee, dim thine eyes and dizzy swum
In darkness, while thy head flames thick and fast
Threw forth, till on the left side op'ning wide,
Likest to thee in shape and count'nance bright,
Then shining heav'nly fair, a goddess armed,
Out of thy head I sprung.[2] Amazement seized
All th' host of Heav'n; back they recoiled afraid
At first, and called me Sin, and for a sign
Portentous held me; but, familiar grown,
I pleased, and with attractive graces won
The most averse—thee chiefly, who, full oft
Thyself in me thy perfect image viewing,
Becam'st enamored; and such joy thou took'st
With me in secret that my womb conceived
A growing burden. Meanwhile war arose,
And fields were fought in Heav'n: wherein remained
(For what could else?) to our Almighty Foe
Clear victory; to our part loss and rout
Through all the Empyrean. Down they fell,
Driven headlong from the pitch° of Heaven, down *field*
Into this deep; and in the general fall
I also: at which time this powerful key
Into my hands was given, with charge to keep
These gates for ever shut, which none can pass
Without my op'ning. Pensive here I sat
Alone; but long I sat not, till my womb,
Pregnant by thee, and now excessive grown,
Prodigious motion felt and rueful throes.
At last this odious offspring whom thou seest,
Thine own begotten, breaking violent way,
Tore through my entrails, that, with fear and pain
Distorted, all my nether shape thus grew
Transformed: but he my inbred enemy
Forth issued, brandishing his fatal dart,
Made to destroy. I fled, and cried out Death!
Hell trembled at the hideous name, and sighed
From all her caves, and back resounded Death!
I fled; but he pursued (though more, it seems,
Inflamed with lust than rage), and, swifter far,
Me overtook, his mother, all dismayed,
And, in embraces forcible and foul
Engendering with me, of that rape begot
These yelling monsters, that with ceaseless cry
Surround me, as thou saw'st—hourly conceived
And hourly born, with sorrow infinite
To me; for, when they list, into the womb
That bred them they return, and howl, and gnaw
My bowels, their repast; then, bursting forth
Afresh, with conscious terrors vex me round,
That rest or intermission none I find.
Before mine eyes in opposition sits
Grim Death, my son and foe, who set them on,
And me, his parent, would full soon devour
For want of other prey, but that he knows
His end with mine involved, and knows that I
Should prove a bitter morsel, and his bane,
Whenever that shall be: so fate pronounced.
But thou, O father, I forewarn thee, shun
His deadly arrow; neither vainly hope
To be invulnerable in those bright arms,
Though tempered heavenly; for that mortal dint,° *power*
Save He who reigns above, none can resist."
She finished; and the subtle fiend his lore
Soon learned, now milder, and thus answered smooth:
"Dear daughter—since thou claim'st me for thy sire,
And my fair son here show'st me, the dear pledge
Of dalliance had with thee in Heav'n, and joys
Then sweet, now sad to mention, through dire change
Befall'n us unforeseen, unthought-of-know,
I come no enemy, but to set free

[1] *portress* Female doorkeeper.

[2] *Out of thy head I sprung* Cf. Athena's birth from the head of Zeus in classical myth.

From out this dark and dismal house of pain
Both him and thee, and all the heav'nly host
Of spirits that, in our just pretences armed,
Fell with us from on high. From them I go
This uncouth errand sole, and one for all
Myself expose, with lonely steps to tread
Th' unfounded deep, and through the void immense
To search, with wandering quest, a place foretold
Should be—and, by concurring signs, ere now
Created vast and round—a place of bliss
In the purlieus° of Heav'n; and therein placed *outskirts*
A race of upstart creatures, to supply
Perhaps our vacant room, though more removed,
Lest Heav'n, surcharged with potent multitude,
Might hap to move new broils.[1] Be this, or aught
Than this more secret, now designed, I haste
To know; and, this once known, shall soon return,
And bring ye to the place where thou and Death
Shall dwell at ease, and up and down unseen
Wing silently the buxom° air, embalmed *healthy*
With odours. There ye shall be fed and filled
Immeasurably; all things shall be your prey."
He ceased; for both seemed highly pleased, and Death
Grinned horrible a ghastly smile, to hear
His famine should be filled, and blessed his maw
Destined to that good hour. No less rejoiced
His mother bad, and thus bespake her sire:
"The key of this infernal pit, by due
And by command of Heav'n's all-powerful King,
I keep, by Him forbidden to unlock
These adamantine gates; against all force
Death ready stands to interpose his dart,
Fearless to be o'ermatched by living might.
But what owe I to His commands above,
Who hates me, and hath hither thrust me down
Into this gloom of Tartarus profound,
To sit in hateful office° here confined, *duty*
Inhabitant of Heav'n and heav'nly born—
Here in perpetual agony and pain,
With terrors and with clamours compassed round
Of mine own brood, that on my bowels feed?
Thou art my father, thou my author, thou
My being gav'st me; whom should I obey
But thee? Whom follow? Thou will bring me soon
To that new world of light and bliss, among
The gods who live at ease, where I shall reign
At thy right hand voluptuous, as beseems
Thy daughter and thy darling, without end."
Thus saying, from her side the fatal key,
Sad instrument of all our woe, she took;
And, towards the gate rolling her bestial train,
Forthwith the huge portcullis high up-drew,
Which, but herself, not all the Stygian powers
Could once have moved; then in the key-hole turns
Th' intricate wards,[2] and every bolt and bar
Of massy iron or solid rock with ease
Unfast'ns. On a sudden op'n fly,
With impetuous recoil and jarring sound,
Th' infernal doors, and on their hinges grate
Harsh thunder, that the lowest bottom shook
Of Erebus.[3] She op'nd; but to shut
Excelled her power: the gates wide op'n stood,
That with extended wings a bannered host,
Under spread ensigns° marching, might pass through *flags*
With horse and chariots ranked in loose array;
So wide they stood, and like a furnace-mouth
Cast forth redounding° smoke and ruddy flame. *copious*
Before their eyes in sudden view appear
The secrets of the hoary deep—a dark
Illimitable ocean, without bound,
Without dimension; where length, breadth, and height,
And time, and place, are lost; where eldest Night
And Chaos, ancestors of nature, hold
Eternal anarchy, amidst the noise
Of endless wars, and by confusion stand.
For Hot, Cold, Moist, and Dry,[4] four champions fierce,
Strive here for mastery, and to battle bring
Their embryon atoms:[5] they around the flag
Of each his faction, in their several clans,
Light-armed or heavy, sharp, smooth, swift, or slow,
Swarm populous, unnumbered as the sands

[1] *Might hap to move new broils* Might chance to begin new wars.

[2] *wards* The tumblers and pin assemblies of a lock, which mate with and are turned by the teeth of a key.

[3] *Erebus* Upper region of Hades.

[4] *Hot, Cold, Moist, and Dry* Personifications of the four classical elements: fire, air, water, and earth.

[5] *Their embryon atoms* Their primeval matter.

Of Barca or Cyrene's torrid soil,[1]
Levied to side with warring winds, and poise
Their lighter wings. To whom these most adhere
He rules a moment: Chaos umpire sits,
And by decision more embroils the fray
By which he reigns: next him, high arbiter,
Chance governs all. Into this wild abyss,
The womb of Nature, and perhaps her grave,
Of neither sea, nor shore, nor air, nor fire,
But all these in their pregnant causes mixed
Confus'dly, and which thus must ever fight,
Unless th' Almighty Maker them ordain
His dark materials to create more worlds—
Into this wild abyss the wary fiend
Stood on the brink of Hell and looked a while,
Pondering his voyage; for no narrow frith° *fjord*
He had to cross. Nor was his ear less pealed° *deafened*
With noises loud and ruinous (to compare
Great things with small) than when Bellona[2] storms
With all her battering engines, bent to raze
Some capital city; or less than if this frame
Of Heav'n were falling, and these elements
In mutiny had from her axle torn
The steadfast Earth. At last his sail-broad vans° *wings*
He spread for flight, and, in the surging smoke
Uplifted, spurns the ground; thence many a league,
As in a cloudy chair, ascending rides
Audacious; but, that seat soon failing, meets
A vast vacuity. All unawares,
Fluttering his pennons° vain, plumb down[3] he drops *wings*
Ten thousand fathom deep, and to this hour
Down had been falling, had not, by ill chance,
The strong rebuff of some tumultuous cloud,
Instinct[4] with fire and nitre, hurried him
As many miles aloft. That fury stayed—
Quenched in a boggy Syrtis,[5] neither sea,
Nor good dry land—nigh foundered,[6] on he fares,
Treading the crude consistence, half on foot,
Half flying; behoves him now both oar and sail.
As when a griffon[7] through the wilderness
With wingèd course, o'er hill or moory dale,
Pursues the Arimaspian,[8] who by stealth
Had from his wakeful custody purloined
The guarded gold; so eagerly the fiend
O'er bog or steep, through strait, rough, dense, or rare,
With head, hands, wings, or feet, pursues his way,
And swims, or sinks, or wades, or creeps, or flies.
At length a universal hubbub wild
Of stunning sounds, and voices all confused,
Borne through the hollow dark, assaults his ear
With loudest vehemence. Thither he plies
Undaunted, to meet there whatever power
Or spirit of the nethermost abyss
Might in that noise reside, of whom to ask
Which way the nearest coast of darkness lies
Bordering on light; when straight behold the throne
Of Chaos, and his dark pavilion spread
Wide on the wasteful° deep! With him enthroned *empty*
Sat sable-vested night, eldest of things,
The consort of his reign; and by them stood
Orcus and Ades, and the dreaded name
Of Demogorgon;[9] Rumour next, and Chance,
And Tumult, and Confusion, all embroiled,
And Discord with a thousand various mouths.
T' whom Satan, turning boldly, thus: "Ye powers
And spirits of this nethermost abyss,
Chaos and ancient Night, I come no spy
With purpose to explore or to disturb
The secrets of your realm; but, by constraint° *necessity*
Wandering this darksome desert, as my way
Lies through your spacious empire up to light,
Alone and without guide, half lost, I seek,
What readiest path leads where your gloomy bounds
Confine° with Heav'n; or, if some other place, *meet*

[1] *Barca or Cyrene's torrid soil* Barca and Cyrene are cities in the Libyan desert surrounded by sand dunes.

[2] *Bellona* Goddess of war in the Roman pantheon.

[3] *plumb down* Straight down.

[4] *Instinct* Shot through.

[5] *Syrtis* Pair of quicksand gulfs on either side of Tripoli; see Book 5 of Pliny the Elder's *Natural History*.

[6] *nigh foundered* Nearly sunk.

[7] *griffon* Fabled beast with the head and wings of an eagle, the body of a lion, a voracious appetite for horses, and a penchant for hoarding gold and treasure.

[8] *Arimaspian* Member of the Arimaspi tribe, said by Herodotus to pilfer the griffons' treasure.

[9] *Orcus* Pluto, Roman god of the underworld; *Ades* Hades, Greek god of the underworld; *Demogorgon* Greek god of the underworld who predates Hades.

From your dominion won, th' ethereal King
Possesses lately, thither to arrive
I travel this profound.° Direct my course: *deep*
Directed, no mean recompense° it brings *reward*
To your behoof,° if I that region lost, *benefit*
All usurpation thence expelled, reduce
To her original darkness and your sway
(Which is my present journey), and once more
Erect the standard° there of ancient Night. *flag*
Yours be th' advantage all, mine the revenge!"
Thus Satan; and him thus the anarch old,[1]
With faltering speech and visage incomposed,
Answered: "I know thee, stranger, who thou art—
That mighty leading angel, who of late
Made head against Heav'n's King, though overthrown.
I saw and heard; for such a numerous host
Fled not in silence through the frighted deep,
With ruin upon ruin, rout on rout,
Confusion worse confounded; and Heav'n-gates
Poured out by millions her victorious bands,
Pursuing. I upon my frontiers here
Keep residence; if all I can will serve
That little which is left so to defend,
Encroached on still through our intestine broils[2]
Weakening the sceptre of old Night: first, Hell,
Your dungeon, stretching far and wide beneath;
Now lately Heav'n and Earth, another world
Hung o'er my realm, linked in a golden chain
To that side Heav'n from whence your legions fell!
If that way be your walk, you have not far;
So much the nearer danger. Go, and speed;
Havoc, and spoil, and ruin, are my gain."
He ceased; and Satan stayed not to reply,
But, glad that now his sea should find a shore,
With fresh alacrity and force renewed
Springs upward, like a pyramid of fire,
Into the wild expanse, and through the shock
Of fighting elements, on all sides round
Environed, wins his way; harder beset
And more endangered than when Argo passed
Through Bosporus betwixt the jostling rocks,
Or when Ulysses on the larboard shunned
Charybdis, and by th' other whirlpool steered.[3]
So he with difficulty and labour hard
Moved on, with difficulty and labour he;
But, he once passed, soon after, when man fell,
Strange alteration! Sin and Death amain,[4]
Following his track (such was the will of Heav'n)
Paved after him a broad and beaten way
Over the dark abyss, whose boiling gulf
Tamely endured a bridge of wondrous length,
From Hell continued, reaching th' utmost orb
Of this frail world; by which the spirits perverse
With easy intercourse[5] pass to and fro
To tempt or punish mortals, except whom
God and good angels guard by special grace.
But now at last the sacred influence
Of light appears, and from the walls of Heav'n
Shoots far into the bosom of dim Night
A glimmering dawn. Here Nature first begins
Her farthest verge,° and Chaos to retire, *border*
As from her outmost works, a broken foe,
With tumult less and with less hostile din;
That Satan with less toil, and now with ease,
Wafts on the calmer wave by dubious light,
And, like a weather-beaten vessel, holds
Gladly the port, though shrouds° and tackle torn; *sails*
Or in the emptier waste, resembling air,
Weighs his spread wings, at leisure to behold
Far off th' empyreal Heav'n, extended wide
In circuit, undetermined square or round,[6]
With opal towers and battlements adorned
Of living sapphire, once his native seat;
And, fast by, hanging in a golden chain,
This pendent world, in bigness as a star

[1] *the anarch old* The old anarchist, i.e., Chaos.

[2] *intestine broils* Civil wars.

[3] *Argo* The ship of Jason and the Argonauts of Greek legend, sailors who faced many challenges in their travels; *the jostling rocks* Huge floating rocks that clashed and ground on one another were a peril passed by Jason and the Argonauts; *Ulysses* Subject of Homer's *Odyssey* and a character in his *Iliad*, a famous wandering king, sailor, and hero; *larboard* The port or left side of a ship; *Charybdis* Terrible whirlpool circumnavigated by Ulysses.

[4] *amain* Moving at full speed.

[5] *intercourse* Entrance.

[6] *undetermined square or round* In other words, the overall shape of Heaven is indiscernible.

Of smallest magnitude close by the moon.[1]
Thither, full fraught with mischievous revenge,
Accursed, and in a cursed hour, he hies.° *goes*

THE END OF THE SECOND BOOK

Argument to Book 3

God sitting on His throne sees Satan flying towards this world, then newly created; shows him to the Son who sat at His right hand; foretells the success of Satan in perverting mankind; clears His own justice and wisdom from all imputation, having created man free and able enough to have withstood his tempter; yet declares His purpose of grace towards Him, in regard he fell not of his own malice, as did Satan, but by him seduced. The Son of God renders praises to His Father for the manifestation of His gracious purpose towards man; but God again declares, that grace cannot be extended towards man without the satisfaction of Divine Justice; man hath offended the Majesty of God by aspiring to Godhead, and therefore with all his progeny devoted to death must die, unless some one can be found sufficient to answer for his offence, and undergo his punishment. The Son of God freely offers himself a ransom for man: the Father accepts Him, ordains His incarnation, pronounces His exaltation above all names in Heaven and Earth; commands all the angels to adore Him; they obey, and hymning to their harps in full choir, celebrate the Father and the Son. Meanwhile Satan alights upon the bare convex of this world's outermost orb; where wandering he first finds a place since called the Limbo of Vanity; what persons and things fly up thither; thence comes to the gate of Heaven, described ascending by stairs, and the waters above the firmament that flow about it: his passage thence to the orb of the Sun; he finds there Uriel the regent of that orb, but first changes himself into the shape of a meaner angel; and pretending a zealous desire to behold the new creation and man whom God had placed here, inquires of him the place of his habitation, and is directed; alights first on Mount Niphates.

[1] *in bigness as a star / Of smallest magnitude close by the moon* Refers to the perceived size of the smallest star in the sky compared to the moon (not the actual size of a star compared to the moon); in other words, very, very small.

from Book 3

Hail, holy light, offspring of Heav'n first-born,
Or of th' eternal coeternal beam
May I express thee unblamed? Since God is light,[2]
And never but in unapproached° light *incomparable*
Dwelt from eternity, dwelt then in thee
Bright effluence of bright essence increate.[3]
Or hear'st thou rather pure ethereal stream,
Whose fountain° who shall tell? Before the sun, *source*
Before the Heav'ns thou wert, and at the voice
Of God, as with a mantle, didst invest
The rising world of waters dark and deep,
Won from the void and formless infinite.
Thee I re-visit now with bolder wing,
Escaped the Stygian pool, though long detained
In that obscure sojourn, while in my flight
Through utter and through middle darkness borne,
With other notes than to th' Orphean[4] lyre
I sung of Chaos and eternal Night;
Taught by the heavenly Muse to venture down
The dark descent, and up to re-ascend,
Though hard and rare: thee I revisit safe,
And feel thy sovereign vital lamp; but thou
Revisit'st not these eyes,[5] that roll in vain
To find thy piercing ray, and find no dawn;
So thick a drop serene[6] hath quenched their orbs,
Or dim suffusion veiled. Yet not the more
Cease I to wander, where the Muses haunt,
Clear spring, or shady grove, or sunny hill;
Smit° with the love of sacred song; but chief *smitten*
Thee, Sion, and the flowery brooks beneath,
That wash thy hallowed feet, and warbling flow,
Nightly I visit: nor sometimes forget
So were I equalled with them in renown,
Thy sov'reign command, that Man should find grace;
Blind Thamyris, and blind Maeonides,

[2] *May I express thee unblam'd* May I call you that without being blamed; *God is light* See 1 John 1.5.

[3] *increate* Not created, always existing.

[4] *Orphean* Orpheus, a musician-hero of Greek myth, visited the underworld to retrieve his wife Eurydice. The notes of his lyre won him safe passage.

[5] *Revisit'st not these eyes* Milton became totally blind in 1652.

[6] *drop serene* Gutta serena, the eye disease Milton had.

And Tiresias, and Phineus,[1] prophets old:
Then feed on thoughts, that voluntary move
Harmonious numbers; as the wakeful bird[2]
Sings darkling,° and in shadiest covert hid *in the dark*
Tunes her nocturnal note. Thus with the year
Seasons return; but not to me returns
Day, or the sweet approach of even or morn,
Or sight of vernal° bloom, or summer's rose, *spring*
Or flocks, or herds, or human face divine;
But cloud instead, and ever-during dark
Surrounds me, from the cheerful ways of men
Cut off, and for the book of knowledge fair
Presented with a universal blank
Of Nature's works to me expunged and razed,
And Wisdom at one entrance quite shut out.[3]
So much the rather thou, celestial Light,
Shine inward, and the mind through all her powers
Irradiate; there plant eyes, all mist from thence
Purge and disperse, that I may see and tell
Of things invisible to mortal sight.
  Now had the Almighty Father from above,
From the pure empyrean where He sits
High throned above all height, bent down His eye
His own works and their works at once to view:
About Him all the sanctities of Heaven[4]
Stood thick as stars, and from His sight received
Beatitude past utterance; on his right
The radiant image of His glory sat,
His only Son; on earth He first beheld
Our two first parents, yet° the only two *thus far*
Of mankind in the happy garden placed
Reaping immortal fruits of joy and love,
Uninterrupted joy, unrivalled love,
In blissful solitude; He then surveyed
Hell and the gulf between, and Satan there
Coasting[5] the wall of Heav'n on this side night
In the dun° air sublime, and ready now *dusky*
To stoop° with wearied wings, and willing feet, *swoop*
On the bare outside of this world, that seemed
Firm land embosomed,° without firmament, *enclosed*
Uncertain which, in ocean or in air.
Him God beholding from His prospect high,
Wherein past, present, future, He beholds,
Thus to His only Son foreseeing spake:
  "Only begotten Son, seest Thou what rage
Transports Our adversary? whom no bounds
Prescribed no bars of Hell, nor all the chains
Heaped on him there, nor yet the main abyss
Wide interrupt, can hold; so bent he seems
On desperate revenge, that shall redound
Upon his own rebellious head. And now,
Through all restraint broke loose, he wings his way
Not far off Heav'n, in the precincts of light,
Directly towards the new created world,
And man there placed, with purpose to assay
If him by force he can destroy, or, worse,
By some false guile pervert; and shall pervert;
For man will hearken to his glozing° lies, *flattering*
And easily transgress the sole command,
Sole pledge of his obedience: so will fall
He and his faithless progeny: Whose fault?
Whose but his own? Ingrate, he had of Me
All he could have; I made him just and right,
Sufficient to have stood, though free to fall.
Such I created all th' ethereal powers
And spirits, both them who stood, and them who
  failed;
Freely they stood who stood, and fell who fell.
Not free, what proof could they have given sincere
Of true allegiance, constant faith, or love,
Where only what they needs must do appeared,
Not what they would? What praise could they receive?
What pleasure I, from such obedience paid,
When Will and Reason (Reason also is choice)
Useless and vain, of freedom both despoiled,
Made passive both, had served necessity,
Not me? They therefore, as to right belonged,
So were created, nor can justly accuse
Their Maker, or their making, or their fate,

[1] *Thamyris* Ancient Greek poet deprived of his sight by the Muses for competing with them; *Maeonides* Homer, the blind author of *The Odyssey* and *The Iliad*; *Tiresias* Greek prophet blinded either by Hera or by Diana; *Phineus* Prophet blinded by the gods for telling too many truthful prophecies.

[2] *wakeful bird* Nightingale.

[3] *And Wisdom at one entrance quite shut out* Information cannot be received as one sense has ceased to operate.

[4] *sanctities of Heaven* Saints.

[5] *Coasting* Following the coast of.

As if predestination over-ruled
Their will disposed by absolute decree
Or high foreknowledge; they themselves decreed
Their own revolt, not I: if I foreknew,
Foreknowledge had no influence on their fault,
Which had no less proved certain unforeknown.
So without least impulse or shadow of fate,
Or aught by me immutably foreseen,
They trespass, authors to themselves in all
Both what they judge and what they choose; for so
I formed them free, and free they must remain,
Till they enthral themselves: I else must change
Their nature, and revoke the high decree
Unchangeable, eternal, which ordained
Their freedom, they themselves ordained their fall.
The first sort by their own suggestion fell,
Self-tempted, self-depraved: Man falls deceived
By the other first: Man therefore shall find grace,
The other none: In mercy and justice both,
Through Heav'n and earth, so shall My glory excel,
But mercy, first and last, shall brightest shine."
Thus while God spake, ambrosial fragrance filled
All Heaven, and in the blessèd spirits elect[1]
Sense of new joy ineffable diffused.
Beyond compare the Son of God was seen
Most glorious; in Him all His Father shone
Substantially expressed; and in His face
Divine compassion visibly appeared,
Love without end, and without measure grace,
Which uttering, thus He to His Father spake:
"O Father, gracious was that word which closed
Thy sovereign sentence, that man should find grace;
For which both Heav'n and earth shall high extol
Thy praises, with the innumerable sound
Of hymns and sacred songs, wherewith Thy throne
Encompassed shall resound Thee ever blest.
For should Man finally be lost, should Man,
Thy creature late so loved, thy youngest son,
Fall circumvented thus by fraud, though joined
With his own folly? That be from Thee far,
That far be from Thee, Father, who art Judge
Of all things made, and judgest only right.
Or shall the adversary thus obtain
His end, and frustrate Thine? Shall he fulfil
His malice, and Thy goodness bring to nought,
Or proud return, though to his heavier doom,
Yet with revenge accomplished, and to Hell
Draw after him the whole race of mankind,
By him corrupted? Or wilt Thou Thyself
Abolish Thy creation, and unmake
For him, what for Thy glory Thou hast made?
So should Thy goodness and Thy greatness both
Be questioned and blasphemed without defence."
To whom the great Creator thus replied:
"O Son, in whom My soul hath chief delight,
Son of My bosom, Son who art alone
My word, My wisdom, and effectual might,
All hast Thou spoken as My thoughts are, all
As My eternal purpose hath decreed;
Man shall not quite be lost, but saved who will;
Yet not of will in him, but grace in Me
Freely vouchsafed;[2] once more I will renew
His lapsed powers, though forfeit; and enthralled
By sin to foul exorbitant desires;
Upheld by Me, yet once more he shall stand
On even ground against his mortal foe;
By Me upheld, that he may know how frail
His fallen condition is, and to Me owe
All his deliv'rance, and to none but Me.
Some I have chosen of peculiar grace,
Elect above the rest; so is My will:
The rest shall hear Me call, and oft be warned
Their sinful state, and to appease betimes
Th' incensèd deity, while offered grace
Invites; for I will clear their senses dark,[3]
What may suffice, and soften stony hearts
To pray, repent, and bring obedience due.
To prayer, repentance, and obedience due,
Though but endeavoured with sincere intent,
Mine ear shall not be slow, Mine eye not shut.
And I will place within them as a guide,
My umpire Conscience; whom if they will hear,
Light after light, well used, they shall attain,
And to the end, persisting, safe arrive.
This My long sufferance, and My day of grace,
They who neglect and scorn, shall never taste;

[1] *spirits elect* Unfallen angels.

[2] *vouchsafed* Given by oath.

[3] *their senses dark* Cf. 1 Corinthians 13.12: "For now we see through a glass, darkly."

But hard be hardened, blind be blinded more,
That they may stumble on, and deeper fall;
And none but such from mercy I exclude.
But yet all is not done; Man disobeying,
Disloyal, breaks his fealty,° and sins — *faith, loyalty*
Against the high supremacy of Heav'n,
Affecting Godhead, and, so losing all,
To expiate his treason hath nought left,
But to destruction sacred and devote,
He, with his whole posterity, must die,
Die he or justice must; unless for him
Some other able, and as willing, pay
The rigid satisfaction, death for death.
Say, heavenly powers, where shall we find such love?
Which of you will be mortal, to redeem
Man's mortal crime, and just the unjust to save,
Dwells in all Heaven charity so dear?"

He asked, but all the heav'nly choir stood mute,
And silence was in Heav'n: on man's behalf
Patron or intercessor none appeared,
Much less that dared upon his own head draw
The deadly forfeiture, and ransom set.
And now without redemption all mankind
Must have been lost, adjudged to death and Hell
By doom severe, had not the Son of God,
In whom the fullness dwells of love divine,
His dearest mediation thus renewed:

"Father, Thy word is past, Man shall find grace;
And shall grace not find means, that finds her way,
The speediest of Thy winged messengers,
To visit all Thy creatures, and to all
Comes unprevented, unimplor'd, unsought?
Happy for Man, so coming; he her aid
Can never seek, once dead in sins, and lost;
Atonement for himself, or offering meet,
Indebted and undone, hath none to bring;
Behold Me then: Me for him, life for life
I offer: on Me let Thine anger fall;
Account Me Man; I for his sake will leave
Thy bosom, and this glory next to Thee
Freely put off, and for him lastly die
Well pleased; on Me let Death wreak all his rage.
Under his gloomy power I shall not long
Lie vanquished. Thou hast giv'n Me to possess
Life in Myself for ever; by Thee I live;
Though now to Death I yield, and am his due,
All that of Me can die, yet, that debt paid,
Thou wilt not leave Me in the loathsome grave
His prey, nor suffer my unspotted soul
For ever with corruption there to dwell;
But I shall rise victorious, and subdue
My vanquisher, spoiled of his vaunted spoil.
Death his death's wound shall then receive, and stoop
Inglorious, of his mortal sting disarmed;[1]
I through the ample air in triumph high
Shall lead Hell captive maugre[2] Hell, and show
The powers of darkness bound. Thou, at the sight
Pleased, out of Heaven shall look down and smile,
While, by Thee raised, I ruin all My foes;
Death last, and with his carcass glut the grave;
Then, with the multitude of My redeemed,
Shall enter Heaven, long absent, and return,
Father, to see Thy face, wherein no cloud
Of anger shall remain, but peace assured
And reconcilement: wrath shall be no more
Thenceforth, but in Thy presence joy entire."

His words here ended; but His meek aspect
Silent yet spake, and breathed immortal love
To mortal men, above which only shone
Filial obedience:[3] as a sacrifice
Glad to be offered, He attends the will
Of His great Father. Admiration seized
All Heav'n, what this might mean, and whither tend,
Wondering; but soon th' Almighty thus replied:

"O Thou in Heav'n and earth the only peace
Found out for mankind under wrath, O Thou
My sole complacence![4] Well Thou know'st how dear
To Me are all My works; nor Man the least,
Though last created, that for him I spare
Thee from My bosom and right hand, to save,
By losing Thee a while, the whole race lost.
Thou, therefore, whom Thou only canst redeem,
Their nature also to Thy nature join;
And be Thyself Man among men on earth,
Made flesh, when time shall be, of virgin seed,

---

1 *Death ... his mortal sting disarmed* See 1 Corinthians 15.55.

2 *maugre* In spite of.

3 *Filial obedience* Proper for a child/parent relationship.

4 *complacence* Here, source of satisfaction.

By wondrous birth; be Thou in Adam's room[1]
The head of all mankind, though Adam's son.
As in him perish all men, so in Thee,
As from a second root, shall be restored
As many as are restored, without Thee none.
His crime makes guilty all his sons; Thy merit,
Imputed, shall absolve them who renounce
Their own both righteous and unrighteous deeds,
And live in Thee transplanted, and from Thee
Receive new life. So Man, as is most just,
Shall satisfy for Man, be judged and die,
And dying rise, and rising with Him raise
His brethren, ransomed with His own dear life.
So heavenly love shall outdo hellish hate,
Giving to death, and dying to redeem,
So dearly to redeem what hellish hate
So easily destroyed, and still destroys
In those who, when they may, accept not grace.
Nor shalt Thou, by descending to assume
Man's nature, lessen or degrade Thine own.
Because Thou hast, though throned in highest bliss
Equal to God, and equally enjoying
God-like fruition, quitted all, to save
A world from utter loss, and hast been found
By merit more than birthright Son of God,
Found worthiest to be so by being good,
Far more than great or high; because in Thee
Love hath abounded more than glory abounds;
Therefore Thy humiliation shall exalt
With Thee Thy manhood also to this throne:
Here shalt thou sit incarnate, here shalt reign
Both God and Man, Son both of God and Man,
Anointed universal King; all power
I give Thee; reign forever, and assume
Thy merits; under Thee, as Head Supreme,
Thrones, princedoms, powers, dominions, I reduce:
All knees to Thee shall bow, of them that bide° *live*
In Heav'n, or earth, or under earth in Hell.
When Thou, attended gloriously from Heav'n,
Shalt in the sky appear, and from Thee send
The summoning arch-angels to proclaim
Thy dread tribunal; forthwith from all winds,
The living, and forthwith the cited dead
Of all past ages, to the general doom
Shall hasten; such a peal shall rouse their sleep.
Then, all Thy saints assembled, Thou shalt judge
Bad men and angels; they, arraigned, shall sink
Beneath Thy sentence; Hell, her numbers full,
Thenceforth shall be forever shut. Meanwhile
The world shall burn, and from her ashes spring
New Heav'n and earth, wherein the just shall dwell,
And, after all their tribulations long,
See golden days, fruitful of golden deeds,
With joy and peace triumphing, and fair truth.
Then Thou Thy regal sceptre shall lay by,
For regal sceptre then no more shall need,
God shall be all in all.[2] But, all ye gods,
Adore Him, who to compass all this dies;
Adore the Son, and honour Him as Me."
No sooner had th' Almighty ceased, but all
The multitude of angels, with a shout
Loud as from numbers without number, sweet
As from blest voices, uttering joy, Heav'n rung
With jubilee, and loud hosannas[3] filled
Th' eternal regions: lowly reverent
Towards either throne[4] they bow, and to the ground
With solemn adoration down they cast
Their crowns inwove with amarant[5] and gold;
Immortal amarant, a flower which once
In Paradise, fast° by the tree of life, *near*
Began to bloom; but soon for man's offence
To Heav'n removed, where first it grew, there grows,
And flowers aloft shading the fount of life,
And where the river of bliss through midst of Heav'n
Rolls o'er Elysian° flowers her amber *paradisiacal*
stream;
With these that never fade the spirits elect
Bind their resplendent locks enwreathed with beams;
Now in loose garlands thick thrown off, the bright
Pavement, that like a sea of jasper shone,
Empurpled with celestial roses smiled.
Then, crowned again, their golden harps they took,

[1] *in Adam's room* Instead of Adam.

[2] *When thou, attended ... be all in all* This account of the end of all things is a paraphrased of the Book of Revelation.

[3] *hosannas* Shouts of fervent and worshipful praise.

[4] *either throne* Both the throne of God and the throne of the Son of God.

[5] *amarant* Amaranthus, a red flower with large leaves that symbolizes undying love.

Harps ever tuned, that glittering by their side
Like quivers hung, and with preamble sweet
Of charming symphony they introduce
Their sacred song, and waken raptures high;
No voice exempt, no voice but well could join
Melodious part, such concord is in Heav'n....

ARGUMENT TO BOOK 4

Satan now in prospect of Eden, and nigh the place where he must now attempt the bold enterprise which he undertook alone against God and man, falls into many doubts with himself, and many passions, fear, envy, and despair; but at length confirms himself in evil, journeys on to Paradise, whose outward prospect and situation is described, overleaps the bounds, sits in the shape of a cormorant on the Tree of Life, as highest in the garden to look about him. The garden described; Satan's first sight of Adam and Eve; his wonder at their excellent form and happy state, but with resolution to work their fall; overhears their discourse, thence gathers that the Tree of Knowledge was forbidden them to eat of, under penalty of death; and thereon intends to found his temptation, by seducing them to transgress: then leaves them a while, to know further of their state by some other means. Meanwhile Uriel descending on a sunbeam warns Gabriel, who had in charge the gate of Paradise, that some evil spirit had escaped the deep, and passed at noon by his sphere in the shape of a good angel down to Paradise, discovered after by his furious gestures in the Mount. Gabriel promises to find him out ere morning. Night coming on, Adam and Eve discourse of going to their rest: their bower described; their evening worship. Gabriel drawing forth his bands of night watch to walk the round of Paradise, appoints two strong angels to Adam's bower, least the evil spirit should be there doing some harm to Adam or Eve sleeping; there they find him at the ear of Eve, tempting her in a dream, and bring him, though unwilling, to Gabriel; by whom questioned, he scornfully answers, prepares resistance, but hindered by a sign from Heaven, flies out of Paradise.

BOOK 4

O, for that warning voice, which he, who saw
Th' Apocalypse, heard cry in Heaven aloud,
Then when the Dragon, put to second rout,[1]
Came furious down to be revenged on men,
Woe to the inhabitants on earth! That now,
While time was,[2] our first parents had been warned
The coming of their secret foe, and 'scaped,
Haply so 'scaped his mortal snare: For now
Satan, now first inflamed with rage, came down,
The tempter ere th' accuser of mankind,
To wreak on innocent frail man his loss
Of that first battle, and his flight to Hell:
Yet, not rejoicing in his speed, though bold
Far off and fearless, nor with cause to boast,
Begins his dire attempt; which nigh the birth
Now rolling boils in his tumultuous breast,
And like a devilish engine back recoils
Upon himself; horror and doubt distract
His troubled thoughts, and from the bottom stir
The Hell within him; for within him Hell
He brings, and round about him, nor from Hell
One step, no more than from himself, can fly
By change of place: Now conscience wakes despair,
That slumbered; wakes the bitter memory
Of what he was, what is, and what must be
Worse; of worse deeds worse sufferings must ensue.
Sometimes towards Eden, which now in his view
Lay pleasant, his grieved look he fixes sad;
Sometimes towards Heav'n, and the full-blazing sun,
Which now sat high in his meridian tower:
Then, much revolving,° thus in sighs began: *pondering*
"O thou that with surpassing glory crowned
Lookest from thy sole dominion like the God
Of this new world; at whose sight all the stars
Hide their diminished heads; to thee I call,
But with no friendly voice, and add thy name,
Of sun to tell thee how I hate thy beams,
That bring to my remembrance from what state
I fell, how glorious once above thy sphere;

[1] *O, for that ... to second rout* See the Book of Revelation, specifically Revelation 1.10.

[2] *That now / While time was* If that had happened now, while there was still time.

Till Pride and worse Ambition threw me down
Warring in Heav'n against Heav'n's matchless King:
Ah, wherefore! He deserved no such return° *repayment*
From me, whom He created what I was
In that bright eminence, and with His good
Upbraided none; nor was His service hard.
What could be less than to afford Him praise,
The easiest recompense, and pay Him thanks,
How due! Yet all His good proved ill in me,
And wrought but malice; lifted up so high
I 'sdained° subjection, and thought one step higher *disdained*
Would set me highest, and in a moment quit
The debt immense of endless gratitude,
So burdensome still paying, still to owe,
Forgetful what from Him I still received,
And understood not that a grateful mind
By owing owes not, but still pays, at once
Indebted and discharged; what burden then
O, had His powerful destiny ordained
Me some inferior angel, I had stood
Then happy; no unbounded hope had raised
Ambition! Yet why not some other power
As great might have aspired, and me, though mean,° *lowly*
Drawn to his part; but other powers as great
Fell not, but stand unshaken, from within
Or from without, to all temptations armed.
Hadst thou the same free will and power to stand?
Thou hadst: whom hast thou then or what to accuse,
But Heav'n's free love dealt equally to all?
Be then his love accursed, since love or hate,
To me alike, it deals eternal woe.
Nay, cursed be thou; since against His thy will
Chose freely what it now so justly rues.
Me miserable! which way shall I fly
Infinite wrath, and infinite despair?
Which way I fly is Hell; myself am Hell;
And, in the lowest deep, a lower deep
Still threatening to devour me opens wide,
To which the Hell I suffer seems a Heav'n.
O, then, at last relent: Is there no place
Left for repentance, none for pardon left?
None left but by submission; and that word
Disdain forbids me, and my dread of shame
Among the spirits beneath, whom I seduced
With other promises and other vaunts
Than to submit, boasting I could subdue
Th' Omnipotent. Ay me! They little know
How dearly I abide° that boast so vain, *bear*
Under what torments inwardly I groan,
While they adore me on the throne of Hell.
With diadem and sceptre high advanced,
The lower still I fall, only supreme
In misery: such joy ambition finds.
But say I could repent, and could obtain,
By act of grace, my former state; how soon
Would height recall high thoughts, how soon unsay
What feigned submission swore? Ease would recant
Vows made in pain, as violent and void.
For never can true reconcilement grow,
Where wounds of deadly hate have pierced so deep:
Which would but lead me to a worse relapse
And heavier fall: so should I purchase dear
Short intermission bought with double smart.
This knows my punisher; therefore as far
From granting He, as I from begging, peace;
All hope excluded thus, behold, instead
Of us outcast, exiled, His new delight,
Mankind created, and for Him this world.
So farewell, hope; and with hope farewell, fear;
Farewell, remorse: all good to me is lost;
Evil, be thou my good; by thee at least
Divided empire with Heav'n's King I hold,
By thee, and more than half perhaps will reign;
As man ere long, and this new world, shall know."
Thus while he spake, each passion dimmed his face
Thrice changed with pale, ire, envy, and despair;
Which marred his borrowed visage,[1] and betrayed
Him counterfeit, if any eye beheld.
For heav'nly minds from such distempers foul
Are ever clear. Whereof he soon aware,
Each perturbation smoothed with outward calm,
Artificer of fraud; and was the first
That practised falsehood under saintly show,

[1] *his borrowed visage* Satan had disguised himself as a "stripling cherub" at the end of Book 3, to fool the angel Uriel into telling him where Earth was.

Deep malice to conceal, couched[1] with revenge:
Yet not enough had practised to deceive
Uriel[2] once warned; whose eye pursued him down
The way he went, and on the Assyrian mount[3]
Saw him disfigured more than could befall
Spirit of happy sort; his gestures fierce
He marked and mad demeanour, then alone,
As he supposed, all unobserved, unseen.
So on he fares, and to the border comes
Of Eden, where delicious Paradise,
Now nearer, crowns with her enclosure green,
As with a rural mound, the champaign head
Of a steep wilderness,[4] whose hairy° sides *forested*
With thicket overgrown, grotesque and wild,
Access denied; and overhead up grew
Insuperable height of loftiest shade,
Cedar, and pine, and fir, and branching palm,
A sylvan scene, and, as the ranks ascend,
Shade above shade, a woody theatre
Of stateliest view. Yet higher than their tops
The verdurous wall of Paradise upsprung;
Which to our general sire° gave prospect large *i.e., Adam*
Into his nether empire neighbouring round.
And higher than that wall a circling row
Of goodliest trees, laden with fairest fruit,
Blossoms and fruits at once of golden hue,
Appeared, with gay enamelled° colours mixed: *vivid*
On which the sun more glad impressed his beams
Than in fair evening cloud, or humid bow,[5]
When God hath showered the earth; so lovely seemed
That landskip:° And of pure now purer air *landscape*
Meets his approach, and to the heart inspires
Vernal delight and joy, able to drive
All sadness but despair: now gentle gales,
Fanning their odoriferous wings, dispense
Native perfumes, and whisper whence they stole
Those balmy spoils. As when to them who fail
Beyond the Cape of Hope, and now are past
Mozambique, off at sea northeast winds blow
Sabean[6] odours from the spicy shore
Of Araby the blest; with such delay
Well pleased they slack their course, and many a
league
Cheered with the grateful smell old ocean smiles:
So entertained those odorous sweets the fiend,
Who came their bane; though with them better
pleased
Than Asmodeus with the fishy fume
That drove him, though enamoured, from the spouse
Of Tobit's son, and with a vengeance sent
From Media post to Egypt,[7] there fast bound.
Now to th' ascent of that steep savage hill
Satan had journeyed on, pensive and slow;
But further way found none, so thick entwined,
As one continued brake,° the undergrowth *thicket*
Of shrubs and tangling bushes had perplexed
All path of man or beast that passed that way.
One gate there only was, and that looked east
On the other side: which when the arch-felon saw,
Due entrance he disdained; and, in contempt,
At one flight bound high over-leaped all bound
Of hill or highest wall, and sheer within
Lights on his feet. As when a prowling wolf,
Whom hunger drives to seek new haunt for prey,
Watching where shepherds pen their flocks at eve
In hurdled cotes[8] amid the field secure,
Leaps o'er the fence with ease into the fold:
Or as a thief, bent to unhoard the cash
Of some rich burgher,° whose substantial *merchant*
doors,
Cross-barred and bolted fast, fear no assault,
In at the window climbs, or o'er the tiles:° *shingles*
So clomb° this first grand thief into God's fold; *climbed*

[1] *couched* Lying closely next to.

[2] *Uriel* Angel standing guard on the sun; the name literally means "fire of God."

[3] *the Assyrian mount* Mount Niphates in Syria, named in Book 3 as Satan's landing place.

[4] *champaign … wilderness* Pastoral meadow at the foot of a steep and wooded slope.

[5] *humid bow* Rainbow.

[6] *Sabean* Exotic; from Sheba, modern-day Yemen.

[7] *Than Asmodeus … post to Egypt* Story from the Apocryphal Book of Tobit, in which the son of Tobit, to win the hand of Sara, defeats the incubus Asmodeus by burning the liver of a certain fish to call the archangel Raphael, who "took the devil, and bound him in the desert of upper Egypt" (Tobit 8.3).

[8] *hurdled cotes* Temporary shelters.

So since into his church lewd hirelings climb.[1]
Thence up he flew, and on the tree of life,
The middle tree and highest there that grew,
Sat like a cormorant; yet not true life
Thereby regained, but sat devising death
To them who lived; nor on the virtue thought
Of that life-giving plant, but only used
For prospect[2] what well used had been the pledge
Of immortality. So little knows
Any, but God alone, to value right
The good before him, but perverts best things
To worst abuse, or to their meanest use.
Beneath him with new wonder now he views,
To all delight of human sense exposed,
In narrow room, nature's whole wealth, yea more,
A Heav'n on Earth: For blissful paradise
Of God the garden was, by Him in the east
Of Eden planted; Eden stretched her line
From Auran° eastward to the royal towers *Israel*
Of great Seleucia,° built by Grecian kings, *Iraq*
Of where the sons of Eden long before
Dwelt in Telassar:[3] In this pleasant soil
His far more pleasant garden God ordained;
Out of the fertile ground He caused to grow
All trees of noblest kind for sight, smell, taste;
And all amid them stood the tree of life,
High eminent, blooming ambrosial fruit
Of vegetable gold; and next to life,
Our death, the tree of knowledge, grew fast by,
Knowledge of good bought dear by knowing ill.
Southward through Eden went a river large,
Nor changed his course, but through the shaggy hill
Passed underneath engulfed; for God had thrown
That mountain as His garden-mould high raised
Upon the rapid current, which, through veins
Of porous earth with kindly thirst up-drawn,
Rose a fresh fountain, and with many a rill
Watered the garden; thence united fell
Down the steep glade, and met the nether flood,
Which from his darksome passage now appears,
And now, divided into four main streams,
Runs diverse, wandering many a famous realm
And country, whereof here needs no account;
But rather to tell how, if art could tell,
How from that sapphire fount the crisped brooks,
Rolling on orient pearl and sands of gold,
With mazy error° under pendant shades *meander*
Ran nectar, visiting each plant, and fed
Flowers worthy of Paradise, which not nice° art *careful*
In beds and curious knots, but nature boon
Poured forth profuse on hill, and dale, and plain,
Both where the morning sun first warmly smote
The open field, and where the unpierced shade
Imbrowned° the noontide bowers: Thus *darkened*
was this place
A happy rural seat of various view;
Groves whose rich trees wept odorous gums and balm,
Others whose fruit, burnished with golden rind,
Hung amiable, Hesperian fables[4] true,
If true, here only, and of delicious taste:
Betwixt them lawns, or level downs, and flocks
Grazing the tender herb, were interposed,
Or palmy hillock; or the flowery lap
Of some irriguous° valley spread her store, *watered*
Flowers of all hue, and without thorn the rose:
Another side, umbrageous grots[5] and caves
Of cool recess, o'er which the mantling° vine *climbing*
Lays forth her purple grape, and gently creeps
Luxuriant; meanwhile murmuring waters fall
Down the slope hills, dispersed, or in a lake,
That to the fringèd bank with myrtle crowned
Her crystal mirror holds, unite their streams.
The birds their choir apply;[6] airs, vernal airs,
Breathing the smell of field and grove, attune
The trembling leaves, while universal Pan,
Knit with the Graces and the Hours in dance,[7]
Led on the eternal spring. Not that fair field

[1] *hirelings* Ministers supported by obligatory tithes or taxes. Milton did not believe in a salaried clergy.

[2] *used / For prospect* Used as a perch.

[3] *Telassar* Province in southeast Syria.

[4] *Hesperian fables* In classical mythology, nymphs called the Hesperides, guarded a tree of golden apples.

[5] *umbrageous grots* Shadowy grottos.

[6] *their choir apply* Sing.

[7] *Pan* Classical god of nature; *Graces* Aglaia, Euphrosyne, and Thalia, sister goddesses of charm and beauty; *Hours* Horae, various goddesses of the hours, seasons, and other aspects of time.

Of Enna,[1] where Proserpine gathering flowers,
Herself a fairer flower by gloomy Dis
Was gathered, which cost Ceres all that pain
To seek her through the world;[2] nor that sweet grove
Of Daphne by Orontes,[3] and the inspired
Castilian spring,[4] might with this Paradise
Of Eden strive; nor that Nyseian[5] isle
Girt with the river Triton,[6] where old Cham,
Whom Gentiles Ammon call and Libyan Jove,[7]
Hid Amalthea, and her florid son
Young Bacchus, from his stepdame Rhea's eye;[8]
Nor where Abassin° kings their issue guard, *Abyssinian*
Mount Amara, though this by some supposed
True Paradise under the Ethiop line[9]
By Nilus' head,[10] enclosed with shining rock,
A whole day's journey high, but wide remote
From this Assyrian garden, where the fiend
Saw, undelighted, all delight, all kind
Of living creatures, new to sight, and strange
Two of far nobler shape, erect and tall,
Godlike erect, with native honour clad
In naked majesty seemed lords of all:
And worthy seemed; for in their looks divine
The image of their glorious Maker shone,
Truth, wisdom, sanctitude severe and pure
(Severe, but in true filial freedom placed),
Whence true authority in men; though both
Not equal, as their sex not equal seemed;
For contemplation he and valour formed;
For softness she and sweet attractive grace;
He for God only, she for God in him:
His fair large front and eye sublime declared
Absolute rule; and hyacinthine[11] locks
Round from his parted forelock manly hung
Clustering, but not beneath his shoulders broad:
She, as a veil, down to the slender waist
Her unadornèd golden tresses wore
Dishevelled, but in wanton ringlets waved
As the vine curls her tendrils, which implied
Subjection, but required with gentle sway,
And by her yielded, by him best received,
Yielded with coy submission, modest pride,
And sweet, reluctant, amorous delay.
Nor those mysterious parts were then concealed;
Then was not guilty shame, dishonest shame
Of nature's works, honour dishonourable,
Sin-bred, how have ye troubled all mankind
With shows instead, mere shows of seeming pure,
And banished from man's life his happiest life,
Simplicity and spotless innocence!
So passed they naked on, nor shunned the sight
Of God or angel; for they thought no ill:
So hand in hand they passed, the loveliest pair,
That ever since in love's embraces met;
Adam the goodliest man of men since born
His sons, the fairest of her daughters Eve.
Under a tuft of shade that on a green
Stood whispering soft, by a fresh fountain side
They sat them down; and, after no more toil
Of their sweet gardening labour than sufficed

[1] *Enna* Meadow in Sicily.

[2] *Proserpine ... world* Proserpine, the daughter of the goddess of agriculture and the harvest, Ceres, was kidnapped by the god of the underworld, Dis (Hades or Pluto). Proserpine's mother went into mourning, thereby bringing winter to the land. Dis agreed to return Proserpine to her mother for half the year; hence, the seasons of summer and winter.

[3] *that sweet ... by Orontes* Daphne was a Naiad, a spirit charged with safekeeping of rivers, streams, and brooks. She was willingly transformed into a laurel tree to avoid Apollo's amorous pursuit; this event was supposed to have happened near the river Orontes, where it crosses through Syria, and to have resulted in a peaceful grotto beneath the transfigured laurel, now sacred to Apollo.

[4] *inspired / Castilian spring* Spring of the Muses on Mount Parnassus.

[5] *Nyseian* Nyseia, an ancient Mediterranean country.

[6] *the river Triton* Modern-day Gazanos River.

[7] *Cham ... Ammon ... Jove* Cham (the Biblical Ham, son of Noah) was sometimes said to be the same as the pagan Ammon and the Lybian version of Jove.

[8] *Hid Amalthea ... stepdame Rhea's eye* Amalthea was impregnated by Ammon, King of Libya and gave birth to Bacchus, god of wine. Since she needed to be hidden from Rhea, Ammon's wife and Uranus's daughter, she was hidden on Nyseia.

[9] *the Ethiop line* The equator.

[10] *By Nilus' head* By the head of the Nile River.

[11] *hyacinthine* Dark colored and shiny, lustrous and thick. The hyacinth is a rich-colored and many-bloomed flower; Hyacinthus was a handsome youth in classical mythology, unintentionally killed by his lover Apollo, who turned him into the flower.

To recommend cool Zephyr,[1] and made ease
More easy, wholesome thirst and appetite
More grateful, to their supper-fruits they fell,
Nectarine fruits which the compliant boughs
Yielded them, side-long as they sat recline
On the soft downy bank damasked with flowers:
The savoury pulp they chew, and in the rind,
Still as they thirsted, scoop the brimming stream;
Nor gentle purpose, nor endearing smiles
Wanted, nor youthful dalliance, as beseems
Fair couple, linked in happy nuptial league,[2]
Alone as they. About them frisking played
All beasts of the earth, since wild, and of all chase
In wood or wilderness, forest or den;
Sporting the lion ramped, and in his paw
Dandled the kid; bears, tigers, ounces, pards,[3]
Gambolled before them; the unwieldy elephant,
To make them mirth, used all his might, and wreathed
His lithe proboscis; close the serpent sly,
Insinuating, wove with Gordian twine[4]
His braided train, and of his fatal guile
Gave proof unheeded; others on the grass
Couched, and now filled with pasture gazing sat,
Or bedward ruminating; for the sun,
Declined, was hasting now with prone career
To th' ocean isles, and in the ascending scale
Of Heav'n the stars that usher evening rose:
When Satan still in gaze, as first he stood,
Scarce thus at length failed speech recovered sad.
"O Hell! What do mine eyes with grief behold!
Into our room of bliss thus high advanced
Creatures of other mould, earth-born perhaps,
Not spirits, yet to heav'nly spirits bright
Little inferior; whom my thoughts pursue
With wonder, and could love, so lively shines
In them divine resemblance, and such grace
The hand that formed them on their shape hath poured.
Ah! Gentle pair, ye little think how nigh
Your change approaches, when all these delights
Will vanish, and deliver ye to woe;
More woe, the more your taste is now of joy;
Happy, but for so happy ill secured
Long to continue, and this high seat your Heav'n
Ill fenced for Heav'n to keep out such a foe
As now is entered; yet no purposed foe
To you, whom I could pity thus forlorn,
Though I unpitied: League with you I seek,
And mutual amity, so strait, so close,
That I with you must dwell, or you with me
Henceforth; my dwelling haply may not please,
Like this fair Paradise, your sense; yet such
Accept your Maker's work; He gave it me,
Which I as freely give: Hell shall unfold,
To entertain you two, her widest gates,
And send forth all her kings; there will be room,
Not like these narrow limits, to receive
Your numerous offspring; if no better place,
Thank Him who puts me loath to this revenge
On you who wrong me not for Him who wronged.
And should I at your harmless innocence
Melt, as I do, yet public reason just,
Honour and empire with revenge enlarged,
By conquering this new world, compels me now
To do what else, though damned, I should abhor."
So spake the fiend, and with necessity,
The tyrant's plea, excused his devilish deeds.
Then from his lofty stand on that high tree
Down he alights among the sportful herd
Of those four-footed kinds, himself now one,
Now other, as their shape served best his end
Nearer to view his prey, and, unespied,
To mark what of their state he more might learn,
By word or action marked. About them round
A lion now he stalks with fiery glare;
Then as a tiger, who by chance hath spied
In some purlieu[5] two gentle fawns at play,
Straight couches close, then, rising, changes oft

[1] *Zephyr* West wind, synonymous with a gentle and pleasant breeze.

[2] *happy nuptial league* Marriage.

[3] *Dandled* Playfully dangled; *kid* Baby goat; *ounces* Lynxes; *pards* Leopards.

[4] *Gordian twine* Inextricable knot, after the Gordian knot of legend, which no one was able to untie. It was undone only by Alexander the Great, who did not attempt to untie it, but instead sliced it in half with his sword.

[5] *purlieu* Forest outskirts.

His couchant° watch, as one who chose his ground, *crouching*
Whence rushing, he might surest seize them both,
Gripped in each paw: when, Adam first of men
To first of women Eve thus moving speech,
Turned him, all ear to hear new utterance flow:
"Sole partner, and sole part, of all these joys,
Dearer thyself than all; needs must the power
That made us, and for us this ample world,
Be infinitely good, and of His good
As liberal and free as infinite;
That raised us from the dust,[1] and placed us here
In all this happiness, who at His hand
Have nothing merited, nor can perform
Aught whereof He hath need; He who requires
From us no other service than to keep
This one, this easy charge, of all the trees
In Paradise that bear delicious fruit
So various, not to taste that only tree
Of knowledge, planted by the tree of life;[2]
So near grows death to life, whate'er death is,
Some dreadful thing no doubt; for well thou knowest
God hath pronounced it death to taste that tree,
The only sign of our obedience left,
Among so many signs of power and rule
Conferred upon us, and dominion giv'n
Over all other creatures that possess
Earth, air, and sea. Then let us not think hard
One easy prohibition, who enjoy
Free leave so large to all things else, and choice
Unlimited of manifold delights:
But let us ever praise Him, and extol
His bounty, following our delightful task,
To prune these growing plants, and tend these flowers,
Which were it toilsome, yet with thee were sweet."
To whom thus Eve replied: "O thou for whom
And from whom I was formed, flesh of thy flesh,
And without whom am to no end, my guide
And head! What thou hast said is just and right.
For we to Him indeed all praises owe,
And daily thanks; I chiefly, who enjoy
So far the happier lot, enjoying thee
Pre-eminent by so much odds, while thou
Like consort to thyself canst nowhere find.
That day I oft remember, when from sleep
I first awaked, and found myself reposed
Under a shade of flowers, much wondering where
And what I was, whence thither brought, and how.
Not distant far from thence a murmuring sound
Of waters issued from a cave, and spread
Into a liquid plain, then stood unmoved
Pure as th' expanse of Heav'n; I thither went
With unexperienced thought, and laid me down
On the green bank, to look into the clear
Smooth lake, that to me seemed another sky.
As I bent down to look, just opposite
A shape within the wat'ry gleam appeared,
Bending to look on me: I started back,
It started back; but pleased I soon returned,
Pleased it returned as soon with answering looks
Of sympathy and love:[3] There I had fixed
Mine eyes till now, and pined with vain desire,
Had not a voice thus warned me; 'What thou seest,
What there thou seest, fair creature, is thyself;
With thee it came and goes: but follow me,
And I will bring thee where no shadow stays
Thy coming, and thy soft embraces—he
Whose image thou art; him thou shalt enjoy
Inseparably thine, to him shalt bear
Multitudes like thyself, and thence be called
Mother of human race.' What could I do,
But follow straight, invisibly thus led?
Till I espied thee, fair indeed and tall,
Under a platane;[4] yet methought less fair,
Less winning soft, less amiably mild,
Than that smooth wat'ry image: back I turned;[5]
Thou following cryedst aloud, 'Return, fair Eve;

[1] *raised us from the dust* See Genesis 2.7.

[2] *not to taste ... tree of life* See Genesis 2.16–17.

[3] *As I bent down ... sympathy and love* The narrative here mirrors the classical myth of Narcissus, a beautiful youth who became captivated by his own reflection and wasted away.

[4] *platane* Plane tree.

[5] *back I turned* The narrative here mirrors the myth of Eurydice, lost when her husband Orpheus took her back from the underworld, but violated his agreement with Pluto by looking back to see if she were following. It also suggests the Biblical story of Lot's wife, who looked back at the destruction of Sodom and Gomorrah and was transformed into a pillar of salt (Genesis 19.26).

Whom flyest thou?[1] Whom thou flyest, of him thou art,
His flesh, his bone; to give thee being I lent
Out of my side to thee, nearest my heart,
Substantial life, to have thee by my side
Henceforth an individual solace dear;
Part of my soul I seek thee, and thee claim
My other half:' With that thy gentle hand
Seized mine: I yielded, and from that time see
How beauty is excelled by manly grace,
And wisdom, which alone is truly fair."
So spake our general mother, and with eyes
Of conjugal attraction unreproved,
And meek surrender, half-embracing leaned
On our first father; half her swelling breast
Naked met his, under the flowing gold
Of her loose tresses hid: he in delight
Both of her beauty, and submissive charms,
Smiled with superior love, as Jupiter
On Juno smiles, when he impregns the clouds
That shed May flowers; and pressed her matron lip
With kisses pure. Aside the devil turned
For envy; yet with jealous leer malign
Eyed them askance, and to himself thus plained.[2]
"Sight hateful, sight tormenting! Thus these two,
Imparadised in one another's arms,
The happier Eden, shall enjoy their fill
Of bliss on bliss; while I to Hell am thrust,
Where neither joy nor love, but fierce desire,
Among our other torments not the least,
Still unfulfilled with pain of longing pines.
Yet let me not forget what I have gained
From their own mouths: all is not theirs, it seems;
One fatal tree there stands, of knowledge called,
Forbidden them to taste: knowledge forbidd'n
Suspicious, reasonless. Why should their Lord
Envy them that? Can it be sin to know?
Can it be death? And do they only stand
By ignorance? Is that their happy state,
The proof of their obedience and their faith?
O fair foundation laid whereon to build
Their ruin! Hence I will excite their minds
With more desire to know, and to reject
Envious commands, invented with design
To keep them low, whom knowledge might exalt
Equal with gods: aspiring to be such,
They taste and die: What likelier can ensue
But first with narrow search I must walk round
This garden, and no corner leave unspied;
A chance but chance may lead where I may meet
Some wandering spirit of Heav'n by fountain side,
Or in thick shade retired, from him to draw
What further would be learned. Live while ye may,
Yet happy pair; enjoy, till I return,
Short pleasures, for long woes are to succeed!"
So saying, his proud step he scornful turned,
But with sly circumspection, and began
Through wood, through waste, o'er hill, o'er dale, his roam
Meanwhile in utmost longitude, where Heav'n
With earth and ocean meets, the setting sun
Slowly descended, and with right aspect
Against the eastern gate of Paradise
Levelled his evening rays: it was a rock
Of alabaster, piled up to the clouds,
Conspicuous far, winding with one ascent
Accessible from earth, one entrance high;
The rest was craggy cliff that overhung
Still as it rose, impossible to climb.
Betwixt these rocky pillars Gabriel[3] sat,
Chief of the angelic guards, awaiting night;
About him exercised heroic games
The unarmed youth of Heav'n, but nigh at hand
Celestial armoury, shields, helms, and spears,
Hung high with diamond flaming, and with gold.
Thither came Uriel, gliding through the even
On a sun-beam, swift as a shooting star
In autumn thwarts the night, when vapours fired[4]
Impress the air, and shows the mariner
From what point of his compass to beware
Impetuous winds: He thus began in haste.
"Gabriel, to thee thy course by lot hath given
Charge and strict watch, that to this happy place
No evil thing approach or enter in.
This day at height of noon came to my sphere

[1] *Whom flyest thou?* From whom are you running?

[2] *plained* Complained, lamented.

[3] *Gabriel* Archangel, messenger of God. His name means "strength of God."

[4] *vapours fired* Shooting stars.

A spirit, zealous, as he seemed, to know
More of th' Almighty's works, and chiefly Man,
God's latest image: I described° his way — *noted*
Bent all on speed, and marked his airy gait;
But in the mount that lies from Eden north,
Where he first lighted, soon discerned his looks
Alien from Heav'n, with passions foul obscured:
Mine eye pursued him still, but under shade
Lost sight of him. One of the banished crew,
I fear, hath ventured from the deep, to raise
New troubles; him thy care must be to find."
To whom the wingèd warrior thus returned:
"Uriel, no wonder if thy perfect sight,
Amid the sun's bright circle where thou sitst,
See far and wide: in at this gate none pass
The vigilance here placed, but such as come
Well known from Heav'n; and since meridian° hour — *noon*
No creature thence: If spirit of other sort,
So minded, have o'er-leaped these earthly bounds
On purpose, hard thou knowest it to exclude
Spiritual substance with corporeal bar.
But if within the circuit of these walks,
In whatsoever shape he lurk, of whom
Thou tellest, by morrow dawning I shall know."
So promised he; and Uriel to his charge
Returned on that bright beam, whose point now raised
Bore him slope downward to the sun now fall'n
Beneath th' Azores;[1] whether the prime orb,
Incredible how swift, had thither rolled
Diurnal, or this less voluble° earth, — *revolving*
By shorter flight to th' east, had left him there[2]
Arraying with reflected purple and gold
The clouds that on his western throne attend.
Now came still evening on, and twilight grey
Had in her sober livery all things clad;
Silence accompanied; for beast and bird,
They to their grassy couch, these to their nests
Were slunk, all but the wakeful nightingale;

[1] *Azores* Islands located in the Atlantic Ocean off the coast of Portugal.

[2] *whether the prime orb ... had left him there* Whether the sun, with amazing speed, circled the earth every day or the earth, less rapid ("voluble"), circled the sun.

She all night long her amorous descant sung;
Silence was pleased. Now glowed the firmament
With living sapphires: Hesperus,[3] that led
The starry host, rode brightest, till the moon,
Rising in clouded majesty, at length
Apparent queen unveiled her peerless light,
And o'er the dark her silver mantle threw.
When Adam thus to Eve: "Fair consort, the hour
Of night, and all things now retired to rest,
Mind us of like repose; since God hath set
Labour and rest, as day and night, to men
Successive; and the timely dew of sleep,
Now falling with soft slumbrous weight, inclines
Our eye-lids: other creatures all day long
Rove idle, unemployed, and less need rest;
Man hath his daily work of body or mind
Appointed, which declares his dignity,
And the regard of Heav'n on all his ways;
While other animals unactive range,
And of their doings God takes no account.
Tomorrow, ere fresh morning streak the east
With first approach of light, we must be risen,
And at our pleasant labour, to reform
Yon flowery arbours, yonder alleys green,
Our walk at noon, with branches overgrown,
That mock our scant manuring, and require
More hands than ours to lop their wanton growth:
Those blossoms also, and those dropping gums,
That lie bestrown, unsightly and unsmooth,
Ask riddance, if we mean to tread with ease;
Meanwhile, as nature wills, night bids us rest."
To whom thus Eve, with perfect beauty adorned:
"My author and disposer, what thou bidst
Unargued I obey: So God ordains;
God is thy law, thou mine: to know no more
Is woman's happiest knowledge, and her praise.
With thee conversing I forget all time;
All seasons, and their change, all please alike.
Sweet is the breath of morn, her rising sweet,
With charm of earliest birds: pleasant the sun,
When first on this delightful land he spreads
His orient beams, on herb, tree, fruit, and flower,
Glistering with dew; fragrant the fertile earth
After soft showers; and sweet the coming on

[3] *Hesperus* The evening star.

Of grateful ev'ning mild; then silent night,
With this her solemn bird, and this fair moon,
And these the gems of Heaven, her starry train:
But neither breath of morn, when she ascends
With charm of earliest birds; nor rising sun
On this delightful land; nor herb, fruit, flower,
Glist'ring with dew; nor fragrance after showers;
Nor grateful ev'ning mild; nor silent night,
With this her solemn bird, nor walk by moon,
Or glittering starlight, without thee is sweet.
But wherefore all night long shine these? For whom
This glorious sight, when sleep hath shut all eyes?"
To whom our general ancestor replied:
"Daughter of God and man, accomplished Eve,
These have their course to finish round the earth,
By morrow ev'ning, and from land to land
In order, though to nations yet unborn,
Ministring light prepared, they set and rise;
Lest total darkness should by night regain
Her old possession, and extinguish life
In nature and all things; which these soft fires
Not only enlighten, but with kindly heat
Of various influence foment[1] and warm,
Temper or nourish, or in part shed down
Their stellar virtue on all kinds that grow
On earth, made hereby apter to receive
Perfection from the sun's more potent ray.
These then, though unbeheld in deep of night,
Shine not in vain; nor think, though men were none,
That Heav'n would want spectators, God want praise:
Millions of spiritual creatures walk the earth
Unseen, both when we wake, and when we sleep:
All these with ceaseless praise His works behold
Both day and night: how often from the steep
Of echoing hill or thicket have we heard
Celestial voices to the midnight air,
Sole, or responsive each to other's note,
Singing their great Creator? Oft in bands
While they keep watch, or nightly rounding walk,
With heav'nly touch of instrumental sounds
In full harmonic number joined, their songs
Divide the night, and lift our thoughts to Heaven."
Thus talking, hand in hand alone they passed
On to their blissful bower: it was a place
Chosen by the Sovereign Planter,[2] when He framed
All things to Man's delightful use; the roof
Of thickest covert was inwoven shade
Laurel and myrtle, and what higher grew
Of firm and fragrant leaf; on either side
Acanthus, and each odorous bushy shrub,
Fenced up the verdant wall; each beauteous flower,
Iris all hues, roses, and jessamine,° *jasmine*
Reared high their flourished heads between, and wrought
Mosaic; underfoot the violet,
Crocus, and hyacinth, with rich inlay
Broidered the ground, more coloured than with stone
Of costliest emblem. Other creature here,
Bird, beast, insect, or worm, durst enter none,
Such was their awe of Man. In shadier bower
More sacred and sequestered, though but feigned,
Pan or Sylvanus never slept, nor Nymph
Nor Faunus[3] haunted. Here, in close recess,
With flowers, garlands, and sweet-smelling herbs,
Espousèd° Eve decked first her nuptial bed; *married*
And heav'nly choirs the hymenaean[4] sung,
What day the genial angel to our sire
Brought her in naked beauty more adorned,
More lovely than Pandora, whom the Gods
Endowed with all their gifts, and O! Too like
In sad event, when to the unwiser son
Of Japhet brought by Hermes, she ensnared
Mankind with her fair looks, to be avenged
On him who had stole Jove's authentic° fire.[5] *primal*
Thus, at their shady lodge arrived, both stood,
Both turned, and under open sky adored
The God that made both sky, air, earth, and Heaven,
Which they beheld, the moon's resplendent globe,

[1] *foment* Excite, cause to develop.

[2] *the Sovereign Planter* God.

[3] *Sylvanus* Roman god of forests, fields, and herding; *Nymph* Nature spirit; *Faunus* Roman god of nature and fertility.

[4] *hymenaean* Wedding song.

[5] *Pandora* Created and given to Epimetheus, the brother of Prometheus, to punish Prometheus for having stolen fire from the gods and given it to humans. Pandora's dowry was a jar that, when opened, released all the ills and cares of the world to roam free and plague humankind. However, one thing remained, Hope; *the unwiser son / Of Japhet* Prometheus, whose father (the Titan Iapetus) was identified with Noah's son Japhet; *Hermes* Greek messenger god; Roman Mercury.

And starry pole: "Thou also madest the night,
Maker omnipotent, and Thou the day,
Which we, in our appointed work employed,
Have finished, happy in our mutual help
And mutual love, the crown of all our bliss
Ordained by Thee; and this delicious place
For us too large, where Thy abundance wants
Partakers, and uncropt falls to the ground.
But Thou hast promised from us two a race
To fill the earth, who shall with us extol
Thy goodness infinite, both when we wake,
And when we seek, as now, thy gift of sleep."
  This said unanimous, and other rites
Observing none, but adoration pure
Which God likes best, into their inmost bower
Handed they went; and, eased the putting off
These troublesome disguises[1] which we wear,
Straight side by side were laid; nor turned, I ween,
Adam from his fair spouse, nor Eve the rites
Mysterious of connubial love refused:
Whatever hypocrites austerely talk
Of purity, and place, and innocence,
Defaming as impure what God declares
Pure, and commands to some,[2] leaves free to all.
Our Maker bids increase;[3] who bids abstain
But our destroyer, foe to God and man?
Hail, wedded love, mysterious law, true source
Of human offspring, sole propriety
In Paradise of all things common else!
By thee adulterous lust was driv'n from men
Among the bestial herds to range; by thee
Founded in reason, loyal, just, and pure,
Relations dear, and all the charities
Of father, son, and brother, first were known.
Far be it, that I should write thee sin or blame,
Or think thee unbefitting holiest place,
Perpetual fountain of domestic sweets,
Whose bed is undefiled and chaste pronounced,
Present, or past, as saints and patriarchs used.
Here love his golden shafts employs, here lights
His constant lamp, and waves his purple wings,
Reigns here and revels; not in the bought smile
Of harlots, loveless, joyless, unendeared,
Casual fruition; nor in court-amours,
Mixed dance, or wanton mask, or midnight ball,
Or serenade, which the starved lover sings
To his proud fair, best quitted with disdain.
These, lulled by nightingales, embracing slept,
And on their naked limbs the flowery roof
Showered roses, which the morn repaired. Sleep on,
Blest pair! And, O! Yet happiest, if ye seek
No happier state, and know to know no more!
  Now had night measured with her shadowy cone
Halfway up hill this vast sublunar vault,[4]
And from their ivory port the cherubim
Forth issuing at th' accustomed hour stood armed
To their night watches in warlike parade,
When Gabriel to his next in power thus spake.
  "Uzziel,[5] half these draw off, and coast the south
With strictest watch; these other wheel the north,[6]
Our circuit meets full west." As flame they part
Half wheeling to the shield, half to the spear.[7]
From these, two strong and subtle spirits he called
That near him stood, and gave them thus in charge.
  "Ithuriel and Zephon,[8] with winged speed
Search through this garden, leave unsearched no nook,
But chiefly where those two fair creatures lodge,
Now laid perhaps asleep secure of° harm. *unsuspecting*
This evening from the sun's decline arrived
Who° tells of some infernal spirit seen *One who*
Hitherward bent (who could have thought?) escaped
The bars of Hell, on errand bad no doubt:
Such where ye find, seize fast, and hither bring."

[1] *These troublesome disguises* Clothes.

[2] *commands to some* See 1 Corinthians 7.2.

[3] *Our Maker bids increase* See Genesis 9.7.

[4] *night measured ... vault* With the sun below the horizon, the earth's globe casts a conical shadow that arches across the horizon. This shadow has ascended halfway to its zenith (midnight), which makes the time 9:00 pm.

[5] *Uzziel* "My strength is God" (Hebrew). A human name in the Bible, but an angel in rabbinic tradition.

[6] *coast the south / ... wheel the north* Starting at the eastern gate, Uzziel sends half his troops to check the garden perimeter to the south, the other half to the north; they will meet again due west.

[7] *to the shield ... to the spear* To the left (shield hand) and right (spear hand).

[8] *Ithuriel and Zephon* "Discovery of God" and "Searcher" respectively (Hebrew). Their names reflect their roles in the narrative. Zephon is a biblical name (human, not an angel); Ithuriel is not biblical, but appears in apocryphal traditions.

So saying, on he led his radiant files,
Dazzling the moon; these to the bower direct
In search of whom they sought: him there they found
Squat like a toad, close at the ear of Eve;
Assaying by his devilish art to reach
The organs of her fancy, and with them forge
Illusions as he list,° phantasms and dreams, *desires*
Or if, inspiring° venom, he might taint *breathing*
Th' animal spirits that from pure blood arise
Like gentle breaths from rivers pure, thence raise
At least distempered,° discontented thoughts, *unbalanced*
Vain hopes, vain aims, inordinate desires
Blown up with high conceits° engend'ring pride. *ideas*
Him thus intent Ithuriel with his spear
Touched lightly; for no falsehood can endure
Touch of celestial temper, but returns
Of force to its own likeness: up he starts
Discovered and surprised. As when a spark
Lights on a heap of nitrous powder,° laid *gunpowder*
Fit for the tun° some magazine° to store *cask / storehouse*
Against a rumored war, the smutty° grain *black*
With sudden blaze diffused, enflames the air:
So started up in his own shape the fiend.
Back stepped those two fair angels half amazed
So sudden to behold the grisly king;
Yet thus, unmoved with fear, accost him soon.
"Which of those rebel spirits adjudged to Hell
Com'st thou, escaped thy prison, and transformed,
Why sat'st thou like an enemy in wait
Here watching at the head of these that sleep?"
"Know ye not then," said Satan, filled with scorn,
"Know ye not me? Ye knew me once no mate
For you, there sitting where ye durst not soar;
Not to know me argues° yourselves unknown, *indicates*
The lowest of your throng; or if ye know,
Why ask ye, and superfluous begin
Your message, like to end as much in vain?"
To whom thus Zephon, answering scorn with scorn.
"Think not, revolted spirit, thy shape the same,
Or undiminished brightness, to be known
As when thou stood'st in Heaven upright and pure;
That glory then, when thou no more wast good,
Departed from thee, and thou resemblest now
Thy sin and place of doom obscure° and foul. *dark*
But come, for thou, be sure, shalt give account
To him who sent us, whose charge is to keep
This place inviolable, and these from harm."
So spake the cherub, and his grave rebuke
Severe in youthful beauty, added grace
Invincible: abashed the Devil stood,
And felt how awful° goodness is, and saw *awe-inspiring*
Virtue in her shape how lovely, saw, and pined
His loss; but chiefly to find here observed
His lustre visibly impaired; yet seemed
Undaunted. "If I must contend," said he,
"Best with the best, the sender not the sent,
Or all at once; more glory will be won,
Or less be lost." "Thy fear," said Zephon bold,
"Will save us trial what the least can do
Single against thee wicked, and thence weak."
The fiend replied not, overcome with rage;
But like a proud steed reined, went haughty on,
Champing his iron curb: to strive or fly
He held it vain; awe from above had quelled
His heart, not else dismayed. Now drew they nigh
The western point, where those half-rounding guards
Just met, and closing stood in squadron joined
Awaiting next command. To whom their chief
Gabriel from the front thus called aloud.
"O friends, I hear the tread of nimble feet
Hasting this way, and now by glimpse discern
Ithuriel and Zephon through the shade,° *trees*
And with them comes a third of regal port,° *bearing*
But faded splendor wan;° who by his gait *gloomy*
And fierce demeanour seems the Prince of Hell,
Not likely to part hence without contest;
Stand firm, for in his look defiance lours."° *scowls*
He scarce had ended, when those two approached
And brief related whom they brought, where found,
How busied, in what form and posture couched.
To whom with stern regard thus Gabriel spake.
"Why hast thou, Satan, broke the bounds prescribed
To thy transgressions, and disturbed the charge
Of others, who approve not to transgress
By thy example, but have power and right
To question thy bold entrance on this place;
Employed it seems to violate sleep, and those
Whose dwelling God hath planted here in bliss?"

To whom thus Satan with contemptuous brow.
"Gabriel, thou hadst in Heaven th' esteem of wise,[1]
And such I held thee; but this question asked
Puts me in doubt. Lives there who loves his pain?
Who would not, finding way, break loose from Hell,
Though thither doomed? Thou wouldst thyself, no doubt,
And boldly venture to whatever place
Farthest from pain, where thou might'st hope to change
Torment with ease, and soonest recompense° *repay*
Dole° with delight, which in this place I sought; *Sorrow*
To thee no reason; who know'st only good,
But evil hast not tried: and wilt object
His will who bound us? Let him surer bar
His iron gates, if he intends our stay
In that dark durance:° thus much what was asked. *confinement*
The rest is true, they found me where they say;
But that implies not violence or harm."
Thus he in scorn. The warlike angel moved,° *angry*
Disdainfully half smiling thus replied.
"O loss of one in Heaven to judge of wise,° *wisdom*
Since Satan fell, whom folly overthrew,
And now returns him from his prison 'scaped,
Gravely in doubt whether to hold them wise
Or not, who ask what boldness brought him hither
Unlicensed from his bounds in Hell prescribed;
So wise he judges it to fly from pain
However,° and to 'scape his punishment. *In whatever way*
So judge thou still, presumptuous, till the wrath,
Which thou incurr'st by flying, meet thy flight
Sevenfold, and scourge that wisdom back to Hell,
Which taught thee yet no better, that no pain
Can equal anger infinite provoked.
But wherefore thou alone? Wherefore with thee
Came not all Hell broke loose? Is pain to them
Less pain, less to be fled, or thou than they
Less hardy to endure? Courageous chief,
The first in flight from pain, hadst thou alleged
To thy deserted host this cause of flight,
Thou surely hadst not come sole fugitive."
To which the fiend thus answered frowning stern.
"Not that I less endure, or shrink from pain,
Insulting angel, well thou know'st I stood° *withstood*
Thy fiercest, when in battle to thy aide
The blasting volleyed thunder made all speed
And seconded thy else° not dreaded spear. *otherwise*
But still thy words at random, as before,
Argue thy inexperience what behooves° *is proper*
From° hard assays° and ill successes past *After / attempts*
A faithful leader, not to hazard all
Through ways of danger by himself untried,
I therefore, I alone first undertook
To wing the desolate abyss, and spy
This new created world, whereof in Hell
Fame° is not silent, here in hope to find *Rumor*
Better abode, and my afflicted powers° *downcast forces*
To settle here on earth, or in mid air;
Though for possession put to try° once more *test*
What thou and thy gay[2] legions dare against;
Whose easier business were to serve their Lord
High up in Heaven, with songs to hymn his throne,
And practiced distances[3] to cringe, not fight."
To whom the warrior angel, soon replied.
"To say and straight unsay, pretending first
Wise to fly pain, professing next the spy,
Argues no leader, but a liar traced,° *discovered*
Satan, and couldst thou faithful add? O name,
O sacred name of faithfulness profaned!
Faithful to whom? To thy rebellious crew?
Army of fiends, fit body to fit head;
Was this your discipline and faith engaged,
Your military obedience, to dissolve
Allegiance to th' acknowledged Power Supreme?
And thou sly hypocrite, who now wouldst seem
Patron of liberty, who more than thou
Once fawned, and cringed, and servilely adored
Heaven's awful° Monarch? Wherefore but in hope *awe-inspiring*
To dispossess him, and thyself to reign?
But mark what I areed° thee now, avant;° *advise / depart*
Fly thither whence thou fled'st: if from this hour
Within these hallowed limits thou appear,
Back to th' infernal pit I drag thee chained,
And seal thee so, as henceforth not to scorn
The facile° gates of Hell too slightly barred." *yielding*
So threatened he, but Satan to no threats

[1] *esteem of wise* Reputation of being wise.

[2] *gay* Showy; like courtiers.

[3] *practiced distances* I.e., they practiced judging distance by courtly bowing, not sword fighting.

Gave heed, but waxing° more in rage replied. *growing*
"Then when I am thy captive talk of chains,
Proud limitary° cherub, but ere then *boundary-guarding*
Far heavier load thyself expect to feel
From my prevailing arm, though Heaven's King
Ride on thy wings, and thou with thy compeers,° *fellows*
Used to the yoke, draw'st his triumphant wheels
In progress through the road of Heaven star-paved."[1]
While thus he spake, th' angelic squadron bright
Turned fiery red, sharp'ning in mooned horns
Their phalanx,[2] and began to hem him round
With ported[3] spears, as thick as when a field
Of Ceres[4] ripe for harvest waving bends
Her bearded grove of ears, which way the wind
Sways them; the careful° plowman doubting *apprehensive*
stands
Lest on the threshing floor his hopeful sheaves
Prove chaff.[5] On th' other side Satan alarmed[6]
Collecting all his might dilated° stood, *inflated*
Like Tenerife or Atlas[7] unremoved:° *immovable*
His stature reached the sky, and on his crest
Sat Horror plumed; nor wanted° in his grasp *lacked*
What seemed both spear and shield: now dreadful deeds
Might have ensued, nor only Paradise
In this commotion, but the starry cope° *canopy*
Of Heaven perhaps, or all the elements
At least had gone to rack,° disturbed and torn *ruin*
With violence of this conflict, had not soon
Th' Eternal to prevent such horrid fray
Hung forth in Heaven his golden scales, yet seen
Betwixt Astrea and the Scorpion sign,[8]
Wherein all things created first he weighed,
The pendulous round Earth with balanced air
In counterpoise, now ponders° all events, *weighs*
Battles and realms: in these he put two weights
The sequel° each of parting and of fight; *consequences*
The latter quick up flew,[9] and kicked the beam;
Which Gabriel spying, thus bespake the fiend.
"Satan, I know thy strength, and thou know'st mine,
Neither our own but given; what folly then
To boast what arms can do, since thine no more
Than Heaven permits, nor mine, though doubled now
To trample thee as mire:° for proof look up, *mud*
And read thy lot° in yon celestial sign *fate*
Where thou art weighed, and shown how light, how weak,
If thou resist." The fiend looked up and knew
His mounted scale aloft: nor more; but fled
Murmuring, and with him fled the shades of night.

ARGUMENT TO BOOK 5

Morning approached, Eve relates to Adam her troublesome dream; he likes it not, yet comforts her: they come forth to their day labours: their morning hymn at the door of their bower. God to render man inexcusable sends Raphael to admonish him of his obedience, of his free estate, of his enemy near at hand; who he is, and why his enemy, and whatever else may avail Adam to know. Raphael comes down to Paradise, his appearance described, his coming discerned by Adam afar off sitting at the door of his bower; he goes out to meet him, brings him to his lodge, entertains him with the choicest fruits of Paradise got together by Eve; their discourse at table: Raphael performs his message, minds Adam of his state and of his enemy; relates at Adam's request who that enemy is, and how he came to be so,

---

[1] *progress ... star-paved* Triumphal procession: Satan compares angels serving the divine to the prisoners who pulled the chariots of triumphant generals in the classical world.

[2] *sharp'ning ... phalanx* The angels surround Satan in a crescent-shaped military formation.

[3] *ported* Held at the ready, slanted in front of them.

[4] *Ceres* Classical goddess of agriculture. Here, grain.

[5] *chaff* Husks. The useless, discarded parts of grain.

[6] *alarmed* Called to arms.

[7] *Tenerife* Mountain in the Canary Islands, reputed in Milton's time the highest in the world; *Atlas* Mountain in Morocco, and the name of the Titan from Greek myth sentenced to hold up the world as punishment for rebelling against the gods.

[8] *golden scales ... sign* Milton identifies these heavenly scales with the autumnal zodiac sign Libra, which lies between Virgo (associated with Astrea, the goddess of Justice) and Scorpio.

[9] *The latter ... flew* The scale representing fighting (desired by Satan) is lighter, and thus found wanting (cf. Daniel 5.27). The scale representing the consequences of preventing the fight weighs more, and is thus more desirable. In a similar scene from Homer's *Iliad*, Zeus balances the fates of the Trojans and the Greeks, but in that scene, it is the loser's scale that sinks down, to death.

beginning from his first revolt in Heaven, and the occasion thereof; how he drew his legions after him to the parts of the North, and there incited them to rebel with him, persuading all but only Abdiel a seraph, who in argument dissuades and opposes him, then forsakes him.

Argument to Book 6

Raphael continues to relate how Michael and Gabriel were sent forth to battle against Satan and his angels. The first fight described: Satan and his powers retire under night: he calls a council, invents devilish engines, which in the second day's fight put Michael and his angels to some disorder; but they at length pulling up mountains overwhelmed both the force and machines of Satan: yet the tumult not so ending, God on the third day sends Messiah His Son, for whom He had reserved the glory of that victory: He in the power of His Father coming to the place, and causing all His legions to stand still on either side, with His chariot and thunder driving into the midst of His enemies, pursues them unable to resist towards the wall of Heaven; which opening, they leap down with horror and confusion into the place of punishment prepared for them in the deep: Messiah returns with triumph to His Father.

Argument to Book 7

Raphael at the request of Adam relates how and wherefore this world was first created; that God, after the expelling of Satan and his angels out of Heaven, declared His pleasure to create another world and other creatures to dwell therein; sends His Son with glory and attendance of angels to perform the work of creation in six days: the angels celebrate with hymns the performance thereof, and His re-ascension into Heaven.

from Book 7

Descend from Heav'n, Urania,[1] by that name
If rightly thou art called, whose voice divine
Following, above th' Olympian hill I soar,
Above the flight of Pegasean[2] wing!
The meaning, not the name, I call: for thou
Nor of the Muses nine, nor on the top
Of old Olympus dwell'st; but, Heavenly-born,
Before the hills appeared, or fountain flowed,
Thou with eternal wisdom didst converse,
Wisdom thy sister, and with her didst play
In presence of th' Almighty Father, pleased
With thy celestial song. Up led by thee
Into the Heav'n of Heav'ns I have presumed,
An earthly guest, and drawn empyreal air,
Thy tempering: with like safety guided down
Return me to my native element:
Lest from this flying steed unreined (as once
Bellerophon,[3] though from a lower clime).° *region*
Dismounted, on the Aleian field[4] I fall,
Erroneous° there to wander, and forlorn. *directionless*
Half yet remains unsung, but narrower bound
Within the visible diurnal sphere;
Standing on earth, not rapt° above the pole, *transported*
More safe I sing with mortal voice, unchanged
To hoarse or mute, though fall'n on evil days,
On evil days though fall'n, and evil tongues;
In darkness, and with dangers compassed round,
And solitude; yet not alone, while thou
Visitest my slumbers nightly, or when morn
Purples the east: still govern thou my song,
Urania, and fit audience find, though few.
But drive far off the barbarous dissonance
Of Bacchus and his revellers, the race
Of that wild rout that tore the Thracian bard
In Rhodope, where woods and rocks had ears
To rapture, till the savage clamour drowned
Both harp and voice; nor could the Muse defend

[1] *Urania* Classical Muse of astronomy and later, of religious poetry.

[2] *Pegasean* Referring to Pegasus, winged horse of Greek myth, a symbol of poetic effort. A strike of his hoof was said to have started the sacred spring of the Muses on Mount Helicon.

[3] *Bellerophon* Rider of Pegasus, who was thrown by the winged horse when he tried to fly to the summit of Mount Olympus. Cursed because of his arrogance, he lived out the rest of his days blind and alone; no mortal dared befriend him for fear of drawing the negative attention of the gods.

[4] *Aleian field* Bellerophon's landing site.

Her son.[1] So fail not thou, who thee implores:
For thou art heav'nly, she an empty dream....

Argument to Book 8

Adam inquires concerning celestial motions, is doubtfully answered, and exhorted to search rather things more worthy of knowledge: Adam assents, and still desirous to detain Raphael, relates to him what he remembered since his own creation, his placing in Paradise, his talk with God concerning solitude and fit society, his first meeting and nuptials with Eve, his discourse with the angel thereupon; who after admonitions repeated departs.

Argument to Book 9

Satan having compassed the Earth, with meditated guile returns as a mist by night into Paradise, enters into the serpent sleeping. Adam and Eve in the morning go forth to their labours, which Eve proposes to divide in several places, each labouring apart: Adam consents not, alleging the danger, lest that enemy, of whom they were forewarned, should attempt her found alone: Eve loath to be thought not circumspect or firm enough, urges her going apart, the rather desirous to make trial of her strength; Adam at last yields; the serpent finds her alone; his subtle approach, first gazing, then speaking, with much flattery extolling Eve above all other creatures. Eve wondering to hear the serpent speak, asks how he attained to human speech and such understanding not till now; the serpent answers, that by tasting of a certain tree in the garden he attained both to speech and reason, till then void of both: Eve requires him to bring her to that tree, and finds it to be the Tree of Knowledge forbidden: the Serpent now grown bolder, with many wiles and arguments induces her at length to eat; she pleased with the taste deliberates awhile whether to impart thereof to Adam or not, at last brings him of the fruit, relates what persuaded her to eat thereof: Adam at first amazed, but perceiving her lost, resolves through vehemence of love to perish with her; and extenuating the trespass, eats also of the fruit: the effects thereof in them both; they seek to cover their nakedness, then fall to variance and accusation of one another.

Book 9

No more of talk where God or angel guest
With man, as with his friend, familiar used,
To sit indulgent, and with him partake
Rural repast; permitting him the while
Venial discourse unblamed. I now must change
Those notes to tragic; foul distrust, and breach
Disloyal on the part of man, revolt,
And disobedience: on the part of Heav'n
Now alienated, distance and distaste,
Anger and just rebuke, and judgement given,
That brought into this world a world of woe,
Sin and her shadow Death, and Misery
Death's harbinger. Sad task, yet argument
Not less but more heroic than the wrath
Of stern Achilles on his foe pursued
Thrice fugitive about Troy wall;[2] or rage
Of Turnus for Lavinia disespoused;[3]
Or Neptune's ire, or Juno's, that so long
Perplexed the Greek, and Cytherea's son:[4]
If answerable style I can obtain
Of my celestial patroness, who deigns[5]

[1] *tore the Thracian bard ... the Muse defend / Her son* These lines allude to the death of Orpheus who, disconsolate after losing his wife for the second time, wandered Thrace playing tunes so sad they made wild animals, stones, and trees weep. He met a frenzied group of Maenads, female followers of Bacchus, whose screams drowned out the song of Orpheus so that they would not be affected by it. They then tore him apart, and not even Orpheus's mother, the Muse Calliope, could stop them. It was said that his head floated down the river, still singing.

[2] *Achilles ... Troy wall* Achilles, a Greek hero at Troy, chased the Trojan hero Hector three times around the walls of Troy before bringing him down, and then dragged the corpse around the city to dispirit its defenders.

[3] *Turnus for Lavinia disespoused* Turnus, a chieftain of the Rutuli people, is the foremost suitor for the hand of Lavinia, daughter of King Latinus, when Aeneas arrives in the latter half of *The Aeneid*. Latinus chooses to grant Lavinia's hand to Aeneas. Turnus then declares war, is slaughtered, and his people are defeated.

[4] *Or Neptune's ire ... Cytherea's son* Neptune, god of the sea, tormented Odysseus ("the Greek"); Juno tormented Aeneas, the son of Venus (who is also known as Cythera, after Cyprus, her purported first home).

[5] *deigns* Chooses to give.

Her nightly visitation unimplored,
And dictates to me slumbering; or inspires
Easy my unpremeditated verse:
Since first this subject for heroic song
Pleased me long choosing, and beginning late;
Not sedulous° by nature to incite *active*
Wars, hitherto the only argument
Heroic deemed chief mastery to dissect
With long and tedious havoc fabled knights
In battles feigned; the better fortitude
Of patience and heroic martyrdom
Unsung; or to describe races and games,
Or tilting furniture,[1] emblazoned shields,
Impresas quaint,[2] caparisons° and steeds, *horse armor*
Bases and tinsel trappings, gorgeous knights
At joust and tournament; then marshalled feast
Served up in hall with sewers° and *servers*
seneschals; ° *stewards*
The skill of artifice or office mean,[3]
Not that which justly gives heroic name
To person, or to poem. Me, of these
Nor skilled nor studious, higher argument
Remains; sufficient of itself to raise
That name, unless an age too late, or cold
Climate, or years damp my intended wing
Depressed; and much they may, if all be mine,
Not hers, who brings it nightly to my ear.
The sun was sunk, and after him the star
Of Hesperus, whose office is to bring
Twilight upon the earth, short arbiter
Twixt day and night, and now from end to end
Night's hemisphere had veiled the horizon round:
When Satan, who late fled before the threats
Of Gabriel out of Eden, now improved[4]
In meditated fraud and malice, bent
On man's destruction, maugre what might hap
Of heavier on himself, fearless returned
By night he fled, and at midnight returned
From compassing° the earth; cautious of day, *circling*
Since Uriel, regent of the sun, descried
His entrance, and forewarned the cherubim
That kept their watch; thence full of anguish driven,
The space of seven continued nights he rode
With darkness; thrice the equinoctial line
He circled; four times crossed the car of night
From pole to pole, traversing each colure;[5]
On the eighth returned; and, on the coast averse° *opposite*
From entrance or cherubic watch, by stealth
Found unsuspected way. There was a place,
Now not, though sin, not time, first wrought the change,
Where Tigris,[6] at the foot of Paradise,
Into a gulf shot under ground, till part
Rose up a fountain by the tree of life:
In with the river sunk, and with it rose
Satan, involved in rising mist; then sought
Where to lie hid; sea he had searched, and land,
From Eden over Pontus and the pool
Maeotis, up beyond the river Ob;
Downward as far antarctic; and in length,
West from Orontes to the ocean barred
At Darien; thence to the land where flows
Ganges and Indus:[7] Thus the orb he roamed
With narrow search; and with inspection deep
Considered every creature, which of all
Most opportune might serve his wiles; and found
The serpent subtlest beast of all the field.
Him after long debate, irresolute
Of thoughts revolved, his final sentence° chose *decision*
Fit vessel, fittest imp° of fraud, in whom *shoot, slip*
To enter, and his dark suggestions hide
From sharpest sight: for, in the wily snake
Whatever sleights, none would suspicious mark,
As from his wit and native subtlety
Proceeding; which, in other beasts observed,

[1] *tilting furniture* Lances or heavy spears.

[2] *Impresas quaint* Complex heraldic designs.

[3] *skill of artifice or office mean* Skill of craftsman or manual worker.

[4] *improved* Strengthened, better able to carry out.

[5] *colure* Conventional cartographic dissection of the globe by two longitudinal lines, perpendicular at the poles and dividing the earth into four sections like the segments of an orange.

[6] *Tigris* Tigris River, originating in eastern Turkey and flowing southeast through Iraq to join the Euphrates River before spilling into the Persian Gulf.

[7] *Pontus* The Black Sea; *the pool / Maeotis* Sea of Azov, the northern arm of the Black Sea; *river Ob* River in Siberia, in northeastern Russia; *Orontes* River originating in northern Lebanon and flowing north through Syria and Turkey to empty into the Mediterranean Sea; *Darien* Panama, in South America; *Ganges and Indus* Ganges and Indus Rivers, the principal rivers of India.

Doubt might beget of diabolic pow'r
Active within, beyond the sense of brute.
Thus he resolved, but first from inward grief
His bursting passion into plaints thus poured:
"O Earth, how like to Heav'n, if not preferred
More justly, seat worthier of gods, as built
With second thoughts, reforming what was old!
For what God, after better, worse would build?
Terrestrial Heav'n, danced round by other Heav'ns
That shine, yet bear their bright officious lamps,
Light above light, for thee alone, as seems,
In thee concentring all their precious beams
Of sacred influence! As God in Heav'n
Is centre, yet extends to all; so thou,
Centring, receivest from all those orbs: in thee,
Not in themselves, all their known virtue appears
Productive in herb, plant, and nobler birth
Of creatures animate with gradual life
Of growth, sense, reason, all summed up in man.
With what delight could I have walked thee round,
If I could joy in aught, sweet interchange
Of hill, and valley, rivers, woods, and plains,
Now land, now sea and shores with forest crowned,
Rocks, dens, and caves! But I in none of these
Find place or refuge; and the more I see
Pleasures about me, so much more I feel
Torment within me, as from the hateful siege
Of contraries: all good to me becomes
Bane, and in Heav'n much worse would be my state.
But neither here seek I, no nor in Heav'n
To dwell, unless by mastering Heav'n's Supreme;
Nor hope to be myself less miserable
By what I seek, but others to make such
As I, though thereby worse to me redound:° *return*
For only in destroying I find ease
To my relentless thoughts; and, him destroyed,
Or won to what may work his utter loss,
For whom all this was made, all this will soon
Follow, as to him linked in weal° or woe; *prosperity*
In woe then; that destruction wide may range:
To me shall be the glory sole among
The infernal powers, in one day to have marred
What He, Almighty styled, six nights and days
Continued making; and who knows how long
Before had been contriving? Though perhaps
Not longer than since I, in one night, freed
From servitude inglorious well nigh half
Th' angelic name, and thinner left the throng
Of His adorers: He, to be avenged,
And to repair His numbers thus impaired,
Whether such virtue spent of old now failed
More angels to create, if they at least
Are His created, or, to spite us more,
Determined to advance into our room
A creature formed of earth, and him endow,
Exalted from so base original,
With Heav'nly spoils, our spoils. What He decreed,
He effected; Man He made, and for him built
Magnificent this world, and earth his seat,
Him lord pronounced; and, O indignity!
Subjected to his service angel-wings,
And flaming ministers to watch and tend
Their earthly charge: of these the vigilance
I dread; and, to elude, thus wrapt in mist
Of midnight vapour glide obscure, and pry
In every bush and brake, where hap may find
The serpent sleeping; in whose mazy folds
To hide me, and the dark intent I bring.
O foul descent! That I, who erst contended
With Gods to sit the highest, am now constrained
Into a beast; and, mixed with bestial slime,
This essence to incarnate and imbrute,
That to the height of deity aspired!
But what will not ambition and revenge
Descend to? Who aspires, must down as low
As high he soared; obnoxious, first or last,
To basest things. Revenge, at first though sweet,
Bitter ere long, back on itself recoils:
Let it; I reck° not, so it light well aimed, *care*
Since higher I fall short, on him who next
Provokes my envy, this new favourite
Of Heav'n, this man of clay, son of despite,
Whom, us the more to spite, his Maker raised
From dust: spite then with spite is best repaid."
So saying, through each thicket dank or dry,
Like a black mist low-creeping, he held on
His midnight-search, where soonest he might find
The serpent; him fast-sleeping soon he found
In labyrinth of many a round self-rolled,
His head the midst, well stored with subtle wiles:

Not yet in horrid shade or dismal den,
Nor nocent° yet; but, on the grassy herb, *harmful*
Fearless unfeared he slept: in at his mouth
The devil entered; and his brutal sense,
In heart or head, possessing, soon inspired
With act intelligential; but his sleep
Disturbed not, waiting close th' approach of morn.
Now, when as sacred light began to dawn
In Eden on the humid flowers, that breathed
Their morning incense, when all things that breathe
From the Earth's great altar send up silent praise
To the Creator, and His nostrils fill
With grateful smell, forth came the human pair,
And joined their vocal worship to the choir
Of creatures wanting voice; that done, partake
The season prime for sweetest scents and airs:
Then commune, how that day they best may ply
Their growing work: for much their work out-grew
The hands' dispatch of two gardening so wide,
And Eve first to her husband thus began:
"Adam, well may we labour still to dress
This garden, still to tend plant, herb, and flower,
Our pleasant task enjoined; but, till more hands
Aid us, the work under our labour grows
Luxurious by restraint; what we by day
Lop overgrown, or prune, or prop, or bind,
One night or two with wanton growth derides
Tending to wild. Thou therefore now advise,
Or hear what to my mind first thoughts present:
Let us divide our labours; thou, where choice
Leads thee, or where most needs, whether to wind
The woodbine round this arbour, or direct
The clasping ivy where to climb; while I,
In yonder spring of roses intermixed
With myrtle, find what to redress till noon:
For, while so near each other thus all day
Our task we choose, what wonder if so near
Looks intervene and smiles, or object new
Casual discourse draw on; which intermits
Our day's work, brought to little, though begun
Early, and th' hour of supper comes unearned?"
To whom mild answer Adam thus returned:
"Sole Eve, associate sole, to me beyond
Compare above all living creatures dear!
Well hast thou motioned, well thy thoughts
employed,
How we might best fulfil the work which here
God hath assigned us; nor of me shalt pass
Unpraised: for nothing lovelier can be found
In woman, than to study household good,
And good works in her husband to promote.
Yet not so strictly hath our Lord imposed
Labour, as to debar° us when we need *constrain*
Refreshment, whether food, or talk between,
Food of the mind, or this sweet intercourse
Of looks and smiles; for smiles from Reason flow,
To brute denied, and are of Love the food;
Love, not the lowest end of human life.
For not to irksome toil, but to delight,
He made us, and delight to reason joined.
These paths and bowers doubt not but our joint hands
Will keep from wilderness with ease, as wide
As we need walk, till younger hands ere long
Assist us; But, if much converse perhaps
Thee satiate, to short absence I could yield:
For solitude sometimes is best society,
And short retirement urges sweet return.
But other doubt possesses me, lest harm
Befall thee severed from me; for thou knowest
What hath been warned us, what malicious foe
Envying our happiness, and of his own
Despairing, seeks to work us woe and shame
By sly assault; and somewhere nigh at hand
Watches, no doubt, with greedy hope to find
His wish and best advantage, us asunder;
Hopeless to circumvent us joined, where each
To other speedy aid might lend at need:
Whether his first design be to withdraw
Our fealty from God, or to disturb
Conjugal love, than which perhaps no bliss
Enjoyed by us excites his envy more;
Or this, or worse, leave not the faithful side
That gave thee being, still shades thee, and protects.
The wife, where danger or dishonour lurks,
Safest and seemliest by her husband stays,
Who guards her, or with her the worst endures."
To whom the virgin majesty of Eve,
As one who loves, and some unkindness meets,

With sweet austere composure thus replied:
"Offspring of Heaven and Earth, and all Earth's lord!
That such an enemy we have, who seeks
Our ruin, both by thee informed I learn,
And from the parting Angel[1] over-heard,
As in a shady nook I stood behind,
Just then returned at shut of evening flowers.
But, that thou shouldst my firmness therefore doubt
To God or thee, because we have a foe
May tempt it, I expected not to hear.
His violence thou fearest not, being such
As we, not capable of death or pain,
Can either not receive, or can repel.
His fraud is then thy fear; which plain infers
Thy equal fear, that my firm faith and love
Can by his fraud be shaken or seduced;
Thoughts, which how found they harbour in thy breast,
Adam, mis-thought of her to thee so dear?"
To whom with healing words Adam replied:
"Daughter of God and Man, immortal Eve!
For such thou art; from sin and blame entire:
Not diffident of thee do I dissuade
Thy absence from my sight, but to avoid
Th' attempt itself, intended by our foe.
For he who tempts, though in vain, at least asperses[2]
The tempted with dishonour foul; supposed
Not incorruptible of faith, not proof
Against temptation: Thou thyself with scorn
And anger wouldst resent the offered wrong,
Though ineffectual found: misdeem not then,
If such affront I labour to avert
From thee alone, which on us both at once
The enemy, though bold, will hardly dare;
Or daring, first on me th' assault shall light.
Nor thou his malice and false guile contemn;
Subtle he needs must be, who could seduce
Angels; nor think superfluous others' aid.
I, from the influence of thy looks, receive
Access in every virtue; in thy sight
More wise, more watchful, stronger, if need were
Of outward strength; while shame, thou looking on,
Shame to be overcome or over-reached,
Would utmost vigour raise, and raised unite.
Why shouldst not thou like sense within thee feel
When I am present, and thy trial choose
With me, best witness of thy virtue tried?"
So spake domestic Adam in his care
And matrimonial love; but Eve, who thought
Less attributed to her faith sincere,
Thus her reply with accent sweet renewed:
"If this be our condition, thus to dwell
In narrow circuit straitened by a foe,
Subtle or violent, we not endued
Single with like defence, wherever met;
How are we happy, still in fear of harm?
But harm precedes not sin: only our foe,
Tempting, affronts us with his foul esteem
Of our integrity: his foul esteem
Sticks no dishonour on our front, but turns
Foul on himself; then wherefore shunned or feared
By us? Who rather double honour gain
From his surmise proved false; find peace within,
Favour from Heav'n, our witness, from the event.
And what is faith, love, virtue, unassayed
Alone, without exterior help sustained?
Let us not then suspect our happy state
Left so imperfect by the Maker wise,
As not secure to single or combined.
Frail is our happiness, if this be so,
And Eden were no Eden, thus exposed."
To whom thus Adam fervently replied.
"O woman, best are all things as the will
Of God ordained them: His creating hand
Nothing imperfect or deficient left
Of all that he created, much less Man,
Or aught that might his happy state secure,
Secure from outward force; within himself
The danger lies, yet lies within his power:
Against his will he can receive no harm.
But God left free the Will; for what obeys
Reason, is free; and Reason He made right,
But bid her well beware, and still erect;[3]

[1] *the parting Angel* Raphael, the angel who visits Adam and Eve in Books Four through Eight, and warns them of the danger they are about to face.

[2] *asperses* Bespatters, besprinkles, here someone's reputation.

[3] *bid her ... still erect* Advised her to be careful, and to remain vigilant.

Lest, by some fair-appearing good surprised,
She dictate false; and mis-inform the will
To do what God expressly hath forbid.
Not then mistrust, but tender love, enjoins,
That I should mind thee oft; and mind thou me.
Firm we subsist, yet possible to swerve;
Since Reason not impossibly may meet
Some specious object by the foe suborned,
And fall into deception unaware,
Not keeping strictest watch, as she was warned.
Seek not temptation then, which to avoid
Were better, and most likely if from me
Thou sever trial will come unsought.
Wouldst thou approve thy constancy, approve
First thy obedience; the other who can know,
Not seeing thee attempted, who attest?
But, if thou think, trial unsought may find
Us both securer than thus warned thou seemest,
Go; for thy stay, not free, absents thee more;
Go in thy native innocence, rely
On what thou hast of virtue; summon all!
For God towards thee hath done his part, do thine."
So spake the patriarch of mankind; but Eve
Persisted; yet submiss, though last, replied:
"With thy permission then, and thus forewarned
Chiefly by what thy own last reasoning words
Touched only; that our trial, when least sought,
May find us both perhaps far less prepared,
The willinger I go, nor much expect
A foe so proud will first the weaker seek;
So bent, the more shall shame him his repulse."
Thus saying, from her husband's hand her hand
Soft she withdrew; and, like a wood-nymph light,
Oread or dryad, or of Delia's train,[1]
Betook her to the groves; but Delia's self
In gait surpassed, and goddess-like deport,° *composure*
Though not as she with bow and quiver armed,
But with such gard'ning tools as art yet rude,
Guiltless of fire, had formed, or angels brought.
To Pales, or Pomona, thus adorned,
Likest she seemed, Pomona when she fled
Vertumnus,[2] or to Ceres in her prime,
Yet virgin of Proserpina from Jove.
Her long with ardent look his eye pursued
Delighted, but desiring more her stay.
Oft he to her his charge of quick return
Repeated; she to him as oft engaged
To be returned by noon amid the bower,
And all things in best order to invite
Noontide repast, or afternoon's repose.
O much deceived, much failing, hapless Eve,
Of thy presumed return! Event perverse!
Thou never from that hour in Paradise
Foundst either sweet repast, or sound repose;
Such ambush, hid among sweet flowers and shades,
Waited with hellish rancour imminent
To intercept thy way, or send thee back
Despoiled of innocence, of faith, of bliss!
For now, and since first break of dawn, the fiend,
Mere serpent in appearance, forth was come;
And on his quest, where likeliest he might find
The only two of mankind, but in them
The whole included race, his purposed prey.
In bower and field he sought, where any tuft
Of grove or garden-plot more pleasant lay,
Their tendance, or plantation for delight;
By fountain or by shady rivulet
He sought them both, but wished his hap might find
Eve separate; he wished, but not with hope
Of what so seldom chanced; when to his wish,
Beyond his hope, Eve separate he spies,
Veiled in a cloud of fragrance, where she stood,
Half spied, so thick the roses blushing round
About her glowed, oft stooping to support
Each flower of slender stalk, whose head, though gay
Carnation, purple, azure, or specked with gold,
Hung drooping unsustained; them she upstays
Gently with myrtle band, mindless the while
Herself, though fairest unsupported flower,
From her best prop so far, and storm so nigh.
Nearer he drew, and many a walk traversed
Of stateliest covert, cedar, pine, or palm;
Then voluble and bold, now hid, now seen,
Among thick-woven arborets, and flowers

[1] *Oread ... dryad* Nature spirits from Greek mythology; *Delia* Roman virgin goddess of the moon and the hunt.

[2] *Pales ... Pomona ... Vertumnus* Goddess of pastures, goddess of orchards, and god of gardens and the change of seasons, respectively.

Imbordered on each bank, the hand of Eve:
Spot more delicious than those gardens feigned
Or of revived Adonis,[1] or renowned
Alcinous,[2] host of old Laertes' son;
Or that, not mystick, where the sapient king
Held dalliance with his fair Egyptian spouse.[3]
Much he the place admired, the person more.
As one who long in populous city pent,
Where houses thick and sewers annoy the air,
Forth issuing on a summer's morn, to breathe
Among the pleasant villages and farms
Adjoined, from each thing met conceives delight;
The smell of grain, or tedded grass, or kine,[4]
Or dairy, each rural sight, each rural sound;
If chance, with nymph-like step, fair virgin pass,
What pleasing seemed, for her now pleases more;
She most, and in her look sums all delight:
Such pleasure took the serpent to behold
This flowery plat,° the sweet recess of Eve *plot, patch of ground*
Thus early, thus alone: Her heav'nly form
Angelic, but more soft, and feminine,
Her graceful innocence, her every air
Of gesture, or least action, overawed
His malice, and with rapine sweet bereaved
His fierceness of the fierce intent it brought:
That space the evil one abstracted stood
From his own evil, and for the time remained
Stupidly good; of enmity disarmed,
Of guile, of hate, of envy, of revenge:
But the hot Hell that always in him burns,
Though in mid Heav'n, soon ended his delight,
And tortures him now more, the more he sees
Of pleasure, not for him ordained: then soon
Fierce hate he recollects, and all his thoughts
Of mischief, gratulating, thus excites:

"Thoughts, whither have ye led me! With what sweet
Compulsion thus transported, to forget
What hither brought us! Hate, not love; nor hope
Of Paradise for Hell, hope here to taste
Of pleasure; but all pleasure to destroy,
Save what is in destroying; other joy
To me is lost. Then, let me not let pass
Occasion which now smiles; behold alone
The woman, opportune to all attempts,
Her husband, for I view far round, not nigh,
Whose higher intellectual more I shun,
And strength, of courage haughty, and of limb
Heroic built, though of terrestrial mould;
Foe not informidable! Exempt from wound,
I not; so much hath Hell debased, and pain
Enfeebled me, to what I was in Heav'n.
She fair, divinely fair, fit love for Gods!
Not terrible, though terror be in love
And beauty, not approached by stronger hate,
Hate stronger, under show of love well feigned;
The way which to her ruin now I tend."

So spake the enemy of mankind, enclosed
In serpent, inmate bad, and toward Eve
Addressed his way: not with indented wave,
Prone on the ground, as since; but on his rear,
Circular base of rising folds, that towered
Fold above fold, a surging maze! His head
Crested aloft, and carbuncle[5] his eyes;
With burnished neck of verdant gold, erect
Amidst his circling spires, that on the grass
Floated redundant: pleasing was his shape
And lovely; never since of serpent-kind
Lovelier, not those that in Illyria changed,
Hermione and Cadmus, or the god
In Epidaurus; nor to which transformed
Ammonian Jove, or Capitoline, was seen;
He with Olympias; this with her who bore
Scipio, the height of Rome.[6] With tract oblique

[1] *Adonis* Beloved of Venus, goddess of love. He was slain by a boar but was turned to a flower. He became a cult figure. His "gardens" were miniature gardens, symbols, says Erasmus, of evanescence.

[2] *Alcinous* Alcinous, King of the Phaeacians, owned a fabulous garden visited by Odysseus, son of Laertes, in Homer's *Odyssey*.

[3] *the sapient king ... spouse* Solomon the Wise and the daughter of the King of Egypt (see 1 Kings).

[4] *tedded* Mown, as for hay; *kine* Cattle.

[5] *carbuncle* Ruby.

[6] *those that in Illyria ... Rome Hermione and Cadmus* Citizens of Illyria changed into serpents: he for killing a sacred snake, she out of love for Cadmus; *the God / In Epidaurus* Aesculapius, god of healing, who appeared at his temple in Epidaurus in the form of a snake; *Ammonian Jove, or Capitoline* Both names refer to Jove, but different instances of his shape-shifting to impregnate (continued)

At first, as one who sought access, but feared
To interrupt, sidelong he works his way.
As when a ship, by skilful steersmen wrought
Nigh river's mouth or foreland, where the wind
Veers oft, as oft so steers, and shifts her sail:
So varied he, and of his tortuous train
Curled many a wanton wreath in sight of Eve,
To lure her eye; she, busied, heard the sound
Of rustling leaves, but minded not, as used
To such disport before her through the field,
From every beast; more duteous at her call,
Than at Circean call the herd disguised.[1]
He, bolder now, uncalled before her stood,
But as in gaze admiring: oft he bowed
His turret crest, and sleek enamelled neck,
Fawning; and licked the ground whereon she trod.
His gentle dumb expression turned at length
The eye of Eve to mark his play; he, glad
Of her attention gained, with serpent-tongue
Organic, or impulse of vocal air,
His fraudulent temptation thus began:
"Wonder not, sov'reign mistress, if perhaps
Thou canst, who art sole wonder! Much less arm
Thy looks, the heaven of mildness, with disdain,
Displeased that I approach thee thus, and gaze
Insatiate; I thus single; nor have feared
Thy awful brow, more awful thus retired.
Fairest resemblance of thy Maker fair,
Thee all things living gaze on, all things thine
By gift, and thy celestial beauty adore
With ravishment beheld! There best beheld,
Where universally admired; but here
In this enclosure wild, these beasts among,
Beholders rude, and shallow to discern
Half what in thee is fair, one man except,
Who sees thee? And what is one? Who should be seen
A goddess among gods, adored and served
By angels numberless, thy daily train."

So glozed the tempter, and his proem tuned:[2]
Into the heart of Eve his words made way,
Though at the voice much marvelling; at length,
Not unamazed, she thus in answer spake:
"What may this mean? Language of man pronounced
By tongue of brute, and human sense expressed?
The first, at least, of these I thought denied
To beasts; whom God, on their creation-day,
Created mute to all articulate sound:
The latter I demur; for in their looks
Much reason, and in their actions, oft appears.
Thee, serpent, subtlest beast of all the field
I knew, but not with human voice endued;
Redouble then this miracle, and say,
How cam'st thou speakable of mute, and how
To me so friendly grown above the rest
Of brutal kind, that daily are in sight?
Say, for such wonder claims attention due."
To whom the guileful tempter thus replied,
"Empress of this fair world, resplendent Eve!
Easy to me it is to tell thee all
What thou commandest; and right thou shouldst be obeyed:
I was at first as other beasts that graze
The trodden herb, of abject thoughts and low,
As was my food; nor aught but food discerned
Or sex, and apprehended nothing high:
Till, on a day roving the field, I chanced
A goodly tree far distant to behold
Loaden with fruit of fairest colours mixed,
Ruddy and gold: I nearer drew to gaze;
When from the boughs a savoury odour blown,
Grateful to appetite, more pleased my sense
Than smell of sweetest fennel, or the teats
Of ewe or goat dropping with milk at even,
Unsucked of lamb or kid, that tend their play.
To satisfy the sharp desire I had
Of tasting those fair apples, I resolved
Not to defer; hunger and thirst at once,
Powerful persuaders, quickened at the scent
Of that alluring fruit, urged me so keen.
About the mossy trunk I wound me soon;
For, high from ground, the branches would require

women with famous conqueror children; *Olympias ... Scipio* Olympias was Alexander the Great's mother, and Scipio was a great Roman conqueror-hero. Both men were supposed to have been begotten by Jove in the form of a snake.

[1] *Circean call the herd disguised* Circe was a sorceress who transformed men into animals.

[2] *glozed* Flattered; *proem* Prelude or introduction.

Thy utmost reach or Adam's: Round the tree
All other beasts that saw, with like desire
Longing and envying stood, but could not reach.
Amid the tree now got, where plenty hung
Tempting so nigh, to pluck and eat my fill
I spared not; for, such pleasure till that hour,
At feed or fountain, never had I found.
Sated at length, ere long I might perceive
Strange alteration in me, to degree
Of reason in my inward powers; and speech
Wanted not long; though to this shape retained.
Thenceforth to speculations high or deep
I turned my thoughts, and with capacious mind
Considered all things visible in Heav'n,
Or Earth, or middle; all things fair and good:
But all that fair and good in thy divine
Semblance, and in thy beauty's heav'nly ray,
United I beheld; no fair to thine
Equivalent or second, which compelled
Me thus, though importune perhaps, to come
And gaze, and worship thee of right declared
Sov'reign of creatures, universal dame!"
    So talked the spirited sly snake; and Eve,
Yet more amazed, unwary thus replied,
    "Serpent, thy overpraising leaves in doubt
The virtue of that fruit, in thee first proved:
But say, where grows the tree? From hence how far?
For many are the trees of God that grow
In Paradise, and various, yet unknown
To us; in such abundance lies our choice,
As leaves a greater store of fruit untouched,
Still hanging incorruptible, till men
Grow up to their provision, and more hands
Help to disburden nature of her birth."
    To whom the wily adder, blithe and glad:
"Empress, the way is ready, and not long;
Beyond a row of myrtles, on a flat,
Fast by a fountain, one small thicket past
Of blowing myrrh and balm: if thou accept
My conduct, I can bring thee thither soon."
    "Lead then," said Eve. He, leading, swiftly rolled
In tangles, and made intricate seem straight,
To mischief swift. Hope elevates, and joy
Brightens his crest; as when a wandering fire,
Compact of unctuous vapour, which the night
Condenses, and the cold environs round,
Kindled through agitation to a flame,
Which oft, they say, some evil spirit attends,
Hovering and blazing with delusive light,
Misleads th' amazed night-wanderer from his way
To bogs and mires, and oft through pond or pool;
There swallowed up and lost, from succour far.
So glistered the dire snake, and into fraud
Led Eve, our credulous mother, to the tree
Of prohibition, root of all our woe;
Which when she saw, thus to her guide she spake:
    "Serpent, we might have spared our coming
        hither,
Fruitless to me, though fruit be here to excess,
The credit of whose virtue rest with thee;
Wondrous indeed, if cause of such effects.
But of this tree we may not taste nor touch;
God so commanded, and left that command
Sole daughter of His voice; the rest, we live
Law to ourselves; our reason is our law."
    To whom the tempter guilefully replied:
"Indeed! Hath God then said that of the fruit
Of all these garden-trees ye shall not eat,
Yet lords declared of all in earth or air?"
    To whom thus Eve, yet sinless: "Of the fruit
Of each tree in the garden we may eat;
But of the fruit of this fair tree amidst
The garden, God hath said, 'ye shall not eat
Thereof, nor shall ye touch it, lest ye die.'"
    She scarce had said, though brief, when now more
        bold
The tempter, but with show of zeal and love
To Man, and indignation at his wrong,
New part puts on; and, as to passion moved,
Fluctuates disturbed, yet comely and in act
Raised, as of some great matter to begin.
As when of old some orator renowned,
In Athens or free Rome, where eloquence
Flourished, since mute to some great cause addressed,
Stood in himself collected; while each part,
Motion, each act, won audience ere the tongue;
Sometimes in height began, as no delay
Of preface brooking, through his zeal of right:
So standing, moving, or to height up grown,
The tempter, all impassioned, thus began:

"O sacred, wise, and wisdom-giving plant,
Mother of science!° Now I feel thy power *knowledge*
Within me clear; not only to discern
Things in their causes, but to trace the ways
Of highest agents, deemed however wise.
Queen of this universe! Do not believe
Those rigid threats of death: ye shall not die:
How should you? By the fruit? It gives you life
To knowledge; by the threat'ner? Look on me,
Me, who have touched and tasted; yet both live,
And life more perfect have attained than fate
Meant me, by vent'ring higher than my lot.
Shall that be shut to Man, which to the beast
Is open? Or will God incense His ire
For such a petty trespass and not praise
Rather your dauntless virtue, whom the pain
Of death denounced, whatever thing death be,
Deterred not from achieving what might lead
To happier life, knowledge of good and evil;
Of good, how just? Of evil, if what is evil
Be real, why not known, since easier shunned?
God therefore cannot hurt ye, and be just;
Not just, not God; not feared then, nor obeyed:
Your fear itself of death removes the fear.
Why then was this forbid? Why, but to awe;
Why, but to keep ye low and ignorant,
His worshippers? He knows that in the day
Ye eat thereof, your eyes that seem so clear,
Yet are but dim, shall perfectly be then
Opened and cleared, and ye shall be as gods,
Knowing both good and evil, as they know.
That ye shall be as gods, since I as man,
Internal man, is but proportion meet;
I, of brute, human; ye, of human, gods.
So ye shall die perhaps, by putting off
Human, to put on gods; death to be wished,
Though threatened, which no worse than this can bring.
And what are gods, that man may not become
As they, participating godlike food?
The gods are first, and that advantage use
On our belief, that all from them proceeds:
I question it; for this fair earth I see,
Warmed by the sun, producing every kind;
Them, nothing: if they all things, who enclosed
Knowledge of good and evil in this tree,
That whoso eats thereof, forthwith attains
Wisdom without their leave? And wherein lies
The offence, that man should thus attain to know?
What can your knowledge hurt Him, or this tree
Impart against His will, if all be His?
Or is it envy? And can envy dwell
In heav'nly breasts? These, these, and many more
Causes import your need of this fair fruit.
Goddess human, reach then, and freely taste!"

He ended; and his words, replete with guile,
Into her heart too easy entrance won:
Fixed on the fruit she gazed, which to behold
Might tempt alone; and in her ears the sound
Yet rung of his persuasive words, impregned
With reason, to her seeming, and with truth:
Meanwhile the hour of noon drew on, and waked
An eager appetite, raised by the smell
So savoury of that fruit, which with desire,
Inclinable now grown to touch or taste,
Solicited her longing eye; yet first
Pausing a while, thus to herself she mused:

"Great are thy virtues, doubtless, best of fruits,
Though kept from man, and worthy to be admired;
Whose taste, too long forborne, at first assay
Gave elocution to the mute, and taught
The tongue not made for speech to speak thy praise:
Thy praise He also, who forbids thy use,
Conceals not from us, naming thee the tree
Of knowledge, knowledge both of good and evil;
Forbids us then to taste! But His forbidding
Commends thee more, while it infers the good
By thee communicated, and our want:
For good unknown sure is not had; or, had
And yet unknown, is as not had at all.
In plain then, what forbids He but to know,
Forbids us good, forbids us to be wise?
Such prohibitions bind not. But, if death
Bind us with after-bands, what profits then
Our inward freedom? In the day we eat
Of this fair fruit, our doom is, we shall die!
How dies the serpent? He hath eaten and lives,
And knows, and speaks, and reasons, and discerns,
Irrational till then. For us alone
Was death invented? Or to us denied

This intellectual food, for beasts reserved?
For beasts it seems: yet that one beast which first
Hath tasted envies not, but brings with joy
The good befallen him, author unsuspect,
Friendly to man, far from deceit or guile.
What fear I then? Rather, what know to fear
Under this ignorance of good and evil,
Of God or death, of law or penalty?
Here grows the cure of all, this fruit divine,
Fair to the eye, inviting to the taste,
Of virtue to make wise: what hinders then
To reach, and feed at once both body and mind?"
So saying, her rash hand in evil hour
Forth reaching to the fruit, she plucked, she ate!
Earth felt the wound; and nature from her seat,
Sighing through all her works, gave signs of woe,
That all was lost. Back to the thicket slunk
The guilty serpent; and well might; for Eve,
Intent now wholly on her taste, nought else
Regarded; such delight till then, as seemed,
In fruit she never tasted, whether true
Or fancied so, through expectation high
Of knowledge; nor was godhead from her thought.
Greedily she engorged without restraint,
And knew not eating death. Satiate at length,
And heightened as with wine, jocund and boon,
Thus to herself she pleasingly began:
"O sov'reign, virtuous, precious of all trees
In Paradise! Of operation blest
To sapience, hitherto obscured, infamed.
And thy fair fruit let hang, as to no end
Created; but henceforth my early care,
Not without song, each morning, and due praise,
Shall tend thee, and the fertile burden ease
Of thy full branches offered free to all;
Till, dieted by thee, I grow mature
In knowledge, as the gods, who all things know;
Though others envy what they cannot give:
For, had the gift been theirs, it had not here
Thus grown. Experience, next, to thee I owe,
Best guide; not following thee, I had remained
In ignorance; thou openest wisdom's way,
And givest access, though secret she retire.
And I perhaps am secret: Heav'n is high,
High, and remote to see from thence distinct
Each thing on Earth; and other care perhaps
May have diverted from continual watch
Our great Forbidder, safe with all His spies
About Him. But to Adam in what sort
Shall I appear? Shall I to him make known
As yet my change, and give him to partake
Full happiness with me, or rather not,
But keeps the odds of knowledge in my power
Without copartner? So to add what wants
In female sex, the more to draw his love,
And render me more equal; and perhaps,
A thing not undesirable, sometime
Superior; for, inferior, who is free?
This may be well: but what if God have seen,
And death ensue? Then I shall be no more!
And Adam, wedded to another Eve,
Shall live with her enjoying, I extinct;
A death to think! Confirmed then I resolve,
Adam shall share with me in bliss or woe:
So dear I love him, that with him all deaths
I could endure, without him live no life."
So saying, from the tree her step she turned;
But first low reverence done, as to the power
That dwelt within, whose presence had infused
Into the plant sciential sap, derived
From nectar, drink of Gods. Adam the while,
Waiting desirous her return, had wove
Of choicest flowers a garland, to adorn
Her tresses, and her rural labours crown;
As reapers oft are wont their harvest-queen.
Great joy he promised to his thoughts, and new
Solace in her return, so long delayed:
Yet oft his heart, divine of something ill,
Misgave him; he the faltering measure felt;
And forth to meet her went, the way she took
That morn when first they parted: by the tree
Of knowledge he must pass; there he her met,
Scarce from the tree returning; in her hand
A bough of fairest fruit, that downy smiled,
New gathered, and ambrosial smell diffused.
To him she hasted; in her face excuse
Came prologue, and apology too prompt;
Which, with bland words at will, she thus addressed:
"Hast thou not wondered, Adam, at my stay?
Thee I have missed, and thought it long, deprived

Thy presence; agony of love till now
Not felt, nor shall be twice; for never more
Mean I to try, what rash untried I sought,
The pain of absence from thy sight. But strange
Hath been the cause, and wonderful to hear:
This tree is not, as we are told, a tree
Of danger tasted, nor to evil unknown
Op'ning the way, but of divine effect
To open eyes, and make them gods who taste;
And hath been tasted such. The serpent wise,
Or not restrained as we, or not obeying,
Hath eaten of the fruit; and is become,
Not dead, as we are threatened, but thenceforth
Endued with human voice and human sense,
Reasoning to admiration; and with me
Persuasively hath so prevailed, that I
Have also tasted, and have also found
Th' effects to correspond; opener mine eyes,
Dim erst, dilated spirits, ampler heart,
And growing up to godhead; which for thee
Chiefly I sought, without thee can despise.
For bliss, as thou hast part, to me is bliss;
Tedious, unshared with thee, and odious soon.
Thou therefore also taste, that equal lot
May join us, equal joy, as equal love;
Lest, thou not tasting, different degree
Disjoin us, and I then too late renounce
Deity for thee, when fate will not permit."
Thus Eve with countenance blithe her story told;
But in her cheek distemper flushing glowed.
On th' other side Adam, soon as he heard
The fatal trespass done by Eve, amazed,
Astonied° stood and blank, while horror chill *astonished*
Ran through his veins, and all his joints relaxed;
From his slack hand the garland wreathed for Eve
Down dropt, and all the faded roses shed:
Speechless he stood and pale, till thus at length
First to himself he inward silence broke.
"O fairest of creation, last and best
Of all God's works, creature in whom excelled
Whatever can to sight or thought be formed,
Holy, divine, good, amiable, or sweet!
How art thou lost! How on a sudden lost,
Defaced, deflowered, and now to death devote!
Rather, how hast thou yielded to transgress
The strict forbiddance, how to violate
The sacred fruit forbidden! Some cursed fraud
Of enemy hath beguiled thee, yet unknown,
And me with thee hath ruined; for with thee
Certain my resolution is to die:
How can I live without thee! How forego
Thy sweet converse, and love so dearly joined,
To live again in these wild woods forlorn!
Should God create another Eve, and I
Another rib afford, yet loss of thee
Would never from my heart; no. No, I feel
The link of nature draw me: flesh of flesh,
Bone of my bone thou art, and from thy state
Mine never shall be parted, bliss or woe."
So having said, as one from sad dismay
Recomforted, and after thoughts disturbed
Submitting to what seemed remediless,
Thus in calm mood his words to Eve he turned.
"Bold deed thou hast presumed, advent'rous Eve,
And peril great provoked, who thus hast dared,
Had it been only coveting to eye
That sacred fruit, sacred to abstinence,
Much more to taste it under ban to touch.
But past who can recall, or done undo?
Not God omnipotent, nor fate; yet so
Perhaps thou shalt not die, perhaps the fact
Is not so heinous now, foretasted fruit,
Profaned first by the serpent, by him first
Made common, and unhallowed, ere our taste;
Nor yet on him found deadly; yet he lives;
Lives, as thou saidst, and gains to live, as man,
Higher degree of life; inducement strong
To us, as likely tasting to attain
Proportional ascent; which cannot be
But to be gods, or angels, demi-gods.
Nor can I think that God, Creator wise,
Though threat'ning, will in earnest so destroy
Us His prime creatures, dignified so high,
Set over all His works; which in our fall,
For us created, needs with us must fail,
Dependent made; so God shall uncreate,
Be frustrate, do, undo, and labour lose;
Not well conceived of God, who, though His power
Creation could repeat, yet would be loth
Us to abolish, lest the adversary

Triumph, and say; 'Fickle their state whom God
Most favours; who can please Him long? Me first
He ruined, now Mankind; whom will He next?'
Matter of scorn, not to be given the foe.
However I with thee have fixed my lot,
Certain to undergo like doom: If death
Consort with thee, death is to me as life;
So forcible within my heart I feel
The bond of nature draw me to my own;
My own in thee, for what thou art is mine;
Our state cannot be severed; we are one,
One flesh; to lose thee were to lose myself."
So Adam; and thus Eve to him replied:
"O glorious trial of exceeding love,
Illustrious evidence, example high!
Engaging me to emulate; but, short
Of thy perfection, how shall I attain,
Adam, from whose dear side I boast me sprung,
And gladly of our union hear thee speak,
One heart, one soul in both; whereof good proof
This day affords, declaring thee resolved,
Rather than death, or aught than death more dread,
Shall separate us, linked in love so dear,
To undergo with me one guilt, one crime,
If any be, of tasting this fair fruit;
Whose virtue for of good still good proceeds,
Direct, or by occasion, hath presented
This happy trial of thy love, which else
So eminently never had been known?
Were it I thought death menaced would ensue
This my attempt, I would sustain alone
The worst, and not persuade thee, rather die
Deserted, than oblige thee with a fact
Pernicious to thy peace; chiefly assured
Remarkably so late of thy so true,
So faithful, love unequalled: but I feel
Far otherwise th' event; not death, but life
Augmented, opened eyes, new hopes, new joys,
Taste so divine, that what of sweet before
Hath touched my sense, flat seems to this, and harsh.
On my experience, Adam, freely taste,
And fear of death deliver to the winds."
So saying, she embraced him, and for joy
Tenderly wept; much won, that he his love
Had so ennobled, as of choice to incur
Divine displeasure for her sake, or death.
In recompense for such compliance bad
Such recompense best merits from the bough
She gave him of that fair enticing fruit
With liberal hand: he scrupled° not to eat, *hesitated*
Against his better knowledge; not deceived,
But fondly overcome with female charm.
Earth trembled from her entrails, as again
In pangs; and Nature gave a second groan;
Sky loured; and, muttering thunder, some sad drops
Wept at completing of the mortal sin
Original: while Adam took no thought,
Eating his fill; nor Eve to iterate
Her former trespass feared, the more to soothe
Him with her loved society; that now,
As with new wine intoxicated both,
They swim in mirth, and fancy that they feel
Divinity within them breeding wings,
Wherewith to scorn the earth: but that false fruit
Far other operation first displayed,
Carnal desire inflaming; he on Eve
Began to cast lascivious eyes; she him
As wantonly repaid; in lust they burn:
Till Adam thus 'gan° Eve to dalliance move: *began*
"Eve, now I see thou art exact of taste,
And elegant, of sapience no small part;
Since to each meaning savour we apply,
And palate call judicious; I the praise
Yield thee, so well this day thou hast purveyed.
Much pleasure we have lost, while we abstained
From this delightful fruit, nor known till now
True relish, tasting; if such pleasure be
In things to us forbidden, it might be wished,
For this one tree had been forbidden ten.
But come, so well refreshed, now let us play,
As meet is, after such delicious fare;
For never did thy beauty, since the day
I saw thee first and wedded thee, adorned
With all perfections, so inflame my sense
With ardour to enjoy thee, fairer now
Than ever; bounty of this virtuous tree!"
So said he, and forbore not glance or toy
Of amorous intent; well understood
Of Eve, whose eye darted contagious fire.
Her hand he seized; and to a shady bank,

Thick over-head with verdant roof embowered,
He led her nothing loth; flowers were the couch,
Pansies, and violets, and asphodel,
And hyacinth; Earth's freshest softest lap.
There they their fill of love and love's disport
Took largely, of their mutual guilt the seal,
The solace of their sin; till dewy sleep
Oppressed them, wearied with their amorous play,
Soon as the force of that fallacious fruit,
That with exhilarating vapour bland
About their spirits had played, and inmost powers
Made err, was now exhaled; and grosser sleep,
Bred of unkindly fumes, with conscious dreams
Encumbered, now had left them; up they rose
As from unrest; and, each the other viewing,
Soon found their eyes how opened, and their minds
How darkened; innocence, that as a veil
Had shadowed them from knowing ill, was gone;
Just confidence, and native righteousness,
And honour, from about them, naked left
To guilty shame; he covered, but his robe
Uncovered more. So rose the Danite strong,
Herculean Samson, from the harlot-lap
Of Philistean Delilah, and waked
Shorn of his strength.[1] They destitute and bare
Of all their virtue, silent, and in face
Confounded, long they sat, as strucken mute:
Till Adam, though not less than Eve abashed,
At length gave utterance to these words constrained:
"O Eve, in evil hour thou didst give ear
To that false worm,° of whomsoever taught *snake*
To counterfeit Man's voice; true in our fall,
False in our promised rising; since our eyes
Opened we find indeed, and find we know
Both good and evil; good lost, and evil got;
Bad fruit of knowledge, if this be to know;
Which leaves us naked thus, of honour void,
Of innocence, of faith, of purity,
Our wonted ornaments now soiled and stained,
And in our faces evident the signs
Of foul concupiscence;° whence evil store; *lust*
Even shame, the last of evils; of the first
Be sure then. How shall I behold the face
Henceforth of God or angel, erst with joy
And rapture so oft beheld? Those heav'nly shapes
Will dazzle now this earthly with their blaze
Insufferably bright. O! Might I here
In solitude live savage; in some glade
Obscured, where highest woods, impenetrable
To star or sun-light, spread their umbrage° broad *shadows*
And brown as evening: Cover me, ye pines!
Ye cedars, with innumerable boughs
Hide me, where I may never see them more!—
But let us now, as in bad plight, devise
What best may for the present serve to hide
The parts of each from other, that seem most
To shame obnoxious, and unseemliest seen;
Some tree, whose broad smooth leaves together sewed,
And girded on our loins, may cover round
Those middle parts; that this newcomer, Shame,
There sit not, and reproach us as unclean."
So counselled he, and both together went
Into the thickest wood; there soon they chose
The fig tree; not that kind for fruit renowned,
But such as at this day, to Indians known,
In Malabar or Decan spreads her arms
Branching so broad and long, that in the ground
The bended twigs take root, and daughters grow
About the mother tree, a pillared shade
High overarched, and echoing walks between:
There oft the Indian herdsman, shunning heat,
Shelters in cool, and tends his pasturing herds
At loop-holes cut through thickest shade: Those leaves
They gathered, broad as Amazonian targe;° *shield*
And, with what skill they had, together sewed,
To gird their waist; vain covering, if to hide
Their guilt and dreaded shame! O, how unlike
To that first naked glory! Such of late
Columbus found the American, so girt
With feathered cincture;° naked else, and wild *belt*
Among the trees on isles and woody shores.
Thus fenced, and, as they thought, their shame in part
Covered, but not at rest or ease of mind,
They sat them down to weep; nor only tears
Rained at their eyes, but high winds worse within
Began to rise, high passions, anger, hate,
Mistrust, suspicion, discord; and shook sore

[1] *So rose the … of his strength* The Biblical hero Samson, whose strength lay in his hair, was undone when it was shorn by his wife, the Philistine Delilah (Judges 16).

Their inward state of mind, calm region once
And full of peace, now tossed and turbulent:
For understanding ruled not, and the will
Heard not her lore; both in subjection now
To sensual appetite, who from beneath
Usurping over sov'reign reason claimed
Superior sway. From thus distempered breast,
Adam, estranged in look and altered style,
Speech intermitted thus to Eve renewed:
"Would thou hadst hearkened to my words, and stayed
With me, as I besought thee, when that strange
Desire of wandering, this unhappy morn,
I know not whence possessed thee; we had° then *would have*
Remained still happy; not, as now, despoiled
Of all our good; shamed, naked, miserable!
Let none henceforth seek needless cause to approve
The faith they owe; when earnestly they seek
Such proof, conclude, they then begin to fail."
To whom, soon moved with touch of blame, thus Eve:
"What words have passed thy lips, Adam severe!
Imputest thou that to my default, or will
Of wandering, as thou call'st it, which who knows
But might as ill have happened thou being by,
Or to thyself perhaps? Hadst thou been there,
Or here the attempt, thou couldst not have discerned
Fraud in the serpent, speaking as he spake;
No ground of enmity between us known,
Why he should mean me ill, or seek to harm.
Was I to have never parted from thy side?
As good have grown there still a lifeless rib.
Being as I am, why didst not thou, the head,
Command me absolutely not to go,
Going into such danger, as thou saidst?
Too facile then, thou didst not much gainsay;
Nay, didst permit, approve, and fair dismiss.
Hadst thou been firm and fixed in thy dissent,
Neither had I transgressed, nor thou with me."
To whom, then first incensed, Adam replied:
"Is this the love, is this the recompense
Of mine to thee, ingrateful Eve! Expressed
Immutable, when thou wert lost, not I;
Who might have lived, and joyed immortal bliss,
Yet willingly chose rather death with thee?
And am I now upbraided as the cause
Of thy transgressing? Not enough severe,
It seems, in thy restraint: what could I more
I warned thee, I admonished thee, foretold
The danger, and the lurking enemy
That lay in wait; beyond this, had been force;
And force upon free will hath here no place.
But confidence then bore thee on; secure
Either to meet no danger, or to find
Matter of glorious trial; and perhaps
I also erred, in overmuch admiring
What seemed in thee so perfect, that I thought
No evil durst attempt thee; but I rue
The error now, which is become my crime,
And thou the accuser. Thus it shall befall
Him, who, to worth in women overtrusting,
Lets her will rule: restraint she will not brook;° *accept*
And, left to herself, if evil thence ensue,
She first his weak indulgence will accuse."
Thus they in mutual accusation spent
The fruitless hours, but neither self-condemning;
And of their vain contest appeared no end.

The End of the Ninth Book

Argument to Book 10

Man's transgression known, the guardian angels forsake Paradise, and return up to Heaven to approve their vigilance, and are approved, God declaring that the entrance of Satan could not be by them prevented. He sends His Son to judge the transgressors, who descends and gives sentence accordingly; then in pity clothes them both, and reascends. Sin and Death sitting till then at the gates of Hell, by wondrous sympathy feeling the success of Satan in this new world, and the sin by Man there committed, resolve to sit no longer confined in Hell, but to follow Satan their sire up to the place of Man: to make the way easier from Hell to this world to and fro, they pave a broad highway or bridge over Chaos, according to the track that Satan first made; then preparing for Earth, they meet him proud of his success returning to Hell; their mutual gratulation. Satan arrives at Pandemonium, in full assembly relates with boasting his success against man; instead of applause is entertained with a general hiss by all his audience, transformed with himself also suddenly into serpents, according to his doom given in Paradise; then deluded with show of the forbidden Tree springing up before them, they greedily reaching to take of the fruit, chew dust and bitter ashes. The proceedings of Sin and Death; God foretells the final victory of His Son over them, and the renewing of all things; but for the present commands His angels to make several alterations in the heavens and elements. Adam more and more perceiving his fallen condition heavily bewails, rejects the condolement of Eve; she persists and at length appeases him: then to evade the curse likely to fall on their offspring, proposes to Adam violent ways, which he approves not, but conceiving better hope, puts her in mind of the late promise made them, that her seed should be revenged on the serpent, and exhorts her with him to seek peace of the offended Deity, by repentance and supplication.

Book 10

Meanwhile the heinous and despiteful act
Of Satan done in Paradise, and how
He, in the serpent, had perverted Eve,
Her husband she, to taste the fatal fruit,
Was known in Heaven; for what can 'scape the eye
Of God all-seeing, or deceive his heart
Omniscient, who in all things wise and just,
Hindered not Satan to attempt the mind
Of man, with strength entire, and free will armed,
Complete to have discovered and repulsed
Whatever wiles of foe or seeming friend.
For still° they knew, and ought to have still remembered — *always*
The high injunction not to taste that fruit,
Whoever tempted; which they not obeying,
Incurred, what could they less, the penalty,
And manifold in sin, deserved to fall.
Up into Heaven from Paradise in haste
Th' angelic guards ascended, mute and sad
For man, for of his state by this° they knew, — *this time*
Much wond'ring how the subtle fiend had stolen
Entrance unseen. Soon as th' unwelcome news
From Earth arrived at Heaven gate, displeased
All were who heard, dim sadness did not spare
That time celestial visages, yet mixed
With pity, violated not their bliss.
About the new-arrived, in multitudes
Th' ethereal people ran, to hear and know
How all befell: they towards the throne supreme
Accountable made haste to make appear
With righteous plea, their utmost vigilance,[1]
And easily approved;° when the most high — *accepted*
Eternal Father from his secret cloud,
Amidst in thunder uttered thus his voice.
"Assembled angels, and ye powers returned
From unsuccessful charge, be not dismayed,
Nor troubled at these tidings from the earth,
Which your sincerest care could not prevent,
Foretold so lately what would come to pass,
When first this tempter crossed the gulf from Hell.
I told ye then he should prevail and speed° — *succeed*
On his bad errand, man should be seduced
And flattered out of all, believing lies
Against his Maker; no decree of mine
Concurring to necessitate his fall,
Or touch with lightest moment[2] of impulse
His free will, to her own inclining left
In even scale. But fallen he is, and now
What rests° but that the mortal sentence pass — *remains*
On his transgression, death denounced° that day, — *proclaimed*
Which he presumes already vain° and void, — *in vain*
Because not yet inflicted, as he feared,
By some immediate stroke; but soon shall find
Forbearance no acquaintance[3] ere day end.
Justice shall not return as bounty scorned.[4]
But whom send I to judge them? Whom but thee
Vicegerent[5] Son, to thee I have transferred
All judgment whether in Heaven, or Earth, or Hell.
Easy it might be seen that I intend

[1] *They towards ... vigilance* The "accountable" angels hasten to plea that they had exercised the utmost vigilance in guarding Eden.

[2] *moment* Small weight or counterweight, to tip the balance.

[3] *Forbearance no acquaintance* Proverbial; a debt has not been repaid just because payment has not yet been requested.

[4] *Justice ... scorned* My justice shall not be scorned like my generosity (bounty) has been.

[5] *Vicegerent* Exercising the powers of a deputy to a sovereign.

Mercy colleague with justice, sending thee
Man's friend his mediator, his designed
Both ransom and redeemer voluntary,
And destined man himself to judge man fallen."
So spake the Father, and unfolding bright
Toward the right hand his glory, on the Son
Blazed forth unclouded deity; he full
Resplendent all his Father manifest
Expressed, and thus divinely answered mild.
"Father Eternal, thine is to decree,
Mine both in Heaven and Earth to do thy will
Supreme, that thou in me thy Son beloved
May'st ever rest well pleased. I go to judge
On Earth these thy transgressors, but thou know'st,
Whoever judged, the worst on me must light,° *fall*
When time shall be, for so I undertook
Before thee; and not repenting, this obtain
Of right, that I may mitigate their doom
On me derived,[1] yet I shall temper so
Justice with mercy, as may illustrate most° *best*
Them fully satisfied, and thee appease.
Attendance none shall need, nor train,° where none *retinue*
Are to behold the judgment, but the judged,
Those two; the third best absent is condemned,
Convict° by flight, and rebel to all law; *Convicted*
Conviction to the serpent none belongs."
Thus saying, from his radiant seat he rose
Of high collateral[2] glory: him Thrones and Powers,
Princedoms, and Dominations ministrant
Accompanied to Heaven gate, from whence
Eden and all the coast° in prospect lay. *surrounding area*
Down he descended strait;° the speed of gods *immediately*
Time counts not,[3] though with swiftest minutes winged.
Now was the sun in western cadence° low *sinking*
From noon, and gentle airs due at their hour
To fan the earth now waked, and usher in
The evening cool, when he from wrath more cool
Came the mild judge and intercessor both
To sentence man: the voice of God they heard
Now walking in the garden, by soft winds
Brought to their ears, while day declined; they heard,
And from his presence hid themselves among
The thickest trees, both man and wife, till God
Approaching, thus to Adam called aloud.
"Where art thou Adam, wont with joy to meet
My coming seen far off? I miss thee here,
Not pleased, thus entertained with solitude,
Where obvious duty erewhile appeared unsought:
Or come I less conspicuous, or what change
Absents thee, or what chance detains? Come forth."
He came, and with him Eve, more loath, though first
To offend, discount'nanced both, and discomposed;
Love was not in their looks, either to God
Or to each other, but apparent guilt,
And shame, and perturbation, and despair,
Anger, and obstinacy, and hate, and guile.
Whence Adam falt'ring long, thus answered brief:
"I heard thee in the garden, and of thy voice
Afraid, being naked, hid myself." To whom
The gracious judge without revile° replied. *reproach*
"My voice thou oft hast heard, and hast not feared,
But still rejoiced, how is it now become
So dreadful to thee? That thou art naked, who
Hath told thee? Hast thou eaten of the tree
Whereof I gave thee charge thou should'st not eat?"
To whom thus Adam sore beset replied.
"O Heaven! In evil strait this day I stand
Before my judge, either to undergo
Myself the total crime, or to accuse
My other self, the partner of my life;
Whose failing, while her faith to me remains,
I should conceal, and not expose to blame
By my complaint; but strict necessity
Subdues me, and calamitous constraint
Lest on my head both sin and punishment,
However insupportable, be all
Devolved;[4] though should I hold my peace, yet thou
Would'st easily detect what I conceal.
This woman whom thou mad'st to be my help,
And gav'st me as thy perfect gift, so good,
So fit, so acceptable, so divine,
That from her hand I could suspect no ill,

[1] *On me derived* I.e., their eventual punishment will be largely diverted onto the redeemer Son.

[2] *collateral* Side-by-side: one of Milton's many ways of expressing the complex and (apparently to him) not quite equivalent relationship between Father and Son.

[3] *Time counts not* I.e., their speed is so fast it cannot be measured.

[4] *Devolved* Caused to fall upon.

And what she did, whatever in itself,
Her doing seemed to justify the deed;
She gave me of the tree, and I did eat."[1]
To whom the sov'reign presence thus replied.
"Was she thy God, that her thou did'st obey
Before his voice, or was she made thy guide,
Superior, or but equal, that to her
Thou did'st resign thy manhood, and the place
Wherein God set thee above her made of thee,
And for thee, whose perfection far excelled
Hers in all real dignity: adorned
She was indeed, and lovely to attract
Thy love, not thy subjection, and her gifts
Were such as under government well seemed,
Unseemly to bear rule, which was thy part° *role*
And person,° hadst thou known thyself aright." *character*
So having said, he thus to Eve in few:° *few words*
"Say woman, what is this which thou hast done?"
To whom sad Eve with shame nigh overwhelmed,
Confessing soon, yet not before her judge
Bold or loquacious, thus abashed replied:
"The serpent me beguiled and I did eat."[2]
Which when the Lord God heard, without delay
To judgment he proceeded on th' accused
Serpent though brute,° unable to transfer *animal*
The guilt on him who made him instrument
Of mischief, and polluted from the end° *purpose*
Of his creation; justly then accursed,
As vitiated in nature: more to know
Concerned not man (since he no further knew)
Nor altered his offence; yet God at last
To Satan first in sin his doom applied
Though in mysterious terms,[3] judged as then best:
And on the serpent thus his curse let fall.
"Because thou hast done this, thou art accurst
Above all cattle, each beast of the field;
Upon thy belly groveling thou shalt go,
And dust shalt eat all the days of thy life.
Between thee and the woman I will put
Enmity, and between thine and her seed;
Her seed shall bruise thy head, thou bruise his heel."
So spake this oracle, then verified
When Jesus son of Mary second Eve,
Saw Satan fall like lightning down from heaven,[4]
Prince of the Air; then rising from his grave
Spoiled Principalities and Powers, triumphed
In open show, and with ascension bright
Captivity led captive through the air,
The realm itself of Satan long usurped,
Whom he shall tread at last under our feet;
Even he who now foretold his fatal bruise,
And to the woman thus his sentence turned.
"Thy sorrow I will greatly multiply
By thy conception; children thou shalt bring
In sorrow forth, and to thy husband's will
Thine shall submit, he over thee shall rule."
On Adam last thus judgment he pronounced.
"Because thou hast hearkened to the voice of thy wife,
And eaten of the tree concerning which
I charged thee, saying, 'Thou shalt not eat thereof,'
Cursed is the ground for thy sake, thou in sorrow
Shalt eat thereof all the days of thy life;
Thorns also and thistles it shall bring thee forth
Unbid, and thou shalt eat th' herb of th' field,
In the sweat of thy face shalt thou eat bread,
Till thou return unto the ground, for thou
Out of the ground wast taken, know thy birth,
For dust thou art, and shalt to dust return."
So judged he man, both Judge and Saviour sent,
And th' instant stroke of death denounced that day
Removed far off; then pitying how they stood
Before him naked to the air, that now
Must suffer change, disdained not to begin
Thenceforth the form of servant to assume,
As when he washed his servants' feet,[5] so now
As father of his family he clad
Their nakedness with skins of beasts, or slain,
Or as the snake with youthful coat repaid;
And thought not much to clothe his enemies:
Nor he their outward only with the skins
Of beasts, but inward nakedness, much more
Opprobrious, with his robe of righteousness,
Arraying covered from his Father's sight.
To him with swift ascent he up returned,

[1] *O Heaven ... eat* Adam's reply expands greatly on Genesis 3.12.

[2] *The serpent ... eat* Eve's reply reproduces that in Genesis 3.13.

[3] *mysterious terms* Mystical or typological (prefigurative) terms.

[4] *Saw Satan ... from heaven* See Luke 10.18–19.

[5] *As when ... servants' feet* See John 13.5.

Into his blissful bosom reassumed
In glory as of old, to him appeased
All, though all-knowing, what had past with man
Recounted, mixing intercession sweet.
Meanwhile ere thus was sinned and judged on Earth,
Within the gates of Hell sat Sin and Death,
In counterview within the gates, that now
Stood open wide, belching outrageous flame
Far into Chaos, since the fiend passed through,
Sin opening, who thus now to Death began.
"O Son, why sit we here each other viewing
Idly, while Satan our great author thrives
In other worlds, and happier seat provides
For us his offspring dear? It cannot be
But that success attends him; if mishap,
Ere this he had returned, with fury driven
By his avengers, since no place like this
Can fit his punishment, or their revenge.
Methinks I feel new strength within me rise,
Wings growing, and dominion given me large
Beyond this deep; whatever draws me on,
Or sympathy, or some connatural force
Powerful at greatest distance to unite
With secret amity things of like kind
By secretest conveyance. Thou my shade
Inseparable must with me along:
For Death from Sin no power can separate.
But lest the difficulty of passing back
Stay his return perhaps over this gulf
Impassable, impervious, let us try
Advent'rous work, yet to thy power and mine
Not unagreeable, to found a path
Over this main[1] from Hell to that new world
Where Satan now prevails, a monument
Of merit high to all th' infernal host,
Easing their passage hence, for intercourse,
Or transmigration,° as their lot shall lead. *migration*
Nor can I miss the way, so strongly drawn
By this new felt attraction and instinct."
Whom thus the meager shadow answered soon.
"Go whither fate and inclination strong
Leads thee, I shall not lag behind, nor err
The way, thou leading, such a scent I draw
Of carnage, prey innumerable, and taste
The savour of death from all things there that live:
Nor shall I to the work thou enterprisest
Be wanting, but afford thee equal aid."
So saying, with delight he snuffed the smell
Of mortal change on Earth. As when a flock
Of ravenous fowl, though many a league remote,
Against the day of battle, to a field,
Where armies lie encamped, come flying, lured
With scent of living carcasses designed
For death, the following day, in bloody fight.
So scented the grim feature,° and upturned *form*
His nostril wide into the murky air,
Sagacious[2] of his quarry from so far.
Then both from out Hell gates into the waste
Wide anarchy of Chaos damp and dark
Flew diverse, and with power (their power was great)
Hovering upon the waters; what they met
Solid or slimy, as in raging sea
Tossed up and down, together crowded drove
From each side shoaling towards the mouth of Hell.
As when two polar winds blowing adverse
Upon the Cronian° Sea, together drive *Arctic*
Mountains of ice, that stop th' imagined way
Beyond Petsora eastward, to the rich
Cathaian Coast.[3] The aggregated soil
Death with his mace petrific, cold and dry,
As with a trident smote, and fixed as firm
As Delos[4] floating once; the rest his look
Bound with Gorgonian rigor[5] not to move,
And with asphaltic slime; broad as the gate,
Deep to the roots of Hell the gathered beach° *stony ridge*
They fastened, and the mole° immense wrought on *causeway*
Over the foaming deep high arched, a bridge
Of length prodigious joining to the wall
Immovable of this now fenceless world
Forfeit to Death; from hence a passage broad,

[1] *main* The "ocean" of Chaos.

[2] *Sagacious* Acutely aware of (by scent).

[3] *imagined way ... Coast* Northwest passage between Siberia (site of the Pechora river) and China.

[4] *Delos* Fabled floating island in the Aegean Sea, chained in place by Neptune.

[5] *Gorgonian rigor* In Greek myth, the beautiful but serpent-haired Medusa, one of the mythical Gorgons, turned those who gazed on her into stone.

Smooth, easy, inoffensive down to Hell.
So, if great things to small may be compared,
Xerxes, the liberty of Greece to yoke,
From Susa his Memnonian palace high
Came to the sea, and over Hellespont
Bridging his way, Europe with Asia joined,
And scourged with many a stroke th' indignant waves.[1]
Now had they brought the work by wondrous art
Pontifical,[2] a ridge of pendent rock
Over the vexed abyss, following the track
Of Satan, to the self same place where he
First lighted from his wing, and landed safe
From out of Chaos to the outside bare
Of this round world: with pins of adamant
And chains they made all fast, too fast they made
And durable; and now in little space
The confines met of empyrean Heaven
And of this world, and on the left hand Hell
With long reach interposed; three sev'ral ways
In sight, to each of these three places led.
And now their way to Earth they had descried,
To Paradise first tending, when behold
Satan in likeness of an angel bright
Betwixt the Centaur and the Scorpion steering
His zenith,[3] while the sun in Aries rose:
Disguised he came, but those his children dear
Their parent soon discerned, though in disguise.
He after Eve seduced, unminded slunk
Into the wood fast by, and changing shape
To observe the sequel, saw his guileful act
By Eve, though all unweeting, seconded
Upon her husband, saw their shame that sought
Vain covertures; but when he saw descend
The Son of God to judge them terrified
He fled, not hoping to escape, but shun
The present, fearing guilty what his wrath
Might suddenly inflict; that past, returned
By night, and listening where the hapless pair
Sat in their sad discourse, and various plaint,
Thence gathered his own doom, which understood
Not instant, but of future time. With joy
And tidings fraught, to Hell he now returned,
And at the brink of Chaos, near the foot
Of this new wondrous pontifice, unhoped
Met who to meet him came, his offspring dear.
Great joy was at their meeting, and at sight
Of that stupendous bridge his joy increased.
Long he admiring stood, till Sin, his fair
Enchanting daughter, thus the silence broke.
"O Parent, these are thy magnific deeds,
Thy trophies, which thou viewest as not thine own,
Thou art their author and prime architect:
For I no sooner in my heart divined,
My heart, which by a secret harmony
Still moves with thine, joined in connection sweet,
That thou on Earth hadst prospered, which thy looks
Now also evidence, but straight I felt
Though distant from the worlds between, yet felt
That I must after thee with this thy son;
Such fatal consequence unites us three:
Hell could no longer hold us in her bounds,
Nor this unvoyageable gulf obscure
Detain from following thy illustrious track.
Thou hast achieved our liberty, confined
Within Hell gates till now, thou us empow'red
To fortify thus far, and overlay
With this portentous bridge the dark abyss.
Thine now is all this world, thy virtue hath won
What thy hands builded not, thy wisdom gained
With odds what war hath lost, and fully avenged
Our foil in Heaven; here thou shalt monarch reign,
There didst not; there let him still victor sway,
As battle hath adjudged, from this new world
Retiring, by his own doom alienated,
And henceforth monarchy with thee divide
Of all things parted by th' empyreal bounds,
His quadrature,[4] from thy orbicular world,
Or try thee now more dang'rous to his throne."
Whom thus the Prince of Darkness answered glad.

[1] *Bridging his way … waves* In order to invade Greece, Xerxes of Persia created a bridge across the Hellespont by laying his ships side by side; when the sea destroyed the bridge he ordered that the waters be whipped.

[2] *Pontifical* Bridge-building (but punning on the Papal title "Pontifex").

[3] *Satan … zenith* Satan had entered the serpent by its mouth; he appears in the sky exiting the tail of the constellation of the serpent Anguis, located between the archer Sagittarius (Milton's "Centaur") and Scorpio.

[4] *quadrature* See Revelation 21.16, where Heaven is described as laid out "four-square."

"Fair daughter, and thou son and grandchild both,
High proof ye now have given to be the race
Of Satan (for I glory in the name,[1]
Antagonist of Heaven's Almighty King)
Amply have merited of me, of all
Th' infernal empire, that so near Heaven's door
Triumphal with triumphal act have met,
Mine with this glorious work, and made one realm
Hell and this world, one realm, one continent
Of easy thoroughfare. Therefore while I
Descend through darkness, on your road with ease
To my associate powers, them to acquaint
With these successes, and with them rejoice,
You two this way, among these numerous orbs
All yours, right down to Paradise descend;
There dwell and reign in bliss, thence on the Earth
Dominion exercise and in the air,
Chiefly on man, sole lord of all declared,
Him first make sure your thrall, and lastly kill.
My substitutes I send ye, and create
Plenipotent° on Earth, of matchless might *Fully powerful*
Issuing from me: on your joint vigor now
My hold of this new kingdom all depends,
Through Sin to Death exposed by my exploit.
If your joint power prevails, th' affairs of Hell
No detriment need fear, go and be strong."
So saying he dismissed them,[2] they with speed
Their course through thickest constellations held
Spreading their bane: the blasted stars looked wan
And planets, planet-struck, real eclipse
Then suffered. Th' other way Satan went down
The causey° to hell gate: on either side *causeway*
Disparted Chaos overbuilt exclaimed,
And with rebounding surge the bars assailed,
That scorned his indignation: through the gate,
Wide open and unguarded, Satan passed,
And all about found desolate; for those
Appointed to sit there had left their charge,
Flown to the upper world; the rest were all
Far to the inland retired, about the walls
Of Pandemonium; city and proud seat
Of Lucifer, so by allusion called
Of that bright star to Satan paragoned;° *compared*
There kept their watch the legions, while the grand
In council sat, solicitous° what chance *anxious to discover*
Might intercept their emperor sent; so he
Departing gave command, and they observed.
As when the Tartar from his Russian foe,
By Astracan,[3] over the snowy plains,
Retires; or Bactrin Sophy,[4] from the horns
Of Turkish crescent, leaves all waste beyond
The realm of Aladule, in his retreat
To Tauris or Casbeen:[5] So these, the late
Heav'n-banished host, left desert utmost Hell[6]
Many a dark league, reduced in careful watch
Round their metropolis; and now expecting
Each hour their great adventurer, from the search
Of foreign worlds: he through the midst unmarked,
In show plebeian angel militant
Of lowest order, passed; and from the door
Of that plutonian[7] hall, invisible
Ascended his high throne; which, under state° *canopy*
Of richest texture spread, at th' upper end
Was placed in regal lustre. Down a while
He sat, and round about him saw unseen:
At last, as from a cloud, his fulgent° head *shining*
And shape star-bright appeared, or brighter; clad
With what permissive glory since his fall
Was left him, or false glitter. All amazed
At that so sudden blaze the Stygian throng
Bent their aspect, and whom they wished beheld,
Their mighty chief returned: loud was th' acclaim:
Forth rushed in haste the great consulting peers,
Raised from their dark divan, and with like joy
Congratulant approached him; who with hand
Silence and with these words attention won:
"Thrones, dominations, princedoms, virtues, powers;
For in possession such, not only of right,
I call ye, and declare ye now; returned
Successful beyond hope, to lead ye forth
Triumphant out of this infernal pit

[1] *name* "Satan" means "adversary" in Hebrew.

[2] *them* Sin and Death, now on their way to Earth.

[3] *Astracan* Modern Astrakhan, a city in the southwest of Russia near the Caspian Sea, originally founded by the Tartars.

[4] *Bactrin Sophy* Shah of Persia.

[5] *Aladule* Armenia; *Tauris ... Casbeen* Cities in northern Iran.

[6] *left desert utmost Hell* Left the outermost reaches of Hell deserted.

[7] *plutonian* Both richly decorated and morbid, deathly; after Pluto, god of the underworld.

Abominable, accursed, the house of woe,
And dungeon of our tyrant: now possess,
As lords, a spacious world, to our native Heaven
Little inferior, by my adventure hard
With peril great achieved. Long were to tell
What I have done; what suffered; with what pain
Voyaged th' unreal, vast, unbounded deep
Of horrible confusion; over which
By Sin and Death a broad way now is paved,
To expedite your glorious march; but I
Toiled out my uncouth passage, forced to ride
Th' intractable abyss, plunged in the womb
Of unoriginal night and Chaos wild;
That, jealous of their secrets, fiercely opposed
My journey strange, with clamorous uproar
Protesting fate supreme; thence how I found
The new created world, which fame in Heav'n
Long had foretold, a fabric wonderful
Of absolute perfection, therein Man
Placed in a Paradise, by our exile
Made happy. Him by fraud I have seduced
From his Creator; and, the more to increase
Your wonder, with an apple; He, thereat
Offended worth your laughter, hath given up
Both His beloved Man, and all His world,
To Sin and Death a prey, and so to us,
Without our hazard, labour, or alarm;
To range in, and to dwell, and over man
To rule, as over all He should have ruled.
True is, me also He hath judged, or rather
Me not, but the brute serpent in whose shape
Man I deceived: that which to me belongs,
Is enmity which He will put between
Me and mankind; I am to bruise his heel;
His seed, when is not set, shall bruise my head:[1]
A world who would not purchase with a bruise,
Or much more grievous pain? Ye have the account
Of my performance: What remains, ye gods,
But up, and enter now into full bliss?"
So having said, a while he stood, expecting
Their universal shout, and high applause,
To fill his ear; when, contrary, he hears
On all sides, from innumerable tongues,
A dismal universal hiss, the sound
Of public scorn; he wondered, but not long
Had leisure, wondering at himself now more,
His visage drawn he felt to sharp and spare;
His arms clung to his ribs; his legs entwining
Each other, till supplanted down he fell
A monstrous serpent on his belly prone,
Reluctant, but in vain; a greater power
Now ruled him, punished in the shape he sinned,
According to his doom: he would have spoke,
But hiss for hiss returnèd with forkèd tongue
To forkèd tongue; for now were all transformed
Alike, to serpents all, as accessories
To his bold riot: dreadful was the din
Of hissing through the hall, thick swarming now
With complicated monsters head and tail,
Scorpion, and asp, and amphisbaena dire,
Cerastes horned, hydrus, and elops drear,
And dipsas (not so thick swarmed once the soil
Bedropt with blood of gorgon, or the isle
Ophiusa);[2] but still greatest he the midst,
Now dragon grown, larger than whom the sun
Engendered in the Pythian Vale or slime,
Huge python, and his power no less he seemed
Above the rest still to retain; they all
Him followed, issuing forth to th' open field,
Where all yet left of that revolted rout,
Heav'n-fall'n, in station stood or just array;
Sublime with expectation when to see
In triumph issuing forth their glorious chief;
They saw, but other sight instead: a crowd
Of ugly serpents; horror on them fell,
And horrid sympathy; for, what they saw,
They felt themselves, now changing; down their arms,
Down fell both spear and shield; down they as fast;
And the dire hiss renewed, and the dire form
Catched by contagion; like in punishment,
As in their crime. Thus was the applause they meant
Turned to exploding hiss, triumph to shame

[1] *I am to bruise … bruise my head* See Genesis 3.15.

[2] *amphisbaena … Ophiusa* *amphisbaena* Mythical serpent with a head at each end of its body; *Cerastes* Legendary four-horned serpent; *hydrus* Hydra, venomous many-headed serpent of classical myth; *elops* Mythical sea snake; *dipsas* Snake whose venom reputedly caused ravenous thirst; *not so / thick swarmed … blood of gorgon* When Perseus slew Medusa, the Gorgon, snakes sprang from every drop of her blood that touched the earth; *Ophiusa* Literally "land of snakes," the island of Rhodes, renowned in legend for its many snakes.

Cast on themselves from their own mouths. There
 stood
A grove hard by, sprung up with this their change,
His will Who reigns above, to aggravate
Their penance, laden with fair fruit, like that
Which grew in Paradise, the bait of Eve
Used by the tempter: on that prospect strange
Their earnest eyes they fixed, imagining
For one forbidden tree a multitude
Now ris'n, to work them further woe or shame;
Yet, parched with scalding thirst and hunger fierce,
Though to delude them sent, could not abstain;
But on they rolled in heaps, and, up the trees
Climbing, sat thicker than the snaky locks
That curled Megaera:[1] greedily they plucked
The fruitage fair to sight, like that which grew
Near that bituminous lake where Sodom flamed;
This more delusive, not the touch, but taste
Deceived; they, fondly thinking to allay
Their appetite with gust, instead of fruit
Chewed bitter ashes, which the offended taste
With spattering noise rejected: oft they assayed,
Hunger and thirst constraining; drugged as oft,
With hatefullest disrelish writhed their jaws,
With soot and cinders filled; so oft they fell
Into the same illusion, not as man
Whom they triumphed once lapsed. Thus were they
 plagued
And worn with famine, long and ceaseless hiss,
Till their lost shape, permitted, they resumed;
Yearly enjoined, some say, to undergo,
This annual humbling certain numbered days,
To dash their pride, and joy, for man seduced.
However some tradition they dispersed
Among the heathen of their purchase got,
And fabled how the serpent, whom they called
Ophion with Eurynome, the wide-
Encroaching Eve perhaps, had first the rule
Of high Olympus, thence by Saturn driven
And Ops, ere yet Dictæan Jove was born.[2]

Meanwhile in Paradise the hellish pair
Too soon arrived, Sin there in power before,
Once actual, now in body, and to dwell
Habitual habitant; behind her Death
Close following pace for pace, not mounted yet
On his pale horse:[3] to whom Sin thus began.
 "Second of Satan sprung, all conquering Death,
What thinkst thou of our empire now, though earned
With travail difficult, not better far
Than still at Hell's dark threshold to have sat watch,
Unnamed, undreaded, and thyself half starved?"
 Whom thus the Sin-born Monster answered soon.
"To me, who with eternal famine pine,
Alike is Hell, or Paradise, or Heaven,
There best, where most with ravin° I may meet; *prey*
Which here, though plenteous, all too little seems
To stuff this maw, this vast unhide-bound corpse."
 To whom th' incestuous mother thus replied.
"Thou therefore on these herbs, and fruits, and flowers
Feed first, on each beast next, and fish, and fowl,
No homely morsels, and whatever thing
The scythe of Time mows down, devour unspared,
Till I in man residing through the race,
His thoughts, his looks, words, actions all infect,
And season him thy last and sweetest prey."
This said, they both betook them several ways,
Both to destroy, or unimmortal make
All kinds, and for destruction to mature
Sooner or later; which th' Almighty seeing,
From his transcendent seat the saints among,
To those bright orders uttered thus his voice.
 "See with what heat these dogs of Hell advance
To waste and havoc yonder world, which I
So fair and good created, and had still
Kept in that state, had not the folly of man
Let in these wasteful Furies, who impute
Folly to me, so doth the Prince of Hell
And his adherents, that with so much ease
I suffer them to enter and possess
A place so heavenly, and conniving seem

[1] *Megaera* One of the classical Furies, avenging underworld goddesses.

[2] *Ophion with … was born* To explain their annual metamorphoses (Milton suggests), the devils spread stories in the ancient world of primordial serpents, such as Ophion (from the Greek word for serpent), who with Eurynome (daughter of the Ocean) ruled Olympus before being driven out by Saturn and his wife Rhea (Ops), parents to Jove (Zeus), who was raised in a cave in Crete near Mount Dicte.

[3] *pale horse* See Revelation 6.8.

To gratify my scornful enemies,
That laugh, as if transported with some fit
Of passion, I to them had quitted° all, *handed over*
At random yielded up to their misrule;
And know not that I called and drew them thither
My Hell-hounds, to lick up the draff and filth
Which man's polluting sin with taint hath shed
On what was pure, till crammed and gorged, nigh burst
With sucked and glutted offal, at one sling
Of thy victorious arm, well-pleasing Son,
Both Sin, and Death, and yawning grave at last
Through Chaos hurled, obstruct the mouth of Hell
Forever, and seal up his ravenous jaws.
Then Heaven and Earth renewed shall be made pure
To sanctity that shall receive no stain:
Till then the curse pronounced on both precedes."
He ended, and the heavenly audience loud
Sung halleluja, as the sound of seas,
Through multitude that sung: "Just are thy ways,
Righteous are thy decrees on all thy works;
Who can extenuate thee? Next, to the Son,
Destined restorer of mankind, by whom
New Heaven and Earth shall to the ages rise,
Or down from Heaven descend." Such was their song,
While the Creator calling forth by name
His mighty angels gave them several charge,
As sorted best with present things. The sun
Had first his precept so to move, so shine,
As might affect the Earth with cold and heat
Scarce tolerable, and from the north to call
Decrepit winter, from the south to bring
Solstitial summer's heat. To the blank° moon *pale*
Her office they prescribed, to th' other five
Their planetary motions and aspects
In sextile, square, and trine, and opposite,[1]
Of noxious efficacy, and when to join
In synod unbenign, and taught the fixed
Their influence malignant when to shower,
Which of them rising with the sun, or falling,
Should prove tempestuous: to the winds they set
Their corners, when with bluster to confound
Sea, air, and shore, the thunder when to roll
With terror through the dark aerial hall.
Some say he bid his angels turn askance
The poles of Earth twice ten degrees and more
From the sun's axle; they with labour pushed
Oblique the centric globe: some say the sun
Was bid turn reins from th' equinoctial road
Like distant breadth to Taurus with the seven
Atlantic sisters, and the Spartan Twins
Up to the Tropic Crab; thence down amain
By Leo and the Virgin and the Scales,
As deep as Capricorn, to bring in change
Of seasons to each clime;[2] else had the spring
Perpetual smiled on Earth with vernant flowers,
Equal in days and nights, except to those
Beyond the polar circles; to them day
Had unbenighted shone, while the low sun
To recompense his distance, in their sight
Had rounded still th' horizon, and not known
Or east or west, which had forbid the snow
From cold Estotiland, and south as far
Beneath Magellan.[3] At that tasted fruit
The sun, as from Thyestean banquet,[4] turned
His course intended; else how had the world
Inhabited, though sinless, more than now,
Avoided pinching cold and scorching heat?
These changes in the heavens, though slow, produced
Like change on sea and land, sideral[5] blast,

[1] *sextile ... opposite* Terms for the four "aspects" or degrees of planetary position: respectively, 60°, 90°, 120°, and 180°. In astrology, planetary aspect shaped planetary influence: as a consequence of the Fall, the angels teach the planets and stars how to exert malignant influences, including weather.

[2] *Some say ... each clime* Seasonal change is caused by the tilt of the earth's axis about 23° ("twice ten degrees and more") relative to the sun. Milton presents both ways of achieving the identical effect, without deciding between them: the angels either tilted the earth from its formerly "centric" (centered) orbit around the "sun's axle" (if the universe is heliocentric), or they shifted the sun's circuit around the earth so that it moved at an oblique angle to the celestial equator, through the path Milton then traces through the Zodiac (if the universe were geocentric).

[3] *Except to those ... Magellan* In the eternal spring before the Fall, days and nights were always equal in length except at the poles, where the sun would never set and there would be no snow even in northern Labrador ("Estotiland") or south of the Strait of Magellan.

[4] *Thyestean banquet* Referring to Seneca's tragedy *Thyestes*, where the sun changes course to avoid the sight of Thyestes unknowingly eating his sons.

[5] *sideral* Usually "sidereal": pertaining to stars. Apparently referring to winds or storms on earth thought to be caused by these post-Fall changes in the heavens.

Vapour, and mist, and exhalation hot,
Corrupt and pestilent: now from the north
Of Norumbega, and the Samoed shore
Bursting their brazen dungeon, armed with ice
And snow and hail and stormy gust and flaw,
Boreas and Caecias and Argestes loud
And Thrascias rend the woods and seas upturn;
With adverse blast upturns them from the south
Notus and Afer black with thund'rous clouds
From Serraliona; thwart of these as fierce
Forth rush the Levant and the ponent° winds *western*
Eurus and Zephyr with their lateral noise,
Sirocco, and Libecchio.[1] Thus began
Outrage from lifeless things; but Discord first
Daughter of Sin, among th' irrational,
Death introduced through fierce antipathy:
Beast now with beast 'gan war, and fowl with fowl,
And fish with fish; to graze the herb° all leaving, *grass*
Devoured each other; nor stood much in awe
Of Man, but fled him; or, with countenance grim,
Glared on him passing. These were from without
The growing miseries, which Adam saw
Already in part, though hid in gloomiest shade,
To sorrow abandoned, but worse felt within;
And, in a troubled sea of passion tossed,
Thus to disburden sought with sad complaint:
"O miserable of happy! Is this the end
Of this new glorious world, and me so late
The glory of that glory, who now become
Accursed, of blessèd? Hide me from the face
Of God,[2] whom to behold was then my height
Of happiness: yet well, if here would end
The misery; I deserved it, and would bear
My own deservings; but this will not serve:
All that I eat or drink, or shall beget,
Is propagated curse. O voice, once heard
Delightfully, 'increase and multiply,'[3]

[1] *Norumbega ... Libecchio* A catalogue of winds let loose by the Fall, some associated with far-flung geographical points of origin. Boreas, Caecias, Argestes, and Thrascias are northern winds, from North America ("Norumbega") and Siberia ("Samoed shore"). They clash with the southern winds Notus and Afer, from Sierra Leone, and various cross-winds from the east and west named Levant, Eurus, Zephyr, Sirocco, and Libecchio.

[2] *Hide me from the face / Of God* See Psalm 27.9.

[3] *increase and multiply* See Genesis 9.7.

Now death to hear! For what can I increase,
Or multiply, but curses on my head?
Who of all ages to succeed, but, feeling
The evil on him brought by me, will curse
My head? 'Ill fare our ancestor impure,
For this we may thank Adam!' But his thanks
Shall be the execration: so, besides
Mine own that bide upon me, all from me
Shall with a fierce reflux on me rebound;
On me, as on their natural centre, light
Heavy, though in their place. O fleeting joys
Of Paradise, dear bought with lasting woes!
Did I request Thee, Maker, from my clay
To mould me man? Did I solicit Thee
From darkness to promote me, or here place
In this delicious garden? As my will
Concurred not to my being, it were but right
And equal to reduce me to my dust;
Desirous to resign and render back
All I received; unable to perform
Thy terms too hard, by which I was to hold
The good I sought not. To the loss of that,
Sufficient penalty, why hast Thou added
The sense of endless woes? Inexplicable
Thy justice seems; yet to say truth, too late,
I thus contest; then should have been refused
Those terms whatever, when they were proposed:
Thou didst accept them; wilt thou enjoy the good,
Then cavil[4] the conditions? And though God
Made thee without thy leave, what if thy son
Prove disobedient, and reproved, retort,
'Wherefore didst thou beget me? I sought it not.'
Wouldst thou admit for his contempt of thee
That proud excuse? Yet him not thy election° *choice*
But natural necessity begot.
God made thee of choice His own, and of His own
To serve Him, thy reward was of His grace,
Thy punishment then justly is at His will.
Be it so, for I submit, His doom is fair,
That dust I am, and shall to dust return.
O welcome hour whenever! Why delays
His hand to execute what His decree
Fixed on this day? Why do I overlive,
Why am I mocked with death, and lengthened out

[4] *cavil* Raise unnecessary objections.

To deathless pain? How gladly would I meet
Mortality my sentence, and be earth
Insensible! How glad would lay me down
As in my mother's lap! There I should rest,
And sleep secure; His dreadful voice no more
Would thunder in my ears; no fear of worse
To me, and to my offspring, would torment me
With cruel expectation. Yet one doubt
Pursues me still, lest all I cannot die;
Lest that pure breath of life, the spirit of man
Which God inspired, cannot together perish
With this corporeal clod; then, in the grave,
Or in some other dismal place, who knows
But I shall die a living death? O thought
Horrid, if true! Yet why? It was but breath
Of life that sinned; what dies but what had life
And sin? The body properly had neither,
All of me then shall die: let this appease
The doubt, since human reach no further knows.
For though the Lord of all be infinite,
Is His wrath also? Be it, man is not so,
But mortal doomed. How can He exercise
Wrath without end on man, whom death must end?
Can He make deathless death? That were to make
Strange contradiction, which to God Himself
Impossible is held; as argument
Of weakness, not of power. Will He draw out,
For anger's sake, finite to infinite,
In punished man, to satisfy His rigour,
Satisfied never? That were to extend
His sentence beyond dust and nature's law;
By which all causes else, according still
To the reception of their matter, act;
Not to the extent of their own sphere. But say
That death be not one stroke, as I supposed,
Bereaving sense, but endless misery
From this day onward; which I feel begun
Both in me, and without me; and so last
To perpetuity; ay me, that fear
Comes thundering back with dreadful revolution
On my defenceless head; both death and I
Am found eternal, and incorporate both;
Nor I on my part single; in me all
Posterity stands cursed: fair patrimony
That I must leave ye, sons; o were I able
To waste it all myself, and leave ye none!
So disinherited, how would you bless
Me, now your curse! Ah, why should all mankind,
For one man's fault, thus guiltless be condemned,
It guiltless? But from me what can proceed,
But all corrupt; both mind and will depraved
Not to do only, but to will the same
With me? How can they then acquitted stand
In sight of God? Him, after all disputes,
Forced I absolve: all my evasions vain,
And reasonings, though through mazes, lead me still
But to my own conviction: first and last
On me, me only, as the source and spring
Of all corruption, all the blame lights due;
So might the wrath. Fond wish! Couldst thou support
That burden, heavier than the earth to bear;
Than all the world much heavier, though divided
With that bad woman? Thus, what thou desirest,
And what thou fearest, alike destroys all hope
Of refuge, and concludes thee miserable
Beyond all past example and future;
To Satan only like both crime and doom.
O Conscience! Into what abyss of fears
And horrors hast thou driven me; out of which
I find no way, from deep to deeper plunged!"
    Thus Adam to himself lamented loud,
Through the still night; not now, as ere man fell,
Wholesome, and cool, and mild, but with black air
Accompanied; with damps, and dreadful gloom;
Which to his evil conscience represented
All things with double terror: on the ground
Outstretched he lay, on the cold ground; and oft
Cursed his creation; Death as oft accused
Of tardy execution, since denounced
The day of his offence. "Why comes not Death,"
Said he, "with one thrice-acceptable stroke
To end me? Shall Truth fail to keep her word,
Justice divine not hasten to be just?
But death comes not at call; justice divine
Mends not her slowest pace for prayers or cries,
O woods, O fountains, hillocks, dales, and bowers!
With other echo late I taught your shades
To answer, and resound far other song."
Whom thus afflicted when sad Eve beheld,
Desolate where she sat, approaching nigh,

Soft words to his fierce passion she assayed:
But her with stern regard he thus repelled.
"Out of my sight, thou serpent! That name best
Befits thee with him leagued, thyself as false
And hateful; nothing wants, but that thy shape,
Like his, and colour serpentine, may show
Thy inward fraud; to warn all creatures from thee
Henceforth; lest that too heav'nly form, pretended
To hellish falsehood, snare them! But for thee
I had persisted happy; had not thy pride
And wandering vanity, when least was safe,
Rejected my forewarning, and disdained
Not to be trusted; longing to be seen,
Though by the Devil himself; him overweening
To over-reach; but, with the serpent meeting,
Fooled and beguiled; by him thou, I by thee
To trust thee from my side; imagined wise,
Constant, mature, proof against all assaults;
And understood not all was but a show,
Rather than solid virtue; all but a rib
Crooked by nature, bent, as now appears,
More to the part sinister, from me drawn;
Well if thrown out, as supernumerary
To my just number found. O why did God,
Creator wise, that peopled highest Heav'n
With spirits masculine,[1] create at last
This novelty on earth, this fair defect
Of nature, and not fill the world at once
With men, as angels, without feminine;
Or find some other way to generate
Mankind? This mischief had not been befallen,
And more that shall befall; innumerable
Disturbances on earth through female snares,
And strait conjunction with this sex: for either
He never shall find out fit mate, but such
As some misfortune brings him, or mistake;
Or whom he wishes most shall seldom gain
Through her perverseness, but shall see her gained
By a far worse; or, if she love, withheld
By parents; or his happiest choice too late
Shall meet, already linked and wedlock-bound
To a fell adversary, his hate or shame:
Which infinite calamity shall cause
To human life, and household peace confound."
He added not, and from her turned; but Eve,
Not so repulsed, with tears that ceased not flowing
And tresses all disordered, at his feet
Fell humble; and, embracing them, besought
His peace, and thus proceeded in her plaint:
"Forsake me not thus, Adam, witness Heav'n
What love sincere, and reverence in my heart
I bear thee, and unweeting° have offended, *unwitting*
Unhappily deceived! Thy suppliant
I beg, and clasp thy knees; bereave me not,
Whereon I live, thy gentle looks, thy aid,
Thy counsel, in this uttermost distress,
My only strength and stay: forlorn of thee,
Whither shall I betake me, where subsist?
While yet we live, scarce one short hour perhaps,
Between us two let there be peace; both joining,
As joined in injuries, one enmity
Against a foe by doom express[2] assigned us,
That cruel serpent. On me exercise not
Thy hatred for this misery befallen;
On me already lost, me than thyself
More miserable! Both have sinned; but thou
Against God only; I against God and thee;
And to the place of judgement will return,
There with my cries importune Heaven; that all
The sentence, from thy head removed, may light
On me, sole cause to thee of all this woe;
Me, me only, just object of His ire!"
She ended weeping; and her lowly plight,
Immoveable, till peace obtained from fault
Acknowledged and deplored, in Adam wrought
Commiseration. Soon his heart relented
Towards her, his life so late, and sole delight,
Now at his feet submissive in distress;
Creature so fair his reconcilement seeking,
His counsel, whom she had displeased, his aid:
As one disarmed, his anger all he lost,
And thus with peaceful words upraised her soon:
"Unwary, and too desirous, as before,
So now of what thou know'st not, who desir'st
The punishment all on thyself; alas!
Bear thine own first, ill able to sustain
His full wrath, whose thou feelest as yet least part,

[1] *that peopled ... masculine* Adam's anger against Eve leads him to forget that angels have no gender (as Raphael had informed him).

[2] *doom express* Specific judgment.

And my displeasure bearest so ill. If prayers
Could alter high decrees, I to that place
Would speed before thee, and be louder heard,
That on my head all might be visited;
Thy frailty and infirmer sex forgiv'n,
To me committed, and by me exposed.
But rise, let us no more contend, nor blame
Each other, blamed enough elsewhere; but strive
In offices of love, how we may light'n
Each other's burden, in our share of woe;
Since this day's death denounced, if aught I see,
Will prove no sudden, but a slow-paced evil;
A long day's dying, to augment our pain;
And to our seed (O hapless seed!) derived."
    To whom thus Eve, recovering heart, replied:
"Adam, by sad experiment I know
How little weight my words with thee can find,
Found so erroneous; thence by just event
Found so unfortunate. Nevertheless,
Restored by thee, vile as I am, to place
Of new acceptance, hopeful to regain
Thy love, the sole contentment of my heart
Living or dying, from thee I will not hide
What thoughts in my unquiet breast are risen,
Tending to some relief of our extremes,
Or end; though sharp and sad, yet tolerable,
As in our evils, and of easier choice.
If care of our descent perplex us most,
Which must be born to certain woe, devoured
By Death at last; and miserable it is
To be to others cause of misery,
Our own begotten, and of our loins to bring
Into this cursèd world a woeful race,
That after wretched life must be at last
Food for so foul a monster; in thy power
It lies, yet ere conception to prevent
The race unblest, to being yet unbegot.
Childless thou art, childless remain: so Death
Shall be deceived his glut, and with us two
Be forced to satisfy his rav'nous maw.
But if thou judge it hard and difficult,
Conversing, looking, loving, to abstain
From love's due rights, nuptial embraces sweet;
And with desire to languish without hope,
Before the present object languishing
With like desire; which would be misery
And torment less than none of what we dread;
Then, both ourselves and seed at once to free
From what we fear for both, let us make short,
Let us seek Death, or he not found, supply
With our own hands his office on ourselves;
Why stand we longer shivering under fears,
That show no end but death, and have the power,
Of many ways to die the shortest choosing,
Destruction with destruction to destroy."
    She ended here, or vehement despair
Broke off the rest: so much of death her thoughts
Had entertained, as dyed her cheeks with pale.
But Adam, with such counsel nothing swayed,
To better hopes his more attentive mind
Labouring had raised; and thus to Eve replied:
    "Eve, thy contempt of life and pleasure seems
To argue in thee something more sublime
And excellent than what thy mind contemns;
But self-destruction therefore sought, refutes
That excellence thought in thee; and implies,
Not thy contempt, but anguish and regret
For loss of life and pleasure overloved.
Or if thou covet death as utmost end
Of misery, so thinking to evade
The penalty pronounced; doubt not but God
Hath wiselier armed His vengeful ire, than so
To be forestalled; much more I fear lest Death,
So snatched, will not exempt us from the pain
We are by doom to pay; rather, such acts
Of contumacy° will provoke the highest *contempt*
To make death in us live. Then let us seek
Some safer resolution, which methinks
I have in view, calling to mind with heed
Part of our sentence, that thy seed shall bruise
The serpent's head; piteous amends! Unless
Be meant, whom I conjecture, our grand foe,
Satan; who, in the serpent, hath contrived
Against us this deceit: to crush his head
Would be revenge indeed, which will be lost
By death brought on ourselves, or childless days
Resolved, as thou proposest; so our foe
Shall 'scape his punishment ordained, and we
Instead shall double ours upon our heads.
No more be mentioned then of violence

Against ourselves; and wilful barrenness,
That cuts us off from hope; and savours only
Rancour and pride, impatience and despite,° *ill-will*
Reluctance° against God and His just yoke *resistance*
Laid on our necks. Remember with what mild
And gracious temper He both heard, and judged,
Without wrath or reviling; we expected
Immediate dissolution, which we thought
Was meant by death that day; when lo, to thee
Pains only in child-bearing were foretold,
And bringing forth; soon recompensed with joy,
Fruit of thy womb: On me the curse aslope
Glanced on the ground; with labour I must earn
My bread; what harm? Idleness had been worse;
My labour will sustain me; and, lest cold
Or heat should injure us, His timely care
Hath, unbesought, provided; and His hands
Clothed us unworthy, pitying while He judged;
How much more, if we pray Him, will His ear
Be open, and His heart to pity incline,
And teach us further by what means to shun
The inclement seasons, rain, ice, hail, and snow!
Which now the sky, with various face, begins
To show us in this mountain; while the winds
Blow moist and keen, shattering the graceful locks
Of these fair spreading trees; which bids us seek
Some better shroud, some better warmth to cherish
Our limbs benumbed, ere this diurnal star
Leave cold the night, how we His gathered beams
Reflected may with matter sere foment;[1]
Or, by collision of two bodies, grind
The air attrite to fire; as late the clouds
Jostling, or pushed with winds, rude in their shock,
Tine[2] the slant lightning; whose thwart flame, driv'n down
Kindles the gummy bark of fir or pine;
And sends a comfortable heat from far,
Which might supply the sun. Such fire to use,
And what may else be remedy or cure
To evils which our own misdeeds have wrought,
He will instruct us praying, and of grace
Beseeching Him; so as we need not fear
To pass commodiously this life, sustained
By Him with many comforts, till we end
In dust, our final rest and native home.
What better can we do than, to the place
Repairing where He judged us, prostrate fall
Before Him reverent; and there confess
Humbly our faults, and pardon beg, with tears
Watering the ground, and with our sighs the air
Frequenting, sent from hearts contrite, in sign
Of sorrow unfeigned, and humiliation meek?
Undoubtedly He will relent, and turn
From His displeasure; in whose look serene,
When angry most He seemed and most severe,
What else but favour, grace, and mercy shone?"
So spake our father penitent; nor Eve
Felt less remorse: they, forthwith to the place
Repairing where He judged them, prostrate fell
Before Him reverent; and both confessed
Humbly their faults, and pardon begged; with tears
Watering the ground, and with their sighs the air
Frequenting, sent from hearts contrite, in sign
Of sorrow unfeigned, and humiliation meek.

The End of the Tenth Book

Argument to Book 11

The Son of God presents to His Father the prayers of our first parents now repenting, and intercedes for them: God accepts them, but declares that they must no longer abide in Paradise; sends Michael with a band of cherubim to dispossess them; but first to reveal to Adam future things: Michael's coming down. Adam shows to Eve certain ominous signs; he discerns Michael's approach, goes out to meet him: the Angel denounces their departure. Eve's lamentation. Adam pleads, but submits: the Angel leads him up to a high hill, sets before him in vision what shall happen till the Flood.

Argument to Book 12

The angel Michael continues from the Flood to relate what shall succeed; then, in the mention of

[1] *with matter sere foment* With dry material, focus the beams of light (so as to make fire).

[2] *Tine* Branch, as of a fork; i.e., forked lightning is coming through the clouds.

Abraham, comes by degrees to explain, who that Seed of the Woman shall be, which was promised Adam and Eve in the Fall; His incarnation, death, resurrection, and ascension; the state of the Church till His second coming. Adam greatly satisfied and recomforted by these relations and promises descends the hill with Michael; wakens Eve, who all this while had slept, but with gentle dreams composed to quietness of mind and submission. Michael in either hand leads them out of Paradise, the fiery sword waving behind them, and the cherubim taking their stations to guard the place.

from Book 12

...

So spake th' archangel Michael;[1] then paused,
As at the world's great period;[2] and our sire,
Replete with joy and wonder, thus replied:
"O goodness infinite, goodness immense!
That all this good of evil shall produce,
And evil turn to good; more wonderful
Than that which by creation first brought forth
Light out of darkness! Full of doubt I stand,
Whether I should repent me now of sin
By me done, and occasioned; or rejoice
Much more, that much more good thereof shall spring;
To God more glory, more goodwill to men
From God, and over wrath grace shall abound.
But say, if our Deliverer up to Heaven
Must re-ascend, what will betide the few
His faithful, left among the unfaithful herd,
The enemies of truth? Who then shall guide
His people, who defend? Will they not deal
Worse with His followers than with Him they dealt?"
"Be sure they will," said th' angel; "but from Heaven
He to His own a comforter will send,
The promise of the Father, who shall dwell
His Spirit within them; and the law of faith,
Working through love, upon their hearts shall write,
To guide them in all truth; and also arm
With spiritual armour, able to resist
Satan's assaults, and quench his fiery darts;
What man can do against them, not afraid,
Though to the death; against such cruelties
With inward consolations recompensed,
And oft supported so as shall amaze
Their proudest persecutors: for the Spirit,
Poured first on His apostles, whom He sends
To evangelize the nations, then on all
Baptized, shall them with wondrous gifts endue
To speak all tongues, and do all miracles,
As did their Lord before them. Thus they win
Great numbers of each nation to receive
With joy the tidings brought from Heav'n. At length
Their ministry performed, and race well run,
Their doctrine and their story written left,
They die; but in their room, as they forewarn,
Wolves shall succeed for teachers, grievous wolves,[3]
Who all the sacred mysteries of Heav'n
To their own vile advantages shall turn
Of lucre and ambition; and the truth
With superstitions and traditions taint,
Left only in those written records pure,
Though not but by the Spirit understood.
Then shall they seek to avail themselves of names,
Places, and titles, and with these to join
Secular power; though feigning still to act
By spiritual, to themselves appropriating
The Spirit of God, promised alike and giv'n
To all believers; and, from that pretence,
Spiritual laws by carnal power shall force
On every conscience; laws which none shall find
Left them enrolled, or what the Spirit within
Shall on the heart engrave. What will they then
But force the Spirit of Grace itself, and bind
His consort Liberty; what, but unbuild
His living temples, built by faith to stand,
Their own faith, not another's? For, on earth,
Who against faith and conscience can be heard
Infallible? Yet many will presume:
Whence heavy persecution shall arise
On all, who in the worship persevere
Of Spirit and Truth; the rest, far greater part,
Will deem in outward rites and specious forms

[1] *So spake th' archangel Michael* Michael has just assured Adam of humanity's eventual redemption and salvation.

[2] *world's great period* End of the world.

[3] *grievous wolves* See Acts 20.29.

Religion satisfied; Truth shall retire
Bestuck with slanderous darts, and works of faith
Rarely be found. So shall the world go on,
To good malignant, to bad men benign;
Under her own weight groaning; till the day
Appear of respiration to the just,
And vengeance to the wicked, at return
Of him so lately promised to thy aid,
The woman's seed; obscurely then foretold,
Now ampler known thy Saviour and thy Lord;
Last, in the clouds, from Heav'n to be revealed
In glory of the Father, to dissolve
Satan with his perverted world; then raise
From the conflagrant mass, purged and refined,
New heav'ns, new earth, ages of endless date,
Founded in righteousness, and peace, and love;
To bring forth fruits, joy and eternal bliss."
He ended; and thus Adam last replied:
"How soon hath thy prediction, seer blest,
Measured this transient world, the race of time,
Till time stand fixed! Beyond is all abyss,
Eternity, whose end no eye can reach.
Greatly instructed I shall hence depart;
Greatly in peace of thought; and have my fill
Of knowledge, what this vessel can contain;
Beyond which was my folly to aspire.
Henceforth I learn that to obey is best,
And love with fear the only God; to walk
As in His presence; ever to observe
His Providence; and on Him sole depend,
Merciful over all His works, with good
Still overcoming evil, and by small
Accomplishing great things, by things deemed weak
Subverting worldly strong, and worldly wise
By simply meek: that suffering for truth's sake
Is fortitude to highest victory,
And, to the faithful, death the gate of life.
Taught this by His example, whom I now
Acknowledge my Redeemer ever blest."
To whom thus also th' angel last replied:
"This having learned, thou hast attained the sum
Of wisdom; hope no higher, though all the stars
Thou knewest by name, and all th' ethereal powers,
All secrets of the deep, all Nature's works,
Or works of God in Heaven, air, earth, or sea,
And all the riches of this world enjoyedst,
And all the rule, one empire; only add
Deeds to thy knowledge answerable; add faith,
Add virtue, patience, temperance; add love,
By name to come called charity, the soul
Of all the rest: then wilt thou not be loth
To leave this Paradise, but shalt possess
A Paradise within thee, happier far.
Let us descend now therefore from this top
Of speculation; for the hour precise
Exacts our parting hence; and see the guards,
By me encamped on yonder hill, expect
Their motion; at whose front a flaming sword,
In signal of remove, waves fiercely round:[1]
We may no longer stay. Go, waken Eve;
Her also I with gentle dreams have calmed
Portending good, and all her spirits composed
To meek submission: thou, at season fit,
Let her with thee partake what thou hast heard;
Chiefly what may concern her faith to know,
The great deliverance by her seed to come
(For by the woman's seed) on all mankind:
That ye may live, which will be many days,
Both in one faith unanimous, though sad,
With cause, for evils past; yet much more cheered
With meditation on the happy end."
He ended, and they both descend the hill;
Descended, Adam to the bower, where Eve
Lay sleeping, ran before; but found her waked;
And thus with words not sad she him received:
"Whence thou returnest, and whither wentest, I
know;
For God is also in sleep; and dreams advise,
Which He hath sent propitious, some great good
Presaging, since with sorrow and heart's distress
Wearied I fell asleep: but now lead on;
In me is no delay; with thee to go,
Is to stay here; without thee here to stay,
Is to go hence unwilling; thou to me
Art all things under Heav'n, all places thou,
Who for my wilful crime art banished hence.
This further consolation yet secure
I carry hence; though all by me is lost,
Such favour I unworthy am vouchsafed,

[1] *a flaming sword ... waves fiercely round* See Genesis 3.24.

By me the promised seed shall all restore."
So spake our mother Eve; and Adam heard
Well pleased, but answered not: for now, too nigh
Th' archangel stood; and, from the other hill
To their fixed station, all in bright array
The cherubim descended; on the ground
Gliding meteorous, as ev'ning mist
Ris'n from a river o'er the marish° glides, *marsh*
And gathers ground fast at the labourer's heel
Homeward returning. High in front advanced,
The brandished sword of God before them blazed,
Fierce as a comet; which with torrid heat,
And vapour as the Libyan air adust,
Began to parch that temperate clime; whereat
In either hand the hastening angel caught
Our lingering parents, and to the eastern gate
Led them direct, and down the cliff as fast
To the subjected plain; then disappeared.
They, looking back, all the eastern side beheld
Of Paradise, so late their happy seat,
Waved over by that flaming brand; the gate
With dreadful faces thronged, and fiery arms.
Some natural tears they dropt, but wiped them soon;
The world was all before them, where to choose
Their place of rest, and Providence their guide.
They, hand in hand, with wand'ring steps and slow,
Through Eden took their solitary way.

THE END

—1667, 1674

In Context

Illustrating *Paradise Lost*

The first illustrated edition of *Paradise Lost* was that of 1688—the fourth published edition. Twelve illustrations appear in the edition (one per book). Of these, seven are attributed to John Baptist Medina and one to Bernard Lens; four are anonymous.

Many illustrated editions of the poem appeared in the eighteenth and nineteenth centuries; among the most notable are those illustrated by Francis Hayman (c. 1707–76), by William Blake (1757–1827), and by John Martin (1789–1854). Two illustrations from each of these editions are reproduced below, together with two from the 1688 edition.

Illustrations to Book 5 and Book 12 (1688).

Francis Hayman, illustrations to Book 2 and Book 4 (1749).

William Blake, illustrations to Book 6 and Book 9 (1808).

John Martin, illustrations to Book 1 and Book 9 (1824).

Samson Agonistes

The biblical story of Samson seems an almost inevitable subject for Milton to address after the Restoration of 1660, when England abandoned its experiment in republicanism and welcomed back both the monarchy and the state church. Samson's initial situation in the poem echoes repeatedly with Milton's likely sense of his own situation: blind and no longer in a position of power; ruled by an enemy with an entertainment-loving aristocracy, politically powerful clergy, and emptily ceremonial religion; disappointed in his countrymen because they preferred "bondage with ease" over "strenuous liberty" (line 271); and questioning his apparent failure to fulfill his divinely appointed role of national liberator. *Samson Agonistes* (1671) addresses matters that Milton had explored throughout *Paradise Lost* (1667) and other works, questions that pressed insistently on the imagination of all who were unhappy with the changes wrought by the Restoration. How do we respond to the experience of defeat, and to fears of having been abandoned by the divine? How do we know when our actions accord with divine will, or when they are fueled instead by our fallen desires and weaknesses? At what point do accommodation and compromise with an enemy become a failure of will? What constitutes true heroism? To what extent is violence justified in the cause of freedom?

Samson Agonistes was first published in a volume with *Paradise Regained* in 1671, four years after the first edition of *Paradise Lost.* While there was some speculation decades ago that *Samson Agonistes* was written before *Paradise Lost,* the consensus now overwhelmingly favors a date of composition in the later 1660s, after Milton had completed both *Paradise Lost* and *Paradise Regained.* Scholars note that *Samson Agonistes* appears to contain several topical allusions to post-Restoration events, and that the poem engages throughout with the language of Restoration debates on political and religious accommodation. Furthermore, its daringly experimental prosody suggests that Milton wrote the poem late in his career. In *Samson Agonistes,* Milton abandons the regularly maintained blank verse of *Paradise Lost* and *Paradise Regained* and employs varying line lengths, mixes blank verse with lyric rhyme, and takes such liberties with scansion that the poem often has the feel of modern "free verse." To most scholars, the poetry of *Samson Agonistes* seems the culminating literary expression of a poet who had already demonstrated his mastery of traditional forms and felt free to abandon convention to create the poetic effects he desired. Finally, for many readers as well as scholars, the resonant last line of *Samson Agonistes*—"And calm of mind all passion spent"—offers a cathartic conclusion to a literary career devoted to passionate engagement with the most fundamental aspects of the human condition.

As Milton notes in his preface, *Samson Agonistes* is a "dramatic poem": while it takes the form of drama, specifically of ancient Greek tragedy, and has been performed successfully in staged readings, it was never intended for the stage. The poem opens with Samson already blinded and enslaved, bemoaning his condition, questioning the events that had reduced him to such a pitiful state. He reminds us that he had once been a great warrior, consecrated to God from birth and divinely appointed to deliver Israel from its bondage under the Philistines. But he had betrayed the secret of his unconquerable strength to his Philistine wife Dalila, and she in turn had betrayed him to the Philistines once she had rendered him temporarily powerless by cutting his hair. A series of discussions then ensues between Samson and various visitors: a Chorus of fellow tribesmen, his wife Dalila, his father Manoa, the Philistine giant Harapha, and a Public Officer. The poem ends when Samson is commanded to entertain his captors by performing feats of strength at a religious festival; he concludes his performance by pulling down the building's pillars, killing himself along with the Philistine social, political, military, and religious elite. As in Greek tragedy, the concluding violence takes place offstage and is reported by a messenger.

Milton freely expands on the biblical account, adding and omitting details, telling the story in his own way for his own purposes. But what these purposes might be is a question that has generated considerable debate. To many modern readers, the biblical Samson can seem more a thuggish trickster figure from folklore than a proper national hero. A long tradition of Christian commentary, however, has interpreted Samson as a prefiguration of Christ, a "type" of the self-sacrificing and regenerate savior. Is that how Milton presents him? While some scholars argue that *Samson Agonistes* offers an unambiguous drama of spiritual regeneration, others argue instead that Milton's Samson is a failed Old Testament hero whose actions contrast with the true heroism of Jesus in *Paradise Regained*, the poem with which *Samson Agonistes* was originally published. One difficulty of *Samson Agonistes* is that Milton's choice of the dramatic form deprives readers of the helpfully omniscient narrative voices of *Paradise Lost* or the Bible. Did God really give "to the man despotic power / Over his female in due awe" (lines 1054–55), as the Chorus claims, or is it more the case, as Dalila notes, that "In argument with men a woman ever / Goes by the worse, whatever be her cause" (lines 903–04)? Each claim is self-evidently true to its speaker, but the poem requires readers to judge between them. When Samson feels "Some rousing motions" within himself (line 1382) as he heads toward suicidal slaughter, are readers confident that his actions are prompted by God? The biblical account makes divine approval explicit; in Milton's presentation, Samson's sudden and unexplained shift in strategy may invite questions. Similarly, when the Messenger describes Samson as inclining his head "as one who prayed" (line 1637), is Samson praying, or simply inclining his head *like* somebody who prays? If Samson's violence is divinely justified, why does Milton take such care to make the slaughter more socially selective than it was in the biblical account? Is the poem ultimately a call to revolution, a vindication of revolution, or a repudiation of revolution?

The heated struggles of scholars with this poem and with one another fittingly reflect the poem's central subject: Samson's struggle to understand himself. "Agonistes" is the Greek word for an athlete competing in the Olympic games, and Milton's appropriation of the word for use in a biblical context adds the resonance of Christian spiritual struggle as well as the physical agonies of Christ. In addition, "agon" was the term used in ancient Greek drama for a verbal contest between two characters. In each "agon" or dialogic encounter with a figure from his life, Samson also struggles with some element within himself: the voice of tribal wisdom in the Chorus, the fame-loving sensualist in Dalila, the strong man who delights in violence in Harapha, the compromiser in his father Manoa. Because the dramatic form gives each visitor his or her say without explicit narratorial framing, the reader consequently spends the poem in Samson's position. We too are blind, reliant on the Chorus to introduce us to each visitor; we listen to and judge a succession of persuasive voices, wrestling with what these encounters mean. We conclude with the catharsis of vicarious slaughter, the purging of untempered passion, and the promise of "peace and consolation." But Milton seems deliberately to leave readers of *Samson Agonistes* with as many questions as answers. What exactly has been won, and at what cost?

⌘⌘⌘

pauses, they may be called alloeostropha.[1] Division into act and scene referring chiefly to the stage (to which this work never was intended) is here omitted.

It suffices if the whole drama be found not produced beyond the fifth act.[2] Of the style and uniformity, and that commonly called the plot, whether intricate or explicit,[3] which is nothing indeed but such economy, or disposition of the fable as may stand best with verisimilitude and decorum, they only will best judge who are not unacquainted with Aeschylus, Sophocles, and Euripides, the three tragic poets unequalled yet by any, and the best rule to all who endeavour to write tragedy. The circumscription of time wherein the whole drama begins and ends, is according to ancient rule,[4] and best example, within the space of twenty-four hours.

The Argument

Samson made captive, blind, and now in the prison at Gaza, there to labour as in a common workhouse, on a festival day, in the general cessation from labour, comes forth into the open air, to a place nigh, somewhat retired there to sit a while and bemoan his condition. Where he happens at length to be visited by certain friends and equals of his tribe, which make the Chorus, who seek to comfort him what they can; then by his old father Manoa, who endeavours the like, and withal tells him his purpose to procure his liberty by ransom; lastly, that this feast was proclaimed by the Philistines as a day of thanksgiving for their deliverance from the hands of Samson, which yet more troubles him. Manoa then departs to prosecute his endeavour with the Philistian lords for Samson's redemption; who in the meanwhile is visited by other persons; and lastly by a public officer to require his coming to the feast before the lords and people, to play or show his strength in their presence; he at first refuses, dismissing the public officer with absolute denial to come; at length persuaded inwardly that this was from God, he yields to go along with him, who came now the second time with great threatenings to fetch him; the Chorus yet remaining on the place, Manoa returns full of joyful hope, to procure ere long his son's deliverance: in the midst of which discourse an Hebrew comes in haste confusedly at first; and afterward more distinctly relating the catastrophe, what Samson had done to the Philistines, and by accident to himself; wherewith the tragedy ends.

The Persons

Samson
Manoa, the father of Samson
Dalila his wife
Harapha of Gath
Public Officer
Messenger
Chorus of Danites[5]

The Scene: before the prison in Gaza

Samson. A little onward lend thy guiding hand
To these dark steps, a little further on;
For yonder bank hath choice of sun or shade,
There I am wont to sit, when any chance
Relieves me from my task of servile toil,
Daily in the common prison else enjoined me,
Where I a prisoner chained, scarce freely draw
The air imprisoned also, close and damp,
Unwholesome draught: but here I feel amends,
The breath of heaven fresh-blowing, pure and sweet,
With day-spring° born; here leave me to respire. *daybreak*
This day a solemn feast the people hold
To Dagon[6] their sea-idol, and forbid
Laborious works, unwillingly this rest

[1] *alloeostropha* Greek: of irregular strophes or stanzas.

[2] *It suffices ... fifth act* That is, while the poem lacks act and scene divisions, it still follows the traditional rules of drama by not extending its action past the concluding fifth-act catharsis.

[3] *intricate or explicit* Complex or simple (alluding to Aristotle's discussion in *Poetics* 10).

[4] *ancient rule* Aristotle observed in *Poetics* 5 that the action of tragedies generally took place within a span of twenty-four hours, but this unity of time only became a "rule" among Renaissance neo-classicists.

[5] *Danites* Members of the tribe to which Manoa and Samson belonged (see Judges 13.2).

[6] *Dagon* The Philistines' principal god, described in *Paradise Lost* as a "sea-monster, upward man / And downward fish" (1.462–63).

Their superstition yields me; hence with leave
Retiring from the popular noise, I seek
This unfrequented place to find some ease,
Ease to the body some, none to the mind
From restless thoughts, that like a deadly swarm
Of hornets armed, no sooner found alone,
But rush upon me thronging, and present
Times past, what once I was, and what am now.
O wherefore was my birth from heaven foretold
Twice by an angel, who at last in sight
Of both my parents all in flames ascended
From off the altar, where an offering burned,
As in a fiery column charioting
His godlike presence, and from some great act
Or benefit revealed to Abraham's race?[1]
Why was my breeding ordered and prescribed
As of a person separate to God,[2]
Designed for great exploits, if I must die
Betrayed, captived, and both my eyes put out,
Made of my enemies the scorn and gaze;
To grind in brazen fetters under task
With this heaven-gifted strength? O glorious strength
Put to the labour of a beast, debased
Lower than bond-slave! Promise was that I
Should Israel from Philistian yoke deliver;
Ask for this great deliverer now, and find him
Eyeless in Gaza at the mill with slaves,
Himself in bonds under Philistian yoke;
Yet stay, let me not rashly call in doubt
Divine prediction; what if all foretold
Had been fulfilled but through mine own default,
Whom have I to complain of but my self?
Who this high gift of strength committed to me,
In what part lodged, how easily bereft me,
Under the seal of silence could not keep,
But weakly to a woman must reveal it,
O'ercome with importunity and tears.
O impotence of mind, in body strong!
But what is strength without a double share
Of wisdom, vast, unwieldy, burdensome,
Proudly secure, yet liable to fall
By weakest subtleties, not made to rule,
But to subserve where wisdom bears command.
God, when he gave me strength, to show withal
How slight the gift was, hung it in my hair.
But peace, I must not quarrel with the will
Of highest dispensation, which herein
Haply had ends above my reach to know:
Suffices that to me strength is my bane,
And proves the source of all my miseries;
So many, and so huge, that each apart
Would ask a life to wail, but chief of all,
O loss of sight, of thee I most complain!
Blind among enemies, O worse than chains,
Dungeon, or beggary, or decrepit age!
Light, the prime work of God, to me is extinct,
And all her various objects of delight
Annulled, which might in part my grief have eased,
Inferior to the vilest now become
Of man or worm; the vilest here excel me,
They creep, yet see, I dark in light exposed
To daily fraud, contempt, abuse and wrong,
Within doors, or without, still as a fool,
In power of others, never in my own;
Scarce half I seem to live, dead more than half.
O dark, dark, dark, amid the blaze of noon,
Irrecoverably dark, total eclipse
Without all hope of day!
O first-created beam, and thou great word,
Let there be light, and light was over all;
Why am I thus bereaved thy prime decree?
The sun to me is dark
And silent as the moon,
When she deserts the night
Hid in her vacant interlunar cave.[3]
Since light so necessary is to life,
And almost life itself, if it be true
That light is in the soul,
She all in every part; why was the sight
To such a tender ball as the eye confined?
So obvious° and so easy to be quenched, *vulnerable*
And not as feeling through all parts diffused,

[1] *O wherefore ... race?* For the circumstances of Samson's birth, see Judges 13.3–5 and 10–23.

[2] *separate to God* Samson is a Nazarite, a person set apart by ascetic vows to serve the divine: see Numbers 6.1–21 and Judges 13.4–7.

[3] *silent as the moon ... interlunar cave* Silent in the sense of dark, vacant in the sense of idle or at leisure; in classical lore, the moon rested in a cave during the period of darkness between old and new moons.

That she might look at will through every pore?
Then had I not been thus exiled from light;
As in the land of darkness yet in light,
To live a life half dead, a living death,
And buried; but O yet more miserable!
My self, my sepulchre, a moving grave,
Buried, yet not exempt
By privilege of death and burial
From worst of other evils, pains and wrongs,
But made hereby obnoxious° more *exposed*
To all the miseries of life,
Life in captivity
Among inhuman foes.
But who are these? For with joint pace I hear
The tread of many feet steering this way;
Perhaps my enemies who come to stare
At my affliction, and perhaps to insult,
Their daily practice to afflict me more.
Chorus. This, this is he; softly a while,
Let us not break in upon him;
O change beyond report, thought, or belief!
See how he lies at random, carelessly diffused,° *sprawled*
With languished head unpropped,
As one past hope, abandoned,
And by himself given over;
In slavish habit, ill-fitted weeds
O'er-worn and soiled;
Or do my eyes misrepresent? Can this be he,
That heroic, that renowned,
Irresistible Samson? Whom unarmed
No strength of man, or fiercest wild beast could withstand;
Who tore the lion, as the lion tears the kid,
Ran on embattled armies clad in iron,
And weaponless himself,
Made arms ridiculous, useless the forgery
Of brazen shield and spear, the hammered cuirass,° *breastplate*
Chalybean tempered steel,[1] and frock of mail
Adamantean proof;[2]
But safest he who stood aloof,
When insupportably his foot advanced,
In scorn of their proud arms and warlike tools,
Spurned them to death by troops. The bold Ascalonite[3]
Fled from his lion ramp, old warriors turned
Their plated backs under his heel;
Or grovelling soiled their crested helmets in the dust.
Then with what trivial weapon came to hand,
The jaw of a dead ass, his sword of bone,
A thousand foreskins[4] fell, the flower of Palestine
In Ramath-lechi famous to this day:
Then by main force pulled up, and on his shoulders bore
The gates of Azza,° post, and massy bar *Gaza (variant form)*
Up to the hill by Hebron, seat of giants old,
No journey of a Sabbath day,[5] and loaded so;
Like whom the Gentiles feign to bear up heaven.[6]
Which shall I first bewail,
Thy bondage or lost sight,
Prison within prison
Inseparably dark?
Thou art become (O worst imprisonment!)
The dungeon of thy self; thy soul
(Which men enjoying sight oft without cause complain)
Imprisoned now indeed,
In real darkness of the body dwells,
Shut up from outward light
To incorporate with gloomy night;
For inward light alas
Puts forth no visual beam.
O mirror of our fickle state,
Since man on earth unparalleled!
The rarer thy example stands,
By how much from the top of wondrous glory,
Strongest of mortal men,
To lowest pitch of abject fortune thou art fallen.
For him I reckon not in high estate
Whom long descent of birth

[1] *Chalybean tempered steel* The Chalybes were a Black Sea tribe famous in the classical period for their work in iron and steel.

[2] *Adamantean proof* Capable of resisting adamant, a fabled mineral hard as diamond.

[3] *Ascalonite* Ascalon was a Philistine city.

[4] *foreskins* Synecdoche for the uncircumcised Philistines.

[5] *No journey of a Sabbath day* The Chorus indulges in epic understatement: Jewish law restricted travel on the Sabbath to about a mile (give or take a half-mile); Samson carried the heavy city gates about forty miles.

[6] *whom the Gentiles ... bear up heaven* Atlas, one of the Titans in Greek myth.

Or the sphere of fortune raises;
But thee whose strength, while virtue was her mate,
Might have subdued the earth,
Universally crowned with highest praises.
Samson. I hear the sound of words, their sense the air
Dissolves unjointed ere it reach my ear.
Chorus. He speaks, let us draw nigh. Matchless in might,
The glory late of Israel, now the grief;
We come thy friends and neighbours not unknown
From Eshtaol and Zora's fruitful vale
To visit or bewail thee, or if better,
Counsel or consolation we may bring,
Salve to thy sores; apt words have power to swage
The tumours of a troubled mind,
And are as balm to festered wounds.
Samson. Your coming, friends, revives me, for I learn
Now of my own experience, not by talk,
How counterfeit a coin they are who friends
Bear in their superscription (of the most
I would be understood): in prosperous days
They swarm, but in adverse withdraw their head
Not to be found, though sought. Ye see, O friends,
How many evils have enclosed me round;
Yet that which was the worst now least afflicts me,
Blindness, for had I sight, confused with shame,
How could I once look up, or heave the head,
Who like a foolish pilot have shipwrecked
My vessel trusted to me from above,
Gloriously rigged; and for a word, a tear,
Fool, have divulged the secret gift of God
To a deceitful woman: tell me friends,
Am I not sung and proverbed for a fool
In every street, do they not say, how well
Are come upon him his deserts? Yet why?
Immeasurable strength they might behold
In me, of wisdom nothing more than mean;
This with the other should, at least, have paired,
These two proportioned ill drove me transverse.° *off course*
Chorus. Tax not divine disposal, wisest men
Have erred, and by bad women been deceived;
And shall again, pretend they ne'er so wise.
Deject not then so overmuch thy self,
Who hast of sorrow thy full load besides;
Yet truth to say, I oft have heard men wonder
Why thou shouldst wed Philistian women rather
Than of thine own tribe fairer, or as fair,
At least of thy own nation, and as noble.
Samson. The first I saw at Timna, and she pleased
Me, not my parents, that I sought to wed,
The daughter of an infidel: they knew not
That what I motioned was of God; I knew
From intimate impulse, and therefore urged
The marriage on; that by occasion hence
I might begin Israel's deliverance,
The work to which I was divinely called;
She proving false, the next I took to wife
(O that I never had! fond wish too late)
Was in the vale of Sorec, Dalila,
That specious monster, my accomplished snare.
I thought it lawful from my former act,
And the same end; still watching to oppress
Israel's oppressors: of what now I suffer
She was not the prime cause, but I my self,
Who vanquished with a peal of words (O weakness!)
Gave up my fort of silence to a woman.
Chorus. In seeking just occasion to provoke
The Philistine, thy country's enemy,
Thou never wast remiss, I bear thee witness:
Yet Israel still serves with all his sons.
Samson. That fault I take not on me, but transfer
On Israel's governors, and heads of tribes,
Who seeing those great acts which God had done
Singly by me against their conquerors
Acknowledged not, or not at all considered
Deliverance offered: I on the other side
Used no ambition to commend my deeds,
The deeds themselves, though mute, spoke loud the doer;
But they persisted deaf, and would not seem
To count them things worth notice, till at length
Their lords the Philistines with gathered powers
Entered Judea seeking me, who then
Safe to the rock of Etham was retired,
Not flying, but forecasting in what place
To set upon them, what advantaged best;
Meanwhile the men of Judah to prevent
The harass of their land, beset me round;
I willingly on some conditions came
Into their hands, and they as gladly yield me
To the uncircumcised a welcome prey,
Bound with two cords; but cords to me were threads

Touched with the flame: on their whole host I flew
Unarmed, and with a trivial weapon felled
Their choicest youth; they only lived who fled.
Had Judah that day joined, or one whole tribe,
They had by this possessed the towers of Gath,
And lorded over them whom now they serve;
But what more oft in nations grown corrupt,
And by their vices brought to servitude,
Than to love bondage more than liberty,
Bondage with ease than strenuous liberty;
And to despise, or envy, or suspect
Whom God hath of his special favour raised
As their deliverer; if he aught begin,
How frequent to desert him, and at last
To heap ingratitude on worthiest deeds?
Chorus. Thy words to my remembrance bring
How Succoth and the fort of Penuel
Their great deliverer contemned,
The matchless Gideon[1] in pursuit
Of Madian and her vanquished kings:
And how ingrateful Ephraim[2]
Had dealt with Jephtha, who by argument,
Not worse than by his shield and spear
Defended Israel from the Ammonite,
Had not his prowess quelled their pride
In that sore battle when so many died
Without reprieve adjudged to death,
For want of well pronouncing *shibboleth.*
Samson. Of such examples add me to the roll;
Me easily indeed mine may neglect,
But God's proposed deliverance not so.
Chorus. Just are the ways of God,
And justifiable to men;
Unless there be who think not God at all,
If any be, they walk obscure;° *in darkness*
For of such doctrine never was there school,
But the heart of the fool,[3]
And no man therein doctor but himself.
Yet more there be who doubt his ways not just,
As to his own edicts, found contradicting,
Then give the reins to wandering thought,
Regardless of his glory's diminution;
Till by their own perplexities involved
They ravel more, still less resolved,
But never find self-satisfying solution.
As if they would confine the interminable,
And tie him to his own prescript,
Who made our laws to bind us, not himself,
And hath full right to exempt
Whom so it pleases him by choice
From national obstriction,[4] without taint
Of sin, or legal debt;
For with his own laws he can best dispense.
He would not else who never wanted means,
Nor in respect of the enemy just cause
To set his people free,
Have prompted this heroic Nazarite,
Against his vow of strictest purity,
To seek in marriage that fallacious bride,
Unclean, unchaste.
Down Reason then, at least vain reasonings down,
Though Reason here aver
That moral verdict quits her of unclean:
Unchaste was subsequent,[5] her stain not his.
But see here comes thy reverend sire
With careful step, locks white as down,
Old Manoa: advise
Forthwith how thou ought'st to receive him.
Samson. Ay me, another inward grief awaked,
With mention of that name renews the assault.
Manoa. Brethren and men of Dan, for such ye seem,
Though in this uncouth° place; if old respect, *unfamiliar*
As I suppose, towards your once gloried friend,
My son now captive, hither hath informed

[1] *Gideon* See Judges 8.4–9; the Israelites in Succoth and Penuel refused to provide Gideon and his army with supplies as they pursued the remaining leaders of a recently defeated Midian (here, Madian) force.

[2] *Ephraim* See Judges 11.12–33, 12.1–6; after the men of Ephraim refused to help Jephtha fight the Ammonites, Jephtha slaughtered them in retribution; his men afterward identified any Ephraimite fugitives by their distinctive pronunciation of the Hebrew word "shibboleth" (meaning an ear of grain).

[3] *the heart of the fool* "The fool hath said in his heart, There is no God" (Psalms 14.1).

[4] *obstriction* Legal obligation, in this case not to marry a Gentile (from Deuteronomy 7.3).

[5] *Unchaste was subsequent* See Judges 14.20; Samson's first wife, the woman of Timna, was given to his companion after Samson rejected her.

Your younger feet, while mine cast back with age
Came lagging after; say if he be here.
Chorus. As signal now in low dejected state,
As erst in highest, behold him where he lies.
Manoa. O miserable change! Is this the man,
That invincible Samson, far renowned,
The dread of Israel's foes, who with a strength
Equivalent to angels walked their streets,
None offering fight; who single combatant
Duelled their armies ranked in proud array,
Himself an army, now unequal match
To save himself against a coward armed
At one spear's length. O ever-failing trust
In mortal strength! and O what not in man
Deceivable and vain! Nay what thing good
Prayed for, but often proves our woe, our bane?
I prayed for children, and thought barrenness
In wedlock a reproach; I gained a son,
And such a son as all men hailed me happy;
Who would be now a father in my stead?
O wherefore did God grant me my request,
And as a blessing with such pomp adorned?
Why are his gifts desirable, to tempt
Our earnest prayers, then given with solemn hand
As graces, draw a scorpion's tail behind?
For this did the angel twice descend? For this
Ordained thy nurture holy, as of a plant;
Select, and sacred, glorious for a while,
The miracle of men: then in an hour
Ensnared, assaulted, overcome, led bound,
Thy foes' derision, captive, poor, and blind
Into a dungeon thrust, to work with slaves?
Alas methinks whom God hath chosen once
To worthiest deeds, if he through frailty err,
He should not so o'erwhelm, and as a thrall
Subject him to so foul indignities,
Be it but for honour's sake of former deeds.
Samson. Appoint[1] not heavenly disposition, father,
Nothing of all these evils hath befall'n me
But justly; I my self have brought them on,
Sole author I, sole cause: if aught seem vile,
As vile hath been my folly, who have profaned
The mystery of God given me under pledge
Of vow, and have betrayed it to a woman,
A Canaanite, my faithless enemy.
This well I knew, nor was at all surprised,
But warned by oft experience: did not she
Of Timna first betray me, and reveal
The secret wrested from me in her highth
Of nuptial love professed, carrying it straight
To them who had corrupted her, my spies,
And rivals? In this other was there found
More faith? Who also in her prime of love,
Spousal embraces, vitiated with gold,
Though offered only, by the scent conceived
Her spurious first-born, treason against me?
Thrice she assayed with flattering prayers and sighs,
And amorous reproaches to win from me
My capital[2] secret, in what part my strength
Lay stored, in what part summed, that she might know:
Thrice I deluded her, and turned to sport
Her importunity, each time perceiving
How openly, and with what impudence
She purposed to betray me, and (which was worse
Than undissembled hate) with what contempt
She sought to make me traitor to my self;
Yet the fourth time, when mustering all her wiles,
With blandished parleys, feminine assaults,
Tongue-batteries, she surceased not day nor night
To storm me over-watched, and wearied out.
At times when men seek most repose and rest,
I yielded, and unlocked her all my heart,
Who with a grain of manhood well resolved
Might easily have shook off all her snares:
But foul effeminacy held me yoked
Her bond-slave; O indignity, O blot
To honour and religion! servile mind
Rewarded well with servile punishment!
The base degree to which I now am fall'n,
These rags, this grinding, is not yet so base
As was my former servitude, ignoble,
Unmanly, ignominious, infamous,
True slavery, and that blindness worse than this,
That saw not how degenerately I served.
Manoa. I cannot praise thy marriage choices, son,
Rather approved them not; but thou didst plead

[1] *Appoint* Both blame, and limit or prescribe.

[2] *capital* Pun: not only his most important and furthermore lethal secret, but a secret pertaining to his head ("capital" derives from the Latin for "head").

Divine impulsion prompting how thou might'st
Find some occasion to infest° our foes. *harass*
I state not that; this I am sure; our foes
Found soon occasion thereby to make thee
Their captive, and their triumph; thou the sooner
Temptation found'st, or over-potent charms
To violate the sacred trust of silence
Deposited within thee; which to have kept
Tacit, was in thy power. True; and thou bear'st
Enough, and more the burden of that fault;
Bitterly hast thou paid, and still art paying
That rigid score. A worse thing yet remains,
This day the Philistines a popular feast
Here celebrate in Gaza, and proclaim
Great pomp, and sacrifice, and praises loud
To Dagon, as their god who hath delivered
Thee Samson bound and blind into their hands,
Them out of thine, who slew'st them many a slain.
So Dagon shall be magnified, and God,
Besides whom is no god, compared with idols,
Disglorified, blasphemed, and had in scorn
By the idolatrous rout amidst their wine;
Which to have come to pass by means of thee,
Samson, of all thy sufferings think the heaviest,
Of all reproach the most with shame that ever
Could have befall'n thee and thy father's house.
Samson. Father, I do acknowledge and confess
That I this honour, I this pomp have brought
To Dagon, and advanced his praises high
Among the heathen round; to God have brought
Dishonour, obloquy, and oped the mouths
Of idolists, and atheists; have brought scandal
To Israel, diffidence of God, and doubt
In feeble hearts, propense enough before
To waver, or fall off and join with idols;
Which is my chief affliction, shame and sorrow,
The anguish of my soul, that suffers not
Mine eye to harbour sleep, or thoughts to rest.
This only hope relieves me, that the strife
With me hath end; all the contest is now
'Twixt God and Dagon; Dagon hath presumed,
Me overthrown, to enter lists with God,
His deity comparing and preferring
Before the God of Abraham. He, be sure,
Will not connive,° or linger, thus provoked, *be tolerant*
But will arise and his great name assert:
Dagon must stoop, and shall ere long receive
Such a discomfit, as shall quite despoil him
Of all these boasted trophies won on me,
And with confusion blank his worshippers.
Manoa. With cause this hope relieves thee, and these words
I as a prophecy receive: for God,
Nothing more certain, will not long defer
To vindicate the glory of his name
Against all competition, nor will long
Endure it, doubtful whether God be Lord,
Or Dagon. But for thee what shall be done?
Thou must not in the meanwhile here forgot
Lie in this miserable loathsome plight
Neglected. I already have made way
To some Philistian lords, with whom to treat
About thy ransom: well they may by this
Have satisfied their utmost of revenge
By pains and slaveries, worse than death inflicted
On thee, who now no more canst do them harm.
Samson. Spare that proposal, father, spare the trouble
Of that solicitation; let me here,
As I deserve, pay on my punishment;
And expiate, if possible, my crime,
Shameful garrulity. To have revealed
Secrets of men, the secrets of a friend,
How heinous had the fact been, how deserving
Contempt, and scorn of all, to be excluded
All friendship, and avoided as a blab,
The mark of fool set on his front! But I
God's counsel have not kept, his holy secret
Presumptuously have published, impiously,
Weakly at least, and shamefully: a sin
That Gentiles in their parables condemn
To their abyss and horrid pains confined.
Manoa. Be penitent and for thy fault contrite,
But act not in thy own affliction, son,
Repent the sin, but if the punishment
Thou canst avoid, self-preservation bids;
Or the execution leave to high disposal,
And let another hand, not thine, exact
Thy penal forfeit from thy self; perhaps
God will relent, and quit thee all his debt;
Who evermore approves and more accepts

(Best pleased with humble and filial submission)
Him who imploring mercy sues for life,
Than who self-rigorous chooses death as due;
Which argues over-just, and self-displeased
For self-offence, more than for God offended.
Reject not then what offered means, who knows
But God hath set before us, to return thee
Home to thy country and his sacred house,
Where thou may'st bring thy off'rings, to avert
His further ire, with prayers and vows renewed.
Samson. His pardon I implore; but as for life,
To what end should I seek it? When in strength
All mortals I excelled, and great in hopes
With youthful courage and magnanimous thoughts
Of birth from heaven foretold and high exploits,
Full of divine instinct, after some proof
Of acts indeed heroic, far beyond
The sons of Anak,[1] famous now and blazed,
Fearless of danger, like a petty god
I walked about admired of all and dreaded
On hostile ground, none daring my affront.
Then swoll'n with pride into the snare I fell
Of fair fallacious looks, venereal trains,
Softened with pleasure and voluptuous life;
At length to lay my head and hallowed pledge
Of all my strength in the lascivious lap
Of a deceitful concubine who shore me
Like a tame wether,[2] all my precious fleece,
Then turned me out ridiculous, despoiled,
Shaven, and disarmed among my enemies.
Chorus. Desire of wine and all delicious drinks,
Which many a famous warrior overturns,
Thou couldst repress, nor did the dancing ruby
Sparkling, out-poured, the flavour, or the smell,
Or taste that cheers the heart of gods and men,
Allure thee from the cool crystalline stream.[3]
Samson. Wherever fountain or fresh current flowed
Against the eastern ray, translucent, pure
With touch ethereal of heaven's fiery rod
I drank, from the clear milky juice[4] allaying
Thirst, and refreshed; nor envied them the grape
Whose heads that turbulent liquor fills with fumes.
Chorus. O madness, to think use of strongest wines
And strongest drinks our chief support of health,
When God with these forbidden made choice to rear
His mighty champion, strong above compare,
Whose drink was only from the liquid brook.
Samson. But what availed this temperance, not complete
Against another object more enticing?
What boots it at one gate to make defence,
And at another to let in the foe,
Effeminately vanquished? By which means,
Now blind, disheartened, shamed, dishonoured, quelled,
To what can I be useful, wherein serve
My nation, and the work from heaven imposed,
But to sit idle on the household hearth,
A burdenous drone; to visitants a gaze,
Or pitied object, these redundant° locks *abundant*
Robustious to no purpose clustering down,
Vain monument of strength; till length of years
And sedentary numbness craze my limbs
To a contemptible old age obscure.
Here rather let me drudge and earn my bread,
Till vermin or the draff of servile food
Consume me, and oft-invocated death
Hasten the welcome end of all my pains.
Manoa. Wilt thou then serve the Philistines with that gift
Which was expressly given thee to annoy them?
Better at home lie bed-rid, not only idle,
Inglorious, unemployed, with age outworn.
But God who caused a fountain at thy prayer
From the dry ground to spring, thy thirst to allay
After the brunt of battle, can as easy
Cause light again within thy eyes to spring,
Wherewith to serve him better than thou hast;
And I persuade me so; why else this strength
Miraculous yet remaining in those locks?
His might continues in thee not for naught,
Nor shall his wondrous gifts be frustrate thus.

[1] *sons of Anak* Giants (from Numbers 13.33).

[2] *wether* Castrated ram.

[3] *Desire of wine ... stream* As a Nazarite, Samson had taken a vow to abstain from alcohol (Judges 13.4).

[4] *clear milky juice* Clear, pure water. Milton also describes water from a stream as "milky" in *Paradise Lost* 5.306. The usage suggests the conception of the earth as mother.

Samson. All otherwise to me my thoughts portend,
That these dark orbs no more shall treat with light,
Nor the other light of life continue long,
But yield to double darkness nigh at hand:
So much I feel my genial spirits droop,
My hopes all flat, nature within me seems
In all her functions weary of herself;
My race of glory run, and race of shame,
And I shall shortly be with them that rest.
Manoa. Believe not these suggestions which proceed
From anguish of the mind and humours black,[1]
That mingle with thy fancy. I however
Must not omit a father's timely care
To prosecute the means of thy deliverance
By ransom or how else: meanwhile be calm,
And healing words from these thy friends admit.
Samson. O that torment should not be confined
To the body's wounds and sores
With maladies innumerable
In heart, head, breast, and reins;° *kidneys*
But must secret passage find
To the inmost mind,
There exercise all his fierce accidents,
And on her purest spirits prey,
As on entrails, joints, and limbs,
With answerable pains, but more intense,
Though void of corporal sense.
My griefs not only pain me
As a lingering disease,
But finding no redress, ferment and rage,
Nor less than wounds immedicable
Rankle, and fester, and gangrene,
To black mortification.
Thoughts my tormentors armed with deadly stings
Mangle my apprehensive tenderest parts,
Exasperate, exulcerate, and raise
Dire inflammation which no cooling herb
Or med'cinal liquor can assuage,
Nor breath of vernal air from snowy alp.
Sleep hath forsook and given me o'er
To death's benumbing opium as my only cure.
Thence faintings, swoonings of despair,
And sense of heaven's desertion.

[1] *humours black* Black bile, one of the four humors of Renaissance medical psychology and thought to produce melancholy.

I was his nursling once and choice delight,
His destined from the womb,
Promised by heavenly message twice descending.
Under his special eye
Abstemious I grew up and thrived amain;
He led me on to mightiest deeds
Above the nerve of mortal arm
Against the uncircumcised, our enemies.
But now hath cast me off as never known,
And to those cruel enemies,
Whom I by his appointment had provoked,
Left me all helpless with the irreparable loss
Of sight, reserved alive to be repeated
The subject of their cruelty, or scorn.
Nor am I in the list of them that hope;
Hopeless are all my evils, all remediless;
This one prayer yet remains, might I be heard,
No long petition, speedy death,
The close of all my miseries, and the balm.
Chorus. Many are the sayings of the wise
In ancient and in modern books enrolled;
Extolling patience as the truest fortitude;[2]
And to the bearing well of all calamities,
All chances incident to man's frail life
Consolatories writ
With studied argument, and much persuasion sought
Lenient of grief and anxious thought,
But with the afflicted in his pangs their sound
Little prevails, or rather seems a tune,
Harsh, and of dissonant mood from his complaint,
Unless he feel within
Some source of consolation from above;
Secret refreshings, that repair his strength,
And fainting spirits uphold.
 God of our fathers, what is man!
That thou towards him with hand so various,
Or might I say contrarious,
Temper'st thy providence through his short course,
Not evenly, as thou rul'st
The angelic orders and inferior creatures mute,
Irrational and brute.
Nor do I name of men the common rout,

[2] *patience as the truest fortitude* Milton himself expressed this "wise" saying in a "modern book": see *Paradise Lost* 9.31–33 and 12.569–70.

That wand'ring loose about
Grow up and perish, as the summer fly,
Heads without name no more remembered,
But such as thou hast solemnly elected,
With gifts and graces eminently adorned
To some great work, thy glory,
And people's safety, which in part they effect:
Yet toward these thus dignified, thou oft
Amidst their height of noon,
Changest thy countenance, and thy hand with no regard
Of highest favours past
From thee on them, or them to thee of service.
Nor only dost degrade them, or remit
To life obscured, which were a fair dismission,
But throw'st them lower than thou didst exalt
them high,
Unseemly falls in human eye,
Too grievous for the trespass or omission,
Oft leav'st them to the hostile sword
Of heathen and profane, their carcasses
To dogs and fowls a prey, or else captived:
Or to the unjust tribunals, under change of times,
And condemnation of the ingrateful multitude.[1]
If these they scape, perhaps in poverty
With sickness and disease thou bow'st them down,
Painful diseases and deformed,
In crude° old age; *premature*
Though not disordinate, yet causeless suffering
The punishment of dissolute days, in fine,
Just or unjust, alike seem miserable,
For oft alike, both come to evil end.
So deal not with this once thy glorious champion,
The image of thy strength, and mighty minister.
What do I beg? How hast thou dealt already?
Behold him in this state calamitous, and turn
His labours, for thou canst, to peaceful end.
But who is this, what thing of sea or land?
Female of sex it seems,
That so bedecked, ornate, and gay,
Comes this way sailing
Like a stately ship
Of Tarsus, bound for th' isles
Of Javan or Gadier[2]
With all her bravery on, and tackle trim,
Sails filled, and streamers waving,
Courted by all the winds that hold them play,
An amber scent of odorous perfume
Her harbinger, a damsel train behind;
Some rich Philistian matron she may seem,
And now at nearer view, no other certain
Than Dalila thy wife.

Samson. My wife, my traitress, let her not come near me.

Chorus. Yet on she moves, now stands and eyes thee
fixed,
About t' have spoke, but now, with head declined
Like a fair flower surcharged with dew, she weeps
And words addressed seem into tears dissolved,
Wetting the borders of her silken veil:
But now again she makes address to speak.

Dalila. With doubtful feet and wavering resolution
I came, still dreading thy displeasure, Samson,
Which to have merited, without excuse,
I cannot but acknowledge; yet if tears
May expiate (though the fact more evil drew
In the perverse event than I foresaw)
My penance hath not slackened, though my pardon
No way assured. But conjugal affection
Prevailing over fear, and timorous doubt
Hath led me on desirous to behold
Once more thy face, and know of thy estate.
If aught in my ability may serve
To lighten what thou suffer'st, and appease
Thy mind with what amends is in my power,
Though late, yet in some part to recompense
My rash but more unfortunate misdeed.

Samson. Out, out hyena; these are thy wonted arts,
And arts of every woman false like thee,
To break all faith, all vows, deceive, betray,
Then as repentant to submit, beseech,
And reconcilement move with feigned remorse,
Confess, and promise wonders in her change,

[1] *their carcasses ... ingrateful multitude* This passage partly echoes Homer's description of those who died in the Trojan war (*Iliad* 1.4–5). Most readers also hear an allusion to the fates of parliamentary leaders at the Restoration: those who remained alive were tried and several imprisoned or executed, and the bodies of some deceased regicides were exhumed and displayed to the public.

[2] *Tarsus* The location of the biblical Tarshish is disputed, but Milton appears to side with those who place it in Cicilia (modern-day Turkey), cf. *Paradise Lost* 1.200; *Javan* Greek islands (cf. *Paradise Lost* 1.508); *Gadier* Cadiz.

Not truly penitent, but chief to try
Her husband, how far urged his patience bears,
His virtue or weakness which way to assail:
Then with more cautious and instructed skill
Again transgresses, and again submits;
That wisest and best men full oft beguiled
With goodness principled not to reject
The penitent, but ever to forgive,
Are drawn to wear out miserable days,
Entangled with a poisonous bosom snake,
If not by quick destruction soon cut off
As I by thee, to ages an example.
Dalila. Yet hear me Samson; not that I endeavour
To lessen or extenuate my offence,
But that on the other side, if it be weighed
By itself, with aggravations not surcharged,
Or else with just allowance counterpoised,
I may, if possible, thy pardon find
The easier towards me, or thy hatred less.
First granting, as I do, it was a weakness
In me, but incident to all our sex,
Curiosity, inquisitive, importune
Of secrets, then with like infirmity
To publish them, both common female faults:
Was it not weakness also to make known
For importunity, that is for naught,
Wherein consisted all thy strength and safety?
To what I did thou show'dst me first the way.
But I to enemies revealed, and should not.
Nor shouldst thou have trusted that to woman's frailty:
Ere I to thee, thou to thy self wast cruel.
Let weakness then with weakness come to parle
So near related, or the same of kind,
Thine forgive mine; that men may censure thine
The gentler, if severely thou exact not
More strength from me, than in thy self was found.
And what if love, which thou interpret'st hate,
The jealousy of love, powerful of sway
In human hearts, nor less in mine towards thee,
Caused what I did? I saw thee mutable
Of fancy, feared lest one day thou wouldst leave me
As her at Timna, sought by all means therefore
How to endear, and hold thee to me firmest:
No better way I saw than by importuning
To learn thy secrets, get into my power
Thy key of strength and safety: thou wilt say,
Why then revealed? I was assured by those
Who tempted me, that nothing was designed
Against thee but safe custody, and hold:
That made for me; I knew that liberty
Would draw thee forth to perilous enterprises,
While I at home sat full of cares and fears
Wailing thy absence in my widowed bed;
Here I should still enjoy thee day and night
Mine and love's prisoner, not the Philistines',
Whole to myself, unhazarded abroad,
Fearless at home of partners in my love.
These reasons in love's law have passed for good,
Though fond and reasonless to some perhaps;
And love hath oft, well meaning, wrought much woe,
Yet always pity or pardon hath obtained.
Be not unlike all others, not austere
As thou art strong, inflexible as steel.
If thou in strength all mortals dost exceed,
In uncompassionate anger do not so.
Samson. How cunningly the sorceress displays
Her own transgressions, to upbraid me mine!
That malice not repentance brought thee hither,
By this appears: I gave, thou say'st, the example,
I led the way; bitter reproach, but true,
I to myself was false ere thou to me,
Such pardon therefore as I give my folly,
Take to thy wicked deed: which when thou seest
Impartial, self-severe, inexorable,
Thou wilt renounce thy seeking, and much rather
Confess it feigned, weakness is thy excuse,
And I believe it, weakness to resist
Philistian gold: if weakness may excuse,
What murderer, what traitor, parricide,
Incestuous, sacrilegious, but may plead it?
All wickedness is weakness: that plea therefore
With God or man will gain thee no remission.
But love constrained thee; call it furious rage
To satisfy thy lust: love seeks to have love;
My love how couldst thou hope, who took'st the way
To raise in me inexpiable hate,
Knowing, as needs I must, by thee betrayed?
In vain thou striv'st to cover shame with shame,
Or by evasions thy crime uncover'st more.
Dalila. Since thou determin'st weakness for no plea

In man or woman, though to thy own condemning,
Hear what assaults I had, what snares besides,
What sieges girt me round, ere I consented;
Which might have awed the best-resolved of men,
The constantest to have yielded without blame.
It was not gold, as to my charge thou lay'st,
That wrought with me: thou know'st the magistrates
And princes of my country came in person,
Solicited, commanded, threatened, urged,
Adjured by all the bonds of civil duty
And of religion, pressed how just it was,
How honourable, how glorious to entrap
A common enemy, who had destroyed
Such numbers of our nation: and the priest[1]
Was not behind, but ever at my ear,
Preaching how meritorious with the gods
It would be to ensnare an irreligious
Dishonourer of Dagon: what had I
To oppose against such powerful arguments?
Only my love of thee held long debate;
And combated in silence all these reasons
With hard contest: at length that grounded maxim
So rife and celebrated in the mouths
Of wisest men; that to the public good
Private respects must yield; with grave authority
Took full possession of me and prevailed;
Virtue, as I thought, truth, duty so enjoining.
Samson. I thought where all thy circling wiles
would end;
In feigned religion, smooth hypocrisy.
But had thy love, still odiously pretended,
Been, as it ought, sincere, it would have taught thee
Far other reasonings, brought forth other deeds.
I before all the daughters of my tribe
And of my nation chose thee from among
My enemies, loved thee, as too well thou knew'st,
Too well, unbosomed all my secrets to thee,
Not out of levity, but overpowered
By thy request, who could deny thee nothing;
Yet now am judged an enemy. Why then
Didst thou at first receive me for thy husband?
Then, as since then, thy country's foe professed:
Being once a wife, for me thou wast to leave
Parents and country; nor was I their subject,
Nor under their protection but my own,
Thou mine, not theirs: if aught against my life
Thy country sought of thee, it sought unjustly,
Against the law of nature, law of nations,
No more thy country, but an impious crew
Of men conspiring to uphold their state
By worse than hostile deeds, violating the ends
For which our country is a name so dear;
Not therefore to be obeyed. But zeal moved thee;
To please thy gods thou didst it; gods unable
To acquit themselves and prosecute their foes
But by ungodly deeds, the contradiction
Of their own deity, gods cannot be:
Less therefore to be pleased, obeyed, or feared,
These false pretexts and varnished colours failing,
Bare in thy guilt how foul must thou appear!
Dalila. In argument with men a woman ever
Goes by the worse, whatever be her cause.
Samson. For want of words no doubt, or lack of breath,
Witness when I was worried with thy peals.
Dalila. I was a fool, too rash, and quite mistaken
In what I thought would have succeeded best.
Let me obtain forgiveness of thee, Samson,
Afford me place to show what recompense
Towards thee I intend for what I have misdone,
Misguided; only what remains past cure
Bear not too sensibly,° nor still insist *keenly*
To afflict thy self in vain: though sight be lost,
Life yet hath many solaces, enjoyed
Where other senses want not their delights
At home in leisure and domestic ease,
Exempt from many a care and chance to which
Eyesight exposes daily men abroad.
I to the lords will intercede, not doubting
Their favourable ear, that I may fetch thee
From forth this loathsome prison-house, to abide
With me, where my redoubled love and care
With nursing diligence, to me glad office,
May ever tend about thee to old age
With all things grateful cheered, and so supplied,
That what by me thou hast lost thou least shalt miss.
Samson. No, no, of my condition take no care;
It fits not; thou and I long since are twain;
Nor think me so unwary or accursed
To bring my feet again into the snare

[1] *priest* One of Milton's additions to the biblical account.

Where once I have been caught; I know thy trains
Though dearly to my cost, thy gins, and toils;[1]
Thy fair enchanted cup, and warbling charms[2]
No more on me have power, their force is nulled,
So much of adder's wisdom[3] I have learnt
To fence my ear against thy sorceries.
If in my flower of youth and strength, when all men
Loved, honoured, feared me, thou alone could hate me
Thy husband, slight me, sell me, and forgo me;
How wouldst thou use me now, blind, and thereby
Deceivable, in most things as a child
Helpless, thence easily contemned, and scorned,
And last neglected? How wouldst thou insult
When I must live uxorious to thy will
In perfect thraldom, how again betray me,
Bearing my words and doings to the lords
To gloss upon, and censuring, frown or smile?
This jail I count the house of liberty
To thine° whose doors my feet shall never enter. *compared to thine*

Dalila. Let me approach at least, and touch thy hand.

Samson. Not for thy life, lest fierce remembrance wake
My sudden rage to tear thee joint by joint.
At distance I forgive thee, go with that;
Bewail thy falsehood, and the pious works
It hath brought forth to make thee memorable
Among illustrious women, faithful wives:
Cherish thy hastened widowhood with the gold
Of matrimonial treason: so farewell.

Dalila. I see thou art implacable, more deaf
To prayers, than winds and seas, yet winds to seas
Are reconciled at length, and sea to shore:
Thy anger, unappeasable, still rages,
Eternal tempest never to be calmed.
Why do I humble thus myself, and suing
For peace, reap nothing but repulse and hate?
Bid go with evil omen and the brand
Of infamy upon my name denounced?
To mix with thy concernments I desist
Henceforth, nor too much disapprove my own.
Fame if not double-faced is double-mouthed,
And with contrary blast proclaims most deeds,
On both his wings, one black, the other white,
Bears greatest names in his wild airy flight.
My name perhaps among the circumcised
In Dan,[4] in Judah, and the bordering tribes,
To all posterity may stand defamed,
With malediction mentioned, and the blot
Of falsehood most unconjugal traduced.
But in my country where I most desire,
In Ecron, Gaza, Asdod, and in Gath[5]
I shall be named among the famousest
Of women, sung at solemn festivals,
Living and dead recorded, who to save
Her country from a fierce destroyer, chose
Above the faith of wedlock-bands, my tomb
With odours visited and annual flowers.
Not less renowned than in Mount Ephraim,
Jael,[6] who with inhospitable guile
Smote Sisera sleeping through the temples nailed.
Nor shall I count it heinous to enjoy
The public marks of honour and reward
Conferred upon me, for the piety
Which to my country I was judged to have shown.
At this whoever envies or repines
I leave him to his lot, and like my own.

Chorus. She's gone, a manifest serpent by her sting
Discovered in the end, till now concealed.

Samson. So let her go, God sent her to debase me,
And aggravate my folly who committed
To such a viper his most sacred trust
Of secrecy, my safety, and my life.

---

[1] *I know thy … and toils* General terms from hunting for traps, snares, or lures.

[2] *enchanted cup, and warbling charms* An allusion to Circe in Homer's *Odyssey*, whose magical potions turned Odysseus's men into pleasure-loving voluptuaries and then into swine; possibly also an allusion to the sirens, whose beautiful songs led men to their deaths.

[3] *adder's wisdom* Deafness. The proverbial deafness of adders derived from Psalms 58.4–5: "they are like the deaf adder that stoppeth her ear; which will not hearken to the voice of charmers, charming never so wisely."

[4] *Dan* Home of the Danites, Samson's tribe.

[5] *Ecron, Gaza, Asdod … Gath* Four of the five main Philistine cities.

[6] *Jael* See Judges 4.17–24; Jael, the wife of Heber the Kenite, gave refuge to the Canaanite general Sisera as he fled an Israelite force led by Barak, but then murdered him as he slept by hammering a tent peg into his temple. She was praised in song by Deborah and Barak (Judges 5.24–31); Dalila imagines her people, the Philistines, celebrating her in similar fashion.

Chorus. Yet beauty, though injurious, hath strange power,
After offence returning, to regain
Love once possessed, nor can be easily
Repulsed, without much inward passion felt
And secret sting of amorous remorse.
Samson. Love-quarrels oft in pleasing concord end,
Not wedlock-treachery endangering life.
Chorus. It is not virtue, wisdom, valour, wit,
Strength, comeliness of shape, or amplest merit
That woman's love can win or long inherit;° *possess*
But what it is, hard is to say,
Harder to hit
(Which way soever men refer it),
Much like thy riddle,[1] Samson, in one day
Or seven, though one should musing sit;
If any of these or all, the Timnian bride
Had not so soon preferred
Thy paranymph,[2] worthless to thee compared,
Successor in thy bed,
Nor both so loosely disallied
Their nuptials, nor this last so treacherously
Had shorn the fatal harvest of thy head.
Is it for that such outward ornament
Was lavished on their sex, that inward gifts
Were left for haste unfinished, judgment scant,
Capacity not raised to apprehend
Or value what is best
In choice, but oftest to affect the wrong?
Or was too much of self-love mixed,
Of constancy no root infixed,
That either they love nothing, or not long?
Whate'er it be, to wisest men and best
Seeming at first all heavenly under virgin veil,
Soft, modest, meek, demure,
Once joined, the contrary she proves, a thorn
Intestine,° far within defensive arms *internal*
A cleaving mischief, in his way to virtue
Adverse and turbulent, or by her charms
Draws him awry enslaved
With dotage, and his sense depraved
To folly and shameful deeds which ruin ends.
What pilot so expert but needs must wreck
Embarked with such a steers-mate at the helm?
Favoured of heaven who finds
One virtuous rarely found,
That in domestic good combines:
Happy that house! His way to peace is smooth:
But virtue which breaks through all opposition,
And all temptation can remove,
Most shines and most is acceptable above.
Therefore God's universal law
Gave to the man despotic power
Over his female in due awe,
Nor from that right to part an hour,
Smile she or lour:
So shall he least confusion draw
On his whole life, not swayed
By female usurpation,[3] nor dismayed.
But had we best retire, I see a storm?
Samson. Fair days have oft contracted wind and rain.
Chorus. But this another kind of tempest brings.
Samson. Be less abstruse, my riddling days are past.
Chorus. Look now for no enchanting voice, nor fear
The bait of honeyed words; a rougher tongue
Draws hitherward, I know him by his stride,
The giant Harapha of Gath,[4] his look
Haughty as is his pile high-built and proud.
Comes he in peace? What wind hath blown him hither
I less conjecture than when first I saw
The sumptuous Dalila floating this way:
His habit carries peace, his brow defiance.
Samson. Or peace or not, alike to me he comes.
Chorus. His fraught° we soon shall know, he now arrives. *freight, business*
Harapha. I come not Samson, to condole thy chance,
As these perhaps, yet wish it had not been,
Though for no friendly intent. I am of Gath,
Men call me Harapha, of stock renowned
As Og or Anak and the Emims old

[1] *thy riddle* See Judges 14.12–18.

[2] *paranymph* Groomsman or "best man" at a wedding: see Judges 14.20, which is silent about the bride's preferences and indicates only that she was "given to" Samson's companion after Samson left her in anger.

[3] *not swayed ... usurpation* An allusion to 1 Timothy 2.12–13: "But I suffer not a woman to teach, nor to usurp authority over the man, but to be in silence."

[4] *Harapha* Not in the biblical story of Samson, but modeled on Goliath; the name derives from the Hebrew word for giant.

That Kiriathaim[1] held, thou know'st me now
If thou at all art known.[2] Much I have heard
Of thy prodigious might and feats performed
Incredible to me, in this displeased,
That I was never present on the place
Of those encounters, where we might have tried
Each other's force in camp or listed field:° *tiltyard*
And now am come to see of whom such noise
Hath walked about, and each limb to survey,
If thy appearance answer loud report.
Samson. The way to know were not to see but taste.
Harapha. Dost thou already single° me? I thought *challenge*
Gyves° and the mill had tamed thee. O that fortune *shackles*
Had brought me to the field where thou art famed
To have wrought such wonders with an ass's jaw;
I should have forced thee soon wish other arms,
Or left thy carcass where the ass lay thrown:
So had the glory of prowess been recovered
To Palestine, won by a Philistine
From the unforeskinned race, of whom thou bear'st
The highest name for valiant acts; that honour
Certain to have won by mortal duel from thee,
I lose, prevented by thy eyes put out.
Samson. Boast not of what thou wouldst have done, but do
What then thou wouldst, thou seest it in thy hand.
Harapha. To combat with a blind man I disdain,
And thou hast need much washing to be touched.
Samson. Such usage as your honourable lords
Afford me assassinated° and betrayed, *attacked treacherously*
Who durst not with their whole united powers
In fight withstand me single and unarmed,
Nor in the house with chamber ambushes
Close-banded durst attack me, no not sleeping,
Till they had hired a woman with their gold
Breaking her marriage faith to circumvent me.
Therefore without feigned shifts let be assigned
Some narrow place enclosed, where sight may give thee,
Or rather flight, no great advantage on me;
Then put on all thy gorgeous arms, thy helmet
And brigandine of brass, thy broad habergeon,
Vantbrace and greaves, and gauntlet,[3] add thy spear
A weaver's beam, and seven-times-folded shield,[4]
I only with an oaken staff will meet thee,
And raise such outcries on thy clattered iron,
Which long shall not withhold me from thy head,
That in a little time while breath remains thee,
Thou oft shalt wish thyself at Gath to boast
Again in safety what thou wouldst have done
To Samson, but shalt never see Gath more.
Harapha. Thou durst not thus disparage glorious arms
Which greatest heroes have in battle worn,
Their ornament and safety, had not spells
And black enchantments, some magician's art
Armed thee or charmed thee strong, which thou from heaven
Feign'dst at thy birth was given thee in thy hair,
Where strength can least abide, though all thy hairs
Were bristles ranged like those that ridge the back
Of chafed wild boars or ruffled porcupines.
Samson. I know no spells, use no forbidden arts;
My trust is in the living God who gave me
At my nativity this strength, diffused
No less through all my sinews, joints and bones,
Than thine, while I preserved these locks unshorn,
The pledge of my unviolated vow.
For proof hereof, if Dagon be thy god,
Go to his temple, invocate his aid
With solemnest devotion, spread before him
How highly it concerns his glory now
To frustrate and dissolve these magic spells,

[1] *Og or Anak and the Emims* Biblical giants (Numbers 13.33, Deuteronomy 2.10–11, 3.11); *Kiriathaim* Home to the Emims (Genesis 14.5).

[2] *thou know'st me … art known* Echoing Satan in *Paradise Lost,* when Ithuriel and Zephon discover him in Eden and demand his identity: "Not to know me argues yourselves unknown" (4.830), Satan haughtily replies.

[3] *brigandine* Body armor; *habergeon* Sleeveless coat of mail; *Vantbrace* Armor for the forearm; *greaves* Armor for the shin; *gauntlet* Armor for the hand.

[4] *weaver's beam* Large wooden roller on a loom; the comparison echoes the description of Goliath's spear in 1 Samuel 17.7; *seven-times-folded shield* Shield of oxhide folded seven times, like the shields of classical heroes Ajax (*Iliad* 7.220) and Turnus (*Aeneid* 12.925).

Which I to be the power of Israel's God
Avow, and challenge Dagon to the test,
Offering to combat thee his champion bold,
With the utmost of his godhead seconded:
Then thou shalt see, or rather to thy sorrow
Soon feel, whose God is strongest, thine or mine.
Harapha. Presume not on thy God, whate'er he be,
Thee he regards not, owns not, hath cut off
Quite from his people, and delivered up
Into thy enemies' hand, permitted them
To put out both thine eyes, and fettered send thee
Into the common prison, there to grind
Among the slaves and asses thy comrades,
As good for nothing else, no better service
With those thy boisterous locks, no worthy match
For valour to assail, nor by the sword
Of noble warrior, so to stain his honour,
But by the barber's razor best subdued.
Samson. All these indignities, for such they are
From thine, these evils I deserve and more,
Acknowledge them from God inflicted on me
Justly, yet despair not of his final pardon
Whose ear is ever open; and his eye
Gracious to readmit the suppliant;
In confidence whereof I once again
Defy thee to the trial of mortal fight,
By combat to decide whose god is God,
Thine or whom I with Israel's sons adore.
Harapha. Fair honour that thou dost thy God, in trusting
He will accept thee to defend his cause,
A murderer, a revolter, and a robber.
Samson. Tongue-doughty giant, how dost thou prove me these?
Harapha. Is not thy nation subject to our lords?
Their magistrates confessed it, when they took thee
As a league-breaker and delivered bound
Into our hands: for hadst thou not committed
Notorious murder on those thirty men
At Ascalon, who never did thee harm,
Then like a robber stripp'dst them of their robes?
The Philistines, when thou hadst broke the league,
Went up with armèd powers thee only seeking,
To others did no violence nor spoil.
Samson. Among the daughters of the Philistines
I chose a wife, which argued me no foe;
And in your city held my nuptial feast:
But your ill-meaning politician lords,
Under pretence of bridal friends and guests,
Appointed to await me thirty spies,
Who threatening cruel death constrained the bride
To wring from me and tell to them my secret,
That solved the riddle which I had proposed.
When I perceived all set on enmity,
As on my enemies, wherever chanced,
I used hostility, and took their spoil
To pay my underminers in their coin.
My nation was subjected to your lords.
It was the force of conquest; force with force
Is well ejected when the conquered can.
But I a private person, whom my country
As a league-breaker gave up bound, presumed
Single rebellion and did hostile acts.
I was no private but a person raised
With strength sufficient and command from heaven
To free my country; if their servile minds
Me their deliverer sent would not receive,
But to their masters gave me up for naught,
The unworthier they; whence to this day they serve.
I was to do my part from heaven assigned,
And had performed it if my known offence
Had not disabled me, not all your force:
These shifts refuted, answer thy appellant
Though by his blindness maimed for high attempts,
Who now defies thee thrice to single fight,
As a petty enterprise of small enforce.
Harapha. With thee a man condemned, a slave enrolled,
Due by the law to capital punishment?
To fight with thee no man of arms will deign.
Samson. Cam'st thou for this, vain boaster, to survey me,
To descant on my strength, and give thy verdict?
Come nearer, part not hence so slight informed;
But take good heed my hand survey not thee.
Harapha. O Baal-zebub! Can my ears unused
Hear these dishonours, and not render death?
Samson. No man withholds thee, nothing from thy hand

Fear I incurable; bring up thy van,[1]
My heels are fettered, but my fist is free.
Harapha. This insolence other kind of answer fits.
Samson. Go baffled coward, lest I run upon thee,
Though in these chains, bulk without spirit vast,
And with one buffet lay thy structure low,
Or swing thee in the air, then dash thee down
To the hazard of thy brains and shattered sides.
Harapha. By Astaroth[2] ere long thou shalt lament
These braveries in irons loaden on thee.
Chorus. His giantship is gone somewhat crestfall'n,
Stalking with less unconscionable[3] strides,
And lower looks, but in a sultry chafe.
Samson. I dread him not, nor all his giant-brood,
Though fame divulge him father of five sons
All of gigantic size, Goliah[4] chief.
Chorus. He will directly to the lords, I fear,
And with malicious counsel stir them up
Some way or other yet further to afflict thee.
Samson. He must allege some cause, and offered fight
Will not dare mention, lest a question rise
Whether he durst accept the offer or not,
And that he durst not plain enough appeared.
Much more affliction than already felt
They cannot well impose, nor I sustain;
If they intend advantage of my labours,
The work of many hands, which earns my keeping
With no small profit daily to my owners.
But come what will, my deadliest foe will prove
My speediest friend, by death to rid me hence,
The worst that he can give, to me the best.
Yet so it may fall out, because their end
Is hate, not help to me, it may with mine
Draw their own ruin who attempt the deed.
Chorus. Oh how comely it is and how reviving
To the spirits of just men long oppressed!
When God into the hands of their deliverer
Puts invincible might
To quell the mighty of the earth, the oppressor,
The brute and boisterous force of violent men
Hardy and industrious to support
Tyrannic power, but raging to pursue
The righteous and all such as honour truth;
He all their ammunition
And feats of war defeats
With plain heroic magnitude of mind
And celestial vigour armed,
Their armouries and magazines contemns,
Renders them useless, while
With wingèd expedition
Swift as the lightning glance he executes
His errand on the wicked, who surprised
Lose their defence distracted and amazed.
But patience is more oft the exercise
Of saints, the trial of their fortitude,
Making them each his own deliverer,
And victor over all
That tyranny or fortune can inflict;
Either of these is in thy lot,
Samson, with might endued
Above the sons of men; but sight bereaved
May chance to number thee with those
Whom patience finally must crown.
This idol's day hath been to thee no day of rest,
Labouring thy mind
More than the working day thy hands,
And yet perhaps more trouble is behind.
For I descry this way
Some other tending, in his hand
A sceptre or quaint° staff he bears, *elaborate or elegant*
Comes on amain, speed in his look.
By his habit° I discern him now *clothing*
A public officer, and now at hand.
His message will be short and voluble.° *rapid*
Officer. Hebrews, the prisoner Samson here I seek.
Chorus. His manacles remark him, there he sits.
Officer. Samson, to thee our lords thus bid me say:
This day to Dagon is a solemn feast,
With sacrifices, triumph, pomp, and games;
Thy strength they know surpassing human rate,
And now some public proof thereof require
To honour this great feast, and great assembly;
Rise therefore with all speed and come along,
Where I will see thee heartened and fresh clad

[1] *van* Vanguard, the foremost division of an army; i.e., start your attack.

[2] *Astaroth* Ancient goddess (also Ashtoreth, Astarte, Ishtar, etc.).

[3] *less unconscionable* Less excessive, shorter.

[4] *Goliah* Goliath (see 1 Samuel 17 and 2 Samuel 19–22).

To appear as fits before the illustrious lords.
Samson. Thou know'st I am an Hebrew, therefore tell them,
Our law forbids at their religious rites
My presence; for that cause I cannot come.
Officer. This answer, be assured, will not content them.
Samson. Have they not sword-players, and every sort
Of gymnic artists, wrestlers, riders, runners,
Jugglers and dancers, antics, mummers, mimics,
But they must pick me out with shackles tired,
And over-laboured at their public mill,
To make them sport with blind activity?
Do they not seek occasion of new quarrels
On my refusal to distress me more,
Or make a game of my calamities?
Return the way thou cam'st, I will not come.
Officer. Regard thyself, this will offend them highly.
Samson. Myself? My conscience and internal peace.
Can they think me so broken, so debased
With corporal servitude, that my mind ever
Will condescend to such absurd commands?
Although their drudge, to be their fool or jester,
And in my midst of sorrow and heart-grief
To show them feats, and play before their god,
The worst of all indignities, yet on me
Joined with extreme contempt? I will not come.
Officer. My message was imposed on me with speed,
Brooks no delay: is this thy resolution?
Samson. So take it with what speed thy message needs.
Officer. I am sorry what this stoutness will produce.
Samson. Perhaps thou shalt have cause to sorrow indeed.
Chorus. Consider, Samson; matters now are strained
Up to the highth, whether to hold or break;
He's gone, and who knows how he may report
Thy words by adding fuel to the flame?
Expect another message more imperious,
More lordly thundering than thou well wilt bear.
Samson. Shall I abuse this consecrated gift
Of strength, again returning with my hair
After my great transgression, so requite
Favour renewed, and add a greater sin
By prostituting holy things to idols;
A Nazarite in place abominable
Vaunting my strength in honour to their Dagon?
Besides, how vile, contemptible, ridiculous,
What act more execrably unclean, profane?
Chorus. Yet with this strength thou serv'st the Philistines,
Idolatrous, uncircumcised, unclean.
Samson. Not in their idol-worship, but by labour
Honest and lawful to deserve my food
Of those who have me in their civil power.
Chorus. Where the heart joins not, outward acts defile not.
Samson. Where outward force constrains, the sentence holds:
But who constrains me to the temple of Dagon,
Not dragging? The Philistian lords command.
Commands are no constraints. If I obey them,
I do it freely; venturing to displease
God for the fear of man, and man prefer,
Set God behind: which in his jealousy
Shall never, unrepented, find forgiveness.
Yet that he may dispense with me or thee
Present in temples at idolatrous rites
For some important cause, thou need'st not doubt.
Chorus. How thou wilt here come off surmounts my reach.
Samson. Be of good courage, I begin to feel
Some rousing motions in me which dispose
To something extraordinary my thoughts.
I with this messenger will go along,
Nothing to do, be sure, that may dishonour
Our law, or stain my vow of Nazarite.
If there be aught of presage in the mind,
This day will be remarkable in my life
By some great act, or of my days the last.
Chorus. In time thou hast resolved, the man returns.
Officer. Samson, this second message from our lords
To thee I am bid say. Art thou our slave,
Our captive, at the public mill our drudge,
And dar'st thou at our sending and command
Dispute thy coming? Come without delay;
Or we shall find such engines to assail
And hamper thee, as thou shalt come of force,
Though thou wert firmlier fastened than a rock.
Samson. I could be well content to try their art,
Which to no few of them would prove pernicious.
Yet knowing their advantages too many,
Because they shall not trail me through their streets

Like a wild beast, I am content to go.
Masters' commands come with a power resistless
To such as owe them absolute subjection;
And for a life who will not change his purpose?
(So mutable are all the ways of men)
Yet this be sure, in nothing to comply
Scandalous or forbidden in our law.
Officer. I praise thy resolution, doff these links:
By this compliance thou wilt win the lords
To favour, and perhaps to set thee free.
Samson. Brethren farewell, your company along
I will not wish, lest it perhaps offend them
To see me girt with friends; and how the sight
Of me as of a common enemy,
So dreaded once, may now exasperate them
I know not. Lords are lordliest in their wine;
And the well-feasted priest then soonest fired
With zeal, if aught religion seem concerned:
No less the people on their holy-days
Impetuous, insolent, unquenchable;
Happen what may, of me expect to hear
Nothing dishonourable, impure, unworthy
Our God, our law, my nation, or my self,
The last of me or no I cannot warrant.
Chorus. Go, and the Holy One
Of Israel be thy guide
To what may serve his glory best, and spread his name
Great among the heathen round:
Send thee the angel of thy birth, to stand
Fast by thy side, who from thy father's field
Rode up in flames after his message told
Of thy conception, and be now a shield
Of fire; that spirit that first rushed on thee
In the camp of Dan
Be efficacious in thee now at need.
For never was from heaven imparted
Measure of strength so great to mortal seed,
As in thy wondrous actions hath been seen.
But wherefore comes old Manoa in such haste
With youthful steps? Much livelier than erewhile
He seems: supposing here to find his son,
Or of him bringing to us some glad news?
Manoa. Peace with you brethren; my inducement hither
Was not at present here to find my son,
By order of the lords new parted hence
To come and play before them at their feast.
I heard all as I came, the city rings
And numbers thither flock, I had no will,
Lest I should see him forced to things unseemly.
But that which moved my coming now, was chiefly
To give ye part with me what hope I have
With good success to work his liberty.
Chorus. That hope would much rejoice us to partake
With thee; say reverend sire, we thirst to hear.
Manoa. I have attempted one by one the lords
Either at home, or through the high street passing,
With supplication prone and father's tears
To accept of ransom for my son their prisoner,
Some much averse I found and wondrous harsh,
Contemptuous, proud, set on revenge and spite;
That part most reverenced Dagon and his priests,
Others more moderate seeming, but their aim
Private reward, for which both god and state
They easily would set to sale; a third
More generous far and civil, who confessed
They had enough revenged, having reduced
Their foe to misery beneath their fears,
The rest was magnanimity to remit,
If some convenient ransom were proposed.
What noise or shout was that? It tore the sky.
Chorus. Doubtless the people shouting to behold
Their once great dread, captive, and blind before them,
Or at some proof of strength before them shown.
Manoa. His ransom, if my whole inheritance
May compass it, shall willingly be paid
And numbered down: much rather I shall choose
To live the poorest in my tribe, than richest,
And he in that calamitous prison left.
No, I am fixed not to part hence without him.
For his redemption all my patrimony,
If need be, I am ready to forgo
And quit: not wanting him, I shall want nothing.
Chorus. Fathers are wont to lay up for their sons,
Thou for thy son art bent to lay out all;
Sons wont to nurse their parents in old age,
Thou in old age car'st how to nurse thy son,
Made older than thy age through eyesight lost.
Manoa. It shall be my delight to tend his eyes,
And view him sitting in the house, ennobled

With all those high exploits by him achieved,
And on his shoulders waving down those locks,
That of a nation armed the strength contained:
And I persuade me God had not permitted
His strength again to grow up with his hair
Garrisoned round about him like a camp
Of faithful soldiery, were not his purpose
To use him further yet in some great service,
Not to sit idle with so great a gift
Useless, and thence ridiculous about him.
And since his strength with eyesight was not lost,
God will restore him eyesight to his strength.
Chorus. Thy hopes are not ill founded nor seem vain
Of his delivery, and thy joy thereon
Conceived, agreeable to a father's love,
In both which we, as next,[1] participate.
Manoa. I know your friendly minds and—O what noise!
Mercy of heaven what hideous noise was that!
Horribly loud unlike the former shout.
Chorus. Noise call you it or universal groan
As if the whole inhabitation perished,
Blood, death, and deathful deeds are in that noise,
Ruin, destruction at the utmost point.
Manoa. Of ruin[2] indeed methought I heard the noise,
O it continues, they have slain my son.
Chorus. Thy son is rather slaying them, that outcry
From slaughter of one foe could not ascend.
Manoa. Some dismal accident it needs must be;
What shall we do, stay here or run and see?
Chorus. Best keep together here, lest running thither
We unawares run into danger's mouth.
This evil on the Philistines is fall'n,
From whom could else a general cry be heard?
The sufferers then will scarce molest us here,
From other hands we need not much to fear.
What if his eyesight (for to Israel's God
Nothing is hard) by miracle restored,
He now be dealing dole among his foes,
And over heaps of slaughtered walk his way?
Manoa. That were a joy presumptuous to be thought.
Chorus. Yet God hath wrought things as incredible
For his people of old; what hinders now?
Manoa. He can I know, but doubt to think he will;
Yet hope would fain subscribe, and tempts belief.
A little stay will bring some notice hither.
Chorus. Of good or bad so great, of bad the sooner;
For evil news rides post, while good news baits.° *travels slowly*
And to our wish I see one hither speeding,
An Hebrew, as I guess, and of our tribe.
Messenger. O whither shall I run, or which way fly
The sight of this so horrid spectacle
Which erst my eyes beheld and yet behold;
For dire imagination still pursues me.
But providence or instinct of nature seems,
Or reason though disturbed, and scarce consulted
To have guided me aright, I know not how,
To thee first reverend Manoa, and to these
My countrymen, whom here I knew remaining,
As at some distance from the place of horror,
So in the sad event too much concerned.
Manoa. The accident was loud, and here before thee
With rueful cry, yet what it was we hear not,
No preface needs, thou seest we long to know.
Messenger. It would burst forth, but I recover breath
And sense distract, to know well what I utter.
Manoa. Tell us the sum, the circumstance defer.
Messenger. Gaza yet stands, but all her sons are fall'n,
All in a moment overwhelmed and fall'n.
Manoa. Sad, but thou know'st to Israelites not saddest
The desolation of a hostile city.
Messenger. Feed on that first, there may in grief be surfeit.
Manoa. Relate by whom.
Messenger. By Samson.
Manoa. That still lessens
The sorrow, and converts it nigh to joy.
Messenger. Ah Manoa I refrain, too suddenly
To utter what will come at last too soon;
Lest evil tidings with too rude irruption
Hitting thy agèd ear should pierce too deep.
Manoa. Suspense in news is torture, speak them out.
Messenger. Then take the worst in brief, Samson is dead.
Manoa. The worst indeed, O all my hope's defeated
To free him hence! But death who sets all free
Hath paid his ransom now and full discharge.
What windy joy this day had I conceived

[1] *as next* As next of kin (as fellow Danites).

[2] *ruin* With the Latin sense of fall or collapse (as of a building).

Hopeful of his delivery, which now proves
Abortive as the first-born bloom of spring
Nipped with the lagging rear of winter's frost.
Yet ere I give the reins to grief, say first,
How died he? Death to life is crown or shame.
All by him fell thou say'st, by whom fell he,
What glorious hand gave Samson his death's wound?
Messenger. Unwounded of his enemies he fell.
Manoa. Wearied with slaughter then or how? Explain.
Messenger. By his own hands.
Manoa. Self-violence? What cause
Brought him so soon at variance with himself
Among his foes?
Messenger. Inevitable cause
At once both to destroy and be destroyed;
The edifice where all were met to see him
Upon their heads and on his own he pulled.
Manoa. O lastly over-strong against thyself!
A dreadful way thou took'st to thy revenge.
More than enough we know; but while things yet
Are in confusion, give us if thou canst,
Eye-witness of what first or last was done,
Relation more particular and distinct.
Messenger. Occasions drew me early to this city,
And as the gates I entered with sunrise,
The morning trumpets festival proclaimed
Through each high street: little I had dispatched
When all abroad was rumoured that this day
Samson should be brought forth to show the people
Proof of his mighty strength in feats and games;
I sorrowed at his captive state, but minded
Not to be absent at that spectacle.
The building was a spacious theatre
Half round on two main pillars vaulted high,
With seats where all the lords and each degree
Of sort,° might sit in order to behold; *rank*
The other side was open, where the throng
On banks and scaffolds under sky might stand;[1]
I among these aloof obscurely stood.
The feast and noon grew high, and sacrifice
Had filled their hearts with mirth, high cheer, and wine,
When to their sports they turned. Immediately
Was Samson as a public servant brought,
In their state livery clad; before him pipes
And timbrels, on each side went armèd guards,
Both horse and foot before him and behind
Archers, and slingers, cataphracts and spears.[2]
At sight of him the people with a shout
Rifted the air clamouring their god with praise,
Who had made their dreadful enemy their thrall.
He patient but undaunted where they led him,
Came to the place, and what was set before him
Which without help of eye might be assayed,
To heave, pull, draw, or break, he still performed
All with incredible, stupendious force,
None daring to appear antagonist.
At length for intermission sake they led him
Between the pillars; he his guide requested
(For so from such as nearer stood we heard)
As over-tired to let him lean a while
With both his arms on those two massy pillars
That to the archèd roof gave main support.
He unsuspicious led him; which when Samson
Felt in his arms, with head a while inclined,
And eyes fast fixed he stood, as one who prayed,
Or some great matter in his mind revolved.
At last with head erect thus cried aloud,
Hitherto, lords, what your commands imposed
I have performed, as reason was, obeying,
Not without wonder or delight beheld.
Now of my own accord such other trial
I mean to show you of my strength, yet greater;
As with amaze shall strike all who behold.
This uttered, straining all his nerves he bowed,
As with the force of winds and waters pent,
When mountains tremble, those two massy pillars
With horrible convulsion to and fro,
He tugged, he shook, till down they came and drew
The whole roof after them, with burst of thunder
Upon the heads of all who sat beneath,
Lords, ladies, captains, counsellors, or priests,
Their choice nobility and flower, not only
Of this but each Philistian city round
Met from all parts to solemnize this feast.
Samson with these immixed, inevitably

[1] *The other side … stand* See Judges 16.27 and line 1659 below. In the biblical account, the general audience of men and women sits on the building's roof (and so dies when Samson pulls down the pillars).

[2] *cataphracts* Armored soldiers; *spears* Spearmen.

Pulled down the same destruction on himself;
The vulgar[1] only scaped who stood without.
Chorus. O dearly-bought revenge, yet glorious!
Living or dying thou hast fulfilled
The work for which thou wast foretold
To Israel, and now li'st victorious
Among thy slain self-killed
Not willingly, but tangled in the fold,
Of dire necessity, whose law in death conjoined
Thee with thy slaughtered foes in number more
Than all thy life had slain before.
Semichorus. While their hearts were jocund and sublime,
Drunk with idolatry, drunk with wine,
And fat regorged of bulls and goats,
Chanting their idol, and preferring
Before our living dread who dwells
In Silo his bright sanctuary:
Among them he a spirit of frenzy sent,
Who hurt their minds,
And urged them on with mad desire
To call in haste for their destroyer;
They only set on sport and play
Unweetingly importuned
Their own destruction to come speedy upon them.
So fond are mortal men
Fall'n into wrath divine,
As their own ruin on themselves to invite,
Insensate left, or to sense reprobate,
And with blindness internal struck.
Semichorus. But he though blind of sight,
Despised and thought extinguished quite,
With inward eyes illuminated
His fiery virtue roused
From under ashes into sudden flame,
And as an evening dragon[2] came,
Assailant on the perchèd roosts,
And nests in order ranged
Of tame villatic° fowl; but as an eagle *barnyard*
His cloudless thunder bolted on their heads.
So virtue given for lost,
Depressed, and overthrown, as seemed,
Like that self-begotten bird
In the Arabian woods embossed,
That no second knows nor third,
And lay erewhile a holocaust,
From out her ashy womb now teemed,
Revives, reflourishes, then vigorous most
When most unactive deemed,
And though her body die, her fame survives,
A secular bird ages of lives.[3]
Manoa. Come, come, no time for lamentation now,
Nor much more cause, Samson hath quit himself
Like Samson, and heroically hath finished
A life heroic, on his enemies
Fully revenged, hath left them years of mourning,
And lamentation to the sons of Caphtor[4]
Through all Philistian bounds. To Israel
Honour hath left, and freedom, let but them
Find courage to lay hold on this occasion,
To himself and father's house eternal fame;
And which is best and happiest yet, all this
With God not parted from him, as was feared,
But favouring and assisting to the end.
Nothing is here for tears, nothing to wail
Or knock the breast, no weakness, no contempt,
Dispraise, or blame, nothing but well and fair,
And what may quiet us in a death so noble.
Let us go find the body where it lies
Soaked in his enemies' blood, and from the stream
With lavers° pure, and cleansing herbs wash off *washbasins*
The clotted gore. I with what speed the while
(Gaza is not in plight to say us nay)
Will send for all my kindred, all my friends
To fetch him hence and solemnly attend
With silent obsequy and funeral train
Home to his father's house: there will I build him
A monument, and plant it round with shade

[1] *vulgar* Common people. See Judges 16.28–31 and lines 1609–10 above; Milton alters the biblical account by restricting the slaughter to the Philistines' social, political, military, and religious elite.

[2] *as an evening dragon* Like a serpent, assailing roosting fowl despite the darkness of night.

[3] *self-begotten bird ... of lives* The phoenix, supposed as existing only one at a time and reborn periodically out of its own ashes; *embossed* Imbosked, hidden in a wood; *holocaust* Sacrifice consumed by fire; *secular* Living for an age or ages.

[4] *sons of Caphtor* The Philistines, described in the Bible as coming originally from a place called Caphtor.

Of laurel ever green, and branching palm,
With all his trophies hung, and acts enrolled
In copious legend, or sweet lyric song.
Thither shall all the valiant youth resort,
And from his memory inflame their breasts
To matchless valour, and adventures high:
The virgins also shall on feastful days
Visit his tomb with flowers, only bewailing
His lot unfortunate in nuptial choice,
From whence captivity and loss of eyes.
Chorus. All is best, though we oft doubt,
What the unsearchable dispose
Of highest wisdom brings about,
And ever best found in the close.
Oft he seems to hide his face,
But unexpectedly returns
And to his faithful champion hath in place
Bore witness gloriously; whence Gaza mourns
And all that band them to resist
His uncontrollable intent,
His servants he with new acquist
Of true experience from this great event
With peace and consolation hath dismissed,
And calm of mind all passion spent.
—1671

In Context

The Biblical Version of the Samson Story

The primary source for *Samson Agonistes* is the account of Samson's life as presented in Judges 13–16. Milton dramatizes the account, focusing the poem's narrative "present" on a relatively short passage (Judges 16.21–30) but drawing freely on details elsewhere in the biblical narrative. A careful comparison of the biblical text with Milton's version of the story raises many interesting interpretative questions. The version presented here is the King James or Authorized translation, first published in 1611, though Milton was familiar with a wide range of versions and commentaries in various languages, including the original Hebrew.

Judges 13–16

13 And the children of Israel did evil again in the sight of the LORD; and the LORD delivered
them into the hand of the Philistines forty years.
2 And there was a certain man of Zorah, of the family of the Danites, whose name was Manoah;
and his wife was barren, and bare not. 3 And the angel of the LORD appeared unto the woman, and
said unto her, Behold now, thou art barren, and bearest not: but thou shalt conceive, and bear a
son. 4 Now therefore beware, I pray thee, and drink not wine nor strong drink, and eat not any
unclean thing: 5 For, lo, thou shalt conceive, and bear a son; and no razor shall come on his head:
for the child shall be a Nazarite unto God from the womb: and he shall begin to deliver Israel out
of the hand of the Philistines. 6 Then the woman came and told her husband, saying, A man of God
came unto me, and his countenance was like the countenance of an angel of God, very terrible: but
I asked him not whence he was, neither told he me his name: 7 But he said unto me, Behold, thou
shalt conceive, and bear a son; and now drink no wine nor strong drink, neither eat any unclean
thing: for the child shall be a Nazarite to God from the womb to the day of his death.
8 Then Manoah intreated the LORD, and said, O my Lord, let the man of God which thou
didst send come again unto us, and teach us what we shall do unto the child that shall be born. 9
And God hearkened to the voice of Manoah; and the angel of God came again unto the woman as
she sat in the field: but Manoah her husband was not with her. 10 And the woman made haste, and
ran, and shewed her husband, and said unto him, Behold, the man hath appeared unto me, that
came unto me the other day. 11 And Manoah arose, and went after his wife, and came to the man,
and said unto him, Art thou the man that spakest unto the woman? And he said, I am. 12 And
Manoah said, Now let thy words come to pass. How shall we order the child, and how shall we do
unto him? 13 And the angel of the LORD said unto Manoah, Of all that I said unto the woman let
her beware. 14 She may not eat of any thing that cometh of the vine, neither let her drink wine or
strong drink, nor eat any unclean thing: all that I commanded her let her observe.
15 And Manoah said unto the angel of the LORD, I pray thee, let us detain thee, until we shall
have made ready a kid for thee. 16 And the angel of the LORD said unto Manoah, Though thou
detain me, I will not eat of thy bread: and if thou wilt offer a burnt offering, thou must offer it unto
the LORD. For Manoah knew not that he was an angel of the LORD. 17 And Manoah said unto
the angel of the LORD, What is thy name, that when thy sayings come to pass we may do thee
honour? 18 And the angel of the LORD said unto him, Why askest thou thus after my name, seeing
it is secret? 19 So Manoah took a kid with a meat offering, and offered it upon a rock unto the

LORD: and the angel did wonderously; and Manoah and his wife looked on. [20] For it came to pass, when the flame went up toward heaven from off the altar, that the angel of the LORD ascended in the flame of the altar. And Manoah and his wife looked on it, and fell on their faces to the ground.

[21] But the angel of the LORD did no more appear to Manoah and to his wife. Then Manoah knew that he was an angel of the LORD. [22] And Manoah said unto his wife, We shall surely die, because we have seen God. [23] But his wife said unto him, If the LORD were pleased to kill us, he would not have received a burnt offering and a meat offering at our hands, neither would he have shewed us all these things, nor would as at this time have told us such things as these. [24] And the woman bare a son, and called his name Samson: and the child grew, and the LORD blessed him. [25] And the Spirit of the LORD began to move him at times in the camp of Dan between Zorah and Eshtaol.

14 And Samson went down to Timnath, and saw a woman in Timnath of the daughters of the Philistines. [2] And he came up, and told his father and his mother, and said, I have seen a woman in Timnath of the daughters of the Philistines: now therefore get her for me to wife. [3] Then his father and his mother said unto him, Is there never a woman among the daughters of thy brethren, or among all my people, that thou goest to take a wife of the uncircumcised Philistines? And Samson said unto his father, Get her for me; for she pleaseth me well.

[4] But his father and his mother knew not that it was of the LORD, that he sought an occasion against the Philistines: for at that time the Philistines had dominion over Israel.

[5] Then went Samson down, and his father and his mother, to Timnath, and came to the vineyards of Timnath: and, behold, a young lion roared against him. [6] And the Spirit of the LORD came mightily upon him, and he rent him as he would have rent a kid, and he had nothing in his hand: but he told not his father or his mother what he had done. [7] And he went down, and talked with the woman; and she pleased Samson well. [8] And after a time he returned to take her, and he turned aside to see the carcase of the lion: and, behold, there was a swarm of bees and honey in the carcase of the lion. [9] And he took thereof in his hands, and went on eating, and came to his father and mother, and he gave them, and they did eat: but he told not them that he had taken the honey out of the carcase of the lion.

[10] So his father went down unto the woman: and Samson made there a feast; for so used the young men to do. [11] And it came to pass, when they saw him, that they brought thirty companions to be with him. [12] And Samson said unto them, I will now put forth a riddle unto you: if ye can certainly declare it me within the seven days of the feast, and find it out, then I will give you thirty sheets and thirty change of garments: [13] But if ye cannot declare it me, then shall ye give me thirty sheets and thirty change of garments. And they said unto him, Put forth thy riddle, that we may hear it. [14] And he said unto them,

> Out of the eater came forth meat,
> and out of the strong came forth sweetness.

And they could not in three days expound the riddle.

[15] And it came to pass on the seventh day, that they said unto Samson's wife, Entice thy husband, that he may declare unto us the riddle, lest we burn thee and thy father's house with fire: have ye called us to take that we have? is it not so? [16] And Samson's wife wept before him, and said, Thou dost but hate me, and lovest me not: thou hast put forth a riddle unto the children of my people, and hast not told it me. And he said unto her, Behold, I have not told it my father nor my mother, and shall I tell it thee? [17] And she wept before him the seven days, while their feast lasted: and it came to pass on the seventh day, that he told her, because she lay sore upon him: and she

told the riddle to the children of her people. [18] And the men of the city said unto him on the seventh day before the sun went down,

> What is sweeter than honey?
> And what is stronger than a lion?

And he said unto them,

> If ye had not plowed with my heifer,
> ye had not found out my riddle.

[19] And the Spirit of the LORD came upon him, and he went down to Ashkelon, and slew thirty men of them, and took their spoil, and gave change of garments unto them which expounded the riddle. And his anger was kindled, and he went up to his father's house. [20] But Samson's wife was given to his companion, whom he had used as his friend.

15 But it came to pass within a while after, in the time of wheat harvest, that Samson visited his wife with a kid; and he said, I will go in to my wife into the chamber. But her father would not suffer him to go in. [2] And her father said, I verily thought that thou hadst utterly hated her; therefore I gave her to thy companion: is not her younger sister fairer than she? take her, I pray thee, instead of her. [3] And Samson said concerning them, Now shall I be more blameless than the Philistines, though I do them a displeasure. [4] And Samson went and caught three hundred foxes, and took firebrands, and turned tail to tail, and put a firebrand in the midst between two tails. [5] And when he had set the brands on fire, he let them go into the standing corn of the Philistines, and burnt up both the shocks, and also the standing corn, with the vineyards and olives. [6] Then the Philistines said, Who hath done this? And they answered, Samson, the son in law of the Timnite, because he had taken his wife, and given her to his companion. And the Philistines came up, and burnt her and her father with fire. [7] And Samson said unto them, Though ye have done this, yet will I be avenged of you, and after that I will cease. [8] And he smote them hip and thigh with a great slaughter: and he went down and dwelt in the top of the rock Etam.

[9] Then the Philistines went up, and pitched in Judah, and spread themselves in Lehi. [10] And the men of Judah said, Why are ye come up against us? And they answered, To bind Samson are we come up, to do to him as he hath done to us. [11] Then three thousand men of Judah went to the top of the rock Etam, and said to Samson, Knowest thou not that the Philistines are rulers over us? what is this that thou hast done unto us? And he said unto them, As they did unto me, so have I done unto them. [12] And they said unto him, We are come down to bind thee, that we may deliver thee into the hand of the Philistines. And Samson said unto them, Swear unto me, that ye will not fall upon me yourselves. [13] And they spake unto him, saying, No; but we will bind thee fast, and deliver thee into their hand: but surely we will not kill thee. And they bound him with two new cords, and brought him up from the rock.

[14] And when he came unto Lehi, the Philistines shouted against him: and the Spirit of the LORD came mightily upon him, and the cords that were upon his arms became as flax that was burnt with fire, and his bands loosed from off his hands. [15] And he found a new jawbone of an ass, and put forth his hand, and took it, and slew a thousand men therewith. [16] And Samson said,

> With the jawbone of an ass,
> heaps upon heaps,
> with the jaw of an ass
> have I slain a thousand men.

17 And it came to pass, when he had made an end of speaking, that he cast away the jawbone out of his hand, and called that place Ramathlehi.

18 And he was sore athirst, and called on the LORD, and said, Thou hast given this great deliverance into the hand of thy servant: and now shall I die for thirst, and fall into the hand of the uncircumcised? 19 But God clave an hollow place that was in the jaw, and there came water thereout; and when he had drunk, his spirit came again, and he revived: wherefore he called the name thereof Enhakkore, which is in Lehi unto this day. 20 And he judged Israel in the days of the Philistines twenty years.

16 Then went Samson to Gaza, and saw there an harlot, and went in unto her. 2 And it was told the Gazites, saying, Samson is come hither. And they compassed him in, and laid wait for him all night in the gate of the city, and were quiet all the night, saying, In the morning, when it is day, we shall kill him. 3 And Samson lay till midnight, and arose at midnight, and took the doors of the gate of the city, and the two posts, and went away with them, bar and all, and put them upon his shoulders, and carried them up to the top of an hill that is before Hebron.

4 And it came to pass afterward, that he loved a woman in the valley of Sorek, whose name was Delilah. 5 And the lords of the Philistines came up unto her, and said unto her, Entice him, and see wherein his great strength lieth, and by what means we may prevail against him, that we may bind him to afflict him; and we will give thee every one of us eleven hundred pieces of silver. 6 And Delilah said to Samson, Tell me, I pray thee, wherein thy great strength lieth, and wherewith thou mightest be bound to afflict thee. 7 And Samson said unto her, If they bind me with seven green withes that were never dried, then shall I be weak, and be as another man. 8 Then the lords of the Philistines brought up to her seven green withes which had not been dried, and she bound him with them. 9 Now there were men lying in wait, abiding with her in the chamber. And she said unto him, The Philistines be upon thee, Samson. And he brake the withes, as a thread of tow is broken when it toucheth the fire. So his strength was not known.

10 And Delilah said unto Samson, Behold, thou hast mocked me, and told me lies: now tell me, I pray thee, wherewith thou mightest be bound. 11 And he said unto her, If they bind me fast with new ropes that never were occupied, then shall I be weak, and be as another man. 12 Delilah therefore took new ropes, and bound him therewith, and said unto him, The Philistines be upon thee, Samson. And there were liers in wait abiding in the chamber. And he brake them from off his arms like a thread.

13 And Delilah said unto Samson, Hitherto thou hast mocked me, and told me lies: tell me wherewith thou mightest be bound. And he said unto her, If thou weavest the seven locks of my head with the web. 14 And she fastened it with the pin, and said unto him, The Philistines be upon thee, Samson. And he awaked out of his sleep, and went away with the pin of the beam, and with the web.

15 And she said unto him, How canst thou say, I love thee, when thine heart is not with me? thou hast mocked me these three times, and hast not told me wherein thy great strength lieth. 16 And it came to pass, when she pressed him daily with her words, and urged him, so that his soul was vexed unto death; 17 That he told her all his heart, and said unto her, There hath not come a razor upon mine head; for I have been a Nazarite unto God from my mother's womb: if I be shaven, then my strength will go from me, and I shall become weak, and be like any other man.

18 And when Delilah saw that he had told her all his heart, she sent and called for the lords of the Philistines, saying, Come up this once, for he hath shewed me all his heart. Then the lords of the Philistines came up unto her, and brought money in their hand. 19 And she made him sleep upon her knees; and she called for a man, and she caused him to shave off the seven locks of his head; and she began to afflict him, and his strength went from him. 20 And she said, The Philistines be upon thee, Samson. And he awoke out of his sleep, and said, I will go out as at other times

before, and shake myself. And he wist not that the LORD was departed from him. 21 But the
Philistines took him, and put out his eyes, and brought him down to Gaza, and bound him with
fetters of brass; and he did grind in the prison house. 22 Howbeit the hair of his head began to grow
again after he was shaven.

23 Then the lords of the Philistines gathered them together for to offer a great sacrifice unto
Dagon their god, and to rejoice: for they said, Our god hath delivered Samson our enemy into our
hand. 24 And when the people saw him, they praised their god: for they said, Our god hath
delivered into our hands our enemy, and the destroyer of our country, which slew many of us. 25
And it came to pass, when their hearts were merry, that they said, Call for Samson, that he may
make us sport. And they called for Samson out of the prison house; and he made them sport: and
they set him between the pillars. 26 And Samson said unto the lad that held him by the hand, Suffer
me that I may feel the pillars whereupon the house standeth, that I may lean upon them. 27 Now
the house was full of men and women; and all the lords of the Philistines were there; and there were
upon the roof about three thousand men and women, that beheld while Samson made sport.

28 And Samson called unto the LORD, and said, O Lord God, remember me, I pray thee, and
strengthen me, I pray thee, only this once, O God, that I may be at once avenged of the Philistines
for my two eyes. 29 And Samson took hold of the two middle pillars upon which the house stood,
and on which it was borne up, of the one with his right hand, and of the other with his left. 30 And
Samson said, Let me die with the Philistines. And he bowed himself with all his might; and the
house fell upon the lords, and upon all the people that were therein. So the dead which he slew at
his death were more than they which he slew in his life. 31 Then his brethren and all the house of
his father came down, and took him, and brought him up, and buried him between Zorah and
Eshtaol in the burying place of Manoah his father. And he judged Israel twenty years.

Reading Poetry

WHAT IS A POEM?

Most of us know what a poem is when we see one. Still, even poets find it difficult to define a poem, or poetry. In a lecture on "The Name and Nature of Poetry" (1933), the English poet A.E. Housman stated that he could "no more define poetry than a terrier can define a rat"; however, he added, "we both recognize the object by the symptoms which it provokes in us." Housman knew he was in the presence of poetry if he experienced a shiver down the spine, or "a constriction of the throat and a precipitation of water to the eyes." Implicit in Housman's response is a recognition that we have to go beyond mere formal characteristics—stanzas, rhymes, rhythms—if we want to know what poetry is, or why it differs from prose. Poetry both represents and *creates* emotions in a highly condensed way. Therefore, any definition of the genre needs to consider, as much as possible, the impact of poetry on us as readers or listeners.

Worth consideration too is the role of the listener or reader not only as passive recipient of a poem, but also as an active participant in its performance. Poetry is among other things the locus for a communicative exchange. A section below deals with the sub-genre of performance poetry, but in a very real sense all poetry is subject to performance. Poems are to be read aloud as well as on the page, and both in sensing meaning and in expressing sound the reader plays a vital role in bringing a poem to life, no matter how long dead its author may be; as W.H. Auden wrote memorably of his fellow poet W.B. Yeats, "the words of a dead man / Are modified in the guts of the living."

For some readers, poetry is, in William Wordsworth's phrase, "the breath and finer spirit of all knowledge" ("Preface" to the *Lyrical Ballads*). They look to poetry for insights into the nature of human experience, and expect elevated thought in carefully-wrought language. In contrast, other readers distrust poetry that seems moralistic or didactic. "We hate poetry that has a palpable design upon us," wrote John Keats to his friend J.H. Reynolds; rather, poetry should be "great & unobtrusive, a thing which enters into one's soul, and does not startle it or amaze it with itself but with its subject." The American poet Archibald MacLeish took Keats's idea a step further: in his poem "Ars Poetica" he suggested that "A poem should not mean / But be." MacLeish was not suggesting that a poem should lack meaning, but rather that meaning should inhere in the poem's expressive and sensuous qualities, not in some explicit statement or versified idea.

Whatever we look for in a poem, the infinitude of forms, styles, and subjects that make up the body of literature we call "poetry" is, in the end, impossible to capture in a definition that would satisfy all readers. All we can do, perhaps, is to agree that a poem is a discourse that is characterized by a heightened attention to language, form, and rhythm, by an expressiveness that works through figurative rather than literal modes, and by a capacity to stimulate our imagination and arouse our feelings.

THE LANGUAGE OF POETRY

To speak of "the language of poetry" implies that poets make use of a vocabulary that is somehow different from the language of everyday life. In fact, all language has the capacity to be "poetic," if by poetry we understand a use of language to which some special importance is attached. The ritualistic utterances of religious ceremonies sometimes have this force; so do the skipping rhymes of children in the schoolyard. We can distinguish such uses of language from the kind of writing we find in, say, a computer user's manual: the author of the manual can describe a given function in a variety of ways, whereas the magic of the skipping rhyme can be invoked only by getting the right words in the right order. So with the poet: he or she chooses particular words in a particular order; the *way* the poet speaks is as important to our understanding as what is said. This doesn't mean that an instruction manual couldn't have poetic qualities—indeed, modern poets have created "found" poems from even less likely materials—but it does mean that in poetry there is an intimate relation amongst language, form, and meaning, and that the writer deliberately structures and manipulates language to achieve very particular ends.

THE BEST WORDS IN THE BEST ORDER

Wordsworth provides us with a useful example of the way that poetry can invest quite ordinary words with a high emotional charge:

> No motion has she now, no force,
> She neither hears nor sees;
> Rolled round in earth's diurnal course
> With rocks, and stones, and trees.

To paraphrase the content of this stanza from "A Slumber Did My Spirit Seal," "she" is dead and buried. But the language and structures used here give this prosaic idea great impact. For example, the regular iambic meter of the two last lines conveys something of the inexorable motion of the earth and of Lucy embedded in it; the monosyllabic last line is a grim reminder of her oneness with objects in nature; the repeated negatives in the first two lines drive home the irreparable destructiveness of death; the alliteration in the third and fourth lines gives a tangible suggestion of roundness, circularity, repetition in terms of the earth's shape and motion, suggesting a cycle in which death is perhaps followed by renewal. Even the unusual word "diurnal" (which would not have seemed so unusual to Wordsworth's readers) seems "right" in this context; it lends more weight to the notion of the earth's perpetual movement than its mundane synonym "daily" (which, besides, would not scan here). It is difficult to imagine a change of any kind to these lines; they exemplify another attempted definition of poetry, this time by Wordsworth's friend Samuel Taylor Coleridge: "the best words in the best order" (*Table Talk*, 1827).

POETIC DICTION AND THE ELEVATED STYLE

Wordsworth's diction in the "Lucy" poem cited above is a model of clarity; he has chosen language that, in its simplicity and bluntness, conveys the strength of the speaker's feelings far more strongly than an elaborate description of grief in more conventionally "poetic" language might have done. Wordsworth, disturbed by what he felt was a deadness and artificiality in the poetry of his day, sought to "choose incidents and situations from common life" and to describe them in "a selection of language really used by men" ("Preface" to *Lyrical Ballads*). His plan might seem an implicit reproach of the "raised" style, the elevated diction of epic poetry we associate with John Milton's *Paradise Lost*:

> Anon out of the earth a fabric huge
> Rose like an exhalation, with the sound
> Of dulcet symphonies and voices sweet,

Built like a temple, where pilasters round
Were set, and Doric pillars overlaid
With golden architrave; nor did there want
Cornice or frieze, with bossy sculptures graven;
The roof was fretted gold.

(*Paradise Lost* I.710–17)

At first glance this passage, with its Latinate vocabulary and convoluted syntax, might seem guilty of inflated language and pretentiousness. However, Milton's description of the devils' palace in Hell deliberately seeks to distance us from its subject in order to emphasize the scale and sublimity of the spectacle, far removed from ordinary human experience. In other words, language and style in *Paradise Lost* are well adapted to suit a particular purpose, just as they are in "A Slumber Did My Spirit Seal," though on a wholly different scale. Wordsworth criticized the poetry of his day, not because of its elevation, but because the raised style was too often out of touch with its subject; in his view, the words did not bear any significant relation to the "truths" they were attempting to depict.

"PLAIN" LANGUAGE IN POETRY

Since Wordsworth's time, writers have been conscious of a need to narrow the apparent gap between "poetic" language and the language of everyday life. In much of the poetry of the past century, especially free verse, we can observe a growing approximation to speech—even to conversation—in the diction and rhythms of poetry. This may have something to do with the changed role of the poet, who today has discarded the mantle of teacher or prophet that was assumed by poets of earlier times, and who is ready to admit all fields of experience and endeavor as appropriate for poetry. The modern poet looks squarely at life, and can often find a provoking beauty in even the meanest of objects.

We should not assume, however, that a greater concern with the "ordinary," with simplicity, naturalness, and clarity, means a reduction in complexity or suggestiveness. A piece such as Stevie Smith's "Mother, Among the Dustbins," for all the casual and playful domesticity of some of its lines, skilfully evokes a range of emotions and sense impressions defying simple paraphrase.

IMAGERY, SYMBOLISM, AND FIGURES OF SPEECH

The language of poetry is grounded in the objects and phenomena that create sensory impressions. Sometimes the poet renders these impressions quite literally, in a series of *images* that seek to recreate a scene in the reader's mind:

Only a man harrowing clods
In a slow silent walk
With an old horse that stumbles and nods
Half asleep as they stalk.

Only thin smoke without flame
From the heaps of couch-grass;
Yet this will go onward the same
Though Dynasties pass.

Yonder a maid and her wight
Come whispering by:
War's annals will cloud into night
Ere their story die.

(Thomas Hardy, "In Time of 'The Breaking of Nations'")

Here, the objects of everyday life are re-created with sensory details designed to evoke in us the sensations or responses felt by the speaker viewing the scene. At the same time, the writer invests the objects with such significance that the poem's meaning extends beyond the literal to the symbolic: that is, the images come to stand for something much larger than the objects they represent. Hardy's poem moves from the presentation of stark images of rural life to a sense of their timelessness. By the last stanza we see the ploughman, the burning grass, and the maid and her companion as symbols of recurring human actions and motives that defy the struggles and conflicts of history.

IMAGISM

The juxtaposition of clear, forceful images is associated particularly with the Imagist movement that flourished at the beginning of the twentieth century. Its chief representatives (in their early work) were the American poets H.D. and Ezra Pound, who defined an image as "that which represents an intellectual and emotional complex in an instant of time." Pound's two-line poem "In a Station of the Metro" provides a good example of the Imagists' goal of representing emotions or impressions through the use of concentrated images:

The apparition of these faces in the crowd,
Petals on a wet, black bough.

As in a Japanese *haiku,* a form that strongly influenced the Imagists, the poem uses sharp, clear, concrete details to evoke both a sensory impression and the emotion or the atmosphere of the scene. Though the Imagist movement itself lasted only a short time (from about 1912 to 1917), it had a far-reaching influence on modern poets such as T. S. Eliot, and William Carlos Williams.

FIGURES OF SPEECH

Imagery often works together with figurative expression to extend and deepen the meaning or impact of a poem. "Figurative" language means language that is metaphorical, not literal or referential. Through "figures of speech" such as metaphor and simile, metonymy, synecdoche, and personification, the writer may alter the ordinary, denotative meanings of words in order to convey greater force and vividness to ideas or impressions, often by showing likenesses between unlike things.

With *simile*, the poet makes an explicit comparison between the subject (called the *tenor*) and another object or idea (known as the *vehicle*), using "as" or "like":

It is a beauteous evening, calm and free,
The holy time is quiet as a Nun
Breathless with adoration. …

In this opening to a sonnet, Wordsworth uses a visual image of a nun in devout prayer to convey in concrete terms the less tangible idea of evening as a "holy time." The comparison also introduces an emotional dimension, conveying something of the feeling that the scene induces in the poet. The simile can thus illuminate and expand meaning in a compact way. The poet may also extend the simile to elaborate at length on any points of likeness.

In *metaphor*, the comparison between tenor and vehicle is implied: connectives such as "like" are omitted, and a kind of identity is created between the subject and the term with which it is being compared. Thus in John Donne's "The Good-Morrow," a lover asserts the endless joy that he and his beloved find in each other:

> My face in thine eye, thine in mine appears,
> And true plain hearts do in the faces rest;
> Where can we find two better hemispheres,
> Without sharp north, without declining west?

Here the lovers are transformed into "hemispheres," each of them a half of the world not subject to the usual natural phenomena of wintry cold ("sharp north") or the coming of night ("declining west"). Thus, they form a perfect world in balance, in which the normal processes of decay or decline have been arrested. Donne renders the abstract idea of a love that defies change in pictorial and physical terms, making it more real and accessible to us. The images here are all the more arresting for the degree of concentration involved; it is not merely the absence of "like" or "as" that gives the metaphor such direct power, but the fusion of distinct images and emotions into a new idea.

Personification is the figure of speech in which the writer endows abstract ideas, inanimate objects, or animals with human characteristics. In other words, it is a type of implied metaphorical comparison in which aspects of a non-human subject are compared to the feelings, appearance, or actions of a human being. In the second stanza of his ode "To Autumn," Keats personifies the concept of autumnal harvesting in the form of a woman, "sitting careless on a granary floor, / Thy hair soft-lifted by the winnowing wind." Personification may also help to create a mood, as when Thomas Gray attributes human feelings to a hooting owl in "Elegy Written in a Country Church-Yard"; using such words as "moping" and "complain," Gray invests the bird's cries with the quality of human melancholy:

> … from yonder ivy-mantled tow'r
> The moping owl does to the moon complain
> Of such, as wand'ring near her secret bow'r,
> Molest her ancient solitary reign.

In his book *Modern Painters* (1856), the English critic John Ruskin criticized such attribution of human feelings to objects in nature. Calling this device the "pathetic fallacy," he objected to what he saw as an irrational distortion of reality, producing "a falseness in all our impressions of external things." Modern criticism, with a distrust of any notions of an objective "reality," tends to use Ruskin's term as a neutral label simply to describe instances of extended personification of natural objects.

Apostrophe, which is closely related to personification, has the speaker directly addressing a non-human object or idea as if it were a sentient human listener. Blake's "The Sick Rose," Shelley's "Ode to the West Wind" and his ode "To a Sky-Lark" all employ apostrophe, personifying the object addressed. Keats's "Ode on a Grecian Urn" begins by apostrophizing the urn ("Thou still unravish'd bride of quietness"), then addresses it in a series of questions and reflections through which the speaker attempts to unravel the urn's mysteries.

Apostrophe also appeals to or addresses a person who is absent or dead. W. H. Auden's lament "In Memory of W. B. Yeats" apostrophizes both the earth in which Yeats is to be buried ("Earth, receive an honoured guest") and the dead poet himself ("Follow, poet, follow right / To the bottom of the night …"). Religious prayers offer an illustration of the usefulness of apostrophe, since they are direct appeals from an earth-bound supplicant to an invisible god. The suggestion of strong emotion associated with such appeals is a common feature of apostrophe in poetry also, especially poetry with a religious theme, like Donne's "Holy Sonnets" (e.g., "Batter My Heart, Three-Personed God").

Metonymy and *synecdoche* are two closely related figures of speech that further illustrate the power of metaphorical language to convey meaning more intensely and vividly than is possible with prosaic statement. *Metonymy* (from the Greek, meaning "change of name") involves referring to an object or concept by substituting the name of another object or concept with which it is usually associated: for example, we might speak of "the Crown" when we mean the monarch, or describe the U.S. executive branch as "the White House." When the writer uses only part of something to signify the whole, or an individual to represent a class, we have an instance of *synecdoche*: T. S. Eliot provides an example in "The Love Song of J. Alfred Prufrock" when a crab is described as "a pair of ragged claws." Similarly, synecdoche is present in Milton's contemptous term "blind mouths" to describe the "corrupted clergy" he attacks in "Lycidas."

Dylan Thomas employs both metonymy and synecdoche in his poem "The Hand That Signed the Paper":

The hand that signed the paper felled a city;
Five sovereign fingers taxed the breath,
Doubled the globe of dead and halved a country;
These five kings did a king to death.

The mighty hand leads to a sloping shoulder,
The finger joints are cramped with chalk;
A goose's quill has put an end to murder
That put an end to talk.

The hand that signed the treaty bred a fever,
And famine grew, and locusts came;
Great is the hand that holds dominion over
Man by a scribbled name.

The five kings count the dead but do not soften
The crusted wound nor stroke the brow;
A hand rules pity as a hand rules heaven;
Hands have no tears to flow.

The "hand" of the poem is evidently a synecdoche for a great king who enters into treaties with friends and foes to wage wars, conquer kingdoms, and extend his personal power—all at the expense of his suffering subjects. The "goose quill" of the second stanza is a metonymy, standing for the pen used to sign the treaty or the death warrant that brings the war to an end.

Thomas's poem is an excellent example of the power of figurative language, which, by its vividness and concentrated force, can add layers of meaning to a poem, make abstract ideas concrete, and intensify the poem's emotional impact.

THE POEM AS PERFORMANCE: WRITER AND PERSON

Poetry is always dramatic. Sometimes the drama is explicit, as in Robert Browning's monologues, in which we hear the voice of a participant in a dialogue; in "My Last Duchess" we are present as the Duke reflects on the portrait of his late wife for the benefit of a visitor who has come to negotiate on behalf of the woman who is to become the Duke's next wife. Or we listen with amusement and pity as the dying Bishop addresses his venal and unsympathetic sons and tries to bargain with them for a fine burial ("The Bishop Orders His Tomb at St. Praxed's"). In such poems, the notion of a speaking voice is paramount: the speaker is a personage in a play, and the poem a means of conveying plot and character.

Sometimes the drama is less apparent, and takes the form of a plea, or a compliment, or an argument addressed to a silent listener. In Donne's "The Flea" we can infer from the poem the situation that has called it forth: a lover's advances are being rejected by his beloved, and his poem is an argument intended to overcome her reluctance by means of wit and logic. We can see a similar example in Marvell's "To His Coy Mistress": here the very shape of the poem, its three-paragraph structure, corresponds to the stages of the speaker's argument as he presents an apparently irrefutable line of reasoning. Much love poetry has this kind of background as its inspiration; the yearnings or lamentations of the lover are part of an imagined scene, not merely versified reflections about an abstraction called "love."

Meditative or reflective poetry can be dramatic too. Donne's "Holy Sonnets" are pleas from a tormented soul struggling to find its god; Tennyson's "In Memoriam" follows the agonized workings of a mind tracing a path from grief and anger to acceptance and renewed hope.

We should never assume that the speaker, the "I" of the poem, is simply a voice for the writer's own views. The speaker in W. H. Auden's "To an Unknown Citizen," presenting a summary of the dead citizen's life, appears to be an official spokesperson for the society which the citizen served ("Our report on his union"; "Our researchers ..." etc.). The speaker's words are laudatory, yet we perceive immediately that Auden's own views of this society are anything but approving. The speaker seems satisfied with the highly regimented nature of his society, one in which every aspect of the individual's life is under scrutiny and subject to correction. The only things necessary to the happiness of the "Modern Man," it seems, are "A phonograph, a radio, a car, and a frigidaire." The tone here is subtly ironic, an irony created by the gap between the imagined speaker's perception and the real feelings of the writer.

PERFORMANCE POETRY

Poetry began as an oral art, passed on in the form of chants, myths, ballads, and legends recited to an audience of listeners rather than readers. Even today, the dramatic qualities of a poem may extend beyond written text. "Performance poets" combine poetry and stagecraft in presenting their work to live audiences. Dramatic uses of voice, rhythm, body movement, music, and sometimes other visual effects make the "text" of the poem multi-dimensional. For example, Edith Sitwell's poem-sequence *Façade* (1922) was originally set to music: Sitwell read from behind a screen, while a live orchestra played. This performance was designed to enhance the verbal and rhythmic qualities of her poetry:

Beneath the flat and paper sky
The sun, a demon's eye
Glowed through the air, that mask of glass;
All wand'ring sounds that pass

Seemed out of tune, as if the light
Were fiddle-strings pulled tight.
The market-square with spire and bell
Clanged out the hour in Hell.
(from *Façade*)

By performing their poetry, writers can also convey cultural values and traditions. The cultural aspect of performance is central to Black poetry, which originates in a highly oral tradition of folklore and storytelling. From its roots in Africa, this oral tradition has been manifested in the songs and stories of slaves, in spirituals, in the jazz rhythms of the Twenties and the Thirties and in the rebelliousness of reggae and of rap. Even when it remains "on the page," much Black poetry written in the oral tradition has a compelling rhythmic quality. The lines below from Linton Kwesi Johnson's "Mi Revalueshanary Fren," for example, blur the line between spoken poetry and song. Johnson often performs his "dub poetry" against reggae or hip-hop musical backings.

yes, people powa jus a showa evry howa
an evrybady claim dem democratic
but some a wolf an some a sheep
an dat is problematic

The chorus of Johnson's poems, with its constant repetitions, digs deeply into the roots of African song and chant. Its performance qualities become clearer when the poem is read aloud:

Husak
e ad to go
Honnicka
e ad to go
Chowcheskhu
e ad to go
Just like apartied
will av to go

To perform a poem is one way to see and hear poetry as multi-dimensional, cultural, historical, and often also political. Performance is also another way to discover how poetic "meaning" can be constructed in the dynamic relation between speaker and listener.

TONE: THE SPEAKER'S ATTITUDE

In understanding poetry, it is helpful to imagine a poem as having a "voice." The voice may be close to the poet's own, or that of an imagined character, a *persona* adopted by the poet. The tone of the voice will reveal the speaker's attitude to the subject, thus helping to shape our understanding and response. In speech we can indicate our feelings by raising or lowering our voices, and we can accompany words with physical actions. In writing, we must try to convey the tonal inflections of the speaking voice through devices of language and rhythm, through imagery and figures of speech, and through allusions and contrasts.

THE IRONIC TONE

Housman's poem "Terence, This Is Stupid Stuff" offers a useful example of ways in which manipulating tone can reinforce meaning. When Housman, presenting himself in the poem as "Terence," imagines himself to be criticized for writing gloomy poems, his response to his critics takes the form of an ironic alternative: perhaps they should stick to drinking ale:

Oh, many a peer of England brews
Livelier liquor than the Muse,
And malt does more than Milton can
To justify God's ways to man.

The tone here is one of heavy scorn. The speaker is impatient with those who refuse to look at the realities of life and death, and who prefer to take refuge in simple-minded pleasure. The ludicrous comparisons, first between the brewers who have been made peers of England and the classical Muse of poetry, then between malt and Milton, create a sense of disproportion and ironic tension; the explicit allusion to *Paradise Lost* ("To justify God's ways to man") helps to drive home the poet's bitter recognition that his auditors are part of that fallen world depicted by Milton, yet unable or unwilling to acknowledge their harsh condition. The three couplets that follow offer a series of contrasts: in each case, the first line sets up a pleasant expectation and the second dashes it with a blunt reminder of reality:

Ale, man, ale's the stuff to drink
For fellows whom it hurts to think:
Look into the pewter pot
To see the world as the world's not.
And faith, 'tis pleasant till 'tis past:
The mischief is that 'twill not last.

These are all jabs at the "sterling lads" who would prefer to lie in "lovely muck" and not think about the way the world is. Housman's sardonic advice is all the more pointed for its sharp and ironic tone.

POETIC FORMS

In poetry, language is intimately related to form, which is the structuring of words within identifiable patterns. In prose we speak of phrases, sentences, and paragraphs; in poetry, we identify structures by lines, stanzas, or complete forms such as the sonnet or the ode (though poetry in complete or blank verse has paragraphs of variable length, not formal stanzas: see below).

Rightly handled, the form enhances expression and meaning, just as a frame can define and enhance a painting or photograph. Unlike the photo frame, however, form in poetry is an integral part of the whole work. At one end of the scale, the term "form" may describe the *epic,* the lengthy narrative governed by such conventions as division into books, a lofty style, and the interplay between human and supernatural characters. At the other end lies the *epigram*, a witty and pointed saying whose distinguishing characteristic is its brevity, as in Alexander Pope's famous couplet,

I am his Highness' dog at Kew;
Pray tell me sir, whose dog are you?

Between the epic and the epigram lie many other poetic forms, such as the sonnet, the ballad, or the ode. "Form" may also describe stanzaic patterns like *couplets* and *quatrains.*

"FIXED FORM" POEMS

The best-known poetic form is probably the sonnet, the fourteen-line poem inherited from Italy (the word itself is from the Italian *sonetto*, little song or sound). Within those fourteen lines, whether the poet chooses the "Petrarchan" rhyme scheme or the "English" form (see below in the section on "Rhyme"), the challenge is to develop an idea or situation that must find its statement and its resolution within the strict confines of the sonnet frame. Typically, there is an initial idea, description, or statement of feeling, followed by a "turn" in the thought that takes the reader by surprise, or that casts the situation in an unexpected light. Thus in Sonnet 130, "My Mistress' Eyes Are Nothing Like the Sun," William Shakespeare spends the first three quatrains apparently disparaging his lover in a series of unfavorable comparisons—"If snow be white, why then her breasts are dun"—but in the closing couplet his point becomes clear:

And yet, by heaven, I think my love as rare
As any she belied with false compare.

In other words, the speaker's disparaging comparisons have really been parodies of sentimental clichés which falsify reality; his mistress has no need of the exaggerations or distortions of conventional love poetry.

Other foreign forms borrowed and adapted by English-language poets include the *ghazal* and the *pantoum.* The *ghazal,* strongly associated with classical Urdu literature, originated in Persia and Arabia and was brought to the Indian subcontinent in the twelfth century. It consists of a series of couplets held together by a refrain, a simple rhyme scheme (a/a, b/a, c/a, d/a…), and a common rhythm, but only loosely related in theme or subject. Some English-language practitioners of the form have captured the epigrammatic quality of the ghazal, but most do not adhere to the strict pattern of the classical form.

The *pantoum*, based on a Malaysian form, was imported into English poetry via the work of nineteenth-century French poets. Typically it presents a series of quatrains rhyming *abab*, linked by a pattern of repetition in which the second and fourth lines of a quatrain become the first and third lines of the stanza that follows. In the poem's final stanza, the pattern is reversed: the second line repeats the third line of the first stanza, and the last line repeats the poem's opening line, thus creating the effect of a loop.

Similar to the pantoum in the circularity of its structure is the *villanelle,* originally a French form, with five *tercets* and a concluding *quatrain* held together by only two rhymes (aba, aba, aba, aba, aba, abaa) and by a refrain that repeats the first line at lines 6, 12, and 18, while the third line of the first tercet reappears as lines 9, 15, and 19. With its interlocking rhymes and elaborate repetitions, the villanelle can create a variety of tonal effects, ranging from lighthearted parody to the sonorous and earnest exhortation of Dylan Thomas's "Do Not Go Gentle Into That Good Night."

STANZAIC FORMS

Recurring formal groupings of lines within a poem are usually described as "stanzas." Both the recurring and the formal aspects of stanzaic forms are important; it is a common misconception to think that any group of lines in a poem, if it is set off by line spaces, constitutes a stanza. If such a group of lines is not patterned as one of a recurring group sharing similar formal characteristics, however, then it may be more appropriate to refer to such irregular groupings in the way we do for prose—as paragraphs. A ballad is typically divided into stanzas; a prose poem or a poem written in free verse, on the other hand, will rarely be divided into stanzas.

A stanza may be identified by the number of lines and the patterns of rhyme repeated in each grouping. One of the simpler traditional forms is the *ballad stanza*, with its alternating four and three-foot lines and its *abcb* rhyme scheme. Drawing on this form's association with medieval ballads and legends, Keats produces the eerie mystery of "La Belle Dame Sans Merci":

I saw pale kings and princes too,
Pale warriors, death-pale were they all;
They cried—"La Belle Dame sans Merci
Hath thee in thrall!"

Such imitations are a form of literary allusion; Keats uses a traditional stanza form to remind us of poems like "Sir Patrick Spens" or "Barbara Allen" to dramatize the painful thralldom of love by placing it within a well-known tradition of ballad narratives with similar forms and themes.

The four-line stanza, or *quatrain*, may be used for a variety of effects: from the elegiac solemnity of Gray's "Elegy Written in a Country Churchyard" to the apparent lightness and simplicity of some of Emily Dickinson's poems. Tennyson used a rhyming quatrain to such good effect in *In Memoriam* that the form he employed (four lines of iambic tetrameter rhyming *abba*) is known as the "In Memoriam stanza."

Other commonly used forms of stanza include the *rhyming couplet*, *terza rima*, *ottava rima*, *rhyme royal*, and the *Spenserian stanza*. Each of these is a rhetorical unit within a longer whole, rather like a paragraph within an essay. The poet's choice among such forms is dictated, at least in part, by the effects that each may produce. Thus the *rhyming couplet* often expresses a complete statement within two lines, creating a sense of density of thought, of coherence and closure; it is particularly effective where the writer wishes to set up contrasts, or to achieve the witty compactness of epigram:

Of all mad creatures, if the learn'd are right,
It is the slaver kills, and not the bite.
A fool quite angry is quite innocent:
Alas! 'tis ten times worse when they repent.

(from Pope, "Epistle to Dr. Arbuthnot")

Ottava rima, as its Italian name implies, is an eight-line stanza, with the rhyme scheme *abababcc*. Like the sonnet, it is long enough to allow the development of a single thought in some detail and complexity, with a concluding couplet that may extend the central idea or cast it in a wholly unexpected light. W.B. Yeats uses this stanza form in "Sailing to Byzantium" and "Among Schoolchildren." Though much used by Renaissance poets, it is particularly associated with George Gordon, Lord Byron's *Don Juan*, in which the poet exploits to the full its potential for devastating irony and bathos. It is long enough to allow the development of a single thought in some detail and complexity; the concluding couplet can then, sonnet-like, turn that thought upon its head, or cast it in a wholly unexpected light:

Sagest of women, even of widows, she
    Resolved that Juan should be quite a paragon,
And worthy of the noblest pedigree
    (His sire was of Castile, his dam from Aragon).
Then for accomplishments of chivalry,
    In case our lord the king should go to war again,
He learned the arts of riding, fencing, gunnery,
And how to scale a fortress—or a nunnery.

(*Don Juan* I.38)

FREE VERSE

Not all writers want the order and symmetry—some might say the restraints and limitations—of traditional forms, and many have turned to *free verse* as a means of liberating their thoughts and feelings. Deriving its name from the French "vers libre" made popular by the French Symbolistes at the end of the nineteenth century, free verse is characterized by irregularity of metre, line length, and rhyme. This does not mean that it is without pattern; rather, it tends to follow more closely than other forms the unforced rhythms and accents of natural speech, making calculated use of spacing, line breaks, and "cadences," the rhythmic units that govern phrasing in speech.

Free verse is not a modern invention. Milton was an early practitioner, as was Blake; however, it was the great modern writers of free verse—first Walt Whitman, then Pound, Eliot, and William Carlos Williams (interestingly, all Americans, at least originally)—who gave this form a fluidity and flexibility that could free the imagination to deal with any kind of feeling or experience. Perhaps because it depends so much more than traditional forms upon the individual intuitions of the poet, it is the form of poetic structure most commonly found today. The best practitioners recognize that free verse, like any other kind of poetry, demands clarity, precision, and a close connection between technique and meaning.

PROSE POETRY

At the furthest extreme from traditional forms lies poetry written in prose. Contradictory as this label may seem, the two have much in common. Prose has at its disposal all the figurative devices available to poetry, such as metaphor, personification, or apostrophe; it may use structuring devices such as verbal repetition or parallel syntactical structures; it can draw on the same tonal range, from pathos to irony. The difference is that prose poetry accomplishes its ends in sentences and paragraphs, rather than lines or stanzas. First given prominence by the French poet Charles Baudelaire (*Petits Poèmes en prose*, 1862), the form is much used to present fragments of heightened sensation, conveyed through vivid or impressionistic description. It draws upon such prosaic forms as journal entries, lists, even footnotes. Prose poetry should be distinguished from "poetic prose," which may be found in a variety of settings (from the King James Bible to the fiction of Jeanette Winterson); the distinction—which not all critics would accept—appears to lie in the writer's intention.

Christan Bok's *Eunoia* is an interesting example of the ways in which a writer of prose poetry may try to balance the demands of each medium. *Eunoia* is an avowedly experimental work in which each chapter is restricted to the use of a single vowel. The text is governed by a series of rules described by the author in an afterword; they include a requirement that all chapters "must allude to the art of writing. All sentences must accent internal rhyme through the use of syntactical parallelism. The text must exhaust the lexicon for each vowel, citing at least 98% of the available repertoire...." Having imposed such constraints upon the language and form of the work, Bok then sets himself the task of showing that "even under such improbable conditions of duress, language can still express an uncanny, if not sublime, thought." The result is a surrealistic narrative that blends poetic and linguistic devices to almost hypnotic effect.

THE POEM AS A MATERIAL OBJECT

Both free verse and prose poetry pay attention in different ways to the poem as a living thing on the printed page. But the way in which poetry is presented in material form is an important part of the existence of almost any form of poetry. In the six volumes of this anthology the material form of the poem is highlighted by the inclusion of a number of facsimile reproductions of poems of other eras in their earliest extant material form.

RHYTHM AND SCANSION

When we read poetry, we often become aware of a pattern of rhythm within a line or set of lines. The formal analysis of that rhythmic pattern, or "metre," is called *scansion.* The verb "to scan" may carry different meanings, depending upon the context: if the *critic* "scans" a line, he or she is attempting to determine the metrical pattern in which it is cast; if the *line* "scans," we are making the observation that the line conforms to particular metrical rules. Whatever the context, the process of scansion is based on the premise that a line of verse is built on a pattern of stresses, a recurring set of more or less regular beats established by the alternation of light and heavy accents in syllables and words. The rhythmic pattern so distinguished in a given poem is said to be the "metre" of that poem. If we find it impossible to identify any specific metrical pattern, the poem is probably an example of free verse.

QUANTITATIVE, SYLLABIC, AND ACCENTUAL-SYLLABIC VERSE

Although we owe much of our terminology for analyzing or describing poetry to the Greeks and Romans, the foundation of our metrical system is quite different from theirs. They measured a line of verse by the duration of sound ("quantity") in each syllable, and by the combination of short and long syllables. Such poetry is known as *quantitative* verse.

Unlike Greek or Latin, English is a heavily accented language. Thus poetry of the Anglo-Saxon period, such as *Beowulf,* was *accentual:* that is, the lines were based on a fixed number of accents, or stresses, regardless of the number of syllables in the line:

> Oft Scyld Scefing   sceapena þreatum
> monegum maegþum   meodosetla ofteah.

Few modern poets have written in the accentual tradition. A notable exception was Gerard Manley Hopkins, who based his line on a pattern of strong stresses that he called "sprung rhythm." Hopkins experimented with rhythms and stresses that approximate the accentual quality of natural speech; the result is a line that is emphatic, abrupt, even harsh in its forcefulness:

> I caught this morning morning's minion, kingdom of daylight's dauphin, dapple-dawn-drawn
>   Falcon, in his riding

Of the rolling level underneath him steady air ....
(from "The Windhover")

Under the influence of French poetry, following the Norman invasion of the eleventh century, English writers were introduced to *syllabic* prosody: that is, poetry in which the number of syllables is the determining factor in the length of any line, regardless of the number of stresses or their placement. A few modern writers have successfully produced syllabic poetry.

However, the accentual patterns of English, in speech as well as in poetry, were too strongly ingrained to disappear. Instead, the native accentual practice combined with the imported syllabic conventions to produce the *accentual-syllabic* line, in which the writer works with combinations of stressed and unstressed syllables in lines of equal syllabic length. Geoffrey Chaucer was the first great writer to employ the accentual-syllabic line in English poetry:

Ther was also a Nonne, a Prioresse,
That of hir smiling was ful simple and coy.
Hir gretteste ooth was but by sainté Loy,
And she was clepéd Madame Eglantine.
(from *The Canterbury Tales*)

The fundamental pattern here is the ten-syllable line (although the convention of sounding the final "e" at the end of a line in Middle English verse sometimes produces eleven syllables). Each line contains five stressed syllables, each of which alternates with one or two unstressed syllables. This was to become the predominant metre of poetry in English until the general adoption of free verse in the twentieth century.

IDENTIFYING POETIC METER

Conventionally, meter is established by dividing a line into roughly equal parts, based on the rise and fall of the rhythmic beats. Each of these divisions, conventionally marked by a bar, is known as a "foot," and within the foot there will be a combination of stressed and unstressed syllables, indicated by the prosodic symbols / (stressed) and x (unstressed).

I know | that I | shall meet | my fate
Somewhere | among | the clouds | above ...
(from Yeats, "An Irish Airman Foresees His Death")

To describe the meter used in a poem, we must first determine what kind of foot predominates, and then count the number of feet in each line. To describe the resultant meter we use terminology borrowed from classical prosody. In identifying the meter of English verse we commonly apply the following labels:

iambic (x /): a foot with one weak stress followed by one strong stress

("Look home | ward, Ang | el, now, | and melt | with ruth")

trochaic (/ x): strong followed by weak

("Ty | ger! Ty | ger! bur | ning bright")

anapaestic (x x /): two weak stresses, followed by a strong

("I have passed | with a nod | of the head")

dactylic (/ x x): strong stress followed by two weak

("Hickory | dickory | dock")

spondaic (/ /): two strong stresses

("If hate | killed men,| Brother | Lawrence,
God's blood,| would not | mine kill | you?")

We also use classical terms to describe the number of feet in a line. Thus, a line with one foot is *monometer*; with two feet, *dimeter*; three feet, *trimeter*; four feet, *tetrameter*; five feet, *pentameter*; and six feet, *hexameter*.

Scansion of the two lines from Yeats's "Irish Airman" quoted above shows that the predominant foot is iambic (x /), that there are four feet to each line, and that the poem is therefore written in *iambic tetrameters*. The first foot of the second line, however, may be read as a trochee ("Somewhere"); the variation upon the iambic norm here is an example of *substitution*, a means whereby the writer may avoid the monotony that would result from adhering too closely to a set rhythm. We very quickly build up an expectation about the dominant meter of a poem; the poet will sometimes disturb that expectation by changing the beat, and so through substitution create a pleasurable tension in our awareness.

The prevailing meter in English poetry is iambic, since the natural rhythm of spoken English is predominantly iambic. Nonetheless, poets may employ other rhythms where it suits their purpose. Thus W.H. Auden can create a solemn tone by the use of a trochaic meter(/ x):

Earth, receive an honoured guest;
William Yeats is laid to rest:
Let the Irish vessel lie
Emptied of its poetry.

The same meter may be much less funereal, as in Ben Jonson's song "*To Celia*":

Come, my Celia, let us prove,
While we may, the sports of love.
Time will not be ours forever;
He, at length, our good will sever.

The sense of greater pace in this last example derives in part from the more staccato phrasing, and also from the greater use of monosyllabic words. A more obviously lilting, dancing effect is obtained from anapaestic rhythm (x x /):

I sprang to the stirrup, and Joris, and he;
I galloped, Dirck galloped, we galloped all three.
"Good speed!" cried the watch, as the gatebolts undrew;
"Speed!" echoed the wall to us galloping through.
(from *Browning*, "How They Brought the Good News from Ghent to Aix")

Coleridge wittily captured the varying effects of different meters in "Metrical Feet: Lesson for a Boy," which the poet wrote for his sons, and in which he marked the stresses himself:

Trochee trips from long to short;
From long to long in solemn sort
Slow Spondee stalks; strong foot! yet ill able
Ever to come up with Dactyl trisyllable.
Iambics march from short to long:—
With a leap and a bound the swift Anapaests throng....

A meter which often deals with serious themes is unrhymed iambic pentameter, also known as *blank verse*. This is the meter of Shakespeare's plays, notably his great tragedies; it is the meter, too, of Milton's *Paradise Lost*, to which it lends a desired sonority and magnificence; and of Wordsworth's "Lines Composed a Few Miles above Tintern Abbey," where the flexibility of the meter allows the writer to move by turns from description, to narration, to philosophical reflection.

RHYME, CONSONANCE, ASSONANCE, AND ALLITERATION

Perhaps the most obvious sign of poetic form is rhyme: that is, the repetition of syllables with the same or similar sounds. If the rhyme words are placed at the end of the line, they are known as *end-rhymes*. The opening stanza of Housman's "To an Athlete Dying Young" has two pairs of end-rhymes:

The time you won your town the *race*
We chaired you through the market-*place*;
Man and boy stood cheering *by*,
And home we brought you shoulder-*high*.

Words rhyming within a line are *internal rhymes*, as in the first and third lines of this stanza from Coleridge's "The Rime of the Ancient Mariner":

The fair breeze *blew*, the white foam *flew*
The furrow followed free;
We were the *first* that ever *burst*
Into that silent sea.

When, as is usually the case, the rhyme occurs in a stressed syllable, it is known as a *masculine rhyme*; if the rhyming word ends in an unstressed syllable, it is referred to as *feminine*. The difference is apparent in the opening stanzas of Alfred Tennyson's poem "The Lady of Shalott," where the first stanza establishes the basic iambic meter with strong stresses on the rhyming words:

On either side the river *lie*
Long fields of barley and of *rye*,
That clothe the wold and meet the *sky*;
And through the field the road runs *by*
To many-towered Camelot ...

In the second stanza Tennyson changes to trochaic lines, ending in unstressed syllables and feminine rhymes:

Willows whiten, aspens *quiver*,
Little breezes dusk and *shiver*
Through the wave that runs *forever*
By the island in the *river*
Flowing down to Camelot.

Not only does Tennyson avoid monotony here by his shift to feminine rhymes, he also darkens the mood by using words that imply a contrast with the bright warmth of day—"quiver," "dusk," "shiver"—in preparation for the introduction of the "silent isle" that embowers the Lady.

NEAR RHYMES

Most of the rhymes in "The Lady of Shalott" are exact, or "*perfect*" rhymes. However, in the second of the stanzas just quoted, it is evident that "forever" at the end of the third line is not a "perfect" rhyme; rather, it is an instance of "*near*" or "*slant*" rhyme. Such "*imperfect*" rhymes are quite deliberate; indeed, two stanzas later we find the rhyming sequence "early," "barley," "cheerly," and "clearly," followed by the rhymes "weary," "airy," and "fairy." As with the introduction of feminine rhymes, such divergences from one dominant pattern prevent monotony and avoid a too-mechanical sing-song effect.

More importantly, near-rhymes have an oddly unsettling effect, perhaps because they both raise and frustrate our expectation of a perfect rhyme. Their use certainly gives added emphasis to the words at the end of these chilling lines from Wilfred Owen's "*Strange Meeting*":

For by my glee might many men have laughed,
And of my weeping something had been left,
Which must die now. I mean the truth untold,
The pity of war, the pity war distilled.
Now men will go content with what we spoiled,
Or, discontent, boil bloody, and be spilled.

CONSONANCE AND ASSONANCE

In Owen's poem, the near-rhymes "laughed / left" and "spoiled / spilled" are good examples of *consonance*, which pairs words with similar consonants but different intervening vowels. Other examples from Owen's poem include "groined / groaned," "hall / Hell," "years / yours," and "mystery / mastery."

Related to consonance as a linking device is *assonance*, the echoing of similar vowel sounds in the stressed syllables of words with differing consonants (lane/hail, penitent/reticence). A device favored particularly by descriptive poets, it appears often in the work of the English Romantics, especially Shelley and Keats, and their great Victorian successor Tennyson, all of whom had a good ear for the musical quality of language. In the following passage, Tennyson makes effective use of repeated "o" and "ow" sounds to suggest the soft moaning of the wind as it spreads the seed of the lotos plant:

The Lotos blooms below the barren peak,
The Lotos blows by every winding creek;

All day the wind breathes low with mellower tone;
Through every hollow cave and alley lone
Round and round the spicy downs the yellow Lotos dust is blown.

(from "The Lotos-Eaters")

ALLITERATION

Alliteration connects words which have the same initial consonant. Like consonance and rhyme, alliteration adds emphasis, throwing individual words into strong relief, and lending force to rhythm. This is especially evident in the work of Gerard Manley Hopkins, where alliteration works in conjunction with the heavy stresses of *sprung rhythm*:

Brute beauty and valour and act, oh, air, pride, plume, here
Buckle! AND the fire that breaks from thee then, a billion
Times told lovelier, more dangerous, O my chevalier!

(from "The Windhover")

Like assonance, alliteration is useful in descriptive poetry, reinforcing an impression or mood through repeated sounds:

Thou on whose stream, 'mid the steep sky's commotion,
Loose clouds like Earth's decaying leaves are shed,
Shook from the tangled boughs of Heaven and Ocean ....

(from Percy Shelley, "Ode to the West Wind")

The repetition of "s" and "sh" sounds conveys the rushing sound of a wind that drives everything before it. This effect is also an example of *onomatopoeia*, a figure of speech in which the sound of the words seems to echo the sense.

RHYME AND POETIC STRUCTURE

Rhyme may play a central role in the structure of a poem. This is particularly apparent in the *sonnet* form, where the expression of the thought is heavily influenced by the poet's choice of rhyme-scheme. The "English" or "Shakespearean" sonnet has three quatrains rhyming *abab*, *cdcd*, *efef*, and concludes with a rhyming couplet, *gg*. This pattern lends itself well to the statement and restatement of an idea, as we find, for example, in Shakespeare's sonnet "That time of year thou mayst in me behold." Each of the quatrains presents an image of decline or decay—a tree in winter, the coming of night, a dying fire; the closing couplet then relates these images to the thought of an impending separation and attendant feelings of loss.

The organization of the "Italian" or "Petrarchan" sonnet, by contrast, hinges on a rhyme scheme that creates two parts, an eight-line section (the *octave*) typically rhyming *abbaabba*, and a concluding six-line section (the *sestet*) rhyming *cdecde* or some other variation. In the octave, the writer describes a thought or feeling; in the sestet, the writer may elaborate upon that thought, or may introduce a sudden "turn" or change of direction. A good example of the Italian form is Donne's "Batter My Heart, Three-Personed God."

The rhyming pattern established at the beginning of a poem is usually followed throughout; thus the opening sets up an expectation in the reader, which the poet may sometimes play on by means of an unexpected or surprising rhyme. This is especially evident in comic verse, where peculiar or unexpected rhymes can contribute a great deal to the comic effect:

> I shoot the Hippopotamus
> with bullets made of platinum,
> Because if I use leaden ones
> his hide is sure to flatten 'em.
>
> (Hilaire Belloc, "The Hippopotamus")

Finally, one of the most obvious yet important aspects of rhyme is its sound. It acts as a kind of musical punctuation, lending verse an added resonance and beauty. And as anyone who has ever had to learn poetry by heart will testify, the sound of rhyme is a powerful aid to memorization and recall, from helping a child to learn numbers—

> One, two,
> Buckle my shoe,
> Three, four,
> Knock at the door—

—to selling toothpaste through an advertising jingle in which the use of rhyme drives home the identity of a product:

> You'll wonder where the yellow went,
> When you brush your teeth with Pepsodent.

OTHER FORMS WITH INTERLOCKING RHYMES

Other forms besides the sonnet depend upon rhyme for their structural integrity. These include the *rondeau*, a poem of thirteen lines in three stanzas, with two half lines acting as a refrain, and having only two rhymes. The linking effect of rhyme is also essential to the three-line stanza called *terza rima*, the form chosen by Shelley for his "Ode to the West Wind," where the rhyme scheme (*aba, bcb, cdc* etc.) gives a strong sense of forward movement. But a poet need not be limited to particular forms to use interlocking rhyme schemes.

THE POET'S TASK

The poet's task, in Sir Philip Sidney's view, is to move us to virtue and well-doing by coming to us with

> words set in delightful proportion, either accompanied with, or prepared for, the well-enchanting skill of music; and with a tale forsooth he cometh unto you, with a tale which holdeth children from play, and old men from the chimney corner; and pretending no more,

> doth intend the winning of the mind from wickedness to virtue: even as the child is often brought to take most wholesome things by hiding them in such other as have a pleasant taste.
> (*The Defence of Poesy,* 1593)

Modern poets have been less preoccupied with the didactic or moral force of poetry, its capacity to win the mind to virtue; nonetheless, like their Renaissance counterparts, they view poetry as a means to understanding, a point of light in an otherwise dark universe. To Robert Frost, a poem "begins in delight and ends in wisdom":

> It begins in delight, it inclines to the impulse, it assumes direction with the first line laid down, it runs a course of lucky events, and ends in a clarification of life—not necessarily a great clarification, such as sects and cults are founded on, but in a momentary stay against confusion.
> ("The Figure a Poem Makes," *Collected Poems,* 1939)

Rhyme and metre are important tools at the poet's disposal, and can be valuable aids in developing thought as well as in creating rhythmic or musical effects. However, the technical skills needed to turn a good line or create metrical complexities should not be confused with the ability to write good poetry. Sidney wryly observes in his *Defence of Poesy* that "there have been many excellent poets that never versified, and now swarm many versifiers that need never answer to the name of poets.…it is not rhyming and versing that maketh a poet, no more than a long gown maketh an advocate." Technical virtuosity may arouse our admiration, but something else is needed to bring that "constriction of the throat and … precipitation of water to the eyes" that A.E. Housman speaks about. What that "something" is will always elude definition, and is perhaps best left for readers and listeners to determine for themselves through their own encounters with poetry.

Maps

ORKNEYS & SHETLANDS
N
W
E
S
SUTHERLAND
CAITHNESS
HEBRIDES
CROMARTY
ROSS
ELGIN
BANFF
NAIRN
ISLE OF SKYE
WESTERN ISLES
INVERNESS
ABERDEEN
SCOTLAND
KINCARDINE
North Sea
Atlantic Ocean
FORFAR
ARGYLL
PERTH
CLACKMANNAN
KINROSS
FIFE
Firth of Forth
STIRLING
HADDINGTON
LOTHIAN
RENFREW
BERWICK
LANARK
PEEBLES
SELKIRK
ROXBURGH
BUTE
AYR
NORTHUMBERLAND
North Channel
DUMFRIES
ANTRIM (1560)
COLERAINE (1585)
DONEGAL (1585)
(ULSTER)
KIRKCUDBRIGHT
WIGTOWN
CUMBERLAND
DURHAM
Donegal Bay
TYRONE (1585)
FERMANAGH (1585)
ARMAGH (1560)
DOWN (1560)
CUMBRIA
SLIGO (1576)
LEITRIM (1583)
MONAGHAN (1585)
ISLE OF MAN
(CONNAUGHT)
CAVAN (1579)
YORKSHIRE
MAYO (1576)
ROSCOMMON (1569)
LONGFORD
LOUTH
ENGLAND
GALWAY (1569)
IRELAND
WESTMEATH (1542)
MEATH
Irish Sea
(LEINSTER)
KING'S COUNTY (1556)
KILDARE
DUBLIN
LANCASHIRE
ANGLESEY
GALWAY (1569)
LINCOLNSHIRE
QUEEN'S COUNTY (1557)
WICKLOW (1560)
FLINT
DENBIGH (1536)
CHESHIRE
DERBY
NOTTINGHAM
CLARE (1560)
CARNARVON
The Wash
CARLOW
MERIONETH
RUTLAND
TIPPERARY
STAFFORD
SHROPSHIRE
NORFOLK
KILKENNY
LEICESTER
HUNTINGDON
LIMERICK
MONTGOMERY (1536)
WEXFORD
WARWICK
(MUNSTER)
RADNOR
NORTHAMPTON
CAMBRIDGE
SUFFOLK
KERRY
CORK
WATERFORD
CARDIGAN
WORCESTER
St. George's Channel
BRECKNOCK (1536)
BEDFORD
WALES
HEREFORD
PEMBROKE
CARMATHEN
OXFORD
BUCKINGHAM
HERTFORD
ESSEX
MONMOUTH (1536)
GLOUCESTER
London
GLAMORGAN
BERKSHIRE
MIDDLESEX
WILTSHIRE
SURREY
KENT
SOMERSET
HAMPSHIRE
SUSSEX
Strait of Dover
DEVON
DORSET
ISLE OF WIGHT
CORNWALL
English Channel
ISLES OF SCILLY
COUNTIES OF THE BRITISH ISLES

THE BRITISH ISLES

THE LONDON AREA
Finchley
Harrow
EPPING FOREST
Twyford Abbey
London
Tower
Westminster
Chelsea
Woolwich
Greenwich
Battersea
Deptford
Richmond
Twickenham
Dartford
Kingston
Wimbledon
Sydenham
Hampton Court
Merton

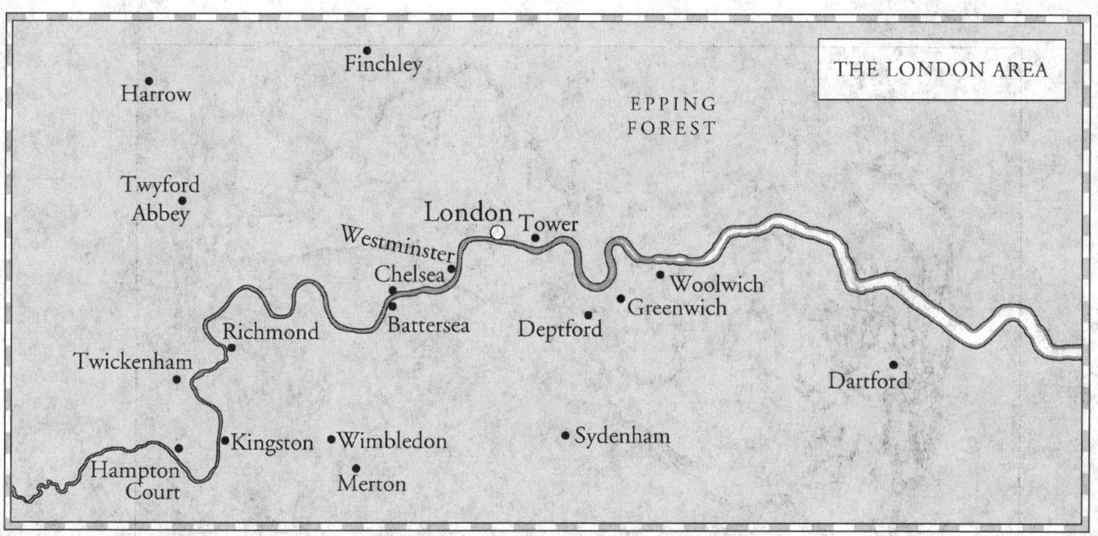

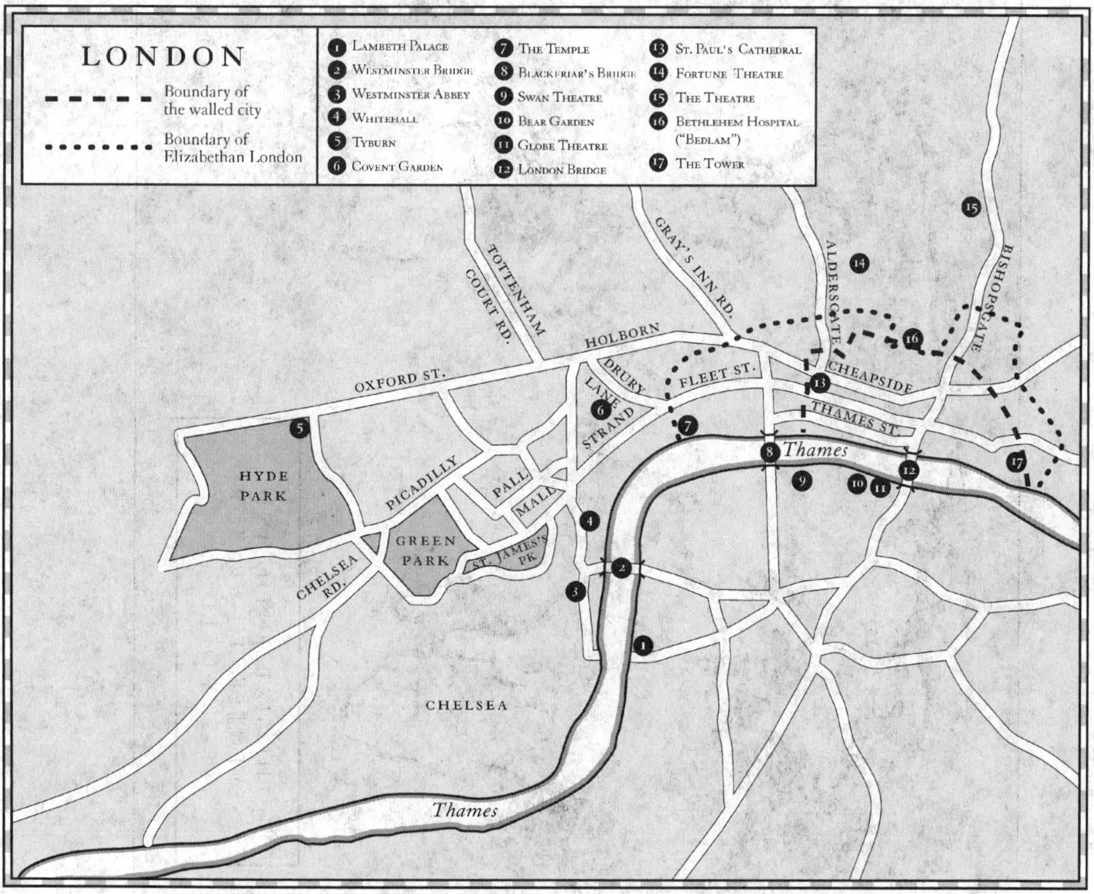

LONDON
Boundary of the walled city
Boundary of Elizabethan London
1 Lambeth Palace
2 Westminster Bridge
3 Westminster Abbey
4 Whitehall
5 Tyburn
6 Covent Garden
7 The Temple
8 Blackfriar's Bridge
9 Swan Theatre
10 Bear Garden
11 Globe Theatre
12 London Bridge
13 St. Paul's Cathedral
14 Fortune Theatre
15 The Theatre
16 Bethlehem Hospital ("Bedlam")
17 The Tower
Tottenham Court Rd.
Gray's Inn Rd.
Aldersgate
Bishopsgate
Holborn
Oxford St.
Drury Lane
Fleet St.
Cheapside
Thames St.
Strand
Thames
Hyde Park
Picadilly
Pall Mall
Green Park
St. James's Pk
Chelsea Rd.
Chelsea
Thames

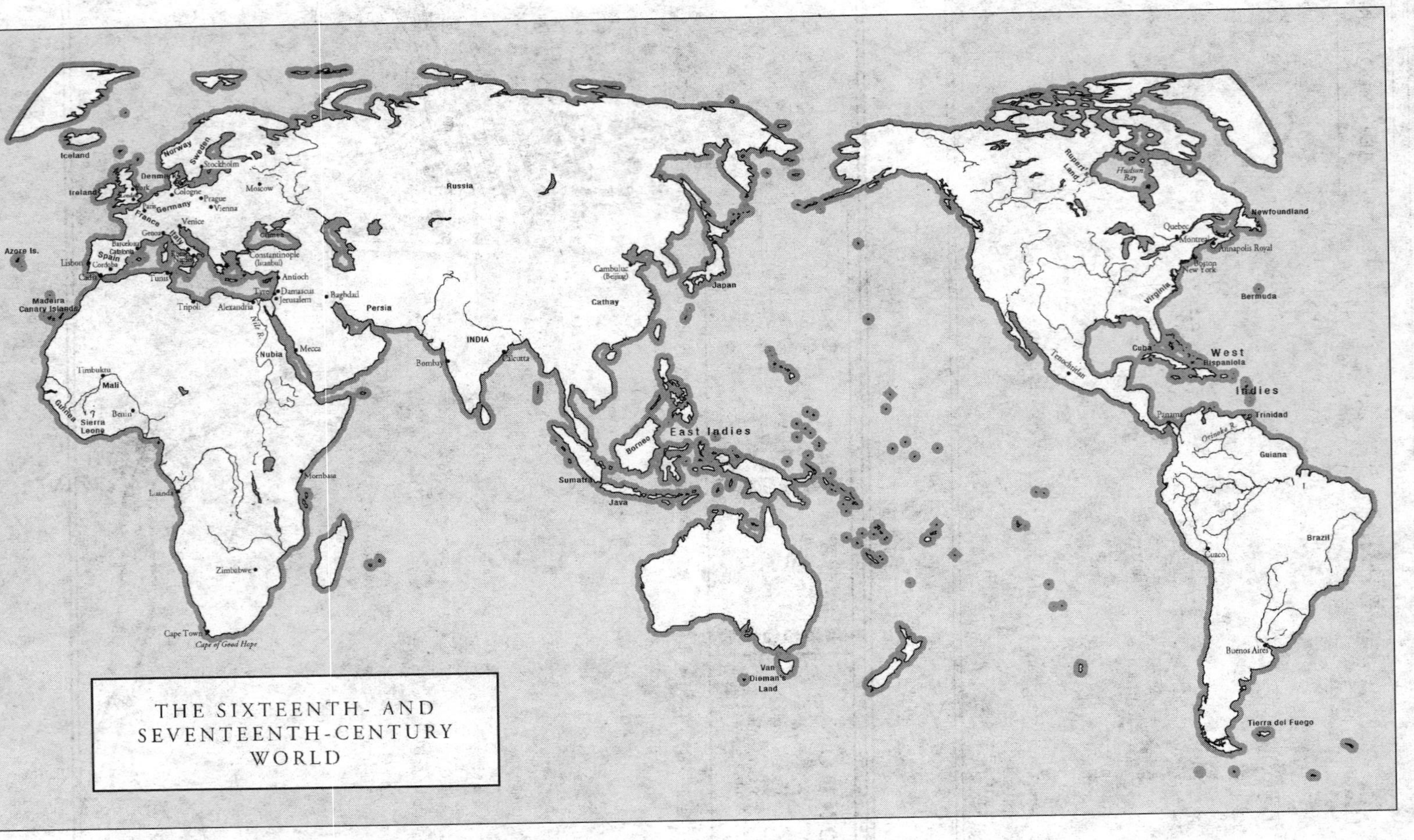
THE SIXTEENTH- AND
SEVENTEENTH-CENTURY
WORLD
Iceland
Ireland
Azore Is.
Madeira
Canary Islands
Lisbon
Cadiz
Spain
Cordoba
Catalonia
Barcelona
France
Paris
Germany
Cologne
Prague
Vienna
Venice
Genoa
Italy
Norway
Sweden
Stockholm
Moscow
Russia
Constantinople
(Istanbul)
Antioch
Tyre
Damascus
Jerusalem
Baghdad
Persia
Tunis
Tripoli
Alexandria
Nile R.
Nubia
Mecca
Timbuktu
Mali
Guinea
Sierra
Leone
Benin
Luanda
Mombasa
Zimbabwe
Cape Town
Cape of Good Hope
INDIA
Bombay
Calcutta
Cambuluc
(Beijing)
Cathay
Japan
Sumatra
Java
Borneo
East Indies
Van
Dieman's
Land
Rupert's
Land
Hudson
Bay
Quebec
Montreal
Annapolis Royal
Newfoundland
Boston
New York
Virginia
Bermuda
Tenochtitlan
Cuba
West
Hispaniola
Indies
Panama
Trinidad
Orinoko R.
Guiana
Brazil
Cuzco
Buenos Aires
Tierra del Fuego

Monarchs and Prime Ministers of Great Britain

MONARCHS

House of Wessex

Egbert (Ecgberht)	829–39
Æthelwulf	839–58
Æthelbald	858–60
Æthelbert	860–66
Æthelred I	866–71
Alfred the Great	871–99
Edward the Elder	899–924
Athelstan	924–40
Edmund I	940–46
Edred (Eadred)	946–55
Edwy (Eadwig)	955–59
Edgar	959–75
Edward the Martyr	975–78
Æthelred II (the Unready)	978–1016
Edmund II (Ironside)	1016

Danish Line

Canute (Cnut)	1016–35
Harold I (Harefoot)	1035–40
Hardecanute	1040–42

Wessex Line, Restored

Edward the Confessor	1042–66
Harold II	1066

Norman Line

William I (the Conqueror)	1066–87
William II (Rufus)	1087–1100
Henry I (Beauclerc)	1100–35
Stephen	1135–54

Harold II

William I

MONARCHS

Plantagenet, Angevin Line

Henry II	1154–89
Richard I (Coeur de Lion)	1189–99
John (Lackland)	1199–1216
Henry III	1216–72
Edward I (Longshanks)	1272–1307
Edward II	1307–27
Edward III	1327–77
Richard II	1377–99

Henry VIII

Plantagenet, Lancastrian Line

Henry IV	1399–1413
Henry V	1413–22
Henry VI	1422–61

Plantagenet, Yorkist Line

Edward IV	1461–83
Edward V	1483
Richard III	1483–85

House of Tudor

Henry VII	1485–1509
Henry VIII	1509–47
Edward VI	1547–53
Mary I	1553–58
Elizabeth I	1558–1603

Mary I

House of Stuart

James I	1603–25
Charles I	1625–49
(The Commonwealth)	1649–60
Oliver Cromwell	1649–58
Richard Cromwell	1658–59

MONARCHS

HOUSE OF STUART, RESTORED

Charles II	1660–85
James II	1685–88

HOUSE OF ORANGE AND STUART

William III and Mary II	1689–94
William III	1694–1702

HOUSE OF STUART

Anne	1702–14

HOUSE OF BRUNSWICK, HANOVER LINE

George I	1714–27
George II	1727–60
George III	1760–1820

George, Prince of Wales, Prince Regent

PRIME MINISTERS

George III

Sir Robert Walpole (Whig)	1721–42
Earl of Wilmington (Whig)	1742–43
Henry Pelham (Whig)	1743–54
Duke of Newcastle (Whig)	1754–56
Duke of Devonshire (Whig)	1756–57
Duke of Newcastle (Whig)	1757–62
Earl of Bute (Tory)	1762–63
George Grenville (Whig)	1763–65
Marquess of Rockingham (Whig)	1765–66
William Pitt the Elder (Earl of Chatham) (Whig)	1766–68
Duke of Grafton (Whig)	1768–70
Frederick North (Lord North) (Tory)	1770–82
Marquess of Rockingham (Whig)	1782
Earl of Shelburne (Whig)	1782–83
Duke of Portland	1783
William Pitt the Younger (Tory)	1783–1801
Henry Addington (Tory)	1801–04
William Pitt the Younger (Tory)	1804–06
William Wyndham Grenville (Baron Grenville) (Whig)	1806–07

MONARCHS		PRIME MINISTERS	
		Duke of Portland (Whig)	1807–09
George, Prince of Wales, Prince Regent	1811–20	Spencer Perceval (Tory)	1809–12
		Earl of Liverpool (Tory)	1812–27
George IV	1820–30		
		George Canning (Tory)	1827
		Viscount Goderich (Tory)	1827–28
		Duke of Wellington (Tory)	1828–30
William IV	1830–37		
		Earl Grey (Whig)	1830–34
		Viscount Melbourne (Whig)	1834
Victoria	1837–1901		
		Sir Robert Peel (Tory)	1834–35
		Viscount Melbourne (Whig)	1835–41
		Sir Robert Peel (Tory)	1841–46
		Lord John Russell (later Earl) (Liberal)	1846–52
		Earl of Derby (Con.)	1852
		Earl of Aberdeen (Tory)	1852–55
		Viscount Palmerston (Lib.)	1855–58
		Earl of Derby (Con.)	1858–59
		Viscount Palmerston (Lib.)	1859–65
		Earl Russell (Liberal)	1865–66
		Earl of Derby (Con.)	1866–68
		Benjamin Disraeli (Con.)	1868
		William Gladstone (Lib.)	1868–74
		Benjamin Disraeli (Con.)	1874–80
		William Gladstone (Lib.)	1880–85
		Marquess of Salisbury (Con.)	1885–86
		William Gladstone (Lib.)	1886
HOUSE OF SAXE-COBURG-GOTHA		Marquess of Salisbury (Con.)	1886–92
Edward VII	1901–10	William Gladstone (Lib.)	1892–94
		Earl of Rosebery (Lib.)	1894–95
		Marquess of Salisbury (Con.)	1895–1902
		Arthur Balfour (Con.)	1902–05
		Sir Henry Campbell-Bannerman (Lib.)	1905–08
		Herbert Asquith (Lib.)	1908–15
HOUSE OF WINDSOR			
George V	1910–36		
		Herbert Asquith (Lib.)	1915–16

Victoria

MONARCHS		PRIME MINISTERS	
		Andrew Bonar Law (Con.)	1922–23
		Stanley Baldwin (Con.)	1923–24
		James Ramsay MacDonald (Labour)	1924
		Stanley Baldwin (Con.)	1924–29
		James Ramsay MacDonald (Labour)	1929–31
		James Ramsay MacDonald (Labour)	1931–35
		Stanley Baldwin (Con.)	1935–37
Edward VIII	1936	Neville Chamberlain (Con.)	1937–40
George VI	1936–52	Winston Churchill (Con.)	1940–45
		Winston Churchill (Con.)	1945
		Clement Attlee (Labour)	1945–51
Elizabeth II	1952–	Sir Winston Churchill (Con.)	1951–55
		Sir Anthony Eden (Con.)	1955–57
		Harold Macmillan (Con.)	1957–63
		Sir Alex Douglas-Home (Con.)	1963–64
		Harold Wilson (Labour)	1964–70
		Edward Heath (Con.)	1970–74
		Harold Wilson (Labour)	1974–76
		James Callaghan (Labour)	1976–79
		Margaret Thatcher (Con.)	1979–90
		John Major (Con.)	1990–97
		Tony Blair (Labour)	1997–2007
		Gordon Brown (Labour)	2007–10
		David Cameron (Con.)	2010–

Winston Churchill

Glossary of Terms

Accent: the natural emphasis (stress) speakers place on a syllable.

Accentual Verse: poetry in which a line is measured only by the number of accents or stresses, not by the number of syllables.

Accentual-Syllabic Verse: the most common metrical system in traditional English verse, in which a line is measured by the number of syllables and by the pattern of accented (stressed) and unaccented (unstressed) syllables.

Aesthetes: members of a late nineteenth-century movement that valued "art for art's sake"—for its purely aesthetic qualities, as opposed to valuing art for the moral content it may convey, for the intellectual stimulation it may provide, or for a range of other qualities.

Alexandrine: a line of verse that is 12 syllables long. In English verse, the alexandrine is always an iambic hexameter: that is, it has six iambic feet. The most-often quoted example is the second line in a couplet from Alexander Pope's "Essay on Criticism" (1711): "A needless Alexandrine ends the song / That, like a wounded snake, drags its slow length along." See also *Spenserian stanza.*

Allegory: a narrative with both a literal meaning and secondary, often symbolic meaning or meanings. Allegory frequently employs personification to give concrete embodiment to abstract concepts or entities, such as feelings or personal qualities. It may also present one set of characters or events in the guise of another, using implied parallels for the purposes of satire or political comment, as in John Dryden's poem "Absalom and Achitophel."

Alliteration: the grouping of words with the same initial consonant (e.g., "break, blow, burn, and make me new"). The repetition of sound acts as a connector. See also *assonance* and *consonance.*

Alliterative Verse: poetry that employs alliteration of stressed syllables in each line as its chief structural principle.

Allusion: a reference, often indirect or unidentified, to a person, thing, or event. A reference in one literary work to another literary work, whether to its content or its form, also constitutes an allusion.

Ambiguity: an "opening" of language created by the writer to allow for multiple meanings or differing interpretations. In literature, ambiguity may be deliberately employed by the writer to enrich meaning; this differs from any unintentional, unwanted, ambiguity in non-literary prose.

Amphibrach: a metrical foot with three syllables, the second of which is stressed: x / x (e.g., sensation).

Analogy: a broad term that refers to our processes of noting similarities among things or events. Specific forms of analogy in poetry include *simile* and *metaphor* (see below).

Anapaest: a metrical foot containing two unstressed syllables followed by one stressed syllable: xx/ (e.g., underneath, intervene).

Anglican Church / Church of England: formed after Henry VIII's break with Rome in the 1530s, the Church of England had acquired a permanently Protestant cast by the 1570s. There has remained considerable variation within the Church, however, with distinctions often drawn among High Church, Broad Church, and Latitudinarian. At one extreme High Church Anglicans (some of whom prefer to be known as "Anglo-Catholics") prefer relatively elaborate church rituals not dissimilar in form to those of the Roman Catholic Church and place considerable emphasis on church hierarchy, while in the other direction Latitudinarians prefer relatively informal religious services and tend far more towards egalitarianism.

Antistrophe: from Greek drama, the chorus's countermovement or reply to an initial movement (strophe). See *ode* below.

Apostrophe: a figure of speech (a trope; see figures of speech below) in which a writer directly addresses an object—or a dead or absent person—as if the imagined audience were actually listening.

Archetype: in literature and mythology, a recurring idea, symbol, motif, character, or place. To some scholars and psychologists, an archetype represents universal human thought-patterns or experiences.

Assonance: the repetition of identical or similar vowel sounds in stressed syllables in which the surrounding consonants are different: for example, "shame" and "fate"; "gale" and "cage"; or the long "i" sounds in "Beside the pumice isle..."

Aubade: a lyric poem that greets or laments the arrival of dawn.

Ballad: a folk song, or a poem originally recited to an audience, which tells a dramatic story based on legend or history.

Ballad Stanza: a quatrain with alternating four-stress and three-stress lines, rhyming *abcb*. A variant is "common measure," in which the alternating lines are strictly iambic, and rhyme *abab*.

Ballade: a fixed form most commonly characterized by only three rhymes, with an 8-line stanza rhyming *ababbcbc* and an envoy rhyming *bcbc*. Both Chaucer and Dante Gabriel Rossetti ("Ballad of the Dead Ladies") adopted this form.

Baroque: powerful and heavily ornamented in style. "Baroque" is a term from the history of visual art and of music that is sometimes also used to describe certain literary styles, such as that of Richard Crashaw.

Bathos: an anticlimactic effect brought about by a writer's descent from an elevated subject or tone to the ordinary or trivial.

Benedictine Rule: set of instructions for monastic communities, composed by Saint Benedict of Nursia (died c. 457).

Blank Verse: unrhymed lines written in iambic pentameter, a form introduced to English verse by Henry Howard, Earl of Surrey, in his translation of parts of Virgil's *Aeneid* in 1547.

Bombast: inappropriately inflated or grandiose language.

Broadside: individual sheet of paper printed on only one side. From the sixteenth through to the eighteenth centuries broadsides of a variety of different sorts (e.g., ballads, political tracts, short satires) were sold on the streets.

Broken Rhyme: in which a multi-syllable word is split at the end of a line and continued onto the next, to allow an end-rhyme with the split syllable.

Burlesque: satire of a particularly exaggerated sort, particularly that which ridicules its subject by emphasising its vulgar or ridiculous aspects.

Caesura: a pause or break in a line of verse occurring where a phrase, clause, or sentence ends, and indicated in scansion by the mark II. If it occurs in the middle of the line, it is known as a "medial" caesura.

Canon: in literature, those works that are commonly accepted as possessing authority or importance. In practice, "canonical" texts or authors are those that are discussed most frequently by scholars and taught most frequently in university courses.

Canto: a sub-section of a long (usually epic) poem.

Canzone: a short song or poem, with stanzas of equal length and an envoy.

Carpe Diem: Latin (from Horace) meaning "seize the day." The idea of enjoying the moment is a common one in Renaissance love poetry. See, for example, Marvell's "To His Coy Mistress."

Catalexis: the omission of unstressed syllables from a line of verse (such a line is referred to as "catalectic"). In iambic verse it is usually the first syllable of the line that is omitted; in trochaic, the last. For example, in the first stanza of Housman's "To an Athlete Dying Young" the third line is catalectic: i.e., it has dropped the first, unstressed syllable called for by the poem's iambic tetrameter form: "The time you won your town the race / We chaired you through the market-place; / Man and boy stood cheering by, / And home we brought you shoulder-high."

Catharsis: the arousal through the performance of a dramatic tragedy of "emotions of pity and fear" to a point where "purgation" or "purification" occurs and the feelings are released or transformed. The concept was developed by Aristotle in his *Poetics* from an ancient Greek medical concept, and adapted by him into an aesthetic principle.

Chiasmus: a figure of speech (a scheme) that reverses word order in successive parallel clauses. If the word order is A-B-C in the first clause, it becomes C-B-A in the second: for example, Donne's line "She is all states, and all princes, I" ("The Sun Rising") incorporates this reversal (though with an ellipsis).

Classical: originating in or relating to ancient Greek or Roman culture. As commonly conceived, *classical* implies a strong sense of formal order. The term *neoclassical* is often used with reference to literature of the Restoration and eighteenth century that was strongly influenced by ancient Greek and Roman models.

Closet Drama: a play (typically in verse) written for private performance. The term came into use in the first half of the nineteenth century.

Colored Narrative: alternative term for *free indirect discourse.*

Comedy: as a literary term, used originally to denote that class of ancient Greek drama in which the action ends happily. More broadly the term has been used to describe a wide variety of literary forms of a more or less light-hearted character.

***Commedia dell'arte*:** largely improvised comic performances conducted by masked performers and involving considerable physical activity. The genre of *commedia dell'arte* originated in Italy in the sixteenth century; it was influential throughout Europe for more than two centuries thereafter.

Commonwealth: from the fifteenth century, a term roughly equivalent to the modern "state," but tending to emphasize the commonality of interests among all citizens. In the seventeenth century Britain was named a commonwealth under Oliver Cromwell. In the twentieth century, the term came to be applied to associations of many nations; the British Commonwealth became the successor to the British Empire.

Conceit: an unusually elaborate metaphor or simile that extends beyond its original tenor and vehicle, sometimes becoming a "master" analogy for the entire poem (see, for example, Donne's "The Flea," and Robert Frost's sonnet "She is as in a field a silken tent"). Ingenious or fanciful images and comparisons were especially popular with the metaphysical poets of the seventeenth century, giving rise to the term "metaphysical conceit."

Concrete Poetry: an experimental form, most popular during the 1950s and 60s, in which the printed type itself forms a visual image of the poem's key words or ideas. See also *pattern poetry, assonance.*

Connotation: the implied, often unspoken meaning(s) of a given word, as distinct from its denotation, or literal meaning. Connotations may have highly emotional undertones and are usually culturally specific.

Conservative Party: See *Political Parties.*

Consonance: the pairing of words with similar initial and ending consonants, but with different vowel sounds (live/love, wander/wonder). See also *alliteration.*

Convention: aesthetic approach, technique, or practice accepted as characteristic and appropriate for a particular form. It is a convention of certain sorts of plays, for example, that the characters speak in blank verse, of other sorts of plays that characters speak in rhymed couplets, and of still other sorts of dramatic performances that characters frequently break into song to express their feelings.

Couplet: a pair of rhyming lines, usually in the same meter. If they form a complete unit of thought and are grammatically complete, the lines are known as a closed couplet. See also *heroic couplet* below.

Dactyl: a metrical foot containing one strong stress followed by two weak stresses: / xx (e.g., muttering, helplessly). A minor form known as "double dactyls" makes use of this meter for humorous purposes, e.g., "Jiggery pokery" or "Higgledy Piggledy."

Denotation: See *connotation* above.

Devolution: process through which a degree of political power was transferred in the late twentieth and early twenty-first centuries from the British government to assemblies in Scotland and in Wales.

Dialogue: words spoken by characters to one another. (When a character is addressing him or her self or the audience directly, the words spoken are referred to as a *monologue*.)

Diction: word choice. Whether the diction of a literary work (or of a literary character) is colloquial, conversational, formal, or of some other type contributes significantly to the tone of the text as well as to characterization.

Didacticism: aesthetic approach emphasizing moral instruction.

Dimeter: a poetic line containing two metrical feet.

Dirge: a song or poem that mourns someone's death. See also *elegy* and *lament* below.

Disestablishmentarianism: movement opposing an official state-supported religion, in particular the Church of England in that role.

Dissonance: harsh, unmusical sounds or rhythms which poets may use deliberately to achieve certain effects.

Dramatic Irony: this form of irony occurs when the audience's reception of a speech by a character on the stage is affected by the possession by the audience of information not available to the character.

Dramatic Monologue: a lyric poem that takes the form of an utterance by a single person addressing a silent listener. The speaker may be an historical personage (as in some of Robert Browning's dramatic monologues), a figure drawn from myth or legend (as in some of Tennyson's), or an entirely imagined figure, as in Webster's "A Castaway."

Dub Poetry: a form of protest poetry originating in Jamaica, with its roots in dance rhythms, especially reggae, and often accompanied in performance by drums and music. See also *rap* and *hip-hop*.

Duple Foot: A duple foot of poetry has two syllables. The possible duple forms are iamb (in which the stress is on the second of the two syllables), trochee (in which the stress is on the first of the two syllables), spondee (in which both are stressed equally), and pyrrhic (in which both syllables are unstressed).

Eclogue: now generally used simply as an alternative name for a pastoral poem. In classical times and in the early modern period, however, an *eclogue* (or *idyll*) was a specific type of pastoral poem—a dialogue or dramatic monologue involving rustic characters. (The other main sub-genre of the pastoral was the *georgic.*)

Elegiac Stanza: a quatrain of iambic pentameters rhyming *abab*, often used in poems meditating on death or sorrow. The best-known example is Thomas Gray's "Elegy Written in a Country Churchyard."

Elegy: a poem which formally mourns the death of a particular person (e.g., Tennyson's "In Memoriam") or in which the poet meditates on other serious subjects (e.g., Gray's "Elegy"). See also *dirge.*

Elision: omitting or suppressing a letter or an unstressed syllable at the beginning or end of a word, so that a line of verse may conform to a given metrical scheme. For example, the three syllables at the beginning of Shakespeare's sonnet 129 are reduced to two by the omission of the first vowel: "Th' expense of spirit in a waste of shame." See also *syncope.*

Ellipsis: the omission of a word or words necessary for the complete grammatical construction of a sentence, but not necessary for our understanding of the sentence.

End-Rhyme: See *rhyme.*

End-stopped: a line of poetry is said to be end-stopped when the end of the line coincides with a natural pause in the syntax, such as the conclusion of a sentence; e.g., in this couplet from Pope's "Essay on Criticism," both lines are end-stopped: "A little learning is a dangerous thing; / Drink deep, or taste not the Pierian spring." Compare this with *enjambement.*

Enjambement: the "running-on" of the sense from one line of poetry to the next, with no pause created by punctuation or syntax. (The more commonly found alternative is referred to as an *end-stopped line.*)

Envoy (Envoi): a stanza or half-stanza that forms the conclusion of certain French poetic forms, such as the *sestina* or the *ballade.* It often sums up or comments upon what has gone before.

Epic: a lengthy narrative poem, often divided into books and sub-divided into cantos. It generally celebrates heroic deeds or events, and the style tends to be lofty and grand. Examples in English include Spenser's *The Faerie Queene* and Milton's *Paradise Lost.*

Epic Simile: an elaborate simile, developed at such length that the vehicle of the comparison momentarily displaces the primary subject with which it is being compared.

Epigram: a very short poem, sometimes in closed couplet form, characterized by pointed wit.

Epigraph: a quotation placed at the beginning of a discourse to indicate or foreshadow the theme.

Epiphany: a moment at which matters of significance are suddenly illuminated for a literary character (or for the reader), typically triggered by something small and seemingly of little import. The term first came into wide currency in connection with the fiction of James Joyce.

Episodic Plot: plot comprising a variety of episodes that are only loosely connected by threads of story material (as opposed to plots that present one or more continually unfolding narratives where successive episodes build one on another).

Epithalamion: a poem celebrating a wedding. The best-known example in English is probably Edmund Spenser's "Epithalamion" (1595).

Eulogy: text expressing praise, especially for a distinguished person recently deceased.

Euphemism: mode of expression through which aspects of reality considered to be vulgar, crudely physical, or unpleasant are referred to indirectly rather than named explicitly. A variety of euphemisms exist for the processes of urination and defecation; *passed away* is often used as a euphemism for *died.* (The word *euphemism* has the same root as *Euphuism* (see below), but has taken on a different meaning.)

Euphony: pleasant, musical sounds or rhythms—the opposite of dissonance.

Euphuism: In the late sixteenth century John Lyly published a prose romance, *Euphues*, which employed a style that featured long sentences filled with balanced phrases and clauses, many of them adding little to the content. This highly mannered style was popular in the court of Elizabeth I for a few years following the publication of Lyly's famous work, and the style became known as *Euphuism*.

European Union: (EU) Group of nations formed in 1993 as the successor to the European Economic Community (Common Market). Britain first applied for membership in the latter in 1961; at first its efforts to join were blocked by the French government, but in 1973 Prime Minister Edward Heath successfully negotiated Britain's entry into the group. Britain has resisted some moves towards full integration with the European community, in particular retaining its own currency when other European nations adopted the Euro on 1 January 2002.

Exchequer: In earlier eras, the central royal financial office, responsible for receiving and keeping track of crown revenues. In later eras, part of the bureaucracy equivalent to the Ministry of Finance in Canada or the Treasury in the United States (the modern post of Chancellor of the Exchequer is equivalent to the American post of Secretary of the Treasury, the Canadian post of Minister of Finance or the Australian post of Treasurer).

Exposition: the setting out of material in an ordered form, either in speech or in writing. In a play those parts of the action that do not occur on stage but are rather recounted by the characters are frequently described as being presented in exposition. Similarly, when the background narrative is filled in near the beginning of a novel, such material is often described as having been presented in exposition. Somewhat confusingly, however, the term "expository prose" is usually used with reference not to fiction but to the setting forth of arguments or descriptions in the context of essays or other works of prose non-fiction.

Eye-Rhyme: See *rhyme* below.

Feminine Ending: the ending of a line of poetry on an "extra," and, especially, on an unstressed syllable. See, for example, the first line of Keat's "Ode on a Grecian Urn": "A thing of beauty is a joy forever," a line of iambic pentameter in which the final foot is an amphibrach rather than an iamb.

Feminine Rhyme: See *rhyme* below.

Figures of Speech: deliberate, highly concentrated uses of language to achieve particular purposes or effects on an audience. There are two kinds of figures: schemes and tropes. Schemes involve changes in word-sound and word-order, such as *alliteration* and *chiasmus.* Tropes play on our understandings of words to extend, alter, or transform meaning, as in *metaphor* and *personification.*

First-Person Narrative: narrative recounted using *I* and *me.* See also *narrative perspective.*

Fixed Forms: the term applied to a number of poetic forms and stanzaic patterns, many derived from French models, such as *ballade, rondeau, sestina, triolet,* and *villanelle.* Other "fixed forms" include the *sonnet, rhyme royal, haiku,* and *ottava rima.*

Folio: largest of several sizes of book page commonly used in the first few centuries after the introduction of the printing press. A folio size results from sheets of paper of at least 14 inches by 20 inches being folded in half (a folio page size will thus be at least 7 inches by 10 inches). When the same sheet is folded twice a quarto is produced, and when it is folded 3 times an octavo.

Foot: a unit of a line of verse which contains a particular combination of stressed and unstressed syllables. Dividing a line into metrical feet (*iambs, trochees,* etc.), then counting the number of feet per line, is part of *scansion.* See also *meter.*

Franklin: in the late medieval period, a landholder of free status, but ranking below the gentry.

Free Indirect Discourse: in prose fiction, commentary in which a seemingly objective and omniscient narrative voice assumes the point of view of one or more characters. When we hear through the third person narrative voice of Jane Austen's *Pride and Prejudice,* for example, that Mr. Darcy "was the proudest, most disagreeable man in the world, and every body hoped that he would never come there again," the narrative voice has assumed the point of view of "every body" in the community; we as readers are not meant to take it that Mr. Darcy is indeed the most disagreeable man in the world. Similarly, in the following passage from the same novel, we are likely to take it to read it as being the view of the character Charlotte that marriage is "the only honourable provision for well-educated young women of small fortune," not to take it to be an objective statement of perceived truth on the part of the novel's third person narrative voice:

> [Charlotte's] reflections were in general satisfactory. Mr. Collins to be sure was neither sensible nor agreeable; his society was irksome, and his attachment to her must be imaginary. But still he would be her husband. Without thinking highly either of men or of matrimony, marriage had always been her object; it was the only honourable provision for well-educated young women of small fortune, and however uncertain of giving happiness, must be their pleasantest preservative from want.

The term free indirect discourse may also be applied to situations in which it may not be entirely clear if the thoughts expressed emanate from the character, the narrator, or some combination of the two. (In the above-quoted passage expressing Charlotte's thoughts, indeed, some might argue that the statement concerning marriage should be taken as the expression of a belief that the narrative voice shares, at least in part.)

Free Verse: poetry that does not follow any regular meter, line length, or rhyming scheme. In many respects, though, free verse follows the complex natural "rules" and rhythmic patterns (or cadences) of speech.

Gaelic: Celtic language, variants of which are spoken in Ireland and Scotland.

Genre: a particular literary form. The concept of genre may be used with different levels of generality. At the most general, poetry, drama, and prose fiction are distinguished as separate genres. At a lower level of generality various sub-genres are frequently distinguished, such as (within drama) comedy and tragedy, or, at a still lower level of generality, Elizabethan domestic tragedy, Edwardian drawing-room comedy, and so on.

Georgic: (from Virgil's *Georgics*) a poem that celebrates the natural wealth of the countryside and advises how to cultivate and live in harmony with it. Pope's *Windsor Forest* and James Thomson's *Seasons* are classed as georgics. They were often said to make up, with eclogues, the two alliterative forms of pastoral poetry.

Ghazal: derived from Persian and Indian precedents, the ghazal presents a series of thoughts in closed couplets joined by a simple rhyme-scheme: *ab bb cb eb fb*, etc.

Gothic: in architecture and the visual arts, a term used to describe styles prevalent from the twelfth to the fourteenth centuries, but in literature a term used to describe work with a sinister or grotesque tone that seeks to evoke a sense of terror on the part of the reader or audience. Gothic literature originated as a genre in the eighteenth century with works such as Horace Walpole's *The Castle of Otranto*. To some extent the notion of the medieval itself then carried with it associations of the dark and the grotesque, but from the beginning an element of intentional exaggeration (sometimes verging on self-parody) attached itself to the genre. The Gothic trend of youth culture that began in the late twentieth century is less clearly associated with the medieval, but shares with the various varieties of Gothic literature (from Walpole in the eighteenth century, to Bram Stoker in the early twentieth, to Stephen King and Anne Rice in the late twentieth) a fondness for the sensational and the grotesque, as well as a propensity to self-parody.

Guilds: non-clerical associations that arose in the late Anglo-Saxon period, devoted both to social purposes (such as the organization of feasts for the members) and to piety. In the later medieval period guilds developed strong associations with particular occupations.

Haiku: a Japanese form, using three unrhymed lines of five, seven, and five syllables. Conventionally, it uses precise, concentrated images to suggest states of feeling.

Heptameter: a line containing seven metrical feet.

Heroic Couplet: a pair of rhymed iambic pentameters, so called because the form was much used in seventeenth and eighteenth-century poems and plays on heroic subjects.

Hexameter: a line containing six metrical feet.

Home Rule: movement dedicated to making Ireland politically independent from Britain.

Horatian Ode: inspired by the work of the Roman poet Horace, an ode that is usually calm and meditative in tone, and homostrophic (i.e., having regular stanzas) in form. Keats's odes are English examples.

House of Commons: elected legislative body, in Britain currently consisting of six hundred and fifty-nine members of Parliament. See also *Parliament*.

House of Lords: the "Upper House" of the British Houses of Parliament. Since the nineteenth century the House of Lords has been far less powerful than the elected House of Commons. The House of Lords is currently made up of both hereditary peers (Lords whose title is passed on from generation to generation) and life peers. As a result of legislation enacted by the Labour government of Tony Blair, the role of hereditary peers in Parliament is being phased out.

Humors: The four humors were believed in until the sixteenth and seventeenth centuries to be elements in the makeup of all humans; a person's temperament was thought to be determined by the way in which the humors were combined. When the *choleric* humor was dominant, the person would tend towards anger; when the *sanguine* humor was dominant, towards pleasant affability; when the *phlegmatic* humor was dominant, towards a cool and calm attitude and/or a lack of feeling or enthusiasm; and when the *melancholic* humor was dominant, towards withdrawal and melancholy.

Hymn: a song whose theme is usually religious, in praise of divinity. Literary hymns may praise more secular subjects.

Hyperbole: a *figure of speech* (a trope) that deliberately exaggerates or inflates meaning to achieve particular effects, such as the irony in A.E. Housman's claim (from "Terence, this is stupid stuff") that "malt does more than Milton can / To justify God's ways to man."

Iamb: the most common metrical foot in English verse, containing one unstressed syllable followed by a stressed syllable: x / (e.g., between, achieve).

Idyll: traditionally, a short pastoral poem that idealizes country life, conveying impressions of innocence and happiness.

Image: the recreation in words of objects perceived by the senses, sometimes thought of as "pictures," although other senses besides sight are involved. Besides this literal application, the term also refers more generally to the descriptive effects of figurative language, especially in *metaphor* and *simile*.

Imagism: a poetic movement that was popular mainly in the second decade of the twentieth century. The goal of Imagist poets (such as H.D. and Ezra Pound in their early work) was to represent emotions or impressions through highly concentrated imagery.

In Memoriam Stanza: a four-line stanza in iambic tetrameter, rhyming *abba*: the type of stanza used by Tennyson in *In Memoriam*.

Incantation: a chant or recitation of words that are believed to have magical power. A poem can achieve an "incantatory" effect through a compelling rhyme scheme and other repetitive patterns.

Interlocking Rhyme: See *rhyme*.

Internal Rhyme: See *rhyme*.

Irony: a subtle form of humor in which a statement is understood to convey a quite different (and often entirely opposite) meaning. A writer achieves this by carefully making sure that the statement occurs in a context which undermines or twists the statement's "literal" meaning. *Hyperbole* and *litotes* are often used for ironic effect. *Sarcasm* is a particularly strong or crude form of irony (usually spoken), in which the meaning is conveyed largely by the tone of voice adopted; something said sarcastically is meant clearly to imply its opposite.

Labour Party: See *Political Parties*.

Lament: a poem which expresses profound regret or grief either because of a death, or because of the loss of a former, happier state.

Language Poetry: a movement that defies the usual lyric and narrative conventions of poetry, and that challenges the structures and codes of everyday language. Often seen as both politically and aesthetically subversive, its roots lie in the works of modernist writers like Ezra Pound and Gertrude Stein.

Liberal Party: See *Political Parties*.

Litotes: a *figure of speech* (a trope) in which a writer deliberately uses understatement to highlight the importance of an argument, or to convey an ironic attitude.

Liturgical Drama: drama based on and/or incorporating text from the liturgy—the text recited during religious services.

Lollard: member of the group of radical Christians that took its inspiration from the ideas of John Wyclif (c. 1330–84). The Lollards, in many ways precursors of the Protestant Reformation, advocated making the Bible available to all, and dedication to the principles of evangelical poverty in imitation of Christ.

Luddites: protestors against the mechanization of industry on the grounds that it was leading to the loss of employment and to an increase in poverty. In the years 1811 to 1816 there were several Luddite protests in which machines were destroyed.

Lyric: a poem, usually short, expressing an individual speaker's feelings or private thoughts. Originally a song performed with accompaniment on a lyre, the lyric poem is often noted for musicality of rhyme and rhythm. The lyric genre includes a variety of forms, including the *sonnet*, the *ode*, the *elegy*, the *madrigal*, the *aubade*, the *dramatic monologue*, and the *hymn*.

Madrigal: a lyric poem, usually short and focusing on pastoral or romantic themes. A madrigal is often set to music.

Masculine Ending: a metrical line ending on a stressed syllable. *Masculine Rhyme*: see *rhyme*.

Masque: an entertainment typically combining music and dance, with a limited script, extravagant costumes and sets, and often incorporating spectacular special effects. Masques, which were performed before court audiences in the early seventeenth century, often focused on royal themes and frequently drew on classical mythology.

Mass: Within Christianity, a church service that includes the sacrament of the Eucharist (Holy Communion), in which bread and wine are consumed which are believed by those of many Christian denominations to have been transubstantiated into the body and blood of Christ. Anglicans (Episcopalians) are more likely to believe the bread and wine merely symbolizes the body and blood.

Melodrama: originally a term used to describe nineteenth-century-plays featuring sensational story lines and a crude separation of characters into moral categories, with the pure and virtuous pitted against evil villains. Early melodramas employed background music throughout the action of the play as a means of heightening the emotional response of the audience. By extension, certain sorts of prose fictions or poems are often described as having melodramatic elements.

Metaphor: a *figure of speech* (in this case, a trope) in which a comparison is made or identity is asserted between two unrelated things or actions without the use of "like" or "as." The primary subject is known as the *tenor*; to illuminate its nature, the writer links it to wholly different images, ideas, or actions referred to as the *vehicle*. Unlike a *simile*, which is a direct comparison of two things, a metaphor "fuses" the separate qualities of two things, creating a new idea. For example, Shakespeare's "Let slip the dogs of war" is a metaphorical statement. The tenor, or primary subject, is "war"; the vehicle of the metaphor is the image of hunting dogs released from their leash. The line fuses the idea of war with the qualities of ravening bloodlust associated with hunting dogs.

Metaphysical Poets: a group of seventeenth-century English poets, notably Donne, Cowley, Marvell, and Herbert, who employed unusual difficult imagery and *conceits* (see above) in order to develop intellectual and religious themes. The term was first applied to these writers to mark as far-fetched their use of philosophical and scientific ideas in a poetic context.

Meter: the pattern of stresses, syllables, and pauses that constitutes the regular rhythm of a line of verse. The meter of a poem written in the English accentual-syllabic tradition is determined by identifying the stressed and unstressed syllables in a line of verse, and grouping them into recurring units known as feet. See *accent*, *accentual-syllabic*, *caesura*, *elision*, and *scansion*. For some of the better known meters, see *iamb*, *trochee*, *dactyl*, *anapaest*, and *spondee*. See also *monometer*, *dimeter*, *trimeter*, *tetrameter*, *pentameter*, and *hexameter*.

Methodist: Protestant denomination formed in the eighteenth century as part of the religious movement led by John and Charles Wesley. Originally a movement within the Church of England, Methodism entailed enthusiastic evangelism, a strong emphasis on free will, and a strict regimen of Christian living.

Metonymy: a *figure of speech* (a trope), meaning "change of name," in which a writer refers to an object or idea by substituting the name of another object or idea closely associated with it: for example, the substitution of "crown" for monarchy, "the press" for journalism, or "the pen" for writing. *Synecdoche* (see below) is a kind of metonymy.

Mock-heroic: a style applying the elevated diction and vocabulary of epic poetry to low or ridiculous subjects. An example is Alexander Pope's "The Rape of the Lock."

Monologue: words spoken by a character to him or herself or to an audience directly.

Monometer: a line containing one metrical foot.

Mood: This can describe the writer's attitude, implied or expressed, towards the subject (see *tone* below); or it may refer to the atmosphere that a writer creates in a passage of description or narration.

Motif: an idea, image, action, or plot element that recurs throughout a literary work, creating new levels of meaning and strengthening structural coherence. The term is taken from music, where it describes recurring melodies or themes. See also *theme*.

Narrative Perspective: in fiction, the point of view from which the story is narrated. A first-person narrative is recounted using *I* and *me*, whereas a third person narrative is recounted using *he*, *she*, *they*, and so on. When a narrative is written in the third person and the narrative voice evidently "knows" all that is being done and thought, the story is typically described as being recounted by an "omniscient narrator."

Neoclassical: adapted from or substantially influenced by the cultures of ancient Greece and Rome. The term *neoclassical* is often used to describe the ideals of Restoration and eighteenth-century writers and artists who looked to ancient Greek and Roman civilization for models.

Nobility: privileged class, the members of which are distinguished by the holding of titles. Dukes, Marquesses, Earls, Viscounts, and Barons (in that order of precedence) are all holders of hereditary titles—that is to say, in the British patrilineal tradition, titles passed on from generation to generation to the eldest son. The title of Baronet, also hereditary, was added to this list by James I. Holders of non-hereditary titles include Knights and Dames.

Nonconformist: general term used to describe one who does subscribe to the Church of England.

Nonsense Verse: light, humorous poetry which contradicts logic, plays with the absurd, and invents words for amusing effects. Lewis Carroll is one of the best-known practitioners of nonsense verse.

Octave: also known as "octet," the first eight lines in an Italian/Petrarchan sonnet, rhyming *abbaabba*. See also *sestet* and *sonnet*.

Octosyllabic: a line of poetry with eight syllables, as in iambic tetrameter.

Ode: originally a classical poetic form, used by the Greeks and Romans to convey serious themes. English poetry has evolved three main forms of ode: the Pindaric (imitative of the odes of the Greek poet Pindar); the Horatian (modeled on the work of the Roman writer Horace); and the irregular ode.

The Pindaric ode was an irregular stanza in English, has a tripartite structure of "strophe," "antistrophe," and "epode" (meaning turn, counterturn, and stand), modeled on the songs and movements of the Chorus in Greek drama. The Horatian ode is more personal, reflective, and literary, and employs a pattern of repeated stanzas. The irregular ode, as its name implies, avoids a recurrent stanza pattern, and is sometimes irregular in line length also (see, for example, Wordsworth's "Ode: Intimations of Immortality").

Onomatopoeia: a *figure of speech* (a scheme) in which a word "imitates" a sound, or in which the sound of a word seems to reflect its meaning.

Ottava Rima: an 8-line stanza, usually in iambic pentameter, with the rhyme scheme *abababcc*. For an example, see Byron's *Don Juan*, or Yeats's "Sailing to Byzantium."

Oxymoron: a *figure of speech* (a trope) in which two words whose meanings seem contradictory are placed together, a paradox: for example, the phrase "darkness visible," from Milton's *Paradise Lost*.

Paean: a triumphant, celebratory song, often associated with a military victory.

Pale: in the medieval period, term for a protective zone around a fortress. As of the year 1500 three of these had been set up to guard frontiers of territory controlled by England—surrounding Calais in France, Berwick-upon-Tweed on the Scottish frontier, and Dublin in Ireland. The Dublin Pale was the largest of the three, and the term remained in use for a longer period there.

Pantoum: a poem in linked quatrains that rhyme *abab*. The second and fourth lines of one stanza are repeated as the first and third lines of the stanza that follows. In the final stanza the pattern is reversed: the second line repeats the third line of the first stanza, the fourth and final line repeats the first line of the first stanza.

Parliament: in Britain, the legislative body, comprising both the House of Commons and the House of Lords. Since the eighteenth century, the most powerful figure in the British government has been the Prime Minister rather than the monarch, the House of Commons has been the dominant body in Parliament, and members of the House of Commons have been organized in political parties. Since the mid-nineteenth century the effective executive in the British Parliamentary system has been the Cabinet, each member of which is typically in charge of a department of government. Unlike the American system, the British Parliamentary system (sometimes called the "Westminster system," after the location of the Houses of Parliament) brings together the executive and legislative functions of government, with the Prime Minister leading the government party in the House of Commons as well as directing the cabinet. By convention it is understood that the House of Lords will not contravene the wishes of the House of Commons in any fundamental way, though the "Upper House," as it is often referred to, may sometimes modify or reject legislation.

Parody: a close, usually mocking imitation of a particular literary work, or of the well-known style of a particular author, in order to expose or magnify weaknesses. Parody is a form of satire—that is, humor that may ridicule and scorn its object.

Pastiche: a discourse which borrows or imitates other writers' characters, forms, style, or ideas. Unlike a parody, a pastiche is usually intended as a compliment to the original writer.

Pastoral: in general, pertaining to country life; in prose, drama, and poetry, a stylized type of writing that idealizes the lives and innocence of country people, particularly shepherds and shepherdesses. Also see *eclogue, georgic, idyll,* above.

Pastoral Elegy: a poem in which the poet uses the pastoral style to lament the death of a friend, usually represented as a shepherd. Milton's "Lycidas" provides a good example of the form, including its use of such conventions as an invocation of the muse and a procession of mourners.

Pathetic Fallacy: a form of personification in which inanimate objects are given human emotions: for example, rain clouds "weeping." The word "fallacy" in this connection is intended to suggest the distortion of reality or the false emotion that may result from an exaggerated use of personification.

Pathos: the emotional quality of a discourse; or the ability of a discourse to appeal to our emotions. It is usually applied to the mood conveyed by images of pain, suffering, or loss that arouse feelings of pity or sorrow in the reader.

Pattern Poetry: a predecessor of modern concrete poetry, in which the shape of the poem on the page is intended to suggest or imitate an aspect of the poem's subject. George Herbert's "Easter Wings" is an example of pattern poetry.

Penny Dreadful: Victorian term for a cheap and poorly produced work of short fiction, usually of a sensational nature.

Pentameter: a line of verse containing five metrical feet.

Performance Poetry: poetry composed primarily for oral performance, often very theatrical in nature. See also *dub poetry* and *rap*.

Persona: the assumed identity or "speaking voice" that a writer projects in a discourse. The term "persona" literally means "mask." Even when a writer speaks in the first person, we should be aware that the attitudes or opinions we hear may not necessarily be those of the writer in real life.

Personification: a *figure of speech* (a trope), also known as "prosopopoeia," in which a writer refers to inanimate objects, ideas, or animals as if they were human, or creates a human figure to represent an abstract entity such as Philosophy or Peace.

Petrarchan Sonnet: the earliest form of the sonnet, also known as the Italian sonnet, with an 8-line octave and a 6-line sestet. The Petrarchan sonnet traditionally focuses on love and descriptions of physical beauty.

Phoneme: a linguistic term denoting the smallest unit of sound that it is possible to distinguish. The words *fun* and *phone* each have three phonemes, though one has three letters and one has five. (Each makes up a single syllable.)

Pindaric: See *ode*.

Plot: the organization of story materials within a literary work. The order in which story material is presented (especially causes and consequences); the inclusion of elements that allow or encourage the reader or audience to form expectations as to what is likely to happen; the decision to present some story material through exposition rather than in more extended form as part of the main action of the narrative—all these are matters of plotting.

Political Parties: The party names "Whig" and "Tory" began to be used in the late seventeenth century; before that time members of the House of Commons acted individually or through shifting and very informal factions. At first the Whigs and Tories had little formal organization either, but by the mid-eighteenth century parties had acknowledged leaders, and the leader of the party with the largest number of members in the House of Commons had begun to be recognized as the Prime Minister. The Tories evolved into the modern Conservative Party, and the Whigs into the Liberal Party. In the late nineteenth century the Labour Party was formed in an effort to provide better representation in Parliament for the working class, and since the 1920s Labour and the Conservatives have alternated as the party of government, with the Liberals reduced to third-party status. (Since 1988, when the Liberals merged with a breakaway faction from Labour known as the Social Democrats, this third party has been named the Liberal Democrats.)

Pre-Raphaelites: originally a group of Victorian artists and writers, formed in 1848. Their goal was to revive what they considered the simpler, fresher, more natural art that existed before Raphael (1483-1520). The poet Dante Gabriel Rossetti was one of the founders of the group.

Presbyterian: term applied to a group of Protestants (primarily English and Scottish) who advocated replacing the traditional hierarchical church in which bishops and archbishops governed lower level members of the clergy with a system in which all presbyters (or ministers) would be equal. The Presbyterians, originally led by John Knox, were strongly influenced by the ideas of John Calvin.

Prose Poem: a poetic discourse that uses prose formats (e.g., it may use margins and paragraphs rather than line breaks or stanzas) yet is written with the kind of attention to language, rhythm and cadence that characterizes verse.

Prosody: the study and analysis of meter, rhythm, rhyme, stanzaic pattern, and other devices of versification.

Protagonist: the central character in a literary work.

Prothalamion: a wedding song; a term coined by the poet Edmund Spenser, adapted from "epithalamion" (see above).

Public School: See *schools* below.

Pun: a play on words, in which a word with two or more distinct meanings, or two words with similar sounds, may create humorous ambiguities. Also known as *paranomasia*.

Puritan: term, originally applied only in a derogatory fashion but later widely accepted as descriptive, referring to those in England who favored religious reforms that went beyond those instituted as part of the Protestant Reformation, or, more generally, who were more forceful and uncompromising in pressing for religious purity both within the Church and in society as a whole.

Pyrrhic: a metrical foot containing two weak stresses: xx.

Quadrivium: group of four academic subjects (arithmetic, astronomy, geometry, and music) that made up part of the university coursework in the Middle Ages. There were studied after the more basic subjects of the *Trivium.*

Quantitative Meter: a metrical system used by Greek and Roman poets, in which a line of verse was measured by the "quantity," or length of sound of each syllable. A foot was measured in terms of syllables classed as long or short.

Quantity: duration of syllables in poetry. The line "There is a Garden in her face" (the first line from the poem of the same name by Thomas Campion) is characterized by the short quantities of the syllables. The last line of Thomas Hardy's "During Wind and Rain" has the same number of syllables as the line by Campion, but the quantities of the syllables are much longer—in other words, the line take much longer to say: "Down their carved names the rain drop ploughs."

Quatrain: a four-line stanza, usually rhymed.

Quintet: a five-line stanza. Sometimes given as *quintain.*

Rap: originally coined to describe informal conversation, "rap" now usually describes a style of performance poetry in which a poet will chant rhymed verse, sometimes improvised and usually with musical accompaniment that has a heavy beat.

Realism: as a literary term, the presentation through literature of material closely resembling real life. As notions both of what constitutes "real life" and of how it may be most faithfully represented in literature have varied widely, "realism" has taken a variety of meanings. The term *naturalistic* has sometimes been used a synonym for *realistic*; *naturalism* originated in the nineteenth century as a term denoting a form of realism focusing in particular on grim, unpleasant, or ugly aspects of the real.

Refrain: one or more words or lines repeated at regular points throughout a poem, often at the end of each stanza or group of stanzas. Sometimes a whole stanza may be repeated to create a refrain, like the chorus in a song.

Reggae: a style of heavily-rhythmic music from the West Indies with lyrics that are colloquial in language and often anti-establishment in content and flavor. First popularized in the 1960s and 1970s, reggae has had a lasting influence on performance poetry, rap, and dub.

Rhetoric: in classical Greece and Rome, the art of persuasion and public speaking. From the Middle Ages onwards, the study of rhetoric gave greater attention to style, particularly figures of speech. Today in poetics, the term rhetoric may encompass not only figures of speech, but also the persuasive effects of forms, sounds and word choices.

Rhyme: the repetition of identical or similar sounds, usually in pairs and generally at the ends of metrical lines.

End-rhyme: a rhyming word or syllable at the end of a line.

Eye Rhyme: rhyming that pairs words whose spellings are alike but whose pronunciations are different: for example, though/slough.

Feminine Rhyme: a two-syllable (also known as "double") rhyme. The first syllable is stressed and the second unstressed: for example, hasty/tasty. See also *triple rhyme* below.

Interlocking Rhyme: the repetition of rhymes from one stanza to the next, creating links that add to the poem's continuity and coherence. Examples may be found in Shelley's use of *terza rima* in "Ode to the West Wind" and in Dylan Thomas's villanelle "Do Not Go Gentle Into That Good Night."

Internal Rhyme: the placement of rhyming words within lines so that at least two words in a line rhyme with each other.

Masculine Rhyme: a correspondence of sound between the final stressed syllables at the end of two or more lines, as in grieve/leave, arr-ive/sur-vive.

Slant Rhyme: an imperfect or partial rhyme (also known as "near" or "half" rhyme) in which the final consonants of stressed syllables match but the vowel sounds do not. E.g., spoiled / spilled, taint / stint.

Triple Rhyme: a three-syllable rhyme in which the first syllable of each rhyme-word is stressed and the other two unstressed (e.g., lottery / coterie).

True Rhyme: a rhyme in which everything but the initial consonant matches perfectly in sound and spelling.

Rhyme Royal: a stanza of seven iambic pentameters, with a rhyme-scheme of *ababbcc*. This is also known as the Chaucerian stanza, as Chaucer was the first English poet to use this form. See also *septet.*

Rhythm: in speech, the arrangement of stressed and unstressed syllables creates units of sound. In song or verse, these units usually form a regular rhythmic pattern, a kind of beat, described in prosody as *meter.*

Romanticism: a major social and cultural movement, originating in Europe, that shaped much of Western artistic thought in the late eighteenth and nineteenth centuries. Opposing the ideal of controlled, rational order of the Enlightenment, Romanticism emphasizes the importance of spontaneous self-expression, emotion, and personal experience in producing art. In Romanticism, the "natural" is privileged over the conventional or the artificial.

Rondeau: a fifteen-line poem, generally octosyllabic, with only two rhymes throughout its three stanzas, and an unrhymed refrain at the end of the ninth and fifteenth lines, repeating part of the opening line.

Sarcasm: See *irony.*

Satire: literary work designed to make fun of or seriously criticize its subject. According to many literary theories of the Renaissance and neoclassical periods, the ridicule through satire of a certain sort of behavior may function for the reader or audience as a corrective of such behavior.

Scansion: the formal analysis of patterns of rhythm and rhyme in poetry. Each line of verse will have a certain number of fairly regular "beats" consisting of alternating stressed and unstressed syllables. To "scan" a poem is to count the beats in each line, to mark stressed and unstressed syllables and indicate their combination into "feet," to note pauses, and to identify rhyme schemes with letters of the alphabet.

Scheme: See *figures of speech*.

Schools: In the sixteenth and seventeenth centuries the different forms of school in England included Cathedral schools (often founded with a view to the education of members of the choir); grammar schools (often founded by towns or by guilds, and teaching a much broader curriculum than the modern sense of "grammar" might suggest, private schools, operated by private individuals out of private residences; and public schools, which (like the private schools and the grammar schools) operated independent of any church authority, but unlike the grammar schools and private schools were organized as independent charities, and often offered free education. Over the centuries certain of these public schools, while remaining not-for-profit institutions, began to accept fee-paying students and to adopt standards that made them more and more exclusive. In the eighteenth and nineteenth century attendance at such prestigious public boarding schools as Eton, Westminster, and Winchester had become almost exclusively the preserve of the upper classes; by the nineteenth century such "public" schools were the equivalent of private schools in North America. Though a few girls attended some early grammar schools, the greater part of this educational system was for boys only. Though a number of individuals of earlier periods were concerned to increase the number of private schools for girls, the movement to create a parallel girls' system of public schools and grammar schools dates from the later nineteenth century.

Septet: a stanza containing seven lines.

Serf: in the medieval period, a person of unfree status, typically engaged in working the land.

Sestet: a six-line stanza that forms the second grouping of lines in an Italian / Petrarchan sonnet, following the octave. See *sonnet* and *sestina.*

Sestina: an elaborate unrhymed poem with six 6-line stanzas and a 3-line envoy.

Shire: originally a multiple estate; since the late medieval period a larger territory forming an administrative unit—also referred to as a county.

Simile: a *figure of speech* (a trope) which makes an explicit comparison between a particular object and another object or idea that is similar in some (often unexpected) way. A simile always uses "like" or "as" to signal the connection. Compare with *metaphor* above.

Sonnet: a highly structured lyric poem, which normally has fourteen lines of iambic pentameter. We can distinguish four major variations of the sonnet.

Italian/Petrarchan: named for the 14th-century Italian poet Petrarch, has an octave rhyming *abbaabba*, and a sestet rhyming *cdecde*, or *cdcdcd* (other arrangements are possible here). Usually, a turn in argument takes place between octave and sestet.

Miltonic: developed by Milton and similar to the Petrarchan in rhyme scheme, but eliminating the turn after the octave, thus giving greater unity to the poem's structure of thought.

Shakespearean: often called the English sonnet, this form has three quatrains and a couplet. The quatrains rhyme internally but do not interlock: *abab cdcd efef gg*. The turn may occur after the second quatrain, but is usually revealed in the final couplet. Shakespeare's sonnets are the best-known examples of this form.

Spenserian: after Edmund Spenser, who developed the form in his sonnet cycle *Amoretti*. This sonnet form has three quatrains linked through interlocking rhyme, and a separately rhyming couplet: *abab bcbc cdcd ee*.

Speaker: in the late medieval period, a member of the Commons in Parliament who spoke on behalf of that entire group. (The Commons first elected a Speaker in 1376.) In later eras the role of Speaker became one of chairing debates in the House of Commons and arbitrating disputes over matters of procedure.

Spenserian Stanza: a nine-line stanza, with eight iambic pentameters and a concluding alexandrine, rhyming *ababbcbcc*.

Spondee: a metrical foot containing two strong stressed syllables: // (e.g., blind mouths).

Sprung Rhythm: a modern variation of accentual verse, created by the English poet Gerard Manley Hopkins, in which rhythms are determined largely by the number of strong stresses in a line, without regard to the number of unstressed syllables. Hopkins felt that sprung rhythm more closely approximated the natural rhythms of speech than did conventional poetry.

Stanza: any lines of verse that are grouped together in a poem and separated from other similarly-structured groups by a space. In metrical poetry, stanzas share metrical and rhyming patterns; however, stanzas may also be formed on the basis of thought, as in irregular odes. Conventional stanza forms include the *tercet*, the *quatrain*, *rhyme royal*, the *Spenserian stanza*, the *ballad stanza*, and *ottava rima*.

Stream of Consciousness: narrative technique that attempts to convey in prose fiction a sense of the progression of the full range of thoughts and sensations occurring within a character's mind. Twentieth-century pioneers in the use of the stream of consciousness technique include Dorothy Richardson, Virginia Woolf, and James Joyce.

Stress: See *accent*.

Strophe: the first stanza in a Pindaric ode. This is followed by an *antistrophe* (see above), which presents the same metrical pattern and rhyme scheme, and finally by an *epode*, differing in meter from the preceding stanzas. Upon completion of this "triad," the entire sequence can recur. *Strophe* may also describe a stanza or other subdivision in other kinds of poem.

Sublime: a concept, most popular in eighteenth-century England, of the qualities of grandeur, power, and awe that may be inherent in or produced by undomesticated nature or great art. The sublime was thought of as higher and loftier than something that is merely beautiful.

Subplot: a line of story that is subordinate to the main storyline of a narrative. (Note that properly speaking a subplot is a category of story material, not of plot.)

Substitution: a deliberate change from the dominant pattern of stresses in a line of verse to create emphasis or variation. Thus the first line of Shakespeare's sonnet "'Shall I compare thee to a summer's day?' is decidedly iambic in meter (x / x / x / x / x /), whereas the second line substitutes a trochee (/ x) in the opening foot: "Thou art more lovely and more temperate."

Subtext: implied or suggested meaning of a passage of text, or of an entire work.

Syllabic Verse: poetry in which the length of a line is measured solely by the number of syllables, regardless of accents or patterns of stress.

Syllable: vocal sound or group of sounds forming a unit of speech; a syllable may be formed with a single effort of articulation. Some syllables consist of a single phoneme (e.g., the word *I*, or the first syllable in the word *u*-ni-ty) but others may be made up of several phonemes (as with one-syllable words such as *lengths*, *splurged*, and *through*). By contrast, the much shorter words *ago*, *any*, and *open* each have two syllables.

Symbol: a word, image, or idea that represents something more, or other, than for what it at first appears to stand. Like metaphor, the symbol extends meaning; but while the tenor and vehicle of metaphor are bound in a specific relationship, a symbol may have a range of connotations. For example, the image of a rose may call forth associations of love, passion, transience, fragility, youth and beauty, among others. Depending upon the context, such an image could be interpreted in a variety of ways, as in Blake's lyric, "The Sick Rose." Though this power of symbolic representation characterizes all language, poetry most particularly endows the concrete imagery evoked through language with a larger meaning. Such meaning is implied rather than explicitly stated; indeed, much of the power of symbolic language lies in the reader's ability to make meaningful sense of it.

Syncope: in poetry, the dropping of a letter or syllable from the middle of a word, as in "trav'ler." Such a contraction allows a line to stay within a metrical scheme. See also *catalexis* and *elision*.

Synecdoche: a kind of *metonymy* in which a writer substitutes the name of a part of something to signify the whole: for example, "sail" for ship or "hand" for a member of the ship's crew.

Tercet: a group, or stanza, of three lines, often linked by an interlocking rhyme scheme as in *terza rima*. See also *triplet*.

Terza Rima: an arrangement of tercets interlocked by a rhyme scheme of *aba bcb cdc ded*, etc., and ending with a couplet that rhymes with the second-last line of the final tercet (for example, *efe, ff*). See, for example, Percy Shelley's "Ode to the West Wind."

Tetrameter: a line of poetry containing four metrical feet.

Theme: the governing idea of a discourse, conveyed through the development of the subject, and through the recurrence of certain words, sounds, or metrical patterns. See also *motif*.

Third-Person Narrative: See *narrative perspective*.

Tone: the writer's attitude toward a given subject or audience, as expressed though an authorial persona or "voice." Tone can be projected through particular choices of wording, imagery, figures of speech, and rhythmic devices. Compare *mood.*

Tories: See *Political Parties.*

Tragedy: in the traditional definition originating in discussions of ancient Greek drama, a serious narrative recounting the downfall of the protagonist. More loosely, the term has been applied to a wide variety of literary forms in which the tone is predominantly a dark one and the narrative does not end happily.

Transcendentalism: a philosophical movement that influenced such Victorian writers as Thomas Carlyle and Robert Browning. Also a mode of Romantic thought, Transcendentalism places the supernatural and the natural within one great Unity and believes that each individual person embodies aspects of the divine.

Trimeter: a line of poetry containing three metrical feet.

Triolet: a French form in which the first line appears three times in a poem of only eight lines. The first line is repeated at lines 4 and 7; the second line is repeated in line 8. The triolet has only two rhymes: *abaaabab.*

Triple Foot: poetic foot of three syllables. The possible varieties of triple foot are the anapest (in which two unstressed syllables are followed by a stressed syllable), the dactyl (in which a stressed syllable is followed by two unstressed lines), and the mollossus (in which all three syllables are stressed equally). English poetry tends to use duple rhythms far more frequently than triple rhythms.

Triplet: a group of three lines with the same end-rhyme, much used by eighteenth-century poets to vary or punctuate the flow of couplets. See also *tercet.*

Trivium: group of three academic subjects (dialectic, grammar, and rhetoric) that were part of the university curriculum in the Middle Ages. Their study precedes that of the more advanced subjects of the *quadrivium.*

Trochee: a metrical foot containing one strong stress followed by one weak stress: / x (heaven, lover).

Trope: any figure of speech that plays on our understandings of words to extend, alter, or transform "literal" meaning. Common tropes include *metaphor, simile, personification, hyperbole, metonymy, oxymoron, synecdoche,* and *irony.* See also *figures of speech,* above.

Turn (Italian "volta"): the point in a *sonnet* where the mood or argument changes. The turn may occur between the octave and sestet, i.e., after the eighth line, or in the final couplet, depending on the kind of sonnet.

Unities: Many literary theorists of the late sixteenth through late eighteenth centuries held that a play should ideally be presented as representing a single place, and confining the action to a single day and a single dominant event. They disapproved of plots involving gaps or long periods of time, shifts in place, or subplots. These concepts, which came to be referred to as the unities of space, time, and action, were based on a misreading of classical authorities (principally of Aristotle).

***Vers de societé*:** French: literally, "verse about society." The term originated with poetry written by aristocrats and upper-middle-class poets that specifically disavows the ambition of creating "high art" while treating the concerns of their own group in verse forms that demonstrate a high degree of formal control (e.g., artful rhymes, surprising turns of diction).

Vers libre (French): See *free verse* above.

Verse: a general term for works of poetry, usually referring to poems that incorporate some kind of metrical structure. The term may also describe a line of poetry, though more frequently it is applied to a stanza.

Villanelle: a poem usually consisting of 19 lines, with five 3-line stanzas (tercets) rhyming *aba*, and a concluding quatrain rhyming *abaa*. The first and third lines of the first tercet are repeated at fixed intervals throughout the rest of the poem. See, for example, Dylan Thomas's "Do Not Go Gentle Into That Good Night."

Whigs: See *Political Parties*.

Workhouse: public institution in which the poor were provided with a minimal level of sustenance and with lodging in exchange for work performed. Early workhouses were typically administered by individual parishes. In 1834 a unified system covering all of England and Wales was put into effect.

Zeugma: a *figure of speech* (trope) in which one word links or "yokes" two others in the same sentence, often to comic or ironic effect. For example, a verb may govern two objects, as in Pope's line "Or stain her honour, or her new brocade."

Permissions Acknowledgments

Aesop, *Aesop's Fables*, Trans. Laura Gibbs. Oxford University Press, 2002. Reproduced by permission of the publisher.

Horace, *Satires and Epistles of Horace*. Trans. Smith Palmer Bovie. (Chicago: © University of Chicago Press, 1959).

"If this, our life, be less than but a day," and "When you are very old, by candle's flame": from LYRICS OF THE FRENCH RENAISSANCE: MAROT, DU BELLAY, RONSARD translated by Norman R. Shapiro, © Yale University Press, 2002. Reproduced with permission of the publisher.

Lucian, "The Dream, or The Cock." Reprinted by permission of the publishers and the Trustees of the Loeb Classical Library from LUCIAN: VOLUME II, Loeb Classical Library ® Volume 54, translated by A.M. Harmon, Cambridge, Mass.: Harvard University Press, 1915. The Loeb Classical Library ® is a registered trademark of the President and Fellows of Harvard College.

Marlowe, Christopher. *The Tragical History of Dr. Faustus*, edited by Michael Keefer. Reproduced with permission of the editor.

Stuart, Mary: Assorted letters from LETTERS AND POEMS edited and translated by Clifford Bax. (New York: Philosophical Library, 1947).

"When in my weeping I inquire of Love": from WOMEN POETS OF THE ITALIAN RENAISSANCE: COURTLY LADIES AND COURTESANS, translated by Laura Anna Stortoni and Mary Prentice Lillie (New York: Italica Press, 1997). Reproduced with permission of the publisher.

Illustration Credits

Cover: Reproduced by permission of The Royal Collection © 2005 Her Majesty Queen Elizabeth II. Page 12: Reproduced by permission of the National Portrait Gallery, London. Page 86: Reproduced by permission of the National Portrait Gallery, London. Page 107: Reproduced by permission of the National Portrait Gallery, London. Page 117: Reproduced by permission of the National Portrait Gallery, London. Page 254: Reproduced by permission of the National Portrait Gallery, London. Page 334: Reproduced by permission of the National Portrait Gallery, London. Page 335: Reproduced by permission of the National Portrait Gallery, London. Page 744: Reproduced by kind permission of Viscount De L'Isle from his private collection at Penshurst Place. Page 755: Reproduced by permission of the National Portrait Gallery, London. Page 806: Reproduced by permission of the National Portrait Gallery, London.

Information on translations used is provided in footnotes at the beginning of selections. Copyright permission to reproduce material translated or edited for this anthology (and material reproduced or adapted here that originally appeared in other books published by Broadview Press) may be sought from Broadview.

The publisher has endeavored to contact rights holders of all copyright material and would appreciate receiving any information as to errors or omissions.

Index of First Lines

Index of Authors and Titles